ANGLES OF VISION

Reading, Writing, and the Study of Literature

ANGLES OF VISION

Reading, Writing, and the Study of Literature

Arthur W. Biddle and Toby Fulwiler

University of Vermont

Mary Jane Dickerson

James Howe

Tony Magistrale

Ghita Orth

Sidney Poger

Allen Shepherd

William A. Stephany

Richard Sweterlitsch

Robyn Warhol

McGraw-Hill, Inc.

New York St. Louis San Francisco Auckland Bogotá
Caracas Lisbon London Madrid Mexico Milan Montreal
New Delhi Paris San Juan Singapore
Sydney Tokyo Toronto

This book was developed by STEVEN PENSINGER, Inc.

ANGLES OF VISION
Reading, Writing, and the Study of Literature

Acknowledgments appear on pages 1783–1794, and on this page by reference.

5 6 7 8 9 0 DOC DOC 9 0 9

ISBN 0-07-005214-X

This book was set in Janson Text by ComCom, Inc.
The editors were Steve Pensinger and Scott Amerman;
the designer was Jo Jones;
the cover was designed by Robin Hoffmann;
the production supervisor was Richard A. Ausburn.
R. R. Donnelley & Sons Company was printer and binder.

This book is printed on acid-free paper.

Library of Congress Cataloging-in-Publication Data

Angles of vision: reading, writing, and the study of literature /
Arthur W. Biddle and Toby Fulwiler, editors; contributing authors,
Mary Jane Dickerson . . . [et al.].
p. cm.
ISBN 0-07-005214-X
1. College readers. 2. English language—Rhetoric.
3. Literature—Collections. I. Biddle, Arthur W. II. Fulwiler,
Toby, (date). III. Dickerson, Mary Jane.
PE1417.A54 1992
808—dc20 91-36839

ABOUT THE AUTHORS

Arthur W. Biddle has taught American literature and writing at the University of Vermont since 1970. He is co-editor with Toby Fulwiler of *Reading, Writing, and the Study of Literature.* His latest project is *The Thinking Book: Critical Thinking Across the Curriculum* (with John Clarke). He admits, though, that getting his poem "Grandfather" published in this book is one of his proudest achievements.

Toby Fulwiler directs the writing program at the University of Vermont where he teaches courses in composition and American literature. He is the author of both *College Writing* and *Teaching With Writing*, the editor of *The Journal Book,* and the co-editor (with Arthur Biddle) of *Reading, Writing, and the Study of Literature.* He is especially interested in the intersection of composition studies with the teaching of literature.

Mary Jane Dickerson, born in North Carolina and educated at the University of North Carolina at Greensboro and at Chapel Hill, has been teaching literature and writing in the University of Vermont's English Department since 1966. She has published articles on American fiction about a range of subjects, from Jean Toomer to William Faulkner. Currently, she is writing a book about American autobiography as a cultural dialogue.

James Howe has been teaching English at the University of Vermont since 1964. He has published books on essay writing and on the plays of Christopher Marlowe. His current project is a study of William Shakespeare's plays, which have also been his teaching specialty for the past few years.

Tony Magistrale is associate professor of English at the University of Vermont. He is the author of several books and articles on American literature and composition. Among his most recent publications are a collection of essays entitled *The Shining Reader,* which he edited for Starmont House, and a critical introduction to Wanda Coleman's poetry, which appeared in the Fall 1989 issue of *Black American Literature Forum.*

Ghita Orth teaches literature and creative writing at the University of Vermont. She has published a book of poetry, *The Music Of What Happens,* and her work has appeared in a number of journals. Having completed the manuscript of a second collection of poems, she is currently collaborating with Allen Shepherd and David Huddle on a fiction text designed primarily for creative writing classes.

Sidney Poger teaches a variety of courses at the University of Vermont, including modern poetry, detective fiction, and genre studies. He has published essays on many poets, including William Cullen Bryant, W. B. Yeats, T. S. Eliot, W. H. Auden, Hart Crane, and

John Montague. He is the author of "Writing About Poetry" in *Reading, Writing, and the Study of Literature.* He is currently at work on a study of moral displacement in detective fiction.

Allen Shepherd teaches nineteenth- and twentieth-century American literature at the University of Vermont. He has published fiction, poetry, and personal, critical, and scholarly articles in American, Canadian, and European journals. With Arthur W. Biddle, he contributed a chapter on fiction to *Reading, Writing, and the Study of Literature* (1989) and is editing, with David Huddle and Ghita Orth, *About These Stories: A Reader for Writers.*

William A. Stephany has been at the University of Vermont since 1968, where he teaches courses on the Middle Ages and on the Bible as literature, as well as a range of introductory literature courses. Most of his scholarly publications, including a book, are on Dante's *Commedia.*

Richard Sweterlitsch, an assistant professor of folklore and English at the University of Vermont since 1974, teaches courses in American literature, ballad and legend, folklore, and advanced composition. He has published essays on the use of journal writing in folklore classes, proverbs in traditional ballads, lake monsters, and outlaw-heroes, and has cowritten the award-winning video documentary *On My Own: The Traditions of Daisy Turner.*

Robyn Warhol, an associate professor of English at the University of Vermont, specializes in feminist theory, narratology, and nineteenth-century fiction. She has published essays on George Eliot, Elizabeth Gaskell, and Harriet Beecher Stowe. She is the author of *Gendered Interventions: Narrative Discourse in the Victorian Novel* and co-editor of *Feminisms: An Anthology of Feminist Literary Theory and Criticism.*

of responding to the literature; many examples of student writing are also given. One multipart assignment asks students to write collaboratively about poetry by starting off with song lyrics. Elsewhere in the poetry chapter students learn about sonnets, for instance, not only by reading the introduction but also by writing about what distinguishes the sonnet in their eyes from other forms of poetry. They then write a sonnet of their own and may even choose to write a parody in sonnet form. Students view the sonnet, then, from a variety of angles. Our uses of informal writing are supported by five substantial chapters devoted specifically to writing about literature: critical essays, personal essays, imaginative essays, essay exams, and researched papers.

4. While many anthologies either ignore the essay or treat it half-heartedly, *Angles of Vision* accords the essay equal status as a major genre along with fiction, poetry, and drama. The act of writing an essay sets conversations into motion—conversations between writer and reader, and a larger social conversation between self and society. The concept of voice leads us to explore the presence of the author in the essay and some of the available options—voices of meditation, of response, of dissent, of explanation, of storytelling. The readings, ranging from the classic to the contemporary, support and develop this approach.

ACKNOWLEDGMENTS

The authors wish to thank the many people who helped us write this book. At the top of any list would be our students, many of whose responses are included. Steve Pensinger, our editor at McGraw-Hill, is one of the best in the business; he knew when we needed help—and gave it—and when to leave us alone. We are grateful to the team at McGraw-Hill who helped produce the book: Scott Amerman, the editing supervisor; Jo Jones, the designer; and Rich Ausburn, the production supervisor. Josie Winch and Jennifer Gordon, our student assistants, cheerfully did the work nobody else wanted to do. We are grateful too for the suggestions made by Jean Cerrington Bauso, Peace College; Bruce Biederwell, University of California—Los Angeles; Barbara Bilson, Santa Monica College; David L. Cowles, Brigham Young University; Richard Dietrich, University of South Florida; Paula Feldman, University of South Carolina; Kelley Griffith, University of North Carolina—Greensboro; Richard Harrison, Kilgore College; John Hoey, State University of New York—Geneseo; Glenda A. Hudson, California State University—Bakersfield; Jodi A. Johnson, Los Angeles Pierce College; Lois Lyles, San Francisco State University; Susan Peck MacDonald, University of California—San Diego; Mbulelo Mzamane, University of Vermont; and Michael J. Rossi, Merrimack College.

Arthur W. Biddle

Toby Fulwiler

PREFACE

We wrote *Angles of Vision* to help college students learn to read and write about literature. In some ways our book resembles other anthologies, with the inclusion of the traditional genres of poetry, drama, and fiction and the representation of well-known writers and works. But here is how it differs:

1. You will hear the varied voices of the eleven authors who wrote the essays in this anthology. Each section was written by a different team, speaking in their own voices from their own experiences and presenting individual, yet solid, approaches to each genre. In the introduction to fiction, for example, we explore the nature of fiction by examining successive drafts of a story by David Huddle. Readers hear the voices of students discussing the story, actually questioning Huddle about why he handled things as he did, and they hear his explanations and reconsiderations based on students' ideas. As they listen to these conversations, readers come to realize that a piece of literature is an organic creation of a human mind. Further, by looking closely at Huddle's story in this way, students learn how to carry on their own conversations with a work of fiction, the questions to ask, the answers to seek.

Throughout the book our critical perspectives range from formalistic to reader response to new historical, but without forcing the critical issues. We value close reading of texts while validating the knowledge and experience students bring with them.

2. In selecting authors and works for *Angles of Vision* we have sought to include a great diversity of material not commonly represented in more traditional collections—works by Chicano(a)-American, African-American, and native American writers; works by South American, African, and Asian authors; as well as much greater representation of women's voices. Among the builders of a diverse American culture are Chicano-Americans Guillermo Gómez-Peña and Rolando Hinojosa-Smith; African-Americans Alice Walker, Gloria Naylor, James Baldwin, Langston Hughes, Zora Neale Hurston, Gwendolyn Brooks, Martin Luther King, Jr., Imamu Baraka, Wanda Coleman, Robert Hayden, Nikki Giovanni, Lorraine Hansberry, Charles Fuller, Claude McKay, Ishmael Reed, AI (Florence Ogawa); and native American Louise Erdrich. Some of the international writers represented are Yukio Mishima (Japan), Rony V. Diaz (Philippines), João Guimarães Rosa (Brazil), Gabriel García Márquez (Colombia), Julia Alvarez (Dominican Republic), Léopold Sédar-Senghor and David Mamdessi Diop (Senegal), Abioseh Nicol (Sierra Leone), Augostnho Neto and Antonio Jacinto (Angola), Gaberiel Pkara and Hadiza Lantana Ampah (Nigeria), David Rubadiri and Jack Mapanje (Malawi), Okot p'Bitek (Uganda), Felix Mnthali (Zambia), Leila Djabali (Algeria), and Kofi Awonoor (Ghana).

3. *Angles of Vision* emphasizes writing as well as reading. As Sid Poger remarked of the poetry chapter, "We focus on how to read poetry and understand it through the writing process." Throughout we are as concerned with "writing to learn" as with "learning to write." Chapter authors offer a rich variety of suggestions for informal writing as a means

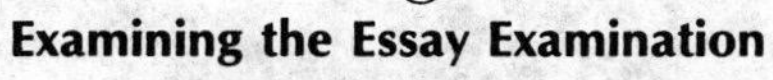

CHAPTER 4 735

Reading Script into Play

James R. Howe and William A. Stephany

PREFACE

We wrote *Angles of Vision* to help college students learn to read and write about literature. In some ways our book resembles other anthologies, with the inclusion of the traditional genres of poetry, drama, and fiction and the representation of well-known writers and works. But here is how it differs:

1. You will hear the varied voices of the eleven authors who wrote the essays in this anthology. Each section was written by a different team, speaking in their own voices from their own experiences and presenting individual, yet solid, approaches to each genre. In the introduction to fiction, for example, we explore the nature of fiction by examining successive drafts of a story by David Huddle. Readers hear the voices of students discussing the story, actually questioning Huddle about why he handled things as he did, and they hear his explanations and reconsiderations based on students' ideas. As they listen to these conversations, readers come to realize that a piece of literature is an organic creation of a human mind. Further, by looking closely at Huddle's story in this way, students learn how to carry on their own conversations with a work of fiction, the questions to ask, the answers to seek.

Throughout the book our critical perspectives range from formalistic to reader response to new historical, but without forcing the critical issues. We value close reading of texts while validating the knowledge and experience students bring with them.

2. In selecting authors and works for *Angles of Vision* we have sought to include a great diversity of material not commonly represented in more traditional collections—works by Chicano(a)-American, African-American, and native American writers; works by South American, African, and Asian authors; as well as much greater representation of women's voices. Among the builders of a diverse American culture are Chicano-Americans Guillermo Gómez-Peña and Rolando Hinojosa-Smith; African-Americans Alice Walker, Gloria Naylor, James Baldwin, Langston Hughes, Zora Neale Hurston, Gwendolyn Brooks, Martin Luther King, Jr., Imamu Baraka, Wanda Coleman, Robert Hayden, Nikki Giovanni, Lorraine Hansberry, Charles Fuller, Claude McKay, Ishmael Reed, AI (Florence Ogawa); and native American Louise Erdrich. Some of the international writers represented are Yukio Mishima (Japan), Rony V. Diaz (Philippines), João Guimarães Rosa (Brazil), Gabriel García Márquez (Colombia), Julia Alvarez (Dominican Republic), Léopold Sédar-Senghor and David Mamdessi Diop (Senegal), Abioseh Nicol (Sierra Leone), Augostnho Neto and Antonio Jacinto (Angola), Gaberiel Pkara and Hadiza Lantana Ampah (Nigeria), David Rubadiri and Jack Mapanje (Malawi), Okot p'Bitek (Uganda), Felix Mnthali (Zambia), Leila Djabali (Algeria), and Kofi Awonoor (Ghana).

3. *Angles of Vision* emphasizes writing as well as reading. As Sid Poger remarked of the poetry chapter, "We focus on how to read poetry and understand it through the writing process." Throughout we are as concerned with "writing to learn" as with "learning to write." Chapter authors offer a rich variety of suggestions for informal writing as a means

of responding to the literature; many examples of student writing are also given. One multipart assignment asks students to write collaboratively about poetry by starting off with song lyrics. Elsewhere in the poetry chapter students learn about sonnets, for instance, not only by reading the introduction but also by writing about what distinguishes the sonnet in their eyes from other forms of poetry. They then write a sonnet of their own and may even choose to write a parody in sonnet form. Students view the sonnet, then, from a variety of angles. Our uses of informal writing are supported by five substantial chapters devoted specifically to writing about literature: critical essays, personal essays, imaginative essays, essay exams, and researched papers.

4. While many anthologies either ignore the essay or treat it half-heartedly, *Angles of Vision* accords the essay equal status as a major genre along with fiction, poetry, and drama. The act of writing an essay sets conversations into motion—conversations between writer and reader, and a larger social conversation between self and society. The concept of voice leads us to explore the presence of the author in the essay and some of the available options—voices of meditation, of response, of dissent, of explanation, of storytelling. The readings, ranging from the classic to the contemporary, support and develop this approach.

ACKNOWLEDGMENTS

The authors wish to thank the many people who helped us write this book. At the top of any list would be our students, many of whose responses are included. Steve Pensinger, our editor at McGraw-Hill, is one of the best in the business; he knew when we needed help—and gave it—and when to leave us alone. We are grateful to the team at McGraw-Hill who helped produce the book: Scott Amerman, the editing supervisor; Jo Jones, the designer; and Rich Ausburn, the production supervisor. Josie Winch and Jennifer Gordon, our student assistants, cheerfully did the work nobody else wanted to do. We are grateful too for the suggestions made by Jean Cerrington Bauso, Peace College; Bruce Biederwell, University of California—Los Angeles; Barbara Bilson, Santa Monica College; David L. Cowles, Brigham Young University; Richard Dietrich, University of South Florida; Paula Feldman, University of South Carolina; Kelley Griffith, University of North Carolina—Greensboro; Richard Harrison, Kilgore College; John Hoey, State University of New York—Geneseo; Glenda A. Hudson, California State University—Bakersfield; Jodi A. Johnson, Los Angeles Pierce College; Lois Lyles, San Francisco State University; Susan Peck MacDonald, University of California—San Diego; Mbulelo Mzamane, University of Vermont; and Michael J. Rossi, Merrimack College.

Arthur W. Biddle

Toby Fulwiler

PRELUDE

Reading and Writing in College

Arthur W. Biddle and Toby Fulwiler

> When I was young, reading and writing were great because I felt like a big person. As I grew older, I realized that all this fun was getting harder.
>
> *Krista, first-year college student*

If you like to read and write, find these activities easy, and do them well, you'll have a good time in college literature classes. As Chris, a sophomore in one of our classes, wrote in his journal: "When I'm in the right mood, and have the right book, it goes down like cream. In 11th grade, my English teacher told us to pretend to be the characters in the book. I made it through one of Russell Baker's stories being a paper boy." However, for many students, not all reading "goes down like cream." Bill, a freshman, explained his attitude this way: "I've never liked reading, especially textbook reading. I don't think I've ever read a book for pleasure except when I was younger. . . . If I read a book I like, I don't mind reading at all, but I guess that's kind of silly because nobody likes to read a book he doesn't like." Meanwhile, Julie, another sophomore, told us: "As far back as I can remember, I have always preferred reading to writing. I think it's because I always found reading easy—I could always sit down and just read for hours (if a book was interesting) without even being told."

When we asked students in this same class about writing, we found mixed opinions as well. Hollis, a junior, told us what many of our students said: "I like to write, but it's very difficult for me unless I like what I am writing about." Peter, a freshman, said he enjoyed writing except in the "college application mode. You know, 'What was your most rewarding nonacademic activity?' or 'Write an essay telling us something about yourself.' That's the kind of writing I can't deal with." Students usually like to write about subjects they choose and in forms with which they are familiar. No surprises here.

In other words, if you are like some of our students, you bring with you mixed emotions toward reading and writing about various kinds of literature. While most of you have positive experiences reading and writing in private, many of you have some negative

experiences when one or the other is assigned in school. In the rest of this essay, we'd like to look more closely first at reading and then at writing, and see if we can't make a sort of peace between our private needs as readers and writers and the more public demands of the academic community.

THE WAY YOU'RE SUPPOSED TO READ

The way you're *supposed* to read fiction, poetry, and drama in order to understand them—as you need to do in order to write essays and examinations about them or discuss them in class—goes something like this: You sit at your desk, text in front of you, notebook open, pen poised. As you read, you mark important passages in the text; you summarize main ideas and trace recurrent themes in your notebook. You look up in a dictionary, encyclopedia, or glossary all words, names, and ideas you do not understand. And if you are reading a novel or poem or a play, you pay particular attention to certain technical elements of the text.

Susan, a seasoned student of literary study, describes the *shoulds* of fiction reading this way: "I have learned that there are a lot of things to look for when I read. For example, who is narrating? Does the narrator change? What is the author's style? What is the point of view from which the story is told? When I read, however, I don't always like to look for these things. I just like to read for the sake of reading. I don't like to read into stories as much as my former professors have done." While Susan clearly knows *how* she's supposed to read and *what* she's supposed to look for, a part of her rebels and wants to read more intuitively or impressionistically, with less deliberately analytical attention than some of her teachers have insisted on.

College students are not alone in rebelling against the kind of academic toughness that good reading is supposed to entail. In fact, one of the contributing authors in this volume confessed in his journal:

> When I read strictly for myself, late at night in bed or through sunglasses on the beach, I violate most of the rules I learned about how to read well. When an image or incident triggers a memory, I let myself daydream and wander off with it. When I don't know what a word means, I skip it. When I find the plot slow moving, I skim until things pick up again. When I'm not in the mood for one book, I start another, and again another. Right now I'm reading about 7 books, 3 magazines, and a couple of catalogues. I no longer consider it a moral obligation to start a book at the beginning, to avoid peeking at the end, or to finish it once started.
>
> To remember something that strikes me as especially interesting, I write a note in the margin, dog-ear a page, or sometimes read the passage out loud to my wife. But I seldom trace plot, character, theme, or symbol methodically from page to page, beginning to end. Often I am confident that I understand the meaning of what I've read—but am not always sure that I could write a coherent essay about it.

Don't misunderstand—we're not making fun of either approach to reading, the rigorously academic or the casually private. It is not our purpose in this book to give you either negative lessons or simplistic formulas about reading literature. We think that serious reading in the academic community is, in many important ways, quite compatible with private enjoyment—but some adjustments may be useful. Reading itself is a complex intellectual activity, governed by conventions and not reducible to foolproof rules. We read, in other words, as members of one or several communities with certain assumptions and expectations that inevitably influence our reading. We do this—consciously or unconsciously—whether we read on the beach or in the classroom.

READING TO UNDERSTAND

The authors of this book no longer believe that we, or anybody else for that matter, will ever perfectly understand the central meaning of the stories, poems, or plays we read, no matter how well we prepare ourselves. Each reader brings to any reading a background unique socially, economically, religiously, politically, esthetically, and intellectually. In other words, our personal history, even our present mood, influences our responses, and so makes each reading to some significant extent our own.

A few simple examples will show what we mean. Last semester, when one of our classes read John Steinbeck's novel about dispossessed farmers, *The Grapes of Wrath,* one student saw reflected in the plight of Steinbeck's Okies her own family's difficulties holding onto their Vermont dairy farm. Another student, a practicing Christian, found meaning in the parallels and dissonances between the lives of several characters and the biblical accounts of Jesus's life. Which reading was "correct"? Both? Neither? This is obviously an unfair question. As these readers were responding to the words of *The Grapes of Wrath,* they were collaborating with Steinbeck in the creation of a text. We believe that in a very real sense any text is created anew—written if you like—by the reader.

Not only does each reader bring something different to a work, but each rereading is different. The second time around, we build on that initial reading, noticing things that escaped us earlier, seeing indications of what is to come, finding patterns impossible to discern the first time. Too, we have become different readers than we were before, and if months or years have passed, we may have changed so significantly that the work itself no longer is the same. In fact, when we reread, we usually find it easier to follow the rules of good reading because we know so much better what the work is about.

It is not restating the obvious to suggest that we read anything better when it is already familiar to us. Consequently, we cannot make sense of any text—literary, scientific, or otherwise—if we don't already know what most of the words, concepts, and formulas mean. Any literature is approachable only because it builds on what we already know. We can understand old characters such as Polonius, Lady Macbeth, and Othello because they have traits we have seen in people we already know. We understand younger characters such as Ophelia, Holden Caulfield, and Huck Finn because we have felt some of what they feel. The trick for an author is to give us enough of what we already understand in order to lead us where we have no firsthand knowledge—be it medieval Denmark, Pencey Prep, or aboard a raft on the Mississippi River.

So, in a very real sense, when we read a poem, play, or short story, a part of what we

read we already know. From that vantage of familiarity we view the rest, the unknown. Ideally, we can engage the piece on a personal, as well as an academic, level and so make it *our own.* If we cannot do this, cannot identify with the narrator, or some character or character trait, or some aspect of the situation, we may have difficulty enjoying the work or understanding it well enough to profit from it.

READING CRITICALLY

While it's true that each of us reads every poem, play, or story a little differently from everyone else, it's also true that authors don't write them that way. That is, authors use their own private experience to convey particular ideas, themes, and images to readers, hoping that if they write especially well, readers will take from the texts exactly what the authors intend. So, though you and your classmate and teacher might disagree on precisely what William Carlos Williams meant when he wrote the poem that looks like a note taped to a refrigerator ("This Is Just to Say"), we can be fairly certain that he, Williams, had some idea when he called it a poem and had it published. The poem is about *something* more or less, not about *anything* at all. The same is true, of course, for every writer in this collection, from William Shakespeare to Alice Walker. In fact, these authors are in here *because* there has been a consensus among many in the literate community that they excel in conveying interesting ideas especially well.

Carefully crafted literature, then, is not open to any and every interpretation we feel like applying to it. Yes, we *can* say that Williams' poem is really about men landing on Mars or women playing soccer or lovers having a quarrel, but we'll have a hard time convincing others to believe us (there are, for instance no words that mention Mars or soccer or quarrelsome lovers). So though we come to literature from different places and experiences, the best literature constructs make-believe worlds in which we all for a while dwell. This is one of the main reasons why English classes exist in the first place: to help students learn why certain poems, plays, and stories earn critical acclaim from culture to culture, year to year.

Reading *critically* generally means reading with such care and attention to the form, theme, and language of a given work that the reader is likely to come close to understanding something of the reason why the author composed it.

Perhaps you have noticed that when English teachers discuss literature in class or ask you to write papers about it, there is seldom only one correct interpretation. And perhaps you have also noticed that some interpretations are clearly considered better than others—usually because they are supported by more direct evidence from the text. There are no *right* answers, but some are more supportable than others.

READING AS A WRITER

Everyone who reads this book is a writer. Everyone who wrote this book is a reader. Of course. We have found that when you *read as a writer,* your relationship to the text changes. What do we mean *read as a writer?* Well, first, understand that you, we, and Mark Twain don't come from three different planets. We all struggle to get control of an idea, to find the words that belong to that idea, and then to present that idea in those words intelligibly and, we hope, with a little grace. Those stories, poems, and plays in magazines and textbooks were written by human beings just like us. You've probably written a story or two, maybe some poetry, certainly a lot of papers. So have we. Realizing that published words were written by men and women pretty much like yourself may not be a great revelation, but it can change the way you read, the attention you pay to words and works, and, in turn, the way you actually write. Here's what we mean:

Humanity. The visitor to William Faulkner's home in Oxford, Mississippi, will find on the desk in his study a clear sign of the great writer's humanity—a blue and white plastic Vick's inhaler. The author of "Barn Burning" and *The Sound and the Fury* sometimes suffered from nasal congestion! To read as a writer, it helps to know that even the greatest authors are mortal—that they catch cold and that they were once students and apprentices as we are now.

Comparing notes, the authors of this volume find themselves well aware of their own failings and imperfections as writers. We know too well that nothing we write is ever perfect—yet we do write books and articles and get them published. So too, we reason, must the great writers often feel about the limits of their own powers. And this realization—like the Vick's inhaler—helps reduce those giants to human size. If you've ever seen an author's early manuscript drafts, you know of the professional's willingness to revise and edit. As a student of literature, eventually you come to understand that any text is a "made" object, that it didn't spring full-blown from the mind of God or the muse of poetry. There was never any inevitability about it. It was probably sweated over, rewritten, and discussed just as your best writing is, and the printed version we study may be the third or the thirtieth rewrite.

Asking Questions. As writers ourselves, we've become aware that almost all written works originate as responses to certain questions or problems. Behind virtually everything we write is a question. Behind a shopping list is the question, "What do we need at the store?" Behind a letter home is the question, "How are you?" or "How am I?" Behind a laboratory report is the question, "What happened?" Sometimes, of course, the piece of writing doesn't answer the question well, or tries to answer a group of questions all at once, or asks still more questions. However, looked at this way, most pieces of writing make more sense and seem more approachable and understandable. Much of the writing in this book asks questions about the experience of being a human being on this planet, some of the hardest questions to answer about work and play, love and death, good and evil. What you read most often, of course, are the answers or attempts at answers. Since the questions are usually implied, seldom stated outright, a good reading strategy is to see if you can locate the question the piece tries to answer. This writer's approach to reading will give you a focus and even invite you to predict what will happen next in the story or play.

Finding Answers. When we write something ourselves, we struggle to answer a question or solve a problem. Of course, it doesn't always work out the way we intend. But watching ourselves work helps us to understand the efforts of other writers. We've also learned where many of those structured answers come from—the writing itself. We've come to realize that the very act of composing is an answer-creating, problem-solving activity. Writers often discover their answers in the process of writing. More than one novelist has told about characters "taking over" and creating a new direction for the second half of a book.

How does this help you as a reader? It lets you know that if you want to figure out a particularly puzzling part of what you're reading, you too should write and see what solutions you discover. As readers, we are still writers. We can use writing to solve reading problems. Our experience as writers also tells us that there is usually more than one answer to any given question. The story that ends one way might have ended differently had the author been in another mood, place, or time. The modern sonnet might have been done in free verse. Hamlet might have survived Act V. Realizing this, the reader-as-writer knows that the author has made choices, that these choices produce certain effects, and that other choices might have been made and would have produced different effects.

Seeing Words. The writer's struggle to write is frequently a struggle to find the right words. Sometimes they come, and just as often they don't. Consider the genius of those who bat better than .500. As a writer, you can appreciate the way a word just fits, seems to be the only word that will do. Sometimes when you recognize one of these words on the page, you get the feeling that you know how pleased the author must have been to find it. Walt Whitman's description of the live oak "solitary in a wide flat space, *uttering* joyous leaves all its life" and Emily Dickinson's "certain *slant* of light, winter afternoons" induce a little shiver of rightness. You'll have your own favorites, of course. When you read with an awareness of how you and other writers select words, you'll understand better the writer's craft.

Hearing Rhythms. In our own struggle to construct sentences and paragraphs that sound fluid to the ear, we appreciate better the same struggle in the writers we read. We notice constructions that work, that have a particular balance, that are deliberately parallel (as we are making this one), that see long sentences set off by short ones. As writers ourselves, we marvel at the apparent ease with which a James Joyce or Gwendolyn Brooks pulls these off. Of course, we never know for sure whether they rolled easily off the author's pen or whether he or she struggled as we so often do. One of the best ways to judge the rhythms of your own writing is to read it aloud to yourself, listening for pleasing rhythms, changing awkward ones.

Tracing Themes. In our own writing, we search for just the right pattern or repetition or other signal to keep readers clearly on the track. We may rearrange sections to make this happen and feel good when it works out, especially in longer pieces in which holding parts together is especially difficult. Then when we become readers, we look harder to see how other authors accomplish the same thing. Sometimes, of course, the search is made more difficult because the theme is subtly embedded in the text, as it is in a James Joyce short story, for instance, where little seems to happen. So we learn to reread such texts to discover what else is there.

Noticing Starts, Stops, Transitions, and Conventions. The writer as reader is far more likely to notice how other writers handle even the elementary problems of composition. If you always have trouble with first lines in whatever you write, you're more likely to notice how published authors start their pieces. You may read with awe a line like "Call me Ishmael," and at other times wonder, "Why did he start there?" You dig deeper into the work and begin to second-guess the author. You might notice how a key word at the end of one paragraph prepares you for what is coming in the next (or deliberately does not). You see this because you too work hard at transitions. And even the smaller matters, such as how white space allows the writer a sharp break in continuity (as it does on this page), how semicolons pull related sentences together, how good titles set up reader expectations (or the effects of sentence fragments such as this one). Readers who are also writers observe these and many other composition tricks because they are thinking about how they too might use them in their own writing.

Rereading and Rewriting. We've discovered that when writing something fairly long and complicated, we need to reread our work to know where it has been and where it needs to go next. If we have that problem *as writers,* is it any wonder that we also have it as readers? Many lengthy and complex works need more than one reading to make complete sense. The first time through is full of surprises—turns of plot, quirks of character, rediscovered memories and associations. In other words, we're so busy *having* the reading experience that there is little opportunity to reflect on or interpret that experience. It is understandable that the first time through a novel, play, or poem we have difficulty seeing close internal relationships and structural and symbolic subtleties. So, we plan on rereading the great texts as carefully and curiously as we do our own.

WRITING AS A READER

The same kinds of *shoulds* surround writing as reading. That is, many students have come to believe that writing privately is one thing, but writing for an academic public quite something else. Melissa, a sophomore, describes it this way in her journal: "Writing, Writing, Writing! Umm, I love it, but I'm told that I'm not allowed to use the verb "to be." I've also been told to never use "never" and never use "always"! Write with description. Action verbs are best." Writing for an academic audience *is,* of course, different from writing for oneself, but maybe not quite in the way Melissa describes.

In the last section we discussed the concept of reading as a writer. In this section, we'd like to explore the other side of that coin, "writing as a reader." We write as readers in at least three distinct ways: First, when we learn how and in what contexts and with what struggles the great works were created, we also learn about our own writing. Second, we need to remember that much of what we write is directed ultimately at other readers whose needs we must anticipate. Third, we write to please ourselves, using all the techniques at our disposal to help generate prose and poetry that satisfies our own sense of rightness. Let's look at each of these perspectives in turn.

Lessons from the Pros

One of the problems with literary study is the distance we often feel between those who write the great works of literature and the rest of us who write *about* them. That's why it can be helpful to remember that the great writers themselves were once students of other great writers, and that they too worked hard on their writing to get it just right. When you read the finished works of William Wordsworth, Joyce Carol Oates, and Arthur Miller, keep in mind that these writers filled notebook after notebook with observations and ideas that only later, and sometimes after many drafts, bore fruit as the finished works we so celebrate today. Keep in mind also that many published authors had mentors—friends, spouses, teachers, editors—who helped them clarify and refine their ideas, images, and characters.

Learning to write well—and continuing to do so—is often a messy, frustrating business. Once you've mastered the conventions and forms of written composition, you need to remember that each time you set out to write something new—a critical essay, a personal narrative, a research proposal, or a poem—each time you need to start all over to develop and order your ideas, always asking "have I said this as clearly, concisely, believably, or gracefully, as possible?"

Most of us who have learned to write with some competence consider writing a fairly unpredictable, multistage process, in which we need to find and capture ideas in the first place, develop them in some reasonably clear sequence according to some reasonably clear logic, support them with good examples remembered or researched, and make sure the whole composition is written in a style appropriate to the audience and purpose. Along the way, many of us have learned to rely on the same tricks that helped Wordsworth, Oates and Miller: to record our insights and observations informally in notebooks or journals; to begin writing before we have fully developed our ideas, trusting that the act of writing itself will help work them out; to plan to write more than one draft of anything important; to receive a little help from our friends; and to edit ceaselessly to get the final product just right. We've also learned that there are few guarantees in the act of writing: Sometimes ideas that seemed brilliant in the shower or on the jogging path look pale on paper; at other times, ideas that start out routinely develop into something quite original and pleasing.

So it may help you, as it helps us, occasionally to remember that writing well wasn't necessarily any easier for the pros than it is for us and that the techniques that helped them may help us as well.

Writing for Other Readers

When we write for other readers, we need to write with care, with courtesy, with doubt, and with empathy for our audience. We write carefully that they may follow the thread of our thought and not be thrown off by distractions. We write courteously out of respect for our readers and in order to be taken seriously. And we write with doubt, anticipating that our readers will be curious and ask questions. We'll look briefly at some of the techniques writers use when they think carefully about their readers.

Conventions. Writers who use the standard conventions of written English treat their readers with respect and care. At the same time, they usually guarantee a fair hearing for whatever they have to say. To misuse the conventions, whether punctuation, spelling, grammar, or format, is to violate your readers' expectations and therefore to distract them. This is not to say that the violation of expectations has no place in writing, for we know it does. Just keep in mind that when it's done by a Walt Whitman, a Joan Didion, or an e. e. cummings, it's done deliberately and with purpose. So, know what you're doing.

Information and Explanation. In writing notes to ourselves, we often use shorthand and abbreviations because we fill in the rest from our heads. But as soon as we begin writing to others, we start asking: How much do my readers already know? What else will they need in order to understand me? Many college students writing to academic audiences don't know how much to assume of their readers. If you are not sure, we recommend that you err by providing too much information rather than too little. When you mention literary works, at least the first time, give full titles, authors, and dates. When you use literary terminology or concepts (like *point of view, existentialism,* or *pastoral*), either define them or make sure your examples do that for you.

Evidence. As you write, try to consider the kind of evidence *you* require in order to believe someone or to be persuaded to accept their perspective. As a reader yourself, you may find that you are seldom convinced by vague generalities or unsupported assertions—at least we seldom are. This means that when you write personal narrative, remember to create belief by supplying concrete detail of character and situation from remembered experience: the score of the game, the words spoken, the dishes served. When you write critical essays, give specific evidence from texts or documented support from experts: to prove that Hamlet is in full control of his wits you might cite his plan for the play-within-a-play. And when you write imaginatively, support your imaginings with details and facts—or the illusions of details and facts: realistic dialogue, the items in a desk drawer, perhaps a telling physical feature like a droopy eye.

Language and Style. The language in which we write makes it easy for our readers to understand us, or it doesn't. It demonstrates our understanding of our subject, or our ignorance. When we write letters to friends, we use a fairly informal talky style. When we write term papers for a Shakespeare professor, we adopt a more formal, analytical style. (And when we write books for college students, we try to fall somewhere in between.) In thinking about who is going to read our writing (our audience), we adjust word choice, sentence structure, perhaps even punctuation and paragraphing to match our intentions with their expectations.

Transitions. The more we become attuned to the needs of our audience, the more important become the little words that connect one sentence to another by showing the relationship between ideas—words like *so, thus, then, however, meanwhile, nevertheless, and, but, first, next, last, on the one hand, in other words, in addition, finally.* These words do not always show up the first time we write a draft, when we're worried more about getting the basic ideas down. But as we rework drafts to make our text as clear as possible, we add signals and cues like these to point readers—as unmistakably as we can—in the right direction.

Documentation. Documentation is another reader courtesy, necessary whenever the writer uses the words, data, or ideas of another. Through in-text references or footnotes, we tell where to find all the assertions and expert opinions used to support our arguments. We explain who said what, where, and when. Readers who are curious can trace these references and find out still more. The *MLA Handbook for Writers of Research Papers* (third edition) contains explanations of how to document your work in literature classes.

Titles and Headings. We're amazed at how often novice writers ignore some of their most powerful tools—titles and headings. A good title (both descriptive and provocative, if possible) not only announces your subject, but creates a favorable attitude toward your piece. Section headings (like those you see in this chapter) guide your reader through an essay. We find that creating subheads *as we write* helps us understand where we are in our writing task, tells us where to go next, and even gives us a marked block of text to relocate elsewhere if revision demands it.

Writing for Ourselves

Our first audience is always ourselves. Remember this, especially when you're blocked or confused or uncertain of exactly what you want to say. At such times, it can actually be a hindrance to worry about your audience. Instead, you must ask yourself: Where do *I* want to go? What is the point *I* want to make in the first place? Do *I* understand where my text leads so far? Where does it need to go next?

While we have been describing writing that is primarily academic, we think the same suggestions hold true for imaginative writing—maybe even more so. Before a fiction writer can worry too much about "reader cues," she or he needs to be pretty certain that his or her "writer cues" are in order; in other words, the writer needs to see *for himself or herself* that the character development is consistent, the setting true to imagination or memory, the plot one the writer believes in. Before a poet can think about potential reader responses to images, rhymes, or rhythms, he or she first has to see them in his or her own eye, hear them with his or her own ear to test their ring of truth. As writers, we are readers, first and last—readers of our own language, whether it be directed through letters to family and friends, through essays to teachers, or through journals, intended from the outset to stay quite close to ourselves.

HOW TO READ THIS BOOK

As you may have figured out by now, we think the best way to *read* the many selections in this anthology is to talk and write about them. Human beings take language in, by reading, seeing, or listening, but that is only part of the way to full understanding. They go the rest of the way when they turn it over for themselves, in their own words, and try to describe what it says to them.

As you will see when you read the Introductions to Poetry, Fiction, Drama, and the Essay, we frequently encourage you to write about the works in order to better understand them. Write to question them. Write to discover how they connect with your personal life. Write to try out an interpretation. Write to see if your critical reading matches the reading of others. Write to communicate to someone else what you have found. Write to create a similar work yourself. Or write, as some of the authors in this book must have done, simply to have fun.

One of our favorite ways of writing about literature is in a personal journal or notebook where your primary audience is really yourself. This is the kind of writing you don't necessarily even show to anybody else, but which helps you figure out what the reading is all about, how it works, and why it was perhaps assigned in the first place. For this reason we have included a chapter on "Journal Writing" right up front in this book: it's the best writing to be doing *while* you are reading, providing a handy place to jot down a reference, an idea, a memory even before you have finished this or that work. We have made suggestions for journal-writing topics throughout the different sections of the book. These would be good places to start; however, we also believe the most useful entries you will write will be those you invent for yourself.

CHAPTER

ONE

Journal Writing

Toby Fulwiler

> For me the journal is not simply a place to record my thoughts, but a place to develop them more objectively; it acts as sort of a mirror for my ideas.

When we write about anything, we learn it better. In fact, I think the most important reason to write in the first place is for ourselves, for what happens in our own minds when we make concrete our otherwise scattered and fragmentary thought. Finding words, generating sentences, constructing paragraphs is also our way of finding, generating, and constructing the meaning of our world. In other words, one of the most powerful reasons for writing is not to convey a message *to* someone else, but to find out for ourselves that we have a message and that we understand its shape and content.

This is where journals come in: they are notebooks kept by writers and thinkers primarily for themselves as a means of methodically locating, collecting, and making sense of their own thoughts. When we write to ourselves, as we do in journals, diaries, and notebooks, we concentrate on what *we* are thinking about, rather than the shape of our words or how some distant audience will react to them.

ASSIGNED JOURNALS

Journals written for college classes differ from private diaries written for yourself. While historically the two terms have been used interchangeably, today we can make a useful distinction between them: diaries are personal notebooks that contain private thoughts, memories, feelings, dreams—things of importance to the writer and nobody else. Journals, however, have a more limited focus; they center more on the point where writers' personal lives meet their intellectual and social lives—in this case, centering on that meeting as it takes place in the study of literature.

If your English teacher has asked you to keep a journal, it is probably with the hope that you will use it to locate, collect, and make sense of your thoughts about the content of your literature class: about your reactions to the novels, plays, or poems; about your role in class discussions; about your candid reactions to particular lectures; about first ideas for writing assignments and later thoughts on revising those assignments; about connections between this course and others you are taking. And about the personal connections you may make between this course and the rest of your life—whatever they may be.

It might also help to separate journals from class notebooks. Unlike diaries, class notebooks contain almost nothing at all that is personal, being filled as they are with other people's ideas: lecture and discussion notes, copied quotations, next week's assignments, and so on. These notebooks are especially useful to help you pass examinations, but that's about it. Think of your journal as a cross between a diary (subjective) and a class notebook (objective): in the journal you write about the object of study from your own personal perspective—and you write primarily to yourself. Here's how I might diagram that difference:

DIARY-------JOURNAL--------CLASS NOTEBOOK

The key difference between a diary kept exclusively for yourself and a journal assigned for a class is obvious: your professor will probably want to look at your journal from time to time. She or he may want to look through it to see what you are thinking about William Shakespeare, Herman Melville, or Nikki Giovanni. If your teacher wants to look at your journal, chances are good that it is not to grade it in any conventional sense. More likely, the teacher wants to see if you have written regularly, often, and at length, about ideas related to the course. I cannot, of course, guarantee that your teacher will look at it this way. That is simply how most English teachers I know use journals. You'll have to check with your teacher to be sure.

Students commonly have questions about journals; they wonder about the mix of public and private expected in an assigned journal. In fact, one student, Missy, described her concern this way:

> 9/3 For three years now I've kept a journal on my own—a personal one, that I sort of talk to when I'm troubled or confused about things. It's like talking to a friend who just listens with great patience and never argues with me. But now I'm supposed to keep one for my English class and I'm not sure how that will work—I don't see how I can write personal things in a book that my professor is going to read. How can a journal be both personal and kept for a class at the same time?

These are good questions. In the rest of this chapter, I will try to lay out the territory of the journal to make clear what it might look like, how it might work, and what you might put in it.

UNASSIGNED JOURNALS

It is entirely possible that your literature instructor has not asked you to keep a journal—or has made it a recommendation and intends to do nothing specifically or formally with it. In either case, the journal is one assignment you may choose to do yourself, independent of any instructional intention. Few of us would write other academic assignments on our own—term papers, for instance—without being required to. But many people do elect to keep journals because they are both intellectually useful and easy to do.

As a literature student, you will find that personal notebooks (sometimes called journals and sometimes diaries) have a long and respected literary history. Some authors even became famous because they wrote private accounts of their lives: Samuel Pepys's *Diary* remains one of the liveliest accounts of seventeenth-century England in existence; James Boswell's eighteenth-century *London Journal* is as famous as anything else he wrote. Many of us know Anaïs Nin only because of the *Diaries* in which she describes life in mid-twentieth-century Paris. Some journals, such as those by William Byrd and William Bradford in the seventeenth century, are especially useful for their historical information about the settlement of colonial America—as were the nineteenth-century journals of the explorers Lewis and Clark.

As a teacher of nineteenth-century American literature, I can attest to the centrality of journals to the lives of some of our best writers. Those of Ralph Waldo Emerson and Henry David Thoreau contain nearly all the germinal ideas and language for their later well-known masterpieces. *Walden,* in fact, retains many of the characteristics of an actual journal; it takes readers chronologically through the cycle of a year, from summer to spring. Journals, diaries, and letters are also interesting because they provide crucial insights into the personalities of complex writers.

Journals are worth your while for another reason: they really do help you sort out your ideas while you are taking the course. They help you understand what you are reading, which in turn helps you participate with more confidence in class discussion. They help you prepare for exams, because whenever you write about an idea, you improve your chances of remembering it. And they help if you have formal papers to write, because they let you try out and play with ideas before you commit them to the judgment to which essays and term papers are usually subjected.

Then too, journals prove to be documents worth saving and rereading at other times in your life. Sometimes the real value of a journal isn't even apparent until months or years later, when the writer or the writer's family finds it a remarkable record of thought frozen in time, revealing as do photograph albums a person at another stage of development. Every time I reread an old journal of mine I find it a benchmark against which to measure my current life. Having kept journals on and off since I was a college sophomore, I have lots of benchmarks.

For some time now, I have asked students in my American literature classes to keep journals to help them understand the books, authors, ideas, and environment that constitutes literary study. In general, I have found the journals to be the best writing assignment I give: the frequent writing both in class and out allows all of us time to find and share insights. My students seem to like the noncompetitive climate journals encourage; I enjoy the way journals let me see my students' more candid reactions to the books they read in the course.

In the rest of this chapter, I will share with you some of the uses my students have found for journals in their study of American literature. I trust that students of any literary period or genre may find good ideas here.

WRITING ABOUT READING

One specific way to use your journal is to write about everything you read. Keep your journal with your books, and every time you read a chapter or an article, jot down your reaction to what you just read. Don't worry about sounding profound; try instead to pin down and express what interests or annoys you or makes your curious or confused. Write honestly in your own voice. If you have a little more time, reflect on why you reacted as you did—why were you excited, angry, bored, empathetic, sympathetic? In the following entry, David writes about his first encounter with Herman Melville's long novel *Moby Dick:*

> Moby has begun. It's nice to be reading a story again instead of the transcendentalists. . . . I actually had a lot of fun with Ralph, Hank, and Walt, but I'm ready for a novel. Herman says some cool things right from the start. He is fascinated with water. . . .

I hear the voice of the David I know in class—a bright and good-humored sophomore. In this entry he writes as he talks, easily and with a slight irreverence, yet showing he's read the work and is ready to talk about it in his own terms.

In the process of reading, it's always a good idea to guess and conjecture about what's going on, because that helps you keep track of what you read, as well as read with more focus. In the following entry, also about *Moby Dick,* Susan expresses her apprehensions about how the novel will end:

> It's an awful thing to say, but I wish Starbuck had killed Ahab with that musket. If Ahab is shot there will be only one life lost, but since Starbuck decides not to do it, I have a feeling the whole crew will be lost because of Ahab's vengeance.

When several of my students read this short William Carlos Williams poem their readings differed greatly:

This Is Just to Say

I have eaten
the plums
that were in
the icebox

and which
you were probably
saving
for breakfast

Forgive me
they were delicious
so sweet
and so cold

John wrote the following first response in his journal:

> A very simple poem. It's a note telling someone he ate the plums that were in the ice box. I can't believe this is poetry, it is usually so hard to understand.

Eric, though equally confused, wrote much harder to make sense of the poem, asking many questions along the way.

> The title of this poem seems to be begging for an apology. Maybe for eating the plums. But then if it is I think I missed the point. It seems too damn simple. What are the plums supposed to represent? Why does he apologize by saying he couldn't resist their sweetness and coldness? Is it supposed to be a love poem? Are ''plums, breakfast, delicious, sweet,'' all allusions to sex? I think he needs a bigger club to hit me over the head with.

Which of these is a better journal entry? From a teacher's perspective, we could actually say that John didn't struggle very hard to understand why this was a poem and settled for his first response. From a teacher's perspective, we could say that Eric struggled *too hard,* trying to fit it into poetic traditions that it does not easily fit. However, a better answer might be that each writer used his journal in a way that was useful to him. We would actually hope that as they each read other poems, John would sometimes ask more questions, Eric sometimes relax and simply enjoy them. Journals are good places to do both.

ANSWERING

Sometimes your journal is a good place to try answering questions, those you pose yourself and those posed by your teacher. In the following entry Robin, a freshman, writes in response to a first-day question: "How do you learn?"

> I learn through reading which gives me a general description of a subject and gives me the tools to begin discussing that subject. Once I have a basic idea I learn best by watching . . . and talking about the subject with another person. I learn and remember best through exciting experiences such as my trip to Jamaica. . . .

Later in this same journal, Robin writes her way to an answer about whether or not the world of Edgar Allan Poe was a *real* world:

> Haven't we all at one time or another experienced a nagging conscience from guilt or shame (''Black Cat'')? And isn't the external appearance of someone or something often a reflection of the inner person's feeling or attitudes (''House of Usher'')? So, even though these horror stories were gruesome and sometimes difficult to comprehend, I think Poe in his own way was trying to tell us something about his feelings and something about the real world.

Robin's *answer* comes from relating her experience of reading Poe to something (she doesn't tell what, nor need she) that she has experienced in the past. By connecting *through writing* Poe's fiction to her own reality, she increases both her understanding and her chances of remembering later what she has read. And by inserting the parenthetical notes, she reminds herself (and shows me) what she was thinking about—a useful reference to have a few weeks from now, when the specific idea that prompted this entry has faded.

ASKING

Throughout the course of our normal day, we run a lot of questions and problems through our head, most having to do with things that bother us personally, some having to do with what we are studying. Keeping a journal provides a place to collect these questions (both personal and academic), to articulate them precisely, and with luck, to lead answers. Recording such questions provides you with a focus for your reading and something to talk with teacher or classmates about. In the following example, Marcia generates questions from her reading of *Walden:*

> I was rather confused at the beginning of this chapter. What is the deal with the conversation between the Hermit and Thoreau?
>
> What really caught my attention was the specific description of the fight between the black and the red ants. In this chapter is Thoreau trying to put his friends (wild animals) on the same line as those people in the village?

Marcia uses her journal to wonder about what she reads. The more she does this, the better will be her chances of asking for clarification in class or, better still, of writing her way to her own answers. In journals, it's a good idea to write "I'm confused" when you are—and to take guesses at resolving that confusion. I often suggest that my poetry students use their journals to write about the lines in the poem they *least* understand—which, of course, usually leads to some kind of understanding.

At other times the journal will serve as a place to think through questions posed by your teacher before you need to make a public statement. In the following example, I asked another one of those first-day general questions to find out how my students would define "the humanities"; here is how Jennifer started her journal entry:

> A definition of the Humanities? Kind of a tough question. I really didn't have any idea before class discussion today. A dictionary definition probably wouldn't help either. They never do. So I guess by remembering what was said I'll have to think of something myself. . . .

Notice that this journal writer uses her natural voice, almost like her speaking voice. We think best in comfortable language, so I'm pleased that Jennifer will give the thinking all her attention and let the language take care of itself.

SEEING

Writing about what you see helps you see it better. This is true of a scientist in a chemistry laboratory, a biologist out in the field, or a literary scholar examining texts line by line. Writing the observation (1) focuses it, (2) makes the sighting more precise, and (3) actually pushes the visual toward the conceptual.

In the following entry, Richard responds to my question about the nature of the detail on the first page of the Edgar Allan Poe story "The Fall of the House of Usher":

> The mood of the entire first paragraph is such that we feel the impending doom of this guy's situation. Even in the first sentences he seems to be buried, in a sense, in his own living tomb—dark, dreary, soundless, the clouds hanging over him ''oppressively.'' His first glance at the house of Usher leaves such a sense of horror, with its bleak walls and eye-like windows. . . . What stood out to me most though was his personification of the house. . . . Roderick Usher pretty much mirrors the house, and all those descriptive words about the house hold true for Roderick as well.

By writing out both paraphrases and direct quotations of what he found on the page, Richard "sees" that page better. Even if he never rereads this entry, writing it out has increased his chances of understanding and remembering that Poe passage for a long time to come. A good exercise? Write all you can in your journal about what you find on the first page of a novel, story, or essay. It's a good way to train yourself to read closely.

CONNECTING AND EXTENDING

One of the best things you can do with a journal is make connections between what you are reading and other parts of your life—your home life or your school life. In the following entry Margaret has read Gwendolyn Brooks's poem "We Real Cool" (see p. 611) and in trying to make sense of its unusual structure, discovers something else:

> I still wonder what the structure has to do with anything. . . . Maybe he wants you to know that these boys stick together through thick and thin. . . . Actually, it doesn't even have to be boys. All it says is ''The Pool Players, Seven at the Golden Shovel.'' There could be girls in this bunch too. Our stereotypes just don't let me think that girls hang around somewhere playing pool. . . . I used to play all the time and so did my sisters, but we never played anywhere other than at home. That's kind of weird.

What is especially interesting here is that Margaret's writing—the fact that she was doing it—led her to an insight about the poem and her own cultural stereotypes.

Another kind of connection occurs when you use your literature journal to comment on your other classes. Sometimes you will see parallels between the history, philosophy, religion, and literature of a period, such as those which existed in Concord, Massachusetts, in the 1840s and 1850s. At other times the connections will be less central, but the act of regular writing will help you see them. In the following entry, Sam reflects on his learning in a business class before going on to write about Benjamin Franklin:

> I can't believe how time consuming my BSAD 60 (accounting) class is. The teacher knows his stuff but he goes way too fast. It reminds me of what we talked

about in class yesterday. It's hard to learn if you have to write and think at the same time. Back to Ben. . . .

You don't keep a literature journal for purposes of writing like this, but sometimes a quick reflection clears your mind and lets you concentrate better on the business at hand—in this case, paying attention to Ben Franklin.

RETHINKING

Journals can help you see and re-see your own ideas, and in the process help you to modify and extend them in new and different directions. Look at Bobby's entry as she tries to make sense out of Emily Dickinson's poem "I Heard a Fly Buzz When I Died":

Boy . . . I was on the wrong track with Emily Dickinson completely!! Completely!! I was—I felt rushed and summarized her—how ridiculous. I didn't even read this poem on page 111. . . . It helps so much to try to take a poem literally—first. I was jumping to profound conclusions.

OK. So in this poem nothing happens. Nothing happens in the sense that she doesn't get at enlightenment as expected. You know she is rather anxious for this expectation but fails at following it through. I cannot believe how much there is in this little poem. She ends her poem pessimistically, yet . . . she begins it optimistically because of her anxiety to reach her enlightenment—her death.

Sometimes the act of writing an observation in your journal causes you to rethink on the spot. You read your own words and see them from a distance not possible when they float loosely in your head, and sometimes you simply take them back, muttering "That's not what I meant at all." For example, Trey wrote the following as he analyzed a short story by Edgar Allan Poe:

The first thing that struck me about ''The Black Cat'' was Poe's opening paragraph. Poe has this quirk about telling us that what he is about to say is so horrible that it's extremely hard to believe. Well, I think it's unnecessary because in the first place it didn't <u>really</u> happen. So we're going to believe just the same with or without the opening paragraph.

Wait a minute, I don't know what I just wrote. I think that paragraph does a lot, it explains the narrator's feelings <u>now</u> so when we go back in time we understand the narrator more. ANYWAY, in the story Poe did some amazing things. . . .

Both Bobby and Trey were prolific writers; each of their journals approached two hundred pages. By making the writing part of their daily routine, they increased the chances of both catching and generating insights about whatever they chose as topics.

CONVERSATIONS

If you are asked to keep a journal by a teacher, chances are she or he will look at it occasionally to see your concerns, and whether or not the class is making sense to you. You can use the journal as well to initiate a dialogue between you and your instructor about things that do concern you but that you haven't time to talk about in person. Here is a snatch of conversation that occurred between Missy and me in an advanced writing class:

MISSY: Look, I want to learn to write well. I want to squeeze as much learning out of this class as possible. Because it means something to me and I care a lot about it. I'm not motivated—at least not like this—by a grade. O.K.? Is the air clear? I want to learn as much of this stuff as I can and semesters are short! So I write hard and I think hard about it a lot . . ., and need the same degree of feedback.

TOBY: Fair enough. You write seriously in here and I'll write seriously back. I agree with you. Too much so-called dialogue between teacher and student is perfunctory or required or something other than real talk shared between people thinking and learning together. Thanks for the candid note!

Sometimes students give me suggestions in their journals, often about the way I'm handling some assigned reading. In Bill's American literature journal, I found this entry:

> Before starting to write on Moby Dick, I would like to make a special request . . . . that you maybe give a second thought to assigning a 500 page book like Moby Dick in the last few weeks of classes.

Bill actually expressed this sentiment aloud in class, and as a class, we talked it through. In truth, next time I assigned *Moby Dick* I *did* think twice about assigning it late in the term and moved it up a week in the schedule. Of course, journals are not letters; they are written primarily to oneself. But in the somewhat artificial learning environment called school, they may accomplish some of the expressive communication between teacher and student usually reserved for the more formal medium of letters or the more informal one of talk.

WHAT JOURNALS LOOK LIKE

Here are a few suggestions for keeping a journal. Keep in mind that a journal is, fundamentally, a collection of thoughts captured at different moments in time. Remember too that a teacher who requires a journal may want it to be done in a particular way. If not, here are some suggestions that work well:

1. Buy a small looseleaf notebook and divide it into several sections. Use one section to collect your reading notes; use another to write whatever else you are thinking about the course, reactions to class discussion and the like; use yet another section for personal ideas, reflections, and feelings that have nothing to do with the course. If you like, make up other sections for things like scrapbook clippings, profound observations about other classes, and any other categories of ideas you want to keep track of or wrestle with. I like the partitions in my journal because they help me organize my thoughts and my life; yet I know others

insist on keeping all the entries together, the unifying principle being simply the chronology of the dates.

2. Write often, regularly, and at length. I write as frequently as I can in my journal, sometimes in the morning with a cup of coffee, sometimes before I go to bed. I intend to write every day, but often that doesn't work out: sometimes I skip a day; other days I write twice. I have learned that the habit of regular writing increases my chances of finding and developing ideas, but it's a haphazard process. Sometimes I think I have a lot to say and nothing much comes out; sometimes I start to write strictly from habit and surprise myself with good ideas. Authors like Ernest Hemingway disciplined themselves to write daily, regardless of inspiration, for essentially the same reason: the discipline will make it more likely that if something is there, you'll find it. I give myself a full new page for each entry, if only to suggest that I have lots of space with which to play.

3. Write in your most natural voice. The journal is the place where a writer can relax and concentrate on *what* she or he is writing about rather than *how*. There's a good reason for this: the degree to which we worry about matters of form, grammar, mechanics, or style is the degree to which we are distracted from the naked thought before us. Worry about clean, nice-looking, organized language in other places; in the journal, stick with what matters most to you as a thinker and writer.

4. Write double entries. A wonderful idea described by Ann Berthoff in *Forming, Thinking, Writing* (Hayden, 1978) is the double-entry notebook. It works like this: write only on the right-hand pages of your journal; keep the left page blank. Periodically—once or twice a week—return to your earlier entries and comment on them, expanding, modifying, arguing as the purpose suits you. In other words, on left-hand pages adjacent to right-hand entries, write about your former writing and develop a dialogue with your past self. It's amazing to see how ideas change even within the span of a week, if we make writing a regular habit.

5. Index your journal. A former teacher, Dixie Goswami, taught me this trick. At the end of the semester, put in page numbers, titles for each entry, a contents, and write an introduction. This will make your journal a nice-looking, organized document to share with a professor—if he or she wants to see it—but the real purpose is once again for yourself. The act of reviewing and organizing the journal takes you once again through nineteenth-century American or seventeenth-century British authors, now from more distance. Rereading and re-seeing your journal in this fashion is quite simply one of the best synthesizing activities I know of to prepare well for both final examination and further literary study.

One final note: Journal writing is essentially whatever you make it. Of all the modes of writing described in this book, this one gives you the greatest freedom to make it what you want. If you are studying literature, you will probably write a lot about your reading; if you are studying composition or creative writing, what you write about will be virtually unlimited. In any case, the journal is your territory—explore it, map its boundaries, and cultivate it well.

CHAPTER

TWO

Fiction: The Story of a Story

Allen Shepherd and Ghita Orth

Introduction

In thinking about how we would share ideas about reading, interpreting, and evaluating fiction with you in this chapter, we decided to have you join us in a conversation with a talented fiction writer and some of our interested students who have been studying fiction. So we invited David Huddle to share with us a story that we could look at and talk about in some detail. Our other collaborators, students from an Introduction to Literature class, have read Huddle's story, talked about it in class, written about it, and had the unusual opportunity to discuss it with the author. Through this chapter, you will be able to participate in these activities as we investigate the whole process of fiction writing.

This chapter, then, is the story of a story, one called "Summer of the Magic Show." We will study this story for the same reasons we would study any other piece of literature—to help us understand it better; we want to discover what it says and how it says it. We especially want to understand why the story affects the reader the way it does, and to see if we can participate in the creative process that made the story in the first place.

An active reader often has a conversation with a text and, through that text, with the author. In this instance, because we have the author on hand to talk to, we have the opportunity for an unusually complete and revealing conversation.

Huddle, our chapter's writer in residence, says he writes fiction as a way of understanding, of finding out what he knows. His stories communicate to their readers what has evolved in that process of discovering meaning, a process not very different from that of anyone trying to make sense of some aspect of his or her world by writing about it.

The story that follows, "Summer of the Magic Show," began with an experience that Huddle had as a teenager in a small town in rural Virginia when a girl he knew slightly came to dinner at his home. It became the germ of a story because he remembered it so vividly, because it had stayed with him over the years for reasons he didn't quite grasp but wanted to understand.

But Huddle is a fiction writer, and fiction, as we know, is imagined, "made up." How can stories that use autobiographical experience as material be called "fiction"? John Cheever, an American short-story writer, maintained that the role of autobiography in fiction is precisely the role of reality in dreams. Certainly we can say that before storytellers can begin to create a believable fictional world, they must know something of what the real world is like—from close observation, from what they read or hear about, or from their personal histories. Out of their sense of how real people may think, feel, and live in the world, they make their fictions. Huddle believes it is incidental that many of his stories have autobiographical sources. He feels no obligation to the actual facts once a story has begun. Like all fiction, his stories investigate not the truth of facts but the truths of shared human experience.

In "Summer of the Magic Show," for example, some incidents actually happened and some were invented. When you read this story, however, all of its details will probably seem equally "real." They are real to us because Huddle has been able to find their essential truth through writing about them, an act in which we participate through thoughtful reading. The reading of fiction, then, like its writing, can be an imaginative process of discovering meaning.

You will realize when you read "Summer of the Magic Show" that fiction is the most natural, familiar, and accessible of literary forms. It is also, like other art forms, ultimately mysterious; that is, we can go only so far in explaining it. But from the "once upon a time" of childhood, we do *know* about fiction and almost instinctively understand what makes a good story.

* * * * *

Summer of the Magic Show

My father did the best he could with a custom my mother invented without consulting him. She didn't consult me either, but since it was something she was doing for me, as she saw it, she didn't need to know what I thought about it. On my birthday I was to ask a girl to our house for dinner.

To put it in straightforward terms, girls made my father uncomfortable. He was a courtly man. When we ate in the dining room, which was when we had company, he stood and held my mother's chair for her until she came to sit down. He spoke with elaborate courtesy to all the women on my mother's side of the family and said yes ma'am and no ma'am to most of them. In fact, I always felt that in the presence of women, my mother excepted, my father was never himself. He limited his conversation to expressing agreement with the people around him or to asking questions of them. If questioned himself, he phrased his replies in such a way as to generalize or abstract whatever he was telling, so that his opinions, in this voice, were dull, his experiences hardly worth mentioning. My father was a man who had once faced an old tool shed full of rattlesnakes, who had been shot at by union strikers, who had taken a knife away from Bernard Seeger at a high school dance, but around women, especially around the women who came to our house as company, my father took on the personality of someone who'd stayed indoors and eaten nothing but cheese sandwiches all his life.

And it was a formidable girl who came to our house that first time, on my fourteenth birthday: Jean Sharp. She was from Palm Beach, and even though she was only thirteen, she must have thought Rosemary was as far back in the wilderness as anybody ever went. She had very fine dark hair, a small nose and mouth, a lanky frame, and no breasts whatsoever. I mowed her grandmother's lawn in those summers when she used to visit Rosemary, and that summer, when I finished the mowing, old Mrs. Sharp had me come in for lemonade while she paid me, coaxed some conversation out of me while I stood sweating in her kitchen, and then when it looked like Jean and I might be able to carry on by ourselves, suggested that we go into the living room and play cards. Jean taught me cribbage while sitting forward on the sofa with her back very straight, her knees bent and together, her ankles crossed. Jean wore sundresses all that summer, and they emphasized her flatchestedness, but there was something about her in those dresses, her thin shoulders maybe, that was sexy in an otherworldly kind of way. Her fingers playing the cards or moving the pegs on the cribbageboard held my attention some of the time, and her soft voice, her precise diction, made me feel I was learning something every time she spoke to me. My father probably hadn't seen Jean more than a couple of times in all her summers of visiting her grandmother in Rosemary, but when he heard she was coming to our house for my birthday dinner, his face showed that he dreaded it, and I sort of knew why. I dreaded it, too. It was one thing to play cards with her over lemonade in her grandmother's cool, dark living room, and another to have her come to eat with us at our dining room table.

That was the summer of my brother's magic show, and Jean was who he'd picked to be the floating lady. I was one of his assistants, the one in fact who pulled the chair out from under Jean's feet so that, after wobbling just a little bit, she floated in the air under my brother's spell, and he passed a hoop from her feet to her head and then back again to show there were no strings holding her up. I was always embarrassed standing there to one side, watching. I thought there was a chance I'd see up Jean's dress, and Jean was a girl whose dress I didn't want to see up.

My brother, the magician, was delighted she was coming to have dinner with us. Even back then he had this hyperbolic way of talking about people: Happy Sult was the greatest drum major in the history of our high school, or Jack Fleming was the second greatest steel guitar player in southwest Virginia, things like that. About Jean I heard him telling our mother in the kitchen, "She's truly beautiful, don't you think?" This was just before Jean's grandmother drove her up there, and my father and I exchanged glances in the living room when we heard Duncan talking like that. We knew Jean wasn't "truly beautiful." Truly beautiful was Esther Williams, Jane Russell, Anita Ekberg. Jean was just a girl who was visiting in our town. Duncan didn't have to exaggerate what she was, but we were used to him, and my father and I were both grateful to him for doing most of the talking when Jean first walked into the house.

She had on another sundress, this one white with a sort of primly high front to it. It set off her tanned shoulders and face, her dark hair. Something about the way that dress fit her at the arms bothered me, though; it made a loose place where, I knew, if you looked at the right angle, you'd have seen her breast, or what should have been her breast. There were girls at school whose dresses I'd tried to look up and whose breasts I'd strained my neck trying to get a peek at, but they weren't like Jean. I didn't want to see into her dress, but sitting beside her at the table, I could hardly help noticing that opening every time I cast my eyes in her direction. To make things worse, I became aware of the sounds my father made as he ate. Courtly man that he was, his table manners, or rather the things that went on between him and the food on his plate, were pretty crude. He took large bites of things, and there was a kind of liquid inhaling noise that went with each bite. Often he chewed with his mouth open, so that you could hear it, and he liked to roll the food around in his mouth so that he made sloshing noises. Over the years I thought a good deal about my father's way of eating, and my conclusion was that it resulted from his courtliness: his way of signaling to my mother that he liked the food was to make eating noises that expressed his liking for it, his gratitude to her for cooking it for him. The noises had to be loud enough for her to hear him at the opposite end of the table, and I expect they were that evening, even though he was holding back on Jean's account. The open place in Jean's dress, my father's eating noises, and my brother's exaggerated chattering—he was telling us all what a great pianist Alan Peltier was even though he couldn't read a note of music—all of these elements had me on the verge of a nervous collapse there on the occasion of my fourteenth birthday when Jean suddenly got choked on a sip of iced tea.

She was all right, of course. Nobody ever died of iced tea going down the wrong way, at least not that I know of, and you would think the incident—Jean gasping and coughing into her napkin, my father and brother and I rising to pound on her back, though not one of us was going to touch those elegant shoulders unless she got really serious about her choking, my mother coming around the table and saying, Oh, you poor dear, you poor thing—you'd think the incident would have humanized us all. It didn't. There was a short moment after Jean had recovered and we'd all gone back to our places when nobody made a sound, one of those embarrassing lulls in the conversation that usually are broken by somebody's giggling. In this case my mother managed a feeble, "Well . . . ," and then we had more silence before we fell back to eating and my father's mouth noises commenced again. The main difference was that now I could hardly bear Jean's presence. Sitting beside her I lost my appetite.

That was the last angel food cake with pink icing that my mother ever made for my birthday, though I have never stopped thinking of it as the only legitimate kind of cake for a birthday. I think my mother must also have experienced some kind of turning at the moment of Jean Sharp's choking that summer evening at our house, the white curtains at the three bay windows of our dining room not even slightly stirring and enough light still lingering in the yard outside so that fireflies had not come out yet, the frogs and crickets were keeping quiet, and even the bats that lived in the unused side of our chimney hadn't begun their darting in the air all around our house.

My brother's magic show was a success later that summer, and I never had to look up Jean's dress in our rehearsals or in our performances of the floating lady trick. One night there were some whistles and a few lewd calls at her from the audience, because of course the young men and boys of our town resented her as they would have resented almost any visitor, especially a pretty girl, from Palm Beach or anywhere else. But by then I had reached a state of serene objectivity about Jean Sharp. I didn't like to be around her, but I continued to think that I ought to be attracted to her. The *didn't* and the *ought to* canceled each other out, and I felt nothing. One night Herky Thompson and Marcy Pless, a distant cousin of Jean's, took us with them on a double-date to the drive in. (Marcy's mother made them do it.) Jean and I sat stiffly in the back seat doing our best to concentrate on *Rio Grande* while Herky and Marcy coiled around each other in Marcy's corner of the front seat. I snuck an arm around Jean—she was wearing a sweater—and though I know she was aware of my arm, I felt no loosening of her good posture, no impulse on her part to lean my way. At the time I resented her for that coldness, but since then I've decided that hers was the greater sensitivity: she felt no real affection or desire in that arm behind her, those fingers lightly touching her shoulder; she didn't respond because I didn't offer her any part of myself to which she could respond.

My brother never understood why I didn't more avidly pursue "The Exquisite Miss Sharp," as he had taken to calling her, and I wouldn't have been inclined to explain it to him even if I had understood my feelings about her. It was my father who gave me the most comfort in that time, my father who seemed to understand what was going on even if I didn't. After the birthday dinner we all sat for an excruciating length of time in the living room, and I found myself copying my father's manner. I agreed with things my brother said, things my mother said, and especially things Jean said. When the rhythm of conversation demanded that I say something, I asked Jean a question about Palm Beach.

When my father stood up to signal that he wished the occasion to be over, I was the first one to rise and second his motion. Standing by the car he instructed Jean and me to ride in the back seat while he drove us to her grandmother's. By that time the fireflies were out, the bats were swooping over our heads, and there was a lovely fragrance over the whole yard, but Jean seemed glad to be climbing into the car. When he saw that she and I weren't going to have too much to say to each other on the drive across the ridge and around town, my father turned on the radio. I've always been grateful to him for that, because I know for a fact that he hated the car radio, especially the hillbilly and rhythm & blues stations that were all we could get at night in our part of the country. I walked Jean up onto her grandmother's front porch, said a quickly retreating goodnight, and scuttled back to sit in the front seat with my father. In his kindness he neither asked me anything nor said a word to me. He turned off the radio of course, and he took his time driving back home. The two of us were quiet the whole way, watching the road in the headlights and occasionally glancing out our side windows at the dark. Then, at exactly the same moment, though our tunes were different, we each began whistling through our teeth.

* * * * *

Although Huddle, like the rest of us, writes to make discoveries about his world, he knows, as we do, that there are readers out there who will be responding to the results of that process, asking and answering questions. What, for example, are some questions you might have about the story? What kinds of responses do you have to it?

INFORMAL WRITING

Does the story in this draft seem complete? Self-sustaining? Are there any things you want to know more about? If so, what?

RESPONDING TO THE STORY

Reading and writing are, as we've said, reciprocal activities; writer and reader touch each other through the text with which they are both involved. For Huddle, readers are important contributors to the revising phase of his process of composition. He calls them his "helpers."

When Huddle completed this draft of "Summer of the Magic Show," he turned it over to such "helpers"—first to friends and fellow writers. Huddle says that sharing his drafts with his peers for their responses (an activity many of us may be familiar with) gives him the chance to gain some distance from his work, to re-see it objectively from another's perspective.

One of Huddle's colleagues, for example, responded to "Summer of the Magic Show" this way: "I like this because of its size—because in less than nine full pages it is complete." Huddle, in fact, was pleased with the story for the same reason.

Another fellow writer, however, had reservations. She wrote on Huddle's typed draft, "I would urge you only to re-write somewhat—and amplify—the brother's character (which seems too swiftly and obliquely drawn). Otherwise, this is a fine story." How does Huddle feel about this kind of response, with its implied criticism and suggestions for improvement? "I'm always willing to listen to suggestions," he says, explaining further that such comments often open up the story for him. Like considered responses to any piece of writing, they can raise new possibilities for the material that the writer might not otherwise have recognized.

In the same spirit, Huddle regularly sends stories out to magazines and journals. He hopes, of course, that they will be accepted for publication, but is ready to use rejections as part of his process of re-thinking and re-seeing a story. For example, Huddle sent "Summer of the Magic Show" to *The Atlantic Monthly,* a prestigious literary magazine. Although he received a personal note rather than the far more common printed rejection slip, a compliment many writers would be delighted with, this was the reply: "The writing is lovely and this is very funny in spots. But the whole seems to us slight and low-key." He also sent the manuscript to *Yankee Magazine,* a journal of regional interests, and again it was returned. This editor explained, "We find 'Summer of the Magic Show' appealing but inconclusive. Please continue to send your work."

Why, then, didn't Huddle just toss the story into the nearest wastebasket, as we might have been tempted to? Because he knew that such criticism could be helpful to him, challenging him to make the story as good as he could make it through revision. As do most writers, Huddle values such readers' responses as part of his writing process; they enable him to send his work out into the world again, stronger for the rewriting it may have undergone.

As fiction's general, nonprofessional, readers, your attentive responses are also a major concern to fiction writers; you are their audience. In fact, student readers of this draft of "Summer of the Magic Show" wrote responses very similar to those of Huddle's more professional "helpers."

Tim, for example, liked the draft: "I enjoy extremely *short* stories," he wrote. "In my opinion, this story is complete." Darlene, however, disagreed: "I think we need to know more about Duncan, and also the narrator's relationships with the other characters." She also felt, as the editors had, that "the story leaves you wondering about a lot of things."

Many students were puzzled by the story's title, which, Nathan wrote, "suggests more emphasis on the magic show. But this draft emphasizes the way the narrator realizes that he is more like his father than he thought before." Jennifer, however, seemed to discover a connection between story and title as she wrote about the problem: "I didn't really understand why the author picked this title when I first looked at the story. Now I see some symbolism, if not irony, in the title. Literally there is a magic show in the story, but what happens between the father and the son is somewhat magical in that they begin to understand each other."

The process of writing about the story provided Jennifer with a way of discovering meanings in it, but it is not only in writing *answers* to questions about a piece of fiction that we can find out how the piece works and what it may be saying. We can also *ask* questions of the story as we read, and test potential answers as we wonder aloud in our writing. For example, Chris wrote, "The plot could be interesting; however, does it concern a boy's relationship to his father or a boy having adolescent apprehension about girls? Perhaps it is about male-female relationships and reactions to one another, but if so, where does the big brother fit in?" In posing and thinking through these questions, Chris is approaching the story's thematic concerns while also figuring out what, for him, keeps it from seeming unified. Similarly, Alex asked, "Is Jean's choking some sort of awakening for the narrator? The revelation at the end is very vague—what has caused the narrator's feelings?"

Some students, in fact, thought this version of "Summer of the Magic Show" was weak primarily because it didn't seem to provide them with ways of answering such questions to their satisfaction. Elizabeth wrote, "I didn't feel I had enough information to really get a handle on the story. I'd like to know more about the father, and why the boy thought one side of his dad was suppressed around women. I also would like to know more about the mother. And why is the boy so preoccupied with Jean's chest (which she doesn't really have)?"

All thoughtful readers who ask questions of a story and, like these students, look for answers in the text, participate actively in the discovery of meaning in fiction. They join in conversation with writers like Huddle just as his peers and editors did earlier when they read this story and wrote out their reactions to it.

The students whose responses we quote here read Huddle's story after they had spent some weeks reading other stories, and both talking and writing about them. In these weeks they had come to understand a lot about how fiction works, how it communicates meaning. Looking closely at this first version of "Summer of the Magic Show" will suggest ways of becoming this kind of informed, active reader.

EXAMINING THE STORY

By the end of the story's first paragraph, Huddle has introduced four characters—the narrator, his father, his mother, and the girl who is coming to dinner. Huddle has also intimated a possible basis of conflict—that the mother has acted without consulting either the father or her son the narrator. We may imagine (as would happen in some families) that father and son will attempt some resistance. And we may wonder what will happen to the poor girl, who presumably doesn't know about any of this. And shouldn't the boy be able to do what he wants to on his own birthday? In any event, Huddle has set the hook in the reader—we want to read on to find out what happens.

What leads most readers to want to read on are *character* and *plot.* We become interested in characters, the people in fiction, and we want to know what is going to happen to them. When we talk about *plot* we are concerned with the order in which the fiction writer presents what happens. Why does Huddle begin where he begins? Plot also refers to causation: why do things happen the way they do? *Story* refers to all that happens. From the first paragraph it may seem that the mother has plans for her husband and son—to socialize or in some other way improve them.

Character

To aid us in discussing the many different kinds of characters encountered in fiction, we ought to review some standard terminology. The British novelist and essayist E. M. Forster invented the terms *round* and *flat* character. A round character is three-dimensional and humanly complex; such a character may surprise the reader while still maintaining credibil-

ity. A flat character, on the other hand, is two-dimensional, essentially simple, and embodies a single idea or quality. Because there is comparatively little to know about the flat character, he or she is likely to be thoroughly predictable. The term flat is not necessarily negative in connotation, however, for it may be desirable to display only one aspect of a character, to portray, for example, the jealous wife or the loving grandmother.

A *static* character does not change or develop. A *dynamic* character, by contrast, does evolve under the pressure of events, and we recognize the consequences of events upon the character. A *universal* character is both understandable and appealing to all readers, regardless of time or place—a tall order. The universal character will display emotions common to all cultures—love, jealousy, courage—and will engage in actions broadly meaningful. Hemingway's Cuban fisherman, Santiago, of *The Old Man and the Sea,* may qualify. After almost three months without a catch, he ventures alone far out into the Gulf, where he hooks and finally kills a gigantic marlin, but loses it to the sharks, in a universal drama.

Traditionally character has been regarded as the most important component of fiction. How does a writer go about developing a character in fiction? In "Summer of the Magic Show" we listen to our adult narrator recalling—we may even say re-creating—his fourteen-year-old younger self, dramatizing the traumas of male adolescence. We learn, that is, what sort of person he was and what sort of person he has since become. We begin to form an opinion by listening to his *speech,* the words themselves, the rhythm of the sentences, the state of mind they reveal. The narrator's *language* is colloquial, relaxed, reflective, and carefully chosen. He certainly has a gift for phrase-making, as evidenced in his description of his father in the presence of women who came to the house as company: ". . . he took on the personality of someone who'd stayed indoors and eaten nothing but cheese sandwiches all his life."

Everything about Duncan, the narrator's brother, which embarrassed and antagonized the narrator is epitomized in Duncan's phrase for Jean, "The Exquisite Miss Sharp." "Exaggerated chattering" the narrator calls it, and we know what he means. The rather surprising failure of the narrator's mother on the occasion of Jean's choking, a failure of tact, self-possession, coping, is registered in one word: ". . . my mother managed a feeble, 'well.' . . ." Speech, then, set down as monologue or dialogue, is a principal means of character development. We do want to know what people sound like, what they say, or alternatively, what they cannot find to say.

Physical description is another effective means of character development. The character whose description matters most is Jean Sharp; because the narrator is so intensely and ambivalently aware of her, we are offered a precise physical description. "She had very fine dark hair, a small nose and mouth, a lanky frame, and no breasts whatsoever." How she makes the narrator feel is registered in further description: ". . . and her soft voice, her precise diction, made me feel I was learning something every time she spoke to me." Although the narrator's mother sets the plot in motion and his brother provides a kind of negative stimulus, it is only Jean Sharp and his father who are sufficiently important to merit physical description. About the father what matters most, until the end of the story, are his table manners, which are vividly recounted. "He took large bites of things, and there was a kind of liquid inhaling noise that went with each bite. Often he chewed with his mouth open, so that you could hear it, and he liked to roll the food around in his mouth so that he made sloshing noises." Outside of context, this passage certainly makes the father seem wonderfully unattractive. In context, however, we see (and hear) it as a manifestation of his considered politeness, of his country courtliness, and of the narrator's heightened sensitivity.

It is surely by seeing a character in *action* that we most readily and naturally come to understand him or her. Think of the moment when all members of the family stand watching Jean Sharp choking on her iced tea. In this case it is their failure or inability to act which characterizes them. Why don't they do or say something? Is it because they aren't particularly demonstrative people? Is it because this is an awkward moment and they are embarrassed—for her and for themselves? Is it because they all have ambivalent feelings about Jean Sharp choking? Is it because even though they know it's not her fault, they still wish she would just stop?

Or think of the revealing power of *gesture*—the narrator at the drive-in theater putting his arm around Jean. What happens? Absolutely nothing: ". . . though I knew she was aware of my arm, I felt no loosening of her good posture, no impulse on her part to lean my way." Although he didn't feel so at the time, the narrator later concludes that Jean's nonresponse was wholly justified, that she sensed he was giving nothing of himself and deserved nothing in return.

Plot

Good writers don't need plots which are dramatic or violent or even entertaining in order to gain and hold our interest. You could say that the plot of "Summer of the Magic Show" hinges upon things which don't happen, beginning with the mother's not consulting either her husband or son before inventing a custom. And the father is not truly himself but a cheese-sandwich-eater around women, nor do father, mother, or their two sons respond appropriately to poor Jean Sharp choking on her iced tea.

Ultimately Huddle's plot seems to dramatize and celebrate intuitive understanding and shared response—all of this on the last page of the story. We see the process begin as the narrator's father "stood up to signal that he wished the occasion to be over, and I was the first to rise and second his motion." Father has resumed his expected directive role, making things happen the way they ought to happen. This notion is confirmed in the next sentence: "Standing by the car he instructed Jean and me to ride in the back while he drove us to her grandmother's." However briefly, all is once more right with and in the narrator's world, even as to the resumption of natural rhythms, which were seemingly suspended when Jean and the others suffered through dinner. Thus concerning the ride to Jean's grandmother's we read in the next sentence, "By that time the fireflies were out, the bats were swooping over our heads, and there was a lovely fragrance over the whole yard, . . ."

What makes a plot move, what glues the events together, is the kind of tension called *conflict.* One of the opposing forces involved in the conflict is likely to be the central character, generally called the *protagonist.* The other force, or forces, which may be essentially external or essentially internal, include (1) another character (generally called the *antagonist*) or group of characters, (2) the forces of nature or the power of the universe, (3) society or culture, and (4) an aspect of the character's own personality or value system. With the exception of the second listed source, all seem to enter into this story's conflict. With father and son alone together at story's end, whistling different tunes but at the same moment, the tension of conflict has been eased, at least for the time being, providing a certain satisfaction for both the characters and the reader. The resolution, however, is certainly not definitive. On reflection the satisfaction may seem somehow hollow because it joins the narrator and his father in not entirely positive ways in relation to women.

Thinking about how Huddle carries us to his climactic duet, we realize that in structuring the plot he has managed *time* very carefully. The title of the story gives us a chronological frame: it is the "Summer of the Magic Show," which is also the summer of the narrator's fourteenth birthday. Within that summer, of course, Huddle focuses upon only a few exemplary scenes.

Let's take a moment and see just how Huddle organizes the story's time scheme, and then try to determine why. Why does he cut and chop, magnify and expand? In the first two paragraphs he sets up the immediate situation and describes the narrator's father's rather puzzling behavior. The father is almost heroic (as intimated by his prowess with snakes, guns, and knives) but is also nearly pathetic (the cheese-sandwich man). Is it possible that the two aspects of the man can be made to fit together? With the third paragraph the focus shifts to Jean Sharp, who is introduced as a "formidable girl"; we learn of the narrator's earlier encounters with her "in those summers when she used to visit Rosemary. . . ." Toward the end of the paragraph, we learn that both father and son dread the current prospect of her coming to dinner. Male solidarity of a sort is established.

With paragraph 4, Huddle takes a chronological step sideways, so to speak, and associates Jean Sharp with the narrator's brother. Because we see the title appear in the text, we pay close attention: "That was the summer of my brother's magic show, and Jean was who he'd picked to be the floating lady." For some reason Huddle does not seem much interested in developing the magic show at this point, however, and at the beginning of the next paragraph he makes brother Duncan simply one of the family waiting for formidable Jean Sharp's arrival. Duncan actually seems to look forward to her coming, but of course it's not his birthday.

Through the following long paragraph (number 6) Huddle dramatizes the narrator's several causes of acute embarrassment: "[t]he open place in Jean's dress, my father's eating noises, and my brother's exaggerated chattering. . . ." The choking scene fills the next paragraph, which leaves us wondering why the narrator is so repulsed by Jean's gasping and coughing over the iced tea. Why? Probably because, by behaving in so common a fashion, she has destroyed his image of her as a superior being. In short, illogical as it may seem to us, he feels that she has failed him and thus he cannot forgive her.

It is the unnaturalness of this unexpected occurrence that keys the images in the next paragraph. In the dining room the curtains do not stir, while outside the fireflies aren't visible and the frogs and crickets are silent and the bats are still asleep. One would almost expect that soon the earth will stand still and the sun will go out. With the beginning of paragraph 9, Huddle reintroduces the brother and the performance of the magic show and expounds further on the narrator's ambivalent feelings for Jean Sharp. The paragraph provides summary, one remembered scene at the drive-in theater, and then returns us to the traumatic birthday party at which, finally, the father recovers his paternal authority. "It was my father," Huddle writes, "who gave me the most comfort in that time, my father who seemed to understand what was going on even if I didn't."

If plot is the significant order of events in a narrative, what can we say about how Huddle organizes time in "Summer of the Magic Show"? We can say that this story, like most short stories, deals with a relatively short period of time. We can say further that Huddle develops one focal scene of what can't be more than an hour—the narrator's birthday party. Before that scene, he provides some reflections, unrelated to a specific time, about the narrator's father. The opening paragraphs of the story in which the father appears in a seemingly negative or indeterminate light are balanced by the final paragraphs, which are wholly specific as to time, and in which the father—decisive, tactful, kind—is redeemed in his son's sight.

There are of course a number of other ways of arranging time in fiction. The simplest is exemplified in the story organized in unbroken linear fashion, or *chronological order.* Such a story begins, say, when the characters get up in the morning and ends when they go to bed at night. We know about the *flashback,* a way of presenting exposition dramatically, typically by means of characters' recollections. A Latin term sometimes encountered is *in medias res,* which means, literally, in the middle of things. It refers to the practice of opening a story in the middle of the action and then providing information about the beginning of the action. If Huddle had wanted to employ this technique in "Summer of the Magic Show," he might have opened with Jean Sharp choking on her iced tea.

INFORMAL WRITING

Plot and Character

1. Can you remember, or invent, an incident that involves some kind of conflict? Write a rough outline of what happens in it.
2. Who are the characters involved? What are they like? Jot down some notes about them.

Point of View

One of the most crucial decisions a writer makes is which point of view to employ in telling a story. You're probably familiar with the terms "first-person" and "third-person" narration. First-person point of view features an "I" who is a character in the story he or she tells. Huddle begins, you remember, with "My father did the best he could with a custom my mother invented without consulting him. She didn't consult me either, . . ." Because it is a character who is doing the narrating, we prefer the term *character-narrator,* rather than first-person narrator, to describe this method of narration. This term reminds us that the narrator is a participant in the story's action.

Writers and critics commonly believe that the use of the character-narrator creates a sense of immediacy or authenticity, of a story being conveyed directly, without screening or editing. The character-narrator can see and know only what is humanly possible. Such a narrator, that is, cannot read other characters' minds or know what's going on a mile away. He or she may speculate, as Huddle's narrator does, but he can't be wholly sure, for instance, of what Jean Sharp is thinking. From the beginning of Huddle's story, however, it is apparent that the *retrospective narrator* is looking back over many years and that he is relating to us something that he has had time to consider carefully. Near the end of the story, for example, he tells us about how disappointingly Jean Sharp responded to his arm around her shoulder:

> At the time I resented her for that coldness, but since then I've decided that hers was the greater sensitivity: she felt no real affection or desire in that arm behind her, those fingers lightly touching her shoulder; she didn't respond because I didn't offer her any part of myself to which she could respond.

This is a fairly elaborate analysis, and it probably seems persuasive because over the years the narrator has changed his mind: he now believes that he was at fault, that Jean Sharp was perfectly justified in what she did, or didn't do.

Huddle leads us to believe that his narrator is a man whose experience and intelligence and perceptiveness we can depend on. He is a *reliable* narrator. If, however, the narrator were

fourteen, we would probably have some doubts as to how dependable a witness he would be. Such an *unreliable* narrator may be affected by the limitations of youth and inexperience.

In selecting a *tense,* as in selecting a point of view, a fiction writer really has only two choices. Huddle has made the more conventional choice, using the *past tense.* Most stories are written in the past tense, which is easier for the writer to manage and which confers on the narrative a seeming objectivity. Think how different the story would be if told in the *present tense,* as more and more fiction has been over the past twenty years. We as readers would experience the story at the same rate the fourteen-year-old narrator would experience it. Such reflective, conclusive passages as the one quoted above would be impossible, but a present-tense narrative would probably make the action seem more immediate; things would seem to happen more quickly.

In using the past tense, Huddle seems to have made the right decision. So too in using a character-narrator rather than third-person perspective. There are two kinds of third-person perspective. One is *total omniscience.* In total omniscience, the story is told as if it were seen through the eyes of a god; the totally omniscient narrator, that is, may tell what every character thinks, what is happening in distant places, as well as what is going to happen in the future. Total omniscience is seldom encountered in twentieth-century fiction. In much modern fiction, the narrator's knowledge is likely to be consciously limited; for example, the narrator may focus on what one character thinks and perceives. That character provides the central consciousness of the *limited omniscient* form of third-person point of view.

If Huddle had written the story employing the *limited omniscient* point of view, it would be substantially different. Would it have worked as well? Consider this alteration: "His father did the best he could with a custom his mother invented without consulting him. She didn't consult her son either. . . ." Even with just part of the first sentence recast in the third person, differences between points of view begin to be apparent. Limited omniscience seems to convey detachment, authority, coherence, and comprehension on the part of the narrator. But what Huddle is writing about in "Summer of the Magic Show" is an ongoing process of discovery. The story represents the narrator as he was at age fourteen, and as he is now, a good many years later. The narration allows us to register both the storm and stress of adolescence and the fond, amused recollections of adulthood. But what the adult narrator realizes is that he certainly did not understand then and probably does not wholly understand now why these people—his father and mother and brother and Jean Sharp and his younger self—behaved as they did.

INFORMAL WRITING

Point of View

1. Try writing a paragraph that begins to narrate the incident you outlined earlier as told by a character narrator. Now write one as told by a third-person narrator.
2. Which seems more effective to you? Why?

Style

Style has been described as the sum of all the choices an author makes. The aspects of style we will be most concerned with include: (1) diction, (2) abstract and concrete language, (3) imagery, (4) syntax, and (5) tone. Let's take a look at one exemplary passage from the story's second paragraph.

> *My father* was a man *who* had once faced an old tool shed full of rattlesnakes, *who* had been shot at by union strikers, *who* had taken a knife away from Bernard Seeger at a high school dance, *but around women,* especially *around women who* came to our house as company, *my father* took on the personality of someone *who'd* stayed indoors and eaten nothing but cheese sandwiches all his life (emphasis added).

First, the matter of *diction* (word choice). Although we are accustomed to giving close attention to the language of poetry, often we ignore the actual words in which prose fiction is written. Huddle's diction is commonplace and *concrete.* We read about a tool shed and a high school dance and cheese sandwiches. These are not intellectually *abstract* terms; instead as *imagery* they appeal to our five senses.

The passage quoted is all one sentence, seventy-one words long, but it's easily understood. The secret is in the *syntax* (sentence structure), principally in the parallel construction Huddle uses. The pattern is "My father . . . who . . . who . . . who . . . but around women . . . around women who . . . my father . . . who." Notice how particular the descriptions of the father's history are: this is a man who has triumphed over deadly snakes and murderous gunfire and a knife-wielder named Bernard Seeger. We don't know why he was in the tool shed or what led the strikers to shoot at him or who Bernard Seeger is, but that doesn't matter. Probably as a child the narrator heard the stories on a number of occasions. The part of the sentence after "but" establishes a second, puzzling, seemingly contradictory aspect of the narrator's father's personality; around women he is a virtual nonentity, a man who scarcely seems capable of venturing outside or eating solid food.

In this passage Huddle is not directly recounting events as they happened: he is not composing a detailed chronological account such as you might find in a newspaper article. Instead the narrator is trying to understand, and thus he pauses, muses, tries to make sense of his father's personality.

Tone, the last element of style we will be concerned with, designates the attitudes toward the subject and toward the audience implied in a literary work. How can tone be identified—what do you look for? Think of what the narrator tells us about: his fourteenth birthday, Jean Sharp, his family, how it all worked out, what conclusions he's come to since then. How does he feel about this? How does he tell us about it? He looks back fondly, though not sentimentally, as we hear in the story's first paragraph. Sentimentality, as usually understood, implies exaggeration, simplification, an overindulgence in emotion which strikes us as false. The narrator, as we discover in the story, does indeed love his father, with good reason, but there is no sentimental exaggeration of that affection, no pulling for a response from the reader to be found in the story's first sentence: *"My father did the best he could* with a custom my mother invented without consulting him." Father is a man like other men; like his son, as the narrator discovers.

Throughout "Summer of the Magic Show" we read of home and family, love and security. We learn of an adolescent's acute embarrassment, but observe that the narrator sustained no permanent damage. He thinks his father and his mother and his brother and he should have behaved better when Jean Sharp choked on the iced tea. What he says is ". . . you'd think the incident would have humanized us all." But even (or particularly) in their inability to be their best selves, the narrator and his family are all recognizably human. He understands the people better now than he did then, or thinks he does. The story ends affirmatively insofar as a mystery of sorts is solved: how one man can be both heroic and inept; and how, remarkably as it then seemed, the narrator and his father are really quite similar, in their generally good intentions, their unease and ambivalence, their relief at being alone together. This last scene also illustrates *irony.* Irony in fiction refers to the recognition that reality is different from appearance. Thus, for example, father and son together whistling through their teeth. The appearance may be one of triumphant male solidarity, but what we suspect is that, in reality, they are mightily relieved to have survived the evening with that "formidable girl," Jean Sharp.

INFORMAL WRITING

Style

1. What kind of language would be best suited to the material and the narrative voice you have chosen in the previous writing suggestions? Why?
2. What attitude do you have toward the incident you are writing about? Do you see it as comic? Serious? Frightening? Pleasant? Ironic? Something other than these?
3. Considering your answers to these questions, write a page that continues your narration and illustrates the style and tone you have chosen.

Setting

So as to simplify and clarify discussions of fiction—how it gets written as well as how it gets read—we are in the habit of partitioning character from plot and plot from point of view, when, as we well know, everything is going on simultaneously and is related to everything else. So it is with *setting,* usually defined as where the story happens, the background against which the action of a narrative occurs. Fair enough, particularly if we add *atmosphere,* which implies mood or emotional aura.

What can we say about the setting of "Summer of the Magic Show"? Is it important? How does it relate to other components of the story? It's a small town named Rosemary, located in southwestern Virginia; it is where our narrator was born and brought up, and you get the impression he hasn't been many other places. What about the name of the town itself? If you look in the dictionary, you find that rosemary is a fragrant shrub, used in cooking and perfume making. It is also said to be an emblem of fidelity or constancy or remembrance. We may well imagine that Huddle, in choosing this name for the narrator's home town, means to suggest something about the kind of life lived there.

Jean Sharp, as we discover, comes from Palm Beach, a resort associated with the rich and famous, and, as Huddle writes, "even though she was only thirteen, she must have thought Rosemary was as far back in the wilderness as anybody ever went." In the narrator, then, we have a small-town boy, not very experienced, shy, uneasy with girls—particularly with this girl. Why? Because she's from Palm Beach, she is cosmopolitan, sophisticated, "sexy in an otherworldy kind of way." You can see that Huddle is setting up a familiar kind of conflict, country vs. city, and that where the story happens is closely connected to character and plot.

Huddle carefully differentiates among three more limited settings. Most significant and longest occupied is the dining room of the narrator's home, scene of the traumatic birthday party. Huddle does not describe the dining room, as he might have done—table, chairs, sideboard, chandelier, wallpaper, woodwork, carpet. What he is interested in, rather, is how it felt to the narrator, the mood of the place on that occasion. Then there is, for the sake of contrast, the second setting, the Rosemary home of Jean Sharp's grandmother, where the narrator remembers standing in the kitchen on an earlier occasion before being paid for cutting the grass, offered lemonade by Jean's grandmother, and led in to play cribbage with Jean. The situation—set up by the grandmother and featuring Jean—may not seem too different from the birthday party, but it "was one thing to play cards with her over lemonade in her grandmother's cool, dark living room, and another to have her come to eat with us at our dining room table."

The third specific setting is the car, in which Jean is at last delivered home. We don't receive any of the usual information about the car—make, model, year, or color. The only fact about the car which matters is that it has a radio, which the narrator's father hates but nonetheless turns on, thereby rescuing his grateful son (not to mention himself) from the necessity of conversation or the agony of silence. What's important about the car, then, is its atmosphere, or emotional aura, which passes from strain to relief.

INFORMAL WRITING

Setting

1. Where does the incident you are describing take place? Is its location important? How or why?
2. Continue writing your narration including the kinds of details that would make this setting and atmosphere clear to a reader.

Symbolism

Of all the components of fiction, the one which often seems to produce the greatest interpretive problems is *symbolism.* For openers, we should consider what symbols are, how they are identified, and what significance they have. A symbol is a figure of speech which combines a literal, concrete quality with a suggestive, abstract dimension. Thus a flag, the Stars and Stripes, is a concrete object which stands for the United States. Symbols are often said to be of two types—the universal and the particular. An example of the universal symbol is the long journey which suggests the course of human life. A symbol of more limited application is the bull, which may be understood to represent a rising and active stock market.

Symbols are functional, not decorative. It's also the case that much first-rate fiction has no symbolic content whatsoever. To assume, then, as some people do, that a symbol is always hiding in there somewhere, but that with sufficient determination and ingenuity it can be hunted down, is a serious interpretive misconception.

After all this prologue, what about "Summer of the Magic Show"? Does it contain any symbols? And how do you recognize a symbol? Careful reading and common sense are the most important requirements. Sometimes symbolic significance is quite readily accessible through speech, gesture, and action. For example, consider the narrator's birthday cake. "That," he says, "was the last angel food cake with pink icing that my mother ever made for my birthday, though I have never stopped thinking of it as the only legitimate kind of cake for a birthday." Note that the narrator is very explicit about the meaning to him of angel food cake with pink icing. Indeed we may begin to think of the birthday cake as a symbol primarily because it is given such specific attention, beyond what might seem called for on a literal level. And consider the other symbolic dimension: after his fourteenth birthday, his mother made him no more such cakes. What does this suggest? Perhaps that she thought her son was too old for an angel food cake with pink icing. Perhaps she found memories of the day embarrassing. We don't know—Huddle doesn't tell us. What he does tell us is that that day marked the end of something, that it was a rite of passage—for him a significant event in the process of growing up. The fact that he still wants such cakes also tells us something about the narrator.

Symbolism in fiction depends for its effectiveness on the reader's making apt associations, grasping the ways in which symbols may expand and deepen meaning. Symbols make good literary sense only when considered in the overall context provided by a piece of fiction. So it is with the last sentence of the story. "Then, at exactly the same moment, though our tunes were different, we each began whistling through our teeth." Two males, whistling in the dark, to keep up their courage. In this image of father and son, who are different, yet much alike, Huddle epitomizes his narrator's most important discovery. Symbols such as the whistling pair don't abstractly stand for other things but are themselves concretely part of a larger whole. That is, through Huddle's use of such symbolic action, we better understand the whole of the story, see the whole thing in a new perspective. As an interpreter of fiction, then, you're involved with putting things together, seeing the story in more than one dimension.

INFORMAL WRITING

Symbolism

1. Are there any concrete objects, actions, etc., related to the incident you are writing about that might have symbolic implications?
2. As your narration progresses, try to present these objects, actions, etc., if there are any, in ways that would help your reader understand the significance of the incident.

Theme

What, ultimately, a story means or is about we may refer to as its *thematic concerns.* How do we go about formulating the thematic concerns of a piece of fiction? What do we look for? Themes in fiction, the central ideas of the work, are usually expressed through character, action, and image. Ask yourself what has happened to the principal character or characters. Have they made discoveries? What kinds of changes do you see in their circumstances? Important actions, we need to remember, aren't necessarily physical or dramatic; some fiction is primarily cerebral and the principal action is intellectual or emotional. Consider, as you are formulating a story's theme, what kinds of images predominate.

What about the thematic concerns of "Summer of the Magic Show"? This is certainly a story about family. We can say further that it's a story about discovery, the narrator finding out about himself, not very happily, through Jean Sharp. He also finds out about himself, more positively, through his father. What does he find out? As our narrator looks back on his fourteen-year-old self and Jean Sharp, he sees a boy who was awkward, embarrassed, naive—none of these capital offenses. He also recognizes his adolescent ambivalence, that he had been both attracted to and repulsed by Jean, that he had been a little afraid of her. Neither of the two family males available to him as models of behavior with women really suited him. His brother seemed affected and his father incompetent; thus, in effect, the narrator had had to make it up as he went along. He tried briefly to emulate the drive-in moves of Herky, but he wasn't Herky and Jean certainly wasn't Marcy. At the end of the story, he is surprised at and grateful for his father's wordless understanding, but clearly something more is to be hoped for than such defensive male solidarity. At fourteen the narrator sensed other more fulfilling possibilities, but he felt himself overmatched by Jean Sharp.

The meanings of substantial fiction are not reducible to simple, explicit statements, handy moral guides, or codified popular wisdom. "Summer of the Magic Show," for example, isn't just an anti-feminist parable about the need for male solidarity. We understand that serious fiction does not offer instruction in the same sense that an editorial or a sermon or a book review does. It is for this reason that the plural form, "thematic concerns," rather than the singular "theme," seems a more accurate way of identifying the multiple meanings or central ideas of a piece of good fiction. The plural form accords better with the sense that we as readers have about the story, that it deals with a number of concerns, not just one. The plural also leaves room for the ambiguity and mystery which fiction writers are interested in exploring through the act of storytelling.

INFORMAL WRITING

Theme

1. When you have completed your telling of the incident, you will have written a story. Is it one in which the initial conflict has been resolved? How so? In which any of the characters have changed? How so?
2. Although you probably did not begin to write your story with the intention of conveying a "theme," the various choices you made when asking yourself questions during the writing process, as well as the story's ending and its characters' change or lack of change, will say something to a reader. Take a step back and ask yourself—what is my story *about?* What does it seem to *say* on these issues? What *ideas* might it be communicating? Now try to resee and revise your story to make it as effective as possible in conveying these thematic concerns.
3. Write a title for your story that will draw the reader's attention to its central focus.

RESEEING THE STORY

After receiving early reactions to "Summer of the Magic Show," Huddle kept thinking about the story. It wasn't until he made a visit home to Virginia, however, that it became clear to him what the story might still become. He was about to ask his brother (on whom the character Duncan was loosely based) to read it when he realized that there was much more to that memorable summer than he had included in his nine-page draft. He felt much as Nathan did when he read the story and found it lacking "in the area of the brother's magic show" and its significance. Huddle says he thought of his brother's reading the story and knew there was a great deal more that had to be written. Another connection between reader and writer thus played an important part in Huddle's producing a major revision of "Summer of the Magic Show," one that may at first seem to be an entirely new story.

This version of "Summer of the Magic Show" is the one that David Huddle published in his second fiction collection *Only the Little Bone.* It did not, however, spring polished and complete from his typewriter. None of our "finished" writing does. Instead, the story went through a number of drafts and one published version before Huddle was satisfied that it was as strong and effective as he could then make it.

Tense

During this period of tinkering and revising—one that took weeks rather than the few days that had produced the shorter version of the story—Huddle again asked for reactions from his peers. In successive drafts he responded to these as well as to his own re-thinking of the material.

One of the earliest changes Huddle made was in the tense in which the story was told. The first typescript of this longer version of "Summer of the Magic Show" was written in the present tense. Huddle then went through the entire manuscript and, in ink, altered the verbs to the past tense.

"Writing a story in the present tense," Huddle explains, "creates a kind of intense trance and generates more detail for me. It's a trick that allows me really to get back into the past and capture all its specific details." But Huddle never considered leaving the story in the present tense. That narrative approach suggests incidents are being recorded as they occur and makes readers feel they are watching unprocessed data unreel before their eyes. For example, Huddle originally wrote, "[Duncan's] turn of mind this summer is such that everything that comes his way must be drawn into the magic show. . . . He doesn't get out of the car, but while I am talking to [Jean] on the porch I can feel Duncan staring at us through the car window."

"Summer of the Magic Show," however, is concerned with a coming to terms with remembered boyhood events. Notice the different effect of the revision: "[Duncan's] turn of mind that summer was such that everything that came his way had to be drawn into the magic show. . . . He didn't get out of the car, but while I was talking to [Jean] on the porch, I could feel Duncan staring at us through the car window." Huddle explains, "By changing the narration to past tense, I could suggest that these events had been processed and considered by an older narrator who's now confronting their implications and significances."

This kind of revision illustrates the way Huddle goes about making a piece of fiction. In an approach that we can usefully apply to much of our own writing, Huddle sees two separate processes involved in his writing a story. He calls the first the "generating" process. "Accept what comes to you when you're writing," he explains. "While writing a first draft I'll use any method that works (writing in the present tense, for example) to generate as much detailed material as possible. Then, because I believe that revision is fifty percent of writing, I begin the second, or 'editing,' process. Now I try to prune, focus, and control the raw material."

Overwriting

"I always overwrite in early drafts," Huddle says, and the various typescripts of this story show a continuing pattern of cutting down and tightening. "I dropped descriptions of Duncan's friends at college and his previous dates, for instance, in the editing phase." Details are crucial to the making of a credible fictional world, but only those details that count. For example, when, after Susan's departure, Reed tells us he "noticed then how skinny [Duncan] was, how the sun had burned his neck and arms," those descriptive details are important in their emphasis on Duncan's vulnerability.

Paragraphs

Similarly, in those first drafts Huddle the generator produced lengthy paragraphs, many nearly a page long. Huddle the editor, however, recognizes how paragraphing can affect the pace of prose. "Facing a solid page of unparagraphed writing," Huddle says, "makes readers feel they have to plow their way through a dense mass of information without a rest. I divided those long units into shorter ones so the story would move more quickly."

In doing so, Huddle was also responding to a suggestion from a colleague who had commented on an early draft: "Seems like you're not using the 'punctuating' abilities of your paragraphs to create rhythms and suspense. . . . Somehow I felt often that the paragraphs were being run together." Again Huddle considered the reactions of his readers as an integral part of his revising process.

Responses

He also again sent the story out to magazines. *The New Yorker* sent it back with a note saying, "Sorry. We're not publishing much reminiscent fiction these days." Unlike the earlier letters of rejection Huddle received, this one was unhelpful. "It didn't present any comments on the work itself that might allow me to make it stronger." If you have ever been disappointed by having a graded paper returned to you with no indication of how it might be altered or improved, you know how a writer needs and values constructive criticism.

Undeterred, Huddle submitted the story elsewhere. Finally, the editor of *Grand Street,* a literary journal, wrote, "I'll be happy to publish 'Summer of the Magic Show'," but then he added, "if you'll cut out the first paragraph." The revising of the story was not yet over.

The offending opening read: "The strangest thing my brother ever did, that I know about, happened, he assures me, on a night, in a place, that was as dark as the inside of a beating heart." It had already received some negative responses from Huddle's "helpers," and now he cut it entirely. The revised story as published in *Grand Street* began with the more direct, less melodramatic sentence with which it opens here: "One October night in his second year at the University of Virginia, my brother persuaded a young woman to drive him to a scenic overlook at the top of Afton Mountain."

Only a few further changes, all minimal, were made before "Summer of the Magic Show" was included in Huddle's book as the finished work you will read. The result of the lengthy generating/editing process was a new story that incorporated the shorter original version but now contained what Huddle calls "more, and more complicated, thematic issues."

A fellow fiction writer who read the final draft called it "a delightful story, deeper, more luminous than the first draft . . . . I was a little worried because I had liked it so much in its shorter version, I thought you might have overwritten it. But no, this is the whole story." Will you agree?

Things to think about as you read

• Does the title still seem appropriate for the story? More so? Less so? Why?

- How does the new opening paragraph make clear that the focus of the story has shifted in this version? From what to what?
- What do the new details about plans and preparations for the magic show add to your understanding of Reed? Of Duncan? Do they alter your prior perceptions of these characters? If so, how?
- How has Huddle made the transition from the new material about Susan's visit to the material presented in the original version of the story? What do you sense the thematic connections between the "core" story and the added material to be?
- Rather than simply taking the original story of Reed and Jean and plunking it "as is" into its new surroundings, Huddle makes a number of revisions in the shorter version when he places it in its new context. Find and list a few of these; considering the story as a whole, why do you think Huddle might have made each of these changes? Does each seem necessary? Why or why not? (For example, in this version Reed explains *why* he found Jean "repulsive" after the choking incident—is this addition important here? If so, why?)
- Which of the two versions of "Summer of the Magic Show" do you like better? Why? Which do you think is the better/stronger/more effective story? Why?

DAVID HUDDLE

(1942–)

Summer of the Magic Show

About the Author: David Huddle, fiction writer, poet, and essayist, was born in Roanoke, Virginia, and grew up in the small town of Ivanhoe. He graduated from the University of Virginia and the MFA programs of Hollins College and Columbia University, and is a veteran of the Vietnam war. Huddle's first collection of stories, *A Dream with No Stump Roots in It,* appeared in 1975. Since then he has published two more story collections, *Only the Little Bone* (1986) and *The High Spirits* (1989), two volumes of poetry, *Paper Boy* (1979) and *Stopping by Home* (1988) (see his poem in Chapter 3), as well as numerous articles and essays. A recipient of two NEA fellowships, Huddle teaches writing and literature at the University of Vermont and the Bread-loaf School of English.

One October night in his second year at the University of Virginia, my brother persuaded a young woman to drive him to a scenic overlook at the top of Afton Mountain. They sat in the dark car a few moments, but they didn't talk. The young woman lit a cigarette just before they both climbed out. There were no stars, no moon, no street or house or car lights.

And they stayed quiet. The woman leaned against her car's front fender, crossed one arm in front of her, held the cigarette near her face, and kept her eyes on Duncan.

It was so dark, Duncan says, he could step away from her only a pace and a half and still see her face and her blond hair. He took a white handkerchief from his jacket pocket—U. Va. students wore coats and ties then—shook the folds out, and held it at arm's length from himself.

A rifle-shot went off not ten yards from them, so loud that Duncan, who knew it was coming, says he couldn't help flinching. The young woman yelped, crouched, dropped her cigarette, crossed her arms in front of her face to protect herself. Duncan had been too startled to notice if the handkerchief had flapped or not, but it had the bullet hole through it, and he carried it over to show to the young woman. He made the desired impression on her: that night so frightened her that she moved away from Charlottesville, where she'd lived most of her life.

Duncan says he regrets what he did. He had arranged for his friend Bobby Langston to wait with his squirrel-rifle up there on the Skyline Drive, and he was lucky Bobby had his night vision and was such an accurate shot as to be able to hit that handkerchief, dark as it was. With the shot, Duncan stopped wanting to harm the woman, but by then, of course, he had already done it. I regret knowing the story and what it tells about him.

Back when he was fourteen, Duncan was taller than anybody in our town—six-five—and thin, but very strong. No matter how much needling he took from the coaches over at Madison High School, he wouldn't play basketball or football for them. Duncan was an intellectual, and he was an innocent boy. He was pale and hairy, wore glasses, was not what anybody'd call handsome. He never really had a date until his senior year of high school.

He was the smartest one ever to come out of our town. No one begrudged him his brains, though my father often shook his head over what he called "the ways Duncan chooses to put his intelligence to use." Duncan's passion was magic. When he was thirteen he found an old *Tarbell Correspondence Course for the Apprentice Magician* in my grandparents' attic, and he read through the year's worth of lessons in about a week.

He put on his first magic show, in our living room, for Uncle Jack and Aunt Mary Alice. I remember that he messed up the Mystical Multiplying Balls, dropped one of the hollow shells right in the middle of his audience and had to stoop, humiliatingly, and pick it up. But he went on, and when he finished the show my parents and aunt and uncle applauded. What else could they do? They didn't know it was going to have a permanent effect on him.

Duncan went on doing tricks for the kids on the bus, who thought he was a freak, and for the kids in his homeroom, who were happy to have him pass the time for them, and so on, until finally Mrs. Pug Jones promised him five dollars if he'd come to Buntsy's birthday party and keep the kids from tearing her house apart. When he came back from Buntsy's party, Duncan showed me the five-dollar bill and said that now he was a professional.

The time I was closest to Duncan was the summer between his first and second years in engineering school at the University of Virginia. He was a National Merit Scholar, the only one we'd had from our whole county. He'd gotten a summer job running the scales for Pendleton over at the rock quarry, and he'd decided to put on a magic show for the town of Rosemary. He told us his plans and started working on us at the supper Mother fixed to celebrate his homecoming from Charlottesville. He wanted my mother to get the Ladies' Aid to sponsor him and my father to talk to the Superintendent of Schools to get him the use of the auditorium. My mother was still a little intoxicated from seeing the Lawn and the Rotunda at the University of Virginia when she drove up there to get him. My father gave Duncan his old slow shake of the head, but he didn't say no. It was a supper where Duncan did all the talking anyway, which was his right, having managed not to flunk out of school like everybody else from Rosemary who went away to college. The plans he told us about for the show were modest ones, a lot of card tricks and sleight-of-hand stuff he'd been practicing for his roommate, Will Greenwood. My father and I packed in the steak and mashed potatoes and peas that were Duncan's celebration supper, and my mother listened to his newly sophisticated talk, hardly touching what was on her plate.

Duncan just assumed I'd help him with the magic show, but that didn't bother me. I had nothing else to do that summer except mow yards for the three or four people in town who wanted them mowed. Rosemary probably had more houses in it that were surrounded by packed-down dirt, with chickens pecking in the dust and dogs under the porch, than it had houses with grass around them. Even the people who were willing to pay me to cut their grass were doing me a favor. So was Duncan, who pronounced me his "stage manager and first assistant."

The more Duncan thought about it—mostly while he was wearing a hard hat and making check-marks on a clipboard over at the rock quarry—the more he realized card tricks and sleight-of-hand wouldn't be good enough for his show. We had to have more illusions, a Chinese Disappearing Cabinet, a Flaming Omelet Bowl that changed the fire into dozens of silk scarves and then changed them into two white doves, a Guillotined Girl, and a Floating Lady. He talked my grandfather into helping him weld together an elaborate device of heavy pipes that he needed for the Floating Lady. He set me to work building, according to diagrams he drew, the Chinese Cabinet. He saw Toots Polk down at the post office one morning, and he persuaded her to be his Guillotined Girl. While he was at it, he asked her if she wouldn't mind doing a few of her dance numbers.

He decided I'd do a couple of trumpet solos, too, just to balance out Toots's tap-dancing. I'd gotten to be pretty good at "It's Cherry Pink and Apple Blossom White." Duncan said I could do that one and one more. I chose "Tammy," which in my opinion I played with a great deal of feeling.

On weekends when Duncan didn't have to work for Pendleton, he and I spent most of the day in the empty schoolhouse, building and painting flats for the set, working on the lighting, blocking out the show. There was a battered upright school piano in there, below and to the right of the stage. I plunked around on that when things got slow. Duncan always asked me to play one of the two songs he liked to sing, "Old Man River" and "Unchained Melody." He stood at center stage and bellowed out the words at the top of his voice, but he held himself formally, as if he had on white tie and tails. At least once every time he and I were in there alone, he had a go at "Unchained Melody."

Duncan had been getting letters from Charlottesville, and he'd mentioned a woman's name in connection with the theater group for which he had done some lighting work. So it wasn't quite a surprise when he announced that Susan O'Meara would be visiting us for a week at the beginning of July.

Susan was twenty-two. Duncan was eighteen. She smoked and wore jeans, men's shirts untucked, and no makeup; what her blond hair looked like didn't seem to matter to her. She drove up to our house one afternoon in a beat-up white Ford. She got there before Duncan had come home from the rock quarry, and right off she told Mother that it was so damn hot in that car, could she please take a bath? I couldn't remember when a woman had ever said *damn* in front of my mother; it startled me to have a strange woman come into our house and go straight upstairs to take a bath. I waited for a sign from Mother, but she remained calm. I was dumbfounded at supper that evening, halfway through my first piece of fried chicken, when I looked and saw, first, that Susan O'Meara was cutting hers with a knife and fork, and then that Mother and Duncan were doing the same with theirs. My father and I stuck to our usual method, but neither of us went beyond our second piece.

Susan talked about the heat in Charlottesville, about her father, who was a doctor, about her mother, who taught biology at St. Ann's. Susan said *damn* again during the meal; then during dessert she laughed and said she had recently told David Weiss of the Virginia Players to go to hell.

I figured my mother was bound to correct that kind of talk at her supper table, but they all went on eating their berry pie, and I was the only one who drowned his in sugar and milk—my mother had given my father a look when he reached for the cream pitcher.

Duncan, for once, wasn't saying much, but he sure was listening to every word Susan spoke. Finally the two of them excused themselves and left the house to go to the drive-in. When I stepped to the window to see which one of them was going to drive, Mother snapped at me to stop spying on them. I saw Duncan open the door of her Ford and Susan climb in on the driver's side.

I waited around the table hoping to hear some interesting opinions of Susan from one or the other of my parents, but they offered nothing. My father did have seconds on the berry pie, and this time he treated himself to plenty of sugar and milk. I asked them straight out, "What do you think of her?"

It was one of the most reasonable questions I'd ever asked them, but I didn't get an answer. What I did get was a look from each of them, neither of which I understood. Then they gave each other another look, and I didn't understand that either.

On the weekend Susan, in her jeans and a sweatshirt, worked over at the schoolhouse with Duncan and me. Mostly she sat in the second row, dangling her feet over the wooden back of the seat in front of her, smoking, and offering suggestions to Duncan. Anything I had to say he had always only half-listened to, but he took notes when Susan told him something. Once she climbed up on a ladder to examine some of the lights above the stage. For a long while she shouted down remarks for Duncan, who stood holding the ladder and gazing up at her.

She wasn't rude to me or to my father, but she dealt with us as if we were photographs of Duncan's cute little brother and his old codger of a father. She never asked us questions the way she sometimes did Mother.

On the last evening she spent with us, Susan wore this little diamond ring Duncan had bought her with his Pendleton money. It couldn't have been anything but the smallest stone they had at Smith's Jewelers, but it probably cost Duncan every cent he had in his savings account at the time. I wouldn't have noticed it if I hadn't caught Mother with her eye on it during the meal.

Obviously Duncan and Susan meant for the rest of us to understand that they were engaged, but for some reason neither of them said anything aloud about it. My father and I weren't about to say anything on our own, and so it was up to my mother to mention it if anybody was going to, and she chose not to. It was as if since nobody gave voice to it, the engagement hadn't really come about. There was the ring on Susan's finger—she chewed her nails, by the way—but without any words being spoken there was no engagement. That last night I did notice a way Susan had of widening her eyes when she talked that made me understand just for an instant what Duncan saw in her, "one of the most brilliant minds in Albemarle County," as he put it.

Next morning, to see her leave, I snuck out of bed and knelt by the window. It was early because Duncan had to go to work at the quarry. My mother and Duncan and Susan all came out to the car together. Mother gave Susan a sort of official kiss on the cheek, so measured that I imagined she must have thought about it all through their breakfast, and Susan had to hold her cigarette away from Mother with her free hand. Then Mother went back inside, Susan stamped out her cigarette in our driveway, and she and Duncan went into this farewell embrace and kiss. I was surprised at how embarrassed I felt to be seeing it, though I confess it was exactly what I had come to the window to see. Maybe I thought

it was going to be funny or sexy, but it was neither of those, and I can't really say what it was. When Susan climbed in behind the steering wheel, Duncan leaned in to kiss her goodbye again. And when she was gone, with the dust from her car still hanging above the driveway, Duncan stood out there alone with his hands in his pockets, toeing at something on the ground. I noticed then how skinny he was, how the sun had burnt his neck and arms.

This was the same morning my mother decided, as she put it, "to inaugurate a custom for the good of our family." She meant to correct the social behavior of my father and me, who had not gracefully carried off Susan O'Meara's visit. Mother didn't ask us what we thought about it, and we knew from her tone of voice not to argue. She commissioned me to ask a girl to our house for my birthday supper. Every birthday, she said, a girl should be invited.

To put it in straightforward terms, girls made my father uncomfortable. Susan O'Meara had come close to paralyzing him. He was a courtly man. When we sat in the dining room, which was when we had company, he stood and held my mother's chair for her until she came in to sit down. He spoke with elaborate courtesy to all the women on my mother's side of the family and said *yes ma'am* and *no ma'am* to most of them. In fact, I felt that in the presence of women, my mother excepted, my father was never himself. He limited his conversation to expressing agreement with the people around him or to asking questions of them. If questioned himself, he phrased his replies in such a way as to generalize or abstract whatever he was telling, so that his opinions in this voice were dull, his experiences hardly worth mentioning. My father was a man who had faced an old toolshed full of rattlesnakes, had been shot at by union strikers, had taken a knife away from Bernard Seeger at a high-school dance, but around women who came to our house as company, and especially around Susan O'Meara that past week, my father took on the personality of somebody who'd stayed indoors all his life and eaten nothing but cheese sandwiches.

I didn't resent my mother's decision, as perhaps I might have any other summer. I had noticed that my parents treated Duncan like a grownup while Susan was in the house; I knew a girl who was almost as formidable as Susan: Jean Sharp. She was from Palm Beach, Florida. Even though she was only thirteen, I'd heard her say things that showed she thought Rosemary, Virginia, was far back in the wilderness.

I was Jean's grandmother's yard-boy. When I finished mowing her yard, old Mrs. Sharp had me come inside for lemonade before she paid me. While I stood there, sweating in her kitchen, she coaxed some conversation out of me, then some out of Jean standing in the kitchen doorway. Jean had very fine dark hair, a small nose and mouth, a lanky frame. When Jean and I gave the appearance of being able to talk with each other, Mrs. Sharp handed me the money and suggested that we go into the living room and play cards. Jean taught me cribbage while sitting forward on the sofa with her back very straight, her knees bent and together, her ankles crossed. All that summer Jean had worn sundresses; they emphasized her flat-chestedness, but there was something about her in those dresses, her thin shoulders maybe, that was sexy. Her fingers playing the cards or moving the pegs on the cribbage board held my attention. Her soft voice, her precise diction, made me feel I was learning something every time she spoke to me.

My father had seen Jean only a few times in all her summers of visiting her grandmother in Rosemary, but he knew about her. When my mother and I talked it through to the conclusion that Jean was the one I would ask to my fourteenth-birthday supper, my father's face showed that he dreaded it. I dreaded it, too, a little bit.

Duncan, of course, when he heard about it, got a bright idea. His turn of mind that summer was one where everything that came to his attention had to be connected in some way to his magic show. He would ask Jean to be his Floating Lady. He was so excited about the notion that he drove me up to old Mrs. Sharp's house that Saturday so I could ask Jean to the supper and so he could get a fresh look at her to see how she'd work on stage. He didn't get out of the car, but while I was talking to Jean on her grandmother's front porch I could feel Duncan staring at us from the car window. Then, driving up to the schoolhouse, Duncan chattered away about Jean, how it was great she was so thin and wouldn't be likely to break down the Floating Lady apparatus, as we'd both joked that Toots might have done, and how Jean's "ethereal face," as he put it, would appeal to the audience. He'd stopped thinking about a Rosemary audience, which would be made up mostly of a bunch of antsy, loud-mouthed, bad-smelling, runny-nosed kids, Jeep Alley, Big-Face Limeberry, Thelma Darby and all her freckle-faced family, Mr. and Mrs. Pug Jones and Buntsy, people like that. Duncan was thinking about *audience* in the way they probably thought about it in Charlottesville.

He had this hyperbolic way of talking about everybody: Will Greenwood was the greatest drum major in the history of his high school, Bobby Langston was a fearless and diabolical genius, and so on. About Jean Sharp, I heard him telling our mother in the kitchen, "She's truly beautiful, don't you think?" This was on my birthday, just before Jean's grandmother drove her up to our house, and my father and I, in the living room, exchanged glances when we heard Duncan talking like that. We knew Jean wasn't "truly beautiful." She was just a girl who was visiting in our town. Duncan didn't have to exaggerate what she was just because he wanted her to be in his show. But my father and I were used to his ways that summer. We were grateful to him for doing most of the talking when Jean first walked into our house.

She had on another sundress, this one white with a sort of primly high front to it. It set off her tanned shoulders and face, her dark hair. Something about the way that dress fit her at the arms bothered me, though. It made a loose place where, I knew, if I looked at the right angle, I'd see her breast, or what should have been her breast.

There were girls in my classes at school whose breasts or bras I'd strained my neck trying to get a peek at, but they weren't like Jean. I didn't want to see into her dress, but sitting beside her at the table, I could hardly help noticing that opening every time I cast my eyes in her direction. To make things worse, I became aware of the sounds my father was making as he ate.

Courtly man though he was, his table manners, or rather the things that went on between him and the food on his plate, were pretty crude. He took large bites of things, and there was a kind of liquid inhaling noise that went with each bite. Often he chewed with his mouth open, so that you could hear it, and he liked to roll the food around in his mouth so that he made sloshing noises. It bothered me even though I knew why he did it. It was the result of his courtliness: his way of signaling to my mother that he liked the food was to make eating noises that expressed his pleasure, his gratitude to her for cooking the food for him. The noises had to be loud enough for her to hear him at the opposite end of the table, and I expect they were that evening, even though I knew he was holding back on Jean's account.

I was thinking about asking to be excused when suddenly Duncan asked Jean if she would be his Floating Lady, and she choked on a sip of iced tea.

She was all right, of course. Nobody ever died of iced tea going down the wrong way, at least not that I know of, and you would think the incident—Jean gasping and coughing into her napkin, my father and brother and I rising and coming around behind her chair, ready to pound on her back (though not one of us was going to touch those elegant shoulders unless she got really serious about her choking), my mother coming around the table, too, carrying her napkin for some reason and saying, "Oh, you poor dear, you poor thing"—you'd think the incident would have humanized us all. It didn't. There was a short moment after Jean recovered and we'd all gone back to our places when nobody made a sound, one of those embarrassing lulls in the conversation that are usually broken by somebody's polite giggle. In this case my mother managed a feeble "Well . . .," and then we had more silence before we fell back to eating, and my father's mouth noises recommenced.

After a while Jean managed to squeak out to Duncan that, yes, she would be happy to be his Floating Lady, and he was released from responsibility for her condition. He went on with his inflated jabbering about the show. But because she had made such a red-faced, watery-eyed, spluttering spectacle of herself, she who was as serene as a piece of sculpture in every other circumstance of my seeing her, Jean now was repulsive to me. Sitting beside her, I lost my appetite.

My mother must also have experienced some kind of pivotal moment that summer evening when Jean Sharp choked in our dining room. That was the last angel food cake with pink icing she ever made for my birthday, though I have never stopped thinking of it as the only legitimate kind of birthday cake.

Next morning, as usual, Duncan and I walked down to the post office where I waited with him while he waited for his ride to Pendleton's quarry. It was an occasion for talking about the magic show. He'd glance at his letter from Susan, if he got one. Then, when he left, I'd take my parents' mail back up the hill to our house.

That morning, though, Duncan had to sign for a little package from Susan. He opened it while he and I were discussing what we were going to do about the kids who'd go around behind the schoolhouse to try to peek in the windows and cracks in the doors to see how the tricks worked. All of a sudden he was holding the diamond ring in his fingers, and I was looking at it, and it was registering on both of us what that meant.

"Aw God, Duncan," I said, "that's a shame." I didn't know what else to say. I wanted to put my arm around his shoulder, but we weren't that kind of a family, and this was in the post office anyway. So I just got out of there as quick as I could and left him standing there staring at the ring with no expression on his face.

I guess he went to work, though I don't know how he got through the day. He came home at the regular time, and he sat with us at the table in the kitchen where we ate supper. But he just dangled his fork over his food and wouldn't eat, wouldn't talk. We'd gotten used to all his jabber-jabber, as my father called it, and the three of us had a hard time filling up the silence. We'd have understood if he'd called off the show. We'd have even understood if he'd taken the car out, gotten drunk, and run it up the side of a tree—there was a tradition of that kind of behavior in our county.

But Duncan was his own man. He worked harder than ever on the magic show, and he said what was necessary to make me work harder on it, too. We'd begun rehearsing in earnest. It wasn't fun for us anymore, what with him losing his temper and going off to sulk when one of us made a mistake. "There is no margin for error in magic," he spat at me once when I lost my balance on the tiny little platform of the Chinese Disappearing Cabinet and put a foot down where the whole audience would have seen it.

Toots asked him to leave the auditorium while she ran through her tap numbers. She said they weren't magic, and she didn't want to know what he thought if she made a mistake.

I was surprised when he agreed to leave, and I found that my pleasure in watching the little shimmering of her thighs increased with Duncan out of the room. When I went outside to tell him Toots was finished, I saw him walking over at the far end of the red-dirt elementary-school playground. He had his head down, and I first thought maybe he was crying and then that maybe he was thinking real hard about something. But then I could see little puffs of red dust coming up from his footsteps, and I knew he was stomping the ground, was raging to himself. I went back inside and waited for him to come back in on his own.

I had become a good deal more objective about Jean Sharp by that time. I didn't like to be around her, but I continued to think that I ought to be attracted to her. She was prettier in the face than Toots Polk, and I knew I ought to like looking at her just as much as I liked looking at Toots. But I didn't. The *didn't* and the *ought to* canceled each other out, and I felt nothing.

One night Herky Thompson and Toots took Jean and me out with them on a double date to the drive-in. (Toots's mother made them do it, I expect, because she didn't trust Herky, who was from Piney.) After dark, Jean and I sat in the back seat doing our best to concentrate on *Miss Tatlock's Millions* while Herky and Toots coiled around each other in Toots's corner of the front seat.

I snuck my arm around Jean—she was wearing a sweater—and though I knew she was aware of my arm, I felt no loosening of her good posture, no impulse on her part to lean my way. At the time I resented her for that coldness, but later I decided that she was in the right: she felt no real affection or desire in that arm behind her, those fingers lightly touching her shoulder. She didn't respond because I didn't offer her any part of myself to which she could respond.

All through the final rehearsals Duncan growled at us and cursed under his breath and once put his fist through one of the flats so that we had to repair it. Jean and Toots and I had grown frightened of him. Jean, who rarely said much, told Toots and me that she thought he was going to scare the audience right out of their seats. Toots nodded. I thought about telling them how it had been, earlier in the summer, when Duncan and I had performed "Unchained Melody" to the empty auditorium, but I didn't.

I opened the show out in front of the curtain, ignoring the giggles that Thelma Darby started in the audience when I stepped into the spotlight. I couldn't see past the first row anyway, though my father had passed back the word that we had a full house. I lifted my trumpet and silenced everybody with "It's Cherry Pink and Apple Blossom White."

I finished, the curtain opened, and there was "Duncan the Great" standing in his tuxedo at center stage with Toots a step or two to the side holding the top hat out of which shortly Duncan would yank the three-pound white rabbit I'd bought from Gilmer Hyatt two weeks ago. But he had time for small talk, or "patter," as magicians call it, before the trick. In the most lighthearted tone I'd ever heard him use, he paid me a compliment: "That's Reed Bryant, my brother, ladies and gentlemen, and isn't he some musician?" I got another feeble little round of applause, along with a couple of jeers that I ignored.

Jean really didn't have many duties for the show. She assisted Duncan for a couple of little tricks, but she didn't have any talents that we really needed; so she spent a lot of time standing around near me when I was offstage. Sometimes it was pitch dark back there when Duncan was doing one of the tricks with flames or working with a deck of cards in the spotlight out front. I could feel Jean standing there with me and reminding me of how much I dreaded the Floating Lady trick.

Toots and I were both assistants for that one. We were to pull the chairs out from each end of the Floating Lady's little platform. Toots was at Jean's head, and I was at her feet. I'd bargained with Toots to trade sides, but Duncan hadn't allowed it. I had to get back to the lighting board immediately after the trick to douse the lights, and so it had to be the feet side for me. I had been anxious all through the rehearsals when Jean had worn shorts or slacks, because I knew that in the performance she was to wear a dress. There was a good chance I'd have to see all the way to the north pole, whether I wanted to or not, and in front of half the town of Rosemary. In any circumstance Jean was a girl up whose dress I did not want to see.

The apparatus for the Floating Lady was heavy and elaborate, because of course it had to hold the lady up, but it had to be so cleverly arranged and concealed that the audience couldn't see it or imagine how it might be set up. Duncan had to brace himself against part of it and stand so that he hid one huge black pipe from the audience. Even then there had to be a four-by-four post holding that thing down behind the rear curtain and braced against the top of a window well. In rehearsal, Toots and I had laughed because all those pipes looked so crude to us that we couldn't believe anybody would ever be fooled. Duncan assured us that the trick would work.

In the performance Duncan and Toots and I were sweating out there under the lights. When Jean in her yellow sundress walked out on stage, she was loudly and somewhat lewdly cheered, but then something about her appearance quieted the audience right down. She really did appear to fall under Duncan's hypnotic spell when he had her sit and then lie down on the platform. Toots fixed Jean's dark hair to lie prettily at the side of her head, and Jean's face and body became waxen, spiritless.

A hush came down over the audience when Toots removed the first chair. Duncan, standing directly behind her, kept his hands held high over Jean while she lay there, and he looked like a crazy preacher held in a spell himself. I looked up at his face then, just before I was to pull my chair. Duncan was charged with some kind of emotion I'd never seen in anybody. I knew that part of it must have had to do with Susan O'Meara, but another part of it was willing that illusion into being: Jean Sharp was by God going to float in the air on the stage of Rosemary Elementary School!

With exaggerated wariness, I removed my chair. Jean wobbled a little bit. Then she held steady. A noise came from the audience, as if everyone had inhaled at once. Clarence Shinault, who'd gone through seventh grade with Duncan, said clearly from way in the back, "Gah-odd *damn,* Duncan."

Gravely, Duncan passed the hoop, with agonizing slowness, from Jean's feet to her head and then back again from her head to her feet. Then he held the hoop up for everyone to see. The applause came just when it should have, Toots and I put our chairs back under the platform, Jean awoke from her spell, smiled, and began climbing down while I skipped back to the lighting board. The trick was over, and I couldn't remember whether or not I'd seen up Jean's dress.

In the week or two before he went back to Charlottesville, thanks to his success with the show, Duncan recovered some of his good spirits. Once he even asked me why I wasn't trying to see more of "The Exquisite Miss Sharp," as he had taken to calling her. I wouldn't have been inclined to explain it to him even if I had understood my feelings about her and even if he had been free enough of his own troubles to be more than halfway interested.

It was my father who gave me the most comfort in that time. Even earlier in the summer he'd started helping me, at the end of the terrible birthday supper when my mother had herded us all into the living room to chat with Jean before she went home. We sat there for an excruciating length of time. I found myself copying my father's manner. I agreed with things Duncan said, things my mother said, and especially with any slight remark of Jean's. Once, the rhythm of conversation demanded that I say something, and so I asked Jean a question about Palm Beach, then pretended to listen while she, with much graceful gesturing of her slender arms and hands, tried to make us understand where in the city she lived and how far that was from the actual beach.

When my father stood up to signal that he wished the occasion to be over, I was the first one to rise and second his motion. Duncan wanted to ride with us on the way over to Jean's grandmother's house so that he could tell her more about the magic show. I'd have been glad to have him along, but my mother put a hand on his sleeve, and he said that, well, now he remembered he had a letter he had to write before he went to sleep.

Outside, standing by the car, my father instructed Jean and me to ride in the back seat. By that time the fireflies were out, the bats were swooping over our heads, it was warm, and there was the scent of honeysuckle over the whole yard, but Jean seemed glad to be climbing into the car. When my father saw that she and I weren't going to have much to say to each other on the drive across the ridge and around the town, he turned on the radio. I've always been grateful to him for that, because I know for a fact that he hated the car radio, especially the hillbilly and rhythm & blues stations that were all we could get at night in our part of the country.

In the cool air I walked Jean up onto her grandmother's front porch, said a quickly retreating goodnight, and scuttled back to sit in the front seat with my father. In his kindness he neither asked me anything nor said a word to me. He'd turned off the radio, and he took his time driving back home. The two of us were quiet, except once when we came to a place where we could see a light way up on the hill at our house.

I said, "I'll bet that's the light in Duncan's room," and my father chuckled and said yes, he guessed Duncan was writing that letter to Charlottesville. That was the night before Duncan got the ring back in the mail from Susan O'Meara, and it was several months before the night he sent Bobby Langston with his squirrel-rifle up on Afton Mountain to wait for him and Susan. It was almost a full year before Duncan flunked out of the University of Virginia. That night, sitting at his bedside table to write that letter to Susan, all Duncan knew that was coming to him was his magic show. My father and I kept driving slowly around the ridge, both he and I watching the road in the headlights and occasionally glancing out our side windows at the dark. Then, at almost exactly the same moment, though our tunes were different, we each began whistling through our teeth.

. . . .

WRITING ABOUT THE STORY

Students in the Introduction to Literature class discovered a lot about the longer version of "Summer of the Magic Show" when they thought through questions about it, and asked some of their own. Christine wasn't quite sure why the actual magic show was now presented so fully, but she noted that the additional details showed "Duncan's real talent for magic."

Since Duncan's showmanship and flair for the dramatic is a significant element in the story's opening scene, Huddle's detailed depiction of this "talent" emphasizes an important aspect of his character. In fact, Julie wrote, "I like the longer version more because it explains more about why the title came to be 'Summer of the Magic Show'," and added, "Duncan becomes the focal character of the story instead of the father and the narrator." Many students noted this seeming shift in emphasis in the longer version; some, like Sheri, found this distracting. She explained, "The expansion of the story seems to have changed the focus, thereby obscuring the original theme."

When David Huddle visited the English 11 class, he was asked about this issue—the interrelation of the story's characters and its thematic concerns. He explained that although on the surface Duncan was the most important character, in his view, nonetheless, "with a first-person narration the story always belongs to the narrator." Thus, for Huddle, Reed and Jean are most central; "the story shows what that summer meant to Reed, but in terms of what it meant to Duncan."

"Well," you may be thinking, "now that I know what its author says the story is about, I know all about the story. I don't have to be an 'active reader' at all." That's how Lisa felt when she read the more explicit choking scene now in "Summer of the Magic Show." "By saying why the narrator found Jean repulsive," Lisa wrote, "Huddle didn't allow the reader any freedom of interpretation."

No matter what a writer knows or tells us about his work, however, it is the work itself that speaks to us most strongly. Because a story acquires a life of its own separate from whatever its writer's purposes and intentions may have been, it is to the words on the page, and the way they affect us, that the informed reader turns for understanding. Trust the tale, not the teller.

In his careful reading of this tale, for example, Nathan discovered that "by bringing in the relationship between Duncan and Susan, Huddle allows Reed to see what a relationship is like." From his personal involvement with the text itself, rather than from explanatory statements by its writer or narrator, Nathan came to his own insights about the story. Huddle later reinforced these when he told the class that for him "Summer of the Magic Show" is about "one brother teaching another, and the difficulty all three men have trying to relate to women in human terms."

Most students in the literature class liked the challenges of the longer, more complex version. Although Tim felt that "the longer draft has added amounts of information that are not necessary," this was a minority view. "The boy was a much more believable character," Sam wrote, "when I understood the rest of the people around him."

The longer "Summer of the Magic Show" thus led these students to critical considerations of how the various elements of fiction, like character, were working together in it to communicate meaning. Whereas in their informal writing they had worked through the process of drafting a story of their own, now they asked analytical questions of Huddle's story and found some answers in his text. Here are some of the kinds of questions you might be raising about the story, thinking about, writing about, informally, or as the beginning of a critical analysis.

Thinking about character—suggestions for writing

- In the now detailed description of the magic show itself, how would you describe Reed's role? Jean's? Duncan's? How does this new information enrich our sense of these characters as individuals? In relation to each other?

Thinking about plot—suggestions for writing

- The opening incident in the story, referred to again in the final paragraph, is a shocking one. Does Duncan's behavior seem credible to you? Why? Why not? Does Susan's? Why? Why not?

Thinking about point of view—suggestions for writing

- Huddle's decision to use a character narration limits Reed to being an outside observer of Duncan and Susan's relationship. What effect does this perspective have on your sense of that relationship? Since the relationship is obviously important in this version of the story, do you think retaining this point of view was a misjudgment on Huddle's part?

Thinking about style—suggestions for writing

- After reading a draft, one of Huddle's colleagues suggested changes in the style of the story; he did not make them. Compare the proposed recasting below to the third paragraph on page 48.

  "During the performance, Toots and I were perspiring under the hot lights. We'd been working quickly and with much energy; all three of us were excited. When Jean walked out on stage she was cheered loudly and lewdly, but something about her appearance made the audience become quiet. She seemed to be hypnotized by Duncan when he requested that she sit and then lie down on the platform. Toots arranged Jean's hair attractively, and Jean's face and body seemed to become pale and without liveliness." Do you think Huddle was right not to make the suggested revisions? Why? Why not?

Thinking about setting—suggestions for writing

- Look carefully at the last two paragraphs of the story—why do you think Huddle chose this setting of the drive home for the story's closing scene? Would the scene have had a different effect if it had been set on Jean's porch? In the Bryants' house? How so?

Thinking about symbolism—suggestions for writing

- The magic show holds a central place in the story, as well as in Reed's memories of that significant summer—can it be seen as symbolic or metaphoric in any way? How so?

Thinking about theme—suggestions for writing

- If one of the concerns of the first draft of the story was male/female, paternal/maternal roles, has that thematic focus been changed with the inclusion of Duncan and Susan here? How so? Has it been enlarged? How so?

There were a variety of responses to these questions in the Introduction to Literature class; the students in your class probably also have different opinions about the story and how it works. None of the questions here have one "right" answer. For example, thinking about the plot, Sheri found Susan's reaction to the shooting incident "overexaggerated." Elizabeth, too, didn't think her behavior was "credible." Others disagreed; Sam and Julie could accept Susan's terror as believable. Which of these opposing opinions is more persuasive, and how can we possibly choose between them?

We can begin by saying that neither view is "wrong," but we can also notice the kinds of evidence on which these students are basing their conclusions. Sam and Julie make their judgments in terms of their understanding of human nature. Sam wrote, "I would have thought Susan would have acted a bit more calmly, but anyone who's been shot at could

react strongly." "Susan," according to Julie, "was probably nervous at the top of Afton Mountain. She should have asked Duncan why he wanted to drive up."

These assumptions are certainly accurate in terms of what Sam and Julie understand about the way most people would behave in potentially dangerous circumstances. Susan O'Meara, however, is a specific *character* whom we can observe closely during the course of the story. Sheri and Elizabeth were thus surprised by her response when they examined it in the light of the text. Sheri wrote, "The way Susan is portrayed in the story gives the impression that she controls most situations and always maintains her own self-assuredness. It is conceivable that she would not fall apart, even in that particular situation."

Elizabeth had a slightly different reason for her opinion, but one that is also based on what she has come to understand of the story: "If Susan knew Duncan and understood his personality, I doubt she'd go through such a drastic reaction to his little plan. She would probably not have put it past him to do such a thing." Perhaps, then, Huddle wants us to wonder if Susan is really as self-assured and knowledgeable as she appears to the young Reed.

Although there obviously are no "right" or "wrong" answers to a question which asks for a reader's opinion about a story, those views that return to the text itself for support are more convincing. Conclusions that are grounded in specific evidence from the story, rather than in generalizations about life, seem more valid and persuasive interpretations of the work.

They also bring the reader closer to discovering its thematic concerns. Many students found Duncan's behavior in the opening scene believable, despite its outrageousness. It seemed consistent with what they had come to know of him. "Duncan's behavior is believable," Sam wrote, "because he has always been interested in creating an effect on people. This was a reason he was involved with magic. He liked to know something the audience didn't. His act with Susan was just another trick."

This understanding of Duncan's personality as presented in the story led many students to recognize the effectiveness of Huddle's choice of point of view. Alex commented, "Reed does not lead me to believe that he is in any way unstable or untrustworthy. This is not just an account of events but a person telling me a story of his experience, as a friend might."

Alex could think of Reed as a friend without losing sight of his function as a character-narrator; he could respond to Reed in human terms while also considering his role in the story. Looking at a story as a crafted piece of fiction that can be analyzed, examined closely, and evaluated need not reduce our sense of its characters as people, or lessen our pleasure in entering their fictional worlds. As Tim wrote praising Huddle's choice of narrator, "I like to see how younger people view the world in which they live." Careful reading of "Summer of the Magic Show" allows him to do just that.

TALKING WITH THE WRITER

We posed one more question to the English II class: What would you want to ask David Huddle about this story and/or his process of revision?

Just as you probably do, the students had many questions for the author of "Summer of the Magic Show." When Huddle visited the class, they had the unusual opportunity to ask them directly, an opportunity that you can share here.

"What is the meaning of the gun scene?" Craig wanted to know after puzzling over the question of its credibility. Huddle admitted this scene was the "most dubious" even to him, but said that he wanted the reader to consider "how a nice guy like Duncan, a role model, could carry out a moderately despicable act." For Huddle the opening scene sets forth a major premise about the character; he hoped the story itself would then demonstrate what led Duncan to this moment. Considering the student insights about this scene quoted earlier, he seems to have been successful.

Lisa asked Huddle why he had included such specific references to the University of Virginia, its Rotunda, etc. For her these details created "an amateurish tone." He responded that he wanted the story to have a "Virginia flavor," to be rooted in a particular time and place, and for its setting to have a strong sense of reality. "Why did Duncan fail out of U. Va.?" Elizabeth wondered. Huddle replied, "A star in high school who flunks college is more interesting," reminding us that "Summer of the Magic Show" is crafted fiction, not raw autobiography.

But "How do you keep autobiographical writing from turning into a journal entry no one will understand but you?" Alex wanted to know. Huddle explained that he begins by writing for himself, not a public audience. "Then," he said, "you use readers to help you get a perspective on the material, to help you make it as good a *story* as you can."

In this chapter we have seen how that kind of creative process produced "Summer of the Magic Show" over many months. Because Huddle was then using a typewriter for his drafts, all of the changes he made along the way have been preserved in his sequence of manuscripts. Now, however, like many of us, he writes on a computer. Alex asked, "How does computer composing work for you?" Huddle said that the computer relieves him from much of the drudgery of revising. Because he can make changes more readily with a word processor, he is more willing to take chances and try new approaches in early drafts. He feels freed by the possibilities that writing on a computer provides. It may be harder to trace the evolution of a Huddle story now that his typewriter is obsolete, but, like those of us who write on computers, he can now generate material more freely and edit it more easily.

"Summer of the Magic Show" was a long time in the making before its final publication in Huddle's book; still, Nathan wanted to know if Huddle was completely satisfied with the story as it appears here. Surprisingly, or perhaps not so surprisingly, Huddle said no—there was still one change that he would make if he ever had the chance to republish the story in another collection.

One reason his answer is surprising is that this version of "Summer of the Magic Show" was very highly regarded by reviewers of Huddle's book, *Only the Little Bone.*

Lucas Carpenter, writing in *Newsday,* called the collection "the work of a writer thoroughly at home with the craft of short fiction. Through his portrayal of the haltingly maturing Reed Bryant and his all-too-human family, Huddle achieves a solid and pleasing sense of unity that makes affirmation possible." In *The Cleveland Plain Dealer,* James R. Frakes said Huddle's "strength [is] unblinking vision and compassion," and singled out "Summer of the Magic Show" for special praise as "shudderingly right and accurate."

The story was so well thought of that it was included in an anthology, *New Stories from the South: The Year's Best, 1986.* The book reviewer of the St. Louis *Post Dispatch* found "Summer of the Magic Show" "the best of all the stories" in that collection, explaining:

> It is about illusion on many different levels, about the illusions of a magician but also about those that control our lives, the sleights of hand that operate in our relationships, the wires and props between men and women and in families, and what happens when we see the truth.

Seeing the truth and sharing it with his readers through his craft is what makes Huddle such an effective fiction writer. That, and his unwillingness to settle for anything less than the best writing he is capable of.

Perhaps, then, it is *not* so surprising that Huddle still wasn't entirely satisfied with the published—and praised—"Summer of the Magic Show." When he began to read the story aloud to audiences at writing workshops, schools, and colleges, he "heard" it in a new way. As a reader now himself, he was dissatisfied with the brief passage in which Susan is introduced. As a writer, he wished he might someday have the chance to change it.

We gave him that chance. At our request, David Huddle has made that final revision of "Summer of the Magic Show" for this chapter. The newly written material is printed here for the first time.

Here is the original passage (from page 42), followed by Huddle's recasting more than two years after the "completion" of the story.

Original

Susan was twenty-two. Duncan was eighteen. She smoked and wore jeans, men's shirts untucked, and no makeup; what her blond hair looked like didn't seem to matter to her. She drove up to our house one afternoon in a beat-up white Ford. She got there before Duncan had come home from the rock quarry, and right off she told Mother that it was so damn hot in that car, could she please take a bath.

Revision

Susan was twenty-two. Duncan was eighteen. One afternoon before Duncan had come home from the rock quarry, Susan drove up to our house in a beat-up white Ford. When she got out of the car and spoke to mother and me, she kept her cigarette in her mouth. She had on jeans, a man's untucked shirt and no makeup, and apparently what her blond hair looked like didn't matter to her. Right off she told Mother that it was so damn hot in that car, could she please take a bath?

A close look at the revision and what it may accomplish can show much about how fiction works. What is your response to it?

- The alteration seems principally tinkering, a reordering, with nothing of consequence added or deleted. Why, then, would Huddle wish to make it? What, if anything, does it accomplish?
- Why do you think he considers this an improvement over the original? Do you agree? Why or why not?
- What does the fact that Huddle thought this change important enough to make two years after the story appeared in his book suggest about writing fiction? About reading fiction?

We asked the students in the literature class what they thought. Elizabeth felt the new passage "made for a clearer picture" and related a more coherent "chain of events." "The alterations made the section stronger," Sheri wrote, "giving the reader a clearer, more direct idea of Susan's personality." Nathan noted *how* the revision accomplishes this: "Instead of simply saying 'she smoked,' Huddle tells us that 'she kept her cigarette in her mouth.' This is a much better way of letting us know what Susan is like."

Huddle thinks the new version is better for the same reasons. He says, "I didn't like the way Susan was described before she shows up. I wanted the reader to *see* her and follow the scene visually." The revision, therefore, allows Huddle to *show,* not tell—to give a "clearer picture." Fiction communicates best in scenes rather than summary; Susan now enters the story in an ongoing scene. As Nathan put it, "Huddle now integrates his description of her with the description of her arriving at Duncan's house."

Here, as with his prior alterations of the story, Huddle has made his work stronger by standing back from it and seeing it anew. "Revision," after all, comes from the Latin words meaning "to see again." Sheri might be speaking about anyone who understands writing as a process when she said of Huddle, "Now that he is removed from the intensity of writing, he is able to clarify his own perceptions and more effectively convey his images."

Elizabeth came to a similar conclusion: "Writing fiction is a process in which changes for improvement can always be made. An author who has set some work aside for a while can look back at it and make those changes." Putting it another way, Alex wrote "Despite the fact that a work is 'complete,' it really never is complete. Fiction is exactly what the word suggests—a product of the imagination. Since fiction comes from the imagination and the imagination is endless, then a piece of fiction is endless as well."

And what can this revision tell us about the *reading* of fiction? Nathan wrote, "This suggests that a reader should always ask questions about a work to try and understand the work better. By asking questions, a reader of fiction can make a work more understandable just as a writer revises a work to make it better in his/her mind."

The idea that a writer never "finishes" a work can be troubling to a reader, however. Alex pointed out that "once one is accustomed to a story, it can be pretty frustrating to think that it could change drastically at the whim of the author." He went on to ask himself a question: "Is this to suggest that a reader should never accept fiction as permanent—unchanging?" And, as he wrote, he found the answer. "Yes. If one wants factual writing he/she should read biographies etc. A work of the imagination is as elusive as the imagination itself." Elusive yes, and rich with the possibilities of interpretation and the pleasures of understanding.

PARTICIPATING IN FICTION

As you read the stories in this anthology, these questions may lead you into a conversation with them, and thus help you to respond and relate to them more closely through discussion, informal writing, or critical analyses.

Plot and Character

1. Who are the story's central characters? What are they like? What details in the story lead you to see them this way?
2. What seems to be the story's central conflict? How is the time scheme of events organized? Is the conflict resolved at the conclusion of the story? Are you satisfied with this ending?

Point of View

1. What is the story's point of view? Why might the writer have chosen this focus of narration rather than some other? What is its effect?
2. If there is a character-narrator, is he/she reliable? What makes you come to this conclusion?

Style

1. How might you describe the kind of language used to tell the story, considering diction, imagery, syntax, etc.? What is the effect of this style?
2. What seems to be the story's tone? What in the story leads you to this assumption?

Setting

1. What is the setting of the story? How/why is it important?
2. How might you describe the story's atmosphere? What in the story creates it?

Symbolism

1. Is there any object, event, action, etc., in the story that seems to be functioning symbolically? If so, what makes you think so?
2. What might it suggest/symbolize in this context? How does it help you to understand the story as a whole?

Theme

1. Have the story's characters undergone any changes or made any discoveries? If so, how and why? If not, why not?
2. What does the story seem to be "about"? What are the central ideas/issues with which it is concerned? What are some things it seems to *say* on these issues through its plot, characters, point of view, style, setting, symbolism?

LOUISE ERDRICH

(1954–)

Fleur

About the Author: Louise Erdrich is a Native American short-story writer, novelist, and poet, who grew up near the Turtle Mountain Chippewa Reservation in North Dakota. She teaches at Dartmouth College, and has published *Jacklight* (1984), a collection of poems, and three volumes of fiction, *Love Medicine* (1984), *The Beet Queen* (1986), and *Tracks* (1988), all of which depict Native American culture.

The first time she drowned in the cold and glassy waters of Lake Turcot, Fleur Pillager was only a girl. Two men saw the boat tip, saw her struggle in the waves. They rowed over to the place she went down, and jumped in. When they dragged her over the gunwales, she was cold to the touch and stiff, so they slapped her face, shook her by the heels, worked her arms back and forth, and pounded her back until she coughed up lake water. She shivered all over like a dog, then took a breath. But it wasn't long afterward that those two men disappeared. The first wandered off, and the other, Jean Hat, got himself run over by a cart.

It went to show, my grandma said. It figured to her, all right. By saving Fleur Pillager, those two men had lost themselves.

The next time she fell in the lake, Fleur Pillager was twenty years old and no one touched her. She washed onshore, her skin a dull dead gray, but when George Many Women bent to look closer, he saw her chest move. Then her eyes spun open, sharp black riprock, and she looked at him. "You'll take my place," she hissed. Everybody scattered and left her there, so no one knows how she dragged herself home. Soon after that we noticed Many Women changed, grew afraid, wouldn't leave his house, and would not be forced to go near water. For his caution, he lived until the day that his sons brought him a new tin bathtub. Then the first time he used the tub he slipped, got knocked out, and breathed water while his wife stood in the other room frying breakfast.

Men stayed clear of Fleur Pillager after the second drowning. Even though she was good-looking, nobody dared to court her because it was clear that Misshepeshu, the waterman, the monster, wanted her for himself. He's a devil, that one, love-hungry with desire and maddened for the touch of young girls, the strong and daring especially, the ones like Fleur.

Our mothers warn us that we'll think he's handsome, for he appears with green eyes, copper skin, a mouth tender as a child's. But if you fall into his arms, he sprouts horns, fangs, claws, fins. His feet are joined as one and his skin, brass scales, rings to the touch. You're fascinated, cannot move. He casts a shell necklace at your feet, weeps gleaming chips that harden into mica on your breasts. He holds you under. Then he takes the body of a lion or a fat brown worm. He's made of gold. He's made of beach moss. He's a thing of dry foam, a thing of death by drowning, the death a Chippewa cannot survive.

Unless you are Fleur Pillager. We all knew she couldn't swim. After the first time, we thought she'd never go back to Lake Turcot. We thought she'd keep to herself, live quiet, stop killing men off by drowning in the lake. After the first time, we thought she'd keep the good ways. But then, after the second drowning, we knew that we were dealing with something much more serious. She was haywire, out of control. She messed with evil, laughed at the old women's advice, and dressed like a man. She got herself into some half-forgotten medicine, studied ways we shouldn't talk about. Some say she kept the finger of a child in her pocket and a powder of unborn rabbits in a leather thong around her neck. She laid the heart of an owl on her tongue so she could see at night, and went out, hunting, not even in her own body. We know for sure because the next morning, in the snow or dust, we followed the tracks of her bare feet and saw where they changed, where the claws sprang out, the pad broadened and pressed into the dirt. By night we heard her chuffing cough, the bear cough. By day her silence and the wide grin she threw to bring down our guard made us frightened. Some thought that Fleur Pillager should be driven off the reservation, but not a single person who spoke like this had the nerve. And finally, when people were just about to get together and throw her out, she left on her own and didn't come back all summer. That's what this story is about.

During that summer, when she lived a few miles south in Argus, things happened. She almost destroyed that town.

When she got down to Argus in the year of 1920, it was just a small grid of six streets on either side of the railroad depot. There were two elevators, one central, the other a few miles west. Two stores competed for the trade of the three hundred citizens, and three churches quarreled with one another for their souls. There was a frame building for Lutherans, a heavy brick one for Episcopalians, and a long narrow shingled Catholic church. This last had a tall slender steeple, twice as high as any building or tree.

No doubt, across the low, flat wheat, watching from the road as she came near Argus on foot, Fleur saw that steeple rise, a shadow thin as a needle. Maybe in that raw space it drew her the way a lone tree draws lightning. Maybe, in the end, the Catholics are to blame. For if she hadn't seen that sign of pride, that slim prayer, that marker, maybe she would have kept walking.

But Fleur Pillager turned, and the first place she went once she came into town was to the back door of the priest's residence attached to the landmark church. She didn't go there for a handout, although she got that, but to ask for work. She got that too, or the town got her. It's hard to tell which came out worse, her or the men or the town, although the upshot of it all was that Fleur lived.

The four men who worked at the butcher's had carved up about a thousand carcasses between them, maybe half of that steers and the other half pigs, sheep, and game animals like deer, elk, and bear. That's not even mentioning the chickens, which were beyond counting. Pete Kozka owned the place, and employed Lily Veddar, Tor Grunewald, and my stepfather, Dutch James, who had brought my mother down from the reservation the year before she disappointed him by dying. Dutch took me out of school to take her place. I kept house half the time and worked the other in the butcher shop, sweeping floors, putting sawdust down, running a hambone across the street to a customer's bean pot or a package of sausage to the corner. I was a good one to have around because until they needed me, I was invisible. I blended into the stained brown walls, a skinny, big-nosed girl with staring eyes. Because I could fade into a corner or squeeze beneath a shelf, I knew everything, what the men said when no one was around, and what they did to Fleur.

Kozka's Meats served farmers for a fifty-mile area, both to slaughter, for it had a stock pen and a chute, and to cure the meat by smoking it or spicing it in sausage. The storage locker was a marvel, made of many thicknesses of brick, earth insulation, and Minnesota timber, lined inside with sawdust and vast blocks of ice cut from Lake Turcot, hauled down from home each winter by horse and sledge.

A ramshackle board building, part slaughterhouse, part store, was fixed to the low, thick square of the lockers. That's where Fleur worked. Kozka hired her for her strength. She could lift a haunch or carry a pole of sausages without stumbling, and she soon learned cutting from Pete's wife, a string-thin blonde who chain-smoked and handled the razor-sharp knives with nerveless precision, slicing close to her stained fingers. Fleur and Fritzie Kozka worked afternoons, wrapping their cuts in paper, and Fleur hauled the packages to the lockers. The meat was left outside the heavy oak doors that were only opened at 5:00 each afternoon, before the men ate supper.

Sometimes Dutch, Tor, and Lily ate at the lockers, and when they did I stayed too, cleaned floors, restoked the fires in the front smokehouses, while the men sat around the squat cast-iron stove spearing slats of herring onto hardtack bread. They played long games of poker or cribbage on a board made from the planed end of a salt crate. They talked and I listened, although there wasn't much to hear since almost nothing ever happened in Argus. Tor was married, Dutch had lost my mother, and Lily read circulars. They mainly discussed about the auctions to come, equipment, or women.

Every so often, Pete Kozka came out front to make a whist, leaving Fritzie to smoke cigarettes and fry raised doughnuts in the back room. He sat and played a few rounds but kept his thoughts to himself. Fritzie did not tolerate him talking behind her back, and the one book he read was the New Testament. If he said something, it concerned weather or a surplus of sheep stomachs, a ham that smoked green or the markets for corn and wheat. He had a good-luck talisman, the opal-white lens of a cow's eye. Playing cards, he rubbed it between his fingers. That soft sound and the slap of cards was about the only conversation.

Fleur finally gave them a subject.

Her cheeks were wide and flat, her hands large, chapped, muscular. Fleur's shoulders were broad as beams, her hips fishlike, slippery, narrow. An old green dress clung to her waist, worn thin where she sat. Her braids were thick like the tails of animals, and swung against her when she moved, deliberately, slowly in her work, held in and half-tamed, but only half. I could tell, but the others never saw. They never looked into her sly brown eyes or noticed her teeth, strong and curved and very white. Her legs were bare, and since she padded around in beadwork moccasins they never saw that her fifth toes were missing. They never knew she'd drowned. They were blinded, they were stupid, they only saw her in the flesh.

And yet it wasn't just that she was a Chippewa, or even that she was a woman, it wasn't that she was good-looking or even that she was alone that made their brains hum. It was how she played cards.

Women didn't usually play with men, so the evening that Fleur drew a chair up to the men's table without being so much as asked, there was a shock of surprise.

"What's this," said Lily. He was fat, with a snake's cold pale eyes and precious skin, smooth and lily-white, which is how he got his name. Lily had a dog, a stumpy mean little bull of a thing with a belly drum-tight from eating pork rinds. The dog liked to play cards just like Lily, and straddled his barrel thighs through games of stud, rum poker, vingt-un. The dog snapped at Fleur's arm that first night, but cringed back, its snarl frozen, when she took her place.

"I thought," she said, her voice soft and stroking, "you might deal me in."

There was a space between the heavy bin of spiced flour and the wall where I just fit. I hunkered down there, kept my eyes open, saw her black hair swing over the chair, her feet solid on the wood floor. I couldn't see up on the table where the cards slapped down, so after they were deep in their game I raised myself up in the shadows, and crouched on a sill of wood.

I watched Fleur's hands stack and ruffle, divide the cards, spill them to each player in a blur, rake them up and shuffle again. Tor, short and scrappy, shut one eye and squinted the other at Fleur. Dutch screwed his lips around a wet cigar.

"Gotta see a man," he mumbled, getting up to go out back to the privy. The others broke, put their cards down, and Fleur sat alone in the lamplight that glowed in a sheen across the push of her breasts. I watched her closely, then she paid me a beam of notice for the first time. She turned, looked straight at me, and grinned the white wolf grin a Pillager turns on its victims, except that she wasn't after me.

"Pauline there," she said, "how much money you got?"

We'd all been paid for the week that day. Eight cents was in my pocket.

"Stake me," she said, holding out her long fingers. I put the coins in her palm and then I melted back to nothing, part of the walls and tables. It was a long time before I understood that the men would not have seen me no matter what I did, how I moved. I wasn't anything like Fleur. My dress hung loose and my back was already curved, an old woman's. Work had roughened me, reading made my eyes sore, caring for my mother before she died had hardened my face. I was not much to look at, so they never saw me.

When the men came back and sat around the table, they had drawn together. They shot each other small glances, stuck their tongues in their cheeks, burst out laughing at odd moments, to rattle Fleur. But she never minded. They played their vingt-un, staying even as Fleur slowly gained. Those pennies I had given her drew nickels and attracted dimes until there was a small pile in front of her.

Then she hooked them with five-card draw, nothing wild. She dealt, discarded, drew, and then she sighed and her cards gave a little shiver. Tor's eye gleamed, and Dutch straightened in his seat.

"I'll pay to see that hand," said Lily Veddar.

Fleur showed, and she had nothing there, nothing at all.

Tor's thin smile cracked open, and he threw his hand in too.

"Well, we know one thing," he said, leaning back in his chair, "the squaw can't bluff."

With that I lowered myself into a mound of swept sawdust and slept. I woke up during the night, but none of them had moved yet, so I couldn't either. Still later, the men must have gone out again, or Fritzie come out to break the game, because I was lifted, soothed, cradled in a woman's arms and rocked so quiet that I kept my eyes shut while Fleur rolled me into a closet of grimy ledgers, oiled paper, balls of string, and thick files that fit beneath me like a mattress.

The game went on after work the next evening. I got my eight cents back five times over, and Fleur kept the rest of the dollar she'd won for a stake. This time they didn't play so late, but they played regular, and then kept going at it night after night. They played poker now, or variations, for one week straight, and each time Fleur won exactly one dollar, no more and no less, too consistent for luck.

By this time, Lily and the other men were so lit with suspense that they got Pete to join the game with them. They concentrated, the fat dog sitting tense in Lily Veddar's lap,

Tor suspicious, Dutch stroking his huge square brow, Pete steady. It wasn't that Fleur won that hooked them in so, because she lost hands too. It was rather that she never had a freak hand or even anything above a straight. She only took on her low cards, which didn't sit right. By chance, Fleur should have gotten a full or flush by now. The irritating thing was she beat with pairs and never bluffed, because she couldn't, and still she ended up each night with exactly one dollar. Lily couldn't believe, first of all, that a woman could be smart enough to play cards, but even if she was, that she would then be stupid enough to cheat for a dollar a night. By day I watched him turn the problem over, his hard white face dull, small fingers probing at his knuckles, until he finally thought he had Fleur figured out as a bit-time player, caution her game. Raising the stakes would throw her.

More than anything now, he wanted Fleur to come away with something but a dollar. Two bits less or ten more, the sum didn't matter, just so he broke her streak.

Night after night she played, won her dollar, and left to stay in a place that just Fritzie and I knew about. Fleur bathed in the slaughtering tub, then slept in the unused brick smokehouse behind the lockers, a windowless place tarred on the inside with scorched fats. When I brushed against her skin I noticed that she smelled of the walls, rich and woody, slightly burnt. Since that night she put me in the closet I was no longer afraid of her, but followed her close, stayed with her, became her moving shadow that the men never noticed, the shadow that could have saved her.

August, the month that bears fruit, closed around the shop, and Pete and Fritzie left for Minnesota to escape the heat. Night by night, running, Fleur had won thirty dollars, and only Pete's presence had kept Lily at bay. But Pete was gone now, and one payday, with the heat so bad no one could move but Fleur, the men sat and played and waited while she finished work. The cards sweat, limp in their fingers, the table was slick with grease, and even the walls were warm to the touch. The air was motionless. Fleur was in the next room boiling heads.

Her green dress, drenched, wrapped her like a transparent sheet. A skin of lakeweed. Black snarls of veining clung to her arms. Her braids were loose, half-unraveled, tied behind her neck in a thick loop. She stood in steam, turning skulls through a vat with a wooden paddle. When scraps boiled to the surface, she bent with a round tin sieve and scooped them out. She'd filled two dishpans.

"Ain't that enough now?" called Lily. "We're waiting." The stump of a dog trembled in his lap, alive with rage. It never smelled me or noticed me above Fleur's smoky skin. The air was heavy in my corner, and pressed me down. Fleur sat with them.

"Now what do you say?" Lily asked the dog. It barked. That was the signal for the real game to start.

"Let's up the ante," said Lily, who had been stalking this night all month. He had a roll of money in his pocket. Fleur had five bills in her dress. The men had each saved their full pay.

"Ante a dollar then," said Fleur, and pitched hers in. She lost, but they let her scrape along, cent by cent. And then she won some. She played unevenly, as if chance was all she had. She reeled them in. The game went on. The dog was stiff now, poised on Lily's knees, a ball of vicious muscle with its yellow eyes slit in concentration. It gave advice, seemed to sniff the lay of Fleur's cards, twitched and nudged. Fleur was up, then down, saved by a scratch. Tor dealt seven cards, three down. The pot grew, round by round, until it held all the money. Nobody folded. Then it all rode on one last card and they went silent. Fleur

picked hers up and blew a long breath. The heat lowered like a bell. Her card shook, but she stayed in.

Lily smiled and took the dog's head tenderly between his palms.

"Say, Fatso," he said, crooning the words, "you reckon that girl's bluffing?"

The dog whined and Lily laughed. "Me, too," he said, "let's show." He swept his bills and coins into the pot and then they turned their cards over.

Lily looked once, looked again, then he squeezed the dog up like a fist of dough and slammed it on the table.

Fleur threw her arms out and drew the money over, grinning that same wolf grin that she'd used on me, the grin that had them. She jammed the bills in her dress, scooped the coins up in waxed white paper that she tied with string.

"Let's go another round," said Lily, his voice choked with burrs. But Fleur opened her mouth and yawned, then walked out back to gather slops for the one big hog that was waiting in the stock pen to be killed.

The men sat still as rocks, their hands spread on the oiled wood table. Dutch had chewed his cigar to damp shreds, Tor's eye was dull. Lily's gaze was the only one to follow Fleur. I didn't move. I felt them gathering, saw my stepfather's veins, the ones in his forehead that stood out in anger. The dog had rolled off the table and curled in a knot below the counter, where none of the men could touch it.

Lily rose and stepped out back to the closet of ledgers where Pete kept his private stock. He brought back a bottle, uncorked and tipped it between his fingers. The lump in his throat moved, then he passed it on. They drank, quickly felt the whiskey's fire, and planned with their eyes things they couldn't say out loud.

When they left, I followed. I hid out back in the clutter of broken boards and chicken crates beside the stock pen, where they waited. Fleur could not be seen at first, and then the moon broke and showed her, slipping cautiously along the rough board chute with a bucket in her hand. Her hair fell, wild and coarse, to her waist, and her dress was a floating patch in the dark. She made a pig-calling sound, rang the tin pail lightly against the wood, froze suspiciously. But too late. In the sound of the ring Lily moved, fat and nimble, stepped right behind Fleur and put out his creamy hands. At his first touch, she whirled and doused him with the bucket of sour slops. He pushed her against the big fence and the package of coins split, went clinking and jumping, winked against the wood. Fleur rolled over once and vanished in the yard.

The moon fell behind a curtain of ragged clouds, and Lily followed into the dark muck. But he tripped, pitched over the huge flank of the pig, who lay mired to the snout, heavily snoring. I sprang out of the weeds and climbed the side of the pen, stuck like glue. I saw the sow rise to her neat, knobby knees, gain her balance, and sway, curious, as Lily stumbled forward. Fleur had backed into the angle of rough wood just beyond, and when Lily tried to jostle past, the sow tipped up on her hind legs and struck, quick and hard as a snake. She plunged her head into Lily's thick side and snatched a mouthful of his shirt. She lunged again, caught him lower, so that he grunted in pained surprise. He seemed to ponder, breathing deep. Then he launched his huge body in a swimmer's dive.

The sow screamed as his body smacked over hers. She rolled, striking out with her knife-sharp hooves, and Lily gathered himself upon her, took her foot-long face by the ears and scraped her snout and cheeks against the trestles of the pen. He hurled the sow's tight skull against an iron post, but instead of knocking her dead, he merely woke her from her dream.

She reared, shrieked, drew him with her so that they posed standing upright. They bowed jerkily to each other, as if to begin. Then his arms swung and flailed. She sank her black fangs into his shoulder, clasping him, dancing him forward and backward through the pen. Their steps picked up pace, went wild. The two dipped as one, box-stepped, tripped each other. She ran her split foot through his hair. He grabbed her kinked tail. They went down and came up, the same shape and then the same color, until the men couldn't tell one from the other in that light and Fleur was able to launch herself over the gates, swing down, hit gravel.

The men saw, yelled, and chased her at a dead run to the smokehouse. And Lily too, once the sow gave up in disgust and freed him. That is where I should have gone to Fleur, saved her, thrown myself on Dutch. But I went stiff with fear and couldn't unlatch myself from the trestles or move at all. I closed my eyes and put my head in my arms, tried to hide, so there is nothing to describe but what I couldn't block out, Fleur's hoarse breath, so loud it filled me, her cry in the old language, and my name repeated over and over among the words.

The heat was still dense the next morning when I came back to work. Fleur was gone but the men were there, slack-faced, hung over. Lily was paler and softer than ever, as if his flesh had steamed on his bones. They smoked, took pulls off a bottle. It wasn't noon yet. I worked awhile, waiting shop and sharpening steel. But I was sick, I was smothered, I was sweating so hard that my hands slipped on the knives, and I wiped my fingers clear of the greasy touch of the customers' coins. Lily opened his mouth and roared once, not in anger. There was no meaning to the sound. His boxer dog, sprawled limp beside his foot, never lifted its head. Nor did the other men.

They didn't notice when I stepped outside, hoping for a clear breath. And then I forgot them because I knew that we were all balanced, ready to tip, to fly, to be crushed as soon as the weather broke. The sky was so low that I felt the weight of it like a yoke. Clouds hung down, witch teats, a tornado's green-brown cones, and as I watched one flicked out and became a delicate probing thumb. Even as I picked up my heels and ran back inside, the wind blew suddenly, cold, and then came rain.

Inside, the men had disappeared already and the whole place was trembling as if a huge hand was pinched at the rafters, shaking it. I ran straight through, screaming for Dutch or for any of them, and then I stopped at the heavy doors of the lockers, where they had surely taken shelter. I stood there a moment. Everything went still. Then I heard a cry building in the wind, faint at first, a whistle and then a shrill scream that tore through the walls and gathered around me, spoke plain so I understood that I should move, put my arms out, and slam down the great iron bar that fit across the hasp and lock.

Outside, the wind was stronger, like a hand held against me. I struggled forward. The bushes tossed, the awnings flapped off storefronts, the rails of porches rattled. The odd cloud became a fat snout that nosed along the earth and sniffled, jabbed, picked at things, sucked them up, blew them apart, rooted around as if it was following a certain scent, then stopped behind me at the butcher shop and bored down like a drill.

I went flying, landed somewhere in a ball. When I opened my eyes and looked, stranger things were happening.

A herd of cattle flew through the air like giant birds, dropping dung, their mouths opened in stunned bellows. A candle, still lighted, blew past, and tables, napkins, garden tools, a whole school of drifting eyeglasses, jackets on hangers, hams, a checkerboard, a lampshade, and at last the sow from behind the lockers, on the run, her hooves a blur, set free, swooping, diving, screaming as everything in Argus fell apart and got turned upside down, smashed, and thoroughly wrecked.

Days passed before the town went looking for the men. They were bachelors, after all, except for Tor, whose wife had suffered a blow to the head that made her forgetful. Everyone was occupied with digging out, in high relief because even though the Catholic steeple had been torn off like a peaked cap and sent across five fields, those huddled in the cellar were unhurt. Walls had fallen, windows were demolished, but the stores were intact and so were the bankers and shop owners who had taken refuge in their safes or beneath their cash registers. It was a fair-minded disaster, no one could be said to have suffered much more than the next, at least not until Fritzie and Pete came home.

Of all the businesses in Argus, Kozka's Meats had suffered worst. The boards of the front building had been split to kindling, piled in a huge pyramid, and the shop equipment was blasted far and wide. Pete paced off the distance the iron bathtub had been flung—a hundred feet. The glass candy case went fifty, and landed without so much as a cracked pane. There were other surprises as well, for the back rooms where Fritzie and Pete lived were undisturbed. Fritzie said the dust still coated her china figures, and upon her kitchen table, in the ashtray, perched the last cigarette she'd put out in haste. She lit it up and finished it, looking through the window. From there, she could see that the old smokehouse Fleur had slept in was crushed to a reddish sand and the stockpens were completely torn apart, the rails stacked helter-skelter. Fritzie asked for Fleur. People shrugged. Then she asked about the others and, suddenly, the town understood that three men were missing.

There was a rally of help, a gathering of shovels and volunteers. We passed boards from hand to hand, stacked them, uncovered what lay beneath the pile of jagged splinters. The lockers, full of the meat that was Pete and Fritzie's investment, slowly came into sight, still intact. When enough room was made for a man to stand on the roof, there were calls, a general urge to hack through and see what lay below. But Fritzie shouted that she wouldn't allow it because the meat would spoil. And so the work continued, board by board, until at last the heavy oak doors of the freezer were revealed and people pressed to the entry. Everyone wanted to be the first, but since it was my stepfather lost, I was let go in when Pete and Fritzie wedged through into the sudden icy air.

Pete scraped a match on his boot, lit the lamp Fritzie held, and then the three of us stood still in its circle. Light glared off the skinned and hanging carcasses, the crates of wrapped sausages, the bright and cloudy blocks of lake ice, pure as winter. The cold bit into us, pleasant at first, then numbing. We must have stood there a couple of minutes before we saw the men, or more rightly, the humps of fur, the iced and shaggy hides they wore, the bearskins they had taken down and wrapped around themselves. We stepped closer and tilted the lantern beneath the flaps of fur into their faces. The dog was there, perched among them, heavy as a doorstop. The three had hunched around a barrel where the game was still laid out, and a dead lantern and an empty bottle, too. But they had thrown down their last hands and hunkered tight, clutching one another, knuckles raw from beating at the door they had also attacked with hooks. Frost stars gleamed off their eyelashes and the stubble of their beards. Their faces were set in concentration, mouths open as if to speak some careful thought, some agreement they'd come to in each other's arms.

Power travels in the bloodlines, handed out before birth. It comes down through the hands, which in the Pillagers were strong and knotted, big, spidery, and rough, with sensitive fingertips good at dealing cards. It comes through the eyes, too, belligerent, darkest brown, the eyes of those in the bear clan, impolite as they gaze directly at a person.

In my dreams, I look straight back at Fleur, at the men. I am no longer the watcher on the dark sill, the skinny girl.

The blood draws us back, as if it runs through a vein of earth. I've come home and, except for talking to my cousins, live a quiet life. Fleur lives quiet too, down on Lake Turcot with her boat. Some say she's married to the waterman, Misshepeshu, or that she's living in shame with white men or windigos, or that she's killed them all. I'm about the only one here who ever goes to visit her. Last winter, I went to help out in her cabin when she bore the child, whose green eyes and skin the color of an old penny made more talk, as no one could decide if the child was mixed blood or what, fathered in a smokehouse, or by a man with brass scales, or by the lake. The girl is bold, smiling in her sleep, as if she knows what people wonder, as if she hears the old men talk, turning the story over. It comes up different every time and has no ending, no beginning. They get the middle wrong too. They only know that they don't know anything.

MARY ROBISON

(1949–)

I Get By

About the Author: Mary Robison was born in Washington, D.C., and educated at Johns Hopkins University (M. A., 1977). A frequent contributor of short stories to *The New Yorker,* she has also published novels, among them *Oh!* (1981). She teaches in the Department of Creative Writing at Harvard University.

Right after the windup of the memorial service, there in the hospital chapel that evening in February, the principal of the elementary school where my husband, Kit, had taught approached me. Enough of a crowd had gathered and passed that I had to inch over and strain to hear him, because the chapel doors had opened. From down the hall there were metal bed and tray noises, buzzers and dings, and doctor-paging voices, as my husband's mourners made their exit.

My mother-in-law, Rennie, still sat in the pew behind me, arm-rocking the baby, who was sounding little pleas. The principal was talking to me. "I think I've found a replacement for Kit," he said.

I had to let that remark hang there for a beat. He meant another teacher. He was either too cruel or too vacant a person to have prefaced it in some way. He said, "Her name's Andrea Dennis. Came down from Danbury for interviews this afternoon. Knocked us sideways, actually. You two might get in touch."

I said, "Isn't that nice."

My kids, Ben and Bibi, helped me up from the pew. The principal mentioned he'd tried to call with his condolences. Possibly he had; I had unplugged all three of our phones.

After we got home, Ben and Bibi lingered in the back yard. It was snowing by now—a

friendly snow, scurrying in the floodlights behind the house. Rennie took over the couch. She had the baby and our whole stack of pastel sympathy cards. "Going to *read* these," she said, as though someone ought to do more than open the envelopes and nod, acknowledging the signatures.

I warmed a bottle of formula in hot tap water, and watched my children through the window over the sinks. Bibi had fitted into the tire swing somehow. She is broad-bottomed at eighteen. The swing's rope, knotted around a limb of the weeping willow tree, was stiff with ice.

Ben was only a few feet away, urinating onto a bump of snow. I had to look twice, to be sure. He was eleven, *almost* eleven, and peeing in view of his sister.

Bibi had just colored her hair, but I wasn't ready to accept her as a champagne blonde yet. She looks *familiar*, I'd think, whenever I happened onto her.

The Saturday morning we learned about Kit, the Old Hadham police visited. So did two station wagons from television news teams. I took a confirming call from the idiot aircraft-company people who'd rented Kit the light plane in which he died. After the call, I snapped the telephones out of their plastic jacks, and Bibi chain-locked the door of the upstairs bathroom and stripped away the hair color nature had given her.

I met Andrea Dennis. I was at the school, sorting through two decades' worth of teacher paraphernalia, looking for anything personal in classroom cupboards and in Kit's mammoth oakwood desk. I found a comb, his reading glasses, a Swiss Army knife, and a hardback copy of "Smiley's People," bookmarked halfway. This was on a school day, but after classes had adjourned. Andrea pushed open the heavy door and found me. She introduced herself in an inquiring way: "I'm Andrea?"

We talked some. We didn't say anything I thought to commit to memory. I spilled Elmer's Glue all over. The white glue moved thickly across the desk blotter. "I'd better take care of that," Andrea said. "Let me fetch a sponge or something, from the lounge."

I used to be entirely comfortable in the staff-and-faculty lounge.

Old Hadham Elementary had gone up in '64. Inside and out, the building was an architectural oddity. Kit's classroom (he'd had half of sixth grade), for instance, was in the shape of a semicircle. His huge desk and his roller chair faced out from the straight wall. The room had three rising rows of student chairs with attached laminated writing arms. The floor was covered with jewel-blue linoleum. The curved wall wore a band of pale corkboard.

In the couple of weeks Andrea Dennis had been teaching, she'd tacked up stuff for the lull between Valentine's Day and St. Patrick's Day. There were pen-and-ink drawings that looked like student self-portraits to me. Some printed quotes were pinned up—sayings of statesmen and explorers. There were two science charts: one explaining the pollination of a flower, the other an illustration of polar and equatorial weather movements. Left over from Kit's days here were the usual flags—Old Glory and the Connecticut state flag—and some empty hamster cages with empty water fonts and play wheels. I planned to leave all those behind, of course, as well as Kit's globe, showing the continents and oceans in their proper cloudy colors. Kit hated globes with countries done in pink or purple.

I had to admit Andrea Dennis was an appealing woman. She had clearly put a lot of clever thought and effort into presenting herself at her best. She had on a touch-me-please cashmere sweater and a soft wool-blend skirt with a lining that rustled. Her sheer nylons gleamed. She had hair long enough to toss.

I had noticed something about us. Whenever I mentioned Kit, I nodded at his desk.

When Andrea referred to him once, she gestured north. Toward the forest where the plane fell?

I hung around for fifteen minutes. Andrea didn't return with the sponge. Anyway, the glue had hardened by now. I pictured her yakking away with young Mr. Mankiewicz or flirting with old Mr. Sonner.

I packed Kit's things into a blue nylon gym bag. I bundled up and walked home—a matter of a mile or so—in the road. My part of Connecticut has no proper sidewalks. I kept stumbling. Ever since the baby, and then especially after what happened to Kit, I had been sleeping sporadically and then only in short spurts. That was part of the reason I'd been so clumsy and had flubbed with the glue. My getup was pretty cockeyed, too. I had forgotten to wear socks, and yet the shoelaces on my Nikes were triple-bow-tied. Beneath my parka, my sweater was lumpy and had the smell of Johnson's baby products, as did the whole interior of our beautiful saltbox house when I got there—baby oil, baby powder, baby's softened-fabric bunting. Everywhere I looked was bright with baby things, baby artifacts.

I went into the kitchen, grateful for Rennie, who'd tidied up. Rennie had almost never stayed with us when Kit was alive. We'd seldom gone to see her. She lived alone on what had once been an apple orchard, near Darien. She cared for the big central house there, and there were two barns and two brown outbuildings on the land. Her husband had long ago put himself into a V.A. hospital. He was a troubled, haunted man. I had witnessed some behavior. He'd sit for long afternoons with his head in his hands. He would roam searchingly over the yards and meadows. He'd seem to hide beside the shadowy brown barns. Other times, he'd pitch and splatter hard apples furiously against the fallen-in stone walls around the borders of the orchard. Thinking of him, I made a bet with myself that I hoped I wouldn't win. I bet that Rennie connected Kit's accident with his father's illness. That would have been unfair.

March came. We'd get a couple more snowstorms in Old Hadham, I suspected. Spring wouldn't arrive in any decided way for weeks and weeks. But I was seeing new grass and there was dry pavement. April would be breathtaking along our road. There'd be arbutus, hepaticas, downy yellow violets. In the living room, Rennie had sections of the local evening newspaper strewn around. The baby was in the playpen, wadding and tearing a Super Duper coupon page.

"Where's the baby's dolly?" I asked Rennie.

She said, "Ask Ben."

"Ben? Ben has Susie Soft Sounds?" But I didn't call up to Ben. Every day, it seemed, there was more about him and Bibi that I didn't care to know.

They had identical rooms, across the hall from each other—identical except that Bibi's wallpaper showed jazz dancers against a mint-green background, whereas Ben's had ponies grazing in a field. The night before, I had happened past the rooms and heard Bibi say, from behind Ben's door, "I am safely buzzed." Next I heard the pop-tab open what I assumed was a beer can.

"That's your *third!*" Ben had whispered.

Another curious moment was when I noticed something in among Bibi's hand laundry; she had borrowed my pushup bra.

Bibi talked a lot about Andrea Dennis these days. Andrea, it turned out, sometimes snacked after school at the Nutmeg Tea and Sandwich Shop, where Bibi waited tables. It seemed as if Andrea was always with someone I knew well, or had known. I could never

resist saying, "Really? What did she have on? Did she look tired? Who picked up the check? Did they have desserts or entrées? Did she have that fruit cup?"

I was driving home from the lawyers'. The airplane company's insurance people had investigated and decided to settle some money on me. I liked it about the money, but what I wanted just now was my bed, pillows, the electric blanket. For three days, a quiet sleet had been falling on Old Hadham.

The car's windshield wiper on my side suddenly locked taut on a diagonal. A film formed immediately on my part of the glass. I tried the squirters, but all I got was blue fluid congealing with the ice at the base of the windshield. I maneuvered down Willow, on Old Hadham's steepest hill—a plunger that had been only cursorily sanded. There was a car not far ahead, and a truck on my tail, no shoulder. I had to tip my head out the driver's window to see. Meanwhile, Rennie was smiling, half asleep. The baby said a noise very much like "Why?" I had something close to nausea suddenly: suddenly missing Kit.

The baby woke me. It was an April morning, pre-dawn. I was groggy, but I had a sweet dream still playing in my head—some of the dream's color and its melody—as I heated water for the formula and started coffee. "Here we come!" Rennie said, and drove the baby's castered crib into the kitchen. Rennie was oddly cheerful, giddy. Her taffeta robe was on inside out. She sat down and swayed the crib and sang some ballad about whaling boats and messmates, with a line about the lowland sea.

To distract the baby, Rennie had dropped a fat nest of pink excelsior into the crib—a leftover from Easter baskets. I was a little afraid the baby would eat the pink cellophane, so I intended to snatch it away. But for now the excelsior ball rolled back and forth with the crib's movement, and with Rennie's song and what rhythms there were of my lingering dream.

When the baby was asleep, we two sipped coffee. I figured Rennie would be stepping out onto the porch for sunrise, as she sometimes did, but instead she said she wanted to talk about her son, about Kit. I told her what I knew was true—that his character faults included overconfidence and impulsiveness. I said that he had received flying lessons and his license. But whatever his license signified, he hadn't been ready, not competent, to solo-pilot a plane.

A lot of Old Hadham showed up at Chicwategue Park for Memorial Day. Some people brought picnic dinners and thermoses or coolers of drinks. The high school's brass-and-drum corps was there to do shows. There were two burros roped to a post for the little kids to ride around a guided circle.

Chicwategue Park had ducks on a pond, and a pair of swans—the town favorites—who'd made it through the winter, and bronze statues of Revolutionary War generals, and, in the center, a white-painted, lacy-looking gazebo. On the soccer fields beyond the woods, there would be footraces and other competitions throughout the day. Rennie had given Ben a two-year-old boxer she'd purchased through a newspaper ad, and Ben had entered himself and Reebok in the Frisbee contest.

I set up camp on a faded quilt with the baby. Rennie took Bibi to gamble away some of her waitress tips from the Nutmeg at the bingo tables. Watching them go, I noticed Andrea Dennis over by the penny-toss place—sporty and pretty in spotless sky-blue sweats, with a balloon on a ribbon looped at her wrist. She and Bibi greeted each other like classmates, with a hug.

Bibi's appearance looked to me like a screaming-out-loud reaction to Andrea Dennis. Bibi had whacked her fake-blond hair into bristles and points, and her face was dusted with chalky makeup. Her lips looked almost black, and the tank top and jeans she wore were black. Still, Andrea was giving Bibi approving looks and nods.

But if Bibi's getups scared people, at least her manner had improved. That morning at breakfast, I'd overheard her saying to Ben, "Relax and sit still. I'll fix you a fresh glass of orange juice."

Now Ben's name was called over the P.A. system. I carried the baby and trailed Ben and Reebok over to the starting stripe on the Frisbee-competition field. Ben had the dog's collar in one hand and his yellow Frisbee in the other. Ben was down on one knee and the dog was trembling with excitement as they waited for the judge's signal to begin their routine.

At the whistle, the dog bolted away down the field. Ben stood up and let fly. His first couple of tries were long, too fast throws, and the Frisbee sailed yards over Reebok's head. The dog wasn't paying attention anyhow. On their third and last turn, Reebok watched as he ran, then leaped, fishtailed, and chomped the disk, but only after it had ricocheted twice off the dirt. At the gazebo, the Frisbee judge held up a card, giving Ben and Reebok a "4" rating.

Andrea Dennis strolled over to us. She introduced herself to the baby and sort of shook hands with him. Ben and the dog came over. Ben's young face was bright, but I couldn't tell if it was from excitement or embarrassment.

Andrea said, "Man, you got robbed! Your dog flew six feet straight up. What do they *want?* They should've given you guys a special award."

Ben absorbed this. I knew that on the car ride home he would relive Reebok's last effort for Bibi and Rennie. He'd say he got robbed.

I asked him to watch the baby a minute—to make sure the kid didn't crawl away, go swimming after the swans, or filch anyone's barbecued spareribs.

I clapped a hand on the smooth blue sweatshirt material on Andrea's shoulder.

"What did I do?" Andrea said, and I said, "A lot."

We walked along together by the rows of blankets and the outdoor furniture that bordered the competition fields. We said hello to people—fellow-teachers of Andrea's, the families of some of her students, old friends of mine.

I was thinking how to tell her that she had been an important distraction for me—maybe even a necessary one. She'd been someone safe for me to focus on while the reality of having no Kit was so fierce. I realized I couldn't make my interest in her into anything polite or easy to explain. I said, "Generally, thanks, Andrea," and I told her how great she looked in her blue.

ALICE ADAMS

(1926–)

Tide Pools

About the Author: Alice Adams is a West Coast (San Francisco) writer whose work reflects her southern childhood (Virginia, North Carolina), eastern education (Radcliffe College), and extensive travels (Europe). She has published five novels and three short-story collections. More than a dozen of her stories have appeared in *Prize Stories: The O. Henry Awards.*

For some years I lived alone in a small white clapboard house, up on a high wooded bluff above the Mississippi River, which I could hardly see—so far down, glimpsed through thick vines and trees, and so narrow just there.

This was near Minneapolis, where I was an assistant professor at a local college. Teaching marine biology. And I thought quite a lot about the irony of my situation—a sea specialty in the landlocked Midwest. (I am from Santa Barbara, California, originally, which may explain quite a bit.)

During those Minnesota years, despite professional business, a heavy teaching load, labs, conferences, friends, and a few sporadic love affairs, I was often lonely, an embarrassing condition to which I would never have admitted. Still, and despite my relative isolation, at that time I regarded the telephone as an enemy, its shrill, imperative sound an interruption even to loneliness. When my phone rang I did not anticipate a friendly chat. For one thing, most of my friends and lovers were also hardworking professionals, not much given to minor social exchange.

Thus, on a summer night about a year ago, a rare warm clear twilight, reminding me of Southern California, I was far from pleased at the sound of the telephone. I had just taken a bath and finished dressing; I was going out to dinner with a man I had met recently, whom I thought I liked. (Was he calling to break the date? Native distrust has not helped my relationships with men, nor with women.) We were going out to celebrate my birthday, actually, but I did not imagine that the ringing phone meant someone calling with congratulations, my birthday not being something that I generally talk about.

What I first heard on picking up that alien instrument was the hollow, whirring sound that meant a long-distance call, and I thought, How odd, what a strange hour for business. Then, as I said hello, and hello again, I heard silence. At last a female voice came on, very slurred. But then words formed. "Judith? Have I got Miss Judith Mallory? *Doctor* Mallory?"

"Yes—"

"Judy, is that you, truly? Truly Jude? Judy, do you know who this is?" An excited, drunken voice, its cadence ineradicably familiar to me—and only one person has ever called me Jude. It was Jennifer Cartwright, my closest early-childhood friend, my almost inseparable pal—whom I had not heard from or about for more than twenty years, not since we both left Santa Barbara, where we grew up together, or tried to.

I asked her, "Jennifer, how are you? Where are you? What are you doing now?"

"Well, I'm back in our house, you know. I've come back home. I've been here since Mother died, and I guess I'm doing O.K. Oh Judy, it's really you! I'm so happy . . ."

Happy was the last thing that Jennifer sounded, though; her voice was almost tearful.

"Oh, Jennifer." I was assailed by an overwhelming affection for my friend, mixed with sadness over whatever ailed her just now, including being so drunk. I had not even known that her mother was dead. Nicola—Nickie Cartwright, whom I had also cared about a lot.

My own parents had both been dead for some time, which is one reason I had had no news from Santa Barbara. Also, since they died of so-called alcohol-related ailments, I was perhaps unreasonably alarmed at Jennifer's condition. A nervous stomach, which is no stomach at all for booze, had kept me, if unwillingly, abstemious.

"And oh!" Jennifer's voice sounded indeed much happier now. "I forgot to say happy birthday. Judy, Jude, happy happy birthday! Every year I think of you today, even if I haven't ever called you."

"You're so good to remember," I told her. "But really, tell me how you are."

"Oh, you tell me! First off, you tell me just what you have on." Such a perfect Jennifer question—or Nickie: Nickie, too, would have asked me what I was wearing, in order to see me, and to check on how I was.

To please Jennifer I should have described a beautiful, colorful dress, but a lack of imagination, I believe, has kept me honest; I tend to tell the truth. My former (only) husband observed that I had a very literal mind, and he might have been right, as he was with a few other accurate accusations. In any case, I told Jennifer, "Just a sweater and some pants. My uniform, I guess. But they're both new. Black. Actually, I'm going out to dinner. This man I met—"

Jennifer began to laugh, her old prolonged, slow, appreciative laugh, and I thought, Well, maybe she's not so drunk. Just a little tipsy, maybe, and overexcited.

"Oh, Jude." Jennifer was laughing still. "You're going out on a date, and we're so old. But you sound like you're about sixteen, and wearing something pink and gauzy."

Rational, sober person that I am, I could have cried.

But Jennifer went on in a conversational, much less drunken way. "I think about you so much," she said. "And everything back then. All the fun we had. Of course, since I've moved back here it's all easier to remember."

"I'm really sorry to hear about Nickie," I told her.

"Well, just one more terrible thing. Everyone gets cancer, it seems like to me. Honestly, Jude, sometimes I think being grown up really sucks, don't you? To use a word I truly hate."

"Well, I guess."

"Your parents die, and your husbands turn out bad. And your kids—oh, don't even talk to me about kids."

Her voice trailed off into a total silence, and I thought, Oh dear, she's fallen asleep at the telephone, out there in California, in that house I know so very well. The house right next door to the house where my parents and I used to live—in fact, its architectural twin—on what was called the Santa Barbara Gold Coast, up above the sea. I wondered what room Jennifer was in—her own room, in bed, I hoped. I called out "Jennifer!" over all that space, Minnesota to California. Calling out over time, too, over many years.

Her laugh came on again. "Oh, Jude, you thought I'd gone to sleep. But I hadn't, I was just lying here thinking. In Mother and Dad's big old bed. You remember?"

"Oh, of course I do." And with a rush I remembered the Sunday morning when Jennifer and I had run into the Cartwrights' bedroom, I guess looking for the Sunday papers, and there were blond Scott and blonder Nickie in their tousled nightclothes, lying back among a paleblue tangle of sheets. Not making love, although I think we must have caught them soon after love. They may have moved apart as we came in; Scott's hand still lingered in Nickie's bright, heavy uncombed hair. At the time, I was mostly struck by their sleepy affection for each other, so clearly present. I can see it now, those particular smiles, all over their pale morning faces.

The room, with its seascape view, was almost identical to my parents' bedroom, and their view. My parents slept in narrow, separate beds. They were silent at home except when they drank, which loosened them up a little, though it never made them anywhere near affectionate with each other.

In any case, I surely remembered the Cartwrights' broad, blue-sheeted carved-mahogany bed.

I asked Jennifer, "Your father—Scott died too?" Although I think I knew that he must have. But I used to see Scott Cartwright as the strongest man I ever knew, as well as the most glamorous, with his golfer's tan, and his stride.

"Just after your mother died. They were all so young, weren't they? Dad had a stroke on the golf course, but maybe that's the best way to go. Poor Mother was sick for years. Oh, Judy, it's all so scary. I hate to think about it."

She had begun to trail off again, and partly to keep her awake, in contact, I asked her if she had married more than once; I thought I had heard her say "husbands," plural, but it was hard to tell, with her vagueness, slurring.

But "Oh, three times!" Jennifer told me. "Each one worse. I never seem to learn." But she sounded cheerful, and next she began to laugh. "You will not believe what their names were," she said. "Tom, Dick, and Harry. That's the truth. Well, not actually the whole truth—I can't lie to my best old favorite friend. The whole truth is, the first two were Tom and Dick, and so when I went and got married the third time I had to call him Harry, even if his name was Jack."

I laughed—I had always laughed a lot with Jennifer—but at the same time I was thinking that people from single, happy marriages are supposed to marry happily themselves. They are not supposed to make lonely, drunken phone calls to old, almost forgotten friends.

Mostly, though, I was extremely pleased—elated, even—to have heard from Jennifer at all, despite the bad signs, the clear evidence that she was not in very good shape. As we hung up a few minutes later I was aware of smiling to myself, the happy recipient of a happy birthday present. And like most especially welcome, sensitive presents, this gift from Jennifer was something that I had not known I needed, but that now I could no longer do without: a friend for talking to.

I went out for dinner with my new beau in a rare lighthearted mood, but I may have seemed more than a little abstracted: I was thinking of Jennifer, her parents, and California.

When Jennifer and I were friends, all that time ago, I truly loved her, but I also coveted almost everything about her: her golden curls, small plump hands, her famously sunny disposition, but most especially and most secretly I envied her her parents. I wanted them to be mine.

I have since learned (hasn't everyone?) that this is a common fantasy; Freud tells us that many children believe they have somehow ended up with the wrong set of parents. But at the time I naturally did not know this; guiltily I felt that only I had such an evil wish, to be rid of my own parents and moved in with another set. If it could somehow be proved, I thought, that I had been stolen by this dark and sombre couple with whom I lived, while all along I was really a Cartwright child—then I would be perfectly happy. And if Jennifer's parents were mine, then of course Jennifer and I would be truly sisters, as so often we spoke of wishing that we were.

From the moment I saw them, even before seeing Jennifer, I was drawn to Scott and Nickie Cartwright, a tanned couple getting out of a new wood-panelled station wagon to look at a house for sale, the house next door to our house. I liked their bright splashy clothes, and the easy, careless way they walked and laughed; I wanted them to be the people to buy that house.

I thought that they looked too young to be parents; that they turned out to have a little girl just my age was a marvellous surprise, a bonus, as it were.

My own parents did not like the look of the Cartwrights, at first. "Lots of flash" was my Vermont mother's succinct summation; and my father's: "That garden they're buying needs plenty of solid work. I hope they know it." But fairly soon the four grownups took to dropping in on each other for a cup of coffee or a Coke, maybe, during the day; and at night they all got together for drinks. The Cartwrights, from St. Louis, had a sort of loose-style hospitality to which even my fairly stiff-mannered parents responded.

What must initially have won my stern parents' approval, though, was the Cartwrights' total dedication to their garden. Even before actually moving in they began to spend their weekends digging among the dahlias, pruning hibiscus, trimming orange blossoms, and probing the roots of ivy. And once they lived there, all during the week beautiful Nickie in her short red shorts could be observed out clipping boxwoods, often mowing the lawn. And watering everything.

On weekends, around dusk if not sooner, the four of them would start in on their Tom Collinses, Gin Rickeys, or fruity concoctions with rum. Eventually one of the grownups (usually Nickie Cartwright) would remember that Jennifer and I should have some supper, and the two men (probably) would go out for some fried clams or pizza. Later on they would pretty much forget all about us, which was fine with Jennifer and me; we could stay up as long as we liked, giggling and whispering.

All the grownups that I knew at that time drank; it was what I assumed grownups did when they got together. Jennifer and I never discussed this adult habit, and "drunk" is not a word we would have used to describe our parents, ever. "Drunk" meant a sort of clownish, TV-cartoon behavior.

My parents as they drank simply talked too much; they told what seemed to me very long dull stories having to do with Santa Barbara history, early architects, all that. The Cartwrights, being younger, listened politely; Nickie laughed a lot, and they sat very close together.

Certainly my parents were never clownish or even loud; God knows they were not. In a bitter, tight-mouthed way they might argue at breakfast; a few times (this was the worst of all) I could hear my mother crying late at night, all by herself.

Because I had never heard them do so, I believed that the Cartwrights never argued, and I was sure that beautiful happy Nickie Cartwright never cried, and maybe she did not.

In the days that succeeded that first phone call from Jennifer, I thought considerably about her, about her parents, and mine. With terrible vividness I remembered the strength of my yearning for the Cartwrights, and I was assailed—again!—by the sheer intensity of all that childhood emotion, my earliest passions and guilts and despairs.

Quite as vividly, though, I also remembered the simple fun that we used to have, Jennifer and I, as children, especially on the beach. Since I had always lived there in Santa Barbara, on the California coast, and the Cartwrights were originally from inland Missouri, I was Jennifer's guide to the seashore. Bravely kicking our sneakers into tide pools, Jennifer and I uncovered marvels: tiny hermit crabs, long swaying seaweed, all purple. Anemones. Jennifer would squeal at dead fish, in a high, squeamish way, as I pretended not to mind them.

I also showed Jennifer the more sophisticated pleasures of State Street, the ice-cream parlors and the hot-dog stands. As we both grew up a little I pointed out the stores. Tweeds & Weeds, my mother's favorite, was always too conservative for the Cartwright ladies, though. Nickie loved frills and lots of colors; she dressed herself and Jennifer in every shade of pink to tangerine. My mother ordered almost all of my clothes from the Liliputian Bazaar, at Best & Co.

Undoubtedly the tide pools and my happy fascination with them to a great extent determined my later choice of a career, although a desire to displease and/or shock my parents must have figured largely also. Biology to them connoted sex, which in a general way they were against.

And possibly in some way of my own I made the same connection. In any case, I am forced to say that so far I have shone neither professionally nor in a romantic way. I did achieve a doctorate, and some years later an assistant professorship, at relatively early ages, but I do not feel that I will ever be truly distinguished.

As one of my more kindly professors put it, my interest in marine biology could be called aesthetic rather than scientific. I excel at drawing—urchins, starfish, snails.

As to my romantic history, it got off to a shaky start, so to speak, with my marriage to a fellow-biologist, a man who after two years of me announced that colleagues should not be married to each other. (This could be true, but it had been his idea, originally.) He left me for a kindergarten teacher in Chicago, where his next teaching job happened to be. I became involved with an elderly musicologist, who was married; later with a graduate student in Speech and Drama, who, I came to believe, used coke, a lot of it.

Three men, then—my husband and two subsequent lovers—who presented certain problems. However, surely I do, too? I am hardly "problem-free" or even especially easy to get along with. I am moody, hypersensitive, demanding.

In any case, these days as far as men are concerned I am running scared.

After that first birthday call, Jennifer telephoned again, and again. She seemed to have an unerring instinct for the right time to call, not an easy feat with me. (I once knew a man who always called me when I was brushing my teeth; I used to think that if I really wanted to hear from him I had only to get out my toothbrush.) In Jennifer's case, though, it may have been that I was simply so glad to hear from her.

I gathered that her present life was quite reclusive; she did not seem to know where anyone else whom we had known was now. I gathered, too, that she was quite "comfortably off," to use an old phrase of my mother's. My mother thought "rich" a vulgar word, and perhaps it is. Anyway, I was very glad that Jennifer was comfortable.

As I got used to talking to Jennifer again, sometimes I would find myself scolding her. You should get out more, take walks, get exercise, I would say. Go swimming—there must be a pool around. And what about vitamins? Do you eat enough? And Jennifer would laugh in her amiable way, and say she was sure I was absolutely right.

Jennifer's memory for long-gone days was extraordinary, though. She reminded me of the day we decided that to be kidnapped would be a thrilling adventure. We put on our best dresses and paraded slowly up and down State Street, conversing in loud voices about how rich (we liked the word) our parents were. Yachts, Spanish castles, trips on the Queen Mary, penthouses in New York—we mentioned all the things the movies had informed us rich people had, and did.

"You had on your striped linen," Jennifer perfectly recalled, "and I was wearing my lavender dotted swiss." She laughed her prolonged, slow chuckle. "We just couldn't understand why no one picked us up. Rich and adorable as we were. You remember, Jude?"

Well, I would not have remembered, but Jennifer brought it all back to me, along with our beach walks, the beautiful tide pools, the white sand, the rocks.

I began to look forward to those phone calls. I felt more and more that my connection with Jennifer was something that I had badly missed for years.

I believe I would have enjoyed talking to Jennifer under almost any circumstances, probably, but that particular fall and winter were bad times for me—and seemingly the rest of the world: Ethiopia, Nicaragua. In the American Midwest, where I was, unemployment was rife, and terrible. And to make everything worse the snows came early that year—heavy, paralyzing.

In a personal way, that snowed-in, difficult winter, things were especially bad: I was not getting along at all with my latest beau, the man who came to take me out to dinner on the night of Jennifer's first phone call. This was particularly depressing since we had got off to a very, very good start—not fireworks, not some spectacular blaze that I would have known to distrust, but many quiet tastes in common, including cats (he had five, an intensely charming fact, I thought, and they all were beautiful tabbies). The truth was that we were quite a lot alike, he and I. Not only our tastes but our defects were quite similar: we were both wary, nervy, shy. Very likely we both needed more by way of contrasting personality—although his former wife had been a successful actress, flamboyant, a great beauty, and that had not worked out too well, either. In any case, we further had in common the fact of being veterans of several mid-life love affairs, both knowing all too well the litany of the condition of not getting along. We exhibited a lessening of interest in each other in identical ways: an increase in our courtesy level. We pretended surprise and pleasure at the sound of each other's voice on the phone; with excruciating politeness we made excuses not to see each other. (At times it occurred to me that in some awful way I was becoming my parents—those super-polite role models.) And then we stopped talking altogether, my lover and I.

The next year was to be my sabbatical from the college, and none of my plans seemed to be working out in that direction, either. Nothing available at Woods Hole, nothing in San Diego. Or Berkeley, or Stanford.

Around March, with everything still going bad and no signs of spring, I realized that I had not heard from Jennifer for several weeks. Some instinct had all along advised me that I should wait to be called, I should not call Jennifer. Now, however, I did; I dialled the number in Santa Barbara. (Easy enough to come by: Jennifer, an unlikely feminist, had returned to her maiden name.)

It was not a good conversation. Jennifer was very drunk, although it was only about six at night, California time. She was drunk and sad and apologetic, over everything. She was extremely polite, but I felt that she was not even certain who I was; I could have been almost anyone. Any stranger, even, who happened to call, selling magazine subscriptions or offering chances to buy tax-free municipal bonds.

I was seriously worried, and after a little time I came to certain serious decisions.

I did the following things, in more or less this order:

I made an appointment and went to see the head of my department, and after some conversation, some argument, we struck up a bargain, of sorts: I would be granted a year's leave of absence (this involved less pay than a sabbatical, which was one of my selling points), and in return for this great favor I would teach an extra section of the general-science course for freshmen on my return.

I put up a notice on the bookstore bulletin board about renting out my house; from a great many applicants (probably I should have asked for more money) I selected a nice young couple from the music department. The only problem was that two people in the house would need all my small space; I would have to store everything but the furniture.

Through a national real-estate outfit I located a real-estate agent in Santa Barbara, who (this seemed an omen, a sure sign that I was on the right track) had a listing just a couple of houses down from Jennifer's—a garage apartment, mercifully cheap.

I called Jennifer, and as though it were a joke I said that I was coming out for a year, to take care of her.

And that is where I am now, and what I am doing. My apartment is in an alley half a block from Jennifer's house, the Cartwright house—and of course from my parents' house, too, the house that I sold when they died: my money for graduate school. My apartment is tiny, but since I am not there much, no matter. I have room for my drawing board, shelves of books and stacked papers; and outside there is a tiny scrap of a yard, where a neighbor cat comes to visit occasionally (he is beautiful—a pale-gray, long-eared, most delicate-footed creature).

I am beginning to run into a problem with space for clothes, though. When I first got here Jennifer was so depressed, she said, by the darkness of my wardrobe ("Judy, you can't go around like that, not out here, in those professor clothes") that we have done a lot of State Street shopping, by way of brightening up my look. "But you're wonderful in that red silk," Jennifer insisted.

Jennifer herself, for a person who drinks or who has drunk that much, looks remarkably well. Needless to say, I was more than a little nervous about seeing her again: how would she look? I was so scared, in fact, that I gave very little thought to how I would look to her, and I think actually I am the one who has aged more. Jennifer is thin, a little frail and shaky on her feet, that is true, but her skin is still good, fine and pink, and her eyes are blue and clear. She just looks like a very, very pretty woman, of a certain age.

The first few weeks of my stay I made all the obvious suggestions having to do with drink: the Betty Ford place, or A.A., or just a plain good doctor. Well, Jennifer refused to go to anything, as I might have known she would—she has always been extremely stubborn. She even says that her doctor says she is perfectly all right. Two explanations for that last occur to me: (1) she does not tell her doctor, or did not, how much she really drinks, or (2) the doctor himself is an alcoholic; I've heard that a lot of them are.

I have made a couple of strong advances, though. One is in terms of nutrition. I have instituted a heavy regimen of vitamins, and also I do most of the shopping and cooking. I go down to the docks for fresh fish, and on Saturday mornings there is a Farmers' Market, with lovely California vegetables and fruits. We eat very well, and I am sure that Jennifer eats a lot more with me around.

Another considerable advance is that Jennifer has entirely given up hard liquor, and now only drinks wine, white wine. In her big blue Ford station wagon we drive down to the new liquor store just off State Street. A handsome, bright-brassy, airy space. We walk around among the wooden crates and bins and shelves of bottles. This particular store deals mostly in California wines, and there are always some interesting new labels. New wineries keep turning up all over the state, even in very unlikely places, like San Luis Obispo or San Diego. We laugh at some of the names, which are often a little outlandish: Witches' Wish? And we admire the designs of the labels. We have even come to conclude that there is a definite correlation between beautiful labels and first-rate wines. Vichon, for example, one of our favorites, has an especially pretty picture on its bottle.

One of the best aspects of this whole venture for me is my discovery that after all I really can drink wine, with no ill effects. When I first came out I would have one glass of

wine at dinner, to keep Jennifer company, as it were. Then sometimes two, then sometimes another at home.

And now, in the late afternoons, though still too early to start over to the Cartwrights'—to Jennifer's house—I begin to think how nice a cool dry glass of wine would taste, and then I think, Well, why not? This is, after all, a sort of vacation for me. And so I pour myself one. I take the wine outside. I sit in one of the half-collapsed but still quite comfortable rattan chairs, in my tiny yard with its minute view of the evening sea, the sky, the burning sun. I sip, and in a peaceful way I contemplate my return to Santa Barbara.

I almost never think about my parents, or those old unhappy days spent here with them, growing up. Our family house has been remodelled almost beyond recognition, for which I am grateful. Only very infrequently do I feel its presence as that of a ghost, looming there just next to the Cartwright house.

I do not worry in the way that I used to about my career—that career, teaching at Minnesota. Marine biology. Sometimes I think I could stay right here forever (someone else could take on the freshman sections), and maybe get into something entirely new. I could walk on the beach and make sketches. (I do that already, of course; I mean I could do it in a more programmatic way.) Maybe someday I would be good enough to have a show, and maybe sell some. Or I could give drawing lessons at some local school. I might even, as we say, *meet someone.* Some nice young bearded man, with leftist views and a fondness for cats. A farmer, maybe; he might wander into the market some Saturday morning, with some lovely artichokes.

Jennifer and I have agreed that I should be the one to keep our store of wine, despite my small quarters. The bottles are stacked in silly places all over my rooms, some under the bed, for example. When I start over to Jennifer's house at dinnertime I just bring along one bottle; in that way I can keep a check on Jennifer's intake. Which is now down to a couple of glasses a day, I believe.

It is interesting and to me a little spooky to see how entirely unchanged the Cartwright house is. Everything is just the same, but since it all looks, as always, brightly new—the fabrics on the upholstered furniture, for instance the cushions and draperies—everything must in fact *be* new. Jennifer must have gone out and found duplicates to replace all the worn-out stuff—and with such precision. What trouble she must have gone to, getting everything just right, getting Nickie's look! Including the flourishing garden, now tended by a nice Japanese couple.

All I said was that it looked really great, what a relief it was to see so little changed—which I know must have pleased Jennifer. She would not have wanted the extreme nature of her pursuit to be mentioned.

As I thought in Minneapolis about coming out here, one of my many conscious or semiconscious fears (worries about Jennifer's looks and her general health naturally being foremost) was a nagging, shadowy worry that as Jennifer and I talked it would somehow come out that Nickie and Scott had been less than the happy, fair, affectionate couple I used to see, and to long for. Heaven knows we would talk a lot, endless talk, and without (probably) coming out and saying so (Jennifer is unusually discreet) she might let me know that sometimes they, like my own parents, used to have recriminatory breakfasts, silences, bitterness. Maybe, even, handsome Scott had affairs, and Nickie cried. That would be a more usual, contemporary ending to their story—and in some circles it would "explain" Jennifer.

But from what Jennifer did say, that sad version would seem not to have taken place; according to her, the sadness was of quite another sort. "My mother was so upset when Dad died she just never got over it, never at all" is what Jennifer said. "Never even looked at anyone else, and you know how pretty she always was."

Well, I do remember how pretty Nickie was, and I can accept that version of her life, I guess. In fact, I would rather: it is what I thought I saw.

"I sometimes wonder if I got married so many times to be just the opposite," Jennifer once mused. "Not to depend on any one person in that way."

"Well, maybe" was all I could contribute. But then I added, "And my parents didn't get along, so I only dared try it once?"

"Lord, who knows?" Jennifer laughed.

Often, as we talked, new memories would assail one or the other of us.

"Do you remember the surprise you planned for Scott one time, on his birthday? The *real* surprise?" I asked Jennifer one night.

She seemed not to, and so I told her: "You led him on into the house when he got home from work, and you told him that you'd found what he'd like better than anything in the world. You brought him to the door of the back-hall closet, and when he opened it up there was Nickie, laughing and jumping out to hug and kiss you both."

"Oh, *yes!*" cried Jennifer. "I'd forgotten that, and how could I forget? But you see what I mean, Judy, Jude? Who could ever come up with a relationship like that?"

Who indeed? Most surely not I, I reflected.

But mostly Jennifer and I are not so serious. Our dinners are fun. We remember school friends, boys, our teachers; we go over and over the people we knew and the times we had back then, just remembering and laughing. Not deeply, intellectually scrutinizing, as I might have with other friends, at another time.

Jennifer subscribes to all the fashion magazines, and sometimes sitting there at dinner we may just leaf through a couple. Most of the newest styles are quite ugly, if not downright ludicrous, we are agreed. But every now and then there will be something really pretty; we will make a note to check it out in the downtown stores.

Jennifer has not taken a newspaper for years, and since I have been out here I have not really read one, either. I find it a great relief, in fact, not to know just how awful things have become. How entirely out of control the whole terrifying world is.

We did at first go over some of the unfortunate events of both our marriages, and in a discreet way I told her about my love affairs. I found that, recounting them to Jennifer, I could make them really funny. She liked the story about the man who always called when I was brushing my teeth, and she appreciated my version of my most recent relationship, the man and I becoming more and more polite as we liked each other less. She told me a couple of funny stories about her husbands, though I think their names are what she most likes to remember.

Jennifer does not talk about her children, except to say that she has three of them, all moved East. Three girls. Two work in New York, one lives on a farm in Vermont—no grandchildren that she has mentioned—and since she never seems to hear from her daughters I would guess that they don't get along. But I never ask.

By the time we have finished our dinner, our bottle of wine, we are both rather sleepy. We get up from the table, and together we walk out to the front hall. Jennifer opens the door, we say good night; we kiss, and I go outside and listen for the sound of the lock behind me.

I walk the short, safe distance down the road to my apartment.

If the weather is nice, a warm night, I may sit outside for a while, something I could almost never have done in Minnesota. Maybe I will have one more glass of wine. Maybe red, a good zinfandel, for sleep.

Just sitting there, sipping my wine, I think a lot, and one of my conclusions has been that, all things considered, even living alone, I really feel better and better out here, and I think I have never been so happy in my life.

The visitor cat must by now be on to my habits, for sometimes at these moments I will feel the sudden warm brush of his arching back against my leg. I reach to stroke him. He allows this, responding with a loud purr—and then, as suddenly as he appeared, with a quick leap out into the dark he is gone.

ROLANDO HINOJOSA-SMITH

(1929–)

Sometimes It Just Happens That Way; That's All

About the Author: Rolando Hinojosa-Smith, son of a Mexican-American father and an Anglo-American mother, grew up in the southern Rio Grande Valley of Texas. He is presently a professor of English at the University of Texas at Austin. His eight books dramatize the history and cultural conflict of the fictional Belkin County, Texas, through the lives of two cousins. His first published volume was *Estampas del Valle y otras obras/ Sketches of the Valley and Other Works* (1973).

Excerpt from the *Klail City Enterprise-News* (March 15, 1970)

Klail City. (Special) Baldemar Cordero, 30, of 169 South Hidalgo Street, is in the city jail following a row in a bar in the city's Southside. Cordero is alleged to have fatally stabbed Arnesto Tamez, also 30, over the affections of one of the "hostesses" who works there.

No bail had been set at press time.

*One of Those Things**

What can I tell you? The truth's the truth, and there's no dodging it, is there? It's a natural fact: I killed Ernesto Tamez, and I did it right there at the *Aquí me quedo.*[1] And how can I deny it? But don't come asking me for no details; not just yet, anyway, 'cause I'm not all that sure just how it did happen—and that's God's truth, and no one else's, as we say. That's right; Neto Tamez is gone and like the Bible says: I can see, and I can hear.

But that's the way it goes, I guess. He's laid out there somewhere, and just yesterday late afternoon it was that me and my brother-in-law, Beto Castañeda, he married my

---

*Editor's note: This cassette recording of Balde Cordero's statements has been reproduced faithfully using conventional spelling where necessary. What matters here is the content, not the form. March 16, 1970, Klail City Workhouse.

[1]Here I'll stay.

sister Marta, you know . . . well, there we were, the two of us drinking, laughing, cuttin' up, and just having ourselves a time, when up pops Ernesto Tamez just like Old Nick himself: swearing and cursing like always, and I got the first blast, but I let it go like I usually . . . like I always do . . . Oh, well . . . Anyway, he kept it up, but it didn't bother me none; and that's the truth, too.

You knew Tamez, didn't you? What am I saying? Of course, you did. Remember that time at Félix Champión's place? Someone came up and broke a bottle of beer, full, too; broke it right backside Ernesto's head, someone did. Ol' Ernesto'd broken a mirror, remember? He'd taken this beer bottle and just let go at that mirror, he did. Well'p, I sure haven't forgotten, and I always kept my eyes open; no telling what he'd do next. I wouldn't step aside, of course, but I wouldn't turn my attention away from him, see?

Well, it was like I said: there we were, Beto and me, we'd hoist a few until we'd run out of cash, or we'd get beer bent, but that was it: none o' that cadging free drinks for us; when we got the money, we drink. When we don't, we don't, and that's it.

Now, I've known Tamez—the whole family, in fact—since primary school and when they lived out in Rebaje; there was Joaquín—he's the oldest, and he wound up marrying or had to anyway, Jovita de Anda. You know her? Now, before she married Joaquín, Jovita was about as hard to catch as a cold in the month of February. She straightened out, though; and fast, too. Then there's Emilio; he's the second in line; he got that permanent limp o'his after he slipped and then fell off a refrigerator car that was standing off the old Mo-Pac line over by that pre-cooler run by Chico Fernández. The last one's Bertita; she's the only girl in the family, and she married one of those hard workin' Leal boys. Took her out of Klail City faster 'n anything you ever saw: he set himself up out in West Texas—Muleshoe, I think it was—and being the worker he was, why, he turned many a shiny penny: Good for him is what I say: he earned it. Bertita's no bargain, I'll say that, but she wasn't a bad woman, either. Ernesto was something, though; from the beginning. I'll tell you this much: I put up with a lot—and took a lot, too. For years. But sometimes something happens, you know. And when it does, well . . .

There's no room for lying, Hinojosa; you've known me, and you've known my folks for a long time . . . Well, as I was saying, Beto and I started drinking at the *San Diego,* from there we showed up at the *Diamond*—the *old Diamond* over on Third—stayed there a while, and we were still on our feet, so we made for the *Blue Bar* after that. We would've stayed there, too, 'cept for the Reyna brothers who showed up. There's usually trouble for somebody when they're around, and that's no secret, no, sir. What they do is they'll drink a beer or two, at the most, but that's about it, 'cause they only drink to cover up the grass they've been popping . . . But you know that already . . . Cops that don't know 'em come up, smell the brew, and they figure the Reynas are drunk, not high. But everybody else knows; don Manuel, for one, he knows. Anyway, as soon as the Reynas showed up at the *Blue Bar,* Beto and I moved on; that's the way to avoid trouble; get out of there, 'cause trouble'll cross your way, and fast. As for Anselmo Reyna, well, I guess he learned his when I looked him down at the *Diamond* that one time; he learned his, all right. But there they were at the *Blue Bar,* higher'n a cat's back, so we got out o'there, and then went on over to the *Aquí me quedo.*

That's really something, isn't it? I mean, if the Reynas hadn't-a showed up at the *Blue Bar,* why, nothing would've happened later on, right? But that's not right either, is it? 'Cause when something's bound to happen, it'll happen; and right on schedule, too. Shoot! That was going to be Ernesto's last night in the Valley, and I was chosen to see to it: just like that.

One. Two. Three. No two ways is there? . . . Although . . . well, I mean, it boils down to this: I killed a human being. Who'd a thought it?

It's funny, Hinojosa . . . I kind of remember the why but not the when of it all. I mean, I've been sworn at, cussed at, but I always let that kind of stuff go by, know what I mean? But then, too . . . to actually have someone come-right-up-to-you like this here, come right up to you, see, point blank kind-a, and, and, ah, added to which I'd been drinking some and Ernesto there had been breaking 'em for me for a long time, and me, remembering a lot o' past crap he'd dumped on me, and him being a coward and all, yeah, he was, always counting on his brothers for everything, so . . . there it was—we went after it. Finally. After all these years.

Later on it I think it was that Beto told me about the blood and about how it just jumped out and got on my arms, and shirt, 'n face, and all over . . . Beto also said I didn't blink an eye or anything; I just stood there, he said. All I remember now is that I didn't hear a word; nothing. Not the women, or the screaming . . . Nothing; not even the guys who came a-running. Nothing. I could see 'em, though, but that's all.

Sometime later, I don't know when or for how long, but sometime later. I walked on out to the street and stood on the curb there, and noticed a family in a house across the way just sitting down and watching TV; they looked peaceful there, y'know what I mean? Innocent-like. Why, they had no idea . . . of what had . . . and here I was, why, I'd been just as innocent a few minutes before . . . You, ah, you understand what I'm saying? . . . I'll say this, though, that talk about life and death is something serious. I mean, it's . . . it's . . . Shoot, I don't even know *what* I'm tryin' to say here . . .

Did I ever tell you that Ernesto—and this was in front of a lot o' people, now—did I ever tell you he cut in every chance he got? Just like that. He'd cut in on a girl I was dancing with, or just take her away from me. All the time. Over at *El Farol* and the other places . . . Well, he did. One other time, he told a dance girl that I had come down with a dose of the clap. Can you beat that? He was always up to something—and then something happened, and I killed him. Justlikethat. Not because of that one thing, no. Jesus! It just happens, that's all. One o' those things, I guess . . . Maybe I shouldn't've waited so long; maybe I should've cut his water off sooner, and then perhaps this wouldn't've happened . . . Ahhhh, who'm I kidding? What's done's done, and that's it.

Well, last night just tore it for me, though; he swore right at me—no mistake there—and he laughed at me, too. And then, like talking into a microphone, he said I didn't have the balls to stand up to him. Right there, in front of everybody again. Now, I had put up with a lot of crap, and I have. From friends, too, 'cause I can then swear or say some things myself, but it's all part of the game—but not with him. Ever. I didn't say a word. Not one; I sure didn't. I just looked at him, but I didn't move or do or say anything; I'm telling you I just stood there. Damfool probably thought I was afraid of him. Well, that was his mistake, and now mine, too, I guess. He kept it up—wouldn't stop, not for a minute. Then, to top it off, he brings one of the dance girls over and says to her, to me, to everybody there, that he'd looked me down a hundred times or more; looked me down, and that I had taken it—'cause I was scared. Chicken, he said. The dance girl, she didn't know what to say, what to do; she was half-scared, and embarrassed, too, I'll warrant . . . But she just stood there as he held on to her . . . by the wrist . . . I think the music stopped or something. I remember, or I think I do, anyway, that there was a buzz or a buzzer going off somewhere, like I was wearing a beehive instead of that hat of mine. Does that make sense? I heard that buzzing, see, and the hissing, raspy voice of that damfool, and then I saw that fixed, idiotic smile o'

that dance girl, and then—suddenly, yeah—in a rush, see; suddenly a scream, a yell, a, a shriek-like, and I saw Ernesto sliding, slippin' sort-a, in a heap . . . and falling away . . . falling, eh?

Now, I do recall I took a deep breath, and the buzzing sort-a-stopped and I remember walking outside, to the sidewalk, and then I spotted that family I told you about, the one watching TV. And standing there, I looked at my left hand: I was carrying that pearl-handled knife that Pa Albino had given me when I was up in Michigan.

I went back inside the place, 'n then I went out again. I didn't even think of running away. What for? And where? Everybody knew me. Shoot. The second time I walked back in, I noticed that the cement floor had been hosed down, scrubbed clean. Not a trace-a blood either, not on the floor, or anywhere. They'd taken Ernesto out back, where they keep the warm beer and the snacks, next to the toilet there. When don Manuel came in, I gave him the knife, and then I went to the sidewalk, to the side of the place . . . I got sick, and then I couldn't stop coughing. I finally got in don Manuel's car, 'n I waited for him. When he got through in there, he brought me here . . . straight to jail . . . That old man probably went home to see my Ma, right? Well . . .

Anyway, early this morning, one of his kids brought me some coffee, and he waited until I finished the pot. You know . . . I've tried to fix, to set down in my mind, when it was that I buried my knife in that damfool. But I just can't remember . . . I just can't you know . . . And try as I may, too. It could be I just don't *want* to remember, right?

Anyway, Beto was here just before you came in . . . He's on his way to the District Attorney's office to give a deposition, he says. I'll tell you how I feel right now: I feel bad. I can't say how I'll feel later on, but for now, I do, I feel really bad, you know. That stuff about no use crying over spilled milk and all that, that's just talk, and nothing more. I feel terrible. I killed a . . . and when I think about it, real slow, I feel bad . . . Real bad . . .

I was wrong—dead wrong, I know; but if Ernesto was to insult me again, I'd probably go after him again. The truth is . . . The truth is one never learns.

Look, I'm not trying to tire you out on this—I keep saying the same thing over and over, but that's all I can talk about. But thanks for coming over. And thanks for the cigarettes, okay? Look, maybe—just maybe, now—maybe one of these days I'll know why I killed him—but he was due and bound to get it someday, wasn't he? All I did was to hurry it up a bit . . . You see? There I go again . . .

Oh, and before I forget, will you tell Mr. Royce that I won't be in tomorrow . . . and remind him I got one week's pay coming to me. Will you see to that?

I'll see you, Hinojosa . . . and thanks, okay?

*Marta, and What She Knows**

. . . what happened was that when Pa Albino died up in Michigan as a result of that accident at the pickle plant, Balde decided we'd all spend the winter there in Michigan till we heard about the settlement one way or 'nother. Right off, then, that contractor who brought us up from the Valley, he tried to skin us there and then and so Balde had to threaten him so he'd do right by us. So, with what little we got out of him, Balde hired us a lawyer to sue Turner Pickle Company. He was a young one that lawyer, but a good one: he won the case, and

*Cassette dated March 17, 1970.

that pickle company, well, they had to pay up for damages, as they call them. Now, when that was settled, we paid what we owed there in Saginaw, and with what we had left from that, well, we used it to see us through the winter months there while we looked around for another contractor to bring us back or to live up in Michigan while some work or other turned up. By this time, Beto was calling on me but not in a formal way. You see, we, Ma and I, we were still in mourning on account o' Pa, and . . . well, you know how that is . . .

You've known Balde since he was a kid, and, as Pa used to say: What can I tell you? Ma's been laid up with paralysis for years, but with all that, she's never missed a trip up North. Well, there we were with other mexicano families from Texas, stuck up in Saginaw, Michigan and waiting for winter to set in and looking for work. Any type of work; whatever it was, it didn't matter. Balde was the first one to land a job: he got himself hired on as a night man at the bay port there. Not too much after that, he put in a good word for Beto, and that way they worked together. Later on, but you know this, Beto and I got married. At that time, Balde must've been twenty-seven years old, and he could have had his pick of any Valley girl there or anywhere else, but because of Ma's condition, and the lack-a money, 'n first one thing and then 'nother, well, you know how that goes sometimes. So, we've been back in the Valley for some two years now, and I guess Balde stopped looking. But you know him; he's a good man; he was raised solid, and no one begrudges the beer or two or whatever many he has on Saturdays: he won't fight, and that's it. He won't say why he won't fight, but I, Ma 'n me, we know why: we'd be hurting, that's why. I'll tell you this, too: he's put up with a lot. A lot . . . but that's because he's always thinking o' Ma and me, see?

Once, and just the once, and by chance, too, I did hear that Balde laid it to one of the Reyna brothers, and no holds barred from what I heard . . . but this wasn't ever brought up here at the house.

You know, it's really hard to say what I felt or even *how* I felt when I first heard about what had happened to Neto Tamez. At first I couldn't . . . I couldn't bring myself to believe it, to picture it . . . I . . . I just couldn't imagine that my brother Balde . . . that he would kill someone. I'm not saying this 'cause he's a saint or something like that, no, not a-tall. But I will say this: it must've been something terrible; horrible, even. Something he just couldn't swallow; put up with. It cost him; I mean, Balde had to hold back for a long time, and he held back, for a long time . . . Holding it in all that time just got to him. It must have.

And, too, it could be that Ernesto went too far that time; too far. Beto had told me, or tried to, in his way, he tried to tell me about some of the stuff Neto Tamez was doing, or saying, and all of it against Balde; trouble is that Beto's not much of a talker, and he keeps everything inside, too, just like Balde does . . . As far as me getting any news out o' Balde, well . . . all he ever brought home was a smile on his face. I'll say this, though, once in a while he'd be as serious and as quiet as anything you'd ever want to see; I wasn't about to ask him anything, no sir, I wasn't about to do that. At any rate, what with tending to Ma here, caring for both of the men of the house, and you add the wash and the cooking, and the sewing, and what not, hooh! I've got enough to do here without worrying about gossip.

I'm not pretending to be an angel here either, but what I do know is all second-hand. What I picked up from Beto or from some of my women friends who'd call, or from what I could pick up here and there from Balde. I'm telling you what I could piece out or what I would come up with by adding two and two together, but I don't really know; like I told you, I don't have that much to go on.

Now, the whole world and its first cousin know that Neto Tamez was always picking and backbiting and just making life miserable for him . . . Well, everybody else knows how Balde put up with it, too. I'll say again that if Balde didn't put a muzzle on him right away, it was because Balde was thinking-a Ma 'n me. And that's the truth. What people don't know is why Neto did what he did against my brother.

Listen to this: back when we were in junior high, Neto Tamez would send me love notes; yes, back then. And he'd follow me home, too. To top this, he'd bully some kids to act as his messenger boys. Yes, he would. Now, I'd never paid attention to him, mind you, and I never gave him any ground to do so, either. The girls'd tell me that Neto wouldn't even let other boys come near me 'n he acted as if he owned me or something like that. This happened a long time ago, a-course, and I'd never breathe a word of it to Balde; but! the very first time I learned that Neto Tamez was giving my brother a hard time, I knew or thought I knew why he was doing it. I don't really know if Balde knew or not, though, but like Beto says: anything's possible.

Some girlfriends of mine once told me that at *La Golondrina* and *El farolito,* you know, those kind-a places . . . Anyway, the girls said that Neto insulted Balde right in front of everybody; a lotta times, too. You know, he'd cut in or just up and walk away with whatever girl Balde had at the time . . . or Neto'd say something nasty, anything, anything to make Balde's life a complete misery. On and on, see? Now, I'm not saying Neto Tamez would actually follow him from place to place, no, I'm not saying that at all; but what I *am* saying is that Neto'd never lose the opportunity . . . I mean the opportunity to push 'n shove, embarrass him until Balde would just have to get up and leave the place, see? You've got to keep in mind that living in the same town, in the same neighborhood, almost, and then to have to put up with all sorts of garbage, why, that's enough to tempt and drive a saint to madness. I swear it would, and Balde's no saint. So many's the time Balde'd come home, not say a word, and drinking or not, he'd come in, kiss Ma as he always did, and he'd sit and talk a while and then go out to the porch and have himself a smoke. Why, compared to Balde, my Beto's a walking-talking chatterbox . . .

The Tamezes are a peculiar bunch of people, you know. When they used to live out in Rebaje, it looked as if they were forever into something with someone, the neighbors, anybody. I remember the time Joaquín had to get married to Jovita de Anda; don Servando Tamez barred all the doors to the house, and then he wouldn't let the de Andas in; they couldn't even attend the wedding, and that was *it.* They say that old Mister de Anda . . . don Marcial . . . the little candyman? Well, they say he cried and just like a baby 'cause he wouldn't get to see his only daughter get married. I remember, too, that Emilio, one leg shorter 'n the other by that time, was marching up and down in front of their house like he was a soldier or something . . .

It was a good thing that poor doña Tula Tamez had passed away and was buried up in Bascom by that time, 'cause she'd-a been mortified with the goings on in that house . . . I swear. About the only thing to come out-a that house was Bertita, and oh! did she have a case on Balde. For years, too. She finally married Ramiro Leal; you know him, do you? His folks own the tortilla machine . . .

Well, anyway, yesterday, just about the time you went to see Balde at the jailhouse, don Manuel Guzmán showed up here. He said he'd come just to say hello to Ma, but that was just an excuse: what he really said was for us not to worry about the law and the house. Isn't that something? Why, I've seen that man dole out kicks, head buttings, and a haymaker or two to every troublemaker here in Klail, and then, bright 'n early, one of his kids'll bring coffee to whoever it is that winds up in jail that weekend. I'll say this, too, though: the streets in Klail have never been safer, and I know that for a fact. Anyway, just as he was about to leave, don Manuel told me that Ma 'n me that we could draw our groceries from the Torres' grocery store down the way. Don Manuel and Pa Albino go back a long time, you know; from the Revolution, I think.

Things are going to get tight around here without Balde, but Ma 'n me we still have Beto here, and . . . My only hope is that the Tamezes don't come looking for Beto 'cause that'll really put us under without a man in the house. Beto's at the Court House just now; he had to go and make a statement, they said.

Oh, Mr. Hinojosa, I just don't know where all of this is going to take us . . . But God'll provide . . . He's got to.

ROMEO HINOJOSA

Attorney at Law

420 South Cerralvo Tel. 843-1640

The following is a deposition, in English, made by Beto Casañeda, today, March 17, 1970, in the office of Mr. Robert A. Chapman, Assistant District Attorney for Belken County.

The aforementioned officer of the court gave me a copy of the statement as part of the testimony in the trial of *The State of Texas v. Cordero* set for August 23 of this year in the court of Judge Harrison Phelps who presides in the 139th District Court.

Romero Hinojosa

March 17, 1970

A Deposition Freely Given

on this seventeenth day of March, 1970, by Mr. Gilberto Castañeda in room 218 of the Belken County Court House was duly taken, witnessed, and signed by Miss Helen Chacón, a legal interpreter and acting assistant deputy recorder for said County, as part of a criminal investigation assigned to Robert A. Chapman, assistant district attorney for the same County.

It is understood that Mr. Castañeda is acting solely as a deponent and is not a party to any civil or criminal investigation, proceeding, or violation which may be alluded to in this deposition.

"Well, my name is Gilberto Castañeda, and I live at 169 South Hidalgo Street here in Klail. It is not my house; it belong to my mother-in-law, but I have live there since I marry Marta (Marta Cordero Castañeda, 169 South Hidalgo Street, Klail City) about three years ago.

"I am working at the Royce-Fedders tomato packing shed as a grader. My brother-in-law, Balde Cordero, work there too. He pack tomatoes and don't get pay for the hour, he get pay for what he pack and since I am a grader I make sure he get the same class tomato and that way he pack faster; he just get a tomato with the right hand, and he wrap it with the left. He pack a lug of tomatoes so fast you don't see it, and he does it fast because I am a good grader.

"Balde is a good man. His father, don Albino, my father-in-law who die up in Saginaw, Michigan when Marta and I, you know, go together . . . well, Balde is like don Albino, you understand? A good man. A right man. Me, I stay an orphan and when the Mejías take me when my father and my mother die in that train wreck—near Flora? don Albino tell the Mejías I must go to the school. I go to First Ward Elementary where Mr. Gold is principal. In First Ward I am a friend of Balde and there I meet Marta too. Later, when I grow up I don't visit the house too much because of Marta, you know what I mean? Anyway, Balde is my friend and I have know him very well . . . maybe more than nobody else. He's a good man.

"Well, last night Balde and I took a few beers in some of the places near where we live. We drink a couple here and a couple there, you know, and we save the *Aquí me quedo* on South Missouri for last. It is there that I tell Balde a joke about the drunk guy who is going to his house and he hear the clock in the corner make two sounds. You know that one? Well, this drunk guy he hear the clock go bong-bong and he say that the clock is wrong for it give one o'clock two time. Well, Balde think that is funny . . . Anyway, when I tell the joke in Spanish it's better. Well, there we were drinking a beer when Ernesto Tamez comes. Ernesto Tamez is like a woman, you know? Everytime he get in trouble he call his family to help him . . . that is the way it is with him. Well, that night he bother Balde again. More than one time Balde has stop me when Tamez begin to insult. That Balde is a man of patience. This time Ernesto bring a *vieja* (woman) and Balde don't say nothing, nothing, nothing. What happens is that things get spooky, you know. Ernesto talking and *burlándose de él* (ridiculing him) and at the same time he have the poor woman by the arm. And then something happen. I don't know what happen, but something and fast.

"I don't know. I really don't know. It all happen so fast; the knife, the blood squirt all over my face and arms, the woman try to get away, a loud really loud scream, not a *grito* (local Mexican yell) but more a woman screaming, you know what I mean? and then Ernesto fall on the cement.

"Right there I look at Balde and his face is like a mask in asleep, you understand? No angry, no surprise, nothing. In his left hand he have the knife and he shake his head before he walk to the door. Look, it happen so fast no one move for a while. Then Balde come in and go out of the place and when don Manuel (Manuel Guzmán, constable for precinct 21) come in, Balde just hand over the knife. Lucas Barrón, you know, El Chorreao (a nickname) well, he wash the blood and sweep the floor before don Manuel get there. Don Manuel just shake his head and tell Balde to go to the car and wait. Don Manuel he walk to the back to see Ernesto and on the way out one of the women, I think it is *la güera Balín* (Amelia Cortez, 23, no known address, this city), try to make a joke, but don Manuel he say *no estés chingando* (shut the hell up, or words to that effect) and after that don Manuel go about his own business. Me, I go to the door but all I see is Balde looking at a house across the street and he don't even know I come to say goodbye. Anyway, this morning a little boy of don Manuel say for me to come here and here I am."

Further deponent sayeth not.
Sworn to before me, this
17th day of March, 1970

/s/ ______________________ /s/ ______________________

Helen Chacón
Acting Asst. Deputy Recorder
Belken County

Gilberto Castañeda

1983

GLORIA NAYLOR

(1950–)

Etta Mae Johnson

About the Author: Gloria Naylor, black American writer, was born in New York City, and has had a varied working and academic life, serving as a missionary for the Jehovah's Witnesses (1968–1975) and (1975–1981) as a telephone operator at various hotels in New York City, while attending Brooklyn College (B.A., 1981). Since that time she has taught at Yale University and published three novels, of which the first, *The Women of Brewster Place: A Novel in Seven Stories* (1982), won the American Book Award in 1983.

The unpainted walls of the long rectangular room were soaked with the smell of greasy chicken and warm, headless beer. The brown and pink faces floated above the trails of used cigarette smoke like bodiless carnival balloons. The plump yellow woman with white gardenias pinned to the side of her head stood with her back pressed against the peeling sides of the baby grand and tried to pierce the bloated hum in the room with her thin scratchy voice. Undisturbed that she remained for the most part ignored, she motioned for the piano player to begin.

It wasn't the music or the words or the woman that took that room by its throat until it gasped for air—it was the pain. There was a young southern girl, Etta Johnson, pushed up in a corner table, and she never forgot. The music, the woman, the words.

I love my man
I'm a lie if I say I don't
I love my man
I'm a lie if I say I don't
But I'll quit my man
I'm a lie if I say I won't

My man wouldn't give me no breakfast
Wouldn't give me no dinner
Squawked about my supper
Then he put me out of doors

Had the nerve to lay
A matchbox to my clothes
I didn't have so many
But I had a long, long, way to go

Children bloomed on Brewster Place during July and August with their colorful shorts and tops plastered against gold, ebony, and nut-brown legs and arms; they decorated the street, rivaling the geraniums and ivy found on the manicured boulevard downtown. The summer heat seemed to draw the people from their cramped apartments onto the stoops, as it drew the tiny drops of perspiration from their foreheads and backs.

The apple-green Cadillac with the white vinyl roof and Florida plates turned into Brewster like a greased cobra. Since Etta had stopped at a Mobil station three blocks away to wash off the evidence of a hot, dusty 1200-mile odyssey home, the chrome caught the rays of the high afternoon sun and flung them back into its face. She had chosen her time well.

The children, free from the conditioned restraints of their older counterparts, ran along the sidewalks flanking this curious, slow-moving addition to their world. Every eye on the block, either openly or covertly, was on the door of the car when it opened. They were rewarded by the appearance of a pair of white leather sandals attached to narrow ankles and slightly bowed, shapely legs. The willow-green sundress, only ten minutes old on the short chestnut woman, clung to a body that had finished a close second in its race with time. Large two-toned sunglasses hid the weariness that had defied the freshly applied mascara and burnt-ivory shadow. After taking twice the time needed to stretch herself, she reached into the back seat of the car and pulled out her plastic clothes bag and Billie Holiday albums.

The children's curiosity reached the end of its short life span, and they drifted back to their various games. The adults sucked their teeth in disappointment, and the more envious felt self-righteousness twist the corners of their mouths. It was only Etta. Looked like she'd done all right by herself—this time around.

Slowly she carried herself across the street—head high and eyes fixed unwaveringly on her destination. The half-dozen albums were clutched in front of her chest like cardboard armor.

There ain't nothing I ever do
Or nothing I ever say
That folks don't criticize me
But I'm going to do
Just what I want to, anyway
And don't care just what people say
If I should take a notion
To jump into the ocean
Ain't nobody's business if I do . . .

Any who bothered to greet her never used her first name. No one called Etta Mae "Etta," except in their minds; and when they spoke to each other about her, it was Etta Johnson; but when they addressed her directly, it was always Miss Johnson. This baffled her because she knew what they thought about her, and she'd always call them by their first

names and invited them to do the same with her. But after a few awkward attempts, they'd fall back into the pattern they were somehow comfortable with. Etta didn't know if this was to keep the distance on her side or theirs, but it was there. And she had learned to tread through these alien undercurrents so well that to a casual observer she had mastered the ancient secret of walking on water.

Mattie sat in her frayed brocade armchair, pushed up to the front window, and watched her friend's brave approach through the dusty screen. Still toting around them oversized records, she thought. That woman is a puzzlement.

Mattie rose to open the door so Etta wouldn't have to struggle to knock with her arms full. "Lord, child, thank you," she gushed, out of breath. "The younger I get, the higher those steps seem to stretch."

She dumped her load on the sofa and swept off her sunglasses. She breathed deeply of the freedom she found in Mattie's presence. Here she had no choice but to be herself. The carefully erected decoys she was constantly shuffling and changing to fit the situation were of no use here. Etta and Mattie went way back, a singular term that claimed co-knowledge of all the important events in their lives and almost all of the unimportant ones. And by rights of this possession, it tolerated no secrets.

"Sit on down and take a breather. Must have been a hard trip. When you first said you were coming, I didn't expect you to be driving."

"To tell the truth, I didn't expect it myself, Mattie. But Simeon got very ornery when I said I was heading home, and he refused to give me the money he'd promised for my plane fare. So I said, just give me half and I'll take the train. Well, he wasn't gonna even do that. And Mattie, you know I'll be damned if I was coming into this city on a raggedy old Greyhound. So one night he was by my place all drunk up and snoring, and as kindly as you please, I took the car keys and registration and so here I am."

"My God, woman! You stole the man's car?"

"Stole—nothing. He owes me that and then some."

"Yeah, but the police don't wanna hear that. It's a wonder the highway patrol ain't stopped you before now."

"They ain't stopped me because Simeon didn't report it."

"How you know that?"

"His wife's daddy is the sheriff of that county." Laughter hung dangerously on the edge of the two women's eyes and lips.

"Yeah, but he could say you picked his pockets."

Etta went to her clothes bag and pulled out a pair of pink and red monogrammed shorts. "I'd have to be a damned good pickpocket to get away with all this." The laughter lost its weak hold on their mouths and went bouncing crazily against the walls of the living room.

Them that's got, shall get
Them that's not, shall lose
So the Bible says
And it still is news

Each time the laughter would try to lie still, the two women would look at each other and send it hurling between them, once again.

Mama may have
Papa may have
But God bless the child
That's got his own
That's got his own

"Lord, Tut, you're a caution." Mattie wiped the tears off her cheeks with the back of a huge dark hand.

Etta was unable to count the years that had passed since she had heard someone call her that. Look a' that baby gal strutting around here like a bantam. You think she'd be the wife of King Tut. The name had stayed because she never lost the walk. The washed-out grime and red mud of backwoods Rock Vale, Tennessee, might wrap itself around her bare feet and coat the back of her strong fleshy legs, but Etta always had her shoulders flung behind her collarbone and her chin thrust toward the horizon that came to mean everything Rock Vale did not.

Etta spent her teenage years in constant trouble. Rock Vale had no place for a black woman who was not only unwilling to play by the rules, but whose spirit challenged the very right of the game to exist. The whites in Rock Vale were painfully reminded of this rebellion when she looked them straight in the face while putting in her father's order at the dry goods store, when she reserved her sirs and mams for those she thought deserving, and when she smiled only if pleased, regardless of whose presence she was in. That Johnson gal wasn't being an uppity nigger, as talk had it; she was just being herself.

Southern trees bear strange fruit
Blood on the leaves and blood at the root
Black bodies swinging
In the southern breeze
Strange fruit hanging
From the poplar trees

But Rutherford County wasn't ready for Etta's blooming independence, and so she left one rainy summer night about three hours ahead of dawn and Johnny Brick's furious pursuing relatives. Mattie wrote and told her they had waited in ambush for two days on the county line, and then had returned and burned down her father's barn. The sheriff told Mr. Johnson that he had gotten off mighty light—considering. Mr. Johnson thought so, too. After reading Mattie's letter, Etta was sorry she hadn't killed the horny white bastard when she had the chance.

Rock Vale had followed her to Memphis, Detroit, Chicago, and even to New York. Etta soon found out that America wasn't ready for her yet—not in 1937. And so along with the countless other disillusioned, restless children of Ham with so much to give and nowhere to give it, she took her talents to the street. And she learned to get over, to hook herself to any promising rising black star, and when he burnt out, she found another.

Her youth had ebbed away quickly under the steady pressure of the changing times, but she was existing as she always had. Even if someone had bothered to stop and tell her that the universe had expanded for her, just an inch, she wouldn't have known how to shine alone.

Etta and Mattie had taken totally different roads that with all of their deceptive winding had both ended up on Brewster Place. Their laughter now drew them into a conspiratorial circle against all the Simeons outside of that dead-end street, and it didn't stop until they were both weak from the tears that flowed down their faces.

"So," Mattie said, blowing her nose on a large cotton handkerchief, "trusting you stay out of jail, what you plan on doing now?"

"Child, I couldn't tell you." Etta dropped back down on the couch. "I should be able to get a coupla thousand for the car to tide me over till another business opportunity comes along."

Mattie raised one eyebrow just a whisper of an inch. "Ain't it time you got yourself a regular job? These last few years them *business opportunities* been fewer and farther between."

Etta sucked her small white teeth. "A job doing what? Come on, Mattie, what kind of experience I got? Six months here, three there. I oughta find me a good man and settle down to live quiet in my old age." She combed her fingers confidently through the thick sandy hair that only needed slight tinting at the roots and mentally gave herself another fifteen years before she had to worry about this ultimate fate.

Mattie, watching the creeping tiredness in her eyes, gave her five. "You done met a few promising ones along the way, Etta."

"No, honey, it just seemed so. Let's face it, Mattie. All the good men are either dead or waiting to be born."

"Why don't you come to meeting with me tonight. There's a few settle-minded men in our church, some widowers and such. And a little prayer wouldn't hurt your soul one bit."

"I'll thank you to leave my soul well alone, Mattie Michael. And if your church is so full of upright Christian men, why you ain't snagged one yet?"

"Etta, I done banked them fires a long time ago, but seeing that you still keeping up steam . . ." Her eyes were full of playful kindness.

"Just barely, Mattie, just barely."

And laughter rolled inside of 2E, once again.

"Etta, Etta Mae!" Mattie banged on the bathroom door. "Come on out now. You making me late for the meeting."

"Just another second, Mattie. The church ain't gonna walk away."

"Lord," Mattie grumbled, "she ain't bigger than a minute, so it shouldn't take more than that to get ready."

Etta came out of the bathroom in an exaggerated rush. "My, my, you the most impatient Christian I know."

"Probably, the only Christian you know." Mattie refused to be humored as she bent to gather up her sweater and purse. She turned and was stunned with a barrage of colors. A huge white straw hat reigned over layers of gold and pearl beads draped over too much bosom and too little dress. "You plan on dazzling the Lord, Etta?"

"Well, honey," Etta said, looking down the back of her stocking leg to double-check for runs, "last I heard, He wasn't available. You got more recent news?"

"Um, um, um." Mattie pressed her lips together and shook her head slowly to swallow down the laughter she felt crawling up her throat. Realizing she wasn't going to succeed,

she quickly turned her face from Etta and headed toward the door. "Just bring your blasphemin' self on downstairs. I done already missed morning services waiting on you today."

Canaan Baptist Church, a brooding, ashen giant, sat in the middle of a block of rundown private homes. Its multi-colored, dome-shaped eyes glowered into the darkness. Fierce clapping and thunderous organ chords came barreling out of its mouth. Evening services had begun.

Canaan's congregation, the poor who lived in a thirty-block area around Brewster Place, still worshiped God loudly. They could not afford the refined, muted benediction of the more prosperous blacks who went to Sinai Baptist on the northern end of the city, and because each of their requests for comfort was so pressing, they took no chances that He did not hear them.

When Israel was in Egypt's land
Let my people go
Oppressed so hard, they could not stand
Let my people go

The words were as ancient as the origin of their misery, but the tempo had picked up threefold in its evolution from the cotton fields. They were now sung with the frantic determination of a people who realized that the world was swiftly changing but for some mystic, complex reason their burden had not.

God said to go down
Go down
Brother Moses
Brother Moses
To the shore of the great Nile River

The choir clapped and stomped each syllable into a devastating reality, and just as it did, the congregation reached up, grabbed the phrase, and tried to clap and stomp it back into oblivion.

Go to Egypt
Go to Egypt
Tell Pharaoh
Tell Pharaoh
Let my people go

Etta entered the back of the church like a reluctant prodigal, prepared at best to be amused. The alien pounding and the heat and the dark glistening bodies dragged her back, back past the cold ashes of her innocence to a time when pain could be castrated on the sharp edges of iron-studded faith. The blood rushed to her temples and began to throb in unison with the musical pleas around her.

Yes, my God is a mighty God
Lord, deliver

And he set old Israel free
Swallowed that Egyptian army
Lord, deliver
With the waves of the great Red Sea

Etta glanced at Mattie, who was swaying and humming, and she saw that the lines in her face had almost totally vanished. She had left Etta in just that moment for a place where she was free. Sadly, Etta looked at her, at them all, and was very envious. Unaccustomed to the irritating texture of doubt, she felt tears as its abrasiveness grated over the fragile skin of her life. Could there have been another way?

The song ended with a huge expulsion of air, and the congregation sat down as one body.

"Come on, let's get us a seat." Mattie tugged her by the arm.

The grizzled church deacon with his suit hanging loosely off his stooped shoulders went up to the pulpit to read the church business.

"That's one of the widowers I was telling you about," Mattie whispered, and poked Etta.

"Unmm." The pressure on her arm brought Etta back onto the uncomfortable wooden pew. But she didn't want to stay there, so she climbed back out the window, through the glass eyes of the seven-foot Good Shepherd, and started again the futile weaving of invisible ifs and slippery mights into an equally unattainable past.

The scenes of her life reeled out before her with the same aging script; but now hindsight sat as the omniscient director and had the young star of her epic recite different brilliant lines and make the sort of stunning decisions that propelled her into the cushioned front pews on the right of the minister's podium. There she sat with the deacons' wives, officers of the Ladies' Auxiliary, and head usherettes. And like them, she would wear on her back a hundred pairs of respectful eyes earned the hard way, and not the way she had earned the red sundress, which she now self-consciously tugged up in the front. Was it too late?

The official business completed, the treasurer pulled at his frayed lapels, cleared his throat, and announced the guest speaker for the night.

The man was magnificent.

He glided to the podium with the effortlessness of a well-oiled machine and stood still for an interminable long moment. He eyed the congregation confidently. He only needed their attention for that split second because once he got it, he was going to wrap his voice around their souls and squeeze until they screamed to be relieved. They knew it was coming and waited expectantly, breathing in unison as one body. First he played with them and threw out fine silken threads that stroked their heart muscles ever so gently. They trembled ecstatically at the touch and invited more. The threads multiplied and entwined themselves solidly around the one pulsating organ they had become and tightened slightly, testing them for a reaction.

The "Amen, brothers" and "Yes, Jesus" were his permission to take that short hop from the heart to the soul and lay all pretense of gentleness aside. Now he would have to push and pound with clenched fists in order to be felt, and he dared not stop the fierce rhythm of his voice until their replies had reached that fevered pitch of satisfaction. Yes, Lord—grind out the unheated tenements! Merciful Jesus—shove aside the low-paying boss man. Perfect Father—fill me, fill me till there's no room, no room for nothing else,

not even that great big world out there that exacts such a strange penalty for my being born black.

It was hard work. There was so much in them that had to be replaced. The minister's chest was heaving in long spasms, and the sweat was pouring down his gray temples and rolling under his chin. His rich voice was now hoarse, and his legs and raised arms trembled on the edge of collapse. And as always they were satisfied a half-breath before he reached the end of his endurance. They sat back, limp and spent, but momentarily at peace. There was no price too high for this service. At that instant they would have followed him to do battle with the emperor of the world, and all he was going to ask of them was money for the "Lord's work." And they would willingly give over half of their little to keep this man in comfort.

Etta had not been listening to the message; she was watching the man. His body moved with the air of one who had not known recent deprivation. The tone of his skin and the fullness around his jawline told her that he was well-off, even before she got close enough to see the manicured hands and diamond pinkie ring.

The techniques he had used to brand himself on the minds of the congregation were not new to her. She'd encountered talent like that in poolrooms, nightclubs, grimy second-floor insurance offices, numbers dens, and on a dozen street corners. But here was a different sort of power. The jungle-sharpened instincts of a man like that could move her up to the front of the church, ahead of the deacons' wives and Ladies' Auxiliary, off of Brewster Place for good. She would find not only luxury but a place that complemented the type of woman she had fought all these years to become.

"Mattie, is that your regular minister?" she whispered.

"Who, Reverend Woods? No, he just visits on occasion, but he sure can preach, can't he?"

"What you know about him, he married?"

Mattie cut her eyes at Etta. "I should have figured it wasn't the sermon that moved you. At least wait till after the prayer before you jump all into the man's business."

During the closing song and prayer Etta was planning how she was going to maneuver Mattie to the front of the church and into introducing her to Reverend Woods. It wasn't going to be as difficult as she thought. Moreland T. Woods had noticed Etta from the moment she'd entered the church. She stood out like a bright red bird among the drab morality that dried up the breasts and formed rolls around the stomachs of the other church sisters. This woman was still dripping with the juices of a full-fleshed life—the kind of life he was soon to get up and damn into hell for the rest of the congregation—but how it fitted her well. He had to swallow to remove the excess fluid from his mouth before he got up to preach.

Now the problem was to make his way to the back of the church before she left without seeming to be in a particular hurry. A half-dozen back slaps, handshakes, and thank-you sisters only found him about ten feet up the aisle, and he was growing impatient. However, he didn't dare to turn his neck and look in the direction where he'd last seen her. He felt a hand on his upper arm and turned to see a grim-faced Mattie flanked by the woman in the scarlet dress.

"Reverend Woods, I really enjoyed your sermon," Mattie said.

"Why, thank you, sister—sister?"

"Sister Michael, Mattie Michael." While he was addressing his words to her, the smile he sent over her shoulder to Etta was undeniable.

"Especially the part," Mattie raised her voice a little, "About throwing away temptation to preserve the soul. That was a mighty fine point."

"The Lord moves me and I speak, Sister Michael. I'm just a humble instrument for his voice."

The direction and intent of his smile was not lost to Etta. She inched her way in front of Mattie. "I enjoyed it, too, Reverend Woods. It's been a long time since I heard preaching like that." She increased the pressure of her fingers on Mattie's arm.

"Oh, excuse my manners. Reverend Woods, this is an old friend of mine, Etta Mae Johnson. Etta Mae, Reverend Woods." She intoned the words as if she were reciting a eulogy.

"Please to meet you, Sister Johnson." He beamed down on the small woman and purposely held her hand a fraction longer than usual. "You must be a new member—I don't recall seeing you the times I've been here before."

"Well, no, Reverend, I'm not a member of the congregation, but I was raised up in the church. You know how it is, as you get older sometimes you stray away. But after your sermon, I'm truly thinking of coming back."

Mattie tensed, hoping that the lightning that God was surely going to strike Etta with wouldn't hit her by mistake.

"Well, you know what the Bible says, sister. The angels rejoice more over one sinner who turns around than over ninety-nine righteous ones."

"Yes, indeed, and I'm sure a shepherd like you has helped to turn many back to the fold." She looked up and gave him the full benefit of her round dark eyes, grateful she hadn't put on that third coat of mascara.

"I try, Sister Johnson, I try."

"It's a shame Mrs. Woods wasn't here tonight to hear you. I'm sure she must be mighty proud of your work."

"My wife has gone to her glory, Sister Johnson. I think of myself now as a man alone—rest her soul."

"Yes, rest her soul," Etta sighed.

"Please, Lord, yes," Mattie muttered, giving out the only sincere request among the three. The intensity of her appeal startled them, and they turned to look at her. "Only knows how hard this life is, she's better in the arms of Jesus."

"Yes"—Etta narrowed her eyes at Mattie and then turned back to the minister—"I can testify to that. Being a woman alone, it seems all the more hard. Sometimes you don't know where to turn."

Moreland Woods knew Etta was the type of woman who not only knew which way to turn, but, more often than not, had built her own roads when nothing else was accessible. But he was enjoying this game immensely—almost as much as the growing heat creeping into his groin.

"Well, if I can be of any assistance, Sister Johnson, don't hesitate to ask. I couldn't sleep knowing one of the Lord's sheep is troubled. As a matter of fact, if you have anything you would like to discuss with me this evening, I'd be glad to escort you home."

"I don't have my own place. You see, I'm just up from out of state and staying with my friend Mattie here."

"Well, perhaps we could all go out for coffee."

"Thank you, but I'll have to decline, Reverend," Mattie volunteered before Etta did it for her. "The services have me all tired out, but if Etta wants to, she's welcome."

"That'll be just fine," Etta said.

"Good, good." And now it was his turn to give her the benefit of a mouth full of strong gold-capped teeth. "Just let me say good-bye to a few folks here, and I'll meet you outside."

"Girl, you oughta patent that speed and sell it to the airplane companies," Mattie said outside. " 'After that sermon, Reverend, I'm thinking of coming back'—indeed!"

"Aw, hush your fussing."

"I declare if you had batted them lashes just a little faster, we'd of had a dust storm in there."

"You said you wanted me to meet some nice men. Well, I met one."

"Etta, I meant a man who'd be serious about settling down with you." Mattie was exasperated. "Why, you're going on like a schoolgirl. Can't you see what he's got in mind?"

Etta turned an indignant face toward Mattie. "The only thing I see is that you're telling me I'm not good enough for a man like that. Oh, no, not Etta Johnson. No upstanding decent man could ever see anything in her but a quick good time. Well, I'll tell you something, Mattie Michael. I've always traveled first class, maybe not in the way you'd approve with all your fine Christian principles, but it's done all right by me. And I'm gonna keep going top drawer till I leave this earth. Don't you think I got a mirror? Each year there's a new line to cover. I lay down with this body and get up with it every morning, and each morning it cries for just a little more rest than it did the day before. Well, I'm finally gonna get that rest, and it's going to be with a man like Reverend Woods. And you and the rest of those slack-mouthed gossips on Brewster be damned!" Tears frosted the edges of her last words. "They'll be humming a different tune when I show up there the wife of a big preacher. I've always known what they say about me behind my back, but I never thought you were right in there with them."

Mattie was stunned by Etta's tirade. How could Etta have so totally misunderstood her words? What had happened back there to stuff up her senses to the point that she had missed the obvious? Surely she could not believe that the vibrations coming from that unholy game of charades in the church aisle would lead to something as permanent as marriage? Why, it had been nothing but the opening gestures to a mating dance. Mattie had gone through the same motions at least once in her life, and Etta must have known a dozen variations to it that were a mystery to her. And yet, somehow, back there it had been played to a music that had totally distorted the steps for her friend. Mattie suddenly felt the helplessness of a person who is forced to explain that for which there are no words.

She quietly turned her back and started down the steps. There was no need to defend herself against Etta's accusations. They shared at least a hundred memories that could belie those cruel words. Let them speak for her.

Sometimes being a friend means mastering the art of timing. There is a time for silence. A time to let go and allow people to hurl themselves into their own destiny. And a time to prepare to pick up the pieces when it's all over. Mattie realized that this moment called for all three.

"I'll see ya when you get home, Etta," she threw gently over her shoulder.

Etta watched the bulky figure become slowly enveloped by the shadows. Her angry words had formed a thick mucus in her throat, and she couldn't swallow them down. She started to run into the darkness where she'd seen Mattie disappear, but at that instant Moreland Woods came out of the lighted church, beaming.

He took her arm and helped her into the front seat of his car. Her back sank into the deep upholstered leather, and the smell of the freshly vacuumed carpet was mellow in her nostrils. All of the natural night sounds of the city were blocked by the thick tinted windows and the hum of the air conditioner, but they trailed persistently behind the polished back of the vehicle as it turned and headed down the long gray boulevard.

Smooth road
Clear day
But why am I the only one
Traveling this way
How strange the road to love
Can be so easy
Can there be a detour ahead?

Moreland Woods was captivated by the beautiful woman at his side. Her firm brown flesh and bright eyes carried the essence of nectar from some untamed exotic flower, and the fragrance was causing a pleasant disturbance at the pit of his stomach. He marveled at how excellently she played the game. A less alert observer might have been taken in, but his survival depended upon knowing people, knowing exactly how much to give and how little to take. It was this razor-thin instinct that had catapulted him to the head of his profession and that would keep him there.

And although she cut her cards with a reckless confidence, pushed her chips into the middle of the table as though the supply was unlimited, and could sit out the game until dawn, he knew. Oh, yes. Let her win a few, and then he would win just a few more, and she would be bankrupt long before the sun was up. And then there would be only one thing left to place on the table—and she would, because the stakes they were playing for were very high. But she was going to lose that last deal. She would lose because when she first sat down in that car she had everything riding on the fact that he didn't know the game existed.

And so it went. All evening Etta had been in another world, weaving his tailored suit and the smell of his expensive cologne into a custom-made future for herself. It took his last floundering thrusts into her body to bring her back to reality. She arrived in enough time to feel him beating against her like a dying walrus, until he shuddered and was still.

She kept her eyes closed because she knew when she opened them there would be the old familiar sights around her. To her right would be the plastic-coated nightstand that matched the cheaply carved headboard of the bed she lay in. She felt the bleached coarseness of the sheet under her sweaty back and predicted the roughness of the worn carpet path that led from the bed to the white-tiled bathroom with bright fluorescent lights, sterilized towels, and tissue-wrapped water glasses. There would be two or three small thin rectangles of soap wrapped in bright waxy covers that bore the name of the hotel.

She didn't try to visualize what the name would be. It didn't matter. They were all the same, all meshed together into one lump that rested like an iron ball on her chest. And the expression on the face of this breathing mass to her left would be the same as all the others. She could turn now and go through the rituals that would tie up the evening for them both, but she wanted just one more second of this soothing darkness before she had to face the echoes of the locking doors she knew would be in his eyes.

Etta got out of the car unassisted and didn't bother to turn and watch the taillights as it pulled off down the deserted avenue adjacent to Brewster Place. She had asked him to leave her at the corner because there was no point in his having to make a U-turn in the dead-end street, and it was less than a hundred yards to her door. Moreland was relieved that she had made it easy for him, because it had been a long day and he was anxious to get home and go to sleep. But then, the whole business had gone pretty smoothly after they left the hotel. He hadn't even been called upon to use any of the excuses he had prepared for why it would be a while before he'd see her again. A slight frown crossed his forehead as he realized that she had seemed as eager to get away from him as he had been to leave. Well, he shrugged his shoulders and placated his dented ego, that's the nice part about these worldly women. They understand the temporary weakness of the flesh and don't make it out to be something bigger than it is. They can have a good time without pawing and hanging all onto a man. Maybe I should drop around sometime. He glanced into his rearview mirror and saw that Etta was still standing on the corner, looking straight ahead into Brewster. There was something about the slumped profile of her body, silhouetted against the dim street light, that caused him to press down on the accelerator.

Etta stood looking at the wall that closed off Brewster from the avenues farther north and found it hard to believe that it had been just this afternoon when she had seen it. It had looked so different then, with the August sun highlighting the browns and reds of the bricks and the young children bouncing their rubber balls against its side. Now it crouched there in the thin predawn light, like a pulsating mouth awaiting her arrival. She shook her head sharply to rid herself of the illusion, but an uncanny fear gripped her, and her legs felt like lead. If I walk into this street, she thought, I'll never come back. I'll never get out. Oh, dear God, I am so tired—so very tired.

Etta removed her hat and massaged her tight forehead. Then, giving a resigned sigh, she started slowly down the street. Had her neighbors been out on their front stoops, she could have passed through their milling clusters as anonymously as the night wind. They had seen her come down that street once in a broken Chevy that had about five hundred dollars' worth of contraband liquor in its trunk, and there was even the time she'd come home with a broken nose she'd gotten in some hair-raising escapade in St. Louis, but never had she walked among them with a broken spirit. This middle-aged woman in the wrinkled dress and wilted straw hat would have been a stranger to them.

When Etta got to the stoop, she noticed there was a light under the shade at Mattie's window, and she strained to hear what actually sounded like music coming from behind the screen. Mattie was playing her records! Etta stood very still, trying to decipher the broken air waves into intelligible sound, but she couldn't make out the words. She stopped straining when it suddenly came to her that it wasn't important what song it was—someone was waiting up for her. Someone who would deny fiercely that there had been any concern—just a little indigestion from them fried onions that kept me from sleeping. Thought I'd pass the time by figuring out what you see in all this loose-life music.

Etta laughed softly to herself as she climbed the steps toward the light and the love and the comfort that awaited her.

RAYMOND CARVER

(1938–1988)

Cathedral

About the Author: Raymond Carver, born in Clatskanie, Oregon, studied writing in California and at the University of Iowa Writers' Workshop; he spent a number of years holding a variety of odd jobs to support himself and his family while he wrote. Carver published ten volumes of poetry and short fiction in the last twenty years of his life; *Where I'm Calling From* (1988) is a collection of what he considered his best stories. In his later years Carver taught creative writing and was the recipient of a prestigious MacArthur Fellowship before his death.

This blind man, an old friend of my wife's, he was on his way to spend the night. His wife had died. So he was visiting the dead wife's relatives in Connecticut. He called my wife from his in-laws'. Arrangements were made. He would come by train, a five-hour trip, and my wife would meet him at the station. She hadn't seen him since she worked for him one summer in Seattle ten years ago. But she and the blind man had kept in touch. They made tapes and mailed them back and forth. I wasn't enthusiastic about his visit. He was no one I knew. And his being blind bothered me. My idea of blindness came from the movies. In the movies, the blind moved slowly and never laughed. Sometimes they were led by seeing-eye dogs. A blind man in my house was not something I looked forward to.

That summer in Seattle she had needed a job. She didn't have any money. The man she was going to marry at the end of the summer was in officers' training school. He didn't have any money, either. But she was in love with the guy, and he was in love with her, etc. She'd seen something in the paper: HELP WANTED—*Reading to Blind Man,* and a telephone number. She phoned and went over, was hired on the spot. She'd worked with this blind man all summer. She read stuff to him, case studies, reports, that sort of thing. She helped him organize his little office in the county social-service department. They'd become good friends, my wife and the blind man. How do I know these things? She told me. And she told me somethng else. On her last day in the office, the blind man asked if he could touch her face. She agreed to this. She told me he touched his fingers to every part of her face, her nose—even her neck! She never forgot it. She even tried to write a poem about it. She was always trying to write a poem. She wrote a poem or two every year, usually after something really important had happened to her.

When we first started going out together, she showed me the poem. In the poem, she recalled his fingers and the way they had moved around over her face. In the poem, she talked about what she had felt at the time, about what went through her mind when the blind man touched her nose and lips. I can remember I didn't think much of the poem. Of course, I didn't tell her that. Maybe I just don't understand poetry. I admit it's not the first thing I reach for when I pick up something to read.

Anyway, this man who'd first enjoyed her favors, the officer-to-be, he'd been her childhood sweetheart. So okay. I'm saying that at the end of the summer she let the blind man run his hands over her face, said goodbye to him, married her childhood etc., who was now a commissioned officer, and she moved away from Seattle. But they'd kept in touch, she and the blind man. She made the first contact after a year or so. She called him up one night from an Air Force base in Alabama. She wanted to talk. They talked. He asked her to send him a tape and tell him about her life. She did this. She sent the tape. On the tape, she told the blind man about her husband and about their life together in the military. She told the blind man she loved her husband but she didn't like it where they lived and she didn't like it that he was a part of the military-industrial thing. She told the blind man she'd written a poem and he was in it. She told him that she was writing a poem about what it was like to be an Air Force officer's wife. The poem wasn't finished yet. She was still writing it. The blind man made a tape. He sent her the tape. She made a tape. This went on for years. My wife's officer was posted to one base and then another. She sent tapes from Moody AFB, McGuire, McConnell, and finally Travis, near Sacramento, where one night she got to feeling lonely and cut off from people she kept losing in that moving-around life. She

got to feeling she couldn't go it another step. She went in and swallowed all the pills and capsules in the medicine chest and washed them down with a bottle of gin. Then she got into a hot bath and passed out.

But instead of dying, she got sick. She threw up. Her officer—why should he have a name? he was the childhood sweetheart, and what more does he want?—came home from somewhere, found her, and called the ambulance. In time, she put it all on a tape and sent the tape to the blind man. Over the years, she put all kinds of stuff on tapes and sent the tapes off lickety-split. Next to writing a poem every year, I think it was her chief means of recreation. On one tape, she told the blind man she'd decided to live away from her officer for a time. On another tape, she told him about her divorce. She and I began going out, and of course she told her blind man about it. She told him everything, or so it seemed to me. Once she asked me if I'd like to hear the latest tape from the blind man. This was a year ago. I was on the tape, she said. So I said okay, I'd listen to it. I got us drinks and we settled down in the living room. We made ready to listen. First she inserted the tape into the player and adjusted a couple of dials. Then she pushed a lever. The tape squeaked and someone began to talk in this loud voice. She lowered the volume. After a few minutes of harmless chitchat, I heard my own name in the mouth of this stranger, this blind man I didn't even know! And then this: "From all you've said about him, I can only conclude—" But we were interrupted, a knock at the door, something, and we didn't ever get back to the tape. Maybe it was just as well. I'd heard all I wanted to.

Now this same blind man was coming to sleep in my house.

"Maybe I could take him bowling," I said to my wife. She was at the draining board doing scalloped potatoes. She put down the knife she was using and turned around.

"If you love me," she said, "you can do this for me. If you don't love me, okay. But if you had a friend, any friend, and the friend came to visit, I'd make him feel comfortable." She wiped her hands with the dish towel.

"I don't have any blind friends," I said.

"You don't have *any* friends," she said. "Period. Besides," she said, "goddamn it, his wife's just died! Don't you understand that? The man's lost his wife!"

I didn't answer. She'd told me a little about the blind man's wife. Her name was Beulah. Beulah! That's a name for a colored woman.

"Was his wife a Negro?" I asked.

"Are you crazy?" my wife said. "Have you just flipped or something?" She picked up a potato. I saw it hit the floor, then roll under the stove. "What's wrong with you?" she said. "Are you drunk?"

"I'm just asking," I said.

Right then my wife filled me in with more detail than I cared to know. I made a drink and sat at the kitchen table to listen. Pieces of the story began to fall into place.

Beulah had gone to work for the blind man the summer after my wife had stopped working for him. Pretty soon Beulah and the blind man had themselves a church wedding. It was a little wedding—who'd want to go to such a wedding in the first place?—just the two of them, plus the minister and the minister's wife. But it was a church wedding just the same. It was what Beulah had wanted, he'd said. But even then Beulah must have been carrying the cancer in her glands. After they had been inseparable for eight years—my wife's word, *inseparable*—Beulah's health went into a rapid decline. She died in a Seattle hospital room, the blind man sitting beside the bed and holding on to her hand. They'd married, lived and worked together, slept together—had sex, sure—and then the blind man had to bury her. All this without his having ever seen what the goddamned woman looked like. It was beyond my understanding. Hearing this, I felt sorry for the blind man for a little bit. And then I found myself thinking what a pitiful life this woman must have led. Imagine a woman who could never see herself as she was seen in the eyes of her loved one. A woman who could go on day after day and never receive the smallest compliment from her beloved. A woman whose husband could never read the expression on her face, be it misery or something better. Someone who could wear makeup or not—what difference to him? She could, if she wanted, wear green eyeshadow around one eye, a straight pin in her nostril, yellow slacks and purple shoes, no matter. And then to slip off into death, the blind man's hand on her hand, his blind eyes streaming tears—I'm imagining now—her last thought maybe this: that he never even knew what she looked like, and she on an express to the grave. Robert was left with a small insurance policy and half of a twenty-peso Mexican coin. The other half of the coin went into the box with her. Pathetic.

So when the time rolled around, my wife went to the depot to pick him up. With nothing to do but wait—sure, I blamed him for that—I was having a drink and watching the TV when I heard the car pull into the drive. I got up from the sofa with my drink and went to the window to have a look.

I saw my wife laughing as she parked the car. I saw her get out of the car and shut the door. She was still wearing a smile. Just amazing. She went around to the other side of the car to where the blind man was already starting to get out. This blind man, feature this, he was wearing a full beard! A beard on a blind man! Too much, I say. The blind man reached into the back seat and dragged out a suitcase. My wife took his arm, shut the car door, and, talking all the way, moved him down the drive and then up the steps to the front porch. I turned off the TV. I finished my drink, rinsed the glass, dried my hands. Then I went to the door.

My wife said, "I want you to meet Robert. Robert, this is my husband. I've told you all about him." She was beaming. She had this blind man by his coat sleeve.

The blind man let go of his suitcase and up came his hand.

I took it. He squeezed hard, held my hand, and then he let it go.

"I feel like we've already met," he boomed.

"Likewise," I said. I didn't know what else to say. Then I said, "Welcome. I've heard a lot about you." We began to move then, a little group, from the porch into the living room, my wife guiding him by the arm. The blind man was carrying his suitcase in his other hand. My wife said things like, "To your left here, Robert. That's right. Now watch it, there's a chair. That's it. Sit down right here. This is the sofa. We just bought this sofa two weeks ago."

I started to say something about the old sofa. I'd liked that old sofa. But I didn't say anything. Then I wanted to say something else, small-talk, about the scenic ride along the Hudson. How going *to* New York, you should sit on the right-hand side of the train, and coming *from* New York, the left-hand side.

"Did you have a good train ride?" I said. "Which side of the train did you sit on, by the way?"

"What a question, which side!" my wife said. "What's it matter which side?" she said.

"I just asked," I said.

"Right side," the blind man said. "I hadn't been on a train in nearly forty years. Not since I was a kid. With my folks. That's been a long time. I'd nearly forgotten the sensation.

I have winter in my beard now," he said. "So I've been told, anyway. Do I look distinguished, my dear?" the blind man said to my wife.

"You look distinguished, Robert," she said. "Robert," she said. "Robert, it's just so good to see you."

My wife finally took her eyes off the blind man and looked at me. I had the feeling she didn't like what she saw. I shrugged.

I've never met, or personally known, anyone who was blind. This blind man was late forties, a heavy-set, balding man with stooped shoulders, as if he carried a great weight there. He wore brown slacks, brown shoes, a light-brown shirt, a tie, a sports coat. Spiffy. He also had this full beard. But he didn't use a cane and he didn't wear dark glasses. I'd always thought dark glasses were a must for the blind. Fact was, I wished he had a pair. At first glance, his eyes looked like anyone else's eyes. But if you looked close, there was something different about them. Too much white in the iris, for one thing, and the pupils seemed to move around in the sockets without his knowing it or being able to stop it. Creepy. As I stared at his face, I saw the left pupil turn in toward his nose while the other made an effort to keep in one place. But it was only an effort, for that eye was on the roam without his knowing it or wanting it to be.

I said, "Let me get you a drink. What's your pleasure? We have a little of everything. It's one of our pastimes."

"Bub, I'm a Scotch man myself," he said fast enough in this big voice.

"Right," I said. Bub! "Sure you are. I knew it."

He let his fingers touch his suitcase, which was sitting alongside the sofa. He was taking his bearings. I didn't blame him for that.

"I'll move that up to your room," my wife said.

"No, that's fine," the blind man said loudly. "It can go up when I go up."

"A little water with the Scotch?" I said.

"Very little," he said.

"I knew it," I said.

He said, "Just a tad. The Irish actor, Barry Fitzgerald? I'm like that fellow. When I drink water, Fitzgerald said, I drink water. When I drink whiskey, I drink whiskey." My wife laughed. The blind man brought his hand up under his beard. He lifted his beard slowly and let it drop.

I did the drinks, three big glasses of Scotch with a splash of water in each. Then we made ourselves comfortable and talked about Robert's travels. First the long flight from the West Coast to Connecticut, we covered that. Then from Connecticut up here by train. We had another drink concerning that leg of the trip.

I remembered having read somewhere that the blind didn't smoke because, as speculation had it, they couldn't see the smoke they exhaled. I thought I knew that much and that much only about blind people. But this blind man smoked his cigarette down to the nubbin and then lit another one. This blind man filled his ashtray and my wife emptied it.

When we sat down at the table for dinner, we had another drink. My wife heaped Robert's plate with cube steak, scalloped potatoes, green beans. I buttered him up two slices of bread. I said, "Here's bread and butter for you." I swallowed some of my drink. "Now let us pray," I said, and the blind man lowered his head. My wife looked at me, her mouth agape. "Pray the phone won't ring and the food doesn't get cold," I said.

We dug in. We ate everything there was to eat on the table. We ate like there was no tomorrow. We didn't talk. We ate. We scarfed. We grazed that table. We were into serious eating. The blind man had right away located his foods, he knew just where everything was on his plate. I watched with admiration as he used his knife and fork on the meat. He'd cut two pieces of meat, fork the meat into his mouth, and then go all out for the scalloped potatoes, the beans next, and then he'd tear off a hunk of buttered bread and eat that. He'd follow this up with a big drink of milk. It didn't seem to bother him to use his fingers once in a while, either.

We finished everything, including half a strawberry pie. For a few moments, we sat as if stunned. Sweat beaded on our faces. Finally, we got up from the table and left the dirty plates. We didn't look back. We took ourselves into the living room and sank into our places again. Robert and my wife sat on the sofa. I took the big chair. We had us two or three more drinks while they talked about the major things that had come to pass for them in the past ten years. For the most part, I just listened. Now and then I joined in. I didn't want him to think I'd left the room, and I didn't want her to think I was feeling left out. They talked of things that had happened to them—to them!—these past ten years. I waited in vain to hear my name on my wife's sweet lips: "And then my dear husband came into my life"—something like that. But I heard nothing of the sort. More talk of Robert. Robert had done a little of everything, it seemed, a regular blind jack-of-all-trades. But most recently he and his wife had had an Amway distributorship, from which, I gathered, they'd earned their living, such as it was. The blind man was also a ham radio operator. He talked in his loud voice about conversations he'd had with fellow operators in Guam, in the Philippines, in Alaska, and even in Tahiti. He said he'd have a lot of friends there if he ever wanted to go visit those places. From time to time, he'd turn his blind face toward me, put his hand under his beard, ask me something. How long had I been in my present position? (Three years.) Did I like my work? (I didn't.) Was I going to stay with it? (What were the options?) Finally, when I thought he was beginning to run down, I got up and turned on the TV.

My wife looked at me with irritation. She was heading toward a boil. Then she looked at the blind man and said, "Robert, do you have a TV?"

The blind man said, "My dear, I have two TVs. I have a color set and a black-and-white thing, an old relic. It's funny, but if I turn the TV on, and I'm always turning it on, I turn on the color set. It's funny, don't you think?"

I didn't know what to say to that. I had absolutely nothing to say to that. No opinion. So I watched the news program and tried to listen to what the announcer was saying.

"This is a color TV," the blind man said. "Don't ask me how, but I can tell."

"We traded up a while ago," I said.

The blind man had another taste of his drink. He lifted his beard, sniffed it, and let it fall. He leaned forward on the sofa. He positioned his ashtray on the coffee table, then put the lighter to his cigarette. He leaned back on the sofa and crossed his legs at the ankles.

My wife covered her mouth, and then she yawned. She stretched. She said, "I think I'll go upstairs and put on my robe. I think I'll change into something else. Robert, you make yourself comfortable," she said.

"I'm comfortable," the blind man said.

"I want you to feel comfortable in this house," she said.

"I am comfortable," the blind man said.

After she'd left the room, he and I listened to the weather report and then to the sports roundup. By that time, she'd been gone so long I didn't know if she was going to come back. I thought she might have gone to bed. I wished she'd come back downstairs. I didn't want to be left alone with a blind man. I asked him if he wanted another drink, and he said sure.

Then I asked if he wanted to smoke some dope with me. I said I'd just rolled a number. I hadn't, but I planned to do so in about two shakes.

"I'll try some with you," he said.

"Damn right," I said. "That's the stuff."

I got our drinks and sat down on the sofa with him. Then I rolled us two fat numbers. I lit one and passed it. I brought it to his fingers. He took it and inhaled.

"Hold it as long as you can," I said. I could tell he didn't know the first thing.

My wife came back downstairs wearing her pink robe and her pink slippers.

"What do I smell?" she said.

"We thought we'd have us some cannabis," I said.

My wife gave me a savage look. Then she looked at the blind man and said, "Robert, I didn't know you smoked."

He said, "I do now, my dear. There's a first time for everything. But I don't feel anything yet."

"This stuff is pretty mellow," I said. "This stuff is mild. It's dope you can reason with," I said. "It doesn't mess you up."

"Not much it doesn't, bub," he said, and laughed.

My wife sat on the sofa between the blind man and me. I passed her the number. She took it and toked and then passed it back to me. "Which way is this going?" she said. Then she said, "I shouldn't be smoking this. I can hardly keep my eyes open as it is. That dinner did me in. I shouldn't have eaten so much."

"It was the strawberry pie," the blind man said. "That's what did it," he said, and he laughed his big laugh. Then he shook his head.

"There's more strawberry pie," I said.

"Do you want some more, Robert?" my wife said.

"Maybe in a little while," he said.

We gave our attention to the TV. My wife yawned again. She said, "Your bed is made up when you feel like going to bed, Robert. I know you must have had a long day. When you're ready to go to bed, say so." She pulled his arm. "Robert?"

He came to and said, "I've had a real nice time. This beats tapes, doesn't it?"

I said, "Coming at you," and I put the number between his fingers. He inhaled, held the smoke, and then let it go. It was like he'd been doing it since he was nine years old.

"Thanks, bub," he said. "But I think this is all for me. I think I'm beginning to feel it," he said. He held the burning roach out for my wife.

"Same here," she said. "Ditto. Me, too." She took the roach and passed it to me. "I may just sit here for a while between you two guys with my eyes closed. But don't let me bother you, okay? Either one of you. If it bothers you, say so. Otherwise, I may just sit here with my eyes closed until you're ready to go to bed," she said. "Your bed's made up, Robert, when you're ready. It's right next to our room at the top of the stairs. We'll show you up when you're ready. You wake me up now, you guys, if I fall asleep." She said that and then she closed her eyes and went to sleep.

The news program ended. I got up and changed the channel. I sat back down on the sofa. I wished my wife hadn't pooped out. Her head lay across the back of the sofa, her mouth open. She'd turned so that her robe had slipped away from her legs, exposing a juicy thigh. I reached to draw her robe back over her, and it was then that I glanced at the blind man. What the hell! I flipped the robe open again.

"You say when you want some strawberry pie," I said.

"I will," he said.

I said, "Are you tired? Do you want me to take you up to your bed? Are you ready to hit the hay?"

"Not yet," he said. "No, I'll stay up with you, bub. If that's all right. I'll stay up until you're ready to turn in. We haven't had a chance to talk. Know what I mean? I feel like me and her monopolized the evening." He lifted his beard and he let it fall. He picked up his cigarettes and his lighter.

"That's all right," I said. Then I said, "I'm glad for the company."

And I guess I was. Every night I smoked dope and stayed up as long as I could before I fell asleep. My wife and I hardly ever went to bed at the same time. When I did go to sleep, I had these dreams. Sometimes I'd wake up from one of them, my heart going crazy.

Something about the church and the Middle Ages was on the TV. Not your run-of-the-mill TV fare. I wanted to watch something else. I turned to the other channels. But there was nothing on them, either. So I turned back to the first channel and apologized.

"Bub, it's all right," the blind man said. "It's fine with me. Whatever you want to watch is okay. I'm always learning something. Learning never ends. It won't hurt me to learn something tonight. I got ears," he said.

We didn't say anything for a time. He was leaning forward with his head turned at me, his right ear aimed in the direction of the set. Very disconcerting. Now and then his eyelids drooped and then they snapped open again. Now and then he put his fingers into his beard and tugged, like he was thinking about something he was hearing on the television.

On the screen, a group of men wearing cowls was being set upon and tormented by men dressed in skeleton costumes and men dressed as devils. The men dressed as devils wore devil masks, horns, and long tails. This pageant was part of a procession. The Englishman who was narrating the thing said it took place in Spain once a year. I tried to explain to the blind man what was happening.

"Skeletons," he said. "I know about skeletons," he said, and he nodded.

The TV showed this one cathedral. Then there was a long, slow look at another one. Finally, the picture switched to the famous one in Paris, with its flying buttresses and its spires reaching up to the clouds. The camera pulled away to show the whole of the cathedral rising above the skyline.

There were times when the Englishman who was telling the thing would shut up, would simply let the camera move around over the cathedrals. Or else the camera would tour the countryside, men in fields walking behind oxen. I waited as long as I could. Then I felt I had to say something. I said, "They're showing the outside of this cathedral now. Gargoyles. Little statues carved to look like monsters. Now I guess they're in Italy. Yeah, they're in Italy. There's paintings on the walls of this one church."

"Are those fresco paintings, bub?" he asked, and he sipped from his drink.

I reached for my glass. But it was empty. I tried to remember what I could remember. "You're asking me are those frescoes?" I said. "That's a good question. I don't know."

The camera moved to a cathedral outside Lisbon. The differences in the Portuguese cathedral compared with the French and Italian were not that great. But they were there. Mostly the interior stuff. Then something occurred to me, and I said, "Something has occurred to me. Do you have any idea what a cathedral is? What they look like, that is? Do you follow me? If somebody says cathedral to you, do you have any notion what they're talking about? Do you know the difference between that and a Baptist church, say?"

He let the smoke dribble from his mouth. "I know they took hundreds of workers fifty

or a hundred years to build," he said. "I just heard the man say that, of course. I know generations of the same families worked on a cathedral. I heard him say that, too. The men who began their life's work on them, they never lived to see the completion of their work. In that wise, bub, they're no different from the rest of us, right?" He laughed. Then his eyelids drooped again. His head nodded. He seemed to be snoozing. Maybe he was imagining himself in Portugal. The TV was showing another cathedral now. This one was in Germany. The Englishman's voice droned on. "Cathedrals," the blind man said. He sat up and rolled his head back and forth. "If you want the truth, bub, that's about all I know. What I just said. What I heard him say. But maybe you could describe one to me? I wish you'd do it. I'd like that. If you want to know, I really don't have a good idea."

I stared hard at the shot of the cathedral on the TV. How could I even begin to describe it? But say my life depended on it. Say my life was being threatened by an insane guy who said I had to do it or else.

I stared some more at the cathedral before the picture flipped off into the countryside. There was no use. I turned to the blind man and said, "To begin with, they're very tall." I was looking around the room for clues. "They reach way up. Up and up. Toward the sky. They're so big, some of them, they have to have these supports. To help hold them up, so to speak. These supports are called buttresses. They remind me of viaducts, for some reason. But maybe you don't know viaducts, either? Sometimes the cathedrals have devils and such carved into the front. Sometimes lords and ladies. Don't ask me why this is," I said.

He was nodding. The whole upper part of his body seemed to be moving back and forth.

"I'm not doing so good, am I?" I said.

He stopped nodding and leaned forward on the edge of the sofa. As he listened to me, he was running his fingers through his beard. I wasn't getting through to him, I could see that. But he waited for me to go on just the same. He nodded, like he was trying to encourage me. I tried to think what else to say. "They're really big," I said. "They're massive. They're built of stone. Marble, too, sometimes. In those olden days, when they built cathedrals, men wanted to be close to God. In those olden days, God was an important part of everyone's life. You could tell this from their cathedral-building. I'm sorry," I said, "but it looks like that's the best I can do for you. I'm just not good at it."

"That's all right, bub," the blind man said. "Hey, listen. I hope you don't mind my asking you. Can I ask you something? Let me ask you a simple question, yes or no. I'm just curious and there's no offense. You're my host. But let me ask if you are in any way religious? You don't mind my asking?"

I shook my head. He couldn't see that, though. A wink is the same as a nod to a blind man. "I guess I don't believe in it. In anything. Sometimes it's hard. You know what I'm saying?"

"Sure, I do," he said.

"Right," I said.

The Englishman was still holding forth. My wife sighed in her sleep. She drew a long breath and went on with her sleeping.

"You'll have to forgive me," I said. "But I can't tell you what a cathedral looks like. It just isn't in me to do it. I can't do any more than I've done."

The blind man sat very still, his head down, as he listened to me.

I said, "The truth is, cathedrals don't mean anything special to me. Nothing. Cathedrals. They're something to look at on late-night TV. That's all they are."

It was then that the blind man cleared his throat. He brought something up. He took a handkerchief from his back pocket. Then he said, "I get it, bub. It's okay. It happens. Don't worry about it," he said. "Hey, listen to me. Will you do me a favor? I got an idea. Why don't you find us some heavy paper? And a pen. We'll do something. We'll draw one together. Get us a pen and some heavy paper. Go on, bub, get the stuff," he said.

So I went upstairs. My legs felt like they didn't have any strength in them. They felt like they did after I'd done some running. In my wife's room, I looked around. I found some ballpoints in a little basket on her table. And then I tried to think where to look for the kind of paper he was talking about.

Downstairs, in the kitchen, I found a shopping bag with onion skins in the bottom of the bag. I emptied the bag and shook it. I brought it into the living room and sat down with it near his legs. I moved some things, smoothed the wrinkles from the bag, spread it out on the coffee table.

The blind man got down from the sofa and sat next to me on the carpet.

He ran his fingers over the paper. He went up and down the sides of the paper. The edges, even the edges. He fingered the corners.

"All right," he said. "All right, let's do her."

He found my hand, the hand with the pen. He closed his hand over my hand. "Go ahead, bub, draw," he said. "Draw. You'll see. I'll follow along with you. It'll be okay. Just begin now like I'm telling you. You'll see. Draw," the blind man said.

So I began. First I drew a box that looked like a house. It could have been the house I lived in. Then I put a roof on it. At either end of the roof, I drew spires. Crazy.

"Swell," he said. "Terrific. You're doing fine," he said. "Never thought anything like this could happen in your lifetime, did you, bub? Well, it's a strange life, we all know that. Go on now. Keep it up."

I put in windows with arches. I drew flying buttresses. I hung great doors. I couldn't stop. The TV station went off the air. I put down the pen and closed and opened my fingers. The blind man felt around over the paper. He moved the tips of his fingers over the paper, all over what I had drawn, and he nodded.

"Doing fine," the blind man said.

I took up the pen again, and he found my hand. I kept at it. I'm no artist. But I kept drawing just the same.

My wife opened up her eyes and gazed at us. She sat up on the sofa, her robe hanging open. She said, "What are you doing? Tell me, I want to know."

I didn't answer her.

The blind man said, "We're drawing a cathedral. Me and him are working on it. Press hard," he said to me. "That's right. That's good," he said. "Sure. You got it, bub. I can tell. You didn't think you could. But you can, can't you? You're cooking with gas now. You know what I'm saying? We're going to really have us something here in a minute. How's the old arm?" he said. "Put some people in there now. What's a cathedral without people?"

My wife said, "What's going on? Robert, what are you doing? What's going on?"

"It's all right," he said to her. "Close your eyes now," the blind man said to me.

I did it. I closed them just like he said.

"Are they closed?" he said. "Don't fudge."

"They're closed," I said.

"Keep them that way," he said. He said, "Don't stop now. Draw."

So we kept on with it. His fingers rode my fingers as my hand went over the paper. It was like nothing else in my life up to now.

Then he said, "I think that's it. I think you got it," he said. "Take a look. What do you think?"

But I had my eyes closed. I thought I'd keep them that way for a little longer. I thought it was something I ought to do.

"Well?" he said. "Are you looking?"

My eyes were still closed. I was in my house. I knew that. But I didn't feel like I was inside anything.

"It's really something," I said.

DAVID QUAMMEN

(1948–)

Walking Out

About the Author: David Quammen, born in Cincinnati, has earned degrees at Yale and, as a Rhodes Scholar, at Oxford. He is the author of three novels, one volume of short stories, and two collections of natural history essays. His monthly column, "Natural Acts," appears in the periodical *Outside.*

As the train rocked dead at Livingston he saw the man, in a worn khaki shirt with button flaps buttoned, arms crossed. The boy's hand sprang up by reflex, and his face broke into a smile. The man smiled back gravely, and nodded. He did not otherwise move. The boy turned from the window and, with the awesome deliberateness of a fat child harboring reluctance, began struggling to pull down his bag. His father would wait on the platform. First sight of him had reminded the boy that nothing was simple enough now for hurrying.

They drove in the old open Willys toward the cabin beyond town. The windshield of the Willys was up, but the fine cold sharp rain came into their faces, and the boy could not raise his eyes to look at the road. He wore a rain parka his father had handed him at the station. The man, protected by only the khaki, held his lips strung in a firm silent line that seemed more grin than wince. Riding through town in the cold rain, open topped and jaunty, getting drenched as though by necessity, was—the boy understood vaguely—somehow in the spirit of this season.

"We have a moose tag," his father shouted.

The boy said nothing. He refused to care what it meant, that they had a moose tag.

"I've got one picked out. A bull. I've stalked him for two weeks. Up in the Crazies. When we get to the cabin, we'll build a good roaring fire." With only the charade of a pause, he added, "Your mother." It was said like a question. The boy waited. "How is she?"

"All right, I guess." Over the jeep's howl, with the wind stealing his voice, the boy too had to shout.

"Are you friends with her?"

"I guess so."

"Is she still a beautiful lady?"

"I don't know. I guess so. I don't know that."

"You must know that. Is she starting to get wrinkled like me? Does she seem worried and sad? Or is she just still a fine beautiful lady? You must know that."

"She's still a beautiful lady, I guess."

"Did she tell you any messages for me?"

"She said . . . she said I should give you her love," the boy lied, impulsively and clumsily. He was at once embarrassed that he had done it.

"Oh," his father said. "Thank you, David."

They reached the cabin on a mile of dirt road winding through meadow to a spruce grove. Inside, the boy was enwrapped in the strong syncretic smell of all seasonal mountain cabins: pine resin and insect repellent and a mustiness suggesting damp bathing trunks stored in a drawer. There were yellow pine floors and ropework throw rugs and a bead curtain to the bedroom and a castiron cook stove with none of the lids or handles missing and a pump in the kitchen sink and old issues of *Field and Stream,* and on the mantel above where a fire now finally burned was a picture of the boy's grandfather, the railroad telegrapher, who had once owned the cabin. The boy's father cooked a dinner of fried ham, and though the boy did not like ham he had expected his father to cook canned stew or Spam, so he said nothing. His father asked him about school and the boy talked and his father seemed to be interested. Warm and dry, the boy began to feel safe from his own anguish. Then his father said:

"We'll leave tomorrow around ten."

Last year on the boy's visit they had hunted birds. They had lived in the cabin for six nights, and each day they had hunted pheasant in the wheat stubble, or blue grouse in the woods, or ducks along the irrigation slews. The boy had been wet and cold and miserable at times, but each evening they returned to the cabin and to the boy's suitcase of dry clothes. They had eaten hot food cooked on a stove, and had smelled the cabin smell, and had slept together in a bed. In six days of hunting, the boy had not managed to kill a single bird. Yet last year he had known that, at least once a day, he would be comfortable, if not happy. This year his father planned that he should not even be comfortable. He had said in his last letter to Evergreen Park, before the boy left Chicago but when it was too late for him not to leave, that he would take the boy camping in the mountains, after big game. He had pretended to believe that the boy would be glad.

The Willys was loaded and moving by ten minutes to ten. For three hours they drove, through Big Timber, and then north on the highway, and then back west again on a logging road that took them winding and bouncing higher into the mountains. Thick cottony streaks of white cloud hung in among the mountaintop trees, light and dense dollops against the bulking sharp dark olive, as though in a black-and-white photograph. They followed the gravel road for an hour, and the boy thought they would soon have a flat tire or break an axle. If they had a flat, the boy knew, his father would only change it and drive on until they had the second, farther from the highway. Finally they crossed a creek and his father plunged the Willys off into a bed of weeds.

His father said, "Here."

The boy said, "Where?"

"Up that little drainage. At the head of the creek."

"How far is it?"

"Two or three miles."

"Is that where you saw the moose?"

"No. That's where I saw the sheepman's hut. The moose is farther. On top."

"Are we going to sleep in a hut? I thought we were going to sleep in a tent."

"No. Why should we carry a tent up there when we have a perfectly good hut?"

The boy couldn't answer that question. He thought now that this might be the time when he would cry. He had known it was coming.

"I don't much want to sleep in a hut," he said, and his voice broke with the simple honesty of it, and his eyes glazed. He held his mouth tight against the trembling.

As though something had broken in him too, the boy's father laid his forehead down on the steering wheel, against his knuckles. For a moment he remained bowed, breathing exhaustedly. But he looked up again before speaking.

"Well, we don't have to, David."

The boy said nothing.

"It's an old sheepman's hut made of logs, and it's near where we're going to hunt, and we can fix it dry and good. I thought you might like that. I thought it might be more fun than a tent. But we don't have to do it. We can drive back to Big Timber and buy a tent, or we can drive back to the cabin and hunt birds, like last year. Whatever you want to do. You have to forgive me the kind of ideas I get. I hope you will. We don't have to do anything that you don't want to do."

"No," the boy said. "I want to."

"Are you sure?"

"No," the boy said. "But I just want to."

They bushwhacked along the creek, treading a thick soft mixture of moss and humus and needles, climbing upward through brush. Then the brush thinned and they were ascending an open creek bottom, thirty yards wide, darkened by fir and cedar. Farther, and they struck a trail, which led them upward along the creek. Farther still, and the trail received a branch, then another, then forked.

"Who made this trail? Did the sheepman?"

"No," his father said. "Deer and elk."

Gradually the creek's little canyon narrowed, steep wooded shoulders funneling closer on each side. For a while the game trails forked and converged like a maze, but soon again there were only two branches, and finally one, heavily worn. It dodged through alder and willow, skirting tangles of browned raspberry, so that the boy and his father could never see more than twenty feet ahead. When they stopped to rest, the boy's father unstrapped the .270 from his pack and loaded it.

"We have to be careful now," he explained. "We may surprise a bear."

Under the cedars, the creek bottom held a cool dampness that seemed to be stored from one winter to the next. The boy began at once to feel chilled. He put on his jacket, and they continued climbing. Soon he was sweating again in the cold.

On a small flat where the alder drew back from the creek, the hut was built into one bank of the canyon, with the sod of the hillside lapping out over its roof. The door was a low dark opening. Forty or fifty years ago, the boy's father explained, this hut had been built and used by a Basque shepherd. At that time there had been many Basques in Montana, and they had run sheep all across this ridge of the Crazies. His father forgot to explain what a Basque was, and the boy didn't remind him.

They built a fire. His father had brought sirloin steaks and an onion for dinner, and the boy was happy with him about that. As they ate, it grew dark, but the boy and his father had stocked a large comforting pile of naked deadfall. In the darkness, by firelight, his father made chocolate pudding. The pudding had been his father's surprise. The boy sat on a piece of canvas and added logs to the fire while his father drank coffee. Sparks rose on the heat and the boy watched them climb toward the cedar limbs and the black pools of sky. The pudding did not set.

"Do you remember your grandfather, David?"

"Yes," the boy said, and wished it were true. He remembered a funeral when he was three.

"Your grandfather brought me up on this mountain when I was seventeen. That was the last year he hunted." The boy knew what sort of thoughts his father was having. But he knew also that his own home was in Evergreen Park, and that he was another man's boy now, with another man's name, though this indeed was his father. "Your grandfather was fifty years older than me."

The boy said nothing.

"And I'm thirty-four years older than you."

"And I'm only eleven," the boy cautioned him.

"Yes," said his father. "And someday you'll have a son and you'll be forty years older than him, and you'll want so badly for him to know who you are that you could cry."

The boy was embarrassed.

"And that's called the cycle of life's infinite wisdom," his father said, and laughed at himself unpleasantly.

"What did he die of?" the boy asked, desperate to escape the focus of his father's rumination.

"He was eighty-seven then. Christ. He was tired." The boy's father went silent. Then he shook his head, and poured himself the remaining coffee.

Through that night the boy was never quite warm. He slept on his side with his knees drawn up, and this was uncomfortable but his body seemed to demand it for warmth. The hard cold mountain earth pressed upward through the mat of fir boughs his father had laid, and drew heat from the boy's body like a pallet of leeches. He clutched the bedroll around his neck and folded the empty part at the bottom back under his legs. Once he woke to a noise. Though his father was sleeping between him and the door of the hut, for a while the boy lay awake, listening worriedly, and then woke again on his back to realize time had passed. He heard droplets begin to hit the canvas his father had spread over the sod roof of the hut. But he remained dry.

He rose to the smell of a fire. The tarp was rigid with sleet and frost. The firewood and the knapsacks were frosted. It was that gray time of dawn before any blue and, through the branches above, the boy was unable to tell whether the sky was murky or clear. Delicate sheet ice hung on everything, but there was no wetness. The rain seemed to have been hushed by the cold.

"What time is it?"

"Early yet."

"How early?" The boy was thinking about the cold at home as he waited outside on 96th Street for his school bus. That was the cruelest moment of his day, but it seemed a benign and familiar part of him compared to this.

"Early. I don't have a watch. What difference does it make, David?"

"Not any."

After breakfast they began walking up the valley. His father had the .270, and the boy carried an old Winchester .30-30, with open sights. The walking was not hard, and with this gentle exercise in the cold morning the boy soon felt fresh and fine. Now I'm hunting for

moose with my father, he told himself. That's just what I'm doing. Few boys in Evergreen Park had ever been moose hunting with their fathers in Montana, he knew. I'm doing it now, the boy told himself.

Reaching the lip of a high meadow, a mile above the shepherd's hut, they had not seen so much as a magpie.

Before them, across hundreds of yards, opened a smooth lake of tall lifeless grass, browned by September drought and killed by the frosts and beginning to rot with November's rain. The creek was here a deep quiet channel of smooth curves overhung by the grass, with a dark surface like heavy oil. When they had come fifty yards into the meadow, his father turned and pointed out to the boy a large ponderosa pine with a forked crown that marked the head of their creek valley. He showed the boy a small aspen grove midway across the meadow, toward which they were aligning themselves.

"Near the far woods is a beaver pond. The moose waters there. We can wait in the aspens and watch the whole meadow without being seen. If he doesn't come, we'll go up another canyon, and check again on the way back."

For an hour, and another, they waited. The boy sat with his hands in his jacket pockets, bunching the jacket tighter around him, and his buttocks drew cold moisture from the ground. His father squatted on his heels like a country man, rising periodically to inspect the meadow in all directions. Finally he stood up; he fixed his stare on the distant fringe of woods and, like a retriever, did not move. He said, "David."

The boy stood beside him. His father placed a hand on the boy's shoulder. The boy saw a large dark form rolling toward them like a great slug in the grass.

"Is it the moose?"

"No," said his father. "That is a grizzly bear, David. An old male grizzly."

The boy was impressed. He sensed an aura of power and terror and authority about the husky shape, even at two hundred yards.

"Are we going to shoot him?"

"No."

"Why not?"

"We don't have a permit," his father whispered. "And because we don't want to."

The bear plowed on toward the beaver pond for a while, then stopped. It froze in the grass and seemed to be listening. The boy's father added: "That's not hunting for the meat. That's hunting for the fear. I don't need the fear. I've got enough in my life already."

The bear turned and moiled off quickly through the grass. It disappeared back into the far woods.

"He heard us."

"Maybe," the boy's father said. "Let's go have a look at that beaver pond."

A sleek furred carcass lay low in the water, swollen grotesquely with putrescence and coated with glistening blowflies. Four days, the boy's father guessed. The moose had been shot at least eighteen times with a .22 pistol. One of its eyes had been shot out; it had been shot twice in the jaw; and both quarters on the side that lay upward were ruined with shots. Standing up to his knees in the sump, the boy's father took the trouble of counting the holes, and probing one of the slugs out with his knife. That only made him angrier. He flung the lead away.

For the next three hours, with his father withdrawn into a solitary and characteristic bitterness, the boy felt abandoned. He did not understand why a moose would be slaughtered with a light pistol and left to rot. His father did not bother to explain; like the bear, he seemed to understand it as well as he needed to. They walked on, but they did not really hunt.

They left the meadow for more pine, and now tamarack, naked tamarack, the yellow needles nearly all down and going ginger where they coated the trail. The boy and his father hiked along a level path into another canyon, this one vast at the mouth and narrowing between high ridges of bare rock. They crossed and recrossed the shepherd's creek, which in this canyon was a tumbling free-stone brook. Following five yards behind his father, watching the cold, unapproachable rage that shaped the line of the man's shoulders, the boy was miserably uneasy because his father had grown so distant and quiet. They climbed over deadfalls blocking the trail, skirted one boulder large as a cabin, and blundered into a garden of nettles that stung them fiercely through their trousers. They saw fresh elk scat, and they saw bear, diarrhetic with late berries. The boy's father eventually grew bored with brooding, and showed the boy how to stalk. Before dusk that day they had shot an elk.

An open and gently sloped hillside, almost a meadow, ran for a quarter mile in quaking aspen, none over fifteen feet tall. The elk was above. The boy's father had the boy brace his gun in the notch of an aspen and take the first shot. The boy missed. The elk reeled and bolted down and his father killed it before it made cover. It was a five-point bull. They dressed the elk out and dragged it down to the cover of large pines, near the stream, where they would quarter it tomorrow, and then they returned under twilight to the hut.

That night even the fetal position could not keep the boy warm. He shivered wakefully for hours. He was glad that the following day, though full of walking and butchery and oppressive burdens, would be their last in the woods. He heard nothing. When he woke, through the door of the hut he saw whiteness like bone.

Six inches had fallen, and it was still snowing. The boy stood about in the campsite, amazed. When it snowed three inches in Evergreen Park, the boy would wake before dawn to the hiss of sand trucks and the ratchet of chains. Here there had been no warning. The boy was not much colder than he had been yesterday, and the transformation of the woods seemed mysterious and benign and somehow comic. He thought of Christmas. Then his father barked at him.

His father's mood had also changed, but in a different way; he seemed serious and hurried. As he wiped the breakfast pots clean with snow, he gave the boy orders for other chores. They left camp with two empty pack frames, both rifles, and a handsaw and rope. The boy soon understood why his father felt pressure of time: it took them an hour to climb the mile to the meadow. The snow continued. They did not rest until they reached the aspens.

"I had half a mind at breakfast to let the bull lie and pack us straight down out of here," his father admitted. "Probably smarter and less trouble in the long run. I could have come back on snowshoes next week. But by then it might be three feet deep and starting to drift. We can get two quarters out today. That will make it easier for me later." The boy was surprised by two things: that his father would be so wary in the face of a gentle snowfall and that he himself would have felt disappointed to be taken out of the woods that morning. The air of the meadow teemed with white.

"If it stops soon, we're fine," said his father.

It continued.

The path up the far canyon was hard climbing in eight inches of snow. The boy fell once, filling his collar and sleeves, and the gun-sight put a small gouge in his chin. But he was not discouraged. That night they would be warm and dry at the cabin. A half mile on and he came up beside his father, who had stopped to stare down at dark splashes of blood.

Heavy tracks and a dragging belly mark led up to the scramble of deepening red, and away. The tracks were nine inches long and showed claws. The boy's father knelt. As the boy watched, one shining maroon splotch the size of a saucer sank slowly beyond sight into the snow. The blood was warm.

Inspecting the tracks carefully, his father said, "She's got a cub with her."

"What happened?"

"Just a kill. Seems to have been a bird. That's too much blood for a grouse, but I don't see signs of any four-footed creature. Maybe a turkey." He frowned thoughtfully. "A turkey without feathers. I don't know. What I dislike is coming up on her with a cub." He drove a round into the chamber of the .270.

Trailing red smears, the tracks preceded them. Within fifty feet they found the body. It was half-buried. The top of its head had been shorn away, and the cub's brains had been licked out.

His father said "Christ," and plunged off the trail. He snapped at the boy to follow closely.

They made a wide crescent through brush and struck back after a quarter mile. His father slogged ahead in the snow, stopping often to stand holding his gun ready and glancing around while the boy caught up and passed him. The boy was confused. He knew his father was worried, but he did not feel any danger himself. They met the trail again, and went on to the aspen hillside before his father allowed them to rest. The boy spat on the snow. His lungs ached badly.

"Why did she do that?"

"She didn't. Another bear got her cub. A male. Maybe the one we saw yesterday. Then she fought him for the body, and she won. We didn't miss them by much. She may even have been watching. Nothing could put her in a worse frame of mind."

He added: "If we so much as see her, I want you to pick the nearest big tree and start climbing. Don't stop till you're twenty feet off the ground. I'll stay down and decide whether we have to shoot her. Is your rifle cocked?"

"No."

"Cock it, and put on the safety. She may be a black bear and black bears can climb. If she comes up after you, lean down and stick your gun in her mouth and fire. You can't miss."

He cocked the Winchester, as his father had said.

They angled downhill to the stream, and on to the mound of their dead elk. Snow filtered down steadily in purposeful silence. The boy was thirsty. It could not be much below freezing, he was aware, because with the exercise his bare hands were comfortable, even sweating between the fingers.

"Can I get a drink?"

"Yes. Be careful you don't wet your feet. And don't wander anywhere. We're going to get this done quickly."

He walked the few yards, ducked through the brush at streamside, and knelt in the snow to drink. The water was painful to his sinuses and bitterly cold on his hands. Standing again, he noticed an animal body ahead near the stream bank. For a moment he felt sure it was another dead cub. During that moment his father called:

"David! Get up here right now!"

The boy meant to call back. First he stepped closer to turn the cub with his foot. The touch brought it alive. It rose suddenly with a high squealing growl and whirled its head like a snake and snapped. The boy shrieked. The cub had his right hand in its jaws. It would not release.

It thrashed senselessly, working its teeth deeper and tearing flesh with each movement. The boy felt no pain. He knew his hand was being damaged and that realization terrified him and he was desperate to get the hand back before it was ruined. But he was helpless. He sensed the same furious terror racking the cub that he felt in himself, and he screamed at the cub almost reasoningly to let him go. His screams scared the cub more. Its head snatched back and forth. The boy did not think to shout for his father. He did not see him or hear him coming.

His father moved at full stride in a slowed laboring run through the snow, saying nothing and holding the rifle he did not use, crossed the last six feet still gathering speed, and brought his right boot up into the cub's belly. That kick seemed to lift the cub clear of the snow. It opened its jaws to another shrill piggish squeal, and the boy felt dull relief on his hand, as though his father had pressed open the blades of a spring trap with his foot. The cub tumbled once and disappeared over the stream bank, then surfaced downstream, squalling and paddling. The boy looked at his hand and was horrified. He still had no pain, but the hand was unrecognizable. His fingers had been peeled down through the palm like flaps on a banana. Glands at the sides of his jaw threatened that he would vomit, and he might have stood stupidly watching the hand bleed if his father had not grabbed him.

He snatched the boy by the arm and dragged him toward a tree without even looking at the boy's hand. The boy jerked back in angry resistance as though he had been struck. He screamed at his father. He screamed that his hand was cut, believing his father did not know, and as he screamed he began to cry. He began to feel hot throbbing pain. He began to worry about the blood he was losing. He could imagine his blood melting red holes in the snow behind him and he did not want to look. He did not want to do anything until he had taken care of his hand. At that instant he hated his father. But his father was stronger. He all but carried the boy to a tree.

He lifted the boy. In a voice that was quiet and hurried and very unlike the harsh grip with which he had taken the boy's arm, he said:

"Grab hold and climb up a few branches as best you can. Sit on a limb and hold tight and clamp the hand under your other armpit, if you can do that. I'll be right back to you. Hold tight because you're going to get dizzy." The boy groped desperately for a branch. His father supported him from beneath, and waited. The boy clambered. His feet scraped at the trunk. Then he was in the tree. Bark flakes and resin were stuck to the raw naked meat of his right hand. His father said:

"Now here, take this. Hurry."

The boy never knew whether his father himself had been frightened enough to forget for that moment about the boy's hand, or whether his father was still thinking quite clearly. His father may have expected that much. By the merciless clarity of his own standards, he may have expected that the boy should be able to hold onto a tree, and a wound, and a rifle, all with one hand. He extended the stock of the Winchester toward the boy.

The boy wanted to say something, but his tears and his fright would not let him gather a breath. He shuddered, and could not speak. "David," his father urged. The boy reached for the stock and faltered and clutched at the trunk with his good arm. He was crying and gasping, and he wanted to speak. He was afraid he would fall out of the tree. He released his grip once again, and felt himself tip. His father extended the gun higher, holding the barrel. The boy swung out his injured hand, spraying his father's face with blood. He reached and he tried to close torn dangling fingers around the stock and he pulled the trigger.

The bullet entered low on his father's thigh and shattered the knee and traveled down the shin bone and into the ground through his father's heel.

His father fell, and the rifle fell with him. He lay in the snow without moving. The boy thought he was dead. Then the boy saw him grope for the rifle. He found it and rolled onto his stomach, taking aim at the sow grizzly. Forty feet up the hill, towering on hind legs, she canted her head to one side, indecisive. When the cub pulled itself up a snowbank from the stream, she coughed at it sternly. The cub trotted straight to her with its head low. She knocked it off its feet with a huge paw, and it yelped. Then she turned quickly. The cub followed.

The woods were silent. The gunshot still echoed awesomely back to the boy but it was an echo of memory, not sound. He felt nothing. He saw his father's body stretched on the snow and he did not really believe he was where he was. He did not want to move: he wanted to wake. He sat in the tree and waited. The snow fell as gracefully as before.

His father rolled onto his back. The boy saw him raise himself to a sitting position and look down at the leg and betray no expression, and then slump back. He blinked slowly and lifted his eyes to meet the boy's eyes. The boy waited. He expected his father to speak. He expected his father to say *Shinny down using your elbows and knees and get the first-aid kit and boil water and phone the doctor. The number is taped to the dial.* His father stared. The boy could see the flicker of thoughts behind his father's eyes. His father said nothing. He raised his arms slowly and crossed them over his face, as though to nap in the sun.

The boy jumped. He landed hard on his feet and fell onto his back. He stood over his father. His hand dripped quietly onto the snow. He was afraid that his father was deciding to die. He wanted to beg him to reconsider. The boy had never before seen his father hopeless. He was afraid.

But he was no longer afraid of his father.

Then his father uncovered his face and said, "Let me see it."

They bandaged the boy's hand with a sleeve cut from the other arm of his shirt. His father wrapped the hand firmly and split the sleeve end with his deer knife and tied it neatly in two places. The boy now felt searing pain in his torn palm, and his stomach lifted when he thought of the damage, but at least he did not have to look at it. Quickly the plaid flannel bandage began to soak through maroon. They cut a sleeve from his father's shirt to tie over the wound in his thigh. They raised the trouser leg to see the long swelling bruise down the calf where he was hemorrhaging into the bullet's tunnel. Only then did his father realize that he was bleeding also from the heel. The boy took off his father's boot and placed a half-clean handkerchief on the insole where the bullet had exited, as his father instructed him. Then his father laced the boot on again tightly. The boy helped his father to stand. His father tried a step, then collapsed in the snow with a blasphemous howl of pain. They had not known that the knee was shattered.

The boy watched his father's chest heave with the forced sighs of suffocating frustration, and heard the air wheeze through his nostrils. His father relaxed himself with the breathing, and seemed to be thinking. He said,

"You can find your way back to the hut."

The boy held his own breath and did not move.

"You can, can't you?"

"But I'm not. I'm not going alone. I'm only going with you."

"All right, David, listen carefully," his father said. "We don't have to worry about freezing. I'm not worried about either of us freezing to death. No one is going to freeze in the woods in November, if he looks after himself. Not even in Montana. It just isn't that cold. I have matches and I have a fresh elk. And I don't think this weather is going to get any worse. It may be raining again by morning. What I'm concerned about is the bleeding. If I spend too much time and effort trying to walk out of here, I could bleed to death.

"I think your hand is going to be all right. It's a bad wound, but the doctors will be able to fix it as good as new. I can see that. I promise you that. You'll be bleeding some too, but if you take care of that hand it won't bleed any more walking than if you were standing still. Then you'll be at the doctor's tonight. But if I try to walk out on this leg it's going to bleed and keep bleeding and I'll lose too much blood. So I'm staying here and bundling up warm and you're walking out to get help. I'm sorry about this. It's what we have to do.

"You can't possibly get lost. You'll just follow this trail straight down the canyon the way we came up, and then you'll come to the meadow. Point yourself toward the big pine tree with the forked crown. When you get to that tree you'll find the creek again. You may not be able to see it, but make yourself quiet and listen for it. You'll hear it. Follow that down off the mountain and past the hut till you get to the jeep."

He struggled a hand into his pocket. "You've never driven a car, have you?"

The boy's lips were pinched. Muscles in his cheeks ached from clenching his jaws. He shook his head.

"You can do it. It isn't difficult." His father held up a single key and began telling the boy how to start the jeep, how to work the clutch, how to find reverse and then first and then second. As his father described the positions on the floor shift the boy raised his swaddled right hand. His father stopped. He rubbed at his eye sockets, like a man waking.

"Of course," he said. "All right. You'll have to help me."

Using the saw with his left hand, the boy cut a small forked aspen. His father showed the boy where to trim it so that the fork would reach just to his armpit. Then they lifted him to his feet. But the crutch was useless on a steep hillside of deep grass and snow. His father leaned over the boy's shoulders and they fought the slope for an hour.

When the boy stepped in a hole and they fell, his father made no exclamation of pain. The boy wondered whether his father's knee hurt as badly as his own hand. He suspected it hurt worse. He said nothing about his hand, though several times in their climb it was twisted or crushed. They reached the trail. The snow had not stopped, and their tracks were veiled. His father said:

"We need one of the guns. I forgot. It's my fault. But you'll have to go back down and get it."

The boy could not find the tree against which his father said he had leaned the .270, so he went toward the stream and looked for blood. He saw none. The imprint of his father's body was already softened beneath an inch of fresh silence. He scooped his good hand through the snowy depression and was startled by cool slimy blood, smearing his fingers like phlegm. Nearby he found the Winchester.

"The lucky one," his father said. "That's all right. Here." He snapped open the breach and a shell flew and he caught it in the air. He glanced dourly at the casing, then cast it aside in the snow. He held the gun out for the boy to see, and with this thumb let the hammer down one notch.

"Remember?" he said. "The safety."

The boy knew he was supposed to feel great shame, but he felt little. His father could no longer hurt him as he once could, because the boy was coming to understand him. His father could not help himself. He did not want the boy to feel contemptible, but he needed him to, because of the loneliness and the bitterness and the boy's mother; and he could not help himself.

After another hour they had barely traversed the aspen hillside. Pushing the crutch away in angry frustration, his father sat in the snow. The boy did not know whether he was thinking carefully of how they might get him out, or still laboring with the choice against despair. The light had wilted to something more like moonlight than afternoon. The sweep of snow had gone gray, depthless, flat, and the sky warned sullenly of night. The boy grew restless. Then it was decided. His father hung himself piggyback over the boy's shoulders, holding the rifle. The boy supported him with elbows crooked under his father's knees. The boy was tall for eleven years old, and heavy. The boy's father weighed 164 pounds.

The boy walked.

He moved as slowly as drifting snow: a step, then time, then another step. The burden at first seemed to him overwhelming. He did not think he would be able to carry his father far.

He took the first few paces expecting to fall. He did not fall, so he kept walking. His arms and shoulders were not exhausted as quickly as he had thought they would be, so he kept walking. Shuffling ahead in the deep powder was like carrying one end of an oak bureau up stairs. But for a surprisingly long time the burden did not grow any worse. He found balance. He found rhythm. He was moving.

Dark blurred the woods, but the snow was luminous. He could see the trail well. He walked.

"How are you, David? How are you holding up?"

"All right."

"We'll stop for a while and let you rest. You can set me down here." The boy kept walking. He moved so ponderously, it seemed after each step that he had stopped. But he kept walking.

"You can set me down. Don't you want to rest?"

The boy did not answer. He wished that his father would not make him talk. At the start he had gulped for air. Now he was breathing low and regularly. He was watching his thighs slice through the snow. He did not want to be disturbed. After a moment he said, "No."

He walked. He came to the cub, shrouded beneath new snow, and did not see it, and fell over it. His face was smashed deep into the snow by his father's weight. He could not move. But he could breathe. He rested. When he felt his father's thigh roll across his right hand, he remembered the wound. He was lucky his arms had been pinned to his sides, or the hand might have taken the force of their fall. As he waited for his father to roll himself clear, the boy noticed the change in temperature. His sweat chilled him quickly. He began shivering.

His father had again fallen in silence. The boy knew that he would not call out or even mention the pain in his leg. The boy realized that he did not want to mention his hand. The blood soaking the outside of his flannel bandage had grown sticky. He did not want to think of the alien tangle of flesh and tendons and bones wrapped inside. There was pain, but he kept the pain at a distance. It was not *his* hand any more. He was not counting on ever having it back. If he was resolved about that, then the pain was not his either. It was merely pain of which he was aware. His good hand was numb.

"We'll rest now."

"I'm not tired," the boy said. "I'm just getting cold."

"We'll rest," said his father. "I'm tired."

Under his father's knee, the boy noticed, was a cavity in the snow, already melted away by fresh blood. The dark flannel around his father's thigh did not appear sticky. It gleamed.

His father instructed the boy how to open the cub with the deer knife. His father stood on one leg against a deadfall, holding the Winchester ready, and glanced around on all sides as he spoke. The boy used his left hand and both his knees. He punctured the cub low in the belly, to a soft squirting sound, and sliced upward easily. He did not gut the cub. He merely cut out a large square of belly meat. He handed it to his father, in exchange for the rifle.

His father peeled off the hide and left the fat. He sawed the meat in half. One piece he rolled up and put in his jacket pocket. The other he divided again. He gave the boy a square thick with glistening raw fat.

"Eat it. The fat too. Especially the fat. We'll cook the rest farther on. I don't want to build a fire here and taunt Momma."

The meat was chewy. The boy did not find it disgusting. He was hungry.

His father sat back on the ground and unlaced the boot from his good foot. Before the boy understood what he was doing, he had relaced the boot. He was holding a damp wool sock.

"Give me your left hand." The boy held out his good hand, and his father pulled the sock down over it. "It's getting a lot colder. And we need that hand."

"What about yours? We need your hands too. I'll give you my—"

"No, you won't. We need your feet more than anything. It's all right. I'll put mine inside your shirt."

He lifted his father, and they went on. The boy walked.

He moved steadily through cold darkness. Soon he was sweating again, down his ribs and inside his boots. Only his hands and ears felt as though crushed in a cold metal vise. But his father was shuddering. The boy stopped.

His father did not put down his legs. The boy stood on the trail and waited. Slowly he released his wrist holds. His father's thighs slumped. The boy was careful about the wounded leg. His father's grip over the boy's neck did not loosen. His fingers were cold against the boy's bare skin.

"Are we at the hut?"

"No. We're not even to the meadow."

"Why did you stop?" his father asked.

"It's so cold. You're shivering. Can we build a fire?"

"Yes," his father said hazily. "We'll rest. What time is it?"

"We don't know," the boy said. "We don't have a watch."

The boy gathered small deadwood. His father used the Winchester stock to scoop snow away from a boulder, and they placed the fire at the boulder's base. His father broke up pine twigs and fumbled dry toilet paper from his breast pocket and arranged the wood, but by then his fingers were shaking too badly to strike a match. The boy lit the fire. The boy stamped down the snow, as his father instructed, to make a small ovenlike recess before the fire boulder. He cut fir boughs to floor the recess. He added more deadwood. Beyond the invisible clouds there seemed to be part of a moon.

"It stopped snowing," the boy said.

"Why?"

The boy did not speak. His father's voice had sounded unnatural. After a moment his father said:

"Yes, indeed. It stopped."

They roasted pieces of cub meat skewered on a green stick. Dripping fat made the fire spatter and flare. The meat was scorched on the outside and raw within. It tasted as good as any meat the boy had ever eaten. They burned their palates on hot fat. The second stick smoldered through before they had noticed, and that batch of meat fell in the fire. The boy's father cursed once and reached into the flame for it and dropped it and clawed it out, and then put his hand in the snow. He did not look at the blistered fingers. They ate. The boy saw that both his father's hands had gone clumsy and almost useless.

The boy went for more wood. He found a bleached deadfall not far off the trail, but with one arm he could only break up and carry small loads. They lay down in the recess together like spoons, the boy nearer the fire. They pulled fir boughs into place above them, resting across the snow. They pressed close together. The boy's father was shivering spastically now, and he clenched the boy in a fierce hug. The boy put his father's hands back inside his own shirt. The boy slept. He woke when the fire faded and added more wood and slept. He woke again and tended the fire and changed places with his father and slept. He slept less soundly with his father between him and the fire. He woke again when his father began to vomit.

The boy was terrified. His father wrenched with sudden vomiting that brought up cub meat and yellow liquid and blood and sprayed them across the snow by the grayish-red glow of the fire and emptied his stomach dry and then would not release him. He heaved on pathetically. The boy pleaded to be told what was wrong. His father could not or would not answer. The spasms seized him at the stomach and twisted the rest of his body taut in ugly jerks. Between the attacks he breathed with a wet rumbling sound deep in his chest, and did not speak. When the vomiting subsided, his breathing stretched itself out into long bubbling sighs, then shallow gasps, then more liquidy sighs. His breath caught and froth rose in his throat and into his mouth and he gagged on it and began vomiting again. The boy thought his father would choke. He knelt beside him and held him and cried. He could not see his father's face well and he did not want to look closely while the sounds that were coming from inside his father's body seemed so unhuman. The boy had never been more frightened. He wept for himself, and for his father. He knew from the noises and movements that his father must die. He did not think his father could ever be human again.

When his father was quiet, he went for more wood. He broke limbs from the deadfall with fanatic persistence and brought them back in bundles and built the fire up bigger. He nestled his father close to it and held him from behind. He did not sleep, though he was not awake. He waited. Finally he opened his eyes on the beginnings of dawn. His father sat up and began to spit.

"One more load of wood and you keep me warm from behind and then we'll go."

The boy obeyed. He was surprised that his father could speak. He thought it strange now that his father was so concerned for himself and so little concerned for the boy. His father had not even asked how he was.

The boy lifted his father, and walked.

Sometime while dawn was completing itself, the snow had resumed. It did not filter down soundlessly. It came on a slight wind at the boy's back, blowing down the canyon. He felt as though he were tumbling forward with the snow into a long vertical shaft. He tumbled slowly. His father's body protected the boy's back from being chilled by the wind. They were both soaked through their clothes. His father was soon shuddering again.

The boy walked. Muscles down the back of his neck were sore from yesterday. His arms ached, and his shoulders and thighs, but his neck hurt him most. He bent his head forward against the weight and the pain, and he watched his legs surge through the snow. At his stomach he felt the dull ache of hunger, not as an appetite but as an affliction. He thought of the jeep. He walked.

He recognized the edge of the meadow but through the snowladen wind he could not see the cluster of aspens. The snow became deeper where he left the wooded trail. The direction of the wind was now variable, sometimes driving snow into his face, sometimes whipping across him from the right. The grass and snow dragged at his thighs, and he moved by stumbling forward and then catching himself back. Twice he stepped into small overhung fingerlets of the stream, and fell violently, shocking the air from his lungs and once nearly spraining an ankle. Farther out into the meadow, he saw the aspens. They were a hundred yards off to his right. He did not turn directly toward them. He was afraid of crossing more hidden creeks on the intervening ground. He was not certain now whether the main channel was between him and the aspen grove or behind him to the left. He tried to project from the canyon trail to the aspens and on to the forked pine on the far side of the meadow, along what he remembered as almost a straight line. He pointed himself toward the far edge, where the pine should have been. He could not see a forked crown. He could not even see trees. He could see only a vague darker corona above the curve of white. He walked.

He passed the aspens and left them behind. He stopped several times with the wind rasping against him in the open meadow, and rested. He did not set his father down. His father was trembling uncontrollably. He had not spoken for a long time. The boy wanted badly to reach the far side of the meadow. His socks were soaked and his boots and cuffs were glazed with ice. The wind was chafing his face and making him dizzy. His thighs felt as if they had been bruised with a club. The boy wanted to give up and set his father down and whimper that this had gotten to be very unfair; and he wanted to reach the far trees. He did not doubt which he would do. He walked.

He saw trees. Raising his head painfully, he squinted against the rushing flakes. He did not see the forked crown. He went on, and stopped again, and craned his neck, and squinted. He scanned a wide angle of pines, back and forth. He did not see it. He turned his body and his burden to look back. The snow blew across the meadow and seemed, whichever way he turned, to be streaking into his face. He pinched his eyes tighter. He could still see the aspens. But he could not judge where the canyon trail met the meadow. He did not know from just where he had come. He looked again at the aspens, and then ahead to the pines. He considered the problem carefully. He was irritated that the forked ponderosa did not show itself yet, but not worried. He was forced to estimate. He estimated, and went on in that direction.

When he saw a forked pine it was far off to the left of his course. He turned and marched toward it gratefully. As he came nearer, he bent his head up to look. He stopped. The boy was not sure that this was the right tree. Nothing about it looked different, except the thick cakes of snow weighting its limbs, and nothing about it looked especially familiar. He had seen thousands of pine trees in the last few days. This was one like the others. It definitely had a forked crown. He entered the woods at its base.

He had vaguely expected to join a trail. There was no trail. After two hundred yards he was still picking his way among trees and deadfalls and brush. He remembered the shepherd's creek that fell off the lip of the meadow and led down the first canyon. He turned and retraced his tracks to the forked pine.

He looked for the creek. He did not see it anywhere near the tree. He made himself quiet, and listened. He heard nothing but wind, and his father's tremulous breathing.

"Where is the creek?"

His father did not respond. The boy bounced gently up and down, hoping to jar him alert.

"Where is the creek? I can't find it."

"What?"

"We crossed the meadow and I found the tree but I can't find the creek. I need you to help."

"The compass is in my pocket," his father said.

He lowered his father into the snow. He found the compass in his father's breast pocket, and opened the flap, and held it level. The boy noticed with a flinch that his right thigh was smeared with fresh blood. For an instant he thought he had a new wound. Then he realized that the blood was his father's. The compass needle quieted.

"What do I do?"

His father did not respond. The boy asked again. His father said nothing. He sat in the snow and shivered.

The boy left his father and made random arcs within sight of the forked tree until he found a creek. They followed it onward along the flat and then where it gradually began sloping away. The boy did not see what else he could do. He knew that this was the wrong creek. He hoped that it would flow into the shepherd's creek, or at least bring them out on the same road where they had left the jeep. He was very tired. He did not want to stop. He did not care any more about being warm. He wanted only to reach the jeep, and to save his father's life.

He wondered whether his father would love him more generously for having done it. He wondered whether his father would ever forgive him for having done it.

If he failed, his father could never again make him feel shame, the boy thought naively. So he did not worry about failing. He did not worry about dying. His hand was not bleeding, and he felt strong. The creek swung off and down to the left. He followed it, knowing that he was lost. He did not want to reverse himself. He knew that turning back would make him feel confused and desperate and frightened. As long as he was following some pathway, walking, going down, he felt strong.

That afternoon he killed a grouse. He knocked it off a low branch with a heavy short stick that he threw like a boomerang. The grouse fell in the snow and floundered and the boy ran up and plunged on it. He felt it thrashing against his chest. He reached in and it nipped him and he caught it by the neck and squeezed and wrenched mercilessly until long after it stopped writhing. He cleaned it as he had seen his father clean grouse and built a small fire with matches from his father's breast pocket and seared the grouse on a stick. He fed his father. His father could not chew. The boy chewed mouthfuls of grouse, and took the chewed gobbets in his hand, and put them into his father's mouth. His father could swallow. His father could no longer speak.

The boy walked. He thought of his mother in Evergreen Park, and at once he felt queasy and weak. He thought of his mother's face and her voice as she was told that her son was lost in the woods in Montana with a damaged hand that would never be right, and with his father, who had been shot and was unconscious and dying. He pictured his mother receiving the news that her son might die himself, unless he could carry his father out of the woods and find his way to the jeep. He saw her face change. He heard her voice. The boy had to stop. He was crying. He could not control the shape of his mouth. He was not crying with true sorrow, as he had in the night when he held his father and thought his father would die; he was crying in sentimental self-pity. He sensed the difference. Still he cried.

He must not think of his mother, the boy realized. Thinking of her could only weaken him. If she knew where he was, what he had to do, she could only make it impossible for him to do it. He was lucky that she knew nothing, the boy thought.

No one knew what the boy was doing, or what he had yet to do. Even the boy's father no longer knew. The boy was lucky. No one was watching, no one knew, and he was free to be capable.

The boy imagined himself alone at his father's grave. The grave was open. His father's casket had already been lowered. The boy stood at the foot in his black Christmas suit, and his hands were crossed at his groin, and he was not crying. Men with shovels stood back from the grave, waiting for the boy's order for them to begin filling it. The boy felt a horrible swelling sense of joy. The men watched him, and he stared down into the hole. He knew it was a lie. If his father died, the boy's mother would rush out to Livingston and have him buried and stand at the grave in a black dress and veil squeezing the boy to her side like he was a child. There was nothing the boy could do about that. All the more reason he must keep walking.

Then she would tow the boy back with her to Evergreen Park. And he would be standing on 96th Street in the morning dark before his father's cold body had even begun to grow alien and decayed in the buried box. She would drag him back, and there would be nothing the boy could do. And he realized that if he returned with his mother after the burial, he would never again see the cabin outside Livingston. He would have no more summers and no more Novembers anywhere but in Evergreen Park.

The cabin now seemed to be at the center of the boy's life. It seemed to stand halfway between this snowbound creek valley and the train station in Chicago. It would be his cabin soon.

The boy knew nothing about his father's will, and he had never been told that legal ownership of the cabin was destined for him. Legal ownership did not matter. The cabin might be owned by his mother, or sold to pay his father's debts, or taken away by the state, but it would still be the boy's cabin. It could only forever belong to him. His father had been telling him *Here, this is yours. Prepare to receive it.* The boy had sensed that much. But he had been threatened, and unwilling. The boy realized now that he might be resting warm in the cabin in a matter of hours, or he might never see it again. He could appreciate the justice of that. He walked.

He thought of his father as though his father were far away from him. He saw himself in the black suit at the grave, and he heard his father speak to him from aside: *That's good. Now raise your eyes and tell them in a man's voice to begin shoveling. Then turn away and walk slowly back down the hill. Be sure you don't cry. That's good.* The boy stopped. He felt his glands quiver, full of new tears. He knew that it was a lie. His father would never be there to congratulate him. His father would never know how well the boy had done.

He took deep breaths. He settled himself. Yes, his father would know somehow, the boy believed. His father had known all along. His father knew.

He built the recess just as they had the night before, except this time he found flat space between a stone back and a large fallen cottonwood trunk. He scooped out the snow, he laid boughs, and he made a fire against each reflector. At first the bed was quite warm. Then the

melt from the fires began to run down and collect in the middle, forming a puddle of wet boughs under them. The boy got up and carved runnels across the packed snow to drain the fires. He went back to sleep and slept warm, holding his father. He rose again each half hour to feed the fires.

The snow stopped in the night, and did not resume. The woods seemed to grow quieter, settling, sighing beneath the new weight. What was going to come had come.

The boy grew tired of breaking deadwood and began walking again before dawn and walked for five more hours. He did not try to kill the grouse that he saw because he did not want to spend time cleaning and cooking it. He was hurrying now. He drank from the creek. At one point he found small black insects like winged ants crawling in great numbers across the snow near the creek. He stopped to pinch up and eat thirty or forty of them. They were tasteless. He did not bother to feed any to his father. He felt he had come a long way down the mountain. He thought he was reaching the level now where there might be roads. He followed the creek, which had received other branches and grown to a stream. The ground was flattening again and the drainage was widening, opening to daylight. As he carried his father, his head ached. He had stopped noticing most of his other pains. About noon of that day he came to the fence.

It startled him. He glanced around, his pulse drumming suddenly, preparing himself at once to see the long empty sweep of snow and broken fence posts and thinking of Basque shepherds fifty years gone. He saw the cabin and the smoke. He relaxed, trembling helplessly into laughter. He relaxed, and was unable to move. Then he cried, still laughing. He cried shamelessly with relief and dull joy and wonder, for as long as he wanted. He held his father, and cried. But he set his father down and washed his own face with snow before he went to the door.

He crossed the lot walking slowly, carrying his father. He did not now feel tired.

The young woman's face was drawn down in shock and revealed at first nothing of friendliness.

"We had a jeep parked somewhere, but I can't find it," the boy said. "This is my father."

They would not talk to him. They stripped him and put him before the fire wrapped in blankets and started tea and made him wait. He wanted to talk. He wished they would ask him a lot of questions. But they went about quickly and quietly, making things warm. His father was in the bedroom.

The man with the face full of dark beard had telephoned for a doctor. He went back into the bedroom with more blankets, and stayed. His wife went from room to room with hot tea. She rubbed the boy's naked shoulders through the blanket, and held a cup to his mouth, but she would not talk to him. He did not know what to say to her, and he could not move his lips very well. But he wished she would ask him some questions. He was restless, thawing in silence before the hearth.

He thought about going back to their own cabin soon. In his mind he gave the bearded man directions to take him and his father home. It wasn't far. It would not require much of the man's time. They would thank him, and give him an elk steak. Later he and his father would come back for the jeep. He could keep his father warm at the cabin as well as they were doing here, the boy knew.

While the woman was in the bedroom, the boy overheard the bearded man raise his voice:

"He what?"

"He carried him out," the woman whispered.

"What do you mean, carried him?"

"Carried him. On his back. I saw."

"Carried him from where?"

"Where it happened. Somewhere on Sheep Creek, maybe."

"Eight miles?"

"I know."

"Eight miles? How could he do that?"

"I don't know. I suppose he couldn't. But he did."

The doctor arrived in half an hour, as the boy was just starting to shiver. The doctor went into the bedroom and stayed five minutes. The woman poured the boy more tea and knelt beside him and hugged him around the shoulders.

When the doctor came out, he examined the boy without speaking. The boy wished the doctor would ask him some questions, but he was afraid he might be shivering too hard to answer in a man's voice. While the doctor touched him and probed him and took his temperature, the boy looked the doctor directly in the eye, as though to show him he was really all right.

The doctor said:

"David, your father is dead. He has been dead for a long time. Probably since yesterday."

"I know that," the boy said.

ANN BEATTIE

(1947–)

The Burning House

About the Author: Ann Beattie was born in Washington, D.C. She began writing fiction in graduate school (M.A., University of Connecticut, 1970) and has published novels, including *Falling in Place* (1980), and stories, many of which have appeared in *The New Yorker.* She is often identified as speaking for her own generation of the 1960s.

Freddy Fox is in the kitchen with me. He has just washed and dried an avocado seed I don't want, and he is leaning against the wall, rolling a joint. In five minutes, I will not be able to count on him. However: he started late in the day, and he has already brought in wood for the fire, gone to the store down the road for matches, and set the table. "You mean you'd know this stuff was Limoges even if you didn't turn the plate over?" he called from the dining room. He pretended to be about to throw one of the plates into the kitchen, like a Frisbee. Sam, the dog, believed him and shot up, kicking the rug out behind him and skidding forward before he realized his error; it was like the Road Runner tricking Wile E. Coyote into going over the cliff for the millionth time. His jowls sank in disappointment.

"I see there's a full moon," Freddy says. "There's just nothing that can hold a candle to nature. The moon and the stars, the tides and the sunshine—and we just don't stop for long enough to wonder at it all. We're so engrossed in ourselves." He takes a very long drag on the joint. "We stand and stir the sauce in the pot instead of going to the window and gazing at the moon."

"You don't mean anything personal by that, I assume."

"I love the way you pour cream in a pan. I like to come up behind you and watch the sauce bubble."

"No, thank you," I say. "You're starting late in the day."

"My responsibilities have ended. You don't trust me to help with the cooking, and I've already brought in firewood and run an errand, and this very morning I exhausted myself by taking Mr. Sam jogging with me, down at Putnam Park. You're sure you won't?"

"No, thanks," I say. "Not now, anyway."

"I love it when you stand over the steam coming out of a pan and the hairs around your forehead curl into damp little curls."

My husband, Frank Wayne, is Freddy's half brother. Frank is an accountant. Freddy is closer to me than to Frank. Since Frank talks to Freddy more than he talks to me, however, and since Freddy is totally loyal, Freddy always knows more than I know. It pleases me that he does not know how to stir sauce; he will start talking, his mind will drift, and when next you look the sauce will be lumpy, or boiling away.

Freddy's criticism of Frank is only implied. "What a gracious gesture to entertain his friends on the weekend," he says.

"Male friends," I say.

"I didn't mean that you're the sort of lady who doesn't draw the line. I most certainly did not mean that," Freddy says. "I would even have been surprised if you had taken a toke of this deadly stuff while you were at the stove."

"O.K.," I say, and take the joint from him. Half of it is left when I take it. Half an inch is left after I've taken two drags and given it back.

"More surprised still if you'd shaken the ashes into the saucepan."

"You'd tell people I'd done it when they'd finished eating, and I'd be embarrassed. You can do it, though. I wouldn't be embarrassed if it was a story you told on yourself."

"You really understand me," Freddy says. "It's moonmadness, but I have to shake just this little bit in the sauce. I have to do it."

He does it.

Frank and Tucker are in the living room. Just a few minutes ago, Frank returned from getting Tucker at the train. Tucker loves to visit. To him, Fairfield County is as mysterious as Alaska. He brought with him from New York a crock of mustard, a jeroboam of champagne, cocktail napkins with a picture of a plane flying over a building on them, twenty egret feathers ("You cannot get them anymore—strictly illegal," Tucker whispered to me), and, under his black cowboy hat with the rhinestone-studded chin strap, a toy frog that hopped when wound. Tucker owns a gallery in SoHo, and Frank keeps his books. Tucker is now stretched out in the living room, visiting with Frank, and Freddy and I are both listening.

". . . so everything I've been told indicates that he lives a purely Jekyll-and-Hyde existence. He's twenty years old, and I can see that since he's still living at home he might not want to flaunt his gayness. When he came into the gallery, he had his hair slicked back—just with water, I got close enough to sniff—and his mother was all but holding his hand. So fresh-scrubbed. The stories I'd heard. Anyway, when I called, his father started looking for the number where he could be reached on the Vineyard—very irritated, because I didn't know James, and if I'd just phoned James I could have found him in a flash.

He's talking to himself, looking for the number, and I say, 'Oh, did he go to visit friends or—' and his father interrupts and says, 'He was going to a gay pig roast. He's been gone since Monday.' *Just like that.*"

Freddy helps me carry the food out to the table. When we are all at the table, I mention the young artist Tucker was talking about. "Frank says his paintings are really incredible," I say to Tucker.

"Makes Estes look like an Abstract Expressionist," Tucker says. "I want that boy. I really want that boy."

"You'll get him," Frank says. "You get everybody you go after."

Tucker cuts a small piece of meat. He cuts it small so that he can talk while chewing. "Do I?" he says.

Freddy is smoking at the table, gazing dazedly at the moon centered in the window. "After dinner," he says, putting the back of his hand against his forehead when he sees that I am looking at him, "we must all go to the lighthouse."

"If only *you* painted," Tucker says. "I'd want you."

"You couldn't have me," Freddy snaps. He reconsiders. "That sounded halfhearted, didn't it? Anybody who wants me can have me. This is the only place I can be on Saturday night where somebody isn't hustling me."

"Wear looser pants," Frank says to Freddy.

"This is so much better than some bar that stinks of cigarette smoke and leather. Why do I do it?" Freddy says. "Seriously—do you think I'll ever stop?"

"Let's not be serious," Tucker says.

"I keep thinking of this table as a big boat, with dishes and glasses rocking on it," Freddy says.

He takes the bone from his plate and walks out to the kitchen, dripping sauce on the floor. He walks as though he's on the deck of a wave-tossed ship. "Mr. Sam!" he calls, and the dog springs up from the living-room floor, where he had been sleeping; his toenails on the bare wood floor sound like a wheel spinning in gravel. "You don't have to beg," Freddy says. "Jesus, Sammy—I'm just giving it to you."

"I hope there's a bone involved," Tucker says, rolling his eyes to Frank. He cuts another tiny piece of meat. "I hope your brother does understand why I couldn't keep him on. He was good at what he did, but he also might say just *anything* to a customer. You have to believe me that if I hadn't been extremely embarrassed more than once I never would have let him go."

"He should have finished school," Frank says, sopping up sauce on his bread. "He'll knock around a while longer, then get tired of it and settle down to something."

"You think I died out here?" Freddy calls. "You think I can't hear you?"

"I'm not saying anything I wouldn't say to your face," Frank says.

"I'll tell you what I wouldn't say to your face," Freddy says. "You've got a swell wife and kid and dog, and you're a snob, and you take it all for granted."

Frank puts down his fork, completely exasperated. He looks at me.

"He came to work once this stoned," Tucker says. *"Comprenez-vous?"*

"You like me because you feel sorry for me," Freddy says.

He is sitting on the concrete bench outdoors, in the area that's a garden in the springtime. It is early April now—not quite spring. It's very foggy out. It rained while we

were eating, and now it has turned mild. I'm leaning against a tree, across from him, glad it's so dark and misty that I can't look down and see the damage the mud is doing to my boots.

"Who's his girlfriend?" Freddy says.

"If I told you her name, you'd tell him I told you."

"Slow down. What?"

"I won't tell you, because you'll tell him that I know."

"He knows you know."

"I don't think so."

"How did you find out?"

"He talked about her. I kept hearing her name for months, and then we went to a party at Garner's, and she was there, and when I said something about her later he said, 'Natalie who?' It was much too obvious. It gave the whole thing away."

He sighs. "I just did something very optimistic," he says. "I came out here with Mr. Sam and he dug up a rock and I put the avocado seed in the hole and packed dirt on top of it. Don't say it—I know: can't grow outside, we'll still have another snow, even if it grew, the next year's frost would kill it."

"He's embarrassed," I say. "When he's home, he avoids me. But it's rotten to avoid Mark, too. Six years old, and he calls up his friend Neal to hint that he wants to go over there. He doesn't do that when we're here alone."

Freddy picks up a stick and pokes around in the mud with it. "I'll bet Tucker's after that painter personally, not because he's the hottest thing since pancakes. That expression of his—it's always the same. Maybe Nixon really loved his mother, but with that expression who could believe him? It's a curse to have a face that won't express what you mean."

"Amy!" Tucker calls. "Telephone."

Freddy waves goodbye to me with the muddy stick. " 'I am not a crook,' " Freddy says. "Jesus Christ."

Sam bounds halfway toward the house with me, then turns and goes back to Freddy.

It's Marilyn, Neal's mother, on the phone.

"Hi," Marilyn says. "He's afraid to spend the night."

"Oh, no," I say. "He said he wouldn't be."

She lowers her voice. "We can try it out, but I think he'll start crying."

"I'll come get him."

"I can bring him home. You're having a dinner party, aren't you?"

I lower my voice. "Some party. Tucker's here. J.D. never showed up."

"Well," she says. "I'm sure that what you cooked was good."

"It's so foggy out, Marilyn. I'll come get Mark."

"He can stay. I'll be a martyr," she says, and hangs up before I can object.

Freddy comes into the house, tracking in mud. Sam lies in the kitchen, waiting for his paws to be cleaned. "Come on," Freddy says, hitting his hand against his thigh, having no idea what Sam is doing. Sam gets up and runs after him. They go into the small downstairs bathroom together. Sam loves to watch people urinate. Sometimes he sings, to harmonize with the sound of the urine going into the water. There are footprints and pawprints everywhere. Tucker is shrieking with laughter in the living room. ". . . he says, he says to the other one, 'Then, dearie, have you ever played *spin* the bottle?' " Frank's and Tucker's laughter drowns out the sound of Freddy peeing in the bathroom. I turn on the water in the kitchen sink, and it drowns out all the noise. I begin to scrape the dishes.

Tucker is telling another story when I turn off the water: ". . . that it was Onassis in the Anvil, and nothing would talk him out of it. They told him Onassis was dead, and he thought they were trying to make him think he was crazy. There was nothing to do but go along with him, but, God—he was trying to goad this poor old fag into fighting about Stavros Niarchos. You know—Onassis's *enemy.* He thought it was *Onassis.* In the *Anvil."* There is a sound of a glass breaking. Frank or Tucker puts *John Coltrane Live in Seattle* on the stereo and turns the volume down low. The bathroom door opens. Sam runs into the kitchen and begins to lap water from his dish. Freddy takes his little silver case and his rolling papers out of his shirt pocket. He puts a piece of paper on the kitchen table and is about to sprinkle grass on it, but realizes just in time that the paper has absorbed water from a puddle. He balls it up with his thumb, flicks it to the floor, puts a piece of rolling paper where the table's dry and shakes a line of grass down it. "You smoke this," he says to me. "I'll do the dishes."

"We'll both smoke it. I'll wash and you can wipe."

"I forgot to tell them I put ashes in the sauce," he says.

"I wouldn't interrupt."

"At least he pays Frank ten times what any other accountant for an art gallery would make," Freddy says.

Tucker is beating his hand on the arm of the sofa as he talks, stomping his feet. ". . . so he's trying to feel him out, to see if this old guy with the dyed hair knew *Maria Callas.* Jesus! And he's so out of it he's trying to think what opera singers are called, and instead of coming up with *'diva'* he comes up with *'duenna.'* At this point, Larry Betwell went up to him and tried to calm him down, and he breaks into song—some aria or something that Maria Callas was famous for. Larry told him he was going to lose his *teeth* if he didn't get it together, and . . ."

"He spends a lot of time in gay hangouts, for not being gay," Freddy says.

I scream and jump back from the sink, hitting the glass I'm rinsing against the faucet, shattering green glass everywhere.

"What?" Freddy says. "Jesus Christ, what is it?"

Too late, I realize what it must have been that I saw: J.D. in a goat mask, the puckered pink plastic lips against the window by the kitchen sink.

"I'm sorry," J.D. says, coming through the door and nearly colliding with Frank, who has rushed into the kitchen. Tucker is right behind him.

"Oooh," Tucker says, feigning disappointment, "I thought Freddy smooched her."

"I'm sorry," J.D. says again. "I thought you'd know it was me."

The rain must have started again, because J.D. is soaking wet. He has turned the mask around so that the goat's head stares out from the back of his head. "I got lost," J.D. says. He has a farmhouse upstate. "I missed the turn. I went miles. I missed the whole dinner, didn't I?"

"What did you do wrong?" Frank asks.

"I didn't turn left onto 58. I don't know why I didn't realize my mistake, but I went *miles.* It was raining so hard I couldn't go over twenty-five miles an hour. Your driveway is all mud. You're going to have to push me out."

"There's some roast left over. And salad, if you want it," I say.

"Bring it in the living room," Frank says to J.D. Freddy is holding out a plate to him. J.D. reaches for the plate. Freddy pulls it back. J.D. reaches again, and Freddy is so stoned that he isn't quick enough this time—J.D. grabs it.

"I thought you'd know it was me," J.D. says. "I apologize." He dishes salad onto the plate. "You'll be rid of me for six months, in the morning."

"Where does your plane leave from?" Freddy says.

"Kennedy."

"Come in here!" Tucker calls. "I've got a story for you about Perry Dwyer down at the Anvil last week, when he thought he saw Aristotle Onassis."

"Who's Perry Dwyer?" J.D. says.

"That is not the point of the story, dear man. And when you're in Cassis, I want you to look up an American painter over there. Will you? He doesn't have a phone. Anyway—I've been tracking him, and I know where he is now, and I am *very* interested, if you would stress that with him, to do a show in June that will be *only* him. He doesn't answer my letters."

"Your hand is cut," J.D. says to me.

"Forget it," I say. "Go ahead."

"I'm sorry," he says. "Did I make you do that?"

"Yes, you did."

"Don't keep your finger under the water. Put pressure on it to stop the bleeding."

He puts the plate on the table. Freddy is leaning against the counter, staring at the blood swirling in the sink, and smoking the joint all by himself. I can feel the little curls on my forehead that Freddy was talking about. They feel heavy on my skin. I hate to see my own blood. I'm sweating. I let J.D. do what he does; he turns off the water and wraps his hand around my second finger, squeezing. Water runs down our wrists.

Freddy jumps to answer the phone when it rings, as though a siren just went off behind him. He calls me to the phone, but J.D. steps in front of me, shakes his head no, and takes the dish towel and wraps it around my hand before he lets me go.

"Well," Marilyn says. "I had the best of intentions, but my battery's dead."

J.D. is standing behind me, with his hand on my shoulder.

"I'll be right over," I say. "He's not upset now, is he?"

"No, but he's dropped enough hints that he doesn't think he can make it through the night."

"O.K.," I say. "I'm sorry about all of this."

"Six years old," Marilyn says. "Wait till he grows up and gets that feeling."

I hang up.

"Let me see your hand," J.D. says.

"I don't want to look at it. Just go get me a Band-Aid, please."

He turns and goes upstairs. I unwrap the towel and look at it. It's pretty deep, but no glass is in my finger. I feel funny; the outlines of things are turning yellow. I sit in the chair by the phone. Sam comes and lies beside me, and I stare at his black-and-yellow tail, beating. I reach down with my good hand and pat him, breathing deeply in time with every second pat.

"Rothko?" Tucker says bitterly, in the living room. "Nothing is great that can appear on greeting cards. Wyeth is that way. Would 'Christina's World' look bad on a cocktail napkin? You know it wouldn't."

I jump as the phone rings again. "Hello?" I say, wedging the phone against my shoulder with my ear, wrapping the dish towel tighter around my hand.

"Tell them it's a crank call. Tell them anything," Johnny says. "I miss you. How's Saturday night at your house?"

"All right," I say. I catch my breath.

"Everything's all right here, too. Yes indeed. Roast rack of lamb. Friend of Nicole's who's going to Key West tomorrow had too much to drink and got depressed because he thought it was raining in Key West, and I said I'd go in my study and call the National Weather Service. Hello, Weather Service. How are you?"

J.D. comes down from upstairs with two Band-Aids and stands beside me, unwrapping one. I want to say to Johnny, "I'm cut. I'm bleeding. It's no joke."

It's all right to talk in front of J.D., but I don't know who else might overhear me.

"I'd say they made the delivery about four this afternoon," I say.

"This is the church, this is the steeple. Open the door, and see all the people," Johnny says. "Take care of yourself. I'll hang up and find out if it's raining in Key West."

"Late in the afternoon," I say. "Everything is fine."

"Nothing is fine," Johnny says. "Take care of yourself."

He hangs up. I put the phone down, and realize that I'm still having trouble focusing, the sight of my cut finger made me so light-headed. I don't look at the finger again as J.D. undoes the towel and wraps the Band-Aids around my finger.

"What's going on in here?" Frank says, coming into the dining room.

"I cut my finger," I say. "It's O.K."

"You did?" he says. He looks woozy—a little drunk. "Who keeps calling?"

"Marilyn. Mark changed his mind about staying all night. She was going to bring him home, but her battery's dead. You'll have to get him. Or I will."

"Who called the second time?" he says.

"The oil company. They wanted to know if we got our delivery today."

He nods. "I'll go get him, if you want," he says. He lowers his voice. "Tucker's probably going to whirl himself into a tornado for an encore," he says, nodding toward the living room. "I'll take him with me."

"Do you want me to go get him?" J.D. says.

"I don't mind getting some air," Frank says. "Thanks, though. Why don't you go in the living room and eat your dinner?"

"You forgive me?" J.D. says.

"Sure," I say. "It wasn't your fault. Where did you get that mask?"

"I found it on top of a Goodwill box in Manchester. There was also a beautiful old birdcage—solid brass."

The phone rings again. I pick it up. "Wouldn't I love to be in Key West with you," Johnny says. He makes a sound as though he's kissing me and hangs up.

"Wrong number," I say.

Frank feels in his pants pocket for the car keys.

J.D. knows about Johnny. He introduced me, in the faculty lounge, where J.D. and I had gone to get a cup of coffee after I registered for classes. After being gone for nearly two years, J.D. still gets mail at the department—he said he had to stop by for the mail anyway, so he'd drive me to campus and point me toward the registrar's. J.D. taught English; now he does nothing. J.D. is glad that I've gone back to college to study art again, now that Mark is in school. I'm six credits away from an M.A. in art history. He wants me to think about myself, instead of thinking about Mark all the time. He talks as though I could roll Mark out on a string and let him fly off, high above me. J.D.'s wife and son died in a car crash. His son was Mark's age. "I wasn't prepared," J.D. said when we were driving over that day.

He always says this when he talks about it. "How could you be prepared for such a thing?" I asked him. "I am now," he said. Then, realizing he was acting very hardboiled, made fun of himself. "Go on," he said, "punch me in the stomach. Hit me as hard as you can." We both knew he wasn't prepared for anything. When he couldn't find a parking place that day, his hands were wrapped around the wheel so tightly that his knuckles turned white.

Johnny came in as we were drinking coffee. J.D. was looking at his junk mail—publishers wanting him to order anthologies, ways to get free dictionaries.

"You are so lucky to be out of it," Johnny said, by way of greeting. "What do you do when you've spent two weeks on *Hamlet* and the student writes about Hamlet's good friend Horchow?"

He threw a blue book into J.D.'s lap. J.D. sailed it back.

"Johnny," he said, "this is Amy."

"Hi, Amy," Johnny said.

"You remember when Frank Wayne was in graduate school here? Amy's Frank's wife."

"Hi, Amy," Johnny said.

J.D. told me he knew it the instant Johnny walked into the room—he knew that second that he should introduce me as somebody's wife. He could have predicted it all from the way Johnny looked at me.

For a long time J.D. gloated that he had been prepared for what happened next—that Johnny and I were going to get together. It took me to disturb his pleasure in himself—me, crying hysterically on the phone last month, not knowing what to do, what move to make next.

"Don't do anything for a while. I guess that's my advice," J.D. said. "But you probably shouldn't listen to me. All I can do myself is run away, hide out. I'm not the learned professor. You know what I believe. I believe all that wicked fairy-tale crap: your heart will break, your house will burn."

Tonight, because he doesn't have a garage at his farm, J.D. has come to leave his car in the empty half of our two-car garage while he's in France. I look out the window and see his old Saab, glowing in the moonlight. J.D. has brought his favorite book, *A Vision,* to read on the plane. He says his suitcase contains only a spare pair of jeans, cigarettes, and underwear. He is going to buy a leather jacket in France, at a store where he almost bought a leather jacket two years ago.

In our bedroom there are about twenty small glass prisms hung with fishing line from one of the exposed beams; they catch the morning light, and we stare at them like a cat eyeing catnip held above his head. Just now, it is 2 A.M. At six-thirty, they will be filled with dazzling color. At four or five, Mark will come into the bedroom and get in bed with us. Sam will wake up, stretch, and shake, and the tags on his collar will clink, and he will yawn and shake again and go downstairs, where J.D. is asleep in his sleeping bag and Tucker is asleep on the sofa, and get a drink of water from his dish. Mark has been coming into our bedroom for about a year. He gets onto the bed by climbing up on a footstool that horrified me when I first saw it—a gift from Frank's mother: a footstool that says "Today Is the First Day of the Rest of Your Life" in needlepoint. I kept it in a closet for years, but it occurred to me that it would help Mark get up onto the bed, so he would not have to make a little leap and possibly skin his shin again. Now Mark does not disturb us when he comes into the bedroom, except that it bothers me that he has reverted to sucking his thumb. Sometimes he lies in bed with his cold feet against my leg. Sometimes, small as he is, he snores.

Somebody is playing a record downstairs. It's the Velvet Underground—Lou Reed, in a dream or swoon, singing "Sunday Morning." I can barely hear the whispering and tinkling of the record. I can only follow it because I've heard it a hundred times.

I am lying in bed, waiting for Frank to get out of the bathroom. My cut finger throbs. Things are going on in the house even though I have gone to bed; water runs, the record plays. Sam is still downstairs, so there must be some action.

I have known everybody in the house for years, and as time goes by I know them all less and less. J.D. was Frank's adviser in college. Frank was his best student, and they started to see each other outside of class. They played handball. J.D. and his family came to dinner. We went there. That summer—the summer Frank decided to go to graduate school in business instead of English—J.D.'s wife and son deserted him in a more horrible way, in that car crash. J.D. has quit his job. He has been to Las Vegas, to Colorado, New Orleans, Los Angeles, Paris twice; he tapes post cards to the walls of his living room. A lot of the time, on the weekends, he shows up at our house with his sleeping bag. Sometimes he brings a girl. Lately, not. Years ago, Tucker was in Frank's therapy group in New York, and ended up hiring Frank to work as the accountant for his gallery. Tucker was in therapy at the time because he was obsessed with foreigners. Now he is also obsessed with homosexuals. He gives fashionable parties to which he invites many foreigners and homosexuals. Before the parties he does TM and yoga, and during the parties he does Seconals and isometrics. When I first met him, he was living for the summer in his sister's house in Vermont while she was in Europe, and he called us one night, in New York, in a real panic because there were wasps all over. They were "hatching," he said—big, sleepy wasps that were everywhere. We said we'd come; we drove all through the night to get to Brattleboro. It was true: there were wasps on the undersides of plates, in the plants, in the folds of curtains. Tucker was so upset that he was out behind the house, in the cold Vermont morning, wrapped like an Indian in a blanket, with only his pajamas on underneath. He was sitting in a lawn chair, hiding behind a bush, waiting for us to come.

And Freddy—"Reddy Fox," when Frank is feeling affectionate toward him. When we first met, I taught him to ice-skate and he taught me to waltz; in the summer, at Atlantic City, he'd go with me on a roller coaster that curved high over the waves. I was the one—not Frank—who would get out of bed in the middle of the night and meet him at an all-night deli and put my arm around his shoulders, the way he put his arm around my shoulders on the roller coaster, and talk quietly to him until he got over his latest anxiety attack. Now he tests me, and I retreat: this man he picked up, this man who picked him up, how it feels to have forgotten somebody's name when your hand is in the back pocket of his jeans and you're not even halfway to your apartment. Reddy Fox—admiring my new red silk blouse, stroking his fingertips down the front, and my eyes wide, because I could feel his fingers on my chest, even though I was holding the blouse in front of me on a hanger to be admired. All those moments, and all they meant was that I was fooled into thinking I knew these people because I knew the small things, the personal things.

Freddy will always be more stoned than I am, because he feels comfortable getting stoned with me, and I'll always be reminded that he's more lost. Tucker knows he can come to the house and be the center of attention; he can tell all the stories he knows, and we'll never tell the story we know about him hiding in the bushes like a frightened dog. J.D. comes back from his trips with boxes full of post cards, and I look at all of them as though they're photographs taken by him, and I know, and he knows, that what he likes about them is their flatness—the unreality of them, the unreality of what he does.

Last summer, I read *The Metamorphosis* and said to J.D., "Why did Gregor Samsa wake up a cockroach?" His answer (which he would have toyed over with his students forever) was "Because that's what people expected of him."

They make the illogical logical. I don't do anything, because I'm waiting, I'm on hold (J.D.); I stay stoned because I know it's better to be out of it (Freddy); I love art because I myself am a work of art (Tucker).

Frank is harder to understand. One night a week or so ago, I thought we were really attuned to each other, communicating by telepathic waves, and as I lay in bed about to speak I realized that the vibrations really existed: they were him, snoring.

Now he's coming into the bedroom, and I'm trying again to think what to say. Or ask. Or do.

"Be glad you're not in Key West," he says. He climbs into bed.

I raise myself up on one elbow and stare at him.

"There's a hurricane about to hit," he says.

"What?" I say. "Where did you hear that?"

"When Reddy Fox and I were putting the dishes away. We had the radio on." He doubles up his pillow, pushes it under his neck. "Boom goes everything," he says. "Bam. Crash. Poof." He looks at me. "You look shocked." He closes his eyes. Then, after a minute or two, he murmurs, "Hurricanes upset you? I'll try to think of something nice."

He is quiet for so long that I think he has fallen asleep. Then he says, "Cars that run on water. A field of flowers, none alike. A shooting star that goes slow enough for you to watch. Your life to do over again." He has been whispering in my ear, and when he takes his mouth away I shiver. He slides lower in the bed for sleep. "I'll tell you something really amazing," he says. "Tucker told me he went into a travel agency on Park Avenue last week and asked the travel agent where he should go to pan for gold, and she told him."

"Where did she tell him to go?"

"I think somewhere in Peru. The banks of some river in Peru."

"Did you decide what you're going to do after Mark's birthday?" I say.

He doesn't answer me. I touch him on the side, finally.

"It's two o'clock in the morning. Let's talk about it another time."

"You picked the house, Frank. They're your friends downstairs. I used to be what you wanted me to be."

"They're your friends, too," he says. "Don't be paranoid."

"I want to know if you're staying or going."

He takes a deep breath, lets it out, and continues to lie very still.

"Everything you've done is commendable," he says. "You did the right thing to go back to school. You tried to do the right thing by finding yourself a normal friend like Marilyn. But your whole life you've made one mistake—you've surrounded yourself with men. Let me tell you something. All men—if they're crazy, like Tucker, if they're gay as the Queen of the May, like Reddy Fox, even if they're just six years old—I'm going to tell you something about them. Men think they're Spider-Man and Buck Rogers and Superman. You know what we all feel inside that you don't feel? That we're going to the stars."

He takes my hand. "I'm looking down on all of this from space," he whispers. "I'm already gone."

T. ALAN BROUGHTON

(1936–)

Duck Season

About the Author: T. Alan Broughton, born in Bryn Mawr, Pennsylvania, began publishing fiction and poetry in 1964, after studying music at the Juilliard School, and English at Harvard, Swarthmore, and the University of Washington. Since then he has published four novels (the first, *A Family Gathering,* appeared in 1977), six volumes of poetry, and a collection of short stories, *The Jesse Tree* (1988). Broughton, a recipient of both NEA and Guggenheim fellowships, teaches writing at the University of Vermont and co-directs its Writers' Workshop Program.

Gracie turned on her side to look at the clock. She could tell by the way the sun glowed through a frozen gauze around the bottom of the windowpane that a hard frost had come at last. This fall had been unusually mild, but all night the wind had shaken and battered the house, ripping away the warm, rainy weather. The leaves would be scattered now all over the lawn and streets. The sun kept dimming and bursting back, and she could smell the cold, cloud-tossed day, smoke from the neighbor's fireplace. Later she would go to the window to see it all.

Below, the phone rang and was immediately answered. They had fixed the one by her bed so it could not ring. Someone was up, and the kids would not be quiet for long. Except George. They said he had been sleeping more than usual. Len would be happy about the cold weather. Duck hunting began soon, and he was worried that the birds would not be flocking in time, like last year when the season was almost over before the flights began, great wedges of geese straggling over the house, ducks skimming across the already frozen pond, but too late. Last week he had been up to the lake with Bert to set up the blind and had described how the boat had stuck in the mud because the lake was so low, and he had lost a boot trying to push out of the muck.

She and Len had fought for years over the duck hunting. And he never understood how she felt. She could not make him see how obsessed he became, how for all those weeks he would be thinking nothing but ducks, ducks, ducks—neglecting the children, not listening to her. Even when he made love his touches were so vague and remote that she started turning away from him because she would rather have no lover than be fondled by a spook. Cleaning his guns, getting up at three A.M. to drive off and meet Bert, turning those bright-feathered creatures into broken-necked and disheveled lumps, their feathers blowing around the lawn for weeks, tracked in by the kids—she had tried to break him of all that, once even threatened to take the kids and go somewhere else for the whole season. He set that jaw the way he always did when he was angry, stared with one eyebrow lifted, and said, "Is that so?" But she never expected Len to settle arguments with words. He mistrusted them, and halfway through, before walking away, he would say, "You can make anything sound right, even when you know better."

She turned slowly onto her back. Len thought he was so strong, but he was only stubborn. He nearly crushed the house once to avoid taking her advice. He was cutting down the white pine that had died by the fence. She had been in the kitchen, looked out the window, and any fool could tell that the limbs were longer toward the house, and more of them too, but there he was chopping as if he thought it would fall the other way. She

had gone out on the stoop and told him so, and he had stared back and then said loud enough so all the neighbors were bound to hear, *It'll damn well fall the way I want it to, woman,* and she watched from the kitchen again as the ax beat furiously into the cut. The tree wavered, drifting toward the house, and then there he was, as if he thought he were Samson, right in the way and pushing back against it, and if a burst of wind from the right direction had not come he would have been crushed. But he was lucky and only lost a section of fence. Afterwards they did not talk about it.

Here he was getting ready to hunt again, as if it were just any fall. *Mother's here,* he had said. *She can get the kids off to school, and I'm always back by late morning.* Now that he slept in another room so he would not bother her or not be kept awake by her, she would not see or hear him get up, would not watch through half-sleeping eyes his naked form drawing on layer after layer of clothes, that stealthy way he would pause by her bed before he left as though at least thinking of kissing her, and then he would be gone. In those days she would not get back to sleep, would worry all morning, the TV kept low so she would be sure to hear the car popping gravel in the driveway when he returned—because always the part she could not tell him was how she had read about the awful accidents with guns, or people falling out of their boats in the freezing water. Even Len's father had almost drowned once fishing when his hip boots filled, dragging him down. But that was not a fair way to argue, that was weak. Besides she did not want him to think she worried that much, not about him when he was so stubborn and inconsiderate. Sometimes he would not even come into the house but would stalk off to work at the garage, angry because he had not shot anything, angry at her as if she had made it that way.

Sometimes when her pain was light and she had space to reflect dispassionately, she felt sorry that everyone around her should have to wait and wait, but at other times she would be irritated at them, would want to say as she finally did to his mother one evening, *I can't bear to watch you sit around like this. Can't you go do something?* But no one wanted to talk about it. Not even she was allowed to mention some things. Once she had said to Len, *I'm going to die soon. Stop trying to pretend,* but he looked at her as if she had betrayed him, and she did not use the word again.

Looking at the clock had become a habit, part of her boredom, but she could not help turning again. Those hands and numbers measured out light and dark, but only to click off the present, foretelling nothing, and to know where they were going was as impossible as trying to tell the tick from tock. Some nights that was her main pastime.

"Gracie?" Len leaned in, his hand on the doorknob. He was wearing a clean, white shirt, an unknotted tie dangling loosely from the open collar.

"It's Sunday, isn't it? I forgot."

He came all the way in and sat on the edge of the bed. He had nicked his chin shaving.

"Yes. Mother's not going, though."

"You'll take the kids?"

"They missed last Sunday. Father Rivard was asking about them."

"Did you wake Georgie? You mustn't let him sleep so late. Mother says he goes to bed early too. That shirt's missing a button."

He looked down at his midriff. He was lean and hard-muscled, and most of the friends his age bulged out a little at their gut, but not Len, and he was proud of that.

"It won't show when my jacket's on."

"Don't let Mother put Betsey into that silly pinafore she gave her. The child hates it and thinks her friends are making fun of her."

His hand felt heavy and hot, and she shifted hers under it.

"Mother will bring up some breakfast soon." He stood looking out the door into the hallway. "Father Rivard was asking if he should stop by. If you'd like to talk with him."

"I don't think so, thanks."

Not her religion, after all. She had done her part by encouraging her children in it, and going to Mass and learning about it all, but there was one thing she did not have to do—she did not have to believe it.

"You'll be back soon?"

"Soon as we can." He stooped so suddenly to kiss her on the mouth that he was almost gone before she could kiss him back.

"Let me see the children all dressed up."

She could hear him calling into the hallway below, the clatter and thump as they raced up the stairs, and suddenly all three were pushing against each other on the threshold. "Georgie, brush that hair down before you go."

He swung in awkwardly, a tie choked up much too tightly against his throat, those hands and wrists and arms dangling out of the cuffs of a shirt his body had abruptly outgrown. He was too tall for a nine-year-old, and she knew that made him vulnerable to teasing at school.

"Come here."

He went to the edge of the bed and stood with his knees pressing the mattress.

"Now bend down."

He leaned stiffly toward her, his sleepy face sullen. She put a hand on his brow, ran it over his cheek.

"Are you feeling all right?"

"Yes."

"He's got Africa sleeping sickness, Gramma says," and Betsey laughed.

She was in that awful pinafore. Gracie felt the old resentment rise hotly in her, then evaporate. What did it matter? Betsey did not seem to care today. It was something between Len's mother and herself.

"Don't be silly. It's because he's growing very fast."

When Gracie glanced at Adele she could see that her oldest child had decided to be a lady that morning. She had her hair drawn back tightly and was wearing a hint of eyeshade which ordinarily Gracie would have told her to remove, but she knew there was no time now, and Len was calling from downstairs.

"Go on." She noticed how relieved they were to turn and go. "Georgie."

He paused. She saw his whole figure then on the threshold, the pants hiked up, the shoes turned in slightly at the toes, but also the stark, clear look of his eyes, mouth open, and she knew he was not sleeping because he was worrying about her. But there was nothing she could say to help him. And she remembered once when she had driven past his school and had seen a child standing at the closed door of the building, waiting for recess to end, not playing with the other children, and suddenly she had realized that was her child, the bewildered look on his face coming out of a life entirely separate from hers, and she had driven on quickly, hoping he had not seen her. Now all of them were that way, further and further away from her, and sometimes even the children seemed to look at her from a huge distance.

"Do brush your hair," she murmured. He nodded and was gone.

She liked many things about the church: the neat, washed aura of the congregation, the incense, Father Rivard's voice which was clear and carried the words well. Even if she kept herself separate from some last part of it, she liked the way Len was solemn, would kneel so totally that she knew he felt a power she could not hope to admit with such severity. But somewhere back of it all for her were those monotonous Sundays when she was a child and living with her grandmother, and they would dress up and go to The Church of the Redeemer. She knew perfectly well they were going only because good families were supposed to do that, and if they lingered afterwards it was to be certain they had been sufficiently seen. She probably should have let Len tell Father Rivard to come, and she almost called him back but heard the door slam and the truck starting and she thought no, I couldn't, I could not pretend anyway, and she was falling asleep which happened often now. She did not try to stop it.

But woke with pain, remembering she had not taken her pills. She had been dreaming that someone was sawing her in half. She was in the magician's box, and he was stooped out of sight, groaning as he jerked the saw back and forth, but the trick was not working and the saw was actually beginning to cut into her. Then the magician's voice became her own, and she saw Len's mother standing there.

"Your pills." She helped Gracie sit up enough to swallow them down.

Gracie was sweating, the pain made everything blurred, and she concentrated on not getting sick because then the pills would fail and they would have to call the nurse to give her a shot, and she was tired of her body being kneaded and poked and cut. She tried to focus on the hand that stroked her forehead. She tried not to moan. She hated that—it did no good. But she could not help it.

After a while the pain began to ease.

"What's the time?"

"Almost 11:30."

"They should be home."

"They'll be a little late this morning."

"Why?"

"I forgot to say your father called last night. He'll be up next weekend to see you. You know, he has his fall reunion then too, so he'll stay here in town and drive over to the college."

Next weekend. So far away. But she could almost laugh. How typical of him to work out everything so conveniently—a visit and his yearly class reunion. He always seemed to need some small excuse to see her.

"Next time he calls, wake me."

Her mother smiled. Gracie knew they would not.

"Some breakfast?"

"I can't."

They never argued with her anymore.

"Mother." She put a hand on her arm. "Promise me something."

The woman's hand fluttered up, past the glasses that tilted to one side, and jabbed at her hair. But the phone was ringing downstairs, and she stood. "I'll take it down there."

Of course they were not going to make promises. They had their lives to live, and again she resented them bitterly, even though she knew it was childish. How she longed to say something fine and noble to Len. She had even made up a whole speech one night to tell him the next day about how it was important for him and the kids that he go on and find another woman and re-marry, but damn it all, she could not. She would never forgive him for that hanging around with Harriet Martin, although he said it was only "casual fun" because she was in the hospital for a month having difficulties before Betsey was born and he had gotten lonely. Men. As if she had not been lonely in that ward with a bunch of women she did not know because the hospital was way over in New Hampshire. Len and Harriet had gone to bars together so often that people in town began to talk, and one night when she had been with him he had run the truck off the road into Carson's field. Old Carson had towed them out with his tractor. Thank God the simpering, frizz-haired woman had moved away. At least he would not marry her. But Len always had an eye for women. When she and Len were driving down the street she would watch him turn slightly to take in more of some little number walking the sidewalk. If he had played around, why should she be so big and brave and make him feel good now about moving on? He would do it anyway if he wanted. He would do it anyway.

She turned to the clock. Noon. They were late. The windows were rattling again as the wind picked up, and once she was sure she saw some leaves whirl as high as she was. But the sun was bright, falling warmly on the end of her bed. Slowly, pushing with her hands against the mattress, she eased her back up against the headboard. It was too big a bed for her alone, almost too much to get out of. She tried to toss back the covers but they only folded down halfway, enough to show her bare legs, and she could not stand to look at them anymore, almost entirely reduced to bone and sinew. Strange how little the bones were when you saw them clearly. She swung her legs over the edge, braced herself, and put her weight on them, turning so that she could lean with both hands on the bed, and then she worked her way down to the foot where she paused to catch her breath. Groping object by object she made her way to a chair set close to the window for her, and she eased into it. She could not sit there long before the edge would begin to bite into her thighs and her legs would go to sleep.

How wild and abandoned the lawn looked! The wind was still gusting, unmown grass clumped up through scattered piles of leaves, and a torn, patched light was strewn everywhere. A huge limb of their neighbor's elm had fallen, crushing a length of the fence and almost reaching to the garage. And the children might have been playing there. She had asked the Farnsworths again and again to have the tree cut down, all but dead for two years now, but they kept saying how expensive the job would be and how it was coming down limb by limb anyway. Now Len would have something to say about that, she hoped. But it had been a fine tree, tall and bell-shaped, and old Mr. Farnsworth could remember when it was barely ten feet tall. Trees, trees, she loved them. The nice thing about their house was how even though they were in the middle of town there were trees everywhere—maples and ash and the big willow in back that Georgie fell out of two years ago and broke his wrist, and she loved waking at night to hear the wind lash through them before a storm, or in the morning opening her eyes to green and the flit of birds. She missed the pine, though, and had asked Len to plant a new one, but he never got around to it. White pines had a sound when even the smallest motions of air went through them that was like no other tree.

The truck turned in off the dirt road, rolled slowly over the potholes and ridges of their driveway. They were crowded into the cab, except Georgie who would be sitting in the back, pretending he really was not cold at all, probably getting some oil or dirt stain all over his new overcoat. She folded her hands. They were all there together. But she wanted to touch or hear them. She sat absolutely still. The truck rocked through a hole and stopped. What if it were like this forever, if when you died it was only a frozen photograph, a picture of the distance going nowhere?

The door swung open. Adele and Betsey raced after Georgie who had the newspaper clutched under his arm. Another person was in the cab with Len, and for a few moments they sat there, the windshield, mottled by light, concealing their faces, and then he stepped out and came around to help her down and it was Lissy Farnsworth. Slowly the two of them strolled over the lawn to where the fence was broken, Lissy mincing on her toes in high-heeled shoes, and Len took her elbow as she stepped over the debris into her parents' yard. They stood talking for a while. When had Lissy come home? She had moved to Syracuse at least two years ago.

Probably they had all gone to church together, and then driven around for a while afterwards, maybe stopped at Russell's for a soda with the kids when they bought the paper. It was obvious why Lissy was there. He was letting the kids begin to get used to her. He had known her, after all, since they were in High School together. Gracie rose slowly, one hand on the windowsill, started to turn away, but could not move fast enough. Len glanced up and waved, but she saw nothing on his face to indicate he was at all sorry. Stubborn, he would have his way even in this, and she was damned if she would say anything about it to him.

Later she tried to eat the soup Len brought her. She agreed the kids should be allowed to go to the movies that afternoon. It was so boring to lift the spoon. She tasted nothing.

"You saw the big limb fell?" he said.

She nodded.

"I guess I'll have a talk with old man Farnsworth after all."

She stared at him, but he was glancing through the newspaper that he had brought up with him, and from time to time he read her an item.

"That's all I can do," she said weakly, and he took away the bowl so she could lie down again.

The newspaper rustled, the wind battered, voices of arguing carried up from downstairs, and she dozed again, waking slowly to see one of the girls standing by her bed in a hazy light, and she felt feverish.

"We're going to the movies now, Mom. But we don't want to sit with Georgie. Please, will you tell him to sit somewhere else? He's always laughing at the wrong times and saying silly things in the serious parts to show off."

"Betsey." Her tongue was awkward as the clapper of a bell. "If you don't pay attention he won't bother you. I want you to be patient. You're the oldest and you have to help."

She saw the odd look on her daughter's face. What she was saying about George could not cause that expression.

"Do wipe off that eyeshade, won't you? I said you could buy it, but not wear it in public. It looks tacky."

"Yes, Mother."

That was more like it, the sullen pout, the glance at her father who simply said, "Do what your mother says," and she left, walking heavily.

Gracie turned on her back. "I do hate that make-up. She's such a beautiful child," and then she realized she had called her Betsey and yet it was Adele. No wonder she had looked so puzzled. Lord, she could not keep anything straight anymore. But no space was left for thinking. Like an enormous, slow wave breaking over her, the pain surged in, not sharp or anything she could cry out against, but a great dull blow that tried to crush and then scatter her body.

For a long time she hovered, tossing in a huge wind where she was forcing her mind to gather the parts of her body. Her body had done this to her, had cut sinew and bone, and was scattering into a thousand fragments, and when she reached, either they parted like water before her grasp or else the wind whirled them further away. Even her voice sank like rain into the needles under the pine trees. For a moment she hated her body. Why was it doing this to her? She had been so good to it, and she wanted to cry with frustration, but the wind broke into her gaping mouth, almost taking her mind with it, and so she closed tightly and concentrated, beginning slowly by some force that still lived in the back of her head to bring the parts together again, and as if they were leaves that she could make come down off the trees to her, she gathered them, leaves of flesh that were hands and feet and strange cells she did not know, then which she recognized as the cancerous ones they had shown her long ago in the slides, and yes, if that was necessary to give a little more time, she would even accept them. Dimly she saw the outline of the trunk and branches of a wide tree, diaphanous and silver, its bark shining as if iced with white fire. The tree fell toward her, or was she gently falling into it?

Her eyes cleared. Len was bent near the window. He was cleaning his guns and now she could smell the oil. She decided she had never smelled anything so fine, which almost made her laugh—she used to hate the oil because it meant duck season again.

"Len."

He looked up.

"It was very bad."

"Do you need a shot?"

"No."

He drew the cloth through again. His hands kept moving but he was looking at her.

"Do you remember that time you took me to the blind?" she asked.

He nodded. She closed her eyes. They had argued fiercely going there. She had made him take her because she said she wanted to be alone with him and why didn't he ever take her hunting, why always Bert? Because she couldn't hunt, never used a gun, he had said, and that was dangerous. Before dawn the lake was dark and bitter cold, a wind knifing at them as they rowed out to the blind, and Len was stiffly silent, would not even tell her where to sit in the boat but only pointed with a gloved hand. In the blind she had no idea what to do, but stood where he told her while he put out the decoys. The wind let up, and off on the shore a barred owl hooted. She had been much colder than she ever remembered being, and lonely because he stood so completely apart from her, still trying to keep something private. Suddenly it was dawn as if someone had shot the sky open and the light bled in. Guns blasted distantly near the island. The land had shattered upward, thousands of dark fragments rising in confusion in the light, raucous with terror.

The geese, he said, and slowly they formed into circles higher and higher, and then wedged off toward the horizon.

In the near dark she could see the decoys bobbing, so real that she thought he must shoot now. He stiffened, the gun rising slowly, although she saw nothing, but then heard the whistling and flutter. She could not catch her breath for a long time after the gun went off. He spun, his shoulder jolted her, *Get down,* he muttered, and she knelt against the poles. She did not know him, this fierce, wheeling block of shadow that loaded and fired, and she plugged her ears with her fingers.

The light was still dim when he stepped down into the boat to retrieve the ducks. She lost sight of him against the black land, hearing for a while the thunk of a bird against the bottom or a slight splash as he stepped out into the shallow water. Then silence, and a light in the sky that seemed never to increase.

Len? she had called tentatively to him across the layers of darkness.

What if out there he had lurched into a deep spot, his boots filling, him struggling silently, dragged down even without a cry? She was going to call again but she shrieked. Something had her by the leg, was pulling her toward the boat slip. She toppled, and he was holding her, easing her down into the boat.

He was laughing. *Scared?*

How she hated him for one wild moment, and then his hands held her so tightly, the boat rocked so crazily under them that she began to laugh too, and they had to sit down together, almost tipping over.

Look, he said. Ten ducks were lumped there, and he held them up one by one. They climbed back into the blind and sat on the platform. He took out the flask of whiskey he had brought. The sun came up into a clear, fall day, and after they finished the bottle she did not mind the cold at all.

Now she shifted her head on the pillow, wishing she could see Len's face more clearly. It must be late afternoon, almost time to turn the lights on.

"You won't take George hunting yet, will you? He's only nine."

"My dad took me out first when I was five. The sooner he learns, the better."

"One more year. You could wait till he's ten."

He did not answer.

"I'm thirsty."

She heard him put down the gun, saw his body moving toward the bathroom door, but never remembered having the water because she walked into a curtain of darkness that tangled around her.

But when she woke, although she was too weak to pull herself up in bed, she saw everything clearly—the small lamp on the dresser casting a dim light onto the corners and edges of things, the window shades pulled. She could hear nothing and decided it must be late. Even the wind had stopped. She breathed deeply, in and out. For a moment she wanted nothing to interrupt this peace, afraid even to move again. Finally she looked at the clock. 10:30. They would all be in bed but Len.

The front door closed solidly. Probably he would have been outside, looking at the weather. He usually did that before going to bed. She heard him coming slowly up the stairs, then down the corridor. She had to decide whether to pretend she was asleep or not. She turned to stare at the door. He came in and sat on the edge of the bed.

"It's clear as anything." He looked so tired. "And there'll be a good frost tonight. The nurse was here. Do you remember?"

"Len, tell me. What were you doing this morning?"

"We went to church."

"Why were you so late coming home?"

"We had some things to do."

"I saw her with you. Level with me. I need to know."

He rose slowly from the bed and walked to the lamp.

"Is there anything you want me to fetch? I'd better be getting some sleep since I promised Jimmy I'd start work on his car early in the morning."

She stared at that set jaw, the heavy, battered hand on the lamp. How she wanted to slap him once across the face, anything but this silence.

"Tell me if it's her."

The light snapped out.

"I know you all went to church together and then you were driving around and that's why you took so long."

"She was walking back and we gave her a lift."

"Why were you late?"

His voice was so low that she had to strain to hear the words that tumbled out.

"We went to see Father Rivard afterwards. His suggestion. He called and said it might be easier and I'd already asked him because your mother couldn't and someone had to explain, Gracie. Someone who could do it right. I couldn't."

"Do what?"

He was moving closer in the dark. His legs touched the bed.

"Tell them about dying. About how you're going to die."

She did not answer. She heard him take off his shoes. He lay down beside her and for the first time in months she reached out and his whole body was there, and even though it hurt her arm when he lay on it, she made him lie closer and hold her so that his breath was in her ear.

"I'm sorry." But as she was speaking she heard and said, "Listen, listen, it's the geese," and they held perfectly still, breathless for a long while, listening to the scattered craking, the high birds calling to each other across the dark, and then he was weeping and she held on with all her strength.

BARRY HANNAH

(1942–)

Testimony of Pilot

About the Author: A native Mississippian, Barry Hannah is presently writer-in-residence at the University of Mississippi, at Oxford. He has published novels, among them *Geronimo Rex* (1972) and *Ray* (1980), and short-story collections, among them *Airships* (1978), and screenplays.

When I was ten, eleven and twelve, I did a good bit of my play in the backyard of a three-story wooden house my father had bought and rented out, his first venture into real estate. We lived right across the street from it, but over here was the place to do your real play. Here there was a harrowed but overgrown garden, a vine-swallowed fence at the back end, and beyond the fence a cornfield which belonged to someone else. This was not the country. This was the town, Clinton, Mississippi, between Jackson on the east and Vicksburg on the west. On this lot stood a few water oaks, a few plum bushes, and much overgrowth of honeysuckle vine. At the very back end, at the fence, stood three strong nude chinaberry trees.

In Mississippi it is difficult to achieve a vista. But my friends and I had one here at the back corner of the garden. We could see across the cornfield, see the one lone tin-roofed house this side of the railroad tracks, then on across the tracks many other bleaker houses with rustier tin roofs, smoke coming out of the chimneys in the late fall. This was nigger-town. We had binoculars and could see the colored children hustling about and perhaps a hopeless sow or two with her brood enclosed in a tiny boarded-up area. Through the binoculars one afternoon in October we watched some men corner and beat a large hog on the brain. They used an ax and the thing kept running around, head leaning toward the ground, for several minutes before it lay down. I thought I saw the men laughing when it finally did. One of them was staggering, plainly drunk to my sight from three hundred yards away. He had the long knife. Because of that scene I considered Negroes savage cowards for a good five more years of my life. Our maid brought some sausage to my mother and when it was put in the pan to fry, I made a point of running out of the house.

I went directly across the street and to the back end of the garden behind the apartment house we owned, without my breakfast. That was Saturday. Eventually, Radcleve saw me. His parents had him mowing the yard that ran alongside my dad's property. He clicked off the power mower and I went over to his fence, which was storm wire. His mother maintained handsome flowery grounds at all costs; she had a leafmold bin and St. Augustine grass as solid as a rug.

Radcleve himself was a violent experimental chemist. When Radcleve was eight, he threw a whole package of .22 shells against the sidewalk in front of his house until one of them went off, driving lead fragments into his calf, most of them still deep in there where the surgeons never dared tamper. Radcleve knew about the sulfur, potassium nitrate and charcoal mixture for gunpowder when he was ten. He bought things through the mail when he ran out of ingredients in his chemistry sets. When he was an infant, his father, a quiet man who owned the Chevrolet agency in town, bought an entire bankrupt sporting-goods store, and in the middle of their backyard he built a house, plain-painted and neat, one room and a heater, where Radcleve's redundant toys forevermore were kept—all the possible toys he would need for boyhood. There were things in there that Radcleve and I were not mature enough for and did not know the real use of. When we were eleven, we uncrated the new Dunlop golf balls and went on up a shelf for the tennis rackets, went out in the middle of his yard, and served new golf ball after new golf ball with blasts of the rackets over into the cornfield, out of sight. When the strings busted we just went in and got another racket. We were absorbed by how a good smack would set the heavy little pills on an endless flight. Then Radcleve's father came down. He simply dismissed me. He took Radcleve into the house and covered his whole body with a belt. But within the week Radcleve had invented the mortar. It was a steel pipe into which a flashlight battery fit perfectly, like a bullet into a muzzle. He had drilled a hole for the fuse of an M-80 firecracker at the base, for the charge. It was a grand cannon, set up on a stack of bricks at the back of my dad's property, which was the free place to play. When it shot, it would back up violently with thick smoke and you could hear the flashlight battery whistling off. So that morning when I ran out of the house protesting the hog sausage, I told Radcleve to bring over the mortar. His ma and dad were in Jackson for the day, and he came right over with the pipe, the batteries and the M-80 explosives. He had two gross of them.

Before, we'd shot off toward the woods to the right of niggertown. I turned the bricks to the left; I made us a very fine cannon carriage pointing toward niggertown. When Radcleve appeared, he had two pairs of binoculars around his neck, one pair a newly plundered German unit as big as a brace of whiskey bottles. I told him I wanted to shoot for that house where we saw them killing the pig. Radcleve loved the idea. We singled out the house with heavy use of the binoculars.

There were children in the yard. Then they all went in. Two men came out of the back door. I thought I recognized the drunkard from the other afternoon. I helped Radcleve fix the direction of the cannon. We estimated the altitude we needed to get down there. Radcleve put the M-80 in the breech with its fuse standing out of the hole. I dropped the flashlight battery in. I lit the fuse. We backed off. The M-80 blasted off deafeningly, smoke rose, but my concentration was on that particular house over there. I brought the binoculars up. We waited six or seven seconds. I heard a great joyful wallop on tin. "We've hit him on the first try, the first try!" I yelled. Radcleve was ecstatic. "Right on his roof!" We bolstered up the brick carriage. Radcleve remembered the correct height of the cannon exactly. So we fixed it, loaded it, lit it and backed off. The battery landed on the roof, blat, again, louder. I looked to see if there wasn't a great dent or hole in the roof. I could not understand why niggers weren't pouring out distraught from that house. We shot the mortar again and again, and always our battery hit the tin roof. Sometimes there was only a dull thud, but other times there was a wild distress of tin. I was still looking through the binoculars, amazed that the niggers wouldn't even come out of their house to see what was hitting their roof. Radcleve was on to it better than me. I looked over at him and he had the huge German binocs much lower than I did. He was looking straight through the cornfield, which was all bare and open, with nothing left but rotten stalks. "What we've been hitting is the roof of that house just this side of the tracks. White people live in there," he said.

I took up my binoculars again. I looked around the yard of that white wooden house on this side of the tracks, almost next to the railroad. When I found the tin roof, I saw four significant dents in it. I saw one of our batteries lying in the middle of a sort of crater. I took the binoculars down into the yard and saw a blond middle-aged woman looking our way.

"Somebody's coming up toward us. He's from that house and he's got, I think, some sort of fancy gun with him. It might be an automatic weapon."

I ran my binoculars all over the cornfield. Then, in a line with the house, I saw him. He was coming our way but having some trouble with the rows and dead stalks of the cornfield.

"That is just a boy like us. All he's got is a saxophone with him," I told Radcleve. I had recently got in the school band, playing drums, and had seen all the weird horns that made up a band.

I watched this boy with the saxophone through the binoculars until he was ten feet from us. This was Quadberry. His name was Ard, short for Arden. His shoes were foot-square wads of mud from the cornfield. When he saw us across the fence and above him, he stuck out his arm in my direction.

"My dad says stop it!"

"We weren't doing anything," says Radcleve.

"Mother saw the smoke puff up from here. Dad has a hangover."

"A what?"

"It's a headache from indiscretion. You're lucky he does. He's picked up the poker to rap on you, but he can't move further the way his head is."

"What's your name? You're not in the band," I said, focusing on the saxophone.

"It's Ard Quadberry. Why do you keep looking at me through the binoculars?"

It was because he was odd, with his hair and its white ends, and his Arab nose, and now his name. Add to that the saxophone.

"My dad's a doctor at the college. Mother's a musician. You better quit what you're doing. . . . I was out practicing in the garage. I saw one of those flashlight batteries roll off the roof. Could I see what you shoot 'em with?"

"No," said Radcleve. Then he said: "If you'll play that horn."

Quadberry stood out there ten feet below us in the field, skinny, feet and pants booted with black mud, and at his chest the slung-on, very complex, radiant horn.

Quadberry began sucking and licking the reed. I didn't care much for this act, and there was too much desperate oralness in his face when he began playing. That was why I chose the drums. One had to engage himself like suck's revenge with a horn. But what Quadberry was playing was pleasant and intricate. I was sure it was advanced, and there was no squawking, as from the other eleven-year-olds on sax in the band room. He made the end with a clean upward riff, holding the final note high, pure and unwavering.

"Good!" I called to him.

Quadberry was trying to move out of the sunken row toward us, but his heavy shoes were impeding him.

"Sounded like a duck. Sounded like a girl duck," said Radcleve, who was kneeling down and packing a mudball around one of the M-80s. I saw and I was an accomplice, because I did nothing. Radcleve lit the fuse and heaved the mudball over the fence. An M-80 is a very serious firecracker; it is like the charge they use to shoot up those sprays six hundred feet on July Fourth at country clubs. It went off, this one, even bigger than most M-80s.

When we looked over the fence, we saw Quadberry all muck specks and fragments of stalks. He was covering the mouthpiece of his horn with both hands. Then I saw there was blood pouring out of, it seemed, his right eye. I thought he was bleeding directly out of his eye.

"Quadberry?" I called.

He turned around and never said a word to me until I was eighteen. He walked back holding his eye and staggering through the cornstalks. Radcleve had him in the binoculars. Radcleve was trembling . . . but intrigued.

"His mother just screamed. She's running out in the field to get him."

I thought we'd blinded him, but we hadn't. I thought the Quadberrys would get the police or call my father, but they didn't. The upshot of this is that Quadberry had a permanent white space next to his right eye, a spot that looked like a tiny upset crown.

I went from sixth through half of twelfth grade ignoring him and that wound. I was coming on as a drummer and a lover, but if Quadberry happened to appear within fifty feet of me and my most tender, intimate sweetheart, I would duck out. Quadberry grew up just like the rest of us. His father was still a doctor—professor of history—at the town college; his mother was still blond, and a musician. She was organist at an Episcopalian church in Jackson, the big capital city ten miles east of us.

As for Radcleve, he still had no ear for music, but he was there, my buddy. He was repentant about Quadberry, although not so much as I. He'd thrown the mud grenade over the fence only to see what would happen. He had not really wanted to maim. Quadberry had played his tune on the sax, Radcleve had played his tune on the mud grenade. It was just a shame they happened to cross talents.

Radcleve went into a long period of nearly nothing after he gave up violent explosives. Then he trained himself to copy the comic strips, *Steve Canyon* to *Major Hoople,* until he became quite a versatile cartoonist with some very provocative new faces and bodies that were gesturing intriguingly. He could never fill in the speech balloons with the smart words they needed. Sometimes he would pencil in "Err" or "What?" in the empty speech places. I saw him a great deal. Radcleve was not spooked by Quadberry. He even once asked Quadberry what his opinion was of his future as a cartoonist. Quadberry told Radcleve that if he took all his cartoons and stuffed himself with them, he would make an interesting dead man. After that, Radcleve was shy of him too.

When I was a senior we had an extraordinary band. Word was we had outplayed all the big A.A.A. division bands last April in the state contest. Then came news that a new blazing saxophone player was coming into the band as first chair. This person had spent summers in Vermont in music camps, and he was coming in with us for the concert season. Our director, a lovable aesthete named Richard Prender, announced to us in a proud silent moment that the boy was joining us tomorrow night. The effect was that everybody should push over a seat or two and make room for this boy and his talent. I was annoyed. Here I'd been with the band and had kept hold of the taste among the whole percussion section. I could play rock and jazz drum and didn't even really need to be here. I could be in Vermont too, give me a piano and a bass. I looked at the kid on first sax, who was going to be supplanted tomorrow. For two years he had thought he was the star, then suddenly enters this boy who's three times better.

The new boy was Quadberry. He came in, but he was meek, and when he tuned up he put his head almost on the floor, bending over trying to be inconspicuous. The girls in the band had wanted him to be handsome, but Quadberry refused and kept himself in such hiding among the sax section that he was neither handsome, ugly, cute or anything. What he was was pretty near invisible, except for the bell of his horn, the all-but-closed eyes, the Arabian nose, the brown hair with its halo of white ends, the desperate oralness, the giant reed punched into his face, and hazy Quadberry, loving the wound in a private dignified ecstasy.

I say dignified because of what came out of the end of his horn. He was more than what Prender had told us he would be. Because of Quadberry, we could take the band arrangement of Ravel's *Bolero* with us to the state contest. Quadberry would do the saxophone solo. He would switch to alto sax, he would do the sly Moorish ride. When he played, I heard the sweetness, I heard the horn which finally brought human *talk* into the realm of music. It could sound like the mutterings of a field nigger, and then it could get up into inhumanly careless beauty, it could get among mutinous helium bursts around Saturn. I already loved *Bolero* for the constant drum part. The percussion was always there, driving along with the subtly increasing triplets, insistent, insistent, at last outraged and trying to steal the whole show from the horns and the others. I knew a large boy with dirty blond hair, name of Wyatt, who played viola in the Jackson Symphony and sousaphone in our band—one of the rare closet transmutations of my time—who was forever claiming to have discovered the central *Bolero* one Sunday afternoon over FM radio as he had seven distinct sexual moments with a certain B., girl flutist with black bangs and skin like mayonnaise, while the drums of Ravel carried them on and on in a ceremony of Spanish sex. It was agreed by all the canny in the band that *Bolero* was exactly the piece to make the band soar—now especially as we had Quadberry, who made his walk into the piece like an actual lean Spanish bandit. This boy could blow his horn. He was, as I had suspected, a genius. His solo was not quite the same as the New York Phil's saxophonist's, but it was better. It came in and was with us. It entered my spine and, I am sure, went up the skirts of the girls. I had almost deafened myself playing drums in the most famous rock and jazz band in the state, but I could hear the voice that went through and out that horn. It sounded like a very troubled forty-year-old man, a man who had had his brow in his hands a long time.

The next time I saw Quadberry up close, in fact the first time I had seen him up close since we were eleven and he was bleeding in the cornfield, was in late February. I had only three classes this last semester, and went up to the band room often, to loaf and complain and keep up my touch on the drums. Prender let me keep my set in one of the instrument rooms, with a tarpaulin thrown over it, and I would drag it out to the practice room and whale away. Sometimes a group of sophomores would come up and I would make them marvel, whaling away as if not only deaf but blind to them, although I wasn't at all. If I saw a sophomore girl with exceptional bod or face, I would do miracles of technique I never knew were in me. I would amaze myself. I would be threatening Buddy Rich and Sam Morello. But this time when I went into the instrument room, there was Quadberry on one side, and, back in a dark corner, a small ninth-grade euphonium player whose face was all red. The little boy was weeping and grinning at the same time.

"Queerberry," the boy said softly.

Quadberry flew upon him like a demon. He grabbed the boy's collar, slapped his face, and yanked his arm behind him in a merciless wrestler's grip, the one that made them bawl on TV. Then the boy broke it and slugged Quadberry in the lips and ran across to my side of the room. He said "Queerberry" softly again and jumped for the door. Quadberry plunged across the room and tackled him on the threshold. Now that the boy was under him, Quadberry pounded the top of his head with his fist made like a mallet. The boy kept calling him "Queerberry" throughout this. He had not learned his lesson. The boy seemed to be going into concussion, so I stepped over and touched Quadberry, telling him to quit. Quadberry obeyed and stood up off the boy, who crawled on out into the band room. But once more the boy looked back with a bruised grin, saying "Queerberry." Quadberry made a move toward him, but I blocked it.

"Why are you beating up on this little guy?" I said. Quadberry was sweating and his eyes were wild with hate; he was a big fellow now, though lean. He was, at six feet tall, bigger than me.

"He kept calling me Queerberry."

"What do you care?" I asked.

"I care," Quadberry said, and left me standing there.

We were to play at Millsaps College Auditorium for the concert. It was April. We got on the buses, a few took their cars, and were a big tense crowd getting over there. To Jackson was only a twenty-minute trip. The director, Prender, followed the bus in his Volkswagen. There was a thick fog. A flashing ambulance, snaking the lanes, piled into him head on. Prender, who I would imagine was thinking of *Bolero* and hearing the young horn voices in his band—perhaps he was dwelling on Quadberry's spectacular gypsy entrance, or perhaps he was meditating on the percussion section, of which I was the king—passed into the airs of band-director heaven. We were told by the student director as we set up on the stage. The student director was a senior from the town college, very much afflicted, almost to the point of drooling, by a love and respect for Dick Prender, and now afflicted by a heartbreaking esteem for his ghost. As were we all.

I loved the tough and tender director awesomely and never knew it until I found myself bawling along with all the rest of the boys of the percussion. I told them to keep setting up, keep tuning, keep screwing the stands together, keep hauling in the kettledrums. To just quit and bawl seemed a betrayal to Prender. I caught some girl clarinetists trying to flee the stage and go have their cry. I told them to get the hell back to their section. They obeyed me. Then I found the student director. I had to have my say.

"Look. I say we just play *Bolero* and junk the rest. That's our horse. We can't play *Brighton Beach* and *Neptune's Daughter*. We'll never make it through them. And they're too happy."

"We aren't going to play anything," he said. "Man, to play is filthy. Did you ever hear Prender play piano? Do you know what a cool man he was in all things?"

"We play. He got us ready, and we play."

"Man, you can't play any more than I can direct. You're bawling your face off. Look out there at the rest of them. Man, it's a herd, it's a weeping herd."

"What's wrong? Why aren't you pulling this crowd together?" This was Quadberry, who had come up urgently. "I got those little brats in my section sitting down, but we've got people abandoning the stage, tearful little finks throwing their horns on the floor."

"I'm not directing," said the mustached college man.

"Then get out of here. You're weak, weak!"

"Man, we've got teen-agers in ruin here, we got sorrowville. Nobody can—"

"Go ahead. Do your number. Weak out on us."

"Man, I—"

Quadberry was already up on the podium, shaking his arms.

"We're right here! The band is right here! Tell your friends to get back in their seats. We're doing *Bolero.* Just put *Bolero* up and start tuning. *I'm* directing. I'll be right here in front of you. You look at *me!* Don't you dare quit on Prender. Don't you dare quit on me. You've got to be heard. *I've* got to be heard. Prender wanted me to be heard. I am the star, and I say we sit down and blow."

And so we did. We all tuned and were burning low for the advent into *Bolero,* though we couldn't believe that Quadberry was going to remain with his saxophone strapped to him and conduct us as well as play his solo. The judges, who apparently hadn't heard about Prender's death, walked down to their balcony desks.

One of them called out "Ready" and Quadberry's hand was instantly up in the air, his fingers hard as if around the stem of something like a torch. This was not Prender's way, but it had to do. We went into the number cleanly and Quadberry one-armed it in the conducting. He kept his face, this look of hostility, at the reeds and the trumpets. I was glad he did not look toward me and the percussion boys like that. But he must have known we would be constant and tasteful because I was the king there. As for the others, the soloists especially, he was scaring them into excellence. Prender had never got quite this from them. Boys became men and girls became women as Quadberry directed us through *Bolero.* I even became a bit better of a man myself, though Quadberry did not look my way. When he turned around toward the people in the auditorium to enter on his solo, I knew it was my baby. I and the drums were the metronome. That was no trouble. It was talent to keep the metronome ticking amidst any given chaos of sound.

But this keeps one's mind occupied and I have no idea what Quadberry sounded like on his sax ride. All I know is that he looked grief-stricken and pale, and small. Sweat had popped out on his forehead. He bent over extremely. He was wearing the red brass-button jacket and black pants, black bow tie at the throat, just like the rest of us. In this outfit he bent over his horn almost out of sight. For a moment, before I caught the glint of his horn through the music stands, I thought he had pitched forward off the stage. He went down so far to do his deep oral thing, his conducting arm had disappeared so quickly, I didn't know but what he was having a seizure.

When *Bolero* was over, the audience stood up and made meat out of their hands applauding. The judges themselves applauded. The band stood up, bawling again, for Prender and because we had done so well. The student director rushed out crying to embrace Quadberry, who eluded him with his dipping shoulders. The crowd was still clapping insanely. I wanted to see Quadberry myself. I waded through the red backs, through the bow ties, over the white bucks. Here was the first-chair clarinetist, who had done his bit like an angel; he sat close to the podium and could hear Quadberry.

"Was Quadberry good?" I asked him.

"Are you kidding? These tears in my eyes, they're for how good he was. He was too good. I'll never touch my clarinet again." The clarinetist slung the pieces of his horn into their case like underwear and a toothbrush.

I found Quadberry fitting the sections of his alto in the velvet holds of his case.

"Hooray," I said. "Hip damn hooray for you."

Arden was smiling too, showing a lot of teeth I had never seen. His smile was sly. He knew he had pulled off a monster unlikelihood.

"Hip hip hooray for me," he said. "Look at her. I had the bell of the horn almost smack in her face."

There was a woman of about thirty sitting in the front row of the auditorium. She wore a sundress with a drastic cleavage up front; looked like something that hung around New Orleans and kneaded your heart to death with her feet. She was still mesmerized by Quadberry. She bore on him with a stare and there was moisture in her cleavage.

"You played well."

"Well? Play well? Yes."

He was trying not to look at her directly. Look at *me,* I beckoned to her with full face: I was the *drums.* She arose and left.

"I was walking downhill in a valley, is all I was doing," said Quadberry. "Another man, a wizard, was playing my horn." He locked his sax case. "I feel nasty for not being able to cry like the rest of them. Look at them. Look at them crying."

True, the children of the band were still weeping, standing around the stage. Several moms and dads had come up among them, and they were misty-eyed too. The mixture of grief and superb music had been unbearable.

A girl in tears appeared next to Quadberry. She was a majorette in football season and played third-chair sax during the concert season. Not even her violent sorrow could take the beauty out of the face of this girl. I had watched her for a number of years—her alertness to her own beauty, the pride of her legs in the majorette outfit—and had taken out her younger sister, a second-rate version of her and a wayward overcompensating nymphomaniac whom several of us made a hobby out of pitying. Well, here was Lilian herself crying in Quadberry's face. She told him that she'd run off the stage when she heard about Prender, dropped her horn and everything, and had thrown herself into a tavern across the street and drunk two beers quickly for some kind of relief. But she had come back through the front doors of the auditorium and sat down, dizzy with beer, and seen Quadberry, the miraculous way he had gone on with *Bolero.* And now she was eaten up by feelings of guilt, weakness, cowardice.

"We didn't miss you," said Quadberry.

"Please forgive me. Tell me to do something to make up for it."

"Don't breathe my way, then. You've got beer all over your breath."

"I want to talk to you."

"Take my horn case and go out, get in my car, and wait for me. It's the ugly Plymouth in front of the school bus."

"I know," she said.

Lilian Field, this lovely teary thing, with the rather pious grace of her carriage, with the voice full of imminent swoon, picked up Quadberry's horn case and her own and walked off the stage.

I told the percussion boys to wrap up the packing. Into my suitcase I put my own gear and also managed to steal drum keys, two pairs of brushes, a twenty-inch Turkish cymbal, a Gretsch snare drum that I desired for my collection, a wood block, kettledrum mallets, a tuning harp and a score sheet of *Bolero* full of marginal notes I'd written down straight from the mouth of Dick Prender, thinking I might want to look at the score sheet sometime in the future when I was having a fit of nostalgia such as I am having right now as I write this. I had never done any serious stealing before, and I was stealing for my art. Prender was dead, the band had done its last thing of the year, I was a senior. Things were finished at the high school. I was just looting a sinking ship. I could hardly lift the suitcase. As I was pushing it across the stage, Quadberry was there again.

"You can ride back with me if you want to."

"But you've got Lilian."

"Please ride back with me . . . us. Please."

"Why?"

"To help me get rid of her. Her breath is full of beer. My father always had that breath. Every time he was friendly, he had that breath. And she looks a great deal like my mother." We were interrupted by the Tupelo band director. He put his baton against Quadberry's arm.

"You were big with *Bolero,* son, but that doesn't mean you own the stage."

Quadberry caught the end of the suitcase and helped me with it out to the steps behind the auditorium. The buses were gone. There sat his ugly ocher Plymouth; it was a failed, gay, experimental shade from the Chrysler people. Lilian was sitting in the front seat wearing her shirt and bow tie, her coat off.

"Are you going to ride back with me?" Quadberry said to me.

"I think I would spoil something. You never saw her when she was a majorette. She's not stupid, either. She likes to show off a little, but she's not stupid. She's in the History Club."

"My father has a doctorate in history. She smells of beer."

I said, "She drank two cans of beer when she heard about Prender."

"There are a lot of other things to do when you hear about death. What I did, for example. She ran away. She fell to pieces."

"She's waiting for us," I said.

"One damned thing I am never going to do is drink."

"I've never seen your mother up close, but Lilian doesn't look like your mother. She doesn't look like anybody's mother."

I rode with them silently to Clinton. Lilian made no bones about being disappointed I was in the car, though she said nothing. I knew it would be like this and I hated it. Other girls in town would not be so unhappy that I was in the car with them. I looked for flaws in Lilian's face and neck and hair, but there weren't any. Couldn't there be a mole, an enlarged pore, too much gum on a tooth, a single awkward hair around the ear? No. Memory, the whole lying opera of it, is killing me now. Lilian was faultless beauty, even sweating, even and especially in the white man's shirt and the bow tie clamping together her collar, when one knew her uncomfortable bosoms, her poor nipples. . . .

"Don't take me back to the band room. Turn off here and let me off at my house," I said to Quadberry. He didn't turn off.

"Don't tell Arden what to do. He can do what he wants to," said Lilian, ignoring me and speaking to me at the same time. I couldn't bear her hatred. I asked Quadberry to please just stop the car and let me out here, wherever he was: this front yard of the mobile home would do. I was so earnest that he stopped the car. He handed back the keys and I dragged my suitcase out of the trunk, then flung the keys back at him and kicked the car to get it going again.

My band came together in the summer. We were the Bop Fiends . . . that was our name. Two of them were from Ole Miss, our bass player was from Memphis State, but when we got together this time, I didn't call the tenor sax, who went to Mississippi Southern, because Quadberry wanted to play with us. During the school year the college boys and I fell into minor groups to pick up twenty dollars on a weekend, playing dances for the Moose Lodge, medical-student fraternities in Jackson, teen-age recreation centers in Greenwood, and such as that. But come summer we were the Bop Fiends again, and the price for us went up to $1,200 a gig. Where they wanted the best rock and bop and they had some bread, we were called. The summer after I was a senior, we played in Alabama, Louisiana and Arkansas. Our fame was getting out there on the interstate route.

This was the summer that I made myself deaf.

Years ago Prender had invited down an old friend from a high school in Michigan. He asked me over to meet the friend, who had been a drummer with Stan Kenton at one time and was now a band director just like Prender. This fellow was almost totally deaf and he warned me very sincerely about deafing myself. He said there would come a point when you had to lean over and concentrate all your hearing on what the band was doing and that was the time to quit for a while, because if you didn't you would be irrevocably deaf like him in a month or two. I listened to him but could not take him seriously. Here was an oldish man who had his problems. My ears had ages of hearing left. Not so. I played the drums so loud the summer after I graduated from high school that I made myself, eventually, stone deaf.

We were at, say, the National Guard Armory in Lake Village, Arkansas, Quadberry out in front of us on the stage they'd built. Down on the floor were hundreds of sweaty teen-agers. Four girls in sundresses, showing what they could, were leaning on the stage with broad ignorant lust on their minds. I'd play so loud for one particular chick, I'd get absolutely out of control. The guitar boys would have to turn the volume up full blast to compensate. Thus I went deaf. Anyhow, the dramatic idea was to release Quadberry on a very soft sweet ballad right in the middle of a long ear-piercing run of rock-and-roll tunes. I'd get out the brushes and we would astonish the crowd with our tenderness. By August, I was so deaf I had to watch Quadberry's fingers changing notes on the saxophone, had to use my eyes to keep time. The other members of the Bop Fiends told me I was hitting out of time. I pretended I was trying to do experimental things with rhythm when the truth was I simply could no longer hear. I was no longer a tasteful drummer, either. I had become deaf through lack of taste.

Which was—taste—exactly the quality that made Quadberry wicked on the saxophone. During the howling, during the churning, Quadberry had taste. The noise did not affect his personality; he was solid as a brick. He could blend. Oh, he could hoot through his horn when the right time came, but he could do supporting roles for an hour. Then, when we brought him out front for his solo on something like "Take Five," he would play with such light blissful technique that he even eclipsed Paul Desmond. The girls around the stage did not cause him to enter into excessive loudness or vibrato.

Quadberry had his own girl friend now, Lilian back at Clinton, who put all the sundressed things around the stage in the shade. In my mind I had congratulated him for getting up next to this beauty, but in June and July, when I was still hearing things a little, he never said a word about her. It was one night in August, when I could hear nothing and was driving him to his house, that he asked me to turn on the inside light and spoke in a retarded deliberate way. He knew I was deaf and counted on my being able to read lips.

"Don't . . . make . . . fun . . . of her . . . or me. . . . We . . . think . . . she . . . is . . . in trouble."

I wagged my head. Never would I make fun of him or her. She detested me because I had taken out her helpless little sister for a few weeks, but I would never think there was anything funny about Lilian, for all her haughtiness. I only thought of this event as monumentally curious.

"No one except you knows," he said.

"Why did you tell me?"

"Because I'm going away and you have to take care of her. I wouldn't trust her with anybody but you."

"She hates the sight of my face. Where are you going?"

"Annapolis."

"You aren't going to any damned Annapolis."

"That was the only school that wanted me."

"You're going to play your saxophone on a boat?"

"I don't know what I'm going to do."

"How . . . how can you just leave her?"

"She wants me to. She's very excited about me at Annapolis. William [this is my name], there is no girl I could imagine who has more inner sweetness than Lilian."

I entered the town college, as did Lilian. She was in the same chemistry class I was. But she was rows away. It was difficult to learn anything, being deaf. The professor wasn't a pantomimer—but finally he went to the blackboard with the formulas and the algebra of problems, to my happiness. I hung in and made a B. At the end of the semester I was swaggering around the grade sheet he'd posted. I happened to see Lilian's grade. She'd only made a C. Beautiful Lilian got only a C while I, with my handicap, had made a B.

It had been a very difficult chemistry class. I had watched Lilian's stomach the whole way through. It was not growing. I wanted to see her look like a watermelon, make herself an amazing mother shape.

When I made the B and Lilian made the C, I got up my courage and finally went by to see her. She answered the door. Her parents weren't home. I'd never wanted this office of watching over her as Quadberry wanted me to, and this is what I told her. She asked me into the house. The rooms smelled of nail polish and pipe smoke. I was hoping her little sister wasn't in the house, and my wish came true. We were alone.

"You can quit watching over me."

"Are you pregnant?"

"No." Then she started crying. "I wanted to be. But I'm not."

"What do you hear from Quadberry?"

She said something, but she had her back to me. She looked to me for an answer, but I had nothing to say. I knew she'd said something, but I hadn't heard it.

"He doesn't play the saxophone anymore," she said.

This made me angry.

"Why not?"

"Too much math and science and navigation. He wants to fly. That's what his dream is now. He wants to get into an F-something jet."

I asked her to say this over and she did. Lilian really was full of inner sweetness, as Quadberry had said. She understood that I was deaf. Perhaps Quadberry had told her.

The rest of the time in her house I simply witnessed her beauty and her mouth moving.

I went through college. To me it is interesting that I kept a B average and did it all deaf, though I know this isn't interesting to people who aren't deaf. I loved music, and never heard it. I loved poetry, and never heard a word that came out of the mouths of the visiting poets who read at the campus. I loved my mother and dad, but never heard a sound they made. One Christmas Eve, Radcleve was back from Ole Miss and threw an M-80 out in the street for old times' sake. I saw it explode, but there was only a pressure in my ears. I was at parties when lusts were raging and I went home with two girls (I am medium handsome) who lived in apartments of the old two-story 1920 vintage, and I took my shirt off and made love to them. But I have no real idea what their reaction was. They were stunned and all smiles when I got up, but I have no idea whether I gave them the last pleasure or not. I hope I did. I've always been partial to women and have always wanted to see them satisfied till their eyes popped out.

Through Lilian I got the word that Quadberry was out of Annapolis and now flying jets off the *Bonhomme Richard,* an aircraft carrier headed for Vietnam. He telegrammed her that he would set down at the Jackson airport at ten o'clock one night. So Lilian and I were out there waiting. It was a familiar place to her. She was a stewardess and her loops were mainly in the South. She wore a beige raincoat, had red sandals on her feet; I was in a black turtleneck and corduroy jacket, feeling significant, so significant I could barely stand it. I'd already made myself the lead writer at Gordon-Marx Advertising in Jackson. I hadn't seen Lilian in a year. Her eyes were strained, no longer the bright blue things they were when she was a pious beauty. We drank coffee together. I loved her. As far as I knew, she'd been faithful to Quadberry.

He came down in an F-something Navy jet right on the dot of ten. She ran out on the airport pavement to meet him. I saw her crawl up the ladder. Quadberry never got out of the plane. I could see him in his blue helmet. Lilian backed down the ladder. Then Quadberry had the cockpit cover him again. He turned the plane around so its flaming red end was at us. He took it down the runway. We saw him leap out into the night at the middle of the runway going west, toward San Diego and the *Bonhomme Richard.* Lilian was crying.

"What did he say?" I asked.

"He said, 'I am a dragon. America the beautiful, like you will never know.' He wanted to give you a message. He was glad you were here."

"What was the message?"

"The same thing. 'I am a dragon. America the beautiful, like you will never know.' "

"Did he say anything else?"

"Not a thing."

"Did he express any love toward you?"

"He wasn't Ard. He was somebody with a sneer in a helmet."

"He's going to war, Lilian."

"I asked him to kiss me and he told me to get off the plane, he was firing up and it was dangerous."

"Arden is going to war. He's just on his way to Vietnam and he wanted us to know that.

It wasn't just him he wanted us to see. It was him in the jet he wanted us to see. He *is* that black jet. You can't kiss an airplane."

"And what are we supposed to do?" cried sweet Lilian.

"We've just got to hang around. He didn't have to lift off and disappear straight up like that. That was to tell us how he isn't with us anymore."

Lilian asked me what she was supposed to do now. I told her she was supposed to come with me to my apartment in the old 1920 Clinton place where I was. I was supposed to take care of her. Quadberry had said so. His six-year-old directive was still working.

She slept on the fold-out bed of the sofa for a while. This was the only bed in my place. I stood in the dark in the kitchen and drank a quarter bottle of gin on ice. I would not turn on the light and spoil her sleep. The prospect of Lilian asleep in my apartment made me feel like a chaplain on a visit to the Holy Land; I stood there getting drunk, biting my tongue when dreams of lust burst on me. That black jet Quadberry wanted us to see him in, its flaming rear end, his blasting straight up into the night at mid-runway—what precisely was he wanting to say in this stunt? Was he saying remember him forever or forget him forever? But I had my own life and was neither going to mother-hen it over his memory nor his old sweetheart. What did he mean, *America the beautiful, like you will never know?* I, William Howly, knew a goddamn good bit about America the beautiful, even as a deaf man. Being deaf had brought me up closer to people. There were only about five I knew, but I knew their mouth movements, the perspiration under their noses, their tongues moving over the crowns of their teeth, their fingers on their lips. Quadberry, I said, you don't have to get up next to the stars in your black jet to see America the beautiful.

I was deciding to lie down on the kitchen floor and sleep the night, when Lilian turned on the light and appeared in her panties and bra. Her body was perfect except for a tiny bit of fat on her upper thighs. She'd sunbathed herself so her limbs were brown, and her stomach, and the instinct was to rip off the white underwear and lick, suck, say something terrific into the flesh that you discovered.

She was moving her mouth.

"Say it again slowly."

"I'm lonely. When he took off in his jet, I think it meant he wasn't ever going to see me again. I think it meant he was laughing at both of us. He's an astronaut and he spits on us."

"You want me on the bed with you?" I asked.

"I know you're an intellectual. We could keep on the lights so you'd know what I said."

"You want to say things? This isn't going to be just sex?"

"It could never be just sex."

"I agree. Go to sleep. Let me make up my mind whether to come in there. Turn out the lights."

Again the dark, and I thought I would cheat not only Quadberry but the entire Quadberry family if I did what was natural.

I fell asleep.

Quadberry escorted B-52s on bombing missions into North Vietnam. He was catapulted off the *Bonhomme Richard* in his suit at 100 degrees temperature, often at night, and put the F-8 on all it could get—the tiny cockpit, the immense long two-million-dollar fuselage, wings, tail and jet engine, Quadberry, the genius master of his dragon, going up to twenty thousand feet to be cool. He'd meet with the big B-52 turtle of the air and get in a position, his cockpit glowing with green and orange lights, and turn on his transistor radio. There was only one really good band, never mind the old American rock-and-roll from Cambodia, and that was Red Chinese opera. Quadberry loved it. He loved the nasal horde in the finale, when the peasants won over the old fat dilettante mayor. Then he'd turn the jet around when he saw the squatty abrupt little fires way down there after the B-52s had dropped their diet. It was a seven-hour trip. Sometimes he slept, but his body knew when to wake up. Another thirty minutes and there was his ship waiting for him out in the waves.

All his trips weren't this easy. He'd have to blast out in daytime and get with the B-52s, and a SAM missile would come up among them. Two of his mates were taken down by these missiles. But Quadberry, as on saxophone, had endless learned technique. He'd put his jet perpendicular in the air and make the SAMs look silly. He even shot down two of them. Then, one day in daylight, a MIG came floating up level with him and his squadron. Quadberry couldn't believe it. Others in the squadron were shy, but Quadberry knew where and how the MIG could shoot. He flew below the cannons and then came in behind it. He knew the MIG wanted one of the B-52s and not mainly him. The MIG was so concentrated on the fat B-52 that he forgot about Quadberry. It was really an amateur suicide pilot in the MIG. Quadberry got on top of him and let down a missile, rising out of the way of it. The missile blew off the tail of the MIG. But then Quadberry wanted to see if the man got safely out of the cockpit. He thought it would be pleasant if the fellow got out with his parachute working. Then Quadberry saw that the fellow wanted to collide his wreckage with the B-52, so Quadberry turned himself over and cannoned, evaporated the pilot and cockpit. It was the first man he'd killed.

The next trip out, Quadberry was hit by a ground missile. But his jet kept flying. He flew it a hundred miles and got to the sea. There was the *Bonhomme Richard,* so he ejected. His back was snapped but, by God, he landed right on the deck. His mates caught him in their arms and cut the parachute off him. His back hurt for weeks, but he was all right. He rested and recuperated in Hawaii for a month.

Then he went off the front of the ship. Just like that, his F-6 plopped in the ocean and sank like a rock. Quadberry saw the ship go over him. He knew he shouldn't eject just yet. If he ejected now he'd knock his head on the bottom and get chewed up in the motor blades. So Quadberry waited. His plane was sinking in the green and he could see the hull of the aircraft carrier getting smaller, but he had oxygen through his mask and it didn't seem that urgent a decision. Just let the big ship get over. Down what later proved to be sixty feet, he pushed the ejection button. It fired him away, bless it, and he woke up ten feet under the surface swimming against an almost overwhelming body of underwater parachute. But two of his mates were in a helicopter, one of them on the ladder to lift him out.

Now Quadberry's back was really hurt. He was out of this war and all wars for good.

Lilian, the stewardess, was killed in a crash. Her jet exploded with a hijacker's bomb, an inept bomb which wasn't supposed to go off, fifteen miles out of Havana; the poor pilot, the poor passengers, the poor stewardesses were all splattered like flesh sparklers over the water just out of Cuba. A fisherman found one seat of the airplane. Castro expressed regrets.

Quadberry came back to Clinton two weeks after Lilian and the others bound for Tampa were dead. He hadn't heard about her. So I told him Lilian was dead when I met him at the airport. Quadberry was thin and rather meek in his civvies—a gray suit and an out-of-style tie. The white ends of his hair were not there—the halo had disappeared—because his hair was cut short. The Arab nose seemed a pitiable defect in an ash-whiskered face that was beyond anemic now. He looked shorter, stooped. The truth was he was sick, his back was killing him. His breath was heavy-laden with airplane martinis and in his limp

right hand he held a wet cigar. I told him about Lilian. He mumbled something sideways that I could not possibly make out.

"You've got to speak right at me, remember? Remember me, Quadberry?"

"Mom and Dad of course aren't here."

"No. Why aren't they?"

"He wrote me a letter after we bombed Hué. Said he hadn't sent me to Annapolis to bomb the architecture of Hué. He had been there once and had some important experience—French-kissed the queen of Hué or the like. Anyway, he said I'd have to do a hell of a lot of repentance for that. But he and Mom are separate people. Why isn't *she* here?"

"I don't know."

"I'm not asking you the question. The question is to God."

He shook his head. Then he sat down on the floor of the terminal. People had to walk around. I asked him to get up.

"No. How is old Clinton?"

"Horrible. Aluminum subdivisions, cigar boxes with four thin columns in front, thick as a hive. We got a turquoise water tank; got a shopping center, a monster Jitney Jungle, fifth-rate teenyboppers covering the place like ants." Why was I being so frank just now, as Quadberry sat on the floor downcast, drooped over like a long weak candle? "It's not our town anymore, Ard. It's going to hurt to drive back into it. Hurts me every day. Please get up."

"And Lilian's not even over there now."

"No. She's a cloud over the Gulf of Mexico. You flew out of Pensacola once. You know what beauty those pink and blue clouds are. That's how I think of her."

"Was there a funeral?"

"Oh, yes. Her Methodist preacher and a big crowd over at Wright Ferguson funeral home. Your mother and father were there. Your father shouldn't have come. He could barely walk. Please get up."

"Why? What am I going to do, where am I going?"

"You've got your saxophone."

"Was there a coffin? Did you all go by and see the pink or blue cloud in it?" He was sneering now as he had done when he was eleven and fourteen and seventeen.

"Yes, they had a very ornate coffin."

"Lilian was the Unknown Stewardess. I'm not getting up."

"I said you still have your saxophone."

"No, I don't. I tried to play it on the ship after the last time I hurt my back. No go. I can't bend my neck or spine to play it. The pain kills me."

"Well, *don't* get up, then. Why am I asking you to get up? I'm just a deaf drummer, too vain to buy a hearing aid. Can't stand to write the ad copy I do. Wasn't I a good drummer?"

"Superb."

"But we can't be in this condition forever. The police are going to come and make you get up if we do it much longer."

The police didn't come. It was Quadberry's mother who came. She looked me in the face and grabbed my shoulders before she saw Ard on the floor. When she saw him she yanked him off the floor, hugging him passionately. She was shaking with sobs. Quadberry was gathered to her as if he were a rope she was trying to wrap around herself. Her mouth was all over him. Quadberry's mother was a good-looking woman of fifty. I simply held her purse. He cried out that his back was hurting. At last she let him go.

"So now we walk," I said.

"Dad's in the car trying to quit crying," said his mother.

"This is nice," Quadberry said. "I thought everything and everybody was dead around here." He put his arms around his mother. "Let's all go off and kill some time together." His mother's hair was on his lips. "You?" he asked me.

"Murder the devil out of it," I said.

I pretended to follow their car back to their house in Clinton. But when we were going through Jackson, I took the North 55 exit and disappeared from them, exhibiting a great amount of taste, I thought. I would get in their way in this reunion. I had an unimprovable apartment on Old Canton Road in a huge plaster house, Spanish style, with a terrace and ferns and yucca plants, and a green door where I went in. When I woke up I didn't have to make my coffee or fry my egg. The girl who slept in my bed did that. She was Lilian's little sister, Esther Field. Esther was pretty in a minor way and I was proud how I had tamed her to clean and cook around the place. The Field family would appreciate how I lived with her. I showed her the broom and the skillet, and she loved them. She also learned to speak very slowly when she had to say something.

•

Esther answered the phone when Quadberry called me seven months later. She gave me his message. He wanted to know my opinion on a decision he had to make. There was this Dr. Gordon, a surgeon at Emory Hospital in Atlanta, who said he could cure Quadberry's back problem. Quadberry's back was killing him. He was in torture even holding up the phone to say this. The surgeon said there was a seventy-five/twenty-five chance. Seventy-five that it would be successful, twenty-five that it would be fatal. Esther waited for my opinion. I told her to tell Quadberry to go over to Emory. He'd got through with luck in Vietnam, and now he should ride it out in this petty back operation.

Esther delivered the message and hung up.

"He said the surgeon's just his age; he's some genius from Johns Hopkins Hospital. He said this Gordon guy has published a lot of articles on spinal operations," said Esther.

"Fine and good. All is happy. Come to bed."

I felt her mouth and her voice on my ears, but I could hear only a sort of loud pulse from the girl. All I could do was move toward moisture and nipples and hair.

Quadberry lost his gamble at Emory Hospital in Atlanta. The brilliant surgeon his age lost him. Quadberry died. He died with his Arabian nose up in the air.

That is why I told this story and will never tell another.

TONI CADE BAMBARA

(1939–)

Gorilla, My Love

About the Author: Toni Cade Bambara was born in New York City and educated at Queens College, the University of Florence, and the City College of the City University of New York. She has worked as a social investigator for the New York State Department of Welfare, as a visiting professor of Afro-American Studies at Stephens College, and as a consultant on women's studies at Emory University. Since 1971, she has been writer-in-residence at Spelman College in Atlanta. Among her fiction is *The Sea Birds Are Still Alive: Collected Stories* (1977).

That was the year Hunca Bubba changed his name. Not a change up, but a change back, since Jefferson Winston Vale was the name in the first place. Which was news to me cause he'd been my Hunca Bubba my whole lifetime, since I couldn't manage Uncle to save my life. So far as I was concerned it was a change completely to somethin soundin very geographical weatherlike to me, like somethin you'd find in a almanac. Or somethin you'd run across when you sittin in the navigator seat with a wet thumb on the map crinkly in your lap, watching the roads and signs so when Granddaddy Vale say "Which way, Scout," you got sense enough to say take the next exit or take a left or whatever it is. Not that Scout's my name. Just the name Granddaddy call whoever sittin in the navigator seat. Which is usually me cause I don't feature sittin in the back with the pecans. Now, you figure pecans all right to be sittin with. If you thinks so, that's your business. But they dusty sometime and make you cough. And they got a way of slidin around and dippin down sudden, like maybe a rat in the buckets. So if you scary like me, you sleep with the lights on and blame it on Baby Jason and, so as not to waste good electric, you study the maps. And that's how come I'm in the navigator seat most times and get to be called Scout.

So Hunca Bubba in the back with the pecans and Baby Jason, and he in love. And we got to hear all this stuff about this woman he in love with and all. Which really ain't enough to keep the mind alive, though Baby Jason got no better sense than to give his undivided attention and keep grabbin at the photograph which is just a picture of some skinny woman in a countrified dress with her hand shot up to her face like she shame fore cameras. But there's a movie house in the background which I ax about. Cause I am a movie freak from way back, even though it do get me in trouble sometime.

Like when me and Big Brood and Baby Jason was on our own last Easter and couldn't go to the Dorset cause we'd seen all the Three Stooges they was. And the RKO Hamilton was closed readying up for the Easter Pageant that night. And the West End, the Regun and the Sunset was too far, less we had grownups with us which we didn't. So we walk up Amsterdam Avenue to the Washington and *Gorilla, My Love* playin, they say, which suit me just fine, though the "my love" part kinda drag Big Brood some. As for Baby Jason, shoot, like Granddaddy say, he'd follow me into the fiery furnace if I say come on. So we go in and get three bags of Havmore potato chips which not only are the best potato chips but the best bags for blowing up and bustin real loud so the matron come trottin down the aisle with her chunky self, flashin that flashlight dead in your eye so you can give her some lip, and if she answer back and you already finish seein the show anyway, why then you just turn the place out. Which I love to do, no lie. With Baby Jason kickin at the seat in front, egging me on, and Big Brood mumblin bout what fiercesome things we goin do. Which means me. Like when the big boys come up on us talking bout Lemme a nickel. It's me that hide the money. Or when the bad boys in the park take Big Brood's Spaudeen way from him. It's me that jump on they back and fight awhile. And it's me that turns out the show if the matron get too salty.

So the movie come on and right away it's this churchy music and clearly not about no gorilla. Bout Jesus. And I am ready to kill, not cause I got anything gainst Jesus. Just that when you fixed to watch a gorilla picture you don't wanna get messed around with Sunday School stuff. So I am mad. Besides, we see this raggedy old brown film *King of Kings* every year and enough's enough. Grownups figure they can treat you just anyhow. Which burns me up. There I am, my feet up and my Havmore potato chips really salty and crispy and two jawbreakers in my lap and the money safe in my shoe from the big boys, and here comes this Jesus stuff. So we all go wild. Yellin, booin, stompin and carryin on. Really to wake the

man in the booth up there who musta went to sleep and put on the wrong reels. But no, cause he holler down to shut up and then he turn the sound up so we really gotta holler like crazy to even hear ourselves good. And the matron ropes off the children section and flashes her light all over the place and we yell some more and some kids slip under the rope and run up and down the aisle just to show it take more than some dusty ole velvet rope to tie us down. And I'm flingin the kid in front of me's popcorn. And Baby Jason kickin seats. And it's really somethin. Then here come the big and bad matron, the one they let out in case of emergency. And she totin that flashlight like she gonna use it on somebody. This here the colored matron Brandy and her friends call Thunderbuns. She do not play. She do not smile. So we shut up and watch the simple ass picture.

Which is not so simple as it is stupid. Cause I realize that just about anybody in my family is better than this god they always talking about. My daddy wouldn't stand for nobody treatin any of us that way. My mama specially. And I can just see it now, Big Brood up there on the cross talkin bout Forgive them Daddy cause they don't know what they doin. And my Mama say Get on down from there you big fool, whatcha think this is, playtime? And my Daddy yellin to Granddaddy to get him a ladder cause Big Brood actin the fool, his mother side of the family showin up. And my mama and her sister Daisy jumpin on them Romans beatin them with they pocketbooks. And Hunca Bubba tellin them folks on they knees they better get out the way and go get some help or they goin to get trampled on. And Granddaddy Vale sayin Leave the boy alone, if that's what he wants to do with his life we ain't got nothin to say about it. Then Aunt Daisy givin him a taste of that pocketbook, fussin bout what a damn fool old man Granddaddy is. Then everybody jumpin in his chest like the time Uncle Clayton went in the army and came back with only one leg and Granddaddy say something stupid about that's life. And by this time Big Brood off the cross and in the park playin handball or skully or somethin. And the family in the kitchen throwin dishes at each other, screamin bout if you hadn't done this I wouldn't had to do that. And me in the parlor trying to do my arithmetic yellin Shut it off.

Which is what I was yellin all by myself which make me a sittin target for Thunderbuns. But when I yell We want our money back, that gets everybody in chorus. And the movie windin up with this heavenly cloud music and the smart-ass up there in his hole in the wall turns up the sound again to drown us out. Then there comes Bugs Bunny which we already seen so we know we been had. No gorilla my nuthin. And Big Brood say Awwww sheeet, we goin to see the manager and get our money back. And I know from this we business. So I brush the potato chips out of my hair which is where Baby Jason like to put em, and I march myself up the aisle to deal with the manager who is a crook in the first place for lyin out there sayin *Gorilla, My Love* playin. And I never did like the man cause he oily and pasty at the same time like the bad guy in the serial, the one that got a hideout behind a push-button bookcase and play "Moonlight Sonata" with gloves on. I knock on the door and I am furious. And I am alone, too. Cause Big Brood suddenly got to go so bad even though my mama told us bout goin in them nasty bathrooms. And I hear him sigh like he disgusted when he get to the door and see only a little kid there. And now I'm really furious cause I get so tired grownups messin over kids just cause they little and can't take em to court. What is it, he say to me like I lost my mittens or wet on myself or am somebody's retarded child. When in reality I am the smartest kid P.S. 186 ever had in its whole lifetime and you can ax anybody. Even them teachers that don't like me cause I won't sing them Southern songs or back off when they tell me my questions are out of order. And cause my Mama come up there in a minute when them teachers start playin the dozens behind colored folks. She stalk in with her hat pulled down bad and that Persian lamb coat draped back over one hip on account of she got her fist planted there so she can talk that talk which gets us all hypnotized, and teacher be comin undone cause she know this could be her job and her behind cause Mama got pull with the Board and bad by her own self anyhow.

So I kick the door open wider and just walk right by him and sit down and tell the man about himself and that I want my money back and that goes for Baby Jason and Big Brood too. And he still trying to shuffle me out the door even though I'm sittin which shows him for the fool he is. Just like them teachers do fore they realize Mama like a stone on that spot and ain't backin up. So he ain't gettin up off the money. So I was forced to leave, takin the matches from under his ashtray, and set a fire under the candy stand, which closed the raggedy ole Washington down for a week. My Daddy had the suspect it was me cause Big Brood got a big mouth. But I explained right quick what the whole thing was about and I figured it was even-steven. Cause if you say Gorilla, My Love, you suppose to mean it. Just like when you say you goin to give me a party on my birthday, you gotta mean it. And if you say me and Baby Jason can go South pecan haulin with Granddaddy Vale, you better not be comin up with no stuff about the weather look uncertain or did you mop the bathroom or any other trickified business. I mean even gangsters in the movies say My word is my bond. So don't nobody get away with nothin far as I'm concerned. So Daddy put his belt back on. Cause that's the way I was raised. Like my Mama say in one of them situations when I won't back down, Okay Badbird, you right. Your point is well-taken. Not that Badbird my name, just what she say when she tired arguin and know I'm right. And Aunt Jo, who is the hardest head in the family and worse even than Aunt Daisy, she say, You absolutely right Miss Muffin, which also ain't my real name but the name she gave me one time when I got some medicine shot in my behind and wouldn't get up off her pillows for nothin. And even Granddaddy Vale—who got no memory to speak of, so sometime you can just plain lie to him, if you want to be like that—he say, Well if that's what I said, then that's it. But this name business was different they said. It wasn't like Hunca Bubba had gone back on his word or anything. Just that he was thinkin bout gettin married and was usin his real name now. Which ain't the way I saw it at all.

So there I am in the navigator seat. And I turn to him and just plain ole ax him. I mean I come right on out with it. No sense goin all around that barn the old folks talk about. And like my mama say, Hazel—which is my real name and what she remembers to call me when she bein serious—when you got somethin on your mind, speak up and let the chips fall where they may. And if anybody don't like it, tell em to come see your mama. And Daddy look up from the paper and say, You hear your mama good, Hazel. And tell em to come see me first. Like that. That's how I was raised.

So I turn clear round in the navigator seat and say, "Look here, Hunca Bubba or Jefferson Windsong Vale or whatever your name is, you gonna marry this girl?"

"Sure am," he say, all grins.

And I say, "Member that time you was baby-sittin me when we lived at four-o-nine and there was this big snow and Mama and Daddy got held up in the country so you had to stay for two days?"

And he say, "Sure do."

"Well. You remember how you told me I was the cutest thing that ever walked the earth?"

"Oh, you were real cute when you were little," he say, which is suppose to be funny. I am not laughin.

"Well. You remember what you said?"

And Grandaddy Vale squintin over the wheel and axin Which way, Scout. But Scout is busy and don't care if we all get lost for days.

"Watcha mean, Peaches?"

"My name is Hazel. And what I mean is you said you were going to marry *me* when I grew up. You were going to wait. That's what I mean, my dear Uncle Jefferson." And he don't say nuthin. Just look at me real strange like he never saw me before in life. Like he lost in some weird town in the middle of night and lookin for directions and there's no one to ask. Like it was me that messed up the maps and turned the road posts round. "Well, you said it, didn't you?" And Baby Jason lookin back and forth like we playin ping-pong. Only I ain't playin. I'm hurtin and I can hear that I am screamin. And Grandaddy Vale mumblin how we never gonna get to where we goin if I don't turn around and take my navigator job serious.

"Well, for cryin out loud, Hazel, you just a little girl. And I was just teasin."

" 'And I was just teasin,' " I say back just how he said it so he can hear what a terrible thing it is. Then I don't say nuthin. And he don't say nuthin. And Baby Jason don't say nuthin nohow. Then Granddaddy Vale speak up. "Look here, Precious, it was Hunca Bubba what told you them things. This here, Jefferson Winston Vale." And Hunca Bubba say, "That's right. That was somebody else. I'm a new somebody."

"You a lying dawg," I say, when I meant to say treacherous dog, but just couldn't get hold of the word. It slipped away from me. And I'm crying and crumplin down in the seat and just don't care. And Granddaddy say to hush and steps on the gas. And I'm losin my bearins and don't even know where to look on the map cause I can't see for cryin. And Baby Jason cryin too. Cause he is my blood brother and understands that we must stick together or be forever lost, what with grown-ups playing change-up and turnin you round every which way so bad. And don't even say they sorry.

JOYCE CAROL OATES

(1938–)

Where Are You Going, Where Have You Been?

About the Author: Joyce Carol Oates was born in Lockport, New York, and published her first collection of stories, *By the North Gate,* in 1963. Since then she has written twenty novels and fourteen short story collections, as well as plays, volumes of poetry, criticism, and non-fiction prose, a reflection of the variety of her interests and concerns. Now a teacher of creative writing at Princeton University, Oates received the National Book Award in 1970 for her novel *Them.*

For Bob Dylan

Her name was Connie. She was fifteen and she had a quick nervous giggling habit of craning her neck to glance into mirrors, or checking other people's faces to make sure her own was all right. Her mother, who noticed everything and knew everything and who hadn't much reason any longer to look at her own face, always scolded Connie about it.

"Stop gawking at yourself, who are you? You think you're so pretty?" she would say. Connie would raise her eyebrows at these familiar complaints and look right through her mother, into a shadowy vision of herself as she was right at that moment: she knew she was pretty and that was everything. Her mother had been pretty once too, if you could believe those old snapshots in the album, but now her looks were gone and that was why she was always after Connie.

"Why don't you keep your room clean like your sister? How've you got your hair fixed—what the hell stinks? Hair spray? You don't see your sister using that junk."

Her sister June was twenty-four and still lived at home. She was a secretary in the high school Connie attended, and if that wasn't bad enough—with her in the same building—she was so plain and chunky and steady that Connie had to hear her praised all the time by her mother and her mother's sisters. June did this, June did that, she saved money and helped clean the house and cooked and Connie couldn't do a thing, her mind was all filled with trashy daydreams. Their father was away at work most of the time and when he came home he wanted supper and he read the newspaper at supper and after supper he went to bed. He didn't bother talking much to them, but around his bent head Connie's mother kept picking at her until Connie wished her mother was dead and she herself was dead and it was all over. "She makes me want to throw up sometimes," she complained to her friends. She had a high, breathless, amused voice which made everything she said sound a little forced, whether it was sincere or not.

There was one good thing: June went places with girl friends of hers, girls who were just as plain and steady as she, and so when Connie wanted to do that her mother had no objections. The father of Connie's best girl friend drove the girls the three miles to town and left them off at a shopping plaza, so that they could walk through the stores or go to a movie, and when he came to pick them up again at eleven he never bothered to ask what they had done.

They must have been familiar sights, walking around that shopping plaza in their shorts and flat ballerina slippers that always scuffed the sidewalk, with charm bracelets jingling on their thin wrists; they would lean together to whisper and laugh secretly if someone passed by who amused or interested them. Connie had long dark blond hair that drew anyone's eye to it, and she wore part of it pulled up on her head and puffed out and the rest of it she let fall down her back. She wore a pull-over jersey blouse that looked one way when she was at home and another way when she was away from home. Everything about her had two sides to it, one for home and one for anywhere that was not home: her walk that could be childlike and bobbing, or languid enough to make anyone think she was hearing music in her head, her mouth which was pale and smirking most of the time, but bright and pink on these evenings out, her laugh which was cynical and drawling at home—"Ha, ha, very funny"—but high-pitched and nervous anywhere else, like the jingling of the charms on her bracelet.

Sometimes they did go shopping or to a movie, but sometimes they went across the highway, ducking fast across the busy road, to a drive-in restaurant where older kids hung out. The restaurant was shaped like a big bottle, though squatter than a real bottle, and on its cap was a revolving figure of a grinning boy who held a hamburger aloft. One night in mid-summer they ran across, breathless with daring, and right away someone leaned out a car window and invited them over, but it was just a boy from high school they didn't like. It made them feel good to be able to ignore him. They went up through the maze of parked and cruising cars to the bright-lit, fly-infested restaurant, their faces pleased and expectant

as if they were entering a sacred building that loomed out of the night to give them what haven and what blessing they yearned for. They sat at the counter and crossed their legs at the ankles, their thin shoulders rigid with excitement, and listened to the music that made everything so good: the music was always in the background like music at a church service, it was something to depend upon.

A boy named Eddie came in to talk with them. He sat backwards on his stool, turning himself jerkily around in semi-circles and then stopping and turning again, and after a while he asked Connie if she would like something to eat. She said she did and so she tapped her friend's arm on her way out—her friend pulled her face up into a brave droll look—and Connie said she would meet her at eleven, across the way. "I just hate to leave her like that," Connie said earnestly, but the boy said that she wouldn't be alone for long. So they went out to his car and on the way Connie couldn't help but let her eyes wander over the windshields and faces all around her, her face gleaming with a joy that had nothing to do with Eddie or even this place; it might have been the music. She drew her shoulders up and sucked in her breath with the pure pleasure of being alive, and just at that moment she happened to glance at a face just a few feet from hers. It was a boy with shaggy black hair, in a convertible jalopy painted gold. He stared at her and then his lips widened into a grin. Connie slit her eyes at him and turned away, but she couldn't help glancing back and there he was still watching her. He wagged a finger and laughed and said, "Gonna get you, baby," and Connie turned away again without Eddie noticing anything.

She spent three hours with him, at the restaurant where they ate hamburgers and drank Cokes in wax cups that were always sweating, and then down an alley a mile or so away, and when he left her off at five to eleven only the movie house was still open at the plaza. Her girl friend was there, talking with a boy. When Connie came up the two girls smiled at each other and Connie said, "How was the movie?" and the girl said, "*You* should know." They rode off with the girl's father, sleepy and pleased, and Connie couldn't help but look at the darkened shopping plaza with its big empty parking lot and its signs that were faded and ghostly now, and over at the drive-in restaurant where cars were still circling tirelessly. She couldn't hear the music at this distance.

Next morning June asked her how the movie was and Connie said, "So-so."

She and that girl and occasionally another girl went out several times a week that way, and the rest of the time Connie spent around the house—it was summer vacation—getting in her mother's way and thinking, dreaming, about the boys she met. But all the boys fell back and dissolved into a single face that was not even a face, but an idea, a feeling, mixed up with the urgent insistent pounding of the music and the humid night air of July. Connie's mother kept dragging her back to the daylight by finding things for her to do or saying, suddenly, "What's this about the Pettinger girl?"

And Connie would say nervously, "Oh, her. That dope." She always drew thick clear lines between herself and such girls, and her mother was simple and kindly enough to believe her. Her mother was so simple, Connie thought, that it was maybe cruel to fool her so much. Her mother went scuffling around the house in old bedroom slippers and complained over the telephone to one sister about the other, then the other called up and the two of them complained about the third one. If June's name was mentioned her mother's tone was approving, and if Connie's name was mentioned it was disapproving. This did not really mean she disliked Connie and actually Connie thought that her mother preferred her to June because she was prettier, but the two of them kept up a pretense of exasperation, a sense that they were tugging and struggling over something of little value to either of them. Sometimes, over coffee, they were almost friends, but something would come up—some vexation that was like a fly buzzing suddenly around their heads—and their faces went hard with contempt.

One Sunday Connie got up at eleven—none of them bothered with church—and washed her hair so that it could dry all day long, in the sun. Her parents and sister were going to a barbecue at an aunt's house and Connie said no, she wasn't interested, rolling her eyes to let her mother know just what she thought of it. "Stay home alone then," her mother said sharply. Connie sat out back in a lawn chair and watched them drive away, her father quiet and bald, hunched around so that he could back the car out, her mother with a look that was still angry and not at all softened through the windshield, and in the back seat poor old June all dressed up as if she didn't know what a barbecue was, with all the running yelling kids and the flies. Connie sat with her eyes closed in the sun, dreaming and dazed with the warmth about her as if this were a kind of love, the caresses of love, and her mind slipped over onto thoughts of the boy she had been with the night before and how nice he had been, how sweet it always was, not the way someone like June would suppose but sweet, gentle, the way it was in movies and promised in songs; and when she opened her eyes she hardly knew where she was, the back yard ran off into weeds and a fence-line of trees and behind it the sky was perfectly blue and still. The asbestos "ranch house" that was now three years old startled her—it looked small. She shook her head as if to get awake.

It was too hot. She went inside the house and turned on the radio to drown out the quiet. She sat on the edge of her bed, barefoot, and listened for an hour and a half to a program called XYZ Sunday Jamboree, record after record of hard, fast, shrieking songs she sang along with, interspersed by exclamations from "Bobby King": "An' look here you girls at Napoleon's—Son and Charley want you to pay real close attention to this song coming up!"

And Connie paid close attention herself, bathed in a glow of slow-pulsed joy that seemed to rise mysteriously out of the music itself and lay languidly about the airless little room, breathed in and breathed out with each gentle rise and fall of her chest.

After a while she heard a car coming up the drive. She sat up at once, startled, because it couldn't be her father so soon. The gravel kept crunching all the way in from the road—the driveway was long—and Connie ran to the window. It was a car she didn't know. It was an open jalopy, painted a bright gold that caught the sunlight opaquely. Her heart began to pound and her fingers snatched at her hair, checking it, and she whispered "Christ. Christ," wondering how bad she looked. The car came to a stop at the side door and the horn sounded four short taps as if this were a signal Connie knew.

She went into the kitchen and approached the door slowly, then hung out the screen door, her bare toes curling down off the step. There were two boys in the car and now she recognized the driver: he had shaggy, shabby black hair that looked crazy as a wig and he was grinning at her.

"I ain't late, am I?" he said.

"Who the hell do you think you are?" Connie said.

"Toldja I'd be out, didn't I?"

"I don't even know who you are."

She spoke sullenly, careful to show no interest or pleasure, and he spoke in a fast bright monotone. Connie looked past him to the other boy, taking her time. He had fair brown hair, with a lock that fell onto his forehead. His sideburns gave him a fierce, embarrassed look, but so far he hadn't even bothered to glance at her. Both boys wore sunglasses. The driver's glasses were metallic and mirrored everything in miniature.

"You wanta come for a ride?" he said.

Connie smirked and let her hair fall loose over one shoulder.

"Don'tcha like my car? New paint job," he said. "Hey."

"What?"

"You're cute."

She pretended to fidget, chasing flies away from the door.

"Don'tcha believe me, or what?" he said.

"Look, I don't even know who you are," Connie said in disgust.

"Hey, Ellie's got a radio, see. Mine's broke down." He lifted his friend's arm and showed her the little transistor the boy was holding, and now Connie began to hear the music. It was the same program that was playing inside the house.

"Bobby King?" she said.

"I listen to him all the time. I think he's great.

"He's kind of great," Connie said reluctantly.

"Listen, that guy's *great.* He knows where the action is."

Connie blushed a little, because the glasses made it impossible for her to see just what this boy was looking at. She couldn't decide if she liked him or if he was just a jerk, and so she dawdled in the doorway and wouldn't come down or go back inside. She said, "What's all that stuff painted on your car?"

"Can'tcha read it?" He opened the door very carefully, as if he was afraid it might fall off. He slid out just as carefully, planting his feet firmly on the ground, the tiny metallic world in his glasses slowing down like gelatine hardening and in the midst of it Connie's bright green blouse. "This here is my name, to begin with," he said. ARNOLD FRIEND was written in tarlike black letters on the side, with a drawing of a round grinning face that reminded Connie of a pumpkin, except it wore sunglasses. "I wanta introduce myself, I'm Arnold Friend and that's my real name and I'm gonna be your friend, honey, and inside the car's Ellie Oscar, he's kinda shy." Ellie brought his transistor radio up to his shoulder and balanced it there. "Now these numbers are a secret code, honey," Arnold Friend explained. He read off the numbers 33, 19, 17 and raised his eyebrows at her to see what she thought of that, but she didn't think much of it. The left rear fender had been smashed and around it was written, on the gleaming gold background: DONE BY CRAZY WOMAN DRIVER. Connie had to laugh at that. Arnold Friend was pleased at her laughter and looked up at her. "Around the other side's a lot more—you wanta come and see them?"

"No."

"Why not?"

"Why should I?"

"Don'tcha wanta see what's on the car? Don'tcha wanta go for a ride?"

"I don't know."

"Why not?"

"I got things to do."

"Like what?"

"Things."

He laughed as if she had said something funny. He slapped his thighs. He was standing in a strange way, leaning back against the car as if he were balancing himself. He wasn't tall, only an inch or so taller than she would be if she came down to him. Connie liked the way he was dressed, which was the way all of them dressed: tight faded jeans stuffed into black, scuffed boots, a belt that pulled his waist in and showed how lean he was, and a white pull-over shirt that was a little soiled and showed the hard small muscles of his arms and shoulders. He looked as if he probably did hard work, lifting and carrying things. Even his neck looked muscular. And his face was a familiar face, somehow: the jaw and chin and cheeks slightly darkened, because he hadn't shaved for a day or two, and the nose long and hawk-like, sniffing as if she were a treat he was going to gobble up and it was all a joke.

"Connie, you ain't telling the truth. This is your day set aside for a ride with me and you know it," he said, still laughing. The way he straightened and recovered from his fit of laughing showed that it had been all fake.

"How do you know what my name is?" she said suspiciously.

"It's Connie."

"Maybe and maybe not."

"I know my Connie," he said, wagging his finger. Now she remembered him even better, back at the restaurant, and her cheeks warmed at the thought of how she sucked in her breath just at the moment she passed him—how she must have looked to him. And he had remembered her. "Ellie and I come out here especially for you," he said. "Ellie can sit in back. How about it?"

"Where?"

"Where what?"

"Where're we going?"

He looked at her. He took off the sunglasses and she saw how pale the skin around his eyes was, like holes that were not in shadow but instead in light. His eyes were chips of broken glass that catch the light in an amiable way. He smiled. It was as if the idea of going for a ride somewhere, to some place, was a new idea to him.

"Just for a ride, Connie sweetheart."

"I never said my name was Connie," she said.

"But I know what it is. I know your name and all about you, lots of things," Arnold Friend said. He had not moved yet but stood still leaning back against the side of his jalopy. "I took a special interest in you, such a pretty girl, and found out all about you like I know your parents and sister are gone somewheres and I know where and how long they're going to be gone, and I know who you were with last night, and your best girl friend's name is Betty. Right?"

He spoke in a simple lilting voice, exactly as if he were reciting the words to a song. His smile assured her that everything was fine. In the car Ellie turned up the volume on his radio and did not bother to look around at them.

"Ellie can sit in the back seat," Arnold Friend said. He indicated his friend with a casual jerk of his chin, as if Ellie did not count and she should not bother with him.

"How'd you find out all that stuff?" Connie said.

"Listen: Betty Schultz and Tony Fitch and Jimmy Pettinger and Nancy Pettinger," he said, in a chant. "Raymond Stanley and Bob Hutter—"

"Do you know all those kids?"

"I know everybody."

"Look, you're kidding. You're not from around here."

"Sure."

"But—how come we never saw you before?"

"Sure you saw me before," he said. He looked down at his boots, as if he were a little offended. "You just don't remember."

"I guess I'd remember you," Connie said.

"Yeah?" He looked up at this, beaming. He was pleased. He began to mark time with the music from Ellie's radio, tapping his fists lightly together. Connie looked away from his smile to the car, which was painted so bright it almost hurt her eyes to look at it. She looked at that name, ARNOLD FRIEND. And up at the front fender was an expression that was familiar—MAN THE FLYING SAUCERS. It was an expression kids had used the year before, but didn't use this year. She looked at it for a while as if the words meant something to her that she did not yet know.

"What're you thinking about? Huh?" Arnold Friend demanded. "Not worried about your hair blowing around in the car, are you?"

"No."

"Think I maybe can't drive good?"

"How do I know?"

"You're a hard girl to handle. How come?" he said. "Don't you know I'm your friend? Didn't you see me put my sign in the air when you walked by?"

"What sign?"

"My sign." And he drew an X in the air, leaning out toward her. They were maybe ten feet apart. After his hand fell back to his side the X was still in the air, almost visible. Connie let the screen door close and stood perfectly still inside it, listening to the music from her radio and the boy's blend together. She stared at Arnold Friend. He stood there so stiffly relaxed, pretending to be relaxed, with one hand idly on the door handle as if he were keeping himself up that way and had no intention of ever moving again. She recognized most things about him, the tight jeans that showed his thighs and buttocks and the greasy leather boots and the tight shirt, and even that slippery friendly smile of his, that sleepy dreamy smile that all the boys used to get across ideas they didn't want to put into words. She recognized all this and also the singsong way he talked, slightly mocking, kidding, but serious and a little melancholy, and she recognized the way he tapped one fist against the other in homage to the perpetual music behind him. But all these things did not come together.

She said suddenly, "Hey, how old are you?"

His smile faded. She could see then that he wasn't a kid, he was much older—thirty, maybe more. At this knowledge her heart began to pound faster.

"That's a crazy thing to ask. Can'tcha see I'm your own age?"

"Like hell you are."

"Or maybe a couple years older, I'm eighteen."

"Eighteen?" she said doubtfully.

He grinned to reassure her and lines appeared at the corners of his mouth. His teeth were big and white. He grinned so broadly his eyes became slits and she saw how thick the lashes were, thick and black as if painted with a black tarlike material. Then he seemed to become embarrassed, abruptly, and looked over his shoulder at Ellie. *"Him,* he's crazy," he said. "Ain't he a riot, he's a nut, a real character." Ellie was still listening to the music. His sunglasses told nothing about what he was thinking. He wore a bright orange shirt unbuttoned halfway to show his chest, which was a pale, bluish chest and not muscular like

Arnold Friend's. His shirt collar was turned up all around and the very tips of the collar pointed out past his chin as if they were protecting him. He was pressing the transistor radio up against his ear and sat there in a kind of daze, right in the sun.

"He's kinda strange," Connie said.

"Hey, she says you're kinda strange! Kinda strange!" Arnold Friend cried. He pounded on the car to get Ellie's attention. Ellie turned for the first time and Connie saw with shock that he wasn't a kid either—he had a fair hairless face, cheeks reddened slightly as if the veins grew too close to the surface of his skin, the face of a forty-year-old baby. Connie felt a wave of dizziness rise in her at this sight and she stared at him as if waiting for something to change the shock of the moment, make it all right again. Ellie's lips kept shaping words, mumbling along with the words blasting in his ear.

"Maybe you two better go away," Connie said faintly.

"What? How come?" Arnold Friend cried. "We come out here to take you for a ride. It's Sunday." He had the voice of the man on the radio now. It was the same voice, Connie thought. "Don'tcha know it's Sunday all day and honey, no matter who you were with last night today you're with Arnold Friend and don't you forget it!—Maybe you better step out here," he said, and this last was in a different voice. It was a little flatter, as if the heat was finally getting to him.

"No. I got things to do."

"Hey."

"You two better leave."

"We ain't leaving until you come with us."

"Like hell I am—"

"Connie, don't fool around with me. I mean, I mean, don't fool *around,"* he said, shaking his head. He laughed incredulously. He placed his sunglasses on top of his head, carefully, as if he were indeed wearing a wig, and brought the stems down behind his ears. Connie stared at him, another wave of dizziness and fear rising in her so that for a moment he wasn't even in focus but was just a blur, standing there against his gold car, and she had the idea that he had driven up the driveway all right but had come from nowhere before that and belonged nowhere and that everything about him and even about the music that was so familiar to her was only half real.

"If my father comes and sees you—"

"He ain't coming. He's at a barbecue."

"How do you know that?"

"Aunt Tillie's. Right now they're—uh—they're drinking. Sitting around," he said vaguely, squinting as if he were staring all the way to town and over to Aunt Tillie's backyard. Then the vision seemed to get clear and he nodded energetically. "Yeah. Sitting around. There's your sister in a blue dress, huh? And high heels, the poor sad bitch—nothing like you, sweetheart! And your mother's helping some fat woman with the corn, they're cleaning the corn—husking the corn—"

"What fat woman?" Connie cried.

"How do I know what fat woman. I don't know every goddam fat woman in the world!" Arnold Friend laughed.

"Oh, that's Mrs. Hornby. . . . Who invited her?" Connie said. She felt a little lightheaded. Her breath was coming quickly.

"She's too fat. I don't like them fat. I like them the way you are, honey," he said, smiling sleepily at her. They stared at each other for a while, through the screen door. He said

softly, "Now what you're going to do is this: you're going to come out that door. You're going to sit up front with me and Ellie's going to sit in the back, the hell with Ellie, right? This isn't Ellie's date. You're my date. I'm your lover, honey."

"What? You're crazy—"

"Yes, I'm your lover. You don't know what that is but you will," he said. "I know that too. I know all about you. But look: it's real nice and you couldn't ask for nobody better than me, or more polite. I always keep my word. I'll tell you how it is, I'm always nice at first, the first time. I'll hold you so tight you won't think you have to try to get away or pretend anything because you'll know you can't. And I'll come inside you where it's all secret and you'll give in to me and you'll love me—"

"Shut up! You're crazy!" Connie said. She backed away from the door. She put her hands against her ears as if she'd heard something terrible, something not meant for her. "People don't talk like that, you're crazy," she muttered. Her heart was almost too big now for her chest and its pumping made sweat break out all over her. She looked out to see Arnold Friend pause and then take a step toward the porch lurching. He almost fell. But, like a clever drunken man, he managed to catch his balance. He wobbled in his high boots and grabbed hold of one of the porch posts.

"Honey?" he said. "You still listening?"

"Get the hell out of here!"

"Be nice, honey. Listen."

"I'm going to call the police—"

He wobbled again and out of the side of his mouth came a fast spat curse, an aside not meant for her to hear. But even this "Christ!" sounded forced. Then he began to smile again. She watched this smile come, awkward as if he were smiling from inside a mask. His whole face was a mask, she thought wildly, tanned down onto his throat but then running out as if he had plastered make-up on his face but had forgotten about his throat.

"Honey—? Listen, here's how it is. I always tell the truth and I promise you this: I ain't coming in that house after you."

"You better not! I'm going to call the police if you—if you don't—"

"Honey," he said, talking right through her voice, "honey, I'm not coming in there but you are coming out here. You know why?"

She was panting. The kitchen looked like a place she had never seen before, some room she had run inside but which wasn't good enough, wasn't going to help her. The kitchen window had never had a curtain, after three years, and there were dishes in the sink for her to do—probably—and if you ran your hand across the table you'd probably feel something sticky there.

"You listening, honey? Hey?"

"—going to call the police—"

"Soon as you touch the phone I don't need to keep my promise and can come inside. You won't want that."

She rushed forward and tried to lock the door. Her fingers were shaking. "But why lock it," Arnold Friend said gently, talking right into her face. "It's just a screen door. It's just nothing." One of his boots was at a strange angle, as if his foot wasn't in it. It pointed out to the left, bent at the ankle. "I mean, anybody can break through a screen door and glass and wood and iron or anything else if he needs to, anybody at all and specially Arnold Friend. If the place got lit up with a fire honey you'd come running out into my arms, right into my arms and safe at home—like you knew I was your lover and'd stopped fooling around. I don't mind a nice shy girl but I don't like no fooling around." Part of those words were spoken with a slight rhythmic lilt, and Connie somehow recognized them—the echo of a song from last year, about a girl rushing into her boy friend's arms and coming home again—

Connie stood barefoot on the linoleum floor, staring at him. "What do you want?" she whispered.

"I want you," he said.

"What?"

"Seen you that night and thought, that's the one, yes sir. I never needed to look any more."

"But my father's coming back. He's coming to get me. I had to wash my hair first—" She spoke in a dry, rapid voice, hardly raising it for him to hear.

"No, your daddy is not coming and yes, you had to wash your hair and you washed it for me. It's nice and shining and all for me, I thank you, sweetheart," he said, with a mock bow, but again he almost lost his balance. He had to bend and adjust his boots. Evidently his feet did not go all the way down; the boots must have been stuffed with something so that he would seem taller. Connie stared out at him and behind him Ellie in the car, who seemed to be looking off toward Connie's right, into nothing. This Ellie said, pulling the words out of the air one after another as if he were just discovering them, "You want me to pull out the phone?"

"Shut your mouth and keep it shut," Arnold Friend said, his face red from bending over or maybe from embarrassment because Connie had seen his boots. "This ain't none of your business."

"What—what are you doing? What do you want?" Connie said. "If I call the police they'll get you, they'll arrest you—"

"Promise was not to come in unless you touch that phone, and I'll keep that promise," he said. He resumed his erect position and tried to force his shoulders back. He sounded like a hero in a movie, declaring something important. He spoke too loudly and it was as if he were speaking to someone behind Connie. "I ain't made plans for coming in that house where I don't belong but just for you to come out to me, the way you should. Don't you know who I am?"

"You're crazy," she whispered. She backed away from the door but did not want to go into another part of the house, as if this would give him permission to come through the door. "What do you. . . . You're crazy, you . . ."

"Huh? What're you saying, honey?"

Her eyes darted everywhere in the kitchen. She could not remember what it was, this room.

"This is how it is, honey: you come out and we'll drive away, have a nice ride. But if you don't come out we're gonna wait till your people come home and then they're all going to get it."

"You want that telephone pulled out?" Ellie said. He held the radio away from his ear and grimaced, as if without the radio the air was too much for him.

"I toldja shut up, Ellie," Arnold Friend said, "you're deaf, get a hearing aid, right? Fix yourself up. This little girl's no trouble and's gonna be nice to me, so Ellie keep to yourself, this ain't your date—right? Don't hem in on me. Don't hog. Don't crush. Don't bird dog. Don't trail me," he said in a rapid meaningless voice, as if he were running through all the expressions he'd learned but was no longer sure which one of them was in style, then

rushing on to new ones, making them up with his eyes closed, "Don't crawl under my fence, don't squeeze in my chipmunk hole, don't sniff my glue, suck my popsicle, keep your own greasy fingers on yourself!" He shaded his eyes and peered in at Connie, who was backed against the kitchen table. "Don't mind him honey he's just a creep. He's a dope. Right? I'm the boy for you and like I said you come out here nice like a lady and give me your hand, and nobody else gets hurt, I mean, your nice old bald-headed daddy and your mummy and your sister in her high heels. Because listen: why bring them in this?"

"Leave me alone," Connie whispered.

"Hey, you know that old woman down the road, the one with the chickens and stuff—you know her?"

"She's dead!"

"Dead? What? You know her?" Arnold Friend said.

"She's dead—"

"Don't you like her?"

"She's dead—she's—she isn't here any more—"

"But don't you like her, I mean, you got something against her? Some grudge or something?" Then his voice dipped as if he were conscious of a rudeness. He touched the sunglasses perched on top of his head as if to make sure they were still there. "Now you be a good girl."

"What are you going to do?"

"Just two things, or maybe three," Arnold Friend said. "But I promise it won't last long and you'll like me that way you get to like people you're close to. You will. It's all over for you here, so come on out. You don't want your people in any trouble, do you?"

She turned and bumped against a chair or something, hurting her leg, but she ran into the back room and picked up the telephone. Something roared in her ear, a tiny roaring, and she was so sick with fear that she could do nothing but listen to it—the telephone was clammy and very heavy and her fingers groped down to the dial but were too weak to touch it. She began to scream into the phone, into the roaring. She cried out, she cried for her mother, she felt her breath start jerking back and forth in her lungs as if it were something Arnold Friend were stabbing her with again and again with no tenderness. A noisy sorrowful wailing rose all about her and she was locked inside it the way she was locked inside the house.

After a while she could hear again. She was sitting on the floor with her wet back against the wall.

Arnold Friend was saying from the door, "That's a good girl. Put the phone back."

She kicked the phone away from her.

"No, honey. Pick it up. Put it back right."

She picked it up and put it back. The dial tone stopped.

"That's a good girl. Now you come outside."

She was hollow with what had been fear, but what was now just an emptiness. All that screaming had blasted it out of her. She sat, one leg cramped under her, and deep inside her brain was something like a pinpoint of light that kept going and would not let her relax. She thought, I'm not going to see my mother again. She thought, I'm not going to sleep in my bed again. Her bright green blouse was all wet.

Arnold Friend said, in a gentle-loud voice that was like a stage voice, "The place where you came from ain't there any more, and where you had in mind to go is cancelled out. This place you are now—inside your daddy's house—is nothing but a cardboard box I can knock down any time. You know that and always did know it. You hear me?"

She thought, I have got to think. I have to know what to do.

"We'll go out to a nice field, out in the country here where it smells so nice and it's sunny," Arnold Friend said. "I'll have my arms around you so you won't need to try to get away and I'll show you what love is like, what it does. The hell with this house! It looks solid all right," he said. He ran a fingernail down the screen and the noise did not make Connie shiver, as it would have the day before. "Now put your hand on your heart, honey. Feel that? That feels solid too but we know better, be nice to me, be sweet like you can because what else is there for a girl like you but to be sweet and pretty and give in?—and get away before her people come back?"

She felt her pounding heart. Her hand seemed to enclose it. She thought for the first time in her life that it was nothing that was hers, that belonged to her, but just a pounding, living thing inside this body that wasn't really hers either.

"You don't want them to get hurt," Arnold Friend went on. "Now get up, honey. Get up all by yourself."

She stood.

"Now turn this way. That's right. Come over here to me—Ellie, put that away, didn't I tell you? You dope. You miserable creepy dope," Arnold Friend said. His words were not angry but only part of an incantation. The incantation was kindly. "Now come out through the kitchen to me honey and let's see a smile, try it, you're a brave sweet little girl and now they're eating corn and hotdogs cooked to bursting over an outdoor fire, and they don't know one thing about you and never did and honey you're better than them because not a one of them would have done this for you."

Connie felt the linoleum under her feet; it was cool. She brushed her hair back out of her eyes. Arnold Friend let go of the post tentatively and opened his arms for her, his elbows pointing in toward each other and his wrists limp, to show that this was an embarrassed embrace and a little mocking, he didn't want to make her self-conscious.

She put out her hand against the screen. She watched herself push the door slowly open as if she were safe back somewhere in the other doorway, watching this body and this head of long hair moving out into the sunlight where Arnold Friend waited.

"My sweet little blue-eyed girl," he said, in a half-sung sigh that had nothing to do with her brown eyes but was taken up just the same by the vast sunlit reaches of the land behind him and on all sides of him, so much land that Connie had never seen before and did not recognize except to know that she was going to it.

YUKIO MISHIMA

(1925–1970)

Swaddling Clothes

TRANSLATED BY IVAN MORRIS

About the Author: Yukio Mishima, Japanese fiction writer and dramatist, was born Kimitake Hiraoka. Under his pen name he became a major figure in modern Japanese literature; he was also an actor and director, and a public promoter of traditional Japanese values. His works include short fiction collections, novels including *Confessions of a Mask* (1949), *The Sailor Who Fell from Grace with the Sea* (1963), and the tetralogy *The Sea of Fertility,* the last volume of which was

published in 1970. In that year Mishima publicly committed ritual suicide, apparently as a political statement.

He was always busy, Toshiko's husband. Even tonight he had to dash off to an appointment, leaving her to go home alone by taxi. But what else could a woman expect when she married an actor—an attractive one? No doubt she had been foolish to hope that he would spend the evening with her. And yet he must have known how she dreaded going back to their house, unhomely with its Western-style furniture and with the bloodstains still showing on the floor.

Toshiko had been oversensitive since girlhood: that was her nature. As the result of constant worrying she never put on weight, and now, an adult woman, she looked more like a transparent picture than a creature of flesh and blood. Her delicacy of spirit was evident to her most casual acquaintance.

Earlier that evening, when she had joined her husband at a night club, she had been shocked to find him entertaining friends with an account of "the incident." Sitting there in his American-style suit, puffing at a cigarette, he had seemed to her almost a stranger.

"It's a fantastic story," he was saying, gesturing flamboyantly as if in an attempt to outweigh the attractions of the dance band. "Here this new nurse for our baby arrives from the employment agency, and the very first thing I notice about her is her stomach. It's enormous—as if she had a pillow stuck under her kimono! No wonder, I thought, for I soon saw that she could eat more than the rest of us put together. She polished off the contents of our rice bin like that. . . ." He snapped his fingers. " 'Gastric dilation'—that's how she explained her girth and her appetite. Well, the day before yesterday we heard groans and moans coming from the nursery. We rushed in and found her squatting on the floor, holding her stomach in her two hands, and moaning like a cow. Next to her our baby lay in his cot, scared out of his wits and crying at the top of his lungs. A pretty scene, I can tell you!"

"So the cat was out of the bag?" suggested one of their friends, a film actor like Toshiko's husband.

"Indeed it was! And it gave me the shock of my life. You see, I'd completely swallowed that story about 'gastric dilation.' Well, I didn't waste any time. I rescued our good rug from the floor and spread a blanket for her to lie on. The whole time the girl was yelling like a stuck pig. By the time the doctor from the maternity clinic arrived, the baby had already been born. But our sitting room was a pretty shambles!"

"Oh, that I'm sure of!" said another of their friends, and the whole company burst into laughter.

Toshiko was dumbfounded to hear her husband discussing the horrifying happening as though it were no more than an amusing incident which they chanced to have witnessed. She shut her eyes for a moment and all at once she saw the newborn baby lying before her; on the parquet floor the infant lay, and his frail body was wrapped in bloodstained newspapers.

Toshiko was sure that the doctor had done the whole thing out of spite. As if to emphasize his scorn for this mother who had given birth to a bastard under such sordid conditions, he had told his assistant to wrap the baby in some loose newspapers, rather than proper swaddling. This callous treatment of the newborn child had offended Toshiko. Overcoming her disgust at the entire scene, she had fetched a brand-new piece of flannel from her cupboard and, having swaddled the baby in it, had lain him carefully in an armchair.

This all had taken place in the evening after her husband had left the house. Toshiko had told him nothing of it, fearing that he would think her oversoft, oversentimental; yet the scene had engraved itself deeply in her mind. Tonight she sat silently thinking back on it, while the jazz orchestra brayed and her husband chatted cheerfully with his friends. She knew that she would never forget the sight of the baby, wrapped in stained newspapers and lying on the floor—it was a scene fit for a butchershop. Toshiko, whose own life had been spent in solid comfort, poignantly felt the wretchedness of the illegitimate baby.

I am the only person to have witnessed its shame, the thought occurred to her. The mother never saw her child lying there in its newspaper wrappings, and the baby itself of course didn't know. I alone shall have to preserve that terrible scene in my memory. When the baby grows up and wants to find out about his birth, there will be no one to tell him, so long as I preserve silence. How strange that I should have this feeling of guilt! After all, it was I who took him up from the floor, swathed him properly in flannel, and laid him down to sleep in the armchair.

They left the night club and Toshiko stepped into the taxi that her husband had called for her. "Take this lady to Ushigomé," he told the driver and shut the door from the outside. Toshiko gazed through the window at her husband's smiling face and noticed his strong, white teeth. Then she leaned back in the seat, oppressed by the knowledge that their life together was in some way too easy, too painless. It would have been difficult for her to put her thoughts into words. Through the rear window of the taxi she took a last look at her husband. He was striding along the street toward his Nash car, and soon the back of his rather garish tweed coat had blended with the figures of the passers-by.

The taxi drove off, passed down a street dotted with bars and then by a theatre, in front of which the throngs of people jostled each other on the pavement. Although the performance had only just ended, the lights had already been turned out and in the half dark outside it was depressingly obvious that the cherry blossoms decorating the front of the theatre were merely scraps of white paper.

Even if that baby should grow up in ignorance of the secret of his birth, he can never become a respectable citizen, reflected Toshiko, pursuing the same train of thoughts. Those soiled newspaper swaddling clothes will be the symbol of his entire life. But why should I keep worrying about him so much? Is it because I feel uneasy about the future of my own child? Say twenty years from now, when our boy will have grown up into a fine, carefully educated young man, one day by a quirk of fate he meets that other boy, who then will also have turned twenty. And say that the other boy, who has been sinned against, savagely stabs him with a knife. . . .

It was a warm, overcast April night, but thoughts of the future made Toshiko feel cold and miserable. She shivered on the back seat of the car.

No, when the time comes I shall take my son's place, she told herself suddenly. Twenty years from now I shall be forty-three. I shall go to that young man and tell him straight out about everything—about his newspaper swaddling clothes, and about how I went and wrapped him in flannel.

The taxi ran along the dark wide road that was bordered by the park and by the Imperial Palace moat. In the distance Toshiko noticed the pin pricks of light which came from the blocks of tall office buildings.

Twenty years from now that wretched child will be in utter misery. He will be living a desolate, hopeless, poverty-stricken existence—a lonely rat. What else could happen to a baby who has had such a birth? He'll be wandering through the streets by himself, cursing his father, loathing his mother.

No doubt Toshiko derived a certain satisfaction from her somber thoughts: she tortured herself with them without cease. The taxi approached Hanzomon and drove past the compound of the British Embassy. At that point the famous rows of cherry trees were spread out before Toshiko in all their purity. On the spur of the moment she decided to go and view the blossoms by herself in the dark night. It was a strange decision for a timid and unadventurous young woman, but then she was in a strange state of mind and she dreaded the return home. That evening all sorts of unsettling fancies had burst open in her mind.

She crossed the wide street—a slim, solitary figure in the darkness. As a rule when she walked in the traffic Toshiko used to cling fearfully to her companion, but tonight she darted alone between the cars and a moment later had reached the long narrow park that borders the Palace moat. Chidorigafuchi, it is called—the Abyss of the Thousand Birds.

Tonight the whole park had become a grove of blossoming cherry trees. Under the calm cloudy sky the blossoms formed a mass of solid whiteness. The paper lanterns that hung from wires between the trees had been put out; in their place electric light bulbs, red, yellow, and green, shone dully beneath the blossoms. It was well past ten o'clock and most of the flower-viewers had gone home. As the occasional passers-by strolled through the park, they would automatically kick aside the empty bottles or crush the waste paper beneath their feet.

Newspapers, thought Toshiko, her mind going back once again to those happenings. Bloodstained newspapers. If a man were ever to hear of that piteous birth and know that it was he who had lain there, it would ruin his entire life. To think that I, a perfect stranger, should from now on have to keep such a secret—the secret of a man's whole existence. . . .

Lost in these thoughts, Toshiko walked on through the park. Most of the people still remaining there were quiet couples; no one paid her any attention. She noticed two people sitting on a stone bench beside the moat, not looking at the blossoms, but gazing silently at the water. Pitch black it was, and swathed in heavy shadows. Beyond the moat the somber forest of the Imperial Palace blocked her view. The trees reached up, to form a solid dark mass against the night sky. Toshiko walked slowly along the path beneath the blossoms hanging heavily overhead.

On a stone bench, slightly apart from the others, she noticed a pale object—not, as she had at first imagined, a pile of cherry blossoms, nor a garment forgotten by one of the visitors to the park. Only when she came closer did she see that it was a human form lying on the bench. Was it, she wondered, one of those miserable drunks often to be seen sleeping in public places? Obviously not, for the body had been systematically covered with newspapers, and it was the whiteness of those papers that had attracted Toshiko's attention. Standing by the bench, she gazed down at the sleeping figure.

It was a man in a brown jersey who lay there, curled up on layers of newspapers, other newspapers covering him. No doubt this had become his normal night residence now that spring had arrived. Toshiko gazed down at the man's dirty, unkempt hair, which in places had become hopelessly matted. As she observed the sleeping figure wrapped in its newspapers, she was inevitably reminded of the baby who had lain on the floor in its wretched swaddling clothes. The shoulder of the man's jersey rose and fell in the darkness in time with his heavy breathing.

It seemed to Toshiko that all her fears and premonitions had suddenly taken concrete form. In the darkness the man's pale forehead stood out, and it was a young forehead, though carved with the wrinkles of long poverty and hardship. His khaki trousers had been slightly pulled up; on his sockless feet he wore a pair of battered gym shoes. She could not see his face and suddenly had an overmastering desire to get one glimpse of it.

She walked to the head of the bench and looked down. The man's head was half buried in his arms, but Toshiko could see that he was surprisingly young. She noticed the thick eyebrows and the fine bridge of his nose. His slightly open mouth was alive with youth.

But Toshiko had approached too close. In the silent night the newspaper bedding rustled, and abruptly the man opened his eyes. Seeing the young woman standing directly beside him, he raised himself with a jerk, and his eyes lit up. A second later a powerful hand reached out and seized Toshiko by her slender wrist.

She did not feel in the least afraid and made no effort to free herself. In a flash the thought had struck her. Ah, so the twenty years have already gone by! The forest of the Imperial Palace was pitch dark and utterly silent.

ABIOSEH NICOL

(1924–)

As the Night the Day

About the Author: Abioseh Nicol, born in Sierra Leone, is a fiction writer and historian who, since 1972, has been an Honorary Fellow at Cambridge University, England. Nicol, a physician, also has served as United Nations Ambassador for Sierra Leone and Under Secretary General of the United Nations. In addition to novels and short stories, he has published studies of African nationalism.

Kojo and Bandele walked slowly across the hot green lawn, holding their science manuals with moist fingers. In the distance they could hear the junior school collecting in the hall of the main school building, for singing practice. Nearer, but still far enough, their classmates were strolling towards them. The two reached the science block and entered it. It was a low building set apart from the rest of the high school which sprawled on the hillside of the African savanna. The laboratory was a longish room and at one end they saw Basu, another boy, looking out of the window, his back turned to them. Mr. Abu, the ferocious laboratory attendant, was not about. The rows of multicoloured bottles looked inviting. A bunsen burner soughed loudly in the heavy weary heat. Where the tip of the light-blue triangle of flame ended, a shimmering plastic transparency started. One could see the restless hot air moving in the minute tornado. The two African boys watched it, interestedly, holding hands.

"They say it is hotter inside the flame than on its surface," Kojo said, doubtfully. "I wonder how they know."

"I think you mean the opposite; let's try it ourselves," Bandele answered.

"How?"

"Let's take the temperature inside."

"All right, here is a thermometer. You do it."

"It says ninety degrees now. I shall take the temperature of the outer flame first, then you can take the inner yellow one."

Bandele held the thermometer gently forward to the flame and Kojo craned to see. The thin thread of quicksilver shot upward within the stem of the instrument with swift malevolence and there was a slight crack. The stem had broken. On the bench the small bulbous drops of mercury which had spilled from it shivered with glinting, playful malice

and shuddered down to the cement floor, dashing themselves into a thousand shining pieces, some of which coalesced again and shook gaily as if with silent laughter.

"Oh my God!" whispered Kojo hoarsely.

"Shut up!" Bandele said, imperiously, in a low voice.

Bandele swept the few drops on the bench into his cupped hand and threw the blob of mercury down the sink. He swept those on the floor under an adjoining cupboard with his bare feet. Then, picking up the broken halves of the thermometer, he tiptoed to the waste bin and dropped them in. He tiptoed back to Kojo, who was standing petrified by the blackboard.

"See no evil, hear no evil, speak no evil," he whispered to Kojo.

It all took place in a few seconds. Then the rest of the class started pouring in, chattering and pushing each other. Basu, who had been at the end of the room with his back turned to them all the time, now turned round and limped laboriously across to join the class, his eyes screwed up as they always were.

The class ranged itself loosely in a semicircle around the demonstration platform. They were dressed in the school uniform of white shirt and khaki shorts. Their official age was around sixteen although, in fact, it ranged from Kojo's fifteen years to one or two boys of twenty-one.

Mr. Abu, the laboratory attendant, came in from the adjoining store and briskly cleaned the blackboard. He was a retired African sergeant from the Army Medical Corps and was feared by the boys. If he caught any of them in any petty thieving, he offered them the choice of a hard smack on the bottom or of being reported to the science masters. Most boys chose the former as they knew the matter would end there with no protracted interviews, moral recrimination, and an entry in the conduct book.

The science master stepped in and stood on his small platform. A tall, thin, dignified Negro, with greying hair and silver-rimmed spectacles badly fitting on his broad nose and always slipping down, making him look avuncular. "Vernier" was his nickname as he insisted on exact measurement and exact speech "as fine as a vernier scale," he would say, which measured, of course, things in thousandths of a millimetre. Vernier set the experiments for the day and demonstrated them, then retired behind the *Church Times* which he read seriously in between walking quickly down the aisles of lab. benches, advising boys. It was a simple heat experiment to show that a dark surface gave out more heat by radiation than a bright surface.

During the class, Vernier was called away to the telephone and Abu was not about, having retired to the lavatory for a smoke. As soon as a posted sentinel announced that he was out of sight, minor pandemonium broke out. Some of the boys raided the store. The wealthier ones swiped rubber tubing to make catapults and to repair bicycles, and helped themselves to chemicals for developing photographic films. The poorer boys were in deadlier earnest and took only things of strict commercial interest which could be sold easily in the market. They emptied stuff into bottles in their pockets. Soda for making soap, magnesium sulphate for opening medicine, salt for cooking, liquid paraffin for women's hairdressing, and fine yellow iodoform powder much in demand for sprinkling on sores. Kojo protested mildly against all this. "Oh, shut up!" a few boys said. Sorie, a huge boy who always wore a fez indoors and who, rumour said, had already fathered a child, commanded respect and some leadership in the class. He was sipping his favourite mixture of diluted alcohol and bicarbonate—which he called "gin and fizz"—from a beaker. "Look here, Kojo, you are getting out of hand. What do you think our parents pay taxes and school fees for?

For us to enjoy—or to buy a new car every year for Simpson?" The other boys laughed. Simpson was the European headmaster, feared by the small boys, adored by the boys in the middle school, and liked, in a critical fashion, with reservations, by some of the senior boys and African masters. He had a passion for new motor-cars, buying one yearly.

"Come to think of it," Sorie continued to Kojo, "you must take something yourself, then we'll know we are safe." "Yes, you must," the other boys insisted. Kojo gave in and, unwillingly, took a little nitrate for some gunpowder experiments which he was carrying out at home.

"Someone!" the look-out called.

The boys dispersed in a moment. Sorie swilled out his mouth at the sink with some water. Mr Abu, the lab. attendant, entered and observed the innocent collective expression of the class. He glared round suspiciously and sniffed the air. It was a physics experiment, but the place smelled chemical. However, Vernier came in then. After asking if anyone was in difficulties, and finding that no one could momentarily think up anything, he retired to his chair and settled down to an article on Christian reunion, adjusting his spectacles and thoughtfully sucking an empty tooth-socket.

Towards the end of the period, the class collected around Vernier and gave in their results, which were then discussed. One of the more political boys asked Vernier: if dark surfaces gave out more heat, was that why they all had black faces in West Africa? A few boys giggled. Basu looked down and tapped his clubfoot embarrassedly on the floor. Vernier was used to questions of this sort from the senior boys. He never committed himself as he was getting near retirement and his pension, and became more guarded each year. He sometimes even feared that Simpson had spies among the boys.

"That may be so, although the opposite might be more convenient."

Everything in science had a loophole, the boys thought, and said so to Vernier.

"Ah! that is what is called research," he replied, enigmatically.

Sorie asked a question. Last time, they had been shown that an electric spark with hydrogen and oxygen atoms formed water. Why was not that method used to provide water in town at the height of the dry season when there was an acute water shortage?

"It would be too expensive," Vernier replied, shortly. He disliked Sorie, not because of his different religion, but because he thought that Sorie was a bad influence and also asked ridiculous questions.

Sorie persisted. There was plenty of water during the rainy season. It could be split by lightning to hydrogen and oxygen in October and the gases compressed and stored, then changed back to water in March during the shortage. There was a faint ripple of applause from Sorie's admirers.

"It is an impracticable idea," Vernier snapped.

The class dispersed and started walking back across the hot grass. Kojo and Bandele heaved sighs of relief and joined Sorie's crowd which was always the largest.

"Science is a bit of a swindle," Sorie was saying. "I do not for a moment think that Vernier believes any of it himself," he continued. "Because, if he does, why is he always reading religious books?"

"Come back, all of you, come back!" Mr Abu's stentorian voice rang out, across to them.

They wavered and stopped. Kojo kept walking on in a blind panic.

"Stop," Bandele hissed across. "You fool." He stopped, turned and joined the returning crowd, closely followed by Bandele. Abu joined Vernier on the platform. The loose semicircle of boys faced them.

"Mr Abu just found this in the waste bin," Vernier announced, grey with anger. He held up the two broken halves of the thermometer. "It must be due to someone from this class as the number of thermometers was checked before being put out."

A little wind gusted in through the window and blew the silence heavily this way and that.

"Who?"

No one answered. Vernier looked round and waited.

"Since no one has owned up, I am afraid I shall have to detain you for an hour after school as punishment," said Vernier.

There was a murmur of dismay and anger. An important soccer house-match was scheduled for that afternoon. Some boys put their hands up and said that they had to play in the match.

"I don't care," Vernier shouted. He felt, in any case, that too much time was devoted to games and not enough to work.

He left Mr Abu in charge and went off to fetch his things from the main building.

"We shall play 'Bible and Key'," Abu announced as soon as Vernier had left. Kojo had been afraid of this and new beads of perspiration sprang from his troubled brow. All the boys knew the details. It was a method of finding out a culprit by divination. A large doorkey was placed between the leaves of a Bible at the New Testament passage where Ananias and Sapphira were struck dead before the Apostles for lying, and the Bible suspended by two bits of string tied to both ends of the key. The combination was held up by someone and the names of all present were called out in turn. When that of the sinner was called, the Bible was expected to turn round and round violently and fall.

Now Abu asked for a Bible. Someone produced a copy. He opened the first page and then shook his head and handed it back. "This won't do," he said, "it's a Revised Version; only the genuine Word of God will give us the answer."

An Authorized King James Version was then produced and he was satisfied. Soon he had the contraption fixed up. He looked round the semicircle from Sorie at one end, through the others, to Bandele, Basu, and Kojo at the other, near the door.

"You seem to have an honest face," he said to Kojo. "Come and hold it." Kojo took the ends of the string gingerly with both hands, trembling slightly.

Abu moved over to the low window and stood at attention, his sharp profile outlined against the red hibiscus flowers, the green trees, and the molten sky. The boys watched anxiously. A black-bodied lizard scurried up a wall and started nodding its pink head with grave impartiality.

Abu fixed his ageing bloodshot eyes on the suspended Bible. He spoke hoarsely and slowly:

"Oh, Bible, Bible, on a key,
Kindly tell it unto me,
By swinging slowly round and true,
To whom this sinful act is due. . . ."

He turned to the boys and barked out their names in a parade-ground voice, beginning with Sorie and working his way round, looking at the Bible after each name.

To Kojo, trembling and shivering as if ice-cold water had been thrown over him, it seemed as if he had lost all power and that some gigantic being stood behind him holding up his tired aching elbows. It seemed to him as if the key and Bible had taken on a life of their own, and he watched with fascination the whole combination moving slowly, jerkily, and rhythmically in short arcs as if it had acquired a heart-beat.

"Ayo Sogbenri, Sonnir Kargbo, Oji Ndebu." Abu was coming to the end now. "Tommy Longe, Ajayi Cole, Bandele Fagb . . ."

Kojo dropped the Bible. "I am tired," he said, in a small scream. "I am tired."

"Yes, he is," Abu agreed, "but we are almost finished; only Bandele and Basu are left."

"Pick up that book, Kojo, and hold it up again." Bandele's voice whipped through the air with cold fury. It sobered Kojo and he picked it up.

"Will you continue please with my name, Mr Abu?" Bandele asked, turning to the window.

"Go back to your place quickly, Kojo," Abu said. "Vernier is coming. He might be vexed. He is a strongly religious man and so does not believe in the Bible-and-Key ceremony."

Kojo slipped back with sick relief, just before Vernier entered.

In the distance the rest of the school were assembling for closing prayers. The class sat and stood around the blackboard and demonstration bench in attitudes of exasperation, resignation, and self-righteous indignation. Kojo's heart was beating so loudly that he was surprised no one else heard it.

"Once to every man and nation
Comes the moment to decide . . ."

The closing hymn floated across to them, interrupting the still afternoon.

Kojo got up. He felt now that he must speak the truth, or life would be intolerable ever afterwards. Bandele got up swiftly before him. In fact, several things seemed to happen all at the same time. The rest of the class stirred. Vernier looked up from a book review which he had started reading. A butterfly, with black and gold wings, flew in and sat on the edge of the blackboard, flapping its wings quietly and waiting too.

"Basu was here first before any of the class," Bandele said firmly.

Everyone turned to Basu, who cleared his throat.

"I was just going to say so myself, sir," Basu replied to Vernier's inquiring glance.

"Pity you had no thought of it before," Vernier said, dryly. "What were you doing here?"

"I missed the previous class, so I came straight to the lab. and waited. I was over there by the window, trying to look at the blue sky. I did not break the thermometer, sir."

A few boys tittered. Some looked away. The others muttered. Basu's breath always smelt of onions, but although he could play no games, some boys liked him and were kind to him in a tolerant way.

"Well if you did not, someone did. We shall continue with the detention."

Vernier noticed Abu standing by. "You need not stay, Mr Abu," he said to him. "I shall close up. In fact, come with me now and I shall let you out through the back gate."

He went out with Abu.

When he had left, Sorie turned to Basu and asked mildly:

"You are sure you did not break it?"

"No, I didn't."

"He did it," someone shouted.

"But what about the Bible-and-key?" Basu protested. "It did not finish. Look at him." He pointed to Bandele.

"I was quite willing for it to go on," said Bandele. "You were the only one left."

Someone threw a book at Basu and said, "Confess!"

Basu backed on to a wall. "To God, I shall call the police if anyone strikes me," he cried fiercely.

"He thinks he can buy the police," a voice called.

"That proves it," someone shouted from the back.

"Yes, he must have done it," the others said, and they started throwing books at Basu. Sorie waved his arm for them to stop, but they did not. Books, corks, boxes of matches rained on Basu. He bent his head and shielded his face with his bent arm.

"I did not do it, I swear I did not do it. Stop it, you fellows," he moaned over and over again. A small cut had appeared on his temple and he was bleeding. Kojo sat quietly for a while. Then a curious hum started to pass through him, and his hands began to tremble, his armpits to feel curiously wetter. He turned round and picked up a book and flung it with desperate force at Basu, and then another. He felt somehow that there was an awful swelling of guilt which he could only shed by punishing himself through hurting someone. Anger and rage against everything different seized him, because if everything and everyone had been the same, somehow he felt nothing would have been wrong and they would all have been happy. He was carried away now by a torrent which swirled and pounded. He felt that somehow Basu was in the wrong, must be in the wrong, and if he hurt him hard enough he would convince the others and therefore himself that he had not broken the thermometer and that he had never done anything wrong. He groped for something bulky enough to throw, and picked up the Bible.

"Stop it," Vernier shouted through the open doorway. "Stop it, you hooligans, you beasts."

They all became quiet and shamefacedly put down what they were going to throw. Basu was crying quietly and hopelessly, his thin body shaking.

"Go home, all of you, go home. I am ashamed of you." His black face shone with anger. "You are an utter disgrace to your nation and to your race."

They crept away, quietly, uneasily, avoiding each other's eyes, like people caught in a secret passion.

Vernier went to the first-aid cupboard and started dressing Basu's wounds.

Kojo and Bandele came back and hid behind the door, listening. Bandele insisted that they should.

Vernier put Basu's bandaged head against his waistcoat and dried the boy's tears with his handkerchief, gently patting his shaking shoulders.

"It wouldn't have been so bad if I had done it, sir," he mumbled, snuggling his head against Vernier, "but I did not do it. I swear to God I did not."

"Hush, hush," said Vernier comfortingly.

"Now they will hate me even more," he moaned.

"Hush, hush."

"They've missed the football match and now they will never talk to me again, oh-ee, oh-ee, why have I been so punished?"

"As you grow older," Vernier advised, "you must learn that men are punished not always for what they do, but often for what people think they will do, or for what they are. Remember that and you will find it easier to forgive them. 'To thine own self be true!' "

Vernier ended with a flourish, holding up his clenched fist in a mock dramatic gesture, quoting from the Shakespeare examination set-book for the year and declaiming to the dripping taps and empty benches and still afternoon, to make Basu laugh.

Basu dried his eyes and smiled wanly and replied: " 'And it shall follow as the night the day.' Hamlet, Act One, Scene Three, Polonius to Laertes."

"There's a good chap. First Class Grade One. I shall give you a lift home."

Kojo and Bandele walked down the red laterite road together, Kojo dispiritedly kicking stones into the gutter.

"The fuss they made over a silly old thermometer," Bandele began.

"I don't know, old man, I don't know," Kojo said impatiently.

They had both been shaken by the scene in the empty lab. A thin invisible wall of hostility and mistrust was slowly rising between them.

"Basu did not do it, of course," Bandele said.

Kojo stopped dead in his tracks. "Of course he did not do it," he shouted; "we did it."

"No need to shout, old man. After all, it was your idea."

"It wasn't," Kojo said furiously. "You suggested we try it."

"Well, you started the argument. Don't be childish." They tramped on silently, raising small clouds of dust with their bare feet.

"I should not take it too much to heart," Bandele continued. "That chap Basu's father hoards foodstuff like rice and palm oil until there is a shortage and then sells them at high prices. The police are watching him."

"What has that got to do with it?" Kojo asked.

"Don't you see, Basu might quite easily have broken that thermometer. I bet he has done things before that we have all been punished for." Bandele was emphatic.

They walked on steadily down the main road of the town, past the Syrian and Lebanese shops crammed with knick-knacks and rolls of cloth, past a large Indian shop with dull red carpets and brass trays displayed in its windows, carefully stepping aside in the narrow road as the British officials sped by in cars to their hill-station bungalows for lunch and siesta.

Kojo reached home at last. He washed his feet and ate his main meal for the day. He sat about heavily and restlessly for some hours. Night soon fell with its usual swiftness, at six, and he finished his homework early and went to bed.

Lying in bed he rehearsed again what he was determined to do the next day. He would go up to Vernier:

"Sir," he would begin, "I wish to speak with you privately."

"Can it wait?" Vernier would ask.

"No, sir," he would say firmly, "as a matter of fact it is rather urgent."

Vernier would take him to an empty classroom and say, "What is troubling you, Kojo Ananse?"

"I wish to make a confession, sir. I broke the thermometer yesterday." He had decided he would not name Bandele; it was up to the latter to decide whether he would lead a pure life.

Vernier would adjust his slipping glasses up his nose and think. Then he would say: "This is a serious matter, Kojo. You realize you should have confessed yesterday?"

"Yes, sir, I am very sorry."

"You have done great harm, but better late than never. You will, of course, apologize in front of the class and particularly to Basu who has shown himself a finer chap than all of you."

"I shall do so, sir."

"Why have you come to me now to apologize? Were you hoping that I would simply forgive you?"

"I was hoping you would, sir. I was hoping you would show your forgiveness by beating me."

Vernier would pull his glasses up his nose again. He would move his tongue inside his mouth reflectively. "I think you are right. Do you feel you deserve six strokes or nine?"

"Nine, sir."

"Bend over!"

Kojo had decided he would not cry because he was almost a man.

Whack! Whack!

Lying in bed in the dark thinking about it all as it would happen tomorrow, he clenched his teeth and tensed his buttocks in imaginary pain.

Whack! Whack!! Whack!!!

Suddenly, in his little room, under his thin cotton sheet, he began to cry. Because he felt the sharp lancing pain already cutting into him. Because of Basu and Simpson and the thermometer. For all the things he wanted to do and be which would never happen. For all the good men they had told them about, Jesus Christ, Mohammed, and George Washington who never told a lie. For Florence Nightingale and David Livingstone. For Kagawa, the Japanese man, for Gandhi, and for Kwegyir Aggrey, the African. Oh-ee, oh-ee. Because he knew he would never be as straight and strong and true as the school song said they should be. He saw, for the first time, what this thing would be like, becoming a man. He touched the edge of an inconsolable eternal grief. Oh-ee, oh-ee; always, he felt, always I shall be a disgrace to the nation and the race.

His mother passed by his bedroom door, slowly dragging her slippered feet as she always did. He pushed his face into his wet pillow to stifle his sobs, but she had heard him. She came in and switched on the light.

"What is the matter with you, my son?"

He pushed his face farther into his pillow.

"Nothing," he said, muffled and choking.

"You have been looking like a sick fowl all afternoon," she continued.

She advanced and put the back of her moist cool fingers against the side of his neck.

"You have got fever," she exclaimed. "I'll get something from the kitchen."

When she had gone out, Kojo dried his tears and turned the dry side of the pillow up. His mother reappeared with a thermometer in one hand and some quinine mixture in the other.

"Oh, take it away, take it away," he shouted, pointing to her right hand and shutting his eyes tightly.

"All right, all right," she said, slipping the thermometer into her bosom.

He is a queer boy, she thought, with pride and a little fear as she watched him drink the clear bitter fluid.

She then stood by him and held his head against her broad thigh as he sat up on the low bed, and she stroked his face. She knew he had been crying but did not ask him why, because she was sure he would not tell her. She knew he was learning, first slowly and now quickly, and she would soon cease to be his mother and be only one of the womenfolk in the family. Such a short time, she thought, when they are really yours and tell you everything. She sighed and slowly eased his sleeping head down gently.

The next day Kojo got to school early, and set to things briskly. He told Bandele that he was going to confess but would not name him. He half hoped he would join him. But Bandele had said, threateningly, that he had better not mention his name, let him go and be a Boy Scout on his own. The sneer strengthened him and he went off to the lab. He met Mr Abu and asked for Vernier. Abu said Vernier was busy and what was the matter, anyhow.

"I broke the thermometer yesterday," Kojo said in a businesslike manner.

Abu put down the glassware he was carrying.

"Well, I never!" he said. "What do you think you will gain by this?"

"I broke it," Kojo repeated.

"Basu broke it," Abu said impatiently. "Sorie got him to confess and Basu himself came here this morning and told the science master and myself that he knew now that he had knocked the thermometer by mistake when he came in early yesterday afternoon. He had not turned round to look, but he had definitely heard a tinkle as he walked by. Someone must have picked it up and put it in the waste bin. The whole matter is settled, the palaver finished."

He tapped a barometer on the wall and, squinting, read the pressure. He turned again to Kojo.

"I should normally have expected him to say so yesterday and save you boys missing the game. But there you are," he added, shrugging and trying to look reasonable, "you cannot hope for too much from a Syrian boy."

MARY LAVIN

(1912–)

Frail Vessel

About the Author: Mary Lavin was born in Walpole, Massachusetts, but at ten moved with her family to Ireland where she later made her reputation as a fiction writer, publishing numerous short story collections as well as two novels and a children's book. As in her first volume, *Tales from Bective Bridge* (1942), Lavin takes as her subjects the people and places of her adopted country; she has been the recipient of the Gregory Medal established by William Butler Yeats to be "the supreme award of the Irish nation."

Who would have thought, as they stood together at their mother's graveside, that they would both be married within the year? Why, Liddy was only sixteen then! Wasn't it partly for her sake that she and Daniel had gone on with the arrangements for their own marriage?

Bedelia was at a loss. Wasn't it partly to give her little sister a home; a real family life again; and prevent a repetition of what happened with Alice that she was getting married at all. People knew that was the reason for her haste. They appreciated the fact that she wasn't in a position to postpone her marriage. And anyway, taking into consideration the

precarious position of the business, and the fact that it would have collapsed years ago only for Daniel's good management, everyone sympathized with the necessity for an immediate formal settlement. There was certainly no disrespect intended towards the dead!

But Liddy! She was absolutely shocked to find that Liddy had no regard at all: for the living or the dead.

Naturally she—Bedelia—was opposed to this other marriage. She made every effort to persuade Liddy to wait a while. But she soon saw her efforts were useless.

Whatever had come over Liddy no good was to be got of her at all. She was like a person that was light in the head.

And as for Alphonsus O'Brien, Bedelia could make nothing out of him from the start. To begin with she never could stand solicitors, anyway. You could never feel at ease with them. They were always too clever for you, no matter what you did. Then, she never could think of Alphonsus O'Brien as anything but a stranger. And what else was he?

He was only a few months in the town; a total stranger, with no connections—and no office you might say, except the use of a room at the Central Hotel. He was a kind of laughing-stock right from the start, sitting inside the hotel window and not a soul ever darkening the door. He made no effort to get to know the people either. Their Liddy was the only one he ever saluted!

Daniel used to laugh at her.

"He must expect to get a lot of business out of you, Liddy," he said.

That was the whole trouble: they treated the thing as a joke, both she and Daniel. And indeed, Liddy took it all as a joke, too, in the start.

No one in their senses would have believed that it could turn into anything serious. No one on earth could have foreseen that a young girl would have lost her head to an old fellow like that.

Not that Alphonsus was so old: it was more that he was odd than anything else: but he was certainly a bit old for a man who was said to have just qualified.

"Just qualified!" she cried. "But he's grey!"

Daniel, however, was able to explain things. He said probably O'Brien had been a law clerk.

"They have a hard time—it's harder that way. So he mightn't be as old as he looks."

As a matter of fact Daniel was right, Alphonsus was a lot younger than he looked, but all the same it never occurred to her that there could be anything romantic about him. And the day that Liddy got so red, when they were passing the Central Hotel, she simply could not account for it.

They had been out for a walk together, she and Liddy, and they were coming home. They were talking about Bedelia's own wedding, as a matter of fact, when she noticed suddenly that Liddy wasn't paying attention. And when she looked at her she saw that she was blushing.

Whatever for? That was her first thought, and she looked around the street. It could only be some boy, she supposed, and she couldn't help feeling annoyed because Liddy seemed too much of a child for that kind of thing. But although she scanned the street up and down there wasn't a soul in sight except Alphonsus O'Brien standing at the hotel door. It simply did not occur to her to attribute those blushes to him; she contented herself by thinking that they were due to embarrassment at the way the child was teased about him.

How differently she would have acted if there was a boy in the street that day, a young man that is to say. If there was anyone presentable at all in sight it would have been a

warning to her. And although she was nearly distracted those days, with plans for her own wedding, she would have kept a better eye on Liddy.

As things were, however, she did not give the incident another thought.

She did notice, however, that Mr O'Brien had taken to standing a lot at the door of the hotel, because when she paused to look out the window occasionally she saw him there.

"He's coming out of his shell," she said to Daniel.

Daniel was dressing the window in the gable-end at the time, and she was looking over his shoulder into the street.

Daniel shook his head. "You'd feel sorry for him," he said. "He can't be doing much of a practice."

She felt a bit sorry for him herself, but as Liddy came into the shop just then she thought she'd make her laugh.

"We're looking out at your friend Mr O'Brien," she said. "He's always standing in the doorway of the hotel. Maybe he's got a job as hotel porter."

"That must be it," said Liddy. And she laughed.

Yes: Liddy laughed at him, too. That deceived them completely.

If she had shown the slightest annoyance or taken his part in any way they might have been suspicious. But she deceived them completely. Either that, or she really and truly still regarded the whole thing as a joke at that time. She certainly didn't take his first proposal seriously. And no wonder!

As it happened, Bedelia herself was at the window, that day, and she saw him lean out as Liddy was passing and catch her by the plait.

She little knew what he had said to her!

"Well, Liddy?" she said, when the girl came running into the shop. "I saw you!" She was partly disapproving; partly amused.

"But you didn't hear what he said to me!" cried Liddy. "He told me to go home and ask you when you'd let me marry him!"

"Well, the cheek of him!" she cried. "I didn't think he had it in him to make a joke." Because, of course, they took it as a joke, both of them.

But when it became a regular thing for him to pull Liddy's plait every time she went up or down the street, Bedelia felt obliged to speak to her.

Liddy didn't take it well, either. She noticed that at once, and for the first time she felt uneasy.

"After all, Liddy, you must remember that I stand in your mother's place. And I think this thing is going beyond a joke."

But her words were truer than she knew: it was already beyond a joke.

And when Liddy paid no heed to her, but continued to hang about the hotel door laughing and talking to the fellow, Bedelia had to resort to threats. They were upstairs at the time, in the big parlour over the shop. Bedelia jerked her head in the direction of the Central Hotel.

"If this thing doesn't stop, Liddy, I'll have to speak to Mr O'Brien!"

That was all she said, and indeed she hadn't any intention of carrying out such a threat. But to her surprise Liddy said nothing. Something odd about the silence made her look sharply at her.

Liddy's face was covered with blushes.

"I think he wants to speak to you, too, Bedelia," she said. Bedelia saw that her hands were trembling.

"To speak to me?" She was astonished.

Liddy's head was bent, but with a great effort she forced herself to look her in the face. "I think he's coming to see you"—she said—"today!"

Today?

But suddenly Liddy could control herself no longer.

"Oh, Bedelia!" she cried. And Bedelia honestly could not tell whether she was crying or laughing. "Oh, Bedelia—you know the way he was always going on—about asking you if you'd let him marry me—you remember we thought he was joking—didn't we? Well—he wasn't!"

Bedelia could only gasp. And then, before she had time to get over the shock there was a loud rap on the hall door.

Never in her life was she thrown into such flurry. She stared at Liddy.

Liddy's blushes had died away.

"I expect that's him now," she said, coolly, calmly, as if it were the most natural thing in the world.

In the few minutes before she went down to the little front parlour to see her prospective brother-in-law, Bedelia tried to gather her thoughts together.

She was absolutely bewildered. What was she to say to this strange man—this absolute stranger?

Her first impulse was to run down the backstairs and call Daniel in from the shop. Daniel would know how to deal with the situation. But as she decided to do so, some impulse made her turn back to the main stairs. It didn't seem fair to drag Daniel into it. Anyway, she doubted if he would be much use in this kind of situation. Daniel's talent was for figures; for keeping books and attending to the financial side of things. Of course, there was a financial side to this situation too, she realized. How was this fellow going to support a wife? Where was he going to bring his wife to live?

All these questions ran through her head as she stood where Liddy had left her, but it was only her mind that was working: her practical common-sense mind, but what she felt about the matter she did not know: as to feeling, she was absolutely numb.

But as she stood there in the middle of her room, her eyes fell on the plain serge suit which was intended for her own wedding, it had just that day come from the dressmaker, and she was suddenly shot through and through with irritation. Why did this business about Liddy have to blow up on the verge of her own wedding?

Goodness knows, she hadn't expected much fuss to be made about her own marriage, what with not being out of mourning, and Daniel having always lived in the house anyway; but it did seem a bit unfair to have all this excitement blow up around Liddy.

Two rare, very rare, and angry tears squeezed out of Bedelia's pale eyes, and fell down her plain round cheeks. Because, of course, mourning or no mourning, a young girl like Liddy wasn't likely to get married in serge!

Bedelia felt just like as if a mean trick had been played on her! After all I've done for her! she thought. After being a mother to her! But this last thought made her feel more bitter than ever because it seemed to her suddenly that it was a measure of the difference between them as brides.

Already she could imagine the fuss there would be over Liddy—the exclamations and the sighs of pity and admiration. Such a lovely bride!

Whereas when she—oh, but it was so unfair because never at any time did she regard her own marriage as anything but a practical expedient. It was only that she hadn't counted on being up against this comparison. It was that she minded.

But here Bedelia called herself to order. Of course a lot depended upon when the others intended to bring their affairs to a head.

After all, Alphonsus O'Brien couldn't have much money. Perhaps he only wanted her sanction to his suit? It might be years before they could get married.

Yes, of course. Of course. She was letting her imagination run away with her: it would probably be years before poor O'Brien would take the final step.

Hastily running across the landing to her bedroom, and dipping the corner of her towel into the ewer of water on her washstand, Bedelia rubbed her face all over and darted a look into the mirror.

Smart and all as she was, Liddy might be old enough by the time her beau was in a position to lead her up to the altar!

She ran down the stairs.

It was when she was at the bottom of the stairs that another aspect of the situation struck Bedelia.

It was all very well for Daniel and herself to be making a home for Liddy when they regarded her as a child—but how would things be after this!

Even if this had never occurred it might have been more awkward than she realized to have another person in the house with them right from the start—and another woman above all.

For the first time in her life, a bashful feeling came over Bedelia at the thought of the night that Daniel would move out of the little return-room on the back-landing, where he had slept since he was a young apprentice, and with his old alarm clock under his arm, take up his position in her room.

It was only then—only at the last minute, with her hand on the knob of the parlour door, that it came over her that things might not be so bad at all. And in any case what could she do about it? If they were bent on getting married, who could stop them?

It was all settled. It had taken less than five minutes, and yet all was arranged. Daniel had even been sent for and although he was as much taken by surprise as anyone, he was more or less brought around to Alphonsus O'Brien's viewpoint.

That was what came of being a solicitor. Bedelia supposed. They were so able. But I'll never like him, she thought. He could build a nest in my ear.

And that was tantamount to what her new brother-in-law proposed to do.

It seemed that Liddy had told him about the little house at the end of the street that they owned; it was unoccupied, tumbling down, in fact, but it never seemed worth while repairing, for the small rent they would get for it.

It would be just the thing for them, Alphonsus said. With a bit of paint, and something done to the bad spot on the roof it would do until they had time to find something better: something more suitable.

"And it's so pretty," cried Liddy. "I always thought it was a dear little house! I used to peep in through the shutters and wish I could go and live in it"—she turned and smiled at Alphonsus—"all by myself," she said.

But Bedelia had enough without that. Such soppiness: and in front of Daniel. Well,

Liddy might like to play the love-bird, but there was no getting away from the fact that the romantic Mr O'Brien was almost grey—whereas Daniel had a head of hair like an infant. She turned around to Alphonsus on an impulse.

"It's a wonder you never married before now, Mr O'Brien," she said, and she looked archly at him to conceal the malice in her voice.

Perhaps he saw through her, because he put out his hand and drew Liddy nearer.

"I suppose I was waiting for Liddy, here," he said, and it was impossible to know whether he was serious or whether he was joking.

And it crossed Bedelia's mind that that was the same mixed way in which he had wormed himself into Liddy's affections: by mixing up sentiment and mockery. It was a kind of cheating, she thought. Nowadays people didn't go on with nonsense like that about waiting for the right person—and being the only one in the world for each other. There was nothing like that between herself and Daniel! Daniel certainly didn't go down on his knees to her! She would have thought he was daft if he did.

But all the same, as she looked at Alphonsus, she felt that he was the kind of a man who could fall down in front of a girl as a kind of a joke—and she'd know he was joking or partly joking—but all the same it would bring a kind of sweetness into her life.

But Bedelia brought herself to order again.

Alphonsus had reached for his hat and they had to see him to the door.

Bedelia made the first reference to what had gone before.

"Well, everyone to his own taste," she said, after the door was closed and they were back in the downstairs parlour. "Although I must say I don't know how on earth you can bear that sloppy manner." Liddy looked up nervously. "You know what I mean," said Bedelia impatiently. She tried to think of something sloppy he said, but it was like trying to remember a smell—she could only remember that it was sloppy. But at last she laid hold on one phrase he had used. "You know—all that rubbish he went on with—about you being the only one in the world for him—and that he was waiting all those years for you. How can you stand that kind of talk? It's so meaningless."

Liddy had caught up the tablecloth and was just about to spread it, but instead she lifted it up high, high as her face almost as if it were a veil behind which she smiled, a little, dreamy, secretive smile.

"Oh, Bedelia, *I* knew what he meant," she said, and then, over the edge of the cloth, her eyes seemed to implore something from Bedelia—but Bedelia turned aside: really this sentimentality was more than she could bear. Her eyes narrowed.

"Liddy," she said sharply, "I hope"—she paused—"you know how I have always felt towards you, like a mother"—she caught herself up—"well anyway, like a guardian," she corrected, "but perhaps lately with my own plans taking up so much of my time I may not have given you as much supervision as I used—as much as you should have had perhaps—I can only hope that you haven't abused your freedom in any way?"

But Liddy had spread the cloth on the table and was bending across it smoothing out the folds. Had she been listening at all? Bedelia gave a clap with her hands.

"What I mean is that I hope you haven't made yourself cheap in any way? Men don't usually speak so sentimentally, unless—well, unless a girl has let them become—well—familiar!"

After she said the word she was a little daunted herself by its force, but to her surprise at first, and then to her unspeakable irritation, Liddy didn't realize its implications at all.

"Oh, but that's just it, Bedelia! I wanted to tell you! We've become *so* familiar really. Isn't it funny, and to think that we only know each other for a few weeks, and that this is the first time we've ever been together inside a house." She gave a little high-pitched laugh. And yes—Bedelia could hardly bear it—she hugged herself. "And yet I feel as if we knew each other for years and years." A rapt look came in her face. "Bedelia! you don't mind my saying it, do you, because you want me to be happy, don't you? But I feel more familiar with him than with you! I do, really! I know it sounds queer, but it's true—" She paused as if she was trying to think of some way to make herself clearer. Then her face lit up. She didn't see the danger signals in Bedelia's face.

"Do you know what I was thinking last night?" she cried. For a minute she paused—to take courage?—and then she rushed on. "In bed," she said softly, "I was thinking about when I was small and used to sleep with you in your big brass bed. Oh, I used to love it, you know that! I used to be lonely when I got a room of my own: I was never able to go to sleep for ages, and I couldn't warm up for hours! But all the same, even when I loved sleeping with you—you don't mind my telling you this, do you?—I used to hate if your—I used to hate if my—I mean I couldn't bear it if our feet touched!"

But here, Liddy's faint heart failed her again, and she had to rush over to Bedelia.

"You don't mind my telling you, do you?"

Bedelia drew back. She did mind. She didn't want to hear it. It sounded a lot of rubbish to her, but still, in spite of everything, she was curious.

"I must say I don't see the point!" she said coldly.

Liddy brightened.

"Oh, I'm coming to the point," she cried. "It's that although I never saw Alphonsus without his shoes and stockings on, of course, it came into my mind—last night in bed—that I wouldn't mind a bit if our feet touched—his and mine, you know—after we were married I mean!"

It was said. She had said it. For a minute her face was radiant. Then she looked at Bedelia.

"Oh, Bedelia! What's the matter?" She couldn't understand the look on the other's face. "You're not hurt, are you?"

"Hurt?" Bedelia put out her two hands. "Keep back from me," she shouted. "Hurt, indeed! Disgusted would be more like it! Such talk from a young girl. Do you want to know what I think? Well, I think you're daft!"

The sisters were both married six months when Liddy came back to the old house one afternoon and passing through the shop with only a word for Daniel, went straight upstairs to Bedelia's room over the shop.

"I want to ask you something, Bedelia," she said, straight away, without preamble. "Will you let us off your share of the rent of the little house—it's such a small sum to you and—well, it's not so small to us—and I know you were only charging us something as a formality—to make us feel independent and all that—but the fact of the matter is—" nervously she had run on without stopping ever since she came into the room, but as Bedelia, who was sitting at the window, stood up, she broke off—Bedelia was looking so queerly at her.

"Why, Liddy," she said, "I must say this is very surprising. Not that the rent means anything to Daniel and me—you're quite right about that—as a matter of fact Daniel was saying only the other day that no rent would compensate us for the loss of store-space—

though mind you, Liddy, I would never have mentioned that if you didn't bring up the matter yourself—but as I was saying, it isn't a question of money—you know that—you know the standard of living in this house, and you know your little contribution wouldn't go far to maintain it! And it hasn't changed, I can tell you that, although I must say Daniel is very particular about my keeping accounts—"

But marriage had quickened Liddy's perceptions.

"You're not going to let us off?" she whispered, not caring that she was interrupting. Was she going to run from the room? Bedelia put out her hand.

"Wait a minute, Liddy," she cried. "Don't be so hasty. I didn't refuse you, did I?" She saw with relief that Liddy had come back into the room. "I was taken by surprise, that's all. It's such a wretched little house—I thought perhaps that you were going to tell me that you'd found something better—you know it was never supposed to be anything but a stop-gap. I thought you'd be out of it long ago, but of course, if Alphonsus hasn't been able to better his position—if indeed as it seems—he's come down a peg instead—well then I think the least he could do would be to come and see me himself and not leave you to do his begging for him."

"Begging! Oh!"

For a minute it was Liddy's stricken face that swam in front of Bedelia, but the next minute she could hardly believe that it was her own little sister who drew herself up all of a sudden, her eyes blazing, her voice a scorpion.

"I'm very glad he didn't come to you, Bedelia," she said. "I wouldn't like anyone, much less Alphonsus, to be hurt like you've hurt me. But before I go, I want you to know one thing—Alphonsus didn't send me. He didn't even know I was coming. And he had no idea of what I was going to ask you." She softened for a minute. "I was going to pretend you suggested it yourself," she said, almost in a whisper. Then she drew herself up again. "I'm sorry I bothered you, Bedelia. Forgive me."

At the door she paused.

"Please don't say anything about this to anyone, Bedelia. After all, we are sisters." She half turned away and then she turned back again. "And just in case you might change your mind, I want you to know I couldn't accept now."

It was the last cut hit Bedelia hardest, because it was just what she was going to do. She already regretted her attitude, and she was at that very minute planning how she'd scribble a note when Liddy was gone and send it up the street after her; to overtake her before she was inside the door of the wretched little house.

But as if she read her mind, Liddy looked at her sadly.

"You see, I couldn't ever pretend now that you had done it of your own accord. It would be telling him a real lie, not just managing things a little bit, making things easy—like I meant it to be!"

She was gone.

"Liddy!"

Bedelia made her way clumsily to the door after her, but she could hear her light feet on the stairs. The next minute she heard the door clapped shut. There was no question of going after her. Bedelia was heavy with child.

It was two months later. Bedelia was once again sitting in the big parlour upstairs, and she was thinking of Liddy. Except when she caught glimpses of her in the street, she had not seen her since she ran down the stairs, and out of the house, her pathetic request ungranted.

Oh, how could she have refused that miserably small favour? How could she have refused her anything: Liddy, her little sister. Only, of course, it wasn't really Liddy she wanted to refuse that day, it was O'Brien. It was him she wanted to humiliate. Oh, how she had grown to hate that fellow. How had she ever consented to his taking Liddy away from her, because, after the tepid experiences of marriage with Daniel, Bedelia had begun to feel, no matter what, no one can ever be as near to you as your own flesh and blood. And although poor Liddy didn't seem to have discovered that fact yet, it only made Bedelia feel more drawn to her, and recalled all her old feelings of motherliness for the child! For to Bedelia as she herself grew heavier in pregnancy, Liddy, when she glimpsed her in the streets, seemed as childish as ever—thinner, if possible, than before she was married.

Oh, what had possessed her that she didn't make more effort to keep her at home?

This was the question that Bedelia asked herself over and over again, and not only did she completely forget the last minute impulse of selfishness that had activated her decision, but she was beginning to think she had erred by being too selfless. And they were both the losers. Liddy's loss was only too obvious, but it was very hard for Bedelia to sit and think of all the help the girl would have been to her in these last few months. To think of the way she could run up and down stairs, and stretch for things, and stoop for things. It would be so different from asking the maids to do things: they were so curious. It nearly drove her into a rage when she caught them covertly glancing at her swollen abdomen.

Vain regrets weren't much use, however, and the most she could hope was that something or other would break Liddy's resolve, and that she would call now and again like she did when she was first married. It wouldn't be the same as having her at hand all the time, and it was irritating the way she kept looking at the clock, but it would be better than nothing. But Liddy's last fling as she ran out the door was to the effect that she'd never set foot in the place again.

It was just as she was thinking of those bitter words that Bedelia heard the footsteps on the stairs, the unmistakable light little steps of Liddy.

There was something wrong though. She sat upright and her hand went to her heart. Always, she was susceptible to wild premonitions of trouble when she heard those flying feet, coming along a passage or as now, upon the stairs. But as she strained to get to her feet, she suddenly sank back again into the chair. For just as the protective waters within her lapped around her embryonic son, securing him from hurt, so in her heart and mind a protective instinct warned her against giving way to shock or distress.

Whatever it was that was wrong, it was not her concern; unless indirectly. She must not let herself become upset. She sat still.

"Oh, Bedelia!"

It was an exclamation, not a greeting; it was a sigh, a gasp, as the young woman entered the room, and closing the door, sank back against it as if exhausted. But the next minute she drew herself together, and even gave a self-critical little smile.

"I never thought I'd set foot in your house again, Bedelia," she said, and to Bedelia there was something preposterously conscious and independent in the words, but the next minute Liddy's voice broke, and a more familiar dependent note came into it.

"But I had to come, Bedelia," she cried. "I had no one else to turn to—no one."

Oh, what satisfaction that last word gave Bedelia.

"Well, what's the matter," she said briskly. "But don't stand there—come in—sit down."

Obediently Liddy moved forward into the room and sat down on the edge of a chair, but almost at once she stood up again.

"It's Alphonsus," she said. "We're in such trouble, Bedelia."

Bedelia tried to look more surprised than she felt.

"It was all my fault, really," cried Liddy. "Only for the way he's always trying to make things easier for me it would never have happened."

Bedelia always hated vagueness.

"What wouldn't have happened?" she asked, sharply.

But it was clear Liddy didn't know how to begin her story.

"Well, you see," she said falteringly, "when we got married Alphonsus wanted to do everything he could to increase his income and so he took on an insurance agency—temporarily, of course, although lots of solicitors do it. He thought he might work it up a bit and that it would bring in a little regular money until his practice grew—you needn't look so contemptuous, Bedelia"—she interrupted suddenly—"the commission wasn't very much, but Alphonsus's idea was to get as many as we could and last month"—here a weak note of pride came into her voice—"last month he collected eleven premiums totalling forty-seven pounds."

Weak and watery as was that little note of pride, it angered Bedelia.

"I presume the forty-seven pounds was the amount of the premiums, not the commission," she said.

"Oh, the premiums of course," said Liddy, somewhat flatter, "the commission was only—"

But here she paused, and almost as if some inspired voice had given her the cue she needed, just at the moment when it had seemed utterly impossible to go on with the story—she threw out her hands and rushed on eagerly.

"That was the beginning of it all," she cried. "The insurance company gives a percentage on each premium but the agent is supposed to make out the amounts himself, subtract his commission, and forward the balance to the head office—it's not fair you know, really—they have such a staff up there and everything, while poor Alphonsus has no one to do anything for him—not yet, I mean."

At this point the voice of the celestial prompter grew faint. Liddy hesitated, "And so he got things a bit mixed up—only in arrears really, but—" Here, however, the voice of the celestial prompter failed utterly. But Bedelia had heard enough.

"Do you mean to tell me he laid hands on it all—the policy money as well as the commission?" she cried, and in spite of nature's elaborate provisions against such contingency, Bedelia's heart began to palpitate, and a pulse began to beat in her temple. She wasn't so indirectly affected at all. She thought it was some trouble that would affect O'Brien only—or at worst the two of them. But if the fellow had converted this money to his own use—newspaper phrases flashed to her mind—well then he might easily bring disgrace on them all.

"Well, answer me! Did he?" she cried.

Although she herself was in a fury, she didn't like the way Liddy's face was quivering.

"I'll have to know sooner or later," she said, more kindly, "you may as well tell me."

But Liddy was crying.

"It's the way you put it," she stammered. "As if he was a thief—"

Bedelia bit back the retort she would liked to have made, and instead she shrugged her shoulders.

"Well," she said then, "what do you want me to do?"

As if she had been running blindly down a wrong pathway and suddenly through the blinding branches had seen another way, the right way, Liddy ran back to Bedelia.

"Oh, Bedelia, all we need is to get an advance on the money—it isn't as if we had to ask you for it outright—it's not even a loan really, because the minute the premiums become due again we'll hand the commission straight over to you—of course it will take a little while, I expect, for it to accrue into the full amount, but you can see, can't you, that it's hardly a loan at all—just an advance."

"Advance—accrue! You've got very glib with financial phrases, I see."

Liddy smiled, or tried to smile. She had foreknown that it would be part of her purgatory to humour Bedelia.

"I've become quite a book-keeper," she said, but as Bedelia said nothing, she looked at her sharply, and then drew back. "You're not going to give it to us!" she said. "I can see by your eyes you're not," and she began to back away from those cold eyes, as from something destructive.

But she didn't go farther than the door, against which she shrank back exhausted. For where could she go?

Bedelia, however, had risen to her feet.

Although she didn't believe the other had strength or spirit left to do what she did last time, flounce away in a temper, she just wasn't going to take any chances this time, and going over to a chest of drawers she took out a black tin box.

Liddy knew that box. There was no need to say anything: Bedelia left it down on the table and let back the lid.

"How much did you say?" she said.

But Liddy was crying; silly hysterical tears.

"Forty-seven—oh, and the commission—I forgot that—but we might be able to make that up ourselves—Oh, Bedelia, I knew you wouldn't fail me—I was only afraid on account of that other time I came about the rent—and that's another thing—I wanted to tell you—you were right about that too—I told Alphonsus and he said you were right, that I shouldn't have asked you: not without telling him, anyway. Oh, you're so good—so kind—"

But Bedelia plunged her hand into the box.

"I'd like to get this settled," she said. "I want to lock the box again. How much did you say?"

"Oh, dear—how much?"

Liddy tried to wipe away the silly tears, tried to think, to calculate. On her fingers she counted up a few figures and then she threw up her hands.

"I'll have to ask Alphonsus," she said. "You see, there's no immediate hurry: the inspector won't be here until the afternoon: I'll have plenty of time to get Alphonsus to make up the amount." She paused. "I'll get him to write it down so I won't forget it," she said.

She wanted Bedelia to see that she was going to be efficient about the whole thing right from the start.

"Liddy, I want to talk to you. Sit down."

Bedelia's voice was so odd that Liddy's eyes flew to the table, as if in doubt of all that had gone before, but no: the box was still there, with the bundle of notes in it held with tape. And to corroborate her previous words, Bedelia was stripping off note after note and counting them, forty, forty-five, fifty. But still, there was that strange, cold note in her voice.

"Sit down," she said again.

Liddy sat down.

"I want to ask you something, Liddy. If I didn't give you this money, what were you going to do?"

For a minute there was silence, then Liddy spoke so low Bedelia had to bend her head to hear her.

"Alphonsus would have to go away," she said in a little dead voice, "until he gathered up the money somewhere," she added with a little more, but not much more, life. Then she looked up straight into Bedelia's eyes. "He would have to go on the four o'clock train this afternoon," she said.

"And leave you to face the music?"

Like a weal from a whiplash the red ran into the younger woman's face. But it was the flush of courage, not shame.

"They couldn't do anything to me," she said, and then she sprang to her feet. "Why are you torturing me like this?" she cried. "Are you going to give it to me or not? Because I don't care! Do you hear that! I don't mind the disgrace. It couldn't be much worse than this. And in any case you'll come in for your share too. Do you think people won't know you refused us!"

"Hush, hush. Stop shouting! Who said I refused you? I didn't refuse you anything. I'm giving it to you," and without finishing the counting, feverishly, anything at all to stop her, Bedelia began to stuff the notes into her hands. "It's only that I want to do my best for you, Liddy. Surely you must know that," she cried, and as she felt the other soften again she led her over to the chair once more. "Liddy," she said softly, tenderly. "Liddy, I want you to ask yourself something. Do you believe in your heart of hearts that Alphonsus will never do this again?"

What is weakness? What is strength? Liddy had stood up to every taunt and vilification, but she wasn't proof against this tenderness.

"Oh, Bedelia," she cried, and she began to cry again.

So many tears; she had shed so many and so many kinds, silly tears, tears of temper and tears of bewilderment, but these were tears of defeat. "I don't know," she said.

"Well, look here!" Bedelia took her hands. "This is the way I see it—I'm going to give you this money, but it's not enough to do just that, I want to do more for you. I want to help your poor husband if I can—help him to help himself, I mean."

Liddy didn't follow.

"Now, listen carefully to me," said Bedelia. "You spoke when I first agreed to help you of conferring with Alphonsus; well, that, I am afraid, I can't allow. This is going to be a matter between you and me"—she paused—"between you and me and the insurance company. I mean Alphonsus is not to know anything at all about it. In fact"—here her voice became so cold and measured that it was as if she were carving the words for ever into the mind of the other—"in fact—he won't know because he will be gone on the four o'clock train. Do you follow?"

No, no! She didn't follow, it would seem, from the way she pressed her hands over her face. But when she took them down again it was clear she partly understood.

"But why?" she cried.

"It will test him out, Liddy. Can't you see that?" she cried. "The other way would be making things too easy for him: it would be doing him harm; moral harm. But this way you save his name—you hand the money over to the company, with some excuse—you might even consider having the agency transferred to your name—but that's another matter—you must let Alphonsus think that it has to be paid back—let him think that he has to send back the money, bit by bit, if necessary, until the whole thing is cleared. And in that way—"

But as at that moment the clock struck three; the sisters both started.

"Is this the only condition on which you'll give the money, Bedelia?" said Liddy quietly.

Bedelia's eyes ran over every cranny of the other's face. For a minute she was almost afraid of what she was doing: afraid of the strain she was putting on the woman in front of her, so thin, so white; so beaten-looking.

But when she had got rid of O'Brien, for a while anyway, and had taken her back into her own care again, it seemed that she could make up to her, make more than amends for what she had to do now. Why, if there were nothing more gained than the opportunity—even for a few months—of feeding her properly and seeing that she had warmer clothes—there would be something to be said for her action.

Why, she could come home again, for the present. And with that thought Bedelia became so pleased that all vestige of doubt vanished from her mind, and she sank back into her chair.

And when, at that minute a button popped off her dress and rolled under the table, she caught herself up in the act of stooping for it. Liddy could do that.

It was two hours later when Liddy came back. The train had gone. Bedelia heard it give a short whistle as it went under the railway bridge at the end of the town, and then a long clear blast as it cut its way into the wide open country beyond the town.

Only a few minutes afterwards there was a noise outside the parlour door, a sound of something heavy bumping, now against the stair treads, now against the banister.

"In the name of God, what is that noise?" cried Bedelia. She thought it was one of the servants.

It was Liddy, and dragging after her, as she came in the door, was their father's big portmanteau that she had taken to carry her things when she left to be married.

"What on earth have you got in the portmanteau," cried Bedelia. She hadn't thought Liddy would have taken her up so quickly about coming back.

"You're welcome, of course," she said, when Liddy, taken aback, began to explain. "I hope there's a bed ready for you, that's all," she said. "You know I can't do anything. I'm doing more than I ought already." But as she saw Liddy's face fall, she tried to be warmer. "It's all right, you know," she said, "it's all right. I meant you to come, only I thought you'd have to make arrangements. I thought it would take you a few days to settle your things, but I dare say you wouldn't have much to attend to in that little poke-hole of a place—"

"Oh, I have lots to do," said Liddy proudly. "I've nothing done at all, I'll have to go back during the daytime, but—" she paused, and involuntarily her glance travelled towards the high window in the gable where the clouds could be seen foregathering in heavy masses on the western horizon.

Bedelia understood, but some unanalysed association of ideas irritated her.

"I thought it was only spinsters that were afraid at night!" she said, but at the same time, prompted by a movement in her body, she knew she must not make those remarks.

If she was to get anything out of the situation; if she was to get some return for taking her back into the house, she'd have to learn not to show those petty vexations.

"Put down that heavy suitcase," she said abruptly.

Was she a fool that she was still holding it all the time, dragging her down to one side?

"Come over to the fire, can't you?" she said, "and sit down. You're tired, I expect. You're very white-looking. When did you eat anything? Are you hungry?"

She was trying to be considerate, but all her questions were irrelevant compared with the one expected question that she could not bring herself to ask. Ask it she must, however.

"Well—how did he go off?" she said abruptly.

For her only answer the tears welled into Liddy's eyes.

"Oh, come now—it's not as bad as all that. You took the only course open to you, you know that!"

But as Liddy's tears still fell silently, Bedelia stood up and looked down at her.

"Oh come, now," she said more kindly. "You'll be hearing from him in a few days: you may have a letter tomorrow if he gets to his destination in time to catch the post tonight—"

As she spoke, however, a new aspect of the thing occurred to her.

"By the way, I didn't ask where he went? Has he any people; any friends or relatives? We never heard of any, I know that," she added quickly, "but I suppose everyone in the world has somewhere to creep when they get into trouble. What's that?"

Liddy had spoken at last, but so softly; only a whisper, that the other had to bend down close to hear her.

"Like I crept back here," that was what she said.

Bedelia looked at her. Was she being clever; trying to get out of telling his whereabouts?

"You didn't say where he was going," she persisted doggedly. "Are you afraid to divulge his whereabouts in case something else comes to light about him? I'd hardly give him away—now!"

It was cruel, but it wasn't cruel enough to make Liddy open her mouth. Bedelia stood over her.

"Perhaps you don't know yourself," said Bedelia, moving nearer to her until she was directly over her like a prosecutor.

But she had to stand back suddenly as Liddy got to her feet unsteadily and swayed forward with her hand on her stomach.

"I think I'm going to be sick, Bedelia," she said, with a mawkish irrelevance.

It was such a shock. Bedelia gave a shout.

"Not on the carpet," she screamed, and frantically she pulled out a handkerchief from her sleeve. "Here, take this—try to swallow. Breathe—take a deep breath—it will pass off in a minute."

So it did; it was only a gust of nausea.

Liddy handed back the handkerchief and tried to smile bleakly through her tears.

"I'm all right now," she said.

It was Bedelia who looked bad now; she sank down on a chair.

"I must say it's a queer way it took you!" she said crossly, and she placed her hand on her own stomach. "You gave me such a start."

Liddy saw the enormity of her offence.

"It must have been the portmanteau," she said apologetically, "the weight of it, I mean," she said, and then gulping she came to a quick decision. "I didn't tell you, Bedelia," she said, "but I'm not supposed to lift anything heavy just now—"

"Good God!"

Heavy and all as she was, awkward and clumsy, Bedelia was on her feet again in an instant.

"You don't mean—" Oh, but it was absolutely—oh, but absolutely unbelievable. It was the last straw. Why, she felt as if she had been tricked—as if between them they had made a fool of her, Liddy and O'Brien, both of them. "Why didn't you tell me this before now?"

she screamed, and as she screamed one question, others swarmed in her mind. What use would the creature be to her in this condition?

This condition: it revolted her to think of the two of them—two of them!—in the same condition, in the one house—one as useless as the other as the days went on.

And this other brat when he was born—what was going to become of him? Would she and Daniel have to rear him too, as well as their own? And for how long?

Before her mind's eye, she saw the face of Alphonsus O'Brien but it was as ever inscrutable.

She swung around. She forgot all her other questions.

"Might I ask one thing," she cried. "Did he know about this when he embezzled the funds, or did it come as a glorious surprise to him afterwards?"

Liddy hesitated for a minute before she answered, but her tears had dried, and she was looking steadily into Bedelia's eyes.

"He didn't know," she said calmly. "He doesn't know even now! I didn't tell him at all!"

"You didn't what?" Bedelia's voice had gone; she could say nothing now except in a shrill scream.

"I didn't tell him," Liddy repeated quietly. Her voice was growing in confidence. "I was going to tell him the very night—the night he had to tell me about the money and so I didn't tell him after all!"

"Why?"

"I wanted to keep it till—"

Anyone—anyone, even Bedelia, could see what she waited for; the hope that the clouds would be dispelled and the sun would shine again, and her secret be given its golden due.

Even Bedelia could see that was why she waited: could see but could not endure the sight.

"You fool," she cried. "There may be a time for sentimentality of that kind, but this wasn't the time! You let him get away without knowing the full extent of his responsibilities. What in the name of God were you thinking about?"

Liddy's mind, however, was in no confusion.

"I knew what I was doing, Bedelia," she said. "I wouldn't have told him for anything. I wouldn't have made things harder for him. He mightn't have been able to make up his mind if he knew—or not so quickly, anyway."

Just like the day she announced that he wanted to marry her there was a radiance and glory about her that Bedelia could not but perceive. Nor could she see whence came this ambience, or why it should be her due.

"I must say it's easy to be noble at the expense of others," she said. "Have you thought about us—about me and my husband? It was one thing to have you here—for a while—by yourself—till he sent for you—you might even have been some help in the house—Daniel would have been only too pleased, but how will he take it now—when I have to tell him we're saddled with rearing another man's brat! And for how long? That's the question."

It was the all-important question.

Yet Liddy never seemed to have pondered it at all. Her body, beautiful, frail even in its fertility, was still a vessel for some secret happiness Bedelia never knew, and although she hadn't known it, what she wanted, all the time, was to break it. She thrust herself forward, thrust her face, that was swollen with the strain she had undergone into the face, still so serene, in front of her.

"Do you know what I think?" she cried. "I think you've seen the last of him—do you hear me—the last of him!"

But she couldn't make out whether Liddy had heard or not. Certainly her reply, which came in a whisper, was absolutely inexplicable.

"Even so!" Liddy whispered. "Even so!"

JOÃO GUIMARÃES ROSA

(1908–1967)

The Third Bank of the River

ENGLISH TRANSLATION BY WILLIAM GROSSMAN

About the Author: João Guimarães Rosa, born in Brazil, served in various European countries as a member of Brazil's diplomatic corps, and, before his death, held a high position in the Ministry of Foreign Affairs. He was also considered his country's foremost fiction writer, publishing three collections of short stories, a two-volume edition of novellas, and a novel, *The Devil to Pay in the Backlands.* In 1963, he was made a member of the Brazilian Academy of Letters.

My father was a dutiful, orderly, straightforward man. And according to several reliable people of whom I inquired, he had had these qualities since adolescence or even childhood. By my own recollection, he was neither jollier nor more melancholy than the other men we knew. Maybe a little quieter. It was mother, not father, who ruled the house. She scolded us daily—my sister, my brother, and me. But it happened one day that father ordered a boat.

He was very serious about it. It was to be made specially for him, of mimosa wood. It was to be sturdy enough to last twenty or thirty years and just large enough for one person. Mother carried on plenty about it. Was her husband going to become a fisherman all of a sudden? Or a hunter? Father said nothing. Our house was less than a mile from the river, which around there was deep, quiet, and so wide you couldn't see across it.

I can never forget the day the rowboat was delivered. Father showed no joy or other emotion. He just put on his hat as he always did and said goodbye to us. He took along no food or bundle of any sort. We expected mother to rant and rave, but she didn't. She looked very pale and bit her lip, but all she said was:

"If you go away, stay away. Don't ever come back!"

Father made no reply. He looked gently at me and motioned me to walk along with him. I feared mother's wrath, yet I eagerly obeyed. We headed toward the river together. I felt bold and exhilarated, so much so that I said:

"Father, will you take me with you in your boat?"

He just looked at me, gave me his blessing, and, by a gesture, told me to go back. I made as if to do so but, when his back was turned, I ducked behind some bushes to watch him. Father got into the boat and rowed away. Its shadow slid across the water like a crocodile, long and quiet.

Father did not come back. Nor did he go anywhere, really. He just rowed and floated across and around, out there in the river. Everyone was appalled. What had never happened, what could not possibly happen, was happening. Our relatives, neighbors, and friends came over to discuss the phenomenon.

Mother was ashamed. She said little and conducted herself with great composure. As a consequence, almost everyone thought (though no one said it) that father had gone insane. A few, however, suggested that father might be fulfilling a promise he had made to God or to a saint, or that he might have some horrible disease, maybe leprosy, and that he left for the sake of the family, at the same time wishing to remain fairly near them.

Travelers along the river and people living near the bank on one side or the other reported that father never put foot on land, by day or night. He just moved about on the river, solitary, aimless, like a derelict. Mother and our relatives agreed that the food which he had doubtless hidden in the boat would soon give out and that then he would either leave the river and travel off somewhere (which would be at least a little more respectable) or he would repent and come home.

How far from the truth they were! Father had a secret source of provisions: me. Every day I stole food and brought it to him. The first night after he left, we all lit fires on the shore and prayed and called to him. I was deeply distressed and felt a need to do something more. The following day I went down to the river with a loaf of corn bread, a bunch of bananas, and some bricks of raw brown sugar. I waited impatiently a long, long hour. Then I saw the boat, far off, alone, gliding almost imperceptibly on the smoothness of the river. Father was sitting in the bottom of the boat. He saw me but he did not row toward me or make any gesture. I showed him the food and then I placed it in a hollow rock on the river bank; it was safe there from animals, rain, and dew. I did this day after day, on and on and on. Later I learned, to my surprise, that mother knew what I was doing and left food around where I could easily steal it. She had a lot of feelings she didn't show.

Mother sent for her brother to come and help on the farm and in business matters. She had the schoolteacher come and tutor us children at home because of the time we had lost. One day, at her request, the priest put on his vestments, went down to the shore, and tried to exorcise the devils that had got into my father. He shouted that father had a duty to cease his unholy obstinacy. Another day she arranged to have two soldiers come and try to frighten him. All to no avail. My father went by in the distance, sometimes so far away he could barely be seen. He never replied to anyone and no one ever got close to him. When some newspapermen came in a launch to take his picture, father headed his boat to the other side of the river and into the marshes, which he knew like the palm of his hand but in which other people quickly got lost. There in his private maze, which extended for miles, with heavy foliage overhead and rushes on all sides, he was safe.

We had to get accustomed to the idea of father's being out on the river. We had to but we couldn't, we never could. I think I was the only one who understood to some degree what our father wanted and what he did not want. The thing I could not understand at all was how he stood the hardship. Day and night, in sun and rain, in heat and in the terrible midyear cold spells, with his old hat on his head and very little other clothing, week after week, month after month, year after year, unheedful of the waste and emptiness in which his life was slipping by. He never set foot on earth or grass, on isle or mainland shore. No doubt he sometimes tied up the boat at a secret place, perhaps at the tip of some island, to get a little sleep. He never lit a fire or even struck a match and he had no flashlight. He took only a small part of the food that I left in the hollow rock—not enough, it seemed to me, for survival. What could his state of health have been? How about the continual drain on his energy, pulling and pushing the oars to control the boat? And how did he survive the annual floods, when the river rose and swept along with it all sorts of dangerous objects—branches of trees, dead bodies of animals—that might suddenly crash against his little boat?

He never talked to a living soul. And we never talked about him. We just thought. No,

we could never put our father out of mind. If for a short time we seemed to, it was just a lull from which we would be sharply wakened by the realization of his frightening situation.

My sister got married, but mother didn't want a wedding party. It would have been a sad affair, for we thought of him every time we ate some especially tasty food. Just as we thought of him in our cozy beds on a cold, stormy night, out there, alone and unprotected, trying to bail out the boat with only his hands and a gourd. Now and then someone would say that I was getting to look more and more like my father. But I knew that by then his hair and beard must have been shaggy and his nails long. I pictured him thin and sickly, black with hair and sunburn, and almost naked despite the articles of clothing I occasionally left for him.

He didn't seem to care about us at all. But I felt affection and respect for him, and, whenever they praised me because I had done something good, I said:

"My father taught me to act that way."

It wasn't exactly accurate but it was a truthful sort of lie. As I said, father didn't seem to care about us. But then why did he stay around there? Why didn't he go up the river or down the river, beyond the possibility of seeing us or being seen by us? He alone knew the answer.

My sister had a baby boy. She insisted on showing father his grandson. One beautiful day we all went down to the river bank, my sister in her white wedding dress, and she lifted the baby high. Her husband held a parasol above them. We shouted to father and waited. He did not appear. My sister cried; we all cried in each other's arms.

My sister and her husband moved far away. My brother went to live in a city. Times changed, with their usual imperceptible rapidity. Mother finally moved too; she was old and went to live with her daughter. I remained behind, a leftover. I could never think of marrying. I just stayed there with the impedimenta of my life. Father, wandering alone and forlorn on the river, needed me. I knew he needed me, although he never even told me why he was doing it. When I put the question to people bluntly and insistently, all they told me was that they heard that father had explained it to the man who made the boat. But now this man was dead and nobody knew or remembered anything. There was just some foolish talk, when the rains were especially severe and persistent, that my father was wise like Noah and had the boat built in anticipation of a new flood; I dimly remember people saying this. In any case, I would not condemn my father for what he was doing. My hair was beginning to turn gray.

I have only sad things to say. What bad had I done, what was my great guilt? My father always away and his absence always with me. And the river, always the river, perpetually renewing itself. The river, always. I was beginning to suffer from old age, in which life is just a sort of lingering. I had attacks of illness and of anxiety. I had a nagging rheumatism. And he? Why, why was he doing it? He must have been suffering terribly. He was so old. One day, in his failing strength, he might let the boat capsize; or he might let the current carry it downstream, on and on, until it plunged over the waterfall to the boiling turmoil below. It pressed upon my heart. He was out there and I was forever robbed of my peace. I am guilty of I know not what, and my pain is an open wound inside me. Perhaps I would know—if things were different. I began to guess what was wrong.

Out with it! Had I gone crazy? No, in our house that word was never spoken, never through all the years. No one called anybody crazy, for nobody is crazy. Or maybe everybody. All I did was go there and wave a handkerchief. So he would be more likely to

see me. I was in complete command of myself. I waited. Finally he appeared in the distance, there, then over there, a vague shape sitting in the back of the boat. I called to him several times. And I said what I was so eager to say, to state formally and under oath. I said it as loud as I could:

"Father, you have been out there long enough. You are old. . . . Come back, you don't have to do it anymore. . . . Come back, and I'll go instead. Right now, if you want. Any time. I'll get into the boat. I'll take your place."

And when I had said this my heart beat more firmly.

He heard me. He stood up. He maneuvered with his oars and headed the boat toward me. He had accepted my offer. And suddenly I trembled, down deep. For he had raised his arm and waved—the first time in so many, so many years. And I couldn't . . . In terror, my hair on end, I ran, I fled madly. For he seemed to come from another world. And I'm begging forgiveness, begging, begging.

I experienced the dreadful sense of cold that comes from deadly fear, and I became ill. Nobody ever saw or heard about him again. Am I a man, after such a failure? I am what never should have been. I am what must be silent. I know it is too late. I must stay in the deserts and unmarked plains of my life, and I fear I shall shorten it. But when death comes I want them to take me and put me in a little boat in this perpetual water between the long shores; and I, down the river, lost in the river, inside the river . . . the river . . .

JOHN UPDIKE

(1932–)

A Sense of Shelter

About the Author: John Updike grew up in Shillington, Pennsylvania, renamed Olinger in his fictional recreations of his early years in such collections as *Pigeon Feathers* (1962). He has published more than three dozen books—poetry, criticism, and memoirs in addition to short stories and novels. Updike's fiction has won numerous awards, including the Pulitzer Prize in 1981 for *Rabbit Is Rich* and in 1991 for *Rabbit at Rest.*

Snow fell against the high school all day, wet big-flaked snow that did not accumulate well. Sharpening two pencils, William looked down on a parking lot that was a blackboard in reverse, car tires had cut smooth arcs of black into the white, and wherever a school bus had backed around, it had left an autocratic signature of two *V*'s. The snow, though at moments it whirled opaquely, could not quite bleach these scars away. The temperature must be exactly 32°. The window was open a crack, and a canted pane of glass lifted outdoor air into his face, coating the cedarwood scent of pencil shavings with the transparent odor of the wet window sill. With each revolution of the handle his knuckles came within a fraction of an inch of the tilted glass, and the faint chill this proximity breathed on them sharpened his already acute sense of shelter.

The sky behind the shreds of snow was stone-colored. The murk inside the high classroom gave the air a solidity that limited the overhead radiance to its own vessels; six globes of dull incandescence floated on the top of a thin sea. The feeling the gloom gave him was not gloomy but joyous: he felt they were all sealed in, safe; the colors of cloth were dyed deeper, the sound of whispers was made more distinct, the smells of tablet paper and wet shoes and varnish and face powder pierced him with a vivid sense of possession. These were his classmates sealed in, his, the stupid as well as the clever, the plain as well as the lovely, his enemies as well as his friends, his. He felt like a king and seemed to move to his seat between the bowed heads of subjects that loved him less than he loved them. His seat was sanctioned by tradition; for twelve years he had sat at the rear of classrooms, William Young, flanked by Marsha Wyckoff and Andy Zimmerman. Once there had been two Zimmermans, but one went to work in his father's greenhouse, and in some classes—Latin and Trig—there were none, and William sat at the edge of the class as if on the lip of a cliff, and Marsha Wyckoff became Marvin Wolf or Sandra Wade, but it was always the same desk, whose surface altered from hour to hour but from whose blue-stained ink-hole his mind could extract, like a chain of magicians' handkerchiefs, a continuity of years. As a senior he was a kind of king, and as a teacher's pet another kind, a puppet king, who gathered in appointive posts and even, when the moron vote split between two football heroes, some elective ones. He was not popular, he had never had a girl, his intense friends of childhood had drifted off into teams and gangs, and in large groups—when the whole school, for instance, went in the fall to the beautiful, dung-and-cotton-candy-smelling county fair—he was always an odd man, without a seat on the bus home. But exclusion is itself a form of inclusion. He even had a nickname: Mip, because he stuttered. Taunts no longer much frightened him; he had come late into his physical inheritance, but this summer it had arrived, and he at last stood equal with his enormous, boisterous parents, and had to unbutton his shirt cuffs to get his wrists through them, and discovered he could pick up a basketball with one hand. So, his long legs blocking two aisles, he felt regal even in size and, almost trembling with happiness under the high globes of light beyond whose lunar glow invisible snowflakes were drowning on the gravel roof of his castle, believed that the long delay of unpopularity had been merely a consolidation, that he was at last strong enough to make his move. Today he would tell Mary Landis he loved her.

He had loved her ever since, a fat-faced tomboy with freckles and green eyes, she deftly stole his rubber-lined schoolbag on the walk back from second grade along Jewett Street and outran him—simply had better legs. The superior speed a boy was supposed to have failed to come; his kidneys burned with panic. In front of the grocery store next to her home she stopped and turned. She was willing to have him catch up. This humiliation on top of the rest was too much to bear. Tears broke in his throat; he spun around and ran home and threw himself on the floor of the front parlor, where his grandfather, feet twiddling, perused the newspaper and soliloquized all morning. In time the letter slot rustled, and the doorbell rang, and Mary gave his mother the schoolbag and the two of them politely exchanged whispers. Their voices had been to him, lying there on the carpet with his head wrapped in his arms, indistinguishable. Mother had always liked Mary. From when she had been a tiny girl dancing along the hedge on the end of an older sister's arm, Mother had liked her. Out of all the children that flocked, similar as pigeons, through the neighborhood, Mother's heart had reached out with claws and fastened on Mary. He never took the schoolbag to school again, had refused to touch it. He supposed it was still in the attic, still faintly smelling of sweet pink rubber.

Fixed high on the plaster like a wren clinging to a barn wall, the buzzer sounded the two-minute signal. In the middle of the classroom Mary Landis stood up, a Monitor badge pinned to her belly. Her broad red belt was buckled with a brass bow and arrow. She wore a lavender sweater with the sleeves pushed up to expose her forearms, a delicately cheap effect. Wild stories were told about her; perhaps it was merely his knowledge of these that put the hardness in her face. Her eyes seemed braced for squinting and their green was frosted. Her freckles had faded. William thought she laughed less this year; now that she was in the Secretarial Course and he in the College Preparatory, he saw her in only one class a day, this one, English. She stood a second, eclipsed at the thighs by Jack Stephens' zebra-striped shoulders, and looked back at the class with a stiff worn glance, as if she had seen the same faces too many times before. Her habit of perfect posture emphasized the angularity she had grown into. There was a nervous edge, a boxiness in her bones, that must have been waiting all along under the childish fat. Her eye sockets were deeply indented and her chin had a prim square set that seemed in the murky air tremulous and defiant. Her skirt was cut square and straight. Below the waist she was lean; the legs that had outrun him were still athletic; she starred at hockey and cheerleading. Above, she was abundant: so stacked her spine curved backwards to keep her body balanced. She turned and in switching up the aisle encountered a boy's leg thrown into her path. She coolly looked down until it withdrew. She was used to such attentions. Her pronged chest poised, Mary proceeded out the door, and someone she saw in the hall made her smile, a wide smile full of warmth and short white teeth, and love scooped at William's heart. He would tell her.

In another minute, the second bell rasped. Shuffling through the perfumed crowds to his next class, he crooned to himself in the slow, over-enunciated manner of the Negro vocalist who had brought the song back this year:

"Lah-vender blue, dilly dilly,
Lavendih gree-heen;
Eef I were king, dilly dilly,
You would: be queen."

The song gave him an exultant sliding sensation that intertwined with the pleasures of his day. He knew all the answers, he had done all the work, the teachers called upon him only to rebuke the ignorance of the others. In Trig and Soc Sci both it was this way. In gym, the fourth hour of the morning, he, who was always picked near the last, startled his side by excelling at volleyball, leaping like a madman, shouting like a bully. The ball felt light as a feather against his big bones. His hair in wet quills from the shower, he walked in the icy air to Luke's Luncheonette, where he ate three hamburgers in a booth with three juniors. There was Barry Kruppman, a tall, thyroid-eyed boy who came on the school bus from the country town of Bowsville and who was an amateur hypnotist; he told the tale of a Portland, Oregon, businessman who under hypnosis had been taken back through sixteen reincarnations to the condition of an Egyptian concubine in the household of a high priest of Isis. There was his friend Lionel Griffin, a pudgy simp whose blond hair puffed out above his ears in two slick waxed wings. He was rumored to be a fairy, and in fact did seem most excited by the transvestite aspect of the soul's transmigration. And there was Lionel's girl Virginia, a drab little mystery who chain-smoked Herbert Tareytons and never said anything. She had sallow skin and smudged eyes and Lionel kept jabbing her and shrieking, making William wince. He would rather have sat with members of his own class, who filled the other booths, but he would have had to force himself on them. These juniors admired him and welcomed his company. He asked, "Wuh-well, was he ever a c-c-c-cockroach, like Archy?"

Kruppman's face grew intense; his furry lids dropped down over the bulge of his eyes, and when they drew back, his pupils were as small and hard as BBs. "That's the really interesting thing. There was this gap, see, between his being a knight under Charlemagne and then a sailor on a ship putting out from Macedonia—that's where Yugoslavia is now—in the time of Nero; there was this gap, when the only thing the guy would do was walk around the office snarling and growling, see, like this." Kruppman worked his blotched ferret face up into a snarl and Griffin shrieked. "He tried to bite one of the assistants and they think that for six hundred years"—the uncanny, unhealthy seriousness of his whisper hushed Griffin momentarily—"for six hundred years he just was a series of wolves. Probably in the German forests. You see, when he was in Macedonia"—his whisper barely audible—"he murdered a woman."

Griffin squealed in ecstasy and cried, "Oh, Kruppman! Kruppman, how you do go on!" and jabbed Virginia in the arm so hard a Herbert Tareyton jumped from her hand and bobbled across the Formica table. William gazed over their heads in pain.

The crowds at the soda counter had thinned so that when the door to the outside opened he saw Mary come in and hesitate there for a second where the smoke inside and the snow outside swirled together. The mixture made a kind of—Kruppman's ridiculous story had put the phrase in his head—wolf-weather, and she was just a gray shadow caught in it alone. She bought a pack of cigarettes from Luke and went out again, a kerchief around her head, the pneumatic thing above the door hissing behind her. For a long time, always in fact, she had been at the center of whatever gang was the one: in the second grade the one that walked home up Jewett Street together, and in the sixth grade the one that went bicycling as far away as the quarry and the Rentschler estate and played touch football Saturday afternoons, and in the ninth grade the one that went roller-skating at Candlebridge Park with the tenth-grade boys, and in the eleventh grade the one that held parties lasting past midnight and that on Sundays drove in caravans as far as Philadelphia and back. And all the while there had been a succession of boy friends, first Jack Stephens and Fritz March in their class and then boys a grade ahead and then Barrel Lord, who was a senior when they were sophomores and whose name was in the newspapers all football season, and then this last summer someone out of the school altogether, a man she met while working as a waitress in the city of Alton. So this year her weekends were taken up, and the party gang carried on as if she had never existed, and nobody saw her much except in school and when she stopped by in Luke's to buy a pack of cigarettes. Her silhouette against the big window had looked wan, her head hooded, her face nibbled by light, her fingers fiddling on the veined counter with her coins. He yearned to reach out, to comfort her, but he was wedged deep in the shrill booths, between the jingling guts of the pinball machine and the hillbilly joy of the jukebox. The impulse left him with a disagreeable feeling. He had loved her too long to want to pity her; it endangered the investment of worship on which he had not yet realized any return.

The two hours of the school afternoon held Latin and a study hall. In study hall, while the five people at the table with him played tic-tac-toe and sucked cough drops and yawned, he did all his homework for the next day. He prepared thirty lines of Vergil, Aeneas in the Underworld. The study hall was a huge low room in the basement of the building; its coziness crept into Tartarus. On the other side of the fudge-colored wall the circular saw in the woodworking shop whined and gasped and then whined again; it bit off pieces of wood with a rising, somehow terrorized inflection—bzzzz*zup!* He solved ten problems in trigonometry. His mind cut neatly through their knots and separated them, neat stiff squares of answer, one by one from the long but finite plank of problems that connected Plane Geometry with Solid. Lastly, as the snow on a ragged slant drifted down into the cement pits outside the steel-mullioned windows, he read a short story by Edgar Allan Poe. He closed the book softly on the pleasing sonority of its final note of horror, gazed at the red, wet, menthol-scented inner membrane of Judy Whipple's yawn, rimmed with flaking pink lipstick, and yielded his conscience to the snug sense of his work done, of the snow falling, of the warm minutes that walked through their shelter so slowly. The perforated acoustic tiling above his head seemed the lining of a long tube that would go all the way: high school merging into college, college into graduate school, graduate school into teaching at a college—section man, assistant, associate, *full* professor, possessor of a dozen languages and a thousand books, a man brilliant in his forties, wise in his fifties, renowned in his sixties, revered in his seventies, and then retired, sitting in the study lined with acoustical books until the time came for the last transition from silence to silence, and he would die, like Tennyson, with a copy of *Cymbeline* beside him on the moon-drenched bed.

After school he had to go to Room 101 and cut a sports cartoon into a stencil for the school paper. He liked the building best when it was nearly empty, when the casual residents—the rural commuters, the do-nothings, the trash—had cleared out. Then the janitors went down the halls sowing seeds of red wax and making an immaculate harvest with broad brooms, gathering all the fluff and hairpins and wrappers and powder that the animals had dropped that day. The basketball team thumped in the hollow gymnasium; the cheerleaders rehearsed behind drawn curtains on the stage. In Room 101 two empty-headed typists with stripes bleached into their hair banged away between giggles and mistakes. At her desk Mrs. Gregory, the faculty sponsor, wearily passed her pencil through misspelled news copy on tablet paper. William took the shadow box from the top of the filing cabinet and the styluses and little square plastic shading screens from their drawer and the stencil from the closet where the typed stencils hung, like fragile scarves, on hooks. B-BALLERS BOW, 57-42, was the headline. He drew a tall b-baller bowing to a stumpy pagan idol, labelled "W" for victorious Weiserton High, and traced it in the soft blue wax with the fine loop stylus. His careful breath grazed his knuckles. His eyebrows frowned while his heart bobbed happily on the giddy prattle of the typists. The shadow box was simply a black frame holding a pane of glass and lifted at one end by two legs so the light bulb, fitted in a tin tray, could slide under; it was like a primitive lean-to sheltering a fire. As he worked, his eyes smarting, he mixed himself up with the light bulb, felt himself burning under a slanting roof upon which a huge hand scratched. The glass grew hot; the danger in the job was pulling the softened wax with your damp hand, distorting or tearing the typed letters. Sometimes the center of an *o* stuck to your skin like a bit of blue confetti. But he was expert and cautious. He returned the things to their places feeling airily tall, heightened by Mrs. Gregory's appreciation, which she expressed by keeping her back turned, in effect stating that other staff members were undependable but William did not need to be watched.

In the hall outside Room 101 only the shouts of a basketball scrimmage reverberated; the chant of the cheerleaders had been silenced. Though he had done everything, he felt reluctant to leave. Neither of his parents—both worked—would be home yet, and this building was as much his home. He knew all its nooks. On the second floor of the annex, beyond the art room, there was a strange, narrow boys' lavatory that no one ever seemed to use. It was here one time that Barry Kruppman tried to hypnotize him and cure his stuttering. Kruppman's voice purred and his irises turned tiny in the bulging whites and for a moment William felt himself lean backward involuntarily, but he was distracted by the

bits of bloodshot pink in the corners of these portentous eyes; the folly of giving up his will to an intellectual inferior occurred to him; he refused to let go and go under, and perhaps therefore his stuttering had continued.

The frosted window at the end of the long room cast a watery light on the green floor and made the porcelain urinals shine like slices of moon. The semi-opacity of this window gave the room's air of secrecy great density. William washed his hands with exaggerated care, enjoying the lavish amount of powdered soap provided for him in this castle. He studied his face in the mirror, making infinitesimal adjustments to attain the absolutely most flattering angle, and then put his hands below his throat to get their strong, long-fingered beauty into the picture. As he walked toward the door he sang, closing his eyes and gasping as if he were a real Negro whose entire career depended upon this recording:

"Who—told me so, dilly dilly,
Who told me soho?
Aii told myself, dilly dilly,
I told: me so."

When he emerged into the hall it was not empty: one girl walked down its varnished perspective toward him, Mary Landis, a scarf on her head and books in her arms. Her locker was up here, on the second floor of the annex. His own was in the annex basement. A tickling sensation that existed neither in the medium of sound nor of light crowded against his throat. She flipped the scarf back from her hair and in a conversational voice that carried well down the clean planes of the hall said, "Hi, Billy." The name came from way back, when they were both children, and made him feel small but brave.

"Hi. How are you?"

"Fine." Her smile broadened out from the *F* of this word.

What was so funny? Was she really, as it seemed, pleased to see him? "Du-did you just get through cheer-cheer-cheer-leading?"

"Yes. Thank God. *Oh* she's so awful. She makes us do the same stupid locomotives for every cheer; I told her, no wonder nobody cheers any more."

"This is M-M-Miss Potter?" He blushed, feeling that he made an ugly face in getting past the *M.* When he got caught in the middle of a sentence the constriction was somehow worse. He admired the way words poured up her throat, distinct and petulant.

"Yes, Potbottom Potter," she said, "she's just aching for a man and takes it out on us. I wish she would get one. Honestly, Billy, I have half a mind to quit. I'll be so glad when June comes, I'll never set foot in this idiotic building again."

Her lips, pale with the lipstick worn off, crinkled bitterly. Her face, foreshortened from the height of his eyes, looked cross as a cat's. It a little shocked him that poor Miss Potter and this kind, warm school stirred her to what he had to take as actual anger; this grittiness in her was the first abrasive texture he had struck today. Couldn't she see around teachers, into their fatigue, their poverty, their fear? It had been so long since he had spoken to her, he wasn't sure how coarse she had become. "Don't quit," he brought out of his mouth at last. "It'd be n-n-n-nuh—it'd be nothing without you."

He pushed open the door at the end of the hall for her and as she passed under his arm she looked up and said, "Why, aren't you sweet?"

The stairwell, all asphalt and iron, smelled of galoshes. It felt more secret than the hall,

more specially theirs; there was something magical in its shifting multiplicity of planes as they descended that lifted the spell on his tongue, so that words came as quickly as his feet pattered on the steps.

"No I mean it," he said, "you're really a beautiful cheerleader. But then you're beautiful period."

"I've skinny legs."

"Who told you that?"

"Somebody."

"Well *he* wasn't very sweet."

"No."

"Why do you hate this poor old school?"

"Now Billy. You know you don't care about this junky place any more than I do."

"I love it. It breaks my heart to hear you say you want to get out, because then I'll never see you again."

"You don't care, do you?"

"Why sure I care; you *know*"—their feet stopped; they had reached bottom, the first-floor landing, two brass-barred doors and a grimy radiator—"I've always li-loved you."

"You don't mean that."

"I do too. It's ridiculous but there it is. I wanted to tell you today and now I have."

He expected her to laugh and go out the door, but instead she showed an unforseeable willingness to discuss this awkward matter. He should have realized before this that women enjoy being talked to. "It's a very silly thing to say," she asserted tentatively.

"I don't see why," he said, fairly bold now that he couldn't seem more ridiculous, and yet picking his words with a certain strategic care. "It's not *that* silly to love somebody, I mean what the hell. Probably what's silly is not to do anything about it for umpteen years but then I never had an opportunity, I thought."

He set his books down on the radiator and she set hers down beside his. "What kind of opportunity were you waiting for?"

"Well, see, that's it; I didn't know." He wished, in a way, she would go out the door. But she had propped herself against the wall and plainly awaited more talking. "Yuh-you were such a queen and I was such a nothing and I just didn't really want to presume." It wasn't very interesting; it puzzled him that she seemed to be interested. Her face had grown quite stern, the mouth very small and thoughtful, and he made a gesture with his hands intended to release her from the bother of thinking about it; after all, it was just a disposition of his heart, nothing permanent or expensive; perhaps it was just his mother's idea anyway. Half in impatience to close the account, he asked, "Will you marry me?"

"You don't want to marry me," she said. "You're going to go on and be a great man."

He blushed in pleasure; is this how she saw him, is this how they all saw him; as worthless now, but in time a great man? Had his hopes always been on view? He dissembled, saying, "No I'm not. But anyway, you're great now. You're so pretty, Mary."

"Oh, Billy," she said, "if you were me for just one day you'd hate it."

She said this rather blankly, watching his eyes; he wished her voice had shown more misery. In his world of closed surfaces a panel, carelessly pushed, had opened, and he hung in this openness paralyzed, unable to think what to say. Nothing he could think of quite fit the abruptly immense context. The radiator cleared its throat; its heat made, in the intimate volume just this side of the doors on whose windows the snow beat limply, a provocative

snugness; he supposed he should try, and stepped forward, his hands lifting toward her shoulders. Mary sidestepped between him and the radiator and put the scarf back on. She lifted the cloth like a broad plaid halo above her head and then wrapped it around her chin and knotted it so she looked, in her red galoshes and bulky coat, like a peasant woman in a movie of Europe. With her thick hair swathed, her face seemed pale and chunky, and when she recradled the books in her arms her back bent humbly under the point of the kerchief. "It's too hot in here," she said. "I've got to wait for somebody." The disconnectedness of the two statements seemed natural in the fragmented atmosphere his stops and starts had produced. She bucked the brass bar with her shoulder and the door slammed open; he followed her into the weather.

"For the person who thinks your legs are too skinny?"

"Uh-huh." As she looked up at him a snowflake caught on the lashes of one eye. She jerkily rubbed that cheek on the shoulder of her coat and stamped a foot, splashing slush. Cold water gathered on the back of his thin shirt. He put his hands in his pockets and pressed his arms against his sides to keep from shivering.

"Thuh-then you wo-won't marry me?" His wise instinct told him the only way back was by going forward, through absurdity.

"We don't know each other," she said.

"My God," he said. "Why not? I've known you since I was two."

"What do you know about me?"

This awful seriousness of hers; he must dissolve it. "That you're not a virgin." But instead of making her laugh this made her face go dead and turned it away. Like beginning to kiss her, it was a mistake; in part, he felt grateful for his mistakes. They were like loyal friends who are nevertheless embarrassing. "What do you know about *me?"* he asked, setting himself up for a finishing insult but dreading it. He hated the stiff feel of his smile between his cheeks; glimpsed, as if the snow were a mirror, how hateful he looked.

"That you're basically very nice."

Her returning good for evil blinded him to his physical discomfort, set him burning with regret. "Listen," he said, "I did love you. Let's at least get that straight."

"You never loved anybody," she said. "You don't know what it is."

"O.K." he said. "Pardon me."

"You're excused."

"You better wait in the school," he told her. "He's-eez-eez going to be a long time."

She didn't answer and walked a little distance, toeing out in the childish Dutch way common to the women in this county, along the slack cable that divided the parking lot from the softball field. One bicycle, rusted as if it had been there for years, leaned in the rack, its fenders supporting airy crescents of white.

The warmth inside the door felt heavy. William picked up his books and ran his pencil along the black ribs of the radiator before going down the stairs to his locker in the annex basement. The shadows were thick at the foot of the steps; suddenly it felt late, he must hurry and get home. He was seized by the irrational fear that they were going to lock him in. The cloistered odors of paper, sweat, and, from the woodshop at the far end of the basement hall, sawdust no longer flattered him. The tall green double lockers appeared to study him critically through the three air slits near their tops. When he opened his locker, and put his books on his shelf, below Marvin Wolf's, and removed his coat from his hook, his self seemed to crawl into the long dark space thus made vacant, the humiliated ugly, educable self. In answer to a flick of his great hand the steel door weightlessly floated shut and through the length of his body he felt so clean and free he smiled. Between now and the happy future predicted for him he had nothing, almost literally nothing, to do.

GABRIEL GARCÍA MÁRQUEZ

(1928–)

Balthazar's Marvelous Afternoon

About the Author: Winner of the 1982 Nobel Prize for Literature, Gabriel García Márquez was born in Aratacata, Colombia, where he was brought up in extreme poverty, the oldest of twelve children. Aside from his literary endeavors, he has been employed in South America and Europe as journalist and film reviewer. For a decade ending in 1968 García Márquez worked as a publicist, screen writer, and press agent for Fidel Castro. *One Hundred Years of Solitude* (1967) is his best-known novel.

The cage was finished. Balthazar hung it under the eave, from force of habit, and when he finished lunch everyone was already saying that it was the most beautiful cage in the world. So many people came to see it that a crowd formed in front of the house, and Balthazar had to take it down and close the shop.

"You have to shave," Ursula, his wife, told him. "You look like a Capuchin."

"It's bad to shave after lunch," said Balthazar.

He had two weeks' growth, short, hard, and bristly hair like the mane of a mule, and the general expression of a frightened boy. But it was a false expression. In February he was thirty; he had been living with Ursula for four years, without marrying her and without having children, and life had given him many reasons to be on guard but none to be frightened. He did not even know that for some people the cage he had just made was the most beautiful one in the world. For him, accustomed to making cages since childhood, it had been hardly any more difficult than the others.

"Then rest for a while," said the woman. "With that beard you can't show yourself anywhere."

While he was resting, he had to get out of his hammock several times to show the cage to the neighbors. Ursula had paid little attention to it until then. She was annoyed because her husband had neglected the work of his carpenter's shop to devote himself entirely to the cage, and for two weeks had slept poorly, turning over and muttering incoherencies, and he hadn't thought of shaving. But her annoyance dissolved in the face of the finished cage. When Balthazar woke up from his nap, she had ironed his pants and a shirt; she had put them on a chair near the hammock and had carried the cage to the dining table. She regarded it in silence.

"How much will you charge?" she asked.

"I don't know," Balthazar answered. "I'm going to ask for thirty pesos to see if they'll give me twenty."

"Ask for fifty," said Ursula. "You've lost a lot of sleep in these two weeks. Furthermore, it's rather large. I think it's the biggest cage I've ever seen in my life."

Balthazar began to shave.

"Do you think they'll give me fifty pesos?"

"That's nothing for Mr. Chepe Montiel, and the cage is worth it," said Ursula. "You should ask for sixty."

The house lay in the stifling shadow. It was the first week of April and the heat seemed less bearable because of the chirping of the cicadas. When he finished dressing, Balthazar opened the door to the patio to cool off the house, and a group of children entered the dining room.

The news had spread. Dr. Octavio Giraldo, an old physician, happy with life but tired of his profession, thought about Balthazar's cage while he was eating lunch with his invalid wife. On the inside terrace, where they put the table on hot days, there were many flowerpots and two cages with canaries. His wife liked birds, and she liked them so much that she hated cats because they could eat them up. Thinking about her, Dr. Giraldo went to see a patient that afternoon, and when he returned he went by Balthazar's house to inspect the cage.

There were a lot of people in the dining room. The cage was on display on the table: with its enormous dome of wire, three stories inside, with passageways and compartments especially for eating and sleeping and swings in the space set aside for the birds' recreation, it seemed like a small-scale model of a gigantic ice factory. The doctor inspected it carefully, without touching it, thinking that in effect the cage was better than its reputation, and much more beautiful than any he had ever dreamed of for his wife.

"This is a flight of the imagination," he said. He sought out Balthazar among the group of people and, fixing his maternal eyes on him, added, "You would have been an extraordinary architect."

Balthazar blushed.

"Thank you," he said.

"It's true," said the doctor. He was smoothly and delicately fat, like a woman who had been beautiful in her youth, and he had delicate hands. His voice seemed like that of a priest speaking Latin. "You wouldn't even need to put birds in it," he said, making the cage turn in front of the audience's eyes as if he were auctioning it off. "It would be enough to hang it in the trees so it could sing by itself." He put it back on the table, thought a moment, looking at the cage, and said:

"Fine, then I'll take it."

"It's sold," said Ursula.

"It belongs to the son of Mr. Chepe Montiel," said Balthazar. "He ordered it specially."

The doctor adopted a respectful attitude.

"Did he give you the design?"

"No," said Balthazar. "He said he wanted a large cage, like this one, for a pair of troupials."

The doctor looked at the cage.

"But this isn't for troupials."

"Of course it is, Doctor," said Balthazar, approaching the table. The children surrounded him. "The measurements are carefully calculated," he said, pointing to the different compartments with his forefinger. Then he struck the dome with his knuckles, and the cage filled with resonant chords.

"It's the strongest wire you can find, and each joint is soldered outside and in," he said.

"It's even big enough for a parrot," interrupted one of the children.

"That it is," said Balthazar.

The doctor turned his head.

"Fine, but he didn't give you the design," he said. "He gave you no exact specifications, aside from making it a cage big enough for troupials. Isn't that right?"

"That's right," said Balthazar.

"Then there's no problem," said the doctor. "One thing is a cage big enough for troupials, and another is this cage. There's no proof that this one is the one you were asked to make."

"It's this very one," said Balthazar, confused. "That's why I made it."

The doctor made an impatient gesture.

"You could make another one," said Ursula, looking at her husband. And then, to the doctor: "You're not in any hurry."

"I promised it to my wife for this afternoon," said the doctor.

"I'm very sorry, Doctor," said Balthazar, "but I can't sell you something that's sold already."

The doctor shrugged his shoulders. Drying the sweat from his neck with a handkerchief, he contemplated the cage silently with the fixed, unfocused gaze of one who looks at a ship which is sailing away.

"How much did they pay you for it?"

Balthazar sought out Ursula's eyes without replying.

"Sixty pesos," she said.

The doctor kept looking at the cage. "It's very pretty." He sighed. "Extremely pretty." Then, moving toward the door, he began to fan himself energetically, smiling, and the trace of that episode disappeared forever from his memory.

"Montiel is very rich," he said.

In truth, José Montiel was not as rich as he seemed, but he would have been capable of doing anything to become so. A few blocks from there, in a house crammed with equipment, where no one had ever smelled a smell that couldn't be sold, he remained indifferent to the news of the cage. His wife, tortured by an obsession with death, closed the doors and windows after lunch and lay for two hours with her eyes opened to the shadow of the room, while José Montiel took his siesta. The clamor of many voices surprised her there. Then she opened the door to the living room and found a crowd in front of the house, and Balthazar with the cage in the middle of the crowd, dressed in white, freshly shaved, with that expression of decorous candor with which the poor approach the houses of the wealthy.

"What a marvelous thing!" José Montiel's wife exclaimed, with a radiant expression, leading Balthazar inside. "I've never seen anything like it in my life," she said, and added, annoyed by the crowd which piled up at the door:

"But bring it inside before they turn the living room into a grandstand."

Balthazar was no stranger to José Montiel's house. On different occasions, because of his skill and forthright way of dealing, he had been called in to do minor carpentry jobs. But he never felt at ease among the rich. He used to think about them, about their ugly and argumentative wives, about their tremendous surgical operations, and he always experienced a feeling of pity. When he entered their houses, he couldn't move without dragging his feet.

"Is Pepe home?" he asked.

He had put the cage on the dining-room table.

"He's at school," said José Montiel's wife. "But he shouldn't be long," and she added, "Montiel is taking a bath."

In reality, José Montiel had not had time to bathe. He was giving himself an urgent alcohol rub, in order to come out and see what was going on. He was such a cautious man that he slept without an electric fan so he could watch over the noises of the house while he slept.

"Adelaide!" he shouted. "What's going on?"

"Come and see what a marvelous thing!" his wife shouted.

José Montiel, obese and hairy, his towel draped around his neck, appeared at the bedroom window.

"What is that?"

"Pepe's cage," said Balthazar.

His wife looked at him perplexedly.

"Whose?"

"Pepe's," replied Balthazar. And then, turning toward José Montiel, "Pepe ordered it."

Nothing happened at that instant, but Balthazar felt as if someone had just opened the bathroom door on him. José Montiel came out of the bedroom in his underwear.

"Pepe!" he shouted.

"He's not back," whispered his wife, motionless.

Pepe appeared in the doorway. He was about twelve, and had the same curved eyelashes and was as quietly pathetic as his mother.

"Come here," José Montiel said to him. "Did you order this?"

The child lowered his head. Grabbing him by the hair, José Montiel forced Pepe to look him in the eye.

"Answer me."

The child bit his lip without replying.

"Montiel," whispered his wife.

José Montiel let the child go and turned toward Balthazar in a fury. "I've very sorry, Balthazar," he said. "But you should have consulted me before going on. Only to you would it occur to contract with a minor." As he spoke, his face recovered its serenity. He lifted the cage without looking at it and gave it to Balthazar.

"Take it away at once, and try to sell it to whomever you can," he said. "Above all, I beg you not to argue with me." He patted him on the back and explained, "The doctor has forbidden me to get angry."

The child had remained motionless, without blinking, until Balthazar looked at him uncertainly with the cage in his hand. Then he emitted a guttural sound, like a dog's growl, and threw himself on the floor screaming.

José Montiel looked at him, unmoved, while the mother tried to pacify him. "Don't even pick him up," he said. "Let him break his head on the floor, and then put salt and lemon on it so he can rage to his heart's content." The child was shrieking tearlessly while his mother held him by the wrists.

"Leave him alone," José Montiel insisted.

Balthazar observed the child as he would have observed the death throes of a rabid animal. It was almost four o'clock. At that hour, at his house, Ursula was singing a very old song and cutting slices of onion.

"Pepe," said Balthazar.

He approached the child, smiling, and held the cage out to him. The child jumped up, embraced the cage which was almost as big as he was, and stood looking at Balthazar through the wirework without knowing what to say. He hadn't shed one tear.

"Balthazar," said José Montiel softly. "I told you already to take it away."

"Give it back," the woman ordered the child.

"Keep it," said Balthazar. And then, to José Montiel: "After all, that's what I made it for."

José Montiel followed him into the living room.

"Don't be foolish, Balthazar," he was saying, blocking his path. "Take your piece of furniture home and don't be silly. I have no intention of paying you a cent."

"It doesn't matter," said Balthazar. "I made it expressly as a gift for Pepe. I didn't expect to charge anything for it."

As Balthazar made his way through the spectators who were blocking the door, José Montiel was shouting in the middle of the living room. He was very pale and his eyes were beginning to get red.

"Idiot!" he was shouting. "Take your trinket out of here. The last thing we need is for some nobody to give orders in my house. Son of a bitch!"

In the pool hall, Balthazar was received with an ovation. Until that moment, he thought that he had made a better cage than ever before, that he'd had to give it to the son of José Montiel so he wouldn't keep crying, and that none of these things was particularly important. But then he realized that all of this had a certain importance for many people, and he felt a little excited.

"So they gave you fifty pesos for the cage."

"Sixty," said Balthazar.

"Score one for you," someone said. "You're the only one who has managed to get such a pile of money out of Mr. Chepe Montiel. We have to celebrate."

They bought him a beer, and Balthazar responded with a round for everybody. Since it was the first time he had ever been out drinking, by dusk he was completely drunk, and he was talking about a fabulous project of a thousand cages, at sixty pesos each, and then of a million cages, till he had sixty million pesos. "We have to make a lot of things to sell to the rich before they die," he was saying, blind drunk. "All of them are sick, and they're going to die. They're so screwed up they can't even get angry any more." For two hours he was paying for the jukebox, which played without interruption. Everybody toasted Balthazar's health, good luck, and fortune, and the death of the rich, but at mealtime they left him alone in the pool hall.

Ursula had waited for him until eight, with a dish of fried meat covered with slices of onion. Someone told her that her husband was in the pool hall, delirious with happiness, buying beers for everyone, but she didn't believe it, because Balthazar had never got drunk. When she went to bed, almost at midnight, Balthazar was in a lighted room where there were little tables, each with four chairs, and an outdoor dance floor, where the plovers were walking around. His face was smeared with rouge, and since he couldn't take one more step, he thought he wanted to lie down with two women in the same bed. He had spent so much that he had had to leave his watch in pawn, with the promise to pay the next day. A moment later, spread-eagled in the street, he realized that his shoes were being taken off, but he didn't want to abandon the happiest dream of his life. The women who passed on their way to five-o'clock Mass didn't dare look at him, thinking he was dead.

RONY V. DIAZ

(1932–)

Death in a Sawmill

About the Author: Rony V. Diaz, Philippine fiction writer, grew up in a rural area where his father managed a lumber mill. Before his country gained its independence as a nation in 1946, Diaz lived under its wartime occupation by the Japanese. He began to publish fiction after studying at the University of Quezon City and Indiana University.

You can cleave a rock with it. It is the iron truth. That was not an accident. That was a murder. Yes, a murder. That impotent bastard, Rustico, murdered Rey.

You have seen the chain that holds the dogs that keep the logs on the carriage in place. Well, that chain is controlled by a lever which is out of the way and unless that lever has been released, the chain cannot whip out like a crocodile's tail and hurl a man to the whirling, circular saw.

I was down at our sawmill last summer to hunt. As soon as school was out, I took a bus for Lemery where I boarded a sailboat for Abra de Ilog. Inong met me at the pier with one of the trucks of the sawmill and took me down.

The brazen heat of summer writhed on the yard of the sawmill which was packed hard with red sawdust.

My father met me at the door of the canteen. He took my bags and led me in. I shouldered my sheathed carbine and followed. The canteen was a large frame house made of unplaned planks. My father's room was behind the big, barred store where the laborers of the sawmill bought their supplies. The rough walls of the small room looked like stiffened pelts.

My father deposited my bags on a cot and then turned to me. "I've asked the assistant sawyer, Rey Olbes, to guide you."

The machines of the sawmill were dead. Only the slow, ruthless grinding of the cables of the winches could be heard.

"No work today?" I asked my father.

"A new batch of logs arrived from the interior and the men are arranging them for sawing."

Then a steamwhistle blew.

"They are ready to saw," my father explained.

The steam machine started and built solid walls of sound that crashed against the frame house. Then I heard the saw bite into one of the logs. Its locust-like trill spangled the air.

"You'll get used to the noise," my father said. "I've some things to attend to. I'll see you at lunchtime." He turned about and walked out of the room, shutting the door after him.

I lay on the cot with my clothes on and listened to the pounding of the steam engine and the taut trill of the circular saw. After a while I dozed off.

After lunch, I walked out of the canteen and crossed the yard to the engine house. It was nothing more than a roof over an aghast collection of soot-blackened, mud-plastered balky engines. Every inch of ground was covered with sour-smelling sawdust. The steam engine had stopped but two naked men were still stoking the furnace of the boilers with kerfs and cracked slabs. Their bodies shone with sweat. I skirted the boilers and went past

the cranes, tractors and trucks to the south end of the sawmill. A deep lateral pit, filled with kerfs, flitches and rejects, isolated like a moat the sawmill from the jungle. Near the pit, I saw Rey. He was sitting on a log deck. When he saw me, he got up and walked straight to me.

"Are you Rustico?" I asked.

"No, I'm Rey Olbes," he answered.

"I'm Eddie," I said, "my father sent me."

He was a tall, sun-blackened young man. He had an unusually long neck and his head was pushed forward like a horse's. His skin was as grainy as moist whetstone. He stopped and picked up a canter and stuck it on the ground and leaned on it. Then he switched his head like a stallion to shake back into place a damp lock of hair that had fallen over his left eye. His manner was easy and deliberate.

"Your father told me you wanted to go hunting," he said slowly, his chin resting in the groove of his hands folded on the butt end of the canter. "Tomorrow is Sunday. Would you like to hunt tomorrow?"

"Yes, we can hunt tomorrow."

Inside the engine shed the heat curled like live steam. It swathed my body like a shirt. "It's hot here," I said. "Do you always stay here after work?"

"No, not always."

Then I saw a woman emerge from behind one of the cranes. She was wearing a gray silk dress. She walked toward us rapidly.

"Rey!" she bugled.

Rey dropped the canter and turned swiftly about. The woman's dress clung damply to her body. She was fair; her lips were feverish and she had a shock of black electric hair.

She faced Rey. "Have you seen Rustico?"

"No," Rey answered. There was a small fang of frenzy in his voice.

"Tonight?" the woman asked.

Rey glanced at me and then looked at the woman. He reverted to his slow, deliberate manner as he said: "Dida, this is Eddie. The son of the boss."

Dida stared at me with frenetic eyes. She did not say anything.

"He's a hunter too," Rey continued.

Then I saw a man striding toward us. He walked hunched, his arms working like the claws of a crab. Tiny wings of sawdust formed around his heels. He was a small squat man, musclebound and graceless. He came to us and looked around angrily. He faced the woman and barked: "Go home, Dida."

"I was looking for you, Rustico," Dida remonstrated.

"Go home!" he commanded hoarsely.

Dida turned around, sulking, and walked away. She disappeared behind the boilers and the furnace that rose in the shed like enormous black tumors. Rustico set himself squarely like a boxer before Rey and demanded almost in a whisper: "Why don't you keep away from her?"

Rey looked at him coldly and answered mockingly: "You have found a fertile *kaingin.* Why don't you start planting?"

"Why you insolent son of the mother of whores!" Rustico screamed. He reached down to the ground for the canter and poised it before Rey like a harpoon. I bounded forward and grappled with Rustico. I was able to wrest the canter from him. He pushed me. I sank to the sawdust; Rustico leapt forward to heel me on the jaw. Rey held him.

"Keep calm," Rey shouted. "That is the son of Mang Pepe."

Rey released him and Rustico dropped his arms to his sides. He looked suddenly very tired. He continued to stare at me with eyes that reflected yellow flecks of light. I got up slowly. What a bastard, I thought. Rustico wheeled about and strode to the whistlebox. He opened it and tugged at the cord. The steamwhistle screamed like a stuck pig.

"All right, men," he yelled. "It's time. Load the skids and let us start working."

Rey picked up his canter and walked toward the log carriage. Rustico was supervising the loading of the log deck. He was as precise and stiff as a derrick as he switched levers and pulled clamps. He sparked like a starter and the monstrous conglomeration of boilers, furnaces, steam machines, cranes and winches came alive. I walked away.

When I reached the door of the canteen, I heard the teeth of the circular saw swarm into a log like a flight of locusts.

The next day, Rey, carrying a light rifle, came to the canteen. He pushed open the door with his foot and entered the barred room. He stood near my father's table. His eyes shifted warily. Then he looked at me and said: "Get ready."

"I did not bring birdshot," I said.

"I thought you wanted to go after deer?" he asked.

I was surprised because I knew that here deer were hunted only at night, with headlamps and buckshot. The shaft of the lamps always impaled a deer on the black wall of night and the hunter could pick it off easily.

"Now? This morning?" I asked.

"Why not? We are not going after spirits."

"All right. You are the guide." I dragged the gunbag from under the cot and unsheathed my carbine. I rammed the magazine full with shells, pushed it in, and got up. "Let's go."

We entered the forest from the west end of the sawmill and followed a wide tractor path to a log station about four kilometers from the sawmill. The forest was alive with the palaver of monkeys, the call of the birds and the whack of the wind. Then we struck left uphill and climbed steadily for about an hour. The trail clambered up the brush. At the top of the rise, the trail turned at an angle and we moved across the shoulder of an *ipil-ipil* ridge.

Rey walked rapidly and evenly, his head pushed forward, until we reached the drop of the trail. I looked down into a valley walled on all sides by cliffs that showed red and blue-gray gnashes. Streaks of brown and green were palmed across the valley. Islands of dark-green scrubs rose above the level rush of yellow-green grass. On the left side of the valley, a small river fed clay-red water to a grove of trees. At the north end, the valley flattened and sky dropped low, filling the valley with white light and making it look like the open mouth of the jungle, sucking at one of the hot, white, impalpable breasts of the sun. We descended into the valley.

Rey's manner changed. He became tense. He walked slowly, half-crouched, his eyes searching the ground. He examined every mound, bush and rock. Once he stopped; he bent and picked up a small rock. The rock had been recently displaced. He raised his hand to feel the wind and then he backtracked for several yards and crept diagonally to a small clump of brush. I followed behind him.

"Urine," he said. The ground near his feet was wet. "Work in a cartridge," he told me, "and follow as noiselessly as possible." I pulled back the bolt of my rifle.

We crept on half-bent knees toward a grove of trees. Rey, carrying his rifle in the crook of his arm, was swaying gently like a weather vane. I looked around. I saw nothing save the

trees that rode to the sky like smoke and the tall grass that swirled with the breeze. Rey was intent.

Then he stopped and stiffened.

"Remove the safety," he whispered. I heard the safety of Rey's rifle click off. I pushed mine off.

"There is your deer," he said in a low voice. We were still crouched. "Near the base of that tree with a dead branch. Only its head is visible but its shoulder is somewhere near that dry patch of leaves. Shoot through that. Do not move until I tell you to do so."

I did not see the deer until it moved. It turned its head toward us. Its antlers were as brown as the dead branch of the tree. The deer regarded us for a long time. Then it dropped its head and quickly raised it again. We did not move. The deer, reassured, stepped diffidently out of the shadows.

"Now!" Rey said, falling to his knees. The deer stopped and looked at us, its antlers scuffling against the leaves. I raised my rifle and fired. The deer went high in the air. Then, dropping its head, it crashed through the trees and vanished.

"Your aim was too high," he told me quietly. He was still on his knees. "Too high," he said softly. "But you got him."

He stood up slowly, pushed down the safety of his rifle and walked toward the grove of low trees.

We found the deer. It was stretched out on the ground. Its neck was arched upward as though it had tried to raise its body with its head after the bullet had ripped a hump of flesh off its back. Blood had spread like a fan around its head. Rey sat down on the ground and dug out of his pocket a small knife. He cut an incision at the base of the deer's neck. He stood and picked the deer up by its hind legs. Blood spurted out of the cut vein.

"You got your deer," he said. "Let's turn back."

Rey hauled the deer up and carried it around his neck like a yoke.

I felt my nerves tingle with triumph. The earth was soaking up the blood slowly. I had a crazy urge to mash my body with the blood. I felt that it would seep into my body and temper my spirit now forging hot with victory. I looked at Rey. He was smiling at me. In a strained voice I said: "I'll try to do this alone."

"You'll learn," he said. "The forest will surely outlive you."

We walked out of the valley.

After about an hour's walk, we came to a *kaingin.* Rey was sweating. We crossed the charred ground. At the edge of the *kaingin,* Rey stopped. He turned around. The deer had stiffened on his shoulders.

"This used to be deer country," he said. We surveyed the black stumps and half-burned branches that lay strewn on the ground. The bare soil looked rusty.

"You know these parts very well, don't you," I asked.

"I grew up here. I was a logger for your father before I became a sawyer."

His rifle slipped from his arm. I picked it up and carried it for him.

"It is the sawmill," Rey continued. "It is the sawmill that opened the forest. The sawmill has thinned the jungle miles around." I stared at him. He continued meditatively, veins showing on his long powerful neck, "But I do not think they can tame the forest. Unless they can discover the seed of the wilderness and destroy it, this place is not yet done for."

"Don't you like your job in the sawmill?" I asked.

He shot a glance at me and grimaced. "I do not complain. You do not have to tell this

to your father but Rustico is making my stay very trying. You saw what happened yesterday."

"Yes," I said. "What made him so mad?"

Rey did not answer. We crossed a gully and worked our way to the end of a dry river bed before he answered. The shale crumbled under our feet. The trees that grew along the bank of the river were caught by a net of vines. Rey, yoked by the deer, was now panting. Under a *kalumpit* tree, he threw his burden down and sank to the ground.

"You know why?" he asked. "Because his wife is pregnant."

"Dida? So?"

"He's impotent."

The revelation struck me like a slap.

"And he suspects you," I asked tentatively, unsure now of my footing.

"He knows. Dida told him."

"Why doesn't he leave her then," I said, trying to direct the talk away from Rey.

"He wouldn't! He'd chain Dida to keep her!" Rey flared.

I shut my mouth. It was noon when we reached the sawmill.

Late that afternoon we left to shoot fruit bats. Rey knew a place where we could shoot them as they flew off their roost. He had several tubes of birdshot and a shotgun.

It was almost eight o'clock when we returned. We followed the road to the sawmill. The shacks of the laborers were built along the road. Near the motor pool, a low grass hut stood. We passed very close to this hut and we heard suppressed, angry voices. "That is Rustico's hut," Rey said.

I heard Rustico's voice. He sounded strangled. "I want you to drop that baby!" The words were spewed out like sand. "Let me go!" Dida screamed. I heard a table or a chair go. It crashed to the floor. "I'll kill you," Rustico threatened. "Do it then! Do it!" The yellow wings of light that had sprouted from a kerosene lamp trembled violently.

Rey quickened his steps. He was carrying a bunch of dead bats. One of the bats had dropped, its wings spread. It looked like a black gule on Rey's side.

The next morning, I heard from the men who were huddled near the door of the canteen that Dida had run away. She had hitched a ride to town on one of the trucks.

I was eating breakfast in the store with my father when Rustico entered. He approached my father carefully as though his feet hurt. Then he stood before us and looked meekly at my father. He was gray.

"Mang Pepe," he began very slowly, "I want to go to the town. I will be back this afternoon or early tomorrow morning."

"Surely," my father said. "Inong is driving a load of lumber to the pier. You can go with him."

"Thank you," he said and left at once.

After breakfast, my father called in Lino, the foreman. "Tell Rey to take charge of the sawing today. Rustico is going to town. We've to finish this batch. A new load is arriving this afternoon.

"Rey left early this morning," Lino said. "He said he will be back tomorrow morning."

"Devil's lightning!" my father fumed. "Why didn't he tell me! Why is everybody so anxious to go to town?"

"You were still asleep when he left, Mang Pepe," Lino said.

"These beggars are going to hold up our shipment this week!" my father flared. "Eddie," my father whirled to face me, "look for Rustico and tell him that he cannot leave until Rey returns. We've to finish all the devil's logs before all these lightning-struck beggars pack up and leave!"

I walked out of the canteen to look for Rustico. I searched all the trucks first and then the engine house. I found him sitting on the log carriage. He was shredding an unlighted cigarette.

"My father said he is sorry but you cannot leave until Rey comes back from the town. We have a lot of work to do here. A new load of logs is expected this afternoon." I spoke rapidly.

He got up on the carriage and leaned on the chain that held the log clamps. He acted very tired.

"It is all right," he said. "I've plenty of time." He spat out a ragged stalk of spittle. "Plenty of time." I turned about to go but he called me back.

He looked at me for a long time and then asked: "You are Rey's friend. What has he been saying about me?"

"Nothing much," I lied. "Why?"

"Nothing much!" he screamed, jumping off the carriage. His dun face had become very red. "He told you about my wife, didn't he? He delights in telling that story to everybody." He seized a lever near the brake of the carriage and yanked it down. The chain lashed out and fell rattling to the floor.

Rustico tensed. He stared at the chain as though it were a dead snake. "Now look at that chain," he said very slowly.

He mounted the carriage again, kicked the clamps into place and pulled at the chain. The chain tightened. He cranked the lever up and locked it.

He was trembling as he unlocked the lever and pulled it down with both hands. The chain lashed out again like a crocodile tail.

"Just look at that chain," he mused.

ALBERTO MORAVIA

(1907–)

The Secret

ENGLISH TRANSLATION BY HELENE CANTARELLA

About the Author: Alberto Moravia is the pseudonym of Alberto Pincherle, a prolific Italian short-story writer and novelist, and recognized leader of the neo-realist school of writing that emerged after World War II. His fiction, including *The Woman of Rome* (1947), is noted for its realism and emphasis on sexuality as a means of character development.

Don't talk to me about secrets! I had one—and it was the kind that weighs on your conscience like a nightmare.

I am a truck driver. One beautiful spring morning, while hauling a load of lava rock from a quarry near Campagnano to Rome, I ran square into a man who was coming in the opposite direction on a motor bike. It was right at the 25 Kilometer marker on the old Cassia road. Through no fault of his, either. I had kept going on the wrong side of the road long after having passed a car, and I was speeding; he was on the right, where he belonged, and going slow. The truck hit him so hard that I barely had time to see something black fly

through the blue air and then fall and lie still and black against the soft whiteness of a daisy field. The motor bike lay on the other side of the road, its wheels in the air, like a dead bug.

Lowering my head, I stepped down hard on the gas. I tore down the road to Rome and dropped my load at the yard.

The next day the papers carried the news: So-and-so, forty-three years old, a jobber by trade, leaving a wife and several children, had been run down at Kilometer 25 of the Cassia road and instantly killed. Nobody knew who had struck him. The hit-and-run driver had fled the scene of the accident like a coward. That's exactly what the paper said: *like a coward.* Except for those three little words that burned a hole in my brain, it didn't take more than four lines to report on what was, after all, only the death of a man.

During the next couple of days, I could think of nothing else. I know that I am only a truck driver, but who can claim that truck drivers have no conscience? A truck driver has a lot of time to mull over his own private business, during the long hours behind the wheel or lying in the truck's sleeping berth. And when, as in my case, that private business is not all it ought to be, thinking can get to be really pretty tough.

One thing in particular kept nagging at me. I just couldn't understand why I hadn't stopped, why I hadn't tried to help the poor guy. I lived the scene over and over again. I would be gauging the distances again before passing that car; I would feel my foot pressing down hard on the accelerator. Then the man's body would come flying up in front of my windshield . . . and at this point I would deliberately block out the picture, as you do at the movies, and I would think, "Now, jam on your brakes, jump down, run into the field, pick him up, put him in the bed of the truck and rush him to Santo Spirito Hospital. . . ."

But, you poor fool, you're just dreaming again. I had *not* stopped, I had driven straight on, with head lowered like a bull after a goring. To make a long story short, the more I thought about that split second when I had stepped on the gas instead of jamming on the brakes, the less I could make it out. Cowardice—that was the word for it all right. But why does a man who has, or at least thinks he has guts, turn into a coward without a moment's warning? That stumped me. Yet the cold hard facts were there: the dead man was really dead; that split second when I might have stopped had passed and was now sinking farther and farther away and no one would ever be able to bring it back. I was no longer the Gino who had passed that car but another Gino who had killed a man and then had run away.

I lay awake nights over it. I grew gloomy and silent and after a while everybody shied away from me at the yard and after work: nobody wants to pass the time with a kill-joy. So I carried my secret around as if it were a hot diamond that you can't entrust to anyone or plant anywhere.

Then, after a while, I began thinking about it less and less and I can even say that there came a time when I didn't think about it at all. But the secret was still stowed away deep down inside me and it weighed on my conscience and kept me from enjoying life. I often thought that I would have felt better if I could have told somebody about it. I wasn't exactly looking for approval—I realized there was no pardon for what I had done—but if I could have told this secret of mine I would have thrown off part of its dead weight onto somebody else who would have helped me carry it. But who could I tell it to? To my friends at the yard? They had other things to worry about. To my family? I had none, being a foundling. My girl friend? She would have been the logical person because, as everybody knows, women are good at understanding you and giving you sympathy when you need it, but unfortunately, I had no girl friend.

II

One Sunday in May I went walking outside the Rome city gates with a girl I had met some time before when I had given her and one of her friends a lift in my truck. She had told me her name and address, and I had seen her again a couple of times. We had enjoyed each other's company, and she had made it clear that she liked me and would be willing to go out with me.

Her name was Iris. She was a lady's maid in the house of some wealthy woman who had lots of servants. I had fallen from the start for her serious little oval face and those great big sad gray eyes of hers. In short, here was just the girl for me in the present circumstances. After we had had a cup of coffee at the Exposition Grounds, with all those columns around us, she finally agreed in her shy, silent, and gentle way to go and sit with me in a meadow not far from St. Paul's Gate, where you get a good view of the Tiber and of the new apartment houses lined up on the opposite bank. She had spread out a handkerchief on the grass to keep her skirt from getting dirty and she sat quietly, her legs tucked under her, her hands in her lap, gazing across at the big white buildings on the other side of the river.

I noticed that there were lots of daisies in the grass around us; and like a flash I remembered the soft whiteness of those other daisies among which, just a month earlier, I had seen lying still and dead the man I had struck down. I don't know what got into me but suddenly I couldn't hold back the urge to tell her my secret. If I tell her, I thought, I'll get rid of the load on my chest. She wasn't one of those dizzy, empty-headed girls who, after you've told them a secret, make you feel so much worse than you did before, that you could kick yourself hard for having spilled all you know. She was a nice, understanding person who had doubtless had her share of knocks in life—and they must have been pretty rough knocks if the sad little look on her face meant anything. Just to break the ice, I said to her, in an offhand way:

"What are you thinking about, Iris?"

She was just raising her hand to choke back a yawn. Perhaps she was tired. She said: "Nothing."

I didn't let that answer get me down but quickly went on. "Iris, you know that I like you a lot, don't you? That's why I feel that I shouldn't hide anything from you. You've got to know everything about me. Iris, I've got a secret."

She kept on looking at the tall buildings on the other side of the river, all the while fingering a little red lump on her chin, a tiny spring pimple.

"What secret?" she asked.

With an effort I got it out: "I've killed a man."

She didn't move but kept on poking gently at her chin. Then she shivered all over, as though she had finally understood. "You've killed a man? And you tell me about it just like that?"

"And how else do you expect me to tell you?"

She said nothing. She seemed to be looking for something on the ground. I went on. "Let's get this thing straight. I didn't mean to kill him."

Suddenly she found what she wanted: picking a long blade of grass, she put it into her mouth and began chewing on it, thoughtfully. Then, hurriedly, but without hiding anything, I told her about the accident, bringing out the part about my cowardice. I got pretty wrought up in spite of myself, but already I was beginning to feel relieved. I concluded:

"Now tell me what you think about all this."

She kept munching on her blade of grass and didn't say a word.

I insisted. "I'll bet that now you can't stand the sight of me."

I saw her shrug her shoulders, lightly. "And why shouldn't I be able to stand the sight of you?"

"Well, I don't know. After all, it was my fault that poor guy got killed."

"And it bothers you?"

"Yes. Terribly." Suddenly, my throat closed tight as if over a hard knot of tears. "I feel as if I can't go on living. No man can go on living if he thinks he's a coward."

"Was it in the papers?"

"Yes. They gave it four lines. Just to say he had been killed and that nobody knew who had hit him."

Suddenly she asked, "What time is it?"

"Five-fifteen."

Another silence. "Listen, Iris, what does a man have to do to find out what's going on in that mind of yours?"

She shifted the blade of grass from one corner of her mouth to the other and said frankly, "Well, if you must know, there's nothing on my mind. I feel good and I'm not thinking about anything."

I couldn't believe my ears. I protested. "It can't be! You must have been thinking something about something. I'm sure of it."

I saw her smile, faintly. "Well, as a matter of fact, I was thinking about something. But if I tell you, you'll never believe it."

Hopefully, I asked, "Was it about me?"

"Good heavens, no! It had absolutely nothing to do with you!"

"What was it, then?"

She said slowly, "It was just one of those things that only women think about. I was looking at my shoes and seeing that they have holes in them. I was thinking that there is a big clearance sale on in Via Cola di Rienzo and that I've got to go there tomorrow and buy myself a pair of new shoes. There . . . are you satisfied?"

This time I shut up like a clam, my face dark and brooding. She noticed it and exclaimed: "Oh, dear! You're not mad, are you?"

I couldn't help blurting out: "Sure, I'm mad. Damn mad. Here I tell you the secret of my life, and it makes so little impression on you I wonder why I didn't keep it to myself!"

This bothered her a bit. "No," she said, "I'm glad you told me about it. It really did make an impression on me."

"Well, what kind of an impression?"

She thought it over and then said, scrupulously, "Well, I'm sorry that such a thing had to happen to you. It must have been awful!"

"Is that all you've got to say?"

"I also think," she added, fingering the pimple on her chin, "that it's only right it should bother you."

"Why?"

"Well, you said so yourself. You ought to have stopped to help him but you didn't."

"Then you think I am a coward?"

"A coward? Well, yes . . . and then no. After all, a thing like that could happen to anybody."

"But you just said that I ought to have stopped!"

"You should have; but you didn't . . ."

At this point I saw her glance down at something in the daisies. "Oh, look! How pretty!"

It was an insect, a green and gold beetle, resting on the white petals of a daisy. Suddenly I felt as if I were emptied out—almost as if that secret over which I had agonized so long had vanished in the spring air, carried away, lightly, like the white butterflies that were flitting around in pairs in the sunlight.

Yet with one dogged last hope, I asked: "But tell me, Iris, in your opinion, was I right or wrong not to stop?"

"You were right and you were wrong. Of course, you ought to have stopped. After all, you had run into him. But, on the other hand, what good would it have done if you had? He was dead by that time anyway and you would probably have got into a terrible mess. You were both right and wrong."

After these words, a thought flashed through my mind. "This is the end of Iris. I'll never take her out again. I thought she was a bright, understanding girl. Instead, she is really nothing but a half-wit. Enough is enough." I jumped to my feet.

"Come on, let's go," I said. "Otherwise, we'll be late for the movies."

Once inside the theater, in the dark, she slipped her hand into mine, forcing her fingers through mine. I didn't budge. The film was a love story, a real tear-jerker. When the lights went on at the end I saw that her big gray eyes were filled with tears and that her cheeks were wet. "I just can't help it," she said, patting her face dry with a handkerchief. "Pictures like this always make me want to cry."

Afterwards we went into a bar and ordered coffee. She pressed so close to me that our bodies touched. Just as the *espresso* machine let off a loud stream of steam, she said softly, "You know that I really like you, don't you?" staring at me with those great big beautiful eyes of hers.

I felt like answering: "Fine. You really like me, but you'll let me carry the whole weight of my secret alone!" Instead, I said nothing.

Now I understood that from her, as from everybody else, I could ask only for affection, nothing more than that.

I answered with a sigh, "I like you a lot, too."

But already she had stopped listening to me. She was peering at herself in the mirror behind the bar, absorbed and concerned as she fingered the little red lump on her chin.

FLANNERY O'CONNOR

(1925–1964)

Good Country People

About the Author: Flannery O'Connor, novelist, short story writer and critic, was born in Georgia and, except for short periods, lived there till her death. After studying at the University of Iowa's Writers' Workshop, she published a volume of short fiction and two novels, *Wise Blood* (1952) and *The Violent Bear It Away* (1960). A second story collection, *Everything That Rises Must Converge* (1965), was published after her death and in 1971 her *Complete Stories* was posthumously honored with the National Book Award.

Besides the neutral expression that she wore when she was alone, Mrs. Freeman had two others, forward and reverse, that she used for all her human dealings. Her forward expression was steady and driving like the advance of a heavy truck. Her eyes never swerved to left or right but turned as the story turned as if they followed a yellow line down the center of it. She seldom used the other expression because it was not often necessary for her to retract a statement, but when she did, her face came to a complete stop, there was an almost imperceptible movement of her black eyes, during which they seemed to be receding, and then the observer would see that Mrs. Freeman, though she might stand there as real as several grain sacks thrown on top of each other, was no longer there in spirit. As for getting anything across to her when this was the case, Mrs. Hopewell had given it up. She might talk her head off. Mrs. Freeman could never be brought to admit herself wrong on any point. She would stand there and if she could be brought to say anything, it was something like, "Well, I wouldn't of said it was and I wouldn't of said it wasn't," or letting her gaze range over the top kitchen shelf where there was an assortment of dusty bottles, she might remark, "I see you ain't ate many of them figs you put up last summer."

They carried on their most important business in the kitchen at breakfast. Every morning Mrs. Hopewell got up at seven o'clock and lit her gas heater and Joy's. Joy was her daughter, a large blonde girl who had an artificial leg. Mrs. Hopewell thought of her as a child though she was thirty-two years old and highly educated. Joy would get up while her mother was eating and lumber into the bathroom and slam the door, and before long, Mrs. Freeman would arrive at the back door. Joy would hear her mother call, "Come on in," and then they would talk for a while in low voices that were indistinguishable in the bathroom. By the time Joy came in, they had usually finished the weather report and were on one or the other of Mrs. Freeman's daughters, Glynese or Carramae. Joy called them Glycerin and Caramel. Glynese, a redhead, was eighteen and had many admirers; Carramae, a blonde, was only fifteen but already married and pregnant. She could not keep anything on her stomach. Every morning Mrs. Freeman told Mrs. Hopewell how many times she had vomited since the last report.

Mrs. Hopewell liked to tell people that Glynese and Carramae were two of the finest girls she knew and that Mrs. Freeman was a *lady* and that she was never ashamed to take her anywhere or introduce her to anybody they might meet. Then she would tell how she had happened to hire the Freemans in the first place and how they were a godsend to her and how she had had them four years. The reason for her keeping them so long was that they were not trash. They were good country people. She had telephoned the man whose name they had given as a reference and he had told her that Mr. Freeman was a good farmer but that his wife was the nosiest woman ever to walk the earth. "She's got to be into everything," the man said. "If she don't get there before the dust settles, you can bet she's dead, that's all. She'll want to know all your business. I can stand him real good," he had said, "but me nor my wife neither could have stood that woman one more minute on this place." That had put Mrs. Hopewell off for a few days.

She had hired them in the end because there were no other applicants but she had made up her mind beforehand exactly how she would handle the woman. Since she was the type who had to be into everything, then, Mrs. Hopewell had decided, she would not only let her be into everything, she would *see to it* that she was into everything—she would give her the responsibility of everything, she would put her in charge. Mrs. Hopewell had no bad qualities of her own but she was able to use other people's in such a constructive way that she never felt the lack. She had hired the Freemans and she had kept them four years.

Nothing is perfect. This was one of Mrs. Hopewell's favorite sayings. Another was:

that is life! And still another, the most important, was: well, other people have their opinions too. She would make these statements, usually at the table, in a tone of gentle insistence as if no one held them but her, and the large hulking Joy, whose constant outrage had obliterated every expression from her face, would stare just a little to the side of her, her eyes icy blue, with the look of someone who has achieved blindness by an act of will and means to keep it.

When Mrs. Hopewell said to Mrs. Freeman that life was like that, Mrs. Freeman would say, "I always said so myself." Nothing had been arrived at by anyone that had not first been arrived at by her. She was quicker than Mr. Freeman. When Mrs. Hopewell said to her after they had been on the place a while, "You know, you're the wheel behind the wheel," and winked, Mrs. Freeman had said, "I know it. I've always been quick. It's some that are quicker than others."

"Everybody is different," Mrs. Hopewell said.

"Yes, most people is," Mrs. Freeman said.

"It takes all kinds to make the world."

"I always said it did myself."

The girl was used to this kind of dialogue for breakfast and more of it for dinner; sometimes they had it for supper too. When they had no guest they ate in the kitchen because that was easier. Mrs. Freeman always managed to arrive at some point during the meal and to watch them finish it. She would stand in the doorway if it were summer but in the winter she would stand with one elbow on top of the refrigerator and look down on them, or she would stand by the gas heater, lifting the back of her skirt slightly. Occasionally she would stand against the wall and roll her head from side to side. At no time was she in any hurry to leave. All this was very trying on Mrs. Hopewell but she was a woman of great patience. She realized that nothing is perfect and that in the Freemans she had good country people and that if, in this day and age, you get good country people, you had better hang onto them.

She had had plenty of experience with trash. Before the Freemans she had averaged one tenant family a year. The wives of these farmers were not the kind you would want to be around you for very long. Mrs. Hopewell, who had divorced her husband long ago, needed someone to walk over the fields with her; and when Joy had to be impressed for these services, her remarks were usually so ugly and her face so glum that Mrs. Hopewell would say, "If you can't come pleasantly, I don't want you at all," to which the girl, standing square and rigid-shouldered with her neck thrust slightly forward, would reply, "If you want me, here I am—LIKE I AM."

Mrs. Hopewell excused this attitude because of the leg (which had been shot off in a hunting accident when Joy was ten). It was hard for Mrs. Hopewell to realize that her child was thirty-two now and that for more than twenty years she had had only one leg. She thought of her still as a child because it tore her heart to think instead of the poor stout girl in her thirties who had never danced a step or had any *normal* good times. Her name was really Joy but as soon as she was twenty-one and away from home, she had had it legally changed. Mrs. Hopewell was certain that she had thought and thought until she had hit upon the ugliest name in any language. Then she had gone and had the beautiful name, Joy, changed without telling her mother until after she had done it. Her legal name was Hulga.

When Mrs. Hopewell thought the name, Hulga, she thought of the broad blank hull of a battleship. She would not use it. She continued to call her Joy to which the girl responded but in a purely mechanical way.

Hulga had learned to tolerate Mrs. Freeman, who saved her from taking walks with her mother. Even Glynese and Carramae were useful when they occupied attention that might otherwise have been directed at her. At first she had thought she could not stand Mrs. Freeman for she had found that it was not possible to be rude to her. Mrs. Freeman would take on strange resentments and for days together she would be sullen but the source of her displeasure was always obscure; a direct attack, a positive leer, blatant ugliness to her face—these never touched her. And without warning one day, she began calling her Hulga.

She did not call her that in front of Mrs. Hopewell who would have been incensed but when she and the girl happened to be out of the house together, she would say something and add the name Hulga to the end of it, and the big spectacled Joy-Hulga would scowl and redden as if her privacy had been intruded upon. She considered the name her personal affair. She had arrived at it first purely on the basis of its ugly sound and then the full genius of its fitness had struck her. She had a vision of the name working like the ugly sweating Vulcan who stayed in the furnace and to whom, presumably, the goddess had to come when called. She saw it as the name of her highest creative act. One of her major triumphs was that her mother had not been able to turn her dust into Joy, but the greater one was that she had been able to turn it herself into Hulga. However, Mrs. Freeman's relish for using the name only irritated her. It was as if Mrs. Freeman's beady steel-pointed eyes had penetrated far enough behind her face to reach some secret fact. Something about her seemed to fascinate Mrs. Freeman and then one day Hulga realized that it was the artificial leg. Mrs. Freeman had a special fondness for the details of secret infections, hidden deformities, assaults upon children. Of diseases, she preferred the lingering or incurable. Hulga had heard Mrs. Hopewell give her the details of the hunting accident, how the leg had been literally blasted off, how she had never lost consciousness. Mrs. Freeman could listen to it any time as if it had happened an hour ago.

When Hulga stumped into the kitchen in the morning (she could walk without making the awful noise but she made it—Mrs. Hopewell was certain—because it was ugly-sounding), she glanced at them and did not speak. Mrs. Hopewell would be in her red kimono with her hair tied around her head in rags. She would be sitting at the table, finishing her breakfast and Mrs. Freeman would be hanging by her elbow outward from the refrigerator, looking down at the table. Hulga always put her eggs on the stove to boil and then stood over them with her arms folded, and Mrs. Hopewell would look at her—a kind of indirect gaze divided between her and Mrs. Freeman—and would think that if she would only keep herself up a little, she wouldn't be so bad looking. There was nothing wrong with her face that a pleasant expression wouldn't help. Mrs. Hopewell said that people who looked on the bright side of things would be beautiful even if they were not.

Whenever she looked at Joy this way, she could not help but feel that it would have been better if the child had not taken the Ph.D. It had certainly not brought her out any and now that she had it, there was no more excuse for her to go to school again. Mrs. Hopewell thought it was nice for girls to go to school to have a good time but Joy had "gone through." Anyhow, she would not have been strong enough to go again. The doctors had told Mrs. Hopewell that with the best of care, Joy might see forty-five. She had a weak heart. Joy had made it plain that if it had not been for this condition, she would be far from these red hills and good country people. She would be in a university lecturing to people who knew what she was talking about. Mrs. Hopewell could very well picture her there, looking like a scarecrow and lecturing to more of the same. Here she went about all day in a six-year-old skirt and a yellow sweat shirt with a faded cowboy on a horse embossed on it. She thought this was funny; Mrs. Hopewell thought it was idiotic and showed simply that she was still a child. She was brilliant but she didn't have a grain of sense. It seemed to Mrs. Hopewell that every year she grew less like other people and more like herself—bloated, rude, and squint-eyed. And she said such strange things! To her own mother she had said—without warning, without excuse, standing up in the middle of a meal with her face purple and her mouth half full—"Woman! do you ever look inside? Do you ever look inside and see what you are *not?* God!" she had cried sinking down again and staring at her plate, "Malebranche was right: we are not our own light. We are not our own light!" Mrs. Hopewell had no idea to this day what brought that on. She had only made the remark, hoping Joy would take it in, that a smile never hurt anyone.

The girl had taken the Ph.D. in philosophy and this left Mrs. Hopewell at a complete loss. You could say, "My daughter is a nurse," or "My daughter is a school teacher," or even, "My daughter is a chemical engineer." You could not say, "My daughter is a philosopher." That was something that had ended with the Greeks and Romans. All day Joy sat on her neck in a deep chair, reading. Sometimes she went for walks but she didn't like dogs or cats or birds or flowers or nature or nice young men. She looked at nice young men as if she could smell their stupidity.

One day Mrs. Hopewell had picked up one of the books the girl had just put down and opening it at random, she read, "Science, on the other hand, has to assert its soberness and seriousness afresh and declare that it is concerned solely with what-is. Nothing—how can it be for science anything but a horror and a phantasm? If science is right, then one thing stands firm: science wishes to know nothing of nothing. Such is after all the strictly scientific approach to Nothing. We know it by wishing to know nothing of Nothing." These words had been underlined with a blue pencil and they worked on Mrs. Hopewell like some evil incantation in gibberish. She shut the book quickly and went out of the room as if she were having a chill.

This morning when the girl came in, Mrs. Freeman was on Carramae. "She thrown up four times after supper," she said, "and was up twict in the night after three o'clock. Yesterday she didn't do nothing but ramble in the bureau drawer. All she did. Stand up there and see what she could run up on."

"She's got to eat," Mrs. Hopewell muttered, sipping her coffee, while she watched Joy's back at the stove. She was wondering what the child had said to the Bible salesman. She could not imagine what kind of a conversation she could possibly have had with him.

He was a tall gaunt hatless youth who had called yesterday to sell them a Bible. He had appeared at the door, carrying a large black suitcase that weighted him so heavily on one side that he had to brace himself against the door facing. He seemed on the point of collapse but he said in a cheerful voice, "Good morning, Mrs. Cedars!" and set the suitcase down on the mat. He was not a bad-looking young man though he had on a bright blue suit and yellow socks that were not pulled up far enough. He had prominent face bones and a streak of sticky-looking brown hair falling across his forehead.

"I'm Mrs. Hopewell," she said.

"Oh!" he said, pretending to look puzzled but with his eyes sparkling, "I saw it said 'The Cedars,' on the mailbox so I thought you was Mrs. Cedars!" and he burst out in a pleasant laugh. He picked up the satchel and under cover of a pant, he fell forward into her hall. It was rather as if the suitcase had moved first, jerking him after it. "Mrs. Hopewell!" he said and grabbed her hand. "I hope you are well!" and he laughed again and then all at once his face sobered completely. He paused and gave her a straight earnest look and said, "Lady, I've come to speak of serious things."

"Well, come in," she muttered, none too pleased because her dinner was almost ready. He came into the parlor and sat down on the edge of a straight chair and put the suitcase between his feet and glanced around the room as if he were sizing her up by it. Her silver gleamed on the two sideboards; she decided he had never been in a room as elegant as this.

"Mrs. Hopewell," he began, using her name in a way that sounded almost intimate, "I know you believe in Christian service."

"Well yes," she murmured.

"I know," he said and paused, looking very wise with his head cocked on one side, "that you're a good woman. Friends have told me."

Mrs. Hopewell never liked to be taken for a fool. "What are you selling?" she asked.

"Bibles," the young man said and his eye raced around the room before he added, "I see you have no family Bible in your parlor, I see that is the one lack you got!"

Mrs. Hopewell could not say, "My daughter is an atheist and won't let me keep the Bible in the parlor." She said, stiffening slightly, "I keep my Bible by my bedside." This was not the truth. It was in the attic somewhere.

"Lady," he said, "the word of God ought to be in the parlor."

"Well, I think that's a matter of taste," she began. "I think . . ."

"Lady," he said, "for a Christian, the word of God ought to be in every room in the house besides in his heart. I know you're a Christian because I can see it in every line of your face."

She stood up and said, "Well, young man, I don't want to buy a Bible and I smell my dinner burning."

He didn't get up. He began to twist his hands and looking down at them, he said softly, "Well lady, I'll tell you the truth—not many people want to buy one nowadays and besides, I know I'm real simple. I don't know how to say a thing but to say it. I'm just a country boy." He glanced up into her unfriendly face. "People like you don't like to fool with country people like me!"

"Why!" she cried, "good country people are the salt of the earth! Besides, we all have different ways of doing, it takes all kinds to make the world go 'round. That's life!"

"You said a mouthful," he said.

"Why, I think there aren't enough good country people in the world!" she said, stirred. "I think that's what's wrong with it!"

His face had brightened. "I didn't inraduce myself," he said. "I'm Manley Pointer from out in the country around Willohobie, not even from a place, just from near a place."

"You wait a minute," she said. "I have to see about my dinner." She went out to the kitchen and found Joy standing near the door where she had been listening.

"Get rid of the salt of the earth," she said, "and let's eat."

Mrs. Hopewell gave her a pained look and turned the heat down under the vegetables. "*I* can't be rude to anybody," she murmured and went back into the parlor.

He had opened the suitcase and was sitting with a Bible on each knee.

"You might as well put those up," she told him. "I don't want one."

"I appreciate your honesty," he said. "You don't see any more real honest people unless you go way out in the country."

"I know," she said, "real genuine folks!" Through the crack in the door she heard a groan.

"I guess a lot of boys come telling you they're working their way through college," he said, "but I'm not going to tell you that. Somehow," he said, "I don't want to go to college.

I want to devote my life to Christian service. See," he said, lowering his voice, "I got this heart condition. I may not live long. When you know it's something wrong with you and you may not live long, well then, lady . . ." He paused, with his mouth open, and stared at her.

He and Joy had the same condition! She knew that her eyes were filling with tears but she collected herself quickly and murmured, "Won't you stay for dinner? We'd love to have you!" and was sorry the instant she heard herself say it.

"Yes mam," he said in an abashed voice, "I would sher love to do that!"

Joy had given him one look on being introduced to him and then throughout the meal had not glanced at him again. He had addressed several remarks to her, which she had pretended not to hear. Mrs. Hopewell could not understand deliberate rudeness, although she lived with it, and she felt she had always to overflow with hospitality to make up for Joy's lack of courtesy. She urged him to talk about himself and he did. He said he was the seventh child of twelve and that his father had been crushed under a tree when he himself was eight years old. He had been crushed very badly, in fact, almost cut in two and was practically not recognizable. His mother had got along the best she could by hard working and she had always seen that her children went to Sunday School and that they read the Bible every evening. He was now nineteen year old and he had been selling Bibles for four months. In that time he had sold seventy-seven Bibles and had the promise of two more sales. He wanted to become a missionary because he thought that was the way you could do most for people. "He who losest his life shall find it," he said simply and he was so sincere, so genuine and earnest that Mrs. Hopewell would not for the world have smiled. He prevented his peas from sliding onto the table by blocking them with a piece of bread which he later cleaned his plate with. She could see Joy observing sidewise how he handled his knife and fork and she saw too that every few minutes, the boy would dart a keen appraising glance at the girl as if he were trying to attract her attention.

After dinner Joy cleared the dishes off the table and disappeared and Mrs. Hopewell was left to talk with him. He told her again about his childhood and his father's accident and about various things that had happened to him. Every five minutes or so she would stifle a yawn. He sat for two hours until finally she told him she must go because she had an appointment in town. He packed his Bibles and thanked her and prepared to leave, but in the doorway he stopped and wrung her hand and said that not on any of his trips had he met a lady as nice as her and he asked if he could come again. She had said she would always be happy to see him.

Joy had been standing in the road, apparently looking at something in the distance, when he came down the steps toward her, bent to the side with his heavy valise. He stopped where she was standing and confronted her directly. Mrs. Hopewell could not hear what he said but she trembled to think what Joy would say to him. She could see that after a minute Joy said something and that then the boy began to speak again, making an excited gesture with his free hand. After a minute Joy said something else at which the boy began to speak once more. Then to her amazement, Mrs. Hopewell saw the two of them walk off together, toward the gate. Joy had walked all the way to the gate with him and Mrs. Hopewell could not imagine what they had said to each other, and she had not yet dared to ask.

Mrs. Freeman was insisting upon her attention. She had moved from the refrigerator to the heater so that Mrs. Hopewell had to turn and face her in order to seem to be listening. "Glynese gone out with Harvey Hill again last night," she said. "She had this sty."

"Hill," Mrs. Hopewell said absently, "is that the one who works in the garage?"

"Nome, he's the one that goes to chiropracter school," Mrs. Freeman said. "She had this sty. Been had it two days. So she says when he brought her in the other night he says, 'Lemme get rid of that sty for you,' and she says, 'How?' and he says, 'You just lay yourself down across the seat of that car and I'll show you.' So she done it and he popped her neck. Kept on a-popping it several times until she made him quit. This morning," Mrs. Freeman said, "she ain't got no sty. She ain't got no traces of a sty."

"I never heard of that before," Mrs. Hopewell said.

"He ast her to marry him before the Ordinary," Mrs. Freeman went on, "and she told him she wasn't going to be married in no *office*."

"Well, Glynese is a fine girl," Mrs. Hopewell said, "Glynese and Carramae are both fine girls."

"Carramae said when her and Lyman was married Lyman said it sure felt sacred to him. She said he said he wouldn't take five hundred dollars for being married by a preacher."

"How much would he take?" the girl asked from the stove.

"He said he wouldn't take five hundred dollars," Mrs. Freeman repeated.

"Well we all have work to do," Mrs. Hopewell said.

"Lyman said it just felt more sacred to him," Mrs. Freeman said. "The doctor wants Carramae to eat prunes. Says instead of medicine. Says them cramps is coming from pressure. You know where I think it is?"

"She'll be better in a few weeks," Mrs. Hopewell said.

"In the tube," Mrs. Freeman said. "Else she wouldn't be as sick as she is."

Hulga had cracked her two eggs into a saucer and was bringing them to the table along with a cup of coffee that she had filled too full. She sat down carefully and began to eat, meaning to keep Mrs. Freeman there by questions if for any reason she showed an inclination to leave. She could perceive her mother's eye on her. The first roundabout question would be about the Bible salesman and she did not wish to bring it on. "How did he pop her neck?" she asked.

Mrs. Freeman went into a description of how he had popped her neck. She said he owned a '55 Mercury but that Glynese said she would rather marry a man with only a '36 Plymouth who would be married by a preacher. The girl asked what if he had a '32 Plymouth and Mrs. Freeman said what Glynese had said was a '36 Plymouth.

Mrs. Hopewell said there were not many girls with Glynese's common sense. She said what she admired in those girls was their common sense. She said that reminded her that they had a nice visitor yesterday, a young man selling Bibles. "Lord," she said, "he bored me to death but he was so sincere and genuine I couldn't be rude to him. He was just good country people, you know," she said, "—just the salt of the earth."

"I seen him walk up," Mrs. Freeman said, "and then later—I seen him walk off," and Hulga could feel the slight shift in her voice, the slight insinuation, that he had not walked off alone, had he? Her face remained expressionless but the color rose into her neck and she seemed to swallow it down with the next spoonful of egg. Mrs. Freeman was looking at her as if they had a secret together.

"Well, it takes all kinds of people to make the world go 'round," Mrs. Hopewell said. "It's very good we aren't all alike."

"Some people are more alike than others," Mrs. Freeman said.

Hulga got up and stumped, with about twice the noise that was necessary, into her room and locked the door. She was to meet the Bible salesman at ten o'clock at the gate.

She had thought about it half the night. She had started thinking of it as a great joke and then she had begun to see profound implications in it. She had lain in bed imagining dialogues for them that were insane on the surface but that reached below to depths that no Bible salesman would be aware of. Their conversation yesterday had been of this kind.

He had stopped in front of her and had simply stood there. His face was bony and sweaty and bright, with a little pointed nose in the center of it, and his look was different from what it had been at the dinner table. He was gazing at her with open curiosity, with fascination, like a child watching a new fantastic animal at the zoo, and he was breathing as if he had run a great distance to reach her. His gaze seemed somehow familiar but she could not think where she had been regarded with it before. For almost a minute he didn't say anything. Then on what seemed an insuck of breath, he whispered, "You ever ate a chicken that was two days old?"

The girl looked at him stonily. He might have just put this question up for consideration at the meeting of a philosophical association. "Yes," she presently replied as if she had considered it from all angles.

"It must have been mighty small!" he said triumphantly and shook all over with little nervous giggles, getting very red in the face, and subsiding finally into his gaze of complete admiration, while the girl's expression remained exactly the same.

"How old are you?" he asked softly.

She waited some time before she answered. Then in a flat voice she said, "Seventeen."

His smiles came in succession like waves breaking on the surface of a little lake. "I see you got a wooden leg," he said. "I think you're real brave. I think you're real sweet."

The girl stood blank and solid and silent.

"Walk to the gate with me," he said. "You're a brave sweet little thing and I liked you the minute I seen you walk in the door."

Hulga began to move forward.

"What's you name?" he asked, smiling down on the top of her head.

"Hulga," she said.

"Hulga," he murmured, "Hulga. Hulga. I never heard of anybody name Hulga before. You're shy, aren't you, Hulga?" he asked.

She nodded, watching his large red hand on the handle of the giant valise.

"I like girls that wear glasses," he said. "I think a lot. I'm not like these people that a serious thought don't ever enter their heads. It's because I may die."

"I may die too," she said suddenly and looked up at him. His eyes were very small and brown, glittering feverishly.

"Listen," he said, "don't you think some people was meant to meet on account of what all they got in common and all? Like they both think serious thoughts and all?" He shifted the valise to his other hand so that the hand nearest her was free. He caught hold of her elbow and shook it a little. "I don't work on Saturday," he said. "I like to walk in the woods and see what Mother Nature is wearing. O'er the hills and far away. Pic-nics and things. Couldn't we go on a pic-nic tomorrow? Say yes, Hulga," he said and gave her a dying look as if he felt his insides about to drop out of him. He had even seemed to sway slightly toward her.

During the night she had imagined that she seduced him. She imagined that the two of them walked on the place until they came to the storage barn beyond the two back fields and there, she imagined, that things came to such a pass that she very easily seduced him and that then, of course, she had to reckon with his remorse. True genius can get an idea across even to an inferior mind. She imagined that she took his remorse in hand and changed it into a deeper understanding of life. She took all his shame away and turned it into something useful.

She set off for the gate at exactly ten o'clock, escaping without drawing Mrs. Hopewell's attention. She didn't take anything to eat, forgetting that food is usually taken on a picnic. She wore a pair of slacks and a dirty white shirt, and as an afterthought, she had put some Vapex on the collar of it since she did not own any perfume. When she reached the gate no one was there.

She looked up and down the empty highway and had the furious feeling that she had been tricked, that he had only meant to make her walk to the gate after the idea of him. Then suddenly he stood up, very tall, from behind a bush on the opposite embankment. Smiling, he lifted his hat which was new and wide-brimmed. He had not worn it yesterday and she wondered if he had bought it for the occasion. It was toast-colored with a red and white band around it and was slightly too large for him. He stepped from behind the bush still carrying the black valise. He had on the same suit and the same yellow socks sucked down in his shoes from walking. He crossed the highway and said, "I knew you'd come!"

The girl wondered acidly how he had known this. She pointed to the valise and asked, "Why did you bring your Bibles?"

He took her elbow, smiling down on her as if he could not stop. "You can never tell when you'll need the word of God, Hulga," he said. She had a moment in which she doubted that this was actually happening and then they began to climb the embankment. They went down into the pasture toward the woods. The boy walked lightly by her side, bouncing on his toes. The valise did not seem to be heavy today; he even swung it. They crossed half the pasture without saying anything and then, putting his hand easily on the small of her back, he asked softly, "Where does your wooden leg join on?"

She turned an ugly red and glared at him and for an instant the boy looked abashed. "I didn't mean you no harm," he said. "I only meant you're so brave and all. I guess God takes care of you."

"No," she said, looking forward and walking fast, "I don't even believe in God."

At this he stopped and whistled. "No!" he exclaimed as if he were too astonished to say anything else.

She walked on and in a second he was bouncing at her side, fanning with his hat. "That's very unusual for a girl," he remarked, watching her out of the corner of his eye. When they reached the edge of the wood, he put his hand on her back again and drew her against him without a word and kissed her heavily.

The kiss, which had more pressure than feeling behind it, produced that extra surge of adrenalin in the girl that enables one to carry a packed trunk out of a burning house, but in her, the power went at once to the brain. Even before he released her, her mind, clear and detached and ironic anyway, was regarding him from a great distance, with amusement but with pity. She had never been kissed before and she was pleased to discover that it was an unexceptional experience and all a matter of the mind's control. Some people might enjoy drain water if they were told it was vodka. When the boy, looking expectant but uncertain, pushed her gently away, she turned and walked on, saying nothing as if such business, for her, were common enough.

He came along panting at her side, trying to help her when he saw a root that she might trip over. He caught and held back the long swaying blades of thorn vine until she had passed beyond them. She led the way and he came breathing heavily behind her. Then they came out on a sunlit hillside, sloping softly into another one a little smaller. Beyond, they could see the rusted top of the old barn where the extra hay was stored.

The hill was sprinkled with small pink weeds. "Then you ain't saved?" he asked suddenly, stopping.

The girl smiled. It was the first time she had smiled at him at all. "In my economy," she said, "I'm saved and you are damned but I told you I didn't believe in God."

Nothing seemed to destroy the boy's look of admiration. He gazed at her now as if the fantastic animal at the zoo had put its paw through the bars and given him a loving poke. She thought he looked as if he wanted to kiss her again and she walked on before he had the chance.

"Ain't there somewheres we can sit down sometime?" he murmured, his voice softening toward the end of the sentence.

"In that barn," she said.

They made for it rapidly as if it might slide away like a train. It was a large two-story barn, cool and dark inside. The boy pointed up the ladder that led into the loft and said, "It's too bad we can't go up there."

"Why can't we?" she asked.

"Yer leg," he said reverently.

The girl gave him a contemptuous look and putting both hands on the ladder, she climbed it while he stood below, apparently awestruck. She pulled herself expertly through the opening and then looked down at him and said, "Well, come on if you're coming," and he began to climb the ladder, awkwardly bringing the suitcase with him.

"We won't need the Bible," she observed.

"You never can tell," he said, panting. After he had got into the loft, he was a few seconds catching his breath. She had sat down in a pile of straw. A wide sheath of sunlight, filled with dust particles, slanted over her. She lay back against a bale, her face turned away, looking out the front opening of the barn where hay was thrown from a wagon into the loft. The two pink-speckled hillsides lay back against a dark ridge of woods. The sky was cloudless and cold blue. The boy dropped down by her side and put one arm under her and the other over her and began methodically kissing her face, making little noises like a fish. He did not remove his hat but it was pushed far enough back not to interfere. When her glasses got in his way, he took them off of her and slipped them into his pocket.

The girl at first did not return any of the kisses but presently she began to and after she had put several on his cheek, she reached his lips and remained there, kissing him again and again as if she were trying to draw all the breath out of him. His breath was clear and sweet like a child's and the kisses were sticky like a child's. He mumbled about loving her and about knowing when he first seen her that he loved her, but the mumbling was like the sleepy fretting of a child being put to sleep by his mother. Her mind, throughout this, never stopped or lost itself for a second to her feelings. "You ain't said you love me none," he whispered finally, pulling back from her. "You got to say that."

She looked away from him off into the hollow sky and then down at a black ridge and then down farther into what appeared to be two green swelling lakes. She didn't realize he had taken her glasses but this landscape could not seem exceptional to her for she seldom paid any close attention to her surroundings.

"You got to say it," he repeated. "You got to say you love me."

She was always careful how she committed herself. "In a sense," she began, "if you use the word loosely, you might say that. But it's not a word I use. I don't have illusions. I'm one of those people who see *through* to nothing."

The boy was frowning. "You got to say it. I said it and you got to say it," he said.

The girl looked at him almost tenderly. "You poor baby," she murmured. "It's just as well you don't understand," and she pulled him by the neck, face-down, against her. "We are all damned," she said, "but some of us have taken off our blindfolds and see that there's nothing to see. It's a kind of salvation."

The boy's astonished eyes looked blankly through the ends of her hair. "Okay," he almost whined, "but do you love me or don'tcher?"

"Yes," she said and added, "in a sense. But I must tell you something. There mustn't be anything dishonest between us." She lifted his head and looked him in the eye. "I am thirty years old," she said. "I have a number of degrees."

The boy's look was irritated but dogged. "I don't care," he said. "I don't care a thing about what all you done. I just want to know if you love me or don'tcher?" and he caught her to him and wildly planted her face with kisses until she said, "Yes, yes."

"Okay then," he said, letting her go. "Prove it."

She smiled, looking dreamily out on the shifty landscape. She had seduced him without even making up her mind to try. "How?" she asked, feeling that he should be delayed a little.

He leaned over and put his lips to her ear. "Show me where your wooden leg joins on," he whispered.

The girl uttered a sharp little cry and her face instantly drained of color. The obscenity of the suggestion was not what shocked her. As a child she had sometimes been subject to feelings of shame but education had removed the last traces of that as a good surgeon scrapes for cancer; she would no more have felt it over what he was asking than she would have believed in his Bible. But she was as sensitive about the artificial leg as a peacock about his tail. No one ever touched it but her. She took care of it as someone else would his soul, in private and almost with her own eyes turned away. "No," she said.

"I known it," he muttered, sitting up. "You're just playing me for a sucker."

"Oh no no!" she cried. "It joins on at the knee. Only at the knee. Why do you want to see it?"

The boy gave her a long penetrating look. "Because," he said, "it's what makes you different. You ain't like anybody else."

She sat staring at him. There was nothing about her face or her round freezing-blue eyes to indicate that this had moved her; but she felt as if her heart had stopped and left her mind to pump her blood. She decided that for the first time in her life she was face to face with real innocence. This boy, with an instinct that came from beyond wisdom, had touched the truth about her. When after a minute, she said in a hoarse high voice, "All right," it was like surrendering to him completely. It was like losing her own life and finding it again, miraculously, in his.

Very gently he began to roll the slack leg up. The artificial limb, in a white sock and brown flat shoe, was bound in a heavy material like canvas and ended in an ugly jointure where it was attached to the stump. The boy's face and his voice were entirely reverent as he uncovered it and said, "Now show me how to take it off and on."

She took it off for him and put it back on again and then he took it off himself, handling it as tenderly as if it were a real one. "See!" he said with a delighted child's face. "Now I can do it myself!"

"Put it back on," she said. She was thinking that she would run away with him and that every night he would take the leg off and every morning put it back on again. "Put it back on," she said.

"Not yet," he murmured, setting it on its foot out of her reach. "Leave it off for a while. You got me instead."

She gave a little cry of alarm but he pushed her down and began to kiss her again. Without the leg she felt entirely dependent on him. Her brain seemed to have stopped thinking altogether and to be about some other function that it was not very good at. Different expressions raced back and forth over her face. Every now and then the boy, his eyes like two steel spikes, would glance behind him where the leg stood. Finally she pushed him off and said, "Put it back on me now."

"Wait," he said. He leaned the other way and pulled the valise toward him and opened it. It had a pale blue spotted lining and there were only two Bibles in it. He took one of these out and opened the cover of it. It was hollow and contained a pocket flask of whiskey, a pack of cards, and a small blue box with printing on it. He laid these out in front of her one at a time in an evenly spaced row, like one presenting offerings at the shrine of a goddess. He put the blue box in her hand. THIS PRODUCT TO BE USED ONLY FOR THE PREVENTION OF DISEASE, she read, and dropped it. The boy was unscrewing the top of the flask. He stopped and pointed, with a smile, to the deck of cards. It was not an ordinary deck but one with an obscene picture on the back of each card. "Take a swig," he said, offering her the bottle first. He held it in front of her, but like one mesmerized, she did not move.

Her voice when she spoke had an almost pleading sound. "Aren't you," she murmured, "aren't you just good country people?"

The boy cocked his head. He looked as if he were just beginning to understand that she might be trying to insult him. "Yeah," he said, curling his lip slightly, "but it ain't held me back none. I'm as good as you any day in the week."

"Give me my leg," she said.

He pushed it farther away with his foot. "Come on now, let's begin to have us a good time," he said coaxingly. "We ain't got to know one another good yet."

"Give me my leg!" she screamed and tried to lunge for it but he pushed her down easily.

"What's the matter with you all of a sudden?" he asked, frowning as he screwed the top on the flask and put it quickly back inside the Bible. "You just a while ago said you didn't believe in nothing. I thought you was some girl!"

Her face was almost purple. "You're a Christian!" she hissed. "You're a fine Christian! You're just like them all—say one thing and do another. You're a perfect Christian, you're . . ."

The boy's mouth was set angrily. "I hope you don't think," he said in a lofty indignant tone, "that I believe in that crap! I may sell Bibles but I know which end is up and I wasn't born yesterday and I know where I'm going!"

"Give me my leg!" she screeched. He jumped up so quickly that she barely saw him sweep the cards and the blue box back into the Bible and throw the Bible into the valise. She saw him grab the leg and then she saw it for an instant slanted forlornly across the inside of the suitcase with a Bible at either side of its opposite ends. He slammed the lid shut and snatched up the valise and swung it down the hole and then stepped through himself.

When all of him had passed but his head, he turned and regarded her with a look that no longer had any admiration in it. "I've gotten a lot of interesting things," he said. "One time I got a woman's glass eye this way. And you needn't to think you'll catch me because Pointer ain't really my name. I use a different name at every house I call at and don't stay nowhere long. And I'll tell you another thing, Hulga," he said, using the name as if he didn't think much of it, "you ain't so smart. I been believing in nothing ever since I was born!" and then the toast-colored hat disappeared down the hole and the girl was left, sitting on the straw in the dusty sunlight. When she turned her churning face toward the opening, she saw his blue figure struggling successfully over the green speckled lake.

Mrs. Hopewell and Mrs. Freeman, who were in the back pasture, digging up onions, saw him emerge a little later from the woods and head across the meadow toward the highway. "Why, that looks like that nice dull young man that tried to sell me a Bible yesterday," Mrs. Hopewell said, squinting. "He must have been selling them to the Negroes back in there. He was so simple," she said, "but I guess the world would be better off if we were all that simple."

Mrs. Freeman's gaze drove forward and just touched him before he disappeared under the hill. Then she returned her attention to the evil-smelling onion shoot she was lifting from the ground. "Some can't be that simple," she said. "I know I never could."

FRANK O'CONNOR

(1903–1966)

First Confession

About the Author: Frank O'Connor, Irish fiction writer, critic, poet, and translator of Gaelic poetry, was born Michael O'Donovan in Cork. Using O'Connor as his pen name while working as a civil servant, he published numerous books rooted in Ireland's culture, history, and landscape, and in his own autobiographical experience. *Guests of the Nation,* his first collection of short stories, was published in 1931.

All the trouble began when my grandfather died and my grandmother—my father's mother—came to live with us. Relations in the one house are a strain at the best of times, but, to make matters worse, my grandmother was a real old countrywoman and quite unsuited to the life in town. She had a fat, wrinkled old face, and, to Mother's great indignation, went round the house in bare feet—the boots had her crippled, she said. For dinner she had a jug of porter and a pot of potatoes with—sometimes—a bit of salt fish, and she poured out the potatoes on the table and ate them slowly, with great relish, using her fingers by way of a fork.

Now, girls are supposed to be fastidious, but I was the one who suffered most from this. Nora, my sister, just sucked up to the old woman for the penny she got every Friday out of the old-age pension, a thing I could not do. I was too honest, that was my trouble; and when I was playing with Bill Connell, the sergeant-major's son, and saw my grandmother steering up the path with the jug of porter sticking out from beneath her shawl I was mortified. I made excuses not to let him come into the house, because I could never be sure what she would be up to when we went in.

When Mother was at work and my grandmother made the dinner I wouldn't touch it. Nora once tried to make me, but I hid under the table from her and took the bread-knife with me for protection. Nora let on to be very indignant (she wasn't, of course, but she knew

Mother saw through her, so she sided with Gran) and came after me. I lashed out at her with the bread-knife, and after that she left me alone. I stayed there till Mother came in from work and made my dinner, but when Father came in later Nora said in a shocked voice: "Oh, Dadda, do you know what Jackie did at dinnertime?" Then, of course, it all came out; Father gave me a flaking; Mother interfered, and for days after that he didn't speak to me and Mother barely spoke to Nora. And all because of that old woman! God knows, I was heart-scalded.

Then, to crown my misfortunes, I had to make my first confession and communion. It was an old woman called Ryan who prepared us for these. She was about the one age with Gran; she was well-to-do, lived in a big house on Montenotte, wore a black cloak and bonnet, and came every day to school at three o'clock when we should have been going home, and talked to us of hell. She may have mentioned the other place as well, but that could only have been by accident, for hell had the first place in her heart.

She lit a candle, took out a new half-crown, and offered it to the first boy who would hold one finger—only one finger!—in the flame for five minutes by the school clock. Being always very ambitious I was tempted to volunteer, but I thought it might look greedy. Then she asked were we afraid of holding one finger—only one finger!—in a little candle flame for five minutes and not afraid of burning all over in roasting hot furnaces for all eternity. "All eternity! Just think of that! A whole lifetime goes by and it's nothing, not even a drop in the ocean of your sufferings." The woman was really interesting about hell, but my attention was all fixed on the half-crown. At the end of the lesson she put it back in her purse. It was a great disappointment; a religious woman like that, you wouldn't think she'd bother about a thing like a half-crown.

Another day she said she knew a priest who woke one night to find a fellow he didn't recognize leaning over the end of his bed. The priest was a bit frightened—naturally enough—but he asked the fellow what he wanted, and the fellow said in a deep, husky voice that he wanted to go to confession. The priest said it was an awkward time and wouldn't it do in the morning, but the fellow said that last time he went to confession, there was one sin he kept back, being ashamed to mention it, and now it was always on his mind. Then the priest knew it was a bad case, because the fellow was after making a bad confession and committing a mortal sin. He got up to dress, and just then the cock crew in the yard outside, and—lo and behold!—when the priest looked round there was no sign of the fellow, only a smell of burning timber, and when the priest looked at his bed didn't he see the print of two hands burned in it? That was because the fellow had made a bad confession. This story made a shocking impression on me.

But the worst of all was when she showed us how to examine our conscience. Did we take the name of the Lord, our God, in vain? Did we honor our father and our mother? (I asked her did this include grandmothers and she said it did.) Did we love our neighbors as ourselves? Did we covet our neighbor's goods? (I thought of the way I felt about the penny that Nora got every Friday.) I decided that, between one thing and another, I must have broken the whole ten commandments, all on account of that old woman, and so far as I could see, so long as she remained in the house I had no hope of ever doing anything else.

I was scared to death of confession. The day the whole class went I let on to have a toothache, hoping my absence wouldn't be noticed; but at three o'clock, just as I was feeling safe, along comes a chap with a message from Mrs. Ryan that I was to go to confession myself on Saturday and be at the chapel for communion with the rest. To make it worse, Mother couldn't come with me and sent Nora instead.

Now, that girl had ways of tormenting me that Mother never knew of. She held my

hand as we went down the hill, smiling sadly and saying how sorry she was for me, as if she were bringing me to the hospital for an operation.

"Oh, God help us!" she moaned. "Isn't it a terrible pity you weren't a good boy? Oh, Jackie, my heart bleeds for you! How will you ever think of all your sins? Don't forget you have to tell him about the time you kicked Gran on the shin."

"Lemme go!" I said, trying to drag myself free of her. "I don't want to go to confession at all."

"But sure, you'll have to go to confession, Jackie," she replied in the same regretful tone. "Sure, if you didn't, the parish priest would be up to the house, looking for you. 'Tisn't, God knows, that I'm not sorry for you. Do you remember the time you tried to kill me with the bread-knife under the table? And the language you used to me? I don't know what he'll do with you at all, Jackie. He might have to send you up to the bishop."

I remember thinking bitterly that she didn't know the half of what I had to tell—if I told it. I knew I couldn't tell it, and understood perfectly why the fellow in Mrs. Ryan's story made a bad confession; it seemed to me a great shame that people wouldn't stop criticizing him. I remember that steep hill down to the church, and the sunlit hillsides beyond the valley of the river, which I saw in the gaps between the houses like Adam's last glimpse of Paradise.

Then, when she had maneuvered me down the long flight of steps to the chapel yard, Nora suddenly changed her tone. She became the raging malicious devil she really was.

"There you are!" she said with a yelp of triumph, hurling me through the church door. "And I hope he'll give you the penitential psalms, you dirty little caffler."

I knew then I was lost, given up to eternal justice. The door with the colored-glass panels swung shut behind me, the sunlight went out and gave place to deep shadow, and the wind whistled outside so that the silence within seemed to crackle like ice under my feet. Nora sat in front of me by the confession box. There were a couple of old women ahead of her, and then a miserable-looking poor devil came and wedged me in at the other side, so that I couldn't escape even if I had the courage. He joined his hands and rolled his eyes in the direction of the roof, muttering aspirations in an anguished tone, and I wondered had he a grandmother too. Only a grandmother could account for a fellow behaving in that heartbroken way, but he was better off than I, for he at least could go and confess his sins; while I would make a bad confession and then die in the night and be continually coming back and burning people's furniture.

Nora's turn came, and I heard the sound of something slamming, and then her voice as if butter wouldn't melt in her mouth, and then another slam, and out she came. God, the hypocrisy of women! Her eyes were lowered, her head was bowed, and her hands were joined very low down on her stomach, and she walked up the aisle to the side altar looking like a saint. You never saw such an exhibition of devotion; and I remembered the devilish malice with which she had tormented me all the way from our door, and wondered were all religious people like that, really. It was my turn now. With the fear of damnation in my soul I went in, and the confessional door closed of itself behind me.

It was pitch-dark and I couldn't see priest or anything else. Then I really began to be frightened. In the darkness it was a matter between God and me, and He had all the odds. He knew what my intentions were before I even started; I had no chance. All I had ever been told about confession got mixed up in my mind, and I knelt to one wall and said: "Bless me, father, for I have sinned; this is my first confession." I waited for a few minutes, but nothing happened, so I tried it on the other wall. Nothing happened there either. He had me spotted all right.

It must have been then that I noticed the shelf at about one height with my head. It was really a place for grown-up people to rest their elbows, but in my distracted state I thought it was probably the place you were supposed to kneel. Of course, it was on the high side and not very deep, but I was always good at climbing and managed to get up all right. Staying up was the trouble. There was room only for my knees, and nothing you could get a grip on but a sort of wooden moulding a bit above it. I held on to the moulding and repeated the words a little louder, and this time something happened all right. A slide was slammed back; a little light entered the box, and a man's voice said: "Who's there?"

" 'Tis me, father," I said for fear he mightn't see me and go away again. I couldn't see him at all. The place the voice came from was under the moulding, about level with my knees, so I took a good grip of the moulding and swung myself down till I saw the astonished face of a young priest looking up at me. He had to put his head on one side to see me, and I had to put mine on one side to see him, so we were more or less talking to one another upside-down. It struck me as a queer way of hearing confessions, but I didn't feel it my place to criticize.

"Bless me, father, for I have sinned; this is my first confession," I rattled off all in one breath, and swung myself down the least shade more to make it easier for him.

"What are you doing up there?" he shouted in an angry voice, and the strain the politeness was putting on my hold of the moulding, and the shock of being addressed in such an uncivil tone, were too much for me. I lost my grip, tumbled, and hit the door an unmerciful wallop before I found myself flat on my back in the middle of the aisle. The people who had been waiting stood up with their mouths open. The priest opened the door of the middle box and came out, pushing his biretta back from his forehead; he looked something terrible. Then Nora came scampering down the aisle.

"Oh, you dirty little caffler!" she said. "I might have known you'd do it. I might have known you'd disgrace me. I can't leave you out of my sight for one minute."

Before I could even get to my feet to defend myself she bent down and gave me a clip across the ear. This reminded me that I was so stunned I had even forgotten to cry, so that people might think I wasn't hurt at all, when in fact I was probably maimed for life. I gave a roar out of me.

"What's all this about?" the priest hissed, getting angrier than ever and pushing Nora off me. "How dare you hit the child like that, you little vixen?"

"But I can't do my penance with him, father," Nora cried, cocking an outraged eye up at him.

"Well, go and do it, or I'll give you some more to do," he said, giving me a hand up. "Was it coming to confession you were, my poor man?" he asked me.

" 'Twas, father," said I with a sob.

"Oh," he said respectfully, "a big hefty fellow like you must have terrible sins. Is this your first?"

" 'Tis, father," said I.

"Worse and worse," he said gloomily. "The crimes of a life-time. I don't know will I get rid of you at all today. You'd better wait now till I'm finished with these old ones. You can see by the looks of them they haven't much to tell."

"I will, father," I said with something approaching joy.

The relief of it was really enormous. Nora stuck out her tongue at me from behind his back, but I couldn't even be bothered retorting. I knew from the very moment that man opened his mouth that he was intelligent above the ordinary. When I had time to think, I saw how right I was. It only stood to reason that a fellow confessing after seven years would

have more to tell than people that went every week. The crimes of a lifetime, exactly as he said. It was only what he expected, and the rest was the cackle of old women and girls with their talk of hell, the bishop, and the penitential psalms. That was all they knew. I started to make my examination of conscience, and barring the one bad business of my grandmother it didn't seem so bad.

The next time, the priest steered me into the confession box himself and left the shutter back the way I could see him get in and sit down at the further side of the grille from me.

"Well, now," he said, "what do they call you?"

"Jackie, father," said I.

"And what's a-trouble to you, Jackie?"

"Father," I said, feeling I might as well get it over while I had him in good humor, "I had it all arranged to kill my grandmother."

He seemed a bit shaken by that, all right, because he said nothing for quite a while.

"My goodness," he said at last, "that'd be a shocking thing to do. What put that into your head?"

"Father," I said, feeling very sorry for myself, "she's an awful woman."

"Is she?" he asked. "What way is she awful?"

"She takes porter, father," I said, knowing well from the way Mother talked of it that this was a mortal sin, and hoping it would make the priest take a more favorable view of my case.

"Oh, my!" he said, and I could see he was impressed.

"And snuff, father," said I.

"That's a bad case, sure enough, Jackie," he said.

"And she goes round in her bare feet, father," I went on in a rush of self-pity, "and she knows I don't like her, and she gives pennies to Nora and none to me, and my da sides with her and flakes me, and one night I was so heart-scalded I made up my mind I'd have to kill her."

"And what would you do with the body?" he asked with great interest.

"I was thinking I could chop that up and carry it away in a barrow I have," I said.

"Begor, Jackie," he said, "do you know you're a terrible child?"

"I know, father," I said, for I was just thinking the same thing myself. "I tried to kill Nora too with a bread-knife under the table, only I missed her."

"Is that the little girl that was beating you just now?" he asked.

" 'Tis, father."

"Someone will go for her with a bread-knife one day, and he won't miss her," he said rather cryptically. "You must have great courage. Between ourselves, there's a lot of people I'd like to do the same to but I'd never have the nerve. Hanging is an awful death."

"Is it, father?" I asked with the deepest interest—I was always very keen on hanging. "Did you ever see a fellow hanged?"

"Dozens of them," he said solemnly. "And they all died roaring."

"Jay!" I said.

"Oh, a horrible death!" he said with great satisfaction. "Lots of the fellows I saw killed their grandmothers too, but they all said 'twas never worth it."

He had me there for a full ten minutes talking, and then walked out the chapel yard with me. I was genuinely sorry to part with him, because he was the most entertaining character I'd ever met in the religious line. Outside, after the shadow of the church, the

sunlight was like the roaring of waves on a beach; it dazzled me; and when the frozen silence melted and I heard the screech of trams on the road my heart soared. I knew now I wouldn't die in the night and come back, leaving marks on my mother's furniture. It would be a great worry to her, and the poor soul had enough.

Nora was sitting on the railing, waiting for me, and she put on a very sour puss when she saw the priest with me. She was mad jealous because a priest had never come out of the church with her.

"Well," she asked coldly, after he left me, "what did he give you?"

"Three Hail Marys," I said.

"Three Hail Marys," she repeated incredulously. "You mustn't have told him anything."

"I told him everything," I said confidently.

"About Gran and all?"

"About Gran and all."

(All she wanted was to be able to go home and say I'd made a bad confession.)

"Did you tell him you went for me with the bread-knife?" she asked with a frown.

"I did to be sure."

"And he only gave you three Hail Marys?"

"That's all."

She slowly got down from the railing with a baffled air. Clearly, this was beyond her. As we mounted the steps back to the main road she looked at me suspiciously.

"What are you sucking?" she asked.

"Bullseyes."

"Was it the priest gave them to you?"

" 'Twas."

"Lord God," she wailed bitterly, "some people have all the luck! 'Tis no advantage to anybody trying to be good. I might just as well be a sinner like you."

JAMES BALDWIN

(1924–1987)

Sonny's Blues

About the Author: James Baldwin was born in New York City, the son of a minister. Many of his novels, short stories, and especially his essays, confront the black experience in an America troubled by social and racial inequalities. Baldwin's first novel, *Go Tell It on the Mountain* (1953), was followed by five others, a collection of short fiction, *Going to Meet The Man* (1965), and four books of essays. He died in France.

I read about it in the paper, in the subway, on my way to work. I read it, and I couldn't believe it, and I read it again. Then perhaps I just stared at it, at the newsprint spelling out his name, spelling out the story. I stared at it in the swinging lights of the subway car, and in the faces and bodies of the people, and in my own face, trapped in the darkness which roared outside.

It was not to be believed and I kept telling myself that, as I walked from the subway

station to the high school. And at the same time I couldn't doubt it. I was scared, scared for Sonny. He became real to me again. A great block of ice got settled in my belly and kept melting there slowly all day long, while I taught my classes algebra. It was a special kind of ice. It kept melting, sending trickles of ice water all up and down my veins, but it never got less. Sometimes it hardened and seemed to expand until I felt my guts were going to come spilling out or that I was going to choke or scream. This would always be at a moment when I was remembering some specific thing Sonny had once said or done.

When he was about as old as the boys in my classes his face had been bright and open, there was a lot of copper in it; and he'd had wonderfully direct brown eyes, and great gentleness and privacy. I wondered what he looked like now. He had been picked up the evening before, in a raid on an apartment downtown, for peddling and using heroin.

I couldn't believe it: but what I meant by that is that I couldn't find any room for it anywhere inside me. I had kept it outside me for a long time. I hadn't wanted to know. I had had suspicions, but I didn't name them, I kept putting them away. I told myself that Sonny was wild, but he wasn't crazy. And he'd always been a good boy, he hadn't ever turned hard or evil or disrespectful, the way kids can, so quick, especially in Harlem. I didn't want to believe that I'd ever see my brother going down, coming to nothing, all that light in his face gone out, in the condition I'd already seen so many others. Yet it had happened and here I was, talking about algebra to a lot of boys who might, every one of them for all I knew, be popping off needles every time they went to the head. Maybe it did more for them than algebra could.

I was sure that the first time Sonny had ever had horse, he couldn't have been much older than these boys were now. These boys, now, were living as we'd been living then, they were growing up with a rush and their heads bumped abruptly against the low ceiling of their actual possibilities. They were filled with rage. All they really knew were two darknesses, the darkness of their lives, which was now closing in on them, and the darkness of the movies, which had blinded them to that other darkness, and in which they now, vindictively, dreamed, at once more together than they were at any other time, and more alone.

When the last bell rang, the last class ended, I let out my breath. It seemed I'd been holding it for all that time. My clothes were wet—I may have looked as though I'd been sitting in a steam bath, all dressed up all afternoon. I sat alone in the classroom a long time. I listened to the boys outside, downstairs, shouting and cursing and laughing. Their laughter struck me for perhaps the first time. It was not the joyous laughter which—God knows why—one associates with children. It was mocking and insular, its intent was to denigrate. It was disenchanted, and in this, also, lay the authority of their curses. Perhaps I was listening to them because I was thinking about my brother and in them I heard my brother. And myself.

One boy was whistling a tune, at once very complicated and very simple, it seemed to be pouring out of him as though he were a bird, and it sounded very cool and moving through all that harsh, bright air, only just holding its own through all those other sounds.

I stood up and walked over to the window and looked down into the courtyard. It was the beginning of the spring and the sap was rising in the boys. A teacher passed through them every now and again, quickly, as though he or she couldn't wait to get out of that courtyard, to get those boys out of their sight and off their minds. I started collecting my stuff. I thought I'd better get home and talk to Isabel.

The courtyard was almost deserted by the time I got downstairs. I saw this boy standing in the shadow of a doorway, looking just like Sonny. I almost called his name. Then I saw that it wasn't Sonny, but somebody we used to know, a boy from around our block. He'd been Sonny's friend. He'd never been mine, having been too young for me, and, anyway, I'd never liked him. And now, even though he was a grown-up man, he still hung around that block, still spent hours on the street corners, was always high and raggy. I used to run into him from time to time and he'd often work around to asking me for a quarter or fifty cents. He always had some real good excuse too, and I always gave it to him, I don't know why.

But now, abruptly I hated him. I couldn't stand the way he looked at me, partly like a dog, partly like a cunning child. I wanted to ask him what the hell he was doing in the school courtyard.

He sort of shuffled over to me, and he said, "I see you got the papers. So you already know about it."

"You mean about Sonny? Yes, I already know about it. How come they didn't get you?"

He grinned. It made him repulsive and it also brought to mind what he'd looked like as a kid. "I wasn't there. I stay away from them people."

"Good for you." I offered him a cigarette and I watched him through the smoke. "You come all the way down here just to tell me about Sonny?"

"That's right." He was sort of shaking his head and his eyes looked strange, as though they were about to cross. The bright sun deadened his damp dark brown skin and it made his eyes look yellow and showed up the dirt in his kinked hair. He smelled funky. I moved a little way away from him and I said, "Well, thanks. But I already know about it and I got to get home."

"I'll walk you a little ways," he said. We started walking. There were a couple of kids still loitering in the courtyard and one of them said good night to me and looked strangely at the boy beside me.

"What're you going to do?" he asked me. "I mean, about Sonny?"

"Look. I haven't seen Sonny for over a year. I'm not sure I'm going to do anything. Anyway, what the hell *can* I do?"

"That's right," he said quickly, "ain't nothing you can do. Can't much help old Sonny no more, I guess."

It was what I was thinking and so it seemed to me he had no right to say it.

"I'm surprised at Sonny, though," he went on—he had a funny way of talking, he looked straight ahead as though he were talking to himself—"I thought Sonny was a smart boy, I thought he was too smart to get hung."

"I guess he thought so too," I said sharply, "and that's how he got hung. And how about you? You're pretty goddamn smart, I bet."

Then he looked directly at me, just for a minute. "I ain't smart," he said. "If I was smart, I'd have reached for a pistol a long time ago."

"Look. Don't tell *me* your sad story, if it was up to me, I'd give you one." Then I felt guilty—guilty, probably, for never having supposed that the poor bastard *had* a story of his own, much less a sad one, and I asked, quickly, "What's going to happen to him now?"

He didn't answer this. He was off by himself some place. "Funny thing," he said, and from his tone we might have been discussing the quickest way to get to Brooklyn, "when I saw the papers this morning, the first thing I asked myself was if I had anything to do with it. I felt sort of responsible."

I began to listen more carefully. The subway station was on the corner, just before us, and I stopped. He stopped, too. We were in front of a bar and he ducked slightly, peering in, but whoever he was looking for didn't seem to be there. The juke box was blasting away with something black and bouncy and I half watched the barmaid as she danced her way from the juke box to her place behind the bar. And I watched her face as she laughingly responded to something someone said to her, still keeping time to the music. When she smiled one saw the little girl, one sensed the doomed, still struggling woman beneath the battered face of the semi-whore.

"I never *give* Sonny nothing," the boy said finally, "but a long time ago I come to school high and Sonny asked me how it felt." He paused, I couldn't bear to watch him, I watched the barmaid, and I listened to the music which seemed to be causing the pavement to shake. "I told him it felt great." The music stopped, the barmaid paused and watched the juke box until the music began again. "It did."

All this was carrying me some place I didn't want to go. I certainly didn't want to know how it felt. It filled everything, the people, the houses, the music, the dark, quicksilver barmaid, with menace, and this menace was their reality.

"What's going to happen to him now?" I asked again.

"They'll send him away some place and they'll try to cure him." He shook his head. "Maybe he'll even think he's kicked the habit. Then they'll let him loose"—he gestured, throwing his cigarette into the gutter. "That's all."

"What do you mean that's *all?*"

But I knew what he meant.

"I *mean,* that's *all.*" He turned his head and looked at me, pulling down the corners of his mouth. "Don't you know what I mean?" he asked, softly.

"How the hell *would* I know what you mean?" I almost whispered it, I don't know why.

"That's right," he said to the air, "how would *he* know what I mean?" He turned toward me again, patient and calm, and yet I somehow felt him shaking, shaking as though he were going to fall apart. I felt that ice in my guts again, the dread I'd felt all afternoon; and again I watched the barmaid, moving about the bar, washing glasses, and singing. "Listen. They'll let him out and then it'll just start all over again. That's what I mean."

"You mean—they'll let him out. And then he'll just start working his way back in again. You mean he'll never kick the habit. Is that what you mean?"

"That's right," he said cheerfully. "*You* see what I mean."

"Tell me," I said at last, "why does he want to die? He must want to die, he's killing himself, why does he want to die?"

He looked at me in surprise. He licked his lips. "He don't want to die. He wants to live. Don't nobody want to die, ever."

Then I wanted to ask him—too many things. He could not have answered, or if he had, I could not have borne the answers. I started walking. "Well, I guess it's none of my business."

"It's going to be rough on old Sonny," he said. We reached the subway station. "This is your station?" he asked. I nodded. I took one step down. "Damn!" he said suddenly. I looked up at him. He grinned again. "Damn it if I didn't leave all my money home. You ain't got a dollar on you, have you? Just for a couple of days, is all."

All at once something inside gave and threatened to come pouring out of me. I didn't hate him any more. I felt that in another moment I'd start crying like a child.

"Sure," I said. "Don't sweat." I looked in my wallet and didn't have a dollar, I only had five. "Here," I said. "That hold you?"

He didn't look at it—he didn't want to look at it. A terrible closed look came over his face, as though he were keeping the number on the bill a secret from him and me. "Thanks," he said, and now he was dying to see me go. "Don't worry about Sonny. Maybe I'll write him or something."

"Sure," I said. "You do that. So long."

"Be seeing you," he said. I went on down the steps.

And I didn't write Sonny or send him anything for a long time. When I finally did, it was just after my little girl died, he wrote me back a letter which made me feel like a bastard.

Here's what he said:

Dear brother,

You don't know how much I needed to hear from you. I wanted to write you many a time but I dug how much I must have hurt you and so I didn't write. But now I feel like a man who's been trying to climb up out of some deep, real deep and funky hole and just saw the sun up there, outside. I got to get outside.

I can't tell you much about how I got here. I mean I don't know how to tell you. I guess I was afraid of something or I was trying to escape from something and you know I have never been very strong in the head (smile). I'm glad Mama and Daddy are dead and can't see what's happened to their son and I swear if I'd known what I was doing I would never have hurt you so, you and a lot of other fine people who were nice to me and who believed in me.

I don't want you to think it had anything to do with me being a musician. It's more than that. Or maybe less than that. I can't get anything straight in my head down here and I try not to think about what's going to happen to me when I get outside again. Sometime I think I'm going to flip and *never* get outside and sometime I think I'll come straight back. I tell you one thing, though, I'd rather blow my brains out than go through this again. But that's what they all say, so they tell me. If I tell you when I'm coming to New York and if you could meet me, I sure would appreciate it. Give my love to Isabel and the kids and I was sure sorry to hear about little Gracie. I wish I could be like Mama and say the Lord's will be done, but I don't know it seems to me that trouble is the one thing that never does get stopped and I don't know what good it does to blame it on the Lord. But maybe it does some good if you believe it.

Your brother,
Sonny

Then I kept in constant touch with him and I sent him whatever I could and I went to meet him when he came back to New York. When I saw him many things I thought I had forgotten came flooding back to me. This was because I had begun, finally, to wonder about Sonny, about the life that Sonny lived inside. This life, whatever it was, had made him older and thinner and it had deepened the distant stillness in which he had always moved. He looked very unlike my baby brother. Yet, when he smiled, when we shook hands, the baby brother I'd never known looked out from the depths of his private life, like an animal waiting to be coaxed into the light.

"How you been keeping?" he asked me.

"All right. And you?"

"Just fine." He was smiling all over his face. "It's good to see you again."

"It's good to see you."

The seven years' difference in our ages lay between us like a chasm: I wondered if these years would ever operate between us as a bridge. I was remembering, and it made it hard to catch my breath, that I had been there when he was born; and I had heard the first words he had ever spoken. When he started to walk, he walked from our mother straight to me. I caught him just before he fell when he took the first steps he ever took in this world.

"How's Isabel?"

"Just fine. She's dying to see you."

"And the boys?"

"They're fine, too. They're anxious to see their uncle."

"Oh, come on. You know they don't remember me."

"Are you kidding? Of course they remember you."

He grinned again. We got into a taxi. We had a lot to say to each other, far too much to know how to begin.

As the taxi began to move, I asked, "You still want to go to India?"

He laughed. "You still remember that. Hell, no. This place is Indian enough for me."

"It used to belong to them," I said.

And he laughed again. "They damn sure knew what they were doing when they got rid of it."

Years ago, when he was around fourteen, he'd been all hipped on the idea of going to India. He read books about people sitting on rocks, naked, in all kinds of weather, but mostly bad, naturally, and walking barefoot through hot coals and arriving at wisdom. I used to say that it sounded to me as though they were getting away from wisdom as fast as they could. I think he sort of looked down on me for that.

"Do you mind," he asked, "if we have the driver drive alongside the park? On the west side—I haven't seen the city in so long."

"Of course not," I said. I was afraid that I might sound as though I were humoring him, but I hoped he wouldn't take it that way.

So we drove along, between the green of the park and the stony, lifeless elegance of hotels and apartment buildings, toward the vivid, killing streets of our childhood. These streets hadn't changed, though housing projects jutted up out of them now like rocks in the middle of a boiling sea. Most of the houses in which we had grown up had vanished, as had the stores from which we had stolen, the basements in which we had first tried sex, the rooftops from which we had hurled tin cans and bricks. But houses exactly like the houses of our past yet dominated the landscape, boys exactly like the boys we once had been found themselves smothering in these houses, came down into the streets for light and air and found themselves encircled by disaster. Some escaped the trap, most didn't. Those who got out always left something of themselves, behind, as some animals amputate a leg and leave it in the trap. It might be said, perhaps, that I had escaped, after all, I was a school teacher; or that Sonny had, he hadn't lived in Harlem for years. Yet, as the cab moved uptown through streets which seemed, with a rush, to darken with dark people, and as I covertly studied Sonny's face, it came to me that what we both were seeking through our separate cab windows was that part of ourselves which had been left behind. It's always at the hour of trouble and confrontation that the missing member aches.

We hit 110th Street and started rolling up Lenox Avenue. And I'd known this avenue all my life, but it seemed to me again, as it had seemed on the day I'd first heard about Sonny's trouble, filled with a hidden menace which was its very breath of life.

"We almost there," said Sonny.

"Almost." We were both too nervous to say anything more.

We live in a housing project. It hasn't been up long. A few days after it was up it seemed uninhabitably new, now, of course, it's already rundown. It looks like a parody of the good, clean, faceless life—God knows the people who live in it do their best to make it a parody. The beat-looking grass lying around isn't enough to make their lives green, the hedges will never hold out the streets, and they know it. The big windows fool no one, they aren't big enough to make space out of no space. They don't bother with the windows, they watch the TV screen instead. The playground is most popular with the children who don't play at jacks, or skip rope, or roller skate, or swing, and they can be found in it after dark. We moved in partly because it's not too far from where I teach, and partly for the kids; but it's really just like the houses in which Sonny and I grew up. The same things happen, they'll have the same things to remember. The moment Sonny and I started into the house I had the feeling that I was simply bringing him back into the danger he had almost died trying to escape.

Sonny has never been talkative. So I don't know why I was sure he'd be dying to talk to me when supper was over the first night. Everything went fine, the oldest boy remembered him, and the youngest boy liked him, and Sonny had remembered to bring something for each of them; and Isabel, who is really much nicer than I am, more open and giving, had gone to a lot of trouble about dinner and was genuinely glad to see him. And she's always been able to tease Sonny in a way that I haven't. It was nice to see her face so vivid again and to hear her laugh and watch her make Sonny laugh. She wasn't, or, anyway, she didn't seem to be, at all uneasy or embarrassed. She chatted as though there were no subject which had to be avoided and she got Sonny past his first, faint stiffness. And thank God she was there, for I was filled with that icy dread again. Everything I did seemed awkward to me, and everything I said sounded freighted with hidden meaning. I was trying to remember everything I'd heard about dope addiction and I couldn't help watching Sonny for signs. I wasn't doing it out of malice. I was trying to find out something about my brother. I was dying to hear him tell me he was safe.

"Safe!" my father grunted, whenever Mama suggested trying to move to a neighborhood which might be safer for children. "Safe, hell! Ain't no place safe for kids, nor nobody."

He always went on like this, but he wasn't, ever, really as bad as he sounded, not even on weekends, when he got drunk. As a matter of fact, he was always on the lookout for "something a little better," but he died before he found it. He died suddenly, during a drunken weekend in the middle of the war, when Sonny was fifteen. He and Sonny hadn't ever got on too well. And this was partly because Sonny was the apple of his father's eye. It was because he loved Sonny so much and was frightened for him, that he was always fighting with him. It doesn't do any good to fight with Sonny. Sonny just moves back, inside himself, where he can't be reached. But the principal reason that they never hit it off is that they were so much alike. Daddy was big and rough and loud-talking, just the opposite of Sonny, but they both had—that same privacy.

Mama tried to tell me something about this, just after Daddy died. I was home on leave from the army.

This was the last time I ever saw my mother alive. Just the same, this picture gets all mixed up in my mind with pictures I had of her when she was younger. The way I always see her is the way she used to be on a Sunday afternoon, say, when the old folks were talking after the big Sunday dinner. I always see her wearing pale blue. She'd be sitting on the sofa.

And my father would be sitting in the easy chair, not far from her. And the living room would be full of church folks and relatives. There they sit, in chairs all around the living room, and the night is creeping up outside, but nobody knows it yet. You can see the darkness growing against the window-panes and you hear the street noises every now and again, or maybe the jangling beat of a tambourine from one of the churches close by, but it's real quiet in the room. For a moment nobody's talking, but every face looks darkening, like the sky outside. And my mother rocks a little from the waist, and my father's eyes are closed. Everyone is looking at something a child can't see. For a minute they've forgotten the children. Maybe a kid is lying on the rug, half asleep. Maybe somebody's got a kid in his lap and is absent-mindedly stroking the kid's head. Maybe there's a kid, quiet and big-eyed, curled up in a big chair in the corner. The silence, the darkness coming, and the darkness in the faces frightens the child obscurely. He hopes that the hand which strokes his forehead will never stop—will never die. He hopes that there will never come a time when the old folks won't be sitting around the living room, talking about where they've come from, and what they've seen, and what's happened to them and their kinfolk.

But something deep and watchful in the child knows that this is bound to end, is already ending. In a moment someone will get up and turn on the light. Then the old folks will remember the children and they won't talk any more that day. And when light fills the room, the child is filled with darkness. He knows that every time this happens he's moved just a little closer to that darkness outside. The darkness outside is what the old folks have been talking about. It's what they've come from. It's what they endure. The child knows that they won't talk any more because if he knows too much about what's happening to *them,* he'll know too much too soon, about what's going to happen to *him.*

The last time I talked to my mother, I remember I was restless. I wanted to get out and see Isabel. We weren't married then and we had a lot to straighten out between us.

There Mama sat, in black, by the window. She was humming an old church song, *Lord you brought me from a long ways off.* Sonny was out somewhere. Mama kept watching the streets.

"I don't know," she said, "if I'll ever see you again, after you go off from here. But I hope you'll remember the things I tried to teach you."

"Don't talk like that," I said, and smiled. "You'll be here a long time yet."

She smiled, too, but she said nothing. She was quiet for a long time. And I said, "Mama, don't you worry about nothing. I'll be writing all the time, and you be getting the checks. . . ."

"I want to talk to you about your brother," she said, suddenly. "If anything happens to me he ain't going to have nobody to look out for him."

"Mama," I said, "ain't nothing going to happen to you *or* Sonny. Sonny's all right. He's a good boy and he's got good sense."

"It ain't a question of his being a good boy," Mama said, "nor of his having good sense. It ain't only the bad ones, nor yet the dumb ones that gets sucked under." She stopped, looking at me. "Your Daddy once had a brother," she said, and she smiled in a way that made me feel she was in pain. "You didn't never know that, did you?"

"No," I said, "I never knew that," and I watched her face.

"Oh, yes," she said, "your Daddy had a brother." She looked out of the window again. "I know you never saw your Daddy cry. But *I* did—many a time, through all these years."

I asked her, "What happened to his brother? How come nobody's ever talked about him?"

This was the first time I ever saw my mother look old.

"His brother got killed," she said, "when he was just a little younger than you are now. I knew him. He was a fine boy. He was maybe a little full of the devil, but he didn't mean nobody no harm."

Then she stopped and the room was silent, exactly as it had sometimes been on those Sunday afternoons. Mama kept looking out into the streets.

"He used to have a job in the mill," she said, "and, like all young folks, he just liked to perform on Saturday nights. Saturday nights, him and your father would drift around to different places, go to dances and things like that, or just sit around with people they knew, and your father's brother would sing, he had a fine voice, and play along with himself on his guitar. Well, this particular Saturday night, him and your father was coming home from some place, and they were both a little drunk and there was a moon that night, it was bright like day. Your father's brother was feeling kind of good, and he was whistling to himself, and he had his guitar slung over his shoulder. They was coming down a hill and beneath them was a road that turned off from the highway. Well, your father's brother, being always kind of frisky, decided to run down this hill, and he did, with his guitar banging and clanging behind him, and he ran across the road, and he was making water behind a tree. And your father was sort of amused at him and he was still coming down the hill, kind of slow. Then he heard a car motor and that same minute his brother stepped from behind the tree, into the road, in the moonlight. And he started to cross the road. And your father started to run down the hill, he says he don't know why. This car was full of white men. They was all drunk, and when they seen your father's brother they let out a great whoop and holler and they aimed the car straight at him. They was having fun, they just wanted to scare him, the way they do sometimes, you know. But they was drunk. And I guess the boy, being drunk, too, and scared, kind of lost his head. By the time he jumped it was too late. Your father says he heard his brother scream when the car rolled over him, and he heard the wood of that guitar when it give, and he heard them strings go flying, and he heard them white men shouting, and the car kept on a-going and it ain't stopped till this day. And, time your father got down the hill, his brother weren't nothing but blood and pulp."

Tears were gleaming on my mother's face. There wasn't anything I could say.

"He never mentioned it," she said, "because I never let him mention it before you children. Your Daddy was like a crazy man that night and for many a night thereafter. He says he never in his life seen anything as dark as that road after the lights of that car had gone away. Weren't nothing, weren't nobody on that road, just your Daddy and his brother and that busted guitar. Oh, yes. Your Daddy never did really get right again. Till the day he died he weren't sure but that every white man he saw was the man that killed his brother."

She stopped and took out her handkerchief and dried her eyes and looked at me.

"I ain't telling you all this," she said, "to make you scared or bitter or to make you hate nobody. I'm telling you this because you got a brother. And the world ain't changed."

I guess I didn't want to believe this. I guess she saw this in my face. She turned away from me, toward the window again, searching those streets.

"But I praise my Redeemer," she said at last, "that He called your Daddy home before me. I ain't saying it to throw no flowers at myself, but, I declare, it keeps me from feeling too cast down to know I helped your father get safely through this world. Your father always acted like he was the roughest, strongest man on earth. And everybody took him to be like that. But if he hadn't had *me* there—to see his tears!"

She was crying again. Still I couldn't move. I said, "Lord, Lord, Mama, I didn't know it was like that."

"Oh, honey," she said, "there's a lot that you don't know. But you are going to find it out." She stood up from the window and came over to me. "You got to hold on to your brother," she said, "and don't let him fall, no matter what it looks like is happening to him and no matter how evil you gets with him. You going to be evil with him many a time. But don't you forget what I told you, you hear?"

"I won't forget," I said. "Don't you worry, I won't forget. I won't let nothing happen to Sonny."

My mother smiled as though she were amused at something she saw in my face. Then, "You may not be able to stop nothing from happening. But you got to let him know you's *there.*"

Two days later I was married, and then I was gone. And I had a lot of things on my mind and I pretty well forgot my promise to Mama until I got shipped home on a special furlough for her funeral.

And, after the funeral, with just Sonny and me alone in the empty kitchen, I tried to find out something about him.

"What do you want to do?" I asked him.

"I'm going to be a musician," he said.

For he had graduated, in the time I had been away, from dancing to the juke box to finding out who was playing what, and what they were doing with it, and he had bought himself a set of drums.

"You mean, you want to be a drummer?" I somehow had the feeling that being a drummer might be all right for other people but not for my brother Sonny.

"I don't think," he said, looking at me very gravely, "that I'll ever be a good drummer. But I think I can play a piano."

I frowned. I'd never played the role of the older brother quite so seriously before, had scarcely ever, in fact, *asked* Sonny a damn thing. I sensed myself in the presence of something I didn't really know how to handle, didn't understand. So I made my frown a little deeper as I asked: "What kind of musician do you want to be?"

He grinned. "How many kinds do you think there are?"

"Be *serious,*" I said.

He laughed, throwing his head back, and then looked at me. "I *am* serious."

"Well, then, for Christ's sake, stop kidding around and answer a serious question. I mean, do you want to be a concert pianist, or want to play classical music and all that, or—or what?" Long before I finished he was laughing again. "For Christ's *sake,* Sonny!"

He sobered, but with difficulty. "I'm sorry. But you sound so—*scared!*" and he was off again.

"Well, you may think it's funny now, baby, but it's not going to be so funny when you have to make your living at it, let me tell you *that.*" I was furious because I knew he was laughing at me and I didn't know why.

"No," he said, very sober now, and afraid, perhaps, that he'd hurt me, "I don't want to be a classical pianist. That isn't what interests me. I mean"—he paused, looking hard at me, as though his eyes would help me to understand, and then gestured helplessly, as though perhaps his hand would help—"I mean, I'll have a lot of studying to do, and I'll have to study *everything,* but, I mean, I want to play *with*—jazz musicians." He stopped. "I want to play jazz," he said.

Well, the word had never before sounded as heavy, as real, as it sounded that afternoon in Sonny's mouth. I just looked at him and I was probably frowning a real frown by this time. I simply couldn't see why on earth he'd want to spend his time hanging around nightclubs, clowning around on bandstands, while people pushed each other around a dance floor. It seemed—beneath him, somehow. I had never thought about it before, had never been forced to, but I suppose I had always put jazz musicians in a class with what Daddy called "goodtime people."

"Are you *serious?*"

"Hell, *yes,* I'm serious."

He looked more helpless than ever, and annoyed, and deeply hurt.

I suggested helpfully: "You mean—like Louis Armstrong?"

His face closed as though I'd struck him. "No. I'm not talking about none of that old-time, down home crap."

"Well, look Sonny, I'm sorry, don't get mad. I just don't altogether get it, that's all. Name somebody—you know, a jazz musician you admire."

"Bird."

"Who?"

"Bird! Charlie Parker! Don't they teach you nothing in the god-damn army?" I lit a cigarette. I was surprised and then a little amused to discover that I was trembling. "I've been out of touch," I said. "You'll have to be patient with me. Now. Who's this Parker character?"

"He's just one of the greatest jazz musicians alive," said Sonny, sullenly, his hands in his pockets, his back to me. "Maybe *the* greatest," he added, bitterly, "that's probably why *you* never heard of him."

"All right," I said, "I'm ignorant. I'm sorry. I'll go out and buy all the cat's records right away, all right?"

"It don't," said Sonny, with dignity, "make any difference to me. I don't care what you listen to. Don't do me no favors."

I was beginning to realize that I'd never seen him so upset before. With another part of my mind I was thinking that this would probably turn out to be one of those things kids go through and that I shouldn't make it seem important by pushing it too hard. Still, I didn't think it would do any harm to ask: "Doesn't all this take a lot of time? Can you make a living at it?"

He turned back to me and half leaned, half sat, on the kitchen table. "Everything takes time," he said, "and—well, yes, sure, I can make a living at it. But what I don't seem to be able to make you understand is that it's the only thing I want to do."

"Well, Sonny," I said gently, "you know people can't always do exactly what they *want* to do—"

"*No,* I don't know that," said Sonny, surprising me. "I think people *ought* to do what they want to do, what else are they alive for?"

"You are getting to be a big boy," I said desperately, "it's time you started thinking about your future."

"I'm thinking about my future," said Sonny, grimly. "I think about it all the time."

I gave up. I decided, if he didn't change his mind, that we could always talk about it later. "In the meantime," I said, "you got to finish school." We had already decided that he'd have to move in with Isabel and her folks. I knew this wasn't the ideal arrangement because Isabel's folks are inclined to be dicty and they hadn't especially wanted Isabel to marry me. But I didn't know what else to do. "And we have to get you fixed up at Isabel's."

There was a long silence. He moved from the kitchen table to the window. "That's a terrible idea. You know it yourself."

"Do you have a *better* idea?"

He just walked up and down the kitchen for a minute. He was as tall as I was. He had started to shave. I suddenly had the feeling that I didn't know him at all.

He stopped at the kitchen table and picked up my cigarettes. Looking at me with a kind of mocking, amused defiance, he put one between his lips. "You mind?"

"You smoking already?"

He lit the cigarette and nodded, watching me through the smoke. "I just wanted to see if I'd have the courage to smoke in front of you." He grinned and blew a great cloud of smoke to the ceiling. "It was easy." He looked at my face. "Come on, now. I bet you was smoking at my age, tell the truth."

I didn't say anything but the truth was on my face, and he laughed. But now there was something very strained in his laugh. "Sure. And I bet that ain't all you was doing."

He was frightening me a little. "Cut the crap," I said. "We already decided that you was going to go and live at Isabel's. Now what's got into you all of a sudden?"

"*You* decided it," he pointed out. "*I* didn't decide nothing." He stopped in front of me, leaning against the stove, arms loosely folded. "Look, brother. I don't want to stay in Harlem no more, I really don't." He was very earnest. He looked at me, then over toward the kitchen window. There was something in his eyes I'd never seen before, some thoughtfulness, some worry all his own. He rubbed the muscle of one arm. "It's time I was getting out of here."

"Where do you want to *go,* Sonny?"

"I want to join the army. Or the navy, I don't care. If I say I'm old enough, they'll believe me."

Then I got mad. It was because I was so scared. "You must be crazy. You goddamn fool, what the hell do you want to go and join the *army* for?"

"I just told you. To get out of Harlem."

"Sonny, you haven't even finished *school.* And if you really want to be a musician, how do you expect to study if you're in the *army?*"

He looked at me, trapped, and in anguish. "There's ways. I might be able to work out some kind of deal. Anyway, I'll have the G.I. Bill when I come out."

"*If* you come out." We stared at each other. "Sonny, please. Be reasonable. I know the setup is far from perfect. But we got to do the best we can."

"I ain't learning nothing in school," he said. "Even when I go." He turned away from me and opened the window and threw his cigarette out into the narrow alley. I watched his back. "At least, I ain't learning nothing you'd want me to learn." He slammed the window so hard I thought the glass would fly out, and turned back to me. "And I'm sick of the stink of these garbage cans!"

"Sonny," I said, "I know how you feel. But if you don't finish school now, you're going to be sorry later that you didn't." I grabbed him by the shoulders. "And you only got another year. It ain't so bad. And I'll come back and I swear I'll help you do *whatever* you want to do. Just try to put up with it till I come back. Will you please do that? For me?

He didn't answer and he wouldn't look at me.

"Sonny. You hear me?"

He pulled away. "I hear you. But you never hear anything *I* say."

I didn't know what to say to that. He looked out of the window and then back at me. "OK," he said, and sighed. "I'll try."

Then I said, trying to cheer him up a little, "They got a piano at Isabel's. You can practice on it."

And as a matter of fact, it did cheer him up for a minute. "That's right," he said to himself. "I forgot that." His face relaxed a little. But the worry, the thoughtfulness, played on it still, the way shadows play on a face which is staring into the fire.

But I thought I'd never hear the end of that piano. At first, Isabel would write me, saying how nice it was that Sonny was so serious about his music and how, as soon as he came in from school, or wherever he had been when he was supposed to be at school, he went straight to that piano and stayed there until suppertime. And, after supper, he went back to that piano and stayed there until everybody went to bed. He was at the piano all day Saturday and all day Sunday. Then he bought a record player and started playing records. He'd play one record over and over again, all day long sometimes, and he'd improvise along with it on the piano. Or he'd play one section of the record, one chord, one change, one progression, then he'd do it on the piano. Then back to the record. Then back to the piano.

Well, I really don't know how they stood it. Isabel finally confessed that it wasn't like living with a person at all, it was like living with sound. And the sound didn't make any sense to her, didn't make any sense to any of them—naturally. They began, in a way, to be afflicted by this presence that was living in their home. It was as though Sonny were some sort of god, or monster. He moved in an atmosphere which wasn't like theirs at all. They fed him and he ate, he washed himself, he walked in and out of their door; he certainly wasn't nasty or unpleasant or rude, Sonny isn't any of those things; but it was as though he were all wrapped up in some cloud, some fire, some vision all his own; and there wasn't any way to reach him.

At the same time, he wasn't really a man yet, he was still a child, and they had to watch out for him in all kinds of ways. They certainly couldn't throw him out. Neither did they dare to make a great scene about that piano because even they dimly sensed, as I sensed, from so many thousands of miles away, that Sonny was at that piano playing for his life.

But he hadn't been going to school. One day a letter came from the school board and Isabel's mother got it—there had, apparently, been other letters but Sonny had torn them up. This day, when Sonny came in, Isabel's mother showed him the letter and asked where he'd been spending his time. And she finally got it out of him that he'd been down in Greenwich Village, with musicians and other characters, in a white girls' apartment. And this scared her and she started to scream at him and what came up, once she began—though she denies it to this day—was what sacrifices they were making to give Sonny a decent home and how little he appreciated it.

Sonny didn't play the piano that day. By evening, Isabel's mother had calmed down but then there was the old man to deal with, and Isabel herself. Isabel says she did her best to be calm but she broke down and started crying. She says she just watched Sonny's face. She could tell, by watching him, what was happening with him. And what was happening was that they penetrated his cloud, they had reached him. Even if their fingers had been a thousand times more gentle than human fingers ever are, he could hardly help feeling that they had stripped him naked and were spitting on that nakedness. For he also had to see that his presence, that music, which was life or death to him, had been torture for them and that they had endured it, not at all for his sake, but only for mine. And Sonny couldn't take that. He can take it a little better today than he could then but he's still not very good at it and, frankly, I don't know anybody who is.

The silence of the next few days must have been louder than the sound of all the music ever played since time began. One morning, before she went to work, Isabel was in his room for something and she suddenly realized that all of his records were gone. And she knew for certain that he was gone. And he was. He went as far as the navy would carry him. He finally sent me a postcard from some place in Greece and that was the first I knew that Sonny was still alive. I didn't see him any more until we were both back in New York and the war had long been over.

He was a man by then, of course, but I wasn't willing to see it. He came by the house from time to time, but we fought almost every time we met. I didn't like the way he carried himself, loose and dreamlike all the time, and I didn't like his friends, and his music seemed to be merely an excuse for the life he led. It sounded just that weird and disordered.

Then we had a fight, a pretty awful fight, and I didn't see him for months. By and by I looked him up, where he was living, in a furnished room in the Village, and I tried to make it up. But there were lots of other people in the room and Sonny just lay on his bed, and he wouldn't come downstairs with me, and he treated these other people as though they were his family and I weren't. So I got mad and then he got mad, and then I told him that he might just as well be dead as live the way he was living. Then he stood up and he told me not to worry about him any more in life, that he *was* dead as far as I was concerned. Then he pushed me to the door and the other people looked on as though nothing were happening, and he slammed the door behind me. I stood in the hallway, staring at the door. I heard somebody laugh in the room and then the tears came to my eyes. I started down the steps, whistling to keep from crying, I kept whistling to myself, *You going to need me, baby, one of these cold, rainy days.*

I read about Sonny's trouble in the spring. Little Grace died in the fall. She was a beautiful little girl. But she only lived a little over two years. She died of polio and she suffered. She had a slight fever for a couple of days, but it didn't seem like anything and we just kept her in bed. And we would certainly have called the doctor, but the fever dropped, she seemed to be all right. So we thought it had just been a cold. Then, one day, she was up, playing, Isabel was in the kitchen fixing lunch for the two boys when they'd come in from school, and she heard Grace fall down in the living room. When you have a lot of children you don't always start running when one of them falls, unless they start screaming or something. And, this time, Grace was quiet. Yet, Isabel says that when she heard that *thump* and then that silence, something happened in her to make her afraid. And she ran to the living room and there was little Grace on the floor, all twisted up, and the reason she hadn't screamed was that she couldn't get her breath. And when she did scream, it was the worst sound, Isabel says, that she'd ever heard in all her life, and she still hears it sometimes in her dreams. Isabel will sometimes wake me up with a low, moaning, strangled sound and I have to be quick to awaken her and hold her to me and where Isabel is weeping against me seems a mortal wound.

I think I may have written Sonny the very day that little Grace was buried. I was sitting in the living room in the dark, by myself, and I suddenly thought of Sonny. My trouble made his real.

One Saturday afternoon, when Sonny had been living with us, or, anyway, been in our house, for nearly two weeks, I found myself wandering aimlessly about the living room, drinking from a can of beer, and trying to work up the courage to search Sonny's room. He was out, he was usually out whenever I was home, and Isabel had taken the children to see their grandparents. Suddenly I was standing still in front of the living room window,

watching Seventh Avenue. The idea of searching Sonny's room made me still. I scarcely dared to admit to myself what I'd be searching for. I didn't know what I'd do if I found it. Or if I didn't.

On the sidewalk across from me, near the entrance to a barbecue joint, some people were holding an old-fashioned revival meeting. The barbecue cook, wearing a dirty white apron, his *conked* hair reddish and metallic in the pale sun, and a cigarette between his lips, stood in the doorway, watching them. Kids and older people paused in their errands and stood there, along with some older men and a couple of very tough-looking women who watched everything that happened on the avenue, as though they owned it, or were maybe owned by it. Well, they were watching this, too. The revival was being carried on by three sisters in black, and a brother. All they had were their voices and their Bibles and a tambourine. The brother was testifying and while he testified two of the sisters stood together, seeming to say, amen, and the third sister walked around with the tambourine outstretched and a couple of people dropped coins into it. Then the brother's testimony ended and the sister who had been taking up the collection dumped the coins into her palm and transferred them to the pocket of her long black robe. Then she raised both hands, striking the tambourine against the air, and then against one hand, and she started to sing. And the two other sisters and the brother joined in.

It was strange, suddenly, to watch, though I had been seeing these street meetings all my life. So, of course, had everybody else down there. Yet, they paused and watched and listened and I stood still at the window. *"Tis the old ship of Zion,"* they sang, and the sister with the tambourine kept a steady, jangling beat, *"it has rescued many a thousand!"* Not a soul under the sound of their voices was hearing this song for the first time, not one of them had been rescued. Nor had they seen much in the way of rescue work being done around them. Neither did they especially believe in the holiness of the three sisters and the brother, they knew too much about them, knew where they lived, and how. The woman with the tambourine, whose voice dominated the air, whose face was bright with joy, was divided by very little from the woman who stood watching her, a cigarette between her heavy, chapped lips, her hair a cuckoo's nest, her face scarred and swollen from many beatings, and her black eyes glittering like coal. Perhaps they both knew this, which was why, when, as rarely, they addressed each other, they addressed each other as Sister. As the singing filled the air the watching, listening faces underwent a change, the eyes focusing on something within; the music seemed to soothe a poison out of them; and time seemed, nearly, to fall away from the sullen, belligerent, battered faces, as though they were fleeing back to their first condition, while dreaming of their last. The barbecue cook half shook his head and smiled, and dropped his cigarette and disappeared into his joint. A man fumbled in his pockets for change and stood holding it in his hand impatiently, as though he had just remembered a pressing appointment further up the avenue. He looked furious. Then I saw Sonny, standing on the edge of the crowd. He was carrying a wide, flat notebook with a green cover, and it made him look, from where I was standing, almost like a schoolboy. The coppery sun brought out the copper in his skin, he was very faintly smiling, standing very still. Then the singing stopped, the tambourine turned into a collection plate again. The furious man dropped in his coins and vanished, so did a couple of the women, and Sonny dropped some change in the plate, looking directly at the woman with a little smile. He started across the avenue, toward the house. He has a slow, loping walk, something like the way Harlem hipsters walk, only he's imposed on this his own half-beat. I had never really noticed it before.

I stayed at the window, both relieved and apprehensive. As Sonny disappeared from my sight, they began singing again. And they were still singing when his key turned in the lock.

"Hey," he said.

"Hey, yourself. You want some beer?"

"No. Well, maybe." But he came up to the window and stood beside me, looking out. "What a warm voice," he said.

They were singing *If I could only hear my mother pray again!*

"Yes," I said, "and she can sure beat that tambourine."

"But what a terrible song," he said, and laughed. He dropped his notebook on the sofa and disappeared into the kitchen. "Where's Isabel and the kids?"

"I think they went to see their grandparents. You hungry?"

"No." He came back into the living room with his can of beer. "You want to come some place with me tonight?"

I sensed, I don't know how, that I couldn't possibly say no. "Sure. Where?"

He sat down on the sofa and picked up his notebook and started leafing through it. "I'm going to sit in with some fellows in a joint in the Village."

"You mean, you're going to play, tonight?"

"That's right." He took a swallow of his beer and moved back, to the window. He gave me a sidelong look. "If you can stand it."

"I'll try," I said.

He smiled to himself and we both watched as the meeting across the way broke up. The three sisters and the brother, heads bowed, were singing *God be with you till we meet again.* The faces around them were very quiet. Then the song ended. The small crowd dispersed. We watched the three women and the lone man walk slowly up the avenue.

"When she was singing before," said Sonny, abruptly, "her voice reminded me for a minute of what heroin feels like sometimes—when it's in your veins. It makes you feel sort of warm and cool at the same time. And distant. And—and sure." He sipped his beer, very deliberately not looking at me. I watched his face. "It makes you feel—in control. Sometimes you've got to have that feeling."

"Do you?" I sat down slowly in the easy chair.

"Sometimes." He went to the sofa and picked up his notebook again. "Some people do."

"In order," I asked, "to play?" And my voice was very ugly, full of contempt and anger.

"Well"—he looked at me with great, troubled eyes, as though, in fact, he hoped his eyes would tell me things he could never otherwise say—"they *think* so. And *if* they think so—!"

"And what do *you* think?" I asked.

He sat on the sofa and put his can of beer on the floor. "I don't know," he said, and I couldn't be sure if he were answering my question or pursuing his thoughts. His face didn't tell me. "It's not so much to *play.* It's to *stand* it, to be able to make it at all. On any level." He frowned and smiled: "In order to keep from shaking to pieces."

"But these friends of yours," I said, "they seem to shake themselves to pieces pretty goddamn fast."

"Maybe." He played with the notebook. And something told me that I should curb my tongue, that Sonny was doing his best to talk, that I should listen. "But of course you only know the ones that've gone to pieces. Some don't—or at least they haven't *yet* and that's just about all *any* of us can say." He paused. "And then there are some who just live, really, in hell, and they know it and they see what's happening, and they go right on. I don't know."

He sighed, dropped the notebook, folded his arms. "Some guys, you can tell from the way they play, they on something *all* the time. And you can see that, well, it makes something real for them. But of course," he picked up his beer from the floor and sipped it and put the can down again, "they *want* to, too, you've got to see that. Even some of them that say they don't—*some,* not all."

"And what about you?" I asked—I couldn't help it. "What about you? Do *you* want to?"

He stood up and walked to the window and remained silent for a long time. Then he sighed. "Me," he said. Then: "While I was downstairs before, on my way here, listening to that woman sing, it struck me all of a sudden how much suffering she must have had to go through—to sing like that. It's *repulsive* to think you have to suffer that much."

I said: "But there's no way not to suffer—is there, Sonny?"

"I believe not," he said and smiled, "but that's never stopped anyone from trying." He looked at me. "Has it?" I realized, with this mocking look, that there stood between us, forever, beyond the power of time or forgiveness, the fact that I had held silence—so long!—when he had needed human speech to help him. He turned back to the window. "No, there's no way not to suffer. But you try all kinds of ways to keep from drowning in it, to keep on top of it, and to make it seem—well, like *you.* Like you did something, all right, and now you're suffering for it. You know?" I said nothing. "Well you know," he said, impatiently, "why *do* people suffer? Maybe it's better to do something to give it a reason, *any* reason."

"But we just agreed," I said, "that there's no way not to suffer. Isn't it better, then, just to—take it?"

"But nobody just takes it," Sonny cried, "that's what I'm telling you! *Everybody* tries not to. You're just hung up on the *way* some people try—its not *your* way!"

The hair on my face began to itch, my face felt wet. "That's not true," I said, "that's not true. I don't give a damn what other people do, I don't even care how they suffer. I just care how *you* suffer." And he looked at me. "Please believe me," I said. "I don't want to see you—die—trying not to suffer."

"I won't," he said flatly, "die trying not to suffer. At least, not any faster than anybody else."

"But there's no need," I said, trying to laugh, "is there? in killing yourself."

I wanted to say more, but I couldn't. I wanted to talk about will power and how life could be—well, beautiful. I wanted to say that it was all within; but was it? or, rather, wasn't that exactly the trouble? And I wanted to promise that I would never fail him again. But it would all have sounded—empty words and lies.

So I made the promise to myself and prayed that I would keep it.

"It's terrible sometimes, inside," he said, "that's what's the trouble. You walk these streets, black and funky and cold, and there's not really a living ass to talk to, and there's nothing shaking, and there's no way of getting it out—that storm inside. You can't talk it and you can't make love with it, and when you finally try to get with it and play it, you realize *nobody's* listening. So *you've* got to listen. You got to find a way to listen."

And then he walked away from the window and sat on the sofa again, as though all the wind had suddenly been knocked out of him. "Sometimes you'll do *anything* to play, even cut your mother's throat." He laughed and looked at me. "Or your brother's." Then he sobered. "Or your own." Then: "Don't worry. I'm all right now and I think I'll *be* all right. But I can't forget—where I've been. I don't mean just the physical place I've been, I mean where I've *been.* And *what* I've been."

"What have you been, Sonny?" I asked.

He smiled—but sat sideways on the sofa, his elbow resting on the back, his fingers playing with his mouth and chin, not looking at me. "I've been something I didn't recognize, didn't know I could be. Didn't know anybody could be." He stopped, looking inward, looking helplessly young, looking old. "I'm not talking about it now because I feel *guilty* or anything like that—maybe it would be better if I did, I don't know. Anyway, I can't really talk about it. Not to you, not to anybody," and now he turned and faced me. "Sometimes, you know and it was actually when I was most *out* of the world. I felt that I was in it, that I was *with* it, really, and I could play or I didn't really have to *play,* it just came out of me, it was there. And I don't know how I played, thinking about it now, but I know I did awful things, those times, sometimes, to people. Or it wasn't that I *did* anything to them—it was that they weren't real." He picked up the beer can; it was empty; he rolled it between his palms: "And other times—well, I needed a fix, I needed to find a place to lean, I needed to clear a space to *listen*—and I couldn't find it, and I—went crazy, I did terrible things to *me,* I was terrible *for* me." He began pressing the beer can between his hands, I watched the metal begin to give. It glittered, as he played with it, like a knife, and I was afraid he would cut himself, but I said nothing. "Oh well. I can never tell you. I was all by myself at the bottom of something, stinking and sweating and crying and shaking, and I smelled it, you know? *my* stink, and I thought I'd die if I couldn't get away from it and yet, all the same, I knew that everything I was doing was just locking me in with it. And I didn't know," he paused, still flattening the beer can, "I didn't know, I still *don't* know, something kept telling me that maybe it was good to smell your own stink, but I didn't think that *that* was what I'd been trying to do—and—who can stand it?" and he abruptly dropped the ruined beer can, looking at me with a small, still smile, and then rose, walking to the window as though it were the lodestone rock. I watched his face, he watched the avenue. "I couldn't tell you when Mama died—but the reason I wanted to leave Harlem so bad was to get away from drugs. And then, when I ran away, that's what I was running from—really. When I came back, nothing had changed, *I* hadn't changed, I was just—older." And he stopped drumming with his fingers on the windowpane. The sun had vanished, soon darkness would fall. I watched his face. "It can come again," he said, almost as though speaking to himself. Then he turned to me. "It can come again," he repeated. "I just want you to know that."

"All right," I said, at last. "So it can come again. All right."

He smiled, but the smile was sorrowful. "I had to try to tell you," he said.

"Yes," I said. "I understand that."

"You're my brother," he said, looking straight at me, and not smiling at all.

"Yes," I repeated, "yes. I understand that."

He turned back to the window, looking out. "All that hatred down there," he said, "all that hatred and misery and love. It's a wonder it doesn't blow the avenue apart."

We went to the only nightclub on a short, dark street, downtown. We squeezed through the narrow, chattering, jam-packed bar to the entrance of the big room, where the bandstand was. And we stood there for a moment, for the lights were very dim in this room and we couldn't see. Then, "Hello, boy," said a voice and an enormous black man, much older than Sonny or myself, erupted out of all that atmospheric lighting and put an arm around Sonny's shoulder. "I been sitting right here," he said, "waiting for you."

He had a big voice, too, and heads in the darkness turned toward us.

Sonny grinned and pulled a little away, and said, "Creole, this is my brother. I told you about him."

Creole shook my hand. "I'm glad to meet you, son," he said, and it was clear that he was glad to meet me *there,* for Sonny's sake. And he smiled, "You got a real musician in *your* family," and he took his arm from Sonny's shoulder and slapped him, lightly, affectionately, with the back of his hand.

"Well. Now I've heard it all," said a voice behind us. This was another musician, and a friend of Sonny's, a coal-black, cheerful-looking man, built close to the ground. He immediately began confiding to me, at the top of his lungs, the most terrible things about Sonny, his teeth gleaming like a lighthouse and his laugh coming up out of him like the beginning of an earthquake. And it turned out that everyone at the bar knew Sonny, or almost everyone; some were musicians, working there, or nearby, or not working, some were simply hangers-on, and some were there to hear Sonny play. I was introduced to all of them and they were all very polite to me. Yet, it was clear that, for them, I was only Sonny's brother. Here, I was in Sonny's world. Or, rather: his kingdom. Here, it was not even a question that his veins bore royal blood.

They were going to play soon and Creole installed me, by myself, at a table in a dark corner. Then I watched them, Creole, and the little black man, and Sonny, and the others, while they horsed around, standing just below the bandstand. The light from the bandstand spilled just a little short of them and, watching them laughing and gesturing and moving about, I had the feeling that they, nevertheless, were being most careful not to step into that circle of light too suddenly: that if they moved into the light too suddenly, without thinking, they would perish in flame. Then, while I watched, one of them, the small, black man, moved into the light and crossed the bandstand and started fooling around with his drums. Then—being funny and being, also, extremely ceremonious—Creole took Sonny by the arm and led him to the piano. A woman's voice called Sonny's name and a few hands started clapping. And Sonny, also being funny and being ceremonious, and so touched, I think, that he could have cried, but neither hiding it nor showing it, riding it like a man, grinned, and put both hands to his heart and bowed from the waist.

Creole then went to the bass fiddle and a lean, very bright-skinned brown man jumped up on the bandstand and picked up his horn. So there they were, and the atmosphere on the bandstand and in the room began to change and tighten. Someone stepped up to the microphone and announced them. Then there were all kinds of murmurs. Some people at the bar shushed others. The waitress ran around, frantically getting in the last orders, guys and chicks got closer to each other, and the lights on the bandstand, on the quartet, turned to a kind of indigo. Then they all looked different there. Creole looked about him for the last time, as though he were making certain that all his chickens were in the coop, and then he—jumped and struck the fiddle. And there they were.

All I know about music is that not many people ever really hear it. And even then, on the rare occasions when something opens within, and the music enters, what we mainly hear, or hear corroborated, are personal, private, vanishing evocations. But the man who creates the music is hearing something else, is dealing with the roar rising from the void and imposing order on it as it hits the air. What is evoked in him, then, is of another order, more terrible because it has no words, and triumphant, too, for that same reason. And his triumph, when he triumphs, is ours. I just watched Sonny's face. His face was troubled, he was working hard, but he wasn't with it. And I had the feeling that, in a way, everyone on the bandstand was waiting for him, both waiting for him and pushing him along. But as I began to watch Creole, I realized that it was Creole who held them all back. He had them on a short rein. Up there, keeping the beat with his whole body, wailing on the fiddle, with his eyes half closed, he was listening to everything, but he was listening to Sonny. He was

having a dialogue with Sonny. He wanted Sonny to leave the shoreline and strike out for the deep water. He was Sonny's witness that deep water and drowning were not the same thing—he had been there, and he knew. And he wanted Sonny to know. He was waiting for Sonny to do the things on the keys which would let Creole know that Sonny was in the water.

And, while Creole listened, Sonny moved, deep within, exactly like someone in torment. I had never before thought of how awful the relationship must be between the musician and his instrument. He has to fill it, this instrument, with the breath of life, his own. He has to make it do what he wants it to do. And a piano is just a piano. It's made out of so much wood and wires and little hammers and big ones, and ivory. While there's only so much you can do with it, the only way to find this out is to try; to try and make it do everything.

And Sonny hadn't been near a piano for over a year. And he wasn't on much better terms with his life, not the life that stretched before him now. He and the piano stammered, started one way, got scared, stopped; started another way, panicked, marked time, started again; then seemed to have found a direction, panicked again, got stuck. And the face I saw on Sonny I'd never seen before. Everything had been burned out of it, and, at the same time, things usually hidden were being burned in, by the fire and fury of the battle which was occuring in him up there.

Yet, watching Creole's face as they neared the end of the first set, I had the feeling that something had happened, something I hadn't heard. Then they finished, there was scattered applause, and then, without an instant's warning, Creole started into something else, it was almost sardonic, it was *Am I Blue.* And, as though he commanded, Sonny began to play. Something began to happen. And Creole let out the reins. The dry, low, black man said something awful on the drums, Creole answered, and the drums talked back. Then the horn insisted, sweet and high, slightly detached perhaps, and Creole listened, commenting now and then, dry, and driving, beautiful and calm and old. Then they all came together again, and Sonny was part of the family again. I could tell this from his face. He seemed to have found, right there beneath his fingers, a damn brand-new piano. It seemed that he couldn't get over it. Then, for awhile, just being happy with Sonny, they seemed to be agreeing with him that brand-new pianos certainly were a gas.

Then Creole stepped forward to remind them that what they were playing was the blues. He hit something in all of them, he hit something in me, myself, and the music tightened and deepened, apprehension began to beat the air. Creole began to tell us what the blues were all about. They were not about anything very new. He and his boys up there were keeping it new, at the risk of ruin, destruction, madness, and death, in order to find new ways to make us listen. For, while the tale of how we suffer, and how we are delighted, and how we may triumph is never new, it always must be heard. There isn't any other tale to tell, it's the only light we've got in all this darkness.

And this tale, according to that face, that body, those strong hands on those strings, has another aspect in every country, and a new depth in every generation. Listen, Creole seemed to be saying, listen. Now these are Sonny's blues. He made the little black man on the drums know it, and the bright, brown man on the horn. Creole wasn't trying any longer to get Sonny in the water. He was wishing him Godspeed. Then he stepped back, very slowly, filling the air with the immense suggestion that Sonny speak for himself.

Then they all gathered around Sonny and Sonny played. Every now and again one of them seemed to say, amen. Sonny's fingers filled the air with life, his life. But that life contained so many others. And Sonny went all the way back, he really began with the spare, flat statement of the opening phrase of the song. Then he began to make it his. It was very beautiful because it wasn't hurried and it was no longer a lament. I seemed to hear with what burning he had made it his, with what burning we had yet to make it ours, how we could cease lamenting. Freedom lurked around us and I understood, at last, that he could help us to be free if we would listen, that he would never be free until we did. Yet, there was no battle in his face now. I heard what he had gone through, and would continue to go through until he came to rest in earth. He had made it his: that long line, of which we knew only Mama and Daddy. And he was giving it back, as everything must be given back, so that, passing through death, it can live forever. I saw my mother's face again, and felt, for the first time, how the stones of the road she had walked on must have bruised her feet. I saw the moonlit road where my father's brother died. And it brought something else back to me, and carried me past it, I saw my little girl again and felt Isabel's tears again, and I felt my own tears begin to rise. And I was yet aware that this was only a moment, that the world waited outside, as hungry as a tiger, and that trouble stretched above us, longer than the sky.

Then it was over. Creole and Sonny let out their breath, both soaking wet, and grinning. There was a lot of applause and some of it was real. In the dark, the girl came by and I asked her to take drinks to the bandstand. There was a long pause, while they talked up there in the indigo light and after awhile I saw the girl put a Scotch and milk on top of the piano for Sonny. He didn't seem to notice it, but just before they started playing again he sipped from it and looked toward me, and nodded. Then he put it back on top of the piano. For me, then, as they began to play again, it glowed and shook above my brother's head like the very cup of trembling.

LANGSTON HUGHES

(1902–1967)

One Friday Morning

About the Author: Langston Hughes, black American short-story writer, novelist, poet (see page 591), playwright, essayist, editor, and autobiographer, was a leader of the Harlem Renaissance of the 1920s. Among his principal works are *Not without Laughter* (novel, 1930), *I Wonder as I Wander* (autobiography, 1956), and *Simple's Uncle Sam* (short fiction, 1965).

The thrilling news did not come directly to Nancy Lee, but it came in little indirections that finally added themselves up to one tremendous fact: she had won the prize! But being a calm and quiet young lady, she did not say anything, although the whole high school buzzed with rumors, guesses, reportedly authentic announcements on the part of students who had no right to be making announcements at all—since no student really knew yet who had won this year's art scholarship.

But Nancy Lee's drawing was so good, her lines so sure, her colors so bright and harmonious, that certainly no other student in the senior art class at George Washington High was thought to have very much of a chance. Yet you never could tell. Last year nobody had expected Joe Williams to win the Artist Club scholarship with that funny

modernistic water color he had done of the high-level bridge. In fact, it was hard to make out there was a bridge until you had looked at the picture a long time. Still, Joe Williams got the prize, was feted by the community's leading painters, club women, and society folks at a big banquet at the Park-Rose Hotel, and was now an award student at the Art School—the city's only art school.

Nancy Lee Johnson was a colored girl, a few years out of the South. But seldom did her high-school classmates think of her as colored. She was smart, pretty, and brown, and fitted in well with the life of the school. She stood high in scholarship, played a swell game of basketball, had taken part in the senior musical in a soft, velvety voice, and had never seemed to intrude or stand out, except in pleasant ways, so it was seldom even mentioned—her color.

Nancy Lee sometimes forgot she was colored herself. She liked her classmates and her school. Particularly she liked her art teacher, Miss Dietrich, the tall red-haired woman who taught her law and order in doing things; and the beauty of working step by step until a job is done; a picture finished; a design created; or a block print carved out of nothing but an idea and a smooth square of linoleum, inked, proofs made, and finally put down on paper—clean, sharp, beautiful, individual, unlike any other in the world, thus making the paper have a meaning nobody else could give it except Nancy Lee. That was the wonderful thing about true creation. You made something nobody else on earth could make—but you.

Miss Dietrich was the kind of teacher who brought out the best in her students—but their own best, not anybody else's copied best. For anybody else's best, great though it might be, even Michelangelo's, wasn't enough to please Miss Dietrich, dealing with the creative impulses of young men and women living in an American city in the Middle West, and being American.

Nancy Lee was proud of being American, a Negro American with blood out of Africa a long time ago, too many generations back to count. But her parents had taught her the beauties of Africa, its strength, its song, its mighty rivers, its early smelting of iron, its building of the pyramids, and its ancient and important civilizations. And Miss Dietrich had discovered for her the sharp and humorous lines of African sculpture, Benin, Congo, Makonde. Nancy Lee's father was a mail carrier, her mother a social worker in a city settlement house. Both parents had been to Negro colleges in the South. And her mother had gotten a further degree in social work from a Northern university. Her parents were, like most Americans, simple, ordinary people who had worked hard and steadily for their education. Now they were trying to make it easier for Nancy Lee to achieve learning than it had been for them. They would be very happy when they heard of the award to their daughter—yet Nancy did not tell them. To surprise them would be better. Besides, there had been a promise.

Casually, one day, Miss Dietrich asked Nancy Lee what color frame she thought would be best on her picture. That had been the first inkling.

"Blue," Nancy Lee said. Although the picture had been entered in the Artist Club contest a month ago, Nancy Lee did not hesitate in her choice of a color for the possible frame, since she could still see her picture clearly in her mind's eye—for that picture waiting for the blue frame had come out of her soul, her own life, and had bloomed into miraculous being with Miss Dietrich's help. It was, she knew, the best water color she had painted in her four years as a high-school art student, and she was glad she had made something Miss Dietrich liked well enough to permit her to enter in the contest before she graduated.

It was not a modernistic picture in the sense that you had to look at it a long time to understand what it meant. It was just a simple scene in the city park on a spring day, with the trees still leaflessly lacy against the sky, the new grass fresh and green, a flag on a tall pole in the center, children playing, and an old Negro woman sitting on a bench with her head turned. A lot for one picture, to be sure, but it was not there in heavy and final detail like a calendar. Its charm was that everything was light and airy, happy like spring, with a lot of blue sky, paper-white clouds, and air showing through. You could tell that the old Negro woman was looking at the flag, and that the flag was proud in the spring breeze, and that the breeze helped to make the children's dresses billow as they played.

Miss Dietrich had taught Nancy Lee how to paint spring, people, and a breeze on what was only a plain white piece of paper from the supply closet. But Miss Dietrich had not said make it like any other spring-people-breeze ever seen before. She let it remain Nancy Lee's own. That is how the old Negro woman happened to be there looking at the flag—for in her mind the flag, the spring, and the woman formed a kind of triangle holding a dream Nancy Lee wanted to express. White stars on a blue field, spring, children, ever-growing life, and an old woman. Would the judges at the Artist Club like it?

One wet, rainy April afternoon Miss O'Shay, the girls' vice-principal, sent for Nancy Lee to stop by her office as school closed. Pupils without umbrellas or raincoats were clustered in doorways, hoping to make it home between showers. Outside the skies were gray. Nancy Lee's thoughts were suddenly gray, too.

She did not think she had done anything wrong, yet that tight little knot came in her throat just the same as she approached Miss O'Shay's door. Perhaps she had banged her locker too often and too hard. Perhaps the note in French she had written to Sallie halfway across the study hall just for fun had never gotten to Sallie but into Miss O'Shay's hands instead. Or maybe she was failing in some subject and wouldn't be allowed to graduate. Chemistry! A pang went through the pit of her stomach.

She knocked on Miss O'Shay's door. That familiarly solid and competent voice said, "Come in."

Miss O'Shay had a way of making you feel welcome, even if you came to be expelled.

"Sit down, Nancy Lee Johnson," said Miss O'Shay. "I have something to tell you." Nancy Lee sat down. "But I must ask you to promise not to tell anyone yet."

"I won't, Miss O'Shay," Nancy Lee said, wondering what on earth the principal had to say to her.

"You are about to graduate," Miss O'Shay said. "And we shall miss you. You have been an excellent student, Nancy, and you will not be without honors on the senior list, as I am sure you know."

At that point there was a light knock on the door. Miss O'Shay called out, "Come in," and Miss Dietrich entered. "May I be a part of this, too?" she asked, tall and smiling.

"Of course," Miss O'Shay said. "I was just telling Nancy Lee what we thought of her. But I hadn't gotten around to giving her the news. Perhaps, Miss Dietrich, you'd like to tell her yourself."

Miss Dietrich was always direct. "Nancy Lee," she said, "your picture has won the Artist Club scholarship."

The slender brown girl's eyes widened, her heart jumped, then her throat tightened again. She tried to smile, but instead tears came to her eyes.

"Dear Nancy Lee," Miss O'Shay said, "we are so happy for you." The elderly white woman took her hand and shook it warmly while Miss Dietrich beamed with pride.

Nancy Lee must have danced all the way home. She never remembered quite how she got there through the rain. She hoped she had been dignified. But certainly she hadn't stopped to tell anybody her secret on the way. Raindrops, smiles, and tears mingled on her brown cheeks. She hoped her mother hadn't yet gotten home and that the house was empty. She wanted to have time to calm down and look natural before she had to see anyone. She didn't want to be bursting with excitement—having a secret to contain.

Miss O'Shay's calling her to the office had been in the nature of a preparation and a warning. The kind, elderly vice-principal said she did not believe in catching young ladies unawares, even with honors, so she wished her to know about the coming award. In making acceptance speeches she wanted her to be calm, prepared, not nervous, overcome, and frightened. So Nancy Lee was asked to think what she would say when the scholarship was conferred upon her a few days hence, both at the Friday morning high-school assembly hour, when the announcement would be made, and at the evening banquet of the Artist Club. Nancy Lee promised the vice-principal to think calmly about what she would say.

Miss Dietrich had then asked for some facts about her parents, her background, and her life, since such material would probably be desired for the papers. Nancy Lee had told her how, six years before, they had come up from the Deep South, her father having been successful in achieving a transfer from the one post office to another, a thing he had long sought in order to give Nancy Lee a chance to go to school in the North. Now they lived in a modest Negro neighborhood, went to see the best plays when they came to town, and had been saving to send Nancy Lee to art school, in case she were permitted to enter. But the scholarship would help a great deal, for they were not rich people.

"Now Mother can have a new coat next winter," Nancy Lee thought, "because my tuition will all be covered for the first year. And once in art school, there are other scholarships I can win."

Dreams began to dance through her head, plans and ambitions, beauties she would create for herself, her parents, and the Negro people—for Nancy Lee possessed a deep and reverent race pride. She could see the old woman in her picture (really her grandmother in the South) lifting her head to the bright stars on the flag in the distance. A Negro in America! Often hurt, discriminated against, sometimes lynched—but always there were the stars on the blue body of the flag. Was there any other flag in the world that had so many stars? Nancy Lee thought deeply, but she could remember none in all the encyclopedias or geographies she had ever looked into.

"Hitch your wagon to a star," Nancy Lee thought, dancing home in the rain. "Who were our flag-makers?"

Friday morning came, the morning when the world would know—her high-school world, the newspaper world, her mother and dad. Dad could not be there at the assembly to hear the announcement, nor see her prize picture displayed on the stage, nor to listen to Nancy Lee's little speech of acceptance, but Mother would be able to come, although Mother was much puzzled as to why Nancy Lee was so insistent she be at school on that particular Friday morning.

When something is happening, something new and fine, something that will change your very life, it is hard to go to sleep at night for thinking about it, and hard to keep your heart from pounding, or a strange little knot of joy from gathering in your throat. Nancy Lee had taken her bath, brushed her hair until it glowed, and had gone to bed thinking about the next day, the big day, when before three thousand students, she would be the one student honored, her painting the one painting to be acclaimed as the best of the year from all the art classes of the city. Her short speech of gratitude was ready. She went over it in her mind, not word for word (because she didn't want it to sound as if she had learned it by heart), but she let the thoughts flow simply and sincerely through her consciousness many times.

When the president of the Artist Club presented her with the medal and scroll of the scholarship award, she would say:

"Judges and members of the Artist Club. I want to thank you for this award that means so much to me personally and through me to my people, the colored people of this city, who, sometimes, are discouraged and bewildered, thinking that color and poverty are against them. I accept this award with gratitude and pride, not for myself alone, but for my race that believes in American opportunity and American fairness—and the bright stars in our flag. I thank Miss Dietrich and the teachers who made it possible for me to have the knowledge and training that lie behind this honor you have conferred upon my painting. When I came here from the South a few years ago, I was not sure how you would receive me. You received me well. You have given me a chance and helped me along the road I wanted to follow. I suppose the judges know that every week here at assembly the students of this school pledge allegiance to the flag. I shall try to be worthy of that pledge, and of the help and friendship and understanding of my fellow citizens of whatever race or creed, and of our American dream of 'Liberty and justice for all!' "

That would be her response before the students in the morning. How proud and happy the Negro pupils would be, perhaps almost as proud as they were of the one colored star on the football team. Her mother would probably cry with happiness. Thus Nancy Lee went to sleep dreaming of a wonderful tomorrow.

The bright sunlight of an April morning woke her. There was breakfast with her parents—their half-amused and puzzled faces across the table, wondering what could be this secret that made her eyes so bright. The swift walk to school; the clock in the tower almost nine; hundreds of pupils streaming into the long, rambling old building that was the city's largest high school; the sudden quiet of the homeroom after the bell rang; then the teacher opening her record book to call the roll. But just before she began, she looked across the room until her eyes located Nancy Lee.

"Nancy," she said, "Miss O'Shay would like to see you in her office, please."

Nancy Lee rose and went out while the names were being called and the word *present* added its period to each name. Perhaps, Nancy Lee thought, the reporters from the papers had already come. Maybe they wanted to take her picture before assembly, which wasn't until ten o'clock. (Last year they had had the photograph of the winner of the award in the morning papers as soon as the announcement had been made.)

Nancy Lee knocked at Miss O'Shay's door.

"Come in."

The vice-principal stood at her desk. There was no one else in the room. It was very quiet.

"Sit down, Nancy Lee," she said. Miss O'Shay did not smile. There was a long pause. The seconds went by slowly. "I do not know how to tell you what I have to say," the elderly woman began, her eyes on the papers on her desk. "I am indignant and ashamed for myself and for this city." Then she lifted her eyes and looked at Nancy Lee in the neat blue dress, sitting there before her. "You are not to receive the scholarship this morning."

Outside in the hall the electric bells announcing the first period rang, loud and interminably long. Miss O'Shay remained silent. To the brown girl there in the chair, the

room grew suddenly smaller, smaller, smaller, and there was no air. She could not speak.

Miss O'Shay said, "When the committee learned that you were colored, they changed their plans."

Still Nancy Lee said nothing, for there was no air to give breath to her lungs.

"Here is the letter from the committee, Nancy Lee." Miss O'Shay picked it up and read the final paragraph to her.

" 'It seems to us wiser to arbitrarily rotate the award among the various high schools of the city from now on. And especially in this case since the student chosen happens to be colored, a circumstance which unfortunately, had we known, might have prevented this embarrassment. But there have never been any Negro students in the local art school, and the presence of one there might create difficulties for all concerned. We have high regard for the quality of Nancy Lee Johnson's talent, but we do not feel it would be fair to honor it with the Artist Club award.' " Miss O'Shay paused. She put the letter down.

"Nancy Lee, I am very sorry to have to give you this message."

"But my speech," Nancy Lee said, "was about. . . ." The words stuck in her throat. ". . . about America. . . ."

Miss O'Shay had risen; she turned her back and stood looking out the window at the spring tulips in the school yard.

"I thought, since the award would be made at assembly right after our oath of allegiance," the words tumbled almost hysterically from Nancy Lee's throat now, "I would put part of the flag salute in my speech. You know, Miss O'Shay, that part about 'liberty and justice for all.' "

"I know," said Miss O'Shay, slowly facing the room again. "But America is only what we who believe in it make it. I am Irish. You may not know, Nancy Lee, but years ago we were called the dirty Irish, and mobs rioted against us in the big cities, and we were invited to go back where we came from. But we didn't go. And we didn't give up, because we believed in the American dream, and in our power to make that dream come true. Difficulties, yes. Mountains to climb, yes. Discouragements to face, yes. Democracy to make, yes. That is it, Nancy Lee! We still have in this world of ours democracy to *make.* You and I, Nancy Lee. But the premise and the base are here, the lines of the Declaration of Independence and the words of Lincoln are here, and the stars in our flag. Those who deny you this scholarship do not know the meaning of those stars, but it's up to us to make them know. As a teacher in the public schools of this city, I myself will go before the school board and ask them to remove from our system the offer of any prizes or awards denied to any student because of race or color."

Suddenly Miss O'Shay stopped speaking. Her clear, clear blue eyes looked into those of the girl before her. The woman's eyes were full of strength and courage. "Lift up your head, Nancy Lee, and smile at me."

Miss O'Shay stood against the open window with the green lawn and the tulips beyond, the sunlight tangled in her gray hair, her voice an electric flow of strength to the hurt spirit of Nancy Lee. The Abolitionists who believed in freedom when there was slavery must have been like that. The first white teachers who went into the Deep South to teach the freed slaves must have been like that. All those who stand against ignorance, narrowness, hate, and mud on stars must be like that.

Nancy Lee lifted her head and smiled. The bell for assembly rang. She went through the long hall filled with students, toward the auditorium.

"There will be other awards," Nancy Lee thought. "There're schools in other cities.

This won't keep me down. But when I'm a woman, I'll fight to see that these things don't happen to other girls as this has happened to me. And men and women like Miss O'Shay will help me."

She took her seat among the seniors. The doors of the auditorium closed. As the principal came onto the platform, the students rose and turned their eyes to the flag on the stage.

One hand went to the heart, the other outstretched toward the flag. Three thousand voices spoke. Among them was the voice of a dark girl whose cheeks were suddenly wet with tears, ". . . one nation indivisible, with liberty and justice for all."

"That is the land we must make," she thought.

EUDORA WELTY

(1909–)

Powerhouse

About the Author: Eudora Welty was born in Jackson, Mississippi, where she still lives. She was educated at Mississippi State College for Women, the University of Wisconsin, and the Columbia University School of Business. She has published short stories and novels, essays and reviews, and a volume of photographs. Among her principal volumes are *Losing Battles* (1970) and *The Optimist's Daughter* (1972), novels, and *The Eye of the Story* (1978), essays on writing.

Powerhouse is playing!

He's here on tour from the city—"Powerhouse and His Keyboard"—"Powerhouse and His Tasmanians"—think of the things he calls himself! There's no one in the world like him. You can't tell what he is. "Nigger man"?—he looks more Asiatic, monkey, Jewish, Babylonian, Peruvian, fanatic, devil. He has pale gray eyes, heavy lids, maybe horny like a lizard's, but big glowing eyes when they're open. He has African feet of the greatest size, stomping, both together, on each side of the pedals. He's not coal black—beverage colored—looks like a preacher when his mouth is shut, but then it opens—vast and obscene. And his mouth is going every minute: like a monkey's when it looks for something. Improvising, coming on a light and childish melody—*smooch*—he loves it with his mouth.

Is it possible that he could be this! When you have him there performing for you, that's what you feel. You know people on a stage—and people of a darker race—so likely to be marvelous, frightening.

This is a white dance. Powerhouse is not a show-off like the Harlem boys, not drunk, not crazy—he's in a trance; he's a person of joy, a fanatic. He listens as much as he performs, a look of hideous, powerful rapture on his face. Big arched eyebrows that never stop traveling, like a Jew's—wandering-Jew eyebrows. When he plays he beats down piano and seat and wears them away. He is in motion every moment—what could be more obscene? There he is with his great head, fat stomach, and little round piston legs, and long yellow-sectioned strong big fingers, at rest about the size of bananas. Of course you know how he sounds—you've heard him on records—but still you need to see him. He's going all the time, like skating around the skating rink or rowing a boat. It makes everybody crowd around, here in the shadowless steel-trussed hall with the rose-like posters of Nelson Eddy

and the testimonial for the mind-reading horse in handwriting magnified five hundred times. Then all quietly he lays his fingers on a key with the promise and serenity of a sibyl touching the book.

Powerhouse is so monstrous he sends everybody into oblivion. When any group, any performers, come to town, don't people always come out and hover near, leaning inward about them, to learn what it is? What is it? Listen. Remember how it was with the acrobats. Watch them carefully, hear the least word, especially what they say to one another, in another language—don't let them escape you; it's the only time for hallucination, the last time. They can't stay. They'll be somewhere else this time tomorrow.

Powerhouse has as much as possible done by signals. Everybody, laughing as if to hide a weakness, will sooner or later hand him up a written request. Powerhouse reads each one, studying with a secret face: that is the face which looks like a mask—anybody's; there is a moment when he makes a decision. Then a light slides under his eyelids, and he says, "92!" or some combination of figures—never a name. Before a number the band is all frantic, misbehaving, pushing, like children in a schoolroom, and he is the teacher getting silence. His hands over the keys, he says sternly, "You-all ready? You-all ready to do some serious walking?"—waits—then, STAMP. Quiet. STAMP, for the second time. This is absolute. Then a set of rhythmic kicks against the floor to communicate the tempo. Then, O Lord! say the distended eyes from beyond the boundary of the trumpets, Hello and good-by, and they are all down the first note like a waterfall.

This note marks the end of any known discipline. Powerhouse seems to abandon them all—he himself seems lost—down in the song, yelling up like somebody in a whirlpool—not guiding them—hailing them only. But he knows, really. He cries out, but he must know exactly. "Mercy! . . . What I say! . . . Yeah!" And then drifting, listening—"Where that skin beater?"—wanting drums, and starting up and pouring it out in the greatest delight and brutality. On the sweet pieces such a leer for everybody! He looks down so benevolently upon all our faces and whispers the lyrics to us. And if you could hear him at this moment on "Marie, the Dawn is Breaking"! He's going up the keyboard with a few fingers in some very derogatory triplet routine, he gets higher and higher, and then he looks over the end of the piano, as if over a cliff. But not in a show-off way—the song makes him do it.

He loves the way they all play, too—all those next to him. The far section of the band is all studious, wearing glasses, every one—they don't count. Only those playing around Powerhouse are the real ones. He has a bass fiddler from Vicksburg, black as pitch, named Valentine, who plays with his eyes shut and talking to himself, very young: Powerhouse has to keep encouraging him. "Go on, go on, give it up, bring it on out there!" When you heard him like that on records, did you know he was really pleading?

He calls Valentine out to take a solo.

"What you going to play?" Powerhouse looks out kindly from behind the piano; he opens his mouth and shows his tongue, listening.

Valentine looks down, drawing against his instrument, and says without a lip movement, " 'Honeysuckle Rose.' "

He has a clarinet player named Little Brother, and loves to listen to anything he does. He'll smile and say, "Beautiful!" Little Brother takes a step forward when he plays and stands at the very front, with the whites of his eyes like fishes swimming. Once when he played a low note, Powerhouse muttered in dirty praise, "He went clear downstairs to get that one!"

After a long time, he holds up the number of fingers to tell the band how many choruses still to go—usually five. He keeps his directions down to signals.

It's a bad night outside. It's a white dance, and nobody dances, except a few straggling jitterbugs and two elderly couples. Everybody just stands around the band and watches Powerhouse. Sometimes they steal glances at one another, as if to say, Of course, you know how it is with *them*—Negroes—band leaders—they would play the same way, giving all they've got, for an audience of one. . . . When somebody, no matter who, gives everything, it makes people feel ashamed for him.

Late at night they play the one waltz they will ever consent to play—by request, "Pagan Love Song." Powerhouse's head rolls and sinks like a weight between his waving shoulders. He groans, and his fingers drag into the keys heavily, holding on to the notes, retrieving. It is a sad song.

"You know what happened to me?" says Powerhouse.

Valentine hums a response, dreaming at the bass.

"I got a telegram my wife is dead," says Powerhouse, with wandering fingers.

"Uh-huh?"

His mouth gathers and forms a barbarous O while his fingers walk up straight, unwillingly, three octaves.

"Gypsy? Why how come her to die, didn't you just phone her up in the night last night long distance?"

"Telegram say—here the words: Your wife is dead." He puts 4/4 over the 3/4.

"Not but four words?" This is the drummer, an unpopular boy named Scoot, a disbelieving maniac.

Powerhouse is shaking his vast cheeks. "What the hell was she trying to do? What was she up to?"

"What name has it got signed, if you got a telegram?" Scoot is spitting away with those wire brushes.

Little Brother, the clarinet player, who cannot now speak, glares and tilts back.

"Uranus Knockwood is the name signed." Powerhouse lifts his eyes open. "Ever heard of him?" A bubble shoots out on his lip like a plate on a counter.

Valentine is beating slowly on with his palm and scratching the strings with his long blue nails. He is fond of a waltz. Powerhouse interrupts him.

"I don't know him. Don't know who he is." Valentine shakes his head with the closed eyes.

"Say it again."

"Uranus Knockwood."

"That ain't Lenox Avenue."

"It ain't Broadway."

"Ain't ever seen it wrote out in any print, even for horse racing."

"Hell, that's on a star, boy, ain't it?" Crash of the cymbals.

"What the hell was she up to?" Powerhouse shudders. "Tell me, tell me, tell me." He makes triplets, and begins a new chorus. He holds three fingers up.

"You say you got a telegram." This is Valentine, patient and sleepy, beginning again.

Powerhouse is elaborate. "Yas, the time I go out, go way downstairs along a long cor-ri-dor to where they puts us: coming back along the cor-ri-dor: steps out and hands me a telegram: Your wife is dead."

"Gypsy?" The drummer like a spider over his drums.

"Aaaaaaaa!" shouts Powerhouse, flinging out both powerful arms for three whole beats to flex his muscles, then kneading a dough of bass notes. His eyes glitter. He plays the piano like a drum sometimes—why not?

"Gypsy? Such a dancer?"

"Why you don't hear it straight from your agent? Why it ain't come from headquarters? What you been doing, getting telegrams in the *corridor,* signed nobody?"

They all laugh. End of that chorus.

"What time is it?" Powerhouse calls. "What the hell place is this? Where is my watch and chain?"

"I hang it on you," whimpers Valentine. "It still there."

There it rides on Powerhouse's great stomach, down where he can never see it.

"Sure did hear some clock striking twelve while ago. Must be *midnight."*

"It going to be intermission," Powerhouse declares, lifting up his finger with the signet ring.

He draws the chorus to an end. He pulls a big Northern hotel towel out of the deep pocket in his vast, special-cut tux pants and pushes his forehead into it.

"If she went and killed herself!" he says with a hidden face. "If she up and jumped out that window!" He gets to his feet, turning vaguely, wearing the towel on his head.

"Ha, ha!"

"Sheik, sheik!"

"She wouldn't do that." Little Brother sets down his clarinet like a precious vase, and speaks. He still looks like an East Indian queen, implacable, divine, and full of snakes. "You ain't going to expect people doing what they says over long distance."

"Come on!" roars Powerhouse. He is already at the back door, he has pulled it wide open, and with a wild, gathered-up face is smelling the terrible night.

Powerhouse, Valentine, Scoot and Little Brother step outside into the drenching rain.

"Well, they emptying buckets," says Powerhouse in a mollified voice. On the street he holds his hands out and turns up the blanched palms like sieves.

A hundred dark, ragged, silent, delighted Negroes have come around from under the eaves of the hall, and follow wherever they go.

"Watch out Little Brother don't shrink," says Powerhouse. "You just the right size now, clarinet don't suck you in. You got a dry throat, Little Brother, you in the desert?" He reaches into the pocket and pulls out a paper of mints. "Now hold 'em in your mouth—don't chew 'em. I don't carry around nothing without limit."

"Go in that joint and have beer," says Scoot, who walks ahead.

"Beer? Beer? You know what beer is? What do they say is beer? What's beer? Where I been?"

"Down yonder where it say World Café—that do?" They are in Negrotown now.

Valentine patters over and holds open a screen door warped like a sea shell, bitter in the wet, and they walk in, stained darker with the rain and leaving footprints. Inside, sheltered dry smells stand like screens around a table covered with a red-checkered cloth, in the center of which flies hang onto an obelisk-shaped ketchup bottle. The midnight walls are checkered again with admonishing "Not Responsible" signs and black-figured, smoky calendars. It is a waiting, silent, limp room. There is a burned-out-looking nickelodeon and

right beside it a long-necked wall instrument labeled "Business Phone, Don't Keep Talking." Circled phone numbers are written up everywhere. There is a worn-out peacock feather hanging by a thread to an old, thin, pink, exposed light bulb, where it slowly turns around and around, whoever breathes.

A waitress watches.

"Come here, living statue, and get all this big order of beer we fixing to give."

"Never seen you before anywhere." The waitress moves and comes forward and slowly shows little gold leaves and tendrils over her teeth. She shoves up her shoulders and breasts. "How I going to know who you might be? Robbers? Coming in out of the black of night right at midnight, setting down so big at my table?"

"Boogers," says Powerhouse, his eyes opening lazily as in a cave.

The girl screams delicately with pleasure. O Lord, she likes talk and scares.

"Where you going to find enough beer to put out on this here table?"

She runs to the kitchen with bent elbows and sliding steps.

"Here's a million nickels," says Powerhouse, pulling his hand out of his pocket and sprinkling coins out, all but the last one, which he makes vanish like a magician.

Valentine and Scoot take the money over to the nickelodeon, which looks as battered as a slot machine, and read all the names of the records out loud.

"Whose 'Tuxedo Junction'?" asks Powerhouse.

"You know whose."

"Nickelodeon, I request you please to play 'Empty Bed Blues' and let Bessie Smith sing."

Silence: they hold it like a measure.

"Bring me all those nickels on back here," says Powerhouse. "Look at that! What you tell me the name of this place?"

"White dance, week night, raining, Alligator, Mississippi, long ways from home."

"Uh-huh."

"Sent for You Yesterday and Here You Come Today" plays.

The waitress, setting the tray of beer down on a back table, comes up taut and apprehensive as a hen. "Says in the kitchen, back there putting their eyes to little hole peeping out, that you is Mr. Powerhouse. . . . They knows from a picture they seen."

"They seeing right tonight, that is him," says Little Brother.

"You him?"

"That is him in the flesh," says Scoot.

"Does you wish to touch him?" asks Valentine. "Because he don't bite."

"You passing through?"

"Now you got everything right."

She waits like a drop, hands languishing together in front.

"Little-Bit, ain't you going to bring the beer?"

She brings it, and goes behind the cash register and smiles, turning different ways. The little fillet of gold in her mouth is gleaming.

"The Mississippi River's here," she says once.

Now all the watching Negroes press in gently and bright-eyed through the door, as many as can get in. One is a little boy in a straw sombrero which has been coated with aluminum paint all over.

Powerhouse, Valentine, Scoot and Little Brother drink beer, and their eyelids come

together like curtains. The wall and the rain and the humble beautiful waitress waiting on them and the other Negroes watching enclose them.

"Listen!" whispers Powerhouse, looking into the ketchup bottle and slowly spreading his performer's hands over the damp, wrinkling cloth with the red squares. "Listen how it is. My wife gets missing me. Gypsy. She goes to the window. She looks out and sees you know what. Street. Sign saying Hotel. People walking. Somebody looks up. Old man. She looks down, out the window. Well? . . . *Sssst! Plooey!* What she do? Jump out and bust her brains all over the world."

He opens his eyes.

"That's it," agrees Valentine. "You gets a telegram."

"Sure she misses you," Little Brother adds.

"No, it's night time." How softly he tells them! "Sure. It's the night time. She say, What do I hear? Footsteps walking up the hall? That him? Footsteps go on off. It's not me. I'm in Alligator, Mississippi, she's crazy. Shaking all over. Listens till her ears and all grow out like old music-box horns but still she can't hear a thing. She says, All right! I'll jump out the window then. Got on her nightgown. I know that nightgown, and her thinking there. Says, Ho hum, all right, and jumps out the window. Is she mad at me! Is she crazy! She don't leave *nothing* behind her!"

"Ya! Ha!"

"Brains and insides everywhere, Lord, Lord."

All the watching Negroes stir in their delight, and to their higher delight he says affectionately, "Listen! Rats in here."

"That must be the way, boss."

"Only, naw, Powerhouse, that ain't true. That sound too *bad.*"

"Does? I even know who finds her," cries Powerhouse. "That no-good pussyfooted crooning creeper, that creeper that follow around after me, coming up like weeds behind me, following around after me everything I do and messing around on the trail I leave. Bets my numbers, sings my songs, gets close to my agent like a Betsy-bug; when I going out he just coming in. I got him now! I got my eye on him."

"Know who he is?"

"Why it's that old Uranus Knockwood!"

"Ya! Ha!"

"Yeah, and he coming now, he going to find Gypsy. There he is, coming around that corner, and Gypsy kadoodling down, oh-oh, watch out! *Ssssst! Plooey!* See, there she is in her little old nightgown, and her insides and brains all scattered round."

A sigh fills the room.

"Hush about her brains. Hush about her insides."

"Ya! Ha! You talking about her brains and insides—old Uranus Knockwood," says Powerhouse, "look down and say Jesus! He say, Look here what I'm walking round in!"

They all burst into halloos of laughter. Powerhouse's face looks like a big hot iron stove.

"Why, he picks her up and carries her off!" he says.

"Ya! Ha!"

"Carries her *back* around the corner. . . ."

"Oh, Powerhouse!"

"You know him."

"Uranus Knockwood!"

"Yeahhh!"

"He take our wives when we gone!"

"He come in when we goes out!"

"Uh-huh!"

"He go out when we comes in!"

"Yeahhh!"

"He standing behind the door!"

"Old Uranus Knockwood."

"You know him."

"Middle-size man."

"Wears a hat."

"That's him."

Everybody in the room moans with pleasure. The little boy in the fine silver hat opens a paper and divides out a jelly roll among his followers.

And out of the breathless ring somebody moves forward like a slave, leading a great logy Negro with bursting eyes, and says, "This here is Sugar-Stick Thompson, that dove down to the bottom of July Creek and pulled up all those drowned white people fall out of a boat. Last summer, pulled up fourteen."

"Hello," says Powerhouse, turning and looking around at them all with his great daring face until they nearly suffocate.

Sugar-Stick, their instrument, cannot speak; he can only look back at the others.

"Can't even swim. Done it by holding his breath," says the fellow with the hero.

Powerhouse looks at him seekingly.

"I his half brother," the fellow puts in.

They step back.

"Gypsy say," Powerhouse rumbles gently again, looking at *them*, " 'What is the use? I'm gonna jump out so far—so far. . . .' *Sssst—!*"

"Don't, boss, don't do it agin," says Little Brother.

"It's awful," says the waitress. "I hates that Mr. Knockwoods. All that the truth?"

"Want to see the telegram I got from him?" Powerhouse's hand goes to the vast pocket.

"Now wait, now wait, boss." They all watch him.

"It must be the real truth," says the waitress, sucking in her lower lip, her luminous eyes turning sadly, seeking the windows.

"No, babe, it ain't the truth." His eyebrows fly up, and he begins to whisper to her out of his vast oven mouth. His hand stays in his pocket. "Truth is something worse, I ain't said what, yet. It's something hasn't come to me, but I ain't saying it won't. And when it does, then want me to tell you?" He sniffs all at once, his eyes come open and turn up, almost too far. He is dreamily smiling.

"Don't, boss, don't, Powerhouse!"

"Oh!" the waitress screams.

"Go on git out of here!" bellows Powerhouse, taking his hand out of his pocket and clapping after her red dress.

The ring of watchers breaks and falls away.

"Look at that! Intermission is up," says Powerhouse.

He folds money under a glass, and after they go out, Valentine leans back in and drops a nickel in the nickelodeon behind them, and it lights up and begins to play "The Goona Goo." The feather dangles still.

"Take a telegram!" Powerhouse shouts suddenly up into the rain over the street. "Take a answer. Now what was that name?"

They get a little tired.

"Uranus Knockwood."

"You ought to know."

"Yas? Spell it to me."

They spell it all the ways it could be spelled. It puts them in a wonderful humor.

"Here's the answer. I got it right here. 'What in the hell you talking about? Don't make any difference: I gotcha.' Name signed: Powerhouse."

"That going to reach him, Powerhouse?" Valentine speaks in a maternal voice.

"Yas, yas."

All hushing, following him up the dark street at a distance, like old rained-on black ghosts, the Negroes are afraid they will die laughing.

Powerhouse throws back his vast head into the steaming rain, and a look of hopeful desire seems to blow somehow like a vapor from his own dilated nostrils over his face and bring a mist to his eyes.

"Reach him and come out the other side."

"That's it, Powerhouse, that's it. You got him now."

Powerhouse lets out a long sigh.

"But ain't you going back there to call up Gypsy long distance, the way you did last night in that other place? I seen a telephone. . . . Just to see if she there at home?"

There is a measure of silence. That is one crazy drummer that's going to get his neck broken some day.

"No," growls Powerhouse. "No! How many thousand times tonight I got to say No?"

He holds up his arm in the rain.

"You sure-enough unroll your voice some night, it about reach up yonder to her," says Little Brother, dismayed.

They go on up the street, shaking the rain off and on them like birds.

Back in the dance hall, they play "San" (99). The jitterbugs start up like windmills stationed over the floor, and in their orbits—one circle, another, a long stretch and a zigzag—dance the elderly couples with old smoothness, undisturbed and stately.

When Powerhouse first came back from intermission, no doubt full of beer, they said, he got the band tuned up again in his own way. He didn't strike the piano keys for pitch—he simply opened his mouth and gave falsetto howls—in A, D and so on—they tuned by him. Then he took hold of the piano, as if he saw it for the first time in his life, and tested it for strength, hit it down in the bass, played an octave with his elbow, lifted the top, looked inside, and leaned against it with all his might. He sat down and played it for a few minutes with outrageous force and got it under his power—a bass deep and coarse as a sea net—then produced something glimmering and fragile, and smiled. And who could ever remember any of the things he says? They are just inspired remarks that roll out of his mouth like smoke.

They've requested "Somebody Loves Me," and he's already done twelve or fourteen choruses, piling them up nobody knows how, and it will be a wonder if he ever gets through. Now and then he calls and shouts, " 'Somebody loves me! Somebody loves me, I wonder who!' " His mouth gets to be nothing but a volcano. "I wonder who!"

"Maybe . . ." He uses all his right hand on a trill.

"Maybe . . ." He pulls back his spread fingers and looks out upon the place where he is. A vast, impersonal and yet furious grimace transfigures his wet face.

". . . Maybe it's you!"

WILLIAM FAULKNER

(1897–1962)

Barn Burning

About the Author: William Faulkner was born and died in Mississippi; he lived most of his life at Oxford. During his Nobel Prize–winning career he wrote twenty-odd novels and scores of short stories, along with two volumes of poetry and a number of screen plays. Much of his fiction is situated in his own invented southern preserve, Yoknapatawpha County, Mississippi. Among his principal novels are *The Sound and the Fury* (1929), *As I Lay Dying* (1936), and *The Hamlet* (1940).

The store in which the Justice of the Peace's court was sitting smelled of cheese. The boy, crouched on his nail keg at the back of the crowded room, knew he smelled cheese, and more: from where he sat he could see the ranked shelves close-packed with the solid, squat, dynamic shapes of tin cans whose labels his stomach read, not from the lettering which meant nothing to his mind but from the scarlet devils and the silver curve of fish—this, the cheese which he knew he smelled and the hermetic meat which his intestines believed he smelled coming in intermittent gusts momentary and brief between the other constant one, the smell and sense just a little of fear because mostly of despair and grief, the old fierce pull of blood. He could not see the table where the Justice sat and before which his father and his father's enemy (*our enemy* he thought in that despair; *ourn! mine and hisn both! He's my father!*) stood, but he could hear them, the two of them that is, because his father had said no word yet:

"But what proof have you, Mr. Harris?"

"I told you. The hog got into my corn. I caught it up and sent it back to him. He had no fence that would hold it. I told him so, warned him. The next time I put the hog in my pen. When he came to get it I gave him enough wire to patch up his pen. The next time I put the hog up and kept it. I rode down to his house and saw the wire I gave him still rolled on to the spool in his yard. I told him he could have the hog when he paid me a dollar pound fee. That evening a nigger came with the dollar and got the hog. He was a strange nigger. He said, 'He say to tell you wood and hay kin burn.' I said, 'What?' 'That whut he say to tell you,' the nigger said. 'Wood and hay kin burn.' That night my barn burned. I got the stock out but I lost the barn."

"Where is the nigger? Have you got him?"

"He was a strange nigger, I tell you. I don't know what became of him."

"But that's not proof. Don't you see that's not proof?"

"Get that boy up here. He knows." For a moment the boy thought too that the man meant his older brother until Harris said, "Not him. The little one. The boy," and, crouching, small for his age, small and wiry like his father, in patched and faded jeans even too small for him, with straight, uncombed, brown hair and eyes gray and wild as storm

scud, he saw the men between himself and the table part and become a lane of grim faces, at the end of which he saw the Justice, a shabby, collarless, graying man in spectacles, beckoning him. He felt no floor under his bare feet; he seemed to walk beneath the palpable weight of the grim turning faces. His father, still in his black Sunday coat donned not for the trial but for the moving, did not even look at him. *He aims for me to lie,* he thought, again with that frantic grief and despair. *And I will have to do hit.*

"What's your name, boy?" the Justice said.

"Colonel Sartoris Snopes," the boy whispered.

"Hey?" the Justice said. "Talk louder. Colonel Sartoris? I reckon anybody named for Colonel Sartoris in this country can't help but tell the truth, can they?" The boy said nothing. *Enemy! Enemy!* he thought; for a moment he could not even see, could not see that the Justice's face was kindly nor discern that his voice was troubled when he spoke to the man named Harris: "Do you want me to question this boy?" But he could hear, and during those subsequent long seconds while there was absolutely no sound in the crowded little room save that of quiet and intent breathing it was as if he had swung outward at the end of a grape vine, over a ravine, and at the top of the swing had been caught in a prolonged instant of mesmerized gravity, weightless in time.

"No!" Harris said violently, explosively. "Damnation! Send him out of here!" Now time, the fluid world, rushed beneath him again, the voices coming to him again through the smell of cheese and sealed meat, the fear and despair and the old grief of blood:

"This case is closed. I can't find against you, Snopes, but I can give you advice. Leave this country and don't come back to it."

His father spoke for the first time, his voice cold and harsh, level, without emphasis: "I aim to. I don't figure to stay in a country among people who . . ." he said something unprintable and vile, addressed to no one.

"That'll do," the Justice said. "Take your wagon and get out of this country before dark. Case dismissed."

His father turned, and he followed the stiff black coat, the wiry figure walking a little stiffly from where a Confederate provost's man's musket ball had taken him in the heel on a stolen horse thirty years ago, followed the two backs now, since his older brother had appeared from somewhere in the crowd, no taller than the father but thicker, chewing tobacco steadily, between the two lines of grim-faced men and out of the store and across the worn gallery and down the sagging steps and among the dogs and half-grown boys in the mild May dust, where as he passed a voice hissed:

"Barn burner!"

Again he could not see, whirling; there was a face in a red haze, moonlike, bigger than the full moon, the owner of it half again his size, he leaping in the red haze toward the face, feeling no blow, feeling no shock when his head struck the earth, scrabbling up and leaping again, feeling no blow this time either and tasting no blood, scrabbling up to see the other boy in full flight and himself already leaping into pursuit as his father's hand jerked him back, the harsh, cold voice speaking above him: "Go get in the wagon."

It stood in a grove of locusts and mulberries across the road. His two hulking sisters in their Sunday dresses and his mother and her sister in calico and sunbonnets were already in it, sitting on and among the sorry residue of the dozen and more movings which even the boy could remember—the battered stove, the broken beds and chairs, the clock inlaid with mother-of-pearl, which would not run, stopped at some fourteen minutes past two o'clock of a dead and forgotten day and time, which had been his mother's dowry. She was

crying, though when she saw him she drew her sleeve across her face and began to descend from the wagon. "Get back," the father said.

"He's hurt. I got to get some water and wash his . . ."

"Get back in the wagon," his father said. He got in too, over the tail-gate. His father mounted to the seat where the older brother already sat and struck the gaunt mules two savage blows with the peeled willow, but without heat. It was not even sadistic; it was exactly that same quality which in later years would cause his descendants to over-run the engine before putting a motor car into motion, striking and reining back in the same movement. The wagon went on, the store with its quiet crowd of grimly watching men dropped behind; a curve in the road hid it. *Forever* he thought. *Maybe he's done satisfied now, now that he has* . . . stopping himself, not to say it aloud even to himself. His mother's hand touched his shoulder.

"Does hit hurt?" she said.

"Naw," he said. "Hit don't hurt. Lemme be."

"Can't you wipe some of the blood off before hit dries?"

"I'll wash to-night," he said. "Lemme be, I tell you."

The wagon went on. He did not know where they were going. None of them ever did or ever asked, because it was always somewhere, always a house of sorts waiting for them a day or two days or even three days away. Likely his father had already arranged to make a crop on another farm before he . . . Again he had to stop himself. He (the father) always did. There was something about his wolflike independence and even courage when the advantage was at least neutral which impressed strangers, as if they got from his latent ravening ferocity not so much a sense of dependability as a feeling that his ferocious conviction in the rightness of his own actions would be of advantage to all whose interest lay with his.

That night they camped, in a grove of oaks and beeches where a spring ran. The nights were still cool and they had a fire against it, of a rail lifted from a nearby fence and cut into lengths—a small fire, neat, niggard almost, a shrewd fire; such fires were his father's habit and custom always, even in freezing weather. Older, the boy might have remarked this and wondered why not a big one; why should not a man who had not only seen the waste and extravagance of war, but who had in his blood an inherent voracious prodigality with material not his own, have burned everything in sight? Then he might have gone a step farther and thought that that was the reason: that niggard blaze was the living fruit of nights passed during those four years in the woods hiding from all men, blue or gray, with his strings of horses (captured horses, he called them). And older still, he might have divined the true reason: that the element of fire spoke to some deep mainspring of his father's being, as the element of steel or of powder spoke to other men, as the one weapon for the preservation of integrity, else breath were not worth the breathing, and hence to be regarded with respect and used with discretion.

But he did not think this now and he had seen those same niggard blazes all his life. He merely ate his supper beside it and was already half asleep over his iron plate when his father called him, and once more he followed the stiff back, the stiff and ruthless limp, up the slope and on to the starlit road where, turning, he could see his father against the stars but without face or depth—a shape black, flat, and bloodless as though cut from tin in the iron folds of the frockcoat which had not been made for him, the voice harsh like tin and without heat like tin:

"You were fixing to tell them. You would have told him."

He didn't answer. His father struck him with the flat of his hand on the side of the head, hard but without heat, exactly as he had struck the two mules at the store, exactly as he would strike either of them with any stick in order to kill a horse fly, his voice still without heat or anger: "You're getting to be a man. You got to learn. You got to learn to stick to your own blood or you ain't going to have any blood to stick to you. Do you think either of them, any man there this morning, would? Don't you know all they wanted was a chance to get at me because they knew I had them beat? Eh?" Later, twenty years later, he was to tell himself, "If I had said they wanted only truth, justice, he would have hit me again." But now he said nothing. He was not crying. He just stood there. "Answer me," his father said.

"Yes," he whispered. His father turned.

"Get on to bed. We'll be there tomorrow."

Tomorrow they were there. In the early afternoon the wagon stopped before a paintless two-room house identical almost with the dozen others it had stopped before even in the boy's ten years, and again, as on the other dozen occasions, his mother and aunt got down and began to unload the wagon, although his two sisters and his father and brother had not moved.

"Likely hit ain't fitten for hawgs," one of the sisters said.

"Nevertheless, fit it will and you'll hog it and like it," his father said. "Get out of them chairs and help your Ma unload."

The two sisters got down, big, bovine, in a flutter of cheap ribbons; one of them drew from the jumbled wagon bed a battered lantern, the other a worn broom. His father handed the reins to the older son and began to climb stiffly over the wheel. "When they get unloaded, take the team to the barn and feed them." Then he said, and at first the boy thought he was still speaking to his brother: "Come with me."

"Me?" he said.

"Yes," his father said. "You."

"Abner," his mother said. His father paused and looked back—the harsh level stare beneath the shaggy, graying, irascible brows.

"I reckon I'll have a word with the man that aims to begin tomorrow owning me body and soul for the next eight months."

They went back up the road. A week ago—or before last night, that is—he would have asked where they were going, but not now. His father had struck him before last night but never before had he paused afterward to explain why; it was as if the blow and the following calm, outrageous voice still rang, repercussed, divulging nothing to him save the terrible handicap of being young, the light weight of his few years, just heavy enough to prevent his soaring free of the world as it seemed to be ordered but not heavy enough to keep him footed solid in it, to resist it and try to change the course of its events.

Presently he could see the grove of oaks and cedars and the other flowering trees and shrubs where the house would be, though not the house yet. They walked beside a fence massed with honeysuckle and Cherokee roses and came to a gate swinging open between two brick pillars, and now, beyond a sweep of drive, he saw the house for the first time and at that instant he forgot his father and the terror and despair both, and even when he remembered his father again (who had not stopped) the terror and despair did not return. Because, for all the twelve movings, they had sojourned until now in a poor country, a land of small farms and fields and houses, and he had never seen a house like this before. *Hit's big as a courthouse* he thought quietly, with a surge of peace and joy whose reason he could not have thought into words, being too young for that: *They are safe from him. People whose lives are a part of this peace and dignity are beyond his touch, he no more to them than a buzzing wasp: capable of stinging for a little moment but that's all; the spell of this peace and dignity rendering even the barns and stable and cribs which belong to it impervious to the puny flames he might contrive* . . . this, the peace and joy, ebbing for an instant as he looked again at the stiff black back, the stiff and implacable limp of the figure which was not dwarfed by the house, for the reason that it had never looked big anywhere and which now, against the serene columned backdrop, had more than ever that impervious quality of something cut ruthlessly from tin, depthless, as though, sidewise to the sun, it would cast no shadow. Watching him, the boy remarked the absolutely undeviating course which his father held and saw the stiff foot come squarely down in a pile of fresh droppings where a horse had stood in the drive and which his father could have avoided by a simple change of stride. But it ebbed only for a moment, though he could not have thought this into words either, walking on in the spell of the house, which he could even want but without envy, without sorrow, certainly never with that ravening and jealous rage which unknown to him walked in the ironlike black coat before him: *Maybe he will feel it too. Maybe it will even change him now from what maybe he couldn't help but be.*

They crossed the portico. Now he could hear his father's stiff foot as it came down on the boards with clocklike finality, a sound out of all proportion to the displacement of the body it bore and which was not dwarfed either by the white door before it, as though it had attained to a sort of vicious and ravening minimum not to be dwarfed by anything—the flat, wide, black hat, the formal coat of broadcloth which had once been black but which had now that friction-glazed greenish cast of the bodies of old house flies, the lifted sleeve which was too large, the lifted hand like a curled claw. The door opened so promptly that the boy knew the Negro must have been watching them all the time, an old man with neat grizzled hair, in a linen jacket, who stood barring the door with his body, saying, "Wipe yo foots, white man, fo you come in here. Major ain't home nohow."

"Get out of my way, nigger," his father said, without heat too, flinging the door back and the Negro also and entering, his hat still on his head. And now the boy saw the prints of the stiff foot on the doorjamb and saw them appear on the pale rug behind the machine-like deliberation of the foot which seemed to bear (or transmit) twice the weight which the body compassed. The Negro was shouting "Miss Lula! Miss Lula!" somewhere behind them, then the boy, deluged as though by a warm wave by a suave turn of the carpeted stair and a pendant glitter of chandeliers and a mute gleam of gold frames, heard the swift feet and saw her too, a lady—perhaps he had never seen her like before either—in a gray, smooth gown with lace at the throat and an apron tied at the waist and the sleeves turned back, wiping cake or biscuit dough from her hands with a towel as she came up the hall, looking not at his father at all but at the tracks on the blond rug with an expression of incredulous amazement.

"I tried," the Negro cried. "I tole him to . . ."

"Will you please go away?" she said in a shaking voice. "Major de Spain is not at home. Will you please go away?"

His father had not spoken again. He did not speak again. He did not even look at her. He just stood stiff in the center of the rug, in his hat, the shaggy iron-gray brows twitching slightly above the pebble-colored eyes as he appeared to examine the house with brief deliberation. Then with the same deliberation he turned; the boy watched him pivot on the good leg and saw the stiff foot drag around the arc of the turning, leaving a final long and fading smear. His father never looked at it, he never once looked down at the rug. The

Negro held the door. It closed behind them, upon the hysteric and indistinguishable woman-wail. His father stopped at the top of the steps and scraped his boot clean on the edge of it. At the gate he stopped again. He stood for a moment, planted stiffly on the stiff foot, looking back at the house. "Pretty and white, ain't it?" he said. "That's sweat. Nigger sweat. Maybe it ain't white enough yet to suit him. Maybe he wants to mix some white sweat with it."

Two hours later the boy was chopping wood behind the house within which his mother and aunt and the two sisters (the mother and aunt, not the two girls, he knew that; even at this distance and muffled by walls the flat loud voices of the two girls emanated an incorrigible idle inertia) were setting up the stove to prepare a meal, when he heard the hooves and saw the linen-clad man on a fine sorrel mare, whom he recognized even before he saw the rolled rug in front of the Negro youth following on a fat bay carriage horse—a suffused, angry face vanishing, still at full gallop, beyond the corner of the house where his father and brother were sitting in the two tilted chairs; and a moment later, almost before he could have put the axe down, he heard the hooves again and watched the sorrel mare go back out of the yard, already galloping again. Then his father began to shout one of the sisters' names, who presently emerged backward from the kitchen door dragging the rolled rug along the ground by one end while the other sister walked behind it.

"If you ain't going to tote, go on and set up the wash pot," the first said.

"You, Sarty!" the second shouted. "Set up the wash pot!" His father appeared at the door, framed against that shabbiness, as he had been against that other bland perfection, impervious to either, the mother's anxious face at his shoulder.

"Go on," the father said. "Pick it up." The two sisters stopped, broad, lethargic; stooping, they presented an incredible expanse of pale cloth and a flutter of tawdry ribbons.

"If I thought enough of a rug to have to git hit all the way from France I wouldn't keep hit where folks coming in would have to tromp on hit," the first said. They raised the rug.

"Abner," the mother said. "Let me do it."

"You go back and git dinner," his father said. "I'll tend to this."

From the woodpile through the rest of the afternoon the boy watched them, the rug spread flat in the dust beside the bubbling wash pot, the two sisters stooping over it with that profound and lethargic reluctance, while the father stood over them in turn, implacable and grim, driving them though never raising his voice again. He could smell the harsh homemade lye they were using; he saw his mother come to the door once and look toward them with an expression not anxious now but very like despair; he saw his father turn, and he fell to with the axe and saw from the corner of his eye his father raise from the ground a flattish fragment of field stone and examine it and return to the pot, and this time his mother actually spoke: "Abner. Abner. Please don't. Please, Abner."

Then he was done too. It was dusk; the whippoorwills had already begun. He could smell coffee from the room where they would presently eat the cold food remaining from the mid-afternoon meal, though when he entered the house he realized they were having coffee again probably because there was a fire on the hearth, before which the rug now lay spread over the backs of the two chairs. The tracks of his father's foot were gone. Where they had been were now long, water-cloudy scoriations resembling the sporadic course of a lilliputian mowing machine.

It still hung there while they ate the cold food and then went to bed, scattered without order or claim up and down the two rooms, his mother in one bed, where his father would later lie, the older brother in the other, himself, the aunt, and the two sisters on pallets on the floor. But his father was not in bed yet. The last thing the boy remembered was the depthless, harsh silhouette of the hat and coat bending over the rug and it seemed to him that he had not even closed his eyes when the silhouette was standing over him, the fire almost dead behind it, the stiff foot prodding him awake. "Catch up the mule," his father said.

When he returned with the mule his father was standing in the black door, the rolled rug over his shoulder. "Ain't you going to ride?" he said.

"No. Give me your foot."

He bent his knee into his father's hand, the wiry, surprising power flowed smoothly, rising, he rising with it, on to the mule's bare back (they had owned a saddle once; the boy could remember it though not when or where) and with the same effortlessness his father swung the rug up in front of him. Now in the starlight they retraced the afternoon's path, up the dusty road rife with honeysuckle, through the gate and up the black tunnel of the drive to the lightless house, where he sat on the mule and felt the rough warp of the rug drag across his thighs and vanish.

"Don't you want me to help?" he whispered. His father did not answer and now he heard again that stiff foot striking the hollow portico with that wooden and clocklike deliberation, that outrageous overstatement of the weight it carried. The rug, hunched, not flung (the boy could tell that even in the darkness) from his father's shoulder struck the angle of wall and floor with a sound unbelievably loud, thunderous, then the foot again, unhurried and enormous; a light came on in the house and the boy sat, tense, breathing steadily and quietly and just a little fast, though the foot itself did not increase its beat at all, descending the steps now; now the boy could see him.

"Don't you want to ride now?" he whispered. "We kin both ride now," the light within the house altering now, flaring up and sinking. *He's coming down the stairs now,* he thought. He had already ridden the mule up beside the horse block; presently his father was up behind him and he doubled the reins over and slashed the mule across the neck, but before the animal could begin to trot the hard, thin arm came around him, the hard, knotted hand jerking the mule back to a walk.

In the first red rays of the sun they were in the lot, putting plow gear on the mules. This time the sorrel mare was in the lot before he heard it at all, the rider collarless and even bareheaded, trembling, speaking in a shaking voice as the woman in the house had done, his father merely looking up once before stooping again to the hame he was buckling, so that the man on the mare spoke to his stooping back:

"You must realize you have ruined that rug. Wasn't there anybody here, any of your women . . ." he ceased, shaking, the boy watching him, the older brother leaning now in the stable door, chewing, blinking slowly and steadily at nothing apparently. "It cost a hundred dollars. But you never had a hundred dollars. You never will. So I'm going to charge you twenty bushels of corn against your crop. I'll add it in your contract and when you come to the commissary you can sign it. That won't keep Mrs. de Spain quiet but maybe it will teach you to wipe your feet off before you enter her house again."

Then he was gone. The boy looked at his father, who still had not spoken or even looked up again, who was now adjusting the logger-head in the hame.

"Pap," he said. His father looked at him—the inscrutable face, the shaggy brows beneath which the gray eyes glinted coldly. Suddenly the boy went toward him, fast, stopping as suddenly. "You done the best you could!" he cried. "If he wanted hit done different why didn't he wait and tell you how? He won't git no twenty bushels! He won't git none! We'll gether hit and hide hit! I kin watch . . ."

"Did you put the cutter back in that straight stock like I told you?"

"No, sir," he said.

"Then go do it."

That was Wednesday. During the rest of that week he worked steadily, at what was within his scope and some which was beyond it, with an industry that did not need to be driven nor even commanded twice; he had this from his mother, with the difference that some at least of what he did he liked to do, such as splitting wood with the half-size axe which his mother and aunt had earned, or saved money somehow, to present him with at Christmas. In company with the two older women (and on one afternoon, even one of the sisters), he built pens for the shoat and the cow which were a part of his father's contract with the landlord, and one afternoon, his father being absent, gone somewhere on one of the mules, he went to the field.

They were running a middle buster now, his brother holding the plow straight while he handled the reins, and walking beside the straining mule, the rich black soil shearing cool and damp against his bare ankles, he thought *Maybe this is the end of it. Maybe even that twenty bushels that seems hard to have to pay for just a rug will be a cheap price for him to stop forever and always from being what he used to be;* thinking, dreaming now, so that his brother had to speak sharply to him to mind the mule. *Maybe he even won't collect the twenty bushels. Maybe it will all add up and balance and vanish—corn, rug, fire; the terror and grief; the being pulled two ways like between two teams of horses—gone, done with for ever and ever.*

Then it was Saturday; he looked up from beneath the mule he was harnessing and saw his father in the black coat and hat. "Not that," his father said. "The wagon gear." And then, two hours later, sitting in the wagon bed behind his father and brother on the seat, the wagon accomplished a final curve, and he saw the weathered paintless store with its tattered tobacco- and patent-medicine posters and the tethered wagons and saddle animals below the gallery. He mounted the gnawed steps behind his father and brother, and there again was the lane of quiet, watching faces for the three of them to walk through. He saw the man in spectacles sitting at the plank table and he did not need to be told this was a Justice of the Peace; he sent one glare of fierce, exultant, partisan defiance at the man in collar and cravat now, whom he had seen but twice before in his life, and that on a galloping horse, who now wore on his face an expression not of rage but of amazed unbelief which the boy could not have known was at the incredible circumstance of being sued by one of his own tenants, and came and stood against his father and cried at the Justice. "He ain't done it! He ain't burnt . . ."

"Go back to the wagon," his father said.

"Burnt?" the Justice said. "Do I understand this rug was burned too?"

"Does anybody here claim it was?" his father said. "Go back to the wagon." But he did not, he merely retreated to the rear of the room, crowded as that other had been, but not to sit down this time, instead, to stand pressing among the motionless bodies, listening to the voices:

"And you claim twenty bushels of corn is too high for the damage you did to the rug?"

"He brought the rug to me and said he wanted the tracks washed out of it. I washed the tracks out and took the rug back to him."

"But you didn't carry the rug back to him in the same condition it was in before you made the tracks on it."

His father did not answer, and now for perhaps, half a minute there was no sound at all save that of breathing, the faint, steady suspiration of complete and intent listening.

"You decline to answer that, Mr. Snopes?" Again his father did not answer. "I'm going to find against you, Mr. Snopes. I'm going to find that you were responsible for the injury to Major de Spain's rug and hold you liable for it. But twenty bushels of corn seems a little high for a man in your circumstances to have to pay. Major de Spain claims it cost a hundred dollars. October corn will be worth about fifty cents. I figure that if Major de Spain can stand a ninety-five dollar loss on something he paid cash for, you can stand a five-dollar loss you haven't earned yet. I hold you in damages to Major de Spain to the amount of ten bushels of corn over and above your contract with him, to be paid out of your crop at gathering time. Court adjourned."

It had taken no time hardly, the morning was but half begun. He thought they would return home and perhaps back to the field, since they were late, far behind all other farmers. But instead his father passed on behind the wagon, merely indicating with his hand for the older brother to follow with it, and crossed the road toward the blacksmith shop opposite, pressing on after his father, overtaking him, speaking, whispering up at the harsh, calm face beneath the weathered hat: "He won't git no ten bushels neither. He won't git one. We'll . . ." until his father glanced for an instant down at him, the face absolutely calm, the grizzled eyebrows tangled above the cold eyes, the voice almost pleasant, almost gentle:

"You think so? Well, we'll wait till October anyway."

The matter of the wagon—the setting of a spoke or two and the tightening of the tires—did not take long either, the business of the tires accomplished by driving the wagon into the spring branch behind the shop and letting it stand there, the mules nuzzling into the water from time to time, and the boy on the seat with the idle reins, looking up the slope and through the sooty tunnel of the shed where the slow hammer rang and where his father sat on an upended cypress bolt, easily, either talking or listening, still sitting there when the boy brought the dripping wagon up out of the branch and halted it before the door.

"Take them on to the shade and hitch," his father said. He did so and returned. His father and the smith and a third man squatting on his heels inside the door were talking, about crops and animals; the boy, squatting too in the ammoniac dust and hoof-parings and scales of rust, heard his father tell a long and unhurried story out of the time before the birth of the older brother even when he had been a professional horsetrader. And then his father came up beside him where he stood before a tattered last year's circus poster on the other side of the store, gazing rapt and quiet at the scarlet horses, the incredible poisings and convolutions of tulle and tights and the painted leers of comedians, and said, "It's time to eat."

But not at home. Squatting beside his brother against the front wall, he watched his father emerge from the store and produce from a paper sack a segment of cheese and divide it carefully and deliberately into three with his pocket knife and produce crackers from the same sack. They all three squatted on the gallery and ate, slowly, without talking; then in the store again, they drank from a tin dipper tepid water smelling of the cedar bucket and of living beech trees. And still they did not go home. It was a horse lot this time, a tall rail fence upon and along which men stood and sat and out of which one by one horses were led, to be walked and trotted and then cantered back and forth along the road while the slow swapping and buying went on and the sun began to slant westward, they—the three of them—watching and listening, the older brother with his muddy eyes and his steady, inevitable tobacco, the father commenting now and then on certain of the animals, to no one in particular.

It was after sundown when they reached home. They ate supper by lamplight, then, sitting on the doorstep, the boy watched the night fully accomplish, listening to the

whippoorwills and the frogs, when he heard his mother's voice: "Abner! No! No! Oh, God. Oh, God. Abner!" and he rose, whirled, and saw the altered light through the door where a candle stub now burned in a bottle neck on the table and his father, still in the hat and coat, at once formal and burlesque as though dressed carefully for some shabby and ceremonial violence, emptying the reservoir of the lamp back into the five-gallon kerosene can from which it had been filled, while the mother tugged at his arm until he shifted the lamp to the other hand and flung her back, not savagely or viciously, just hard, into the wall, her hands flung out against the wall for balance, her mouth open and in her face the same quality of hopeless despair as had been in her voice. Then his father saw him standing in the door.

"Go to the barn and get that can of oil we were oiling the wagon with," he said. The boy did not move. Then he could speak.

"What . . ." he cried. "What are you . . ."

"Go get that oil," his father said. "Go."

Then he was moving, running, outside the house, toward the stable: this the old habit, the old blood which he had not been permitted to choose for himself, which had been bequeathed him willy nilly and which had run for so long (and who knew where, battening on what of outrage and savagery and lust) before it came to him. *I could keep on,* he thought. *I could run on and on and never look back, never need to see his face again. Only I can't. I can't,* the rusted can in his hand now, the liquid sploshing in it as he ran back to the house and into it, into the sound of his mother's weeping in the next room, and handed the can to his father.

"Ain't you going to even send a nigger?" he cried. "At least you sent a nigger before!"

This time his father didn't strike him. The hand came even faster than the blow had, the same hand which had set the can on the table with almost excruciating care flashing from the can toward him too quick for him to follow it, gripping him by the back of his shirt and on to tiptoe before he had seen it quit the can, the face stooping at him in breathless and frozen ferocity, the cold, dead voice speaking over him to the older brother who leaned against the table, chewing with that steady, curious, sidewise motion of cows:

"Empty the can into the big one and go on. I'll catch up with you."

"Better tie him up to the bedpost," the brother said.

"Do like I told you," the father said. Then the boy was moving, his bunched shirt and the hard, bony hand between his shoulder-blades, his toes just touching the floor, across the room and into the other one, past the sisters sitting with spread heavy thighs in the two chairs over the cold hearth, and to where his mother and aunt sat side by side on the bed, the aunt's arms about his mother's shoulders.

"Hold him," the father said. The aunt made a startled movement. "Not you," the father said. "Lennie. Take hold of him. I want to see you do it." His mother took him by the wrist. "You'll hold him better than that. If he gets loose don't you know what he is going to do? He will go up yonder." He jerked his head toward the road. "Maybe I'd better tie him."

"I'll hold him," his mother whispered.

"See you do then." Then his father was gone, the stiff foot heavy and measured upon the boards, ceasing at last.

Then he began to struggle. His mother caught him in both arms, he jerking and wrenching at them. He would be stronger in the end, he knew that. But he had no time to wait for it. "Lemme go!" he cried. "I don't want to have to hit you!"

"Let him go!" the aunt said. "If he don't go, before God, I am going up there myself!"

"Don't you see I can't?" his mother cried. "Sarty! Sarty! No! No! Help me, Lizzie!"

Then he was free. His aunt grasped at him but it was too late. He whirled, running, his mother stumbled forward on to her knees behind him, crying to the nearer sister: "Catch him, Net! Catch him!" But that was too late too, the sister (the sisters were twins, born at the same time, yet either of them now gave the impression of being, encompassing as much living meat and volume and weight as any other two of the family) not yet having begun to rise from the chair, her head, face, alone merely turned, presenting to him in the flying instant an astonishing expanse of young female features untroubled by any surprise even, wearing only an expression of bovine interest. Then he was out of the room, out of the house, in the mild dust of the starlit road and the heavy rifeness of honeysuckle, the pale ribbon unspooling with terrific slowness under his running feet, reaching the gate at last and turning in, running, his heart and lungs drumming, on up the drive toward the lighted house, the lighted door. He did not knock, he burst in, sobbing for breath, incapable for the moment of speech; he saw the astonished face of the Negro in the linen jacket without knowing when the Negro had appeared.

"De Spain!" he cried, panted. "Where's . . ." then he saw the white man too emerging from a white door down the hall. "Barn!" he cried. "Barn!"

"What?" the white man said. "Barn?"

"Yes!" the boy cried. "Barn!"

"Catch him!" the white man shouted.

But it was too late this time too. The Negro grasped his shirt, but the entire sleeve, rotten with washing, carried away, and he was out that door too and in the drive again, and had actually never ceased to run even while he was screaming into the white man's face.

Behind him the white man was shouting, "My horse! Fetch my horse!" and he thought for an instant of cutting across the park and climbing the fence into the road, but he did not know the park nor how high the vine-massed fence might be and he dared not risk it. So he ran on down the drive, blood and breath roaring; presently he was in the road again though he could not see it. He could not hear either: the galloping mare was almost upon him before he heard her, and even then he held his course, as if the very urgency of his wild grief and need must in a moment more find him wings, waiting until the ultimate instant to hurl himself aside and into the weed-choked roadside ditch as the horse thundered past and on, for an instant in furious silhouette against the stars, the tranquil early summer night sky which, even before the shape of the horse and rider vanished, stained abruptly and violently upward: a long, swirling roar incredible and soundless, blotting the stars, and he springing up and into the road again, running again, knowing it was too late yet still running even after he heard the shot and an instant later, two shots, pausing now without knowing he had ceased to run, crying "Pap! Pap!", running again before he knew he had begun to run, stumbling, tripping over something and scrabbling up again without ceasing to run, looking backward over his shoulder at the glare as he got up, running on among the invisible trees, panting, sobbing, "Father! Father!"

At midnight he was sitting on the crest of a hill. He did not know it was midnight and he did not know how far he had come. But there was no glare behind him now and he sat now, his back toward what he had called home for four days anyhow, his face toward the dark woods which he would enter when breath was strong again, small, shaking steadily in the chill darkness, hugging himself into the remainder of his thin, rotten shirt, the grief and despair now no longer terror and fear but just grief and despair. *Father. My father,* he thought. "He was brave!" he cried suddenly, aloud but not loud, no more than a whisper. "He was! He was in the war! He was in Colonel Sartoris' cav'ry!" not knowing that his father had gone

to that war a private in the fine old European sense, wearing no uniform, admitting the authority of and giving fidelity to no man or army or flag, going to war as Malbrouck himself did: for booty—it meant nothing and less than nothing to him if it were enemy booty or his own.

The slow constellations wheeled on. It would be dawn and then sun-up after a while and he would be hungry. But that would be tomorrow and now he was only cold, and walking would cure that. His breathing was easier now and he decided to get up and go on, and then he found that he had been asleep because he knew it was almost dawn, the night almost over. He could tell that from the whippoorwills. They were everywhere now among the dark trees below him, constant and inflectioned and ceaseless, so that, as the instant for giving over to the day birds drew nearer and nearer, there was no interval at all between them. He got up. He was a little stiff, but walking would cure that too as it would the cold, and soon there would be the sun. He went on down the hill, toward the dark woods within which the liquid silver voices of the birds called unceasing—the rapid and urgent beating of the urgent and quiring heart of the late spring night. He did not look back.

ZORA NEALE HURSTON

(1903–1960)

The Gilded Six-Bits

About the Author: Zora Neale Hurston, black folklorist and fiction writer, was born in Eatonville, Florida. She attended Morgan State College and Howard University and won a scholarship to Barnard College, where she studied with the anthropologist Franz Boas before beginning a career as a folklorist. In addition to two folklore studies, she published short stories, four novels, among them *Their Eyes Were Watching God* (1937), and an autobiography.

It was a Negro yard around a Negro house in a Negro settlement that looked to the payroll of the G. and G. Fertilizer works for its support.

But there was something happy about the place. The front yard was parted in the middle by a sidewalk from gate to doorstep, a sidewalk edged on either side by quart bottles driven neck down into the ground on a slant. A mess of homey flowers planted without a plan but blooming cheerily from their helter-skelter places. The fence and house were white-washed. The porch and steps scrubbed white.

The front door stood open to the sunshine so that the floor of the front room could finish drying after its weekly scouring. It was Saturday. Everything clean from the front gate to the privy house. Yard raked so that the strokes of the rake would make a pattern. Fresh newspaper cut in fancy edge on the kitchen shelves.

Missie May was bathing herself in the galvanized washtub in the bedroom. Her dark-brown skin glistened under the soapsuds that skittered down from her washrag. Her stiff young breasts thrust forward aggressively, like broad-based cones with the tips lacquered in black.

She heard men's voices in the distance and glanced at the dollar clock on the dresser.

"Humph! Ah'm way behind time t'day! Joe gointer be heah 'fore Ah git mah clothes on if Ah don't make haste."

She grabbed the clean meal sack at hand and dried herself hurriedly and began to dress. But before she could tie her slippers, there came the ring of singing metal on wood. Nine times.

Missie May grinned with delight. She had not seen the big tall man come stealing in the gate and creep up the walk grinning happily at the joyful mischief he was about to commit. But she knew that it was her husband throwing silver dollars in the door for her to pick up and pile beside her plate at dinner. It was this way every Saturday afternoon. The nine dollars hurled into the open door, he scurried to a hiding place behind the Cape jasmine bush and waited.

Missie May promptly appeared at the door in mock alarm.

"Who dat chunkin' money in mah do'way?" she demanded. No answer from the yard. She leaped off the porch and began to search the shrubbery. She peeped under the porch and hung over the gate to look up and down the road. While she did this, the man behind the jasmine darted to the chinaberry tree. She spied him and gave chase.

"Nobody ain't gointer be chunkin' money at me and Ah not do 'em nothing'," she shouted in mock anger. He ran around the house with Missie May at his heels. She overtook him at the kitchen door. He ran inside but could not close it after him before she crowded in and locked with him in a rough-and-tumble. For several minutes the two were a furious mass of male and female energy. Shouting, laughing, twisting, turning, tussling, tickling each other in the ribs; Missie May clutching onto Joe and Joe trying, but not too hard, to get away.

"Missie May, take yo' hand out mah pocket!" Joe shouted out between laughs.

"Ah ain't, Joe, not lessen you gwine gimme whateve' it is good you got in yo' pocket. Turn it go, Joe, do. Ah'll tear yo' clothes."

"Go on tear 'em. You de one dat pushes de needles round heah. Move yo' hand, Missie May."

"Lemme git dat paper sack out yo' pocket. Ah bet it's candy kisses."

"Tain't. Move yo' hand. Woman ain't got no business in a man's clothes nohow. Go way."

Missie May gouged way down and gave an upward jerk and triumphed.

"Unhhunh! Ah got it! It 'tis so candy kisses. Ah knowed you had somethin' for me in yo' clothes. Now Ah got to see whut's in every pocket you got."

Joe smiled indulgently and let his wife go through all of his pockets and take out the things that he had hidden there for her to find. She bore off the chewing gum, the cake of sweet soap, the pocket handkerchief as if she had wrested them from him, as if they had not been bought for the sake of this friendly battle.

"Whew! dat play-fight done got me all warmed up!" Joe exclaimed. "Got me some water in de kittle?"

"Yo' water is on de fire and yo' clean things is cross de bed. Hurry up and wash yo'self and git changed so we kin eat. Ah'm hongry." As Missie said this, she bore the steaming kettle into the bedroom.

"You ain't hongry, sugar," Joe contradicted her. "Youse jes' a little empty. Ah'm de one whut's hongry. Ah could eat up camp meetin', back off'ssociation, and drink Jurdan dry. Have it on de table when Ah git out de tub."

"Don't you mess wid mah business, man. You git in yo' clothes. Ah'm a real wife, not no dress and breath. Ah might not look lak one, but if you burn me, you won't git a thing but wife ashes."

Joe splashed in the bedroom and Missie May fanned around in the kitchen. A fresh red-and-white checked cloth on the table. Big pitcher of buttermilk beaded with pale drops of butter from the churn. Hot fried mullet, crackling bread, ham hock atop a mound of string beans and new potatoes, and perched on the windowsill a pone of spicy potato pudding.

Very little talk during the meal but that little consisted of banter that pretended to deny affection but in reality flaunted it. Like when Missie May reached for a second helping of the tater pone. Joe snatched it out of her reach.

After Missie May had made two or three unsuccessful grabs at the pan, she begged, "Aw, Joe, gimme some mo' dat tater pone."

"Nope, sweetenin' is for us menfolks. Y'all pritty lil frail eels don't need nothin' lak dis. You too sweet already."

"Please, Joe."

"Naw, naw. Ah don't want you to git no sweeter than whut you is already. We goin' down de road a lil piece t'night so you go put on yo' Sunday-go-to-meetin' things."

Missie May looked at her husband to see if he was playing some prank. "Sho nuff, Joe?"

"Yeah. We goin' to de ice cream parlor."

"Where de ice cream parlor at, Joe?"

"A new man done come heah from Chicago and he done got a place and took and opened it up for a ice cream parlor, and bein' as it's real swell, Ah wants you to be one de first ladies to walk in dere and have some set down."

"Do Jesus, Ah ain't knowed nothin' 'bout it. Who de man done it?"

"Mister Otis D. Slemmons, of spots and places—Memphis, Chicago, Jacksonville, Philadelphia and so on."

"Dat heavyset man wid his mouth full of gold teeths?"

"Yeah. Where did you see 'im at?"

"Ah went down to de sto' tuh git a box of lye and Ah seen 'im standin' on de corner talkin' to some of de mens, and Ah come on back and went to scrubbin' de floor, and he passed and tipped his hat whilst Ah was scourin' de steps. Ah thought Ah never seen *him* befo'."

Joe smiled pleasantly. "Yeah, he's up-to-date. He got de finest clothes as ever seen on a colored man's back."

"Aw, he don't look no better in his clothes than you do in yourn. He got a puzzlegut on 'im and he so chuckleheaded he got a pone behind his neck."

Joe looked down at his own abdomen and said wistfully: "Wisht Ah had a build on me lak he got. He ain't puzzlegutted, honey. He jes' got a corperation. Dat make 'm look lak a rich white man. All rich mens is got some belly on 'em."

"Ah seen de pitchers of Henry Ford and he's a spare-built man and Rockefeller look lak he ain't got but one gut. But Ford and Rockefeller and dis Slemmons and all de rest kin be as many-gutted as dey please, Ah's satisfied wid you jes' lak you is, baby. God took pattern after a pine tree and built you noble. Youse a pritty man, and if Ah knowed any way to make you mo' pritty still Ah'd take and do it."

Joe reached over gently and toyed with Missie May's ear. "You jes' say dat cause you love me, but Ah know Ah can't hold no light to Otis D. Slemmons. Ah ain't never been nowhere and Ah ain't got nothin' but you."

Missie May got on his lap and kissed him and he kissed back in kind. Then he went on. "All de women's is crazy 'bout 'im everywhere he go."

"How you know dat, Joe?"

"He tole us so hisself."

"Dat don't make it so. His mouf is cut crossways, ain't it? Well, he kin lie jes' lak anybody else."

"Good Lawd, Missie! You womens sho is hard to sense into things. He's got a five-dollar gold piece for a stickpin and he got a ten-dollar gold piece on his watch chain and his mouf is jes' crammed full of gold teeths. Sho wisht it wuz mine. And whut make it so cool, he got money 'cumulated. And womens give it all to 'im."

"Ah don't see whut de womens see on 'im. Ah wouldn't give 'im a wink if de sheriff wuz after 'im."

"Well, he tole us how de white womens in Chicago give 'im all dat gold money. So he don't 'low nobody to touch it at all. Not even put day finger on it. Dey tole 'im not to. You kin make 'miration at it, but don't tetch it."

"Whyn't he stay up dere where dey so crazy 'bout 'im?"

"Ah reckon dey done made 'im vast-rich and he wants to travel some. He says dey wouldn't leave 'im hit a lick of work. He got mo' lady people crazy 'bout him than he kin shake a stick at."

"Joe, Ah hates to see you so dumb. Dat stray nigger jes' tell y'all anything and y'all b'lieve it."

"Go 'head on now, honey, and put on yo' clothes. He talkin' 'bout his pritty womens—Ah want 'im to see *mine.*"

Missie May went off to dress and Joe spent the time trying to make his stomach punch out like Slemmon's middle. He tried the rolling swagger of the stranger, but found that his tall bone-and-muscle stride fitted ill with it. He just had time to drop back into his seat before Missie May came in dressed to go.

On the way home that night Joe was exultant. "Didn't Ah say ole Otis was swell? Can't he talk Chicago talk? Wuzn't dat funny whut he said when great big fat ole Ida Armstrong come in? He asked me, 'Who is dat broad wid de forte shake?' Dat's a new word. Us always thought forty was a set of figgers but he showed us where it means a whole heap of things. Sometimes he don't say forty, he jes' say thirty-eight and two and dat mean de same thing. Know whut he tole me when Ah wuz payin' for our ice cream? He say, 'Ah have to hand it to you, Joe. Dat wife of yours is jes' thirty-eight and two. Yessuh, she's forte!' Ain't he killin'?"

"He'll do in case of a rush. But he sho is got uh heap uh gold on 'im. Dat's de first time Ah ever seed gold money. It lookted good on him sho nuff, but it'd look a whole heap better on you."

"Who, me? Missie May, youse crazy! Where would a po' man lak me git gold money from?"

Missie May was silent for a minute, then she said, "Us might find some goin' long de road some time. Us could."

"Who would be losin' gold money round heah? We ain't even seen none dese white folks wearin' no gold money on dey watch chain. You must be figgerin' Mister Packard or Mister Cadillac goin' pass through heah."

"You don't know whut been lost 'round heah. Maybe somebody way back in memorial times lost they gold money and went on off and it ain't never been found. And then if we wuz to find it, you could wear some 'thout havin' no gang of womens lak dat Slemmons say he got."

Joe laughed and hugged her. "Don't be so wishful 'bout me. Ah'm satisfied de way Ah is. So long as Ah be yo' husband, Ah don't keer 'bout nothin' else. Ah'd ruther all de other womens in de world to be dead than for you to have de toothache. Less we go to bed and git our night rest."

It was Saturday night once more before Joe could parade his wife in Slemmons's ice cream parlor again. He worked the night shift and Saturday was his only night off. Every other evening around six o'clock he left home, and dying dawn saw him hustling home around the lake, where the challenging sun flung a flaming sword from east to west across the trembling water.

That was the best part of life—going home to Missie May. Their white-washed house, the mock battle on Saturday, the dinner and ice cream parlor afterwards, church on Sunday nights when Missie outdressed any woman in town—all, everything, was right.

One night around eleven the acid ran out at the G. and G. The foreman knocked off the crew and let the steam die down. As Joe rounded the lake on his way home, a lean moon rode the lake in a silver boat. If anybody had asked Joe about the moon on the lake, he would have said he hadn't paid it any attention. But he saw it with his feelings. It made him yearn painfully for Missie. Creation obsessed him. He thought about children. They had been married more than a year now. They had money put away. They ought to be making little feet for shoes. A little boy child would be about right.

He saw a dim light in the bedroom and decided to come in through the kitchen door. He could wash the fertilizer dust off himself before presenting himself to Missie May. It would be nice for her not to know that he was there until he slipped into his place in bed and hugged her back. She always liked that.

He eased the kitchen door open slowly and silently, but when he went to set his dinner bucket on the table he bumped it into a pile of dishes, and something crashed to the floor. He heard his wife gasp in fright and hurried to reassure her.

"Iss me, honey. Don't git skeered."

There was a quick, large movement in the bedroom. A rustle, a thud, and a stealthy silence. The light went out.

What? Robbers? Murderers? Some varmint attacking his helpless wife, perhaps. He struck a match, threw himself on guard and stepped over the doorsill into the bedroom.

The great belt on the wheel of Time slipped and eternity stood still. By the match light he could see the man's legs fighting with his breeches in his frantic desire to get them on. He had both chance and time to kill the intruder in his helpless condition—half in and half out of his pants—but he was too weak to take action. The shapeless enemies of humanity that live in the hours of Time had waylaid Joe. He was assaulted in his weakness. Like Samson awakening after his haircut. So he just opened his mouth and laughed.

The match went out and he struck another and lit the lamp. A howling wind raced across his heart, but underneath its fury he heard his wife sobbing and Slemmons pleading for his life. Offering to buy it with all that he had. "Please, suh, don't kill me. Sixty-two dollars at de sto'. Gold money."

Joe just stood. Slemmons looked at the window, but it was screened. Joe stood out like a rough-backed mountain between him and the door. Barring him from escape, from sunrise, from life.

He considered a surprise attack upon the big clown that stood there laughing like a chessy cat. But before his fist could travel an inch, Joe's own rushed out to crush him like a battering ram. Then Joe stood over him.

"Git into you' damn rags, Slemmons, and dat quick."

Slemmons scrambled to his feet and into his vest and coat. As he grabbed his hat, Joe's fury overrode his intentions and he grabbed at Slemmons with his left hand and struck at him with his right. The right landed. The left grazed the front of his vest. Slemmons was knocked a somersault into the kitchen and fled through the open door. Joe found himself alone with Missie May, with the golden watch charm clutched in his left fist. A short bit of broken chain dangled between his fingers.

Missie May was sobbing. Wails of weeping without words. Joe stood, and after a while he found out that he had something in his hand. And then he stood and felt without thinking and without seeing with his natural eyes. Missie May kept on crying and Joe kept on feeling so much, and not knowing what to do with all his feelings, he put Slemmons's watch charm in his pants pocket and took a good laugh and went to bed.

"Missie May, whut you cryin' for?"

"Cause Ah love you so hard and Ah know you don't love *me* no mo'."

Joe sank his face into the pillow for a spell, then he said huskily, "You don't know de feelings of dat yet, Missie May."

"Oh Joe, honey, he said he wuz gointer give me dat gold money and he jes' kept on after me—"

Joe was very still and silent for a long time. Then he said, "Well, don't cry no mo', Missie May. Ah got yo' gold piece for you."

The hours went past on their rusty ankles. Joe still and quiet on one bed rail and Missie May wrung dry of sobs on the other. Finally the sun's tide crept upon the shore of night and drowned all its hours. Missie May with her face stiff and streaked towards the window saw the dawn come into her yard. It was day. Nothing more. Joe wouldn't be coming home as usual. No need to fling open the front door and sweep off the porch, making it nice for Joe. Never no more breakfast to cook; no more washing and starching of Joe's jumper-jackets and pants. No more nothing. So why get up?

With this strange man in her bed, she felt embarrassed to get up and dress. She decided to wait till he had dressed and gone. Then she would get up, dress quickly and be gone forever beyond reach of Joe's looks and laughs. But he never moved. Red light turned to yellow, then white.

From beyond the no-man's land between them came a voice. A strange voice that yesterday had been Joe's.

"Missie May, ain't you gonna fix me no breakfus'?"

She sprang out of bed. "Yeah, Joe. Ah didn't reckon you wuz hongry."

No need to die today. Joe needed her for a few more minutes anyhow.

Soon there was a roaring fire in the cookstove. Water bucket full and two chickens killed. Joe loved fried chicken and rice. She didn't deserve a thing and good Joe was letting her cook him some breakfast. She rushed hot biscuits to the table as Joe took his seat.

He ate with his eyes in his plate. No laughter, no banter.

"Missie May, you ain't eatin' yo' breakfus'."

"Ah don't choose none, Ah thank yuh."

His coffee cup was empty. She sprang to refill it. When she turned from the stove and bent to set the cup beside Joe's plate, she saw the yellow coin on the table between them.

She slumped into her seat and wept into her arms.

Presently Joe said calmly, "Missie May, you cry too much. Don't look back lak Lot's wife and turn to salt."

The sun, the hero of every day, the impersonal old man that beams as brightly on death

as on birth, came up every morning and raced across the blue dome and dipped into the sea of fire every morning. Water ran downhill and birds nested.

Missie knew why she didn't leave Joe. She couldn't. She loved him too much, but she could not understand why Joe didn't leave her. He was polite, even kind at times, but aloof.

There were no more Saturday romps. No ringing silver dollars to stack beside her plate. No pockets to rifle. In fact, the yellow coin in his trousers was like a monster hiding in the cave of his pockets to destroy her.

She often wondered if he still had it, but nothing could have induced her to ask nor yet to explore his pockets to see for herself. Its shadow was in the house whether or no.

One night Joe came home around midnight and complained of pains in the back. He asked Missie to rub him down with liniment. It had been three months since Missie had touched his body and it all seemed strange. But she rubbed him. Grateful for the chance. Before morning youth triumphed and Missie exulted. But the next day, as she joyfully made up their bed, beneath her pillow she found the piece of money with the bit of chain attached.

Alone to herself, she looked at the thing with loathing, but look she must. She took it into her hands with trembling and saw first thing that it was no gold piece. It was a gilded half dollar. Then she knew why Slemmons had forbidden anyone to touch his gold. He trusted village eyes at a distance not to recognize his stickpin as a gilded quarter, and his watch charm as a four-bit piece.

She was glad at first that Joe had left it there. Perhaps he was through with her punishment. They were man and wife again. Then another thought came clawing at her. He had come home to buy from her as if she were any woman in the longhouse. Fifty cents for her love. As if to say that he could pay as well as Slemmons. She slid the coin into his Sunday pants pocket and dressed herself and left his house.

Halfway between her house and the quarters she met her husband's mother, and after a short talk she turned and went back home. Never would she admit defeat to that woman who prayed for it nightly. If she had not the substance of marriage she had the outside show. Joe must leave *her*. She let him see she didn't want his old gold four-bits, too.

She saw no more of the coin for some time though she knew that Joe could not help finding it in his pocket. But his health kept poor, and he came home at least every ten days to be rubbed.

The sun swept around the horizon, trailing its robes of weeks and days. One morning as Joe came in from work, he found Missie May chopping wood. Without a word he took the ax and chopped a huge pile before he stopped.

"You ain't got no business choppin' wood, and you know it."

"How come? Ah been choppin' it for de last longest."

"Ah ain't blind. You makin' feet for shoes."

"Won't you be glad to have a lil baby chile, Joe?"

"You know dat 'thout astin' me."

"Iss gointer be a boy chile and de very spit of you."

"You reckon, Missie May?"

"Who else could it look lak?"

Joe said nothing, but he thrust his hand deep into his pocket and fingered something there.

It was almost six months later Missie May took to bed and Joe went and got his mother to come wait on the house.

Missie May was delivered of a fine boy. Her travail was over when Joe came in from work one morning. His mother and the old women were drinking great bowls of coffee around the fire in the kitchen.

The minute Joe came into the room his mother called him aside.

"How did Missie May make out?" he asked quickly.

"Who, dat gal? She strong as a ox. She gointer have plenty mo'. We done fixed her wid de sugar and lard to sweeten her for de nex' one."

Joe stood silent awhile.

"You ain't ask 'bout de baby, Joe. You oughter be mighty proud cause he sho is de spittin' image of yuh, son. Dat's yourn all right, if you never git another one, dat un is yourn. And you know Ah'm mighty proud too, son, cause Ah never thought well of you marrying' Missie May cause her ma used tuh fan her foot round right smart and Ah been mighty skeered dat Missie May wuz gointer git misput on her road."

Joe said nothing. He fooled around the house till late in the day, then, just before he went to work, he went and stood at the foot of the bed and asked his wife how she felt. He did this every day during the week.

On Saturday he went to Orlando to make his market. It had been a long time since he had done that.

Meat and lard, meal and flour, soap and starch. Cans of corn and tomatoes. All the staples. He fooled around town for a while and bought bananas and apples. Way after while he went around to the candy store.

"Hello, Joe," the clerk greeted him. "Ain't seen you in a long time."

"Nope, Ah ain't been heah. Been round in spots and places."

"Want some of them molasses kisses you always buy?"

"Yessuh." He threw the gilded half dollar on the counter. "Will dat spend?"

"Whut is it, Joe? Well, I'll be doggone! A gold-plated four-bit piece. Where'd you git it, Joe?"

"Offen a stray nigger dat come through Eatonville. He had it on his watch chain for a charm—goin' round making out iss gold money. Ha ha! He had a quarter on his tiepin and it wuz all golded up too. Tryin' to fool people. Makin' out he so rich and everything. Ha! Ha! Tryin' to tole off folkses wives from home."

"How did you git it, Joe? Did he fool you, too?"

"Who, me? Naw suh! He ain't fooled me none. Know whut Ah done? He come round me wid his smart talk. Ah hauled off and knocked 'im down and took his old four-bits away from 'im. Gointer buy my wife some good ole lasses kisses wid it. Gimme fifty cents worth of dem candy kisses."

"Fifty cents buys a mighty lot of candy kisses, Joe. Why don't you split it up and take some chocolate bars, too? They eat good, too."

"Yessuh, dey do, but Ah wants all dat in kisses. Ah got a lil boy chile home now. Tain't a week old yet, but he kin suck a sugar tit and maybe eat one them kisses hisself."

Joe got his candy and left the store. The clerk turned to the next customer. "Wisht I could be like these darkies. Laughin' all the time. Nothin' worries 'em."

Back in Eatonville, Joe reached his own front door. There was the ring of singing metal on wood. Fifteen times. Missie May couldn't run to the door, but she crept there as quickly as she could.

"Joe Banks, Ah hear you chunkin' money in mah do'way. You wait till Ah got mah strength back and Ah'm gointer fix you for dat."

SHERWOOD ANDERSON

(1876–1941)

Death in the Woods

About the Author: Sherwood Anderson was a novelist and short-story writer. He was born in Camden, Ohio, and completed his education at 14. He is best known for *Winesburg, Ohio* (1919), a collection of interrelated stories of small-town life, and the novel *Poor White* (1920), which examines the effects of technological change on American society.

I

She was an old woman and lived on a farm near the town in which I lived. All country and small-town people have seen such old women, but no one knows much about them. Such an old woman comes into town driving an old worn-out horse or she comes afoot carrying a basket. She may own a few hens and have eggs to sell. She brings them in a basket and takes them to a grocer. There she trades them in. She gets some salt pork and some beans. Then she gets a pound or two of sugar and some flour.

Afterwards she goes to the butcher's and asks for some dog-meat. She may spend ten or fifteen cents, but when she does she asks for something. Formerly the butchers gave liver to anyone who wanted to carry it away. In our family we were always having it. Once one of my brothers got a whole cow's liver at the slaughterhouse near the fair grounds in our town. We had it until we were sick of it. It never cost a cent. I have hated the thought of it ever since.

The old farm woman got some liver and a soup-bone. She never visited with anyone, and as soon as she got what she wanted she lit out for home. It made quite a load for such an old body. No one gave her a lift. People drive right down a road and never notice an old woman like that.

There was such an old woman who used to come into town past our house one summer and fall when I was a young boy and was sick with what was called inflammatory rheumatism. She went home later carrying a heavy pack on her back. Two or three large gaunt-looking dogs followed at her heels.

The old woman was nothing special. She was one of the nameless ones that hardly anyone knows, but she got into my thoughts. I have just suddenly now, after all these years, remembered her and what happened. It is a story. Her name was Grimes, and she lived with her husband and son in a small unpainted house on the bank of a small creek four miles from town.

The husband and son were a tough lot. Although the son was but twenty-one, he had already served a term in jail. It was whispered about that the woman's husband stole horses and ran them off to some other county. Now and then, when a horse turned up missing, the man had also disappeared. No one ever caught him. Once, when I was loafing at Tom Whitehead's livery-barn, the man came there and sat on the bench in front. Two or three other men were there, but no one spoke to him. He sat for a few minutes and then got up and went away. When he was leaving he turned around and stared at the men. There was a look of defiance in his eyes. "Well, I have tried to be friendly. You don't want to talk to me. It has been so wherever I have gone in this town. If, some day, one of your fine horses turns up missing, well, then what?" He did not say anything actually. "I'd like to bust one

of you on the jaw," was about what his eyes said. I remember how the look in his eyes made me shiver.

The old man belonged to a family that had had money once. His name was Jake Grimes, had owned a sawmill when the country was new, and had made money. Then he got to drinking and running after women. When he died there wasn't much left.

Jake blew in the rest. Pretty soon there wasn't any more lumber to cut and his land was nearly all gone.

He got his wife off a German farmer, for whom he went to work one June day in the wheat harvest. She was a young thing then and scared to death. You see, the farmer was up to something with the girl—she was, I think, a bound girl and his wife had her suspicions. She took it out on the girl when the man wasn't around. Then, when the wife had to go off to town for supplies, the farmer got after her. She told young Jake that nothing really ever happened, but he didn't know whether to believe it or not.

He got her pretty easy himself, the first time he was out with her. He wouldn't have married her if the German farmer hadn't tried to tell him where to get off. He got her to go riding with him in his buggy one night when he was threshing on the place, and then he came for her the next Sunday night.

She managed to get out of the house without her employer's seeing, but when she was getting into the buggy he showed up. It was almost dark, and he just popped up suddenly at the horse's head. He grabbed the horse by the bridle and Jake got out his buggy-whip.

They had it out all right! The German was a tough one. Maybe he didn't care whether his wife knew or not. Jake hit him over the face and shoulders with the buggy-whip, but the horse got to acting up and he had to get out.

Then the two men went for it. The girl didn't see it. The horse started to run away and went nearly a mile down the road before the girl got him stopped. Then she managed to tie him to a tree beside the road. (I wonder how I know all this. It must have stuck in my mind from small-town tales when I was a boy.) Jake found her there after he got through with the German. She was huddled up in the buggy seat, crying, scared to death. She told Jake a lot of stuff, how the German had tried to get her, how he chased her once into the barn, how another time, when they happened to be alone in the house together, he tore her dress open clear down the front. The German, she said, might have got her that time if he hadn't heard his old woman drive in at the gate. She had been off to town for supplies. Well, she would be putting the horse in the barn. The German managed to sneak off to the fields without his wife seeing. He told the girl he would kill her if she told. What could she do? She told a lie about ripping her dress in the barn when she was feeding the stock. I remember now that she was a bound girl and did not know where her father and mother were. Maybe she did not have any father. You know what I mean.

Such bound children were often enough cruelly treated. They were children who had no parents, slaves really. There were very few orphan homes then. They were legally bound into some home. It was a matter of pure luck how it came out.

II

She married Jake and had a son and daughter, but the daughter died.

Then she settled down to feed stock. That was her job. At the German's place she had cooked the food for the German and his wife. The wife was a strong woman with big hips and worked most of the time in the fields with her husband. She fed them and fed the cows

in the barn, fed the pigs, the horses and the chickens. Every moment of every day, as a young girl, was spent feeding something.

Then she married Jake Grimes and he had to be fed. She was a slight thing, and when she had been married for three or four years, and after the two children were born, her slender shoulders became stooped.

Jake always had a lot of big dogs around the house, that stood near the unused sawmill near the creek. He was always trading horses when he wasn't stealing something and had a lot of poor bony ones about. Also he kept three or four pigs and a cow. They were all pastured in the few acres left of the Grimes place and Jake did little enough work.

He went into debt for a threshing outfit and ran it for several years, but it did not pay. People did not trust him. They were afraid he would steal the grain at night. He had to go a long way off to get work and it cost too much to get there. In the winter he hunted and cut a little firewood, to be sold in some nearby town. When the son grew up he was just like the father. They got drunk together. If there wasn't anything to eat in the house when they came home the old man gave his old woman a cut over the head. She had a few chickens of her own and had to kill one of them in a hurry. When they were all killed she wouldn't have any eggs to sell when she went to town, and then what would she do?

She had to scheme all her life about getting things fed, getting the pigs fed so they would grow fat and could be butchered in the fall. When they were butchered her husband took most of the meat off to town and sold it. If he did not do it first the boy did. They fought sometimes and when they fought the old woman stood aside trembling.

She had got the habit of silence anyway—that was fixed. Sometimes, when she began to look old—she wasn't forty yet—and when the husband and son were both off, trading horses or drinking or hunting or stealing, she went around the house and the barnyard muttering to herself.

How was she going to get everything fed?—that was her problem. The dogs had to be fed. There wasn't enough hay in the barn for the horses and the cow. If she didn't feed the chickens how could they lay eggs? Without eggs to sell how could she get things in town, things she had to have to keep the life of the farm going? Thank heaven, she did not have to feed her husband—in a certain way. That hadn't lasted long after their marriage and after the babies came. Where he went on his long trips she did not know. Sometimes he was gone from home for weeks, and after the boy grew up they went off together.

They left everything at home for her to manage and she had no money. She knew no one. No one ever talked to her in town. When it was winter she had to gather sticks of wood for her fire, had to try to keep the stock fed with very little grain.

The stock in the barn cried to her hungrily, the dogs followed her about. In the winter the hens laid few enough eggs. They huddled in the corners of the barn and she kept watching them. If a hen lays an egg in the barn in the winter and you do not find it, it freezes and breaks.

One day in winter the old woman went off to town with a few eggs and the dogs followed her. She did not get started until nearly three o'clock and the snow was heavy. She hadn't been feeling very well for several days and so she went muttering along, scantily clad, her shoulders stooped. She had an old grain bag in which she carried her eggs, tucked away down in the bottom. There weren't many of them, but in winter the price of eggs is up. She would get a little meat in exchange for the eggs, some salt pork, a little sugar, and some coffee perhaps. It might be the butcher would give her a piece of liver.

When she had got to town and was trading in her eggs the dogs lay by the door outside.

She did pretty well, got the things she needed, more than she had hoped. Then she went to the butcher and he gave her some liver and some dog-meat.

It was the first time anyone had spoken to her in a friendly way for a long time. The butcher was alone in his shop when she came in and was annoyed by the thought of such a sick-looking old woman out on such a day. It was bitter cold and the snow, that had let up during the afternoon, was falling again. The butcher said something about her husband and her son, swore at them, and the old woman stared at him, a look of mild surprise in her eyes as he talked. He said that if either the husband or the son were going to get any of the liver or the heavy bones with scraps of meat hanging to them that he had put into the grain bag, he'd see him starve first.

Starve, eh? Well, things had to be fed. Men had to be fed, and the horses that weren't any good but maybe could be traded off, and the poor thin cow that hadn't given any milk for three months.

Horses, cows, pigs, dogs, men.

III

The old woman had to get back before darkness came if she could. The dogs followed at her heels, sniffing at the heavy grain bag she had fastened on her back. When she got to the edge of town she stopped by a fence and tied the bag on her back with a piece of rope she had carried in her dress-pocket for just that purpose. That was an easier way to carry it. Her arms ached. It was hard when she had to crawl over fences and once she fell over and landed in the snow. The dogs went frisking about. She had to struggle to get to her feet again, but she made it. The point of climbing over the fences was that there was a short cut over a hill and through a woods. She might have gone around by the road, but it was a mile farther that way. She was afraid she couldn't make it. And then, besides, the stock had to be fed. There was a little hay left and a little corn. Perhaps her husband and son would bring some home when they came. They had driven off in the only buggy the Grimes family had, a rickety thing, a rickety horse hitched to the buggy, two other rickety horses led by halters. They were going to trade horses, get a little money if they could. They might come home drunk. It would be well to have something in the house when they came back.

The son had an affair on with a woman at the county seat, fifteen miles away. She was a rough enough woman, a tough one. Once, in the summer, the son had brought her to the house. Both she and the son had been drinking. Jake Grimes was away and the son and his woman ordered the old woman about like a servant. She didn't mind much; she was used to it. Whatever happened she never said anything. That was her way of getting along. She had managed that way when she was a young girl at the German's and ever since she had married Jake. That time her son brought his woman to the house they stayed all night, sleeping together just as though they were married. It hadn't shocked the old woman, not much. She had got past being shocked early in life.

With the pack on her back she went painfully along across an open field, wading in the deep snow, and got into the woods.

There was a path, but it was hard to follow. Just beyond the top of the hill, where the woods was thickest, there was a small clearing. Had someone once thought of building a house there? The clearing was as large as a building lot in town, large enough for a house and a garden. The path ran along the side of the clearing, and when she got there the old woman sat down to rest at the foot of a tree.

It was a foolish thing to do. When she got herself placed, the pack against the tree's trunk, it was nice, but what about getting up again? She worried about that for a moment and then quietly closed her eyes.

She must have slept for a time. When you are about so cold you can't get any colder. The afternoon grew a little warmer and the snow came thicker than ever. Then after a time the weather cleared. The moon even came out.

There were four Grimes dogs that had followed Mrs. Grimes into town, all tall gaunt fellows. Such men as Jake Grimes and his son always keep just such dogs. They kick and abuse them, but they stay. The Grimes dogs, in order to keep from starving, had to do a lot of foraging for themselves, and they had been at it while the old woman slept with her back to the tree at the side of the clearing. They had been chasing rabbits in the woods and in adjoining fields and in their ranging had picked up three other farm dogs.

After a time all the dogs came back to the clearing. They were excited about something. Such nights, cold and clear and with a moon, do things to dogs. It may be that some old instinct, come down from the time when they were wolves and ranged the woods in packs on winter nights, comes back into them.

The dogs in the clearing, before the old woman, had caught two or three rabbits and their immediate hunger had been satisfied. They began to play, running in circles in the clearing. Round and round they ran, each dog's nose at the tail of the next dog. In the clearing, under the snow-laden trees and under the wintry moon they made a strange picture, running thus silently, in a circle their running had beaten in the soft snow. The dogs made no sound. They ran around and around in the circle.

It may have been that the old woman saw them doing that before she died. She may have awakened once or twice and looked at the strange sight with dim old eyes.

She wouldn't be very cold now, just drowsy. Life hangs on a long time. Perhaps the old woman was out of her head. She may have dreamed of her girlhood, at the German's, and before that, when she was a child and before her mother lit out and left her.

Her dreams couldn't have been very pleasant. Not many pleasant things had happened to her. Now and then one of the Grimes dogs left the running circle and came to stand before her. The dog thrust his face close to her face. His red tongue was hanging out.

The running of the dogs may have been a kind of death ceremony. It may have been that the primitive instinct of the wolf, having been aroused in the dogs by the night and the running, made them somehow afraid.

"Now we are no longer wolves. We are dogs, the servants of men. Keep alive, man! When man dies we become wolves again."

When one of the dogs came to where the old woman sat with her back against the tree and thrust his nose close to her face he seemed satisfied and went back to run with the pack. All the Grimes dogs did it at some time during the evening, before she died. I knew all about it afterward, when I grew to be a man, because once in a woods in Illinois, on another winter night, I saw a pack of dogs act just like that. The dogs were waiting for me to die as they had waited for the old woman that night when I was a child, but when it happened to me I was a young man and had no intention whatever of dying.

The old woman died softly and quietly. When she was dead and when one of the Grimes dogs had come to her and had found her dead all the dogs stopped running.

They gathered about her.

Well, she was dead now. She had fed the Grimes dogs when she was alive, what about now?

There was the pack on her back, the grain bag containing the piece of salt pork, the liver the butcher had given her, the dog-meat, the soup bones. The butcher in town, having been suddenly overcome with a feeling of pity, had loaded her grain bag heavily. It had been a big haul for the old woman.

It was a big haul for the dogs now.

IV

One of the Grimes dogs sprang suddenly out from among the others and began worrying the pack on the old woman's back. Had the dogs really been wolves that one would have been the leader of the pack. What he did, all the others did.

All of them sank their teeth into the grain bag the old woman had fastened with ropes to her back.

They dragged the old woman's body out into the open clearing. The worn-out dress was quickly torn from her shoulders. When she was found, a day or two later, the dress had been torn from her body clear to the hips, but the dogs had not touched her body. They had got the meat out of the grain bag, that was all. Her body was frozen still when it was found, and the shoulders were so narrow and the body so slight that in death it looked like the body of some charming young girl.

Such things happened in towns of the Middle West, on farms near town, when I was a boy. A hunter out after rabbits found the old woman's body and did not touch it. Something, the beaten round path in the little snow-covered clearing, the silence of the place, the place where the dogs had worried the body trying to pull the grain bag away or tear it open—something startled the man and he hurried off to town.

I was in Main Street with one of my brothers who was town newsboy and who was taking the afternoon papers to the stores. It was almost night.

The hunter came into a grocery and told his story. Then he went to a hardware shop and into a drugstore. Men began to gather on the sidewalks. Then they started out along the road to the place in the woods.

My brother should have gone on about his business of distributing papers but he didn't. Everyone was going to the woods. The undertaker went and the town marshal. Several men got on a dray and rode out to where the path left the road and went into the woods, but the horses weren't very sharply shod and slid about on the slippery roads. They made no better time than those of us who walked.

The town marshal was a large man whose leg had been injured in the Civil War. He carried a heavy cane and limped rapidly along the road. My brother and I followed at his heels, and as we went other men and boys joined the crowd.

It had grown dark by the time we got to where the old woman had left the road but the moon had come out. The marshal was thinking there might have been a murder. He kept asking the hunter questions. The hunter went along with his gun across his shoulders, a dog following at his heels. It isn't often a rabbit hunter has a chance to be so conspicuous. He was taking full advantage of it, leading the procession with the town marshal. "I didn't see any wounds. She was a beautiful young girl. Her face was buried in the snow. No, I didn't know her." As a matter of fact, the hunter had not looked closely at the body. He had been frightened. She might have been murdered and someone might spring out from behind a tree and murder him. In a woods, in the late afternoon, when the trees are all bare and there is white snow on the ground, when all is silent, something creepy steals over the mind and body. If something strange or uncanny has happened in the neighborhood all you think about is getting away from there as fast as you can.

The crowd of men and boys had got to where the old woman had crossed the field and went, following the marshal and the hunter, up the slight incline and into the woods.

My brother and I were silent. He had his bundle of papers in a bag slung across his shoulder. When he got back to town he would have to go on distributing his papers before he went home to supper. If I went along, as he had no doubt already determined I should, we would both be late. Either mother or our older sister would have to warm our supper.

Well, we would have something to tell. A boy did not get such a chance very often. It was lucky we just happened to go into the grocery when the hunter came in. The hunter was a country fellow. Neither of us had ever seen him before.

Now the crowd of men and boys had got to the clearing. Darkness comes quickly on such winter nights, but the full moon made everything clear. My brother and I stood near the tree, beneath which the old woman had died.

She did not look old, lying there in that light, frozen and still. One of the men turned her over in the snow and I saw everything. My body trembled with some strange mystical feeling and so did my brother's. It might have been the cold.

Neither of us had ever seen a woman's body before. It may have been the snow, clinging to the frozen flesh, that made it look so white and lovely, so like marble. No woman had come with the party from town; but one of the men, he was the town blacksmith, took off his overcoat and spread it over her. Then he gathered her into his arms and started off to town, all the others following silently. At that time no one knew who she was.

V

I had seen everything, had seen the oval in the snow, like a miniature race track, where the dogs had run, had seen how the men were mystified, had seen the white bare young-looking shoulders, had heard the whispered comments of the men.

The men were simply mystified. They took the body to the undertaker's, and when the blacksmith, the hunter, the marshal and several others had got inside they closed the door. If father had been there perhaps he could have got in, but we boys couldn't.

I went with my brother to distribute the rest of his papers and when we got home it was my brother who told the story.

I kept silent and went to bed early. It may have been I was not satisfied with the way he told it.

Later, in the town, I must have heard other fragments of the old woman's story. She was recognized the next day and there was an investigation.

The husband and son were found somewhere and brought to town and there was an attempt to connect them with the woman's death, but it did not work. They had perfect enough alibis.

However, the town was against them. They had to get out. Where they went I never heard.

I remember only the picture there in the forest, the men standing about, the naked girlish-looking figure, face down in the snow, the tracks made by the running dogs and the clear cold winter sky above. White fragments of clouds were drifting across the sky. They went racing across the little open space among the trees.

The scene in the forest had become for me, without my knowing it, the foundation for the real story I am now trying to tell. The fragments, you see, had to be picked up slowly, long afterwards.

Things happened. When I was a young man I worked on the farm of a German. The hired-girl was afraid of her employer. The farmer's wife hated her.

I saw things at that place. Once later, I had a half-uncanny, mystical adventure with dogs in an Illinois forest on a clear, moonlit winter night. When I was a schoolboy, and on a summer day, I went with a boy friend out along a creek some miles from town and came to the house where the old woman had lived. No one had lived in the house since her death. The doors were broken from the hinges; the window lights were all broken. As the boy and I stood in the road outside, two dogs, just roving farm dogs no doubt, came running around the corner of the house. The dogs were tall, gaunt fellows and came down to the fence and glared through at us, standing in the road.

The whole thing, the story of the old woman's death, was to me as I grew older like music heard from far off. The notes had to be picked up slowly one at a time. Something had to be understood.

The woman who died was one destined to feed animal life. Anyway, that is all she ever did. She was feeding animal life before she was born, as a child, as a young woman working on the farm of the German, after she married, when she grew old and when she died. She fed animal life in cows, in chickens, in pigs, in horses, in dogs, in men. Her daughter had died in childhood and with her one son she had no articulate relations. On the night when she died she was hurrying homeward, bearing on her body food for animal life.

She died in the clearing in the woods and even after her death continued feeding animal life.

You see it is likely that, when my brother told the story, that night when we got home and my mother and sister sat listening, I did not think he got the point. He was too young and so was I. A thing so complete has its own beauty.

I shall not try to emphasize the point. I am only explaining why I was dissatisfied then and have been ever since. I speak of that only that you may understand why I have been impelled to try to tell the simple story over again.

ERNEST HEMINGWAY

(1899–1961)

Soldier's Home

About the Author: Born in Oak Park, Illinois, Ernest Hemingway while still in his teens worked as a journalist on the *Kansas City Star* and served briefly at the Italian front in World War I, until he was badly wounded. After the war he lived as an expatriate in Paris, working still as a journalist but writing fiction as well. His early successes included a volume of short stories, *In Our Time* (1925), and two novels, *The Sun Also Rises* (1926) and *A Farewell to Arms* (1929). He also wrote poems, plays, and a memoir. He was awarded the Nobel Prize for Literature in 1954. Since his death by suicide, several novels have been posthumously published.

Krebs went to the war from a Methodist college in Kansas. There is a picture which shows him among his fraternity brothers, all of them wearing exactly the same height and style collar. He enlisted in the Marines in 1917 and did not return to the United States until the second division returned from the Rhine in the summer of 1919.

There is a picture which shows him on the Rhine with two German girls and another corporal. Krebs and the corporal look too big for their uniforms. The German girls are not beautiful. The Rhine does not show in the picture.

By the time Krebs returned to his home town in Oklahoma the greeting of heroes was over. He came back much too late. The men from the town who had been drafted had all been welcomed elaborately on their return. There had been a great deal of hysteria. Now the reaction had set in. People seemed to think it was rather ridiculous for Krebs to be getting back so late, years after the war was over.

At first Krebs, who had been at Belleau Wood, Soissons, the Champagne, St. Mihiel and in the Argonne did not want to talk about the war at all. Later he felt the need to talk but no one wanted to hear about it. His town had heard too many atrocity stories to be thrilled by actualities. Krebs found that to be listened to at all he had to lie, and after he had done this twice he, too, had a reaction against the war and against talking about it. A distaste for everything that had happened to him in the war set in because of the lies he had told. All of the times that had been able to make him feel cool and clear inside himself when he thought of them; the times so long back when he had done the one thing, the only thing for a man to do, easily and naturally, when he might have done something else, now lost their cool, valuable quality and then were lost themselves.

His lies were quite unimportant lies and consisted in attributing to himself things other men had seen, done or heard of, and stating as facts certain apocryphal incidents familiar to all soldiers. Even his lies were not sensational at the pool room. His acquaintances, who had heard detailed accounts of German women found chained to machine guns in the Argonne forest and who could not comprehend, or were barred by their patriotism from interest in, any German machine gunners who were not chained, were not thrilled by his stories.

Krebs acquired the nausea in regard to experience that is the result of untruth or exaggeration, and when he occasionally met another man who had really been a soldier and they talked a few minutes in the dressing room at a dance he fell into the easy pose of the old soldier among other soldiers: that he had been badly, sickeningly frightened all the time. In this way he lost everything.

During this time, it was late summer, he was sleeping late in bed, getting up to walk down town to the library to get a book, eating lunch at home, reading on the front porch until he became bored and then walking down through the town to spend the hottest hours of the day in the cool dark of the pool room. He loved to play pool.

In the evening he practiced on his clarinet, strolled down town, read and went to bed. He was still a hero to his two young sisters. His mother would have given him breakfast in bed if he had wanted it. She often came in when he was in bed and asked him to tell her about the war, but her attention always wandered. His father was non-committal.

Before Krebs went away to the war he had never been allowed to drive the family motor car. His father was in the real estate business and always wanted the car to be at his command when he required it to take clients out into the country to show them a piece of farm property. The car always stood outside the First National Bank building where his father had an office on the second floor. Now, after the war, it was still the same car.

Nothing was changed in the town except that the young girls had grown up. But they lived in such a complicated world of already defined alliances and shifting feuds that Krebs did not feel the energy or the courage to break into it. He liked to look at them, though. There were so many good-looking young girls. Most of them had their hair cut short. When he went away only little girls wore their hair like that or girls that were fast. They all wore sweaters and shirt waists with round Dutch collars. It was a pattern. He liked to look at them from the front porch as they walked on the other side of the street. He liked to watch them walking under the shade of the trees. He liked the round Dutch collars above their sweaters. He liked their silk stockings and flat shoes. He liked their bobbed hair and the way they walked.

When he was in town their appeal to him was not very strong. He did not like them when he saw them in the Greek's ice cream parlor. He did not want them themselves really. They were too complicated. There was something else. Vaguely he wanted a girl but he did not want to have to work to get her. He would have liked to have a girl but he did not want to have to spend a long time getting her. He did not want to get into the intrigue and the politics. He did not want to have to do any courting. He did not want to tell any more lies. It wasn't worth it.

He did not want any consequences. He did not want any consequences ever again. He wanted to live along without consequences. Besides he did not really need a girl. The army had taught him that. It was all right to pose as though you had to have a girl. Nearly everybody did that. But it wasn't true. You did not need a girl. That was the funny thing. First a fellow boasted how girls mean nothing to him, that he never thought of them, that they could not touch him. Then a fellow boasted that he could not get along without girls, that he had to have them all the time, that he could not go to sleep without them.

That was all a lie. It was all a lie both ways. You did not need a girl unless you thought about them. He learned that in the army. Then sooner or later you always got one. When you were really ripe for a girl you always got one. You did not have to think about it. Sooner or later it would come. He had learned that in the army.

Now he would have liked a girl if she had come to him and not wanted to talk. But here at home it was all too complicated. He knew he could never get through it all again. It was not worth the trouble. That was the thing about French girls and German girls. There was not all this talking. You couldn't talk much and you did not need to talk. It was simple and you were friends. He thought about France and then he began to think about Germany. On the whole he had liked Germany better. He did not want to leave Germany. He did not want to come home. Still, he had come home. He sat on the front porch.

He liked the girls that were walking along the other side of the street. He liked the look of them much better than the French girls or the German girls. But the world they were in was not the world he was in. He would like to have one of them. But it was not worth it. They were such a nice pattern. He liked the pattern. It was exciting. But he would not go through all the talking. He did not want one badly enough. He liked to look at them all, though. It was not worth it. Not now when things were getting good again.

He sat there on the porch reading a book on the war. It was a history and he was reading about all the engagements he had been in. It was the most interesting reading he had ever done. He wished there were more maps. He looked forward with a good feeling to reading all the really good histories when they would come out with good detail maps. Now he was really learning about the war. He had been a good soldier. That made a difference.

One morning after he had been home about a month his mother came into his bedroom and sat on the bed. She smoothed her apron.

"I had a talk with your father last night, Harold," she said, "and he is willing for you to take the car out in the evenings."

"Yeah?" said Krebs, who was not fully awake. "Take the car out? Yeah?"

"Yes. Your father has felt for some time that you should be able to take the car out in the evenings whenever you wished but we only talked it over last night."

"I'll bet you made him," Krebs said.

"No. It was your father's suggestion that we talk the matter over."

"Yeah. I'll bet you made him," Krebs sat up in bed.

"Will you come down to breakfast, Harold?" his mother said.

"As soon as I get my clothes on," Krebs said.

His mother went out of the room and he could hear her frying something downstairs while he washed, shaved and dressed to go down into the dining-room for breakfast. While he was eating breakfast his sister brought in the mail.

"Well, Hare," she said. "You old sleepy-head. What do you ever get up for?"

Krebs looked at her. He liked her. She was his best sister.

"Have you got the paper?" he asked.

She handed him the Kansas City *Star* and he shucked off its brown wrapper and opened it to the sporting page. He folded the *Star* open and propped it against the water pitcher with his cereal dish to steady it, so he could read while he ate.

"Harold," his mother stood in the kitchen doorway, "Harold, please don't muss up the paper. Your father can't read his *Star* if it's been mussed."

"I won't muss it," Krebs said.

His sister sat down at the table and watched him while he read.

"We're playing indoor over at school this afternoon," she said. "I'm going to pitch."

"Good," said Krebs. "How's the old wing?"

"I can pitch better than lots of the boys. I tell them all you taught me. The other girls aren't much good."

"Yeah?" said Krebs.

"I tell them all you're my beau. Aren't you my beau, Hare?"

"You bet."

"Couldn't your brother really be your beau just because he's your brother?"

"I don't know."

"Sure you know. Couldn't you be my beau, Hare, if I was old enough and if you wanted to?"

"Sure. You're my girl now."

"Am I really your girl?"

"Sure."

"Do you love me?"

"Uh, huh."

"Will you love me always?"

"Sure."

"Will you come over and watch me play indoor?"

"Maybe."

"Aw, Hare, you don't love me. If you loved me, you'd want to come over and watch me play indoor."

Kreb's mother came into the dining-room from the kitchen. She carried a plate with two fried eggs and some crisp bacon on it and a plate of buckwheat cakes.

"You run along, Helen," she said. "I want to talk to Harold."

She put the eggs and bacon down in front of him and brought in a jug of maple syrup for the buckwheat cakes. Then she sat down across the table from Krebs.

"I wish you'd put down the paper a minute, Harold," she said.

Krebs took down the paper and folded it.

"Have you decided what you are going to do yet, Harold?" his mother said, taking off her glasses.

"No," said Krebs.

"Don't you think it's about time?" His mother did not say this in a mean way. She seemed worried.

"I hadn't thought about it," Krebs said.

"God has some work for everyone to do," his mother said. "There can be no idle hands in His Kingdom."

"I'm not in His Kingdom," Krebs said.

"We are all of us in His Kingdom."

Krebs felt embarrassed and resentful as always.

"I've worried about you so much, Harold," his mother went on. "I know the temptations you must have been exposed to. I know how weak men are. I know what your own dear grandfather, my own father, told us about the Civil War and I have prayed for you. I pray for you all day long, Harold."

Krebs looked at the bacon fat hardening on his plate.

"Your father is worried, too," his mother went on. "He thinks you have lost your ambition, that you haven't got a definite aim in life. Charley Simmons, who is just your age, has a good job and is going to be married. The boys are all settling down; they're all determined to get somewhere; you can see that boys like Charley Simmons are on their way to being really a credit to the community."

Krebs said nothing.

"Don't look that way, Harold," his mother said. "You know we love you and I want to tell you for your own good how matters stand. Your father does not want to hamper your freedom. He thinks you should be allowed to drive the car. If you want to take some of the nice girls out riding with you, we are only too pleased. We want you to enjoy yourself. But you are going to have to settle down to work, Harold. Your father doesn't care what you start in at. All work is honorable as he says. But you've got to make a start at something. He asked me to speak to you this morning and then you can stop in and see him at his office."

"Is that all?" Krebs said.

"Yes. Don't you love your mother, dear boy?"

"No," Krebs said.

His mother looked at him across the table. Her eyes were shiny. She started crying.

"I don't love anybody," Krebs said.

It wasn't any good. He couldn't tell her, he couldn't make her see it. It was silly to have said it. He had only hurt her. He went over and took hold of her arm. She was crying with her head in her hands.

"I didn't mean it," he said. "I was just angry at something. I didn't mean I didn't love you."

His mother went on crying. Krebs put his arm on her shoulder.

"Can't you believe me, mother?"

His mother shook her head.

"Please, please, mother. Please believe me."

"All right," his mother said chokily. She looked up at him. "I believe you, Harold."

Krebs kissed her hair. She put her face up to him.

"I'm your mother," she said. "I held you next to my heart when you were a tiny baby."

Krebs felt sick and vaguely nauseated.

"I know, Mummy," he said. "I'll try and be a good boy for you."

"Would you kneel and pray with me, Harold?" his mother asked.

They knelt down beside the dining-room table and Kreb's mother prayed.

"Now, you pray, Harold," she said.

"I can't," Krebs said.

"Try, Harold."

"I can't."

"Do you want me to pray for you?"

"Yes."

So his mother prayed for him and then they stood up and Krebs kissed his mother and went out of the house. He had tried so to keep his life from being complicated. Still, none of it had touched him. He had felt sorry for his mother and she had made him lie. He would go to Kansas City and get a job and she would feel all right about it. There would be one more scene maybe before he got away. He would not go down to his father's office. He would miss that one. He wanted his life to go smoothly. It had just gotten going that way. Well, that was all over now, anyway. He would go over to the schoolyard and watch Helen play indoor baseball.

DAVID HERBERT LAWRENCE

(1885–1930)

The Horse Dealer's Daughter

About the Author: David Herbert Lawrence, English fiction writer, poet, and critic, was born the son of a Nottinghamshire miner. Although trained as a teacher, he instead devoted himself to a literary career that led him to travel in Europe and America; after his death, his ashes were buried in Taos, New Mexico, where he had spent some of his later years. Lawrence's first novel, *Sons and Lovers,* appeared in 1913, and was followed by *Women in Love* (1920) and *Lady Chatterley's Lover* (1928) among others, as well as numerous short stories, poems, and essays.

"Well, Mabel, and what are you going to do with yourself?" asked Joe, with foolish flippancy. He felt quite safe himself. Without listening for an answer, he turned aside, worked a grain of tobacco to the tip of his tongue, and spat it out. He did not care about anything, since he felt safe himself.

The three brothers and the sister sat round the desolate breakfast table, attempting some sort of desultory consultation. The morning's post had given the final tap to the family fortune, and all was over. The dreary dining-room itself, with its heavy mahogany furniture, looked as if it were waiting to be done away with.

But the consultation amounted to nothing. There was a strange air of ineffectuality about the three men, as they sprawled at table, smoking and reflecting vaguely on their own condition. The girl was alone, a rather short, sullen-looking young woman of twenty-seven. She did not share the same life as her brothers. She would have been good-looking, save for the impassive fixity of her face, "bull-dog," as her brothers called it.

There was a confused tramping of horses' feet outside. The three men all sprawled round in their chairs to watch. Beyond the dark hollybushes that separated the strip of lawn from the high-road, they could see a cavalcade of shire horses swinging out of their own yard, being taken for exercise. This was the last time. These were the last horses that would go through their hands. The young men watched with critical, callous look. They were all frightened at the collapse of their lives, and the sense of disaster in which they were involved left them no inner freedom.

Yet they were three fine, well-set fellows enough. Joe, the eldest, was a man of thirty-three, broad and handsome in a hot, flushed way. His face was red, he twisted his black moustache over a thick finger, his eyes were shallow and restless. He had a sensual way of uncovering his teeth when he laughed, and his bearing was stupid. Now he watched the horses with a glazed look of helplessness in his eyes, a certain stupor of downfall.

The great draught-horses swung past. They were tied head to tail, four of them, and they heaved along to where a lane branched off from the highroad, planting their great hoofs floutingly in the fine black mud, swinging their great rounded haunches sumptuously, and trotting a few sudden steps as they were led into the lane, round the corner. Every movement showed a massive, slumbrous strength, and a stupidity which held them in subjection. The groom at the head looked back, jerking the leading rope. And the cavalcade moved out of sight up the lane, the tail of the last horse bobbed up tight and stiff, held out taut from the swinging great haunches as they rocked behind the hedges in a motion like sleep.

Joe watched with glazed hopeless eyes. The horses were almost like his own body to him. He felt he was done for now. Luckily he was engaged to a woman as old as himself, and therefore her father, who was steward of a neighboring estate, would provide him with a job. He would marry and go into harness. His life was over, he would be a subject animal now.

He turned uneasily aside, the retreating steps of the horses echoing in his ears. Then, with foolish restlessness, he reached for the scraps of bacon-rind from the plates, and making a faint whistling sound, flung them to the terrier that lay against the fender. He watched the dog swallow them, and waited till the creature looked into his eyes. Then a faint grin came on his face, and in a high, foolish voice he said:

"You won't get much more bacon, shall you, you little bitch?"

The dog faintly and dismally wagged its tail, then lowered its haunches, circled round, and lay down again.

There was another helpless silence at the table. Joe sprawled uneasily in his seat, not willing to go till the family conclave was dissolved. Fred Henry, the second brother, was erect, clean-limbed, alert. He had watched the passing of the horses with more sangfroid. If he was an animal, like Joe, he was an animal which controls, not one which is controlled. He was master of any horse, and he carried himself with a well-tempered air of mastery. But he was not master of the situations of life. He pushed his coarse brown moustache upwards, off his lip, and glanced irritably at his sister, who sat impassive and inscrutable.

"You'll go and stop with Lucy for a bit, shan't you?" he asked. The girl did not answer.

"I don't see what else you can do," persisted Fred Henry.

"Go as a skivvy," Joe interpolated laconically.

The girl did not move a muscle.

"If I was her, I should go in for training for a nurse," said Malcolm, the youngest of

them all. He was the baby of the family, a young man of twenty-two, with a fresh, jaunty *museau.*

But Mabel did not take any notice of him. They had talked at her and round her for so many years, that she hardly heard them at all.

The marble clock on the mantelpiece softly chimed the half-hour, the dog rose uneasily from the hearthrug and looked at the party at the breakfast table. But still they sat on in ineffectual conclave.

"Oh, all right," said Joe suddenly, apropos of nothing. "I'll get a move on."

He pushed back his chair, straddled his knees with a downward jerk, to get them free, in horsey fashion, and went to the fire. Still he did not go out of the room; he was curious to know what the others would do or say. He began to charge his pipe, looking down at the dog and saying, in a high, affected voice:

"Going wi' me? Going wi' me are ter? Tha'rt goin' further than tha counts on just now, dost hear?"

The dog faintly wagged its tail, the man stuck out his jaw and covered his pipe with his hands, and puffed intently, losing himself in the tobacco, looking down all the while at the dog with an absent brown eye. The dog looked up at him in mournful distrust. Joe stood with his knees stuck out, in real horsey fashion.

"Have you had a letter from Lucy?" Fred Henry asked of his sister.

"Last week," came the neutral reply.

"And what does she say?"

There was no answer.

"Does she *ask* you to go and stop there?" persisted Fred Henry.

"She says I can if I like."

"Well, then, you'd better. Tell her you'll come on Monday."

This was received in silence.

"That's what you'll do then, is it?" said Fred Henry, in some exasperation.

But she made no answer. There was a silence of futility and irritation in the room. Malcolm grinned fatuously.

"You'll have to make up your mind between now and next Wednesday," said Joe loudly, "or else find yourself lodgings on the kerbstone."

The face of the young woman darkened, but she sat on immutable.

"Here's Jack Fergusson!" exclaimed Malcolm, who was looking aimlessly out of the window.

"Where?" exclaimed Joe, loudly.

"Just gone past."

"Coming in?"

Malcolm craned his neck to see the gate.

"Yes," he said.

There was a silence. Mabel sat on like one condemned, at the head of the table. Then a whistle was heard from the kitchen. The dog got up and barked sharply. Joe opened the door and shouted:

"Come on."

After a moment a young man entered. He was muffled up in overcoat and a purple woollen scarf, and his tweed cap, which he did not remove, was pulled down on his head. He was of medium height, his face was rather long and pale, his eyes looked tired.

"Hello, Jack! Well, Jack!" exclaimed Malcolm and Joe. Fred Henry merely said, "Jack."

"What's doing?" asked the newcomer, evidently addressing Fred Henry.

"Same. We've got to be out by Wednesday. Got a cold?"

"I have—got it bad, too."

"Why don't you stop in?"

"*Me* stop in? When I can't stand on my legs, perhaps I shall have a chance." The young man spoke huskily. He had a slight Scotch accent.

"It's a knock-out, isn't it?" said Joe, boisterously, "if a doctor goes round croaking with a cold. Looks bad for the patients, doesn't it?"

The young doctor looked at him slowly.

"Anything the matter with *you,* then?" he asked sarcastically.

"Not as I know of. Damn your eyes, I hope not. Why?"

"I thought you were very concerned about the patients, wondered if you might be one yourself."

"Damn it, no, I've never been patient to no flaming doctor, and hope I never shall be," returned Joe.

At this point Mabel rose from the table, and they all seemed to become aware of her existence. She began putting the dishes together. The young doctor looked at her, but did not address her. He had not greeted her. She went out of the room with the tray, her face impassive and unchanged.

"When are you off then, all of you?" asked the doctor.

"I'm catching the eleven-forty," replied Malcolm. "Are you goin' down wi' th' trap, Joe?"

"Yes, I've told you I am going down wi' th' trap, haven't I?"

"We'd better be getting her in then. So long, Jack, if I don't see you before I go," said Malcolm, shaking hands.

He went out, followed by Joe, who seemed to have his tail between his legs.

"Well, this is the devil's own," exclaimed the doctor, when he was left alone with Fred Henry. "Going before Wednesday, are you."

"That's the orders," replied the other.

"Where, to Northampton?"

"That's it."

"The devil!" exclaimed Fergusson, with quiet chagrin.

And there was silence between the two.

"All settled up, are you?" asked Fergusson.

"About."

There was another pause.

"Well, I shall miss yer, Freddy, boy," said the young doctor.

"And I shall miss thee, Jack," returned the other.

"Miss you like hell," mused the doctor.

Fred Henry turned aside. There was nothing to say. Mabel came in again, to finish clearing the table.

"What are *you* going to do, then, Miss Pervin?" asked Fergusson. "Going to your sister's are you?"

Mabel looked at him with her steady, dangerous eyes, that always made him uncomfortable, unsettling his superficial ease.

"No," she said.

"Well, what in the name of fortune are *you* going to do? Say what you mean to do," cried Fred Henry, with futile intensity.

But she only averted her head, and continued her work. She folded the white tablecloth, and put on the chenile cloth.

"The sulkiest bitch that ever trod!" muttered her brother.

But she finished her task with perfectly impassive face, the young doctor watching her interestedly all the while. Then she went out.

Fred Henry stared after her, clenching his lips, his blue eyes fixing in sharp antagonism, as he made a grimace of sour exasperation.

"You could bray her into bits, and that's all you'd get out of her," he said in a small, narrowed tone.

The doctor smiled faintly.

"What's she *going* to do, then?" he asked.

"Strike me if I know!" returned the other.

There was a pause. Then the doctor stirred.

"I'll be seeing you to-night, shall I?" he said to his friend.

"Ay—where's it to be? Are we going over to Jessdale?"

"I don't know. I've got such a cold on me. I'll come round to the Moon and Stars, anyway."

"Let Lizzie and May miss their night for once, eh?"

"That's it—if I feel as I do now."

"All's one—"

The two young men went through the passage and down to the back door together. The house was large, but it was servantless now, and desolate. At the back was a small bricked house-yard, and beyond that a big square, gravelled fine and red, and having stables on two sides. Sloping, dank, winter-dark fields stretched away on the open sides.

But the stables were empty. Joseph Pervin, the father of the family, had been a man of no education, who had become a fairly large horse dealer. The stables had been full of horses, there was a great turmoil and come-and-go of horses and of dealers and grooms. Then the kitchen was full of servants. But of late things had declined. The old man had married a second time, to retrieve his fortunes. Now he was dead and everything was gone to the dogs, there was nothing but debt and threatening.

For months, Mabel had been servantless in the big house, keeping the home together in penury for her ineffectual brothers. She had kept house for ten years. But previously it was with unstinted means. Then, however brutal and coarse everything was, the sense of money had kept her proud, confident. The men might be foul-mouthed, the women in the kitchen might have bad reputations, her brothers might have illegitimate children. But so long as there was money, the girl felt herself established and brutally proud, reserved.

No company came to the house, save dealers and coarse men. Mabel had no associates of her own sex, after her sister went away. But she did not mind. She went regularly to church, she attended to her father. And she lived in the memory of her mother, who had died when she was fourteen, and whom she had loved. She had loved her father, too, in a different way, depending upon him, and feeling secure in him, until at the age of fifty-four he married again. And then she had set hard against him. Now he had died and left them all hopelessly in debt.

She had suffered badly during the period of poverty. Nothing, however, could shake the curious sullen, animal pride that dominated each member of the family. Now, for Mabel, the end had come. Still she would not cast about her. She would follow her own way just the same. She would always hold the keys of her own situation. Mindless and persistent, she endured from day to day. What should she think? Why should she answer anybody? It was enough that this was the end and there was no way out. She need not pass any more darkly along the main street of the small town, avoiding every eye. She need not demean herself any more, going into the shops and buying the cheapest food. This was at an end. She thought of nobody, not even of herself. Mindless and persistent, she seemed in a sort of ecstasy to be coming nearer to her fulfilment, her own glorification, approaching her dead mother, who was glorified.

In the afternoon she took a little bag, with shears and sponge and a small scrubbing brush, and went out. It was a grey, wintry day, with saddened, dark green fields and an atmosphere blackened by the smoke of foundries not far off. She went quickly, darkly along the causeway, heeding nobody, through the town to the churchyard.

There she always felt secure, as if no one could see her, although as a matter of fact she was exposed to the stare of every one who passed along under the churchyard wall. Nevertheless, once under the shadow of the great looming church, among the graves, she felt immune from the world, reserved within the thick churchyard wall as in another country.

Carefully she clipped the grass from the grave, and arranged the pinky white, small chrysanthemums in the tin cross. When this was done, she took an empty jar from a neighbouring grave, brought water, and carefully, most scrupulously sponged the marble head-stone and the coping-stone.

It gave her sincere satisfaction to do this. She felt in immediate contact with the world of her mother. She took minute pains, went through the park in a state bordering on pure happiness, as if in performing this task she came into a subtle, intimate connection with her mother. For the life she followed here in the world was far less real than the world of death she inherited from her mother.

The doctor's house was just by the church. Fergusson, being a mere hired assistant, was slave to the country-side. As he hurried now to attend to the out-patients in the surgery, glancing across the graveyard with his quick eye, he saw the girl at her task at the grave. She seemed so intent and remote, it was like looking into another world. Some mystical element was touched in him. He slowed down as he walked, watching her as if spell-bound.

She lifted her eyes, feeling him looking. Their eyes met. And each looked away again at once, each feeling, in some way, found out by the other. He lifted his cap and passed on down the road. There remained distinct in his consciousness, like a vision, the memory of her face, lifted from the tombstone in the churchyard, and looking at him with slow, large, portentous eyes. It *was* portentous, her face. It seemed to mesmerize him. There was a heavy power in her eyes which laid hold of his whole being, as if he had drunk some powerful drug. He had been feeling weak and done before. Now the life came back into him, he felt delivered from his own fretted, daily self.

He finished his duties at the surgery as quickly as might be, hastily filling up the bottle of the waiting people with cheap drugs. Then, in perpetual haste, he set off again to visit several cases in another part of his round, before tea-time. At all times he preferred to walk if he could, but particularly when he was not well. He fancied the motion restored him.

The afternoon was falling. It was grey, deadened, and wintry, with a slow, moist, heavy coldness sinking in and deadening all the faculties. But why should he think or notice? He hastily climbed the hill and turned across the dark green fields, following the black cinder-track. In the distance, across a shallow dip in the country, the small town was clustered like smouldering ash, a tower, a spire, a heap of low, raw, extinct houses. And on the nearest fringe of the town, sloping into the dip, was Oldmeadow, the Pervins' house. He could see the stables and the outbuildings distinctly, as they lay towards him on the slope. Well, he would not go there many more times! Another resource would be lost to him, another place gone: the only company he cared for in the alien, ugly little town he was losing. Nothing but work, drudgery, constant hastening from dwelling to dwelling among the colliers and the ironworkers. It wore him out, but at the same time he had a craving for it. It was a stimulant to him to be in the homes of the working people, moving as it were through the innermost body of their life. His nerves were excited and gratified. He could come so near, into the very lives of the rough, inarticulate, powerfully emotional men and women. He grumbled, he said he hated the hellish hole. But as a matter of fact it excited him, the contact with the rough, strongly-feeling people was a stimulant applied direct to his nerves.

Below Oldmeadow, in the green, shallow, soddened hollow of fields lay a square, deep pond. Roving across the landscape, the doctor's quick eye detected a figure in black passing through the gate of the field, down towards the pond. He looked again. It would be Mabel Pervin. His mind suddenly became alive and attentive.

Why was she going down there? He pulled up on the path on the slope above, and stood staring. He could just make sure of the small black figure moving in the hollow of the failing day. He seemed to see her in the midst of such obscurity, that he was like a clairvoyant, seeing rather with the mind's eye than with ordinary sight. Yet he could see her positively enough, whilst he kept his eye attentive. He felt, if he looked away from her, in the thick, ugly falling dusk, he would lose her altogether.

He followed her minutely as she moved, direct and intent, like something transmitted rather than stirring in voluntary activity, straight down the field towards the pond. There she stood on the bank for a moment. She never raised her head. Then she waded slowly into the water.

He stood motionless as the small black figure walked slowly and deliberately towards the centre of the pond, very slowly, gradually moving deeper into the motionless water, and still moving forward as the water got up to her breast. Then he could see her no more in the dusk of the dead afternoon.

"There!" he exclaimed. "Would you believe it?"

And he hastened straight down, running over the wet, soddened fields, pushing through the hedges, down into the depression of callous wintry obscurity. It took him several minutes to come to the pond. He stood on the bank, breathing heavily. He could see nothing. His eyes seemed to penetrate the dead water. Yes, perhaps that was the dark shadow of her black clothing beneath the surface of the water.

He slowly ventured into the pond. The bottom was deep, soft clay, he sank in, and the water clasped dead cold round his legs. As he stirred he could smell the cold, rotten clay that fouled up into the water. It was objectionable in his lungs. Still, repelled and yet not heeding, he moved deeper into the pond. The cold water rose over his thighs, over his loins, upon his abdomen. The lower part of his body was all sunk in the hideous cold element. And the bottom was so deeply soft and uncertain, he was afraid of pitching with his mouth underneath. He could not swim, and was afraid.

He crouched a little, spreading his hands under the water and moving them round, trying to feel for her. The dead cold pond swayed upon his chest. He moved again, a little deeper, and again, with his hands underneath, he felt all around the water. And he touched her clothing. But it evaded his fingers. He made a desperate effort to grasp it.

And so doing he lost his balance and went under, horribly, suffocating in the foul earthy water, struggling madly for a few moments. At last, after what seemed an eternity, he got his footing, rose again into the air and looked around. He gasped, and knew he was in the world. Then he looked at the water. She had risen near him. He grasped her clothing, and drawing her nearer, turned to take his way to land again.

He went very slowly, carefully, absorbed in the slow progress. He rose higher, climbing out of the pond. The water was now only about his legs; he was thankful, full of relief to be out of the clutches of the pond. He lifted her and staggered on to the bank, out of the horror of wet, grey clay.

He laid her down on the bank. She was quite unconscious and running with water. He made the water come from her mouth, he worked to restore her. He did not have to work very long before he could feel the breathing begin again in her; she was breathing naturally. He worked a little longer. He could feel her live beneath his hands; she was coming back. He wiped her face, wrapped her in his overcoat, looked round into the dim, dark grey world, then lifted her and staggered down the bank and across the fields.

It seemed an unthinkably long way, and his burden so heavy he felt he would never get to the house. But at last he was in the stable-yard, and then in the house-yard. He opened the door and went into the house. In the kitchen he laid her down on the hearth-rug, and called. The house was empty. But the fire was burning in the grate.

Then again he kneeled to attend to her. She was breathing regularly, her eyes were wide open and as if conscious, but there seemed something missing in her look. She was conscious in herself, but unconscious of her surroundings.

He ran upstairs, took blankets from a bed, and put them before the fire to warm. Then he removed her saturated, earthy-smelling clothing, rubbed her dry with a towel, and wrapped her naked in the blankets. Then he went into the dining-room, to look for spirits. There was a little whisky. He drank a gulp himself, and put some into her mouth.

The effect was instantaneous. She looked full into his face, as if she had been seeing him for some time, and yet had only just become conscious of him.

"Dr. Fergusson?" she said.

"What?" he answered.

He was divesting himself of his coat, intending to find some dry clothing upstairs. He could not bear the smell of the dead, clayey water, and he was mortally afraid for his own health.

"What did I do?" she asked.

"Walked into the pond," he replied. He had begun to shudder like one sick, and could hardly attend to her. Her eyes remained full on him, he seemed to be going dark in his mind, looking back at her helplessly. The shuddering became quieter in him, his life came back in him, dark and unknowing, but strong again.

"Was I out of my mind?" she asked, while her eyes were fixed on him all the time.

"Maybe, for the moment," he replied. He felt quiet, because his strength had come back. The strange fretful strain had left him.

"Am I out of my mind now?" she asked.

"Are you?" he reflected a moment. "No," he answered truthfully. "I don't see that you are." He turned his face aside. He was afraid now, because he felt dazed, and felt dimly that her power was stronger than his, in this issue. And she continued to look at him fixedly all the time. "Can you tell me where I shall find some dry things to put on?" he asked.

"Did you dive into the pond for me?" she asked.

"No," he answered. "I walked in. But I went in overhead as well."

There was silence for a moment. He hesitated. He very much wanted to go upstairs to get into dry clothing. But there was another desire in him. And she seemed to hold him. His will seemed to have gone to sleep, and left him, standing there slack before her. But he felt warm inside himself. He did not shudder at all, though his clothes were sodden on him.

"Why did you?" she asked.

"Because I didn't want you to do such a foolish thing," he said.

"It wasn't foolish," she said, still gazing at him as she lay on the floor, with a sofa cushion under her head. "It was the right thing to do. *I* knew best, then."

"I'll go and shift these wet things," he said. But still he had not the power to move out of her presence, until she sent him. It was as if she had the life of his body in her hands, and he could not extricate himself. Or perhaps he did not want to.

Suddenly she sat up. Then she became aware of her own immediate condition. She felt the blankets about her, she knew her own limbs. For a moment it seemed as if her reason were going. She looked round, with wild eye, as if seeking something. He stood still with fear. She saw her clothing lying scattered.

"Who undressed me?" she asked, her eyes resting full and inevitable on his face.

"I did," he replied, "to bring you round."

For some moments she sat and gazed at him awfully, her lips parted.

"Do you love me, then?" she asked.

He only stood and stared at her, fascinated. His soul seemed to melt.

She shuffled forward on her knees, and put her arms around him, round his legs, as he stood there, pressing her breasts against his knees and thighs, clutching him with strange, convulsive certainty, pressing his thighs against her, drawing him to her face, her throat, as she looked up at him with flaring, humble eyes of transfiguration, triumphant in first possession.

"You love me," she murmured, in strange transport, yearning and triumphant and confident. "You love me. I know you love me, I know."

And she was passionately kissing his knees, through the wet clothing, passionately and indiscriminately kissing his knees, his legs, as if unaware of everything.

He looked down at the tangled wet hair, the wild, bare, animal shoulders. He was amazed, bewildered, and afraid. He had never thought of loving her. He had never wanted to love her. When he rescued her and restored her, he was a doctor, and she was a patient. He had had no single personal thought of her. Nay, this introduction of the personal element was very distasteful to him, a violation of his professional honour. It was horrible to have her there embracing his knees. It was horrible. He revolted from it, violently. And yet—and yet—he had not the power to break away.

She looked at him again, with the same supplication of powerful love, and that same transcendent, frightening light of triumph. In view of the delicate flame which seemed to come from her face like a light, he was powerless. And yet he had never intended to love her. He had never intended. And something stubborn in him could not give way.

"You love me," she repeated, in a murmur of deep rhapsodic assurance. "You love me."

Her hands were drawing him, drawing him down to her. He was afraid, even a little horrified. For he had, really, no intention of loving her. Yet her hands were drawing him towards her. He put out his hand quickly to steady himself, and grasped her bare shoulder. A flame seemed to burn the hand that grasped her soft shoulder. He had no intention of loving her: his whole will was against his yielding. It was horrible. And yet wonderful was the touch of her shoulders, beautiful the shining of her face. Was she perhaps mad? He had a horror of yielding to her. Yet something in him ached also.

He had been staring away at the door, away from her. But his hand remained on her shoulder. She had gone suddenly very still. He looked down at her. Her eyes were now wide with fear, with doubt, the light was dying from her face, a shadow of terrible grayness was returning. He could not bear the touch of her eyes' question upon him, and the look of death behind the question.

With an inward groan he gave way, and let his heart yield towards her. A sudden gentle smile came on his face. And her eyes, which never left his face, slowly, slowly filled with tears. He watched the strange water rise in her eyes, like some slow fountain coming up. And his heart seemed to burn and melt away in his breast.

He could not bear to look at her any more. He dropped on his knees and caught her head with his arms and pressed her face against his throat. She was very still. His heart, which seemed to have broken, was burning with a kind of agony in his breast. And he felt her slow, hot tears wetting his throat. But he could not move.

He felt the hot tears wet his neck and the hollows of his neck, and he remained motionless, suspended through one of man's eternities. Only now it had become indispensable to him to have her face pressed close to him; he could never let her go again. He could never let her head go away from the close clutch of his arm. He wanted to remain like that for ever, with his heart hurting him in a pain that was also life to him. Without knowing, he was looking down on her damp, soft brown hair.

Then, as it were suddenly, he smelt the horrid stagnant smell of that water. And at the same moment she drew away from him and looked at him. Her eyes were wistful and unfathomable. He was afraid of them, and he fell to kissing her, not knowing what he was doing. He wanted her eyes not to have that terrible, wistful, unfathomable look.

When she turned her face to him again, a faint delicate flush was glowing, and there was again dawning that terrible shining of joy in her eyes, which really terrified him, and yet which he now wanted to see, because he feared the look of doubt still more.

"You love me?" she said, rather faltering.

"Yes." The word cost him a painful effort. Not because it wasn't true. But because it was too newly true, the *saying* seemed to tear open again his newly-torn heart. And he hardly wanted it to be true, even now.

She lifted her face to him, and he bent forward and kissed her on the mouth, gently, with the one kiss that is an eternal pledge. And as he kissed her his heart strained again in his breast. He never intended to love her. But now it was over. He had crossed over the gulf to her, and all that he had left behind had shrivelled and become void.

After the kiss, her eyes again slowly filled with tears. She sat still, away from him, with her face dropped aside, and her hands folded in her lap. The tears fell very slowly. There was complete silence. He too sat there motionless and silent on the hearthrug. The strange pain of his heart that was broken seemed to consume him. That he should love her? That this was love! That he should be ripped open in this way! Him, a doctor! How they would all jeer if they knew! It was agony to him to think they might know.

In the curious naked pain of the thought he looked again to her. She was sitting there drooped into a muse. He saw a tear fall, and his heart flared hot. He saw for the first time that one of her shoulders was quite uncovered, one arm bare, he could see one of her small breasts; dimly, because it had become almost dark in the room.

"Why are you crying?" he asked, in an altered voice.

She looked up at him, and behind her tears the consciousness of her situation for the first time brought a dark look of shame to her eyes.

"I'm not crying, really," she said, watching him half frightened.

He reached his hand, and softly closed it on her bare arm.

"I love you! I love you!" he said in a soft, low vibrating voice, unlike himself.

She shrank, and dropped her head. The soft, penetrating grip of his hand on her arm distressed her. She looked up at him.

"I want to go," she said. "I want to go and get you some dry things."

"Why?" he said. "I'm all right."

"But I want to go," she said. "And I want you to change your things."

He released her arm, and she wrapped herself in the blanket, looking at him rather frightened. And still she did not rise.

"Kiss me," she said wistfully.

He kissed her, but briefly, half in anger.

Then, after a second, she rose nervously, all mixed up in the blanket. He watched her in confusion, as she tried to extricate herself and wrap herself up so that she could walk. He watched her relentlessly, as she knew. And as she went, the blanket trailing, and as he saw a glimpse of her feet and her white leg, he tried to remember her as she was when he had wrapped her in the blanket. But then he didn't want to remember, because she had been nothing to him then, and his nature revolted from remembering her as she was when she was nothing to him.

A tumbling, muffled noise from within the dark house startled him. Then he heard her voice:—"There are clothes." He rose and went to the foot of the stairs, and gathered up the garments she had thrown down. Then he came back to the fire, to rub himself down and dress. He grinned at his own appearance when he had finished.

The fire was sinking, so he put on coal. The house was now quite dark, save for the light of a street-lamp that shone in faintly from beyond the holly trees. He lit the gas with matches he found on the mantlepiece. Then he emptied the pockets of his own clothes, and threw all his wet things in a heap into the scullery. After which he gathered up her sodden clothes, gently, and put them in a separate heap on the copper-top in the scullery.

It was six o'clock on the clock. His own watch had stopped. He ought to go back to the surgery. He waited, and still she did not come down. So he went to the foot of the stairs and called:

"I shall have to go."

Almost immediately he heard her coming down. She had on her best dress of black voile, and her hair was tidy, but still damp. She looked at him—and in spite of herself, smiled.

"I don't like you in those clothes," she said.

"Do I look a sight?" he answered.

They were shy of one another.

"I'll make you some tea," she said.

"No, I must go."

"Must you?" And she looked at him again with the wide, strained, doubtful eyes. And again, from the pain of his breast, he knew how he loved her. He went and bent to kiss her, gently, passionately, with his heart's painful kiss.

"And my hair smells so horrible," she murmured in distraction. "And I'm so awful, I'm so awful! Oh, no, I'm too awful." And she broke into bitter, heartbroken sobbing. "You can't want to love me, I'm horrible."

"Don't be silly, don't be silly," he said, trying to comfort her, kissing her, holding her in his arms. "I want you, I want to marry you, we're going to be married, quickly, quickly—tomorrow if I can."

But she only sobbed terribly, and cried:

"I feel awful. I feel awful. I feel I'm horrible to you."

"No, I want you, I want you," was all he answered, blindly, with that terrible intonation which frightened her almost more than her horror lest he should *not* want her.

KATHERINE MANSFIELD

(1888–1923)

The Garden Party

About the Author: Katherine Mansfield was born in New Zealand, later settled in England, and died in France. Many of her short stories are set in New Zealand and reflect her childhood experiences and social concerns. Her best-known collections are *Bliss* (1920), *The Garden Party* (1922), and *The Dove's Nest* (1923). Mansfield's *Collected Stories* appeared in 1945, and volumes of her letters and her journal have also been published in the years since her death.

And after all the weather was ideal. They could not have had a more perfect day for a garden-party if they had ordered it. Windless, warm, the sky without a cloud. Only the blue was veiled with a haze of light gold, as it is sometimes in early summer. The gardener had been up since dawn, mowing the lawns and sweeping them, until the grass and the dark flat rosettes where the daisy plants had been seemed to shine. As for the roses, you could not help feeling they understood that roses are the only flowers that impress people at garden-parties; the only flowers that everybody is certain of knowing. Hundreds, yes, literally hundreds, had come out in a single night; the green bushes bowed down as though they had been visited by archangels.

Breakfast was not yet over before the men came to put up the marquee.

"Where do you want the marquee put, mother?"

"My dear child, it's no use asking me. I'm determined to leave everything to you children this year. Forget I am your mother. Treat me as an honored guest."

But Meg could not possibly go and supervise the men. She had washed her hair before breakfast, and she sat drinking her coffee in a green turban, with a dark wet curl stamped on each cheek. Jose, the butterfly, always came down in a silk petticoat and a kimono jacket.

"You'll have to go, Laura; you're the artistic one."

Away Laura flew, still holding her piece of bread-and-butter. It's so delicious to have an excuse for eating out of doors, and besides, she loved having to arrange things; she always felt she could do it so much better than anybody else.

Four men in their shirt-sleeves stood grouped together on the garden path. They carried staves covered with rolls of canvas, and they had big tool-bats slung on their backs. They looked impressive. Laura wished now that she had not got the bread-and-butter, but there was nowhere to put it, and she couldn't possibly throw it away. She blushed and tried to look severe and even a little bit short-sighted as she came up to them.

"Good morning," she said, copying her mother's voice. But that sounded so fearfully affected that she was ashamed, and stammered like a little girl. "Oh—er—have you come—is it about the marquee?"

"That's right, miss," said the tallest of the men, a lanky, freckled fellow, and he shifted his tool-bag, knocked back his straw hat and smiled down at her. "That's about it."

His smile was so easy, so friendly that Laura recovered. What nice eyes he had, small, but such a dark blue! And now she looked at the others, they were smiling too. "Cheer up, we won't bite," their smile seemed to say. How very nice workmen were! And what a beautiful morning! She mustn't mention the morning; she must be businesslike. The marquee.

"Well, what about the lily-lawn? Would that do?"

And she pointed to the lily-lawn with the hand that didn't hold the bread-and-butter. They turned, they stared in the direction. A little fat chap thrust out his under-lip, and the tall fellow frowned.

"I don't fancy it," said he. "Not conspicuous enough. You see, with a thing like a marquee," and he turned to Laura in his easy way, "you want to put it somewhere where it'll give you a bang slap in the eye, if you follow me."

Laura's upbringing made her wonder for a moment whether it was quite respectful of a workman to talk to her of bangs slap in the eye. But she did quite follow him.

"A corner of the tennis-court," she suggested. "But the band's going to be in one corner."

"H'm, going to have a band, are you?" said another of the workmen. He was pale. He had a haggard look as his dark eyes scanned the tennis-court. What was he thinking?

"Only a very small band," said Laura gently. Perhaps he wouldn't mind so much if the band was quite small. But the tall fellow interrupted.

"Look here, miss, that's the place. Against those trees. Over there. That'll do fine."

Against the karakas. Then the karaka-trees would be hidden. And they were so lovely, with their broad, gleaming leaves, and their clusters of yellow fruit. They were like trees you imagined growing on a desert island, proud, solitary, lifting their leaves and fruits to the sun in a kind of silent splendor. Must they be hidden by a marquee?

They must. Already the men had shouldered their staves and were making for the place. Only the tall fellow was left. He bent down, pinched a sprig of lavender, put his thumb and forefinger to his nose and snuffed up the smell. When Laura saw that gesture she forgot all about the karakas in her wonder at him caring for things like that—caring for the smell of lavender. How many men that she knew would have done such a thing? Oh, how extraordinarily nice workmen were, she thought. Why couldn't she have workmen for friends rather than the silly boys she danced with and who came to Sunday night supper? She would get on much better with men like these.

It's all the fault, she decided, as the tall fellow drew something on the back of an envelope, something that was to be looped up or left to hang, of these absurd class distinctions. Well, for her part, she didn't feel them. Not a bit, not an atom. . . . And now there came the chock-chock of wooden hammers. Some one whistled, some one sang out,

"Are you right there, matey?" "Matey!" The friendliness of it, the—the—Just to prove how happy she was, just to show the tall fellow how at home she felt, and how she despised stupid conventions, Laura took a big bite of her bread-and-butter as she stared at the little drawing. She felt just like a work-girl.

"Laura, Laura, where are you? Telephone, Laura!" a voice cried from the house.

"Coming!" Away she skimmed, over the lawn, up the path, up the steps, across the veranda, and into the porch. In the hall her father and Laurie were brushing their hats ready to go to the office.

"I say, Laura," said Laurie very fast, "you might just give a squiz at my coat before this afternoon. See if it wants pressing."

"I will," said she. Suddenly she couldn't stop herself. She ran at Laurie and gave him a small, quick squeeze. "Oh, I do love parties, don't you?" gasped Laura.

"Ra-ther," said Laurie's warm, boyish voice, and he squeezed his sister too, and gave her a gentle push. "Dash off to the telephone, old girl."

The telephone. "Yes, yes; oh yes. Kitty? Good morning, dear. Come to lunch? Do, dear. Delighted of course. It will only be a very scratch meal—just the sandwich crusts and broken meringue-shells and what's left over. Yes, isn't it a perfect morning? Your white? Oh, I certainly should. One moment—hold the line. Mother's calling." And Laura sat back. "What, mother? Can't hear."

Mrs. Sheridan's voice floated down the stairs. "Tell her to wear that sweet hat she had on last Sunday."

"Mother says you're to wear that *sweet* hat you had on last Sunday. Good. One o'clock. Bye-bye."

Laura put back the receiver, flung her arms over her head, took a deep breath, stretched and let them fall. "Huh," she sighed, and the moment after the sigh she sat up quickly. She was still, listening. All the doors in the house seemed to be open. The house was alive with soft, quick steps and running voices. The green baize door that led to the kitchen regions swung open and shut with a muffled thud. And now there came a long, chuckling absurd sound. It was the heavy piano being moved on its stiff castors. But the air! If you stopped to notice, was the air always like this? Little faint winds were playing chase, in at the tops of the windows, out at the doors. And there were two tiny spots of sun, one on the inkpot, one on a silver photograph frame, playing too. Darling little spots. Especially the one on the inkpot lid. It was quite warm. A warm little silver star. She could have kissed it.

The front door bell pealed, and there sounded the rustle of Sadie's print skirt on the stairs. A man's voice murmured; Sadie answered, careless, "I'm sure I don't know. Wait. I'll ask Mrs. Sheridan."

"What is it, Sadie?" Laura came into the hall.

"It's the florist, Miss Laura."

It was, indeed. There, just inside the door, stood a wide, shallow tray full of pots of pink lilies. No other kind. Nothing but lilies—canna lilies, big pink flowers, wide open, radiant, almost frighteningly alive on bright crimson stems.

"O-oh, Sadie!" said Laura, and the sound was like a little moan. She crouched down as if to warm herself at that blaze of lilies; she felt they were in her fingers, on her lips, growing in her breast.

"It's some mistake," she said faintly. "Nobody ever ordered so many. Sadie, go and find mother."

But at that moment Mrs. Sheridan joined them.

"It's quite right," she said calmly. "Yes, I ordered them. Aren't they lovely?" She pressed Laura's arm. "I was passing the shop yesterday, and I saw them in the window. And I suddenly thought for once in my life I shall have enough canna lilies. The garden-party will be a good excuse."

"But I thought you said you didn't mean to interfere," said Laura. Sadie had gone. The florist's man was still outside at his van. She put her arm round her mother's neck and gently, very gently, she bit her mother's ear.

"My darling child, you wouldn't like a logical mother, would you? Don't do that. Here's the man."

He carried more lilies still, another whole tray.

"Bank them up, just inside the door, on both sides of the porch, please," said Mrs. Sheridan. "Don't you agree, Laura?"

"Oh, I *do,* mother."

In the drawing-room Meg, Jose and good little Hans had at last succeeded in moving the piano.

"Now, if we put this chesterfield against the wall and move everything out of the room except the chairs, don't you think?"

"Quite."

"Hans, move these tables into the smoking-room, and bring a sweeper to take these marks off the carpet and—one moment, Hans—" Jose loved giving orders to the servants, and they loved obeying her. She always made them feel they were taking part in some drama. "Tell mother and Miss Laura to come here at once."

"Very good, Miss Jose."

She turned to Meg. "I want to hear what the piano sounds like, just in case I'm asked to sing this afternoon. Let's try over 'This Life is Weary.' "

Pom! Ta-ta-ta *Tee*-ta! The piano burst out so passionately that Jose's face changed. She clasped her hands. She looked mournfully and enigmatically at her mother and Laura as they came in.

This Life is *Wee*-ary,
A Tear—a Sigh.
A Love that *Chan*-ges,
This Life is *Wee*-ary,
A Tear—a Sigh.
A Love that *Chan*-ges,
And then . . . Goodbye!

But at the word "Goodbye," and although the piano sounded more desperate than ever, her face broke into a brilliant, dreadfully unsympathetic smile.

"Aren't I in good voice, mummy?" she beamed.

This Life is *Wee*-ary,
Hope comes to Die.
A Dream—a *Wa*-kening.

But now Sadie interrupted them. "What is it, Sadie?"

"If you please, m'm, cook says have you got the flags for the sandwiches?"

"The flags for the sandwiches, Sadie?" echoed Mrs. Sheridan dreamily. And the children knew by her face that she hadn't got them. "Let me see." And she said to Sadie firmly, "Tell cook I'll let her have them in ten minutes."

Sadie went.

"Now, Laura," said her mother quickly. "Come with me into the smoking-room. I've got the names somewhere on the back of an envelope. You'll have to write them out for me. Meg, go upstairs this minute and take that wet thing off your head. Jose, run and finish dressing this instant. Do you hear me, children, or shall I have to tell your father when he comes home to-night? And—and, Jose, pacify cook if you do go into the kitchen, will you? I'm terrified of her this morning."

The envelope was found at last behind the dining-room clock, though how it had got there Mrs. Sheridan could not imagine.

"One of you children must have stolen it out of my bag, because I remember vividly—cream cheese and lemon-curd. Have you done that?"

"Yes."

"Egg and—" Mrs. Sheridan held the envelope away from her. "It looks like mice. It can't be mice, can it?"

"Olive, pet," said Laura, looking over her shoulder.

"Yes, of course, olive. What a horrible combination it sounds. Egg and olive."

They were finished at last, and Laura took them off to the kitchen. She found Jose there pacifying the cook, who did not look at all terrifying.

"I have never seen such exquisite sandwiches," said Jose's rapturous voice. "How many kinds did you say there were, cook? Fifteen?"

"Fifteen, Miss Jose."

"Well, cook, I congratulate you."

Cook swept up crusts with the long sandwich knife, and smiled broadly.

"Godber's has come," announced Sadie, issuing out of the pantry. She had seen the man pass the window.

That meant the cream puffs had come. Godber's were famous for their cream puffs. Nobody ever thought of making them at home.

"Bring them in and put them on the table, my girl," ordered cook.

Sadie brought them in and went back to the door. Of course Laura and Jose were far too grown-up to really care about such things. All the same, they couldn't help agreeing that the puffs looked very attractive. Very. Cook began arranging them, shaking off the extra icing sugar.

"Don't they carry one back to all one's parties?" said Laura.

"I suppose they do," said practical Jose, who never liked to be carried back. "They look beautifully light and feathery, I must say."

"Have one each, my dears," said cook in her comfortable voice. "Yer ma won't know."

Oh, impossible. Fancy cream puffs so soon after breakfast. The very idea made one shudder. All the same, two minutes later Jose and Laura were licking their fingers with that absorbed inward look that only comes from whipped cream.

"Let's go into the garden, out by the back way," suggested Laura. "I want to see how the men are getting on with the marquee. They're such awfully nice men."

But the back door was blocked by cook, Sadie, Godber's man and Hans.

Something had happened.

"Tuk-tuk-tuk," clucked cook like an agitated hen. Sadie had her hand clapped to her

cheek as though she had toothache. Hans's face was screwed up in the effort to understand. Only Godber's man seemed to be enjoying himself; it was his story.

"What's the matter? What's happened?"

"There's been a horrible accident," said Cook. "A man killed."

"A man killed! Where? How? When?"

But Godber's man wasn't going to have his story snatched from under his very nose.

"Know those little cottages just below here, miss?" Know them? Of course, she knew them. "Well, there's a young chap living there, name of Scott, a carter. His horse shied at a traction-engine, corner of Hawke Street this morning, and he was thrown out on the back of his head. Killed."

"Dead!" Laura stared at Godber's man.

"Dead when they picked him up," said Godber's man with relish. "They were taking the body home as I come up here." And he said to the cook, "He's left a wife and five little ones."

"Jose, come here." Laura caught hold of her sister's sleeve and dragged her through the kitchen to the other side of the green baize door. There she paused and leaned against it. "Jose!" she said, horrified, "however are we going to stop everything?"

"Stop everything, Laura!" cried Jose in astonishment. "What do you mean?"

"Stop the garden-party, of course." Why did Jose pretend?

But Jose was still more amazed. "Stop the garden-party? My dear Laura, don't be so absurd. Of course we can't do anything of the kind. Nobody expects us to. Don't be so extravagant."

"But we can't possibly have a garden-party with a man dead just outside the front gate."

That really was extravagant, for the little cottages were in a lane to themselves at the very bottom of a steep rise that led up to the house. A broad road ran between. True, they were far too near. They were the greatest possible eyesore, and they had no right to be in that neighborhood at all. They were little mean dwellings painted a chocolate brown. In the garden patches there was nothing but cabbage stalks, sick hens and tomato cans. The very smoke coming out of their chimneys was poverty-stricken. Little rags and shreds of smoke, so unlike the great silvery plumes that uncurled from the Sheridans' chimneys. Washerwomen lived in the lane and sweeps and a cobbler, and a man whose house-front was studded all over with minute bird-cages. Children swarmed. When the Sheridans were little they were forbidden to set foot there because of the revolting language and of what they might catch. But since they were grown up, Laura and Laurie on their prowls sometimes walked through. It was disgusting and sordid. They came out with a shudder. But still one must go everywhere; one must see everything. So through they went.

"And just think of what the band would sound like to that poor woman," said Laura.

"Oh, Laura!" Jose began to be seriously annoyed. "If you're going to stop a band playing every time some one has an accident, you'll lead a very strenuous life. I'm every bit as sorry about it as you. I feel just as sympathetic." Her eyes hardened. She looked at her sister just as she used to when they were little and fighting together. "You won't bring a drunken workman back to life by being sentimental," she said softly.

"Drunk! Who said he was drunk?" Laura turned furiously on Jose. She said, just as they had used to say on those occasions, "I'm going straight up to tell mother."

"Do, dear," cooed Jose.

"Mother, can I come into your room?" Laura turned the big glass doorknob.

"Of course, child. Why, what's the matter? What's given you such a color?" And Mrs. Sheridan turned round from her dressing-table. She was trying on a new hat.

"Mother, a man's been killed," began Laura.

"Not in the garden?" interrupted her mother.

"No, no!"

"Oh, what a fright you gave me!" Mrs. Sheridan sighed with relief, and took off the big hat and held it on her knees.

"But listen, mother," said Laura. Breathless, half-choking, she told the dreadful story. "Of course, we can't have our party, can we?" she pleaded. "The band and everybody arriving. They'd hear us, mother; they're nearly neighbors!"

To Laura's astonishment her mother behaved just like Jose; it was harder to bear because she seemed amused. She refused to take Laura seriously.

"But, my dear child, use your common sense. It's only by accident we've heard of it. If some one had died there normally—and I can't understand how they keep alive in those poky little holes—we should still be having our party, shouldn't we?"

Laura had to say "yes" to that, but she felt it was all wrong. She sat down on her mother's sofa and pinched the cushion frill.

"Mother, isn't it really terribly heartless of us?" she asked.

"Darling!" Mrs. Sheridan got up and came over to her, carrying the hat. Before Laura could stop her she had popped it on. "My child!" said her mother, "the hat is yours. It's made for you. It's much too young for me. I have never seen you look such a picture. Look at yourself!" And she held up her hand-mirror.

"But, mother," Laura began again. She couldn't look at herself; she turned aside.

This time Mrs. Sheridan lost patience just as Jose had done.

"You are being very absurd, Laura," she said coldly. "People like that don't expect sacrifices from us. And it's not very sympathetic to spoil everybody's enjoyment as you're doing now."

"I don't understand," said Laura, and she walked quickly out of the room into her own bedroom. There, quite by chance, the first thing she saw was this charming girl in the mirror, in her black hat trimmed with gold daisies, and a long black velvet ribbon. Never had she imagined she could look like that. Is mother right? she thought. And now she hoped her mother was right. Am I being extravagant? Perhaps it was extravagant. Just for a moment she had another glimpse of that poor woman and those little children, and the body being carried into the house. But it all seemed blurred, unreal, like a picture in the newspaper. I'll remember it again after the party's over, she decided. And somehow that seemed quite the best plan. . . .

Lunch was over by half-past one. By half-past two they were all ready for the fray. The green-coated band had arrived and was established in a corner of the tennis-court.

"My dear!" trilled Kitty Maitland, "aren't they too like frogs for words? You ought to have arranged them round the pond with the conductor in the middle on a leaf."

Laurie arrived and hailed them on his way to dress. At the sight of him Laura remembered the accident again. She wanted to tell him. If Laurie agreed with the others, then it was bound to be all right. And she followed him into the hall.

"Laurie!"

"Hallo!" He was half-way upstairs, but when he turned round and saw Laura he suddenly puffed out his cheeks and goggled his eyes at her. "My word, Laura! You do look stunning," said Laurie, "What an absolutely topping hat!"

Laura said faintly "Is it?" and smiled up at Laurie, and didn't tell him after all.

Soon after that people began coming in streams. The band struck up; the hired waiters ran from the house to the marquee. Wherever you looked there were couples strolling, bending to the flowers, greeting, moving on over the lawn. They were like bright birds that had alighted in the Sheridan's garden for this one afternoon, on their way to—where? Ah, what happiness it is to be with people who all are happy, to press hands, press cheeks, smile into eyes.

"Darling Laura, how well you look!"

"What a becoming hat, child!"

"Laura, you look quite Spanish. I've never seen you look so striking."

And Laura, glowing, answered softly, "Have you had tea? Won't you have an ice? The passion-fruit ices really are rather special." She ran to her father and begged him. "Daddy darling, can't the band have something to drink?"

And the perfect afternoon slowly ripened, slowly faded, slowly its petals closed.

"Never a more delightful garden-party . . ." "The greatest success . . ." "Quite the most . . ."

Laura helped her mother with the good-byes. They stood side by side in the porch till it was all over.

"All over, all over, thank heaven," said Mr. Sheridan. "Round up the others, Laura. Let's go and have some fresh coffee. I'm exhausted. Yes, it's been very successful. But oh, these parties, these parties! Why will you children insist on giving parties!" And they all of them sat down in the deserted marquee.

"Have a sandwich, daddy dear. I wrote the flag."

"Thanks." Mr. Sheridan took a bite and the sandwich was gone. He took another. "I suppose you didn't hear of a beastly accident that happened today?" he said.

"My dear," said Mrs. Sheridan, holding up her hand, "we did. It nearly ruined the party. Laura insisted we should put it off."

"Oh, mother!" Laura didn't want to be teased about it.

"It was a horrible affair all the same," said Mr. Sheridan. "The chap was married too. Lived just below in the lane, and leaves a wife and half a dozen kiddies, so they say."

An awkward little silence fell. Mrs. Sheridan fidgeted with her cup. Really, it was very tactless of father . . .

Suddenly she looked up. There on the table were all those sandwiches, cakes, puffs, all uneaten, all going to be wasted. She had one of her brilliant ideas.

"I know," she said. "Let's make up a basket. Let's send that poor creature some of this perfectly good food. At any rate, it will be the greatest treat for the children. Don't you agree? And she's sure to have neighbors calling in and so on. What a point to have it all ready prepared. Laura!" She jumped up. "Get me the big basket out of the stairs cupboard."

"But, mother, do you really think it's a good idea?" said Laura.

Again, how curious, she seemed to be different from them all. To take scraps from their party. Would the poor woman really like that?

"Of course! What's the matter with you today? An hour or two ago you were insisting on us being sympathetic, and now—"

Oh, well! Laura ran for the basket. It was filled, it was heaped by her mother.

"Take it yourself, darling," said she. "Run down just as you are. No, wait, take the arum lilies too. People of that class are so impressed by arum lilies."

"The stems will ruin her lace frock," said practical Jose.

So they would. Just in time. "Only the basket, then. And, Laura!"—her mother followed her out of the marquee—"don't on any account—"

"What, mother?"

No, better not put such ideas into the child's head! "Nothing! Run along."

It was just growing dusky as Laura shut their garden gates. A big dog ran by like a shadow. The road gleamed white, and down below in the hollow the little cottages were in deep shade. How quiet it seemed after the afternoon. Here she was going down the hill to somewhere where a man lay dead, and she couldn't realize it. Why couldn't she? She stopped a minute. And it seemed to her that kisses, voices, tinkling spoons, laughter, the smell of crushed grass were somehow inside her. She had no room for anything else. How strange! She looked up at the pale sky, and all she thought was, "Yes, it was the most successful party."

Now the broad road was crossed. The lane began, smoky and dark. Women in shawls and men's tweed caps hurried by. Men hung over the palings; the children played in the doorways. A low hum came from the mean little cottages. In some of them there was a flicker of light, and a shadow, crab-like, moved across the window. Laura bent her head and hurried on. She wished now she had put on a coat. How her frock shone! And the big hat with the velvet streamer—if only it was another hat! Were the people looking at her? They must be. It was a mistake to have come; she knew all along it was a mistake. Should she go back even now?

No, too late. This was the house. It must be. A dark knot of people stood outside. Beside the gate an old, old woman with a crutch sat in a chair, watching. She had her feet on a newspaper. The voices stopped as Laura drew near. The group parted. It was as though she was expected, as though they had known she was coming here.

Laura was terribly nervous. Tossing the velvet ribbon over her shoulder, she said to a woman standing by, "Is this Mrs. Scott's house?" and the woman, smiling queerly, said, "It is, my lass."

Oh, to be away from this! She actually said, "Help me, God," as she walked up the tiny path and knocked. To be away from those staring eyes, or to be covered up in anything, one of those women's shawls even. I'll just leave the basket and go, she decided. I shan't even wait for it to be emptied.

Then the door opened. A little woman in black showed in the gloom.

Laura said, "Are you Mrs. Scott?" But to her horror the woman answered, "Walk in please, miss," and she was shut in the passage.

"No," said Laura, "I don't want to come in. I only want to leave this basket. Mother sent—"

The little woman in the gloomy passage seemed not to have heard her. "Step this way, please, miss," she said in an oily voice, and Laura followed her.

She found herself in a wretched little low kitchen, lighted by a smoky lamp. There was a woman sitting before the fire.

"Em," said the little creature who had let her in. "Em! It's a young lady." She turned to Laura. She said meaningly, "I'm 'er sister, Miss. You'll excuse 'er, won't you?"

"Oh, but of course!" said Laura. "Please, please don't disturb her. I—I only want to leave—"

But at that moment the woman at the fire turned round. Her face, puffed up, red, with swollen eyes and swollen lips, looked terrible. She seemed as though she couldn't understand why Laura was there. What did it mean? Why was this stranger standing in the kitchen with a basket? What was it all about? And the poor face puckered up again.

"All right, my dear," said the other. "I'll thank the young lady."

And again she began, "You'll excuse her, miss, I'm sure," and her face, swollen too, tried an oily smile.

Laura only wanted to get out, to get away. She was back in the passage. The door opened. She walked straight through into the bedroom, where the dead man was lying.

"You'd like a look at 'im, wouldn't you?" said Em's sister, and she brushed past Laura over to the bed. "Don't be afraid, my lass—" and now her voice sounded fond and sly, and fondly she drew down the sheet—" 'e looks a picture. There's nothing to show. Come along, my dear."

Laura came.

There lay a young man, fast asleep—sleeping so soundly, so deeply, that he was far, far away from them both. Oh, so remote, so peaceful. He was dreaming. Never wake him up again. His head was sunk in the pillow, his eyes were closed; they were blind under the closed eyelids. He was given up to his dream. What did garden-parties and baskets and lace frocks matter to him? He was far from all those things. He was wonderful, beautiful. While they were laughing and while the band was playing, this marvel had come to the lane. Happy . . . happy. . . . All is well, said that sleeping face. This is just as it should be. I am content.

But all the same you had to cry, and she couldn't go out of the room without saying something to him. Laura gave a loud childish sob.

"Forgive my hat," she said.

And this time she didn't wait for Em's sister. She found her way out of the door, down the path, past all those dark people. At the corner of the lane she met Laurie.

He stepped out of the shadow. "Is that you, Laura?"

"Yes."

"Mother was getting anxious. Was it all right?"

"Yes, quite. Oh, Laurie!" She took his arm, she pressed up against him.

"I say, you're not crying, are you?" asked her brother.

Laura shook her head. She was.

Laurie put his arm round her shoulder. "Don't cry," he said in his warm, loving voice. "Was it awful?"

"No," sobbed Laura. "It was simply marvelous. But, Laurie—" She stopped, she looked at her brother. "Isn't life," she stammered, "isn't life—" But what life was she couldn't explain. No matter. He quite understood.

"Isn't it, darling?" said Laurie.

JAMES JOYCE

(1882–1941)

Eveline

About the Author: James Joyce, born in Dublin, left Ireland at twenty. Although he spent the rest of his life on the European continent, the city of his birth was always at the center of his fiction—*Dubliners* (1914), short stories, and the novels *Portrait of the Artist as a Young Man* (1916), *Ulysses* (1922), and *Finnegans Wake* (1939). Best known for his innovative fiction, Joyce also published poetry and *Exiles,* a play. He died in Zurich.

She sat at the window watching the evening invade the avenue. Her head was leaned against the window curtains and in her nostrils was the odour of dusty cretonne. She was tired.

Few people passed. The man out of the last house passed on his way home; she heard his footsteps clacking along the concrete pavement and afterwards crunching on the cinder path before the new red houses. One time there used to be a field there in which they used to play every evening with other people's children. Then a man from Belfast bought the field and built houses in it—not like their little brown houses but bright brick houses with shining roofs. The children of the avenue used to play together in that field—the Devines, the Waters, the Dunns, little Keogh the cripple, she and her brothers and sisters. Ernest, however, never played: he was too grown up. Her father used often to hunt them in out of the field with his blackthorn stick; but usually little Keogh used to keep *nix* and call out when he saw her father coming. Still they seemed to have been rather happy then. Her father was not so bad then; and besides, her mother was alive. That was a long time ago; she and her brothers and sisters were all grown up; her mother was dead. Tizzie Dunn was dead, too, and the Waters had gone back to England. Everything changes. Now she was going to go away like the others, to leave her home.

Home! She looked round the room, reviewing all its familiar objects which she had dusted once a week for so many years, wondering where on earth all the dust came from. Perhaps she would never see again those familiar objects from which she had never dreamed of being divided. And yet during all those years she had never found out the name of the priest whose yellowing photograph hung on the wall above the broken harmonium beside the coloured print of the promises made to Blessed Margaret Mary Alacoque. He had been a school friend of her father. Whenever he showed the photograph to a visitor her father used to pass it with a casual word:

—He is in Melbourne now.

She had consented to go away, to leave her home. Was that wise? She tried to weigh each side of the question. In her home anyway she had shelter and food; she had those whom she had known all her life about her. Of course she had to work hard both in the house and at business. What would they say of her in the Stores when they found out that she had run away with a fellow? Say she was a fool, perhaps; and her place would be filled up by advertisement. Miss Gavan would be glad. She had always had an edge on her, especially whenever there were people listening.

—Miss Hill, don't you see these ladies are waiting?

—Look lively, Miss Hill, please.

She would not cry many tears at leaving the Stores.

But in her new home, in a distant unknown country, it would not be like that. Then she would be married—she, Eveline. People would treat her with respect then. She would not be treated as her mother had been. Even now, though she was over nineteen, she sometimes felt herself in danger of her father's violence. She knew it was that that had given her the palpitations. When they were growing up he had never gone for her, like he used to go for Harry and Ernest, because she was a girl; but latterly he had begun to threaten her and say what he would do to her only for her dead mother's sake. And now she had nobody to protect her. Ernest was dead and Harry, who was in the church decorating business, was nearly always down somewhere in the country. Besides, the invariable squabble for money on Saturday nights had begun to weary her unspeakably. She always gave her entire wages—seven shillings—and Harry always sent up what he could but the trouble was to get any money from her father. He said she used to squander the money, that she

had no head, that he wasn't going to give her his hard-earned money to throw about the streets, and much more, for he was usually fairly bad of a Saturday night. In the end he would give her the money and ask her had she any intention of buying Sunday's dinner. Then she had to rush out as quickly as she could and do her marketing, holding her black leather purse tightly in her hand as she elbowed her way through the crowds and returning home late under her load of provisions. She had hard work to keep the house together and to see that the two young children who had been left to her charge went to school regularly and got their meals regularly. It was hard work—a hard life—but now that she was about to leave it she did not find it a wholly undesirable life.

She was about to explore another life with Frank. Frank was very kind, manly, open-hearted. She was to go away with him by the night-boat to be his wife and to live with him in Buenos Ayres where he had a home waiting for her. How well she remembered the first time she had seen him; he was lodging in a house on the main road where she used to visit. It seemed a few weeks ago. He was standing at the gate, his peaked cap pushed back on his head and his hair tumbled forward over a face of bronze. Then they had come to know each other. He used to meet her outside the Stores every evening and see her home. He took her to see *The Bohemian Girl* and she felt elated as she sat in an unaccustomed part of the theatre with him. He was awfully fond of music and sang a little. People knew that they were courting and, when he sang about the lass that loves a sailor, she always felt pleasantly confused. He used to call her Poppens out of fun. First of all it had been an excitement for her to have a fellow and then she had begun to like him. He had tales of distant countries. He had started as a deck boy at a pound a month on a ship of the Allan Line going out to Canada. He told her the names of the ships he had been on and the names of the different services. He had sailed through the Straits of Magellan and he told her stories of the terrible Patagonians. He had fallen on his feet in Buenos Ayres, he said, and had come over to the old country just for a holiday. Of course, her father had found out the affair and had forbidden her to have anything to say to him.

—I know these sailor chaps, he said.

One day he had quarrelled with Frank and after that she had to meet her lover secretly.

The evening deepened in the avenue. The white of two letters in her lap grew indistinct. One was to Harry; the other was to her father. Ernest had been her favourite but she liked Harry too. Her father was becoming old lately, she noticed; he would miss her. Sometimes he could be very nice. Not long before, when she had been laid up for a day, he had read her out a ghost story and made toast for her at the fire. Another day, when their mother was alive, they had all gone for a picnic to the Hill of Howth. She remembered her father putting on her mother's bonnet to make the children laugh.

Her time was running out but she continued to sit by the window, leaning her head against the window curtain, inhaling the odour of dusty cretonne. Down far in the avenue she could hear a street organ playing. She knew the air. Strange that it should come that very night to remind her of the promise to her mother, her promise to keep the home together as long as she could. She remembered the last night of her mother's illness; she was again in the close dark room at the other side of the hall and outside she heard a melancholy air of Italy. The organ-player had been ordered to go away and given sixpence. She remembered her father strutting back into the sickroom saying:

—Damned Italians! coming over here!

As she mused the pitiful vision of her mother's life laid its spell on the very quick of her being—that life of commonplace sacrifices closing in final craziness. She trembled as she heard again her mother's voice saying constantly with foolish insistence:

—Derevaun Seraun! Derevaun Seraun!

She stood up in a sudden impulse of terror. Escape! She must escape! Frank would save her. He would give her life, perhaps love, too. But she wanted to live. Why should she be unhappy? She had a right to happiness. Frank would take her in his arms, fold her in his arms. He would save her.

She stood among the swaying crowd in the station at the North Wall. He held her hand and she knew that he was speaking to her, saying something about the passage over and over again. The station was full of soldiers with brown baggages. Through the wide doors of the sheds she caught a glimpse of the black mass of the boat, lying in beside the quay wall, with illumined portholes. She answered nothing. She felt her cheek pale and cold and, out of a maze of distress, she prayed to God to direct her, to show her what was her duty. The boat blew a long mournful whistle into the mist. If she went, to-morrow she would be on the sea with Frank, steaming towards Buenos Ayres. Their passage had been booked. Could she still draw back after all he had done for her? Her distress awoke a nausea in her body and she kept moving her lips in silent fervent prayer.

A bell clanged upon her heart. She felt him seize her hand:

—Come!

All the seas of the world tumbled about her heart. He was drawing her into them: he would drown her. She gripped with both hands at the iron railing.

—Come!

No! No! No! It was impossible. Her hands clutched the iron in frenzy. Amid the seas she sent a cry of anguish!

—Eveline! Evvy!

He rushed beyond the barrier and called to her to follow. He was shouted at to go on but he still called to her. She set her white face to him, passive, like a helpless animal. Her eyes gave him no sign of love or farewell or recognition.

CHARLOTTE PERKINS GILMAN

(1860–1935)

The Yellow Wallpaper

About the Author: Charlotte Perkins Gilman was born in Hartford, Connecticut. During her lifetime she was known for such pioneering studies of women's role in society as *Women and Economics* (1898). Gilman's concern with both public and domestic issues affecting women is also reflected in her fiction, first collected only after her death in *The Charlotte Perkins Gilman Reader* (1979).

It is very seldom that mere ordinary people like John and myself secure ancestral halls for the summer.

A colonial mansion, a hereditary estate, I would say a haunted house and reach the height of romantic felicity—but that would be asking too much of fate!

Still I will proudly declare that there is something queer about it.

Else, why should it be let so cheaply? And why have stood so long untenanted?

John laughs at me, of course, but one expects that.

John is practical in the extreme. He has no patience with faith, an intense horror of superstition, and he scoffs openly at any talk of things not to be felt and seen and put down in figures.

John is a physician, and *perhaps*—(I would not say it to a living soul, of course, but this is dead paper and a great relief to my mind)—*perhaps* that is one reason I do not get well faster.

You see, he does not believe I am sick! And what can one do?

If a physician of high standing, and one's own husband, assures friends and relatives that there is really nothing the matter with one but temporary nervous depression—a slight hysterical tendency—what is one to do?

My brother is also a physician, and also of high standing, and he says the same thing.

So I take phosphates or phosphites—whichever it is—and tonics, and air and exercise, and journeys, and am absolutely forbidden to "work" until I am well again.

Personally, I disagree with their ideas.

Personally, I believe that congenial work, with excitement and change, would do me good.

But what is one to do?

I did write for a while in spite of them; but it *does* exhaust me a good deal—having to be so sly about it, or else meet with heavy opposition.

I sometimes fancy that in my condition, if I had less opposition and more society and stimulus—but John says the very worst thing I can do is to think about my condition, and I confess it always makes me feel bad.

So I will let it alone and talk about the house.

The most beautiful place! It is quite alone, standing well back from the road, quite three miles from the village. It makes me think of English places that you read about, for there are hedges and walls and gates that lock, and lots of separate little houses for the gardeners and people.

There is a *delicious* garden! I never saw such a garden—large and shady, full of box-bordered paths, and lined with long grape-covered arbors with seats under them.

There were greenhouses, but they are all broken now.

There was some legal trouble, I believe, something about the heirs and co-heirs; anyhow, the place has been empty for years.

That spoils my ghostliness, I am afraid, but I don't care—there is something strange about the house—I can feel it.

I even said so to John one moonlight evening, but he said what I felt was a draught, and shut the window.

I get unreasonably angry with John sometimes. I'm sure I never used to be so sensitive. I think it is due to this nervous condition.

But John says if I feel so I shall neglect proper self-control; so I take pains to control myself—before him, at least, and that makes me very tired.

I don't like our room a bit. I wanted one downstairs that opened onto the piazza and had roses all over the window, and such pretty old-fashioned chintz hangings! But John would not hear of it.

He said there was only one window and not room for two beds, and no near room for him if he took another.

He is very careful and loving, and hardly lets me stir without special direction.

I have a schedule prescription for each hour in the day; he takes all care from me, and so I feel basely ungrateful not to value it more.

He said he came here solely on my account, that I was to have perfect rest and all the air I could get. "Your exercise depends on your strength, my dear," said he, "and your food somewhat on your appetite; but air you can absorb all the time." So we took the nursery at the top of the house.

It is a big, airy room, the whole floor nearly, with windows that look all ways, and air and sunshine galore. It was nursery first, and then playroom and gymnasium, I should judge, for the windows are barred for little children, and there are rings and things in the walls.

The paint and paper look as if a boys' school had used it. It is stripped off—the paper—in great patches all around the head of my bed, about as far as I can reach, and in a great place on the other side of the room low down. I never saw a worse paper in my life. One of those sprawling, flamboyant patterns committing every artistic sin.

It is dull enough to confuse the eye in following, pronounced enough constantly to irritate and provoke study, and when you follow the lame uncertain curves for a little distance they suddenly commit suicide—plunge off at outrageous angles, destroy themselves in unheard-of contradictions.

The color is repellent, almost revolting: a smouldering unclean yellow, strangely faded by the slow-turning sunlight. It is a dull yet lurid orange in some places, a sickly sulphur tint in others.

No wonder the children hated it! I should hate it myself if I had to live in this room long.

There comes John, and I must put this away—he hates to have me write a word.

We have been here two weeks, and I haven't felt like writing before, since that first day.

I am sitting by the window now, up in this atrocious nursery, and there is nothing to hinder my writing as much as I please, save lack of strength.

John is away all day, and even some nights when his cases are serious.

I am glad my case is not serious!

But these nervous troubles are dreadfully depressing.

John does not know how much I really suffer. He knows there is no reason to suffer, and that satisfies him.

Of course it is only nervousness. It does weigh on me so not to do my duty in any way!

I meant to be such a help to John, such a real rest and comfort, and here I am a comparative burden already!

Nobody would believe what an effort it is to do what little I am able—to dress and entertain, and order things.

It is fortunate Mary is so good with the baby. Such a dear baby!

And yet I *cannot* be with him, it makes me so nervous.

I suppose John never was nervous in his life. He laughs at me so about this wallpaper!

At first he meant to repaper the room, but afterward he said that I was letting it get the better of me, and that nothing was worse for a nervous patient than to give way to such fancies.

He said that after the wallpaper was changed it would be the heavy bedstead, and then the barred windows, and then that gate at the head of the stairs, and so on.

"You know the place is doing you good," he said, "and really, dear, I don't care to renovate the house just for a three months' rental."

"Then do let us go downstairs," I said. "There are such pretty rooms there."

Then he took me in his arms and called me a blessed little goose, and said he would go down cellar, if I wished, and have it whitewashed into the bargain.

But he is right enough about the beds and windows and things.

It is as airy and comfortable a room as anyone need wish, and, of course, I would not be so silly as to make him uncomfortable just for a whim.

I'm really getting quite fond of the big room, all but that horrid paper.

Out of one window I can see the garden—those mysterious deep-shaded arbors, the riotous old-fashioned flowers, and bushes and gnarly trees.

Out of another I get a lovely view of the bay and a little private wharf belonging to the estate. There is a beautiful shaded lane that runs down there from the house. I always fancy I see people walking in these numerous paths and arbors, but John has cautioned me not to give way to fancy in the least. He says that with my imaginative power and habit of story-making, a nervous weakness like mine is sure to lead to all manner of excited fancies, and that I ought to use my will and good sense to check the tendency. So I try.

I think sometimes that if I were only well enough to write a little it would relieve the press of ideas and rest me.

But I find I get pretty tired when I try.

It is so discouraging not to have any advice and companionship about my work. When I get really well, John says we will ask Cousin Henry and Julia down for a long visit; but he says he would as soon put fireworks in my pillow-case as to let me have those stimulating people about now.

I wish I could get well faster.

But I must not think about that. This paper looks to me as if it *knew* what a vicious influence it had!

There is a recurrent spot where the pattern lolls like a broken neck and two bulbous eyes stare at you upside down.

I get positively angry with the impertinence of it and the everlastingness. Up and down and sideways they crawl, and those absurd unblinking eyes are everywhere. There is one place where two breadths didn't match, and the eyes go all up and down the line, one a little higher than the other.

I never saw so much expression in an inanimate thing before, and we all know how much expression they have! I used to lie awake as a child and get more entertainment and terror out of blank walls and plain furniture than most children could find in a toy-store.

I remember what a kindly wink the knobs of our big old bureau used to have, and there was one chair that always seemed like a strong friend.

I used to feel that if any of the other things looked too fierce I could always hop into that chair and be safe.

The furniture in this room is no worse than inharmonious, however, for we had to bring it all from downstairs. I suppose when this was used as a playroom they had to take the nursery things out, and no wonder! I never saw such ravages as the children have made here.

The wallpaper, as I said before, is torn off in spots, and it sticketh closer than a brother—they must have had perseverance as well as hatred.

Then the floor is scratched and gouged and splintered, the plaster itself is dug out here and there, and this great heavy bed, which is all we found in the room, looks as if it had been through the wars.

But I don't mind it a bit—only the paper.

There comes John's sister. Such a dear girl as she is, and so careful of me! I must not let her find me writing.

She is a perfect and enthusiastic housekeeper, and hopes for no better profession. I verily believe she thinks it is the writing which made me sick!

But I can write when she is out, and see her a long way off from these windows.

There is one that commands the road, a lovely shaded winding road, and one that just looks off over the country. A lovely country, too, full of great elms and velvet meadows.

This wallpaper has a kind of sub-pattern in a different shade, a particularly irritating one, for you can only see it in certain lights, and not clearly then.

But in the places where it isn't faded and where the sun is just so—I can see a strange, provoking, formless sort of figure that seems to skulk about behind that silly and conspicuous front design.

There's sister on the stairs!

Well, the Fourth of July is over! The people are all gone, and I am tired out. John thought it might do me good to see a little company, so we just had Mother and Nellie and the children down for a week.

Of course I didn't do a thing. Jennie sees to everything now.

But it tired me all the same.

John says if I don't pick up faster he shall send me to Weir Mitchell in the fall.

But I don't want to go there at all. I had a friend who was in his hands once, and she says he is just like John and my brother, only more so!

Besides, it is such an undertaking to go so far.

I don't feel as if it was worthwhile to turn my hand over for anything, and I'm getting dreadfully fretful and querulous.

I cry at nothing, and cry most of the time.

Of course I don't when John is here, or anybody else, but when I am alone.

And I am alone a good deal just now. John is kept in town very often by serious cases, and Jennie is good and lets me alone when I want her to.

So I walk a little in the garden or down that lovely lane, sit on the porch under the roses, and lie down up here a good deal.

I'm getting really fond of the room in spite of the wallpaper. Perhaps *because* of the wallpaper.

It dwells in my mind so!

I lie here on this great immovable bed—it is nailed down, I believe—and follow that pattern about by the hour. It is as good as gymnastics, I assure you. I start, we'll say, at the bottom, down in the corner over there where it has not been touched, and I determine for the thousandth time that I *will* follow that pointless pattern to some sort of a conclusion.

I know a little of the principle of design, and I know this thing was not arranged on any laws of radiation, or alternation, or repetition, or symmetry, or anything else that I ever heard of.

It is repeated, of course, by the breadths, but not otherwise.

Looked at in one way, each breadth stands alone; the bloated curves and flourishes—a kind of "debased Romanesque" with delirium tremens go waddling up and down in isolated columns of fatuity.

But, on the other hand, they connect diagonally, and the sprawling outlines run off in great slanting waves of optic horror, like a lot of wallowing sea-weeds in full chase.

The whole thing goes horizontally, too, at least it seems so, and I exhaust myself trying to distinguish the order of its going in that direction.

They have used a horizontal breadth for a frieze, and that adds wonderfully to the confusion.

There is one end of the room where it is almost intact, and there, when the crosslights fade and the low sun shines directly upon it, I can almost fancy radiation after all—the interminable grotesque seems to form around a common center and rush off in headlong plunges of equal distraction.

It makes me tired to follow it. I will take a nap, I guess.

I don't know why I should write this.

I don't want to.

I don't feel able.

And I know John would think it absurd. But I *must* say what I feel and think in some way—it is such a relief!

But the effort is getting to be greater than the relief.

Half the time now I am awfully lazy, and lie down ever so much. John says I mustn't lose my strength, and has me take cod liver oil and lots of tonics and things, to say nothing of ale and wine and rare meat.

Dear John! He loves me very dearly, and hates to have me sick. I tried to have a real earnest reasonable talk with him the other day, and tell him how I wish he would let me go and make a visit to Cousin Henry and Julia.

But he said I wasn't able to go, nor able to stand it after I got there; and I did not make out a very good case for myself, for I was crying before I had finished.

It is getting to be a great effort for me to think straight. Just this nervous weakness, I suppose.

And dear John gathered me up in his arms, and just carried me upstairs and laid me on the bed, and sat by me and read to me till it tired my head.

He said I was his darling and his comfort and all he had, and that I must take care of myself for his sake, and keep well.

He says no one but myself can help me out of it, that I must use my will and self-control and not let any silly fancies run away with me.

There's one comfort—the baby is well and happy, and does not have to occupy this nursery with the horrid wallpaper.

If we had not used it, that blessed child would have! What a fortunate escape! Why, I wouldn't have a child of mine, an impressionable little thing, live in such a room for worlds.

I never thought of it before, but it is lucky that John kept me here after all; I can stand it so much easier than a baby, you see.

Of course I never mention it to them any more—I am too wise—but I keep watch for it all the same.

There are things in that wallpaper that nobody knows about but me, or ever will.

Behind that outside pattern the dim shapes get clearer every day.

It is always the same shape, only very numerous.

And it is like a woman stooping down and creeping about behind that pattern. I don't like it a bit. I wonder—I begin to think—I wish John would take me away from here!

It is so hard to talk with John about my case, because he is so wise, and because he loves me so.

But I tried it last night.

It was moonlight. The moon shines in all around just as the sun does.

I hate to see it sometimes, it creeps so slowly, and always comes in by one window or another.

John was asleep and I hated to waken him, so I kept still and watched the moonlight on that undulating wallpaper till I felt creepy.

The faint figure behind seemed to shake the pattern, just as if she wanted to get out.

I got up softly and went to feel and see if the paper *did* move, and when I came back John was awake.

"What is it, little girl?" he said. "Don't go walking about like that—you'll get cold."

I thought it was a good time to talk, so I told him that I really was not gaining here, and that I wished he would take me away.

"Why, darling!" said he. "Our lease will be up in three weeks, and I can't see how to leave before.

"The repairs are not done at home, and I cannot possibly leave town just now. Of course, if you were in any danger, I could and would, but you really are better, dear, whether you can see it or not. I am a doctor, dear, and I know. You are gaining flesh and color, your appetite is better, I feel really much easier about you."

"I don't weigh a bit more," said I, "nor as much; and my appetite may be better in the evening when you are here but it is worse in the morning when you are away!"

"Bless her little heart!" said he with a big hug. "She shall be as sick as she pleases! But now let's improve the shining hours by going to sleep, and talk about it in the morning!"

"And you won't go away?" I asked gloomily.

"Why, how can I, dear? It is only three weeks more and then we will take a nice little trip of a few days while Jennie is getting the house ready. Really, dear, you are better!"

"Better in body perhaps—" I began, and stopped short, for he sat up straight and looked at me with such a stern, reproachful look that I could not say another word.

"My darling," said he, "I beg of you, for my sake and for our child's sake, as well as for your own, that you will never for one instant let that idea enter your mind! There is nothing so dangerous, so fascinating, to a temperament like yours. It is a false and foolish fancy. Can you not trust me as a physician when I tell you so?"

So of course I said no more on that score, and we went to sleep before long. He thought I was asleep first, but I wasn't, and lay there for hours trying to decide whether that front pattern and the back pattern really did move together or separately.

On a pattern like this, by daylight, there is a lack of sequence, a defiance of law, that is a constant irritant to a normal mind.

The color is hideous enough, and unreliable enough, and infuriating enough, but the pattern is torturing.

You think you have mastered it, but just as you get well under way in following, it turns a back-somersault and there you are. It slaps you in the face, knocks you down, and tramples upon you. It is like a bad dream.

The outside pattern is a florid arabesque, reminding one of a fungus. If you can imagine a toadstool in joints, an interminable string of toadstools, budding and sprouting in endless convolutions—why, that is something like it.

That is, sometimes!

There is one marked peculiarity about this paper, a thing nobody seems to notice but myself, and that is that it changes as the light changes.

When the sun shoots in through the east window—I always watch for that first long, straight ray—it changes so quickly that I never can quite believe it.

That is why I watch it always.

By moonlight—the moon shines in all night when there is a moon—I wouldn't know it was the same paper.

At night in any kind of light, in twilight, candlelight, lamplight, and worst of all by moonlight, it becomes bars! The outside pattern, I mean, and the woman behind it is as plain as can be.

I didn't realize for a long time what the thing was that showed behind, that dim sub-pattern, but now I am quite sure it is a woman.

By daylight she is subdued, quiet. I fancy it is the pattern that keeps her so still. It is so puzzling. It keeps me quiet by the hour.

I lie down ever so much now. John says it is good for me, and to sleep all I can.

Indeed he started the habit by making me lie down for an hour after each meal.

It is a very bad habit, I am convinced, for you see, I don't sleep.

And that cultivates deceit, for I don't tell them I'm awake—oh, no!

The fact is I am getting a little afraid of John.

He seems very queer sometimes, and even Jennie has an inexplicable look.

It strikes me occasionally, just as a scientific hypothesis, that perhaps it is the paper!

I have watched John when he did not know I was looking, and come into the room suddenly on the most innocent excuses, and I've caught him several times *looking at the paper!* And Jennie too. I caught Jennie with her hand on it once.

She didn't know I was in the room, and when I asked her in a quiet, a very quiet voice, with the most restrained manner possible, what she was doing with the paper, she turned around as if she had been caught stealing, and looked quite angry—asked me why I should frighten her so!

Then she said that the paper stained everything it touched, that she had found yellow smooches on all my clothes and John's and she wished we would be more careful!

Did not that sound innocent? But I know she was studying that pattern, and I am determined that nobody shall find it out but myself!

Life is very much more exciting now than it used to be. You see, I have something more to expect, to look forward to, to watch. I really do eat better, and am more quiet than I was.

John is so pleased to see me improve! He laughed a little the other day, and said I seemed to be flourishing in spite of my wallpaper.

I turned it off with a laugh. I had no intention of telling him it was *because* of the wallpaper—he would make fun of me. He might even want to take me away.

I don't want to leave now until I have found it out. There is a week more, and I think that will be enough.

I'm feeling so much better!

I don't sleep much at night, for it is so interesting to watch developments; but I sleep a good deal during the day time.

In the daytime it is tiresome and perplexing.

There are always new shoots on the fungus, and new shades of yellow all over it. I cannot keep count of them, though I have tried conscientiously.

It is the strangest yellow, that wallpaper! It makes me think of all the yellow things I ever saw—not beautiful ones like buttercups, but old, foul, bad yellow things.

But there is something else about the paper—the smell! I noticed it the moment we came into the room, but with so much air and sun it was not bad. Now we have had a week of fog and rain, and whether the windows are open or not, the smell is here.

It creeps all over the house.

I find it hovering in the dining-room, skulking in the parlor, hiding in the hall, lying in wait for me on the stairs.

It gets into my hair.

Even when I go to ride, if I turn my head suddenly and surprise it—there is that smell!

Such a peculiar odor, too! I have spent hours in trying to analyze it, to find what it smelled like.

It is not bad—at first—and very gentle, but quite the subtlest, most enduring odor I ever met.

In this damp weather it is awful. I wake up in the night and find it hanging over me.

It used to disturb me at first. I thought seriously of burning the house—to reach the smell.

But now I am used to it. The only thing I can think of that it is like is the *color* of the paper! A yellow smell.

There is a very funny mark on this wall, low down, near the mopboard. A streak that runs round the room. It goes behind every piece of furniture, except the bed, a long, straight, even *smooch,* as if it had been rubbed over and over.

I wonder how it was done and who did it, and what they did it for. Round and round and round—round and round and round—it makes me dizzy!

I really have discovered something at last.

Through watching so much at night, when it changes so, I have finally found out.

The front pattern *does* move—and no wonder! The woman behind shakes it!

Sometimes I think there are a great many women behind, and sometimes only one, and she crawls around fast, and her crawling shakes it all over.

Then in the very bright spots she keeps still, and in the very shady spots she just takes hold of the bars and shakes them hard.

And she is all the time trying to climb through. But nobody could climb through that pattern—it strangles so; I think that is why it has so many heads.

They get through and then the pattern strangles them off and turns them upside down, and makes their eyes white!

If those heads were covered or taken off it would not be half so bad.

I think that woman gets out in the daytime!

And I'll tell you why—privately—I've seen her!

I can see her out of every one of my windows!

It is the same woman, I know, for she is always creeping, and most women do not creep by daylight.

I see her in that long shaded lane, creeping up and down. I see her in those dark grape arbors, creeping all around the garden.

I see her on that long road under the trees, creeping along, and when a carriage comes she hides under the blackberry vines.

I don't blame her a bit. It must be very humiliating to be caught creeping by daylight!

I always lock the door when I creep by daylight. I can't do it at night, for I know John would suspect something at once.

And John is so queer now that I don't want to irritate him. I wish he would take another room! Besides, I don't want anybody to get that woman out at night but myself.

I often wonder if I could see her out of all the windows at once.

But, turn as fast as I can, I can only see out of one at one time.

And though I always see her, she *may* be able to creep faster than I can turn! I have watched her sometimes away off in the open country, creeping as fast as a cloud shadow in a wind.

If only that top pattern could be gotten off from the under one! I mean to try it, little by little.

I have found out another funny thing, but I shan't tell it this time! It does not do to trust people too much.

There are only two more days to get this paper off, and I believe John is beginning to notice. I don't like the look in his eyes.

And I heard him ask Jennie a lot of professional questions about me. She had a very good report to give.

She said I slept a good deal in the daytime.

John knows I don't sleep very well at night, for all I'm so quiet!

He asked me all sorts of questions, too, and pretended to be very loving and kind.

As if I couldn't see through him!

Still, I don't wonder he acts so, sleeping under this paper for three months.

It only interests me, but I feel sure John and Jennie are affected by it.

Hurrah! This is the last day, but it is enough. John is to stay in town over night, and won't be out until this evening.

Jennie wanted to sleep with me—the sly thing; but I told her I should undoubtedly rest better for a night all alone.

That was clever, for really I wasn't alone a bit! As soon as it was moonlight and that poor thing began to crawl and shake the pattern, I got up and ran to help her.

I pulled and she shook. I shook and she pulled, and before morning we had peeled off yards of that paper.

A strip about as high as my head and half around the room.

And then when the sun came and that awful pattern began to laugh at me, I declared I would finish it today!

We go away tomorrow, and they are moving all my furniture down again to leave things as they were before.

Jennie looked at the wall in amazement, but I told her merrily that I did it out of pure spite at the vicious thing.

She laughed and said she wouldn't mind doing it herself, but I must not get tired.

How she betrayed herself that time!

But I am here, and no person touches this paper but Me—not *alive!*

She tried to get me out of the room—it was too patent! But I said it was so quiet and empty and clean now that I believed I would lie down again and sleep all I could, and not to wake me even for dinner—I would call when I woke.

So now she is gone, and the servants are gone, and the things are gone, and there is nothing left but that great bedstead nailed down, with the canvas mattress we found on it.

We shall sleep downstairs tonight, and take the boat home tomorrow.

I quite enjoy the room, now it is bare again.

How those children did tear about here!

This bedstead is fairly gnawed!

But I must get to work.

I have locked the door and thrown the key down into the front path.

I don't want to go out, and I don't want to have anybody come in, till John comes.

I want to astonish him.

I've got a rope up here that even Jennie did not find. If that woman does get out, and tries to get away, I can tie her!

But I forgot I could not reach far without anything to stand on!

This bed will *not* move!

I tried to lift and push it until I was lame, and then I got so angry I bit off a little piece at one corner—but it hurt my teeth.

Then I peeled off all the paper I could reach standing on the floor. It sticks horribly and the pattern just enjoys it! All those strangled heads and bulbous eyes and waddling fungus growths just shriek with derision!

I am getting angry enough to do something desperate. To jump out of the window would be admirable exercise, but the bars are too strong even to try.

Besides I wouldn't do it. Of course not. I know well enough that a step like that is improper and might be misconstrued.

I don't like to *look* out of the windows even—there are so many of those creeping women, and they creep so fast.

I wonder if they all come out of that wallpaper as I did?

But I am securely fastened now by my well-hidden rope—you don't get *me* out in the road there!

I suppose I shall have to get back behind the pattern when it comes night, and that is hard!

It is so pleasant to be out in this great room and creep around as I please!

I don't want to go outside. I won't, even if Jennie asks me to.

For outside you have to creep on the ground, and everything is green instead of yellow.

But here I can creep smoothly on the floor, and my shoulder just fits in that long smooch around the wall, so I cannot lose my way.

Why, there's John at the door!

It is no use, young man, you can't open it!

How he does call and pound!

Now he's crying to Jennie for an axe.

It would be a shame to break down that beautiful door!

"John, dear!" said I in the gentlest voice. "The key is down by the front steps, under a plantain leaf!"

That silenced him for a few moments.

Then he said, very quickly indeed, "Open the door, my darling!"

"I can't," said I. "The key is down by the front door under a plantain leaf!" And then I said it again, several times, very gently and slowly, and said it so often that he had to go and see, and he got it of course, and came in. He stopped short by the door.

"What is the matter?" he cried. "For God's sake, what are you doing!"

I kept on creeping just the same, but I looked at him over my shoulder.

"I've got out at last," said I, "in spite of you and Jane. And I've pulled off most of the paper, so you can't put me back!"

Now why should that man have fainted? But he did, and right across my path by the wall, so that I had to creep over him every time!

AMBROSE BIERCE

(1842–1914?)

An Occurrence at Owl Creek Bridge

About the Author: Ambrose Bierce fought through the Civil War, attaining the rank of major in the Union Army. Although his collected works run to twelve volumes, it is his stories of the war, which feature disillusion, disgust, and defeat, that sustain his present-day reputation. In 1913, Bierce disappeared in Mexico.

I

A man stood upon a railroad bridge in Northern Alabama, looking down into the swift waters twenty feet below. The man's hands were behind his back, the wrists bound with a cord. A rope loosely encircled his neck. It was attached to a stout cross-timber above his head, and the slack fell to the level of his knees. Some loose boards laid upon the sleepers supporting the metals of the railway supplied a footing for him and his executioners—two private soldiers of the Federal army, directed by a sergeant, who in civil life may have been a deputy sheriff. At a short remove upon the same temporary platform was an officer in the uniform of his rank, armed. He was a captain. A sentinel at each end of the bridge stood with his rifle in the position known as 'support,' that is to say, vertical in front of the left shoulder, the hammer resting on the forearm thrown straight across the chest—a formal and unnatural position, enforcing an erect carriage of the body. It did not appear to be the duty of these two men to know what was occurring at the centre of the bridge; they merely blockaded the two ends of the foot plank which traversed it.

Beyond one of the sentinels nobody was in sight; the railroad ran straight away into a forest for a hundred yards, then, curving, was lost to view. Doubtless there was an outpost further along. The other bank of the stream was open ground—a gentle acclivity crowned with a stockade of vertical tree trunks, loop-holed for rifles, with a single embrasure through which protruded the muzzle of a brass cannon commanding the bridge. Midway of the slope between bridge and fort were the spectators—a single company of infantry in line, at 'parade rest,' the butts of the rifles on the ground, the barrels inclining slightly backward against the right shoulder, the hands crossed upon the stock. A lieutenant stood at the right of the line, the point of his sword upon the ground, his left hand resting upon his right. Excepting the group of four at the centre of the bridge not a man moved. The company faced the bridge, staring stonily, motionless. The sentinels, facing the banks of the stream, might have been statues to adorn the bridge. The captain stood with folded arms, silent, observing the work of his subordinates but making no sign. Death is a dignitary who, when he comes announced, is to be received with formal manifestations of respect, even by those most familiar with him. In the code of military etiquette silence and fixity are forms of deference.

The man who was engaged in being hanged was apparently about thirty-five years of age. He was a civilian, if one might judge from his dress, which was that of a planter. His features were good—a straight nose, firm mouth, broad forehead, from which his long, dark hair was combed straight back, falling behind his ears to the collar of his well-fitting frock coat. He wore a moustache and pointed beard, but no whiskers; his eyes were large and dark grey and had a kindly expression which one would hardly have expected in one whose neck was in the hemp. Evidently this was no vulgar assassin. The liberal military code makes provision for hanging many kinds of people, and gentlemen are not excluded.

The preparations being complete, the two private soldiers stepped aside and each drew away the plank upon which he had been standing. The sergeant turned to the captain, saluted and placed himself immediately behind that officer, who in turn moved apart one pace. These movements left the condemned man and the sergeant standing on the two ends of the same plank, which spanned three of the cross-ties of the bridge. The end upon which the civilian stood almost, but not quite, reached a fourth. This plank had been held in place by the weight of the captain; it was now held by that of the sergeant. At a signal from the former, the latter would step aside, the plank would tilt and the condemned man go down between two ties. The arrangement commended itself to his judgment as simple and effective. His face had not been covered nor his eyes bandaged. He looked a moment at his 'unsteadfast footing,' then let his gaze wander to the swirling water of the stream racing madly beneath his feet. A piece of dancing driftwood caught his attention and his eyes followed it down the current. How slowly it appeared to move! What a sluggish stream!

He closed his eyes in order to fix his last thoughts upon his wife and children. The water, touched to gold by the early sun, the brooding mists under the banks at some distance down the stream, the fort, the soldiers, the piece of drift—all had distracted him. And now he became conscious of a new disturbance. Striking through the thought of his dear ones was a sound which he could neither ignore nor understand, a sharp, distinct, metallic percussion like the stroke of a blacksmith's hammer upon the anvil; it had the same ringing quality. He wondered what it was, and whether immeasurably distant or near by—it seemed both. Its recurrence was regular, but as slow as the tolling of a death knell. He awaited each stroke with impatience and—he knew not why—apprehension. The intervals of silence grew progressively longer; the delays became maddening. With their greater infrequency the sounds increased in strength and sharpness. They hurt his ear like the thrust of a knife; he feared he would shriek. What he heard was the ticking of his watch.

He unclosed his eyes and saw again the water below him. 'If I could free my hands,' he thought, 'I might throw off the noose and spring into the stream. By diving I could evade the bullets, and, swimming vigorously, reach the bank, take to the woods, and get away home. My home, thank God, is as yet outside their lines; my wife and little ones are still beyond the invader's farthest advance.'

As these thoughts, which have here to be set down in words, were flashed into the doomed man's brain rather than evolved from it, the captain nodded to the sergeant. The sergeant stepped aside.

II

Peyton Farquhar was a well-to-do planter, of an old and highly-respected Alabama family. Being a slave owner, and, like other slave owners, a politician, he was naturally an original secessionist and ardently devoted to the Southern cause. Circumstances of an imperious nature which it is unnecessary to relate here, had prevented him from taking service with the gallant army which had fought the disastrous campaigns ending with the fall of Corinth, and he chafed under the inglorious restraint, longing for the release of his energies, the larger life of the soldier, the opportunity for distinction. That opportunity, he felt, would come, as it comes to all in war time. Meanwhile he did what he could. No service was too humble for him to perform in aid of the South, no adventure too perilous for him to undertake if consistent with the character of a civilian who was at heart a soldier, and who in good faith and without too much qualification assented to at least a part of the frankly villainous dictum that all is fair in love and war.

One evening while Farquhar and his wife were sitting on a rustic bench near the entrance to his grounds, a grey-clad soldier rode up to the gate and asked for a drink of water. Mrs. Farquhar was only too happy to serve him with her own white hands. While she was gone to fetch the water, her husband approached the dusty horseman and inquired eagerly for news from the front.

'The Yanks are repairing the railroads,' said the man, 'and are getting ready for another advance. They have reached the Owl Creek bridge, put it in order, and built a stockade on the other bank. The commandant has issued an order, which is posted everywhere, declaring that any civilian caught interfering with the railroad, its bridges, tunnels, or trains, will be summarily hanged. I saw the order.'

'How far is it to the Owl Creek bridge?' Farquhar asked.

'About thirty miles.'

'Is there no force on this side the creek?'

'Only a picket post half a mile out, on the railroad, and a single sentinel at this end of the bridge.'

'Suppose a man—a civilian and student of hanging—should elude the picket post and perhaps get the better of the sentinel,' said Farquhar, smiling, "what could he accomplish?'

The soldier reflected. 'I was there a month ago,' he replied. 'I observed that the flood of last winter had lodged a great quantity of driftwood against the wooden pier at this end of the bridge. It is now dry and would burn like tow.'

The lady had now brought the water, which the soldier drank. He thanked her ceremoniously, bowed to her husband, and rode away. An hour later, after nightfall, he repassed the plantation, going northward in the direction from which he had come. He was a Federal scout.

III

As Peyton Farquhar fell straight downward through the bridge, he lost consciousness and was as one already dead. From this state he was awakened—ages later, it seemed to him—by the pain of a sharp pressure upon his throat, followed by a sense of suffocation. Keen, poignant agonies seemed to shoot from his neck downward through every fibre of his body and limbs. These pains appeared to flash along well-defined lines of ramification, and to beat with an inconceivably rapid periodicity. They seemed like streams of pulsating fire heating him to an intolerable temperature. As to his head, he was conscious of nothing but a feeling of fullness—of congestion. These sensations were unaccompanied by thought. The intellectual part of his nature was already effaced; he had power only to feel, and feeling was torment. He was conscious of motion. Encompassed in a luminous cloud, of which he was now merely the fiery heart, without material substance, he swung through unthinkable arcs of oscillation, like a vast pendulum. Then all at once, with terrible suddenness, the light about him shot upward with the noise of a loud plash; a frightful roaring was in his ears, and all was cold and dark. The power of thought was restored; he knew that the rope had broken and he had fallen into the stream. There was no additional strangulation; the noose about his neck was already suffocating him, and kept the water from his lungs. To die of hanging at the bottom of a river!—the idea seemed to him ludicrous. He opened his eyes in the blackness and saw above him a gleam of light, but how distant, how inaccessible! He was still sinking, for the light became fainter and fainter until it was a mere glimmer. Then it began to grow and brighten, and he knew that he was rising toward the surface—knew it with reluctance, for he was now very comfortable. 'To be hanged and drowned,' he thought, 'that is not so bad; but I do not wish to be shot. No; I will not be shot; that is not fair.'

He was not conscious of an effort, but a sharp pain in his wrist apprised him that he was trying to free his hands. He gave the struggle his attention, as an idler might observe the feat of a juggler, without interest in the outcome. What splendid effort!—what magnificent, what superhuman strength! Ah, that was a fine endeavour! Bravo! The cord fell away; his arms parted and floated upward, the hands dimly seen on each side in the growing light. He watched them with a new interest as first one and then the other pounced upon the noose at his neck. They tore it away and thrust it fiercely aside, its undulations resembling those of a water-snake. 'Put it back, put it back!' He thought he shouted these words to his hands, for the undoing of the noose had been succeeded by the direst pang which he had yet experienced. His neck ached horribly; his brain was on fire; his heart, which had been fluttering faintly, gave a great leap, trying to force itself out at his mouth. His whole body was racked and wrenched with an insupportable anguish! But his disobedient hands gave no heed to the command. They beat the water vigorously with quick, downward strokes, forcing him to the surface. He felt his head emerge; his eyes were blinded by the sunlight; his chest expanded convulsively, and with a supreme and crowning agony his lungs engulfed a great draught of air, which instantly he expelled in a shriek!

He was now in full possession of his physical senses. They were, indeed, preternaturally keen and alert. Something in the awful disturbance of his organic system had so exalted and refined them that they made record of things never before perceived. He felt the ripples upon his face and heard their separate sounds as they struck. He looked at the forest on the bank of the stream, saw the individual trees, the leaves and the veining of each leaf—saw the very insects upon them, the locusts, the brilliant-bodied flies, the grey spiders stretching their webs from twig to twig. He noted the prismatic colors in all the dewdrops upon a million blades of grass. The humming of the gnats that danced above the eddies of the stream, the beating of the dragon flies' wings, the strokes of the water spiders' legs, like oars which had lifted their boat—all these made audible music. A fish slid along beneath his eyes and he heard the rush of its body parting the water.

He had come to the surface facing down the stream; in a moment the visible world seemed to wheel slowly round, himself the pivotal point, and he saw the bridge, the fort, the soldiers upon the bridge, the captain, the sergeant, the two privates, his executioners. They were in silhouette against the blue sky. They shouted and gesticulated, pointing at him; the captain had drawn his pistol, but did not fire; the others were unarmed. Their movements were grotesque and horrible, their forms gigantic.

Suddenly he heard a sharp report and something struck the water smartly within a few inches of his head, spattering his face with spray. He heard a second report, and saw one of the sentinels with his rifle at his shoulder, a light cloud of blue smoke rising from the muzzle. The man in the water saw the eye of the man on the bridge gazing into his own through the sights of the rifle. He observed that it was a grey eye, and remembered having read that grey eyes were keenest and that all famous marksmen had them. Nevertheless, this one had missed.

A counter swirl had caught Farquhar and turned him half round; he was again looking into the forest on the bank opposite the fort. The sound of a clear, high voice in a monotonous sing song now rang out behind him and came across the water with a distinctness that pierced and subdued all other sounds, even the beating of the ripples in his ears. Although no soldier, he had frequented camps enough to know the dread significance of that deliberate, drawling, aspirated chant; the lieutenant on shore was taking a part in the morning's work. How coldly and pitilessly—with what an even, calm intonation, presaging and enforcing tranquillity in the men—with what accurately-measured intervals fell those cruel words:

'Attention, company. . . . Shoulder arms. . . . Ready. . . . Aim. . . . Fire.'

Farquhar dived—dived as deeply as he could. The water roared in his ears like the voice of Niagara, yet he heard the dulled thunder of the volley, and rising again toward the surface, met shining bits of metal, singularly flattened, oscillating slowly downward. Some of them touched him on the face and hands, then fell away, continuing their descent. One lodged between his collar and neck; it was uncomfortably warm, and he snatched it out.

As he rose to the surface, gasping for breath, he saw that he had been a long time under water; he was perceptibly farther down stream—nearer to safety. The soldiers had almost finished reloading; the metal ramrods flashed all at once in the sunshine as they were drawn from the barrels, turned in the air, and thrust into their sockets. The two sentinels fired again, independently and ineffectually.

The hunted man saw all this over his shoulder; he was now swimming vigorously with the current. His brain was as energetic as his arms and legs; he thought with the rapidity of lightning.

'The officer,' he reasoned, 'will not make that martinet's error a second time. It is as easy to dodge a volley as a single shot. He has probably already given the command to fire at will. God help me, I cannot dodge them all!'

An appalling plash within two yards of him, followed by a loud rushing sound, *diminuendo,* which seemed to travel back through the air to the fort and died in an explosion which stirred the very river to its deeps! A rising sheet of water, which curved over him, fell down upon him, blinded him, strangled him! The cannon had taken a hand in the game. As he shook his head free from the commotion of the smitten water, he heard the deflected shot humming through the air ahead, and in an instant it was cracking and smashing the branches in the forest beyond.

'They will not do that again,' he thought; 'the next time they will use a charge of grape. I must keep my eye upon the gun; the smoke will apprise me—the report arrives too late; it lags behind the missile. It is a good gun.'

Suddenly he felt himself whirled round and round—spinning like a top. The water, the banks, the forest, the now distant bridge, fort and men—all were commingled and blurred. Objects were represented by their colors only; circular horizontal streaks of color—that was all he saw. He had been caught in a vortex and was being whirled on with a velocity of advance and gyration which made him giddy and sick. In a few moments he was flung upon the gravel at the foot of the left bank of the stream—the southern bank—and behind a projecting point which concealed him from his enemies. The sudden arrest of his motion, the abrasion of one of his hands on the gravel, restored him and he wept with delight. He dug his fingers into the sand, threw it over himself in handfuls and audibly blessed it. It looked like gold, like diamonds, rubies, emeralds; he could think of nothing beautiful which it did not resemble. The trees upon the bank were giant garden plants; he noted a definite order in their arrangement, inhaled the fragrance of their blooms. A strange, roseate light shone through the spaces among their trunks, and the wind made in their branches the music of æolian harps. He had no wish to perfect his escape, was content to remain in that enchanting spot until retaken.

A whizz and rattle of grapeshot among the branches high above his head roused him from his dream. The baffled cannoneer had fired him a random farewell. He sprang to his feet, rushed up the sloping bank, and plunged into the forest.

All that day he travelled, laying his course by the rounding sun. The forest seemed interminable; nowhere did he discover a break in it, not even a woodman's road. He had not known that he lived in so wild a region. There was something uncanny in the revelation.

By nightfall he was fatigued, footsore, famishing. The thought of his wife and children urged him on. At last he found a road which led him in what he knew to be the right direction. It was as wide and straight as a city street, yet it seemed untraveled. No fields bordered it, no dwelling anywhere. Not so much as the barking of a dog suggested human habitation. The black bodies of the great trees formed a straight wall on both sides, terminating on the horizon in a point, like a diagram in a lesson in perspective. Overhead, as he looked up through this rift in the wood, shone great golden stars looking unfamiliar and grouped in strange constellations. He was sure they were arranged in some order which had a secret and malign significance. The wood on either side was full of singular noises, among which—once, twice, and again—he distinctly heard whispers in an unknown tongue.

His neck was in pain, and, lifting his hand to it, he found it horribly swollen. He knew that it had a circle of black where the rope had bruised it. His eyes felt congested; he could no longer close them. His tongue was swollen with thirst; he relieved its fever by thrusting it forward from between his teeth into the cool air. How softly the turf had carpeted the untravelled avenue! He could no longer feel the roadway beneath his feet!

Doubtless, despite his suffering, he fell asleep while walking, for now he sees another scene—perhaps he has merely recovered from a delirium. He stands at the gate of his own home. All is as he left it, and all bright and beautiful in the morning sunshine. He must have travelled the entire night. As he pushes open the gate and passes up the wide white walk, he sees a flutter of female garments; his wife, looking fresh and cool and sweet, steps down from the vernadah to meet him. At the bottom of the steps she stands waiting, with a smile of ineffable joy, an attitude of matchless grace and dignity. Ah, how beautiful she is! He springs forward with extended arms. As he is about to clasp her, he feels a stunning blow upon the back of the neck; a blinding white light blazes all about him, with a sound like the shock of a cannon—then all is darkness and silence!

Peyton Farquhar was dead; his body, with a broken neck, swung gently from side to side beneath the timbers of the Owl Creek bridge.

ANTON CHEKHOV

(1860–1904)

A Dead Body

ENGLISH TRANSLATION BY ROBERT PAYNE

About the Author: Anton Chekhov, grandson of a serf, was born in the Russian provincial town of Taganrog and died at Badenweiler, Germany. He wrote fiction (over 800 stories), nonfiction, and plays, of which *The Cherry Orchard* is perhaps best known. He was also a medical doctor.

A calm August night. The mist rose slowly from the fields, covering everything within view with a dull-colored winding sheet. When lit by the moon, the mist gave the impression of a quiet and limitless expanse of ocean, and at another time it resembled an immense white wall. The air was damp and chilly, and the morning still far away. There was a fire blazing a step or two beyond the pathway running along the edge of the forest. Near the small fire, under a young oak, lay a dead body covered from head to foot with a clean white linen sheet, and there was a small wooden icon lying on the dead man's chest. Beside the dead body, almost sitting in the pathway, were "the watchers," two peasants who were performing one of the most disagreeable and uninviting tasks ever given to peasants. One was a tall youngster with a faint mustache and thick black bushy eyebrows, wearing bast shoes and a tattered sheepskin jacket, his feet stretched out in front of him, as he sat in the damp grass. He was trying to make time go faster by getting down to work. His long neck was bent, and he wheezed loudly while he whittled a spoon from a big curved chunk of wood. The other was a small, thin pock-marked peasant with an ancient face, a scant mustache, and a little goatee beard. His hands had fallen on his knees, and he gazed listlessly and motionlessly into the flames.

The small pile of faggots that lay between them blazed up and threw a red glare on their faces. It was very quiet. The only sound came from the scraping of the knife on the wood and the crackling of the damp faggots in the flames.

"Don't fall asleep, Syoma," the young man said.

"Me? No, I'm not falling asleep," stammered the man with a goatee.

"That's good. It's hard sitting here alone, I'd get frightened. Talk to me, Syoma."

"I wouldn't know . . ."

"Oh, you're a strange fellow, Syomushka! Some people laugh, invent stories, and sing songs, but you—God knows what to make of you. You sit there like a scarecrow in a potato field and stare at the flames. You don't know how to put words together. . . . You're plain scared of talking. You must be getting on for fifty, but you've no more sense than a baby. Aren't you sorry you are such a fool?"

"Reckon so," said the man with a goatee gloomily.

"Well, we're sorry too. Wouldn't you say so? There you are, a good solid fellow, don't drink too much, and the only trouble is that you haven't a brain in your head. Still, if the good Lord afflicted you by making you witless, there's no reason why you shouldn't try to pick up some glimmerings of intelligence, is there? Make an effort, Syoma. . . . If someone speaks a good word and you don't understand it, you ought to try to fathom it, get the sense of it somehow, keep on thinking and concentrating. If there's anything you don't understand, you should make an effort and think over exactly what it means. Do you understand me? Just make an effort! If you don't get some sense into your head, you'll die an idiot, you'll be the least important man in the world."

Suddenly a long-drawn-out moaning sound was heard from the direction of the forest. There was the sound of something being torn from the top of a tree, slithering down and rustling among the leaves, and falling to the ground, followed by a dull echo. The young man shuddered and looked searchingly at his companion.

"It's only an owl running after little birds," Syoma said gloomily.

"I'd have thought it was time for the birds to be flying to warm countries now."

"Yes, that's true."

"And the dawns are getting cold now—there's a chill in the air. Birds, too—cranes, for example—they feel the cold, they're delicate things. When it's cold like this, they die. Me, I'm not a crane, but I'm frozen. Put some more wood on!"

Syoma rose and vanished in the dark undergrowth. While he was wandering through the undergrowth, snapping off dry twigs, his companion shielded his eyes with his hands, shivering at every sound. Syoma brought back an armful of wood and threw it on the fire. Little tongues of flame licked the black twigs uncertainly, and then suddenly, as though at a word of command, the flames leapt up and enveloped their faces in a deep purple glow; and the pathway, and the white linen sheet which showed the dead man's hands and feet in relief, and the icon, all these shone with the same deep purple glow. The watchers remained silent. The young man bent his neck still lower and went back to work more nervously than ever. Meanwhile the old man with the goatee sat motionless, never taking his eyes from the fire.

"Oh, ye that love not Zion shall be ashamed in the face of the Lord!"—the silence of the night was suddenly broken by a high falsetto voice, and soft footsteps.

Into the purple firelight there emerged the dark figure of a man wearing a broad-brimmed hat and the short cassock of a monk, carrying a birch-bark sack on his shoulders.

"Thy will be done, O Lord! O Holy Mother!" he sang in a voice grown hoarse. "I saw the fire in the depths of night, and my soul leapt for joy! At first, I told myself they were keeping watch over horses, and then I told myself, it cannot be so, for there are no horses. Then, said I, they were thieves waiting to pounce upon some rich Lazarus, and then it crossed my mind they were gypsies preparing to sacrifice victims to their idols. My soul again leapt for joy! I said to myself: Go then, Theodosy, thou servant of God, receive a martyr's crown! So I flew to the fire on the gentle wings of a moth. Now I stand before you, and examine your physiognomies, and judge your souls, and I conclude you are neither thieves nor heathens! Peace be upon you!"

"Good evening to you."

"Dear brethren in God, pray tell me where I can find Makukhinsky's brickyard?"

"It's not far. Straight down the road, and after a mile and a half you'll come to Ananova, which is our village. Turn right at the village, Father, follow the riverbank, and keep on going till you reach the brickyard. It's two miles from Ananova."

"God give you health! . . . Tell me, why are you sitting here?"

"We are keeping watch. Look over there—there's a dead body."

"Eh, what's that? A dead body! Holy Mother!"

When the stranger saw the white sheet and the icon, he shivered so violently that his legs involuntarily made little hopping motions. This unexpected sight produced an overwhelming effect. He shrank within himself and was rooted to the spot, his eyes glazed, his mouth wide open. For three minutes he remained completely silent, as though he could not believe his eyes, and then he muttered: "O Lord, O Holy Mother! I was wandering abroad and giving offense to none, and now am I consigned to punishment. . . ."

"What are you?" the young man asked. "Are you a member of the clergy?"

"No, no . . . I wander from one monastery to another. Do you know by chance Mikhail Polikarpich? He runs the brickyard, and I'm his nephew. . . . Thy will be done, O Lord! . . . What are you doing here?"

"We are the watchers. They told us to watch him."

"Yes, yes," muttered the man in the cassock, running his hands over his eyes. "Tell me—the dead man—where did he come from?"

"He was passing by."

"Well, such is life! So it is, dear brethren, and now I must go on my way. I'm all

confused. I tell you, I'm more frightened of the dead than of anything else. And it comes to me that when he was living, no one paid any attention to him, and now that he is dead and delivered over to corruption, we tremble before him as though he were a great conqueror or a high official of the Church. . . . Such is life! . . . Tell me, was he murdered?"

"Christ knows! Maybe he was murdered, maybe he just died."

"Yes, yes. So it is! And who knows, dear brethren, even now his soul may be tasting the delights of Paradise."

"No, his soul is still clinging close to his body," the young man said. "It doesn't leave the body for three days."

"Hm, yes! How cold it is, eh? My teeth are chattering. . . . How do I go? Straight ahead, eh?"

"Till you reach the village, and then you turn to the right, by the river."

"By the river, eh? Why am I standing here? I must get going. Good-by, dear brethren!"

The man in the cassock took four or five steps along the path, and then stood still.

"I forgot to give a kopeck for the funeral," he said. "You are good religious people. May I—is it right for me to leave the money?"

"You should know best, since you go about from one monastery to another. Suppose he died a natural death—then it will go for the good of his soul. If he didn't, then it's a sin."

"That's true. Maybe he killed himself, and so I had better keep the money. Oh, so much evil in the world! Even if you gave me a thousand rubles, I wouldn't stay here. . . . Farewell, brothers!"

Slowly the man in the cassock moved away, and again he stood still.

"I don't know what to do," he muttered. "It's terrible to be staying here by the fire and waiting for daybreak, and it's terrible to be going along the road. I'll be haunted by him—he'll come out of the shadows! God is punishing me! I've walked for four hundred miles, and nothing ever happened to me, and now I am close to home, and there's all this misery. I can't go on. . . ."

"You're right. It's terrible."

"I'm not afraid of wolves. I'm not afraid of robbers, or the dark, but I'm afraid of the dead. I'm terrified, and that's the truth! Dear good religious brethren, I beg you on my knees to see me to the village."

"We have to stay with the body."

"Dear brethren, no one will ever know. Truly, no one will see you coming with me. God will reward you a hundredfold. You with a beard—come with me! Do me that kindness! Why doesn't he talk?"

"He hasn't got much sense," the young man said.

"Come with me, friend. I'll give you five kopecks!"

"I might, for five kopecks," the young man said, scratching the back of his head. "It's against orders, though. If Syoma, the poor fool, will stay here, then I'll come. Syoma, do you mind staying here alone?"

"I don't mind," the fool said.

"All right. Let's go."

So the young man rose and went with the man wearing a cassock, and soon the sound of their steps and the talk died away into the night.

Syoma closed his eyes and fell into a gentle sleep. The fire gradually went out, and soon the dead body was lost among great shadows.

HERMAN MELVILLE

(1819–1891)

The Paradise of Bachelors and the Tartarus of Maids

About the Author: Herman Melville was born into an established merchant family in New York City. The five years that Melville spent at sea formed the largest part of his literary capital, generating most of his novels, notably *Moby Dick* (1851) and *Billy Budd* (posthumously published in 1924), as well as some of his short stories. Inspired by the Civil War, Melville turned to poetry in his early forties. He died, largely forgotten, in New York.

I. The Paradise of Bachelors

It lies not far from Temple Bar.

Going to it, by the usual way, is like stealing from a heated plain into some cool, deep glen, shady among harboring hills.

Sick with the din and soiled with the mud of Fleet Street—where the Benedick tradesmen are hurrying by, with ledgerlines ruled along their brows, thinking upon rise of bread and fall of babies—you adroitly turn a mystic corner—not a street—glide down a dim, monastic way, flanked by dark, sedate, and solemn piles, and still wending on, give the whole careworn world the slip, and, disentangled, stand beneath the quiet cloisters of the Paradise of Bachelors.

Sweet are the oases in Sahara; charming the isle-groves of August prairies; delectable pure faith amidst a thousand perfidies; but sweeter, still more charming, most delectable, the dreamy Paradise of Bachelors, found in the stony heart of stunning London.

In mild meditation pace the cloisters; take your pleasure, sip your leisure, in the garden waterward; go linger in the ancient library; go worship in the sculptured chapel; but little have you seen, just nothing do you know, not the sweet kernel have you tasted, till you dine among the banded Bachelors, and see their convivial eyes and glasses sparkle. Not dine in bustling commons, during term-time, in the hall; but tranquilly, by private hint, at a private table; some fine Templar's hospitably invited guest.

Templar? That's a romantic name. Let me see. Brian de Bois Guilbert was a Templar, I believe. Do we understand you to insinuate that those famous Templars still survive in modern London? May the ring of their armed heels be heard, and the rattle of their shields, as in mailed prayer the monk-knights kneel before the consecrated Host? Surely a monk-knight were a curious sight picking his way along the Strand, his gleaming corselet and snowy surcoat spattered by an omnibus. Long-bearded, too, according to his order's rule; his face fuzzy as a pard's; how would the grim ghost look among the crop-haired, close-shaven citizens? We know indeed—sad history recounts it—that a moral blight tainted at last this sacred Brotherhood. Though no sworded foe might out-skill them in the fence, yet the worm of luxury crawled beneath their guard, gnawing the core of knightly troth, nibbling the monastic vow, till at last the monk's austerity relaxed to wassailing, and the sworn knights-bachelors grew to be but hypocrites and rakes.

But for all this, quite unprepared were we to learn that Knights-Templars (if at all in being) were so entirely secularized as to be reduced from carving out immortal fame in

glorious battling for the Holy Land, to the carving of roast mutton at a dinner-board. Like Anacreon, do these degenerate Templars now think it sweeter far to fall in banquet than in war? Or, indeed, how can there be any survival of that famous order? Templars in modern London! Templars in their red-cross mantles smoking cigars at the Divan! Templars crowded in a railway train, till, stacked with steel helmet, spear, and shield, the whole train looks like one elongated locomotive!

No. The genuine Templar is long since departed. Go view the wondrous tombs in the Temple Church; see there the rigidly-haughty forms stretched out, with crossed arms upon their stilly hearts, in everlasting and undreaming rest. Like the years before the flood, the bold Knights-Templars are no more. Nevertheless, the name remains, and the nominal society, and the ancient grounds, and some of the ancient edifices. But the iron heel is changed to a boot of patent leather; the long two-handed sword to a one-handed quill; the monk-giver of gratuitous ghostly counsel now counsels for a fee; the defender of the sarcophagus (if in good practice with his weapon) now has more than one case to defend; the vowed opener and clearer of all highways leading to the Holy Sepulchre, now has it in particular charge to check, to clog, to hinder, and embarrass all the courts and avenues of Law; the knight-combatant of the Saracen, breasting spear-points at Acre, now fights lawpoints in Westminster Hall. The helmet is a wig. Struck by Time's enchanter's wand, the Templar is to-day a Lawyer.

But, like many others tumbled from proud glory's height—like the apple, hard on the bough but mellow on the ground—the Templar's fall has but made him all the finer fellow.

I dare say those old warrior-priests were but gruff and grouty at the best; cased in Birmingham hardware, how could their crimped arms give yours or mine a hearty shake? Their proud, ambitious, monkish souls clasped shut, like horn-book missals; their very faces clapped in bomb-shells; what sort of genial men were these? But best of comrades, most affable of hosts, capital diner is the modern Templar. His wit and wine are both of sparkling brands.

The church and cloisters, courts and vaults, lanes and passages, banquet-halls, refectories, libraries, terraces, gardens, broad walks, domiciles, and dessert-rooms, covering a very large space of ground, and all grouped in central neighborhood, and quite sequestered from the old city's surrounding din; and everything about the place being kept in most bachelor-like particularity, no part of London offers to a quiet wight so agreeable a refuge.

The Temple is indeed a city by itself. A city with all the best appurtenances, as the above enumeration shows. A city with a park to it, and flower-beds, and a river-side—the Thames flowing by as openly, in one part, as by Eden's primal garden flowed the mild Euphrates. In what is now the Temple Garden the old Crusaders used to exercise their steeds and lances; the modern Templars now lounge on the benches beneath the trees, and, switching their patent-leather boots, in gay discourse exercise at repartee.

Long lines of stately portraits in the banquet-halls, show what great men of mark—famous nobles, judges, and Lord Chancellors—have in their time been Templars. But all Templars are not known to universal fame; though, if the having warm hearts and warmer welcomes, full minds and fuller cellars, and giving good advice and glorious dinners, spiced with rare divertisements of fun and fancy, merit immortal mention, set down, ye muses, the names of R. F. C. and his imperial brother.

Though to be a Templar, in the one true sense, you must needs be a lawyer, or a student at the law, and be ceremoniously enrolled as member of the order, yet as many such, though Templars, do not reside within the Temple's precincts, though they may have their offices there, just so, on the other hand, there are many residents of the hoary old domiciles who are not admitted Templars. If being, say, a lounging gentleman and bachelor, or a quiet, unmarried, literary man, charmed with the soft seclusion of the spot, you much desire to pitch your shady tent among the rest in this serene encampment, then you must make some special friend among the order, and procure him to rent, in his name, but at your charge, whatever vacant chamber you may find to suit.

Thus, I suppose, did Dr. Johnson, that nominal Benedick and widower but virtual bachelor, when for a space he resided here. So, too, did that undoubted bachelor and rare good soul, Charles Lamb. And hundreds more, of sterling spirits, Brethren of the Order of Celibacy, from time to time have dined, and slept, and tabernacled here. Indeed, the place is all a honeycomb of offices and domiciles. Like any cheese, it it quite perforated through and through in all directions with the snug cells of bachelors. Dear, delightful spot! Ah! when I bethink me of the sweet hours there passed, enjoying such genial hospitalities beneath those time-honored roofs, my heart only finds due utterance through poetry; and, with a sigh, I softly sing, "Carry me back to old Virginny!"

Such then, at large, is the Paradise of Bachelors. And such I found it one pleasant afternoon in the smiling month of May, when, sallying from my hotel in Trafalgar Square, I went to keep my dinner appointment with that fine Barrister, Bachelor, and Bencher, R.F.C. (he *is* the first and second, and *should be* the third; I hereby nominate him), whose card I kept fast pinched between my gloved forefinger and thumb, and every now and then snatched still another look at the pleasant address inscribed beneath the name. "No.—, Elm Court, Temple."

At the core he was a right bluff, care-free, right comfortable, and most companionable Englishman. If on a first acquaintance he seemed reserved, quite icy in his air—patience; this champagne will thaw. And if it never do, better frozen champagne than liquid vinegar.

There were nine gentlemen, all bachelors, at the dinner. One was from "No.—, King's Bench Walk, Temple"; a second, third, and fourth, and fifth, from various courts or passages christened with some similarly rich resounding syllables. It was indeed a sort of Senate of the Bachelors, sent to this dinner from widely scattered districts, to represent the general celibacy of the Temple. Nay, it was, by representation, a Grand Parliament of the best Bachelors in universal London; several of those present being from distant quarters of the town, noted immemorial seats of lawyers and unmarried men—Lincoln's Inn, Furnival's Inn; and one gentleman, upon whom I looked with a sort of collateral awe, hailed from the spot where Lord Verulam once abode a bachelor—Gray's Inn.

The apartment was well up toward heaven. I know not how many strange old stairs I climbed to get to it. But a good dinner, with famous company, should be well earned. No doubt our host had his dining-room so high with a view to secure the prior exercise necessary to the due relishing and digesting of it.

The furniture was wonderfully unpretending, old, and snug. No new shining mahogany, sticky with undried varnish; no uncomfortably luxurious ottomans, and sofas too fine to use, vexed you in this sedate apartment. It is a thing which every sensible American should learn from every sensible Englishman, that glare and glitter, gim cracks and gewgaws, are not indispensable to domestic solacement. The American Benedick snatches, down-town, a tough chop in a gilded show-box; the English bachelor leisurely dines at home on that incomparable South Down of his, off a plain deal board.

The ceiling of the room was low. Who wants to dine under the dome of St. Peter's? High ceilings! If that is your demand, and the higher the better, and you be so very tall, then go dine out with the topping giraffe in the open air.

In good time the nine gentlemen sat down to nine covers, and soon were fairly under way.

If I remember right, ox-tail soup inaugurated the affair. Of a rich russet hue, its agreeable flavor dissipated my first confounding of its main ingredient with teamsters' gads and the rawhides of ushers. (By way of interlude, we here drank a little claret.) Neptune's was the next tribute rendered—turbot coming second; snow-white, flaky, and just gelatinous enough, not too turtleish in its unctuousness.

(At this point we refreshed ourselves with a glass of sherry.) After these light skirmishers had vanished, the heavy artillery of the feast marched in, led by that well-known English generalissimo, roast beef. For aides-de-camp we had a saddle of mutton, a fat turkey, a chicken-pie, and endless other savory things; while for avant-couriers came nine silver flagons of humming ale. This heavy ordnance having departed on the track of the light skirmishers, a picked brigade of game-fowl encamped upon the board, their camp-fires lit by the ruddiest of decanters.

Tarts and puddings followed, with innumerable niceties; then cheese and crackers. (By way of ceremony, simply, only to keep up good old fashions, we here each drank a glass of good old port.)

The cloth was now removed; and, like Blucher's army coming in at the death on the field of Waterloo, in marched a fresh detachment of bottles, dusty with their hurried march.

All these manœuvrings of the forces were superintended by a surprising old field-marshal (I can not school myself to call him by the inglorious name of waiter), with snowy hair and napkin, and a head like Socrates. Amidst all the hilarity of the feast, intent on important business, he disdained to smile. Venerable man!

I have above endeavored to give some slight schedule of the general plan of operations. But any one knows that a good, genial diner is a sort of pell-mell, indiscriminate affair, quite baffling to detail in all particulars. Thus, I spoke of taking a glass of claret, and a glass of sherry, and a glass of port, and a mug of ale—all at certain specific periods and times. But those were merely the state bumpers, so to speak. Innumerable impromptu glasses were drained between the periods of those grand imposing ones.

The nine bachelors seemed to have the most tender concern for each other's health. All the time, in flowing wine, they most earnestly expressed their sincerest wishes for the entire well-being and lasting hygiene of the gentleman on the right and on the left. I noticed that when one of these kind bachelors desired a little more wine (just for his stomach's sake, like Timothy), he would not help himself to it unless some other bachelor would join him. It seemed held something indelicate, selfish, and unfraternal, to be seen taking a lonely, unparticipated glass. Meantime, as the wine ran apace, the spirits of the company grew more and more to perfect genialness and unconstraint. They related all sorts of pleasant stories. Choice experiences in their private lives were now brought out, like choice brands of Moselle or Rhenish, only kept for particular company. One told us how mellowly he lived when a student at Oxford; with various spicy anecdotes of most frank-hearted noble lords, his liberal companions. Another bachelor, a gray-headed man, with a sunny face, who, by his own account, embraced every opportunity of leisure to cross over into the Low Countries, on sudden tours of inspection of the fine old Flemish architecture there—this learned, white-haired, sunny-faced old bachelor excelled in his descriptions of the elaborate

splendors of those old guild-halls, town-halls, and stadthold-houses, to be seen in the land of the ancient Flemings. A third was a great frequenter of the British Museum, and knew all about scores of wonderful antiquities, of Oriental manuscripts, and costly books without a duplicate. A fourth had lately returned from a trip to Old Granada, and, of course, was full of Saracenic scenery. A fifth had a funny case in law to tell. A sixth was erudite in wines. A seventh had a strange characteristic anecdote of the private life of the Iron Duke, never printed, and never before announced in any public or private company. An eighth had lately been amusing his evenings, now and then, with translating a comic poem of Pulci's. He quoted for us the more amusing passages.

And so the evening slipped along, the hours told, not by a water-clock, like King Alfred's, but a wine-chronometer. Meantime the table seemed a sort of Epsom Heath; a regular ring, where the decanters galloped round. For fear one decanter should not with sufficient speed reach his destination, another was sent express after him to hurry him; and then a third to hurry the second; and so on with a fourth and fifth. And throughout all this nothing loud, nothing unmannerly, nothing turbulent. I am quite sure, from the scrupulous gravity and austerity of his air, that had Socrates, the field-marshal, perceived aught of indecorum in the company he served, he would have forthwith departed without giving warning. I afterward learned that, during the repast, an invalid bachelor in an adjoining chamber enjoyed his first sound refreshing slumber in three long, weary weeks.

It was the very perfection of quiet absorption of good living, good drinking, good feeling, and good talk. We were a band of brothers. Comfort—fraternal, household comfort, was the grand trait of the affair. Also, you could plainly see that these easy-hearted men had no wives or children to give an anxious thought. Almost all of them were travelers, too; for bachelors alone can travel freely, and without any twinges of their consciences touching desertion of the fireside.

The thing called pain, the bugbear styled trouble—those two legends seemed preposterous to their bachelor imaginations. How could men of liberal sense, ripe scholarship in the world, and capacious philosophical and convivial understandings—how could they suffer themselves to be imposed upon by such monkish fables? Pain! Trouble! As well talk of Catholic miracles. No such thing.—Pass the sherry, sir.—Pooh, pooh! Can't be!—The port, sir, if you please. Nonsense; don't tell me so.—The decanter stops with you, sir, I believe.

And so it went.

Not long after the cloth was drawn our host glanced significantly upon Socrates, who, solemnly stepping to a stand, returned with an immense convolved horn, a regular Jericho horn, mounted with polished silver, and otherwise chased and curiously enriched; not omitting two life-like goats' heads, with four more horns of solid silver, projecting from opposite sides of the mouth of the noble main horn.

Not having heard that our host was a performer on the bugle, I was surprised to see him lift this horn from the table, as if he were about to blow an inspiring blast. But I was relieved from this, and set quite right as touching the purposes of the horn, by his now inserting his thumb and forefinger into its mouth; whereupon a slight aroma was stirred up, and my nostrils were greeted with the smell of some choice Rappee. It was a mull of snuff. It went the rounds. Capital idea this, thought I, of taking snuff about this juncture. This goodly fashion must be introduced among my countrymen at home, further ruminated I.

The remarkable decorum of the nine bachelors—a decorum not to be affected by any quantity of wine—a decorum unassailable by any degree of mirthfulness—this was again

set in a forcible light to me, by now observing that, though they took snuff very freely, yet not a man so far violated the proprieties, or so far molested the invalid bachelor in the adjoining room as to indulge himself in a sneeze. The snuff was snuffed silently, as if it had been some fine innoxious powder brushed off the wings of butterflies.

But fine though they be, bachelors' dinners, like bachelors' lives, can not endure forever. The time came for breaking up. One by one the bachelors took their hats, and two by two, and arm-in-arm they descended, still conversing, to the flagging of the court; some going to their neighboring chambers to turn over the *Decameron* ere retiring for the night; some to smoke a cigar, promenading in the garden on the cool river-side; some to make for the street, call a hack, and be driven snugly to their distant lodgings.

I was the last lingerer.

"Well," said my smiling host, "what do you think of the Temple here, and the sort of life we bachelors make out to live in it?"

"Sir," said I, with a burst of admiring candor—"Sir, this is the very Paradise of Bachelors!"

II. The Tartarus of Maids

It lies not far from Woedolor Mountain in New England. Turning to the east, right out from among bright farms and sunny meadows, nodding in early June with odorous grasses, you enter ascendingly among bleak hills. These gradually close in upon a dusky pass, which, from the violent Gulf Stream of air unceasingly driving between its cloven walls of haggard rock, as well as from the tradition of a crazy spinster's hut having long ago stood somewhere hereabouts, is called the Mad Maid's Bellows-pipe.

Winding along at the bottom of the gorge is a dangerously narrow wheel-road, occupying the bed of a former torrent. Following this road to its highest point, you stand as within a Dantean gateway. From the steepness of the walls here, their strangely ebon hue, and the sudden contraction of the gorge, this particular point is called the Black Notch. The ravine now expandingly descends into a great, purple, hopper-shaped hollow, far sunk among many Plutonian, shaggy-wooded mountains. By the country people this hollow is called the Devil's Dungeon. Sounds of torrents fall on all sides upon the ear. These rapid waters unite at last in one turbid brick-colored stream, boiling through a flume among enormous boulders. They call this strange-colored torrent Blood River. Gaining a dark precipice it wheels suddenly to the west, and makes one maniac spring of sixty feet into the arms of a stunted wood of gray-haired pines, between which it thence eddies on its further way down to the invisible low lands.

Conspicuously crowning a rocky bluff high to one side, at the cataract's verge, is the ruin of an old saw-mill, built in those primitive times when vast pines and hemlocks superabounded throughout the neighboring region. The black-mossed bulk of those immense, rough-hewn, and spike-knotted logs, here and there tumbled all together, in long abandonment and decay, or left in solitary, perilous projection over the cataract's gloomy brink, impart to this rude wooden ruin not only much of the aspect of one of rough-quarried stone, but also a sort of feudal, Rhineland and Thurmberg look, derived from the pinnacled wildness of the neighboring scenery.

Not far from the bottom of the Dungeon stands a large white-washed building, relieved, like some great whited sepulchre, against the sullen background of mountain side firs, and other hardy evergreens, inaccessibly rising in grim terraces for some two thousand feet.

The building is a paper-mill.

Having embarked on a large scale in the seedsman's business (so extensively and broadcast, indeed, that at length my seeds were distributed through all the Eastern and Northern States, and even fell into the far soil of Missouri and the Carolinas), the demand for paper at my place became so great that the expenditure soon amounted to a most important item in the general account. It need hardly be hinted how paper comes into use with seedsmen, as envelopes. These are mostly made of yellowish paper, folded square; and when filled, are all but flat, and being stamped, and superscribed with the nature of the seeds contained, assume not a little the appearance of business-letters ready for the mail. Of these small envelopes I used an incredible quantity—several hundreds of thousands in a year. For a time I had purchased my paper from the wholesale dealers in a neighboring town. For economy's sake, and partly for the adventure of the trip, I now resolved to cross the mountains, some sixty miles, and order my future paper at the Devil's Dungeon paper-mill.

The sleighing being uncommonly fine toward the end of January, and promising to hold so for no small period, in spite of the bitter cold I started one gray Friday noon in my pung, well fitted with buffalo and wolf robes; and spending one night on the road, next noon came in sight of Woedolor Mountain.

The far summit fairly smoked with frost; white vapors curled up from its white-wooded top, as from a chimney. The intense congelation made the whole country look like one petrifaction. The steel shoes of my pung craunched and gritted over the vitreous, chippy snow, as if it had been broken glass. The forests here and there skirting the route, feeling the same all-stiffening influence, their inmost fibres penetrated with the cold, strangely groaned—not in the swaying branches merely, but likewise in the vertical trunk—as the fitful gusts remorselessly swept through them. Brittle with excessive frost, many colossal tough-grained maples, snapped in twain like pipestems, cumbered the unfeeling earth.

Flaked all over with frozen sweat, white as a milky ram, his nostrils at each breath sending forth two horn-shaped shoots of heated respiration, Black, my good horse, but six years old, started at a sudden turn, where, right across the track—not ten minutes fallen—an old distorted hemlock lay, darkly undulatory as an anaconda.

Gaining the Bellows-pipe, the violent blast, dead from behind, all but shoved my high-backed pung up-hill. The gust shrieked through the shivered pass, as if laden with lost spirits bound to the unhappy world. Ere gaining the summit, Black, my horse, as if exasperated by the cutting wind, slung out with his strong hind-legs, tore the light pung straight up-hill, and sweeping grazingly through the narrow notch, sped downward madly past the ruined saw-mill. Into the Devil's Dungeon horse and cataract rushed together.

With might and main, quitting my seat and robes, and standing backward, with one foot braced against the dashboard, I rasped and churned the bit, and stopped him just in time to avoid collision, at a turn, with the bleak nozzle of a rock, couchant like a lion in the way—a roadside rock.

At first I could not discover the paper-mill.

The whole hollow gleamed with the white, except, here and there, where a pinnacle of granite showed one windswept angle bare. The mountains stood pinned in shrouds—a pass of Alpine corpses. Where stands the mill? Suddenly a whirring, humming sound broke upon my ear. I looked, and there, like an arrested avalanche, lay the large whitewashed factory. It was subordinately surrounded by a cluster of other and smaller buildings, some of which, from their cheap, blank air, great length, gregarious windows, and comfortless expression, no doubt were boarding-houses of the operatives. A snow-white hamlet amidst

the snows. Various rude, irregular squares and courts resulted from the somewhat picturesque clusterings of these buildings, owing to the broken, rocky nature of the ground, which forbade all method in their relative arrangement. Several narrow lanes and alleys, too, partly blocked with snow fallen from the roof, cut up the hamlet in all directions.

When, turning from the traveled highway, jingling with bells of numerous farmers—who, availing themselves of the fine sleighing, were dragging their wood to market—and frequently diversified with swift cutters dashing from inn to inn of the scattered villages—when, I say, turning from that bustling main-road, I by degrees wound into the Mad Maid's Bellows-pipe, and saw the grim Black Notch beyond, then something latent, as well as something obvious in the time and scene, strangely brought back to my mind my first sight of dark and grimy Temple Bar. And when Black, my horse, went darting through the Notch, perilously grazing its rocky wall, I remembered being in a runaway London omnibus, which in much the same sort of style, though by no means at an equal rate, dashed through the ancient arch of Wren. Though the two objects did by no means completely correspond, yet this partial inadequacy but served to tinge the similitude not less with the vividness than the disorder of a dream. So that, when upon reining up at the protruding rock I at last caught sight of the quaint groupings of the factory-buildings and with the traveled highway and the Notch behind, found myself all alone, silently and privily stealing through deep-cloven passages into this sequestered spot, and saw the long, high-gabled main factory edifice, with a rude tower—for hoisting heavy boxes—at one end, standing among its crowded outbuildings and boarding-houses, as the Temple Church amidst the surrounding offices and dormitories, and when the marvelous retirement of this mysterious mountain nook fastened its whole spell upon me, then, what memory lacked, all tributary imagination furnished, and I said to myself, "This is the very counterpart of the Paradise of Bachelors, but snowed upon, and frost-painted to a sepulchre."

Dismounting and warily picking my way down the dangerous declivity—horse and man both sliding now and then upon the icy ledges—at length I drove, or the blast drove me, into the largest square, before one side of the main edifice. Piercingly and shrilly the shotted blast blew by the corner; and redly and demoniacally boiled Blood River at one side. A long wood-pile, of many scores of cords, all glittering in mail of crusted ice, stood crosswise in the square. A row of horse-posts, their north sides plastered with adhesive snow, flanked the factory wall. The bleak frost packed and paved the square as with some ringing metal.

The inverted similitude recurred—"The sweet, tranquil Temple garden, with the Thames bordering its green beds," strangely meditated I.

But where are the gay bachelors?

Then, as I and my horse stood shivering in the wind-spray, a girl ran from a neighboring dormitory door, and throwing her thin apron over her bare head, made for the opposite building.

"One moment, my girl; is there no shed hereabouts which I may drive into?"

Pausing, she turned upon me a face pale with work and blue with cold; an eye supernatural with unrelated misery.

"Nay," faltered I, "I mistook you. Go on; I want nothing."

Leading my horse close to the door from which she had come, I knocked. Another pale, blue girl appeared, shivering in the doorway as, to prevent the blast, she jealously held the door ajar.

"Nay, I mistake again. In God's name shut the door. But hold, is there no man about?"

That moment a dark-complexioned, well-wrapped personage passed, making for the factory door, and spying him coming, the girl rapidly closed the other one.

"Is there no horse-shed here, sir?"

"Yonder, the wood-shed," he replied, and disappeared inside the factory.

With much ado I managed to wedge in horse and pung between the scattered piles of wood all sawn and split. Then, blanketing my horse, and piling my buffalo on the blanket's top, and tucking in its edges well around the breast-band and breeching, so that the wind might not strip him bare, I tied him fast, and ran lamely for the factory door, stiff with frost, and cumbered with my driver's dreadnaught.

Immediately I found myself standing in a spacious place intolerably lighted by long rows of windows, focusing inward the snowy scene without.

At rows of blank-looking counters sat rows of blank-looking girls, with blank, white folders in their blank hands, all blankly folding blank paper.

In one corner stood some huge frame of ponderous iron, with a vertical thing like a piston periodically rising and falling upon a heavy wooden block. Before it—its tame minister—stood a tall girl, feeding the iron animal with half-quires of rose-hued note-paper which, at every downward dab of the piston-like machine, received in the corner the impress of a wreath of roses. I looked from the rosy paper to the pallid cheek, but said nothing.

Seated before a long apparatus, strung with long, slender strings like any harp, another girl was feeding it with foolscap sheets which, so soon as they curiously traveled from her on the cords, were withdrawn at the opposite end of the machine by a second girl. They came to the first girl blank; they went to the second girl ruled.

I looked upon the first girl's brow, and saw it was young and fair; I looked upon the second girl's brow, and saw it was ruled and wrinkled. Then, as I still looked, the two—for some small variety to the monotony—changed places; and where had stood the young, fair brow, now stood the ruled and wrinkled one.

Perched high upon a narrow platform, and still higher upon a high stool crowning it, sat another figure serving some other iron animal; while below the platform sat her mate in some sort of reciprocal attendance.

Not a syllable was breathed. Nothing was heard but the low, steady overruling hum of the iron animals. The human voice was banished from the spot. Machinery—that vaunted slave of humanity—here stood menially served by human beings, who served mutely and cringingly as the slave serves the Sultan. The girls did not so much seem accessory wheels to the general machinery as mere cogs to the wheels.

All this scene around me was instantaneously taken in at one sweeping glance—even before I had proceeded to unwind the heavy fur tippet from around my neck. But as soon as this fell from me, the dark-complexioned man, standing close by, raised a sudden cry, and seizing my arm, dragged me out into the open air, and without pausing for a word instantly caught up some congealed snow and began rubbing both my cheeks.

"Two white spots like the whites of your eyes," he said; "man, your cheeks are frozen."

"That may well be," muttered I; " 'tis some wonder the frost of the Devil's Dungeon strikes in no deeper. Rub away."

Soon a horrible, tearing pain caught at my reviving cheeks. Two gaunt blood-hounds, one on each side, seemed mumbling them. I seemed Actæon.

Presently, when all was over, I re-entered the factory, made known my business,

concluded it satisfactorily, and then begged to be conducted throughout the place to view it.

"Cupid is the boy for that," said the dark-complexioned man. "Cupid!" and by this odd fancy-name calling a dimpled, red-cheeked, spirited-looking, forward little fellow who was rather impudently, I thought, gliding about among the passive-looking girls—like a goldfish through hueless waves—yet doing nothing in particular that I could see, the man bade him lead the stranger through the edifice.

"Come first and see the water-wheel," said this lively lad, with the air of boyishly-brisk importance.

Quitting the folding-room, we crossed some damp, cold boards, and stood beneath a great wet shed, incessantly showering with foam, like the green barnacled bow of some East Indiaman in a gale. Round and round here went the enormous revolutions of the dark colossal water-wheel, grim with its one immutable purpose.

"This sets our whole machinery a-going, sir; in every part of all these buildings; where the girls work and all."

I looked, and saw that the turbid waters of Blood River had not changed their hue by coming under the use of man.

"You make only blank paper; no printing of any sort, I suppose? All blank paper, don't you?"

"Certainly; what else should a paper-factory make?"

The lad here looked at me as if suspicious of my common-sense.

"Oh, to be sure!" said I, confused and stammering; "it only struck me as so strange that red waters should turn out pale chee—paper, I mean."

He took me up a wet and rickety stair to a great light room, furnished with no visible thing but rude, manger-like receptacles running all round its sides; and up to these mangers, like so many mares haltered to the rack, stood rows of girls. Before each was vertically thrust up a long, glittering scythe, immovably fixed at bottom to the manger-edge. The curve of the scythe, and its having no snath to it, made it look exactly like a sword. To and fro, across the sharp edge, the girls forever dragged long strips of rags, washed white, picked from baskets at one side; thus ripping asunder every seam, and converting the tatters almost into lint. The air swam with the fine, poisonous particles, which from all sides darted, subtilely, as motes in sunbeams, into the lungs.

"This is the rag-room," coughed the boy.

"You find it rather stifling here," coughed I in answer; "but the girls don't cough."

"Oh, they are used to it."

"Where do you get such hosts of rags?" picking up a handful from a basket.

"Some from the country round about; some from far over sea—Leghorn and London."

" 'Tis not unlikely, then," murmured I, "that among these heaps of rags there may be some old shirts, gathered from the dormitories of the Paradise of Bachelors. But the buttons are all dropped off. Pray, my lad, do you ever find any bachelor's buttons hereabouts?"

"None grow in this part of the country. The Devil's Dungeon is no place for flowers."

"Oh!" you mean the *flowers* so called—the Bachelor's Buttons?"

"And was not that what you asked about? Or did you mean the gold bosom-buttons of our boss, Old Bach, as our whispering girls all call him?"

"The man, then, I saw below is a bachelor, is he?"

"Oh, yes, he's a Bach."

"The edges of those swords, they are turned outward from the girls, if I see right; but their rags and fingers fly so, I can not distinctly see."

"Turned outward."

Yes, murmured I to myself; I see it now; turned outward; and each erected sword is so borne, edge-outward, before each girl. If my reading fails me not, just so, of old, condemned state-prisoners went from the hall of judgment to their doom: an officer before, bearing a sword, its edge turned outward, in significance of their fatal sentence. So, through consumptive pallors of this blank, raggy life, go these white girls to death.

"Those scythes look very sharp," again turning toward the boy.

"Yes; they have to keep them so. Look!"

That moment two of the girls, dropping their rags, plied each a whetstone up and down the swordblade. My unaccustomed blood curdled at the sharp shriek of the tormented steel.

Their own executioners; themselves whetting the very swords that slay them, meditated I.

"What makes those girls so sheet-white, my lad?"

"Why"—with a roguish twinkle, pure ignorant drollery, not-knowing heartlessness—"I suppose the handling of such white bits of sheets all the time makes them so sheety."

"Let us leave the rag-room now, my lad."

More tragical and more inscrutably mysterious than any mystic sight, human or machine, throughout the factory, was the strange innocence of cruel-heartedness in this usage-hardened boy.

"And now," said he, cheerily, "I suppose you want to see our great machine, which cost us twelve thousand dollars only last autumn. That's the machine that makes the paper, too. This way, sir."

Following him, I crossed a large, bespattered place, with two great round vats in it, full of a white, wet, woolly-looking stuff, not unlike the albuminous part of an egg, soft-boiled.

"There," said Cupid, tapping the vats carelessly, "these are the first beginnings of the paper, this white pulp you see. Look how it swims bubbling round and round, moved by the paddle here. From hence it pours from both vats into that one common channel yonder, and so goes, mixed up and leisurely, to the great machine. And now for that."

He led me into a room, stifling with a strange, blood-like, abdominal heat, as if here, true enough, were being finally developed the germinous particles lately seen.

Before me, rolled out like some long Eastern manuscript, lay stretched one continuous length of iron framework—multitudinous and mystical, with all sorts of rollers, wheels, and cylinders, in slowly-measured and unceasing motion.

"Here first comes the pulp now," said Cupid, pointing to the highest end of the machine. "See; first it pours out and spreads itself upon this wide, sloping board; and then—look—slides, thin and quivering, beneath the first roller there. Follow on now, and see it as it slides from under that to the next cylinder. There; see how it has become just a very little less pulpy now. One step more, and it grows still more to some slight consistence. Still another cylinder, and it is so knitted—though as yet mere dragon-fly wing—that it forms an air-bridge here, like a suspended cobweb, between two more separated rollers; and flowing over the last one, and under again, and doubling about there out of sight for a minute among all those mixed cylinders you indistinctly see, it reappears here, looking now at last a little less like pulp and more like paper, but still quite delicate and defective yet awhile. But—a little further onward, sir, if you please—here now, at this further point, it puts on something of a real look, as if it might turn out to be something you might possibly handle in the end. But it's not yet done, sir. Good way to travel yet, and plenty more of cylinders must roll it."

"Bless my soul!" said I, amazed at the elongation, interminable convolutions, and deliberate slowness of the machine; "it must take a long time for the pulp to pass from end to end and come out paper."

"Oh! not so long," smiled the precocious lad, with a superior and patronizing air; "only nine minutes. But look; you may try it for yourself. Have you a bit of paper? Ah! here's a bit on the floor. Now mark that with any word you please, and let me dab it on here, and we'll see how long before it comes out at the other end."

"Well, let me see," said I, taking out my pencil; "come, I'll mark it with your name."

Bidding me take out my watch, Cupid adroitly dropped the inscribed slip on an exposed part of the incipient mass.

Instantly my eye marked the second-hand on my dial-plate.

Slowly I followed the slip, inch by inch; sometimes pausing for full half a minute as it disappeared beneath inscrutable groups of the lower cylinders, but only gradually to emerge again; and so, on, and on, and on—inch by inch; now in open sight, sliding along like a freckle on the quivering sheet; and then again wholly vanished; and so, on, and on, and on—inch by inch; all the time the main sheet growing more and more to final firmness—when, suddenly, I saw a sort of paper-fall, not wholly unlike a water-fall; a scissory sound smote my ear, as of some cord being snapped; and down dropped an unfolded sheet of perfect foolscap with my "Cupid" half faded out of it, and still moist and warm.

My travels were at an end, for here was the end of the machine.

"Well, how long was it?" said Cupid.

"Nine minutes to a second," replied I, watch in hand.

"I told you so."

For a moment a curious emotion filled me, not wholly unlike that which one might experience at the fulfillment of some mysterious prophecy. But how absurd, thought I again; the thing is a mere machine, the essence of which is unvarying punctuality and precision.

Previously absorbed by the wheels and cylinders, my attention was now directed to a sad-looking woman standing by.

"That is rather an elderly person so silently tending the machine-end here. She would not seem wholly used to it either."

"Oh," knowingly whispered Cupid, through the din, "she only came last week. She was a nurse formerly. But the business is poor in these parts, and she's left it. But look at the paper she is piling there."

"Aye, foolscap," handling the piles of moist, warm sheets, which continually were being delivered into the woman's waiting hands. "Don't you turn out anything but foolscap at this machine?"

"Oh, sometimes, but not often, we turn out finer work—cream-laid and royal sheets, we call them. But foolscap being in chief demand, we turn out foolscap most."

It was very curious. Looking at that blank paper continually dropping, dropping, dropping, my mind ran on in wonderings of those strange uses to which those thousand sheets eventually would be put. All sorts of writings would be writ on those now vacant things—sermons, lawyers' briefs, physicians' prescriptions, love-letters, marriage certificates, bills of divorce, registers of births, death-warrants, and so on, without end. Then, recurring back to them as they here lay all blank, I could not but bethink me of that celebrated comparison of John Locke, who, in demonstration of his theory that man had no innate ideas, compared the human mind at birth to a sheet of blank paper; something destined to be scribbled on, but what sort of characters no soul might tell.

Pacing slowly to and fro along the involved machine, still humming with its play, I was struck as well by the inevitability as the evolvement-power in all its motions.

"Does that thin cobweb there," said I, pointing to the sheet in its more imperfect stage, "does that never tear or break? It is marvelous fragile, and yet this machine it passes through is so mighty."

"It never is known to tear a hair's point."

"Does it never stop—get clogged?"

"No. It *must* go. The machinery makes it go just *so;* just that very way, and at that very pace you there plainly *see* it go. The pulp can't help going."

Something of awe now stole over me, as I gazed upon this inflexible iron animal. Always, more or less, machinery of this ponderous, elaborate sort strikes, in some moods, strange dread into the human heart, as some living, panting Behemoth might. But what made the thing I saw so specially terrible to me was the metallic necessity, the unbudging fatality which governed it. Though, here and there, I could not follow the thin, gauzy veil of pulp in the course of its more mysterious or entirely invisible advance, yet it was indubitable that, at those points where it eluded me, it still marched on in unvarying docility to the autocratic cunning of the machine. A fascination fastened on me. I stood spell-bound and wandering in my soul. Before my eyes—there, passing in slow procession along the wheeling cylinders, I seemed to see, glued to the pallid incipience of the pulp, the yet more pallid faces of all the pallid girls I had eyed that heavy day. Slowly, mournfully, beseechingly, yet unresistingly, they gleamed along, their agony dimly outlined on the imperfect paper, like the print of the tormented face on the handkerchief of Saint Veronica.

"Halloa! the heat of the room is too much for you," cried Cupid, staring at me.

"No—I am rather chill, if anything."

"Come out, sir—out—out," and, with the protecting air of a careful father, the precocious lad hurried me outside.

In a few moments, feeling revived a little, I went into the folding-room—the first room I had entered, and where the desk for transacting business stood, surrounded by the blank counters and blank girls engaged at them.

"Cupid here has led me a strange tour," said I to the dark-complexioned man before mentioned, whom I had ere this discovered not only to be an old bachelor, but also the principal proprietor. "Yours is a most wonderful factory. Your great machine is a miracle of inscrutable intricacy."

"Yes, all our visitors think it so. But we don't have many. We are in a very out-of-the-way corner here. Few inhabitants, too. Most of our girls come from far-off villages."

"The girls," echoed I, glancing round at their silent forms. "Why is it, sir, that in most factories, female operatives, of whatever age, are indiscriminately called girls, never women?"

"Oh! as to that—why, I suppose, the fact of their being generally unmarried—that's the reason, I should think. But it never struck me before. For our factory here, we will not have married women; they are apt to be off-and-on too much. We want none but steady workers: twelve hours to the day, day after day, through the three hundred and sixty-five days, excepting Sundays, Thanksgiving, and Fast-days. That's our rule. And so, having no married women, what females we have are rightly enough called girls."

"Then these are all maids," said I, while some pained homage to their pale virginity made me involuntarily bow.

"All maids."

Again the strange emotion filled me.

"Your cheeks look whitish yet, sir," said the man, gazing at me narrowly. "You must be careful going home. Do they pain you at all now? It's a bad sign, if they do."

"No doubt, sir," answered I, "when once I have got out of the Devil's Dungeon, I shall feel them mending."

"Ah, yes; the winter air in valleys, or gorges, or any sunken place, is far colder and more bitter than elsewhere. You would hardly believe it now, but it is colder here then at the top of Woedolor Mountain."

"I dare say it is, sir. But time presses me; I must depart."

With that, remuffling myself in dread-naught and tippet, thrusting my hands into my huge seal-skin mittens, I sallied out into the nipping air, and found poor Black, my horse, all cringing and doubled up with the cold.

Soon, wrapped in furs and meditations, I ascended from the Devil's Dungeon.

At the Black Notch I paused, and once more bethought me of Temple Bar. Then, shooting through the pass, all alone with inscrutable nature, I exclaimed—Oh! Paradise of Bachelors! and oh! Tartarus of Maids!

EDGAR ALLAN POE

(1809–1849)

The Fall of the House of Usher

About the Author: Edgar Allan Poe edited a number of literary periodicals and published poetry (see Chapter 3), fiction, criticism, and other nonfiction. He is regarded as one of the principal developers of the modern short story, and as among the founders of the detective story, the science fiction story, and the story of psychological analysis.

Son cœur est un luth suspendu;
Sitôt qu'on le touche il résonne.
—De Béranger

During the whole of a dull, dark, and soundless day in the autumn of the year, when the clouds hung oppressively low in the heavens, I had been passing alone, on horseback, through a singularly dreary tract of country; and at length found myself, as the shades of the evening drew on, within view of the melancholy House of Usher. I know not how it was—but, with the first glimpse of the building, a sense of insufferable gloom pervaded my spirit. I say insufferable; for the feeling was unrelieved by any of that half-pleasurable, because poetic, sentiment, with which the mind usually receives even the sternest natural images of the desolate or terrible. I looked upon the scene before me—upon the mere house, and the simple landscape features of the domain, upon the bleak walls, upon the vacant eye-like windows, upon a few rank sedges, and upon a few white trunks of decayed trees—with an utter depression of soul which I can compare to no earthly sensation more properly than to the after-dream of the reveller upon opium: the bitter lapse into everyday life, the hideous dropping off of the veil. There was an iciness, a sinking, a sickening of the heart, an unredeemed dreariness of thought which no goading of the imagination could torture into aught of the sublime. What was it—I paused to think—what was it that so unnerved me in the contemplation of the House of Usher? It was a mystery all insoluble; nor could I grapple with the shadowy fancies that crowded upon me as I pondered. I was forced to fall back upon the unsatisfactory conclusion, that while, beyond doubt, there *are* combinations of very simple natural objects which have the power of thus affecting us, still the analysis of this power lies among considerations beyond our depth. It was possible, I reflected, that a mere different arrangement of the particulars of the scene, of the details of the picture, would be sufficient to modify, or perhaps to annihilate its capacity for sorrowful impression; and, acting upon this idea, I reined my horse to the precipitous brink of a black and lurid tarn that lay in unruffled lustre by the dwelling, and gazed down—but with a shudder even more thrilling than before—upon the remodelled and inverted images of the gray sedge, and the ghastly tree-stems, and the vacant and eye-like windows.

Nevertheless, in this mansion of gloom I now proposed to myself a sojourn of some weeks. Its proprietor, Roderick Usher, had been one of my boon companions in boyhood; but many years had elapsed since our last meeting. A letter, however, had lately reached me in a distant part of the country—a letter from him—which, in its wildly importunate nature, had admitted of no other than a personal reply. The MS. gave evidence of nervous agitation. The writer spoke of acute bodily illness, of a mental disorder which oppressed him, and of an earnest desire to see me, as his best, and indeed his only personal friend, with a view of attempting, by the cheerfulness of my society, some alleviation of his malady. It was the manner in which all this, and much more, was said—it was the apparent *heart* that went with his request—which allowed me no room for hesitation; and I accordingly obeyed forthwith what I still considered a very singular summons.

Although, as boys, we had been even intimate associates, yet I really knew little of my friend. His reserve had been always excessive and habitual. I was aware, however, that his very ancient family had been noted, time out of mind, for a peculiar sensibility of temperament, displaying itself, through long ages, in many works of exalted art, and manifested, of late, in repeated deeds of munificent yet unobtrusive charity, as well as in a passionate devotion to the intricacies, perhaps even more than to the orthodox and easily recognizable beauties, of musical science. I had learned, too, the very remarkable fact, that the stem of the Usher race, all time-honored as it was, had put forth, at no period, any enduring branch; in other words, that the entire family lay in the direct line of descent, and had always, with very trifling and very temporary variation, so lain. It was this deficiency, I considered, while running over in thought the perfect keeping of the character of the premises with the accredited character of the people, and while speculating upon the possible influence which the one, in the long lapse of centuries, might have exercised upon the other—it was this deficiency, perhaps, of collateral issue, and the consequent undeviating transmission, from sire to son, of the patrimony with the name, which had, at length, so identified the two as to merge the original title of the estate in the quaint and equivocal appellation of the "House of Usher"—an appellation which seemed to include, in the minds of the peasantry who used it, both the family and the family mansion.

I have said that the sole effect of my somewhat childish experiment, that of looking down within the tarn, had been to deepen the first singular impression. There can be no doubt that the consciousness of the rapid increase of my superstition—for why should I not so term it?—served mainly to accelerate the increase itself. Such, I have long known, is the paradoxical law of all sentiments having terror as a basis. And it might have been for this reason only, that, when I again uplifted my eyes to the house itself, from its image in the pool, there grew in my mind a strange fancy—a fancy so ridiculous, indeed, that I but mention it to show the vivid force of the sensations which oppressed me. I had so worked upon my imagination as really to believe that about the whole mansion and domain there hung an atmosphere peculiar to themselves and their immediate vicinity: an atmosphere which had no affinity with the air of heaven, but which had reeked up from the decayed trees, and the gray wall, and the silent tarn: a pestilent and mystic vapor, dull, sluggish, faintly discernible, and leaden-hued.

Shaking off from my spirit what *must* have been a dream, I scanned more narrowly the real aspect of the building. Its principal feature seemed to be that of an excessive antiquity. The discoloration of ages had been great. Minute fungi overspread the whole exterior, hanging in a fine tangled webwork from the eaves. Yet all this was apart from any extraordinary dilapidation. No portion of the masonry had fallen; and there appeared to be a wild inconsistency between its still perfect adaptation of parts and the crumbling condition of the individual stones. In this there was much that reminded me of the specious totality of old wood-work which has rotted for long years in some neglected vault, with no disturbance from the breath of the external air. Beyond this indication of extensive decay, however, the fabric gave little token of instability. Perhaps the eye of a scrutinizing observer might have discovered a barely perceptible fissure, which, extending from the roof of the building in front, made its way down the wall in a zigzag direction, until it became lost in the sullen waters of the tarn.

Noticing these things, I rode over a short causeway to the house. A servant in waiting took my horse, and I entered the Gothic archway of the hall. A valet, of stealthy step, thence conducted me, in silence, through many dark and intricate passages in my progress to the *studio* of his master. Much that I encountered on the way contributed, I know not how, to heighten the vague sentiments of which I have already spoken. While the objects around me—while the carvings of the ceilings, the sombre tapestries of the walls, the ebon blackness of the floors, and the phantasmagoric armorial trophies which rattled as I strode, were but matters to which, or to such as which, I had been accustomed from my infancy—while I hesitated not to acknowledge how familiar was all this—I still wondered to find how unfamiliar were the fancies which ordinary images were stirring up. On one of the staircases, I met the physician of the family. His countenance, I thought, wore a mingled expression of low cunning and perplexity. He accosted me with trepidation and passed on. The valet now threw open a door and ushered me into the presence of his master.

The room in which I found myself was very large and lofty. The windows were long, narrow, and pointed, and at so vast a distance from the black oaken floor as to be altogether inaccessible from within. Feeble gleams of encrimsoned light made their way through the trellised panes, and served to render sufficiently distinct the more prominent objects around; the eye, however, struggled in vain to reach the remoter angles of the chamber, or the recesses of the vaulted and fretted ceiling. Dark draperies hung upon the walls. The general furniture was profuse, comfortless, antique, and tattered. Many books and musical instruments lay scattered about, but failed to give any vitality to the scene. I felt that I breathed an atmosphere of sorrow. An air of stern, deep, and irredeemable gloom hung over and pervaded all.

Upon my entrance, Usher arose from a sofa on which he had been lying at full length, and greeted me with a vivacious warmth which had much in it, I at first thought, of an overdone cordiality—of the constrained effort of the *ennuyé* man of the world. A glance, however, at his countenance, convinced me of his perfect sincerity. We sat down; and for some moments, while he spoke not, I gazed upon him with a feeling half of pity, half of awe. Surely, man had never before so terribly altered, in so brief a period, as had Roderick Usher! It was with difficulty that I could bring myself to admit the identity of the wan being before me with the companion of my early boyhood. Yet the character of his face had been at all times remarkable. A cadaverousness of complexion; an eye large, liquid, and luminous beyond comparison, lips somewhat thin and very pallid, but of a surpassingly beautiful curve; a nose of a delicate Hebrew model, but with a breadth of nostril unusual in similar formations; a finely moulded chin, speaking, in its want of prominence, of a want of moral energy; hair of a more than web-like softness and tenuity; these features, with an inordinate expansion above the regions of the temple, made up altogether a countenance not easily to be forgotten. And now in the mere exaggeration of the prevailing character of these features, and of the expression they were wont to convey, lay so much of change that I doubted to whom I spoke. The now ghastly pallor of the skin, and the now miraculous lustre of the eye, above all things startled and even awed me. The silken hair, too, had been suffered to grow all unheeded, and as, in its wild gossamer texture, it floated rather than fell about the face, I could not, even with effort, connect its Arabesque expression with any idea of simple humanity.

In the manner of my friend I was at once struck with an incoherence, an inconsistency; and I soon found this to arise from a series of feeble and futile struggles to overcome an habitual trepidancy, an excessive nervous agitation. For something of this nature I had indeed been prepared, no less by his letter, than by reminiscences of certain boyish traits, and by conclusions deduced from his peculiar physical conformation and temperament. His action was alternately vivacious and sullen. His voice varied rapidly from a tremulous indecision (when the animal spirits seemed utterly in abeyance) to that species of energetic concision—that abrupt, weighty, unhurried, and hollow-sounding enunciation—that leaden, self-balanced and perfectly modulated guttural utterance, which may be observed in the lost drunkard, or the irreclaimable eater of opium, during the periods of his most intense excitement.

It was thus that he spoke of the object of my visit, of his earnest desire to see me, and of the solace he expected me to afford him. He entered, at some length, into what he conceived to be the nature of his malady. It was, he said, a constitutional and a family evil, and one for which he despaired to find a remedy—a mere nervous affection, he immediately added, which would undoubtedly soon pass off. It displayed itself in a host of unnatural sensations. Some of these, as he detailed them, interested and bewildered me; although, perhaps, the terms, and the general manner of the narration had their weight. He suffered much from a morbid acuteness of the senses; the most insipid food was alone endurable; he could wear only garments of certain texture; the odors of all flowers were oppressive; his eyes were tortured by even a faint light; and there were but peculiar sounds, and these from stringed instruments, which did not inspire him with horror.

To an anomolous species of terror I found him a bounden slave. 'I shall perish,' said he, 'I *must* perish in this deplorable folly. Thus, thus, and not otherwise, shall I be lost. I dread the events of the future, not in themselves, but in their results. I shudder at the thought of any, even the most trivial, incident, which may operate upon this intolerable agitation of soul. I have, indeed, no abhorrence of danger, except in its absolute effect—in terror. In this unnerved—in this pitiable condition, I feel that the period will sooner or later arrive when I must abandon life and reason together, in some struggle with the grim phantasm, FEAR.'

I learned, moreover, at intervals, and through broken and equivocal hints, another singular feature of his mental condition. He was enchained by certain superstitious impressions in regard to the dwelling which he tenanted, and whence, for many years, he had never ventured forth—in regard to an influence whose suppositious force was conveyed in terms too shadowy here to be re-stated—an influence which some peculiarities in the mere form and substance of his family mansion, had, by dint of long sufferance, he said, obtained over his spirit—an effect which the *physique* of the gray walls and turrets, and of the dim tarn into which they all looked down, had, at length, brought about upon the *morale* of his existence.

He admitted, however, although with hesitation, that much of the peculiar gloom which thus afflicted him could be traced to a more natural and far more palpable origin—to the severe and long-continued illness, indeed to the evidently approaching dissolution, of a tenderly beloved sister—his sole companion for long years, his last and only relative on earth. 'Her decease,' he said, with a bitterness which I can never forget, 'would leave him (him the hopeless and the frail) the last of the ancient race of the Ushers.' While he spoke, the lady Madeline (for so was she called) passed slowly through a remote portion of the apartment, and, without having noticed my presence, disappeared. I regarded her with an utter astonishment not unmingled with dread, and yet I found it impossible to account for such feelings. A sensation of stupor oppressed me, as my eyes followed her retreating steps. When a door, at length, closed upon her, my glance sought instinctively and eagerly the countenace of the brother; but he had buried his face in his hands, and I could only perceive that a far more than ordinary wanness had overspread the emaciated fingers through which trickled many passionate tears.

The disease of the lady Madeline had long baffled the skill of her physicians. A settled apathy, a gradual wasting away of the person, and frequent although transient affections of a partially cataleptical character, were the unusual diagnosis. Hitherto she had steadily borne up against the pressure of her malady, and had not betaken herself finally to bed; but, on the closing in of the evening of my arrival at the house, she succumbed (as her brother told me at night with inexpressible agitation) to the prostrating power of the destroyer; and I learned that the glimpse I had obtained of her person would thus probably be the last I should obtain—that the lady, at least while living, would be seen by me no more.

For several days ensuing, her name was unmentioned by either Usher or myself: and during this period I was busied in earnest endeavors to alleviate the melancholy of my friend. We painted and read together; or I listened, as if in a dream, to the wild improvisations of his speaking guitar. And thus, as a closer and still closer intimacy admitted me more unreservedly into the recesses of his spirit, the more bitterly did I perceive the futility of all attempt at cheering a mind from which darkness, as if an inherent positive quality, poured forth upon all objects of the moral and physical universe, in one unceasing radiation of gloom.

I shall ever bear about me a memory of the many solemn hours I thus spent alone with the master of the House of Usher. Yet I should fail in any attempt to convey an idea of the exact character of the studies, or of the occupations, in which he involved me, or led me the way. An excited and highly distempered ideality threw a sulphureous lustre over all. His long improvised dirges will ring forever in my ears. Among other things, I hold painfully in mind a certain singular perversion and amplification of the wild air of the last waltz of Von Weber. From the paintings over which his elaborate fancy brooded, and which grew, touch by touch, into vaguenesses at which I shuddered the more thrillingly, because I shuddered knowing not why;—from these paintings (vivid as their images now are before me) I would in vain endeavor to educe more than a small portion which should lie within the compass of merely written words. By the utter simplicity, by the nakedness of his designs, he arrested and overawed attention. If ever mortal painted an idea, that mortal was Roderick Usher. For me at least, in the circumstances then surrounding me, there arose out of the pure abstractions which the hypochondriac contrived to throw upon his canvas, an intensity of intolerable awe, no shadow of which felt I ever yet in the contemplation of the certainly glowing yet too concrete reveries of Fuseli.

One of the phantasmagoric conceptions of my friend, partaking not so rigidly of the spirit of abstraction, may be shadowed forth, although feebly, in words. A small picture presented the interior of an immensely long and rectangular vault or tunnel, with low walls, smooth, white, and without interruption or device. Certain accessory points of the design served well to convey the idea that this excavation lay at an exceeding depth below the surface of the earth. No outlet was observed in any portion of its vast extent, and no torch, or other artificial source of light was discernible; yet a flood of intense rays rolled throughout, and bathed the whole in a ghastly and inappropriate splendor.

I have just spoken of that morbid condition of the auditory nerve which rendered all music intolerable to the sufferer, with the exception of certain effects of stringed instruments. It was, perhaps, the narrow limits to which he thus confined himself upon the guitar, which gave birth, in great measure, to the fantastic character of his performances. But the fervid *facility* of his *impromptus* could not be so accounted for. They must have been, and were, in the notes, as well as in the words of his wild fantasias (for he not unfrequently accompanied himself with rhymed verbal improvisations), the result of that intense mental collectedness and concentration to which I have previously alluded as observable only in particular moments of the highest artificial excitement. The words of one of these rhapsodies I have easily remembered. I was, perhaps, the more forcibly impressed with it, as he gave it, because, in the under or mystic current of its meaning, I fancied that I perceived, and for the first time, a full consciousness on the part of Usher, of the tottering of his lofty reason upon her throne. The verses, which were entitled "The Haunted Palace," ran very nearly, if not accurately, thus:

In the greenest of our valleys
   By good angels tenanted,
Once a fair and stately palace—
   Radiant palace—reared its head.
In the monarch Thought's dominion,
   It stood there!
Never seraph spread a pinion
   Over fabric half so fair!

Banners yellow, glorious, golden,
   On its roof did float and flow
(This—all this—was in the olden
   Time long ago)
And every gentle air that dallied,
   In that sweet day,
Along the ramparts plumed and pallid,
   A wingèd odor went away.

Wanderers in that happy valley,
  Through two luminous windows, saw
Spirits moving musically
  To a lute's well-tunèd law,
Round about a throne where, sitting,
  Porphyrogene!
In state his glory well befitting,
  The ruler of the realm was seen.

And all with pearl and ruby glowing
  Was the fair palace door,
Through which came flowing, flowing, flowing,
  And sparkling evermore,
A troop of Echoes, whose sweet duty
  Was but to sing,
In voices of surpassing beauty,
  The wit and wisdom of their king.

But evil things, in robes of sorrow,
  Assailed the monarch's high estate;
(Ah, let us mourn!—for never morrow
  Shall dawn upon him, desolate!)
And round about his home the glory
  That blushed and bloomed
Is but a dim-remembered story
  Of the old time entombed.

And travellers, now, within that valley,
  Through the red-litten windows see
Vast forms that move fantastically
  To a discordant melody;
While, like a ghastly rapid river,
  Through the pale door
A hideous throng rush out forever,
  And laugh—but smile no more.

I well remember that suggestions arising from this ballad led us into a train of thought wherein there became manifest an opinion of Usher's which I mention not so much on account of its novelty, (for other men have thought thus), as on account of the pertinacity with which he maintained it. This opinion, in its general form, was that of the sentience of all vegetable things. But, in his disordered fancy, the idea had assumed a more daring character, and trespassed, under certain conditions, upon the kingdom of inorganization. I lack words to express the full extent, or the earnest *abandon* of his persuasion. The belief, however, was connected (as I have previously hinted) with the gray stones of the home of his forefathers. The conditions of the sentience had been here, he imagined, fulfilled in the method of collocation of these stones—in the order of their arrangement, as well as in that of the many *fungi* which overspread them, and of the decayed trees which stood around—

above all, in the long undisturbed endurance of this arrangement, and in its reduplication in the still waters of the tarn. Its evidence—the evidence of the sentience—was to be seen, he said, (and I here started as he spoke), in the gradual yet certain condensation of an atmosphere of their own about the waters and the walls. The result was discoverable, he added, in that silent, yet importunate and terrible influence which for centuries had moulded the destinies of his family, and which made *him* what I now saw him—what he was. Such opinions need no comment, and I will make none.

Our books—the books which, for years, had formed no small portion of the mental existence of the invalid—were, as might be supposed, in strict keeping with this character of phantasm. We pored together over such works as the *Ververt et Chartreuse* of Gresset; the *Belphegor* of Machiavelli; the *Heaven and Hell* of Swedenborg; the *Subterranean Voyage of Nicholas Klimm* by Holberg; the *Chiromancy* of Robert Flud, of Jean D'Indaginé, and of De la Chambre; the *Journey into the Blue Distance* of Tieck; and the *City of the Sun* of Campanella. One favorite volume was a small octavo edition of the *Directorium Inquisitorum,* by the Dominican Eymeric de Gironne; and there were passages in Pomponius Mela, about the old African Satyrs and Aegipans, over which Usher would sit dreaming for hours. His chief delight, however, was found in the perusal of an exceedingly rare and curious book in quarto Gothic—the manual of a forgotten church—the *Vigilæ Mortuorum Secundum Chorum Ecclesiæ Maguntinæn.*

I could not help thinking of the wild ritual of this work, and of its probable influence upon the hypochondriac, when, one evening, having informed me abruptly that the lady Madeline was no more, he stated his intention of preserving her corpse for a fortnight, (previously to its final interment), in one of the numerous vaults within the main walls of the building. The worldly reason, however, assigned for this singular proceeding, was one which I did not feel at liberty to dispute. The brother had been led to his resolution (so he told me) by consideration of the unusual character of the malady of the deceased, of certain obtrusive and eager inquiries on the part of her medical men, and of the remote and exposed situation of the burial-ground of the family, I will not deny that when I called to mind the sinister countenance of the person whom I met upon the staircase, on the day of my arrival at the house, I had no desire to oppose what I regarded as at best but a harmless, and by no means an unnatural, precaution.

At the request of Usher, I personally aided him in the arrangements for the temporary entombment. The body having been encoffined, we two alone bore it to its rest. The vault in which we placed it (and which had been so long unopened that our torches, half smothered in its oppressive atmosphere, gave us little opportunity for investigation) was small, damp, and entirely without means of admission for light; lying, at great depth, immediately beneath that portion of the building in which was my own sleeping apartment. It had been used, apparently, in remote feudal times, for the worst purposes of a donjon-keep, and, in later days, as a place of deposit for powder, or some other highly combustible substance, as a portion of its floor, and the whole interior of a long archway through which we reached it, were carefully sheathed with copper. The door, of massive iron, had been, also, similarly protected. Its immense weight caused an unusually sharp grating sound, as it moved upon its hinges.

Having deposited our mournful burden upon tressels within this region of horror, we partially turned aside the yet unscrewed lid of the coffin, and looked upon the face of the tenant. A striking similitude between the brother and sister now first arrested my attention; and Usher, divining, perhaps, my thoughts, murmured out some few words from which I

learned that the deceased and himself had been twins, and that sympathies of a scarcely intelligible nature had always existed between them. Our glances, however, rested not long upon the dead—for we could not regard her unawed. The disease which had thus entombed the lady in the maturity of youth, had left, as usual in all maladies of a strictly cataleptical character, the mockery of a faint blush upon the bosom and the face, and that suspiciously lingering smile upon the lip which is so terrible in death. We replaced and screwed down the lid, and, having secured the door of iron, made our way, with toil, into the scarcely less gloomy apartments of the upper portion of the house.

And now, some days of bitter grief having elapsed, an observable change came over the features of the mental disorder of my friend. His ordinary manner had vanished. His ordinary occupations were neglected or forgotten. He roamed from chamber to chamber with hurried, unequal, and objectless step. The pallor of his countenance had assumed, if possible, a more ghastly hue—but the luminousness of his eye had utterly gone out. The once occasional huskiness of his tone was heard no more; and a tremulous quaver, as if of extreme terror, habitually characterized his utterance. There were times, indeed, when I thought his unceasingly agitated mind was laboring with some oppressive secret, to divulge which he struggled for the necessary courage. At times, again, I was obliged to resolve all into the mere inexplicable vagaries of madness, for I beheld him gazing upon vacancy for long hours, in an attitude of the profoundest attention, as if listening to some imaginary sound. It was no wonder that his condition terrified—that it infected me. I felt creeping upon me, by slow yet certain degrees, the wild influences of his own fantastic yet impressive superstitions.

It was, especially, upon retiring to bed late in the night of the seventh or eighth day after the placing of the lady Madeline within the donjon, that I experienced the full power of such feelings. Sleep came not near my couch, while the hours waned and waned away. I struggled to reason off the nervousness which had dominion over me. I endeavored to believe that much, if not all of what I felt, was due to the bewildering influence of the gloomy furniture of the room—of the dark and tattered draperies, which, tortured into motion by the breath of a rising tempest, swayed fitfully to and fro upon the walls, and rustled uneasily about the decorations of the bed. But my efforts were fruitless. An irrepressible tremor gradually pervaded my frame; and, at length, there sat upon my very heart an incubus of utterly causeless alarm. Shaking this off with a gasp and a struggle, I uplifted myself upon the pillows, and, peering earnestly within the intense darkness of the chamber, hearkened—I know not why, except that an instinctive spirit prompted me—to certain low and indefinite sounds which came, through the pauses of the storm, at long intervals I knew not whence. Overpowered by an intense sentiment of horror, unaccountable yet unendurable, I threw on my clothes with haste (for I felt that I should sleep no more during the night), and endeavored to arouse myself from the pitiable condition into which I had fallen, by pacing rapidly to and fro through the apartment.

I had taken but few turns in this manner, when a light step on an adjoining staircase arrested my attention. I presently recognized it as that of Usher. In an instant afterward he rapped, with a gentle touch, at my door, and entered, bearing a lamp. His countenance was, as usual, cadaverously wan—but, moreover, there was a species of mad hilarity in his eyes—an evidently restrained *hysteria* in his whole demeanor. His air appalled me—but anything was preferable to the solitude which I had so long endured, and I even welcomed his presence as a relief.

'And you have not seen it?' he said abruptly, after having stared about him for some moments in silence—'you have not then seen it?—but, stay! you shall.' Thus speaking, and having carefully shaded his lamp, he hurried to one of the casements and threw it freely open to the storm.

The impetuous fury of the entering gust nearly lifted us from our feet. It was, indeed, a tempestuous yet sternly beautiful night, and one wildly singular in its terror and its beauty. A whirlwind had apparently collected its force in our vicinity; for there were frequent and violent alterations in the direction of the wind; and the exceeding density of the clouds (which hung so low as to press upon the turrets of the house) did not prevent our perceiving the life-like velocity with which they flew careering from all points against each other, without passing away into the distance. I say that even their exceeding density did not prevent our perceiving this; yet we had no glimpse of the moon or stars, nor was there any flashing forth of the lightning. But the under surfaces of the huge masses of agitated vapor, as well as all terrestrial objects immediately around us, were glowing in the unnatural light of a faintly luminous and distinctly visible gaseous exhalation which hung about and enshrouded the mansion.

'You must not—you shall not behold this!' said I, shudderingly, to Usher, as I led him, with a gentle violence, from the window to a seat. 'These appearances, which bewilder you, are merely electrical phenomena not uncommon—or it may be that they have their ghastly origin in the rank miasma of the tarn. Let us close this casement; the air is chilling and dangerous to your frame. Here is one of your favorite romances. I will read, and you shall listen;—and so we will pass away this terrible night together.'

The antique volume which I had taken up was the *Mad Trist* of Sir Launcelot Canning; but I had called it a favorite of Usher's more in sad jest than in earnest; for, in truth, there is little in its uncouth and unimaginative prolixity which could have had interest for the lofty and spiritual ideality of my friend. It was, however, the only book immediately at hand; and I indulged a vague hope that the excitement which now agitated the hypochondriac might find relief (for the history of mental disorder is full of similar anomalies) even in the extremeness of the folly which I should read. Could I have judged, indeed, by the wild overstrained air of vivacity with which he hearkened, or apparently hearkened, to the words of the tale, I might well have congratulated myself upon the success of my design.

I had arrived at that well-known portion of the story where Ethelred, the hero of the *Trist,* having sought in vain for peaceable admission into the dwelling of the hermit, proceeds to make good an entrance by force. Here, it will be remembered, the words of the narrative run thus:

> And Ethelred, who was by nature of a doughty heart, and who was now mighty withal, on account of the powerfulness of the wine which he had drunken, waited no longer to hold parley with the hermit, who, in sooth, was of an obstinate and maliceful turn, but, feeling the rain upon his shoulders, and fearing the rising of the tempest, uplifted his mace outright, and, with blows, made quickly room in the plankings of the door for his gauntleted hand; and now pulling therewith sturdily, he so cracked, and ripped, and tore all asunder, that the noise of the dry and hollow-sounding wood alarmed and reverberated throughout the forest.

At the termination of this sentence I started, and for a moment, paused; for it appeared to me (although I at once concluded that my excited fancy had deceived me)—it appeared

to me that, from some very remote portion of the mansion, there came, indistinctly, to my ears, what might have been, in its exact similarity of character, the echo (but a stifled and dull one certainly) of the very cracking and ripping sound which Sir Launcelot had so particularly described. It was, beyond doubt, the coincidence alone which had arrested my attention; for, amid the rattling of the sashes of the casements, and the ordinary commingled noises of the still increasing storm, the sound, in itself, had nothing, surely, which should have interested or disturbed me. I continued the story:

> But the good champion Ethelred, now entering within the door, was sore enraged and amazed to perceive no signal of the maliceful hermit; but, in the stead thereof, a dragon of a scaly and prodigious demeanor, and of a fiery tongue, which sate in guard before a palace of gold, with a floor of silver; and upon the wall there hung a shield of shining brass with this legend enwritten—
>
> Who entereth herein, a conqueror hath bin;
> Who slayeth the dragon, the shield he shall win;
>
> And Ethelred uplifted his mace, and struck upon the head of the dragon, which fell before him, and gave up his pesty breath, with a shriek so horrid and harsh, and withal so piercing, that Ethelred had fain to close his ears with his hands against the dreadful noise of it, the like whereof was never before heard.

Here again I paused abruptly, and now with a feeling of wild amazement—for there could be no doubt whatever that, in this instance, I did actually hear (although from what direction it proceeded I found it impossible to say) a low and apparently distant, but harsh, protracted, and most unusual screaming or grating sound—the exact counterpart of what my fancy had already conjured up for the dragon's unnatural shriek as described by the romancer.

Oppressed, as I certainly was, upon the occurrence of the second and most extraordinary coincidence, by a thousand conflicting sensations, in which wonder and extreme terror were predominant, I still retained sufficient presence of mind to avoid exciting, by any observation, the sensitive nervousness of my companion. I was by no means certain that he had noticed the sounds in question; although, assuredly, a strange alteration had, during the last few minutes, taken place in his demeanor. From a position fronting my own, he had gradually brought round his chair, so as to sit with his face to the door of the chamber; and thus I could but partially perceive his features, although I saw that his lips trembled as if he were murmuring inaudibly. His head had dropped upon his breast—yet I knew that he was not asleep, from the wide and rigid opening of the eye as I caught a glance of it in profile. The motion of his body, too, was at variance with this idea—for he rocked from side to side with a gentle yet constant and uniform sway. Having rapidly taken notice of all this, I resumed the narrative of Sir Launcelot, which thus proceeded:

> And now, the champion, having escaped from the terrible fury of the dragon, bethinking himself of the brazen shield, and of the breaking up of the enchantment which was upon it, removed the carcass from out of the way before him, and approached valorously over the silver pavement of the castle to where the shield was upon the wall; which in sooth tarried not for his

full coming, but fell down at his feet upon the silver floor, with a mighty great and terrible ringing sound.

No sooner had these syllables passed my lips, than—as if a shield of brass had indeed, at the moment, fallen heavily upon a floor of silver—I became aware of a distinct, hollow, metallic and clangorous yet apparently muffled reverberation. Completely unnerved, I leaped to my feet; but the measured rocking movement of Usher was undisturbed. I rushed to the chair in which he sat. His eyes were bent fixedly before him, and throughout his whole countenance there reigned a stony rigidity. But as I placed my hand upon his shoulder, there came a strong shudder over his whole person; a sickly smile quivered about his lips; and I saw that he spoke in a low, hurried, and gibbering murmur, as if unconscious of my presence. Bending closely over him, I at length drank in the hideous import of his words.

'Not hear it?—yes, I hear it, and *have* heard it. Long—long—long—many minutes, many hours, many days, have I heard it—yet I dared not—oh, pity me, miserable wretch that I am!—I dared not—I *dared* not speak! *We have put her living in the tomb!* Said I not that my senses were acute? I *now* tell you that I heard her first feeble movements in the hollow coffin. I heard them—many, many days ago—yet I dared not—*I dared not speak!* And now—to-night—Ethelred—ha! ha!—the breaking of the hermit's door, and the death-cry of the dragon, and the clangor of the shield!—say, rather, the rending of her coffin, and the grating of the iron hinges of her prison, and her struggles within the coppered archway of the vault! Oh whither shall I fly? Will she not be here anon? Is she not hurrying to upbraid me for my haste? Have I not heard her footstep on the stair? Do I not distinguish that heavy and horrible beating of her heart? MADMAN!' here he sprang furiously to his feet, and shrieked out his syllables, as if in the effort he were giving up his soul—*'Madman! I tell you that she now stands without the door!'*

As if in the superhuman energy of his utterance there had been found the potency of a spell, the huge antique panels to which the speaker pointed, threw slowly back, upon the instant, their ponderous and ebony jaws. It was the work of the rushing gust—but then without those doors there DID stand the lofty and enshrouded figure of the lady Madeline of Usher. There was blood upon her white robes, and the evidence of some bitter struggle upon every portion of her emaciated frame. For a moment she remained trembling and reeling to and fro upon the threshold—then, with a low moaning cry, fell heavily inward upon the person of her brother, and in her violent and now final death-agonies, bore him to the floor a corpse, and a victim to the terrors he had anticipated.

From that chamber, and from that mansion, I fled aghast. The storm was still abroad in all its wrath as I found myself crossing the old causeway. Suddenly there shot along the path a wild light, and I turned to see whence a gleam so unusual could have issued; for the vast house and its shadows were alone behind me. The radiance was that of the full, setting, and blood-red moon which now shone vividly through that once barely-discernible fissure of which I have before spoken as extending from the roof of the building, in a zigzag direction, to the base. While I gazed, this fissure rapidly widened—there came a fierce breath of the whirlwind—the entire orb of the satellite burst at once upon my sight—my brain reeled as I saw the mighty walls rushing asunder—there was a long tumultuous shouting sound like the voice of a thousand waters—and the deep and dank tarn at my feet closed sullenly and silently over the fragments of the HOUSE OF USHER.

NATHANIEL HAWTHORNE

(1804–1864)

My Kinsman, Major Molineux

About the Author: Nathaniel Hawthorne was born in Salem, Massachusetts, where his family had lived for generations. He published numerous historical and allegorical tales, some nonfiction, and five novels (or "romances," as he termed them), of which *The Scarlet Letter* (1850) and *The House of the Seven Gables* (1851) are most widely read.

After the kings of Great Britain had assumed the right of appointing the colonial governors, the measures of the latter seldom met with the ready and general approbation which had been paid to those of their predecessors, under the original charters. The people looked with most jealous scrutiny to the exercise of power which did not emanate from themselves, and they usually rewarded their rulers with slender gratitude for the compliances by which, in softening their instructions from beyond the sea, they had incurred the reprehension of those who gave them. The annals of Massachusetts Bay will inform us, that of six governors in the space of about forty years from the surrender of the old charter, under James II., two were imprisoned by a popular insurrection; a third, as Hutchinson inclines to believe, was driven from the province by the whizzing of a musket-ball; a fourth, in the opinion of the same historian, was hastened to his grave by continual bickerings with the House of Representatives; and the remaining two, as well as their successors, till the Revolution, were favored with few and brief intervals of peaceful sway. The inferior members of the court party, in times of high political excitement, led scarcely a more desirable life. These remarks may serve as a preface to the following adventures, which chanced upon a summer night, not far from a hundred years ago. The reader, in order to avoid a long and dry detail of colonial affairs, is requested to dispense with an account of the train of circumstances that had caused much temporary inflammation of the popular mind.

It was near nine o'clock of a moonlight evening, when a boat crossed the ferry with a single passenger, who had obtained his conveyance at that unusual hour by the promise of an extra fare. While he stood on the landing-place, searching in either pocket for the means of fulfilling his agreement, the ferryman lifted a lantern, by the aid of which, and the newly risen moon, he took a very accurate survey of the stranger's figure. He was a youth of barely eighteen years, evidently country-bred, and now, as it should seem, upon his first visit to town. He was clad in a coarse gray coat, well worn, but in excellent repair; his under garments were durably constructed of leather, and fitted tight to a pair of serviceable and well-shaped limbs; his stockings of blue yarn were the incontrovertible work of a mother or a sister; and on his head was a three-cornered hat, which in its better days had perhaps sheltered the graver brow of the lad's father. Under his left arm was a heavy cudgel, formed of an oak sapling, and retaining a part of the hardened root; and his equipment was completed by a wallet, not so abundantly stocked as to incommode the vigorous shoulders on which it hung. Brown, curly hair, well-shaped features, and bright, cheerful eyes were nature's gifts, and worth all that art could have done for his adornment.

The youth, one of whose names was Robin, finally drew from his pocket the half of a little province bill of five shillings, which, in the depreciation of that sort of currency, did but satisfy the ferryman's demand, with the surplus of a sexangular piece of parchment, valued at three pence. He then walked forward into the town, with as light a step as if his day's journey had not already exceeded thirty miles, and with as eager an eye as if he were entering London city, instead of the little metropolis of a New England colony. Before Robin had proceeded far, however, it occurred to him that he knew not whither to direct his steps; so he paused, and looked up and down the narrow street, scrutinizing the small and mean wooden buildings that were scattered on either side.

"This low hovel cannot be my kinsman's dwelling," thought he, "nor yonder old house, where the moonlight enters at the broken casement; and truly I see none hereabouts that might be worthy of him. It would have been wise to inquire my way of the ferryman, and doubtless he would have gone with me, and earned a shilling from the Major for his pains. But the next man I meet will do as well."

He resumed his walk, and was glad to perceive that the street now became wider, and the houses more respectable in their appearance. He soon discerned a figure moving on moderately in advance, and hastened his steps to overtake it. As Robin drew nigh, he saw that the passenger was a man in years, with a full periwig of gray hair, a wide-skirted coat of dark cloth, and silk stockings rolled above his knees. He carried a long and polished cane, which he struck down perpendicularly before him, at every step; and at regular intervals he uttered two successive hems, of a peculiarly solemn and sepulchral intonation. Having made these observations, Robin laid hold of the skirt of the old man's coat, just when the light from the open door and windows of a barber's shop fell upon both their figures.

"Good evening to you, honored sir, said he, making a low bow, and still retaining his hold of the skirt. "I pray you tell me whereabouts is the dwelling of my kinsman, Major Molineux."

The youth's question was uttered very loudly; and one of the barbers, whose razor was descending on a well-soaped chin, and another who was dressing a Ramillies wig, left their occupations, and came to the door. The citizen, in the mean time, turned a long-favored countenance upon Robin, and answered him in a tone of excessive anger and annoyance. His two sepulchral hems, however, broke into the very centre of his rebuke, with most singular effect, like a thought of the cold grave obtruding among wrathful passions.

"Let go my garment, fellow! I tell you, I know not the man you speak of. What! I have authority, I have—hem, hem—authority; and if this be the respect you show for your betters, your feet shall be brought acquainted with the stocks by daylight, to-morrow morning!"

Robin released the old man's skirt, and hastened away, pursued by an ill-mannered roar of laughter from the barber's shop. He was at first considerably surprised by the result of his question, but, being a shrewd youth, soon thought himself able to account for the mystery.

"This is some country representative," was his conclusion, "who has never seen the inside of my kinsman's door, and lacks the breeding to answer a stranger civilly. The man is old, or verily—I might be tempted to turn back and smite him on the nose. Ah, Robin, Robin! even the barber's boys laugh at you for choosing such a guide! You will be wiser in time, friend Robin."

He now became entangled in a succession of crooked and narrow streets, which crossed each other, and meandered at no great distance from the water-side. The smell of tar was obvious to his nostrils, the masts of vessels pierced the moonlight above the tops of the buildings, and the numerous signs, which Robin paused to read, informed him that he was near the centre of business. But the streets were empty, the shops were closed, and lights were visible only in the second stories of a few dwelling-houses. At length, on the corner of a narrow lane, through which he was passing, he beheld the broad countenance of a British hero swinging before the door of an inn, whence proceeded the voices of many guests. The casement of one of the lower windows was thrown back, and a very thin curtain permitted Robin to distinguish a party at supper, round a well-furnished table. The fragrance of the good cheer steamed forth into the outer air, and the youth could not fail to recollect that the last remnant of his travelling stock of provision had yielded to his morning appetite, and that noon had found and left him dinnerless.

"O, that a parchment three-penny might give me a right to sit down at yonder table!" said Robin, with a sigh. "But the Major will make me welcome to the best of his victuals; so I will even step boldly in, and inquire my way to his dwelling."

He entered the tavern, and was guided by the murmur of voices and the fumes of tobacco to the public-room. It was a long and low apartment, with oaken walls, grown dark in the continual smoke, and a floor which was thickly sanded, but of no immaculate purity. A number of persons—the larger part of whom appeared to be mariners, or in some way connected with the sea—occupied the wooden benches, or leather-bottomed chairs, conversing on various matters, and occasionally lending their attention to some topic of general interest. Three or four little groups were draining as many bowls of punch, which the West India trade had long since made a familiar drink in the colony. Others, who had the appearance of men who lived by regular and laborious handicraft, preferred the insulated bliss of an unshared potation, and became more taciturn under its influence. Nearly all, in short, evinced a predilection for the Good Creature in some of its various shapes, for this is a vice to which, as Fast-day sermons of a hundred years ago will testify, we have a long hereditary claim. The only guests to whom Robin's sympathies inclined him were two or three sheepish countrymen, who were using the inn somewhat after the fashion of a Turkish caravansary; they had gotten themselves into the darkest corner of the room, and, heedless of the Nicotian atmosphere, were supping on the bread of their own ovens, and the bacon cured in their own chimney-smoke. But though Robin felt a sort of brotherhood with these strangers, his eyes were attracted from them to a person who stood near the door, holding whispered conversation with a group of ill-dressed associates. His features were separately striking almost to grotesqueness, and the whole face left a deep impression on the memory. The forehead bulged out into a double prominence, with a vale between; the nose came boldly forth in an irregular curve, and its bridge was of more than a finger's breadth; the eyebrows were deep and shaggy, and the eyes glowed beneath them like fire in a cave.

While Robin deliberated of whom to inquire respecting his kinsman's dwelling, he was accosted by the innkeeper, a little man in a stained white apron, who had come to pay his professional welcome to the stranger. Being in the second generation from a French Protestant, he seemed to have inherited the courtesy of his parent nation; but no variety of circumstances was ever known to change his voice from the one shrill note in which he now addressed Robin.

"From the country, I presume, sir?" said he, with a profound bow. "Beg leave to congratulate you on your arrival, and trust you intend a long stay with us. Fine town here, sir, beautiful buildings, and much that may interest a stranger. May I hope for the honor of your commands in respect to supper?"

"The man sees a family likeness! The rogue has guessed that I am related to the Major!" thought Robin, who had hitherto experienced little superfluous civility.

All eyes were now turned on the country lad, standing at the door, in his worn three-cornered hat, gray coat, leather breeches, and blue yarn stockings, leaning on an oaken cudgel, and bearing a wallet on his back.

Robin replied to the courteous innkeeper, with such an assumption of confidence as befitted the Major's relative. "My honest friend," he said, "I shall make it a point to patronize your house on some occasion, when"—here he could not help lowering his voice—"when I may have more than a parchment three-pence in my pocket. My present business," continued he, speaking with lofty confidence, "is merely to inquire my way to the dwelling of my kinsman, Major Molineux."

There was a sudden and general movement in the room, which Robin interpreted as expressing the eagerness of each individual to become his guide. But the innkeeper turned his eyes to a written paper on the wall, which he read, or seemed to read, with occasional recurrences to the young man's figure.

"What have we here?" said he, breaking his speech into little dry fragments. " 'Left the house of the subscriber, bounden servant, Hezekiah Mudge,—had on, when he went away, gray coat, leather breeches, master's third-best hat. One pound currency reward to whosoever shall lodge him in any jail of the province.' Better trudge, boy, better trudge!"

Robin had begun to draw his hand towards the lighter end of the oak cudgel, but a strange hostility in every countenance induced him to relinquish his purpose of breaking the courteous innkeeper's head. As he turned to leave the room, he encountered a sneering glance from the bold-featured personage whom he had before noticed; and no sooner was he beyond the door, than he heard a general laugh, in which the innkeeper's voice might be distinguished, like the dropping of small stones into a kettle.

"Now, is it not strange," thought Robin, with his usual shrewdness,—"is it not strange that the confession of an empty pocket should outweigh the name of my kinsman, Major Molineux? O, if I had one of those grinning rascals in the woods, where I and my oak sapling grew up together, I would teach him that my arm is heavy, though my purse be light!"

On turning the corner of the narrow lane, Robin found himself in a spacious street, with an unbroken line of lofty houses on each side, and a steepled building at the upper end, whence the ringing of a bell announced the hour of nine. The light of the moon, and the lamps from the numerous shop-windows, discovered people promenading on the pavement, and amongst them Robin hoped to recognize his hitherto inscrutable relative. The result of his former inquiries made him unwilling to hazard another, in a scene of such publicity, and he determined to walk slowly and silently up the street, thrusting his face close to that of every elderly gentleman, in search of the Major's lineaments. In his progress, Robin encountered many gay and gallant figures. Embroidered garments of showy colors, enormous periwigs, gold-laced hats, and silver-hilted swords glided past him and dazzled his optics. Travelled youths, imitators of the European fine gentlemen of the period, trod jauntily along, half dancing to the fashionable tunes which they hummed, and making poor Robin ashamed of his quiet and natural gait. At length, after many pauses to examine the gorgeous display of goods in the shop-windows, and after suffering some rebukes for the impertinence of his scrutiny into people's faces, the Major's kinsman found himself near the steepled building, still unsuccessful in his search. As yet, however, he had seen only one side of the thronged street; so Robin crossed, and continued the same sort of inquisition down the opposite pavement, with stronger hopes than the philosopher seeking an honest man, but with no better fortune. He had arrived about midway towards the lower end, from which his course began, when he overheard the approach of some one who struck down a cane on the flag-stones at every step, uttering, at regular intervals, two sepulchral hems.

"Mercy on us!" quoth Robin, recognizing the sound.

Turning a corner, which chanced to be close at his right hand, he hastened to pursue his researches in some other part of the town. His patience now was wearing low, and he seemed to feel more fatigue from his rambles since he crossed the ferry, than from his journey of several days on the other side. Hunger also pleaded loudly within him, and Robin began to balance the propriety of demanding, violently, and with lifted cudgel, the necessary guidance from the first solitary passenger whom he should meet. While a resolution to this effect was gaining strength, he entered a street of mean appearance, on either side of which a row of ill-built houses was straggling towards the harbor. The moonlight fell upon no passenger along the whole extent, but in the third domicile which Robin passed there was a half-opened door, and his keen glance detected a woman's garment within.

"My luck may be better here," said he to himself.

Accordingly, he approached the door, and beheld it shut closer as he did so; yet an open space remained, sufficing for the fair occupant to observe the stranger, without a corresponding display on her part. All that Robin could discern was a strip of scarlet petticoat, and the occasional sparkle of an eye, as if the moonbeams were trembling on some bright thing.

"Pretty mistress," for I may call her so with a good conscience, thought the shrewd youth, since I know nothing to the contrary,—"my sweet pretty mistress, will you be kind enough to tell me whereabouts I must seek the dwelling of my kinsman, Major Molineux?"

Robin's voice was plaintive and winning, and the female, seeing nothing to be shunned in the handsome country youth, thrust open the door, and came forth into the moonlight. She was a dainty little figure, with a white neck, round arms, and a slender waist, at the extremity of which her scarlet petticoat jutted out over a hoop, as if she were standing in a balloon. Moreover, her face was oval and pretty, her hair dark beneath the little cap, and her bright eyes possessed a sly freedom, which triumphed over those of Robin.

"Major Molineux dwells here," said this fair woman.

Now, her voice was the sweetest Robin had heard that night, the airy counterpart of a stream of melted silver; yet he could not help doubting whether that sweet voice spoke Gospel truth. He looked up and down the mean street, and then surveyed the house before which they stood. It was a small, dark edifice of two stories, the second of which projected over the lower floor; and the front apartment had the aspect of a shop for petty commodities.

"Now, truly, I am in luck," replied Robin, cunningly, "and so indeed is my kinsman, the Major, in having so pretty a housekeeper. But I prithee trouble him to step to the door; I will deliver him a message from his friends in the country, and then go back to my lodgings at the inn."

"Nay, the Major has been abed this hour or more," said the lady of the scarlet petticoat; "and it would be to little purpose to disturb him tonight, seeing his evening draught was of the strongest. But he is a kind-hearted man, and it would be as much as my life's worth to let a kinsman of his turn away from the door. You are the good old gentleman's very picture, and I could swear that was his rainy-weather hat. Also he has garments very much resembling those leather small-clothes. But come in, I pray, for I bid you hearty welcome in his name."

So saying, the fair and hospitable dame took our hero by the hand; and the touch was light, and the force was gentleness, and though Robin read in her eyes what he did not hear in her words, yet the slender-waisted woman in the scarlet petticoat proved stronger than the athletic country youth. She had drawn his half-willing footsteps nearly to the threshold, when the opening of a door in the neighborhood startled the Major's housekeeper, and, leaving the Major's kinsman, she vanished speedily into her own domicile. A heavy yawn preceded the appearance of a man, who, like the Moonshine of Pyramus and Thisbe, carried a lantern, needlessly aiding his sister luminary in the heavens. As he walked sleepily up the street, he turned his broad, dull face on Robin, and displayed a long staff, spiked at the end.

"Home, vagabond, home!" said the watchman, in accents that seemed to fall asleep as soon as they were uttered. "Home, or we'll set you in the stocks, by peep of day!"

"This is the second hint of the kind," thought Robin. "I wish they would end my difficulties, by setting me there to-night."

Nevertheless, the youth felt an instinctive antipathy towards the guardian of midnight order, which at first prevented him from asking his usual question. But just when the man was about to vanish behind the corner, Robin resolved not to lose the opportunity, and shouted lustily after him,—

"I say, friend! will you guide me to the house of my kinsman, Major Molineux?"

The watchman made no reply, but turned the corner and was gone; yet Robin seemed to hear the sound of drowsy laughter stealing along the solitary street. At that moment, also, a pleasant titter saluted him from the open window above his head; he looked up, and caught the sparkle of a saucy eye; a round arm beckoned to him, and next he heard light footsteps descending the staircase within. But Robin, being of the household of a New England clergyman, was a good youth, as well as a shrewd one; so he resisted temptation, and fled away.

He now roamed desperately, and at random, through the town, almost ready to believe that a spell was on him, like that by which a wizard of his country had once kept three pursuers wandering, a whole winter night, within twenty paces of the cottage which they sought. The streets lay before him, strange and desolate, and the lights were extinguished in almost every house. Twice, however, little parties of men, among whom Robin distinguished individuals in outlandish attire, came hurrying along; but though on both occasions they paused to address him, such intercourse did not at all enlighten his perplexity. They did but utter a few words in some language of which Robin knew nothing, and perceiving his inability to answer, bestowed a curse upon him in plain English, and hastened away. Finally, the lad determined to knock at the door of every mansion that might appear worthy to be occupied by his kinsman, trusting that perseverance would overcome the fatality that had hitherto thwarted him. Firm in this resolve, he was passing beneath the walls of a church, which formed the corner of two streets, when, as he turned into the shade of its steeple, he encountered a bulky stranger, muffled in a cloak. The man was proceeding with the speed of earnest business, but Robin planted himself full before him, holding the oak cudgel with both hands across his body as a bar to further passage.

"Halt, honest man, and answer me a question," said he, very resolutely. "Tell me, this instant, whereabouts is the dwelling of my kinsman, Major Molineux!"

"Keep your tongue between your teeth, fool, and let me pass!" said a deep, gruff voice, which Robin partly remembered. "Let me pass, I say, or I'll strike you to the earth!"

"No, no, neighbor!" cried Robin, flourishing his cudgel, and then thrusting its larger end close to the man's muffled face. "No, no, I'm not the fool you take me for, nor do you pass till I have an answer to my question. Whereabouts is the dwelling of my kinsman, Major Molineux?"

The stranger, instead of attempting to force his passage, stepped back into the moonlight, unmuffled his face, and stared full into that of Robin.

"Watch here an hour, and Major Molineux will pass by," said he.

Robin gazed with dismay and astonishment on the unprecedented physiognomy of the speaker. The forehead with its double prominence, the broad hooked nose, the shaggy eyebrows, and fiery eyes were those which he had noticed at the inn, but the man's complexion had undergone a singular, or, more properly, a twofold change. One side of the face blazed an intense red, while the other was black as midnight, the division line being in the broad bridge of the nose; and a mouth which seemed to extend from ear to ear was black or red, in contrast to the color of the cheek. The effect was as if two individual devils, a fiend of fire and a fiend of darkness, had united themselves to form this infernal visage. The stranger grinned in Robin's face, muffled his party-colored features, and was out of sight in a moment.

"Strange things we travellers see!" ejaculated Robin.

He seated himself, however, upon the steps of the church-door, resolving to wait the appointed time for his kinsman. A few moments were consumed in philosophical speculations upon the species of man who had just left him; but having settled this point shrewdly, rationally, and satisfactorily, he was compelled to look elsewhere for his amusement. And first he threw his eyes along the street. It was of more respectable appearance than most of those into which he had wandered, and the moon, creating, like the imaginative power, a beautiful strangeness in familiar objects, gave something of romance to a scene that might not have possessed it in the light of day. The irregular and often quaint architecture of the houses, some of whose roofs were broken into numerous little peaks, while others ascended, steep and narrow, into a single point, and others again were square; the pure snow-white of some of their complexions, the aged darkness of others, and the thousand sparklings, reflected from bright substances in the walls of many; these matters engaged Robin's attention for a while, and then began to grow wearisome. Next he endeavored to define the forms of distant objects, starting away, with almost ghostly indistinctness, just as his eye appeared to grasp them; and finally he took a minute survey of an edifice which stood on the opposite side of the street, directly in front of the church-door, where he was stationed. It was a large, square mansion, distinguished from its neighbors by a balcony, which rested on tall pillars, and by an elaborate Gothic window, communicating therewith.

"Perhaps this is the very house I have been seeking," thought Robin.

Then he strove to speed away the time, by listening to a murmur which swept continually along the street, yet was scarcely audible, except to an unaccustomed ear like his; it was a low, dull, dreamy sound, compounded of many noises, each of which was at too great a distance to be separately heard. Robin marvelled at this snore of a sleeping town, and marvelled more whenever its continuity was broken by now and then a distant shout, apparently loud where it originated. But altogether it was a sleep-inspiring sound, and, to shake off its drowsy influence, Robin arose, and climbed a window-frame, that he might view the interior of the church. There the moonbeams came trembling in, and fell down upon the deserted pews, and extended along the quiet aisles. A fainter yet more awful radiance was hovering around the pulpit, and one solitary ray had dared to rest upon the open page of the great Bible. Had nature, in that deep hour, become a worshipper in the house which man had builded? Or was that heavenly light the visible sanctity of the place,—visible because no earthly and impure feet were within the walls? The scene made Robin's heart shiver with a sensation of loneliness stronger than he had ever felt in the remotest depths of his native woods; so he turned away, and sat down again before the door.

There were graves around the church, and now an uneasy thought obtruded into Robin's breast. What if the object of his search, which had been so often and so strangely thwarted, were all the time mouldering in his shroud? What if his kinsman should glide through yonder gate, and nod and smile to him in dimly passing by?

"O that any breathing thing were here with me!" said Robin.

Recalling his thoughts from this uncomfortable track, he sent them over forest, hill, and stream, and attempted to imagine how that evening of ambiguity and weariness had been spent by his father's household. He pictured them assembled at the door, beneath the tree, the great old tree, which had been spared for its huge twisted trunk, and venerable shade, when a thousand leafy brethren fell. There, at the going down of the summer sun, it was his father's custom to perform domestic worship, that the neighbors might come and join with him like brothers of the family, and that the wayfaring man might pause to drink at that fountain, and keep his heart pure by freshening the memory of home. Robin distinguished the seat of every individual of the little audience; he saw the good man in the midst, holding the Scriptures in the golden light that fell from the western clouds; he beheld him close the book and all rise up to pray. He heard the old thanksgivings for daily mercies, the old supplications for their continuance, to which he had so often listened in weariness, but which were now among his dear remembrances. He perceived the slight inequality of his father's voice when he came to speak of the absent one; he noted how his mother turned her face to the broad and knotted trunk; how his elder brother scorned, because the beard was rough upon his upper lip, to permit his features to be moved; how the younger sister drew down a low hanging branch before her eyes; and how the little one of all, whose sports had hitherto broken the decorum of the scene, understood the prayer for her playmate, and burst into clamorous grief. Then he saw them go in at the door; and when Robin would have entered also, the latch tinkled into its place, and he was excluded from his home.

"Am I here, or there?" cried Robin, starting; for all at once, when his thoughts had become visible and audible in a dream, the long, wide, solitary street shone out before him.

He aroused himself, and endeavored to fix his attention steadily upon the large edifice which he had surveyed before. But still his mind kept vibrating between fancy and reality; by turns, the pillars of the balcony lengthened into the tall, bare stems of pines, dwindled down to human figures, settled again into their true shape and size, and then commenced a new succession of changes. For a single moment, when he deemed himself awake, he could have sworn that a visage—one which he seemed to remember, yet could not absolutely name as his kinsman's—was looking towards him from the Gothic window. A deeper sleep wrestled with and nearly overcame him, but fled at the sound of footsteps along the opposite pavement. Robin rubbed his eyes, discerned a man passing at the foot of the balcony, and addressed him in a loud, peevish, and lamentable cry.

"Hallo, friend! must I wait here all night for my kinsman, Major Molineux?"

The sleeping echoes awoke, and answered the voice; and the passenger, barely able to discern a figure sitting in the oblique shade of the steeple, traversed the street to obtain a nearer view. He was himself a gentleman in his prime, of open, intelligent, cheerful, and altogether prepossessing countenance. Perceiving a country youth, apparently homeless and without friends, he accosted him in a tone of real kindness, which had become strange to Robin's ears.

"Well, my good lad, why are you sitting here?" inquired he. "Can I be of service to you in any way?"

"I am afraid not, sir," replied Robin, despondingly; "yet I shall take it kindly, if you'll answer me a single question. I've been searching, half the night, for one Major Molineux; now, sir, is there really such a person in these parts, or am I dreaming?"

"Major Molineux! The name is not altogether strange to me," said the gentleman, smiling. "Have you any objection to telling me the nature of your business with him?"

Then Robin briefly related that his father was a clergyman, settled on a small salary, at a long distance back in the country, and that he and Major Molineux were brothers' children. The Major, having inherited riches, and acquired civil and military rank, had visited his cousin, in great pomp, a year or two before; had manifested much interest in Robin and an elder brother, and, being childless himself, had thrown out hints respecting the future establishment of one of them in life. The elder brother was destined to succeed to the farm which his father cultivated in the interval of sacred duties; it was therefore determined that Robin should profit by his kinsman's generous intentions, especially as he seemed to be rather the favorite, and was thought to possess other necessary endowments.

"For I have the name of being a shrewd youth," observed Robin, in this part of his story.

"I doubt not you deserve it," replied his new friend, good-naturedly; "but pray proceed."

"Well, sir, being nearly eighteen years old, and well grown, as you see," continued Robin, drawing himself up to his full height, "I thought it high time to begin the world. So my mother and sister put me in handsome trim, and my father gave me half the remnant of his last year's salary, and five days ago I started for this place, to pay the Major a visit. But, would you believe it, sir! I crossed the ferry a little after dark, and have yet found nobody that would show me the way to his dwelling; only, an hour or two since, I was told to wait here, and Major Molineux would pass by."

"Can you describe the man who told you this?" inquired the gentleman.

"O, he was a very ill-favored fellow, sir," replied Robin, "with two great bumps on his forehead, a hook nose, fiery eyes; and, what struck me as the strangest, his face was of two different colors. Do you happen to know such a man, sir?"

"Not intimately," answered the stranger, "but I chanced to meet him a little time previous to your stopping me. I believe you may trust his word, and that the Major will very shortly pass through this street. In the meantime, as I have a singular curiosity to witness your meeting, I will sit down here upon the steps, and bear you company."

He seated himself accordingly, and soon engaged his companion in animated discourse. It was but of brief continuance, however, for a noise of shouting, which had long been remotely audible, drew so much nearer that Robin inquired its cause.

"What may be the meaning of this uproar?" asked he. "Truly, if your town be always as noisy, I shall find little sleep, while I am an inhabitant."

"Why, indeed, friend Robin, there do appear to be three or four riotous fellows abroad to-night," replied the gentleman. "You must not expect all the stillness of your native woods, here in our streets. But the watch will shortly be at the heels of these lads, and—"

"Ay, and set them in the stocks by peep of day," interrupted Robin, recollecting his own encounter with the drowsy lantern-bearer. "But, dear sir, if I may trust my ears, an army of watchmen would never make head against such a multitude of rioters. There were at least a thousand voices went up to make that one shout."

"May not a man have several voices, Robin, as well as two complexions?" said his friend.

"Perhaps a man may; but Heaven forbid that a woman should!" responded the shrewd youth, thinking of the seductive tones of the Major's housekeeper.

The sounds of a trumpet in some neighboring street now became so evident and continual, that Robin's curiosity was strongly excited. In addition to the shouts, he heard frequent bursts from many instruments of discord, and a wild and confused laughter filled up the intervals. Robin rose from the steps, and looked wistfully towards a point whither several people semed to be hastening.

"Surely some prodigious merry-making is going on," exclaimed he. "I have laughed very little since I left home, sir, and should be sorry to lose an opportunity. Shall we step round the corner by that darkish house, and take our share of the fun?"

"Sit down again, sit down, good Robin," replied the gentleman, laying his hand on the skirt of the gray coat. "You forget that we must wait here for your kinsman; and there is reason to believe that he will pass by, in the course of a very few moments."

The near approach of the uproar had now disturbed the neighborhood; windows flew open on all sides; and many heads, in the attire of the pillow, and confused by sleep suddenly broken, were protruded to the gaze of whoever had leisure to observe them. Eager voices hailed each other from house to house, all demanding the explanation, which not a soul could give. Half-dressed men hurried towards the unknown commotion, stumbling as they went over the stone steps that thrust themselves into the narrow foot-walk. The shouts, the laughter, and the tuneless bray, the antipodes of music, came onwards with increasing din, till scattered individuals, and then denser bodies, began to appear round a corner at the distance of a hundred yards.

"Will you recognize your kinsman, if he passes in this crowd?" inquired the gentleman.

"Indeed, I can't warrant it, sir; but I'll take my stand here, and keep a bright lookout," answered Robin, descending to the outer edge of the pavement.

A mighty stream of people now emptied into the street, and came rolling slowly towards the church. A single horseman wheeled the corner in the midst of them, and close behind him came a band of fearful wind-instruments, sending forth a fresher discord, now that no intervening buildings kept it from the ear. Then a redder light disturbed the moonbeams, and a dense multitude of torches shone along the street, concealing, by their glare, whatever object they illuminated. The single horseman, clad in a military dress, and bearing a drawn sword, rode onward as the leader, and, by his fierce and variegated countenance, appeared like war personified; the red of one cheek was an emblem of fire and sword; the blackness of the other betokened the mourning that attends them. In his train were wild figures in the Indian dress, and many fantastic shapes without a model, giving the whole march a visionary air, as if a dream had broken forth from some feverish brain, and were sweeping visibly through the midnight streets. A mass of people, inactive, except as applauding spectators, hemmed the procession in; and several women ran along the side-walk, piercing the confusion of heavier sounds with their shrill voices of mirth or terror.

"The double-faced fellow has his eye upon me," muttered Robin, with an indefinite but an uncomfortable idea that he was himself to bear a part in the pageantry.

The leader turned himself in the saddle, and fixed his glance full upon the country youth, as the steed went slowly by. When Robin had freed his eyes from those fiery ones, the musicians were passing before him, and the torches were close at hand; but the unsteady brightness of the latter formed a veil which he could not penetrate. The rattling of wheels over the stones sometimes found its way to his ear, and confused traces of a human form appeared at intervals, and then melted into the vivid light. A moment more, and the leader thundered a command to halt: the trumpets vomited a horrid breath, and then held their peace; the shouts and laughter of the people died away, and there remained only a universal hum, allied to silence. Right before Robin's eyes was an uncovered cart. There the torches blazed the brightest, there the moon shone out like day, and there, in tar-and-feathery dignity, sat his kinsman, Major Molineux!

He was an elderly man, of large and majestic person, and strong, square features, betokening a steady soul; but steady as it was, his enemies had found means to shake it. His face was pale as death, and far more ghastly; the broad forehead was contracted in his agony, so that his eyebrows formed one grizzled line; his eyes were red and wild, and the foam hung white upon his quivering lip. His whole frame was agitated by a quick and continual tremor, which his pride strove to quell, even in those circumstances of overwhelming humiliation. But perhaps the bitterest pang of all was when his eyes met those of Robin; for he evidently knew him on the instant, as the youth stood witnessing the foul disgrace of a head grown gray in honor. They stared at each other in silence, and Robin's knees shook, and his hair bristled, with a mixture of pity and terror. Soon, however, a bewildering excitement began to seize upon his mind; the preceding adventures of the night, the unexpected appearance of the crowd, the torches, the confused din and the hush that followed, the spectre of his kinsman reviled by that great multitude,—all this, and, more than all, a perception of tremendous ridicule in the whole scene, affected him with a sort of mental inebriety. At that moment a voice of sluggish merriment saluted Robin's ears; he turned instinctively, and just behind the corner of the church stood the lantern-bearer, rubbing his eyes, and drowsily enjoying the lad's amazement. Then he heard a peal of laughter like the ringing of silvery bells; a woman twitched his arm, a saucy eye met his, and he saw the lady of the scarlet petticoat. A sharp, dry cachinnation appealed to his memory, and, standing on tiptoe in the crowd, with his white apron over his head, he beheld the courteous little innkeeper. And lastly, there sailed over the heads of the multitude a great, broad laugh, broken in the midst by two sepulchral hems; thus, "Haw, haw, haw,—hem, hem,—haw, haw, haw, haw!"

The sound proceeded from the balcony of the opposite edifice, and thither Robin turned his eyes. In front of the Gothic window stood the old citizen, wrapped in a wide gown, his gray periwig exchanged for a nightcap, which was thrust back from his forehead, and his silk stockings hanging about his legs. He supported himself on his polished cane in a fit of convulsive merriment, which manifested itself on his solemn old features like a funny inscription on a tombstone. Then Robin seemed to hear the voices of the barbers, of the guests of the inn, and of all who had made sport of him that night. The contagion was spreading among the multitude, when, all at once, it seized upon Robin, and he sent forth a shout of laughter that echoed through the street;—every man shook his sides, every man emptied his lungs, but Robin's shout was the loudest there. The cloud-spirits peeped from their silvery islands, as the congregated mirth went roaring up the sky! The Man in the Moon heard the far bellow. "Oho," quoth he, "the old earth is frolicsome to-night!"

When there was a momentary calm in that tempestuous sea of sound, the leader gave the sign, the procession resumed its march. On they went, like fiends that throng in mockery around some dead potentate, mighty no more, but majestic still in his agony. On they went, in counterfeited pomp, in senseless uproar, in frenzied merriment, trampling all on an old man's heart. On swept the tumult, and left a silent street behind.

"Well, Robin, are you dreaming?" inquired the gentleman, laying his hand on the youth's shoulder.

Robin started, and withdrew his arm from the stone post to which he had instinctively clung, as the living stream rolled by him. His cheek was somewhat pale, and his eye not quite as lively as in the earlier part of the evening.

"Will you be kind enough to show me the way to the ferry?" said he, after a moment's pause.

"You have, then, adopted a new subject of inquiry?" observed his companion, with a smile.

"Why, yes, sir," replied Robin, rather dryly. "Thanks to you, and to my other friends, I have at last met my kinsman, and he will scarce desire to see my face again. I begin to grow weary of a town life, sir. Will you show me the way to the ferry?"

"No, my good friend Robin,—not to-night, at least," said the gentleman. "Some few days hence, if you wish it, I will speed you on your journey. Or, if you prefer to remain with us, perhaps, as you are a shrewd youth, you may rise in the world without the help of your kinsman, Major Molineux."

DAVID HILBERG

(1967–   )

Mask

About the Author: David Hilberg, born in Burlington, Vermont, was a junior mathematics major at the University of Vermont when he wrote "Mask." The idea for the story had come to him more than two years earlier, but it was in a creative writing class that he began to develop it through copious notes, preliminary drafts, and numerous revisions. Ultimately Hilberg discarded several introductory pages to begin with the confrontation between Alex and his father; he also abandoned his notes prescribing Alex's character traits to let Alex develop through interaction with his father, and refocused the story on one climactic event rather than the three originally planned. The result of this writing/revising process is published here for the first time.

Alex waited in the living room. He was walking around and around the border of the carpet, alternately glancing at his watch and staring at the blank, white walls.

The apartment was unfurnished. Though a little larger than the last, and much closer to work, it did not feel comfortable, and would not feel so until Alex had combed many a flea market and raided all the thrift stores. He would be out hunting right now, in fact, except his father had invited himself over.

(But what could he have said? "No, Father, it's best you not visit your son's new apartment"? Better to lose a day of shopping.)

He stopped circling the carpet at 5:59 and started toward the door to let his father in. The bell rang as he swung the door open; Mr. Pontopoulos stood waiting. Tall and dark-complected, he was an older version of his son, but distinguished himself with a black beard and the beginnings of a pot-belly. He wore his formal tails, which indicated he'd come directly from work; Alex stepped back to let him pass and, indeed, the black outfit exuded the sickly-sweet perfume of the Funeral Home.

Mr. Pontopoulos strode into the livingroom, stopping in the center of the carpet. He surveyed the barren walls, his right hand stroking the trim, jet beard, and the back of his left pinning the tail coat to the small of his back. He considered the boxes of books, the worn sofa, and the curtainless windows, then turned sharply.

"Alexander?"

"I was thinking . . ." Alex began, "Father, I was thinking of something modern—perhaps a Picasso poster. Perhaps—"

"Perhaps a Parmigianino painting!" Pontopoulos boomed. "Or at least, a print." He turned back to study the dimensions of the opposite wall.

"Father," Alex sighed, "I answer questions about vacuums for a living—I can afford a poster."

Pontopoulos whirled. "Alexander!" he exclaimed with astonished impatience. "I will *help* you buy a painting. What are you now, twenty-eight? You are not a teenager. This is not a 'pad'. You should decorate appropriately."

Alex was thinking, "Yes, I am twenty-eight, and my father still tells me how to run my life." What he said was, "Yes, Father, you're probably right. Something classy." And then, "May I take your coat?"

But Mr. Pontopoulos was already heading for the kitchen.

"Alexander," he called back, "Your kitchen is underequipped!"

Alex came through the doorway.

"You cannot survive," his father continued, "without either a wife or a microwave oven, and seeing as you lack the former . . ."—he let the words sink in—"you really have no choice but to obtain the latter."

"Speaking of wives," Alex said, smiling, "You're just as eligible as I am, Father, so—" He stifled himself abruptly: his father was not smiling. Indeed, Mr. Pontopoulos's jaw and brow were set, and his gaze so cold no microwave could have thawed it.

Alex's smile disintegrated. "Well," he murmured after a pause, "a microwave would save me time."

Mr. Pontopoulos shot back, "Of course it would," and walked into the bathroom. He was out almost immediately, his thin eyebrows raised.

"A *kitty*-litter, Alexander? You have a *kitty*-cat?"

"No, Father," Alex replied wearily, "I don't have a cat. But I was going to stop at the animal shelter after work tomorrow."

"Alexander," Mr. Pontopoulos began, in his I'm-sorry-to-lecture-but-you-evidently-need-it tone of voice, "Pets are for children. Kittens for kiddies." He stopped, and when Alex didn't reply, continued, "But you miss your little dog, hey? Somehow I still think you need a wife." A smile traced his lips.

Shame enveloped Alex like a fever, and he stared at the black-and-white checkerboard of the kitchen floor. He knew his father was wrong: wrong about pets, and wrong to humiliate him in his own home. He buried his hurt and anger, however, and fairly whispered, "Come see the bedroom."

It was the one room he had attempted to furnish completely, and decorate in a coordinated fashion. "This will redeem me," he thought, and as he opened the door the scent of fresh paint and incense escaped into the hallway. Alex walked to the center of the room and turned around, looking at his father as if to say, "Well? What do you think?"

The senior Pontopoulos stood at the edge of the rug, absorbing his surroundings.

The bedding, rug, and drapes all played variations on a theme of verdant hues; the walls, a bright lime, sported reproductions of Gaugin and Rousseau; African violets graced the night table and dresser, and spider plants hung in the windows. The crowning detail, however, was the set of masks—three ancient, wooden, African tribal masks—that hung in a line above the head of Alex's bed.

They were enough alike so that one would have said all were carved by the same craftsman: all were about a foot high, stained clay red, and possessed solid eyes and dagger-teeth. Yet each also bore its own ritual scars, its own searching eyes, and a uniquely contorted mouth.

Mr. Pontopoulos's gaze found the masks and remained fixed on them. "Real?" he asked, his eyes still not leaving the artifacts.

"Yes," Alex answered, "They're real. Real, but retired."

He had bought them in a pawn shop: not from the proprietor, but from a black man—a black man in white shoes with grey creeping up his sideburns, who was making a big show of disappointment over the price the proprietor was offering him. Alex hadn't offered much more, but the man had accepted (perhaps out of spite) and handed the boxful to him on the spot. They became friends, in that moment of conspiracy, thwarting the peeved proprietor behind the counter. As they walked out of the pawnship, the man said to Alex, "Don't let them expressions scare you, son. They can't do nothin'. They're all used up, like me. Retired."

Alex was not relieved to hear this: he hadn't been apprehensive in the first place. Rather, he had seen the masks and, fascinated by their primitive intensity, had resolved to obtain them, budget or no.

"And what were they, before?" Alex asked, "Before retirement?"

"Oh," replied the man, " a couple-hunnerd years ago they was summat to be respected. You put 'em on, dance aroun', you became an animal. An *animal.* I imagine that old shaman's brew helped, though," he chuckled. "Find your old animal spirit pretty quick with that stuff."

"Undoubtedly," said Alex, and handed him a company business card on which he had written his own name and telephone extension. "Call me if you ever have vacuum troubles," Alex said, because he didn't know what else to offer in return for the kindness he had felt done him.

"Take care of them masks!" the man admonished, and thus they had parted.

"So what do you think?" Alex asked, hoping to elicit from his father some praise for the room which had been so painstakingly adorned.

"I think," said Mr. Pontopoulos, his eyes still on the masks, "they may actually be genuine." He stared hard at the scarred faces, and they stared back, their gaze every bit as intent as his own.

Pontopoulos did not remark on the spider plants, or the African violets, or the way the curtains matched the rug, but simply turned from the masks and exited the room, with Alex following. As they passed the bathroom, Mr. Pontopoulos shook his head. "A kitty," he spat, "a kitty. Alexander, you could have at least decided on another dog."

"The landlord—" Alex began, but his father was not listening. Mr. Pontopoulos was letting himself out.

As soon as he was gone, Alex threw away the litter box, angrily forcing it down the chute to the building incinerator. He unboxed books the rest of the evening, then went to bed at 10:00; many vacuum-related questions awaited him in the morning. Though

feeling secure in the jungle chamber he had created, with the masks ever watchful above his head, Alex had trouble falling asleep: he could not let go of the events of his father's visit.

As he finally slipped from consciousness, his thoughts all became intertwined: "Pets are for kiddies . . . cats . . . Your kitchen is not genuine . . . underequipped pad . . . You need a wife you cannot survive without your little dog, hey?"

Alex had a dream. He was outside on a sunny summer day, visiting his mother's grave, except somehow it was his dog's grave. He was standing by his father, a picture of solemnity as he contemplated the grave of his wife. Alex thought of his dog, and a lump rose in his throat. He swallowed hard, but the lump was still there, and he thought how he would never hold his dog again. Tears came to his eyes. He blinked a few times and bit his lip, but when the tears kept forming and his sinuses got tight he let out a whine, and then a sob, and then he bent down and hugged the gravestone and bawled as only a child can bawl, barely stopping to catch a breath. "Neverever," he wailed, "Neverever hold him again!" His father bent down and said sharply, "Quiet, Alexander! It's such a beautiful day and you cry. You're a big boy, but you cry for a dog."

He wasn't finished crying: he went on and on, his cheeks thoroughly wetted, his nose running, the tears flowing down and dripping off his chin. They tickled the corners of his nostrils. They slid down across his upper lip and into his mouth, stinging his tongue with salt. He closed his mouth, but the tears stung where he had bitten his lower lip. Squeezing his eyes shut, he sobbed against the warm granite of the gravestone.

When Alex awoke, his eyelids didn't want to open. He assumed more sleep was in order; in any case, the alarm clock hadn't yet sounded. The dawn's insistent sunbeams, however, filtering red through his eyelids, prevented him from drifting off again.

Yet his eyes didn't open naturally, and wouldn't open when he tried what he supposed were his lid muscles. Furthermore, his jaws would not part for the yawn rising within him, and midway through he had to stifle it, leaving his tongue with a cramp and his eustachian tubes very dissatisfied. "Am I dreaming?" Alex wondered. He rolled over on his stomach, but there was something between his face and the pillowcase. "My God!" thought Alex, frantically propping himself up on his elbows and feeling his face. He did not contact soft eyebrows, or the skin of his nose, or one night's whisker growth, but instead encountered a hard, sandpapery surface. He tapped it with one fingernail.

"But that's not wood," he thought, for it had occurred to him that one of the African masks might have, in mischief or loneliness, jumped his face in the night.

Whatever it was, he was determined to get it off. Although it evidently possessed nostril holes, he was beginning to feel suffocated. "Oh, jeez," he thought, patting his unsolicited faceplate, "jeez oh jeez oh jeez." He carefully felt around the edges of the carapace. It seemed to extend from sideburn to sideburn and chin to eyebrows. After some more gingerly exploration, he was able to dig a finger under it at each temple.

It came away cleanly, aside from keeping a few eyelashes. Alex hardly noticed the loss, however, he was so glad at being able to blink again, to see his green, sun-warmed room, to open his mouth and fill his lungs, to pucker his lips and then stretch them back over his teeth. . . . He would have taken several pleasurable minutes just arranging his face in leering grins, but the object in his hands pressed his curiosity.

It was indeed a mask of sorts, though not a shaman's mask or a Halloween mask. It was white: inside, fairly smooth though not polished; outside, crystalline, as if made of sand. Its features matched his exactly, though the expression reflected a very sad mood. In fact, he realized, it most resembled one of those masks one sees on theatrical posters: the mask of tragedy. And it had come from his face!

Should he call his doctor?

No: Shaken though he was, he could not picture himself explaining what had happened. Besides, what if it turned out he had a rare disease? "Oh, yes," the doctor would say, "spontaneous nocturnal superectodermal sclerosis. Often misdiagnosed. Leads to harelips, bug eyes, large pores, and mustaches on women."

Alex didn't think it was worth the risk.

He walked over to the mirror above the dresser and slowly put the mask to his face, feeling how its inner surface accepted his nose, molded his lips and pressed his eyelids. He lowered it slightly, peeking over the top. The reflection was of a ghost in a plaid nightshirt.

Alex wanted desperately to call someone—to tell somebody about this bizarre occurrence. He realized, however, that he had no one to call.

He held the white mask in the sunlight, tilting it and watching the surface sparkle, then carefully laid it in a dresser drawer, nestled in his underwear.

In the shower, Alex puzzled over the vizard that had appeared on his face in the night. He suspected the African Trio in its origin, but could not fathom its purpose. The water beat down on his face, and to his surprise, it tasted sweet. He rushed the remainder of his shower and, still dripping, headed to the bedroom, where he retrieved the mask. Touching his tongue to its nose, he confirmed his hypothesis: it was made of salt.

The dream returned to him, and he sat on the bed, recollecting.

"That's not what happened, though," he finally said, aloud. "It wasn't like that at all."

Some fifteen years ago his dog had indeed died, struck by a pick-up he had been chasing on one of the backroads in Alex's hometown. From the moment poor Panayotis was found, Alex's father had taken charge. Although Mr. Pontopoulos was the manager of the Reddier Funeral Home, and therefore not inclined to involve himself deeply with any one particular funeral, he made it his personal project to see that Alex's dog was dispatched in the most expert manner. Had the treadmarks from the truck tires read "Dispose of Properly," Mr. Pontopoulos could not have been induced to do a more thorough job: Everything from the type of casket to the color of the flowers at the ceremony was painstakingly planned, with Alex's approval being asked at every step of the way, as if he were a bonafide Reddier client. In fact, as Alex recalled, the only things he had not been asked were how he felt about his best friend dying, and whether he wanted a new dog.

When the funerary ceremony came, Mr. Pontopoulos and all the employees of the Reddier Funeral Home stood around the closed hardwood casket, admiring the carpentry and commenting on the floral arrangements. Alex was quite numb. He had been too young to attend his mother's funeral, so didn't really know how to act at this one. Following his father's example, he just stood, hands behind his back, gazing at the casket.

"It could have been a cardboard box in a corner of the backyard," Alex mused, "and it would have been more of a funeral than that."

He had to get to work.

Myriad housewives and househusbands were at this very moment discovering they had thrown away their vacuum cleaners' instruction booklets before learning how to change the bags. Even as Alex trotted to the bus stop, operators would be patching through calls to Amtech Customer Service from people whose vacuums wheezed when they should have whined, snored when they should have roared, or, worst of all, puffed when they should have sucked.

"I wish," thought Alex as he stared out the bus window, "there was no such thing as wall-to-wall carpeting, and everyone took rugs outside and pounded them with a broom." His private motto was "Nature abhors a vacuum—especially if it's an Amtech."

When he arrived at work, however, Customer Service wasn't bustling, and his extension rang only sporadically. He found himself thinking about the mask at home in his bureau, and then about his father. Then he got mad. "You don't find a wife because you're lonely," he muttered to his coffee mug. "You find a pet." He regretted throwing away the litterbox.

After work, Alex left the Amtech Building and started walking down the avenue. Passing the pawnshop, he scanned the window for pet supplies. Seeing none, he continued on to Pam's Pets.

Alex entered Pam's with a purpose. He planned only to pick up a litterbox and travel carrier, then hop a bus to the animal shelter. He made the fatal error, however, of looking in on the kittens playing in their cages.

"Bred for cuteness," said a man standing near him, "Don't be sucked in."

"Oh, I won't," Alex replied. There was some poor creature at the local humane society who needed him.

"Yeah," the man returned, "just keep staring. You'll last about as long as a lump of butter in a microwave."

Funny you should put it that way, Alex thought.

He handed the man a business card. "Pet hair," Alex said, "is a cinch for an Amtech."

The man moved down to look at the birds.

Alex returned his attention to the kittens, who were for the most part batting at each other's tails or yawning in typically cute fashion. One, however, intrigued him: A black short-hair with cream-colored stomach and paws, and alert gold eyes. She sat, staring across the wire of the cage door, and studied Alex even as Alex studied her. The card said "Anne," and while Alex thought it unusual that a pet shop animal would have already been named, he couldn't really blame them for not allowing this one to remain anonymous.

Anne looked at him, and he looked at Anne.

"When it's like this with a person," Alex thought, "then I'll get married. Until then, I've got to have this cat."

He looked around, and a saleslady approached. She was a quick-moving, full-bodied woman with auburn hair and green eyes, and as she strode up to him, Alex read her nametag. It was the owner, Pam herself.

"You're taking my favorite, aren't you?" Pam asked, opening the cage door and lifting out the kitten before Alex even responded. "Guess so," Alex said, "but you can come visit her if you like." He had begun it as a joke, but by the time he had said it, he realized he meant it.

"Yeah, OK," Pam laughed, giving Anne a one-fingered head scratch. "Just be sure this little one doesn't come visiting *me!*" She then proceeded to sell Alex a leash and collar, as well as some overpriced cat food, in addition to the carrier and litter box he had come for in the first place.

"There goes the microwave," Alex thought, handing Pam his credit card. "My kitchen will just have to be underequipped."

The next few weeks passed smoothly. Alex managed to furnish most of his living quarters (in spite of Anne, who did her best to promote entropy in the apartment), Mr. Pontopoulos did not announce any more visits (which made Alex suspect his father to be allergic to cats), and Alex was not having any more mask-inducing dreams. (Once in his sleep he had felt suffocated, but when he awoke it was only the kitten lying on his face.)

In addition, Pam's Pets put Alex on its preferred customer mailing list. Lately, Alex was finding a lot of excuses to visit Pam's. If it wasn't a catnip toy to distract Anne from the spiderplants, then it was a scratching post to save the sofa, or a new squeaky rubber mouse to replace the one lost behind the refrigerator. He always left the store with something.

When he could, Alex engaged Pam in lengthy discussions on various pressing matters: the question of flea collars versus powders, the merits of canned food over dry, or the advantages of clay litter as opposed to alfalfa pellets. Pam, however, seemed to know what was going on; one Saturday afternoon, after Alex had tied her up for half an hour in a debate over currycombs, she excused herself to the storeroom, telling him to return five minutes before closing.

At exactly five to nine, Alex entered Pam's Pets. A clerk was sweeping the floor as Pam totaled the day's receipts.

Seeing the broom, Alex blurted out, "Oh, do you need a vacuum? If you do—"

"That's all right," Pam called from behind the counter, "we just sweep and mop. Some of the animals are really bothered by vacuums." "Anne chases the rug attachment."

Pam smiled, and continued her accounting. Alex loved the way her eyes crinkled when she smiled.

A minute passed. Alex stood awkwardly before the counter. "Listen," he began, "can I help out? Clean the aquariums, restock the birdfeed? Something?"

Pam reached under the counter and handed him a telephone directory. "Here. You can check the restaurants—make reservations for 9:30."

Alex gazed stupidly at the telephone book and felt his face getting hot. He looked up at Pam and saw that she, too, was blushing. They looked at one another bashfully.

Then they traded closed-lipped smiles, and Alex asked, "Do you like Chinese?"

He had been going out with Pam for a month when, one Saturday, the doorbell rang, and Alex found himself staring at a black man with white shoes and an empty box under his arm.

"I got vacuum troubles," said the man, a broad grin on his face.

Alex invited him in and, glancing at the empty box, returned, "I think I can help you, sir, but where's your vacuum?"

The man pressed his hand to his heart. "In here, son."

Alex needed no prompting. He went to his jungle chamber and took down the masks from above the bed.

"I'm grateful," said the man, as they placed the masks in the box. He reached into his pocket. "I can give you what you gave me—"

Alex waved his hands. "Already paid for, sir, already paid in full." He then took from the top of the bookcase a flat wooden box, opening it to reveal a white mask on black velvet. He thereupon related the story of the salt mask, and when he was finished telling it the old man said, "Don't doubt it, son. Don't doubt it a bit."

"Then you lied." It was Alex's turn to grin. He looked at the African masks in their cardboard box. "They aren't quite retired, are they?"

"Well, neither am I, son. Neither am I."

Alex was never sure what he had meant by that.

Mr. Pontopoulos was horrified to hear Alex no longer had the masks, and berated him at the earliest opportunity. "That was not smart, Alexander. They were probably worth a lot of money."

Alex thought about that for a moment, then stared into the eyes of the man in black tails. "It seemed the right thing to do at the time," he replied, but Pontopoulos only "hmphed."

On Fiction

EUDORA WELTY

Place in Fiction

Place is one of the lesser angels that watch over the racing hand of fiction, perhaps the one that gazes benignly enough from off to one side, while others, like character, plot, symbolic meaning, and so on, are doing a good deal of wing-beating about her chair, and feeling, who in my eyes carries the crown, soars highest of them all and rightly relegates place into the shade. Nevertheless, it is this lowlier angel that concerns us here. There have been signs that she has been rather neglected of late; maybe she could do with a little petitioning.

What place has place in fiction? It might be thought so modest a one that it can be taken for granted: the location of a novel; to use a term of the day, it may make the novel "regional." The term, like most terms used to pin down a novel, means little; and Henry James said there isn't any difference between "the English novel" and "the American novel," since there are only two kinds of novels at all, the good and the bad. Of course Henry James didn't stop there, and we all hate generalities, and so does place. Yet as soon as we step down from the general view to the close and particular, as writers must and readers may and teachers well know how to, and consider what good writing may be, place can be seen, in her own way, to have a great deal to do with that goodness, if not to be responsible for it. How so?

First, with the goodness—validity—in the raw material of writing. Second, with the goodness in the writing itself—the achieved world of appearance, through which the novelist has his whole say and puts his whole case. There will still be the lady, always, who dismissed *The Ancient Mariner* on grounds of implausibility. Third, with the goodness—the worth—in the writer himself: place is where he has his roots, place is where he stands; in his experience out of which he writes, it provides the base of reference; in his work, the point of view. Let us consider place in fiction in these three wide aspects.

Wide, but of course connected—vitally so. And if in some present-day novels the connection has apparently slipped, that makes a fresh reason for us to ponder the subject of place. For novels, besides being the pleasantest things imaginable, are powerful forces on the side. Mutual understanding in the world being nearly always, as now, at low ebb, it is comforting to remember that it is through art that one country can nearly always speak reliably to another, if the other can hear at all. Art, though, is never the voice of a country; it is an even more precious thing, the voice of the individual, doing its best to speak, not comfort of any sort, indeed, but truth. And the art that speaks it most unmistakably, most directly, most variously, most fully, is fiction; in particular, the novel.

Why? Because the novel from the start has been bound up in the local, the "real," the present, the ordinary day-to-day of human experience. Where the imagination comes in is in directing the use of all this. That use is endless, and there are only four words, of all the millions we've hatched, that a novel rules out: "Once upon a time." They make a story a fairy tale by the simple sweep of the remove—by abolishing the present and the place where we are instead of conveying them to us. Of course we shall have some sort of fairy tale with us always—just now it is the historical novel. Fiction is properly at work on the here and now, or the past made here and now; for in novels *we* have to be there. Fiction provides the ideal texture through which the feeling and meaning that permeate our own personal, present lives will best show through. For in his theme—the most vital and important part of the work at hand—the novelist has the blessing of the inexhaustible subject: you and me. You and me, here. Inside that generous scope and circumference—who could ask for anything more?—the novel can accommodate practically anything on earth; and has abundantly done so. The novel so long as it be *alive* gives pleasure, and must always give pleasure, enough to stave off the departure of the Wedding Guest forever, except for that one lady.

It is by the nature of itself that fiction is all bound up in the local. The internal reason for that is surely that *feelings* are bound up in place. The human mind is a mass of associations—associations more poetic even than actual. I say, "The Yorkshire Moors," and you will say, *"Wuthering Heights,"* and I have only to murmur, "If Father were only alive—" for you to come back with "We could go to Moscow," which certainly is not even so. The truth is, fiction depends for its life on place. Location is the crossroads of circumstance, the proving ground of "What happened? Who's here? Who's coming?"—and that is the heart's field.

Unpredictable as the future of any art must be, one condition we may hazard about writing: of all the arts, it is the one least likely to cut the cord that binds it to its source. Music and dancing, while originating out of place—groves!—and perhaps invoking it still to minds pure or childlike, are no longer bound to dwell there. Sculpture exists out in empty space: that is what it commands and replies to. Toward painting, place, to be so highly visible, has had a curious and changing relationship. Indeed, wasn't it when landscape invaded painting, and painting was given, with the profane content, a narrative content, that this worked to bring on a revolution to the art? Impressionism brought not the likeness-to-life but the mystery of place onto canvas; it was the method, not the subject, that told this. Painting and writing, always the closest two of the sister arts (and in ancient Chinese days only the blink of an eye seems to have separated them), have each a still closer connection with place than they have with each other; but a difference lies in their respective requirements of it, and even further in the way they use it—the written word being ultimately as different from the pigment as the note of the scale is from the chisel.

One element, which has just been mentioned, is surely the underlying bond that connects all the arts with place. All of them celebrate its mystery. Where does this mystery lie? Is it in the fact that place has a more lasting identity than we have, and we unswervingly tend to attach ourselves to identity? Might the magic lie partly, too, in the *name* of the place—since that is what *we* gave it? Surely, once we have it named, we have put a kind of poetic claim on its existence; the claim works even out of sight—may work forever sight unseen. The Seven Wonders of the World still give us this poetic kind of gratification. And notice we do not say simply "The Hanging Gardens"—that would leave them dangling out of reach and dubious in nature; we say "The Hanging Gardens of Babylon," and there they are, before our eyes, shimmering and garlanded and exactly elevated to the Babylonian measurement.

Edward Lear tapped his unerring finger on the magic of place in the limerick. There's something unutterably convincing about that Old Person of Sparta who had twenty-five sons and one darta, and it is surely beyond question that he fed them on snails and weighed

them in scales, because we know where that Old Person is *from*—Sparta! We certainly do not need further to be told his *name.* "Consider the source." Experience has ever advised us to base validity on point of origin.

Being shown how to locate, to place, any account is what does most toward *making* us believe it, not merely allowing us to, may the account be the facts or a lie; and that is where place in fiction comes in. Fiction is a lie. Never in its inside thoughts, always in its outside dress.

Some of us grew up with the china night-light, the little lamp whose lighting showed its secret and with that spread enchantment. The outside is painted with a scene, which is one thing; then, when the lamp is lighted, through the porcelain sides a new picture comes out through the old, and they are seen as one. A lamp I knew of was a view of London till it was lit; but then it was the Great Fire of London, and you could go beautifully to sleep by it. The lamp alight is the combination of internal and external, glowing at the imagination as one; and so is the good novel. Seeing that these inner and outer surfaces do lie so close together and so implicit in each other, the wonder is that human life so often separates them, or appears to, and it takes a good novel to put them back together.

The good novel should be steadily alight, revealing. Before it can hope to be that, it must of course be steadily visible from its outside, presenting a continuous, shapely, pleasing and finished surface to the eye.

The sense of a story when the visibility is only partial or intermittent is as endangered as Eliza crossing the ice. Forty hounds of confusion are after it, the black waters of disbelief open up between its steps, and no matter which way it jumps it is bound to slip. Even if it has a little baby moral in its arms, it is more than likely a goner.

The novel must get Eliza across the ice; what it means—the way it proceeds—is always in jeopardy. It must be given a surface that is continuous and unbroken, never too thin to trust, always in touch with the senses. Its world of experience must be at every step, through every moment, within reach as the world of appearance.

This makes it the business of writing, and the responsibility of the writer, to disentangle the significant—in character, incident, setting, mood, everything—from the random and meaningless and irrelevant that in real life surround and beset it. It is a matter of his selecting and, by all that implies, of changing "real" life as he goes. With each word he writes, he acts—as literally and methodically as if he hacked his way through a forest and blazed it for the word that follows. He makes choices at the explicit demand of this one present story; each choice implies, explains, limits the next, and illuminates the one before. No two stories ever go the same way, although in different hands one story might possibly go any one of a thousand ways; and though the woods may look the same from outside, it is a new and different labyrinth every time. What tells the author his way? Nothing at all but what he knows inside himself: the same thing that hints to him afterward how far he has missed it, how near he may have come to the heart of it. In a working sense, the novel and its place have become one: work has made them, for the time being, the same thing, like the explorer's tentative map of the known world.

The reason why every word you write in a good novel is a lie, then, is that it is written expressly to serve the purpose; if it does not apply, it is fancy and frivolous, however, specially dear to the writer's heart. Actuality, it is true, is an even bigger risk to the novel than fancy writing is, being frequently even more confusing, irrelevant, diluted and generally far-fetched than ill-chosen words can make it. Yet somehow, the world of appearance in the novel has got to *seem* actuality. Is there a reliable solution to the problem? Place being

brought to life in the round before the reader's eye is the readiest and gentlest and most honest and natural way this can be brought about, I think; every instinct advises it. The moment the place in which the novel happens is accepted as true, through it will begin to glow, in a kind of recognizable glory, the feeling and thought that inhabited the novel in the author's head and animated the whole of his work.

Besides furnishing a plausible abode for the novel's world of feeling, place has a good deal to do with making the characters real, that is, themselves, and keeping them so. The reason is simply that, as Tristram Shandy observed, "We are not made of glass, as characters on Mercury might be." Place *can* be transparent, or translucent: not people. In real life we have to express the things plainest and closest to our minds by the clumsy word and the half-finished gesture; the chances are our most usual behavior makes sense only in a kind of daily way, because it has become familiar to our nearest and dearest, and still demands their constant indulgence and understanding. It is our describable outside that defines us, willy-illy, to others, that may save us, or destroy us, in the world; it may be our shield against chaos, our mask against exposure; but whatever it is, the move we make in the place we live has to signify our intent and meaning.

Then think how unprotected the poor character in a novel is, into whose mind the author is inviting us to look—unprotected and hence surely unbelievable! But no, the author has expressly seen to believability. Though he must know all, again he works with illusion. Just as the world of a novel is more highly selective than that of real life, so character in a novel is much more definite, less shadowy than our own, in order that we may believe in it. This is not to say that the character's scope must be limited; it is our vision of it that is guided. It is a kind of phenomenon of writing that the likeliest character has first to be enclosed inside the bounds of even greater likelihood, or he will fly to pieces. Paradoxically, the more narrowly we can examine a fictional character, the greater he is likely to loom up. We must see him set to scale in his proper world to know his size. Place, then, has the most delicate control over character too: by confining character, it defines it.

Place in fiction is the named, identified, concrete, exact and exacting, and therefore credible, gathering spot of all that has been felt, is about to be experienced, in the novel's progress. Location pertains to feeling; feeling profoundly pertains to place; place in history partakes of feeling, as feeling about history partakes of place. Every story would be another story, and unrecognizable as art, if it took up its characters and plot and happened somewhere else. Imagine *Swann's Way* laid in London, or *The Magic Mountain* in Spain, or *Green Mansions* in the Black Forest. The very notion of moving a novel brings ruder havoc to the mind and affections than would a century's alteration in its time. It is only too easy to conceive that a bomb that could destroy all trace of places as we know them, in life and through books, could also destroy all feelings as we know them, so irretrievably and so happily are recognition, memory, history, valor, love, all the instincts of poetry and praise, worship and endeavor, bound up in place. From the dawn of man's imagination, place has enshrined the spirit; as soon as man stopped wandering and stood still and looked about him, he found a god in that place; and from then on, that was where the god abided and spoke from if ever he spoke.

Feelings are bound up in place, and in art, from time to time, place undoubtedly works upon genius. Can anyone well explain otherwise what makes a given dot on the map come passionately alive, for good and all, in a novel—like one of those novae that suddenly blaze with inexplicable fire in the heavens? What brought a *Wuthering Heights* out of Yorkshire, or a *Sound and the Fury* out of Mississippi?

If place does work upon genius, how does it? It may be that place can focus the gigantic, voracious eye of genius and bring its gaze to point. Focus then means awareness, discernment, order, clarity, insight—they are like the attributes of love. The act of focusing itself has beauty and meaning; it is the act that, continued in, turns into mediation, into poetry. Indeed, as soon as the least of us stands still, that is the moment something extraordinary is seen to be going on in the world. The drama, old beyond count as it is, is no older than the first stage. Without the amphitheatre around it to persuade the ear and bend the eye upon a point, how could poetry ever have been spoken, how have been heard? Man is articulate and intelligible only when he begins to communicate inside the strict terms of poetry and reason. Symbols in the end, both are permanent forms of the act of focusing.

Surely place induces poetry, and when the poet is extremely attentive to what is there, a meaning may even attach to his poem out of the spot on earth where it is spoken, and the poem signify the more because it does spring so wholly out of its place, and the sap has run up into it as into a tree.

But we had better confine ourselves here to prose. And then, to take the most absolutely unfanciful novelist of them all, it is to hear him saying, *"Madame Bovary—c'est moi."* And we see focusing become so intent and aware and conscious in this most "realistic" novel of them all as to amount to fusion. Flaubert's work is indeed of the kind that is embedded immovably as rock in the country of its birth. If, with the slicers of any old (or new) criticism at all, you were to cut down through *Madame Bovary,* its cross section would still be the same as the cross section of that living earth, in texture, color, composition, all; which would be no surprise to Flaubert. For such fusion always means accomplishment no less conscious than it is gigantic—effort that must exist entirely as its own reward. We all know the letter Flaubert wrote when he had just found, in the morning paper, in an account of a minister's visit to Rouen, a phrase in the Mayor's speech of welcome

> which I had written the day before, textually, in my *Bovary* . . . Not only were the idea and the words the same, but even the rhythm of the style. It's things like this that give me pleasure . . . Everything one invents is true, you may be perfectly sure of that! Poetry is as precise as geometry . . . And besides, after reaching a certain point, one no longer makes any mistakes about the things of the soul. My poor Bovary, without a doubt, is suffering and weeping this very instant in twenty villages of France.

And now that we have come to the writer himself, the question of place resolves itself into the point of view. In this changeover from the objective to the subjective, wonderful and unexpected variations may occur.

Place, to the writer at work, is seen in a frame. Not an empty frame, a brimming one. Point of view is a sort of burning-glass, a product of personal experience and time; it is burnished with feelings and sensibilities, charged from moment to moment with the sun-points of imagination. It is an instrument—one of intensification; it acts, it behaves, it is temperamental. We have seen that the writer must accurately choose, combine, superimpose upon, blot out, shake up, alter the outside world for one absolute purpose, the good of his story. To do this, he is always seeing double, two pictures at once in his frame, his and the world's, a fact that he constantly comprehends; and he works best in a state of constant and subtle and unfooled reference between the two. It is his clear intention—his passion, I should say—to make the reader see only one of the pictures—the author's—under the pleasing illusion that it is the world's; this enormity is the accomplishment of a good story. I think it likely that at the moment of the writer's highest awareness of, and

responsiveness to, the "real" world, his imagination's choice (and miles away it may be from actuality) comes closest to being infallible for his purpose. For the spirit of things is what is sought. No blur of inexactness, no cloud of vagueness, is allowable in good writing; from the first seeing to the last putting down, there must be steady lucidity and uncompromise of purpose. I speak, of course, of the ideal.

One of the most important things the young writer comes to see for himself is that point of view *is* an instrument, not an end in itself, that is useful as a glass, and not as a mirror to reflect a dear and pensive face. Conscientiously used, point of view will discover, explore, see through—it may sometimes divine and prophesy. Misused, it turns opaque almost at once and gets in the way of the book. And when the good novel is finished, its cooled outside shape, what Sean O'Faolàin has called "the veil of reality," has all the burden of communicating that initial, spontaneous, overwhelming, driving charge of personal inner feeling that was the novel's reason for being. The measure of this representation of life corresponds most tellingly with the novel's life expectancy: whenever its world of outside appearance grows dim or false to the eye, the novel has expired.

Establishing a chink-proof world of appearance is not only the first responsibility of the writer; it is the primary step in the technique of every sort of fiction: lyric and romantic, of course; the "realistic," it goes without saying; and other sorts as well. Fantasy itself must touch ground with at least one toe, and ghost stories must have one foot, so to speak, in the grave. The black, squat, hairy ghosts of M. R. James come right out of Cambridge. Only fantasy's stepchild, poor science-fiction, does not touch earth anywhere; and it is doubtful already if happenings entirely confined to outer space are ever going to move us, or even divert us for long. Satire, engaged in its most intellectual of exercises, must first of all establish an impeccable *locus operandi;* its premise is the kingdom where certain rules apply. The countries Gulliver visits are the systems of thought and learning Swift satirizes made visible one after the other and set in operation. But while place in satire is a purely artificial construction, set up to be knocked down, in humor place becomes its most revealing and at the same time is itself the most revealed. This is because humor, it seems to me, of all forms of fiction, entirely accepts place for what it is.

"Spotted Horses," by William Faulkner, is a good case in point. At the same time that this is just about Mr. Faulkner's funniest story, it is the most thorough and faithful picture of a Mississippi crossroads hamlet that you could ever hope to see. True in spirit, it is also true to everyday fact. Faulkner's art, which often lets him shoot the moon, tells him when to be literal too. In all its specification of detail, both mundane and poetic, in its complete adherence to social fact (which nobody knows better than Faulkner, surely, in writing today), by its unerring aim of observation as true as the sights of a gun would give, but Faulkner has no malice, only compassion; and even and also in the joy of those elements of harlequinade-fantasy that the spotted horses of the title bring in—in all that shining fidelity to place lies the heart and secret of this tale's comic glory.

Faulkner is, of course, the triumphant example in America today of the mastery of place in fiction. Yoknapatawpha County, so supremely and exclusively and majestically and totally itself, is an everywhere, but only because Faulkner's first concern is for what comes first—Yoknapatawpha, his own created world. I am not sure, as a Mississippian myself, how widely it is realized and appreciated that these works of such marvelous imaginative power can also stand as works of the carefulest and purest representation. Heightened, of course: their specialty is they are twice as true as life, and that is why it takes a genius to write them. "Spotted Horses" may not have happened yet; if it had, some others might have tried to make a story of it; but "Spotted Horses" could happen tomorrow—that is one of its glories. It could happen today or tomorrow at any little crossroads hamlet in Mississippi; the whole combination of irresistibility is there. We have the Snopses ready, the Mrs. Littlejohns ready, nice Ratliff and the Judge ready and sighing, the clowns, sober and merry, settled for the evening retrospection of it in the cool dusk of the porch; and the Henry Armstids armed with their obsessions, the little periwinkle-eyed boys armed with their indestructibility; the beautiful, overweening spring, too, the moonlight on the pear trees from which the mockingbird's song keeps returning; and the little store and the fat boy to steal and steal away at its candy. There are undoubtedly spotted horses too, in the offing—somewhere in Texas this minute, straining toward the day. After Faulkner has told it, it is easy for one and all to look back and see it.

Faulkner, simply, knew it already; it is a different kind of knowledge from Flaubert's, and proof could not add much to it. He was born knowing, or rather learning, or rather prophesying, all that and more; and having it all together at one time available while he writes is one of the marks of his mind. If there *is* any more in Mississippi than is engaged and dilated upon, and made twice as real as it used to be and applies now to the world, in the one story "Spotted Horses," then we would almost rather not know it—but I don't bet a piece of store candy that there is. In Faulkner's humor, even more measurably than in his tragedy, it is all there.

It may be going too far to say that the exactness and concreteness and solidity of the real world achieved in a story correspond to the intensity of feeling in the author's mind and to the very turn of his heart; but there lies the secret of our confidence in him.

Making reality real is art's responsibility. It is a practical assignment, then, a self-assignment: to achieve, by a cultivated sensitivity for observing life, a capacity for receiving its impressions, a lonely, unremitting, unaided, unaidable vision, and transferring this vision without distortion to it onto the pages of a novel, where, if the reader is so persuaded, it will turn into the reader's illusion. How bent on this peculiar joy we are, reader and writer, willingly to practice, willingly to undergo, this alchemy for it!

What is there, then, about place that is transferable to the pages of a novel? The best things—the explicit things: physical texture. And as place has functioned between the writer and his material, so it functions between the writer and reader. Location is the ground conductor of all the currents of emotion and belief and moral conviction that charge out from the story in its course. These charges need the warm, hard earth underfoot, the light and lift of air, the stir and play of mood, the softening bath of atmosphere that give the likeness-to-life that life needs. Through the story's translation and ordering of life, the unconvincing raw material becomes the very heart's familiar. Life *is* strange. Stories hardly make it more so; with all they are able to tell and surmise, they make it more believably, more inevitably so.

I think the sense of place is as essential to good and honest writing as a logical mind; surely they are somewhere related. It is by knowing where you stand that you grow able to judge where you are. Place absorbs our earliest notice and attention, it bestows on us our original awareness; and our critical powers spring up from the study of it and the growth of experience inside it. It perseveres in bringing us back to earth when we fly too high. It never really stops informing us, for it is forever astir, alive, changing, reflecting, like the mind of man itself. One place comprehended can make us understand other places better. Sense of place gives equilibrium; extended, it is sense of direction too. Carried off we might be in spirit, and should be, when we are reading or writing something good; but it is the sense of place going with us still that is the ball of golden thread to carry us there and back and in every sense of the word to bring us home.

What can place *not* give? Theme. It can present theme, show it to the last detail—but place is forever illustrative: it is a picture of what man has done and imagined, it is his visible past, result. Human life is fiction's only theme.

Should the writer, then, write about home? It is both natural and sensible that the place where we have our roots should become the setting, the first and primary proving ground, of our fiction. Location, however, is not simply to be used by the writer—it is to be discovered, as each novel itself, in the act of writing, is discovery. Discovery does not imply that the place is new, only that we are. Place is as old as the hills. Kilroy at least has been there, and left his name. Discovery, not being a matter of writing our name on a wall, but of seeing what that wall is, and what is over it, is a matter of vision.

One can no more say, "To write stay home," than one can say, "To write leave home." It is the writing that makes its own rules and conditions for each person. And though place is home, it is for the writer writing simply *locus*. It is where the particular story he writes can be pinned down, the circle it can spin through and keep the state of grace, so that for the story's duration the rest of the world suspends its claim upon it and lies low as the story in peaceful extension, the *locus* fading off into the blue.

Naturally, it is the very breath of life, whether one writes a word of fiction or not, to go out and see what is to be seen of the world. For the artist to be unwilling to move, mentally or spiritually or physically, out of the familiar is a sign that spiritual timidity or poverty or decay has come upon him; for what is familiar will then have turned into all that is tyrannical.

One can only say: writers must always write best of what they know, and sometimes they do it by staying where they know it. But not for safety's sake. Although it is in the words of a witch—or all the more because of that—a comment of Hecate's in *Macbeth* is worth our heed: "Security / Is mortal's chiefest enemy." In fact, when we think in terms of the spirit, which are the terms of writing, is there a conception more stupefying than that of security? Yet writing of what you know has nothing to do with security: what is more dangerous? How can you go out on a limb if you do not know your own tree? No art ever came out of not risking your neck. And risk—experiment—is a considerable part of the joy of doing, which is the lone, simple reason all writers of serious fiction are willing to work as hard as they do.

The open mind and the receptive heart—which are at last and with fortune's smile the informed mind and the experienced heart—are to be gained anywhere, any time, without necessarily moving an inch from any present address. There must surely be as many ways of seeing a place as there are pairs of eyes to see it. The impact happens in so many different ways.

It may be the stranger within the gates whose eye is smitten by the crucial thing, the essence of life, the moment or act in our long-familiar midst that will forever define it. The inhabitant who has taken his fill of a place and gone away may look back and see it for good, from afar, still there in his mind's eye like a city over the hill. It was in the New Zealand stories, written eleven thousand miles from home and out of homesickness, that Katherine Mansfield came into her own. Joyce transplanted not his subject but himself while writing about it, and it was as though he had never left it at all: there it was, still in his eye, exactly the way he had last seen it. From the Continent he wrote the life of Dublin as it was then into a book of the future, for he went translating his own language of it on and on into a country of its own, where it set up a kingdom as renowned as Prester John's. Sometimes two places, two countries, are brought to bear on each other, as in E. M. Forster's work, and the heart of the novel is heard beating most plainly, most passionately, most personally when two places are at meeting point.

There may come to be new places in our lives that are second spiritual homes—closer to us in some ways, perhaps, than our original homes. But the home tie is the blood tie. And had it meant nothing to us, any other place thereafter would have meant less, and we would carry no compass inside ourselves to find home ever, anywhere at all. We would not even guess what we had missed.

It is noticeable that those writers who for their own good reasons push out against their backgrounds nearly always passionately adopt the new one in their work. Revolt itself is a reference and tribute to the potency of what is left behind. The substitute place, the adopted country, is sometimes a very much stricter, bolder, or harsher one than the original, seldom more lax or undemanding—showing that what was wanted was structure, definition, rigidity—perhaps these were wanted, and understanding was not.

Hemingway in our time has sought out the formal and ruthless territories of the world, archaic ones often, where there are bullfight arenas, theatres of hunting and war, places with a primitive, or formidable, stripped-down character, with implacable codes, with inscrutable justices and inevitable retributions. But whatever the scene of his work, it is the *places* that never are hostile. People give pain, are callous and insensitive, empty and cruel, carrying with them no pasts as they promise no futures. But place heals the hurt, soothes the outrage, fills the terrible vacuum that these human beings make. It heals actively, and the response is given consciously, with the ardent care and explicitness, respect and delight of a lover, when fishing streams or naming over streets becomes almost something of the lover's secret language—as the careful conversations between characters in Hemingway bear hints of the secret language of hate. The response to place has the added intensity that comes with the place's not being native or taken for granted, but found, chosen; thereby is the rest more heavily repudiated. It is the response of the aficionado; the response, too, is adopted. The title "A Clean Well Lighted Place" is just what the human being is not, for Hemingway, and perhaps it is the epitome of what man would like to find in his fellow-man but never has yet, says the author, and never is going to.

We see that point of view is hardly a single, unalterable vision, but a profound and developing one of great complexity. The vision itself may move in and out of its material, shuttle-fashion, instead of being simply turned on it, like a telescope on the moon. Writing is an expression of the writer's own peculiar personality, could not help being so. Yet in reading great works one feels that the finished piece transcends the personal. All writers great and small must sometimes have felt that they have become part of what they wrote even more than it still remains a part of them.

When I speak of writing from where you have put down roots, it may be said that what I urge is "regional" writing. "Regional," I think, is a careless term, as well as a condescending one, because what it does is fail to differentiate between the localized raw material of life and its outcome as art. "Regional" is an outsider's term; it has no meaning for the insider who is doing the writing, because as far as he knows he is simply writing about life. Jane Austen, Emily Brontë, Thomas Hardy, Cervantes, Turgenev, the authors of the books of the Old Testament, all confined themselves to regions, great or small—but are they regional? Then who from the start of time has not been so?

It may well be said that all work springing out of such vital impulse from its native soil has certain things in common. But what signifies is that these are not the little things that it takes a fine-tooth critic to search out, but the great things, that could not be missed or mistaken, for they are the beacon lights of literature.

It seems plain that the art that speaks most clearly, explicitly, directly and passionately from its place of origin will remain the longest understood. It is through place that we put out roots, wherever birth, chance, fate or our traveling selves set us down; but where those roots reach toward—whether in America, England or Timbuktu—is the deep and running vein, eternal and consistent and everywhere purely itself, that feeds and is fed by the human understanding. The challenge to writers today, I think, is not to disown any part of our heritage. Whatever our theme in writing, it is old and tried. Whatever our place, it has been visited by the stranger, it will never be new again. It is only the vision that can be new; but that is enough.

FLANNERY O'CONNOR

The Nature and Aim of Fiction

I understand that this is a course called "How the Writer Writes," and that each week you are exposed to a different writer who holds forth on the subject. The only parallel I can think of to this is having the zoo come to you, one animal at a time; and I suspect that what you hear one week from the giraffe is contradicted the next week by the baboon.

My own problem in thinking what I should say to you tonight has been how to interpret such a title as "How the Writer Writes." In the first place, there is no such thing as THE writer, and I think that if you don't know that now, you should by the time such a course as this is over. In fact, I predict that it is the one thing you can be absolutely certain of learning.

But there is a widespread curiosity about writers and how they work, and when a writer talks on this subject, there are always misconceptions and mental rubble for him to clear away before he can even begin to see what he wants to talk about. I am not, of course, as innocent as I look. I know well enough that very few people who are supposedly interested in writing are interested in writing well. They are interested in publishing something, and if possible in making a "killing." They are interested in being a writer, not in writing. They are interested in seeing their names at the top of something printed, it matters not what. And they seem to feel that this can be accomplished by learning certain things about working habits and about markets and about what subjects are currently acceptable.

If this is what you are interested in, I am not going to be of much use to you. I feel that the external habits of the writer will be guided by his common sense or his lack of it and by his personal circumstances; and that these will seldom be alike in two cases. What interests the serious writer is not external habits but what Maritain calls, "the habit of art"; and he explains that "habit" in this sense means a certain quality or virtue of the mind. The scientist has the habit of science; the artist, the habit of art.

Now I'd better stop here and explain how I'm using the word *art*. Art is a word that immediately scares people off, as being a little too grand. But all I mean by art is writing something that is valuable in itself and that works in itself. The basis of art is truth, both in matter and in mode. The person who aims after art in his work aims after truth, in an imaginative sense, no more and no less. St. Thomas said that the artist is concerned with the good of that which is made; and that will have to be the basis of my few words on the subject of fiction.

Now you'll see that this kind of approach eliminates many things from the discussion. It eliminates any concern with the motivation of the writer except as this finds its place inside the work. It also eliminates any concern with the reader in his market sense. It also eliminates that tedious controversy that always rages between people who declare that they write to express themselves and those who declare that they write to fill their pocketbooks, if possible.

In this connection I always think of Henry James. I know of no writer who was hotter after the dollar than James was, or who was more of a conscientious artist. It is true, I think, that these are times when the financial rewards for sorry writing are much greater than those for good writing. There are certain cases in which, if you can only learn to write poorly enough, you can make a great deal of money. But it is not true that if you write well, you won't get published at all. It is true that if you want to write well and live well at the same time, you'd better arrange to inherit money or marry a stockbroker or a rich woman who can operate a typewriter. In any case, whether you write to make money or to express your soul or to insure civil rights or to irritate your grandmother will be a matter for you and your analyst, and the point of departure for this discussion will be the good of the written work.

The kind of written work I'm going to talk about is story-writing, because that's the only kind I know anything about. I'll call any length of fiction a story, whether it be a novel or a shorter piece, and I'll call anything a story in which specific characters and events influence each other to form a meaningful narrative. I find that most people know what a story is until they sit down to write one. Then they find themselves writing a sketch with an essay woven through it, or an essay with a sketch woven through it, or an editorial with a character in it, or a case history with a moral, or some other mongrel thing. When they realize that they aren't writing stories, they decide that the remedy for this is to learn something that they refer to as the "technique of the short story" or "the technique of the novel." Technique in the minds of many is something rigid, something like a formula that you impose on the material; but in the best stories it is something organic, something that grows out of the material, and this being the case, it is different for every story of any account that has ever been written.

I think we have to begin thinking about stories at a much more fundamental level, so I want to talk about one quality of fiction which I think is its least common denominator—the fact that it is concrete—and about a few of the qualities that follow from this. We will be concerned in this with the reader in his fundamental human sense, because the nature of fiction is in large measure determined by the nature of our perceptive apparatus. The beginning of human knowledge is through the senses, and the fiction writer begins where human perception begins. He appeals through the senses, and you cannot appeal to the senses with abstractions. It is a good deal easier for most people to state an abstract idea than to describe and thus re-create some object that they actually see. But the world of the fiction writer is full of matter, and this is what the beginning fiction writers are very loath to create. They are concerned primarily with unfleshed ideas and emotions. They are apt to be reformers and to want to write because they are possessed not by a story but by the bare bones of some abstract notion. They are conscious of problems, not of people, of questions and issues, not of the texture of existence, of case histories and of everything that has a sociological smack, instead of with all those concrete details of life that make actual the mystery of our position on earth.

The Manicheans separated spirit and matter. To them all material things were evil. They sought pure spirit and tried to approach the infinite directly without any mediation of matter. This is also pretty much the modern spirit, and for the sensibility infected with it, fiction is hard if not impossible to write because fiction is so very much an incarnational art.

One of the most common and saddest spectacles is that of a person of really fine sensibility and acute psychological perception trying to write fiction by using these qualities alone. This type of writer will put down one intensely emotional or keenly perceptive sentence after the other, and the result will be complete dullness. The fact is that the materials of the fiction writer are the humblest. Fiction is about everything human and we are made out of dust, and if you scorn getting yourself dusty, then you shouldn't try to write fiction. It's not a grand enough job for you.

Now when the fiction writer finally gets this idea through his head and into his habits, he begins to realize what a job of heavy labor the writing of fiction is. A lady who writes, and whom I admire very much, wrote me that she had learned from Flaubert that it takes at least three activated sensuous strokes to make an object real; and she believes that this is connected with our having five senses. If you're deprived of any of them, you're in a bad way, but if you're deprived of more than two at once, you almost aren't present.

All the sentences in *Madame Bovary* could be examined with wonder, but there is one in particular that always stops me in admiration. Flaubert has just shown us Emma at the piano with Charles watching her. He says, "She struck the notes with aplomb and ran from top to bottom of the keyboard without a break. Thus shaken up, the old instrument, whose strings buzzed, could be heard at the other end of the village when the window was open, and often the bailiff's clerk, passing along the highroad, bareheaded and in list slippers, stopped to listen, his sheet of paper in his hand."

The more you look at a sentence like that, the more you can learn from it. At one end of it, we are with Emma and this very solid instrument "whose strings buzzed," and at the other end of it we are across the village with this very concrete clerk in his list slippers. With regard to what happens to Emma in the rest of the novel, we may think that it makes no difference that the instrument has buzzing strings or that the clerk wears list slippers and has a piece of paper in his hand, but Flaubert had to create a believable village to put Emma in. It's always necessary to remember that the fiction writer is much less *immediately* concerned with grand ideas and bristling emotions than he is with putting list slippers on clerks.

Now of course this is something that some people learn only to abuse. This is one reason that strict naturalism is a dead end in fiction. In a strictly naturalistic work the detail is there because it is natural to life, not because it is natural to the work. In a work of art we can be extremely literal, without being in the least naturalistic. Art is selective, and its truthfulness is the truthfulness of the essential that creates movement.

The novel works by a slower accumulation of detail than the short story does. The short story requires more drastic procedures than the novel because more has to be accomplished in less space. The details have to carry more immediate weight. In good fiction, certain of the details will tend to accumulate meaning from the story itself, and when this happens, they become symbolic in their action.

Now the word *symbol* scares a good many people off, just as the word *art* does. They seem to feel that a symbol is some mysterious thing put in arbitrarily by the writer to frighten the common reader—sort of a literary Masonic grip that is only for the initiated. They seem to think that it is a way of saying something that you aren't actually saying, and so if they can be got to read a reputedly symbolic work at all, they approach it as if it were a problem in algebra. Find *x*. And when they do find or think they find this abstraction, *x*, then they go off with an elaborate sense of satisfaction and the notion that they have "understood" the story. Many students confuse the *process* of understanding a thing with understanding it.

I think that for the fiction writer himself, symbols are something he uses simply as a matter of course. You might say that these are details that, while having their essential place in the literal level of the story, operate in depth as well as on the surface, increasing the story in every direction.

I think the way to read a book is always to see what happens, but in a good novel, more always happens than we are able to take in at once, more happens than meets the eye. The mind is led on by what it sees into the greater depths that the book's symbols naturally suggest. This is what is meant when critics say that a novel operates on several levels. The truer the symbol, the deeper it leads you, the more meaning it opens up. To take an example from my own book, *Wise Blood,* the hero's rat-colored automobile is his pulpit and his coffin as well as something he thinks of as a means of escape. He is mistaken in thinking that it is a means of escape, of course, and does not really escape his predicament until the car is destroyed by the patrolman. The car is a kind of death-in-life symbol, as his blindness is a life-in-death symbol. The fact that these meanings are there makes the book significant. The reader may not see them but they have their effect on him nonetheless. This is the way the modern novelist sinks, or hides, his theme.

The kind of vision the fiction writer needs to have, or to develop, in order to increase the meaning of his story is called anagogical vision, and that is the kind of vision that is able to see different levels of reality in one image or one situation. The medieval commentators on Scripture found three kinds of meaning in the literal level of the sacred text: one they called allegorical, in which one fact pointed to another; one they called tropological, or moral, which had to do with what should be done; and one they called anagogical, which had to do with the Divine life and our participation in it. Although this was a method applied to biblical exegesis, it was also an attitude toward all of creation, and a way of reading nature which included most possibilities, and I think it is this enlarged view of the human scene that the fiction writer has to cultivate if he is ever going to write stories that have any chance of becoming a permanent part of our literature. It seems to be a paradox that the larger and more complex the personal view, the easier it is to compress it into fiction.

People have a habit of saying, "What is the theme of your story?" and they expect you to give them a statement: "The theme of my story is the economic pressure of the machine on the middle class"—or some such absurdity. And when they've got a statement like that, they go off happy and feel it is no longer necessary to read the story.

Some people have the notion that you read the story and then climb out of it into the meaning, but for the fiction writer himself the whole story is the meaning, because it is an experience, not an abstraction.

Now the second common characteristic of fiction follows from this, and it is that fiction is presented in such a way that the reader has the sense that it is unfolding around him. This doesn't mean he has to identify himself with the character or feel compassion for the character or anything like that. It just means that fiction has to be largely presented rather than reported. Another way to say it is that though fiction is a narrative art, it relies heavily on the element of drama.

The story is not as extreme a form of drama as the play, but if you know anything about the history of the novel, you know that the novel as an art form has developed in the direction of dramatic unity.

The major difference between the novel as written in the eighteenth century and the novel as we usually find it today is the disappearance from it of the author. Fielding, for example, was everywhere in his own work, calling the reader's attention to this point and that, directing him to give his special attention here or there, clarifying this and that incident for him so that he couldn't possibly miss the point. The Victorian novelists did this, too. They were always coming in, explaining and psychologizing about their characters. But along about the time of Henry James, the author began to tell his story in a different way. He began to let it come through the minds and eyes of the characters themselves, and he sat behind the scenes, apparently disinterested. By the time we get to James Joyce, the author is nowhere to be found in the book. The reader is on his own, floundering around in the thoughts of various unsavory characters. He finds himself in the middle of a world apparently without comment.

But it is from the kind of world the writer creates, from the kind of character and detail he invests it with, that a reader can find the intellectual meaning of a book. Once this is found, however, it cannot be drained off and used as a substitute for the book. As the late John Peale Bishop said: "You can't say Cézanne painted apples and a tablecloth and have said what Cézanne painted." The novelist makes his statements by selection, and if he is any good, he selects every word for a reason, every detail for a reason, every incident for a reason, and arranges them in a certain time-sequence for a reason. He demonstrates something that cannot possibly be demonstrated any other way than with a whole novel.

Art forms evolve until they reach their ultimate perfection, or until they reach some state of petrifaction, or until some new element is grafted on and a new art form made. But however the past of fiction has been or however the future will be, the present state of the case is that a piece of fiction must be very much a self-contained dramatic unit.

This means that it must carry its meaning inside it. It means that any abstractly expressed compassion or piety or morality in a piece of fiction is only a statement added to it. It means that you can't make an inadequate dramatic action complete by putting a statement of meaning on the end of it or in the middle of it or at the beginning of it. It means that when you write fiction you are speaking *with* character and action, not *about* character and action. The writer's moral sense must coincide with his dramatic sense.

It's said that when Henry James received a manuscript that he didn't like, he would return it with the comment, "You have chosen a good subject and are treating it in a straightforward manner." This usually pleased the person getting the manuscript back, but it was the worst thing that James could think of to say, for he knew, better than anybody else, that the straightforward manner is seldom equal to the complications of the good subject. There may never be anything new to say, but there is always a new way to say it, and since, in art, the way of saying a thing becomes a part of what is said, every work of art is unique and requires fresh attention.

It's always wrong of course to say that you can't do this or you can't do that in fiction. You can do anything you can get away with, but nobody has ever gotten away with much.

I believe that it takes a rather different type of disposition to write novels than to write

short stories, granted that both require fundamentally fictional talents. I have a friend who writes both, and she says that when she stops a novel to work on short stories, she feels as if she has just left a dark wood to be set upon by wolves. The novel is a more diffused form and more suited to those who like to linger along the way; it also requires a more massive energy. For those of us who want to get the agony over in a hurry, the novel is a burden and a pain. But no matter which fictional form you are using, you are writing a story, and in a story something has to happen. A perception is not a story, and no amount of sensitivity can make a story-writer out of you if you just plain don't have a gift for telling a story.

But there's a certain grain of stupidity that the writer of fiction can hardly do without, and this is the quality of having to stare, of not getting the point at once. The longer you look at one object, the more of the world you see in it; and it's well to remember that the serious fiction writer always writes about the whole world, no matter how limited his particular scene. For him, the bomb that was dropped on Hiroshima affects life on the Oconee River, and there's not anything he can do about it.

People are always complaining that the modern novelist has no hope and that the picture he paints of the world is unbearable. The only answer to this is that people without hope do not write novels. Writing a novel is a terrible experience, during which the hair often falls out and the teeth decay. I'm always highly irritated by people who imply that writing fiction is an escape from reality. It is a plunge into reality and it's very shocking to the system. If the novelist is not sustained by a hope of money, then he must be sustained by a hope of salvation, or he simply won't survive the ordeal.

People without hope not only don't write novels, but what is more to the point, they don't read them. They don't take long looks at anything, because they lack the courage. The way to despair is to refuse to have any kind of experience, and the novel, of course, is a way to have experience. The lady who only read books that improved her mind was taking a safe course—and a hopeless one. She'll never know whether her mind is improved or not, but should she ever, by some mistake, read a great novel, she'll know mighty well that something is happening to her.

A good many people have the notion that nothing happens in modern fiction and that nothing is supposed to happen, that it is the style now to write a story in which nothing happens. Actually, I think more happens in modern fiction—with less furor on the surface—than has ever happened in fiction before. A good example of this is a story by Caroline Gordon called "Summer Dust." It's in a collection of her stories called *The Forest of the South,* which is a book that repays study.

"Summer Dust" is divided into four short sections, which don't at first appear to have any relation between them and which are minus any narrative connection. Reading the story is at first rather like standing a foot away from an impressionistic painting, then gradually moving back until it comes into focus. When you reach the right distance, you suddenly see that a world has been created—and a world in action—and that a complete story has been told, by a wonderful kind of understatement. It has been told more by showing what happens around the story than by touching directly on the story itself.

You may say that this requires such an intelligent and sophisticated reader that it is not worth writing, but I'm rather inclined to think that it is more a false sophistication that prevents people from understanding this kind of story than anything else. Without being naturalistic in the least, a story like "Summer Dust" is actually much closer in form to life than a story that follows a narrative sequence of events.

The type of mind that can understand good fiction is not necessarily the educated

mind, but it is at all times the kind of mind that is willing to have its sense of mystery deepened by contact with reality, and its sense of reality deepened by contact with mystery. Fiction should be both canny and uncanny. In a good deal of popular criticism, there is the notion operating that all fiction has to be about the Average Man, and has to depict average ordinary everyday life, that every fiction writer must produce what used to be called "a slice of life." But if life, in that sense, satisfied us, there would be no sense in producing literature at all.

Conrad said that his aim as a fiction writer was to render the highest possible justice to the visible universe. That sounds very grand, but it is really very humble. It means that he subjected himself at all times to the limitations that reality imposed, but that reality for him was not simply coextensive with the visible. He was interested in rendering justice to the visible universe because it suggested an invisible one, and he explained his own intentions as a novelist in this way:

> . . . and if the [artist's] conscience is clear, his answer to those who in the fullness of a wisdom which looks for immediate profit, demand specifically to be edified, consoled, amused; who demand to be promptly improved, or encouraged, or frightened, or shocked or charmed, must run thus: My task which I am trying to achieve is, by the power of the written word, to make you hear, to make you feel—it is, before all, to make you *see.* That—and no more, and it is everything. If I succeed, you shall find there, according to your deserts, encouragement, consolation, fear, charm, all you demand—and, perhaps, also that glimpse of truth for which you have forgotten to ask.

You may think from all I say that the reason I write is to make the reader see what I see, and that writing fiction is primarily a missionary activity. Let me straighten this out.

Last spring I talked here, and one of the girls asked me, "Miss O'Connor, why do you write?" and I said, "Because I'm good at it," and at once I felt a considerable disapproval in the atmosphere. I felt that this was not thought by the majority to be a high-minded answer; but it was the only answer I could give. I had not been asked why I write the way I do, but why I write at all; and to that question there is only one legitimate answer.

There is no excuse for anyone to write fiction for public consumption unless he has been called to do so by the presence of a gift. It is the nature of fiction not to be good for much unless it is good in itself.

A gift of any kind is a considerable responsibility. It is a mystery in itself, something gratuitous and wholly undeserved, something whose real uses will probably always be hidden from us. Usually the artist has to suffer certain deprivations in order to use his gift with integrity. Art is a virtue of the practical intellect, and the practice of any virtue demands a certain asceticism and a very definite leaving-behind of the niggardly part of the ego. The writer has to judge himself with a stranger's eye and a stranger's severity. The prophet in him has to see the freak. No art is sunk in the self, but rather, in art the self becomes self-forgetful in order to meet the demands of the thing seen and the thing being made.

I think it is usually some form of self-inflation that destroys the free use of a gift. This may be the pride of the reformer or the theorist, or it may only be that simple-minded self-appreciation which uses its own sincerity as a standard of truth. If you have read the very vocal writers from San Francisco, you may have got the impression that the first thing you must do in order to be an artist is to loose yourself from the bonds of reason, and thereafter, anything that rolls off the top of your head will be of great value. Anyone's unrestrained feelings are considered worth listening to because they are unrestrained and because they are feelings.

St. Thomas called art "reason in making." This is a very cold and very beautiful definition, and if it is unpopular today, this is because reason has lost ground among us. As grace and nature have been separated, so imagination and reason have been separated, and this always means an end to art. The artist uses his reason to discover an answering reason in everything he sees. For him, to be reasonable is to find, in the object, in the situation, in the sequence, the spirit which makes it itself. This is not an easy or simple thing to do. It is to intrude upon the timeless, and that is only done by the violence of a single-minded respect for the truth.

It follows from all this that there is no technique that can be discovered and applied to make it possible for one to write. If you go to a school where there are classes in writing, these classes should not be to teach you how to write, but to teach you the limits and possibilities of words and the respect due them. One thing that is always with the writer—no matter how long he has written or how good he is—is the continuing process of learning how to write. As soon as the writer "learns to write," as soon as he knows what he is going to find, and discovers a way to say what he knew all along, or worse still, a way to say nothing, he is finished. If a writer is any good, what he makes will have its source in a realm much larger than that which his conscious mind can encompass and will always be a greater surprise to him than it can ever be to his reader.

I don't know which is worse—to have a bad teacher or no teacher at all. In any case, I believe the teacher's work should be largely negative. He can't put the gift into you, but if he finds it there, he can try to keep it from going in an obviously wrong direction. We can learn how not to write, but this is a discipline that does not simply concern writing itself but concerns the whole intellectual life. A mind cleared of false emotion and false sentiment and egocentricity is going to have at least those roadblocks removed from its path. If you don't think cheaply, then there at least won't be the quality of cheapness in your writing, even though you may not be able to write well. The teacher can try to weed out what is positively bad, and this should be the aim of the whole college. Any discipline can help your writing: logic, mathematics, theology, and of course and particularly drawing. Anything that helps you to see, anything that makes you look. The writer should never be ashamed of staring. There is nothing that doesn't require his attention.

We hear a great deal of lamentation these days about writers having all taken themselves to the colleges and universities where they live decorously instead of going out and getting firsthand information about life. The fact is that anybody who has survived his childhood has enough information about life to last him the rest of his days. If you can't make something out of a little experience, you probably won't be able to make it out of a lot. The writer's business is to contemplate experience, not to be merged in it.

Everywhere I go I'm asked if I think the universities stifle writers. My opinion is that they don't stifle enough of them. There's many a best-seller that could have been prevented by a good teacher. The idea of being a writer attracts a good many shiftless people, those who are merely burdened with poetic feelings or afflicted with sensibility. Granville Hicks, in a recent review of James Jones' novel, quoted Jones as saying, "I was stationed at Hickham Field in Hawaii when I stumbled upon the works of Thomas Wolfe, and his home life seemed so similar to my own, his feelings about himself so similar to mine about myself, that I realized I had been a writer all my life without knowing it or having written." Mr.

Hicks goes on to say that Wolfe did a great deal of damage of this sort but that Jones is a particularly appalling example.

Now in every writing class you find people who care nothing about writing, because they think they are already writers by virtue of some experience they've had. It is a fact that if, either by nature or training, these people can learn to write badly enough, they can make a great deal of money, and in a way it seems a shame to deny them this opportunity; but then, unless the college is a trade school, it still has its responsibility to truth, and I believe myself that these people should be stifled with all deliberate speed.

Presuming that the people left have some degree of talent, the question is what can be done for them in a writing class. I believe the teacher's work is largely negative, that it is largely a matter of saying "This doesn't work because . . ." or "This does work because . . ." The *because* is very important. The teacher can help you understand the nature of your medium, and he can guide you in your reading. I don't believe in classes where students criticize each other's manuscripts. Such criticism is generally composed in equal parts of ignorance, flattery, and spite. It's the blind leading the blind, and it can be dangerous. A teacher who tries to impose a way of writing on you can be dangerous too. Fortunately, most teachers I've known were too lazy to do this. In any case, you should beware of those who appear overenergetic.

In the last twenty years the colleges have been emphasizing creative writing to such an extent that you almost feel that any idiot with a nickel's worth of talent can emerge from a writing class able to write a competent story. In fact, so many people can now write competent stories that the short story as a medium is in danger of dying of competence. We want competence, but competence by itself is deadly. What is needed is the vision to go with it, and you do not get this from a writing class.

CHAPTER

THREE

Why Poetry Matters: Singing a New Song, Dancing an Old Dance

Sidney Poger and Tony Magistrale

Introduction

SECTION I: WHY POETRY?

INFORMAL WRITING 1

What is the first poem you remember reading? Describe your feelings toward that poem and what you remember of the experience in reading it.

Nancy, a student in Tony Magistrale's literature class, wrote in her journal:

> I like to read novels and stories—I've always liked English—but something happens to me when we get to poetry. I just don't feel very confident taking poems apart. I never seem to get it right. Also, I guess I like reading straight narratives because they are more directly relevant to my life and the world I know about. Poetry too often is too far removed—it never really seems to be about the world I live in, but is confined instead to the poet's alone.

Both writers of this chapter asked ourselves how we were first introduced to poetry. Sid Poger remembers:

There was always a lot of reading around my house; as the youngest by five years, I was thrown even more on the company of books than I would have been in many other families. My mother was always singing the songs she remembered from her European homeland and which are now part of my deepest subconscious, that collection of memories from which I will never be able to escape and which make up the central and indestructible part of myself. These songs may have been part of the process by which I came to poetry.

The first poetry I remember came from A. A. Milne. I had loved Winnie-The-Pooh and The House at Pooh Corner, which were among my first books. Since I wanted these stories to go on, I turned to the poetry of When We Were Very Young and Now We Are Six, an age I have remained stuck at for a long time. I remember when they were changing the guard at Buckingham Palace, and when the king complained, ''I do like a little bit of butter for my bread.'' I still can recite bits of ''James James Robinson Robinson Wetherbee George Dupree / Took good care of his mother, though he was only three.'' But what first woke me to the possibilities of poetry was a small poem called ''The Mirror'' which was not like the other poems for children, but was really a small lyric, a description of nature, and a mood piece. Here, I think I remember, I found something different, something I liked and wanted to know more about. In short, I said to myself, Here is poetry.

On the other hand, Tony Magistrale recalls:

My earliest memories of poetry date back to early adolescence—my own primitive writings emerging as part balm and part pressure cooker release from the tensions and mixed signals of an American boy. Some of the early poems I wrote were painfully derivative—from Schiller and St. John of the Cross (I always interpreted his religious laments in secular, usually sexual, terms) to the rock lyrics of the day, particularly the Beatles. Poetry supplied this nervous child-man with his first awkward voice against the forces of chaos and confusion that are the natural inheritances of adolescence.

As I look back on these early poems, I don't remember them as pleasant exercises. These were statements of pain and betrayal, of loss and limitation. But the act of writing about these painful experiences also gave me a degree of control over them that would not have been possible without the voice of poetry. Poetry taught me something most of my high school classmates never quite grasped: that language matters, and that words are often all we have.

What Does Poetry Look Like?

One student in an ''Introduction to Literature'' course wrote in his journal: ''Reading poetry is like licking sandpaper.''

One day in class, Nancy, who had found poetry too removed from her life, talked about the kind of music she listens to. She named popular groups and artists—Talking Heads, Bruce Springsteen, The Rolling Stones—but then told the class her favorite songs were performed by Jim Morrison and the Doors, a rock group that claimed an enormous following during the late sixties and early seventies. Nancy's favorite song by the Doors is "L.A. Woman": "It had a good beat," she wrote, "and you could dance to it all night long."

Tony pressed a little further. What about the words? Didn't they add in some way to her appreciation of the song? She agreed cautiously. He asked her to repeat some of them from memory and, after coaxing from several classmates, Nancy reluctantly recalled:

I see your hair is burning
Hills are full of fire
If they say I never loved you
You know they are a liar
Driving down the freeway
Midnight alleys roam
Cops in cars, the topless bars
Never saw a woman so alone.

Tony wrote these words on the blackboard. Then he asked Nancy what she thought they meant. With assistance from some of the other members of the class, Nancy concluded that this was a song about the city of Los Angeles, and, more important, that Morrison seemed to have mixed feelings about it. Other members of the class asked: What were these mixed feelings and why did he have them? Why did the singer personify the city as a woman? What were the characteristics that precisely defined this city for a listener?

It was clear after this class discussion that many of the same topics the class had encountered the week before in its consideration of e. e. cummings, Robinson Jeffers, and Robert Frost—consistent metaphors, visual imagery, the importance of diction—were equally applicable to words that Nancy had heard at least a hundred times, but had never before considered as poetry.

If song lyrics are like poetry, and Nancy had little trouble with lyrics, why does she have trouble with poetry? Perhaps she never got comfortable with poetry. In distinguishing between prose and poetry in her journal, Nancy acknowledged that one reason she prefers prose to poetry is a matter of confidence: She feels quite comfortable engaging novels and stories, and, one assumes, song lyrics, but she considers poetry an alien form. As she wrote in her journal, "I never seem to get it right."

What caused this perception? Why do students feel this way? Students have to deal in class with some poems that are either too complex or irrelevant to the stuff of which their lives are made. Some students may never have received the right kind of help in learning how to read a poem carefully—connecting and ordering the individual lines to produce a developing meaning in the reader's mind. For others, perhaps, the whole idea of poetry was never emphasized as an enterprise of enjoyment and fun, like listening to popular music, but instead treated as a classroom task that reduced the poem to the formal study of poetics (meter, rhyme schemes, etc.) or simple memorization.

Teachers are experienced at analyzing poems, at identifying metaphors, investigating a rhyme scheme, exploring the stanzaic form. "Teachers, they can do it," students seem to feel, "but I can't." But teachers were students once, too, and had some of the same problems. They can be viewed as people who have done this before, not as people gifted with the

power of reading poetry from birth. No one inherits such a gift; understanding poetry is a skill that can be learned.

The Poetry of Song

As Nancy illustrated in the lines she remembered from "L.A. Woman," poetry is all around us, in music, in advertising, in political slogans. It needs only to be recognized and acknowledged. Poetry has always fulfilled some deep and persistent need of humankind, we know of no culture that has been without it. Science has replaced art in telling us about the real conditions in the world around us. On the other hand, although science and technology may explain with objectivity the reasons for death or thunderstorms, science is silent on the terror of death or the emotional response human beings often share in seeing lightning or hearing thunder. To understand these feelings, to give them some universal sympathy, we must turn to art, to song, to poetry. A description of light reflected from the bottoms of clouds that characterizes a winter afternoon is not the same as Dickinson's poem, "There's a Certain Slant of Light," which describes not the light but its effect on the human observer (see p. 411). A major goal of good poetry in every language is to find words that speak directly to the reader, that educate emotions and feelings, allowing you to learn something about yourself and to articulate what you feel. The first step in overcoming the alienation and the mystification that are too often associated with the study of poetry is an awareness on your part that the art form is worthy of your understanding.

Perhaps one explanation for Nancy's inability or unwillingness to see the words of "L.A. Woman" as poetry is her reluctance to distinguish between the words and the music. "L.A. Woman" is, first and foremost, a song. The words of this song are attended with fierce guitar riffs that sound like a motorcycle revving its motor. But, just as the song has a musical rhythm that inspired Nancy to describe it as having "a good beat and you could dance to it all night long," the words themselves possess an inherent rhythm that works independently of the song's guitars. Removing the lyrics from their context may change their meaning; still, the words have meanings in themselves. Notice, first of all, that each of the lines in the song possesses a similar, regular beat. A pattern connects these individual lines: They are roughly the same length on the page, each line contains about the same number of words, and each line takes the same amount of time to say. Because this is a song, which has a break at the end of each line, one stops at the end of each line for a breath. Poems often don't conclude at the ends of lines and verses because they don't have to blend with melody: They create their own.

We have two kinds of memory; one is for melody, the other for words. We can stroll and hum, pace to a marching song, or run to the tune of a Walkman. Melodies may stir some of our deepest memories. When Sid visits his mother in a nursing home, she remains locked in herself. When he asks a direct question or touches her hand, she looks up and asks, "Who are you?" or "Who am I?" Once, he began to sing a Yiddish melody she used to sing around the house during the sunny afternoons of his childhood. His mother smiled, and for a moment sang along with him. Her eyes lit up, and she was communicating beyond words. When they finished the song, she sank back into her imprisoned self.

If Sid's mother could be called back to herself by the sound of a deeply remembered melody, music can call to our minds things we can scarcely call up any other way. A collection of notes speaks to us beyond words. When we add the words to the song, the impact seems greater. The tunes themselves are like people who need walkers to get around: They aren't always remembered on their own, but the additional support makes them stronger and more independent.

Song as Poetry

The words in a poem have to do the work of both words and melody in a song. They not only make the piece memorable by communicating on the verbal level, but they also supply the music. Devices such as alliteration, the repetition of initial consonants, help us to remember words like "That fearfull sound of 'Fire!' and 'Fire!' / Let no man know is my Desire." This line from Anne Bradstreet's "Upon the Burning of Our House" (see p. 500) which emphasizes the fear she felt when she heard the alarm, gives pleasure apart from its meaning; like music, it sounds nice. So does the old fairy-tale line, "Fee, fi, fo, fum." But Bradstreet's line does mean something, and the meaning is underscored by the musical qualities; both sound and meaning are an aid to understanding as well as to memory. This is true of W. H. Auden's "Doom is deeper and darker than any sea dingle" as well as any of the slogans we hear every night on TV.

What makes the lines Nancy quoted from "L.A. Woman" poetry? The words of the poem describe something, the city of Los Angeles, in imaginative terms. Morrison knows the value of using language in an exciting manner: The annual fall fires of the vegetation growing on the sides of the hills surrounding Los Angeles, for example, suggest a woman's auburn hair. At any rate, the city itself is described through feminine images, encouraging the reader/listener to think of Los Angeles in a context that is uniquely human. Since Morrison is a man, the city as a woman intensifies the feelings of love and separation that the song implies. Since he wrote this song in the sixties, it may reflect a sexist bias insofar as Morrison makes a connection between the sexual aspects of urban life and a woman. Morrison seems to feel an attraction to, and a repulsion from, the feminine qualities of the city he describes.

Why does Morrison employ these comparisons? It's what we all do when we try to explain something to someone else. We don't always want to say, "You had to be there." We want to say something that will make the listener feel that he or she was really there. What we do is try to compare the unfamiliar with the familiar, or to make a new connection between things that were familiar before but are now being put together in new ways. For example, when someone asks you how shark steak tastes, you might say, "Here's a piece on my plate; try it yourself." But, without the actual steak there, you might say, "It tastes like tuna but less oily."

Words don't describe only physical things like the tastes of food; they describe our deepest emotions, our broadest experiences. Like other language, poetry works through comparisons. The Scottish poet Robert Burns writes, "O my luve's like a red, red rose." How? we might ask. Is she red in color, does she have thorns, will she be revived by rain? We know that this kind of literal comparison isn't what Burns means. He means his love is as beautiful as a rose, in its perfection; she overcomes the senses as the perfume of the rose does. In another mood, Burns might have suggested that his love's beauty would not last, that she carries a worm of destruction within that would destroy her life (as Blake suggests in "The Sick Rose," see p. 485), or that her thorns might drive the lover away. The poet chooses carefully which quality of the rose he wishes to use to communicate his feelings.

Metaphor and Simile In literature we call these comparisons metaphors or similes. Although many commentators on poetry suggest there are real differences between them—the difference between being the same and looking the same, for example—despite their separate names, they really aren't very different. One basic difference, however, is that similes use explicit comparison words such as "like," "as," "than," "similar to," "resembles," or "seems"; metaphors don't. They imply a comparison, with the figurative word substituted for the literal term. But both devices take an experience and define it in terms of some other experience. We may not know what the evening looks like that T.S. Eliot describes at the beginning of "The Lovesong of J. Alfred Prufrock,"

> Let us go then, you and I,
> When the evening is spread out against the sky
> Like a patient etherised upon a table,

but we might have known, had we lived in 1920, what being under ether felt like, as Sid remembers the smell of ether from the operation to remove his tonsils when he was five years old. Among the traditional objects most commonly used as one of the elements for comparison are the rose, the moon, and the sun. These comparisons, traditional or not, are controlled partially by their context and partially by the language in which they are couched.

Langston Hughes, in "Dream Deferred," uses a series of comparisons to build up feeling toward an accumulation of America's indifference to its black population.

> What happens to a dream deferred?
>
> Does it dry up
> like a raisin in the sun?
> Or fester like a sore—
> And then run?
> Does it stink like rotten meat?
> Or crust and sugar over—
> like a syrupy sweet?
>
> Maybe it just sags
> like a heavy load.
>
> *Or does it explode?*

Why does Hughes load the poem with a series of similes? The "dream deferred" refers to the position of black people in America, and each of the similes Hughes uses in this poem speaks directly to a state that, within this racial context, is restrictive or unattractive. For example, the raisin is not meant to be sweet, but the idea of a grape withering in the sun. Similarly, the sore runs, the meat rots, the sugar turns syrupy. These states occur because they have been left unattended too long and thus the connection to the failure of America to address adequately its relations to a racial minority. All that is left is a metaphor, the implicit comparison to a bomb in the last line that is a prediction of the explosion to come.

Good poetry always works for economy and clarity as well as the ability to be understood, opting for conciseness and precision. When trying to describe the shark steak to someone who has never tasted it, we described what it tasted like—like tuna—and how it differed from that familiar thing—it is less oily. This standard two-part method of comparison—what it is like, what it is unlike—is not always spelled out in poetry. The poet may explore only one part of the formal comparison to express his ideas and feelings.

Diction Like the language of Jim Morrison, the language of poetry is precise, exact, and sharp. Leaving aside the metaphoric quality of Morrison's language, of the burning hillsides suggesting a red-haired woman, there are the suggestive meanings of the **diction**.* Imagine "L.A. Woman" rewritten as "Los Angeles Person":

"L.A. Woman"	"Los Angeles Person"
I see your hair is burning	I perceive your tresses aflame,
Hills are full of fire	Conflagration covers low mountains,
If they say I never loved you	If observers say our love is false
You know they are a liar	They don't know what they claim.
Driving down the freeway	Riding through the landscape
Midnight alleys roam	Darkest passageways lead,
Cops in cars, the topless bars	While policemen patrol, sleaze gains control,
Never saw a woman so alone.	No person so abandoned has been seen.

The idea hasn't been changed much, since the **denotation**, or dictionary meaning, of the words hasn't changed much. "I perceive your tresses aflame" means the same thing as "I see your hair is burning" to the dictionary or to the person studying English for the first time. But the **connotations**, or secondary meanings, are quite different. Morrison's lyric is clear and unequivocal: You know how he feels. His city, which is like a woman, inspires loneliness; he shakes his head over how alone she can be. But a "person"—isn't a woman a person? Isn't a woman seen to be abandoned the same as a lone woman? These questions arise from examining the choice of diction. It is a different thing, and reflects a different level of speech, to refer to a dog as a mutt, a hound, a bitch, a bulldog, a collie, a miniature poodle, an AKC registered purebred, or a Bichon Frise. Jim Morrison was careful to select a diction that suggests a familiarity with parts of the city like the familiarity of a country singer with his beloved homestead; poets are as careful to choose their words and to talk about things they know.

Rhyme Morrison also chose his words by how their sounds match. We all recognize the advantages of rhyme, which consists of a close similarity or identity of sounds between accented syllables. A regular rhyme consists of the repetition of the last stressed vowel and all following consonants, as "soon," "June," "honeymoon." Many ads and jingles employ rhymes with great success. Morrison does the same thing with "fire" and "liar," even though he has to make a lot of people—"they"—into a single person—"a liar"—in order to make the match work. Morrison even uses slant rhyme—where the words almost, but don't quite, match, such as "roam" and "alone," emphasizing the woman's separateness, her nonmatching. There are all kinds of ways of matching words—by initial consonant, by final consonant, by last long vowel—and not all of them come at the ends of lines. Morrison rhymes "cars" and "bars" in the same line (a move that also affects the rhythm) partly to surprise us and partly to encourage us to wait until the end, where we already expect a rhyme, to find a conclusion to the verse.

---

*Terms in boldface are defined in the glossary at the end of the book.

INFORMAL WRITING 2

In your journal, describe one of the following in two ways to a visitor from Mars (or from some other place outside our world): high heels, Superman, Twinkies, Tupperware. The first time, do not use any comparisons. The second time, use them. Which do you prefer? Why?

INFORMAL WRITING 3

Describe one of the objects listed in the assignment above in four lines of poetry.

INFORMAL WRITING 4

Examine the comparisons in the Langston Hughes poem above. Can you think of other comparisons to describe what Hughes is getting at? Can you substitute for the last line with another metaphor? Does it work as well?

The Pleasures of the Poem

One of the great pleasures of studying poetry, like that of singing popular songs, is to discover the way in which the meaning and the melody fit one another. Once you have become familiar with a poem and decided how all the devices work, how the consonants echo one another, how the rhymes pick up and repeat sounds, how the rhythms create the emphases of meaning, you are ready, like a singer, to perform. Sid describes it in this way:

> Whenever I teach poems, I always take time to read them aloud. Like a picture, a poem can be discussed within a single class, all the devices still held in mind, and the listener can perceive how they all work together in performance. A painting can be looked at, inch by square inch, color, brush stroke, composition, massing, and all be brought together by stepping back and viewing the entire composition. A performance of a poem can do the same thing.
>
> Every time I read a poem to a class, I can tell if I have not prepared properly because I stumble over the words as I perform the poem. When it goes well, however, like a singer, I am moved through my own performance, feeling lost, triumphant, sly, as the poem directs. My class, students tell me, feels the same way. When colleagues tell me that I missed my calling, that I should have been a singer, I remind them that I am.

The pleasures of performing poems are not reserved to the teacher alone, nor are the pleasures of singing reserved only for the singer. You can enjoy doing both. After going to a movie or seeing a live musical, we go home humming the melodies, singing the lyrics. Nancy reminded us earlier that she learned the words to "L.A. Woman" while "dancing to them all night long." After reading some poems, you can perform them for yourselves (or for your roommates).

There are rules for reading poetry aloud just as there are rules for singing songs. The words should be clearly pronounced, the most important ones emphasized, and the meaning respected. Too singsong a rhythm should be avoided. Don't stop at the ends of lines unless punctuation or meaning forces you to. If forced to choose between a regular rhythm and a clear meaning, you should always choose clarity. Don't worry about being too loud or too soft; the meaning of the words will dictate how loudly the poem should be read. We do not shout an intimate love poem nor whisper a call to arms.

INFORMAL WRITING 5

Read a poem selected for class discussion aloud, to yourself or your roommates. In your journal answer the following questions. What did you learn from such a "performance"? What did you hear? Did your appreciation for the poem change in any way after reading it aloud? Why? How?

INFORMAL WRITING 6

Choose a paragraph of prose from a newspaper or magazine. Rewrite the paragraph, changing words and form, so that it looks like a poem. After you have done this, in a journal entry make note of the aspects you elected to change: How and where did you reshape the paragraph? Which words did you eliminate? Why did you put it in this particular poetic form? Is it a poem now?

But the pleasures of performing and of listening are not the only goals of studying poetry. Language used in complex ways describes our life and our experiences most exactly. It speaks to us not only in meaning, but in the satisfaction we feel when the melody and the meaning combine in a way that is a surprise and a continual delight.

Nancy hadn't considered all these aspects when she chose "L.A. Woman" as her favorite song. Neither did she try to separate the words from the music. She just liked it; listening to the song made her feel pleasure. Poetry works the same way. We read a poem, like any of those in this book, and we like it. We want to learn about poems, to find out why they give pleasure. Poems tell us about life, they shape experience, they show the reader that an individual's deepest experiences are not necessarily different from those of other people. When the reader tries to figure these devices out, he or she asks *how* they work to determine just how good the poems are. Even if he or she does not want to perform Jim Morrison's "L.A. Woman," the reader may want to know the tune, sing the lyrics over, and try variations to see how they work. Even if we don't want to write poetry, finding out how poems work increases our pleasure in reading them and introduces us to the highest and most pleasurable forms of language.

SECTION II: THE NARRATIVE OF POETRY

Studying the devices of poetry may do all the things we just claimed. Nevertheless, you might ask, why can't we just enjoy it, as we enjoy other arts? Can't we say, "I don't know much about poetry but I know what I like?" Whenever we get interested in something, we want to know more about it. Our interest piques our curiosity, and our curiosity leads us to new knowledge. When we study anything—a musical composition, a chemical equation, the human body, poetry—our effort to understand it better usually increases our appreciation for whatever it is that we are studying.

Poems may not be as difficult to understand as you think. All of us, at one time or another, get impatient. We may not understand all the nuances of a particular song's meaning—or appreciate them until we've listened to it so often others think we're crazy—but we know if it's a love song or a fight song and whether it's happy or sad. We know the

same thing when we first encounter a poem. We read it and come to some conclusion about its subject: A man is trying to convince a woman that he's in love with her, or someone is concerned about the approach of death. Knowing the subject, we conclude that we don't react favorably to poems about death, or we like the way the man talks to the woman. It is when we like it that we try to find out how the parts work.

Perhaps that's why we should learn as much as we can about poetic devices. Not that we want to learn so we can pass the knowledge on to others (although teachers love to do that) but so we can find out more for ourselves and enjoy reading poetry more. Most people do not go out of their way to say, "Look at that rhyme scheme" or "That's a great metaphor," but a lot can be seen by discovering how the rhyme scheme helps to make sense of the poem. By studying the devices of poetry, you won't get to the end of the process; you won't learn all there is to know. You'll only learn how to start. From there on, your own interest will take you farther.

INFORMAL WRITING 7

One of the ways to start, especially as you get more and more into the technical devices, is to use your journal to see what you can find out about how things work. Look back in your journals to see if you can find examples of personification (see the definition directly below), alliteration (see p. 417 above), and metaphor (see p. 418 above). When you used these figures, you were working in the language of poetry.

INFORMAL WRITING 8

Using the paragraph you selected from a newspaper or magazine in Informal Writing 6, alter the lines to include examples of personification, alliteration, and metaphor.

Figurative Language

Personification "The snow had fallen off the hedge dog. When Danny had come down it had only been a harmless lump of snow outside the playground. Now it stood revealed, an incongruous splash of green in all the eye-watering whiteness. It was sitting up, as if to beg a sweet or a scrap." Everyone knows that a hedge is not able to move—it is merely a sculptured piece of vegetation. But in Stephen King's novel *The Shining*, the hedge, shaped in the form of a dog, actually moves—as if it were not merely sticks and leaves, but flesh and bone. **Personification** does not mean merely making someone or something into a person, but giving any animal, object, or concept human attributes. Keats personifies the season in the second stanza of "To Autumn" (see p. 517) when he suggests the season is like a farm worker, but like one we've never seen. The worker dozes, he watches the cider pressings, but does not do any active work. The personification applies not only to the season, but also to the reader, who recognizes what he or she would want to be doing in the midst of autumn: staring and dreaming. Donald Finkel, in "They" (see p. 657), personifies trees and the machines that eat their limbs and eliminate sawdust.

The impulse to use personification comes from our tendency to see things in human terms. If, in an abstracted stupor, we bump into a tree or a telephone pole, our tendency is to say "Stupid tree" or, more politely, "Excuse me." Since we are human, our imaginations, when we identify with inanimate objects, tend to animate them, making them living beings, if not human ones.

The ancient Greeks thought that every tree was animated by a living spirit; any harm committed to the tree might well bring harm to the perpetrator. Chop down that tree, and the naiad who inhabits it, or one of her relatives, will bring vengeance down on you. Poets today are more restrained in their use of this device. Too much personification leads toward sentimentality, and the direct address to inanimate objects may become tiresome.

Used carefully, personification can control the development of a song or a poem. The singer can call a city a woman, and describe a landscape of burning hills as a red-headed woman. And we believe him. In fact, the city becomes all the more real because of this identification.

Allusion An allusion is a reference to a person, place, or event outside the poem, to a symphony, a sculpture, a TV show, or another literary work, that the audience may or may not understand. In one of the most popular movies of all time, *E.T.: The Extraterrestrial,* E.T. receives the initial idea to contact his distant planet when he hears the phrase "Phone Home" on a television commercial for Bell Telephone. The phrase "Phone Home," which becomes a kind of refrain throughout the film, is an allusion both E.T. and the audience watching the film understand. Alluding to its own original allusion, Bell Industries followed the success of *E.T.* with another commercial, of E.T.'s face repeating the phrase, "Phone Home." In this second commercial, however, America's favorite alien is exhorting the human audience to follow his example.

One of the problems confronting someone who reads a poem is that he or she doesn't always know what the poet or his contemporaries knew. To understand the opening of T. S. Eliot's "The Love Song of J. Alfred Prufrock," one should be acquainted with the effects of ether. When Eliot began his most famous poem, *The Waste Land,* with the lines,

April is the cruellest month, breeding
Lilacs out of the dead land

he wanted to suggest that the annual rebirth that occurs in spring can be painful to those who do not want to be reminded of the possibilities of life. He also expected some of his readers to remember the poems they had run into that, in contrast to his, praised spring for its powers. (Eliot made sure they would recognize a number of his allusions by writing footnotes to his poem.) He probably thought specifically of the beginning of Chaucer's *Canterbury Tales* (rendered here in modern English):

When April with his showers sweet
Has pierced the drought of March to the root
And bathed every vine in such liquid
That engenders the flower through its power . . .
Then people long to go on pilgrimages.

When William Carlos Williams in his poem *Paterson* wanted to make fun of Eliot and his famous opening, he asked: "Who is it spoke of April? Some/insane engineer" (*Paterson* 169). He knew that readers of modern poetry would think of Eliot when they saw the word "April," and he wanted to add some suggestions of Eliot's personality. Eliot, who had worked in a bank and as head of a publishing house, was meticulous in his details, so that he might be recognized as an "engineer" by his readers. Williams exaggerates the meticulousness into insanity, so that the reader would smile at the characterization. For those who recognize the allusion, it is a powerful, shorthand way of characterizing Eliot; for those who do not, it remains a minor puzzle.

One of the problems you will have is that lots of allusions are to events of the distant

past or to books you may not have read. So editors invented footnotes, which direct your eye to the bottom of the page and tell you, with a sureness of tone that may put you off, that *this* is what the allusion means. If the text does not provide footnotes to explain allusions, use a dictionary, a bible, an encyclopedia, or a handbook of mythology to see what you can find. Sometimes only part of what you find is useful; sometimes none of it. What you should do, before even looking up an allusion, is to read the poem through and see what you make of it. Then look at the footnote or in the reference book. If the information makes sense, think about how the allusion deepens the poem. If it doesn't add something to your understanding, ignore it since you're not ready to use that meaning yet. Or, better yet, ask your instructor, who will probably be able to explain the allusion more fully so that you can see how it works within the poem. Sometimes your instructor may not have recognized that an allusion is being made; you will make your instructor see new things in the poem. By contributing to the instructor's knowledge of the poem, you may also be contributing to the way your instructor teaches the poem in the future.

Imagery Imagery signifies all objects and qualities of sense perception, which, as one of our students writes, make us "picture it, hear it, or even smell it." It also appeals to the senses of touch and taste. "The images in our mind are the thing that is the reader's connection with the poem," she adds. Since "the point of reading poetry is to get a mental picture of the actions or ideas described in the poems," writes another student, "without imagery, the poem does nothing." While this view may be extreme, it does suggest how central imagery is to poetry. Words like "burning" and "fire" in "L.A. Woman" carry a feeling of heat and suggest that the woman has red hair. A number of additional words about fire may also suggest the smell of smoke, the burning in the eyes as the smoke irritates them, the heat if one approaches too closely. Some poets overwhelm their readers with a large number of images, as Keats does in "Ode to a Nightingale."

> O, for a draught of vintage! that hath been
>   *Cooled* a long age in the *deep-delved* earth,
> *Tasting* of Flora and the *country green,*
>   *Dance,* and Provençal *song,* and *sunburnt mirth!*
> O for a beaker full of the *warm* South,
>   Full of the true, the *blushful* Hippocrene,
>   With *beaded bubbles winking* at the brim,
>   And *purple-stainéd* mouth;
> That I might *drink,* and leave the world *unseen,*
> And with thee *fade away* into the *forest dim.*

The italicized words all refer to the senses. "Cooled" and "deep-delved" call up the coolness of the earth, especially in a cave or at the bottom of a hole. The taste of flowers personified in a goddess named Flora, grass, dance, and song, are all mixed together, with the addition of "sunburnt mirth" to add another flavor to the draught. The warmth of the South contrasts with the coolness of the earth. The bubbles that wink also leave a stain on the mouth. All of this is summed up in the word "drink." After the poet drinks, his senses are overcome so that he feels himself fading away into something only half-seen. One appreciative student suggests, "Imagery awakens my senses and keeps me tuned in to the poem, being able to see, hear, feel, smell, and taste whatever is being described."

Some poems depend on language that evokes a single sense—Williams's "The Red Wheelbarrow." Wallace Stevens emphasizes the feeling of cold when he transforms himself (or his reader) into "The Snow Man" (see p. 557). Edgar Allan Poe suggests four different moods through emphasizing the differences in the sounds of four different kinds of bells in his poem "The Bells" (see p. 524).

Images force you into participating in the process of creation. If you watch a TV program or a film, you more passively allow the colors and sounds to overwhelm your senses. Once the stimulus disappears, so does the sensual appeal. The stimulus of a film makes us go back to see it again; all one must do to recall Keats's draught is to recall the words of the poem.

INFORMAL WRITING 9

Write in your journal about the colors and sounds you observe in a TV show or in a film. How do these images help to convey the meaning? Can you recall the stimuli long after viewing the film?

INFORMAL WRITING 10

In Matthew Arnold's "Dover Beach" (see p. 538), or in some other poem selected by your instructor, find examples of personification, allusion, and imagery.

INFORMAL WRITING 11

Make two lists: one, of colors; the other, of sounds. After the lists are completed, match colors to sounds. Write a line of poetry where one of the colors is linked to one of the sounds into a complete thought or image.

Symbol Symbol is a difficult term, partly because it is so familiar. A symbol is anything that, while it acts within the texture of the poem, also stands for something else. It can be read both literally and metaphorically. A symbol is not limited to a single meaning, but can suggest a number of meanings at the same time. We have all seen *conventional symbols,* about which we seldom think but that communicate clearly and simply, such as a banner with a hammer and sickle, which is a piece of cloth that also represents the Soviet Union; a large foam rubber hand with the index finger raised in triumph while its wearer chants "We're number one" at a college football game; or a flashing light atop an ambulance or a fire engine, which represents an urgency for which we must give way. Our feelings toward these symbols may differ; for example, when you see in the rear-view mirror a police car that starts flashing its light. If you've been speeding, your reaction is different than if you have been obeying the speed limit and someone has just cut in front of you going fifteen or twenty miles over the limit.

We must take care, as readers, both to see what the poet suggests by his or her words and to examine the effects in our heads triggered by the words. Although a symbol has the capacity to suggest different things to different people at different times, it is not unlimited in its suggestions. If I like my Aunt Millie, who always wears a bright green hat, I may like any mention of bright green. The response of the reader is important for understanding a poem, but it should be typical of the responses of other readers. Norman Bates of Alfred Hitchcock's film *Psycho* or Freddy Krugger of *Nightmare on Elm Street* would not be a typical reader; if we examined Bates's responses to a poem about mothers, or, for that matter, a poem about young females in the shower, we might find out a great deal about Bates. But his responses won't help in understanding the poem. Examining our own reactions, insofar as they are typical, helps us to complete the creative process.

A symbol, which is a way of seeing rather than a way of saying, can be very subtle. It exists within a realistic context. In Frost's "Mending Wall," there really is a wall.

Before I built a wall I'd ask to know
What I was walling in or walling out,
And to whom I was like to give offense.

It is real enough to have its boulders tumbled in the sun and have to be repaired every year. Both men, the speaker and his neighbor, have to lift the stubborn rocks and balance them on top of the wall. But is a wall a good thing or not? When Frost read to college audiences, he used to say, "I was very fair. Twice I said 'Something there is that doesn't love a wall' and twice I said, 'Good fences make good neighbors.' What could be fairer than that?" But readers of that poem know that they are to look on the wall as an unnecessary thing. "My apple trees will never get across / And eat the cones under his pines, I tell him." What harm can come that a wall needs to keep out? Besides, we all know that there *is* something that knocks down walls, even if it is only frost heaves. But, would any of us like to see all those stone walls destroyed? Aren't they part of the rustic charm of Frost's New England landscape? And aren't walls *sometimes* necessary to preserve some degree of privacy? Frost may also be suggesting that without *some* walls, it is impossible to maintain good friendships; that's just the way human beings are, especially New Englanders who have grown accustomed to harsh and isolating winters. So we don't know how we feel about the wall in the poem. Symbols are elusive; they always have to be located within their context before we can come to any conclusions about them. We have to see the context before we can see the symbol. By looking at Frost's wall, we can suggest that it stands for some connecting, as well as dividing, device. If it makes good neighbors, it must be part of what makes them get along. At the same time, what wants it down is something that is trying to remove barriers. Beginning readers often jump to interpreting a symbol without having considered how it is presented. A symbol is normally an important item in the poem, one that is examined or presented in some way that suggests it means more than it first appears to. It is always better to be a bit reluctant about interpreting symbols rather than jumping in without examining the surface or the literal meaning of the poem.

Technical Devices

Rhythm One of our students calls rhythm "the heartbeat of a poem." Like a heartbeat, it does not always go at exactly the same pace, but varies as pressure varies. Once a poet or songwriter establishes a basic beat or meter, he or she can develop variations that deepen the meaning and delight the reader or listener. You may wonder what difference it makes, but Nancy answered that question for us when she said "L.A. Woman" has a good beat. She may not have known how to describe the beat, or how Morrison played variations against its regularity, but she was affected by it. If she wanted to dance to the song, she would have to know about the beat. We may not want to dance to every poem, but we should at least know how the steps might be done.

Although all poems have rhythm, only some have **meter**, or a recurrence of regular beats. The process of determining the meter of a poem is called **scansion**, which consists of analyzing the component feet, and pauses, in a line. Traditional English poetic meters are based on stressed syllables, not on words. Every time we speak, we stress some syllables

in contrast to others. We say "to *day,*" not "*to* day" [italics indicate stress]. One says *in* can *des* cent, stressing the third syllable the most, and the first syllable less, and the second and fourth least of all. Many people have found that not all stressed syllables have the same amount of stress—some prosodists have identified as many as five separate levels of stress—but that kind of distinction can, and should, be left to specialists. All we have to be concerned with is whether a syllable is stressed in relation to its neighbors. The rhythm sets up a pattern, within a line, between lines, or between stanzas, whose contrast makes them more interesting. For example, the first two lines of "L.A. Woman" contrast in that the first begins and ends with an unstressed syllable; the second line begins and ends with a stressed syllable:

> I see your hair is burning
> Hills are full of fire

A similar pattern is seen in the fifth and sixth lines, although the first line begins with a stressed syllable:

> Driving down the freeway
> Midnight alleys roam

The last two lines contrast in that one is divided into two parts separated by a comma; the last line goes on without a break:

> Cops in cars, the topless bars
> Never saw a woman so alone.

INFORMAL WRITING 12

Choose any poem from the anthology. Count the number of stresses by making a V of your thumb and index finger. Put your chin into the V and read the words aloud. Every time your chin wiggles, you have a stress. Note the way the stress falls into some more or less regular pattern. Does this stress pattern have anything to do with the meaning of the poem you have chosen?

INFORMAL WRITING 13

Go back to the color–sound line of poetry you just wrote. Can you change the stresses in that line to alter the meaning?

Robert Frost, a very skillful user of meter, in the opening stanza of "The Death of the Hired Man," demonstrates how stress can be used to emphasize certain dramatic phrases. Mary is waiting for Warren to return in order to alert him, and the reader, to some news. Frost emphasizes the news by placing it into half lines set off by periods. These half lines are the only spoken words in this stanza. They are also full of stressed sounds, in contrast to the more hurried, less stressed words of the rest of the paragraph. Reading the stanza aloud, with attention to the rhythm, shows how important those stressed phrases are.

> Mary sat musing on the lamp-flame at the table
> Waiting for Warren. When she heard his step,
> She ran on tip-toe down the darkened passage
> To meet him in the doorway with the news

And put him on his guard. 'Silas is back.'
She pushed him outward with her through the door
And shut it after her. 'Be kind,' she said.
She took the market things from Warren's arms
And set them on the porch, then drew him down
To sit beside her on the wooden steps.

Frost's use of rhythm is based on the alternation of stressed and unstressed syllables to emphasize certain phrases. Wanda Coleman, in her poem "HUH," uses a series of rhythms that contribute to meaning.

whatcha gonna do girl
get married. let me see the ring. It's only glass

Definitions of Metrical Terms

FOOT PATTERNS

iambic foot unstressed syllable followed by a stressed syllable, as "Whose *woods* these *are,* I *think* I *know*"

trochaic foot stressed syllable followed by an unstressed syllable, as "*Once upon* a *mid*night *drear*y"

anapestic foot two unstressed syllables followed by a stressed syllable, as "The Assyrian came *down* like the *wolf* on the *fold*"

dactylic foot a stressed syllable followed by two unstressed syllables, as "*Lift* her up *ten*derly"

spondaic foot two stressed syllables, a rare but emphatic foot, as "think upon it I *dare not*"

LINE NUMBERS

monometer one foot—"Adam / Had em"

dimeter two feet—"I have eaten"

trimeter three feet—"He kindly stopped for me"

tetrameter four feet—"Because I could not stop for Death"

pentameter five feet—"To be or not to be: that is the question"

hexameter six feet—"That like a wounded snake drags its slow length along"

These terms are used to describe lines, such as *iambic pentameter* for a five-foot line made up of iambic feet. But few poems are completely regular, so that a poem made up mostly of iambic feet would be called iambic despite the occasional trochaic or anapestic foot. What you do is count the number of feet as closely as you can and see which foot predominates, and you know the meter. Then you should explore why the poet varies his rhythm.

We should notice that no combination of feet is inherently solemn or happy, gay or melancholy. Tone is derived from a combination of meaning, diction, context, meter, speed, and other musical devices.

but it look like a whole lot of diamond. he only a boy
but he look like a whole lot of man. you only a
child but you look like a whole lot of woman
it's only the world and it's a whole lot of trouble
whatcha gonna do girl when the weddin's thru
and the moon's wine turns to vinegar
whatcha gonna do when you got no one but you
and baby to feed. whatcha gonna do
when the sun go down and the wind move in to stay?

The rhythm of this poem is tied to common, everyday street speech. Coleman starts this poem by asking a short question. The question expands into a series of declarations, and these declarations in turn suggest a trap that the woman in the poem will not be able to escape. If you read the poem aloud, you will discover that the rhythms of the poem force the words to speed up as you get further along. One of the reasons for this is that the rhythmical units get longer—short questions, longer declarations, even longer disaster. The rhythms of the poem highlight the poem's meaning. The world threatens the temporary bliss the woman experiences as her wedding day approaches. Although the poem is filled with the trappings of marital happiness and apparent security, no sooner does Coleman mention such elements than she deliberately undercuts them. The rhythms emphasize this process of undercutting.

Meter Meter, or the recurrence of a rhythmic pattern, gives us the beat, so we can follow the song; rhythm, the recurrence of stressed and unstressed syllables, indicates the important words as Jim Morrison does. With stresses indicated by italics, "L.A. Woman" might be scanned like this:

I *see* your *hair* is *burn*ing
Hills are *full* of *fire*
If they *say* I *ne*ver *loved* you
You *know* they *are* a *liar*
*Dri*ving *down* the *free*way
*Mid*night *al*leys *roam*
Cops in *cars,* the *top*less *bars*
*Ne*ver saw a *wo*man so a*lone.*

While the melody helps to create these stresses, we can discover through a cursory examination that the song is written in lines containing three metric feet. We can't tell whether the feet are iambic or trochaic or exactly what the rhythm of the last line is, but we do discover a pattern in the words that gives pleasure and meaning.

Rhyme Rhyme is the close similarity or identity of sounds between accented syllables. Normally, a rhyme consists of the repetition of the last stressed vowel and all following consonants (shuttlecock, stock, rock, flock). We like to hear these sounds in some regular pattern, especially at the emphatic ends of lines, and sometimes we wonder if the poet can keep up what he or she has started. Tom Lehrer, a satiric songster, has a series of rhymes about the possibility of sex when we are growing old:

An awful debility,
A lessened utility,
A loss of mobility
Is a strong possibility.
In all probability
I'll lose my virility
And you your fertility
And desirability,
And this liability
Of total sterility
Will lead to hostility
And a sense of futility.
So let's act with agility
While we still have facility,
Or we'll soon reach senility
And lose the ability.

We wonder how long Lehrer can go on with this rhyme; then he changes the tune and switches to a new rhyme.

We not only derive pleasure from rhyme, but we also feel a sense of completeness. For example, in Dickinson's "Because I Could Not Stop for Death,"

Because I could not stop for Death—
He kindly stopped for me—
The Carriage held but just Ourselves—
And Immortality—

the rhyme of "Me" and "Immortality" completes the stanza; we waited for some such signal that the stanza would end. The rhyme, like the rhythm, also helps sometimes to emphasize the ideas; the speaker (me) and Immortality are linked by the rhyme. Since Immortality overcomes death, Death is left alone, a kind caller who gives one a lift but who will be left alone at the end. The rhymes may suggest that those who believe in God's power for eternal life know that they will be immortal and overcome death.

Rhymes are either stressed, as Dickinson's are, or unstressed, as when there is a similar unstressed syllable following the last stressed vowel: "tenderly," "slenderly," as in Thomas Hood's "The Bridge of Sighs." Stressed rhyme (which used to be called masculine rhyme) emphasizes the ending with impact; unstressed (which used to be called feminine rhyme) is often used for comic effect, as in "The Lovesong of J. Alfred Prufrock":

I have seen the moment of my greatness flicker,
I have seen the eternal Footman hold my coat, and snicker.

If rhyme gives us a sense of pleasure in regularity or completeness, it also holds other delights. Sometimes, as in Poe's "The Raven," there is internal rhyme, when the middle and end of a line use the same sound ("Once upon a midnight dreary, while I pondered weak and weary"). Sometimes there are slant or off rhymes that echo a sound without repeating it. When we expect to find a full and satisfying end rhyme and are given an inexact one, we may be disappointed but we may also discover some difference in meaning emphasized by the rhyme or some pleasure in a minor key where we expected a major one. Morrison uses "alone" and "roam" as slant rhymes to bring his song to its conclusion: The lack of a perfect rhyme may stress the *alone*ness—uncoupled, unmatched.

Although Dickinson uses a great number of slant rhymes, such as in her poem "There's a Certain Slant of Light," she is not one who "can't get the rhyme right," as the character Rita says in the play and film *Educating Rita.* Dickinson alternates slant rhymes with regular rhymes as if to warn us that whatever is going on on the surface, something else is going on under the surface for which we are not prepared.

There's a certain Slant of light,
Winter Afternoons—
That oppresses. like the Heft
Of Cathedral Tunes—

Heavenly Hurt, it gives us—
We can find no scar,
But internal difference,
Where the Meanings, are—

None may teach it—Any—
'Tis the Seal Despair—
An imperial affliction
Sent us of the Air—

When it comes, the Landscape listens—
Shadows—hold their breath—
When it goes, 'tis like the Distance
On the look of Death—

The regular rhymes, in the even-numbered lines, round things off in the expected way: After*noons*-T*unes,* sc*ar*-*are,* Desp*air*-*Air,* br*eath*-D*eath.* These may not be the most cheerful of words but they do satisfy our expectations and sense of completeness. The other rhymes disturb us, not by their meanings, but by the unexpected repetition of partial sounds: ligh*t*-Hef*t,* gives u*s*-differen*ce,* *A*ny-*a*ffliction, liste*ns*-Dista*nce.* Each of these words echoes the sound of another in a way that, although it may not call attention to itself, impresses the reader. Jim Morrison rhymes r*oa*m-al*o*ne. These sounds are close enough, especially as they are sung, not to disturb us, but they would if the last line were something like "Never saw a woman so steamed." The effect would be different, and part of that difference can be attributed to the rhyme.

Some poets have largely turned away from the more regular rhyme patterns, partly to soften what some of them condemned as the artificiality of the traditional ways of writing poetry. Poets wanted to "make it new," as Ezra Pound wrote, and to try to say things accurately seemed to contemporary poets to work against the traditional forms. The poets sought to mirror the lives of contemporary people—their poems often used language the way people *actually talked* and were written on themes contemporary people found important to their lives. Even avoiding traditional rhyme, however, many poets used the less intrusive slant rhymes or took advantage of other kinds of verbal music. In our own time, many poets have returned to traditional devices, reveling in the rediscovery of older forms.

Repeated sounds Repeated sounds are the way a poet approximates the work of the musician. We've already talked about alliteration (see p. 417 above), the repetition of initial identical consonant sounds. There are names for other kinds of sound repetitions. Consonance is the repetition of consonants usually within a stressed or final syllable; assonance, the repetition of vowel sounds usually in a stressed or final syllable. Both consonance and assonance are powerful devices that, like rhyme, can link words and their ideas or can emphasize them, or, as one student writes, "unify words with meanings." "*R*ide a *r*ed ho*r*se" shows consonance, "stroll down a d*a*rk *a*lley" assonance (italics indicate sound repetition). Sometimes the poet gets quite fancy and uses consonance and assonance at the same time. (This also emphasizes the different vowel sounds Auden uses.) " 'O where are you going?' said reader to rider," " 'O do you imagine,' said fearer to farer," " 'O what was that bird,' said horror to hearer." Auden had a good time making these up in "The Three Companions," and we have a good time playing with the patterns when we read it aloud or to ourselves.

One student offered, "This has nothing to do with poetry but my favorite line in the movie *Broadcast News* is said by Albert Brooks about William Hurt's character.

> "An awful lot of alliteration from an anxious anchor."

It's really the only line that has stuck with me from the movie. Maybe that's what alliteration does for poetry, too. It makes certain parts of the poem stay with the reader more than other parts." She helps us by saying that her comment has nothing to do with poetry, but then shows that it does.

Morrison uses assonance in "L.A. Woman" when the initial words "Driving" and "Midnight" repeat the same *i* sounds. In another line "cops" and "topless" repeat the same *o* and *s* sounds in a line that already has the internal rhyme "cars" and "bars." We recognize that in songs, these help to carry the melody and emphasize the beat. But we don't recognize these devices; normally, we just say, "That sounds good." One of the things we do with poetry when we try to see how it works is to listen to how the sounds echo each other and figure out why the poem sounds good.

A student said this about sound devices. They

> connect one line to the next and they unify individual lines. These devices help me stay in tune with the poem. They make more vivid pictures or references to things we as the reader can relate to. These devices emphasize the words they appear in. These devices are the underlining melody of the poem. They are what makes the poem ''sing'' for us. These sound devices appeal to our hearing much like a song does. They provide a musical pattern that helps convey the author's or speaker's attitude.

INFORMAL WRITING 14

Look through some of your favorite magazines and newspapers (don't forget your college paper) for examples of sound devices in advertisements. How are repeated sounds used to call attention to the product? Do these sounds give you pleasure so that you might repeat them to someone else, thereby making the ad even more effective by reaching more people? Make a journal entry addressing some of these questions.

INFORMAL WRITING 15

Compose a jingle to sell something or write a poetic parody of the ad you have just uncovered.

Tone and atmosphere When we speak of tone in poetry we mean much the same thing as when we speak of tone of voice. When someone says to you, "Don't talk to me in that tone," what she means is that your attitude has to be changed: Your hostility is showing. If you change your tone of voice, she will listen to you. Tone, formally defined, is an author's attitude toward the subject and the audience. Take the hostile tone referred to above. Does this mean the speaker is hostile to her audience, to what she has to do, or to her subject because she knows that she has to do something she doesn't like, such as taking out the garbage? It could refer to any of these or to a combination of all of them at the same time.

Often to define the tone is to discover the theme. Suckling's "Out Upon It!" (see p. 500) is such an exaggeration. The speaker in the poem seems to say, "Look at me, I have already loved longer than anyone in history, three whole days, and, if nothing comes up to disturb the relationship, I may love another three days." We recognize the allusion to traditional poems that swear eternal love. More people love three whole days than love for eternity, Suckling seems to say, and the joy he feels in love is reflected in his tone of exaggeration. Housman's "Terence, This Is Stupid Stuff" (see p. 544) uses one tone in its first stanza, when Terence's friends address him, and another in the rest of the poem, when he addresses them. But there are shifts in Terence's tone as when he praises beer, then describes its aftereffects—waking up in a ditch, discovering that his situation has not changed, life is the same, and his clothes are wet. His warning, in his tale of Mithridates, is basically serious, but it retains some of the lightness of the earlier, lighter parts of the poem by retaining their form.

One of the most important aspects of tone is **irony**, a recognition of a reality different from the masking appearance, where two views of the same thing are presented simultaneously. This term is defined as saying one thing and meaning another. There are various kinds of irony. Dramatic irony, for example, refers to a condition in which one of the actors on a stage does not know as much about his situation as the audience does, and so tells them something whose meaning he is unawaie of. In a poem, the speaker can give off an air of being pleased with himself even when his subject is mournful, as in A. E. Housman's "When I Was One-and-Twenty" (see p. 545). In this poem the speaker bemoans the fact that his love has broken his heart, but he sounds pleased with his experience, which, if not common to us all, is one with which we can sympathize. His acknowledgment of the truth of his experience suggests that he is older and wiser. But we suspect that he, who thinks he has learned a great deal by his experience, will make other mistakes of which he will be as proud as he is of this one. Dickinson's "I Like to See It Lap the Miles" (see p. 487) is an ironic comment on progress in the form of the newly developing railroad. Her pretended breathless wonder at the exploits of the train belies the fact that the train, she points out, like progress in our time, ends up right back where it started. The train may be "omnipotent" but its strength doesn't accomplish anything.

Atmosphere is closely related to, or may even be part of, tone. It is the air, the impression, given off by the work. It is a mood established in part by the setting or landscape. In Whitman's "Out of the Cradle, Endlessly Rocking" (see p. 533) the setting of the

seashore, where the boy hides and listens to the singing of the bird, creates an atmosphere in which the boy can learn what the sea has to tell him.

INFORMAL WRITING 16

Choose two poems from the anthology with contrasting tones or atmospheres. Write a journal entry in which you compare these elements and their effects on meaning.

INFORMAL WRITING 17

Take one of your earlier poetic fragments and see if you can change the atmosphere by adding (or altering) the descriptive details of the setting.

Experiments in form What we've been discussing so far are the parts of the poem. We have referred to the repeated devices of meter and rhyme that together make up a stanza, a couplet, or a sonnet. These are examples of a closed form, one whose parts contribute to a predetermined structure. There are variations of closed forms, as there are in the heroic couplet, an iambic pentameter set of two rhyming lines that contain a single thought and are end-stopped; the rhyming couplet, which consists of two lines of any length that rhyme but are not necessarily end-stopped; and the couplet, any two lines; or some variation of the couplet form that has not been given its own proper name. Closed forms include the sonnet, the sestina, the vilanelle, and other traditional forms.

An open form such as free verse claims that it is "free" of the restrictions of meter as well as of rhyme. When popularized by Walt Whitman, the form was a radical departure from the poetic norm. But it was not free of any kind of rhythm or structure; Whitman himself used many devices to unify his poems. Best known of the free verse experimentalists in our century is e. e. cummings. His experiments in form appeal to the eye, instead of making the traditional poetic, and musical, appeal to the ear. Some of these play off traditional forms, such as "next to of course god america i," a normally formed sonnet that doesn't look like one. Others suggest their meaning through their arrangement on the page. In defining loneliness as a leaf falling from a tree, cummings reproduces the leaf's movement:

l(a

le
af
fa

ll

s)
one
l

iness

This poem does not appeal to the ear: Reading it aloud does not help. We appreciate this poem when we recognize the relationship of its parts as seen on the page. Your recognition that a leaf falling symbolizes loneliness is the first part of that recognition. Even the parts of the word are broken up to suggest that loneliness. The placement of "one" in a single line emphasizes that loneliness comes from being one, without other company. Experiments like cummings' have led the way to concrete poetry, which consists of visual shapes that suggest meaning, like the poem that prints OVE on one side of the page and R on the other. Free verse is not easier to write because it is free of traditional rules; it is often harder, because the rhythm of ideas and language is not reenforced by traditional rules and the form is governed largely by the pressure of the ideas.

Students in Sid's class divided about equally in their preferences for either closed or open forms. One noted that the closed form "forces the poet to find just the right word or phrase and most of the time it forces the poet to condense what he is saying." Another suggested that the closed form "is easier to follow, and, therefore, easier to understand. It probably is harder to write, but that isn't my concern." A third objected to being let loose, with no form to guide him: "I just don't like the feeling of uncertainty I get when reading an open form."

Others praised the freedom of the open form, and many suggested that a closed form is easier to read but more difficult to write because of the restrictions of form. One student claimed that an open form poem can be more interesting because "the form itself can be related to the subject of the poem; it can further the poem's meaning." Another suggested a contrast between the two forms:

> Reading an open form poem is like being presented with a problem with no fixed method to solve it. With a closed form poem, it is much like being given steps to follow. These steps allow the reader to follow the poem more easily and grasp its full meaning.

The students were divided in their preferences, but there is no inherent advantage in either form. The open form is not as easy as it looks because one has to find one's own form each time to fit the subject. The closed form is more familiar to readers but it requires a sharp sense of meeting a restriction, making a virtue of necessity, and triumphing over all obstacles.

INFORMAL WRITING 18: COLLABORATIVE WRITING ABOUT POETRY

Working with one or two of your classmates, choose the lyrics from any popular song. Phase 1: Write in your journal individually about any aspect of this song covered by the chapter you have just read (e.g., sound, rhythm, meter). Phase 2: Read your journal entries to one another and decide on a plan to write about these lyrics. Phase 3: Write a collaborative paper that expands on this approach.

SECTION III: SO WHAT DOES IT ALL MEAN?

Where does all of this get us? After the analysis, the counting of feet, the examination of rhymes, what we have is the remains of a poem, which resemble the parts of a car engine, spread on the floor. As parts, they do not do anything; assembled, they make the car go. A poem has a purpose, too: to communicate something, to express some thematic concern or meaning toward which the parts contribute. Like the songwriter, the short story writer, the novelist, the dramatist, and the essayist, the poet wants to use everything he or she can to communicate something. After first reading a poem, you should have some idea of what it is getting at. Sometimes, you may not feel sure of the meaning, just as the first time you hear a song you may not feel sure what it is about. One of the things you can do, with both song and poem, is to listen to it again. Then, look at how the parts work. As you examine the parts, see how each one works with the others to contribute to meaning. In Herrick's "To the Virgins, To Make Much of Time" (see p. 475), the thematic concern is the Latin admonition, *carpe diem,* "seize the day." The meaning of the poem is that, like a rosebud or a day, woman's beauty will fade before long. Therefore, a beautiful woman should enjoy her beauty before it fades with age.

Let's examine two sonnets and ask some questions about them, to see how the parts of this closed form contribute to their theme and meaning. Sonnets, though short, are not easy. Because the form is so traditional, and because the poet consciously works in a living tradition, sonnets are not the easiest poems to deal with. They are full of rules, which are followed or broken in ways that help to establish the meaning of the poem. They refer to other sonnets partly through the popularity of the form, so that one who reads a sonnet would be likely to have read others. Often, writers will tackle the sonnet just to show how contemporary they can be with an older form in a dazzling display of skill. So they are good illustrations of a closed form, and tough but fun to consider. Perhaps we can demystify the process of analysis and see that a poem, like a song, is something to enjoy, hum, and even dance to.

By definition, all sonnets are fourteen lines long. The meter is normally iambic pentameter. There are two basic types of sonnets, Petrarchan and Shakespearean, normally identified by their rhyme schemes. We use a quasi-algebraic convention for using letters to express the relationships among rhyme words. Lines that rhyme with each other are assigned the same letters. The first line is assigned the letter *a,* and all words that rhyme with it are assigned the same letter. The next rhyming word is assigned the letter *b,* and all subsequent words with the same sound are assigned the same letter. In the Petrarchan sonnet the first eight lines are rhymed *abba abba.* The last six lines have a rhyme scheme that differs sharply from the octet—*cdcdcd* and *cdecde* are two common patterns, but others are often found. A Shakespearean sonnet is made up of three quatrains and a couplet, invariably rhymed as follows: *abab cdcd efef gg.* Usually the rhymed couplet at the end is a summary of the concerns of the sonnet. Another important distinction between the two forms is that the Petrarchan sonnet is divided into an argument—which occupies the first eight lines—and a contrasting argument or observation, which occupies the last six lines. Thus, the contrast in rhyme helps establish the contrast in argument. See Wordsworth's "The World Is Too Much with Us" (p. 513) for an example of a Petrarchan sonnet. The Shakespearean sonnet is divided into three quatrains and a summary couplet, which suggests a logical argument that flows from beginning to end. While the form of the argument is another structural device, it is also one that is often altered.

Let's look at one of Shakespeare's sonnets.

That time of year thou may'st in me behold

That time of year thou may'st in me behold
When yellow leaves, or none, or few, do hang
Upon those boughs which shake against the cold,
Bare ruined choirs where late the sweet birds sang.

In me thou see'st the twilight of such day
As after sunset fadeth in the west,
Which by-and-by black night doth take away,
Death's second self that seals up all in rest.
In me thou see'st the glowing of such fire
That on the ashes of his youth doth lie,
As the deathbed whereon it must expire,
Consumed with that which it was nourished by.
This thou perceiv'st, which makes thy love more strong,
To love that well which thou must leave ere long.

This poem is concerned with the consciousness of the approach of death. Each of the quatrains presents a metaphor for the age of the speaker, for something coming to an end. In the first quatrain his age is compared to a season of the year, autumn after the leaves have fallen. In the second, his age is compared to the twilight as the day draws to a close. In the third, his age is compared to a dying fire, now mostly ashes. Although these events are parallel, each takes place more swiftly than the one before it. A season takes more time than twilight; a fire dies more quickly than the light after the sunset. From these comparisons, the writer draws a conclusion that he expresses in the final couplet.

The writer thinks this meaning, which we remember each time we say goodbye to someone we may never see again, or when we say goodbye at the approach of death, is an important, nay, a universal, one. He draws his conclusion from the clear set of metaphors he has made, in which each comparison centers on a smaller amount of time: season, day, fire. This sense of hurry impels us into agreeing with the poem's conclusion. Each of the comparisons, contained in a complete stanza, is underlined by an end stop, so that the reader pauses at the clearly demarcated conclusion of the quatrain. However, the thought does not conclude until the conclusion of the poem. We come to accept the conclusion at the same time as the poem is over.

We may also notice that the sonnet seems to accept the conclusions of the quatrains because the speaker knows his life is ending. His conclusion is that we love more strongly what we will soon lose. But the last two lines are said positively and persuasively, as if the entire poem were made to induce the listener to love something more strongly than he or she did before (since the sonnet is part of a sequence about two lovers, it may be another way of proving the speaker's love). But there is a break in logic: The couplet at the end does not rise from the argument that came before. The three quatrains present a series of metaphors for a time of life; nowhere do they present any argument about loving well what one will soon lose. Indeed, one may ignore what one is going to lose; that conclusion would also suit the logic of the three quatrains. During autumn, the birds that gather may look forward to their flight south; the sunset may mark the magnificent punctuation of one day, but another comes tomorrow; the fire, out of fuel, may even feel comfort in dying. As logical a conclusion might be, "This thou perceiv'st, 'cause I will soon be gone / To say adieu to what you've known so long." But the reader gives more assent to Shakespeare's conclusion than to the one we've just suggested because of the weight of the movement of the poem.

INFORMAL WRITING 19

Which of the two conclusions do you agree with? Is Shakespeare's poem an acceptance of death or a protest against the loss of what one loves? Do you think the knowledge of losing something you care for makes you care for it more? Does Shakespeare say we love things

more at the end, or that we appear to care more because of our knowledge that life will soon be over? How do you feel about the questions he raises? Imagine yourself coming on the knowledge that you will soon die. How might that knowledge change your ways?

Contemporary sonnets follow traditional rules, but speak more to what we understand of our own lives. Louis Simpson speaks of love, not in Shakespeare's indirect way, but directly, in language that is more accessible to a modern reader:

Summer Storm

In that so sudden summer storm they tried
Each bed, couch, closet, carpet, car-seat, table,
Both river banks, five fields, a mountain side,
Covering as much ground as they were able.

A lady, coming on them in the dark
In a white fixture, wrote to the newspapers
Complaining of the statues in the park.
By Cupid, but they cut some pretty capers!

The envious oxen in still rings would stand
Ruminating. Their sweet incessant plows
I think had changed the contours of the land
And made two modest conies move their house.

God rest them well, and firmly shut the door.
Now they are married Nature breathes once more.

The speed of the opening of the poem makes us feel as if we have been overtaken by a sudden storm, as the lovers are in the poem. In a literal storm, we would seek protection from the pelting rain. But the storm of passion, which suddenly sweeps them away, is quickly seen as metaphoric. The violence of the desire of the lovers is echoed in the number of places they make love, all specified in the last three lines of the first stanza. Like the storm sweeping down, thundering, lightning, and raining, the lovers fill the world with their loving. They not only make love through all the secluded nooks of nature—it's exhausting trying to follow them—but even in the less secluded park, where they are discovered by an irate lady, and in the populated field, where the oxen watch, chewing their day's grazing and slowly turning over in their minds what they witness, and the rabbits (conies), famous fornicators, who modestly make way for the more passionate pair who have altered the very landscape with their loving. The rabbits even move their house, either because of the disturbing sounds that come from the lovers or because they want a quieter, more modest neighborhood. Remember, sonnets often say more than one thing, which adds to the difficulty, as well as the joy, of reading them. An alternate reading of this stanza is that even the oxen, who have made the conies move through their plowing of the earth, stare in wonderment at the plowing of the ground by the two eager lovers.

This passion is described in language whose form reinforces the meaning of the words. The swiftness of the first line is made more swift by the alliteration of the soft and continuing "s" sound in "sudden summer storm." The second line, in contrast, is made up of a series of nouns, each set off by a comma and each slowed down by the hard alliterative sounds such as the hard "c" of "couch, closet, carpet, car-seat." The first line is without sharp contrasts in stress; the second line is full of sharply stressed words. The stress of the third line is looser than the second, and the fourth line is more relaxed still, the stanza finally coming to rest at the period at the end of the stanza. The first stanza, the most remarkable in this poem, carries us into the storm of passion. The second and third stanzas are more descriptive of those who view the lovers, lady and animals, rather than describing the storm within the lovers themselves. The final couplet, when we take leave of the lovers and "firmly shut the door," marks the return to normal, to a world not of storms, but of the quiet that reigns after the storm is through. It is also a subtle comment on marriage—that marriage brings with it a domesticity that robs the world (and the lovers) of passion's thunder.

We do not have to tick the rhyme scheme off on our fingers, or make mechanical comparisons to Shakespeare's "That Time of Year," to recognize that these poems have the same form. We don't even have to recognize the form to think Simpson's description of the first throes of passion a fine one. But if we know that Shakespeare's sonnets are concerned with love, and if we see the three quatrain and couplet arrangement, we know that Simpson wants us to recall the form of the earlier poem. As we are aware of echoes of other songs during Harry Connick, Jr.'s improvised jazz or scat singing, so we are aware both of what is Simpson and of the manner in which Simpson alludes to Shakespeare. Simpson implies that Shakespeare's descriptions of love are too artificial. It may be the difference between the formal dance, or waltz, and "dirty dancing," where bodies touch more than at wrist and waist.

All this examination of technique serves to fill out our comprehension of the poem. All the scansion and counting of rhyme schemes should lead not only to a greater understanding of the way the poem works, but, as in this poem, to some idea of the nature of passion. Simpson's poem may seem more relevant to our lives because it shows passion in a more modern way, shows how we ourselves may be shaped by it and what attitudes others might have toward it. But Shakespeare's is just as contemporary. Each of us must still note the approach of death in the conclusion of seasons and days.

All the studying of devices should lead to greater understanding. Diagrams of dance steps, notes of music on a page, tell someone how to perform the piece. But we are not all experts; what we have to do is put the notes to music, feel the rhythm in our feet and bodies. That's the only way to learn a new song and dance, and isn't that what it's all about?

INFORMAL WRITING 20

There are several sonnets by the poet Claude McKay in this book (see pp. 577–579). Choose one, and discuss why you think McKay elected to use the sonnet form to present his thematic concerns. Does McKay's use of the sonnet bear any resemblance or relation to what you have written about other sonnets in this anthology? If so, how? If not, why not?

INFORMAL WRITING 21

Read Chapter 8, "Imaginative Writing and Risk Taking," by William Stephany (see page 1739). Pay particular attention to the student poem "The Good Toro." After reading several of the sonnets in this anthology, write an imitation or a parody of one of them.

What a Poem Means: Writing about Poetry

Ralph Waldo Emerson, the nineteenth-century American writer, once observed that when he read an essay or a novel, he found himself focusing on the way in which sentences were arranged in paragraphs. In contrast, whenever he read a poem, his attention was drawn to the importance of each individual word: Every one of them mattered. This is a good way to begin thinking about poetry, as a collection of words, each of which communicates something. The arrangement of words in prose has as its purpose the communication of an idea that is larger than the individual words; in poetry, the words stand on their own, each contributing in its own way to communication. Analyzing a poem is like analyzing a computer program—the smallest elements are extremely important. How a poem is written—from the form it takes on the page to the diction it incorporates, even its punctuation (or lack thereof)—is *always* relevant to what a poem means.

One way to begin writing about a poem is to consider the way that it looks. As Emerson has reminded us, we read a poem differently than a play, an essay, or narrative fiction. It would stand to reason, then, that we should also write about poems in ways that would somehow be different from writing about these other genres. Because reading poetry requires a greater amount of patience and closer attention to details, students often get ideas for writing about poetry when they are drawn to the use of a particular word or the appearance of a certain image that can be traced throughout the poem. In writing about "Phenomenal Woman" (see p. 444) for example, Aimée was drawn to Maya Angelou's use of physical description to help expand the definition of femininity developed in the poem.

> Throughout the poem Angelou exemplifies the new age of feminism where women no longer need to reject everything feminine in order to conform to a man's world. The poet raises the consciousness of all women by posing alternatives to that ideal. A ''phenomenal woman'' does not have to be asexual or suppress her femininity. Her secrets are also found in ''the reach of [her] arms . . . The span of [her] hips . . . the stride in [her] step . . . The click of [her] heels.'' The poem joins together the inner spirituality of a woman with her physical aspects to give a more complete composite. . . . Angelou is proud of the ''inner mysteries'' that make her a phenomenal woman, but if you look at what these mysteries are, you'll see they are not so magical or even mysterious. They are, instead, the everyday things that we don't pay much attention to unless someone points them out.

Maybe this is what all the best poems ask us to do—pay attention to the little details, "the everyday things" that are too easily overlooked in our headlong rush to "greater" pursuits. Writing about poetry should be like a warm spring walk in a luxurious garden: It will not do to rush to get to the other side, for then you will miss things—the colors, the smells, the relationship of individual flowers to the garden's larger patterns. If a poem works, even the smallest thing you notice and choose to write about represents the essence of what the poem is about.

Conversations (Poems with Questions)

ELOISE KLEIN HEALY

(1943–   )

Los Angeles

Like an older sister who wasn't quite as pretty
you were never expected to become much,
only to settle your larger body into the practicality
of middle age.
You were never expected to be charming
like the younger one
who could enchant.
There was something about your proportions
that was indelicate—your more abundant waist.
She always had the poetic suitors who
came to visit.
You always answered the door.

Nobody expected it
and you never told about
the lover who met you
loose and large
in the late afternoon
and loved you all night,
completely out of proportion.

QUESTION

Compare this poem to the portrait of Los Angeles in Morrison's song (see page 415). Based on evidence from both the song and the poem, how do the writers differ in their description of the city?

RONALD KOERTGE

(1940–   )

Two Men

and two women were racing. Sometimes
a man won, sometimes a woman.

In the course of this event, the contestants
grew fond of one another. The men
were ashamed of themselves, however,
and each chose a wife.

Now the teams raced. Sometimes one team
won, sometimes the other.

"Let's make this more interesting,"
said the men and they gave one of the women
a Norge and a Hoover and a Singer to carry.
The other had to hold a baby and every
so often douche or shave her legs without
stopping and without putting down the baby.
Sometimes one of the women won, sometimes
the other.

"Let's get in on this," said the men
and they sprinted to the wire, looking back
over their shoulders and laughing.

"It's all over," they said, "we won."
But the women kept on
coming.

QUESTIONS

Why does this poem revolve around the theme of a race? How does this contribute to a statement about men and women? Their changing places and roles in society?

LISEL MUELLER

(1924–   )

A Voice from Out of the Night

Remember me, I was a celebrity,
the famous beauty. All mirrors confirmed me,
the panel of judges ogled me
and cast a unanimous vote.
I was asked my opinion
on marriage, men, abortion,
the use of liquor and drugs;
that was a long time ago.

When my voice deepened
and a bristle

appeared under my chin,
when my blond hair
developed gray roots
and my waist thickened,
the rumors started.
When my legs became sticks
and small brown toads
spotted the backs of my hands,
everyone believed them.
I was accused of devouring children
and mutilating men;
they said I smelled of old age
and strong home remedies.
They cast me into the forest
but come to me secretly, in the dark,
in their times of trouble.
What could I have done to convince them
I was not guilty?
Loss of beauty was all
the proof they needed.

Young wives in love with your men,
kissing your babies: this
could be a warning, but what is the use?
Husbands will flee you,
sons will turn on you,
daughters will throw up their hands
and cry, "Not me! Not me!"

QUESTION

The social emphasis on a woman's physical beauty is at the center of this poem. In this context, why does the poet ask, "What could I have done to convince them I was not guilty?"

PAUL ZIMMER

(1934–)

Zimmer in Grade School

In grade school I wondered
Why I had been born
To wrestle in the ashy puddles,
With my square nose
Streaming mucus and blood,

My knuckles puffed from combat
And the old nun's ruler.
I feared everything: God,
Learning and my schoolmates.
I could not count, spell or read.
My report card proclaimed
These scarlet failures.
My parents wrang their loving hands.
My guardian angel wept constantly.

But I could never hide anything.
If I peed my pants in class
The puddle was always quickly evident.
My worst mistakes were at
The blackboard for Jesus and all
The saints to see.
Even now
When I hide behind elaborate mask
It is always known that I am Zimmer,
The one who does the messy papers
And fractures all his crayons,
Who spits upon the radiators
And sits all day in shame
Outside the office of the principal.

QUESTIONS

How much is Zimmer to blame for his "scarlet failures" in this poem? Is it Zimmer or his school which is the real failure?

MAYA ANGELOU

(1928–   )

Phenomenal Woman

Pretty women wonder where my secret lies.
I'm not cute or built to suit a fashion model's size
But when I start to tell them,
They think I'm telling lies.
I say,
It's in the reach of my arms,
The span of my hips,
The stride of my step,
The curl of my lips.
I'm a woman

Phenomenally.
Phenomenal woman,
That's me.

I walk into a room
Just as cool as you please,
And to a man,
The fellows stand or
Fall down on their knees.
Then they swarm around me,
A hive of honey bees.
I say,
It's the fire in my eyes,
And the flash of my teeth,
The swing in my waist,
And the joy in my feet.
I'm a woman
Phenomenally.
Phenomenal woman,
That's me.

Men themselves have wondered
What they see in me.
They try so much
But they can't touch
My inner mystery.
When I try to show them
They say they still can't see.
I say,
It's in the arch of my back,
The sun of my smile,
The ride of my breasts,
The grace of my style.
I'm a woman
Phenomenally.
Phenomenal woman,
That's me.

Now you understand
Just why my head's not bowed.
I don't shout or jump about
Or have to talk real loud.
When you see me passing
It ought to make you proud.
I say,
It's in the click of my heels,
The bend of my hair,

the palm of my hand,
The need for my care.
'Cause I'm a woman
Phenomenally.
Phenomenal woman,
That's me.

QUESTIONS

Why does the poet insist that men "can't touch/My inner mystery"? Does the poem supply information to explain why this separation exists?

LANGSTON HUGHES

(1902–1967)

Freedom's Plow

When a man starts out with nothing,
When a man starts out with his hands
Empty, but clean,
When a man starts out to build a world,
He starts first with himself
And the faith that is in his heart—
The strength there,
The will there to build.

First in the heart is the dream.
Then the mind starts seeking a way.
His eyes look out on the world,
On the great wooded world,
On the rich soil of the world,
On the rivers of the world.

The eyes see there materials for building,
See the difficulties, too, and the obstacles.
The hand seeks tools to cut the wood,
To till the soil, and harness the power of the waters.
Then the hand seeks other hands to help,
A community of hands to help—
Thus the dream becomes not one man's dream alone,
But a community dream.
Not my dream alone, but *our* dream.
Not my world alone,
But *your world and my world,*
Belonging to all the hands who build.

A long time ago, but not too long ago,
Ships came from across the sea
Bringing Pilgrims and prayer-makers,
Free men and indentured servants,
Slave men and slave masters, all new—
To a new world, America!

With billowing sails the galleons came
Bringing men and dreams, women and dreams.
In little bands together,
Heart reaching out to heart,
Hand reaching out to hand,
They began to build our land.
Some were free hands
Seeking a greater freedom,
Some were indentured hands
Hoping to find their freedom,
Some were slave hands
Guarding in their hearts the seed of freedom.
But the word was there always:
FREEDOM.
Down into the earth went the plow
In the free hands and the slave hands,
In indentured hands and adventurous hands,
Turning the rich soil went the plow in many hands
That planted and harvested the food that fed
And the cotton that clothed America.
Clang against the trees went the ax in many hands
That hewed and shaped the rooftops of America.
Splash into the rivers and the seas went the boat-hulls
That moved and transported America.
Crack went the whips that drove the horses
Across the plains of America.
Free hands and slave hands,
Indentured hands, adventurous hands,
White hands and black hands
Held the plow handles,
Ax handles, hammer handles,
Launched the boats and whipped the horses
That fed and housed and moved America.
Thus together through labor,
All these hands made America.
Labor! Out of labor came the villages
And the towns that grew to cities.
Labor! Out of labor came the rowboats
And the sailboats and the steamboats,
Came the wagons, stage coaches,

Out of labor came the factories,
Came the foundries, came the railroads,
Came the marts and markets, shops and stores,
Came the mighty products moulded, manufactured,
Sold in shops, piled in warehouses,
Shipped the wide world over:
Out of labor—white hands and black hands—
Came the dream, the strength, the will,
And the way to build America.
Now it is Me here, and You there.
Now it's Manhattan, Chicago,
Seattle, New Orleans,
Boston and El Paso—
Now it is the U.S.A.

A long time ago, but not too long ago, a man said:

> ALL MEN ARE CREATED EQUAL . . .
> ENDOWED BY THEIR CREATOR
> WITH CERTAIN INALIENABLE RIGHTS . . .
> AMONG THESE LIFE, LIBERTY
> AND THE PURSUIT OF HAPPINESS.

His name was Jefferson. There were slaves then,
But in their hearts the slaves believed him, too,
And silently took for granted
That what he said was also meant for them.
It was a long time ago,
But not so long ago at that, Lincoln said:

> NO MAN IS GOOD ENOUGH
> TO GOVERN ANOTHER MAN
> WITHOUT THAT OTHER'S CONSENT.

There were slaves then, too,
But in their hearts the slaves knew
What he said must be meant for every human being—
Else it had no meaning for anyone.
Then a man said:

> BETTER TO DIE FREE,
> THAN TO LIVE SLAVES.

He was a colored man who had been a slave
But had run away to freedom.
And the slaves knew
What Frederick Douglass said was true.

With John Brown at Harpers Ferry, Negroes died.
John Brown was hung.
Before the Civil War, days were dark,
And nobody knew for sure
When freedom would triumph.
"Or if it would," thought some.
But others knew it had to triumph.
In those dark days of slavery,
Guarding in their hearts the seed of freedom,
The slaves made up a song:

KEEP YOUR HAND ON THE PLOW!
HOLD ON!

That song meant just what it said: *Hold on!*
Freedom will come!

KEEP YOUR HAND ON THE PLOW!
HOLD ON!

Out of war, it came, bloody and terrible!
But it came!
Some there were, as always,
Who doubted that the war would end right,
That the slaves would be free,
Or that the union would stand.
But now we know how it all came out.
Out of the darkest days for a people and a nation,
We know now how it came out.
There was light when the battle clouds rolled away.
There was a great wooded land,
And men united as a nation.
America is a dream.
The poet says it was promises.
The people say it *is* promises—that will come true.
The people do not always say things out loud,
Nor write them down on paper.
The people often hold
Great thoughts in their deepest hearts
And sometimes only blunderingly express them,
Haltingly and stumbling say them,
And faultily put them into practice.
The people do not always understand each other.
But there is, somewhere there,
Always the *trying* to understand,
And the *trying* to say,
"You are a man. Together we are building our land."

America!
Land created in common,
Dream nourished in common,
Keep your hand on the plow! Hold on!
If the house is not yet finished,
Don't be discouraged, builder!
If the fight is not yet won,
Don't be weary, soldier!
The plan and the pattern is here,
Woven from the beginning
Into the warp and woof of America:

ALL MEN ARE CREATED EQUAL.

NO MAN IS GOOD ENOUGH
TO GOVERN ANOTHER MAN WITHOUT
THAT OTHER'S CONSENT.

BETTER DIE FREE,
THAN LIVE SLAVES.

Who said those things? Americans!
Who owns those words? America!
Who is America? You, me!
We are America!
To the enemy who would conquer us from without,
We say, NO!
To the enemy who would divide
and conquer us from within,
We say, NO!

FREEDOM!
BROTHERHOOD!
DEMOCRACY!

To all the enemies of these great words:
We say, NO!

A long time ago,
An enslaved people heading toward freedom
Made up a song:
Keep Your Hand On The Plow! Hold On!
That plow plowed a new furrow
Across the field of history.
Into that furrow the freedom seed was dropped.
From that seed a tree grew, is growing, will ever grow.
That tree is for everybody,

For all America, for all the world.
May its branches spread and its shelter grow
Until all races and all peoples know its shade.

KEEP YOUR HAND ON THE PLOW!
HOLD ON!

QUESTION

This is an optimistic poem about the evolution of racial equality in America. Hughes wrote this poem in the 1960s. Since then, what evidence could you present either to support or refute Hughes's belief that racial harmony is inevitable?

GWENDOLYN BROOKS

(1917–)

The Lovers of the Poor

arrive. The Ladies from the Ladies' Betterment League
Arrive in the afternoon, the late light slanting
In diluted gold bars across the boulevard brag
Of proud, seamed faces with mercy and murder hinting
Here, there, interrupting, all deep and debonair,
The pink paint on the innocence of fear;
Walk in a gingerly manner up the hall.
Cutting with knives served by their softest care,
Served by their love, so barbarously fair.
Whose mothers taught: You'd better not be cruel!
You had better not throw stones upon the wrens!
Herein they kiss and coddle and assault
Anew and dearly in the innocence
With which they baffle nature. Who are full,
Sleek, tender-clad, fit, fiftyish, a-glow, all
Sweetly abortive, hinting at fat fruit,
Judge it high time that fiftyish fingers felt
Beneath the lovelier planes of enterprise.
To resurrect. To moisten with milky chill.
To be a random hitching-post or plush.
To be, for wet eyes, random and handy hem.
Their guild is giving money to the poor.
The worthy poor. The very very worthy
And beautiful poor. Perhaps just not too swarthy?
Perhaps just not too dirty nor too dim
Nor—passionate. In truth, what they could wish
Is—something less than derelict or dull.

Not staunch enough to stab, though, gaze for gaze!
God shield them sharply from the beggar-bold!
The noxious needy ones whose battle's bald
Nonetheless for being voiceless, hits one down.
　　But it's all so bad! and entirely too much for them.
The stench; the urine, cabbage, and dead beans,
Dead porridges of assorted dusty grains,
The old smoke, *heavy* diapers, and, they're told,
Something called chitterlings. The darkness. Drawn
Darkness, or dirty light. The soil that stirs.
The soil that looks the soil of centuries.
And for that matter the *general* oldness. Old
Wood. Old marble. Old tile. Old old old.
Not homekind Oldness! Not Lake Forest, Glencoe.
Nothing is sturdy, nothing is majestic,
There is no quiet drama, no rubbed glaze, no
Unkillable infirmity of such
A tasteful turn as lately they have left,
Glencoe, Lake Forest, and to which their cars
Must presently restore them. When they're done
With dullards and distortions of this fistic
Patience of the poor and put-upon.
　　They've never seen such a make-do-ness as
Newspaper rugs before! In this, this "flat,"
Their hostess is gathering up the oozed, the rich
Rugs of the morning (tattered! the bespattered. . . .)
Readies to spread clean rugs for afternoon.
Here is a scene for you. The Ladies look,
In horror, behind a substantial citizeness
Whose trains clank out across her swollen heart.
Who, arms akimbo, almost fills a door.
All tumbling children, quilts dragged to the floor
And tortured thereover, potato peelings, soft-
Eyed kitten, hunched-up, haggard, to-be-hurt.
　　Their League is allotting largesse to the Lost.
But to put their clean, their pretty money, to put
Their money collected from delicate rose-fingers
Tipped with their hundred flawless rose-nails seems . . .
　　They own Spode, Lowestoft, candelabra,
Mantels, and hostess gowns, and sunburst clocks,
Turtle soup, Chippendale, red satin "hangings,"
Aubussons and Hattie Carnegie. They Winter
In Palm Beach; cross the Water in June; attend,
When suitable, the nice Art Institute;
Buy the right books in the best bindings; saunter
On Michigan, Easter mornings, in sun or wind.
Oh Squalor! This sick four-story hulk, this fibre

With fissures everywhere! Why, what are bringings
Of loathe-love largesse? What shall peril hungers
So old old, what shall flatter the desolate?
Tin can, blocked fire escape and chitterling
And swaggering seeking youth and the puzzled wreckage
Of the middle passage, and urine and stale shames
And, again, the porridges of the underslung
And children children children. Heavens! That
Was a rat, surely, off there, in the shadows? Long
And long-tailed? Gray? The Ladies from the Ladies'
Betterment League agree it will be better
To achieve the outer air that rights and steadies,
To hie to a house that does not holler, to ring
Bells elsetime, better presently to cater
To no more Possibilities, to get
Away. Perhaps the money can be posted.
Perhaps they two may choose another Slum!
Some serious sooty half-unhappy home!—
Where loathe-love likelier may be invested.
        Keeping their scented bodies in the center
Of the hall as they walk down the hysterical hall,
They allow their lovely skirts to graze no wall,
Are off at what they manage of a canter,
And, resuming all the clues of what they were,
Try to avoid inhaling the laden air.

QUESTIONS

Why is the poet so antagonistic toward women who are at least concerned enough about poverty to try and do something about it? Is this a poem that is critical toward acts of charity? All acts of charity, or just certain kinds?

DON L. LEE

(1942–   )

a poem to complement other poems

change.
life if u were a match i wd light u into something beautiful. change.
change.
for the better into a realreal together thing. change, from a make believe
nothing on corn meal and water. change.
change. from the last drop to the first, maxwellhouse did. change.
change was a programmer for IBM, thought him was a brown computor.
  change.

colored is something written on southern outhouses. change.
grayhound did, i mean they got rest rooms on buses. change.
change.
change nigger.
saw a nigger hippy, him wanted to be different. changed.
saw a nigger liberal, him wanted to be different. changed.
saw a nigger conservative, him wanted to be different. changed.
niggers don't u know that niggers are different. change.
a doublechange. nigger wanted a double zero in front of his name; a
license to kill,
niggers are licensed to be killed. change. a negro: something pigs eat.
change. i say change into a realblack righteous aim. like i don't play
saxophone but that doesn't mean i don't dig 'trane.' change.
change.
hear u coming but yr/steps are too loud. change. even a lamp post
changes nigger.
change, stop being an instant yes machine. change.
niggers don't change they just grow. that's a change; bigger & better
niggers.
change, into a necessary blackself.
change, like a gas meter gets higher.
change, like a blues song talking about a righteous tomorrow.
change, like a tax bill getting higher.
change, like a good sister getting better.
change, like knowing wood will burn. change.
know the realenemy.
change,
change nigger: standing on the corner, thought him was cool. him still
standing there. it's winter time, him cool.
change,
know the realenemy.
change: him wanted to be a TV star. him is. ten o'clock news.
wanted, wanted. nigger stole some lemon & lime popsicles,
thought them were diamonds.
change nigger change.
know the realenemy.
change: is u is or is u aint. change. now now change. for the better
change.
read a change. live a change. read a blackpoem. change. be the
realpeople.
change. blackpoems
will change:
know the realenemy. change. know the realenemy. change yr/enemy
change know the real
change know the realenemy change, change, know the realenemy, the
realenemy, the real
realenemy change your the enemies/change your change your change
your enemy change

your enemy. know the realenemy, the world's enemy. know them know them know them the
realenemy change your enemy change your change change change your enemy change change
change change your change change change
your
mind nigger.

QUESTIONS

Read this poem out loud. Notice how often Lee repeats certain words and phrasings. How do these repetitions contribute to the way in which you read the poem? How do they contribute to the poem's meaning?

MERIDEL LESUEUR

(1900–)

The Village

The Village has always lain in the path of the conqueror.
The villages of Viet Nam, of Africa, of Peru and Brazil,
of Ireland, Spain, Mexico, Cuba, Haiti, Iowa, New
Mexico, Thailand, look up in anger at the sky filled with
fire, at napalm burning crops and skin, and still
they plunder the Village and the Villagers.
The Puritans plundered villages from coast to coast;
drove the Cherokees on the Trail of Tears, threw smallpox
infected clothes into the Mandan villages, Kit Carson
drove the Navajos off their lands into the concentration
camps; north of Trinidad, Colorado, you can see the
monument over the Black Hole of Ludlow, a tent village
burned by Rockefeller. Cortez marched over the bodies
of the Indian villages, destroyed from Ohio to Tierra del
Fuego; Hearst left a village of skulls at the mines of Potosí.
My family fled the Irish villages taken over for sheep
runs for the mills of Newcastle. My Iowa village is owned
by absentee landlords now. Name Lidice, the villages
of pogroms, Guernica; from the Big Horn to Viet Nam—
the Massacre of Wounded Knee to the Mekong Delta,
the same Village—our Village.

QUESTIONS

What is the significance of the poem's final line: "the same village—our Village"? How does it connect to the varied historical references the poet cites from around the world?

DAVID HUDDLE

(1942–)

Going, 1960–1970

1.

My roommate in Charlottesville
was from Youngstown, Ohio,
a doctor's son, whose parents
took us to Farmington Country
Club and drove me home once
in a Cadillac, first one
except Barnett's hearse
that'd ever been
in our driveway.

2.

First airplane
I ever rode was south
to Fort Jackson, South Carolina,
for basic training, but a train
took me north again
to Baltimore, and I was used
to that.

3.

Monika Litskus
was a Polish girl I danced with
in Stuttgart bars, and hell,
we might have gotten married
if I'd have known
a language to ask
her in.

4.

I took a ferry
from Landau, Denmark,
to Göteborg, Sweden, and there
was tax-free liquor on board
that got all those crazy Swedes

mean drunk and fighting,
and even though that
was on the North Sea
it reminded me
of home.

5.

I spent a Thanksgiving
in Luxembourg City, but it
was raining, so I didn't see
much except a skinned rabbit
and a deer carcass hanging outside
somebody's butcher shop,
and they'd written me
from home that
my grandfather
was sick.

6.

I surprised Mother
while she was ironing,
hadn't told anybody I was coming
home on my way west of Hawaii,
wore my khakis and spitshined
boots over to see Grandad.
He had his shirt off, trying
to shave sitting down
in front of a mirror.
He'd cut himself
3 or 4 times he was
shaking so bad.

7.

Helicopters
flew me in
to an old, cracked
French-built tennis court
near the capital city of
Binh Chanh Province
so that one Asian
could beat up
another one

under my
super-
vision.

8.

Drunk on a back street
in Tokyo well after midnight
I was cussed out in perfect English
for something I was only partially
aware of being guilty of by
the most beautiful whore
I'd ever seen.

9.

Marines told me
some things they'd done
but in Bangkok I didn't want
to start trading that kind of stories
because, Christ, for eleven dollars
you could spend a night
and a day with a woman
you'd dream about years
later.

10.

I had a plan
for when I was discharged
of spending the night in the best
hotel San Francisco had to offer
and laying down $100 for some
good-smelling California girl,
but funny thing was I went
straight to the airport
and caught the first
flight home.

11.

He was still alive
though they'd kept him off
whiskey all that time, and he
was delighted I'd drive him to

the Wytheville liquor store where
they spoke to him by name and he bought
five fifths of I. W. Harper, had me carry
the package and hide it in the car trunk,
but even though we met her at the door
and lied we'd been to the optometrist's,
Grandmama found those bottles
before he even got a sip,
went out and on rocks
behind the garage
broke every
god damn
one.

12.

In white tie
and tails my father
danced the first two
times in his life, first
with my bride and then with
her mother. There were close
to 300 people watching, and he
kept a smile on his face, got
through it just fine. I felt
like kissing him because I'd
been through enough of a
war to know courage
when I saw it.

13.

I was up there
going to Columbia
and drinking cocktails
with writers who knew my name,
but when Mother called
that morning and gave me the news,
he'd got up around five,
gone in to pee,
died standing there
(not a joke! not a joke!),
fell wedging his head
between the bathtub and the wall,
my father working
almost an hour getting him out,

knowing all that time
his father was gone,
the only thing I could think
was I have to
get a haircut,
I have to
drive down there,
I have to
go down.

14.

It was sunny and cold,
but I didn't feel anything,
I was like something cut
out of a sheet of tin,
and then I saw my father
take off his glasses,
doing what I'd never
in 30 years seen him do,
and swab at his eyes,
and I felt a hurt snap
through my whole body,
wanted just for that instant
to plunge down with him
into that grave, going down
into black dirt, keep going
down with him the rest
of my life.

QUESTION

How is this poem, so centered on foreign and exotic locations and travel, also about "home" and the memory of it?

WANDA COLEMAN
(1945–)

Rape

THANX, KIKA WARFIELD

i am here to help you

he laughed. and his partner laughed. she squeezed
her palms/triggers. their uniforms bled

the laughter became screams of horror and she
dragged the bodies of the white blond cop and
his chinese bunky down stairs
and buried them in her eyes/hatred
sprang up and blossomed

talk about it

tell me every detail, said the doctor
they broke in on me. every detail. they took me
in the bedroom, one at a time. next detail
i was scared they'd find my purse—i lied about
having no money. detail, detail. they undressed me,
asked me to tell them how it felt. did it feel
good? yes. did you cum? they were gentle lovers
did you cum? yes. both times? yes

the boyfriend

came in. she was feeling shrunken dirty suicide
she hadn't douched. the wetness still pouring
out/a sticky riverlet on her inner thighs
he got indignant. why didn't she call the police
why didn't she call her mama. why didn't she die
fighting. she remained silent. he asked her where
it happened. she showed him the spot. he
pulled down his pants, forced her back onto the sheets
i haven't cleaned up, she whined. but he was
full saddle hard dicking and cumming torrents

the two burglars

kicked the door in. she woke. she thought, he's
drunk again. she slipped into her thin pink
gown, got up and went to see. it wasn't him. we
have guns, the dark one announced
there's no one here but me and the kids she said

there was little

for them to steal. the dark one took her into
the bedroom while his partner searched. he turned
out the lights and stripped. he laid her gently on
the bed. this is my name. when you cum, call
my name. she agreed. and he entered. your pussy's
hot and tight. where's your old man? he's
a fool not to be here with you. you're pretty
you're soft. you fuck good. kiss me. and she did

as told. we don't want to hurt you. you like
the way i kiss. tell the truth. it's good,
she said and after a while she moaned his name

the other one

came in and took off his clothes in the dark
i'm really sorry to do this, he said, but
i can't help myself. strange, she thought. such
polite rapists. i wonder if they'll kill me
somehow it must make them care enough not
to kill me. he told her his name and sucked
hungry at her nipples, parted her legs
he was very thick long hard. his friend's seed
eased the pain. i want your tongue he said
give me your tongue. she gave and gave
jesus! he cried and shot into her, long spastic jerks
he trembled and fell into her arms. shit
that was good

in the kitchen

her few valuables were piled neatly mid-floor
she promised not to call the police
what could they do, save her?
the other one, the jesus-man took her typewriter
and put it back, and all the other stuff they
had planned to take. even the television

here is my number, said the dark one
when you get lonely, call

and she walked

them to the door. the dark one took her in his arms
kissed her goodbye

she waited

until she was sure they wouldn't
come back and kill

she picked up the phone

and made the mistake of thinking the world
would understand

QUESTIONS

Coleman has written a painful and violent poem about a painful and violent event. Yet we are told by the woman speaker in the poem that she is assaulted by "polite rapists." Is there evidence in the poem that these men are indeed "polite," and, if so, why do you think Coleman chose to portray them this way?

WALLACE STEVENS

(1879–1955)

The Emperor of Ice-Cream

Call the roller of big cigars,
The muscular one, and bid him whip
In kitchen cups concupiscent curds.
Let the wenches dawdle in such dress
As they are used to wear, and let the boys
Bring flowers in last month's newspapers.
Let be be finale of seem.
The only emperor is the emperor of ice-cream.

Take from the dresser of deal,
Lacking the three glass knobs, that sheet
On which she embroidered fantails once
And spread it so as to cover her face.
If her horny feet protrude, they come
To show how cold she is, and dumb.
Let the lamp affix its beam.
The only emperor is the emperor of ice-cream.

QUESTION

Why does Stevens choose a title, so evocative of happiness and children, so apparently at odds with a poem about death and loss?

Companions (Paired Poems with Questions)

THOMAS HARDY

(1840–1928)

The Darkling Thrush

I leant upon a coppice[1] gate
  When Frost was specter-gray,
And Winter's dregs made desolate
  The weakening eye of day.
The tangled bine-stems[2] scored the sky
  Like strings of broken lyres,
And all mankind that haunted nigh
  Had sought their household fires.

The land's sharp features seemed to be
  The Century's corpse outleant,[3]
His crypt the cloudy canopy,
  The wind his death-lament.
The ancient pulse of germ and birth
  Was shrunken hard and dry,
And every spirit upon earth
  Seemed fervorless as I.

At once a voice arose among
  The bleak twigs overhead
In a full-hearted evensong
  Of joy illimited;
An aged thrush, frail, gaunt, and small,
  In blast-beruffled plume,
Had chosen thus to fling his soul
  Upon the growing gloom.

So little cause for carolings
  Of such ecstatic sound
Was written on terrestrial things
  Afar or nigh around.

---

[1]**coppice** small woods or thicket. [2]**bine stems** stems of vines. [3]**outleant** stretched out

That I could think there trembled through
His happy good-night air
Some blessed Hope, whereof he knew
And I was unaware.

JOHN KEATS

(1795–1821)

Ode to a Nightingale

I

My heart aches, and a drowsy numbness pains
My sense, as though of hemlock I had drunk,
Or emptied some full opiate to the drains
One minute past, and Lethe-wards had sunk:
'Tis not through envy of thy happy lot,
But being too happy in thine happiness,—
That thou, light-wingèd Dryad of the trees,
In some melodious plot
Of beechen green, and shadows numberless,
Singest of summer in full-throated ease.

II

O, for a draught of vintage! that hath been
Cooled a long age in the deep-delved earth,
Tasting of Flora and the country green,
Dance, and Provençal song, and sunburnt mirth!
O for a beaker full of the warm South,
Full of the true, the blushful Hippocrene,
With beaded bubbles winking at the brim,
And purple-stainèd mouth;
That I might drink, and leave the world unseen,
And with thee fade away into the forest dim:

III

Fade far away, dissolve, and quite forget
What thou among the leaves hast never known,

The weariness, the fever, and the fret
  Here, where men sit and hear each other groan;
Where palsy shakes a few, sad, last grey hairs,
  Where youth grows pale, and spectre-thin, and dies;
    Where but to think is to be full of sorrow
      And leaden-eyed despairs,
    Where Beauty cannot keep her lustrous eyes,
      Or new Love pine at them beyond tomorrow.

IV

Away! away! for I will fly to thee,
  Not charioted by Bacchus and his pards°, leopards
But on the viewless wings of Poesy,
  Though the dull brain perplexes and retards:
Already with thee! tender is the night,
  And haply the Queen-Moon is on her throne,
    Clustered around by all her starry Fays°; fairies
      But here there is no light,
  Save what from heaven is with the breezes blown
      Through verdurous glooms and winding mossy ways.

V

I cannot see what flowers are at my feet,
  Nor what soft incense hangs upon the boughs,
But, in embalmèd darkness, guess each sweet
  Wherewith the seasonable month endows
The grass, the thicket, and the fruit-tree wild;
  White hawthorn, and the pastoral eglantine;
    Fast fading violets covered up in leaves;
      And mid-May's eldest child,
The coming musk-rose, full of dewy wine,
    The murmurous haunt of flies on summer eves.

VI

Darkling I listen; and, for many a time
  I have been half in love with easeful Death,
Called him soft names in many a musèd rhyme,
  To take into the air my quiet breath;
Now more than ever seems it rich to die,
  To cease upon the midnight with no pain,
    While thou art pouring forth thy soul abroad
      In such an ecstasy!
  Still wouldst thou sing, and I have ears in vain—
    To thy high requiem become a sod.

VII

Thou wast not born for death, immortal Bird!
No hungry generations tread thee down;
The voice I hear this passing night was heard
In ancient days by emperor and clown:
Perhaps the self-same song that found a path
Through the sad heart of Ruth, when, sick for home,
She stood in tears amid the alien corn;
The same that oft-times hath
Charmed magic casements, opening on the foam
Of perilous seas, in faery lands forlorn.

VIII

Forlorn! the very word is like a bell
To toll me back from thee to my sole self!
Adieu! the fancy cannot cheat so well
As she is famed to do, deceiving elf.
Adieu! adieu! thy plaintive anthem fades
Past the near meadows, over the still stream,
Up the hill-side; and now 'tis buried deep
In the next valley-glades:
Was it a vision, or a waking dream?
Fled is that music:—Do I wake or sleep? ■

QUESTIONS

1. Why do the poets choose birds for their messengers?
2. Which poet's view of life is more optimistic? Why?

■ EMILY DICKINSON

(1830–1886)

Because I could not stop for Death

Because I could not stop for Death—
He kindly stopped for me—
The Carriage held but just Ourselves—
And Immortality.

We slowly drove—He knew no haste
And I had put away
My labor and my leisure too,
For His Civility—

We passed the School, where Children strove
At Recess—in the Ring—
We passed the Fields of Gazing Grain—
We passed the Setting Sun—

Or rather—He passed Us—
The Dews drew quivering and chill—
For only Gossamer, my Gown—
My Tippet°—only Tulle[1]— scarf

We paused before a House that seemed
A Swelling of the Ground—
The Roof was scarcely visible—
The Cornice—in the Ground—

Since then—'tis Centuries—and yet
Feels shorter than the Day
I first surmised the Horses' Heads
Were toward Eternity—

SYLVIA PLATH

(1932–1963)

Death & Co.

Two, of course there are two.
It seems perfectly natural now—
The one who never looks up, whose eyes are lidded
And balled, like Blake's,
Who exhibits

The birthmarks that are his trademark—
The scald scar of water,
The nude
Verdigris of the condor.
I am red meat. His beak

Claps sidewise: I am not his yet.
He tells me how badly I photograph.

BECAUSE I COULD NOT STOP FOR DEATH [1]**Tulle** thin net of silk.

He tells me how sweet
The babies look in their hospital
Icebox, a simple

Frill at the neck,
Then the flutings of their Ionian
Death-gowns,
Then two little feet.
He does not smile or smoke.

The other does that,
His hair long and plausive.
Bastard
Masturbating a glitter,
He wants to be loved.

I do not stir.
The frost makes a flower,
The dew makes a star,
The dead bell,
The dead bell.

Somebody's done for. ■

QUESTIONS

1. Why does each poet suggest Death is a suitor? Is their portrait of death as revealed in these poems related to the fact that both these poets are women?
2. Can you find the qualities of each of Plath's personifications in Dickinson's poem?

■

EDGAR ALLAN POE

(1809–1849)

Eldorado[1]

Gaily bedight,[2]
A gallant knight,
In sunshine and in shadow,
Had journeyed long,
Singing a song,
In search of Eldorado.

ELDORADO [1]**Eldorado** Spanish for "the gilded one." [2]**bedight** decked out.

But he grew old—
This knight so bold—
And o'er his heart a shadow
Fell as he found
No spot of ground
That looked like Eldorado.

And, as his strength
Failed him at length,
He met a pilgrim shadow—
"Shadow," said he,
"Where can it be—
This land of Eldorado?"

"Over the Mountains
Of the Moon,
Down the Valley of the Shadow,
Ride, boldly ride,"
The shade replied,—
"If you seek for Eldorado!"

JOHN KEATS

(1795–1821)

La Belle Dame sans Merci[1]

O what can ail thee, Knight at arms,
Alone and palely loitering?
The sedge has withered from the Lake
And no birds sing!

O what can ail thee, Knight at arms,
So haggard, and so woebegone?
The squirrel's granary is full
And the harvest's done.

I see a lily on thy brow
With anguish moist and fever dew,
And on thy cheeks a fading rose
Fast withereth too.

"I met a Lady in the Meads,° meadows
Full beautiful, a faery's child,

LA BELLE DAME SANS MERCI [1]French: "The beautiful woman without pity."

Her hair was long, her foot was light
And her eyes were wild.

"I made a Garland for her head,
And bracelets too, and fragrant Zone;° girdle
She looked at me as she did love
And made sweet moan.

"I set her on my pacing steed
And nothing else saw all day long,
For sidelong would she bend and sing
A faery's song.

"She found me roots of relish sweet,
And honey wild, and manna dew,
And sure in language strange she said
'I love thee true.'

"She took me to her elfin grot
And there she wept and sighed full sore,
And there I shut her wild wild eyes
With kisses four.

"And there she lulléd me asleep,
And there I dreamed, Ah Woe betide!
The latest dream I ever dreamt
On the cold hill side.

"I saw pale kings and princes too,
Pale warriors, death-pale were they all;
They cried, "La Belle Dame sans Merci
Hath thee in thrall!"

"I saw their starved lips in the gloam,
With horrid warning gaped wide,
And I awoke, and found me here,
On the cold hill's side.

"And this is why I sojourn here,
Alone and palely loitering,
Though the sedge is wither'd from the lake,
And no birds sing." ■

QUESTIONS

1. Why do both poets choose to set their poems in medieval costume when both are nineteenth-century poets?
2. Distinguish between the two searchers, one of whom still boldly rides, the other who just mopes around the hillside. Which is better off?

GEORGE GORDON, LORD BYRON

(1788–1824)

The Destruction of Sennacherib[1]

1

The Assyrian came down like the wolf on the fold,
And his cohorts were gleaming in purple and gold;
And the sheen of their spears was like stars on the sea,
When the blue wave rolls nightly on deep Galilee.

2

Like the leaves of the forest when summer is green,
That host with their banners at sunset were seen:
Like the leaves of the forest when autumn hath blown,
That host on the morrow lay withered and strown.

3

For the Angel of Death spread his wings on the blast,
And breathed in the face of the foe as he passed;
And the eyes of the sleepers waxed deadly and chill,
And their hearts but once heaved, and forever grew still!

4

And there lay the steed with his nostril all wide,
But through it there rolled not the breath of his pride;
And the foam of his gasping lay white on the turf,
And cold as the spray of the rock-beating surf.

5

And there lay the rider distorted and pale,
With the dew on his brow, and the rust on his mail:
And the tents were all silent, the banners alone,
The lances unlifted, the trumpet unblown.

6

And the widows of Ashur° are loud in their wail, Assyria
And the idols are broke in the temple of Baal;
And the might of the Gentile, unsmote by the sword,
Hath melted like snow in the glance of the Lord!

THE DESTRUCTION OF SENNACHERIB [1]**Sennacherib** Assyrian king whose army was destroyed by an angel.

OGDEN NASH

(1902–1971)

Very Like a Whale

One thing that literature would be greatly the better for
Would be a more restricted employment by authors of simile and metaphor.
Authors of all races, be they Greeks, Romans, Teutons or Celts.
Can't seem just to say that anything is the thing it is but have to go out of their way to say that it is like something else.
What does it mean when we are told
That the Assyrian came down like a wolf on the fold?
In the first place, George Gordon Byron had had enough experience
To know that it probably wasn't just one Assyrian, it was a lot of Assyrians.
However, as too many arguments are apt to induce apoplexy and thus hinder longevity,
We'll let it pass as one Assyrian for the sake of brevity.
Now then, this particular Assyrian, the one whose cohorts were gleaming in purple and gold.
Just what does the poet mean when he says he came down like a wolf on the fold?
In heaven and earth more than is dreamed of in our philosophy there are a great many things,
But I don't imagine that among them there is a wolf with purple and gold cohorts or purple and gold anythings.
No, no, Lord Byron, before I'll believe that this Assyrian was actually like a wolf I must have some kind of proof:
Did he run on all fours and did he have a hairy tail and a big red mouth and big white teeth and did he say Woof woof woof?
Frankly I think it very unlikely, and all you were entitled to say, at the very most,
Was that the Assyrian cohorts came down like a lot of Assyrian cohorts about to destroy the Hebrew host.
But that wasn't fancy enough for Lord Byron, oh dear me no, he had to invent a lot of figures of speech and then interpolate them.
With the result that whenever you mention Old Testament soldiers to people they say Oh yes, they're the ones that a lot of wolves dressed up in gold and purple ate them.
That's the kind of thing that's being done all the time by poets, from Homer to Tennyson:
They're always comparing ladies to lilies and veal to venison.
How about the man who wrote,
Her little feet stole in and out like mice beneath her petticoat?
Wouldn't anybody but a poet think twice
Before stating that his girl's feet were mice?

Then they always say things like that after a winter storm
The snow is a white blanket. Oh it is, is it, all right then, you sleep
  under a six-inch blanket of snow and I'll sleep under a half-inch
  blanket of unpoetical blanket material and we'll see which one keeps
  warm.
And after that maybe you'll begin to comprehend dimly
What I meant by too much metaphor and simile. ■

QUESTIONS

1. Are Nash's comments on Byron's use of metaphor true?
2. Nash's title is taken from the conversation between Hamlet and Polonious in Shakespeare's play *Hamlet* (see Chapter 4). Are metaphors something mad, as Polonious suggests?
3. Why do poets employ metaphors to begin with?

■ ANDREW MARVELL

(1621–1678)

To His Coy Mistress

Had we but world enough, and time,
This coyness, lady, were no crime.
We would sit down, and think which way
To walk, and pass our long love's day.
Thou by the Indian Ganges' side
Shoudst rubies find; I by the tide
Of Humber[1] would complain. I would
Love you ten years before the flood,
And you should, if you please, refuse
Till the conversion of the Jews.[2]
My vegetable love should grow
Vaster than empires and more slow;
An hundred years should go to praise
Thine eyes, and on thy forehead gaze;
Two hundred to adore each breast,
But thirty thousand to the rest;
An age at least to every part,
And the last age should show your heart.
For, lady, you deserve this state,
Nor would I love at lower rate.
But at my back I always hear

TO HIS COY MISTRESS [1]**Humber** river in England. [2]**till the conversion of the Jews** until the end of the world.

Time's wingèd chariot hurrying near;
And yonder all before us lie
Deserts of vast eternity.
Thy beauty shall no more be found;
Nor, in thy marble vault, shall sound
My echoing song; then worms shall try
That long-preserved virginity,
And your quaint honor turn to dust,
And into ashes all my lust:
The grave's a fine and private place,
But none, I think, do there embrace.
  Now therefore, while the youthful hue
Sits on thy skin like morning glow,
And while thy willing soul transpires
At every pore with instant fires,
Now let us sport us while we may,
And now, like amorous birds of prey,
Rather at once our time devour
Than languish in his slow-chapped° power. slow-jawed
Let us roll all our strength and all
Our sweetness up into one ball,
And tear our pleasures with rough strife
Thorough the iron gates of life:
Thus, though we cannot make our sun
Stand still, yet we will make him run.

ROBERT HERRICK

(1591–1674)

To the Virgins, To Make Much of Time

Gather ye rosebuds while ye may,
  Old time is still a-flying;
And this same flower that smiles today,
  Tomorrow will be dying.

The glorious lamp of heaven, the sun,
  The higher he's a-getting,
The sooner will his race be run,
  And nearer he's to setting.

That age is best which is the first,
  When youth and blood are warmer,
But being spent, the worse, and worst
  Times still succeed the former.

Then be not coy, but use your time,
And while ye may, go marry:
For having lost but once your prime,
You may forever tarry.

ARCHIBALD MacLEISH

(1892–1982)

You, Andrew Marvell

And here face down beneath the sun
And here upon earth's noonward height
To feel the always coming on
The always rising of the night:

To feel creep up the curving east
The earthly chill of dusk and slow
Upon those under lands the vast
And ever climbing shadow grow

And strange at Ecbatan[1] the trees
Take leaf by leaf the evening strange
The flooding dark about their knees
The mountains over Persia change

And now at Kermanshah[2] the gate
Dark empty and the withered grass
And through the twilight now the late
Few travelers in the westward pass

And Baghdad darken and the bridge
Across the silent river gone
And through Arabia the edge
Of evening widen and steal on

And deepen on Palmyra's[3] street
The wheel rut in the ruined stone
And Lebanon fade out and Crete
High through the clouds and overblown

And over Sicily the air
Still flashing with the landward gulls

YOU, ANDREW MARVELL [1]**Ectaban** ancient name of Hamadan. [2]**Kermanshah** a city in western Iran. [3]**Palmyra** ancient city in central Syria.

And loom and slowly disappear
The sails above the shadowy hulls

And Spain go under and the shore
Of Africa the gilded sand
And evening vanish and no more
The low pale light across the land

Nor now the long light on the sea:

And here face downward in the sun
To feel how swift how secretly
The shadow of the night comes on . . . ■

QUESTIONS

1. Both of the first two are seduction poems. What is the difference in point of view of their arguments?
2. How does the MacLeish poem change or emphasize the feelings about time in the other two poems?

■

WALLACE STEVENS

(1879–1955)

So-And-So Reclining on Her Couch

On her side, reclining on her elbow.
This mechanism, this apparition,
Suppose we call it Projection A.

She floats in air at the level of
The eye, completely anonymous,
Born, as she was, at twenty-one,

Without lineage or language, only
The curving of her hip, as motionless gesture,
Eyes dripping blue, so much to learn.

If just above her head there hung,
Suspended in air, the slightest crown
Of Gothic prong and practick bright,

The suspension, as in solid space,
The suspending hand withdrawn, would be
An invisible gesture. Let this be called

Projection B. To get at the thing
Without gestures is to get at it as
Idea. She floats in the contention, the flux

Between the thing as idea and
The idea as thing. She is half who made her.
This is the final Projection, C.

The arrangement contains the desire of
The artist. But one confides in what has no
Concealed creator. One walks easily

The unpainted shore, accepts the world
As anything but sculpture. Good-bye,
Mrs. Pappadopoulos, and thanks.

TONY MAGISTRALE

(1952–)

Vanishing Point

1

M. Benni appears in my little office
and crosses long nyloned legs
precisely at the knee.
She comes to talk American literature,
but I am thinking renaissance art,
of Uccello obsessed in his studio
searching for vanishing points,
currents of energy obeying mathematical laws—
the narrow center of creation
at the nexus of paint and being.
I am beginning to understand his fascination;
I have discovered the vanishing point
of this office.
M. Benni's legs
are lines of perpendiculars
unfolding forever beneath a chair
at the center of ceiling and floor.
They pull on the solid forms
in my office, and if not
for the hidden tyrants,
gravity and repression,

the entire contents of this bare cubicle
—books, journals, desk, and professor
would be sucked down deep into a vortex of perfection.

II

M. Benni wants to know exactly why
American writers are drunkneuroticself-
destructivepervertedwomen-
haters. I tell her
because American women are simply not
sympathetic like Italian women.
M. Benni wants to know exactly why
I insist on pronouncing
arrivedérci
like an American. I ask her
exactly what does that mean
but she has vanished
up from the chair and gone,
sweeping the oxygen
out of the room. ■

QUESTIONS

1. What is the role of perspective and the concept of a vanishing point in each of these poems?
2. Stevens contrasts his model with his imagined world of art; Magistrale, with the awareness of different perspectives. What creates the difference?

■ BEN JONSON

(1572–1637)

Still to be neat, still to be dressed

Still to be neat, still to be dressed,
As you were going to a feast;
Still to be powdered, still perfumed:
Lady, it is to be presumed,
Though art's hid causes are not found,
All is not sweet, all is not sound.

Give me a look, give me a face,
That makes simplicity a grace;
Robes loosely flowing, hair as free:

Such sweet neglect more taketh me
Than all the adulteries of art;
They strike mine eyes, but not my heart.

ROBERT HERRICK

(1591–1674)

Delight in Disorder

A sweet disorder in the dress
Kindles in clothes a wantonness.
A lawn° about the shoulders thrown — scarf of fine linen
Into a fine distractiön;
An erring lace, which here and there
Enthralls the crimson stomacher;° — cummerbund
A cuff neglectful, and thereby
Ribbons to flow confusedly;
A winning wave, deserving note,
In the tempestuous petticoat;
A careless shoestring, in whose tie
I see a wild civility;
Do more bewitch me than when art
Is too precise in every part. ■

QUESTIONS

1. How do these poets use form to create their arguments?
2. Which style of beauty do you prefer, and why?

■ THEODORE ROETHKE

(1908–1963)

The Waking

I wake to sleep, and take my waking slow.
I feel my fate in what I cannot fear.
I learn by going where I have to go.

We think by feeling. What is there to know?
I hear my being dance from ear to ear.
I wake to sleep, and take my waking slow.

Of those so close beside me, which are you?
God bless the Ground! I shall walk softly there,
And learn by going where I have to go.

Light takes the Tree; but who can tell us how?
The lowly worm climbs up a winding stair;
I wake to sleep, and take my waking slow.

Great Nature has another thing to do
To you and me; so take the lively air,
And, lovely, learn by going where to go.

This shaking keeps me steady. I should know.
What falls away is always. And is near.
I wake to sleep, and take my waking slow.
I learn by going where I have to go.

DYLAN THOMAS

(1914–1953)

Do Not Go Gentle into That Good Night

Do not go gentle into that good night,
Old age should burn and rave at close of day;
Rage, rage against the dying of the light.

Though wise men at their end know dark is right,
Because their words had forked no lightning they
Do not go gentle into that good night.

Good men, the last wave by, crying how bright
Their frail deeds might have danced in a green bay,
Rage, rage against the dying of the light.

Wild men who caught and sang the sun in flight,
And learn, too late, they grieved it on its way,
Do not go gentle into that good night.

Grave men, near death, who see with blinding sight
Blind eyes could blaze like meteors and be gay,
Rage, rage against the dying of the light.

And you, my father, there on the sad height,
Curse, bless, me now with your fierce tears, I pray.
Do not go gentle into that good night.
Rage, rage against the dying of the light.

QUESTIONS

1. How does each poet use the intricate form of the villanelle to make his point?
2. Why do the tones of these two poems contrast?

WILLIAM CARLOS WILLIAMS

(1883–1963)

This Is Just to Say

I have eaten
the plums
that were in
the icebox

and which
you were probably
saving
for breakfast

Forgive me
they were delicious
so sweet
and so cold

KENNETH KOCH

(1925–)

Variations on a Theme by William Carlos Williams

1

I chopped down the house that you had been saving to live in next summer.
I am sorry, but it was morning, and I had nothing to do
and its wooden beams were so inviting.

2

We laughed at the hollyhocks together
and then I sprayed them with lye.
Forgive me. I simply do not know what I am doing.

3

I gave away the money that you had been saving to live on for the next ten years.
The man who asked for it was shabby
and the firm March wind on the porch was so juicy and cold.

4

Last evening we went dancing and I broke your leg.
Forgive me. I was clumsy, and
I wanted you here in the wards, where I am the doctor! ■

QUESTIONS

1. Williams has written in *Paterson V*, "Poetry is language charged with emotion. It's words, rhythmically organized." Does that definition fit Williams's poem?
2. Does the Koch poem make fun of Williams, pay tribute to Williams, or call into question the poetical qualities of what Williams writes?

■

E. E. CUMMINGS

(1894–1962)

raise the shade will youse dearie?

raise the shade
will youse dearie?
rain
wouldn't that

get yer goat but
we don't care do
we dearie we should
worry about the rain

huh
dearie?
yknow
i'm

sorry for awl the
poor girls that
gets up god
knows when every

day of their
lives
aint you,
oo-oo. dearie

not so
hard dear

you're killing me

WANDA COLEMAN

(1945–)

Sweet Mama Wanda Tells Fortunes for a Price

dark stairs
me walking up them
the room
is cold
i am here to fuck
then go back
to the streets

he sighs
touches
likes my lips
my cocoa thighs
we lay down
the bed yields
he comes off calling mama

outside
i count my cash
it's been a good night
the street is cold
i head east

i am hungry
i smile

i know what tomorrow
is all about ■

QUESTIONS

1. Contrast the attitudes of both these prostitutes.
2. How does race or class affect the language patterns in which these poems were written as well as the attitudes of the women?

■ WILLIAM BLAKE

(1757–1827)

The Sick Rose

O Rose, thou art sick.
The invisible worm
That flies in the night
In the howling storm

Has found out thy bed
Of crimson joy,
And his dark secret love
Does thy life destroy.

ROBERT BURNS

(1759–1796)

A Red, Red Rose

O my luve's like a red, red rose,
That's newly sprung in June;
O my luve's like the melodie
That's sweetly played in tune.

As fair art thou, my bonnie lass,
So deep in luve am I;
And I will luve thee still, my dear,
Till a' the seas gang dry.

Till a' the seas gang dry, my dear,
And the rocks melt wi' the sun:
O I will love thee still, my dear,
While the sands o' life shall run.

And fare thee weel, my only luve,
And fare thee weel awhile!
And I will come again, my luve,
Though it were ten thousand
mile. ■

QUESTIONS

1. Blake uses a single metaphor to organize his poem; Burns a series of metaphors. How is this choice affected by the thematic concerns of the poems?
2. The rose is a conventional symbol for love and beauty. How do both poets use or play off that expected meaning?

■ WALT WHITMAN

(1819–1892)

To a Locomotive in Winter

Thee for my recitative,
Thee in the driving storm even as now, the snow the winter-day declining,
Thee in thy panoply, thy measur'd dual throbbing and thy beat convulsive,
Thy black cylindric body, golden brass and silvery steel,
Thy ponderous side-bars, parallel and connecting rods, gyrating, shuttling at thy sides,
Thy metrical, now swelling pant and roar, now tapering in the distance,
Thy great protruding head-light fix'd in front,
Thy long, pale, floating vapor-pennants, tinged with delicate purple,
The dense and murky clouds out-belching from thy smoke-stack,
Thy knitted frame, thy springs and valves, the tremulous twinkle of thy wheels,
Thy train of cars behind, obedient, merrily following,
Through gale or calm, now swift, now slack, yet steadily careering;
Type of the modern—emblem of motion and power—pulse of the continent,
For once come serve the Muse and merge in verse, even as here I see thee,
With storm and buffeting gusts of wind and falling snow,

By day thy warning ringing bell to sound its notes,
By night thy silent signal lamps to swing.

Fierce-throated beauty!
Roll through my chant with all thy lawless music, thy swinging lamps at night,
Thy madly-whistled laughter, echoing, rumbling like an earthquake, rousing all,
Law of thyself complete, thine own track firmly holding,
(No sweetness debonair of tearful harp or glib piano thine,)
Thy trills of shrieks by rocks and hills return'd,
Launch'd o'er the prairies wide, across the lakes,
To the free skies unpent and glad and strong.

EMILY DICKINSON

(1830–1886)

I Like to See It Lap the Miles

I like to see it lap the Miles—
And lick the Valleys up—
And stop to feed itself at Tanks—
And then—prodigious step

Around a Pile of Mountains—
And supercilious peer
In Shanties—by the sides of Roads—
And then a Quarry pare

To fit its Ribs
And crawl between
Complaining all the while
In horrid—hooting stanza—
Then chase itself down Hill—

And neigh like Boanerges[1]—
Then—punctual as a Star
Stop—docile and omnipotent
At its own stable door—

■

I LIKE TO SEE IT LAP THE MILES [1]**Boanerges** Son of Thunder, name of a racehorse.

QUESTIONS

1. Both nineteenth-century American poets look at the invention of the railroad and celebrate it. What is the difference between their attitudes?
2. How does the form of these poems affect these attitudes?

THOMAS HARDY

(1840–1928)

The Man He Killed

"Had he and I but met
By some old ancient inn,
We should have sat us down to wet
Right many a nipperkin!

"But ranged as infantry,
And staring face to face,
I shot at him as he at me,
And killed him in his place.

"I shot him dead because—
Because he was my foe,
Just so: my foe of course he was;
That's clear enough; although

"He thought he'd 'list, perhaps,
Off-hand-like—just as I—
Was out of work—had sold his traps—
No other reason why.

"Yes; quaint and curious war is!
You shoot a fellow down
You'd treat, if met where any bar is,
Or help to half-a-crown."

WILFRED OWEN

(1893–1918)

Strange Meeting

It seemed that out of battle I escaped
Down some profound dull tunnel, long since scooped
Through granites which titanic wars had groined.

Yet also there encumbered sleepers groaned,
Too fast in thought or death to be bestirred.
Then, as I probed them, one sprang up, and stared
With piteous recognition in fixed eyes,
Lifting distressful hands, as if to bless.
And by his smile, I knew that sullen hall,—
By his dead smile I knew we stood in Hell.

With a thousand pains that vision's face was grained;
Yet no blood reached there from the upper ground,
And no guns thumped, or down the flues made moan.
"Strange friend," I said, "here is no cause to mourn."
"None," said the other, "save the undone years,
The hopelessness. Whatever hope is yours,
Was my life also; I went hunting wild
After the wildest beauty in the world,
Which lies not calm in eyes, or braided hair,
But mocks the steady running of the hour,
And if it grieves, grieves richlier than here.
For by my glee might many men have laughed,
And of my weeping something had been left,
Which must die now. I mean the truth untold,
The pity of war, the pity war distilled.
Now men will go content with what we spoiled,
Or, discontent, boil bloody, and be spilled.
They will be swift with swiftness of the tigress.
None will break ranks, though nations trek from progress.
Courage was mine, and I had mystery,
Wisdom was mine, and I had mastery:
To miss the march of this retreating world
Into vain citadels that are not walled.
Then, when much blood had clogged their chariot-wheels,
I would go up and wash them from sweet wells,
Even with truths that lie too deep for taint.
I would have poured my spirit without stint
But not through wounds; not on the cess° of war. waste
Foreheads of men have bled where no wounds were.

"I am the enemy you killed, my friend.
I knew you in this dark: for so you frowned
Yesterday through me as you jabbed and killed.
I parried; but my hands were loath and cold.
Let us sleep now. . . ." ■

QUESTIONS

1. Does the greater formality of Owen's poem make it more affecting?
2. What is the difference between ending one poem in a world in which one is puzzled and ending the other in the land of the dead, told by two ghosts?

WOLE SOYINKA

(1934–)

Massacre, October '66

WRITTEN IN TEGEL

Shards of sunlight touch me here
Shredded in willows. Through stained-glass
Fragments on the lake I sought to reach
A mind at silt-bed

The lake stayed cold
I swam in an October flush of dying leaves
The gardener's labour flew in seasoned scrolls
Lettering the wind

Swept from painted craft
A mockery of waves remarked this idyll sham
I trod on acorns; each shell's detonation
Aped the skull's uniqueness.

Came sharper reckoning—
This favoured food of hogs cannot number high
As heads still harshly crop to whirlwinds
I have briefly fled

The oak rains a hundred more
A kind confusion to arithmetics of death:
Time to watch autumn the removal man
Dust down rare canvases

To let a loud resolve of passion
Fly to a squirrel, burnished light and copper fur
A distant stance without the lake's churchwindows
And for a stranger, love.

A host of acorns fell, silent
As they are silenced all, whose laughter
Rose from such indifferent paths, oh God
They are not strangers all

Whose desecration mocks the word
Of peace—*salaam aleikun*[1]—not strangers any

[1] ***salaam aleikun*** peace be with you.

Brain of thousands pressed asleep to pig fodder—
Shun pork the unholy—cries the priest.

I borrow seasons of an alien land
In brotherhood of ill, pride of race around me
Strewn in sunlit shards. I borrow alien lands
To stay the season of a mind.

SEAMUS HEANEY

(1939–)

Requiem for the Croppies[1]

The pockets of our great coats full of barley—
No kitchens on the run, no striking camp—
We moved quick and sudden in our own country.
The priest lay behind ditches with the tramp.
A people, hardly marching—on the hike—
We found new tactics happening each day:
We'd cut through reins and rider with the pike
And stampede cattle into infantry,
Then retreat through hedges where cavalry must be thrown.
Until, on Vinegar Hill, the fatal conclave.
Terraced thousands died, shaking scythes at cannon.
The hillside blushed, soaked in our broken wave.
They buried us without shroud or coffin
And in August the barley grew up out of the grave. ■

QUESTIONS

1. How does each of these poets deal with the theme of struggle?
2. How does each of these poets deal with official authority?

REQUIEM FOR THE CROPPIES [1]**Croppies** Irish soldiers with cropped hair.

Chronology of Poems

ANONYMOUS

Timor Mortis

In what estate so ever I be
Timor mortis conturbat me.[1]

As I went on a merry morning,
I heard a bird both weep and sing.
This was the tenor of her talking:
"Timor mortis conturbat me."

I asked that bird what she meant.
"I am a musket° both fair and gent;° — male sparrow hawk/gentle
For dread of death I am all shent:
Timor mortis conturbat me.

"When I shall die, I know no day;
What country or place I cannot say;
Wherefore this song sing I may:
Timor mortis conturbat me.

"Jesu Christ, when he should die,
To his Father he gan say,
'Father,' he said, 'in Trinity,
Timor mortis conturbat me.'

"All Christian people, behold and see:
This world is but a vanity
And replete with necessity.
Timor mortis conturbat me.

"Wake I or sleep, eate or drink,
When I on my last end do think,
For greate fear my soul do shrink:
Timor mortis conturbat me.

"God grant us grace him for to serve,
And be at our end when we sterve,° — die
And from the fiend he us preserve.
Timor mortis conturbat me.

[1] ***Timor mortis conturbat me*** The fear of death disturbs me.

ANONYMOUS

Western Wind

Western wind, when will thou blow,
  The small rain down can rain?
Christ, if my love were in my arms
  And I in my bed again!

ANONYMOUS

Get Up and Bar the Door

1

It fell about the Martinmas[1] time,
  And a gay time it was then,
When our goodwife got puddings to make,
  And she's boiled them in the pan.

2

The wind sae° cauld blew south and north, *so*
  And blew into the floor;
Quoth our goodman to our goodwife,
  "Gae° out and bar the door." *go*

3

"My hand is in my hussyfskap.° *domestic chores*
  Goodman, as ye may see;
An° it should nae be barred this hundred year, *if*
  It s'° no be barred for me." *shall*

4

They made a paction 'tween them twa,
  They made it firm and sure,
That the first word whae'er should speak,
  Should rise and bar the door.

GET UP AND BAR THE DOOR [1]**Martinmas** a church festival on November 11 in honor of St. Martin.

5

Then by there came two gentlemen,
At twelve o'clock at night,
And they could neither see house nor hall,
Nor coal nor candle-light.

6

"Now whether is this a rich man's house,
Or whether is it a poor?"
But ne'er a word wad° ane o' them speak, would
For barring of the door.

7

And first they ate the white puddings,
And then they ate the black;
Though muckle° thought the goodwife to hersel, much
Yet ne'er a word she spak.

8

Then said the one unto the other,
"Here, man, tak ye my knife;
Do ye tak aff° the auld man's beard, off
And I'll kiss the goodwife."

9

"But there's nae water in the house,
And what shall we do then?"
"What ails ye at the pudding-broo,° broth
That boils into the pan?"

10

O up then started our goodman,
An angry man was he:
"Will ye kiss my wife before my een,° eyes
And scad° me wi' pudding-bree?"° scald/broth

11

Then up and started our goodwife,
Gied° three skips on the floor: to give
"Goodman, you've spoken the foremost word,
Get up and bar the door."

WILLIAM SHAKESPEARE

(1564–1616, England)

My mistress' eyes are nothing like the sun

My mistress' eyes are nothing like the sun;
Coral is far more red than her lips' red;
If snow be white, why then her breasts are dun;
If hairs be wires, black wires grow on her head.
I have seen roses damasked,° red and white, unveiled
But no such roses see I in her cheeks;
And in some perfumes is there more delight
Than in the breath that from my mistress reeks.
I love to hear her speak, yet well I know
That music hath a far more pleasing sound;
I grant I never saw a goddess go;
My mistress, when she walks, treads on the ground.
And yet, by heaven, I think my love as rare
As any she belied with false compare.

Shall I compare thee to a summer's day

Shall I compare thee to a summer's day?
Thou art more lovely and more temperate:
Rough winds do shake the darling buds of May,
And summer's lease hath all too short a date;
Sometime too hot the eye of heaven shines,
And often is his gold complexion dimm'd;
And every fair from fair sometime declines,
By chance or nature's changing course untrimm'd:
But thy eternal summer shall not fade
Nor lose possession of that fair thou ow'st;
Nor shall Death brag thou wand'rest in his shade,
When in eternal lines to time thou grow'st;
So long as men can breathe or eyes can see,
So long lives this, and this gives life to thee.

Let me not to the marriage of true minds

Let me not to the marriage of true minds
Admit impediments Love is not love
Which alters when it alteration finds,
Or bends with the remover to remove:

Oh, no! it is an ever-fixéd mark,
That looks on tempests and is never shaken;
It is the star to every wandering bark,° — sailing vessel
Whose worth's unknown, although his height be taken.
Love's not Time's fool, though rosy lips and cheeks
Within his bending sickle's compass come;
Love alters not with his brief hours and weeks,
But bears it out even to the edge of doom.
If this be error and upon me proved,
I never writ, nor no man ever loved.

JOHN DONNE

(1572–1631, England)

At the round earth's imagined corners, blow

At the round earth's imagined corners, blow
Your trumpets, angels; and arise, arise
From death, you numberless infinities
Of souls, and to your scattered bodies go;
All whom the flood did, and fire shall, o'erthrow,
All whom war, dearth, age, agues, tyrannies,
Despair, law, chance hath slain, and you whose eyes
Shall behold God, and never taste death's woe.
But let them sleep, Lord, and me mourn a space;
For, if above all these, my sins abound,
It's late to ask abundance of Thy grace
When we are there. Here on this lowly ground,
Teach me how to repent; for that's as good
As if Thou hadst sealed my pardon with Thy blood.

Death, be not proud

Death, be not proud, though some have calléd thee
Mighty and dreadful, for thou are not so;
For those whom thou think'st thou dost overthrow
Die not, poor Death, nor yet canst thou kill me.
From rest and sleep, which but thy pictures be,
Much pleasure; then from thee much more must flow,
And soonest our best men with thee do go,
Rest of their bones, and soul's delivery.
Thou art slave to fate, chance, kings, and desperate men,
And dost with poison, war, and sickness dwell,
And poppy or charms can make us sleep as well

And better than thy stroke; why swell'st thou then?
One short sleep past, we wake eternally
And death shall be no more; Death, thou shalt die.

Batter my heart, three-personed God

Batter my heart, three-personed God; for You
As yet but knock, breathe, shine, and seek to mend;
That I may rise and stand, o'erthrow me, and bend
Your force to break, blow, burn, and make me new.
I, like an usurped town, to another due,
Labor to admit You, but O, to no end;
Reason, Your viceroy in me, me should defend,
But is captívéd, and proves weak or untrue.
Yet dearly I love You, and would be lovéd fain°, wish
But am betrothed unto Your enemy.
Divorce me, untie or break that knot again;
Take me to You, imprison me, for I,
Except You enthrall me, never shall be free,
Nor ever chaste, except You ravish me.

Song

Go, and catch a falling star,
    Get with child a mandrake root,[1]
Tell me, where all past years are,
    Or who cleft the devil's foot,
Teach me to hear mermaids singing
Or to keep off envy's stinging,
        And find
        What wind
Serves to advance an honest mind.

If thou beest born to strange sights,
    Things invisible to see,
Ride ten thousand days and nights,
    Till age snow white hairs on thee;
Thou, when thou return'st, wilt tell me
All strange wonders that befell thee,
        And swear,
        No where
Lives a woman true, and fair.

SONG [1]**mandrake root** a plant whose roots resemble a pregnant woman from the waist down.

If thou find'st one, let me know:
  Such a pilgrimage were sweet.
Yet do not, I would not go,
  Though at next door we might meet:
Though she were true when you met her,
And last till you write your letter,
    Yet she
    Will be
False, ere I come, to two, or three.

BEN JONSON

(1573–1637, England)

On Gut

Gut eats all day and lechers all the night;
So all his meat he tasteth over twice;
And, striving so to double his delight,
He makes himself a thoroughfare of vice.
Thus in his belly can he change a sin:
Lust it comes out, that gluttony went in.

Epitaph on Salomon Pavy, a Child of Queen Elizabeth's Chapel

Weep with me, all you that read
  This little story,
And know, for whom a tear you shed,
  Death's self is sorry.
'Twas a child, that so did thrive
  In grace and feature,
As Heaven and Nature seemed to strive
  Which owned the creature.
Years he numbered scarce thirteen
  When Fates turned cruel,
Yet three filled zodiacs° had he been — three years
  The stage's jewel,
And did act, what now we moan,
  Old men so duly,
As, sooth, the Parcae° thought him one, — fates
  He played so truly.

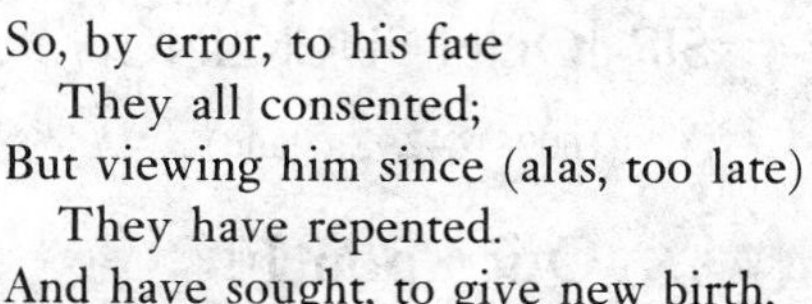

So, by error, to his fate
They all consented;
But viewing him since (alas, too late)
They have repented.
And have sought, to give new birth,
In baths to steep him;
But, being so much too good for earth
Heaven vows to keep him.

Song: To Celia

Drink to me only with thine eyes,
And I will pledge with mine;
Or leave a kiss but in the cup,
And I'll not look for wine.
The thirst that from the soul doth rise,
Doth ask a drink divine:
But might I of Jove's nectar sup,
I would not change for thine.

I sent thee late a rosy wreath,
Not so much honoring thee,
As giving it a hope, that there
It could not withered be.
But thou thereon did'st only breathe,
And sent'st it back to me;
Since when it grows and smells, I swear,
Not of itself, but thee.

ROBERT HERRICK

(1591–1674, England)

Upon Julia's Clothes

Whenas in silks my Julia goes,
Then, then, methinks, how sweetly flows
That liquefaction of her clothes.
Next, when I cast mine eyes, and see
That brave vibration, each way free,
O, how that glittering taketh me!

SIR JOHN SUCKLING

(1609–1642, England)

Out upon It!

Out upon it! I have loved
Three whole days together;
And am like to love three more,
If it prove fair weather.

Time shall molt away his wings,
Ere he shall discover
In the whole wide world again
Such a constant lover.

But the spite on 't is, no praise
Is due at all to me:
Love with me had made no
stays° — limits
Had it any been but she.

Had it any been but she,
And that very face,
There had been at least ere this
A dozen dozen in her place.

ANNE BRADSTREET

(1612–1672, Colonial America)

Upon the Burning of Our House

In silent night when rest I took,
For sorrow near I did not look,
I wakened was with thundering noise
And piteous shrieks of dreadful voice.
That fearful sound of "Fire!" and "Fire!"
Let no man know is my Desire.

I, starting up, the light did spy,
And to my God my heart did cry
To strengthen me in my distress
And not to leave me succorless.° — helpless
Then coming out beheld a space,
The flame consume my dwelling place.

And, when I could no longer look,
I blest His name that gave and took,

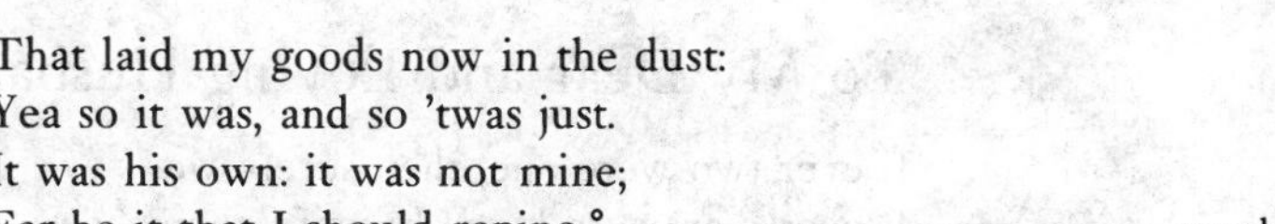

That laid my goods now in the dust:
Yea so it was, and so 'twas just.
It was his own: it was not mine;
Far be it that I should repine.° complain

He might of all justly bereft,
But yet sufficient for us left.
When by the ruins oft I passed,
My sorrowing eyes aside did cast,
And here and there the places spy
Where oft I sat, and long did lie.

Here stood that trunk, and there that chest;
There lay that store I counted best:
My pleasant things in ashes lie,
And them behold no more shall I.
Under thy roof no guest shall sit,
Nor at thy table eat a bit.

No pleasant tale shall e'er be told,
Nor things recounted done of old.
No candle e'er shall shine in thee,
Nor bridegroom's voice e'er heard shall be.
In silence ever shalt thou lie;
Adieu, adieu; all's vanity.

Then straight I 'gin my heart to chide,
And did thy wealth on earth abide?
Didst fix thy hope on mould'ring dust?
The arm of flesh didst make thy trust?
Raise up thy thoughts above the sky,
That dunghill mists away may fly.

Thou hast an house on high erect,
Fram'd by that mighty Architect,
With glory richly furnished,
Stands permanent, though this be fled.
It's purchased, and paid for, too,
By Him who hath enough to do.

A prize so vast as is unknown,
Yet, by his gift, is made thine own.
There's wealth enough, I need no more;
Farewell my pelf,° farewell my store. money, wealth
The world no longer let me love,
My hope and treasure lies above.

To My Dear and Loving Husband

If ever two were one, then surely we.
If ever man were loved by wife, then thee;
If ever wife was happy in a man,
Compare with me ye women if you can.
I prize thy love more than whole mines of gold,
Or all the riches that the East doth hold.
My love is such that rivers cannot quench,
Nor ought but love from thee give recompense.
Thy love is such I can no way repay;
The heavens reward thee manifold, I pray.
Then while we live, in love let's so persever,
That when we live no more we may live ever.

ALEXANDER POPE

(1688–1744, England)

Engraved on the Collar of a Dog Which I Gave to His Royal Highness

I am his Highness' dog at Kew;
Pray tell me, sir, whose dog are you?

THOMAS GRAY

(1716–1771, England)

Ode: On the Death of a Favorite Cat, Drowned in a Tub of Goldfishes

'Twas on a lofty vase's side,
Where China's gayest art had dyed
  The azure flowers that blow;° blossom
Demurest of the tabby kind,
The pensive Selima, reclined,
  Gazed on the lake below.

Her conscious tail her joy declared;
The fair round face, the snowy beard,
  The velvet of her paws,
Her coat, that with the tortoise vies,

Her ears of jet, and emerald eyes,
She saw; and purred applause.

Still had she gazed; but 'midst the tide
Two angel forms were seen to glide,
The genii° of the stream: guardian spirits
Their scaly armor's Tyrian hue
Through richest purple to the view
Betrayed a golden gleam.

The hapless nymph with wonder saw:
A whisker first and then a claw,
With many an ardent wish,
She stretched in vain to reach the prize.
What female heart can gold despise?
What cat's averse to fish?

Presumptuous maid! with looks intent
Again she stretched, again she bent,
Nor knew the gulf between.
(Malignant Fate sat by and smiled)
The slippery verge her feet beguiled,
She tumbled headlong in.

Eight times emerging from the flood
She mewed to every watery god,
Some speedy aid to send.
No dolphin came, no Nereid stirred;
Nor cruel Tom, nor Susan heard;
A favorite has no friend!

From hence, ye beauties, undeceived,
Know, one false step is ne'er retrieved,
And be with caution bold.
Not all that tempts your wandering eyes
And heedless hearts, is lawful prize;
Nor all that glisters, gold.

WILLIAM BLAKE

(1757–1827, England)

The Lamb

Little Lamb, who made thee?
Dost thou know who made thee?
Gave thee life & bid thee feed,

By the stream & o'er the mead;
Gave thee clothing of delight,
Softest clothing wooly bright;
Gave thee such a tender voice,
Making all the vales rejoice!
   Little Lamb who made thee?
   Dost thou know who made thee?

   Little Lamb I'll tell thee,
   Little Lamb I'll tell thee!
He is calléd by thy name,
For he calls himself a Lamb:
He is meek & he is mild,
He became a little child:
I a child & thou a lamb,
We are calléd by his name.
   Little Lamb God bless thee.
   Little Lamb God bless thee.

The Tyger

Tyger! Tyger! burning bright
In the forests of the night,
What immortal hand or eye
Could frame thy fearful symmetry?

In what distant deeps or skies
Burnt the fire of thine eyes?
On what wings dare he aspire?
What the hand, dare seize the fire?

And what shoulder, & what art,
Could twist the sinews of thy heart?
And when thy heart began to beat,
What dread hand? & what dread feet?

What the hammer? what the chain?
In what furnace was thy brain?
What the anvil? what dread grasp
Dare its deadly terrors clasp?

When the stars threw down their spears,
And water'd heaven with their tears,
Did he smile his work to see?
Did he who made the Lamb make thee?

Tyger! Tyger! burning bright
In the forests of the night,
What immortal hand or eye
Dare frame thy fearful symmetry?

London

I wander thro' each charter'd° street, mapped-out
Near where the charter'd Thames does flow,
And mark in every face I meet
Marks of weakness, marks of woe.

In every cry of every man,
In every Infant's cry of fear,
In every voice, in every ban,
The mind-forg'd manacles I hear.

How the Chimney-sweeper's cry
Every blackning Church appalls;
And the hapless Soldier's sigh
Runs in blood down Palace walls.

But most thro' midnight streets I hear
How the youthful Harlot's curse
Blasts the new-born Infant's tear,
And blights with plagues the Marriage hearse.

ROBERT BURNS

(1759–1796, Scotland)

John Anderson, My Jo

John Anderson my jo,° John, joy
When we were first acquent,
Your locks were like the raven,
Your bonie brow was brent;
But now your brow is beld, John,
Your locks are like the snow;
But blessings on your frosty
pow,° head
John Anderson, my jo.

John Anderson my jo, John,
We clamb° the hill thegither; climbed

And mony a canty° day, John, merry
  We've had wi' ane anither:
Now we maun totter down, John,
  And hand in hand we'll go,
And sleep thegither at the foot,
  John Anderson, my jo.

AMELIA ALDERSON OPIE

(1769–1853, United States)

Song

A YOUTH for Jane with ardour sighed,
  The maid with sparkling eye;
But to his vows she still replied,
  'I'll hear you by and by.'

'Suspense,' he cries, 'my bloom decays,
  And bids my spirits fly;
Now hear my vows:'. . . . but still she says
  'I'll hear you by and by.'

At length her frowns his love subdue,
  He shuns her scornful eye,
And Emma seeks, who'll hear him woo
  Both now and by and by.

And soon to church he leads the maid,
  When, lo! he sees draw nigh
The now repentant fair who said
  She'd hear him by and by.

'Hear me,' she cries: 'no more in vain
  Thy heart for me shall sigh!'. . . .
'I'm busy now,' said he. . . . 'but, Jane,
  I'll hear you by and by.'

The Despairing Wanderer

OH! 'tis an hour to misery dear!
No noise but dashing waves I hear,
Save hollow blasts that rush around,
For Midnight reigns with horrors crowned.

Lo! clouds in swarthy grandeur sweep
Portentous o'er the troubled deep:
O'er the tall rocks' majestic heads,
Lo! billowy vapour slowly spreads,
While Fancy, as she marks its swell,
Around it throws her magic spell:. . . .
And see! fantastic shapes seem near,
The rocks with added height appear,
And from the mist, to seek the tide,
Gigantic figures darkly glide;
While, with quick step and hurried mien,
Pale Terror leads the shadowy scene.
Again loud blasts I shuddering hear,
Which seem to Fancy's listening ear
To toll some shipwrecked sailor's knell!
Of fear, of grief, of death, they tell.
Perhaps they bade yon foaming tide
Unheard-of-misery scatter wide.
Hail! dread idea, fancy-taught, ...
To me with gloomy pleasure fraught!
I should rejoice the world to see
Distressed, distracted, lost, like me.

Oh! why is phrensy called a curse?
I deem the sense of misery worse:
Come, Madness, come! though pale with fear
Be joy's flushed cheek when thou art near,
On thee I eager glances bend;
Despair, O Madness, calls thee friend!
Come, with thy visions cheer my gloom, ...
Spread o'er my cheek thy feverish bloom,
To my weak form thy strength impart,
From my sunk eye thy lightnings dart!
O come, and on the troubled air
Throw rudely my disordered hair;
Arm me with thy supporting pride,
Let me all ills, all fears deride!
O bid me roam in tattered vest,
Bare to the wintry wind my breast,
Horrors with dauntless eye behold,
And stalk in fancied greatness bold!
Let me, from yonder frowning rock,
With thy shrill scream the billows mock;
With fearless step ascend the steep,
That totters o'er the encroaching deep;
And while the swelling main along
Blue lightning's awful splendors throng, ...

And while upon the foaming tide
Danger and Death in triumph ride,
And thunder rends the ear of Night,
Rousing the form of pale Affright, ...
Let me the mountain torrent quaff,
And midst the war of nature. . . . laugh!

FELICIA DOROTHEA BROWNE

(1793–1835, United States)

Woman on the Field of Battle

Where hath not woman stood,
Strong in affection's might? a reed, upborne
By an o'ermastering current!

Gentle and lovely form,
What didst thou here,
When the fierce battle-storm
Bore down the spear?

Banner and shiver'd crest,
Beside thee strown,
Tell, that amidst the best,
Thy work was done!

Yet strangely, sadly fair,
O'er the wild scene,
Gleams, through its golden hair,
That brow serene.

Low lies the stately head,—
Earth-bound the free;
How gave those haughty dead
A place to thee?

Slumberer! *thine* early bier
Friends should have crown'd,
Many a flower and tear
Shedding around.

Soft voices, clear and young,
Mingling their swell,
Should o'er thy dust have sung
Earth's last farewell.

Sisters, above the grave
  Of thy repose,
Should have bid violets wave
  With the white rose.

Now must the trumpet's note,
  Savage and shrill,
For requiem o'er thee float,
  Thou fair and still!

And the swift charger sweep,
  In full career,
Trampling thy place of sleep,—
  Why camest thou here?

Why?—ask the true heart why
  Woman hath been
Ever, where brave men die,
  Unshrinking seen?

Unto this harvest ground
  Proud reapers came,—
Some, for that stirring sound,
  A warrior's name;

Some, for the stormy play
  And joy of strife;
And some, to fling away
  A weary life;—

But thou, pale sleeper, thou,
  With the slight frame,
And the rich locks, whose glow
  Death cannot tame;

Only one thought, one power,
  Thee could have led,
So, through the tempest's hour,
  To lift thy head!

Only the true, the strong,
  The love, whose trust
Woman's deep soul too long
  Pours on the dust!

The Dreaming Child

Alas! what kind of grief should thy years know?
Thy brow and cheek are smooth as waters be
When no breath troubles them.

BEAUMONT AND FLETCHER

AND is there sadness in *thy* dreams, my boy?
What should the cloud be made of?—blessed child!
Thy spirit, borne upon a breeze of joy,
All day hath ranged through sunshine, clear, yet mild:

And now thou tremblest!—wherefore?—in *thy* soul
There lies no past, no future.—Thou hast heard
No sound of presage from the distance roll,
Thy heart bears traces of no arrowy word.

From thee no love hath gone; thy mind's young eye
Hath look'd not into Death's, and thence become
A questioner of mute Eternity,
A weary searcher for a viewless home:

Nor hath thy sense been quicken'd unto pain,
By feverish watching for some step beloved;
Free are thy thoughts, an ever-changeful train,
Glancing like dewdrops, and as lightly moved.

Yet now, on billows of strange passion toss'd,
How art thou wilder'd in the cave of sleep!
My gentle child! 'midst what dim phantoms lost,
Thus in mysterious anguish dost thou weep?

Awake! they sadden me—those early tears,
First gushings of the strong dark river's flow,
That *must* o'ersweep thy soul with coming years
Th' unfathomable flood of human woe!

Awful to watch, ev'n rolling through a dream,
Forcing wild spray-drops but from childhood's eyes!
Wake, wake! as yet *thy* life's transparent stream
Should wear the tinge of none but summer skies.

Come from the shadow of those realms unknown,
Where now thy thoughts dismay'd and darkling rove;
Come to the kindly region all thine own,
The home, still bright for thee with guardian love.

Happy, fair child! that yet a mother's voice
Can win thee back from visionary strife!—
Oh! shall *my* soul, thus waken'd to rejoice,
Start from the dreamlike wilderness of life?

The Last Tree of the Forest

Whisper, thou Tree, thou lonely Tree,
One, where a thousand stood!
Well might proud tales be told by thee,
Last of the solemn wood!

Dwells there no voice amidst thy boughs,
With leaves yet darkly green?
Stillness is round, and noontide glows—
Tell us what thou hast seen.

"I have seen the forest shadows lie
Where men now reap the corn;
I have seen the kingly chase rush by,
Through the deep glades at morn.

"With the glance of many a gallant spear,
And the wave of many a plume,
And the bounding of a hundred deer,
It hath lit the woodland's gloom.

"I have seen the knight and his train ride past,
With his banner borne on high;
O'er all my leaves there was brightness cast
From his gleaming panoply.

"The Pilgrim at my feet hath laid
His palm branch 'midst the flowers,
And told his beads, and meekly pray'd,
Kneeling, at vesper-hours.

"And the merry-men of wild and glen,
In the green array they wore,
Have feasted here with the red wine's cheer,
And the hunter's song of yore.

"And the minstrel, resting in my shade,
Hath made the forest ring

With the lordly tales of the high Crusade,
Once loved by chief and king.

"But now the noble forms are gone,
That walk'd the earth of old;
The soft wind hath a mournful tone,
The sunny light looks cold.

"There is no glory left us now,
Like the glory with the dead:—
I would that where they slumber low
My latest leaves were shed!"

Oh! Thou dark Tree, thou lonely Tree,
That mournest for the past!
A peasant's home in thy shades I see,
Embower'd from every blast.

A lovely and a mirthful sound
Of laughter meets mine ear;
For the poor man's children sport around
On the turf, with nought to fear.

And roses lend that cabin's wall
A happy summer-glow;
And the open door stands free to all,
For it recks not of a foe.

And the village bells are on the breeze,
That stirs thy leaf, dark Tree!
How can I mourn, 'midst things like these,
For the stormy past, with thee?

WILLIAM WORDSWORTH

(1770–1850, England)

A Slumber Did My Spirit Seal

A slumber did my spirit seal;° cushion, overprotect
I had no human fears:
She seemed a thing that could not feel
The touch of earthly years.

No motion has she now, no force;
She neither hears nor sees;
Rolled round in earth's diurnal° course, daily
With rocks, and stones, and trees.

I Wandered Lonely As a Cloud

I wandered lonely as a cloud
That floats on high o'er vales and hills,
When all at once I saw a crowd,
A host, of golden daffodils;
Beside the lake, beneath the trees,
Fluttering and dancing in the breeze.

Continuous as the stars that shine
And twinkle on the milky way,
They stretched in never-ending line
Along the margin of a bay:
Ten thousand saw I at a glance,
Tossing their heads in sprightly dance.

The waves beside them danced; but they
Outdid the sparkling waves in glee;
A poet could not but be gay,
In such a jocund° company; happy
I gazed—and gazed—but little thought
What wealth the show to me had brought:

For oft, when on my couch I lie
In vacant or in pensive mood,
They flash upon that inward eye
Which is the bliss of solitude;
And then my heart with pleasure fills,
And dances with the daffodils.

The World Is Too Much with Us

The world is too much with us; late and soon,
Getting and spending, we lay waste our powers;
Little we see in Nature that is ours;
We have given our hearts away, a sordid boon!° gift
This Sea that bares her bosom to the moon,
The winds that will be howling at all hours,
And are up-gathered now like sleeping flowers,
For this, for everything, we are out of tune;
It moves us not.—Great God! I'd rather be
A Pagan suckled in a creed outworn;
So might I, standing on this pleasant lea,

Have glimpses that would make me less forlorn;
Have sight of Proteus[1] rising from the sea;
Or hear old Triton[2] blow his wreathéd horn.

SAMUEL TAYLOR COLERIDGE

(1772–1834, England)

Kubla Khan

OR A VISION IN A DREAM, A FRAGMENT

In Xanadu did Kubla Khan
A stately pleasure-dome decree:
Where Alph, the sacred river, ran
Through caverns measureless to man
  Down to a sunless sea.
So twice five miles of fertile ground
With walls and towers were girdled round:
And there were gardens bright with sinuous rills,
Where blossomed many an incense-bearing tree;
And here were forests ancient as the hills,
Enfolding sunny spots of greenery.

But oh! that deep romantic chasm which slanted
Down the green hill athwart a cedarn cover!
A savage place! as holy and enchanted
As e'er beneath a waning moon was haunted
By woman wailing for her demon-lover!
And from this chasm, with ceaseless turmoil seething,
As if this earth in fast thick pants were breathing,
A mighty fountain momently was forced:
Amid whose swift half-intermitted burst
Huge fragments vaulted like rebounding hail,
Or chaffy grain beneath the thresher's flail:
And 'mid these dancing rocks at once and ever
It flung up momently the sacred river.
Five miles meandering with a mazy motion
Through wood and dale the sacred river ran,
Then reached the caverns measureless to man,
And sank in tumult to a lifeless ocean:

THE WORLD IS TOO MUCH WITH US [1]**Proteus** Greek god who changes shape to imitate things in nature. [2]**Triton** Greek sea god whose horn calms the waves.

And 'mid this tumult Kubla heard from far
Ancestral voices prophesying war!
The shadow of the dome of pleasure
Floated midway on the waves;
Where was heard the mingled measure
From the fountain and the caves.
It was a miracle of rare device,
A sunny pleasure-dome with caves of ice!

A damsel with a dulcimer
In a vision once I saw:
It was an Abyssinian maid,
And on her dulcimer she played,
Singing of Mount Abora.
Could I revive within me
Her symphony and song,
To such a deep delight 'twould win me,
That with music loud and long,
I would build that dome in air,
That sunny dome! those caves of ice!
And all who heard should see them there,
And all should cry, Beware! Beware!
His flashing eyes, his floating hair!
Weave a circle round him thrice,
And close your eyes with holy dread,
For he on honey-dew hath fed,
And drunk the milk of Paradise.

GEORGE GORDON, LORD BYRON

(1788–1824, England)

When a Man Hath No Freedom to Fight For at Home

When a man hath no freedom to fight for at home,
Let him combat for that of his neighbors;
Let him think of the glories of Greece and of Rome,
And get knocked on his head for his labors.

To do good to mankind is the chivalrous plan,
And is always as nobly requited;
Then battle for freedom wherever you can,
And, if not shot or hanged, you'll get knighted.

PERCY BYSSHE SHELLEY

(1792–1822, England)

Ozymandias[1]

I met a traveler from an antique land
Who said: Two vast and trunkless legs of stone
Stand in the desert . . . Near them, on the sand,
Half sunk, a shattered visage lies, whose frown,
And wrinkled lip, and sneer of cold command,
Tell that its sculptor well those passions read
Which yet survive, stamped on these lifeless things,
The hand that mocked them, and the heart that fed:
And on the pedestal these words appear:
"My name is Ozymandias, king of kings:
Look on my works, ye Mighty, and despair!"
Nothing beside remains. Round the decay
Of that colossal wreck, boundless and bare
The lone and level sands stretch far away.

JOHN KEATS

(1795–1821, England)

On First Looking into Chapman's[1] Homer

Much have I traveled in the realms of gold,
And many goodly states and kingdoms seen;
Round many western islands have I been
Which bards in fealty° to Apollo hold. allegiance
Oft of one wide expanse had I been told
That deep-browed Homer ruled as his demesne;° domain
Yet did I never breathe its pure serene° atmosphere
Till I heard Chapman speak out loud and bold:
Then felt I like some watcher of the skies
When a new planet swims into his ken;
Or like stout Cortez[2] when with eagle eyes
He stared at the Pacific—and all his men
Looked at each other with a wild surmise—
Silent, upon a peak in Darien.

OZYMANDIAS [1]**Ozymandias** another mane for Rameses II, Pharoah of Egypt. *ON FIRST LOOKING INTO CHAPMAN'S HOMER* [1]**Chapman** translator of Homer's epics. [2]**Cortez** Keats forgot his history; it was Balboa he meant.

To Autumn

I

Season of mists and mellow fruitfulness,
Close bosom-friend of the maturing sun;
Conspiring with him how to load and bless
With fruit the vines that round the thatch-eves run;
To bend with apples the mossed cottage-trees,
And fill all fruit with ripeness to the core;
To swell the gourd, and plump the hazel shells
With a sweet kernel; to set budding more,
And still more, later flowers for the bees,
Until they think warm days will never cease,
For Summer has o'er-brimmed their clammy cells.

II

Who hath not seen thee oft amid thy store?
Sometimes whoever seeks abroad may find
Thee sitting careless on a granary floor,
Thy hair soft-lifted by the winnowing wind;
Or on a half-reaped furrow sound asleep,
Drowsed with the fume of poppies, while thy hook
Spares the next swath and all its twinèd flowers:
And sometimes like a gleaner thou dost keep
Steady thy laden head across a brook;
Or by a cider-press, with patient look,
Thou watchest the last oozings hours by hours.

III

Where are the songs of Spring? Aye, where are they?
Think not of them, thou hast thy music too,—
While barred clouds bloom the soft-dying day,
And touch the stubble-plains with rosy hue;
Then in a wailful choir the small gnats mourn
Among the river sallows,° borne aloft — willows
Or sinking as the light wind lives or dies;
And full-grown lambs loud bleat from hilly bourn;
Hedge-crickets sing; and now with treble soft
The red-breast whistles from a garden-croft;
And gathering swallows twitter in the skies.

MARY HOWITT

(1799–1888, United States)

Childhood

Oh, when I was a little child,
  My life was full of pleasure;
I had four-and-twenty living things,
  And many another treasure.

But chiefest was my sister dear,
  Oh, how I loved my sister!
I never played at all with joy,
  If from my side I missed her.

I can remember many a time,
  Up in the morning early,—
Up in the morn by break of day,
  When summer dews hung pearly;

Out in the fields what joy it was,
  While the cowslip yet was bending,
To see the large round moon grow dim,
  And the early lark ascending!

I can remember, too, we rose
  When the winter stars shone brightly;
'Twas an easy thing to shake off sleep
  From spirits strong and sprightly.

How beautiful were those winter skies,
  All frosty-bright and unclouded,
And the garden-trees, like cypresses,
  Looked black, in the darkness shrouded!

Then the deep, deep snows were beautiful,
  That fell through the long night stilly,
When behold, at morn, like a silent plain,
  Lay the country wild and hilly!

And the fir-trees down by the garden side,
  In their blackness towered more stately;
And the lower trees were feathered with snow,
  That were bare and brown so lately.

And then, when the rare hoar-frost would come,
'Twas all like a dream of wonder,
When over us grew the crystal trees,
And the crystal plants grew under!

The garden all was enchanted land;
All silent and without motion,
Like a sudden growth of the stalactite,
Or the corallines of ocean!

'Twas all like a fairy forest then,
Where the diamond cards were growing,
And within each branch the emerald green
And the ruby red were glowing.

I remember many a day we spent
In the bright hay-harvest meadow;
The glimmering heat of the noonday ground,
And the hazy depth of shadow.

I can remember, as to-day
The corn-field and the reaping,
The rustling of the harvest-sheaves,
And the harvest-wain's upheaping:

I can feel this hour as if I lay
Adown 'neath the hazel bushes,
And as if we wove, for pastime wild,
Our grenadier-caps of rushes.

And every flower within that field
To my memory's eye comes flitting,
The chiccory-flower, like a blue cockade,
For a fairy-knight befitting.

The willow-herb by the water side,
With its fruit-like scent so mellow;
The gentian blue on the marly hill,
And the snap-dragon white and yellow.

I know where the hawthorn groweth red;
Where pink grows the way-side yarrow;
I remember the wastes of woad and broom,
And the shrubs of the red rest-harrow.

I know where the blue geranium grows,
And the stork's-bill small and musky;

Where the rich osmunda groweth brown,
  And the wormwood white and dusky.

There was a forest anigh our home,—
  A forest so old and hoary;
How we loved in its ancient glooms to be,
  And remember its bygone story!

We sate in the shade of its mighty trees,
  When the summer noon was glowing
And heard in the depths of its undergroth
  The pebbly waters flowing.

We quenched our thirst at the forest-well;
  We ate of the forest berry;
And the time we spent in the good greenwood,
  Like the times of song, were merry.

We had no crosses then, no cares;
  We were children like yourselves then;
And we danced and sang, and made us mirth,
  Like the dancing moonlight elves then!

The Spider and the Fly

AN APOLOGUE
A NEW VERSION OF AN OLD STORY

"WILL you walk into my parlor?" said the Spider to the Fly,
"'Tis the prettiest little parlor that ever you did spy;
The way into my parlor is up a winding stair,
And I've many curious things to show when you are there."
"Oh no, no," said the little Fly, "to ask me is in vain,
For who goes up your winding stair can ne'er come down again."

"I'm sure you must be weary, dear, with soaring up so high;
Will you rest upon my little bed?" said the Spider to the Fly.
"There are pretty curtains drawn around; the sheets are fine and thin,
And if you like to rest awhile, I'll snugly tuck you in!"
"Oh no, no," said the little Fly, "for I've often heard it said,
They never, never wake again, who sleep upon your bed!"

Said the cunning Spider to the Fly, "Dear friend, what can I do,
To prove the warm affection I've always felt for you?

I have within my pantry good store of all that's nice;
I'm sure you're very welcome—will you please to take a slice?"
"Oh no, no," said the little Fly, "kind sir, that cannot be,
I've heard what's in your pantry, and I do not wish to see!"

"Sweet creature!" said the Spider, "you're witty and you're wise,
How handsome are your gauzy wings, how brilliant are your eyes!
I've a little looking-glass upon my parlor shelf,
If you'll step in one moment, dear, you shall behold yourself."
"I thank you, gentle sir," she said, "for what you're pleased to say,
And bidding you good morning now, I'll call another day."

The Spider turned him round about, and went into his den,
For well he knew the silly Fly would soon come back again:
So he wove a subtle web, in a little corner sly,
And set his table ready, to dine upon the Fly.
Then he came out to his door again, and merrily did sing,
"Come hither, hither, pretty Fly, with the pearl and silver wing;
Your robes are green and purple—there's a crest upon your head;
Your eyes are like the diamond bright, but mine are dull as lead!"
Alas, alas! how very soon this silly little Fly,
Hearing his wily, flattering words, came slowly flitting by;
With buzzing wings she hung aloft, then near and nearer drew,
Thinking only of her brilliant eyes, and green and purple hue—
Thinking only of her crested head—poor foolish thing! At last,
Up jumped the cunning Spider, and fiercely held her fast.
He dragged her up his winding stair, into his dismal den,
Within his little parlor—but she ne'er came out again!

And now, dear little children, who may this story read,
To idle, silly, flattering words, I pray you ne'er give heed;
Unto an evil counsellor, close heart, and ear, and eye,
And take a lesson from this tale, of the Spider and the Fly.

ELIZABETH BARRETT BROWNING

(1806–1861, England)

How Do I Love Thee?

How do I love thee? Let me count the ways.
I love thee to the depth and breadth and height
My soul can reach, when feeling out of sight
For the ends of Being and ideal Grace.
I love thee to the level of everyday's

Most quiet need, by sun and candle-light.
I love thee freely, as men strive for Right;
I love thee purely, as they turn from Praise.
I love thee with the passion put to use
In my old griefs, and with my childhood's faith.
I love thee with a love I seemed to lose
With my lost saints—I love thee with the breath,
Smiles, tears, of all my life!—and, if God choose,
I shall but love thee better after death.

OLIVER WENDELL HOLMES

(1809–1894, United States)

The Height of the Ridiculous

I wrote some lines once on a time
 In wondrous merry mood,
And thought, as usual, men would say
 They were exceeding good.

They were so queer, so very queer,
 I laughed as I would die;
Albeit, in the general way,
 A sober man am I.

I called my servant, and he came;
 How kind it was of him
To mind a slender man like me,
 He of the mighty limb!

"These to the printer," I exclaimed,
 And, in my humorous way,
I added, (as a trifling jest,)
 "There'll be the devil to pay."

He took the paper, and I watched,
 And saw him peep within;
At the first line he read, his face
 Was all upon the grin.

He read the next; the grin grew broad,
 And shot from ear to ear;
He read the third; a chuckling noise
 I now began to hear.

The fourth; he broke into a roar;
    The fifth; his waistband split;
The sixth; he burst five buttons off,
    And tumbled in a fit.

Ten days and nights, with sleepless eye,
    I watched that wretched man,
And since, I never dare to write
    As funny as I can.

EDGAR ALLAN POE

(1809–1849, United States)

Annabel Lee

It was many and many a year ago,
        In a kingdom by the sea,
That a maiden there lived whom you may know
        By the name of Annabel Lee;
And this maiden she lived with no other thought
        Than to love and be loved by me.

She was a child and *I* was a child,
        In this kingdom by the sea,
But we loved with a love that was more than love—
        I and my Annabel Lee—
With a love that the wingéd seraphs of Heaven
        Coveted her and me.

And this was the reason that, long ago,
        In this kingdom by the sea,
A wind blew out of a cloud by night
        Chilling my Annabel Lee;
So that her highborn kinsmen came
        And bore her away from me,
To shut her up in a sepulchre
        In this kingdom by the sea.

The angels, not half so happy in Heaven,
        Went envying her and me:
Yes! that was the reason (as all men know,
        In this kingdom by the sea)
That the wind came out of the cloud, chilling
        And killing my Annabel Lee.

But our love it was stronger by far than the love
Of those who were older than we—
Of many far wiser than we—
And neither the angels in Heaven above
Nor the demons down under the sea,
Can ever dissever my soul from the soul
Of the beautiful Annabel Lee:

For the moon never beams without bringing me dreams
Of the beautiful Annabel Lee;
And the stars never rise but I see the bright eyes
Of the beautiful Annabel Lee;
And so, all the night-tide, I lie down by the side
Of my darling, my darling, my life and my bride,
In her sepulchre there by the sea—
In her tomb by the side of the sea.

The Bells

I.

Hear the sledges with the bells—
Silver bells!
What a world of merriment their melody foretells!
How they tinkle, tinkle, tinkle,
In the icy air of night!
While the stars that oversprinkle
All the heavens, seem to twinkle
With a crystalline delight;
Keeping time, time, time,
In a sort of Runic rhyme,
To the tintinnabulation that so musically wells
From the bells, bells, bells, bells,
Bells, bells, bells—
From the jingling and the tinkling of the bells.

II.

Hear the mellow wedding bells—
Golden bells!
What a world of happiness their harmony foretells!
Through the balmy air of night
How they ring out their delight!—

From the molten-golden notes,
And all in tune,
What a liquid ditty floats
To the turtle-dove that listens, while she gloats
On the moon!
Oh, from out the sounding cells,
What a gush of euphony voluminously wells!
How it swells!
How it dwells
On the Future!—how it tells
Of the rapture that impels
To the swinging and the ringing
Of the bells, bells, bells—
Of the bells, bells, bells, bells,
Bells, bells, bells—
To the rhyming and the chiming of the bells!

III.

Hear the loud alarum bells—
Brazen bells!
What a tale of terror, now, their turbulency tells!
In the startled ear of night
How they scream out their affright!
Too much horrified to speak,
They can only shriek, shriek,
Out of tune,
In a clamorous appealing to the mercy of the fire,
In a mad expostulation with the deaf and frantic fire,
Leaping higher, higher, higher,
With a desperate desire,
And a resolute endeavor
Now—now to sit, or never,
By the side of the pale-faced moon.
Oh, the bells, bells, bells!
What a tale their terror tells
Of Despair!
How they clang, and clash, and roar!
What a horror they outpour
On the bosom of the palpitating air!
Yet the ear, it fully knows,
By the twanging
And the clanging,
How the danger ebbs and flows;
Yet the ear distinctly tells,

In the jangling
And the wrangling,
How the danger sinks and swells,
By the sinking or the swelling in the anger of the bells—
Of the bells,—
Of the bells, bells, bells, bells,
Bells, bells, bells—
In the clamor and the clangor of the bells!

IV.

Hear the tolling of the bells—
Iron bells!
What a world of solemn thought their monody compels!
In the silence of the night,
How we shiver with affright
At the melancholy menace of their tone!
For every sound that floats
From the rust within their throats
Is a groan.
And the people—ah, the people—
They that dwell up in the steeple,
All alone,
And who tolling, tolling, tolling,
In that muffled monotone,
Feel a glory in so rolling
On the human heart a stone—
They are neither man nor woman—
They are neither brute nor human—
They are Ghouls:—
And their king it is who tolls:—
And he rolls, rolls, rolls,
Rolls
A pæan from the bells!
And his merry bosom swells
With the pæan of the bells!
And he dances, and he yells;
Keeping time, time, time,
In a sort of Runic rhyme,
To the pæan of the bells—
Of the bells:—
Keeping time, time, time,
In a sort of Runic rhyme,
To the throbbing of the bells—
Of the bells, bells, bells—
To the sobbing of the bells;

Keeping time, time, time,
As he knells, knells, knells,
In a happy Runic rhyme,
To the rolling of the bells—
Of the bells, bells, bells—
To the rolling of the bells—
Of the bells, bells, bells, bells,
Bells, bells, bells—
To the moaning and the groaning of the bells.

ALFRED, LORD TENNYSON

(1809–1892, England)

Ulysses

It little profits that an idle king,
By this still hearth, among these barren crags,
Matched with an aged wife, I mete and dole
Unequal laws unto a savage race,
That hoard, and sleep, and feed, and know not me.
I cannot rest from travel; I will drink
Life to the lees. All times I have enjoyed
Greatly, have suffered greatly, both with those
That loved me, and alone, on shore, and when
Through scudding drifts the rainy Hyades[1]
Vext the dim sea. I am become a name;
For always roaming with a hungry heart
Much have I seen and known—cities of men
And manners, climates, councils, governments,
Myself not least, but honored of them all,—
And drunk delight of battle with my peers,
Far on the ringing plains of windy Troy.
I am a part of all that I have met;
Yet all experience is an arch wherethrough
Gleams that untraveled world whose margin fades
For ever and for ever when I move.
How dull it is to pause, to make an end,
To rust unburnished, not to shine in use!
As though to breathe were life! Life piled on life
Were all too little and of one to me
Little remains; but every hour is saved

ULYSSES [1]**Hyades** stars that signal rain.

From that eternal silence, something more,
A bringer of new things; and vile it were
For some three suns to store and hoard myself,
And this gray spirit yearning in desire
To follow knowledge like a sinking star,
Beyond the utmost bound of human thought.
This is my son, mine own Telemachus,
To whom I leave the scepter and the isle,
Well-loved of me discerning to fulfill
This labor, by slow prudence to make mild
A rugged people, and through soft degrees
Subdue them to the useful and the good.
Most blameless is he, centered in the sphere
Of common duties, decent not to fail
In offices of tenderness, and pay
Meet adoration to my household gods,
When I am gone. He works his work, I mine.
There lies the port; the vessel puffs her sail;
There gloom the dark, broad seas. My mariners,
Souls that have toiled, and wrought, and thought with me,
That ever with a frolic welcome took
The thunder and the sunshine, and opposed
Free hearts, free foreheads—you and I are old;
Old age hath yet his honor and his toil.
Death closes all; but something ere the end,
Some work of noble note, may yet be done,
Not unbecoming men that strove with gods.
The lights begin to twinkle from the rocks;
The long day wanes, the slow moon climbs; the deep
Moans round with many voices. Come, my friends,
'Tis not too late to seek a newer world.
Push off, and sitting well in order smite
The sounding furrows, for my purpose holds
To sail beyond the sunset, and the baths
Of all the western stars, until I die.
It may be that the gulfs will wash us down;
It may be we shall touch the Happy Isles,[2]
And see the great Achilles, whom we knew.
Though much is taken, much abides; and though
We are not now that strength which in old days
Moved earth and heaven, that which we are, we are,
One equal temper of heroic hearts,
Made weak by time and fate, but strong in will
To strive, to seek, to find, and not to yield.

---

[2]**Happy Isles** home of heroes after death.

Now Sleeps the Crimson Petal

Now sleeps the crimson petal, now the white;
Nor waves the cypress in the palace walk;
Nor winks the gold fin in the porphyry font.
The firefly wakens; waken thou with me.

Now droops the milk-white peacock like a ghost,
And like a ghost she glimmers on to me.

Now lies the Earth all Danaë[1] to the stars,
And all thy heart lies open unto me.

Now slides the silent meteor on, and leaves
A shining furrow, as thy thoughts in me.

Now folds the lily all her sweetness up,
And slips into the bosom of the lake.
So fold thyself, my dearest, thou, and slip
Into my bosom and be lost in me.

The Eagle

Fragment

He clasps the crag with crooked hands;
Close to the sun in lonely lands,
Ringed with the azure world, he stands.

The wrinkled sea beneath him crawls;
He watches from his mountain walls,
And like a thunderbolt he falls.

ROBERT BROWNING

(1812–1889, England)

My Last Duchess

Ferrara

That's my last Duchess painted on the wall,
Looking as if she were alive. I call
That piece a wonder, now; Frà Pandolf's hands

NOW SLEEPS THE CRIMSON PETAL [1]**Danaë** Greek maiden kept in a locked tower who was visited by Zeus in the form of a shower of gold.

Worked busily a day, and there she stands.
Will 't please you sit and look at her? I said
"Frà Pandolf" by design, for never read
Strangers like you that pictured countenance,
The depth and passion of its earnest glance,
But to myself they turned (since none puts by
The curtain I have drawn for you, but I)
And seemed as they would ask me, if they durst,
How such a glance came there; so, not the first
Are you to turn and ask thus. Sir, 'twas not
Her husband's presence only, called that spot
Of joy into the Duchess' cheek; perhaps
Frà Pandolf chanced to say, "Her mantle laps
Over my lady's wrist too much," or "Paint
Must never hope to reproduce the faint
Half-flush that dies along her throat." Such stuff
Was courtesy, she thought, and cause enough
For calling up that spot of joy. She had
A heart—how shall I say?—too soon made glad,
Too easily impressed; she liked whate'er
She looked on, and her looks went everywhere.
Sir, 'twas all one! My favor at her breast,
The dropping of the daylight in the West,
The bough of cherries some officious fool
Broke in the orchard for her, the white mule
She rode with round the terrace—all and each
Would draw from her alike the approving speech,
Or blush, at least. She thanked men,—good! but thanked
Somehow—I know not how—as if she ranked
My gift of a nine-hundred-years-old name
With anybody's gift. Who'd stoop to blame
This sort of trifling? Even had you skill
In speech—which I have not—to make your will
Quite clear to such an one, and say, "Just this
Or that in you disgusts me; here you miss,
Or there exceed the mark."—and if she let
Herself be lessoned so, nor plainly set
Her wits to yours, forsooth, and made excuse—
E'en then would be some stooping; and I choose
Never to stoop. Oh, sir, she smiled, no doubt,
Whene'er I passed her; but who passed without
Much the same smile? This grew; I gave commands;
Then all smiles stopped together. There she stands
As if alive. Will 't please you rise? We'll meet
The company below, then. I repeat,
The Count your master's known munificence
Is ample warrant that no just pretense
Of mine for dowry will be disallowed;

Though his fair daughter's self, as I avowed
At starting, is my object. Nay, we'll go
Together down, sir. Notice Neptune, though,
Taming a sea-horse, thought a rarity,
Which Claus of Innsbruck cast in bronze for me!

Home-Thoughts, From Abroad

1

Oh, to be in England
Now that April's there,
And whoever wakes in England
Sees, some morning, unaware,
That the lowest boughs and the brushwood sheaf
Round the elm-tree bole are in tiny leaf,
While the chaffinch sings on the orchard bough
In England—now!

2

And after April, when May follows,
And the whitethroat builds, and all the swallows!
Hark, where my blossomed pear-tree in the hedge
Leans to the field and scatters on the clover
Blossoms and dewdrops—at the bent spray's edge—
That's the wise thrush; he sings each song twice over,
Lest you should think he never could recapture
The first fine careless rapture!
And though the fields look rough with hoary dew
All will be gay when noontide wakes anew
The buttercups, the little children's dower
—Far brighter than this gaudy melon-flower!

HERMAN MELVILLE

(1819–1891, United States)

A Utilitarian View of the Monitor's Fight

Plain be the phrase, yet apt the verse,
More ponderous than nimble;
For since grimed War here laid aside

His Orient pomp, 'twould ill befit
Overmuch to ply
The rhyme's barbaric cymbal.

Hail to victory without the gaud
Of glory; zeal that needs no fans
Of banners; plain mechanic power
Plied cogently in War now placed—
Where War belongs—
Among the trades and artisans.

Yet this was battle, and intense—
Beyond the strife of fleets heroic;
Deadlier, closer, calm 'mid storm;
No passion; all went on by crank,
Pivot, and screw,
And calculations of caloric.

Needless to dwell; the story's known.
The ringing of those plates on plates
Still ringeth round the world—
The clangor of that blacksmiths' fray.
The anvil-din
Resounds this message from the Fates:

War shall yet be, and to the end;
But war-paint shows the streaks of weather;
War yet shall be, but warriors.
Are now but operatives; War's made
Less grand than Peace,
And a singe runs through lace and feather.

WALT WHITMAN

(1819–1892, United States)

When I Heard the Learn'd Astronomer

When I heard the learn'd astronomer,
When the proofs, the figures, were ranged in columns before me,
When I was shown the charts and diagrams, to add, divide, and measure them,
When I sitting heard the astronomer where he lectured with much applause in the lecture-room,
How soon unaccountable I became tired and sick,

Till rising and gliding out I wander'd off by myself,
In the mystical moist night-air, and from time to time,
Look'd up in perfect silence at the stars.

Out of the Cradle Endlessly Rocking

Out of the cradle endlessly rocking,
Out of the mocking-bird's throat, the musical shuttle,
Out of the Ninth-month midnight,
Over the sterile sands and the fields beyond, where the child leaving his bed wander'd alone, bareheaded, barefoot,
Down from the shower'd halo,
Up from the mystic play of shadows twining and twisting as if they were alive,
Out from the patches of briers and blackberries,
From the memories of the bird that chanted to me,
From your memories sad brother, from the fitful risings and fallings I heard,
From under that yellow half-moon late-risen and swollen as if with tears,
From those beginning notes of yearning and love there in the mist,
From the thousand responses of my heart never to cease,
From the myriad thence-arous'd words,
From the word stronger and more delicious than any,
From such as now they start the scene revisiting,
As a flock, twittering, rising, or overhead passing,
Borne hither, ere all eludes me, hurriedly,
A man, yet by these tears a little boy again,
Throwing myself on the sand, confronting the waves,
I, chanter of pains and joys, uniter of here and hereafter,
Taking all hints to use them, but swiftly leaping beyond them,
A reminiscence sing.

Once Paumanok,[1]
When the lilac-scent was in the air and Fifth-month grass was growing,
Up this seashore in some briers,
Two feather'd guests from Alabama, two together,
And their nest, and four light-green eggs spotted with brown,
And every day the he-bird to and fro near at hand,
And every day the she-bird crouch'd on her nest, silent, with bright eyes,
And every day I, a curious boy, never too close, never disturbing them,
Cautiously peering, absorbing, translating.

OUT OF THE CRADLE ENDLESSLY ROCKING [1]**Paumanok** American Indian name for Long Island.

Shine! shine! shine!
Pour down your warmth, great sun!
While we bask, we two together.

Two together!
Winds blow south, or winds blow north,
Day come white, or night come black,
Home, or rivers and mountains from home,
Singing all time, minding no time,
While we two keep together.

Till of a sudden,
May-be kill'd, unknown to her mate,
One forenoon the she-bird crouch'd not on the nest,
Nor return'd that afternoon, nor the next,
Nor ever appear'd again.

And thenceforward all summer in the sound of the sea,
And at night under the full of the moon in calmer weather,
Over the hoarse surging of the sea,
Or flitting from brier to brier by day,
I saw, I heard at intervals the remaining one, the he-bird,
The solitary guest from Alabama.

Blow! blow! blow!
Blow up sea-winds along Paumanok's shore;
I wait and I wait till you blow my mate to me.

Yes, when the stars glisten'd,
All night along on the prong of a moss-scallop'd stake,
Down almost amid the slapping waves,
Sat the lone singer wonderful causing tears.

He call'd on his mate,
He pour'd forth the meanings which I of all men know.

Yes my brother I know,
The rest might not, but I have treasur'd every note,
For more than once dimly down to the beach gliding,
Silent, avoiding the moonbeams, blending myself with the shadows,
Recalling now the obscure shapes, the echoes, the sounds and sight after their sorts,
The white arms out in the breakers tirelessly tossing,
I, with bare feet, a child, the wind wafting my hair,
Listen'd long and long.

Listen'd to keep, to sing, now translating the notes,
Following you my brother.

Soothe! soothe! soothe!
Close on its wave soothes the wave behind,
And again another behind embracing and lapping, every one close,
But my love soothes not me, not me.

Low hangs the moon, it rose late,
It is lagging—O I think it is heavy with love, with love.

O madly the sea pushes upon the land,
With love, with love.

O night! do I not see my love fluttering out among the breakers?
What is that little black thing I see there in the white?

Loud! loud! loud!
Loud I call to you, my love!
High and clear I shoot my voice over the waves,
Surely you must know who is here, is here,
You must know who I am, my love.

Low-hanging moon!
What is that dusky spot in your brown yellow?
O it is the shape, the shape of my mate!
O moon do not keep her from me any longer.

Land! land! O land!
Whichever way I turn, O I think you could give me my mate back again if you only would,
For I am almost sure I see her dimly whichever way I look.

O rising stars!
Perhaps the one I want so much will rise, will rise with some of you.

O throat! O trembling throat!
Sound clearer through the atmosphere!
Pierce the woods, the earth,
Somewhere listening to catch you must be the one I want.

Shake out carols!
Solitary here, the night's carols!
Carols of lonesome love! death's carols!
Carols under that lagging, yellow, waning moon!
O under that moon where she droops almost down into the sea!
O reckless despairing carols.

But soft! sink low!
Soft! let me just murmur,
And do you wait a moment you husky-nois'd sea,
For somewhere I believe I heard my mate responding to me,
So faint, I must be still, be still to listen,
But not altogether still, for then she might not come immediately to me.

Hither my love!
Here I am! here!
With this just-sustain'd note I announce myself to you,
This gentle call is for you my love, for you.

Do not be decoy'd elsewhere,
That is the whistle of the wind, it is not my voice,
That is the fluttering, the fluttering of the spray,
Those are the shadows of leaves.

O darkness! O in vain!
O I am very sick and sorrowful.

O brown halo in the sky near the moon, drooping upon the sea!
O troubled reflection in the sea!
O throat! O throbbing heart!
And I singing uselessly, uselessly all the night.

O past! O happy life! O songs of joy!
In the air, in the woods, over fields,
Loved! loved! loved! loved! loved!
But my mate no more, no more with me!
We two together no more.

The aria sinking,
All else continuing, the stars shining,
The winds blowing, the notes of the bird continuous echoing,
With angry moans the fierce old mother incessantly moaning,
On the sands of Paumanok's shore gray and rustling,
The yellow half-moon enlarged, sagging down, drooping, the face of the sea almost touching,
The boy ecstatic, with his bare feet the waves, with his hair the atmosphere dallying,
The love in the heart long pent, now loose, now at last tumultuously bursting,
The aria's meaning, the ears, the soul, swiftly depositing,
The strange tears down the cheeks coursing,
The colloquy there, the trio, each uttering,
The undertone, the savage old mother incessantly crying.

To the boy's soul's questions sullenly timing, some drown'd secret hissing,
To the outsetting bard.

Demon or bird! (said the boy's soul,)
Is it indeed toward your mate you sing? or is it really to me?
For I, that was a child, my tongue's use sleeping, now I have heard you,
Now in a moment I know what I am for, I awake,
And already a thousand singers, a thousand songs, clearer, louder and more sorrowful than yours,
A thousand warbling echoes have started to life within me, never to die.

O you singer solitary, singing by yourself, projecting me,
O solitary me listening, never more shall I cease perpetuating you,
Never more shall I escape, never more the reverberations,
Never more the cries of unsatisfied love be absent from me,
Never again leave me to be the peaceful child I was before what there in the night,
By the sea under the yellow and sagging moon,
The messenger there arous'd, the fire, the sweet hell within,
The unknown want, the destiny of me.

O give me the clew! (it lurks in the night here somewhere,)
O if I am to have so much, let me have more!
A word then, (for I will conquer it,)
The word final, superior to all,
Subtle, sent up—what is it?—I listen:
Are you whispering it, and have been all the time, you sea-waves?
Is that it from your liquid rims and wet sands?

Whereto answering, the sea,
Delaying not, hurrying not,
Whisper'd me through the night, and very plainly before daybreak,
Lisp'd to me the low and delicious word death,
And again, death, death, death, death,
Hissing melodious, neither like the bird nor like my arous'd child's heart,
But edging near as privately for me rustling at my feet,
Creeping thence steadily up to my ears and laving me softly all over,
Death, death, death, death, death.

Which I do not forget,
But fuse the song of my dusky demon and brother,
That he sang to me in the moonlight on Paumanok's gray beach,
With the thousand responsive songs at random,
My own songs awaked from that hour,
And with them the key, the word up from the waves,
The word of the sweetest song and all songs,

That strong and delicious word which, creeping to my feet,
(Or like some old crone rocking the cradle, swathed in sweet garments, bending aside,)
The sea whisper'd me.

A Noiseless Patient Spider

A noiseless patient spider,
I mark'd where on a little promontory it stood isolated,
Mark'd how to explore the vacant vast surrounding,
It launch'd forth filament, filament, filament, out of itself,
Ever unreeling them, ever tirelessly speeding them.

And you O my soul where you stand,
Surrounded, detached, in measureless oceans of space,
Ceaselessly musing, venturing, throwing, seeking the spheres to connect them,
Till the bridge you will need be form'd, till the ductile anchor hold,
Till the gossamer thread you fling catch somewhere, O my soul.

MATTHEW ARNOLD

(1822–1888, England)

Dover Beach

The sea is calm tonight.
The tide is full, the moon lies fair
Upon the straits;—on the French coast the light
Gleams and is gone; the cliffs of England stand,
Glimmering and vast, out in the tranquil bay.
Come to the window, sweet is the night-air!

Only, from the long line of spray
Where the sea meets the moon-blanched land,
Listen! you hear the grating roar
Of pebbles which the waves draw back, and fling,
At their return, up the high strand,
Begin, and cease, and then again begin,
With tremulous cadence slow, and bring
The eternal note of sadness in.

Sophocles long ago
Heard it on the Ægæan, and it brought
Into his mind the turbid ebb and flow
Of human misery; we
Find also in the sound a thought,
Hearing it by this distant northern sea.

The Sea of Faith
Was once, too, at the full, and round earth's shore
Lay like the folds of a bright girdle furled.
But now I only hear
Its melancholy, long, withdrawing roar,
Retreating, to the breath
Of the night-wind, down the vast edges drear
And naked shingles of the world.

Ah, love, let us be true
To one another! for the world, which seems
To lie before us like a land of dreams,
So various, so beautiful, so new,
Hath really neither joy, nor love, nor light,
Nor certitude, nor peace, nor help for pain;
And we are here as on a darkling plain
Swept with confused alarms of struggle and flight,
Where ignorant armies clash by night.

EMILY DICKINSON

(1830–1886, United States)

A Bird came down the Walk—

A Bird came down the Walk—
He did not know I saw—
He bit an Angleworm in halves
And ate the fellow, raw,

And then he drank a Dew
From a convenient Grass—
And then hopped sidewise to the Wall
To let a Beetle pass—

He glanced with rapid eyes
That hurried all around—

They looked like frightened Beads, I thought—
He stirred his Velvet Head

Like one in danger, Cautious,
I offered him a Crumb
And he unrolled his feathers
And rowed him softer home—

Than Oars divide the Ocean,
Too silver for a seam—
Or Butterflies, off Banks of Noon
Leap, plashless as they swim.

I heard a Fly buzz—when I died—

I heard a Fly buzz—when I died—
The Stillness in the Room
Was like the Stillness in the Air—
Between the Heaves of Storm—

The Eyes around—had wrung them dry—
And Breaths were gathering firm
For that last Onset—when the King
Be witnessed—in the Room—

I willed my Keepsakes—Signed away
What portion of me be
Assignable—and then it was
There interposed a Fly—

With Blue—uncertain stumbling Buzz—
Between the light—and me—
And then the Windows failed—and then
I could not see to see—

A narrow Fellow in the Grass

A narrow Fellow in the Grass
Occasionally rides—
You may have met Him—did you not
His notice sudden is—

The Grass divides as with a Comb—
A spotted shaft is seen—

And then it closes at your feet
And opens further on—

He likes a Boggy Acre
A Floor too cool for Corn—
Yet when a Boy, and Barefoot—
I more than once at Noon
Have passed, I thought, a Whip lash
Unbraiding in the Sun
When stooping to secure it
It wrinkled, and was gone—

Several of Nature's People
I know, and they know me—
I feel for them a transport
Of cordiality—

But never met this Fellow
Attended, or alone
Without a tighter breathing
And Zero at the Bone—

Tell all the Truth but tell it slant—

Tell all the Truth but tell it slant—
Success in Circuit lies
Too bright for our infirm Delight
The Truth's superb surprise
As Lightning to the Children eased
With explanation kind
The Truth must dazzle gradually
Or every man be blind—

THOMAS HARDY

(1840–1928, England)

"Ah, Are You Digging on My Grave?"

"Ah, are you digging on my grave
  My beloved one?—planting rue?"
—"No: yesterday he went to wed
One of the brightest wealth has bred,

'It cannot hurt her now,' he said,
  'That I should not be true.' "

"Then who is digging on my grave?
  My nearest, dearest kin?"
—"Ah, no: they sit and think, 'What use!
What good will planting flowers produce?
No tendance of her mound can loose
  Her spirit from Death's gin.' "

"But someone digs upon my grave?
  My enemy?—prodding sly?"
—"Nay: when she heard you had passed the Gate
That shuts on all flesh soon or late,
She thought you no more worth her hate,
  And cares not where you lie."

"Then, who is digging on my grave?
  Say—since I have not guessed!"
—"O it is I, my mistress dear.
Your little dog, who still lives near,
And much I hope my movements here
  Have not disturbed your rest?"

"Ah, yes! *You* dig upon my grave. . . .
  Why flashed it not on me
That one true heart was left behind!
What feeling do we ever find
To equal among human kind
  A dog's fidelity!"

"Mistress, I dug upon your grave
  To bury a bone, in case
I should be hungry near this spot
When passing on my daily trot.
I am sorry, but I quite forgot
  It was your resting-place."

In Church

"And now to God the Father," he ends,
And his voice thrills up to the topmost tiles:
Each listener chokes as he bows and bends,
And emotion pervades the crowded aisles.

Then the preacher glides to the vestry-door,
And shuts it, and thinks he is seen no more.

The door swings softly ajar meanwhile,
And a pupil of his in the Bible class,
Who adores him as one without gloss or guile,
Sees her idol stand with a satisfied smile
And reënact at the vestry-glass
Each pulpit gesture in deft dumb-show
That had moved the congregation so.

A. E. HOUSMAN

(1859–1936, England)

Loveliest of Trees

Loveliest of trees, the cherry now
Is hung with bloom along the bough,
And stands about the woodland ride
Wearing white for Eastertide.

Now, of my threescore years and ten,
Twenty will not come again,
And take from seventy springs a score,
It only leaves me fifty more.

And since to look at things in bloom
Fifty springs are little room,
About the woodlands I will go
To see the cherry hung with snow.

With Rue My Heart Is Laden

With rue my heart is laden
For golden friends I had,
For many a rose-lipt maiden
And many a lightfoot lad.

By brooks too broad for leaping
The lightfoot boys are laid;
The rose-lipt girls are sleeping
In fields where roses fade.

Terence, This Is Stupid Stuff

"Terence, this is stupid stuff;
You eat your victuals fast enough;
There can't be much amiss, 'tis clear,
To see the rate you drink your beer.
But oh, good Lord, the verse you make,
It gives a chap the belly-ache.
The cow, the old cow, she is dead;
It sleeps well, the hornèd head:
We poor lads, 'tis our turn now
To hear such tunes as killed the cow.
Pretty friendship 'tis to rhyme
Your friends to death before their time
Moping melancholy mad:
Come, pipe a tune to dance to, lad."

Why, if 'tis dancing you would be,
There's brisker pipes than poetry.
Say, for what were hop-yards meant,
Or why was Burton built on Trent?
Oh, many a peer of England brews
Livelier liquor than the Muse,
And malt does more than Milton can
To justify God's ways to man.
Ale, man, ale's the stuff to drink
For fellows whom it hurts to think:
Look into the pewter pot
To see the world as the world's not.
And faith, 'tis pleasant till 'tis past:
The mischief is that 'twill not last.
Oh, I have been to Ludlow fair
And left my necktie God knows where,
And carried half way home, or near,
Pints and quarts of Ludlow beer:
Then the world seemed none so bad,
And I myself a sterling lad:
And down in lovely muck I've lain,
Happy till I woke again.
Then I saw the morning sky:
Heigho, the tale was all a lie:
The world, it was the old world yet.
I was I, my things were wet.
And nothing now remained to do
But begin the game anew.

Therefore, since the world has still
Much good, but much less good than ill,
And while the sun and moon endure
Luck's a chance, but trouble's sure,
I'd face it as a wise man would,
And train for ill and not for good.
'Tis true, the stuff I bring for sale
Is not so brisk a brew as ale:
Out of a stem that scored the hand
I wrung it in a weary land.
But take it: if the smack is sour,
The better for the embittered hour;
It should do good to heart and head
When your soul is in my soul's stead;
And I will friend you, if I may,
In the dark and cloudy day.

There was a king reigned in the East:
There, when kings will sit to feast,
They get their fill before they think
With poisoned meat and poisoned drink.
He gathered all that springs to birth
From the many-venomed earth;
First a little, thence to more,
He sampled all her killing store;
And easy, smiling, seasoned sound,
Sate the king when healths went round.
They put arsenic in his meat
And stared aghast to watch him eat:
They poured strychnine in his cup
And shook to see him drink it up:
They shook, they stared as white's their shirt:
Them it was their poison hurt.
—I tell the tale that I heard told.
Mithridates, he died old.

When I Was One-and-Twenty

When I was one-and-twenty
  I heard a wise man say,
"Give crowns and pounds and guineas
  But not your heart away:
Give pearls away and rubies
  But keep your fancy free."

But I was one-and-twenty,
  No use to talk to me.

When I was one-and-twenty
  I heard him say again,
"The heart out of the bosom
  Was never given in vain:
'Tis paid with sighs a-plenty
  And sold for endless rue."
And I am two-and-twenty,
  And oh, 'tis true, 'tis true.

WILLIAM BUTLER YEATS

(1865–1939, Ireland)

The Lake Isle of Innisfree

I will arise and go now, and go to Innisfree,
And a small cabin build there, of clay and wattles made;
Nine bean rows will I have there, a hive for the honey bee,
    And live alone in the bee-loud glade.

And I shall have some peace there, for peace comes dropping slow,
Dropping from the veils of the morning to where the cricket sings;
There midnight's all a glimmer, and noon a purple glow.
    And evening full of the linnet's wings.

I will arise and go now, for always night and day
I hear lake water lapping with low sounds by the shore:
While I stand on the roadway, or on the pavements gray,
    I hear it in the deep heart's core.

The Wild Swans at Coole[1]

The trees are in their autumn beauty,
The woodland paths are dry,
Under the October twilight the water
Mirrors a still sky;

THE WILD SWANS AT COOLE [1]**Coole** Coole Park, an estate in the west of Ireland where Yeats often visited.

Upon the brimming water among the stones
Are nine and fifty swans.

The nineteenth Autumn has come upon me
Since I first made my count;
I saw, before I had well finished,
All suddenly mount
And scatter, wheeling, in great broken rings
Upon their clamorous wings.

I have looked upon those brilliant creatures,
And now my heart is sore.
All's changed since I, hearing at twilight,
The first time on this shore,
The bell-beat of their wings above my head,
Trod with a lighter tread.

Unwearied still, lover by lover,
They paddle in the cold,
Companionable streams or climb the air;
Their hearts have not grown old;
Passion or conquest, wander where they will,
Attend upon them still.

But now they drift on the still water
Mysterious, beautiful;
Among what rushes will they build,
By what lake's edge or pool
Delight men's eyes, when I awake some day
To find they have flown away?

A Prayer for My Daughter

Once more the storm is howling, and half hid
Under this cradle-hood and coverlid
My child sleeps on. There is no obstacle
But Gregory's wood and one bare hill
Whereby the haystack- and roof-levelling wind,
Bred on the Atlantic, can be stayed;
And for an hour I have walked and prayed
Because of the great gloom that is in my mind.

I have walked and prayed for this young child an hour
And heard the sea-wind scream upon the tower,
And under the arches of the bridge, and scream

In the elms above the flooded stream;
Imagining in excited reverie
That the future years had come,
Dancing to a frenzied drum,
Out of the murderous innocence of the sea.

May she be granted beauty and yet not
Beauty to make a stranger's eye distraught,
Or hers before a looking-glass, for such,
Being made beautiful overmuch,
Consider beauty a sufficient end,
Lose natural kindness and maybe
The heart-revealing intimacy
That chooses right, and never find a friend.

Helen being chosen found life flat and dull
And later had much trouble from a fool,
While that great Queen, that rose out of the spray,
Being fatherless could have her way
Yet chose a bandy-leggèd smith for man.
It's certain that fine women eat
A crazy salad with their meat
Whereby the Horn of Plenty is undone.

In courtesy I'd have her chiefly learned;
Hearts are not had as a gift but hearts are earned
By those that are not entirely beautiful;
Yet many, that have played the fool
For beauty's very self, has charm made wise,
And many a poor man that has roved,
Loved and thought himself beloved,
From a glad kindness cannot take his eyes.

May she become a flourishing hidden tree
That all her thoughts may like the linnet be,
And have no business but dispensing round
Their magnanimities of sound,
Nor but in merriment begin a chase,
Nor but in merriment a quarrel.
O may she live like some green laurel
Rooted in one dear perpetual place.

My mind, because the minds that I have loved,
The sort of beauty that I have approved,
Prosper but little, has dried up of late,
Yet knows that to be choked with hate
May well be of all evil chances chief.
If there's no hatred in a mind

Assault and battery of the wind
Can never tear the linnet from the leaf.

An intellectual hatred is the worst,
So let her think opinions are accursed.
Have I not seen the loveliest woman born
Out of the mouth of Plenty's horn,
Because of her opinionated mind
Barter that horn and every good
By quiet natures understood
For an old bellows full of angry wind?

Considering that, all hatred driven hence,
The soul recovers radical innocence
And learns at last that it is self-delighting,
Self-appeasing, self-affrighting,
And that its own sweet will is Heaven's will;
She can, though every face should scowl
And every windy quarter howl
Or every bellows burst, be happy still.

And may her bridegroom bring her to a house
Where all's accustomed, ceremonious:
For arrogance and hatred are the wares
Peddled in the thoroughfares.
How but in custom and in ceremony
Are innocence and beauty born?
Ceremony's a name for the rich horn,
And custom for the spreading laurel tree.

Lapis Lazuli[1]

(For Harry Clifton)

I have heard that hysterical women say
They are sick of the palette and fiddle-bow,
Of poets that are always gay,
For everybody knows or else should know
That if nothing drastic is done
Aeroplane and Zeppelin will come out,
Pitch like King Billy[2] bomb-balls in
Until the town lie beaten flat.

LAPIS LAZULI [1]**lapis lazuli** a deep blue semiprecious stone. [2]**King Billy** King William III who destroyed the Catholic forces at the Battle of the Boyne.

All perform their tragic play,
There struts Hamlet, there is Lear,
That's Ophelia, that Cordelia;
Yet they, should the last scene be there,
The great stage curtain about to drop,
If worthy their prominent part in the play,
Do not break up their lines to weep.
They know that Hamlet and Lear are gay;
Gaiety transfiguring all that dread.
All men have aimed at, found and lost;
Black out; Heaven blazing into the head:
Tragedy wrought to its uttermost.
Though Hamlet rambles and Lear rages,
And all the drop-scenes drop at once
Upon a hundred thousand stages,
It cannot grow by an inch or an ounce.

On their own feet they came, or on shipboard,
Camelback, horseback, ass-back, mule-back,
Old civilizations put to the sword.
Then they and their wisdom went to rack:
No handiwork of Callimachus,[3]
Who handled marble as if it were bronze,
Made draperies that seemed to rise
When sea-wind swept the corner, stands;
His long lamp-chimney shaped like the stem
Of a slender palm, stood but a day;
All things fall and are built again,
And those that build them again are gay.

Two Chinamen, behind them a third,
Are carved in lapis lazuli,
Over them flies a long-legged bird,
A symbol of longevity;
The third, doubtless a serving-man,
Carries a musical instrument.
Every discoloration of the stone,
Every accidental crack or dent,
Seems a water-course or an avalanche,
Or lofty slope where it still snows
Though doubtless plum or cherry-branch
Sweetens the little half-way house
Those Chinamen climb towards, and I
Delight to imagine them seated there;

[3]**Callimachus** Greek sculptor.

There, on the mountain and the sky,
On all the tragic scene they stare.
One asks for mournful melodies;
Accomplished fingers begin to play.
Their eyes mid many wrinkles, their eyes,
Their ancient, glittering eyes, are gay.

The Circus Animals' Desertion

1

I sought a theme and sought for it in vain,
I sought it daily for six weeks or so.
Maybe at last, being but a broken man,
I must be satisfied with my heart, although
Winter and summer till old age began
My circus animals were all on show,
Those stilted boys, that burnished chariot,
Lion and woman and the Lord knows what.

2

What can I but enumerate old themes?
First that sea-rider Oisin[1] led by the nose
Through three enchanted islands, allegorical dreams,
Vain gaiety, vain battle, vain repose,
Themes of the embittered heart, or so it seems,
That might adorn old songs or courtly shows;
But what cared I that set him on to ride,
I, starved for the bosom of his faery bride?

And then a counter-truth filled out its play,
The Countess Cathleen[2] was the name I gave it;
She, pity-crazed, had given her soul away,
But masterful Heaven had intervened to save it.
I thought my dear must her own soul destroy,
So did fanaticism and hate enslave it,
And this brought forth a dream and soon enough
This dream itself had all my thought and love.

THE CIRCUS ANIMALS' DESERTION [1]**Oisin** Irish mythological figure. [2]***The Countess Cathleen*** a play by Yeats.

And when the Fool and Blind Man stole the bread
Cuchulain fought the ungovernable sea;[3]
Heart-mysteries there, and yet when all is said
It was the dream itself enchanted me:
Character isolated by a deed
To engross the present and dominate memory.
Players and painted stage took all my love,
And not those things that they were emblems of.

3

Those masterful images because complete
Grew in pure mind, but out of what began?
A mound of refuse or the sweeping of a street,
Old kettles, old bottles, and a broken can,
Old iron, old bones, old rags, that raving slut
Who keeps the till. Now that my ladder's gone,
I must lie down where all the ladders start,
In the foul rag-and-bone shop of the heart.

EDWIN ARLINGTON ROBINSON

(1869–1935, United States)

Richard Cory

Whenever Richard Cory went down town,
  We people on the pavement looked at him:
He was a gentleman from sole to crown,
  Clean favored, and imperially slim.

And he was always quietly arrayed,
  And he was always human when he talked;
But still he fluttered pulses when he said,
  "Good-morning," and he glittered when he walked.

And he was rich—yes, richer than a king—
  And admirably schooled in every grace:
In fine, we thought that he was everything
  To make us wish that we were in his place.

THE CIRCUS ANIMALS' DESERTION [3]in Yeats's play *On Baile's Strand.*

So on we worked, and waited for the light,
And went without the meat, and cursed the bread;
And Richard Cory, one calm summer night,
Went home and put a bullet through his head.

Mr. Flood's Party

Old Eben Flood, climbing alone one night
Over the hill between the town below
And the forsaken upland hermitage
That held as much as he should ever know
On earth again of home, paused warily.
The road was his with not a native near;
And Eben, having leisure, said aloud,
For no man else in Tilbury Town to hear:

"Well, Mr. Flood, we have the harvest moon
Again, and we may not have many more;
The bird is on the wing, the poet says,
And you and I have said it here before.
Drink to the bird." He raised up to the light
The jug that he had gone so far to fill,
And answered huskily: "Well, Mr. Flood,
Since you propose it, I believe I will."

Alone, as if enduring to the end
A valiant armor of scarred hopes outworn,
He stood there in the middle of the road
Like Roland's ghost winding a silent horn.[1]
Below him, in the town among the trees,
Where friends of other days had honored him,
A phantom salutation of the dead
Rang thinly till old Eben's eyes were dim.

Then, as a mother lays her sleeping child
Down tenderly, fearing it may awake,
He set the jug down slowly at his feet
With trembling care, knowing that most things break;
And only when assured that on firm earth
It stood, as the uncertain lives of men
Assuredly did not, he paced away,
And with his hand extended paused again:

MR. FLOOD'S PARTY [1]In *Chanson de Roland,* Roland blows his horn to summon help at the moment of his death.

"Well, Mr. Flood, we have not met like this
In a long time; and many a change has come
To both of us, I fear, since last it was
We had a drop together. Welcome home!"
Convivially returning with himself,
Again he raised the jug up to the light:
And with an acquiescent quaver said:
"Well, Mr. Flood, if you insist, I might.

"Only a very little, Mr. Flood—
For auld lang syne. No more, sir; that will do."
So, for the time, apparently it did,
And Eben evidently thought so too;
For soon amid the silver loneliness
Of night he lifted up his voice and sang,
Secure, with only two moons listening,
Until the whole harmonious landscape rang—

"For auld lang syne." The weary throat gave out,
The last word wavered; and the song being done,
He raised again the jug regretfully
And shook his head, and was again alone.
There was not much that was ahead of him,
And there was nothing in the town below—
Where strangers would have shut the many doors
That many friends had opened long ago.

WALTER DE LA MARE

(1873–1956, England)

The Listeners

"Is there anybody there?" said the Traveller,
  Knocking on the moonlit door;
And his horse in the silence champed the grasses
  Of the forest's ferny floor:
And a bird flew up out of the turret,
  Above the Traveller's head:
And he smote upon the door again a second time;
  "Is there anybody there?" he said.
But no one descended to the Traveller;
  No head from the leaf-fringed sill

Leaned over and looked into his grey eyes,
  Where he stood perplexed and still.
But only a host of phantom listeners
  That dwelt in the lone house then
Stood listening in the quiet of the moonlight
  To that voice from the world of men:
Stood thronging the faint moonbeams on the dark stair,
  That goes down to the empty hall,
Hearkening in an air stirred and shaken
  By the lonely Traveller's call.
And he felt in his heart their strangeness,
  Their stillness answering his cry,
While his horse moved, cropping the dark turf,
  'Neath the starred and leafy sky;
For he suddenly smote on the door, even
  Louder, and lifted his head:—
"Tell them I came, and no one answered,
  That I kept my word," he said.
Never the least stir made the listeners,
  Though every word he spake
Fell echoing through the shadowiness of the still house
  From the one man left awake:
Ay, they heard his foot upon the stirrup,
  And the sound of iron on stone,
And how the silence surged softly backward,
  When the plunging hoofs were gone.

Silver

Slowly, silently, now the moon
Walks the night in her silver shoon;
This way, and that, she peers, and sees
Silver fruit upon silver trees;
One by one the casements catch
Her beams beneath the silvery thatch;
Couched in his kennel, like a log,
With paws of silver sleeps the dog;
From their shadowy cote the white breasts peep
Of doves in a silver-feathered sleep:
A harvest mouse goes scampering by,
With silver claws and a silver eye;
And moveless fish in the water gleam,
By silver reeds in a silver stream.

ROBERT FROST

(1874–1963, United States)

Stopping by Woods on a Snowy Evening

Whose woods these are I think I know.
His house is in the village though;
He will not see me stopping here
To watch his woods fill up with snow.

My little horse must think it queer
To stop without a farmhouse near
Between the woods and frozen lake
The darkest evening of the year.

He gives his harness bells a shake
To ask if there is some mistake.
The only other sound's the sweep
Of easy wind and downy flake.

The woods are lovely, dark and deep,
But I have promises to keep,
And miles to go before I sleep,
And miles to go before I sleep.

The Silken Tent

She is as in a field a silken tent
At midday when a sunny summer breeze
Has dried the dew and all its ropes relent,
So that in guys it gently sways at ease,
And its supporting central cedar pole,
That is its pinnacle to heavenward
And signifies the sureness of the soul,
Seems to owe naught to any single cord,
But strictly held by none, is loosely bound
By countless silken ties of love and thought
To everything on earth the compass round,
And only by one's going slightly taut
In the capriciousness of summer air
Is of the slightest bondage made aware.

Design

I found a dimpled spider, fat and white,
On a white heal-all, holding up a moth
Like a white piece of rigid satin cloth—
Assorted characters of death and blight
Mixed ready to begin the morning right,
Like the ingredients of a witches' broth—
A snow-drop spider, a flower like a froth,
And dead wings carried like a paper kite.

What had that flower to do with being white,
The wayside blue and innocent heal-all?
What brought the kindred spider to that height,
Then steered the white moth thither in the night?
What but design of darkness to appall?—
If design govern in a thing so small.

WALLACE STEVENS

(1879–1955, United States)

The Snow Man

One must have a mind of winter
To regard the frost and the boughs
Of the pine-trees crusted with snow;

And have been cold a long time
To behold the junipers shagged with ice,
The spruces rough in the distant glitter

Of the January sun; and not to think
Of any misery in the sound of the wind,
In the sound of a few leaves,

Which is the sound of the land
Full of the same wind
That is blowing in the same bare place

For the listener, who listens in the snow,
And, nothing himself, beholds
Nothing that is not there and the nothing that is.

Anecdote of the Jar

I placed a jar in Tennessee,
And round it was, upon a hill.
It made the slovenly wilderness
Surround that hill.

The wilderness rose up to it,
And sprawled around, no longer wild.
The jar was round upon the ground
And tall and of a port in air.

It took dominion everywhere.
The jar was gray and bare.
It did not give of bird or bush,
Like nothing else in Tennessee.

The Motive for Metaphor

You like it under the trees in autumn,
Because everything is half dead.
The wind moves like a cripple among the leaves
And repeats words without meaning.

In the same way, you were happy in spring,
With the half colors of quarter-things,
The slightly brighter sky, the melting clouds,
The single bird, the obscure moon—

The obscure moon lighting an obscure world
Of things that would never be quite expressed,
Where you yourself were never quite yourself
And did not want nor have to be,

Desiring the exhilarations of changes:
The motive for metaphor, shrinking from
The weight of primary noon,
The A B C of being,

The ruddy temper, the hammer
Of red and blue, the hard sound—
Steel against intimation—the sharp flash,
The vital, arrogant, fatal, dominant X.

WILLIAM CARLOS WILLIAMS

(1883–1963, United States)

Danse Russe

If I when my wife is sleeping
and the baby and Kathleen
are sleeping
and the sun is a flame-white disc
in silken mists
above shining trees,—
if I in my north room
dance naked, grotesquely
before my mirror
waving my shirt round my head
and singing softly to myself:
"I am lonely, lonely.
I was born to be lonely,
I am best so!"
If I admire my arms, my face
my shoulders, flanks, buttocks
against the yellow drawn shades,—

Who shall say I am not
the happy genius of my household?

At the Ball Game

The crowd at the ball game
is moved uniformly

by a spirit of uselessness
which delights them—

all the exciting detail
of the chase

and the escape, the error
the flash of genius—

all to no end save beauty
the eternal—

So in detail they, the crowd,
are beautiful

for this
to be warned against

saluted and defied—
It is alive, venomous

it smiles grimly
its words cut—

The flashy female with her
mother, gets it—

The Jew gets it straight—it
is deadly, terrifying—

It is the Inquisition, the
Revolution

It is beauty itself
that lives

day by day in them
idly—

This is
the power of their faces

It is summer, it is the solstice
the crowd is

cheering, the crowd is laughing
in detail

permanently, seriously
without thought

The Dance

In Breughel's great picture, The Kermess,
the dancers go round, they go round and
around, the squeal and the blare and the
tweedle of bagpipes, a bugle and fiddles
tipping their bellies (round as the thick-
sided glasses whose wash they impound)
their hips and their bellies off balance

to turn them. Kicking and rolling about
the Fair Grounds, swinging their butts, those
shanks must be sound to bear up under such
rollicking measures, prance as they dance
in Breughel's great picture, The Kermess.

Tract

I will teach you my townspeople
how to perform a funeral
for you have it over a troop
of artists—
unless one should scour the world—
you have the ground sense necessary.

See! the hearse leads.
I begin with a design for a hearse.
For Christ's sake not black—
nor white either—and not polished!
Let it be weathered—like a farm wagon—
with gilt wheels (this could be
applied fresh at small expense)
or no wheels at all:
a rough dray to drag over the ground.

Knock the glass out!
My God—glass, my townspeople!
For what purpose? Is it for the dead
to look out or for us to see
how well he is housed or to see
the flowers or the lack of them—
or what?
To keep the rain and snow from him?
He will have a heavier rain soon:
pebbles and dirt and what not.
Let there be no glass—
and no upholstery, phew!
and no little brass rollers
and small easy wheels on the bottom—
my townspeople what are you thinking of?

A rough plain hearse then
with gilt wheels and no top at all.
On this the coffin lies
by its own weight.
No wreaths please—

especially no hot house flowers.
Some common memento is better,
something he prized and is known by:
his old clothes—a few books perhaps—
God knows what! You realize
how we are about these things
my townspeople—
something will be found—anything
even flowers if he had come to that.
So much for the hearse.

For heaven's sake though see to the driver!
Take off the silk hat! In fact
that's no place at all for him—
up there unceremoniously
dragging our friend out to his own dignity!
Bring him down—bring him down!
Low and inconspicuous! I'd not have him ride
on the wagon at all—damn him—
the undertaker's understrapper!
Let him hold the reins
and walk at the side
and inconspicuously too!

Then briefly as to yourselves:
Walk behind—as they do in France,
seventh class, or if you ride
Hell take curtains! Go with some show
of inconvenience; sit openly—
to the weather as to grief.
Or do you think you can shut grief in?
What—from us? We who have perhaps
nothing to lose? Share with us
share with us—it will be money
in your pockets.
Go now
I think you are ready.

D. H. LAWRENCE

(1885–1930, England)

Piano

Softly, in the dusk, a woman is singing to me;
Taking me back down the vista of years, till I see
A child sitting under the piano, in the boom of the tingling strings
And pressing the small, poised feet of a mother who smiles as she sings.

In spite of myself, the insidious mastery of song
Betrays me back, till the heart of me weeps to belong
To the old Sunday evenings at home, with winter outside
And hymns in the cosy parlour, the tinkling piano our guide.

So now it is vain for the singer to burst into clamour
With the great black piano appassionato. The glamour
Of childish days is upon me, my manhood is cast
Down in the flood of remembrance, I weep like a child for the past.

Snake

A snake came to my water-trough
On a hot, hot day, and I in pyjamas for the heat,
To drink there.

In the deep, strange-scented shade of the great dark carob-tree
I came down the steps with my pitcher
And must wait, must stand and wait, for there he was at the trough
  before me.

He reached down from a fissure in the earth-wall in the gloom
And trailed his yellow-brown slackness soft-bellied down, over the edge
  of the stone trough
And rested his throat upon the stone bottom,
And where the water had dripped from the tap, in a small clearness,
He sipped with his straight mouth,
Softly drank through his straight gums, into his slack long body,
Silently.

Someone was before me at my water-trough,
And I, like a second comer, waiting.

He lifted his head from his drinking, as cattle do,
And looked at me vaguely, as drinking cattle do,
And flickered his two-forked tongue from his lips, and mused a moment,
And stooped and drank a little more,
Being earth-brown, earth-golden from the burning bowels of the earth
On the day of Sicilian July, with Etna[1] smoking.

The voice of my education said to me
He must be killed,

SNAKE [1]**Etna** volcanic mountain in Sicily.

For in Sicily the black, black snakes are innocent, the gold are venomous.

And voices in me said, If you were a man
You would take a stick and break him now, and finish him off.

But must I confess how I liked him,
How glad I was he had come like a guest in quiet, to drink at my water-trough
And depart peaceful, pacified, and thankless,
Into the burning bowels of this earth?

Was it cowardice, that I dared not kill him?
Was it perversity, that I longed to talk to him?
Was it humility, to feel so honoured?
I felt so honoured.

And yet those voices:
If you were not afraid, you would kill him!
And truly I was afraid, I was most afraid,
But even so, honoured still more
That he should seek my hospitality
From out the dark door of the secret earth.

He drank enough
And lifted his head, dreamily, as one who has drunken,
And flickered his tongue like a forked night on the air, so black;
Seeming to lick his lips,
And looked around like a god, unseeing, into the air,
And slowly turned his head,
And slowly, very slowly, as if thrice adream,
Proceeded to draw his slow length curving round
And climb again the broken bank of my wall-face.

And as he put his head into that dreadful hole,
And as he slowly drew up, snake-easing his shoulders, and entered farther,
A sort of horror, a sort of protest against his withdrawing into that horrid black hole,
Deliberately going into the blackness, and slowly drawing himself after,
Overcame me now his back was turned.

I looked round, I put down my pitcher,
I picked up a clumsy log
And threw it at the water-trough with a clatter.

I think it did not hit him,
But suddenly that part of him that was left behind convulsed in
  undignified haste,
Writhed like lightning, and was gone
Into the black hole, the earth-lipped fissure in the wall-front,
At which, in the intense still noon, I stared with fascination.

And immediately I regretted it.
I thought how paltry, how vulgar, what a mean act!
I despised myself and the voices of my accursed human education.

And I thought of the albatross,[2]
And I wished he would come back, my snake.

For he seemed to me again like a king,
Like a king in exile, uncrowned in the underworld,
Now due to be crowned again.

And so, I missed my chance with one of the lords
Of life.
And I have something to expiate;
A pettiness.

EZRA POUND

(1885–1972, United States)

In a Station of the Metro

The apparition of these faces in the crowd;
Petals on a wet, black bough.

ROBINSON JEFFERS

(1887–1962, United States)

To the Stone-Cutters

Stone-cutters fighting time with marble, you foredefeated
Challengers of oblivion
Eat cynical earnings, knowing rock splits, records fall down,

---

SNAKE [2]**albatross** a bird whose death brings a curse in Coleridge's "Rime of the Ancient Mariner."

The square-limbed Roman letters
Scale in the thaws, wear in the rain.
  The poet as well
Builds his monument mockingly;
For man will be blotted out, the blithe earth die, the brave sun
Die blind and blackened to the heart:
Yet stones have stood for a thousand years, and pained thoughts found
The honey of peace in old poems.

Hurt Hawks

1

The broken pillar of the wing jags from the clotted shoulder,
The wing trails like a banner in defeat,
No more to use the sky forever but live with famine
And pain a few days: cat nor coyote
Will shorten the week of waiting for death, there is game without talons.
He stands under the oak-bush and waits
The lame feet of salvation; a night he remembers freedom
And flies in a dream, the dawns ruin it.
He is strong and pain is worse to the strong, incapacity is worse.
The curs of the day come and torment him
At distance, no one but death the redeemer will humble that head,
The intrepid readiness, the terrible eyes.
The wild God of the world is sometimes merciful to those
That ask mercy, not often to the arrogant.
You do not know him, you communal people, or you have forgotten
  him;
Intemperate and savage, the hawk remembers him;
Beautiful and wild, the hawks, and men that are dying, remember him.

II

I'd sooner, except the penalties, kill a man than a hawk; but the great
  redtail
Had nothing left but unable misery
From the bone too shattered for mending, the wing that trailed under his
  talons when he moved.
We had fed him six weeks, I gave him freedom,
He wandered over the foreland hill and returned in the evening, asking
  for death,
Not like a beggar, still eyed with the old

Implacable arrogance. I gave him the lead gift in the twilight.
    What fell was relaxed,
Owl-downy, soft feminine feathers; but what
Soared: the fierce rush: the night-herons by the flooded river cried fear at
  its rising
Before it was quite unsheathed from reality.

MARIANNE MOORE

(1887–1972, United States)

Poetry

I, too, dislike it: there are things that are important beyond all this fiddle.
  Reading it, however, with a perfect contempt for it, one discovers in
  it after all, a place for the genuine.[1]
    Hands that can grasp, eyes
    that can dilate, hair that can rise
      if it must, these things are important not because a

high-sounding interpretation can be put upon them but because they are
  useful. When they become so derivative as to become unintelligible,
  the same thing may be said for all of us, that we
    do not admire what
    we cannot understand: the bat
      holding on upside down or in quest of something to

eat, elephants pushing, a wild horse taking a roll, a tireless wolf under
  a tree, the immovable critic twitching his skin like a horse that feels a
    flea, the base-
  ball fan, the statistician—
  nor is it valid
      to discriminate against 'business documents and

school-books'; all these phenomena are important. One must make a dis-
    tinction
  however: when dragged into prominence by half poets, the result is
  not
    poetry,
  nor till the poets among us can be
    'literalists of
    the imagination'—above
      insolence and triviality and can present

POETRY [1]In the final version, Moore ended the poem here.

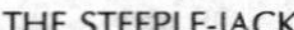

for inspection, 'imaginary gardens with real toads in them', shall we have
it. In the meantime, if you demand on the one hand,
the raw material of poetry in
all its rawness and
that which is on the other hand
genuine, you are interested in poetry.

The Steeple-Jack

Dürer[1] would have seen a reason for living
in a town like this, with eight stranded whales
to look at; with the sweet sea air coming into your house
on a fine day, from water etched
with waves as formal as the scales
on a fish.

One by one in two's and three's, the seagulls keep
flying back and forth over the town clock,
or sailing around the lighthouse without moving their wings—
rising steadily with a slight
quiver of the body—or flock
mewing where

a sea the purple of the peacock's neck is
paled to greenish azure as Dürer changed
the pine green of the Tyrol to peacock blue and guinea
gray. You can see a twenty-five-
pound lobster; and fish nest arranged
to dry. The

whirlwind fife-and-drum of the storm bends the salt
marsh grass, disturbs stars in the sky and the
star on the steeple; it is a privilege to see so
much confusion. Disguised by what
might seem the opposite, the sea-
side flowers and

trees are favored by the fog so that you have
the tropics at first hand: the trumpet vine,
foxglove, giant snapdragon, a salpiglossis that has

THE STEEPLE-JACK [1]**Dürer** Albrecht Dürer, German painter.

spots and stripes; morning-glories, gourds,
    or moon-vines trained on fishing twine
at the back door:

cattails, flags, blueberries and spiderwort,
    striped grass, lichens, sunflowers, asters, daisies—
yellow and crab-claw ragged sailors with green bracts—toad-plant,
petunias, ferns; pink lilies, blue
    ones, tigers; poppies; black sweet-peas.
The climate

is not right for the banyan, frangipani, or
    jack-fruit trees; or for exotic serpent
life. Ring lizard and snakeskin for the foot, if you see fit;
but here they've cats, not cobras, to
    keep down the rats. The diffident
little newt
with white pin-dots on black horizontal spaced-
    out bands lives here; yet there is nothing that
ambition can buy or take away. The college student
named Ambrose sits on the hillside
    with his not-native books and hat
and sees boats

at sea progress white and rigid as if in
    a groove. Liking an elegance of which
the source is not bravado, he knows by heart the antique
sugar-bowl shaped summerhouse of
    interlacing slats, and the pitch
of the church

spire, not true, from which a man in scarlet lets
    down a rope as a spider spins a thread;
he might be part of a novel, but on the sidewalk a
sign says C. J. Poole, Steeple Jack,
    in black and white; and one in red
and white says

Danger. The church portico has four fluted
    columns, each a single piece of stone, made
modester by whitewash. This would be a fit haven for
waifs, children, animals, prisoners,
    and presidents who have repaid
sin-driven

senators by not thinking about them. The
    place has a schoolhouse, a post-office in a

store, fish-houses, hen-houses, a three-masted schooner on
the stocks. The hero, the student,
the steeple jack, each in his way,
is at home.

It could not be dangerous to be living
in a town like this, of simple people,
who have a steeple-jack placing danger signs by the church
while he is gilding the solid-
pointed star, which on a steeple
stands for hope.

T. S. ELIOT

(1888–1965, United States)

The Hippopotamus

And when this epistle is read among you, cause that it be read also in the church of the Laodiceans.

The broad-backed hippopotamus
Rests on his belly in the mud;
Although he seems so firm to us
He is merely flesh and blood.

Flesh and blood is weak and frail,
Susceptible to nervous shock;
While the True Church can never fail
For it is based upon a rock.

The hippo's feeble steps may err.
In compassing material ends,
While the True Church need never stir
To gather in its dividends.

The 'potamus can never reach
The mango on the mango-tree;
But fruits of pomegranate and peach
Refresh the Church from over sea.

At mating time the hippo's voice
Betrays inflexions hoarse and odd,
But every week we hear rejoice
The Church, at being one with God.

The hippopotamus's day
Is passed in sleep; at night he hunts;
God works in a mysterious way—
The Church can sleep and feed at once.

I saw the 'potamus take wing
Ascending from the damp savannas,
And quiring angels round him sing
The praise of God, in loud hosannas.

Blood of the Lamb shall wash him clean
And him shall heavenly arms enfold,
Among the saints he shall be seen
Performing on a harp of gold.

He shall be washed as white as snow,
By all the martyr'd virgins kist,
While the True Church remains below
Wrapt in the old miasmal mist.

Preludes

I

The winter evening settles down
With smell of steaks in passageways.
Six o'clock.
The burnt-out ends of smoky days.
And now a gusty shower wraps
The grimy scraps
Of withered leaves about your feet
And newspapers from vacant lots;
The showers beat
On broken blinds and chimney-pots,
And at the corner of the street
A lonely cab-horse steams and stamps.
And then the lighting of the lamps.

II

The morning comes to consciousness
Of faint stale smells of beer
From the sawdust-trampled street

With all its muddy feet that press
To early coffee-stands.
With the other masquerades
That time resumes,
One thinks of all the hands
That are raising dingy shades
In a thousand furnished rooms.

III

You tossed a blanket from the bed,
You lay upon your back, and waited;
You dozed, and watched the night revealing
The thousand sordid images
Of which your soul was constituted;
They flickered against the ceiling.
And when all the world came back
And the light crept up between the shutters
And you heard the sparrows in the gutters,
You had such a vision of the street
As the street hardly understands;
Sitting along the bed's edge, where
You curled the papers from your hair,
Or clasped the yellow soles of feet
In the palms of both soiled hands.

IV

His soul stretched tight across the skies
That fade behind a city block,
Or trampled by insistent feet
At four and five and six o'clock;
And short square fingers stuffing pipes,
And evening newspapers, and eyes
Assured of certain certainties,
The conscience of a blackened street
Impatient to assume the world.

I am moved by fancies that are curled
Around these images, and cling:
The notion of some infinitely gentle
Infinitely suffering thing.

Wipe your hand across your mouth, and laugh;
The worlds revolve like ancient women
Gathering fuel in vacant lots.

The Love Song of J. Alfred Prufrock

S'io credessi che mia risposta fosse
a persona che mai tornasse al mondo,
questa fiamma staria senza più scosse.
Ma per ciò che giammai di questo fondo
non tornò vivo alcun, s'i'odo il vero,
senza tema d'infamia ti rispondo.[1]

Let us go then, you and I,
When the evening is spread out against the sky
Like a patient etherised upon a table;
Let us go, through certain half-deserted streets,
The muttering retreats
Of restless nights in one-night cheap hotels
And sawdust restaurants with oyster-shells:
Streets that follow like a tedious argument
Of insidious intent
To lead you to an overwhelming question . . .
Oh, do not ask, 'What is it?'
Let us go and make our visit.

In the room the women come and go
Talking of Michelangelo.

The yellow fog that rubs its back upon the window-panes,
The yellow smoke that rubs its muzzle on the window-panes,
Licked its tongue into the corners of the evening,
Lingered upon the pools that stand in drains,
Let fall upon its back the soot that falls from chimneys,
Slipped by the terrace, made a sudden leap,
And seeing that it was a soft October night,
Curled once about the house, and fell asleep.

And indeed there will be time
For the yellow smoke that slides along the street
Rubbing its back upon the window-panes;
There will be time, there will be time
To prepare a face to meet the faces that you meet;
There will be time to murder and create,
And time for all the works and days of hands
That lift and drop a question on your plate;
Time for you and time for me,

[1]These lines are from Dante's *Inferno*: "If I thought I was speaking to someone who would go back to the world, this [tongue of flame] would speak no more."

And time yet for a hundred indecisions,
And for a hundred visions and revisions,
Before the taking of a toast and tea.

In the room the women come and go
Talking of Michelangelo.

And indeed there will be time
To wonder, 'Do I dare?' and, 'Do I dare?'
Time to turn back and descend the stair,
With a bald spot in the middle of my hair—
(They will say: 'How his hair is growing thin!')
My morning coat, my collar mounting firmly to the chin,
My necktie rich and modest, but asserted by a simple pin—
(They will say: 'But how his arms and legs are thin!')
Do I dare
Disturb the universe?
In a minute there is time
For decisions and revisions which a minute will reverse.

For I have known them all already, known them all—
Have known the evenings, mornings, afternoons,
I have measured out my life with coffee spoons;
I know the voices dying with a dying fall
Beneath the music from a farther room.
  So how should I presume?

And I have known the eyes already, known them all—
The eyes that fix you in a formulated phrase,
And when I am formulated, sprawling on a pin,
When I am pinned and wriggling on the wall,
Then how should I begin
To spit out all the butt-ends of my days and ways?
  And how should I presume?

And I have known the arms already, known them all—
Arms that are braceleted and white and bare
(But in the lamplight, downed with light brown hair!)
Is it perfume from a dress
That makes me so digress?
Arms that lie along a table, or wrap about a shawl.
  And should I then presume?
  And how should I begin?

Shall I say, I have gone at dusk through narrow streets
And watched the smoke that rises from the pipes
Of lonely men in shirt-sleeves, leaning out of windows? . . .

I should have been a pair of ragged claws
Scuttling across the floors of silent seas.

And the afternoon, the evening, sleeps so peacefully!
Smoothed by long fingers,
Asleep . . . tired . . . or it malingers,
Stretched on the floor, here beside you and me.
Should I, after tea and cakes and ices,
Have the strength to force the moment to its crisis?
But though I have wept and fasted, wept and prayed,
Though I have seen my head (grown slightly bald) brought in upon a platter,
I am no prophet—and here's no great matter;
I have seen the moment of my greatness flicker,
And I have seen the eternal Footman hold my coat, and snicker,
And in short, I was afraid.

And would it have been worth it, after all,
After the cups, the marmalade, the tea,
Among the porcelain, among some talk of you and me,
Would it have been worth while,
To have bitten off the matter with a smile,
To have squeezed the universe into a ball
To roll it towards some overwhelming question,
To say: "I am Lazarus, come from the dead,
Come back to tell you all, I shall tell you all"—
If one, settling a pillow by her head,
Should say: "That is not what I meant at all.
That is not it, at all."

And would it have been worth it, after all,
Would it have been worth while,
After the sunsets and the dooryards and the sprinkled streets,
After the novels, after the teacups, after the skirts that trail along the floor—

And this, and so much more?—
It is impossible to say just what I mean!
But as if a magic lantern threw the nerves in patterns on a screen:
Would it have been worth while
If one, settling a pillow or throwing off a shawl,
And turning toward the window, should say:
"That is not it at all,
That is not what I meant, at all."

No! I am not Prince Hamlet, nor was meant to be;
Am an attendant lord, one that will do

To swell a progress, start a scene or two,
Advise the prince; no doubt, an easy tool,
Deferential, glad to be of use,
Politic, cautious, and meticulous;
Full of high sentence, but a bit obtuse;
At times, indeed, almost ridiculous—
Almost, at times, the Fool.

I grow old . . . I grow old . . .
I shall wear the bottoms of my trousers rolled.

Shall I part my hair behind? Do I dare to eat a peach?
I shall wear white flannel trousers, and walk upon the beach.
I have heard the mermaids singing, each to each.

I do not think that they will sing to me.

I have seen them riding seaward on the waves
Combing the white hair of the waves blown back
When the wind blows the water white and black.

We have lingered in the chambers of the sea
By sea-girls wreathed with seaweed red and brown
Till human voices wake us, and we drown.

JOHN CROWE RANSOM

(1888–1974, United States)

Bells for John Whiteside's Daughter

There was such speed in her little body,
And such lightness in her footfall,
It is no wonder her brown study° reverie
Astonishes us all.

Her wars were bruited° rumored
We looked among orchard trees and beyond
Where she took arms against her shadow,
Or harried unto the pond

The lazy geese, like a snow cloud
Dripping their snow on the green grass,
Tricking and stopping, sleepy and proud,
Who cried in goose, Alas,

For the tireless heart within the little
Lady with rod that made them rise
From their noon apple-dreams and scuttle
Goose-fashion under the skies!

But now go the bells, and we are ready,
In one house we are sternly stopped
To say we are vexed at her brown study,
Lying so primly propped.

Piazza Piece

—I am a gentleman in a dustcoat trying
To make you hear. Your ears are soft and small
And listen to an old man not at all.
They want the young men's whispering and sighing.
But see the roses on your trellis dying
And hear the spectral singing of the moon;
For I must have my lovely lady soon,
I am a gentleman in a dustcoat trying.

—I am a lady young in beauty waiting
Until my truelove comes, and then we kiss.
But what grey man among the vines is this
Whose words are dry and faint as in a dream?
Back from my trellis, Sir, before I scream!
I am a lady young in beauty waiting.

CLAUDE McKAY

(1890–1948, United States)

The White House[1]

Your door is shut against my tightened face,
And I am sharp as steel with discontent;
But I possess the courage and the grace
To bear my anger proudly and unbent.

THE WHITE HOUSE [1]**the white house** not a reference to the President's residence in Washington.

The pavement slabs burn loose beneath my feet,
A chafing savage, down the decent street;
And passion rends my vitals as I pass,
Where boldly shines your shuttered door of glass.
Oh, I must search for wisdom every hour,
Deep in my wrathful bosom sore and raw,
And find in it the superhuman power
To hold me to the letter of your law!
Oh, I must keep my heart inviolate
Against the potent poison of your hate.

America

Although she feeds me bread of bitterness,
And sinks into my throat her tiger's tooth,
Stealing my breath of life, I will confess
I love this cultured hell that tests my youth!
Her vigor flows like tides into my blood,
Giving me strength erect against her hate.
Her bigness sweeps my being like a flood.
Yet as a rebel fronts a king in state,
I stand within her walls with not a shred
Of terror, malice, not a word of jeer.
Darkly I gaze into the days ahead,
And see her might and granite wonders there,
Beneath the touch of Time's unerring hand,
Like priceless treasures sinking in the sand.

The Harlem Dancer

Applauding youths laughed with young prostitutes
And watched her perfect, half-clothed body sway;
Her voice was like the sound of blended flutes
Blown by black players upon a picnic day.
She sang and danced on gracefully and calm,
The light gauze hanging loose about her form;
To me she seemed a proudly-swaying palm
Grown lovelier for passing through a storm.
Upon her swarthy neck black shiny curls
Luxuriant fell; and tossing coins in praise,
The wine-flushed, bold-eyed boys, and even the girls,
Devoured her shape with eager, passionate gaze;
But looking at her falsely-smiling face,
I knew her self was not in that strange place.

If We Must Die

If we must die, let it not be like hogs
Hunted and penned in an inglorious spot,
While round us bark the mad and hungry dogs,
Making their mock at our accursed lot.
If we must die, O let us nobly die,
So that our precious blood may not be shed
In vain; then even the monsters we defy
Shall be constrained to honor us though dead!
O kinsmen! we must meet the common foe!
Though far outnumbered let us show us brave,
And for their thousand blows deal one deathblow!
What though before us lies the open grave?
Like men we'll face the murderous, cowardly pack,
Pressed to the wall, dying, but fighting back!

Baptism

Into the furnace let me go alone;
Stay you without in terror of the heat.
I will go naked in—for thus 'tis sweet—
Into the weird depths of the hottest zone.
I will not quiver in the frailest bone,
You will not note a flicker of defeat;
My heart shall tremble not its fate to meet,
My mouth give utterance to any moan.
The yawning oven spits forth fiery spears;
Red aspish tongues shout wordlessly my name.
Desire destroys, consumes my mortal fears,
Transforming me into a shape of flame.
I will come out, back to your world of tears,
A stronger soul within a finer frame.

ARCHIBALD MacLEISH

(1892–1982, United States)

Ars Poetica

A poem should be palpable and mute
As a globed fruit

Dumb
As old medallions to the thumb

Silent as the sleeve-worn stone
Of casement ledges where the moss has grown—

A poem should be wordless
As the flight of birds

A poem should be motionless in time
As the moon climbs

Leaving, as the moon releases
Twig by twig the night-entangled trees,

Leaving, as the moon behind the winter leaves,
Memory by memory the mind—

A poem should be motionless in time
As the moon climbs

A poem should be equal to:
Not true

For all the history of grief
An empty doorway and a maple leaf

For love
The leaning grasses and two lights above the sea—

A poem should not mean
But be.

Memorial Rain

Ambassador Puser the ambassador
Reminds himself in French, felicitous tongue,
What these (young men no longer) lie here for
In rows that once, and somewhere else, were young—

All night in Brussels the wind had tugged at my door:
I had heard the wind at my door and the trees strung
Taut, and to me who had never been before
In that country it was a strange wind blowing
Steadily, stiffening the walls, the floor,
The roof of my room. I had not slept for knowing
He too, dead, was a stranger in that land
And felt beneath the earth in the wind's flowing

A tightening of roots and would not understand,
Remembering lake winds in Illinois,
That strange wind. I had felt his bones in the sand
Listening.

—Reflects that these enjoy
Their country's gratitude, that deep repose,
That peace no pain can break, no hurt destroy,
That rest, that sleep—

At Ghent the wind rose.
There was a smell of rain and a heavy drag
Of wind in the hedges but not as the wind blows
Over fresh water when the waves lag
Foaming and the willows huddle and it will rain:
I felt him waiting.

—Indicates the flag
Which (may he say) enisles in Flanders' plain
This little field these happy, happy dead
Have made America—

In the ripe grain
The wind coiled glistening, darted, fled,
Dragging its heavy body: at Waereghem
The wind coiled in the grass above his head:
Waiting—listening—

—Dedicates to them
This earth their bones have hallowed, this last gift
A grateful country—

Under the dry grass stem
The words are blurred, are thickened, the words sift
Confused by the rasp of the wind, by the thin grating
Of ants under the grass, the minute shift
And tumble of dusty sand separating
From dusty sand. The roots of the grass strain,
Tighten, the earth is rigid, waits—he is waiting—

And suddenly, and all at once, the rain!

The people scatter, they run into houses, the wind
Is trampled under the rain, shakes free, is again
Trampled. The rain gathers, running in thinned
Spurts of water that ravel in the dry sand
Seeping into the sand under the grass roots, seeping

Between cracked boards to the bones of a clenched hand:
The earth relaxes, loosens; he is sleeping,
He rests, he is quiet, he sleeps in a strange land.

The End of the World

Quite unexpectedly as Vasserot
The armless ambidextrian was lighting
A match between his great and second toe
And Ralph the lion was engaged in biting
The neck of Madame Sossman while the drum
Pointed, and Teeny was about to cough
In waltz-time swinging Jocko by the thumb—
Quite unexpectedly the top blew off:

And there, there overhead, there, there, hung over
Those thousands of white faces, those dazed eyes,
There in the starless dark the poise, the hover,
There with vast wings across the canceled skies,
There in the sudden blackness the black pall
Of nothing, nothing, nothing—nothing at all.

WILFRED OWEN

(1893–1918, England)

Anthem for Doomed Youth

What passing-bells for these who die as cattle?
  —Only the monstrous anger of the guns.
  Only the stuttering rifles' rapid rattle
Can patter out their hasty orisons.° prayers
No mockeries now for them; no prayers nor bells;
  Nor any voice of mourning save the choirs,—
The shrill, demented choirs of wailing shells;
  And bugles calling for them from sad shires.

What candles may be held to speed them all?
  Not in the hands of boys but in their eyes
Shall shine the holy glimmers of goodbyes.
  The pallor of girls' brows shall be their pall;
Their flowers the tenderness of patient minds,
And each slow dusk a drawing-down of blinds.

Dulce et Decorum Est[1]

Bent double, like old beggars under sacks,
Knock-kneed, coughing like hags, we cursed through sludge,
Till on the haunting flares we turned our backs
And towards our distant rest began to trudge.
Men marched asleep. Many had lost their boots
But limped on, blood-shod. All went lame; all blind;
Drunk with fatigue; deaf even to the hoots
Of tired, outstripped Five-Nines that dropped behind.

Gas! GAS! Quick, boys!—An ecstasy of fumbling,
Fitting the clumsy helmets just in time;
But someone still was yelling out and stumbling,
And flound'ring like a man in fire or lime . . .
Dim, through the misty panes and thick green light,
As under a green sea, I saw him drowning.

In all my dreams, before my helpless sight,
He plunges at me, guttering, choking, drowning.

If in some smothering dreams you too could pace
Behind the wagon that we flung him in,
And watch the white eyes writhing in his face,
His hanging face, like a devil's sick of sin;
If you could hear, at every jolt, the blood
Come gargling from the froth-corrupted lungs,
Obscene as cancer, bitter as the cud
Of vile, incurable sores on innocent tongues,—
My friend, you would not tell with such high zest
To children ardent for some desperate glory,
The old Lie: Dulce et decorum est
Pro patria mori.

E. E. CUMMINGS

(1894–1962, United States)

in Just—

in Just—
spring   when the world is mud-
luscious the little
lame balloonman

DULCE ET DECORUM EST [1]Latin: "It is sweet and fitting to die for one's country."

whistles far and wee

and eddieandbill come
running from marbles and
piracies and it's
spring

when the world is puddle-wonderful

the queer
old balloonman whistles
far and wee
and bettyandisbel come dancing

from hopscotch and jump-rope and

it's
spring
and
the

goat-footed

balloonMan whistles
far
and
wee

next to of course god america i

"next to of course god america i
love you land of the pilgrims' and so forth oh
say can you see by the dawn's early my
country 'tis of centuries come and go
and are no more what of it we should worry
in every language even deafanddumb
thy sons acclaim your glorious name by gorry
by jingo by gee by gosh by gum
why talk of beauty what could be more beaut-
iful than these heroic happy dead
who rushed like lions to the roaring slaughter
they did not stop to think they died instead
then shall the voice of liberty be mute?"

He spoke. And drank rapidly a glass of water

the Cambridge ladies who live in furnished souls

the Cambridge ladies who live in furnished souls
are unbeautiful and have comfortable minds
(also, with the church's protestant blessings
daughters, unscented shapeless spirited)
they believe in Christ and Longfellow, both dead,
are invariably interested in so many things—
at the present writing one still finds
delighted fingers knitting for the is it Poles?
perhaps. While permanent faces coyly bandy
scandal of Mrs. N and Professor D
. . . . the Cambridge ladies do not care, above
Cambridge if sometimes in its box of
sky lavender and cornerless, the
moon rattles like a fragment of angry candy

she being Brand

she being Brand

-new;and you
know consequently a
little stiff i was
careful of her and (having

thoroughly oiled the universal
joint tested my gas felt of
her radiator made sure her springs were O.

K.)i went right to it flooded-the-carburetor cranked her

up,slipped the
clutch (and then somehow got into reverse she
kicked what
the hell) next
minute i was back in neutral tried and

again slo-wly;bare,ly nudge.   ing(my

lev-er Right-
oh and her gears being in
A 1 shape passed

from low through
second-in-to-high like
greasedlightning)just as we turned the corner of Divinity

avenue i touched the accelerator and give

her the juice,good

                    (it
was the first ride and believe i we was
happy to see how nice she acted right up to
the last minute coming back down by the Public
Gardens i slammed on
the

internalexpanding
&
externalcontracting
brakes Bothatonce and

brought allofher tremB
-ling
to a:dead.

stand-
;Still)

if everything happens that can't be done

if everything happens that can't be done
(and anything's righter
than books
could plan)
the stupidest teacher will almost guess
(with a run
skip
around we go yes)
there's nothing as something as one

one hasn't a why or because or although
(and buds know better
than books
don't grow)
one's anything old being everything new
(with a what

which
around we come who)
one's everyanything so

so world is a leaf so tree is a bough
(and birds sing sweeter
than books
tell how)
so here is away and so your is a my
(with a down
up
around again fly)
forever was never till now

now i love you and you love me
(and books are shuter
than books
can be)
and deep in the high that does nothing but fall
(with a shout
each
around we go all)
there's somebody calling who's we

we're anything brighter than even the sun
(we're everything greater
than books
might mean)
we're everyanything more than believe
(with a spin
leap
alive we're alive)
we're wonderful one times one

ALLEN TATE

(1899–1979, United States)

Ode to the Confederate Dead

Row after row with strict impunity
The headstones yield their names to the element,
The wind whirrs without recollection;

In the riven troughs the splayed leaves
Pile up, of nature the casual sacrament
To the seasonal eternity of death;
Then driven by the fierce scrutiny
Of heaven to their election in the vast breath,
They sough the rumour of mortality.

Autumn is desolation in the plot
Of a thousand acres where these memories grow
From the inexhaustible bodies that are not
Dead, but feed the grass row after rich row.
Think of the autumns that have come and gone!—
Ambitious November with the humors of the year,
With a particular zeal for every slab,
Staining the uncomfortable angels that rot
On the slabs, a wing chipped here, an arm there:
The brute curiosity of an angel's stare
Turns you, like them, to stone,
Transforms the heaving air
Till plunged to a heavier world below
You shift your sea-space blindly
Heaving, turning like the blind crab.

Dazed by the wind, only the wind
The leaves flying, plunge

You know who have waited by the wall
The twilight certainty of an animal,
Those midnight restitutions of the blood
You know—the immitigable pines, the smoky frieze
Of the sky, the sudden call: you know the rage,
The cool pool left by the mounting flood,
Of muted Zeno and Parmenides.[1]
You who have waited for the angry resolution
Of those desires that should be yours tomorrow,
You know the unimportant shrift of death
And praise the vision
And praise the arrogant circumstance
Of those who fall
Rank upon rank, hurried beyond decision—
Here by the sagging gate, stopped by the wall.

Seeing, seeing only the leaves
Flying, plunge and expire

---

[1]**Zeno and Parmenides** Greek philosophers.

Turn your eyes to the immoderate past,
Turn to the inscrutable infantry rising
Demons out of the earth—they will not last.
Stonewall, Stonewall, and the sunken fields of hemp,
Shiloh, Antietam, Malvern Hill, Bull Run.[2]
Lost in the orient of the thick-and-fast
You will curse the setting sun.

Cursing only the leaves crying
Like an old man in a storm

You hear the shout, the crazy hemlocks point
With troubled fingers, to the silence which
Smothers you, a mummy, in time.

The hound bitch
Toothless and dying, in a musty cellar
Hears the wind only.

Now that the salt of their blood
Stiffens the saltier oblivion of the sea,
Seals the malignant purity of the flood,
What shall we who count our days and bow
Our heads with a commemorial woe
In the ribboned coats of grim felicity,
What shall we say of the bones, unclean,
Whose verdurous anonymity will grow?
The ragged arms, the ragged heads and eyes
Lost in these acres of the insane green?
The gray lean spiders come, they come and go;
In a tangle of willows without light
The singular screech-owl's tight
Invisible lyric seeds the mind
With the furious murmur of their chivalry.

We shall say only the leaves
Flying, plunge and expire

We shall say only the leaves whispering
In the improbable mist of nightfall
That flies on multiple wing;
Night is the beginning and the end
And in between the ends of distraction
Waits mute speculation, the patient curse

[2]These are all battles of the Civil War.

That stones the eyes, or like the jaguar leaps
For his own image in a jungle pool, his victim.

What shall we say who have knowledge
Carried to the heart? Shall we take the act
To the grave? Shall we, more hopeful, set up the grave
In the house? The ravenous grave?

Leave now
The shut gate and the decomposing wall:
The gentle serpent, green in the mulberry bush,
Riots with his tongue through the hush—
Sentinel of the grave who counts us all!

HART CRANE

(1899–1932, United States)

from Voyages

II

—And yet this great wink of eternity,
Or rimless floods, unfettered leewardings,
Samite[1] sheeted and processioned where
Her undinal vast belly moonward bends,
Laughing the wrapt inflections of our love;

Take this Sea, whose diapason knells
On scrolls of silver snowy sentences,
The sceptred terror of whose sessions rends
As her demeanors motion well or ill,
All but the pieties of lovers' hands.

And onward, as bells off San Salvador
Salute the crocus lustres of the stars,
In these poinsettia meadows of her tides,—
Adagios[2] of islands, O my Prodigal,
Complete the dark confessions her veins spell.

VOYAGES [1]**samite** a rich silk fabric. [2]**adagios** slow graceful divisions of a musical composition.

Mark how her turning shoulders wind the hours,
And hasten while her penniless rich palms
Pass superscription of bent foam and wave,—
Hasten, while they are true,—sleep, death, desire,
Close round one instant in one floating flower.

Bind us in time, O Seasons clear, and awe.
O minstrel galleons of Carib fire,
Bequeath us to no earthly shore until
Is answered in the vortex of our grave
The seal's wide spindrift[3] gaze toward paradise.

LANGSTON HUGHES

(1902–1967, United States)

I, Too

I, too, sing America.

I am the darker brother.
They send me to eat in the kitchen
When company comes,
But I laugh,
And eat well,
And grow strong.

Tomorrow,
I'll sit at the table
When company comes.
Nobody'll dare
Say to me,
"Eat in the kitchen,"
Then.

Besides,
They'll see how beautiful I am
And be ashamed—

I, too, am America.

VOYAGES [3]**spindrift** filled with blown sea spray.

STEVIE SMITH

(1902–1971, England)

Not Waving But Drowning

Nobody heard him, the dead man,
But still he lay moaning:
I was much further out than you thought
And not waving but drowning.

Poor chap, he always loved larking
And now he's dead
It must have been too cold for him his heart gave way,
They said.

Oh, no no no, it was too cold always
(Still the dead one lay moaning)
I was much too far out all my life
And not waving but drowning.

Our Bog is Dood

Our Bog is dood, our Bog is dood,
They lisped in accents mild,
But when I asked them to explain
They grew a little wild.
How do you know your Bog is dood
My darling little child?

We know because we wish it so
That is enough, they cried,
And straight within each infant eye
Stood up the flame of pride,
And if you do not think it so
You shall be crucified.

Then tell me, darling little ones,
What's dood, suppose Bog is?
Just what we think, the answer came,
Just what we think it is.
They bowed their heads. Our Bog is ours
And we are wholly his.

But when they raised them up again
They had forgotten me
Each one upon each other glared
In pride and misery
For what was dood, and what their Bog
They never could agree.

Oh sweet it was to leave them then,
And sweeter not to see,
And sweetest of all to walk alone
Beside the encroaching sea,
The sea that soon should drown them all,
That never yet drowned me.

RICHARD EBERHART

(1904– , United States)

Long Term Suffering

There will be no examination in Long Term Suffering,
The course will come to an end as planned.
I have found that examinations are useless,
We have altogether too short a time to spend.

Time, ladies and gentlemen, is the great examiner.
I have discovered that this is true.
It is what you write as you go through the course
Is the only determinant and determinator of you.

Long Term Suffering is for those of all ages
In our tussling University, our bulging classroom.
It may be that I will profess near madness,
It may be that you will write out your doom.

All that you will have at the end of the course
Is writings you indite, or poems you make,
If you make them. Words, words in a sea flow;
At any rate, a lot of heartbreak.

Save your papers. It may be that years later,
Forty, maybe, you would like to look back
At your course in Long Term Suffering,
And note how strangely you had to act.

Reading Room, The New York Public Library

In the reading room in the New York Public Library
All sorts of souls were bent over silence reading the past,
Or the present, or maybe it was the future, persons
Devoted to silence and the flowering of the imagination,
When all of a sudden I saw my love,
She was a faun with light steps and brilliant eye
And she came walking among the tables and rows of persons,

Straight from the forest to the center of New York,
And nobody noticed, or raised an eyelash.
These were fixed on imaginary splendours of the past,
Or of the present, or maybe of the future, maybe
Something as seductive as the aquiline nose
Of Eleanor of Aquitaine, or Cleopatra's wrist-locket in Egypt,
Or maybe they were thinking of Juliana of Norwich.

The people of this world pay no attention to the fauns
Whether of this world or of another, but there she was,
All gaudy pelt, and sleek, gracefully moving,
Her amber eye was bright among the porticoes,
Her delicate ears were raised to hear of love,
Her lips had the appearance of green grass
About to be trodden, and her shanks were smooth and sleek.

Everybody was in the splendor of his imagination,
Nobody paid any attention to this splendour
Appearing in the New York Public Library,
Their eyes were on China, India, Arabia, or the Balearics,
While my faun was walking among the tables and eyes
Inventing their world of life, invisible and light,
In silence and sweet temper, loving the world.

LÉOPOLD SÉDAR-SENGHOR

(1906–   , Senegal)

Visit

I dream in the intimate semi-darkness of an afternoon.
I am visited by the fatigues of the day,
The deceased of the year, the souvenirs of the decade,
Like the procession of the dead in the village on the horizon of the
shallow sea.

It is the same sun bedewed with illusions,
The same sky unnerved by hidden presences,
The same sky feared by those who have a reckoning with the dead.
And suddenly my dead draw near to me. . . .

New York

(FOR JAZZ ORCHESTRA: TRUMPET SOLO)

1

New York! At first I was confused by your beauty, by those great golden long-legged girls.
So shy at first before your blue metallic eyes, your frosted smile
So shy. And the anguish in the depths of skyscraper streets
Lifting eyes hawkhooded to the sun's eclipse.
Sulphurous your light and livid the towers with heads that thunderbolt the sky
The skyscrapers which defy the storms with muscles of steel and stone-glazed hide.
But two weeks on the bare sidewalks of Manhattan
—At the end of the third week the fever seizes you with the pounce of a leopard
Two weeks without rivers or fields, all the birds of the air
Falling sudden and dead on the high ashes of flat rooftops.
No smile of a child blooms, his hand refreshed in my hand,
No mother's breast, but only nylon legs. Legs and breasts that have no sweat nor smell.
No tender word for there are no lips, only artificial hearts paid for in hard cash
And no book where wisdom may be read. The painter's palette blossoms with crystals of coral.
Nights of insomnia oh nights of Manhattan! So agitated by flickering lights, while motor-horns howl of empty hours
And while dark waters carry away hygienic loves, like rivers flooded with the corpses of children.

2

Now is the time of signs and reckonings
New York! Now is the time of manna and hyssop.
You must but listen to the trombones of God, let your heart beat in the rhythm of blood, your blood.
I saw in Harlem humming with noise with stately colours and flamboyant smells

—It was teatime at the house of the seller of pharmaceutical products—
I saw them preparing the festival of night for escape from the day.
I proclaim night more truthful than the day.
It was the pure hour when in the streets God makes the life that goes back beyond memory spring up
All the amphibious elements shining like suns.
Harlem Harlem! Now I saw Harlem! A green breeze of corn springs up from the pavements ploughed by the naked feet of dancers
Bottoms waves of silk and sword-blade breasts, water-lily ballets and fabulous masks.
At the feet of police-horses roll the mangoes of love from low houses.
And I saw along the sidewalks streams of white rum streams of black milk in the blue fog of cigars.
I saw the sky in the evening snow cotton-flowers and seraphims' wings and sorcerers' plumes.
Listen New York! Oh listen to your male voice of brass vibrating with oboes, the anguish choked with tears falling in great clots of blood
Listen to the distant beating of your nocturnal heart, rhythm and blood of the tom-tom, tom-tom blood and tom-tom.

3

New York! I say to you: New York let black blood flow into your blood
That it may rub the rust from your steel joints, like an oil of life.
That it may give to your bridges the bend of buttocks and the suppleness of creepers.
Now return the most ancient times, the unity recovered, the reconciliation of the Lion the Bull and the Tree
Thought linked to act, ear to heart, sign to sense.
There are your rivers murmuring with scented crocodiles and mirage-eyed manatees. And no need to invent the Sirens.
But it is enough to open the eyes to the rainbow of April
And the ears, above all the ears, to God who out of the laugh of a saxophone created the heaven and the earth in six days.
And the seventh day he slept the great sleep of the Negro.

W. H. AUDEN

(1907–1973, England)

As I Walked Out One Evening

As I walked out one evening,
Walking down Bristol Street,
The crowds upon the pavement
Were fields of harvest wheat.

And down by the brimming river
I heard a lover sing
Under an arch of the railway:
"Love has no ending.

"I'll love you, dear, I'll love you
Till China and Africa meet,
And the river jumps over the mountain
And the salmon sing in the street,

"I'll love you till the ocean
Is folded and hung up to dry
And the seven stars go squawking
Like geese about the sky.

"The years shall run like rabbits,
For in my arms I hold
The Flower of the Ages,
And the first love of the world."

But all the clocks in the city
Began to whirr and chime:
"O let not Time deceive you,
You cannot conquer Time.

"In the burrows of the Nightmare
Where Justice naked is,
Time watches from the shadow
And coughs when you would kiss.

"In headaches and in worry
Vaguely life leaks away.
And Time will have his fancy
To-morrow or to-day.

"Into many a green valley
Drifts the appalling snow;
Time breaks the threaded dances
And the diver's brilliant bow.

"O plunge your hands in water,
Plunge them in up to the wrist;
Stare, stare in the basin
And wonder what you've missed.

"The glacier knocks in the cupboard,
The desert sighs in the bed,

And the crack in the tea-cup opens
  A lane to the land of the dead.

"Where the beggars raffle the banknotes
  And the Giant is enchanting to Jack,
And the Lily-white Boy is a Roarer,
  And Jill goes down on her back.

"O look, look in the mirror,
  O look in your distress;
Life remains a blessing
  Although you cannot bless.

"O stand, stand at the window
  As the tears scald and start;
You shall love your crooked neighbour
  With your crooked heart."

It was late, late in the evening,
  The lovers they were gone;
The clocks had ceased their chiming,
  And the deep river ran on.

O what is that sound which so thrills the ear

O what is that sound which so thrills the ear
  Down in the valley drumming, drumming?
Only the scarlet soldiers, dear,
    The soldiers coming.

O what is that light I see flashing so clear
  Over the distance brightly, brightly?
Only the sun on their weapons, dear,
    As they step lightly.

O what are they doing with all that gear;
  What are they doing this morning, this morning?
Only the usual manoeuvres, dear,
    Or perhaps a warning.

O why have they left the road down there;
  Why are they suddenly wheeling, wheeling?
Perhaps a change in the orders, dear;
    Why are you kneeling?

O haven't they stopped for the doctor's care;
  Haven't they reined their horses, their horses?
Why, they are none of them wounded, dear,
    None of these forces.

O is it the parson they want with white hair;
  Is it the parson, is it, is it?
No, they are passing his gateway, dear,
    Without a visit.

O it must be the farmer who lives so near;
  It must be the farmer so cunning, so cunning?
They have passed the farm already, dear,
    And now they are running.

O where are you going? stay with me here!
  Were the vows you swore me deceiving, deceiving?
No, I promised to love you, dear,
    But I must be leaving.

O it's broken the lock and splintered the door,
  O it's the gate where they're turning, turning;
Their feet are heavy on the floor
    And their eyes are burning.

Musée des Beaux Arts

About suffering they were never wrong,
The old Masters: how well they understood
Its human position: how it takes place
While someone else is eating or opening a window or just walking dully along;
How, when the aged are reverently, passionately waiting
For the miraculous birth, there always must be
Children who did not specially want it to happen, skating
On a pond at the edge of the wood:
They never forgot
That even the dreadful martyrdom must run its course
Anyhow in a corner, some untidy spot
Where the dogs go on with their doggy life and the torturer's horse
Scratches its innocent behind on a tree.

In Breughel's *Icarus,* for instance: how everything turns away
Quite leisurely from the disaster; the ploughman may
Have heard the splash, the forsaken cry,

But for him it was not an important failure; the sun shone
As it had to on the white legs disappearing into the green
Water, and the expensive delicate ship that must have seen
Something amazing, a boy falling out of the sky,
Had somewhere to get to and sailed calmly on.

The Shield of Achilles

She looked over his shoulder
    For vines and olive trees,
Marble well-governed cities
    And ships upon untamed seas,
But there on the shining metal
    His hands had put instead
An artificial wilderness
    And a sky like lead.

A plain without a feature, bare and brown,
    No blade of grass, no sign of neighborhood,
Nothing to eat and nowhere to sit down,
    Yet, congregated on its blankness, stood
    An unintelligible multitude,
A million eyes, a million boots in line,
Without expression, waiting for a sign.

Out of the air a voice without a face
    Proved by statistics that some cause was just
In tones as dry and level as the place:
    No one was cheered and nothing was discussed;
    Column by column in a cloud of dust
They marched away enduring a belief
Whose logic brought them, somewhere else, to grief.

She looked over his shoulder
    For ritual pieties,
White flower-garlanded heifers,
    Libation and sacrifice,
But there on the shining metal
    Where the altar should have been,
She saw by his flickering forge-light
    Quite another scene.

Barbed wire enclosed an arbitrary spot
    Where bored officials lounged (one cracked a joke)
And sentries sweated for the day was hot:
    A crowd of ordinary decent folk
    Watched from without and neither moved nor spoke

As three pale figures were led forth and bound
To three posts driven upright in the ground.

The mass and majesty of this world, all
   That carries weight and always weighs the same
Lay in the hands of others; they were small
   And could not hope for help and no help came:
   What their foes liked to do was done, their shame
Was all the worst could wish; they lost their pride
And died as men before their bodies died.

She looked over his shoulder
   For athletes at their games,
Men and women in a dance
   Moving their sweet limbs
Quick, quick, to music,
   But there on the shining shield
His hands had set no dancing-floor
   But a weed-choked field.

A ragged urchin, aimless and alone,
   Loitered about that vacancy; a bird
Flew up to safety from his well-aimed stone:
   That girls are raped, that two boys knife a third,
   Were axioms to him, who'd never heard
Of any world where promises were kept,
Or one could weep because another wept.

The thin-lipped armorer,
   Hephaestos, hobbled away,
Thetis of the shining breasts
   Cried out in dismay
At what the god had wrought
   To please her son, the strong
Iron-hearted man-slaying Achilles
   Who would not live long.

THEODORE ROETHKE

(1908–1963, United States)

My Papa's Waltz

The whiskey on your breath
Could make a small boy dizzy;
But I hung on like death:
Such waltzing was not easy.

We romped until the pans
Slid from the kitchen shelf;
My mother's countenance
Could not unfrown itself.

The hand that held my wrist
Was battered on one knuckle;
At every step you missed
My right ear scraped a buckle.

You beat time on my head
With a palm caked hard by dirt,
Then waltzed me off to bed
Still clinging to your shirt.

Frau Bauman, Frau Schmidt, and Frau Schwartze

Gone the three ancient ladies
Who creaked on the greenhouse ladders,
Reaching up white strings
To wind, to wind
The sweet-pea tendrils, the smilax,
Nasturtiums, the climbing
Roses, to straighten
Carnations, red
Chrysanthemums; the stiff
Stems, jointed like corn,
They tied and tucked,—
These nurses of nobody else.
Quicker than birds, they dipped
Up and sifted the dirt;
They sprinkled and shook;
They stood astride pipes,
Their skirts billowing out wide into tents,
Their hands twinkling with wet;
Like witches they flew along rows
Keeping creation at ease;
With a tendril for needle
They sewed up the air with a stem;
They teased out the seed that the cold kept asleep,—
All the coils, loops, and whorls.
They trellised the sun; they plotted for more than themselves.

I remember how they picked me up, a spindly kid,
Punching and poking my thin ribs
Till I lay in their laps, laughing,
Weak as a whiffet;° insignificant person
Now, when I'm alone and cold in my bed,
They still hover over me,
These ancient leathery crones,
With their bandannas stiffened with sweat,
And their thorn-bitten wrists,
And their snuff-laden breath blowing lightly over me in my first sleep.

STEPHEN SPENDER

(1909– , England)

Rough

My parents kept me from children who were rough
Who threw words like stones and who wore torn clothes.
Their thighs showed through rags. They ran in the street.
And climbed cliffs and stripped by the country streams.

I feared more than tigers their muscles like iron
Their jerking hands and their knees tight on my arms.
I feared the salt-coarse pointing of those boys
Who copied my lisp behind me on the road.

They were lithe, they sprang out behind hedges
Like dogs to bark at my world. They threw mud
While I looked the other way, pretending to smile.
I longed to forgive them, but they never smiled.

ELIZABETH BISHOP

(1911–1979, United States)

The Fish

I caught a tremendous fish
And held him beside the boat
half out of water, with my hook
fast in the corner of his mouth.
He didn't fight.
He hadn't fought at all.

He hung a grunting weight,
battered and venerable
and homely. Here and there
his brown skin hung in strips
like ancient wallpaper,
and its pattern of darker brown
was like wallpaper:
shapes like full-blown roses
stained and lost through age.
He was speckled with barnacles,
fine rosettes of lime,
and infested
with tiny white sea-lice,
and underneath two or three
rags of green weed hung down.
While his gills were breathing in
the terrible oxygen
—the frightening gills,
fresh and crisp with blood,
I thought of the coarse white flesh
packed in like feathers,
the big bones and the little bones,
the dramatic reds and blacks
of his shiny entrails,
and the pink swim-bladder
like a big peony.
I looked into his eyes
which were far larger than mine
but shallower, and yellowed,
the irises backed and packed
with tarnished tinfoil
seen through the lenses
of old scratched isinglass.[1]
They shifted a little, but not
to return my stare.
—It was more like the tipping
of an object toward the light.
I admired his sullen face,
the mechanism of his jaw,
and then I saw
that from his lower lip
—if you could call it a lip—
grim, wet, and weaponlike,
hung five old pieces of fish-line,

---

[1]**isinglass** semi-transparent substance used for windows.

or four and a wire leader
with the swivel still attached,
with all their five big hooks
grown firmly in his mouth.
A green line, frayed at the end
where he broke it, two heavier lines,
and a fine black thread
still crimped from the strain and snap
when it broke and he got away.
Like medals with their ribbons
frayed and wavering,
a five-haired beard of wisdom
trailing from his aching jaw.
I stared and stared
and victory filled up
the little rented boat,
from the pool of bilge
where oil had spread a rainbow
around the rusted engine
to the bailer rusted orange,
the sun-cracked thwarts,
the oarlocks on their strings,
the gunnels—until everything
was rainbow, rainbow, rainbow!
And I let the fish go.

ROBERT HAYDEN

(1913–1988, United States)

Those Winter Sundays

Sundays too my father got up early
and put his clothes on in the blueblack cold,
then with cracked hands that ached
from labor in the weekday weather made
banked fires blaze. No one ever thanked him.

I'd wake and hear the cold splintering, breaking.
When the rooms were warm, he'd call,
and slowly I would rise and dress,
fearing the chronic angers of that house,

Speaking indifferently to him,
who had driven out the cold

and polished my good shoes as well.
What did I know, what did I know
of love's austere and lonely offices?

Frederick Douglass

When it is finally ours, this freedom, this liberty, this beautiful
and terrible thing, needful to man as air,
usable as earth; when it belongs at last to all,
when it is truly instinct, brain matter, diastole, systole,
reflex action; when it is finally won; when it is more
than the gaudy mumbo jumbo of politicians,
this man, this Douglass, this former slave, this Negro
beaten to his knees, exiled, visioning a world
where none is lonely, none hunted, alien,
this man, superb in love and logic, this man
shall be remembered. Oh, not with statues' rhetoric,
not with legends and poems and wreaths of bronze alone,
but with the lives grown out of his life, the lives
fleshing his dream of the beautiful, needful thing.

DYLAN THOMAS

(1914–1953, Wales)

Fern Hill

Now as I was young and easy under the apple boughs
About the lilting house and happy as the grass was green,
   The night above the dingle starry,
      Time let me hail and climb
   Golden in the heydays of his eyes,
And honoured among wagons I was prince of the apple towns
And once below a time I lordly had the trees and leaves
      Trail with daisies and barley
   Down the rivers of the windfall light.

And as I was green and carefree, famous among the barns
About the happy yard and singing as the farm was home,
   In the sun that is young once only,
      Time let me play and be
   Golden in the mercy of his means,

And green and golden I was huntsman and herdsman, the calves
Sang to my horn, the foxes on the hills barked clear and cold,
And the sabbath rang slowly
In the pebbles of the holy streams.

All the sun long it was running, it was lovely, the hay
Fields high as the house, the tunes from the chimneys, it was air
And playing, lovely and watery
And fire green as grass.
And nightly under the simple stars
As I rode to sleep the owls were bearing the farm away,
All the moon long I heard, blessed among stables, the
nightjars° nightbirds
Flying with the ricks,° and the horses haystacks
Flashing into the dark.

And then to awake, and the farm, like a wanderer white
With the dew, come back, the cock on his shoulder: it was all
Shining, it was Adam and maiden,
The sky gathered again
And the sun grew round that very day.
So it must have been after the birth of the simple light
In the first, spinning place, the spellbound horses walking warm
Out of the whinnying green stable
On to the fields of praise.

And honoured among foxes and pheasants by the gay house
Under the new made clouds and happy as the heart was long,
In the sun born over and over,
I ran my heedless ways,
My wishes raced through the house high hay
And nothing I cared, at my sky blue trades, that time allows
In all his tuneful turning so few and such morning songs
Before the children green and golden
Follow him out of grace,

Nothing I cared, in the lamb white days, that time would take me
Up to the swallow thronged loft by the shadow of my hand,
In the moon that is always rising,
Nor that riding to sleep
I should hear him fly with the high fields
And wake to the farm forever fled from the childless land.
Oh as I was young and easy in the mercy of his means,
Time held me green and dying
Though I sang in my chains like the sea.

HENRY REED

(1914– , England)

Naming of Parts

Today we have naming of parts. Yesterday,
We had daily cleaning. And tomorrow morning,
We shall have what to do after firing. But today,
Today we have naming of parts. Japonica
Glistens like coral in all of the neighbouring gardens,
And today we have naming of parts.

This is the lower sling swivel. And this
Is the upper sling swivel, whose use you will see,
When you are given your slings. And this is the piling swivel,
Which in your case you have not got. The branches
Hold in the gardens their silent, eloquent gestures,
Which in our case we have not got.

This is the safety-catch, which is always released
With an easy flick of the thumb. And please do not let me
See anyone using his finger. You can do it quite easy
If you have any strength in your thumb. The blossoms
Are fragile and motionless, never letting anyone see
Any of them using their finger.

And this you can see is the bolt. The purpose of this
Is to open the breech, as you see. We can slide it
Rapidly backwards and forwards: we call this
Easing the spring. And rapidly backwards and forwards
The early bees are assaulting and fumbling the flowers:
They call it easing the Spring.

They call it easing the Spring: it is perfectly easy
If you have any strength in your thumb: like the bolt,
And the breech, and the cocking-piece, and the point of balance,
Which in our case we have not got; and the almond-blossom
Silent in all of the gardens and the bees going backwards and forwards,
For today we have naming of parts.

Judging Distances

Not only how far away, but the way that you say it
Is very important. Perhaps you may never get
The knack of judging a distance, but at least you know

How to report on a landscape: the central sector,
The right of arc and that, which we had last Tuesday,
And at least you know

That maps are of time, not place, so far as the army
Happens to be concerned—the reason being,
Is one which need not delay us. Again, you know
There are three kinds of tree, three only, the fir and the poplar,
And those which have bushy tops too; and lastly
That things only seem to be things.

A barn is not called a barn, to put it more plainly,
Or a field in the distance, where sheep may be safely grazing.
You must never be over-sure. You must say, when reporting:
At five o'clock in the central sector is a dozen
Of what appear to be animals; whatever you do,
Don't call the bleeders *sheep*.

I am sure that's quite clear; and suppose, for the sake of example,
The one at the end, asleep, endeavors to tell us
What he sees over there to the west, and how far away,
After first having come to attention. There to the west,
On the fields of summer the sun and the shadows bestow
Vestments of purple and gold.

The still white swellings are like a mirage in the heat,
And under the swaying elms a man and a woman
Lie gently together. Which is, perhaps, only to say
That there is a row of houses to the left of arc,
And that under some poplars a pair of what appears to be humans
Appear to be loving.

Well that, for an answer, is what we might rightly call
Moderately satisfactory only, the reason being,
Is that two things have been omitted, and those are important.
The human beings, now: in what direction are they,
And how far away, would you say? And do not forget
There may be dead ground in between.

There may be dead ground in between; and I may not have got
The knack of judging a distance; I will only venture
A guess that perhaps between me and the apparent lovers,
(Who, incidentally, appear by now to have finished,)
At seven o'clock from the houses, is roughly a distance
Of about one year and a half.

GWENDOLYN BROOKS

(1917– , United States)

kitchenette building

We are things of dry hours and the involuntary plan,
Grayed in, and gray. "Dream" makes a giddy sound, not strong
Like "rent," "feeding a wife," "satisfying a man."

But could a dream send up through onion fumes
Its white and violet, fight with fried potatoes
And yesterday's garbage ripening in the hall,
Flutter, or sing an aria down these rooms

Even if we were willing to let it in,
Had time to warm it, keep it very clean,
Anticipate a message, let it begin?

We wonder. But not well! not for a minute!
Since Number Five is out of the bathroom now,
We think of lukewarm water, hope to get in it.

the mother

Abortions will not let you forget.
You remember the children you got that you did not get,
The damp small pulps with a little or with no hair,
The singers and workers that never handled the air.
You will never neglect or beat
Them, or silence or buy with a sweet.
You will never wind up the sucking-thumb
Or scuttle off ghosts that come.
You will never leave them, controlling your luscious sigh,
Return for a snack of them, with gobbling mother-eye.

I have heard in the voices of the wind the voices of my dim
killed children.
I have contracted. I have eased
My dim dears at the breasts they could never suck.
I have said, Sweets, if I sinned, if I seized
Your luck
And your lives from your unfinished reach,
If I stole your births and your names,
Your straight baby tears and your games,
Your stilted or lovely loves, your tumults, your marriages,
aches, and your deaths,

If I poisoned the beginnings of your breaths,
Believe that even in my deliberateness I was not deliberate.
Though why should I whine,
Whine that the crime was other than mine?—
Since anyhow you are dead.
Or rather, or instead,
You were never made.
But that too, I am afraid,
Is faulty: oh, what shall I say, how is the truth to be said?
You were born, you had body, you died.
It is just that you never giggled or planned or cried.

Believe me, I loved you all.
Believe me, I knew you, though faintly, and I loved, I loved you
All.

We Real Cool

THE POOL PLAYERS.
SEVEN AT THE GOLDEN SHOVEL.

We real cool. We
Left school. We

Lurk late. We
Strike straight. We

Sing sin. We
Thin gin. We

Jazz June. We
Die soon.

The Blackstone Rangers

I

AS SEEN BY DISCIPLINES

There they are
Thirty at the corner.
Black, raw, ready.
Sores in the city
that do not want to heal.

II
THE LEADERS

Jeff. Gene. Geronimo. And Bop.
They cancel, cure and curry.
Hardly the dupes of the downtown thing
the cold bonbon,
The rhinestone thing. And hardly
in a hurry.
Hardly Belafonte, King,
Black Jesus, Stokely, Malcolm X or Rap.
Bungled trophies.
Their country is a Nation on no map.

Jeff, Gene, Geronimo and Bop
in the passionate noon,
in bewitching night
are the detailed men, the copious men.
They curry, cure,
they cancel, cancelled images whose Concerts
are not divine, vivacious; the different tins
are intense last entries; pagan argument;
translations of the night.

The Blackstone bitter bureaus
(bureaucracy is footloose) edit, fuse
unfashionable damnations and descent;
and exulting, monstrous hand on monstrous hand,
construct, strangely, a monstrous pearl or grace.

III
GANG GIRLS
A RANGERETTE

Gang Girls are sweet exotics.
Mary Ann
uses the nutrients of her orient,
but sometimes sighs for Cities of blue and jewel
beyond her Ranger rim of Cottage Grove
(Bowery Boys, Disciples, Whip-Birds will
dissolve no margins, stop no savory sanctities.)

Mary is
a rose in a whiskey glass.

Mary's
Februaries shudder and are gone. Aprils

fret frankly, lilac hurries on.
Summer is a hard irregular ridge.
October looks away.
And that's the Year!
Save for her bugle-love.
Save for the bleat of not-obese devotion.
Save for Somebody Terribly Dying, under
the philanthropy of robins. Save for her Ranger
bringing
an amount of rainbow in a string-drawn bag.

"Where did you get the diamond?" Do not ask:
but swallow, straight, the spirals of his flask
and assist him at your zipper; pet his lips
and help him clutch you.

Love's another departure.
Will there be any arrivals, confirmations?
Will there be gleaming?

Mary, the Shakedancer's child
from the rooming-flat, pants carefully, peers at
her laboring lover. . . .
Mary! Mary Ann!
Settle for sandwiches! settle for stocking caps!
for sudden blood, aborted carnival,
the props and niceties of non-loneliness—
the rhymes of Leaning.

ROBERT LOWELL

(1917–1977, United States)

For the Union Dead

"Relinquunt Omnia Servare Rem Publicam."[1]

The old South Boston Aquarium stands
in a Sahara of snow now. Its broken windows are boarded.
The bronze weathervane cod has lost half its scales.
The airy tanks are dry.

FOR THE UNION DEAD [1]"They give up everything to save the Republic."

Once my nose crawled like a snail on the glass;
my hand tingled
to burst the bubbles
drifting from the noses of the cowed, compliant fish.

My hand draws back. I often sigh still
for the dark downward and vegetating kingdom
of the fish and reptile. One morning last March,
I pressed against the new barbed and galvanized

fence on the Boston Common. Behind their cage,
yellow dinosaur steamshovels were grunting
as they cropped up tons of mush and grass
to gouge their underworld garage.

Parking spaces luxuriate like civic
sandpiles in the heart of Boston.
A girdle of orange, Puritan-pumpkin colored girders
braces the tingling Statehouse,

shaking over the excavations, as it faces Colonel Shaw
and his bell-cheeked Negro infantry
on St. Gaudens' shaking Civil War relief,
propped by a plank splint against the garage's earthquake.

Two months after marching through Boston,
half the regiment was dead;
at the dedication,
William James could almost hear the bronze Negroes breathe.

Their monument sticks like a fishbone
in the city's throat.
Its Colonel is as lean
as a compass-needle.

He has an angry wrenlike vigilance,
a greyhound's gentle tautness;
he seems to wince at pleasure,
and suffocate for privacy.

He is out of bounds now. He rejoices in man's lovely,
peculiar power to choose life and die—
when he leads his black soldiers to death,
he cannot bend his back.

On a thousand small town New England greens,
the old white churches hold their air

of sparse, sincere rebellion; frayed flags
quilt the graveyards of the Grand Army of the Republic.

The stone statues of the abstract Union Soldier
grow slimmer and younger each year—
wasp-waisted, they doze over muskets
and muse through their sideburns . . .

Shaw's father wanted no monument
except the ditch,
where his son's body was thrown
and lost with his "niggers."

The ditch is nearer.
There are no statues for the last war here;
on Boylston Street, a commercial photograph
shows Hiroshima boiling

over a Mosler Safe, the "Rock of Ages"
that survived the blast. Space is nearer.
When I crouch to my television set,
the drained faces of Negro school-children rise like balloons.

Colonel Shaw
is riding on his bubble,
he waits
for the blesséd break.

The Aquarium is gone. Everywhere,
giant finned cars nose forward like fish;
a savage servility
slides by on grease.

Jonathan Edwards in Western Massachusetts

Edwards' great millstone and rock
of hope has crumbled, but the square
white houses of his flock
stand in the open air,

out in the cold,
like sheep outside the fold.
Hope lives in doubt.
Faith is trying to do without

faith. In western Massachusetts,
I could almost feel the frontier
crack and disappear.
Edwards thought the world would end there.

We know how the world will end,
but where is paradise, each day farther
from the Pilgrim's blues for England
and the Promised Land.

Was it some country house
that seemed as if it were
Whitehall, if the Lord were there?
so nobly did he live.

Gardens designed
that the breath of flowers in the wind,
or crushed underfoot,
came and went like warbling music?

Bacon's great oak grove
he refused to sell,
when he fell,
saying, "Why should I sell my feathers?"

Ah paradise! Edwards,
I would be afraid
to meet you there as a shade.
We move in different circles.

As a boy, you built a booth
in a swamp for prayer;
lying on your back,
you saw the spiders fly,

basking at their ease,
swimming from tree to tree—
so high, they seemed tacked to the sky.
You knew they would die.

Poor country Berkeley at Yale,
you saw the world was soul,
the soul of God! The soul
of Sarah Pierrepont!

So filled with delight in the Great Being,
she hardly cared for anything—

walking the fields, sweetly singing,
conversing with some one invisible.

Then God's love shone in sun, moon and stars,
on earth, in the waters,
in the air, in the loose winds,
which used to greatly fix your mind.

Often she saw you come home from a ride
or a walk, your coat dotted with thoughts
you had pinned there
on slips of paper.

You gave
her Pompey, a Negro slave,
and eleven children.
Yet people were spiders

in your moment of glory,
at the Great Awakening[1]—"Alas, how many
in this very meeting house are more than likely
to remember my discourse in hell!"

The meeting house remembered!
You stood on stilts in the air,
but you fell from your parish.
"All rising is by a winding stair."

On my pilgrimage to Northampton,
I found no relic,
except the round slice of an oak
you are said to have planted.

It was flesh-colored, new,
and a common piece of kindling,
only fit for burning.
You too must have been green once.

White wig and black coat,
all cut from one cloth,
and designed
like your mind!

[1]**the Great Awakening** eighteenth-century American religious revival partly inspired by Jonathan Edwards.

I love you faded,
old, exiled and afraid
to leave your last flock, a dozen
Houssatonic Indian children;

afraid to leave
all your writing, writing, writing,
denying the Freedom of the Will.[2]
You were afraid to be president

of Princeton, and wrote:
"My deffects are well known;
I have a constitution
peculiarly unhappy:

flaccid solids,
vapid, sizzy, scarse fluids,
causing a childish weakness,
a low tide of spirits.

I am contemptible,
stiff and dull.

Why should I leave behind
my delight and entertainment,
those studies
that have swallowed up my mind?"

NAOMI REPLANSKY

(1918– , United States)

The Mistress Addresses the Wife

Do not tremble, wife,
When you think of me.
Your castle may be sand
But I am not the sea.

Nor am I a refuge,
Nor am I a throne.
I am the dark streets
A man walks alone.

JONATHAN EDWARDS IN WESTERN MASSACHUSETTS [2]**"Freedom of the Will"** an essay by Edwards.

Alone, alone he walks,
And he sings at will,
And at will departs,
And my streets are still.

Though at moments I
Heard his helpless cry,
It was not you he yielded
In that yielding sigh.

Guilt ties my tongue,
Rage makes you blind.
Let your eyes just once
Fasten upon mine.

LAWRENCE FERLINGHETTI

(1919– , United States)

Lost Parents

It takes a fast car
                    to lead a double life
in these days of short-distance love affairs
   when he has far-out lovers in
                              three different locations
   and a date with each one
                        at least twice a week
   a little simple arithmetic shows
            what a workout he's engaged in
   crossing & recrossing the city
         from bedroom to patio to swimming pool
the ignition key hot
      and the backseat a jumble of clothes
                              for different life-styles
a surfboard on the roof
   and a copy of Kahlil Gibran or Rod McKuen
                              under the dashboard
         next to the Indian music casettes
   packs of Tarot and the I-Ching
                    crammed into the glove compartment
   along with old traffic tickets
                         and hardpacks of Kents
      dents attesting to the passion
                              of his last lover

And his answering service
catching him on the freeway
between two calls or two encounter groups
and the urgent message left
with an unlisted number to call Carol
about the bottle of fine wine
he forgot to pick up
and deliver to the gallery
for the reception at nine
While she shuttles to her gynecologist
and will meet him later
between two other numbers
male or female
including his wife
who also called twice
wanting to know where he's been
and what he's done
with their throw-away children
who
left to their own devices
in a beach house at Malibu
grew up and dropped out into Nothing
in a Jungian search
for lost parents
their own age

Constantly Risking Absurdity

Constantly risking absurdity
and death
whenever he performs
above the heads
of his audience
the poet like an acrobat
climbs on rime
to a high wire of his own making
and balancing on eyebeams
above a sea of faces
paces his way
to the other side of day

performing entrechats
and sleight-of-foot tricks
and other high theatrics
and all without mistaking
any thing
for what it may not be

For he's the super realist
who must perforce perceive
taut truth
before the taking of each stance or step
in his supposed advance
toward that still higher perch
where Beauty stands and waits
with gravity
to start her death-defying leap
And he
a little charleychaplinman
who may or may not catch
her fair eternal form
spreadeagled in the empty air
of existence

AUGOSTNHO NETO

(1921–1979, Angola)

African Poem

There on the horizon
the fire
and the dark silhouettes of the imbondeiro trees
with their arms raised
in the air the green smell of burnt palm trees

On the road
the line of Bailundo porters
groaning under their loads of crueira

in the room
the sweet sweet-eyed mulatress
retouching her face with rouge and rice-powder
the woman under her many clothes moving her hips
on the bed

the sleepless man thinking
of buying knives and forks to eat with at a table

On the sky the reflections
of the fire
and the silhouette of the blacks at the drums
with their arms raised
in the air the warm tune of marimbas

On the road the porters
in the room the mulatress
on the bed the sleepless man

The burning coals consuming
consuming with fire
the warm country of the horizons.

The Grieved Lands

The grieved lands of Africa
in the tearful woes of ancient and modern slave
in the degrading sweat of impure dance
of other seas
grieved

The grieved lands of Africa
in the infamous sensation of the stunning perfume of the flower
crushed in the forest
by the wickedness of iron and fire
the grieved lands

The grieved lands of Africa
in the dream soon undone in jinglings of gaolers' keys
and in the stifled laughter and victorious voice of laments
and in the unconscious brilliance of hidden sensations
of the grieved lands of Africa

Alive
in themselves and with us alive

They bubble up in dreams
decked with dances by baobabs over balances
by the antelope
in the perpetual alliance of everything that lives

They shout out the sound of life
shout it
even the corpses thrown up by the Atlantic
in putrid offering of incoherence and death
and in the clearness of rivers

They live
the grieved lands of Africa
in the harmonious sound of consciences
contained in the honest blood of men
in the strong desire of men
in the sincerity of men
in the pure and simple rightness of the stars' existence

They live
the grieved lands of Africa
because we are living
and are imperishable particles
of the grieved lands of Africa.

GABRIEL OKARA

(1921– , Nigeria)

Piano and Drums

When at break of day at a riverside
I hear jungle drums telegraphing
the mystic rhythm, urgent, raw
like bleeding flesh, speaking of
primal youth and the beginning,
I see the panther ready to pounce,
the leopard snarling about to leap
and the hunters crouch with spears poised;

And my blood ripples, turns torrent,
topples the years and at once I'm
in my mother's lap a suckling;
at once I'm walking simple
paths with no innovations,
rugged, fashioned with the naked
warmth of hurrying feet and groping hearts
in green leaves and wild flowers pulsing.

Then I hear a wailing piano
solo speaking of complex ways
in tear-furrowed concerto;
of faraway lands
and new horizons with

coaxing diminuendo, counterpoint,
crescendo. But lost in the labyrinth
of its complexities, it ends in the middle
of a phrase at a daggerpoint.

And I, lost in the morning mist
of an age at a riverside, keep
wandering in the mystic rhythm
of jungle drums and the concerto.

Once Upon a Time

Once upon a time, son,
they used to laugh with their hearts
and laugh with their eyes;
but now they only laugh with their teeth,
while their ice-block-cold eyes
search behind my shadow.

There was a time indeed
they used to shake hands with their hearts;
but that's gone, son.
Now they shake hands without hearts
while their left hands search
my empty pockets.

"Feel at home," "Come again,"
they say, and when I come
again and feel
at home, once, twice,
there will be no thrice—
for then I find doors shut on me.

So I have learned many things, son.
I have learned to wear many faces
like dresses—homeface,
officeface, streetface, hostface, cock-
tailface, with all their conforming smiles
like a fixed portrait smile.

And I have learned too
to laugh with only my teeth
and shake hands without my heart.
I have also learned to say, "Goodbye,"
when I mean "Goodriddance";
to say "Glad to meet you,"
without being glad; and to say "It's been
nice talking to you," after being bored.

But believe me, son.
I want to be what I used to be
when I was like you. I want
to unlearn all these muting things.
Most of all, I want to relearn
how to laugh, for my laugh in the mirror
shows only my teeth like a snake's bare fangs!

So show me, son,
how to laugh; show me how
I used to laugh and smile
once upon a time when I was like you.

PHILIP LARKIN

(1922–1985, England)

Church Going

Once I am sure there's nothing going on
I step inside, letting the door thud shut.
Another church: matting, seats, and stone,
And little books; sprawlings of flowers, cut
For Sunday, brownish now; some brass and stuff
Up at the holy end; the small neat organ;
And a tense, musty, unignorable silence,
Brewed God knows how long. Hatless, I take off
My cycle-clips in awkward reverence,

Move forward, run my hand around the font.
From where I stand, the roof looks almost new—
Cleaned, or restored? Someone would know: I don't.
Mounting the lectern, I peruse a few
Hectoring large-scale verses, and pronounce
"Here endeth" much more loudly than I'd meant.
The echoes snigger briefly. Back at the door

I sign the book, donate an Irish sixpence.
Reflect the place was not worth stopping for.

Yet stop I did: in fact I often do,
And always end much at a loss like this,
Wondering what to look for; wondering, too,
When churches fall completely out of use
What we shall turn them into, if we shall keep
A few cathedrals chronically on show,
Their parchment, plate and pyx[1] in locked cases,
And let the rest rent-free to rain and sheep.
Shall we avoid them as unlucky places?

Or, after dark, will dubious women come
To make their children touch a particular stone;
Pick simples[2] for a cancer; or on some
Advised night see walking a dead one?
Power of some sort or other will go on
In games, in riddles, seemingly at random;
But superstition, like belief, must die,
And what remains when disbelief has gone?
Grass, weedy pavement, brambles, buttress, sky,

A shape less recognisable each week,
A purpose more obscure. I wonder who
Will be the last, the very last, to seek
This place for what it was, one of the crew
That tap and jot and know what rood-lofts[3] were?
Some ruin-bibber, randy for antique,
Or Christmas-addict, counting on a whiff
Of gown-and-bands and organ-pipes and myrrh?
Or will he be my representative,

Bored, uninformed, knowing the ghostly silt
Dispersed, yet tending to this cross of ground
Through suburb scrub because it held unsplit
So long and equably what since is found
Only in separation—marriage, and birth,
And death, and thoughts of these—for whom was built
This special shell? For, though I've no idea
What this accoutred frowsty barn is worth,
It pleases me to stand in silence here;

[1]**pyx** sacred objects. [2]**simples** medicinable herbs. [3]**rood-lofts** galley above the altar which supports a cross.

A serious house on serious earth it is,
In whose blent air all our compulsions meet,
Are recognised, and robed as destinies.
And that much never can be obsolete,
Since someone will forever be surprising
A hunger in himself to be more serious,
And gravitating with it to this ground,
Which, he once heard, was proper to grow wise in,
If only that so many dead lie round.

This Be the Verse

They fuck you up, your mum and dad.
  They may not mean to, but they do.
They fill you with the faults they had
  And add some extra, just for you.

But they were fucked up in their turn
  By fools in old-style hats and coats,
Who half the time were soppy-stern
  And half at one another's throats.

Man hands on misery to man.
  It deepens like a coastal shelf.
Get out as early as you can,
  And don't have any kids yourself.

A Study of Reading Habits

When getting my nose in a book
Cured most things short of school,
It was worth ruining my eyes
To know I could still keep cool,
And deal out the old right hook
To dirty dogs twice my size.

Later, with inch-thick specs,
Evil was just my lark:
Me and my cloak and fangs
Had ripping times in the dark.
The women I clubbed with sex!
I broke them up like meringues.

Don't read much now: the dude
Who lets the girl down before
The hero arrives, the chap
Who's yellow and keeps the store,
Seem far too familiar. Get stewed:
Books are a load of crap.

HOWARD MOSS

(1922–1987, United States)

The Refrigerator

The argument of the refrigerator wakes me.
It is trying to tell me it doesn't want to be cold,
It never wanted to be cold, it didn't choose
This life where everyone around it hates it.
"People only use me for their own convenience,"
It says. With a shudder, it starts off again,
Undergoing an electrical seizure,
Rambling on about its hurts and troubles:
People think it's heartless, stolid, frigid,
When, deep down, it craves for warmth and wants . . .
Well, it hesitates to say it, but
All it *really* wants is to be a stove.
Oh, how it dreams each night of the paired
Gas jets switching on their tropical blue,
The swoosh just after the match catches on,
The rectangular, passionate grid of flame
In the oven, the romance of changing things
Into other things. "The egg of the Real
Becoming the soufflé of the Ideal—
That's what I call the creative life."

"You perform an important function," I say,
"Without you, where would we be, these days . . ."
"Yes, yes, I know," it impatiently replies,
"But do you"—pause—"think I'm attractive?"
My silence, I fear, gives the show away.
"Of course," I stumble on, "for what you do,
You're remarkably well made, so few things work . . ."
Coldly, it opens, then slams its door.
"I didn't mean . . ." I say. But it will not respond.
At midnight, with a premeditated click,
It detaches itself from the circuits of the world,

Manages to shut itself off completely,
And gives up the ghost. By morning, all is lost.
"Damn it," I say to my coffee, black
(The milk's turned sour overnight),
"Unfulfillment's claimed yet another victim,"
Just as the stove speaks up to say,
"Do you think? . . . I hear . . . in the frozen north . . ."

CONSTANCE URDANG

(1922– , United States)

Safe Places

The retreat to Vermont was orderly at first
Everybody expecting to find
At the end of the macadam, the old dirt road
Leading back into childhood
Expecting the luster of the farmhouse windows
As firelight burnished twilight
To make up for all they had lost
All they had left behind

So they marched like an army of refugees
Carrying lamps and birdcages, mattresses and clocks,
Flowing along the highways of Vermont
Calmly as a river

But something went wrong

The simple hills that, from a plane
Look smooth and domesticated
Turned rough and wild;
Bears lurched through the wood
Travellers who wandered from the road
Lost all direction, starving, or seeing ghosts

Even the road grew treacherous.
As night fell, and neighbors
Eyed one another with suspicion
The safe places retreated from Vermont
Northward to Canada and the frozen void,
Or lay behind them, maybe, in the ruined cities.

RICHARD HUGO

(1923–1982, United States)

Landscapes

If I painted, I'd paint landscapes. In museums
I stop often at van Ruysdael, and the wind he painted
high in European oaks gives license to my style.
I move the barn two feet. I curve the hill down
more dramatic. I put a woman on the hill against
the light, calling me to dinner. The wind I paint
is low and runs the grass down dancing to the sea.

In no time I have aged the barn stark gray.
Obviously, my cows hate no one. My wife
across the field stays carved out solid on the sky.
My tossed kiss stings her through the waves of heat
plowed dirt gives off in August. My tossed worm
drifts beneath the cutbank where I know trout wait.
As long as wind is pouring, my paint keeps farming green.

When wind stops, men come smiling with the mortgage.
They send me the eviction notice, postage due.
My cows are thin and failing. My deaf wife snarls
and claws the chair. The creek turns putrid.
I said fifty years moss on the roof is lovely.
It rots the roof. Oaks ache but cannot stir.
I call van Ruysdael from my knees on the museum floor.

In uniforms like yours you'll never understand.
Why these questions? The bank was wrong. The farm
is really mine. Even now along these pale green halls
I hear van Ruysdael's wind. Please know I rearranged things
only slightly, barn and hill. This is real: the home
that warps in August and the man inside who sold it
long ago, forgot he made the deal and will not move.

DENISE LEVERTOV

(1923–   , United States)

Libation

Raising our glasses, smilingly
we wish one another not luck
but happiness. After half a lifetime

with and without luck,
we know we need more than luck.
It makes no difference that we're drinking
tomato juice, not wine or whiskey—
we know what we mean,
and the red juice of those virtuous
vegetable-fruits is something we both enjoy.
I remember your wonder, as at a miracle,
finding them growing on sturdy vines
in my old aunt and uncle's sun-room
ripe to pluck at the breakfast table!
We were twenty-three, and unappeasably hungry . . .

We agree on tomatoes, then—and happiness?
yes, that too: we mean growth, branching,
leafing, yielding blossoms and fruit and the sharp odor
of dreams.

We mean knowing someone as deeply,
no, deeper, than we've known each other,
we mean being known. We are wishing each other
the luck not to need luck. I mill
some pepper into my juice, though,
and salt in the ancient gesture; and what would be wrong
with tipping out half a glass
for the gods?
We smile.
After these months of pain we begin
to admit our new lives have begun.

HARVEY SHAPIRO

(1924– , United States)

Riding Westward

It's holiday night
And crazy Jews are on the road,
Finished with fasting and high on prayer.
On either side of the Long Island Expressway
The lights go spinning
Like the twin ends of my tallis.
I hope I can make it to Utopia Parkway
Where my father lies at the end of his road.
And then home to Brooklyn.

Jews, departure from the law
Is equivalent to death.
Shades, we greet each other.
Darkly, on the Long Island Expressway,
Where I say my own prayers for the dead,
Crowded in Queens, remembered in Queens,
As far away as Brooklyn. Cemeteries
Break against the City like seas,
A white froth of tombstones
Or like schools of herring, still desperate
To escape the angel of death.
Entering the City, you have to say
Memorial prayers as he slides overhead
Looking something like my father approaching
The Ark as the gates close on the Day of Atonement
Here in the car and in Queens and in Brooklyn.

MAXINE KUMIN

(1925– , United States)

After Love

Afterwards, the compromise.
Bodies resume their boundaries.

These legs, for instance, mine.
Your arms take you back in.

Spoons of our fingers, lips
admit their ownership.

The bedding yawns, a door
blows aimlessly ajar

and overhead, a plane
singsongs coming down.

Nothing is changed, except
there was a moment when

the wolf, the mongering wolf
who stands outside the self

lay lightly down, and slept.

DONALD JUSTICE

(1925–   , United States)

Men at Forty

Men at forty
Learn to close softly
The doors to rooms they will not be
Coming back to.
At rest on a stair landing,
They feel it moving
Beneath them now like the deck of a ship,
Though the swell is gentle.

And deep in mirrors
They rediscover
The face of the boy as he practices tying
His father's tie there in secret

And the face of that father,
Still warm with the mystery of lather.
They are more fathers than sons themselves now.
Something is filling them, something

That is like the twilight sound
Of the crickets, immense,
Filling the woods at the foot of the slope
Behind their mortgaged houses.

A. R. AMMONS

(1926–   , United States)

Corsons Inlet

I went for a walk over the dunes again this morning
to the sea,
then turned right along
    the surf
                rounded a naked headland
                and returned

    along the inlet shore:

it was muggy sunny, the wind from the sea steady and high,
crisp in the running sand,
some breakthroughs of sun
but after a bit

continuous overcast:

the walk liberating, I was released from forms,
from the perpendiculars,
straight lines, blocks, boxes, binds
of thought
into the hues, shadings, rises, flowing bends and blends
of sight:

I allow myself eddies of meaning:
yield to a direction of significance
running
like a stream through the geography of my work:
you can find
in my sayings
swerves of action
like the inlet's cutting edge:
there are dunes of motion,
organizations of grass, white sandy paths of remembrance
in the overall wandering of mirroring mind:

but Overall is beyond me: is the sum of these events
I cannot draw, the ledger I cannot keep, the accounting
beyond the account:

in nature there are few sharp lines: there are areas of
primrose
more or less dispersed;
disorderly orders of bayberry; between the rows
of dunes,
irregular swamps of reeds,
though not reeds alone, but grass, bayberry, yarrow, all . . .
predominantly reeds:

I have reached no conclusions, have erected no boundaries,
shutting out and shutting in, separating inside
from outside: I have
drawn no lines:
as

manifold events of sand
change the dune's shape that will not be the same shape
tomorrow.

so I am willing to go along, to accept
the becoming
thought to stake off no beginnings or ends, establish
      no walls:

by transitions the land falls from grassy dunes to creek
to undercreek: but there are no lines, though
   change in that transition is clear
   as any sharpness: but "sharpness" spread out,
allowed to occur over a wider range
than mental lines can keep:

the moon was full last night: today, low tide was low:
black shoals of mussels exposed to the risk
of air
and earlier, of sun,
waved in and out with the waterline, waterline inexact,
caught always in the event of change:
   a young mottled gull stood free on the shoals
   and ate
to vomiting: another gull, squawking possession, cracked a crab,
picked out the entrails, swallowed the soft-shelled legs, a ruddy
turnstone running in to snatch leftover bits:

risk is full: every living thing in
siege: the demand is life, to keep life: the small
white blacklegged egret, how beautiful, quietly stalks and spears
      the shallows, darts to shore
                  to stab—what? I couldn't
   see against the black mudflats—a frightened
   fiddler crab?

      the news to my left over the dunes and
reeds and bayberry clumps was
      fall: thousands of tree swallows
      gathering for flight:
      an order held
      in constant change: a congregation
rich with entropy: nevertheless, separable, noticeable
   as one event,
         not chaos: preparations for

flight from winter,
cheet, cheet, cheet, cheet, wings rifling the green clumps,
beaks
at the bayberries
  a perception full of wind, flight, curve,
  sound:
  the possibility of rule as the sum of rulelessness:
the "field" of action
with moving, incalculable center:

in the smaller view, order tight with shape:
blue tiny flowers on a leafless weed: carapace of crab:
snail shell:
    pulsations of order
    in the bellies of minnows: orders swallowed,
broken down, transferred through membranes
to strengthen larger orders: but in the large view, no
lines or changeless shapes: the working in and out, together
    and against, of millions of events: this,
        so that I make
        no form
        formlessness:

orders as summaries, as outcomes of actions override
or in some way result, not predictably (seeing me gain
the top of a dune,
the swallows
could take flight—some other fields of bayberry
    could enter fall
    berryless) and there is serenity:

    no arranged terror: no forcing of image, plan,
or thought:
no propaganda, no humbling of reality to precept:

terror pervades but is not arranged, all possibilities
of escape open: no route shut, except in
  the sudden loss of all routes:

    I see narrow orders, limited tightness, but will
not run to that easy victory:
    still around the looser, wider forces work:
    I will try
  to fasten into order enlarging grasps of disorder, widening

scope, but enjoying the freedom that
Scope eludes my grasp, that there is no finality of vision,
that I have perceived nothing completely,
that tomorrow a new walk is a new walk.

ROBERT BLY

(1926– , United States)

from The Teeth Mother Naked at Last

II

Excellent Roman knives slip along the ribs.

A stronger man starts to jerk up the strips of flesh.

"Let's hear it again, you believe in the Father, the Son, and the Holy Ghost?"

A long scream unrolls.

More.

"From the political point of view, democratic institutions are being built in Vietnam, wouldn't you agree?"

A green parrot shudders under the fingernails.
Blood jumps in the pocket.
The scream lashes like a tail.

"Let us not be deterred from our task by the voices of dissent. . . ."

The whines of the jets
pierce like a long needle.

As soon as the President finishes his press conference, black wings carry off the words,
bits of flesh still clinging to them.
The ministers lie, the professors lie, the television lies, the priests lie. . . .
These lies mean that the country wants to die.

Lie after lie starts out into the prairie grass,
like enormous caravans of Conestoga wagons. . . .

And a long desire for death flows out, guiding the enormous
caravans from beneath,
stringing together the vague and foolish words.
It is a desire to eat death,
to gobble it down,
to rush on it like a cobra with mouth open.
It's a desire to take death inside,
to feel it burning inside, pushing out velvety hairs,
like a clothes brush in the intestines—

This is the thrill that leads the President on to lie.

These lies are only the longing we all feel to die.
It is the longing for someone to come and take you by the
hand to where they all are sleeping:
where the Egyptian pharaohs are asleep, and your own
mother,
and all those disappeared children, who used to go around
with you in the rings at grade school. . . .

Do not be angry at the President—he is longing to take in
his hand
the locks of death hair—
to meet his own children dead, or unborn. . . .
He is drifting sideways toward the dusty places
Now the Chief Executive enters; the press conference
begins:
First the President lies about the date the Appalachian
Mountains rose.
Then he lies about the population of Chicago, then he lies
about the weight of the adult eagle, then about the
acreage of the Everglades.

He lies about the number of fish taken every year in the
Arctic, he has private information about which city *is* the
capital of Wyoming, he lies about the birthplace of
Attila the Hun.

He lies about the composition of the amniotic fluid, and he
insists that Luther was never a German, and that only
the Protestants sold indulgences,

That Pope Leo X *wanted* to reform the church, but the
"liberal elements" prevented him,

that the Peasants' War was fomented by Italians from the North.

And the Attorney General lies about the time the sun sets.

W. D. SNODGRASS

(1926– , United States)

A Flat One

Old Fritz, on this rotating bed
For seven wasted months you lay
Unfit to move, shrunken, gray,
No good to yourself or anyone
But to be babied—changed and bathed and fed.
At long last, that's all done.

Before each meal, twice every night,
We set pads on your bedsores, shut
Your catheter tube off, then brought
The second canvas-and-black-iron
Bedframe and clamped you in between them, tight,
Scared, so we could turn

You over. We washed you, covered you,
Cut up each bite of meat you ate;
We watched your lean jaws masticate
As ravenously your useless food
As thieves at hard labor in their chains chew
Or insects in the wood.

Such pious sacrifice to give
You all you could demand of pain:
Receive this haddock's body, slain
For you, old tyrant; take this blood
Of a tomato, shed that you might live.
You had that costly food.

You seem to be all finished, so
We'll plug your old recalcitrant anus
And tie up your discouraged penis
In a great, snow-white bow of gauze.

We wrap you, pin you, and cart you down below,
Below, below, because

Your credit has finally run out.
On our steel table, trussed and carved,
You'll find this world's hardworking, starved
Teeth working in your precious skin.
The earth turns, in the end, by turn about
And opens to take you in.

Seven months gone down the drain; thank God
That's through. Throw out the four-by-fours,
Swabsticks, the thick salve for bedsores,
Throw out the diaper pads and drug
Containers, pile the bedclothes in a wad,
And rinse the cider jug

Half-filled with the last urine. Then
Empty out the cotton cans,
Autoclave the bowls and spit pans,
Unhook the pumps and all the red
Tubes—catheter, suction, oxygen;
Next, wash the empty bed.

—All this Dark Age machinery
On which we had tormented you
To life. Last, we collect the few
Belongings: snapshots, some odd bills,
Your mail, and half a pack of Luckies we
Won't light you after meals.

That made your life seem bearable.
You still whispered you would not die.
Yet in the nights I heard you cry
Like a whipped child; in fierce old age
You whimpered, tears stood on your gun-metal
Blue cheeks shaking with rage

And terror. So much pain would fill
Your room that when I left I'd pray
That if I came back the next day
I'd find you gone. You stayed for me—
Nailed to your own rapacious, stiff self-will.
You've shook loose, finally.

They'd say this was a worthwhile job
Unless they tried it. It is mad

To throw our good lives after bad;
Waste time, drugs, and our minds, while strong
Men starve. How many young men did we rob
To keep you hanging on?

I can't think we did *you* much good.
Well, when you died, none of us wept.
You killed for us, and so we kept
You, because we need to earn our pay.
No. We'd still have to help you try. We would
Have killed for you today.

Old man, these seven months you've lain
Determined—not that you would live—
Just to not die. No one would give
You one chance you could ever wake
From that first night, much less go well again,
Much less go home and make

Your living; how could you hope to find
A place for yourself in all creation?—
Pain was your only occupation.
And pain that should content and will
A man to give it up, nerved you to grind
Your clenched teeth, breathing, till

Your skin broke down, your calves went flat
And your legs lost all sensation. Still,
You took enough morphine to kill
A strong man. Finally, nitrogen
Mustard: you could last two months after that;
It would kill you then.

Even then you wouldn't quit.
Old soldier, yet you must have known
Inside the animal had grown
Sick of the world, made up its mind
To stop. Your mind ground on its separate
Way, merciless and blind,

Into these last weeks when the breath
Would only come in fits and starts
That puffed out your sections like the parts
Of some enormous, damaged bug.
You waited, not for life, not for your death,
Just for the deadening drug

ALLEN GINSBERG

(1926– , United States)

To Aunt Rose

Aunt Rose—now—might I see you
with your thin face and buck tooth smile and pain
of rheumatism—and a long black heavy shoe
for your bony left leg
limping down the long hall in Newark on the running carpet
past the black grand piano
in the day room
where the parties were
and I sang Spanish loyalist[1] songs
in a high squeaky voice
(hysterical) the committee listening
while you limped around the room
collected the money—

Aunt Honey, Uncle Sam, a stranger with a cloth arm
in his pocket
and huge young bald head
of Abraham Lincoln Brigade[2]

—your long sad face
your tears of sexual frustration
(what smothered sobs and bony hips
under the pillows of Osborne Terrace)
—the time I stood on the toilet seat naked
and you powdered my thighs with calamine
against the poison ivy—my tender
and shamed first black curled hairs
what were you thinking in secret heart then
knowing me a man already—
and I an ignorant girl of family silence on the thin pedestal
of my legs in the bathroom—Museum of Newark.

Aunt Rose
Hitler is dead, Hitler is in Eternity; Hitler is with
Tamburlane and Emily Brontë

Though I see you walking still, a ghost on Osborne Terrace
down the long dark hall to the front door
limping a little with a pinched smile

---

[1]**loyalist** for the defenders of the Spanish government, 1936. [2]**Abraham Lincoln Brigade** American volunteers who fought in Spain during the Spanish Civil War.

in what must have been a silken
flower dress
welcoming my father, the Poet, on his visit to Newark
—see you arriving in the living room
dancing on your crippled leg
and clapping hands his book
had been accepted by Liveright° — publisher

Hitler is dead and Liveright's gone out of business
The Attic of the Past and *Everlasting Minute* are out of print
Uncle Harry sold his last silk stocking
Claire quit interpretive dancing school
Buba° sits a wrinkled monument in Old — Grandmother (Yiddish)
Ladies Home blinking at new babies

last time I saw you was the hospital
pale skull protruding under ashen skin
blue veined unconscious girl
in an oxygen tent
the war in Spain has ended long ago
Aunt Rose

A Supermarket in California

What thoughts I have of you tonight, Walt Whitman, for I walked down the streets under the trees with a headache self-conscious looking at the full moon.

In my hungry fatigue, and shopping for images, I went into the neon fruit supermarket, dreaming of your enumerations!

What peaches and what penumbras? Whole families shopping at night! Aisles full of husbands! Wives in the avocados, babies in the tomatoes!—and you, García Lorca,[1] what were you doing down by the watermelons?

I saw you, Walt Whitman, childless, lonely old grubber, poking among the meats in the refrigerator and eyeing the grocery boys.

I heard you asking questions of each: Who killed the pork chops? What price bananas? Are you my Angel?

I wandered in and out of the brilliant stacks of cans following you, and followed in my imagination by the store detective.

We strode down the open corridors together in our solitary fancy tasting artichokes, possessing every frozen delicacy, and never passing the cashier.

A SUPERMARKET IN CALIFORNIA [1]**García Lorca** an early twentieth-century Spanish poet and dramatist.

Where are we going, Walt Whitman? The doors close in an hour. Which way does your beard point tonight?
(I touch your book and dream of our odyssey in the supermarket and feel absurd.)
Will we walk all night through solitary streets? The trees add shade to shade, lights out in the houses, we'll both be lonely.
Will we stroll dreaming of the lost America of love past blue automobiles in driveways, home to our silent cottage?
Ah, dear father, graybeard, lonely old courage-teacher, what America did you have when Charon quit poling his ferry and you got out on a smoking bank and stood watching the boat disappear on the black waters of Lethe?

RALPH POMEROY

(1926– , United States)

Looking at the Empire State Building

It is still The Tallest Building in the World.
(Although they are already busy changing that.)
Coming as I do from the Great Plains,
it has been my Holy Mountain from the beginning.
When it disappears past clouds, I imagine
the gods holding a picnic—for once
happily masked from our stares.

At night when the top is lighted
I see it as my Holy Volcano
and the biggest penny-bank anywhere.
It is the only present I would ever
have liked to give Jean Harlow.
Planes and birds are known to crash into it.

I can't help expecting any minute
to see poor King Kong fall from the dirigible mast
or spot lovely Melisande leaning out from an upper floor
to let down her long golden hair.

DAVID MAMDESSI DIOP

(1927–1960, Senegal)

The Vultures

In those days
When civilization kicked us in the face
When holy water slapped our cringing brows

The vultures built in the shadow of their talons
The bloodstained monument of tutelage
In those days
There was painful laughter on the metallic hell of the roads
And the monotonous rhythm of the paternoster
Drowned the howling on the plantations
O the bitter memories of extorted kisses
Of promises broken at the point of a gun
Of foreigners who did not seem human
Who knew all the books but did not know love
But we whose hands fertilize the womb of the earth
In spite of your songs of pride
In spite of the desolate villages of torn Africa
Hope was preserved in us as in a fortress
And from the mines of Swaziland to the factories of Europe
Spring will be reborn under our bright steps.

GALWAY KINNELL

(1927– , United States)

from The Dead Shall Be Raised Incorruptible

In the Twentieth Century of my trespass on earth,
having exterminated one billion heathens,
heretics, Jews, Moslems, witches, mystical seekers,
black men, Asians, and Christian brothers,
every one of them for his own good,

a whole continent of red men for living in unnatural community
and at the same time having relations with the land,
one billion species of animals for being sub-human,
and ready to take on the bloodthirsty creatures from the other planets,
I, Christian man, groan out this testament of my last will.
I give my blood fifty parts polystyrene,
twenty-five parts benzene, twenty-five parts good old gasoline,
to the last bomber pilot aloft, that there shall be one acre
in the dull world where the kissing flower may bloom,
which kisses you so long your bones explode under its lips.

My tongue goes to the Secretary of the Dead
to tell the corpses, "I'm sorry, fellows,
the killing was just one of those things
difficult to pre-visualize—like a cow,
say, getting hit by lightning."

My stomach, which has digested
four hundred treaties giving the Indians
eternal right to their land, I give to the Indians,
I throw in my lungs which have spent four hundred years
sucking in good faith on peace pipes.

My soul I leave to the bee
that he may sting it and die, my brain
to the fly, his back the hysterical green color of slime,
that he may suck on it and die, my flesh to the advertising man,
the anti-prostitute, who loathes human flesh for money.

I assign my crooked backbone
to the dice maker, to chop up into dice,
for casting lots as to who shall see his own blood
on his shirt front and who his brother's,
for the race isn't to the swift but to the crooked.

To the last man surviving on earth
I give my eyelids worn out by fear, to wear
in his long nights of radiation and silence,
so that his eyes can't close, for regret
is like tears seeping through closed eyelids.

I give the emptiness my hand: the pinkie picks no more noses,
slag clings to the black stick of the ring finger,
a bit of flame jets from the tip of the fuck-you finger,
the first finger accuses the heart, which has vanished,
on the thumb stump wisps of smoke ask a ride into the emptiness.

In the Twentieth Century of my nightmare
on earth, I swear on my chromium testicles
to this testament
and last will
of my iron will, my fear of love, my itch for money, and my madness.

JAMES WRIGHT

(1927–1980, United States)

Lying in a Hammock at William Duffy's Farm in Pine Island, Minnesota

Over my head, I see the bronze butterfly,
Asleep on the black trunk,
Blowing like a leaf in green shadow.

Down the ravine behind the empty house,
The cowbells follow one another
Into the distances of the afternoon.
To my right,
In a field of sunlight between two pines,
The droppings of last year's horses
Blaze up into golden stones.
I lean back, as the evening darkens and comes on.
A chicken hawk floats over, looking for home.
I have wasted my life.

KEITH WILSON

(1927– , United States)

The Arrival of My Mother

She got off, according to the diary,
dressed in a lovely beaded gown, fresh
from Washington with sixteen trunks of ballgowns,
chemises, blouses (4 Middie), shoes and assorted
lingerie. She was at that time about 25, old
for an unmarried woman. Her stiff mother was at
her side, she also wildly overdressed for New Mexico
sun and wind.

What must she have thought, seeing my uncle standing,
hat in hand in the dust of that lonely train house,
cracked yellow paint, faded letters of welcome
for passengers that rarely come?

The buckboard was waiting and they rode out into
the darkness of evening toward the tent, the half
built frame homestead house, wind dying as the sun
sank, birdcries stilled.

I see her now outshooting my father and me, laughing
at our pride and embarrassment. My sister as good a
shot, waiting her turn. Or that picture of her
on horseback, in Eastern riding clothes beside the Pecos.
A picnic when I was small and how my father lifted me up

to her and she carefully walked the horse around rock
and sand.

I suppose she finally arrived in New Mexico
in the April of one year when my sister and I sat beside
a rented bed, each holding one of her hands and watched
her eyes grow childlike, unmasked as a *kachina*
entering the final *kiva* of this Dance. The graceful
the slim laughing woman of my childhood. The old mother
heavy with her years slipped away and the woods of New
England dimmed as these dry hills ripened and caught
her last breath, drums, drums should have beaten
for the arrival of my mother.

PHILIP LEVINE

(1928– , United States)

My Son and I

In a coffee house at 3 am
and he believes
I'm dying. Outside the wind
moves along the streets
of New York City picking up
abandoned scraps of newspapers
and tiny messages of hope
no one hears. He's dressed
in worn corduroy pants
and shirts over shirts,
and his hands are stained
as mine once were
with glue, ink, paint.
A brown stocking cap
hides the thick blond hair
so unlike mine. For forty
minutes he's tried not
to cry. How are his brothers?
I tell him I don't know,
they have grown away
from me. We are Americans
and never touch on this
stunned earth where a boy

sees his life fly past
through a car window. His mother?
She is deaf and works
in the earth for days, hearing
the dirt pray and guiding
the worm to its feasts. Why
do I have to die? Why
do I have to sit before him
no longer his father, only
a man? Because the given
must be taken, because
we hunger before we eat,
because each small spark
must turn to darkness.
As we said when we were kids
and knew the names of everything
. . . just because. I reach
across the table and take
his left hand in mine.
I have no blessing. I can
tell him how I found
the plum blossom before
I was thirty, how once
in a rooming house in Alicante
a man younger than I,
an Argentine I barely understood,
sat by me through the night
while my boy Teddy cried out
for help, and how when he slept
at last, my friend wept
with thanks in the cold light.
I can tell him that his hand
sweating in mine can raise
the Lord God of Stones,
bring down the Republic of Lies,
and hold a spoon. Instead
I say it's late, and he pays
and leads me back
through the empty streets
to the Earle Hotel, where
the room sours with the mould
of old Bibles dumped down
the air-shaft. In my coat
I stand alone in the dark
waiting for something,
a flash of light, a song,

a remembered sweetness
from all the lives I've lost.
Next door the TV babbles
on and on, and I give up
and sway toward the bed
in a last chant before dawn.

DONALD HALL

(1928– , United States)

Kicking the Leaves

1

Kicking the leaves, October, as we walk home together
from the game, in Ann Arbor,
on a day the color of soot, rain in the air;
I kick at the leaves of maples,
reds of seventy different shades, yellow
like old paper; and poplar leaves, fragile and pale;
and elm leaves, flags of a doomed race.
I kick at the leaves, making a sound I remember
as the leaves swirl upward from my boot,
and flutter; and I remember
Octobers walking to school in Connecticut,
wearing corduroy knickers that swished
with a sound like leaves; and a Sunday buying
a cup of cider at a roadside stand
on a dirt road in New Hampshire; and kicking the leaves,
autumn 1955 in Massachusetts, knowing
my father would die when the leaves were gone.

2

Each fall in New Hampshire, on the farm
where my mother grew up, a girl in the country,
my grandfather and grandmother
finished the autumn work, taking the last vegetables in
from the cold fields, canning, storing roots and apples
in the cellar under the kitchen. Then my grandfather
raked leaves against the house
as the final chore of autumn.
One November I drove up from college to see them.

We pulled big rakes, as we did when we hayed in summer,
pulling the leaves against the granite foundations
around the house, on every side of the house,
and then, to keep them in place, we cut spruce boughs
and laid them across the leaves,
green on red, until the house
was tucked up, ready for snow
that would freeze the leaves in tight, like a stiff skirt.
Then we puffed through the shed door,
taking off boots and overcoats, slapping our hands,
and sat in the kitchen, rocking, and drank
black coffee my grandmother made,
three of us sitting together, silent, in gray November.

3

One Saturday when I was little, before the war,
my father came home at noon from his half day at the office
and wore his Bates sweater, black on red,
with the crossed hockey sticks on it, and raked beside me
in the back yard, and tumbled in the leaves with me,
laughing, and carried me, laughing, my hair full of leaves,
to the kitchen window
where my mother could see us, and smile, and motion
to set me down, afraid I would fall and be hurt.

4

Kicking the leaves today, as we walk home together
from the game, among crowds of people
with their bright pennants, as many and bright as leaves,
my daughter's hair is the red-yellow color
of birch leaves, and she is tall like a birch,
growing up, fifteen, growing older; and my son
flamboyant as maple, twenty,
visits from college, and walks ahead of us, his step
springing, impatient to travel
the woods of the earth. Now I watch them
from a pile of leaves beside this clapboard house
in Ann Arbor, across from the school
where they learned to read,
as their shapes grow small with distance, waving,
and I know that I
diminish, not them, as I go first
into the leaves, taking
the step they will follow, Octobers and years from now.

5

This year the poems came back, when the leaves fell.
Kicking the leaves, I heard the leaves tell stories,
remembering, and therefore looking ahead, and building
the house of dying. I looked up into the maples
and found them, the vowels of bright desire.
I thought they had gone forever
while the bird sang *I love you, I love you*
and shook its black head
from side to side, and its red eye with no lid,
through years of winter, cold
as the taste of chicken wire, the music of cinder block.

6

Kicking the leaves, I uncover the lids of graves.
My grandfather died at seventy-seven, in March
when the sap was running; and I remember my father
twenty years ago,
coughing himself to death at fifty-two in the house
in the suburbs. Oh, how we flung
leaves in the air! How they tumbled and fluttered around us,
like slowly cascading water, when we walked together
in Hamden, before the war, when Johnson's Pond
had not surrendered to houses, the two of us
hand in hand, and in the wet air the smell of leaves
burning;
and in six years I will be fifty-two.

7

Now I fall, now I leap and fall
to feel the leaves crush under my body, to feel my body
buoyant in the ocean of leaves, the night of them,
night heaving with death and leaves, rocking like the ocean.
Oh, this delicious falling into the arms of leaves,
into the soft laps of leaves!
Face down, I swim into the leaves, feathery,
breathing the acrid odor of maple, swooping
in long glides to the bottom of October—
where the farm lies curled against winter, and soup steams
its breath of onion and carrot
onto damp curtains and windows; and past the windows
I see the tall bare maple trunks and branches, the oak
with its few brown weathery remnant leaves,

and the spruce trees, holding their green.
Now I leap and fall, exultant, recovering
from death, on account of death, in accord with the dead,
the smell and taste of leaves again,
and the pleasure, the only long pleasure, of taking a place
in the story of leaves.

Names of Horses

All winter your brute shoulders strained against collars, padding
and steerhide over the ash hames, to haul
sledges of cordwood for drying through spring and summer,
for the Glenwood stove next winter, and for the simmering range.

In April you pulled cartloads of manure to spread on the fields,
dark manure of Holsteins, and knobs of your own clustered with oats.
All summer you mowed the grass in meadow and hayfield, the mowing
machine
clacketing beside you, while the sun walked high in the morning;

and after noon's heat, you pulled a clawed rake through the same acres,
gathering stacks, and dragged the wagon from stack to stack,
and the built hayrack back, up hill to the chaffy barn,
three loads of hay a day from standing grass in the morning.

Sundays you trotted the two miles to church with the light load
of a leather quartertop buggy, and grazed in the sound of hymns.
Generation on generation, your neck rubbed the windowsill
of the stall, smoothing the wood as the sea smooths glass.

When you were old and lame, when your shoulders hurt bending to
graze,
one October the man who fed you and kept you, and harnessed you
every morning,
led you through corn stubble to sandy ground above Eagle Pond,
and dug a hole beside you where you stood shuddering in your skin,

and lay the shotgun's muzzle on the boneless hollow behind your ear,
and fired the slug into your brain, and felled you into your grave,
shoveling sand to cover you, setting goldenrod upright above you,
where by next summer a dent in the ground made your monument.

For a hundred and fifty years, in the pasture of dead horses,
roots of pine trees pushed through the pale curves of your ribs,

yellow blossoms flourished above you in autumn, and in winter
frost heaved your bones in the ground—old toilers, soil makers:

O Roger, Mackerel, Riley, Ned, Nellie, Chester, Lady Ghost.

ANNE SEXTON

(1928–1974, United States)

All My Pretty Ones

All my pretty ones?
Did you say all? O hell-kite! All?
What! all my pretty chickens and their dam
At one fell swoop? . . .
I cannot but remember such things were,
That were most precious to me.
—Macbeth

Father, this year's jinx rides us apart
where you followed our mother to her cold slumber,
a second shock boiling its stone to your heart,
leaving me here to shuffle and disencumber
you from the residence you could not afford:
a gold key, your half of a woollen mill,
twenty suits from Dunne's, an English Ford,
the love and legal verbiage of another will,
boxes of pictures of people I do not know.
I touch their cardboard faces. They must go.

But the eyes, as thick as wood in this album,
hold me. I stop here, where a small boy
waits in a ruffled dress for someone to come . . .
for this soldier who holds his bugle like a toy
or for this velvet lady who cannot smile.
Is this your father's father, this commodore
in a mailman suit? My father, time meanwhile
has made it unimportant who you are looking for.
I'll never know what these faces are all about.
I lock them into their book and throw them out.

This is the yellow scrapbook that you began
the year I was born; as crackling now and wrinkly
as tobacco leaves: clippings where Hoover outran
the Democrats, wiggling his dry finger at me

and Prohibition; news where the *Hindenburg*[1] went
down and recent years when you went flush
on war. This year, solvent but sick, you meant
to marry that pretty widow in a one-month rush.
But before you had that second chance, I cried
on your fat shoulder. Three days later you died.

These are the snapshots of marriage, stopped in places.
Side by side at the rail toward Nassau now;
here, with the winner's cup at the speedboat races,
here, in tails at the Cotillion, you take a bow,
here, by our kennel of dogs with their pink eyes,
running like show-bred pigs in their chain-link pen;
here, at the horseshow where my sister wins a prize;
and here, standing like a duke among groups of men.
Now I fold you down, my drunkard, my navigator,
my first lost keeper, to love or look at later.

I hold a five-year diary that my mother kept
for three years, telling all she does not say
of your alcoholic tendency. You overslept,
she writes. My God, father, each Christmas Day
with your blood, will I drink down your glass
of wine? The diary of your hurly-burly years
goes to my shelf to wait for my age to pass.
Only in this hoarded span will love persevere.
Whether you are pretty or not, I outlive you.
bend down my strange face to yours and forgive you.

Woman with Girdle

Your midriff sags toward your knees;
your breasts lie down in air,
their nipples as uninvolved
as warm starfish.
You stand in your elastic case,
still not giving up the new-born
and the old-born cycle.
Moving, you roll down the garment,
down that pink snapper and hoarder,
as your belly, soft as pudding,
slops into the empty space;

ALL MY PRETTY ONES [1]**Hindenberg** a blimp that crashed on its maiden flight.

down, over the surgeon's careful mark,
down over hips, those head cushions
and mouth cushions,
slow motion like a rolling pin,
over crisp hairs, that amazing field
that hides your genius from your patron;
over thighs, thick as young pigs,
over knees like saucers,
over calves, polished as leather,
down toward the feet.
You pause for a moment,
tying your ankles into knots.
Now you rise,
a city from the sea,
born long before Alexandria was,
straightway from God you have come
into your redeeming skin.

JOHN MONTAGUE

(1929– , Ireland)

The Cage

My father, the least happy
man I have known. His face
retained the pallor
of those who work underground:
the lost years in Brooklyn
listening to a subway
shudder the earth.

But a traditional Irishman
who (released from his grille
in the Clark St. I.R.T.)[1]
drank neat whiskey until
he reached the only element
he felt at home in
any longer: brute oblivion.

And yet picked himself
up, most mornings,

THE CAGE [1]**I.R.T.** "*I*nterborough *R*apid *T*ransit," a New York City subway system.

to march down the street
extending his smile
to all sides of the good
(non-negro) neighbourhood
belled by St. Teresa's church.

When he came back
we walked together
across fields of Garvaghey[2]
to see hawthorn on the summer
hedges, as though
he had never left;
a bend of the road

which still sheltered
primroses. But we
did not smile in
the shared complicity
of a dream, for when
weary Odysseus returns
Telemachus must leave.

Often as I descend
into subway or underground
I see his bald head behind
the bars of the small booth;
the mark of an old car
accident beating on his
ghostly forehead.

DONALD FINKEL

(1929– , United States)

They

are at the end of our street now cutting down trees
a scream like a seven foot locust
they have cut off another

THE CAGE [2]**Garvaghey** a town in Ireland.

neatly at the pavement
never again will the pin-oak threaten a taxi
will the ash lie in wait to fall on a child

it is a good time for this
the sun is bright
the plane has only just begun
to sprout little shoots from under her fingernails
never again will she dance
her terrible saraband in the tornado
the sweet gum trembles
bristling with tiny mines like brown sea urchins
never again will he drop them on the walk
to menace the sensible shoes of mailmen

they have brought a machine that eats trees
that shits sawdust
they cut off limbs to feed it
snarling it chews the pale green fingers of the plane
the pin-oak's wrinkled elbows and knees
they fill truck after truck with the dust
in the schoolyard now they are cutting down the children
I hear their screams
first at the ankles
it is nothing then to sever
their soles from the asphalt
there is no danger their falling
on the school and crushing it

I have invented a machine that shoots words
I type faster and faster
I cannot keep up with them
in front of the house now they are cutting the rosebush
vainly she scratches their hands like a drowning kitten
they are cutting the grass
scythes in their wheels they race over our lawn
flashing in the sun like the chariots of the barbarians
the grass blades huddle whimpering
there is no place to go
it is spring and the street is alive
with the clamor of motors
the laughter of saws

ADRIENNE RICH

(1929– , United States)

Aunt Jennifer's Tigers

Aunt Jennifer's tigers prance across a screen,
Bright topaz denizens of a world of green.
They do not fear the men beneath the tree;
They pace in sleek chivalric certainty.

Aunt Jennifer's fingers fluttering through her wool
Find even the ivory needle hard to pull.
The massive weight of Uncle's wedding band
Sits heavily upon Aunt Jennifer's hand.

When Aunt is dead, her terrified hands will lie
Still ringed with ordeals she was mastered by.
The tigers in the panel that she made
Will go on prancing, proud and unafraid.

DAVID RUBADIRI

(1930– , Malawi)

An African Thunderstorm

From the west
Clouds come hurrying with the wind
Turning
Sharply
Here and there
Like a plague of locusts
Whirling
Tossing up things on its tail
Like a madman chasing nothing.

Pregnant clouds
Ride stately on its back
Gathering to perch on hills
Like dark sinister wings;

The Wind whistles by
And trees bend to let it pass.

In the village
Screams of delighted children
Toss and turn
In the din of whirling wind,
Women—
Babies clinging on their backs—
Dart about
In and out
Madly
The Wind whistles by
Whilst trees bend to let it pass.
Clothes wave like tattered flags
Flying off
To expose dangling breasts
As jaggered blinding flashes
Rumble, tremble, and crack
Amidst the smell of fired smoke
And the pelting march of the storm.

GARY SNYDER

(1930– , United States)

The Bath

Washing Kai in the sauna,
The kerosene lantern set on a box
  outside the ground-level window,
Lights up the edge of the iron stove and the
  washtub down on the slab
Steaming air and crackle of waterdrops
  brushed by on the pile of rocks on top
He stands in warm water
Soap all over the smooth of his thigh and stomach
  "Gary don't soap my hair!"
  —his eye-sting fear—
  the soapy hand feeling

through and around the globes and curves of his body
up in the crotch,
And washing-tickling out the scrotum, little anus,
his penis curving up and getting hard
as I pull back skin and try to wash it
Laughing and jumping, flinging arms around,
I squat all naked too,
is this our body?

Sweating and panting in the stove-steam hot-stone
cedar-planking wooden bucket water-splashing
kerosene lantern-flicker wind-in-the-pines-out
sierra forest ridges night—
Masa comes in, letting fresh cool air
sweep down from the door
a deep sweet breath
And she tips him over gripping neatly, one knee down
her hair falling hiding one whole side of
shoulder, breast, and belly,
Washes deftly Kai's head-hair
as he gets mad and yells—
The body of my lady, the winding valley spine,
the space between the thighs I reach through,
cup her curving vulva arch and hold it from behind,
a soapy tickle a hand of grail
The gates of Awe
That open back a turning double-mirror world of
wombs in wombs, in rings,
that start in music,
is this our body?

The hidden place of seed
The veins net flow across the ribs, that gathers
milk and peaks up in a nipple—fits
our mouth—
The sucking milk from this our body sends through
jolts of light; the son, the father,
sharing mother's joy
That brings a softness to the flower of the awesome
open curling lotus gate I cup and kiss
As Kai laughs at his mother's breast he now is weaned
from, we
wash each other,
this our body

Kai's little scrotum up close to his groin,
the seed still tucked away, that moved from us to him
In flows that lifted with the same joys forces
as his nursing Masa later,
playing with her breast,
Or me within her,
Or him emerging,
this is our body:

Clean, and rinsed, and sweating more, we stretch
out on the redwood benches hearts all beating
Quiet to the simmer of the stove,
the scent of cedar
And then turn over,
murmuring gossip of the grasses,
talking firewood,
Wondering how Gen's napping, how to bring him in
soon wash him too—
These boys who love their mother
who loves men, who passes on
her sons to other women;

The cloud across the sky. The windy pines.
the trickle gurgle in the swampy meadow

this is our body.

Fire inside and boiling water on the stove
We sigh and slide ourselves down from the benches
wrap the babies, step outside,

black night & all the stars.

Pour cold water on the back and thighs
Go in the house—stand steaming by the center fire
Kai scampers on the sheepskin
Gen standing hanging on and shouting,

"Bao! bao! bao! bao! bao!"

This is our body. Drawn up crosslegged by the flames
drinking icy water
hugging babies, kissing bellies,

Laughing on the Great Earth

Come out from the bath.

ROBERT WINNER

(1930– , United States)

Miss Alderman

By the high steel hospital bed
a thousand miles from anyone I knew,
she sat while I slept;
Miss Alderman, night duty student nurse
with auburn hair, blue eyes, a perfect body.

Sixteen, just inside girl hunger,
paralyzed, sleeping on my side,
I dreamt of her in my fever,
my spine like a broken chair
on one of their broken Southern porches.

Coming out of sick half-sleep, I found her
pressing my face with her parted lips.
Desire leaped in me, all my body
helpless to respond like a sack of gravel.
I could see her breast.
A warm deep wave of her carried me off.
She kissed me, fondled me; she cared enough
to want to give me
some of that womanly fire
which haunts my manhood,
heals me, makes things right.

It haunts me now, that only chance with her,
that tenderness
lost to me in some provincial Southern city,
a nurse still maybe, or a housewife.

I knew it was no more
than kindness
by the blank calm way
she fixed her hair at the mirror
and scraped her lipstick
with her fingernail
and buttoned her dress
afterwards.

JOHN ENGELS

(1931–   , United States)

Vivaldi in Early Fall

O this is what it is to be
Vivaldi, in September, in my
forty-eighth year, the pines
just beginning to sing
on the hillsides, the rivers
coloring with the first rains
(which are, as usual, precisely
on time). And there is also

this young girl, who, each year,
I bring into my mind,
making it to be that if she knew
by what measure I considered her,
she would turn and look at me and smile,
thinking, "It is the priest again,
the one with red hair, who is said
to make music, and who—as every year—
has gone a little sweetly crazy,

and I think he may love how I am today
in my blue dress." And she
is right. In September I am moved
to the melancholy theme: I like to make the cello
sing with the pines, be on the verge
of the thunderously sad. And, as always,
at this time I would like to make the melody

go on forever, but cannot, being cursed
to disdain my narrow lusts
and sorrows. I have never said
that with me an innocent angel
is alone at work: it may be
I exercise the murderous grace.
But in September, the face of God
passes through my walls to show me
how the motion of song sleeps
at the center of the world, as, indeed,
among the Angels, innocent of time. I hear

at this time every year the voice that loves me
crying out *return, return!* and I do, I round
on the beginning in full belief:
and the girl is gone, having never breathed
as I breathe, in the weary
exactitude of matter. The song
stops at the certain moment
of its growth. It is
the truth of me, not any lie
that I imagine, and I
can do nothing with it. Still,

it is autumn, and over the whole world
the air resumes its liveliness; and I,
Vivaldi, possessed of love and confidence
in measure wonderful to me, I seek
to magnify the text: *viola, bassoon, cello,*
it is as if the trees have broken into song,
and the song roots, blossoms, thrusts
deep toward the still center, overspreads
the sky like a million breathing leaves.

ETHERIDGE KNIGHT

(1933– , United States)

The Idea of Ancestry

1

Taped to the wall of my cell are 47 pictures: 47 black
faces: my father, mother, grandmothers (1 dead), grand
fathers (both dead), brothers, sisters, uncles, aunts,
cousins (1st & 2nd), nieces, and nephews. They stare
across the space at me sprawling on my bunk. I know
their dark eyes, they know mine. I know their style,
they know mine. I am all of them, they are all of me;
they are farmers, I am a thief, I am me, they are thee.

I have at one time or another been in love with my mother,
1 grandmother, 2 sisters, 2 aunts (1 went to the asylum),
and 5 cousins. I am now in love with a 7 yr old niece
(she sends me letters written in large block print, and
her picture is the only one that smiles at me).

I have the same name as 1 grandfather, 3 cousins, 3 nephews,
and 1 uncle. The uncle disappeared when he was 15, just took
off and caught a freight (they say). He's discussed each year
when the family has a reunion, he causes uneasiness in
the clan, he is an empty space. My father's mother, who is 93
and who keeps the Family Bible with everybody's birth dates
(and death dates) in it, always mentions him. There is no
place in her Bible for "whereabouts unknown."

2

Each Fall the graves of my grandfathers call me, the brown
hills and red gullies of mississippi send out their electric
messages, galvanizing my genes. Last yr/like a salmon quitting
the cold ocean—leaping and bucking up his birthstream/I
hitchhiked my way from L.A. with 16 caps in my pocket and a
monkey on my back. and I almost kicked it with the kinfolks.
I walked barefooted in my grandmother's backyard/I smelled the old
land and the woods/I sipped cornwhiskey from fruit jars with the men/
I flirted with the women/I had a ball till the caps ran out
and my habit came down. That night I looked at my grandmother
and split/my guts were screaming for junk/but I was almost
contented/I had almost caught up with me.
(The next day in Memphis I cracked a croaker's crib for a fix.)

This yr there is a gray stone wall damming my stream, and when
the falling leaves stir my genes, I pace my cell or flop on my bunk
and stare at 47 black faces across the space. I am all of them,
they are all of me, I am me, they are thee, and I have no sons
to float in the space between

OKOT P'BITEK

(1931– , Uganda)

The Graceful Giraffe Cannot Become a Monkey

My husband tells me
I have no ideas
Of modern beauty.
He says
I have stuck
To old-fashioned hair-styles.

He says
I am stupid and very backward,
That my hair-style
Makes him sick
Because I am dirty.
It is true
I cannot do my hair
As white women do.

Listen,
My father comes from Payira,
My mother is a woman of Koc!
I am a true Acoli
I am not a half-caste
I am not a slave girl;
My father was not brought home
By the spear
My mother was not exchanged
For a basket of millet.

Ask me what beauty is
To the Acoli
And I will tell you;
I will show it to you
If you give me a chance!

You once saw me,
You saw my hair-style
And you admired it,
And the boys loved it.
At the arena
Boys surrounded me
And fought for me.

My mother taught me
Acoli hair fashions;
Which fits the kind
Of hair of the Acoli,
And the occasion.

Listen,
Ostrich plumes differ
From chicken feathers,
A monkey's tail
Is different from that of the giraffe,
The crocodile's skin
Is not like the guinea-fowl's,
And the hippo is naked, and hairless.

The hair of the Acoli
Is different from that of the Arabs;
The Indians' hair
Resembles the tail of the horse;
It is like sisal strings
And needs to be cut
With scissors.
It is black,
And is different from that of white women.

A white woman's hair
Is soft like silk;
It is light
And brownish like
That of the brown monkey,
And is very different from mine.
A black woman's hair
Is thick and curly;
It is true
Ringworm sometimes eats up

A little girl's hair
And this is terrible;
But when hot porridge
Is put on the head
And the dance is held
Under the sausage-fruit tree
And the youths have sung

You, Ringworm,
Who is eating Duka's hair
Here is your porridge,

Then the girl's hair
Begins to grow again
And the girl is pleased.

*

No one, except wizards
And women who poison others
Leaves her hair untrimmed!
And the men
Do not leave their chins
To grow bushy
Like the lion's neck,
Like the chin
Of a billy-goat,
So that they look
Like wild beasts.

They put hot ash
On the hair
Below the belly-button
And pluck it up,
And they pluck the hair on their face
And the hair of the armpits.

When death has occurred
Women leave their hair uncombed!
They remove all beads
And necklaces,
Because they are mourning
Because of sorrows.
The woman who adorns herself

When others are wailing
Is the killer!
She comes to the funeral
To congratulate herself.
When you go to dance
You adorn yourself for the dance,
If your string-skirt
Is ochre-red
You do your hair
With ochre,
And you smear your body
With red oil
And you are beautifully red all over!
If you put on a black string-skirt
You do your hair with *akuku*
Your body shines with simsim oil
And the tattoos on your chest
And on your back
Glitter in the evening sun.
And the healthy sweat
On your bosom
Is like the glassy fruits of *ocuga.*

Young girls
Whose breasts are just emerging
Smear *shea* butter on their bodies,
The beautiful oil from Labwor-omor.

The aroma is wonderful
And their white teeth sparkle
As they sing
And dance fast
Among the dancers
Like small fish
In a shallow stream.

Butter from cows' milk
Or the fat from edible rats
Is cooked together with *lakura*
Or *atika;*
You smear it on your body today
And the aroma
Lasts until the next day.

And when you balance on your head
A beautiful water-pot

Or a new basket
Or a long-necked jar
Full of honey,
Your long neck
Resembles the *alwiri* spear.

And as you walk along the pathway
On both sides
The *obiya* grasses are flowering
And the *pollok* blossoms
And the wild white lilies
Are shouting silently
To the bees and butterflies!

And as the fragrance
Of the ripe wild berries
Hooks the insects and little birds,
As the fishermen hook the fish
And pull them up mercilessly,

The young men
From the surrounding villages,
And from across many streams,
They come from beyond the hills
And the wide plains,
They surround you
And bite off their ears
Like jackals.

And when you go
To the well
Or into the freshly burnt woodlands
To collect the red *oceyu,*
Or to cut *oduggu* shrubs,
You find them
Lurking in the shades
Like the leopardess with cubs.

*

Ocol tells me
That I like dirt.
He says
Shea butter causes
Skin diseases.

He says, Acoli adornments
Are old-fashioned and unhealthy.
He says I soil his white shirt
If I touch him,
My husband treats me
As if I am suffering from
The 'Don't touch me' disease!

He says that I make his bed-sheets dirty
And his bed smelly.
Ocol says
I look extremely ugly
When I am fully adorned
For the dance!

When I walk past my husband
He hisses like a wounded *ororo* snake
Choking with vengeance.
He has vowed
That he will never touch
My hands again.

My husband
Is in love with Tina
The woman with the large head;
Ocol dies for Clementine
Ocol never sleeps.
For the beautiful one
Who has read!

When the beautiful one
With whom I share my husband
Returns from cooking her hair
She resembles
A chicken
That has fallen into a pond;
Her hair looks
Like the python's discarded skin.

They cook their hair
With hot iron
And pull it hard
So that it may grow long.
Then they rope the hair
On wooden pens
Like a billy-goat

Brought for the sacrifice
Struggling to free itself.

They fry their hair
In boiling oil
As if it were locusts,
And the hair sizzles
It cries aloud in sharp pain
As it is pulled and stretched.
And the vigorous and healthy hair
Curly, springy and thick
That glistens in the sunshine
Is left listless and dead
Like the elephant grass
Scorched brown by the fierce
February sun.
It lies lifeless
Like the sad and dying banana leaves
On a hot and windless afternoon.

The beautiful woman
With whom I share my husband
Smears black shoe-polish
On her hair
To blacken it
And to make it shine,
She washes her hair
With black ink;

But the thick undergrowth
Rejects the shoe-polish
And the ink
And it remains untouched
Yellowish, greyish
Like the hair of the grey monkey.

There is much water
In my husband's house
Cold water and hot water.
You twist a cross-like handle
And water gushes out
Hot and steaming
Like the urine
Of the elephant.

You twist another cross-like handle;
It is cold water,

Clean like the cooling fresh waters
From the streams
Of Lututuru hills.
But the woman
With whom I share my husband
Does not wash her head;
The head of the beautiful one
Smells like rats
That have fallen into the fireplace.

And she uses
Powerful perfumes
To overcome the strange smells,
As they treat a pregnant coffin!
And the different smells
Wrestle with one another
And the smell of the shoe-polish
Mingles with them.
Clementine has many headkerchiefs,
Beautiful headkerchiefs of many colours.
She ties one on her head
And it covers up
The rot inside;

She ties the knot
On her forehead
And arranges the edges
With much care
So that it covers
Her ears
As well as the bold forehead
That jumps sparks
When lightning has splashed,
And hurls back sunlight
More powerfully than a mirror!

Sometimes she wears
The hair of some dead woman
Of some white woman
Who died long ago
And she goes with it
To the dance!
What witchcraft!

Shamelessly, she dances
Holding the shoulder of my husband,
The hair of a dead woman

On her head,
The body of the dead woman
Decaying in the tomb!

One night
The ghost of the dead woman
Pulled away her hair
From the head of the wizards
And the beautiful one
Fell down
And shook with shame
She shook
As if the angry ghost
Of the white woman
Had entered her head.

*

Ocol, my friend
Look at my skin
It is smooth and black.
And my boy friend
Who plays the *nanga*
Sings praises to it.

I am proud of the hair
With which I was born
And as no white woman
Wishes to do her hair
Like mine,
Because she is proud

Of the hair with which she was born,
I have no wish
To look like a white woman.

No leopard
Would change into a hyena,
And the crested crane
Would hate to be changed
Into the bold-headed,
Dung-eating vulture,
The long-necked and graceful giraffe
Cannot become a monkey.

Let no one
Uproot the Pumpkin.

ANTONIO JACINTO

(1932– , Angola)

Monangamba

On that big estate there is no rain
it's the sweat of my brow that waters the crops:

On that big estate there is coffee ripe
and that cherry-redness
is drops of my blood turned sap.

The coffee will be roasted,
ground, and crushed,
will turn black, black with the colour of the *contratado*.[1]

Black with the colour of the *contratado!*

Ask the birds that sing,
the streams in carefree wandering
and the high wind from inland:

Who gets up early? Who goes to toil?
Who is it carries on the long road
the hammock or bunch of kernels?
Who reaps and for pay gets scorn
rotten maize, rotten fish,
ragged clothes, fifty *angolares*[2]
beating for biting back?
Who?

Who makes the millet grow

and the orange groves to flower?
—Who?

Who gives the money for the boss to buy
cars, machinery, women
and Negro heads for motors?

Who makes the white man prosper,
grow big-bellied—get much money?
—Who?

---

[1]***contratado*** contract laborer. [2]***angolores*** unit of money.

And the birds that sing,
the streams in carefree wandering
and the high wind from inland
will answer:

—Monangambeeee. . . .

Ah! Let me at least climb the palm trees
Let me drink wine, palm wine
and fuddled by my drunkness forget

—Monangambeeee. . . .

Poem of Alienation

This is not yet my poem
the poem of my soul and of my blood
no
I still lack knowledge and power to write my poem
the great poem I feel already turning in me

My poem wanders aimlessly
in the bush or in the city
in the voice of the wind
in the surge of the sea
in the Aspect and the Being

My poem steps outside
wrapped in showy cloths
selling itself
selling
'lemons, buy my le-e-e-emons'

My poem runs through the streets
with a putrid cloth pad on its head
offering itself
offering

'mackerel, sardine, sprats
fine fish, fine fi-i-i-sh . . .'

My poem trudges the streets
'here J'urnal' 'Dai-i-i-ly'
and no newspaper yet carries my poem

My poem goes into the cafés
'lott'ry draw-a tomorra lott'ry draw-a tomorra'
and the draw of my poem
wheel as it wheels
whirl as it whirls
never changes
'lott'ry draw-a tomorra
lott'ry draw-a tomorra'

My poem comes from the township
on Saturdays bring the washing
on Mondays take the washing
on Saturdays surrender the washing and surrender self
on Mondays surrender self and take the washing

My poem is in the suffering
of the laundress's daughter
shyly
in the closed room
of a worthless boss idling
to build up an appetite for the violation

My poem is the prostitute
in the township at the broken door of her hut
'hurry hurry
pay your money
come and sleep with me'

My poem lightheartedly plays at ball
in a crowd where everyone is a servant
and shouts
'offside goal goal'

My poem is a contract worker
goes to the coffee fields to work
the contract is a burden
that is hard to load
'contract wor-r-r-ker'

My poem walks barefoot in the street

SYLVIA PLATH

(1932–1963, United States)

Daddy

You do not do, you do not do
Any more, black shoe
In which I have lived like a foot
For thirty years, poor and white,
Barely daring to breathe or Achoo.

Daddy, I have had to kill you.
You died before I had time—
Marble-heavy, a bag full of God,
Ghastly statue with one grey toe
Big as a Frisco seal

And a head in the freakish Atlantic
Where it pours bean green over blue
In the waters off beautiful Nauset.
I used to pray to recover you.
Ach, du[1]

In the German tongue, in the Polish town
Scraped flat by the roller
Of wars, wars, wars.
But the name of the town is common.
My Polack friend

Says there are a dozen or two.
So I never could tell where you
Put your foot, your root,
I never could talk to you.
The tongue stuck in my jaw.

It stuck in a barb wire snare.
Ich, ich, ich, ich,[2]
I could hardly speak.
I thought every German was you.
And the language obscene

An engine, an engine
Chuffing me off like a Jew.
A Jew to Dachau, Auschwitz, Belsen.

---

[1]***Ach, du*** German: "Ah, you." [2]***Ich, ich, ich, ich*** German: "I, I, I, I."

I began to talk like a Jew.
I think I may well be a Jew.

The snows of the Tyrol, the clear beer of Vienna
Are not very pure or true.
With my gypsy ancestress and my weird luck
And my Taroc pack and my Taroc pack
I may be a bit of a Jew.

I have always been scared of *you,*
With your Luftwaffe,[3] your gobbledygoo.
And your neat moustache
And your Aryan eye, bright blue.
Panzer-man, panzer-man, O You—

Not God but a swastika
So black no sky could squeak through.
Every woman adores a Fascist,
The boot in the face, the brute
Brute heart of a brute like you.

You stand at the blackboard, daddy,
In the picture I have of you,
A cleft in your chin instead of your foot
But no less a devil for that, no not
Any less the black man who

Bit my pretty red heart in two.
I was ten when they buried you.
At twenty I tried to die
And get back, back, back to you.
I thought even the bones would do.

But they pulled me out of the sack,
And they stuck me together with glue.
And then I knew what to do.
I made a model of you,
A man in black with a Meinkampf[4] look

And a love of the rack and the screw.
And I said I do, I do.
So daddy, I'm finally through.
The black telephone's off at the root,
The voices just can't worm through.

---

[3]**Luftwaffe** Nazi air force. [4]***Meinkampf*** reference to Adolf Hitler's autobiography, *My Struggle.*

If I've killed one man, I've killed two—
The vampire who said he was you
And drank my blood for a year,
Seven years, if you want to know.
Daddy, you can lie back now.

There's a stake in your fat black heart
And the villagers never liked you.
They are dancing and stamping on you.
They always *knew* it was you.
Daddy, daddy, you bastard, I'm through.

FELIX MNTHALI

(1933– , Zambia)

The Stranglehold of English Lit.

(FOR MOLARA OGUNDIPE-LESLIE)

Those questions, sister,
those questions
stand
stab
jab
and gore
too close to the centre!

For if we had asked
why Jane Austen's people
carouse all day
and do no work

would Europe in Africa
have stood
the test of time?
and would she still maul
the flower of our youth
in the south?
Would she?

Your elegance of deceit,
Jane Austen,
lulled the sons and daughters
of the dispossessed
into a calf-love
with irony and satire
around imaginary people.

While history went on mocking
the victims of branding irons
and sugar-plantations
that made Jane Austen's people
wealthy beyond compare!

Eng. Lit., my sister,
was more than a cruel joke—
it was the heart
of alien conquest.

LEILA DJABALI

(1933– , Algeria)

For My Torturer, Lieutenant D——

TRANSLATED FROM THE FRENCH BY ANITA BARROWS

You slapped me—
no one had ever slapped me—
electric shock
and then your fist
and your filthy language
I bled too much to be able to blush
All night long
a locomotive in my belly
rainbows before my eyes
It was as if I were eating my mouth
drowning my eyes
I had hands all over me
and felt like smiling.

Then one morning a different soldier came
You were as alike as two drops of blood.
Your wife, lieutenant—
Did she stir the sugar in your coffee?
Did your mother dare to tell you you looked well?
Did you run your fingers through your kids' hair?

IMAMU BARAKA

(1934– , United States)

Poem for Half White College Students

Who are you, listening to me, who are you
listening to yourself? Are you white or
black, or does that have anything to do
with it? Can you pop your fingers to no
music, except those wild monkies go on
in your head, can you jerk, to no melody,
except finger poppers get it together
when you turn from starchecking to checking
yourself. How do you sound, your words, are they
yours? The ghost you see in the mirror, is it really
you, can you swear you are not an imitation greyboy,
can you look right next to you in that chair, and swear,
that the sister you have your hand on is not really
so full of Elizabeth Taylor, Richard Burton is
coming out of her ears. You may even have to be Richard
with a white shirt and face, and four million negroes
think you cute, you may have to be Elizabeth Taylor, old lady,
if you want to sit up in your crazy spot dreaming about dresses,
and the sway of certain porters' hips. Check yourself, learn who it is
speaking, when you make some ultrasophisticated point, check yourself,
when you find yourself gesturing like Steve McQueen, check it out, ask
in your black heart who it is you are, and is that image black or white,

you might be surprised right out the window, whistling dixie on the way
in

WOLE SOYINKA

(1934– , Nigeria)

Telephone Conversation

The price seemed reasonable, location
Indifferent. The landlady swore she lived
Off premises. Nothing remained
But self-confession. 'Madam,' I warned,
'I hate a wasted journey—I am African.'
Silence. Silenced transmission of
Pressurized good-breeding. Voice, when it came,
Lipstick coated, long gold-rolled
Cigarette-holder pipped. Caught I was, foully.
'HOW DARK?' . . . I had not misheard. . . . 'ARE YOU LIGHT
OR VERY DARK?' Button B. Button A. Stench
Of rancid breath of public hide-and-speak.
Red booth. Red pillar-box. Red double-tiered
Omnibus squelching tar. It *was* real! Shamed
By ill-mannered silence, surrender
Pushed dumbfoundment to beg simplification.
Considerate she was, varying the emphasis—
'ARE YOU DARK? OR VERY LIGHT?' Revelation came.
'You mean—like plain or milk chocolate?'
Her assent was clinical, crushing in its light
Impersonality. Rapidly, wave-length adjusted,
I chose. 'West African sepia'—and as afterthought,
'Down in my passport.' Silence for spectroscopic
Flight of fancy, till truthfulness clanged her accent
Hard on the mouthpiece. 'WHAT'S THAT?' conceding
'DON'T KNOW WHAT THAT IS.' 'Like brunette.'
'THAT'S DARK, ISN'T IT?' 'Not altogether.
Facially, I am brunette, but madam, you should see
The rest of me. Palm of my hand, soles of my feet
Are a peroxide blonde. Friction, caused—
Foolishly madam—by sitting down, has turned
My bottom raven black—One moment madam!'—sensing
Her receiver rearing on the thunderclap
About my ears—'Madam,' I pleaded, 'wouldn't you rather
See for yourself?'

PAUL ZIMMER

(1934– , United States)

Zimmer Envying Elephants

I have a wide, friendly face
Like theirs, yet I can't hang
My nose like a fractured arm
Nor flap my dishpan ears.
I can't curl my canine teeth,
Swing my tail like a filthy tassel,
Nor make thunder without lightning.

But I'd like to thud amply around
For a hundred years or more,
Stuffing an occasional tree top
Into my mouth, screwing hugely for
Hours at a time, gaining weight,
And slowly growing a few hairs.

Once in a while I'd charge a power pole
Or smash a wall down just to keep
Everybody loose and at a distance.

What Zimmer Would Be

When asked, I used to say,
"I want to be a doctor."
Which is the same thing
As a child saying,
"I want to be a priest,"
Or
"I want to be a magician,"
Which is the laying
Of hands, the vibrations,
The rabbit in the hat,
Or the body in the cup,
The curing of the sick
And the raising of the dead.

"Fix and fix, you're all better,"
I would say
To the neighborhood wounded
As we fought the world war
Through the vacant lots of Ohio.
"Fix and fix, you're all better,"
And they would rise
To fight again.
But then
I saw my aunt die slowly of cancer
And a man struck down by a car.

All along I had really
Wanted to be a poet,
Which is, you see, almost
The same thing as saying,
"I want to be a doctor,"
"I want to be a priest,"
Or
"I want to be a magician."
All along, without realizing it,
I had wanted to be a poet.

Fix and fix, you're all better.

The Day Zimmer Lost Religion

The first Sunday I missed Mass on purpose
I waited all day for Christ to climb down
Like a wiry flyweight from the cross and
Club me on my irreverent teeth, to wade into
My blasphemous gut and drop me like a
Red hot thurible, the devil roaring in
Reserved seats until he got the hiccups.

It was a long cold way from the old days
When cassocked and surpliced I mumbled Latin
At the old priest and rang his obscure bell.
A long way from the dirty wind that blew
The soot like venial sins across the school yard
Where God reigned as a threatening,
One-eyed triangle high in the fleecy sky.

The first Sunday I missed Mass on purpose
I waited all day for Christ to climb down
Like the playground bully, the cuts and mice
Upon his face agleam, and pound me
Till my irreligious tongue hung out.
But of course He never came, knowing that
I was grown up and ready for Him now.

KOFI AWONOOR

(1935– , Ghana)

Song of War

I shall sleep in white calico;
War has come upon the sons of men
And I shall sleep in calico;
Let the boys go forward,
Kpli and his people should go forward;
Let the white man's guns boom,
We are marching forward;
We all shall sleep in calico.

When we start, the ground shall shake;
The war is within our very huts;
Cowards should fall back
And live at home with the women;
They who go near our wives
While we are away in battle
Shall lose their calabashes when we come.

Where has it been heard before
That a snake has bitten a child
In front of its own mother;
The war is upon us
It is within our very huts
And the sons of men shall fight it
Let the white man's guns boom
And its smoke cover us
We are fighting them to die.

We shall die on the battlefield
We shall like death at no other place,
Our guns shall die with us
And our sharp knives shall perish with us
We shall die on the battlefield.

The Weaver Bird

The weaver bird built in our house
And laid its eggs on our only tree
We did not want to send it away
We watched the building of the nest
And supervised the egg-laying.
And the weaver returned in the guise of the owner
Preaching salvation to us that owned the house
They say it came from the west
Where the storms at sea had felled the gulls
And the fishers dried their nets by lantern light
Its sermon is the divination of ourselves
And our new horizons limit at its nest
But we cannot join the prayers and answers of the communicants.
We look for new homes every day,
For new altars we strive to rebuild
The old shrines defiled by the weaver's excrement.

The First Circle

1

the flat end of sorrow here
two crows fighting over New Year's Party
leftovers. From my cell, I see a cold
hard world.

2

So this is the abscess that
hurts the nation—
jails, torture, blood
and hunger.
One day it will burst;
it must burst.

3

When I heard you were taken
we speculated, those of us at large
where you would be
in what nightmare will you star?

That night I heard the moans
wondering whose child could now
be lost in the cellars of oppression.
Then you emerged, tall, and bloody-eyed.

It was the first time
I wept.

MARGARET PIERCY

(1936– , United States)

To the Pay Toilet

You strop my anger, especially
when I find you in restaurant or bar
and pay for the same liquid, coming and going.
In bus depots and airports and turnpike plazas
some woman is dragging in with three kids hung off her
shrieking their simple urgency like gulls.
She's supposed to pay for each of them
and the privilege of not dirtying the corporate floor.
Sometimes a woman in a uniform's on duty
black or whatever the prevailing bottom is
getting thirty cents an hour to make sure
no woman sneaks her full bladder under a door.
Most blatantly you shout that waste of resources
for the greatest good of the smallest number
where twenty pay toilets line up glinty clean
and at the end of the row one free toilet
oozes from under its crooked door,
while a row of weary women carrying packages and babies
wait and wait and wait to do
what only the dead find unnecessary.

BRENDAN KENNELLY

(1936– , Ireland)

The Silent Pits

When all is said and done, not much is done and said.
Moving among the living hordes,
Resurrecting some version of the dead

To flesh them out again with sagging words
Is, given the silent pits, a bit of a game
I learned to play while still a boy
Dreaming of a hole blown in the sky
Through which I'd glimpse the god without a name,
The deft maker of silences, the quiet one
Who asks nothing but absolute attention
And in return puzzles the puzzled mind
Permitting, though, the sight of a cheeky pigeon
Beaking for crumbs among stones in July sun,
Committed to the search, taking what he can find.

ARTHUR W. BIDDLE

(1936– , United States)

Grandfather

It began yesterday in Venice
at the pastry shop that bears your name
(yours, not mine, father of my mother),
the shop I happened upon in the humid afternoon.

"Si, si, in Treviso are many of our name.
I thought you looked like one of us,"
the baker offered,
then proudly posed for snapshots.

Now I feel your being
—present and past—
as the train carries me from that city,
past the mountain wall
you regarded with hot eyes.

Was that your house
that one gaping roofless
there across the field?
This your soil
where vines of grapes sink roots
and inch along wired paths?

You tore your feet
from the earth of your valley,
put mountains at your back,
followed your own path

to the land of young men
and younger women,
the land that never quite became your own.
You never spoke of the old place
in the language harsh and alien.

Finally, nearing ninety,
waiting in the parking lot of the suburban mall,
your heart burst.

Welcome home, grandfather,
welcome home.

GHITA ORTH

(1936– , United States)

What Didn't Happen in Arizona

She stands at an exit ramp
of the Interstate on a flat
beige plain of brush and dust.

In no direction is there anything
except this band of asphalt
joining nothing to nothing.

Far in the background clouds
daubed by some power plant
drift without connection

to the sky. She is by herself
at this roadside by choice—
husband and daughter have driven

over the bridge that marks
the interchange, the one rise
generous enough to hide a car.

She will smoke a cigarette
while he will take a picture,
their daughter will still sleep

curled in the backseat burrow
of duffels and suitcases
with a Walkman playing.

She has no fear that he might
leave her here, rather that she
will vanish in the only place

she'd ever been so perfectly
alone that disappearing seems
as likely as it is impossible.

She stands and waits in that
vacant landscape for a blue
Ford truck with a smiling Indian

at the wheel, waits for an R.V.
splashed with bumper stickers—
I LOVE RETIREMENT, *Disney World*—

waits for a station wagon or
a tour bus, or a van covered
entirely in psychedelic swirls.

She waits for the one who must
surely pass, and slow, and back up,
and scoop her quickly into the trunk

so that her husband will return
to the place she was and find
it emptied, will drive long

into the night while their daughter
sleeps, marveling at how she managed
to disappear there in a flat land

with no cars, no hiding places,
and only manufactured clouds.
Then their bronze Honda rises

into the frame of sky and scrub.
She sticks her thumb out. Her husband
laughs, waves, drives past, stops.

And she runs to get inside a space
so filled with what belongs to her
that she can hardly breathe.

Secrets of the Rain Forest

About one-inch long and translucent, the glass frog barely casts a shadow, making it hard to see. Its bones are green, and the visible red vein leads to its heart.

PHOTO CAPTION IN THE *N.Y. TIMES*

Glass frog, I need you
to tell my daughter,
in whatever small spare
notes you can manage
with that sheer throat,
the joys of barely
casting a shadow.

Tell her, who would walk
the high school hallways
etching footprints
deep in the vinyl tiles,
burning handprints
into the locker doors,
who would leave a spoor
of woman-scent blatant
enough for anyone to find
her even blindfolded,
but does not yet know how,
tell her the blessings
of being hard to see.
Describe the safety
of the small green leaf,
how you nestle into it
with your gelid fingers
swollen at the tips
like an embryo's
while the predators—
flecked snakes, fluorescent
lizards—must pass you by.

Explain the pleasures
of green bones, how
yours are pliant twigs
hid in the twistings
of low moist brush, how
they can blend against
the old mossed bark
of monkeypod or fig
and not be trampled.

And then, show her
your vulnerable belly
holding the light
like a candled egg.
Show her that loud red
line of vein arrowing
straight to the heart,
dangerously visible
as the one that will
surely lead her
in some furtive tangle
of sweaty dark
to give herself away.

ISHMAEL REED

(1938– , United States)

badman of the guest professor

FOR JOE OVERSTREET, DAVID HENDERSON, ALBERT AYLER & D MYSTERIOUS "H" WHO CUT UP D REMBRANDTS

1

you worry me whoever you are
i know you didn't want me to
come here but here i am just
d same; hi-jacking yr stagecoach,
hauling in yr pocket watches & mak
ing you hoof it all d way to
town. black bart, a robber w/an
art; i left some curses in d cash
box so youll know its me

listen man, i cant help it if
yr thing is over, kaputs,
   finis
no matter how you slice it dick
you are done. a dead duck all out
of quacks; d nagging hiccup dat
goes on & on w/out a simple glass
   of water for relief

2

youve been teaching shakespeare for
20 years only to find d joke
   on you
d eavesdropping rascal who got it

in d shins because he didnt know
enough to keep his feet behind d cur
tains; a sad-sacked head served on a
platter in titus andronicus or falstaff
  too fat to make a go of it
  anymore

3

its not my fault dat yr tradition
was knocked off wop style & left in
d alley w/pricks in its mouth. i
read abt it in d papers but it was no
  skin off my nose
wasnt me who opened d gates & allowed
d rustlers to slip thru unnoticed. you
ought to do something abt yr security or
  mend yr fences partner
dont look at me if all dese niggers
are ripping it up like deadwood dick;
doing art d way its never been done, mak
ing wurlitzer sorry he made d piano dat
will drive mozart to d tennis
  courts
making smith-corona feel like d red
faced university dat has just delivered china
  some 50 e-leben h bomb experts

i didnt deliver d blow dat drove d
abstract expressionists to mi ladies
linoleum where dey sleep beneath tons of
wax & dogshit & d muddy feet of children or
because some badassed blackpainter done sent
french impressionism to d walls of highrise
  lobbies where dey belong is not my fault
martha graham will never do d jerk
shes a sweet ol soul but her hips
cant roll; as stiff as d greek
statues she loves so much

4

dese are d reasons you did me nasty
j alfred prufrock, d trick you pull
ed in d bookstore today; stand in d
corner no peaches for a week, u lemon

u must blame me because yr wife is
ugly. 86-d by a thousand discriminating

saunas. dats why you did dat sneaky thing
i wont tell d townsfolk because u hv
to live here and im just passing thru

5

you got one thing right tho. i did say
dat everytime i read william faulkner i
go to sleep. when i read hemmingway i
wish dat one of dem bulls wd hv jumped d
fence & gored his fingers so dat he wdnt hv
taken up so much
good space

fitzgerald wdnt hv known a gangster if one
had snatched zelda & made her a moll tho
she wd hv been grateful i bet

bonnie of clyde wrote d saga of suicide
sal just as d feds were closing in. it is
worth more than d collected works of ts
eliot a trembling anglican whose address
is now d hell dat thrilled him so
last word from down there he was open
ing a publishing co dat will bore d
devil back to paradise

6

& by d way did you hear abt grammar?
cut to ribbons in a photo finish by
stevie wonder, a blindboy who dances
on a heel. he just came out of d slang
& broke it down before millions.
it was bloody murder

7

to make a long poem shorter—3 things
moleheaded lame w/ 4 or 5 eyes
1) yr world is riding off into d sunset
2) d chips are down & nobody will chance yr i.o.u.s
3) d last wish was a fluke so now you hv to return to be-
ing a fish
p.s. d enchantment has worn off

dats why you didn't like my reading list right?
it didn't include anyone on it dat you cd in
vite to a cocktail party & shoot a lot of
bull right?

so you want to take it out on my hide   right?
well i got news for you professor nothing—i
am my own brand while you must be d fantasy of
a japanese cartoonist

a strangekind of dinosaurmouse
i can see it all now. d leaves
are running low. its d eve of
extinction & dere are no holes to
accept yr behind. you wander abt yr
long neck probing a tree. you think
its a tree but its really a trap. a
cry of victory goes up in d kitchen of
d world. a pest is dead. a prehis
toric pest at dat. really funnytime
prehistoric pest whom we will lug into
a museum to show everyone how really funny
you are   yr fate wd make a good
scenario but d plot is between you &
charles darwin. you know, whitefolkese
business

as is said. im passing thru. just sing
ing my song. get along little doggie &
jazz like dat. word has it dat a big gold
shipment is coming to californy. i hv to
ride all night if im to meet my pardners
dey want me to help score d ambush

ED OCHESTER

(1939–   , United States)

The Gift

One day
as I was lying on the lawn
dreaming of the Beautiful
and my wife was justifiably bitching
out the window
at my shiftlessness and
the baby was screaming
because I wouldn't let him
eat my cigarettes,
a tiger cat leaped over the fence,
smiled at my wife,
let the baby pull his tail,

hummed like a furry dynamo
as I stroked him.

My wife took the car to get him some food,
my son began to sing his wordless song,
and I wrote a poem in the sand.

Now God give every man who's hopeless
a beautiful wife,
an infant son who sings,
and the gift of a sweet-faced cat.

SEAMUS HEANEY

(1939– , Ireland)

Mid-Term Break

I sat all morning in the college sick bay
Counting bells knelling classes to a close.
At two o'clock our neighbours drove me home.

In the porch I met my father crying—
He had always taken funerals in his stride—
And Big Jim Evans saying it was a hard blow.

The baby cooed and laughed and rocked the pram
When I came in, and I was embarrassed
By old men standing up to shake my hand

And tell me they were 'sorry for my trouble.'
Whispers informed strangers I was the eldest,
Away at school, as my mother held my hand

In hers and coughed out angry tearless sighs.
At ten o'clock the ambulance arrived
With the corpse, stanched and bandaged by the nurses.

Next morning I went up into the room. Snowdrops
And candles soothed the bedside; I saw him
For the first time in six weeks. Paler now,

Wearing a poppy bruise on his left temple,
He lay in the four foot box as in his cot.
No gaudy scars, the bumper knocked him clear.

A four foot box, a foot for every year.

Death of a Naturalist

All year the flax-dam[1] festered in the heart
Of the townland; green and heavy headed
Flax had rotted there, weighted down by huge sods.
Daily it sweltered in the punishing sun.
Bubbles gargled delicately, bluebottles° flies
Wove a strong gauze of sound around the smell.
There were dragon-flies, spotted butterflies,
But best of all was the warm thick slobber
Of frogspawn that grew like clotted water
In the shade of the banks. Here, every spring
I would fill jampotfuls of the jellied
Specks to range on window-sills at home,
On shelves at school, and wait and watch until
The fattening dots burst into nimble-
Swimming tadpoles. Miss Walls would tell us how
The daddy frog was called a bullfrog
And how he croaked and how the mammy frog
Laid hundreds of little eggs and this was
Frogspawn. You could tell the weather by frogs too
For they were yellow in the sun and brown
In rain.

Then one hot day when fields were rank
With cowdung in the grass the angry frogs
Invaded the flax-dam; I ducked through hedges
To a coarse croaking that I had not heard
Before. The air was thick with a bass chorus.
Right down the damn gross-bellied frogs were cocked
On sods; their loose necks pulsed like sails. Some hopped:
The slap and plop were obscene threats. Some sat
Poised like mud grenades, their blunt heads farting.
I sickened, turned, and ran. The great slime kings
Were gathered there for vengeance and I knew
That if I dipped my hand the spawn would clutch it.

Digging

Between my finger and my thumb
The squat pen rests; snug as a gun.

DEATH OF A NATURALIST [1]**flax-dam** dam made of fiber, which crosses a stream.

Under my window, a clean rasping sound
When the spade sinks into gravelly ground:
My father, digging. I look down

Till his straining rump among the flowerbeds
Bends low, comes up twenty years away
Stooping in rhythm through potato drills
Where he was digging.

The coarse boot nestled on the lug, the shaft
Against the inside knee was levered firmly.
He rooted out tall tops, buried the bright edge deep
To scatter new potatoes that we picked
Loving their cool hardness in our hands.

By God, the old man could handle a spade.
Just like his old man.

My grandfather cut more turf in a day
Than any other man on Toner's bog.
Once I carried him milk in a bottle
Corked sloppily with paper. He straightened up
To drink it, then fell to right away
Nicking and slicing neatly, heaving sods
Over his shoulder, going down and down
For the good turf. Digging.

The cold smell of potato mould, the squelch and slap
Of soggy peat, the curt cuts of an edge
Through living roots awaken in my head.
But I've no spade to follow men like them.

Between my finger and my thumb
The squat pen rests.
I'll dig with it.

RONALD KOERTGE

(1940– , United States)

Orientation Week

and a family of two is exploring the Student Union.
Dad is all decked out in the shirt she bought with
her own money. Joyce is wearing snug cutoffs and
her freshman breasts stir as she walks.

Dad knows that all the boys plan to slip some LSD
in her cocoa as soon as he is out of sight. He
takes in the monsters, their hair down to there,
a fuselage in every pair of pants.

Worse than he expected, certainly not the eunuchs
and mild wethers[1] that he hoped for. And where is
The Jake Barnes Dormitory?

He sees them do it to her even as they stand by the
car. Worse, he sees her ask for it, coaxing with
her expensive teeth. Why can't he
lock those vivid hips in her room?
Follow her everywhere, revolvers drawn?
Punch a few of those furry bastards in the chops?

So he does what he can—lips to chaste brow, hand
to bare arm saying,

Good-by now. Be good.

Panty Hose

A little after 5:00 the curb in front of
the Bank of America is rich with typists
holding their cold elbows and waiting for
boys who are pale and hairy, who play a
little guitar, always have some good dope
and do not work.

These girls in their panty hose are sowing
their wild oats now because soon each will
leave the hair and the ribs-that-show
for their legacy, the movie Mom ran every
day of their lives.

Already they hate their husbands for sucking
up to big shots, for voting Republican
and pointing out creeps in vans. They will
never love anybody like they do the one
who is always late. They will never look
up and down the street so eagerly, not

ORIENTATION WEEK [1]**wethers** a castrated male sheep.

even when dinner is ice-cold and someone
in a new Country Squire has just been
involved in a terrible crash.

For My Daughter

She often lies with her hands behind her head
in a San Quentin pose, arms forming a pair
of small empty wings.

She does not slip from the bath in a loose
towel, according Follies' glimpses
of rump and thigh. She does lumber by
in a robe of immense dunciness.

Her dates are fixed up or blind
often, like specimens, behind thick glass.
She leaves late, returns by twelve, afraid
perhaps that she will turn into
something worse.

She comes to me and wants to know what to do.
I say I do not know.
She comes to me and wants to know if it will
ever be all right.
I say Yes but it will take a long time.

SHARON OLDS

(1942–   , United States)

Sex Without Love

How do they do it, the ones who make love
without love? Beautiful as dancers,
gliding over each other like ice-skaters
over the ice, fingers hooked
inside each other's bodies, faces
red as steak, wine, wet as the
children at birth whose mothers are going to
give them away. How do they come to the
come to   the come to the   God   come to the
still waters, and not love

the one who came there with them, light
rising slowly as steam off their joined
skin? These are the true religious,
the purists, the pros, the ones who will not
accept a false Messiah, love the
priest instead of the God. They do not
mistake the lover for their own pleasure,
they are like great runners: they know they are alone
with the road surface, the cold, the wind,
the fit of their shoes, their over-all cardio-
vascular health—just factors, like the partner
in the bed, and not the truth, which is the
single body alone in the universe
against its own best time.

DAVID HUDDLE

(1942– , United States)

Stopping by Home

1.

Five times since July my father
has been hospitalized. He's home
today, sitting up at his desk
in bathrobe, pajamas, slippers.
I am embarrassed, I want him
fat again, in khakis that smell
like sweat, cigarette smoke, carbide,

ignoring me because he'd rather
work the crossword puzzle, alone
or pretending to be, than risk
in those minutes before supper
finding out what meanness I'd been
up to. He's thin now. And pale.
Waiting to hear what's on my mind.

2.

In the summer in the hospital
he sat on the bed's edge clutching
that formica table they crank up

and put your food tray on. He coughed
up white mucus, took oxygen
from a thin green tube, couldn't sleep,
couldn't lie back and breathe. He

and my mother thought it was all
finished the day he got medicine
to make him relax, make him sleep,
then couldn't sit up because he'd lost
his strength but couldn't breathe lying
back. They rang for the nurse, but he
passed through something you couldn't see.

3.

They say his hair turned white. It's true,
it's grayer than it was, almost
white. He can't read much now, has no
power of concentration, mind
strays. Today he talks about friends
who've died, relatives long gone.
In a photograph he points out

which ones are dead now. "But you
and Lester Waller and Tom Pope
and George Schreiber and James Payne—so
many still alive," I remind
him. He seems not to hear and bends
to put the picture away. "Some
still around," he says, "yes, no doubt."

4.

My mother wants us to talk. This
is what she always wants, her sons
sitting around with their dad, talk
being evidence of love, she
thinks. My evenings home from school,
the army, New York, or Vermont,
she'd leave the room for us to do it.

We always argued politics.
Didn't intend to, but reasons
came to us. Once he said I ought
to go to Russia if the
things I said were really true,

and I walked out. Words are too hard
for us now. We'll just have to sit.

5.

Their lives in that house before he got too sick must have been
so filled with silence that even when a truck would pass
on the highway down the hill they would listen. Those
clear sunny days of May and June she sat with him
on the front porch where sometimes the soft wind
rustled in that hackberry that's grown
so high now. I hold an infant

recollection of the sun
warming the three of us,
their holding me so
close between them
I knew then
what home
meant.

6.

So
if I
care so much
about them I
have to sit up here
a thousand miles away
and write myself back home, why

not look for a job down there, try
to find some town close enough to say,
"I'm going to see them," drive over there
and walk in the door and not even surprise
them, sit down with them and talk, maybe stay for lunch,
say an easy goodbye and leave without feeling like
I betrayed them, and I will never find my way back home.

7.

Night comes down, the winter sky
momentarily ecstatic,
then stunned, bruised, ruined with pain, dark. . .

Coal on the fire, our old habits
keep us still, without lights, sitting
until the study's bay window
yields maybe one moving tree branch.

Then Mother rises, breathes a sigh
for all three of us when she flicks
on the overhead light. The dog barks
lightly in its sleep. We blink. It's
not late. His fingers shake setting
his watch. Before us are the slow
hours, each breath he takes a chance.

8.

At six we move from the study
to the living room for the news,
the weather report our excuse.
The man draws snow over the whole
Northeast, freely uses the word
blizzard, and I stand up before
he's finished and say I think I

better keep driving north, maybe
I can beat that storm. "But son, you
just got here." Mother's hurt. He's used
to my skedaddling ways, and so
makes himself grin, offers his hand
for me to shake and at the door
we say our word for love. Good-bye.

9.

I scuttle out into the dark
and drive 300 miles north, numb,
knowing that I hurt but not able
to register it, a busted
speedometer on a car that
hurtles forward. In the morning
I get what's coming to me. Snow

starts in Pennsylvania, slick
stuff on those mountains south of Scranton,
the interstate a long white table
of ice, everything blasted
white. Wind and drifts in those high flat

stretches near nowhere. Endless dream
of losing control, moving through snow.

10.

Tell me whose parents don't get old.
Your father's sick, and you can't stand
to be around him and help him
die or get well, whichever it
turns out he's going to do. Well,
son, you deserve to drive through snow,
wind and freezing cold, past Hometown,

Port Jervis, Newburgh, Kingston. No
decent motel would have you, can't
stop, can't give your old man an arm
to help him walk into the next
room. Albany says go to hell,
keep driving, boy, get your ass home
where you've got children of your own.

ALTA

(1942– , United States)

I Never Saw a Man in a Negligee

i'm frigid when I wear see thru negligees
my almost good figure looks good half hidden,
nipples the only hard bumps on my body & men
are sposed to sigh and go ooh & rub their hands
all over the filmy thing recalling norman mailer
& raquel welch & god knows who.
it never occurred to me to dress that way for women.
we'd pull off our cotton pants & go to it. so i figured,
if women can want the Real Me, men have to too. 2 times
i wore special fucky gowns, you know the type, one look
& he turns off the football game (but they never do)
& i was so busy being dainty & smelling fresh i couldnt
hump, couldnt wiggle, couldnt sweat, couldnt scream & you know
damn well i couldnt come.
but when i romp ass in a wrinkly blue shirt smelling like printers ink
or slightly soggy slacks after playing with babies,
then the happy human of me wants lovins, & rolls around with glee
rolling up, under, over&over o whee.

I Don't Have No Bunny Tail on My Behind

i don't have no bunny tail on my behind.
i'm a sister of the blood taboo.

my throat's too tight to swallow.
must be because i'm scared to death. i'm scared to live.
how do i get thru the day? the night?
guts, fella. that's how
what are your perversions to me?
what do i care you want sadistic broads in black boots,
cigarettes up your asshole?
what do i care?
that's our child sleeping in that blue crib

how did it feel:
that cigarette up my nose?
how did it feel?
you grimacing "does it hurt, baby? does it hurt?"
how did it feel to curse your pretty smile,
pray blindness strike your ice blue eyes?
how did it feel to curse: may you never know joy.
i hate your very soul.

i swore to avenge all the wasted dead, the caged wives.
what vengeance could answer our pain, our fury?
i hope i find out before i die.
in my cunt is blood & i always want it to be your blood.
i hope you bleed 5 days every month. i hope your strength drains down
the toilet.

you're afraid of me.
you laugh. you hit me.
you're running scared, man.
our voodoo dolls are all worn out.

yes i hate you.
yes i want your cock

off.
yes i want your blood & balls to spill
like my monthly payment in blood.
yes i want you to beat off in shame,
afraid to call me.
yes i want you dead.
when i was married i prayed to be a widow.
there are still wives. they are still preying.

yes i want you to flinch when i laugh
flinch when i laugh
my teeth tearing your heart, knowing your love is poisoned,
you cannot wash clean,
knowing the earth & i will outlive you.
you are a dying breed, you & your penis guns,
your joyless fucks, you are dying,
you are dying,
the curse of every wicked witch be upon your heart.
i could not hate you more if hatred were my bones.

The Art of Enforced Deprivation

i remember back in hi school
corliss & i were practicing dancing
i was the boy: my hand was round
her waist & the other hand holding her
hand. (that was how we danced back in those days)
her breast was poking me right there & i thot
"wow! boys sure get the good part!"

i looked at her face to see
if it felt as good to her as it did to me
but she wouldnt look at me.
i still dont know.

ELLEN BRYANT VOIGT

(1943– , United States)

The Lotus Flowers

The surface of the pond was mostly green—
bright green algae reaching out from the banks,
then the mass of waterlilies, their broad round leaves
rim to rim, each white flower spreading
from the center of a green saucer.
We teased and argued, choosing the largest,
the sweetest bloom, but when the rowboat
lumbered through and rearranged them,
we found the plants were anchored, the separate
muscular stems descending in the dense water—
only the most determined put her hand

into that frog-slimed pond
to wrestle with a flower. Back and forth
we pumped across the water, in twos and threes,
full of brave adventure. On the marshy shore,
the others hollered for their turns,
or at the hem of where we pitched the tents
gathered firewood—
this was wilderness,
although the pond was less than half an acre
and we could still see the grand magnolias
in the village cemetery, their waxy
white conical blossoms gleaming in the foliage.
A dozen girls, the oldest only twelve, two sisters
with their long braids, my shy neighbor,
someone squealing without interruption:
all we didn't know about the world buoyed us,
as the frightful water sustained and moved the flowers
tethered at a depth we couldn't see.

In the late afternoon, before they'd folded
into candles on the dark water,
I went to fill the bucket at the spring.
Deep in the pines, exposed tree roots
formed a natural arch, a cave of black loam.
I raked off the skin of leaves and needles,
leaving a pool so clear and shallow
I could count the pebbles
on the studded floor. The sudden cold
splashing up from the bucket to my hands
made me want to plunge my hand in—
and I held it under, feeling the shock that wakes
and deadens, watching first my fingers,
then the ledge beyond me,
the snake submerged and motionless,
the head propped on its coils the way a girl
crosses her arms before her on the sill
and rests her chin there.
Lugging the bucket
back to the noisy clearing, I found nothing changed,
the boat still rocked across the pond,
the fire straggled and cracked as we fed it
branches and debris into the night,
leaning back on our pallets—
spokes in a wheel—learning the names of the many
constellations, learning how each fixed
cluster took its name:

not from the strongest light, but from the pattern
made by stars of lesser magnitude,
so like the smaller stars we rowed among.

NIKKI GIOVANNI

(1943– , United States)

My Poem

i am 25 years old
black female poet
wrote a poem asking
nigger can you kill
if they kill me
it won't stop
the revolution

i have been robbed
it looked like they knew
that i was to be hit

they took my tv
my two rings
my piece of african print
and my two guns
if they take my life
it won't stop
the revolution

my phone is tapped
my mail is opened
they've caused me to turn
on all my old friends
and all my new lovers
if i hate all black
people
and all negroes
it won't stop
the revolution

i'm afraid to tell
my roommate where i'm going

and scared to tell
people if i'm coming
if i sit here
for the rest
of my life
if won't stop
the revolution

if i never write
another poem
or short story
if i flunk out
of grad school
if my car is reclaimed
and my record player
won't play
and if i never see
a peaceful day
or do a meaningful
black thing
it won't stop
the revolution

the revolution
is in the streets
and if i stay on
the 5th floor
it will go on
if i never do
anything
it will go on

The True Import of Present Dialogue: Black vs. Negro

(For Peppi, Who Will Ultimately Judge Our Efforts)

Nigger
Can you kill
Can you kill
Can a nigger kill

Can a nigger kill a honkie
Can a nigger kill the Man
Can you kill nigger
Huh? nigger can you
kill
Do you know how to draw blood
Can you poison
Can you stab-a-jew
Can you kill huh? nigger
Can you kill
Can you run a protestant down with your
'68 El Dorado
(that's all they're good for anyway)
Can you kill
Can you piss on a blond head
Can you cut it off
Can you kill
A nigger can die
We ain't got to prove we can die
We got to prove we can kill
They sent us to kill
Japan and Africa
We policed europe
Can you kill
Can you kill a white man
Can you kill the nigger
in you
Can you make your nigger mind
die
Can you kill your nigger mind
And free your black hands to
strangle
Can you kill
Can a nigger kill
Can you shoot straight and
Fire for good measure
Can you splatter their brains in the street
Can you kill them
Can you lure them to bed to kill them
We kill in Viet Nam
for them
We kill for UN & NATO & SEATO & US
And everywhere for all alphabet but
BLACK
Can we learn to kill WHITE for BLACK
Learn to kill niggers
Learn to be Black men

JACK MAPANJE

(1945– , Malawi)

On Being Asked to Write a Poem for 1979

Without kings and warriors occasional verse fails

Skeletal Kampuchea children staring, cold
Stubborn Irish children throwing grenades
These are objects too serious for verse,
Crushed Soweto children clutching their entrails
Then in verse bruised, mocks

Today no poet sufficiently asks why dying children
Stare or throw bombs. And why should we
Compute painful doubts that will forever occupy us?
Talking oil-crises in our eight-cylinder cars
Is enough travesty . . .

The year of the child must make no difference then
Where tadpoles are never allowed to grow into frogs!

WANDA COLEMAN

(1946– , United States)

Women of my Color

i follow the curve of his penis
and go down

there is a peculiar light in which women
of my color are regarded by men

being on the bottom where pressures
are greatest is least desirable
would be better to be dead i
sometimes think

there is a peculiar light in which women
of my race are regarded by black men
as saints
as mothers
as sisters
as whores

but mostly as the enemy

it's not our fault   we are victims
who have chosen to struggle and stay alive

there is a peculiar light in which women
of my race are regarded by white men
                                        as exotic
                                        as enemy

but mostly as whores

it's enough to make me cry
but i don't

following the curve of his penis
i go down

will i ever see
the sun?

Drone

i am a clerk
i am a medical billing clerk
i sit here all day and type
the same type of things all day long
insurance claim forms
for people who suffer chronic renal failure
fortunately these people i rarely see
these are hard core cases
most of them are poor, black or latin
they are cases most other doctors refuse
they are problem cases
some of them have complications like heroin abuse
some of them are very young
most of them have brief charts
which means they died within a year of beginning treatment
sometimes a patient gets worried about his or her
coverage and calls the office
i refer them to the dialysis unit case worker
a few of the patients do bad things. for instance
some of them might refuse treatment as scheduled
sometimes they get drunk and call up
the nurses or attendants and curse them out

sometimes they try to fight the attendants
because they feel neglected/afraid
sometimes they wait until the last minute
to show up and it is the last minute
most of the patients, good patients,
quietly expire
i retire their charts to the inactive file
a few more claims i won't be typing up anymore
they are quickly replaced by others black, latin or poor
i make out crisp new charts
and the process starts all over again
the cash flows and flows and flows
so that the doctors can feed their race horses
and play tennis and pay the captains of their yachts
and keep up their children's college tuition and
trusts and maintain their luxury cars
for this service i am paid a subsistance salary
i come in here each morning
and bill the government for the people by the people
for these patients
i sit here and type
is what i do and that's very important
day after day/adrift in the river of forms
that flows between my desk and the computer that
prints out the checks
there are few problems here. i am a very good clerk
i sit here all day and type
i am a medical billing clerk
i am a clerk
i clerk

Doing Battle with the Wolf

1.

i drip blood
on my way to and from work
i drip blood
down the aisles while shopping at the supermarket
i drip blood
standing in line at the bank
filling my tank at the gas station
visiting my man in prison
buying money orders at the post office

driving the kids to school
walking to bed at night
i drip blood

an occasional transfusion arrives in the mail
or i find plasma in the streets
an occasional vampire flashes my way
but they don't take much
my enemy is the wolf
who eats even the mind

the wolf will come for me sooner or later
i know this
the wolf makes no sexual distinctions
i am the right color
he has a fetish for black meat and
frequently hunts with his mate along side him

he follows my trail of blood

i drip blood for hours
go to the bathroom and apply bandages
i've bled enough
it's my monthly bleeding of poison
getting it out of my system
watching it as it flows from the
open sore of my body into the toilet stool
making a red ring
so pretty
flushing it away—red swirls
a precious painful price i pay

my man cannot protect me
the wolf has devoured most of my friends
i watched them die horribly
saw the
raw hunks of meat skin bone
swallowed
watched as full, the wolf crept away
to sleep

2.

the wolf has a beautiful coat
it is white and shimmers in moonlight/a coat of diamonds
his jaws are power

teeth sharp as guns glisten against his red tongue
down around his feet the fur is dirty with the caked blood of my friends

i smile
i never thought it would come to this

scratching
scratching at my door
scratching to get in

howls howls howls
my children are afraid
i send them to hide in the bedroom

scratch scratch scratch
the door strains
howl howl howl
cries of my children "mama! mama! who is it?"

i am ready
—armed with my spear inherited from my father as he from his mother
(who was a psychic) as she from her father (who was a runaway slave) as he
from his mother (who married the tribal witch doctor)—me—african warrior
imprisoned inside my barely adequate female form
determined
i open the door
a snarl
he lunges
the spear
against his head
he falls back
to prepare for second siege
i wait
the door will not close
i do not see the wolf
my children scream
i wait
look down
am wounded
drip blood
cannot move
or apply bandages
must wait
wolf howls and the roar of police sirens

AI (FLORENCE OGAWA)

(1947– United States)

Why Can't I Leave You?

You stand behind the old black mare,
dressed as always in that red shirt,
stained from sweat, the crying of the armpits,
that will not stop for anything,
stroking her rump, while the barley goes unplanted.
I pick up my suitcase and set it down,
as I try to leave you again.
I smooth the hair back from your forehead.
I think with your laziness and the drought too,
you'll be needing my help more than ever.
You take my hands, I nod
and go to the house to unpack,
having found another reason to stay.

I undress, then put on my white lace slip
for you to take off, because you like that
and when you come in, you pull down the straps
and I unbutton your shirt.
I know we can't give each other any more
or any less than what we have.
There is safety in that, so much
that I can never get past the packing,
the begging you to please, if I can't make you happy,
come close between my thighs
and let me laugh for you from my second mouth.

JULIA ALVAREZ

(1950– , Dominican Republic)

Homecoming

When my cousin Carmen married, the guards
at her father's *finca* took the guests' bracelets
and wedding rings and put them in an armored truck
for safekeeping while wealthy, dark-skinned men,
their plump, white women and spoiled children
bathed in a river whose bottom had been cleaned
for the occasion. She was Uncle's only daughter,

and he wanted to show her husband's family,
a bewildered group of sunburnt Minnesotans,
that she was valued. He sat me at their table
to show off my English, and when he danced with me,
fondling my shoulder blades beneath my bridesmaid's gown
as if they were breasts, he found me skinny
but pretty at seventeen, and clever.
Come back from that cold place, Vermont, he said,
all this is yours! Over his shoulder
a dozen workmen hauled in blocks of ice
to keep the champagne lukewarm and stole
glances at the wedding cake, a dollhouse duplicate
of the family *rancho,* the shutters marzipan,
the cobbles almonds. A maiden aunt housekept,
touching up whipped cream roses with a syringe
of eggwhites, rescuing the groom when the heat
melted his chocolate shoes into the frosting.
On too much rum Uncle led me across the dance floor,
dusted with talcum for easy gliding, a smell
of babies underfoot. He twirled me often,
excited by my pleas of dizziness, teasing me,
saying that my merengue had lost its Caribbean.
Above us, Chinese lanterns strung between posts
came on and one snapped off and rose
into a purple postcard sky.
A grandmother cried: *The children all grow up too fast.*
The Minnesotans finally broke loose and danced a Charleston
and were pronounced good gringos with latino hearts.
The little sister, freckled with a week of beach,
her hair as blonde as movie stars, was asked
by maids if they could touch her hair or skin,
and she backed off, until it was explained to her,
they meant no harm. *This is all yours,*
Uncle whispered, pressing himself into my dress.
The workmen costumed in their workclothes danced
a workman's jig. The maids went by with trays
of wedding bells and matchbooks monogrammed
with Dick's and Carmen's names. It would be years
before I took the courses that would change my mind
in schools paid for by sugar from the fields around us,
years before I could begin to comprehend
how one does not see the maids when they pass by. . . .
—It was too late, or early, to be wise—
The sun was coming up beyond the amber waves
of cane, the roosters crowed, the band struck up
Las Mañanitas, a morning serenade. I had a vision
that I blamed on the champagne:

the fields around us were burning. At last
a yawning bride and groom got up and cut
the wedding cake, but everyone was full
of drink and eggs, roast pig, and rice and beans.
Except the maids and workmen,
sitting on stoops behind the sugar house,
ate with their fingers from their open palms
windows, shutters, walls, pillars, doors,
made from the cane they had cut in the fields.

Dusting

Each morning I wrote my name
on the dusty cabinet, then crossed
the dining table in script, scrawled
in capitals on the backs of chairs,
practising signatures like scales
while Mother followed, squirting
linseed from a burping can
into a crumpled-up flannel.

She erased my fingerprints
from the bookshelf and rocker,
polished mirrors on the desk
scribbled with my alphabets.
My name was swallowed in the towel
with which she jeweled the table tops.
The grain surfaced in the oak
and the pine grew luminous.
But I refused with every mark
to be like her, anonymous.

GREG DELANTY

(1958– , Ireland)

Out of the Ordinary

Skin-head pigeons strut in a gang
along the road's white line
& fly from under a fuming cop car.
Lazy, contented sea gulls catch rides
on the conveyor belt of a river—

Others glide & hover in the slow air
of a busking tin whistle player
as if conjured from his upside-down hat.
Singing thrushes play on the fret board
of electric wires & sparrows
arrow upward, seemingly desperate
to enter heaven, not noticing heaven
has descended to the ordinary
as we saunter along Union Quay.

HADIZA LANTANA AMPAH

(1964–   , Nigeria)

When the Clouds Gather

When the clouds gather
and the heat passes away
and the earth brings
forth fruits, Maryama
fresh as paint will be
taken home to her husband.
When the clouds gather
and the heat passes away
and the earth brings
forth fruits, Maryama
will make her husband's
bed as warm as wool.
When the clouds gather
and the heat passes away
and the earth brings
forth fruits, Maryama
will be as fruitful as a vine
and her children like olive plants.
When the clouds gather
and the heat passes away
and the earth brings
forth fruits, Maryama
will watch them bloom
like flowers in Summer.
When the clouds gather
and the heat passes away
and the earth brings
forth fruits, Maryama
will watch them fly

high like an eagle.
When the rain clouds gather
and the heat passes away
and the earth brings
forth fruits, Maryama
old as the hills will
be watched over like
the flower that withers away.
When the clouds gather
and the heat passes away
and the earth brings
forth fruits, Maryama
will finally be toasted into the soil, for the worms
skilful in the art of anatomy . . .
When the clouds gather.

On Poetry

WILLIAM WORDSWORTH

(1770–1850)

Preface to *Lyrical Ballads*

About the Author: William Wordsworth is generally considered to be the father of English romantic poetry. In the essay "Preface to *Lyrical Ballads*" (1802) Wordsworth outlines his definition of poetry and creates an elaborate comparison between poetry and prose. This definition has strongly affected the way we all look at poetry.

The first volume of these poems has already been submitted to general perusal. It was published, as an experiment, which, I hoped, might be of some use to ascertain, how far, by fitting to metrical arrangement a selection of the real language of men in a state of vivid sensation, that sort of pleasure and that quantity of pleasure may be imparted, which a poet may rationally endeavour to impart. . . .

It is supposed, that by the act of writing in verse an author makes a formal engagement that he will gratify certain known habits of association; that he not only thus apprizes the reader that certain classes of ideas and expressions will be found in his book, but that others will be carefully excluded. This exponent or symbol held forth by metrical language must in different eras of literature have excited very different expectations: for example, in the age of Catullus, Terence, and Lucretius and that of Statius or Claudian;[1] and in our own country, in the age of Shakespeare and Beaumont and Fletcher, and that of Donne and Cowley, or Dryden, or Pope. I will not take upon me to determine the exact import of the promise which by the act of writing in verse an author, in the present day, makes to his reader; but I am certain, it will appear to many persons that I have not fulfilled the terms of an engagement thus voluntarily contracted. They who have been accustomed to the gaudiness and inane phraseology of many modern writers, if they persist in reading this book to its conclusion, will, no doubt, frequently have to struggle with feelings of strangeness and awkwardness: they will look round for poetry, and will be induced to inquire by what species of courtesy these attempts can be permitted to assume that title. I hope therefore the reader will not censure me, if I attempt to state what I have proposed to myself to perform; and also (as far as the limits of a preface will permit), to explain some of the chief reasons which have determined me in the choice of my purpose: that at least he may be spared any unpleasant feeling of disappointment, and that I myself may be protected from the most dishonourable accusation which can be brought against an author, namely, that of an indolence which prevents him from endeavouring to ascertain what is his duty, or, when his duty is ascertained, prevents him from performing it.

---

[1]Stratius wrote naturally and simply; Claudian wrote artificially.

The principal object, then, which I proposed to myself in these poems was to choose incidents and situations from common life and to relate or describe them, throughout, as far as was possible, in a selection of language really used by men; and, at the same time, to throw over them a certain colouring of imagination, whereby ordinary things should be presented to the mind in an unusual way; and, further, and above all, to make these incidents and situations interesting by tracing in them, truly though not ostentatiously, the primary laws of our nature: chiefly, as far as regards the manner in which we associate ideas in a state of excitement. Low and rustic life was generally chosen, because in that condition, the essential passions of the heart find a better soil in which they can attain their maturity, are less under restraint, and speak a plainer and more emphatic language; because in that condition of life our elementary feelings co-exist in a state of greater simplicity, and, consequently, may be more accurately contemplated, and more forcibly communicated; because the manners of rural life germinate from those elementary feelings; and, from the necessary character of rural occupations, are more easily comprehended; and are more durable; and lastly, because in that condition the passions of men are incorporated with the beautiful and permanent forms of nature. The language, too, of these men is adopted (purified indeed from what appear to be its real defects, from all lasting and rational causes of dislike or disgust) because such men hourly communicate with the best objects from which the best part of language is originally derived; and because, from their rank in society and the sameness and narrow circle of their intercourse, being less under the influence of social vanity they convey their feelings and notions in simple and unelaborated expressions. Accordingly, such a language, arising out of repeated experience and regular feelings, is a more permanent, and a far more philosophical language, than that which is frequently substituted for it by poets, who think that they are conferring honour upon themselves and their art, in proportion as they separate themselves from the sympathies of men, and indulge in arbitrary and capricious habits of expression, in order to furnish food for fickle tastes, and fickle appetites, of their own creation.

I cannot, however, be insensible of the present outcry against the triviality and meanness both of thought and language, which some of my contemporaries have occasionally introduced into their metrical compositions; and I acknowledge, that this defect, where it exists, is more dishonourable to the writer's own character than false refinement or arbitrary innovation, though I should contend at the same time that it is far less pernicious in the sum of its consequences. From such verses the poems in these volumes will be found distinguished at least by one mark of difference, that each of them has a worthy *purpose.* Not that I mean to say, that I always began to write with a distinct purpose formally conceived; but I believe that my habits of meditation have so formed my feelings, as that my descriptions of such objects as strongly excite those feelings, will be found to carry along with them a *purpose.* If in this opinion I am mistaken, I can have little right to the name of a poet. For all good poetry is the spontaneous overflow of powerful feelings: but though this be true, poems to which any value can be attached, were never produced on any variety of subjects but by a man, who being possessed of more than usual organic sensibility, had also thought long and deeply. For our continued influxes of feeling are modified and directed by our thoughts, which are indeed the representatives of all our past feelings; and, as by contemplating the relation of these general representatives to each other we discover what is really important to men, so, by the repetition and continuance of this act, our feelings will be connected with important subjects, till at length, if we be originally possessed of much sensibility, such habits of mind will be produced, that, by obeying blindly and mechanically

the impulses of those habits, we shall describe objects, and utter sentiments, of such a nature and in such connection with each other, that the understanding of the being to whom we address ourselves, if he be in a healthful state of association, must necessarily be in some degree enlightened, and his affections ameliorated. . . .

I will not suffer a sense of false modesty to prevent me from asserting, that I point my reader's attention to this mark of distinction, far less for the sake of these particular poems than from the general importance of the subject. The subject is indeed important! For the human mind is capable of being excited without the application of gross and violent stimulants; and he must have a very faint perception of its beauty and dignity who does not know this, and who does not further know, that one being is elevated above another, in proportion as he possesses this capability. It has therefore appeared to me, that to endeavour to produce or enlarge this capability is one of the best services in which, at any period, a writer can be engaged; but this service, excellent at all times, is especially so at the present day. For a multitude of causes, unknown to former times, are now acting with a combined force to blunt the discriminating powers of the mind, and unfitting it for all voluntary exertion to reduce it to a state of almost savage torpor. The most effective of these causes are the great national events which are daily taking place, and the increasing accumulation of men in cities, where the uniformity of their occupations produces a craving for extraordinary incident, which the rapid communication of intelligence hourly gratifies. To this tendency of life and manners the literature and theatrical exhibitions of the country have conformed themselves. The invaluable works of our elder writers, I had almost said the works of Shakespeare and Milton, are driven into neglect by frantic novels, sickly and stupid German tragedies, and deluges of idle and extravagant stories in verse.—When I think upon this degrading thirst after outrageous stimulation, I am almost ashamed to have spoken of the feeble effort with which I have endeavoured to counteract it; and, reflecting upon the magnitude of the general evil, I should be oppressed with no dishonourable melancholy, had I not a deep impression of certain inherent and indestructible qualities of the human mind, and likewise of certain powers in the great and permanent objects that act upon it which are equally inherent and indestructible; and did I not further add to this impression a belief, that the time is approaching when the evil will be systematically opposed, by men of greater powers, and with far more distinguished success.

Having dwelt thus long on the subjects and aim of these poems, I shall request the reader's permission to apprize him of a few circumstances relating to their *style,* in order, among other reasons, that I may not be censured for not having performed what I never attempted. The reader will find that personifications of abstract ideas rarely occur in these volumes; and, I hope, are utterly rejected as an ordinary device to elevate the style, and raise it above prose. I have proposed to myself to imitate, and, as far as is possible, to adopt the very language of men; and assuredly such personifications do not make any natural or regular part of that language. They are, indeed, a figure of speech occasionally prompted by passion, and I have made use of them as such; but I have endeavoured utterly to reject them as a mechanical device of style, or as a family language which writers in metre seem to lay claim to by prescription. I have wished to keep my reader in the company of flesh and blood, persuaded that by so doing I shall interest him. I am, however, well aware that others who pursue a different track may interest him likewise; I do not interfere with their claim, I only wish to prefer a different claim of my own. There will also be found in these volumes little of what is usually called poetic diction; I have taken as much pains to avoid it as others ordinarily take to produce it; this I have done for the reason already alleged, to bring my language near to the language of men, and further, because the pleasure which I have proposed to myself to impart is of a kind very different from that which is supposed by many persons to be the proper object of poetry. . . .

If in a poem there should be found a series of lines, or even a single line, in which the language, though naturally arranged and according to the strict laws of metre, does not differ from that of prose, there is a numerous class of critics, who, when they stumble upon these prosaisms as they call them, imagine that they have made a notable discovery, and exult over the poet as over a man ignorant of his own profession. Now these men would establish a canon of criticism which the reader will conclude he must utterly reject, if he wishes to be pleased with these volumes. And it would be a most easy task to prove to him, that not only the language of a large portion of every good poem, even of the most elevated character, must necessarily, except with reference to the metre, in no respect differ from that of good prose, but likewise that some of the most interesting parts of the best poems will be found to be strictly the language of prose, when prose is well written. . . .

Taking up the subject, then, upon general grounds, I ask what is meant by the word poet? What is a poet? To whom does he address himself? And what language is to be expected from him? He is a man speaking to men: a man, it is true, endued with more lively sensibility, more enthusiasm and tenderness, who has a greater knowledge of human nature, and a more comprehensive soul, than are supposed to be common among mankind; a man pleased with his own passions and volitions, and who rejoices more than other men in the spirit of life that is in him; delighting to contemplate similar volitions and passions as manifested in the goings-on of the universe, and habitually impelled to create them where he does not find them. To these qualities he has added a disposition to be affected more than other men by absent things as if they were present; an ability of conjuring up in himself passions, which are indeed far from being the same as those produced by real events, yet (especially in those parts of the general sympathy which are pleasing and delightful) do more nearly resemble the passions produced by real events, than any thing which, from the motions of their own minds merely, other men are accustomed to feel in themselves; whence, and from practice, he has acquired a greater readiness and power in expressing what he thinks and feels, and especially those thoughts and feelings which, by his own choice, or from the structure of his own mind, arise in him without immediate external excitement.

But, whatever portion of this faculty we may suppose even the greatest poet to possess, there cannot be a doubt but that the language which it will suggest to him, must, in liveliness and truth, fall far short of that which is uttered by men in real life, under the actual pressure of those passions, certain shadows of which the poet thus produces, or feels to be produced, in himself. However exalted a notion we would wish to cherish of the character of a poet, it is obvious, that, while he describes and imitates passions, his situation is altogether slavish and mechanical, compared with the freedom and power of real and substantial action and suffering. So that it will be the wish of the poet to bring his feelings near to those of the persons whose feelings he describes, nay, for short spaces of time perhaps, to let himself slip into an entire delusion, and even confound and identify his own feelings with theirs; modifying only the language which is thus suggested to him, by a consideration that he

describes for a particular purpose, that of giving pleasure. Here, then, he will apply the principle on which I have so much insisted, namely, that of selection; on this he will depend for removing what would otherwise be painful or disgusting in the passion; he will feel that there is no necessity to trick out or to elevate nature: and, the more industriously he applies this principle, the deeper will be his faith that no words, which his fancy or imagination can suggest, will be to be compared with those which are the emanations of reality and truth.

But it may be said by those who do not object to the general spirit of these remarks, that, as it is impossible for the poet to produce upon all occasions language as exquisitely fitted for the passion as that which the real passion itself suggests, it is proper that he should consider himself as in the situation of a translator, who deems himself justified when he substitutes excellences of another kind for those which are unattainable by him; and endeavours occasionally to surpass his original, in order to make some amends for the general inferiority to which he feels that he must submit. But this would be to encourage idleness and unmanly despair. Further, it is the language of men who speak of what they do not understand; who talk of poetry as of a matter of amusement and idle pleasure; who will converse with us as gravely about a *taste* for poetry, as they express it, as if it were a thing as indifferent as a taste for rope-dancing, or frontiniac[2] or sherry. Aristotle, I have been told, hath said, that poetry is the most philosophic of all writing: it is so: its object is truth, not individual and local, but general, and operative; not standing upon external testimony, but carried alive into the heart by passion; truth which is its own testimony, which gives strength and divinity to the tribunal to which it appeals, and receives them from the same tribunal. Poetry is the image of man and nature. The obstacles which stand in the way of the fidelity of the biographer and historian, and of their consequent utility, are incalculably greater than those which are to be encountered by the poet who has an adequate notion of the dignity of his art. The poet writes under one restriction only, namely, that of the necessity of giving immediate pleasure to a human being possessed of that information which may be expected from him, not as a lawyer, a physician, a mariner, an astronomer or a natural philosopher, but as a man. Except this one restriction, there is no object standing between the poet and the image of things; between this, and the biographer and historian there are a thousand.

Nor let this necessity of producing immediate pleasure be considered as a degradation of the poet's art. It is far otherwise. It is an acknowledgment of the beauty of the universe, an acknowledgment the more sincere because it is not formal, but indirect; it is a task light and easy to him who looks at the world in the spirit of love: further, it is a homage paid to the native and naked dignity of man, to the grand elementary principle of pleasure, by which he knows, and feels, and lives, and moves. We have no sympathy but what is propagated by pleasure: I would not be misunderstood; but wherever we sympathize with pain it will be found that the sympathy is produced and carried on by subtle combinations with pleasure. We have no knowledge, that is, no general principles drawn from the contemplation of particular facts, but what has been built up by pleasure, and exists in us by pleasure alone. The man of science, the chemist and mathematician, whatever difficulties and disgusts they may have had to struggle with, know and feel this. However painful may be the objects with which the anatomist's knowledge is connected, he feels that his knowledge is pleasure; and where he has no pleasure he has no knowledge. What then does the

---

[2]**frontiniac** a sweet wine.

poet? He considers man and the objects that surround him as acting and reacting upon each other, so as to produce an infinite complexity of pain and pleasure; he considers man in his own nature and in his ordinary life as contemplating this with a certain quantity of immediate knowledge, with certain convictions, intuitions, and deductions which by habit become of the nature of intuitions; he considers him as looking upon this complex scene of ideas and sensations, and finding every where objects that immediately excite in him sympathies which, from the necessities of his nature, are accompanied by an overbalance of enjoyment.

To this knowledge which all men carry about with them, and to these sympathies in which without any other discipline than that of our daily life we are fitted to take delight, the poet principally directs his attention. He considers man and nature as essentially adapted to each other, and the mind of man as naturally the mirror of the fairest and most interesting qualities of nature. And thus the poet, prompted by this feeling of pleasure which accompanies him through the whole course of his studies, converses with general nature with affections akin to those, which, through labour and length of time, the man of science has raised up in himself, by conversing with those particular parts of nature which are the objects of his studies. The knowledge both of the poet and the man of science is pleasure; but the knowledge of the one cleaves to us as a necessary part of our existence, our natural and unalienable inheritance; the other is a personal and individual acquisition, slow to come to us, and by no habitual and direct sympathy connecting us with our fellow-beings. The man of science seeks truth as a remote and unknown benefactor; he cherishes and loves it in his solitude: the poet, singing a song in which all human beings join with him, rejoices in the presence of truth as our visible friend and hourly companion. Poetry is the breath and finer spirit of all knowledge; it is the impassioned expression which is in the countenance of all science. Emphatically may it be said of the poet, as Shakespeare hath said of man, 'that he looks before and after.' . . .

The poet thinks and feels in the spirit of the passions of men. How, then, can his language differ in any material degree from that of all other men who feel vividly and see clearly? It might be *proved* that it is impossible. But supposing that this were not the case, the poet might then be allowed to use a peculiar language, when expressing his feelings for his own gratification, or that of men like himself. But poets do not write for poets alone, but for men. Unless therefore we are advocates for that admiration which depends upon ignorance, and that pleasure which arises from hearing what we do not understand, the poet must descend from this supposed height, and, in order to excite rational sympathy, he must express himself as other men express themselves. . . .

To this, by such as are unconvinced by what I have already said, it may be answered, that a very small part of the pleasure given by poetry depends upon the metre, and that it is injudicious to write in metre, unless it be accompanied with the other artificial distinctions of style with which metre is usually accompanied, and that by such deviation more will be lost from the shock which will be thereby given to the reader's associations, than will be counterbalanced by any pleasure which he can derive from the general power of numbers. In answer to those who still contend for the necessity of accompanying metre with certain appropriate colours of style in order to the accomplishment of its appropriate end, and who also, in my opinion, greatly underrate the power of metre in itself, it might perhaps, as far as relates to these poems, have been almost sufficient to observe, that poems are extant, written upon more humble subjects, and in a more naked and simple style than I have aimed at, which poems have continued to give pleasure from generation to genera-

tion. Now, if nakedness and simplicity be a defect, the fact here mentioned affords a strong presumption that poems somewhat less naked and simple are capable of affording pleasure at the present day; and, what I wished *chiefly* to attempt, at present, was to justify myself for having written under the impression of this belief. . . .

If I had undertaken a systematic defence of the theory upon which these poems are written, it would have been my duty to develop the various causes upon which the pleasure received from metrical language depends. Among the chief of these causes is to be reckoned a principle which must be well known to those who have made any of the arts the object of accurate reflection; I mean the pleasure which the mind derives from the perception of similitude in dissimilitude. This principle is the great spring of the activity of our minds, and their chief feeder. From this principle the direction of the sexual appetite, and all the passions connected with it take their origin: it is the life of our ordinary conversation; and upon the accuracy with which similitude in dissimilitude, and dissimilitude in similitude are perceived, depend our taste and our moral feelings. It would not have been a useless employment to have applied this principle to the consideration of metre, and to have shown that metre is hence enabled to afford much pleasure, and to have pointed out in what manner that pleasure is produced. But my limits will not permit me to enter upon this subject, and I must content myself with a general summary.

I have said that poetry is the spontaneous overflow of powerful feelings: it takes its origin from emotion recollected in tranquillity: the emotion is contemplated till by a species of reaction the tranquillity gradually disappears, and an emotion, kindred to that which was before the subject of contemplation, is gradually produced, and does itself actually exist in the mind. In this mood successful composition generally begins, and in a mood similar to this it is carried on; but the emotion, of whatever kind and in whatever degree, from various causes is qualified by various pleasures, so that in describing any passions whatsoever, which are voluntarily described, the mind will upon the whole be in a state of enjoyment. Now, if nature be thus cautious in preserving in a state of enjoyment a being thus employed, the poet ought to profit by the lesson thus held forth to him, and ought especially to take care, that whatever passions he communicates to his reader, those passions, if his reader's mind be sound and vigorous, should always be accompanied with an overbalance of pleasure. . . .

I have one request to make of my reader, which is, that in judging these poems he would decide by his own feelings genuinely, and not by reflection upon what will probably be the judgment of others. How common is it to hear a person say, 'I myself do not object to this style of composition or this or that expression, but to such and such classes of people it will appear mean or ludicrous.' This mode of criticism, so destructive of all sound unadulterated judgment, is almost universal: I have therefore to request, that the reader would abide independently by his own feelings, and that if he finds himself affected he would not suffer such conjectures to interfere with his pleasure.

If an author by any single composition has impressed us with respect for his talents, it is useful to consider this as affording a presumption, that, on other occasions where we have been displeased, he nevertheless may not have written ill or absurdly; and, further, to give him so much credit for this one composition as may induce us to review what has displeased us with more care than we should otherwise have bestowed upon it. This is not only an act of justice, but in our decisions upon poetry especially, may conduce in a high degree to the improvement of our own taste: for an *accurate* taste in poetry, and in all the other arts, as Sir Joshua Reynolds[3] has observed, is an *acquired* talent, which can only be produced by thought and a long continued intercourse with the best models of composition. This is mentioned, not with so ridiculous a purpose as to prevent the most inexperienced reader from judging for himself (I have already said that I wish him to judge for himself), but merely to temper the rashness of decision, and to suggest, that, if poetry be a subject on which much time has not been bestowed, the judgment may be erroneous; and that in many cases it necessarily will be so.

I know that nothing would have so effectually contributed to further the end which I have in view as to have shown of what kind the pleasure is, and how that pleasure is produced, which is confessedly produced by metrical composition essentially different from that which I have here endeavoured to recommend: for the reader will say that he has been pleased by such composition; and what can I do more for him? The power of any art is limited; and he will suspect, that, if I propose to furnish him with new friends, it is only upon condition of his abandoning his old friends. Besides, as I have said, the reader is himself conscious of the pleasure which he has received from such composition, composition to which he has peculiarly attached the endearing name of poetry; and all men feel an habitual gratitude, and something of an honourable bigotry for the objects which have long continued to please them: we not only wish to be pleased, but to be pleased in that particular way in which we have been accustomed to be pleased. There is a host of arguments in these feelings; and I should be the less able to combat them successfully, as I am willing to allow, that, in order entirely to enjoy the poetry which I am recommending, it would be necessary to give up much of what is ordinarily enjoyed. But, would my limits have permitted me to point out how this pleasure is produced, I might have removed many obstacles, and assisted my reader in perceiving that the powers of language are not so limited as he may suppose; and that it is possible that poetry may give other enjoyments, of a purer, more lasting, and more exquisite nature. This part of my subject I have not altogether neglected; but it has been less my present aim to prove, that the interest excited by some other kinds of poetry is less vivid, and less worthy of the nobler powers of the mind, than to offer reasons for presuming, that, if the object which I have proposed to myself were adequately attained, a species of poetry would be produced, which is genuine poetry; in its nature well adapted to interest mankind permanently, and likewise important in the multiplicity and quality of its moral relations.

ROBERT FROST

(1874–1963)

The Figure a Poem Makes

About the Author: Robert Frost, one of the great American poets of the twentieth century, in "The Figure a Poem Makes," describes poetry through a series of metaphors that, if not definitions, get to the heart of the poetic experience. For Frost poetry is a way of living as well as seeing, a way of imposing form over the complex materials of our lives.

---

 [3]**Sir Joshua Reynolds** eighteenth-century English portrait painter.

Abstraction is an old story with the philosophers, but it has been like a new toy in the hands of the artists of our day. Why can't we have any one quality of poetry we choose by itself? We can have in thought. Then it will go hard if we can't in practice. Our lives for it.

Granted no one but a humanist much cares how sound a poem is if it is only *a* sound. The sound is the gold in the ore. Then we will have the sound out alone and dispense with the inessential. We do till we make the discovery that the object in writing poetry is to make all poems sound as different as possible from each other, and the resources for that of vowels, consonants, punctuation, syntax, words, sentences, meter are not enough. We need the help of context—meaning—subject matter. That is the greatest help towards variety. All that can be done with words is soon told. So also with meters—particularly in our language where there are virtually but two, strict iambic and loose iambic. The ancients with many were still poor if they depended on meters for all tune. It is painful to watch our sprung-rhythmists straining at the point of omitting one short from a foot for relief from monotony. The possibilities for tune from the dramatic tones of meaning struck across the rigidity of a limited meter are endless. And we are back in poetry as merely one more art of having something to say, sound or unsound. Probably better if sound, because deeper and from wider experience.

Then there is this wildness whereof it is spoken. Granted again that it has an equal claim with sound to being a poem's better half. If it is a wild tune, it is a poem. Our problem then is, as modern abstractionists, to have the wildness pure; to be wild with nothing to be wild about. We bring up as aberrationists, giving way to undirected associations and kicking ourselves from one chance suggestion to another in all directions as of a hot afternoon in the life of a grasshopper. Theme alone can steady us down. Just as the first mystery was how a poem could have a tune in such a straightness as meter, so the second mystery is how a poem can have wildness and at the same time a subject that shall be fulfilled.

It should be of the pleasure of a poem itself to tell how it can. The figure a poem makes. It begins in delight and ends in wisdom. The figure is the same as for love. No one can really hold that the ecstasy should be static and stand still in one place. It begins in delight, it inclines to the impulse, it assumes direction with the first line laid down, it runs a course of lucky events, and ends in a clarification of life—not necessarily a great clarification, such as sects and cults are founded on, but in a momentary stay against confusion. It has denouement. It has an outcome that though unforeseen was predestined from the first image of the original mood—and indeed from the very mood. It is but a trick poem and no poem at all if the best of it was thought of first and saved for the last. It finds its own name as it goes and discovers the best waiting for it in some final phrase at once wise and sad—the happy-sad blend of the drinking song.

No tears in the writer, no tears in the reader. No surprise for the writer, no surprise for the reader. For me the initial delight is in the surprise of remembering something I didn't know I knew. I am in a place, in a situation, as if I had materialized from cloud or risen out of the ground. There is a glad recognition of the long lost and the rest follows. Step by step the wonder of unexpected supply keeps growing. The impressions most useful to my purpose seem always those I was unaware of and so made no note of at the time when taken, and the conclusion is come to that like giants we are always hurling experience ahead of us to pave the future with against the day when we may want to strike a line of purpose across it for somewhere. The line will have the more charm for not being mechanically straight. We enjoy the straight crookedness of a good walking stick. Modern instruments of precision are being used to make things crooked as if by eye and hand in the old days.

I tell how there may be a better wildness of logic than of inconsequence. But the logic is backward, in retrospect, after the act. It must be more felt than seen ahead like prophecy. It must be a revelation, or a series of revelations, as much for the poet as for the reader. For it to be that there must have been the greatest freedom of the material to move about in it and to establish relations in it regardless of time and space, previous relation, and everything but affinity. We prate of freedom. We call our schools free because we are not free to stay away from them till we are sixteen years of age. I have given up my democratic prejudices and now willingly set the lower classes free to be completely taken care of by the upper classes. Political freedom is nothing to me. I bestow it right and left. All I would keep for myself is the freedom of my material—the condition of body and mind now and then to summons aptly from the vast chaos of all I have lived through.

Scholars and artists thrown together are often annoyed at the puzzle of where they differ. Both work from knowledge; but I suspect they differ most importantly in the way their knowledge is come by. Scholars get theirs with conscientious thoroughness along projected lines of logic; poets theirs cavalierly and as it happens in and out of books. They stick to nothing deliberately, but let what will stick to them like burrs where they walk in the fields. No acquirement is on assignment, or even self-assignment. Knowledge of the second kind is much more available in the wild free ways of wit and art. A school boy may be defined as one who can tell you what he knows in the order in which he learned it. The artist must value himself as he snatches a thing from some previous order in time and space into a new order with not so much as a ligature clinging to it of the old place where it was organic.

More than once I should have lost my soul to radicalism if it had been the originality it was mistaken for by its young converts. Originality and initiative are what I ask for my country. For myself the originality need be no more than the freshness of a poem run in the way I have described: from delight to wisdom. The figure is the same as for love. Like a piece of ice on a hot stove the poem must ride on its own melting. A poem may be worked over once it is in being, but may not be worried into being. Its most precious quality will remain its having run itself and carried away the poet with it. Read it a hundred times: it will forever keep its freshness as a metal keeps its fragrance. It can never lose its sense of a meaning that once unfolded by surprise as it went.

CHAPTER

FOUR

Reading Script into Play

James R. Howe and William A. Stephany

Introduction

Drama differs in several basic ways from the other literary genres in this book. Unlike the author of a poem or story or essay, the playwright does not intend his or her words primarily to be *read* in private, but to be *heard* as they are spoken by actors on a stage. Reading a play in private will always be in some respect an unnatural act. A play's primary space is not your bedroom or the library, but the theater, where it can be staged by a group of players before a live audience. When we read a play, therefore, we should be aware of what we are missing: the infectiousness of being in the theater and sharing a communal experience, the power which comes from seeing a tangibly "real" performance by live actors, and the challenge of being confronted by someone else's idea of how the play should be presented.

However, both this book and the course for which you are reading it ask you to perform exactly this kind of unnatural act. This is partly because there are compensations for what is lost in reading a play rather than watching it in a theater. When we read, we can stop to make marginal jottings, or turn back a few pages (or a few acts) to check on the accuracy of our memory of an earlier moment—things we cannot do in the theater. As readers, we have the leisure to consider alternative interpretations of a line, a character, a scene, even of the play as a whole. As readers, we are even able to make the decisions that a director has already made for us when we go to the theater. In fact, readers are *required* to direct their own play: to imagine its actors and actresses, its costumes and setting, while at the same time responding as its audience as well. Unless we do this, we cannot fully comprehend the play.

This is part of the reason why reading a play is so challenging. We have to make decisions, but without many of the specifically narrative clues that might help us if we were

reading fiction; and we do not have the *dramatic* clues—tone of voice or facial expression or bodily gestures—which would help us if we saw the play acted in a theater. If we look at the beginning of William Shakespeare's *Hamlet,* for example, we are immediately confronted with the following stage direction and dialogue:

Elsinore. A platform before the castle.
[FRANCISCO at his post. Enter to him BERNARDO.]

BER. Who's there?
FRAN. Nay, answer me. Stand, and unfold yourself.
BER. Long live the King!
FRAN. Bernardo?
BER. He.
FRAN. You come most carefully upon the hour.

If we were sitting in an audience watching a performance of the play, we would see a soldier standing or walking alertly, and then another soldier entering and encountering him. From his costume, his posture, and perhaps from the setting (if, for example, it were made to represent the ramparts of a castle), we would guess that the first is on guard duty, a guess that is confirmed by the first line, the sentry's traditional query, "Who's there?"

However, the situation seems reversed. Francisco, as the guard on duty, is the one who is supposed to challenge others, yet it is the newcomer, Bernardo, who challenges *him.* (This role reversal is much easier to "get" when we see a performance, than when we read these lines.) This situation is also odd in another way: Bernardo, as the soldier who will relieve Francisco, should *expect* Francisco to be at his post. He shouldn't be surprised to find him there, so why would he have to ask, "Who's there?" Who else would be there?

Francisco's response, the second line of the play, shows that he recognizes this question as a departure from normal ritual. "Nay, answer *me,*" he insists, and then he issues the sentry's formal challenge: "Stand, and unfold yourself," that is, stop advancing and identify yourself. With his response, "Long live the King," Bernardo apparently gives the password and is recognized. The little crisis passes, but we are left with questions. Why is Bernardo so nervous? Whom did he expect Francisco to be? Why is Francisco so jumpy, especially since Bernardo has arrived to relieve him right on schedule? It turns out that they are expecting a ghost who has appeared to them twice already at about this hour. (Since it's the ghost of the recently deceased king, it adds a level of irony to Bernardo's password.) Later in this scene, when the ghost arrives, they will have questions about how to deal with it, and the air of mystery will build throughout the play. Broken or misleading ceremonies will also repeat themselves. Indeed, this is a *play* of questions and mysteries, and its first two lines put us immediately into its atmosphere.

In asking ourselves such questions and responding to this atmosphere, we would be reacting to the play as it is enacted before us by specific actors under the guidance of a specific director on a specific occasion. These questions are intensified when we read the play, rather than when we see it performed. Instead of responding to a play as acted, we need to imagine for ourselves the meaning of each speech, the tone of voice of the speakers, the physical postures and gestures they might assume, and ultimately the significance of what is said. We have to figure out for ourselves how every speech sounds and looks, and

only then can we begin to answer that first set of questions. All this is very demanding, but unless we do it, for us this script will not become a play.

CONVENTIONS OF DRAMATIC SCRIPTS

To do this kind of reading, we need to be familiar with some of the conventions of dramatic writing—some of the rules of the playwright's game. By far the greatest part of any script will consist of the **dialogue** to be spoken by the actors. The brief excerpt from the beginning of *Hamlet* presents us with a typical example of the primary conventions of script writing and also with the special problem we face in reading a play. Remember that a script is written for people who wish to stage the play, not for the theater audience and not for a reading audience, and it is the needs of those who will stage the play that determine the form of a script. The two major conventions are the following:

1. Individual actors need to know when one character's speech ends and another's begins, so the playwright's convention is to place the new speaking character's name before each speech. This practice allows actors to scan down the page and easily locate their next speaking part.
2. Sometimes, the playwright will provide the player with a **stage direction**. Usually, these directions to the players will be printed in italics, to set them off from the words to be spoken. Stage directions are the playwright's primary means (apart from dialogue) of communicating with the people who are putting on the play. They might give instructions to the players or to the music director or to the costume designer. They might even, like the lengthy stage direction that precedes Tom's first speech in *The Glass Menagerie* (see page 1178), provide elaborate instructions to the set designer about how the stage should be constructed.

HOW CONVENTIONS WORK: THE READER'S CHALLENGE

The central problem confronting every playwright is how to communicate to an audience through dialogue alone, without the luxury of a narrative voice to serve as intermediary. The writer's intellectual attitudes or thematic concerns need to be expressed indirectly, filtered through the language and actions of characters interacting on a stage.

Sometimes, however, playwrights try to find alternative ways to communicate directly to an audience. In Shakespeare's day, for example, playwrights used the aside and the soliloquy. In an *aside,* a player turns toward the members of the audience and says something perfectly audible to them, but supposedly not audible to anyone on stage. Since the audience is farther from the speaker than are the other characters onstage, this situation is clearly not realistic. Also, by speaking to the audience rather than to the other characters, a player erases the boundaries of the play and enters the world of the audience, momentarily destroying the comfortable distance which usually separates us from the fictional space of the stage. However, this is a "convention" which the audience at that time came to the theater prepared to accept. In another Shakespearean convention, the *soliloquy,* a character who is alone onstage speaks aloud about his or her emotional or psychic state for the

audience to overhear. Both of these conventions are designed to provide the audience with necessary information about how characters are thinking or feeling, often about their otherwise concealed motivation. They allow the dramatist temporarily to exercise the power available to a fiction writer who is using an omniscient point of view (using a narrator to present information about the character which no single individual can know). While these devices seem artificial to us, they may have been as invisibly "conventional" to audiences in an earlier age as our modern high-tech equivalent of the voice-over: An actor stares off moodily, his recorded voice speaks, and we accept the convention that we are able to overhear his "inner voice."

These are exceptional devices, however, and quickly seem silly if overused. Normally, both dramatist and audience have to accept and cope with the limits of dramatic form, and this requires sensitivity to detail by both of them. Writers have to let detail communicate for them through indirection, and readers, therefore, need to be alert to detail in order to understand. In fact, the hardest part of reading a play, as opposed to a novel or short story, is the absence of a narrator's voice standing between us and the dialogue. This is the drama reader's special challenge. Stage directions telling the actor how the character feels or moves or looks sometimes help, but usually we are dependent upon context to answer such questions. Our clue may be the way another character reacts to the first character's words. As if to anger? To irony? To joking? We need to infer from such reactions how the original line might have been delivered. But then how dependable is *that* character? Do you trust his or her reactions? You will need to read the entire play to feel secure about a character's identity.

The following dialogue occurs early in Lorraine Hansberry's play *A Raisin in the Sun.* The play is set in the 1950s, in an apartment on Chicago's black south side. Ruth is a mother, Travis her ten- or eleven-year-old son. By reading this passage very carefully, we will see some of the inferences we might draw about these characters' relationship and, more specifically, about the tensions of this particular morning's before-school conversation. After the passage we will give you an example of one way of reading it; we will try to show how much we can learn by reading between the lines as well as by reading the lines themselves, by taking into account what is suggested as well as what is directly stated.

RUTH Sit down and have your breakfast, Travis.
TRAVIS Mama, this is Friday. *(Gleefully)* Check coming tomorrow, huh?
RUTH You get your mind off money and eat your breakfast.
TRAVIS *(Eating)* This is the morning we supposed to bring fifty cents to school.
RUTH Well, I ain't got no fifty cents this morning.
TRAVIS Teacher says we have to.
RUTH I don't care what teacher say. I ain't got it. Eat your breakfast, Travis.
TRAVIS I *am* eating.
RUTH Hush up now and just eat!

(The boy gives her an exasperated look for her lack of understanding, and eats grudgingly.)

TRAVIS You think Grandmama would have it?
RUTH No! And I want you to stop asking your grandmother for money, you hear me?
TRAVIS *(Outraged)* Gaaaleee! I don't ask her, she just gimme it sometimes!
RUTH Travis Willard Younger—I got too much on me this morning to be—

TRAVIS Maybe Daddy—

RUTH *Travis!*

(The boy hushes abruptly. They are both quiet and tense for several seconds.)

TRAVIS *(Presently)* Could I maybe go carry some groceries in front of the supermarket for a little while after school then?

RUTH Just hush, I said. *(Travis jabs his spoon into his cereal bowl viciously, and rests his head in anger upon his fists.)* If you through eating, you can get up over there and make up your bed.

(The boy obeys stiffly and crosses the room, almost mechanically, to the bed and more or less carefully folds the covering. He carries the bedding into his mother's room and returns with his books and cap.)

TRAVIS *(Sulking and standing apart from her unnaturally)* I'm gone.

RUTH *(Looking up from the stove to inspect him automatically)* Come here. *(He crosses to her and she studies his head.)* If you don't take this comb and fix this here head, you better! *(Travis puts down his books with a great sigh of oppression, and crosses to the mirror. His mother mutters under her breath about his "slubbornness.")* 'Bout to march out of here with that head looking just like chickens slept in it! I just don't know where you get your slubborn ways. . . . And get your jacket, too. Looks chilly out this morning.

TRAVIS *(With conspicuously brushed hair and jacket)* I'm gone.

RUTH Get carfare and milk money— *(Waving one finger)* —and not a single penny for no caps, you hear me?

TRAVIS *(With sullen politeness)* Yes'm.

(He turns in outrage to leave. His mother watches after him as in his frustration he approaches the door almost comically. When she speaks to him, her voice has become a very gentle tease.)

RUTH *(Mocking; as she thinks he would say it)* Oh, Mama makes me so mad sometimes, I don't know what to do! *(She waits and continues to his back as he stands stock-still in front of the door.)* I wouldn't kiss that woman good-bye for nothing in this world this morning! *(The boy finally turns around and rolls his eyes at her, knowing the mood has changed and he is vindicated; he does not, however, move toward her yet.)* Not for nothing in this world! *(She finally laughs aloud at him and holds out her arms to him and we see that it is a way between them, very old and practiced. He crosses to her and allows her to embrace him warmly but keeps his face fixed with masculine rigidity. She holds him back from her presently and looks at him and runs her fingers over the features of his face. With utter gentleness—)* Now—whose little old angry man are you?

TRAVIS *(The masculinity and gruffness start to fade at last.)* Aw gaalee—Mama . . .

RUTH *(Mimicking)* Aw—gaaaaalleeeee, Mama! *(She pushes him, with rough playfulness and finality, toward the door.)* Get on out of here or you going to be late.

TRAVIS *(In the face of love, new aggressiveness)* Mama, could I *please* go carry groceries?

RUTH Honey, it's starting to get so cold evenings.

The first thing you might notice about this dialogue is the enormous range of emotions that Travis goes through in a short period of time. His first words are spoken "gleefully," but it's downhill from there. In the ensuing dialogue, Ruth expresses unyielding hostility, and Travis's ongoing reactions are specified in the stage directions: He goes from "exasperated" to "outraged" to "sulking"; he "rests his head in anger upon his fists," utters "a great sigh of oppression," and answers "with sullen politeness." It is unusual to have so many specific stage directions about how a character should react. Maybe Hansberry felt the need to offer more guidance to a child actor than a more experienced actor would need (or want). Whatever the reason, it allows us to be unusually confident about how Travis is reacting and therefore to draw uncommonly secure inferences about his mother's actions on the basis of those reactions.

If you were to look only at Ruth's speeches, you might decide that she is a model of bad parenting. In fact, until she turns playful and loving when Travis approaches the door to leave, Ruth's speeches consist of nothing but directives and putdowns. In these few speeches, she issues seventeen separate commands; four times she directly denies or negates what Travis says; twice she throws in statements apparently calculated to make him feel guilty (about how much she's "got on her" this morning and about his "slubborness"); and twice she resorts to naked power, once calling on him by all three names—Travis Willard Younger—and then cutting him off in midsentence with the italicized and exclamation-pointed *"Travis!"* She seems wholly insensitive to his potential embarrassment in not being able to produce the fifty cents that his teacher expects. Her barrage begins with "Sit down and have your breakfast," and it ends with "not a single penny for no caps, you hear me," and in between it never relents for a moment.

Is this her normal behavior? Is this the way they usually interact? We can never be certain, of course, but it would seem doubtful. Travis seems too spontaneous at the start of the dialogue, too resourceful in the middle (in suggesting that he hustle work at the supermarket), too trusting and open to her affection at the end, to be a habitually abused child. We wonder then what could have triggered this apparently abnormal hostility from a normally loving mother. If this were a transcript of real conversation, the answer might not be significant. Everybody has bad days, and we all tolerate occasional slumps in those we love and depend upon. But this isn't life; it's a play. This isn't conversation; it's dialogue, and we expect dialogue to matter. After all, these words didn't just happen. Someone chose them to be here, and it's fair for us to ask why. To do this, we have to draw inferences.

One approach is to try to isolate what it was that first set Ruth up for the attack. Perhaps it's because both of Travis's first two speeches concern money, the mysterious check that's expected tomorrow and the fifty cents he needs in school. His apparently innocent remarks about money seem to touch some submerged anxiety in his mother, and she lashes out. We know even this early in the play that money is a problem for the Younger family. In the opening moments of the play, we've seen that Travis sleeps on the living room sofa and that the family shares a common bathroom in the hall with at least one other apartment. And yet Ruth's reaction seems so extreme that something specific, something beyond everyday anxiety about poverty, seems to be working on her. Let's try a different line of questioning. Look back at those specific moments when Ruth seemed to pull rank on Travis, when she resorted to unanswerable power, cutting him off in midthought by using his name as the verbal equivalent of a slap. Those moments would be even more arresting, even more painful, if we saw them onstage. What prompted them? On each occasion, they are Ruth's response to her son's mentioning other family members who might give him the money he wants. We need to read the rest of the play to see how this approach might begin to open up our understanding of Ruth's behavior. As it turns out, the family is in the midst of a very specific financial dilemma, one that centers on another mother-son relationship, between exactly those two absent figures, Grandmama and Daddy, who are really in the background throughout this dialogue between Ruth and Travis. We don't yet know everything that's going on, but because Hansberry has written with such care, if we're alert readers, we can infer what her thematic concerns are. In a way that is not yet clear to us, but already hinted at, maternal love and the anger and frustration of children will be at the center of this play.

We might also notice that the words of Ruth and Travis in this brief exchange seem very realistic. Our first reaction is likely to be that Hansberry "got it right." More than just sounding true to life, though, these words are crafted into a remarkably concise introduction to some of the main aspects of the play's characters, plot, and thematic concerns, almost like an overture at the beginning of a piece of music. This brief episode demonstrates the way a well-crafted play has the power to reach out into our world and at the same time to reverberate within its own. It can do this for us, however, only if we play our part as readers and draw intelligent inferences from the way characters speak and interact.

Writing Assignments

As this chapter continues, you will read several passages which are introduced by the italicized words *Informal Writing.* Each of them contains a suggestion for informal writing—writing that is not necessarily done for a grade. Your instructor might assign some or you may choose to do them on your own or with a group of other students. They are designed to help you learn to read plays better by working out your observations and ideas through the process of writing. A journal would be a good place in which to collect them, because there you can refer to them and build on them when it seems helpful.

There are three different kinds of writing assignments in this chapter. The first asks you to write about yourself, to remember or imagine yourself in situations like the ones in the sample dramatic passages we study. These writings are intended to help you connect your own experiences with those of the characters, to see how important in your own life are the issues which the characters face in the play. This kind of understanding, in turn, should help you imagine what kind of people and situations a particular play presents. The second kind is more analytical. It asks you to do for yourself the kind of inferential reading that we exemplify in our model readings in this chapter. It should prove to yourself that you can do it, that writing it out helps you to do it, and that you can generate your own ideas and questions by yourself, or with other students. The third kind of writing is imaginative. You will learn the conventions, limitations, and potential of dramatic form by writing dialogue in various forms and styles.

At the end of this chapter, you will find more extended notes on informal writing. Then, in the anthology section, just before the plays themselves, you will find more analytic questions leading in another direction: toward more formal modes of writing. When you use them, remember that both the informal suggestions and the formal questions are intended to be general, to apply to virtually any play you happen to read.

Informal Writing: Think back to a specific brief moment from your childhood when you interacted with a member of your family, a moment no longer than the length of the exchange between Ruth and Travis. It does not need to be a painful moment, but it should be one that affected you emotionally in a powerful way. As you look back upon it now, in the light of whom you have become, can you see a way in which that moment expresses something more important than you could then have recognized? Important, perhaps, for what it reveals about you or the other person or your relationship or your values or your family's values? Write a brief dialogue in which you try to capture both the feeling of that moment as you experienced it and also what you now see as its significance. Write it in the dialogue–stage direction form we have been discussing.

Informal Writing: Read aloud to a friend the dialogue you have just written. Did you "get it right"? Do the speeches sound the way you imagine yourself and the other person really sounded? If not, what would you need to change to make it seem "right"? Perhaps add more slang terms, for example? A more informal brand of language? Revise the passage so that it catches the *flavor* of the scene you remember as truthfully as possible.

EXPOSITION

To illustrate more fully how a reader can draw inferences from the dialogue of a play, we will now look at the way a particular play in this anthology, *Lysistrata,* approaches a challenge which every playwright faces, the challenge of **exposition**. This term is traditionally used to refer to the problem of how to provide background information about the play's plot and character, information that an audience must have in order to understand what is going on.

To explore this issue as fully as we can, we will provide a model reading of a slightly longer passage than the one we studied from *A Raisin in the Sun,* most of the first episode of *Lysistrata.* However, we want to emphasize that this model is meant to be an example of how a reading *can* be done; it is definitely *not* intended as "the correct reading." Rather, it is a model of a *method,* a *process* which you must go through for yourself, a process that will probably lead you to different answers than ours, and in fact to questions different from the ones we ask here.

Lysistrata is one of the best-known comedies that have survived from ancient Greece. It was written by Aristophanes, the only writer of comedies whose work has survived from the fifth century B.C., the golden age of ancient Greek drama. The play begins when the title character walks on stage. She is joined by her friend Kalonike, and the two of them converse until, at the end of our excerpt, groups of women enter from two different directions to meet them. In the rest of the scene, not included here, Lysistrata details the two parts of her plan to end the war which has been raging throughout Greece for a generation: The young women will go on a "marriage strike," denying their husbands sex until they agree to stop fighting, and the older women will seize the city treasury on the Akropolis, making it impossible for the men to go on financing the war.

Begin by reading the prologue from *Lysistrata* straight through to get a feel for it. As you do, notice how Aristophanes whets our curiosity, how he gets us to want to know more than we do, how he keeps us interested by refusing to satisfy our desire for knowledge too quickly.

PROLOGUE

[*Athens; a public square; early morning;* LYSISTRATA *sola*]

LYSISTRATA: If someone had invited them to a festival—
of Bacchos, say; or to Pan's shrine, or to Aphroditê's
over at Kôlias—, you couldn't get through the streets,
what with the drums and the dancing. But now,
not a woman in sight!
Except—oh, yes!

[*Enter* KALONIKE]

Here's one of my neighbors, at last. Good
morning, Kalonikê.
KALONIKE: Good morning, Lysistrata.
Darling,
don't frown so! You'll ruin your face!
LYSISTRATE: Never mind my face.
Kalonikê,
the way we women behave! Really, I don't blame the men
for what they say about us.
KALONIKE: No; I imagine they're right.
LYSISTRATA: For example: I call a meeting
to think out a most important matter—and what happens?
The women all stay in bed!
KALONIKE: Oh, they'll be along.
It's hard to get away, you know: a husband, a cook,
a child . . . Home life can be *so* demanding!
LYSISTRATA: What I have in mind is even more demanding.
KALONIKE: Tell me: what is it?
LYSISTRATA: It's big.
KALONIKE: Goodness! *How* big?
LYSISTRATA: Big enough for all of us.
KALONIKE: But we're not all here!
LYSISTRATA: We would be, if *that's* what was up!
No, Kalonikê,
this is something I've been turning over for nights,
long sleepless nights.
KALONIKE: It must be getting worn down, then,
if you've spent so much time on it.
LYSISTRATA: Worn down or not,
it comes to this: Only we women can save Greece!
KALONIKE: Only we women? Poor Greece!
LYSISTRATA: Just the same,
it's up to us. First we must liquidate
the Peloponnesians—

KALONIKE: Fun, fun!
LYSISTRATA: —and then the Boiotians.
KALONIKE: Oh! But not those heavenly eels!
LYSISTRATA: You needn't worry.
I'm not talking about eels.—But here's the point:
If we can get the women from those places—
all those Boiotians and Peloponnesians—
to join us women here, why, we can save
all Greece!
KALONIKE: But dearest Lysistrata!
How can women do a thing so austere, so
political? We belong at home. Our only armor's
our perfumes, our saffron dresses and
our pretty little shoes!
LYSISTRATA: Exactly. Those
transparent dresses, the saffron, the
perfume, those pretty shoes—
KALONIKE: Oh?
LYSISTRATA: Not a single man would lift
his spear—
KALONIKE: I'll send my dress to the dyer's tomorrow!
LYSISTRATA: —or grab a shield—
KALONIKE: The sweetest little negligé—
LYSISTRATA: —or haul out his sword.
KALONIKE: I know where I can buy
the dreamiest sandals!
LYSISTRATA: Well, so you see. Now, shouldn't
the women have come?
KALONIKE: Come? They should have *flown!*
LYSISTRATA: Athenians are always late.
But imagine!
There's no one here from the South Shore, or from Sálamis.
KALONIKE: Things are hard over in Sálamis, I swear.
They have to get going at dawn.
LYSISTRATA: And nobody from Acharnai.
I thought they'd be here hours ago.
KALONIKE: Well, you'll get
that awful Theagenês woman: she'll be
a sheet or so in the wind.
But look!
Someone at last! Can you see who they are?

The first thing you might notice as the play opens is how little we know. The stage directions are minimal: We know only that this represents a square in Athens. When Lysistrata enters, it is as though we pick her up in midthought in a soliloquy. Whom does she mean by "them?" Why should they be expected to be here "now"? Yet even in these opening lines, although their main effect is to leave us in mystery, Lysistrata begins to provide the details that will enable us to understand what is happening: She complains that, although the other women are quick to turn out for parties, festivals, and orgies (in honor of Aphrodite or Bacchos or Pan), there is now "not a woman in sight" (5). We do not learn why this is upsetting until their meeting is mentioned in line 12; the importance of this meeting waits until line 24: "Only we women can save Greece!" However, as each increment of information is given us, we want to know more. Knowing the importance of this meeting, we still do not know the precise reason for calling it in the first place. How can Greek survival depend on this meeting? Aristophanes feeds us information slowly, keeping us in suspense. While Aristophanes withholds most of this information at the beginning of the play, however, he is providing something else: information about the characters. Lysistrata sums up a general prejudice against women: When "a most important matter" turns up, "the women all stay in bed" (13–14). Women are regarded as superficial, lazy, and self-indulgent. At first glance, Kalonike might seem to be an exception to this view since she has shown up, and almost on time. But her first lines are, "Darling, / don't frown so! You'll ruin your face!" (7–8). She seems more concerned with Lysistrata's attractiveness than with her friend's feeling of frustration. Both characters are women, but they seem preoccupied with putting women (including themselves) down.

Kalonike makes excuses for the women who have not shown up by describing how the limited social roles available to them interfere with independent action. For her, women are wives and cooks and mothers, and those obligations come first, before such other activities as, for example, attending meetings (15–16). We might wonder whether this excuse implies social criticism or is just a statement about the inescapable realities of feminine identity in Greek society.

Next these two women collaborate in a joke about the bigness of the "thing" for which Kalonike suddenly imagines Lysistrata to have called all Greek women together. Lysistrata has a big plan in mind which has kept her from sleeping, but Kalonike turns it into a sexual pun. Lysistrata herself acknowledges that all women are united in their love for that: All the women would be here "if *that's* what was up!" (20). It sounds as though these women are characterizing themselves and all other women as wanting only one thing, sexual satisfaction.

As the scene goes on, however, Lysistrata seems to change. She does not deny her interest in sex, but she also claims to be interested in saving her country, and she claims that its survival depends on Greek women (24). In her following lines she mentions a series of areas in Greece (27–31), all of them on one side or the other in the ongoing war between her city, Athens, and its rival, Sparta. Lysistrata wants to unite women from all parts of Greece in order to end the war (32–33).

Kalonike's speeches, however, provide a constant counterpoint. Lysistrata talks nobly, but Kalonike reminds us of the view (here held by a woman!) that if Greece must depend on women, "Poor Greece!" (25). Her response to the possible liquidation of the Peloponnesians and Boiotians is a lament for a lost sensory pleasure—the eels that come from there (28). Her description of typical women sitting around in their "armor"—"our perfumes, our saffron dresses and / our pretty little shoes" (35–37)—makes us wonder if women are capable of anything but servitude or sexual allurement. She and those like her seem mentally imprisoned; she is willing to be limited to her biological drives and her male-imposed social roles.

Informal Writing: It is tempting to look down on these characters for having accepted their limiting social roles. However, if we think about it, we might find that we aren't much different. For example, you might ask yourself who you think *you* are? How do you define yourself? Is there a part of you that you can separate from the roles you play? You have been given the role of student, and of your parents' child, and of woman or man, and many more as well. Other roles you may choose for yourself. Focus on any one of these roles you play. Did you pick it for yourself, or was it given to you? Now that you're playing it, how does it restrict your freedom? If you abandoned it, what would be the effect? How would it change you and your sense of who you are? How would it affect other people who are close to you?

Informal Writing: Think back to the dialogue which we suggested that you write several pages ago. Try to find a connection between that experience and the role you have just been thinking about. Don't force it, but if the connection seems to be there, revise the dialogue to make this connection clearer.

Lysistrata is different. Although she acknowledges her own sexuality, she refuses to be limited by it. Like Kalonike, she knows that men too have sexual drives; unlike Kalonike, she seems to see this as an opportunity for action, rather than a condemnation to subservience. She has, therefore, devised a plan, and although we don't yet know its full details, we are beginning to gather enough information to be able to speculate about it. Let us examine some of the hints we have received.

Lysistrata says that she (and the other women she has called to the meeting) will use the very symbols of their female subservience, their sexually suggestive clothing, to teach men not to fight: "Exactly. Those / transparent dresses, the saffron, the / perfume, those pretty shoes / . . ." (37–39) will be the very things which will stop men from using their spears, shields, and swords (39–42). She will use the implements of their enslavement to set them free. Women's alleged weakness—"I don't blame the men / for what they say about us" (10–11)—the aspect of female identity which men use to demean them, will be used to control men. The war between the sexes will become more than just a metaphor for sexual or romantic gamesmanship; it will become an actual confrontation of power between men and women. Using their sexual attractiveness as their weapon, they will engage in a battle designed to end fighting.

At the end of this part of the opening scene, the situation is beginning to clarify, but we are still left with many questions. Can women, through political action, re-create themselves according to a set of ideals, and achieve a self-determined identity? Or, even if they can, is this dramatic premise still at some level a cruel antifeminist joke? What are we to think of women who use their sexual attractiveness as a military tactic? Will the play go further, and question whether women have a value beyond biological utility? Will it question whether men do? Might this play be less about the conflict of men against women, and more about humanity regardless of gender? We need to read on in order to figure out the fundamental tone which colors the play's central dramatic situation.

However, we can say at this point that the play is raising questions which are still important to us today. Feminist literary analysis, for example, has as its main concern the question of gender roles in a particular society: What roles are open to a woman or to a man? Who decides what these roles are? What options are open to a man or a woman in coping with them? We should also remember that sometimes a play remains open-ended, that it may not give a clear answer to the questions that it raises. Instead, a play might present issues in a way which challenges each of us to think out our own answers for ourselves. In this case, to a large degree it's up to the director—up to you—to decide how you read this script and what kind of play you make it into.

In doing so, you will, of course, do your best to determine whether the author, here Aristophanes, is implying a thematic attitude toward the characters and the social roles they are playing. If a character seems happy with a limiting social role, is the author encouraging or discouraging that attitude, or simply showing the way things are? Complicating the question in this case is the fact that *Lysistrata* is a play written by a male dramatist in a society where only males were eligible for citizenship. Knowing this, do you think that Lysistrata and Kalonike are right about what women most want? Or are they just expressing the author's typical male fantasy?

Informal Writing: Practice the inferential method of reading which we have modeled for Lysistrata by doing your own, similar reading of the first episode of any other play in this anthology. In doing so, your first step will be to read carefully with a pencil in hand, underlining key words, drawing lines connecting words and ideas that seem to talk to each other, jotting your own ideas in the margins. Once you've begun to assemble your evidence in this way, try organizing it into topics and categories. As you do so, and then as you actually write your sentences and paragraphs, be open to the possibility of discovering previously unforeseen connections and relationships in the scene. Writing is not just the process of transcribing what you know; it is also the process of discovering what you know.

THE STRUCTURE OF A PLAY: SCENES AND ACTS

When we read whole plays rather than short episodes, we encounter more complex aspects of dramatic structure. In general, a play's dialogue is divided into units called **scenes**. A scene consists of the action that is staged for an audience as if in a single physical space and during an unbroken period of time. The specific form that this dramatic convention will take is, like others, often dictated by the physical nature of the stage for which a play is written. On the modern stage, change of scene is sometimes marked off by the raising of a curtain at its beginning and the lowering of a curtain at its end, sometimes by changing the lighting, most obviously perhaps by turning all stage lights off to show that one scene has ended and back on when a new one begins.

Earlier stages, which lacked these modern devices, had others available. For example, the theaters in ancient Greece and in Shakespeare's London did not have curtains to separate actors from audience, and, since plays were staged outdoors in daylight, they had no opportunity to manipulate lighting. A scene in this type of play begins when characters walk onto an unoccupied stage, and it ends when all the characters leave (or are carried off) so that the stage is again unoccupied. During the time that a group of characters remains onstage, the setting is fixed, and the amount of time that passes in the theater more or less corresponds to the amount of time depicted from the lives of the characters. According to the conventions of Shakespeare's theater, when new characters enter a previously emptied stage to start a new scene, the play has probably moved to a different imagined time and a different imagined space. (Usually, but not always. The first few lines of the new scene will usually let us know.)

The ancient Greek theater was similar, with one difference: the presence of a Chorus. This was a group of actors which moved and spoke in unison and which represented some group of people affected by the play's actions. Early in the play, they entered their area of the theater, between the audience and the main actors, and they remained there until the end. Scenes in Greek drama, therefore, are marked by the entrances and exits of the main characters and by the songs and dances performed by the Chorus during the intervals when the acting area is otherwise empty. Since the acting area was never totally empty in a classical Greek play, however, most plays are set in only one place and enact fictional events that take more or less the amount of time required to enact them.

No matter how a scene may be marked off by the conventions of a particular stage, however, one essential fact about it is always true: It is the playwright's basic compositional unit. As such, it has a reason for being in the play, and it has probably been arranged very carefully to accomplish its objectives. It is always a good idea, therefore, to ask yourself when a scene is over what has just happened. What did you know at the beginning of the scene, and what do you now know that is different? How do characters change in the scene? On the basis of what? Events? Words? Errors in judgment? How does the plot develop in this scene? In other words, just what has happened here?

In addition to examining what happens in individual scenes, you might ask how the scenes are interrelated. The way this is phrased might seem to prejudice the case by presupposing that the parts *are* interrelated, but for most plays this will be a reasonable assumption. For example, are there ways in which one episode might help you understand another which occurs just before or just after it? **Juxtaposition**, literally "placing beside," is the term for this structural device. If you were to take the dialogue between Ruth and Travis, which we excerpted earlier in this chapter, and place it in its original context within *A Raisin in the Sun,* you would find an example of juxtaposition. Immediately before the first words we quoted, Walter, Ruth's husband and Travis's father, exited from the stage (and their apartment) to go out to the bathroom in the hall; immediately after the last words we quoted, Walter reenters. The entire episode between mother and son is framed by this reminder of the family's inadequate housing and by an ongoing awareness that Walter, whose situation is in some ways similar to his son's, will soon be returning to his own breakfast.

Scenes are also sometimes combined into larger units called *acts.* Modern plays are often divided into acts to define intermissions when the audience can stretch, get something to drink, find a bathroom. Playwrights are likely to shape their material so the audience will reach this breaking point with a sense that the play has reached a climax. In traditional plays such as those of Shakespeare, however, acts are essentially textual, not dramatic, units. As you *read* a Shakespearean play, you may be aware of acts, but nothing happens on stage to signal to a theater audience that one act has ended and another begun. Still, if the units are logically intended by the playwright—and since every one of Shakespeare's plays has exactly the same number of acts, five, you can guess that he probably did think and compose in these terms—you can ask questions about acts that are similar to those we asked about scenes. What movements of plot and what developments of character occur within the act? How does the act fit into the structure of the play as a whole? Do the scenes within the same act seem to reinforce each other?

Finally, do all the events presented in a play move toward the resolution of one action, or does the play have one or more *subplots?* You will find that such subplots often illuminate the main plot, by presenting either a reinforcing parallel action or an ironically contrastive one. When there is a subplot, you might look for a close thematic relationship between it and the main plot. If there is no such relationship, you might consider why the playwright is violating this expected structure. What effect is achieved?

Informal Writing: Take one of the passages of dialogue you have already written and expand it into a scene. Or write new dialogue which portrays an important moment in your past, then expand it. The goal of this expansion will be to generate movement or change toward an imagined or actually remembered conclusion, even a climax, to a moment that clarifies the importance of the passage presented in the original dialogue. For example, a second character could react to the situation you have already presented in dialogue form: She might learn something about herself, or about the other character, or even about the world. Or she could do something that provokes a response which is even more powerful and revealing than the original dialogue itself. For example, one of the characters might see her situation so clearly that she actually decides to change her life. It is not necessary, by the way, to be slavishly faithful to the details of your biography. If you change or invent the "facts" in order to be true to a fictional experience, you are discovering the normal working method of writers of drama (as well as of fiction).

Informal Writing: As an alternative to the suggestion above, you could write a completely new scene which either reinforces or contrasts with an idea in the original scene you wrote. Imagine this new scene to be part of the same play, enacted in sequence with your first scene. By placing these two passages side by side, you could undercut the original, or you could make it stronger; you could show that its situation applies only to one time and place, or suggest that it is always true. Try your own hand at juxtaposition.

THE TWO MASKS: TRAGEDY AND COMEDY

When we move from scenes and acts to a consideration of complete plays, it is useful to know about their most common traditional forms, **comedy** and **tragedy**. Even plays which seem very different from one another are often variations on one or both of these basic forms. Since *Lysistrata,* the play we have most recently been looking at, is a comedy, we might consider that **genre** first.

In comedy, of course we expect laughter and a happy ending. However, there are at least three kinds of laughter. It is possible to laugh *with* a character whom we like or admire; if this character triumphs at the end, for example, we might laugh in celebration. On the other hand, when we laugh *at* characters, it is usually because of some incongruity in behavior: because they are not as good or as clever or as moral as they think they are, or as they should be. This kind of comedy, which shows us the characters' vice or foolishness—and, if we are honest, often shows us our own as well—is *satire.* Characters are held up to some standard of social or moral behavior and found wanting. Writers of satire have usually claimed that they are motivated by a desire to reform the behavior being satirized. Their motivations can be more complex, however. Sometimes people excluded from power satirize those in power to express their moral outrage and frustration over *not* being able to accomplish reform. A third kind of laughter is not so much *with* or *at* anything; it is neither celebratory nor judgmental. Instead, it seems to come out of the sheer need to express ourselves through laughter. What happens onstage is so crazy, so incongruous to

our normal view of reality, that the world seems turned upside down. It seems so exaggerated that its resemblance to our normal world is almost lost. A play that provokes this kind of laughter is called *farce.* The laughter itself can signal our recognition of a whole *world* out of kilter, not just a character. Comedy, therefore, can be philosophical, and it can be escapist. It can express a wide range of emotions. It can present a world of miracles, or a world of horrors. It can make us laugh in joy or in ironic despair.

Since we know that **tragedy** is different, that it will be "sad," we might think at first that it is the opposite of comedy. Actually, they are near cousins. They give us very similar information, but they approach that information differently. Both remind us of our human weaknesses, but comedy has us laughing at them instead of crying, shows us how our weaknesses make our triumphs fragile, instead of how they can lead to catastrophe. At the end of a comedy, we often sense that the happy ending of Act Five would fall apart into tragedy if there were an Act Six. By the end of a tragedy, we often sense that the destructive forces in the play have been spent and that in a sixth act new life could begin. Comedy may be seen as the sequel to tragedy, tragedy the sequel to comedy. They are different sides of the same coin.

They do have important differences, though. Whereas there is likely to be a group of equally important characters in classical comedy, most of whom will be common people like us, in tragedy one character will be the primary focal point, and, particularly in Greek and Shakespearean tragedy, this character will be heroic, larger than normal life size. Whereas in classical comedy most characters will be reintegrated into society, in classical tragedy the main character is isolated from society throughout (by accomplishment or status at the beginning, by suffering at the end). Usually, the society is sick and can return to health only with the exile or death of the hero or heroine. Whereas comedy typically distances us from the characters so that we can laugh at them, tragedy sobers us by bringing us close to the main character in sympathy so that we too experience the pain.

There are other qualities of tragedy which it is also useful for us to examine. For instance, the Greek philosopher Aristotle defined tragedy as the imitation of a unified and significant action which involves the fall of a great or representative person. However much the times and the nature of theater have changed (and however much people disagree about how to interpret aspects of Aristotle's analysis), this definition remains the basis for discussions of tragedy. At the start, the hero is likely to be a figure of power and authority, and at the end to be powerless, humbled, dependent, rejected—and usually dead. For Aristotle, however, although the fall may be sad, it need not be considered either good or bad, but simply the way life is. It is a reminder to us that good things do not always last; that when things look best, the worst may be coming; that most of the time we are blind to this reality; and that this blindness is one of our principal weaknesses.

Its effect on its audience, says Aristotle, is purgative. It provides us with a **katharsis**, to use the Greek word that has been adopted into English, a purgation of pity and terror. In classical tragedy, these emotions are heightened throughout a play which is likely to seem relentless in its forces, inexorable in its chain of causally interrelated actions, until finally the built-up tension is released in the play's climactic moment. For Aristotle, typically, we pity the hero or heroine for suffering an unmerited misfortune due to frailty or error; or due to inherent and inevitable human limitations; or perhaps due to what might be called "askewness," to being somehow unsynchronized with the world, or with fate, or just simply with the way of things. It is not necessarily a moral issue at all; no "fatal flaw" is required. It is just that the main character intended one thing, but something else happened, and the cause of this "something else" is also the source of our terror or fear, the second of the emotions which Aristotle identifies as particularly "purged" by tragedy. The forces which act on this main character act in our lives also; this fate could just as easily happen to us. And so we are led to see what the main character did not see, at least not until it was too late: our human blindness. In katharsis, then, we are purged not only of pity and terror but also of our superficial way of seeing the world. We may be prepared to see the paradox of much tragedy—that suffering, shame, and even evil can result in good: in self-recognition, in moral reform, even in exaltation. The great person, exposed to great pain, is challenged to live up to the fullest human possibilities.

Informal Writing: Rethink the scene you were asked to write a few pages ago in terms of how it might fit into a comedy or a tragedy. (Think of how the "same" scene would differ in these two contexts.) Imagine the story line for the full play, then revise the scene so that it will perform a specific function in your tragedy or comedy.

Informal Writing: Alternatively, write a new scene based on an important moment in your past, one that reveals something crucial about you, or one that helped cause an important change or realization. Imagine how this scene fits into the story line of a full play, either comedy or tragedy, and revise it to make it perform a specific function in this play.

Comedy and tragedy provide complementary perspectives on life and complementary dramatic forms to express them in. Yet because the form of a play helps to define (and therefore limit) what a playwright can think and feel and express, many playwrights in the twentieth century have felt the need to change these generic conventions. Recent playwrights have been influenced by philosophical uncertainty about why people and their world behave as they do, as well as by new thinking about the importance of class, gender, and ethnic identity. The traditional generic forms were based on assumptions about these issues which are now often in question, so that modern writers have sometimes felt the need to modify the classical genres to express their new ideas, sometimes actually creating new dramatic forms by combining elements from each of the older ones.

For example, modern writers of tragedy have not been comfortable with traditional assumptions of aristocratic or upper-class superiority. Often, therefore, they have attempted to make a common or typical person into the main character, and this, in turn, requires a redefinition of what a hero or heroine is and also a redefinition of the notion of tragedy itself. In his *Poetics,* Aristotle presupposed that serious drama would focus on events in the life of a "great man," someone with the power to shape events in the surrounding world. The discovery of limits to this power is in fact one of the common outcomes of the plot of traditional tragedy. A twentieth-century Marxist writer such as Bertold Brecht, however, is likely to begin with the assumption that society imposes inescapable restraints on human freedom, and that social and economic forces by and large shape human "personality," and therefore that there is no such thing as a hero. In addition, in comedy as well as tragedy, the optimistic Judeo-Christian beliefs that suffering can be educative, that it can remind us of our natural virtues, even that we can know the way we ought to behave and what we ought to believe, are often viewed with suspicion. The pain of tragedy and the laughter of comedy now often seem to be based on disillusionment instead of the discovery of wisdom or social harmony. Indeed, when a playwright follows traditional forms in this modern era, it is frequently to express disbelief in them and in the assumptions they seem to imply about

our world. Experiments with combined forms often portray the horrors of life that were traditionally the subject of tragedy and provoke the laughter we used to associate with comedy. This results sometimes in a disillusioned view of a world without clear meaning: Whatever happens, happens at random, by chance as much as by intention, and therefore without pattern or goal. Whatever happens, that is, often seems **absurd**.

This widespread desire on the part of playwrights to alter or escape traditional dramatic forms has led them to a new consciousness of dramatic form itself, and to experiments in how to manipulate it to get audience responses which are different from the traditional ones. In an apparent tragedy, for example, a playwright might deliberately make the "hero" unsympathetic, or might create a world full of contradictions so that we cannot know what to sympathize with or what to value. In other plays, the characters might speak self-consciously about themselves as characters in a play, reminding us in the audience that they are invented things, not real people; that we are watching a pretense of reality, not a scene from real life. At the same time these plays, by breaking the boundaries between pretense and reality, encourage us to see ourselves as being somehow like these invented characters. Each of these kinds of plays is disconcerting: Our normal expectations of what happens in a theater are deliberately challenged. Instead of becoming emotionally involved with the characters, we are distanced from them. They become objects of contemplation rather than fellow humans, but they may force us to become objects of our own contemplation as well. In general, modern playwrights are less interested in presenting traditional values than in forcing us to think about ourselves and our world by presenting that world, as well as the theater in which it appears, in unfamiliar terms.

One implication of this consciousness of genres applies to all plays in all ages: Because we have more or less predictable expectations when we go to a tragedy, and different but equally predictable ones when we anticipate a comedy, a playwright can deliberately manipulate these expectations. Sometimes it is the subtle difference between what the playwright gives us and what we expected that provides a play with its particular twist of meaning. This is true even for plays from ancient Greece. For example, if *Lysistrata* seems to get us to laugh at women, is this done so that we will see how stupid our prejudices are? Might this be why *women* put themselves down at the start of that play? There are usually several possibilities, so be alert.

THE LANGUAGE OF DRAMA

At this point, let us leave the comedy *Lysistrata* 2,000 years behind and turn to the beginning of Shakespeare's tragedy *Othello.* The biggest difference we will notice at first will not be in dramatic form, but in language. At first, the language of *Othello* will seem more difficult than that of *Lysistrata* because we printed *Lysistrata* in modern English translation, while Shakespeare's play is presented here more or less in the language of its earliest performance in 1604. In fact, however, the language is not so different as it seems. It is the ancestor of our own modern English, and after you have worked with it for a short time, you will see its resemblances to ours; gradually, you will feel at home with it.

The advantage to reading Shakespeare's original language is that it is extremely rich. Earlier in this chapter, we compared drama to narrative fiction, but there are also ways in which it is similar to poetry. Not only does Shakespeare write in poetic form (his blank verse line usually has ten syllables and five stresses) but he also writes with the kind of verbal compression and intensity that we associate with lyric poetry. He offers a particularly

clear example of an idea we have been discussing throughout this chapter: that there are indirect uses of language which say more, not less, and say it powerfully.

Shakespeare, then, offers us a good reason to present another model reading, this time of the opening two-thirds of the first scene of *Othello.* As you will quickly see, many of its words and phrases suggest more than one meaning, each of which may be important: Shakespeare often says two or three things at the same time. Also, he sometimes uses an image early in a scene or a play, then builds on that image later by clustering a variety of related images around it, or by using the same image again and again in different situations, so that its meaning changes or develops as the scene goes on. The following passage offers a rich opportunity to observe the power of poetic language in a play.

The play opens with the stage direction, *"Enter* Roderigo *and* Iago." All we have are the names of two characters, and we do not even have this much in performance, where we just see the two characters walk onstage in midconversation. Whatever else we are to learn about these characters—including their names—we will need to figure out for ourselves through the words the players speak to each other. Among the things we learn in this way is that two men are talking to each other at night in a street in the Italian city of Venice, just outside the house of a prominent citizen named Brabantio (74–78). The principal action of this part of the scene occurs when they conclude their conversation, and rouse him from his sleep (78–81).

At this point, we ask you to read the first 115 lines of *Othello*:

ACT I

SCENE I. *Venice. A Street.*

[*Enter* RODERIGO *and* IAGO.]

ROD. Tush, never tell me. I take it much unkindly
That thou, Iago, who hast had my purse
As if the strings were thine, shouldst know of this.
IAGO. 'Sblood, but you will not hear me.
If ever I did dream of such a matter,
Abhor me.
ROD. Thou told'st me thou didst hold him in thy hate.
IAGO. Despise me if I do not. Three great ones of the city,
In personal suit to make me his Lieutenant,
Off-capped to him. And, by the faith of man,
I know my price, I am worth no worse a place.
But he, as loving his own pride and purposes,
Evades them, with a bombast circumstance
Horribly stuffed with epithets of war.
And, in conclusion,
Nonsuits my mediators, for, "Certes," says he,
"I have already chose my officer."

And what was he?
Forsooth, a great arithmetician,
One Michael Cassio, a Florentine,
A fellow almost damned in a fair wife,
That never set a squadron in the field,
Nor the division of a battle knows
More than a spinster, unless the bookish theoric,
Wherein the toged Consuls can propose
As masterly as he—mere prattle without practice
Is all his soldiership. But he, sir, had the election.
And I, of whom his eyes had seen the proof
At Rhodes, at Cyprus, and on other grounds
Christian and heathen, must be beleed and calmed
By debitor and creditor. This countercaster,
He, in good time, must his Lieutenant be,
And I—God bless the mark!—his Moorship's Ancient.
ROD. By Heaven, I rather would have been his hangman.
IAGO. Why, there's no remedy. 'Tis the curse of service,
Preferment goes by letter and affection,
And not by old gradation, where each second
Stood heir to the first. Now, sir, be judge yourself
Whether I in any just term am affined
To love the Moor.
ROD. I would not follow him, then.
IAGO. Oh, sir, content you,
I follow him to serve my turn upon him.
We cannot all be masters, nor all masters
Cannot be truly followed. You shall mark
Many a duteous and knee-crooking knave
That doting on his own obsequious bondage
Wears out his time, much like his master's ass,
For naught but provender, and when he's old, cashiered.
Whip me such honest knaves. Others there are
Who, trimmed in forms and visages of duty,
Keep yet their hearts attending on themselves,
And throwing but shows of service on their lords
Do well thrive by them, and when they have lined their coats
Do themselves homage. These fellows have some soul,
And such a one do I profess myself. For, sir,
It is as sure as you are Roderigo,
Were I the Moor, I would not be Iago.
In following him, I follow but myself.
Heaven is my judge, not I for love and duty,
But seeming so, for my peculiar end.
For when my outward action doth demonstrate
The native act and figure of my heart
In compliment extern, 'tis not long after

But I will wear my heart upon my sleeve
For daws to peck at. I am not what I am.

ROD. What a full fortune does the thick-lips owe
If he can carry't thus!

IAGO. Call up her father,
Rouse him. Make after him, poison his delight,
Proclaim him in the streets. Incense her kinsmen,
And though he in a fertile climate dwell,
Plague him with flies. Though that his joy be joy,
Yet throw such changes of vexation on't
As it may lose some color.

ROD. Here is her father's house, I'll call aloud.

IAGO. Do, with like timorous accent and dire yell
As when, by night and negligence, the fire
Is spied in populous cities.

ROD. What ho, Brabantio! Signior Brabantio, ho!

IAGO. Awake! What ho, Brabantio! Thieves! Thieves! Thieves!
Look to your house, your daughter and your bags!
Thieves! Thieves!

[BRABANTIO *appears above, at a window.*]

BRA. What is the reason of this terrible summons?
What is the matter there?

ROD. Signior, is all your family within?

IAGO. Are your doors locked?

BRA. Why, wherefore ask you this?

IAGO. 'Zounds, sir, you're robbed. For shame, put on your gown,
Your heart is burst, you have lost half your soul.
Even now, now, very now, an old black ram
Is tupping your white ewe. Arise, arise,
Awake the snorting citizens with the bell,
Or else the Devil will make a grandsire of you.
Arise, I say.

BRA. What, have you lost your wits?

ROD. Most reverend signior, do you know my voice?

BRA. Not I. What are you?

ROD. My name is Roderigo.

BRA. The worser welcome.
I have charged thee not to haunt about my doors.
In honest plainness thou hast heard me say
My daughter is not for thee, and now, in madness,
Being full of supper and distempering draughts,
Upon malicious bravery dost thou come
To start my quiet.

ROD. Sir, sir, sir—

BRA. But thou must needs be sure

My spirit and my place have in them power
To make this bitter to thee.
ROD. Patience, good sir.
BRA. What tell'st thou me of robbing? This is Venice,
My house is not a grange.
ROD. Most grave Brabantio,
in simple and pure soul I come to you.
IAGO. 'Zounds, sir, you are one of those that will not serve God if the Devil bid you. Because we come to do you service and you think we are ruffians, you'll have your daughter covered with a Barbary horse, you'll have your nephews neigh to you, you'll have coursers for cousins, and jennets for germans.
BRA. What profane wretch art thou?
IAGO. I am one, sir, that comes to tell you your daughter and the Moor are now making the beast with two backs.

After you have read this part of the scene through, you can return to look for the details that might help you to figure out more precisely just what has happened and what we have learned in this brief bit of stage business—and it is an enormous amount that Shakespeare gets done here. This is a classic example of "dramatic compression," the feeling that a great deal of telling detail is packed into the matter of a few minutes. Let us look again at the opening lines:

ROD. Tush, never tell me. I take it much unkindly
That thou, Iago, who hast had my purse
As if the strings were thine, shouldst know of this.
IAGO. 'Sblood, but you will not hear me.
If ever I did dream of such a matter,
Abhor me.

As in *Lysistrata,* the play begins with an air of mystery; the two characters are apparently in the middle of an ongoing conversation, and we have no idea what it is that they are talking about. We would understand more if we knew what "this" refers to in line 3, presumably the same thing referred to by the other character in line 5 as "such a matter," but they are so intent in their dialogue that neither of them stops to fill us in. This is like conversation in real life, but it is hard on us as readers.

In fact, the specific matter that concerns them is not even mentioned again until lines 66–67: "What a full fortune does the thick-lips owe / If he can carry't thus!" And even here we *still* don't know what would constitute this "full fortune" or what it is that he needs to carry off. Not until lines 88–89 do we begin to figure things out, when Iago cries to Brabantio, "Even now, now, very now, an old black ram / Is tupping your white ewe." The title character, the Moor, an older black man, is at this very moment having sex with a younger white woman, Brabantio's daughter, a relationship which Iago assumes the father does not know about and would not approve of.

Clearly, this situation is potentially explosive. No wonder it has preoccupied Iago and Roderigo since the beginning of the play. But apparently Shakespeare does not yet want our full attention on this, the major premise of the plot. Instead, like Aristophanes, he puts our attention on the two characters who open the play. Why? What can we learn of them

before the action makes its decisive shift to involve Brabantio after line 67? We need to go back to the play's beginning and see what their dialogue tells us.

Shakespeare makes us feel that we are breaking into the middle of an important conversation. Roderigo's first three lines show anger. He seems to have trusted Iago, and now he feels betrayed because of something Iago has just told him a moment ago, just before the play began. It is natural for us to concentrate, to try to figure out where we are in this tense exchange between two men who seem to have been friends. Iago's first speech frustrates our hope for an explanation: He protests his innocence and teases us with a reference to what he has been talking about just before the play began. "You're just not listening to me," he says. "I never dreamed that such a thing would happen." What thing? Roderigo still seems to feel betrayed. In saying, "Thou toldst me thou didst hold him in thy hate," he suggests that Iago is a hypocrite, that Iago's alleged hatred of "him" has been called into question by "this." We are still puzzled.

Iago's response, the first lengthy speech of the play (lines 8–33), fixes this mysterious "him" character in the center of our attention, even though he is not onstage. Iago reassures Roderigo that he does hate "him" and with good reason: Iago is evidently a soldier who wanted to be promoted to lieutenant, second in command of Othello's army (8–17). Instead, Michael Cassio, a military theoretician with no practical experience in battle, gets the promotion, and Iago is given what to him is the insultingly lower rank of "his Moorship's Ancient" or, as we would say, his Ensign (18–33). Iago's anger, apparent in his derisively invented term "his Moorship" (apparent because it mocks the term "his worship"), seems to persuade Roderigo that Iago is telling the truth. His response suggests that he is sympathetic to the injustice Iago feels: "By heaven, I rather would have been his hangman," than his ancient. The tension between them has been resolved by their common reassertion of their hatred for "him," the title character.

Having successfully calmed Roderigo, Iago next generalizes about the corruption of the modern world, where "Preferment goes by letter and affection," by favoritism and whim, rather than by experience, by seniority. He concludes (38–40) by asking Roderigo to judge whether he should feel any obligation "to love the Moor." In response, Roderigo responds, "I would not follow him, then." However, although this response is what Iago expects, it also suggests a difference between the two men. At one level, Roderigo's line may suggest an upperclass insensitivity to the needs of someone who has to work his way up the ladder of promotion rung by rung. A secondary effect of his words is to make Iago defensive. How can he keep his dignity if he serves a person he hates, one who allegedly mistreats him?

Iago's self-defense (lines 41–65) is extremely odd. He begins, "I follow him to serve my turn upon him," and ends, "I am not what I am." He describes himself as a hypocrite, a person who pretends loyalty to his master but who actually has none. His justification is found in his previous speech: Since he is unjustly treated, he himself is justified in being unjust, or at least deceptive, in return. Surprisingly, he goes further: "Whip me such honest knaves" as those who are true and loyal servants. It would be one thing to say they are stupid, that they will be mistreated in this corrupt modern age. But whip them? For honesty? What kind of man is this Iago? He goes further still: It is the hypocrites, people like himself, who "have some soul." It's not just that he *justifies* hypocrisy. He actually *praises* it. He seems to be as corrupt as the new world against which he just finished complaining.

What are we to think of Iago? If he boasts that he would lie to Othello about his loyalty, can we believe what he tells Roderigo about his hatred? Can we believe anything a character like this says? for example, about Othello's unfairness? or about the corruption of

the age? or even about his own motives? On the other hand, this speech seems to be a completely honest statement about himself. Who would praise his own hypocrisy except a person who was telling the truth? That is clearly what Roderigo thinks, and we might too. It is as if Iago were baring his soul both to Roderigo and to us. It is not actually a *soliloquy,* but in this respect the speech is like one. And, typically, we like a person who is honest with us about himself. Since we are taken into Iago's confidence, just as Roderigo is, we too might like him and even trust him. He seems somehow honest in his dishonesty, leaving us a little uncertain about how we feel. We need to delay deciding while we gather more information.

As his attention turns toward Brabantio, his words convey a new degree of venom: "Call up her father, / Rouse him. Make after him, poison his delight" (67–68). Is it Brabantio or Othello whose delight he would poison? To whom does "his" refer? Remember his complaint about the unfairness of the age he lives in. There may be a general ill will here, not just against Othello. And when the "poison" is joined to the image of an emergency like a city fire (76–77), we sense his urgency in wanting to spread the alarm, wanting to spread "poison" all through the aristocratic world of Venice.

When he finally tells Brabantio—and us, too, at last—what the subject of the whole scene has been so far, his terms are even more venomous: "an old black ram / Is tupping your white ewe." He is a racist, or at least he deliberately appeals to the racist feelings of Brabantio, emphasizing the difference between Othello's blackness and his daughter's whiteness. And he describes their mating as unnatural, as bestial (a ram and a ewe). A little later, he uses the bestial imagery in grotesquely playful ways, turning it into an extended metaphor of the Moor as an Arabian stallion and adorning the figure of speech thickly with alliteration: "You'll have your daughter cover'd with a Barbary horse, you'll have your nephews neigh to you; you'll have coursers for cousins, and gennets for germans" (110–112). ("Gennets" and "germans" are exotic words for horses and relatives.) In his next speech he again mentions "your daughter and the Moor" as "making the beast with two backs" (114–115). He seems obsessed with the idea that their sexuality is gross, crude, and unnatural.

By this point in the scene, we have figured out the situation that Roderigo and Iago have been talking about, and we have also discovered a number of things about Iago: that he seems appealing and honest (or at least open) to us and Roderigo, and that he claims to be angered both by general social injustice, and by personal injustice. These qualities might tempt us to be sympathetic. But we also learn that he is angered by his thwarted ambition and wants revenge; that he is a self-serving hypocrite; that he is a racist; and we might begin to suspect (from his overactive imagination) that he is also obsessed with Desdemona as a sexual object. He is envious not only of Othello's position in the army but also of his position with Desdemona. In general, he is envious of Othello's *power.*

IMAGERY

We know these things from what he says, but also from the way he says them. Part of this way of speaking is his use of *imagery.* Words and phrases like "poison," "old black ram," and "the beast with two backs" do not just express an idea but express it in a way which gives it sensory content, which makes the idea powerful to us by implicitly comparing it to something we can imagine.

At this point, let us take advantage of one of the prerogatives we have as readers of this play that would not be available to us if we were watching it in a theater. Let us backtrack and focus on some of the imagery which has already been used in the first scene. At lines 66–67, Roderigo says:

> What a full fortune does the thick-lips owe [i.e., own]
> If he can carry't thus!

Earlier, we saw either that Iago is a racist, or that he is appealing to the racism of Brabantio. We also saw that Roderigo is an aristocrat (he seemed not to understand Iago's problem about thwarted ambition when he said, "I would not follow him then" at line 40). Roderigo now shows that he, too, like the senator Brabantio, and probably also like Iago, seems to be a racist. This seems to be a *society* of racists.

Moreover, notice what Iago shouts up at the senator, Desdemona's father: "Awake! What ho, Brabantio! Thieves! Thieves! Thieves! / Look to your house, your daughter and your bags! / Thieves! Thieves!" (79–81). When Brabantio comes to the window, this imagery of theft continues: "Are your doors lock'd" (line 85)? And again: " 'Zounds, sir, y'are robb'd! For shame, put on your gown" (86). On our first reading of the play, we are probably confused at this point. Has Brabantio really been a victim of robbery? As we are about to learn, only one thing has been taken from him: his daughter. We might ask, then, what this implies about a father's relationship to his daughter. Under what legal circumstances can a father be "robbed" of her? Would this be true for a wife also?

We have learned from this imagery that a person who is white and male believes himself to have all the rights and power in this society. Perhaps this helps explain why the three characters in this first scene seem so bitter toward the as-yet-unnamed Othello. He is black, and he has both the power and the woman that each of the three white men wants, in their different ways, to possess.

Informal Writing: Return to one of the scenes that you have written as an "Informal Writing." Alternatively, write a new passage of dialogue between two characters based on a crucial event in your past. Now read this scene or passage carefully, as though it were written by Shakespeare, staying alert to the nuance of your specific language. Are there places where you find that your words speak to each other, places where your imagery or figurative language seems of a piece? Try to see ways in which you might revise the dialogue to achieve this effect more fully. Revise it with particular emphasis on the specific words selected and the way they speak to each other, so that your main points are implied more powerfully.

Informal Writing: Read the opening scene of another play in this anthology, taking careful note of images which are repeated or built on, and of phrases which echo or answer other phrases. Try paraphrasing the meaning of these images and phrases into explicit statements. If some of them are difficult to paraphrase, try to explain why this might be. How is language working to produce meaning in these phrases?

The imagery in *Othello* has opened an issue that is a tremendous problem not only for blacks and women but also for white men. If we pause to think about the dynamics of power, we will realize that people who have power, even such great power as to be able to possess other people, define themselves by their ability to live up to that power. As a result, they have to protect it; otherwise, they risk losing their status and maybe even their sense of identity. Status, then, can be a burden as well as an advantage. With it comes insecurity. Iago's question, "Are your doors lock'd?" goes to the heart of the white male ego: Iago's emphasis on blackness, on "an old black ram" who is also "the Devil" (91) who threatens miscegenation, who not only steals Brabantio's property but pollutes the blood of his family—who steals his family's honor—completes the threat to white patriarchal society.

This portrait of a whole society, accomplished in only 115 lines, makes us curious about this black man, this white woman, and their love. Together, they seem powerful enough to threaten the entire city. It will be exciting to see them onstage.

A RETROSPECTIVE VIEW OF THE MODEL READINGS

We could ask many other questions about this scene. For instance, ask what kind of person would defy her entire society for love? We could also speculate about the immense pressure this racist and sexist society will put on a black man and a runaway white woman who have married each other, and what this might do to their relationship. But we have done enough to make the point we intended, the point that we have been making throughout this introduction: that in reading plays, we need to be alert to the tiniest hints of information, to ask questions about them, to maintain a running dialogue with the lines, to test ideas. We need to remember that reading is an act of imagination, although a disciplined one; that if a play is worth rereading, several lines of investigation will usually be possible. We can take off with one of them for a while, and then we can check them against later words. If we find that our first reaction no longer makes sense, we can shelve that line of thought and start another. That is the advantage we readers have over the theater audience.

At the same time, we need to imagine ourselves as directors in the theater as we read. We have to imagine what the play looks like, how it feels and sounds, as well as what its meanings are. In fact, sometimes the most important suggestion about meaning will be precisely that, the way it looks and feels and sounds as you imagine it in a theater. In this way we convert our script into a play.

DO IT YOURSELF: WRITING ABOUT DRAMA

We want to repeat a main idea of this chapter, the idea that is behind all our informal writing suggestions and many of our comments on plays. You can empower yourself as a student to learn how to learn on your own. A primary method for doing this learning is to write about the plays you read. Nothing helps your reading more than writing. It helps you do the work of questioning, interpreting, and staging these plays. For this reason, we want to encourage you to continue to use writing as a means of discovering and clarifying your own ideas about the plays you read, in this course and after it.

As we said before, we are not necessarily referring here to traditional formal assigned papers, although writing of this sort is important and will almost certainly be involved in most literature courses. In fact, at the beginning of the next part of this section on drama, we have included a long set of questions which are specifically designed to help you think about how to analyze plays, and from that analysis, how to discover topics and theses for precisely this formal, assigned kind of writing. But the kind of writing we are proposing to you here is different. It is informal because, assigned or not, written for your professor to see or not, it is primarily undertaken for *your* sake, in an effort to articulate for yourself precisely what you feel and think, and why, as a result of reading these plays. It is your place perhaps to second-guess yourself, to think again, to try on new ideas and new ways of thinking. It can be valuable for your professor to see this writing—to see how much you're thinking, and to help guide you in doing it. But writing of this sort does not *need* to be assigned in order to be valuable. It does not need to be graded in order to be validated. You and your friends might simply decide to do it because it is useful in your work of learning.

In this spirit, we suggest some general ways of engaging yourself with your play by writing. Some of these ways will be familiar because examples of them have been used in the suggestions for informal writing that we have already made. Others are new.

1. Take any one of the general questions about drama from the section that precedes the plays themselves (just after this section), and write about it with specific reference to the play you are reading.
2. Keep a reading journal as you work your way through a play. Write a page or so in response to each act of a play as you finish it. Here, instead of beginning with a specific traditional question, you might begin by asking yourself why you liked or did not like the act, or you might write to clarify why it is that you feel confused by a scene or by a character's role. Sometimes, if you can figure out why you are confused, you aren't confused any more.
3. Imagine that you will produce and direct a particular play on a stage. Ask yourself what effect you want the play to make on the audience, and then write out the staging details which will help the play achieve that effect. Include information about costumes, lighting, stage sets, props, backdrop painting, stage size and shape, the nature of the actors, special effects (visual or auditory), and whatever else occurs to you that will help. You might ask yourself if you could get the same effect with less material, if you can make more efficient use of fewer resources. Obviously, you are being asked to think of the relationship between the things on the stage and the audience, and you are also being asked to choose one effect rather than some others as your preferred interpretation of this play.
4. Play with literary form. Rewrite a scene as if it were narrative (for example, a short story or a biography). In doing so, you will need to ask yourself questions like, what would be the most effective point of view to adopt? Should the narrator be one of the characters, telling the story in the first person? If so, what would be the narrator's limitations of knowledge? (Your story would be very different if narrated by Roderigo rather than by Iago; by Kalonike rather than by Lysistrata.) Having answered that question, you then have another challenge: Can you create a consistent voice for your narrator?
5. Create your own audience for your writing, one that does not necessarily include your teacher, at least not at every stage in the writing process. Sympathetic and supportive teachers often form an important part of a writer's audience, but they are by no means the whole of it. For example, exchange your writing with a friend in the class. Every

writer we know of—that's *every* writer—shows his or her written work to friends while the writing is in process, in order to get some feedback about what works and what does not. Let yourself have the fun of doing what professional writers do. Better still, get together with a group of students and exchange your work with each other in collaborative learning. In academic circles, we often encourage people to pursue individual, isolated learning experiences, and academic writing is often undertaken in that way, but it doesn't have to be, and maybe it *shouldn't* be. Writing can be—maybe *ought* to be—a means of communication and of self-definition and self-actualization. Writers who come to love their craft are often part of a group of writers who give each other support and constructive criticism. If you and other students in your class form that kind of group for yourselves as you write about drama, you might be amazed at what happens.

An Anthology of Plays

QUESTIONS ABOUT DRAMA

Our hope, in providing you with model readings of parts of several plays, has been to suggest by example the kinds of questions that a dramatic text might raise for you as readers, and also the kinds of responses you might make to such questions. In addition, we have suggested ways of using informal writing to help you in this process. As a further help, we list below a series of questions which can be applied to nearly any play. Although some will be more useful than others for a particular script, the test of their usefulness will be the same for each: Does your answer lead you to ask still another question, so that you become engaged in an ongoing process of questioning? They are valuable only if they do this, if they stimulate your curiosity to think more and more deeply about the play.

You should know that we have wrestled with the problem of whether to provide you with this list of questions. Our fear is that they will seem to provide a complete list of things to check, so that you can run through each question, give it a short answer, and think you have mastered the play. They do provide a list of things to be aware of, but this list will serve its purpose only if it provokes you to ask questions of the play, to enter into dialogue with it, to discover other issues which are not listed here because they are unique to the particular play which you are reading now. For example, if you were to question the meaning of the "raisin" image in *A Raisin in the Sun,* your questions should lead you beyond raisins to other images, to other actions, and finally to possible meanings in the play as a whole. Your answer should be the starting point for a series of further questions.

It is in this spirit that we offer the following *general* questions to help you figure out for yourself what *specific* questions you need to raise about any given play. Use them as questions to write about in your journals, as questions to bring to class for discussion, and as the basis for discovering ideas, topics, and theses to be used in longer, formal papers about the plays. We have phrased these questions in general terms so that you can use them in a variety of ways.

Questions about Plot and Structure

1. What is the principal *conflict* in the play? Does it involve an internal conflict in one character? Or one character against another? Or one group against another? Or an individual or a group against nature? Against some person or force larger than nature? (A clue to the conflict: the characters are most interested in and perform most of their actions because of it. They fight against it; they strive for it; they escape it; in their dialogue, they are preoccupied with it.)
2. Is the play *unified?* When we have finished reading it, can we look back and see that all its episodes somehow moved in the same direction, toward the same final meaning or dramatic effect? Does each incident seem to grow logically out of some preceding incident and lead naturally to what follows? Is there a part that seems *not* to fit this sense of the well-made play? Sometimes parts fit into the whole in unexpected ways, to give it a twist of meaning that is surprising. Consider the possibility that the part

which *seems* not to fit may be the most important part of the play, and not the playwright's mistake. See if you can find a way to read the play that makes this "strange" part logical. *Warning:* Sometimes the parts may fit together too easily; the problems in the plot might be solved so much more easily than in real life that you can't believe in its resolution. The play might seem forced and unnatural. Often, this kind of imposed and superficial order masks a profoundly unresolved social, psychological, or artistic problem—possibly an issue which the playwright doesn't know how to deal with fully. Are there places in the play when a complex problem is resolved so simplistically or so tidily that you end up questioning whether so simple or tidy a resolution is possible (or desirable)?

3. Traditionally (since Aristotle) people have spoken of moments of "reversal" in drama, where the fortunes of a tragic character take a decisively downward turn or where the fortunes of a comic character begin to rise. Is there such a moment in this play?
4. Traditionally (since Aristotle) people have spoken of moments of "discovery" or "recognition" in drama, where a main character learns the significance of a person or thing or situation previously unknown or inadequately understood. Is there such a moment in this play?

Questions about Character

5. A character whose personality seems to evolve is sometimes called a **developing character**. Is there any such character in the play you are reading? What kind of change happens in this character? Is it a change in personality or attitude, in opinion or values or ideals, in personality, perhaps in behavior? Is it a large one or a small one? What causes this change? For example, the cause might be an event, or it could just be something another character says. How is this change presented dramatically? Does it seem natural: is it consistent with the character's attitudes or behavior prior to this change? Does it seem adequately motivated?
6. Another possibility is that the change is only apparent, that what seems to be a new mode of behavior is actually rooted in the depths of the character as previously presented. Instead of a developing character, do we have one who is really just revealing his or her true character more fully than before? A complex character who seems realistic is usually either a developing or a **revealed character**. In the case of these revealed characters, it is not they who change so much as our perception of them: we regard them in one way at first, but as more is revealed about them, our first impression changes, and in retrospect we reconsider our earlier impressions of them. When we recognize characters in this way, they strike us as familiar because this is the way we perceive the other people with whom we regularly interact. Think about the people in class with you right now. Has it happened that your first impression of any of them has changed as the semester has progressed? If so, do you think this is because they have changed? Or because, as you have gotten to know them better, you have modified your initial perception? Characters in plays are often "revealed" in just this way, so that early episodes need to be reinterpreted later, in the light of the events that follow.
7. Does the play you are reading make use of **contrasting characters**? In particular, are minor characters ever left relatively undeveloped so that, instead of attracting attention primarily to themselves, they can focus on some complementary or contrasting

aspect of the more developed main characters? A character so used is often called a **foil** of the major character. The metaphor comes from jewelry making, where a piece of gold foil placed behind a transluscent gem intensifies and reflects the light that passes through it, in this way showing off the gem with greater clarity than it has by itself. Perhaps Travis could be said to serve this function in *A Raisin in the Sun,* acting as a foil for his father Walter.

Questions about Language and Texture

8. Is there some consistent strain of **imagery** in the play's figurative language, especially in its metaphors and similes? If so, is it merely decorative, or is it functional as well? Does it, for example, reinforce, modify, or in some other way illuminate an aspect of plot, character, or theme? Think, for example, of the racist images which both Iago and Roderigo use to refer to Othello, and of the imagery of robbery and theft which is used to refer to Brabantio's daughter's elopement. What might the nature of the play's imagery reveal about the characters who use them and about the thematic concerns of the author who wrote them?
9. Are any of the objects (or characters) in the play dealt with in a way that suggests that they might be **symbols**? We need to be very careful about how we use this term. A symbol is not, for example, an abstraction. Just the opposite, it is a concrete object which gains specific conceptual or emotional value because of the way it is used or talked about. This meaning is not inherent in the object, but grows from the way it operates in the play, and in general a symbol will reinforce or help refine the play's effect and meaning. Ordinarily, it will *not* provide some secret clue to a meaning that would be otherwise inaccessible. Think, for example, about the collection of glass animals from which *The Glass Menagerie* takes its title. They serve at a literal level to help define the interior decor of the play's domestic setting, but as the play progresses, they gradually take on a central significance which reinforces any interpretation of Laura and of the play. Even a character's name can sometimes imply thematic significance. Be careful not to push these possibilities too far, but sometimes the point seems inescapable. Lysistrata, for example, means "disbander of the armies" in Greek.
10. Irony in a play can be verbal or situational, but there is another kind of irony so characteristic of drama that it is called **dramatic irony**. This is the term used to describe the situation when we in the audience know details that some of the characters on stage do not know. By showing us a character's ignorance of the full truth of a situation, for example, it can be used to demonstrate that character's blindness. In tragedy, this blindness could lead to the catastrophe, as it does in *Oedipus Rex* and *Othello;* in comedy, it causes us to laugh at the fool.

Other Questions

11. The **setting** of a play will usually be significant; be careful to avoid treating it superficially. It is usually easy to identify, but it is harder to analyze its importance. This is not the only reason for considering it seriously, however. For example, in the case of *Lysistrata,* the play's action is set on the same hill where it was first staged. Its subject is in some sense the Athenian audience which watches the play, a fact which must figure into our calculations about its tone and meaning.

12. **Titles** are carefully chosen by playwrights. What does the title of the play you are reading suggest about its meaning? For example, Lorraine Hansberry's title, *A Raisin in the Sun,* is an allusion to a specific poem (see page 418) whose meaning can be applied to the play. Playwrights will almost always choose titles that will imply what matters in their plays.
13. The final—and perhaps most difficult—questions will be about meaning, about significance. What are the play's **thematic concerns**? We refer you to the analogous discussion in the fiction section (page 36) for more on this topic, but we will add this much. A play usually reveals most of its significance through indirection, since the author cannot manipulate narrative voice for emphasis. However, sometimes the playwright will state the play's intentions directly, in a character's dialogue. Therefore, be especially alert to moments in the play that seem undramatic: lengthy speeches that seem especially "talky," that express generalizations about thematic concerns without furthering the action very much. However, we also need to remember that even a "talky" character does not necessarily speak for the author. Playwrights can be tricky, and that's part of the fun of constructing your plays from their scripts.

THE GREEK THEATER

The theater in ancient Greece was communal, the one in Athens, for example, providing seats (stone benches) for all 16,000 of its citizens. Set in an open-air amphitheater, its center was a circular acting area which was nearly surrounded by the semicircular rings of audience rising above it. This central acting area was bare, with neither scenery nor artificial lighting. The modern theater's visual separation of players from audience by footlights and spotlights, for instance, did not exist. Since the lighting for the stage and the audience was the same, the actors were embedded, as it were, within their community—the audience with whom they shared the same natural light. As a result, these ancient Greek actors were in a unique position to represent their community, its history and legends, its ideas and beliefs, even its skepticism about these beliefs. In this theater, the most important ideas of Greek society were made part of public life and public debate.

This playing area had a strong sense of the sacred. Its actors were privileged to enact the intertwined religious and social heritage of their community. Indeed, as if to emphasize this point, the theater itself was always dedicated to a god. In Athens, site of the first performances of both of the Greek plays in this text, the god was Dionysus; his theater was on the side of the hill of rock whose smoothed top was called the *Akropolis,* the site of the city's major government and religious buildings, chief among them the Parthenon, the temple of the city's patron goddess Athena. If one drew a straight line from the center of the acting area through the center of the audience, this line would cross the Akropolis to the Parthenon and lead directly within to the huge statue of the goddess herself. The nature and placement of the theater were strongly linked to the belief structure of its society.

Within a performance, this sense of community was further reinforced by the Chorus, a group of actors who chanted and danced in unison and who represented either the citizens as a whole, or a particular and significant part of the citizens (the elders, the women, etc.). The dramatic style of the plays produced in this theater was in some respects more like a religious ritual than real life. The action alternates between the songs of the Chorus and

the scenes in which a very limited number of characters speak to each other in dialogue. Sophocles is generally credited with the innovation of adding a third actor onstage; previously only two characters at a time were represented. The leader of the Chorus, the Choragos, acting as the group's representative, could also engage in dialogue with the main characters. When a passage of dialogue is completed, the characters leave the stage and the Chorus comes forward to comment upon it. Frequently, its point of view is the cue for our own reactions, since it often seems to provide something of a model response to the play's action.

Since the Chorus never left its area during the play and was always present before the audience, once the play's fictional time and place were established, they did not change. If the imagined space is established as the public area outside of the Palace of King Oedipus in Thebes, that is what it remains throughout the duration of the play. How could it change if the Chorus remains always present outside his door? This convention is usually referred to as *unity of place.* In addition, the amount of time imagined to have elapsed during the play is identical to the amount of time it takes to enact the play. If the play lasts for two hours, it depicts two hours from the life of the hero. This second convention is usually referred to as *unity of time.* The result of this spatial and temporal focus is that Greek plays typically depict a single climactic moment from the life of the hero. His or her whole life turns on the events of a few minutes, but those minutes imply the events of a lifetime—or more, as in the case of Oedipus where the significant events began before his life was conceived.

A Greek play presents no violent action and uses no sets; we see below us only a series of scenes in which two, or sometimes three, men on a bare stone circle speak from behind face masks whose expressions are set in extremes of human emotions. They represent types of people as much as they do individuals. What we hear them speak is poetry, not realistic speech. The plots of those plays, particularly in tragedy, are likely to be taken from traditional legends, so that suspense is not a major concern: the audience knows the ending in advance. Our interest is not so much in how the action will turn out but in the new twist that the playwright gives the familiar material, the new nuances of meaning he teases from it. As modern readers coming to these plays for the first time, we must concentrate on *how* things happen as much as on what it is that happens.

SOPHOCLES

(496?–406 B.C.)

Oedipus Rex

AN ENGLISH VERSION BY DUDLEY FITTS AND ROBERT FITZGERALD

About the Author: Sophocles was the most famous of ancient Greek tragic playwrights. During the century of Athens' political rise, he served the city in a variety of political, military, and religious roles, but he was best known as a prolific and innovative playwright. Of the 123 plays attributed to him by ancient accounts, 7 have survived.

About the Play: *Oedipus Rex* is the best known of Sophocles' plays. Indeed, because it was the primary example cited by Aristotle in his *Poetics,* it has remained central to thinking about the nature of tragedy as well. The legend of Oedipus was well known to the ancient Greeks. To avoid fulfilling the prophecy that he would kill his father and marry his mother, his parents sent him away to Corinth to die when he was still a helpless infant. However, he was discovered, saved, and brought up in the royal household of Corinth where, hearing the prophecy and believing his foster parents to be his true parents, he himself ran away to avoid fulfilling the prophecy. When the play opens, Oedipus has become king of Thebes and—as the ancient Greek audience well knew—has also fulfilled the prophecy. While running away from his predicted fate, he had encountered and killed a stranger who turned out to be Laios, his true father. When he arrived at Thebes, he had solved the riddle of the Sphinx and thereby destroyed this monster. The riddle had been, What walks on four legs at dawn, on two legs at noon, and on three legs at sunset? The answer to the riddle is "a person," who crawls on all fours in infancy, walks upright in maturity, and with the aid of a staff in old age. For ridding the city of its oppressor, the grateful city offered him marriage to its widowed queen, his mother Iokaste.

This is a play, then, about a man who was faced with a terrible prophecy about his fate, who has done everything he can to avoid this fate, and who has made himself a king entirely by his own abilities. It raises some of the most troubling issues of human existence: the relationship between fate (or destiny, or the circumstances to which we are born) and free will, our ability to create our own destiny; the relationship of the present to the past and the future; the difficulty of our knowing what is true of the future or of the present, of the world or even of ourselves; the difficulty and consequences of coming to terms with the truth once we discover it. We could say that these issues are universal because we must all deal with them. (The answer to the Sphinx's riddle also suggests that something universal is involved.) Part of the appeal of this play is that it faces them directly, simply, without extraneous local concerns and without pretending that they are easier to solve than they are. It is this toughness in dealing with the hard aspects of life which gives this play its realism; we feel that if anything positive is suggested by the end, that affirmation is fairly earned. Life is not, in this play, made to seem easier than it is.

One of the play's thematic patterns requires particular comment. The character Teiresias is a blind prophet; he cannot see, yet he knows the truth about the future and the past. Although in the present he has the identity of an old man, in the past he has also been a woman. Through him, the play seems to imply that truth is beyond sight, sex and gender, that to see truly one must not be distracted by the superficial appearances of normal sight or by worldly desires (such as are exemplified by the desire one sex feels for the other). This becomes clearest in the unusual concentration of tragic effects; the climax of the play coincides with both its catastrophe (the scene in which unmerited suffering is meted out) and its recognition scene (in which we and, in this case, the hero recognize his true identity). In this scene, Oedipus finds a way to enact for himself the full implications of the issues which Teiresias embodies.

CHARACTERS

OEDIPUS
A PRIEST
CREON
TEIRESIAS
IOCASTÊ
MESSENGER
SHEPHERD OF LAÏOS
SECOND MESSENGER
CHORUS OF THEBAN ELDERS

Scene. *Before the palace of* OEDIPUS, *King of Thebes. A central door and two lateral doors open onto a platform which runs the length of the façade. On the platform, right and left, are altars; and three steps lead down into the "orchestra," or chorus-ground. At the beginning of the action these steps are crowded by* SUPPLIANTS *who have brought branches and chaplets of olive leaves and who lie in various attitudes of despair.* OEDIPUS *enters.*

PROLOGUE

OEDIPUS. My children, generations of the living
In the line of Kadmos,° nursed at his ancient hearth:
Why have you strewn yourselves before these altars
In supplication, with your boughs and garlands?
The breath of incense rises from the city
With a sound of prayer and lamentation.
Children,
I would not have you speak through messengers,
And therefore I have come myself to hear you—
I, Oedipus, who bear the famous name.
(To a PRIEST.*)* You, there, since you are eldest in the company,
Speak for them all, tell me what preys upon you,
Whether you come in dread, or crave some blessing:
Tell me, and never doubt that I will help you
In every way I can; I should be heartless
Were I not moved to find you suppliant here.
PRIEST. Great Oedipus, O powerful King of Thebes!
You see how all the ages of our people
Cling to your altar steps: here are boys
Who can barely stand alone, and here are priests
By weight of age, as I am a priest of God,
And young men chosen from those yet unmarried;
As for the others, all that multitude,
They wait with olive chaplets in the squares,
At the two shrines of Pallas,° and where Apollo°
Speaks in the glowing embers.
Your own eyes
Must tell you: Thebes is in her extremity
And cannot lift her head from the surge of death.
A rust consumes the buds and fruits of the earth;
The herds are sick; children die unborn,
And labor is vain. The god of plague and pyre
Raids like detestable lightning through the city,
And all the house of Kadmos is laid waste,
All emptied, and all darkened: Death alone

---

[2]**Kadmos** legendary founder of Thebes. [24]**Pallas** Athena, goddess of wisdom. [24]**Apollo** god of poetry and prophecy.

Battens upon the misery of Thebes.
You are not one of the immortal gods, we know;
Yet we have come to you to make our prayer
As to the man of all men best in adversity
And wisest in the ways of God. You saved us
From the Sphinx,° that flinty singer, and the tribute
We paid to her so long; yet you were never
Better informed than we, nor could we teach you:
It was some god breathed in you to set us free.

Therefore, O mighty King, we turn to you:
Find us our safety, find us a remedy,
Whether by counsel of the gods or the men.
A king of wisdom tested in the past
Can act in a time of troubles, and act well.
Noblest of men, restore
Life to your city! Think how all men call you
Liberator for your triumph long ago;
Ah, when your years of kingship are remembered,
Let them not say *We rose, but later fell—*
Keep the State from going down in the storm!
Once, years ago, with happy augury,
You brought us fortune; be the same again!
No man questions your power to rule the land:
But rule over men, not over a dead city!
Ships are only hulls, citadels are nothing,
When no life moves in the empty passageways.

OEDIPUS. Poor children! You may be sure I know
All that you longed for in your coming here.
I know that you are deathly sick; and yet,
Sick as you are, not one is as sick as I.
Each of you suffers in himself alone
His anguish, not another's; but my spirit
Groans for the city, for myself, for you.

I was not sleeping, you are not waking me.
No, I have been in tears for a long while
And in my restless thought walked many ways.
In all my search, I found one helpful course,
And that I have taken: I have sent Creon,
Son of Menoikeus, brother of the Queen,
To Delphi, Apollo's place of revelation,
To learn there, if he can,
What act or pledge of mine may save the city.

---

39 **The Sphinx** a monster with a lion's body, birds' wings, and woman's face.

I have counted the days, and now, this very day,
I am troubled, for he has overstayed his time.
What is he doing? He has been gone too long.
Yet whenever he comes back, I should do ill
To scant whatever hint the god may give.

PRIEST. It is a timely promise. At this instant
They tell me Creon is here.

OEDIPUS. O Lord Apollo!
May his news be fair as his face is radiant!

PRIEST. It could not be otherwise: he is crowned with bay,
The chaplet is thick with berries.

OEDIPUS. We shall soon know;
He is near enough to hear us now.

Enter CREON.

O Prince:
Brother: son of Menoikeus:
What answer do you bring us from the god?

CREON. It is favorable. I can tell you, great afflictions
Will turn out well, if they are taken well.

OEDIPUS. What was the oracle? These vague words
Leave me still hanging between hope and fear.

CREON. Is it your pleasure to hear me with all these
Gathered around us? I am prepared to speak,
But should we not go in?

OEDIPUS. Let them all hear it.
It is for them I suffer, more than myself.

CREON. Then I will tell you what I heard at Delphi.
In plain words
The god commands us to expel from the land of Thebes
An old defilement that it seems we shelter.
It is a deathly thing, beyond expiation.
We must not let it feed upon us longer.

OEDIPUS. What defilement? How shall we rid ourselves of it?

CREON. By exile or death, blood for blood. It was
Murder that brought the plague-wind on the city.

OEDIPUS. Murder of whom? Surely the god has named him?

CREON. My lord: long ago Laïos was our king,
Before you came to govern us.

OEDIPUS. I know;
I learned of him from others; I never saw him.

CREON. He was murdered; and Apollo commands us now
To take revenge upon whoever killed him.

OEDIPUS. Upon whom? Where are they? Where shall we find a clue
To solve that crime, after so many years?
CREON. Here in this land, he said.
If we make enquiry,
We may touch things that otherwise escape us.
OEDIPUS. Tell me: Was Laïos murdered in his house,
Or in the fields, or in some foreign country?
CREON. He said he planned to make a pilgrimage.
He did not come home again.
OEDIPUS. And was there no one,
No witness, no companion, to tell what happened?
CREON. They were all killed but one, and he got away
So frightened that he could remember one thing only.
OEDIPUS. What was that one thing? One may be the key
To everything, if we resolve to use it.
CREON. He said that a band of highwaymen attacked them,
Outnumbered them, and overwhelmed the King.
OEDIPUS. Strange, that a highwayman should be so daring—
Unless some faction here bribed him to do it.
CREON. We thought of that. But after Laïos' death
New troubles arose and we had no avenger.
OEDIPUS. What troubles could prevent your hunting down the killers?
CREON. The riddling Sphinx's song
Made us deaf to all mysteries but her own.
OEDIPUS. Then once more I must bring what is dark to light.
It is most fitting that Apollo shows,
As you do, this compunction for the dead.
You shall see how I stand by you, as I should,
To avenge the city and the city's god,
And not as though it were for some distant friend,
But for my own sake, to be rid of evil.
Whoever killed King Laïos might—who knows?—
Decide at any moment to kill me as well.
By avenging the murdered king I protect myself.
Come, then, my children: leave the altar steps,
Lift up your olive boughs!
One of you go
And summon the people of Kadmos to gather here.
I will do all that I can; you may tell them that.

Exit a PAGE.

So, with the help of God,
We shall be saved—or else indeed we are lost.
PRIEST. Let us rise, children. It was for this we came,
And now the King has promised it himself.

Phoibos° has sent us an oracle; may he descend
Himself to save us and drive out the plague.

Exeunt OEDIPUS *and* CREON *into the palace by the central door. The* PRIEST *and the* SUPPLIANTS *disperse right and left. After a short pause the* CHORUS *enters the orchestra.*

PÁRODOS°

Strophe 1

CHORUS. What is God singing in his profound
Delphi of gold and shadow?
What oracle for Thebes, the sunwhipped city?
Fear unjoints me, the roots of my heart tremble.
Now I remember, O Healer, your power, and wonder;
Will you send doom like a sudden cloud, or weave it
Like nightfall of the past?
Speak, speak to us, issue of holy sound:
Dearest to our expectancy: be tender!

Antistrophe 1

Let me pray to Athenê, the immortal daughter of Zeus,
And to Artemis her sister
Who keeps her famous throne in the market ring,
And to Apollo, bowman at the far butts of heaven—

O gods, descend! Like three streams leap against
The fires of our grief, the fires of darkness;
Be swift to bring us rest!

As in the old time from the brilliant house
Of air you stepped to save us, come again!

Strophe 2

Now our afflictions have no end,
Now all our stricken host lies down
And no man fights off death with his mind;

The noble plowland bears no grain,
And groaning mothers cannot bear—

152**Phoibos** Phoebus Apollo, the sun god. °**Párodos** sung as the chorus enters the stage area. Presumably they sang the *strophe* while dancing from right to left and the antistrophe as they reversed direction.

See, how our lives like birds take wing.
Like sparks that fly when a fire soars,
To the shore of the god of evening.

Antistrophe 2

The plague burns on, it is pitiless,
Though pallid children laden with death
Lie unwept in the stony ways,
And old gray women by every path
Flock to the strand about the altars

There to strike their breasts and cry
Worship of Phoibos in wailing prayers:
Be kind, God's golden child!

Strophe 3

There are no swords in this attack by fire,
No shields, but we are ringed with cries.
Send the besieger plunging from our homes
Into the vast sea-room of the Atlantic
Or into the waves that foam eastward of Thrace—
For the day ravages what the night spares—

Destroy our enemy, lord of the thunder!
Let him be riven by lightning from heaven!

Antistrophe 3

Phoibos Apollo, stretch the sun's bowstring,
That golden cord, until it sing for us,
Flashing arrows in heaven!
                                        Artemis,° Huntress,
Race with flaring lights upon our mountains!
O scarlet god, O golden-banded brow,
O Theban Bacchos° in a storm of Maenads,°

Enter OEDIPUS, *center.*

Whirl upon Death, that all the Undying hate!
Come with blinding cressets, come in joy!

---

[45]**Artemis** goddess of hunting and chastity. [48]**Bacchos . . . Maenads** god of wine and revelry with his attendants.

SCENE I

OEDIPUS. Is this your prayer? It may be answered. Come,
Listen to me, act as the crisis demands,
And you shall have relief from all these evils.

Until now I was a stranger to this tale,
As I had been a stranger to the crime.
Could I track down the murderer without a clue?
But now, friends,
As one who became a citizen after the murder,
I make this proclamation to all Thebans:
If any man knows by whose hand Laïos, son of Labdakos,
Met his death, I direct that man to tell me everything,
No matter what he fears for having so long withheld it.
Let it stand as promised that no further trouble
Will come to him, but he may leave the land in safety.

Moreover: If anyone knows the murderer to be foreign,
Let him not keep silent: he shall have his reward from me.
However, if he does conceal it; if any man
Fearing for his friend or for himself disobeys this edict,
Hear what I propose to do:

I solemnly forbid the people of this country,
Where power and throne are mine, ever to receive that man
Or speak to him, no matter who he is, or let him
Join in sacrifice, lustration, or in prayer.
I decree that he be driven from every house,

Being, as he is, corruption itself to us: the Delphic
Voice of Zeus has pronounced this revelation.
Thus I associate myself with the oracle
And take the side of the murdered king.

As for the criminal, I pray to God—
Whether it be a lurking thief, or one of a number—
I pray that that man's life be consumed in evil and wretchedness.
And as for me, this curse applies no less
If it should turn out that the culprit is my guest here,
Sharing my hearth.
You have heard the penalty.
I lay it on you now to attend to this
For my sake, for Apollo's, for the sick
Sterile city that heaven has abandoned.
Suppose the oracle had given you no command:
Should this defilement go uncleansed for ever?

You should have found the murderer: your king,
A noble king, had been destroyed!
Now I,
Having the power that he held before me,
Having his bed, begetting children there
Upon his wife, as he would have, had he lived—
Their son would have been my children's brother,
If Laïos had had luck in fatherhood!
(But surely ill luck rushed upon his reign)—
I say I take the son's part, just as though
I were his son, to press the fight for him
And see it won! I'll find the hand that brought
Death to Labdakos' and Polydoros' child,
Heir of Kadmos' and Agenor's line.
And as for those who fail me,
May the gods deny them the fruit of the earth,
Fruit of the womb, and may they rot utterly!
Let them be wretched as we are wretched, and worse!
For you, for loyal Thebans, and for all
Who find my actions right, I pray the favor
Of justice, and of all the immortal gods.

CHORAGOS. Since I am under oath, my lord, I swear
I did not do the murder, I cannot name
The murderer. Might not the oracle
That has ordained the search tell where to find him?

OEDIPUS. An honest question. But no man in the world
Can make the gods do more than the gods will.

CHORAGOS. There is one last expedient—

OEDIPUS. Tell me what it is.
Though it seem slight, you must not hold it back.

CHORAGOS. A lord clairvoyant to the lord Apollo,
As we all know, is the skilled Teiresias.
One might learn much about this from him, Oedipus.

OEDIPUS. I am not wasting time:
Creon spoke of this, and I have sent for him—
Twice, in fact; it is strange that he is not here.

CHORAGOS. The other matter—that old report—seems useless.

OEDIPUS. Tell me. I am interested in all reports.

CHORAGOS. The King was said to have been killed by highwaymen.

OEDIPUS. I know. But we have no witnesses to that.

CHORAGOS. If the killer can feel a particle of dread,
Your curse will bring him out of hiding!

OEDIPUS. No.
The man who dared that act will fear no curse.

Enter the blind seer TEIRESIAS, *led by a* PAGE.

CHORAGOS. But there is one man who may detect the criminal.
This is Teiresias, this is the holy prophet
In whom, alone of all men, truth was born.

OEDIPUS. Teiresias: seer: student of mysteries,
Of all that's taught and all that no man tells,
Secrets of Heaven and secrets of the earth:
Blind though you are, you know the city lies
Sick with plague; and from this plague, my lord,
We find that you alone can guard or save us.

Possibly you did not hear the messengers?
Apollo, when we sent to him,
Sent us back word that this great pestilence
Would lift, but only if we established clearly
The identity of those who murdered Laïos.
They must be killed or exiled.
Can you use
Birdflight or any art of divination
To purify yourself, and Thebes, and me
From this contagion? We are in your hands.
There is no fairer duty
Than that of helping others in distress.

TEIRESIAS. How dreadful knowledge of the truth can be
When there's no help in truth! I knew this well,
But did not act on it: else I should not have come.

OEDIPUS. What is troubling you? Why are your eyes so cold?

TEIRESIAS. Let me go home. Bear your own fate, and I'll
Bear mine. It is better so: trust what I say.

OEDIPUS. What you say is ungracious and unhelpful
To your native country. Do not refuse to speak.

TEIRESIAS. When it comes to speech, your own is neither temperate
Nor opportune. I wish to be more prudent.

OEDIPUS. In God's name, we all beg you—

TEIRESIAS. You are all ignorant.
No; I will never tell you what I know.
Now it is my misery; then, it would be yours.

OEDIPUS. What! You do know something, and will not tell us?
You would betray us all and wreck the State?

TEIRESIAS. I do not intend to torture myself, or you.
Why persist in asking? You will not persuade me.

OEDIPUS. What a wicked old man you are! You'd try a stone's
Patience! Out with it! Have you no feeling at all?

TEIRESIAS. You call me unfeeling. If you could only see
The nature of your own feelings . . .

OEDIPUS. Why,
Who would not feel as I do? Who could endure
Your arrogance toward the city?

TEIRESIAS. What does it matter!
Whether I speak or not, it is bound to come.
OEDIPUS. Then, if "it" is bound to come, you are bound to tell me.
TEIRESIAS. No, I will not go on. Rage as you please.
OEDIPUS. Rage? Why not!
And I'll tell you what I think:
You planned it, you had it done, you all but
Killed him with your own hands: if you had eyes,
I'd say the crime was yours, and yours alone.
TEIRESIAS. So? I charge you, then,
Abide by the proclamation you have made:
From this day forth
Never speak again to these men or to me;
You yourself are the pollution of this country.
OEDIPUS. You dare say that! Can you possibly think you have
Some way of going free, after such insolence?
TEIRESIAS. I have gone free. It is the truth sustains me.
OEDIPUS. Who taught you shamelessness? It was not your craft.
TEIRESIAS. You did. You made me speak. I did not want to.
OEDIPUS. Speak what? Let me hear it again more clearly.
TEIRESIAS. Was it not clear before? Are you tempting me?
OEDIPUS. I did not understand it. Say it again.
TEIRESIAS. I say that you are the murderer whom you seek.
OEDIPUS. Now twice you have spat out infamy. You'll pay for it!
TEIRESIAS. Would you care for more? Do you wish to be really angry?
OEDIPUS. Say what you will. Whatever you say is worthless.
TEIRESIAS. I say you live in hideous shame with those
Most dear to you. You cannot see the evil.
OEDIPUS. It seems you can go on mouthing like this for ever.
TEIRESIAS. I can, if there is power in truth.
OEDIPUS. There is:
But not for you, not for you,
You sightless, witless, senseless, mad old man!
TEIRESIAS. You are the madman. There is no one here
Who will not curse you soon, as you curse me.
OEDIPUS. You child of endless night! You cannot hurt me
Or any other man who sees the sun.
TEIRESIAS. True: it is not from me your fate will come.
That lies within Apollo's competence,
As it is his concern.
OEDIPUS. Tell me:
Are you speaking for Creon, or for yourself?
TEIRESIAS. Creon is no threat. You weave your own doom.
OEDIPUS. Wealth, power, craft of statesmanship!
Kingly position, everywhere admired!
What savage envy is stored up against these,
If Creon, whom I trusted, Creon my friend,

For this great office which the city once
Put in my hands unsought—if for this power
Creon desires in secret to destroy me!

He has brought this decrepit fortune-teller, this
Collector of dirty pennies, this prophet fraud—
Why, he is no more clairvoyant than I am!
Tell us:
Has your mystic mummery ever approached the truth?
When that hellcat the Sphinx was performing here,
What help were you to these people?
Her magic was not for the first man who came along:
It demanded a real exorcist. Your birds—
What good were they? or the gods, for the matter of that?
But I came by,
Oedipus, the simple man, who knows nothing—
I thought it out for myself, no birds helped me!
And this is the man you think you can destroy,
That you may be close to Creon when he's king!
Well, you and your friend Creon, it seems to me,
Will suffer most. If you were not an old man,
You would have paid already for your plot.

CHORAGOS. We cannot see that his words or yours
Have been spoken except in anger, Oedipus,
And of anger we have no need. How can God's will
Be accomplished best? That is what most concerns us.

TEIRESIAS. You are a king. But where argument's concerned
I am your man, as much a king as you.
I am not your servant, but Apollo's.
I have no need of Creon to speak for me.

Listen to me. You mock my blindness, do you?
But I say that you, with both your eyes, are blind:
You cannot see the wretchedness of your life,
Nor in whose house you live, no, nor with whom.
Who are your father and mother? Can you tell me?
You do not even know the blind wrongs
That you have done them, on earth and in the world below.
But the double lash of your parents' curse will whip you
Out of this land some day, with only night
Upon your precious eyes.
Your cries then—where will they not be heard?
What fastness of Kithairon will not echo them?
And that bridal-descant of yours—you'll know it then,
The song they sang when you came here to Thebes

And found your misguided berthing.
All this, and more, that you cannot guess at now,
Will bring you to yourself among your children.
Be angry, then. Curse Creon. Curse my words.
I tell you, no man that walks upon the earth
Shall be rooted out more horribly than you.

OEDIPUS. Am I to bear this from him?—Damnation
Take you! Out of this place! Out of my sight!

TEIRESIAS. I would not have come at all if you had not asked me.

OEDIPUS. Could I have told that you'd talk nonsense, that
You'd come here to make a fool of yourself, and of me?

TEIRESIAS. A fool? Your parents thought me sane enough.

OEDIPUS. My parents again!—Wait: who were my parents?

TEIRESIAS. This day will give you a father, and break your heart.

OEDIPUS. Your infantile riddles! Your damned abracadabra!

TEIRESIAS. You were a great man once at solving riddles.

OEDIPUS. Mock me with that if you like; you will find it true.

TEIRESIAS. It was true enough. It brought about your ruin.

OEDIPUS. But if it saved this town?

TEIRESIAS. *(to the* PAGE*).* Boy, give me your hand.

OEDIPUS. Yes, boy; lead him away.
—While you are here
We can do nothing. Go; leave us in peace.

TEIRESIAS. I will go when I have said what I have to say.
How can you hurt me? And I tell you again:
The man you have been looking for all this time,
The damned man, the murderer of Laïos,
That man is in Thebes. To your mind he is foreignborn,
But it will soon be shown that he is a Theban,
A revelation that will fail to please.

A blind man,
Who has his eyes now; a penniless man, who is rich now;
And he will go tapping the strange earth with his staff;
To the children with whom he lives now he will be
Brother and father—the very same; to her
Who bore him, son and husband—the very same
Who came to his father's bed, wet with his father's blood.

Enough. Go think that over.
If later you find error in what I have said,
You may say that I have no skill in prophecy.

Exit TEIRESIAS, *led by his* PAGE. OEDIPUS *goes into the palace.*

ODE I°

Strophe 1

CHORUS. The Delphic stone of prophecies
Remembers ancient regicide
And a still bloody hand.
That killer's hour of flight has come.
He must be stronger than riderless
Courses of untiring wind,
For the son of Zeus° armed with his father's thunder
Leaps in lightning after him;
And the Furies° follow him, the sad Furies.

Antistrophe 1

Holy Parnossos' peak of snow
Flashes and blinds that secret man,
That all shall hunt him down:
Though he may roam the forest shade
Like a bull gone wild from pasture
To rage through glooms of stone.
Doom comes down on him; flight will not avail him;
For the world's heart calls him desolate,
And the immortal Furies follow, for ever follow.

Strophe 2

But now a wilder thing is heard
From the old man skilled at hearing Fate in the
wingbeat of a bird.
Bewildered as a blown bird, my soul hovers and cannot find
Foothold in this debate, or any reason or rest of mind.
But no man ever brought—none can bring
Proof of strife between Thebes' royal house,
Labdakos' line,° and the son of Polybos;°
And never until now has any man brought word
Of Laïos' dark death staining Oedipus the King.

Antistrophe 2

Divine Zeus and Apollo hold
Perfect intelligence alone of all tales ever told;
And well though this diviner works, he works in his own night;

°**Ode** a poetic song sung by the chorus. [7]**son of Zeus** Apollo. [9]**the Furies** three women spirits who punished evildoers. [25]**Labdakos' line** his descendants. [25]**Polybos** King of Corinth who adopted Oedipus as an infant.

No man can judge that rough unknown or trust in second sight,
For wisdom changes hands among the wise.
Shall I believe my great lord criminal
At a raging word that a blind old man let fall?
I saw him, when the carrion woman faced him of old,
Prove his heroic mind! These evil words are lies.

SCENE II

CREON. Men of Thebes:
I am told that heavy accusations
Have been brought against me by King Oedipus.
I am not the kind of man to bear this tamely.

If in these present difficulties
He holds me accountable for any harm to him
Through anything I have said or done—why, then,
I do not value life in this dishonor.
It is not as though this rumor touched upon
Some private indiscretion. The matter is grave.
The fact is that I am being called disloyal
To the State, to my fellow citizens, to my friends.

CHORAGOS. He may have spoken in anger, not from his mind.

CREON. But did you not hear him say I was the one
Who seduced the old prophet into lying?

CHORAGOS. The thing was said; I do not know how seriously.

CREON. But you were watching him! Were his eyes steady?
Did he look like a man in his right mind?

CHORAGOS. I do not know.
I cannot judge the behavior of great men.
But here is the King himself.

Enter OEDIPUS.

OEDIPUS. So you dared come back.
Why? How brazen of you to come to my house,
You murderer!
Do you think I do not know
That you plotted to kill me, plotted to steal my throne?
Tell me, in God's name: am I coward, a fool,
That you should dream you could accomplish this?
A fool who could not see your slippery game?
A coward, not to fight back when I saw it?
You are the fool, Creon, are you not? hoping
Without support or friends to get a throne?
Thrones may be won or bought: you could do neither.

CREON. Now listen to me. You have talked; let me talk, too.
You cannot judge unless you know the facts.
OEDIPUS. You speak well: there is one fact; but I find it hard
To learn from the deadliest enemy I have.
CREON. That above all I must dispute with you.
OEDIPUS. That above all I will not hear you deny.
CREON. If you think there is anything good in being stubborn
Against all reason, then I say you are wrong.
OEDIPUS. If you think a man can sin against his own kind
And not be punished for it, I say you are mad.
CREON. I agree. But tell me: what have I done to you?
OEDIPUS. You advised me to send for that wizard, did you not?
CREON. I did. I should do it again.
OEDIPUS. Very well. Now tell me:
How long has it been since Laïos—
CREON. What of Laïos?
OEDIPUS. Since he vanished in that onset by the road?
CREON. It was long ago, a long time.
OEDIPUS. And this prophet,
Was he practicing here then?
CREON. He was; and with honor, as now.
OEDIPUS. Did he speak of me at that time?
CREON. He never did;
At least, not when I was present.
OEDIPUS. But . . . the enquiry?
I suppose you held one?
CREON. We did, but we learned nothing.
OEDIPUS. Why did the prophet not speak against me then?
CREON. I do not know; and I am the kind of man
Who holds his tongue when he has no facts to go on.
OEDIPUS. There's one fact that you know, and you could tell it.
CREON. What fact is that? If I know it, you shall have it.
OEDIPUS. If he were not involved with you, he could not say
That it was I who murdered Laïos.
CREON. If he says that, you are the one that knows it!—
But now it is my turn to question you.
OEDIPUS. Put your questions. I am no murderer.
CREON. First, then: You married my sister?
OEDIPUS. I married your sister.
CREON. And you rule the kingdom equally with her?
OEDIPUS. Everything that she wants she has from me.
CREON. And I am the third, equal to both of you?
OEDIPUS. That is why I call you a bad friend.
CREON. No. Reason it out, as I have done.
Think of this first. Would any sane man prefer
Power, with all a king's anxieties,
To that same power and the grace of sleep?

Certainly not I.
I have never longed for the king's power—only his rights.
Would any wise man differ from me in this?
As matters stand, I have my way in everything
With your consent, and no responsibilities.
If I were king, I should be a slave to policy.
How could I desire a scepter more
Than what is now mine—untroubled influence?
No, I have not gone mad; I need no honors,
Except those with the perquisites I have now.
I am welcome everywhere; every man salutes me,
And those who want your favor seek my ear,
Since I know how to manage what they ask.
Should I exchange this ease for that anxiety?
Besides, no sober mind is treasonable.
I hate anarchy
And never would deal with any man who likes it.

Test what I have said. Go to the priestess
At Delphi, ask if I quoted her correctly.
And as for this other thing: if I am found
Guilty of treason with Teiresias,
Then sentence me to death! You have my word
It is a sentence I should cast my vote for—
But not without evidence!
                    You do wrong
When you take good men for bad, bad men for good.
A true friend thrown aside—why, life itself
Is not more precious!
                    In time you will know this well:
For time, and time alone, will show the just man,
Though scoundrels are discovered in a day.

CHORAGOS. This is well said, and a prudent man would ponder it.
Judgments too quickly formed are dangerous.

OEDIPUS. But is he not quick in his duplicity?
And shall I not be quick to parry him?
Would you have me stand still, hold my peace, and let
This man win everything, through my inaction?

CREON. And you want—what is it, then? To banish me?

OEDIPUS. No, not exile. It is your death I want,
So that all the world may see what treason means.

CREON. You will persist, then? You will not believe me?

OEDIPUS. How can I believe you?

CREON. Then you are a fool.

OEDIPUS. To save myself?

CREON. In justice, think of me.

OEDIPUS. You are evil incarnate.

CREON. But suppose that you are wrong?
OEDIPUS. Still I must rule.
CREON. But not if you rule badly.
OEDIPUS. O city, city!
CREON. It is my city, too!
CHORAGOS. Now, my lords, be still. I see the Queen,
Iocastê, coming from her palace chambers;
And it is time she came, for the sake of you both.
This dreadful quarrel can be resolved through her.

Enter IOCASTÊ.

IOCASTÊ. Poor foolish men, what wicked din is this?
With Thebes sick to death, is it not shameful
That you should rake some private quarrel up?

(To OEDIPUS.*)*

Come into the house.
—And you, Creon, go now:
Let us have no more of this tumult over nothing.
CREON. Nothing? No, sister: what your husband plans for me
Is one of two great evils: exile or death.
OEDIPUS. He is right.
Why, woman, I have caught him squarely
Plotting against my life.
CREON. No! Let me die
Accurst if ever I have wished you harm!
IOCASTÊ. Ah, believe it, Oedipus!
In the name of the gods, respect this oath of his
For my sake, for the sake of these people here!

Strophe 1

CHORAGOS. Open your mind to her, my lord. Be ruled by her, I beg you!
OEDIPUS. What would you have me do?
CHORAGOS. Respect Creon's word. He has never spoken like a fool,
And now he has sworn an oath.
OEDIPUS. You know what you ask?
CHORAGOS. I do.
OEDIPUS. Speak on, then.
CHORAGOS. A friend so sworn should not be baited so,
In blind malice, and without final proof.
OEDIPUS. You are aware, I hope, that what you say
Means death for me, or exile at the least.

Strophe 2

CHORAGOS. No, I swear by Helios, first in Heaven!
May I die friendless and accurst,
The worst of deaths, if ever I meant that!
It is the withering fields
That hurt my sick heart:
Must we bear all these ills,
And now your bad blood as well?
OEDIPUS. Then let him go. And let me die, if I must,
Or be driven by him in shame from the land of Thebes.
It is your unhappiness, and not his talk,
That touches me.
As for him—
Wherever he is, I will hate him as long as I live.
CREON. Ugly in yielding, as you were ugly in rage!
Natures like yours chiefly torment themselves.
OEDIPUS. Can you not go? Can you not leave me?
CREON. I can.
You do not know me; but the city knows me,
And in its eyes I am just, if not in yours.

Exit CREON.

Antistrophe 1

CHORAGOS. Lady Iocastê, did you not ask the King to go to his chambers?
IOCASTÊ. First tell me what has happened.
CHORAGOS. There was suspicion without evidence; yet it rankled
As even false charges will.
IOCASTÊ. On both sides?
CHORAGOS. On both.
IOCASTÊ. But what was said?
CHORAGOS. Oh let it rest, let it be done with!
Have we not suffered enough?
OEDIPUS. You see to what your decency has brought you:
You have made difficulties where my heart saw none.

Antistrophe 2

CHORAGOS. Oedipus, it is not once only I have told you—
You must know I should count myself unwise
To the point of madness, should I now forsake you—
You, under whose hand,
In the storm of another time,
Our dear land sailed out free.
But now stand fast at the helm!

IOCASTÊ. In God's name, Oedipus, inform your wife as well:
Why are you so set in this hard anger?
OEDIPUS. I will tell you, for none of these men deserves
My confidence as you do. It is Creon's work,
His treachery, his plotting against me.
IOCASTÊ. Go on, if you can make this clear to me.
OEDIPUS. He charges me with the murder of Laïos.
IOCASTÊ. Has he some knowledge? Or does he speak from hearsay?
OEDIPUS. He would not commit himself to such a charge,
But he has brought in that damnable soothsayer
To tell his story.
IOCASTÊ. Set your mind at rest.
If it is a question of soothsayers, I tell you
That you will find no man whose craft gives knowledge
Of the unknowable.
Here is my proof:

An oracle was reported to Laïos once
(I will not say from Phoibos himself, but from
His appointed ministers, at any rate)
That his doom would be death at the hands of his own son—
His son, born of his flesh and of mine!
Now, you remember the story: Laïos was killed
By marauding strangers where three highways meet;
But his child had not been three days in this world
Before the King had pierced the baby's ankles
And left him to die on a lonely mountainside.

Thus, Apollo never caused that child
To kill his father, and it was not Laïos' fate
To die at the hands of his son, as he had feared.
This is what prophets and prophecies are worth!
Have no dread of them.
It is God himself
Who can show us what he wills, in his own way.
OEDIPUS. How strange a shadowy memory crossed my mind,
Just now while you were speaking; it chilled my heart.
IOCASTÊ. What do you mean? What memory do you speak of?
OEDIPUS. If I understand you, Laïos was killed
At a place where three roads meet.
IOCASTÊ. So it was said;
We have no later story.
OEDIPUS. Where did it happen?
IOCASTÊ. Phokis, it is called: at a place where the Theban Way
Divides into the roads towards Delphi and Daulia.
OEDIPUS. When?

IOCASTÊ. We had the news not long before you came
And proved the right to your succession here.
OEDIPUS. Ah, what net has God been weaving for me?
IOCASTÊ. Oedipus! Why does this trouble you?
OEDIPUS. Do not ask me yet.
First, tell me how Laïos looked, and tell me
How old he was.
IOCASTÊ. He was tall, his hair just touched
With white; his form was not unlike your own.
OEDIPUS. I think that I myself may be accurst
By my own ignorant edict.
IOCASTÊ.
You speak strangely.
It makes me tremble to look at you, my King.
OEDIPUS. I am not sure that the blind man cannot see.
But I should know better if you were to tell me—
IOCASTÊ. Anything—though I dread to hear you ask it.
OEDIPUS. Was the King lightly escorted, or did he ride
With a large company, as a ruler should?
IOCASTÊ. There were five men with him in all: one was a herald;
And a single chariot, which he was driving.
OEDIPUS. Alas, that makes it plain enough!
But who—
Who told you how it happened?
IOCASTÊ. A household servant,
The only one to escape.
OEDIPUS. And is he still
A servant of ours?
IOCASTÊ. No; for when he came back at last
And found you enthroned in the place of the dead king,
He came to me, touched my hand with his, and begged
That I would send him away to the frontier district
Where only the shepherds go—
As far away from the city as I could send him.
I granted his prayer; for although the man was a slave,
He had earned more than this favor at my hands.
OEDIPUS. Can he be called back quickly?
IOCASTÊ. Easily.
But why?
OEDIPUS. I have taken too much upon myself
Without enquiry; therefore I wish to consult him.
IOCASTÊ. Then he shall come.
But am I not one also
To whom you might confide these fears of yours!
OEDIPUS. That is your right; it will not be denied you,
Now least of all; for I have reached a pitch
Of wild foreboding. Is there anyone

To whom I should sooner speak?
Polybos of Corinth is my father.
My mother is a Dorian: Meropê.
I grew up chief among the men of Corinth
Until a strange thing happened—
Not worth my passion, it may be, but strange.

At a feast, a drunken man maundering in his cups
Cries out that I am not my father's son!

I contained myself that night, though I felt anger
And a sinking heart. The next day I visited
My father and mother, and questioned them. They stormed,
Calling it all the slanderous rant of a fool;
And this relieved me. Yet the suspicion
Remained always aching in my mind;
I knew there was talk; I could not rest;
And finally, saying nothing to my parents,
I went to the shrine at Delphi.
The god dismissed my question without reply;
He spoke of other things.
Some were clear,
Full of wretchedness, dreadful, unbearable:
As, that I should lie with my own mother, breed
Children from whom all men would turn their eyes;
And that I should be my father's murderer.

I heard all this, and fled. And from that day
Corinth to me was only in the stars
Descending in that quarter of the sky,
As I wandered farther and farther on my way
To a land where I should never see the evil
Sung by the oracle. And I came to this country
Where, so you say, King Laïos was killed.
I will tell you all that happened there, my lady.

There were three highways
Coming together at a place I passed;
And there a herald came towards me, and a chariot
Drawn by horses, with a man such as you describe
Seated in it. The groom leading the horses
Forced me off the road at his lord's command;
But as this charioteer lurched over towards me
I struck him in my rage. The old man saw me
And brought his double goad down upon my head
As I came abreast.
He was paid back, and more!

Swinging my club in this right hand I knocked him
Out of his car, and he rolled on the ground.
I killed him.

I killed them all.
Now if that stranger and Laïos were—kin,
Where is a man more miserable than I?
More hated by the gods? Citizen and alien alike
Must never shelter me or speak to me—
I must be shunned by all.
And I myself
Pronounced this malediction upon myself!

Think of it: I have touched you with these hands,
These hands that killed your husband. What defilement!

Am I all evil, then? It must be so,
Since I must flee from Thebes, yet never again
See my own countrymen, my own country,
For fear of joining my mother in marriage
And killing Polybos, my father.
Ah,
If I was created so, born to this fate,
Who could deny the savagery of God?
O holy majesty of heavenly powers!
May I never see that day! Never!
Rather let me vanish from the race of men
Than know the abomination destined me!

CHORAGOS. We too, my lord, have felt dismay at this.
But there is hope: you have yet to hear the shepherd.

OEDIPUS. Indeed, I fear no other hope is left me.

IOCASTÊ. What do you hope from him when he comes?

OEDIPUS. This much:
If his account of the murder tallies with yours,
Then I am cleared.

IOCASTÊ. What was it that I said
Of such importance?

OEDIPUS. Why, "marauders," you said,
Killed the King, according to this man's story.
If he maintains that still, if there were several,
Clearly the guilt is not mine: I was alone.
But if he says one man, singlehanded, did it,
Then the evidence all points to me.

IOCASTÊ. You may be sure that he said there were several;
And can he call back that story now? He cannot.
The whole city heard it as plainly as I.

But suppose he alters some detail of it:
He cannot ever show that Laïos' death
Fulfilled the oracle: for Apollo said
My child was doomed to kill him; and my child—
Poor baby!—it was my child that died first.

No. From now on, where oracles are concerned,
I would not waste a second thought on any.

OEDIPUS. You may be right.
But come: let someone go
For the shepherd at once. This matter must be settled.

IOCASTÊ. I will send for him.
I would not wish to cross you in anything,
And surely not in this.—Let us go in.

Exeunt into the palace.

ODE II

Strophe 1

CHORUS. Let me be reverent in the ways of right,
Lowly the paths I journey on;
Let all my words and actions keep
The laws of the pure universe
From highest Heaven handed down.
For Heaven is their bright nurse,
Those generations of the realms of light;
Ah, never of mortal kind were they begot,
Nor are they slaves of memory, lost in sleep:
Their Father is greater than Time, and ages not.

Antistrophe 1

The tyrant is a child of Pride
Who drinks from his great sickening cup
Recklessness and vanity,
Until from his high crest headlong
He plummets to the dust of hope.
That strong man is not strong.
But let no fair ambition be denied;
May God protect the wrestler for the State
In government, in comely policy,
Who will fear God, and on His ordinance wait.

Strophe 2

Haughtiness and the high hand of disdain
Tempt and outrage God's holy law;
And any mortal who dares hold
No immortal Power in awe
Will be caught up in a net of pain:
The price for which his levity is sold.
Let each man take due earnings, then,
And keep his hands from holy things,
And from blasphemy stand apart—
Else the crackling blast of heaven
Blows on his head, and on his desperate heart;
Though fools will honor impious men,
In their cities no tragic poet sings.

Antistrophe 2

Shall we lose faith in Delphi's obscurities,
We who have heard the world's core
Discredited, and the sacred wood
Of Zeus at Elis praised no more?
The deeds and the strange prophecies
Must make a pattern yet to be understood.
Zeus, if indeed you are lord of all,
Throned in light over night and day,
Mirror this in your endless mind:
Our masters call the oracle
Words on the wind, and the Delphic vision blind!
Their hearts no longer know Apollo,
And reverence for the gods has died away.

SCENE III

Enter IOCASTÊ.

IOCASTÊ. Princes of Thebes, it has occurred to me
To visit the altars of the gods, bearing
These branches as a suppliant, and this incense.
Our King is not himself: his noble soul
Is overwrought with fantasies of dread,
Else he would consider
The new prophecies in the light of the old.
He will listen to any voice that speaks disaster,
And my advice goes for nothing.

She approaches the altar, right.

To you, then, Apollo,
Lycean lord, since you are nearest, I turn in prayer.
Receive these offerings, and grant us deliverance
From defilement. Our hearts are heavy with fear
When we see our leader distracted, as helpless sailors
Are terrified by the confusion of their helmsman.

Enter MESSENGER.

MESSENGER. Friends, no doubt you can direct me:
Where shall I find the house of Oedipus,
Or, better still, where is the King himself?
CHORAGOS. It is this very place, stranger; he is inside.
This is his wife and mother of his children.
MESSENGER. I wish her happiness in a happy house,
Blest in all the fulfillment of her marriage.
IOCASTÊ. I wish as much for you: your courtesy
Deserves a like good fortune. But now, tell me:
Why have you come? What have you to say to us?
MESSENGER. Good news, my lady, for your house and your husband.
IOCASTÊ. What news? Who sent you here?
MESSENGER. I am from Corinth.
The news I bring ought to mean joy for you,
Though it may be you will find some grief in it.
IOCASTÊ. What is it? How can it touch us in both ways?
MESSENGER. The people of Corinth, they say,
Intend to call Oedipus to be their king.
IOCASTÊ. But old Polybos—is he not reigning still?
MESSENGER. No. Death holds him in his sepulchre.
IOCASTÊ. What are you saying? Polybos is dead?
MESSENGER. If I am not telling the truth, may I die myself.
IOCASTÊ *(to a* MAIDSERVANT*)*. Go in, go quickly; tell this to your master.

O riddlers of God's will, where are you now!
This was the man whom Oedipus, long ago,
Feared so, fled so, in dread of destroying him—
But it was another fate by which he died.

Enter OEDIPUS, *center.*

OEDIPUS. Dearest Iocastê, why have you sent for me?
IOCASTÊ. Listen to what this man says, and then tell me
What has become of the solemn prophecies.
OEDIPUS. Who is this man? What is his news for me?
IOCASTÊ. He has come from Corinth to announce your father's death!
OEDIPUS. Is it true, stranger? Tell me in your own words.
MESSENGER. I cannot say it more clearly: the King is dead.

OEDIPUS. Was it by treason? Or by an attack of illness?
MESSENGER. A little thing brings old men to their rest.
OEDIPUS. It was sickness, then?
MESSENGER. Yes, and his many years.
OEDIPUS. Ah!
Why should a man respect the Pythian hearth,° or
Give heed to the birds that jangle above his head?
They prophesied that I should kill Polybos,
Kill my own father; but he is dead and buried,
And I am here—I never touched him, never,
Unless he died in grief for my departure,
And thus, in a sense, through me. No. Polybos
Has packed the oracles off with him underground.
They are empty words.
IOCASTÊ. Had I not told you so?
OEDIPUS. You had; it was my faint heart that betrayed me.
IOCASTÊ. From now on never think of those things again.
OEDIPUS. And yet—must I not fear my mother's bed?
IOCASTÊ. Why should anyone in this world be afraid,
Since Fate rules us and nothing can be foreseen?
A man should live only for the present day.
Have no more fear of sleeping with your mother:
How many men, in dreams, have lain with their mothers!
No reasonable man is troubled by such things.
OEDIPUS. That is true; only—
If only my mother were not still alive!
But she is alive. I cannot help my dread.
IOCASTÊ. Yet this news of your father's death is wonderful.
OEDIPUS. Wonderful. But I fear the living woman.
MESSENGER. Tell me, who is this woman that you fear?
OEDIPUS. It is Meropê, man; the wife of King Polybos.
MESSENGER. Meropê? Why should you be afraid of her?
OEDIPUS. An oracle of the gods, a dreadful saying.
MESSENGER. Can you tell me about it or are you sworn to silence?
OEDIPUS. I can tell you, and I will.
Apollo said through his prophet that I was the man
Who should marry his own mother, shed his father's blood
With his own hands. And so, for all these years
I have kept clear of Corinth, and no harm has come—
Though it would have been sweet to see my parents again.
MESSENGER. And is this the fear that drove you out of Corinth?
OEDIPUS. Would you have me kill my father?
MESSENGER. As for that
You must be reassured by the news I gave you.

---

[52]**Pythian hearth** Delphi, also called Pytho because a large dragon, the Python, had guarded the chasm at Delphi until Apollo killed it and established his oracle on the site.

OEDIPUS. If you could reassure me, I would reward you.
MESSENGER. I had that in mind, I will confess: I thought
I could count on you when you returned to Corinth.
OEDIPUS. No: I will never go near my parents again.
MESSENGER. Ah, son, you still do not know what you are doing—
OEDIPUS. What do you mean? In the name of God tell me!
MESSENGER. —If these are your reasons for not going home.
OEDIPUS. I tell you, I fear the oracle may come true.
MESSENGER. And guilt may come upon you through your parents?
OEDIPUS. That is the dread that is always in my heart.
MESSENGER. Can you not see that all your fears are groundless?
OEDIPUS. How can you say that? They are my parents, surely?
MESSENGER. Polybos was not your father.
OEDIPUS. Not my father?
MESSENGER. No more your father than the man speaking to you.
OEDIPUS. But you are nothing to me!
MESSENGER. Neither was he.
OEDIPUS. Then why did he call me son?
MESSENGER. I will tell you:
Long ago he had you from my hands, as a gift.
OEDIPUS. Then how could he love me so, if I was not his?
MESSENGER. He had no children, and his heart turned to you.
OEDIPUS. What of you? Did you buy me? Did you find me by chance?
MESSENGER. I came upon you in the crooked pass of Kithairon.
OEDIPUS. And what were you doing there?
MESSENGER. Tending my flocks.
OEDIPUS. A wandering shepherd?
MESSENGER. But your savior, son, that day.
OEDIPUS. From what did you save me?
MESSENGER. Your ankles should tell you that.
OEDIPUS. Ah, stranger, why do you speak of that childhood pain?
MESSENGER. I cut the bonds that tied your ankles together.
OEDIPUS. I have had the mark as long as I can remember.
MESSENGER. That was why you were given the name you bear.°
OEDIPUS. God! Was it my father or my mother who did it?
Tell me!
MESSENGER. I do not know. The man who gave you to me
Can tell you better than I.
OEDIPUS. It was not you that found me, but another?
MESSENGER. It was another shepherd gave you to me.
OEDIPUS. Who was he? Can you tell me who he was?
MESSENGER. I think he was said to be one of Laïos' people.
OEDIPUS. You mean the Laïos who was king here years ago?
MESSENGER. Yes; King Laïos; and the man was one of his herdsmen.
OEDIPUS. Is he still alive? Can I see him?

---

116 **name you bear** "Oedipus" means "swollen-foot."

MESSENGER. These men here
Know best about such things.
OEDIPUS. Does anyone here
Know this shepherd that he is talking about?
Have you seen him in the fields, or in the town?
If you have, tell me. It is time things were made plain.
CHORAGOS. I think the man he means is that same shepherd
You have already asked to see. Iocastê perhaps
Could tell you something.
OEDIPUS. Do you know anything
About him, Lady? Is he the man we have summoned?
Is that the man this shepherd means?
IOCASTÊ. Why think of him?
Forget this herdsman. Forget it all.
This talk is a waste of time.
OEDIPUS. How can you say that,
When the clues to my true birth are in my hands?
IOCASTÊ. For God's love, let us have no more questioning!
Is your life nothing to you?
My own is pain enough for me to bear.
OEDIPUS. You need not worry. Suppose my mother a slave,
And born of slaves: no baseness can touch you.
IOCASTÊ. Listen to me, I beg you: do not do this thing!
OEDIPUS. I will not listen; the truth must be made known.
IOCASTÊ. Everything that I say is for your own good!
OEDIPUS. My own good
Snaps my patience, then: I want none of it.
IOCASTÊ. You are fatally wrong! May you never learn who you are!
OEDIPUS. Go, one of you, and bring the shepherd here.
Let us leave this woman to brag of her royal name.
IOCASTÊ. Ah, miserable!
That is the only word I have for you now.
That is the only word I can ever have.

Exit into the palace.

CHORAGOS. Why has she left us, Oedipus? Why has she gone
In such a passion of sorrow? I fear this silence:
Something dreadful may come of it.
OEDIPUS. Let it come!
However base my birth, I must know about it.
The Queen, like a woman, is perhaps ashamed
To think of my low origin. But I
Am a child of luck; I cannot be dishonored.
Luck is my mother; the passing months, my brothers,
Have seen me rich and poor.
If this is so,

How could I wish that I were someone else?
How could I not be glad to know my birth?

ODE III

Strophe

CHORUS. If ever the coming time were known
To my heart's pondering,
Kithairon, now by Heaven I see the torches
At the festival of the next full moon,
And see the dance, and hear the choir sing
A grace to your gentle shade:
Mountain where Oedipus was found,
O mountain guard of a noble race!
May the god who heals us lend his aid,
And let that glory come to pass
For our king's cradling-ground.

Antistrophe

Of the nymphs that flower beyond the years,
Who bore you, royal child,
To Pan of the hills or the timberline Apollo,
Cold in delight where the upland clears,
Or Hermês for whom Kyllenê's heights° are piled?
Or flushed as evening cloud,
Great Dionysos, roamer of mountains,
He—was it he who found you there,
And caught you up in his own proud
Arms from the sweet god-ravisher
Who laughed by the Muses' fountains?

SCENE IV

OEDIPUS. Sirs: though I do not know the man,
I think I see him coming, this shepherd we want:
He is old, like our friend here, and the men
Bringing him seem to be servants of my house.
But you can tell, if you have ever seen him.

Enter SHEPHERD *escorted by servants.*

---

[16]**Kyllenê's heights** holy mountain, birthplace of Hermes, messenger of the gods.

CHORAGOS. I know him, he was Laïos' man. You can trust him.
OEDIPUS. Tell me first, you from Corinth: is this the shepherd
We were discussing?
MESSENGER. This is the very man.
OEDIPUS *(to* SHEPHERD*)*. Come here. No, look at me. You must answer
Everything I ask.—You belonged to Laïos?
SHEPHERD. Yes: born his slave, brought up in his house.
OEDIPUS. Tell me: what kind of work did you do for him?
SHEPHERD. I was a shepherd of his, most of my life.
OEDIPUS. Where mainly did you go for pasturage?
SHEPHERD. Sometimes Kithairon, sometimes the hills near-by.
OEDIPUS. Do you remember ever seeing this man out there?
SHEPHERD. What would he be doing there? This man?
OEDIPUS. This man standing here. Have you ever seen him before?
SHEPHERD. No. At least, not to my recollection.
MESSENGER. And that is not strange, my lord. But I'll refresh
His memory: he must remember when we two
Spent three whole seasons together, March to September,
On Kithairon or thereabouts. He had two flocks;
I had one. Each autumn I'd drive mine home
And he would go back with his to Laïos' sheepfold.—
Is this not true, just as I have described it?
SHEPHERD. True, yes; but it was all so long ago.
MESSENGER. Well, then: do you remember, back in those days
That you gave me a baby boy to bring up as my own?
SHEPHERD. What if I did? What are you trying to say?
MESSENGER. King Oedipus was once that little child.
SHEPHERD. Damn you, hold your tongue!
OEDIPUS. No more of that!
It is your tongue needs watching, not this man's.
SHEPHERD. My King, my Master, what is it I have done wrong?
OEDIPUS. You have not answered his question about the boy.
SHEPHERD. He does not know . . . He is only making trouble . . .
OEDIPUS. Come, speak plainly, or it will go hard with you.
SHEPHERD. In God's name, do not torture an old man!
OEDIPUS. Come here, one of you; bind his arms behind him.
SHEPHERD. Unhappy king! What more do you wish to learn?
OEDIPUS. Did you give this man the child he speaks of?
SHEPHERD. I did.
And I would to God I had died that very day.
OEDIPUS. You will die now unless you speak the truth.
SHEPHERD. Yet if I speak the truth, I am worse than dead.
OEDIPUS. Very well; since you insist upon delaying—
SHEPHERD. No! I have told you already that I gave him the boy.
OEDIPUS. Where did you get him? From your house?
From somewhere else?
SHEPHERD. Not from mine, no. A man gave him to me.

OEDIPUS. Is that man here? Do you know whose slave he was?
SHEPHERD. For God's love, my King, do not ask me any more!
OEDIPUS. You are a dead man if I have to ask you again.
SHEPHERD. Then . . . Then the child was from the palace of Laïos.
OEDIPUS. A slave child? or a child of his own line?
SHEPHERD. Ah, I am on the brink of dreadful speech!
OEDIPUS. And I of dreadful hearing. Yet I must hear.
SHEPHERD. If you must be told, then . . .
They said it was Laïos' child,
But it is your wife who can tell you about that.
OEDIPUS. My wife!—Did she give it to you?
SHEPHERD. My lord, she did.
OEDIPUS. Do you know why?
SHEPHERD. I was told to get rid of it.
OEDIPUS. An unspeakable mother!
SHEPHERD. There had been prophecies . . .
OEDIPUS. Tell me.
SHEPHERD. It was said that the boy would kill his own father.
OEDIPUS. Then why did you give him over to this old man?
SHEPHERD. I pitied the baby, my King.
And I thought that this man would take him far away
To his own country.
He saved him—but for what a fate!
For if you are what this man says you are,
No man living is more wretched than Oedipus.
OEDIPUS. Ah God!
It was true!
All the prophecies!
—Now,
O Light, may I look on you for the last time!
I, Oedipus,
Oedipus, damned in his birth, in his marriage damned,
Damned in the blood he shed with his own hand!

He rushes into the palace.

ODE IV

Strophe 1

CHORUS. Alas for the seed of men.
What measure shall I give these generations
That breathe on the void and are void
And exist and do not exist?

Who bears more weight of joy
Than mass of sunlight shifting in images,

Or who shall make his thought stay on
That down time drifts away?

Your splendor is all fallen.

O naked brow of wrath and tears,
O change of Oedipus!
I who saw your days call no man blest—
Your great days like ghósts góne.

Antistrophe 1

That mind was a strong bow.
Deep, how deep you drew it then, hard archer,
At a dim fearful range,
And brought dear glory down!

You overcame the stranger—
The virgin with her hooking lion claws—
And though death sang, stood like a tower
To make pale Thebes take heart.

Fortress against our sorrow!

Divine king, giver of laws,
Majestic Oedipus!
No prince in Thebes had ever such renown,
No prince won such grace of power.

Strophe 2

And now of all men ever known
Most pitiful is this man's story:
His fortunes are most changed, his state
Fallen to a low slave's
Ground under bitter fate.

O Oedipus, most royal one!
The great door that expelled you to the light
Gave at night—ah, gave night to your glory:
As to the father, to the fathering son.

All understood too late.

How could that queen whom Laïos won,
The garden that he harrowed at his height,
Be silent when that act was done?

Antistrophe 2

But all eyes fail before time's eye,
All actions come to justice there.
Though never willed, though far down the deep past,
Your bed, your dread sirings,
Are brought to book at last.
Child by Laïos doomed to die,
Then doomed to lose that fortunate little death,
Would God you never took breath in this air
That with my wailing lips I take to cry:

For I weep the world's outcast.

I was blind, and now I can tell why:
Asleep, for you had given ease of breath
To Thebes, while the false years went by.

EXODOS

Enter, from the palace, SECOND MESSENGER.

SECOND MESSENGER. Elders of Thebes, most honored in this land,
What horrors are yours to see and hear, what weight
Of sorrow to be endured, if, true to your birth,
You venerate the line of Labdakos!
I think neither Istros nor Phasis, those great rivers,
Could purify this place of the corruption
It shelters now, or soon must bring to light—
Evil not done unconsciously, but willed.

The greatest griefs are those we cause ourselves.
CHORAGOS. Surely, friend, we have grief enough already;
What new sorrow do you mean?
SECOND MESSENGER. The Queen is dead.
CHORAGOS. Iocastê? Dead? But at whose hand?
SECOND MESSENGER. Her own.
The full horror of what happened you cannot know,
For you did not see it; but I, who did, will tell you
As clearly as I can how she met her death.

When she had left us,
In passionate silence, passing through the court,
She ran to her apartment in the house,
Her hair clutched by the fingers of both hands.
She closed the doors behind her; then, by that bed

Where long ago the fatal son was conceived—
That son who should bring about his father's death—
We heard her call upon Laïos, dead so many years,
And heard her wail for the double fruit of her marriage,
A husband by her husband, children by her child.

Exactly how she died I do not know:
For Oedipus burst in moaning and would not let us
Keep vigil to the end: it was by him
As he stormed about the room that our eyes were caught.
From one to another of us he went, begging a sword,
Cursing the wife who was not his wife, the mother
Whose womb had carried his own children and himself.
I do not know: it was none of us aided him,
But surely one of the gods was in control!
For with a dreadful cry
He hurled his weight, as though wrenched out of himself,
At the twin doors: the bolts gave, and he rushed in.
And there we saw her hanging, her body swaying
From the cruel cord she had noosed about her neck.
A great sob broke from him heartbreaking to hear,
As he loosed the rope and lowered her to the ground.

I would blot out from my mind what happened next!
For the King ripped from her gown the golden brooches
That were her ornament, and raised them, and plunged them down
Straight into his own eyeballs, crying, "No more,
No more shall you look on the misery about me,
The horrors of my own doing! Too long you have known
The faces of those whom I should never have seen,
Too long been blind to those for whom I was searching!
From this hour, go in darkness!" And as he spoke,
He struck at his eyes—not once, but many times;
And the blood spattered his beard,
Bursting from his ruined sockets like red hail.

So from the unhappiness of two this evil has sprung,
A curse on the man and woman alike. The old
Happiness of the house of Labdakos
Was happiness enough: where is it today?
It is all wailing and ruin, disgrace, death—all
The misery of mankind that has a name—
And it is wholly and for ever theirs.

CHORAGOS. Is he in agony still? Is there no rest for him?

SECOND MESSENGER. He is calling for someone to lead him to the gates
So that all the children of Kadmos may look upon

His father's murderer, his mother's—no,
I cannot say it!
And then he will leave Thebes,
Self-exiled, in order that the curse
Which he himself pronounced may depart from the house.
He is weak, and there is none to lead him,
So terrible is his suffering.
But you will see:
Look, the doors are opening; in a moment
You will see a thing that would crush a heart of stone.

The central door is opened; OEDIPUS, *blinded, is led in.*

CHORAGOS. Dreadful indeed for men to see.
Never have my own eyes
Looked on a sight so full of fear.

Oedipus!
What madness came upon you, what daemon
Leaped on your life with heavier
Punishment than a mortal man can bear?
No: I cannot even
Look at you, poor ruined one.
And I would speak, question, ponder,
If I were able. No.
You make me shudder.
OEDIPUS. God. God.
Is there a sorrow greater?
Where shall I find harbor in this world?
My voice is hurled far on a dark wind.
What has God done to me?
CHORAGOS. Too terrible to think of, or to see.

Strophe 1

OEDIPUS. O cloud of night,
Never to be turned away: night coming on,
I cannot tell how: night like a shroud!
My fair winds brought me here.
Oh God. Again
The pain of the spikes where I had sight,
The flooding pain
Of memory, never to be gouged out.
CHORAGOS. This is not strange.
You suffer it all twice over, remorse in pain,
Pain in remorse.

Antistrophe 1

OEDIPUS. Ah dear friend
Are you faithful even yet, you alone?
Are you still standing near me, will you stay here,
Patient, to care for the blind?
The blind man!
Yet even blind I know who it is attends me,
By the voice's tone—
Though my new darkness hide the comforter.
CHORAGOS. Oh fearful act!
What god was it drove you to rake black
Night across your eyes?

Strophe 2

OEDIPUS. Apollo. Apollo. Dear
Children, the god was Apollo.
He brought my sick, sick fate upon me.
But the blinding hand was my own!
How could I bear to see
When all my sight was horror everywhere?
CHORAGOS. Everywhere; that is true.
OEDIPUS. And now what is left?
Images? Love? A greeting even,
Sweet to the senses? Is there anything?
Ah, no, friends: lead me away.
Lead me away from Thebes.
Lead the great wreck
And hell of Oedipus, whom the gods hate.
CHORAGOS. Your fate is clear, you are not blind to that.
Would God you had never found it out!

Antistrophe 2

OEDIPUS. Death take the man who unbound
My feet on that hillside
And delivered me from death to life! What life?
If only I had died,
This weight of monstrous doom
Could not have dragged me and my darlings down.
CHORAGOS. I would have wished the same.
OEDIPUS. Oh never to have come here
With my father's blood upon me! Never
To have been the man they call his mother's husband!
Oh accurst! Oh child of evil,

To have entered that wretched bed—
the selfsame one!
More primal than sin itself, this fell to me.
CHORAGOS. I do not know how I can answer you.
You were better dead than alive and blind.
OEDIPUS. Do not counsel me any more. This punishment
That I have laid upon myself is just.
If I had eyes,
I do not know how I could bear the sight
Of my father, when I came to the house of Death,
Or my mother: for I have sinned against them both
So vilely that I could not make my peace
By strangling my own life.
Or do you think my children,
Born as they were born, would be sweet to my eyes?
Ah never, never! Nor this town with its high walls,
Nor the holy images of the gods.
For I,
Thrice miserable—Oedipus, noblest of all the line
Of Kadmos, have condemned myself to enjoy
These things no more, by my own malediction
Expelling that man whom the gods declared
To be a defilement in the house of Laïos.
After exposing the rankness of my own guilt,
How could I look men frankly in the eyes?
No, I swear it,
If I could have stifled my hearing at its source,
I would have done it and made all this body
A tight cell of misery, blank to light and sound:
So I should have been safe in a dark agony
Beyond all recollection.
Ah Kithairon!
Why did you shelter me? When I was cast upon you,
Why did I not die? Then I should never
Have shown the world my execrable birth.

Ah Polybos! Corinth, city that I believed
The ancient seat of my ancestors: how fair
I seemed, your child! And all the while this evil
Was cancerous within me!
For I am sick
In my daily life, sick in my origin.

O three roads, dark ravine, woodland and way
Where three roads met you, drinking my father's blood,
My own blood, spilled by my own hand: can you remember

The unspeakable things I did there, and the things
I went on from there to do?
O marriage, marriage!
The act that engendered me, and again the act
Performed by the son in the same bed—
Ah, the net
Of incest, mingling fathers, brothers, sons,
With brides, wives, mothers: the last evil
That can be known by men: no tongue can say
How evil!
No. For the love of God, conceal me
Somewhere far from Thebes; or kill me; or hurl me
Into the sea, away from men's eyes for ever.
Come, lead me. You need not fear to touch me.
Of all men, I alone can bear this guilt.

Enter CREON.

CHORAGOS. We are not the ones to decide; but Creon here
May fitly judge of what you ask. He only
Is left to protect the city in your place.
OEDIPUS. Alas, how can I speak to him? What right have I
To beg his courtesy whom I have deeply wronged?
CREON. I have not come to mock you, Oedipus,
Or to reproach you, either.

(To ATTENDANTS.*)*

—You, standing there:
If you have lost all respect for man's dignity,
At least respect the flame of Lord Helios:
Do not allow this pollution to show itself
Openly here, an affront to the earth
And Heaven's rain and the light of day. No, take him
Into the house as quickly as you can.
For it is proper
That only the close kindred see his grief.
OEDIPUS. I pray you in God's name, since your courtesy
Ignores my dark expectation, visiting
With mercy this man of all men most execrable:
Give me what I ask—for your good, not for mine.
CREON. And what is it that you would have me do?
OEDIPUS. Drive me out of this country as quickly as may be
To a place where no human voice can ever greet me.
CREON. I should have done that before now—only,
God's will had not been wholly revealed to me.

OEDIPUS. But his command is plain: the parricide
Must be destroyed. I am that evil man.
CREON. That is the sense of it, yes; but as things are,
We had best discover clearly what is to be done.
OEDIPUS. You would learn more about a man like me?
CREON. You are ready now to listen to the god.
OEDIPUS. I will listen. But it is to you
That I must turn for help. I beg you, hear me.
The woman in there—
Give her whatever funeral you think proper:
She is your sister.
—But let me go, Creon!
Let me purge my father's Thebes of the pollution
Of my living here, and go out to the wild hills,
To Kithairon, that has won such fame with me,
The tomb my mother and father appointed for me,
And let me die there, as they willed I should.
And yet I know
Death will not ever come to me through sickness
Or in any natural way: I have been preserved
For some unthinkable fate. But let that be.
As for my sons, you need not care for them.
They are men, they will find some way to live.
But my poor daughters, who have shared my table,
Who never before have been parted from their father—
Take care of them, Creon; do this for me.
And will you let me touch them with my hands
A last time, and let us weep together?
Be kind, my lord,
Great prince, be kind!
Could I but touch them,
They would be mine again, as when I had my eyes.

Enter ANTIGONÊ *and* ISMENÊ, *attended.*

Ah, God!
Is it my dearest children I hear weeping?
Has Creon pitied me and sent my daughters?
CREON. Yes, Oedipus: I knew that they were dear to you
In the old days, and know you must love them still.
OEDIPUS. May God bless you for this—and be a friendlier
Guardian to you than he has been to me!

Children, where are you?
Come quickly to my hands: they are your brother's—
Hands that have brought your father's once clear eyes
To this way of seeing—

Ah dearest ones,
I had neither sight nor knowledge then, your father
By the woman who was the source of his own life!
And I weep for you—having no strength to see you—,
I weep for you when I think of the bitterness
That men will visit upon you all your lives.
What homes, what festivals can you attend
Without being forced to depart again in tears?
And when you come to marriageable age,
Where is the man, my daughters, who would dare
Risk the bane that lies on all my children?
Is there any evil wanting? Your father killed
His father; sowed the womb of her who bore him;
Engendered you at the fount of his own existence!
That is what they will say of you.
Then, whom
Can you ever marry? There are no bridegrooms for you,
And your lives must wither away in sterile dreaming.
O Creon, son of Menoikeus!
You are the only father my daughters have,
Since we, their parents, are both of us gone for ever.
They are your own blood: you will not let them
Fall into beggary and loneliness;
You will keep them from the miseries that are mine!
Take pity on them; see, they are only children,
Friendless except for you. Promise me this,
Great Prince, and give me your hand in token of it.

CREON *clasps his right hand.*

Children:
I could say much, if you could understand me,
But as it is, I have only this prayer for you:
Live where you can, be as happy as you can—
Happier, please God, than God has made your father!

CREON. Enough. You have wept enough. Now go within.
OEDIPUS. I must; but it is hard.
CREON. Time eases all things.
OEDIPUS. But you must promise—
CREON. Say what you desire.
OEDIPUS. Send me from Thebes!
CREON. God grant that I may!
OEDIPUS. But since God hates me . . .
CREON. No, he will grant your wish.
OEDIPUS. You promise?
CREON. I cannot speak beyond my knowledge.
OEDIPUS. Then lead me in.
CREON. Come now, and leave your children.

OEDIPUS. No! Do not take them from me!
CREON. Think no longer
That you are in command here, but rather think
How, when you were, you served your own destruction.

Exeunt into the house all but the CHORUS; *the* CHORAGOS *chants directly to the audience.*

CHORAGOS. Men of Thebes: look upon Oedipus.
This is the king who solved the famous riddle
And towered up, most powerful of men
No mortal eyes but looked on him with envy.
Yet in the end ruin swept over him.
Let every man in mankind's frailty
Consider his last day; and let none
Presume on his good fortune until he find
Life, at his death, a memory without pain.

ARISTOPHANES

(450?–380? B.C.)

Lysistrata

TRANSLATED BY DUDLEY FITTS

About the Author: Aristophanes is the only ancient Greek comic playwright whose work has survived—thirteen plays produced between 425 and 388. They frequently make fun of contemporary political and intellectual figures, and, though often wildly obscene and farcical, they usually deal with serious and controversial subjects in Athenian society.

About the Play: *Lysistrata* was produced in the middle of the great Pelopponesian War between the city states of Athens and Sparta, with most of the Greek world involved by alliance with one side or the other. From the local Athenian point of view, it was a very bad time; their economy had been severely weakened by their recent unsuccessful attack on Sicily, one which had also undermined confidence in Athenian civic idealism, and they were feeling militarily threatened. The play seems to attack those attitudes of Greek citizens—its males—which not only produce this society but also make war its natural expression. Indeed, Aristophanes may have focused on war to examine the main destructive forces within Athens and, implicitly, within all Greece.

As we saw in the drama introduction, however, his central emphasis is on the issue of gender. War is a political expression of the attitude of machismo which Greek men also express in their relationship toward women. By dealing with gender issues in the context of war, Aristophanes can show simultaneously how destructive sexism is and how futile war is. However, although his female characters hold up men and their "heroic" nature to ridicule, Aristophanes' full intentions are uncertain. Are women less aggressive than men in this play? Or is it mainly their weapons which are different? Are women out for peace and equality, or for taking power from men so that they can have it for themselves? Are they for peace because peace is more sane than war, or because in peace women have a better chance at power? At the end the military situation has changed, but has there been a change in the relations between men and women? What is the cost of the final settlement?

More questions may be raised when we consider some of the qualities of the society for

which this play was produced, and what these qualities might imply about its members. For example, male heads of household were the only ones eligible to be citizens and to vote in democratic Athens. Menial work, including personal and domestic services, was not done by Athenians but by women and by slaves from other states. Only men acted on the stage. There is some uncertainty still about whether women were even allowed to see comedy in the theater. In other words, we should imagine ancient Athens as an extraordinarily proud, sexist, racist, male-dominated culture. In this theater in this society at this time, when the supporters of war would be feeling unusually defensive, can we take what a male playwright says about women's potential power over men and against war at face value? Perhaps. But perhaps we can see it with equal ease as a male joke at women's expense: this is what *they* think; look how ridiculous they are. We cannot know how Aristophanes intended his play, nor how his audience received it. What is clear is that through his satire Aristophanes raises issues about gender and about social organization that are still among our central concerns today.

PERSONS REPRESENTED:

LYSISTRATA
KALONIKE
MYRRHINE
LAMPITO
CHORUS
COMMISSIONER
KINESIAS
SPARTAN HERALD
SPARTAN AMBASSADOR
A SENTRY

Scene: *Athens. First, a public square; later, beneath the walls of the Akropolis; later, a courtyard within the Akropolis.*

Until the éxodos,° *the* CHORUS *is divided into two hemichori:° the first, of Old Men; the second, of Old Women. Each of these has its* KORYPHAIOS.° *In the* éxodos, *the hemichori return as Athenians and Spartans.*

The supernumeraries include the BABY SON *of Kinêsias;* STRATYLLIS, *a member of the hemichorus of Old Women; various individual speakers, both Spartan and Athenian.*

PROLOGUE

[*Athens; a public square; early morning;* LYSISTRATA *sola*]

LYSISTRATA:

If someone had invited them to a festival—
of Bacchos, say; or to Pan's shrine, or to Aphroditê's
over at Kôlias—, you couldn't get through the streets,

°**exodos** the final scene. °**hemichori** two half-choruses, one of men (^{m}) and one of women (^{w}). °**koryphaios** leader or spokesperson of the Chorus.

what with the drums and the dancing. But now,
not a woman in sight!
Except—oh, yes!

[*Enter* KALONIKE]

Here's one of my neighbors, at last. Good
morning, Kalonikê.

KALONIKE:
Good morning, Lysistrata.
Darling,
don't frown so! You'll ruin your face!

LYSISTRATA:
Never mind my face.
Kalonikê,
the way we women behave! Really, I don't blame the men
for what they say about us.

KALONIKE:
No; I imagine they're right.

LYSISTRATA:
For example: I call a meeting
to think out a most important matter—and what happens?
The women all stay in bed!

KALONIKE:
Oh, they'll be along.
It's hard to get away, you know: a husband, a cook,
a child . . . Home life can be *so* demanding!

LYSISTRATA:
What I have in mind is even more demanding.

KALONIKE:
Tell me: what is it?

LYSISTRATA:
It's big.

KALONIKE:
Goodness! *How* big?

LYSISTRATA:
Big enough for all of us.

KALONIKE:
But we're not all here!

LYSISTRATA:
We would be, if *that*'s what was up!
No, Kalonikê,
this is something I've been turning over for nights,
long sleepless nights.

KALONIKE:
It must be getting worn down, then,
if you've spent so much time on it.

LYSISTRATA:
Worn down or not,
it comes to this: Only we women can save Greece!

KALONIKE:
Only we women? Poor Greece!

LYSISTRATA:
Just the same,
it's up to us. First, we must liquidate
the Peloponnesians—

KALONIKE:
Fun, fun!

LYSISTRATA:
—and then the Boiotians.

KALONIKE:
Oh! But not those heavenly eels!

LYSISTRATA:
You needn't worry.
I'm not talking about eels.—But here's the point:
If we can get the women from those places—
all those Boiotians and Peloponnesians—
to join us women here, why, we can save
all Greece!

KALONIKE:
But dearest Lysistrata!
How can women do a thing so austere, so
political? We belong at home. Our only armor's
our perfumes, our saffron dresses and
our pretty little shoes!

LYSISTRATA:
Exactly. Those
transparent dresses, the saffron, the
perfume, those pretty shoes—

KALONIKE: Oh?

LYSISTRATA:
Not a single man would lift
his spear—

KALONIKE:
I'll send my dress to the dyer's tomorrow!

LYSISTRATA:
—or grab a shield—

KALONIKE:
The sweetest little negligée—

LYSISTRATA:
—or haul out his sword.

KALONIKE:
I know where I can buy
the dreamiest sandals!

LYSISTRATA:

Well, so you see. Now, shouldn't
the women have come?

KALONIKE:

Come? They should have *flown!*

LYSISTRATA:

Athenians are always late.
But imagine!
There's no one here from the South Shore, or from Sálamis.

KALONIKE:

Things are hard over in Sálamis, I swear.
They have to get going at dawn.

LYSISTRATA:

And nobody from Acharnai.
I thought they'd be here hours ago.

KALONIKE:

Well, you'll get
that awful Theagenês woman: she'll be
a sheet or so in the wind.
But look!
Someone at last! Can you see who they are?

[*Enter* MYRRHINE *and other women*]

LYSISTRATA:

They're from Anagyros.

KALONIKE:

They certainly are.
You'd know them anywhere, by the scent.

MYRRHINE:

Sorry to be late, Lysistrata.
Oh come,
don't scowl so. Say something!

LYSISTRATA:

My dear Myrrhinê,
what is there to say? After all,
you've been pretty casual about the whole thing.

MYRRHINE:

Couldn't find
my girdle in the dark, that's all.
But what *is*
'the whole thing'?

KALONIKE:

No, we've got to wait
for those Boiotians and Peloponnesians.

LYSISTRATA:
That's more like it.—But, look!
Here's Lampitô!

[*Enter* LAMPITO *with women from Sparta*]

LYSISTRATA:
Darling Lampitô,
how pretty you are today! What a nice color!
Goodness, you look as though you could strangle a bull!

LAMPITO:
Ah think Ah could! It's the work-out
in the gym every day: and, of co'se that dance of ahs°
where y' kick yo' own tail.

KALONIKE:
What an adorable figure!

LAMPITO:
Lawdy,° when y' touch me lahk that,
Ah feel lahk a heifer at the altar!

LYSISTRATA:
And this young lady?
Where is she from?

LAMPITO:
Boiotia. Social-Register type.

LYSISTRATA:
Ah. 'Boiotia of the fertile plain.'

KALONIKE:
And if you look,
you'll find the fertile plain has just been mowed.

LYSISTRATA:
And this lady?

LAMPITO:
Hagh, wahd, handsome. She comes from
Korinth.

KALONIKE:
High and wide's the word for it.

LAMPITO:
Which one of you
called this heah meeting, and why?

LYSISTRATA:
I did.

---

[67]**that dance of ahs** Athenian girls were brought up in seclusion. In Sparta, however, girls were expected to participate in athletic exercises. The "dance" referred to here is the strenuous *bibasis,* in which the executant must strike her buttocks with her heels. (Fitts) [69]**Lawdy** She swears "by the Two," which, in Sparta, meant the Heavenly Twins, Kastor and Polydeukes. The Athenian "by the Two" was reserved to women only, and referred to Demeter and Persephone. (Fitts)

LAMPITO:

Well, then, tell us:

What's up?

MYRRHINE:

Yes, darling, what *is* on your mind, after all?

LYSISTRATA:

I'll tell you. —But first, one little question.

MYRRHINE:

Well?

LYSISTRATA:

It's your husbands. Fathers of your children. Doesn't it bother you
that they're always off with the Army? I'll stake my life,
not one of you has a man in the house this minute!

KALONIKE:

Mine's been in Thrace the last five months, keeping an eye
on that General.°

MYRRHINE:

Mine's been in Pylos for seven.

LAMPITO:

And mahn,
whenever he gets a *dis*charge, he goes raht back
with that li'l ole shield of his, and enlists again!

LYSISTRATA:

And not the ghost of a lover to be found!
From the very day the war began—
those Milesians!
I could skin them alive!
—I've not seen so much, even,
as one of those leather consolation prizes.—
But there! What's important is: If I've found a way
to end the war, are you with me?

MYRRHINE:

I should *say* so!
Even if I have to pawn my best dress and
drink up the proceeds.°

KALONIKE:

Me, too! Even if they split me
right up the middle, like a flounder.

LAMPITO:

Ah'm shorely with you.
Ah'd crawl up Taÿgetos on mah knees
if that'd bring peace.

---

[84]**that General** His name was Eukrates, and [Scholiast] describes him as "an Athenian general, for sale, a traitor, and a mercenary." (Fitts) [94]**drink up the proceeds** The Athenian women were frequently satirized as being heavy drinkers. The joke here, such as it is, depends upon a rhetorical trope by which the expected conclusion of a sentence is twisted into an unexpected incongruity. Thus, one would have expected Myrrhine to say that she would pawn her best dress and contribute the proceeds to the Cause. (Fitts)

LYSISTRATA:
All right, then; here it is:
Women! Sisters!
If we really want our men to make peace,
we must be ready to give up—
MYRRHINE:
Give up what?
Quick, tell us!
LYSISTRATA:
But *will* you?
MYRRHINE:
We will, even if it kills us.
LYSISTRATA:
Then we must give up going to bed with our men.

[*Long silence*]

Oh? So now you're sorry? Won't look at me?
Doubtful? Pale? All teary-eyed?
But come: be frank with me.
Will you do it, or not? Well? Will you do it?
MYRRHINE:
I couldn't. No.
Let the war go on.
KALONIKE:
Nor I. Let the war go on.
LYSISTRATA:
You, you little flounder,
ready to be split up the middle?
KALONIKE:
Lysistrata, no!
I'd walk through fire for you—you *know* I would!—, but don't
ask us to give up *that!* Why, there's nothing like it!
LYSISTRATA:
And you?
BOIOTIAN:
No. I must say *I'd* rather walk through fire.
LYSISTRATA:
What an utterly perverted sex we women are!
No wonder poets write tragedies about us.
There's only one thing we can think of.
But you from Sparta:
if you stand by me, we may win yet! Will you?
It means so much!
LAMPITO:
Ah sweah, it means *too* much!
By the Two Goddesses, it does! Asking a girl

to sleep—Heaven knows how long!—in a great big bed
with nobody there but herself! But Ah'll stay with you!
Peace comes first!

LYSISTRATA:
Spoken like a true Spartan!

KALONIKE:
But if—
oh dear!
—if we give up what you tell us to,
will there *be* any peace?

LYSISTRATA:
Why, mercy, of course there will!
We'll just sit snug in our very thinnest gowns,
perfumed and powdered from top to bottom, and those men
simply won't stand still! And when we say No,
they'll go out of their minds! And there's your peace.
You can take my word for it.

LAMPITO:
Ah seem to remember
that Colonel Menelaos threw his sword away
when he saw Helen's breast° all bare.

KALONIKE:
But, goodness me!
What if they just get up and leave us?

LYSISTRATA:
In that case
we'll have to fall back on ourselves, I suppose.
But they won't.

KALONIKE:
I must say that's not much help. But
what if they drag us into the bedroom?

LYSISTRATA:
Hang on to the door.

KALONIKE:
What if they slap us?

LYSISTRATA:
If they do, you'd better give in.
But be sulky about it. Do I have to teach you how?
You know there's no fun for men when they have to force you.
There are millions of ways of getting them to see reason.
Don't you worry: a man
doesn't like it unless the girl co-operates.

---

[129]**when he saw Helen's breast** An allusion to Euripides' Andromache, 627, sqq; where Menelaos, about to stab his faithless wife, is overcome by her beauty and drops his sword. (Fitts)

KALONIKE:
I suppose so. Oh, all right. We'll go along.

LAMPITO:
Ah imagine us Spahtans can arrange a peace. But you
Athenians! Why, you're just war-mongerers!

LYSISTRATA:
Leave that to me.
I know how to make them listen.

LAMPITO:
Ah don't see how.
After all, they've got their boats; and there's lots of money
piled up in the Akropolis.

LYSISTRATA:
The Akropolis? Darling,
we're taking over the Akropolis today!
That's the older women's job. All the rest of us
are going to the Citadel to sacrifice—you understand me?
And once there, we're in for good!

LAMPITO:
Whee! Up the rebels!
Ah can see you're a good strat*ee*gist.

LYSISTRATA:
Well, then, Lampitô,
what we have to do now is take a solemn oath.

LAMPITO:
Say it. We'll sweah.

LYSISTRATA:
This is it.
—But where's our Inner Guard?
—Look, Guard: you see this shield?
Put it down here. Now bring me the victim's entrails.

KALONIKE:
But the oath?

LYSISTRATA:
You remember how in Aischylos' *Seven*°
they killed a sheep and swore on a shield? Well, then?

KALONIKE:
But I don't see how you can swear for peace on a shield.

LYSISTRATA:
What else do you suggest?

KALONIKE:
Why not a white horse?
We could swear by that.

---

155 **Aischylos' Seven** One of the plays of the tragedian Aischylos was *Seven Against Thebes*.

LYSISTRATA:

And where will you get a white horse?

KALONIKE:

I never thought of that. *What* can we do?

LYSISTRATA:

I have it!

Let's set this big black wine-bowl on the ground
and pour in a gallon or so of Thasian, and swear
not to add one drop of water.

LAMPITO:

Ah lahk *that* oath!

LYSISTRATA:

Bring the bowl and the wine-jug.

KALONIKE:

Oh, what a simply *huge* one!

LYSISTRATA:

Set it down. Girls, place your hands on the gift-offering.
O Goddess of Persuasion! And thou, O Loving-cup
Look upon this our sacrifice, and
be gracious!

KALONIKE:

See the blood spill out. How red and pretty it is!

LAMPITO:

And Ah must say it smells good.

MYRRHINE:

Let me swear first!

KALONIKE:

No, by Aphroditê, we'll match for it!

LYSISTRATA:

Lampitô: all of you women: come, touch the bowl,
and repeat after me—remember, this is an oath—:
I WILL HAVE NOTHING TO DO WITH MY HUSBAND OR MY LOVER

KALONIKE:

I will have nothing to do with my husband or my lover

LYSISTRATA:

THOUGH HE COME TO ME IN PITIABLE CONDITION

KALONIKE:

Though he come to me in pitiable condition
(Oh Lysistrata! This is killing me!)

LYSISTRATA:

IN MY HOUSE I WILL BE UNTOUCHABLE

KALONIKE:

In my house I will be untouchable

LYSISTRATA:

IN MY THINNEST SAFFRON SILK

KALONIKE:

In my thinnest saffron silk

LYSISTRATA:
AND MAKE HIM LONG FOR ME.

KALONIKE:
And make him long for me.

LYSISTRATA:
I WILL NOT GIVE MYSELF

KALONIKE:
I will not give myself

LYSISTRATA:
AND IF HE CONSTRAINS ME

KALONIKE:
And if he constrains me

LYSISTRATA:
I WILL BE COLD AS ICE AND NEVER MOVE

KALONIKE:
I will be cold as ice and never move

LYSISTRATA:
I WILL NOT LIFT MY SLIPPERS TOWARD THE CEILING

KALONIKE:
I will not lift my slippers toward the ceiling

LYSISTRATA:
OR CROUCH ON ALL FOURS LIKE THE LIONESS IN THE CARVING

KALONIKE:
Or crouch on all fours like the lioness in the carving

LYSISTRATA:
AND IF I KEEP THIS OATH LET ME DRINK FROM THIS BOWL

KALONIKE:
And if I keep this oath let me drink from this bowl

LYSISTRATA:
IF NOT, LET MY OWN BOWL BE FILLED WITH WATER.

KALONIKE:
If not, let my own bowl be filled with water.

LYSISTRATA:
You have all sworn?

MYRRHINE: We have.

LYSISTRATA: Then thus
I sacrifice the victim.

[*Drinks largely*]

KALONIKE: Save some for us!
Here's to you, darling, and to you, and to you!

[*Loud cries off-stage*]

LAMPITO:
What's all *that* whoozy-goozy?

LYSISTRATA:

Just what I told you.
The older women have taken the Akropolis.
Now you, Lampitô,
rush back to Sparta. We'll take care of things here. Leave
these girls here for hostages.
The rest of you,
up to the Citadel: and mind you push in the bolts.

KALONIKE:

But the men? Won't they be after us?

LYSISTRATA:

Just you leave
the men to me. There's not fire enough in the world,
or threats either, to make me open these doors
except on my own terms.

KALONIKE:

I hope not, by Aphroditê!
After all,
we've got a reputation for bitchiness to live up to.

[*Exeunt*]

PÁRODOS:° CHORAL EPISODE

[*The hillside just under the Akropolis. Enter* CHORUS OF OLD MEN *with burning torches and braziers; much puffing and coughing.*]

KORYPHAIOS^{m}:

Forward march, Drakês, old friend: never you mind
that damn big log banging hell down on your back.

STROPHE°

CHORUS^{m}:

There's this to be said for longevity:
You see things you thought that you'd never see.
Look, Strymodôros, who would have thought it?
We've caught it—
the New Feminity!
The wives of our bosom, our board, our bed—
Now, by the gods, they've gone ahead
And taken the Citadel (Heaven knows why!),

°**parodos** entry of the Chorus. °**strophe, antistrophe** During the strophe, one section of its song or chant, the Chorus moves toward one side of the orchestral place; in the next section, the antistrophe, the Chorus moves back in the opposite direction.

Profanèd the sacred statuar-y,°
And barred the doors,
The subversive whores!

KORYPHAIOS[m]:
Shake a leg there, Philûrgos, man: the Akropolis or bust!
Put the kindling around here. We'll build one almighty big
bonfire for the whole bunch of bitches, every last one;
and the first we fry will be old Lykôn's woman.

Antistrophe

CHORUS[m]:
They're not going to give me the old horse-laugh!
No, by Deméter, they won't pull this off!
Think of Kleómenês: even he
Didn't go free
till he brought me his stuff.
A good man he was, all stinking and shaggy,
Bare as an eel except for the bag he
Covered his rear with. God, what a mess!
Never a bath in six years, I'd guess.
Pure Sparta, man!
He also ran.

KORYPHAIOS[m]:
That was a siege, friends! Seventeen ranks strong
we slept at the Gate. And shall we not do as much
against these women, whom God and Euripides hate?
If we don't, I'll turn in my medals from Marathon.

Strophe 2

CHORUS[m]:
Onward and upward! A little push,
And we're there.
Ouch, my shoulders! I could wish
For a pair
Of good strong oxen. Keep your eye
On the fire there, it mustn't die.
Akh! Akh!
The smoke would make a cadaver cough!

Antistrophe 2

Holy Heraklês, a hot spark
Bit my eye!

---

10 **the sacred statuary** The august statue of Athena Polias, which fell from heaven upon the Akropolis. (Fitts)

Damn this hellfire, damn this work!
So say I.
Onward and upward just the same.
(Lachês, remember the Goddess: for shame!)
Akh! Akh!
The smoke would make a cadaver cough!

KORYPHAIOS[m]:

At last (and let us give suitable thanks to God
for his infinite mercies) I have managed to bring
my personal flame to the common goal. It breathes, it lives.
Now, gentlemen, let us consider. Shall we insert
the torch, say, into the brazier, and thus extract
a kindling brand? And shall we then, do you think,
push on to the gate like valiant sheep? On the whole, yes.
But I would have you consider this, too: if they—
I refer to the women—should refuse to open,
what then? Do we set the doors afire
and smoke them out? At ease, men. Meditate.
Akh, the smoke! Woof! What we really need
is the loan of a general or two from the Samos Command.
At least we've got this lumber off our backs.
That's something. And now let's look to our fire.

O Pot, brave Brazier, touch my torch with flame!
Victory, Goddess, I invoke thy name!
Strike down these paradigms of female pride,
And we shall hang our trophies up inside.

[*Enter* CHORUS OF OLD WOMEN *on the walls of the Akropolis, carrying jars of water*]

KORYPHAIOS[w]:

Smoke, girls, smoke! There's smoke all over the place!
Probably fire, too. Hurry, girls! Fire! Fire!

Strophe 1

CHORUS[w]:

Nikodikê, run!
Or Kalykê's done
To a turn, and poor Kritylla's
Smoked like a ham.
Damn
These old men! Are we too late?
I nearly died down at the place
Where we fill our jars:
Slaves pushing and jostling—
Such a hustling
I never saw in all my days.

Antistrophe 1

But here's water at last.
Haste, sisters, haste!
Slosh it on them, slosh it down,
The silly old wrecks!
Sex
Almighty! What they want's
A hot bath? Good. Send one down.
Athêna of Athens town,
Trito-born!° Helm of Gold!
Cripple the old
Firemen! Help us help them drown!

[*The* OLD MEN *capture a woman,* STRATYLLIS.]

STRATYLLIS:
Let me go! Let me go!

KORYPHAIOS[w]:
You walking corpses,
have you no shame?

KORYPHAIOS[m]:
I wouldn't have believed it!
An army of women in the Akropolis!

KORYPHAIOS[w]:
So we scare you, do we? Grandpa, you've seen
only our pickets yet!

KORYPHAIOS[m]:
Hey, Phaidrias!
Help me with the necks of these jabbering hens!

KORYPHAIOS[w]:
Down with your pots, girls! We'll need both hands
if these antiques attack us.

KORYPHAIOS[m]:
Want your face kicked in?

KORYPHAIOS[w]:
Want your balls chewed off?

KORYPHAIOS[m]:
Look out! I've got a stick!

KORYPHAIOS[w]:
You lay a half-inch of your stick on Stratyllis,
and you'll never stick again!

KORYPHAIOS[m]:
Fall apart!

---

88 **Trito-born!** Name for Athena, who, according to some accounts, was born near Lake Tritonis, in Libya. (Fitts)

KORYPHAIOS[w]:
I'll spit up your guts!
KORYPHAIOS[m]:
Euripides!° Master!
How well you knew women!
KORYPHAIOS[w]:
Listen to him! Rhodippê,
up with the pots!
KORYPHAIOS[m]:
Demolition of God,
what good are your pots?
KORYPHAIOS[w]:
You refugee from the tomb,
what good is your fire?
KORYPHAIOS[m]:
Good enough to make a pyre
to barbecue you!
KORYPHAIOS[w]:
We'll squizzle your kindling!
KORYPHAIOS[m]:
You think so?
KORYPHAIOS[w]:
Yah! Just hang around a while!
KORYPHAIOS[m]:
Want a touch of my torch?
KORYPHAIOS[w]:
It needs a good soaping.
KORYPHAIOS[m]:
How about you?
KORYPHAIOS[w]:
Soap for a senile bridegroom!
KORYPHAIOS[m]:
Senile? Hold your trap!
KORYPHAIOS[w]:
Just *you* try to hold it!
KORYPHAIOS[m]:
The yammer of women!
KORYPHAIOS[w]:
Oh is that so?
You're not in the jury room now, you know.
KORYPHAIOS[m]:
Gentlemen, I beg you, burn off that woman's hair!
KORYPHAIOS[w]:
Let it come down!

---

102 **Euripides** a Greek writer of tragedies, sometimes thought to be somewhat cynical or disrespectful.

[*They empty their pots on the men.*]

KORYPHAIOS^{m}:
What a way to drown!

KORYPHAIOS^{w}:
Hot, hey?

KORYPHAIOS^{m}:
Say,
enough!

KORYPHAIOS^{w}:
Dandruff
needs watering. I'll make you
nice and fresh.

KORYPHAIOS^{m}:
For God's sake, you,
hold off!

SCENE I

[*Enter a* COMMISSIONER *accompanied by four constables*]

COMMISSIONER:
These degenerate women! What a racket of little drums,
what a yapping for Adonis on every house-top!
It's like the time in the Assembly when I was listening
to a speech—out of order, as usual—by that fool
Demostratos, all about troops for Sicily,°
that kind of nonsense—
and there was his wife
trotting around in circles howling
Alas for Adonis!—
and Demostratos insisting
we must draft every last Zakynthian that can walk—
and his wife up there on the roof,
drunk as an owl, yowling
Oh weep for Adonis!—
and that damned ox Demostratos
mooing away through the rumpus. That's what we get
for putting up with this wretched woman-business!

KORYPHAIOS^{m}:
Sir, you haven't heard the half of it. They laughed at us!
Insulted us! They took pitchers of water
and nearly drowned us! We're still wringing out our clothes,
for all the world like unhousebroken brats.

5**troops for Sicily** A reference to the elaborate Sicilian Expedition (415 B.C.), in which Athens suffered a calamitous defeat from which she never recovered. (Fitts)

COMMISSIONER:

Serves you right, by Poseidon!
Whose fault is it if these women-folk of ours
get out of hand? We coddle them,
we teach them to be wasteful and loose. You'll see a husband
go into a jeweler's. 'Look,' he'll say,
'jeweler,' he'll say, 'you remember that gold choker
'you made for my wife? Well, she went to a dance last night
'and broke the clasp. Now, I've got to go to Sálamis,
'and can't be bothered. Run over to my house tonight,
'will you, and see if you can put it together for her.'
Or another one
goes to a cobbler—a good strong workman, too,
with an awl that was never meant for child's play. 'Here,'
he'll tell him, 'one of my wife's shoes is pinching
'her little toe. Could you come up about noon
'and stretch it out for her?'
Well, what do you expect?
Look at me, for example. I'm a Public Officer,
and it's one of my duties to pay off the sailors.
And where's the money? Up there in the Akropolis!
And those blasted women slam the door in my face!
But what are we waiting for?
—Look here, constable,
stop sniffing around for a tavern, and get us
some crowbars. We'll force their gates! As a matter of fact,
I'll do a little forcing myself.

[*Enter* LYSISTRATA, *above, with* MYRRHINE, KALONIKE, *and the* BOIOTIAN.]

LYSISTRATA:

No need of forcing.
Here I am, of my own accord. And all this talk
about locked doors—! We don't need locked doors,
but just the least bit of common sense.

COMMISSIONER:

Is that so, ma'am!
—Where's my constable?
—Constable,
arrest that woman, and tie her hands behind her.

LYSISTRATA:

If he touches me, I swear by Artemis
there'll be one scamp dropped from the public pay-roll tomorrow!

COMMISSIONER:

Well, constable? You're not afraid, I suppose? Grab her,
two of you, around the middle!

KALONIKE:

No, by Pándrosos!°

Lay a hand on her, and I'll jump on you so hard
your guts will come out the back door!

COMMISSIONER:

That's what *you* think!

Where's the sergeant?—Here, you: tie up that trollop first,
the one with the pretty talk!

MYRRHINE:

By the Moon-Goddess,

just try! They'll have to scoop you up with a spoon!

COMMISSIONER:

Another one!

Officer, seize that woman!

I swear

I'll put an end to this riot!

BOIOTIAN:

By the Taurian,

one inch closer, you'll be one screaming bald-head!

COMMISSIONER:

Lord, what a mess! And my constables seem ineffective.
But—women get the best of us? By God, no!

—Skythians!

Close ranks and forward march!

LYSISTRATA:

'Forward,' indeed!

By the Two Goddesses, what's the sense in *that?*
They're up against four companies of women
armed from top to bottom.

COMMISSIONER:

Forward, my Skythians!

LYSISTRATA:

Forward, yourselves, dear comrades!
You grainlettucebeanseedmarket girls!
You garlicandonionbreadbakery girls!
Give it to 'em! Knock 'em down! Scratch 'em!
Tell 'em what you think of 'em!

[*General mêlée; the Skythians yield*]

—Ah, that's enough!

Sound a retreat: good soldiers don't rob the dead.

COMMISSIONER:

A nice day *this* has been for the police!

---

[52]**Pandrosos** In myth, priestess of Athena who jumped from the Akropolis to her death.

LYSISTRATA:

Well, there you are.—Did you really think we women would be driven like slaves? Maybe now you'll admit that a woman knows something about spirit.

COMMISSIONER:

Spirit enough, especially spirits in bottles! Dear Lord Apollo!

KORYPHAIOS ^{m}:

Your Honor, there's no use talking to them. Words mean nothing whatever to wild animals like these. Think of the sousing they gave us! and the water was not, I believe, of the purest.

KORYPHAIOS ^{w}:

You shouldn't have come after us. And if you try it again, you'll be one eye short!—Although, as a matter of fact, what I like best is just to stay at home and read, like a sweet little bride: never hurting a soul, no, never going out. But if you *must* shake hornets' nests, look out for the hornets.

Strophe 1

CHORUS ^{m}:

Of all the beasts that God hath wrought
What monster's worse than woman?
Who shall encompass with his thought
Their guile unending? No man.

They've seized the Heights, the Rock, the Shrine—
But to what end? I wot not.
Sure there's some clue to their design!
Have you the key? I thought not.

KORYPHAIOS ^{m}:

We might question them, I suppose. But I warn you, sir, don't believe anything you hear! It would be un-Athenian not to get to the bottom of this plot.

COMMISSIONER:

Very well. My first question is this: Why, so help you God, did you bar the gates of the Akropolis?

LYSISTRATA:

Why? To keep the money, of course. No money, no war.

COMMISSIONER:

You think that money's the cause of war?

LYSISTRATA:

I do.

Money brought about that Peisandros business°
and all the other attacks on the State. Well and good!
They'll not get another cent here!

COMMISSIONER:
And what will you do?

LYSISTRATA:
What a question! From now on, we intend
to control the Treasury.

COMMISSIONER:
Control the Treasury!

LYSISTRATA:
Why not? Does that seem strange? After all,
we control our household budgets.

COMMISSIONER:
But that's different!

LYSISTRATA:
'Different'? What do you mean?

COMMISSIONER:
I mean simply this:
it's the Treasury that pays for National Defense.

LYSISTRATA:
Unnecessary. We propose to abolish war.

COMMISSIONER:
Good God.—And National Security?

LYSISTRATA:
Leave that to us.

COMMISSIONER:
You?

LYSISTRATA:
Us.

COMMISSIONER: We're done for, then!

LYSISTRATA:
Never mind.
We women will save you in spite of yourselves.

COMMISSIONER:
What nonsense!

LYSISTRATA:
If you like. But you must accept it, like it or not.

COMMISSIONER:
Why, this is downright subversion!

LYSISTRATA:
Maybe it is.
But we're going to save you, Judge.

---

[104]**that Peisandros business** Peisandros, an Athenian politician credited with responsibility for the overthrow of democracy, was condemned for treason *in absentia.*

COMMISSIONER:
I don't *want* to be saved.

LYSISTRATA:
Tut. The death-wish. All the more reason.

COMMISSIONER:
But the idea
of women bothering themselves about peace and war!

LYSISTRATA:
Will you listen to me?

COMMISSIONER:
Yes. But be brief, or I'll—

LYSISTRATA:
This is no time for stupid threats.

COMMISSIONER:
By the gods,
I can't stand any more!

AN OLD WOMAN:
Can't stand? Well, well.

COMMISSIONER:
That's enough out of you, you old buzzard!
Now, Lysistrata: tell me what you're thinking.

LYSISTRATA:
Glad to.
Ever since this war began
We women have been watching you men, agreeing with you,
keeping our thoughts to ourselves. That doesn't mean
we were happy: we weren't, for we saw how things were going;
but we'd listen to you at dinner
arguing this way and that.
—Oh you, and your big
Top Secrets!—
And then we'd grin like little patriots
(though goodness knows we didn't feel like grinning) and ask you:
'Dear, did the Armistice come up in Assembly today?'
And you'd say, 'None of your business! Pipe down!', you'd say.
And so we would.

AN OLD WOMAN:
I wouldn't have, by God!

COMMISSIONER:
You'd have taken a beating, then!
—Go on.

LYSISTRATA:
Well, we'd be quiet. But then, you know, all at once
you men would think up something worse than ever.
Even *I* could see it was fatal. And, 'Darling,' I'd say,
'have you gone completely mad?' And my husband would look at me
and say, 'Wife, you've got your weaving to attend to.

'Mind your tongue, if you don't want a slap. "War's
'"a man's affair"!'°

COMMISSIONER:
Good words, and well pronounced.

LYSISTRATA:
You're a fool if you think so.
It was hard enough
to put up with all this banquet-hall strategy.
But then we'd hear you out in the public square:
'Nobody left for the draft-quota here in Athens?'
you'd say; and, 'No,' someone else would say, 'not a man!'
And so we women decided to rescue Greece.
You might as well listen to us now: you'll have to, later.

COMMISSIONER:
You rescue Greece? Absurd.

LYSISTRATA:
You're the absurd one.

COMMISSIONER:
You expect me to take orders from a woman?
I'd die first!

LYSISTRATA:
Heavens, if that's what's bothering you, take my veil,
here, and wrap it around your poor head.

KALONIKE:
Yes,
and you can have my market-basket, too.
Go home, tighten your girdle, do the washing, mind
your beans! 'War's
a woman's affair'!

KORYPHAIOS [W]:
Ground pitchers! Close ranks!

Antistrophe

CHORUS [W]:
This is a dance that I know well,
My knees shall never yield.
Wobble and creak I may, but still
I'll keep the well-fought field.

Valor and grace march on before,
Love prods us from behind.
Our slogan is EXCELSIOR,
Our watchword SAVE MANKIND.

---

145 **"War's / a man's affair"** quoted from *Iliad* VI:492; Hektor to Andromache. (Fitts)

KORYPHAIOS [W]:

Women, remember your grandmothers! Remember
that little old mother of yours, what a stinger she was!
On, on, never slacken. There's a strong wind astern!

LYSISTRATA:

O Erôs of delight! O Aphroditê! Kyprian!°
If ever desire has drenched our breasts or dreamed
in our thighs, let it work so now on the men of Hellas
that they shall tail us through the land, slaves, slaves
to Woman, Breaker of Armies!

COMMISSIONER:

And if we do?

LYSISTRATA:

Well, for one thing, we shan't have to watch you
going to market, a spear in one hand, and heaven knows
what in the other.

KALONIKE:

Nicely said, by Aphroditê!

LYSISTRATA:

As things stand now, you're neither men nor women.
Armor clanking with kitchen pans and pots—
you sound like a pack of Korybantês!°

COMMISSIONER:

A man must do what a man must do.

LYSISTRATA:

So I'm told.
But to see a General, complete with Gorgon-shield,
jingling along the dock to buy a couple of herrings!

KALONIKE:

I saw a Captain the other day—lovely fellow he was,
nice curly hair—sitting on his horse; and—can you believe it?—
he'd just bought some soup, and was pouring it into his helmet!
And there was a soldier from Thrace
swishing his lance like something out of Euripides,
and the poor fruit-store woman got so scared
that she ran away and let him have his figs free!

COMMISSIONER:

All this is beside the point.
Will you be so kind
as to tell me how you mean to save Greece?

LYSISTRATA:

Of course.
Nothing could be simpler.

---

[172]**Kyprian** Aphrodite was thought to have a special association with Cyprus. She is therefore sometimes called "the Cyprian." [182]**Korybantes** Priests of the Great Mother goddess in Phrygia; their celebrations of worship took the form of orgiastic dance.

COMMISSIONER:

I assure you, I'm all ears.

LYSISTRATA:

Do you know anything about weaving?
Say the yarn gets tangled: we thread it
this way and that through the skein, up and down,
until it's free. And it's like that with war.
We'll send our envoys
up and down, this way and that, all over Greece,
until it's finished.

COMMISSIONER:

Yarn? Thread? Skein?
Are you out of your mind? I tell you,
war is a serious business.

LYSISTRATA:

So serious
that I'd like to go on talking about weaving.

COMMISSIONER:

All right. Go ahead.

LYSISTRATA:

The first thing we have to do
is to wash our yarn, get the dirt out of it.
You see? Isn't there too much dirt here in Athens?
You must wash those men away.
Then our spoiled wool—
that's like your job-hunters, out for a life
of no work and big pay. Back to the basket,
citizens or not, allies or not,
or friendly immigrants.
And your colonies?
Hanks of wool lost in various places. Pull them
together, weave them into one great whole,
and our voters are clothed for ever.

COMMISSIONER:

It would take a woman
to reduce state questions to a matter of carding and weaving.

LYSISTRATA:

You fool! Who were the mothers whose sons sailed off
to fight for Athens in Sicily?

COMMISSIONER:

Enough!
I beg you, do not call back those memories.

LYSISTRATA:

And then,
instead of the love that every woman needs,
we have only our single beds, where we can dream
of our husbands off with the Army.

Bad enough for wives!
But what about our girls, getting older every day,
and older, and no kisses?

COMMISSIONER:
Men get older, too.

LYSISTRATA:
Not in the same sense.
A soldier's discharged,
and he may be bald and toothless, yet he'll find
a pretty young thing to go to bed with.
But a woman!
Her beauty is gone with the first grey hair.
She can spend her time
consulting the oracles and the fortune-tellers,
but they'll never send her a husband.

COMMISSIONER:
Still, if a man can rise to the occasion—

LYSISTRATA:
Rise? Rise, yourself!

[*Furiously*]

Go invest in a coffin!
You've money enough.
I'll bake you
a cake for the Underworld.
And here's your funeral
wreath!

[*She pours water upon him.*]

MYRRHINE:
And here's another!

[*More water*]

KALONIKE:
And here's
my contribution!

[*More water*]

LYSISTRATA:
What are you waiting for?
All aboard Styx Ferry!
Charôn's calling for you!
It's sailing-time: don't disrupt the schedule!

COMMISSIONER:

The insolence of women! And to me!
No, by God, I'll go back to town and show
the rest of the Commission what might happen to them.

[*Exit* COMMISSIONER]

LYSISTRATA:

Really, I suppose we should have laid out his corpse
on the doorstep, in the usual way.
But never mind.
We'll give him the rites of the dead tomorrow morning.

[*Exit* LYSISTRATA *with* MYRRHINE *and* KALONIKE.]

PARÁBASIS:° CHORAL EPISODE

Ode 1

KORYPHAIOS^{m}:

Sons of Liberty, awake! The day of glory is at hand.

CHORUS^{m}:

I smell tyranny afoot, I smell it rising from the land.
I scent a trace of Hippias, I sniff upon the breeze
A dismal Spartan hogo that suggests King Kleisthenês.
Strip, strip for action, brothers!
Our wives, aunts, sisters, mothers
Have sold us out: the streets are full of godless female rages.
Shall we stand by and let our women confiscate our wages?

Epirrhema° 1

KORYPHAIOS^{m}:

Gentlemen, it's a disgrace to Athens, a disgrace
to all that Athens stands for, if we allow these grandmas
to jabber about spears and shields and making friends
with the Spartans. What's a Spartan? Give me a wild wolf
any day. No. They want the Tyranny back, I suppose.
Are we going to take that? No. Let us look like
the innocent serpent, but be the flower under it,
as the poet sings. And just to begin with,
I propose to poke a number of teeth
down the gullet of that harridan over there.

°**parabasis** The poet addresses the audience through the agency of the Chorus. °**epirrhema** a satiric speech on current affairs.

Antode 1

KORYPHAIOS[w]:

Oh, is that so? When you get home, your own mammá won't know you!

CHORUS[w]:

Who do you think we are, you senile bravos? Well, I'll show you.
I bore the sacred vessels° in my eighth year, and at ten
I was pounding out the barley° for Athêna Goddess; then
 They made me Little Bear
 At the Braunonian Fair;
I'd held the Holy Basket° by the time I was of age,
The Blessed Dry Figs had adorned my plump décolletage.

Antepirrhema 1

KORYPHAIOS[w]:

A 'disgrace to Athens', am I, just at the moment
I'm giving Athens the best advice she ever had?
Don't I pay taxes to the State? Yes, I pay them
in baby boys. And what do you contribute,
you impotent horrors? Nothing but waste: all
our Treasury,° dating back to the Persian Wars,
gone! rifled! And not a penny out of your pockets!
Well, then? Can you cough up an answer to that?
Look out for your own gullet, or you'll get a crack
from this old brogan that'll make your teeth see stars!

Ode 2

CHORUS[m]:

Oh insolence!
Am I unmanned?
Incontinence!
Shall my scarred hand
Strike never a blow
To curb this flow-
ing female curse?

Leipsydrion!°
Shall I betray

---

[21]**I bore the vessels** Annually, four girls of high birth, between the ages of seven and eleven, were appointed acolytes to Athena in the Akropolis. (Fitts) [22]**I was pounding out the barley** At the age of ten, an aristocratic girl was eligible to be chosen as Mill-maid; her duty was to grind the sacred grain for Athena. (Fitts) [25]**the Holy Basket** The highest distinction of all. According to [Scholiast], the baskets containing objects sacred to Athena were of gold. (Fitts) [32]**our Treasury** A sum of money, originally contributed by Athens and her allies, intended to finance an extension of the sea-war against Persia. Since the failure of the Sicilian Expedition, the contributions of the allies had fallen off; and the fund itself was now being raided by Athenian politicians. (Fitts) [44]**Leipsydrion** Site of an Attic fort on its border with Boiotia.

The laurels won
On that great day?
Come, shake a leg,
Shed old age, beg
The years reverse!

Epirrhema 2

KORYPHAIOS[m]:

Give them an inch, and we're done for! We'll have them
launching boats next and planning naval strategy,
sailing down on us like so many Artemisias.
Or maybe they have ideas about the cavalry.
That's fair enough, women are certainly good
in the saddle. Just look at Mikôn's paintings,
all those Amazons wrestling with all those men!
On the whole, a straitjacket's their best uniform.

Antode 2

CHORUS[w]:

Tangle with me,
And you'll get cramps.
Ferocity
'S no use now, Gramps!
By the Two,
I'll get through
To you wrecks yet!

I'll scramble your eggs,
I'll burn your beans,
With my two legs.
You'll see such scenes
As never yet
Your two eyes met.
A curse? You bet!

Antepirrhema 2

KORYPHAIOS[w]:

If Lampitô stands by me, and that delicious Theban girl,
Ismênia—what good are *you?* You and your seven
Resolutions! Resolutions? Rationing Boiotian eels
and making our girls go without them at Hekatê's Feast!
That was statesmanship! And we'll have to put up with it
and all the rest of your decrepit legislation
until some patriot—God give him strength!—
grabs you by the neck and kicks you off the Rock.

SCENE II

[*Re-enter* LYSISTRATA *and her lieutenants*]

KORYPHAIOS^{W} [*Tragic tone*]:
Great Queen, fair Architect of our emprise,
Why lookst thou on us with foreboding eyes?

LYSISTRATA:
The behavior of these idiotic women!
There's something about the female temperament
that I can't bear!

KORYPHAIOS^{W}:
What in the world do you mean?

LYSISTRATA:
Exactly what I say.

KORYPHAIOS^{W}:
What dreadful thing has happened?
Come, tell us: we're all your friends.

LYSISTRATA:
It isn't easy
to say it; yet, God knows, we can't hush it up.

KORYPHAIOS^{W}:
Well, then? Out with it!

LYSISTRATA:
To put it bluntly,
we're dying to get laid.

KORYPHAIOS^{W}:
Almighty God!

LYSISTRATA:
Why bring God into it?—No, it's just as I say.
I can't manage them any longer: they've gone man-crazy,
they're all trying to get out.
Why, look:
one of them was sneaking out the back door
over there by Pan's cave,° another
was sliding down the walls with rope and tackle;
another was climbing aboard a sparrow, ready to take off
for the nearest brothel—I dragged *her* back by the hair!
They're all finding some reason to leave.
Look there!
There goes another one.
—Just a minute, you!
Where are you off to so fast?

FIRST WOMAN:
I've got to get home.
I've a lot of Milesian wool, and the worms are spoiling it.

---

[15]**Pan's cave** A grotto on the north side of the Akropolis, beneath the walls. (Fitts)

LYSISTRATA:

Oh bother you and your worms! Get back inside!

FIRST WOMAN:

I'll be back right away, I swear I will.
I just want to get it stretched out on my bed.

LYSISTRATA:

You'll do no such thing. You'll stay right here.

FIRST WOMAN:

And my wool?
You want it ruined?

LYSISTRATA:

Yes, for all I care.

SECOND WOMAN:

Oh dear! My lovely new flax from Amorgos—
I left it at home, all uncarded!

LYSISTRATA:

Another one!
And all she wants is someone to card her flax.
Get back in there!

SECOND WOMAN:

But I swear by the Moon-Goddess,
the minute I get it done, I'll be back!

LYSISTRATA:

I say No.
If you, why not all the other women as well?

THIRD WOMAN:

O Lady Eileithyia! Radiant goddess! Thou
intercessor for women in childbirth! Stay, I pray thee,
oh stay this parturition. Shall I pollute
a sacred spot?

LYSISTRATA:

And what's the matter with *you?*

THIRD WOMAN:

I'm having a baby—any minute now.

LYSISTRATA:

But you weren't pregnant yesterday.

THIRD WOMAN:

Well, I am today.
Let me go home for a midwife, Lysistrata:
there's not much time.

LYSISTRATA:

I never heard such nonsense.
What's that bulging under your cloak?

THIRD WOMAN:

A little baby boy.

LYSISTRATA:

It certainly isn't. But it's something hollow,
like a basin or—Why, it's the helmet of Athêna!
And you said you were having a baby.

THIRD WOMAN:

Well, I am! So there!

LYSISTRATA:

Then why the helmet?

THIRD WOMAN:

I was afraid that my pains
might begin here in the Akropolis; and I wanted
to drop my chick into it, just as the dear doves do.

LYSISTRATA:

Lies! Evasions!—But at least one thing's clear:
you can't leave the place before your purification.

THIRD WOMAN:

But I can't stay here in the Akropolis! Last night I dreamed
of the Snake.°

FIRST WOMAN:

And those horrible owls,° the noise they make!
I can't get a bit of sleep; I'm just about dead.

LYSISTRATA:

You useless girls, that's enough: Let's have no more lying.
Of course you want your men. But don't you imagine
that they want you just as much? I'll give you my word,
their nights must be pretty hard.
Just stick it out!
A little patience, that's all, and our battle's won.
I have heard an Oracle. Should you like to hear it?

FIRST WOMAN:

An Oracle? Yes, tell us!

LYSISTRATA:

Here is what it says:
WHEN SWALLOWS SHALL THE HOOPOE SHUN
AND SPURN HIS HOT DESIRE,
ZEUS WILL PERFECT WHAT THEY'VE BEGUN
AND SET THE LOWER HIGHER.

FIRST WOMAN:

Does that mean we'll be on top?

LYSISTRATA:

BUT IF THE SWALLOWS SHALL FALL OUT
AND TAKE THE HOOPOE'S BAIT,

---

52 **the Snake** This divine snake was the Guardian of the Temple, the peculiar Safeguard of the Akropolis. He never appeared, but each month a succulent cake was set out for him, and it always vanished overnight. (Fitts)
52 **those horrible owls** The Owl was sacred to Athena. (Fitts)

A CURSE MUST MARK THEIR HOUR OF DOUBT,
INFAMY SEAL THEIR FATE.

THIRD WOMAN:
I swear, *that* Oracle's all too clear.

FIRST WOMAN:
Oh the dear gods!

LYSISTRATA:
Let's not be downhearted, girls. Back to our places!
The god has spoken. How can we possibly fail him?

[*Exit* LYSISTRATA *with the dissident women*]

CHORAL EPISODE

Strophe

CHORUS[m]:
I know a little story that I learned way back in school
Goes like this:
Once upon a time there was a young man—and no fool—
Named Melanion; and his
One aversi-on was marriage. He loathed the very thought.
So he ran off to the hills, and in a special grot
Raised a dog, and spent his days
Hunting rabbits. And it says
That he never never never did come home.
It might be called a refuge *from* the womb.
All right,
all right,
all right!
We're as bright as young Melanion, and we hate the very sight
Of you women!

A MAN:
How about a kiss, old lady?

A WOMAN:
Here's an onion for your eye!

A MAN:
A kick in the guts, then?

A WOMAN:
Try, old bristle-tail, just try!

A MAN:
Yet they say Myronidês
On hands and knees
Looked just as shaggy fore and aft as I.

Antistrophe

CHORUS[W]:
Well, *I* know a little story, and it's just as good as yours.
Goes like this:
Once there was a man named Timon—a rough diamond, of course,
And that whiskery face of his
Looked like murder in the shrubbery. By God, he was a son
Of the Furies, let me tell you! And what did he do but run
From the world and all its ways,
Cursing mankind! And it says
That his choicest execrations as of then
Were leveled almost wholly at *old* men.
All right,
all right,
all right!
But there's one thing about Timon: he could always stand the sight
Of us women.

A WOMAN:
How about a crack in the jaw, Pop?

A MAN:
I can take it, Ma—no fear!

A WOMAN:
How about a kick in the face?

A MAN:
You'd reveal your old caboose?

A WOMAN:
What I'd show,
I'll have you know,
Is an instrument you're too far gone to use.

SCENE III

[*Re-enter* LYSISTRATA]

LYSISTRATA:
Oh, quick, girls, quick! Come here!

A WOMAN:
What is it?

LYSISTRATA:
A man.
A man simply bulging with love.
O Kyprian Queen,
O Paphian, O Kythereian! Hear us and aid us!

A WOMAN:
Where is this enemy?

LYSISTRATA:
Over there, by Demêter's shrine.

A WOMAN:
Damned if he isn't. But who *is* he?

MYRRHINE:
My husband.
Kinêsias.

LYSISTRATA:
Oh then, get busy! Tease him! Undermine him!
Wreck him! Give him everything—kissing, tickling, nudging,
whatever you generally torture him with—: give him everything
except what we swore on the wine we would not give.

MYRRHINE:
Trust me.

LYSISTRATA:
I do. But I'll help you get him started.
The rest of you women, stay back.

[*Enter* KINESIAS]

KINESIAS:
Oh God! Oh my God!
I'm stiff from lack of exercise. All I can do to stand up.

LYSISTRATA:
Halt! Who are you, approaching our lines?

KINESIAS:
Me? I.

LYSISTRATA:
A man?

KINESIAS:
You have eyes, haven't you?

LYSISTRATA:
Go away.

KINESIAS:
Who says so?

LYSISTRATA:
Officer of the Day.

KINESIAS:
Officer, I beg you,
by all the gods at once, bring Myrrhinê out.

LYSISTRATA:
Myrrhinê? And who, my good sir, are you?

KINESIAS:
Kinêsias. Last name's Pennison. Her husband.

LYSISTRATA:
Oh, of course. I beg your pardon. We're glad to see you.
We've heard so much about you. Dearest Myrrhinê
is always talking about 'Kinêsias'—never nibbles an egg
or an apple without saying
'Here's to Kinêsias!'

KINESIAS: Do you really mean it?

LYSISTRATA:
I do.
When we're discussing men, she always says
'Well, after all, there's nobody like Kinêsias!'

KINESIAS:
Good God.—Well, then, please send her down here.

LYSISTRATA:
And what do *I* get out of it?

KINESIAS:
A standing promise.

LYSISTRATA:
I'll take it up with her.

[*Exit* LYSISTRATA]

KINESIAS:
But be quick about it!
Lord, what's life without a wife? Can't eat. Can't sleep.
Every time I go home, the place is so empty, so
insufferably sad. Love's killing me. Oh,
hurry!

[*Enter* MANES, *a slave, with* KINESIAS' *baby; the voice of* MYRRHINE *is heard off-stage.*]

MYRRHINE:
But of course I love him! Adore him!—But no,
he hates love. No. I won't go down.

[*Enter* MYRRHINE, *above*]

KINESIAS:
Myrrhinê!
Darlingest Myrrhinette! Come down quick!

MYRRHINE:
Certainly not.

KINESIAS:
Not? But why, Myrrhinê?

MYRRHINE:
Why? You don't need me.

KINESIAS:

Need you? My God, *look* at me!

MYRRHINE:

So long!

[*Turns to go*]

KINESIAS:

Myrrhinê, Myrrhinê, Myrrhinê!
If not for my sake, for our child!

[*Pinches* BABY]

—All right, you: pipe up!

BABY:

Mummie! Mummie! Mummie!

KINESIAS:

You hear that?
Pitiful, I call it. Six days now
with never a bath; no food; enough to break your heart!

MYRRHINE:

My darlingest child! What a father *you* acquired!

KINESIAS:

At least come down for his sake.

MYRRHINE:

I suppose I must.
Oh, this mother business!°

[*Exit*]

KINESIAS:

How pretty she is! And younger!
The harder she treats me, the more bothered I get.

[MYRRHINE *enters, below*]

MYRRHINE:

Dearest child,
you're as sweet as your father's horrid. Give me a kiss.

KINESIAS:

Now don't you see how wrong it was to get involved
in this scheming League of women? It's bad
for us both.

MYRRHINE:

Keep your hands to yourself!

---

[44]**Oh, this mother business!** a parody of Euripides, *Iph. Aul.* 917. (Fitts)

KINESIAS:

But our house going to rack and ruin?

MYRRHINE:

I don't care.

KINESIAS:

And your knitting all torn to pieces by the chickens? Don't you care?

MYRRHINE:

Not at all.

KINESIAS:

And our debt to Aphroditê? Oh, *won't* you come back?

MYRRHINE:

No.—At least, not until you men make a treaty and stop this war.

KINESIAS:

Why, I suppose that might be arranged.

MYRRHINE:

Oh? Well, I suppose I might come down then. But meanwhile, I've sworn not to.

KINESIAS:

Don't worry.—Now, let's have fun.

MYRRHINE:

No! Stop it! I said no!

—Although, of course, I *do* love you.

KINESIAS:

I know you do. Darling Myrrhinê: come, shall we?

MYRRHINE:

Are you out of your mind? In front of the child?

KINESIAS:

Take him home, Manês.

[*Exit* MANES *with* BABY]

There. He's gone.

Come on! There's nothing to stop us now.

MYRRHINE:

You devil! But where?

KINESIAS:

In Pan's cave. What could be snugger than that?

MYRRHINE:

But my purification before I go back to the Citadel?

KINESIAS:

Wash in the Klepsydra.

MYRRHINE:

And my oath?

KINESIAS:

Leave the oath to me.
After all, I'm the man.

MYRRHINE:

Well . . . if you say so.
I'll go find a bed.

KINESIAS:

Oh, bother a bed! The ground's good enough for me.

MYRRHINE:

No. You're a bad man, but you deserve something better than dirt.

[*Exit* MYRRHINE]

KINESIAS:

What a love she is! And how thoughtful!

[*Re-enter* MYRRHINE]

MYRRHINE:

Here's your bed.
Now let me get my clothes off.
But, good horrors!
We haven't a mattress.

KINESIAS:

Oh, forget the mattress!

MYRRHINE:

No.
Just lying on blankets? Too sordid.

KINESIAS:

Give me a kiss.

MYRRHINE:

Just a second.

[*Exit* MYRRHINE]

KINESIAS:

I swear, I'll explode!

[*Re-enter* MYRRHINE]

MYRRHINE:

Here's your mattress.
I'll just take my dress off.
But look—
where's our pillow?

KINESIAS:

I don't *need* a pillow!

MYRRHINE:

Well, *I* do.

[*Exit* MYRRHINE]

KINESIAS:

I don't suppose even Heraklês
would stand for this!

[*Re-enter* MYRRHINE]

MYRRHINE:

There we are. Ups-a-daisy!

KINESIAS:

So we are. Well, come to bed.

MYRRHINE:

But I wonder:
is everything ready now?

KINESIAS:

I can swear to that. Come, darling!

MYRRHINE:

Just getting out of my girdle.
But remember, now,
what you promised about the treaty.

KINESIAS:

Yes, yes, yes!

MYRRHINE:

But no coverlet!

KINESIAS:

Damn it, I'll be
your coverlet!

MYRRHINE:

Be right back.

[*Exit* MYRRHINE]

KINESIAS: This girl and her coverlets
will be the death of me.

[*Re-enter* MYRRHINE]

MYRRHINE:
Here we are. Up you go!

KINESIAS:
Up? I've been up for ages.

MYRRHINE:
Some perfume?

KINESIAS:
No, by Apollo!

MYRRHINE:
Yes, by Aphroditê!
I don't care whether you want it or not.

[*Exit* MYRRHINE]

KINESIAS:
For love's sake, hurry!

[*Re-enter* MYRRHINE]

MYRRHINE:
Here, in your hand. Rub it right in.

KINESIAS:
Never cared for perfume.
And this is particularly strong. Still, here goes.

MYRRHINE:
What a nitwit I am! I brought you the Rhodian bottle.

KINESIAS:
Forget it.

MYRRHINE:
No trouble at all. You just wait here.

[*Exit* MYRRHINE]

KINESIAS:
God damn the man who invented perfume!

[*Re-enter* MYRRHINE]

MYRRHINE:
At last! The right bottle!

KINESIAS:
I've got the rightest
bottle of all, and it's right here waiting for you.
Darling, forget everything else. Do come to bed.

MYRRHINE:

Just let me get my shoes off.
—And, by the way,
you'll vote for the treaty?

KINESIAS:

I'll think about it.

[MYRRHINE *runs away*]

There! That's done it! The damned woman,
she gets me all bothered, she half kills me,
and off she runs! What'll I do? Where
can I get laid?
—And you, little prodding pal,
who's going to take care of *you?* No, you and I
had better get down to old Foxdog's Nursing Clinic.

CHORUS [m]:

Alas for the woes of man, alas
Specifically for you.
She's brought you to a pretty pass:
What are you going to do?
Split, heart! Sag, flesh! Proud spirit, crack!
Myrrhineê's got you on your back.

KINESIAS:

The agony, the protraction!

KORYPHAIOS [m]:

Friend,
What woman's worth a damn?
They bitch us all, world without end.

KINESIAS:

Yet they're so damned sweet, man!

HERALD:

A man after mah own haht! Seh, Ah thank you.

[*Exit* HERALD]

CHORAL EPISODE

Strophe

CHORUS [m]:

Oh these women! Where will you find
A slavering beast that's more unkind?
Where a hotter fire?
Give me a panther, any day.
He's not so merciless as they,
And panthers don't conspire.

Antistrophe

CHORUS[w]:

We may be hard, you silly old ass,
But who brought you to this stupid pass?
You're the ones to blame.
Fighting with us, your oldest friends,
Simply to serve your selfish ends—
Really, you have no shame!

KORYPHAIOS[m]:

No, I'm through with women for ever.

KORYPHAIOS[w]:

If you say so.
Still, you might put some clothes on. You look too absurd
standing around naked. Come, get into this cloak.

KORYPHAIOS[m]:

Thank you; you're right. I merely took it off
because I was in such a temper.

KORYPHAIOS[w]:

That's much better.
Now you resemble a man again.
Why have you been so horrid?
And look: there's some sort of insect in your eye.
Shall I take it out?

KORYPHAIOS[m]:

An insect, is it? So that's
what's been bothering me. Lord, yes: take it out!

KORYPHAIOS[w]:

You might be more polite.
—But, heavens!
What an enormous mosquito!

KORYPHAIOS[m]:

You've saved my life.
That mosquito was drilling an artesian well
in my left eye.

KORYPHAIOS[w]:

Let me wipe
those tears away.—And now: one little kiss?

KORYPHAIOS[m]:

No, no kisses.

KORYPHAIOS[w]:

You're so difficult.

KORYPHAIOS[m]:

You impossible women! How you do get around us!
The poet was right: Can't live with you, or without you.
But let's be friends.
And to celebrate, you might join us in an Ode.

Strophe 1

CHORUS[m and w]:

Let it never be said
That my tongue is malicious:
Both by word and by deed
I would set an example that's noble and gracious.
We've had sorrow and care
Till we're sick of the tune.
Is there anyone here
Who would like a small loan?
My purse is crammed,
As you'll soon find;
And you needn't pay me back if the Peace gets signed.

Strophe 2

I've invited to lunch
Some Karystian rips—
An esurient bunch,
But I've ordered a menu to water their lips.
I can still make soup
And slaughter a pig.
You're all coming, I hope?
But a bath first, I beg!
Walk right up
As though you owned the place,
And you'll get the front door slammed to in your face.

SCENE V

[*Enter* SPARTAN AMBASSADOR, *with entourage*]

KORYPHAIOS[m]:

The Commission has arrived from Sparta.
How oddly
they're walking!
Gentlemen, welcome to Athens!
How is life in Lakonia?

AMBASSADOR:

Need we discuss that?
Simply use your eyes.

CHORUS[m]:

The poor man's right:
What a sight!

AMBASSADOR:

Words fail me.
But come, gentlemen, call in your Commissioners,
and let's get down to a Peace.

CHORAGOS^{m}:

The state we're in! Can't bear a stitch below the waist. It's a kind of pelvic paralysis.

COMMISSIONER:

Won't somebody call Lysistrata? —Gentlemen, we're no better off than you.

AMBASSADOR:

So I see.

A SPARTAN:

Seh, do y'all feel a certain strain early in the morning?

AN ATHENIAN:

I do, sir. It's worse than a strain. A few more days, and there's nothing for us but Kleisthenês, that broken blossom.

CHORAGOS^{m}:

But you'd better get dressed again. You know these people going around Athens with chisels, looking for statues° of Hermês.

ATHENIAN:

Sir, you are right.

SPARTAN:

He certainly is! Ah'll put mah own clothes back on.

[*Enter* ATHENIAN COMMISSIONERS]

COMMISSIONER:

Gentlemen from Sparta, welcome. This is a sorry business.

SPARTAN: [*To one of his own group:*]

Colonel, we got dressed just in time. Ah sweah. if they'd seen us the way we were, there'd have been a new wah between the states.

COMMISSIONER:

Shall we call the meeting to order? Now, Lakonians, what's your proposal?

AMBASSADOR:

We propose to consider peace.

COMMISSIONER:

Good. That's on our minds, too. —Summon Lysistrata. We'll never get anywhere without her.

---

[16]**looking for statues** The statues were the Hermai, stone posts set up in various parts of Athens. Just before the sailing of the Sicilian Expedition, a group of anonymous vandals mutilated these statues with chisels. This and the women's Adonis-dirge were considered unhappy auguries. (Fitts)

AMBASSADOR:

Lysistrata?

Summon Lysis-*any*body!° Only, summon!

KORYPHAIOS [m]:

No need to summon:

here she is, herself.

[*Enter* LYSISTRATA]

COMMISSIONER:

Lysistrata! Lion of women!
This is your hour to be
hard and yielding, outspoken and shy, austere and
gentle. You see here
the best brains of Hellas (confused, I admit,
by your devious charming) met as one man
to turn the future over to you.

LYSISTRATA:

That's fair enough,
unless you men take it into your heads
to turn to each other instead of to us. But I'd know
soon enough if you did.
—Where is Reconciliation?
Go, some of you: bring her here.

[*Exeunt two women*]

And now, women,
lead the Spartan delegates to me: not roughly
or insultingly, as our men handle them, but gently,
politely, as ladies should. Take them by the hand,
or by anything else if they won't give you their hands.

[*The* SPARTANS *are escorted over.*]

There.—The Athenians next, by any convenient handle.

[*The* ATHENIANS *are escorted.*]

Stand there, please.—Now, all of you, listen to me.

[*During the following speech the two women re-enter, carrying an enormous statue of a naked girl; this is* RECONCILIATION.]

---

[26]**Summon Lysis-anybody!** He actually says "Lysistratos," grasping at random for a name. Lysistrata's name means Dissolver of Armies. (Fitts)

I'm only a woman, I know; but I've a mind,
and, I think, not a bad one: I owe it to my father
and to listening to the local politicians.
So much for that.
Now, gentlemen,
since I have you here, I intend to give you a scolding.
We are all Greeks.
Must I remind you of Thermopylai, of Olympia,
of Delphoi? names deep in all our hearts?
Are they not a common heritage?
Yet you men
go raiding through the country from both sides,
Greek killing Greek, storming down Greek cities—
and all the time the Barbarian across the sea
is waiting for his chance!
—That's my first point.

AN ATHENIAN:
Lord! I can hardly contain myself.

LYSISTRATA:
As for you Spartans:
Was it so long ago that Perikleidês
came here to beg our help? I can see him still,
his grey face, his sombre gown. And what did he want?
An army from Athens. All Messênê
was hot at your heels, and the sea-god splitting your land.
Well, Kimôn and his men,
four thousand strong, marched out and saved all Sparta.
And what thanks do we get? You come back to murder us.

AN ATHENIAN:
They're aggressors, Lysistrata!

A SPARTAN:
Ah admit it.
When Ah look at those laigs, Ah sweah Ah'll aggress mahself!

LYSISTRATA:
And you, Athenians: do you think you're blameless?
Remember that bad time when we were helpless,
and an army came from Sparta,
and that was the end of the Thessalian menace,
the end of Hippias and his allies.
And that was Sparta,
and only Sparta; but for Sparta, we'd be
cringing slaves today, not free Athenians.

[From this point, the male responses are less to LYSISTRATA *than to the statue.]*

A SPARTAN:
A well shaped speech.

AN ATHENIAN:

Certainly it has its points.

LYSISTRATA:

Why are we fighting each other? With all this history
of favors given and taken, what stands in the way
of making peace?

AMBASSADOR:

Spahta is ready, ma'am,
so long as we get that place back.

LYSISTRATA:

What place, man?

AMBASSADOR:

Ah refer to Pylos.

COMMISSIONER:

Not a chance, by God!

LYSISTRATA:

Give it to them, friend.

COMMISSIONER:

But—what shall we have to bargain with?

LYSISTRATA:

Demand something in exchange.

COMMISSIONER:

Good idea.—Well, then:
Cockeville first, and the Happy Hills, and the country
between the Legs of Mégara.

AMBASSADOR:

Mah government objects.

LYSISTRATA:

Over-ruled. Why fuss about a pair of legs?

[*General assent. The statue is removed.*]

AN ATHENIAN:

I want to get out of these clothes and start my plowing.

A SPARTAN:

Ah'll fertilize mahn first, by the Heavenly Twins!

LYSISTRATA:

And so you shall,
once you've made peace. If you are serious,
go, both of you, and talk with your allies.

COMMISSIONER:

Too much talk already. No, we'll stand together.
We've only one end in view. All that we want
is our women; and I speak for our allies.

AMBASSADOR:

Mah government concurs.

AN ATHENIAN:
So does Karystos.

LYSISTRATA:
Good.—But before you come inside
to join your wives at supper, you must perform
the usual lustration. Then we'll open
our baskets for you, and all that we have is yours.
But you must promise upright good behavior
from this day on. Then each man home with his woman!

AN ATHENIAN:
Let's get it over with.

A SPARTAN:
Lead on. Ah follow.

AN ATHENIAN:
Quick as a cat can wink!

[*Exeunt all but the* CHORUSES]

Antistrophe 1

CHORUS[W]:

Embroideries ánd
Twinkling ornaments ánd
Pretty dresses—I hand
Them all over to you, and with never a qualm.
They'll be nice for your daughters
On festival days
When the girls bring the Goddess
The ritual prize.
Come in, one and all:
Take what you will.
I've nothing here so tightly corked that you can't make it spill.

Antistrophe 2

You may search my house,
But you'll not find
The least thing of use,
Unless your two eyes are keener than mine.
Your numberless brats
Are half starved? and your slaves?
Courage, grandpa! I've lots
Of grain left, and big loaves.
I'll fill your guts,
I'll go the whole hog;
But if you come too close to me, remember: 'ware the dog!

[*Exeunt* CHORUSES]

ÉXODOS

[*A* DRUNKEN CITIZEN *enters, approaches the gate, and is halted by a sentry.*]

CITIZEN:
Open. The. Door.
SENTRY:
Now, friend, just shove along!
—So you want to sit down. If it weren't such an old joke,
I'd tickle your tail with this torch. Just the sort of gag
this audience appreciates.
CITIZEN:
I. Stay. Right. Here.
SENTRY:
Get away from there, or I'll scalp you! The gentlemen from Sparta
are just coming back from dinner.

[*Exit* CITIZEN; *the general company re-enters; the two* CHORUSES *now represent* SPARTANS *and* ATHENIANS.]

A SPARTAN:
Ah must say,
Ah never tasted better grub.
AN ATHENIAN:
And those Lakonians!
They're gentlemen, by the Lord! Just goes to show,
a drink to the wise is sufficient.
COMMISSIONER:
And why not?
A sober man's an ass.
Men of Athens, mark my words: the only efficient
Ambassador's a drunk Ambassador. Is that clear?
Look: we go to Sparta,
and when we get there we're dead sober. The result?
Everyone cackling at everyone else. They make speeches;
and even if we understand, we get it all wrong
when we file our reports in Athens. But today—!
Everybody's happy. Couldn't tell the difference
between *Drink to Me Only* and
The Star-Spangled Athens.
What's a few lies,
washed down in good strong drink?

[*Re-enter the* DRUNKEN CITIZEN]

SENTRY:
God almighty,
he's back again!
CITIZEN:
I. Resume. My. Place.

A SPARTAN: [*To an* ATHENIAN]

Ah beg yo', seh,
take yo' instrument in yo' hand and play for us.
Ah'm told
yo' understand the in*tri*cacies of the floot?
Ah'd lahk to execute a song and dance
in honor of Athens,
and, of cohse, of Spahta.

CITIZEN:

Toot. On. Your. Flute.

[*The following song is a solo—an aria—accompanied by the flute. The* CHORUS OF SPARTANS *begins a slow dance.*]

A SPARTAN:

O Memory,
Let the Muse speak once more
In my young voice. Sing glory.
Sing Artemision's shore,
Where Athens fluttered the Persians. *Alalai,*
Sing glory, that great
Victory! Sing also
Our Leonidas and his men,
Those wild boars, sweat and blood
Down in a red drench. Then, then
The barbarians broke, though they had stood
Numberless as the sands before!

O Artemis,
Virgin Goddess, whose darts
Flash in our forests: approve
This pact of peace and join our hearts,
From this day on, in love.
Huntress, descend!

LYSISTRATA:

All that will come in time.
But now, Lakonians,
take home your wives. Athenians, take yours.
Each man be kind to his woman; and you, women,
be equally kind. Never again, pray God,
shall we lose our way in such madness.

KORYPHAIOS[a]:

And now
let's dance our joy.

[*From this point the dance becomes general.*]

CHORUS[a]:

Dance, you Graces
Artemis, dance
Dance, Phoibos, Lord of dancing
Dance,
In a scurry of Maenads,° Lord Dionysos
Dance, Zeus Thunderer
Dance, Lady Hera
Queen of the Sky
Dance, dance, all you gods
Dance witness everlasting of our pact
Evohí Evohé
Dance for the dearest
the Bringer of Peace
Deathless Aphroditê!

COMMISSIONER:

Now let us have another song from Sparta.

CHORUS[s]:

From Taÿgetos, from Taÿgetos,
Lakonian Muse, come down.
Sing to the Lord Apollo
Who rules Amyklai Town.

Sing Athêna of the House of Brass!°
Sing Lêda's Twins,° that chivalry
Resplendent on the shore
Of our Eurôtas; sing the girls
That dance along before:

Sparkling in dust their gleaming feet,
Their hair a Bacchant fire,
And Lêda's daughter, thyrsos raised,
Leads their triumphant choir.

CHORUSES [s and a]:

Evohé!
Evohaí!
Evohé!
We pass
Dancing
dancing
to greet
Athêna of the House of Brass.

---

[56]**Maenads** women who are followers of the cult of Dionysos, god of wine and natural fertility in all its forms. [69]**Athena of the House of Brass** This famous temple stood on the Akropolis of Sparta. [70]**Leda's Twins** Castor and Pollydeukes, sons of Leda and Zeus, famous for bravery and for skill in warfare; sometimes called the Dioscuri.

SHAKESPEARE AND HIS THEATER

William Shakespeare, English actor and poet and the world's best-known playwright, was born in Stratford-Upon-Avon in 1564, twelve years before the construction of the first permanent theater building since those of the Roman Empire a thousand years earlier. By the time of his death in 1616, he had written all or part of thirty-eight plays. Although the two appearing here, *Hamlet* (1600–1601) and *Othello* (1604), are both tragedies, he also wrote many comedies, history plays, and romances, and experimented widely with dramatic form.

Shakespeare's Globe Theater was built in 1599, just in time for the first production of *Hamlet* about a year later. Although we are not certain about all of its details, the consensus is that it was a circular or octagonal building and that its inside walls held three tiers of roofed galleries for the more privileged part of the audience. The rest of the viewers stood or sat on the floor of the theater, in the open air. The stage thrust itself out about halfway across this theater space, so that it was ringed on three sides by its audience. There was no restriction about who could go to the theater, and it could accommodate perhaps three thousand people. These facts, coupled with the additional ones that it was a daylight and a repertory theater (a set series of plays were enacted in rotation by the same company of actors), make it a community theater somewhat like the Greek.

However, there were also important differences. Although all actors were males (highly trained boys enacted female roles), they did not wear masks. Although the stories were often borrowed from other writers, the audience did not usually know the ending in advance. There was therefore interest in the individuality of a character, and in the suspense value of a plot, at the same time that important public ideas could be discussed as they had been in the Greek theater. Because of a system of official censorship, however, it is uncertain how much freedom a playwright had in the expression of ideas. Some plays from this period surely presented attitudes toward God, gender roles, ethnicity, and monarchy which served as propaganda supporting the views of the reigning monarch. Sometimes, however, it seems that Shakespeare presents a more critical and unsympathetic attitude toward the customs and beliefs of his age than we might expect from these conditions.

WILLIAM SHAKESPEARE

(1564–1616)

Hamlet

EDITED, WITH NOTES, BY G.B. HARRISON

About the Play: Hamlet seems to be an idealistic college student caught in an evil or at least mysterious world who is given a morally complex task: in Act One, the ghost of his dead father asks him to kill his murderer. The moral complexity of this demand is intensified by the fact that the murderer is Claudius, the man who is also Hamlet's stepfather and the king. Killing, even in revenge, is against the law of the church. Seeking private revenge violates the law of the land. Killing of a relative violates the kinship code. And killing the king in Shakespeare's age was considered an outrage, a sacrilege against God's anointed representative. The ghost has called upon Hamlet to act in a way that breaks powerful social, ecclesiastical, and political taboos.

In tiptoeing through this moral minefield, Hamlet behaves in a generally sympathetic way. And yet he treats the only women in the play brutishly, continually reprimands himself for delaying the vengeance he seems to believe in, unfeelingly kills his girlfriend's father and two old school friends, and at times seems literally out of his mind. It is often tempting to consider him too weak for his mission, misogynist, even villainous. This uncertainty about the character Hamlet is echoed in the play. Near the end of Act One he warns his friend Horatio that he will sometimes "put an antic disposition on" (1.5.172), that he will sometimes pretend to be mad. In Act Two, several characters make different guesses about why he seems so disturbed. All this may encourage us too to join the game of psychoanalyzing Hamlet. In addition, he is also playing a deadly cat and mouse game with Claudius—he wants to be certain of his guilt before acting—and the heightened tension of the plot reinforces our desire to understand the character.

Yet as often as he speaks obliquely, he also speaks rationally, most obviously when talking to the players or when talking about playing. Part of his game is setting up the play within the play in 3.2, which reenacts crucial elements of what happened before *Hamlet* opened and influences everything which follows. In fact, there is much playing in this play, and on several levels. Polonius teaches his son Laertes how to seem the ideal man (1.3), then instructs Reynaldo on how to spy on him (2.1), while at the same time he himself is acting for Claudius as a spy on Hamlet. Rosencrantz and Guildenstern, and even Ophelia, are also recruited in this spy game. In one way or another, Hamlet will be implicated in the deaths of them all.

As a result, the play keeps its focus on the difference between "seeming" of various kinds and the reality behind it. At the center of this motif is Hamlet, who is not only the subject of everybody else's speculations, but of his own. He is uncertain about what to do, or even whether he wants to live. Moreover, his play within the play reminds us that the whole of *Hamlet* is also make-believe, while at the same time showing us that the little make-believe in its middle, "The Murder of Gonzago," exercises actual power which affects the characters who produce and who watch it. This is, then, a philosophical play as well as a crime drama, one which questions the nature of reality, and which questions whether we can know anything with certainty in a world of misleading appearances.

The relations of parents and children are also an important element in this play. There are three father-and-son pairs, as well as one daughter and one mother. It is interesting to contrast the ways in which the parents in three different families treat their children, and perhaps even more important to see the contrasts among the ways the children respond to their parents. The most complex of these familial situations is Hamlet's; contrasting his with the others' is likely to clarify our understanding of him and of the play.

DRAMATIS PERSONAE

CLAUDIUS, *King of Denmark*
HAMLET, *son to the late, and nephew to the present King*
POLONIUS, *Lord Chamberlain*
HORATIO, *friend to Hamlet*
LAERTES, *son to Polonius*
VOLTIMAND
CORNELIUS
ROSENCRANTZ
GUILDENSTERN
OSRIC
A GENTLEMAN
} *courtiers*
A PRIEST
MARCELLUS
BERNARDO
} *officers*

FRANCISCO, *a soldier*
REYNALDO, *servant to Polonius*
PLAYERS
TWO CLOWNS, *gravediggers*
FORTINBRAS, *Prince of Norway*
A CAPTAIN
ENGLISH AMBASSADORS

GERTRUDE, *Queen of Denmark, and mother to Hamlet*

OPHELIA, *daughter to Polonius*
LORDS, LADIES, OFFICERS, SOLDIERS, SAILORS, MESSENGERS, *and other* ATTENDANTS

GHOST *of Hamlet's father*

SCENE—*Denmark.*

ACT I

SCENE I. *Elsinore. A platform° before the castle.*

[FRANCISCO *at his post. Enter to him* BERNARDO.]

BER. Who's there?
FRAN. Nay, answer me. Stand, and unfold yourself.°
BER. Long live the King!°
FRAN. Bernardo?
BER. He.
FRAN. You come most carefully upon your hour.
BER. 'Tis now struck twelve. Get thee to bed, Francisco.
FRAN. For this relief much thanks. 'Tis bitter cold,
And I am sick at heart.
BER. Have you had quiet guard?
FRAN. Not a mouse stirring.
BER. Well, good night.
If you do meet Horatio and Marcellus,
The rivals° of my watch, bid them make haste.
FRAN. I think I hear them. Stand, ho! Who is there?

[*Enter* HORATIO *and* MARCELLUS.]

HOR. Friends to this ground.
MAR. And liegemen° to the Dane.
FRAN. Give you good night.

Act I, Sc. i: s.d., platform: the level place on the ramparts where the cannon were mounted. **2. unfold yourself:** reveal who you are. **3. Long . . . King:** probably the password for the night. **13. rivals:** partners. **15. liegemen:** loyal subjects.

MAR. Oh, farewell, honest soldier.
Who hath relieved you?
FRAN. Bernardo hath my place.
Give you good night.

[*Exit.*]

MAR. Holloa! Bernardo!
BER. Say,
What, is Horatio there?
HOR. A piece of him.
BER. Welcome, Horatio. Welcome, good Marcellus.
MAR. What, has this thing appeared again tonight?
BER. I have seen nothing.
MAR. Horatio says 'tis but our fantasy,°
And will not let belief take hold of him
Touching this dreaded sight twice seen of us.
Therefore I have entreated him along
With us to watch the minutes of this night,
That if again this apparition come,
He may approve our eyes° and speak to it.
HOR. Tush, tush, 'twill not appear.
BER. Sit down awhile,
And let us once again assail your ears,
That are so fortified against our story,
What we have two nights seen.
HOR. Well, sit we down,
And let us hear Bernardo speak of this.
BER. Last night of all,
When yond same star that's westward from the pole°
Had made his course to illume° that part of heaven
Where now it burns, Marcellus and myself,
The bell then beating one—

[*Enter* GHOST.]

MAR. Peace, break thee off. Look where it comes again!
BER. In the same figure, like the King that's dead.
MAR. Thou art a scholar.° Speak to it, Horatio.
BER. Looks it not like the King? Mark it, Horatio.
HOR. Most like. It harrows° me with fear and wonder.
BER. It would be spoke to.
MAR. Question it, Horatio.

---

23. fantasy: imagination. **29. approve our eyes:** verify what we have seen. **36. pole:** Polestar. **37. illume:** light. **42. scholar:** As Latin was the proper language in which to address and exorcise evil spirits, a scholar was necessary. **44. harrows:** distresses; lit., plows up.

HOR. What art thou that usurp'st this time of night,
Together with° that fair and warlike form
In which the majesty of buried Denmark°
Did sometimes march? By Heaven I charge thee, speak!
MAR. It is offended.
BER. See, it stalks away!
HOR. Stay! Speak, speak! I charge thee, speak!

[*Exit* GHOST.]

MAR. 'Tis gone, and will not answer.
BER. How now, Horatio! You tremble and look pale.
Is not this something more than fantasy?
What think you on 't?
HOR. Before my God, I might not this believe
Without the sensible and true avouch
Of mine own eyes.°
MAR. Is it not like the King?
HOR. As thou art to thyself.
Such was the very armor he had on
When he the ambitious Norway combated.
So frowned he once when, in an angry parle,°
He smote the sledded Polacks° on the ice
'Tis strange.
MAR. Thus twice before, and jump at this dead hour,°
With martial stalk hath he gone by our watch.
HOR. In what particular thought to work I know not,
But in the gross and scope° of my opinion
This bodes some strange eruption° to our state.
MAR. Good now, sit down and tell me, he that knows,
Why this same strict and most observant watch
So nightly toils° the subject° of the land;
And why such daily cast of brazen cannon
And foreign mart° for implements of war;
Why° such impress° of shipwrights, whose sore task
Does not divide the Sunday from the week;
What might be toward,° that this sweaty haste
Doth make the night joint laborer with the day.
Who is 't that can inform me?

---

47. Together with: i.e., appearing in. **48. majesty . . . Denmark:** the dead King. **57–58. Without . . . eyes:** unless my own eyes had vouched for it. **sensible:** perceived by my senses. **62. parle:** parley. **63. sledded Polacks:** There has been much controversy about this phrase. Q1 and Q2 read "sleaded Pollax," F1 reads "sledded Pollax." Either the late King smote his heavy (leaded) poleax on the ice, or else he attacked the Poles in their sledges. There is no further reference to this incident. **65. jump . . . hour:** just at deep midnight. **68. gross . . . scope:** general conclusion. **69. eruption:** violent disturbance. **72. toils:** wearies. **subject:** subjects. **74. foreign mart:** purchase abroad. **75–78. Why . . . day:** i.e., workers in shipyards and munition factories are working night shifts and Sundays. **impress:** conscription. **toward:** in preparation.

HOR. That can I,
At least the whisper goes so. Our last King,
Whose image even but now appeared to us,
Was, as you know, by Fortinbras of Norway,
Thereto pricked° on by a most emulate° pride,
Dared to the combat, in which our valiant Hamlet—
For so this side of our known world esteemed him—
Did slay this Fortinbras. Who° by a sealed compact,°
Well ratified by law and heraldry,°
Did forfeit, with his life, all those his lands
Which he stood seized of° to the conqueror.
Against the which, a moiety competent°
Was gagèd° by our King, which had returned
To the inheritance of Fortinbras
Had he been vanquisher, as by the same covenant
And carriage of the article designed°
His fell to Hamlet. Now, sir, young Fortinbras,
Of unimprovèd mettle° hot and full,
Hath in the skirts° of Norway here and there
Sharked° up a list of lawless resolutes,°
For food and diet,° to some enterprise
That hath a stomach° in 't. Which is no other—
As it doth well appear unto our state—
But to recover of us, by strong hand
And terms compulsatory,° those foresaid lands
So by his father lost. And this, I take it,
Is the main motive of our preparations,
The source of this our watch and the chief head°
Of this posthaste and romage° in the land.

BER. I think it be no other but e'en so.
Well may it sort° that this portentous figure
Comes armèd through our watch, so like the King
That was and is the question of these wars.

HOR. A mote° it is to trouble the mind's eye.
In the most high and palmy° state of Rome,
A little ere the mightiest Julius fell,
The graves stood tenantless, and the sheeted° dead
Did squeak and gibber° in the Roman streets.

---

83. pricked: spurred. **emulate:** jealous. **86–95. Who . . . Hamlet:** i.e., before the combat it was agreed that the victor should win the lands of the vanquished. **86. sealed compact:** formal agreement. **87. heraldry:** The heralds were responsible for arranging formal combats. **89. seized of:** possessed of, a legal term. **90. moiety competent:** adequate portion. **91. gaged:** pledged. **94. carriage . . . designed:** fulfillment of the clause in the agreement. **96. unimproved mett'e:** untutored, wild material, nature. **97. skirts:** outlying parts. **98. Sharked:** collected indiscriminately, as a shark bolts its prey. **lawless resolutes:** gangsters. **99. diet:** maintenance. **100. stomach:** resolution. **103. terms compulsatory:** force. **106. chief head:** main purpose. **107. posthaste . . . romage:** urgency and bustle. **109. Well . . . sort:** it would be a natural reason. **112. mote:** speck of dust. **113. palmy:** flourishing. **115. sheeted:** in their shrouds. **116. gibber:** utter strange sounds.

As stars° with trains of fire and dews of blood,
Disasters° in the sun, and the moist star°
Upon whose influence Neptune's empire stands
Was sick almost to doomsday with eclipse.
And even the like precurse° of fierce events,
As harbingers° preceding still the fates
And prologue to the omen° coming on,
Have Heaven and earth together demonstrated
Unto our climatures° and countrymen.

[*Re-enter* GHOST.]

But soft, behold! Lo where it comes again!
I'll cross it,° though it blast me. Stay, illusion!
If thou hast any sound, or use of voice,
Speak to me.
If° there be any good thing to be done
That may to thee do ease and grace to me,°
Speak to me.
If thou art privy to° thy country's fate,
Which, happily,° foreknowing may avoid,
Oh, speak!
Or if thou hast uphoarded in thy life
Extorted° treasure in the womb of earth,
For which, they say, you spirits oft walk in death,
Speak of it. Stay, and speak!

[*The cock crows.*°]

Stop it, Marcellus.
MAR. Shall I strike at it with my partisan?
HOR. Do, if it will not stand.
BER. 'Tis here!
HOR. 'Tis here!
MAR. 'Tis gone!

[*Exit* GHOST.]

---

117. As stars: The sense of the passage is here broken; possibly a line has been omitted after l. 116. **118. Disasters:** unlucky signs. **moist star:** the moon, which influences the tides. **121. precurse:** forewarning. **122. harbingers:** forerunners. The harbinger was an officer of the Court who was sent ahead to make the arrangements when the Court went on progress. **123. omen:** disaster. **125. climatures:** regions. **127. cross it:** stand in its way. **130–39. If . . . speak:** In popular belief there were four reasons why the spirit of a dead man should *walk:* (a) to reveal a secret, (b) to utter a warning, (c) to reveal concealed treasure, (d) to reveal the manner of its death. Horatio thus adjures the ghost by three potent reasons, but before he can utter the fourth the cock crows. **131. grace to me:** bring me into a state of spiritual grace. **133. privy to:** have secret knowledge of. **134. happily:** by good luck. **137. Extorted:** evilly acquired. **139. s.d., cock crows:** i.e., a sign that dawn is at hand. See ll. 147–64.

We do it wrong, being so majestical,
To offer it the show of violence,
For it is as the air invulnerable,
And our vain blows malicious mockery.

BER. It was about to speak when the cock crew.

HOR. And then it started like a guilty thing
Upon a fearful° summons. I have heard
The cock, that is the trumpet to the morn,
Doth with his lofty and shrill-sounding throat
Awake the god of day, and at his warning,
Whether in sea or fire, in earth or air,
The extravagant and erring° spirit hies
To his confine.° And of the truth herein
This present object made probation.°

MAR. It faded on the crowing of the cock.
Some say that ever 'gainst° that season comes
Wherein Our Saviour's birth is celebrated,
The bird of dawning singeth all night long.
And then, they say, no spirit dare stir abroad,
The nights are wholesome, then no planets° strike,
No fairy takes° nor witch hath power to charm,
So hallowed and so gracious is the time.

HOR. So have I heard and do in part believe it.
But look, the morn, in russet mantle clad,
Walks o'er the dew of yon high eastward hill.
Break we our watch up, and by my advice
Let us impart what we have seen tonight
Unto young Hamlet, for upon my life,
This spirit, dumb to us, will speak to him.
Do you consent we shall acquaint him with it,
As needful in our loves, fitting our duty?

MAR. Let's do 't, I pray. And I this morning know
Where we shall find him most conveniently.

[*Exeunt.*]

SCENE II. *A room of state in the castle.*

[*Flourish.° Enter the* KING, QUEEN, HAMLET, POLONIUS, LAERTES, VOLTIMAND, CORNELIUS, LORDS, *and* ATTENDANTS.]

---

149. fearful: causing fear. **154. extravagant . . . erring:** both words mean "wandering." **155. confine:** place of confinement. **156. probation:** proof. **158. 'gainst:** in anticipation of. **162. planets:** Planets were supposed to bring disaster. **163. takes:** bewitches.

Sc. ii: s.d., Flourish: fanfare of trumpets.

KING. Though yet of Hamlet our dear brother's death
The memory be green,° and that it us befitted
To bear our hearts in grief and our whole kingdom
To be contracted in one brow of woe,°
Yet so far hath discretion° fought with nature°
That we with wisest sorrow think on him,
Together with remembrance of ourselves.
Therefore our sometime sister,° now our Queen,
The imperial jointress° to this warlike state,
Have we, as 'twere with a defeated joy—
With an auspicious and a dropping eye,°
With mirth in funeral and with dirge in marriage,
In equal scale weighing delight and dole°—
Taken to wife. Nor have we herein barred
Your better wisdoms,° which have freely gone
With this affair along. For all, our thanks.
Now follows that you know. Young Fortinbras,
Holding a weak supposal° of our worth,
Or thinking by our late dear brother's death
Our state to be disjoint and out of frame,
Colleagued with the dream of his advantage,°
He hath not failed to pester us with message
Importing the surrender of those lands
Lost by his father, with all bonds of law,°
To our most valiant brother. So much for him.
Now for ourself, and for this time of meeting.
Thus much the business is: We have here writ
To Norway, uncle of young Fortinbras—
Who, impotent and bedrid, scarcely hears
Of this his nephew's purpose—to suppress
His further gait° herein, in that the levies,
The lists° and full proportions,° are all made
Out of his subject.° And we here dispatch
You, good Cornelius, and you, Voltimand,
For bearers of this greeting to old Norway,
Giving to you no further personal power
To business with the King more than the scope°

---

2. **green:** fresh. 4. **contracted . . . woe:** i.e., every subject's forehead should be puckered with grief. 5. **discretion:** common sense. **nature:** natural sorrow. 8. **sister:** sister-in-law. 9. **jointress:** partner by marriage. 11. **auspicious . . . eye:** an eye at the same time full of joy and of tears. 13. **dole:** grief. 14–15. **barred . . . wisdoms:** i.e., in taking this step we have not shut out your advice. As is obvious throughout the play, the Danes chose their King by election and not by right of birth. See V.ii.65, 366. 18. **weak supposal:** poor opinion. 21. **Colleagued . . . advantage:** uniting himself with this dream that here was a good opportunity. 24. **with . . . law:** legally binding, as already explained in ll. 80–95 above. 31. **gait:** progress. 32. **lists: rosters. proportions:** military establishments. 33. **subject:** subjects. 37. **scope:** limit.

Of these delated articles° allow.
Farewell, and let your haste commend° your duty.
COR. & VOLT. In that and all things will we show our duty.
KING. We doubt it nothing. Heartily farewell.

[*Exeunt* VOLTIMAND *and* CORNELIUS.]

And now, Laertes, what's the news with you?
You told us of some suit°—what is 't, Laertes?
You cannot speak of reason to the Dane
And lose your voice. What wouldst thou beg, Laertes,
That shall not be my offer, not thy asking?
The head is not more native° to the heart,
The hand more instrumental° to the mouth,
Than is the throne of Denmark to thy father.
What wouldst thou have, Laertes?
LAER. My dread° lord,
Your leave and favor to return to France,
From whence though willingly I came to Denmark
To show my duty in your coronation,
Yet now, I must confess, that duty done,
My thoughts and wishes bend again toward France
And bow them to your gracious leave and pardon.
KING. Have you your father's leave? What says Polonius?
POL. He hath, my lord, wrung from me my slow leave
By laborsome petition, and at last
Upon his will° I sealed my hard consent.°
I do beseech you give him leave to go.
KING. Take thy fair hour, Laertes, time be thine,
And thy best graces spend° it at thy will!
But now, my cousin° Hamlet, and my son—
HAML. [*Aside*] A little more than kin and less than kind.°
KING. How is it that the clouds still hang on you?
HAML. Not so, my lord. I am too much i' the sun.
QUEEN. Good Hamlet, cast thy nighted color° off,
And let thine eye look like a friend on Denmark.
Do not forever with thy vailèd lids°
Seek for thy noble father in the dust.

38. delated articles: detailed instructions. Claudius is following usual diplomatic procedure. Ambassadors sent on a special mission carried with them a letter of introduction and greeting to the King of the foreign Court and detailed instructions to guide them in the negotiations. **39. commend:** display; lit., recommend. **43. suit:** petition. **47. native:** closely related. **48. instrumental:** serviceable. **50. dread:** dreaded, much respected. **60. will:** desire. **sealed . . . consent:** agreed to, but with great reluctance. **63. best . . . spend:** i.e., use your time well. **64. cousin:** kinsman. The word was used for any near relation. **65. A . . . kind:** too near a relation (uncle-father) and too little natural affection. **kind:** affectionate. **68. nighted color:** black. Hamlet alone is in deep mourning; the rest of the Court wear gay clothes. **70. vailed lids:** lowered eyelids.

Thou know'st 'tis common—all that lives must die,
Passing through nature to eternity.
HAML. Aye, madam, it is common.
QUEEN. If it be,
Why seems it so particular with thee?
HAML. Seems, madam! Nay, it is. I know not "seems."
'Tis not alone my inky cloak, good Mother,
Nor customary suits of solemn black,
Nor windy suspiration of forced breath—
No, nor the fruitful river° in the eye,
Nor the dejected havior of the visage,°
Together with all forms, moods, shapes of grief—
That can denote me truly. These indeed seem,
For they are actions that a man might play.°
But I have that within which passeth show,
These but the trappings° and the suits of woe.
KING. 'Tis sweet and commendable in your nature, Hamlet,
To give these mourning duties to your father.
But you must know your father lost a father,
That father lost, lost his, and the survivor bound
In filial obligation for some term
To do obsequious sorrow.° But to perséver
In obstinate condolement° is a course
Of impious stubbornness, 'tis unmanly grief.
It shows a will most incorrect to Heaven,
A heart unfortified,° a mind impatient,
An understanding simple and unschooled.
For what we know must be and is as common
As any the most vulgar° thing to sense,
Why should we in our peevish opposition
Take it to heart? Fie! 'Tis a fault to Heaven,
A fault against the dead, a fault to nature,
To reason most absurd, whose common theme
Is death of fathers, and who still hath cried,
From the first corse° till he that died today,
"This must be so." We pray you throw to earth
This unprevailing° woe, and think of us
As of a father. For let the world take note,
You are the most immediate° to our throne,
And with no less nobility of love
Than that which dearest father bears his son

---

80. fruitful river: stream of tears. **81. dejected . . . visage:** downcast countenance. **84. play:** act, as in a play. **86. trappings:** ornaments. **92. obsequious sorrow:** the sorrow usual at funerals. **93. obstinate condolement:** lamentation disregarding the will of God. **96. unfortified:** not strengthened with the consolation of religion. **99. vulgar:** common. **105. corse:** corpse. There is unconscious irony in this remark, for the first corpse was that of Abel, also slain by his brother. **107. unprevailing:** futile. **109. most immediate:** next heir.

Do I impart toward you. For your intent
In going back to school° in Wittenberg,
It is most retrograde° to our desire.
And we beseech you bend you° to remain
Here in the cheer and comfort of our eye,
Our chiefest courtier, cousin, and our son.
QUEEN. Let not thy mother lose her prayers, Hamlet.
I pray thee, stay with us, go not to Wittenberg.
HAML. I shall in all my best obey you, madam.
KING. Why, 'tis a loving and a fair reply.
Be as ourself in Denmark. Madam, come,
This gentle and unforced accord of Hamlet
Sits smiling to my heart. In grace whereof,
No jocund health that Denmark drinks today
But the great cannon° to the clouds shall tell,
And the King's rouse° the Heaven shall bruit° again,
Respeaking earthly thunder. Come away.

[*Flourish. Exeunt all but* HAMLET.]

HAML. Oh, that this too too solid flesh would melt,
Thaw, and resolve itself into a dew!
Or that the Everlasting had not fixed
His canon° 'gainst self-slaughter! Oh, God! God!
How weary, stale, flat, and unprofitable
Seem to me all the uses° of this world!
Fie on 't, ah, fie! 'Tis an unweeded garden,
That grows to seed, things rank° and gross in nature
Possess it merely.° That it should come to this!
But two months dead! Nay, not so much, not two.
So excellent a King, that was, to this,
Hyperion° to a satyr.° So loving to my mother
That he might not beteem° the winds of heaven
Visit her face too roughly. Heaven and earth!
Must I remember? Why, she would hang on him
As if increase of appetite had grown
By what it fed on. And yet within a month—
Let me not think on 't.—Frailty, thy name is woman!—
A little month, or ere those shoes were old
With which she followed my poor father's body,
Like Niobe° all tears.—Why she, even she—

---

113. school: university. **114. retrograde:** contrary. **115. bend you:** incline. **126. great cannon:** This Danish custom of discharging cannon when the King proposed a toast was much noted by Englishmen. **127. rouse:** deep drink. **bruit:** sound loudly, echo. **132. canon:** rule, law. **134. uses:** ways. **136. rank:** coarse. **137. merely:** entirely. **140. Hyperion:** the sun god. **satyr:** a creature half man, half goat—ugly and lecherous. **141. beteem:** allow. **149. Niobe:** She boasted of her children, to the annoyance of the goddess Artemis, who slew them all. Thereafter Niobe became so sorrowful that she changed into a rock everlastingly dripping water.

Oh, God! A beast that wants discourse of reason°
Would have mourned longer—married with my uncle,
My father's brother, but no more like my father
Than I to Hercules. Within a month,
Ere yet the salt of most unrighteous tears
Had left the flushing in her gallèd° eyes,
She married. Oh, most wicked speed, to post°
With such dexterity° to incestuous sheets!
It is not, nor it cannot, come to good.
But break, my heart, for I must hold my tongue!

[*Enter* HORATIO, MARCELLUS, *and* BERNARDO.]

HOR. Hail to your lordship!
HAML. I am glad to see you well.
Horatio—or I do forget myself.
HOR. The same, my lord, and your poor servant ever.
HAML. Sir, my good friend—I'll change that name° with you.
And what make you from Wittenberg, Horatio?
Marcellus?
MAR. My good lord?
HAML. I am very glad to see you. [*To* BERNARDO]
Good even, sir.
But what, in faith, make you from Wittenberg?
HOR. A truant disposition, good my lord.
HAML. I would not hear your enemy say so,
Nor shall you do my ear that violence
To make it truster of your own report
Against yourself. I know you are no truant.
But what is your affair in Elsinore?
We'll teach you to drink deep° ere you depart.
HOR. My lord, I came to see your father's funeral.
HAML. I pray thee do not mock me, fellow student.
I think it was to see my mother's wedding.
HOR. Indeed, my lord, it followed hard upon.
HAML. Thrift, thrift, Horatio! The funeral baked meats
Did coldly furnish forth the marriage tables.°
Would I had met my dearest° foe in Heaven
Or ever I had seen that day, Horatio!
My father!—Methinks I see my father.
HOR. Oh, where, my lord?
HAML. In my mind's eye, Horatio.

---

150. wants . . . reason: is without ability to reason. **155. galled:** sore. **156. post:** hasten. **157. dexterity:** nimbleness. **164. that name:** i.e., friend. **175. drink deep:** For more on the drunken habits of the Danes, see I.iv.8–38. **180–81. Thrift . . . tables:** they hurried on the wedding for economy's sake, so that the remains of food served at the funeral might be used cold for the wedding. **baked meats:** feast. **182. dearest:** best-hated.

HOR. I saw him once. He was a goodly King.
HAML. He was a man, take him for all in all.
I shall not look upon his like again.
HOR. My lord, I think I saw him yesternight.
HAML. Saw? Who?
HOR. My lord, the King your father.
HAML. The King my father!
HOR. Season your admiration° for a while
With an attent° ear till I may deliver,
Upon the witness of these gentlemen,
This marvel to you.
HAML. For God's love, let me hear.
HOR. Two nights together had these gentlemen,
Marcellus and Bernardo, on their watch
In the dead vast and middle of the night,°
Been thus encountered. A figure like your father,
Armed at point exactly, cap-a-pie,°
Appears before them and with solemn march
Goes slow and stately by them. Thrice he walked
By their oppressed and fear-surprisèd eyes
Within his truncheon's° length, whilst they, distilled°
Almost to jelly with the act of fear,
Stand dumb, and speak not to him. This to me
In dreadful secrecy impart they did,
And I with them the third night kept the watch.
Where, as they had delivered, both in time,
Form of the thing, each word made true and good,
The apparition comes. I knew your father.
These hands are not more like.
HAML. But where was this?
MAR. My lord, upon the platform where we watched.
HAML. Did you not speak to it?
HOR. My lord, I did,
But answer made it none. Yet once methought
It lifted up it° head and did address
Itself to motion, like as it would speak.
But even then the morning cock crew loud,
And at the sound it shrunk in haste away
And vanished from our sight.
HAML. 'Tis very strange.
HOR. As I do live, my honored lord, 'tis true,
And we did think it writ down in our duty
To let you know of it.

---

192. Season . . . admiration: moderate your wonder. **193. attent:** attentive. **198. dead . . . night:** deep, silent midnight. **200. at . . . cap-a-pie:** complete in every detail, head to foot. **204. truncheon:** a general's staff. **distilled:** melted. **216. it:** its.

HAML. Indeed, indeed, sirs, but this troubles me.
Hold you the watch tonight?
MAR. & BER. We do, my lord.
HAML. Armed, say you?
MAR. & BER. Armed, my lord.
HAML. From top to toe?
MAR. & BER. My lord, from head to foot.
HAML. Then saw you not his face?
HOR. Oh yes, my lord, he wore his beaver° up.
HAML. What, looked he frowningly?
HOR. A countenance more in sorrow than in anger.
HAML. Pale, or red?
HOR. Nay, very pale.
HAML. And fixed his eyes upon you?
HOR. Most constantly.
HAML. I would I had been there.
HOR. It would have much amazed you.
HAML. Very like, very like. Stayed it long?
HOR. While one with moderate haste might tell° a hundred.
MAR. & BER. Longer, longer.
HOR. Not when I saw't.
HAML. His beard was grizzled?° No?
HOR. It was as I have seen it in his life,
A sable silvered.°
HAML. I will watch tonight.
Perchance 'twill walk again.
HOR. I warrant it will.
HAML. If it assume my noble father's person,
I'll speak to it though Hell itself should gape
And bid me hold my peace. I pray you all,
If you have hitherto concealed this sight,
Let it be tenable° in your silence still,
And whatsoever else shall hap tonight,
Give it an understanding, but no tongue.
I will requite° your loves. So fare you well.
Upon the platform, 'twixt eleven and twelve,
I'll visit you.
ALL. Our duty to your Honor.
HAML. Your loves, as mine to you. Farewell.

[*Exeunt all but* HAMLET.]

---

229. beaver: front part of the helmet, which could be raised. **238. tell:** count. **240. grizzled:** gray. **242. sable silvered:** black mingled with white. **248. tenable:** held fast. **251. requite:** repay.

My father's spirit in arms! All is not well.
I doubt° some foul play. Would the night were come!
Till then sit still, my soul. Foul deeds will rise,
Though all the earth o'erwhelm them, to men's eyes.

[*Exit.*]

Scene III. *A room in* POLONIUS'S *house.*

[*Enter* LAERTES *and* OPHELIA.]

LAER. My necessaries° are embarked. Farewell.
And, Sister, as the winds give benefit
And convoy is assistant,° do not sleep,
But let me hear from you.

OPH. Do you doubt that?

LAER. For Hamlet, and the trifling of his favor,°
Hold it a fashion and a toy in blood,°
A violet in the youth of primy° nature,
Forward, not permanent, sweet, not lasting,
The perfume and suppliance of a minute°—
No more.

OPH. No more but so?

LAER. Think it no more.
For Nature crescent does not grow alone
In thews and bulk,° but as this temple° waxes
The inward service of the mind and soul
Grows wide withal. Perhaps he loves you now,
And now no soil nor cautel° doth besmirch
The virtue of his will.° But you must fear,
His greatness weighed,° his will is not his own,
For he himself is subject to his birth.
He may not, as unvalued persons do,
Carve° for himself, for on his choice depends
The safety and health of this whole state,
And therefore must his choice be circumscribed°
Unto the voice and yielding of that body
Whereof he is the head. Then if he says he loves you,
It fits your wisdom so far to believe it
As he in his particular act and place

---

256. doubt: suspect.

Sc. iii: 1. necessaries: baggage. **3. convoy . . . assistant:** means of conveyance is available. **5. favor:** i.e., toward you. **6. toy in blood:** trifling impulse. **7. primy:** springtime; i.e., youthful. **8. perfume . . . minute:** perfume which lasts only for a minute. **11–12. For . . . bulk:** for natural growth is not only in bodily bulk. **12. temple:** i.e., the body. **15. cautel:** deceit. **16. will:** desire. **17. His . . . weighed:** when you consider his high position. **20. Carve:** choose. **22. circumscribed:** restricted.

May give his saying deed, which is no further
Than the main voice of Denmark goes withal.
Then weigh what loss your honor may sustain
If with too credent° ear you list his songs,
Or lose your heart, or your chaste treasure° open
To his unmastered importunity.
Fear it, Ophelia, fear it, my dear sister,
And keep you in the rear° of your affection,
Out of the shot and danger of desire.
The chariest maid is prodigal enough
If she unmask her beauty to the moon.
Virtue itself 'scapes not calumnious strokes.
The canker galls the infants° of the spring
Too oft before their buttons° be disclosed,
And in the morn and liquid dew of youth
Contagious blastments° are most imminent.
Be wary, then, best safety lies in fear.
Youth to itself rebels, though none else near.°

OPH. I shall the effect of this good lesson keep
As watchman to my heart. But, good my brother,
Do not, as some ungracious pastors do,
Show me the steep and thorny way to Heaven
Whilst, like a puffed° and reckless libertine,
Himself the primrose path of dalliance° treads
And recks not his own rede.°

LAER. Oh, fear me not.
I stay too long. But here my father comes.

[*Enter* POLONIUS.]

A double blessing is a double grace,
Occasion smiles° upon a second leave.

POL. Yet here, Laertes! Aboard, aboard, for shame!
The wind sits in the shoulder of your sail
And you are stayed° for. There, my blessing with thee!
And these few precepts in thy memory
Look thou charácter.° Give thy thoughts no tongue,
Nor any unproportioned° thought his act.
Be thou familiar, but by no means vulgar.
Those friends thou hast, and their adoption tried,°

---

30. credent: credulous. **31. chaste treasure:** the treasure of your chastity. **34. in . . . rear:** i.e., farthest from danger. **39. canker . . . infants:** maggot harms the unopened buds. **40. buttons:** buds. **42. Contagious blastments:** infectious blasts. **44. though . . . near:** without anyone else to encourage it. **49. puffed:** panting. **50. primrose . . . dalliance:** i.e., the pleasant way of love-making. **51. recks . . . rede:** takes no heed of his own advice. **54. Occasion smiles:** i.e., here is a happy chance. **57. stayed:** waited. **59. character:** inscribe. **60. unproportioned:** unsuitable. **62. adoption tried:** friendship tested by experience.

Grapple them to thy soul with hoops of steel,
But do not dull thy palm with entertainment°
Of each new-hatched unfledged° comrade. Beware
Of entrance to a quarrel, but being in,
Bear't that the opposèd may beware of thee.
Give every man thy ear, but few thy voice.°
Take each man's censure,° but reserve thy judgment.
Costly thy habit° as thy purse can buy,
But not expressed in fancy°—rich, not gaudy.
For the apparel oft proclaims the man,
And they in France of the best rank and station
Are of a most select and generous chief in that.°
Neither a borrower nor a lender be,
For loan oft loses both itself and friend
And borrowing dulls the edge of husbandry.°
This above all: To thine own self be true,
And it must follow, as the night the day,
Thou canst not then be false to any man.
Farewell. My blessing season° this in thee!

LAER. Most humbly do I take my leave, my lord.

POL. The time invites you. Go, your servants tend.°

LAER. Farewell, Ophelia, and remember well
What I have said to you.

OPH. 'Tis in my memory locked,
And you yourself shall keep the key of it.

LAER. Farewell.

[*Exit.*]

POL. What is't, Ophelia, he hath said to you?

OPH. So please you, something touching the Lord Hamlet.

POL. Marry,° well bethought.°
'Tis told me he hath very oft of late
Given private time to you, and you yourself
Have of your audience been most free and bounteous.
If it be so—as so 'tis put on me,
And that in way of caution—I must tell you
You do not understand yourself so clearly
As it behooves° my daughter and your honor.
What is between you? Give me up the truth.

---

64. dull . . . entertainment: let your hand grow callous with welcome. **65. unfledged:** lit., newly out of the egg, immature. **68. Give . . . voice:** listen to everyone but commit yourself to few. **69. censure:** opinion. **70. habit:** dress. **71. expressed in fancy:** fantastic. **74. Are . . . that:** A disputed line; this is the F1 reading. Q2 reads "Or of the most select and generous, chief in that"; i.e., the best noble and gentle families are very particular in their dress. **generous:** of gentle birth. **77. husbandry:** economy. **81. season:** bring to fruit. **83. tend:** attend. **90. Marry:** Mary, by the Virgin Mary. **well bethought:** well remembered. **97. behooves:** is the duty of.

OPH. He hath, my lord, of late made many tenders°
Of his affection to me.
POL. Affection! Pooh! You speak like a green girl,
Unsifted° in such perilous circumstance.
Do you believe his tenders, as you call them?
OPH. I do not know, my lord, what I should think.
POL. Marry, I'll teach you. Think yourself a baby
That you have ta'en these tenders° for true pay,
Which are not sterling.° Tender yourself more dearly,
Or—not to crack the wind of° the poor phrase,
Running it thus—you'll tender me a fool.
OPH. My lord, he hath importuned me with love
In honorable fashion.
POL. Aye, fashion° you may call it. Go to, go to.
OPH. And hath given countenance to his speech,° my lord,
With almost all the holy vows of Heaven.
POL. Aye, springes° to catch woodcocks.° I do know,
When the blood burns, how prodigal° the soul
Lends the tongue vows. These blazes,° daughter,
Giving more light than heat, extinct in both,
Even in their promise as it is a-making,
You must not take for fire. From this time
Be something scanter of your maiden presence,
Set your entreatments at a higher rate
Than a command to parley.° For Lord Hamlet,
Believe so much in him, that he is young,
And with a larger tether° may he walk
Than may be given you. In few,° Ophelia,
Do not believe his vows, for they are brokers,°
Not of that dye which their investments° show,
But mere implorators° of unholy suits,
Breathing like sanctified and pious bawds°
The better to beguile. This is for all.
I would not, in plain terms, from this time forth
Have you so slander any moment leisure°
As to give words or talk with the Lord Hamlet.
Look to 't, I charge you. Come your ways.
OPH. I shall obey, my lord.

---

99. tenders: offers. **102. Unsifted:** untried. **106–09. tenders . . . tender:** Polonius puns on "tenders," counters (used for money in games); "tender," value; "tender," show. **107. sterling:** true currency. **108. crack . . . of:** i.e., ride to death. **112. fashion:** mere show. **113. given . . . speech:** confirmed his words. **115. springes:** snares. **woodcocks:** foolish birds. **116. prodigal:** extravagantly. **117. blazes:** flashes, quickly extinguished *(extinct)*. **122–23. Set . . . parley:** when you are asked to see him do not regard it as a command to negotiate. **parley:** meeting to discuss terms. **125. tether:** rope by which a grazing animal is fastened to its peg. **126. In few:** in short. **127. brokers:** traveling salesmen. **128. investments:** garments. **129. implorators:** men who solicit. **130. bawds:** keepers of brothels. F1 and Q2 read "bond," an easy misprint for "baud"—the Elizabethan spelling of "bawd." **133. slander . . . leisure:** misuse any moment of leisure.

[*Exeunt.*]

SCENE IV. *The platform*

[*Enter* HAMLET, HORATIO, *and* MARCELLUS.]

HAML. The air bites shrewdly.° It is very cold.
HOR. It is a nipping and an eager° air.
HAML. What hour now?
HOR. I thinks it lacks of twelve.
MAR. No, it is struck.
HOR. Indeed? I heard it not. It then draws near the season
Wherein the spirit held his wont to walk.

[*A flourish of trumpets, and ordnance shot off within.*°]

What doth this mean, my lord?
HAML. The King doth wake° tonight and takes his rouse,°
Keeps wassail,° and the swaggering upspring reels.°
And as he drains his draughts of Rhenish° down,
The kettledrum and trumpet thus bray out
The triumph of his pledge.
HOR. Is it a custom?
HAML. Aye, marry, is 't.
But to my mind, though I am native here
And to the manner born, it is a custom
More honored in the breach than the observance.
This heavy-headed revel° east and west
Makes us traduced and taxed of° other nations.
They clepe° us drunkards, and with swinish phrase
Soil our addition,° and indeed it takes
From our achievements, though performed at height,°
The pith and marrow of our attribute.°
So oft it chances in particular men,
That for some vicious mole° of nature in them,
As in their birth—wherein they are not guilty,
Since nature cannot choose his origin—
By the o'ergrowth of some complexion,°
Oft breaking down the pales° and forts of reason,
Or by some habit that too much o'erleavens°

Sc. iv: 1. shrewdly: bitterly. **2. eager:** sharp. **6. s.d., within:** off stage. **8. wake:** "makes a night of it." **rouse:** See I.ii.127,n. **9. wassail:** revelry. **swaggering . . . reels:** reel in a riotous dance. **10. Rhenish:** Rhine wine. **17. heavy-headed revel:** drinking which produces a thick head. **18. traduced . . . of:** disgraced and censured by. **19. clepe:** call. **20. soil . . . addition:** smirch our honor. **addition: lit.,** title of honor added to a man's name. **21. though . . . height:** though of the highest merit. **22. pith . . . attribute:** essential part of our honor; i.e., we lose the honor due to our achievements because of our reputation for drunkenness. **24. mole:** blemish. **27. o'ergrowth . . . complexion:** some quality allowed to overbalance the rest. **28. pales:** defenses. **29. o'erleavens:** mixes with.

The form of plausive° manners, that these men—
Carrying, I say, the stamp of one defect,
Being Nature's livery,° or Fortune's star°—
Their virtues else—be they as pure as grace,
As infinite as man may undergo—
Shall in the general censure take corruption
From that particular fault. The dram of eale
Doth all the noble substance of a doubt
To his own scandal.°

[*Enter* GHOST.]

HOR. Look, my lord, it comes!

HAML. Angels and ministers of grace defend us!
Be thou a spirit of health or goblin damned,°
Bring with thee airs from Heaven or blasts from Hell,
Be thy intents wicked or charitable,
Thou comest in such a questionable° shape
That I will speak to thee. I'll call thee Hamlet,
King, Father, royal Dane. Oh, answer me!
Let me not burst in ignorance, but tell
Why thy canónized° bones, hearsèd° in death,
Have burst their cerements,° why the sepulcher
Wherein we saw thee quietly inurned°
Hath oped his ponderous and marble jaws
To cast thee up again. What may this mean,
That thou, dead corse, again, in complete steel,°
Revisit'st thus the glimpses of the moon,
Making night hideous, and we fools° of nature
So horridly to shake our disposition°
With thoughts beyond the reaches of our souls?
Say, why is this? Wherefore? What should we do?

[GHOST *beckons* HAMLET.]

---

30. **plausive:** agreeable. 32. **Nature's livery:** i.e., inborn. **Fortune's star:** the result of ill luck. 36–38. **The . . . scandal:** This is the most famous of all disputed passages in Shakespeare's plays. The general meaning is clear: "a small portion of evil brings scandal on the whole substance, however noble." "Eale" is an Elizabethan spelling and pronunciation of "evil," as later in Q2 (II.ii.628); "deale" is the spelling and pronunciation of "Devil." The difficulty lies in "of a doubt," which is obviously a misprint for some such word as "corrupt"; but to be satisfactory it must fit the meter and be a plausible misprint. So far, although many guesses have been made, none is wholly convincing. The best is perhaps "often dout"—often put out. 40. **spirit . . . damned:** a holy spirit or damned fiend. Hamlet, until convinced at the end of the play scene (III.ii.298), is perpetually in doubt whether the ghost which he sees is a good spirit sent to warn him, a devil sent to tempt him into some damnable action, or a hallucination created by his own diseased imagination. See II.ii.627–32. 43. **questionable:** inviting question. 47. **canonized:** buried with full rites according to the canon of the Church. **hearsed:** buried. 48. **cerements:** waxen shroud, used to wrap the bodies of the illustrious dead. 49. **inurned:** buried. 52. **complete steel:** full armor. 54. **fools:** dupes. 55. **disposition:** nature.

HOR. It beckons you to go away with it,
As if it some impartment° did desire
To you alone.
MAR. Look with what courteous action
It waves you to a more removèd ground.
But do not go with it.
HOR. No, by no means.
HAML. It will not speak. Then I will follow it.
HOR. Do not, my lord.
HAML. Why, what should be the fear?
I do not set my life at a pin's fee,°
And for my soul, what can it do to that,
Being a thing immortal as itself?
It waves me forth again. I'll follow it.
HOR. What if it tempt you toward the flood, my lord,
Or to the dreadful summit of the cliff
That beetles o'er° his base into the sea,
And there assume some other horrible form
Which might deprive your sovereignty of reason°
And draw you into madness? Think of it.
The very place puts toys of desperation,°
Without more motive, into every brain
That looks so many fathoms to the sea
And hears it roar beneath.
HAML. It waves me still.
Go on. I'll follow thee.
MAR. You shall not go, my lord.
HAML. Hold off your hands.
HOR. Be ruled. You shall not go.
HAML. My fate cries out,
And makes each petty artery in this body
As hardy as the Nemean lion's nerve.°
Still am I called. Unhand me, gentlemen.
By Heaven, I'll make a ghost of him that lets° me!
I say, away! Go on I'll follow thee.

[*Exeunt* GHOST *and* HAMLET.]

HOR. He waxes desperate with imagination.
MAR. Let's follow. 'Tis not fit thus to obey him.
HOR. Have after. To what issue will this come?
MAR. Something is rotten in the state of Denmark.

59. impartment: communication. **65. fee:** value. **71. beetles o'er:** juts out over. **73. sovereignty of reason:** control of your reason over your actions. **75. toys of desperation:** desperate fancies. **83. Nemean . . . nerve:** sinew of a fierce beast slain by Hercules. **85. lets:** hinders.

HOR. Heaven will direct it.
MAR. Nay, let's follow him.

[*Exeunt.*]

SCENE V. *Another part of the platform.*

[*Enter* GHOST *and* HAMLET.]

HAML. Whither wilt thou lead me? Speak. I'll go no further.
GHOST. Mark me.
HAML. I will.
GHOST. My hour is almost come
When I to sulphurous and tormenting flames
Must render up myself.
HAML. Alas, poor ghost!
GHOST. Pity me not, but lend thy serious hearing
To what I shall unfold.
HAML. Speak. I am bound to hear.
GHOST. So art thou to revenge, when thou shalt hear.
HAML. What?
GHOST. I am thy father's spirit,
Doomed for a certain term to walk the night
And for the day confined to fast in fires
Till the foul crimes done in my days of nature
Are burnt and purged away. But that I am forbid
To tell the secrets of my prison house,
I could a tale unfold whose lightest word
Would harrow up thy soul, freeze thy young blood,
Make thy two eyes, like stars, start from their spheres,
Thy knotted and combinèd° locks to part
And each particular° hair to stand an° end
Like quills upon the fretful porpentine.°
But this eternal blazon° must not be
To ears of flesh and blood. List, list, oh, list!
If thou didst ever thy dear father love—
HAML. Oh, God!
GHOST. Revenge his foul and most unnatural murder.
HAML. Murder!
GHOST. Murder most foul, as in the best° it is,
But this most foul, strange, and unnatural.
HAML. Haste me to know't, that I, with wings as swift
As meditation or the thoughts of love,
May sweep to my revenge.

Sc. v: 18. knotted . . . combined: the hair that lies together in a mass. **19. particular:** individual. **an:** on. **20. porpentine:** porcupine. **21. eternal blazon:** description of eternity. **27. in . . . best:** i.e., murder is foul even when there is a good excuse.

GHOST. I find thee apt,
And duller shouldst thou be than the fat° weed
That roots itself in ease° on Lethe wharf°
Wouldst thou not stir in this. Now, Hamlet, hear.
'Tis given out that, sleeping in my orchard,
A serpent stung me—so the whole ear of Denmark
Is by a forgèd process° of my death
Rankly abused. But know, thou noble youth,
The serpent that did sting thy father's life
Now wears his crown.

HAML. Oh, my prophetic soul!
My uncle!

GHOST. Aye, that incestuous, that adulterate beast,
With witchcraft of his wit, with traitorous gifts—
O wicked wit and gifts, that have the power
So to seduce!—won to his shameful lust
The will of my most seeming-virtuous Queen.
O Hamlet, what a falling-off was there!
From me, whose love was of that dignity
That it went hand in hand even with the vow
I made to her in marriage, and to decline
Upon a wretch whose natural gifts were poor
To those of mine!
But virtue, as it never will be moved
Though lewdness court it in a shape of Heaven,°
So Lust, though to a radiant angel linked,
Will sate itself° in a celestial bed
And prey on garbage.
But soft! Methinks I scent the morning air.
Brief let me be. Sleeping within my orchard,
My custom always of the afternoon,
Upon my secure hour° thy uncle stole
With juice of cursèd hebenon° in a vial,
And in the porches° of my ears did pour
The leperous distillment,° whose effect
Holds such an enmity with blood of man
That swift as quicksilver it courses through
The natural gates and alleys of the body,
And with a sudden vigor it doth posset°
And curd, like eager° droppings into milk,
The thin and wholesome blood. So did it mine,
And a most instant tetter barked° about,

32. fat: thick, slimy, motionless. **33. in ease:** undisturbed. **Lethe wharf:** the bank of Lethe, the river of forgetfulness in the underworld. **37. forged process:** false account. **54. lewdness . . . Heaven:** though wooed by Lust disguised as an angel. **56. sate itself:** gorge. **61. secure hour:** time of relaxation. **62. hebenon:** probably henbane, a poisonous plant. **63. porches:** entrances. **64. leperous distillment:** distillation causing leprosy. **68. posset:** curdle. **69. eager:** acid. **71. tetter barked:** eruption formed a bark.

Most lazarlike,° with vile and loathsome crust,
All my smooth body.
Thus was I, sleeping, by a brother's hand
Of life, of crown, of Queen, at once dispatched—
Cut off even in the blossoms of my sin,°
Unhouseled, disappointed, unaneled,°
No reckoning made, but sent to my account
With all my imperfections on my head.
Oh, horrible! Oh, horrible, most horrible!
If thou hast nature° in thee, bear it not.
Let not the royal bed of Denmark be
A couch for luxury° and damned incest.
But, howsoever thou pursuest this act,
Taint not thy mind, nor let thy soul contrive
Against thy mother aught. Leave her to Heaven
And to those thorns that in her bosom lodge
To prick and sting her. Fare thee well at once!
The glowworm shows the matin° to be near,
And 'gins to pale his uneffectual° fire.
Adieu, adieu, adieu! Remember me.

[*Exit.*]

HAML. O all you host of Heaven! O earth! What else?
And shall I couple Hell? Oh, fie! Hold, hold, my heart,
And you, my sinews, grow not instant old
But bear me stiffly up. Remember thee!
Aye, thou poor ghost, while memory holds a seat
In this distracted globe.° Remember thee!
Yea, from the table° of my memory
I'll wipe away all trivial fond° recórds,
All saws° of books, all forms,° all pressures° past,
That youth and observation copied there,
And thy commandment all alone shall live
Within the book and volume of my brain,
Unmixed with baser matter. Yes, by Heaven!
O most pernicious woman!
O villain, villain, smiling, damnèd villain!
My tables—meet it is I set it down
[*Writing*] That one may smile, and smile, and be a villain.

---

72. lazarlike: like leprosy. **76. Cut . . . sin:** cut off in a state of sin and so in danger of damnation. See III.iii.80–86. **77. Unhouseled . . . unaneled:** without receiving the sacrament, not properly prepared, unanointed—without extreme unction. **81. nature:** natural feelings. **83. luxury:** lust. **89. matin:** morning. **90. uneffectual:** made ineffectual by daylight. **97. globe:** i.e., head. **98. table:** notebook. Intellectual young men carried notebooks in which they recorded good sayings and notable observations. See III.ii.42,n. **99. fond:** trifling. **100. saws:** wise sayings. **forms:** images in the mind. **pressures:** impressions.

At least I'm sure it may be so in Denmark.
So, Uncle, there you are. Now to my word.°
It is "Adieu, adieu! Remember me."
I have sworn 't.

HOR. & MAR. [*Within*] My lord, my lord!

[*Enter* HORATIO *and* MARCELLUS.]

MAR. Lord Hamlet!

HOR. Heaven secure him!

HAML. So be it!

MAR. Illo, ho, ho,° my lord!

HAML. Hillo, ho, ho, boy! Come, bird, come.

MAR. How is 't, my noble lord?

HOR. What news, my lord?

HAML. Oh, wonderful!

HOR. Good my lord, tell it.

HAML. No, you will reveal it.

HOR. Not I, my lord, by Heaven.

MAR. Nor I, my lord.

HAML. How say you, then, would heart of man once think it?
But you'll be secret?

HOR. & MAR. Aye, by Heaven, my lord.

HAML. There's ne'er a villain dwelling in all Denmark
But he's an arrant° knave.

HOR. There needs no ghost, my lord, come from the grave
To tell us this.

HAML. Why, right, you are i' the right.
And so, without more circumstance° at all.
I hold it fit that we shake hands and part—
You as your business and desire shall point you,
For every man hath business and desire,
Such as it is. And for my own poor part,
Look you, I'll go pray.

HOR. These are but wild and whirling° words, my lord.

HAML. I'm sorry they offend you, heartily,
Yes, faith, heartily.

HOR. There's no offense, my lord.

HAML. Yes, by Saint Patrick, but there is, Horatio,
And much offense too. Touching this vision here,
It is an honest° ghost, that let me tell you.
For your desire to know what is between us,
O'ermaster 't as you may. And now, good friends,

---

110. word: cue. **115. Illo . . . ho:** the falconer's cry to recall the hawk. **124. arrant:** out-and-out. **127. circumstance:** ceremony. **133. whirling:** violent. **138. honest:** true. See I.iv.40,n

As you are friends, scholars, and soldiers,
Give me one poor request.
HOR. What is 't, my lord? We will.
HAML. Never make known what you have seen tonight.
HOR. & MAR. My lord, we will not.
HAML. Nay, but swear 't.
HOR. In faith,
My lord, not I.
MAR. Nor I, my lord, in faith.
HAML. Upon my sword.
MAR. We have sworn, my lord, already
HAML. Indeed, upon my sword,° indeed.
GHOST. [*Beneath*] Swear.
HAML. Ah, ha, boy! Say'st thou so? Art thou there, truepenny?°
Come on. You hear this fellow in the cellarage.
Consent to swear.
HOR. Propose the oath, my lord.
HAML. Never to speak of this that you have seen,
Swear by my sword.
GHOST. [*Beneath*] Swear.
HAML. *Hic et ubique?*° Then we'll shift our ground.
Come hither, gentlemen,
And lay your hands again upon my sword.
Never to speak of this that you have heard,
Swear by my sword.
GHOST. [*Beneath*] Swear.
HAML. Well said, old mole! Canst work i' the earth so fast?
A worthy pioner!° Once more remove,° good friends.
HOR. Oh, day and night, but this is wondrous strange!
HAML. And therefore as a stranger give it welcome.
There are more things in Heaven and earth, Horatio,
Than are dreamt of in your philosophy.
But come,
Here, as before, never, so help you mercy,
How strange or odd soe'er I bear myself,
As I perchance hereafter shall think meet
To put an antic disposition° on,
That you, at such times seeing me, never shall,
With arms encumbered° thus, or this headshake,
Or by pronouncing of some doubtful phrase,
As "Well, well, we know," or "We could an if we would,"
Or "If we list to speak," or "There be, an if they might,"

---

148. upon . . . sword: on the cross made by the hilt of the sword; but for soldiers the sword itself was a sacred object. **150. truepenny:** old boy. **156. Hic et ubique:** here and everywhere. **163. pioner:** miner. **remove:** move. **172. antic disposition:** mad behavior. **174. encumbered:** folded.

Or such ambiguous giving out, to note
That you know aught of me. This not to do,
So grace and mercy at your most need help you,
Swear.

GHOST. [*Beneath*] Swear.

HAML. Rest, rest, perturbèd spirit! [*They swear.*] So, gentlemen,
With all my love I do commend me to you.
And what so poor a man as Hamlet is
May do to express his love and friending° to you,
God willing, shall not lack. Let us go in together.
And still your fingers on your lips, I pray.
The time is out of joint. Oh, cursèd spite
That ever I was born to set it right!
Nay, come, let's go together.

[*Exeunt.*]

ACT II

SCENE I. *A room in* POLONIUS'S *house.*

[*Enter* POLONIUS *and* REYNALDO.]

POL. Give him this money and these notes, Reynaldo.

REY. I will, my lord.

POL. You shall do marvelous wisely, good Reynaldo,
Before you visit him, to make inquire
Of his behavior.

REY. My lord, I did intend it.

POL. Marry, well said, very well said. Look you, sir,
Inquire me first what Danskers° are in Paris,
And how, and who, what means,° and where they keep,°
What company, at what expense, and finding
By this encompassment and drift of question°
That they do know my son, come you more nearer
Than your particular demands will touch it.°
Take you, as 'twere, some distant knowledge of him,
As thus, "I know his father and his friends,
And in part him." Do you mark this, Reynaldo?

REY. Aye, very well, my lord.

---

186. friending: friendship.

Act II, Sc. i: 7. Danskers: Danes. **8. what means:** what their income is. **keep:** live. **10. encompassment . . . question:** roundabout method of questioning. **12. your . . . it:** i.e., you won't get at the truth by straight questions.

POL. "And in part him, but," you may say, "not well.
But if 't be he I mean, he's very wild,
Addicted so and so"—and there put on him
What forgeries° you please. Marry, none so rank°
As may dishonor him, take heed of that,
But, sir, such wanton, wild, and usual slips
As are companions noted and most known
To youth and liberty.

REY. As gaming, my lord.

POL. Aye, or drinking, fencing,° swearing, quarreling,
Drabbing.° You may go so far.

REY. My lord, that would dishonor him.

POL. Faith, no, as you may season° it in the charge.
You must not put another scandal on him,
That he is open to incontinency.°
That's not my meaning. But breathe his faults so quaintly°
That they may seem the taints of liberty,
The flash and outbreak of a fiery mind,
A savageness in unreclaimèd° blood,
Of general assault.°

REY. But, my good lord—

POL. Wherefore should you do this?

REY. Aye, my lord,
I would know that.

POL. Marry, sir, here's my drift,°
And I believe it is a fetch of warrant.°
You laying these slight sullies° on my son,
As 'twere a thing a little soiled i' the working,
Mark you,
Your party in converse, him you would sound,
Having ever seen° in the prenominate° crimes
The youth you breathe of guilty, be assured
He closes with you in this consequence°—
"Good sir," or so, or "friend," or "gentleman,"
According to the phrase or the addition°
Of man and country.

REY. Very good, my lord.

---

20. forgeries: inventions. **rank:** gross. **25. fencing:** A young man who haunted fencing schools would be regarded as quarrelsome and likely to belong to the sporting set. **26. Drabbing:** whoring. **28. season:** qualify. **30. open . . . incontinency:** So long as Laertes does his drabbing inconspicuously Polonius would not be disturbed. **31. quaintly:** skillfully. **34. unreclaimed:** naturally wild. **35. Of . . . assault:** common to all men. **37. drift:** intention. **38. fetch . . . warrant:** trick warranted to work. **39. sullies:** blemishes. **43. Having . . . seen:** if ever he has seen. **prenominate:** aforementioned. **45. closes . . . consequence:** follows up with this reply. **47. addition:** title. See I.iv.20.

POL. And then, sir, does he this—he does—
What was I about to say? By the mass, I was about to say something. Where did I leave?
REY. At "closes in the consequence," at "friend or so," and "gentleman."
POL. At "closes in the consequence," aye, marry,
He closes with you thus: "I know the gentleman.
I saw him yesterday, or t'other day,
Or then, or then, with such, or such, and, as you say,
There was a' gaming, there o'ertook in 's rouse,
There falling out at tennis."° Or perchance,
"I saw him enter such a house of sale,"
Videlicet,° a brothel, or so forth.
See you now,
Your bait of falsehood takes this carp of truth.
And thus do we of wisdom and of reach,°
With windlasses° and with assays of bias,°
By indirections find directions out.°
So, by my former lecture and advice,
Shall you my son. You have me, have you not?
REY. My lord, I have.
POL. God be wi'ye, fare ye well.
REY. Good my lord!
POL. Observe his inclination in° yourself.
REY. I shall, my lord.
POL. And let him ply his music.
REY. Well, my lord.
POL. Farewell!

[*Exit* REYNALDO.]

[*Enter* OPHELIA.]

How now, Ophelia! What's the matter?
OPH. Oh, my lord, my lord, I have been so affrighted!
POL. With what, i' the name of God?
OPH. My lord, as I was sewing in my closet,°
Lord Hamlet, with his doublet° all unbraced,
No hat upon his head, his stockings fouled,
Ungartered and down-gyved° to his ankle,
Pale as his shirt, his knees knocking each other,

---

58. tennis: Visitors to France were much impressed by the enthusiasm of all classes of Frenchmen for tennis, which in England was mainly a courtier's game. **60. Videlicet:** namely, "viz." **63. wisdom . . . reach:** of far-reaching wisdom. **64. windlasses:** roundabout methods. **assays of bias:** making our bowl take a curved course. **65. indirections . . . out:** by indirect means come at the direct truth. **70. in:** for. **77. closet:** private room. **78. doublet:** the short close-fitting coat which was braced to the hose by laces. When a man was relaxing or careless of appearance, he *unbraced,* as a modern man takes off his coat or unbuttons his waistcoat. **80. down-gyved:** hanging around his ankles like fetters.

And with a look so piteous in purport
As if he had been loosèd out of Hell
To speak of horrors, he comes before me.
POL. Mad for thy love?
OPH. My lord, I do not know,
But truly I do fear it.
POL. What said he?
OPH. He took me by the wrist and held me hard.
Then goes he to the length of all his arm,
And with his other hand thus o'er his brow,
He falls to such perusal of my face
As he would draw it. Long stayed he so.
At last, a little shaking of mine arm,
And thrice his head thus waving up and down,
He raised a sigh so piteous and profound
As it did seem to shatter all his bulk
And end his being. That done, he lets me go.
And with his head over his shoulder turned,
He seemed to find his way without his eyes;
For out o' doors he went without their helps,
And to the last bended their light on me.
POL. Come, go with me. I will go seek the King.
This is the very ecstasy° of love,
Whose violent property fordoes° itself
And leads the will to desperate undertakings
As oft as any passion under heaven
That does afflict our natures. I am sorry.
What, have you given him any hard words of late?
OPH. No, my good lord, but, as you did command,
I did repel his letters and denied
His access to me.
POL. That hath made him mad.
I am sorry that with better heed and judgment
I had not quoted° him. I feared he did but trifle
And meant to wreck thee, but beshrew° my jealousy!
By Heaven, it is as proper° to our age
To cast beyond ourselves° in our opinions
As it is common for the younger sort
To lack discretion. Come, go we to the King.
This must be known, which, being kept close, might move
More grief to hide than hate to utter love.°
Come.

---

102. ecstasy: frenzy. **103. property fordoes:** natural quality destroys. **112. quoted:** observed carefully. **113. beshrew:** a plague on. **114. proper:** natural. **115. cast . . . ourselves:** be too clever. **118–19. which . . . love:** by being kept secret it may cause more sorrow than it will cause anger by being revealed; i.e., the King and Queen may be angry at the thought of the Prince's marrying beneath his proper rank.

[*Exeunt.*]

SCENE II. *A room in the castle.*

[*Flourish. Enter* KING, QUEEN, ROSENCRANTZ, GUILDENSTERN, *and* ATTENDANTS.]

KING. Welcome, dear Rosencrantz and Guildenstern!
Moreover° that we much did long to see you,
The need we have to use you did provoke
Our hasty sending. Something have you heard
Of Hamlet's transformation—so call it,
Sith° nor the exterior nor the inward man
Resembles that it was. What it should be,
More than his father's death, that thus hath put him
So much from the understanding of himself
I cannot dream of. I entreat you both
That, being of so young days brought up with him
And sith so neighbored to his youth and havior°
That you vouchsafe your rest° here in our Court
Some little time, so by your companies
To draw him on to pleasures, and to gather
So much as from occasion you may glean,
Whether aught to us unknown afflicts him thus
That opened lies within our remedy.°
QUEEN. Good gentlemen, he hath much talked of you,
And sure I am two men there art not living
To whom he more adheres.° If it will please you
To show us so much gentry° and goodwill
As to expend your time with us a while
For the supply and profit of our hope,°
Your visitation shall receive such thanks
As fits a king's remembrance.
ROS. Both your Majesties
Might, by the sovereign power you have of us,
Put your dread pleasures more into command
Than to entreaty.
GUIL. But we both obey,
And here give up ourselves, in the full bent°
To lay our service freely at your feet,
To be commanded.
KING. Thanks, Rosencrantz and gentle Guildenstern.
QUEEN. Thanks, Guildenstern and gentle Rosencrantz.

Sc. ii: 2. Moreover: in addition to the fact that. **6. Sith:** since. **12. neighbored . . . havior:** so near to his youthful manner of living. **13. vouchsafe . . . rest:** consent to stay. **18. opened . . . remedy:** if revealed, might be put right by us. **21. To . . . adheres:** whom he regards more highly. **22. gentry:** courtesy. **24. supply . . . hope:** to bring a profitable conclusion to our hope. **30. in . . . bent:** stretched to our uttermost.

And I beseech you instantly to visit
My too-much-changèd son. Go, some of you,
And bring these gentlemen where Hamlet is.
GUIL. Heavens make our presence and our practices
Pleasant and helpful to him!
QUEEN. Aye, amen!

[*Exeunt* ROSENCRANTZ, GUILDENSTERN, *and some* ATTENDANTS.]

[*Enter* POLONIUS.]

POL. The ambassadors from Norway, my good lord,
Are joyfully returned.
KING. Thou still° hast been the father of good news.
POL. Have I, my lord? I assure my good liege
I hold my duty as I hold my soul,
Both to my God and to my gracious King.
And I do think, or else this brain of mine
Hunts not the trail of policy so sure
As it hath used to do,° that I have found
The very cause of Hamlet's lunacy.
KING. Oh, speak of that. That do I long to hear.
POL. Give first admittance to the ambassadors.
My news shall be the fruit° to that great feast.
KING. Thyself do grace° to them and bring them in.

[*Exit* POLONIUS.]

He tells me, my dear Gertrude, he hath found
The head and source of all your son's distemper.°
QUEEN. I doubt it is no other but the main,°
His father's death and our o'erhasty marriage.
KING. Well, we shall sift him.

[*Re-enter* POLONIUS, *with* VOLTIMAND *and* CORNELIUS.]

Welcome, my good friends!
Say, Voltimand, what from our brother Norway?
VOLT. Most fair return of greetings and desires.
Upon our first,° he sent out to suppress
His nephew's levies, which to him appeared
To be a preparation 'gainst the Polack,
But better looked into, he truly found

---

42. still: always. **47–48. Hunts . . . do:** is not so good at following the scent of political events as it used to be. **52. fruit:** the dessert, which comes at the end of the feast. **53. do grace:** honor; i.e., by escorting them into the royal presence. **55. distemper:** mental disturbance. **56. main:** principal cause. **61. first:** i.e., audience.

It was against your Highness, whereat, grieved
That so his sickness, age, and impotence
Was falsely borne in hand,° sends out arrests
On Fortinbras; which he, in brief, obeys,
Receives rebuke from Norway, and in fine°
Makes vow before his uncle never more
To give the assay of arms° against your Majesty.
Whereon old Norway, overcome with joy,
Gives him three thousand crowns in annual fee
And his commission to employ those soldiers,
So levied as before, against the Polack.
With an entreaty, herein further shown,

[*Giving a paper*]

That it might please you to give quiet pass°
Through your dominions for this enterprise,
On such regards of safety and allowance°
As therein are set down.

KING. It likes° us well,
And at our more considered time we'll read,
Answer, and think upon this business.
Meantime we thank you for your well-took labor.
Go to your rest. At night we'll feast together.
Most welcome home!

[*Exeunt* VOLTIMAND *and* CORNELIUS.]

POL. This business is well ended.
My liege, and madam, to expostulate°
What majesty should be, what duty is,
Why day is day, night night, and time is time,
Were nothing but to waste night, day, and time.
Therefore, since brevity is the soul of wit
And tediousness the limbs and outward flourishes,°
I will be brief. Your noble son is mad.
Mad call I it, for to define true madness,
What is 't but to be nothing else but mad?
But let that go.

QUEEN. More matter, with less art.°

POL. Madam, I swear I use no art at all.
That he is mad, 'tis true. 'Tis true 'tis pity,

---

67. borne in hand: imposed upon. **69. in fine:** in the end. **71. give . . . arms:** make an attack. **77. quiet pass:** unmolested passage. **79. regards . . . allowance:** safeguard and conditions. **80. likes:** pleases. **86. expostulate:** indulge in an academic discussion. **91. flourishes:** ornaments. **95. art:** ornament.

And pity 'tis 'tis true—a foolish figure,°
But farewell it, for I will use no art.
Mad let us grant him, then. And now remains
That we find out the cause of this effect,
Or rather say the cause of this defect,
For this effect defective comes by cause.
Thus it remains and the remainder thus.
Perpend.°
I have a daughter—have while she is mine—
Who in her duty and obedience, mark,
Hath given me this. Now gather and surmise.° [*Reads.*]
"To the celestial, and my soul's idol, the most beautified° Ophelia—"
That's an ill phrase, a vile phrase, "beautified" is a vile phrase. But you shall hear. Thus: [*Reads.*]
"In her excellent white bosom, these," and so forth.

QUEEN. Came this from Hamlet to her?

POL. Good madam, stay awhile, I will be faithful. [*Reads.*]
"Doubt thou the stars are fire,
Doubt that the sun doth move,
Doubt truth to be a liar,
But never doubt I love.
"O dear Ophelia, I am ill at these numbers,° I have not art to reckon my groans, but that I love thee best, O most best, believe it. Adieu.
"Thine evermore, most dear lady, whilst this
machine° is to him, HAMLET."
This in obedience hath my daughter shown me,
And more above, hath his solicitings,
As they fell out by time, by means and place,
All given to mine ear.

KING. But how hath she
Received his love?

POL. What do you think of me?

KING. As of a man faithful and honorable.

POL. I would fain prove so. But what might you think,
When I had seen this hot love on the wing—
As I perceived it, I must tell you that,
Before my daughter told me—what might you
Or my dear Majesty your Queen here think
If I had played the desk or table book,°
Or given my heart awinking, mute and dumb,
Or looked upon this love with idle sight—

---

98. figure: i.e., a figure of speech. **105. Perpend:** note carefully. **108. surmise:** guess the meaning. **109. beautified:** beautiful. **119. numbers:** verses. **122. machine:** i.e., body, an affected phrase. **134. desk . . . book:** i.e., acted as silent go-between (desks and books being natural post offices for a love letter), or been a recipient of secrets but took no action (as desks and notebooks are the natural but inanimate places for keeping secrets).

What might you think? No, I went round° to work,
And my young mistress thus I did bespeak:°
"Lord Hamlet is a Prince, out of thy star.°
This must not be." And then I prescripts° gave her
That she should lock herself from his resort,
Admit no messengers, receive no tokens.
Which done, she took the fruits of my advice.
And he, repulsèd, a short tale to make,
Fell into a sadness, then into a fast,
Thence to a watch, thence into a weakness,
Thence to a lightness,° and by this declension°
Into the madness wherein now he raves
And all we mourn for.

KING. Do you think this?

QUEEN. It may be, very like.

POL. Hath there been such a time, I'd fain know that,
That I have positively said " 'Tis so"
When it proved otherwise?

KING. Not that I know.

POL. [*Pointing to his head and shoulder.*] Take this from this, if this be otherwise.
If circumstances lead me, I will find
Where truth is hid, though it were hid indeed
Within the center.°

KING. How may we try it further?

POL. You know sometimes he walks four hours together
Here in the lobby.

QUEEN. So he does indeed.

POL. At such a time I'll loose° my daughter to him.
Be you and I behind an arras° then.
Mark the encounter. If he love her not,
And be not from his reason fall'n thereon,
Let me be no assistant for a state,
But keep a farm and carters.°

KING. We will try it.

QUEEN. But look where sadly the poor wretch comes reading.

POL. Away, I do beseech you, both away.
I'll board° him presently.

[*Exeunt* KING, QUEEN, *and* ATTENDANTS.]

---

137. round: straight. **138. bespeak:** address. **139. out . . . star:** above your destiny. **140. prescripts:** instructions. **145–47. Fell . . . lightness:** Hamlet's case history, according to Polonius, develops by stages—melancholy, loss of appetite, sleeplessness, physical weakness, mental instability, and finally madness. **147. declension:** decline. **157. center:** the very center of the earth. **160. loose:** turn loose. **161. arras:** tapestry hanging. **165. keep . . . carters:** i.e., turn country squire—like Justice Shallow. See *II Hen IV.* **168. board:** accost.

[*Enter* HAMLET, *reading.*]

Oh, give me leave. How does my good Lord Hamlet?

HAML. Well, God-a-mercy.

POL. Do you know me, my lord?

HAML. Excellent well. You are a fishmonger.°

POL. Not I, my lord.

HAML. Then I would you were so honest a man.

POL. Honest, my lord!

HAML. Aye, sir, to be honest, as this world goes, is to be one man picked out of ten thousand.

POL. That's very true, my lord.

HAML. For if the sun breed maggots° in a dead dog, being a god° kissing carrion°— Have you a daughter?

POL. I have, my lord.

HAML. Let her not walk i' the sun. Conception is a blessing, but not as your daughter may conceive—friend, look to 't.

POL. [*Aside*] How say you by that? Still harping on my daughter. Yet he knew me not at first, he said I was a fishmonger. He is far gone, far gone. And truly in my youth I suffered much extremity for love, very near this. I'll speak to him again.—What do you read, my lord?

HAML. Words, words, words.

POL. What is the matter, my lord?

HAML. Between who?

POL. I mean the matter that you read, my lord.

HAML. Slanders, sir. For the satirical rogue says here that old men have gray beards, that their faces are wrinkled, their eyes purging thick amber and plum-tree gum, and that they have a plentiful lack of wit, together with most weak hams.° All which, sir, though I most powerfully and potently believe, yet I hold it not honesty to have it thus set down; for yourself, sir, should be old as I am if like a crab you could go backward.

POL. [*Aside*] Though this be madness, yet there is method° in't.—Will you walk out of the air, my lord?

HAML. Into my grave.

POL. Indeed, that's out of the air. [*Aside*] How pregnant° sometimes his replies are! A happiness° that often madness hits on, which reason and sanity could not so prosperously be delivered of. I will leave him, and suddenly contrive the means of meeting between him and my daughter.—My honorable lord, I will most humbly take my leave of you.

HAML. You cannot, sir, take from me anything that I will more willingly part withal—except my life, except my life, except my life.

POL. Fare you well, my lord.

HAML. These tedious old fools!

---

172. fishmonger: Hamlet is now in his "antic disposition," enjoying himself by fooling Polonius. **179. sun . . . maggots:** a general belief. Cf. *Ant & Cleo,* II.vii.29–31. **179. god:** Q2 and F1 read "good." **carrion:** flesh. **195. hams:** knee joints. **198. method:** order, sense. **201. pregnant:** apt, meaningful. **202. happiness:** good turn of phrase.

[*Enter* ROSENCRANTZ *and* GUILDENSTERN.]

POL. You go to seek the Lord Hamlet. There he is.

ROS. [*To* POLONIUS] God save you, sir!

[*Exit* POLONIUS.]

GUIL. My honored lord!

ROS. My most dear lord!

HAML. My excellent good friends!° How dost thou, Guildenstern? Ah, Rosencrantz! Good lads, how do you both?

ROS. As the indifferent° children of the earth.

GUIL. Happy in that we are not overhappy.
On Fortune's cap we are not the very button.°

HAML. Nor the soles of her shoe?

ROS. Neither, my lord.

HAML. Then you live about her waist, or in the middle of her favors?

GUIL. Faith, her privates° we.

HAML. In the secret parts of Fortune? Oh, most true, she is a strumpet. What's the news?

ROS. None, my lord, but that the world's grown honest.

HAML. Then is Doomsday near. But your news is not true. Let me question more in particular. What have you, my good friends, deserved at the hands of Fortune, that she sends you to prison hither?

GUIL. Prison, my lord!

HAML. Denmark's a prison.

ROS. Then is the world one.

HAML. A goodly one, in which there are many confines,° wards,° and dungeons, Denmark being one o' the worst.

ROS. We think not so, my lord.

HAML. Why, then 'tis none to you, for there is nothing either good or bad but thinking makes it so. To me it is a prison.

ROS. Why, then your ambition° makes it one. 'Tis too narrow for your mind.

HAML. Oh, God, I could be bounded in a nutshell and count myself a king of infinite space were it not that I have bad dreams.

GUIL. Which dreams indeed are ambition, for the very substance of the ambitious° is merely the shadow of a dream.

HAML. A dream itself is but a shadow.

ROS. Truly, and I hold ambition of so airy and light a quality that it is but a shadow's shadow.

---

214. My . . . friends: As soon as Polonius has gone, Hamlet drops his assumed madness and greets Rosencrantz and Guildenstern naturally. **216. indifferent:** neither too great nor too little. **218. button:** i.e., at the top. **222. privates:** with a pun on "private parts" and "private," not concerned with politics. **232. confines:** places of confinement. **wards:** cells. **237. your ambition:** Rosencrantz is feeling after one possible cause of Hamlet's melancholy—thwarted ambition. **240. substance . . . ambitious:** that on which an ambitious man feeds his fancies.

HAML. Then are our beggars bodies, and our monarchs and outstretched heroes the beggars' shadows.° Shall we to the Court? For, by my fay,° I cannot reason.°

ROS. & GUIL. We'll wait upon you.°

HAML. No such matter. I will not sort° you with the rest of my servants, for, to speak to you like an honest man, I am most dreadfully attended.° But in the beaten way of friendship, what make you at Elsinore?

ROS. To visit you, my lord, no other occasion.

HAML. Beggar that I am, I am even poor in thanks, but I thank you. And sure, dear friends, my thanks are too dear a halfpenny.° Were you not sent for? Is it your own inclining? Is it a free visitation?° Come, deal justly with me. Come, come. Nay, speak.

GUIL. What should we say, my lord?

HAML. Why, anything, but to the purpose.° You were sent for, and there is a kind of confession in your looks which your modesties have not craft enough to color.° I know the good King and Queen have sent for you.

ROS. To what end, my lord?

HAML. That you must teach me. But let me conjure° you, by the rights of our fellowship,° by the consonancy° of our youth, by the obligation of our ever preserved love, and by what more dear a better proposer could charge you withal, be even° and direct with me, whether you were sent for, or no.

ROS. [*Aside to* GUILDENSTERN] What say you?

HAML. [*Aside*] Nay, then, I have an eye of you.—
If you love me, hold not off.

GUIL. My lord, we were sent for.

HAML. I will tell you why. So shall my anticipation prevent your discovery, and your secrecy to the King and Queen molt no feather.° I have of late—but wherefore I know not—lost all my mirth, forgone all custom of exercises, and indeed it goes so heavily with my disposition that this goodly frame the earth seems to me a sterile promontory. This most excellent canopy,° the air, look you, this brave o'erhanging firmament,° this majestical roof fretted° with golden fire—why, it appears no other thing to me than a foul and pestilent congregation of vapors. What a piece of work is a man! How noble in reason! How infinite in faculty!° In form and moving° how express° and admirable! In action how like an angel! In apprehension how like a god! The beauty of the world! The paragon of animals! And yet, to me, what is this quintessence°

245–46. Then . . . shadows: i.e., by your reasoning beggars are the only men of substance, for kings and heroes are by nature ambitious and therefore "the shadows of a dream." outstretched: of exaggerated reputation. **246. fay:** faith. **247. reason:** argue. **248. wait . . . you:** be your servants. **249. sort:** class. **250. dreadfully attended:** my attendants are a poor crowd. **254. too . . . halfpenny:** not worth a halfpenny. **255. free visitation:** voluntary visit. **258. anything . . . purpose:** anything so long as it is not true. **260. color:** conceal. **262. conjure:** make solemn appeal to. **263. fellowship:** comradeship. **263. consonancy:** concord. **265. even:** straight. **271–72. So . . . feather:** i.e., so by my telling you first you will not be obliged to betray the secrets of the King. **prevent:** forestall. **molt no feather:** be undisturbed. **275. canopy:** covering. **276. firmament:** sky. **fretted:** ornamented. **279. faculty:** power of the mind. **moving:** movement. **express:** exact. **281. quintessence:** perfection; the fifth essence, which would be left if the four elements were taken away.

of dust? Man delights not me—no, nor woman neither, though by your smiling you seem to say so.

ROS. My lord, there was no such stuff in my thoughts.

HAML. Why did you laugh, then, when I said "Man delights not me"?

ROS. To think, my lord, if you delight not in man, what lenten entertainment° the players shall receive from you. We coted° them on the way, and hither are they coming to offer you service.

HAML. He that plays the King shall be welcome, His Majesty shall have tribute of me. The adventurous knight shall use his foil and target,° the lover shall not sigh gratis, the humorous man° shall end his part in peace, the clown shall make those laugh whose lungs are tickle o' the sere,° and the lady shall say her mind freely or the blank verse shall halt° for't. What players are they?

ROS. Even those you were wont to take such delight in, the tragedians of the city.

HAML. How chances it they travel? Their residence, both in reputation and profit, was better both ways.°

ROS. I° think their inhibition° comes by the means of the late innovation.°

HAML. Do they hold the same estimation they did when I was in the city? Are they so followed?

ROS. No, indeed are they not.

HAML. How comes it? Do they grow rusty?

ROS. Nay, their endeavor keeps in the wonted pace.° But there is, sir, an eyrie° of children, little eyases,° that cry out on the top of question° and are most tyrannically° clapped for 't. These are now the fashion, and so berattle° the common stages°—so they call them—that many wearing rapiers are afraid of goose quills° and dare scarce come thither.

HAML. What, are they children? Who maintains 'em? How are they escoted?° Will they pursue the quality° no longer than they can sing? Will they not say afterward, if they should grow themselves to common players—as it is most like if their means are no better—their writers do them wrong to make them exclaim against their own succession?°

ROS. Faith, there has been much to-do on both sides, and the nation holds it no sin to tarre° them to controversy. There was for a while no money bid for argument° unless the poet and the player went to cuffs° in the question.

HAML. Is 't possible?

GUIL. Oh, there has been much throwing-about of brains.

HAML. Do the boys carry it away?

---

286. lenten entertainment: meager welcome. **287. coted:** overtook. **290. foil . . . target:** rapier and small shield. **291 humorous man:** the man who specializes in character parts; e.g., Jaques in *AYLI.* **297. are . . . sere:** explode at a touch. The *sere* is part of the trigger mechanism of a gun which if "ticklish" will go off at a touch. **293. halt:** limp. **295–96. Their . . . ways:** i.e., if they stayed in the city, it would bring them more profit and fame. **297–318. I . . . too:** This is one of the several topical references in *Hamlet.* **297. inhibition:** formal prohibition. **297. innovation:** riot. **302. endeavor . . . pace:** they try as hard as ever. **302. eyrie:** nest. **303. eyases:** young hawks. **303. cry . . . question:** either "cry in a shrill voice" or perhaps "cry out the latest detail of the dispute." **304. tyrannically:** outrageously. **304. berattle:** abuse. **305. common stages:** the professional players. The boys acted in "private" playhouses. **306. goose quills:** pens; i.e., of such as Ben Jonson. **307. escoted:** paid. **308. quality:** acting profession. **311. exclaim . . . succession:** abuse the profession to which they will afterward belong. **313. tarre:** urge on to fight; generally used of encouraging a dog. **314. argument:** plot of a play. See III.ii.242. **314. went to cuffs:** boxed each other's ears.

ROS. Aye, that they do, my lord, Hercules and his load° too.

HAML. It is not very strange, for my uncle is King of Denmark, and those that would make mows° at him while my father lived give twenty, forty, fifty, a hundred ducats apiece for his picture in little. 'Sblood,° there is something in this more than natural, if philosophy could find it out.

[Flourish of trumpets within.]

GUIL. There are the players.

HAML. Gentlemen, you are welcome to Elsinore. Your hands. Come then. The appurtenance of welcome is fashion and ceremony.° Let me comply° with you in this garb,° lest my extent° to the 390 players—which, I tell you, must show fairly outward—should more appear like entertainment° than yours. You are welcome. But my uncle-father and aunt-mother are deceived.

GUIL. In what, my dear lord?

HAML. I am but mad north-northwest.° When the wind is southerly,° I know a hawk from a handsaw.°

[Re-enter POLONIUS.*]*

POL. Well be with you, gentlemen!

HAML. Hark you, Guildenstern, and you too—at each ear a hearer. That great baby you see there is not yet out of his swaddling clouts.°

ROS. Happily he's the second time come to them, for they say an old man is twice a child.

HAML. I will prophesy he comes to tell me of the players, mark it. You say right, sir. O' Monday morning, 'twas so indeed.

POL. My lord, I have news to tell you.

HAML. My lord, I have news to tell you. When Roscius° was an actor in Rome—

POL. The actors are come hither, my lord.

HAML. Buzz, buzz!°

POL. Upon my honor—

HAML. Then came each actor on his ass—

POL. The° best actors in the world, either for tragedy, comedy, history, pastoral, pastoral-comical, historical-pastoral, tragical-historical, tragical-comical-historical-pastoral, scene individable° or poem unlimited.° Seneca cannot be too heavy, nor Plautus° too light. For the law of writ° and the liberty,° these are the only men.

---

318. Hercules . . . load: Hercules carrying the globe on his shoulders was the sign of the Globe Playhouse. **320. mows:** grimaces. **321. 'Sblood:** by God's blood. **325. appurtenance . . . ceremony:** that which pertains to welcome is formal ceremony. **325. comply:** use the formality of welcome; i.e., shake hands with you. **326. garb:** fashion. **extent:** outward behavior. **327. entertainment:** welcome. **330. north-northwest:** i.e., 327° (out of 360°) of the compass. **330. wind is southerly:** The south wind was considered unhealthy. **331. hawk . . . handsaw:** Either "handsaw" is a corruption of "heronshaw," heron, or a hawk is a tool like a pickax. The phrase means "I'm not so mad as you think." **334. clouts:** clothes. **340. Roscius:** the most famous of Roman actors. **342. Buzz, buzz:** slang for "stale news." **345–49. The . . . men:** Polonius reads out the accomplishments of the actors from the license which they have presented him. **347. scene individable:** i.e., a play preserving the unities. **347. poem unlimited:** i.e., a play which disregards the rules. **347–48. Seneca . . . Plautus:** the Roman writers of tragedy and comedy with whose plays every educated man was familiar. **348. law of writ:** the critical rules; i.e., classical plays. **liberty:** plays freely written; i.e., "modern" drama.

HAML. O Jephthah,° judge of Israel, what a treasure hadst thou!
POL. What a treasure had he, my lord?
HAML. Why,

"One° fair daughter, and no more,
The which he lovèd passing well."

POL. [*Aside*] Still° on my daughter.
HAML. Am I not i' the right, old Jephthah?
POL. If you call me Jephthah, my lord, I have a daughter that I love passing well.
HAML. Nay, that follows not.
POL. What follows, then, my lord?
HAML. Why,

"As by lot, God wot,"°

and then you know,

"It came to pass, as most like it was—" the first row° of the pious chanson° will show you more, for look where my abridgement° comes.

[*Enter four or five* PLAYERS.]

You are welcome, masters, welcome all. I am glad to see thee well. Welcome, good friends. Oh, my old friend!° Why, thy face is valanced° since I saw thee last. Comest thou to beard° me in Denmark? What, my young lady° and mistress! By 'r Lady, your ladyship is nearer to Heaven than when I saw you last, by the altitude of a chopine.° Pray God your voice, like a piece of uncurrent gold, be not cracked within the ring.° Masters, you are all welcome. We'll e'en to 't like French falconers,° fly at anything we see. We'll have a speech straight. Come, give us a taste of your quality°—come, a passionate speech.

I. PLAY. What speech, my good lord?
HAML. I heard thee speak me a speech once, but it was never acted, or if it was, not above once; for the play, I remember, pleased not the million, 'twas caviar° to the general.° But it was—as I received it, and others, whose judgments in such matters cried in the top of mine°—an excellent play, well digested° in the scenes, set down with as much modesty° as cunning. I remember one said there were no sallets° in the lines to make the matter savory, nor no matter in the phrase that might indict the author of affection,° but called it an honest method, as wholesome as sweet, and by very much more handsome than fine.° One speech in it I chiefly loved. 'Twas Aeneas'

---

350. Jephthah: The story of Jephthah is told in Judges, Chapter II. He vowed that if successful against the Ammonites he would sacrifice the first creature to meet him on his return, which was his daughter. **253–63. One . . . was:** Quotations from a ballad of Jephthah. **355. Still:** always. **361. wot:** knows. **363. row:** line. **pious chanson:** godly poem. **364. abridgement:** entertainment. Cf. *MND,* V.i.39. **366. old friend: i.e.,** the leading player. **367. valanced:** bearded. A valance is a fringe hung round the sides and bottom of a bed. **367. beard:** dare, with a pun on "valanced." **368. young lady:** i.e., the boy who takes the woman's parts. **369. chopine:** lady's shoe with thick cork sole. **370. cracked . . . ring:** Before coins were milled on the rim they were liable to crack. When the crack reached the ring surrounding the device, the coin was no longer valid. **371. French falconers:** They were famous for their skill in hawking. **372. quality:** skill as an actor. **377. caviar:** sturgeon's roe, a Russian delicacy not then appreciated (or known) by any but gourmets. **general:** common herd. **378. cried . . . mine:** surpassed mine. **379. digested:** composed. **modesty:** moderation. **380. sallets:** tasty bits. **381. phrase . . . affection:** nothing in the language which could charge the author with affectation. **383. fine:** subtle.

tale to Dido,° and thereabout of it especially where he speaks of Priam's° slaughter. If it live in your memory, begin at this line—let me see, let me see—

"The rugged Pyrrhus,° like th' Hyrcanian
beast,°—"
It is not so. It begins with "Pyrrhus."
"The° rugged Pyrrhus, he whose sable° arms,
Black as his purpose, did the night resemble
When he lay couchèd in the ominous° horse,°
Hath now this dread and black complexion smeared
With heraldry° more dismal. Head to foot
Now is he total gules, horridly tricked
With blood of fathers, mothers, daughters, sons,
Baked and impasted° with the parching streets
That lend a tyrannous and a damnèd light
To their lord's murder. Roasted in wrath and fire,
And thus o'ersized with coagulate gore,°
With eyes like carbuncles, the hellish Pyrrhus
Old grandsire Priam seeks."
So, proceed you.

POL. 'Fore God, my lord, well spoken, with good accent and good discretion.

I. PLAY. "Anon he finds him
Striking too short at Greeks. His antique sword,
Rebellious to his arm, lies where it falls,
Repugnant to command.° Unequal matched,
Pyrrhus at Priam drives, in rage strikes wide,
But with the whiff and wind of his fell sword
The unnerved father falls. Then senseless Ilium,°
Seeming to feel this blow, with flaming top
Stoops to his base,° and with a hideous crash
Takes prisoner Pyrrhus' ear. For, lo! his sword,
Which was declining° on the milky° head
Of reverend Priam, seemed i' the air to stick.
So as a painted tyrant° Pyrrhus stood,
And like a neutral to his will and matter,°

383–84. Aeneas' . . . Dido: the story of the sack of Troy as told by Aeneas to Dido, Queen of Carthage. The original is in Virgil's *Aeneid.* A similar speech occurs in Marlowe's play *Dido, Queen of Carthage.* **384. Priam:** the old King of Troy. **387. Pyrrhus:** the son of Achilles, one of the Greeks concealed in the Wooden Horse. **387–88. Hyrcanian beast:** the tiger. **390–454. The . . . gods:** The speech may be from some lost play of *Dido and Aeneas,* but more likely it is Shakespeare's own invention. It is written in the heavy elaborate style still popular in the dramas of the Admiral's Men. The first player delivers it with excessive gesture and emotion. **390. sable:** black. **392. ominous:** fateful. **horse:** the Wooden Horse by which a small Greek force was enabled to make a secret entry into Troy. **394. heraldry:** painting. The image of heraldic painting is kept up in *gules* (the heraldic term for red) and *tricked* (painted). **397. impasted:** turned into a crust by the heat of the burning city. **400. o'ersized . . . gore:** covered over with congealed blood. **408. Repugnant to command:** refusing to be used. **411. Ilium:** the citadel of Troy. **413. stoops . . . base:** collapses. **415. declining:** bending toward. **milky:** milk-white. **417. painted tyrant:** as in the painting of a tyrant. **418. neutral . . . matter:** one midway *(neutral)* between his desire *(will)* and action *(matter).*

Did nothing.
But as we often see, against° some storm
A silence in the heavens, the rack° stand still,
The bold winds speechless and the orb° below
As hush as death, anon the dreadful thunder
Doth rend the region°—so after Pyrrhus' pause
Arousèd vengeance sets him new awork.
And never did the Cyclops'° hammers fall
On Mars's armor, forged for proof eterne,°
With less remorse° than Pyrrhus' bleeding sword
Now falls on Priam.
Out, out, thou strumpet, Fortune! All you gods,
In general synod° take away her power,
Break all the spokes and fellies° from her wheel,
And bowl the round nave° down the hill of Heaven
As low as to the fiends!"

POL. This is too long.

HAML. It shall to the barber's, with your beard. Prithee, say on. He's for a jig° or a tale of bawdry, or he sleeps. Say on. Come to Hecuba.

I. PLAY. "But who, oh, who had seen the mobled° Queen—"

HAML. "The mobled Queen"?

POL. That's good, "mobled Queen" is good.

I. PLAY. "Run barefoot up and down, threatening the flames
With bisson rheum,° a clout° upon that head
Where late the diadem stood, and for a robe,
About her lank and all o'erteemèd° loins
A blanket, in the alarm of fear caught up.
Who this had seen, with tongue in venom steeped
'Gainst Fortune's state would treason have pronounced.°
But if the gods themselves did see her then,
When she saw Pyrrhus make malicious sport
In mincing with his sword her husband's limbs,
The instant burst of clamor that she made,
Unless things mortal move them not at all,
Would have made milch° the burning eyes of Heaven
And passion in the gods."

POL. Look whether he has not turned his color and has tears in 's eyes. Prithee, no more.

HAML. 'Tis well; I'll have thee speak out the rest of this soon. Good my lord, will

---

420. against: just before. **421. rack:** the clouds in the upper air. Cf. *Ant & Clco,* IV.xiv.10. **507. orb:** world. **422. orb:** world. **424. region:** the country round. **426. Cyclops':** of Titans, giants who aided Vulcan, the blacksmith god, to make armor for Mars, the war god. **427. proof eterne:** everlasting protection. **428. remorse:** pity. **431. synod:** council. **432. fellies:** the pieces forming the circumference of a wooden wheel. **433. nave:** center of the wheel. **436. jig:** bawdy dance. **438. mobled:** muffled. **442. bisson rheum:** blinding moisture. **clout:** rag. **444. o'erteemed:** exhausted by bearing children; she had borne fifty-two. **446–47. Who . . . pronounced:** anyone who had seen this sight would with bitter words have uttered treason against the tyranny of Fortune. **453. milch:** milky, i.e., dripping moisture.

you see the players well bestowed?° Do you hear, let them be well used, for they are the abstract and brief chronicles of the time.° After your death you were better have a bad epitaph than their ill report while you live.

POL. My lord, I will use them according to their desert.°

HAML. God's bodykins,° man, much better. Use every man after his desert and who shall 'scape whipping? Use them after your own honor and dignity. The less they deserve, the more merit is in your bounty. Take them in.

POL. Come, sirs.

HAML. Follow him, friends. We'll hear a play tomorrow.

[*Exit* POLONIUS *with all the* PLAYERS *but the* FIRST.]

Dost thou hear me, old friend? Can you play *The Murder of Gonzago?*

I. PLAY. Aye, my lord.

HAML. We'll ha 't tomorrow night. You could, for a need, study a speech of some dozen or sixteen lines which I would set down and insert in 't, could you not?

I. PLAY. Aye, my lord.

HAML. Very well. Follow that lord, and look you mock him not.

[*Exit* FIRST PLAYER.]

My good friends, I'll leave you till night. You are welcome to Elsinore.

ROS. Good my lord!

HAML. Aye, so, God be wi' ye!

[*Exeunt* ROSENCRANTZ *and* GUILDENSTERN.]

Now I am alone.
Oh, what a rogue and peasant slave am I!
Is it not monstrous that this player here,
But in a fiction, in a dream of passion,°
Could force his soul so to his own conceit°
That from her working° all his visage wanned,°
Tears in his eyes, distraction° in 's aspect,°
A broken voice, and his whole function° suiting
With forms to his conceit? And all for nothing!
For Hecuba!
What's Hecuba to him or he to Hecuba,
That he should weep for her? What would he do
Had he the motive and the cue for passion

---

458. bestowed: housed. **459. abstract . . . time:** they summarize and record the events of our time. Elizabethan players were often in trouble for too saucily commenting on their betters in plays dealing with history or contemporary events and persons. **461. desert:** rank. **462. God's bodykins:** by God's little body. **480. dream of passion:** imaginary emotion. **481. conceit:** imagination. **482. her working:** i.e., the effect of imagination. **wanned:** went pale. **483. distraction:** frenzy. **aspect:** countenance. **484. function:** behavior.

That I have? He would drown the stage with tears
And cleave the general ear° with horrid speech,
Make mad the guilty and appal the free,°
Confound the ignorant, and amaze indeed
The very faculties of eyes and ears.
Yet I,
A dull and muddy-mettled° rascal, peak,°
Like John-a-dreams,° unpregnant or my cause,°
And can say nothing—no, not for a King
Upon whose property° and most dear life
A damned defeat° was made. Am I a coward?
Who° calls me villain? Breaks my pate across?
Plucks off my beard and blows it in my face?
Tweaks me by the nose? Gives me the lie i' the throat
As deep as to the lungs? Who does me this?
Ha!
'Swounds,° I should take it. For it cannot be
But I am pigeon-livered° and lack gall°
To make oppression bitter, or ere this
I should have fatted all the region kites
With this slave's offal.° Bloody, bawdy villain!
Remorseless, treacherous, lecherous, kindless° villain!
Oh, vengeance!
Why, what an ass am I! This is most brave,
That I, the son of a dear father murdered,
Prompted to my revenge by Heaven and Hell,
Must, like a whore, unpack my heart with words
And fall a-cursing like a very drab,°
A scullion!°
Fie upon 't! Foh! About, my brain! Hum, I have heard
That guilty creatures sitting at a play
Have by the very cunning of the scene
Been struck so to the soul that presently°
They have proclaimed their malefactions;°
For murder, though it have no tongue, will speak
With most miraculous organ. I'll have these players
Play something like the murder of my father
Before mine uncle. I'll observe his looks,
I'll tent° him to the quick. If he but blench,°

---

491. general ear: ears of the audience. **492. free:** innocent. **496. muddy-mettled:** made of mud, not iron. **peak:** mope. **497. John-a-dreams:** "Sleepy Sam." **unpregnant . . . cause:** barren of plans for vengeance. **499. property:** personality, life. **500. defeat:** ruin. **501–504. Who . . . this:** Hamlet runs through all the insults which provoked a resolute man to mortal combat. **pate:** head. **lie . . . throat:** the bitterest of insults. **506. 'Swounds:** by God's wounds. **507. pigeon-livered:** "as gentle as a dove." **gall:** spirit. **509–510. I . . . offal:** before this I would have fed this slave's (i.e., the King's) guts to the kites. **fatted:** made fat. **511. kindless:** unnatural. **517. drab:** "moll." **518. scullion:** the lowest of the kitchen servants. **522. presently:** immediately. **523. proclaimed . . . malefactions:** shouted out their crimes. **528. tent:** probe. See *Cor,* I.ix.31. **blench:** flinch.

I know my course. The spirit that I have seen
May be the Devil, and the Devil hath power
To assume a pleasing shape. Yea, and perhaps
Out of my weakness and my melancholy,
As he is very potent with such spirits,
Abuses me to damn me.° I'll have grounds°
More relative than this.° The play's the thing
Wherein I'll catch the conscience of the King.

[*Exit.*]

ACT III

SCENE I. *A room in the castle.*

[*Enter* KING, QUEEN, POLONIUS, OPHELIA, ROSENCRANTZ, *and* GUILDENSTERN.]

KING. And can you, by no drift of circumstance,°
Get from him why he puts on this confusion,
Grating° so harshly all his days of quiet
With turbulent and dangerous lunacy?
ROS. He does confess he feels himself distracted,
But from what cause he will by no means speak.
GUIL. Nor do we find him forward to be sounded,°
But, with a crafty madness, keeps aloof
When we would bring him on to some confession
Of his true state.
QUEEN. Did he receive you well?
ROS. Most like a gentleman.
GUIL. But with much forcing of his disposition.°
ROS. Niggard of question,° but of our demands
Most free in his reply.
QUEEN. Did you assay him
To any pastime?°
ROS. Madam, it so fell out that certain players
We o'erraught° on the way. Of these we told him,
And there did seem in him a kind of joy
To hear of it. They are about the Court,
And, as I think, they have already order
This night to play before him.

---

534. Abuses . . . me: i.e., deceives me so that I may commit the sin of murder which will bring me to damnation. **grounds:** reasons for action. **535. relative . . . this:** i.e., more convincing than the appearance of a ghost.

Act III. Sc. i: 1. drift of circumstance: circumstantial evidence, hint. **3. grating:** disturbing. **7. forward . . . sounded:** eager to be questioned. **12. much . . . disposition:** making a great effort to be civil to us. **13. Niggard of question:** not asking many questions. **14–15. Did . . . pastime:** did you try to interest him in any amusement. **17. o'erraught:** overtook.

POL. 'Tis most true.
And he beseeched me to entreat your Majesties
To hear and see the matter.

KING. With all my heart, and it doth much content me
To hear him so inclined.
Good gentlemen, give him a further edge,°
And drive his purpose on to these delights.

ROS. We shall, my lord.

[*Exeunt* ROSENCRANTZ *and* GUILDENSTERN.]

KING. Sweet Gertrude, leave us too,
For we have closely° sent for Hamlet hither,
That he, as 'twere by accident, may here
Affront° Ophelia.
Her father and myself, lawful espials,°
Will so bestow ourselves that, seeing unseen,
We may of their encounter frankly judge
And gather by him, as he is behaved,°
If't be the affliction of his love or no
That thus he suffers for.

QUEEN. I shall obey you.
And for your part, Ophelia, I do wish
That your good beauties be the happy cause
Of Hamlet's wildness. So shall I hope your virtues
Will bring him to his wonted way° again,
To both your honors.

OPH. Madam, I wish it may.

[*Exit* QUEEN.]

POL. Ophelia, walk you here. Gracious,° so please you,
We will bestow ourselves. [*To* OPHELIA] Read on this book,°
That show of such an exercise may color
Your loneliness. We are oft to blame in this—
'Tis too much proved—that with devotion's visage°
And pious action we do sugar o'er
The Devil himself.

KING. [*Aside*] Oh, 'tis too true!
How smart a lash that speech doth give my conscience!
The harlot's cheek, beautied with plastering art,

26. edge: encouragement. **29. closely:** secretly. **31. Affront:** encounter. **32. lawful espials:** who are justified in spying on him. **35. by . . . behaved:** from him, from his behavior. **41. wonted way:** normal state. **43. Gracious:** your Majesty—addressed to the King. **44. book:** i.e., of devotions. **47. devotion's visage:** an outward appearance of religion.

Is not more ugly to the thing that helps it°
Than is my deed to my most painted° word.
Oh, heavy burden!

POL. I hear him coming. Let's withdraw, my lord.

[*Exeunt* KING *and* POLONIUS.]

[*Enter* HAMLET.°]

HAML. To be, or not to be—that is the question.
Whether 'tis nobler in the mind to suffer
The slings and arrows of outrageous° fortune,
Or to take arms against a sea° of troubles
And by opposing end them. To die, to sleep—
No more, and by a sleep to say we end
The heartache and the thousand natural shocks
That flesh is heir to. 'Tis a consummation°
Devoutly to be wished. To die, to sleep,
To sleep—perchance to dream. Aye, there's the rub,°
For in that sleep of death what dreams may come
When we have shuffled off this mortal coil°
Must give us pause. There's the respect°
That makes calamity of so long life.°
For who would bear the whips and scorns of time,
The oppressor's wrong, the proud man's contumely°
The pangs of déspised love, the law's delay,
The insolence of office° and the spurns
That patient merit of the unworthy takes,°
When he himself might his quietus° make
With a bare bodkin?° Who would fardels° bear,
To grunt and sweat under a weary life,
But that the dread of something after death,
The undiscovered country from whose bourn°
No traveler returns, puzzles the will,°
And makes us rather bear those ills we have
Than fly to others that we know not of?
Thus° conscience does make cowards of us all,
And thus the native hue° of resolution

---

52. ugly . . . it: i.e., lust, which is the cause of its artificial beauty. **53. painted:** i.e., false. **55. s.d., Enter Hamlet:** In Q1 the King draws attention to Hamlet's approach with the words "See where he comes poring upon a book." Hamlet is again reading, and is too much absorbed to notice Ophelia. **58. outrageous:** cruel. **59. sea:** i.e., an endless turmoil. **63. consummation:** completion. **65. rub:** impediment. **67. shuffled . . . coil:** cast off this fuss of life. **68. respect:** reason. **69. makes . . . life:** makes it a calamity to have to live so long. **71. contumely:** insulting behavior. **73. insolence of office:** insolent behavior of government officials. **73–74. spurns . . . takes:** insults which men of merit have patiently to endure from the unworthy. **75. quietus:** discharge. See Sonnet 126. **76. bodkin:** dagger. **fardels:** burdens, the coolie's pack. **79. bourn:** boundary. **80. will:** resolution, ability to act. **83–88. Thus . . . action:** the religious fear that death may not be the end makes men shrink from heroic actions. **84. native hue:** natural color.

Is sicklied o'er with the pale cast° of thought,
And enterprises of great pitch° and moment
With this regard their currents turn awry
And lose the name of action.°—Soft you now!
The fair Ophelia! Nymph, in thy orisons°
Be all my sins remembered.

OPH. Good my lord,
How does your Honor for this many a day?

HAML. I humbly thank you—well, well, well.

OPH. My lord, I have remembrances of yours
That I have longed long to redeliver.
I pray you now receive them.

HAML. No, not I.
I never gave you aught.

OPH. My honored lord, you know right well you did,
And with them words of so sweet breath composed
As made the things more rich. Their perfume lost,
Take these again, for to the noble mind
Rich gifts wax poor when givers prove unkind.
There, my lord.

HAML. Ha, ha! Are you honest?°

OPH. My lord?

HAML. Are you fair?

OPH. What means your lordship?

HAML. That if you be honest and fair, your honesty should admit no discourse to your beauty.°

OPH. Could beauty, my lord, have better commerce than with honesty?

HAML. Aye, truly, for the power of beauty will sooner transform honesty from what it is to a bawd° than the force of honesty can translate beauty into his likeness. This was sometime a paradox,° but now the time gives it proof. I did love you once.

OPH. Indeed, my lord, you made me believe so.

HAML. You should not have believed me, for virtue cannot so inoculate our old stock but we shall relish° of it. I loved you not.

OPH. I was the more deceived.

HAML. Get thee to a nunnery. Why wouldst thou be a breeder of sinners? I am myself indifferent honest,° but yet I could accuse me of such things that it were better my mother had not borne me. I am very proud, revengeful, ambitious, with more offenses at my beck° than I have thoughts to put them in, imagination to give them shape, or time to act them in. What should such

---

85. cast: color. **86. pitch:** height; used of the soaring flight of a hawk. **87–88. With . . . action:** by brooding on this thought great enterprises are diverted from their course and fade away. **89. orisons:** prayers. **103. honest:** chaste **107–08. That . . . beauty:** if you are chaste and beautiful your chastity should have nothing to do with your beauty—because (so Hamlet thinks in his bitterness) beautiful women are seldom chaste. **111. bawd:** brothel-keeper. **112. paradox:** statement contrary to accepted opinion. **116. relish:** have some trace. **119. indifferent honest:** moderately honorable. **121. at . . . beck:** waiting to come when I beckon.

fellows as I do crawling between heaven and earth? We are arrant knaves all. Believe none of us. Go thy ways to a nunnery.° Where's your father?

OPH. At home, my lord.

HAML. Let the doors be shut upon him, that he may play the fool nowhere but in's own house. Farewell.

OPH. Oh, help him, you sweet Heavens!

HAML. If thou dost marry, I'll give thee this plague for thy dowry: Be thou as chaste as ice, as pure as snow—thou shalt not escape calumny.° Get thee to a nunnery, go. Farewell. Or if thou wilt needs marry, marry a fool, for wise men know well enough what monsters° you make of them. To a nunnery, go, and quickly too. Farewell.

OPH. O heavenly powers, restore him!

HAML. I have heard of your paintings° too, well enough. God hath given you one face and you make yourselves another. You jig,° you amble,° and you lisp,° and nickname God's creatures, and make your wantonness your ignorance.° Go to, I'll no more on't—it hath made me mad. I say we will have no more marriages. Those that are married already, all but one, shall live; the rest shall keep as they are. To a nunnery, go.

[*Exit.*]

OPH. Oh, what a noble mind is here o'erthrown!
The courtier's, soldier's, scholar's, eye, tongue, sword—
The expectancy and rose° of the fair state,
The glass° of fashion and the mold of form,°
The observed of all observers—quite, quite down!
And I, of ladies most deject and wretched,
That sucked the honey of his music vows,
Now see that noble and most sovereign reason,
Like sweet bells jangled, out of tune and harsh,
That unmatched° form and feature of blown° youth
Blasted with ecstasy.° Oh, woe is me,
To have seen what I have seen, see what I see!

[*Re-enter* KING *and* POLONIUS.]

KING. Love! His affections° do not that way tend,
Nor what he spake, though it lacked form a little,
Was not like madness. There's something in his soul

124. nunnery: i.e., a place where she will be removed from temptation. **130. calumny:** slander. **132. monsters:** horned beasts, cuckolds. **135. paintings:** using make-up. **140. jig:** dance lecherously. **amble:** walk artificially. **lisp:** talk affectedly. **137. nickname . . . ignorance:** give things indecent names and pretend to be too simple to understand their meanings. **143. expectancy . . . rose:** bright hope. The rose is used as a symbol for beauty and perfection. Cf. *I Hen IV,* I.iii.175. **144. glass:** mirror. **mold of form:** perfect pattern of manly beauty. **150. unmatched:** unmatchable. **blown:** perfect, like an open flower at its best. **151. Blasted . . . ecstasy:** ruined by madness. **153. affections:** state of mind.

O'er which his melancholy sits on brood,°
And I do doubt the hatch and the disclose°
Will be some danger. Which for to prevent,
I have in quick determination
Thus set it down: He shall with speed to England,
For the demand of our neglected tribute.
Haply° the seas and countries different
With variable objects° shall expel
This something-settled° matter in his heart
Whereon his brains still beating puts him thus
From fashion of himself.° What think you on't?

POL. It shall do well. But yet do I believe
The origin and commencement of his grief
Sprung from neglected love. How now, Ophelia!
You need not tell us what Lord Hamlet said,
We heard it all. My lord, do as you please,
But, if you hold it fit, after the play
Let his Queen mother all alone entreat him
To show his grief. Let her be round° with him,
And I'll be placed, so please you, in the ear
Of all their conference. If she find him not,
To England send him, or confine him where
Your wisdom best shall think.

KING. It shall be so.
Madness in great ones must not unwatched go.

[*Exeunt.*]

SCENE II. *A hall in the castle.*

[*Enter* HAMLET *and* PLAYERS.]

HAML. Speak the speech,° I pray you, as I pronounced it to you, trippingly° on the tongue. But if you mouth° it, as many of your players do, I had as lief° the town crier spoke my lines. Nor do not saw the air too much with your hand, thus, but use all gently. For in the very torrent, tempest, and, as I may say, whirlwind of passion, you must acquire and beget a temperance that may give it smoothness. Oh, it offends me to the soul to hear a robustious° periwig-pated° fellow tear a passion to tatters, to very rags, to split the ears of the

---

156. sits . . . brood: sits hatching. **157. doubt . . . disclose:** suspect the brood which will result. **162. Haply:** perhaps. **163. variable objects:** novel sights. **164. something-settled:** somewhat settled; i.e., not yet incurable. **165–55. puts . . . himself:** i.e., separates him from his normal self. **174. round:** direct.

Sc. ii: 1. the speech: which he has written. See ll. 266–67. The whole passage which follows is Shakespeare's own comment on the actor's art and states the creed and practice of his company as contrasted with the more violent methods of Edward Alleyn and his fellows. **1. trippingly:** smoothly, easily. **2. mouth:** "ham" it. **2. lief:** soon. **6. robustious:** ranting. **6–7. periwig-pated:** wearing a wig.

groundlings,° who for the most part are capable of nothing but inexplicable dumb shows° and noise. I would have such a fellow whipped for o'erdoing Termagant°—it out-Herods Herod. Pray you, avoid it.

I. PLAY. I warrant your Honor.

HAML. Be not too tame neither, but let your own discretion be your tutor. Suit the action to the word, the word to the action, with this special observance, that you o'erstep not the modesty of nature. For anything so overdone is from° the purpose of playing, whose end, both at the first and now, was and is to hold as 'twere the mirror up to Nature—to show Virtue her own feature, scorn her own image, and the very age and body of the time his form and pressure.° Now this overdone or come tardy off, though it make the unskillful laugh, cannot but make the judicious grieve, the censure of the which one° must in your allowance o'erweigh a whole theater of others. Oh, there be players° that I have seen play, and heard others praise—and that highly, not to speak it profanely—that neither having the accent of Christians nor the gait of Christian, pagan, nor man, have so strutted and bellowed that I have thought some of Nature's journeymen° had made men, and not made them well, they imitated humanity so abominably.

I. PLAY. I hope we have reformed that indifferently° with us, sir.

HAML. Oh, reform it altogether. And let those that play your clowns° speak no more than is set down for them. For there be of them that will themselves laugh, to set on some quantity of barren spectators to laugh too, though in the meantime some necessary question of the play be then to be considered. That's villainous, and shows a most pitiful° ambition in the fool that uses it. Go, make you ready.

[*Exeunt* PLAYERS. *Enter* POLONIUS, ROSENCRANTZ, *and* GUILDENSTERN.]

How now, my lord! Will the King hear this piece of work?

POL. And the Queen too, and that presently.

HAML. Bid the players make haste.

[*Exit* POLONIUS.]

Will you two help to hasten them?

ROS. & GUIL. We will, my lord.

---

8. groundlings: the poorer spectators, who stood in the yard of the playhouse. **9. dumb shows:** an old-fashioned dramatic device, still being used by the Admiral's Men: before a tragedy, and sometimes before each act, the characters mimed the action which was to follow. See later, l. 145. **10. Termagant:** God of the Saracens, who, like Herod, was presented in early stage plays as a roaring tyrant. **14. from:** contrary to. **17–18. very . . . pressure:** an exact reproduction of the age. **form:** shape. **pressure:** imprint (of a seal). **19. the . . . one:** i.e., the judicious spectator. **20–21. there . . . players:** An obvious attack on Alleyn. **24. journeymen:** hired workmen, not masters of the trade. **26. indifferently:** moderately. **27. those . . . clowns:** A hit at Will Kempe, the former clown of Shakespeare's company. Q1 adds the passage "And then you have some again that keep one suit of jests, as a man is known by one suit of apparel, and gentlemen quote his jests down in their tables before they come to the play, as thus: 'Cannot you stay till I eat my porridge?' and 'You owe me a quarter's wages,' and 'My coat wants a cullison,' and 'Your beer is sour,' and blabbering with his lips, and thus keeping in his cinquepace of jests, when God knows the warm clown cannot make a jest unless by chance, as the blind man catcheth a hare. Masters tell him of it." **31. pitiful:** contemptible.

[*Exeunt* ROSENCRANTZ *and* GUILDENSTERN.]

HAML. What ho! Horatio!

[*Enter* HORATIO.]

HOR. Here, sweet lord, at your service.

HAML. Horatio, thou art e'en as just a man
As e'er my conversation coped° withal.

HOR. Oh, my dear lord—

HAML. Nay, do not think I flatter
For what advancement° may I hope from thee,
That no revénue hast but thy good spirits
To feed and clothe thee? Why should the poor be flattered?
No, let the candied° tongue lick absurd pomp
And crook the pregnant hinges of the knee
Where thrift may follow fawning.° Dost thou hear?
Since my dear soul was mistress of her choice
And could of men distinguish, her election
Hath sealed° thee for herself. For thou hast been
As one in suffering all that suffers nothing,
A man that fortune's buffets and rewards
Hast ta'en with equal thanks. And blest are those
Whose blood and judgment are so well commingled
That they are not a pipe° for fortune's finger
To sound what stop she please. Give me that man
That is not passion's slave, and I will wear him
In my heart's core—aye, in my heart of heart,
As I do thee. Something too much of this.
There is a play tonight before the King.
One scene of it comes near the circumstance
Which I have told thee of my father's death.
I prithee when thou seest that act afoot,
Even with the very comment° of thy soul
Observe my uncle. If his occulted° guilt
Do not itself unkennel° in one speech
It is a damnèd ghost° that we have seen
And my imaginations are as foul
As Vulcan's° stithy.° Give him heedful note,°
For I mine eyes will rivet to his face,

---

41. coped: met. **43. advancement:** promotion. **46. candied:** sugared over with hypocrisy. **47–48. crook . . . fawning:** bend the ready knees whenever gain will follow flattery. **51. sealed:** set a mark on. **56. pipe:** an instrument that varies its notes. **65. comment:** close observation. **66. occulted:** concealed. **67. unkennel:** come to light; lit., force a fox from his hole. **68. damned ghost:** See II.ii.627. **70. Vulcan:** the blacksmith god. **stithy:** smithy. **heedful note:** careful observation.

And after we will both our judgments join
In censure of his seeming.°

HOR. Well, my lord.
If he steal aught the whilst this play is playing,
And 'scape detecting, I will pay the theft.

HAML. They are coming to the play. I must be idle.°
Get you a place.

[Danish march. A flourish. Enter KING, QUEEN, POLONIUS, OPHELIA, ROSENCRANTZ, GUILDENSTERN, *and other* LORDS *attendant, with the* GUARD *carrying torches.]*

KING. How fares our cousin Hamlet?

HAML. Excellent, i' faith, of the chameleon's dish.
I eat the air, promise-crammed. You cannot feed capons so.°

KING. I have nothing with this answer,° Hamlet.
These words are not mine.

HAML. No, nor mine now.° *[To* POLONIUS*]* My lord, you played once i' the university, you say?

POL. That did I, my lord, and was accounted a good actor.

HAML. What did you enact?

POL. I did enact Julius Caesar. I was killed i' the Capitol. Brutus killed me.

HAML. It was a brute part of him to kill so capital a calf there. Be the players ready?

ROS. Aye, my lord, they stay upon your patience.°

QUEEN. Come hither, my dear Hamlet, sit by me.

HAML. No, good Mother, here's metal more attractive.

POL. *[To the* KING*]* Oh ho! Do you mark that?

HAML. Lady, shall I lie in your lap?

[Lying down at OPHELIA'S *feet]*

OPH. No, my lord.

HAML. I mean, my head upon your lap?

OPH. Aye, my lord.

HAML. Do you think I meant country matters?°

OPH. I think nothing, my lord.

HAML. That's a fair thought to lie between maids' legs.

OPH. What is, my lord?

HAML. Nothing.

OPH. You are merry, my lord.

HAML. Who, I?

OPH. Aye, my lord.

---

73. censure . . . seeming: judgment on his looks. **76. be idle:** seem crazy. **79–80. Excellent . . . so:** Hamlet takes "fare" literally as "what food are you eating." The chameleon was supposed to feed on air. **promise-crammed:** stuffed, like a fattened chicken *(capon)*—but with empty promises. **81. I . . . answer:** I cannot make any sense of your answer. **83. nor . . . now:** i.e., once words have left the lips they cease to belong to the speaker. **89. stay . . . patience:** wait for you to be ready. **97. country matters:** something indecent.

HAML. Oh God, your only jig-maker.° What should a man do but be merry? For look you how cheerfully my mother looks, and my father died within 's two hours.

OPH. Nay, 'tis twice two months, my lord.

HAML. So long? Nay, then, let the Devil wear black, for I'll have a suit of sables.° Oh heavens! Die two months ago, and not forgotten yet? Then there's hope a great man's memory may outlive his life half a year. But, by 'r Lady, he must build churches then, or else shall he suffer not thinking on, with the hobbyhorse,° whose epitaph is "For, oh, for oh, the hobbyhorse is forgot."

[*Hautboys° play. The dumb show enters.° Enter a* KING *and a* QUEEN *very lovingly, the* QUEEN *embracing him and he her. She kneels, and makes show of protestation unto him. He takes her up, and declines his head upon her neck, lays him down upon a bank of flowers. She, seeing him asleep, leaves him. Anon comes in a fellow, takes off his crown, kisses it, and pours poison in the* KING'*s ears, and exit. The* QUEEN *returns, finds the* KING *dead, and makes passionate action. The Poisoner, with some two or three Mutes, comes in again, seeming to lament with her. The dead body is carried away. The Poisoner woos the* QUEEN *with gifts. She seems loath and unwilling awhile, but in the end accepts his love. Exeunt.*]

OPH. What means this, my lord?

HAML. Marry, this is miching mallecho.° It means mischief.

OPH. Belike this show imports the argument° of the play.

[*Enter* PROLOGUE.]

HAML. We shall know by this fellow. The players cannot keep counsel, they'll tell all.

OPH. Will he tell us what this show meant?

HAML. Aye, or any show that you'll show him. Be not you ashamed to show, he'll not shame to tell you what it means.

OPH. You are naught,° you are naught. I'll mark the play.

PRO. For us, and for our tragedy,
Here stooping to your clemency,
We beg your hearing patiently.

HAML. Is this a prologue, or the posy of a ring?°

OPH. 'Tis brief, my lord.

HAML. As woman's love.

[*Enter two* PLAYERS, KING *and* QUEEN.]

---

105. jig-maker: composer of jigs. **109. suit of sables:** a quibble on "sable," black, and "sable," gown trimmed with sable fur, worn by wealthy old gentlemen. **112–13. hobbyhorse:** imitation horse worn by performers in a morris dance, an amusement much disapproved of by the godly. **114. s.d., Hautboys:** oboes. **The dumb show enters:** Critics have been disturbed because this dumb show cannot be exactly paralleled in any other Elizabethan play, and because the King is apparently not disturbed by it. Shakespeare's intention, however, in presenting a play within a play is to produce something stagy and artificial compared with the play proper. Moreover, as Hamlet has already complained, dumb shows were often inexplicable. **115. miching mallecho:** slinking mischief. **116. argument:** plot. She too is puzzled by the dumb show. **122. naught:** i.e., disgusting. **126. posy . . . ring:** It was a pretty custom to inscribe rings with little mottoes or messages, which were necessarily brief.

P. KING. Full° thirty times hath Phoebus' cart° gone round
Neptune's° salt wash and Tellus'° orbèd ground,
And thirty dozen moons with borrowed sheen°
About the world have times twelve thirties been,
Since love our hearts and Hymen° did our hands
Unite commutual° in most sacred bands.

P. QUEEN. So many journeys may the sun and moon
Make us again count o'er ere love be done!
But, woe is me, you are so sick of late,
So far from cheer and from your former state,
That I distrust° you. Yet, though I distrust,
Discomfort you, my lord, it nothing must.
For women's fear and love holds quantity°
In neither aught or in extremity.°
Now what my love is, proof hath made you know,
And as my love is sized, my fear is so.
Where love is great, the littlest doubts are fear,
Where little fears grow great, great love grows there.

P. KING. Faith, I must leave thee,° love, and shortly too,
My operant powers° their functions leave to do.
And thou shalt live in this fair world behind,
Honored, beloved, and haply one as kind
For husband shalt thou—

P. QUEEN. Oh, confound the rest!
Such love must needs be treason in my breast.
In second husband let me be accurst!
None wed the second but who killed the first.

HAML. [*Aside*] Wormwood,° wormwood.

P. QUEEN. The instances° that second marriage move
Are base respects of thrift,° but none of love.
A second time I kill my husband dead
When second husband kisses me in bed.

P. KING. I do believe you think what now you speak,
But what we do determine oft we break.
Purpose is but the slave to memory,
Of violent birth but poor validity,
Which now, like fruit unripe, sticks on the tree
But fall unshaken when they mellow be.
Most necessary 'tis that we forget
To pay ourselves what to ourselves is debt.

129–202. Full . . . twain: The play is deliberately written in crude rhyming verse, full of ridiculous and bombastic phrases. **129. Phoebus' cart:** the chariot of the sun. **130. Neptune:** the sea god. **Tellus:** the earth goddess. **131 borrowed sheen:** light borrowed from the sun. **133 Hymen:** god of marriage. **134. commutual:** mutually. **139. distrust:** am anxious about. **141. quantity:** proportion. **142. In . . . extremity:** either nothing or too much. **147. leave thee:** i.e., die. **148. operant powers:** bodily strength. **155. Wormwood:** bitterness. **156. instances:** arguments. **157. respects of thrift:** considerations of gain.

What to ourselves in passion we propose,
The passion ending, doth the purpose lose.
The violence of either grief or joy
Their own enactures° with themselves destroy.
Where joy most revels, grief doth most lament,
Grief joys, joy grieves, on slender accident.
This world is not for aye,° nor 'tis not strange
That even our loves should with our fortunes change,
For 'tis a question left us yet to prove
Whether love lead fortune or else fortune love.
The great man down, you mark his favorite flies,
The poor advanced makes friends of enemies.
And hitherto doth love on fortune tend,
For who not needs shall never lack a friend,
And who in want a hollow friend doth try
Directly seasons° him his enemy.
But, orderly to end where I begun,
Our wills and fates do so contráry run
That our devices still are overthrown,
Our thoughts are ours, their ends none of our own.
So think thou wilt no second husband wed,
But die thy thoughts when thy first lord is dead.

P. QUEEN. Nor earth to me give food nor Heaven light!
Sport and repose lock from me day and night!
To desperation turn my trust and hope!
An anchor's° cheer in prison be my scope!
Each opposite that blanks° the face of joy
Meet what I would have well and it destroy!
Both here and hence pursue me lasting strife
If, once a widow, ever I be wife!

HAML. If she should break it now!

P. KING. 'Tis deeply sworn. Sweet, leave me here a while.
My spirits grow dull, and fain I would beguile
The tedious day with sleep.

[*Sleeps.*]

P. QUEEN. Sleep rock thy brain,
And never come mischance between us twain!

[*Exit.*]

HAML. Madam, how like you this play?

---

171. enactures: performances. **174. aye:** ever. **183. seasons:** ripens into. **193. anchor:** anchorite, hermit. **194. blanks:** makes pale.

QUEEN. The lady doth protest too much, methinks.
HAML. Oh, but she'll keep her word.
KING. Have you heard the argument?° Is there no offense in 't?
HAML. No, no, they do but jest, poison in jest—no offense i' the world.
KING. What do you call the play?
HAML. *The Mousetrap.*° Marry, how? Tropically.° This play is the image of a murder done in Vienna. Gonzago is the Duke's name, his wife, Baptista. You shall see anon. 'Tis a knavish piece of work, but what o' that? Your Majesty, and we that have free° souls, it touches us not. Let the galled jade wince, our withers are unwrung.°

[*Enter* LUCIANUS.]

This is one Lucianus, nephew to the King.
OPH. You are as good as a chorus,° my lord.
HAML. I could interpret between you and your love, if I could see the puppets dallying.°
OPH. You are keen, my lord, you are keen.
HAML. It would cost you a groaning to take off my edge.
OPH. Still better, and worse.
HAML. So you must take your husbands.° Begin, murderer. Pox, leave thy damnable faces and begin. Come, the croaking raven doth bellow for revenge.
LUC. Thoughts black, hands apt, drugs fit, and time agreeing,
Confederate season, else no creature° seeing,
Thou mixture rank of midnight weeds collected,
With Hecate's ban° thrice blasted, thrice infected,
Thy natural magic and dire property°
On wholesome life usurp immediately.

[*Pours the poison into the sleeper's ear.*]

HAML. He poisons him i' the garden for his estate.° His name's Gonzago. The story is extant, and written in very choice Italian. You shall see anon how the murderer gets the love of Gonzago's wife.
OPH. The King rises.
HAML. What, frighted with false fire!°
QUEEN. How fares my lord?

---

206. argument: plot. When performances were given at Court it was sometimes customary to provide a written or printed synopsis of the story for the distinguished spectators. **209. Mousetrap:** The phrase was used of a device to entice a person to his own destruction (OED). **Tropically:** figuratively, with a pun on "trap." **212. free:** innocent. **212–13. galled . . . unwrung:** let a nag with a sore back flinch when the saddle is put on; our shoulders (being ungalled) feel no pain. **215. chorus:** the chorus sometimes introduced the characters and commented on what was to follow. See, for instance, the Chorus in *Hen V.* **216–17. puppets dallying:** Elizabethan puppets were crude marionettes, popular at fairs. While the figures were put through their motions, the puppet master explained what was happening. **221. So . . . husbands:** i.e., as the marriage service expresses it, "for better, for worse." **224. confederate . . . creature:** the opportunity conspiring with me, no other creature. **226. Hecate's ban:** the curse of Hecate, goddess of witchcraft. **227. property:** nature. **229. estate:** kingdom. **233. false fire:** a mere show.

POL. Give o'er the play.
KING. Give me some light. Away!
POL. Lights, lights, lights!

[*Exeunt all but* HAMLET *and* HORATIO.]

HAML. "Why, let the stricken deer go weep,
The hart ungallèd play,
For some must watch while some must sleep.
Thus runs the world away."
Would not this, sir, and a forest of feathers°—if the rest of my fortunes turn Turk° with me—with two Provincial roses° on my razed° shoes, get me a fellowship° in a cry° of players, sir?
HOR. Half a share.
HAML. A whole one, I.
"For thou dost know, O Damon° dear,
This realm dismantled° was
Of Jove himself, and now reigns here
A very, very—pajock."°
HOR. You might have rhymed.
HAML. O good Horatio, I'll take the ghost's word for a thousand pound. Didst perceive?
HOR. Very well, my lord.
HAML. Upon the talk of the poisoning?
HOR. I did very well note him.
HAML. Ah, ha! Come, some music! Come, the recorders!°
"For if the King like not the comedy,
Why then, belike, he likes it not, perdy."°
Come, some music!

[*Re-enter* ROSENCRANTZ *and* GUILDENSTERN.]

GUIL. Good my lord, vouchsafe me a word with you.
HAML. Sir, a whole history.
GUIL. The King, sir—
HAML. Aye, sir, what of him?
GUIL. Is in his retirement marvelous distempered.°
HAML. With drink, sir?
GUIL. No, my lord, rather with choler.°
HAML. Your wisdom should show itself more richer to signify this to the doctor,

---

242. forest of feathers: set of plumes, much worn by players. **242–43. turn Turk:** turn heathen, and treat me cruelly. **243. Provincial roses:** rosettes, worn on the shoes. **razed:** slashed, ornamented with cuts. **249. fellowship:** partnership. **cry:** pack. **247. Damon:** Damon and Pythias were types of perfect friends. **248. dismantled:** robbed. **250. pajock:** peacock, a strutting, lecherous bird. These verses, and the lines above, may have come from some ballad, otherwise lost. **257. recorders:** wooden pipes. **259. perdy:** by God. **265. distempered:** disturbed; but Hamlet takes the word in its other sense of "drunk." **267. choler:** anger, which Hamlet again pretends to understand as meaning "biliousness."

for for me to put him to his purgation° would perhaps plunge him into far more choler.

GUIL. Good my lord, put your discourse into some frame,° and start not so wildly from my affair.

HAML. I am tame, sir. Pronounce.

GUIL. The Queen your mother, in most great affliction of spirit, hath sent me to you.

HAML. You are welcome.

GUIL. Nay, good my lord, this courtesy is not of the right breed. If it shall please you to make me a wholesome answer, I will do your mother's commandment. If not, your pardon and my return shall be the end of my business.

HAML. Sir, I cannot.

GUIL. What, my lord?

HAML. Make you a wholesome answer, my wit's diseased. But, sir, such answer as I can make you shall command, or rather, as you say, my mother. Therefore no more, but to the matter. My mother, you say—

ROS. Then thus she says. Your behavior hath struck her into amazement and admiration.°

HAML. Oh, wonderful son that can so astonish a mother! But is there no sequel at the heels of this mother's admiration? Impart.

ROS. She desires to speak with you in her closet ere you go to bed.

HAML. We shall obey, were she ten times our mother. Have you any further trade with us?

ROS. My lord, you once did love me.

HAML. So I do still, by these pickers and stealers.°

ROS. Good my lord, what is your cause of distemper? You do surely bar the door upon your own liberty if you deny your griefs° to your friend.

HAML. Sir, I lack advancement.°

ROS. How can that be when you have the voice of the King himself for your succession in Denmark?

HAML. Aye, sir, but "While the grass grows"°—the proverb is something musty.

[*Re-enter* PLAYERS *with recorders.*]

Oh, the recorders! Let me see one. To withdraw° with you—why do you go about to recover the wind° of me, as if you would drive me into a toil?°

GUIL. O my lord, if my duty be too bold, my love is too unmannerly.°

HAML. I do not well understand that. Will you play upon this pipe?

GUIL. My lord, I cannot.

---

269. put . . . purgation: "give him a dose of salts." **271. frame:** shape; i.e., "please talk sense." **286. admiration:** wonder. **293. pickers . . . stealers: i.e.,** hands—an echo from the Christian's duty in the catechism to keep his hands "from picking and stealing." **295. deny . . . griefs:** refuse to tell your troubles. **296. advancement:** promotion. Hamlet harks back to his previous interview with Rosencrantz and Guildenstern. See II.ii.258. **299. While . . . grows:** the proverb ends "the steed starves." **300. withdraw:** go aside. Hamlet leads Guildenstern to one side of the stage. **301. recover . . . wind:** a hunting metaphor; approach me with the wind against you. **302. toil:** net. **303. if . . . unmannerly:** if I exceed my duty by asking these questions, then my affection for you shows lack of manners; i.e., forgive me if I have been impertinent.

HAML. I pray you.

GUIL. Believe me, I cannot.

HAML. I do beseech you.

GUIL. I know no touch of it, my lord.

HAML. It is as easy as lying. Govern these ventages° with your fingers and thumb, give it breath with your mouth, and it will discourse most eloquent music. Look you, these are the stops.

GUIL. But these cannot I command to any utterance of harmony, I have not the skill.

HAML. Why, look you now, how unworthy a thing you make of me! You would play upon me, you would seem to know my stops, you would pluck out the heart of my mystery, you would sound me from my lowest note to the top of my compass—and there is much music, excellent voice, in this little organ—yet cannot you make it speak. 'Sblood, do you think I am easier to be played on than a pipe? Call me what instrument you will, though you can fret° me, you cannot play upon me.

[*Re-enter* POLONIUS.]

God bless you, sir!

POL. My lord, the Queen would speak with you, and presently.

HAML. Do you see yonder cloud that's almost in shape of a camel?

POL. By the mass, and 'tis like a camel indeed.

HAML. Methinks it is like a weasel.

POL. It is backed like a weasel.

HAML. Or like a whale?

POL. Very like a whale.

HAML. Then I will come to my mother by and by. They fool me to the top of my bent.° I will come by and by.

POL. I will say so.

[*Exit* POLONIUS.]

HAML. "By and by" is easily said. Leave me, friends.

[*Exeunt all but* HAMLET.]

'Tis now the very witching time° of night,
When churchyards yawn and Hell itself breathes out
Contagion° to this world. Now could I drink hot blood,
And do such bitter business as the day
Would quake to look on. Soft! Now to my mother.
O heart, lose not thy nature, let not ever

310. ventages: holes, stops. **320. fret:** annoy, with a pun on the frets or bars on stringed instruments by which the fingering is regulated. **329–30. top . . . bent:** See II.ii.30,n. **333. witching time:** when witches perform their foul rites. **335. Contagion:** infection.

The soul of Nero° enter this firm bosom.
Let me be cruel, not unnatural.
I will speak daggers to her, but use none.
My tongue and soul in this be hypocrites,
How in my words soever she be shent,°
To give them seals° never, my soul, consent!

[*Exit.*]

SCENE III. *A room in the castle.*

[*Enter* KING, ROSENCRANTZ, *and* GUILDENSTERN.]

KING. I like him not, nor stands it safe with us
To let his madness range.° Therefore prepare you.
I your commission will forthwith dispatch,
And he to England shall along with you.
The terms of our estate° may not endure
Hazard so near us as doth hourly grow
Out of his lunacies.

GUIL. We will ourselves provide.°
Most holy and religious fear° it is
To keep those many many bodies safe
That live and feed upon your Majesty.

ROS. The single and peculiar° life is bound
With all the strength and armor of the mind
To keep itself from noyance,° but much more
That spirit upon whose weal° depends and rests
The lives of many. The cease of majesty°
Dies not alone, but like a gulf° doth draw
What's near it with it. It is a massy° wheel
Fixed on the summit of the highest mount,
To whose huge spokes ten thousand lesser things
Are mortised° and adjoined; which, when it falls,
Each small annexment, petty consequence,°
Attends° the boisterous ruin. Never alone
Did the King sigh but with a general groan.

KING. Arm you, I pray you, to this speedy voyage,
For we will fetters put upon this fear,
Which now goes too free-footed.

ROS. & GUIL. We will haste us.

---

339. Nero: Nero killed his own mother. Hamlet is afraid that in the interview to come he will lose all self-control. **343. shent:** rebuked. **344. give . . . seals:** ratify words by actions.

Sc. iii: 2. range: roam freely. **5. terms . . . estate:** i.e., one in my position. **7. ourselves provide:** make our preparations. **8. fear:** anxiety. **11. peculiar:** individual. **13. noyance:** injury. **14. weal:** welfare. **15. cease of majesty:** death of a king. **16. gulf:** whirlpool. **17. massy:** massive. **20. mortised:** firmly fastened. **21. annexment . . . consequence:** attachment, smallest thing connected with it. **22. Attends:** waits on, is involved in.

[*Exeunt* ROSENCRANTZ *and* GUILDENSTERN.]

[*Enter* POLONIUS.]

POL. My lord, he's going to his mother's closet.
Behind the arras I'll convey myself
To hear the process.° I'll warrant she'll tax° him home.
And, as you said,° and wisely was it said,
'Tis meet that some more audience than a mother,
Since nature makes them partial, should o'erhear
The speech, of vantage.° Fare you well, my liege.
I'll call upon you ere you go to bed
And tell you what I know.

KING. Thanks, dear my lord.

[*Exit* POLONIUS.]

Oh, my offense is rank,° it smells to Heaven.
It hath the primal eldest curse° upon 't,
A brother's murder. Pray can I not,
Though inclination be as sharp as will.°
My stronger guilt defeats my strong intent,
And like a man to double business bound,
I stand in pause where I shall first begin,
And both neglect. What if this cursèd hand
Were thicker than itself with brother's blood,
Is there not rain enough in the sweet heavens
To wash it white as snow? Whereto serves mercy
But to confront the visage of offense?°
And what's in prayer but this twofold force,
To be forestalled° ere we come to fall
Or pardoned being down? Then I'll look up,
My fault is past. But oh, what form of prayer
Can serve my turn? "Forgive me my foul murder"?
That cannot be, since I am still possessed
Of those effects° for which I did the murder—
My crown, mine own ambition, and my Queen.
May one be pardoned and retain the offense?°
In the corrupted currents° of this world

29. process: proceeding. **tax:** censure. **30. as . . . said:** Actually Polonius himself had said it (III.i.189–93). **33. of vantage:** from a place of vantage: i.e., concealment. **36. rank:** foul. **37. primal . . . curse:** the curse laid upon Cain, the first murderer, who also slew his brother. **39. will:** desire. **47. confront . . . offense:** look crime in the face. **49. forestalled:** prevented. **54. effects:** advantages. **56. offense:** i.e., that for which he has offended. **57. currents:** courses, ways.

Offense's gilded hand may shove by justice,
And oft 'tis seen the wicked prize° itself
Buys out the law. But 'tis not so above.
There is no shuffling, there the action lies
In his true nature,° and we ourselves compelled
Even to the teeth and forehead° of our faults
To give in evidence. What then? What rests?
Try what repentance can. What can it not?
Yet what can it when one cannot repent?
Oh, wretched state! Oh, bosom black as death!
Oh, limèd° soul, that struggling to be free
Art more engaged!° Help, angels! Make assay!°
Bow, stubborn knees, and heart with strings of steel,
Be soft as sinews of the newborn babe!
All may be well.

[*Retires and kneels.*]

[*Enter* HAMLET.]

HAML. Now might I do it pat, now he is praying,
And now I'll do 't. And so he goes to Heaven,
And so am I revenged. That would be scanned:
A villain kills my father, and for that
I, his sole son, do this same villain send
To Heaven.
Oh, this is hire and salary,° not revenge.
He took my father grossly,° full of bread,
With all his crimes broad blown, as flush° as May,
And how his audit° stands who knows save Heaven?
But in our circumstance and course of thought,°
'Tis heavy with him. And am I then revenged,
To take him in the purging of his soul,
When he is fit and seasoned,° for his passage?
No.
Up, sword, and know thou a more horrid hent.°
When he is drunk asleep, or in his rage,
Or in the incestuous pleasure of his bed—
At gaming, swearing, or about some act
That has no relish of salvation in 't—
Then trip him, that his heels may kick at Heaven

---

59. wicked prize: the proceeds of the crime. **61–62. there . . . nature:** in Heaven the case is tried on its own merits. **63. teeth . . . forehead:** i.e., face to face. **68. limed:** caught as in birdlime. **69. engaged:** stuck fast. **assay:** attempt. **79. hire . . . salary:** i.e., a kind action deserving pay. **80. grossly:** i.e., when he was in a state of sin. See I.v.74–80. **81. broad . . . flush:** in full blossom, as luxuriant. **82. audit:** account. **83. circumstance . . . thought:** as it appears to my mind. **86. seasoned:** ripe. **88. hent:** opportunity.

And that his soul may be as damned and black
As Hell, whereto it goes. My mother stays.
This physic but prolongs thy sickly days.

[*Exit.*]

KING [*Rising*] My words fly up, my thoughts remain below.
Words without thoughts never to Heaven go.

[*Exit.*]

SCENE IV. *The* QUEEN'S *closet.*

[*Enter* QUEEN *and* POLONIUS.]

POL. He will come straight. Look you lay home to° him.
Tell him his pranks have been too broad° to bear with,
And that your grace hath screened and stood between
Much heat and him. I'll sconce me° even here.
Pray you, be round with him.
HAML. [*Within*] Mother, Mother, Mother!
QUEEN. I'll warrant you,
Fear me not. Withdraw, I hear him coming.

[POLONIUS *hides behind the arras.*]

[*Enter* HAMLET.]

HAML. Now, Mother, what's the matter?
QUEEN. Hamlet, thou hast thy father much offended.
HAML. Mother, you have my father much offended.
QUEEN. Come, come, you answer with an idle° tongue.
HAML. Go, go, you question with a wicked tongue.
QUEEN. Why, how now, Hamlet!
HAML. What's the matter now?
QUEEN. Have you forgot me?
HAML. No, by the rood,° not so.
You are the Queen, your husband's brother's wife,
And—would it were not so!—you are my mother.
QUEEN. Nay, then, I'll set those to you that can speak.
HAML. Come, come, and sit you down. You shall not budge,
You go not till I set you up a glass°
Where you may see the inmost part of you.

Sc. iv: 1. **lay . . . to:** be strict with. 2. **broad:** unrestrained. Polonius is thinking of the obvious insolence of the remarks about second marriage in the play scene. 4. **sconce me:** hide myself. 11. **idle:** foolish. 14. **rood:** crucifix. 19. **glass:** looking-glass.

QUEEN. What wilt thou do? Thou wilt not murder me?
Help, help, ho!
POL. [*Behind*] What ho! Help, help, help!
HAML. [*Drawing*] How now! A rat? Dead, for a ducat, dead!

[*Makes a pass through the arras.*]

POL. [*Behind*] Oh, I am slain!

[*Falls and dies.*]

QUEEN. Oh me, what hast thou done?
HAML. Nay, I know not. Is it the King?
QUEEN. Oh, what a rash and bloody deed is this!
HAML. A bloody deed! Almost as bad, good Mother,
As kill a king and marry with his brother.
QUEEN. As kill a king!
HAML. Aye, lady, 'twas my word.

[*Lifts up the arras and discovers* POLONIUS.]

Thou wretched, rash, intruding fool, farewell!
I took thee for thy better. Take thy fortune.
Thou find'st to be too busy is some danger.
Leave wringing of your hands. Peace! Sit you down,
And let me wring your heart. For so I shall
If it be made of penetrable stuff,
If damnèd custom have not brassed° it so
That it be proof and bulwark against sense.
QUEEN. What have I done that thou darest wag thy tongue
In noise so rude against me?
HAML. Such an act
That blurs the grace and blush of modesty,
Calls virtue hypocrite, takes off the rose
From the fair forehead of an innocent love,
And sets a blister° there—makes marriage vows
As false as dicers' oaths. Oh, such a deed
As from the body of contraction° plucks
The very soul, and sweet religion makes
A rhapsody of words.° Heaven's face doth glow,
Yea, this solidity and compound mass,°
With tristful visage, as against the doom,°
Is thought-sick at the act.

---

37. brassed: made brazen; i.e., impenetrable. **44. sets a blister:** brands as a harlot. **46. contraction:** the marriage contract. **48. rhapsody of words:** string of meaningless words. **49. solidity . . . mass:** i.e., solid earth. **50. tristful . . . doom:** sorrowful face, as in anticipation of Doomsday.

QUEEN. Aye me, what act
That roars so loud and thunders in the index?°

HAML. Look here upon this picture,° and on this,
The counterfeit presentment° of two brothers.
See what a grace was seated on this brow—
Hyperion's curls, the front° of Jove himself,
An eye like Mars, to threaten and command,
A station° like the herald Mercury°
New-lighted° on a heaven-kissing hill,
A combination° and a form indeed
Where every god did seem to set his seal°
To give the world assurance of a man.
This was your husband. Look you now what follows.
Here is your husband, like a mildewed ear,
Blasting his wholesome brother. Have you eyes?
Could you on this fair mountain leave to feed
And batten° on this moor? Ha! Have you eyes?
You cannot call it love, for at your age
The heyday° in the blood is tame, it's humble,
And waits upon the judgment. And what judgment
Would step from this to this? Sense° sure you have,
Else could you not have motion.° But sure that sense
Is apoplexed;° for madness would not err,
Nor sense to ecstasy° was ne'er so thralled°
But it reserved some quantity of choice
To serve in such a difference.° What devil was't
That thus hath cozened° you at hoodman-blind?°
Eyes without feeling, feeling without sight,
Ears without hands or eyes, smelling sans° all,
Or but a sickly part of one true sense
Could not so mope.°
Oh, shame! Where is thy blush? Rebellious° Hell,
If thou canst mutine° in a matron's bones,
To flaming youth let virtue be as wax
And melt in her own fire. Proclaim no shame
When the compulsive ardor° gives the charge,

---

52. in . . . index: i.e., if the beginning (*index,* i.e., table of contents) is so noisy, what will follow? **53. picture:** Modern producers usually interpret the pictures as miniatures, Hamlet wearing one of his father, Gertrude one of Claudius. In the eighteenth century, wall portraits were used. **54. counterfeit presentment:** portrait. **56. front:** forehead. **58. station:** figure; lit., standing. **Mercury:** messenger of the gods, and one of the most beautiful. **59. New-lighted:** newly alighted. **60. combination:** i.e., of physical qualities. **61. set . . . seal:** guarantee as a perfect man. **67. batten:** glut yourself. **69. heyday:** excitement. **71. Sense:** feeling. **72. motion:** desire. **73. apoplexed:** paralyzed. **74. ecstasy:** excitement, passion. See II.i.102. **thralled:** enslaved. **76. serve . . . difference:** to enable you to see the difference between your former and your present husband. **77. cozened:** cheated. **hoodman-blind:** blind-man's-buff. **79. sans:** without. **81. mope:** be dull. **82–88. Rebellious . . . will:** i.e., if the passion *(Hell)* of a woman of your age is uncontrollable *(rebellious),* youth can have no restraints; there is no shame in a young man's lust when the elderly are just as eager and their reason (which should control desire) encourages them. **83. mutine:** mutiny. **86. compulsive ardor:** compelling lust.

Since frost itself as actively doth burn,
And reason panders° will.

QUEEN. O Hamlet, speak no more.
Thou turn'st mine eyes into my very soul,
And there I see such black and grainèd° spots
As will not leave their tinct.°

HAML. Nay, but to live
In the rank sweat of an enseamèd° bed,
Stewed in corruption, honeying and making love
Over the nasty sty—

QUEEN. Oh, speak to me no more,
These words like daggers enter in my ears.
No more, sweet Hamlet!

HAML. A murderer and a villain,
A slave that is not twentieth part the tithe°
Of your precedent° lord, a vice of kings,°
A cutpurse° of the empire and the rule,
That from a shelf the precious diadem stole
And put it in his pocket!

QUEEN. No more!

HAML. A king of shreds and patches—

[*Enter* GHOST]

Save me, and hover o'er me with your wings,
You heavenly guards! What would your gracious figure?

QUEEN. Alas, he's mad!

HAML. Do you not come your tardy son to chide
That, lapsed in time and passion, lets go by
The important acting of your dread command?°
Oh, say!

GHOST. Do not forget. This visitation
Is but to whet thy almost blunted purpose.
But look, amazement on thy mother sits.
Oh, step between her and her fighting soul.
Conceit° in weakest bodies strongest works.
Speak to her, Hamlet.

HAML. How is it with you, lady?

QUEEN. Alas, how is 't with you
That you do bend your eye on vacancy°

---

88. panders: acts as go-between. **90. grained:** dyed in the grain. **91. tinct:** color. **92. enseamed:** greasy. **97. tithe:** tenth part. **98. precedent:** former, **vice of kings:** caricature of a king. **99. cutpurse:** thief. **107–08. That . . . command:** who has allowed time to pass and passion to cool, and neglects the urgent duty of obeying your dread command. **114. Conceit:** imagination. **117. vacancy:** empty space.

And with the incorporal° air do hold discourse?
Forth at your eyes your spirits wildly peep,
And as the sleeping soldiers in the alarm,
Your bedded° hairs, like life in excrements,°
Start up and stand an° end. O gentle son,
Upon the heat and flame of thy distemper°
Sprinkle cool patience. Whereon do you look?

HAML. On him, on him! Look you how pale he glares!
His form and cause conjoined,° preaching to stones,
Would make them capable.° Do not look upon me,
Lest with this piteous action you convert
My stern effects.° Then what I have to do
Will want true color—tears perchance for blood.

QUEEN. To whom do you speak this?

HAML. Do you see nothing there?

QUEEN. Nothing at all, yet all that is I see.

HAML. Nor did you nothing hear?

QUEEN. No, nothing but ourselves.

HAML. Why, look you there! Look how it steals away!
My father, in his habit as he lived!
Look where he goes, even now, out at the portal!

[*Exit* GHOST.]

QUEEN. This is the very coinage of your brain.
This bodiless creation ecstasy°
Is very cunning in.

HAML. Ecstasy!
My pulse, as yours, doth temperately keep time,
And makes as healthful music. It is not madness
That I have uttered. Bring me to the test
And I the matter will reword, which madness
Would gambol° from. Mother, for love of grace,
Lay not that flattering unction° to your soul,
That not your trespass but my madness speaks.
It will but skin and film the ulcerous place,
Whiles rank corruption, mining° all within,
Infects unseen. Confess yourself to Heaven,
Repent what's past, avoid what is to come,
And do not spread the compost° on the weeds
To make them ranker. Forgive me this my virtue,

---

118. incorporal: bodiless. **121. bedded:** evenly laid. **extrements:** anything that grows out of the body, such as hair or fingernails; here hair. **122. an:** on. **123. distemper:** mental disturbance. **126. form . . . conjoined:** his appearance and the reason for his appearance joined. **127. capable:** i.e., of feeling. **128–29. convert . . . effects:** change the stern action which should follow. **138. ecstasy:** madness. **144. gambol:** start away. **145. unction:** healing ointment. **148. mining:** undermining. **151. compost:** manure.

For in the fatness° of these pursy° times
Virtue itself of vice must pardon beg—
Yea, curb° and woo for leave to do him good.

QUEEN. O Hamlet, thou hast cleft my heart in twain.

HAML. Oh, throw away the worser part of it,
And live the purer with the other half.
Good night. But go not to my uncle's bed.
Assume a virtue if you have it not.
That° monster, custom, who all sense doth eat,
Of habits devil,° is angel yet in this,
That to the use° of actions fair and good
He likewise gives a frock or livery
That aptly° is put on. Refrain tonight,
And that shall lend a kind of easiness
To the next abstinence, the next more easy.
For use almost can change the stamp° of nature,
And either the Devil,° or throw him out
With wondrous potency. Once more, good night.
And when you are desirous to be blest,
I'll blessing beg of you. For this same lord,

[*Pointing to* POLONIUS]

I do repent; but Heaven hath pleased it so,
To punish me with this, and this with me,
That I must be their scourge and minister.
I will bestow° him, and will answer well
The death I gave him. So again good night.
I must be cruel only to be kind.
Thus bad begins, and worse remains behind.
One word more, good lady.

QUEEN. What shall I do?

HAML. Not this, by no means, that I bid you do.
Let the bloat° king tempt you again to bed,
Pinch wanton° on your cheek, call you his mouse,
And let him, for a pair of reechy° kisses
Or paddling in your neck with his damned fingers,
Make you to ravel° all this matter out,
That I essentially am not in madness,
But mad in craft. 'Twere good you let him know.

---

153. fatness: grossness. **pursy:** bloated. **155. curb:** bow low. **161–65. That . . . on:** i.e., custom (bad habits) like an evil monster destroys all sense of good and evil, but yet can become an angel (good habits) when it makes us perform good actions as mechanically as we put on our clothes. **162. devil:** This is the Q2 reading; the passage is omitted in F1. Probably the word should be "evil." **163. use:** practice. **165. aptly:** readily. **168. stamp:** impression. **169. either the Devil:** some verb such as "shame" or "curb" has been omitted. **176. bestow:** get rid of. **182. bloat:** bloated. **183. wanton:** lewdly. **184. reechy:** foul. **186. ravel:** unravel, reveal.

For who that's but a Queen, fair, sober, wise,
Would from a paddock,° from a bat, a gib,°
Such dear concernings° hide? Who would do so?
No, in despite° of sense and secrecy,
Unpeg the basket on the house's top,
Let the birds fly, and like the famous ape,°
To try conclusions,° in the basket creep
And break your own neck down.

QUEEN. Be thou assured if words be made of breath
And breath of life, I have no life to breathe
What thou hast said to me.

HAML. I must to England. You know that?

QUEEN. Alack,
I had forgot. 'Tis so concluded on.

HAML. There's letters sealed, and my two schoolfellows,
Whom I will trust as I will adders fanged,
They bear the mandate.° They must sweep my way,
And marshal me to knavery. Let it work,
For 'tis the sport to have the enginer°
Hoist with his own petar.° And 't shall go hard
But I will delve one yard below their mines
And blow them at the moon: Oh, 'tis most sweet
When in one line two crafts° directly meet.
This man shall set me packing.
I'll lug the guts into the neighbor room.
Mother, good night. Indeed this counselor
Is now most still, most secret, and most grave
Who was in life a foolish prating knave.
Come, sir, to draw toward an end with you.
Good night, Mother.

[*Exeunt severally,°* HAMLET *dragging in* POLONIUS.]

ACT IV

SCENE I. *A room in the castle.*

[*Enter* KING, QUEEN, ROSENCRANTZ, *and* GUILDENSTERN.]

---

190. paddock: toad. **gib:** tomcat. **191. dear concernings:** important matters. **192. despite:** spite. **194. famous ape:** The story is not known, but evidently told of an ape that let the birds out of their cage and, seeing them fly, crept into the cage himself and jumped out, breaking his own neck. **195. try conclusions:** repeat the experiment. **204. mandate:** command. **206. enginer:** engineer. **207. petar:** petard, land mine. **210. crafts:** devices. **217 s.d., Exeunt severally:** i.e., by separate exits. In F1 there is no break here. The King enters as soon as Hamlet has dragged the body away. Q2 marks the break. The act division was first inserted in a quarto of 1676.

KING. There's matter° in these sighs, these profound heaves,
You must translate. 'Tis fit we understand them.
Where is your son?
QUEEN. Bestow this place° on us a little while.

[*Exeunt* ROSENCRANTZ *and* GUILDENSTERN.]

Ah, mine own lord, what have I seen tonight!
KING. What, Gertrude? How does Hamlet?
QUEEN. Mad as the sea and wind when both contend
Which is the mightier. In his lawless fit,
Behind the arras hearing something stir,
Whips out his rapier, cries "A rat, a rat!"
And in this brainish apprehension° kills
The unseen good old man.
KING. Oh, heavy deed!
It had been so with us had we been there.
His liberty is full of threats to all,
To you yourself, to us, to everyone.
Alas, how shall this bloody deed be answered?
It will be laid to us, whose providence°
Should have kept short,° restrained and out of haunt,°
This mad young man. But so much was our love
We would not understand what was most fit,
But, like the owner of a foul disease,
To keep it from divulging° let it feed
Even on the pith° of life. Where is he gone?
QUEEN. To draw apart the body he hath killed,
O'er whom his very madness, like some ore
Among a mineral of metals base,
Shows itself pure. He weeps for what is done.
KING. O Gertrude, come away!
The sun no sooner shall the mountains touch
But we will ship him hence. And this vile deed
We must, with all our majesty and skill,
Both countenance° and excuse. Ho, Guildenstern!

[*Re-enter* ROSENCRANTZ *and* GUILDENSTERN.]

Friends both, go join you with some further aid.
Hamlet in madness hath Polonius slain,
And from his mother's closet hath he dragged him.

Act IV. Sc. i: 1. matter: something serious. **4. Bestow . . . place:** give place, leave us. **11. brainish apprehension:** mad imagination. **17. providence:** foresight. **18. short:** confined. **out of haunt:** away from others. **22. divulging:** becoming known. **23. pith:** marrow. **32. countenance:** take responsibility for.

Go seek him out, speak fair, and bring the body
Into the chapel. I pray you, haste in this.

[*Exeunt* ROSENCRANTZ *and* GUILDENSTERN.]

Come, Gertrude, we'll call up our wisest friends,
And let them know both what we mean to do
And what's untimely done,°
Whose whisper o'er the world's diameter
As level as the cannon to his blank°
Transports his poisoned shot, may miss our name
And hit the woundless air. Oh, come away!
My soul is full of discord and dismay.

[*Exeunt.*]

SCENE II. *Another room in the castle.*

[*Enter* HAMLET.]

HAML. Safely stowed.
ROS. & GUIL. [*Within*] Hamlet! Lord Hamlet!
HAML. But soft, what noise? Who calls on Hamlet?
Oh, here they come.

[*Enter* ROSENCRANTZ *and* GUILDENSTERN.]

ROS. What have you done, my lord, with the dead body?
HAML. Compounded it with dust, whereto 'tis kin.
ROS. Tell us where 'tis, that we may take it thence
And bear it to the chapel.
HAML. Do not believe it.
ROS. Believe what?
HAML. That I can keep your counsel and not mine own. Besides, to be demanded of a sponge! What replication° should be made by the son of a king?
ROS. Take you me for a sponge, my lord?
HAML. Aye, sir, that soaks up the King's countenance,° his rewards, his authorities. But such officers do the King best service in the end. He keeps them, like an ape, in the corner of his jaw, first mouthed, to be last swallowed. When he needs what you have gleaned, it is but squeezing you and, sponge, you shall be dry again.
ROS. I understand you not, my lord.
HAML. I am glad of it. A knavish speech sleeps in a foolish ear.°
ROS. My lord, you must tell us where the body is, and go with us to the King.

---

40. done: A half-line has been omitted. Some editors fill the gap with "So, haply slander." **42. blank:** target.

Sc. ii: 12. replication: answer. **14. countenance:** favor. **20. A . . . ear:** a fool never understands the point of a sinister speech.

HAML. The body is with the King, but the King is not with the body.° The King is a thing—

GUIL. A thing, my lord?

HAML. Of nothing. Bring me to him. Hide fox, and all after.°

[*Exeunt.*]

SCENE III. *Another room in the castle.*

[*Enter* KING, *attended.*]

KING. I have sent to seek him, and to find the body.
How dangerous is it that this man goes loose!
Yet must not we put the strong law on him.
He's loved of the distracted° multitude,
Who like not in their judgment but their eyes;°
And where 'tis so, the offender's scourge° is weighed,
But never the offense. To bear° all smooth and even,
This sudden sending him away must seem
Deliberate pause.° Diseases desperate grown
By desperate appliance are relieved,
Or not at all.

[*Enter* ROSENCRANTZ.]

How now! What hath befall'n?

ROS. Where the dead body is bestowed, my lord,
We cannot get from him.

KING. But where is he?

ROS. Without, my lord, guarded, to know your pleasure.

KING. Bring him before us.

ROS. Ho, Guildenstern! Bring in my lord.

[*Enter* HAMLET *and* GUILDENSTERN.]

KING. Now, Hamlet, where's Polonius?

HAML. At supper.

KING. At supper! Where?

HAML. Not where he eats, but where he is eaten. A certain convocation of politic worms° are e'en at him. Your worm is your only emperor for diet. We fat all creatures else to fat us, and we fat ourselves for maggots. Your fat king and your lean beggar is but variable service,° two dishes, but to one table. That's the end.

---

22. The . . . body: Hamlet deliberately bewilders his companions. **25. Hide . . . after:** a form of the game of hide-and-seek. With these words Hamlet runs away from them.

Sc. iii: 4. distracted: bewildered. **5. like . . . eyes:** whose likings are swayed not by judgment but by looks. **6. scourge:** punishment. **7. bear:** make. **9. Deliberate pause:** the result of careful planning. **21–22. convocation . . . worms:** an assembly of political-minded worms. **24. variable service:** choice of alternatives.

KING. Alas, alas!

HAML. A man may fish with the worm that hath eat of a king, and eat of the fish that hath fed of that worm.

KING. What dost thou mean by this?

HAML. Nothing but to show you how a king may go a progress° through the guts of a beggar.

KING. Where is Polonius?

HAML. In Heaven—send thither to see. If your messenger find him not there, seek him i' the other place yourself. But indeed if you find him not within this month, you shall nose him as you go up the stairs into the lobby.

KING. [*To some* ATTENDANTS] Go seek him there.

HAML. He will stay till you come.

[*Exeunt* ATTENDANTS.]

KING. Hamlet, this deed, for thine especial safety,
Which we do tender,° as we dearly grieve
For that which thou hast done, must send thee hence
With fiery quickness. Therefore prepare thyself.
The bark is ready and the wind at help,°
The associates tend,° and every thing is bent°
For England.

HAML. For England?

KING. Aye, Hamlet.

HAML. Good.

KING. So is it if thou knew'st our purposes.

HAML. I see a cherub that sees them. But, come, for England! Farewell, dear Mother.

KING. Thy loving father, Hamlet.

HAML. My mother. Father and mother is man and wife, man and wife is one flesh, and so, my mother. Come, for England!

[*Exit.*]

KING. Follow him at foot,° tempt° him with speed aboard.
Delay it not, I'll have him hence tonight.
Away! For everything is sealed and done
That else leans on the affair. Pray you make haste.

[*Exeunt* ROSENCRANTZ *and* GUILDENSTERN.]

And, England, if my love thou hold'st at aught—
As my great power thereof may give thee sense,
Since yet thy cicatrice° looks raw and red
After the Danish sword, and thy free awe°

---

30. go a progress: make a state journey. **39. tender:** regard highly. **42. at help:** favorable. **43. associates tend:** your companions are waiting. **bent:** ready. **50. at foot:** at his heels. **tempt:** entice. **56. cicatrice:** scar. There is nothing in the play to explain this incident. **57. free awe:** voluntary submission.

Pays homage to us—thou mayst not coldly set
Our sovereign process,° which imports at full,
By letters congruing° to that effect,
The present° death of Hamlet. Do it, England,
For like the hectic° in my blood he rages,
And thou must cure me. Till I know 'tis done,
Howe'er my haps,° my joys were ne'er begun.

[*Exit.*]

SCENE IV. *A plain in Denmark.*

[*Enter* FORTINBRAS, *a* CAPTAIN *and* SOLDIERS, *marching.*]

FOR. Go, Captain, from me greet the Danish King.
Tell him that by his license Fortinbras
Craves the conveyance of a promised march°
Over his kingdom. You know the rendezvous.
If that His Majesty would aught with us,
We shall express our duty in his eye,°
And let him know so.

CAP. I will do 't, my lord.

FOR. Go softly on.

[*Exeunt* FORTINBRAS *and* SOLDIERS.]

[*Enter* HAMLET, ROSENCRANTZ, GUILDENSTERN, *and others.*]

HAML. Good sir, whose powers° are these?

CAP. They are of Norway, sir.

HAML. How purposed, sir, I pray you?

CAP. Against some part of Poland.

HAML. Who commands them, sir?

CAP. The nephew to old Norway, Fortinbras.

HAML. Goes it against the main° of Poland, sir,
Or for some frontier?

CAP. Truly to speak, and with no addition,°
We go to gain a little patch of ground
That hath in it no profit but the name.
To pay five ducats, five, I would not farm it,

58–59. coldly . . . process: hesitate to carry out our royal command. **60. congruing:** agreeing. **61. present:** immediate. **62. hectic:** fever. **64. Howe'er my haps:** whatever may happen to me.

Sc. iv: 3. Craves . . . march: asks for permission to transport his army, as had already been promised. See II.ii.76–82. **6. in . . . eye:** before his eyes; i.e., in person. **9. powers:** forces. **15. main:** mainland. **17. addition:** exaggeration.

Nor will it yield to Norway or the Pole
A ranker° rate should it be sold in fee.°
HAML. Why, then the Polack never will defend it.
CAP. Yes, it is already garrisoned.
HAML. Two thousand souls and twenty thousand ducats
Will not debate the question of this straw.
This is the imposthume of° much wealth and peace,
That inward breaks, and shows no cause without
Why the man dies. I humbly thank you, sir.
CAP. God be wi' you, sir.

[*Exit.*]

ROS. Will 't please you go, my lord?
HAML. I'll be with you straight. Go a little before.

[*Exeunt all but* HAMLET.]

How° all occasions do inform against° me
And spur my dull revenge! What is a man
If his chief good and market° of his time
Be but to sleep and feed? A beast, no more.
Sure, He that made us with such large discourse,
Looking before and after,° gave us not
That capability and godlike reason
To fust° in us unused. Now whether it be
Bestial oblivion, or some craven scruple
Of thinking too precisely on the event—
A thought which, quartered, hath but one part wisdom
And ever three parts coward—I do not know
Why yet I live to say "This thing's to do,"
Sith I have cause, and will, and strength, and means
To do 't. Examples gross° as earth exhort me.
Witness this army, of such mass and charge,°
Led by a delicate and tender Prince
Whose spirit with divine ambition puffed
Makes mouths at the invisible event,°
Exposing what is mortal and unsure
To all that fortune, death, and danger dare,
Even for an eggshell.° Rightly to be great
Is not to stir without great argument,

---

22. ranker: richer. **in fee:** with possession as freehold. **27. imposthume of:** inward swelling caused by. **32–66. How . . . worth:** The soliloquy and all the dialogue after the exit of Fortinbras are omitted in F1. **32. inform against:** accuse. **34. market:** profit. **36–37. such . . . after:** intelligence that enables us to consider the future and the past. **39. fust:** grow musty. **46. gross:** large. **47. charge:** expense. **50. Makes . . . event:** mocks at the unseen risk. **53. eggshell:** i.e., worthless trifle.

But greatly to find quarrel in a straw
When honor's at the stake.° How stand I then,
That have a father killed, a mother stained,
Excitements of my reason and my blood,
And let all sleep while to my shame I see
The imminent death of twenty thousand men
That for a fantasy and trick° of fame
Go to their graves like beds, fight for a plot
Whereon the numbers cannot try the cause,°
Which is not tomb enough and continent°
To hide the slain? Oh, from this time forth,
My thoughts be bloody or be nothing worth!

[*Exit.*]

SCENE V. *Elsinore. A room in the castle.*

[*Enter* QUEEN, HORATIO, *and a* GENTLEMAN.]

QUEEN. I will not speak with her.
GEN. She is importunate, indeed distract.°
Her mood will needs be pitied.
QUEEN What would she have?
GEN. She speaks much of her father, says she hears
There's tricks° i' the world, and hems° and beats her heart,
Spurns enviously° at straws, speaks things in doubt
That carry but half-sense. Her speech is nothing,
Yet the unshaped use° of it doth move
The hearers to collection.° They aim° at it,
And botch° the words up fit to their own thoughts,
Which, as her winks and nods and gestures yield them,
Indeed would make one think there might be thought,
Though nothing sure, yet much unhappily.
HOR. 'Twere good she were spoken with, for she may strew
Dangerous conjectures in ill-breeding minds.
QUEEN. Let her come in.

[*Exit* GENTLEMAN.]

[*Aside*] To my sick soul, as sin's true nature is,
Each toy° seems prologue to some great amiss.°

53–56. Rightly . . . stake: true greatness is a matter of fighting not for a mighty cause but for the merest trifle when honor is concerned. **61. fantasy . . . trick:** illusion and whim. **63. Whereon . . . cause:** a piece of ground so small that it would not hold the combatants. **64. continent:** large enough to contain.

Sc. v: 2. distract: out of her mind. **5. tricks:** trickery. **hems:** makes significant noises. **6. Spurns enviously:** kicks spitefully. **8. unshaped use:** disorder. **9. collection:** i.e., attempts to find a sinister meaning. **aim:** guess. **10. botch:** patch. **18. toy:** trifle. **amiss:** calamity.

So full of artless jealousy° is guilt,
It spills itself in fearing to be spilt.°

[*Re-enter* GENTLEMAN, *with* OPHELIA.°]

OPH. Where is the beauteous Majesty of Denmark?
QUEEN. How now, Ophelia!
OPH. [*Sings.*]
"How should I your truelove know
From another one?
By his cockle hat° and staff
And his sandal shoon."°
QUEEN. Alas, sweet lady, what imports this song?
OPH. Say you? nay, pray you, mark. [*Sings.*]
"He is dead and gone, lady,
He is dead and gone,
At his head a grass-green turf,
At his heels a stone."
Oh, oh!
QUEEN. Nay, but, Ophelia—
OPH. Pray you, mark. [*Sings.*]
"White his shroud as the mountain snow—"

[*Enter* KING.]

QUEEN. Alas, look here, my lord.
OPH. [*Sings.*]
"Larded° with sweet flowers,
Which bewept to the grave did go
With truelove showers."°
KING. How do you, pretty lady?
OPH. Well, God 'ild° you! They say the owl was a baker's daughter.° Lord, we know what we are but know not what we may be. God be at your table!
KING. Conceit upon her father.
OPH. Pray you let's have no words of this, but when they ask you what it means, say you this [*Sings*]:
"Tomorrow is Saint Valentine's day,°
All in the morning betime,

---

19. artless jealousy: clumsy suspicion. **20. It . . . spilt:** guilt reveals itself by its efforts at concealment. **20. s.d., Re-enter . . . Ophelia:** Q1 notes "Enter Ophelia playing on a lute, and her hair down, singing." **25. cockle hat:** a hat adorned with a cockleshell worn by pilgrims. **26. sandal shoon:** sandals, the proper footwear of pilgrims. **37. Larded:** garnished. **39. truelove showers:** the tears of his faithful love. **41. 'ild (yield):** reward. **owl . . . daughter:** An allusion to a legend that Christ once went into a baker's shop and asked for bread. The baker's wife gave him a piece but was rebuked by her daughter for giving him too much. Thereupon the daughter was turned into an owl. **46. Saint . . . day:** February 14, the day when birds are supposed to mate. According to the old belief the first single man then seen by a maid is destined to be her husband.

And I a maid at your window,
To be your Valentine.
"Then up he rose, and donned his clothes,
And dupped° the chamber door,
Let in the maid, that out a maid
Never departed more."

KING. Pretty Ophelia!

OPH. Indeed, la, without an oath, I'll make an end on 't. [*Sings.*]
"By Gis° and by Saint Charity,
Alack, and fie for shame!
Young men will do 't, if they come to 't,
By cock, they are to blame.
Quoth she, before you tumbled me,
You promised me to wed."
He answers:
"So would I ha' done, by yonder sun,
An thou hadst not come to my bed."

KING. How long hath she been thus?

OPH. I hope all will be well. We must be patient. But I cannot choose but weep to think they should lay him i' the cold ground. My brother shall know of it. And so I thank you for your good counsel. Come, my coach! Good night, ladies, good night, sweet ladies, good night, good night.

[*Exit.*]

KING. Follow her close,° give her good watch, I pray you.

[*Exit* HORATIO.]

Oh, this is the poison of deep grief. It springs
All from her father's death. O Gertrude, Gertrude,
When sorrows come, they come not single spies,°
But in battalions! First, her father slain.
Next, your son gone, and he most violent author°
Of his own just remove. The people muddied,
Thick and unwholesome in their thoughts and whispers,
For good Polonius' death. And we have done but greenly°
In huggermugger° to inter him. Poor Ophelia
Divided from herself and her fair judgment,°
Without the which we are pictures,° or mere beasts.
Last, and as much containing as all these,
Her brother is in secret come from France,
Feeds on his wonder, keeps himself in clouds,

---

51. dupped: opened. **56–59. Gis . . . cock:** for "Jesus" and "God," both words being used instead of the sacred names, like the modern "Jeez" and "Gee." **70. close:** closely. **73. spies:** scouts. **75. author:** cause. **78. done . . . greenly:** shown immature judgment. **79. huggermugger:** secret haste, "any which way." **80. Divided . . . judgment:** no longer able to use her judgment. **81. pictures:** lifeless imitations.

And wants not buzzers° to infect his ear
With pestilent speeches of his father's death,
Wherein necessity, of matter beggared,
Will nothing stick our person to arraign°
In ear and ear. O my dear Gertrude, this,
Like to a murdering piece,° in many places
Gives me superfluous death.

[*A noise within*]

QUEEN. Alack, what noise is this?
KING. Where are my Switzers?° Let them guard the door.

[*Enter another* GENTLEMAN.]

What is the matter?
GEN. Save yourself, my lord.
The ocean, overpeering of his list,°
Eats not the flats° with more impetuous haste
Than young Laertes, in a riotous head,°
O'erbears your officers. The rabble call him lord,
And as the world were now but to begin,
Antiquity forgot, custom not known,
The ratifiers and props of every word,°
They cry "Choose we—Laertes shall be King!"
Caps, hands, and tongues applaud it to the clouds—
"Laertes shall be King, Laertes King!"
QUEEN. How cheerfully on the false trail they cry!
Oh, this is counter,° you false Danish dogs!

[*Noise within*]

KING. The doors are broke.

[*Enter* LAERTES, *armed,* DANES *following.*]

LAER. Where is this King? Sirs, stand you all without.
DANES. No, let's come in.
LAER. I pray you, give me leave.
DANES. We will, we will.

---

85. buzzers: scandalmongers. **87–88. Wherein . . . arraign:** in which, knowing nothing of the true facts, he must necessarily accuse us. **90. murdering piece:** cannon loaded with grapeshot. **92. Switzers:** Swiss bodyguard. **94. overpeering . . . list:** looking over its boundary; i.e., flooding the mainland. **95. Eats . . . flats:** floods not the flat country. **96. in . . . head:** with a force of rioters. **99–100. Antiquity . . . word:** forgetting ancient rule and ignoring old custom, by which all promises must be maintained. **105. counter:** in the wrong direction of the scent.

[*They retire without the door.*]

LAER. I thank you. Keep the door. O thou vile King,
Give me my father!
QUEEN. Calmly, good Laertes.
LAER. That drop of blood that's calm proclaims me bastard,
Cries cuckold° to my father, brands the harlot°
Even here, between the chaste unsmirchèd brows
Of my true mother.
KING. What is the cause, Laertes,
That thy rebellion looks so giantlike?
Let him go, Gertrude. Do not fear° our person.
There's such divinity doth hedge a king°
That treason can but peep° to what it would,
Acts little of his will. Tell me, Laertes,
Why thou art thus incensed. Let him go, Gertrude.
Speak, man.
LAER. Where is my father?
KING. Dead.
QUEEN. But not by him.
KING. Let him demand his fill.
LAER. How came he dead? I'll not be juggled with.
To Hell, allegiance! Vows, to the blackest devil!
Conscience and grace, to the profoundest pit!
I dare damnation. To this point I stand,
That both the worlds I give to negligence.°
Let come what comes, only I'll be revenged
Most thoroughly° for my father.
KING. Who shall stay you?
LAER. My will, not all the world.
And for my means, I'll husband° them so well
They shall go far with little.
KING. Good Laertes,
If you desire to know the certainty
Of your dear father's death, is 't writ in your revenge
That, swoopstake,° you will draw both friend and foe,
Winner and loser?
LAER. None but his enemies.
KING. Will you know them, then?
LAER. To his good friends thus wide I'll ope my arms,
And like the kind life-rendering pelican,°
Repast° them with my blood.

---

113. cuckold: a husband deceived by his wife. **brands . . . harlot:** Convicted harlots were branded with a hot iron. Cf. III.iv.44. **117. fear:** fear for. **118. divinity . . . king:** divine protection surrounds a king as with a hedge. **119. peep:** look over, not break through. **129. That . . . negligence:** I do not care what happens to me in this world or the next. **131. throughly:** thoroughly. **133. husband:** use economically. **137. swoopstake:** "sweeping the board." **141. life-rendering pelican:** The mother pelican was supposed to feed her young with blood from her own breast. **142. Repast:** feed.

KING. Why, now you speak
Like a good child and a true gentleman.
That I am guiltless of your father's death,
And am most sensibly° in grief for it,
It shall as level° to your judgment pierce
As day does to your eye.

DANES. [*Within*] Let her come in.

LAER. How now! What noise is that?

[*Re-enter* OPHELIA.]

O heat, dry up my brains! Tears seven times salt
Burn out the sense and virtue of mine eye!
By Heaven, thy madness shall be paid with weight
Till our scale turn the beam.° O rose of May!°
Dear maid, kind sister, sweet Ophelia!
Oh heavens! Is 't possible a young maid's wits
Should be as mortal as an old man's life?
Nature is fine in love, and where 'tis fine
It sends some precious instance of itself
After the thing it loves.°

OPH. [*Sings.*]
"They bore him barefaced on the bier,
Hey non nonny, nonny, hey nonny,
And in his grave rained many a tear—"
Fare you well, my dove!

LAER. Hadst thou thy wits and didst persuade revenge,
It could not move thus.

OPH. [*Sings.*]
"You must sing down a-down
An you call him a-down-a."
Oh, how the wheel° becomes it! It is the false steward, that stole his master's daughter.

LAER. This nothing's more than matter.°

OPH. There's° rosemary, that's for remembrance—pray you, love, remember. And there is pansies, that's for thoughts.

---

145. sensibly: feelingly. **146. level:** clearly. **153. turn . . . beam:** weigh down the beam of the scale. **rose of May:** perfection of young beauty. See III.i.160. **157–159. Nature . . . loves:** i.e., her love for her father was so exquisite that she has sent her sanity after him. Laertes, especially in moments of emotion, is prone to use highly exaggerated speech. **168. wheel:** explained variously as the spinning wheel, Fortune's wheel, or the refrain. The likeliest explanation is that she breaks into a little dance at the words "You must sing," and that the *wheel* is the turn as she circles round. **170. This . . . matter:** this nonsense means more than sense. **171–177. There's . . . died:** In the language of flowers, each has its peculiar meaning, and Ophelia distributes them appropriately: for her brother rosemary (remembrance) and pansies (thoughts); for the King fennel (flattery) and columbine (thanklessness); for the Queen rue, called also herb o' grace (sorrow), and daisy (light of love). Neither is worthy of violets (faithfulness).

LAER. A document° in madness, thoughts and remembrance fitted.

OPH. There's fennel for you, and columbines. There's rue for you, and here's some for me—we may call it herb of grace o' Sundays. Oh, you must wear your rue with a difference. There's a daisy. I would give you some violets, but they withered all when my father died. They say a' made a good end. [*Sings.*]

"For bonny sweet Robin is all my joy."

LAER. Thought and affliction, passion, Hell itself,
She turns to favor° and to prettiness.

OPH. [*Sings.*]

"And will a' not come again?
And will a' not come again?
No, no, he is dead,
Go to thy deathbed,
He never will come again.

"His beard was as white as snow,
All flaxen was his poll.°
He is gone, he is gone,
And we cast away moan.
God ha' mercy on his soul!"

And of all Christian souls, I pray God. God be wi' you.

[*Exit.*]

LAER. Do you see this, O God?

KING. Laertes, I must commune with your grief,
Or you deny me right. Go but apart,
Make choice of whom your wisest friends you will,
And they shall hear and judge 'twixt you and me.
If by direct or by collateral° hand
They find us touched,° we will our kingdom give,
Our crown, our life, and all that we call ours,
To you in satisfaction. But if not,
Be you content to lend your patience to us
And we shall jointly labor with your soul
To give it due content.

LAER. Let this be so.
His means of death, his obscure funeral,°
No trophy, sword, nor hatchment° o'er his bones,
No noble rite nor formal ostentation,°

173. document: instruction. **180. favor:** charm. **187. flaxen . . . poll:** white as flax was his head. **197. collateral:** i.e., as an accessory. **198. touched:** implicated. **204. obscure funeral:** Men of rank were buried with much ostentation. To bury Polonius "huggermugger" was thus an insult to his memory and to his family. **205. hatchment:** device of the coat of arms carried in a funeral and hung up over the tomb. **206. formal ostentation:** ceremony properly ordered.

Cry to be heard, as 'twere from Heaven to earth,
That I must call 't in question.

KING. So you shall,
And where the offense is let the great ax fall.
I pray you, go with me.

[*Exeunt.*]

SCENE VI. *Another room in the castle.*

[*Enter* HORATIO *and a* SERVANT.]

HOR. What are they that would speak with me?
SER. Seafaring men, sir. They say they have letters for you.
HOR. Let them come in.

[*Exit* SERVANT.]

I do not know from what part of the world
I should be greeted, if not from Lord Hamlet.

[*Enter* SAILORS.]

I. SAIL. God bless you, sir.
HOR. Let Him bless thee too.
I. SAIL. He shall, sir, an 't please Him. There's a letter for you, sir. It comes from the ambassador that was bound for England—if your name be Horatio, as I am let to know it is.

HOR. [*Reads.*] "Horatio, when thou shalt have overlooked° this, give these fellows some means° to the King. They have letters for him. Ere we were two days old at sea, a pirate of very warlike appointment° gave us chase. Finding ourselves too slow of sail, we put on a compelled valor, and in the grapple I boarded them. On the instant they got clear of our ship, so I alone became their prisoner. They have dealt with me like thieves of mercy; but they knew what they did—I am to do a good turn for them. Let the King have the letters I have sent, and repair thou to me with as much speed as thou wouldest fly death. I have words to speak in thine ear will make thee dumb, yet are they much too light for the bore of the matter.° These good fellows will bring thee where I am. Rosencrantz and Guildenstern hold their course for England. Of them I have much to tell thee. Farewell.

"He that thou knowest thine,
"HAMLET"

Sc. vi: 11. overlooked: read. **12. means:** access. **13. appointment:** equipment. **20. too . . . matter:** i.e., words fall short, like a small shot fired from a cannon with too wide a bore.

Come, I will make you way for these your letters,
And do 't the speedier that you may direct me
To him from whom you brought them.

[*Exeunt.*]

SCENE VII. *Another room in the castle.*

[*Enter* KING *and* LAERTES.]

KING. Now must your conscience my acquittance seal,°
And you must put me in your heart for friend,
Sith you have heard, and with a knowing ear,
That he which hath your noble father slain
Pursued my life.
LAER. It well appears. But tell me
Why you proceeded not against these feats,°
So crimeful and so capital° in nature,
As by your safety, wisdom, all things else,
You mainly were stirred up.
KING. Oh, for two special reasons,
Which may to you perhaps seem much unsinewed,°
But yet to me they're strong. The Queen his mother
Lives almost by his looks, and for myself—
My virtue or my plague, be it either which—
She's so conjunctive° to my life and soul
That as the star moves not but° in his sphere,
I could not but by her. The other motive
Why to a public count° I might not go
Is the great love the general gender° bear him,
Who, dipping all his faults in their affection,°
Would, like the spring that turneth wood to stone,°
Convert his gyves to graces.° So that my arrows,
Too slightly timbered° for so loud a wind,
Would have reverted to my bow again
And not where I had aimed them.
LAER. And so have I a noble father lost,
A sister driven into desperate terms,°
Whose worth, if praises may go back again,°

Sc. vii: 1. my . . . seal: acquit me. **6. feats:** acts. **7. capital:** deserving death. **10. unsinewed:** weak, flabby. **14. conjunctive:** joined inseparably. **15. moves . . . but:** moves only in. **17. count:** trial. **18. general gender:** common people. **19. dipping . . . affection:** gilding his faults with their love. **20. like . . . stone:** In several places in England there are springs of water so strongly impregnated with lime that they will quickly cover with stone anything placed under them. **21. Convert . . . graces:** regard his fetters as honorable ornaments. **22. timbered:** shafted. A light arrow is caught by the wind and blown back. **26. terms:** condition. **27. if . . . again:** if one may praise her for what she used to be.

Stood challenger on mount of all the age
For her perfections.° But my revenge will come.
KING. Break not your sleeps for that. You must not think
That we are made of stuff so flat and dull
That we can let our beard be shook with danger
And think it pastime. You shortly shall hear more.°
I loved your father, and we love ourself,
And that, I hope, will teach you to imagine—

[*Enter a* MESSENGER, *with letters.*]

How now! What news?
MESS. Letters, my lord, from Hamlet.
This to your Majesty, this to the Queen.
KING. From Hamlet! Who brought them?
MESS. Sailors, my lord, they say—I saw them not.
They were given me by Claudio, he received them
Of him that brought them.
KING. Laertes, you shall hear them.
Leave us.

[*Exit* MESSENGER.]

[*Reads*]

"High and Mighty, you shall know I am set naked° on your kingdom. Tomorrow shall I beg leave to see your kingly eyes, when I shall, first asking your pardon thereunto, recount the occasion of my sudden and more strange return.

"HAMLET"

What should this mean? Are all the rest come back?
Or is it some abuse,° and no such thing?
LAER. Know you the hand?
KING. 'Tis Hamlet's character.° "Naked!"
And in a postscript here, he says "alone."
Can you advise me?
LAER. I'm lost in it, my lord. But let him come.
It warms the very sickness in my heart
That I shall live and tell him to his teeth
"Thus didest thou."
KING. If it be so, Laertes—
As how should it be so, how otherwise?—
Will you be ruled by me?

28–29. Stood . . . perfections: i.e., her worth challenged the whole world to find one as perfect. **33. hear more:** i.e., when news comes from England that Hamlet is dead. **45. naked:** destitute. **50. abuse:** attempt to deceive. **52. character:** handwriting.

LAER. Aye, my lord,
So you will not o'errule° me to a peace.

KING. To thine own peace. If he be now returned,
As checking at° his voyage, and that he means
No more to undertake it, I will work him
To an exploit now ripe in my device,
Under the which he shall not choose but fall.
And for his death no wind of blame shall breathe,
But even his mother shall uncharge the practice°
And call it accident.

LAER. My lord, I will be ruled;
The rather if you could devise it so
That I might be the organ.°

KING. It falls right.
You have been talked of since your travel much,
And that in Hamlet's hearing, for a quality
Wherein they say you shine. Your sum of parts°
Did not together pluck such envy from him
As did that one, and that in my regard
Of the unworthiest siege.°

LAER. What part is that, my lord?

KING. A very ribbon in the cap of youth,
Yet needful too; for youth no less becomes
The light and careless livery that it wears
Than settled age his sables and his weeds,°
Importing health and graveness. Two months since,
Here was a gentleman of Normandy.
I've seen myself, and served against, the French,
And they can well° on horseback; but this gallant
Had witchcraft in 't, he grew unto his seat,
And to such wondrous doing brought his horse
As had he been incorpsed and deminatured°
With the brave beast. So far he topped my thought°
That I, in forgery of shapes and tricks,°
Come short of what he did.

LAER. A Norman was 't?

KING. A Norman.

LAER. Upon my life, Lamond.

KING. The very same.

---

61. o'errule: command. **63. checking at:** swerving aside from, like a hawk that leaves the pursuit of his prey. **68. uncharge . . . practice:** not suspect that his death was the result of the plot. **71. organ:** instrument. **74. sum of parts:** accomplishments as a whole. **77. siege:** seat, place. **81. sables . . . weeds:** dignified robes. See III.ii.138. **85. can well:** can do well. **88. incorpsed . . . deminatured:** of one body. **89. topped my thought:** surpassed what I could imagine. **90. forgery . . . tricks:** imagination of all kinds of fancy tricks. **shapes:** fancies.

LAER. I know him well. He is the brooch° indeed
And gem of all the nation.

KING. He made confession° of you,
And gave you such a masterly report
For art and exercise in your defense,
And for your rapier most especial,
That he cried out 'twould be a sight indeed
If one could match you. The scrimers° of their nation,
He swore, had neither motion, guard, nor eye
If you opposed them. Sir, this report of his
Did Hamlet so envenom° with his envy
That he could nothing do but wish and beg
Your sudden coming o'er, to play with him.
Now, out of this—

LAER. What out of this, my lord?

KING. Laertes, was your father dear to you?
Or are you like the painting° of a sorrow,
A face without a heart?

LAER. Why ask you this?

KING. Not that I think you did not love your father,
But that I know love is begun by time,
And that I see, in passages of proof,°
Time qualifies° the spark and fire of it.
There lives within the very flame of love
A kind of wick or snuff° that will abate it.
And nothing is at a like goodness still,°
For goodness, growing to a pleurisy,°
Dies in his own too much. That we would do
We should do when we would; for this "would" changes
And hath abatements and delays as many
As there are tongues, are hands, are accidents,
And then this "should" is like a spendthrift° sigh
That hurts by easing. But to the quick o' the ulcer.°
Hamlet comes back. What would you undertake
To show yourself your father's son in deed
More than in words?

LAER. To cut his throat i' the church.°

---

94. brooch: ornament. **96. confession:** report. **101. scrimers:** fencers. **104. envenom:** poison. **109. painting:** i.e., imitation. **113. passages of proof:** experiences which prove. **114. qualifies:** diminishes. **116. snuff:** Before the invention of self-consuming wicks for candles, the wick smoldered and formed a ball of soot which dimmed the light and gave out a foul smoke. **117. still:** always. **118. pleurisy:** fullness. **123. spendthrift:** wasteful, because sighing was supposed to be bad for the blood. **124. quick . . . ulcer:** i.e., to come to the real issue. **quick:** flesh, sensitive part. **127. cut . . . church:** i.e., to commit murder in a holy place, which would bring Laertes in danger of everlasting damnation; no crime could be worse.

KING. No place indeed should murder sanctuarize,°
Revenge should have no bounds. But, good Laertes,
Will you do this, keep close within your chamber.
Hamlet returned shall know you are come home.
We'll put on those° shall praise your excellence
And set a double varnish on the fame
The Frenchman gave you, bring you in fine° together
And wager on your heads. He, being remiss,°
Most generous° and free from all contriving,°
Will not peruse the foils, so that with ease,
Or with a little shuffling, you may choose
A sword unbated,° and in a pass of practice°
Requite him for your father.

LAER. I will do 't,
And for that purpose I'll anoint my sword.
I bought an unction° of a mountebank°
So mortal that but dip a knife in it,
Where it draws blood no cataplasm° so rare,
Collected from all simples° that have virtue
Under the moon,° can save the thing from death
That is but scratched withal. I'll touch my point
With this contagion, that if I gall° him slightly,
It may be death.

KING. Let's further think of this,
Weigh what convenience both of time and means
May fit us to our shape.° If this should fail,
And that our drift look through our bad performance,°
'Twere better not assayed. Therefore this project
Should have a back or second, that might hold
If this did blast in proof.° Soft! Let me see—
We'll make a solemn wager on your cunnings.
I ha 't.
When in your motion you are hot and dry—
As make your bouts° more violent to that end—
And that he calls for drink, I'll have prepared him
A chalice° for the nonce,° whereon but sipping,
If he by chance escape your venomed stuck,°
Our purpose may hold there. But stay, what noise?

---

128. sanctuarize: give sanctuary to. **132. put . . . those:** set on some. **134. fine:** short. **135. remiss:** careless. **136. generous:** noble. **contriving:** plotting. **139. unbated:** not blunted, with a sharp point. **pass of practice:** treacherous thrust. **142. unction:** poison. **mountebank:** quack doctor. **144. cataplasm:** poultice. **145. simples:** herbs. **146. Under . . . moon:** herbs collected by moonlight were regarded as particularly potent. **148. gall:** break the skin. **150–51. Weigh . . . shape:** consider the best time and method of carrying out our plan. **152. drift . . . performance:** intention be revealed through bungling. **155. blast in proof:** break in trial, like a cannon which bursts when being tested. **159. bouts:** attacks, in the fencing match. **161. chalice:** cup. **nonce:** occasion. **162. stuck:** thrust.

[*Enter* QUEEN.]

How now, sweet Queen!
QUEEN. One woe doth tread upon another's heel,
So fast they follow. Your sister's drowned, Laertes.
LAER. Drowned! Oh, where?
QUEEN. There is a willow grows aslant a brook
That shows his hoar° leaves in the glassy stream.
There with fantastic garlands did she come
Of crowflowers, nettles, daisies, and long purples
That liberal° shepherds give a grosser name,
But our cold maids do dead-men's-fingers call them.
There on the pendent° boughs her coronet weeds°
Clambering to hang, an envious sliver° broke,
When down her weedy trophies and herself
Fell in the weeping brook. Her clothes spread wide,
And mermaidlike awhile they bore her up—
Which time she chanted snatches of old tunes,
As one incapable° of her own distress,
Or like a creature native and indued°
Unto that element. But long it could not be
Till that her garments, heavy with their drink,
Pulled the poor wretch from her melodious lay°
To muddy death.
LAER. Alas, then, she is drowned!
QUEEN. Drowned, drowned.
LAER. Too much of water hast thou, poor Ophelia,
And therefore I forbid my tears. But yet
It is our trick°—Nature her custom holds,
Let shame say what it will. When these° are gone,
The woman will be out.° Adieu, my lord.
I have a speech of fire that fain° would blaze
But that this folly douts° it.

[*Exit.*]

KING. Let's follow, Gertrude.
How much I had to do to calm his rage!
Now fear I this will give it start again,
Therefore let's follow.

[*Exeunt.*]

---

169. hoar: gray. The underside of the leaves of the willow are silver-gray. **172. liberal:** coarse-mouthed. **174. pendent:** hanging over the water. **coronet weeds:** wild flowers woven into a crown. **175. envious sliver:** malicious branch. **180. incapable:** not realizing. **181. indued:** endowed; i.e., a creature whose natural home is the water *(element)*. **184. lay:** song. **188–89. But . . . trick:** it is our habit; i.e., to break into tears at great sorrow. **190. these:** i.e., my tears. **191. woman . . . out:** I shall be a man again. **192. fain:** willingly. **193. douts:** puts out.

ACT V

SCENE I. *A churchyard.*

[*Enter two* CLOWNS,° *with spades, etc.*]

1. CLO. Is she to be buried in Christian burial° that willfully seeks her own salvation?

2. CLO. I tell thee she is, and therefore make her grave straight.° The crowner° hath sat on her, and finds it Christian burial.

1. CLO. How can that be, unless she drowned herself in her own defense?

2. CLO. Why, 'tis found so.

1. CLO. It must be "se offendendo,"° it cannot be else. For here lies the point. If I drown myself wittingly,° it argues an act, and an act hath three branches—it is to act, to do, and to perform. Argal,° she drowned herself wittingly.

2. CLO. Nay, but hear you, goodman delver.°

1. CLO. Give me leave. Here lies the water, good. Here stands the man, good. If the man go to this water and drown himself, it is will he, nill he° he goes, mark you that; but if the water come to him and drown him, he drowns not himself. Argal, he that is not guilty of his own death shortens not his own life.

2. CLO. But is this law?

1. CLO. Aye, marry, is 't, crowner's quest° law.

2. CLO. Will you ha' the truth on 't? If this had not been a gentlewoman, she should have been buried out o' Christian burial.

1. CLO. Why, there thou say'st. And the more pity that great folks should have countenance° in this world to drown or hang themselves more than their even° Christian. Come, my spade. There is no ancient gentlemen but gardeners, ditchers, and gravemakers. They hold up° Adam's profession.

2. CLO. Was he a gentleman?

1. CLO. A' was the first that ever bore arms.°

2. CLO. Why, he had none.

1. CLO. What, art a heathen? How dost thou understand the Scripture? The Scripture says Adam digged. Could he dig without arms? I'll put another question to thee. If thou answerest me not to the purpose, confess thyself—

2. CLO. Go to.

1. CLO. What is he that builds stronger than either the mason, the shipwright, or the carpenter?

2. CLO. The gallows-maker, for that frame outlives a thousand tenants.

1. CLO. I like thy wit well, in good faith. The gallows does well, but how does it well? It does well to those that do ill. Now thou dost ill to say the gallows is

---

Act V, Sc. i: s.d., Clowns: countrymen. **1. Christian burial:** Suicides were not allowed burial in consecrated ground, but were buried at crossroads. The gravediggers and the priest are professionally scandalized that Ophelia should be allowed Christian burial solely because she is a lady of the Court. **3. straight:** straightway. **crowner:** coroner. **7. se offendendo:** for *defendendo,* in self-defense. **8. wittingly:** with full knowledge. **9. Argal:** for the Latin *ergo,* therefore. **10. delver:** digger. **12. will he, nill he:** willy-nilly, whether he wishes or not. **16. quest:** inquest. **20. countenance:** favor. **21. even:** fellow. **22. hold up:** support. **24. bore arms:** had a coat of arms—the outward sign of a gentleman.

built stronger than the church; argal, the gallows may do well to thee. To 't again, come.

2. CLO. Who builds stronger than a mason, a shipwright, or a carpenter?

1. CLO. Aye, tell me that, and unyoke.°

2. CLO. Marry, now I can tell.

1. CLO. To 't.

2. CLO. Mass,° I cannot tell.

[*Enter* HAMLET *and* HORATIO, *afar off.*]

1. CLO. Cudgel thy brains no more about it, for your dull ass will not mend his pace with beating, and when you are asked this question next, say "A gravemaker." The houses that he makes last till Doomsday. Go, get thee to Yaughan,° fetch me a stoup° of liquor.

[*Exit* SECOND CLOWN.]

[FIRST CLOWN *digs, and sings.*]

"In youth,° when I did love, did love,
Methought it was very sweet,
To contract; oh, the time, for-a my behoove,°
Oh, methought, there-a was nothing-a meet."

HAML. Has this fellow no feeling of his business, that he sings at grave-making?

HOR. Custom hath made it in him a property of easiness.°

HAML. 'Tis e'en so. The hand of little employment hath the daintier sense.°

1. CLO. [*Sings.*] "But age, with his stealing steps,
Hath clawed me in his clutch,
And hath shipped me until the land°
As if I had never been such."

[*Throws up a skull.*]

HAML. That skull had a tongue in it, and could sing once. How the knave jowls° it to the ground, as if it were Cain's jawbone, that did the first murder! It might be the pate of a politician which this ass now o'erreaches°—one that would circumvent° God, might it not?

HOR. It might, my lord.

HAML. Or of a courtier, which could say "Good morrow, sweet lord! How dost thou, good lord?" This might be my lord Such-a-one that praised my lord Such-a-one's horse when he meant to beg it, might it not?

---

38. unyoke: finish the job, unyoking the plow oxen being the end of the day's work. **41. Mass:** by the mass. **44. Yaughan:** apparently an innkeeper near the Globe Theatre. **45. stoup:** large pot. **46–49. In youth . . . meet:** The song which the gravedigger sings without much care for accuracy or sense was first printed in *Tottel's Miscellany*, 1558. **48. behoove:** benefit. **51. property of easiness:** careless habit. **52. hand . . . sense:** those who have little to do are the most sensitive. **55. shipped . . . land:** shoved me into the ground. **57. jowls:** dashes. **59. o'erreaches:** gets the better of. **60. circumvent:** get around.

HOR. Aye, my lord.

HAML. Why, e'en so. And now my Lady Worm's chapless,° and knocked about the mazzard° with a sexton's spade. Here's fine revolution, an we had the trick to see't. Did these bones cost no more the breeding but to play at loggats° with 'em? Mine ache to think on 't.

1. CLO.

[*Sings.*] "A pickax and a spade, a spade,
For and a shrouding sheet—
Oh, a pit of clay for to be made
For such a guest is meet."

[*Throws up another skull.*]

HAML. There's another. Why may not that be the skull of a lawyer?° Where be his quiddities now, his quillets, his cases, his tenures, and his tricks? Why does he suffer this rude knave now to knock him about the sconce° with a dirty shovel, and will not tell him of his action of battery? Hum! This fellow might be in 's time a great buyer of land, with his statutes, his recognizances, his fines, his double vouchers, his recoveries. Is this the fine° of his fines and the recovery of his recoveries, to have his fine pate full of fine dirt? Will his vouchers vouch him no more of his purchases, and double ones too, than the length and breadth of a pair of indentures? The very conveyances of his lands will hardly lie in this box,° and must the inheritor himself have no more, ha?

HOR. Not a jot more, my lord.

HAML. Is not parchment made of sheepskins?

HOR. Aye, my lord, and of calfskins too.

HAML. They are sheep and calves which seek out assurance in that. I will speak to this fellow. Whose grave's this, sirrah?

1. CLO. Mine, sir. [*Sings.*]

"Oh, a pit of clay for to be made
For such a guest is meet."

HAML. I think it be thine indeed, for thou liest in 't.

1. CLO. You lie out on 't, sir, and therefore 'tis not yours. For my part, I do not lie in 't, and yet it is mine.

HAML. Thou dost lie in 't, to be in 't and say it is thine. 'Tis for the dead, not for the quick, therefore thou liest.

1. CLO. 'Tis a quick lie, sir, 'twill away again, from me to you.

HAML. What man dost thou dig it for?

1. CLO. For no man, sir.

HAML. What woman, then?

---

66. chapless: without jaws. **67. mazzard:** head, a slang word; lit., drinking-bowl. **68. loggats:** a game in which billets of wood or bones were stuck in the ground and knocked over by throwing at them. **74–82. lawyer . . . indentures:** Hamlet strings out a number of the legal phrases loved by lawyers: *quiddities:* subtle arguments; *quillets:* quibbles; *tenures:* titles to property; *tricks:* knavery; *statutes:* bonds; *recognizances:* obligations; *fines:* conveyances; *vouchers:* guarantors; *recoveries:* transfers; *indentures:* agreements. **76. sconce:** head; lit., blockhouse. **79. fine:** ending. **83. box:** coffin.

1. CLO. For none, neither.

HAML. Who is to be buried in 't?

1. CLO. One that was a woman, sir, but, rest her soul, she's dead.

HAML. How absolute° the knave is! We must speak by the card,° or equivocation° will undo us. By the Lord, Horatio, this three years I have taken note of it—the age is grown so picked° that the toe of the peasant comes so near the heel of the courtier, he galls his kibe.° How long hast thou been a grave-maker?

1. CLO. Of all the days i' the year, I came to 't that day that our last King Hamlet o'ercame Fortinbras.

HAML. How long is that since?

1. CLO. Cannot you tell that? Every fool can tell that. It was that very day that young Hamlet was born, he that is mad, and sent into England.

HAML. Aye, marry, why was he sent into England?

1. CLO. Why, because a' was mad. A' shall recover his wits there, or, if a' do not, 'tis no great matter there.

HAML. Why?

1. CLO. 'Twill not be seen in him there—there the men are as mad as he.

HAML. How came he mad?

1. CLO. Very strangely, they say.

HAML. How "strangely"?

1. CLO. Faith, e'en with losing his wits.

HAML. Upon what ground?

1. CLO. Why, here in Denmark. I have been sexton here, man and boy, thirty years.°

HAML. How long will a man lie i' the earth ere he rot?

1. CLO. I' faith, if a' be not rotten before a' die—as we have many pocky° corses nowadays that will scarce hold the laying in—a' will last you some eight year or nine year. A tanner will last you nine year.

HAML. Why he more than another?

1. CLO. Why, sir, his hide is so tanned with his trade that a' will keep out water a great while, and your water is a sore decayer of your whoreson° dead body. Here's a skull now. This skull has lain in the earth three and twenty years.

HAML. Whose was it?

1. CLO. A whoreson mad fellow's it was. Whose do you think it was?

HAML. Nay, I know not.

1. CLO. A pestilence on him for a mad rogue! A' poured a flagon of Rhenish on my head once. This same skull, sir, was Yorick's skull, the King's jester.

HAML. This?

---

109. absolute: exact. **by . . . card:** exactly. The card is the mariner's compass. **equivocation:** speaking with a double sense. The word was much discussed when *Hamlet* was written. **106. picked:** refined. **106–107. toe . . . kibe:** i.e., the peasant follows the courtier so closely that he rubs the courtier's heel into a blister. From about 1598 onward, writers, especially dramatists, often satirized the practice of yeoman farmers grown rich from war profits in sending their awkward sons to London to learn gentlemanly manners. Ben Jonson portrays two specimens in Stephen in *Every Man in His Humour* and Sogliardo in *Every Man out of His Humour.* **124. thirty years:** The Clown's chronology has puzzled critics, for the general impression is that Hamlet was much younger. **126. pocky:** suffering from the pox (venereal disease). **131. whoreson:** bastard, "son of a bitch."

1. CLO. E'en that.

HAML. Let me see.

[*Takes the skull.*]

Alas, poor Yorick! I knew him, Horatio—a fellow of infinite jest, of most excellent fancy. He hath borne me on his back a thousand times, and now how abhorred in my imagination it is! My gorge rises° at it. Here hung those lips that I have kissed I know not how oft. Where be your gibes now? Your gambols? Your songs? Your flashes of merriment that were wont to set the table on a roar? Not one now, to mock your own grinning? Quite chopfallen?° Now get you to my lady's chamber and tell her, let her paint an inch thick, to this favor° she must come—make her laugh at that. Prithee, Horatio, tell me one thing.

HOR. What's that, my lord?

HAML. Dost thou think Alexander looked o' this fashion i' the earth?

HOR. E'en so.

HAML. And smelt so? Pah!

[*Puts down the skull.*]

HOR. E'en so, my lord.

HAML. To what base uses we may return, Horatio! Why may not imagination trace the noble dust of Alexander till he find it stopping a bunghole?°

HOR. 'Twere to consider too curiously° to consider so.

HAML. No, faith, not a jot, but to follow him thither with modesty° enough and likelihood to lead it. As thus: Alexander died, Alexander was buried, Alexander returneth into dust; the dust is earth; of earth we make loam;° and why of that loam, whereto he was converted, might they not stop a beer barrel?

"Imperious Caesar, dead and turned to clay,
Might stop a hole to keep the wind away.
Oh, that that earth which kept the world in awe
Should patch a wall to expel the winter's flaw!"°
But soft! But soft! Aside—here comes the king.

[*Enter* PRIESTS,° *etc., in procession; the corpse of Ophelia,* LAERTES *and* MOURNERS *following;* KING, QUEEN, *their trains, etc.*]

The Queen, the courtiers—Who is this they follow?
And with such maimèd° rites? This doth betoken°

142–43. My . . . rises: I feel sick. **gorge:** throat. **146. chopfallen:** downcast, with a pun on "chapless," (see l. 97). **147. favor:** appearance, especially in the face. **155. bunghole:** the hole in a beer barrel. **156. curiously:** precisely. **157. with modesty:** without exaggeration. **159. loam:** mixture of clay and sand, used in plastering walls. **164. flaw:** blast. **s.d., Enter Priests.** The stage directions in early texts are less elaborate. Q2 notes, curtly, *Enter K.Q. Laertes and the corse.* F1 has *Enter King, Queen, Laertes, and a coffin, with Lords attendant.* Q1 prints *Enter King and Queen, Laertes and other lords, with a Priest after the coffin.* This probably was how the scene was originally staged. The modern directions ignore the whole significance of the "maimed rites"—Ophelia's funeral is insultingly simple. **167. maimed:** curtailed. **betoken:** indicate.

The corse they follow did with desperate hand
Fordo° its own life. 'Twas of some estate.°
Couch° we awhile, and mark.

[*Retiring with* HORATIO.]

LAER. What ceremony else?
HAML. That is Laertes, a very noble youth. Mark.
LAER. What ceremony else?
1. PRIEST. Her obsequies have been as far enlarged
As we have warranty.° Her death was doubtful,
And but that great command o'ersways the order,°
She should in ground unsanctified have lodged
Till the last trumpet; for° charitable prayers,
Shards,° flints, and pebbles should be thrown on her.
Yet here she is allowed her virgin crants,°
Her maiden strewments° and the bringing home
Of bell and burial.
LAER. Must there no more be done?
1. PRIEST. No more be done.
We should profane the service of the dead
To sing a requiem and such rest to her
As to peace-parted souls.°
LAER. Lay her i' the earth.
And from her fair and unpolluted flesh
May violets spring! I tell thee, churlish priest,
A ministering angel shall my sister be
When thou liest howling.
HAML. What, the fair Ophelia!
QUEEN. [*Scattering flowers*] Sweets to the sweet. Farewell!
I hoped thou shouldst have been my Hamlet's wife,
I thought thy bride bed to have decked, sweet maid,
And not have strewed thy grave.
LAER. Oh, treble woe
Fall ten times treble on that cursèd head
Whose wicked deed thy most ingenious sense°
Deprived thee of! Hold off the earth a while
Till I have caught her once more in mine arms.

[*Leaps into the grave.*]

---

169. Fordo: destroy. **estate:** high rank. **170. Couch:** lie down. **174–75. Her . . . warranty:** the funeral rites have been as complete as may be allowed. **176. but . . . order:** if the King's command had not overruled the proper procedure. **178. for:** instead of. **179. Shards:** pieces of broken crockery. **180. crants:** wreaths of flowers—a sign that she had died unwed. **181. maiden strewments:** the flowers strewn on the corpse of a maiden. **186. peace-parted souls:** souls which departed in peace, fortified with the rites of the Church. **196. most . . . sense:** lively intelligence.

Now pile your dust upon the quick° and dead
Till of this flat a mountain you have made
To o'ertop old Pelion° or the skyish° head
Of blue Olympus.

HAML. [*Advancing*] What is he whose grief
Bears such an emphasis? Whose phrase of sorrow
Conjures the wandering stars and makes them stand°
Like wonder-wounded hearers? This is I,
Hamlet the Dane.

[*Leaps into the grave.*]

LAER. The Devil take thy soul!

[*Grappling with him*]

HAML. Thou pray'st not well.
I prithee, take thy fingers from my throat,
For though I am not splenitive° and rash,
Yet have I in me something dangerous,
Which let thy wisdom fear. Hold off thy hand.

KING. Pluck them asunder.

QUEEN. Hamlet, Hamlet!

ALL. Gentlemen—

HOR. Good my lord, be quiet.

[*The* ATTENDANTS *part them, and they come out of the grave.*]

HAML. Why, I will fight with him upon this theme
Until my eyelids will no longer wag.

QUEEN. O my son, what theme?

HAML. I loved Ophelia. Forty thousand brothers
Could not, with all their quantity of love,
Make up my sum. What wilt thou do for her?

KING. Oh, he is mad, Laertes.

QUEEN. For love of God, forbear him.°

HAML. 'Swounds,° show me what thou'lt do.
Woo't weep? Woo't fight? Woo't fast? Woo't tear thyself?
Woo't drink up eisel?° Eat a crocodile?
I'll do 't. Dost thou come here to whine?
To outface° me with leaping in her grave?

---

199. quick: living. **201. Pelion:** When the giants fought against the gods in order to reach Heaven, they tried to pile Mount Pelion and Mount Ossa on Mount Olympus, the highest mountain in Greece. **skyish:** reaching the sky. **205. stand:** stand still. **210. splenitive:** hot-tempered. **222. forbear him:** leave him alone. **223. 'Swounds . . . thou:** Hamlet in his excitement cries out that if Laertes wishes to make extravagant boasts of what he will do to show his sorrow, he will be even more extravagant. **225. eisel:** vinegar. **227. outface:** browbeat.

Be buried quick with her, and so will I.
And if thou prate of mountains, let them throw
Millions of acres on us, till our ground,
Singeing his pate against the burning zone,
Make Ossa° like a wart! Nay, an thou 'lt mouth,
I'll rant as well as thou.

QUEEN. This is mere madness.
And thus awhile the fit will work on him.
Anon, as patient as the female dove
When that her golden couplets° are disclosed,°
His silence will sit drooping.

HAML. Hear you, sir.
What is the reason that you use me thus?
I loved you ever. But it is no matter,
Let Hercules himself do what he may,
The cat will mew and dog will have his day.° [*Exit.*]

KING. I pray thee, good Horatio, wait upon him.

[*Exit* HORATIO.]

[*To* LAERTES] Strengthen your patience in our last night's speech.
We'll put the matter to the present push.°
Good Gertrude, set some watch over your son.
This grave shall have a living monument.°
An hour of quiet shortly shall we see,
Till then, in patience our proceeding be.

[*Exeunt.*]

SCENE II. *A hall in the castle.*

[*Enter* HAMLET *and* HORATIO.]

HAML. So much for this, sir. Now shall you see the other.
You do remember all the circumstance?

HOR. Remember it, my lord!

HAML. Sir, in my heart there was a kind of fighting
That would not let me sleep. Methought I lay
Worse than the mutines in the bilboes.° Rashly,
And praised be rashness for it, let us know,
Our indiscretion sometime serves us well
When our deep plots do pall.° And that should learn° us

---

232. Ossa: See 1. 276, n. **236. couplets:** eggs, of which the dove lays two only. **disclosed:** hatched. **240–41. Let . . . day:** i.e., let this ranting hero have his turn; mine will come sometime. **244. push:** test; lit., thrust of a pike. **246. living monument:** with the double meaning of "lifelike memorial" and "the death of Hamlet."

Sc. ii: 6. mutines . . . bilboes: mutineers in the shackles used on board ship. **9. pall:** fail. **learn:** teach.

There's a divinity that shapes our ends,
Roughhew them how we will.°

HOR. That is most certain.

HAML. Up from my cabin,
My sea gown° scarfed° about me, in the dark
Groped I to find out them,° had my desire,
Fingered their packet, and in fine withdrew
To mine own room again, making so bold,
My fears forgetting manners, to unseal
Their grand commission where I found, Horatio—
Oh royal knavery!—an exact command,
Larded° with many several sorts of reasons,
Importing Denmark's health and England's too,
With, ho! such bugs° and goblins in my life°
That, on the supervise,° no leisure bated,°
No, not to stay the grinding of the ax,
My head should be struck off.

HOR. Is 't possible?

HAML. Here's the commission. Read it at more leisure
But wilt thou hear me how I did proceed?

HOR. I beseech you.

HAML. Being thus benetted round with villainies—
Ere I could make a prologue to my brains,
They had begun the play—I sat me down,
Devised a new commission, wrote it fair.
I once did hold it, as our statists° do,
A baseness to write fair, and labored much
How to forget that learning, but, sir, now
It did me yeoman's service.° Wilt thou know
The effect of what I wrote?

HOR. Aye, good my lord.

HAML. An earnest conjuration from the King,
As England was his faithful tributary,
As love between them like the palm might flourish,
As peace should still her wheaten garland wear
And stand a comma 'tween their amities,°
And many suchlike "Ases"° of great charge,°
That, on the view and knowing of these contents,

10–11. There's . . . will: though we may make the rough beginning, God finishes our designs. **13. sea gown:** a thick coat with a high collar worn by seamen. **scarfed:** wrapped. **14. them:** i.e., Rosencrantz and Guildenstern. **20. Larded:** garnished. **22. bugs:** bugbears. **in my life:** so long as I was alive. **23. supervise:** reading. **bated:** allowed. **33. statists:** statesmen. As scholars who have had to read Elizabethan documents know, the more exalted the writer, the worse his handwriting. As a girl Queen Elizabeth wrote a beautiful script; as Queen her letters are as illegible as any. All but the most confidential documents were copied out in a fair hand by a secretary. **36. yeoman's service:** faithful service. The most reliable English soldiers were yeomen—farmers and their men. **42. stand . . . amities:** be a connecting link of their friendship. **43. "Ases":** Official documents were written in flowery language full of metaphorical clauses beginning with "As." Hamlet puns on "asses." **great charge:** "great weight" and "heavy burden."

Without debatement° further, more or less,
He should the bearers put to sudden death,
Not shriving time allowed.°

HOR. How was this sealed?

HAML. Why, even in that was Heaven ordinant.°
I had my father's signet in my purse,
Which was the model° of that Danish seal—
Folded the writ° up in the form of the other,
Subscribed° it, gave 't the impression,° placed it safely,
The changeling° never known. Now the next day
Was our sea fight, and what to this was sequent°
Thou know'st already.

HOR. So Guildenstern and Rosencrantz go to 't.

HAML. Why, man, they did make love to this employment.
They are not near my conscience, their defeat°
Does by their own insinuation° grow.
'Tis dangerous when the baser nature comes
Between the pass and fell incensèd points
Of mighty opposites.°

HOR. Why, what a King is this!

HAML. Does it not, think'st thee, stand me now upon—
He that hath killed my King and whored my mother,
Popped in between the election and my hopes,°
Thrown out his angle° for my proper° life,
And with such cozenage°—is 't not perfect conscience,
To quit° him with this arm? And is 't not to be damned,
To let this canker° of our nature come
In further evil?

HOR. It must be shortly known to him from England
What is the issue of the business there.

HAML. It will be short. The interim° is mine,
And a man's life's no more than to say "One."
But I am very sorry, good Horatio,
That to Laertes I forgot myself,
For by the image of my cause I see
The portraiture of his. I'll court his favors.
But, sure, the bravery° of his grief did put me
Into a towering passion.

HOR. Peace! Who comes here?

---

45. debatement: argument. **47. Not . . . allowed:** without giving them time even to confess their sins. **48. ordinant:** directing, in control. **50. model:** copy. **51. writ:** writing. **52. Subscribed:** signed. **impression:** of the seal. **53. changeling:** lit., an ugly child exchanged by the fairies for a fair one. **54. sequent:** following. **58. defeat:** destruction. **59. by . . . insinuation:** because they insinuated themselves into this business. **60–62. 'Tis . . . opposites:** it is dangerous for inferior men to interfere in a duel between mighty enemies. **pass:** thrust. **fell:** fierce. **65. Popped . . . hopes:** As is from time to time shown in the play. the Danes chose their King by election. **66. angle:** fishing rod and line. **proper:** own. **67. cozenage:** cheating. **68. quit:** pay back. **69. canker:** maggot. See I.iii.39. **73. interim:** interval; between now and the news from England. **79. bravery:** excessive show.

[*Enter* OSRIC.°]

OSR. Your lordship is right welcome back to Denmark.

HAML. I humbly thank you, sir. Dost know this water fly?°

HOR. No, my good lord.

HAML. Thy state is the more gracious,° for 'tis a vice to know him. He hath much land, and fertile. Let a beast be lord of beasts and his crib shall stand at the King's mess.° 'Tis a chough,° but, as I say, spacious° in the possession of dirt.

OSR. Sweet lord, if your lordship were at leisure, I should impart a thing to you from His Majesty.

HAML. I will receive it, sir, with all diligence of spirit. Put your bonnet to his right use,° 'tis for the head.

OSR. I thank your lordship, it is very hot.

HAML. No, believe me, 'tis very cold. The wind is northerly.

OSR. It is indifferent° cold, my lord, indeed.

HAML. But yet methinks it is very sultry and hot, for my complexion—

OSR. Exceedingly, my lord. It is very sultry, as 'twere—I cannot tell how. But, my lord, His Majesty bade me signify to you that he has laid a great wager on your head. Sir, this is the matter—

HAML. I beseech you, remember—

[HAMLET *moves him to put on his hat.*]

OSR. Nay, good my lord, for mine ease, in good faith. Sir, here is newly come to Court Laertes—believe me, an absolute° gentleman, full of most excellent differences,° of very soft society° and great showing.° Indeed, to speak feelingly° of him, he is the card or calendar of gentry,° for you shall find in him the continent of what part a gentleman would see.°

HAML. Sir,° his definement suffers no perdition in you, though I know to divide him inventorially would dizzy the arithmetic of memory, and yet but yaw neither, in respect of his quick sail. But in the verity of extolment, I take him to be

---

s.d., Osric: Osric is a specimen of the fashionable, effeminate courtier. He dresses prettily and talks the jargon of his class, which at this time affected elaborate and allusive metaphors and at all costs avoided saying plain things plainly. **82. water fly:** a useless little creature that flits about. **84. Thy . . . gracious:** you are in the better state. **85–86. Let . . . mess:** i.e., any man, however low, who has wealth enough will find a good place at Court. **crib:** manager. **mess:** table. **86. chough:** jackdaw. **spacious:** wealthy. **89–90. Put . . . use:** i.e., put your hat on your head. Osric is so nice-mannered that he cannot bring himself to wear his hat in the presence of the Prince. **93. indifferent:** moderately. **100. absolute:** perfect. **101. differences:** qualities peculiar to himself. **soft society:** gentle breeding. **101. great showing:** distinguished appearance. **101–102. feelingly:** with proper appreciation. **102. card . . . gentry:** the very fashion plate of what a gentleman should be. **103. continent . . . see:** all the parts that should be in a perfect gentleman. **104–109. Sir . . . more:** Hamlet retorts in similar but even more extravagant language. This is too much for Osric (and for most modern readers). Hamlet's words may be paraphrased: "Sir, the description of this perfect gentleman loses nothing in your account of him; though I realize that if one were to try to enumerate his excellences, it would exhaust our arithmetic, and yet"—here he changes the image to one of sailing—"we should still lag behind him as he outsails us. But in the true vocabulary of praise, I take him to be a soul of the greatest worth, and his perfume"—i.e., his personal essence—"so scarce and rare that to speak truly of him, the only thing like him is his own reflection in his mirror, and everyone else who tries to follow him merely his shadow." **yaw:** fall off from the course laid. **verity . . . extolment:** in true praise. **infusion:** essence. **semblable:** resemblance. **trace:** follow. **umbrage:** shadow.

a soul of great article, and his infusion of such dearth and rareness as, to make true diction of him, his semblable is his mirror, and who else would trace him, his umbrage—nothing more.

OSR. Your lordship speaks most infallibly of him.

HAML. The concernancy,° sir? Why do we wrap the gentleman in our more rawer breath?°

OSR. Sir?°

HOR. Is 't not possible to understand in another tongue? You will do 't, sir, really.

HAML. What imports the nomination° of this gentleman?

OSR. Of Laertes?

HOR. His purse is empty already, all's golden words are spent.

HAML. Of him, sir.

OSR. I know you are not ignorant—

HAML. I would you did, sir. Yet, in faith, if you did, it would not much approve° me. Well, sir?

OSR. You are not ignorant of what excellence Laertes is—

HAML. I dare not confess that, lest I should compare with him in excellence, but to know a man well were to know himself.

OSR. I mean, sir, for his weapon,° but in the imputation° laid on him by them, in his meed° he's unfellowed.°

HAML. What's his weapon?

OSR. Rapier and dagger.

HAML. That's two of his weapons, but, well.

OSR. The King, sir, hath wagered with him six Barbary horses, against the which he has imponed,° as I take it, six French rapiers and poniards, with their assigns,° as girdle, hanger,° and so—three of the carriages, in faith, are very dear to fancy,° very responsive to° the hilts, most delicate carriages, and of very liberal conceit.°

HAML. What call you the carriages?

HOR. I knew you must be edified by the margent° ere you had done.

OSR. The carriages, sir, are the hangers.

HAML. The phrase would be more germane° to the matter if we could carry a cannon by our sides. I would it might be hangers till then. But, on—six Barbary horses against six French swords, their assigns, and three liberal-conceited carriages. That's the French bet against the Danish. Why is this "imponed," as you call it?

OSR. The King, sir, hath laid, sir, that in a dozen passes between yourself and him, he shall not exceed you three hits. He hath laid on twelve for nine, and it would come to immediate trial if your lordship would vouchsafe the answer.

---

111. concernancy: i.e., what is all this talk about? **111–12. Why . . . breath:** why do we discuss the gentleman with our inadequate voices? **113. Sir:** Osric is completely baffled. **115. nomination:** naming. **120. approve:** commend. **125. his weapon:** i.e., skill with his weapon. **imputation:** reputation. **meed:** merit. **unfellowed:** without an equal. **131. imponed:** laid down as a stake. **132. assigns:** that which goes with them. **hanger:** straps by which the scabbard was hung from the belt. **133. dear to fancy:** of beautiful design. **responsive to:** matching. **134. liberal conceit:** elaborately artistic. **136. edified . . . margent:** informed by the notes. In Shakespeare's time the notes were often printed in the margin. **138. germane:** related.

HAML. How if I answer no?

OSR. I mean, my lord, the opposition of your person in trial.

HAML. Sir, I will walk here in the hall. If it please His Majesty, it is the breathing-time of day with me.° Let the foils be brought, the gentleman willing, and the King hold his purpose, I will win for him an I can. If not, I will gain nothing but my shame and the odd hits.

OSR. Shall I redeliver you e'en so?

HAML. To this effect, sir, after what flourish° your nature will.

OSR. I commend my duty to your lordship.

HAML. Yours, yours.

[*Exit* OSRIC.]

He does well to commend it himself, there are no tongues else for 's turn.

HOR. This lapwing° runs away with the shell on his head.

HAML. He did comply with his dug° before he sucked it. Thus has he—and many more of the same breed that I know the drossy° age dotes on—only got the tune of the time and outward habit of encounter,° a kind of yesty collection° which carries them through and through the most fond° and winnowed° opinions—and do but blow them to their trial, the bubbles are out.°

[*Enter a* LORD.]

LORD. My lord, His Majesty commended him to you by young Osric, who brings back to him that you attend him in the hall. He sends to know if your pleasure hold to play with Laertes, or that you will take longer time.

HAML. I am constant to my purposes, they follow the King's pleasure. If his fitness speaks, mine is ready, now or whensoever, provided I be so able as now.

LORD. The King and Queen and all are coming down.

HAML. In happy time.°

LORD. The Queen desires you to use some gentle entertainment° to Laertes before you fall to play.

HAML. She well instructs me.

[*Exit* LORD.]

HOR. You will lose this wager, my lord.

HAML. I do not think so. Since he went into France I have been in continual practice, I shall win at the odds. But thou wouldst not think how ill all's here about my heart—but it is no matter.

148–49. breathing-time . . . me: time when I take exercise. **153. flourish:** fanfare, elaborate phrasing. **157. lapwing:** a pretty, lively little bird. It is so lively that it can run about the moment it is hatched. **158. did . . . dug:** was ceremonious with the nipple; i.e., behaved in this fantastic way from his infancy. See II.ii.389. **159. drossy:** scummy, frivolous. **160. tune . . . encounter:** i.e., they sing the same tune as everyone else and have the same society manners. **yesty collection:** frothy catchwords. **161. fond:** foolish. **winnowed:** light as chaff. Winnowing is the process of fanning the chaff from the grain. **162. do . . . out:** force them to make sense of their words and they are deflated, as Hamlet has just deflated Osric. **169. In . . . time:** at a good moment. **170. gentle entertainment:** kindly treatment; i.e., be reconciled after the brawl in the churchyard.

HOR. Nay, good my lord—

HAML. It is but foolery, but it is such a kind of gaingiving° as would perhaps trouble a woman.

HOR. If your mind dislike anything, obey it. I will forestall their repair hither and say you are not fit.

HAML. Not a whit, we defy augury.° There's special providence in the fall of a sparrow.° If it be now, 'tis not to come; if it be not to come, it will be now; if it be not now, yet it will come. The readiness is all. Since no man has aught of what he leaves, what is 't to leave betimes? Let be.

[*Enter* KING, QUEEN, LAERTES, *and* LORDS, OSRIC *and other* ATTENDANTS *with foils; a table and flagons of wine on it.*]

KING. Come, Hamlet, come, and take this hand from me.

[*The* KING *puts* LAERTES' *hand into* HAMLET'S.]

HAML. Give me your pardon, sir. I've done you wrong,
But pardon 't, as you are a gentleman.
This presence° knows,
And you must needs have heard, how I am punished
With sore distraction. What I have done
That might your nature, honor, and exception°
Roughly awake, I here proclaim was madness.
Was 't Hamlet wronged Laertes? Never Hamlet.
If Hamlet from himself be ta'en away,°
And when he's not himself does wrong Laertes,
Then Hamlet does it not, Hamlet denies it.
Who does it, then? His madness. If 't be so,
Hamlet is of the faction that is wronged,
His madness is poor Hamlet's enemy.
Sir, in this audience
Let my disclaiming from a purposed evil°
Free me so far in your most generous thoughts
That I have shot mine arrow o'er the house,
And hurt my brother.

LAER. I am satisfied in nature,
Whose motive, in this case, should stir me most
To my revenge. But in my terms of honor
I stand aloof, and will no reconcilement
Till by some elder masters of known honor

---

178. gaingiving: misgiving. **182. augury:** omens. **183. special . . . sparrow:** The idea comes from Matthew 10:29. "Are not two sparrows sold for a farthing? and one of them shall not fall to the ground without your Father." **189. presence:** the whole Court. **192. exception:** resentment. **195. If . . . away:** i.e., Hamlet mad is not Hamlet. **202. Let . . . evil:** let my declaration that I did not intend any harm.

I have a voice and precedent of peace
To keep my name ungored.° But till that time
I do receive your offered love like love
And will not wrong it.

HAML. I embrace it freely,
And will this brother's wager frankly play.
Give us the foils. Come on.

LAER. Come, one for me.

HAML. I'll be your foil,° Laertes. In mine ignorance
Your skill shall, like a star i' the darkest night,
Stick° fiery off indeed.

LAER. You mock me, sir.

HAML. No, by this hand.

KING. Give them the foils, young Osric. Cousin Hamlet,
You know the wager?

HAML. Very well, my lord.
Your Grace has laid the odds o' the weaker side.

KING. I do not fear it, I have seen you both.
But since he is bettered,° we have therefore odds.

LAER. This is too heavy, let me see another.

HAML. This likes° me well. These foils have all a length?°

[*They prepare to play.*]

OSR. Aye, my good lord.

KING. Set me the stoups° of wine upon that table.
If Hamlet give the first or second hit,
Or quit° in answer of the third exchange,
Let all the battlements their ordnance fire.
The King shall drink to Hamlet's better breath,
And in the cup a union° shall he throw
Richer than that which four successive kings
In Denmark's crown have worn. Give me the cups,
And let the kettle° to the trumpet speak,
The trumpet to the cannoneer without,
The cannon to the Heavens, the Heaven to earth,
"Now the King drinks to Hamlet." Come, begin,
And you, the judges, bear a wary eye.

HAML. Come on, sir.

LAER. Come, my lord.

---

211. I . . . ungored: I bear you no grudge so far as concerns my personal feelings, which would most readily move me to vengeance; but as this matter touches my honor, I cannot accept your apology until I have been assured by those expert in matters of honor that I may so do without loss of reputation. **216. foil:** Hamlet puns on the other meaning of foil—tin foil set behind a gem to give it luster. **218. Stick . . . off:** Shine out. **224. bettered:** considered your superior. **226. likes:** pleases. **have . . . length:** are all of equal length. **228. stoups:** drinking-vessels. **231. quit:** strike back. **233. union:** a large pearl. **236. kettle:** kettledrum.

[*They play.*]

HAML. One.
LAER. No.
HAML. Judgment.
OSR. A hit, a very palpable° hit.
LAER. Well, again.
KING. Stay, give me drink. Hamlet, this pearl is thine°—
Here's to thy health.

[*Trumpets sound, and cannon shot off within.*]

Give him the cup.
HAML. I'll play this bout first. Set it by a while. Come.

[*They play.*]

Another hit, what say you?
LAER. A touch, a touch, I do confess.
KING. Our son shall win.
QUEEN. He's fat° and scant of breath.
Here, Hamlet, take my napkin, rub thy brows.
The Queen carouses to thy fortune, Hamlet.
HAML. Good madam!
KING. Gertrude, do not drink.
QUEEN. I will, my lord, I pray you pardon me.

[*She drinks.*]

KING. [*Aside*] It is the poisoned cup, it is too late.
HAML. I dare not drink yet, madam—by and by.
QUEEN. Come, let me wipe thy face.
LAER. My lord, I'll hit him now.
KING. I do not think 't.
LAER. [*Aside*] And yet 'tis almost against my conscience.
HAML. Come, for the third, Laertes. You but dally.°
I pray you pass with your best violence,
I am afeard you make a wanton of me.°
LAER. Say you so? Come on.

[*They play.*]

---

243. palpable: clear. **243. this . . . thine:** With these words the King drops the poisoned pearl into the cup intended for Hamlet. **248. fat:** out of condition. **258. dally:** play. **260. make . . . me:** treat me like a child by letting me win.

OSR. Nothing, neither way.
LAER. Have at you now!

[LAERTES *wounds* HAMLET; *then, in scuffling, they change rapiers, and* HAMLET *wounds* LAERTES.]

KING. Part them, they are incensed.
HAML. Nay, come, again.

[*The* QUEEN *falls.*]

OSR. Look to the Queen there, ho!
HOR. They bleed on both sides. How is it, my lord?
OSR. How is 't, Laertes?
LAER. Why, as a woodcock to mine own springe,° Osric,
I am justly killed with mine own treachery.
HAML. How does the Queen?
KING. She swounds to see them bleed.
QUEEN. No, no, the drink, the drink!—O my dear Hamlet—
The drink, the drink! I am poisoned.

[*Dies.*]

HAML. Oh, villainy! Ho! Let the door be locked.
Treachery! Seek it out.

[LAERTES *falls.*]

LAER. It is here, Hamlet. Hamlet, thou art slain.
No medicine in the world can do thee good,
In thee there is not half an hour of life.
The treacherous instrument is in thy hand,
Unbated and envenomed. The foul practice
Hath turned itself on me. Lo, here I lie
Never to rise again. Thy mother's poisoned.
I can no more. The King, the King's to blame.
HAML. The point envenomed too!
Then, venom, to thy work.

[*Stabs the* KING.]

ALL. Treason! Treason!
KING. Oh, yet defend me, friends, I am but hurt.
HAML. Here, thou incestuous, murderous, damnèd Dane,
Drink off this potion. Is thy union° here?
Follow my mother.

267. springe: snare. **287. union:** pearl, as in 1. 283.

[KING *dies.*]

LAER. He is justly served.
It is a poison tempered° by himself.
Exchange forgiveness with me, noble Hamlet.
Mine and my father's death come not upon thee,°
Nor thine on me!

[*Dies.*]

HAML. Heaven make thee free of it!° I follow thee.
I am dead, Horatio. Wretched Queen, adieu!
You that look pale and tremble at this chance,
That are but mutes or audience to this act,
Had I but time—as this fell° sergeant,° Death,
Is strict in his arrest—oh, I could tell you—
But let it be. Horatio, I am dead,
Thou livest. Report me and my cause aright
To the unsatisfied.°
HOR. Never believe it.
I am more an antique Roman° than a Dane.
Here's yet some liquor left.
HAML. As thou 'rt a man,
Give me the cup. Let go—by Heaven, I'll have 't.
O good Horatio, what a wounded name,
Things standing thus unknown, shall live behind me!
If thou didst ever hold me in thy heart,
Absent thee from felicity a while,
And in this harsh world draw thy breath in pain
To tell my story

[*March afar off, and shot within*]

What warlike noise is this?
OSR. Young Fortinbras, with conquest come from Poland,
To the ambassadors of England gives
This warlike volley.
HAML. Oh, I die, Horatio,
The potent poison quite o'ercrows° my spirit.
I cannot live to hear the news from England,
But I do prophesy the election° lights
On Fortinbras. He has my dying voice.°

---

289. tempered: mixed. **291. come . . . thee:** are not on your head. **292. Heaven . . . it:** God forgive you. **297. fell:** dread. **sergeant:** the officer of the Court who made arrests. **301. unsatisfied:** who do not know the truth. **302. antique Roman:** like Cato and Brutus, who killed themselves rather than survive in a world which was unpleasing to them. **314. o'ercrows:** overpowers. **316. election:** as King of Denmark. See 1. 65 above. **317. voice:** support.

So tell him, with the occurrents, more and less,
Which have solicited.° The rest is silence.

[*Dies.*]

HOR. Now cracks a noble heart. Good night, sweet Prince,
And flights of angels sing thee to thy rest!

[*March within.*]

Why does the drum come hither?

[*Enter* FORTINBRAS, *and the* ENGLISH AMBASSADORS, *with drum, colors, and* ATTENDANTS.]

FOR. Where is this sight?
HOR. What is it you would see?
If aught of woe or wonder, cease your search.
FOR. This quarry cries on havoc.° O proud Death,
What feast is toward° in thine eternal cell
That thou so many princes at a shot
So bloodily hast struck?
1. AMB. The sight is dismal,
And our affairs from England come too late.
The ears are senseless that should give us hearing,
To tell him his commandment is fulfilled,
That Rosencrantz and Guildenstern are dead.
Where should we have our thanks?
HOR. Not from his mouth
Had it the ability of life to thank you.
He never gave commandment for their death.
But since, so jump° upon this bloody question,°
You from the Polack wars, and you from England,
Are here arrived, give order that these bodies
High on a stage be placèd to the view,
And let me speak to the yet unknowing world
How these things came about. So shall you hear
Of carnal, bloody, and unnatural acts,
Of accidental judgments, casual slaughters,
Of deaths put on by cunning and forced cause,
And, in this upshot, purposes mistook
Fall'n on the inventors' heads.° All this can I
Truly deliver.

318–19. occurrents . . . solicited: events great and small which have caused me to act. **325. quarry . . . havoc:** heap of slain denotes a pitiless slaughter. See *Caesar,* III.i.273. **326. toward:** being prepared. **336. jump:** exactly. See I.i.65. **question:** matter. **342–46. carnal . . . heads:** These lines sum up the whole tragedy: Claudius' adultery with Gertrude, his murder of his brother, the death of Ophelia due to an accident, that of Polonius by casual chance, Hamlet's device which caused the deaths of Rosencrantz and Guildenstern, the plan which went awry and caused the deaths of Claudius and Laertes.

FOR. Let us haste to hear it,
And call the noblest to the audience.
For me, with sorrow I embrace my fortune.
I have some rights of memory° in this kingdom,
Which now to claim my vantage° doth invite me.
HOR. Of that I shall have also cause to speak,
And from his mouth whose voice will draw on more.°
But let this same be presently performed,
Even while men's minds are wild, lest more mischance
On plots and errors happen.
FOR. Let four captains
Bear Hamlet, like a soldier, to the stage.
For he was likely, had he been put on,°
To have proved most royally. And for his passage
The soldiers' music and the rites of war
Speak loudly for him.
Take up the bodies. Such a sight as this
Becomes the field, but here shows much amiss.
Go, bid the soldiers shoot.

[*A dead march. Exeunt, bearing off the bodies; after which a peal of ordnance is shot off.*]

Othello

About the Play: This play was produced about three years after *Hamlet.* Although its story is much simpler than the earlier play, the perspectives from which it can be seen are nearly as various. It is, for example, the tragedy of a noble outsider, a princely black African, who achieves great stature in a white European society entirely by his own abilities, becoming commander in chief of the Venetian army. It is also the story of a man not entirely sure of his position in this alien culture, who tries to cement it by marrying a rich white Venetian aristocrat. It is an intense study of what happens to two lovers who depend very greatly on one another, as well as an intense exploration of the psychological implications of race and gender issues on such a couple when they have distanced themselves from their respective societies.

Othello is also the tragedy of his wife, Desdemona, who believes as Othello does that she should be submissive, obedient, and faithful, which she is. But this situation is self-defeating for both of them. It breeds insecurity in Othello, possibly because he doubts that his white wife and new society can fully accept him, and it creates a set of contradictions for Desdemona. She demonstrates her love for Othello by leaving her father without his permission, rebelling against Venetian social values, and so prompting her husband's uncertainty about her present loyalty.

We might ask too about what Iago's motive is in misleading Othello into believing that his wife is unfaithful. This action is also the play's central puzzle: Why does Othello trust his friend

---

350. rights of memory: rights which will be remembered; i.e., with the disappearance of all the family of the original King Hamlet the situation reverts to what it was before the death of Fortinbras' father. See I.i.80–95. **351. vantage:** i.e., my advantage, there being none to dispute my claim. **353. voice . . . more:** i.e., Hamlet's dying voice will strengthen your claim. **358. had . . . on:** had he become King.

more than he does Desdemona, whom he loves? We can see Iago's skilled hypocrisy, but somehow this in itself does not account for his success. We need to ask, how is it that Othello is so ready to believe him?

DRAMATIS PERSONAE

DUKE OF VENICE
BRABANTIO, *a Senator*
OTHER SENATORS
GRATIANO, *brother to Brabantio*
LODOVICO, *kinsman to Brabantio*
OTHELLO, *a noble Moor in the service of the Venetian state*
CASSIO, *his lieutenant*
IAGO, *his ancient*
MONTANO, *Othello's predecessor in the government of Cyprus*
RODERIGO, *a Venetian gentleman*
CLOWN, *servant to Othello*

DESDEMONA, *daughter to Brabantio and wife to Othello*
EMILIA, *wife to Iago*
BIANCA, *mistress to Cassio*

SAILOR, MESSENGER, HERALD, OFFICERS, GENTLEMEN, MUSICIANS, *and* ATTENDANTS

SCENE—*Venice: a seaport in Cyprus.*

ACT I

SCENE 1. *Venice. A street.*

[*Enter* RODERIGO *and* IAGO.]

ROD. Tush, never tell me. I take it much unkindly
That thou, Iago, who hast had° my purse
As if the strings were thine, shouldst know of this.
IAGO. 'Sblood,° but you will not hear me.
If ever I did dream of such a matter,
Abhor me.
ROD. Thou told'st me thou didst hold him in thy hate.
IAGO. Despise me if I do not. Three great ones of the city,
In personal suit° to make me his Lieutenant,
Off-capped° to him. And, by the faith of man,
I know my price, I am worth no worse a place.
But he, as loving his own pride and purposes,

Act 1, Sc. i: 2. had: i.e., used. **4. 'Sblood:** by God's blood. **9. In . . . suit:** making this request in person. **10. Off-capped:** stood cap in hand.

Evades them, with a bombast circumstance°
Horribly stuffed with epithets of war.°
And, in conclusion,
Nonsuits° my mediators, for, "Certes,"° says he,
"I have already chose my officer."
And what was he?
Forsooth, a great arithmetician,°
One Michael Cassio, a Florentine,
A fellow almost damned in a fair wife,°
That never set a squadron in the field,
Nor the division of a battle° knows
More than a spinster, unless the bookish theoric,°
Wherein the toged° Consuls° can propose
As masterly as he—mere prattle without practice
Is all his soldiership. But he, sir, had the election.
And I, of whom his eyes had seen the proof
At Rhodes, at Cyprus, and on other grounds
Christian and heathen, must be beleed° and calmed
By debitor and creditor. This countercaster,°
He, in good time,° must his Lieutenant be,
And I—God bless the mark!°—his Moorship's Ancient.°

ROD. By Heaven, I rather would have been his hangman.

IAGO. Why, there's no remedy. 'Tis the curse of service,
Preferment goes by letter and affection,
And not by old gradation,° where each second
Stood heir to the first. Now, sir, be judge yourself
Whether I in any just term am affined°
To love the Moor.

ROD. I would not follow him, then.

IAGO. Oh, sir, content you,
I follow him to serve my turn upon him.
We cannot all be masters, nor all masters
Cannot be truly followed. You shall mark
Many a duteous and knee-crooking knave
That doting on his own obsequious bondage
Wears out his time, much like his master's ass,

---

13. bombast circumstance: bombastic phrases. Bombast is cotton padding used to stuff out a garment. **14. stuffed . . . war:** padded out with military terms. **16. Nonsuits:** rejects the petition of. **Certes:** assuredly. **19. arithmetician:** Contemporary books on military tactics are full of elaborate diagrams and numerals to explain military formations. Cassio is a student of such books. **21. almost . . . wife:** A much-disputed phrase. There is an Italian proverb, "You have married a fair wife? You are damned." If Iago has this in mind, he means by *almost* that Cassio is about to marry. **23. division . . . battle:** organization of an army. **24. bookish theoric:** student of war; not a practical soldier. **25. toged:** wearing a toga. **Consuls:** councilors. Cf. I.ii.43. **30. beleed:** placed on the lee (or unfavorable) side. **31. countercaster:** calculator (repeating the idea of arithmetician). Counters were used in making calculations. **32. in . . . time:** A phrase expressing indignation. **33. God . . . mark:** An exclamation of impatience. **Ancient:** ensign, the third officer in the company of which Othello is Captain and Cassio Lieutenant. **36–37. Preferment . . . gradation:** promotion comes through private recommendation and favoritism and not by order of seniority. **39. affined:** tied by affection.

For naught but provender, and when he's old, cashiered.°
Whip me such honest knaves. Others there are
Who, trimmed in forms and visages of duty,°
Keep yet their hearts attending on themselves,
And throwing but shows of service° on their lords
Do well thrive by them, and when they have lined their coats
Do themselves homage.° These fellows have some soul,
And such a one do I profess myself. For, sir,
It is as sure as you are Roderigo,
Were I the Moor, I would not be Iago.
In following him, I follow but myself.
Heaven is my judge, not I for love and duty,
But seeming so, for my peculiar° end.
For when my outward action doth demónstrate
The native act and figure of my heart°
In compliment extern,° 'tis not long after
But I will wear my heart upon my sleeve
For daws° to peck at. I am not what I am.°

ROD. What a full fortune° does the thick-lips owe°
If he can carry 't thus!°

IAGO. Call up her father,
Rouse him. Make after him, poison his delight,
Proclaim him in the streets. Incense her kinsmen,
And though he in a fertile climate dwell,
Plague him with flies. Though that his joy be joy,
Yet throw such changes of vexation on 't
As it may lose some color.°

ROD. Here is her father's house, I'll call aloud.

IAGO. Do, with like timorous° accent and dire yell
As when, by night and negligence, the fire
Is spied in populous cities.

ROD. What ho, Brabantio! Signior Brabantio, ho!

IAGO. Awake! What ho, Brabantio! Thieves! Thieves! Thieves!
Look to your house, your daughter and your bags!°
Thieves! Thieves!

[BRABANTIO *appears above, at a window.*]

BRA. What is the reason of this terrible summons?
What is the matter there?

---

48. cashiered: dismissed. The word at this time did not imply dishonorable discharge. **50. trimmed . . . duty:** decking themselves out with the outward forms of loyal service. **52. throwing . . . service:** serving merely in outward show. **54. Do . . . homage:** serve themselves. **homage:** an outward act signifying obedience. **60. peculiar:** particular, personal. **62. native . . . heart:** natural actions and shape of my secret designs. **63. extern:** outward. **65. daws:** jackdaws; i.e., fools. **I . . . am:** i.e., I am in secret a devil. **66. full fortune:** overflowing good luck. **owe:** own. **67. carry't thus:** i.e., bring off this marriage. **72–73. throw . . . color:** cause him some annoyance by way of variety to tarnish his joy. **75. timorous:** terrifying. **80. bags:** moneybags.

ROD. Signior, is all your family within?
IAGO. Are your doors locked?
BRA. Why, wherefore ask you this?
IAGO. 'Zounds,° sir, you're robbed. For shame, put on your gown,°
Your heart is burst, you have lost half your soul.
Even now, now, very now, an old black ram
Is tupping° your white ewe. Arise, arise,
Awake the snorting° citizens with the bell,
Or else the Devil° will make a grandsire of you.
Arise, I say.
BRA. What, have you lost your wits?
ROD. Most reverend signior, do you know my voice?
BRA. Not I. What are you?
ROD. My name is Roderigo.
BRA. The worser welcome.
I have charged thee not to haunt about my doors.
In honest plainness thou hast heard me say
My daughter is not for thee, and now, in madness,
Being full of supper and distempering draughts,°
Upon malicious bravery° dost thou come
To start° my quiet.
ROD. Sir, sir, sir—
BRA. But thou must needs be sure
My spirit and my place have in them power
To make this bitter to thee.
ROD. Patience, good sir.
BRA. What tell'st thou me of robbing? This is Venice,
My house is not a grange.°
ROD. Most grave Brabantio,
In simple and pure soul I come to you.
IAGO. 'Zounds, sir, you are one of those that will not serve God if the Devil bid you. Because we come to do you service and you think we are ruffians, you'll have your daughter covered with a Barbary° horse, you'll have your nephews° neigh to you, you'll have coursers for cousins,° and jennets° for germans.°
BRA. What profane wretch art thou?
IAGO. I am one, sir, that comes to tell you your daughter and the Moor are now making the beast with two backs.
BRA. Thou art a villain.
IAGO. You are—a Senator.
BRA. This thou shalt answer. I know thee, Roderigo.

---

86. 'Zounds: by God's wounds. **gown:** dressing gown. **89. tupping:** covering. **90. snorting:** snoring. **91. Devil:** The Devil in old pictures and woodcuts was represented as black. **99. distempering draughts:** liquor that makes senseless. **100. bravery:** defiance. **101. start:** startle. **106. grange:** lonely farm. **110. Barbary:** Moorish. **111. nephews:** grandsons. **cousins:** near relations. **jennets:** Moorish ponies. **112. germans:** kinsmen.

ROD. Sir, I will answer anything. But I beseech you
If 't be your pleasure and most wise consent,
As partly I find it is, that your fair daughter,
At this odd-even° and dull° watch o' the night,
Transported with no worse nor better guard
But with a knave of common hire, a gondolier,
To the gross clasps of a lascivious Moor—
If this be known to you, and your allowance,°
We then have done you bold and saucy wrongs.
But if you know not this, my manners tell me
We have your wrong rebuke. Do not believe
That from the sense of all civility°
I thus would play and trifle with your reverence.
Your daughter, if you have not given her leave,
I say again, hath made a gross revolt,°
Tying her duty, beauty, wit, and fortunes
In an extravagant° and wheeling° stranger
Of here and everywhere. Straight satisfy yourself.
If she be in her chamber or your house,
Let loose on me the justice of the state
For thus deluding you.

BRA. Strike on the tinder,° ho!
Give me a taper!° Call up all my people!
This accident is not unlike my dream.
Belief of it oppresses me already.
Light, I say! Light!

[*Exit above.*]

IAGO. Farewell, for I must leave you.
It seems not meet, nor wholesome to my place,°
To be produced—as if I stay I shall—
Against the Moor. For I do know the state,
However this may gall° him with some check,°
Cannot with safety cast° him. For he's embarked
With such loud reason to the Cyprus wars,
Which even now stand in act,° that, for their souls,
Another of his fathom° they have none
To lead their business. In which regard,

---

121. odd-even: about midnight. **dull:** heavy, sleepy. **125. your allowance:** by your permission. **129. from . . . civility:** disregarding all sense of decent behavior. **132. gross revolt:** indecent rebellion. **134. extravagant:** vagabond. **wheeling:** wandering. **138. tinder:** the primitive method of making fire, used before the invention of matches. A spark, made by striking flint on steel, fell on the tinder, some inflammable substance such as charred linen, which was blown into flame. **139. taper:** candle. **143. place:** i.e., as Othello's officer. **146. gall:** make sore. **check:** rebuke. **147. cast:** dismiss from service. **149. stand in act:** are on the point of beginning. **150. fathom:** depth.

Though I do hate him as I do Hell pains,
Yet for necessity of present life
I must show out a flag° and sign of love,
Which is indeed but sign. That you shall surely find him,
Lead to the Sagittary° the raisèd search,
And there will I be with him. So farewell.

[*Exit.*]

[*Enter, below,* BRABANTIO, *in his nightgown, and* SERVANTS *with torches.*]

BRA. It is too true an evil. Gone she is,
And what's to come of my despisèd time°
Is naught but bitterness. Now, Roderigo,
Where didst thou see her? Oh, unhappy girl!
With the Moor, say'st thou? Who would be a father!
How didst thou know 'twas she? Oh, she deceives me
Past thought! What said she to you? Get more tapers.
Raise all my kindred. Are they married, think you?
ROD. Truly, I think they are.
BRA. Oh Heaven! How got she out? Oh, treason of the blood!°
Fathers, from hence trust not your daughters' minds
By what you see them act. Are there not charms°
By which the property° of youth and maidhood
May be abused?° Have you not read, Roderigo,
Of some such thing?
ROD. Yes, sir, I have indeed.
BRA. Call up my brother. Oh, would you had had her!
Some one way, some another. Do you know
Where we may apprehend her and the Moor?
ROD. I think I can discover him, if you please
To get good guard and go along with me.
BRA. Pray you, lead on. At every house I'll call,
I may command° at most. Get weapons, ho!
And raise some special officers of night.
On, good Roderigo, I'll deserve your pains.°

[*Exeunt.*]

SCENE II. *Another street.*

[*Enter* OTHELLO, IAGO, *and* ATTENDANTS *with torches.*]

---

154. flag: a sign of welcome. **156. Sagittary:** presumably some building in Venice, not identified, used as a meeting place for the Council. **159. what's . . . time:** the rest of my wretched life. **167. treason . . . blood:** treachery of my own child. **169. charms:** magic spells. **170. property:** nature. **171. abused:** deceived. **179. command:** find supporters. **181. deserve . . . pains:** reward your labor.

IAGO. Though in the trade of war I have slain men,
Yet do I hold it very stuff° o' the conscience
To do no contrivèd° murder. I lack iniquity
Sometimes to do me service. Nine or ten times
I had thought to have yerked° him here under the ribs.
OTH. 'Tis better as it is.
IAGO. Nay, but he prated
And spoke such scurvy and provoking terms
Against your honor
That, with the little godliness I have,
I did full hard forbear him.° But I pray you, sir,
Are you fast° married? Be assured of this,
That the Magnifico° is much beloved,
And hath in his effect° a voice potential
As double as° the Duke's. He will divorce you,
Or put upon you what restraint and grievance
The law, with all his might to enforce it on,
Will give him cable.°
OTH. Let him do his spite.
My services which I have done the signiory°
Shall outtongue his complaints. 'Tis yet to know°—
Which, when I know that boasting is an honor,
I shall promulgate°—I fetch my life and being°
From men of royal siege,° and my demerits°
May speak unbonneted° to as proud a fortune
As this that I have reached. For know, Iago,
But that I love the gentle Desdemona,
I would not my unhousèd° free condition
Put into circumscription and confine°
For the sea's worth. But look! What lights come yond?
IAGO. Those are the raisèd father and his friends.
You were best go in.
OTH. Not I, I must be found.
My parts,° my title, and my perfect° soul
Shall manifest me rightly. Is it they?
IAGO. By Janus,° I think no.

[*Enter* CASSIO, *and certain* OFFICERS *with torches.*]

Sc. ii: 2. stuff: material, nature. **3. contrived:** deliberately planned. **5. yerked:** jabbed. **10. full . . . him:** had a hard job to keep my hands off him. **11. fast:** securely. **12. Magnifico:** the title of the chief men of Venice. **13. in . . . effect:** what he can do. **13–14. potential . . . as:** twice as powerful as. **17. cable:** rope. **18. signiory:** the state of Venice. **19. 'Tis . . . know:** it has still to be made known. **21. promulgate:** proclaim. **fetch . . . being:** am descended. **22. royal siege:** throne. **demerits:** deserts. **23. unbonneted:** A disputed phrase. Usually it means "without a cap"; i.e., in sign that the wearer is standing before a superior. But Othello means that his merits are such that he need show deference to no man. **26. unhoused:** unmarried. **27. confine:** confinement. **31. parts:** abilities. **perfect:** ready. **33. Janus:** the two-faced God of the Romans, an appropriate deity for Iago.

OTH. The servants of the Duke, and my Lieutenant.
The goodness of the night upon you, friends!
What is the news?
CAS. The Duke does greet you, General,
And he requires your haste-posthaste° appearance,
Even on the instant.
OTH. What is the matter, think you?
CAS. Something from Cyprus, as I may divine.
It is a business of some heat. The galleys°
Have sent a dozen sequent° messengers
This very night at one another's heels,
And many of the consuls, raised and met,
Are at the Duke's already. You have been hotly called for
When, being not at your lodging to be found,
The Senate hath sent about three several° quests
To search you out.
OTH. 'Tis well I am found by you.
I will but spend a word here in the house
And go with you.

[*Exit.*]

CAS. Ancient, what makes he here?
IAGO. Faith, he tonight hath boarded a land carrack.°
If it prove lawful prize, he's made forever.
CAS. I do not understand.
IAGO. He's married.
CAS. To who?

[*Re-enter* OTHELLO.]

IAGO. Marry,° to—Come, Captain, will you go?
OTH. Have with you.
CAS. Here comes another troop to seek for you.
IAGO. It is Brabantio. General, be advised,°
He comes to bad intent.

[*Enter* BRABANTIO, RODERIGO, *and* OFFICERS *with torches and weapons.*]

OTH. Holloa! Stand there!
ROD. Signior, it is the Moor.
BRA. Down with him, thief!

---

37. haste-posthaste: with the quickest possible speed. When it was necessary to urge the postboy to greater speed than usual, the letter or dispatch was inscribed "haste, posthaste." The Earl of Essex once inscribed a letter "haste, haste, haste posthaste, haste for life." See App. 17. **40. galleys:** Venetian ships manned and rowed by slaves; the fastest of craft. **41. sequent:** following one after another. **46. several:** separate. **50. carrack:** the largest type of Spanish merchant ship. **53. Marry:** Mary, by the Virgin—with a pun. **55. advised:** careful.

[*They draw on both sides.*]

IAGO. You, Roderigo! Come, sir, I am for you.
OTH. Keep up° your bright swords, for the dew will rust them.
Good signior, you shall more command with years
Than with your weapons.
BRA. O thou foul thief, where hast thou stowed my daughter?
Damned as thou art, thou hast enchanted her.
For I'll refer me to all things of sense°
If she in chains of magic were not bound,
Whether a maid so tender, fair, and happy,
So opposite to marriage that she shunned
The wealthy curlèd darlings of our nation,
Would ever have, to incur a general mock,
Run from her guardage° to the sooty bosom
Of such a thing as thou, to fear, not to delight.
Judge me the world if 'tis not gross in sense°
That thou hast practiced on her with foul charms,
Abused her delicate youth with drugs or minerals
That weaken motion.° I'll have 't disputed on,°
'Tis probable, and palpable° to thinking.
I therefore apprehend and do attach° thee
For an abuser of the world, a practicer
Of arts inhibited and out of warrant.°
Lay hold upon him. If he do resist,
Subdue him at his peril.
OTH. Hold your hands,
Both you of my inclining and the rest.
Were it my cue to fight, I should have known it
Without a prompter. Where will you that I go
To answer this your charge?
BRA. To prison, till fit time
Of law and course of direct session°
Call thee to answer.
OTH. What if I do obey?
How may the Duke be therewith satisfied,
Whose messengers are here about my side
Upon some present° business of the state
To bring me to him?
1. OFF. 'Tis true, most worthy signior.

---

59. Keep up: sheathe. **64. refer . . . sense:** i.e., by every rational consideration. **70. guardage:** guardianship. **72. gross in sense:** i.e., plain to the perception. **75. motion:** sense. **disputed on:** argued in the courts of law. **76. palpable:** clear. **77. attach:** arrest. **79. arts . . . warrant:** forbidden and illegal acts; i.e., magic and witchcraft. **86. course . . . session:** trial in the ordinary courts, where witches and other criminals are tried—and not by special commission as a great man. **90. present:** immediate.

The Duke's in Council, and your noble self
I am sure is sent for.

BRA. How! The Duke in Council!
In this time of the night! Bring him away.
Mine's not an idle° cause. The Duke himself,
Or any of my brothers of the state,
Cannot but feel this wrong as 'twere their own.
For if such actions may have passage free,°
Bondslaves and pagans shall our statesmen be.

[*Exeunt.*]

SCENE III. *A council chamber.*

[*The* DUKE *and* SENATORS *sitting at a table,* OFFICERS *attending.*]

DUKE. There is no composition° in these news°
That gives them credit.

1. SEN. Indeed they are disproportioned.
My letters say a hundred and seven galleys.

DUKE. And mine, a hundred and forty.

2. SEN. And mine, two hundred.
But though they jump not on a just account°—
As in these cases, where the aim reports,°
'Tis oft with difference—yet do they all confirm
A Turkish fleet, and bearing up° to Cyprus.

DUKE. Nay, it is possible enough to judgment.
I do not so secure me in the error,°
But the main article° I do approve
In fearful° sense.

SAILOR. [*Within*] What ho! What ho! What ho!

1. OFF. A messenger from the galleys.

[*Enter* SAILOR.]

DUKE. Now, what's the business?

SAIL. The Turkish preparation makes for Rhodes.
So was I bid report here to the state
By Signior Angelo.

DUKE. How say you by this change?

---

95. idle: trivial. **98. have . . . free:** be freely allowed.

Sc. iii: 1. composition: agreement. **news:** reports. **5. jump . . . account:** do not agree with an exact estimate. **6. aim reports:** i.e., intelligence reports of an enemy's intention often differ in the details. **8. bearing up:** making course for. **10. I . . . error:** I do not consider myself free from danger, because the reports may not all be accurate. **11. main article:** general purport. **12. fearful:** to be feared.

1. SEN. This cannot be,
By no assay of reason.° 'Tis a pageant°
To keep us in false gaze.° When we consider
The importancy of Cyprus to the Turk,
And let ourselves again but understand
That as it more concerns the Turk than Rhodes,
So may he with more facile question bear° it,
For that it stands not in such warlike brace°
But altogether lacks the abilities
That Rhodes is dressed° in—if we make thought of this,
We must not think the Turk is so unskillful
To leave that latest which concerns him first,
Neglecting an attempt of ease and gain
To wake and wage° a danger profitless.
DUKE. Nay, in all confidence, he's not for Rhodes.
1. OFF. Here is more news.

[*Enter a* MESSENGER.]

MESS. The Ottomites,° Reverend and Gracious,
Steering with due course toward the isle of Rhodes,
Have there injointed° them with an after-fleet.°
1. SEN. Aye, so I thought. How many, as you guess?
MESS. Of thirty sail. And now they do restem°
Their backward course, bearing with frank appearance°
Their purposes toward Cyprus. Signior Montano,
Your trusty and most valiant servitor,
With his free duty recommends you thus,°
And prays you to believe him.
DUKE. 'Tis certain then for Cyprus.
Marcus Luccicos, is not he in town?
1. SEN. He's now in Florence.
DUKE. Write from us to him, post-posthaste dispatch.
1. SEN. Here comes Brabantio and the valiant Moor.

[*Enter* BRABANTIO, OTHELLO, IAGO, RODERIGO, *and* OFFICERS.]

DUKE. Valiant Othello, we must straight employ you
Against the general enemy Ottoman.
[*To* BRABANTIO] I did not see you. Welcome, gentle signior,
We lacked your counsel and your help tonight.
BRA. So did I yours. Good your Grace, pardon me,

---

18. assay of reason: reasonable test. **pageant:** show. **19. false gaze:** looking the wrong way. **23. with . . . bear:** take it more easily. **24. brace:** state of defense. **26. dressed:** prepared. **30. wage:** risk. **33. Ottomites:** Turks. **35. injointed:** joined. **after-fleet:** following, second fleet. **37. restem:** steer again. **38. frank appearance:** no attempt at concealment. **41. With . . . thus:** with all due respect thus advises.

Neither my place nor aught I heard of business
Hath raised me from my bed, nor doth the general care
Take hold on me. For my particular° grief
Is of so floodgate° and o'erbearing nature
That it engluts° and swallows other sorrows,
And it is still itself.

DUKE. Why, what's the matter?

BRA. My daughter! Oh, my daughter!

ALL. Dead?

BRA. Aye, to me.
She is abused, stol'n from me and corrupted
By spells and medicines bought of mountebanks.°
For nature so preposterously to err,
Being not deficient, blind, or lame of sense,
Sans° witchcraft could not.

DUKE. Whoe'er he be that in this foul proceeding
Hath thus beguiled your daughter of herself°
And you of her, the bloody book of law
You shall yourself read in the bitter letter
After your own sense—yea, though our proper° son
Stood in your action.

BRA. Humbly I thank your Grace.
Here is the man, this Moor, whom now, it seems,
Your special mandate for the state affairs
Hath hither brought.

ALL. We are very sorry for 't.

DUKE. [*To* OTHELLO] What in your own part can you say to this?

BRA. Nothing but this is so.

OTH. Most potent, grave, and reverend signiors,
My very noble and approved° good masters,
That I have ta'en away this old man's daughter,
It is most true—true, I have married her.
The very head and front° of my offending
Hath this extent, no more. Rude° am I in my speech,
And little blest with the soft phrase of peace.
For since these arms of mine had seven years' pith°
Till now some nine moons wasted, they have used
Their dearest° action in the tented field.
And little of this great world can I speak,
More than pertains to feats of broil and battle,
And therefore little shall I grace my cause

---

55. particular: personal. **56. floodgate:** i.e., like water rushing through an opened sluice. **57. engluts:** swallows. **61. mountebanks:** quack doctors, who dealt in poisons and love potions. Cf. *Haml,* IV.vii.142. **64. Sans:** without. **66. beguiled . . . herself:** cheated your daughter of herself; i.e., caused her to be "beside herself." **69. proper:** own. **77. approved:** tested; i.e., found good masters by experience. **80. front:** forehead. **81. Rude:** rough, uncultured. **83. pith:** marrow. **85. dearest:** most important.

In speaking for myself. Yet, by your gracious patience,
I will a round unvarnished tale° deliver
Of my whole course of love—what drugs, what charms,
What conjuration and what mighty magic—
For such proceeding I am charged withal—
I won his daughter.

BRA. A maiden never bold,
Of spirit so still and quiet that her motion
Blushed at herself,° and she—in spite of nature,
Of years, of country, credit,° everything—
To fall in love with what she feared to look on!
It is a judgment maimed and most imperfect
That will confess° perfection so could err
Against all rules of nature, and must be driven
To find out practices° of cunning Hell
Why this should be. I therefore vouch° again
That with some mixtures° powerful o'er the blood,°
Or with some dram conjured° to this effect,
He wrought upon her.

DUKE. To vouch this is no proof
Without more certain and more overt° test
Than these thin habits° and poor likelihoods°
Of modern seeming° do prefer° against him.

1. SEN. But, Othello, speak.
Did you by indirect and forcèd° courses
Subdue and poison this young maid's affections?
Or came it by request, and such fair question
As soul to soul affordeth?

OTH. I do beseech you
Send for the lady to the Sagittary,
And let her speak of me before her father.
If you do find me foul in her report,
The trust, the office I do hold of you,
Not only take away, but let your sentence
Even fall upon my life.

DUKE. Fetch Desdemona hither.

OTH. Ancient, conduct them, you best know the place.

[*Exeunt* IAGO *and* ATTENDANTS.]

---

90. round . . . tale: direct, unadorned account. **95–96. Of . . . herself:** she was so shy that she blushed at the slightest cause. **motion:** outward behavior. **97. credit:** reputation. **100. will confess:** would believe. **102. practices:** plots. **103. vouch:** declare. **104. mixtures:** drugs. **blood:** passions. **105. conjured:** mixed with spells. **107. overt:** open. **108. thin habits:** slight evidence; lit., thin clothes. **poor likelihoods:** unconvincing charges. **109. modern seeming:** slight suspicion. **prefer:** make a charge against. **111. forced:** unnatural.

And till she come, as truly as to Heaven
I do confess the vices of my blood,
So justly to your grave ears I'll present
How I did thrive in this fair lady's love
And she in mine.

DUKE. Say it, Othello.

OTH. Her father loved me, oft invited me,
Still° questioned me the story of my life
From year to year, the battles, sieges, fortunes,
That I have passed.
I ran it through, even form my boyish days
To the very moment that he bade me tell it.
Wherein I spake of most disastrous chances,°
Of moving accidents° by flood and field,
Of hairbreadth 'scapes i' the imminent deadly breach,°
Of being taken by the insolent foe
And sold to slavery, of my redemption thence,
And portance° in my travels' history.
Wherein of antres° vast and deserts idle,°
Rough quarries, rocks, and hills whose heads touch heaven,
It was my hint° to speak—such was the process.°
And of the cannibals that each other eat,
The anthropophagi,° and men whose heads
Do grow beneath their shoulders.° This to hear
Would Desdemona seriously incline.
But still the house affairs would draw her thence,
Which ever as she could with haste dispatch,
She'd come again, and with a greedy ear
Devour up my discourse. Which I observing,
Took once a pliant° hour and found good means
To draw from her a prayer of earnest heart
That I would all my pilgrimage dilate,°
Whereof by parcels° she had something heard,
But not intentively.° I did consent,
And often did beguile her of° her tears
When I did speak of some distressful stroke
That my youth suffered. My story being done,
She gave me for my pains a world of sighs.
She swore, in faith, 'twas strange, 'twas passing strange,
'Twas pitiful, 'twas wondrous pitiful.

---

129. Still: always, continually. **134. chances:** accidents. **135. accidents:** occurrences. **136. breach:** assault on a city. See Pl. 12a. **139. portance:** bearing. **140. antres:** caves. **idle:** worthless. **142. hint:** occasion. **process:** proceeding, order. **144. anthropophagi:** cannibals. **144–45. men . . . shoulders:** See *Temp,* III.iii.46–47,n. **151. pliant:** suitable. **153. dilate:** relate at length. **154. parcels:** portions. **155. intentively:** intently. **156. beguile . . . of:** draw from her.

She wished she had not heard it, yet she wished
That Heaven had made her° such a man. She thanked me,
And bade me, if I had a friend that loved her,
I should but teach him how to tell my story
And that would woo her. Upon this hint I spake.
She loved me for the dangers I had passed,
And I loved her that she did pity them.
This only is the witchcraft I have used.
Here comes the lady, let her witness it.

[*Enter* DESDEMONA, IAGO, *and* ATTENDANTS.]

DUKE. I think this tale would win my daughter too.
Good Brabantio,
Take up this mangled matter at the best.°
Men do their broken weapons rather use
Than their bare hands.

BRA. I pray you hear her speak.
If she confess that she was half the wooer,
Destruction on my head if my bad blame
Light on the man! Come hither, gentle mistress.
Do you perceive in all this noble company
Where most you owe obedience?

DES. My noble Father,
I do perceive here a divided duty.
To you I am bound for life and education,
My life and education both do learn° me
How to respect you, you are the lord of duty,°
I am hitherto your daughter. But here's my husband,
And so much duty as my mother showed
To you, preferring you before her father
So much I challenge that I may profess
Due to the Moor my lord.

BRA. God be with you! I have done.
Please it your Grace, on to the state affairs.
I had rather to adopt a child than get° it.
Come hither, Moor.
I here do give thee that with all my heart
Which, but thou hast already, with all my heart
I would keep from thee. For your sake, jewel,
I am glad at soul I have no other child,
For thy escape would teach me tyranny,
To hang clogs on them. I have done, my lord.

---

163. her: for her. **173. Take . . . best:** make the best settlement you can of this confused business. **183. learn:** teach. **184. lord of duty:** the man to whom I owe duty. **191. get:** beget.

DUKE. Let me speak like yourself, and lay a sentence°
Which, as a grise° or step, may help these lovers
Into your favor.
When remedies are past, the griefs are ended
By seeing the worst, which late on hopes depended.°
To mourn a mischief that is past and gone
Is the next way to draw new mischief on.
What cannot be preserved when fortune takes,
Patience her injury a mockery makes.°
The robbed that smiles steals something from the thief.
He robs himself that spends a bootless° grief.

BRA. So° let the Turk of Cyprus us beguile,
We lose it not so long as we can smile.
He bears the sentence well that nothing bears
But the free comfort which from thence he hears.
But he bears both the sentence and the sorrow
That, to pay grief, must of poor patience borrow.
These sentences, to sugar or to gall,
Being strong on both sides, are equivocal.
But words are words. I never yet did hear
That the bruised heart was piercèd through the ear.
I humbly beseech you, proceed to the affairs of state.

DUKE. The Turk with a most mighty preparation makes for Cyprus. Othello, the fortitude of the place is best known to you, and though we have there a substitute° of most allowed° sufficiency,° yet opinion, a sovereign mistress of effects, throws a more safer voice on you.° You must therefore be content to slubber° the gloss of your new fortunes with this more stubborn and boisterous expedition.

OTH. The tyrant custom, most grave Senators,
Hath made the flinty and steel couch of war
My thrice-driven° bed of down. I do agnize°
A natural and prompt alacrity
I find in hardness,° and do undertake
These present wars against the Ottomites.
Most humbly therefore bending to your state,
I crave fit disposition for my wife,
Due reference of place° and exhibition,°

---

199. sentence: proverbial saying. **200. grise:** degree, step. **202–03. When . . . depended:** our anxieties end when the feared event happens. **207. Patience . . . makes:** i.e., when we are not unduly disturbed by our misfortunes, we mock Fortune. **209. bootless:** vain. **210–19. So . . . ear:** Brabantio retaliates sarcastically with a few "sentences" of his own: Let the Turk take Cyprus; it is no loss if we smile at it. It is easy enough to produce sententious consolation, it costs nothing; but the man who has to endure both consolation and the sorrow itself must needs be patient. These sentences work both ways; mere words hurt no one. Cf. Leonato's similar outburst, *M Ado,* V.i.3–38. **223. substitute:** deputy commander. **allowed:** admitted. **sufficiency:** efficiency. **223–24. yet . . . you:** yet public opinion, which controls our actions, is such that we regard you as a safer choice. **225. slubber:** tarnish. **229. thrice-driven:** three times refined. **agnize:** confess. **231. hardness:** hardship. **235. Due . . . place:** i.e., that she shall be treated as becomes my wife. **exhibition:** allowance.

With such accommodation and besort°
As levels with her breeding.°
DUKE. If you please,
Be 't at her father's.
BRA. I'll not have it so.
OTH. Nor I.
DES. Nor I. I would not there reside,
To put my father in impatient thoughts
By being in his eye. Most gracious Duke,
To my unfolding° lend your prosperous° ear,
And let me find a charter° in your voice
To assist my simpleness.
DUKE. What would you, Desdemona?
DES. That I did love the Moor to live with him,
My downright violence and storm of fortunes
May trumpet to the world. My heart's subdued
Even to the very quality of my lord.°
I saw Othello's visage in his mind,
And to his honors and his valiant parts
Did I my soul and fortunes consecrate.
So that, dear lords, if I be left behind,
A moth of peace,° and he go to the war,
The rites for which I love him are bereft me,
And I a heavy interim° shall support
By his dear absence. Let me go with him.
OTH. Let her have your voices.
Vouch° with me, Heaven, I therefore beg it not
To please the palate of my appetite,
Nor to comply with heat—the young affects
In me defunct°—and proper satisfaction,
But to be free and bounteous° to her mind.°
And Heaven defend° your good souls, that you think
I will your serious and great business scant
For she is with me. No, when light-winged toys°
Of feathered Cupid seel° with wanton dullness
My speculative and officed instruments,°
That my disports° corrupt and taint my business,
Let housewives make a skillet° of my helm,

---

236. besort: attendants. **237. levels . . . breeding:** as suits her birth. **242. unfolding:** plan; lit., revealing. **prosperous:** favorable. **243. charter:** privilege. **246–49. That . . . lord:** my love for the Moor is publicly shown by the way in which I have violently taken my fortunes in my hands; my heart has become a soldier like my husband. **quality:** profession. **254. moth of peace:** a useless creature living in luxury. **256. interim:** interval. **259. Vouch:** certify. **261–62. young . . . defunct:** in me the passion of youth is dead. **263. bounteous:** generous. **to . . . mind:** Othello repeats Desdemona's claim that this is a marriage of minds. **264. defend:** forbid. **266. toys:** trifles. **267. seel:** close up; a technical term from falconry. See App. 26. **268. speculative . . . instruments:** powers of sight and action; i.e., my efficiency as your general. **269. disports:** amusements. **270. skillet:** saucepan.

And all indign° and base adversities
Make head against° my estimation!°

DUKE. Be it as you shall privately determine,
Either for her stay or going. The affair cries haste,
And speed must answer 't. You must hence tonight.

DES. Tonight, my lord?

DUKE. This night.

OTH. With all my heart.

DUKE. At nine i' the morning here we'll meet again.
Othello, leave some officer behind,
And he shall our commission° bring to you,
With such things else of quality and respect
As doth import you.°

OTH. So please your Grace, my Ancient,
A man he is of honesty and trust.
To his conveyance I assign my wife,
With what else needful your good grace shall think
To be sent after me.

DUKE. Let it be so.
Good night to everyone. [*To* BRABANTIO] And, noble signior,
If virtue no delighted beauty lack,
Your son-in-law is far more fair than black.°

1. SEN. Adieu, brave Moor. Use Desdemona well.

BRA. Look to her, Moor, if thou hast eyes to see.
She has deceived her father, and may thee.°

[*Exeunt* DUKE, SENATORS, OFFICERS, *etc.*]

OTH. My life upon her faith! Honest Iago,
My Desdemona must I leave to thee.
I prithee, let thy wife attend on her,
And bring them after in the best advantage.°
Come, Desdemona, I have but an hour
Of love, of worldly matters and direction,
To spend with thee. We must obey the time.

[*Exeunt* OTHELLO *and* DESDEMONA.]

ROD. Iago!

IAGO. What say'st thou, noble heart?

ROD. What will I do, thinkest thou?

---

271. indign: unworthy. **272. Make . . . against:** overcome. **estimation:** reputation. **279. commission:** formal document of appointment. **280–81. With . . . you:** with other matters that concern your position and honor. **287–88. If . . . black:** if worthiness is a beautiful thing in itself, your son-in-law, though black, has beauty. **290–91. Look . . . thee:** Iago in the background takes note of these words, and later reminds Othello of them with deadly effect. See III.iii.206. **295. in . . . advantage:** at the best opportunity.

IAGO. Why, go to bed and sleep.

ROD. I will incontinently° drown myself.

IAGO. If thou dost, I shall never love thee after. Why, thou silly gentleman!

ROD. It is silliness to live when to live is torment, and then have we a prescription to die when death is our physician.

IAGO. Oh, villainous! I have looked upon the world for four times seven years, and since I could distinguish betwixt a benefit and an injury I never found man that knew how to love himself. Ere I would say I would drown myself for the love of a guinea hen, I would change my humanity with a baboon.

ROD. What should I do? I confess it is my shame to be so fond,° but it is not in my virtue° to amend it.

IAGO. Virtue! A fig! 'Tis in ourselves that we are thus or thus. Our bodies are gardens, to the which our wills° are gardeners. So that if we will plant nettles or sow lettuce, set hyssop and weed up thyme, supply it with one gender° of herbs or distract it with many, either to have it sterile with idleness or manured with industry—why, the power and corrigible° authority of this lies in our wills. If the balance of our lives had not one scale of reason to poise° another of sensuality, the blood and baseness of our natures would conduct us to most preposterous conclusions. But we have reason to cool our raging motions, our carnal stings,° our unbitted° lusts, whereof I take this that you call love to be a sect or scion.°

ROD. It cannot be.

IAGO. It is merely a lust of the blood and a permission of the will. Come, be a man. Drown thyself! Drown cats and blind puppies. I have professed me thy friend, and I confess me knit to thy deserving with cables of perdurable° toughness. I could never better stead° thee than now. Put money in thy purse, follow thou the wars, defeat thy favor with an usurped beard°—I say put money in thy purse. It cannot be that Desdemona should long continue her love to the Moor—put money in thy purse—nor he his to her. It was a violent commencement, and thou shalt see an answerable sequestration°—put but money in thy purse. These Moors are changeable in their wills.—Fill thy purse with money. The food that to him now is as luscious as locusts° shall be to him shortly as bitter as coloquintida.° She must change for youth. When she is sated with his body, she will find the error of her choice. She must have change, she must—therefore put money in thy purse. If thou wilt needs damn thyself, do it a more delicate way than drowning. Make all the money thou canst.° If sanctimony and a frail vow betwixt an erring° barbarian and a supersubtle Venetian be not too hard for my wits and all the tribe of Hell,

---

303. incontinently: immediately. **311. fond:** foolishly in love. **virtue:** manhood. **314. wills:** desires. **315. gender:** kind. **317. corrigible:** correcting, directing. **318. poise:** weigh. **321. carnal stings:** fleshly desires. **321. unbitted:** uncontrolled. **322. sect or scion:** Both words mean a slip taken from a tree and planted to produce a new growth. **326. perdurable:** very hard. **327. stead:** help. **328. defeat . . . beard:** disguise your face by growing a beard. **331. answerable sequestration:** corresponding separation; i.e., reaction. **333. locusts:** It is not known what fruit was called a locust. **334. coloquintida:** known as "bitter apple," a form of gherkin from which a purge was made. **337–38. Make . . . canst:** turn all you can into ready cash. **338. erring:** vagabond.

thou shalt enjoy her—therefore make money. A pox of drowning thyself! It is clean out of the way. Seek thou rather to be hanged in compassing° thy joy than to be drowned and go without her.

ROD. Wilt thou be fast to my hopes if I depend on the issue?

IAGO. Thou art sure of me. Go, make money. I have told thee often, and I retell thee again and again, I hate the Moor. My cause is hearted,° thine hath no less reason. Let us be conjunctive° in our revenge against him. If thou canst cuckold° him, thou dost thyself a pleasure, me a sport. There are many events in the womb of time, which will be delivered. Traverse,° go, provide thy money. We will have more of this tomorrow. Adieu.

ROD. Where shall we meet i' the morning?

IAGO. At my lodging.

ROD. I'll be with thee betimes.°

IAGO. Go to, farewell. Do you hear, Roderigo?

ROD. What say you?

IAGO. No more of drowning, do you hear?

ROD. I am changed. I'll go sell all my land. [*Exit.*]

IAGO. Thus do I ever make my fool my purse,
For I mine own gained knowledge should profane
If I would time expend with such a snipe
But for my sport and profit. I hate the Moor,
And it is thought abroad that 'twixt my sheets
He has done my office. I know not if 't be true,
But I for mere suspicion in that kind
Will do as if for surety. He holds me well,
The better shall my purpose work on him.
Cassio's a proper° man. Let me see now,
To get his place, and to plume up° my will
In double knavery—How, how?—Let's see.—
After some time, to abuse Othello's ear
That he is too familiar with his wife.
He hath a person and a smooth dispose
To be suspected,° framed to make women false.
The Moor is of a free and open nature
That thinks men honest that but seem to be so,
And will as tenderly be led by the nose
As asses are.
I have 't. It is engendered.° Hell and night
Must bring this monstrous birth to the world's light.

[*Exit.*]

---

341. compassing: achieving. **345. hearted:** heartfelt. **346. conjunctive:** united. **347. cuckold:** make him a cuckold. See App. 11. **348. Traverse:** quickstep. **352. betimes:** in good time, early. **366. proper:** handsome. **367. plume up:** glorify. **371–72. He . . . suspected:** an easy way with him that is naturally suspected. **377. engendered:** conceived.

ACT II

SCENE I. *A seaport in Cyprus. An open place near the wharf.*

[*Enter* MONTANO *and two* GENTLEMEN.]

MON. What from the cape can you discern at sea?
1. GENT. Nothing at all. It is a high-wrought flood.°
I cannot 'twixt the heaven and the main°
Descry a sail.
MON. Methinks the wind hath spoke aloud at land,
A fuller blast ne'er shook our battlements.
If it hath ruffianed° so upon the sea,
What ribs of oak, when mountains melt on them,
Can hold the mortise?° What shall we hear of this?
2. GENT. A segregation° of the Turkish fleet.
For do but stand upon the foaming shore,
The chidden billow seems to pelt the clouds,
The wind-shaked surge, with high and monstrous mane,
Seems to cast water on the burning Bear,°
And quench the guards of the ever-fixèd Pole.°
I never did like molestation° view
On the enchafèd° flood.
MON. If that the Turkish fleet
Be not ensheltered and embayed,° they are drowned.
It is impossible to bear it out.

[*Enter a* THIRD GENTLEMAN.]

3. GENT. News, lads! Our wars are done.
The desperate tempest hath so banged the Turks
That their designment halts.° A noble ship of Venice
Hath seen a grievous wreck and sufferance°
On most part of their fleet.
MON. How! Is this true?
3. GENT. The ship is here put in,
A Veronesa. Michael Cassio,
Lieutenant to the warlike Moor Othello,
Is come on shore, the Moor himself at sea,
And is in full commission° here for Cyprus.
MON. I am glad on 't. 'Tis a worthy governor.
3. GENT. But this same Cassio, though he speak of comfort

Act II, Sc. i: 2. high-wrought flood: heavy sea. **3. main:** sea. **7. ruffianed:** played the ruffian. **9. hold . . . mortise:** remain fast joined. **10. segregation:** separation. **14. Bear:** the Great Bear. **15. guards . . . Pole:** stars in the "tail" of the Little Bear constellation. **16. molestation:** disturbance. **17. enchafed:** angry. **18. embayed:** anchored in some bay. **22. designment halts:** plan is made lame. **23. sufferance:** damage. **29. in . . . commission:** with full powers. See I.iii.281–82.

Touching the Turkish loss, yet he looks sadly
And prays the Moor be safe, for they were parted
With foul and violent tempest.

MON. Pray Heavens he be,
For I have served him, and the man commands
Like a full° soldier. Let's to the seaside, ho!
As well to see the vessel that's come in
As to throw out our eyes for brave Othello,
Even till we make the main and the aerial blue
An indistinct regard.°

3. GENT. Come, let's do so.
For every minute is expectancy
Of more arrivance.°

[*Enter* CASSIO.]

CAS. Thanks, you the valiant of this warlike isle
That so approve the Moor! Oh, let the heavens
Give him defense against the elements,
For I have lost him on a dangerous sea.

MON. Is he well shipped?°

CAS. His bark is stoutly timbered, and his pilot
Of very expert and approved allowance.°
Therefore my hopes, not surfeited° to death,
Stand in bold cure.°

[*A cry within:* "A sail, a sail, a sail!"]

[*Enter a* FOURTH GENTLEMAN.]

CAS. What noise?

4. GENT. The town is empty. On the brow o' the sea
Stand ranks of people, and they cry "A sail!"

CAS. My hopes do shape° him for the governor.

[*Guns heard*]

2. GENT. They do discharge their shot of courtesy.
Our friends, at least.

CAS. I pray you, sir, go forth,
And give us truth who 'tis that is arrived.

2. GENT. I shall.

---

36. full: perfect. **39–40. Even . . . regard:** until we can no longer distinguish between sea and sky. **41–42. For . . . arrivance:** every minute more arrivals are expected. **47. well shipped:** in a good ship. **49. approved allowance:** proved skill. **50. surfeited:** sickened. **51. Stand . . . cure:** have every hope of cure. **55. shape:** imagine.

[*Exit.*]

MON. But, good Lieutenant, is your General wived?
CAS. Most fortunately. He hath achieved° a maid
That paragons° description and wild fame,
One that excels the quirks of blazoning pens
And in the essential vesture of creation
Does tire the ingener.°

[*Re-enter* SECOND GENTLEMAN.]

How now! Who has put in?
2. GENT. 'Tis one Iago, Ancient to the General.
CAS. He has had most favorable and happy speed.
Tempests themselves, high seas, and howling winds,
The guttered° rocks, and congregated sands,
Traitors ensteeped° to clog the guiltless keel,
As having sense of beauty, do omit
Their mortal natures,° letting go safely by
The divine Desdemona.
MON. What is she?
CAS. She that I spake of, our great Captain's captain,
Left in the conduct° of the bold Iago,
Whose footing° here anticipates our thoughts
A sennight's° speed. Great Jove, Othello guard,
And swell his sail with thine own powerful breath,
That he may bless this bay with his tall ship,
Make love's quick pants in Desdemona's arms,
Give renewed fire to our extincted° spirits,
And bring all Cyprus comfort.

[*Enter* DESDEMONA, EMILIA, IAGO, RODERIGO, *and* ATTENDANTS.]

Oh, behold,
The riches of the ship is come on shore!
Ye men of Cyprus, let her have your knees.
Hail to thee, lady! And the grace of Heaven,
Before, behind thee, and on every hand,
Enwheel° thee round!
DES. I thank you, valiant Cassio.
What tidings can you tell me of my lord?

---

61. achieved: won. **62. paragons:** surpasses. **63–65. One . . . ingener:** one that is too good for the fancy phrases *(quirks)* of painting pens (i.e., poets) and in her absolute perfection wearies the artist (i.e., the painter). (Cassio is full of gallant phrases and behavior, in contrast to Iago's bluntness.) **ingener:** inventor. **69. guttered:** worn into channels. **70. ensteeped:** submerged. **71–72. omit . . . natures:** forbear their deadly nature. **75. conduct:** escort. **76. footing:** arrival. **77. sennight:** week. **81. extincted:** extinguished. **87. Enwheel:** encompass.

CAS. He is not yet arrived, nor know I aught
But that he's well and will be shortly here.
DES. Oh, but I fear—How lost you company?
CAS. The great contention of the sea and skies
Parted our fellowship.°—But, hark! A sail.

[*A cry within:* "A sail, a sail!" *Guns heard.*]

2. GENT. They give their greeting to the citadel.
This likewise is a friend.
CAS. See for the news.

[*Exit* GENTLEMAN.]

Good Ancient, you are welcome. [*To* EMILIA] Welcome, mistress.
Let it not gall your patience, good Iago,
That I extend my manners.° 'Tis my breeding°
That gives me this bold show of courtesy.°

[*Kissing her.*]

IAGO. Sir, would she give you so much of her lips
As of her tongue she oft bestows on me,
You'd have enough.
DES. Alas, she has no speech.
IAGO. In faith, too much,
I find it still° when I have list° to sleep.
Marry, before your ladyship, I grant,
She puts her tongue a little in her heart
And chides with thinking.
EMIL. You have little cause to say so.
IAGO. Come on, come on. You are pictures° out of doors,
Bells° in your parlors, wildcats in your kitchens,
Saints in your injuries,° devils being offended,
Players in your housewifery, and housewives in your beds.
DES. Oh, fie upon thee, slanderer!
IAGO. Nay, it is true, or else I am a Turk.°
You rise to play, and go to bed to work.
EMIL. You shall not write my praise.
IAGO. No, let me not.
DES. What wouldst thou write of me if thou shouldst praise me?

---

93. fellowship: company. **98. extend my manners:** i.e., salute your wife. **breeding:** bringing-up. **99. bold . . . courtesy:** i.e., of saluting your wife with a kiss—a piece of presumptuous behavior which indicates that Cassio regards himself as Iago's social superior. **104. still:** continuously. **list:** desire. **109. pictures:** i.e., painted and dumb. **110. Bells:** i.e., ever clacking. **111. Saints . . . injuries:** saints when you hurt anyone else. **114. Turk:** heathen.

IAGO. O gentle lady, do not put me to 't,
For I am nothing if not critical.°
DES. Come on, assay.°—There's one gone to the harbor?
IAGO. Aye, madam.
DES. I am not merry, but I do beguile
The thing I am by seeming otherwise.
Come, how wouldst thou praise me?
IAGO. I am about it, but indeed my invention
Comes from my pate as birdlime does from frieze°—
It plucks out brains and all. But my Muse labors,
And thus she is delivered.
If she be fair and wise, fairness and wit,
The one's for use, the other useth it.
DES. Well praised! How if she be black and witty?
IAGO. If she be black, and thereto have a wit,
She'll find a white° that shall her blackness fit.
DES. Worse and worse.
EMIL. How if fair and foolish?
IAGO. She never yet was foolish that was fair,
For even her folly helped her to an heir.

DES. These are old fond paradoxes° to make fools laugh i' the alehouse. What miserable praise hast thou for her that's foul and foolish?

IAGO. There's none so foul, and foolish thereunto,
But does foul pranks which fair and wise ones do.

DES. Oh, heavy ignorance! Thou praisest the worst best. But what praise couldst thou bestow on a deserving woman indeed, one that in the authority of her merit did justly put on the vouch of very malice itself?°

IAGO. She that was ever fair and never proud,
Had tongue at will° and yet was never loud,
Never lacked gold and yet went never gay,
Fled from her wish and yet said "Now I may."
She that, being angered, her revenge being nigh,
Bade her wrong stay and her displeasure fly.
She that in wisdom never was so frail
To change the cod's head for the salmon's tail.°
She that could think and ne'er disclose her mind,
See suitors following and not look behind.
She was a wight, if ever such wight were—
DES. To do what?
IAGO. To suckle fools and chronicle small beer.°

DES. Oh, most lame and impotent conclusion! Do not learn of him, Emilia, though

---

119. critical: bitter. **120. assay:** try. **125–26. my . . . frieze:** my literary effort *(invention)* is as hard to pull out of my head as frieze (cloth with a nap) stuck to birdlime. **133. white:** with a pun on *wight* (l. 159), man, person. **137. fond paradoxes:** foolish remarks, contrary to general opinion. **142–43. one . . . itself:** one so deserving that even malice would declare her good. **145. tongue . . . will:** a ready flow of words. **151. To . . . tail:** to prefer the tail end of a good thing to the head of a poor thing. **156. chronicle . . . beer:** write a whole history about trifles (*small beer:* thin drink).

he be thy husband. How say you, Cassio? Is he not a most profane and liberal° counselor?

CAS. He speaks home,° madam. You may relish° him more in the soldier than in the scholar.

IAGO. [*Aside*] He° takes her by the palm. Aye, well said, whisper. With as little a web as this will I ensnare as great a fly as Cassio. Aye, smile upon her, do, I will gyve° thee in thine own courtship. You say true, 'tis so indeed. If such tricks as these strip you out of your Lieutenantry, it had been better you had not kissed your three fingers° so oft, which now again you are most apt to play the sir° in. Very good, well kissed! An excellent courtesy! 'Tis so indeed. Yet again your fingers to your lips? Would they were clyster pipes° for your sake! [*Trumpet within.*] The Moor! I know his trumpet.

CAS. 'Tis truly so.

DES. Let's meet him and receive him.

CAS. Lo where he comes!

[*Enter* OTHELLO *and* ATTENDANTS.]

OTH. O my fair warrior!°
DES. My dear Othello!
OTH. It gives me wonder great as my content
To see you here before me. O my soul's joy!
If after every tempest come such calms,
May the winds blow till they have wakened death!
And let the laboring bark climb hills of seas
Olympus-high,° and duck again as low
As Hell's from Heaven! If it were now to die,
'Twere now to be most happy, for I fear
My soul hath her content so absolute
That not another comfort like to this
Succeeds in unknown fate.
DES. The Heavens forbid
But that our loves and comforts should increase,
Even as our days do grow!
OTH. Amen to that, sweet powers!
I cannot speak enough of this content.
It stops me here,° it is too much of joy.
And this, and this, the greatest discords be

[*Kissing her*]

That e'er our hearts shall make!

---

158. liberal: gross. **160. home:** to the point. **relish:** appreciate. **162. He . . . sake:** As so often, Shakespeare without using elaborate stage directions exactly indicates the action in the dialogue. Cf. *W Tale,* I.ii.111–18. **164. gyve:** fetter. **166. kissed . . . fingers:** a gesture of gallantry. **167. play . . . sir:** act the fine gentleman. **168. clyster pipes:** an enema syringe. **173. warrior:** because she is a soldier's wife. See I.iii.249. **179. Olympus-high:** high as Olympus, the highest mountain in Greece. **188. here:** i.e., in the heart.

IAGO. [*Aside*] Oh, you are well tuned now,
But I'll set down the pegs° that make this music,
As honest as I am.
OTH. Come, let us to the castle.
News, friends. Our wars are done, the Turks are drowned.
How does my old acquaintance of this isle?
Honey, you shall be well desired in Cyprus,
I have found great love amongst them. O my sweet,
I prattle out of fashion,° and I dote
In mine own comforts. I prithee, good Iago,
Go to the bay and disembark my coffers.°
Bring thou the master° to the citadel.
He is a good one, and his worthiness
Does challenge° much respect. Come, Desdemona,
Once more well met at Cyprus.

[*Exeunt all but* IAGO *and* RODERIGO.]

IAGO. Do thou meet me presently° at the harbor. Come hither. If thou beest valiant—as they say base men being in love have then a nobility in their natures more than is native to them—list me. The Lieutenant tonight watches on the court of guard.° First, I must tell thee this. Desdemona is directly in love with him.

ROD. With him! Why, 'tis not possible.

IAGO. Lay thy finger thus,° and let thy soul be instructed. Mark me with what violence she first loved the Moor, but for° bragging and telling her fantastical lies. And will she love him still for prating? Let not thy discreet heart think it. Her eye must be fed, and what delight shall she have to look on the Devil?° When the blood is made dull with the act of sport, there should be, again to inflame it and to give satiety a fresh appetite, loveliness in favor,° sympathy in years, manners, and beauties, all which the Moor is defective in. Now, for want of these required conveniences, her delicate tenderness will find itself abused, begin to heave the gorge,° disrelish and abhor the Moor. Very nature will instruct her in it and compel her to some second choice. Now, sir, this granted—as it is a most pregnant and unforced position°—who stands so eminently in the degree of this fortune as Cassio does? A knave very voluble, no further conscionable° than in putting on the mere form of civil and humane seeming° for the better compassing of his salt° and most hidden

---

192. set . . . pegs: i.e., make you sing in a different key. A stringed instrument was tuned by the pegs. **198. prattle . . . fashion:** talk idly. **200. coffers:** trunks. **201. master:** captain of the ship. **203. challenge:** claim. **205. presently:** immediately. **207–08. watches . . . guard:** is on duty with the guard. The court of guard meant both the guard itself and the guardroom. **211. finger thus:** i.e., on the lips. **212. but for:** only for. **214. Devil:** See I.i.91,n. **216. favor:** face. **219. heave . . . gorge:** retch. **gorge:** throat. **221. pregnant . . . position:** very significant and probable argument. **223. no . . . conscionable:** who has no more conscience. **224. humane seeming:** courteous appearance. **salt:** lecherous.

loose affection? Why, none, why, none. A slipper° and subtle knave, a finder-out of occasions, that has an eye can stamp and counterfeit advantages,° though true advantage never present itself. A devilish knave! Besides, the knave is handsome, young, and hath all those requisites in him that folly and green° minds look after. A pestilent complete knave, and the woman hath found him already.

ROD. I cannot believe that in her. She's full of most blest condition.°

IAGO. Blest fig's-end!° The wine she drinks is made of grapes. If she had been blest, she would never have loved the Moor. Blest pudding! Didst thou not see her paddle° with the palm of his hand? Didst not mark that?

ROD. Yes, that I did, but that was but courtesy.

IAGO. Lechery, by this hand, an index° and obscure prologue to the history of lust and foul thoughts. They met so near with their lips that their breaths embraced together. Villainous thoughts, Roderigo! When these mutualities° so marshal the way, hard at hand comes the master and main exercise, the incorporate° conclusion. Pish! But, sir, be you ruled by me. I have brought you from Venice. Watch you tonight. For the command, I'll lay 't upon you. Cassio knows you not. I'll not be far from you. Do you find some occasion to anger Cassio, either by speaking too loud, or tainting° his discipline, or from what other course you please which the time shall more favorably minister.°

ROD. Well.

IAGO. Sir, he is rash and very sudden in choler,° and haply° may strike at you. Provoke him, that he may, for even out of that will I cause these of Cyprus to mutiny, whose qualification° shall come into no true taste again but by the displanting° of Cassio. So shall you have a shorter journey to your desires by the means I shall then have to prefer° them, and the impediment most profitably removed without the which there were no expectation of our prosperity.

ROD. I will do this, if I can bring it to any opportunity.

IAGO. I warrant thee. Meet me by and by at the citadel. I must fetch his necessaries ashore. Farewell.

ROD. Adieu.

[*Exit.*]

IAGO. That Cassio loves her, I do well believe it.
That she loves him, 'tis apt and of great credit.°
The Moor, howbeit that I endure him not,
Is of a constant, loving, noble nature,

---

225. slipper: slippery. **226. stamp . . . advantages:** forge false opportunities. **229. green:** inexperienced, foolish. **231. condition:** disposition. **232. Blest fig's-end:** blest nonsense, a phrase used as a substitute in contempt for a phrase just used, as is also *blest pudding* (l.258). **234. paddle:** play. **236. index:** table of contents. **238. mutualities:** mutual exchanges. **240. incorporate:** bodily. **243. tainting:** disparaging. **244. minister:** provide. **246. choler:** anger. **haply:** perhaps. **248. qualification:** appeasement. **249. displanting:** removal. **250. prefer:** promote. **258. apt . . . credit:** likely and very credible.

And I dare think he'll prove to Desdemona
A most dear husband. Now, I do love her too,
Not out of absolute lust, though peradventure
I stand accountant for as great a sin,
But partly led to diet° my revenge
For that I do suspect the lusty Moor
Hath leaped into my seat. The thought whereof
Doth like a poisonous mineral° gnaw my inwards.
And nothing can or shall content my soul
Till I am evened with him, wife for wife.
Or failing so, yet that I put the Moor
At least into a jealousy so strong
That judgment° cannot cure. Which thing to do,
If this poor trash of Venice, whom I trash°
For his quick hunting,° stand the putting-on,°
I'll have our Michael Cassio on the hip,
Abuse him to the Moor in the rank garb°—
For I fear Cassio with my nightcap too—
Make the Moor thank me, love me, and reward me
For making him egregiously° an ass
And practicing upon° his peace and quiet
Even to madness. 'Tis here, but yet confused.
Knavery's plain face is never seen till used.

[*Exit.*]

SCENE II. *A street.*

[*Enter a* HERALD *with a proclamation,* PEOPLE *following.*]

HER. It is Othello's pleasure, our noble and valiant General, that upon certain tidings now arrived, importing the mere perdition° of the Turkish fleet, every man put himself into triumph°—some to dance, some to make bonfires, each man to what sport and revels his addiction° leads him. For, besides these beneficial news, it is the celebration of his nuptial. So much was his pleasure should be proclaimed. All offices° are open, and there is full liberty of feasting from this present hour of five till the bell have told eleven. Heaven bless the isle of Cyprus and our noble General Othello!

[*Exeunt.*]

---

265. diet: feed. **268. poisonous mineral:** corrosive poison. See I.ii.74. **273. judgment:** reason. **274. trash . . . trash:** rubbish . . . discard. **274–75. trash . . . hunting:** Fr reads "trace" and Qr "crush." If the emendation "trash" is correct, it means "hold back from outrunning the pack." Cf. *Temp,* I.ii.81,n. **275. putting-on:** encouraging. **276. rank garb:** gross manner; i.e., by accusing him of being Desdemona's lover. **280. egregiously:** notably. **281. practicing upon:** plotting against.

Sc. ii: 2. mere perdition: absolute destruction. **3. put . . . triumph:** celebrate. **4. addiction:** inclination. **6. offices:** the kitchen and buttery—i.e., free food and drink for all.

SCENE III. *A hall in the castle.*

[*Enter* OTHELLO, DESDEMONA, CASSIO, *and* ATTENDANTS.]

OTH. Good Michael, look you to the guard tonight.
Let's teach ourselves that honorable stop,
Not to outsport discretion.°
CAS. Iago hath direction what to do,
But notwithstanding with my personal eye
Will I look to 't.
OTH. Iago is most honest.
Michael, good night. Tomorrow with your earliest°
Let me have speech with you. Come, my dear love,
The purchase made, the fruits are to ensue—
That profit's yet to come 'tween me and you.
Good night.

[*Exeunt* OTHELLO, DESDEMONA, *and* ATTENDANTS.]

[*Enter* IAGO.]

CAS. Welcome, Iago. We must to the watch.
IAGO. Not this hour, Lieutenant, 'tis not yet ten o' the clock. Our General cast° us thus early for the love of his Desdemona, who let us not therefore blame. He hath not yet made wanton the night with her, and she is sport for Jove.
CAS. She's a most exquisite lady.
IAGO. And, I'll warrant her, full of game.
CAS. Indeed she's a most fresh and delicate creature.
IAGO. What an eye she has. Methinks it sounds a parley to provocation.°
CAS. An inviting eye, and yet methinks right modest.
IAGO. And when she speaks, is it not an alarum° to love?
CAS. She is indeed perfection.
IAGO. Well, happiness to their sheets! Come, Lieutenant, I have a stoup° of wine, and here without are a brace of Cyprus gallants that would fain° have a measure to the health of black Othello.
CAS. Not tonight, good Iago. I have very poor and unhappy brains for drinking. I could well wish courtesy would invent some other custom of entertainment.
IAGO. Oh, they are our friends. But one cup—I'll drink for you.
CAS. I have drunk but one cup tonight, and that was craftily qualified° too, and behold what innovation° it makes here. I am unfortunate in the infirmity, and dare not task° my weakness with any more.
IAGO. What, man! 'Tis a night of revels. The gallants desire it.

Sc. iii: 3. outsport discretion: let the fun go too far. **7. with . . . earliest:** very early. **13. cast:** dismissed. **19. sounds . . . provocation:** invites to a love talk. **21. alarum:** call to arms. **23. stoup:** large drinking vessel. See Pl. 20e. **24. fain:** gladly. **29. craftily qualified:** cunningly mixed. **30. innovation:** revolution, disturbance. **31. task:** burden.

CAS. Where are they?
IAGO. Here at the door. I pray you call them in.
CAS. I'll do 't, but it dislikes° me.

[*Exit.*]

IAGO. If I can fasten but one cup upon him,
With that which he hath drunk tonight already
He'll be as full of quarrel and offense
As my young mistress' dog. Now my sick fool Roderigo,
Whom love hath turned almost the wrong side out,
To Desdemona hath tonight caroused°
Potations pottle-deep,° and he's to watch.
Three lads of Cyprus, noble swelling° spirits
That hold their honors in a wary distance,°
The very elements° of this warlike isle,
Have I tonight flustered with flowing cups,
And they watch too. Now, 'mongst this flock of drunkards,
Am I to put our Cassio in some action
That may offend the isle. But here they come.
If consequence do but approve my dream,°
My boat sails freely, both with wind and stream.

[*Re-enter* CASSIO, *with him* MONTANO *and* GENTLEMEN, SERVANTS *following with wine.*]

CAS. 'Fore God, they have given me a rouse° already.
MON. Good faith, a little one—not past a pint, as I am a soldier.
IAGO. Some wine, ho! [*Sings.*]
"And let me the cannikin° clink, clink,
And let me the cannikin clink.
A soldier's a man,
A life's but a span.°
Why, then let a soldier drink."
Some wine, boys!
CAS. 'Fore God, an excellent song.
IAGO. I learned it in England, where indeed they are most potent in potting.° Your Dane, your German, and your swag-bellied° Hollander—Drink, ho!—are nothing to your English.
CAS. Is your Englishman so expert in his drinking?
IAGO. Why, he drinks you with facility your Dane dead drunk, he sweats not° to

35. dislikes: displeases. **41. caroused:** drunk healths. **42. pottle-deep:** "bottoms up"; a pottle held two quarts. **43. swelling:** bursting with pride. **44. hold . . . distance:** "have a chip on their shoulders." **45. very elements:** typical specimens. **50. If . . . dream:** if what follows proves my dream true. **52. rouse:** a deep drink. **55. cannikin:** drinking pot. See Pl. 20e. **58. span:** lit., the measure between the thumb and little finger of the outstretched hand; about 9 inches. **62. potent in potting:** desperate drinkers. For the Danes' potency in potting see *Haml,* I.iv.8–38. **63. swag-bellied:** with loose bellies. Germans and Dutchmen were almost as famous for drinking as the Danes. **66. sweats not:** has no need to labor excessively.

overthrow your Almain,° he gives your Hollander a vomit° ere the next pottle can be filled.

CAS. To the health of our General!

MON. I am for it, Lieutenant, and I'll do you justice.

IAGO. O sweet England! [*Sings.*]

"King Stephen was a worthy peer,
His breeches cost him but a crown.
He held them sixpence all too dear,°
With that he called the tailor lown.°"He was a wight of high renown,
And thou art but of low degree.
'Tis pride that pulls the country down.
Then take thine auld cloak about thee."

Some wine, ho!

CAS. Why, this is a more exquisite song than the other.

IAGO. Will you hear 't again?

CAS. No, for I hold him to be unworthy of his place that does those things. Well, God's above all, and there be souls must be saved and there be souls must not be saved.

IAGO. It's true, good Lieutenant.

CAS. For mine own part—no offense to the General, nor any man of quality°—I hope to be saved.

IAGO. And so do I too, Lieutenant.

CAS. Aye, but, by your leave, not before me. The Lieutenant is to be saved before the Ancient. Let's have no more of this, let's to our affairs. God forgive us our sins! Gentlemen, let's look to our business. Do not think, gentlemen, I am drunk. This is my Ancient, this is my right hand and this is my left. I am not drunk now, I can stand well enough and speak well enough.

ALL. Excellent well.

CAS. Why, very well, then, you must not think then that I am drunk.

[*Exit.*]

MON. To the platform,° masters. Come, let's set the watch.°

IAGO. You see this fellow that is gone before.
He is a soldier fit to stand by Caesar
And give direction. And do but see his vice.
'Tis to his virtue a just equinox,°
The one as long as the other. 'Tis pity of him.
I fear the trust Othello puts him in
On some odd time° of his infirmity
Will shake this island.

MON. But is he often thus?

---

67. Almain: German. **gives . . . vomit:** drinks as much as will make a Dutchman throw up. **74. sixpence . . . dear:** too dear by sixpence. **75. lown:** lout. **86. quality:** rank. **96. platform:** the level place on the ramparts where the cannon were mounted. **set . . . watch:** mount guard. **100. just equinox:** exact equal. **103. some . . . time:** some time or other.

IAGO. 'Tis evermore the prologue to his sleep.
He'll watch the horologe a double set,°
If drink rock not his cradle.
MON. It were well
The General were put in mind of it.
Perhaps he sees it not, or his good nature
Prizes the virtue that appears in Cassio
And looks not on his evils. Is not this true?

[*Enter* RODERIGO.]

IAGO. [*Aside to him*] How now, Roderigo! I pray you, after the Lieutenant. Go.

[*Exit* RODERIGO.]

MON. And 'tis great pity that the noble Moor
Should hazard such a place as his own second
With one of an ingraft° infirmity.
It were an honest action to say
So to the Moor.
IAGO. Not I, for this fair island.
I do love Cassio well, and would do much
To cure him of this evil—But, hark! What noise?

[*A cry within:* "Help! help!"]

[*Re-enter* CASSIO, *driving in* RODERIGO.]

CAS. 'Zounds! You rogue! You rascal!
MON. What's the matter, Lieutenant?
CAS. A knave teach me my duty!
But I'll beat the knave into a wicker bottle.°
ROD. Beat me!
CAS. Dost thou prate, rogue?

[*Striking* RODERIGO.]

MON. Nay, good Lieutenant,

[*Staying him.*]

I pray you, sir, hold your hand.
CAS. Let me go, sir,
Or I'll knock you o'er the mazzard.°

---

106. watch . . . set: stay awake the clock twice round. **115. ingraft:** engrafted, firmly fixed. **122. But . . . bottle:** One of those bad-tempered threatening phrases which have no very exact meaning, like "I'll knock him into a cocked hat." **wicker bottle:** large bottle covered with wicker, demijohn. **126. mazzard:** head, a slang word.

MON. Come, come, you're drunk.
CAS. Drunk!

[*They fight.*]

IAGO. [*Aside to* RODERIGO] Away, I say. Go out and cry a mutiny.°

[*Exit* RODERIGO.]

Nay, good Lieutenant! God's will, gentlemen!
Help, ho!—Lieutenant—sir—Montano—sir—
Help, masters!—Here's a goodly watch indeed!

[*A bell rings.*]

Who's that that rings the bell?—Diablo,° ho!
The town will rise. God's will, Lieutenant, hold—
You will be shamed forever.

[*Re-enter* OTHELLO *and* ATTENDANTS.]

OTH. What is the matter here?
MON. 'Zounds, I bleed still, I am hurt to the death.

[*Faints.*]

OTH. Hold, for your lives!
IAGO. Hold, ho! Lieutenant—sir—Montano—gentlemen—
Have you forgot all sense of place and duty?
Hold! The General speaks to you. Hold, hold, for shame!
OTH. Why, how now, ho! From whence ariseth this?
Are we turned Turks, and to ourselves do that
Which Heaven hath forbid the Ottomites?
For Christian shame, put by this barbarous brawl.
He that stirs next to carve for his own rage°
Holds his soul light, he dies upon his motion.°
Silence that dreadful bell. It frights the isle
From her propriety.° What is the matter, masters?
Honest Iago, that look'st dead with grieving,
Speak, who began this? On thy love, I charge thee.
IAGO. I do not know. Friends all but now, even now,
In quarter and in terms like bride and groom
Devesting° them for bed. And then, but now,

128. cry . . . mutiny: cry that a mutiny has broken out; i.e., raise a riot. **132. Diablo:** the Devil. **145. carve . . . rage:** to satisfy his hunger for rage. **146. upon . . . motion:** at his first movement. **148. propriety:** natural behavior. **153. Devesting:** taking off their clothes.

As if some planet had unwitted men,°
Swords out, and tilting° one at other's breast
In opposition bloody. I cannot speak
Any beginning to this peevish odds,°
And would in action glorious I had lost
Those legs that brought me to a part of it!

OTH. How comes it, Michael, you are thus forgot?°

CAS. I pray you, pardon me, I cannot speak.

OTH. Worthy Montano, you were wont be civil.°
The gravity and stillness° of your youth
The world hath noted, and your name is great
In mouths of wisest censure.° What's the matter
That you unlace° your reputation thus,
And spend your rich opinion° for the name
Of a night brawler? Give me answer to it.

MON. Worthy Othello, I am hurt to danger.
Your officer, Iago, can inform you—
While I spare speech, which something now offends me—
Of all that I do know. Nor know I aught
By me that's said or done amiss this night,
Unless self-charity° be sometimes a vice,
And to defend ourselves it be a sin
When violence assails us.

OTH. Now, by Heaven,
My blood begins my safer guides to rule,
And passion, having my best judgment collied,°
Assays to lead the way. If I once stir,
Or do but lift this arm, the best of you
Shall sink in my rebuke. Give me to know
How this foul rout° began, who set it on,
And he that is approved° in this offense,
Though he had twinned with me, both at a birth,
Shall lose me. What! In a town of war,
Yet wild, the people's hearts brimful of fear,
To manage° private and domestic quarrel,
In night, and on the court and guard of safety!
'Tis monstrous. Iago, who began 't?

MON. If partially affined, or leagued in office,
Thou dost deliver° more or less than truth,
Thou art no soldier.

IAGO. Touch me not so near.

---

154. planet . . . men: as if some evil star had made men mad. See App. I. **155. tilting:** thrusting. **157. peevish odds:** silly disagreement. **160. are . . . forgot:** have so forgotten yourself. **162. civil:** well behaved. **163. stillness:** staid behavior. **165. censure:** judgment. **166. unlace:** undo. **167. spend . . . opinion:** lose your good reputation. **174. self-charity:** love for oneself. **178. collied:** darkened. **182. rout:** riot, uproar. **183. approved:** proved guilty. **187. manage:** be concerned with. **190–91. If . . . deliver:** if, because you are influenced by partiality or because he is your fellow officer, you report. **affined:** bound.

I had rather have this tongue cut from my mouth
Than it should do offense to Michael Cassio.
Yet I persuade myself to speak the truth
Shall nothing wrong him. Thus it is, General.
Montano and myself being in speech,
There comes a fellow crying out for help,
And Cassio following him with determined sword
To execute upon him. Sir, this gentleman
Steps in to Cassio and entreats his pause.°
Myself the crying fellow did pursue,
Lest by his clamor—as it so fell out—
The town might fall in fright. He, swift of foot,
Outran my purpose, and I returned the rather
For that I heard the clink and fall of swords,
And Cassio high in oath, which till tonight
I ne'er might say before. When I came back—
For this was brief—I found them close together,
At blow and thrust, even as again they were
When you yourself did part them.
More of this matter cannot I report.
But men are men, the best sometimes forget.
Though Cassio did some little wrong to him,
As men in rage strike those that wish them best,
Yet surely Cassio, I believe, received
From him that fled some strange indignity,
Which patience could not pass.

OTH. I know, Iago,
Thy honesty and love doth mince this matter,
Making it light to Cassio. Cassio, I love thee,
But never more be officer of mine.

[Re-enter DESDEMONA, *attended.]*

Look, if my gentle love be not raised up!
I'll make thee an example.

DES. What's the matter?

OTH. All's well now, sweeting.° Come away to bed. *[To* MONTANO, *who is led off]*

Sir, for your hurts, myself will be your surgeon.
Lead him off.
Iago, look with care about the town,
And silence those whom this vile brawl distracted.
Come, Desdemona. 'Tis the soldiers' life
To have their balmy slumbers waked with strife.

201. entreats . . . pause: begs him to stop. **224. sweeting:** sweetheart.

[*Exeunt all but* IAGO *and* CASSIO.]

IAGO. What, are you hurt, Lieutenant?

CAS. Aye, past all surgery.

IAGO. Marry, Heaven forbid!

CAS. Reputation, reputation, reputation! Oh, I have lost my reputation! I have lost the immortal part of myself, and what remains is bestial. My reputation, Iago, my reputation!

IAGO. As I am an honest man, I thought you had received some bodily wound. There is more sense in that than in reputation. Reputation is an idle and most false imposition,° oft got without merit and lost without deserving. You have lost no reputation at all unless you repute yourself such a loser. What, man! There are ways to recover the General again. You are but now cast in his mood,° a punishment more in policy° than in malice—even so as one would beat his offenseless dog to affright an imperious lion.° Sue to him again and he's yours.

CAS. I will rather sue to be despised than to deceive so good a commander with so slight, so drunken, and so indiscreet an officer. Drunk? And speak parrot?° And squabble? Swagger? Swear? And discourse fustian° with one's own shadow? O thou invisible spirit of wine, if thou hast no name to be known by, let us call thee devil!

IAGO. What was he that you followed with your sword? What had he done to you?

CAS. I know not.

IAGO. Is 't possible?

CAS. I remember a mass of things, but nothing distinctly—a quarrel, but nothing wherefore. Oh God, that men should put an enemy in their mouths to steal away their brains! That we should, with joy, pleasance,° revel, and applause, transform ourselves into beasts!

IAGO. Why, but you are now well enough. How came you thus recovered?

CAS. It hath pleased the devil drunkenness to give place to the devil wrath. One unperfectness shows me another, to make me frankly despise myself.

IAGO. Come, you are too severe a moraler.° As the time, the place, and the condition of this country stands, I could heartily wish this had not befallen. But since it is as it is, mend it for your own good.

CAS. I will ask him for my place again, he shall tell me I am a drunkard! Had I as many mouths as Hydra,° such an answer would stop them all. To be now a sensible man, by and by a fool, and presently a beast! Oh, strange! Every inordinate° cup is unblest, and the ingredient is a devil.

IAGO. Come, come, good wine is a good familiar creature, if it be well used. Exclaim no more against it. And, good Lieutenant, I think you think I love you.

---

239. imposition: a quality laid on a man by others. **241–2. cast . . . mood:** dismissed because he is in a bad mood. **242. in policy:** i.e., because he must appear to be angry before the Cypriots. **242–43. even . . . lion:** a proverb meaning that when the lion sees the dog beaten, he will know what is coming to him. **246. speak parrot:** babble. **247. fustian:** nonsense; lit., cheap cloth. **255. pleasance:** a gay time. **260. moraler:** moralizer. **264. Hydra:** a hundred-headed beast slain by Hercules. **266. inordinate:** excessive.

CAS. I have well approved it, sir. I drunk!

IAGO. You or any man living may be drunk at some time, man. I'll tell you what you shall do. Our General's wife is now the General. I may say so in this respect, for that he hath devoted and given up himself to the contemplation, mark, and denotement° of her parts and graces. Confess yourself freely to her, importune her help to put you in your place again. She is of so free, so kind, so apt,° so blessed a disposition, she holds it a vice in her goodness not to do more than she is requested. This broken joint between you and her husband entreat her to splinter° and, my fortunes against any lay° worth naming, this crack of your love shall grow stronger than it was before.

CAS. You advise me well.

IAGO. I protest, in the sincerity of love and honest kindness.

CAS. I think it freely, and betimes in the morning I will beseech the virtuous Desdemona to undertake for me. I am desperate of my fortunes if they check me here.°

IAGO. You are in the right. Good night, Lieutenant, I must to the watch.

CAS. Good night, honest Iago.

[*Exit.*]

IAGO. And what's he then that says I play the villain?
When this advice is free I give and honest,
Probal° to thinking, and indeed the course
To win the Moor again? For 'tis most easy
The inclining Desdemona to subdue
In any honest suit. She's framed° as fruitful
As the free elements.° And then for her
To win the Moor, were 't to renounce his baptism,
All seals and symbols of redeemèd sin,
His soul is so enfettered to her love
That she may make, unmake, do what she list,
Even as her appetite shall play the god
With his weak function.° How am I then a villain
To counsel Cassio to this parallel course,
Directly to his good? Divinity of Hell!
When devils will the blackest sins put on,
They do suggest° at first with heavenly shows,
As I do now. For whiles this honest fool
Plies° Desdemona to repair his fortunes,
And she for him pleads strongly to the Moor,
I'll pour this pestilence into his ear,
That she repeals° him for her body's lust.

---

274. denotement: careful observation. **276. apt:** ready. **279. splinter:** put in splints. **lay:** bet. **283–84. I . . . here:** I despair of my future if my career is stopped short here. **289. Probal:** probable. **292. framed:** made. **293. free elements:** i.e., the air. **299. function:** intelligence. **303. suggest:** seduce. **305. Plies:** vigorously urges. **308. repeals:** calls back.

And by how much she strives to do him good,
She shall undo her credit with the Moor.
So will I turn her virtue into pitch,
And out of her own goodness make the net
That shall enmesh them all.

[*Enter* RODERIGO.]

How now, Roderigo!

ROD. I do follow here in the chase, not like a hound that hunts but one that fills up the cry.° My money is almost spent, I have been tonight exceedingly well cudgeled, and I think the issue will be I shall have so much experience for my pains and so, with no money at all and a little more wit, return again to Venice.

IAGO. How poor are they that have not patience!
What wound did ever heal but by degrees?
Thou know'st we work by wit and not by witchcraft,
And wit depends on dilatory Time.°
Does 't not go well? Cassio hath beaten thee,
And thou by that small hurt hast cashiered Cassio.
Though other things grow fair against the sun,
Yet fruits that blossom first will first be ripe.°
Content thyself awhile. By the mass, 'tis morning.
Pleasure and action make the hours seem short.
Retire thee, go where thou art billeted.
Away, I say. Thou shalt know more hereafter.
Nay, get thee gone. [*Exit* RODERIGO.] Two things are to be done:
My wife must move for° Cassio to her mistress,
I'll set her on,
Myself the while to draw the Moor apart
And bring him jump° when he may Cassio find
Soliciting his wife. Aye, that's the way.
Dull not device° by coldness and delay.

[*Exit.*]

ACT III

SCENE I. *Before the castle.*

[*Enter* CASSIO *and some* MUSICIANS.]

315–16. one . . . cry: See *MND,* IV.i.127–28,n. **323. And . . . Time:** and cleverness must wait for Time, who is in no hurry. **326–27. Though . . . ripe:** though the fruit ripens in the sun, yet the first fruit to ripen will come from the earliest blossoms; i.e., our first plan—to get Cassio cashiered—has succeeded, the rest will soon follow. **333. move for:** petition for. **336. jump:** at the moment, just. **338. Dull . . . device:** do not spoil the plan.

CAS. Masters, play here, I will content your pains°—
Something that's brief, and bid "Good morrow, General."°

[*Music.*]

[*Enter* CLOWN.]

CLO. Why, masters, have your instruments been in Naples,° that they speak i' the nose thus?

I. MUS. How, sir, how?

CLO. Are these, I pray you, wind instruments?

I. MUS. Aye, marry are they, sir.

CLO. Oh, thereby hangs a tail.

I. MUS. Whereby hangs a tale, sir?

CLO. Marry, sir, by many a wind instrument that I know. But, masters, here's money for you. And the General so likes your music that he desires you, for love's sake, to make no more noise with it.

I. MUS. Well, sir, we will not.

CLO. If you have any music that may not be heard, to 't again. But, as they say, to hear music the General does not greatly care.

I. MUS. We have none such, sir.

CLO. Then put up your pipes in your bag, for I'll away. Go, vanish into air, away!

[*Exeunt* MUSICIANS.]

CAS. Dost thou hear, my honest friend?

CLO. No, I hear not your honest friend, I hear you.

CAS. Prithee keep up thy quillets.° There's a poor piece of gold for thee. If the gentlewoman that attends the General's wife be stirring, tell her there's one Cassio entreats her a little favor of speech. Wilt thou do this?

CLO. She is stirring, sir. If she will stir hither, I shall seem to notify unto her.

CAS. Do, good my friend.

[*Exit* CLOWN.]

[*Enter* IAGO.]

In happy time,° Iago.

IAGO. You have not been abed, then?

CAS. Why, no, the day had broke
Before we parted. I have made bold, Iago,
To send in to your wife. My suit to her

Act III, Sc. i: 1. content . . . pains: reward your labor. **2. bid . . . General:** It was a common custom to play or sing a song beneath the bedroom window of a distinguished guest or of a newly wedded couple on the morning after their wedding night. **3. in Naples:** a reference to the Neapolitan (i.e., venereal) disease. **20. keep . . . quillets:** put away your wisecracks. **25. In . . . time:** i.e., I am glad to see you.

Is that she will to virtuous Desdemona
Procure me some access.

IAGO. I'll send her to you presently,
And I'll devise a mean to draw the Moor
Out of the way, that your convérse and business
May be more free.

CAS. I humbly thank you for 't. [*Exit* IAGO.] I never knew
A Florentine more kind° and honest.

[*Enter* EMILIA.]

EMIL. Good morrow, good Lieutenant. I am sorry
For your displeasure,° but all will sure be well.
The General and his wife are talking of it,
And she speaks for you stoutly. The Moor replies
That he you hurt is of great fame in Cyprus
And great affinity,° and that in wholesome wisdom
He might not but° refuse you. But he protests he loves you,
And needs no other suitor but his likings°
To take the safest occasion by the front
To bring you in° again.

CAS. Yet I beseech you
If you think fit, or that it may be done,
Give me advantage of some brief discourse
With Desdemona alone.

EMIL. Pray you, come in.
I will bestow you where you shall have time.
To speak your bosom freely.°

CAS. I am much bound to you.

[*Exeunt.*]

SCENE II. *A room in the castle.*

[*Enter* OTHELLO, IAGO, *and* GENTLEMEN.]

OTH. These letters give, Iago, to the pilot,
And by him do my duties° to the Senate.
That done, I will be walking on the works.°
Repair there to me.

IAGO. Well, my good lord, I'll do 't.

---

36. Florentine . . . kind: Iago is a Venetian. Cassio means: even one of my own people could not have been kinder. **38. your displeasure:** i.e., that Othello is displeased with you. **42. affinity:** kindred. **43. might . . . but:** i.e., he must. **44. likings:** affections. **45–46. safest . . . in:** to take the first opportunity to restore you to your position. **front:** forehead; i.e., to take Time by the forelock. **51. speak . . . freely:** declare what is on your mind.

Sc. ii:2. do . . . duties: express my loyalty. **3. works:** fortifications.

OTH. This fortification, gentlemen, shall we see 't?
GENT. We'll wait upon your lordship.

[*Exeunt.*]

SCENE III. *The garden of the castle.*

[*Enter* DESDEMONA, CASSIO, *and* EMILIA.]

DES. Be thou assured, good Cassio, I will do
All my abilities in thy behalf.
EMIL. Good madam, do. I warrant it grieves my husband
As if the case were his.
DES. Oh, that's an honest fellow. Do not doubt, Cassio,
But I will have my lord and you again
As friendly as you were.
CAS. Bounteous madam,
Whatever shall become of Michael Cassio,
He's never anything but your true servant.
DES. I know't. I thank you. You do love my lord.
You have known him long, and be you well assured
He shall in strangeness stand no farther off
Than in a politic distance.°
CAS. Aye, but, lady,
That policy may either last so long,
Or feed upon such nice and waterish diet,°
Or breed itself so out of circumstance,°
That, I being absent and my place supplied,°
My General will forget my love and service.
DES. Do not doubt° that. Before Emilia here
I give thee warrant of thy place.° Assure thee,
If I do vow a friendship, I'll perform it
To the last article. My lord shall never rest.
I'll watch him tame° and talk him out of patience,
His bed shall seem a school, his board a shrift.°
I'll intermingle every thing he does
With Cassio's suit. Therefore be merry, Cassio,
For thy solicitor shall rather die
Than give thy cause away.

[*Enter* OTHELLO *and* IAGO, *at a distance.*]

Sc. iii: 12–13. He . . . distance: i.e., his apparent coldness to you shall only be so much as his official position demands for reasons of policy. **15. nice . . . diet:** have such weak encouragement. **16. breed . . . circumstance:** become so used to the situation. **17. supplied:** filled by another. **19. doubt:** fear. **20. give . . . place:** guarantee that you will be restored to your position. **23. watch . . . tame:** as wild hawks are made tame by keeping them from sleep. See App. 26. **24. shrift:** place of confession and absolution.

EMIL. Madam, here comes my lord.
CAS. Madam, I'll take my leave.
DES. Nay, stay and hear me speak.
CAS. Madam, not now. I am very ill at ease, unfit for mine own purposes.°
DES. Well, do your discretion.

[*Exit* CASSIO.]

IAGO. Ha! I like not that.
OTH. What dost thou say?
IAGO. Nothing, my lord. Or if—I know not what.
OTH. Was not that Cassio parted from my wife?
IAGO. Cassio, my lord! No, sure, I cannot think it,
That he would steal away so guilty-like,
Seeing you coming.
OTH. I do believe 'twas he.
DES. How now, my lord!
I have been talking with a suitor here,
A man that languishes in your displeasure.
OTH. Who is 't you mean?
DES. Why, your Lieutenant, Cassio. Good my lord,
If I have any grace or power to move you,
His present reconciliation take.°
For if he be not one that truly loves you,
That errs in ignorance and not in cunning,°
I have no judgment in an honest face.
I prithee call him back.
OTH. Went he hence now?
DES. Aye, sooth, so humbled
That he hath left part of his grief with me,
To suffer with him. Good love, call him back.
OTH. Not now, sweet Desdemona, some other time.
DES. But shall 't be shortly?
OTH. The sooner, sweet, for you.
DES. Shall 't be tonight at supper?
OTH. No, not tonight.
DES. Tomorrow dinner then?
OTH. I shall not dine at home.
I meet the captains at the citadel.
DES. Why, then tomorrow night or Tuesday morn,
On Tuesday noon, or night, on Wednesday morn.
I prithee name the time, but let it not
Exceed three days. In faith, he's penitent,

---

32. Unfit . . . purposes: in no condition to plead my own cause. **47. His . . . take:** accept his immediate apology and forgive him. **49. in cunning:** knowingly.

And yet his trespass, in our common reason°—
Save that, they say, the wars must make examples
Out of their best—is not almost° a fault
To incur a private check.° When shall he come?
Tell me, Othello. I wonder in my soul
What you would ask me that I should deny,
Or stand so mammering° on. What! Michael Cassio,
That came a-wooing with you, and so many a time
When I have spoke of you dispraisingly
Hath ta'en your part—to have so much to do
To bring him in! Trust me, I could do much—
OTH. Prithee, no more. Let him come when he will.
I will deny thee nothing.
DES. Why, this is not a boon.°
'Tis as I should entreat you wear your gloves,
Or feed on nourishing dishes, or keep you warm,
Or sue to you to do a peculiar° profit
To your own person. Nay, when I have a suit
Wherein I mean to touch your love indeed,
It shall be full of poise° and difficult weight,°
And fearful to be granted.°
OTH. I will deny thee nothing.
Whereon I do beseech thee grant me this,
To leave me but a little to myself.
DES. Shall I deny you? No. Farewell, my lord.
OTH. Farewell, my Desdemona. I'll come to thee straight.
DES. Emilia, come. Be as your fancies teach you.°
Whate'er you be, I am obedient.

[*Exeunt* DESDEMONA *and* EMILIA.]

OTH. Excellent wretch! Perdition catch my soul
But I do love thee! And when I love thee not,
Chaos° is come again.
IAGO. My noble lord—
OTH. What dost thou say, Iago?
IAGO. Did Michael Cassio,° when you wooed my lady,
Know of your love?
OTH. He did, from first to last. Why dost thou ask?
IAGO. But for a satisfaction of my thought,
No further harm.

---

64. common reason: common sense. **66. not almost:** hardly. **67. check:** rebuke. **70. mammering:** hesitating. **76. boon:** great favor. **79. peculiar:** particular. **82. poise:** weight in the scales. **difficult weight:** hard to estimate. **83. fearful . . . granted:** only granted with a sense of fear. **88. Be . . . you:** please yourself. **92. Chaos:** the utter confusion that existed before order was established in the universe. The idea of order and chaos is worked out elaborately in *Tr & Cr,* I.iii.83–124. **94. Did . . . Cassio:** See App. 22.

OTH. Why of thy thought, Iago?
IAGO. I did not think he had been acquainted with her.
OTH. Oh yes, and went between us very oft.
IAGO. Indeed!
OTH. Indeed! Aye, indeed. Discern'st thou aught in that?
Is he not honest?
IAGO. Honest, my lord!
OTH. Honest! Aye, honest.
IAGO. My lord, for aught I know.
OTH. What dost thou think?
IAGO. Think, my lord!
OTH. Think, my lord!
By Heaven, he echoes me
As if there were some monster in his thought
Too hideous to be shown. Thou dost mean something.
I heard thee say even now thou likedst not that
When Cassio left my wife. What didst not like?
And when I told thee he was of my counsel
In my whole course of wooing, thou criedst "Indeed!"
And didst contract and purse thy brow together
As if thou then hadst shut up in thy brain
Some horrible conceit.° If thou dost love me,
Show me thy thought
IAGO. My lord, you know I love you.
OTH. I think thou dost,
And for° I know thou'rt full of love and honesty
And weigh'st thy words before thou givest them breath,
Therefore these stops of thine fright me the more.
For such things in a false disloyal knave
Are tricks of custom, but in a man that's just
They're close delations,° working from the heart,
That passion cannot rule.
IAGO. For Michael Cassio,
I dare be sworn I think that he is honest.
OTH. I think so too.
IAGO. Men should be what they seem,
Or those that be not, would they might seem none!°
OTH. Certain, men should be what they seem.
IAGO. Why, then I think Cassio's an honest man.
OTH. Nay, yet there's more in this.
I prithee speak to me as to thy thinkings,
As thou dost ruminate, and give thy worst of thoughts
The worst of words.
IAGO. Good my lord, pardon me.

115. conceit: conception, notion. **118. for:** since. **123. close delations:** concealed accusations. **127. seem none:** i.e., not seem to be honest men.

Though I am bound to every act of duty,
I am not bound to that all slaves are free to.
Utter my thoughts? Why, say they are vile and false,
As where's that palace whereinto foul things
Sometimes intrude not? Who has a breast so pure
But some uncleanly apprehensions
Keep leets and law days, and in session sit
With meditations lawful?°

OTH. Thou dost conspire against thy friend, Iago,
If thou but think'st him wronged and makest his ear
A stranger to thy thoughts.

IAGO. I do beseech you—
Though I perchance am vicious in my guess,
As, I confess, it is my nature's plague
To spy into abuses, and oft my jealousy°
Shapes faults that are not—that your wisdom yet,
From one that so imperfectly conceits,°
Would take no notice, nor build yourself a trouble
Out of his scattering° and unsure observance.°
It were not for your quiet nor your good,
Nor for my manhood, honesty, or wisdom,
To let you know my thoughts.

OTH. What dost thou mean?

IAGO. Good name in man and woman, dear my lord,
Is the immediate° jewel of their souls.
Who steals my purse steals trash—'tis something, nothing,
'Twas mine, 'tis his, and has been slave to thousands—
But he that filches from me my good name
Robs me of that which not enriches him
And makes me poor indeed.

OTH. By Heaven, I'll know thy thoughts.

IAGO. You cannot if my heart were in your hand,
Nor shall not whilst 'tis in my custody.

OTH. Ha!

IAGO. Oh, beware, my lord, of jealousy.
It is the green-eyed monster which doth mock°
The meat° it feeds on. That cuckold lives in bliss
Who, certain of his fate, loves not his wronger.°
But, oh, what damnèd minutes tells he o'er
Who dotes, yet doubts, suspects, yet strongly loves!

138–41. Who . . . lawful: whose heart is so pure but that some foul suggestion will sit on the bench alongside lawful thoughts; i.e., foul thoughts will rise even on the most respectable occasions. **leet:** court held by the lord of the manor. **law days:** days when courts sit. **session:** sitting of the court. **147. jealousy:** suspicion. **149. conceits:** conceives, imagines. **151. scattering:** scattered, casual. **observance:** observation. **156. immediate:** most valuable. **166. doth mock:** makes a mockery of. **167. meat:** i.e., victim. **167–68. That . . . wronger:** i.e., the cuckold who hates his wife and knows her falseness is not tormented by suspicious jealousy. See App. II.

OTH. Oh, misery!

IAGO. Poor and content is rich, and rich enough,
But riches fineless° is as poor as winter
To him that ever fears he shall be poor.
Good Heaven, the souls of all my tribe defend
From jealousy!

OTH. Why, why is this?
Think'st thou I'd make a life of jealousy,
To follow still the changes of the moon
With fresh suspicions? No, to be once in doubt
Is once to be resolved.° Exchange me for a goat
When I shall turn the business of my soul
To such exsufflicate and blown surmises,
Matching thy inference.° 'Tis not to make me jealous
To say my wife is fair, feeds well, loves company,
Is free of speech, sings, plays, and dances well.
Where virtue is, these are more virtuous.
Nor from mine own weak merits will I draw
The smallest fear or doubt of her revolt,°
For she had eyes, and chose me. No, Iago,
I'll see before I doubt, when I doubt, prove,
And on the proof, there is no more but this—
Away at once with love or jealousy!

IAGO. I am glad of it, for now I shall have reason
To show the love and duty that I bear you
With franker spirit. Therefore, as I am bound,
Receive it from me. I speak not yet of proof.
Look to your wife. Observe her well with Cassio.
Wear your eye thus, not jealous nor secure.°
I would not have your free and noble nature
Out of self-bounty° be abused, look to 't.
I know our country disposition well.
In Venice° they do let Heaven see the pranks
They dare not show their husbands. Their best conscience
Is not to leave 't undone, but keep 't unknown.

OTH. Dost thou say so?

IAGO. She did deceive her father,° marrying you,
And when she seemed to shake and fear your looks,
She loved them most.

OTH. And so she did.

IAGO. Why, go to, then.

---

173. fineless: limitless. **179–80. to . . . resolved:** whenever I find myself in doubt I at once seek out the truth. **181–83. When . . . inference:** when I shall allow that which concerns me most dearly to be influenced by such trifling suggestions as yours. **exsufflicate:** blown up, like a bubble. **188. revolt:** faithlessness, **198. secure:** overconfident. **200. self-bounty:** natural goodness. **202. In Venice:** Venice was notorious for its loose women; the Venetian courtesans were among the sights of Europe and were much commented upon by travelers. **206. She . . . father:** Iago deliberately echoes Brabantio's parting words. See I.iii.293–94.

She that so young could give out such a seeming
To seel° her father's eyes up close as oak—
He thought 'twas witchcraft—but I am much to blame.
I humbly do beseech you of your pardon
For too much loving you.

OTH. I am bound to thee forever.

IAGO. I see this hath a little dashed your spirits.

OTH. Not a jot, not a jot.

IAGO. I' faith, I fear it has.
I hope you will consider what is spoke
Comes from my love, but I do see you're moved.
I am to pray you not to strain my speech
To grosser issues° nor to larger reach°
Than to suspicion.

OTH. I will not.

IAGO. Should you do so, my lord,
My speech should fall into such vile success°
As my thoughts aim not at. Cassio's my worthy friend.—
My lord, I see you're moved.

OTH. No, not much moved.
I do not think but Desdemona's honest.°

IAGO. Long live she so! And long live you to think so!

OTH. And yet, how nature erring from itself—

IAGO. Aye, there's the point. As—to be bold with you—
Not to affect° many proposed matches°
Of her own clime, complexion, and degree,
Whereto we see in all things nature tends°—
Foh! One may smell in such a will most rank,°
Foul disproportion, thoughts unnatural.
But pardon me. I do not in position
Distinctly speak of her, though I may fear
Her will, recoiling to her better judgment,
May fall to match° you with her country forms,°
And happily° repent.

OTH. Farewell, farewell.
If more thou dost perceive, let me know more.
Set on thy wife to observe. Leave me, Iago.

IAGO. [*Going*] My lord, I take my leave.

OTH. Why did I marry? This honest creature doubtless
Sees and knows more, much more, than he unfolds.

IAGO. [*Returning*] My lord, I would I might entreat your honor

---

210. seel: blind. See I.iii.270,n. **219. grosser issues:** worse conclusions. **larger reach:** i.e., more widely. **222. success:** result. **225. honest:** When applied to Desdemona, "honest" means "chaste," but applied to Iago it has the modern meaning of "open and sincere." **229. affect:** be inclined to. **proposed matches:** offers of marriage. **231. in . . . tends:** i.e., a woman naturally marries a man of her own country, color, and rank. **232. will . . . rank:** desire most lustful. **237. match:** compare. **country forms:** the appearance of her countrymen; i.e., white men. **238. happily:** haply, by chance.

To scan this thing no further. Leave it to time.
Though it be fit that Cassio have his place,
For sure he fills it up with great ability,
Yet if you please to hold him off awhile,
You shall by that perceive him and his means.
Note if your lady strain his entertainment°
With any strong or vehement importunity—
Much will be seen in that. In the meantime,
Let me be thought too busy in my fears—
As worthy cause I have to fear I am—
And hold her free, I do beseech your Honor.

OTH. Fear not my government.°

IAGO. I once more take my leave.

[*Exit.*]

OTH. This fellow's of exceeding honesty,
And knows all qualities,° with a learned spirit,
Of human dealings.° If I do prove her haggard,
Though that her jesses were my dear heartstrings,
I'd whistle her off and let her down the wind
To prey at fortune.° Haply, for I am black
And have not those soft parts of conversation
That chamberers° have, or for I am declined
Into the vale of years—yet that's not much—
She's gone, I am abused, and my relief
Must be to loathe her. Oh, curse of marriage,
That we can call these delicate creatures ours,
And not their appetites! I had rather be a toad
And live upon the vapor of a dungeon
Than keep a corner in the thing I love
For others' uses. Yet, 'tis the plague of great ones,
Prerogatived° are they less than the base.
'Tis destiny unshunnable, like death.
Even then this forkèd plague° is fated to us
When we do quicken.° Desdemona comes.

[*Re-enter* DESDEMONA *and* EMILIA.]

If she be false, oh, then Heaven mocks itself!
I'll not believe 't.

---

250. strain . . . entertainment: urge you to receive him. **256. government:** self-control. **259. qualities:** different kinds. **259–60. with . . . dealings:** with wide experience of human nature. **260–63. If . . . fortune:** Othello keeps up the imagery of falconry throughout. He means: If I find that she is wild, I'll whistle her off the game and let her go where she will, for she's not worth keeping. See App. 26. **haggard:** a wild hawk. **jesses:** the straps attached to a hawk's legs. **265. chamberers:** playboys. **274. Prerogatived:** privileged. **276. forked plague:** i.e., to be a cuckold. **277. quicken:** stir in our mother's womb.

DES. How now, my dear Othello!
Your dinner, and the generous° islanders
By you invited, do attend your presence.
OTH. I am to blame.
DES. Why do you speak so faintly?
Are you not well?
OTH. I have a pain upon my forehead here.
DES. Faith, that's with watching,° 'twill away again.
Let me but bind it hard, within this hour
It will be well.
OTH. Your napkin° is too little,

[*He puts the handkerchief from him, and she drops it.*]

Let it alone. Come, I'll go in with you.
DES. I am very sorry that you are not well.

[*Exeunt* OTHELLO *and* DESDEMONA.]

EMIL. I am glad I have found this napkin.
This was her first remembrance from the Moor.
My wayward° husband hath a hundred times
Wooed me to steal it, but she so loves the token,
For he conjured° her she should ever keep it,
That she reserves it evermore about her
To kiss and talk to. I'll have the work ta'en out,°
And give 't Iago. What he will do with it
Heaven knows, not I.
I nothing but to please his fantasy.°

[*Re-enter* IAGO.]

IAGO. How now! What do you here alone?
EMIL. Do not you chide, I have a thing for you.
IAGO. A thing for me? It is a common thing—
EMIL. Ha!
IAGO. To have a foolish wife.
EMIL. Oh, is that all? What will you give me now
For that same handkerchief?
IAGO. What handkerchief?
EMIL. What handkerchief!
Why, that the Moor first gave to Desdemona,
That which so often you did bid me steal.
IAGO. Hast stol'n it from her?

280. generous: noble, of gentle blood. **285. watching:** lack of sleep. **287. napkin:** handkerchief. **292. wayward:** unaccountable. **294. conjured:** begged with an oath. **296. work . . . out:** pattern copied. **299. fantasy:** whim.

EMIL. No, faith, she let it drop by negligence,
And, to the advantage,° I being here took 't up.
Look, here it is.
IAGO. A good wench. Give it me.
EMIL. What will you do with 't, that you have been so earnest
To have me filch it?
IAGO. [*Snatching it*] Why, what's that to you?
EMIL. If 't be not for some purpose of import,
Give 't me again. Poor lady, she'll run mad
When she shall lack it.
IAGO. Be not acknown on 't,° I have use for it.
Go, leave me.

[*Exit* EMILIA.]

I will in Cassio's lodging lose this napkin,
And let him find it. Trifles light as air
Are to the jealous confirmations strong
As proofs of Holy Writ. This may do something.
The Moor already changes with my poison.
Dangerous conceits are in their natures poisons,
Which at the first are scarce found to distaste,°
But with a little° act upon the blood
Burn like the mines of sulphur. I did say so.°
Look where he comes!

[*Re-enter* OTHELLO.]

Not poppy,° nor mandragora,°
Nor all the drowsy syrups of the world,
Shall ever medicine thee to that sweet sleep
Which thou owedst° yesterday.
OTH. Ha! Ha! False to me?
IAGO. Why, how now, General! No more of that.
OTH. Avaunt!° Be gone! Thous hast set me on the rack.°
I swear 'tis better to be much abused
Than but to know 't a little.
IAGO. How now, my lord!
OTH. What sense had I of her stol'n hours of lust?
I saw 't not, thought it not, it harmed not me.
I slept the next night well, was free and merry.

---

312. to . . . advantage: thereby giving me the opportunity. **319. Be . . . on't:** know nothing about it. **327. distaste:** taste unpleasantly. **328. with a little:** in a little while. **329. I . . . so:** As Iago says this, Othello is seen approaching, with all the signs of his agitation outwardly visible. **330. poppy:** opium. **mandragora:** called also mandrake, a root used as a drug to bring sleep. See Pl. 12e. **333. owedst:** owned, possessed. **335. Avaunt:** be off! **on . . . rack:** i.e., in tormet. See App. 10.

I found not Cassio's kisses on her lips.
He that is robbed, not wanting° what is stol'n,
Let him not know 't and he's not robbed at all.

IAGO. I am sorry to hear this.

OTH. I had been happy if the general camp,
Pioners° and all, had tasted her sweet body,
So I had nothing known. Oh, now forever
Farewell the tranquil mind! Farewell content!
Farewell the plumèd° troop and the big wars
That make ambition virtue! Oh, farewell,
Farewell the neighing steed and the shrill trump,
The spirit-stirring drum, the ear-piercing fife,
The royal banner and all quality,°
Pride, pomp, and circumstance of glorious war!
And, O you mortal engines,° whose rude throats
The immortal Jove's dread clamors counterfeit,°
Farewell! Othello's occupation's gone!

IAGO. Is't possible, my lord?

OTH. Villain, be sure thou prove my love a whore,
Be sure of it, give me the ocular proof.
Or by the worth of man's eternal soul,
Thou hadst been better have been born a dog
Than answer my waked wrath!

IAGO. Is 't come to this?

OTH. Make me to see 't, or at the least so prove it
That the probation° bear no hinge nor loop
To hang a doubt on, or woe upon thy life!

IAGO. My noble lord—

OTH. If thou dost slander her and torture me,
Never pray more, abandon all remorse.°
On horror's head horrors accumulate,
Do deeds to make Heaven weep, all earth amazed,
For nothing canst thou to damnation add
Greater than that.

IAGO. Oh, grace! Oh, Heaven defend me!
Are you a man? Have you a soul or sense?
God be wi' you, take mine office. O wretched fool,
That livest to make thine honesty a vice!
O monstrous world! Take note, take note, O world,
To be direct and honest is not safe.
I thank you for this profit,° and from hence
I'll love no friend, sith° love breeds such offense.

---

342. wanting: missing. **346. Pioners:** pioneers, the lowest type of soldier. **349. plumed:** wearing plumes in the helmet. **353. quality:** military rank. **355. mortal engines:** deadly cannnon. **356. counterfeit:** imitate. **365. probation:** proof. **369. remorse:** pity. **379. profit:** profitable lesson. **380. sith:** since.

OTH. Nay, stay. Thou shouldst be honest.
IAGO. I should be wise, for honesty's a fool,
And loses that it works for.
OTH. By the world,
I think my wife be honest, and think she is not.
I think that thou art just, and think thou art not.
I'll have some proof. Her name, that was as fresh
As Dian's° visage, is now begrimed and black
As mine own face. If there be cords, or knives,
Poison, or fire, or suffocating streams,
I'll not endure it. Would I were satisfied!
IAGO. I see, sir, you are eaten up with passion.
I do repent me that I put it to you.
You would be satisfied?
OTH. Would! Nay, I will.
IAGO. And may, but, how? How satisfied, my lord?
Would you, the supervisor,° grossly gape on?
Behold her topped?
OTH. Death and damnation! Oh!
IAGO. It were a tedious difficulty, I think,
To bring them to that prospect.° Damn them then,
If ever mortal eyes do see them bolster°
More than their own! What then? How then?
What shall I say? Where's satisfaction?
It is impossible you should see this,
Were they as prime° as goats, as hot as monkeys,
As salt° as wolves in pride,° and fools as gross
As ignorance made drunk. But yet I say
If imputation° and strong circumstances,
Which lead directly to the door of truth,
Will give you satisfaction, you may have 't.
OTH. Give me a living° reason she's disloyal.
IAGO. I do not like the office.
But sith I am entered in this cause so far,
Pricked° to 't by foolish honesty and love,
I will go on. I lay with Cassio lately,
And being troubled with a raging tooth,
I could not sleep.
There are a kind of men so loose of soul
That in their sleeps will mutter their affairs.
One of this kind is Cassio.
In sleep I heard him say "Sweet Desdemona,

---

387. Dian: Diana, goddess of chastity. **395. supervisor:** looker-on. **398. prospect:** sight. **399. bolster:** sleep together. **403. prime:** lustful. **404. salt:** eager. **in pride:** in heat. **406. imputation:** probability. **409. living:** tangible. **412. Pricked:** spurred on.

Let us be wary, let us hide our loves."
And then, sir, would he gripe° and wring my hand,
Cry "O sweet creature!" and then kiss me hard,
As if he plucked up kisses by the roots
That grew upon my lips. Then laid his leg
Over my thigh, and sighed and kissed, and then
Cried "Cursed fate that gave thee to the Moor!"

OTH. Oh, monstrous! Monstrous!

IAGO. Nay, this was but his dream,

OTH. But this denoted a foregone conclusion.
'Tis a shrewd doubt,° though it be but a dream.

IAGO. And this may help to thicken other proofs
That do demónstrate thinly.

OTH. I'll tear her all to pieces.

IAGO. Nay, but be wise. Yet we see nothing done.
She may be honest yet. Tell me but this:
Have you not sometimes seen a handkerchief
Spotted with strawberries° in your wife's hand?

OTH. I gave her such a one, 'twas my first gift.

IAGO. I know not that. But such a handkerchief—
I am sure it was your wife's—did I today
See Cassio wipe his beard with.

OTH. If it be that—

IAGO. If it be that, or any that was hers,
It speaks against her with the other proofs.

OTH. Oh, that the slave had forty thousand lives!
One is too poor, too weak, for my revenge.
Now do I see 'tis true. Look here, Iago,
All my fond love thus do I blow to Heaven—
'Tis gone.
Arise, black Vengeance, from thy hollow cell!
Yield up, O Love, thy crown and hearted° throne
To tyrannous hate! Swell, bosom, with thy fraught,°
For 'tis of aspics'° tongues!

IAGO. Yet be content.

OTH. Oh, blood, blood, blood!

IAGO. Patience, I say. Your mind perhaps may change.

OTH. Never, Iago. Like to the Pontic Sea,
Whose icy current and compulsive course
Ne'er feels retiring ebb but keeps due on
To the Propontic and the Hellespont;°

---

421. gripe: grip. **429. shrewd doubt:** bitter suspicion. **435. with strawberries:** with a pattern of strawberries. **448. hearted:** in my heart. **449. fraught:** freight, load. **450. aspic:** asp, a small poisonous snake. See *Ant & Cleo,* V.ii.351–56. **453–56. Like . . . Hellespont:** In Pliny's *Natural History,* translated by Philemon Holland in 1601, it was noted that "the sea Pontus (Black Sea) evermore floweth and runneth out into Propontis (Sea of Marmora) but the sea never returneth back again within Pontus." **Hellespont:** the Dardanelles.

Even so my bloody thoughts, with violent pace,
Shall ne'er look back, ne'er ebb to humble love,
Till that capable° and wide revenge
Swallow them up. Now, by yond marble Heaven,
In the due reverence of a sacred vow

[*Kneels.*]

I here engage° my words.

IAGO. Do not rise yet.

[*Kneels.*]

Witness, you ever burning lights above,
You elements that clip° us round about,
Witness that here Iago doth give up
The execution of his wit, hands, heart,
To wronged Othello's service! Let him command,
And to obey shall be in me remorse,°
What bloody business ever.

[*They rise.*]

OTH. I greet thy love,
Not with vain thanks, but with acceptance bounteous,
And will upon the instant put thee to 't.°
Within these three days let me hear thee say
That Cassio's not alive.

IAGO. My friend is dead. 'Tis done at your request.
But let her live.

OTH. Damn her, lewd minx! Oh, damn her!
Come, go with me apart. I will withdraw,
To furnish me with some swift means of death
For the fair devil. Now art thou my Lieutenant.

IAGO. I am your own forever.

[*Exeunt.*]

SCENE IV. *Before the castle.*

[*Enter* DESDEMONA, EMILIA, *and* CLOWN.]

DES. Do you know, sirrah, where Lieutenant Cassio lies?

CLO. I dare not say he lies anywhere.

---

459. capable: comprehensive, complete. **462. engage:** pledge. **464. elements . . . clip:** skies that embrace, surround. **468. remorse:** solemn obligation. **471. put . . . to't:** put you to the proof.

DES. Why, man?
CLO. He's a soldier, and for one to say a soldier lies is stabbing.
DES. Go to. Where lodges he?
CLO. To tell you where he lodges is to tell you where I lie.
DES. Can anything be made of this?
CLO. I know not where he lodges, and for me to devise a lodging, and say he lies here or he lies there, were to lie in mine own throat.
DES. Can you inquire him out and be edified by report?°
CLO. I will catechize the world for him; that is, make questions and by them answer.
DES. Seek him, bid him come hither. Tell him I have moved my lord on his behalf and hope all will be well.
CLO. to do this is within the compass of man's wit, and therefore I will attempt the doing it.

[*Exit.*]

DES. Where should I lose that handkerchief, Emilia?
EMIL. I know not, madam.
DES. Believe me, I had rather have lost my purse
Full of crusados.° And, but my noble Moor
Is true of mind and made of no such baseness
As jealous creatures are, it were enough
To put him to ill thinking.
EMIL. Is he not jealous?
DES. Who, he? I think the sun where he was born
Drew all such humors° from him.
EMIL. Look where he comes.
DES. I will not leave him now till Cassio
Be called to him.

[*Enter* OTHELLO.]

How is 't with you, my lord?
OTH. Well, my good lady. [*Aside*] Oh, hardness to dissemble!
How do you, Desdemona?
DES. Well, my good lord.
OTH. Give me your hand. This hand is moist,° my lady.
DES. It yet has felt no age nor known no sorrow.
OTH. This argues fruitfulness and liberal heart.
Hot, hot, and moist—this hand of yours requires
A sequester° from liberty, fasting and prayer,
Much castigation, exercise devout.
For here's a young and sweating devil here,

Sc. iv: 9. edified by report: enlightened by the information. Desdemona speaks with mock pomposity. **19. crusados:** small gold Portuguese coins. **24. humors:** moods; lit., dampnesses. **30. moist:** a hot moist palm was believed to show desire. **34. sequester:** separation.

That commonly rebels. 'Tis a good hand,
A frank one.

DES. You may indeed say so,
For 'twas that hand that gave away my heart.

OTH. A liberal° hand. The hearts of old gave hands,
But our new heraldry is hands, not hearts.°

DES. I cannot speak of this. Come now, your promise.

OTH. What promise, chuck?°

DES. I have sent to bid Cassio come speak with you.

OTH. I have a salt and sorry rheum° offends me.
Lend me thy handkerchief.

DES. Here, my lord.

OTH. That which I gave you.

DES. I have it not about me.

OTH. Not?

DES. No indeed, my lord.

OTH. That's a fault.
That handkerchief
Did an Egyptian° to my mother give.
She was a charmer, and could almost read
The thoughts of people. She told her while she kept it
'Twould make her amiable and subdue my father
Entirely to her love, but if she lost it
Or made a gift of it, my father's eye
Should hold her loathed and his spirits should hunt
After new fancies. She dying gave it me,
And bid me, when my fate would have me wive,
To give it her. I did so. And take heed on 't,
Make it a darling like your precious eye.
To lose 't or give 't away were such perdition
As nothing else could match.

DES. Is 't possible?

OTH. 'Tis true. There's magic in the web of it.
A sibyl° that had numbered in the world
The sun to course two hundred compasses
In her prophetic fury° sewed the work.
The worms were hallowed that did breed the silk,

---

39. liberal: overgenerous. **39–40. The . . . hearts:** once love and deeds went together, but now it is all deeds (i.e., faithlessness) and no love. This phrase has been taken as a reference to the order of baronets created by James I in 1611, who bore on their heraldic coats of arms the device of the "bloody hand of Ulster." If so, the lines are a later addition; but the reference is very doubtful. The contrast between hearts (true love and faith) and hands (actions) is natural (see *Lear* I.ii. 72–73). As Othello's passions rise, he ceases to be entirely coherent. **42. chuck:** a term of affection, but not the kind of word with which a person of Othello's dignity would normally address his wife. He is beginning to treat her with contemptuous familiarity. See IV.ii.24. **44. rheum:** common cold. **49. Egyptian:** gypsy. **63. sibyl:** prophetess. **65. fury:** inspiration.

And it was dyed in mummy° which the skillful
Conserved° of maidens' hearts.

DES. Indeed! Is 't true?

OTH. Most veritable, therefore look to 't well.

DES. Then would to God that I had never seen 't.

OTH. Ha! Wherefore?

DES. Why do you speak so startlingly and rash?

OTH. Is 't lost? Is 't gone? Speak, is it out o' the way?

DES. Heaven bless us!

OTH. Say you?

DES. It is not lost, but what an if it were?

OTH. How!

DES. I say it is not lost.

OTH. Fetch 't, let me see it.

DES. Why, so I can, sir, but I will not now.
This is a trick to put me from my suit.
Pray you let Cassio be received again.

OTH. Fetch me the handkerchief. My mind misgives.

DES. Come, come,
You'll never meet a more sufficient man.

OTH. The handkerchief!

DES. I pray talk me of Cassio.

OTH. The handkerchief!

DES. A man that all his time
Hath founded his good fortunes on your love,
Shared dangers with you—

OTH. The handkerchief!

DES. In sooth, you are to blame.

OTH. Away!

[*Exit.*]

EMIL. Is not this man jealous?

DES. I ne'er saw this before.
Sure there's some wonder in this handkerchief.
I am most unhappy in the loss of it.

EMIL. 'Tis not a year or two shows us a man.°
They are all but stomachs and we all but food.
They eat us hungerly, and when they are full
They belch us. Look you, Cassio and my husband.

[*Enter* CASSIO *and* IAGO.]

---

67. mummy: a concoction made from Egyptian mummies. **68. Conserved:** prepared. **97. 'Tis . . . man:** it does not take a couple of years for us to discover the nature of a man; i.e., he soon shows his real nature.

IAGO. There is no other way, 'tis she must do 't.
And, lo, the happiness!° Go and impórtune her.
DES. How now, good Cassio! What's the news with you?
CAS. Madam, my former suit. I do beseech you
That by your virtuous means I may again
Exist, and be a member of his love
Whom I with all the office of my heart
Entirely honor. I would not be delayed.
If my offense be of such mortal kind
That nor my service past nor present sorrows
Nor purposed merit in futurity°
Can ransom me into his love again,
But to know so must be my benefit.
So shall I clothe me in a forced content
And shut myself up in some other course
To Fortune's alms.°
DES. Alas, thrice-gentle Cassio!
My advocation° is not now in tune.
My lord is not my lord, nor should I know him
Were he in favor as in humor altered.°
So help me every spirit sanctified,
As I have spoken for you all my best
And stood within the blank° of his displeasure
For my free speech! You must awhile be patient.
What I can do I will, and more I will
Than for myself I dare. Let that suffice you.
IAGO. Is my lord angry?
EMIL. He went hence but now,
And certainly in strange unquietness.
IAGO. Can he be angry? I have seen the cannon
When it hath blown his ranks into the air,
And, like the Devil, from his very arm
Puffed his own brother, and can he be angry?
Something of moment then. I will go meet him.
There's matter in 't indeed if he be angry.
DES. I prithee do so. [*Exit* IAGO.] Something sure of state,
Either from Venice, or some unhatched practice
Made demonstrable° here in Cyprus to him,
Hath puddled° his clear spirit. And in such cases
Men's natures wrangle with inferior things,

102. And . . . happiness: what good luck, here she is. **111. Nor . . . futurity:** nor my good resolutions for the future. **113–116. But . . . alms:** if I know that Othello will not restore me to my position, it will have this benefit: I shall force myself to be contented and try my luck elsewhere. **Fortune's alms:** what Fortune may give me. **117. advocation:** advocacy, pleading. **119. favor . . . altered:** as changed in face as in mood. **122. blank:** aim. The blank is the bull's-eye of a target. **135–36. unhatched . . . demonstrable:** some plot, not yet matured, which has been revealed. **137. puddled:** muddied, stirred up.

Though great ones are their object.° 'Tis even so,
For let our finger ache and it indues°
Our other healthful members even to that sense
Of pain. Nay, we must think men are not gods,
Nor of them look for such observancy
As fits the bridal.° Beshew me° much, Emilia,
I was, unhandsome warrior° as I am,
Arraigning his unkindness with my soul,
But now I find I had suborned the witness,°
And he's indicted falsely.

EMIL. Pray Heaven it be state matters, as you think,
And no conception nor no jealous toy°
Concerning you.

DES. Alas the day, I never gave him cause!

EMIL. But jealous souls will not be answered so.
They are not ever jealous for the cause,
But jealous for they are jealous. 'Tis a monster
Begot upon itself, born on itself.

DES. Heaven keep that monster from Othello's mind!

EMIL. Lady, amen.

DES. I will go seek him. Cassio, walk hereabout.
If I do find him fit, I'll move your suit,
And seek to effect it to my uttermost.

CAS. I humbly thank your ladyship.

[*Exeunt* DESDEMONA *and* EMILIA.]
[*Enter* BIANCA.]

BIAN. Save you, friend Cassio!

CAS. What make you from° home?
How is it with you, my most fair Bianca?
I' faith, sweet love, I was coming to your house.

BIAN. And I was going to your lodging, Cassio.
What, keep a week away? Seven days and nights?
Eightscore eight hours? And lovers' absent hours,
More tedious than the dial eightscore times?°
Oh, weary reckoning!

CAS. Pardon me, Bianca.
I have this while with leaden thoughts been pressed,

138–39. in . . . object: when men are disturbed by great matters, they show their temper in small things. **140. indues:** endows, pervades. **144. bridal:** honeymoon. **Beshrew me:** plague on me. **145. unhandsome warrior:** clumsy soldier. Desdemona continually thinks of herself as Othello's companion in arms. Cf. I.iii.249ff. **147. suborned . . . witness:** corrupted the evidence; i.e., it is my fault, not his. **150. jealous toy:** silly suspicion. **163. make . . . from:** are you doing away from. **168–69. And . . . times:** when one's lover is absent for a week does it not seem far longer than a hundred and sixty clock hours?

But I shall in a more continuate time°
Strike off this score of absence. Sweet Bianca,

[*Giving her* DESDEMONA'S *handkerchief*]

Take me this work out.°
BIAN. O Cassio, whence came this?
This is some token from a newer friend.
To the felt absence now I feel a cause.
Is't come to this? Well, well.
CAS. Go to, woman!
Throw your vile guesses in the Devil's teeth,
From whence you have them. You are jealous now
That this is from some mistress, some remembrance,
No, by my faith, Bianca.
BIAN. Why, whose is it?
CAS. I know not, sweet. I found it in my chamber.
I like the work well. Ere it be demanded—
As like enough it will—I'd have it copied.
Take it, and do 't, and leave me for this time.
BIAN. Leave you! Wherefore?
CAS. I do attend here on the General,
And think it no addition,° nor my wish,
To have him see me womaned.°
BIAN. Why, I pray you?
CAS. Not that I love you not.
BIAN. But that you do not love me.
I pray you bring me on the way a little,
And say if I shall see you soon at night.
CAS. 'Tis but a little way that I can bring you,
For I attend here. But I'll see you soon.
BIAN. 'Tis very good, I must be circumstanced.°

[*Exeunt.*]

ACT IV

SCENE I. *Cyprus. Before the castle.*

[*Enter* OTHELLO *and* IAGO.]

IAGO. Will you think so?
OTH. Think so, Iago!
IAGO. What,
To kiss in private?

---

172. continuate time: i.e., when my time is not continually being interrupted. **174. Take . . . out:** copy this pattern. **188. addition:** honor. **189. womaned:** with a girl. **195. circumstanced:** put off.

OTH. An unauthorized kiss.
IAGO. Or to be naked with her friend in bed
An hour or more, not meaning any harm?
OTH. Naked in bed, Iago, and not mean harm!
It is hypocrisy against the Devil.°
They that mean virtuously and yet do so,
The Devil their virtue tempts and they tempt Heaven.°
IAGO. So° they do nothing, 'tis a venial° slip.
But if I give my wife a handkerchief—
OTH. What then?
IAGO. Why, then, 'tis hers, my lord, and being hers,
She may, I think, bestow 't on any man.
OTH. She is protectress of her honor too.
May she give that?
IAGO. Her honor is an essence that's not seen.
They have it very oft that have it not.°
But for the handkerchief—
OTH. By Heaven, I would most gladly have forgot it.
Thou said'st—oh, it comes o'er my memory,
As doth the raven o'er the infected house,°
Boding° to all—he had my handkerchief.
IAGO. Aye, what of that?
OTH. That's not so good now.
IAGO. What,
If I had said I had seen him do you wrong?
Or heard him say—as knaves be such abroad,
Who having, by their own importunate suit,
Or voluntary dotage° of some mistress,
Convincèd or supplied° them, cannot choose
But they must blab—
OTH. Hath he said anything?
IAGO. He hath, my lord, but be you well assured,
No more than he'll unswear.
OTH. What hath he said?
IAGO. Faith, that he did—I know not what he did.
OTH. What? What?
IAGO. Lie—
OTH. With her?
IAGO. With her, on her, what you will.

Act IV, Sc. i: 6. hypocrisy . . . Devil: "double-crossing the Devil"; i.e., they are behaving in a most suspicious way. **7–8. They . . . Heaven:** i.e., those who go to bed together and mean no harm are asking the Devil to tempt them, and they make God suspect their innocence. **9. So:** so long as. **venial:** pardonable. **17. They . . . not:** i.e., many are honored who have no honor. **21. As . . . house:** i.e., as a bird of prey waits for its victim to die. **22. Boding:** foretelling evil. **27. dotage:** infatuation. **28. Convinced or supplied:** overcome or satisfied their desires.

OTH. Lie° with her! Lie on her!—We say lie on her when they belie her.—Lie with her! 'Zounds, that's fulsome!° Handkerchief—confessions—handkerchief!—To confess, and be hanged for his labor. First to be hanged, and then to confess. I tremble at it. Nature would not invest herself in such shadowing passion without some instruction.° It is not words that shake me thus. Pish!
Noses, ears, and lips. Is 't possible?—Confess?—
Handkerchief?—Oh, devil!

[*Falls in a trance.*]

IAGO. Work on,
My medicine, work! Thus credulous fools are caught,
And many worthy and chaste dames even thus,
All guiltless, meet reproach. What ho! My lord!
My lord, I say! Othello!

[*Enter* CASSIO.]

How now, Cassio!
CAS. What's the matter?
IAGO. My lord is fall'n into an epilepsy.
This is his second fit, he had one yesterday.
CAS. Rub him about the temples.
IAGO. No, forbear,
The lethargy° must have his quiet course.
If not, he foams at mouth and by and by
Breaks out to savage madness. Look, he stirs.
Do you withdraw yourself a little while,
He will recover straight. When he is gone,
I would on great occasion speak with you.

[*Exit* CASSIO.]

How is it, General? Have you not hurt your head?°
OTH. Dost thou mock me?
IAGO. I mock you! No, by Heaven.
Would you would bear your fortune like a man!
OTH. A hornèd man's a monster and a beast.
IAGO. There's many a beast, then, in a populous city,
And many a civil° monster.
OTH. Did he confess it?
IAGO. Good sir, be a man.

35–41. Lie . . . devil: Othello breaks into incoherent muttering before he falls down in a fit. **36. fulsome:** disgusting. **38–39. Nature . . . instruction:** nature would not fill me with such overwhelming emotion unless there was some cause. **51. lethargy:** epileptic fit. Cf. *II Hen IV*, I.ii.127–29. **57. Have . . . head:** With brutal cynicism Iago asks whether Othello is suffering from cuckold's headache. **62. civil:** sober, well-behaved citizen.

Think every bearded fellow that's but yoked°
May draw with you.° There's millions now alive
That nightly lie in those unproper beds
Which they dare swear peculiar.° Your case is better.
Oh, 'tis the spite of Hell, the Fiend's archmock,
To lip° a wanton in a secure couch°
And to suppose her chaste! No, let me know,
And knowing what I am, I know what she shall be.

OTH. Oh, thou art wise, 'tis certain.

IAGO. Stand you awhile apart,
Confine yourself but in a patient list.°
Whilst you were here o'erwhelmèd with your grief—
A passion most unsuiting such a man—
Cassio came hither. I shifted him away,
And laid good 'scuse upon your ecstasy,°
Bade him anon return and here speak with me,
The which he promisèd. Do but encave° yourself,
And mark the fleers,° the gibes, and notable scorns,
That dwell in every region of his face.
For I will make him tell the tale anew,
Where, how, how oft, how long ago, and when
He hath and is again to cope° your wife.
I say but mark his gesture. Marry, patience,
Or I shall say you are all in all in spleen,°
And nothing of a man.

OTH. Dost thou hear, Iago?
I will be found most cunning in my patience,
But—dost thou hear?—most bloody.

IAGO. That's not amiss,
But yet keep time in all. Will you withdraw?

[OTHELLO *retires.*]

Now will I question Cassio of Bianca,
A housewife° that by selling her desires
Buys herself bread and clothes. It is a creature
That dotes on Cassio, as 'tis the strumpet's plague
To beguile many and be beguiled by one.
He, when he hears of her, cannot refrain
From the excess of laughter. Here he comes.

[*Re-enter* CASSIO.]

---

64. yolked: married. **65. draw . . . you:** lit., be your yoke fellow, share your fate. **66–67. That . . . peculiar:** that lie nightly in beds which they believe are their own but which others have shared. **69. lip:** kiss. **secure couch:** lit., a carefree bed; i.e., a bed which has been used by the wife's lover, but secretly **73. patient list:** confines of patience. **77. ecstasy:** fit. **79. encave:** hide. **80. fleers:** scornful grins. **84. cope:** encounter. **86. spleen:** hot temper. Cf. *I Hen IV,* V.ii.19. **92. housewife:** hussy.

As he shall smile, Othello shall go mad,
And his unbookish° jealousy must construe°
Poor Cassio's smiles, gestures, and light behavior
Quite in the wrong. How do you now, Lieutenant?

CAS. The worser that you give me the addition°
Whose want even kills me.

IAGO. Ply° Desdemona well, and you are sure on 't.
Now, if this suit lay in Bianca's power,
How quickly should you speed!

CAS. Alas, poor caitiff!°

OTH. Look how he laughs already!

IAGO. I never knew a woman love man so.

CAS. Alas, poor rogue! I think, i' faith, she loves me.

OTH. Now he denies it faintly and laughs it out.

IAGO. Do you hear, Cassio?

OTH. Now he impórtunes him
To tell it o'er. Go to. Well said, well said.

IAGO. She gives it out that you shall marry her.
Do you intend it?

CAS. Ha, ha, ha!

OTH. Do you triumph, Roman?° Do you triumph?

CAS. I marry her! What, a customer!° I prithee bear some charity to my wit. Do not think it so unwholesome. Ha, ha, ha!

OTH. So, so, so, so. They laugh that win.°

IAGO. Faith, the cry goes that you shall marry her.

CAS. Prithee say true.

IAGO. I am a very villain else.

OTH. Have you scored° me? Well.

CAS. This is the monkey's own giving out. She is persuaded I will marry her out of her own love and flattery, not out of my promise.

OTH. Iago beckons me, now he begins the story.

CAS. She was here even now. She haunts me in every place. I was the other day talking on the sea bank with certain Venetians, and thither comes the bauble,° and, by this hand, she falls me thus about my neck—

OTH. Crying "O dear Cassio!" as it were. His gesture imports it.

CAS. So hangs and lolls and weeps upon me, so hales° and pulls me. Ha, ha, ha!

OTH. Now he tells how she plucked him to my chamber. Oh, I see that nose of yours, but not that dog I shall throw it to.

CAS. Well, I must leave her company.

---

99. unbookish: unlearned, simple. **construe:** interpret. **102. addition:** title (Lieutenant) which he has lost. **104. Ply:** urge. **106. caitiff:** wretch. **116. triumph, Roman:** The word "triumph" suggests "Roman" because the Romans celebrated their victories with triumphs, elaborate shows, and processions. Cf. *Caesar*, I.i.56. **117. customer:** harlot. **119. They . . . win:** a proverbial saying. See *Temp*, II.i.33. **123. scored:** marked, as with a blow from a whip. **128. bauble:** toy, plaything. **131. hales:** hauls, drags.

IAGO. Before me!° Look where she comes.

CAS. 'Tis such another fitchew!° Marry, a perfumed one.

[*Enter* BIANCA.]

What do you mean by this haunting of me?

BIAN. Let the Devil and his dam° haunt you! What did you mean by that same handkerchief you gave me even now? I was a fine fool to take it. I must take out the work? A likely piece of work, that you should find it in your chamber and not know who left it there! This is some minx's token, and I must take out the work? There, give it your hobbyhorse.° Wheresoever you had it, I'll take out no work on't.

CAS. How now, my sweet Bianca! How now! How now!

OTH. By Heaven, that should be my handkerchief!

BIAN. An° you'll come to supper tonight, you may. An you will not, come when you are next prepared for.

[*Exit.*]

IAGO. After her, after her.

CAS. Faith, I must, she'll rail i' the street else.

IAGO. Will you sup there?

CAS. Faith, I intend so.

IAGO. Well, I may chance to see you, for I would very fain° speak with you.

CAS. Prithee, come, will you?

IAGO. Go to. Say no more.

[*Exit* CASSIO.]

OTH. [*Advancing*] How shall I murder him, Iago?

IAGO. Did you perceive how he laughed at his vice?

OTH. Oh, Iago!

IAGO. And did you see the handkerchief?

OTH. Was that mine?

IAGO. Yours, by this hand. And to see how he prizes the foolish woman your wife! She gave it him, and he hath given it his whore.

OTH. I would have him nine years a-killing. A fine woman! A fair woman! A sweet woman!

IAGO. Nay, you must forget that.

OTH. Aye, let her rot, and perish, and be damned tonight, for she shall not live. No, my heart is turned to stone, I strike it and it hurts my hand. Oh, the world hath not a sweeter creature. She might lie by an emperor's side, and command him tasks.

IAGO. Nay, that's not your way.°

---

135. **Before me:** by my soul, a mild oath. 136. **fitchew:** polecat, a creature most demonstrative in the mating season. 138. **dam:** mother. 142. **hobbyhorse:** harlot. 146. **An:** if. 152. **fain:** gladly. 169. **Nay . . . way:** i.e., don't get soft thoughts about her.

OTH. Hang her! I do but say what she is, so delicate with her needle, an admirable musician—oh, she will sing the savageness out of a bear—of so high and plenteous wit and invention—

IAGO. She's the worse for all this.

OTH. Oh, a thousand thousand times. And then, of so gentle a condition!°

IAGO. Aye, too gentle.

OTH. Nay, that's certain. But yet the pity of it, Iago! O Iago, the pity of it, Iago!

IAGO. If you are so fond° over her iniquity, give her patent° to offend, for if it touch not you, it comes near nobody.

OTH. I will chop her into messes.° Cuckold me!

IAGO. Oh, 'tis foul in her.

OTH. With mine officer!

IAGO. That's fouler.

OTH. Get me some poison, Iago, this night. I'll not expostulate° with her, lest her body and beauty unprovide° my mind again. This night, Iago.

IAGO. Do it not with poison, strangle her in her bed, even the bed she hath contaminated.

OTH. Good, good. The justice of it pleases. Very good.

IAGO. And for Cassio, let me be his undertaker.° You shall hear more by midnight.

OTH. Excellent good.

[*A trumpet within.*]

What trumpet is that same?

IAGO. Something from Venice, sure. 'Tis Lodovico
Come from the Duke. And see, your wife is with him.

[*Enter* LODOVICO, DESDEMONA, *and* ATTENDANTS.]

LOD. God save the worthy General!

OTH. With all my heart, sir.

LOD. The Duke and Senators of Venice greet you.

[*Gives him a letter.*]

OTH. I kiss the instrument° of their pleasures.

[*Opens the letter, and reads.*]

DES. And what's the news, good Cousin Lodovico?

IAGO. I am very glad to see you, signior.
Welcome to Cyprus.

LOD. I thank you. How does Lieutenant Cassio?

IAGO. Lives, sir.

---

174. condition: nature. **177. fond:** foolish. **patent:** a grant by the King of some special privilege. **179. messes:** little pieces. **183. expostulate:** argue. **184. unprovide:** weaken. **188. be . . . undertaker:** undertake to manage his business. In Shakespeare's plays the word does *not* mean "mortician." **194. instrument:** i.e., the official letter which he has just received.

DES. Cousin, there's fall'n between him and my lord
An unkind breach, but you shall make all well.
OTH. Are you sure of that?
DES. My lord?
OTH. [*Reads.*] "This fail you not to do, as you will—"
LOD. He did not call, he's busy in the paper.
Is there division 'twixt my lord and Cassio?
DES. A most unhappy one. I would do much
To atone° them, for the love I bear to Cassio.
OTH. Fire and brimstone!
DES. My lord?
OTH. Are you wise?°
DES. What, is he angry?
LOD. Maybe the letter moved him,
For, as I think, they do command him home,
Deputing Cassio in his government.°
DES. By my troth,° I am glad on 't.
OTH. Indeed!
DES. My lord?
OTH. I am glad to see you mad.
DES. Why, sweet Othello?
OTH. Devil!

[*Striking her.*]

DES. I have not deserved this.
LOD. My lord, this would not be believed in Venice
Though I should swear I saw't. 'Tis very much.°
Make her amends, she weeps.
OTH. O devil, devil!
If that the earth could teem with a woman's tears,
Each drop she falls would prove a crocodile.°
Out of my sight!
DES. I will not stay to offend you.

[*Going.*]

LOD. Truly, an obedient lady.
I do beseech your lordship, call her back.
OTH. Mistress!
DES. My lord?
OTH. What would you with her, sir?
LOD. Who, I, my lord?

---

207. atone: reconcile. **208. Are . . . wise:** i.e., in saying you bear love to Cassio. **212. in . . . government:** in his place as governor. **213. troth:** truth. **217. 'Tis . . . much:** this is too much. **219–20. If . . . crocodile:** if the earth could breed from woman's tears, each tear that she lets fall would become a crocodile. It was believed that the crocodile would cry and sob to attract the sympathetic passer-by, who was then snapped up.

OTH. Aye, you did wish that I would make her turn.
Sir, she can turn and turn, and yet go on
And turn again. And she can weep, sir, weep.
And she's obedient, as you say, obedient,
Very obedient. Proceed you in your tears.
Concerning this, sir—oh, well-painted passion!°—
I am commanded home. Get you away.
I'll send for you anon. Sir, I obey the mandate,
And will return to Venice. Hence, avaunt!

[*Exit* DESDEMONA.]

Cassio shall have my place. And, sir, tonight,
I do entreat that we may sup together.
You are welcome, sir, to Cyprus. Goats and monkeys!

[*Exit.*]

LOD. Is this the noble Moor whom our full Senate
Call all-in-all sufficient? This the nature
Whom passion could not shake? Whose solid virtue
The shot of accident nor dart of chance
Could neither graze nor pierce?
IAGO. He is much changed.
LOD. Are his wits safe? Is he not light of brain?
IAGO. He's that he is. I may not breathe my censure°
What he might be. If what he might he is not,
I would to Heaven he were!°
LOD. What, strike his wife!
IAGO. Faith, that was not so well, yet would I knew
That stroke would prove the worst!
LOD. Is it his use?°
Or did the letters work upon his blood,
And new-create this fault?
IAGO. Alas, alas!
It is not honesty in me to speak
What I have seen and known. You shall observe him,
And his own courses° will denote him so
That I may save my speech. Do but go after,
And mark how he continues.
LOD. I am sorry that I am deceived in him.

[*Exeunt.*]

---

232. well-painted passion: cleverly imitated emotion; *passion* is any violent emotion. **245. censure:** opinion, judgment. **247. I . . . were:** I wish he were the man he ought to be. Once more Iago hints that he is holding back some unpleasant fact. **249. Is . . . use:** does he always behave like this? **254. courses:** ways, behavior.

SCENE II. *A room in the castle.*

[*Enter* OTHELLO *and* EMILIA.]

OTH. You have seen nothing, then?
EMIL. Nor ever heard, nor ever did suspect.
OTH. Yes, you have seen Cassio and she together.
EMIL. But then I saw no harm, and then I heard
Each syllable that breath made up between them.
OTH. What, did they never whisper?
EMIL. Never, my lord.
OTH. Nor send you out o' the way?
EMIL. Never.
OTH. To fetch her fan, her gloves, her mask, nor nothing?
EMIL. Never, my lord.
OTH. That's strange.
EMIL. I durst, my lord, to wager she is honest,
Lay down my soul at stake.° If you think other,
Remove your thought, it doth abuse your bosom.
If any wretch have put this in your head,
Let Heaven requite it with the serpent's curse!°
For if she be not honest, chaste, and true,
There's no man happy, the purest of their wives
Is foul as slander.
OTH. Bid her come hither. Go.

[*Exit* EMILIA.]

She says enough. Yet she's a simple bawd°
That cannot say as much. This is a subtle whore,
A closet° lock and key of villainous secrets.
And yet she'll kneel and pray, I have seen her do 't.

[*Enter* DESDEMONA *with* EMILIA.]

DES. My lord, what is your will?
OTH. Pray, chuck,° come hither.
DES. What is your pleasure?
OTH. Let me see your eyes.
Look in my face.
DES. What horrible fancy's this?
OTH. [*To* EMILIA] Some of your function,° mistress.

Sc. ii: 13. at stake: as the stake, the bet. **16. serpent's curse:** i.e., the curse laid on the serpent in the Garden of Eden. **20. bawd:** keeper of a brothel. **22. closet:** box in which secret papers are kept. **24. chuck:** See III.iv.49,n. **27. Some . . . function:** get about your business; i.e., prostitution. Othello pretends that Emilia is keeper of a brothel and Desdemona one of the women.

Leave procreants alone and shut the door,
Cough, or cry hem, if anybody come.
Your mystery,° your mystery. Nay, dispatch.°

[*Exit* EMILIA.]

DES. Upon my knees, what doth your speech import?
I understand a fury in your words,
But not the words.
OTH. Why, what art thou?
DES. Your wife, my lord, your true and loyal wife.
OTH. Come, swear it, damn thyself,
Lest, being like one of Heaven,° the devils themselves
Should fear to seize thee. Therefore be double-damned.
Swear thou art honest.
DES. Heaven doth truly know it.
OTH. Heaven truly knows that thou art false as Hell.
DES. To whom, my lord? With whom? How am I false?
OTH. O Desdemona! Away! Away! Away!
DES. Alas the heavy day! Why do you weep?
Am I the motive of these tears, my lord?
If haply you my father do suspect
An instrument of this your calling-back,
Lay not your blame on me. If you have lost him,
Why, I have lost him too.
OTH. Had it pleased Heaven
To try me with affliction, had they rained
All kinds of sores and shames on my bare head,
Steeped me in poverty to the very lips,
Given to captivity me and my utmost hopes,
I should have found in some place of my soul
A drop of patience. But, alas, to make me
A fixèd figure for the time of scorn
To point his slow unmoving finger at!°
Yet could I bear that too, well, very well.
But there where I have garnered up my heart,°
Where either I must live or bear no life,
The fountain from the which my current runs
Or else dries up—to be discarded thence!
Or keep it as a cistern for foul toads
To knot and gender° in! Turn thy complexion there,

---

30. mystery: profession. **dispatch:** be quick **36. being . . . Heaven:** because you look like an angel. **54–55. A . . . at:** A difficult image, much discussed. F1 reads "slow and moving finger"; Q1 reads "slow unmoving." Probably it means "a perpetual mark for scorn to point at with motionless finger." **time of scorn:** (perhaps) scorn for all time. **57. garnered . . . heart:** stored the harvest of my love. **62. gender:** mate.

Patience, thou young and rose-lipped cherubin—
Aye, there, look grim as Hell!
DES. I hope my noble lord esteems me honest.
OTH. Oh, aye, as summer flies are in the shambles,°
That quicken even with blowing.° O thou weed,
Who art so lovely fair and smell'st so sweet
That the sense aches at thee, would thou hadst ne'er been born!
DES. Alas, what ignorant sin have I committed?
OTH. Was this fair paper,° this most goodly book,
Made to write "whore" upon? What committed!
Committed! O thou public commoner!°
I should make very forges of my cheeks°
That would to cinders burn up modesty
Did I but speak thy deeds. What committed!
Heaven stops the nose at it, and the moon winks.
The bawdy wind, that kisses all it meets,
Is hushed within the hollow mine° of earth
And will not hear it. What committed!
Impudent strumpet!
DES. By Heaven, you do me wrong.
OTH. Are not you a strumpet?
DES. No, as I am a Christian.
If to preserve this vessel for my lord
From any other foul unlawful touch
Be not to be a strumpet, I am none.
OTH. What, not a whore?
DES. No, as I shall be saved.
OTH. Is 't possible?
DES. Oh, Heaven forgive us!
OTH. I cry you mercy, then.
I took you for that cunning whore of Venice
That married with Othello. [*Raising his voice.*] You, mistress,
That have the office opposite to Saint Peter,°
And keep the gate of Hell!

[*Re-enter* EMILIA.]

You, you, aye, you!
We have done our course, there's money for your pains.
I pray you turn the key, and keep our counsel.°

[*Exit.*]

66. shambles: slaughterhouse. **67. quicken . . . blowing:** come to life as soon as the eggs are laid. **71. fair paper:** i.e., her white body. **73. public commoner:** one who offers herself to all comers. **74. I . . . cheeks:** i.e., my cheeks would be as hot as a forge if I told the truth. **79. hollow mine:** i.e., the cave where the winds were supposed to be kept. **91. office . . . Peter:** St. Peter kept the keys to Heaven. **94. counsel:** i.e., secret.

EMIL. Alas, what does this gentleman conceive?°
How do you, madam? How do you, my good lady?
DES. Faith, half-asleep.
EMIL. Good madam, what's the matter with my lord?
DES. With who?
EMIL. Why, with my lord, madam.
DES. Who is thy lord?
EMIL. He that is yours, sweet lady.
DES. I have none. Do not talk to me, Emilia.
I cannot weep, nor answer have I none
But what should go by water.° Prithee tonight
Lay on my bed my wedding sheets. Remember,
And call thy husband hither.
EMIL. Here's a change indeed!

[*Exit.*]

DES. 'Tis meet I should be used so, very meet.
How have I been behaved that he might stick
The small'st opinion on my least misuse?°

[*Re-enter* EMILIA *with* IAGO.]

IAGO. What is your pleasure, madam? How is 't with you?
DES. I cannot tell. Those that do teach young babes
Do it with gentle means and easy tasks.
He might have chid me so, for, in good faith,
I am a child to chiding.
IAGO. What's the matter, lady?
EMIL. Alas, Iago, my lord hath so bewhored her,
Thrown such despite and heavy terms upon her,
As true hearts cannot bear.
DES. Am I that name, Iago?
IAGO. What name, fair lady?
DES. Such as she says my lord did say I was.
EMIL. He called her whore. A beggar in his drink
Could not have laid such terms upon his callet.°
IAGO. Why did he so?
DES. I do not know. I am sure I am none such.
IAGO. Do not weep, do not weep. Alas the day!
EMIL. Hath she forsook so many noble matches,
Her father and her country and her friends,
To be called whore? Would it not make one weep?

---

95. conceive: imagine. **104. should . . . water:** be expressed in tears. **108–09. How . . . misuse:** what have I done that he could find the smallest reason to find fault with my least mistake? **121. laid . . . callet:** used such words about his moll.

DES. It is my wretched fortune.
IAGO. Beshrew him for 't!
How comes this trick upon him?
DES. Nay, Heaven doth know.
EMIL. I will be hanged if some eternal villain,
Some busy and insinuating rogue,
Some cogging, cozening° slave, to get some office,
Have not devised this slander. I'll be hanged else.
IAGO. Fie, there is no such man, it is impossible.
DES. If any such there be, Heaven pardon him!
EMIL. A halter pardon him! And Hell gnaw his bones!
Why should he call her whore? Who keeps her company?
What place? What time? What form? What likelihood?
The Moor's abused by some most villainous knave,
Some base notorious knave, some scurvy fellow.
O Heaven, that such companions° Thou'dst unfold,°
And put in every honest hand a whip
To lash the rascals naked through the world
Even from the east to the west!
IAGO. Speak withindoor.°
EMIL. Oh, fie upon them! Some such squire° he was
That turned your wit the seamy side without,
And made you to suspect me with the Moor.
IAGO. You are a fool. Go to.°
DES. O good Iago,
What shall I do to win my lord again?
Good friend, go to him, for, by this light of Heaven,
I know not how I lost him. Here I kneel.
If e'er my will did trespass 'gainst his love
Either in discourse of thought or actual deed,
Or that mine eyes, mine ears, or any sense
Delighted them in any other form,
Or that I do not yet, and ever did,
And ever will, though he do shake me off
To beggarly divorcement, love him dearly,
Comfort forswear° me! Unkindness may do much,
And his unkindness may defeat° my life,
But never taint my love. I cannot say "whore,"
It doth abhor me now I speak the word.
To do the act that might the addition° earn
Not the world's mass of vanity° could make me.
IAGO. I pray you be content, 'tis but his humor.

---

132. cogging, cozening: deceiving, cheating. **141. companions:** low creatures. **unfold:** bring to light. **144. Speak withindoor:** don't shout so loud that all the street will hear you. **145. squire:** fine fellow. **148. Go to:** An expression of derision. **159. forswear:** repudiate. **160. defeat:** destroy. **163. addition:** title. Cf. IV.i.105. **164. vanity:** i.e., riches.

The business of the state does him offense,
And he does chide with you.

DES. If 'twere no other—

IAGO. 'Tis but so, I warrant.

[*Trumpets within.*]

Hark how these instruments summon to supper!
The messengers of Venice stay the meat.°
Go in, and weep not, all things shall be well.

[*Exeunt* DESDEMONA *and* EMILIA.]

[*Enter* RODERIGO.]

How now, Roderigo!

ROD. I do not find that thou dealest justly with me.

IAGO. What in the contrary?

ROD. Every day thou daffest° me with some device, Iago, and rather, as it seems to me now, keepest from me all conveniency° than suppliest me with the least advantage of hope. I will indeed no longer endure it, nor am I yet persuaded to put up in peace what already I have foolishly suffered.

IAGO. Will you hear me, Roderigo?

ROD. Faith, I have heard too much, for your words and performances are no kin together.

IAGO. You charge me most unjustly.

ROD. With naught but truth. I have wasted myself out of my means. The jewels you have had from me to deliver to Desdemona would half have corrupted a votarist.° You have told me she hath received them, and returned me expectations and comforts of sudden respect and acquaintance, but I find none.

IAGO. Well, go to, very well.

ROD. Very well! Go to! I cannot go to, man, nor 'tis not very well. By this hand, I say 'tis very scurvy, and begin to find myself fopped° in it.

IAGO. Very well.

ROD. I tell you 'tis not very well. I will make myself known to Desdemona. If she will return me my jewels, I will give over my suit and repent my unlawful solicitation. If not, assure yourself I will seek satisfaction of you.

IAGO. You have said now.°

ROD. Aye, and said nothing but what I protest intendment of doing.

IAGO. Why, now I see there's mettle° in thee, and even from this instant do build on thee a better opinion than ever before. Give me thy hand, Roderigo. Thou hast taken against me a most just exception,° but yet I protest I have dealt most directly in thy affair.

---

170. meat: serving of supper. **175. thou daffest:** you put me aside. Cf. *I Hen IV,* IV.i.96. **176. conveniency:** opportunity. **185. votarist:** one who has taken a vow, here a nun. **189. fopped:** fooled. **194. You . . . now:** or in modern slang, "Oh yeah." **196. mettle:** metal, good stuff. **198. just exception:** reasonable grievance.

ROD. It hath not appeared.

IAGO. I grant indeed it hath not appeared, and your suspicion is not without wit° and judgment. But, Roderigo, if thou hast that in thee indeed which I have greater reason to believe now than ever—I mean purpose, courage, and valor—this night show it. If thou the next night following enjoy not Desdemona, take me from this world with treachery and devise engines° for my life.

ROD. Well, what is it? Is it within reason and compass?

IAGO. Sir, there is especial commission come from Venice to depute Cassio in Othello's place.

ROD. Is that true? Why, then Othello and Desdemona return again to Venice.

IAGO. Oh, no. He goes into Mauritania, and takes away with him the fair Desdemona, unless his abode be lingered here by some accident. Wherein none can be so determinate° as the removing of Cassio.

ROD. How do you mean, "removing of" him?

IAGO. Why, by making him uncapable° of Othello's place, knocking out his brains.

ROD. And that you would have me to do?

IAGO. Aye, if you dare do yourself a profit and a right. He sups tonight with a harlotry,° and thither will I go to him. He knows not yet of his honorable fortune. If you will watch his going thence, which I will fashion to fall out between twelve and one, you may take him at your pleasure. I will be near to second your attempt, and he shall fall between us. Come, stand not amazed at it, but go along with me. I will show you such a necessity in his death that you shall think yourself bound to put it on him. It is now high suppertime, and the night grows to waste. About it.

ROD. I will hear further reason for this.

IAGO. And you shall be satisfied.

[*Exeunt.*]

SCENE III. *Another room in the castle.*

[*Enter* OTHELLO, LODOVICO, DESDEMONA, EMILIA, *and* ATTENDANTS.]

LOD. I do beseech you, sir, trouble yourself no further.

OTH. Oh, pardon me, 'twill do me good to walk.

LOD. Madam, good night. I humbly thank your ladyship.

DES. Your Honor is most welcome.

OTH. Will you walk, sir?

Oh—Desdemona—

DES. My lord?

OTH. Get you to bed on the instant, I will be returned forthwith. Dismiss your attendant there. Look it be done.

DES. I will, my lord.

---

201. wit: wisdom. **205. engines:** instruments of torture. **213. determinate:** decisive. **215. uncapable:** unable to take. **218. harlotry:** harlot.

[*Exeunt* OTHELLO, LODOVICO, *and* ATTENDANTS.]

EMIL. How goes it now? He looks gentler than he did.
DES. He says he will return incontinent.°
He hath commanded me to go to bed,
And bade me to dismiss you.
EMIL. Dismiss me!
DES. It was his bidding, therefore, good Emilia,
Give me my nightly wearing,° and adieu.
We must not now displease him.
EMIL. I would you had never seen him!
DES. So would not I. My love doth so approve° him
That even his stubbornness, his checks, his frowns—
Prithee, unpin me—have grace and favor in them.
EMIL. I have laid those sheets you bade me on the bed.
DES. All's one. Good faith, how foolish are our minds!
If I do die before thee, prithee shroud me
In one of those same sheets.
EMIL. Come, come, you talk.
DES. My mother had a maid called Barbara.
She was in love, and he she loved proved mad
And did forsake her. She had a song of "willow"°—
An old thing 'twas, but it expressed her fortune,
And she died singing it. That song tonight
Will not go from my mind. I have much to do
But to go hang my head all at one side
And sing it like poor Barbara. Prithee, dispatch.
EMIL. Shall I go fetch your nightgown?
DES. No, unpin me here.
This Lodovico is a proper man.
EMIL. A very handsome man.
DES. He speaks well.
EMIL. I know a lady in Venice would have walked barefoot to Palestine for a touch of his nether° lip.
DES. [*Singing*]
"The poor soul sat sighing by a sycamore tree,
Sing all a green willow.
Her hand on her bosom, her head on her knee,
Sing willow, willow, willow.
The fresh streams ran by her, and murmured her moans,
Sing willow, willow, willow.
Her salt tears fell from her, and softened the stones—"
Lay by these— [*Singing*]

Sc. iii: 12. incontinent: immediately. **15. nightly wearing:** nightgown. **18. approve:** commend. **27. willow:** the emblem of the forlorn lover. **38. nether:** lower.

"Sing willow, willow, willow."
Prithee, hie thee, he'll come anon.°— [*Singing*]
"Sing all a green willow must be my garland.
Let nobody blame him, his scorn I approve—"
Nay, that's not next. Hark! Who is 't that knocks?
EMIL. It's the wind.
DES. [*Singing*]
"I called my love false love, but what said he then?
Sing willow, willow, willow.
If I court moe° women, you'll couch with moe men."
So get thee gone, good night. Mine eyes do itch.
Doth that bode weeping?
EMIL. 'Tis neither here nor there.
DES. I have heard it said so. Oh, these men, these men!
Dost thou in conscience think—tell me, Emilia—
That there be women do abuse their husbands
In such gross kind?
EMIL. There be some such, no question.
DES. Wouldst thou do such a deed for all the world?
EMIL. Why, would not you?
DES. No, by this heavenly light!
EMIL. Nor I neither by this heavenly light. I might do 't as well i' the dark.
DES. Wouldst thou do such a deed for all the world?
EMIL. The world's a huge thing. It is a great price
For a small vice.
DES. In troth, I think thou wouldst not.
EMIL. In troth, I think I should, and undo 't when I had done. Marry, I would not do such a thing for a joint ring,° nor for measures of lawn,° nor for gowns, petticoats, nor caps, nor any petty exhibition;° but for the whole world—why, who would not make her husband a cuckold to make him a monarch? I should venture Purgatory for 't.
DES. Beshrew me if I would do such a wrong
For the whole world.
EMIL. Why, the wrong is but a wrong i' the world, and having the world for your labor, 'tis a wrong in your own world and you might quickly make it right.
DES. I do not think there is any such woman.
EMIL. Yes, a dozen, and as many to the vantage°
as would store° the world they played for.
But I do think it is their husbands' faults
If wives do fall. Say that they slack their duties
And pour our treasures into foreign laps,

---

48. anon: soon. **55. moe:** more. **69. joint ring:** ring made in two pieces, a lover's gift. **measures of lawn:** lengths of finest lawn, or as a modern woman would say, "sheer nylon." **70. petty exhibition:** small allowance of money. **78. as . . . vantage:** and more too; *vantage* is that added to the exact weight to give generous measure. **79. store:** stock, fill up.

Or else break out in peevish jealousies,
Throwing restraint° upon us, or say they strike us,
Or scant our former having in despite,°
Why, we have galls,° and though we have some grace,
Yet have we some revenge. Let husbands know
Their wives have sense like them. They see and smell
And have their palates both for sweet and sour,
As husbands have. What is it that they do
When they change us for others? Is it sport?
I think it is. And doth affection breed it?
I think it doth. Is 't frailty that thus errs?
It is so too. And have not we affections,
Desires for sport, and frailty, as men have?
Then let them use us well. Else let them know
The ills we do, their ills instruct us so.
DES. Good night, good night. Heaven me such uses° send,
Not to pick bad from bad, but by bad mend!

[*Exeunt.*]

ACT V

SCENE I. *Cyprus. A street.*

[*Enter* IAGO *and* RODERIGO.]

IAGO. Here, stand behind this bulk,° straight° will he come.
Wear thy good rapier bare, and put it home.
Quick, quick, fear nothing, I'll be at thy elbow.
It makes us, or it mars us. Think on that,
And fix most firm thy resolution.
ROD. Be near at hand, I may miscarry in 't.
IAGO. Here, at thy hand. Be bold, and take thy stand.

[*Retires.*]

ROD. I have no great devotion to the deed,
And yet he hath given me satisfying reasons.
'Tis but a man gone. Forth, my sword. He dies.
IAGO. I have rubbed this young quat° almost to the sense,°
And he grows angry. Now, whether he kill Cassio,
Or Cassio him, or each do kill the other,

---

84. Throwing restraint: putting restraints. **85. scant . . . despite:** for spite cut down our allowance. **86. galls:** bile, the cause of bitterness. **98. uses:** practices.

Act V, Sc. I: 1. bulk: stall outside a shop. **straight:** straightway. **11. quat:** pimple. **to . . . sense:** to the quick, to the raw.

Every way makes my gain. Live Roderigo,
He calls me to a restitution large°
Of gold and jewels that I bobbed° from him
As gifts to Desdemona.
It must not be. If Cassio do remain,
He hath a daily beauty in his life
That makes me ugly,° and besides, the Moor
May unfold° me to him. There stand I in much peril.
No, he must die. Be 't so. I hear him coming.

[*Enter* CASSIO.]

ROD. I know his gait, 'tis he. Villain, thou diest!

[*Makes a pass at* CASSIO.]

CAS. That thrust had been mine enemy indeed
But that my coat is better than thou know'st.°
I will make proof of thine.

[*Draws, and wounds* RODERIGO.]

ROD. Oh, I am slain!

[IAGO *from behind wounds* CASSIO *in the leg, and exit.*]

CAS. I am maimed for ever. Help, ho! Murder!
Murder!

[*Falls.*]

[*Enter* OTHELLO.]

OTH. The voice of Cassio. Iago keeps his word.
ROD. Oh, villain that I am!
OTH. It is even so.
CAS. Oh, help, ho! Light! A surgeon!
OTH. 'Tis he. O brave Iago, honest and just,
That hast such noble sense of thy friend's wrong!
Thou teachest me. Minion,° your dear lies dead,
And your unblest fate hies.° Strumpet, I come!
Forth of my heart those charms, thine eyes, are blotted.
Thy bed lust-stained shall with lust's blood be spotted.

---

15. large: full. **16. bobbed:** cheated. **19–20. He . . . ugly:** by comparison with him I am a poor thing. Iago is conscious of his lack of social graces. **21. unfold:** expose. **25. coat . . . know'st:** i.e., I wear mail under my coat. **33. Minion:** darling, in a bad sense. **34. hies:** comes on quickly.

[*Exit.*]

[*Enter* LODOVICO *and* GRATIANO.]

CAS. What ho! No watch?° No passage?° Murder! Murder!
GRA. 'Tis some mischance, the cry is very direful.
CAS. Oh, help!
LOD. Hark!
ROD. Oh, wretched villain!
LOD. Two or three groan. It is a heavy° night.
These may be counterfeits.° Let's think 't unsafe
To come in to the cry without more help.
ROD. Nobody come? Then shall I bleed to death.
LOD. Hark!

[*Re-enter* IAGO, *with a light.*]

GRA. Here's one comes in his shirt, with light and weapons.
IAGO. Who's there? Whose noise is this that cries on° murder?
LOD. We do not know.
IAGO. Did not you hear a cry?
CAS. Here, here! For Heaven's sake, help me!
IAGO. What's the matter?
GRA. This is Othello's Ancient, as I take it.
LOD. The same indeed, a very valiant fellow.
IAGO. What are you here that cry so grievously?
CAS. Iago? Oh, I am spoiled, undone by villains!
Give me some help.
IAGO. Oh me, Lieutenant! What villains have done this?
CAS. I think that one of them is hereabout,
And cannot make away.
IAGO. Oh, treacherous villains!
[*To* LODOVICO *and* GRATIANO.] What are you there?
Come in and give some help.
ROD. Oh, help me here!
CAS. That's one of them.
IAGO. Oh, murderous slave! Oh, villain!

[*Stabs* RODERIGO.]

ROD. Oh, damned Iago! Oh, inhuman dog!
IAGO. Kill men i' the dark! Where be these bloody thieves?
How silent is this town! Ho! Murder! Murder!
What may you be? Are you of good or evil?

37. watch: police. See Gen. Intro. p. 18a. **No passage:** nobody passing. **42. heavy:** thick. **43. counterfeits:** fakes. **47. cries on:** cries out.

LOD. As you shall prove us, praise us.
IAGO. Signior Lodovico?
LOD. He, sir.
IAGO. I cry you mercy. Here's Cassio hurt by villains.
GRA. Cassio!
IAGO. How is 't, brother?
CAS. My leg is cut in two.
IAGO. Marry, Heaven forbid!
Light, gentlemen. I'll bind it with my shirt.

[*Enter* BIANCA.]

BIAN. What is the matter, ho? Who is 't that cried?
IAGO. Who is 't that cried!
BIAN. Oh, my dear Cassio! My sweet Cassio!
Oh, Cassio, Cassio, Cassio!
IAGO. Oh, notable strumpet! Cassio, may you suspect
Who they should be that have thus mangled you?
CAS. No.
GRA. I am sorry to find you thus. I have been to seek you.
IAGO. Lend me a garter. So. Oh, for a chair,
To bear him easily hence!
BIAN. Alas, he faints! Oh, Cassio, Cassio, Cassio!
IAGO. Gentlemen all, I do suspect this trash
To be a party in this injury.
Patience awhile, good Cassio. Come, come,
Lend me a light. Know we this face or no?
Alas, my friend and my dear countryman
Roderigo? No—yes, sure. Oh Heaven! Roderigo.
GRA. What, of Venice?
IAGO. Even he, sir. Did you know him?
GRA. Know him! Aye.
IAGO. Signior Gratiano? I cry you gentle pardon.°
These bloody accidents must excuse my manners,
That so neglected you.
GRA. I am glad to see you.
IAGO. How do you, Cassio? Oh, a chair, a chair!
GRA. Roderigo!
IAGO. He, he, 'tis he. [*A chair brought in*] Oh, that's well said, the chair.
Some good man bear him carefully from hence.
I'll fetch the General's surgeon. [*To* BIANCA] For you, mistress,
Save you your labor. He that lies slain here, Cassio,
Was my dear friend. What malice was between you?
CAS. None in the world, nor do I know the man.
IAGO. [*To* BIANCA] What, look you pale? Oh, bear him out o' the air.

---

93. I . . . pardon: I beg you kindly pardon me.

[CASSIO *and* RODERIGO *are borne off.*]

Stay you, good gentlemen. Look you pale, mistress?
Do you perceive the gastness° of her eye?
Nay, if you stare, we shall hear more anon.
Behold her well, I pray you look upon her.
Do you see, gentlemen? Nay, guiltiness will speak,
Though tongues were out of use.

[*Enter* EMILIA.]

EMIL. 'Las, what's the matter? What's the matter, husband?
IAGO. Cassio hath here been set on in the dark
By Roderigo, and fellows that are 'scaped.
He's almost slain, and Roderigo dead.
EMIL. Alas, good gentlemen! Alas, good Cassio!
IAGO. This is the fruit of whoring. Prithee, Emilia,
Go know of Cassio where he supped tonight.
What, do you shake at that?
BIAN. He supped at my house, but I therefore shake not.
IAGO. Oh, did he so? I charge you, go with me.
EMIL. Fie, fie upon thee, strumpet!
BIAN. I am no strumpet, but of life as honest
As you that thus abuse me.
EMIL. As I! Foh! Fie upon thee!
IAGO. Kind gentlemen, let's go see poor Cassio dressed.°
Come, mistress, you must tell 's another tale.
Emilia, run you to the citadel,
And tell my lord and lady what hath happened!
Will you go on? I pray. [*Aside*] This is the night
That either makes me or fordoes° me quite.

[*Exeunt.*]

SCENE II. *A bedchamber in the castle.* DESDEMONA *in bed asleep, a light burning.*

[*Enter* OTHELLO.]

OTH. It is the cause,° it is the cause, my soul.
Let me not name it to you, you chaste stars!
It is the cause. Yet I'll not shed her blood,
Nor scar that whiter skin of hers than snow

---

106. gastness: ghastly look. **124. dressed:** i.e., his wound dressed. **129. fordoes:** ruins.

Sc. ii: 1. It . . . cause: The meaning of the opening lines of this speech has been much discussed. The *cause* is Desdemona's supposed faithlessness; Othello, at this moment, sees himself as embodied vengeance, the venger of man betrayed by woman.

And smooth as monumental alabaster.°
Yet she must die, else she'll betray more men.
Put out the light, and then put out the light.
If I quench thee, thou flaming minister,°
I can again thy former light restore,
Should I repent me. But once put out thy light,
Thou cunning'st° pattern of excelling nature,
I know not where is that Promethean heat°
That can thy light relume.° When I have plucked the rose,
I cannot give it vital growth again,
It needs must wither. I'll smell it on the tree.

[*Kissing her*]

Ah, balmy breath, that dost almost persuade
Justice to break her sword! One more, one more.
Be thus when thou art dead, and I will kill thee,
And love thee after. One more, and this the last.
So sweet was ne'er so fatal. I must weep,
But they are cruel tears. This sorrow's heavenly,
It strikes where it doth love. She wakes.
DES. Who's there? Othello?
OTH. Aye, Desdemona.
DES. Will you come to bed, my lord?
OTH. Have you prayed tonight, Desdemona?
DES. Aye, my lord.
OTH. If you bethink yourself of any crime
Unreconciled as yet to Heaven and grace,
Solicit for it straight.
DES. Alas, my lord, what may you mean by that?
OTH. Well, do it, and be brief. I will walk by.
I would not kill thy unpreparèd spirit.
No, Heaven forfend! I would not kill thy soul.°
DES. Talk you of killing?
OTH. Aye, I do.
DES. Then Heaven have mercy on me!
OTH. Amen, with all my heart!
DES. If you say so, I hope you will not kill me.
OTH. Hum!
DES. And yet I fear you, for you are fatal° then
When your eyes roll so. Why I should fear I know not,
Since guiltiness I know not, but yet I feel I fear.

---

5. monumental alabaster: Alabaster is white translucent stone, much used for memorial effigies on Elizabethan tombs. **8. minister:** servant. **11. cunning'st:** most skillfully made. **12. Promethean heat:** fire from Heaven. Prometheus stole fire from Heaven and first gave it to man. **13. relume:** relight. **27–32. If . . . soul:** Othello will be a merciful murderer. Cf. *Haml,* I.v.76–80. **forfend:** forbid. **37. fatal:** deadly.

OTH. Think on thy sins.
DES. They are loves I bear to you.
OTH. Aye, and for that thou diest.
DES. That death's unnatural that kills for loving.
Alas, why gnaw you so your nether lip?
Some bloody passion shakes your very frame.
These are portents,° but yet I hope, I hope,
They do not point on me.
OTH. Peace, and be still!
DES. I will so. What's the matter?
OTH. That handkerchief which I so loved and gave thee
Thou gavest to Cassio.
DES. No, by my life and soul!
Send for the man, and ask him.
OTH. Sweet soul, take heed,
Take heed of perjury, thou art on thy deathbed.
DES. Aye, but not yet to die.
OTH. Yes, presently.°
Therefore confess thee freely of thy sin,
For to deny each article with oath
Cannot remove nor choke the strong conception°
That I do groan withal. Thou art to die.
DES. Then Lord have mercy on me!
OTH. I say amen.
DES. And have you mercy too! I never did
Offend you in my life, never loved Cassio
But with such general warranty° of Heaven
As I might love. I never gave him token.
OTH. By Heaven, I saw my handkerchief in 's hand.
O perjured woman! Thou dost stone° my heart,
And makest me call what I intend to do
A murder, which I thought a sacrifice.
I saw the handkerchief.
DES. He found it, then,
I never gave it him. Send for him hither.
Let him confess a truth.
OTH. He hath confessed.
DES. What, my lord?
OTH. That he hath used thee.
DES. How? Unlawfully?
OTH. Aye.
DES. He will not say so.

---

45. portents: signs foretelling disaster. **52. presently:** at once. **55. conception:** thought. **60. warranty:** permission. **63. stone:** turn to stone.

OTH. No, his mouth is stopped.
Honest Iago hath ta'en order for 't.
DES. Oh, my fear interprets! What, is he dead?
OTH. Had all his hairs been lives, my great revenge
Had stomach for them all.
DES. Alas, he is betrayed, and I undone!
OTH. Out, strumpet! Weep'st thou for him to my face?
DES. Oh, banish me, my lord, but kill me not!
OTH. Down, strumpet!
DES. Kill me tomorrow, let me live tonight!
OTH. Nay, if you strive—
DES. But half an hour!
OTH. Being done, there is no pause.
DES. But while I say one prayer!
OTH. It is too late.

[*He stifles her.*]

EMIL. [*Within*] My lord, my lord! What ho! My lord, my lord!
OTH. What noise is this? Not dead? Not yet quite dead?
I that am cruel am yet merciful,
I would not have thee linger in thy pain.
So, so.
EMIL. [*Within*] What ho! My lord, my lord!
OTH. Who's there?
EMIL. [*Within*] Oh, good my lord, I would speak a word with you!
OTH. Yes, 'tis Emilia. By and by. She's dead.
'Tis like she comes to speak of Cassio's death.
The noise was here. Ha! No more moving?
Still as the grave. Shall she come in? Were 't good?
I think she stirs again. No. What's best to do?
If she come in, she'll sure speak to my wife.
My wife! My wife! What wife? I have no wife.
Oh, insupportable! Oh, heavy hour!
Methinks it should be now a huge eclipse
Of sun and moon, and that the affrighted globe
Should yawn at alteration.°
EMIL. [*Within*] I do beseech you
That I may speak with you, O good my lord!
OTH. I had forgot thee. Oh, come in, Emilia.
Soft, by and by. Let me the curtains° draw.
Where art thou?

---

101. yawn at alteration: gape with wonder at some monstrous change. **104. curtains:** i.e., of the bed. See Pl. 17b.

[*Unlocks the door.*]

[*Enter* EMILIA.]

What's the matter with thee now?
EMIL. Oh, my good lord, yonder 's foul murders done!
OTH. What, now?
EMIL. But now, my lord.
OTH. It is the very error° of the moon.
She comes more nearer earth than she was wont
And makes men mad.
EMIL. Cassio, my lord, hath killed a young Venetian
Called Roderigo.
OTH. Roderigo killed!
And Cassio killed!
EMIL. No, Cassio is not killed.
OTH. Not Cassio killed! Then murder's out of tune,
And sweet revenge grows harsh.
DES. Oh, falsely, falsely murdered!
EMIL. Alas, what cry is that?
OTH. That! What?
EMIL. Out and alas! That was my lady's voice.
Help! Help, ho! Help! O lady, speak again!
Sweet Desdemona! O sweet mistress, speak!
DES. A guiltless death I die.
EMIL. Oh, who hath done this deed?
DES. Nobody, I myself. Farewell.
Commend me to my kind lord. Oh, farewell!

[*Dies.*]

OTH. Why, how should she be murdered?
EMIL. Alas, who knows?
OTH. You heard her say herself it was not I.
EMIL. She said so. I must needs report the truth.
OTH. She's like a liar gone to burning Hell.
'Twas I that killed her.
EMIL. Oh, the more angel she,
And you the blacker devil!
OTH. She turned to folly,° and she was a whore.
EMIL. Thou dost belie her, and thou art a devil.
OTH. She was false as water.
EMIL. Thou art rash as fire to say
That she was false. Oh, she was heavenly true!
OTH. Cassio did top her, ask thy husband else.

---

109. error: wandering out of her proper course. **132. folly:** lewdness.

Oh, I were damned beneath all depth in Hell
But that I did proceed upon just grounds
To this extremity. Thy husband knew it all.
EMIL. My husband!
OTH. Thy husband.
EMIL. That she was false to wedlock?
OTH. Aye, with Cassio. Nay, had she been true,
If Heaven would make me such another world
Of one entire and perfect chrysolite,°
I'd not have sold her for it.
EMIL. My husband!
OTH. Aye, 'twas he that told me first.
An honest man he is, and hates the slime
That sticks on filthy deeds.
EMIL. My husband!
OTH. What needs this iteration,° woman? I say thy husband.
EMIL. Oh, mistress, villainy hath made mocks with love!
My husband say that she was false!
OTH. He, woman.
I say thy husband. Dost understand the word?
My friend, thy husband, honest, honest Iago.
EMIL. If he say so, may his pernicious soul
Rot half a grain a day! He lies to the heart.
She was too fond of her most filthy bargain.
OTH. Ha!
EMIL. Do thy worst.
This deed of thine is no more worthy Heaven
Than thou wast worthy her.
OTH. Peace, you were best.
EMIL. Thou hast not half that power to do me harm
As I have to be hurt. O gull!° O dolt!°
As ignorant as dirt! Thou hast done a deed—
I care not for thy sword, I'll make thee known,
Though I lost twenty lives. Help! Help, ho! Help!
The Moor hath killed my mistress! Murder! Murder!

[*Enter* MONTANO, GRATIANO, IAGO, *and others.*]

MON. What is the matter? How now, General!
EMIL. Oh, are you come, Iago? You have done well,
That men must lay their murders on your neck.
GRA. What is the matter?
EMIL. Disprove this villain, if thou be'st a man.

---

145. chrysolite: a semiprecious stone, usually green in color. **150. iteration:** repetition. **163. gull:** dupe. **dolt:** dull-witted ass.

He says thou told'st him that his wife was false.
I know thou didst not, thou'rt not such a villain.
Speak, for my heart is full.

IAGO. I told him what I thought, and told no more
Than what he found himself was apt° and true.

EMIL. But did you ever tell him she was false?

IAGO. I did.

EMIL. You told a lie, an odious, damnèd lie,
Upon my soul, a lie, a wicked lie!
She false with Cassio! Did you say with Cassio?

IAGO. With Cassio, mistress. Go to, charm your tongue.°

EMIL. I will not charm my tongue, I am bound to speak.
My mistress here lies murdered in her bed.

ALL. Oh, Heavens forfend!

EMIL. And your reports have set the murder on.

OTH. Nay, stare not, masters. It is true indeed.

GRA. 'Tis a strange truth.

MON. Oh, monstrous act!

EMIL. Villainy, villainy, villainy!
I think upon 't. I think I smell 't. Oh, villainy!
I thought so then.° I'll kill myself for grief.
Oh, villainy, villainy!

IAGO. What, are you mad? I charge you, get you home.

EMIL. Good gentlemen, let me have leave to speak.
'Tis proper I obey him, but not now.
Perchance, Iago, I will ne'er go home.

OTH. Oh! Oh! Oh!

[*Falling on the bed.*]

EMIL. Nay, lay thee down and roar,
For thou hast killed the sweetest innocent
That e'er did lift up eye.

OTH. [*Rising*] Oh, she was foul!
I scarce did know you, Uncle. There lies your niece,
Whose breath indeed these hands have newly stopped.
I know this act shows horrible and grim.

GRA. Poor Desdemona! I am glad thy father's dead.
Thy match was mortal° to him, and pure grief
Shore his old thread in twain.° Did he live now,
This sight would make him do a desperate turn—
Yea, curse his better angel from his side,
And fall to reprobation.°

---

177. apt: likely. **183. charm . . . tongue:** be silent. **192. I . . . then:** i.e., I suspected this earlier—as for example when Iago took the handkerchief. See III.iii.313. **205. match . . . mortal:** i.e., grief at this marriage killed him. **206. Shore . . . twain:** cut his thread of life in two. **209. reprobation:** damnation; i.e., by self-murder.

OTH. 'Tis pitiful, but yet Iago knows
That she with Cassio hath the act of shame
A thousand times committed. Cassio confessed it.
And she did gratify his amorous works
With that recognizance° and pledge of love
Which I first gave her, I saw it in his hand.
It was a handkerchief, an antique token
My father gave my mother.
EMIL. Oh, Heaven! Oh, heavenly powers!
IAGO. 'Zounds! Hold your peace.
EMIL. 'Twill out, 'twill out. I peace!
No, I will speak as liberal as the north.°
Let Heaven and men and devils, let them all,
All, all, cry shame against me, yet I'll speak.
IAGO. Be wise, and get you home.
EMIL. I will not.

[IAGO *offers to stab* EMILIA.]

GRA. Fie!
Your sword upon a woman!
EMIL. O thou dull Moor! That handkerchief thou speak'st of
I found by fortune and did give my husband,
For often with a solemn earnestness,
More than indeed belonged to such a trifle,
He begged of me to steal it.
IAGO. Villainous whore!
EMIL. She give it Cassio! No, alas, I found it,
And I did give 't my husband.
IAGO. Filth, thou liest!
EMIL. By Heaven, I do not, I do not, gentlemen.
Oh, murderous coxcomb!° What should such a fool
Do with so good a wife?
OTH. Are there no stones° in Heaven
But what serve for the thunder? Precious villain!

[*He runs at* IAGO. IAGO, *from behind, stabs* EMILIA, *and exit.*]

GRA. The woman falls. Sure, he hath killed his wife.
EMIL. Aye, aye. Oh, lay me by my mistress' side.
GRA. He's gone, but his wife's killed.
MON. 'Tis a notorious villain. Take you this weapon,
Which I have here recovered from the Moor.

214. recognizance: badge, token. **220. liberal . . . north:** as freely as the north wind, which is loud and bitter. **233. coxcomb:** conceited fool. **234. stones:** thunderbolts.

Come, guard the door without, let him not pass,
But kill him rather. I'll after that same villain,
For 'tis a damnèd slave.

[*Exeunt all but* OTHELLO *and* EMILIA.]

OTH. I am not valiant neither.
But every puny whipster° gets my sword.
But why should honor outlive honesty?
Let it go all.

EMIL. What did thy song bode, lady?
Hark, canst thou hear me? I will play the swan,
And die in music.° [*Singing*]
"Willow, willow, willow."
Moor, she was chaste. She loved thee, cruel Moor,
So come my soul to bliss as I speak true.
So speaking as I think, I die, I die.

[*Dies.*]

OTH. I have another weapon in this chamber.
It is a sword of Spain,° the ice brook's temper.°—
Oh, here it is. Uncle, I must come forth.

GRA. [*Within*] If thou attempt it, it will cost thee dear.
Thou hast no weapon, and perforce must suffer.

OTH. Look in upon me then, and speak with me,
Or, naked° as I am, I will assault thee.

[*Re-enter* GRATIANO.]

GRA. What is the matter?

OTH. Behold, I have a weapon,
A better never did itself sustain
Upon a soldier's thigh. I have seen the day
That with this little arm and this good sword
I have made my way through more impediments
Than twenty times your stop. But, oh, vain boast!
Who can control his fate? 'Tis not so now.
Be not afraid, though you do see me weaponed.
Here is my journey's end, here is my butt°
And very sea mark of my utmost sail.°

---

244. whipster: whippersnapper. **247–48. play . . . music:** i.e., I will sing at my death. It was believed that swans sang once only, just before they died. **253. sword of Spain:** Spanish swords and rapiers, from Toledo or Bilbao, were famous. **ice . . . temper:** hardened in ice-cold water. **258. naked:** unarmed. **267. butt:** aim. **268. And . . . sail:** the mark that I have reached the end of my voyage.**sea mark:** a conspicuous object by which the mariner checks his course.

Do you go back dismayed? 'Tis a lost fear.
Man but a rush° against Othello's breast,
And he retires. Where should Othello go?
Now, how dost thou look now? O ill-starred wench!
Pale as thy smock! When we shall meet at compt,°
This look of thine will hurl my soul from Heaven
And fiends will snatch at it. Cold, cold, my girl!
Even like thy chastity. Oh, cursèd slave!
Whip me, ye devils,
From the possession of this heavenly sight!
Blow me about in winds! Roast me in sulphur!
Wash me in steep-down gulfs° of liquid fire!
O Desdemona! Desdemona! Dead!
Oh! Oh! Oh!

[*Enter* LODOVICO, MONTANO, CASSIO *carried in a chair, and* OFFICERS *with* IAGO, *prisoner.*]

LOD. Where is this rash and most unfortunate man?
OTH. That's he that was Othello. Here I am.
LOD. Where is that viper? Bring the villain forth.
OTH. I look down toward his feet,° but that's a fable.
If that thou be'st a devil,° I cannot kill thee.

[*Wounds* IAGO.]

LOD. Wrench his sword from him.
IAGO. I bleed, sir, but not killed.
OTH. I am not sorry neither. I'd have thee live,
For, in my sense, 'tis happiness to die.
LOD. O thou Othello, that wert once so good,
Fall'n in the practice° of a damnèd slave,
What shall be said to thee?
OTH. Why, anything.
An honorable murderer, if you will,
For naught did I in hate, but all in honor.
LOD. This wretch hath part confessed his villainy.
Did you and he consent in Cassio's death?
OTH. Aye.
CAS. Dear General, I never gave you cause.
OTH. I do believe it, and I ask your pardon.
Will you, I pray, demand that demidevil
Why he hath thus ensnared my soul and body?

---

270. Man . . . rush: attack with only a reed. **273. compt:** account; i.e., the Day of Judgment. **280. steep-down gulfs:** sheer whirlpools. **286. toward . . . feet:** i.e., to see if he has the cloven hoof of a devil. **287. If . . . devil:** if you are an evil spirit and no man. **292. Fall'n . . . practice:** destroyed by the plotting.

IAGO. Demand me nothing. What you know, you know.
From this time forth I never will speak word.
LOD. What, not to pray?
GRA. Torments will ope your lips.
OTH. Well, thou dost best.
LOD. Sir, you shall understand what hath befall'n,
Which, as I think, you know not. Here is a letter
Found in the pocket of the slain Roderigo,
And here another. The one of them imports
The death of Cassio to be undertook
By Roderigo.
OTH. Oh, villain!
CAS. Most heathenish and most gross!
LOD. Now here's another discontented paper,
Found in his pocket too. And this, it seems,
Roderigo meant to have sent this damnèd villain
But that, belike, Iago in the interim
Came in and satisfied him.
OTH. Oh, the pernicious caitiff!
How came you, Cassio, by that handkerchief
That was my wife's?
CAS. I found it in my chamber.
And he himself confessed but even now
That there he dropped it for a special purpose
Which wrought to his desire.
OTH. O fool! Fool! Fool!
CAS. There is besides in Roderigo's letter
How he upbraids Iago, that he made him
Brave° me upon the watch, whereon it came
That I was cast.° And even but now he spake
After long seeming dead, Iago hurt him,
Iago set him on.
LOD. You must forsake this room, and go with us.
Your power and your command is taken off,
And Cassio rules in Cyprus. For this slave,
If there be any cunning cruelty
That can torment him much and hold him long,°
It shall be his. You shall close prisoner rest
Till that the nature of your fault be known
To the Venetian state. Come, bring away.
OTH. Soft you,° a word or two before you go.
I have done the state some service, and they know 't.
No more of that. I pray you, in your letters,
When you shall these unlucky deeds relate,

---

326. Brave: dare, insult. **327. cast:** dismissed. **334. hold . . . long:** i.e., in dying. **338. Soft you:** pause awhile.

Speak of me as I am, nothing extenuate,
Nor set down aught in malice. Then must you speak
Of one that loved not wisely but too well,
Of one not easily jealous, but, being wrought,
Perplexed in the extreme, of one whose hand,
Like the base Indian, threw a pearl away
Richer than all his tribe°—of one whose subdued eyes,
Albeit unusèd to the melting mood,
Drop tears as fast as the Arabian trees
Their medicinal gum. Set you down this,
And say besides that in Aleppo once,
Where a malignant and a turbaned Turk
Beat a Venetian and traduced° the state,
I took by the throat the circumcisèd dog
And smote him, thus.

[*Stabs himself.*]

LOD. Oh, bloody period!
GRA. All that's spoke is marred.°
OTH. I kissed thee ere I killed thee. No way but this,
Killing myself, to die upon a kiss.

[*Falls on the bed, and dies.*]

CAS. This did I fear, but thought he had no weapon.
For he was great of heart.
LOD. [*To* IAGO] O Spartan° dog,
More fell° than anguish, hunger, or the sea!
Look on the tragic loading° of this bed,
This is thy work. The object poisons sight,
Let it be hid.° Gratiano, keep the house,
And seize upon the fortunes of the Moor,
For they succeed on you. To you, Lord Governor,
Remains the censure of this hellish villain,
The time, the place, the torture.
Oh, enforce it!
Myself will straight aboard, and to the state
This heavy act with heavy heart relate.

[*Exeunt.*]

347–48. base . . . tribe: A much discussed passage. F1 reads "Iudean" (Judean), and if correct it would refer to Judas Iscariot, who betrayed Jesus. Shakespeare does not elsewhere use the word "Judean," and he does associate India with pearls, as in *Tr & Cr,* I.i.105: "Her bed is India, There she lies a pearl." **354. traduced:** insulted. **357. marred:** spoiled. **361. Spartan:** i.e., hardhearted. **362. fell:** cruel. **363. loading:** burden—the bodies of Desdemona and Othello. **365. Let . . . hid:** At these words the curtains are closed across the inner stage (or chamber, if this scene was acted aloft), concealing all three bodies. See Pl. 5b.

HENRIK IBSEN

(1828–1906)

The Wild Duck

A NEW TRANSLATION BY OTTO REINERT

About the Author: Henrik Ibsen lived in Germany and Italy from 1864 to 1891, and it was from abroad that he wrote most of his best-known works, but his major plays are always set in his native Norway. Because of his exploration of controversial social issues and universal mythic themes, he is often considered one of the founders of a uniquely "modern" drama, and his plays remain influential and are regularly produced a century after their composition. His early works (1850 to 1873) were largely poetic dramas, often set in the historical past or in some mythic realm, but beginning in 1877 he shifted to the "photographic realism" that is usually associated with his mature style, and between 1877 and 1896 he wrote the eleven prose plays upon which his reputation rests as one of the founders of modern drama.

The most common setting for these plays is the interior of a home in his contemporary Norway. This setting provides a classic example of what is often called a "fourth-wall stage": the stage is arranged to look like a room with its furnishings, three of its walls, its windows and doors, all visible, but with the fourth wall—the one through which the audience looks in upon the action—removed. It used to be common, even in Ibsen's own lifetime, to dismiss him as a writer whose primary interest in these plays was in this faithful reproduction of the details of everyday middle-class life and as a writer of so-called problem plays, plays which dramatize some specific, currently controversial social issue. The three plays written immediately before *The Wild Duck* seem to many to give credence to this view: *A Doll's House* (1879), where women's rights are a central issue; *Ghosts* (1881), which deals with the medical and social effects of venereal disease; and *An Enemy of the People* (1883), where a scientist's sense of social responsibility (he's discovered that the water in a local health spa is polluted) risks undermining his town's financial well-being.

About the Play: To treat Ibsen's plays as mere exercises in dramatic journalism is to trivialize some of the most powerful plays ever written, and perhaps the fact that some people did perceive them in this way helps explain some aspects of *The Wild Duck* (1884). The play's main characters are a photographer (who is ineffectual) and a social reformer (who causes social harm), and in the play perceiving the truth about oneself and one's social situation seems potentially devastating. Moreover, while the stage represents a combination photographer's studio and family sitting room and is filled with details from modern bourgeois life, it is dominated by the mysterious attic space behind it, never seen by the audience, where Hjalmar Ekdal and his father have created a pretend wilderness, stocked with felled trees, rabbits to hunt, and, most prominently, the Wild Duck.

The result is that this is a play where seemingly petty domestic issues become intertwined with and expressions of aspects of momentous historical change, played out against a background of mythic significance. The modern industrialism that has created Hjalmar's tawdry, overcrowded urban life was built on the pillaging of state parkland. In the play, the imagination and the world of nature have both been wounded. Do they reassert themselves as indestructible, or do they remain only as maimed grotesques which serve to remind us of what has been lost? What does the play suggest about the possibility for heroic behavior in this world? All of these are questions that can be addressed only through attention to the texture of the play's language.

A good place to start may be with the Wild Duck, perhaps one of the most famous literary symbols in all of dramatic literature. It is clear to anyone who sees or reads the play that the duck means more than herself. She is spoken of so often and in ways that attribute to her a significance beyond the ornithological that there can be no mistaking that she has some larger meaning. Just what that significance is, however, is a matter for discussion. Is her situation analogous to one of the characters? Which one? More than one? Something larger than individual characters in this play? Is there a way in which she expands or brings into focus the larger thematic concerns of the play? Whatever she may mean, there is a way in which this creature, never seen on stage, dominates the play and seems to crystallize its significance.

Two final points about Ibsen's dramatic practice. Unlike most dramatists, he presents his stage directions from the audience's, rather than the players', point of view. As you try to imagine the setting of his play, therefore, remember that if he says there is a door off to the right, he means to the right as we would look in through the fourth wall. (Most playwrights would mean to the right as an actor would look out at the audience through that wall.) The second point has to do with **exposition.** Typically in an Ibsen play, the exposition is deferred. Whereas someone like Shakespeare usually tries to explain to the audience whatever it needs to know by the end of Act One, Ibsen often withholds necessary facts until the final act. Perhaps he is influenced by the then-new *genre* of the mystery story, since this practice does add an element of the "whodunit" to many of Ibsen's plays. They are in this respect the opposite of a play such as *Oedipus Rex,* where the audience knew the plot in advance. If you want to respond to a play like *The Wild Duck* and catch the full effect of its dramatic irony, therefore, it may be necessary for you, even more than with other plays, to reread it.

CHARACTERS

WERLE, *a manufacturer and merchant*
GREGERS WERLE, *his son*
OLD EKDAL
HJALMAR EKDAL, *his son, a photographer*
GINA EKDAL, *Hjalmar's wife*
HEDVIG, *their daughter, fourteen years old*
MRS. SØRBY, *Werle's housekeeper*
RELLING, *a physician*
MOLVIK, *a former student of theology*
GRÅBERG, *a bookkeeper in Werle's office*
PETTERSEN, *Werle's servant*
JENSEN, *a hired waiter*
A FLABBY GENTLEMAN
A THIN-HAIRED GENTLEMAN
A NEARSIGHTED GENTLEMAN
SIX OTHER GENTLEMEN, *Werle's dinner guests*
OTHER HIRED WAITERS

SCENE: *The first act takes place at* WERLE'S; *the other four, in* HJALMAR EKDAL'S *studio.*

ACT I

An expensive-looking and comfortable study in WERLE'S *house; bookcases and upholstered furniture; in the middle of the room a desk with papers and ledgers; lamps with green shades give the room a soft, subdued light. In the rear, open double doors with portieres pulled apart*

reveal a large, elegant drawing room, brightly illuminated by lamps and candles. Front right, a small door to the office wing. Front left, a fireplace with glowing coals in it. Farther back on the left wall, double doors to the dining room.

PETTERSEN, WERLE'S *servant, in livery, and the hired waiter* JENSEN, *in black, are setting the study in order for the guests. In the drawing room, two or three other hired waiters are lighting candles, moving chairs, etc. Sounds of conversation and laughter of many people come from the dining room. Someone signals he wishes to make a speech by touching his glass with his knife. Silence follows, a short speech is made, there are noises of approval, then again conversation.*

PETTERSEN *(lights a lamp by the fireplace and puts a shade on it):* Just listen to that, Jensen. There's the old man now, proposing a long toast to Mrs. Sørby.

JENSEN *(moving an armchair):* Do you think it's true what people say, that the two of 'em—y'know—?

PETTERSEN: Couldn't say.

JENSEN: I bet he used to be quite a goat in the old days.

PETTERSEN: Maybe so.

JENSEN: They say this dinner is for his son.

PETTERSEN: That's right. He came home yesterday.

JENSEN: It's the first I've heard Werle has a son.

PETTERSEN: He has a son, all right. But he's up at the works at Høydal all the time. He hasn't been home as long as I've been here.

A HIRED WAITER *(in the drawing room doorway):* Pst, Pettersen, there's an old fellow here, says he—

PETTERSEN *(under his breath):* Dammit! Can't have anybody in here now!

*(*OLD EKDAL *appears from the right in the drawing room. He is dressed in a shabby old coat with a high collar. Wool mittens. He carries a walking stick and a fur cap in his hand. Under his arm a parcel in thick paper. Dirty, reddish brown wig. Small, gray mustache.)*

PETTERSEN *(going towards him):* Good Lord! What are *you* doing here?

EKDAL *(in the doorway):* Got to get into the office, Pettersen.

PETTERSEN: The office closed an hour ago, and—

EKDAL: They told me that downstairs. But Gråberg is still in there. Be a good boy, Pettersen; let me in this way. *(Points to the small office door.)* Been through here before.

PETTERSEN: Oh well, all right. *(Opens the door.)* But see you go out the other way. We're having guests tonight.

EKDAL: I know, I know—h'm! Thanks a lot, Pettersen, old boy. Good old friend. Thanks. *(Mutters.)* Ass!

(He enters the office. PETTERSEN *closes the door behind him.)*

JENSEN: Is he one of them office people, too?

PETTERSEN: Oh no. He just does some extra copying for them, when they need it. But he's been a fine enough fellow in his day, old Ekdal has.

JENSEN: You know, he sort of looked like that.

PETTERSEN: Oh yes. He used to be a lieutenant.

JENSEN: I'll be damned! A lieutenant!

PETTERSEN: Yessir: Then he got mixed up in some forest deal or something. They say he pretty near ruined Werle once. The two of 'em were partners—owned the Høydal works together. Oh yes, Ekdal and I are good friends. We've had many a drink together at Madam Eriksen's place, we have.

JENSEN: Didn't look to me like he'd have much to buy people drinks with.

PETTERSEN: Good Lord, Jensen. It's my treat, of course. I always say one should be nice to people who've seen better days.

JENSEN: So he went bankrupt?

PETTERSEN: Worse than that. He went to prison.

JENSEN: Prison!

PETTERSEN: Or something.— *(Listens.)* Shhh. They are getting up from the table.

(Servants open the doors to the dining room. MRS. SØRBY *appears, in conversation with a couple of the dinner guests. The rest of the company follows in small groups.* WERLE *is among them. The last to appear are* HJALMAR EKDAL *and* GREGERS WERLE.*)*

MRS. SØRBY *(to the servant, in passing):* Pettersen, tell them to serve the coffee in the music room, will you?

PETTERSEN: Very well, Mrs. Sørby.

(She and the two guests go into the drawing room and disappear, right. PETTERSEN *and* JENSEN *follow them out.)*

A FLABBY GENTLEMAN *(to* A THIN-HAIRED *one):* Phew! That dinner—It was almost too much for me.

THE THIN-HAIRED GENTLEMAN: Oh, I don't know. With a little bit of good will, it's amazing what one can accomplish in three hours.

THE FLABBY GENTLEMAN: Yes, but afterwards, my dear chamberlain!

A THIRD GENTLEMAN: I am told the coffee and liqueurs will be served in the music room.

THE FLABBY GENTLEMAN: Wonderful! Then maybe Mrs. Sørby will play something for us.

THE THIN-HAIRED GENTLEMAN *(in a low voice):* If only she doesn't play us a different tune one of these days.

THE FLABBY GENTLEMAN: Don't worry. Bertha isn't one to let old friends down.

(They laugh and enter the drawing room.)

WERLE *(in a low and troubled voice):* I don't think anybody noticed, Gregers.

GREGERS *(looks at him):* Noticed what?

WERLE: You didn't either?

GREGERS: What?

WERLE: We were thirteen at the table.

GREGERS: Really? Were we thirteen?

WERLE *(with a glance at* HJALMAR EKDAL*):* Usually we are only twelve. *(To the other guests:)* Gentlemen!

(He and the remaining guests, except HJALMAR *and* GREGERS*, leave through the drawing room, rear right.)*

HJALMAR *(who has overheard the conversation):* You shouldn't have invited me, Gregers.

GREGERS: Nonsense! This is supposed to be a party for *me.* Shouldn't I invite my one and only friend?

HJALMAR: But I don't think your father approves. I never come to this house.

GREGERS: So I hear. But I wanted to see you and talk to you.—Well, well, we two old school fellows have certainly drifted apart. It must be sixteen—seventeen years since we saw each other.

HJALMAR: Is it really that long?

GREGERS: It is indeed. And how are you? You look fine. You're almost stout.

HJALMAR: Stout is hardly the word, but I suppose I look a little more manly than I used to.

GREGERS: Yes, you do. Your appearance hasn't suffered any all these years.

HJALMAR *(gloomily):* But the inner man—! Believe me, that's a different story. You know, of course, how utterly everything has collapsed for me and mine since we last met.

GREGERS *(in a lower voice):* How is your father these days?

HJALMAR: I'd just as soon not talk about him. My poor, unfortunate father lives with me, of course. He has no one else in the whole world to turn to. But it is so terribly difficult for me to talk about these things. Tell me rather how you have been—up there at the works.

GREGERS: Lonely—blissfully lonely. I've had all the time in the world to think over all sorts of things.—Here. Let's make ourselves comfortable.

(He sits down in an armchair near the fireplace and gets HJALMAR *to take another chair beside him.)*

HJALMAR *(softly):* All the same, I do want to thank you, Gregers, for inviting me to your father's table. It proves to me you no longer bear me a grudge.

GREGERS *(surprised):* Grudge? What makes you think I ever did?

HJALMAR: You did at first, you know.

GREGERS: When?

HJALMAR: Right after the tragedy. Of course, that was only natural. After all, your own father only escaped by the skin of his teeth. Oh, that terrible old business!

GREGERS: And so I bore you a grudge? Who told you that?

HJALMAR: I know you did, Gregers. Your father said so himself.

GREGERS *(startled):* Father! Really? H'm. So that's why you've never written—not a single word.

HJALMAR: Yes.

GREGERS: Not even when you decided to become a photographer?

HJALMAR: Your father thought it would be better if I didn't write about anything at all.

GREGERS *(looking straight ahead):* Oh well, maybe he was right, at that.—But tell me, Hjalmar—do you feel you have adjusted pretty well to your situation?

HJALMAR *(with a small sigh):* Oh yes, I think I have. Can't say I haven't, anyway. At first, of course, things seemed very strange. My circumstances were so completely different. But then, everything had changed. Father's great, ruinous tragedy—The shame—The disgrace—

GREGERS *(feelingly):* Yes, yes. I see.

HJALMAR: Of course there was no way in which I could pursue my studies. There wasn't a penny left. Rather the opposite; there was debt. Mainly to your father, I think.

GREGERS: H'm—

HJALMAR: Well—then I thought it best to take the bull by the horns and make a clean break with the past—you know, all at once. Your father thought so, too, and since he had been so helpful, and—

GREGERS: Father helped you?

HJALMAR: Yes, surely you know that? Where do you think I got the money to learn photography and to set up my own studio? Things like that are expensive, I can tell you.

GREGERS: And father paid for all that?

HJALMAR: Yes, didn't you know? I understood him to say he had written to you about it.

GREGERS: Not a word that it was *he*. He must have forgotten. We only write business letters. So it was father—!

HJALMAR: It certainly was. But he has never wanted people to know that. It was he who made it possible for me to get married, too. Or maybe—maybe you didn't know that, either?

GREGERS: No! How could I? *(Shakes HJALMAR's arm.)* My dear Hjalmar, I can't tell you how happy all this makes me—and pains me, too. Perhaps I have been unfair to father. In some respects, anyway. For this shows he has a heart, you know. A kind of conscience—

HJALMAR: Conscience?

GREGERS: Or whatever you want to call it. No, really, I can't tell you how glad I am to hear this about father.—So you are married, Hjalmar. That's more than I ever will be. I trust you find yourself happy as a married man?

HJALMAR: Yes, I certainly do. She is as good and competent a wife as any man could ask for. And she is by no means without culture.

GREGERS *(a little taken aback)*: No, of course not.

HJALMAR: Life itself is an education, you see. Being with me every day—And then there are a couple of remarkable men we see quite a lot of. I assure you, you'd hardly recognize Gina.

GREGERS: Gina?

HJALMAR: Yes. Surely you remember her name was Gina?

GREGERS: Whose name? I haven't the slightest idea—

HJALMAR: But don't you remember she was here in the house for a while?

GREGERS *(looks at him)*: Is it Gina Hansen—?

HJALMAR: Of course it is Gina Hansen.

GREGERS: —who kept house for us the last year of mother's illness?

HJALMAR: That's it. But my dear friend, I know for a fact that your father wrote you about my marriage.

GREGERS *(who has risen)*: Yes, so he did, that's true, but not that— *(paces the floor)*. Wait a minute—Yes, he did—now when I think back. But father always writes such short letters. *(Sits down on the arm of the chair.)* Listen, Hjalmar—this interests me—how did you make Gina's acquaintance—your wife, I mean?

HJALMAR: Quite simply. You remember she didn't stay here very long. Everything was so unsettled during your mother's illness. Gina couldn't take that, so she gave notice and moved out. That was the year before your mother died. Or maybe it was the same year.

GREGERS: It was the same year. I was up at Høydal at the time. Then what happened?

HJALMAR: Well, Gina moved in with her mother, Madam Hansen, an excellent, hardworking woman, who ran a small eating place. And she had a room for rent, too. A nice, comfortable room.

GREGERS: Which you were lucky enough to get?

HJALMAR: Yes. Through your father, in fact. And it was there I really learned to know Gina.

GREGERS: And then you got engaged?

HJALMAR: Yes. It's easy for young people to fall in love, you know. H'm—

GREGERS *(gets up, walks up and down):* Tell me—after you'd become engaged, was that when father—I mean, was that when you took up photography?

HJALMAR: That's right. Naturally, I wanted to get married and have a place of my own, the sooner the better. And both your father and I agreed that photography was the best thing I could get into. Gina thought so, too. Oh yes, that was another reason. It so happened that Gina had learned how to retouch.

GREGERS: What a wonderful coincidence.

HJALMAR *(smiling contentedly):* Yes, wasn't it? Don't you think it worked out very well?

GREGERS: Remarkably well, I should say. So father has really been a kind of Providence for you, Hjalmar; hasn't he?

HJALMAR *(moved):* He did not abandon his old friend's son in his days of need. That's one thing about your father: he does have a heart.

MRS. SØRBY *(enters on* WERLE'S *arm):* I don't want to hear another word, my dear sir. You are not to stay in there staring at all those bright lights. It isn't good for you.

WERLE *(letting go of her arm and moving his hand across his eyes):* I almost think you are right.

*(*PETTERSEN *and* JENSEN *enter carrying trays with glasses of punch.)*

MRS. SØRBY *(to the guests in the drawing room):* Gentlemen, if you want a glass of punch, you'll have to take the trouble to come in here.

THE FLABBY GENTLEMAN *(to* MRS. SØRBY*):* Dear Mrs. Sørby, please tell me it isn't so. You have not withdrawn your cherished permission to smoke?

MRS. SØRBY: Yes, Chamberlain. No smoking here in Mr. Werle's own sanctum.

THE THIN-HAIRED GENTLEMAN: And when did you append these harsh paragraphs to the tobacco regulations, Mrs. Sørby?

MRS. SØRBY: After the last dinner, Chamberlain, when certain persons abused their liberties.

THE THIN-HAIRED GENTLEMAN: And will not even the smallest infraction be tolerated, Mrs. Sørby? Really none at all?

MRS. SØRBY: None whatsoever, Chamberlain.

(Most of the guests are gathered in the study. The servants are serving punch.)

WERLE *(to* HJALMAR, *over by a table):* Well, Ekdal, what is that you are looking at?

HJALMAR: Oh, just an album, sir.

THE THIN-HAIRED GENTLEMAN *(moving about):* Ah yes! Photographs! That's your line, of course.

THE FLABBY GENTLEMAN *(seated):* Haven't you brought some of your own along?

HJALMAR: No, I haven't.

THE FLABBY GENTLEMAN: Too bad. Looking at pictures is good for the digestion, you know.

THE THIN-HAIRED GENTLEMAN: And then it would have contributed a mite to the general entertainment.

A NEARSIGHTED GENTLEMAN: And all contributions are gratefully received.

MRS. SØRBY: The chamberlains think that when one has been invited to dinner, one ought to work for one's food, Mr. Ekdal.

THE FLABBY GENTLEMAN: With a cuisine like this that's only a pleasure.

THE THIN-HAIRED GENTLEMAN: Oh well, if it's a question of the struggle for existence—

MRS. SØRBY: You are so right!

(They continue their conversation, laughing and joking.)

GREGERS *(in a low voice):* You must join in, Hjalmar.

HJALMAR *(with a twist of his body):* What am I to say?

THE FLABBY GENTLEMAN: Don't you believe, sir, that Tokay may be considered relatively beneficial to the stomach?

WERLE *(by the fireplace):* I'll guarantee the Tokay you were served tonight, at any rate. It is one of the very best years. I am sure you noticed that yourself.

THE FLABBY GENTLEMAN: Yes, it really was unusually delicate-tasting.

HJALMAR *(hesitantly):* Do the years differ?

THE FLABBY GENTLEMAN *(laughs):* Ah, Mr. Ekdal! Splendid!

WERLE *(with a smile):* I see it is hardly worth while to serve you fine wine.

THE THIN-HAIRED GENTLEMAN: Tokay is like photographs, Mr. Ekdal. Both need sunshine. Or isn't that so?

HJALMAR: Yes, sunshine has something to do with it.

MRS. SØRBY: Just the same with chamberlains. They need sunshine, too—royal sunshine, as the saying goes.

THE THIN-HAIRED GENTLEMAN: Ouch! That's a tired old joke, Mrs. Sørby.

THE NEARSIGHTED GENTLEMAN: The lady will have her fun—

THE FLABBY GENTLEMAN: —and at our expense. *(Wagging his finger.)* Madam Bertha! Madam Bertha!

MRS. SØRBY: But it is true that vintages differ widely sometimes. The older the better.

THE NEARSIGHTED GENTLEMAN: Do you count me among the older vintages?

MRS. SØRBY: Far from it.

THE THIN-HAIRED GENTLEMAN: Well, well! But what about me, Mrs. Sørby?

THE FLABBY GENTLEMAN: And me? What vintages do we belong to?

MRS. SØRBY: I reckon you among the sweet vintages, gentlemen.

(She sips a glass of punch. The chamberlains laugh and flirt with her.)

WERLE: Mrs. Sørby always finds a way out—when she wants to. But gentlemen, you aren't drinking! Pettersen, please see to it that—! Gregers, let's have a glass together.

(GREGERS does not move.)

Won't you join us, Ekdal? I had no opportunity at the table—

(GRÅBERG comes in through the office door.)

GRÅBERG: Beg your pardon, Mr. Werle, but I can't get out.

WERLE: They've locked you in again, eh?

GRÅBERG: Yes, they have, sir. And Flakstad has left with the keys.

WERLE: That's all right. You just come through here.

GRÅBERG: But there is somebody else—
WERLE: Doesn't matter. Come on, both of you.

(GRÅBERG and OLD EKDAL enter from the office.)

WERLE *(involuntarily):* Damn!

(Laughter and talk among the guests cease. HJALMAR gives a start when he sees his father, puts down his glass, and turns away toward the fireplace.)

EDKAL *(does not look up but makes quick little bows to both sides, as he mutters):* Beg pardon. Came the wrong way. Gate's locked. Gate's locked. Beg pardon. *(He and GRÅBERG go out, rear right.)*

WERLE *(between his teeth):* That idiot Gråberg!

GREGERS *(staring, his mouth hanging open, to HJALMAR):* Don't tell me that was—!

THE FLABBY GENTLEMAN: What is it? Who was that?

GREGERS: Nothing. Just the bookkeeper and somebody else.

THE NEARSIGHTED GENTLEMAN *(to HJALMAR):* Did *you* know that man?

HJALMAR: I don't know—I didn't notice—

THE FLABBY GENTLEMAN *(getting up):* What the devil has gotten into everybody? *(He walks over to some other guests, who are talking in low voices.)*

MRS. SØRBY *(whispers to the servant):* Give him something from the kitchen to take home. Something good.

PETTERSEN *(nods his head):* I'll do that, ma'am. *(Goes out.)*

GREGERS *(shocked, in a low voice to HJALMAR):* Then it really was he?

HJALMAR: Yes.

GREGERS: And you stood there and denied him!

HJALMAR *(in a fierce whisper):* But how *could* I—?

GREGERS: —acknowledge your own father?

HJALMAR *(pained):* Oh, if you had been in my place, maybe—

(The low conversation among the guests changes to forced gaiety.)

THE THIN-HAIRED GENTLEMAN *(approaching HJALMAR and GREGERS, in a friendly mood):* Aha! Reminiscing about university days, gentlemen?—Don't you smoke, Mr. Ekdal? Can I give you a light? Oh that's right. We are not allowed—

HJALMAR: Thanks, I don't smoke.

THE FLABBY GENTLEMAN: Don't you have a nice little poem you could recite for us, Mr. Ekdal? You used to do that so beautifully.

HJALMAR: I am sorry. I don't remember any.

THE FLABBY GENTLEMAN: That's a shame. Well, in that case, Balle, what do we do?

(They both walk into the drawing room.)

HJALMAR *(gloomily):* Gregers—I am leaving! You see, when a man has felt Fate's crushing blow—Say goodbye to your father for me.

GREGERS: Yes, of course. Are you going straight home?

HJALMAR: Yes. Why?

GREGERS: I thought I might come up and see you a little later.

HJALMAR: No, don't do that. Not to my home. My home is a gloomy one, Gregers, particularly after a brilliant banquet such as this. We can meet somewhere in town.

MRS. SØRBY *(has come up to them; in a low voice):* Are you leaving, Ekdal?

HJALMAR: Yes.

MRS. SØRBY: Say hello to Gina.

HJALMAR: Thank you. I'll do that.

MRS. SØRBY: Tell her I'll be up to see her one of these days.

HJALMAR: Fine. *(To* GREGERS*)* You stay here. I'll slip out without anybody noticing. *(Drifts off. A little later he goes into the drawing room and out right.)*

MRS. SØRBY *(in a low voice to the servant who has returned):* Well, did you give the old man something?

PETTERSEN: Oh yes. A bottle of brandy.

MRS. SØRBY: Oh dear. Couldn't you have found something better?

PETTERSEN: But Mrs. Sørby, there's nothing he likes better than brandy.

THE FLABBY GENTLEMAN *(in the doorway to the drawing room, with a sheet of music in his hand):* Will you play a duet, Mrs. Sørby?

MRS. SØRBY: Yes, gladly.

THE GUESTS: Good! Good!

(She and all the guests go out rear right. GREGERS *remains standing by the fireplace.* WERLE *is looking for something on the desk and appears to wish to be left alone. Since* GREGERS *does not leave,* WERLE *walks towards the drawing room door.)*

GREGERS: Father, do you have a moment?

WERLE *(stops):* What is it?

GREGERS: I'd like a word with you.

WERLE: Couldn't it wait till we're alone?

GREGERS: No, it can't, for maybe we'll never be alone again.

WERLE *(coming closer):* What does that mean?

(During the following scene, the sound of a piano is faintly heard from the music room.)

GREGERS: How is it that family has been allowed to go to ruin so miserably?

WERLE: I suppose you refer to the Ekdals?

GREGERS: Yes, I do mean the Ekdals. Lieutenant Ekdal was once your close friend.

WERLE: Yes, unfortunately. Too close. I have felt that keenly enough for many years. It was his fault that my good name and reputation, too, were—somewhat tarnished.

GREGERS *(in a low voice):* Was he the only one who was guilty?

WERLE: Who else, do you mean?

GREGERS: The two of you were together on that big purchase of forest land, weren't you?

WERLE: But it was Ekdal who surveyed the area—surveyed it fraudulently. It was he who felled all that timber on state property. He was responsible for everything that went on up there. I didn't know what he was doing.

GREGERS: I doubt that Lieutenant Ekdal himself knew what he was doing.

WERLE: That may well be. The fact remains that he was convicted and I was not.

GREGERS: Yes, I know there were no proofs.

WERLE: Acquittal is acquittal. Why do you want to bring back that miserable old business that gave me gray hairs before my time? Is that what has been on your mind all these years up there? I can assure you, Gregers, here in town that whole story has been forgotten long ago, as far as *I* am concerned.

GREGERS: But what about that unfortunate family?

WERLE: Well, now, exactly what do you want me to do for those people? When Ekdal got out, he was a broken man, beyond help altogether. Some people go to the bottom as soon as they've got some buckshot in them and never come up again. Believe me, Gregers, I've done all I possibly could do, if I didn't want to put myself in a false light and give people occasion for all sorts of talk and suspicion—

GREGERS: Suspicion? I see.

WERLE: I have given Ekdal copying work to do for the office, and I pay him far, far more than he is worth.

GREGERS *(without looking at him):* H'm. I don't doubt that.

WERLE: You are laughing? Don't you think I am telling you the truth? Oh, to be sure, you won't find it in my books. I never enter expenses like that.

GREGERS *(with a cold smile):* No, I suppose there are certain expenses that are better not entered.

WERLE *(puzzled):* What do you mean?

GREGERS *(being brave):* Have you entered what it cost you to let Hjalmar Ekdal learn photography?

WERLE: I? What do you mean—entered?

GREGERS: I know now it was you who paid for it. And I also know it was you who set him up in business—quite comfortably, too.

WERLE: All right! And you still say I have done nothing for the Ekdals! I assure you, Gregers, those people have cost me a pretty penny!

GREGERS: Have you entered those expenses?

WERLE: Why do you ask?

GREGERS: I have my reasons. Listen—at the time you were providing so kindly for your old friend's son, wasn't that just when he was getting married?

WERLE: Damn it, Gregers! How can I remember—! After so many years—!

GREGERS: You wrote me a letter at the time. A business letter, of course. And in a postscript you mentioned very briefly that Hjalmar Ekdal had married one Miss Hansen.

WERLE: That's right. That was her name.

GREGERS: But you did not say anything about Miss Hansen being Gina Hansen, our ex-housekeeper.

WERLE *(with scornful but forced laughter):* No, to tell the truth, it didn't occur to me that you were particularly interested in our ex-housekeeper.

GREGERS: I wasn't. But— *(Lowers his voice.)* somebody else in this house was.

WERLE: What do you mean? *(Flaring up.)* Don't tell me you're referring to me!

GREGERS *(in a low but firm voice):* Yes, I am referring to you.

WERLE: And you dare—! You have the audacity—! How can that ingrate, that—that photographer fellow—how dare he make accusations like that!

GREGERS: Hjalmar hasn't said a word. I don't think he has the faintest suspicion of anything like this.

WERLE: Then where do you get it from? Who could have said a thing like that?

GREGERS: My poor, unfortunate mother. The last time I saw her.

WERLE: Your mother! I might have thought so! You and she—you always stood together. It was she who first turned you against me.

GREGERS: No, it was all she had to go through, till things became too much for her and she died in sheer misery.

WERLE: Oh, nonsense! She didn't have to go through anything! No more than what others have had to, anyway. There's just no way of getting on with morbid, hysterical people—that's something *I* have had to learn! And here you are, with a suspicion like that—dabbling in old rumors and gossip against your own father. Listen here, Gregers. It really seems to me that at your age you might find something more useful to do.

GREGERS: Yes, it is about time.

WERLE: Then maybe your mind would be more at ease than it seems to be now. What is the point of working away, year in and year out, as just an ordinary clerk up there at Høydal, with not so much as a penny beyond regular wages? It's plain silly!

GREGERS: I wish I could believe that.

WERLE: Not that I don't understand, mind you. You want to be independent, don't want to be obliged to me for anything. But right now there is a chance for you to become independent, to be on your own in everything.

GREGERS: Oh? How so?

WERLE: When I wrote you that I needed you here in town right away—h'm—

GREGERS: Yes, what is it you want of me? I've been waiting to hear all day.

WERLE: I am offering you a partnership in the firm.

GREGERS: I! In your firm? As a partner?

WERLE: Yes. That doesn't mean we have to be together all the time. You could take over the business here in town and I could go up to Høydal.

GREGERS: You would want to do that?

WERLE: Well, you see, Gregers. I can't work as well as I used to. I'll have to save my eyes. They are getting weaker.

GREGERS: You have always had weak eyes.

WERLE: Not as bad as now. Besides—there are other things, too, that may make it advisable for me to live up there—for a while, anyway.

GREGERS: Nothing like this has ever even occurred to me.

WERLE: Look here, Gregers. I know there are many things that stand between us. But after all, we are father and son. It seems to me we ought to be able to come to some sort of understanding.

GREGERS: For appearance's sake, I suppose you mean.

WERLE: Well, that would be something, anyway. Think it over, Gregers. Wouldn't that be possible? What do you say?

GREGERS *(looks at him coldly):* There is something behind this.

WERLE: I don't understand.

GREGERS: You want to use me for something.

WERLE: In a relationship as close as ours I suppose one person can always be of use to the other.

GREGERS: Yes. So they say.

WERLE: I want to have you at home with me for a while. I am a lonely man, Gregers. I have always been lonely, but mostly now, when I am getting older. I need somebody around me.

GREGERS: You have Mrs. Sørby.

WERLE: So I do, and she has become almost indispensable to me. She is bright, she has an even temper, she brings life into the house—and I badly need that.

GREGERS: Well, then, everything is just as you want it.

WERLE: Yes, but I am afraid it won't last. A woman in her circumstances can easily have her position misconstrued in the eyes of the world. I'll almost go so far as to say it does a man no good either.

GREGERS: Oh, I don't know. When a man gives the kind of dinner parties you do he can take quite a few liberties.

WERLE: Yes, but what about *her*, Gregers? I am afraid she will not put up with it much longer. And even if she did, even if she ignored what people are saying and all that sort of thing, out of devotion to me—Do you really think, Gregers, you with your strong sense of justice, do you feel it would be—

GREGERS *(interrupting)*: Just tell me this: are you going to marry her?

WERLE: What if I did? What then?

GREGERS: That's what I am asking. What then?

WERLE: Would it displease you very much?

GREGERS: No, not at all.

WERLE: Well, you see, I didn't know—I thought perhaps out of regard for your mother—

GREGERS: I am not given to melodramatics.

WERLE: Well, whether you are or not, you have lifted a stone from my heart. I can't tell you how pleased I am that I can count on your support in this matter.

GREGERS *(looks intently at him)*: Now I see what you want to use me for.

WERLE: Use you for? What an expression!

GREGERS: Let's not be particular in our choice of words—not as long as we're by ourselves, at any rate. *(Laughs.)* So that's it. That's why I had to come to town at all costs. Because of Mrs. Sørby, there are arrangements being made for family life in this house. Touching scene between father and son! That would indeed be something new!

WERLE: I won't have you use that tone!

GREGERS: When were we ever a family here? Never in my memory. But now, of course, there is need for a display of domestic affection. It will look very well to have the son hastening home on wings of filial feeling to attend the aging father's marriage feast. What happens then to all the talk of what the poor, deceased mother had to suffer? It evaporates. Her son takes care of that.

WERLE: Gregers, I don't believe there is anyone you detest as much as me.

GREGERS *(in a low voice)*: I have seen too much of you.

WERLE: You've seen me with your mother's eyes. *(Lowers his voice a little.)* But don't forget that those eyes were—clouded at times.

GREGERS *(his voice trembles)*: I know what you have in mind. But who's to blame for mother's tragic weakness? You and all those—! The last one was that female you palmed off on Hjalmar Ekdal, when you yourself no longer—!

WERLE *(shrugs his shoulders)*: Word for word as if I were hearing your mother.

GREGERS *(paying no attention)*: —and there he is now, with his great, trusting child's soul in the middle of all this deceit—sharing his roof with a woman like that, unaware that what he calls his home is based on a lie! *(Steps closer to* WERLE.*)* When I look back upon all you have done, I seem to see a battlefield strewn with mangled human destinies.

WERLE: I almost think the gap between us is too wide.

GREGERS *(with a formal bow):* So I have observed. That is why I take my hat and leave.
WERLE: You're leaving? The house?
GREGERS: Yes. For now at last I see a mission to live for.
WERLE: What mission is that?
GREGERS: You'd only laugh if I told you.
WERLE: A lonely man doesn't laugh so easily, Gregers.
GREGERS *(pointing to the rear):* Look, father. The chamberlains are playing blindman's buff with Mrs. Sørby.—Goodnight and good-bye.

(He goes out rear right. The sound of people talking, laughing, and playing games can be heard from the drawing room, where the guests are now coming into view.)

WERLE *(mutters scornfully):* Hah—! The fool! And he says he is not melodramatic!

ACT II

(HJALMAR EKDAL's studio, a large attic room. To the right, a slanting roof with skylights, half covered by blue cloth. The entrance door from the hallway is in the far right corner; the door to the living room farther forward on the same wall. There are two doors to the left, as well, with an iron stove between them. In the rear, wide, sliding, double doors. The studio is unpretentious but cozy. Between the two doors on the right and a little out from the wall is a sofa with a table and some chairs in front of it. On the table is a lighted lamp with a shade. Near the wall by the stove is an old armchair. Various pieces of photographic equipment here and there in the room. In the rear, to the left of the sliding doors, a shelf with a few books, bottles with chemical solutions, tools, and some other objects. Photographs, brushes, paper, etc., are lying on the table.

GINA EKDAL sits by the table, sewing. HEDVIG sits on the sofa, reading, her hands shading her eyes, her thumbs in her ears.)

GINA *(glances at HEDVIG a few times, as if secretly anxious):* Hedvig!
HEDVIG *(does not hear.)*
GINA *(louder):* Hedvig!
HEDVIG *(takes away her hands and looks up):* Yes, mother?
GINA: Hedvig, be a good girl. Don't read any more tonight.
HEDVIG: Please, mother, just a little bit longer? Can't I?
GINA: No. I want you to put that book away. Your father doesn't like you to read so much. He never reads at night.
HEDVIG *(closing her book):* Well, father doesn't care much for reading, anyway.
GINA *(puts her sewing aside and picks up a pencil and a small notebook from the table):* Do you remember how much we spent for the butter today?
HEDVIG: One crown and sixty-five øre.
GINA: That's right. *(Writes it down.)* We're using an awful lot of butter in this family. Then there was the sausage and the cheese—let me see— *(writing)* —and the ham— *(mumbles figures while adding up).* Goodness! it does add up—
HEDVIG: And the beer.
GINA: Right. *(Writes.)* It gets terrible expensive, but it can't be helped.

HEDVIG: And you and I didn't need anything hot for supper since father was out.

GINA: No, that's right. That helps some. And I did get eight crowns and fifty øre for the pictures.

HEDVIG: Was it that much?

GINA: Eight-fifty, exactly.

(Silence. GINA *picks up her sewing.* HEDVIG *takes paper and pencil and starts drawing, her left hand shading her eyes.)*

HEDVIG: Isn't it nice to think that father is at that big dinner party at Mr. Werle's?

GINA: Can't rightly say he's *his* guest. It was the son who invited him. *(After a pause.)* We have nothing to do with the old man.

HEDVIG: I can't wait till father comes home. He promised to ask Mrs. Sørby if he could take home something good for me.

GINA: Why yes, you can be sure there are plenty of good things in *that* house.

HEDVIG *(still drawing):* Besides, I think I am a little bit hungry, too.

*(*OLD EKDAL *enters right rear, the brown paper parcel under his arm, another parcel in his coat pocket.)*

GINA: So late you are today, Grandpa.

EKDAL: They'd locked the office. Had to wait for Gråberg. And then I had to go through—h'm—

HEDVIG: Did they give you any more copying to do, Grandpa?

EKDAL: This whole parcel. Look.

GINA: That's nice.

HEDVIG: And you've got another one in your pocket.

EKDAL: What? Oh never mind. That's nothing. *(Puts his walking stick away in the corner.)* This will keep me busy a long time, Gina. *(Slides one of the double doors half open.)* Shhh! *(Peeks into the attic for a while, then he cautiously slides the door shut. Chuckling.)* They're sound asleep the whole lot of 'em. And she herself's in the basket.

HEDVIG: Are you sure she won't be cold in that basket, Grandpa?

EKDAL: Cold? With all that straw? Don't you worry about *that. (Goes towards the door left rear.)* There are matches, aren't there?

GINA: On the dresser.

*(*EKDAL *goes into his room.)*

HEDVIG: It's nice that he got all that new work to do.

GINA: Yes, poor old thing. It will give him a little spending money.

HEDVIG: And he won't be able to stay down at that awful Madam Eriksen's all morning.

GINA: No; there's that, too.

HEDVIG: Do you think they're still at the table?

GINA: Lord knows. Could be.

HEDVIG: Just think of all that delicious food. I'm sure he'll be in a good mood when he comes home. Don't you think so, mother?

GINA: Yes, but what if we could tell him we'd rented the room. Wouldn't that be nice?

HEDVIG: But we don't need that tonight.

GINA: Oh yes we do. We could always use the money. The room is no good to us as it is.

HEDVIG: No, I mean that father will be in a good mood tonight, anyway. It's better to have the room for some other time.

GINA *(looking at her):* You like it when you have something nice to tell father when he comes home nights, don't you?

HEDVIG: It makes things more pleasant.

GINA *(reflectively):* Yes, I guess you're right about that.

(OLD EKDAL enters from his room, heads for the kitchen door, left front.)

GINA *(turning half around in her chair):* Do you need anything in the kitchen, Grandpa?

EKDAL: Yes. But don't you get up. *(Goes out.)*

GINA: I hope he isn't fooling around with the fire out there. *(After a while.)* Hedvig, go out and see what he's doing.

(OLD EKDAL enters with a pitcher of hot water.)

HEDVIG: Getting hot water, Grandpa?

EKDAL: That's right. Got some writing to do, but the ink's as thick as gruel. H'm—

GINA: But hadn't you better have supper first? It's all ready for you in your room.

EKDAL: Never mind supper, Gina. I tell you I'm busy. I don't want anybody coming in to me. Not anybody. H'm.

(He goes into his room. GINA and HEDVIG look at each other.)

GINA *(in a low voice):* I can't think where he got the money from. Can you?

HEDVIG: From Gråberg, maybe.

GINA: No, it wouldn't be that. Gråberg always gives me the money.

HEDVIG: Maybe he got a bottle on credit.

GINA: Him! Who'd give him credit?

(HJALMAR EKDAL, in overcoat and gray hat, enters right.)

GINA *(throws down her sewing, gets up):* Heavens, Ekdal! Home already?

HEDVIG *(getting up at the same time):* Father? So soon!

HJALMAR *(lays down his hat):* Most of them seemed to be leaving now.

HEDVIG: Already?

HJALMAR: Well, it was a dinner party, you know. *(Takes his coat off.)*

GINA: Let me help you.

HEDVIG: Me too. *(They help him off with his coat. GINA hangs it up in the rear.)* Were there many there, father?

HJALMAR: Not too many. About twelve or fourteen at the table.

GINA: Did you get to talk to all of them?

HJALMAR: Oh yes, a little. Though Gregers kept me engaged most of the evening.

GINA: Is he as ugly as he used to be?

HJALMAR: Well—I suppose nobody would call him handsome. Is father back?

HEDVIG: Yes, he is in there writing.
HJALMAR: Did he say anything?
GINA: No. About what?
HJALMAR: He didn't mention—? I thought I heard he'd been with Gråberg. I think I'll go in to him for a moment.
GINA: No, you'd better not.
HJALMAR: Why not? Did he say he didn't want to see me?
GINA: He doesn't want to see anybody.
HEDVIG *(making signs to her)*: Ahem!
GINA *(doesn't notice)*: He's gotten himself some hot water.
HJALMAR: Ah! So he is—
GINA: Looks that way.
HJALMAR: Ah yes—my poor old white-haired father. Let him enjoy his little pleasures as best he can.

(OLD EKDAL, a lighted pipe in his mouth, enters in an old smoking jacket.)

EKDAL: Home again? Thought it was you I heard talking.
HJALMAR: Yes. I just came back.
EKDAL: Guess you didn't see me, did you?
HJALMAR: No, but they told me you'd gone through, so I thought I'd catch up with you.
EKDAL: H'm. That's good of you, Hjalmar. Who were they—all those people?
HJALMAR: Oh—all sorts. Chamberlain Flor and Chamberlain Balle and Chamberlain Kaspersen and chamberlain this and that. I don't know—
EKDAL *(nodding his head)*: Hear that, Gina? He's been with nothing but chamberlains all evening.
GINA: Yes, I hear as they've become quite fancy in that house now.
HEDVIG: Did the chamberlains sing, father? Or recite poetry?
HJALMAR: No. They just talked nonsense. They wanted *me* to recite, though, but I didn't want to.
EKDAL: They couldn't get you to, eh?
GINA: Seems to me you might have done that.
HJALMAR: No. I don't see any reason why one has to oblige every Tom, Dick, and Harry all the time. *(Walks up and down.)* At any rate, I won't.
EKDAL: No point in being too obliging, you know. That's Hjalmar for you.
HJALMAR: I don't see why *I* always have to be the one who provides entertainment on the rare occasions when I am out for dinner. Let the others exert themselves for a change. Those fellows go from one big meal to the next, stuffing themselves day in and day out. Let *them* do something for all the food they are getting!
GINA: You didn't tell them that though, did you?
HJALMAR *(humming a little)*: Well, I don't know about that. They were told a thing or two.
EKDAL: The chamberlains?
HJALMAR: Mmm— *(Casually.)* Then we had a little controversy over Tokay wine.
EKDAL: Tokay, no less! Say, that's a fine wine!
HJALMAR *(stops his walking)*: It *may* be a fine wine. But let me tell you: not all the vintages are equally fine. It depends on how much sunshine the grapes get.
GINA: If you don't know everything—!
EKDAL: And they quarreled with that?

HJALMAR: They tried to, but then it was pointed out to them that it was the same way with chamberlains. Not all vintages are equally fine among chamberlains, either—so they were told.

GINA: Goodness! What you don't think of!

EKDAL: Heh-heh! So they got that to put in their pipe.

HJALMAR: Right to their face. That's how they got it.

EKDAL: Gina, d'ye hear that? He gave it to them right to their face!

GINA: Right to their face! Imagine!

HJALMAR: Yes, but I don't want you to talk about it. One doesn't talk about such things. Of course, the whole thing was done in the friendliest possible way. They are all of them pleasant, easy-going people. Why should I hurt them? No!

EKDAL: Right to their face, though—

HEDVIG *(ingratiatingly):* It's so nice to see you all dressed up, father. You look very well in tails.

HJALMAR: Yes, don't you think so? And it really fits me perfectly. As if it were tailor-made. Possibly a trifle tight in the armpits, that's all. Help me, Hedvig. *(Takes his dinner jacket off.)* I'd rather wear my own coat. Where is it, Gina?

GINA: Here it is. *(Helps him on with it.)*

HJALMAR: There now! Be sure to have Molvik get his suit back first thing in the morning.

GINA *(putting the clothes away):* I'll take care of it.

HJALMAR *(stretching):* Aaahh. This feels cozier after all. And this kind of loose-fitting, casual wear is really more in keeping with my whole appearance; don't you think so, Hedvig?

HEDVIG: Oh yes, father!

HJALMAR: Especially when I tie my neckcloth with loose, flying ends—like this? What do you think?

HEDVIG: Yes, it goes extremely well with your mustache. And with your curls, too.

HJALMAR: I'd hardly call my hair curly. Wavy, rather.

HEDVIG: Yes, for the curls are so large.

HJALMAR: Waves, really.

HEDVIG *(after a moment, pulling his sleeve):* Father?

HJALMAR: What is it?

HEDVIG: Oh, you know very well what it is!

HJALMAR: I certainly don't.

HEDVIG *(laughing and pleading):* Oh come on, father! Don't tease me!

HJALMAR: But what is it?

HEDVIG *(shaking him):* Father! Give it to me! You know, you promised me. Something good to eat.

HJALMAR: Oh, dear! I completely forgot!

HEDVIG: You are only teasing, father. Shame on you! Where is it?

HJALMAR: No, honest, I really did forget. But wait a moment. I have something else for you, Hedvig. *(Goes and searches his coat pockets.)*

HEDVIG *(jumps up and down, clapping her hands):* Oh mother, mother!

GINA: See what I mean? If you just give him time—

HJALMAR *(with a piece of paper):* Here it is.

HEDVIG: That? But that's just a piece of paper.

HJALMAR: It's the menu, Hedvig, the entire menu. Look here. It says "Menu." That means what you get to eat.

HEDVIG: Haven't you anything else for me?

HJALMAR: I tell you, I forgot all about it. But take my word for it: it's not such a great treat, all that rich food. You just sit down and read the menu, now, and I'll tell you later what the things taste like. Here you are, Hedvig.

HEDVIG *(swallowing her tears):* Thank you.

(She sits down but doesn't read. GINA *signals to her.* HJALMAR *notices.)*

HJALMAR *(pacing the floor):* It is really unbelievable all the things a father is supposed to keep in mind. And if he forgets the smallest item—! Long faces right away. Oh well. One gets used to that, too. *(Stops by the stove where* OLD EKDAL *is sitting.)* Have you looked at them tonight, father?

EKDAL: I certainly have! She's in the basket!

HJALMAR: No! Really? In the basket? She is getting used to it then, I guess.

EKDAL: Didn't I tell you she would? But look, Hjalmar, there are still a few things—

HJALMAR: —improvements, yes, I know.

EKDAL: They've got to be done.

HJALMAR: Right. Let's talk about it now, father. Come over here to the sofa.

EKDAL: All right. H'm. Guess I want to fill my pipe first, though. Need to clean it, too—h'm— *(Goes into his room.)*

GINA *(with a smile, to* HJALMAR*):* Cleaning his pipe—

HJALMAR: Oh well, Gina—let him. The poor shipwrecked old man.—About those improvements—We'd better get to them tomorrow.

GINA: You won't have time tomorrow, Ekdal.

HEDVIG *(interrupting):* Oh, yes, mother.

GINA: For remember those prints you were going to retouch? They came for 'em again today.

HJALMAR: I see. It's those prints again, is it? Well, they'll get done. You can be sure of that. Perhaps there are some new orders come in, too?

GINA: Not a thing, worse luck. Tomorrow I've got only those two portraits I told you about.

HJALMAR: Is that all? Well, if one doesn't exert oneself, what can you expect?

GINA: But what can I do? I advertise in the papers all I can, seems to me.

HJALMAR: The papers, the papers—you see yourself how far that gets us. I suppose there hasn't been anyone to look at the room, either?

GINA: No, not yet.

HJALMAR: Just as I thought. Well, no—if one doesn't *do* anything—One has to make a real effort, Gina!

HEDVIG *(going to him):* Shall I get your flute, father?

HJALMAR: No, not the flute. *I* need no pleasures. *(Paces up and down.)* You'll see if I don't work tomorrow! You don't need to worry about *that!* You can be sure I shall work as long as my strength holds out—

GINA: But Ekdal, dear—I didn't mean it that way.

HEDVIG: How about a bottle of beer, father?

HJALMAR: Not at all. I don't need anything— *(Stops.)* Beer? Did you say beer?

HEDVIG *(brightly):* Yes, father; lovely, cool beer.

HJALMAR: Oh well—all right—since you insist, I suppose you may bring me a bottle.

GINA: Yes, do that. That'll be nice and cozy.

*(*HEDVIG *runs towards the kitchen door.)*

HJALMAR *(by the stove, stops her, looks at her, takes her by the head and presses her to him):* Hedvig! Hedvig!

HEDVIG *(happy, in tears):* Oh father! You are so sweet and good!

HJALMAR: No, no, don't say that. There I was—seated at the rich man's table—gorging myself on his ample fare—and I couldn't even remember—

GINA *(seated by the table):* Nonsense, Ekdal.

HJALMAR: It is not nonsense. But you must not reckon too strictly. You know I love you, regardless.

HEDVIG *(throwing her arms around him):* And we love you, father, so much, so much!

HJALMAR: And if I am unreasonable at times, remember—God forgive me—remember I am a man beset by a host of sorrows. Well, well! *(Drying his eyes.)* No beer at such a moment. Give me my flute.

(HEDVIG runs to the shelf and fetches it.)

HJALMAR: Thank you. There now. With my flute in my hand and you two around me—ah!

(HEDVIG sits down by the table next to GINA. HJALMAR walks back and forth, playing a Bohemian folk dance. He plays loudly but in slow tempo and with pronounced sentiment.)

HJALMAR *(interrupts his playing, gives his left hand to GINA, and says with strong emotion):* Our home may be mean and humble, Gina. But it is our home. And I say to you both: here dwells contentment!

(He resumes his playing. Presently there is a knock on the door.)

GINA *(getting up):* Shh, Ekdal. I think somebody's coming.

HJALMAR *(putting the flute back on the shelf):* Yes, yes of course. Somebody would—

(GINA goes to open the door.)

GREGERS WERLE *(out in the hall):* I beg your pardon—

GINA *(taking a step back):* Oh!

GREGERS: —isn't this where Mr. Ekdal lives, the photographer?

GINA: Yes, it is.

HJALMAR *(going to the door):* Gregers! So you did come, after all. Come in.

GREGERS *(entering):* I told you I wanted to see you.

HJALMAR: But tonight—? Have you left the party?

GREGERS: Both party and home. Good evening, Mrs. Ekdal. I don't know if you recognize me.

GINA: Oh yes. Young Mr. Werle isn't hard to recognize.

GREGERS: No, for I look like my mother, and you remember her, I am sure.

HJALMAR: You have left your home?

GREGERS: Yes. I have taken a room at a hotel.

HJALMAR: Really?—Well, since you're here, take off your coat and sit down.

GREGERS: Thanks. *(Removes his overcoat. He has changed clothes and is now dressed in a plain, gray suit, of somewhat unfashionable cut.)*

HJALMAR: Here on the sofa. Make yourself comfortable.

(GREGERS *sits down on the sofa,* HJALMAR *on a chair by the table.)*

GREGERS *(looking around):* So this is your residence, Hjalmar. This is where you live.
HJALMAR: This is the studio, as you can see.
GINA: It's roomier in here, so this is where we mostly keep ourselves.
HJALMAR: The apartment we had before was really nicer than this, but there is one big advantage here: we have plenty of space.
GINA: And we have a room across the hallway that we're renting out.
GREGERS *(to* HJALMAR*):* You have lodgers, too?
HJALMAR: No, not yet. These things take time, you see. One has to be on the lookout. *(To* HEDVIG.*)* What about that beer?

(HEDVIG *nods her head and goes out into the kitchen.)*

GREGERS: So that's your daughter.
HJALMAR: Yes, that's Hedvig.
GREGERS: Your only child, isn't she?
HJALMAR: Our only one. Our greatest joy in the world, and *(lowers his voice)* our greatest sorrow, as well.
GREGERS: What are you saying!
HJALMAR: Yes, Gregers, for there is every probability that she'll lose her sight.
GREGERS: Becoming blind!
HJALMAR: Yes. So far, there are only early symptoms, and things may be well with her for some time yet. But the doctor has warned us. It is coming, irresistibly.
GREGERS: But this is nothing less than a tragedy! How do you account for it?
HJALMAR *(with a sigh):* Heredity, most likely.
GREGERS *(struck):* Heredity?
GINA: Ekdal's mother had weak eyes.
HJALMAR: That's what father says. I of course don't remember her.
GREGERS: Poor child. How does she take it?
HJALMAR: Oh, we can't bring ourselves to tell her—I'm sure you can understand that. She suspects nothing. Joyous and carefree, chirping like a little bird, she'll flutter into life's endless night. *(Overcome by emotion.)* Oh Gregers, this is such a terrible burden for me.

(HEDVIG *enters with a tray with beer and glasses. She puts it down on the table.)*

HJALMAR *(stroking her hair):* Thanks. Thank you, Hedvig.
HEDVIG *(puts her arms around his neck and whispers something in his ear.)*
HJALMAR: No. No sandwiches now. *(Looks off.)* That is—unless Gregers wants some?
GREGERS *(with a gesture of refusal):* No. No thanks.
HJALMAR *(still in a melancholic mood):* Oh well, you might as well bring in some, all the same. A crust, if you have one. And plenty of butter, please.
GREGERS *(who has followed her with his eyes):* Otherwise she seems healthy enough.
HJALMAR: Yes, thank God, there is nothing else wrong with her.
GREGERS: I think she is going to look like you, Mrs. Ekdal. How old is she?
GINA: Hedvig is just about fourteen. Her birthday is day after tomorrow.
GREGERS: Quite big for her age, isn't she?

GINA: Yes, she has grown a lot lately.

GREGERS: It's by the children we tell we're growing older ourselves. How long have you two been married now?

GINA: We've been married for—let's see—fifteen years, pretty near.

GREGERS: Just imagine! Has it really been that long?

GINA *(taking notice, looks at him):* It certainly has.

HJALMAR: That's right. Fifteen years, less a few months. *(Changing topic.)* Those must have been long years for you up there at the works, Gregers.

GREGERS: They were long while they lasted. Now afterwards I hardly know where they went.

(OLD EKDAL enters from his room, without his pipe, but with his old-fashioned lieutenant's cap on his head. His walk is a trifle unsteady.)

EKDAL: I'm ready for you now, Hjalmar. Let's talk about this—h'm—What was it again?

HJALMAR *(going towards him):* Father, there's someone here. Gregers Werle. I don't know if you remember him?

EKDAL *(looks at GREGERS, who has stood up):* Werle? That's the son, isn't it? What does he want from me?

HJALMAR: Nothing. He has come to see me.

EKDAL: Then there's nothing wrong?

HJALMAR: Of course not.

EKDAL *(swinging one arm back and forth):* Not that I am scared, mind you, but—

GREGERS *(goes up to him):* I just wanted to bring you greetings from your old hunting grounds, Lieutenant Ekdal.

EKDAL: Hunting grounds?

GREGERS: Yes, the woods up around the Høydal works.

EKDAL: Oh yes, up there. Yes, I used to know that country quite well in the old days.

GREGERS: You were quite a hunter then, weren't you?

EKDAL: Could be. Maybe I was. You're looking at my get-up. I don't ask anybody's permission to wear it in the house. Just as long as I don't go outside—

(HEDVIG brings a plate with open-faced sandwiches, which she puts down on the table.)

HJALMAR: You sit down, father, and have a glass of beer. Help yourself, Gregers.

(EKDAL mutters something and shuffles over to the sofa. GREGERS sits down on a chair next to him; HJALMAR is on the other side of GREGERS. GINA sits some distance from the table, sewing. HEDVIG is standing by her father.)

GREGERS: Do you remember, Lieutenant Ekdal, when Hjalmar and I used to come up and visit you summers and Christmas?

EKDAL: You did? No; can't say as I do. But it's true I used to be a good hunter, if I do say so myself. I've killed bears, too. Nine of 'em.

GREGERS *(looks at him with compassion):* And now your hunting days are over.

EKDAL: Oh—I wouldn't say that. I still go hunting once in a while. Well, yes, not in the old way, of course. For you see, the woods—the woods—the woods—! *(Drinks.)* Nice-looking woods up there now?

GREGERS: Not as in your time. They have cut a great deal.

EKDAL: Cut? *(In a lower voice and as if afraid.)* That's risky business, that is. It has consequences. The woods are vengeful.

HJALMAR *(filling his glass):* Here, father. Have some more.

GREGERS: How can a man like you—such an outdoors man as you used to be—how can you stand living here in the middle of a musty city, within four walls?

EKDAL *(chuckles, glancing at* HJALMAR*):* Oh, it's not so bad here. Not bad at all.

GREGERS: But surely—all the things your soul grew used to up there—? The cool, invigorating breezes? The free life in woods and mountains, among beasts and birds—?

EKDAL *(smiling):* Hjalmar, shall we show it to him?

HJALMAR *(quickly, a little embarrassed):* Oh no, father. Not tonight.

GREGERS: What is it he wants to show me?

HJALMAR: Oh, it's just—something. You can see it some other time.

GREGERS *(continues addressing* OLD EKDAL*):* You see, this is what I had in mind, Lieutenant. Why don't you come up to Høydal with me? I'll probably be going back shortly. I'm sure you could get some copying work to do up there as well. For down here you can't have a thing to cheer you up and keep you occupied.

EKDAL *(looks at him in astonishment):* Don't *I* have—!

GREGERS: Yes, of course, you have Hjalmar. But then he has his own family. And a man like you, who have always loved the outdoors—

EKDAL *(striking the table):* Hjalmar, he *shall* see it!

HJALMAR: But father, do you really think so? It's dark and—

EKDAL: Nonsense. There's a moon. *(Getting up.)* I say he's got to see it. Let me out. Come and help me, Hjalmar!

HEDVIG: Oh yes, father! Do!

HJALMAR *(getting up):* Oh well, all right.

GREGERS *(to* GINA*):* What is it?

GINA: Oh, don't expect anything much.

*(*EKDAL *and* HJALMAR *have gone to the rear of the room. Each of them slides one of the double doors back.* HEDVIG *is helping the old man.* GREGERS *remains standing by the sofa.* GINA *keeps on sewing, paying no attention. Through the opened doors can be seen a big, elongated, irregular-shaped attic, with nooks and corners and a couple of chimneys standing free from the wall. Moonlight falls through several skylights, illuminating some parts of the room, while others are in deep shadow.)*

EKDAL *(to* GREGERS*):* You are welcome to come closer, sir.

GREGERS *(goes up to them):* What is this really?

EKDAL: See for yourself. H'm.

HJALMAR *(somewhat embarrassed):* This is all father's, you understand.

GREGERS *(at the door, peering into the attic):* Do you keep chickens, Lieutenant?

EKDAL: Should say we do. They're roosting now. But you ought to see those chickens in daylight!

HEDVIG: And there is—

EKDAL: Hush, don't say anything yet.

GREGERS: And I see you've got pigeons, too.

EKDAL: Could be we have. We've got pigeons, all right! The roosts are up on the rafters, for pigeons like to be up high, you know.

HJALMAR: They aren't all of them just ordinary pigeons.

EKDAL: Ordinary! I should say not! We've got tumblers and even a couple of pouters. But come over here. Do you see that pen over by the wall?

GREGERS: Yes. What do you use that for?

EKDAL: That's where the rabbits are at night.

GREGERS: Oh? You have rabbits, too, do you?

EKDAL: Damn right we have rabbits! He asks if we have rabbits, Hjalmar! H'm. But now we're coming to the *real* thing. Here we are. Move, Hedvig. You stand here and look down—there; that's right. Now, do you see a basket with straw in it?

GREGERS: Yes, I do. And I see a bird.

EKDAL: H'm—A "bird."

GREGERS: Isn't it a duck?

EKDAL *(offended):* I'd say it's a duck!

HJALMAR: But what kind of duck, do you think?

HEDVIG: It's not just an ordinary duck.

EKDAL: Hush!

GREGERS: And it's not a muscovy duck, either.

EKDAL: No, Mr.—Werle; it's not a muscovy, for it's a wild duck!

GREGERS: Is it really? A wild duck?

EKDAL: That's what it is. The—"bird," as you called it. A wild duck. It's our wild duck.

HEDVIG: *My* wild duck. For it belongs to me.

GREGERS: And it lives here in the attic? It's thriving?

EKDAL: What's so odd about that? She's got a big pail of water to splash around in.

HJALMAR: Fresh water every other day.

GINA *(turning to* HJALMAR*):* Ekdal, please. I'm freezing.

EKDAL: H'm. All right; let's close up. Just as well not to disturb their night's rest, anyway. Help me, Hedvig.

*(*HJALMAR *and* HEDVIG *slide the double doors shut.)*

EKDAL: You can have a good look at her some other time. *(Sits down in the armchair by the stove.)* I'm telling you, they are strange birds, those wild ducks.

GREGERS: But how did you ever catch it, Lieutenant?

EKDAL: I didn't. There's a certain man in this town we can thank for her.

GREGERS *(struck by a thought):* Would that man be my father?

EKDAL: Indeed it is. It's your father, sure enough. H'm.

HJALMAR: Funny you'd guess that, Gregers.

GREGERS: You told me before that you owed a great deal to my father, so I thought that perhaps—

GINA: But we didn't get the duck from Werle himself.

EKDAL: It's Håkon Werle we have to thank for her all the same, Gina. *(To* GREGERS.*)* He was out in a boat, see, and took a shot at her. But he doesn't see so well, your father doesn't. H'm. Anyway, she was only wounded.

GREGERS: I see. She got some buckshot in her.

HJALMAR: Yes. A little.

HEDVIG: Right under the wing, so she couldn't fly.

GREGERS: Then she went to the bottom, I suppose.

EKDAL *(sleepily, his voice muffled):* So it did. Always do that, wild ducks. Dive straight to the

bottom—far as they can, sir. Bite themselves fast in the grasses and roots and weeds and all the other damn stuff down there. And never come up again.

GREGERS: But, Lieutenant, *your* wild duck did.

EKDAL: He had such a wonderfully clever dog, your father. And that dog—it went down and got the duck up.

GREGERS *(to* HJALMAR*)*: And so it came to you?

HJALMAR: Not right away. First your father took it home with him, but it didn't seem to get on too well there, and then he told Pettersen to get rid of it.

EKDAL *(half asleep)*: H'm—Pettersen—Ass—

HJALMAR: That's how we got it, for father knows Pettersen a little, and when he heard about the wild duck, he asked Pettersen to give it to him.

GREGERS: And now it seems perfectly contented in there in the attic.

HJALMAR: Yes, you would hardly believe how well it gets on. It's becoming fat. I think perhaps it's been in there so long that it has forgotten what wild life is like. And that makes all the difference.

GREGERS: I am sure you are right, Hjalmar. The thing to do is never to let it look at sea and sky again.—But I don't think I should stay any longer. I believe your father is asleep.

HJALMAR: Oh, as far as that is concerned—

GREGERS: Oh yes, one thing more. You said you had a room for rent? A vacant room?

HJALMAR: We do. What of it? Do you know anyone who—?

GREGERS: Could I get it?

HJALMAR: You?

GINA: Oh, Mr. Werle, I'm sure *you* don't want to—

GREGERS: Couldn't I have it? If I can, I'll move in first thing in the morning.

HJALMAR: Yes, indeed, with the greatest pleasure.

GINA: No, but Mr. Werle, that's not a room for you.

HJALMAR: Gina! How can you say that?

GINA: It's not large enough or light enough, and—

GREGERS: That doesn't matter, Mrs. Ekdal.

HJALMAR: I think it's quite a nice room myself, and decently furnished, too.

GINA: But remember those two downstairs.

GREGERS: Who are they?

GINA: There's one who used to be a private tutor.

HJALMAR: Molvik is his name. He studied to be a minister once.

GINA: And then there's a doctor, name of Relling.

GREGERS: Relling? I know him slightly. He used to practice up at Høydal.

GINA: They are a couple of real wild characters those two. Out all hours of the night, and when they come home they aren't always—y'know—

GREGERS: One gets used to that sort of thing. I hope I'll be like the wild duck.

GINA: H'm. Well, *I* think you ought to sleep on it first.

GREGERS: I take it you don't really want me in the house, Mrs. Ekdal.

GINA: Good Lord! How can you say a thing like that?

HJALMAR: Yes, Gina. It really does seem very odd of you. *(To* GREGERS.*)* Does this mean you'll be staying in town for a while?

GREGERS *(putting on his overcoat)*: Yes, I think I'll stay.

HJALMAR: But not with your father? What do you intend to do?

GREGERS: If I knew that, Hjalmar, I'd be much better off. But when you're cursed with a name like "Gregers"—and then "Werle" after that—Did you ever hear of an uglier name?

HJALMAR: I don't think it's ugly at all.

GREGERS: Ugh! I feel like spitting in the face of anybody with a name like that. But since it's my cross in life to be Gregers Werle, such as I am—

HJALMAR: Ha-ha! If you weren't Gregers Werle, what would you like to be?

GREGERS: If I could choose, I'd like to be a really clever dog.

GINA: A dog!

HEDVIG *(involuntarily):* Oh no!

GREGERS: Yes, an exceptionally skillful dog—the kind that goes down to the bottom after wild ducks when they've dived down among the weeds and the grass down there in the mud.

HJALMAR: Honestly, Gregers. This makes no sense whatever.

GREGERS: I suppose it doesn't. But tomorrow morning, then, I'll be moving in. *(To* GINA.*)* You won't have any trouble with me; I'll do everything myself. *(To* HJALMAR.*)* The other things we can talk about tomorrow.—Goodnight, Mrs. Ekdal. *(Nods to* HEDVIG.*)* Goodnight!

GINA: Goodnight, Mr. Werle.

HEDVIG: Goodnight.

HJALMAR *(who has lighted a candle):* Wait a moment. I'll see you down. I'm sure it's all dark on the stairs.

*(*GREGERS *and* HJALMAR *go out through the entrance door, right rear.)*

GINA *(staring ahead, her sewing lowered in her lap):* Wasn't it funny all that talk about wanting to be a dog?

HEDVIG: Do you know, mother—I think he really meant something else.

GINA: What would that be?

HEDVIG: No, I coudln't say, but it was just like he had something else in mind all the time.

GINA: You think so? It sure was funny, though.

HJALMAR *(returning):* The lamp was still burning. *(Blows out the candle and sits down.)* Ah, at last it's possible to get a bite to eat. *(Starts on the sandwiches.)* Now do you see what I mean, Gina—about seizing the opportunity?

GINA: What opportunity?

HJALMAR: Well—it was lucky, wasn't it, that we got the room rented? And then to somebody like Gregers, a dear old friend.

GINA: Well, I don't know what to say to that.

HEDVIG: Oh mother, you'll see it will be fun.

HJALMAR: I must say you are strange. First you wanted nothing more than to get a lodger; then when we do, you don't like it.

GINA: I know, Ekdal. If only it had been somebody else. What do you think old Werle will say?

HJALMAR: He? It's none of his business.

GINA: But don't you see that something's bound to be wrong between the two of 'em, since the young one is moving out. Sure you know how those two are.

HJALMAR: That may be so, but—

GINA: And maybe Werle will think you are behind it!

HJALMAR: All right! Let him think that. Oh, by all means, Werle has done a great deal for me—I'm the first to admit it. But that doesn't mean I everlastingly have to let him run my life.

GINA: But Ekdal, dear, it could hurt Grandpa. Perhaps he'll lose what little he's making from working for Gråberg.

HJALMAR: I almost wish he would! Is it not humiliating for a man like me to see his gray-haired father treated like dirt? Ah, but soon now the time will be ripe. I feel it. *(Takes another sandwich.)* As sure as I have a mission in life, it shall be accomplished!

HEDVIG: Oh yes, father!

GINA: Shhh! Don't wake him up.

HJALMAR *(in a lower voice):* I say it again: I *will* accomplish it! The day will come, when— That's why it's such a good thing we got the room rented out, for that makes me more independent. And that's necessary for a man with a mission in life. *(Over by the armchair, with feeling.)* Poor old white-haired father. Trust your Hjalmar. He has broad enough shoulders—powerful shoulders, at any rate. Some day you'll wake up, and— *(to GINA.)* Or don't you believe that?

GINA *(getting up):* Sure I do, but let's first get him to bed.

HJALMAR: Yes, let us.

(They tenderly lift the old man.)

ACT III

(The studio. It is morning. Daylight comes in through the skylight, the blue cloth having been pulled aside.

HJALMAR *sits at the table, retouching a photograph. Several other photographs are lying in front of him. After a while,* GINA, *in coat and hat, enters from outside. She is carrying a covered basket.)*

HJALMAR: Back already, Gina?

GINA: Yes. I'm in a hurry. *(Puts the basket down on a chair and takes off her coat and hat.)*

HJALMAR: Did you look in at Gregers's?

GINA: I did. It looks real nice in there. He fixed up the place real pretty, soon as he moved in.

HJALMAR: Oh?

GINA: Remember, he was to take care of everything himself? Well, he built a fire in the stove, but he hadn't opened the flue, so the whole room got filled with smoke. Phew! It smelled like—

HJALMAR: Oh dear—

GINA: Then do you know what he does? This really beats everything. He wanted to put out the fire, so he pours the water from the wash basin into the stove. The whole floor is sloppy with filth!

HJALMAR: I am sorry.

GINA: I've got the janitor's wife to clean up after him, pig as he is, but the room can't be lived in till this afternoon.

HJALMAR: Where is he now?

GINA: He said he was going out for a while.

HJALMAR: I went in there for a moment, too—right after you had left.

GINA: He told me. You've asked him for breakfast.

HJALMAR: Just a bit of a late morning meal. It's the first day and all. We can hardly do less. I am sure you have something.

GINA: I'll have to find something, at any rate.

HJALMAR: Be sure it's plenty, though. I think Relling and Molvik are coming, too. I ran into Relling on the stairs just now, and so of course I had to—

GINA: So we are to have those two as well.

HJALMAR: Good heavens, one or two more or less—can that make any difference?

EKDAL *(opens his door and looks in)*: Listen, Hjalmar— *(Sees* GINA.*)* Well, never mind.

GINA: Do you want something, Grandpa?

EKDAL: No. It doesn't matter. H'm! *(Goes back inside his room.)*

GINA *(picking up her basket)*: Make sure he doesn't go out.

HJALMAR: Yes, I will.—Say, Gina—how about some herring salad? I believe Relling and Molvik made a night of it again last night.

GINA: If only they don't get here too soon.

HJALMAR: I'm sure they won't. Just take your time.

GINA: Well, all right. Then you can work some in the meantime.

HJALMAR: I *am* working! I'm working as hard as I can!

GINA: All I mean is you'd have it out of the way for later. *(Goes into the kitchen.)*

*(*HJALMAR *picks up the photograph and the brush and works for a while—slowly and with evident distaste.)*

EKDAL *(peeks in, looks around, says in a low voice)*: Pst! Are you busy?

HJALMAR: Yes. I am struggling with these everlasting pictures—

EKDAL: All right, all right. If you're busy, then you're busy. H'm! *(Goes back inside his room. The door remains open.)*

HJALMAR *(works in silence for a while, puts his brush down, walks over to* EKDAL*'s door)*: Are *you* busy, father?

EKDAL *(grumbling inside his room)*: When *you* are busy, *I* am busy! H'm!

HJALMAR: Oh all right. *(Returns to his work.)*

EKDAL *(appears in his door again after a while)*: H'm, Hjalmar, listen—I'm not so *terribly* busy, you know.

HJALMAR: I thought you were writing.

EKDAL: Dammit all! Can't that Gråberg wait a day or two? Didn't think it was a matter of life and death.

HJALMAR: Of course not. And you aren't a slave, after all.

EKDAL: And there is this other job in there—

HJALMAR: Just what I was thinking. Do you want to go in there now? Shall I open the door for you?

EKDAL: Good idea.

HJALMAR *(getting up)*: Then we'd have that job out of the way.

EKDAL: Exactly. It has to be ready for tomorrow, anyway. It *is* tomorrow, isn't it?

HJALMAR: Sure it's tomorrow.

(They slide the double doors open. The morning sun is shining through the skylight. Some pigeons are flying around; others are cooing on their perches. From farther inside the room the chickens are heard clucking once in a while.)

HJALMAR: All right, father. Guess you can go ahead.
EKDAL *(entering the attic):* Aren't you coming?
HJALMAR: Yes, do you know—I almost think I will. *(Notices* GINA *in the kitchen door.)* I? No, I don't have the time. I have to work. But then there is this thing—

(He pulls a cord. A curtain comes down from within the attic. Its lower part is made out of a strip of old sailcloth; its upper part is a piece of stretched-out fish net. The attic floor is now no longer visible.)

HJALMAR *(returns to the table):* Now! Maybe I can have peace for a few minutes.
GINA: Is he fooling around in there again?
HJALMAR: Would you rather he went down to Madam Eriksen? *(Sitting down.)* Do you want anything? I thought you said—
GINA: I just wanted to ask you if you think we can set the table in here?
HJALMAR: Yes. There aren't any appointments this early, are there?
GINA: No—only those two sweethearts who want their picture taken.
HJALMAR: Damn! Couldn't they come some other time!
GINA: Goodness, Ekdal, they'll be here after dinner, when you're asleep.
HJALMAR: Oh, in that case it's all right. Yes, let's eat in here.
GINA: Fine. But there's no hurry with the table. You're welcome to use it some more.
HJALMAR: Can't you see I *am* using it?
GINA: Then you'll be all done for afterwards, you know. *(Goes into the kitchen.)*

(Brief silence.)

EKDAL *(in the door to the attic, inside the fish net):* Hjalmar!
HJALMAR: What?
EKDAL: Afraid we'll have to move the pail, after all.
HJALMAR: What else have I been saying all along?
EKDAL: H'm—h'm—h'm! *(Disappears inside again.)*
HJALMAR *(keeps on working for a moment, glances over towards the attic, half rises, as* HEDVIG *enters from the kitchen. He quickly sits down again):* What do you want?
HEDVIG: Just to be with you, father.
HJALMAR *(after a short while):* Seems to me like you're snooping around. Have you been told to watch me, perhaps?
HEDVIG: No, of course not.
HJALMAR: What is mother doing?
HEDVIG: Mother is in the middle of the herring salad. *(Comes over to the table.)* Isn't there any little thing I can help you with, father?
HJALMAR: Oh no. It is better I do it all alone—as long as my strength lasts. There is no need for you to worry about anything, Hedvig, as long as your father is allowed to keep his health.
HEDVIG: Oh father. I won't have you talk that horrid way. *(She walks around a bit, stops by the opening to the inner room and looks in.)*
HJALMAR: What is he doing in there?
HEDVIG: Looks like a new ladder up to the water pail.
HJALMAR: He'll never manage that by himself! And here I am condemned to sit—!

HEDVIG *(goes to him):* Give me the brush, father. I can do it.

HJALMAR: I won't hear of it. You'll just be ruining your eyes.

HEDVIG: No, I won't. Give me the brush.

HJALMAR *(getting up):* It would only be for a minute or two—

HEDVIG: What possible harm could that do? *(Takes the brush.)* There now. *(Sits down.)* And here is one I can use as model.

HJALMAR: But don't ruin your eyes! Do you hear me? I will not take the responsibility. It's all yours. I'm just telling you.

HEDVIG *(working):* Yes, of course.

HJALMAR: You are really very good at it, Hedvig. It will only be for a few minutes, you understand.

(He slips into the attic by the edge of the curtain. HEDVIG *keeps on working.* HJALMAR *and* EKDAL *can be heard talking behind the curtain.)*

HJALMAR *(appearing inside the net):* Hedvig, please give me the pliers on the shelf. And the chisel. *(Turns around.)* See here, father. Just let me show you what I have in mind first.

*(*HEDVIG *fetches the tools from the shelf and gives them to him.)*

HJALMAR: Thank you. It was a good thing I went in.

(He leaves the doorway. Sounds of carpentering and conversation are heard from inside. HEDVIG *remains watching them. After a while there is a knock on the entrance door. She does not notice.)*

GREGERS *(bareheaded and coatless, enters, stops near the door):* H'm!

HEDVIG *(turns around and walks towards him):* Good morning! Won't you please come in?

GREGERS: Thank you. *(Looks towards the attic.)* You seem to have workmen in the house.

HEDVIG: Oh no. It's just father and Grandpa. I'll tell them you're here.

GREGERS: Please don't. I'd rather wait a while. *(Sits down on the sofa.)*

HEDVIG: It's such a mess in here— *(Begins removing the photographs.)*

GREGERS: Never mind. Are they pictures you are retouching?

HEDVIG: Yes. It is something I help father with.

GREGERS: I hope you won't let me disturb you.

HEDVIG: I won't.

(She moves the things more within her reach and resumes work. GREGERS *watches her in silence.)*

GREGERS: Did the wild duck sleep well last night?

HEDVIG: Yes, thank you. I think so.

GREGERS *(turning towards the attic):* In daylight it looks quite different from last night when there was a moon.

HEDVIG: Yes, it varies so. In the morning it looks different than in the afternoon, and when it rains it looks different than when the sun is shining.

GREGERS: You have noticed that?

HEDVIG: Yes, of course.

GREGERS: Do you too spend much time with the wild duck?

HEDVIG: Yes, when I can.

GREGERS: I suppose you don't have much spare time, though. You are going to school, of course?

HEDVIG: Not any more. Father is afraid I'll ruin my eyes.

GREGERS: Then he reads with you himself?

HEDVIG: He has promised to, but he hasn't had the time yet.

GREGERS: But isn't there anyone else who can help you?

HEDVIG: Well, yes, there is Mr. Molvik, but he isn't always—you know—quite—

GREGERS: You mean he is drunk sometimes.

HEDVIG: I think so.

GREGERS: Well, in that case you have time for many things. And in there, I suppose, it's like a world all its own?

HEDVIG: Yes, quite. And there are so many strange things in there.

GREGERS: There are?

HEDVIG: Yes, there are big closets with books in them, and in many of the books there are pictures.

GREGERS: I see.

HEDVIG: And there is an old desk with drawers and drop-down leaves and a big clock with figures that come out. But the clock doesn't run any more.

GREGERS: So time has stopped in there where the wild duck lives?

HEDVIG: Yes. And there are old coloring sets and that sort of thing, and then all the books.

GREGERS: I expect you read the books.

HEDVIG: Yes, whenever I have a chance. But most of them are in English and I can't read that. But I look at the pictures. There is a great, big book that's called "Harrison's History of London." I think it is a hundred years old. There are ever so many pictures in it. In front it shows a picture of Death with an hourglass and a girl. I think that is horrible. But then there are all the pictures of churches and castles and streets and big ships that sail the seas.

GREGERS: Tell me—where do all those strange things come from?

HEDVIG: There was an old sea captain who used to live here. He brought them home. They called him The Flying Dutchman. And that's odd, I think, for he wasn't a Dutchman at all.

GREGERS: No?

HEDVIG: No. But finally he disappeared at sea, and all the things were left here.

GREGERS: Listen—when you sit in there looking at the pictures, don't you ever want to travel and see the real, big world for yourself?

HEDVIG: Oh no. I want to stay here at home always and help father and mother.

GREGERS: With the photographs?

HEDVIG: Not just with that. Best of all I'd like to learn how to engrave pictures like those in the English books.

GREGERS: H'm. And what does your father say to that?

HEDVIG: I don't think father likes the idea very much. He is funny about things like that. You know, he says I ought to learn basket-weaving and straw-plaiting. But I don't think that sounds like much of anything at all.

GREGERS: No, I don't think it does either.

HEDVIG: Though of course father is quite right in saying that if I had learned basket-weaving I could have made the new basket for the wild duck.

GREGERS: That's true. And that really ought to have been your job, you know.
HEDVIG: Yes. Because it is my wild duck.
GREGERS: So I hear.
HEDVIG: Oh yes. I own it. But father and Grandpa get to borrow it as often as they like.
GREGERS: So? And what do they do with it?
HEDVIG: Oh—they take care of it and build things for it and that sort of thing.
GREGERS: I see. For of course the wild duck is the noblest of all the animals in there.
HEDVIG: Yes, she is, for she is a real, wild bird. And then I feel sorrier for her than for any of the others, because she's all alone, poor thing.
GREGERS: No family, like the rabbits.
HEDVIG: No. And the chickens, they have so many they were little chicks together with. But she is all alone, with none of her own near by. And there is the strange thing about the wild duck. Nobody knows her and nobody knows where she is from.
GREGERS: And she has been down to the depths of the sea.
HEDVIG *(glances quickly at him, suppresses a smile, asks):* Why do you say "the depths of the sea"?
GREGERS: What should I say?
HEDVIG: You could say "the sea bottom" or "the bottom of the sea."
GREGERS: Can't I just as well say "the depths of the sea"?
HEDVIG: Yes, but I think it sounds so strange when other people say "the depths of the sea."
GREGERS: Why is that? Tell me.
HEDVIG: No, I won't, for it is so silly.
GREGERS: I don't think so. Please tell me why you smiled.
HEDVIG: It's because every time I think of what's in there—when it comes into my head all of a sudden, I mean—I always feel that the whole room and everything that's in it are the depths of the sea. But that's silly.
GREGERS: Don't say that.
HEDVIG: Yes, for it's just an old attic, you know.
GREGERS *(looking intently at her):* Are you sure?
HEDVIG *(surprised):* That it's an attic?
GREGERS: Yes. Are you sure it is?

(HEDVIG stares at him in silence, her mouth open in astonishment. GINA enters from the kitchen with linen, silverware, etc., to set the table.)

GREGERS *(getting up):* I am afraid I am too early for you.
GINA: Oh well. You have to be somewhere. Things are almost ready now, anyway. Clear the table, Hedvig.

(During the next scene HEDVIG clears the table and GINA sets it. GREGERS seats himself in the armchair and starts leafing through an album of photographs.)

GREGERS: I understand you know how to retouch, Mrs. Ekdal.
GINA *(looks at him out of the corner of her eye):* That's right.
GREGERS: That was fortunate.
GINA: How—fortunate?
GREGERS: I mean since Ekdal is a photographer.
HEDVIG: Mother knows how to take pictures, too.

GINA: Oh yes, I've had to learn *that* business, all right.
GREGERS: Perhaps it is you who are responsible for the daily routine?
GINA: Yes, when Ekdal himself doesn't have the time—
GREGERS: I suppose he busies himself a great deal with his old father?
GINA: Yes, and then it's not for a man like Ekdal to waste his time taking pictures of everybody and his grandmother.
GREGERS: I quite agree, but since he did choose this as his profession, shouldn't he—?
GINA: You know just as well as I do, Mr. Werle, that Ekdal isn't just one of your common, ordinary photographers.
GREGERS: Of course not, but—nevertheless—

(A shot is heard from the attic.)

GREGERS *(jumps up)*: What was that?
GINA: Ugh! There they go, firing away again!
GREGERS: They shoot, too?
HEDVIG: They go hunting.
GREGERS: What? *(Over by the door to the attic.)* Do you go hunting, Hjalmar?
HJALMAR *(inside the curtain)*: Have you arrived? I didn't know—I've been so busy— *(To* HEDVIG.*)* And you—not letting us know—! *(Comes into the studio.)*
GREGERS: Do you go shooting in the attic?
HJALMAR *(showing him a double-barreled pistol)*: Oh, it's only this old thing.
GINA: You and Grandpa are going to have an accident with that pestol of yours one of these days.
HJALMAR *(irritated)*: I believe I have told you that this kind of firearm is called a pistol.
GINA: I don't see that that makes it any better.
GREGERS: So you have taken up hunting, too, Hjalmar?
HJALMAR: Only a little rabbit hunting now and then. It's mostly for father's sake, you understand.
GINA: Menfolks are strange. They always need something to diverge themselves with.
HJALMAR *(grimly)*: That's right. We always need something to divert ourselves with.
GINA: That's exactly what I'm saying.
HJALMAR: Oh well—! H'm! *(To* GREGERS.*)* Well, you see, we're fortunate in that the attic is situated so that nobody can hear the shots. *(Puts the pistol on the top shelf.)* Don't touch the pistol, Hedvig! Remember, one barrel is loaded!
GREGERS *(peering through the net)*: You have a hunting rifle, too, I see.
HJALMAR: That's father's old gun. It doesn't work any more. There's something wrong with the lock. But it's rather fun to have it around all the same, for we take it apart and clean it once in a while and grease it and put it back together again. It's mostly father, of course, who amuses himself with things like that.
HEDVIG *(standing next to* GREGERS*)*: Now you can get a good look at the wild duck.
GREGERS: I was just looking at it. One wing is drooping a bit, isn't it?
HJALMAR: Well that's not so strange. She was hit, you know.
GREGERS: And she drags her foot a little. Or doesn't she?
HJALMAR: Perhaps a little bit.
HEDVIG: Yes, for that is the foot the dog seized her by.
HJALMAR: But aside from that she has no other hurt or defect, and that's really quite remarkable when you consider that she has a charge of buckshot in her and has been between the teeth of a dog.

GREGERS *(with a glance at* HEDVIG*):* Yes, and been to the depths of the sea—for so long.

HEDVIG *(smiles):* Yes.

GINA *(busy at the table):* Oh yes, that precious wild duck. There sure is enough circumstance made over it.

HJALMAR: H'm. Will you be done setting the table soon?

GINA: In a minute. Hedvig, I need your help. *(*GINA *and* HEDVIG *go into the kitchen.)*

HJALMAR *(in a low voice):* You had better not watch father. He doesn't like it.

(GREGERS *leaves the attic door.)*

HJALMAR: And I ought to close this before the others arrive. *(Shoos the birds away with his hands.)* Shoo! Shoo—you! *(Raising the curtain and sliding the doors back.)* This arrangement is my own invention. It is really quite amusing to fool around with these things and to fix them when they get broken. And it's absolutely necessary to have something like it, for Gina won't stand for rabbits and chickens in the studio.

GREGERS: No, I suppose not. And perhaps the studio is your wife's department?

HJALMAR: I generally leave the daily run of the business to her. That gives me a chance to retire into the living room and give my thoughts to more important things.

GREGERS: What things, Hjalmar?

HJALMAR: I have been wondering why you haven't asked me that before. Or maybe you haven't heard about the invention?

GREGERS: Invention? No.

HJALMAR: Really? You haven't? Oh well—up there in the woods and wilderness—

GREGERS: So you have invented something!

HJALMAR: Not quite yet, but I am working on it. As you can well imagine, when I decided to devote myself to photography it was not my intent to do nothing but take portraits of all sorts of ordinary people.

GREGERS: I suppose not. Your wife just said the same thing.

HJALMAR: I made a pledge to myself that if I were to give my powers to this profession, I would raise it so high that it would become both an art and a science. That is how I decided to make some remarkable invention.

GREGERS: What is it? What does it do?

HJALMAR: Well, Gregers, you must not ask for details just yet. You see, it takes time. And don't think I am driven by vanity. I can truthfully say I am not working for my own sake. Far from it. It is my life's mission that is in my thoughts night and day.

GREGERS: What mission?

HJALMAR: The old man with the silver hair—can you forget him?

GREGERS: Yes, your poor father. But what exactly do you think you can do for him?

HJALMAR: I can resurrect his respect for himself by once again raising the name of Ekdal to fame and honor.

GREGERS: So that is your life's mission.

HJALMAR: Yes. I will rescue that shipwrecked man. For he was shipwrecked the moment the storm broke. During those terrible inquiries he was not himself. The pistol over yonder—the one we use to shoot rabbits with—it has played its part in the tragedy of the Ekdal family.

GREGERS: The pistol? Really?

HJALMAR: When sentence had been pronounced and he was to be confined—he had that pistol in his hand—

GREGERS: He tried to—!

HJALMAR: Yes, but didn't dare. He was a coward. So much of a wreck, so spiritually ruined was he already then. Can you understand it? He, an officer, the killer of nine bears, descended from two lieutenant colonels—I mean one after the other, of course—Can you understand it, Gregers?

GREGERS: I can indeed.

HJALMAR: Not I.—But the pistol came to figure in our family chronicle a second time. When he had begun to wear the garb of gray and sat there behind bolt and bar—oh, those were terrible days for me, believe me. I kept the shades down on both windows. When I looked out, I saw the sun shining as usual. I saw people in the street laughing and talking about nothing. I could not understand it. It seemed to me that all of existence ought to come to a standstill, as during an eclipse of the sun.

GREGERS: I felt that way when mother died.

HJALMAR: In such an hour Hjalmar Ekdal turned the pistol against himself—

GREGERS: You too were thinking of—?

HJALMAR: Yes.

GREGERS: But you did not pull the trigger?

HJALMAR: No. In the decisive moment I won a victory over myself. I remained alive. Take my word for it: it requires courage to go on living in a situation like that.

GREGERS: That depends on how you look at it.

HJALMAR: No, it doesn't. At any rate, it all turned out to be for the best. For soon now I will finish my invention, and when I do, Doctor Relling thinks, as I do myself, that father will be allowed to wear his uniform again. I shall claim that as my only reward.

GREGERS: So it is this business with the uniform that mostly—

HJALMAR: Yes, to be able to wear it again is what he dreams of and longs for. You have no idea how it cuts me to the quick to see him. Whenever we have a little family celebration here, like Gina's and my wedding anniversary or whatever it may be, then the old man appears in his lieutenant's uniform from happier days. But no sooner is there a knock on the door than he scuttles back to his own little room as fast as his old legs will carry him. He doesn't dare to show himself to strangers, you know. A sight like that lacerates a son's heart, Gregers!

GREGERS: About when do you think the invention will be ready?

HJALMAR: Heavens, you must not ask for details like that. An invention, you see, is something you don't altogether control yourself. It is very largely a matter of inspiration—a sudden idea—and it is next to impossible to tell beforehand when that may come.

GREGERS: But it is progressing?

HJALMAR: Certainly, it is progressing. It occupies my thoughts every day. It fills me. Every afternoon, after dinner, I shut myself up in the living room to ponder in peace. I just can't be hurried; it won't do any good. That is what Relling says, too.

GREGERS: And you don't think that all this business in the attic interferes too much, distracts you from your work?

HJALMAR: No, no, no. Quite the contrary. You must not say a thing like that. After all, I cannot everlastingly be pursuing the same exhausting train of thought. I need something else, something to occupy me during the waiting period. The inspiration, the sudden flash of insight, don't you see?—when it comes, it comes.

GREGERS: My dear Hjalmar, I almost think there is something of the wild duck in you.

HJALMAR: The wild duck? How do you mean?

GREGERS: You have plunged down through the sea and got yourself entangled in the grasses on the bottom.

HJALMAR: Are you perhaps referring to the well-nigh fatal shot that lodged in father's wing and hit me, too?

GREGERS: Not to that so much. I won't say you are crippled. But you are in a poisonous marsh, Hjalmar. You have contracted an insidious disease and gone to the bottom to die in the dark.

HJALMAR: I? Die in the dark? Honestly, Gregers. You really shouldn't say such things.

GREGERS: Don't you worry. I'll get you up again. For I, too, have got a mission in life. I found it yesterday.

HJALMAR: That may well be, but I shall ask you kindly to leave me out of it. I assure you that—aside from my easily explainable melancholia, of course—I am as contented a man as anybody could wish to be.

GREGERS: The fact that you are—that is one of the symptoms of the poisoning.

HJALMAR: No, really, Gregers. Please don't talk to me any more about disease and poison. I am not used to that sort of talk. In my house we never discuss unpleasant topics.

GREGERS: That I can well believe.

HJALMAR: No, for it isn't good for me. And there is no marshy air here, as you call it. The roof may be low in the poor photographer's home—I know very well it is—and my lot is lowly. But I am an inventor, and a provider as well. That is what raises me above my humble circumstances.—Ah! Here's lunch!

(GINA and HEDVIG enter with bottles of beer, a decanter of brandy, glasses, and other appurtenances. At the same moment, RELLING and MOLVIK come through the entrance door. Neither one wears hat or coat. MOLVIK is dressed in black.)

GINA *(putting the things down on the table):* Well, you two arrive just in time.

RELLING: Molvik thought he could smell herring salad, and then there was no holding him.—Good morning again, Ekdal.

HJALMAR: Gregers, may I introduce you to Mr. Molvik—And Doctor—that's right, you two already know each other, don't you.

GREGERS: Slightly.

RELLING: Oh yes, young Mr. Werle. We used to do some skirmishing up at the Høydal works. I take it you have just moved in?

GREGERS: This morning.

RELLING: Well, Molvik and I live downstairs, so you don't have far to go for doctor and minister if you need them.

GREGERS: Thank you; maybe I shall. We were thirteen at the table yesterday.

HJALMAR: Come now! Please don't start any of that unpleasantness again!

RELLING: Calm down, Ekdal. You are immune.

HJALMAR: I hope so, for my family's sake.—Sit down. Let's eat, drink, and be merry.

GREGERS: Aren't we going to wait for your father?

HJALMAR: No, he'll eat later in his own room. Do sit down!

(The men seat themselves and begin eating and drinking. GINA and HEDVIG wait on them.)

RELLING: Molvik got pretty high last night, Mrs. Ekdal.

GINA: Again?

RELLING: Didn't you hear me bring him home?

GINA: Can't say I did.

RELLING: That's good, for Molvik was awful last night.

GINA: Is that true, Molvik?

MOLVIK: Let us consign last night's events to oblivion. They do not represent my better self.

RELLING *(to* GREGERS*)*: It comes over him like an irresistible impulse. Then he has to go out and get drunk. You see, Molvik is demonic.

GREGERS: Demonic?

RELLING: That's right. Molvik is demonic.

GREGERS: H'm.

RELLING: And demonic natures aren't made to follow the straight and narrow path. They have to take off for the fields once in a while.—So you still stick it out up at that filthy old place?

GREGERS: So far.

RELLING: Did you ever collect on that claim you went around presenting?

GREGERS: Claim? *(Looks at him and understands.)* Oh I see.

HJALMAR: Have you been a bill collector, Gregers?

GREGERS: Oh nonsense.

RELLING: Oh yes, he has. He went around to all the cottages up there, trying to collect on something he called "the claim of the ideal."

GREGERS: I was young.

RELLING: You're right. You were very young. And the claim of the ideal—you never collected as long as I was up there.

GREGERS: Not since then, either.

RELLING: In that case, I suppose you have been wise enough to reduce the amount somewhat.

GREGERS: Never when I have to do with a real and genuine human being.

HJALMAR: I think that is reasonable enough.—Some butter, Gina.

RELLING: And a piece of bacon for Molvik.

MOLVIK: Ugh! Not bacon!

(There is a knock from inside the door to the attic.)

HJALMAR: Go and open, Hedvig. Father wants to get out.

*(*HEDVIG *opens the door a little.* OLD EKDAL *enters with the skin of a freshly flayed rabbit.* HEDVIG *closes the door after him.)*

EKDAL: Good morning, gentlemen! Good hunting today. Got me a big one.

HJALMAR: And you skinned it yourself, I see.

EKDAL: Salted it, too. It's nice, tender meat, rabbit is. It's sweet, y'know. Tastes like sugar. Good appetite, gentlemen! *(Goes into his room.)*

MOLVIK *(getting up)*: Excuse me—I can't—Got to get downstairs—

RELLING: Drink soda water, you idiot!

MOLVIK: Uh—Uh— *(Hurries out, right rear.)*

RELLING *(to* HJALMAR*)*: Let us drink to the old hunter.

HJALMAR *(touching* RELLING*'s glass with his own)*: For the sportsman on the brink of the grave—yes.

RELLING: For the gray-haired— *(Drinks.)* Tell me, is his hair gray or is it white?

HJALMAR: In between, I think. Though I don't think there are many hairs left on his head at all.

RELLING: Oh well. One can live happily with a wig, too. Ah, yes, Ekdal. You are really a very happy man. You have this beautiful ambition of yours to strive for—

HJALMAR: Believe me, I am striving.

RELLING: Then you have your excellent wife, shuffling about in slippered feet with that comfortable waddle of hers, making things nice and pleasant for you.

HJALMAR: Yes, Gina— *(Nods to her.)* —you are a good companion on life's journey.

GINA: Aw, you don't need to sit there and dissectate me!

RELLING: And your Hedvig, Ekdal.

HJALMAR *(moved):* Ah yes, the child! The child above all. Hedvig, come to me. *(Stroking her hair.)* What day is tomorrow?

HEDVIG *(playfully shaking him):* Oh, stop it, father!

HJALMAR: It's like a knife through my heart, when I consider how little we can do. Just a small celebration here in the attic.

HEDVIG: But that's just the way I like it!

RELLING: You wait till the invention is all done, Hedvig.

HJALMAR: Yes! Then you'll see, Hedvig. I have decided to secure your future. You shall be made comfortable for as long as you live. I will ask for something for you, something or other. That will be the impecunious inventor's sole reward.

HEDVIG *(whispers, her arms around his neck):* Oh you good, sweet father!

RELLING *(to* GREGERS*):* Well, now, don't you think it's nice for a change to sit down to a good table in a happy family circle?

HJALMAR: Yes, I really relish these hours at the table.

GREGERS: I, for one, don't like to breathe marsh air.

RELLING: Marsh air?

HJALMAR: Oh, don't start all that again!

GINA: I'll have you know there is no marsh air here, Mr. Werle. The place is aired every single day.

GREGERS *(leaving the table):* The stench I have in mind you don't get rid of by opening windows.

HJALMAR: Stench!

GINA: Yes, how do you like that, Ekdal!

RELLING: Begging your pardon—it wouldn't by any chance be you yourself who bring the stench with you from the Høydal mines?

GREGERS: It's just like you to call stench what I bring to this house.

RELLING *(walks over to* GREGERS*:)* Listen here, Mr. Werle junior. I strongly suspect that you still carry the claim of the ideal around in your rear pocket.

GREGERS: I carry it in my heart.

RELLING: I don't care where the hell you carry it as long as you don't go bill collecting here while *I* am around.

GREGERS: And if I do so, nevertheless?

RELLING: Then you'll go head first down the stairs. Now you know!

HJALMAR: No, really, Relling—!

GREGERS: Go ahead! Throw me out!

GINA *(interposing):* No, we won't have any of that, Relling. But I will say this to you, Mr.

Werle, that it seems like you are not the right person to come here and talk about stench after what you did to the stove in your room this morning.

(There is a knock on the door.)

HEDVIG: Mother, someone's knocking.
HJALMAR: Oh yes, let's have customers on top of everything else—!
GINA: I'll handle it. *(Opens the door, gives a start, steps back):* Oh dear!

(WERLE, in a fur coat, steps inside.)

WERLE: I beg your pardon, but I am told my son is here.
GINA *(swallowing hard):* Yes sir.
HJALMAR *(closer):* Sir, wouldn't you like to—?
WERLE: Thanks. I just want a word with my son.
GREGERS: Well. Here I am.
WERLE: I want to talk with you in your room.
GREGERS: In my room—? Oh, all right. *(Is about to leave.)*
GINA: Good Lord, no! That's not a fit place!
WERLE: All right; out here in the hall, then. I want to see you alone.
HJALMAR: You may do that right here, Mr. Werle. Relling, come into the living room with me.

(HJALMAR and RELLING go out, right front. GINA takes HEDVIG with her into the kitchen, left front.)

GREGERS *(after a brief silence):* Well. We are alone.
WERLE: You dropped some hints last night. And since you have moved in with the Ekdals, I can only assume that you are planning something or other against me.
GREGERS: I plan to open Hjalmar Ekdal's eyes. He is to see his position as it really is. That's all.
WERLE: Is that the life mission you mentioned yesterday?
GREGERS: Yes. You have left me no other.
WERLE: So you feel it is I who have twisted your mind, Gregers?
GREGERS: You have twisted my whole life. I am not thinking of all that with mother. But it is you I can thank for the fact that I am being haunted and driven by a guilty conscience.
WERLE: Ah, I see. So your conscience is ailing.
GREGERS: I should have opposed you the time you were laying traps for Lieutenant Ekdal. I should have warned him, for I suspected how things were going.
WERLE: Yes, in that case you certainly ought to have said something.
GREGERS: I didn't have the courage. I was a coward—frightened. I felt an unspeakable fear of you—both then and for a long, long time afterwards.
WERLE: That fear appears to have left you now.
GREGERS: Yes, fortunately. What has been done to Old Ekdal, both by me and by—others, for that there is no remedy. But Hjalmar I can rescue from the web of lies and deceit in which he is suffocating.
WERLE: Do you think that is a good thing to do?

GREGERS: I am sure it is.

WERLE: I take it you think Mr. Photographer Ekdal is the kind of man who will be grateful for your friendly services?

GREGERS: Yes! He is that kind of man.

WERLE: H'm. We'll see.

GREGERS: Besides, if I am to continue living, I have to find a way to heal my sick conscience.

WERLE: It will never get well. Your conscience has been sickly from the time you were a child. It's hereditary, Gregers. You have it from your mother. The only inheritance she left you.

GREGERS *(with a contemptuous half smile):* I see you still haven't forgotten your disappointment when you found out mother wasn't rich.

WERLE: Let's not change the subject. Am I to think, then, that you are firmly resolved to guide Hjalmar Ekdal into the path you consider the right one?

GREGERS: Yes. That is my firm intent.

WERLE: In that case I could have saved myself coming all the way up here. For then I suppose there is no point in my asking you to move back home again?

GREGERS: No.

WERLE: And you don't want to join the firm?

GREGERS: No.

WERLE: Very well. But since I am to marry again, your part of the estate will have to be paid you.

GREGERS *(quickly):* No, I don't want that.

WERLE: You don't want it?

GREGERS: I dare not, for my conscience's sake.

WERLE *(after a brief pause):* Are you going back up to Høydal?

GREGERS: No. I consider myself released from your service.

WERLE: But what do you want to do with yourself?

GREGERS: Accomplish my mission. Nothing else.

WERLE: But afterwards? What are you going to live on?

GREGERS: I have saved some of my salary.

WERLE: How long do you think that will last?

GREGERS: I think it will do for the time I have left.

WERLE: What is that supposed to mean?

GREGERS: I won't answer any more questions.

WERLE: Well, goodbye, Gregers.

GREGERS: Goodbye.

(WERLE leaves.)

HJALMAR *(looks in):* Did he leave?

GREGERS: Yes.

(HJALMAR and RELLING enter from the living room, GINA and HEDVIG from the kitchen.)

RELLING: Now that was a very successful breakfast.

GREGERS: Put on your coat, Hjalmar. I want you to take a long walk with me.

HJALMAR: Gladly. What did your father want? Did it have to do with me?

GREGERS: Just come. We'll talk. I'll go and get my coat. *(Goes out.)*

GINA: You shouldn't go with him, Ekdal.

RELLING: No, don't. Stay here.

HJALMAR *(taking his hat and coat):* What! When an old friend feels the need to open his heart for me in private—!

RELLING: But goddamit! Can't you see that the fellow is mad, cracked, insane!

GINA: Yes, listen to Relling. His mother used to have physicological fits, too.

HJALMAR: All the more reason why he needs a friend's alert eyes. *(To* GINA.*)* Be sure to have dinner ready at the usual time. Goodbye. *(Goes out.)*

RELLING: It's nothing less than a disaster that that man didn't go straight to hell down one of the shafts up at Høydal.

GINA: Heavens—! Why do you say that?

RELLING *(mutters):* I have my reasons.

GINA: Do you really think young Werle is crazy?

RELLING: No, unfortunately. He is no madder than most people. He is sick, though.

GINA: What do you think is wrong with him?

RELLING: That I can tell you, Mrs. Ekdal. He suffers from an acute attack of moral integrity.

GINA: Moral integrity?

HEDVIG: Is that a disease?

RELLING: Yes, it is a national disease, but it occurs only sporadically. *(Nods to* GINA.*)* That was a good meal, thank you. *(Goes out.)*

GINA *(troubled, walks up and down):* Ugh! That Gregers Werle—he's always been a weird fish.

HEDVIG *(by the table, looks at her searchingly):* I think this is very strange.

ACT IV

(The studio. Photographs have just been taken. A cloth-covered camera on a tripod, a couple of chairs, and a small table are standing about in the middle of the floor. Afternoon light. The sun is about to disappear. After a while darkness begins to fall.

GINA *stands in the open entrance door with a small box and a wet glass plate in her hand. She is talking to someone not in sight.)*

GINA: Absolutely. When I promise something, I keep it. I'll have the first dozen ready for you on Monday.—Goodbye.

(Sounds of someone descending the stairs. GINA *closes the door, puts the plate inside the box and the box into the camera.)*

HEDVIG *(enters from the kitchen):* Did they leave?

GINA *(putting things in order):* Yes, thank goodness. I finally got rid of them.

HEDVIG: Can you understand why father isn't back yet?

GINA: You're sure he is not down at Relling's?

HEDVIG: No, he is not there. I just went down the kitchen stairs to ask.

GINA: His food is getting cold and everything.

HEDVIG: Yes. And father who is always so particular about having dinner on time.

GINA: Oh well. You'll see he'll be back soon.

HEDVIG: I wish he'd come. Everything seems so strange.

(HJALMAR enters from outside.)

HEDVIG *(towards him):* Father! If you knew how we've been waiting for you!

GINA *(glancing at him):* You've been gone quite some time.

HJALMAR *(without looking at her):* Yes, I suppose I have.

(He starts taking his coat off. GINA and HEDVIG both go to help him. He turns them away.)

GINA: Maybe you and Werle had something to eat some place?

HJALMAR *(hanging up his coat):* No.

GINA *(towards the kitchen door):* I'll get your dinner.

HJALMAR: Never mind. I don't feel like eating now.

HEDVIG *(coming closer):* Are you sick, father?

HJALMAR: Sick? No, I'm not sick—exactly. We had a strenuous walk, Gregers and I.

GINA: You shouldn't do that, Ekdal. You aren't used to it.

HJALMAR: H'm. There are many things in life a man has to get used to. *(Paces up and down.)* Anybody here while I've been gone?

GINA: Only that engaged couple.

HJALMAR: No new appointments?

GINA: No, not today.

HEDVIG: There will be some tomorrow, father, I am sure.

HJALMAR: I hope you are right, for tomorrow I plan to go to work in earnest.

HEDVIG: Tomorrow! But don't you remember what day is tomorrow?

HJALMAR: That's right. Well, then, the day after tomorrow. From now on I'll do everything myself. I want to assume the entire work load.

GINA: Whatever for, Ekdal? That's only making yourself miserable. I'll manage the pictures. You just go on with the invention.

HEDVIG: And the wild duck, father. And the chickens and the rabbits and—

HJALMAR: Don't ever mention all that junk to me again! Starting tomorrow, I'll never more set foot in the attic.

HEDVIG: But father, you promised that tomorrow we're having a celebration—

HJALMAR: H'm. That's right. Day after tomorrow then. That damn wild duck. I'd like to wring its neck!

HEDVIG *(with a cry):* The wild duck!

GINA: Now I've heard everything!

HEDVIG *(shaking him):* But father—it's *my* wild duck!

HJALMAR: That's why I won't do it. I don't have the heart—for your sake, Hedvig. But deep down I feel I ought to do it. I shouldn't harbor under my roof a creature that has been in those hands.

GINA: For heaven's sake! Even if Grandpa *did* get it from that awful Pettersen.

HJALMAR *(walking up and down):* There are certain demands—what shall I call them? Let me say ideal demands—certain claims, that a man disregards only at the peril of his soul.

HEDVIG *(following after him):* But think—the wild duck! That poor wild duck!

HJALMAR *(halts):* Didn't I tell you I'll spare it—for your sake? Not a hair on its head will

be—h'm. Well, as I said, I'll spare it. After all, there are bigger tasks awaiting me. But you ought to go out for a little walk, Hedvig. The twilight is just right for you.

HEDVIG: I don't care to go out now.

HJALMAR: Yes, do. Seems to me you are squinting. The fums in here aren't good for you. The air is close under this roof.

HEDVIG: All right. I'll run down the kitchen stairs and walk around a bit. My hat and coat? Oh yes, in my room. Father, please—don't do anything bad to the wild duck while I'm gone!

HJALMAR: Not a feather shall be plucked from its head. *(Clutches her to him.)* You and I, Hedvig—we two! Be on your way now.

(HEDVIG nods goodbye to her parents and goes out through the kitchen door.)

HJALMAR *(pacing back and forth):* Gina.

GINA: Yes?

HJALMAR: Starting tomorrow—or let's say the day after tomorrow—I'd like to keep account of the housekeeping expenses myself.

GINA: So you want to keep the accounts too, now?

HJALMAR: Keep track of what we take in, at any rate.

GINA: Lord knows, that's easily done!

HJALMAR: One wouldn't think so. It seems to me you make the money go incredibly far. *(Stops and looks at her.)* How do you do it?

GINA: It's because Hedvig and I need so little.

HJALMAR: Is it true that father is overpaid for the copying work he does for Werle?

GINA: I couldn't say about that. I don't know the rates.

HJALMAR: Well, what *does* he get? In round figures.—I want to know.

GINA: It differs. I guess it comes to about what he costs us, plus a little extra in spending money.

HJALMAR: What he costs us! And you haven't told me that!

GINA: No, I couldn't, for you were so happy because he got everything from you.

HJALMAR: And it has really been Werle all the time!

GINA: Oh well. He can afford it.

HJALMAR: Light the lamp!

GINA *(lighting the lamp):* And as far as that is concerned, how do we know it is Werle himself? It may be Gråberg—

HJALMAR: Really, Gina. You know that isn't so. Why do you say a thing like that?

GINA: I don't know. I just thought—

HJALMAR: H'm!

GINA: It wasn't me who got Grandpa all that copying to do. It was Bertha, when she took service there.

HJALMAR: It sounds to me like your voice is trembling.

GINA *(putting the shade on the lamp):* Does it?

HJALMAR: And your hands are shaking. Aren't they?

GINA *(firmly):* You might as well tell me straight, Ekdal. What has he been saying about me?

HJALMAR: Is it true—*can* it be true—that there was some kind of affair between you and Werle while you were in his house?

GINA: That's not so. Not then. He was after me, though. And Mrs. Werle thought there was

something going on, and she made a fuss and a big hullaballoo about it, and she beat me and pulled me around—and so I quit.

HJALMAR: But afterwards—!

GINA: Well, then I went to live with mother. And you see—mother—she wasn't all the woman you thought she was, Ekdal. She talked to me about this, that, and the other. For Werle was a widower by that time—

HJALMAR: And then—?

GINA: You might as well know it, I guess. He didn't give up till he had his way.

HJALMAR *(striking his hands together):* And this is the mother of my child! How could you keep a thing like this from me?

GINA: Yes, I know it was wrong. I should have told you long ago, I suppose.

HJALMAR: You should have told me right away; that's what you should have. Then I would have known what sort of woman you were.

GINA: But would you have married me, irregardless?

HJALMAR: Of course, I wouldn't!

GINA: I didn't think so, and that's why I didn't dare to tell you. I had come to care for you, you know—a whole lot I cared for you. And I just couldn't see making myself as unhappy as all that—

HJALMAR *(walking about):* And this is my Hedvig's mother! And to know that everything I lay my eyes on here *(Kicks a chair.)* —my whole home—I owe to a favored predecessor! Oh, that seducer, that damn Werle!

GINA: Do you regret the fourteen-fifteen years we've had together?

HJALMAR *(fronting her):* Tell me if you haven't felt every day and every hour to be one long agony of repentance for that web of deceitful silence you have woven around me, like a spider? Answer me! Haven't you lived here in perpetual torture of guilt and remorse?

GINA: Bless you, Ekdal! I've been plenty busy with the house and the pictures—

HJALMAR: So you never cast a probing glance at your past?

GINA: No, to tell the truth, I had almost forgotten all those old stories.

HJALMAR: Oh, this dull, apathetic calm! There is something shocking about it. Not even repentant—!

GINA: Just tell me this, Ekdal. What do you think would have become of you if you hadn't got yourself a wife like me?

HJALMAR: Like you—!

GINA: Yes, for you know I have always been more practical and able to cope with things than you. Of course, I am a couple of years older—

HJALMAR: What would have become of me!

GINA: For you've got to admit you weren't living exactly right when you first met me.

HJALMAR: So you call that living wrong! Oh, what do you know about a man's feelings when he sorrows and despairs—especially a man of my fiery temperament.

GINA: No, I guess I don't know. And I don't mean to execrete you for it, either, for you turned into as decent a man as they come as soon as you got a house and a family of your own to take care of. And now we were getting on so nicely here, and Hedvig and I were just thinking that pretty soon we might spend some money on clothes for ourselves.

HJALMAR: Yes, in the swamp of deceit!

GINA: That that fellow ever poked his nose inside here!

HJALMAR: I, too, thought our home a pleasant one. That was a mistake. Where now do I

gather the necessary inner resilience to bring my invention into the world of reality? Perhaps it will die with me. If it does, it will be your past, Gina, that has killed it.

GINA *(on the verge of tears):* Please, Ekdal—don't be saying such things! I that have all my days only tried to make things nice and pleasant for you!

HJALMAR: I ask—what happens now to the breadwinner's dream? As I reclined in there on the sofa, pondering the invention, it came to me that it was going to drain me of my last drop of vitality. I knew that the day the patent was issued and in my hands—that day would be my—my day of farewell. And then it was my dream that you were to live on as the late inventor's well-to-do widow.

GINA *(wiping her tears):* I won't have you talk that way, Ekdal. May the good Lord never let me live the day when I'm your widow!

HJALMAR: Oh what difference does it all make! It is all over now, anyway. Everything!

(GREGERS cautiously opens the entrance door and peers in.)

GREGERS: May I come in?

HJALMAR: Yes, do.

GREGERS *(goes up to them with a beaming, happy face, reaches out his hands to them):* Now, then—you dear people—! *(Looks from one to the other, whispers to HJALMAR:)* It hasn't happened yet?

HJALMAR *(loud):* It has happened.

GREGERS: It has?

HJALMAR: I have lived through the bitterest moment of my life.

GREGERS: But also, I trust, its most exalted one.

HJALMAR: Anyway, it's done and over with.

GINA: May God forgive you, Mr. Werle.

GREGERS *(greatly bewildered):* But I don't understand—!

HJALMAR: What don't you understand?

GREGERS: As crucial a conversation as this—a conversation that is to be the foundation for a whole new way of life—a life, a partnership, in truth and frankness—

HJALMAR: I know. I know it very well.

GREGERS: I was so sure that when I came in here now I would be met with a splendor of revelation shining from both husband and wife. But all I see is this dull, heavy gloom—

GINA: So that's it. *(Removes the lamp shade.)*

GREGERS: You refuse to understand me, Mrs. Ekdal. Well, I suppose you need time. But you, Hjalmar? Surely, you must have felt a higher consecration in this great crisis.

HJALMAR: Of course I did. That is, in a way.

GREGERS: For surely nothing in the world can be compared to finding forgiveness in one's heart for her who has erred and lovingly lifting her up to one's own heights.

HJALMAR: Do you think a man so easily forgets the draught of wormwood I just drained?

GREGERS: An ordinary man, maybe not. But a man like you—!

HJALMAR: Oh, I know. But you must not rush me, Gregers. It takes time.

GREGERS: There is much of the wild duck in you, Hjalmar.

(RELLING has entered.)

RELLING: Ah! Here we go with the wild duck again!

HJALMAR: Mr. Werle's crippled prey—yes.

RELLING: Werle? Is it him you're talking about?

HJALMAR: About him—and about ourselves.

RELLING *(in a low voice, to* GREGERS*):* Damn you to hell!

HJALMAR: What are you saying?

RELLING: I am just expressing an ardent wish that this quack here would betake himself home. If he stays around he is likely to ruin both of you.

GREGERS: Those two cannot be ruined, Mr. Relling. Of Hjalmar I need say nothing. Him we know. But she, too, has surely in the depths of her being something reliable, something of integrity—

GINA *(almost crying):* Why didn't you leave me alone then?

RELLING *(to* GREGERS*):* Is it impertinent to ask exactly what you want in this house?

GREGERS: I want to lay the foundation for a true marriage.

RELLING: So you don't think the Ekdals' marriage is good enough as it is?

GREGERS: I daresay it is as good a marriage as most, unfortunately. But a true marriage it has yet to become.

HJALMAR: You have never had an eye for the claim of the ideal, Relling!

RELLING: Nonsense, boy!—Begging your pardon, Mr. Werle—how many—roughly—how many true marriages have you observed in your life?

GREGERS: Hardly a single one.

RELLING: Nor have I.

GREGERS: But I have seen a number of the other kind. And I have had occasion to witness what havoc a marriage like that can work in a pair of human beings.

HJALMAR: A man's whole moral foundation may crumble under his feet; that's the terrible thing.

RELLING: Well, I can't say I've ever been exactly married, so I can't judge about that. But I do know this, that the child belongs to marriage too. And you had better leave the child alone.

HJALMAR: Oh, Hedvig! My poor Hedvig!

RELLING: Yes—keep Hedvig out of it, you two! You are grown-ups. In God's name, do whatever fool things you like to your marriage. But I am warning you: be careful what you do to Hedvig. If you're not, there is no telling what may happen to her.

HJALMAR: Happen to her!

RELLING: Yes, she may bring a disaster upon herself—and perhaps on others, too.

GINA: But how can you tell about that, Relling?

HJALMAR: Are you saying there is some immediate danger to her eyes?

RELLING: This has nothing whatever to do with her eyes. Hedvig is in a difficult age. She may do all sorts of crazy things.

GINA: I know—she does already. She's taken to fooling around with the woodstove in the kitchen. Playing fire, she calls it. Sometimes I'm scared she'll burn the whole house down.

RELLING: There you are. I knew it.

GREGERS *(to* RELLING*):* But how do you explain a thing like that?

RELLING *(sullenly):* Her voice is changing, sir.

HJALMAR: As long as the child has *me—!* As long as *my* head is above the ground!

(There is a knock on the door.)

GINA: Shhh, Ekdal. There are people outside.

(MRS. SØRBY enters, wearing hat and coat.)

MRS. SØRBY: Good evening!

GINA *(going to her):* Goodness! Is it you, Bertha!

MRS. SØRBY: So it is. Maybe it's inconvenient—?

HJALMAR: Oh by no means! A messenger from *that* house—!

MRS. SØRBY *(to GINA):* Frankly, I had hoped you'd be without your menfolks this time of day. I've just dropped in to have a word with you about something and say goodbye.

GINA: You're going away?

MRS. SØRBY: Tomorrow morning—to Høydal. Mr. Werle left this afternoon. *(Casually, to GREGERS.)* He asked me to say hello.

GINA: Imagine—!

HJALMAR: So Mr. Werle has left? And you are going after him?

MRS. SØRBY: Yes. What do you say to that, Ekdal?

HJALMAR: Look out, is all I say.

GREGERS: I can explain. Father and Mrs. Sørby are getting married.

GINA: Oh Bertha! At long last!

RELLING *(his voice trembling a little):* Surely, this cannot be true?

MRS. SØRBY: Yes, my dear Relling, true it is.

RELLING: You want to get married again?

MRS. SØRBY: That's what it amounts to. Werle has got the license. We'll have a quiet little party up at the works.

GREGERS: I suppose I should tender my felicitations like a good stepson.

MRS. SØRBY: Thank you, if you really mean it. I hope this will be for the best for both Werle and myself.

RELLING: I am sure you have every reason to think it will. Mr. Werle never gets drunk—at least not to my knowledge. Nor do I believe he is in the habit of beating up his wife, like the late lamented horse doctor.

MRS. SØRBY: Let Sørby rest quietly in his grave. He had his good sides, too.

RELLING: Mr. Industrialist Werle has better ones, I am sure.

MRS. SØRBY: At least he has not thrown away what is best in himself. The man who does that must take the consequences.

RELLING: Tonight I'll go out with Molvik.

MRS. SØRBY: Don't do that, Relling. Don't—for my sake.

RELLING: There's nothing else to do. *(To HJALMAR.)* Want to come along?

GINA: No, thank you. Ekdal doesn't go in for excapades like that.

HJALMAR *(angrily, in a half whisper):* For heaven's sake! Keep your mouth shut!

RELLING: Goodbye—Mrs. Werle! *(Goes out.)*

GREGERS *(to MRS. SØRBY):* It appears that you and Doctor Relling know each other quite well?

MRS. SØRBY: Yes, we've known each other for a good many years. At one time it looked as if we might have made a match of it.

GREGERS: I'm sure it was lucky for you that you didn't.

MRS. SØRBY: You may well say that. But I've always been wary of acting on impulse. A woman can't just throw herself away, you know.

GREGERS: Aren't you afraid I'll let my father know about this old acquaintanceship?

MRS. SØRBY: Do you really believe I haven't told him myself?

GREGERS: Oh?

MRS. SØRBY: Your father knows every little thing people might say about me with any show of truth at all. I have told him everything. That was the first thing I did when I realized what his intentions were.

GREGERS: It seems to me you are more than usually frank.

MRS. SØRBY: I have always been frank. For us women that's the best policy.

HJALMAR: What do you say to that, Gina?

GINA: Oh, women differ. Some do it one way, others do it different.

MRS. SØRBY: Well, Gina, in my opinion I have followed the wiser course. And Werle hasn't kept back anything either. You see, that's what mainly brought us together. Now he can sit and talk to me as openly as a child. He has never been able to do that before. A healthy, vigorous man like him—all through his youth and all the best years of his life he had his ears drummed full with angry sermons. And very often sermons about sins he hadn't even committed—according to what I have been told.

GINA: That's the truth.

GREGERS: If you ladies want to pursue that topic any further, I had better absent myself.

MRS. SØRBY: You may just as well stay as far as that's concerned. I won't say another word. I just wanted you to know I haven't kept anything back or played him false in any way. Maybe people will say I am a very fortunate woman, and in a way of course that's true. But I don't think I am getting any more than I am giving. I'll certainly never desert him. And I can be of more service and use to him than anybody else, now that he'll soon be helpless.

HJALMAR: Will he be helpless?

GREGERS *(to* MRS. SØRBY*)*: Don't say anything about that here.

MRS. SØRBY: It can't be kept secret any longer, much as he'd like to. He is going blind.

HJALMAR *(struck)*: Blind? That's strange. He, too?

GINA: Lots of people go blind.

MRS. SØRBY: And I'm sure you can tell yourself what that must mean to a businessman. Well, I'll try to be his eyes, the best I know how.—But I can't stay any longer. I have so much to do right now.—Oh yes, What I wanted to tell you, Ekdal, is that if Werle can be of any service to you, all you need to do is to get in touch with Gråberg.

GREGERS: That is an offer I am sure Hjalmar Ekdal will decline.

MRS. SØRBY: Really? It seems to me he hasn't always been so—

GINA: Yes, Bertha. Ekdal doesn't need to accept anything more from Mr. Werle.

HJALMAR *(slowly, with weight)*: Tell your husband-to-be from me, that in the very near future I intend to go to Mr. Gråberg—

GREGERS: What! You want to do that!

HJALMAR: —I say, go to Mr. Gråberg, and demand an account of the sum I owe his employer. I desire to pay this debt of honor—ha-ha-ha!—let us call it a debt of honor! Enough! I shall pay it all, with five per cent interest.

GINA: But Ekdal—goodness! We don't have that kind of money!

HJALMAR: Be so good as to inform your fiancé that I am working incessantly on my invention. Please tell him that what sustains my mind during this exhausting enterprise is my ambition to free myself from a painful burden of debt. This is why I am an inventor.

The entire proceeds from my invention are to be devoted to liberating myself from the obligation to remunerate your husband-to-be for his expenses on behalf of my family.

MRS. SØRBY: Something has happened here.

HJALMAR: Indeed, something has.

MRS. SØRBY: Well, goodbye. I had something else I wanted to talk to you about, Gina, but that will have to wait till some other time. Goodbye.

(HJALMAR and GREGERS return her greeting silently. GINA sees her to the door.)

HJALMAR: Not beyond the threshold, Gina!

(MRS. SØRBY leaves. GINA closes the door.)

HJALMAR: There, now, Gregers. I have that burdensome debt off my chest.

GREGERS: You soon will, at any rate.

HJALMAR: I believe my attitude must be deemed the proper one.

GREGERS: You are the man I have always taken you to be.

HJALMAR: In certain cases it is impossible to disregard the claims of the ideal. As provider for my family, I am bound, of course, to find my course of action difficult and painful. Believe me, it is no joke for a man situated as I am, without means, to assume a debt of many years' standing—a debt, you might say, covered by the sands of oblivion. But never mind. The man in me demands his rights.

GREGERS *(placing his hand on his shoulder):* Dear Hjalmar—wasn't it a good thing that I came?

HJALMAR: Yes.

GREGERS: That your whole situation was made clear to you—wasn't that a good thing?

HJALMAR *(a bit impatiently):* Of course it was. But there is one thing that shocks my sense of justice.

GREGERS: What is that?

HJALMAR: It is this that—But I don't know that I ought to speak so freely about your father—

GREGERS: Don't let that worry you. Say what you want.

HJALMAR: All right. Well, you see, there is something shocking in the notion that now it's he and not I who realizes the true marriage.

GREGERS: How can you say a thing like that!

HJALMAR: Well, it is. For your father and Mrs. Sørby are about to solemnify a union built on full mutual confidence, on complete, unconditional frankness on both sides. They conceal nothing from each other, there are no deceitful silences, there has been declared, if I may put it so, mutual absolution between them.

GREGERS: Well, what of it?

HJALMAR: Well, then—it's all there! All the difficult conditions you yourself said are prerequisites for the building of a true marriage.

GREGERS: But that's in quite a different way, Hjalmar. Surely, you won't compare either yourself or Gina with those two—? Oh I am sure you know what I mean.

HJALMAR: Yet I can't get away from the thought that in all this there is something that offends my sense of justice. It looks exactly as if there were no just order in the universe.

GINA: Ekdal, for God's sake, don't talk like that!

GREGERS: H'm. Let's not get involved in those issues.

HJALMAR: Though, on the other hand, I do in a way discern fate's ruling finger, too. He is going blind.

GINA: We don't know that yet.

HJALMAR: There is no doubt about it. At least, we ought not to doubt it, for in that very fact lies the proof of just retribution. He did once hoodwink a trusting fellow being.

GREGERS: I am afraid he has hoodwinked many.

HJALMAR: And here comes the inexorable, the inscrutable, claiming Werle's own eyes.

GINA: How you talk! I think it's scary.

HJALMAR: It is salutary at times to contemplate the night side of existence.

(HEDVIG, dressed for the outside, enters. She is happy, breathless.)

GINA: Back so soon?

HEDVIG: Yes. I didn't feel like walking any farther. It was a good thing, too, for I met somebody as I was coming in.

HJALMAR: Mrs. Sørby, I suppose.

HEDVIG: Yes.

HJALMAR *(pacing the floor):* I hope you have seen her for the last time.

(Silence. HEDVIG, troubled, looks from one to the other in order to gauge their mood.)

HEDVIG *(approaching HJALMAR, ingratiatingly):* Father?

HJALMAR: All right—what is it, Hedvig?

HEDVIG: Mrs. Sørby had something for me.

HJALMAR *(halts):* For you?

HEDVIG: Yes. Something for tomorrow.

GINA: Bertha always brings you a little something for your birthday.

HJALMAR: What is it?

HEDVIG: No, you're not to find out now. Mother is to give it to me in the morning, when she brings me breakfast in bed.

HJALMAR: What is all this mystification that I am to be kept in the dark about!

HEDVIG *(quickly):* I'll be glad to let you see it, father. It's a big letter. *(Takes the letter out of her coat pocket.)*

HJALMAR: A letter too?

HEDVIG: The letter is all there is. I suppose the other thing will come later. Just think—a letter! I never got a letter before. And it says "Miss" on the outside of it. *(Reads.)* "Miss Hedvig Ekdal." Just think—that's me!

HJALMAR: Let me see that letter.

HEDVIG: Here you are. *(Hands it to him.)*

HJALMAR: It's Werle's handwriting.

GINA: Are you sure, Ekdal?

HJALMAR: See for yourself.

GINA: How would I know?

HJALMAR: Hedvig? May I open the letter? Read it?

HEDVIG: If you like.

GINA: Not tonight, Ekdal. It's supposed to be for tomorrow.

HEDVIG *(in a low voice):* Please let him read it! It's bound to be something nice, and then father will be in a good mood, and everything will be pleasant again.

HJALMAR: You say I may open it?

HEDVIG: Yes, please, father. I'd like to know what it is about, too.

HJALMAR: Good. *(Opens the envelope, reads the letter inside. Appears confused.)* What *is* this—?

GINA: What does it say?

HEDVIG: Please, father—tell us!

HJALMAR: Be quiet. *(Reads the letter again. He is pale, but his voice is controlled.)* It is a gift letter, Hedvig.

HEDVIG: Imagine! What is it I get?

HJALMAR: Read for yourself.

(HEDVIG goes over to the lamp and reads.)

HJALMAR *(in a low voice, clenches his fists):* The eyes, the eyes! And now that letter!

HEDVIG *(interrupting her reading):* Seems to me like it's Grandpa who gets it.

HJALMAR *(taking the letter away from her):* You, Gina—can you make any sense out of this?

GINA: I don't know a blessed thing about it. Why don't you just tell me?

HJALMAR: Werle writes to Hedvig that her old grandfather no longer needs to trouble himself with the copying work he has been doing, but that he may go to the office every month and draw one hundred crowns—

GREGERS: Aha!

HEDVIG: One hundred crowns, mother! I read that.

GINA: That will be nice for Grandpa.

HJALMAR: —one hundred crowns for as long as he needs it. That means, of course, till he closes his eyes.

GINA: So *he* is all taken care of, poor soul.

HJALMAR: Then it comes. You can't have read that far, Hedvig. After his death, that money will be yours.

HEDVIG: Mine? All of it?

HJALMAR: He writes that the same amount has been set aside for you for the rest of your life. Are you listening, Gina?

GINA: Yes, I hear.

HEDVIG: Just think—all the money I'll be getting! *(Shaking HJALMAR's arm.)* Father! Father! But aren't you glad?

HJALMAR *(going away from her):* Glad! *(Walking about.)* Oh what vistas, what perspectives, open up before me! It is Hedvig he is so generous to!

GINA: Well, she's the one with the birthday.

HEDVIG: And of course you will get it anyway, father! Don't you know I'll give it all to you and mother?

HJALMAR: To mother, yes! That's just it!

GREGERS: Hjalmar, this is a trap being prepared for you.

HJALMAR: You think this may be another trap?

GREGERS: When he was here this morning, he said, "Hjalmar Ekdal is not the man you think he is."

HJALMAR: Not the man—!

GREGERS: "You just wait and see," he said.

HJALMAR: You were to see me selling myself for money—!

HEDVIG: Mother, what *is* all this?

GINA: Go out and take your wraps off.

(HEDVIG, about to cry, goes out into the kitchen.)

GREGERS: Well, Hjalmar—now we shall see who is right—he or I.

HJALMAR *(slowly tearing the letter in two, putting the pieces down on the table):* Here is my answer.

GREGERS: Just as I thought.

HJALMAR *(to GINA, who is standing near the stove; in a low voice):* No more concealment now. If everything was over between you and him when you—came to care for me, as you call it, then why did he make it possible for us to get married?

GINA: I guess he thought he'd make free of the house.

HJALMAR: Just that? He wasn't worried about a certain possibility?

GINA: I don't know what you're talking about.

HJALMAR: I want to know—if your child has the right to live under my roof.

GINA *(drawing herself up, her eyes flashing):* You ask me that!

HJALMAR: Just tell me one thing. Is Hedvig mine or—?—Well?

GINA *(looks at him with cold defiance):* I don't know.

HJALMAR *(with a slight tremble):* You don't know!

GINA: How can I? A woman like me!

HJALMAR *(quietly, turning away from her):* In that case I have nothing more to do in this house.

GREGERS: Think it over, Hjalmar!

HJALMAR *(putting his overcoat on):* For a man like me there is nothing to think over.

GREGERS: Yes, there is ever so much to think over. You three must stay together if you are to attain to the sacrificial spirit of sublime forgivingness.

HJALMAR: I don't want to attain it! Never! Never! My hat! *(Takes his hat.)* My house is in ruins about me. *(Bursts out crying.)* Gregers! I have no child!

HEDVIG *(who has opened the kitchen door):* Father! What are you saying!

GINA: Oh dear!

HJALMAR: Don't come near me, Hedvig! Go far away from me. I can't stand looking at you. Oh those eyes—! Goodbye. *(Is about to go out.)*

HEDVIG *(clings to him, cries):* No! No! Don't leave me!

GINA: Look at the child, Ekdal! Look at the child!

HJALMAR: I will not! I cannot! I must get out—away from all this! *(He tears himself loose from HEDVIG and exits.)*

HEDVIG *(her eyes desperate):* He's leaving us, mother! He's leaving us! He'll never come back!

GINA: Just don't cry, Hedvig. Father will be back. You wait.

HEDVIG *(throws herself sobbing down on the sofa):* No! No! He'll never come back to us any more!

GREGERS: Do you believe I meant all for the best, Mrs. Ekdal?

GINA: Yes, I suppose you did, but God forgive you all the same.

HEDVIG *(on the sofa):* I want to die! What have I done to him, mother? You just have to get him back again!

GINA: Yes, yes, yes; only be quiet. I'll go out and look for him. *(Putting on her coat.)* Perhaps he's gone down to Relling's. But you're not to lie there, bawling like that. Promise?

HEDVIG *(sobbing convulsively):* All right, I'll stop, if only father comes home again.

GREGERS *(to* GINA, *who is leaving):* But would it not be better to let him fight his agony through by himself?

GINA: He can do that afterwards. First we've got to get the child quieted down. *(Goes out.)*

HEDVIG *(sitting up, drying her eyes):* Now you have to tell me what this is all about. Why doesn't father want me any more?

GREGERS: You must not ask that till you're big and grown-up.

HEDVIG *(sobbing):* But I just can't stay as miserable as this all the time till I'm grown up.—But I know what it is. Maybe I'm not really father's child.

GREGERS *(uneasily):* How could that be?

HEDVIG: Mother might have found me. And now perhaps father has found out about it. I have read about things like that.

GREGERS: Well, if it really were so—

HEDVIG: I think he could love me just as much, regardless. More, almost. The wild duck is a gift, too, and I love her very, very much.

GREGERS *(glad to turn the conversation):* Oh yes, the wild duck. Let's talk about the wild duck, Hedvig.

HEDVIG: That poor wild duck. He can't stand the sight of her, either. Just think, he wants to wring her neck!

GREGERS: Oh, I don't think he'll do that.

HEDVIG: No, but he said it. And I think that was horrid of father, for I pray for the wild duck every night, that she may be kept safe from death and all that's evil.

GREGERS *(looks at her):* Do you usually say prayers at night?

HEDVIG: Yes, I do.

GREGERS: Who taught you that?

HEDVIG: Myself, for father was terribly sick once and had leeches on his neck, and then he said that death was his dread companion.

GREGERS: And—?

HEDVIG: So I prayed for him when I went to bed. And I have done so ever since.

GREGERS: And now you pray for the wild duck, too?

HEDVIG: I thought it was best to mention her as well, for she was so sickly when we first got her.

GREGERS: Do you say morning prayers, too?

HEDVIG: Of course not.

GREGERS: Why is that so of course?

HEDVIG: Because it's light in the morning. There's not so much to be afraid of then.

GREGERS: And the wild duck you love so much—your father said he'd like to wring her neck?

HEDVIG: No, he said it would be better for him if he did, but he was going to spare her for my sake. And that was good of him.

GREGERS *(closer to her):* How would it be if you decided to sacrifice the wild duck for *his* sake?

HEDVIG *(getting up):* The wild duck!

GREGERS: What if you willingly gave up the dearest thing in the whole world for him?

HEDVIG: Do you think that would help?

GREGERS: Try it, Hedvig.

HEDVIG *(softly, with shining eyes):* Yes. I want to.

GREGERS: Do you think you have the right kind of strength for doing it?

HEDVIG: I shall ask Grandpa to shoot the wild duck for me.

GREGERS: Yes, do that. But not a word to your mother about this!

HEDVIG: Why not?

GREGERS: She doesn't understand us.

HEDVIG: The wild duck? I'll try it in the morning!

(GINA enters from the hall.)

HEDVIG *(towards her):* Did you find him, mother?

GINA: No, but I found out he's got Relling with him.

GREGERS: Are you sure?

GINA: Yes, the janitor's wife said so. Molvik's with them also.

GREGERS: Just now, when his soul so sorely needs to struggle in solitude—!

GINA *(taking off her coat):* Yes, men are funny. God knows where Relling is taking him! I ran over to Madam Eriksen's, but they aren't there.

HEDVIG *(struggling with her tears):* What if he never comes back!

GREGERS: He'll come back. I'll get word to him tomorrow, and then you'll see *how* he comes back. You count on that, Hedvig, and get a good night's sleep. Goodnight. *(Goes out.)*

HEDVIG *(throws herself sobbing on GINA's neck):* Mother! Mother!

GINA *(patting her back, sighing):* Yes, Relling was right. This is what happens when crazy people come around pestering us with the claim of the ordeal.

ACT V

(The studio. Cold, gray morning light. There is wet snow on the big panes of the skylight. GINA, aproned, with broom and dust cloth in her hand, enters from the kitchen and goes towards the living room door. HEDVIG hurries in from the outside at the same moment.)

GINA *(stops):* Well?

HEDVIG: Yes, mother, I almost think he's down at Relling's—

GINA: What did I tell you!

HEDVIG: —for the janitor's wife said she heard Relling bring two others home with him last night.

GINA: I knew it.

HEDVIG: But what good does it do, if he doesn't come up here to us?

GINA: I want to go down and have a talk with him, anyway.

(OLD EKDAL, in dressing gown and slippers and with his lighted pipe, appears in the door to his room.)

EKDAL: Eh—Hjalmar—? Isn't Hjalmar here?

GINA: No, he is out, Grandpa.

EKDAL: So early? In this blizzard? Well, I can walk by myself in the morning, I can, if it comes to that.

(He slides the attic door open. HEDVIG *helps him. He enters. She closes the door behind him.)*

HEDVIG *(in a low voice):* Mother, what do you think will happen when poor Grandpa hears that father has left us?

GINA: Silly! Grandpa mustn't hear anything about it, of course. It was a good thing he wasn't home last night, during all that hullaballoo.

HEDVIG: Yes, but—

*(*GREGERS *enters.)*

GREGERS: Well? Have you traced him yet?

GINA: They say he's down at Relling's.

GREGERS: At Relling's! Has he really been out with those two?

GINA: It looks like it.

GREGERS: But he is so badly in need of solitude—to find himself in earnest—

GINA: Yes. I should think so, too.

*(*RELLING *enters.)*

HEDVIG *(goes towards him):* Is father with you?

GINA *(at the same time):* Is he down there?

RELLING: He certainly is.

HEDVIG: And you haven't told us!

RELLING: I know. I am a big, bad beast. But I had this other big, bad beast to take care of, too—I mean the demonic one. And after that, I just fell asleep—sound asleep—

GINA: What does Ekdal say today?

RELLING: Not a thing.

HEDVIG: Doesn't he say anything at all?

RELLING: Not a blessed word.

GREGERS: I think I understand that.

GINA: But what is he doing?

RELLING: He is on the sofa, snoring.

GINA: Oh. Yes, Ekdal does snore a lot.

HEDVIG: He's asleep? Can he sleep now?

RELLING: It certainly looks that way.

GREGERS: That's reasonable enough, after the spiritual turmoil he's just been through—

GINA: And he isn't used to be out revelling nights, either.

HEDVIG: It may be a good thing that he is sleeping, mother.

GINA: That's what I am thinking. Anyway, we'd better not wake him up too soon. Thank you, Relling. First of all I've got to clean things up a bit and make the place look nice. Come and help me, Hedvig. *(They go into the living room.)*

GREGERS *(turning to* RELLING*):* Can you account for the present spiritual unrest in Hjalmar Ekdal?

RELLING: To tell you the truth, I haven't noticed any spiritual unrest in him.

GREGERS: What? At such a turning point—When his whole life is acquiring a new basis? How can you think that a personality like Hjalmar Ekdal—?

RELLING: Personality? He? If he ever had any tendency to sprout the kind of abnormal growth you call personality, I can assure you that all roots and tendrils were thoroughly extirpated in his boyhood.

GREGERS: That would indeed be strange, considering the loving upbringing he enjoyed.

RELLING: By those two crackpot, hysterical spinster aunts of his, you mean?

GREGERS: Let me tell you that they were women who never forgot the claim of the ideal—though I suppose you'll just be making fun of me again.

RELLING: No, I'm not in the mood. I do know about them, though. He has often enough held forth about "his soul's two mothers." Personally, I don't think he has much to be grateful to them for. Ekdal's misfortune is that he has always been looked upon as a shining light in his own circle.

GREGERS: And you don't think he is that? I mean, when it comes to depth of soul?

RELLING: I have never noticed it. That his father thought so is one thing. The old lieutenant has been an idiot all his days.

GREGERS: He has all his days been a man with a childlike mind. That is what you don't understand.

RELLING: All right. But after dear, sweet Hjalmar had taken up studying—after a fashion—right away he was the light of the future among his friends, too. He was handsome enough, the rascal—red and white, just the way little shop-girls like the fellows. And he had this sentimental temperament and this warm-hearted voice, and he could give such pretty declamations of other people's poetry and other people's thoughts—

GREGERS *(indignantly)*: Is this Hjalmar Ekdal you are describing?

RELLING: Yes, if you please. For this is what he looks like on the inside, the idol you are prostrating yourself for.

GREGERS: I didn't know I was as blind as all that.

RELLING: Well—not far from it. For you are sick, too, you see.

GREGERS: That is true.

RELLING: Yes it is. And yours is a complicated case. First, there is this pesky integrity fever you're suffering from, and then something worse—you are forever walking around in a delirium of adoration, always looking for something to admire outside of yourself.

GREGERS: Yes, there certainly wouldn't be much point in looking for it within myself.

RELLING: But you are always so hideously wrong about all those big, wonderful flies you see and hear buzzing around you. Once again you have entered a cottage with your claim of the ideal. People here just can't pay.

GREGERS: If this is the way you think of Hjalmar Ekdal, what sort of pleasure can you derive from your constant association with him?

RELLING: Oh well. I am supposed to be a kind of doctor, believe it or not, so the least I can do is to look after the poor patients I share quarters with.

GREGERS: Ah, I see. Hjalmar Ekdal is sick, too?

RELLING: Most people are, worse luck.

GREGERS: And what treatment do you apply in Hjalmar's case?

RELLING: My usual one. I see to it that his vital lie is kept up.

GREGERS: Vital—lie? I am not sure I heard what you said.

RELLING: That's right. I said the vital lie. You see, that's the stimulating principle.

GREGERS: May I ask with what vital lie you have infected Hjalmar?

RELLING: You may not. I never reveal professional secrets to quacks. You are capable of

messing him up for me even more than you have. But the method is proven. I have used it with Molvik, too. I have made him demonic. That's the suppurative I have applied to *his* neck.

GREGERS: But *isn't* he demonic?

RELLING: What the hell does it mean—being demonic? It's just some nonsense I thought of to save his life. If I hadn't, the poor, pitiful swine would have succumbed to self-hatred and despair many a year ago. Not to mention the old lieutenant! Though he has found his own cure.

GREGERS: Lieutenant Ekdal? What about him?

RELLING: What do you think? There he is, the old slayer of bears, chasing rabbits in a dark attic. And yet, there isn't a happier hunter alive than that old man when he is playing with all that junk. The four or five dried-out Christmas trees he has saved are the whole big, wild Høydal forest to him. The rooster and the chickens are wild fowl in the tree tops, and the rabbits bouncing about on the floor are bears he's grappling with—the frisky old sportsman.

GREGERS: Ah, yes—that unfortunate old Lieutenant Ekdal. He has certainly had to compromise the ideals of his youth.

RELLING: While I think of it, Mr. Werle—don't use the foreign word "ideals." We have available a good native one: "lies."

GREGERS: You think the two things are related?

RELLING: About as closely as typhus and putrid fever.

GREGERS: Doctor Relling! I won't give up till I have rescued Hjalmar from your clutches!

RELLING: That might be his bad luck. Take his vital lie away from the average person, and you take his happiness, too. *(To* HEDVIG, *who enters from the living room.)* Well, now, little duck mother. I am going down to see if papa is still in bed pondering that wonderful invention of his. *(Goes out.)*

GREGERS *(approaching* HEDVIG*)*: I can tell from looking at you that it has not yet been accomplished.

HEDVIG: What? Oh, that about the wild duck? No.

GREGERS: Your strength of purpose deserted you, I suppose, when the time for action had come.

HEDVIG: No, it wasn't that. But when I woke up this morning and remembered what we had talked about, it all seemed so strange.

GREGERS: Strange?

HEDVIG: Yes, I don't know—Last night, just at the time—I thought there was something very wonderful about it, but when I had slept and I thought about it again, it didn't seem like anything much.

GREGERS: I see. I could hardly expect you to grow up in this environment without injury to your soul.

HEDVIG: I don't care about that, if only father would come home again.

GREGERS: If only your eyes were opened to what gives life its worth—if only you possessed the true, joyful, brave, sacrificial spirit, then you'd see he'll return. But I still have faith in you, Hedvig. *(Goes out.)*

*(*HEDVIG *walks around aimlessly. She is about to enter the kitchen, when there is a knock on the inside of the door to the attic.* HEDVIG *opens the doors wide enough for* OLD EKDAL *to come out. She shuts them again.)*

EKDAL: H'm. Not much fun taking a walk by yourself, y'know.
HEDVIG: Wouldn't you like to go hunting, Grandpa?
EKDAL: It isn't hunting weather today. Too dark. Can hardly see a thing.
HEDVIG: Don't you ever want to shoot something beside rabbits?
EKDAL: Aren't the rabbits good enough, perhaps?
HEDVIG: Yes, but what about the wild duck?
EKDAL: Haw! So you're scared I'll shoot your wild duck? I'll never do that, Hedvig. Never.
HEDVIG: No, for I bet you don't know how. I've heard it's difficult to shoot wild ducks.
EKDAL: Don't know how! Should say I do!
HEDVIG: How would you do it, Grandpa?—I don't mean *my* wild duck, but another one.
EKDAL: Would try to get a shot in just below the breast; that's the best place. And try to shoot *against* the feathers, not *with*.
HEDVIG: Then they die?
EKDAL: Damn right they do—if you shoot right.—Well, better go in and dress up. H'm. Y'know. H'm— *(Goes into his own room.)*

(HEDVIG waits a moment, glances towards the living room door, stands on tiptoe, takes the double-barreled pistol down from the shelf, looks at it. GINA, with broom and dust cloth, enters from the living room. HEDVIG quickly puts the pistol back, without GINA's noticing.)

GINA: Don't fool with father's things, Hedvig.
HEDVIG *(leaving the shelf)*: I just wanted to straighten up some.
GINA: Why don't you go into the kitchen and see if the coffee is keeping hot? I am taking a tray with me when I go down.

(HEDVIG goes into the kitchen. GINA starts putting the studio in order. After a short while, the door to the outside is hesitantly opened and HJALMAR looks in. He is wearing a coat but no hat. He looks unkempt and unwashed. His eyes are dull and lusterless.)

GINA *(stands staring at him, still with the broom in her hand)*: Bless you, Ekdal—so you did come back, after all!
HJALMAR *(enters, answers in a dull voice)*: I return—only to leave.
GINA: Yes, yes, I suppose. But good Lord! how you look!
HJALMAR: Look?
GINA: And your nice winter coat? I'd say that's done for.
HEDVIG *(in the kitchen door)*: Mother, don't you want me to— *(sees HJALMAR, gives a shout of joy and runs towards him.)* Father! Father!
HJALMAR *(turning away, with a gesture)*: Go away! Go away! *(To GINA.)* Get her away from me, I say!
GINA *(in a low voice)*: Go into the living room, Hedvig.

(HEDVIG leaves silently.)

HJALMAR *(busy, pulling out the table drawer)*: I need my books with me. Where are my books?
GINA: Which books?
HJALMAR: My scientific works, of course—the technical journals I need for my invention.
GINA: *(looking on the shelf)*: Do you mean these over here, with no covers on them?

HJALMAR: Yes, yes, of course.

GINA *(puts a pile of journals down on the table):* Don't you want me to get Hedvig to cut them open for you?

HJALMAR: No. Nobody needs to cut any pages for me.

(Brief silence.)

GINA: So you *are* going to leave us, Ekdal?

HJALMAR *(rummaging among the books):* That goes without saying, I should think.

GINA: All right.

HJALMAR *(violently):* For you can hardly expect me to want to stay where my heart is pierced every single hour of the day!

GINA: God forgive you for thinking so bad of me!

HJALMAR: Proof—!

GINA: Seems to me, you're the one who should bring proof.

HJALMAR: After a past like yours? There are certain claims—I might call them the claims of the ideal—

GINA: What about Grandpa? What is *he* going to do, poor man?

HJALMAR: I know my duty. The helpless one goes with me. I'll go out and make arrangements—H'm. *(Hesitantly.)* Has anybody found my hat on the stairs?

GINA: No. Have you lost your hat?

HJALMAR: I most certainly had it on when I came home last night; there isn't the slightest doubt about that. But now I can't find it.

GINA: Good Lord! Where did you go with those two drunks?

HJALMAR: Oh, don't ask about inessentials. Do you think I'm in a mood for remembering details?

GINA: I only hope you haven't got a cold, Ekdal *(Goes into the kitchen.)*

HJALMAR *(speaking to himself, in a low voice, angrily, as he empties the drawer):* You're a scoundrel, Relling!—A villain is what you are!—Miserable traitor!—I'd gladly see you assassinated—!

(He puts aside some old letters, discovers the torn gift letter from the day before, picks it up and looks at the two pieces, puts them down quickly as GINA *enters.)*

GINA *(putting a tray with food down on the table):* Here's a drop of coffee, if you want it. And some salt meat sandwiches.

HJALMAR *(glancing at the tray):* Salt meat? Never under this roof! True it is, I haven't taken solid nourishment for almost twenty-four hours, but that can't be helped.—My notes! My incipient memoirs! Where is my diary—all my important papers! *(Opens the door to the living room, but steps back.)* If she isn't there, too!

GINA: Heavens, Ekdal. She's got to be somewhere.

HJALMAR: Leave! *(He makes room.* HEDVIG, *scared, enters the studio. With his hand on the door knob; to* GINA.*)* During the last moments I spend in my former home I wish to be spared the sight of intruders— *(Enters the living room.)*

HEDVIG *(starts, asks her mother in a low and trembling voice):* Does that mean me?

GINA: Stay in the kitchen, Hedvig, or no—go to your own room. *(To* HJALMAR, *as she enters*

the living room.) Wait a minute, Ekdal. Don't make such a mess in the dresser. I know where everything is.

HEDVIG *(remains motionless for a moment, in helpless fright, presses her lips together not to cry, clenches her hands, whispers):* The wild duck!

(She tiptoes over to the shelf and takes the pistol down, opens the doors to the inner attic, goes inside, closes behind her. HJALMAR *and* GINA *are heard talking in the living room.)*

HJALMAR *(appears with some notebooks and a pile of old papers, which he puts down on the table):* The bag obviously won't be enough. There are thousands of things I need to take with me!

GINA *(entering with the bag):* Can't you leave most of it behind for the time being and just pick up a clean shirt and some underwear?

HJALMAR: Phew—! These exhausting preparations—! *(Takes off his overcoat and throws it on the sofa.)*

GINA: And there's the coffee getting cold too.

HJALMAR: H'm. *(Without thinking, he takes a sip, and then another one.)*

GINA *(dusting off the back of chairs):* How are you ever going to find a large enough attic for the rabbits?

HJALMAR: You mean I have to drag all those rabbits along, too?

GINA: Grandpa can't do without his rabbits—you know that as well as I do.

HJALMAR: He'll have to get used to that. I shall have to give up higher values in life than a bunch of rabbits.

GINA *(dusting off the shelf):* Shall I put the flute in for you?

HJALMAR: No. No flute for me. But give me my pistol.

GINA: You want that old pestol?

HJALMAR: Yes. My loaded pistol.

GINA *(looking for it):* It's gone. He must have taken it inside with him.

HJALMAR: Is he in the attic?

GINA: Sure, he's in the attic.

HJALMAR: H'm. The lonely grayhead— *(He eats a sandwich, empties his cup of coffee.)*

GINA: If only we hadn't rented that room, you could have moved in there.

HJALMAR: And stay under the same roof as—! Never! Never again!

GINA: But couldn't you stay in the living room for a day or two? There you'd have everything to yourself.

HJALMAR: Not within these walls!

GINA: How about down at Relling's and Molvik's, then?

HJALMAR: Don't mention their names to me! I get sick just thinking about them. Oh no—it's out into the wind and the snowdrifts for me—to walk from house to house seeking shelter for father and myself.

GINA: But you have no hat, Ekdal! You've lost your hat, remember?

HJALMAR: Oh, those two abominations! Rich in nothing but every vice! A hat must be procured. *(Takes another sandwich.)* Arrangements must be made. After all, I don't intend to catch my death. *(Looks for something on the tray.)*

GINA: What are you looking for?

HJALMAR: Butter.

GINA: Just a moment. *(Goes out into the kitchen.)*

HJALMAR *(shouting after her)*: Oh never mind. Dry bread is good enough for me.

GINA *(bringing a plate with butter)*: Here. This is supposed to be freshly churned.

(She pours him another cup of coffee. He sits down on the sofa, puts more butter on his bread, eats and drinks in silence.)

HJALMAR *(after a pause)*: Could I, without being disturbed by anyone—and I mean *anyone*—stay in the living room for a day or two?

GINA: You certainly can, if you want to.

HJALMAR: You see, I don't know how to get all of father's things moved out on such short notice.

GINA: And there is this, too, that first you'd have to tell him that you don't want to live together with the rest of us any more.

HJALMAR *(pushing his cup away)*: Yes, yes—that, too. I shall have to go into all those intricate relationships once again, to explain—I must think, I must have air to breathe, I can't bear all the burdens in one single day.

GINA: Of course not. And in such awful weather too—

HJALMAR *(moving* WERLE'S *letter)*: I notice this piece of paper still lying around.

GINA: Well, *I* haven't touched it.

HJALMAR: Not that it concerns *me*—

GINA: I'm sure *I* don't expect to make use of it—

HJALMAR: Nevertheless, I suppose we shouldn't let it get completely lost. In all the fuss of moving, something might easily—

GINA: I'll take care of it, Ekdal.

HJALMAR: For the gift letter belongs to father, first of all. It's his affair whether he wants to make use of it or not.

GINA: *(with a sigh)*: Yes, poor old Grandpa—

HJALMAR: Just to make sure—Is there any glue?

GINA *(walks over to the shelf)*: Here's a bottle.

HJALMAR: And a brush?

GINA: Here. *(Brings him both.)*

HJALMAR *(picks up a pair of scissors)*: Just a strip of paper on the back— *(Cuts and glues.)* Far be it from me to lay hands on somebody else's property—least of all the property of a poverty-stricken old man.—Well—not on—that other one's, either.—There, now! Leave it to dry for a while. And when it's dry, remove it. I don't want to see that document again—ever!

*(*GREGERS *enters.)*

GREGERS *(a little surprised)*: What? So this is where you are, Hjalmar!

HJALMAR *(quickly gets up)*: Sheer exhaustion drove me to sit down.

GREGERS: And I see you've had breakfast.

HJALMAR: The body, too, makes demands at times.

GREGERS: Well, what have you decided to do?

HJALMAR: For a man like me, there is only one way open. I am in the process of gathering up my most important possessions. Obviously, that takes time.

GINA *(a trifle impatient):* Do you want me to make the living room ready for you, or do you want me to pack the bag?

HJALMAR *(after an irritated glance at* GREGERS*):* Pack—and make the room ready.

GINA *(picking up the bag):* All right. I'll just put in the shirts and those other things. *(She goes into the living room, closing the door behind her.)*

GREGERS *(after a short silence):* I had no idea this would be the end of it. Is it really necessary for you to leave house and home?

HJALMAR *(paces restlessly up and down):* What do you want me to do? I am not made to be unhappy, Gregers. I require peace and security and comfort around me.

GREGERS: But you can have all that, Hjalmar. Just try. It seems to me there is a firm foundation to build upon now. Start all over again. And remember, you still have your invention to live for.

HJALMAR: Oh don't talk about that invention. It may take a long time yet.

GREGERS: So?

HJALMAR: Well, yes, for heaven's sake, what do you expect me to invent, anyway? The others have invented most of it already. It's getting more difficult every day.

GREGERS: But all the labor you have put into it—?

HJALMAR: It was that dissipated Relling who got me started on it.

GREGERS: Relling?

HJALMAR: Yes, it was he who first called attention to my talent for making some fabulous invention or other in photography.

GREGERS: I see. It was Relling—!

HJALMAR: Ah—I have been so wonderfully happy about it. Not so much about the invention itself, but because Hedvig believed in it—believed with all the strength and power of a child's soul.—That is, I *thought* she did—fool as I was.

GREGERS: Can you really think that Hedvig would be false to you?

HJALMAR: I can believe anything now. It is Hedvig who is in the way. She it is who is shutting the sun out of my entire life.

GREGERS: Hedvig? You mean Hedvig? How in the world is she going to be an obstacle?

HJALMAR *(without answering):* I have loved that child more than I can ever say. You have no idea how happy I was whenever I came back to my humble dwelling and she rushed towards me with her sweet, squinting eyes. Ha, credulous fool that I was! She was so unspeakably dear to me—and so I lulled myself into the dream that I was equally dear to her.

GREGERS: You call that a dream?

HJALMAR: How can I tell? I can't get anything out of Gina. Besides, she completely lacks any sense of the ideal aspects of the issue. But to you I can open up, Gregers. It is this terrible doubt—perhaps Hedvig has never really loved me.

GREGERS: Maybe you'll receive proof— *(Listens.)* Shh! What's that? The wild duck?

HJALMAR: It's just quacking. Father's in the attic.

GREGERS: He is! *(Joy lights his face.)* I tell you again, Hjalmar—maybe you will find proof that your poor, misunderstood Hedvig has always loved you!

HJALMAR: Pah! What proof could she give? I dare not trust to mere asseverations.

GREGERS: Surely, Hedvig doesn't know what deceit is.

HJALMAR: Ah, Gregers—that is just what I cannot be certain of. Who knows what Gina and this Mrs. Sørby may have been whispering and scheming? And Hedvig's ears are big enough, believe you me. Maybe that gift letter didn't come as such a surprise to her. It seemed to me I noticed something like that.

GREGERS: Good heavens, Hjalmar! What kind of spirit is this that's taken possession of you!

HJALMAR: I have had my eyes opened. You just wait. It may turn out that the gift letter was just the beginning. Mrs. Sørby has always been very fond of Hedvig, and now, of course, it's in her power to do anything she likes for the child. They can take her away from me what day and hour they choose.

GREGERS: Hedvig will never leave you, Hjalmar. Never.

HJALMAR: Don't be too sure. If they beckon her with their arms full—? And I who have loved her so infinitely much! I, whose greatest joy it was to take her tenderly by the hand and lead her, as one leads a frightened child through a dark and deserted room! Now I feel this painful certainty that the poor photographer in his attic has never really meant very much to her. She has only cleverly managed to keep on good terms with him while she bided her time.

GREGERS: You don't believe this, Hjalmar.

HJALMAR: That is just what is so terrible—I don't know what to believe—I'll never be able to find out! But do you really doubt that I am right? Ah, Gregers, you put too much trust in the claim of the ideal! If those others were to come now, with their ample offerings, and called to the child: Leave him; life awaits you here with us—

GREGERS *(quickly)*: Yes, what then—?

HJALMAR: If then I were to ask her: Hedvig, are you willing to give your life for me? *(Laughs scornfully.)* Oh yes—you'd find out soon enough what answer I'd get!

(A pistol shot is heard from within the attic.)

GREGERS *(with a shout of joy)*: Hjalmar!

HJALMAR: Must he go shooting today—!

GINA *(enters)*: Can't say I like this, Ekdal—Grandpa in there all by himself, banging away.

HJALMAR: I'll take a look—

GREGERS *(agitated, feelingly)*: Wait! Do you know what that was?

HJALMAR: Yes, of course, I do.

GREGERS: No, you don't. But *I* know. It was the proof!

HJALMAR: What proof?

GREGERS: It was a child's sacrifice. She has got your father to shoot the wild duck.

HJALMAR: Shoot the wild duck!

GINA: Heavens—!

HJALMAR: Whatever for?

GREGERS: She wanted to sacrifice to you what she held dearest in the whole world. For then she thought you'd love her again.

HJALMAR *(softly, moved)*: Oh that child!

GINA: What she thinks of!

GREGERS: All she wanted was your love, Hjalmar. Without it, life didn't seem possible to her.

GINA *(struggling with tears)*: *Now,* do you see, Ekdal?

HJALMAR: Gina, where is she?

GINA *(sniffling)*: Poor thing. She is sitting out in the kitchen, I guess.

HJALMAR *(walks to the kitchen door, flings it open, says)*: Hedvig—come! Come to me! *(Looks around.)* No. She isn't here.

GINA: Then she must be in her own room.

HJALMAR *(offstage):* No, she isn't there, either. *(Re-entering the studio.)* She must have gone out.

GINA: Yes, for you know you didn't want to see hide nor hair of her in the house.

HJALMAR: If only she'd come back soon—so I can tell her—Now I feel that everything will be all right, Gregers. Now I think we can start life over again.

GREGERS *(quietly):* I knew it. Restitution would come through the child.

(Old EKDAL appears in the door to his room. He is in full uniform and is buckling on his sabre.)

HJALMAR *(surprised):* Father! You're in there!

GINA: Do you go shooting in your room, now, Grandpa?

EKDAL *(approaches indignantly):* So you're off hunting by yourself, are you Hjalmar?

HJALMAR *(tense, confused):* You mean it wasn't you who fired that shot in the attic just now?

EKDAL: I? Fired? H'm.

GREGERS *(shouts to HJALMAR):* She has shot the wild duck herself!

HJALMAR: What *is* this? *(He hurriedly slides the attic doors open, looks in, gives a loud cry.)* Hedvig!

GINA *(runs to the door):* Oh God! What is it?

HJALMAR *(going inside):* She is lying on the floor!

GREGERS: Lying—! *(Follows HJALMAR inside.)*

GINA *(at the same time):* Hedvig! *(Enters the attic.)* No! No! No!

EKDAL: Ho-ho! So *she* has taken to hunting too, now!

(HJALMAR, GINA, and GREGERS drag HEDVIG into the studio. Her trailing right hand clasps the pistol tightly.)

HJALMAR *(beside himself):* The pistol went off! She's hit! Call for help! Help!

GINA *(running out into the hallway, shouts down):* Relling! Relling! Doctor Relling! Hurry up here, fast as you can!

(HJALMAR and GREGERS put HEDVIG down on the sofa.)

EKDAL *(quietly):* The woods avenge themselves.

HJALMAR *(on his knees beside HEDVIG):* She's coming to now. She is coming to. Oh yes, yes, yes—

GINA *(having returned):* Where's she hit? I can't see a thing.

(RELLING enters hurriedly, followed by MOLVIK. The latter is without vest and tie, his tailcoat thrown open.)

RELLING: What's the matter?

GINA: They say Hedvig has shot herself.

HJALMAR: Come and help us!

RELLING: Shot herself! *(He pulls the table back and begins to examine her.)*

HJALMAR *(still on his knees, looking anxiously at RELLING):* It can't be dangerous, can it, Relling? What, Relling? She hardly bleeds at all. It can't possibly be dangerous?

RELLING: How did this happen?

HJALMAR: Oh, I don't know—

GINA: She was going to shoot the wild duck.

RELLING: The wild duck?

HJALMAR: The pistol must have gone off.

RELLING: H'm. I see.

EKDAL: The woods avenge themselves. But I'm not afraid. *(Enters the attic and closes the doors behind him.)*

HJALMAR: Relling—why don't you say anything?

RELLING: The bullet has entered her chest.

HJALMAR: Yes, but she's coming to!

RELLING: Can't you see that Hedvig is dead?

GINA *(bursts into tears):* Oh, the child, the child—!

GREGERS *(hoarsely):* In the depths of the sea—

HJALMAR *(jumps to his feet):* She must live! I want her to live! For God's sake, Relling—just for a moment—just so I can tell her how unspeakably much I have loved her all the time!

RELLING: Her heart has been pierced. Internal hemorrhage. She died instantly.

HJALMAR: And I who chased her away from me like an animal! Frightened and lonely she crawled into the attic and died for love of me. *(Sobbing.)* Never to be able to make up for it! Never to tell her—! *(Shakes his fists upwards.)* You! You above! If thou art at all—! Why hast thou done this unto me?

GINA: Shhh, shhh. You mustn't make such a fuss. We had no right to keep her, I suppose.

MOLVIK: The child is not dead. It sleepeth.

RELLING: Rubbish!

HJALMAR *(quieting down, walks over to the sofa, looks at* HEDVIG, *his arms crossed):* There she lies, so stiff and still.

RELLING *(trying to release the pistol):* She holds on so tightly, I can't—

GINA: No, no, Relling. Don't break her fingers. Let the pistol be.

HJALMAR: Let her have it with her.

GINA: Yes, let her. But the child isn't going to lie out here for a show. She is going into her own little room, right now. Give me a hand, Ekdal.

*(*HJALMAR *and* GINA *carry* HEDVIG *between them.)*

HJALMAR *(carrying):* Gina, Gina—do you think you can bear this?

GINA: The one has to help the other. Seems to me like now we both have a share in her.

MOLVIK *(raising his arms, muttering):* Praise be the Lord, to dust thou returnest, to dust thou returnest—

RELLING *(whispers):* Shut up, man! You're drunk.

*(*HJALMAR *and* GINA *carry* HEDVIG *through the kitchen door.* RELLING *closes the door behind them.* MOLVIK *slinks quietly out into the hall.)*

RELLING *(goes up to* GREGERS*):* Nobody is going to tell me this was an accident.

GREGERS *(who has remained stunned, moving convulsively):* Who is to say how this terrible thing happened?

RELLING: There were powder burns on her dress. She must have placed the muzzle against her chest and pulled the trigger.

GREGERS: Hedvig has not died in vain. Did you notice how grief released what is great in him?

RELLING: There is a touch of greatness in most of us when we stand in sorrow by a corpse. How long do you think that will last with him?

GREGERS: As if it won't last and grow throughout the rest of his days!

RELLING: Within a year little Hedvig won't be anything to him but an occasion for spouting pretty sentiments.

GREGERS: And you dare say that about Hjalmar Ekdal!

RELLING: Let's talk about this again when the first grass has withered on her grave. You'll hear all about "the child so early taken from the father's heart." You'll see him wallow in sentimentality and self-admiration and self-pity. You just wait!

GREGERS: If you are right and I am wrong, life isn't worth living.

RELLING: Oh, life would be fairly tolerable if only we'd be spared these blasted bill collectors who come around pestering us paupers with the claim of the ideal.

GREGERS *(staring ahead):* In that case I am glad my destiny is what it is.

RELLING: Beg your pardon—what *is* your destiny?

GREGERS *(about to leave):* To be the thirteenth man at the table.

RELLING: The hell it is.

BERTHOLD BRECHT

(1898–1956)

Mother Courage and Her Children

ENGLISH VERSION BY ERIC BENTLEY

About the Author: Berthold Brecht, German poet, director, and playwright, developed an enduring hatred of war while serving as a medical orderly in a German military hospital during World War I. After the war he studied at the University of Munich, and he scored his first major dramatic success in Berlin in 1928 with the Marxist *Threepenny Opera.* As Hitler came to power, Brecht went into exile, going first to the Scandinavian countries, then to Hollywood and Switzerland, before returning to Berlin after World War II.

Brecht tried to invent a new kind of play which could change the consciousness of his audience, one which could change the way his society thought about social issues. He called this new form "epic theater." In it, he tried to deny the audience the possibility of identifying with the characters, tried to force the people in the audience to detach themselves emotionally from the performance so that they would think critically about the issues presented in the plays. In creating his characters, Brecht tried to ignore their so-called universal human traits and to emphasize instead those characteristics which were uniquely produced by a particular past situation. He tried to avoid suspense and climax in his plots, so that we will not concentrate on what happens next but on how events unfold and on what the forces are behind them. The absence of suspense keeps us from losing ourselves in the story so that we can think seriously about the story's ideas and apply them to our own lives. Brecht did not try to make events seem

realistic onstage; the lights and other theatrical necessities were exposed to view, so that the audience would constantly be reminded that it was in a theater, that the play was a make-believe story that posed difficult but crucial questions, and that those questions were what the play was about. To reinforce this effect, characters often speak directly to the audience. When (as often) there is music, sentimental lyrics are undermined by harsh melodies.

About the Play: *Mother Courage* was written in 1939 and first performed in 1941 in Zurich. It was produced in reaction against Hitler and World War II, constructed against the combination of Naziism and capitalism and war which characterized that historical moment. In the title character, instead of expecting consistency, we might look for her contradictions or *in*consistencies. And we might think about how those contradictions are produced and whether they continue to be produced in us today.

CHARACTERS

MOTHER COURAGE
EILIF } *her sons*
SWISS CHEESE }
KATTRIN, *her daughter*
RECRUITING OFFICER
SERGEANT
COOK
COMMANDER
CHAPLAIN
ORDNANCE OFFICER
SERGEANT
YVETTE POTTIER
ONE EYE
SOLDIER
COLONEL
CLERK
OLDER SOLDIER
YOUNGER SOLDIER
FIRST SOLDIER
PEASANT
SECOND SOLDIER
PEASANT WOMAN
SOLDIER, *SINGING*
OLD WOMAN
YOUNG MAN
SOLDIER
LIEUTENANT
OLD PEASANT
FIRST SOLDIER
PEASANT WOMAN
SECOND SOLDIER
YOUNG PEASANT

THE TIME: 1624–1636
THE PLACE: *Sweden, Poland, Germany*

PROLOGUE: *THE SONG OF MOTHER COURAGE*

The wagon of a vivandière.

MOTHER COURAGE *sits on the wagon with her daughter* KATTRIN. *Her sons,* EILIF *and* SWISS CHEESE, *pull the wagon and join in the refrains of the song.* KATTRIN *plays a harmonica.*

Here's Mother Courage and her wagon!
Hey, Captain, let them come and buy!
Beer by the keg! Wine by the flagon!
Let your men drink before they die!
Sabers and swords are hard to swallow:
First you must give them beer to drink.
Then they can face what is to follow—
But let 'em swim before they sink!
Christians, awake! The winter's gone!
The snows depart, the dead sleep on.
And though you may not long survive,
Get out of bed and look alive!

Your men will march till they are dead, sir,
But cannot fight unless they eat.
The blood they spill for you is red, sir,
What fires that blood is my red meat.
For meat and soup and jam and jelly
In this old cart of mine are found:
So fill the hole up in your belly
Before you fill one underground.
Christians, awake! The winter's gone!
The snows depart, the dead sleep on.
And though you may not long survive,
Get out of bed and look alive!

1

SPRING, 1624. IN DALARNA, THE SWEDISH KING GUSTAVUS IS RECRUITING FOR THE CAMPAIGN IN POLAND. THE CANTEEN WOMAN ANNA FIERLING, COMMONLY KNOWN AS MOTHER COURAGE, LOSES A SON.

Highway outside a town. A TOP SERGEANT *and a* RECRUITING OFFICER *stand shivering.*

RECRUITING OFFICER: How the hell can you line up a squadron in *this* place? You know what I keep thinking about, Sergeant? Suicide. I'm supposed to slap four platoons together by the twelfth—four platoons the Chief's asking for! And they're so friendly around here, I'm scared to sleep nights. Suppose I do get my hands on some character and squint at him so I don't notice he's chicken-breasted and has varicose veins. I get him drunk and relaxed, he signs on the dotted line. I pay for the drinks, he steps outside for a minute. I get a hunch I should follow him to the door, and am I right! Off he's

shot like a louse from a scratch. You can't take a man's word any more, Sergeant. There's no loyalty left in the world, no trust, no faith, no sense of honor. I'm losing my confidence in mankind, Sergeant.

SERGEANT: What they could use around here is a good war. What else can you expect with peace running wild all over the place? You know what the trouble with peace is? No organization. And when do you get organization? In a war. Peace is one big waste of equipment. Anything goes, no one gives a damn. See the way they eat? Cheese on rye, bacon on the cheese? Disgusting! How many horses they got in this town? How many young men? Nobody knows! They haven't bothered to count 'em! That's peace for you!!! I been places where they haven't had a war in seventy years and you know what? The people can't remember their own names! They don't know who they are! It takes a war to fix that. In a war, everyone registers, everyone's name's on a list. Their shoes are stacked, their corn's in the bag, you count it all up—cattle, men, *et cetera*—and you take it away! That's the story: no organization, no war!

RECRUITING OFFICER: It's the God's truth.

SERGEANT: Course, a war's like every real good deal: hard to get going. But when it's on the road, it's a pisser—everybody's scared off peace—like a crap-shooter that keeps fading to cover his loss. Course, *until* it gets going, they're just as scared off war—afraid to try anything new.

RECRUITING OFFICER: Look, a wagon! Two women and a couple of young punks. Stop 'em, Sergeant. And if there's nothing doing this time, you won't catch *me* freezing my ass in the April wind.

MOTHER COURAGE *enters on her wagon and with her children as in the prologue.*

MOTHER COURAGE: Good day to you, Sergeant.

SERGEANT *(barring the way):* Good day! Who d'you think you are?

MOTHER COURAGE: Tradespeople.

(She prepares to go.)

SERGEANT: Halt! Where are you from, riffraff?

EILIF: Second Protestant Regiment!

SERGEANT: Where are your papers?

MOTHER COURAGE: Papers?

SWISS CHEESE: But this is Mother Courage!

SERGEANT: Never heard of her. Where'd she get a name like that?

MOTHER COURAGE: In Riga.

EILIF AND SWISS CHEESE *(reciting together):* They call her Mother Courage because she drove through the bombardment of Riga with fifty loaves of bread in her wagon!

MOTHER COURAGE: They were going moldy, I couldn't help myself.

SERGEANT: No funny business! Where are your papers?

MOTHER COURAGE *rummages among papers in a tin box and clambers down from her wagon.*

MOTHER COURAGE: Here, Sergeant! Here's a whole Bible—I got it in Altötting to wrap my cucumbers in. Here's a map of Moravia—God knows if I'll ever get there. And here's

a document saying my horse hasn't got hoof and mouth disease—too bad he died on us, he cost fifteen guilders, thank God I didn't pay it. Is that enough paper?

SERGEANT: Are you making a pass at me? Well, you got another guess coming. You must have a license and you know it.

MOTHER COURAGE: Show a little respect for a lady and don't go telling these grown children of mine I'm making a pass at you. What would I want with you? My license in the Second Protestant Regiment is an honest face—even if *you* wouldn't know how to read it.

RECRUITING OFFICER: Sergeant, we have a case of insubordination on our hands. *(To her:)* Do you know what we need in the army? *(MOTHER COURAGE starts to answer.)* Discipline!

MOTHER COURAGE: I was going to say sausages.

SERGEANT: Name?

MOTHER COURAGE: Anna Fierling.

SERGEANT: So you're all Fierlings.

MOTHER COURAGE: I was talking about me.

SERGEANT: And I was talking about your children.

MOTHER COURAGE: Must they all have the same name? This boy, for instance, I call him Eilif Noyocki—he got the name from his father who told me he was called Koyocki. Or was it Moyocki? Anyhow, the lad remembers him to this day. Only the man he remembers is someone else, a Frenchman with a pointed beard. But he certainly has his father's brains—that man could whip the pants off a farmer's behind before he could turn around. So we all have our own names.

SERGEANT: You're all called something different?

MOTHER COURAGE: Are you pretending you don't get it?

SERGEANT *(pointing at SWISS CHEESE):* He's a Chinese, I suppose.

MOTHER COURAGE: Wrong again. A Swiss.

SERGEANT: After the Frenchman?

MOTHER COURAGE: Frenchman? What Frenchman? Don't confuse the issue, Sergeant, or we'll be here all day. He's a Swiss, but he happens to be called Feyos, a name that has nothing to do with his father, who was called something else—a military engineer, if you please, and a drunkard.

SWISS CHEESE *nods, beaming; even* KATTRIN *smiles.*

SERGEANT: Then how come his name's Feyos?

MOTHER COURAGE: Oh, Sergeant, you have no imagination. *Of course* he's called Feyos: When he came, I was with a Hungarian. He didn't mind. He had a floating kidney, though he never touched a drop. He was a very *honest* man. The boy takes after him.

SERGEANT: But that wasn't his father!

MOTHER COURAGE: I said: he took after him. I call him Swiss Cheese. And that is my daughter Kattrin Haupt, she's half German.

SERGEANT: A nice family, I must say!

MOTHER COURAGE: And we've seen the whole wide world together—this wagon-load and me.

SERGEANT *(writing):* We'll need all that in writing.

RECRUITING OFFICER *(to EILIF):* So you two are the oxen for the wagon? Do they ever let you out of harness?

EILIF: Mother! May I smack him in the puss?

MOTHER COURAGE: You stay where you are. And now, gentlemen, how about a pair of pistols? Or a belt? Sergeant? Yours is worn clean through.

SERGEANT: It's something else *I'm* looking for. These lads of yours are straight as birch-trees. What are such fine specimens doing out of the army?

MOTHER COURAGE *(quickly)*: The soldier's life is not for sons of mine!

RECRUITING OFFICER: Why not? It means money. It means fame. Peddling shoes is woman's work. *(To* EILIF:*)* Step this way and let's see if that's muscle or chicken fat.

MOTHER COURAGE: It's chicken fat. Give him a good hard look, and he'll fall right over.

RECRUITING OFFICER: Well, I hope he doesn't fall on me, that's all. *(He tries to hustle* EILIF *away.)*

MOTHER COURAGE: Let him alone! He's not for you!

RECRUITING OFFICER: He called my face a puss. That is an insult. The two of us will now go settle the affair on the field of honor.

EILIF: Don't worry, Mother, I can handle him.

MOTHER COURAGE: Stay here. You're never happy till you're in a fight. *(To the* OFFICER:*)* He has a knife in his boot and he knows how to use it.

RECRUITING OFFICER: I'll draw it out of him like a milk tooth. *(To* EILIF:*)* Come on, young fellow!

MOTHER COURAGE: Officer, I'll report you to the Colonel, and he'll throw you in jail. His lieutenant is courting my daughter.

SERGEANT *(to* OFFICER*)*: Go easy. *(To* MOTHER COURAGE:*)* What have you got against the service, wasn't his own father a soldier? Didn't you say he died a soldier's death?

MOTHER COURAGE: He's dead all right. But this one's just a baby. You'll lead him like a lamb to the slaughter. I know you. You'll get five guilders for him.

RECRUITING OFFICER *(to* EILIF*)*: First thing you know, you'll have a new cap and high boots, how about it?

EILIF: Not from you, thanks.

MOTHER COURAGE: "Let's you and me go fishing," said the angler to the worm. *(To* SWISS CHEESE:*)* Run and tell everybody they're trying to steal your brother! *(She draws a knife.)* Yes, just you try, and I'll cut you down like dogs! We sell cloth, we sell ham, we are peaceful people!

SERGEANT: You're peaceful all right: your knife proves that. Now tell me, how can we have a war without soldiers?

MOTHER COURAGE: Do they have to be mine?

SERGEANT: So that's the trouble! The war should swallow the pits and spit out the peach, huh? Tsk, tsk, tsk: call yourself Mother Courage and then get scared of the war, your breadwinner? Your sons aren't scared, I know that much.

EILIF: No war can scare me.

SERGEANT: Of course not! Take me. The soldier's life hasn't done *me* any harm, has it? I enlisted at seventeen.

MOTHER COURAGE: You haven't reached seventy.

SERGEANT: I will, though.

MOTHER COURAGE: Above ground?

SERGEANT: Are you trying to rile me, telling me I'll die?

MOTHER COURAGE: Suppose it's the truth? Suppose I see it's your fate? Suppose I *know* you're just a corpse on furlough?

SWISS CHEESE: She can look into the future. Everyone says so.

RECRUITING OFFICER: Then by all means look into the Sergeant's future. It might amuse him.
SERGEANT: I don't believe in that stuff.
MOTHER COURAGE *(obeying the* OFFICER*):* Helmet!

*(*SERGEANT *gives her his helmet.)*

SERGEANT: Anything for a laugh.

MOTHER COURAGE *takes a sheet of parchment and tears it in two.*

MOTHER COURAGE: Eilif, Swiss Cheese, Kattrin! So shall we all be torn asunder if we let ourselves get too deep into this war! *(To the* SERGEANT:*)* I'll give you the bargain rate, and do it for free. Watch! Death is black, so I draw a black cross.
SWISS CHEESE *(pointing to the second piece of parchment):* And the others she leaves blank, see?
MOTHER COURAGE: I fold them, put them in the helmet, and mix 'em up, the way we're all mixed up from our mother's womb on. Now draw!
RECRUITING OFFICER *(to* EILIF*):* I don't take just anybody. I'm choosy. And you've got guts, I like that.
SERGEANT *(after hesitating, fishes around in the helmet):* It's a lot of crap!
SWISS CHEESE *(watching over his shoulder):* The black cross! Oh, his number's up!
SERGEANT *(hoarsely):* You cheated me!
MOTHER COURAGE: You cheated yourself the day you enlisted. And now we must drive on. There isn't a war every day in the week.
SERGEANT: Hell, you're not getting away with this! We're taking that bastard of yours with *us!*
EILIF: I'd like that, mother.
MOTHER COURAGE: Quiet—you Finnish devil, you!
EILIF: And Swiss Cheese wants to be a soldier, too.
MOTHER COURAGE: That's news to me. I see I'll have to draw lots for all three of you. *(She goes to one side to do this.)*
RECRUITING OFFICER *(to* EILIF*):* People've been saying the Swedish soldier is religious. That kind of loose talk has hurt us a lot. One verse of a hymn every Sunday—and then only if you have a voice . . .

MOTHER COURAGE *returns with the slips and puts them in the* SERGEANT*'s helmet.*

MOTHER COURAGE: So they'd desert their old mother, would they, the rascals? They take to war like a cat to cream! Well, there's yours, Eilif, my boy! *(As* EILIF *takes the slip, she snatches it and holds it up.)* See? A cross!
RECRUITING OFFICER *(to* EILIF*):* If you're going to wet your pants, I'll try your kid brother.
MOTHER COURAGE: Take yours, Swiss Cheese. You should be a better bet—you're my *good* boy. *(*SWISS CHEESE *draws.)* Don't tell me it's a cross? Is there no saving you either? Just look, Sergeant—a black cross!
SERGEANT: What I don't see is why *I* got one: I always stay well in the rear. *(To the* OFFICER:*)* It can't be a trick: it gets her own children.
MOTHER COURAGE *(to* KATTRIN*):* Now all I have left is you. You're a cross in yourself but you have a kind heart. *(She holds the helmet up but takes the slip herself.)* Oh dear, there must

be some mistake! Don't be too kind, Kattrin, don't be too kind—there's a black cross in your path! So now you all know: be careful! Be very careful! *(MOTHER COURAGE climbs on her wagon, preparing to leave.)*

RECRUITING OFFICER *(to SERGEANT):* Do something!

SERGEANT: I don't feel too good.

RECRUITING OFFICER: Try doing business with her! *(In a loud voice:)* That belt, Sergeant, you could at least take a look at it! Hey, you, the Sergeant will take the belt!

MOTHER COURAGE: Half a guilder. Worth four times the price.

SERGEANT: It's not even a new one. But there's too much wind here. I'll go look at it behind the wagon.

MOTHER COURAGE: It doesn't seem windy to me.

SERGEANT: Maybe it's worth a half guilder at that. There's silver on it.

MOTHER COURAGE *(now following him eagerly behind the wagon):* A solid six ounces worth!

RECRUITING OFFICER *(to EILIF):* I can let you have some cash in advance, how about it?

EILIF hesitates. MOTHER COURAGE is behind the wagon.

MOTHER COURAGE: Half a guilder then. Quick.

SERGEANT: I still don't see why *I* had to draw a cross. As I told you, I always stay in the rear—it's the only place that's safe. You've ruined my afternoon, Mother Courage.

MOTHER COURAGE: You mustn't take on so. Here. Take a shot of brandy. *(He does.)* And go right on staying in the rear. Half a guilder.

The RECRUITING OFFICER has taken EILIF by the arm and drawn him away.

RECRUITING OFFICER: Ten guilders in advance, and you're a soldier of the king! The women'll be crazy about you, and you can smack me in the puss because I insulted you!

They leave. KATTRIN makes harsh noises.

MOTHER COURAGE: Coming, Kattrin, coming! The Sergeant's just paying his bill. *(She bites the half guilder.)* All money is suspect, Sergeant, but your half guilder is good. Let's go. Where's Eilif?

SWISS CHEESE: Gone with the recruiting officer.

Pause.

MOTHER COURAGE: Oh, you simpleton! *(To KATTRIN:)* You can't speak. You *couldn't* tell me.

SERGEANT: That's life, Mother Courage. Take a shot yourself.

MOTHER COURAGE: You must help your brother now, Kattrin.

Brother and sister get into harness together and pull the wagon. They all move off.

SERGEANT *(looking after them):*

When a war gives you all you earn
One day it may claim something in return!

2

IN THE YEARS 1625 AND 1626 MOTHER COURAGE JOURNEYS THROUGH POLAND IN THE BAGGAGE TRAIN OF THE SWEDISH ARMY. SHE MEETS HER BRAVE SON AGAIN BEFORE WALLHOF CASTLE. OF THE SUCCESSFUL SALE OF A CAPON AND GREAT DAYS FOR THE BRAVE SON.

The tent of the Swedish Commander, and the kitchen next to it. Sound of cannon. In the kitchen: MOTHER COURAGE *and the* COOK. *The* COOK *has a Dutch accent.*

COOK: Sixty hellers—for that paltry piece of poultry?

MOTHER COURAGE: Paltry poultry? He's the fattest fowl you ever saw. I could get sixty hellers for him—this Commander can *eat!*

COOK: They're ten hellers a dozen on every street corner.

MOTHER COURAGE: A capon like that on every street corner? With a siege going on and people all skin and bones? Maybe you can find a field rat some place. I said maybe, because we're all out of them too. All right, then, in a siege, my price for this giant capon is fifty hellers.

COOK: *We're* doing the besieging, it's the other side that's "in a siege"!

MOTHER COURAGE: A fat lot of difference that makes—we don't have a thing to eat either. Look at the farmers round here. They haven't a thing.

COOK: Sure they have. They hide it.

MOTHER COURAGE: They haven't a thing! They're ruined. They're so hungry they dig up roots to eat. I could boil that leather belt of yours and make their mouths water with it. And I'm supposed to let a capon go for forth hellers?

COOK: Thirty. I said thirty hellers.

MOTHER COURAGE: I know *your* problem. If you don't find something to eat and quick, the Commander will cut your fat head off!

COOK: Look! Here's a piece of beef. I am about to roast it. I give you one more chance.

MOTHER COURAGE: Roast it. Go ahead. It's only twelve months old.

COOK: Twelve hours old! Why, only yesterday it was a cow—I saw it running around!

MOTHER COURAGE: Then it must have started stinking before it died.

COOK: I'll cook it five hours if I have to.

MOTHER COURAGE: Put plenty of pepper in.

The SWEDISH COMMANDER, *the* CHAPLAIN, *and* EILIF *enter the tent. The* COMMANDER *claps* EILIF *on the shoulder.*

COMMANDER: In your Commander's tent you go, Eilif, my son, sit at my right hand! Well done, good and faithful servant—you've played the hero in God's own war and you'll get a gold bracelet out of it yet if I have any say in the matter! We come to save their souls and what do they do, the filthy, irreligious sons of bitches? Try to hide their cattle from us—meanwhile stuffing beef into their priests at both ends! But you showed 'em—so here's a can of red wine for you. We'll drink together. *(They do so.)* The chaplain gets the dregs, he's so pious. And now, my hearty, what would you like for dinner?

EILIF: How about a slice of meat?

COOK: Nothing to eat—so he brings company to eat it.

MOTHER COURAGE: Sh!

COMMANDER: Cook! Meat!!

EILIF: Tires you out, skinning peasants. Gives you an appetite.

MOTHER COURAGE: Dear God, it's my Eilif!

COOK: Who?

MOTHER COURAGE: My eldest. It's two years since I saw him. He must be *high* in favor—the Commander inviting him to dinner! And what do you have to eat? Nothing. The Commander's guest wants meat! Take my advice: buy the capon. The price is one hundred hellers.

The COMMANDER *has sat down with* EILIF *and the* CHAPLAIN.

COMMANDER *(roaring):* Dinner, you pig! Or I'll have your head!

COOK: This is blackmail. Give me the damn thing!

MOTHER COURAGE: A paltry piece of poultry like this?

COOK: You were right. Give it here. It's highway robbery, fifty hellers.

MOTHER COURAGE: One hundred hellers. No price is too high for the Commander's guest of honor.

COOK: Well, you might at least pluck the wretched thing till I have a fire going.

MOTHER COURAGE *sits down to pluck the capon.*

MOTHER COURAGE: I can't wait to see his face when he sees me.

COMMANDER: Another glass, my son! It's my favorite Falernian. There's only one keg left but it's worth it to meet a soldier that still believes in God! Our chaplain here only preaches. He hasn't a clue how things get done. So now, Eilif my boy, tell us how you fixed the peasants and grabbed the twenty bullocks.

EILIF: It was like this. I found out the peasants had hidden the oxen in a certain wood. The people from the town were to pick them up there. So I let them go for their oxen in peace—they should know better than me where they are, I said to myself. Meanwhile I made my men crazy for meat. Their rations were short already. I made sure they got shorter. Finally, their mouths would water at the sound of *any* word beginning with M—like mother.

COMMANDER: Smart kid!

EILIF: Not bad. The rest was a snap. Only the peasants had clubs—and outnumbered us three to one. They made a murderous attack on us. Four of them drove me into a clump of trees, knocked my sword from my hand, and screamed: Surrender! What now? I said to myself, they'll make mincemeat of me.

COMMANDER: So what did you do?

EILIF: I laughed.

COMMANDER: You what?

EILIF: I laughed. And so we got to talking. I came right down to business and said: "Twenty guilders an ox is too much, I bid fifteen." Like I wanted to buy. That foxed 'em. So while they were scratching their heads, I reached for my good sword and cut 'em to ribbons. Necessity knows no law, huh?

COMMANDER: What do *you* say, keeper of souls?

CHAPLAIN: Strictly speaking, that saying is not in the Bible. Our Lord made five hundred loaves out of five so that no necessity should arise. So when he told men to love their neighbors, their bellies were full. Things have changed since his day.

COMMANDER *(laughing):* Things have changed! Some wine for those wise words, you old Pharisee! Eilif my boy, you cut them to ribbons in a great cause! As for our fellows, "they were hungry and you gave them to eat!" You don't know how I value a brave soldier like you. *(He points to the map.)* Let's take a look at our position. It isn't all it might be, is it?

MOTHER COURAGE: He must be a very bad commander, this fellow.

COOK: Just a greedy one. Why bad?

MOTHER COURAGE: He says he needs *brave* soldiers. If his plan of campaign was any good, wouldn't plain ordinary soldiers do? Bravery! In a good country, such virtues wouldn't be needed. We could all be cowards and relax.

COMMANDER: I bet your father was a soldier.

EILIF: A very great soldier. My mother warned me about it. In a little song.

COMMANDER: Sing it! *(Roaring:)* Bring that meat!

EILIF: It's called The Fishwife and the Soldier.

THE FISHWIFE AND THE SOLDIER

To a soldier lad comes an old fishwife
    And this old fishwife, says she:
A gun will shoot, a knife will knife,
    You will drown if you fall in the sea.
Keep away from the ice if you want my advice,
    Says the old fishwife, says she.
The soldier laughs and loads his gun
Then grabs his knife and starts to run:
    It's the life of a hero for me!
From the north to the south I shall march through the land
With a knife at my side and a gun in my hand!
    Says the soldier lad, says he.

When the lad defies the fishwife's cries
    The old fishwife, says she:
The young are young, the old are wise,
    You will drown if you fall in the sea.
Don't ignore what I say or you'll rue it one day!
    Says the old fishwife, says she.
But gun in hand and knife at side
The soldier steps into the tide:
    It's the life of a hero for me!
When the new moon is shining on shingle roofs white
We are all coming back, go and pray for that night!
    Says the soldier lad, says he.

And the fishwife old does what she's told:
    Down upon her knees drops she.
When the smoke is gone, the air is cold,

Your heroic deeds won't warm me!
See the smoke, how it goes! May God scatter his foes!
Down upon her knees drops she.
But gun in hand and knife at side
The lad is swept out by the tide:
He floats with the ice to the sea.
And the new moon is shining on shingle roofs white.
But the lad and his laughter are lost in the night:
He floats with the ice to the sea.

The third stanza has been sung by MOTHER COURAGE, *somewhat to the* COMMANDER*'s surprise.*

COMMANDER: What goes on in my kitchen? The liberties they take nowadays!

EILIF *has now left the tent for the kitchen. He embraces his mother.*

EILIF: You! Mother! Where are the others?
MOTHER COURAGE *(still in his arms):* Happy as ducks in a pond. Swiss Cheese is paymaster with the Second Protestant Regiment.
EILIF: Paymaster, eh?
MOTHER COURAGE: At least he isn't in the fighting.
EILIF: Your feet holding up?
MOTHER COURAGE: I have a bit of trouble getting my shoes on in the morning.
COMMANDER *(also in the kitchen by now):* So! You're his mother? I hope you have more sons for me like this young fellow?
EILIF: If I'm not the lucky one! To be the Commander's guest—while you sit listening in the kitchen!
MOTHER COURAGE: I heard you all right. *(She gives him a clout on the ear.)*
EILIF *(grinning):* Because I took the oxen?
MOTHER COURAGE: No. Because you didn't surrender when the four peasants tried to make mincemeat of you! Didn't I teach you to take care of yourself, you Finnish devil, you?

3

THREE YEARS PASS, AND MOTHER COURAGE, WITH PARTS OF A FINNISH REGIMENT, IS TAKEN PRISONER. HER DAUGHTER IS SAVED, HER WAGON LIKEWISE, BUT HER HONEST SON DIES.

A camp. The regimental flag is flying from a pole. Afternoon. MOTHER COURAGE*'s clothes-line is tied to the wagon at one end, to a cannon at the other. She and* KATTRIN *are folding the wash on the cannon. At the same time she is bargaining with an* ORDNANCE OFFICER *over a bag of bullets.* SWISS CHEESE, *wearing his Paymaster's uniform, looks on.* YVETTE POTTIER, *a very good-looking young person, is sewing at a colored hat, a glass of brandy before her. Her red boots are nearby; she is in stocking feet.*

ORDNANCE OFFICER: I'm letting you have the bullets for two guilders. Dirt cheap. 'Cause I need the money. The Colonel's been drinking for three days and we're out of liquor.
MOTHER COURAGE: They're army property. If they find them here, I'll be court-martialled. You sell your bullets, you bastards, and send your men out to fight with nothing to shoot with.

ORDNANCE OFFICER: If you scratch my back, I'll scratch yours.

MOTHER COURAGE: I won't touch army stuff. Not at that price.

ORDNANCE OFFICER: You can resell 'em for five guilders, maybe eight—to the Ordnance Officer of the 4th Regiment. All you have to do is give him a receipt for twelve. He hasn't a bullet left.

MOTHER COURAGE: Why don't you do it yourself?

ORDNANCE OFFICER: I don't trust him: we're friends.

MOTHER COURAGE *(taking the bag, to* KATTRIN*)*: Take it round the back and pay him a guilder and a half. *(As the* OFFICER *starts to protest:)* A guilder and a half! *(*KATTRIN *drags the bag away, the* OFFICER *follows. To* SWISS CHEESE:*)* Here's your underwear. Take care of it. It's October, autumn may come at any time. I don't say it must, but it may. Nothing *must* come, not even the seasons. Only your books *must* balance. Do your books balance, Mr. Paymaster?

SWISS CHEESE: Yes, Mother.

MOTHER COURAGE: Don't forget they made you paymaster because you're honest and so simple you'd never think of running off with the cash. Don't lose that underwear.

SWISS CHEESE: No, Mother. I'll put it under the mattress.

ORDNANCE OFFICER: I'll go with you, Paymaster.

MOTHER COURAGE: Don't teach him any finagling.

THE ORDNANCE OFFICER *and* SWISS CHEESE *leave.*

YVETTE *(waving to the* OFFICER*)*: You might at least say good-bye!

MOTHER COURAGE *(to* YVETTE*)*: I don't like that: he's no company for my Swiss Cheese. But the war's not making a bad start: if I look ahead and make no mistakes, business will be good. *(Noticing the brandy:)* Don't you know you shouldn't drink in the morning—with your sickness and all?

YVETTE: Who says I'm sick? That's a libel!

MOTHER COURAGE: They all say so.

YVETTE: Then they're all liars! I'm desperate, Mother Courage. They avoid me like a stinking fish. Because of those lies! So what am I fixing this hat for? *(She throws it down.)* That's why I drink in the morning. It gives you crow's feet, so what? The whole regiment knows me. I should have stayed home when my first was unfaithful. But pride isn't for the likes of us. You eat dirt or down you go.

MOTHER COURAGE: Don't start in again about your friend Peter Piper and How It All Happened—in front of my innocent daughter.

YVETTE: She's the one that *should* hear it. So she'll get hardened against love.

MOTHER COURAGE: That's something no one ever gets hardened against.

YVETTE: He was an army cook, blond, Dutch, and thin. Kattrin, beware of thin men! I didn't. I didn't even know he'd had another girl before me and she called him Peter Piper because he never took his pipe out of his mouth even in bed—it meant so little to him. *(She sings:)*

THE CAMP FOLLOWER'S SONG

Scarce seventeen was I when
  The foe came to our land
And laid aside his saber
  And took me by the hand.

And we performed by day
The sacred rite of May
And we performed by night
Another sacred rite.
The regiment, well exercised,
Presented arms, then stood at ease,
Then took us off behind the trees
Where we fraternized.

Each of us had her foe and
A cook fell to my lot.
I hated him by daylight
But in the dark did not.
So we perform by day
The sacred rite of May
And we perform by night
That other sacred rite.
The regiment, well exercised,
Presents its arms, then stands at ease,
Then takes us off behind the trees
Where we fraternize.

Ecstasy filled my heart, O
My love seemed heaven-born!
Yet why were people saying
It was not love but scorn?
The springtime's soft amour
Through summer may endure
But swiftly comes the fall
And winter ends it all.
December came. All of the men
Filed past the trees where once we hid
Then quickly marched away and did
Not come back again.

YVETTE: I made the mistake of running after him. I never found him. It's ten years ago now. *(YVETTE goes behind the wagon.)*

MOTHER COURAGE: You're leaving your hat.

YVETTE: For the birds.

MOTHER COURAGE: Let that be a lesson to you, Kattrin: never start anything with a soldier. Love does seem heaven-born, so watch out: they tell you they worship the ground under your feet—did you wash 'em yesterday, while we're on the subject?—then, if you don't look out, you're their slave for life.

The CHAPLAIN comes in with the COOK.

CHAPLAIN: Mother Courage, I bring a message from your son Eilif. The cook came with me—you've made an impression on him.

COOK: Oh, I thought I'd get a little whiff of the breeze.

MOTHER COURAGE: You're welcome to it, but what does Eilif want? I don't have any money!

CHAPLAIN: My message is for his brother, the paymaster.

MOTHER COURAGE: He's not here. He's not anywhere. Look, he is not his brother's paymaster: I won't have him led into temptation! *(She takes money from a purse.)* Give him this. But it's a sin—he's speculating in mother love.

COOK: Maybe not for long. How d'you know he'll come back alive? You're hard, you women. A glass of brandy wouldn't cost you much. But no, you say, no—and six feet under goes your man.

CHAPLAIN: My dear Cook, you talk as if dying for one's beliefs were a misfortune—it is the highest privilege! This is not just any war, remember it is a religious war, and therefore pleasing unto God.

COOK: I see that. In one sense it's a war because of all thre cheating, plunder, rape, and so forth, but it's different from all other wars because it's a religious war and therefore pleasing unto God. At that it does make you thirsty.

CHAPLAIN *(to* MOTHER COURAGE*)*: He says you've bewitched him. He says he dreams about you.

COOK *(lighting his pipe)*: Innocent dreams! I dream of a fair lady dispensing brandy! Stop embarrassing me! The stories you were telling on the way over still have me blushing.

MOTHER COURAGE: I must get you two something to drink, or you'll be making improper advances out of sheer boredom.

CHAPLAIN: That is indeed a temptation—said the Court Chaplain, as he gave way to it. And who is this captivating young person?

MOTHER COURAGE *(looking at Kattrin)*: That is not a captivating young person. That is a respectable young person. *(And she goes with* COOK *and* CHAPLAIN *behind the wagon.)*

MOTHER COURAGE: The trouble with Poland is the Poles. It's true our Swedish king moved in on them with his army—but instead of maintaining the peace the Poles would keep interfering. So their blood is on their own heads, *I* say.

CHAPLAIN: Anyway, since the German Kaiser had enslaved them, King Gustavus had no alternative but to liberate them!

COOK: Just what *I* always say. Your health, Mother Courage, your brandy is first-rate, I'm never mistaken in a face. This war is a religious war.

KATTRIN *watches them go behind the wagon, leaves the washing, picks up the hat, sits, takes up the red boots. The* COOK *sings:*

LUTHER'S HYMN

A mighty fortress is our God
A bulwark never failing.
Our helper He, amid the flood
Of mortal ills prevailing.
For still our ancient Foe
Doth seek to work us woe.
His craft and power are great
And armed with cruel hate
On earth is not his equal.

COOK: And King Gustavus liberated Poland from the Germans. Who could deny it? Then his appetite grew with eating, and he liberated *Germany* from the Germans. Made quite a profit on the deal, I'm told.

CHAPLAIN: That is a calumny! The Swedish king puts religion first!

MOTHER COURAGE: What's more, you eat his bread.

COOK: I don't eat his bread: I bake his bread.

MOTHER COURAGE: He'll never be conquered, that man, and you know why? We all back him up—the little fellows like you and me. Oh yes, to hear the big fellows talk, they're fighting for their beliefs and so on, but if you look into it, you find they're not that silly: they do want to make a profit on the deal. So you and I back them up!

COOK: Surely

CHAPLAIN *(pointing to flag, to* COOK*)*: And as a Dutchman you'd do well to look which flag is flying here!

MOTHER COURAGE: To our Protestant flag!

COOK: A toast!

And now KATTRIN *has begun to strut about with hat and boots on. Suddenly: cannon and shots. Drums.* MOTHER COURAGE, *the* COOK, *and the* CHAPLAIN *rush round to the front of the wagon, the two last with glasses in their hands. The* ORDNANCE OFFICER *and a* SOLDIER *come running for the cannon. They try to push it.*

MOTHER COURAGE: Hey, let me get my wash off that gun!

ORDNANCE OFFICER: Surprise attack! The Catholics! We don't know if we can get away! *(To the* SOLDIER:*)* Bring that gun! *(He runs off.)*

COOK: Good God! I must go to the commander. Mother Courage, I'll be back soon—for a short conversation. *(He rushes off.)*

MOTHER COURAGE: Hey, you're leaving your pipe!

COOK *(off)*: Keep it for me, I'll need it!

MOTHER COURAGE: This *would* happen just when we were making money.

CHAPLAIN: "Blessed are the peacemakers!" A good slogan for wartime. Well, I must be going too. Yes, if the enemy's so close, it can be dangerous. I wish I had a cloak.

MOTHER COURAGE: I'm lending no cloaks. Not even to save a life. I've had experience in that line.

CHAPLAIN: But I'm in special danger—because of my religion!

MOTHER COURAGE *(bringing him a cloak)*: It's against my better judgment. Now run!

CHAPLAIN: Thank you, you're very generous, but on second thought I better stay put. If I run, I might attract attention.

The SOLDIER *is still struggling with the cannon.*

MOTHER COURAGE: Let it alone, you idiot, who's going to pay you for this? *You'll* pay—with your life. Let me keep it for you.

SOLDIER *(running off)*: You're my witness: I tried!

MOTHER COURAGE: I'll swear to that. *(And now she sees* KATTRIN *with the hat and boots.)* Yvette's hat! Take it off this minute! Are you crazy—with the enemy coming? *(She tears it off her head.)* They'll make a whore of you when they see it! And she has the boots on, too, straight from Babylon, I'll soon fix that. *(She pulls at the boots.)* Chaplain, help me with these boots, I'll be right back. *(She runs to the wagon.)*

YVETTE *enters, powdering her face.*

YVETTE: What's this—the Catholics are coming? Where's my hat? Who's been trampling on it? I can't run around in that, what will they think of me? And I've no mirror. *(Coming very close to the* CHAPLAIN:*)* How do I look? Too much powder?

CHAPLAIN: No—er—just right.

YVETTE: And where are my red boots? *(*KATTRIN *is hiding her feet under her skirt.)* I left them here! Must I go barefoot? It's a scandal.

Exit YVETTE. SWISS CHEESE *comes running on with a cash-box. Enter* MOTHER COURAGE, *her hands smeared with ashes.*

MOTHER COURAGE *(to* SWISS CHEESE*)*: What have you got there?

SWISS CHEESE: The regimental cash-box.

MOTHER COURAGE: Throw it away! Your paymastering days are over!

SWISS CHEESE: But they trusted me with it! *(He goes to one side.)*

MOTHER COURAGE *(to the* CHAPLAIN*)*: Take your pastor's coat off, or they'll recognize you, cloak or no cloak. *(She is rubbing ashes into* KATTRIN'S *face.)* Keep still! A little dirt, and you're safe. When a soldier sees a clean face, there's one more whore in the world. That does it. Now stop trembling. Nothing can happen now. *(To* SWISS CHEESE:*)* Where've you put that cash-box?

SWISS CHEESE: I thought I'd just leave it in the wagon.

MOTHER COURAGE: In my wagon?! Why, they'll hang all three of us!

SWISS CHEESE: Somewhere else then. Maybe I'll run away some place.

MOTHER COURAGE: It's too late for that.

CHAPLAIN *(still changing his clothes)*: For Heaven's sake, that Protestant flag!

MOTHER COURAGE *(taking the flag down)*: I've had it twenty-five years. I don't notice it any more.

The sound of cannon grows. Blackout. Three days later. Morning. The cannon is gone. MOTHER COURAGE, KATTRIN, *the* CHAPLAIN, *and* SWISS CHEESE *sit eating anxiously.*

SWISS CHEESE: This is the third day I've sat doing nothing. The sergeant has always been patient with me, but by this time he must be asking himself: Now where is Swiss Cheese with that cash-box?

MOTHER COURAGE: Be glad they're not on the trail.

CHAPLAIN: What about me? I can't even hold service here. It is written: "Out of the abundance of the heart the tongue speaketh"—but woe is me if *my* tongue speaketh!

MOTHER COURAGE: So here you sit—one with his religion, the other with his cash-box! I don't know which is more dangerous.

CHAPLAIN: We're in God's hands now.

MOTHER COURAGE: Oh, I hope we're not as desperate as *that!* But it *is* hard to sleep at night. It'd be easier if you weren't here, Swiss Cheese. All the same I've not done badly.

CHAPLAIN: The milk is good. As for the quantity, we may have to reduce our Swedish appetites somewhat. We are defeated.

MOTHER COURAGE: Who's defeated? There've been cases where a defeat is a victory for the little fellows, it's only their honor that's lost, nothing serious. At that, either victory or defeat can be a costly business. The best thing, *I* say, is for politics to kind of get stuck in the mud. *(To* SWISS CHEESE:*)* Eat!

SWISS CHEESE: I don't like it. How will the sergeant pay the men?

MOTHER COURAGE: Soldiers in flight don't get paid.

SWISS CHEESE: Then they should refuse to flee! No pay, no flight!

MOTHER COURAGE: Swiss Cheese, I've brought you up honest because you're not very bright, but don't overdo it! And now I'm going with the Chaplain to buy a Catholic flag and some meat. *(She disappears into the wagon.)*

CHAPLAIN: She's worried about the cash-box.

SWISS CHEESE: I can get rid of it.

CHAPLAIN: You may be seen. They have spies everywhere. Yesterday one jumped out of the very hole I was relieving myself in. I was so scared I almost broke into a prayer—think how *that* would have given me away! He was a little brute with a patch over one eye.

MOTHER COURAGE *clambers out of the wagon with a basket.*

MOTHER COURAGE *(to* KATTRIN, *holding up the red boots):* You shameless little hussy! She went and switched them—because you called her a captivating young person. *(She puts them in the basket. To* KATTRIN:*)* Stealing Yvette's boots! She at least gets paid for it, you just *enjoy* strutting like a peacock! Save your proud ways for peacetime!

CHAPLAIN: I don't find her proud.

MOTHER COURAGE: I like her when people say, I never even noticed her. I like her when she's a stone in Dalarna, where there's nothing but stones. *(To* SWISS CHEESE:*)* Leave the cash-box where it is, and look after your sister, she needs it. You two are more trouble than a bag of fleas.

MOTHER COURAGE *and the* CHAPLAIN *leave.* KATTRIN *clears the dishes away.*

SWISS CHEESE: Not many days more when you can sit in the sun in your shirtsleeves. *(*KATTRIN *points to a tree.)* Yes, the leaves are yellow already. *(With gestures,* KATTRIN *asks if he wants a drink.)* No, I'm not drinking, I'm thinking. *(Pause.)* Mother says she can't sleep, so I *should* take the cash-box away. I have a place for it: the mole-hole by the river. I can pick it up there—late tonight maybe—and take it to the sergeant. How far can they have fled in three days? The sergeant's eyes'll pop! "You've disappointed me most pleasantly, Swiss Cheese," he'll say, *"I* trust you with the cash-box, and *you* bring it back!" Yes, Kattrin, I *will* have a glass now.

When KATTRIN *gets behind the wagon, two men confront her. One is a* SERGEANT*; the other doffs his hat and flourishes it in a showy greeting; he has a patch over one eye.*

ONE EYE: Morning, young lady! Have you seen a staff officer from the Second Protestant Regiment?

KATTRIN *is terrified and runs away, spilling her brandy. The two men look at each other, see* SWISS CHEESE, *and withdraw.*

SWISS CHEESE *(starting up):* You're spilling it, can't you see where you're going? I don't understand you. Anyway, I must be leaving. That's what I've decided on. *(He stands up. She tries to make him understand the danger he is in. He pushes her away.)* I know you mean well, poor thing, you just can't get it out. And don't worry about the brandy. I'll live to drink so much brandy—what's one glass? *(He takes the cash-box out of the wagon and puts it under his coat.)* I'll be right back, but don't hold me up, or I'll have to scold you. Yes, I know you're trying to help!

He kisses her as she tries to hold him back, and pulls himself free. Exit SWISS CHEESE. KATTRIN *is now desperate. She runs up and down, making little sounds.* MOTHER COURAGE *and* THE CHAPLAIN *return.* KATTRIN *rushes at her mother.*

MOTHER COURAGE: What is it, what is it, control yourself! Have they done something to you? Where's Swiss Cheese? *(To the* CHAPLAIN:*)* And don't you stand around—get that Catholic flag up!

She takes the flag from her basket. The CHAPLAIN *runs it up the pole.*

CHAPLAIN: God bless our Catholic flag!

MOTHER COURAGE: Now calm down, Kattrin, and tell me all about it. What? That little rascal has taken the cash-box away? Oh, he's going to get a good whipping? Now take your time, don't try to talk, use your hands. I don't like that howling—what will the Chaplain think? A man with one eye? Here?

CHAPLAIN: That fellow is an informer. They've captured Swiss Cheese?

KATTRIN *shakes her head, then shrugs her shoulders. Voices off.* ONE EYE *and the same* SERGEANT *bring in* SWISS CHEESE.

SWISS CHEESE: Let me go! I've nothing on me. You're breaking my shoulder. I am innocent!

SERGEANT: This is where he comes from. These are his friends.

MOTHER COURAGE: Us? Since when?

SWISS CHEESE: I was just getting my lunch here. I paid ten hellers for it. Maybe you saw me on that bench. The food was too salty.

MOTHER COURAGE: That's true. He got his lunch here. And it was too salty.

SERGEANT: Are you pretending you don't know him?

MOTHER COURAGE: I can't know all of them.

CHAPLAIN: He sat there like a law-abiding citizen and never opened his mouth except to eat. Which is necessary.

SERGEANT: Who d'you think you are?

MOTHER COURAGE: He's my bartender. And you must be thirsty. I'll bring you some brandy.

SERGEANT: No liquor while on duty. *(To* SWISS CHEESE:*)* You were carrying something. You must have hidden it. We saw the bulge in your shirt.

MOTHER COURAGE: Are you sure it was him?

SWISS CHEESE: I think you mean another fellow. There *was* a fellow with something under his shirt. I saw him.

MOTHER COURAGE: I think so too. It's a misunderstanding. Could happen to anyone. Oh, I know what people are like. I'm Mother Courage and I can tell you this: he looks honest.

SERGEANT: We want the regimental cash-box. And we know the looks of the fellow that's been taking care of it. It's you!

SWISS CHEESE: No! No, it's not!

SERGEANT: If you don't shell out, you're dead, see!
MOTHER COURAGE: Oh, he'd give it to you to save his life, he's not that stupid! Speak up, my boy, the sergeant's giving you one last chance!
SWISS CHEESE: What if I don't have it?
SERGEANT: We'll get it out of you.

ONE EYE and the SERGEANT lead him off.

MOTHER COURAGE *(shouting after them):* He'll tell you! He's not *that* stupid! And don't you break his shoulder!

She runs a little way after them. Blackout. The same evening. The CHAPLAIN and KATTRIN are waiting.

MOTHER COURAGE *(entering):* It's a matter of life and death. But the sergeant will still listen to us. Only he mustn't know it's our Swiss Cheese—or they'll say we helped him. It's just a matter of money. But where can *we* get money? Wasn't Yvette here? I just talked with her. She's picked up a Colonel, and she says he might buy her a canteen business.
CHAPLAIN: You'd sell the wagon, everything?
MOTHER COURAGE: Where else would I get the money for the sergeant?
CHAPLAIN: What are you going to live off?
MOTHER COURAGE: That's just it.

Enter YVETTE with a hoary old COLONEL. She embraces MOTHER COURAGE.

YVETTE: Dear Mrs. Fierling, we meet again! *(Whispering:)* He didn't say no. *(Loud:)* This is my friend, my . . . business adviser. I heard you might want to sell your wagon.
MOTHER COURAGE: I want to pawn it, not sell it. And nothing hasty. You don't find another wagon like this in a hurry.
YVETTE: In that case, I'm not sure I'd be interested. What do *you* think, my dear?
COLONEL: I agree with you, honey bun.
MOTHER COURAGE: It's only for pawn.
YVETTE: But I thought you *had* to have the money?
MOTHER COURAGE: I do have to. But I'd rather run my feet off looking for another offer than just sell. We live off that wagon.
COLONEL: Take it! Take it!
YVETTE: My friend thinks I might take it. *(Turning to him:)* But you think we should buy it outright, don't you?
COLONEL: Oh, I do, bunny, I do!
MOTHER COURAGE: Then you must find one that's for sale.
YVETTE: Yes! We can travel around looking for one! I love going around looking. Especially with you, Poldy!
COLONEL: Really? Do you?
YVETTE: Oh, I love it. I could take weeks of it!
COLONEL: Really? Could you?
YVETTE: If you get the money, when would you pay it back?
MOTHER COURAGE: In two weeks. Maybe one.

YVETTE: I can't make up my mind. Poldy, chéri, advise me! *(Aside to him:)* She'll have to sell, don't worry. That lieutenant—the blond one—remember?—he'll lend me the money. He's crazy about me. He says I remind him of someone. What do you advise?

COLONEL: Oh, I have to warn you against *him:* he's no good, he'll only exploit the situation. I told you, bunny, I told you I'd buy you something? Didn't I tell you that?

YVETTE: I can't let you.

COLONEL: Oh, please, please!

YVETTE: Well, if you think the lieutenant might exploit the situation?

COLONEL: I do think so.

YVETTE: So you advise me to go ahead?

COLONEL: I do, bunny, I do!

YVETTE *(returning to* MOTHER COURAGE*):* My friend says all right: two hundred guilders. And I need a receipt saying the wagon would be mine in two weeks. With everything in it. I'll look it all over right now. The two hundred can wait. *(To the* COLONEL:*)* You go on ahead to the camp. I'll follow.

COLONEL *(helping her up the steps of the wagon):* I'll help you up. Come soon, honey bun. *(Exit* COLONEL.*)*

MOTHER COURAGE: Yvette, Yvette!

YVETTE: There aren't many shoes left.

MOTHER COURAGE: Yvette, this is no time for an inventory, yours or not yours. You promised to talk to the sergeant about Swiss Cheese. There isn't a minute to lose. He's up for court martial one hour from now.

YVETTE: I want to check through these shirts.

MOTHER COURAGE *drags her down the steps by the skirt.*

MOTHER COURAGE: You hyena! Swiss Cheese's life is at stake! And don't say where the money comes from. Pretend he's your sweetheart, or we'll all get it in the neck for helping him.

YVETTE: I arranged to meet One Eye in the bushes. He must be there by now.

CHAPLAIN: And don't give him the whole two hundred. A hundred and fifty should do the trick.

MOTHER COURAGE: You keep your nose out of this! I'm not doing you out of *your* porridge. Now run, and no haggling! Remember his life's at stake! *(She pushes* YVETTE *off.)*

CHAPLAIN: All I meant was: what are we going to live on?

MOTHER COURAGE: I'm counting on that cash-box. At the very least, Swiss Cheese'll get paid out of it.

CHAPLAIN: But d'you think Yvette can manage this?

MOTHER COURAGE: It's in her interest—if I don't pay their two hundred, she won't get the wagon. And she knows the score: she won't have this colonel on the string forever. Kattrin, go clean the knives! And don't you just stand around: wash those glasses: there'll be fifty cavalrymen here tonight . . . . I think they'll let us have him. They're not wolves, they're human and after money. God is merciful and men are bribable—that's how His will is done on earth, I don't know about Heaven.

YVETTE *(entering):* They'll do it for two hundred if you make it snappy. He confessed he'd had the cash-box, they put the thumb screws on him, but he threw it in the river when he saw them coming at him. Shall I go get the money from my colonel?

MOTHER COURAGE: The cash-box in the river? How'll I ever get my two hundred back?

YVETTE: You were expecting to get it from the cash-box? I *would* have been sunk. Mother Courage, if you want your Swiss Cheese, you'll have to pay. Or shall I let the whole thing drop—so you can keep your wagon?

MOTHER COURAGE: Now I *can't* pay two hundred. I must hold on to something. Go say I'll pay one hundred twenty or the deal's off. Even at that I lose the wagon.

YVETTE: One Eye's in a hurry. Looks over his shoulder the whole time. Hadn't I better just give them the two hundred?

MOTHER COURAGE: I have her to think of. She's twenty-five and still no husband. I know what I'm doing. One hundred twenty or no deal.

YVETTE: You know best.

YVETTE runs off. After walking up and down abstractedly, MOTHER COURAGE sits down to help KATTRIN with the knives.

MOTHER COURAGE: I *will* pay two hundred if I have to. With eighty guilders we could pack a hamper and begin over. It won't be the end of the world.

CHAPLAIN: The Bible says: the Lord will provide.

MOTHER COURAGE *(to KATTRIN)*: You must rub them dry.

YVETTE *(re-enters)*: They won't do it. I warned you. He said the drums would roll any second now—and that's the sign they've reached a verdict. I offered one hundred fifty. He didn't even shrug his shoulders.

MOTHER COURAGE: Tell him I'll pay two hundred. Run! *(YVETTE runs, MOTHER COURAGE sits, THE CHAPLAIN has finished the glasses.)* I believe—I haggled too long.

In the distance: a roll of drums. The CHAPLAIN stands up and walks away. MOTHER COURAGE remains seated. It grows dark; it gets light again. MOTHER COURAGE has not moved.

YVETTE *(re-enters, pale)*: You've done it—with your haggling. You can keep your wagon now. He got eleven bullets in him. I don't know why I still bother about you, you don't deserve it, but I just happened to hear they don't think the cash-box is really in the river. They think it's here. And they think you were in with him. I think they're going to bring his body, to see if you give yourself away when you see him. You'd better not know him or we're in for it. And I should tell you straight: they're right behind me. Shall I keep Kattrin out of this? *(MOTHER COURAGE shakes her head.)* Does she know? Maybe she didn't hear the drums or didn't understand.

MOTHER COURAGE: She knows. Bring her.

YVETTE brings KATTRIN who stands by her mother, who takes her hand. Two men come on with a stretcher. There is a sheet over it, and something underneath. Beside them, the SERGEANT. They put the stretcher down.

SERGEANT: There's a man here we don't know the name of, but he has to be registered to keep the records straight. He bought a meal from you. Look at him. See if you know him. *(He draws back the sheet.)* You know him? *(MOTHER COURAGE shakes her head.)* What? You never saw him before he bought that meal? *(MOTHER COURAGE shakes her head.)* Lift him up. Throw him on the garbage dump. He has no one that knows him.

They carry him off.

4

MOTHER COURAGE SINGS THE SONG OF THE GREAT CAPITULATION

Outside an officer's tent. MOTHER COURAGE *waits. A* REGIMENTAL CLERK *looks out of the tent.*

REGIMENTAL CLERK: You want to speak to the captain? I know you. You had a Protestant paymaster with you. He was hiding out. Better make no complaint here.

MOTHER COURAGE: But I'm innocent and if I give up it'll look like I have a bad conscience. They cut my wagon to ribbons with their sabers, and then claimed a fine of five thalers—for nothing, for less than nothing!

REGIMENTAL CLERK *(quietly):* For your own good: keep your mouth shut. We haven't many canteens, so we let you stay in business, especially if you've a bad conscience and have to pay a fine now and then.

MOTHER COURAGE: I'm going to lodge a complaint.

REGIMENTAL CLERK: As you wish. Wait here till the captain is free.

The CLERK *retires into the tent.* A YOUNG SOLDIER *comes storming in.*

YOUNG SOLDIER: Screw the captain! Where is the son of a bitch? Grabbing my reward, spending it on brandy for his whores! I'll rip his belly open!

OLDER SOLDIER *(following him):* Shut your hole, you'll only wind up in the stocks!

YOUNG SOLDIER: I was the only one in the squad who swam the river and *he* grabs the money. I can't even buy me a beer. Come out, you thief, I'll make lamb chops out of you!

OLDER SOLDIER: Holy Christ, he'll destroy himself.

YOUNG SOLDIER *(pulling himself free of the older man):* Let me go or I'll cut you down too!

OLDER SOLDIER: Saved the colonel's horse and didn't get the reward. He's young. He hasn't been at it long.

MOTHER COURAGE: Let him go. He doesn't have to be chained like a dog. Very reasonable to want a reward. Why else should he go to the trouble?

YOUNG SOLDIER: He's in there pouring it down. I done something special: I want the reward!

MOTHER COURAGE: Young man, don't scream at *me,* I have my own problems.

YOUNG SOLDIER: He's whoring on my money and I'm hungry! I'll murder him!

MOTHER COURAGE: You're hungry. You're angry. I understand.

YOUNG SOLDIER: Talking'll get you nowhere. I won't stand for injustice!

MOTHER COURAGE: How long? How long won't you stand for injustice? One hour? Or two? It's a misery to sit in the stocks: especially if you leave it till then to realize you do stand for injustice.

YOUNG SOLDIER: I don't know why I listen to you. Screw that captain!

MOTHER COURAGE: You listen because you know I'm right. Your rage has calmed down already. It was a short one, and you'd need a long one.

YOUNG SOLDIER: Are you trying to tell me I shouldn't ask for the money?

MOTHER COURAGE: Just the opposite. I only say your rage won't last, you'll get nowhere with it. If your rage was a long one. I'd say: go ahead, slice him up. But what's the use—if you don't slice him up? What's the use if you stand there with your tail between your legs?

OLDER SOLDIER: You're quite right: he's crazy.

YOUNG SOLDIER: All right, we'll see whether I slice him up or not. *(He draws his sword.)* When he comes out, I slice him up.

CLERK *(looking out again):* The captain will be right out. *(A military order:)* Be seated!

The YOUNG SOLDIER *sits.*

MOTHER COURAGE: What did I tell you? Oh, they know us inside out. "Be seated!" And we sit. *I'm* no better. Let me tell you about the great capitulation.

THE GREAT CAPITULATION

Long, long ago, a green beginner
I thought myself a special case.
(None of your ordinary, run of the mill girls, with my looks
and my talent and my love of the Higher Things.)
I picked a hair out of my dinner
And put the waiter in his place.
(All or nothing. Anyway, never the second best. I am the
master of my fate. I'll take no orders from no one.)
Then a little bird whispers!
The bird says: "Wait a year or so
And marching with the band you'll go
Keeping in step, now fast, now slow,
And piping out your little spiel.
Then one day the battalions wheel!
And you go down upon your knees
To God Almighty if you please!

My friend, before that year was over
I'd learned to drink their cup of tea.
(Two children round your neck and the price of bread and what all!)
When they were through with me, moreover,
They had me where they wanted me
(You must get in with people. If you scratch my back, I'll
scratch yours. Don't stick your neck out!)
Then a little bird whispers!
The bird says: "Scarce a year or so
And marching with the band she'd go
Keeping in step, now fast, now slow,
And piping out her little spiel.
Then one day the battalions wheel!
And she goes down upon her knees
To God Almighty if you please!"

Our plans are big, our hopes colossal.
We hitch our wagon to a star.
(Where there's a will, there's a way. You can't hold a good man down.)
"We can lift mountains," says the apostle.
And yet: how heavy one cigar!
(You must cut your coat according to your cloth.)
That little bird whispers!

The bird says: "Wait a year or so
And marching with the band we go
Keeping in step, now fast, now slow,
And piping out our little spiel.
Then one day the battalions wheel!
And we go down upon our knees
To God Almighty if you please!"

MOTHER COURAGE: So stay here with your sword drawn, if your anger is big enough. If it isn't, you'd better go.

YOUNG SOLDIER: Aw, shove it! *(He stumbles off, the* OLDER SOLDIER *following him.)*

REGIMENTAL CLERK *(again sticking his head out):* The captain is free now. You can lodge your complaint.

MOTHER COURAGE: I've thought better of it. I'm not complaining.

She leaves. The CLERK *looks after her, shaking his head.*

5

TWO YEARS HAVE PASSED. THE WAR COVERS WIDER AND WIDER TERRITORY. ALWAYS ON THE MOVE, THE LITTLE WAGON CROSSES POLAND, MORAVIA, BAVARIA, ITALY, AND AGAIN BAVARIA. 1631. GENERAL TILLY'S VICTORY AT LEIPZIG COSTS MOTHER COURAGE FOUR SHIRTS.

The wagon stands in a war-ruined village. Victory march in the distance. TWO SOLDIERS *are being served at a counter by* KATTRIN *and* MOTHER COURAGE. *One of them has a woman's fur coat about his shoulders.*

MOTHER COURAGE: What, you can't pay? No money, no schnapps! If they can play victory marches, they should pay their men.

FIRST SOLDIER: I want my schnapps! I arrived too late for plunder. The Chief allowed just one hour to plunder the town. He's not inhuman, he says—so I guess they bought him off.

CHAPLAIN *(staggering in):* There are people in the farmhouse. A whole family. Help me, someone! I need linen.

The SECOND SOLDIER *goes with him.* KATTRIN, *becoming excited, tries to get her mother to bring linen out of the wagon.*

MOTHER COURAGE: I have none. I sold all my bandages to the regiment. I'm not tearing up my officer's shirts for these people.

CHAPLAIN *(over his shoulder):* I said: I need linen!

MOTHER COURAGE *stops* KATTRIN *from entering the wagon.*

MOTHER COURAGE: Not on your life! They have nothing and they pay nothing.

The CHAPLAIN *carries in a* WOMAN.

CHAPLAIN: Why did you stay there—in the line of fire?

WOMAN *(faintly):* Our farm . . .

MOTHER COURAGE: Think they'd ever let go of anything? And now *I'm* supposed to pay. Well, I won't!

FIRST SOLDIER: They're Protestants. Why do they have to be Protestants?

MOTHER COURAGE: Protestant, Catholic, what do they care? It's their farm they're thinking of.

SECOND SOLDIER: Anyway, they're not Protestants. They're Catholics.

FIRST SOLDIER: I guess our cannon don't know the difference.

The CHAPLAIN *brings in a* PEASANT.

PEASANT: My arm's shot.

CHAPLAIN: Where's that linen?

MOTHER COURAGE: I can't give you any. With all I have to pay out in taxes, duties, bribes . . . (KATTRIN *picks up a board and threatens her mother with it, making gurgling sounds.)* Are you out of your mind? Put that board down this minute! I'm giving nothing! *(The* CHAPLAIN *lifts her bodily off the wagon steps, then brings the shirts from the wagon, and tears them in strips.)* My shirts! My officer's shirts!

From the house, the cry of a child in pain.

PEASANT: The child's still in the house.

KATTRIN *runs into the house.*

MOTHER COURAGE: Hey, grab Kattrin, the roof may fall in!

CHAPLAIN: I'm not going back in there.

MOTHER COURAGE: My officer's shirts, half a guilder apiece. I'm ruined! (KATTRIN *comes out with a baby in her arms. To her:)* Never happy till you're dragging babies around! Give it to its mother at once!

KATTRIN *is humming a lullaby to the child.*

CHAPLAIN *(bandaging):* The blood comes through.

MOTHER COURAGE: And, in all this, she's happy as a lark! Stop that music! I don't need music to tell me what victory's like. *(The* FIRST SOLDIER *tries to make off with the bottle he's been drinking from.)* Come back, you! If you want another victory, you'll have to pay for it.

FIRST SOLDIER: But I'm broke.

MOTHER COURAGE *tears the fur coat off his back.*

MOTHER COURAGE: Then leave this. It's stolen goods anyhow.

KATTRIN *rocks the child and raises it high above her head.*

6

THE CATHOLIC GENERAL TILLY IS KILLED BEFORE THE CITY OF INGOLSTADT AND IS BURIED IN STATE. MOTHER COURAGE GIVES HER

VIEWS OF HEROES, AND THE CHAPLAIN SINGS A SONG ABOUT THE DURATION OF THE WAR. KATTRIN GETS THE RED BOOTS AT LAST. THE YEAR IS 1632.

The interior of a canteen tent. The inside part of the counter is seen at the rear. Funeral march in the distance. The CHAPLAIN *and the* REGIMENTAL CLERK *are playing checkers.* MOTHER COURAGE *and* KATTRIN *are taking inventory.*

CHAPLAIN: The funeral procession is just starting out.

MOTHER COURAGE: Pity about the Chief—twenty-two pairs, socks—getting killed that way. They say it was an accident. There was a fog over the fields that morning, and the fog was to blame. He'd been telling his men to fight to the death, and was just riding back to safety when he lost his way in the fog, went forward instead of back, found himself in the thick of the battle, and ran right smack into a bullet. *(A whistle from the counter. She goes over to attend to a soldier.)* It's a disgrace—the way you're all skipping your Commander's funeral.

REGIMENTAL CLERK: They shouldn't have handed out the money before the funeral. Now the men are getting drunk instead of going to it.

CHAPLAIN *(to the* REGIMENTAL CLERK*)*: Don't you have to be there?

REGIMENTAL CLERK: I stayed away because of the rain.

MOTHER COURAGE: It's different for you. The rain might spoil your uniform.

ANOTHER SOLDIER *comes to the counter. He sings:*

BATTLE HYMN

One schnapps, mine host, be quick, make haste!
A soldier's got no time to waste:
He must be shooting, shooting, shooting,
His Kaiser's enemies uprooting!

SOLDIER: A brandy.

Two breasts, my girl, be quick, make haste,
A soldier's got no time to waste:
He must be hating, hating, hating,
He cannot keep his Kaiser waiting!

SOLDIER: Make it a double, this is a holiday.

MOTHER COURAGE: Money first. No, you can't come inside, not with those boots on. Only officers are allowed in here, rain or no rain.

CHAPLAIN *(as the funeral music resumes)*: Now they're filing past the body.

MOTHER COURAGE: I feel sorry for a commander like that—when maybe he had something big in mind, something they'd talk about in times to come, something they'd raise a statue to him for, the conquest of the whole world, for example—Lord, the worms have got into these biscuits!—he works his hands to the bone and then the common riffraff don't support him because all they care about is a jug of beer or a bit of company. Am I right?

CHAPLAIN: You're right, Mother Courage. Till you come to the riffraff. You underestimate them. Take those fellows outside right now, drinking their brandy in the rain, why, they'd fight for a hundred years, one war after another—if necessary, two at a time.

MOTHER COURAGE: Seventeen leather belts.—Then you don't think the war might end?

CHAPLAIN: Because a commander's dead? Don't be childish. Heroes are cheap. There are plenty of others where he came from.

MOTHER COURAGE: I wasn't asking just for the sake of argument. I was wondering if I should buy up a lot of supplies. They happen to be cheap right now. But if the war's going to end, I might just as well forget it.

CHAPLAIN: There are people who think the war's about to end, but I say: you can't be sure it will *ever* end. Oh, it may have to pause occasionally, for breath, as it were. It can even meet with an accident—nothing on this earth is perfect—one can't think of everything—a little oversight and a war may be in the hole and someone's got to pull it out again. That someone is the King or the Emperor or the Pope. But they're such friends in need, this war hasn't got much to worry about: it can look forward to a prosperous future.

MOTHER COURAGE: If I was sure you're right . . .

CHAPLAIN: Think it out for yourself. How *could* the war end?

REGIMENTAL CLERK: I'm from Bohemia. I'd like to get home once in a while. So I'm hoping for peace.

CHAPLAIN: Peace?

REGIMENTAL CLERK: Yes, peace! How can we live without it?

CHAPLAIN: We don't have to. There's peace even in war. War satisfies all needs—even those of peace. I know a song about that. *(He sings:)*

THE ARMY CHAPLAIN'S SONG

Does war, my friend, stop you from drinking?
  Does it not give you bread to chew?
To my old-fashioned way of thinking
  That much at least a war can do.

And even in the thick of slaughter
  A soldier feels the amorous itch
And many a buxom farmer's daughter
  Has lost her virtue in a ditch.

REGIMENTAL CLERK: Maybe. But when shall I get another good night's sleep?

CHAPLAIN: That also has been taken care of.

Somehow we find the bread and brandy
  And finding women is a snap.
And when there is a gutter handy
  We catch a twenty-minute nap.

As for the sleep that lasts forever
  Though it will come in any case
In war more Christian souls than ever
  Reach their eternal resting place.

REGIMENTAL CLERK: And when everyone's dead, the war won't stop even then, I suppose?

CHAPLAIN: Let me finish.

What won't a soldier do in wartime
  His savage lust to satisfy!

But after all, 'twas said aforetime:
Be fruitful, lads, and multiply!

If you ignore this high injunction,
The war will have to stop, my friend:
Perform your biologic function
And then the war need never end!

REGIMENTAL CLERK: You admit the war *could* stop.
CHAPLAIN: Tsk, tsk, tsk. You don't know where God lives. Listen!

Peacemakers shall the earth inherit:
We bless those men of simple worth.
Warmakers have still greater merit:
They *have* inherited the earth.

I'll tell you, my good sir, what peace is:
The hole when all the cheese is gone.
And what is war? This is my thesis:
It's what the world is founded on.

War is like love: it'll always find a way. Why *should* it end?

MOTHER COURAGE: Then I *will* buy those supplies. I'll take your word for it. *(KATTRIN, who has been staring at the CHAPLAIN, suddenly bangs a basket of glasses down on the ground and runs out. MOTHER COURAGE laughs.)* She'll go right on waiting for peace. I promised her she'll get a husband when peace comes. *(She follows KATTRIN.)*

REGIMENTAL CLERK *(standing up)*: You were singing. I win.

MOTHER COURAGE brings KATTRIN back.

MOTHER COURAGE: Be sensible, the war'll go on a bit longer, and we'll make a bit more money—then peace'll be all the nicer. Now you go into the town, it's not ten minutes' walk, and bring the things from the Golden Lion. Just the special things for your trousseau: the rest we can pick up later in the wagon. The Clerk will go with you, you'll be quite safe. Do a good job, and don't lose anything, think of your trousseau! *(KATTRIN ties a kerchief round her head and leaves with the CLERK.)* Now you can chop me a bit of firewood.

The CHAPLAIN takes his coat off and prepares to chop wood.

CHAPLAIN: Properly speaking, I am a pastor of souls, not a woodcutter.
MOTHER COURAGE: But I don't have a soul, and I do need wood.
CHAPLAIN: What's that little pipe you've got there?
MOTHER COURAGE: Just a pipe.
CHAPLAIN: I think it's a very particular pipe.
MOTHER COURAGE: Oh?
CHAPLAIN: The cook's pipe in fact. Our Swedish Commander's cook.
MOTHER COURAGE: If you know, why beat about the bush?
CHAPLAIN: I wondered if *you* knew. It was possible you just rummaged among your belongings and just lit on . . . some pipe.

MOTHER COURAGE: How'd you know that's not it?

CHAPLAIN: It isn't! You did know! *(He brings the axe down on the block.)*

MOTHER COURAGE: What if I did?

CHAPLAIN: Mother Courage, it is my duty to warn you. You are unlikely to see the gentleman again, but that's a blessing. Mother Courage, he did not strike me as trustworthy.

MOTHER COURAGE: Really? He was such a nice man.

CHAPLAIN: Well! So that's what you call a nice man! I do not. *(Again the axe falls.)* Far be it from me to wish him ill, but I cannot, cannot describe him as nice. No, he's a Don Juan, a cunning Don Juan. Just look at that pipe if you don't believe me—it tells all!

MOTHER COURAGE: I see nothing special about this pipe. It's been used, of course . . .

CHAPLAIN: It's been practically bitten through! Oho, he's a wild man! That is the pipe of a wild man! *(The axe falls more violently than ever.)*

MOTHER COURAGE: Now it's my chopping block that's bitten through!

CHAPLAIN: I told you the care of souls was my field. In physical labor my God-given talents find no adequate expression. You haven't heard me preach. Why, I can put such spirit into a regiment with a single sermon that the enemy's a mere flock of sheep to them and their own lives are no more than a smelly old pair of shoes to be instantly thrown away at the thought of final victory! God has given me the gift of tongues! I can preach you out of your senses!

MOTHER COURAGE: But I need my senses. What would I do without them?

CHAPLAIN: Mother Courage, I have often thought that—under a veil of blunt speech—you conceal a heart. You are human, you need warmth.

MOTHER COURAGE: The best way of warming this tent is to chop plenty of firewood.

CHAPLAIN: Seriously, my dear Courage, I sometimes ask myself how it would be if our relationship should be somewhat more firmly cemented. I mean: now the wild wind of war has whirled us so strangely together.

MOTHER COURAGE: The cement's pretty firm already. I cook your meals. And you lend a hand—at chopping firewood, for instance.

The CHAPLAIN *flourishes the axe as he approaches her.*

CHAPLAIN: Oh, you know what I mean by a closer relationship. Let your heart speak!

MOTHER COURAGE: Don't come at me like that with your axe! That'd be *too* close a relationship!

CHAPLAIN: This is no laughing matter. I have given it careful thought.

MOTHER COURAGE: My dear Chaplain, be sensible, I do like you. All I want is for me and mine to get by in this war. Now chop the firewood and we'll be warm in the evenings. What's that? *(*MOTHER COURAGE *stands up.* KATTRIN *enters with a nasty wound above her eye. She is letting everything fall, parcels, leather goods, a drum, etc.)* What happened? Were you attacked? On the way back? It's not serious, only a flesh wound. I'll bandage it up, and you'll be better within a week. Didn't the clerk walk you back? That's because you're a good girl, he thought they'd leave you alone. The wound isn't deep. It will never show. There! *(She has finished the bandage.)* Now I have a little present for you. *(She fishes Yvette's red boots out of a bag.)* See? You always wanted them—now you have them. Put them on before I change my mind. It will never show. Look, the boots have kept well, I cleaned them good before I put them away.

But KATTRIN *leaves the boots alone, and creeps into the wagon.*

CHAPLAIN: I hope she won't be disfigured.

MOTHER COURAGE: There'll be quite a scar. She needn't wait for peace now.

CHAPLAIN: She didn't let them get any of the things.

MOTHER COURAGE: I wish I knew what goes on inside her head. She stayed out all night once—once in all the years. I never did get out of her what happened. *(She picks up the things that* KATTRIN *spilled and angrily sorts them out.)* And this is war! A nice source of income, I must say!

Cannon.

CHAPLAIN: They're lowering the Commander in his grave. A historic moment!

MOTHER COURAGE: It's historic to me all right. She's finished. How would she ever get a husband now? And she's crazy for children. Even her dumbness comes from the war. A soldier stuck something in her mouth when she was little. I'll never see Swiss Cheese again, and where my Eilif is the Good Lord knows. Curse the war!

7

A highway. The Chaplain and Kattrin are pulling the wagon.
It is dirty and neglected, though new goods
are hung around it.

MOTHER COURAGE *(walking beside the wagon, a flask at her waist):* I won't have my war all spoiled for me! Destroys the weak, does it? Well, what does peace do for 'em? Huh? *(She sings* THE SONG OF MOTHER COURAGE:)

So cheer up, boys, the rose is fading!
When victory comes you may be dead!
A war is just the same as trading:
But not with cheese—with steel and lead!
Christians, awake! The winter's gone!
The snows depart, the dead sleep on.
And though you may not long survive
Get out of bed and look alive!

8

IN THE SAME YEAR, THE PROTESTANT KING FELL IN THE BATTLE OF LÜTZEN. THE PEACE THREATENS MOTHER COURAGE WITH RUIN. HER BRAVE SON PERFORMS ONE HEROIC DEED TOO MANY AND COMES TO A SHAMEFUL END.

A camp. Summer morning. In front of the wagon, an OLD WOMAN *and her* SON. *The* SON *drags a large bag of bedding.* MOTHER COURAGE *is inside the wagon.*

MOTHER COURAGE: Must you come at the crack of dawn?

YOUNG MAN: We've been walking all night. Twenty miles. We have to get back today.

MOTHER COURAGE: What do I want with bed feathers? Take them to the town!

YOUNG MAN: At least wait till you see them.

OLD WOMAN: Nothing doing here either. Let's go.

YOUNG MAN: And let 'em sign away the roof over our heads for taxes? Maybe she'll pay three guilders if you throw in that bracelet. *(Bells start ringing.)* Hear that, Mother?

VOICE FROM A DISTANCE: It's peace! The King of Sweden got killed!

MOTHER COURAGE *sticks her head out of the wagon. She hasn't done her hair yet.*

MOTHER COURAGE: Bells? Bells in the middle of the week? *The* CHAPLAIN *crawls out from under the wagon.*

CHAPLAIN: What's that they're shouting?

YOUNG MAN: It's peace.

CHAPLAIN: Peace?!

MOTHER COURAGE: Don't tell me peace has broken out—I've gone and bought all these supplies!

CHAPLAIN *(shouting):* Is it peace?

VOICE: Yes! The war stopped three weeks ago!

CHAPLAIN *(To* MOTHER COURAGE*):* Why else would they ring the bells?

VOICE: A big crowd of Lutherans just arrived—they brought the news.

YOUNG MAN: It's peace, Mother. *(The* OLD WOMAN *collapses.)* What's the matter?

MOTHER COURAGE *(back in the wagon):* Kattrin, it's peace! Put on your black dress, we're going to church, we owe it to Swiss Cheese.

YOUNG MAN: The war's over. *(The* OLD WOMAN *gets up, dazed.)* I'll get the harness shop going again now. Everything will be all right. Father will get his bed back. Can you walk? *(To the* CHAPLAIN*:)* It was the news. She didn't believe there'd ever be peace again. Father always said there would. We'll be going home.
They leave.

MOTHER COURAGE *(from the wagon):* Give them a schnapps!

CHAPLAIN: Too late: they've gone! And who may this be coming over from the camp? If it isn't our Swedish Commander's cook?!

The COOK *comes on, bedraggled, carrying a bundle.*

CHAPLAIN: Mother Courage, a visitor!

MOTHER COURAGE *clambers out of the wagon.*

COOK: I promised to come back, remember? For a short conversation? I didn't forget your brandy, Mrs. Fierling.

MOTHER COURAGE: The Commander's cook! After all these years! Where's Eilif?

COOK: Isn't he here yet? He went on ahead yesterday. He was on his way here.

CHAPLAIN: I'll be putting my pastor's clothes back on. *(He goes behind the wagon.)*

MOTHER COURAGE: Kattrin, Eilif's coming! Bring a glass of brandy for the cook! *(But* KATTRIN *doesn't.)* Oh, pull your hair over your face and forget it, the cook's no stranger! *(To him:)* She won't come out. Peace is nothing to her. It took too long to get here. Here's your schnapps. *(She has got it herself. They sit.)*

COOK: Dear old peace!

MOTHER COURAGE: Dear old peace has broken my neck. On the chaplain's advice I went and bought a lot of supplies. Now everybody's leaving, and I'm holding the baby.

COOK: How could you listen to a windbag like the chaplain? If I'd had the time I'd have warned you against him. But the Catholics were too quick for me. Since when did he become the big wheel around here?

MOTHER COURAGE: He's been doing the dishes and helping me with the wagon.

COOK: And telling you a few of his jokes? He has a most unhealthy attitude to women. He's completely unsound.

MOTHER COURAGE: And you're completely sound?

COOK: And I am completely sound. Your health!

MOTHER COURAGE: Sound! Only one person around here was ever sound, and I never had to slave as I did then. He sold the blankets off the children's beds in autumn. You aren't recommending yourself to me if you claim to be sound.

COOK: Ah well, here we sit, drinking your famous brandy while the bells of peace do ring!

MOTHER COURAGE: I don't see where they're going to find all this pay that's in arrears. Were you people paid?

COOK *(hesitating):* Not exactly. That's why we disbanded. Why stay? I said to myself. Why not look up a couple of friends? So here I am.

MOTHER COURAGE: In other words: you're broke.

COOK *(annoyed by the bells):* I wish they'd stop that racket! I'd like to set myself up in some business.

The CHAPLAIN *enters in his pastor's coat again.*

CHAPLAIN: Pretty good, eh? Just a few moth holes.

COOK: I have a bone to pick with you. You advised a lady to buy superfluous goods on the pretext that the war would never end.

CHAPLAIN: And what business is that of yours?

COOK: It's unprincipled behavior! How dare you interfere with the conduct of other people's businesses?

CHAPLAIN: Who's interfering now, I'd like to know? *(To* MOTHER COURAGE:*)* I was far from suspecting you had to account to *this* gentleman for everything!

MOTHER COURAGE: Now don't get excited. The cook's giving his personal opinion. You can hardly deny your war was a flop.

CHAPLAIN: You are a hyena of the battlefield! You are taking the name of peace in vain!

MOTHER COURAGE: I'm a what, did you say?

CHAPLAIN: A hyena!

COOK: Who insults my girl friend, insults me!

CHAPLAIN: *Your* intentions are only too transparent! *(To* MOTHER COURAGE:*)* But when I see *you* take peace between finger and thumb like a snotty old handkerchief, the humanity in me rebels! You want war, do you? Well, don't you forget the proverb: who sups with the devil must use a long spoon!

MOTHER COURAGE: Remember what one fox said to another that was caught in a trap? "If you stay there, you're just asking for trouble." I'm not in love with war, Mr. Army Chaplain and when it comes to calling people hyenas, you and I part company!

CHAPLAIN: Then why all this grumbling about the peace? Is it just for the junk in your wagon?

MOTHER COURAGE: My goods are not junk. I live off them.

CHAPLAIN: You live off war. Exactly!

COOK: As a grown man, you should know better than to run around advising people. *(To* MOTHER COURAGE:*)* In your situation you should get rid of certain goods at once—before prices sink to zero.

MOTHER COURAGE: That's good advice. I think I'll take it. *(She climbs on to her wagon.)*

COOK: One up for me. Anyway, Chaplain, cockfights are unbecoming to your cloth!

CHAPLAIN: If you don't shut your mouth, I'll murder you, cloth or no cloth!

Enter YVETTE, *wearing black, leaning on a stick. She is much older, fatter, and heavily powdered. Behind her, a* VALET.

YVETTE: Hullo everybody! Is this the Mother Courage establishment?

CHAPLAIN: Quite right. And with whom have we the pleasure?

YVETTE: I am Madam Colonel Starhemberg, good people. Where's Mother Courage?

CHAPLAIN *(calling to the wagon):* Madam Colonel Starhemberg to speak with you!

MOTHER COURAGE: Coming!

YVETTE *(calling):* It's me—Yvette!

MOTHER COURAGE: Yvette!

YVETTE: I've come to see how you're getting on! *(The* COOK *turns round in horror.)* Peter!

COOK: Yvette!

YVETTE: Of all things. How did *you* get here?

COOK: On a cart.

CHAPLAIN: Well! You know each other? Intimately?

YVETTE: I'll say! You're fat.

COOK: For that matter, you're no beanpole.

YVETTE: It's good we've met. Now I can tell you what I think of you, tramp.

CHAPLAIN: Do that. Tell him exactly what you think of him. But wait till Mother Courage comes out.

COOK: Now don't make a scene.

MOTHER COURAGE *comes out, laden with goods.*

MOTHER COURAGE: Yvette! *(They embrace.)* But why are you in mourning?

YVETTE: Doesn't it suit me? My husband, the colonel, died several years ago.

MOTHER COURAGE: The old fellow that nearly bought my wagon?

YVETTE: Nah, not him. His older brother.

MOTHER COURAGE: Good to see one person that got somewhere in this war.

CHAPLAIN: You promised to give us your opinion of this gentleman.

COOK: Now, Yvette, don't make a stink!

MOTHER COURAGE: He's a friend of mine, Yvette.

YVETTE: He's Peter Piper, that's what.

COOK: Cut the nicknames!

MOTHER COURAGE: Peter Piper? The one that turned the girls' heads? I'll have to sit down. And I've been keeping your pipe for you.

CHAPLAIN: And smoking it.

YVETTE: Lucky I can warn you against him. He's a bad lot. You won't find a worse on the whole coast of Flanders. He got more girls in trouble than . . .

COOK: That's a long time ago. It's not true any more.

YVETTE: Stand up when you talk to a lady! How I loved that man, and all the time he was having a little bowlegged brunette. He got her in trouble, too, of course.

COOK: I seem to have brought *you* luck.

YVETTE: Speak when you're spoken to, you hoary ruin! And take care, Mother Courage, this type is dangerous even in decay!

MOTHER COURAGE *(to* YVETTE*)*: Come with me. I must get rid of this stuff before the prices fall.

YVETTE *(to* COOK*)*: Miserable cur!

MOTHER COURAGE: Maybe you can help me at army headquarters—with your contacts.

YVETTE: Damnable whore hunter!

MOTHER COURAGE: Kattrin, church is all off, I'm going to market!

YVETTE: Inveterate seducer!

MOTHER COURAGE *(still to* KATTRIN*)*: When Eilif comes, give him something to drink!

YVETTE: I've put an end to your tricks, Peter Piper, and one day, in a better life than this, the Lord God will reward me! *(She sniffs.)* Come, Mother Courage!

The two leave. Pause.

CHAPLAIN: As our text this morning, let us take the saying: the mills of God grind slowly. And you complain of my jokes!

COOK: I'll be frank with you: I was hoping for a good hot dinner. And now she'll be getting a wrong picture of me. I think I should leave before she comes back.

CHAPLAIN: I think so too.

COOK: Chaplain, peace makes me sick! It's the lot of mankind to perish by fire and sword! Oh, how I wish I was roasting a great fat capon for the Commander—with mustard sauce and those little yellow carrots . . .

CHAPLAIN: Red cabbage. With capon: red cabbage.

COOK: You're right. But he always wanted yellow carrots.

CHAPLAIN: He never understood anything.

COOK: You always put plenty away.

CHAPLAIN: Under protest.

COOK: Anyway, you must admit, those were the days.

CHAPLAIN: Yes, that I might admit.

COOK: And now you've called her a hyena. *You* haven't much future here either . . . What are you staring at?

CHAPLAIN: Why, it's Eilif! *(*EILIF *enters followed by two soldiers with halberds. His hands are fettered. He is white as chalk.)* What happened?

EILIF: Where's my mother?

CHAPLAIN: Gone to the town.

EILIF: They said she was here. I was allowed a last visit.

COOK *(to the soldiers)*: Where are you taking him?

SOLDIER: For a ride.

The OTHER SOLDIER *makes the gesture of throat cutting.*

CHAPLAIN: What has he done?

SOLDIER: He broke in on a peasant. The wife is dead.

CHAPLAIN: Eilif, how could you?

EILIF: It's no different. It's what I did before.

COOK: That was in wartime.

EILIF: Shut your mouth. Can I sit down till she comes?

SOLDIER: No.

CHAPLAIN: It's true. In wartime they honored him for it. He sat at the Commander's right hand. It was bravery. Couldn't we speak with the provost?

SOLDIER: What's the use? Stealing cattle from a peasant, what's brave about that?

COOK: It was just dumb.

EILIF: If I'd been dumb, I'd have starved, smarty.

COOK: So you were bright—and paid for it.

CHAPLAIN: We must bring Kattrin out.

EILIF: Let her alone. Just give me some brandy.

SOLDIER: No.

CHAPLAIN: What shall we tell your mother?

EILIF: Tell her it was no different. Tell her it was the same. Aw, tell her nothing.

The soldiers lead him away.

CHAPLAIN: I'll come with you!

EILIF: I don't need any priest.

CHAPLAIN: You don't know—yet. *(He follows them.)*

COOK: I'll have to tell her, she'll expect to see him.

CHAPLAIN: Tell her he'll be back.

He leaves. The COOK *shakes his head, finally approaches the wagon.*

COOK: Hi! Won't you come out? I'm the cook! Have you got anything to eat in there? *(He looks in.)* She's got a blanket over her head.

Cannon. Re-enter MOTHER COURAGE, *breathless, still carrying her goods.*

MOTHER COURAGE: The peace is over! The war's on again—has been for three days! I didn't get rid of this stuff after all, thank God! The shooting has started in the town already. We must get away. Pack, Kattrin! What's on *your* mind?

COOK: Nothing.

MOTHER COURAGE: But there is. I see it in your face.

COOK: Eilif was here. Only he had to go away again.

MOTHER COURAGE: He was here? Then we'll see him on the march. I'll be with our side this time. How'd he look?

COOK: The same.

MOTHER COURAGE: He'll *never* change. And the war won't get *him,* he's bright. Help me with the packing. *(She starts it.)* Is Eilif in good with the captain? Did he tell you about his heroic deeds?

COOK: He's done one of them over again.

MOTHER COURAGE: Tell me about it later. *(*KATTRIN *appears.)* Kattrin, the peace is over. We're on the move again. *(To the* COOK*:)* What *is* eating you?

COOK: I'll enlist.

MOTHER COURAGE: Where's the Chaplain?

COOK: In the town. With Eilif.

MOTHER COURAGE: Stay with us a while, Cook, I need a bit of help.

COOK: This Yvette matter . . .

MOTHER COURAGE: Hasn't done you any harm in my eyes. Just the opposite. Where there's smoke, there's fire. You'll come?

COOK: I may as well.

MOTHER COURAGE: The twelfth regiment is under way. *(The* COOK *gets into harness with* KATTRIN.*)* Maybe I'll see Eilif before the day is out! Let's go! *(She sings, and the* COOK *joins in the refrain, THE SONG OF MOTHER COURAGE:)*

Up hill, down dale, past dome and steeple,
My wagon always moves ahead.
The war can care for all its people
So long as there is steel and lead.
Though steel and lead are stout supporters
A war needs human beings too.
Report today to your headquarters!
If it's to last, this war needs you!
Christians, awake! The winter's gone!
The snow departs, the dead sleep on.
And though you may not long survive
Get out of bed and look alive!

9

THE RELIGIOUS WAR HAS LASTED SIXTEEN YEARS, AND GERMANY HAS LOST HALF ITS INHABITANTS. THOSE WHO ARE SPARED IN BATTLE DIE BY PLAGUE. OVER ONCE-BLOOMING COUNTRYSIDE HUNGER RAGES. TOWNS ARE BURNED DOWN. WOLVES PROWL THE EMPTY STREETS. IN THE AUTUMN OF 1634 WE FIND MOTHER COURAGE IN THE FICHTELGEBIRGE NOT FAR FROM THE ROAD THE SWEDISH ARMY IS TAKING. WINTER HAS COME EARLY AND IS SEVERE. BUSINESS IS BAD. ONLY BEGGING REMAINS. THE COOK RECEIVES A LETTER FROM UTRECHT AND IS SENT PACKING.

In front of a half-ruined parsonage. Early winter. A grey morning. Gusts of wind. MOTHER COURAGE *and the* COOK *at the wagon in rags.*

COOK: There are no lights. No one is up.

MOTHER COURAGE: But it's a parsonage. The parson'll have to leave his feather bed to go ring the bells. Then he'll have himself some hot soup.

COOK: Where'll he find it? The whole village is starving.

MOTHER COURAGE: Why don't we sing him something?

COOK: Anna, I've had enough. A letter came from Utrecht, did I tell you? My mother died of cholera. The inn is mine. Look! *(He hands her the letter. She glances through it.)*

MOTHER COURAGE: I'm tired of this wandering life. I feel like a butcher's dog, taking meat to the customers and getting none for myself.

COOK: The world's coming to an end.

MOTHER COURAGE: Sometimes I dream of driving through hell with this wagon—and selling brimstone. Or I see myself driving through heaven handing out supplies to wandering souls! If only we could find a place where there's no shooting, me and my children—what's left of 'em—we might rest up a while.

COOK: Why don't we open this inn together? With you or without you, I'm leaving for Utrecht today. Think it over.

MOTHER COURAGE: I must tell Kattrin. Kattrin! *(KATTRIN comes out of the wagon.)* Listen. We're thinking of going to Utrecht, the cook and me. His mother's left him an inn. We'd be sure of our dinner. And you'd have a bed of your own. What about it?

COOK: Anna, I must speak to you alone.

MOTHER COURAGE: Go back in, Kattrin.

KATTRIN *does so.*

COOK: There's a misunderstanding. I hoped I wouldn't have to come right out with it—but if you're bringing her, it's all off.

KATTRIN *is listening—her head sticking out at the back of the wagon.*

MOTHER COURAGE: You want me to leave Kattrin behind?

COOK: There's no room. The inn isn't a place with three counters. If the two of us stand on our hind legs we can earn a living, but three's too many. Let Kattrin keep your wagon.

MOTHER COURAGE: I was thinking she might find a husband in Utrecht.

COOK: At her age? With that scar?

MOTHER COURAGE: Not so loud!

COOK: The customers wouldn't like it!

MOTHER COURAGE: Not so loud, I said!

COOK: There's a light in the parsonage. We'd better sing. Worthy Master Parson, and all within, we shall now sing the song of Solomon, Holy Saint Martin, and other good men who came to a bad end, so you can see we're good folk too, and have a hard time getting by, especially in winter. *(He sings. MOTHER COURAGE joins him in the refrains.)*

THE SONG OF THE WISE AND GOOD

You've heard of wise old Solomon
    You know his history.
He thought so little of this earth
He cursed the hour of his birth
    Declaring: all is vanity.
How very wise was Solomon!
    But ere night came and day did go
This fact was clear to everyone:
    It was his wisdom that had brought him low.
(Better for you if you have none.)

For the virtues are dangerous in this world, you're better off without, you have a nice life—some good hot soup included. We're told to be unselfish and share what we have, but what if we have nothing? Unselfishness is a very rare virtue, it simply doesn't pay.

Unselfish Martin could not bear
His fellow creatures' woes.
He met a beggar in the snows
And gave him half his cloak to wear:
So both of them fell down and froze.
What an unselfish paragon!
But ere night came and day did go
This fact was clear to everyone:
It was unselfishness that brought him low.
(Better for you if you have none.)

That's how it is! We're good, we don't steal, we don't kill, we don't burn the house down, and so, as the song says, we sink lower and lower and there isn't a plate of soup going.

God's Ten Commandments we have kept
And acted as we should.
It has not done us any good.
O you who sit beside a fire
Please help us now: our need is dire!
Strict godliness we've always shown.
But ere night came and day did go
This fact was clear to everyone:
It was our godliness that brought us low.
(Better for you if you have none.)

VOICE *(from above):* You there! Come up! There's some hot soup for you!

MOTHER COURAGE: I couldn't swallow a thing. Was that your last word?

COOK: The inn isn't big enough. We better go up.

MOTHER COURAGE: I'll get Kattrin.

COOK: If there are three of us the parson won't like it. Stick something in your pocket for her.

The COOK *and* MOTHER COURAGE *enter the parsonage.* KATTRIN *climbs out of the wagon with a bundle. Making sure the others have gone, she lays out on a wagon wheel a skirt of her mother's and a pair of the* COOK*'s pants. She has just finished, and picked her bundle up, when* MOTHER COURAGE *comes down with soup for her.*

MOTHER COURAGE: Kattrin! Where do you think you're going? *(She examines the bundle.)* Ah! So you were listening! I told him: nothing doing—he can have his lousy inn. *(Now she sees the skirt and pants.)* Oh, you stupid girl! Now what if I'd seen that, and you'd been gone! *(*KATTRIN *tries to leave. Her mother holds her.)* And don't imagine I sent him packing on your account. It was the wagon. They can't part me from my wagon. Now we'll put the cook's things here where he'll find 'em, that silly man. You and I are leaving. *(She climbs up on the wagon and throws the rest of the* COOK*'s few things down on to the pants.)* There! He's fired! The last man I'll ever take into *this* business! Get into harness, Kattrin. This winter will pass like all the others.

The two women harness themselves to the wagon and start out. A gust of wind. When they have disappeared, the COOK *re-enters, still chewing. He sees his things.*

10

On the highway. MOTHER COURAGE *and* KATTRIN *are pulling the wagon. They come to a prosperous farmhouse. Someone inside is singing.*

THE SONG OF SHELTER

In March a tree we planted
To make the garden gay.
In June we were enchanted:
A lovely rose was blooming
The balmy air perfuming!
Blest of the gods are they
Who have a garden gay!
In June we were enchanted.

When snow falls helter-skelter
And loudly blows the storm
Our farmhouse gives us shelter.
The winter's in a hurry
But we've no cause to worry.
Cosy are we and warm
Though loudly blows the storm:
Our farmhouse gives us shelter.

MOTHER COURAGE *and* KATTRIN *have stopped to listen. They start out again.*

11

JANUARY, 1636. CATHOLIC TROOPS THREATEN THE PROTESTANT TOWN OF HALLE. THE STONES BEGIN TO TALK. MOTHER COURAGE LOSES HER DAUGHTER AND JOURNEYS ONWARD ALONE. THE WAR IS NOT YET NEAR ITS END.

The wagon, very far gone now, stands near a farmhouse with a straw roof. It is night. Out of the wood come a LIEUTENANT *and* THREE SOLDIERS *in full armor.*

LIEUTENANT: And there mustn't be a sound. If anyone yells, cut him down.
FIRST SOLDIER: But we'll have to knock—if we want a guide.
LIEUTENANT: Knocking's a natural noise, it's all right, could be a cow hitting the wall of the cowshed.

The soldiers knock at the farmhouse door. An OLD PEASANT WOMAN *opens. A hand is clapped over her mouth. Two soldiers enter.*

PEASANT'S VOICE: What is it? *(The soldiers bring out an* OLD PEASANT *and his* SON.*)*
LIEUTENANT *(pointing to the wagon on which* KATTRIN *has appeared):* There's another. *(A* SOLDIER *pulls her out.)* Is this everybody?
OLD PEASANT: That's our son.

PEASANT WOMAN: And that's a girl that can't talk. Her mother's in town buying up stocks because the shopkeepers are running away and selling cheap.
OLD PEASANT: They're canteen people.
LIEUTENANT: I'm warning you. Keep quiet. One sound and you'll have a sword in your ribs. I need someone to show us the path to the town. *(Points to the* YOUNG PEASANT:*)* You! Come here!
YOUNG PEASANT: I don't know any path!
SECOND SOLDIER *(grinning):* He don't know any path!
YOUNG PEASANT: I don't help Catholics.
LIEUTENANT *(to* SECOND SOLDIER*):* Show him your sword.
YOUNG PEASANT *(forced to his knees, a sword at his throat):* I'd rather die!
SECOND SOLDIER *(again mimicking):* He'd rather die!
FIRST SOLDIER: We'll soon fix this. *(Walks over to the cowshed.)* Two cows and a bull. Listen, you. If you aren't going to be reasonable, I'll saber your cattle.
YOUNG PEASANT: Not the cattle!
PEASANT WOMAN *(weeping):* Spare the cattle, Captain, or we'll starve!
LIEUTENANT: If he must be stubborn.
FIRST SOLDIER: I think I'll start with the bull.
YOUNG PEASANT *(to his father):* Do I have to? *(The* OLD PEASANT *nods.)* I'll do it.
PEASANT WOMAN: Thank you, thank you, Captain, for sparing us, for ever and ever, Amen.

The OLD PEASANT *stops her going on thanking him.*

FIRST SOLDIER: I knew the bull came first all right!

Led by the YOUNG PEASANT, *the* LIEUTENANT *and the soldiers go on their way.*

OLD PEASANT: What goes on? Nothing good, I guess.
PEASANT WOMAN: Maybe they're just scouts. What are you doing?
OLD PEASANT *(setting a ladder against the roof and climbing up):* I'm seeing if they're alone. *(On the roof:)* Things are moving—all over. I can see armor. And a cannon. There must be more than a regiment. God have mercy on the town and its people!
PEASANT WOMAN: Are there lights in the town?
OLD PEASANT: No, they're all asleep. *(He climbs down.)* It's an attack. They'll all be slaughtered in their beds.
PEASANT WOMAN: The watchman'll give warning.
OLD PEASANT: They must have killed the watchman in the tower on the hill or he'd have sounded his horn before this.
PEASANT WOMAN: If there were more of us . . .
OLD PEASANT: But being that we're alone with that cripple . . .
PEASANT WOMAN: There's nothing we can do, is there?
OLD PEASANT: Nothing.
PEASANT WOMAN: We can't get to the town in the dark.
OLD PEASANT: The whole hillside's swarming with men.
PEASANT WOMAN: We could give a sign?
OLD PEASANT: And be cut down for it?
PEASANT WOMAN: No, there's nothing we can do. *(To* KATTRIN:*)* Pray, poor thing, pray! There's

nothing we can do to stop this bloodshed, so even if you can't talk, at least pray! *He* hears, if no one else does. I'll help you. *(All kneel,* KATTRIN *behind.)* Our Father, which art in Heaven, hear our prayer, let not the town perish with all that lie therein asleep and fearing nothing. Wake them, that they rise and go to the walls and see the foe that comes with fire and sword in the night down the hill and across the fields. God protect our mother and make the watchman not sleep but wake ere it's too late. And save our son-in-law too, O God, he's there with his four children, let them not perish, they're innocent, they know nothing, one of them's not two years old, the eldest is seven. *(*KATTRIN *rises, troubled.)* Heavenly Father, hear us, only Thou canst help us or we die, for we are weak and have no sword nor nothing; we cannot trust our own strength but only Thine, O Lord; we are in Thy hands, our cattle, our farm, and the town too, we're all in Thy hands, and the foe is nigh unto the walls with all his power. *(*KATTRIN, *unperceived, has crept off to the wagon, has taken something out of it, put it under her skirt, and has climbed up the ladder to the roof.)* Be mindful of the children in danger, especially the little ones, be mindful of the old folk who cannot move, and of all Christian souls, O Lord.

OLD PEASANT: And forgive us our trespasses as we forgive them that trespass against us. Amen.

Sitting on the roof, KATTRIN *takes a drum from under her skirt, and starts to beat it.*

PEASANT WOMAN: Heavens, what's she doing?

OLD PEASANT: She's out of her mind!

PEASANT WOMAN: Get her down, quick! *(The* OLD PEASANT *runs to the ladder but* KATTRIN *pulls it up on the roof.)* She'll get us in trouble.

OLD PEASANT: Stop it this minute, you silly cripple!

PEASANT WOMAN: The soldiers'll come!

OLD PEASANT *(looking for stones):* I'll stone you!

PEASANT WOMAN: Have you no pity, don't you have a heart? We have relations there too, four grandchildren. If they find us now, it's the end, they'll stab us to death! *(*KATTRIN *is staring into the far distance, toward the town. She goes on drumming. To the* PEASANT:*)* I told you not to let that sort into the farm. What do *they* care if we lose our cattle?

LIEUTENANT *(running back with soldiers and* YOUNG PEASANT*):* I'll cut you all to bits!

PEASANT WOMAN: We're innocent, sir, we couldn't stop her!

LIEUTENANT: Where's the ladder?

OLD PEASANT: On the roof.

LIEUTENANT *(calling):* Throw down the drum. I order you! *(To peasants:)* You're all in this, but you won't live to tell the tale.

OLD PEASANT: They've been cutting down fir trees around here. If we get a good long trunk we can knock her off the roof.

FIRST SOLDIER *(to the* LIEUTENANT*):* May I make a suggestion? *(He whispers something to the* LIEUTENANT, *who nods. To* KATTRIN:*)* Listen, you! We'll do you a favor. Everyone in that town is gonna get killed. Come down, go with us to the town, show us your mother and we'll spare her.

KATTRIN *replies with more drumming.*

LIEUTENANT *(pushing him away)*: She doesn't trust you, no wonder with your face. *(He calls up to* KATTRIN:*)* Hey, you! Suppose I give you my word? I'm an officer, my word's my bond! *(*KATTRIN *again replies with drumming—harder this time.)* Nothing is sacred to her.

FIRST SOLDIER: They'll sure as hell hear it in the town.

LIEUTENANT: We must make another noise. Louder than that drum. What can we make a noise with?

FIRST SOLDIER: We mustn't make a noise!

LIEUTENANT: A harmless noise, fool, a peacetime noise!

OLD PEASANT: I could start chopping wood.

LIEUTENANT: That's it! *(The* PEASANT *brings his axe and chops away.)* Chop! Chop harder! Chop for your life! It's not enough. *(To* FIRST SOLDIER:*)* You chop too!

OLD PEASANT: I've only one axe.

LIEUTENANT: We must set fire to the farm. Smoke her out.

OLD PEASANT: That's no good, Captain, when they see fire from the town, they'll know everything.

KATTRIN *is laughing now and drumming harder than ever.*

LIEUTENANT: Laughing at us, is she? I'll settle *her* hash if it's the last thing I do. Bring me a musket!

Two soldiers off.

PEASANT WOMAN: I have it, Captain. That's their wagon over there, Captain. If we smash that, she'll stop. It's all they have, Captain.

LIEUTENANT *(to the* YOUNG PEASANT*)*: Smash it! *(Calling:)* If you don't stop that noise, we'll smash up your wagon!

The YOUNG PEASANT *deals the wagon a couple of feeble blows with a board.*

PEASANT WOMAN *(to* KATTRIN*)*: Stop, you little beast!

KATTRIN *stares at the wagon and pauses. Noises of distress come out of her. She goes on drumming.*

LIEUTENANT: Where are those sonsofbitches with that gun?

FIRST SOLDIER: They can't have heard anything in the town or we'd hear their cannon.

LIEUTENANT *(calling)*: They don't hear you. And now we're going to shoot. I'll give you one more chance: throw down that drum!

YOUNG PEASANT *(dropping the board, screaming to* KATTRIN*)*: Don't stop now! Go on, go on, go on!

The soldier knocks him down and stabs him. KATTRIN *starts crying but goes on drumming.*

PEASANT WOMAN: You're killing him!

The soldiers arrive with the gun.

LIEUTENANT: Set it up! *(Calling while the gun is set up on forks:)* Once for all: stop that drumming! *(Still crying,* KATTRIN *is drumming as hard as she can.)* Fire!

The soldiers fire. KATTRIN *is hit. She gives the drum another feeble beat or two, then collapses.*

LIEUTENANT: So that ends the noise.

But the last beats of the drum are lost in the din of cannon from the town. Mingled with the thunder of cannon, alarm-bells are heard in the distance.

FIRST SOLDIER: She made it.

12

Toward morning. The drums and pipes of troops on the march, receding. In front of the wagon MOTHER COURAGE *sits by* KATTRIN*'s body. The* THREE PEASANTS *of the last scene are standing near.*

PEASANT WOMAN: The regiments have all left. No, there's still one to go.
OLD PEASANT *(to* MOTHER COURAGE*)*: You must latch on to it. You'll never get by alone. Hurry!
MOTHER COURAGE: Maybe she's asleep. *(She sings:)*

Lullay, lullay, what's that in the hay?
The neighbor's kids cry but mine are gay.
The neighbor's kids are dressed in dirt:
Your silks were cut from an angel's skirt.
They are all starving: you have a cake;
If it's too stale, you need but speak.
Lullay, lullay, what's rustling there?
One lad fell in Poland. The other is—where?

MOTHER COURAGE: You shouldn't have told her about the children.
OLD PEASANT: If you hadn't gone off to get your cut, maybe it wouldn't have happened.
MOTHER COURAGE: I'm glad she can sleep.
PEASANT WOMAN: She's not asleep, it's time you realized, she's through.
OLD PEASANT: You must get away. There are wolves in these parts. And the bandits are worse.
MOTHER COURAGE *(stands up)*: That's right.
OLD PEASANT: Have you no one left?
MOTHER COURAGE: Yes, my son Eilif.
OLD PEASANT: Find him then, leave *her* to us.
PEASANT WOMAN: We'll give her a proper burial, you needn't worry.
MOTHER COURAGE: Here's a little money for the expenses. *(She harnesses herself to the wagon.)* I hope I can pull the wagon by myself. Yes, I'll manage. There's not much in it now. *(The last regiment is heard passing.)* Hey! Take me with you!

The men are heard singing THE SONG OF MOTHER COURAGE:

Dangers, surprises, devastations—
    The war takes hold and will not quit.

But though it last three generations
  We shall get nothing out of it.
Starvation, filth, and cold enslave us.
  The army robs us of our pay.
Only a miracle can save us
  And miracles have had their day.
    Christians, awake! The winter's gone!
    The snows depart, the dead sleep on.
    And though you may not long survive
    Get out of bed and look alive!

TENNESSEE WILLIAMS

(1911–1983)

The Glass Menagerie

About the Author: Thomas Lanier "Tennessee" Williams was born in Columbus, Mississippi; he attended the University of Missouri and Washington University in St. Louis before completing his bachelor's degree in 1938 at the University of Iowa. Beginning in 1935, he wrote over three dozen plays and won virtually all the major awards a playwright can be given in the United States, including the Pulitzer Prize twice (in 1948 for *A Streetcar Named Desire* and in 1955 for *Cat on a Hot Tin Roof*) and the New York Drama Critics Circle Award four times (the first in 1945 for *The Glass Menagerie*).

About the Play: The beginning of *The Glass Menagerie* introduces several of its central thematic concerns. The first paragraph of Williams's lengthy introductory stage direction expresses a strong attitude toward lower-middle-class society. Set in difficult economic times (the great depression) and featuring a character obsessed with her family's former status, the play seems to emphasize this issue of economic and social class. The first speech of the play itself, however, presents other issues. We are confronted by a narrator, Tom, who tells us that his play is about "truth in the pleasant guise of illusion," and that at least one of the characters, the one who is "most realistic," is also to be used "as a symbol." It would seem to be of the nature of drama that there can be no narrator: The plot is presented by characters interacting on a stage, not by a narrative voice, but Williams seems here to insist on blurring this distinction. This "narrator" emphasizes the relationship between illusion and reality and the symbolic dimension of reality. These ideas (among others) interact in this complex play. For example, Laura and Amanda both seem crippled in their relations with the outside world by their respective illusions, and the whole question of illusion seems somehow connected with questions of social and economic class.

The form of the play itself forces us to focus on the nature of illusion: This is a play with a narrator who fills in information for us. Like an author, he is telling us his story, is having it enacted onstage. (Some of the details of his story are like those in the author's life too: Williams was a shoe salesman in St. Louis in this kind of neighborhood during the depression.) Yet at the same time that he "tells" his story, Tom is a character inside the story. Although this story seems as "real" as stories can when enacted on a stage, it is, as he says, "a memory play." It is all happening inside the mind of Tom the narrator, who is looking back, reliving the experiences of Tom the character. The play becomes a way for him to explain himself and to learn about why he is as he is. From this perspective, the narrator is perhaps less a narrator, than the only "real" character in the play. Laura and Amanda suffered from different versions of blindness from which Tom, the narrator in the present tense, seems to believe he has escaped. Has he? If so, why does he feel compelled to stage this play? Is it, from the point of view of its own fiction, the "truth," or is it, like any memory, only one version of "reality"?

CHARACTERS

AMANDA WINGFIELD, *the mother*
LAURA WINGFIELD, *her daughter*
TOM WINGFIELD, *her son*
JIM O'CONNOR, *the gentleman caller*

SCENE: *An alley in St. Louis.*

PART I. *Preparation for a Gentleman Caller.*
PART II. *The Gentleman Calls.*

TIME: *Now and the Past.*

SCENE ONE

(The Wingfield apartment is in the rear of the building, one of those vast hive-like conglomerations of cellular living-units that flower as warty growths in overcrowded urban centers of lower middle-class population and are symptomatic of the impulse of this largest and fundamentally enslaved section of American society to avoid fluidity and differentiation and to exist and function as one interfused mass of automatism.

The apartment faces an alley and is entered by a fire-escape, a structure whose name is a touch of accidental poetic truth, for all of these huge buildings are always burning with the slow and implacable fires of human desperation. The fire-escape is included in the set—that is, the landing of it and steps descending from it.

The scene is memory and is therefore nonrealistic. Memory takes a lot of poetic license. It omits some details; others are exaggerated, according to the emotional value of the articles it touches, for memory is seated predominantly in the heart. The interior is therefore rather dim and poetic.

At the rise of the curtain, the audience is faced with the dark, grim rear wall of the Wingfield tenement. This building, which runs parallel to the footlights, is flanked on both sides by dark, narrow alleys which run into murky canyons of tangled clotheslines, garbage cans and the sinister latticework of neighboring fire-escapes. It is up and down these side alleys that exterior entrances and exits are made, during the play. At the end of TOM'S *opening commentary, the dark tenement wall slowly reveals (by means of a transparency) the interior of the ground floor Wingfield apartment.*

Downstage is the living room, which also serves as a sleeping room for LAURA, *the sofa unfolding to make her bed. Upstage, center, and divided by a wide arch or second proscenium with transparent faded portieres (or second curtain), is the dining room. In an old-fashioned what-not in the living room are seen scores of transparent glass animals. A blown-up photograph of the father hangs on the wall of the living room, facing the audience, to the left of the archway. It is the face of a very handsome young man in a doughboy's First World War cap. He is gallantly smiling, ineluctably smiling, as if to say, "I will be smiling forever."*

The audience hears and sees the opening scene in the dining room through both the transparent fourth wall of the building and the transparent gauze portieres of the dining-room arch. It is during this revealing scene that the fourth wall slowly ascends, out of sight. This transparent exterior wall is not brought down again until the very end of the play, during TOM'S *final speech.*

The narrator is an undisguised convention of the play. He takes whatever license with dramatic convention as is convenient to his purposes.

TOM *enters dressed as a merchant sailor from alley, stage left, and strolls across the front of the stage to the fire-escape. There he stops and lights a cigarette. He addresses the audience.)*

TOM: Yes, I have tricks in my pocket, I have things up my sleeve. But I am the opposite of a stage magician. He gives you illusion that has the appearance of truth. I give you truth in the pleasant disguise of illusion. To begin with, I turn back time. I reverse it to that quaint period, the thirties, when the huge middle class of America was matriculating in a school for the blind. Their eyes had failed them, or they had failed their eyes, and so they were having their fingers pressed forcibly down on the fiery Braille alphabet of a dissolving economy. In Spain there was revolution. Here there was only shouting and confusion. In Spain there was Guernica. Here there were disturbances of labor, sometimes pretty violent, in otherwise peaceful cities such as Chicago, Cleveland, Saint Louis. . . . This is the social background of the play.

*(*MUSIC.*)*

The play is memory. Being a memory play, it is dimly lighted, it is sentimental, it is not realistic. In memory everything seems to happen to music. That explains the fiddle in the wings. I am the narrator of the play, and also a character in it. The other characters are my mother, Amanda, my sister, Laura, and a gentleman caller who appears in the final scenes. He is the most realistic character in the play, being an emissary from a world of reality that we were somehow set apart from. But since I have a poet's weakness for symbols, I am using this character also as a symbol; he is the long delayed but always expected something that we live for. There is a fifth character in the play who doesn't appear except in this larger-than-life photograph over the mantel. This is our father who left us a long time ago. He was a telephone man who fell in love with long distances; he gave up his job with the telephone company and skipped the light fantastic out of town . . . The last we heard of him was a picture post-card from Mazatlan, on the Pacific coast of Mexico, containing a message of two words—"Hello—Good-bye!" and no address. I think the rest of the play will explain itself. . . .

*(*AMANDA'S *voice becomes audible through the portieres.)*

(LEGEND ON SCREEN: "OÙ SONT LES NEIGES.")

(He divides the portieres and enters the upstage area.)

*(*AMANDA *and* LAURA *are seated at a drop-leaf table. Eating is indicated by gestures without food or utensils.* AMANDA *faces the audience.* TOM *and* LAURA *are seated in profile.)*

(The interior has lit up softly and through the scrim we see AMANDA *and* LAURA *seated at the table in the upstage area.)*

AMANDA *(calling):* Tom?

TOM: Yes, Mother.

AMANDA: We can't say grace until you come to the table!

TOM: Coming, Mother. *(He bows slightly and withdraws, reappearing a few moments later in his place at the table.)*

AMANDA *(to her son):* Honey, don't *push* with your *fingers.* If you have to push with something, the thing to push with is a crust of bread. And chew—chew! Animals have secretions in their stomachs which enable them to digest food without mastication, but human beings are supposed to chew their food before they swallow it down. Eat food leisurely, son, and really enjoy it. A well-cooked meal has lots of delicate flavors that have to be held in the mouth for appreciation. So chew your food and give your salivary glands a chance to function!

*(*TOM *deliberately lays his imaginary fork down and pushes his chair back from the table.)*

TOM: I haven't enjoyed one bite of this dinner because of your constant directions on how to eat it. It's you that makes me rush through meals with your hawk-like attention to every bite I take. Sickening—spoils my appetite—all this discussion of animals' secretion—salivary glands—mastication!

AMANDA *(lightly):* Temperament like a Metropolitan star! *(He rises and crosses downstage.)* You're not excused from the table.

TOM: I'm getting a cigarette.

AMANDA: You smoke too much.

*(*LAURA *rises.)*

LAURA: I'll bring in the blanc mange.

(He remains standing with his cigarette by the portieres during the following.)

AMANDA *(rising):* No, sister, no, sister—you be the lady this time and I'll be the darky.

LAURA: I'm already up.

AMANDA: Resume your seat, little sister—I want you to stay fresh and pretty—for gentlemen callers!

LAURA: I'm not expecting any gentlemen callers.

AMANDA *(crossing out to kitchenette. Airily):* Sometimes they come when they are least expected! Why, I remember one Sunday afternoon in Blue Mountain— *(Enters kitchenette.)*

TOM: I know what's coming!

LAURA: Yes. But let her tell it.

TOM: Again?

LAURA: She loves to tell it.

*(*AMANDA *returns with bowl of dessert.)*

AMANDA: One Sunday afternoon in Blue Mountain—your mother received—*seventeen!*—gentlemen callers! Why, sometimes there weren't chairs enough to accommodate them all. We had to send the nigger over to bring in folding chairs from the parish house.

TOM *(remaining at portieres):* How did you entertain those gentlemen callers?

AMANDA: I understood the art of conversation!

TOM: I bet you could talk.

AMANDA: Girls in those days *knew* how to talk, I can tell you.

TOM: Yes?

(IMAGE: AMANDA AS A GIRL ON A PORCH, GREETING CALLERS.)

AMANDA: They knew how to entertain their gentlemen callers. It wasn't enough for a girl to be possessed of a pretty face and a graceful figure—although I wasn't slighted in either respect. She also needed to have a nimble wit and a tongue to meet all occasions.

TOM: What did you talk about?

AMANDA: Things of importance going on in the world! Never anything coarse or common or vulgar. *(She addresses* TOM *as though he were seated in the vacant chair at the table though he remains by portieres. He plays this scene as though he held the book.)* My callers were gentlemen—all! Among my callers were some of the most prominent young planters of the Mississippi Delta—planters and sons of planters!

*(*TOM *motions for music and a spot of light on* AMANDA.*)*

(Her eyes lift, her face glows, her voice becomes rich and elegiac.)

(SCREEN LEGEND: *"Où sont les neiges."*)

There was young Champ Laughlin who later became vice-president of the Delta Planters Bank. Hadley Stevenson who was drowned in Moon Lake and left his widow one hundred and fifty thousand in Government bonds. There were the Cutrere brothers, Wesley and Bates. Bates was one of my bright particular beaux! He got in a quarrel with that wild Wainright boy. They shot it out on the floor of Moon Lake Casino. Bates was shot through the stomach. Died in the ambulance on his way to Memphis. His widow was also well-provided for, came into eight or ten thousand acres, that's all. She married him on the rebound—never loved her—carried my picture on him the night he died! And there was that boy that every girl in the Delta had set her cap for! That beautiful, brilliant young Fitzhugh boy from Greene County!

TOM: What did he leave his widow?

AMANDA: He never married! Gracious, you talk as though all of my old admirers had turned up their toes to the daisies!

TOM: Isn't this the first you've mentioned that still survives?

AMANDA: That Fitzhugh boy went North and made a fortune—came to be known as the Wolf of Wall Street! He had the Midas touch, whatever he touched turned to gold! And I could have been Mrs. Duncan J. Fitzhugh, mind you! But—I picked your *father!*

LAURA *(rising):* Mother, let me clear the table.

AMANDA: No, dear, you go in front and study your typewriter chart. Or practice your shorthand a little. Stay fresh and pretty!—It's almost time for our gentlemen callers to

start arriving. *(She flounces girlishly toward the kitchenette.)* How many do you suppose we're going to entertain this afternoon?

(TOM throws down the paper and jumps up with a groan.)

LAURA *(alone in the dining room):* I don't believe we're going to receive any, Mother.

AMANDA *(reappearing, airily):* What? No one—not one? You must be joking! *(LAURA nervously echoes her laugh. She slips in a fugitive manner through the half-open portieres and draws them gently behind her. A shaft of very clear light is thrown on her face against the faded tapestry of the curtains.* MUSIC: "THE GLASS MENAGERIE" UNDER FAINTLY. *Lightly.)* Not one gentlemen caller? It can't be true! There must be a flood, there must have been a tornado!

LAURA: It isn't a flood, it's not a tornado, Mother. I'm just not popular like you were in Blue Mountain. . . . *(TOM utters another groan. LAURA glances at him with a faint, apologetic smile. Her voice catching a little.)* Mother's afraid I'm going to be an old maid.

The scene dims out with "Glass Menagerie" music.

SCENE TWO

("Laura, Haven't You Ever Liked Some Boy?"

On the dark stage the screen is lighted with the image of blue roses.

Gradually LAURA's figure becomes apparent and the screen goes out.

The music subsides.

LAURA is seated in the delicate ivory chair at the small claw-foot table.

She wears a dress of soft violet material for a kimono—her hair tied back from her forehead with a ribbon.

She is washing and polishing her collection of glass.

AMANDA appears on the fire-escape steps. At the sound of her ascent, LAURA catches her breath, thrusts the bowl of ornaments away and seats herself stiffly before the diagram of the typewriter keyboard as though it held her spellbound. Something has happened to AMANDA. It is written in her face as she climbs to the landing: a look that is grim and hopeless and a little absurd.

She has on one of those cheap or imitation velvety-looking cloth coats with imitation fur collar. Her hat is five or six years old, one of those dreadful cloche hats that were worn in the late twenties and she is clasping an enormous black patent-leather pocketbook with nickel clasp and initials. This is her full-dress outfit, the one she usually wears to the D.A.R.

Before entering she looks through the door.

She purses her lips, opens her eyes wide, rolls them upward and shakes her head.

Then she slowly lets herself in the door. Seeing her mother's expression LAURA touches her lips with a nervous gesture.)

LAURA: Hello, Mother, I was— *(She makes a nervous gesture toward the chart on the wall. AMANDA leans against the shut door and stares at LAURA with a martyred look.)*

AMANDA: Deception? Deception? *(She slowly removes her hat and gloves, continuing the swift suffering stare. She lets the hat and gloves fall on the floor—a bit of acting.)*

LAURA *(shakily):* How was the D.A.R. meeting? *(AMANDA slowly opens her purse and removes a dainty white handkerchief which she shakes out delicately and delicately touches to her lips and nostrils.)* Didn't you go to the D.A.R. meeting, Mother?

AMANDA *(faintly, almost inaudibly):* —No.—No. *(Then more forcibly.)* I did not have the strength—to go to the D.A.R. In fact, I did not have the courage! I wanted to find a hole in the ground and hide myself in it forever! *(She crosses slowly to the wall and removes the diagram of the typewriter keyboard. She holds it in front of her for a second, staring at it sweetly and sorrowfully—then bites her lips and tears it in two pieces.)*

LAURA *(faintly):* Why did you do that, Mother? *(*AMANDA *repeats the same procedure with the chart of the Gregg Alphabet.)* Why are you—

AMANDA: Why? Why? How old are you, Laura?

LAURA: Mother, you know my age.

AMANDA: I thought that you were an adult; it seems that I was mistaken. *(She crosses slowly to the sofa and sinks down and stares at* LAURA.*)*

LAURA: Please don't stare at me, Mother.

*(*AMANDA *closes her eyes and lowers her head. Count ten.)*

AMANDA: What are we going to do, what is going to become of us, what is the future?

(Count ten.)

LAURA: Has something happened, Mother? *(*AMANDA *draws a long breath and takes out the handkerchief again. Dabbing process.)* Mother, has—something happened?

AMANDA: I'll be all right in a minute. I'm just bewildered— *(Count five.)* —by life. . . .

LAURA: Mother, I wish that you would tell me what's happened!

AMANDA: As you know, I was supposed to be inducted into my office at the D.A.R. this afternoon. *(Image: a swarm of typewriters.)* But I stopped off at Rubicam's Business College to speak to your teachers about your having a cold and ask them what progress they thought you were making down there.

LAURA: Oh. . . .

AMANDA: I went to the typing instructor and introduced myself as your mother. She didn't know who you were. Wingfield, she said. We don't have any such student enrolled at the school! I assured her she did, that you had been going to classes since early in January. "I wonder," she said, "if you could be talking about that terribly shy little girl who dropped out of school after only a few days' attendance?" "No," I said, "Laura, my daughter, has been going to school every day for the past six weeks!" "Excuse me," she said. She took the attendance book out and there was your name, unmistakably printed, and all the dates you were absent until they decided that you had dropped out of school. I still said, "No, there must have been some mistake! There must have been some mix-up in the records!" And she said, "No—I remember her perfectly now. Her hands shook so that she couldn't hit the right keys! The first time we gave a speed-test, she broke down completely—was sick at the stomach and almost had to be carried into the wash-room! After that morning she never showed up any more. We phoned the house but never got any answer—while I was working at Famous and Barr, I suppose, demonstrating those—Oh!" I felt so weak I could barely keep on my feet! I had to sit down while they got me a glass of water! Fifty dollars' tuition, all of our plans—my hopes and ambitions for you—just gone up the spout, just gone up the spout like that. *(*LAURA *draws a long breath and gets awkwardly to her feet. She crosses to the victrola and winds it up.)* What are you doing?

LAURA: Oh! *(She releases the handle and returns to her seat.)*

AMANDA: Laura, where have you been going when you've gone out pretending that you were going to business college?

LAURA: I've just been going out walking.

AMANDA: That's not true.

LAURA: It is. I just went walking.

AMANDA: Walking? Walking? In winter? Deliberately courting pneumonia in that light coat? Where did you walk to, Laura?

LAURA: All sorts of places—mostly in the park.

AMANDA: Even after you'd started catching that cold?

LAURA: It was the lesser of two evils, Mother. *(Image: Winter scene in park.)* I couldn't go back up. I—threw up—on the floor!

AMANDA: From half past seven till after five every day you mean to tell me you walked around in the park, because you wanted to make me think that you were still going to Rubicam's Business College?

LAURA: It wasn't as bad as it sounds. I went inside places to get warmed up.

AMANDA: Inside where?

LAURA: I went in the art museum and the bird-houses at the Zoo. I visited the penguins every day! Sometimes I did without lunch and went to the movies. Lately I've been spending most of my afternoons in the Jewel-box, that big glass house where they raise the tropical flowers.

AMANDA: You did all this to deceive me, just for the deception? *(LAURA looks down.)* Why?

LAURA: Mother, when you're disappointed, you get that awful suffering look on your face, like the picture of Jesus' mother in the museum!

AMANDA: Hush!

LAURA: I couldn't face it.

(Pause. A whisper of strings.)

(LEGEND: *"The crust of humility."*)

AMANDA *(hopelessly fingering the huge pocketbook)*: So what are we going to do the rest of our lives? Stay home and watch the parades go by? Amuse ourselves with the glass menagerie, darling? Eternally play those worn-out phonograph records your father left as a painful reminder of him? We won't have a business career—we've given that up because it gave us nervous indigestion! *(Laughs wearily.)* What is there left but dependency all our lives? I know so well what becomes of unmarried women who aren't prepared to occupy a position. I've seen such pitiful cases in the South—barely tolerated spinsters living upon the grudging patronage of sister's husband or brother's wife!—stuck away in some little mouse-trap of a room—encouraged by one in-law to visit another—little birdlike women without any nest—eating the crust of humility all their life! Is that the future that we've mapped out for ourselves? I swear it's the only alternative I can think of! It isn't a very pleasant alternative, is it? Of course—some girls *do marry*. *(LAURA twists her hands nervously.)* Haven't you ever liked some boy?

LAURA: Yes. I liked one once. *(Rises.)* I came across his picture a while ago.

AMANDA *(with some interest)*: He gave you his picture?

LAURA: No, it's in the year-book.

AMANDA *(disappointed)*: Oh—a high-school boy.

(SCREEN IMAGE: *Jim as high-school hero bearing a silver cup.)*

LAURA: Yes. His name was Jim. (LAURA *lifts the heavy annual from the claw-foot table.)* Here he is in *The Pirates of Penzance.*

AMANDA *(absently):* The what?

LAURA: The operetta the senior class put on. He had a wonderful voice and we sat across the aisle from each other Mondays, Wednesdays and Fridays in the Aud. Here he is with the silver cup for debating! See his grin?

AMANDA *(absently):* He must have had a jolly disposition.

LAURA: He used to call me—Blue Roses.

(IMAGE: *Blue roses.*)

AMANDA: Why did he call you such a name as that?

LAURA: When I had that attack of pleurosis—he asked me what was the matter when I came back. I said pleurosis—he thought that I said Blue Roses! So that's what he always called me after that. Whenever he saw me, he'd holler, "Hello, Blue Roses!" I didn't care for the girl that he went out with. Emily Meisenbach. Emily was the best-dressed girl at Soldan. She never struck me, though, as being sincere . . . It says in the Personal Section—they're engaged. That's—six years ago! They must be married by now.

AMANDA: Girls that aren't cut out for business careers usually wind up married to some nice man. *(Gets up with a spark of revival.)* Sister, that's what you'll do!

(LAURA *utters a startled, doubtful laugh. She reaches quickly for a piece of glass.)*

LAURA: But, Mother—

AMANDA: Yes? *(Crossing to photograph.)*

LAURA *(in a tone of frightened apology):* I'm—crippled!

(IMAGE: *Screen.*)

AMANDA: Nonsense! Laura, I've told you never, never to use that word. Why, you're not crippled, you just have a little defect—hardly noticeable, even! When people have some slight disadvantage like that, they cultivate other things to make up for it—develop charm—and vivacity—and—*charm!* That's all you have to do! *(She turns again to the photograph.)* One thing your father had *plenty of*—was *charm!*

(TOM *motions to the fiddle in the wings.)*

The scene fades out with music.

SCENE THREE

LEGEND ON SCREEN: *"After the fiasco—"*

(TOM *speaks from the fire-escape landing.)*

TOM: After the fiasco at Rubicam's Business College, the idea of getting a gentleman caller for Laura began to play a more important part in Mother's calculations. It became an obsession. Like some archetype of the universal unconscious, the image of the gentleman caller haunted our small apartment. . . . (IMAGE: *Young man at door with flowers.)* An evening at home rarely passed without some allusion to this image, this spectre, this hope. . . . Even when he wasn't mentioned, his presence hung in Mother's preoccupied look and in my sister's frightened, apologetic manner—hung like a sentence passed upon the Wingfields! Mother was a woman of action as well as words. She began to take logical steps in the planned direction. Late that winter and in the early spring—realizing that extra money would be needed to properly feather the nest and plume the bird—she conducted a vigorous campaign on the telephone, roping in subscribers to one of those magazines for matrons called *The Home-maker's Companion,* the type of journal that features the serialized sublimations of ladies of letters who think in terms of delicate cup-like breasts, slim, tapering waists, rich, creamy thighs, eyes like wood-smoke in autumn, fingers that soothe and caress like strains of music, bodies as powerful as Etruscan sculpture.

(SCREEN IMAGE: Glamor *magazine cover.)*

*(*AMANDA *enters with phone on long extension cord. She is spotted in the dim stage.)*

AMANDA: Ida Scott? This is Amanda Wingfield! We *missed* you at the D.A.R. last Monday! I said to myself: She's probably suffering with that sinus condition! How is that sinus condition? Horrors! Heaven have mercy!—You're a Christian martyr, yes, that's what you are, a Christian martyr! Well, I just now happened to notice that your subscription to the *Companion's* about to expire! Yes, it expires with the next issue, honey!—just when that wonderful new serial by Bessie Mae Hopper is getting off to such an exciting start. Oh, honey, it's something that you can't miss! You remember how *Gone With the Wind* took everybody by storm? You simply couldn't go out if you hadn't read it. All everybody *talked* was Scarlett O'Hara. Well, this is a book that critics already compare to *Gone With the Wind.* It's the *Gone With the Wind* of the post-World War generation!—What?—Burning?—Oh, honey, don't let them burn, go take a look in the oven and I'll hold the wire! Heavens—I think she's hung up!

Dim out.

(LEGEND ON SCREEN: *"You think I'm in love with Continental Shoemakers?")*

(Before the stage is lighted, the violent voices of TOM *and* AMANDA *are heard.)*

(They are quarreling behind the portieres. In front of them stands LAURA *with clenched hands and panicky expression.)*

(A clear pool of light on her figure throughout this scene.)

TOM: What in Christ's name am I—
AMANDA *(shrilly):* Don't you use that—

TOM: Supposed to do!
AMANDA: Expression! Not in my—
TOM: Ohhh!
AMANDA: Presence! Have you gone out of your senses?
TOM: I have, that's true, *driven* out!
AMANDA: What is the matter with you, you—big—big—IDIOT!
TOM: Look—I've got *no thing,* no single thing—
AMANDA: Lower your voice!
TOM: In my life here that I can call my OWN! Everything is—
AMANDA: Stop that shouting!
TOM: Yesterday you confiscated my books! You had the nerve to—
AMANDA: I took that horrible novel back to the library—yes! That hideous book by that insane Mr. Lawrence. *(TOM laughs wildly.)* I cannot control the output of diseased minds or people who cater to them— *(TOM laughs still more wildly.)* BUT I WON'T ALLOW SUCH FILTH BROUGHT INTO MY HOUSE! No, no, no, no, no!
TOM: House, house! Who pays rent on it, who makes a slave of himself to—
AMANDA *(fairly screeching):* Don't you DARE to—
TOM: No, no, *I* mustn't say things! *I've* got to just—
AMANDA: Let me tell you—
TOM: I don't want to hear any more! *(He tears the portieres open. The upstage area is lit with a turgid smoky red glow.)*

(AMANDA's hair is in metal curlers and she wears a very old bathrobe, much too large for her slight figure, a relic of the faithless Mr. Wingfield.)

(An upright typewriter and a wild disarray of manuscripts is on the drop-leaf table. The quarrel was probably precipitated by AMANDA's interruption of his creative labor. A chair lying overthrown on the floor.)

(Their gesticulating shadows are cast on the ceiling by the fiery glow.)

AMANDA: You *will* hear more, you—
TOM: No, I won't hear more, I'm going out!
AMANDA: You come right back in—
TOM: Out, out out! Because I'm—
AMANDA: Come back here, Tom Wingfield! I'm not through talking to you!
TOM: Oh, go—
LAURA *(desperately):* —Tom!
AMANDA: You're going to listen, and no more insolence from you! I'm at the end of my patience! *(He comes back toward her.)*
TOM: What do you think I'm at? Aren't I supposed to have any patience to reach the end of, Mother? I know, I know. It seems unimportant to you, what I'm *doing*—what I *want* to do—having a little *difference* between them! You don't think that—
AMANDA: I think you've been doing things that you're ashamed of. That's why you act like this. I don't believe that you go every night to the movies. Nobody goes to the movies night after night. Nobody in their right minds goes to the movies as often as you pretend to. People don't go to the movies at nearly midnight, and movies don't let out

at two A.M. Come in stumbling. Muttering to yourself like a maniac! You get three hours sleep and then go to work. Oh, I can picture the way you're doing down there. Moping, doping, because you're in no condition.

TOM *(wildly):* No, I'm in no condition!

AMANDA: What right have you got to jeopardize your job? Jeopardize the security of us all? How do you think we'd manage if you were—

TOM: Listen! You think I'm crazy *about* the *warehouse? (He bends fiercely toward her slight figure.)* You think I'm in love with the Continental Shoemakers? You think I want to spend fifty-five *years* down there in that—*celotex interior!* with—*fluorescent—tubes!* Look! I'd rather somebody picked up a crowbar and battered out my brains—than go back mornings! I *go!* Every time you come in yelling that God damn *"Rise and Shine!" "Rise and Shine!"* I say to myself, "How *lucky dead* people are!" But I get up. I *go!* For sixty-five dollars a month I give up all that I dream of doing and being *ever!* And you say self—*self's* all I ever think of. Why, listen, if self is what I thought of, Mother, I'd be where he is—GONE! *(Pointing to father's picture.)* As far as the system of transportation reaches! *(He starts past her. She grabs his arm.)* Don't grab at me, Mother!

AMANDA: Where are you going?

TOM: I'm going to the *movies!*

AMANDA: I don't believe that lie!

TOM *(crouching toward her, overtowering her tiny figure. She backs away, gasping):* I'm going to opium dens! Yes, opium dens, dens of vice and criminals' hang-outs, Mother. I've joined the Hogan gang, I'm a hired assassin, I carry a tommy-gun in a violin case! I run a string of cat-houses in the Valley! They call me Killer, Killer Wingfield, I'm leading a double-life, a simple, honest warehouse worker by day, by night, a dynamic *czar* of the *underworld, Mother.* I go to gambling casinos, I spin away fortunes on the roulette table! I wear a patch over one eye and a false mustache, sometimes I put on green whiskers. On those occasions they call me—*El Diablo!* Oh, I could tell you things to make you sleepless! My enemies plan to dynamite this place. They're going to blow us all sky-high some night! I'll be glad, very happy, and so will you! You'll go up, up on a broomstick, over Blue Mountain with seventeen gentlemen callers! You ugly—babbling old—*witch. . . . (He goes through a series of violent, clumsy movements, seizing his overcoat, lunging to the door, pulling it fiercely open. The women watch him, aghast. His arm catches in the sleeve of the coat as he struggles to pull it on. For a moment he is pinioned by the bulky garment. With an outraged groan he tears the coat off again, splitting the shoulder of it, and hurls it across the room. It strikes against the shelf of* LAURA*'s glass collection, there is a tinkle of shattering glass.* LAURA *cries out as if wounded.)*

(MUSIC LEGEND: *"The Glass Menagerie."*)

LAURA *(shrilly): My glass!*—menagerie. . . . *(She covers her face and turns away.)*

(But AMANDA *is still stunned and stupefied by the "ugly witch" so that she barely notices this occurrence. Now she recovers her speech.)*

AMANDA *(in an awful voice):* I won't speak to you—until you apologize! *(She crosses through portieres and draws them together behind her.* TOM *is left with* LAURA. LAURA *clings weakly to the mantel with her face averted.* TOM *stares at her stupidly for a moment. Then he crosses to shelf. Drops awkwardly to his knees to collect the fallen glass, glancing at* LAURA *as if he would speak but couldn't.)*

"The Glass Menagerie" steals in as

THE SCENE DIMS OUT.

SCENE FOUR

(The interior is dark. Faint light in the alley.

A deep-voiced bell in a church is tolling the hour of five as the scene commences.

TOM appears at the top of the alley. After each solemn boom of the bell in the tower, he shakes a little noise-maker or rattle as if to express the tiny spasm of man in contrast to the sustained power and dignity of the Almighty. This and the unsteadiness of his advance make it evident that he has been drinking.

As he climbs the few steps to the fire-escape landing light steals up inside. LAURA appears in night-dress, observing TOM's empty bed in the front room.

TOM fishes in his pockets for the door-key, removing a motley assortment of articles in the search, including a perfect shower of movie-ticket stubs and an empty bottle. At last he finds the key, but just as he is about to insert it, it slips from his fingers. He strikes a match and crouches below the door.)

TOM *(bitterly):* One crack—and it falls through!

(LAURA opens the door.)

LAURA: Tom! Tom, what are you doing?
TOM: Looking for a door-key.
LAURA: Where have you been all this time?
TOM: I have been to the movies.
LAURA: All this time at the movies?
TOM: There was a very long program. There was a Garbo picture and a Mickey Mouse and a travelogue and a newsreel and a preview of coming attractions. And there was an organ solo and a collection for the milk-fund—simultaneously—which ended up in a terrible fight between a fat lady and an usher!
LAURA *(innocently):* Did you have to stay through everything?
TOM: Of course! And, oh, I forgot! There was a big stage show! The headliner on this stage show was Malvolio the Magician. He performed wonderful tricks, many of them, such as pouring water back and forth between pitchers. First it turned to wine and then it turned to beer and then it turned to whiskey. I know it was whiskey it finally turned into because he needed somebody to come up out of the audience to help him, and I came up—both shows! It was Kentucky Straight Bourbon. A very generous fellow, he gave souvenirs. *(He pulls from his back pocket a shimmering rainbow-colored scarf.)* He gave me this. This is his magic scarf. You can have it, Laura. You wave it over a canary cage and you get a bowl of gold-fish. You wave it over the gold-fish bowl and they fly away canaries.... But the wonderfullest trick of all was the coffin trick. We nailed him into a coffin and he got out of the coffin without removing one nail. *(He has come inside.)* There is a trick that would come in handy for me—get me out of this 2 by 4 situation! *(Flops onto bed and starts removing shoes.)*
LAURA: Tom—Shhh!
TOM: What you shushing me for?

LAURA: You'll wake up Mother.

TOM: Goody, goody! Pay 'er back for all those "Rise an' Shines." *(Lies down, groaning.)* You know it don't take much intelligence to get yourself into a nailed-up coffin, Laura. But who in hell ever got himself out of one without removing one nail?

(As if in answer, the father's grinning photograph lights up.)

SCENE DIMS OUT.

(Immediately following: The church bell is heard striking six. At the sixth stroke the alarm clock goes off in AMANDA*'s room, and after a few moments we hear her calling: "Rise and Shine! Rise and Shine! Laura, go tell your brother to rise and shine!")*

TOM *(sitting up slowly):* I'll rise—but I won't shine.

(The light increases.)

AMANDA: Laura, tell your brother his coffee is ready.

*(*LAURA *slips into front room.)*

LAURA: Tom! It's nearly seven. Don't make Mother nervous. *(He stares at her stupidly. Beseechingly.)* Tom, speak to Mother this morning. Make up with her, apologize, speak to her!

TOM: She won't to me. It's her that started not speaking.

LAURA: If you just say you're sorry she'll start speaking.

TOM: Her not speaking—is that such a tragedy?

LAURA: Please—please!

AMANDA *(calling from kitchenette):* Laura, are you going to do what I asked you to do, or do I have to get dressed and go out myself?

LAURA: Going, going—soon as I get on my coat! *(She pulls on a shapeless felt hat with nervous, jerky movement, pleadingly glancing at* TOM*. Rushes awkwardly for coat. The coat is one of* AMANDA*'s, inaccurately made-over, the sleeves too short for* LAURA*.)* Butter and what else?

AMANDA *(entering upstage):* Just butter. Tell them to charge it.

LAURA: Mother, they make such faces when I do that.

AMANDA: Stick and stones may break our bones, but the expression on Mr. Garfinkel's face won't harm us! Tell your brother his coffee is getting cold.

LAURA *(at door):* Do what I asked you, will you, will you, Tom?

(He looks sullenly away.)

AMANDA: Laura, go now or just don't go at all!

LAURA *(rushing out):* Going—going! *(A second later she cries out.* TOM *springs up and crosses to the door.* AMANDA *rushes anxiously in.* TOM *opens the door.)*

TOM: Laura?

LAURA: I'm all right. I slipped, but I'm all right.

AMANDA *(peering anxiously after her):* If anyone breaks a leg on those fire-escape steps, the landlord ought to be sued for every cent he possesses! *(She shuts door. Remembers she isn't speaking and returns to other room.)*

(As TOM *enters listlessly for his coffee, she turns her back to him and stands rigidly facing the window on the gloomy gray vault of the areaway. Its light on her face with its aged but childish features is cruelly sharp, satirical as a Daumier print.)*

(MUSIC UNDER: *"Ave Maria."*)

*(*TOM *glances sheepishly but sullenly at her averted figure and slumps at the table. The coffee is scalding hot; he sips it and gasps and spits it back in the cup. At his gasp,* AMANDA *catches her breath and half turns. Then catches herself and turns back to window.)*

*(*TOM *blows on his coffee, glancing sidewise at his mother. She clears her throat.* TOM *clears his. He starts to rise. Sinks back down again, scratches his head, clears his throat again.* AMANDA *coughs.* TOM *raises his cup in both hands to blow on it, his eyes staring over the rim of it at his mother for several moments. Then he slowly sets the cup down and awkwardly and hesitantly rises from the chair.)*

TOM *(hoarsely):* Mother. I—I apologize. Mother. *(*AMANDA *draws a quick, shuddering breath. Her face works grotesquely. She breaks into childlike tears.)* I'm sorry for what I said, for everything that I said, I didn't mean it.

AMANDA *(sobbingly):* My devotion has made me a witch and so I make myself hateful to my children!

TOM: *No,* you *don't.*

AMANDA: I worry so much, don't sleep, it makes me nervous!

TOM *(gently):* I understand that.

AMANDA: I've had to put up a solitary battle all these years. But you're my right-hand bower! Don't fall down, don't fail!

TOM *(gently):* I try, Mother.

AMANDA *(with great enthusiasm):* Try and you will SUCCEED! *(The notion makes her breathless.)* Why, you—you're just *full* of natural endowments! Both of my children—they're *unusual* children! Don't you think I know it? I'm so—*proud!* Happy and—feel I've—so much to be thankful for but—Promise me one thing, son!

TOM: What, Mother?

AMANDA: Promise, son, you'll—never be a drunkard!

TOM *(turns to her grinning):* I will never be a drunkard, Mother.

AMANDA: That's what frightened me so, that you'd be drinking! Eat a bowl of Purina!

TOM: Just coffee, Mother.

AMANDA: Shredded wheat biscuit?

TOM: No. No, Mother, just coffee.

AMANDA: You can't put in a day's work on an empty stomach. You've got ten minutes—don't gulp! Drinking too-hot liquids makes cancer of the stomach. . . . Put cream in.

TOM: No, thank you.

AMANDA: To cool it.

TOM: No! No, thank you, I want it black.

AMANDA: I know, but it's not good for you. We have to do all that we can to build ourselves up. In these trying times we live in, all that we have to cling to is—each other. . . . That's why it's so important to—Tom, I—I sent out your sister so I could discuss something with you. If you hadn't spoken I would have spoken to you. *(Sits down.)*

TOM *(gently):* What is it, Mother, that you want to discuss?
AMANDA: *Laura!*

*(*TOM *puts his cup down slowly.)*

(LEGEND ON SCREEN: *"Laura."*)

(MUSIC: *"The Glass Menagerie."*)

TOM: —Oh.—Laura . . .

AMANDA *(touching his sleeve):* You know how Laura is. So quiet but—still water runs deep! She notices things and I think she—broods about them. *(*TOM *looks up).* A few days ago I came in and she was crying.

TOM: What about?

AMANDA: You.

TOM: Me?

AMANDA: She has an idea that you're not happy here.

TOM: What gave her that idea?

AMANDA: What gives her any idea? However, you do act strangely. I—I'm not criticizing, understand *that!* I know your ambitions do not lie in the warehouse, that like everybody in the whole wide world—you've had to—make sacrifices, but—Tom—Tom—life's not easy, it calls for—Spartan endurance! There's so many things in my heart that I cannot describe to you! I've never told you but I—*loved* your father. . . .

TOM *(gently):* I know that, Mother.

AMANDA: And you—when I see you taking after his ways! Staying out late—and—well, you *had* been drinking the night you were in that—terrifying condition! Laura says that you hate the apartment and that you go out nights to get away from it! Is that true, Tom?

TOM: No. You say there's so much in your heart that you can't describe to me. That's true of me, too. There's so much in my heart that I can't describe to *you!* So let's respect each other's—

AMANDA: But, why—*why,* Tom—are you always so *restless?* Where do you go to, nights?

TOM: I—go to the movies.

AMANDA: Why do you go to the movies so much, Tom?

TOM: I go to the movies because—I like adventure. Adventure is something I don't have much of at work, so I go to the movies.

AMANDA: But, Tom, you go to the movies *entirely* too *much!*

TOM: I like a lot of adventure.

*(*AMANDA *looks baffled, then hurt. As the familiar inquisition resumes he becomes hard and impatient again.* AMANDA *slips back into her querulous attitude toward him.)*

(IMAGE ON SCREEN: *Sailing vessel with Jolly Roger.*)

AMANDA: Most young men find adventure in their careers.

TOM: Then most young men are not employed in a warehouse.

AMANDA: The world is full of young men employed in warehouses and offices and factories.

TOM: Do all of them find adventure in their careers?

AMANDA: They do or they do without it! Not everybody has a craze for adventure.

TOM: Man is by instinct a lover, a hunter, a fighter, and none of those instincts are given much play at the warehouse!

AMANDA: Man is by instinct! Don't quote instinct to me! Instinct is something that people have got away from! It belongs to animals! Christian adults don't want it!

TOM: What do Christian adults want, then, Mother?

AMANDA: Superior things! Things of the mind and the spirit! Only animals have to satisfy instincts! Surely your aims are somewhat higher than theirs! Than monkeys—pigs—

TOM: I reckon they're not.

AMANDA: You're joking. However, that isn't what I wanted to discuss.

TOM *(rising):* I haven't much time.

AMANDA *(pushing his shoulders):* Sit down.

TOM: You want me to punch in red at the warehouse, Mother?

AMANDA: You have five minutes. I want to talk about Laura.

(LEGEND: *"Plans and Provisions."*)

TOM: All right! What about Laura?

AMANDA: We have to be making plans and provisions for her. She's older than you, two years, and nothing has happened. She just drifts along doing nothing. It frightens me terribly how she just drifts along.

TOM: I guess she's the type that people call home girls.

AMANDA: There's no such type, and if there is, it's a pity! That is unless the home is hers, with a husband!

TOM: What?

AMANDA: Oh, I can see the handwriting on the wall as plain as I see the nose in front of my face! It's terrifying! More and more you remind me of your father! He was out all hours without explanation—Then *left! Good-bye!* And me with a bag to hold. I saw that letter you got from the Merchant Marine. I know what you're dreaming of. I'm not standing here blindfolded. Very well, then. Then *do* it! But not till there's somebody to take your place.

TOM: What do you mean?

AMANDA: I mean that as soon as Laura has got somebody to take care of her, married, a home of her own, independent—why, then you'll be free to go wherever you please, on land, on sea, whichever way the wind blows you! But until that time you've got to look out for your sister. I don't say me because I'm old and don't matter! I say for your sister because she's young and dependent. I put her in business college—a dismal failure! Frightened her so it made her sick to her stomach. I took her over to the Young People's League at the church. Another fiasco. She spoke to nobody, nobody spoke to her. Now all she does is fool with those pieces of glass and play those worn-out records. What kind of a life is that for a girl to lead?

TOM: What can I do about it?

AMANDA: Overcome selfishness! Self, self, self is all that you ever think of! *(TOM springs up and crosses to get his coat. It is ugly and bulky. He pulls on a cap with earmuffs.)* Where is your muffler? Put your wool muffler on! *(He snatches it angrily from the closet and tosses it around his neck and pulls both ends tight.)* Tom! I haven't said what I had in mind to ask you.

TOM: I'm too late to—

AMANDA *(catching his arm—very importunately. Then shyly):* Down at the warehouse, aren't there some—nice young men?

TOM: No!

AMANDA: There *must* be—*some* . . .

TOM: Mother—

(Gesture.)

AMANDA: Find out one that's clean-living—doesn't drink and—ask him out for sister!

TOM: What?

AMANDA: For *sister!* To *meet!* Get *acquainted!*

TOM *(stamping to door):* Oh, my *go-osh!*

AMANDA: Will you? *(He opens door. Imploringly.)* Will you? *(He starts down.)* Will you? *Will* you, dear?

TOM *(calling back):* YES!

(AMANDA closes the door hesitantly and with a troubled but faintly hopeful expression.)

(SCREEN IMAGE: Glamor *magazine cover.)*

(Spot AMANDA at phone.)

AMANDA: Ella Cartwright? This is Amanda Wingfield! How are you, honey? How is that kidney condition? *(Count five.) Horrors! (Count five.)* You're a Christian martyr, yes, honey, that's what you are, a Christian martyr! Well, I just happened to notice in my little red book that your subscription to the *Companion* has just run out! I knew that you wouldn't want to miss out on the wonderful serial starting in this new issue. It's by Bessie Mae Hopper, the first thing she's written since *Honeymoon for Three.* Wasn't that a strange and interesting story? Well, this one is even lovelier, I believe. It has a sophisticated society background. It's all about the horsey set on Long Island!

FADE OUT.

SCENE FIVE

LEGEND ON SCREEN: *"Annunciation." Fade with music.*

(It is early dusk of a spring evening. Supper has just been finished in the Wingfield apartment. AMANDA and LAURA in light colored dresses are removing dishes from the table, in the upstage area, which is shadowy, their movements formalized almost as a dance or ritual, their moving forms as pale and silent as moths.

TOM, in white shirt and trousers, rises from the table and crosses toward the fire-escape.)

AMANDA *(as he passes her):* Son, will you do me a favor?

TOM: What?

AMANDA: Comb your hair! You look so pretty when your hair is combed! *(TOM slouches on sofa with evening paper. Enormous caption "Franco Triumphs.")* There is only one respect in which I would like you to emulate your father.

TOM: What respect is that?

AMANDA: The care he always took of his appearance. He never allowed himself to look untidy. *(He throws down the paper and crosses to fire-escape.)* Where are you going?

TOM: I'm going out to smoke.

AMANDA: You smoke too much. A pack a day at fifteen cents a pack. How much would that amount to in a month? Thirty times fifteen is how much, Tom? Figure it out and you will be astounded at what you could save. Enough to give you a night-school course in accounting at Washington U! Just think what a wonderful thing that would be for you, son!

(TOM is unmoved by the thought.)

TOM: I'd rather smoke. *(He steps out on landing, letting the screen door slam.)*

AMANDA *(sharply):* I know! That's the tragedy of it. . . . *(Alone, she turns to look at her husband's picture.)*

(DANCE MUSIC: *"All the World Is Waiting for the Sunrise!"*)

TOM *(to the audience):* Across the alley from us was the Paradise Dance Hall. On evenings in spring the windows and doors were open and the music came outdoors. Sometimes the lights were turned out except for a large glass sphere that hung from the ceiling. It would turn slowly about and filter the dusk with delicate rainbow colors. Then the orchestra played a waltz or a tango, something that had a slow and sensuous rhythm. Couples would come outside, to the relative privacy of the alley. You could see them kissing behind ash-pits and telephone poles. This was the compensation for lives that passed like mine, without any change or adventure. Adventure and change were imminent in this year. They were waiting around the corner for all these kids. Suspended in the mist over Berchtesgaden, caught in the folds of Chamberlain's umbrella—In Spain there was Guernica! But here there was only hot swing music and liquor, dance halls, bars, and movies, and sex that hung in the gloom like a chandelier and flooded the world with brief, deceptive rainbows. . . . All the world was waiting for bombardments!

(AMANDA turns from the picture and comes outside.)

AMANDA *(sighing).* A fire-escape landing's a poor excuse for a porch. *(She spreads a newspaper on a step and sits down, gracefully and demurely as if she were settling into a swing on a Mississippi veranda.)* What are you looking at?

TOM: The moon.

AMANDA: Is there a moon this evening?

TOM: It's rising over Garfinkel's Delicatessen.

AMANDA: So it is! A little silver slipper of a moon. Have you made a wish on it yet?

TOM: Um-hum.

AMANDA: What did you wish for?

TOM: That's a secret.

AMANDA: A secret, huh? Well, I won't tell mine either. I will be just as mysterious as you.

TOM: I bet I can guess what yours is.

AMANDA: Is my head so transparent?

TOM: You're not a sphinx.

AMANDA: No, I don't have secrets. I'll tell you what I wished for on the moon. Success and happiness for my precious children! I wish for that whenever there's a moon, and when there isn't a moon, I wish for it, too.

TOM: I thought perhaps you wished for a gentleman caller.

AMANDA: Why do you say that?

TOM: Don't you remember asking me to fetch one?

AMANDA: I remember suggesting that it would be nice for your sister if you brought home some nice young man from the warehouse. I think I've made that suggestion more than once.

TOM: Yes, you have made it repeatedly.

AMANDA: Well?

TOM: We are going to have one.

AMANDA: *What?*

TOM: A gentleman caller!

(The annunciation is celebrated with music.)

*(*AMANDA *rises.)*

*(*IMAGE ON SCREEN: *Caller with bouquet.)*

AMANDA: You mean you have asked some nice young man to come over?

TOM: Yep. I've asked him to dinner.

AMANDA: You really did?

TOM: I did!

AMANDA: You did, and did he—*accept?*

TOM: He did!

AMANDA: Well, well—well, well! That's—lovely!

TOM: I thought that you would be pleased.

AMANDA: It's definite, then?

TOM: Very definite.

AMANDA: Soon?

TOM: Very soon.

AMANDA: For heaven's sake, stop putting on and tell me some things, will you?

TOM: What things do you want me to tell you?

AMANDA: *Naturally* I would like to know when he's *coming!*

TOM: He's coming tomorrow.

AMANDA: *Tomorrow?*

TOM: Yep. Tomorrow.

AMANDA: But, Tom!

TOM: Yes, Mother?

AMANDA: Tomorrow gives me no time!

TOM: Time for what?

AMANDA: Preparations! Why didn't you phone me at once, as soon as you asked him, the minute that he accepted? Then, don't you see, I could have been getting ready!

TOM: You don't have to make any fuss.

AMANDA: Oh, Tom, Tom, Tom, of course I have to make a fuss! I want things nice, not sloppy! Not thrown together. I'll certainly have to do some fast thinking, won't I?

TOM: I don't see why you have to think at all.

AMANDA: You just don't know. We can't have a gentleman caller in a pig-sty! All my wedding silver has to be polished, the monogrammed table linen ought to be laundered! The windows have to be washed and fresh curtains put up. And how about clothes? We have to *wear* something, don't we?

TOM: Mother, this boy is no one to make a fuss over!

AMANDA: Do you realize he's the first young man we've introduced to your sister? It's terrible, dreadful, disgraceful that poor little sister has never received a single gentleman caller! Tom, come inside! *[She opens the screen door.]*

TOM: What for?

AMANDA: I want to ask you some things.

TOM: If you're going to make such a fuss, I'll call it off, I'll tell him not to come.

AMANDA: You certainly won't do anything of the kind. Nothing offends people worse than broken engagements. It simply means I'll have to work like a Turk! We won't be brilliant, but we'll pass inspection. Come on inside. *(TOM follows, groaning.)* Sit down.

TOM: Any particular place you would like me to sit?

AMANDA: Thank heavens I've got that new sofa! I'm also making payments on a floor lamp I'll have sent out! And put the chintz covers on, they'll brighten things up! Of course I'd hoped to have these walls re-papered. . . . What is the young man's name?

TOM: His name is O'Connor.

AMANDA: That, of course, means fish—tomorrow is Friday! I'll have that salmon loaf—with Durkee's dressing! What does he do? He works at the warehouse?

TOM: Of course! How else would I—

AMANDA: Tom, he—doesn't drink?

TOM: Why do you ask me that?

AMANDA: Your father *did!*

TOM: Don't get started on that!

AMANDA: He *does* drink, then?

TOM: Not that I know of!

AMANDA: Make sure, be certain! The last thing I want for my daughter's a boy who drinks!

TOM: Aren't you being a little premature? Mr. O'Connor has not yet appeared on the scene!

AMANDA: But will tomorrow. To meet your sister, and what do I know about his character? Nothing! Old maids are better off than wives of drunkards!

TOM: Oh, my God!

AMANDA: Be still!

TOM *(leaning forward to whisper):* Lots of fellows meet girls whom they don't marry!

AMANDA: Oh, talk sensibly, Tom—and don't be sarcastic! *(She has gotten a hairbrush.)*

TOM: What are you doing?

AMANDA: I'm brushing that cow-lick down! What is this young man's position at the warehouse?

TOM *(submitting grimly to the brush and the interrogation):* This young man's position is that of a shipping clerk, Mother.

AMANDA: Sounds to me like a fairly responsible job, the sort of a job *you* would be in if you just had more *get-up.* What is his salary? Have you got any idea?

TOM: I would judge it to be approximately eighty-five dollars a month.

AMANDA: Well—not princely, but—

TOM: Twenty more than I make.

AMANDA: Yes, how well I know! But for a family man, eighty-five dollars a month is not much more than you can just get by on. . . .

TOM: Yes, but Mr. O'Connor is not a family man.

AMANDA: He might be, mightn't he? Some time in the future?

TOM: I see. Plans and provisions.

AMANDA: You are the only young man that I know of who ignores the fact that the future becomes the present, the present the past, and the past turns into everlasting regret if you don't plan for it!

TOM: I will think that over and see what I can make of it.

AMANDA: Don't be supercilious with your mother! Tell me some more about this—what do you call him?

TOM: James D. O'Connor. The D. is for Delaney.

AMANDA: Irish on *both* sides! *Gracious!* And doesn't drink?

TOM: Shall I call him up and ask him right this minute?

AMANDA: The only way to find out about those things is to make discreet inquiries at the proper moment. When I was a girl in Blue Mountain and it was suspected that a young man drank, the girl whose attentions he had been receiving, if any girl *was,* would sometimes speak to the minister of his church, or rather her father would if her father was living, and sort of feel him out on the young man's character. That is the way such things are discreetly handled to keep a young woman from making a tragic mistake!

TOM: Then how did you happen to make a tragic mistake?

AMANDA: That innocent look of your father's had everyone fooled! He *smiled*—the world was *enchanted!* No girl can do worse than put herself at the mercy of a handsome appearance! I hope that Mr. O'Connor is not too good-looking.

TOM: No, he's not too good-looking. He's covered with freckles and hasn't too much of a nose.

AMANDA: He's not right-down homely, though?

TOM: Not right-down homely. Just medium homely, I'd say.

AMANDA: Character's what to look for in a man.

TOM: That's what I've always said, Mother.

AMANDA: You've never said anything of the kind and I suspect you would never give it a thought.

TOM: Don't be suspicious of me.

AMANDA: At least I hope he's the type that's up and coming.

TOM: I think he really goes in for self-improvement.

AMANDA: What reason have you to think so?

TOM: He goes to night school.

AMANDA *(beaming):* Splendid! What does he do, I mean study?

TOM: Radio engineering and public speaking!

AMANDA: Then he has visions of being advanced in the world! Any young man who studies public speaking is aiming to have an executive job some day! And radio engineering? A thing for the future! Both of these facts are very illuminating. Those are the sort of things that a mother should know concerning any young man who comes to call on her daughter. Seriously or—not.

TOM: One little warning. He doesn't know about Laura. I didn't let on that we had dark ulterior motives. I just said, why don't you come have dinner with us? He said okay and that was the whole conversation.

AMANDA: I bet it was! You're eloquent as an oyster. However, he'll know about Laura when he gets here. When he sees how lovely and sweet and pretty she is, he'll thank his lucky stars he was asked to dinner.

TOM: Mother, you mustn't expect too much of Laura.

AMANDA: What do you mean?

TOM: Laura seems all those things to you and me because she's ours and we love her. We don't even notice she's crippled any more.

AMANDA: Don't say crippled! You know that I never allow that word to be used!

TOM: But face facts, Mother. She is and—that's not all—

AMANDA: What do you mean "not all"?

TOM: Laura is very different from other girls.

AMANDA: I think the difference is all to her advantage.

TOM: Not quite all—in the eyes of others—strangers—she's terribly shy and lives in a world of her own and those things make her seem a little peculiar to people outside the house.

AMANDA: Don't say peculiar.

TOM: Face the facts. She is.

(The dance-hall music changes to a tango that has a minor and somewhat ominous tone.)

AMANDA: In what way is she peculiar—may I ask?

TOM *(gently):* She lives in a world of her own—a world of—little glass ornaments, Mother. . . . *(Gets up.* AMANDA *remains holding brush, looking at him, troubled.)* She plays old phonograph records and—that's about all— *(He glances at himself in the mirror and crosses to door.)*

AMANDA *(sharply):* Where are you going?

TOM: I'm going to the movies. *(Out screen door.)*

AMANDA: Not to the movies, every night to the movies! *(Follows quickly to screen door.)* I don't believe you always go to the movies! *(He is gone.* AMANDA *looks worriedly after him for a moment. Then vitality and optimism return and she turns from the door. Crossing to portieres.)* Laura! Laura! *(*LAURA *answers from kitchenette.)*

LAURA: Yes, Mother.

AMANDA: Let those dishes go and come in front! *(*LAURA *appears with dish towel. Gaily.)* Laura, come here and make a wish on the moon!

LAURA *(entering):* Moon—moon?

AMANDA: A little silver slipper of a moon. Look over your left shoulder, Laura, and make a wish! *(*LAURA *looks faintly puzzled as if called out of sleep.* AMANDA *seizes her shoulders and turns her at an angle by the door.)* No! Now, darling, *wish!*

LAURA: What shall I wish for, Mother?

AMANDA *(her voice trembling and her eyes suddenly filling with tears):* Happiness! Good Fortune!

(The violin rises and the stage dims out.)

SCENE SIX

(IMAGE: *High school hero.*)

TOM: And so the following evening I brought Jim home to dinner. I had known Jim slightly in high school. In high school Jim was a hero. He had tremendous Irish good nature and vitality with the scrubbed and polished look of white chinaware. He seemed to move in a continual spotlight. He was a star in basketball, captain of the debating club, president of the senior class and the glee club and he sang the male lead in the annual light operas. He was always running or bounding, never just walking. He seemed always at the point of defeating the law of gravity. He was shooting with such velocity through his adolescence that you would logically expect him to arrive at nothing short of the White House by the time he was thirty. But Jim apparently ran into more interference after his graduation from Soldan. His speed had definitely slowed. Six years after he left high school he was holding a job that wasn't much better than mine.

(IMAGE: *Clerk.*)

He was the only one at the warehouse with whom I was on friendly terms. I was valuable to him as someone who could remember his former glory, who had seen him win basketball games and the silver cup in debating. He knew of my secret practice of retiring to a cabinet of the washroom to work on poems when business was slack in the warehouse. He called me Shakespeare. And while the other boys in the warehouse regarded me with suspicious hostility, Jim took a humorous attitude toward me. Gradually his attitude affected the others, their hostility wore off and they also began to smile at me as people smile at an oddly fashioned dog who trots across their path at some distance.

I knew that Jim and Laura had known each other at Soldan, and I had heard Laura speak admiringly of his voice. I didn't know if Jim remembered her or not. In high school Laura had been as unobtrusive as Jim had been astonishing. If he did remember Laura, it was not as my sister, for when I asked him to dinner, he grinned and said, "You know, Shakespeare, I never thought of you as having folks!"

He was about to discover that I did. . . .

(Light up stage.)

(LEGEND ON SCREEN: *"The Accent of a Coming Foot."*)

(Friday evening. It is about five o'clock of a late spring evening which comes "scattering poems in the sky.")

(A delicate lemony light is in the Wingfield apartment.)

(AMANDA *has worked like a Turk in preparation for the gentleman caller. The results are astonishing. The new floor lamp with its rose-silk shade is in place, a colored paper lantern conceals the broken light fixture in the ceiling, new billowing white curtains are at the windows, chintz covers are on chairs and sofa, a pair of new sofa pillows make their initial appearance.)*

(Open boxes and tissue paper are scattered on the floor.)

*(*LAURA *stands in the middle with lifted arms while* AMANDA *crouches before her, adjusting the hem of the new dress, devout and ritualistic. The dress is colored and designed by memory. The arrangement of* LAURA*'s hair is changed; it is softer and more becoming. A fragile, unearthly prettiness has come out in* LAURA*: she is like a piece of translucent glass touched by light, given a momentary radiance, not actual, not lasting.)*

AMANDA *(impatiently):* Why are you trembling?
LAURA: Mother, you've made me so nervous!
AMANDA: How have I made you nervous?
LAURA: By all this fuss! You make it seem so important!
AMANDA: I don't understand you, Laura. You couldn't be satisfied with just sitting home, and yet whenever I try to arrange something for you, you seem to resist it. *(She gets up.)* Now take a look at yourself. No, wait! Wait just a moment—I have an idea!
LAURA: What is it now?

*(*AMANDA *produces two powder puffs which she wraps in handkerchiefs and stuffs in* LAURA*'s bosom.)*

LAURA: Mother, what are you doing?
AMANDA: They call them "Gay Deceivers"!
LAURA: I won't wear them!
AMANDA: You will!
LAURA: Why should I?
AMANDA: Because, to be painfully honest, your chest is flat.
LAURA: You make it seem like we were setting a trap.
AMANDA: All pretty girls are a trap, a pretty trap, and men expect them to be. *(*LEGEND: "A PRETTY TRAP."*)* Now look at yourself, young lady. This is the prettiest you will ever be! I've got to fix myself now! You're going to be surprised by your mother's appearance! *(She crosses through portieres, humming gaily.)*

*(*LAURA *moves slowly to the long mirror and stares solemnly at herself.)*

(A wind blows the white curtains inward in a slow, graceful motion and with a faint, sorrowful sighing.)

AMANDA *(off stage):* It isn't dark enough yet. *(She turns slowly before the mirror with a troubled look.)*

(LEGEND ON SCREEN: *"This Is My Sister: Celebrate Her with Strings!" Music.)*

AMANDA *(laughing, off):* I'm going to show you something. I'm going to make a spectacular appearance!
LAURA: What is it, Mother?
AMANDA: Possess your soul in patience—you will see! Something I've resurrected from that old trunk! Styles haven't changed so terribly much after all. . . . *(She parts the portieres.)* Now just look at your mother! *(She wears a girlish frock of yellowed voile with a blue silk*

sash. She carries a bunch of jonquils—the legend of her youth is nearly revived. Feverishly.) This is the dress in which I led the cotillion. Won the cakewalk twice at Sunset Hill, wore one spring to the Governor's ball in Jackson! See how I sashayed around the ballroom, Laura? *(She raises her skirt and does a mincing step around the room.)* I wore it on Sundays for my gentlemen callers! I had it on the day I met your father—I had malaria fever all that spring. The change of climate from East Tennessee to the Delta—weakened resistance—I had a little temperature all the time—not enough to be serious—just enough to make me restless and giddy! Invitations poured in—parties all over the Delta!—"Stay in bed," said Mother, "you have fever!"—but I just wouldn't.—I took quinine but kept on going, going!—Evenings, dances!—Afternoons, long, long rides! Picnics—lovely!—So lovely, that country in May.—All lacy with dogwood, literally flooded with jonquils!—That was the spring I had the craze for jonquils. Jonquils became an absolute obsession. Mother said, "Honey, there's no more room for jonquils." And still I kept on bringing in more jonquils. Whenever, wherever I saw them, I'd say, "Stop! Stop! I see jonquils!" I made the young men help me gather the jonquils! It was a joke, Amanda and her jonquils! Finally there were no more vases to hold them, every available space was filled with jonquils. No vases to hold them? All right, I'll hold them myself! And then I— *(She stops in front of the picture. MUSIC.)* met your father! Malaria fever and jonquils and then—this—boy. . . . *(She switches on the rose-colored lamp.)* I hope they get here before it starts to rain. *(She crosses upstage and places the jonquils in bowl on table.)* I gave your brother a little extra change so he and Mr. O'Connor could take the service car home.

LAURA *(with altered look)*: What did you say his name was?

AMANDA: O'Connor.

LAURA: What is his first name?

AMANDA: I don't remember. Oh, yes, I do. It was—Jim!

(LAURA sways slightly and catches hold of a chair.)

(LEGEND ON SCREEN: *"Not Jim!"*)

LAURA *(faintly)*: Not—Jim!

AMANDA: Yes, that was it, it was Jim! I've never known a Jim that wasn't nice!

(MUSIC: *Ominous.*)

LAURA: Are you sure his name is Jim O'Connor?

AMANDA: Yes. Why?

LAURA: Is he the one that Tom used to know in high school?

AMANDA: He didn't say so. I think he just got to know him at the warehouse.

LAURA: There was a Jim O'Connor we both knew in high school— *(Then, with effort.)* If that is the one that Tom is bringing to dinner—you'll have to excuse me, I won't come to the table.

AMANDA: What sort of nonsense is this?

LAURA: You asked me once if I'd ever liked a boy. Don't you remember I showed you this boy's picture?

AMANDA: You mean the boy you showed me in the year book?

LAURA: Yes, that boy.

AMANDA: Laura, Laura, were you in love with that boy?

LAURA: I don't know, Mother. All I know is I couldn't sit at the table if it was him!

AMANDA: It won't be him! It isn't the least bit likely. But whether it is or not, you will come to the table. You will not be excused.

LAURA: I'll have to be, Mother.

AMANDA: I don't intend to humor your silliness, Laura. I've had too much from you and your brother, both! So just sit down and compose yourself till they come. Tom has forgotten his key so you'll have to let them in, when they arrive.

LAURA *(panicky):* Oh, Mother—*you* answer the door!

AMANDA *(lightly):* I'll be in the kitchen—busy!

LAURA: Oh, Mother, please answer the door, don't make me do it!

AMANDA *(crossing into kitchenette):* I've got to fix the dressing for the salmon. Fuss, fuss—silliness!—over a gentleman caller!

(Door swings shut. LAURA *is left alone.)*

(LEGEND: *"Terror!")*

(She utters a low moan and turns off the lamp—sits stiffly on the edge of the sofa, knotting her fingers together.)

(LEGEND ON SCREEN: *"The Opening of a Door!")*

*(*TOM *and* JIM *appear on the fire-escape steps and climb to landing. Hearing their approach,* LAURA *rises with a panicky gesture. She retreats to the portieres.)*

(The doorbell. LAURA *catches her breath and touches her throat. Low drums.)*

AMANDA *(calling):* Laura, sweetheart! The door!

*(*LAURA *stares at it without moving.)*

JIM: I think we just beat the rain.

TOM: Uh-huh. *(He rings again, nervously.* JIM *whistles and fishes for a cigarette.)*

AMANDA *(very, very gaily):* Laura, that is your brother and Mr. O'Connor! Will you let them in, darling?

*(*LAURA *crosses toward kitchenette door.)*

LAURA *(breathlessly):* Mother—you go to the door!

*(*AMANDA *steps out of kitchenette and stares furiously at* LAURA. *She points imperiously at the door.)*

LAURA: Please, please!

AMANDA *(in a fierce whisper):* What is the matter with you, you silly thing?

LAURA *(desperately)*: Please, you answer it, *please!*

AMANDA: I told you I wasn't going to humor you, Laura. Why have you chosen this moment to lose your mind?

LAURA: Please, please, please, you go!

AMANDA: You'll have to go to the door because I can't!

LAURA *(despairingly)*: I can't either!

AMANDA: *Why?*

LAURA: I'm *sick!*

AMANDA: I'm sick, too—of your nonsense! Why can't you and your brother be normal people? Fantastic whims and behavior! *(*TOM *gives a long ring.)* Preposterous goings on! Can you give me one reason— *(Calls out lyrically.)* COMING? JUST ONE SECOND!—why should you be afraid to open a door? Now you answer it, Laura!

LAURA: Oh, oh, oh . . . *(She returns through the portieres. Darts to the victrola and winds it frantically and turns it on.)*

AMANDA: Laura Wingfield, you march right to that door!

LAURA: Yes—yes, Mother!

(A faraway, scratchy rendition of "Dardanella" softens the air and gives her strength to move through it. She slips to the door and draws it cautiously open.)

*(*TOM *enters with the caller,* JIM O'CONNOR.*)*

TOM: Laura, this is Jim. Jim, this is my sister, Laura.

JIM *(stepping inside)*: I didn't know that Shakespeare had a sister!

LAURA *(retreating stiff and trembling from the door)*: How—how do you do?

JIM *(heartily extending his hand)*: Okay!

*(*LAURA *touches it hesitantly with hers.)*

JIM: Your hand's *cold,* Laura!

LAURA: Yes, well—I've been playing the victrola. . . .

JIM: Must have been playing classical music on it! You ought to play a little hot swing music to warm you up!

LAURA: Excuse me—I haven't finished playing the victrola. . . .

(She turns awkwardly and hurries into the front room. She pauses a second by the victrola. Then catches her breath and darts through the portieres like a frightened deer.)

JIM *(grinning)*: What was the matter?

TOM: Oh—with Laura? Laura is—terribly shy.

JIM: Shy, huh? It's unusual to meet a shy girl nowadays. I don't believe you ever mentioned you had a sister.

TOM: Well, now you know. I have one. Here is the *Post Dispatch.* You want a piece of it?

JIM: Uh-huh.

TOM: What piece? The comics?

JIM: Sports! *(Glances at it.)* Ole Dizzy Dean is on his bad behavior.

TOM *(disinterest)*: Yeah? *(Lights cigarette and crosses back to fire-escape door.)*

JIM: Where are *you* going?

TOM: I'm going out on the terrace.

JIM *(goes after him):* You know, Shakespeare—I'm going to sell you a bill of goods!

TOM: What goods?

JIM: A course I'm taking.

TOM: Huh?

JIM: In public speaking! You and me, we're not the warehouse type.

TOM: Thanks—that's good news. But what has public speaking got to do with it?

JIM: It fits you for—executive positions!

TOM: Awww.

JIM: I tell you it's done a helluva lot for me.

(IMAGE: *Executive at desk.*)

TOM: In what respect?

JIM: In every! Ask yourself what is the difference between you an' me and men in the office down front? Brains?—No!—Ability?—No! Then what? Just one little thing—

TOM: What is that one little thing?

JIM: Primarily it amounts to—social poise! Being able to square up to people and hold your own on any social level!

AMANDA *(off stage):* Tom?

TOM: Yes, Mother?

AMANDA: Is that you and Mr. O'Connor?

TOM: Yes, Mother.

AMANDA: Well, you just make yourselves comfortable in there.

TOM: Yes, Mother.

AMANDA: Ask Mr. O'Connor if he would like to wash his hands.

JIM: Aw, no—no—thank you—I took care of that at the warehouse. Tom—

TOM: Yes?

JIM: Mr. Mendoza was speaking to me about you.

TOM: Favorably?

JIM: What do you think?

TOM: Well—

JIM: You're going to be out of a job if you don't wake up.

TOM: I am waking up—

JIM: You show no signs.

TOM: The signs are interior.

(IMAGE ON SCREEN: *The Sailing Vessel with Jolly Roger Again.*)

TOM: I'm planning to change. *(He leans over the rail speaking with quiet exhilaration. The incandescent marquees and signs of the first-run movie houses light his face from across the alley. He looks like a voyager.)* I'm right at the point of committing myself to a future that doesn't include the warehouse and Mr. Mendoza or even a night-school course in public speaking.

JIM: What are you gassing about?

TOM: I'm tired of the movies.

JIM: Movies!

TOM: Yes, movies! Look at them— *(A wave toward the marvels of Grand Avenue.)* All of those glamorous people—having adventures—hogging it all, gobbling the whole thing up! You know what happens? People go to the *movies* instead of *moving!* Hollywood characters are supposed to have all the adventures for everybody in America, while everybody in America sits in a dark room and watches them have them! Yes, until there's a war. That's when adventure becomes available to the masses! *Everyone's* dish, not only Gable's! Then the people in the dark room come out of the dark room to have some adventures themselves—Goody, goody!—It's our turn now, to go to the South Sea Island—to make a safari—to be exotic, far-off!—But I'm not patient. I don't want to wait till then. I'm tired of the *movies* and I am *about* to *move!*

JIM *(incredulously):* Move?

TOM: Yes.

JIM: When?

TOM: Soon!

JIM: Where? Where?

(Theme three music seems to answer the question, while TOM thinks it over. He searches among his pockets.)

TOM: I'm starting to boil inside. I know I seem dreamy, but inside—well, I'm boiling! Whenever I pick up a shoe, I shudder a little thinking how short life is and what I am doing!—Whatever that means. I know it doesn't mean shoes—except as something to wear on a traveler's feet! *(Finds paper.)* Look—

JIM: What?

TOM: I'm a member.

JIM *(reading):* The Union of Merchant Seamen.

TOM: I paid my dues this month, instead of the light bill.

JIM: You will regret it when they turn the lights off.

TOM: I won't be here.

JIM: How about your mother?

TOM: I'm like my father. The bastard son of a bastard! See how he grins? And he's been absent going on sixteen years!

JIM: You're just talking, you drip. How does your mother feel about it?

TOM: Shhh!—Here comes Mother! Mother is not acquainted with my plans!

AMANDA *(enters portieres):* Where are you all?

TOM: On the terrace, Mother.

(They start inside. She advances to them. TOM is distinctly shocked at her appearance. Even JIM blinks a little. He is making his first contact with girlish Southern vivacity and in spite of the night-school course in public speaking is somewhat thrown off the beam by the unexpected outlay of social charm.)

(Certain responses are attempted by JIM but are swept aside by AMANDA's gay laughter and chatter. TOM is embarrassed but after the first shock JIM reacts very warmly. Grins and chuckles, is altogether won over.)

(IMAGE: *Amanda as a girl.*)

AMANDA *(coyly smiling, shaking her girlish ringlets):* Well, well, well, so this is Mr. O'Connor. Introductions entirely unnecessary. I've heard so much about you from my boy. I finally said to him, Tom—good gracious!—why don't you bring this paragon to supper? I'd like to meet this nice young man at the warehouse!—Instead of just hearing him sing your praises so much! I don't know why my son is so stand-offish—that's not Southern behavior! Let's sit down and—I think we could stand a little more air in here! Tom, leave the door open. I felt a nice fresh breeze a moment ago. Where has it gone to? Mmm, so warm already! And not quite summer, even. We're going to burn up when summer really gets started. However, we're having—we're having a very light supper. I think light things are better fo' this time of year. The same as light clothes are. Light clothes an' light food are what warm weather calls fo'. You know our blood gets so thick during th' winter—it takes a while fo' us to *adjust* ou'selves!—when the season changes . . . It's come so quick this year. I wasn't prepared. All of a sudden—heavens! Already summer!—I ran to the trunk an' pulled out this light dress—Terribly old! Historical almost! But feels so good—so good an' co-ol, y'know. . . .

TOM: Mother—

AMANDA: Yes, honey?

TOM: How about—supper?

AMANDA: Honey, you go ask Sister if supper is ready! You know that Sister is in full charge of supper! Tell her you hungry boys are waiting for it. *(To* JIM.*)* Have you met Laura?

JIM: She—

AMANDA: Let you in? Oh, good, you've met already! It's rare for a girl as sweet an' pretty as Laura to be domestic! But Laura is, thank heavens, not only pretty but also very domestic. I'm not at all. I never was a bit. I never could make a thing but angel-food cake. Well, in the South we had so many servants. Gone, gone, gone. All vestige of gracious living! Gone completely! I wasn't prepared for what the future brought me. All of my gentlemen callers were sons of planters and so of course I assumed that I would be married to one and raise my family on a large piece of land with plenty of servants. But man proposes—and woman accepts the proposal!—To vary that old, old saying a little bit—I married no planter! I married a man who worked for the telephone company!—That gallantly smiling gentlemen over there! *(Points to the picture.)* A telephone man who—fell in love with long-distance!—Now he travels and I don't even know where!—But what am I going on for about my—tribulations? Tell me yours—I hope you don't have any! Tom?

TOM *(returning):* Yes, Mother?

AMANDA: Is supper nearly ready?

TOM: It looks to me like supper is on the table.

AMANDA: Let me look— *(She rises prettily and looks through portieres.)* Oh, lovely!—But where is Sister?

TOM: Laura is not feeling well and she says that she thinks she'd better not come to the table.

AMANDA: What?—Nonsense!—Laura? Oh, Laura!

LAURA *(Off stage, faintly):* Yes, Mother.

AMANDA: You really must come to the table. We won't be seated until you come to the table! Come in, Mr. O'Connor. You sit over there, and I'll—Laura? Laura Wingfield! You're keeping us waiting, honey! We can't say grace until you come to the table!

(The back door is pushed weakly open and LAURA *comes in. She is obviously quite faint, her lips trembling, her eyes wide and staring. She moves unsteadily toward the table.)*

(LEGEND: *"Terror!")*

(Outside a summer storm is coming abruptly. The white curtains billow inward at the windows and there is a sorrowful murmur and deep blue dusk.)

*(*LAURA *suddenly stumbles—she catches at a chair with a faint moan.)*

TOM: Laura!

AMANDA: Laura! *(There is a clap of thunder.) (*LEGEND: "AH!"*)* (Despairingly). Why, Laura, you *are* sick, darling! Tom, help your sister into the living room, dear! Sit in the living room, Laura— rest on the sofa. Well! *(To the gentleman caller.)* Standing over the hot stove made her ill!—I told her that it was just too warm this evening, but— *(*TOM *comes back in.* LAURA *is on the sofa.)* Is Laura all right now?

TOM: Yes.

AMANDA: What *is* that? Rain? A nice cool rain has come up! *(She gives the gentleman caller a frightened look.)* I think we may—have grace—now . . . *(*TOM *looks at her stupidly.)* Tom, honey—you say grace!

TOM: Oh . . . "For these and all thy mercies—" *(They bow their heads,* AMANDA *stealing a nervous glance at* JIM. *In the living room* LAURA, *stretched on the sofa, clenches her hand to her lips, to hold back a shuddering sob.)* God's Holy Name be praised—

The scene dims out.

SCENE SEVEN

(A Souvenir.)

(Half an hour later. Dinner is just being finished in the upstage area which is concealed by the drawn portieres.

As the curtain rises LAURA *is still huddled upon the sofa, her feet drawn under her, her head resting on a pale blue pillow, her eyes wide and mysteriously watchful. The new floor lamp with its shade of rose-colored silk gives a soft, becoming light to her face, bringing out the fragile, unearthly prettiness which usually escapes attention. There is a steady murmur of rain, but it is slackening and stops soon after the scene begins; the air outside becomes pale and luminous as the moon breaks out.*

A moment after the curtain rises, the lights in both rooms flicker and go out.)

JIM: Hey, there, Mr. Light Bulb!

*(*AMANDA *laughs nervously.)*

(LEGEND: "SUSPENSION OF A PUBLIC SERVICE.")

AMANDA: Where was Moses when the lights went out? Ha-ha. Do you know the answer to that one, Mr. O'Connor?

JIM: No, Ma'am, what's the answer?

AMANDA: In the dark! (JIM *laughs appreciably.)* Everybody sit still. I'll light the candles. Isn't it lucky we have them on the table? Where's a match? Which of you gentlemen can provide a match?

JIM: Here.

AMANDA: Thank you, sir.

JIM: Not at all, Ma'am!

AMANDA: I guess the fuse has burnt out. Mr. O'Connor, can you tell a burnt-out fuse? I know I can't and Tom is a total loss when it comes to mechanics. (SOUND: *Getting up: Voices recede a little to kitchenette.)* Oh, be careful you don't bump into something. We don't want our gentleman caller to break his neck. Now wouldn't that be a fine howdy-do?

JIM: Ha-ha! Where is the fuse-box?

AMANDA: Right here next to the stove. Can you see anything?

JIM: Just a minute.

AMANDA: Isn't electricity a mysterious thing? Wasn't it Benjamin Franklin who tied a key to a kite? We live in such a mysterious universe, don't we? Some people say that science clears up all the mysteries for us. In my opinion it only creates more! Have you found it yet?

JIM: No, Ma'am. All these fuses look okay to me.

AMANDA: Tom!

TOM: Yes, Mother?

AMANDA: That light bill I gave you several days ago. The one I told you we got the notices about?

TOM: Oh.—Yeah.

(LEGEND: *"Ha!")*

AMANDA: You didn't neglect to pay it by any chance?

TOM: Why, I—

AMANDA: Didn't! I might have known it!

JIM: Shakespeare probably wrote a poem on that light bill, Mrs. Wingfield.

AMANDA: I might have known better than to trust him with it! There's such a high price for negligence in this world!

JIM: Maybe the poem will win a ten-dollar prize.

AMANDA: We'll just have to spend the remainder of the evening in the nineteenth century, before Mr. Edison made the Mazda lamp!

JIM: Candlelight is my favorite kind of light.

AMANDA: That shows you're romantic! But that's no excuse for Tom. Well, we got through dinner. Very considerate of them to let us get through dinner before they plunged us into everlasting darkness, wasn't it, Mr. O'Connor?

JIM: Ha-ha!

AMANDA: Tom, as a penalty for your carelessness you can help me with the dishes.

JIM: Let me give you a hand.

AMANDA: Indeed you will not!

JIM: I ought to be good for something.

AMANDA: Good for something? *(Her tone is rhapsodic.) You?* Why, Mr. O'Connor, nobody, *nobody's* given me this much entertainment in years—as you have!

JIM: Aw, now, Mrs. Wingfield!

AMANDA: I'm not exaggerating, not one bit! But Sister is all by her lonesome. You go keep her company in the parlor! I'll give you this lovely old candelabrum that used to be on the altar at the church of the Heavenly Rest. It was melted a little out of shape when the church burnt down. Lightning struck it one spring. Gypsy Jones was holding a revival at the time and he intimated that the church was destroyed because the Episcopalians gave card parties.

JIM: Ha-ha.

AMANDA: And how about coaxing Sister to drink a little wine? I think it would be good for her! Can you carry both at once?

JIM: Sure. I'm Superman!

AMANDA: Now, Thomas, get into this apron!

(The door of kitchenette swings closed on AMANDA*'s gay laughter; the flickering light approaches the portieres.)*

*(*LAURA *sits up nervously as he enters. Her speech at first is low and breathless from the almost intolerable strain of being alone with a stranger.)*

(THE LEGEND: *"I don't suppose you remember me at all!"*)

(In her first speeches in this scene, before JIM*'s warmth overcomes her paralyzing shyness,* LAURA*'s voice is thin and breathless as though she has just run up a steep flight of stairs.)*

*(*JIM*'s attitude is gently humorous. In playing this scene it should be stressed that while the incident is apparently unimportant, it is to* LAURA *the climax of her secret life.)*

JIM: Hello, there, Laura.

LAURA *(faintly)*: Hello. *(She clears her throat.)*

JIM: How are you feeling now? Better?

LAURA: Yes. Yes, thank you.

JIM: This is for you. A little dandelion wine. *(He extends it toward her with extravagant gallantry.)*

LAURA: Thank you.

JIM: Drink it—but don't get drunk! *(He laughs heartily.* LAURA *takes the glass uncertainly; laughs shyly.)* Where shall I set the candles?

LAURA: Oh—oh, anywhere . . .

JIM: How about here on the floor? Any objections?

LAURA: No.

JIM: I'll spread a newspaper under to catch the drippings. I like to sit on the floor. Mind if I do?

LAURA: Oh, no.

JIM: Give me a pillow?

LAURA: What?

JIM: A pillow!

LAURA: Oh . . . *(Hands him one quickly.)*

JIM: How about you? Don't you like to sit on the floor?

LAURA: Oh—yes.

JIM: Why don't you, then?

LAURA: I—will.

JIM: Take a pillow! *(*LAURA *does. Sits on the other side of the candelabrum.* JIM *crosses his legs and smiles engagingly at her.)* I can't hardly see you sitting way over there.

LAURA: I can—see you.

JIM: I know, but that's not fair, I'm in the limelight. *(*LAURA *moves her pillow closer.)* Good! Now I can see you! Comfortable?

LAURA: Yes.

JIM: So am I. Comfortable as a cow. Will you have some gum?

LAURA: No, thank you.

JIM: I think that I will indulge, with your permission. *(Musingly unwraps it and holds it up.)* Think of the fortune made by the guy that invented the first piece of chewing gum. Amazing, huh? The Wrigley Building is one of the sights of Chicago.—I saw it summer before last when I went up to the Century of Progress. Did you take in the Century of Progress?

LAURA: No, I didn't.

JIM: Well, it was quite a wonderful exposition. What impressed me most was the Hall of Science. Gives you an idea of what the future will be in America, even more wonderful than the present time is! *(Pause. Smiling at her.)* Your brother tells me you're shy. Is that right, Laura?

LAURA: I—don't know.

JIM: I judge you to be an old-fashioned type of girl. Well, I think that's a pretty good type to be. Hope you don't think I'm being too personal—do you?

LAURA *(hastily, out of embarrassment):* I believe I *will* take a piece of gum, if you—don't mind. *(Clearing her throat.)* Mr. O'Connor, have you—kept up with your singing?

JIM: Singing? Me?

LAURA: Yes. I remember what a beautiful voice you had.

JIM: When did you hear me sing?

(Voice off stage in the pause.)

VOICE *(off stage):*

O blow, ye winds, heigh-ho,
A-roving I will go!
  I'm off to my love
  With a boxing glove—
  Ten thousand miles away!

JIM: You say you've heard me sing?

LAURA: Oh, yes! Yes, very often . . . I—don't suppose you remember me—at all?

JIM *(smiling doubtfully):* You know I have an idea I've seen you before. I had that idea soon as you opened the door. It seemed almost like I was about to remember your name. But the name that I started to call you—wasn't a name! And so I stopped myself before I said it.

LAURA: Wasn't it—Blue Roses?

JIM: *(springs up. Grinning):* Blue Roses! My gosh, yes—Blue Roses! That's what I had on my tongue when you opened the door! Isn't it funny what tricks your memory plays? I didn't connect you with the high school somehow or other. But that's where it was; it was high school. I didn't even know you were Shakespeare's sister! Gosh, I'm sorry.

LAURA: I didn't expect you to. You—barely knew me!

JIM: But we did have a speaking acquaintance, huh?

LAURA: Yes, we—spoke to each other.

JIM: When did you recognize me?

LAURA: Oh, right away!

JIM: Soon as I came in the door?

LAURA: When I heard your name I thought it was probably you. I knew that Tom used to know you a little in high school. So when you came in the door—Well, then I was—sure.

JIM: Why didn't you *say* something, then?

LAURA *(breathlessly)*: I didn't know what to say, I was—too surprised!

JIM: For goodness' sakes! You know, this sure is funny!

LAURA: Yes! Yes, isn't it, though . . .

JIM: Didn't we have a class in something together?

LAURA: Yes, we did.

JIM: What class was that?

LAURA: It was—singing—Chorus!

JIM: Aw!

LAURA: I sat across the aisle from you in the Aud.

JIM: Aw.

LAURA: Mondays, Wednesdays and Fridays.

JIM: Now I remember—you always came in late.

LAURA: Yes, it was so hard for me, getting upstairs. I had that brace on my leg—it clumped so loud!

JIM: I never heard any clumping.

LAURA *(wincing at the recollection)*: To me it sounded like—thunder!

JIM: Well, well, well, I never even noticed.

LAURA: And everybody was seated before I came in. I had to walk in front of all those people. My seat was in the back row. I had to go clumping all the way up the aisle with everyone watching!

JIM: You shouldn't have been self-conscious.

LAURA: I know, but I was. It was always such a relief when the singing started.

JIM: Aw, yes, I've placed you now! I used to call you Blue Roses. How was it that I got started calling you that?

LAURA: I was out of school a little while with pleurosis. When I came back you asked me what was the matter. I said I had pleurosis—you thought I said Blue Roses. That's what you always called me after that!

JIM: I hope you didn't mind.

LAURA: Oh, no—I liked it. You see, I wasn't acquainted with many—people. . . .

JIM: As I remember you sort of stuck by yourself.

LAURA: I—I—never had much luck at—making friends.

JIM: I don't see why you wouldn't.

LAURA: Well, I—started out badly.

JIM: You mean being—

LAURA: Yes, it sort of—stood between me—

JIM: You shouldn't have let it!

LAURA: I know, but it did, and—

JIM: You were shy with people!

LAURA: I tried not to be but never could—

JIM: Overcome it?

LAURA: No, I—I never could!

JIM: I guess being shy is something you have to work out of kind of gradually.

LAURA: *(sorrowfully):* Yes—I guess it—

JIM: Takes time!

LAURA: Yes—

JIM: People are not so dreadful when you know them. That's what you have to remember! And everybody has problems, not just you, but practically everybody has got some problems. You think of yourself as having the only problems, as being the only one who is disappointed. But just look around you and you will see lots of people as disappointed as you are. For instance, I hoped when I was going to high school that I would be further along at this time, six years later, than I am now—You remember that wonderful write-up I had in *The Torch?*

LAURA: Yes! *(She rises and crosses to table.)*

JIM: It said I was bound to succeed in anything I went into! *(LAURA returns with the annual.)* Holy Jeez! *The Torch! (He accepts it reverently. They smile across it with mutual wonder. LAURA crouches beside him and they begin to turn through it. LAURA's shyness is dissolving in his warmth.)*

LAURA: Here you are in *Pirates of Penzance!*

JIM: *(wistfully):* I sang the baritone lead in that operetta.

LAURA *(rapidly):* So—*beautifully!*

JIM *(protesting):* Aw—

LAURA: Yes, yes—beautifully—beautifully!

JIM: You heard me?

LAURA: All three times!

JIM: No!

LAURA: Yes!

JIM: All three performances?

LAURA *(looking down):* Yes.

JIM: Why?

LAURA: I—wanted to ask you to—autograph my program.

JIM: Why didn't you ask me to?

LAURA: You were always surrounded by your own friends so much that I never had a chance to.

JIM: You should have just—

LAURA: Well, I—thought you might think I was—

JIM: Thought I might think you was—what?

LAURA: Oh—

JIM *(with reflective relish):* I was beleaguered by females in those days.

LAURA: You were terribly popular!

JIM: Yeah—

LAURA: You had such a—friendly way—

JIM: I was spoiled in high school.

LAURA: Everybody—liked you!

JIM: Including you?

LAURA: I—yes, I—I did, too— *(She gently closes the book in her lap.)*

JIM: Well, well, well!—Give me that program, Laura. *(She hands it to him. He signs it with a flourish.)* There you are—better late than never!

LAURA: Oh, I—what a—surprise!

JIM: My signature isn't worth very much right now. But some day—maybe—it will increase in value! Being disappointed is one thing and being discouraged is something else. I am disappointed but I am not discouraged. I'm twenty-three years old. How old are you?

LAURA: I'll be twenty-four in June.

JIM: That's not old age!

LAURA: No, but—

JIM: You finished high school?

LAURA *(with difficulty)*: I didn't go back.

JIM: You mean you dropped out?

LAURA: I made bad grades in my final examinations. *(She rises and replaces the book and the program. Her voice strained.)* How is—Emily Meisenbach getting along?

JIM: Oh, that kraut-head!

LAURA: Why do you call her that?

JIM: That's what she was.

LAURA: You're not still—going with her?

JIM: I never see her.

LAURA: It said in the Personal Section that you were—engaged!

JIM: I know, but I wasn't impressed by that—propaganda!

LAURA: It wasn't—the truth?

JIM: Only in Emily's optimistic opinion!

LAURA: Oh—

(LEGEND: *"What have you done since high school?"*)

(JIM lights a cigarette and leans indolently back on his elbows smiling at LAURA with a warmth and charm which lights her inwardly with altar candles. She remains by the table and turns in her hands a piece of glass to cover her tumult.)

JIM *(after several reflective puffs on a cigarette)*: What have you done since high school? *(She seems not to hear him.)* Huh? *(LAURA looks up.)* I said what have you done since high school, Laura?

LAURA: Nothing much.

JIM: You must have been doing something these six long years.

LAURA: Yes.

JIM: Well, then, such as what?

LAURA: I took a business course at business college—

JIM: How did that work out?

LAURA: Well, not very—well—I had to drop out, it gave me—indigestion—

(JIM laughs gently.)

JIM: What are you doing now?

LAURA: I don't do anything—much. Oh, please don't think I sit around doing nothing! My glass collection takes up a good deal of my time. Glass is something you have to take good care of.

JIM: What did you say—about glass?

LAURA: Collection I said—I have one— *(She clears her throat and turns away again, acutely shy.)*

JIM: *(abruptly):* You know what I judge to be the trouble with you? Inferiority complex! Know what that is? That's what they call it when someone low-rates himself! I understand it because I had it, too. Although my case was not so aggravated as yours seems to be. I had it until I took up public speaking, developed my voice, and learned that I had an aptitude for science. Before that time I never thought of myself as being outstanding in any way whatsoever! Now I've never made a regular study of it, but I have a friend who says I can analyze people better than doctors that make a profession of it. I don't claim that to be necessarily true, but I can sure guess a person's psychology, Laura! *(Takes out his gum.)* Excuse me, Laura. I always take it out when the flavor is gone. I'll use this scrap of paper to wrap it in. I know how it is to get it stuck on a shoe. Yep—that's what I judge to be your principal trouble. A lack of confidence in yourself as a person. You don't have the proper amount of faith in yourself. I'm basing that fact on a number of your remarks and also on certain observations I've made. For instance that clumping you thought was so awful in high school. You say that you even dreaded to walk into class. You see what you did? You dropped out of school, you gave up an education because of a clump, which as far as I know was practically non-existent! A little physical defect is what you have. Hardly noticeable even! Magnified thousands of times by imagination! You know what my strong advice to you is? Think of yourself as *superior* in some way!

LAURA: In what way would I think?

JIM: Why, man alive, Laura! Just look about you a little. What do you see? A world full of common people! All of 'em born and all of 'em going to die! Which of them has one-tenth of your good points! Or mine! Or anyone else's, as far as that goes—Gosh! Everybody excels in some one thing. Some in many! *(Unconsciously glances at himself in the mirror.)* All you've got to do is discover in *what!* Take me, for instance. *(He adjusts his tie at the mirror.)* My interest happens to lie in electro-dynamics. I'm taking a course in radio engineering at night school, Laura, on top of a fairly responsible job at the warehouse. I'm taking that course and studying public speaking.

LAURA: Ohhhh.

JIM: Because I believe in the future of television! *(Turning back to her.)* I wish to be ready to go up right along with it. Therefore I'm planning to get in on the ground floor. In fact, I've already made the right connections and all that remains is for the industry itself to get under way! Full steam— *(His eyes are starry.)* *Knowledge*—Zzzzzp! *Money*—Zzzzzzp!—*Power!* That's the cycle democracy is built on! *(His attitude is convincingly dynamic.* LAURA *stares at him, even her shyness eclipsed in her absolute wonder. He suddenly grins.)* I guess you think I think a lot of myself!

LAURA: No—o-o-o, I—

JIM: Now how about you? Isn't there something you take more interest in than anything else?

LAURA: Well, I do—as I said—have my—glass collection—

(A peal of girlish laughter from the kitchen.)

JIM: I'm not right sure I know what you're talking about. What kind of glass is it?

LAURA: Little articles of it, they're ornaments mostly! Most of them are little animals made out of glass, the tiniest little animals in the world. Mother calls them a glass menagerie! Here's an example of one, if you'd like to see it! This one is one of the oldest. It's nearly thirteen. *(He stretches out his hand.)* (MUSIC: "THE GLASS MENAGERIE.") Oh, be careful—if you breathe, it breaks!

JIM: I'd better not take it. I'm pretty clumsy with things.

LAURA: Go on, I trust you with him! *(Places it in his palm.)* There now—you're holding him gently! Hold him over the light, he loves the light! You see how the light shines through him?

JIM: It sure does shine!

LAURA: I shouldn't be partial, but he is my favorite one.

JIM: What kind of a thing is this one supposed to be?

LAURA: Haven't you noticed the single horn on his forehead?

JIM: A unicorn, huh?

LAURA: Mmm-hmmm!

JIM: Unicorns, aren't they extinct in the modern world?

LAURA: I know!

JIM: Poor little fellow, he must feel sort of lonesome.

LAURA *(smiling):* Well, if he does he doesn't complain about it. He stays on a shelf with some horses that don't have horns and all of them seem to get along nicely together.

JIM: How do you know?

LAURA *(lightly):* I haven't heard any arguments among them!

JIM *(grinning):* No arguments, huh? Well, that's a pretty good sign! Where shall I set him?

LAURA: Put him on the table. They all like a change of scenery once in a while!

JIM *(stretching):* Well, well, well, well—Look how big my shadow is when I stretch!

LAURA: Oh, oh, yes—it stretches across the ceiling!

JIM *(crossing to door):* I think it's stopped raining. *(Opens fire-escape door.)* Where does the music come from?

LAURA: From the Paradise Dance Hall across the alley.

JIM: How about cutting the rug a little, Miss Wingfield?

LAURA: Oh, I—

JIM: Or is your program filled up? Let me have a look at it. *(Grasps imaginary card.)* Why, every dance is taken! I'll just have to scratch some out. (WALTZ MUSIC: "LA GOLONDRINA.") Ahhh, a waltz! *(He executes some sweeping turns by himself then holds his arms toward* LAURA.*)*

LAURA *(breathlessly):* I—can't dance!

JIM: There you go, that inferiority stuff!

LAURA: I've never danced in my life!

JIM: Come on, try!

LAURA: Oh, but I'd step on you!

JIM: I'm not made out of glass.

LAURA: How—how—how do we start?

JIM: Just leave it to me. You hold your arms out a little.

LAURA: Like this?

JIM: A little bit higher. Right. Now don't tighten up, that's the main thing about it—relax.

LAURA *(laughing breathlessly):* It's hard not to.

JIM: Okay.

LAURA: I'm afraid you can't budge me.

JIM: What do you bet I can't? *(He swings her into motion.)*

LAURA: Goodness, yes, you can!

JIM: Let yourself go, now, Laura, just let yourself go.

LAURA: I'm—

JIM: Come on!

LAURA: Trying!

JIM: Not so stiff—Easy does it!

LAURA: I know but I'm—

JIM: Loosen th' backbone! There now, that's a lot better.

LAURA: Am I?

JIM: Lots, lots better! *(He moves her about the room in a clumsy waltz.)*

LAURA: Oh, my!

JIM: Ha-ha!

LAURA: Oh, my goodness!

JIM: Ha-ha-ha! *(They suddenly bump into the table.* JIM *stops.)* What did we hit on?

LAURA: Table.

JIM: Did something fall off it? I think—

LAURA: Yes.

JIM: I hope that it wasn't the little glass horse with the horn!

LAURA: Yes.

JIM: Aw, aw, aw. Is it broken?

LAURA: Now it is just like all the other horses.

JIM: It's lost its—

LAURA: Horn! It doesn't matter. Maybe it's a blessing in disguise.

JIM: You'll never forgive me. I bet that that was your favorite piece of glass.

LAURA: I don't have favorites much. It's no tragedy, Freckles. Glass breaks so easily. No matter how careful you are. The traffic jars the shelves and things fall off them.

JIM: Still I'm awfully sorry that I was the cause.

LAURA *(smiling):* I'll just imagine he had an operation. The horn was removed to make him feel less—freakish! *(They both laugh.)* Now he will feel more at home with the other horses, the ones that don't have horns . . .

JIM: Ha-ha, that's very funny! *(Suddenly serious.)* I'm glad to see that you have a sense of humor. You know—you're—well—very different! Surprisingly different from anyone else I know! *(His voice becomes soft and hesitant with a genuine feeling.)* Do you mind me telling you that? *(*LAURA *is abashed beyond speech.)* I mean it in a nice way . . . *(*LAURA *nods shyly, looking away.)* You make me feel sort of—I don't know how to put it! I'm usually pretty good at expressing things, but—This is something that I don't know how to say! *(*LAURA *touches her throat and clears it—turns the broken unicorn in her hands.) (Even softer.)* Has anyone ever told you that you were pretty? *(*PAUSE: MUSIC.*) (*LAURA *looks up slowly, with wonder, and shakes her head.)* Well, you are! In a very different way from anyone else. And all the nicer because of the difference, too. *(His voice becomes low and husky.* LAURA *turns away, nearly faint with the novelty of her emotions.)* I wish that you were my sister. I'd teach you to have some confidence in yourself. The different people are not like other people, but being different is nothing to be ashamed of. Because other people are not such wonderful people. They're one hundred times one thousand.

You're one times one! They walk all over the earth. You just stay here. They're common as—weeds, but—you—well, you're—*Blue Roses!*

(IMAGE ON SCREEN: *Blue roses.)*

(Music changes.)

LAURA: But blue is wrong for—roses . . .

JIM: It's right for you—You're—pretty!

LAURA: In what respect am I pretty?

JIM: In all respects—believe me! Your eyes—your hair—are pretty! Your hands are pretty! *(He catches hold of her hand.)* You think I'm making this up because I'm invited to dinner and have to be nice. Oh, I could do that! I could put on an act for you, Laura, and say lots of things without being very sincere. But this time I am. I'm talking to you sincerely. I happened to notice you had this inferiority complex that keeps you from feeling comfortable with people. Somebody needs to build your confidence up and make you proud instead of shy and turning away and—blushing—Somebody ought to—Ought to—*kiss* you, Laura! *(His hand slips slowly up her arm to her shoulder.) (Music swells tumultuously.) (He suddenly turns her about and kisses her on the lips. When he releases her* LAURA *sinks on the sofa with a bright, dazed look.* JIM *backs away and fishes in his pocket for a cigarette.)* (LEGEND ON SCREEN: "SOUVENIR."*)* Stumble-john! *(He lights the cigarette, avoiding her look. There is a peal of girlish laughter from* AMANDA *in the kitchen.* LAURA *slowly raises and opens her hand. It still contains the little broken glass animal. She looks at it with a tender, bewildered expression.)* Stumble-john! I shouldn't have done that—That was way off the beam. You don't smoke, do you? *(She looks up, smiling, not hearing the question. He sits beside her a little gingerly. She looks at him speechlessly—waiting. He coughs decorously and moves a little farther aside as he considers the situation and senses her feelings, dimly, with perturbation. Gently.)* Would you—care for a—mint? *(She doesn't seem to hear him but her look grows brighter even.)* Peppermint—Life Saver? My pocket's a regular drug store—wherever I go . . . *(He pops a mint in his mouth. Then gulps and decides to make a clean breast of it. He speaks slowly and gingerly.)* Laura, you know, if I had a sister like you, I'd do the same thing as Tom. I'd bring out fellows and—introduce her to them. The right type of boys of a type to—appreciate her. Only—well—he made a mistake about me. Maybe I've got no call to be saying this. That may not have been the idea in having me over. But what if it was? There's nothing wrong about that. The only trouble is that in my case—I'm not in a situation to—do the right thing. I can't take down your number and say I'll phone. I can't call up next week and—ask for a date. I thought I had better explain the situation in case you misunderstood it and—hurt your feelings. . . . *(Pause. Slowly, very slowly,* LAURA'S *look changes, her eyes returning slowly from his to the ornament in her palm.)*

*(*AMANDA *utters another gay laugh in the kitchen.)*

LAURA *(faintly):* You—won't—call again?

JIM: No, Laura, I can't. *(He rises from the sofa.)* As I was just explaining, I've—got strings on me, Laura, I've—been going steady! I go out all the time with a girl named Betty. She's a home-girl like you, and Catholic, and Irish, and in a great many ways we—get along

fine. I met her last summer on a moonlight boat trip up the river to Alton, on the *Majestic.* Well—right away from the start it was—love! (LEGEND: LOVE!) *(*LAURA *sways slightly forward and grips the arm of the sofa. He fails to notice, now enrapt in his own comfortable being.)* Being in love has made a new man of me! *(Leaning stiffly forward, clutching the arm of the sofa,* LAURA *struggles visibly with her storm. But* JIM *is oblivious, she is a long way off.)* The power of love is really pretty tremendous! Love is something that—changes the whole world, Laura! *(The storm abates a little and* LAURA *leans back. He notices her again.)* It happened that Betty's aunt took sick, she got a wire and had to go to Centralia. So Tom—when he asked me to dinner—I naturally just accepted the invitation, not knowing that you—that he—that I— *(He stops awkwardly.)* Huh—I'm a stumble-john! *(He flops back on the sofa. The holy candles in the altar of* LAURA*'s face have been snuffed out. There is a look of almost infinite desolation.* JIM *glances at her uneasily.)* I wish that you would—say something. *(She bites her lip which was trembling and then bravely smiles. She opens her hand again on the broken glass ornament. Then she gently takes his hand and raises it level with her own. She carefully places the unicorn in the palm of his hand, then pushes his fingers closed upon it.)* What are you—doing that for? You want me to have him?—Laura? *(She nods.)* What for?

LAURA: A—souvenir . . .

(She rises unsteadily and crouches beside the victrola to wind it up.)

(LEGEND ON SCREEN: *"Things have a way of turning out so badly!")*

(OR IMAGE: *"Gentleman caller waving goodbye!—Gaily.")*

(At this moment AMANDA *rushes brightly back in the front room. She bears a pitcher of fruit punch in an old-fashioned cut-glass pitcher and a plate of macaroons. The plate has a gold border and poppies painted on it.)*

AMANDA: Well, well, well! Isn't the air delightful after the shower? I've made you children a little liquid refreshment. *(Turns gaily to the gentleman caller.)* Jim, do you know that song about lemonade?

"Lemonade, lemonade
  Made in the shade and stirred with a spade—
Good enough for any old maid!"

JIM *(uneasily):* Ha-ha! No—I never heard it.

AMANDA: Why, Laura! You look so serious!

JIM: We were having a serious conversation.

AMANDA: Good! Now you're better acquainted!

JIM *(uncertainly):* Ha-ha! Yes.

AMANDA: You modern young people are much more serious-minded than my generation. I was so gay as a girl!

JIM: You haven't changed, Mrs. Wingfield.

AMANDA: Tonight I'm rejuvenated! The gaiety of the occasion, Mr. O'Connor! *(She tosses her head with a peal of laughter. Spills lemonade.)* Oooo! I'm baptizing myself!

JIM: Here—let me—

AMANDA *(setting the pitcher down):* There now. I discovered we had some maraschino cherries. I dumped them in, juice and all!

JIM: You shouldn't have gone to that trouble, Mrs. Wingfield.

AMANDA: Trouble, trouble? Why it was loads of fun! Didn't you hear me cutting up in the kitchen? I bet your ears were burning! I told Tom how outdone with him I was for keeping you to himself so long a time! He should have brought you over much, much sooner! Well, now that you've found your way, I want you to be a very frequent caller! Not just occasional but all the time. Oh, we're going to have a lot of gay times together! I see them coming! Mmm, just breathe that air! So fresh, and the moon's so pretty! I'll skip back out—I know where my place is when young folks are having a—serious conversation!

JIM: Oh, don't go out, Mrs. Wingfield. The fact of the matter is I've got to be going.

AMANDA: Going, now? You're joking! Why, it's only the shank of the evening, Mr. O'Connor!

JIM: Well, you know how it is.

AMANDA: You mean you're a young workingman and have to keep workingmen's hours. We'll let you off early tonight. But only on the condition that next time you stay later. What's the best night for you? Isn't Saturday night the best night for you workingmen?

JIM: I have a couple of time-clocks to punch, Mrs. Wingfield. One at morning, another one at night!

AMANDA: My, but you *are* ambitious! You work at night, too?

JIM: No, Ma'am, not work but—Betty! *(He crosses deliberately to pick up his hat. The band at the Paradise Dance Hall goes into a tender waltz.)*

AMANDA: Betty? Betty? Who's—Betty! *(There is an ominous cracking sound in the sky.)*

JIM: Oh, just a girl. The girl I go steady with! *(He smiles charmingly. The sky falls.)*

(LEGEND: *"The sky falls."*)

AMANDA *(a long-drawn exhalation):* Ohhhh . . . Is it a serious romance, Mr. O'Connor?

JIM: We're going to be married the second Sunday in June.

AMANDA: Ohhhh—how nice! Tom didn't mention that you were engaged to be married.

JIM: The cat's not out of the bag at the warehouse yet. You know how they are. They call you Romeo and stuff like that. *(He stops at the oval mirror to put on his hat. He carefully shapes the brim and the crown to give a discreetly dashing effect.)* It's been a wonderful evening, Mrs. Wingfield. I guess this is what they mean by Southern hospitality.

AMANDA: It really wasn't anything at all.

JIM: I hope it don't seem like I'm rushing off. But I promised Betty I'd pick her up at the Wabash depot, an' by the time I get my jalopy down there her train'll be in. Some women are pretty upset if you keep 'em waiting.

AMANDA: Yes, I know—The tyranny of women! *(Extends her hand.)* Good-bye, Mr. O'Connor. I wish you luck—and happiness—and success! All three of them, and so does Laura!—Don't you, Laura?

LAURA: Yes!

JIM *(taking her hand):* Good-bye, Laura. I'm certainly going to treasure that souvenir. And don't you forget the good advice I gave you. *(Raises his voice to a cheery shout.)* So long, Shakespeare! Thanks again, ladies—Good night!

(He grins and ducks jauntily out.)

(Still bravely grimacing, AMANDA *closes the door on the gentleman caller. Then she turns back to the room with a puzzled expression. She and* LAURA *don't dare to face each other.* LAURA *crouches beside the victrola to wind it.)*

AMANDA *(faintly):* Things have a way of turning out so badly. I don't believe that I would play the victrola. Well, well—well—Our gentleman caller was engaged to be married! Tom!

TOM *(from back):* Yes, Mother?

AMANDA: Come in here a minute. I want to tell you something awfully funny.

TOM *(enters with macaroon and a glass of the lemonade):* Has the gentleman caller gotten away already?

AMANDA: The gentleman caller has made an early departure. What a wonderful joke you played on us!

TOM: How do you mean?

AMANDA: You didn't mention that he was engaged to be married.

TOM: Jim? Engaged?

AMANDA: That's what he just informed us.

TOM: I'll be jiggered! I didn't know about that.

AMANDA: That seems very peculiar.

TOM: What's peculiar about it?

AMANDA: Didn't you call him your best friend down at the warehouse?

TOM: He is, but how did I know?

AMANDA: It seems extremely peculiar that you wouldn't know your best friend was going to be married!

TOM: The warehouse is where I work, not where I know things about people!

AMANDA: You don't know things anywhere! You live in a dream; you manufacture illusions! *(He crosses to door.)* Where are you going?

TOM: I'm going to the movies.

AMANDA: That's right, now that you've had us make such fools of ourselves. The effort, the preparations, all the expense! The new floor lamp, the rug, the clothes for Laura! All for what? To entertain some other girl's fiancé! Go to the movies, go! Don't think about us, a mother deserted, an unmarried sister who's crippled and has no job! Don't let anything interfere with your selfish pleasure! Just go, go, go—to the movies!

TOM: All right, I will! The more you shout about my selfishness to me the quicker I'll go, and I won't go to the movies!

AMANDA: Go, then! Then go to the moon—you selfish dreamer!

*(*TOM *smashes his glass on the floor. He plunges out on the fire-escape, slamming the door.* LAURA *screams—cut by door.)*

(Dance-hall music up. TOM *goes to the rail and grips it desperately, lifting his face in the chill white moonlight penetrating the narrow abyss of the alley.)*

(LEGEND ON SCREEN: *"And so good-bye . . ."*)

*(*TOM'S *closing speech is timed with the interior pantomime. The interior scene is played as though viewed through soundproof glass.* AMANDA *appears to be making a comforting speech*

to LAURA *who is huddled upon the sofa. Now that we cannot hear the mother's speech, her silliness is gone and she has dignity and tragic beauty.* LAURA*'s dark hair hides her face until at the end of the speech she lifts it to smile at her mother.* AMANDA*'s gestures are slow and graceful, almost dancelike, as she comforts the daughter. At the end of her speech she glances a moment at the father's picture—then withdraws through the portieres. At close of* TOM*'s speech,* LAURA *blows out the candles, ending the play.)*

TOM: I didn't go to the moon, I went much further—for time is the longest distance between two places—Not long after that I was fired for writing a poem on the lid of a shoe-box. I left Saint Louis. I descended the steps of this fire-escape for a last time and followed, from then on, in my father's footsteps, attempting to find in motion what was lost in space—I traveled around a great deal. The cities swept about me like dead leaves, leaves that were brightly colored but torn away from the branches. I would have stopped, but I was pursued by something. It always came upon me unawares, taking me altogether by surprise. Perhaps it was a familiar bit of music. Perhaps it was only a piece of transparent glass—Perhaps I am walking along a street at night, in some strange city, before I have found companions. I pass the lighted window of a shop where perfume is sold. The window is filled with pieces of colored glass, tiny transparent bottles in delicate colors, like bits of a shattered rainbow. Then all at once my sister touches my shoulder. I turn around and look into her eyes . . . Oh, Laura, Laura, I tried to leave you behind me, but I am more faithful than I intended to be! I reach for a cigarette, I cross the street, I run into the movies or a bar, I buy a drink, I speak to the nearest stranger—anything that can blow your candles out! *(*LAURA *bends over the candles.)* —for nowadays the world is lit by lightning! Blow out your candles, Laura—and so good-bye. . . .

(She blows the candles out.)

THE SCENE DISSOLVES.

LORRAINE HANSBERRY

(1930–1965)

A Raisin in the Sun

About the Author: Lorraine Hansberry came from a prominent Chicago family. Her father, a real estate broker, founded one of the first black banks in that city and also, in the face of opposition from white neighbors, successfully carried a case to the U.S. Supreme Court against "restrictive covenants" that would limit access to housing on the basis of race. Her mother was Ward Commissioner for the Republican party. Her Uncle Leo, Professor of African History at Howard University, had a university named after him in Nigeria. During her adolescence, major black intellectual and artistic leaders were regular guests in her family home, most importantly perhaps the philosopher W. E. B. DuBois, the poet Langston Hughes, and the singer-actor-political activist Paul Robeson. Hansberry attended the University of Wisconsin for two years before deciding to study painting at the Art Institute of Chicago. From 1951 to 1955 she wrote

for, and for a time edited, *Freedom,* a magazine founded by Robeson, to which DuBois was a regular contributor. She turned subsequently to the theater, and her first play, *A Raisin in the Sun,* was spectacularly successful on stage and was shortly thereafter made into a motion picture.

Shortly after the opening of her second play on Broadway, *The Sign in Sidney Brustein's Window,* Lorraine Hansberry died of cancer at age thirty-four.

About the Play: The title *A Raisin in the Sun* is an allusion to a poem by Hughes (see Chapter 3). The play won the New York Drama Critics Award for 1959, making Hansberry the youngest playwright, as well as the first black writer, to win the award. The play presents a family at a moment of crisis, when a moment of personal loss paradoxically presents a possibility for material advancement. The humanity and dignity of the characters, the intensity of the plot, and the complexity of the themes combine to make this play a classic of American theater.

What happens to a dream deferred?
Does it dry up
Like a raisin in the sun?
Or fester like a sore—
And then run?
Does it stink like rotten meat?
Or crust and sugar over—
Like a syrupy sweet?

Maybe it just sags
Like a heavy load.

Or does it explode?
—Langston Hughes

CHARACTERS

(*In order of appearance*)

RUTH YOUNGER
TRAVIS YOUNGER
WALTER LEE YOUNGER (BROTHER)
BENEATHA YOUNGER
LENA YOUNGER (MAMA)
JOSEPH ASAGAI
GEORGE MURCHISON
KARL LINDNER
BOBO
MOVING MEN

The action of the play is set in Chicago's Southside, sometime between World War II and the present.

Act I
Scene One: *Friday morning.*
Scene Two: *The following morning.*
Act II
Scene One: *Later, the same day.*
Scene Two: *Friday night, a few weeks later.*

Scene Three: *Moving day, one week later.*
Act III
An hour later.

ACT I

SCENE I

The YOUNGER *living room would be a comfortable and well-ordered room if it were not for a number of indestructible contradictions to this state of being. Its furnishings are typical and undistinguished and their primary feature now is that they have clearly had to accommodate the living of too many people for too many years—and they are tired. Still, we can see that at some time, a time probably no longer remembered by the family (except perhaps for* MAMA*), the furnishings of this room were actually selected with care and love and even hope—and brought to this apartment and arranged with taste and pride.*

That was a long time ago. Now the once loved pattern of the couch upholstery has to fight to show itself from under acres of crocheted doilies and couch covers which have themselves finally come to be more important than the upholstery. And here a table or a chair has been moved to disguise the worn places in the carpet; but the carpet has fought back by showing its weariness, with depressing uniformity, elsewhere on its surface.

Weariness has, in fact, won in this room. Everything has been polished, washed, sat on, used, scrubbed too often. All pretenses but living itself have long since vanished from the very atmosphere of this room.

Moreover, a section of this room, for it is not really a room unto itself, though the landlord's lease would make it seem so, slopes backward to provide a small kitchen area, where the family prepares the meals that are eaten in the living room proper, which must also serve as dining room. The single window that has been provided for these "two" rooms is located in this kitchen area. The sole natural light the family may enjoy in the course of a day is only that which fights its way through this little window.

At left, a door leads to a bedroom which is shared by MAMA *and her daughter,* BENEATHA. *At right, opposite, is a second room (which in the beginning of the life of this apartment was probably a breakfast room) which serves as a bedroom for* WALTER *and his wife,* RUTH.

Time: Sometime between World War II and the present.

Place: Chicago's Southside.

At Rise: It is morning dark in the living room. TRAVIS *is asleep on the make-down bed at center. An alarm clock sounds from within the bedroom at right, and presently* RUTH *enters from that room and closes the door behind her. She crosses sleepily toward the window. As she passes her sleeping son she reaches down and shakes him a little. At the window she raises the shade and a dusky Southside morning light comes in feebly. She fills a pot with water and puts it on to boil. She calls to the boy, between yawns, in a slightly muffled voice.*

RUTH *is about thirty. We can see that she was a pretty girl, even exceptionally so, but now it is apparent that life has been little that she expected, and disappointment has already begun to hang in her face. In a few years, before thirty-five even, she will be known among her people as a "settled woman."*

She crosses to her son and gives him a good, final, rousing shake.

RUTH: Come on now, boy, it's seven thirty! *(Her son sits up at last, in a stupor of sleepiness)* I say hurry up, Travis! You ain't the only person in the world got to use a bathroom! *(The child, a sturdy, handsome little boy of ten or eleven, drags himself out of the bed and almost blindly takes his towels and "today's clothes" from drawers and a closet and goes out to the bathroom, which is in an outside hall and which is shared by another family or families on the same floor.* RUTH *crosses to the bedroom door at right and opens it and calls in to her husband)* Walter Lee! . . . It's after seven thirty! Lemme see you do some waking up in there now! *(She waits)* You better get up from there, man! It's after seven thirty I tell you. *(She waits again)* All right, you just go ahead and lay there and next thing you know Travis be finished and Mr. Johnson'll be in there and you'll be fussing and cussing round here like a madman! And be late too! *(She waits, at the end of patience)* Walter Lee—it's time for you to GET UP!

(She waits another second and then starts to go into the bedroom, but is apparently satisfied that her husband has begun to get up. She stops, pulls the door to, and returns to the kitchen area. She wipes her face with a moist cloth and runs her fingers through her sleep-disheveled hair in a vain effort and ties an apron around her housecoat. The bedroom door at right opens and her husband stands in the doorway in his pajamas, which are rumpled and mismated. He is a lean, intense young man in his middle thirties, inclined to quick nervous movements and erratic speech habits—and always in his voice there is a quality of indictment)

WALTER: Is he out yet?

RUTH: What you mean *out?* He ain't hardly got in there good yet.

WALTER *(wandering in, still more oriented to sleep than to a new day):* Well, what was you doing all that yelling for if I can't even get in there yet? *(Stopping and thinking)* Check coming today?

RUTH: They *said* Saturday and this is just Friday and I hopes to God you ain't going to get up here first thing this morning and start talking to me 'bout no money—'cause I 'bout don't want to hear it.

WALTER: Something the matter with you this morning?

RUTH: No—I'm just sleepy as the devil. What kind of eggs you want?

WALTER: Not scrambled. *(*RUTH *starts to scramble eggs)* Paper come? *(*RUTH *points impatiently to the rolled up* Tribune *on the table, and he gets it and spreads it out and vaguely reads the front page)* Set off another bomb yesterday.

RUTH *(maximum indifference):* Did they?

WALTER *(looking up):* What's the matter with you?

RUTH: Ain't nothing the matter with me. And don't keep asking me that this morning.

WALTER: Ain't nobody bothering you. *(Reading the news of the day absently again)* Say Colonel McCormick is sick.

RUTH *(affecting tea-party interest):* Is he now? Poor thing.

WALTER *(sighing and looking at his watch):* Oh, me. *(He waits)* Now what is that boy doing in that bathroom all this time? He just going to have to start getting up earlier. I can't be being late to work on account of him fooling around in there.

RUTH *(turning on him):* Oh, no he ain't going to be getting up no earlier no such thing! It ain't his fault that he can't get to bed no earlier nights 'cause he got a bunch of crazy good-for-nothing clowns sitting up running their mouths in what is supposed to be his bedroom after ten o'clock at night . . .

WALTER: That's what you mad about, ain't it? The things I want to talk about with my friends just couldn't be important in your mind, could they?

(He rises and finds a cigarette in her handbag on the table and crosses to the little window and looks out, smoking and deeply enjoying this first one)

RUTH *(almost matter of factly, a complaint too automatic to deserve emphasis):* Why you always got to smoke before you eat in the morning?

WALTER *(at the window):* Just look at 'em down there . . . Running and racing to work . . . *(He turns and faces his wife and watches her a moment at the stove, and then, suddenly)* You look young this morning, baby.

RUTH *(indifferently):* Yeah?

WALTER: Just for a second—stirring them eggs. Just for a second it was—you looked real young again. *(He reaches for her; she crosses away. Then, drily)* It's gone now—you look like yourself again!

RUTH: Man, if you don't shut up and leave me alone.

WALTER *(looking out to the street again):* First thing a man ought to learn in life is not to make love to no colored woman first thing in the morning. You all some eeeevil people at eight o'clock in the morning.

(TRAVIS appears in the hall doorway, almost fully dressed and quite wide awake now, his towels and pajamas across his shoulders. He opens the door and signals for his father to make the bathroom in a hurry)

TRAVIS *(watching the bathroom):* Daddy, come on!

(WALTER gets his bathroom utensils and flies out to the bathroom)

RUTH: Sit down and have your breakfast, Travis.

TRAVIS: Mama, this is Friday. *(Gleefully)* Check coming tomorrow, huh?

RUTH: You get your mind off money and eat your breakfast.

TRAVIS *(eating):* This is the morning we supposed to bring the fifty cents to school.

RUTH: Well, I ain't got no fifty cents this morning.

TRAVIS: Teacher say we have to.

RUTH: I don't care what teacher say. I ain't got it. Eat your breakfast, Travis.

TRAVIS: I *am* eating.

RUTH: Hush up now and just eat!

(The boy gives her an exasperated look for her lack of understanding, and eats grudgingly)

TRAVIS: You think Grandmama would have it?

RUTH: No! And I want you to stop asking your grandmother for money, you hear me?

TRAVIS *(outraged):* Gaaaleee! I don't ask her, she just gimme it sometimes!

RUTH: Travis Willard Younger—I got too much on me this morning to be—

TRAVIS: Maybe Daddy—

RUTH: *Travis!*

(The boy hushes abruptly. They are both quiet and tense for several seconds)

TRAVIS *(presently):* Could I maybe go carry some groceries in front of the supermarket for a little while after school then?

RUTH: Just hush, I said. *(TRAVIS jabs his spoon into his cereal bowl viciously, and rests his head in anger upon his fists)* If you through eating, you can get over there and make up your bed.

(The boy obeys stiffly and crosses the room, almost mechanically, to the bed and more or less folds the bedding into a heap, then angrily gets his books and cap)

TRAVIS *(sulking and standing apart from her unnaturally):* I'm gone.

RUTH *(looking up from the stove to inspect him automatically):* Come here. *(He crosses to her and she studies his head)* If you don't take this comb and fix this here head, you better! *(TRAVIS puts down his books with a great sigh of oppression, and crosses to the mirror. His mother mutters under her breath about his "slubbornness")* 'Bout to march out of here with that head looking just like chickens slept in it! I just don't know where you get your slubborn ways . . . And get your jacket, too. Looks chilly out this morning.

TRAVIS *(with conspiciously brushed hair and jacket):* I'm gone.

RUTH: Get carfare and milk money— *(Waving one finger)* —and not a single penny for no caps, you hear me?

TRAVIS *(with sullen politeness):* Yes'm.

(He turns in outrage to leave. His mother watches after him as in his frustration he approaches the door almost comically. When she speaks to him, her voice has become a very gentle tease)

RUTH *(mocking; as she thinks he would say it):* Oh, Mama makes me so mad sometimes, I don't know what to do! *(She waits and continues to his back as he stands stock-still in front of the door)* I wouldn't kiss that woman good-bye for nothing in this world this morning! *(The boy finally turns around and rolls his eyes at her, knowing the mood has changed and he is vindicated; he does not, however, move toward her yet)* Not for nothing in this world! *(She finally laughs aloud at him and holds out her arms to him and we see that it is a way between them, very old and practiced. He crosses to her and allows her to embrace him warmly but keeps his face fixed with masculine rigidity. She holds him back from her presently and looks at him and runs her fingers over the features of his face. With utter gentleness—)* Now—whose little old angry man are you?

TRAVIS *(the masculinity and gruffness start to fade at last):* Aw gaalee—Mama . . .

RUTH *(mimicking):* Aw—gaaaaalleeeee, Mama! *(She pushes him, with rough playfulness and finality, toward the door)* Get on out of here or you going to be late.

TRAVIS *(in the face of love, new aggressiveness):* Mama, could I *please* go carry groceries?

RUTH: Honey, it's starting to get so cold evenings.

WALTER *(coming in from the bathroom and drawing a make-believe gun from a make-believe holster and shooting at his son):* What is it he wants to do?

RUTH: Go carry groceries after school at the supermarket.

WALTER: Well, let him go . . .

TRAVIS *(quickly, to the ally):* I *have* to—she won't gimme the fifty cents . . .

WALTER *(to his wife only):* Why not?

RUTH *(simply, and with flavor):* 'Cause we don't have it.

WALTER *(to RUTH only):* What you tell the boy things like that for? *(Reaching down into his pants with a rather important gesture)* Here, son—

(He hands the boy the coin, but his eyes are directed to his wife's. TRAVIS takes the money happily)

TRAVIS: Thanks, Daddy.

(He starts out. RUTH *watches both of them with murder in her eyes.* WALTER *stands and stares back at her with defiance, and suddenly reaches into his pocket again on an afterthought)*

WALTER *(without even looking at his son, still staring hard at his wife):* In fact, here's another fifty cents . . . Buy yourself some fruit today—or take a taxicab to school or something!

TRAVIS: Whoopee—

(He leaps up and clasps his father around the middle with his legs, and they face each other in mutual appreciation; slowly WALTER LEE *peeks around the boy to catch the violent rays from his wife's eyes and draws his head back as if shot)*

WALTER: You better get down now—and get to school, man.

TRAVIS *(at the door):* O.K. Good-bye.

(He exits)

WALTER *(after him, pointing with pride):* That's *my* boy. *(She looks at him in disgust and turns back to her work)* You know what I was thinking 'bout in the bathroom this morning?

RUTH: No.

WALTER: How come you always try to be so pleasant!

RUTH: What is there to be pleasant 'bout!

WALTER: You want to know what I was thinking 'bout in the bathroom or not!

RUTH: I know what you thinking 'bout.

WALTER *(ignoring her):* 'Bout what me and Willy Harris was talking about last night.

RUTH *(immediately—a refrain):* Willy Harris is a good-for-nothing loudmouth.

WALTER: Anybody who talks to me has got to be a good-for-nothing loudmouth, ain't he? And what you know about who is just a good-for-nothing loudmouth? Charlie Atkins was just a "good-for-nothing loudmouth" too, wasn't he! When he wanted me to go in the dry-cleaning business with him. And now—he's grossing a hundred thousand a year. A hundred thousand dollars a year! You still call *him* a loudmouth!

RUTH *(bitterly):* Oh, Walter Lee . . .

(She folds her head on her arms over the table)

WALTER *(rising and coming to her and standing over her):* You tired, ain't you? Tired of everything. Me, the boy, the way we live—this beat-up hole—everything. Ain't you? *(She doesn't look up, doesn't answer)* So tired—moaning and groaning all the time, but you wouldn't do nothing to help, would you? You couldn't be on my side that long for nothing, could you?

RUTH: Walter, please leave me alone.

WALTER: A man needs for a woman to back him up . . .

RUTH: Walter—

WALTER: Mama would listen to you. You know she listen to you more than she do me and Bennie. She think more of you. All you have to do is just sit down with her when you drinking your coffee one morning and talking 'bout things like you do and— *(He sits down beside her and demonstrates graphically what he thinks her methods and tone should be)* —you just sip your coffee, see, and say easy like that you been thinking 'bout that deal Walter Lee is so interested in, 'bout the store and all, and sip some more coffee, like what you saying ain't really that important to you—And the next thing you know, she be listening good and asking you questions and when I come home—I can tell her the details. This ain't no fly-by-night proposition, baby. I mean we figured it out, me and Willy and Bobo.

RUTH *(with a frown)*: Bobo?

WALTER: Yeah. You see, this little liquor store we got in mind cost seventy-five thousand and we figured the initial investment on the place be 'bout thirty thousand, see. That be ten thousand each. Course, there's a couple of hundred you got to pay so's you don't spend your life just waiting for them clowns to let your license get approved—

RUTH: You mean graft?

WALTER *(frowning impatiently)*: Don't call it that. See there, that just goes to show you what women understand about the world. Baby, don't *nothing* happen for you in this world 'less you pay *somebody* off!

RUTH: Walter, leave me alone! *(She raises her head and stares at him vigorously—then says, more quietly) Eat* your eggs, they gonna be cold.

WALTER *(straightening up from her and looking off)*: That's it. There you are. Man say to his woman: I got me a dream. His woman say: Eat your eggs. *(Sadly, but gaining in power)* Man say: I got to take hold of this here world, baby! And a woman will say: Eat your eggs and go to work. *(Passionately now)* Man say: I got to change my life, I'm choking to death, baby! And his woman say— *(In utter anguish as he brings his fists down on his thighs)* —Your eggs is getting cold!

RUTH *(softly)*: Walter, that ain't none of our money.

WALTER *(not listening at all or even looking at her)*: This morning, I was lookin' in the mirror and thinking about it . . . I'm thirty-five years old; I been married eleven years and I got a boy who sleeps in the living room— *(Very, very quietly)* —and all I got to give him is stories about how rich white people live . . .

RUTH: Eat your eggs, Walter.

WALTER *(slams the table and jumps up)*: —DAMN MY EGGS—DAMN ALL THE EGGS THAT EVER WAS!

RUTH: Then go to work.

WALTER *(looking up at her)*: See—I'm trying to talk to you 'bout myself— *(Shaking his head with the repetition)* —and all you can say is eat them eggs and go to work.

RUTH *(wearily)*: Honey, you never say nothing new. I listen to you every day, every night and every morning, and you never say nothing new. *(Shrugging)* So you would rather *be* Mr. Arnold than be his chauffeur. So—I would *rather* be living in Buckingham Palace.

WALTER: That is just what is wrong with the colored woman in this world . . . Don't understand about building their men up and making 'em feel like they somebody. Like they can do something.

RUTH *(drily, but to hurt)*: There *are* colored men who do things.

WALTER: No thanks to the colored woman.

RUTH: Well, being a colored woman, I guess I can't help myself none.

(She rises and gets the ironing board and sets it up and attacks a huge pile of rough-dried clothes, sprinkling them in preparation for the ironing and then rolling them into tight fat balls)

WALTER *(mumbling):* We one group of men tied to a race of women with small minds!

(His sister BENEATHA *enters. She is about twenty, as slim and intense as her brother. She is not as pretty as her sister-in-law, but her lean, almost intellectual face has a handsomeness of its own. She wears a bright-red flannel nightie, and her thick hair stands wildly about her head. Her speech is a mixture of many things; it is different from the rest of the family's insofar as education has permeated her sense of English—and perhaps the Midwest rather than the South has finally—at last—won out in her inflection; but not altogether, because over all of it is a soft slurring and transformed use of vowels which is the decided influence of the Southside. She passes through the room without looking at either* RUTH *or* WALTER *and goes to the outside door and looks, a little blindly, out to the bathroom. She sees that it has been lost to the Johnsons. She closes the door with a sleepy vengeance and crosses to the table and sits down a little defeated)*

BENEATHA: I am going to start timing those people.

WALTER: You should get up earlier.

BENEATHA *(her face in her hands. She is still fighting the urge to go back to bed):* Really—would you suggest dawn? Where's the paper?

WALTER *(pushing the paper across the table to her as he studies her almost clinically, as though he has never seen her before):* You a horrible-looking chick at this hour.

BENEATHA *(drily):* Good morning, everybody.

WALTER *(senselessly):* How is school coming?

BENEATHA *(in the same spirit):* Lovely. Lovely. And you know, biology is the greatest. *(Looking up at him)* I dissected something that looked just like you yesterday.

WALTER: I just wondered if you've made up your mind and everything.

BENEATHA *(gaining in sharpness and impatience):* And what did I answer yesterday morning—and the day before that?

RUTH *(from the ironing board, like someone disinterested and old):* Don't be so nasty, Bennie.

BENEATHA *(still to her brother):* And the day before that and the day before that!

WALTER *(defensively):* I'm interested in you. Something wrong with that? Ain't many girls who decide—

WALTER *and* BENEATHA *(in unison):* —"to be a doctor."

(Silence)

WALTER: Have we figured out yet just exactly how much medical school is going to cost?

RUTH: Walter Lee, why don't you leave that girl alone and get out of here to work?

BENEATHA *(exits to the bathroom and bangs on the door):* Come on out of there, please!

(She comes back into the room)

WALTER *(looking at his sister intently):* You know the check is coming tomorrow.

BENEATHA *(turning on him with a sharpness all her own):* That money belongs to Mama, Walter, and it's for her to decide how she wants to use it. I don't care if she wants to buy a house or a rocket ship or just nail it up somewhere and look at it. It's hers. Not ours—*hers.*

WALTER *(bitterly):* Now ain't that fine! You just got your mother's interest at heart, ain't you, girl? You such a nice girl—but if Mama got that money she can always take a few thousand and help you through school too—can't she?

BENEATHA: I have never asked anyone around here to do anything for me!

WALTER: No! And the line between asking and just accepting when the time comes is big and wide—ain't it!

BENEATHA *(with fury):* What do you want from me, Brother—that I quit school or just drop dead, which!

WALTER: I don't want nothing but for you to stop acting holy 'round here. Me and Ruth done made some sacrifices for you—why can't you do something for the family?

RUTH: Walter, don't be dragging me in it.

WALTER: You are in it—Don't you get up and go work in somebody's kitchen for the last three years to help put clothes on her back?

RUTH: Oh, Walter—that's not fair . . .

WALTER: It ain't that nobody expects you to get on your knees and say thank you, Brother; thank you, Ruth; thank you, Mama—and thank you, Travis, for wearing the same pair of shoes for two semesters—

BENEATHA *(dropping to her knees):* Well—I *do*—all right?—thank everybody! And forgive me for ever wanting to be anything at all! *(Pursuing him on her knees across the floor)* FORGIVE ME, FORGIVE ME, FORGIVE ME!

RUTH: Please stop it! Your mama'll hear you.

WALTER: Who the hell told you you had to be a doctor? If you so crazy 'bout messing 'round with sick people—then go be a nurse like other women—or just get married and be quiet . . .

BENEATHA: Well—you finally got it said . . . It took you three years but you finally got it said. Walter, give up; leave me alone—it's Mama's money.

WALTER: *He was my father, too!*

BENEATHA: So what? He was mine, too—and Travis's grandfather—but the insurance money belongs to Mama. Picking on me is not going to make her give it to you to invest in any liquor stores— *(Underbreath, dropping into a chair)* —and I for one say, God bless Mama for that!

WALTER *(to* RUTH*):* See—did you hear? Did you hear!

RUTH: Honey, please go to work.

WALTER: Nobody in this house is ever going to understand me.

BENEATHA: Because you're a nut.

WALTER: Who's a nut?

BENEATHA: You—you are a nut. Thee is mad, boy.

WALTER *(looking at his wife and his sister from the door, very sadly):* The world's most backward race of people, and that's a fact.

BENEATHA *(turning slowly in her chair):* And then there are all those prophets who would lead us out of the wilderness— *(*WALTER *slams out of the house)* —into the swamps!

RUTH: Bennie, why you always gotta be pickin' on your brother? Can't you be a little sweeter sometimes? *(Door opens.* WALTER *walks in. He fumbles with his cap, starts to speak, clears throat, looks everywhere but at* RUTH*. Finally:)*

WALTER *(to* RUTH*):* I need some money for carfare.

RUTH *(looks at him, then warms; teasing, but tenderly):* Fifty cents? *(She goes to her bag and gets money)* Here—take a taxi!

*(*WALTER *exits.* MAMA *enters. She is a woman in her early sixties, full-bodied and strong. She is one of those women of a certain grace and beauty who wear it so unobtrusively that it takes a while to notice. Her dark-brown face is surrounded by the total whiteness of her hair, and being a woman who has adjusted to many things in life and overcome many more, her face is full of strength. She has, we can see, wit and faith of a kind that keep her eyes lit and full of interest and expectancy. She is, in a word, a beautiful woman. Her bearing is perhaps most like the noble bearing of the women of the Hereros of Southwest Africa—rather as if she imagines that as she walks she still bears a basket or a vessel upon her head. Her speech, on the other hand, is as careless as her carriage is precise—she is inclined to slur everything—but her voice is perhaps not so much quiet as simply soft)*

MAMA: Who that 'round here slamming doors at this hour?

(She crosses through the room, goes to the window, opens it, and brings in a feeble little plant growing doggedly in a small pot on the window sill. She feels the dirt and puts it back out)

RUTH: That was Walter Lee. He and Bennie was at it again.

MAMA: My children and they tempers. Lord, if this little old plant don't get more sun than it's been getting it ain't never going to see spring again. *(She turns from the window)* What's the matter with you this morning, Ruth? You looks right peaked. You aiming to iron all them things? Leave some for me. I'll get to 'em this afternoon. Bennie honey, it's too drafty for you to be sitting 'round half dressed. Where's your robe?

BENEATHA: In the cleaners.

MAMA: Well, go get mine and put it on.

BENEATHA: I'm not cold, Mama, honest.

MAMA: I know—but you so thin . . .

BENEATHA *(irritably):* Mama, I'm not cold.

MAMA *(seeing the make-down bed as* TRAVIS *has left it):* Lord have mercy, look at that poor bed. Bless his heart—he tries, don't he?

(She moves to the bed TRAVIS *has sloppily made up)*

RUTH: No—he don't half try at all 'cause he knows you going to come along behind him and fix everything. That's just how come he don't know how to do nothing right now—you done spoiled that boy so.

MAMA *(folding bedding):* Well—he's a little boy. Ain't supposed to know 'bout housekeeping. My baby, that's what he is. What you fix for his breakfast this morning?

RUTH *(angrily):* I feed my son, Lena!

MAMA: I ain't meddling— *(Under breath; busy-bodyish)* I just noticed all last week he had cold cereal, and when it starts getting this chilly in the fall a child ought to have some hot grits or something when he goes out in the cold—

RUTH *(furious):* I gave him hot oats—is that all right!

MAMA: I ain't meddling. *(Pause)* Put a lot of nice butter on it? *(*RUTH *shoots her an angry look and does not reply)* He likes lots of butter.

RUTH *(exasperated):* Lena—

MAMA *(to* BENEATHA. MAMA *is inclined to wander conversationally sometimes):* What was you and your brother fussing 'bout this morning?

BENEATHA: It's not important, Mama.

(She gets up and goes to look out at the bathroom, which is apparently free, and she picks up her towels and rushes out)

MAMA: What was they fighting about?

RUTH: Now you know as well as I do.

MAMA *(shaking her head):* Brother still worrying hisself sick about that money?

RUTH: You know he is.

MAMA: You had breakfast?

RUTH: Some coffee.

MAMA: Girl, you better start eating and looking after yourself better. You almost thin as Travis.

RUTH: Lena—

MAMA: Uh-hunh?

RUTH: What are you going to do with it?

MAMA: Now don't you start, child. It's too early in the morning to be talking about money. It ain't Christian.

RUTH: It's just that he got his heart set on that store—

MAMA: You mean that liquor store that Willy Harris want him to invest in?

RUTH: Yes—

MAMA: We ain't no business people, Ruth. We just plain working folks.

RUTH: Ain't nobody business people till they go into business. Walter Lee say colored people ain't never going to start getting ahead till they start gambling on some different kinds of things in the world—investments and things.

MAMA: What done got into you, girl? Walter Lee done finally sold you on investing.

RUTH: No. Mama, something is happening between Walter and me. I don't know what it is—but he needs something—something I can't give him any more. He needs this chance, Lena.

MAMA *(frowning deeply):* But liquor, honey—

RUTH: Well—like Walter say—I spec people going to always be drinking themselves some liquor.

RUTH: Well—whether they drinks it or not ain't none of my business. But whether I go into business selling it to 'em *is,* and I don't want that on my ledger this late in life. *(Stopping suddenly and studying her daughter-in-law)* Ruth Younger, what's the matter with you today? You look like you could fall over right there.

RUTH: I'm tired.

MAMA: Then you better stay home from work today.

RUTH: I can't stay home. She'd be calling up the agency and screaming at them, "My girl didn't come in today—send me somebody! My girl didn't come in!" Oh, she just have a fit . . .

MAMA: Well, let her have it. I'll just call her up and say you got the flu—

RUTH *(laughing):* Why the flu?

MAMA: 'Cause it sounds respectable to 'em. Something white people get, too. They know 'bout the flu. Otherwise they think you been cut up or something when you tell 'em you sick.

RUTH: I got to go in. We need the money.

MAMA: Somebody would of thought my children done all but starved to death the way they talk about money here late. Child, we got a great big old check coming tomorrow.

RUTH *(sincerely, but also self-righteously):* Now that's your money. It ain't got nothing to do with me. We all feel like that—Walter and Bennie and me—even Travis.

MAMA *(thoughtfully, and suddenly very far away):* Ten thousand dollars—

RUTH: Sure is wonderful.

MAMA: Ten thousand dollars.

RUTH: You know what you should do, Miss Lena? You should take yourself a trip somewhere. To Europe or South America or someplace—

MAMA *(throwing up her hands at the thought):* Oh, child!

RUTH: I'm serious. Just pack up and leave! Go on away and enjoy yourself some. Forget about the family and have yourself a ball for once in your life—

MAMA *(drily):* You sound like I'm just about ready to die. Who'd go with me? What I look like wandering 'round Europe by myself?

RUTH: Shoot—these here rich white women do it all the time. They don't think nothing of packing up they suitcases and piling on one of them big steamships and—swoosh!—they gone, child.

MAMA: Something always told me I wasn't no rich white woman.

RUTH: Well—what are you going to do with it then?

MAMA: I ain't rightly decided. *(Thinking. She speaks now with emphasis)* Some of it got to be put away for Beneatha and her schoolin'—and ain't nothing going to touch that part of it. Nothing. *(She waits several seconds, trying to make up her mind about something, and looks at* RUTH *a little tentatively before going on)* Been thinking that we maybe could meet the notes on a little old two-story somewhere, with a yard where Travis could play in the summertime, if we use part of the insurance for a down payment and everybody kind of pitch in. I could maybe take on a little day work again, few days a week—

RUTH *(studying her mother-in-law furtively and concentrating on her ironing, anxious to encourage without seeming to):* Well, Lord knows, we've put enough rent into this here rat trap to pay for four houses by now . . .

MAMA *(looking up at the words "rat trap" and then looking around and leaning back and sighing—in a suddenly reflective mood):* "Rat trap"—yes, that's all it is. *(Smiling)* I remember just as well the day me and Big Walter moved in here. Hadn't been married but two weeks and wasn't planning on living here no more than a year. *(She shakes her head at the dissolved dream)* We was going to set away, little by little, don't you know, and buy a little place out in Morgan Park. We had even picked out the house. *(Chuckling a little)* Looks right dumpy today. But Lord, child, you should know all the dreams I had 'bout buying that house and fixing it up and making me a little garden in the back— *(She waits and stops smiling)* And didn't none of it happen.

(Dropping her hands in a futile gesture)

RUTH *(keeps her head down, ironing):* Yes, life can be a barrel of disappointments, sometimes.

MAMA: Honey, Big Walter would come in here some nights back then and slump down on that couch there and just look at the rug, and look at me and look at the rug and then back at me—and I'd know he was down then . . . really down. *(After a second very long and thoughtful pause; she is seeing back to times that only she can see)* And then, Lord, when I lost that baby—little Claude—I almost thought I was going to lose Big Walter too. Oh, that man grieved hisself! He was one man to love his children.

RUTH: Ain't nothin' can tear at you like losin' your baby.

MAMA: I guess that's how come that man finally worked hisself to death like he done. Like he was fighting his own war with this here world that took his baby from him.

RUTH: He sure was a fine man, all right. I always liked Mr. Younger.

MAMA: Crazy 'bout his children! God knows there was plenty wrong with Walter Younger—hard-headed, mean, kind of wild with women—plenty wrong with him. But he sure loved his children. Always wanted them to have something—be something. That's where Brother gets all these notions, I reckon. Big Walter used to say, he'd get right wet in the eyes sometimes, lean his head back with the water standing in his eyes and say, "Seem like God didn't see fit to give the black man nothing but dreams—but He did give us children to make them dreams seem worth while." *(She smiles)* He could talk like that, don't you know.

RUTH: Yes, he sure could. He was a good man, Mr. Younger.

MAMA: Yes, a fine man—just couldn't never catch up with his dreams, that's all.

(BENEATHA comes in, brushing her hair and looking up to the ceiling, where the sound of a vacuum cleaner has started up)

BENEATHA: What could be so dirty on that woman's rugs that she has to vacuum them every single day?

RUTH: I wish certain young women 'round here who I could name would take inspiration about certain rugs in a certain apartment I could also mention.

BENEATHA *(shrugging)*: How much cleaning can a house need, for Christ's sakes.

MAMA *(not liking the Lord's name used thus)*: Bennie!

RUTH: Just listen to her—just listen!

BENEATHA: Oh, God!

MAMA: If you use the Lord's name just one more time—

BENEATHA *(a bit of a whine)*: Oh, Mama—

RUTH: Fresh—just fresh as salt, this girl!

BENEATHA *(drily)*: Well—if the salt loses its savor—

MAMA: Now that will do. I just ain't going to have you 'round here reciting the scriptures in vain—you hear me?

BENEATHA: How did I manage to get on everybody's wrong side by just walking into a room?

RUTH: If you weren't so fresh—

BENEATHA: Ruth, I'm twenty years old.

MAMA: What time you be home from school today?

BENEATHA: Kind of late. *(With enthusiasm)* Madeline is going to start my guitar lessons today.

(MAMA and RUTH look up with the same expression)

MAMA: Your *what* kind of lessons?

BENEATHA: Guitar.

RUTH: Oh, Father!

MAMA: How come you done taken it in your mind to learn to play the guitar?

BENEATHA: I just want to, that's all.

MAMA *(smiling)*: Lord, child, don't you know what to do with yourself? How long it going to be before you get tired of this now—like you got tired of that little play-acting group you joined last year? *(Looking at RUTH)* And what was it the year before that?

RUTH: The horseback-riding club for which she bought that fifty-five-dollar riding habit that's been hanging in the closet ever since!

MAMA *(to* BENEATHA*)*: Why you got to flit so from one thing to another, baby?

BENEATHA *(sharply)*: I just want to learn to play the guitar. Is there anything wrong with that?

MAMA: Ain't nobody trying to stop you. I just wonders sometimes why you has to flit so from one thing to another all the time. You ain't never done nothing with all that camera equipment you brought home—

BENEATHA: I don't flit! I—I experiment with different forms of expression—

RUTH: Like riding a horse?

BENEATHA: —People have to express themselves one way or another.

MAMA: What is it you want to express?

BENEATHA *(angrily)*: Me! *(*MAMA *and* RUTH *look at each other and burst into raucous laughter)* Don't worry—I don't expect you to understand.

MAMA *(to change the subject)*: Who you going out with tomorrow night?

BENEATHA *(with displeasure)*: George Murchison again.

MAMA *(pleased)*: Oh—you getting a little sweet on him?

RUTH: You ask me, this child ain't sweet on nobody but herself— *(Under breath)* Express herself!

(They laugh)

BENEATHA: Oh—I like George all right, Mama. I mean I like him enough to go out with him and stuff, but—

RUTH *(for devilment)*: What does *and stuff* mean?

BENEATHA: Mind your own business.

MAMA: Stop picking at her now, Ruth. *(She chuckles—then a suspicious sudden look at her daughter as she turns in her chair for emphasis)* What DOES it mean?

BENEATHA *(wearily)*: Oh, I just mean I couldn't ever really be serious about George. He's—he's so shallow.

RUTH: Shallow—what do you mean he's shallow? He's *Rich!*

MAMA: Hush, Ruth.

BENEATHA: I know he's rich. He knows he's rich, too.

RUTH: Well—what other qualities a man got to have to satisfy you, little girl?

BENEATHA: You wouldn't even begin to understand. Anybody who married Walter could not possibly understand.

MAMA *(outraged)*: What kind of way is that to talk about your brother?

BENEATHA: Brother is a flip—let's face it.

MAMA *(to* RUTH*, helplessly)*: What's a flip?

RUTH *(glad to add kindling)*: She's saying he's crazy.

BENEATHA: Not crazy. Brother isn't really crazy yet—he—he's an elaborate neurotic.

MAMA: Hush your mouth!

BENEATHA: As for George. Well. George looks good—he's got a beautiful car and he takes me to nice places and, as my sister-in-law says, he is probably the richest boy I will ever get to know and I even like him sometimes—but if the Youngers are sitting around waiting to see if their little Bennie is going to tie up the family with the Murchisons, they are wasting their time.

RUTH: You mean you wouldn't marry George Murchison if he asked you someday? That pretty, rich thing? Honey, I knew you was odd—

BENEATHA: No I would not marry him if all I felt for him was what I feel now. Besides, George's family wouldn't really like it.

MAMA: Why not?

BENEATHA: Oh, Mama—The Murchisons are honest-to-God-real-*live*-rich colored people, and the only people in the world who are more snobbish than rich white people are rich colored people. I thought everybody knew that. I've met Mrs. Murchison. She's a scene!

MAMA: You must not dislike people 'cause they well off, honey.

BENEATHA: Why not? It makes just as much sense as disliking people 'cause they are poor, and lots of people do that.

RUTH *(a wisdom-of-the-ages manner. To* MAMA*)*: Well, she'll get over some of this—

BENEATHA: Get over it? What are you talking about, Ruth? Listen, I'm going to be a doctor. I'm not worried about who I'm going to marry yet—if I ever get married.

MAMA *and* RUTH: *If!*

MAMA: Now, Bennie—

BENEATHA: Oh, I probably will . . . but first I'm going to be a doctor, and George, for one, still thinks that's pretty funny. I couldn't be bothered with that. I am going to be a doctor and everybody around here better understand that!

MAMA *(kindly)*: 'Course you going to be a doctor, honey, God willing.

BENEATHA *(drily)*: God hasn't got a thing to do with it.

MAMA: Beneatha—that just wasn't necessary.

BENEATHA: Well—neither is God. I get sick of hearing about God.

MAMA: Beneatha!

BENEATHA: I mean it! I'm just tired of hearing about God all the time. What has He got to do with anything? Does he pay tuition?

MAMA: You 'bout to get your fresh little jaw slapped!

RUTH: That's just what she needs, all right!

BENEATHA: Why? Why can't I say what I want to around here, like everybody else?

MAMA: It don't sound nice for a young girl to say things like that—you wasn't brought up that way. Me and your father went to trouble to get you and Brother to church every Sunday.

BENEATHA: Mama, you don't understand. It's all a matter of ideas, and God is just one idea I don't accept. It's not important. I am not going out and be immoral or commit crimes because I don't believe in God. I don't even think about it. It's just that I get tired of Him getting credit for all the things the human race achieves through its own stubborn effort. There simply is no blasted God—there is only man and it is *he* who makes miracles!

*(*MAMA *absorbs this speech, studies her daughter and rises slowly and crosses to* BENEATHA *and slaps her powerfully across the face. After, there is only silence and the daughter drops her eyes from her mother's face, and* MAMA *is very tall before her)*

MAMA: Now—you say after me, in my mother's house there is still God. *(There is a long pause and* BENEATHA *stares at the floor wordlessly.* MAMA *repeats the phrase with precision and cool emotion)* In my mother's house there is still God.

BENEATHA: In my mother's house there is still God.

(A long pause)

MAMA *(walking away from* BENEATHA, *too disturbed for triumphant posture. Stopping and turning back to her daughter):* There are some ideas we ain't going to have in this house. Not long as I am at the head of this family.

BENEATHA: Yes, ma'am.

*(*MAMA *walks out of the room)*

RUTH *(almost gently, with profound understanding):* You think you a woman, Bennie—but you still a little girl. What you did was childish—so you got treated like a child.

BENEATHA: I see. *(Quietly)* I also see that everybody thinks it's all right for Mama to be a tyrant. But all the tyranny in the world will never put a God in the heavens!

(She picks up her books and goes out. Pause)

RUTH *(goes to* MAMA*'s door):* She said she was sorry.

MAMA *(coming out, going to her plant):* They frightens me, Ruth. My children.

RUTH: You got good children, Lena. They just a little off sometimes—but they're good.

MAMA: No—there's something come down between me and them that don't let us understand each other and I don't know what it is. One done almost lost his mind thinking 'bout money all the time and the other done commence to talk about things I can't seem to understand in no form or fashion. What is it that's changing, Ruth.

RUTH *(soothingly, older than her years):* Now . . . you taking it all too seriously. You just got strong-willed children and it takes a strong woman like you to keep 'em in hand.

MAMA *(looking at her plant and sprinkling a little water on it):* They spirited all right, my children. Got to admit they got spirit—Bennie and Walter. Like this little old plant that ain't never had enough sunshine or nothing—and look at it . . .

(She has her back to RUTH, *who has had to stop ironing and lean against something and put the back of her hand to her forehead)*

RUTH *(trying to keep* MAMA *from noticing):* You . . . sure . . . loves that little old thing, don't you? . . .

MAMA: Well, I always wanted me a garden like I used to see sometimes at the back of the houses down home. This plant is close as I ever got to having one. *(She looks out of the window as she replaces the plant)* Lord, ain't nothing as dreary as the view from this window on a dreary day, is there? Why ain't you singing this morning, Ruth? Sing that "No Ways Tired." That song always lifts me up so— *(She turns at last to see that* RUTH *has slipped quietly to the floor, in a state of semiconsciousness)* Ruth! Ruth honey—what's the matter with you . . . Ruth!

Curtain

SCENE II

It is the following morning; a Saturday morning, and house cleaning is in progress at the YOUNGERS. *Furniture has been shoved hither and yon and* MAMA *is giving the kitchen-area walls a washing down.* BENEATHA, *in dungarees, with a handkerchief tied around her face, is spraying*

insecticide into the cracks in the walls. As they work, the radio is on and a Southside disk-jockey program is inappropriately filling the house with a rather exotic saxophone blues. TRAVIS, *the sole idle one, is leaning on his arms, looking out of the window.*

TRAVIS: Grandmama, that stuff Bennie is using smells awful. Can I go downstairs, please?
MAMA: Did you get all them chores done already? I ain't seen you doing much.
TRAVIS: Yes'm—finished early. Where did Mama go this morning?
MAMA *(looking at* BENEATHA*)*: She had to go on a little errand.

(The phone rings. BENEATHA *runs to answer it and reaches it before* WALTER, *who has entered from bedroom)*

TRAVIS: Where?
MAMA: To tend to her business.
BENEATHA: Haylo . . . *(Disappointed)* Yes, he is. *(She tosses the phone to* WALTER, *who barely catches it)* It's Willy Harris again.
WALTER *(as privately as possible under* MAMA*'s gaze)*: Hello, Willy. Did you get the papers from the lawyer? . . . No, not yet. I told you the mailman doesn't get here till ten-thirty . . . No, I'll come there . . . Yeah! Right away. *(He hangs up and goes for his coat)*
BENEATHA: Brother, where did Ruth go?
WALTER *(as he exits)*: How should I know!
TRAVIS: Aw come on, Grandma. Can I go outside?
MAMA: Oh, I guess so. You stay right in front of the house, though, and keep a good lookout for the postman.
TRAVIS: Yes'm. *(He darts into bedroom for stickball and bat, reenters, and sees* BENEATHA *on her knees spraying under the sofa with behind upraised. He edges closer to the target, takes aim, and lets her have it. She screams)* Leave them poor little cockroaches alone, they ain't bothering you none! *(He runs as she swings the spray-gun at him viciously and playfully)* Grandma! Grandma!
MAMA: Look out there, girl, before you be spilling some of that stuff on that child!
TRAVIS *(safely behind the bastion of* MAMA*)*: That's right—look out, now! *(He exits)*
BENEATHA *(drily)*: I can't imagine that it would hurt him—it has never hurt the roaches.
MAMA: Well, little boys' hides ain't as tough as Southside roaches. You better get over there behind the bureau. I seen one marching out of there like Napoleon yesterday.
BENEATHA: There's really only one way to get rid of them, Mama—
MAMA: How?
BENEATHA: Set fire to this building! Mama, where did Ruth go?
MAMA *(looking at her with meaning)*: To the doctor, I think.
BENEATHA: The doctor? What's the matter? *(They exchange glances)* You don't think—
MAMA *(with her sense of drama)*: Now I ain't saying what I think. But I ain't never been wrong 'bout a woman neither.

(The phone rings)

BENEATHA *(at the phone)*: Hay-lo . . . *(Pause, and a moment of recognition)* Well—when did you get back! . . . And how was it? . . . Of course I've missed you—in my way . . . This morning? No . . . house cleaning and all that and Mama hates it if I let people come over when the house is like this . . . You *have?* Well, that's different . . . What is it—Oh, what the hell, come on over . . . Right, see you then. *Arrividerci.*

(She hangs up)

MAMA *(who has listened vigorously, as is her habit):* Who is that you inviting over here with this house looking like this? You ain't got the pride you was born with!

BENEATHA: Asagai doesn't care how houses look, Mama—he's an intellectual.

MAMA: *Who?*

BENEATHA: Asagai—Joseph Asagai. He's an African boy I met on campus. He's been studying in Canada all summer.

MAMA: What's his name?

BENEATHA: Asagai, Joseph. Ah-sah-guy . . . He's from Nigeria.

MAMA: Oh, that's the little country that was founded by slaves way back . . .

BENEATHA: No, Mama—that's Liberia.

MAMA: I don't think I never met no African before.

BENEATHA: Well, do me a favor and don't ask him a whole lot of ignorant questions about Africans. I mean, do they wear clothes and all that—

MAMA: Well, now, I guess if you think we so ignorant 'round here maybe you shouldn't bring your friends here—

BENEATHA: It's just that people ask such crazy things. All anyone seems to know about when it comes to Africa is Tarzan—

MAMA *(indignantly):* Why should I know anything about Africa?

BENEATHA: Why do you give money at church for the missionary work?

MAMA: Well, that's to help save people.

BENEATHA: You mean save them from *heathenism—*

MAMA *(innocently):* Yes.

BENEATHA: I'm afraid they need more salvation from the British and the French.

(RUTH comes in forlornly and pulls off her coat with dejection. They both turn to look at her)

RUTH *(dispiritedly):* Well, I guess from all the happy faces—everybody knows.

BENEATHA: You pregnant?

MAMA: Lord have mercy, I sure hope it's a little old girl. Travis ought to have a sister.

(BENEATHA and RUTH give her a hopeless look for this grandmotherly enthusiasm)

BENEATHA: How far along are you?

RUTH: Two months.

BENEATHA: Did you mean to? I mean did you plan it or was it an accident?

MAMA: What do you know about planning or not planning?

BENEATHA: Oh, Mama.

RUTH *(wearily):* She's twenty years old, Lena.

BENEATHA: Did you plan it, Ruth?

RUTH: Mind your own business.

BENEATHA: It is my business—where is he going to live, on the *roof? (There is silence following*

the remark as the three women react to the sense of it) Gee—I didn't mean that, Ruth, honest. Gee, I don't feel like that at all. I—I think it is wonderful.

RUTH *(dully)*: Wonderful.

BENEATHA: Yes—really.

MAMA *(looking at* RUTH*, worried)*: Doctor say everything going to be all right?

RUTH *(far away)*: Yes—she says everything is going to be fine . . .

MAMA *(immediately suspicious)*: "She"—What doctor you went to?

*(*RUTH *folds over, near hysteria)*

MAMA *(worriedly hovering over* RUTH*)*: Ruth honey—what's the matter with you—you sick?

*(*RUTH *has her fists clenched on her thighs and is fighting hard to suppress a scream that seems to be rising in her)*

BENEATHA: What's the matter with her, Mama?

MAMA *(working her fingers in* RUTH*'s shoulders to relax her)*: She be all right. Women gets right depressed sometimes when they get her way. *(Speaking softly, expertly, rapidly)* Now you just relax. That's right . . . just lean back, don't think 'bout nothing at all . . . nothing at all—

RUTH: I'm all right . . .

(The glassy-eyed look melts and then she collapses into a fit of heavy sobbing. The bell rings)

BENEATHA: Oh, my God—that must be Asagai.

MAMA *(to* RUTH*)*: Come on now, honey. You need to lie down and rest awhile . . . then have some nice hot food.

(They exit, RUTH*'s weight on her mother-in-law.* BENEATHA*, herself profoundly disturbed, opens the door to admit a rather dramatic-looking young man with a large package)*

ASAGAI: Hello, Alaiyo—

BENEATHA *(holding the door open and regarding him with pleasure)*: Hello . . . *(Long pause)* Well—come in. And please excuse everything. My mother was very upset about my letting anyone come here with the place like this.

ASAGAI *(coming into the room)*: You look disturbed too . . . Is something wrong?

BENEATHA *(still at the door, absently)*: Yes . . . we've all got acute ghetto-itus. *(She smiles and comes toward him, finding a cigarette and sitting)* So—sit down! No! Wait! *(She whips the spraygun off sofa where she had left it and puts the cushions back. At last perches on arm of sofa. He sits)* So, how was Canada?

ASAGAI *(a sophisticate)*: Canadian.

BENEATHA *(looking at him)*: Asagai, I'm very glad you are back.

ASAGAI *(looking back at her in turn)*: Are you really?

BENEATHA: Yes—very.

ASAGAI: Why?—you were quite glad when I went away. What happened?

BENEATHA: You went away.

ASAGAI: Ahhhhhhhh.

BENEATHA: Before—you wanted to be so serious before there was time.

ASAGAI: How much time must there be before one knows what one feels?

BENEATHA *(stalling this particular conversation. Her hands presed together, in a deliberately childish gesture):* What did you bring me?

ASAGAI *(handing her the package):* Open it and see.

BENEATHA *(eagerly opening the package and drawing out some records and the colorful robes of a Nigerian woman):* Oh, Asagai! . . . You got them for me! . . . How beautiful . . . and the records too! *(She lifts out the robes and runs to the mirror with them and holds the drapery up in front of herself)*

ASAGAI *(coming to her at the mirror):* I shall have to teach you how to drape it properly. *(He flings the material about her for the moment and stands back to look at her)* Ah—*Oh-pay-gay-day, oh-gbah-mu-shay. (A Yoruba exclamation for admiration)* You wear it well . . . very well . . . mutilated hair and all.

BENEATHA *(turning suddenly):* My hair—what's wrong with my hair?

ASAGAI *(shrugging):* Were you born with it like that?

BENEATHA *(reaching up to touch it):* No . . . of course not.

(She looks back to the mirror, disturbed)

ASAGAI *(smiling):* How then?

BENEATHA: You know prefectly well how . . . as crinkly as yours . . . that's how.

ASAGAI: And it is ugly to you that way?

BENEATHA *(quickly):* Oh, no—not ugly . . . *(More slowly, apologetically)* But it's so hard to manage when it's, well—raw.

ASAGAI: And so to accommodate that—you mutilate it every week?

BENEATHA: It's not mutilation!

ASAGAI *(laughing aloud at her seriousness):* Oh . . . please! I am only teasing you because you are so very serious about these things. *(He stands back from her and folds his arms across his chest as he watches her pulling at her hair and frowning in the mirror)* Do you remember the first time you met me at school? . . . *(He laughs)* You came up to me and you said—and I thought you were the most serious little thing I had ever seen—you said: *(He imitates her)* "Mr. Asagai—I want very much to talk with you. About Africa. You see, Mr. Asagai, I am looking for my *identity!*"

(He laughs)

BENEATHA *(turning to him, not laughing):* Yes—

(Her face is quizzical, profoundly disturbed)

ASAGAI *(still teasing and reaching out and taking her face in his hands and turning her profile to him):* Well . . . it is true that this is not so much a profile of a Hollywood queen as perhaps a queen of the Nile— *(A mock dismissal of the importance of the question)* But what does it matter? Assimilationism is so popular in your country.

BENEATHA *(wheeling, passionately, sharply):* I am not an assimilationist!

ASAGAI *(the protest hangs in the room for a moment and* ASAGAI *studies her, his laughter fad-*

ing): Such a serious one. *(There is a pause)* So—you like the robes? You must take excellent care of them—they are from my sister's personal wardrobe.

BENEATHA *(with incredulity):* You—you sent all the way home—for me?

ASAGAI *(with charm):* For you—I would do much more . . . Well, that is what I came for. I must go.

BENEATHA: Will you call me Monday?

ASAGAI: Yes . . . We have a great deal to talk about. I mean about identity and time and all that.

BENEATHA: Time?

ASAGAI: Yes. About how much time one needs to know what one feels.

BENEATHA: You see! You never understood that there is more than one kind of feeling which can exist between a man and a woman—or, at least, there should be.

ASAGAI *(shaking his head negatively but gently):* No. Between a man and a woman there need be only one kind of feeling. I have that for you . . . Now even . . . right this moment . . .

BENEATHA: I know—and by itself—it won't do. I can find that anywhere.

ASAGAI: For a woman it should be enough.

BENEATHA: I know—because that's what it says in all the novels that men write. But it isn't. Go ahead and laugh—but I'm not interested in being someone's little episode in America or— *(With feminine vengeance)* —one of them! *(ASAGAI has burst into laughter again)* That's funny as hell, huh!

ASAGAI: It's just that every American girl I have known has said that to me. White—black—in this you are all the same. And the same speech, too!

BENEATHA *(angrily):* Yuk, yuk, yuk!

ASAGAI: It's how you can be sure that the world's most liberated women are not liberated at all. You all talk about it too much!

(MAMA enters and is immediately all social charm because of the presence of a guest)

BENEATHA: Oh—Mama—this is Mr. Asagai.

MAMA: How do you do?

ASAGAI *(total politeness to an elder):* How do you do, Mrs. Younger. Please forgive me for coming at such an outrageous hour on a Saturday.

MAMA: Well, you are quite welcome. I just hope you understand that our house don't always look like this. *(Chatterish)* You must come again. I would love to hear all about— *(Not sure of the name)* —your country. I think it's so sad the way our American Negroes don't know nothing about Africa 'cept Tarzan and all that. And all that money they pour into these churches when they ought to be helping you people over there drive out them French and Englishmen done taken away your land.

(The mother flashes a slightly superior look at her daughter upon completion of the recitation)

ASAGAI *(taken aback by this sudden and acutely unrelated expression of sympathy):* Yes . . . yes . . .

MAMA *(smiling at him suddenly and relaxing and looking him over):* How many miles is it from here to where you come from?

ASAGAI: Many thousands.

MAMA *(looking at him as she would* WALTER*):* I bet you don't half look after yourself, being away from your mama either. I spec you better come 'round here from time to time to get yourself some decent home-cooked meals . . .

ASAGAI *(moved):* Thank you. Thank you very much. *(They are all quiet, then—)* Well . . . I must go. I will call you Monday, Alaiyo.

MAMA: What's that he call you?

ASAGAI: Oh—"Alaiyo." I hope you don't mind. It is what you would call a nickname, I think. It is a Yoruba word. I am a Yoruba.

MAMA *(looking at* BENEATHA*):* I—I thought he was from— *(Uncertain)*

ASAGAI *(understanding):* Nigeria is my country. Yoruba is my tribal origin—

BENEATHA: You didn't tell us what Alaiyo means . . . for all I know, you might be calling me Little Idiot or something . . .

ASAGAI: Well . . . let me see . . . I do not know how just to explain it . . . The sense of a thing can be so different when it changes languages.

BENEATHA: You're evading.

ASAGAI: No—really it is difficult . . . *(Thinking)* It means . . . it means One for Whom Bread—Food—Is Not Enough. *(He looks at her)* Is that all right?

BENEATHA *(understanding, softly):* Thank you.

MAMA *(looking from one to the other and not understanding any of it):* Well . . . that's nice . . . You must come see us again—Mr.——

ASAGAI: Ah-sah-guy . . .

MAMA: Yes . . . Do come again.

ASAGAI: Good-bye.

(He exits)

MAMA *(after him):* Lord, that's a pretty thing just went out here! *(Insinuatingly, to her daughter)* Yes, I guess I see why we done commence to get so interested in Africa 'round here. Missionaries my aunt Jenny!

(She exits)

BENEATHA: Oh, Mama! . . .

(She picks up the Nigerian dress and holds it up to her in front of the mirror again. She sets the headdress on haphazardly and then notices her hair again and clutches at it and then replaces the headdress and frowns at herself. Then she starts to wriggle in front of the mirror as she thinks a Nigerian woman might. TRAVIS *enters and stands regarding her)*

TRAVIS: What's the matter, girl, you cracking up?

BENEATHA: Shut up.

(She pulls the headdress off and looks at herself in the mirror and clutches at her hair again and squinches her eyes as if trying to imagine something. Then, suddenly, she gets her raincoat and kerchief and hurriedly prepares for going out)

MAMA *(coming back into the room):* She's resting now. Travis, baby, run next door and ask Miss Johnson to please let me have a little kitchen cleanser. This here can is empty as Jacob's kettle.

TRAVIS: I just came in.

MAMA: Do as you told. *(He exits and she looks at her daughter)* Where you going?

BENEATHA *(halting at the door):* To become a queen of the Nile!

(She exits in a breathless blaze of glory. RUTH *appears in the bedroom doorway)*

MAMA: Who told you to get up?

RUTH: Ain't nothing wrong with me to be lying in no bed for. Where did Bennie go?

MAMA *(drumming her fingers):* Far as I could make out—to Egypt. *(*RUTH *just looks at her)* What time is it getting to?

RUTH: Ten twenty. And the mailman going to ring that bell this morning just like he done every morning for the last umpteen years.

*(*TRAVIS *comes in with the cleanser can)*

TRAVIS: She say to tell you that she don't have much.

MAMA *(angrily):* Lord, some people I could name sure is tight-fisted! *(Directing her grandson)* Mark two cans of cleanser down on the list there. If she that hard up for kitchen cleanser, I sure don't want to forget to get her none!

RUTH: Lena—maybe the woman is just short on cleanser—

MAMA *(not listening):* —Much baking powder as she done borrowed from me all these years, she could of done gone into the baking business!

(The bell sounds suddenly and sharply and all three are stunned—serious and silent—mid-speech. In spite of all the other conversations and distractions of the morning, this is what they have been waiting for, even TRAVIS*, who looks helplessly from his mother to his grandmother.* RUTH *is the first to come to life again)*

RUTH *(to* TRAVIS*): Get down them steps, boy!*

*(*TRAVIS *snaps to life and flies out to get the mail)*

MAMA *(her eyes wide, her hand to her breast):* You mean it done really come?

RUTH *(excited):* Oh, Miss Lena!

MAMA *(collecting herself):* Well . . . I don't know what we all so excited about 'round here for. We known it was coming for months.

RUTH: That's a whole lot different from having it come and being able to hold it in your hands . . . a piece of paper worth ten thousand dollars . . . *(*TRAVIS *bursts back into the room. He holds the envelope high above his head, like a little dancer, his face is radiant and he is breathless. He moves to his grandmother with sudden slow ceremony and puts the envelope into her hands. She accepts it, and then merely holds it and looks at it)* Come on! Open it . . . Lord have mercy, I wish Walter Lee was here!

TRAVIS: Open it, Grandmama!

MAMA *(staring at it):* Now you all be quiet. It's just a check.

RUTH: Open it . . .

MAMA *(still staring at it):* Now don't act silly . . . We ain't never been no people to act silly 'bout no money—

RUTH *(swiftly):* We ain't never had none before—OPEN IT!

(MAMA finally makes a good strong tear and pulls out the thin blue slice of paper and inspects it closely. The boy and his mother study it raptly over MAMA's shoulders)

MAMA: *Travis! (She is counting off with doubt)* Is that the right number of zeros?

TRAVIS: Yes'm . . . ten thousand dollars. Gaalee, Grandmama, you rich.

MAMA *(she holds the check away from her, still looking at it. Slowly her face sobers into a mask of unhappiness):* Ten thousand dollars. *(She hands it to RUTH)* Put it away somewhere, Ruth. *(She does not look at RUTH; her eyes seem to be seeing something somewhere very far off)* Ten thousand dollars they give you. Ten thousand dollars.

TRAVIS *(to his mother, sincerely):* What's the matter with Grandmama—don't she want to be rich?

RUTH *(distractedly):* You go on out and play now, baby. *(TRAVIS exits. MAMA starts wiping dishes absently, humming intently to herself. RUTH turns to her, with kind exasperation)* You've gone and got yourself upset.

MAMA *(not looking at her):* I spec if it wasn't for you all . . . I would just put that money away or give it to the church or something.

RUTH: Now what kind of talk is that. Mr. Younger would just be plain mad if he could hear you talking foolish like that.

MAMA *(stopping and staring off):* Yes . . . he sure would. *(Sighing)* We got enough to do with that money, all right. *(She halts then, and turns and looks at her daughter-in-law hard; RUTH avoids her eyes and MAMA wipes her hands with finality and starts to speak firmly to RUTH)* Where did you go today, girl?

RUTH: To the doctor.

MAMA *(impatiently):* Now, Ruth . . . you know better than that. Old Doctor Jones is strange enough in his way but there ain't nothing 'bout him make somebody slip and call him "she"—like you done this morning.

RUTH: Well, that's what happened—my tongue slipped.

MAMA: You went to see that woman, didn't you?

RUTH *(defensively, giving herself away):* What woman you talking about?

MAMA *(angrily):* That woman who—

(WALTER enters in great excitement)

WALTER: Did it come?

MAMA *(quietly):* Can't you give people a Christian greeting before you start asking about money?

WALTER *(to RUTH):* Did it come? *(RUTH unfolds the check and lays it quietly before him, watching him intently with thoughts of her own. WALTER sits down and grasps it close and counts off the zeros)* Ten thousand dollars— *(He turns suddenly, frantically to his mother and draws some papers out of his breast pocket)* Mama—look. Old Willy Harris put everything on paper—

MAMA: Son—I think you ought to talk to your wife . . . I'll go on out and leave you alone if you want—

WALTER: I can talk to her later—Mama, look—

MAMA: Son—

WALTER: WILL SOMEBODY PLEASE LISTEN TO ME TODAY!

MAMA *(quietly):* I don't 'low no yellin' in this house, Walter Lee, and you know it— *(*WALTER *stares at them in frustration and starts to speak several times)* And there ain't going to be no investing in no liquor stores.

WALTER: But, Mama, you ain't even looked at it.

MAMA: I don't aim to have to speak on that again.

(A long pause)

WALTER: You ain't looked at it and you don't aim to have to speak on that again? You ain't even looked at it and *you* have decided— *(Crumpling his papers)* Well, *you* tell that to my boy tonight when you put him to sleep on the living-room couch . . . *(Turning to* MAMA *and speaking directly to her)* Yeah—and tell it to my wife, Mama, tomorrow when she has to go out of here to look after somebody else's kids. And tell it to *me,* Mama, every time we need a new pair of curtains and I have to watch *you* go out and work in somebody's kitchen. Yeah, you tell me then!

*(*WALTER *starts out)*

RUTH: Where you going?

WALTER: I'm going out!

RUTH: Where?

WALTER: Just out of this house somewhere—

RUTH *(getting her coat):* I'll come too.

WALTER: I don't want you to come!

RUTH: I got something to talk to you about, Walter.

WALTER: That's too bad.

MAMA *(still quietly):* Walter Lee— *(She waits and he finally turns and looks at her)* Sit down.

WALTER: I'm a grown man, Mama.

MAMA: Ain't nobody said you wasn't grown. But you still in my house and my presence. And as long as you are—you'll talk to your wife civil. Now sit down.

RUTH *(suddenly):* Oh, let him go on out and drink himself to death! He makes me sick to my stomach! *(She flings her coat against him and exits to bedroom)*

WALTER *(violently flinging the coat after her):* And you turn mine too, baby! *(The door slams behind her)* That was my biggest mistake—

MAMA *(still quietly):* Walter, what is the matter with you?

WALTER: Matter with me? Aint' nothing the matter with *me!*

MAMA: Yes there is. Something eating you up like a crazy man. Something more than me not giving you this money. The past few years I been watching it happen to you. You get all nervous acting and kind of wild in the eyes— *(*WALTER *jumps up impatiently at her words)* I said sit there now, I'm talking to you!

WALTER: Mama—I don't need no nagging at me today.

MAMA: Seem like you getting to a place where you always tied up in some kind of knot about something. But if anybody ask you 'bout it you just yell at 'em and bust out the house and go out and drink somewheres. Walter Lee, people can't live with that. Ruth's a good, patient girl in her way—but you getting to be too much. Boy, don't make the mistake of driving that girl away from you.

WALTER: Why—what she do for me?

MAMA: She loves you.

WALTER: Mama—I'm going out. I want to go off somewhere and be by myself for a while.

MAMA: I'm sorry 'bout your liquor store, son. It just wasn't the thing for us to do. That's what I want to tell you about—

WALTER: I got to go out, Mama—

(He rises)

MAMA: It's dangerous, son.

WALTER: What's dangerous?

MAMA: When a man goes outside his home to look for peace.

WALTER *(beseechingly):* Then why can't there never be no peace in this house then?

MAMA: You done found it in some other house?

WALTER: No—there ain't no woman! Why do women always think there's a woman somewhere when a man gets restless. *(Picks up the check)* Do you know what this money means to me? Do you know what this money can do for us? *(Puts it back)* Mama—Mama—I want so many things . . .

MAMA: Yes, son—

WALTER: I want so many things that they are driving me kind of crazy . . . Mama—look at me.

MAMA: I'm looking at you. You a good-looking boy. You got a job, a nice wife, a fine boy and—

WALTER: A job. *(Looks at her)* Mama, a job? I open and close car doors all day long. I drive a man around in his limousine and I say, "Yes, sir; no, sir; very good, sir; shall I take the Drive, sir?" Mama, that ain't no kind of job . . . that ain't nothing at all. *(Very quietly)* Mama, I don't know if I can make you understand.

MAMA: Understand what, baby?

WALTER *(quietly):* Sometimes it's like I can see the future stretched out in front of me—just plain as day. The future, Mama. Hanging over there at the edge of my days. Just waiting for me—a big, looming blank space—full of *nothing.* Just waiting for *me.* But it don't have to be. *(Pause. Kneeling beside her chair)* Mama—sometimes when I'm downtown and I pass them cool, quiet-looking restaurants where them white boys are sitting back and talking 'bout things . . . sitting there turning deals worth millions of dollars . . . sometimes I see guys don't look much older than me—

MAMA: Son—how come you talk so much 'bout money?

WALTER *(with immense passion):* Because it is life, Mama!

MAMA *(quietly):* Oh— *(Very quietly)* So now it's life. Money is life. Once upon a time freedom used to be life—now it's money. I guess the world really do change . . .

WALTER: No—it was always money, Mama. We just didn't know about it.

MAMA: No . . . something has changed. *(She looks at him)* You something new, boy. In my time we was worried about not being lynched and getting to the North if we could and how to stay alive and still have a pinch of dignity too . . . Now here come you and

Beneatha—talking 'bout things we ain't never even thought about hardly, me and your daddy. You ain't satisfied or proud of nothing we done. I mean that you had a home; that we kept you out of trouble till you was grown; that you don't have to ride to work on the back of nobody's streetcar—You my children—but how different we done become.

WALTER *(a long beat. He pats her hand and gets up)*: You just don't understand, Mama, you just don't understand.

MAMA: Son—do you know your wife is expecting another baby? *(*WALTER *stands, stunned, and absorbs what his mother has said)* That's what she wanted to talk to you about. *(*WALTER *sinks down into a chair)* This ain't for me to be telling—but you ought to know. *(She waits)* I think Ruth is thinking 'bout getting rid of that child.

WALTER *(slowly understanding)*: —No—no—Ruth wouldn't do that.

MAMA: When the world gets ugly enough—a woman will do anything for her family. *The part that's already living.*

WALTER: You don't know Ruth, Mama, if you think she would do that.

*(*RUTH *opens the bedroom door and stands there a little limp)*

RUTH *(beaten)*: Yes I would too, Walter. *(Pause)* I gave her a five-dollar down payment.

(There is total silence as the man stares at his wife and the mother stares at her son)

MAMA *(presently)*: Well— *(Tightly)* Well—son, I'm waiting to hear you say something . . . *(She waits)* I'm waiting to hear how you be your father's son. Be the man he was . . . *(Pause. The silence shouts)* Your wife say she going to destroy your child. And I'm waiting to hear you talk like him and say we a people who give children life, not who destroys them— *(She rises)* I'm waiting to see you stand up and look like your daddy and say we done give up one baby to poverty and that we ain't going to give up nary another one . . . I'm waiting.

WALTER: Ruth— *(He can say nothing)*

MAMA: If you a son of mine, tell her! *(*WALTER *picks up his keys and his coat and walks out. She continues, bitterly)* You . . . you are a disgrace to your father's memory. Somebody get me my hat!

Curtain

ACT II

SCENE I

TIME: *Later the same day.*

AT RISE: RUTH *is ironing again. She has the radio going. Presently* BENEATHA'*s bedroom door opens and* RUTH'*s mouth falls and she puts down the iron in fascination.*

RUTH: What have we got on tonight!

BENEATHA *(emerging grandly from the doorway so that we can see her thoroughly robed in the*

costume Asagai brought): You are looking at what a well-dressed Nigerian woman wears— *(She parades for* RUTH, *her hair completely hidden by the headdress; she is coquettishly fanning herself with an ornate oriental fan, mistakenly more like Butterfly than any Nigerian that ever was)* Isn't it beautiful? *(She promenades to the radio and, with an arrogant flourish, turns off the good loud blues that is playing)* Enough of this assimilationist junk! *(*RUTH *follows her with her eyes as she goes to the phonograph and puts on a record and turns and waits ceremoniously for the music to come up. Then, with a shout—)* OCOMOGOSIAY!

*(*RUTH *jumps. The music comes up, a lovely Nigerian melody.* BENEATHA *listens, enraptured, her eyes far away—"back to the past." She begins to dance.* RUTH *is dumbfounded)*

RUTH: What kind of dance is that?

BENEATHA: A folk dance.

RUTH *(Pearl Bailey):* What kind of folks do that, honey?

BENEATHA: It's from Nigeria. It's a dance of welcome.

RUTH: Who you welcoming?

BENEATHA: The men back to the village.

RUTH: Where they been?

BENEATHA: How should I know—out hunting or something. Anyway, they are coming back now . . .

RUTH: Well, that's good.

BENEATHA *(with the record):*

Alundi, alundi
Alundi alunya
Jop pu à jeepua
Ang gu soooooooooo

Ai yai yae . . .
Ayehaye—alundi . . .

*(*WALTER *comes in during this performance; he has obviously been drinking. He leans against the door heavily and watches his sister, at first with distaste. Then his eyes look off—"back to the past"—as he lifts both his fists to the roof, screaming)*

WALTER: YEAH . . . AND ETHIOPIA STRETCH FORTH HER HANDS AGAIN! . . .

RUTH *(drily, looking at him):* Yes—and Africa sure is claiming her own tonight. *(She gives them both up and starts ironing again)*

WALTER *(all in a drunken, dramatic shout):* Shut up! . . . I'm digging them drums . . . them drums move me! . . . *(He makes his weaving way to his wife's face and leans in close to her)* In my *heart of hearts*— *(He thumps his chest)* —I am much warrior!

RUTH *(without even looking up):* In your heart of hearts you are much drunkard.

WALTER *(coming away from her and starting to wander around the room, shouting):* Me and Jomo . . . *(Intently, in his sister's face. She has stopped dancing to watch him in this unknown mood)* That's my man, Kenyatta. *(Shouting and thumping his chest)* FLAMING SPEAR! HOT DAMN! *(He is suddenly in possession of an imaginary spear and actively spearing enemies all over the room)* *OCOMOGOSIAY* . . .

BENEATHA *(to encourage* WALTER, *thoroughly caught up with this side of him): OCOMOGOSIAY,* FLAMING SPEAR!

WALTER: THE LION IS WAKING . . . OWIMOWEH!

(He pulls his shirt open and leaps up on the table and gestures with his spear)

BENEATHA: OWIMOWEH!

WALTER *(on the table, very far gone, his eyes pure glass sheets. He sees what we cannot, that he is a leader of his people, a great chief, a descendant of Chaka, and that the hour to march has come):* Listen, my black brothers—

BENEATHA: OCOMOGOSIAY!

WALTER: —Do you hear the waters rushing against the shores of the coastlands—

BENEATHA: OCOMOGOSIAY!

WALTER: —Do you hear the screeching of the cocks in yonder hills beyond where the chiefs meet in council for the coming of the mighty war—

BENEATHA: OCOMOGOSIAY!

(And now the lighting shifts subtly to suggest the world of WALTER*'s imagination, and the mood shifts from pure comedy. It is the inner* WALTER *speaking: the Southside chauffeur has assumed an unexpected majesty)*

WALTER: —Do you hear the beating of the wings of the birds flying low over the mountains and the low places of our land—

BENEATHA: OCOMOGOSIAY!

WALTER: —Do you hear the singing of the women, singing the war songs of our fathers to the babies in the great houses? Singing the sweet war songs! *(The doorbell rings)* OH, DO YOU HEAR, MY *BLACK* BROTHERS!

BENEATHA *(completely gone):* We hear you, Flaming Spear—

*(*RUTH *shuts off the phonograph and opens the door.* GEORGE MURCHISON *enters)*

WALTER: Telling us to prepare for the GREATNESS OF THE TIME! *(Lights back to normal. He turns and sees* GEORGE*)* Black Brother!

(He extends his hand for the fraternal clasp)

GEORGE: Black Brother, hell!

RUTH *(having had enough, and embarrassed for the family):* Beneatha, you got company—what's the matter with you? Walter Lee Younger, get down off that table and stop acting like a fool . . .

*(*WALTER *comes down off the table suddenly and makes a quick exit to the bathroom)*

RUTH: He's had a little to drink . . . I don't know what her excuse is.

GEORGE *(to* BENEATHA*):* Look honey, we're going *to* the theatre—we're not going to be *in* it . . . so go change, huh?

*(*BENEATHA *looks at him and slowly, ceremoniously, lifts her hands and pulls off the headdress. Her hair is close-cropped and unstraightened.* GEORGE *freezes mid-sentence and* RUTH*'s eyes all but fall out of her head)*

GEORGE: What in the name of—

RUTH *(touching* BENEATHA*'s hair):* Girl, you done lost your natural mind? Look at your head!

GEORGE: What have you done to your head—I mean your hair!

BENEATHA: Nothing—except cut it off.

RUTH: Now that's the truth—it's what ain't been done to it! You expect this boy to go out with you with your head all nappy like that?

BENEATHA *(looking at* GEORGE*):* That's up to George. If he's ashamed of his heritage—

GEORGE: Oh, don't be so proud of yourself, Bennie—just because you look eccentric.

BENEATHA: How can something that's natural be eccentric?

GEORGE: That's what being eccentric means—being natural. Get dressed.

BENEATHA: I don't like that, George.

RUTH: Why must you and your brother make an argument out of everything people say?

BENEATHA: Because I hate assimilationist Negroes!

RUTH: Will somebody please tell me what assimila-who-ever means!

GEORGE: Oh, it's just a college girl's way of calling people Uncle Toms—but that isn't what it means at all.

RUTH: Well, what does it mean?

BENEATHA *(cutting* GEORGE *off and staring at him as she replies to* RUTH*):* It means someone who is willing to give up his own culture and submerge himself completely in the dominant, and in this case *oppressive* culture!

GEORGE: Oh, dear, dear, dear! Here we go! A lecture on the African past! On our Great West African Heritage! In one second we will hear all about the great Ashanti empires; the great Songhay civilizations; and the great sculpture of Bénin—and then some poetry in the Bantu—and the whole monologue will end with the word *heritage! (Nastily)* Let's face it, baby, your heritage is nothing but a bunch of raggedy-assed spirituals and some grass huts!

BENEATHA: GRASS HUTS! *(*RUTH *crosses to her and forcibly pushes her toward the bedroom)* See there . . . you are standing there in your splendid ignorance talking about people who were the first to smelt iron on the face of the earth! *(*RUTH *is pushing her through the door)* The Ashanti were performing surgical operations when the English— *(*RUTH *pulls the door to, with* BENEATHA *on the other side, and smiles graciously at* GEORGE. BENEATHA *opens the door and shouts the end of the sentence defiantly at* GEORGE*)* —were still tattooing themselves with blue dragons! *(She goes back inside)*

RUTH: Have a seat, George *(They both sit.* RUTH *folds her hands rather primly on her lap, determined to demonstrate the civilization of the family)* Warm, ain't it? I mean for September. *(Pause)* Just like they always say about Chicago weather: If it's too hot or cold for you, just wait a minute and it'll change. *(She smiles happily at this cliché of clichés)* Everybody say it's got to do with them bombs and things they keep setting off. *(Pause)* Would you like a nice cold beer?

GEORGE: No, thank you. I don't care for beer. *(He looks at his watch)* I hope she hurries up.

RUTH: What time is the show?

GEORGE: It's an eight-thirty curtain. That's just Chicago, though. In New York standard curtain time is eight forty.

(He is rather proud of this knowledge)

RUTH *(properly appreciating it):* You get to New York a lot?

GEORGE *(offhand):* Few times a year.

RUTH: Oh—that's nice. I've never been to New York.

(WALTER enters. We feel he has relieved himself, but the edge of unreality is still with him)

WALTER: New York ain't got nothing Chicago ain't. Just a bunch of hustling people all squeezed up together—being "Eastern."

(He turns his face into a screw of displeasure)

GEORGE: Oh—you've been?

WALTER: *Plenty* of times.

RUTH *(shocked at the lie):* Walter Lee Younger!

WALTER *(staring her down):* Plenty! *(Pause)* What we got to drink in this house? Why don't you offer this man some refreshment. *(To GEORGE)* They don't know how to entertain people in this house, man.

GEORGE: Thank you—I don't really care for anything.

WALTER *(feeling his head; sobriety coming):* Where's Mama?

RUTH: She ain't come back yet.

WALTER *(looking MURCHISON over from head to toe, scrutinizing his carefully casual tweed sports jacket over cashmere V-neck sweater over soft eyelet shirt and tie, and soft slacks, finished off with white buckskin shoes):* Why all you college boys wear them faggoty-looking white shoes?

RUTH: Walter Lee!

(GEORGE MURCHISON ignores the remark)

WALTER *(to RUTH):* Well, they look crazy as hell—white shoes, cold as it is.

RUTH *(crushed):* You have to excuse him—

WALTER: No he don't! Excuse me for what? What you always excusing me for! I'll excuse myself when I needs to be excused! *(A pause)* They look as funny as them black knee socks Beneatha wears out of here all the time.

RUTH: It's the college *style,* Walter.

WALTER: Style, hell. She looks like she got burnt legs or something!

RUTH: Oh, Walter—

WALTER *(an irritable mimic):* Oh, Walter! Oh, Walter! *(To MURCHISON)* How's your old man making out? I understand you all going to buy that big hotel on the Drive? *(He finds a beer in the refrigerator, wanders over to MURCHISON, sipping and wiping his lips with the back of his hand, and straddling a chair backwards to talk to the other man)* Shrewd move. Your old man is all right, man. *(Tapping his head and half winking for emphasis)* I mean he knows how to operate. I mean he thinks *big,* you know what I mean, I mean for a *home,* you know? But I think he's kind of running out of ideas now. I'd like to talk to him. Listen, man, I got some plans that could turn this city upside down. I mean think like he does. *Big.* Invest big, gamble big, hell, lose *big* if you have to, you know what

I mean. It's hard to find a man on this whole Southside who understands my kind of thinking—you dig? *(He scrutinizes* MURCHISON *again, drinks his beer, squints his eyes and leans in close, confidential, man to man)* Me and you ought to sit down and talk sometimes, man. Man, I got me some ideas. . .

MURCHISON *(with boredom):* Yeah—sometimes we'll have to do that, Walter.

WALTER *(understanding the indifference, and offended):* Yeah—well, when you get the time, man. I know you a busy little boy.

RUTH: Walter, please—

WALTER *(bitterly, hurt):* I know ain't nothing in this world as busy as you colored boys with your fraternity pins and white shoes . . .

RUTH *(covering her face with humiliation):* Oh, Walter Lee—

WALTER: I see you all all the time—with the books tucked under your arms—going to your *(British A—a mimic)* clahsses." And for what! What the hell you learning over there? Filling up your heads *(Counting off on his fingers)* —with the sociology and the psychology—but they teaching you how to be a man? How to take over and run the world? They teaching you how to run a rubber plantation or a steel mill? Naw—just to talk proper and read books and wear them faggoty-looking white shoes . . .

GEORGE *(looking at him with distaste, a little above it all):* You're all wacked up with bitterness, man.

WALTER *(intently, almost quietly, between the teeth, glaring at the boy):* And you—ain't you bitter, man? Ain't you just about had it yet? Don't you see no stars gleaming that you can't reach out and grab? You happy?—You contented son-of-a-bitch—you happy? You got it made? Bitter? Man, I'm a volcano. Bitter? Here I am a giant—surrounded by ants! Ants who can't even understand what it is the giant is talking about.

RUTH *(passionately and suddenly):* Oh, Walter—ain't you with nobody!

WALTER *(violently):* No! 'Cause ain't nobody with me! Not even my own mother!

RUTH: Walter, that's a terrible thing to say!

*(*BENEATHA *enters, dressed for the evening in a cocktail dress and earrings, hair natural)*

GEORGE: Well—hey— *(Crosses to* BENEATHA; *thoughtful, with emphasis, since this is a reversal)* You look great!

WALTER *(seeing his sister's hair for the first time):* What's the matter with your head?

BENEATHA *(tired of the jokes now):* I cut it off, Brother.

WALTER *(coming close to inspect it and walking around her):* Well, I'll be damned. So that's what they mean by the African bush . . .

BENEATHA: Ha ha. Let's go, George.

GEORGE *(looking at her):* You know something? I like it. It's sharp. I mean it really is. *(Helps her into her wrap)*

RUTH: Yes—I think so, too. *(She goes to the mirror and starts to clutch at her hair)*

WALTER: Oh no! You leave yours alone, baby. You might turn out to have a pin-shaped head or something!

BENEATHA: See you all later.

RUTH: Have a nice time.

GEORGE: Thanks. Good night. *(Half out the door, he reopens it. To* WALTER*)* Good night, Prometheus!

*(*BENEATHA *and* GEORGE *exit)*

WALTER *(to* RUTH*)*: Who is Prometheus?

RUTH: I don't know. Don't worry about it.

WALTER *(in fury, pointing after* GEORGE*)*: See there—they get to a point where they can't insult you man to man—they got to go talk about something ain't nobody never heard of!

RUTH: How do you know it was an insult? *(To humor him)* Maybe Prometheus is a nice fellow.

WALTER: Prometheus! I bet there ain't even no such thing! I bet that simple-minded clown—

RUTH: Walter—

(She stops what she is doing and looks at him)

WALTER *(yelling)*: Don't start!

RUTH: Start what?

WALTER: Your nagging! Where was I? Who was I with? How much money did I spend?

RUTH *(plaintively)*: Walter Lee—why don't we just try to talk about it . . .

WALTER *(not listening)*: I been out talking with people who understand me. People who care about the things I got on my mind.

RUTH *(wearily)*: I guess that means people like Willy Harris.

WALTER: Yes, people like Willy Harris.

RUTH *(with a sudden flash of impatience)*: Why don't you all just hurry up and go into the banking business and stop talking about it!

WALTER: Why? You want to know why? 'Cause we all tied up in a race of people that don't know how to do nothing but moan, pray and have babies!

(The line is too bitter even for him and he looks at her and sits down)

RUTH: Oh, Walter . . . *(Softly)* Honey, why can't you stop fighting me?

WALTER *(without thinking)*: Who's fighting you? Who even cares about you?

(This line begins the retardation of his mood)

RUTH: Well— *(She waits a long time, and then with resignation starts to put away her things)* I guess I might as well go on to bed . . . *(More or less to herself)* I don't know where we lost it . . . but we have . . . *(Then, to him)* I—I'm sorry about this new baby, Walter. I guess maybe I better go on and do what I started . . . I guess I just didn't realize how bad things was with us . . . I guess I just didn't really realize— *(She starts out to the bedroom and stops)* You want some hot milk?

WALTER: Hot milk?

RUTH: Yes—hot milk.

WALTER: Why hot milk?

RUTH: 'Cause after all that liquor you come home with you ought to have something hot in your stomach.

WALTER: I don't want no milk.

RUTH: You want some coffee then?

WALTER: No, I don't want no coffee. I don't want nothing hot to drink. *(Almost plaintively)* Why you always trying to give me something to eat?

RUTH *(standing and looking at him helplessly)*: What *else* can I give you, Walter Lee Younger?

(She stands and looks at him and presently turns to go out again. He lifts his head and watches her going away from him in a new mood which began to emerge when he asked her "Who cares about you?")

WALTER: It's been rough, ain't it, baby? *(She hears and stops but does not turn around and he continues to her back)* I guess between two people there ain't never as much understood as folks generally thinks there is. I mean like between me and you— *(She turns to face him)* How we gets to the place where we scared to talk softness to each other. *(He waits, thinking hard himself)* Why you think it got to be like that? *(He is thoughtful, almost as a child would be)* Ruth, what is it gets into people ought to be close?

RUTH: I don't know, honey. I think about it a lot.

WALTER: On account of you and me, you mean? The way things are with us. The way something done come down between us.

RUTH: There ain't so much between us, Walter . . . Not when you come to me and try to talk to me. Try to be with me . . . a little even.

WALTER *(total honesty)*: Sometimes . . . sometimes . . . I don't even know how to try.

RUTH: Walter—

WALTER: Yes?

RUTH *(coming to him, gently and with misgiving, but coming to him)*: Honey . . . life don't have to be like this. I mean sometimes people can do things so that things are better . . . You remember how we used to talk when Travis was born . . . about the way we were going to live . . . the kind of house . . . *(She is stroking his head)* Well, it's all starting to slip away from us . . .

(He turns her to him and they look at each other and kiss, tenderly and hungrily. The door opens and MAMA *enters—*WALTER *breaks away and jumps up. A beat)*

WALTER: Mama, where have you been?

MAMA: My—them steps is longer than they used to be. Whew! *(She sits down and ignores him)* How you feeling this evening, Ruth?

*(*RUTH *shrugs, disturbed at having been interrupted and watching her husband knowingly)*

WALTER: Mama, where have you been all day?

MAMA *(still ignoring him and leaning on the table and changing to more comfortable shoes)*: Where's Travis?

RUTH: I let him go out earlier and he ain't come back yet. Boy, is he going to get it!

WALTER: Mama!

MAMA *(as if she has heard him for the first time)*: Yes, son?

WALTER: Where did you go this afternoon?

MAMA: I went downtown to tend to some business that I had to tend to.

WALTER: What kind of business?

MAMA: You know better than to question me like a child, Brother.

WALTER *(rising and bending over the table)*: Where were you, Mama? *(Bringing his fists down and shouting)* Mama, you didn't go do something with that insurance money, something crazy?

(The front door opens slowly, interrupting him, and TRAVIS *peeks his head in, less than hopefully)*

TRAVIS *(to his mother):* Mama, I—

RUTH: "Mama I" nothing! You're going to get it, boy! Get on in that bedroom and get yourself ready!

TRAVIS: But I—

MAMA: Why don't you all never let the child explain hisself.

RUTH: Keep out of it now, Lena.

*(*MAMA *clamps her lips together, and* RUTH *advances toward her son menacingly)*

RUTH: A thousand times I have told you not to go off like that—

MAMA *(holding out her arms to her grandson):* Well—at least let me tell him something. I want him to be the first one to hear . . . Come here, Travis. *(The boy obeys, gladly)* Travis—*(She takes him by the shoulder and looks into his face)* —you know that money we got in the mail this morning?

TRAVIS: Yes'm—

MAMA: Well—what you think your grandmama gone and done with that money?

TRAVIS: I don't know, Grandmama.

MAMA *(putting her finger on his nose for emphasis):* She went out and she bought you a house! *(The explosion comes from* WALTER *at the end of the revelation and he jumps up and turns away from all of them in a fury.* MAMA *continues, to* TRAVIS*)* You glad about the house? It's going to be yours when you get to be a man.

TRAVIS: Yeah—I always wanted to live in a house.

MAMA: All right, gimme some sugar then— *(*TRAVIS *puts his arms around her neck as she watches her son over the boy's shoulder. Then, to* TRAVIS*, after the embrace)* Now when you say your prayers tonight, you thank God and your grandfather—'cause it was him who give you the house—in his way.

RUTH *(taking the boy from* MAMA *and pushing him toward the bedroom):* Now you get out of here and get ready for your beating.

TRAVIS: Aw, Mama—

RUTH: Get on in there— *(Closing the door behind him and turning radiantly to her mother-in-law)* So you went and did it!

MAMA *(quietly, looking at her son with pain):* Yes, I did.

RUTH *(raising both arms classically):* PRAISE GOD! *(Looks at* WALTER *a moment, who says nothing. She crosses rapidly to her husband)* Please, honey—let me be glad . . . you be glad too. *(She has laid her hands on his shoulders, but he shakes himself free of her roughly, without turning to face her)* Oh, Walter . . . home . . . *a home. (She comes back to* MAMA*)* Well—where is it? How big is it? How much it going to cost?

MAMA: Well—

RUTH: When we moving?

MAMA *(smiling at her):* First of the month.

RUTH *(throwing back her head with jubilance):* Praise God!

MAMA *(tentatively, still looking at her son's back turned against her and* RUTH*):* It's—it's a nice house too . . . *(She cannot help speaking directly to him. An imploring quality in her voice, her manner, makes her almost like a girl now)* Three bedrooms—nice big one for you and Ruth. . . . Me and Beneatha still have to share our room, but Travis have one of his

own—and *(With difficulty)* I figure if the—new baby—is a boy, we could get one of them double-decker outfits . . . And there's a yard with a little patch of dirt where I could maybe get to grow me a few flowers . . . And a nice big basement . . .

RUTH: Walter honey, be glad—

MAMA *(still to his back, fingering things on the table):* 'Course I don't want to make it sound fancier than it is . . . It's just a plain little old house—but it's made good and solid—and it will be *ours*. Walter Lee—it makes a difference in a man when he can walk on floors that belong to *him* . . .

RUTH: Where is it?

MAMA *(frightened at this telling):* Well—well—it's out there in Clybourne Park—

(RUTH's radiance fades abruptly, and WALTER finally turns slowly to face his mother with incredulity and hostility)

RUTH: Where?

MAMA *(matter-of-factly):* Four o six Clybourne Street, Clybourne Park.

RUTH: Clybourne Park? Mama, there ain't no colored people living in Clybourne Park.

MAMA *(almost idiotically):* Well, I guess there's going to be some now.

WALTER *(bitterly):* So that's the peace and comfort you went out and bought for us today!

MAMA *(raising her eyes to meet his finally):* Son—I just tried to find the nicest place for the least amount of money for my family.

RUTH *(trying to recover from the shock):* Well—well—'course I ain't one never been 'fraid of no crackers, mind you—but—well, wasn't there no other houses nowhere?

MAMA: Them houses they put up for colored in them areas way out all seem to cost twice as much as other houses. I did the best I could.

RUTH *(struck senseless with the news, in its various degrees of goodness and trouble, she sits a moment, her fists propping her chin in thought, and then she starts to rise, bringing her fists down with vigor, the radiance spreading from cheek to cheek again):* Well—well!—All I can say is—if this is my time in life—*MY* TIME—to say good-bye— *(And she builds with momentum as she starts to circle the room with an exuberant, almost tearfully happy release)* —to these Goddamned cracking walls!— *(She pounds the walls)* —and these marching roaches!— *(She wipes at an imaginary army of marching roaches)* —and this cramped little closet which ain't now or never was no kitchen! . . . then I say it loud and good, HALLELUJAH! AND GOOD-BYE MISERY . . . I DON'T NEVER WANT TO SEE YOUR UGLY FACE AGAIN! *(She laughs joyously, having practically destroyed the apartment, and flings her arms up and lets them come down happily, slowly, reflectively, over her abdomen, aware for the first time perhaps that the life therein pulses with happiness and not despair)* Lena?

MAMA *(moved, watching her happiness):* Yes, honey?

RUTH *(looking off):* Is there—is there a whole lot of sunlight?

MAMA *(understanding):* Yes, child, there's a whole lot of sunlight.

(Long pause)

RUTH *(collecting herself and going to the door of the room TRAVIS is in):* Well—I guess I better see 'bout Travis. *(To MAMA)* Lord, I sure don't feel like whipping nobody today!

(She exits)

MAMA *(the mother and son are left alone now and the mother waits a long time, considering deeply, before she speaks):* Son—you—you understand what I done, don't you? *(WALTER is silent and sullen)* I—I just seen my family falling apart today . . . just falling to pieces in front of my eyes . . . We couldn't of gone on like we was today. We was going backwards 'stead of forwards—talking 'bout killing babies and wishing each other was dead . . . When it gets like that in life—you just got to do something different, push on out and do something bigger . . . *(She waits)* I wish you say something, son . . . I wish you'd say how deep inside you think I done the right thing—

WALTER *(crossing slowly to his bedroom door and finally turning there and speaking measuredly):* What you need me to say you done right for? *You* the head of this family. You run our lives like you want to. It was your money and you did what you wanted with it. So what you need for me to say it was all right for? *(Bitterly, to hurt her as deeply as he knows is possible)* So you butchered up a dream of mine—you—who always talking 'bout your children's dreams . . .

MAMA: Walter Lee—

(He just closes the door behind him. MAMA sits alone, thinking heavily)

Curtain

SCENE II

TIME: *Friday night. A few weeks later.*

AT RISE: *Packing crates mark the intention of the family to move.* BENEATHA *and* GEORGE *come in, presumably from an evening out again.*

GEORGE: O.K. . . . O.K., whatever you say . . . *(They both sit on the couch. He tries to kiss her. She moves away)* Look, we've had a nice evening; let's not spoil it, huh? . . .

(He again turns her head and tries to nuzzle in and she turns away from him, not with distaste but with momentary lack of interest; in a mood to pursue what they were talking about)

BENEATHA: I'm *trying* to talk to you.

GEORGE: We always talk.

BENEATHA: Yes—and I love to talk.

GEORGE *(exasperated; rising):* I know it and I don't mind it sometimes . . . I want you to cut it out, see—The moody stuff, I mean. I don't like it. You're a nice-looking girl . . . all over. That's all you need, honey, forget the atmosphere. Guys aren't going to go for the atmosphere—they're going to go for what they see. Be glad for that. Drop the Garbo routine. It doesn't go with you. As for myself, I want a nice— *(Groping)* — simple *(Thoughtfully)*— sophisticated girl . . . not a poet—O.K.?

(He starts to kiss her, she rebuffs him again and he jumps up)

BENEATHA: Why are you angry, George?

GEORGE: Because this is stupid! I don't go out with you to discuss the nature of "quiet desperation" or to hear all about your thoughts—because the world will go on thinking what it thinks regardless—

BENEATHA: Then why read books? Why go to school?

GEORGE *(with artificial patience, counting on his fingers)*: It's simple. You read books—to learn facts—to get grades—to pass the course—to get a degree. That's all—it has nothing to do with thoughts.

(A long pause)

BENEATHA: I see. *(He starts to sit)* Good night, George.

(GEORGE looks at her a little oddly, and starts to exit. He meets MAMA coming in)

GEORGE: Oh—hello, Mrs. Younger.

MAMA: Hello, George, how you feeling?

GEORGE: Fine—fine, how are you?

MAMA: Oh, a little tired. You know them steps can get you after a day's work. You all have a nice time tonight?

GEORGE: Yes—a fine time. A fine time.

MAMA: Well, good night.

GEORGE: Good night. *(He exits. MAMA closes the door behind her)* Hello, honey. What you sitting like that for?

BENEATHA: I'm just sitting.

MAMA: Didn't you have a nice time?

BENEATHA: No.

MAMA: No? What's the matter?

BENEATHA: Mama, George is a fool—honest. *(She rises)*

MAMA *(hustling around unloading the packages she has entered with. She stops)*: Is he, baby?

BENEATHA: Yes.

(BENEATHA makes up TRAVIS' bed as she talks)

MAMA: You sure?

BENEATHA: Yes.

MAMA: Well—I guess you better not waste your time with no fools.

(BENEATHA looks up at her mother, watching her put groceries in the refrigerator. Finally she gathers up her things and starts into the bedroom. At the door she stops and looks back at her mother)

BENEATHA: Mama—

MAMA: Yes, baby—

BENEATHA: Thank you.

MAMA: For what?

BENEATHA: For understanding me this time.

(She exits quickly and the mother stands, smiling a little, looking at the place where BENEATHA *just stood.* RUTH *enters)*

RUTH: Now don't you fool with any of this stuff, Lena—

MAMA: Oh, I just thought I'd sort a few things out. Is Brother here?

RUTH: Yes.

MAMA *(with concern):* Is he—

RUTH *(reading her eyes):* Yes.

*(*MAMA *is silent and someone knocks on the door.* MAMA *and* RUTH *exchange weary and knowing glances and* RUTH *opens it to admit the neighbor,* MRS. JOHNSON,* *who is a rather squeaky wide-eyed lady of no particular age, with a newspaper under her arm)*

MAMA *(changing her expression to acute delight and a ringing cheerful greeting):* Oh—hello there, Mis' Johnson.

JOHNSON *(This is a woman who decided long ago to be enthusiastic about EVERYTHING in life and she is inclined to wave her wrist vigorously at the height of her exclamatory comments):* Hello there, yourself! H'you this evening, Ruth?

RUTH *(not much of a deceptive type):* Fine, Mis' Johnson, h'you?

JOHNSON: Fine. *(Reaching out quickly, playfully, and patting* RUTH'S *stomach)* Ain't you starting to poke out none yet! *(She mugs with delight at the over-familiar remark and her eyes dart around looking at the crates and packing preparation;* MAMA'S *face is a cold sheet of endurance)* Oh, ain't we getting ready round here, though! Yessir! Lookathere! I'm telling you the Youngers is really getting ready to "move on up a little higher!"—Bless God!

MAMA *(a little drily, doubting the total sincerity of the Blesser):* Bless God.

JOHNSON: He's good, ain't He?

MAMA: Oh yes, He's good.

JOHNSON: I mean sometimes He works in mysterious ways . . . but He works, don't He!

MAMA *(the same):* Yes, he does.

JOHNSON: I'm just soooooo happy for y'all. And this here child— *(About* RUTH*)* looks like she could just pop open with happiness, don't she. Where's all the rest of the family?

MAMA: Bennie's gone to bed—

JOHNSON: Ain't no . . . *(The implication is pregnancy)* sickness done hit you—I hope . . . ?

MAMA: No—she just tired. She was out this evening.

JOHNSON *(all is a coo, an emphatic coo):* Aw—aint' that lovely. She still going out with the little Murchison boy?

MAMA *(drily):* Ummmm huh.

JOHNSON: That's lovely. You sure got lovely children, Younger. Me and Isaiah talks all the time 'bout what fine children you was blessed with. We sure do.

MAMA: Ruth, give Mis' Johnson a piece of sweet potato pie and some milk.

JOHNSON: Oh honey, I can't stay hardly a minute—I just dropped in to see if there was anything I could do. *(Accepting the food easily)* I guess y'all seen the news what's all over the colored paper this week . . .

MAMA: No—didn't get mine yet this week.

*This character and the scene of her visit were cut from the original production and early editions of the play.

JOHNSON *(lifting her head and blinking with the spirit of catastrophe):* You mean you ain't read 'bout them colored people that was bombed out their place out there?

*(*RUTH *straightens with concern and takes the paper and reads it.* JOHNSON *notices her and feeds commentary)*

JOHNSON: Ain't it something how bad these here white folks is getting here in Chicago! Lord, getting so you think you right down in Mississippi! *(With a tremendous and rather insincere sense of melodrama)* 'Course I thinks it's wonderful how our folks keeps on pushing out. You hear some of these Negroes round here talking 'bout how they don't go where they ain't wanted and all that—but not me, honey! *(This is a lie)* Wilhemenia Othella Johnson goes anywhere, any time she feels like it! *(With head movement for emphasis)* Yes I do! Why if we left it up to these here crackers, the poor niggers wouldn't have nothing— *(She clasps her hand over her mouth)* Oh, I always forgets you don't 'low that word in your house.

MAMA *(quietly, looking at her):* No—I don't 'low it.

JOHNSON *(vigorously again):* Me neither! I was just telling Isaiah yesterday when he come using it in front of me—I said, "Isaiah, it's just like Mis' Younger says all the time—"

MAMA: Don't you want some more pie?

JOHNSON: No—no thank you; this was lovely. I got to get on over home and have my midnight coffee. I hear some people say it don't let them sleep but I finds I can't close my eyes right lessen I done had that laaaast cup of coffee . . . *(She waits. A beat. Undaunted)* My Goodnight coffee, I calls it!

MAMA *(with much eye-rolling and communication between herself and* RUTH*):* Ruth, why don't you give Mis' Johnson some coffee.

*(*RUTH *gives* MAMA *an unpleasant look for her kindness)*

JOHNSON *(accepting the coffee):* Where's Brother tonight?

MAMA: He's lying down.

JOHNSON: MMmmmmm, he sure gets his beauty rest, don't he? Good-looking man. Sure is a good-looking man! *(Reaching out to pat* RUTH*'s stomach again)* I guess that's how come we keep on having babies around here. *(She winks at* MAMA*)* One thing 'bout Brother, he always know how to have a *good* time. And soooooo ambitious! I bet it was his idea y'all moving out to Clybourne Park. Lord—I bet this time next month y'all's names will have been in the papers plenty— *(Holding up her hands to mark off each word of the headline she can see in front of her)* "NEGROES INVADE CLYBOURNE PARK—BOMBED!"

MAMA *(she and* RUTH *look at the woman in amazement):* We ain't exactly moving out there to get bombed.

JOHNSON: Oh, honey—you know I'm praying to God every day that don't nothing like that happen! But you have to think of life like it is—and these here Chicago peckerwoods is some baaaad peckerwoods.

MAMA *(wearily):* We done thought about all that, Mis' Johnson.

*(*BENEATHA *comes out of the bedroom in her robe and passes through to the bathroom.* MRS. JOHNSON *turns)*

JOHNSON: Hello there, Bennie!

BENEATHA *(crisply):* Hello, Mrs. Johnson.

JOHNSON: How is school?

BENEATHA *(crisply):* Fine, thank you. *(She goes out.)*

JOHNSON *(insulted):* Getting so she don't have much to say to nobody.

MAMA: The child was on her way to the bathroom.

JOHNSON: I know—but sometimes she act like ain't got time to pass the time of day with nobody ain't been to college. Oh—I ain't criticizing her none. It's just—you know how some of our young people gets when they get a little education. *(MAMA and RUTH say nothing, just look at her)* Yes—well. Well, I guess I better get on home. *(Unmoving)* 'Course I can understand how she must be proud and everything—being the only one in the family to make something of herself. I know just being a chauffeur ain't never satisfied Brother none. He shouldn't feel like that, though. Ain't nothing wrong with being a chauffeur.

MAMA: There's plenty wrong with it.

JOHNSON: What?

MAMA: Plenty. My husband always said being any kind of a servant wasn't a fit thing for a man to have to be. He always said a man's hands was made to make things, or to turn the earth with—not to drive nobody's car for 'em—or— *(She looks at her own hands)* carry they slop jars. And my boy is just like him—he wasn't meant to wait on nobody.

JOHNSON *(rising, somewhat offended):* Mmmmmmmmm. The Youngers is too much for me! *(She looks around)* You sure one proud-acting bunch of colored folks. Well—I always thinks like Booker T. Washington said that time—"Education has spoiled many a good plow hand"—

MAMA: Is that what old Booker T. said?

JOHNSON: He sure did.

MAMA: Well, it sounds just like him. The fool.

JOHNSON *(indignantly):* Well—he was one of our great men.

MAMA: Who said so?

JOHNSON *(nonplussed):* You know, me and you ain't never agreed about some things, Lena Younger. I guess I better be going—

RUTH *(quickly):* Good night.

JOHNSON: Good night. Oh— *(Thrusting it at her)* You can keep the paper! *(With a trill)* 'Night.

MAMA: Good night, Mis' Johnson.

(MRS. JOHNSON exits)

RUTH: If ignorance was gold . . .

MAMA: Shush. Don't talk about folks behind their backs.

RUTH: You do.

MAMA: I'm old and corrupted. *(BENEATHA enters)* You was rude to Mis' Johnson, Beneatha, and I don't like it at all.

BENEATHA *(at her door):* Mama, if there are two things we, as a people, have got to overcome, one is the Klu Klux Klan—and the other is Mrs. Johnson. *(She exits)*

MAMA: Smart aleck.

(The phone rings)

RUTH: I'll get it.

MAMA: Lord, ain't this a popular place tonight.

RUTH *(at the phone):* Hello—Just a minute. *(Goes to door)* Walter, it's Mrs. Arnold. *(Waits. Goes back to the phone. Tense)* Hello. Yes, this is his wife speaking . . . He's lying down now. Yes . . . well, he'll be in tomorrow. He's been very sick. Yes—I know we should have called, but we were so sure he'd be able to come in today. Yes—yes, I'm very sorry. Yes . . . Thank you very much. *(She hangs up.* WALTER *is standing in the doorway of the bedroom behind her)* That was Mrs. Arnold.

WALTER *(indifferently):* Was it?

RUTH: She said if you don't come in tomorrow that they are getting a new man . . .

WALTER: Ain't that sad—ain't that crying sad.

RUTH: She said Mr. Arnold has had to take a cab for three days . . . Walter, you ain't been to work for three days! *(This is a revelation to her)* Where you been, Walter Lee Younger? *(*WALTER *looks at her and starts to laugh)* You're going to lose your job.

WALTER: That's right . . . *(He turns on the radio)*

RUTH: Oh, Walter, and with your mother working like a dog every day—

(A steamy, deep blues pours into the room)

WALTER: That's sad too—Everything is sad.

MAMA: What you been doing for these three days, son?

WALTER: Mama—you don't know all the things a man what got leisure can find to do in this city . . . What's this—Friday night? Well—Wednesday I borrowed Willy Harris' car and I went for a drive . . . just me and myself and I drove and drove . . . Way out . . . way past South Chicago, and I parked the car and I sat and looked at the steel mills all day long. I just sat in the car and looked at them big black chimneys for hours. Then I drove back and I went to the Green Hat. *(Pause)* And Thursday—Thursday I borrowed the car again and I got in it and I pointed it the other way and I drove the other way—for hours—way, way up to Wisconsin, and I looked at the farms. I just drove and looked at the farms. Then I drove back and I went to the Green Hat. *(Pause)* And today—today I didn't get the car. Today I just walked. All over the Southside. And I looked at the Negroes and they looked at me and finally I just sat down on the curb at Thirty-ninth and South Parkway and I just sat there and watched the Negroes go by. And then I went to the Green Hat. You all sad? You all depressed? And you know where I am going right now—

*(*RUTH *goes out quietly)*

MAMA: Oh, Big Walter, is this the harvest of our days?

WALTER: You know what I like about the Green Hat? I like this little cat they got there who blows a sax . . . He blows. He talks to me. He ain't but 'bout five feet tall and he's got a conked head and his eyes is always closed and he's all music—

MAMA *(rising and getting some papers out of her handbag):* Walter—

WALTER: And there's this other guy who plays the piano . . . and they got a sound. I mean they can work on some music . . . They got the best little combo in the world in the Green Hat . . . You can just sit there and drink and listen to them three men play and you realize that don't nothing matter worth a damn, but just being there—

MAMA: I've helped do it to you, haven't I, son? Walter, I been wrong.

WALTER: Naw—you ain't never been wrong about nothing, Mama.

MAMA: Listen to me, now. I say I been wrong, son. That I been doing to you what the rest of the world been doing to you. *(She turns off the radio)* Walter— *(She stops and he looks up slowly at her and she meets his eyes pleadingly)* What you ain't never understood is that I ain't got nothing, don't own nothing, ain't never really wanted nothing that wasn't for you. There ain't nothing as precious to me . . . There ain't nothing worth holding on to, money, dreams, nothing else—if it means—if it means it's going to destroy my boy. *(She takes an envelope out of her handbag and puts it in front of him and he watches her without speaking or moving)* I paid the man thirty-five hundred dollars down on the house. That leaves sixty-five hundred dollars. Monday morning I want you to take this money and take three thousand dollars and put it in a savings account for Beneatha's medical schooling. The rest you put in a checking account—with your name on it. And from now on any penny that come out of it or that go in it is for you to look after. For you to decide. *(She drops her hands a little helplessly)* It ain't much, but it's all I got in the world and I'm putting it in your hands. I'm telling you to be the head of this family from now on like you supposed to be.

WALTER *(stares at the money)*: You trust me like that, Mama?

MAMA: I ain't never stop trusting you. Like I ain't never stop loving you.

(She goes out, and WALTER sits looking at the money on the table. Finally, in a decisive gesture, he gets up, and, in mingled joy and desperation, picks up the money. At the same moment, TRAVIS enters for bed)

TRAVIS: What's the matter, Daddy? You drunk?

WALTER *(sweetly, more sweetly than we have ever known him)*: No, Daddy ain't drunk. Daddy ain't going to never be drunk again. . . .

TRAVIS: Well, good night, Daddy.

(The FATHER has come from behind the couch and leans over, embracing his son)

WALTER: Son, I feel like talking to you tonight.

TRAVIS: About what?

WALTER: Oh, about a lot of things. About you and what kind of man you going to be when you grow up. . . . Son—son, what do you want to be when you grow up?

TRAVIS: A bus driver.

WALTER *(laughing a little)*: A what? Man, that ain't nothing to want to be!

TRAVIS: Why not?

WALTER: 'Cause, man—it ain't big enough—you know what I mean.

TRAVIS: I don't know then. I can't make up my mind. Sometimes Mama asks me that too. And sometimes when I tell her I just want to be like you—she says she don't want me to be like that and sometimes she says she does. . . .

WALTER *(gathering him up in his arms)*: You know what, Travis? In seven years you going to be seventeen years old. And things is going to be very different with us in seven years, Travis. . . . One day when you are seventeen I'll come home—home from my office downtown somewhere—

TRAVIS: You don't work in no office, Daddy.

WALTER: No—but after tonight. After what your daddy gonna do tonight, there's going to be offices—a whole lot of offices. . . .

TRAVIS: What you gonna do tonight, Daddy?

WALTER: You wouldn't understand yet, son, but your daddy's gonna make a transaction . . . a business transaction that's going to change our lives. . . . That's how come one day when you 'bout seventeen years old I'll come home and I'll be pretty tired, you know what I mean, after a day of conferences and secretaries getting things wrong the way they do . . . 'cause an executive's life is hell, man— *(The more he talks the farther away he gets)* And I'll pull the car up on the driveway . . . just a plain black Chrysler, I think, with white walls—no—black tires. More elegant. Rich people don't have to be flashy . . . though I'll have to get something a little sportier for Ruth—maybe a Cadillac convertible to do her shopping in. . . . And I'll come up the steps to the house and the gardener will be clipping away at the hedges and he'll say, "Good evening, Mr. Younger." And I'll say, "Hello, Jefferson, how are you this evening?" And I'll go inside and Ruth will come downstairs and meet me at the door and we'll kiss each other and she'll take my arm and we'll go up to your room to see you sitting on the floor with the catalogues of all the great schools in America around you. . . . All the great schools in the world! And—and I'll say, all right son—it's your seventeenth birthday, what is it you've decided? . . . Just tell me where you want to go to school and you'll *go.* Just tell me, what it is you want to be—and you'll *be* it. . . . Whatever you want to be—Yessir! *(He holds his arms open for* TRAVIS*)* You just name it, son . . . *(*TRAVIS *leaps into them)* and I hand you the world!

*(*WALTER*'s voice has risen in pitch and hysterical promise and on the last line he lifts* TRAVIS *high)*

(Blackout)

SCENE III

TIME: *Saturday, moving day, one week later.*

Before the curtain rises, RUTH*'s voice, a strident, dramatic church alto, cuts through the silence.*

It is, in the darkness, a triumphant surge, a penetrating statement of expectation: "Oh, Lord, I don't feel no ways tired! Children, oh, glory hallelujah!"

As the curtain rises we see that RUTH *is alone in the living room, finishing up the family's packing. It is moving day. She is nailing crates and tying cartons.* BENEATHA *enters, carrying a guitar case, and watches her exuberant sister-in-law.*

RUTH: Hey!

BENEATHA *(putting away the case):* Hi.

RUTH *(pointing at a package):* Honey—look in that package there and see what I found on sale this morning at the South Center. *(*RUTH *gets up and moves to the package and draws out some curtains)* Lookahere—hand-turned hems!

BENEATHA: How do you know the window size out there?

RUTH *(who hadn't thought of that):* Oh—Well, they bound to fit something in the whole house. Anyhow, they was too good a bargain to pass up. *(*RUTH *slaps her head, suddenly remembering something)* Oh, Bennie—I meant to put a special note on that carton over there. That's your mama's good china and she wants 'em to be very careful with it.

BENEATHA: I'll do it.

(BENEATHA *finds a piece of paper and starts to draw large letters on it)*

RUTH: You know what I'm going to do soon as I get in that new house?

BENEATHA: What?

RUTH: Honey—I'm going to run me a tub of water up to here . . . *(With her fingers practically up to her nostrils)* And I'm going to get in it—and I am going to sit . . . and sit . . . and sit in that hot water and the first person who knocks to tell *me* to hurry up and come out—

BENEATHA: Gets shot at sunrise.

RUTH *(laughing happily):* You said it, sister! *(Noticing how large* BENEATHA *is absent-mindedly making the note)* Honey, they ain't going to read that from no airplane.

BENEATHA *(laughing herself):* I guess I always think things have more emphasis if they are big, somehow.

RUTH *(looking up at her and smiling):* You and your brother seem to have that as a philosophy of life. Lord, that man—done changed so 'round here. You know—you know what we did last night? Me and Walter Lee?

BENEATHA: What?

RUTH *(smiling to herself):* We went to the movies. *(Looking at* BENEATHA *to see if she understands)* We went to the movies. You know the last time me and Walter went to the movies together?

BENEATHA: No.

RUTH: Me neither. That's how long it been. *(Smiling again)* But we went last night. The picture wasn't much good, but that didn't seem to matter. We went—and we held hands.

BENEATHA: Oh, Lord!

RUTH: We held hands—and you know what?

BENEATHA: What?

RUTH: When we come out of the show it was late and dark and all the stores and things was closed up . . . and it was kind of chilly and there wasn't many people on the streets . . . and we was still holding hands, me and Walter.

BENEATHA: You're killing me.

(WALTER *enters with a large package. His happiness is deep in him; he cannot keep still with his new-found exuberance. He is singing and wiggling and snapping his fingers. He puts his package in a corner and puts a phonograph record, which he has brought in with him, on the record player. As the music, soulful and sensuous, comes up he dances over to* RUTH *and tries to get her to dance with him. She gives in at last to his raunchiness and in a fit of giggling allows herself to be drawn into his mood. They dip and she melts into his arms in a classic, body-melding "slow drag")*

BENEATHA *(regarding them a long time as they dance, then drawing in her breath for a deeply exaggerated comment which she does not particularly mean):* Talk about—olddddddddd-fashioneddddddd—Negroes!

WALTER *(stopping momentarily):* What kind of Negroes? *(He says this in fun. He is not angry with her today, nor with anyone. He starts to dance with his wife again)*

BENEATHA: Old-fashioned.

WALTER *(as he dances with* RUTH*):* You know, when these *New Negroes* have their convention— *(Pointing at his sister)* —that is going to be the chairman of the Committee on

Unending Agitation. *(He goes on dancing, then stops)* Race, race, race! . . . Girl, I do believe you are the first person in the history of the entire human race to successfully brainwash yourself. *(BENEATHA breaks up and he goes on dancing. He stops again, enjoying his tease)* Damn, even the N double A C P takes a holiday sometimes! *(BENEATHA and RUTH laugh. He dances with RUTH some more and starts to laugh and stops and pantomimes someone over an operating table)* I can just see that chick someday looking down at some poor cat on an operating table and before she starts to slice him, she says . . . *(Pulling his sleeves back maliciously)* "By the way, what are your views on civil rights down there? . . ."

(He laughs at her again and starts to dance happily. The bell sounds)

BENEATHA: Sticks and stones may break my bones but . . . words will never hurt me!

(BENEATHA goes to the door and opens it as WALTER and RUTH go on with the clowning. BENEATHA is somewhat surprised to see a quiet-looking middle-aged white man in a business suit holding his hat and a briefcase in his hand and consulting a small piece of paper)

MAN: Uh—how do you do, miss. I am looking for a Mrs.— *(He looks at the slip of paper)* Mrs. Lena Younger? *(He stops short, struck dumb at the sight of the oblivious WALTER and RUTH)*

BENEATHA *(smoothing her hair with slight embarrassment)*: Oh—yes, that's my mother. Excuse me. *(She closes the door and turns to quiet the other two)* Ruth! Brother! *(Enunciating precisely but soundlessly: "There's a white man at the door!" They stop dancing, RUTH cuts off the phonograph, BENEATHA opens the door. The man casts a curious quick glance at all of them)* Uh—come in please.

MAN *(coming in)*: Thank you.

BENEATHA: My mother isn't here just now. Is it business?

MAN: Yes . . . well, of a sort.

WALTER *(freely, the Man of the House)*: Have a seat. I'm Mrs. Younger's son. I look after most of her business matters.

(RUTH and BENEATHA exchange amused glances)

MAN *(regarding WALTER, and sitting)*: Well—My name is Karl Lindner . . .

WALTER *(stretching out his hand)*: Walter Younger. This is my wife— *(RUTH nods politely)* —and my sister.

LINDNER: How do you do.

WALTER *(amiably, as he sits himself easily on a chair, leaning forward on his knees with interest and looking expectantly into the newcomer's face)*: What can we do for you, Mr. Lindner!

LINDNER *(some minor shuffling of the hat and briefcase on his knees)*: Well—I am a representative of the Clybourne Park Improvement Association—

WALTER *(pointing)*: Why don't you sit your things on the floor?

LINDNER: Oh—yes. Thank you. *(He slides the briefcase and hat under the chair)* And as I was saying—I am from the Clybourne Park Improvement Association and we have had it brought to our attention at the last meeting that you people—or at least your mother—has bought a piece of residential property at— *(He digs for the slip of paper again)* —four o six Clybourne Street . . .

WALTER: That's right. Care for something to drink? Ruth, get Mr. Lindner a beer.

LINDNER *(upset for some reason):* Oh—no, really. I mean thank you very much, but no thank you.

RUTH *(innocently):* Some coffee?

LINDNER: Thank you, nothing at all.

*(*BENEATHA *is watching the man carefully)*

LINDNER: Well, I don't know how much you folks know about our organization. *(He is a gentle man; thoughtful and somewhat labored in his manner)* It is one of these community organizations set up to look after—oh, you know, things like block upkeep and special projects and we also have what we call our New Neighbors Orientation Committee . . .

BENEATHA *(drily):* Yes—and what do they do?

LINDNER *(turning a little to her and then returning the main force to* WALTER*):* Well—it's what you might call a sort of welcoming committee, I guess. I mean they, we—I'm the chairman of the committee—go around and see the new people who move into the neighborhood and sort of give them the lowdown on the way we do things in Clybourne Park.

BENEATHA *(with appreciation of the two meanings, which escape* RUTH *and* WALTER*):* Un-huh.

LINDNER: And we also have the category of what the association calls— *(He looks elsewhere)* —uh—special community problems . . .

BENEATHA: Yes—and what are some of those?

WALTER: Girl, let the man talk.

LINDNER *(with understated relief):* Thank you. I would sort of like to explain this thing in my own way. I mean I want to explain to you in a certain way.

WALTER: Go ahead.

LINDNER: Yes. Well. I'm going to try to get right to the point. I'm sure we'll all appreciate that in the long run.

BENEATHA: Yes.

WALTER: Be still now!

LINDNER: Well—

RUTH *(still innocently):* Would you like another chair—you don't look comfortable.

LINDNER *(more frustrated than annoyed):* No, thank you very much. Please. Well—to get right to the point I— *(A great breath, and he is off at last)* I am sure you people must be aware of some of the incidents which have happened in various parts of the city when colored people have moved into certain areas— *(*BENEATHA *exhales heavily and starts tossing a piece of fruit up and down in the air)* Well—because we have what I think is going to be a unique type of organization in American community life—not only do we deplore that kind of thing—but we are trying to do something about it. *(*BENEATHA *stops tossing and turns with a new and quizzical interest to the man)* We feel— *(gaining confidence in his mission because of the interest in the faces of the people he is talking to)* —we feel that most of the trouble in this world, when you come right down to it— *(He hits his knee for emphasis)* —most of the trouble exists because people just don't sit down and talk to each other.

RUTH *(nodding as she might in church, pleased with the remark):* You can say that again, mister.

LINDNER *(more encouraged by such affirmation):* That we don't try hard enough in this world to understand the other fellow's problem. The other guy's point of view.

RUTH: Now that's right.

*(*BENEATHA *and* WALTER *merely watch and listen with genuine interest)*

LINDNER: Yes—that's the way we feel out in Clybourne Park. And that's why I was elected to come here this afternoon and talk to you people. Friendly like, you know, the way people should talk to each other and see if we couldn't find some way to work this thing out. As I say, the whole business is a matter of *caring* about the other fellow. Anybody can see that you are a nice family of folks, hard working and honest I'm sure. *(*BENEATHA *frowns slightly, quizzically, her head tilted regarding him)* Today everybody knows what it means to be on the outside of *something*. And of course, there is always somebody who is out to take advantage of people who don't always understand.

WALTER: What do you mean?

LINDNER: Well—you see our community is made up of people who've worked hard as the dickens for years to build up that little community. They're not rich and fancy people; just hard-working, honest people who don't really have much but those little homes and a dream of the kind of community they want to raise their children in. Now, I don't say we are perfect and there is a lot wrong in some of the things they want. But you've got to admit that a man, right or wrong, has the right to want to have the neighborhood he lives in a certain kind of way. And at the moment the overwhelming majority of our people out there feel that people get along better, take more of a common interest in the life of the community, when they share a common background. I want you to believe me when I tell you that race prejudice simply doesn't enter into it. It is a matter of the people of Clybourne Park believing, rightly or wrongly, as I say, that for the happiness of all concerned that our Negro families are happier when they live in their *own* communities.

BENEATHA *(with a grand and bitter gesture):* This, friends, is the Welcoming Committee!

WALTER *(dumbfounded, looking at* LINDNER*):* Is this what you came marching all the way over here to tell us?

LINDNER: Well, now we've been having a fine conversation. I hope you'll hear me all the way through.

WALTER *(tightly):* Go ahead, man.

LINDNER: You see—in the face of all the things I have said, we are prepared to make your family a very generous offer . . .

BENEATHA: Thirty pieces and not a coin less!

WALTER: Yeah?

LINDNER *(putting on his glasses and drawing a form out of the briefcase):* Our association is prepared, through the collective effort of our people, to buy the house from you at a financial gain to your family.

RUTH: Lord have mercy, ain't this the living gall!

WALTER: All right, you through?

LINDNER: Well, I want to give you the exact terms of the financial arrangement—

WALTER: We don't want to hear no exact terms of no arrangements. I want to know if you got any more to tell us 'bout getting together?

LINDNER *(taking off his glasses):* Well—I don't suppose that you feel . . .

WALTER: Never mind how I feel—you got any more to say 'bout how people ought to sit down and talk to each other? . . . Get out of my house, man.

(He turns his back and walks to the door)

LINDNER *(looking around at the hostile faces and reaching and assembling his hat and briefcase):* Well—I don't understand why you people are reacting this way. What do you think you are going to gain by moving into a neighborhood where you just aren't wanted and where some elements—well—people can get awful worked up when they feel that their whole way of life and everything they've ever worked for is threatened.

WALTER: Get out.

LINDNER *(at the door, holding a small card):* Well—I'm sorry it went like this.

WALTER: Get out.

LINDNER *(almost sadly regarding* WALTER*):* You just can't force people to change their hearts, son.

(He turns and puts his card on a table and exits. WALTER *pushes the door to with stinging hatred, and stands looking at it.* RUTH *just sits and* BENEATHA *just stands. They say nothing.* MAMA *and* TRAVIS *enter)*

MAMA: Well—this all the packing got done since I left out of here this morning. I testify before God that my children got all the energy of the *dead!* What time the moving men due?

BENEATHA: Four o'clock. You had a caller, Mama.

(She is smiling, teasingly)

MAMA: Sure enough—who?

BENEATHA *(her arms folded saucily):* The Welcoming Committee.

*(*WALTER *and* RUTH *giggle)*

MAMA *(innocently):* Who?

BENEATHA: The Welcoming Committee. They said they're sure going to be glad to see you when you get there.

WALTER *(devilishly):* Yeah, they said they can't hardly wait to see your face.

(Laughter)

MAMA *(sensing their facetiousness):* What's the matter with you all?

WALTER: Ain't nothing the matter with us. We just telling you 'bout the gentleman who came to see you this afternoon. From the Clybourne Park Improvement Association.

MAMA: What he want?

RUTH *(in the same mood as* BENEATHA *and* WALTER*):* To welcome you, honey.

WALTER: He said they can't hardly wait. He said the one thing they don't have, that they just *dying* to have out there is a fine family of fine colored people! *(To* RUTH *and* BENEATHA*)* Ain't that right!

RUTH *(mockingly):* Yeah! He left his card—

BENEATHA *(handing card to* MAMA*):* In case.

*(*MAMA *reads and throws it on the floor—understanding and looking off as she draws her chair up to the table on which she has put her plant and some sticks and some cord)*

MAMA: Father, give us strength. *(Knowingly—and without fun)* Did he threaten us?

BENEATHA: Oh—Mama—they don't do it like that any more. He talked Brotherhood. He said everybody ought to learn how to sit down and hate each other with good Christian fellowship.

(She and WALTER shake hands to ridicule the remark)

MAMA *(sadly)*: Lord, protect us . . .

RUTH: You should hear the money those folks raised to buy the house from us. All we paid and then some.

BENEATHA: What they think we going to do—eat 'em?

RUTH: No, honey, marry 'em.

MAMA *(shaking her head)*: Lord, Lord, Lord . . .

RUTH: Well—that's the way the crackers crumble. *(A beat)* Joke.

BENEATHA *(laughingly noticing what her mother is doing)*: Mama, what are you doing?

MAMA: Fixing my plant so it won't get hurt none on the way . . .

BENEATHA: Mama, you going to take *that* to the new house?

MAMA: Un-huh—

BENEATHA: That raggedy-looking old thing?

MAMA *(stopping and looking at her)*: It expresses ME!

RUTH *(with delight, to BENEATHA)*: So there, Miss Thing!

(WALTER comes to MAMA suddenly and bends down behind her and squeezes her in his arms with all his strength. She is overwhelmed by the suddenness of it and, though delighted, her manner is like that of RUTH and TRAVIS)

MAMA: Look out now, boy! You make me mess up my thing here!

WALTER *(his face lit, he slips down on his knees beside her, his arms still about her)*: Mama . . . you know what it means to climb up in the chariot?

MAMA *(gruffly, very happy)*: Get on away from me now . . .

RUTH *(near the gift-wrapped package, trying to catch WALTER's eye)*: Psst—

WALTER: What the old song say, Mama . . .

RUTH: Walter—Now?

(She is pointing at the package)

WALTER *(speaking the lines, sweetly, playfully, in his mother's face)*: I got wings . . . you got wings . . . All God's Children got wings . . .

MAMA: Boy—get out of my face and do some work . . .

WALTER: When I get to heaven gonna put on my wings,
Gonna fly all over God's heaven . . .

BENEATHA *(teasingly, from across the room)*: Everybody talking 'bout heaven ain't going there!

WALTER *(to RUTH, who is carrying the box across to them)*: I don't know, you think we ought to give her that . . . Seems to me she ain't been very appreciative around here.

MAMA *(eyeing the box, which is obviously a gift)*: What is that?

WALTER *(taking it from RUTH and putting it on the table in front of MAMA)*: Well—what you all think? Should we give it to her?

RUTH: Oh—she was pretty good today.
MAMA: I'll good you—

(She turns her eyes to the box again)

BENEATHA: Open it, Mama.

(She stands up, looks at it, turns and looks at all of them, and then presses her hands together and does not open the package)

WALTER *(sweetly):* Open it, Mama. It's for you. *(MAMA looks in his eyes. It is the first present in her life without its being Christmas. Slowly she opens her package and lifts out, one by one, a brand-new sparkling set of gardening tools. WALTER continues, prodding)* Ruth made up the note—read it . . .
MAMA *(picking up the card and adjusting her glasses):* "To our own Mrs. Miniver—Love from Brother, Ruth and Beneatha." Ain't that lovely . . .
TRAVIS *(tugging at his father's sleeve):* Daddy, can I give her mine now?
WALTER: All right, son. *(TRAVIS flies to get his gift)*
MAMA: Now I don't have to use my knives and forks no more . . .
WALTER: Travis didn't want to go in with the rest of us, Mama. He got his own. *(Somewhat amused)* We don't know what it is . . .
TRAVIS *(racing back in the room with a large hatbox and putting it in front of his grandmother):* Here!
MAMA: Lord have mercy, baby. You done gone and bought your grandmother a hat?
TRAVIS *(very proud):* Open it!

(She does and lifts out an elaborate, but very elaborate, wide gardening hat, and all the adults break up at the sight of it)

RUTH: Travis, honey, what is that?
TRAVIS *(who thinks it is beautiful and appropriate):* It's a gardening hat! Like the ladies always have on in the magazines when they work in their gardens.
BENEATHA *(giggling fiercely):* Travis—we were trying to make Mama Mrs. Miniver—not Scarlett O'Hara!
MAMA *(indignantly):* What's the matter with you all! This here is a beautiful hat! *(Absurdly)* I always wanted me one just like it!

(She pops it on her head to prove it to her grandson, and the hat is ludicrous and considerably oversized)

RUTH: Hot dog! Go, Mama!
WALTER *(doubled over with laughter):* I'm sorry, Mama—but you look like you ready to go out and chop you some cotton sure enough!

(They all laugh except MAMA, out of deference to TRAVIS' feelings)

MAMA *(gathering the boy up to her):* Bless your heart—this is the prettiest hat I ever owned— *(WALTER, RUTH and BENEATHA chime in—noisily, festively and insincerely con-*

gratulating TRAVIS *on his gift)* What are we all standing around here for? We ain't finished packin' yet. Bennie, you ain't packed one book.

(The bell rings)

BENEATHA: That couldn't be the movers . . . it's not hardly two good yet—

*(*BENEATHA *goes into her room.* MAMA *starts for door)*

WALTER *(turning, stiffening):* Wait—wait—I'll get it.

(He stands and looks at the door)

MAMA: You expecting company, son?
WALTER *(just looking at the door):* Yeah—yeah . . .

*(*MAMA *looks at* RUTH*, and they exchange innocent and unfrightened glances)*

MAMA *(not understanding):* Well, let them in, son.
BENEATHA *(from her room):* We need some more string.
MAMA: Travis—you run to the hardware and get me some string cord.

*(*MAMA *goes out and* WALTER *turns and looks at* RUTH. TRAVIS *goes to a dish for money)*

RUTH: Why don't you answer the door, man?
WALTER *(suddenly bounding across the floor to embrace her):* 'Cause sometimes it hard to let the future begin!

(Stooping down in her face)

I got wings! You got wings!
All God's children got wings!

(He crosses to the door and throws it open. Standing there is a very slight little man in a not too prosperous business suit and with haunted frightened eyes and a hat pulled down tightly, brim up, around his forehead. TRAVIS *passes between the men and exits.* WALTER *leans deep in the man's face, still in his jubilance)*

When I get to heaven gonna put on my wings,
Gonna fly all over God's heaven . . .

(The little man just stares at him)

Heaven—

(Suddenly he stops and looks past the little man into the empty hallway)

Where's Willy, man?

BOBO: He ain't with me.

WALTER *(not disturbed):* Oh—come on in. You know my wife.

BOBO *(dumbly, taking off his hat):* Yes—h'you, Miss Ruth.

RUTH *(quietly, a mood apart from her husband already, seeing* BOBO*):* Hello, Bobo.

WALTER: You right on time today . . . Right on time. That's the way! *(He slaps* BOBO *on his back)* Sit down . . . lemme hear.

*(*RUTH *stands stiffly and quietly in back of them, as though somehow she senses death, her eyes fixed on her husband)*

BOBO *(his frightened eyes on the floor, his hat in his hands):* Could I please get a drink of water, before I tell you about it, Walter Lee?

*(*WALTER *does not take his eyes off the man.* RUTH *goes blindly to the tap and gets a glass of water and brings it to* BOBO*)*

WALTER: There ain't nothing wrong, is there?

BOBO: Lemme tell you—

WALTER: Man—didn't nothing go wrong?

BOBO: Lemme tell you—Walter Lee. *(Looking at* RUTH *and talking to her more than to* WALTER*)* You know how it was. I got to tell you how it was. I mean first I got to tell you how it was all the way . . . I mean about the money I put in, Walter Lee . . .

WALTER *(with taut agitation now):* What about the money you put in?

BOBO: Well—it wasn't much as we told you—me and Willy— *(He stops)* I'm sorry, Walter. I got a bad feeling about it. I got a real bad feeling about it . . .

WALTER: Man, what you telling me about all this for? . . . Tell me what happened in Springfield . . .

BOBO: Springfield.

RUTH *(like a dead woman):* What was supposed to happen in Springfield?

BOBO *(to her):* This deal that me and Walter went into with Willy—Me and Willy was going to go down to Springfield and spread some money 'round so's we wouldn't have to wait so long for the liquor license . . . That's what we were going to do. Everybody said that was the way you had to do, you understand, Miss Ruth?

WALTER: Man—what happened down there?

BOBO *(a pitiful man, near tears):* I'm trying to tell you, Walter.

WALTER *(screaming at him suddenly):* THEN TELL ME, GODDAMMIT . . . WHAT'S THE MATTER WITH YOU?

BOBO: Man . . . I didn't go to no Springfield, yesterday.

WALTER *(halted, life hanging in the moment):* Why not?

BOBO *(the long way, the hard way to tell):* 'Cause I didn't have no reasons to . . .

WALTER: Man, what are you talking about!

BOBO: I'm talking about the fact that when I got to the train station yesterday morning—eight o'clock like we planned . . . Man—*Willy didn't never show up.*

WALTER: Why . . . where was he . . . where is he?

BOBO: That's what I'm trying to tell you . . . I don't know . . . I waited six hours . . . I called his house . . . and I waited . . . six hours . . . I waited in that train station six hours

. . . *(Breaking into tears)* That was all the extra money I had in the world . . . *(Looking up at* WALTER *with the tears running down his face)* Man, *Willy is gone.*

WALTER: Gone, what you mean Willy is gone? Gone where? You mean he went by himself. You mean he went off to Springfield by himself—to take care of getting the license—*(Turns and looks anxiously at* RUTH*)* You mean maybe he didn't want too many people in on the business down there? *(Looks to* RUTH *again, as before)* You know Willy got his own ways. *(Looks back to* BOBO*)* Maybe you was late yesterday and he just went on down there without you. Maybe—maybe—he's been callin' you at home tryin' to tell you what happened or something. Maybe—maybe—he just got sick. He's somewhere—he's got to be somewhere. We just got to find him—me and you got to find him. *(Grabs* BOBO *senselessly by the collar and starts to shake him)* We got to!

BOBO *(in sudden angry, frightened agony):* What's the matter with you, Walter! *When a cat take off with your money he don't leave you no road maps!*

WALTER *(turning madly, as though he is looking for* WILLY *in the very room):* Willy! . . . Willy . . . don't do it . . . Please don't do it . . . Man, not with that money . . . Man, please, not with that money . . . Oh, God . . . Don't let it be true . . . *(He is wandering around, crying out for* WILLY *and looking for him or perhaps for help from God)* Man . . . I trusted you . . . Man, I put my life in your hands . . . *(He starts to crumble down on the floor as* RUTH *just covers her face in horror.* MAMA *opens the door and comes into the room, with* BENEATHA *behind her)* Man . . . *(He starts to pound the floor with his fists, sobbing wildly)* THAT MONEY IS MADE OUT OF MY FATHER'S FLESH—

BOBO *(standing over him helplessly):* I'm sorry, Walter . . . *(Only* WALTER*'s sobs reply.* BOBO *puts on his hat)* I had my life staked on this deal, too . . .

(He exits)

MAMA *(to* WALTER*):* Son— *(She goes to him, bends down to him, talks to his bent head)* Son . . . Is it gone? Son, I gave you sixty-five hundred dollars. Is it gone? All of it? Beneatha's money too?

WALTER *(lifting his head slowly):* Mama . . . I never . . . went to the bank at all . . .

MAMA *(not wanting to believe him):* You mean . . . your sister's school money . . . you used that too . . . Walter? . . .

WALTER: Yessss! All of it . . . It's all gone . . .

(There is total silence. RUTH *stands with her face covered with her hands;* BENEATHA *leans forlornly against a wall, fingering a piece of red ribbon from the mother's gift.* MAMA *stops and looks at her son without recognition and then, quite without thinking about it, starts to beat him senselessly in the face.* BENEATHA *goes to them and stops it)*

BENEATHA: Mama!

*(*MAMA *stops and looks at both of her children and rises slowly and wanders vaguely, aimlessly away from them)*

MAMA: I seen . . . him . . . night after night . . . come in . . . and look at that rug . . . and then look at me . . . the red showing in his eyes . . . the veins moving in his head . . . I seen him grow thin and old before he was forty . . . working and working and working like

somebody's old horse . . . killing himself . . . and you—you give it all away in a day— *(She raises her arms to strike him again)*

BENEATHA: Mama—

MAMA: Oh, God . . . *(She looks up to Him)* Look down here—and show me the strength.

BENEATHA: Mama—

MAMA *(folding over)*: Strength . . .

BENEATHA *(plaintively)*: Mama . . .

MAMA: Strength!

Curtain

ACT III

An hour later.

At curtain, there is a sullen light of gloom in the living room, gray light not unlike that which began the first scene of Act One. At left we can see WALTER *within his room, alone with himself. He is stretched out on the bed, his shirt out and open, his arms under his head. He does not smoke, he does not cry out, he merely lies there, looking up at the ceiling, much as if he were alone in the world.*

In the living room BENEATHA *sits at the table, still surrounded by the now almost ominous packing crates. She sits looking off. We feel that this is a mood struck perhaps an hour before, and it lingers now, full of the empty sound of profound disappointment. We see on a line from her brother's bedroom the sameness of their attitudes. Presently the bell rings and* BENEATHA *rises without ambition or interest in answering. It is* ASAGAI, *smiling broadly, striding into the room with energy and happy expectation and conversation.*

ASAGAI: I came over . . . I had some free time. I thought I might help with the packing. Ah, I like the look of packing crates! A household in preparation for a journey! It depresses some people . . . but for me . . . it is another feeling. Something full of the flow of life, do you understand? Movement, progress . . . It makes me think of Africa.

BENEATHA: Africa!

ASAGAI: What kind of a mood is this? Have I told you how deeply you move me?

BENEATHA: He gave away the money, Asagai . . .

ASAGAI: Who gave away what money?

BENEATHA: The insurance money. My brother gave it away.

ASAGAI: Gave it away?

BENEATHA: He made an investment! With a man even Travis wouldn't have trusted with his most worn-out marbles.

ASAGAI: And it's gone?

BENEATHA: Gone!

ASAGAI: I'm very sorry . . . And you, now?

BENEATHA: Me? . . . Me? . . . Me, I'm nothing . . . Me. When I was very small . . . we used to take our sleds out in the wintertime and the only hills we had were the ice-covered stone steps of some houses down the street. And we used to fill them in with snow and make them smooth and slide down them all day . . . and it was very dangerous, you know . . . far too steep . . . and sure enough one day a kid named Rufus came down too fast and hit the sidewalk and we saw his face just split open right there in front

of us . . . And I remember standing there looking at his bloody open face thinking that was the end of Rufus. But the ambulance came and they took him to the hospital and they fixed the broken bones and they sewed it all up . . . and the next time I saw Rufus he just had a little line down the middle of his face . . . I never got over that . . .

ASAGAI: What?

BENEATHA: That that was what one person could do for another, fix him up—sew up the problem, make him all right again. That was the most marvelous thing in the world . . . I wanted to do that. I always thought it was the one concrete thing in the world that a human being could do. Fix up the sick, you know—and make them whole again. This was truly being God . . .

ASAGAI: You wanted to be God?

BENEATHA: No—I wanted to cure. It used to be so important to me. I wanted to cure. It used to matter. I used to care. I mean about people and how their bodies hurt . . .

ASAGAI: And you've stopped caring?

BENEATHA: Yes—I think so.

ASAGAI: Why?

BENEATHA *(bitterly):* Because it doesn't seem deep enough, close enough to what ails mankind! It was a child's way of seeing things—or an idealist's.

ASAGAI: Children see things very well sometimes—and idealists even better.

BENEATHA: I know that's what you think. Because you are still where I left off. You with all your talk and dreams about Africa! You still think you can patch up the world. Cure the Great Sore of Colonialism— *(Loftily, mocking it)* with the Penicillin of Independence—!

ASAGAI: Yes!

BENEATHA: Independence *and then what?* What about all the crooks and thieves and just plain idiots who will come into power and steal and plunder the same as before—only now they will be black and do it in the name of the new Independence—WHAT ABOUT THEM?!

ASAGAI: That will be the problem for another time. First we must get there.

BENEATHA: And where does it end?

ASAGAI: End? Who even spoke of an end? To life? To living?

BENEATHA: An end to misery! To stupidity! Don't you see there isn't any real progress, Asagai, there is only one large circle that we march in, around and around, each of us with our own little picture in front of us—our own little mirage that we think is the future.

ASAGAI: That is the mistake.

BENEATHA: What?

ASAGAI: What you just said—about the circle. It isn't a circle—it is simply a long line—as in geometry, you know, one that reaches into infinity. And because we cannot see the end—we also cannot see how it changes. And it is very odd but those who see the changes—who dream, who will not give up—are called idealists . . . and those who see only the circle—we call *them* the "realists"!

BENEATHA: Asagai, while I was sleeping in that bed in there, people went out and took the future right out of my hands! And nobody asked me, nobody consulted me—they just went out and changed my life!

ASAGAI: Was it your money?

BENEATHA: What?

ASAGAI: Was it your money he gave away?

BENEATHA: It belonged to all of us.

ASAGAI: But did you earn it? Would you have had it at all if your father had not died?

BENEATHA: No.

ASAGAI: Then isn't there something wrong in a house—in a world—where all dreams, good or bad, must depend on the death of a man? I never thought to see *you* like this, Alaiyo. You! Your brother made a mistake and you are grateful to him so that now you can give up the ailing human race on account of it! You talk about what good is struggle, what good is anything! Where are we all going and why are we bothering!

BENEATHA: AND YOU CANNOT ANSWER IT!

ASAGAI *(shouting over her): I LIVE THE ANSWER! (Pause)* In my village at home it is the exceptional man who can even read a newspaper . . . or who ever sees a book at all. I will go home and much of what I will have to say will seem strange to the people of my village. But I will teach and work and things will happen, slowly and swiftly. At times it will seem that nothing changes at all . . . and then again the sudden dramatic events which make history leap into the future. And then quiet again. Retrogression even. Guns, murder, revolution. And I even will have moments when I wonder if the quiet was not better than all that death and hatred. But I will look about my village at the illiteracy and disease and ignorance and I will not wonder long. And perhaps . . . perhaps I will be a great man . . . I mean perhaps I will hold on to the substance of truth and find my way always with the right course . . . and perhaps for it I will be butchered in my bed some night by the servants of empire . . .

BENEATHA: *The martyr!*

ASAGAI *(he smiles):* . . . or perhaps I shall live to be a very old man, respected and esteemed in my new nation . . . And perhaps I shall hold office and this is what I'm trying to tell you, Alaiyo: Perhaps the things I believe now for my country will be wrong and outmoded, and I will not understand and do terrible things to have things my way or merely to keep my power. Don't you see that there will be young men and women— not British soldiers then, but my own black countrymen—to step out of the shadows some evening and slit my then useless throat? Don't you see they have always been there . . . that they always will be. And that such a thing as my own death will be an advance? They who might kill me even . . . actually replenish all that I was.

BENEATHA: Oh, Asagai, I know all that.

ASAGAI: Good! Then stop moaning and groaning and tell me what you plan to do.

BENEATHA: Do?

ASAGAI: I have a bit of a suggestion.

BENEATHA: What?

ASAGAI *(rather quietly for him):* That when it is all over—that you come home with me—

BENEATHA *(staring at him and crossing away with exasperation):* Oh—Asagai—at this moment you decide to be romantic!

ASAGAI *(quickly understanding the misunderstanding):* My dear, young creature of the New World—I do not mean across the city—I mean across the ocean: home—to Africa.

BENEATHA *(slowly understanding and turning to him with murmured amazement):* To Africa?

ASAGAI: Yes! . . . *(Smiling and lifting his arms playfully)* Three hundred years later the African Prince rose up out of the seas and swept the maiden back across the middle passage over which her ancestors had come—

BENEATHA *(unable to play):* To—to Nigeria?

ASAGAI: Nigeria. Home. *(Coming to her with genuine romantic flippancy)* I will show you our mountains and our stars; and give you cool drinks from gourds and teach you the old songs and the ways of our people—and, in time, we will pretend that— *(Very softly)* — you have only been away for a day. Say that you'll come— *(He swings her around and takes her full in his arms in a kiss which proceeds to passion)*

BENEATHA *(pulling away suddenly)*: You're getting me all mixed up—

ASAGAI: Why?

BENEATHA: Too many things—too many things have happened today. I must sit down and think. I don't know what I feel about anything right this minute.

(She promptly sits down and props her chin on her fist)

ASAGAI *(charmed)*: All right, I shall leave you. No—don't get up. *(Touching her, gently, sweetly)* Just sit awhile and think . . . Never be afraid to sit awhile and think. *(He goes to door and looks at her)* How often I have looked at you and said, "Ah—so this is what the New World hath finally wrought . . ."

(He exits. BENEATHA *sits on alone. Presently* WALTER *enters from his room and starts to rummage through things, feverishly looking for something. She looks up and turns in her seat)*

BENEATHA *(hissingly)*: Yes—just look at what the New World hath wrought! . . . Just look! *(She gestures with bitter disgust)* There he is! *Monsieur le petit bourgeois noir*—himself! There he is—Symbol of a Rising Class! Entrepreneur! Titan of the system! *(*WALTER *ignores her completely and continues frantically and destructively looking for something and hurling things to floor and tearing things out of their place in his search.* BENEATHA *ignores the eccentricity of his actions and goes on with the monologue of insult)* Did you dream of yachts on Lake Michigan, Brother? Did you see yourself on that Great Day sitting down at the Conference Table, surrounded by all the mighty bald-headed men in America? All halted, waiting, breathless, waiting for your pronouncements on industry? Waiting for you—Chairman of the Board! *(*WALTER *finds what he is looking for—a small piece of white paper—and pushes it in his pocket and puts on his coat and rushes out without ever having looked at her. She shouts after him)* I look at you and I see the final triumph of stupidity in the world!

(The door slams and she returns to just sitting again. RUTH *comes quickly out of* MAMA*'s room)*

RUTH: Who was that?

BENEATHA: Your husband.

RUTH: Where did he go?

BENEATHA: Who knows—maybe he has an appointment at U.S. Steel.

RUTH *(anxiously, with frightened eyes)*: You didn't say nothing bad to him, did you?

BENEATHA: Bad? Say anything bad to him? No—I told him he was a sweet boy and full of dreams and everything is strictly peachy keen, as the ofay kids say!

*(*MAMA *enters from her bedroom. She is lost, vague, trying to catch hold, to make some sense of her former command of the world, but it still eludes her. A sense of waste overwhelms her gait; a measure of apology rides on her shoulders. She goes to her plant, which has remained*

on the table, looks at it, picks it up and takes it to the window sill and sits it outside, and she stands and looks at it a long moment. Then she closes the window, straightens her body with effort and turns around to her children)

MAMA: Well—ain't it a mess in here, though? *(A false cheerfulness, a beginning of something)* I guess we all better stop moping around and get some work done. All this unpacking and everything we got to do. *(*RUTH *raises her head slowly in response to the sense of the line; and* BENEATHA *in similar manner turns very slowly to look at her mother)* One of you all better call the moving people and tell 'em not to come.

RUTH: Tell 'em not to come?

MAMA: Of course, baby. Ain't no need in 'em coming all the way here and having to go back. They charges for that too. *(She sits down, fingers to her brow, thinking)* Lord, ever since I was a little girl, I always remembers people saying, "Lena—Lena Eggleston, you aims too high all the time. You needs to slow down and see life a little more like it is. Just slow down some." That's what they always used to say down home—"Lord, that Lena Eggleston is a high-minded thing. She'll get her due one day!"

RUTH: No, Lena . . .

MAMA: Me and Big Walter just didn't never learn right.

RUTH: Lena, no! We gotta go. Bennie—tell her . . . *(She rises and crosses to* BENEATHA *with her arms outstretched.* BENEATHA *doesn't respond)* Tell her we can still move . . . the notes ain't but a hundred and twenty-five a month. We got four grown people in this house—we can work . . .

MAMA *(to herself)*: Just aimed too high all the time—

RUTH *(turning and going to* MAMA *fast—the words pouring out with urgency and desperation)*: Lena—I'll work . . . I'll work twenty hours a day in all the kitchens in Chicago . . . I'll strap my baby on my back if I have to and scrub all the floors in America and wash all the sheets in America if I have to—but we got to MOVE! We got to get OUT OF HERE!!

*(*MAMA *reaches out absently and pats* RUTH*'s hand)*

MAMA: No—I sees things differently now. Been thinking 'bout some of the things we could do to fix this place up some. I seen a second-hand bureau over on Maxwell Street just the other day that could fit right there. *(She points to where the new furniture might go.* RUTH *wanders away from her)* Would need some new handles on it and then a little varnish and it look like something brand-new. And—we can put up them new curtains in the kitchen . . . Why this place be looking fine. Cheer us all up so that we forget trouble ever come . . . *(To* RUTH*)* And you could get some nice screens to put up in your room round the baby's bassinet . . . *(She looks at both of them, pleadingly)* Sometimes you just got to know when to give up some things . . . and hold on to what you got. . . .

*(*WALTER *enters from the outside, looking spent and leaning against the door, his coat hanging from him)*

MAMA: Where you been, son?

WALTER *(breathing hard)*: Made a call.

MAMA: To who, son?

WALTER: To The Man. *(He heads for his room)*

MAMA: What man, baby?

WALTER *(stops in the door):* The Man, Mama. Don't you know who The Man is?

RUTH: Walter Lee?

WALTER: *The Man.* Like the guys in the streets say—The Man. Captain Boss—Mistuh Charley . . . Old Cap'n Please Mr. Bossman . . .

BENEATHA *(suddenly):* Lindner!

WALTER: That's right! That's good. I told him to come right over.

BENEATHA *(fiercely, understanding):* For what? What do you want to see him for!

WALTER *(looking at his sister):* We going to do business with him.

MAMA: What you talking 'bout, son?

WALTER: Talking 'bout life, Mama. You all always telling me to see life like it is. Well—I laid in there on my back today . . . and I figured it out. Life just like it is. Who gets and who don't get. *(He sits down with his coat on and laughs)* Mama, you know it's all divided up. Life is. Sure enough. Between the takers and the "tooken." *(He laughs)* I've figured it out finally. *(He looks around at them)* Yeah. Some of us always getting "tooken." *(He laughs)* People like Willy Harris, they don't never get "tooken." And you know why the rest of us do? 'Cause we all mixed up. Mixed up bad. We get to looking 'round for the right and the wrong; and we worry about it and cry about it and stay up nights trying to figure out 'bout the wrong and the right of things all the time . . . And all the time, man, them takers is out there operating, just taking and taking. Willy Harris? Shoot—Willy Harris don't even count. He don't even count in the big scheme of things. But I'll say one thing for old Willy Harris . . . he's taught me something. He's taught me to keep my eye on what counts in this world. Yeah—*(Shouting out a little)* Thanks, Willy!

RUTH: What did you call that man for, Walter Lee?

WALTER: Called him to tell him to come on over to the show. Gonna put on a show for the man. Just what he wants to see. You see, Mama, the man came here today and he told us that them people out there where you want us to move—well they so upset they willing to pay us *not* to move! *(He laughs again)* And—and oh, Mama—you would of been proud of the way me and Ruth and Bennie acted. We told him to get out . . . Lord have mercy! We told the man to get out! Oh, we was some proud folks this afternoon, yeah. *(He lights a cigarette)* We were still full of that old-time stuff . . .

RUTH *(coming toward him slowly):* You talking 'bout taking them people's money to keep us from moving in that house?

WALTER: I ain't just talking 'bout it, baby—I'm telling you that's what's going to happen!

BENEATHA: Oh, God! Where is the bottom! Where is the real honest-to-God bottom so he can't go any farther!

WALTER: See—that's the old stuff. You and that boy that was here today. You all want everybody to carry a flag and a spear and sing some marching songs, huh? You wanna spend your life looking into things and trying to find the right and the wrong part, huh? Yeah. You know what's going to happen to that boy someday—he'll find himself sitting in a dungeon, locked in forever—and the takers will have the key! Forget it, baby! There ain't no causes—there ain't nothing but taking in this world, and he who takes most is smartest—and it don't make a damn bit of difference *how.*

MAMA: You making something inside me cry, son. Some awful pain inside me.

WALTER: Don't cry, Mama. Understand. That white man is going to walk in that door able to write checks for more money than we ever had. It's important to him and I'm going to help him . . . I'm going to put on the show, Mama.

MAMA: Son—I come from five generations of people who was slaves and sharecroppers—but ain't nobody in my family never let nobody pay 'em no money that was a way of telling us we wasn't fit to walk the earth. We ain't never been that poor. *(Raising her eyes and looking at him)* We ain't never been that—dead inside.

BENEATHA: Well—we are dead now. All the talk about dreams and sunlight that goes on in this house. It's all dead now.

WALTER: What's the matter with you all! I didn't make this world! It was give to me this way! Hell, yes, I want me some yachts someday! Yes, I want to hang some real pearls 'round my wife's neck. Ain't she supposed to wear no pearls? Somebody tell me—tell me, who decides which women is suppose to wear pearls in this world. I tell you I am a *man*—and I think my wife should wear some pearls in this world!

(This last line hangs a good while and WALTER *begins to move about the room. The word "Man" has penetrated his consciousness; he mumbles it to himself repeatedly between strange agitated pauses as he moves about)*

MAMA: Baby, how you going to feel on the inside?

WALTER: Fine! . . . Going to feel fine . . . a man . . .

MAMA: You won't have nothing left then, Walter Lee.

WALTER *(coming to her):* I'm going to feel fine, Mama. I'm going to look that son-of-a-bitch in the eyes and say— *(He falters)* —and say, "All right, Mr. Lindner— *(He falters even more)*— that's *your* neighborhood out there! You got the right to keep it like you want! You got the right to have it like you want! Just write the check and—the house is yours." And—and I am going to say— *(His voice almost breaks)* "And you—you people just put the money in my hand and you won't have to live next to this bunch of stinking niggers! . . ." *(He straightens up and moves away from his mother, walking around the room)* And maybe—maybe I'll just get down on my black knees . . . *(He does so;* RUTH *and* BENNIE *and* MAMA *watch him in frozen horror)* "Captain, Mistuh, Bossman— *(Groveling and grinning and wringing his hands in profoundly anguished imitation of the slow-witted movie stereotype)* A-hee-hee-hee! Oh, yassuh boss! Yasssssuh! Great white— *(Voice breaking, he forces himself to go on)* —Father, just gi' ussen de money, fo' God's sake, and we's—we's ain't gwine come out deh and dirty up yo' white folks neighborhood . . ." *(He breaks down completely)* And I'll feel fine! Fine! FINE! *(He gets up and goes into the bedroom)*

BENEATHA: That is not a man. That is nothing but a toothless rat.

MAMA: Yes—death done come in this here house. *(She is nodding, slowly, reflectively)* Done come walking in my house on the lips of my children. You what supposed to be my beginning again. You—what supposed to be my harvest. *(To* BENEATHA*)* You—you mourning your brother?

BENEATHA: He's no brother of mine.

MAMA: What you say?

BENEATHA: I said that that individual in that room is no brother of mine.

MAMA: That's what I thought you said. You feeling like you better than he is today? *(*BENEATHA *does not answer)* Yes? What you tell him a minute ago? That he wasn't a man? Yes?

You give him up for me? You done wrote his epitaph too—like the rest of the world? Well, who give you the privilege?

BENEATHA: Be on my side for once! You saw what he just did, Mama! You saw him—down on his knees. Wasn't it you who taught me to despise any man who would do that? Do what he's going to do?

MAMA: Yes—I taught you that. Me and your daddy. But I thought I taught you something else too . . . I thought I taught you to love him.

BENEATHA: Love him? There is nothing left to love.

MAMA: There is *always* something left to love. And if you ain't learned that, you ain't learned nothing. *(Looking at her)* Have you cried for that boy today? I don't mean for yourself and for the family 'cause we lost the money. I mean for him: what he been through and what it done to him. Child, when do you think is the time to love somebody the most? When they done good and made things easy for everybody? Well then, you ain't through learning—because that ain't the time at all. It's when he's at his lowest and can't believe in hisself 'cause the world done whipped him so! When you starts measuring somebody, measure him right, child, measure him right. Make sure you done taken into account what hills and valleys he come through before he got to wherever he is.

(TRAVIS bursts into the room at the end of the speech, leaving the door open)

TRAVIS: Grandmama—the moving men are downstairs! The truck just pulled up.

MAMA *(turning and looking at him)*: Are they, baby? They downstairs?

(She sighs and sits. LINDNER appears in the doorway. He peers in and knocks lightly, to gain attention, and comes in. All turn to look at him)

LINDNER *(hat and briefcase in hand)*: Uh—hello . . .

(RUTH crosses mechanically to the bedroom door and opens it and lets it swing open freely and slowly as the lights come up on WALTER within, still in his coat, sitting at the far corner of the room. He looks up and out through the room to LINDNER)

RUTH: He's here.

(A long minute passes and WALTER slowly gets up)

LINDNER *(coming to the table with efficiency, putting his briefcase on the table and starting to unfold papers and unscrew fountain pens)*: Well, I certainly was glad to hear from you people. *(WALTER has begun the trek out of the room, slowly and awkwardly, rather like a small boy, passing the back of his sleeve across his mouth from time to time)* Life can really be so much simpler than people let it be most of the time. Well—with whom do I negotiate? You, Mrs. Younger, or your son here? *(MAMA sits with her hands folded on her lap and her eyes closed as WALTER advances. TRAVIS goes closer to LINDNER and looks at the papers curiously)* Just some official papers, sonny.

RUTH: Travis, you go downstairs—

MAMA *(opening her eyes and looking into* WALTER*'s):* No. Travis, you stay right here. And you make him understand what you doing, Walter Lee. You teach him good. Like Willy Harris taught you. You show where our five generations done come to. *(*WALTER *looks from her to the boy, who grins at him innocently)* Go ahead, son— *(She folds her hands and closes her eyes)* Go ahead.

WALTER *(at last crosses to* LINDNER*, who is reviewing the contract):* Well, Mr. Lindner. *(*BENEATHA *turns away)* We called you— *(There is a profound, simple groping quality in his speech)* —because, well, me and my family *(He looks around and shifts from one foot to the other)* Well—we are very plain people . . .

LINDNER: Yes—

WALTER: I mean—I have worked as a chauffeur most of my life—and my wife here, she does domestic work in people's kitchens. So does my mother. I mean—we are plain people . . .

LINDNER: Yes, Mr. Younger—

WALTER *(really like a small boy, looking down at his shoes and then up at the man):* And—uh—well, my father, well, he was a laborer most of his life. . . .

LINDNER *(absolutely confused):* Uh, yes—yes, I understand. *(He turns back to the contract)*

WALTER *(a beat; staring at him):* And my father— *(With sudden intensity)* My father almost *beat a man to death* once because this man called him a bad name or something, you know what I mean?

LINDNER *(looking up, frozen):* No, no, I'm afraid I don't—

WALTER *(a beat. The tension hangs; then* WALTER *steps back from it):* Yeah. Well—what I mean is that we come from people who had a lot of *pride.* I mean—we are very proud people. And that's my sister over there and she's going to be a doctor—and we are very proud—

LINDNER: Well—I am sure that is very nice, but—

WALTER: What I am telling you is that we called you over here to tell you that we are very proud and that this— *(Signaling to* TRAVIS*)* Travis, come here. *(*TRAVIS *crosses and* WALTER *draws him before him facing the man)* This is my son, and he makes the sixth generation of our family in this country. And we have all thought about your offer—

LINDNER: Well, good . . . good—

WALTER: And we have decided to move into our house because my father—my father—he earned it for us brick by brick. *(*MAMA *has her eyes closed and is rocking back and forth as though she were in church, with her head nodding the Amen yes)* We don't want to make no trouble for nobody or fight no causes, and we will try to be good neighbors. And that's *all* we got to say about that. *(He looks the man absolutely in the eyes)* We don't want your money. *(He turns and walks away)*

LINDNER *(looking around at all of them):* I take it then—that you have decided to occupy . . .

BENEATHA: That's what the man said.

LINDNER *(to* MAMA *in her reverie):* Then I would like to appeal to you, Mrs. Younger. You are older and wiser and understand things better, I am sure . . .

MAMA: I am afraid you don't understand. My son said we was going to move and there ain't nothing left for me to say. *(Briskly)* You know how these young folks is nowadays, mister. Can't do a thing with 'em! *(As he opens his mouth, she rises)* Good-bye.

LINDNER *(folding up his materials):* Well—if you are that final about it . . . there is nothing

left for me to say. *(He finishes, almost ignored by the family, who are concentrating on* WALTER LEE. *At the door* LINDNER *halts and looks around)* I sure hope you people know what you're getting into.

(He shakes his head and exits)

RUTH *(looking around and coming to life):* Well, for God's sake—if the moving men are here—LET'S GET THE HELL OUT OF HERE!

MAMA *(into action):* Ain't it the truth! Look at all this here mess. Ruth, put Travis' good jacket on him . . . Walter Lee, fix your tie and tuck your shirt in, you look like somebody's hoodlum! Lord have mercy, where is my plant? *(She flies to get it amid the general bustling of the family, who are deliberately trying to ignore the nobility of the past moment)* You all start on down . . . Travis child, don't go empty-handed . . . Ruth, where did I put that box with my skillets in it? I want to be in charge of it myself . . . I'm going to make us the biggest dinner we ever ate tonight . . . Beneatha, what's the matter with them stockings? Pull them things up, girl . . .

(The family starts to file out as two moving men appear and begin to carry out the heavier pieces of furniture, bumping into the family as they move about)

BENEATHA: Mama, Asagai asked me to marry him today and go to Africa—

MAMA *(in the middle of her getting-ready activity):* He did? You ain't old enough to marry nobody— *(Seeing the moving men lifting one of her chairs precariously)* Darling, that ain't no bale of cotton, please handle it so we can sit in it again! I had that chair twenty-five years . . .

(The movers sigh with exasperation and go on with their work)

BENEATHA *(girlishly and unreasonably trying to pursue the conversation):* To go to Africa, Mama—be a doctor in Africa . . .

MAMA *(distracted):* Yes, baby—

WALTER: *Africa!* What he want you to go to Africa for?

BENEATHA: To practice there . . .

WALTER: Girl, if you don't get all them silly ideas out your head! You better marry yourself a man with some loot . . .

BENEATHA *(angrily, precisely as in the first scene of the play):* What have you got to do with who I marry!

WALTER: Plenty. Now I think George Murchison—

BENEATHA: *George Murchison!* I wouldn't marry him if he was Adam and I was Eve!

*(*WALTER *and* BENEATHA *go out yelling at each other vigorously and the anger is loud and real till their voices diminish.* RUTH *stands at the door and turns to* MAMA *and smiles knowingly)*

MAMA *(fixing her hat at last):* Yeah—they something all right, my children . . .

RUTH: Yeah—they're something. Let's go, Lena.

MAMA *(stalling, starting to look around at the house:)* Yes—I'm coming. Ruth—

RUTH: Yes?

MAMA *(quietly, woman to woman):* He finally come into his manhood today, didn't he? Kind of like a rainbow after the rain . . .

RUTH *(biting her lip lest her own pride explode in front of* MAMA*):* Yes, Lena.

*(*WALTER*'s voice calls for them raucously)*

WALTER *(off stage):* Y'all come on! These people charges by the hour, you know!

MAMA *(waving* RUTH *out vaguely):* All right, honey—go on down. I be down directly.

*(*RUTH *hesitates, then exits.* MAMA *stands, at last alone in the living room, her plant on the table before her as the lights start to come down. She looks around at all the walls and ceilings and suddenly, despite herself, while the children call below, a great heaving thing rises in her and she puts her fist to her mouth to stifle it, takes a final desperate look, pulls her coat about her, pats her hat and goes out. The lights dim down. The door opens and she comes back in, grabs her plant, and goes out for the last time)*

Curtain

BRIAN FRIEL

(1929–)

Philadelphia, Here I Come!

About the Author: Brian Friel, Ireland's best-known living playwright, was born in 1929 in the Northern Irish city of Derry, where he spent most of his life. He has published two books of short stories in addition to many plays, and he is founder of the Field Day Theatre Company in Derry. He now lives over the border in the Republic of Ireland, where he has been named senator, a largely honorific office, in recognition of his literary stature.

About the Play: *Philadelphia, Here I Come!* remains his best-known work. It was first performed in Dublin in 1964, and shortly thereafter in New York on Broadway in 1966 and in London's West End in 1967. The play is set in the home of Gar O'Donnell on the evening before and morning of his emigration to Philadelphia from the small Irish village of Ballybeg. The play is dramatically innovative in having two actors simultaneously portraying Gar, one as his public self, perceived by and interacting with the other characters, and the other as his private self, acknowledged only by his private self (although never looked at by him). Since the audience can hear what the Private Gar says, the effect is at times akin to that of the Shakespearian soliloquy or aside, especially when Private is expressing Public's conscious, but unexpressed, thoughts. At other times, however, Private expresses Gar's repressed unconscious or subconscious emotional reactions to the play's actions, and the effect is closer to that of a post-Freudian version of a Greek chorus. This presentation of the central character's inner and outer psychological state, combined with the flashback technique through which his memories of earlier moments from his life are depicted, allows Friel to present a particularly rich and textured portrayal of individual psychology.

CAST

MADGE	*Housekeeper*
GAR O'DONNELL (PUBLIC) GAR O'DONNELL (PRIVATE)	*Son of the house*
S. B. O'DONNELL	*Gar's father*
KATE DOOGAN/MRS KING	*Daughter of Senator Doogan*
SENATOR DOOGAN	
MASTER BOYLE	*Local teacher*
LIZZY SWEENEY	*Gar's aunt*
CON SWEENEY	*Lizzy's husband*
BEN BURTON	*Friend of the Sweeneys*
NED TOM JOE	*The boys*
CANON MICK O'BYRNE	*The parish priest*

There is an interval at the end of Episode I and at the end of Episode II.

Time: *the present in the small village of Ballybeg in County Donegal, Ireland. The action takes place on the night before, and on the morning of, Gar's departure for Philadelphia.*

When the curtain rises the only part of the stage that is lit is the kitchen, i.e. the portion on the left from the point of view of the audience. It is sparsely and comfortlessly furnished—a bachelor's kitchen. There are two doors; one left which leads to the shop, and one upstage leading to the scullery [off]. Beside the shop door is a large deal table, now set for tea without cloth and with rough cups and saucers. Beside the scullery door is an old-fashioned dresser. On the scullery wall is a large school-type clock.

Stage right, now in darkness, is Gar's bedroom. Both bedroom and kitchen should be moved upstage, leaving a generous apron. Gar's bedroom is furnished with a single bed, a wash-hand basin (crockery jug and bowl), a table with a record-player and records, and a small chest of drawers.

These two areas—kitchen and Gar's bedroom—occupy more than two-thirds of the stage. The remaining portion is fluid: in Episode I, for example, it represents a room in Senator Doogan's home.

The two Gars, Public Gar and Private Gar, are two views of the one man. Public Gar is the Gar that people see, talk to, talk about. Private Gar is the unseen man, the man within, the conscience, the alter ego, the secret thoughts, the id.

Private Gar, the spirit, is invisible to everybody, always. Nobody except Public Gar hears him talk. But even Public Gar, although he talks to Private Gar occasionally, never sees him and never looks at him. *One cannot look at one's alter ego.*

MUSIC

Mendelssohn's Violin Concerto in E Minor, Op. 64
Ceildhe music
'All Round My Hat'—First Verse.
'She Moved through the Fair'—Second Verse.
'California, Here I Come!'
'Give the Woman in the Bed More Porter.'

EPISODE I

[Kitchen in the home of County Councillor S. B. O'Donnell who owns a general shop. As the curtain rises Madge, the housekeeper, enters from the scullery with a tray in her hands and finishes setting the table. She is a woman in her sixties. She walks as if her feet were precious. She pauses on her way past the shop door.]

MADGE Gar! Your tea!
PUBLIC [*off*] Right!

[She finishes setting the table and is about to go to the scullery door when Public Gar marches on stage. He is ecstatic with joy and excitement: tomorrow morning he leaves for Philadelphia.]

GAR [*singing*] 'Philadelphia, here I come, right back where I started from . . .' [*Breaks off and catches Madge*] Come on, Madge! What about an old time waltz!
MADGE Agh, will you leave me alone.

[He holds on to her and forces her to do a few steps as he sings in waltz time.]

PUBLIC 'Where bowers of flowers bloom in the spring'—
MADGE [*struggling*] Stop it! Stop it! You brat you!
PUBLIC Madge, you dance like an angel. [*Suddenly lets her go and springs away from her.*] Oh, but you'd give a fella bad thoughts very quick!
MADGE And the smell of fish of you, you dirty thing!

[He grabs her again and puts his face up to hers, very confidentially.]

PUBLIC Will you miss me?
MADGE Let me on with my work!
PUBLIC The truth!
MADGE Agh, will you quit it, will you?
PUBLIC I'll tickle you till you squeal for mercy.
MADGE Please, Gar . . .
PUBLIC [*tickling her*] Will you miss me, I said?
MADGE I will—I will—I will—I—
PUBLIC That's better. Now tell me: What time is it?
MADGE Agh, Gar—
PUBLIC What time is it?
MADGE [*looking at clock*] Ten past seven.
PUBLIC And what time do I knock off at?
MADGE At seven.
PUBLIC Which means that on my last day with him he got ten minutes overtime out of my hide. [*He releases Madge.*] Instead of saying to me: [*grandly*] 'Gar, my son, since you are leaving me forever, you may have the entire day free,' what does he do? Lines up five packs of flour and says: [*in flat dreary tones*] 'Make them up into two-pound pokes.'
MADGE He's losing a treasure, indeed!

PUBLIC So d'you know what I said to him? I just drew myself up and looked him straight in the eye and said to him: 'Two-pound pokes it will be'—just like that.

MADGE That flattened him.

[*She goes off to the scullery. He stands at the door and talks in to her.*]

PUBLIC And that wasn't it all. At six o'clock he remembered about the bloody pollock, and him in the middle of the Angelus [*stands in imitation of the Father: head bowed, hands on chest. In flat tones*—] 'Behold-the-handmaid-of-the-Lord-Gut-and-salt-them-fish.' So by God I lashed so much salt on those bloody fish that any poor bugger that eats them will die of thirst. But when the corpses are strewn all over Ballybeg, where will I be? In the little old U.S.A.! Yip-eeeeee! [*He swings away from the scullery door and does a few exuberant steps as he sings*—] 'Philadelphia, here I come, rightah backah where Ah started from—'

[*He goes into his bedroom, flings himself down on his bed, rests his head on his hands, and looks at the ceiling. Sings alternate lines of 'Philadelphia'—first half—with Private* [*off*]].

PUBLIC It's all over.

PRIVATE [*off, in echo-chamber voice*] And it's all about to begin. It's all over.

PUBLIC And all about to begin.

PRIVATE [*Now on*] Just think, Gar.

PUBLIC Think . . .

PRIVATE Think. . . . Up in that big bugger of a jet, with its snout pointing straight for the States, and its tail belching smoke over Ireland; and you sitting up at the front [*Public acts this*] with your competent fingers poised over the controls; and then away down below in the Atlantic you see a bloody bugger of an Irish boat out fishing for bloody pollock and—

[*Public nose-dives, engines screaming, machine guns stuttering.*]

PUBLIC Rat-tat-tat-tat-tat-tat-tat-tat-tat-tat.

PRIVATE Abandon ship! Make for the life-boats! Send for Canon Mick O'Byrne!

[*Public gains altitude and nose-dives again.*]

PUBLIC Rat-tat-tat-tat-tat-tat-tat-tat-tat.

PRIVATE To hell with women and children! Say an Act of Contrition!

PUBLIC Yip-eeeee!

[*He finishes taking off the shop coat, rolls it into a bundle, and places it carefully on the floor.*]

PRIVATE It looks as if—I can't see very well from the distance—but it looks as if—yes!—yes!—the free is being taken by dashing Gar O'Donnell [*Public gets back from the coat, poises himself to kick it*], pride of the Ballybeg team. [*In commentator's hushed voice*] O'Donnell is now moving back, taking a slow, calculating look at the goal, I've never seen this boy in the brilliant form he's in today—absolute magic in his feet. He's now in position, running up, and—

[*Public kicks the shop coat into the air.*]

PUBLIC Ya-hoooo! [*Sings and gyrates at same time.*] 'Philah-delph-yah, heah Ah come, rightah backah weah Ah stahted from, boom-boom-boom-boom—'

[*He breaks off suddenly when Private addresses him in sombre tones of a judge.*]

PRIVATE Gareth Mary O'Donnell.

[*Public springs to attention, salutes, and holds this absurd military stance. He is immediately inside his bedroom door, facing it.*]

PUBLIC Sir.
PRIVATE You are full conscious of all the consequences of your decision?
PUBLIC Yessir.
PRIVATE Of leaving the country of your birth, the land of the curlew and the snipe, the Aran sweater and the Irish Sweepstakes?
PUBLIC [*with fitting hesitation*] I-I-I-I have considered all these, Sir.
PRIVATE Of going to a profane, irreligious, pagan country of gross materialism?
PUBLIC I am fully sensitive to this, Sir.
PRIVATE Where the devil himself holds sway, and lust—abhorrent lust—is everywhere indulged in shamelessly?

[*Public winks extravagantly and nudges an imaginary man beside him.*]

PUBLIC Who are you tellin'? [*Poker-stiff again.*] Shamelessly, Sir, shamelessly.

[*Madge has entered from the scullery, carrying an old suitcase and a bundle of clothes.*]

PRIVATE And yet you persist in exposing yourself to these frightful dangers?
PUBLIC I would submit, Sir, that these stories are slightly exaggerated, Sir. For every door that opens—

[*Madge opens the bedroom door.*]

MADGE Oh! You put the heart across me there! Get out of my road, will you, and quit eejiting about!
PUBLIC Madge, you're an aul duck.
MADGE Aye, so. There's the case. And there's a piece of rope for I see the clasp's all rusted. And there's your shirts and your winter vests and your heavy socks. And you'll need to air them shirts before you—Don't put them smelly hands on them!
PUBLIC Sorry!
MADGE See that they're well aired before you put them on. He's said nothing since, I suppose?
PUBLIC Not a word.
PRIVATE The bugger.
MADGE But he hasn't paid you your week's wages?

PUBLIC £3 15*s*—that'll carry me far.

MADGE He'll have something to say then, you'll see. And maybe he'll slip you a couple of extra pounds.

PUBLIC Whether he says good-bye to me or not, or whether he slips me a few miserable quid or not, it's a matter of total indifference to me, Madge.

MADGE Aye, so. Your tea's on the table—but that's a matter of total indifference to me.

PUBLIC Give me time to wash, will you?

MADGE And another thing: just because he doesn't say much doesn't mean that he hasn't feelings like the rest of us.

PUBLIC Say much? He's said nothing!

MADGE He said nothing either when your mother died. It must have been near daybreak when he got to sleep last night. I could hear his bed creaking.

PUBLIC Well to hell with him—

MADGE [*leaving*] Don't come into your tea smelling like a lobster-pot.

PUBLIC If he wants to speak to me he knows where to find me! But I'm damned if I'm going to speak to him first!

[*Madge goes off to the scullery.*]

[*Calling after her*] And you can tell him I said that if you like!

PRIVATE What the hell do you care about him. Screwballs! Skinflint! Skittery Face! You're free of him and his stinking bloody shop. And tomorrow morning, boy, when that little ole plane gets up into the skies, you'll stick your head out the window [*Public acts this*] and spit down on the lot of them!

[*S.B. appears at the shop door. He is in his late sixties. Wears a hat, a good dark suit, collar and tie, black apron. S. B. O'Donnell is a responsible, respectable citizen.*]

S.B. Gar!

[*Public reacts instinctively. Private keeps calm.*]

PRIVATE Let the bugger call.

S.B. [*louder*] Gar!

[*Instinct is stronger than reason: Public rushes to his door and opens it. But as soon as he opens it and looks out at his father he assumes in speech and gesture a surly, taciturn gruffness. He always behaves in this way when he is in his father's company.*]

PUBLIC Aye?

S.B. How many coils of barbed-wire came in on the mail-van this evening?

PUBLIC Two. Or was it 3?

S.B. That's what I'm asking you. It was you that carried them into the yard.

PUBLIC There were two—no, no, no, three—yes, three—or maybe it was . . . was it two?

S.B. Agh!

[*S.B. retires to the shop. Public and Private come back into the bedroom.*]

PRIVATE What sort of a stupid bugger are you? Think, man! You went out and stood yarning to Joe the Post; then you carried one coil into the yard and came out with the sack of spuds for the parochial; then you carried in the second coil . . . and put it in the corner . . . and came out again to the van . . . and . . . [*Public skips into the air.*] Ah, what the hell odds! That's his headache, old Nicodemus! After tomorrow a bloody roll of barbed-wire will be a mere bagatelle to you. [*In cowboy accent.*] Yeah, man. You see tham thar plains stretchin' 's far th'eye can see, man? Well, tham thar plains belongs to Garry the Kid. An' Garry the Kid he don't go in for none of your fancy fencin'. No siree. [*His eye lights on the fresh laundry Madge brought in.*] And what'll you wear on the plane tomorrow, old rooster, eh?

[*Public picks up a clean shirt, holds it to his chest, and surveys himself in the small mirror above his wash-hand basin.*]

Pretty smart, eh?

PUBLIC Pretty smart.

PRIVATE Pretty sharp?

PUBLIC Pretty sharp.

PRIVATE Pretty ou-la-la?

PUBLIC Mais oui.

PRIVATE And not a bad looker, if I may say so.

PUBLIC You may. You may.

PRIVATE [*in heavy U.S. accent*] I'm Patrick Palinakis, president of the biggest chain of biggest hotels in the world. We're glad to have you, Mr O'Donnell.

PUBLIC [*sweet, demure*] And I'm glad to be here, Sir.

PRIVATE Handsomely said, young man. I hope you'll be happy with us and work hard and one day maybe you'll be president of the biggest chain of biggest hotels in the world.

PUBLIC That's my ambition, Sir.

PRIVATE You are twenty-five years of age, Mr O'Donnell?

PUBLIC Correct.

PRIVATE And you spent one year at University College Dublin?

PUBLIC Yes, Sir.

PRIVATE Would you care to tell me why you abandoned your academic career, Mr O'Donnell?

PUBLIC [*with disarming simplicity*] Well, just before I sat my First Arts exam, Sir, I did an old Irish turas, or pilgrimage, where I spent several nights in devout prayer, Sir.

PRIVATE St Patrick's Pilgrimage—on Lough—?

PUBLIC St Harold's Cross, Sir. And it was there that I came to realize that a life of scholarship was not for me. So I returned to my father's business.

PRIVATE Yeah. You mentioned that your father was a businessman. What's his line?

PUBLIC Well, Sir, he has—what you would call—his finger in many pies—retail mostly—general dry goods—assorted patent drugs—hardware—ah—ah—dehydrated fish—men's king-size hose—snuffs from the exotic East . . . of Donegal—a confection for gourmets, known as Peggy's Leg—weedkiller— [*Suddenly breaking off: in his normal accent: rolling on the bed*—] Yahoooooo! It is now sixteen or seventeen years since I saw the Queen of France, then the Dauphiness, at Versailles—

PRIVATE Let's git packin', boy. Let's git that li'l ole saddle bag opened and let's git packin'.

But first let's have a li'l ole music on the li'l ole phonograph. Yeah man. You bet. Ah reckon. Yessir.

[*Public puts a record on the player: First Movement, Mendelssohn's violin concerto. Public is preening himself before his performance, and while he is flexing his fingers and adjusting his bow-tie, Private announces in the reverential tones of a radio announcer*]

The main item in tonight's concert is the first movement of the violin concerto in E minor, opus 64, by Jacob Ludwig Felix Mendelssohn. The orchestra is conducted by Gareth O'Donnell and the soloist is the Ballybeg half-back, Gareth O'Donnell. Music critics throughout the world claim that O'Donnell's simultaneous wielding of baton and bow is the greatest thing since Leather Ass died. Mendelssohn's Violin Concerto, 3rd movement.

[*Private sits demurely on the chair. Public clears his throat. Now Public plays the violin, conducts, plays the violin, conducts, etc. etc. This keeps up for some time. Then Private rises from his chair*]

Agh, come on, come on, come on! Less aul foolin'. To work, old rooster, to work. [*Public stops. Turns player down low and changes from the first to the second movement. Takes a look at the case Madge brought in.*] Ah, hell, how can any bloody bugger head into a jet plane with aul' cardboard rubbish like that! [*Public examines the surface.*] Damnit, maybe you could give it a lick of paint! Or wash it! [*Public spits on the lid and rubs it with his finger.*] God, you'll rub a hole in the damn thing if you're not careful! Maybe aul Screwballs'll slip you a fiver tonight and you can get a new one in Dublin.

PUBLIC What a hope!

[*Public opens the case and sniffs the inside.*]

PRIVATE Oh! Stinks of cat's pee!

[*Public lifts out a sheet of faded newspaper.*]

PUBLIC [*reads*] The *Clarion*—1st January 1937.

PRIVATE Precious medieval manuscript . . . my God, was it? . . . By God it was—the day they were married—and it [*the case*] hasn't been opened since their honeymoon . . . she and old Screwballs off on a side-car to Bundoran for three days. . . .

PUBLIC O God, the Creator and Redeemer of all the faithful, give to the soul of Maire, my mother, the remission of all her sins, that she may obtain. . . .

PRIVATE She was small, Madge says, and wild, and young, Madge says, from a place called Bailtefree beyond the mountains; and her eyes were bright, and her hair was loose, and she carried her shoes under her arm until she came to the edge of the village, Madge says, and then she put them on. . . .

PUBLIC Eternal rest grant unto her, O Lord, and let perpetual light shine. . . .

PRIVATE She was nineteen and he was forty, and he owned a shop, and he wore a soft hat, and she thought he was the grandest gentleman that ever lived, Madge says; and he—he couldn't take his eyes off her, Madge says. . . .

PUBLIC O God, O God the Creator and Redeemer. . . .

PRIVATE And sometimes in that first year, when she was pregnant with you, laddybuck, the other young girls from Bailtefree would call in here to dress up on their way to a dance, Madge says, and her face would light up too, Madge says. . . .

[*Public puts the newspaper carefully inside the folds of a shirt.*]

. . . And he must have known, old Screwballs, he must have known, Madge says, for many a night he must have heard her crying herself to sleep . . . and maybe it was good of God to take her away three days after you were born. . . . [*Suddenly boisterous.*] Damn you, anyhow, for a bloody stupid bastard! It is now sixteen or seventeen years since I saw the Queen of France, then the Dauphiness, at Versailles! And to hell with that bloody mushy fidler!

[*Public goes quickly to the record-player and sings boisterously as he goes.*]

PUBLIC 'Philadelphia, here I come—'

PRIVATE Watch yourself, nut-head. If you let yourself slip that way, you might find that—

PUBLIC '—right back where I started from.'

[*Public has taken off the Mendelssohn and is now searching for another.*]

PRIVATE Something lively! Something bloody animal! A bit of aul thumpety-thump! [*Public puts on the record.*] An' you jist keep atalkin' to you'self all the time, Mistah, 'cos once you stop atalkin' to you'self ah reckon then you jist begin to think kinda crazy things— [*The record begins—Any lively piece of Ceilidhe Band music.*] Ahhhhh!

PUBLIC Yipeeeeeeeee!

[*Public dances up and down the length of his bedroom. Occasionally he leaps high into the air or does a neat bit of foot-work. Occasionally he lilts. Occasionally he talks to different people he meets on the dance floor.*]

Righ-too-del-loo-del-oo-del-oo-del-oo-del-oo-del-ah,
Rum-ta-del-ah-del-ah-del-agh-del-ah-del-ah-del-agh.
Hell of a crowd here the night, eh? Yah-ho!
Man, you're looking powerful! Great!

[*Private sits on the chair and watches. When he speaks his voice is soft. Public pretends not to hear him.*]

PRIVATE Remember—that was Katie's tune. You needn't pretend you have forgotten. And it reminds you of the night the two of you made all the plans, and you thought your heart would burst with happiness.

PUBLIC [*louder*] Tigh-righ-tigh-righ-scal-del-de-da-del-ah, Come on! A dirty big swing! Yaaaaaaaaaaah!

PRIVATE [*quietly, rapidly insisting*] Are you going to take her photograph to the States with you? When are you going to say good-bye to her? Will you write to her? Will you send her cards and photographs? You loved her once, old rooster; you wanted so much to marry her that it was a bloody sickness. Tell me, randy boy; tell me the truth: have you got over that sickness? Do you still love her? Do you still lust after her? Well, do you? Do you? Do you?

PUBLIC Bugger!

[*Public suddenly stops dancing, switches—almost knocks—off the record-player, pulls a wallet out of his hip pocket and produces a snap. He sits and looks at it.*]

PRIVATE Shhhhhhhhhhhhh. . . .

PUBLIC [*softly*] Kate . . . sweet Katie Doogan . . . my darling Kathy Doogan. . . .

PRIVATE [*in same soft tone*] Aul bitch. [*Loudly.*] Rotten aul snobby bitch! Just like her stinking rotten father and mother—a bugger and a buggeress—a buggeroo and a buggerette!

PUBLIC No, no; my fault—all my fault—

PRIVATE [*remembering and recalling tauntingly*] By God, that was a night, boy, eh? By God, you made a right bloody cow's ass of yourself. [*Public goes off right.*] Remember—when was it?—10 months ago?—you had just come back from a walk out the Mill Road, and the pair of you had the whole thing planned: engaged at Christmas, married at Easter, and 14 of a family—7 boys and 7 girls. Cripes, you make me laugh! You bloody-well make me die laughing. You were going to 'develop' the hardware lines and she was going to take charge of the 'drapery'! The drapery! The fishy socks and the shoebox of cotton spools and rusted needles! And you—you were to ask Screwballs for a rise in pay—'in view of your increased responsibilities'! And you were so far gone that night, Laddybuck— [*Public and Kate enter from the left and walk very slowly across the front of the stage. They stop and kiss. Then they move on again.*] —So bloody-well astray in the head with 'love' that you went and blabbed about your secret egg deals that nobody knew anything about—not even Madge! Stupid bloody get! O my God, how you stick yourself I'll never know!

PUBLIC Kate—Kathy—I'm mad about you! I'll never last till Easter! I'll—I'll—I'll bloody-well burst!

[*He catches her again and kisses her.*]

PRIVATE Steady, boy, steady. You know what the Canon says: long passionate kisses in lonely places. . . .

PUBLIC Our daughters'll all be gentle and frail and silly, like you; and our sons—they'll be thick bloody louts, sexy goats, like me, and by God I'll beat the tar out of them!

KATE But £3 15*s*, Gar! We could never live on that.

PUBLIC [*kissing her hair*] Mmmm.

KATE Gar! Listen! Be sensible.

PUBLIC Mmm?

KATE How will we *live?*

PRIVATE [*imitating*] 'How will we *live?*'

PUBLIC Like lords—free house, free light, free fuel, free groceries! And every night at seven when we close—except Saturday; he stays open till damn near midnight on Saturdays, making out bloody bills; and sure God and the world knows that sending out bills here is as hopeless as peeing against the wind.

KATE Gar! No matter what you say we just couldn't live on that much money. It—it's not possible. We'll need to have more security than that.
PUBLIC Maybe he'll die—tonight—of galloping consumption!
KATE Gar. . . .
PUBLIC What's troubling you?

[*He tries to kiss her again and she avoids him.*]

KATE Please. This is serious.
PRIVATE 'Please. This is serious.'
PUBLIC [*irritably*] What is it?
KATE You'll have to see about getting more money.
PUBLIC Of course I'll see about getting more money! Haven't I told you I'm going to ask for a rise?
KATE But will he—?
PUBLIC I'll get it; don't you worry; I'll get it. Besides: [*with dignity*] I have a—a-a source of income that he knows nothing about—that nobody knows nothing about—knows anything about.
KATE [*with joy*] Investments? Like Daddy?
PUBLIC Well . . . sort of . . . [*quickly*]. You know when I go round the country every Tuesday and Thursday in the lorry?
KATE Yes?
PUBLIC Well, I buy eggs direct from the farms and sell them privately to McLaughlin's Hotel— [*winks*] —for a handsome profit— [*quickly*] —but he knows nothing about it.
KATE And how much do you make?
PUBLIC It varies—depending on the time of year.
KATE Roughly.
PUBLIC Oh, anything from 12*s* 6*d* to £1.
KATE Every Tuesday and Thursday?
PUBLIC Every month. [*Grabs her again.*] God, Kate, I can't even wait till Christmas!
KATE Shhhhh.
PUBLIC But I can't. We'll have to get married sooner—next month—next week—
PRIVATE Steady, steady. . . .
PUBLIC Kate . . . my sweet Katie . . . my darling Kathy. . . .

[*They kiss. Suddenly Kate breaks off. Her voice is urgent.*]

KATE We'll go now, rightaway, and tell them.
PUBLIC Who?
KATE Mammy and Daddy. They're at home tonight.

[*She catches his arm and pulls him towards the left.*]

Come on. Quickly. Now, Gar, now.
PUBLIC [*adjusting his tie*] God, Kathy, I'm in no—look at the shoes—the trousers—
KATE What matter. It must be now, Gar, now!

PUBLIC What—what—what'll I say?
KATE That you want their permission to marry me next week.
PUBLIC God, they'll wipe the bloody floor with me!
KATE Gar!

[*She kisses him passionately, quickly, then breaks off and goes. Stage right, now lit. A room in Doogan's house.*]

PUBLIC God, my legs are trembling! Kathy. . . .
KATE Anybody at home? Mammy! Daddy!

[*Public hesitates before entering Doogan's house. Private is at his elbow, prompting him desperately.*]

PRIVATE Mr Doogan . . . —Senator Doogan—I want to ask your permission. . . . O my God! . . .
KATE Yo-ho!
PRIVATE Mrs Doogan, Kate and I have to get married rightaway—Cripes, no!—
KATE Where is everybody! Yo-ho-yo-ho!
PRIVATE If the boys could see you now!

[*Kate comes back to him, gives him a quick kiss on the cheek.*]

KATE Don't look so miserable. Here . . . [*fixes his tie*].
PUBLIC Kathy, maybe we should wait until—until—until next Sunday—
KATE [*earnestly*] Remember, it's up to you, entirely up to you.
DOOGAN [*off*] That you, Kate?
KATE [*rapidly*] You have £20 a week and £5,000 in the bank and your father's about to retire. [*Turning and smiling at Doogan who has now entered.*] Just Gar and I, Daddy. [*Doogan, Lawyer, Senator, middle forties.*]
DOOGAN Hello, Gareth. You're a stranger.
PRIVATE Speak, you dummy you!
KATE [*filling in*] Where's Mammy?
DOOGAN She's watching TV. [*To Gar.*] And how are things with you, Gareth?
PUBLIC Mr Doogan, I want—
PRIVATE Go on.
PUBLIC I won't be staying long.
DOOGAN [*to Kate*] Francis arrived when you were out. Took a few days off and decided to come north.
PRIVATE Cripes!
KATE He—he's—he's here—now?
DOOGAN Inside with your mother. Ask them to join us, will you?

[*Kate gives Public a last significant look.*]

KATE You talk to Daddy, Gar.
PRIVATE God, I will, I will.

[*Kate goes off right.*]

DOOGAN You've met Francis King, haven't you, Gareth?

PUBLIC Yes—yes—

PRIVATE King of the bloody fairies!

DOOGAN We don't want to raise Kate's hopes unduly, but strictly between ourselves there's a good chance that he'll get the new dispensary job here.

PUBLIC Kate's hopes?

DOOGAN Didn't she tell you? No, I can see she didn't. Of course there's nothing official yet; not even what you might call an understanding. But if this post does fall into his lap, well, her mother and I . . . let's say we're living in hope. A fine boy, Francis; and we've known the Kings, oh, since away back. As a matter of fact his father and I were class-fellows at school. . . .

[*Doogan goes on and on. We catch an occasional word. Meantime Private has moved up to Public's elbow.*]

PRIVATE Cripes, man!

DOOGAN . . . and then later at university when he did medicine and I did law, we knocked about quite a bit. . . .

PRIVATE O God, the aul bitch! Cripes, you look a right fool standing there—the father of 14 children!—Get out, you eejit you! Get out! Get out quick before the others come in and die laughing at you! And all the time she must have known—the aul bitch!—And you promised to give her breakfast in bed every morning! And you told her about the egg money!

DOOGAN . . . your father, Gareth?

PRIVATE He's talking to you, thick-skull.

PUBLIC What—what—what's that?

DOOGAN Your father—how is he?

PUBLIC Oh he—he—he's grand, thanks.

PRIVATE Get out! Get out!

PUBLIC Look Mr Doogan, if you'll excuse me, I think I'd better move on—

DOOGAN Aren't you waiting for supper? The others will be along in a moment for—

PUBLIC No, I must run. I've got to make up half-a-hundredweight of sugar bags.

PRIVATE Brilliant!

PUBLIC Say good-bye to—

DOOGAN Certainly—certainly. Oh, Gareth— [*Public pauses*].

[*Awkwardly, with sincerity.*] Kate is our only child, Gareth, and her happiness is all that is important to us—

PRIVATE [*sings*] 'Give the woman in the bed more porter—'

DOOGAN What I'm trying to say is that any decision she makes will be her own—

PRIVATE '—Give the man beside her water, Give the woman in the bed more porter,—'

DOOGAN Just in case you should think that her mother or I were . . . in case you might have the idea. . . .

PUBLIC [*rapidly*] Good night, Mr Doogan.

[*Public rushes off.*]

DOOGAN Good-bye. . . . Gareth.

[*Doogan stands lighting his pipe.*]

KATE [*enters down right of Doogan and sees that Gar is no longer there*] Where's Gar?
DOOGAN He didn't seem anxious to stay.
KATE But didn't he—did he—?
DOOGAN No, he didn't. [*He crosses Kate to exit down right as light fades to black out.*]

[*Black out Doogan's room. Public and Private move back to the bedroom where Public is putting away the photograph and begins washing.*]

PRIVATE [*wearily*] Mrs Doctor Francis King. September 8th. In harvest sunshine. Red carpet and white lilies and Sean Horgan singing 'Bless This House'—and him whipped off to Sligo jail two days later for stealing turf. Honeymoon in Mallorca and you couldn't have afforded to take her to Malahide. By God, Gar, aul sod, it was a sore hoke on the aul prestige, eh? Between ourselves, aul son, in the privacy of the bedroom, between you and me and the wall, as the fella says, has it left a deep scar on the aul skitter of a soul, eh? What I mean to say like, you took it sort of bad, between you and me and the wall, as the fella says—
PUBLIC [*sings*] 'Philadelphia, here I come, right back—"
PRIVATE But then there's more fish in the sea, as the fella says, and they're all the same when they're upside down; and between you and me and the wall, the first thing you would have had to do would have been to give the boot to Daddy Senator. And I'm thinking, Gar, aul rooster, that wouldn't have made you his pet son-in-law. Mister Fair-play Lawyer Senator Doogan—'her happiness is all that is important to us'! You know, of course, that he carries one of those wee black cards in the inside pocket of his jacket, privately printed for him: 'I am a Catholic. In case of accident send for a bishop.' And you know, too, that in his spare time he travels for maternity corsets; and that he's a double spy for the Knights and the Masons; and that he takes pornographic photographs of Mrs D. and sends them anonymously to reverend mothers. And when you think of a bugger like that, you want to get down on your knees and thank God for aul Screwballs. [*Imitating his father's slow speech.*] So you're going to America in the morning, son?

[*Public carries on with his washing and dressing and at the same time does this dialogue.*]

PUBLIC Yes, Father.
PRIVATE Nothing like it to broaden the mind. Man, how I'd love to travel. But there's some it doesn't agree with—like me, there.
PUBLIC In what way, Father?
PRIVATE The bowels, son. Let me move an inch from the house here—and they stall.
PUBLIC No!
PRIVATE Like the time I went to Lough Derg, away back in '35. Not a budge. The bare feet were nothing to the agonies I went through. I was bound up for two full weeks afterwards.
PUBLIC It taught you a lesson.

PRIVATE Didn't it just? Now I wouldn't even think of travelling.
PUBLIC Anchored by the ass.
PRIVATE Bound by the bowels.
PUBLIC Tethered by the toilet. Tragic.

[*Public has now finished dressing. He surveys himself in the mirror.*]

PRIVATE Not bad. Not bad at all. And well preserved for a father of 14 children.
PUBLIC [*in absurd Hollywood style*] Hi, gorgeous! You live in my block?
PRIVATE [*matching the accent*] Yeah, big handsome boy. Sure do.
PUBLIC Mind if I walk you past the incinerator, to the elevator?
PRIVATE You're welcome, slick operator.

[*Public is facing the door of his bedroom. Madge enters the kitchen from the scullery.*]

PUBLIC What'ya say, li'l chick, you and me—you know—I'll spell it out for ya ifya like. [*Winks, and clicks his tongue.*]
PRIVATE You say the cutest things, big handsome boy!
PUBLIC A malted milk at the corner drug-store?
PRIVATE Wow!
PUBLIC A movie at the downtown drive-in?
PRIVATE Wow-wow!
PUBLIC Two hamburgers, two cokes, two slices of blueberry pie?
PRIVATE Wow-wow-wow.
PUBLIC And then in my apartment—

[*Madge enters the bedroom.*]

MADGE Gee, Mary, and Jay! Will you quit them antics!
PUBLIC Well, you should knock anyway before you enter a man's room!
MADGE Man! I bathed you every Saturday night till you were a big lout of fourteen! Your tea's cold waiting. [*She makes towards door.*]

[*She goes into the kitchen. Public and Private follow her.*]

PUBLIC How was I to know that?
MADGE Amn't I hoarse calling you? Dear, but you're in for a cooling when you go across! [*As she passes through the shop door on way to scullery.*] Boss!
PRIVATE [*in imitation*] 'Boss!'

[*She pauses at the scullery door. With shy delight.*]

MADGE I forgot to tell you. Nelly had a wee baby this morning.
PUBLIC Go on!
MADGE A wee girl. 7 lb 4 oz.
PUBLIC How many's that you have now?
MADGE Four grandnieces and three grandnephews. [*Pause.*] And they're going to call this one Madge—at least so she *says.*

PUBLIC I'll send it a—a—a—an elephant out of my first wages! An elephant for wee Madge!

MADGE I had a feeling it would be a wee girl this time. Maybe I'll take a run over on Sunday and square the place up for her. She could do with some help, with seven of them.

PUBLIC You're a brick, Madge.

MADGE Aye, so. [*As she goes to scullery.*] Wee Madge, maybe. . . .

[*Public sits at the table. Private leans against the wall beside him.*]

PRIVATE And now what are you sad about? Just because she lives for those Mulhern children, and gives them whatever few half-pence she has? Madge, Madge, I think I love you more than any of them. Give me a piece of your courage, Madge.

[*S.B. enters from the shop and goes through his nightly routine. He hangs up the shop keys. He looks at his pocket watch and checks its time with the clock on the wall. He takes off his apron, folds it carefully, and leaves it on the back of his chair. Then he sits down to eat. During all these ponderous jobs Private keeps up the following chatter:*]

And here comes your pleasure, your little ray of sunshine. Ladies and Gentlemen, I give you—the one and only—the inimitable—the irrepressible—the irresistible—County Councillor—S—B—O'Donnell! [*Trumpet—hummed—fanfare. Continues in the smooth, unctuous tones of the commentator at a mannequin parade.*] And this time Marie Celeste is wearing a cheeky little head-dress by Pamela of Park Avenue, eminently suitable for cocktail parties, morning coffee, or just casual shopping. It is of brown Viennese felt, and contrasts boldly with the attractive beach ensemble, created by Simon. The pert little apron is detachable— [*S.B. removes apron*] —thank you, Marie Celeste—and underneath we have the tapered Italian-line slacks in ocelot. I would draw your attention to the large collar stud which is highly decorative and can be purchased separately at our boutique. We call this seductive outfit 'Indiscretion'. It can be worn six days a week, in or out of bed. [*In polite tone.*] Have a seat, Screwballs. [*S.B. sits down at the table.*] Thank you. Remove the hat. [*S.B. takes off the hat to say grace. He blesses himself.*] On again. [*Hat on.*] Perfectly trained; the most obedient father I ever had. And now for our nightly lesson in the English language. Repeat slowly after me: Another day over.

S.B. Another day over.

PRIVATE Good. Next phrase. I suppose we can't complain.

S.B. I suppose we can't complain.

PRIVATE Not bad. Now for a little free conversation. But no obscenities, Father dear; the child is only twenty-five. [*S.B. eats in silence. Pause.*] Well, come on, come on! Where's that old rapier wit of yours, the toast of the Ballybeg coffee houses?

S.B. Did you set the rat-trap in the store?

PUBLIC Aye.

PRIVATE [*hysterically*] Isn't he a riot! Oh my God, that father of yours just kills me! But wait—wait—shhh-shhh—

S.B. I didn't find as many about the year.

PRIVATE Ooooh God! Priceless! Beautiful! Delightful! 'I didn't find as many about the year!' Did you ever hear the beat of that? Wonderful! But isn't he in form tonight? But isn't

he? You know, it's not every night that jewels like that, pearls of wisdom on rodent reproduction, drop from those lips! But hold it—hold it—!

[*S.B. takes out a handkerchief, removes his teeth, wraps them in the handkerchief, and puts them in his pocket.*]

[*Private exhales with satisfaction.*]

PRIVATE Ah! That's what we were waiting for; complete informality; total relaxation between intimates. Now we can carry on. Screwballs. [*Pause.*] I'm addressing you, Screwballs.

[*S.B. clears his throat.*]

Thank you. [*As the following speech goes on all trace of humour fades from Private's voice. He becomes more and more intense and it is with an effort that he keeps his voice under control.*] Screwballs, we've eaten together like this for the past twenty-odd years, and never once in all that time have you made as much as one unpredictable remark. Now, even though you refuse to acknowledge the fact, Screwballs, I'm leaving you forever. I'm going to Philadelphia, to work in an hotel. And you know why I'm going, Screwballs, don't you. Because I'm twenty-five, and you treat me as if I were five—I can't order even a dozen loaves without getting your permission. Because you pay me less than you pay Madge. But worse, far worse than that, Screwballs, because—*we embarrass one another.* If one of us were to say, 'You're looking tired' or 'That's a bad cough you have', the other would fall over backways with embarrassment. So tonight d'you know what I want you to do? I want you to make one unpredictable remark, and even though I'll still be on that plane tomorrow morning, I'll have doubts: Maybe I should have stuck it out; maybe the old codger did have feelings; maybe I have maligned the old bastard. So now, Screwballs, say . . . [*thinks*] . . . 'Once upon a time a rainbow ended in our garden' . . . say, 'I like to walk across the White Strand when there's a misty rain falling' . . . say, 'Gar, son—' say, 'Gar, you bugger you, why don't you stick it out here with me for it's not such a bad aul bugger of a place.' Go on. Say it! Say it! Say it!

S.B. True enough. . . .

PUBLIC [*almost inaudibly*] Aye?

S.B. I didn't find as many about the year.

PUBLIC [*roars*] Madge! Madge!

S.B. No need to roar like that.

PUBLIC The-the-the-bread's done. We need more bread.

S.B. You know where it's kept, don't you?

[*Madge at scullery door.*]

PUBLIC Can we have more bread, Madge . . . please. . . .

MADGE Huh! Pity you lost the power of your legs.

PUBLIC I'll—I'll get it myself—it doesn't matter. . . . [*Madge comes over to the table and takes the plate from Public. She gives S.B. a hard look.*]

MADGE [*irony*] The chatting in this place would deafen a body. Won't the house be quiet soon enough—long enough?

[*She shuffles off with the plate.*]

PRIVATE Tick-tock-tick-tock-tick-tock. It is now sixteen or seventeen years since I saw the Queen of France, then the Dauphiness, at Versailles. . . . Go on! What's the next line?

[*S.B. produces a roll of money from his pocket and puts it on the table.*]

S.B. I suppose you'll be looking for your pay.
PUBLIC I earned it.
S.B. I'm not saying you didn't. It's all there—you needn't count it.
PUBLIC I didn't say I was going to count it, did I?
PRIVATE Tick-tock-tick-tock-tick-tock—
PUBLIC More tea?
S.B. Sure you know I never take a second cup.
PRIVATE [*imitating*] 'Sure you know I never take a second cup.' [*Brittle and bright again.*] Okay, okay, okay, it's better this way, Screwballs, isn't it? You can't teach new tricks to two old dogs like us. In the meantime there's a little matter I'd like to discuss with you, Screwballs . . . [*with exaggerated embarrassment*] it's—it's nothing really . . . it's just something I'm rather hesitant to bring up, but I'm advised by the very best Church authorities that you'll be only too glad to discuss it with your son. Admittedly we're both a bit late in attacking the issue now, but—ha—you see—

[*Madge enters with a plate of bread. Private makes a very obvious show of changing the subject.*]

Oh marvellous weather—truly wonderful for the time of year—a real heat wave—all things considered—
MADGE A body couldn't get a word in edgeways with you two!
PRIVATE Madge has such a keen sense of humour, don't you agree? I love people with a sense of humour, don't you? It's the first thing I look for in a person. I seize them by the throat and say to them, 'Have you a sense of humour?' And then, if they have, I feel—I feel *at home* with them immediately. . . . But where was I? Oh, yes—our little talk—I'm beginning to wonder, Screwballs—I suspect—I'm afraid— [*in a rush, ashamed*] —I think I'm a sex-maniac! [*Throws his hands up.*] Please, please don't cry, Screwballs; please don't say anything; and above all please don't stop eating. Just—just let me talk a bit more—let me communicate with someone—that's what they all advise—communicate—pour out your pent-up feelings into a sympathetic ear. So all I ask for the moment is that you listen—just listen to me. As I said, I suspect that that I'm an s.-m. [*Rapidly, in self-defence.*] But I'm not the only one, Screwballs; oh indeed I am not; and all the boys around—some of them are far worse than I am. [*As if he had been asked the question.*] Why? Why do I think we're all s.-m.s? Well, because none of us is married. Because we're never done boasting about the number of hot courts we know—and the point is we're all virgins. Because—

[*Voices off.*]

Shhhh! Someone's coming. Not a word to anybody. This is our secret. Scouts' honour.

[*Enter Master Boyle from the scullery. He is around sixty, white-haired, handsome, defiant. He is shabbily dressed; his eyes, head, hands, arms are constantly moving—he sits for a moment and rises again—he puts his hands in his pocket and takes them out again—his eyes roam around the room but see nothing. S.B. is barely courteous to him.*]

S.B. Oh, good night, Master Boyle. How are you doing?

PUBLIC Master.

BOYLE Sean. Gar. No, no, don't stir. I only dropped in for a second.

PUBLIC Sit over and join us.

BOYLE No. I'm not stopping.

S.B. Here's a seat for you. I was about to go out to the shop anyway to square up a bit.

BOYLE Don't let me hold you back.

S.B. I'll be in again before you leave, Master.

BOYLE If you have work to do. . . .

PRIVATE [*to S.B.*] Ignorant bastard! [*Looking at Boyle.*] On his way to the pub! God, but he's a sorry wreck too, arrogant and pathetic. And yet whatever it is about you. . . .

BOYLE Tomorrow morning, isn't it?

PUBLIC Quarter past seven. I'm getting the mail van the length of Strabane.

BOYLE You're doing the right thing, of course. You'll never regret it. I gather it's a vast restless place that doesn't give a curse about the past; and that's the way things should be. Impermanence and anonymity—it offers great attractions. You've heard about the latest to-do?

PUBLIC Another row with the Canon? I really hadn't heard—

BOYLE But the point is he can't sack me! The organization's behind me and he can't budge me. Still, it's a . . . a bitter victory to hold on to a job when your manager wants rid of you.

PUBLIC Sure everybody knows the kind of the Canon, Master.

BOYLE I didn't tell you, did I, that I may be going out there myself?

PRIVATE Poor bastard.

BOYLE I've been offered a big post in Boston, head of education in a reputable university there. They've given me three months to think it over. What are you going to do?

PUBLIC Work in an hotel.

BOYLE You have a job waiting for you?

PUBLIC In Philadelphia.

BOYLE You'll do all right. You're young and strong and of average intelligence.

PRIVATE Good old Boyle. Get the dig in.

BOYLE Yes, it was as ugly and as squalid as all the other to-dos—before the whole school—the priest and the teacher—dedicated moulders of the mind. You're going to stay with friends?

PUBLIC With Aunt Lizzy.

BOYLE Of course.

PRIVATE Go on. Try him.

PUBLIC You knew her, didn't you, Master?

BOYLE Yes, I knew all the Gallagher girls: Lizzy, Una, Rose, Agnes. . . .

PRIVATE And Maire, my mother, did you love her?

BOYLE A long, long time ago . . . in the past. . . . He comes in to see your father every night, doesn't he?

PUBLIC The Canon? Oh, it's usually much later than this—

BOYLE I think so much about him that—ha—I feel a peculiar attachment for him. Funny, isn't it? Do you remember the Christmas you sent me the packet of cigarettes? And the day you brought me a pot of jam to the digs? It was you, wasn't it?

PRIVATE Poor Boyle—

BOYLE All children are born with generosity. Three months they gave me to make up my mind.

PUBLIC I remember very well—

BOYLE By the way— [*producing a small book*] a—little something to remind you of your old teacher—my poems—

PUBLIC Thank you very much.

BOYLE I had them printed privately last month. Some of them are a bit mawkish but you'll not notice any distinction.

PUBLIC I'm very grateful, Master.

BOYLE I'm not going to give you advice, Gar. Is that clock right? Not that you would heed it even if I did; you were always obstinate—

PRIVATE Tch, tch.

BOYLE But I would suggest that you strike out on your own as soon as you find your feet out there. Don't keep looking back over your shoulder. Be 100 per cent American.

PUBLIC I'll do that.

BOYLE There's an inscription on the fly-leaf. By the way, Gar, you couldn't lend me 10*s* until—ha—I was going to say until next week but you'll be gone by then.

PUBLIC Surely, surely.

BOYLE I seem to have come out without my wallet. . . .

PRIVATE Give him the quid.

[*Public gives over a note. Boyle does not look at it.*]

BOYLE Fine. I'll move on now. Yes, I knew all the Gallagher girls from Bailtefree, long, long ago. Maire and Una and Rose and Lizzy and Agnes and Maire, your mother. . . .

PRIVATE You might have been my father.

BOYLE Oh, another thing I meant to ask you: should you come across any newspapers or magazines over there that might be interested in an occasional poem, perhaps you would send me some addresses—

PUBLIC I'll keep an eye out.

BOYLE Not that I write as much as I should. You know how you get caught up in things. But you have your packing to do, and I'm talking too much as usual.

[*He holds out his hand and they shake hands. He does not release Public's hand.*]

Good luck, Gareth.

PUBLIC Thanks, Master.

BOYLE Forget Ballybeg and Ireland.

PUBLIC It's easier said.

BOYLE Perhaps you'll write me.

PUBLIC I will indeed.
BOYLE Yes, the first year. Maybe the second. I'll—I'll miss you, Gar.
PRIVATE For God's sake get a grip on yourself.
PUBLIC Thanks for the book and for—

[Boyle embraces Public briefly.]

PRIVATE Stop it! Stop it! Stop it!

[Boyle breaks away and goes quickly off through the scullery. He bumps into Madge who is entering.]

MADGE Lord, the speed of him! His tongue out for a drink!
PRIVATE Quick! Into your room!
MADGE God knows I don't blame the Canon for wanting rid of that—

[Public rushes to the bedroom. Private follows.]

Well! The manners about this place!

[She gathers up the tea things. Public stands inside the bedroom door, his hands up to his face. Private stands at his elbow, speaking urgently into his ear.]

PRIVATE Remember—you're going! At 7.15. You're still going! He's nothing but a drunken aul schoolmaster—a conceited, arrogant wash-out!
PUBLIC O God, the Creator and Redeemer of all the faithful—
PRIVATE Get a grip on yourself! Don't be a damned sentimental fool! [*Sings.*] 'Philadelphia, here I come—'
PUBLIC Maire and Una and Rose and Agnes and Lizzy and Maire—
PRIVATE Yessir, you're going to cut a bit of a dash in them thar States! Great big sexy dames and night clubs and high living and films and dances and—
PUBLIC Kathy, my own darling Kathy—
PRIVATE [*sings*] 'Where bowers of flowers bloom in the spring'
PUBLIC I don't—I can't.
PRIVATE [*sings*] 'Each morning at dawning, everything is bright and gay/A sun-kissed miss says Don't be late—' Sing up, man!
PUBLIC I—I—I——
PRIVATE [*sings*] 'That's why I can hardly wait.'
PUBLIC [*sings limply*] 'Philadelphia, here I come.'
PRIVATE That's it, laddybuck!
TOGETHER 'Philadelphia, here I come.'

Curtain

END OF EPISODE I: *First interval.*

EPISODE II

[*A short time later. Public is lying on the bed, his hands behind his head. Private is slumped in the chair, almost as if he were dozing. Public sings absently.*]

PUBLIC [*sings*]

Last night she came to me, she came softly in,
So softly she came that her feet made no din,
And laid her hand on me, and this she did say,
'It will not be long love till our wedding day'.

[*When the singing stops there is a moment of silence. Then, suddenly, Private springs to his feet.*]

PRIVATE What the bloody hell are you at, O'Donnell? Snap out of it, man! Get up and keep active! The devil makes work for idle hands! It is now sixteen or seventeen years since I saw the Queen of France, then the Dauphiness, at Versailles.

[*Public goes off the bed and begins taking clothes from the chest of drawers and putting them into his case.*]

PRIVATE [*lilting to a mad air of his own making*] Ta-ra-del-oo-del-ah-dol-de-dol-de-dol-del-ah— [*continuing as rapidly as he can speak*] —Tell me this and tell me no more: Why does a hen cross the road?
PUBLIC Why?
PRIVATE To get to the other side. Ha-ha! Why does a hen lay an egg?
PUBLIC Why?
PRIVATE Because it can't lay a brick. Yo-ho. Why does a sailor wear a round hat?
PUBLIC Why?
PRIVATE To cover his head. Hee-hee-hee. Nought out of three; very bad for a man of average intelligence. That's the style. Keep working; keep the mind active and well stretched by knowing the best that is thought and written in the world, and you wouldn't call Daddy Senator your father-in-law. [*Sings.*]

Give the woman in the bed more porter
Give the man beside her water
Give the woman in the bed more porter
More porter for the woman in the bed.

[*Confidentially.*] D'you know what I think, laddie; I mean, just looking at you there.
PUBLIC What?
PRIVATE You'd make a hell of a fine President of the United States.

[*Public straightens up and for a second surveys the room with the keen eye of a politician. Relaxes again.*]

PUBLIC Agh!
PRIVATE But you would!

PUBLIC You need to be born an American citizen.
PRIVATE True for you. What about Chairman of General Motors?

[*Public shrugs indifferently.*]

Boss of the Teamsters' Union?

[*Public shrugs his indifference.*]

PRIVATE Hollywood—what about Hollywood?
PUBLIC Not what it was.
PRIVATE Damnit but you're hard to please too. Still, there must be something great in store for you. [*Cracks his fingers at his brainwave.*] The U.S. Senate! Senator Gareth O'Donnell, Chairman of the Foreign Aid Committee!

[*He interviews Public who continues packing his clothes busily.*]

Is there something you would like to say, Senator, before you publish the findings of your committee?
PUBLIC Nothing to say.
PRIVATE Just a few words.
PUBLIC No comment.
PRIVATE Isn't it a fact that suspicion has fallen on Senator Doogan?
PUBLIC Nothing further to add.
PRIVATE Did your investigators not discover that Senator Doogan is the grandfather of fourteen unborn illegitimate children? That he sold his daughter to the king of the fairies for a crock of gold? That a Chinese spy known to the FBI as Screwballs——
PUBLIC Screwballs?
PRIVATE Screwballs.
PUBLIC Describe him.
PRIVATE Tall, blond, athletic-looking——
PUBLIC Military moustache?
PRIVATE —very handsome; uses a diamond-studded cigarette-holder.
PUBLIC Usually accompanied by a dark seductive woman in a low-cut evening gown?
PRIVATE —wears a monocle, fluent command of languages——
PUBLIC But seldom speaks? A man of few words?
PRIVATE —drives a cream convertible, villas in Istanbul, Cairo and Budapest——
PUBLIC [*Declaims*] Merchant Prince, licensed to deal in tobacco——
PRIVATE An' sowl! That's me man! To a T! The point is—what'll we do with him?
PUBLIC Sell him to a harem?
PRIVATE Hide his cascara sagrada?

[*Madge comes into the kitchen to lift the tablecloth.*]

PUBLIC [*serious*] Shhh!
PRIVATE The boys? Is it the boys? To say good-bye?
PUBLIC Shhhh!
PRIVATE It's Madge—aul fluke-feet Madge.

[*They both stand listening to the sound of Madge flapping across the kitchen and out to the scullery.*]

PUBLIC [*calls softly*] Madge.

[*Private drops into the armchair. Public stands listening until the sound has died away.*]

PRIVATE [*wearily*] Off again! You know what you're doing, don't you, laddybuck? Collecting memories and images and impressions that are going to make you bloody miserable; and in a way that's what you want, isn't it?

PUBLIC Bugger!

[*Private springs to his feet again. With forced animation.*]

PRIVATE Bugger's right! Bugger's absolutely correct! Back to the job! Keep occupied. Be methodical.

Eanie-meanie-minie-mow
Catch-the-baby-by-the-toe.

Will all passengers holding immigration visas please come this way.

[*Public produces documents from a drawer. He checks them.*]

PRIVATE Passport?
PUBLIC Passport.
PRIVATE Visa?
PUBLIC Visa.
PRIVATE Vaccination cert.?
PUBLIC Vaccination cert.
PRIVATE Currency?
PUBLIC Eighty dollars
PRIVATE Sponsorship papers?
PUBLIC Signed by Mr Conal Sweeney.
PRIVATE Uncle Con and Aunt Lizzy. Who made the whole thing possible. Read her letter again—strictly for belly-laughs.
PUBLIC [*reads*] Dear Nephew Gar, Just a line to let you know that your Uncle Con and me have finalized all the plans——
PRIVATE Uncle Con and I.
PUBLIC —and we will meet you at the airport and welcome you and bring you to our apartment which you will see is located in a pretty nice locality and you will have the spare room which has TV and air-conditioning and window meshes and your own bathroom with a shower——
PRIVATE Adjacent to RC church. No children. Other help kept.
PUBLIC You will begin at the Emperor Hotel on Monday 23rd which is only about twenty minutes away.
PRIVATE Monsieur, madam.
PUBLIC Con says it is a fine place for to work in and the owner is Mr Patrick Palinakis who is half-Irish——

PRIVATE Patrick.
PUBLIC —and half-Greek.
PRIVATE Palinakis.
PUBLIC His grandfather came from County Mayo.
PRIVATE By the hokey! The Greek from Belmullet!
PUBLIC We know you will like it here and work hard.
PRIVATE [*rapidly*] Monsieur-madam-monsieur-madam-monsieur-madam——
PUBLIC We remember our short trip to Ireland last September with happy thoughts and look forward to seeing you again. Sorry we missed your father that day. We had Ben Burton in to dinner last evening. He sends his regards.
PRIVATE Right sort, Ben.
PUBLIC Until we see you at the airport, all love, Elise.
PRIVATE 'Elise'! Damnit, Lizzy Gallagher, but you came on in the world.
PUBLIC P.S. About paying back the passage money which you mentioned in your last letter—desist!—no one's crying about it.
PRIVATE Aye, Ben Burton was a right skin.
PUBLIC [*remembering*] September 8th.
PRIVATE By God Lizzy was in right talking form that day——
PUBLIC 'You are invited to attend the wedding of Miss Kathleen Doogan of Gortmore House——'
PRIVATE [*snaps*] Shut up, O'Donnell! You've got to quit this moody drivelling! [*Coaxing.*] They arrived in the afternoon; remember? A beautiful quiet harvest day, the sun shining, not a breath of wind; and you were on your best behaviour. And Madge—remember? Madge was as huffy as hell with the carry-on of them, and you couldn't take your eyes off Aunt Lizzy, your mother's sister—so this was your mother's sister—remember?

[*Three people have moved into the kitchen: Con Sweeney, Lizzy Sweeney, and Ben Burton. All three are in the fifty-five to sixty region. Burton is American, the Sweeneys Irish-American. Con Sweeney sits at the kitchen table with Ben Burton. Lizzy moves around in the centre of the kitchen. Public stands at the door of his bedroom. Private hovers around close to Public. The three guests have glasses in their hands. None of them is drunk, but Lizzy is more than usually garrulous. She is a small energetic woman, heavily made-up, impulsive. Con, her husband, is a quiet, patient man. Burton, their friend, sits smiling at his glass most of the time. As she talks Lizzy moves from one to the other, and she has the habit of putting her arm around, or catching the elbow of, the person she is addressing. This constant physical touching is new and disquieting to Public. A long laugh from Lizzy:*]

LIZZY Anyhow, there we are, all sitting like stuffed ducks in the front seat—Una and Agnes and Rose and Mother and me—you know—and mother dickied up in her good black shawl and everything—and up at the altar rails there's Maire all by herself and her shoulders are sorta working—you know—and you couldn't tell whether she was crying or giggling—she was a helluva one for giggling—but maybe she was crying that morning—I don't know——
CON Get on with the story, honey.
LIZZY [*with dignity*] Would you please desist from bustin' in on me?

[*Con spreads his hands in resignation.*]

LIZZY But listen to this—this'll kill you—Mother's here, see? And Agnes is here and I'm here. And Agnes leans across Mother to me—you know—and she says in this helluva loud voice—she says— [*laughs*] —this really does kill me—she says—in this whisper of hers—and you know the size of Bailtefree chapel; couldn't swing a cat in that place— [*Suddenly anxious.*] That chapel's still there, isn't it? It hasn't fell down or nothing, has it?

CON [*dryly*] Unless it fell down within the last couple of hours. We drove up there this morning. Remember?

LIZZY [*relieved*] Yeah. So we did. Fine place. Made me feel kinda—you know—what the hell was I talking about?

BEN Agnes leaned over to you and said——

[*Lizzy puts her arm around him and kisses the crown of his head.*]

LIZZY Thanks, Ben. A great friend with a great memory! I'll tell you, Gar, Ben Burton's one hundred per cent. The first and best friend we made when we went out. [*To Con.*] Right, honey?

CON Right.

LIZZY Way back in '37.

CON '38.

LIZZY [*loudly*] October 23rd, 19 and 37 we sailed for the United States of America. [*Con spreads his hands.*] Nothing in our pockets. No job to go to. And what does Ben do?

CON A guy in a million.

LIZZY He gives us this apartment. He gives us dough. He gives us three meals a day—until bonzo [*Con*] finally gets himself this job. Looks after us like we were his own skin and bone. Right, honey?

CON Right.

LIZZY So don't let nobody say nothing against Ben Burton. Then when he [*Con*] gets this job in this downtown store——

CON First job was with the construction company.

LIZZY Would you please desist? [*Con spreads hands.*] His first job was with Young and Pecks, hauling out them packing cases and things; and then he moved to the construction company, and *then* we got a place of our own.

PUBLIC You were telling us about that morning.

LIZZY What's he talking about?

PUBLIC The day my father and mother got married.

LIZZY That day! Wasn't that something? With the wind howling and the rain slashing about! And Mother, poor Mother, may God be good to her, she thought that just because Maire got this guy with a big store we should all of got guys with big stores. And poor Maire—we were so alike in every way, Maire and me. But he was good to her. I'll say that for S. B. O'Donnell—real good to her. Where the hell is he anyhow? Why will S. B. O'Donnell, my brother-in-law, not meet me?

CON He [*Public*] told you—he's away at a wedding.

LIZZY What wedding?

CON Some local girl and some Dublin doc.

LIZZY What local girl? You think I'm a stranger here or something?

CON [*to Public*] What local girl?

PUBLIC Senator Doogan's daughter.

PRIVATE Kathy.

LIZZY Never heard of him. Some Johnny-hop-up. When did they start having Senators about this place for Gawds sakes?

BEN [*to Public*] You have a senate in Dublin, just like our Senate, don't you?

LIZZY Don't you start telling me nothing about my own country, Ben. You got your own problems to look after. Just you leave me to manage this place, okay?

BEN Sorry, Elise.

LIZZY Ben! [*She kisses the top of his head.*] Only that I'm a good Irish-American Catholic— [*to Public*] and believe me, they don't come much better than that—and only that I'm stuck with Rudolph Valentino [*Con*], I'd take a chance with Ben Burton any day [*kisses him again*], black Lutheran and all that he is.

[*Madge appears at the door of the shop. She refuses to look at the visitors. Her face is tight with disapproval. Her accent is very precise.*]

MADGE Are there any *Clarions* to spare or are they all ordered?

PUBLIC They're all ordered, Madge.

LIZZY Doing big deals out there, honey, huh?

MADGE Thank you, Gareth. [*Madge withdraws.*]

LIZZY 'Thank you, Gareth!' [*She giggles to herself*].

CON Honey! [*To Public.*] You'll think about what we were discussing?

PUBLIC I will, Uncle Con.

CON The job's as good as you'll get and we'd be proud to have you.

LIZZY Don't force him.

CON I'm not forcing him. I'm only telling him.

LIZZY Well now, you've told him—a dozen times. So now desist, will you? [*Con spreads his hands.*]

PUBLIC I will think about it. Really.

LIZZY Sure! Sure! Typical Irish! He will think about it! And while he's thinking about it the store falls in about his head! What age are you? Twenty-four? Twenty-five? What are you waiting for? For S.B. to run away to sea? Until the weather gets better?

CON Honey!

LIZZY I'm talking straight to the kid! He's Maire's boy and I've got an interest in him—the only nephew I have. [*To Ben.*] Am I right or am I wrong?

BEN I'm still up in Bailtefree chapel.

LIZZY Where? [*Confidentially to Con.*] Give him no more to drink. [*Patiently to Ben.*] You're sitting in the home of S. B. O'Donnell and my deceased sister, Maire, Ben.

CON You were telling us a story about the morning they got married, honey, in Bailtefree chapel.

LIZZY Yeah, I know, I know, but you keep busting in on me.

PUBLIC You were about to tell us what Agnes whispered to you.

LIZZY [*crying*] Poor Aggie—dead. Maire—dead. Rose, Una, Lizzy—dead—all gone—all dead and gone. . . .

CON Honey, you're Lizzy.

LIZZY So what?

CON Honey, you're not dead.

LIZZY [*regarding Con cautiously*] You gone senile all of a sudden? [*Confidentially to Ben.*] Give him no more to drink. [*To Con.*] For Gawds sakes who says I'm dead?

BEN You're very much alive, Elise.

[*She goes to him and gives him another kiss.*]

LIZZY Thank you, Ben. A great friend with a great intellect. Only one thing wrong with Ben Burton: he's a black Baptist.

BEN Just for the record, Gar, I'm Episcopalian.

LIZZY Episcopalian—Lutheran—Baptist—what's the difference? As our pastor, Father O'Flaherty, says—'My dear brethren,' he says, 'Let the whole cart-load of them, and the whole zoo of them, be to thee as the Pharisee and the publican.'

CON Honey!

LIZZY But he's still the best friend we have. And we have many good, dear, kind friends in the US. Right, honey?

CON Right.

LIZZY But when it comes to holding a candle to Ben Burton—look—comparisons are—he's not in the halfpenny place with them!

BEN [*laughing*] Bang on, Elise!

LIZZY Am I right or am I wrong?

CON Honey!

LIZZY [*to Public*] And that's why I say to you: America's Gawd's own country. Ben?

BEN Don't ask me. I was born there.

LIZZY What d'ya mean—'Don't ask me'? I am asking you. He should come out or he should not—which is it?

BEN It's just another place to live, Elise. Ireland—America—what's the difference?

LIZZY You tell him, honey. You tell him the set-up we have. [*Now with growing urgency, to Public.*] We have this ground-floor apartment, see, and a car that's air-conditioned, and colour TV, and this big collection of all the Irish records you ever heard, and 15,000 bucks in Federal Bonds—

CON Honey.

LIZZY —and a deep freezer and—and—and a back yard with this great big cherry tree, and squirrels and night-owls and the smell of lavender in the spring and long summer evenings and snow at Christmas and a Christmas tree in the parlour and—and—and——

CON Elise. . . .

LIZZY And it's all so Gawd-awful because we have no one to share it with us. . . . [*She begins to sob.*]

CON [*softly*] It's okay, honey, okay. . . .

LIZZY He's my sister's boy—the only child of five girls of us——

BEN I'll get the car round the front.

[*Ben goes off through the scullery.*]

LIZZY —and we spent a fortune on doctors, didn't we, Connie, but it was no good, and then I says to him [*Con*] , 'We'll go home to Ireland', I says, 'and Maire's boy, we'll offer him everything we have——'

PRIVATE [*terrified*] No. No.

LIZZY '—everything, and maybe we could coax him—you know——' maybe it was sorta bribery—I dunno—but he would have everything we ever gathered——

PRIVATE Keep it! Keep it!

LIZZY —and all the love we had in us——

PRIVATE No! No!

CON Honey, we've a long drive back to the hotel.

LIZZY [*trying to control herself*] That was always the kind of us Gallagher girls, wasn't it . . . either laughing or crying . . . you know, sorta silly and impetuous, shooting our big mouths off, talking too much, not like the O'Donnells—you know—kinda cold——

PRIVATE Don't, man, don't.

CON Your gloves, honey. It's been a heavy day.

LIZZY [*to Public, with uncertain dignity*] Tell your father that we regret we did not have the opportunity for to make his acquaintance again after all these——

PUBLIC [*impetuously*] I want to go to America—if you'll have me——

PRIVATE Laddy!

CON Sure. You think about it, son. You think about it.

PUBLIC Now—as soon as I can, Aunt Lizzy—I mean it—

LIZZY Gar? [*To Con, as if for confirmation.*] Honey?

CON Look, son——

LIZZY To us, Gar? To come to us? To our home?

CON Ben's waiting, Elise.

PUBLIC If you'll have me. . . .

LIZZY If we'll have him, he says; he says if we'll have him! That's why I'm here! That's why I'm half-shot-up! [*She opens her arms and approaches him.*] Oh Gar, my son——

PRIVATE Not yet! Don't touch me yet!

[*Lizzy throws her arms around him and cries happily.*]

LIZZY My son, Gar, Gar, Gar. . . .

PRIVATE [*softly, with happy anguish*] God . . . my God . . . Oh my God. . . .

(BLACK OUT)

[*When the bedroom light goes up Public and Private are there. The kitchen is empty. Public bangs the lid of his case shut and Private stands beside him, jeering at him. While this taunting goes on Public tries to escape by fussing about the room.*]

PRIVATE September 8th, the sun shining, not a breath of wind—and this was your mother's sister—remember. And that's how you were got! Right, honey? Silly and impetuous like a Gallagher! Regrets?

PUBLIC None.

PRIVATE Uncertainties?

PUBLIC None.

PRIVATE Little tiny niggling reservations?

PUBLIC None.

PRIVATE Her grammar?

PUBLIC Shut up!
PRIVATE But, honey, wasn't it something?
PUBLIC Go to hell.
PRIVATE Her vulgarity?
PUBLIC Bugger off.
PRIVATE She'll tuck you into your air-conditioned cot every night.

[*Public, so that he won't hear, begins to whistle 'Philadelphia, Here I Come.'*]

PRIVATE And croon, 'Sleep well, my li'l honey child.' [*Public whistles determinedly.*] She got you soft on account of the day it was, didn't she?

[*Public whistles louder.*]

And because she said you were an O'Donnell—'cold like'.
PUBLIC It is now sixteen or seventeen years since I saw the Queen of France——
PRIVATE But of course when she threw her arms around you—well, well, well!
PUBLIC —then the Dauphiness, at Versailles——
PRIVATE Poor little orphan boy!
PUBLIC Shut up! Shut up!
PRIVATE [*in child's voice*] Ma-ma. . . . Maa-ma.

[*Public flings open the bedroom door and dashes into the kitchen. Private follows behind.*]

PUBLIC Madge!
PRIVATE [*quietly, deliberately*] You don't want to go, laddybuck. Admit it. You don't want to go.

[*Madge enters from the scullery.*]

PUBLIC [*searching for an excuse*] I can't find my coat. I left it in my room.

[*Madge gives him a long, patient look, goes to the nail below the school clock, lifts down the coat, and hands it to him. He takes it from her and goes towards the scullery door.*]

PUBLIC If you would only learn to leave things where you find them you wouldn't be such a bad aul nuisance.

[*Public and Private go off*].

MADGE [*calls*] Don't you dare come home drunk!

[*Public's head appears round the door.*]

PUBLIC [*softly*] I'm going to say good-bye to the boys over a quiet drink or two. And how I spend my nights is a matter entirely for myself.
MADGE 'The Boys!' Couldn't even come here to say good-bye to you on your last night.

PRIVATE Straight to the bone!
PUBLIC Just you mind your business and I'll mind mine.
MADGE How many of them are getting the pension now?
PUBLIC And in case you're in bed when I get back I want a call at half-six.
MADGE The clock'll be set. If you hear it well and good.

[Public disappears. Madge fusses about the kitchen until S.B. enters from the shop. He has a newspaper in his hand and sits at the top of the table. She watches him as he reads. She adjusts a few things. She looks back at him, then suddenly, on the point of tears, she accuses him.]

MADGE You sit there, night after night, year after year, reading that aul paper, and not a tooth in your head! If you had any decency in you at all, you would keep them plates in while there's a lady in your presence!
S.B. *[puzzled]* Eh?
MADGE I mean it. It—it—it—it just drives me mad, the sight of you! *[The tears begin to come.]* And I have that much work to do: the stairs have to be washed down, and the store's to be swept, and your room has to be done out—and—and—I'm telling you I'll be that busy for the next couple of weeks that I won't have time to lift my head!

[She dashes off. S.B. stares after her, then out at the audience. Then, very slowly, he looks down at the paper again—it has been upside down—and turns it right side up. But he can't read. He looks across at Gar's bedroom, sighs, rises, and exits very slowly to the shop. Silence for a second after S.B. leaves. The silence is suddenly shattered by the boisterous arrival of the boys and Gar. We hear their exaggerated laughter and talk outside before they burst in. When they enter they take over the kitchen, sprawling on chairs, hunting for tumblers for the stout they produce from their pockets, taking long, deep pulls on their cigarettes, giving the impression that they are busy, purposeful, randy gents about to embark on some exciting adventure. But their bluster is not altogether convincing. There is something false about it. Tranquility is their enemy: they fight it valiantly. At the beginning of this scene Gar is flattered that the boys have come to him. When they consistently refuse to acknowledge his leaving—or perhaps because he is already spiritually gone from them—his good humour deserts him. He becomes apart from the others. Ned is the leader of the group. Tom is his feed-man, subserviently watching for every cue. Joe, the youngest of the trio, and not yet fully committed to the boys' way of life, is torn between fealty to Ned and Tom and a spontaneous and simple loneliness over Gar's departure. Nothing would suit him better than a grand loud send-off party. But he cannot manage this, and his loyalty is divided. He is patently gauche, innocent, obvious.]

NED There's only one way to put the fear of God up them bastards— *[points to his boot]* —every time—you know where.
JOE Who's the ref, Ned?
TOM Jimmy Pat Barney from Bunmornan. *[Guardedly to Public.]* Where's the aul fella?
PUBLIC Haven't a bloody clue. Probably in the shop. Relax, man.
NED That *[the boot]* or the knee—it's the only game them gets can play; and we can play it too.
TOM *[relaxing]* They've a hell of a forward line all the same, Ned.
NED They'll be in crutches this day week. By God, I can hardly wait to get the studs planted in wee Bagser Doran's face! *[He crashes his fist into the palm of his hand.]*
TOM All the same, Jimmy Pat Barney's the get would put you off very quick.
NED He won't say a word to me. He knows his match when he meets it.

[*Tom laughs appreciatively. Madge appears at the scullery door.*]

MADGE [*coldly*] Just thought I heard somebody whispering. So youse finally made it.

JOE [*holding up glass*] True to our word, Madge, that's us!

PUBLIC [*happily*] They were on their way here when I ran into them.

MADGE Aye, so. [*Ned belches.*] Mister Sweeney, too; gentlemanly as ever.

NED [*slapping his knee*] Come on away over here and I'll take some of the starch out of you, Madge Mulhern. How long is since a fella gripped your knee? Haaaaaaaaaaa!

MADGE None of your smutty talk here, Mister Sweeney. And if the boss comes in and finds them bottles——

PUBLIC I'll keep them in order, Madge.

MADGE 'Boys'! How are you! [*She goes out.*]

TOM [*calling*] You're jealous because you're past it—that's what's wrong with you. Right, Ned?

PUBLIC [*raising glass*] Well, boys, when you're lining out on the pitch, you can think of me, because I'll be thinking of you.

JOE [*earnestly*] Lucky bloody man, Gar. God, I wish I was in your——

NED [*quickly*] By the way, lads, who's the blondie thing I seen at the last Mass on Sunday?

TOM A big red-head?

NED Are you bloody-well deaf! A blondie! She wouldn't be Maggie Hanna's niece, would she?

TOM There was two of them, sitting over near the box?

NED I seen one.

TOM 'Cos they're English. Staying at the hotel. But the big red thing—she's one of Neil McFadden's girls.

NED Annie? Is Annie home?

JOE Aye, she is. So I heard the mammy saying.

NED Bloody great! That's me fixed up for the next two weeks! Were any of youse ever on that job?

JOE No, I wasn't, Ned.

TOM For God's sake, she wouldn't spit on you!

NED Game as they're going, big Annie. But you need the constitution of a horse. I had her for the fortnight she was home last year and she damned near killed me.

PUBLIC Big Annie from up beyond the quarry?

JOE You know, Gar—the one with the squint.

NED [*with dignity*] Annie McFadden has no squint.

PUBLIC Away and take a running race to yourself, Ned.

NED [*with quiet threat*] What do you mean?

PUBLIC You were never out with big Annie McFadden in your puff, man.

NED Are you calling me a liar?

PRIVATE [*wearily*] What's the point.

TOM [*quickly*] Oh, by God, Ned was there, Gar, manys and manys the time. Weren't you, Ned?

PUBLIC Have it your own way.

JOE [*nervously*] And maybe she got the squint straightened out since I saw her last. All the women get the squints straightened out nowadays. Damnit, you could walk from here to Cork nowadays and you wouldn't see a woman with a——

NED I just don't like fellas getting snottery with me, that's all.

[*There follows an uneasy silence during which Private surveys the group.*]

PRIVATE The boys. . . . They weren't always like this, were they? There was a hell of a lot of crack, wasn't there? There was a hell of a lot of laughing, wasn't there?

TOM [*briskly*] Bit of life about the place next week, lads—the Carnival. Too bad you'll miss it, Gar. By God it was a holy fright last year, night after night. [*To Ned.*] Remember?

NED [*sulkily*] Bloody cows, the whole bloody lot of them!

TOM Mind the night with the two wee Greenock pieces?

NED [*thawing*] Aw, stop, stop!

TOM Talk about hot things!

NED Liveliest wee tramps I ever laid!

TOM And the fat one from Dublin you picked up at the dance that night—the one that hauled you down into the ditch!

NED I was never the same since.

TOM [*to Public*] Whatever it is about him [*Ned*], if there's a fast woman in the country, she'll go for Ned first thing. Lucky bugger! [*Pause.*] Aye, lucky bugger!

[*Another brief silence. These silences occur like regular cadences. To defeat them someone always introduces a fresh theme.*]

PUBLIC I'm for off tomorrow, boys.

NED [*indifferently*] Aye, so, so. . . .

TOM Brooklyn, isn't it?

PUBLIC Philadelphia.

TOM Philadelphia. That's where Jimmy Crerand went to, isn't it? Philadelphia. . . .

NED [*quickly*] Mind the night Jimmy and us went down to the caves with them Dublin skivvies that was working up at the Lodge? [*To Public.*] Were you?—No, you weren't with us that night.

JOE Was I there, Ned?

NED You mind the size of Jimmy?—five foot nothing and scared of his shadow.

PUBLIC Best goalie we ever had.

NED One of the women was Gladys and the other was Emmy or something——

TOM Damnit, I mind now! Gladys and Emmy—that was it, Ned!

NED Anyhow the rest of us went in for a swim——

TOM In the bloody pelt!

NED —and your man Jimmy was left in the cave with the women; and what the hell do they do but whip the trousers off him!

JOE No, I wasn't there that night.

NED And the next thing we see is wee Jimmy coming shouting across the White Strand and the two Dublin cows haring after him.

TOM Not a stab on him!

NED —and him squealing at the top of his voice, 'Save me, boys, save me!'

TOM Never drew breath till he reached home!

NED You [*Gar*] missed that night.

TOM 'Save me, boys, save me!'

NED I don't think we went to bed that night at all.

TOM You may be sure we didn't.

NED Powerful.

[*Another silence descends. After a few seconds* Private *speaks.*]

PRIVATE We were all there that night, Ned. And the girls' names were Gladys and Susan. And they sat on the rocks dangling their feet in the water. And we sat in the cave, peeping out at them. And then Jimmy Crerand suggested that we go in for a swim; and we all ran to the far end of the shore; and we splashed about like schoolboys. Then we came back to the cave, and wrestled with one another. And then out of sheer boredom, Tom, you suggested that we take the trousers off Crerand—just to prove how manly we all were. But when Ned started towards Jimmy—five foot nothing, remember?—wee Jimmy squared up and defied not only the brave Ned but the whole lot of us. So we straggled back home, one behind the other, and left the girls dangling their feet in the water. And that was that night.

PUBLIC If the ground's not too hard, you'll do well on Sunday.

NED Hard or soft— [*examining his boot*] —I've a couple of aul scores to settle.

PUBLIC You'll never get as good a half-back as the one you're losing.

NED [*quickly, with pretended interest*] D'you know what I'm thinking? We'd better see about transport.

TOM Damnit, you're right. I'll get the aul fella's van easy enough. Can you get your Charlie's lorry?

NED Just maybe. I'd better try him the night.

JOE What about a song from Gar, boys, before we break up?

NED What time is it?

JOE It's early in the night yet.

TOM Twenty past nine.

NED We'd better move then; Charlie was talking about going to a dance in Ardmore.

TOM Damnit, that's an idea!

JOE We'll all go—a big last night for Gar!

NED Ardmore? Are you mad? Bloody women in that place don't know what they're for!

TOM True for you. Scream their heads off if you laid a hand on them.

NED But I'll tell you what we'll do—call in home first to see Charlie and then go on to the hotel for a dirty big booze-up.

JOE I don't like drinking in that place.

NED Them two English bits—what's their name?

TOM Them strangers? Agh you wouldn't have a chance there. They do nothing but walk and look at weeds and stuff——

NED Who wouldn't have a chance?

TOM I know, Ned. But them two—they're sort of stiff-looking—like—like they worked in a post-office or something.

NED They're women, aren't they?

TOM Damnit, we might! . . . Still I don't know. . . . They knit a lot. . . . [*To Public.*] What d'you think?

JOE I vote we stay here.

PUBLIC And you can count me out. I've an early start.

NED £10 to a shilling I click with one or other of them!

PUBLIC I won't be here to collect my winnings.

NED Come on! Any takers? Never clapped eyes on them and I'm offering ten notes to a bob!

TOM Cripes, I know that look in his eyes!

NED Wise bloody men! The blood's up, lads! Off to the front! Any volunteers for a big booze-up and a couple of women?

TOM Did he say women? Sign me on!

JOE I don't think I'm in form the night, boys——

NED We'll show them a weed or two, eh?

TOM Out to the sand-banks! Get them in the bloody bent!

NED We're away—Wait! Wait!—How much money have you?

[They both produce their money—a fistful of small coins.]

TOM *2s 6d . . . 2s 11d . . . 3s 3d . . . 3s 5½d.*

NED And I have *6s 2d.* It'll have to do. Say a prayer they're fast and thrifty.

TOM Dirty aul brute! Lead the way, Bull!

NED I'm telling you—the blood's up!

TOM Coming, lads?

PUBLIC I'm getting up at half six.

NED [*casually from the door*] So long, Gar. You know the aul rule—If you can't be good. . . .

TOM Send us a pack of them playing cards—the ones with the dirty pictures on the back!

NED And if the women are as easy as the money out there, we might think of joining you. [*To Tom.*] Right, old cock?

TOM Bull on regardless! Yaaaaaaaaaaah!

[They open the door. Ned hesitates and begins taking off the broad leather belt with the huge brass buckle that supports his trousers.]

NED [*shyly, awkwardly*] By the way, Gar, since I'll not see you again before you go——

TOM Hi! What are you at? At least wait till you're sure of the women!

NED [*impatiently to Tom*] Agh, shut up! [*To Public.*] If any of them Yankee scuts try to beat you up some dark night, you can . . . [*now he is very confused and flings the belt across the room to Public*] . . . you know . . . there's a bloody big buckle on it . . . manys a get I scutched with it. . . .

TOM Safe enough, lads: he has braces on as well!

NED I meant to buy you something good, but the aul fella didn't sell the calf to the jobbers last Friday . . . and he could have, the stupid bastard, such a bloody stupid bastard of an aul fella!

PUBLIC [*moved*] Thanks, Ned . . . thanks. . . .

JOE Damnit, I have nothing for you, Gar.

TOM [*quickly*] Are we for the sandbanks or are we not?

NED You'll make out all right over there . . . have a. . . .

TOM I know that look in his eyes!

[Ned wheels rapidly on Tom, gives him a more than playful punch, and says savagely.]

NED Christ, if there's one get I hate, it's you!

[He goes off quickly.]

[*Tom looks uncertainly after him, looks back at Public, and says with dying conviction*:]

TOM The blood's up. . . . Oh by God, when he goes on like that, the . . . the blood's up all right. . . .

[*Tom looks after Ned, then back to Joe and Gar, as if he can't decide which to join, then impetuously he dashes off after Ned, calling*:]

Hi! Ned, Ned, wait for me. . . .

[*There is a silence. Public is looking at the belt. Joe begins to fidget. Now Public becomes aware of him.*]

PUBLIC What the hell are you waiting for?
JOE Damnit, man, like it's your last night and all, and I thought——
PUBLIC Get to hell and run after them.
JOE Sure you know yourself they'll hang about the gable of the hotel and chat and do nothing.
PUBLIC For God's sake, man, those English women will be swept off their feet!
JOE [*uncertainly*] You're taking a hand at me now.
PUBLIC I'm telling you, you're missing the chance of a lifetime.
JOE Maybe—eh?—what d'you think?
PUBLIC Go on! Go on!
JOE God, maybe you're right. You never know what'll happen, eh? You finish that [*drink*] for me! God, maybe we'll click the night! Say a wee prayer we do! Cripes, my blood's up too! Where's my cap?

[*He grabs the cap, dashes to the door, remembers he won't see Gar again.*]

JOE Send us a card, Gar, sometimes, eh?
PUBLIC Surely, Joe.
JOE Lucky bloody man. I wish I was you.
PUBLIC There's nothing stopping you, is there?
JOE Only that the mammy planted sycamore trees last year, and she says I can't go till they're tall enough to shelter the house.
PUBLIC You're stuck for another couple of days, then. Away off with you, man.
JOE Good luck, Gar. And tell Madge that the next time she asks us up for tea we'd bloody well better get it.
PUBLIC She *asked* you?
JOE That's why I was joking her about us keeping our word. As if we wanted tea, for God's sake! But I'd better catch up with the stirk before they do damage . . . So long, aul cock!

[*He runs off.*]

PUBLIC Madge. . . . Oh God. . . .

[*Private moves over beside him. He speaks quickly, savagely at first, spitting out the first three lines. Gradually he softens, until the speech ends almost in a whisper:*]

PRIVATE They're louts, ignorant bloody louts, and you've always known it! And don't pretend you're surprised; because you're not. And you know what they'll do tonight, don't you? They'll shuffle around the gable of the hotel and take an odd furtive peep into the lounge at those English women who won't even look up from their frigid knitting! Many a time you did it yourself, bucko! Aye, and but for Aunt Lizzy and the grace of God, you'd be there tonight, too, watching the lights go out over the village, and hearing the front doors being bolted, and seeing the blinds being raised; and you stamping your feet to keep the numbness from spreading, not wanting to go home, not yet for another while, wanting to hold on to the night although nothing can happen now, nothing at all. . . . Joe and Tom and big, thick, generous Ned. . . . No one will ever know or understand the fun there was; for there *was* fun and there *was* laughing—foolish, silly fun and foolish, silly laughing; but what it was all about you can't remember, can you? Just the memory of it—that's all you have now—just the memory; and even now, even so soon, it is being distilled of all its coarseness; and what's left is going to be precious, precious gold. . . .

[*There is a knock at the door. Public goes off to answer it.*]

KATE [*off*] Hello, Gar.
PRIVATE Kate!
KATE [*on*] This isn't a healthy sign, drinking by yourself.
PRIVATE Talk! Talk!
PUBLIC What—what are you doing here?
KATE I hear you're off to America.
PUBLIC First thing in the morning.
KATE You wouldn't think of calling to say good-bye to your friends, I suppose?
PUBLIC I was going to, but I——
PRIVATE Careful!
PUBLIC —it went clean out of my mind. You know how it is, getting ready. . . .
KATE I understand, Gar.
PRIVATE She's a married woman, you bugger!
KATE Philadelphia?
PUBLIC Yes. Take a seat.
KATE To an aunt, isn't it?
PUBLIC That's right. A sister of mother's.
KATE And you're going to work in a hotel.
PUBLIC You know as much about it as I do.
KATE You know Baile Beag—Small Town.
PUBLIC I'll probably go to night-school as well—you know, at night——
PRIVATE Brilliant.
PUBLIC —do law or medicine or something——
PRIVATE Like hell! First Arts stumped you!
KATE You'll do well, Gar; make a lot of money, and come back here in twenty years' time, and buy the whole village.
PUBLIC Very likely. That's my plan anyhow.
PRIVATE Kate . . . Kathy. . . .
PUBLIC How's your father and mother?

KATE Fine, thanks. And Mr O'Donnell?

PUBLIC Grand, grand. Is Dr King well?

KATE I hear no complaints.

PRIVATE Then the Dauphiness of Versailles. And surely never lighted on this orb, which she hardly seemed to touch, a more delightful vision. I saw her just above the horizon, decorating and cheering the elevated sphere she just began to move in——

PUBLIC [*a shade louder than necessary*] I'll come home when I make my first million, driving a Cadillac and smoking cigars and taking movie-films.

KATE I hope you're very happy there and that life will be good to you.

PUBLIC [*slightly louder*] I'll make sure life's good to me from now on.

KATE Your father'll miss you.

PUBLIC [*rapidly, aggressively*] That's his look out! D'you know something? If I had to spend another week in Ballybeg, I'd go off my bloody head! This place would drive anybody crazy! Look around you, for God's sake! Look at Master Boyle! Look at my father! Look at the Canon! Look at the boys! Asylum cases, the whole bloody lot of them!

PRIVATE [*pained*] Shhhhhhh!

PUBLIC Listen, if someone were to come along to me tonight and say, 'Ballybeg's yours—lock, stock, and barrel,' it wouldn't make that [*cracks his fingers*] much difference to me. If you're not happy and content in a place—then—then—then you're not happy and content in a place! It's as simple as that. I've stuck around this hole far too long. I'm telling you: it's a bloody quagmire, a backwater, a dead-end! And everybody in it goes crazy sooner or later! Everybody!

PRIVATE Shhhhhhhh. . . .

PUBLIC There's nothing about Ballybeg that I don't know already. I hate the place, and every stone, and every rock, and every piece of heather around it! Hate it! Hate it! And the sooner that plane whips me away, the better I'll like it!

KATE It isn't as bad as that, Gar.

PUBLIC You're stuck here! What else can you say!

PRIVATE That'll do!

PUBLIC And you'll die here! But I'm not stuck! I'm free! Free as the bloody wind!

KATE All I meant was——

PUBLIC Answerable to nobody! All this bloody yap about father and son and all this sentimental rubbish about 'homeland' and 'birthplace'—yap! Bloody yap! Impermanence—anonymity—that's what I'm looking for; a vast restless place that doesn't give a damn about the past. To hell with Ballybeg, that's what I say!

PRIVATE Oh, man. . . .

KATE I'd better go. Francis'll be wondering what's keeping me.

PUBLIC [*recklessly*] Tell him I was asking for him.

KATE Good-bye, Gar.

PUBLIC [*in same tone*] Enjoy yourself, Kate. And if you can't be good—you know?

[*Public goes off with Kate.*]

[*Off.*] Be sure to call the first one after me.

[*She is gone. Public returns and immediately buries his face in his hands.*]

PRIVATE Kate . . . sweet Katie Doogan . . . my darling Kathy Doogan. . . .

[*Public uncovers his face and with trembling fingers lights a cigarette and takes a drink. As he does:*]

PRIVATE [*very softly*] Oh my God, steady man, steady—it is now sixteen or seventeen years since I saw the Queen of France, then the Dauphiness, at Versailles, and surely never lighted on this orb—Oh God, Oh my God, those thoughts are sinful— [*sings*] as beautiful Kitty one morning was tripping with a pitcher of milk—

[*Public attempts to whistle his song 'Philadelphia, Here I Come.' He whistles the first phrase and the notes die away. Private keeps on talking while Public attempts to whistle.*]

PRIVATE We'll go now, right away, and tell them—Mammy and Daddy—they're at home tonight—now, Gar, now—it must be now—remember, it's up to you entirely up to you—gut and salt them fish—and they're going to call this one Madge, at least so she *says*—

[*Public makes another attempt to whistle.*]

—a little something to remind you of your old teacher—don't keep looking back over your shoulder, be 100 per cent American—a packet of cigarettes and a pot of jam—seven boys and seven girls—and our daughters'll be all gentle and frail and silly like you—and I'll never wait till Christmas—I'll burst, I'll bloody-well burst—good-bye, Gar, it isn't as bad as that—good-bye, Gar, it isn't as bad as that—good-bye, Gar, it isn't as bad as that—

PUBLIC [*in whispered shout*] Screwballs, say something! Say something, father!

Quick Curtain

END OF EPISODE TWO: *Second interval.*

EPISODE III

PART ONE

[*A short time later. The rosary is being said. Public is kneeling with his back to the audience. S.B. is kneeling facing the audience. Madge is facing the shop door. Private kneels beside Public. Madge is saying her decade, and the other three—S.B. Public and Private—are answering. The words are barely distinct, a monotonous, somnolent drone. After a few moments Private lowers his body until his rear is resting on the backs of his legs. We cannot see Public's face. While Private talks, the rosary goes on.*]

PRIVATE [*relaxing, yawning*] Ah-ho-ho-ho-ho-ho. This time tomorrow night, bucko, you'll be saying the rosary all by yourself—unless Lizzy and Con say it [*joins in a response in American accent*] —Holy Mairy, Mother of Gawd, pray for us sinners now and at the

hour . . . [*He tails off as his mind wanders again.*] No, not this time tomorrow. It's only about half-four in Philadelphia now, and when it's half-nine there it'll be the wee hours of the morning here; and Screwballs'll be curled up and fast asleep in his wee cot— [*To S.B.*] —right, honey? And when he's dreaming, you'll be swaggering down 56th Street on Third at the junction of 29th and Seventh at 81st with this big blonde nuzzling up to you— [*Suddenly kneels erect again and responds in unison with Public. Keeps this up for two or three responses and slowly subsides again.*] You'd need to be careful out there, boy; some of those Yankee women are dynamite. But you'll never marry; never; bachelor's written all over you. Fated to be alone, a man without intimates; something of an enigma. Who is he, this silent one? Where is he from? Where does he go? Every night we see him walking beneath the trees along the bank of the canal, his black cloak swinging behind him, his eyes lost in thought, his servant following him at a respectful distance. [*In reply.*] Who is he? I'll tell you who he is: The Bachelor. All the same, laddybuck, there are compensations in being a bachelor. You'll age slowly and graciously, and then, perhaps, when you're quite old—about forty-three—you'll meet this beautiful girl of nineteen, and you'll fall madly in love. Karin—that's her name—no—ah—ah—Tamara— [*Caressing the word.*] Tamara—grand-daughter of an exiled Russian prince, and you'll be consumed by a magnificent passion; and this night you'll invite her to dinner in your penthouse, and you'll be dressed in a deep blue velvet jacket, and the candles will discover magic fairy lights in her hair, and you'll say to her, 'Tamara,' and she'll incline her face towards you, and close her eyes, and whisper—

[*From a few seconds back the droning prayers have stopped. Now Madge leans over to Public and gives him a rough punch.*]

MADGE Your decade!

[*Private and Public jump erect again and in perfect unison give out their decade. Gradually, as the prayers continue, they relax into their slumped position.*]

PRIVATE When you're curled up in your wee cot, Screwballs, do you dream? Do you ever dream of the past, Screwballs, of that wintry morning in Bailtefree, and the three days in Bundoran? . . .

[*Public stays as he is. Private gets slowly to his feet and moves over to S.B. He stands looking down at him.*]

. . . and of the young, gay girl from beyond the mountains who sometimes cried herself to sleep? [*Softly, nervously, with growing excitement.*] God—maybe—Screwballs—behind those dead eyes and that flat face are there memories of precious moments in the past? My God, have I been unfair to you? Is it possible that you have hoarded in the back of that mind of yours—do you remember—it was an afternoon in May—oh, fifteen years ago—I don't remember every detail but some things are as vivid as can be: the boat was blue and the paint was peeling and there was an empty cigarette packet floating in the water at the bottom between two trout and the left rowlock kept slipping and you had given me your hat and had put your jacket round my shoulders because there had been a shower of rain. And you had the rod in your left hand—I

can see the cork nibbled away from the butt of the rod—and maybe we had been chatting—I don't remember—it doesn't matter—but between us at that moment there was this great happiness, this great joy—you must have felt it too—it was so much richer than a content—it was a great, great happiness, and active, bubbling joy—although nothing was being said—just the two of us fishing on a lake on a showery day—and young as I was I felt, I knew that this was precious, and your hat was soft on the top of my ears—I can feel it—and I shrank down into your coat—and then, then for no reason at all except that you were happy too, you began to sing: [*sings*]

All round my hat I'll wear a green coloured ribbono,
All round my hat for a twelve month and a day.
And if anybody asks me the reason why I wear it,
It's all because my true love is far, far away.

[*The rosary is over. Madge and S.B. get slowly to their feet. Public and Private are not aware that the prayers are finished. S.B. does the nightly job of winding the clock.*]

MADGE Will you take your supper now?
S.B. Any time suits you. [*Madge goes to Public, still kneeling.*]
MADGE And what about St. Martin de Porres?
PUBLIC Mm?

[*He blesses himself hurriedly, in confusion, and gets to his feet.*]

MADGE Supper.
PUBLIC Yes—yes—please, Madge—
MADGE [*going off*] I suppose even the saints must eat now and again, too.

[*Pause. S.B. consults his pocket watch.*]

S.B. What time do you make it?
PUBLIC Quarter to ten.
S.B. It's that anyhow.
PRIVATE Go on! Ask him! He must remember!
S.B. The days are shortening already. Before we know we'll be burning light before closing time.
PRIVATE Go on! Go on!
PUBLIC [*in the churlish, off-hand tone he uses to S.B.*] What ever happened to that aul boat on Lough na Cloc Cor.
S.B. What's that?
PRIVATE Again!
PUBLIC That aul boat that used to be up on Lough na Cloc Cor—an aul blue thing—d'you remember it?
S.B. A boat? Eh? [*Voices off.*] The Canon!
PRIVATE Bugger the Canon!

[*The Canon enters; a lean, white man with alert eyes and a thin mouth. He is talking back to Madge in the scullery.*]

CANON Hee-hee-hee—you're a terrible woman.
S.B. Well, Canon!
CANON That Madge . . . hee-hee-hee.
PUBLIC Good night, Canon.
CANON She says I wait till the rosary's over and the kettle's on . . . hee-hee-hee.
S.B. She's a sharp one, Madge.
CANON 'You wait', says she, 'till the rosary's over and the kettle's on!'
PRIVATE Hee-hee-hee.
S.B. Pay no heed to Madge, Canon.
PRIVATE And how's the O'Donnell family tonight?
CANON And how's the O'Donnell family tonight?

[*Public sits when the Canon sits.*]

S.B. Living away as usual. Not a thing happening.
PRIVATE Liar!
CANON Just so, now, just so.
S.B. Will we have a game now or will we wait till the supper comes in?
CANON We may as well commence, Sean. I see no reason why we shouldn't commence.
S.B. [*setting the board*] Whatever you say, Canon.
CANON Hee-hee-hee. 'You wait', says she, 'till the rosary's over and the kettle's on.'
PRIVATE She's a sharp one, Madge.
S.B. She's a sharp one, Madge.
CANON It'll be getting near your time, Gareth.
PUBLIC Tomorrow morning, Canon.
CANON Just so, now. Tomorrow morning.
PRIVATE Tomorrow morning.
CANON Tomorrow morning.
S.B. Here we are.
CANON Powerful the way time passes, too.
S.B. Black or white, Canon?
CANON [*considering the problem*] Black or white. . . .
PRIVATE Black for the crows and white for the swans.
CANON Black for the crows and white for the swans.
PRIVATE Ha-ha! [*He preens himself at his skill in prophecy.*]
S.B. Have a shot at the black the night.
CANON Maybe I will then.
PRIVATE Can't take the money off you every night.
CANON Can't take the trousers off you every night. Hee-hee-hee.
PRIVATE [*shocked*] Canon O'Byrne!
S.B. You had a great streak of luck last night, I'll grant you that.
CANON [*a major announcement*] D'you know what?
S.B. What's that, Canon?
CANON You'll have rain before morning.
S.B. D'you think so?
CANON It's in the bones. The leg's giving me the odd jab.

S.B. We could do without the rain then.

CANON Before the morning you'll have it.

S.B. Tch tch tch. We get our fill of it here.

CANON The best barometer I know.

S.B. Aye. No want of rain.

CANON Before the morning.

S.B. As if we don't get enough of it.

CANON The jabs are never wrong.

PRIVATE [*wildly excited*] Stop press! News flash! Sensation! We interrupt our programmes to bring you the news that Canon Mick O'Byrne, of Ballybeg, Ireland, has made the confident prediction that *you'll* have rain before the morning! Stand by for further bulletins!

CANON 'You wait', says she, 'till the rosary's over and the kettle's on!'

S.B. Usual stakes, Canon?

CANON I see no reason to alter them.

S.B. What about putting them up—just for the first game?

CANON The thin end of the wedge, eh, as the Bishop says? No, Sean, the way I see it, a half-penny a game'll neither make nor break either of us.

[*Enter Madge with cups of tea and a plate of biscuits.*]

MADGE Have you begun already?

S.B. Shh!

MADGE If it was turkeys or marble clocks they were playing for they couldn't be more serious!

S.B. Quiet!

MADGE Agh!

[*She leaves their tea beside them and brings a cup over to Public. They talk in undertones.*]

MADGE Wouldn't you love to throw it round them!

PUBLIC Scalding hot!

MADGE And raise blisters on their aul bald pates!—God forgive me!

PUBLIC Madge.

MADGE What?

PUBLIC Why don't you take a run over to see the new baby?

MADGE I've more on my mind than that.

PUBLIC I'll put up the jars and wash up these few things.

MADGE And this the last night we'll have you to torment us?

PUBLIC Go on. Go on. We won't start swopping the dirty stories till we get you out of the road.

S.B. Shhhhhhh!

PUBLIC Hurry up. Nelly'll be wondering why you didn't show up.

MADGE Aye, so.

PUBLIC Your own namesake, isn't it?

MADGE So she *says*.

PUBLIC Get a move on. You'll be back before bedtime.
MADGE What d'you think?
PUBLIC Quick!
MADGE I'm away! [*She takes a few steps away and comes back.*] Don't forget: them shirts isn't right aired.

[*Just when she is at the scullery door.*]

PUBLIC Madge.
MADGE What is it?
PRIVATE Don't! Don't!
PUBLIC Why did my mother marry him [*S.B.*] instead of Master Boyle?
MADGE What?
PUBLIC She went with both of them, didn't she?
MADGE She married the better man by far.
PUBLIC But she went with Boyle first, didn't she?
MADGE I've told you before: she went with a dozen—that was the kind of her—she couldn't help herself.
PUBLIC But is that what started Boyle drinking?
MADGE If it was, more fool he. And any other nosing about you want to do, ask the Boss. For you're not going to pump me.

[*She goes off.*]

PRIVATE What the hell had you to go and ask that for! Snap, boy, snap! We want no scenes tonight. Get up and clear out of this because you're liable to get over-excited watching these two dare-devils dicing with death. [*Public takes his cup and goes towards his bedroom.*] Into your survival shelter and brood, brood, brood. [*As if replying to the draught players—who have not noticed his exit.*] No, no, I'm not leaving. Just going in here to have a wee chat with my Chinese mistress.

[*Public goes into his bedroom, leaving the door open. Private stays in the kitchen. Public in the bedroom mimes the actions of Private in the following sequence. Private stands at the table between S.B. and Canon:*]

PRIVATE Canon battling tooth and nail for another half-penny; Screwballs fighting valiantly to retain his trousers! Gripped in mortal combat! County Councillor versus Canon! Screwballs versus Canonballs! [*Stares intently at them.*] Hi, kids! Having fun, kids? [*Gets to his feet, leans his elbow on the table, and talks confidentially into their faces.*] Any chance of a game, huh? Tell me, boys, strictly between ourselves, will you miss me? You will? You really will? But now I want you both to close your eyes—please, my darlings—don't, don't argue—just do as I say—just close your eyes and think of all the truly wonderful times we've had together. Now! What'll we chat about, eh? Let's—chat—about—what? No, Screwballs, not women; not before you-know-who. [*Looking at the Canon.*] Money? Agh, sure, Canon, what interest have you in money? Sure as long as you get to Tenerife for five weeks every winter what interest have you in money? But

I'm wasting my time with you, Canon—Screwballs here is different; there's an affinity between Screwballs and me that no one, literally, no one could understand—except you, Canon [*deadly serious*], because you're warm and kind and soft and sympathetic—all things to all men—because you could translate all this loneliness, this groping, this dreadful bloody buffoonery into Christian terms that will make life bearable for us all. And yet you don't say a word. Why, Canon? Why, arid Canon? Isn't this your job?—to translate? Why don't you speak, then? Prudence arid Canon? Prudence be damned! Christianity isn't prudent—it's insane! Or maybe this just happens to be one of your bad nights— [*suddenly bright and brittle again*] —A pound to a shilling I make you laugh! [*Dancing around, singing to the tune of 'Daisy':*] 'Screwballs, Screwballs, give me your answer do. I'm half crazy all for the love of you. I'm off to Philadelphey, and I'll leave you on the shelfey—'

[*S.B. gives a short dry laugh.*]

PRIVATE A pound you owe me! Money for aul rope! And you, Canon, what about giving us a bar or two?

CANON Aye.

PRIVATE You will? Wonderful! What'll it be? A pop number? An aul Gregorian come-all-ye? A whack out of an aul aria?

CANON I had you cornered.

PRIVATE 'I had you cornered'—I know it! I know it! I know it! okay. [*Sings in the style of a modern crooner.*] I had you cornered / That night in Casablanca / That night you said you loved me—all set? Boys and girls, that top, pop recording star, Kenny O'Byrne and the Ballybeg Buggers in their latest fabulous release, 'I Had You Cornered.'

[*Private stands with head lowered, his foot tapping, his fingers clicking in syncopated rhythm, waiting for the Canon to begin. He keeps this up for a few seconds. Then in time to his own beat he sings very softly, as he goes to the bedroom—*

Should aul acquaintance be forgot
And never brought to min'?
Should aul acquaintance be forgot
And days o' lang-syne?
Yah—ooooo.

[*Public suddenly sits up in bed.*]

Mendelssohn! That's the bugger'll tear the guts out of you! [*Public puts on a recording of the second movement of the violin concerto. Private, now almost frenzied, dashes back to the kitchen.*] Give us a bar or two, Mendelssohn, aul fella. Come on, lad; resin the aul bow and spit on your hands and give us an aul bar!

[*The record begins. Private runs to the table and thrusts his face between the players.*]

Listen! Listen! Listen! D'you hear it? D'you know what the music says? [*To S.B.*] It says that once upon a time a boy and his father sat in a blue boat on a lake on an afternoon in May, and on that afternoon a great beauty happened, a beauty that has haunted the boy ever since, because he wonders now did it really take place or did he imagine it. There are only the two of us, he says; each of us is all the other has; and why can we not even look at each other? Have pity on us, he says; have goddam pity on every goddam bloody man jack of us.

[He comes away from the table and walks limply back to the bedroom. When he gets to the bedroom door he turns, surveys the men.]

To hell with all strong silent men!

[He goes into the bedroom, drops into the chair, and sits motionless. Public sinks back on to the bed again. Silence.]

CANON What's that noise?
S.B. What's that, Canon?
CANON A noise of some sort.
S.B. Is there?

[They listen.]

S.B. I don't hear—
CANON Wait.
S.B. Is it—
CANON It's music—is it?
S.B. Music?
CANON Aye. It's music.
S.B. That'll be Gar then.
CANON Oh.
S.B. Playing them records of his.
CANON Thought I heard something.
S.B. All he asks is to sit in there and play them records all day.
CANON It makes him happy.
S.B. Terrible man for the records.
CANON Just so, now. It'll be getting near his time, he tells me.
S.B. Tomorrow morning.
CANON Tomorrow morning.
S.B. Aye, tomorrow morning. Powerful the way time passes, too.
CANON You wait, says she, till the rosary's over and the kettle's on.
S.B. A sharp one, Madge.
CANON Ah-hah. There's hope for you yet.
S.B. I don't know is there.
CANON No. You're not too late yet.
S.B. Maybe . . . maybe. . . .
CANON No, I wouldn't say die yet—not yet I wouldn't.

Slow Curtain

END OF EPISODE THREE, PART I

PART TWO

[*The small hours of the morning. The kitchen is dimly lit. In the kitchen, just outside the bedroom door, are Gar's cases, and lying across them are his coat, his cap, and a large envelope containing his X-ray and visa. The bedroom is in darkness: just enough light to see Public on the bed and Private in the chair. S.B. comes in from the scullery carrying a cup of tea in his hand. He is dressed in long trousers, a vest, a hat, socks. He moves slowly towards the table, sees the cases, goes over to them, touches the coat, goes back towards the table, and sits there, staring at the bedroom door. He coughs. Immediately Private is awake and Public sits up sleepily in bed.*]

PRIVATE What—what—what's that? [*Relaxing.*] Madge probably. Looking to see is the door bolted.

[*Public gets out of bed and switches on the light. Looks at his watch.*]

You'll not sleep again tonight, laddo.

PUBLIC Bugger.

[*Public looks at himself in the mirror and then sits on edge of bed.*]

PRIVATE Four more hours. This is the last time you'll lie in this bed, the last time you'll look at that pattern [*on the floor*], the last time you'll listen to the silence of Ballybeg, the last time you'll—

PUBLIC Agh, shut up!

PRIVATE It is now sixteen or seventeen years since I saw the Queen of France. Go into the shop, man, and get yourself a packet of aspirin; that'll do the trick. [*Looking up at ceiling.*] Mind if I take a packet of aspirin, Screwballs? Send the bill to the U.S.A., okay? Out you go, boy, and get a clatter of pills!

[*They both go into the kitchen. Public stops dead when he sees S.B. staring at him.*]

PRIVATE My God! Lady Godiva!

PUBLIC Is this where you are?

S.B. Aye—I—I—I—I wasn't sleeping. What has you up?

[*Public goes to where the key of the shop is hung up.*]

PUBLIC I—I wasn't sleeping either. I'll get some aspirins inside.

S.B. It's hard to sleep sometimes. . . .

PUBLIC It is, aye . . . sometimes. . . .

S.B. There's tea in the pot.

PUBLIC Aye?

S.B. If it's a headache you have.

PUBLIC It'll make me no worse anyway.

[*Public goes into the scullery. Private stands at the door and talks into him.*]

PRIVATE Now's your time, boy. The small hours of the morning. Put your head on his shoulder and say, 'How's my wee darling Daddy?'

[*Public puts his head round the door.*]

PUBLIC You take some?

S.B. Sure you know I never take a second cup.

PRIVATE Playing hard to get. Come on, bucko; it's your place to make the move—the younger man. Say—say—say—say, 'Screwballs, with two magnificent legs like that, how is it you were never in show biz?' Say, 'It is now sixteen or seventeen—'—Say—oh my God—say—say something.

[*Public enters with a cup of tea.*]

PUBLIC You'll need a new tyre for the van.

S.B. What one's that?

PUBLIC The back left-hand one. I told you. It's done.

S.B. Aye. So you did.

PUBLIC And—and—

PRIVATE What else?

PUBLIC —and don't forget the fencing posts for McGuire next Wednesday.

S.B. Fencing posts.

PUBLIC Twelve dozen. The milk lorry'll take them. I spoke to Packey.

S.B. Aye. . . . right. . . .

PRIVATE Go on! Keep talking!

PUBLIC And if you're looking for the pliers, I threw them into the tea chest under the counter.

S.B. Which tea chest?

PUBLIC The one near the window.

S.B. Oh, I see—I see. . . .

PRIVATE You're doing grand. Keep at it. It's the silence that's the enemy.

PUBLIC You'll be wanting more plug tobacco. The traveller'll be here this week.

S.B. More plug.

PUBLIC It's finished. The last of it went up to Curran's wake.

S.B. I'll—I'll see about that.

PUBLIC And you'll need to put a new clasp on the lower window—the tinkers are about again.

S.B. Aye?

PUBLIC They were in at dinner time. I got some cans off them.

S.B. I just thought I noticed something shining from the ceiling.

PUBLIC It's the cans then.

S.B. Aye.

PUBLIC That's what it is. I bought six off them.

S.B. They'll not go to loss.

PUBLIC They wanted me to take a dozen but I said six would do us.

S.B. Six is plenty. They don't go as quick as they used to—them cans.

PUBLIC They've all got cookers and ranges and things.

S.B. What's that?

PUBLIC I say they don't buy them now because the open fires are nearly all gone.

S.B. That's it. All cookers and ranges and things these times.

PUBLIC That's why I wouldn't take the dozen.

S.B. You were right, too. Although I mind the time when I got through a couple of dozen a week.

PUBLIC Aye?

S.B. All cans it was then. Maybe you'd sell a kettle at turf-cutting or if there'd be a Yank coming home. . . . [*Pause.*]

PUBLIC Better get these pills and then try to get a couple of hours sleep—

S.B. You're getting the mail-van to Strabane?

[*Public gives him a quick, watchful look.*]

PUBLIC At a quarter past seven.

S.B. [*awkwardly*] I was listening to the weather forecast there . . . moderate westerly winds and occasional showers, it said.

PUBLIC Aye?

S.B. I was thinking it—it—it—it would be a fair enough day for going up in thon plane.

PUBLIC It should be, then.

S.B. Showers—just like the Canon said. . . . And I was meaning to tell you that you should sit at the back. . . .

PRIVATE It is now sixteen or seventeen years—the longest way round's the shortest way home—

S.B. So *he* was saying, too . . . you know there—if there was an accident or anything—it's the front gets it hardest—

PUBLIC I suppose that's true enough.

S.B. So *he* was saying . . . not that I would know—just that he was saying it there. . . .

PRIVATE [*urgently, rapidly*] Now! Now! He might remember—he might. But if he does, my God, laddo—what if he does?

PUBLIC [*with pretended carelessness*] D'you know what kept coming into my mind the day?

S.B. Eh?

PUBLIC The fishing we used to do on Lough na Cloc Cor.

S.B. [*confused, on guard*] Oh, aye, Lough na Cloc Cor—aye—aye—

PUBLIC We had a throw on it every Sunday during the season.

S.B. That's not the day nor yesterday.

PUBLIC [*more quickly*] There used to be a blue boat on it—d'you remember it?

S.B. Many's the fish we took off that same lake.

PUBLIC D'you remember the blue boat?

S.B. A blue one, eh?

PUBLIC I don't know who owned it. But it was blue. And the paint was peeling.

S.B. [*remembering*] I mind a brown one the doctor brought from somewhere up in the—

PUBLIC [*quickly*] It doesn't matter who owned it. It doesn't even matter that it was blue. But d'you remember one afternoon in May—we were up there—the two of us—and it

must have rained because you put your jacket round my shoulders and gave me your hat—

S.B. Aye?

PUBLIC —and it wasn't that we were talking or anything—but suddenly—suddenly you sang 'All Round My Hat I'll Wear a Green Coloured Ribbono'—

S.B. Me?

PUBLIC —for no reason at all except that we—that you were happy. D'you remember? D'you remember?

[There is a pause while S.B. tries to recall.]

S.B. No . . . no, then, I don't. . . .

[Private claps his hands in nervous mockery.]

PRIVATE *[quickly]* There! There! There!

S.B. 'All Round My Hat'? No, I don't think I ever knew that one. It wasn't 'The Flower of Sweet Strabane', was it? That was my song.

PUBLIC It could have been. It doesn't matter.

PRIVATE So now you know: it never happened! Ha-ha-ha-ha-ha.

S.B. 'All Round My Hat'?—that was never one of mine. What does it go like?

PUBLIC I couldn't tell you. I don't know it either.

PRIVATE Ha-ha-ha-ha-ha-ha-ha-ha.

S.B. And you say the boat was blue?

PUBLIC It doesn't matter. Forget it.

S.B. *[justly, reasonably]* There was a brown one belonging to the doctor, and before that there was a wee flat-bottom—but it was green—or was it white? I'll tell you, you wouldn't be thinking of a punt—it could have been blue—one that the curate had down at the pier last summer—

[Private's mocking laughter increases. Public rushes quickly into the shop. Private, still mocking, follows.]

—a fine sturdy wee punt it was, too, and it could well have been the. . . .

[He sees that he is alone and tails off. Slowly he gets to his feet and goes towards the scullery door. He meets Madge entering. She is dressed in outside clothes. She is very weary.]

MADGE What has you up?

S.B. Me? Aw, I took medicine and the cramps wouldn't let me sleep. I thought you were in bed?

MADGE I was over at Nelly's. The place was upside down.

S.B. There's nothing wrong, is there?

MADGE Not a thing.

S.B. The baby's strong and healthy?

MADGE Grand—grand.

S.B. That's all that matters.

MADGE They're going to call it Brigid.

S.B. Brigid—that's a grand name . . . Patrick, Brigid, and Colmcille. . . .

[*She takes off her hat and coat. S.B. hesitates.*]

Madge. . . .

MADGE You'll get a cold padding about in yon rig.

S.B. Madge, I'll manage rightly, Madge, eh?

MADGE Surely you will.

S.B. I'll get one of Charley Bonner's boys to do the van on Tuesdays and Thursdays and I'll manage rightly?

MADGE This place is cold. Away off to bed.

S.B. It's not like in the old days when the whole countryside did with me; I needed the help then. But it's different now. I'll manage by myself now. Eh? I'll manage fine, eh?

MADGE Fine.

S.B. D'you mind the trouble we had keeping him at school just after he turned ten. D'you mind nothing would do him but he'd get behind the counter. And he had this wee sailor suit on him this morning—

MADGE A sailor suit? He never had a sailor suit.

S.B. Oh, he had, Madge. Oh, Madge, he had. I can see him, with his shoulders back, and the wee head up straight, and the mouth, aw, man, as set, and says he this morning, I can hear him saying it, says he, 'I'm not going to school. I'm going into my daddy's business'—you know—all important—and, d'you mind, you tried to coax him to go to school, and not a move you could get out of him, and him as manly looking, and this wee sailor suit as smart looking on him, and—and—and at the heel of the hunt I had to go with him myself, the two of us, hand in hand, as happy as larks—we were that happy, Madge—and him dancing and chatting beside me—mind?—you couldn't get a word in edge-ways with all the chatting he used to go through. . . . Maybe, Madge, maybe it's because I could have been his grandfather, eh?

MADGE I don't know.

S.B. I was too old for her, Madge, eh?

MADGE I don't know. They're a new race—a new world.

S.B. [*leaving*] In the wee sailor suit—all the chatting he used to go through. . . . I don't know either. . . .

MADGE [*looking at case*] Tomorrow'll be sore on him [*Gar*]: his heart'll break tomorrow, and all next week, and the week after maybe. . . . Brigid—aye, it's all right— [*Trying out the sound of the name*] Brigid—Biddy—Biddy Mulhern—Brigid Mulhern—aye—like Madge Mulhern doesn't sound right— [*Trying it out*] —Madge Mulhern—Madge Mulhern—I don't know—it's too aul'fashioned or something. . . . Has he his cap? [*Finds it in the pocket of the coat. Also finds an apple.*] . . . Aye, he has. And an apple, if you don't mind—for all his grief. He'll be all right. That Lizzy one'll look after him well, I suppose, if she can take time off from blatherin'. Garden front and back, and a TV in the house of lords—I'll believe them things when I see them! Never had much time for blatherin' women. . . . [*Remembering.*] An envelope. . . . [*She takes two notes from her pocket, goes to the dresser, and finds an envelope. She puts the money into the envelope, and slips the envelope into the coat pocket.*] That'll get him a cup of tea on the plane.

I had put them two pounds by me to get my feet done on the fair day. But I can wait till next month. From what I hear, there's no big dances between now and then. . . . [*She stands looking at the bedroom door.*] So. I think that's everything. . . . [*She raises her hand in a sort of vague Benediction, then shuffles towards the scullery.*] When the boss was his [*Gar's*] age, he was the very same as him: leppin, and eejitin' about and actin' the clown; as like as two peas. And when he's [*Gar*] the age the boss is now, he'll turn out just the same. And although I won't be here to see it, you'll find that he's learned nothin' in-between times. That's people for you—they'd put you astray in the head if you thought long enough about them.

[*Public and Private enter from the shop.*]

PUBLIC You down too? Turning into a night club, this place.
MADGE I'm only getting back.
PUBLIC Well, how's the new Madge?
MADGE Strong and healthy—and that's all that matters.
MADGE Were you and the boss chatting there?
PUBLIC When's the christening?
MADGE Sunday. After last Mass.
PUBLIC Madge Mulhern. Are you proud?
MADGE I'm just tired, son. Very tired.
PUBLIC You're sure there's nothing wrong, Madge?
MADGE If there was something wrong, wouldn't I tell you?
PRIVATE Of course she would. Who else has she?
PUBLIC Did you tell her she's getting an elephant out of my first wages?
MADGE Aye, so. The jars are up?
PUBLIC They are.
MADGE And the dishes washed?
PUBLIC All done.
MADGE I'll give you a call at half-six, then.
PUBLIC Madge—Madge, you'd let me know if—if he got sick or anything?
MADGE Who else would there be?
PUBLIC Just in case . . . not that it's likely—he'll outlive the whole of us. . . .
MADGE Good night.
PUBLIC Sleep well, Madge.
MADGE Sleep well yourself.

[*Madge goes off. Public and Private watch her shuffle off.*]

PRIVATE Watch her carefully, every movement, every gesture, every little peculiarity: keep the camera whirring; for this is a film you'll run over and over again—Madge Going to Bed On My Last Night At Home. . . . Madge. . . . [*Public and Private go into bedroom.*] God, Boy, why do you have to leave? Why? Why?
PUBLIC I don't know. I—I—I don't know.

Quick Curtain

TOM STOPPARD

(1937–)

Rosencrantz and Guildenstern Are Dead

About the Author: Tom Stoppard was born Tomas Straussler in Zlín, Czechoslovakia, in 1937, and two years later his family moved to Singapore where his father was a company doctor for the Bata shoe company. In 1942, Tomas, his brother, and his mother fled to India in advance of the Japanese invasion, and his father, who remained behind, was killed. In India, his mother married an English army officer named Kenneth Stoppard, the children took his name, and in 1946, after the war, the family returned to England. After graduating from high school, Stoppard worked as a journalist and freelance writer, subsequently turning his attention to writing plays. He has become one of England's most successful playwrights since 1967, when *Rosencrantz and Guildenstern Are Dead* was produced in London by the National Theatre and in New York on Broadway, where the play won both the Tony Award and the Drama Critics Circle Award for Best Play of 1967–68.

About the Play: Any play assumes that its audience brings some kind of knowledge into the theater, but *Rosencrantz* is unusual in assuming that its audience is intimately familiar with another play: Shakespeare's *Hamlet.* Rosencrantz and Guildenstern, minor characters in Shakespeare's play, are the major characters in Stoppard's, which is conceived of as going on at the same time. Characters from Shakespeare's play enter Stoppard's stage from time to time speaking lines from *Hamlet* and reminding us of what is going on in that parallel dramatic world. Many of the play's thematic concerns are the same as those in *Hamlet:* questions of individual freedom and identity and direction; the relationship of death to human morality and significance; and speculation about the nature of dramatic artifice, especially through the dramatization of playing within the play.

Rosencrantz, however, often presents these notions as farce, in a style closer in spirit to Monty Python or the Marx Brothers than to Shakespeare. For example, at the start of the play, at the same time that the Ghost walks in *Hamlet* ominously suggesting that the natural order has been disturbed, Rosencrantz and Guildenstern flip a coin again and again, and it keeps coming up unfailingly heads—the laws of probability, if not of nature, have been suspended. Rosencrantz, however, is too caught up in winning to notice that anything is unusual, so the episode seems comic rather than serious. This play often seems tongue in cheek, but it raises and explores profound philosophical and literary questions nonetheless. In this regard it resembles the theater of the absurd, a dramatic style current in the 1950s and 1960s. This style was often minimalist in dialogue, however; it used as few words as possible, usually very simple ones. *Rosencrantz,* by contrast, is a celebration of language, filled with puns, allusions, incantatory rhythms, and intellectual jokes. More than an appendage to *Hamlet,* it is a major play in its own right.

CHARACTERS

ROSENCRANTZ
GUILDENSTERN
THE PLAYER
TRAGEDIANS
HAMLET
OPHELIA
CLAUDIUS

GERTRUDE
POLONIUS

ACT ONE

TWO ELIZABETHANS passing the time in a place without any visible character.

They are well dressed—hats, cloaks, sticks and all.

Each of them has a large leather money bag.

GUILDENSTERN's bag is nearly empty.

ROSENCRANTZ's bag is nearly full.

The reason being: they are betting on the toss of a coin, in the following manner: GUILDENSTERN (hereafter "GUIL") takes a coin out of his bag, spins it, letting it fall. ROSENCRANTZ (hereafter "ROS") studies it, announces it as "heads" (as it happens) and puts it into his own bag. Then they repeat the process. They have apparently been doing this for some time.

The run of "heads" is impossible, yet ROS betrays no surprise at all—he feels none. However, he is nice enough to feel a little embarrassed at taking so much money off his friend. Let that be his character note.

GUIL is well alive to the oddity of it. He is not worried about the money, but he is worried by the implications; aware but not going to panic about it—his character note.

GUIL sits. ROS stands (he does the moving, retrieving coins).

GUIL spins. ROS studies coin.

ROS: Heads.

He picks it up and puts it in his bag. The process is repeated.

Heads.

Again.

Heads.

Again.

Heads.

Again.

Heads.

GUIL *(flipping a coin):* There is an art to the building up of suspense.

ROS: Heads.

GUIL *(flipping another):* Though it can be done by luck alone.

ROS: Heads.

GUIL: If that's the word I'm after.

ROS *(raises his head at* GUIL*):* Seventy-six—love.

GUIL gets up but has nowhere to go. He spins another coin over his shoulder without looking at it, his attention being directed at his environment or lack of it.

Heads.

GUIL: A weaker man might be moved to re-examine his faith, if in nothing else at least in the law of probability. *(He slips a coin over his shoulder as he goes to look upstage.)*

ROS: Heads.

GUIL, examining the confines of the stage, flips over two more coins as he does so, one by one of course. ROS announces each of them as "heads."

GUIL *(musing):* The law of probability, it has been oddly asserted, is something to do with the proposition that if six monkeys *(he has surprised himself)* . . . if six monkeys were . . .

ROS: Game?

GUIL: Were they?

ROS: Are you?

GUIL *(understanding):* Game. *(Flips a coin.)* The law of averages, if I have got this right, means that if six monkeys were thrown up in the air for long enough they would land on their tails about as often as they would land on their—

ROS: Heads. *(He picks up the coin.)*

GUIL: Which even at first glance does not strike one as a particularly rewarding speculation, in either sense, even without the monkeys. I mean you wouldn't *bet* on it. I mean *I* would, but *you* wouldn't. . . . *(As he flips a coin.)*

ROS: Heads.

GUIL: Would you? *(Flips a coin.)*

ROS: Heads.

Repeat.

Heads. *(He looks up at* GUIL*—embarrassed laugh.)* Getting a bit of a bore, isn't it?

GUIL *(coldly):* A bore?

ROS: Well . . .

GUIL: What about the suspense?

ROS *(innocently)*: What suspense?

Small pause.

GUIL: It must be the law of diminishing returns. . . . I feel the spell about to be broken. *(Energizing himself somewhat. He takes out a coin, spins it high, catches it, turns it over on to the back of his other hand, studies the coin—and tosses it to* ROS. *His energy deflates and he sits.)*

Well, it was an even chance . . . if my calculations are correct.

ROS: Eighty-five in a row—beaten the record!

GUIL: Don't be absurd.

ROS: Easily!

GUIL *(angry)*: Is that *it,* then? Is that all?

ROS: What?

GUIL: A new record? Is that as far as you are prepared to go?

ROS: Well . . .

GUIL: No questions? Not even a pause?

ROS: You spun them yourself.

GUIL: Not a flicker of doubt?

ROS *(aggrieved, aggressive)*: Well, I won—didn't I?

GUIL *(approaches him—quieter)*: And if you'd lost? If they'd come down against you, eighty-five times, one after another, just like that?

ROS *(dumbly)*: Eighty-five in a row? *Tails?*

GUIL: Yes! What would you think?

ROS *(doubtfully)*: Well. . . . *(Jocularly.)* Well, I'd have a good look at your coins for a start!

GUIL *(retiring)*: I'm relieved. At least we can still count on self-interest as a predictable factor. . . . I suppose it's the last to go. Your capacity for trust made me wonder if perhaps . . . you, alone . . . *(He turns on him suddenly, reaches out a hand.)* Touch.

ROS *clasps his hand.* GUIL *pulls him up to him.*

GUIL *(more intensely)*: We have been spinning coins together since— *(He releases him almost as violently.)* This is not the first time we have spun coins!

ROS: Oh no—we've been spinning coins for as long as I remember.

GUIL: How long is that?

ROS: I forget. Mind you—eighty-five times!

GUIL: Yes?

ROS: It'll take some beating, I imagine.

GUIL: Is *that* what you imagine? Is that it? No *fear?*

ROS: Fear?

GUIL *(in fury—flings a coin on the ground)*: *Fear!* The crack that might flood your brain with light!

ROS: Heads. . . . *(He puts it in his bag.)*

GUIL *sits despondently. He takes a coin, spins it, lets it fall between his feet. He looks at it, picks it up, throws it to* ROS, *who puts it in his bag.*

GUIL *takes another coin, spins it, catches it, turns it over onto his other hand, looks at it, and throws it to* ROS, *who puts it in his bag.*

GUIL *takes a third coin, spins it, catches it in his right hand, turns it over onto his left wrist, lobs it in the air, catches it with his left hand, raises his left leg, throws the coin up under it, catches it and turns it over on the top of his head, where it sits.* ROS *comes, looks at it, puts it in his bag.*

ROS: I'm afraid—
GUIL: So am I.
ROS: I'm afraid it isn't your day.
GUIL: I'm afraid it is.

Small pause.

ROS: Eighty-nine.
GUIL: It must be indicative of something, besides the redistribution of wealth. *(He muses.)* List of possible explanations. One: I'm willing it. Inside where nothing shows, I am the essence of a man spinning double-headed coins; and betting against himself in private atonement for an unremembered past. *(He spins a coin at* ROS.*)*
ROS: Heads.
GUIL: Two: time has stopped dead, and the single experience of one coin being spun once has been repeated ninety times. . . . *(He flips a coin, looks at it, tosses it to* ROS.*)* On the whole, doubtful. Three: divine intervention, that is to say, a good turn from above concerning him, cf. children of Israel, or retribution from above concerning me, cf. Lot's wife. Four: a spectacular vindication of the principle that each individual coin spun individually *(he spins one)* is as likely to come down heads as tails and therefore should cause no surprise each individual time it does. *(It does. He tosses it to* ROS.*)*
ROS: I've never known anything like it!
GUIL: And a syllogism: One, he has never known anything like it. Two, he has never known anything to write home about. Three, it is nothing to write home about. . . . Home . . . What's the first thing you remember?
ROS: Oh, let's see. . . . The first thing that comes into my head, you mean?
GUIL: No—the first thing you remember.
ROS: Ah. *(Pause.)* No, it's no good, it's gone. It was a long time ago.
GUIL *(patient but edged)*: You don't get my meaning. What is the first thing after all the things you've forgotten?
ROS: Oh I see. *(Pause.)* I've forgotten the question.

GUIL *leaps up and paces.*

GUIL: Are you happy?
ROS: What?
GUIL: Content? At ease?
ROS: I suppose so.
GUIL: What are you going to do now?
ROS: I don't know. What do you want to do?
GUIL: I have no desires. None. *(He stops pacing dead.)* There was a messenger . . . that's right. We were sent for. *(He wheels at* ROS *and raps out:)* Syllogism the second: One, probability is a factor which operates within natural forces. Two, probability is not operating as a factor. Three, we are now within un-, sub- or supernatural forces. Discuss. *(*ROS *is suitably startled. Acidly.)* Not too heatedly.
ROS: I'm sorry I—What's the matter with you?
GUIL: The scientific approach to the examination of phenomena is a defence against the pure emotion of fear. Keep tight hold and continue while there's time. Now—counter to the previous syllogism: tricky one, follow me carefully, it may prove a comfort. If we

postulate, and we just have, that within un-, sub- or supernatural forces *the probability is* that the law of probability will not operate as a factor, then we must accept that the probability of the *first* part will not operate as a factor, in which case the law of probability *will* operate as a factor within un-, sub- or supernatural forces. And since it obviously hasn't been doing so, we can take it that we are not held within un-, sub- or supernatural forces after all; in all probability, that is. Which is a great relief to me personally. *(Small pause.)* Which is all very well, except that— *(He continues with tight hysteria, under control.)* We have been spinning coins together since I don't know when, and in all that time (if it *is* all that time) I don't suppose either of us was more than a couple of gold pieces up or down. I hope that doesn't sound surprising because its very unsurprisingness is something I am trying to keep hold of. The equanimity of your average tosser of coins depends upon a law, or rather a tendency, or let us say a probability, or at any rate a mathematically calculable chance, which ensures that he will not upset himself by losing too much nor upset his opponent by winning too often. This made for a kind of harmony and a kind of confidence. It related the fortuitous and the ordained into a reassuring union which we recognized as nature. The sun came up about as often as it went down, in the long run, and a coin showed heads about as often as it showed tails. Then a messenger arrived. We had been sent for. Nothing else happened. Ninety-two coins spun consecutively have come down heads ninety-two consecutive times . . . and for the last three minutes on the wind of a windless day I have heard the sound of drums and flute. . . .

ROS *(cutting his fingernails):* Another curious scientific phenomenon is the fact that the fingernails grow after death, as does the beard.

GUIL: What?

ROS *(loud):* Beard!

GUIL: But you're not dead.

ROS *(irritated):* I didn't say they *started* to grow after death! *(Pause, calmer.)* The fingernails also grow before birth, though *not* the beard.

GUIL: *What?*

ROS *(shouts):* Beard! What's the matter with you? *(Reflectively.)* The toenails, on the other hand, never grow at all.

GUIL *(bemused):* The toenails never grow at all?

ROS: Do they? It's a funny thing—I cut my fingernails all the time, and every time I think to cut them, they need cutting. Now, for instance. And yet, I never, to the best of my knowledge, cut my toenails. They ought to be curled under my feet by now, but it doesn't happen. I never think about them. Perhaps I cut them absent-mindedly, when I'm thinking of something else.

GUIL *(tensed up by this ranbling):* Do you remember the first thing that happened today?

ROS *(promptly):* I woke up, I suppose. *(Triggered.)* Oh—I've got it now—that man, a foreigner, he woke us up—

GUIL: A messenger. *(He relaxes, sits.)*

ROS: That's it—pale sky before dawn, a man standing on his saddle to bang on the shutters—shouts—What's all the row about?! Clear off!—But then he called our names. You remember that—this man woke us up.

GUIL: Yes.

ROS: We were sent for.

GUIL: Yes.

ROS: That's why we're here. *(He looks round, seems doubtful, then the explanation.)* Travelling.

GUIL: Yes.

ROS *(dramatically):* It was urgent—a matter of extreme urgency, a royal summons, his very words: official business and no questions asked—lights in the stable-yard, saddle up and off headlong and hotfoot across the land, our guides outstripped in breakneck pursuit of our duty! Fearful lest we come too late!!

Small pause.

GUIL: Too late for what?

ROS: How do I know? We haven't got there yet.

GUIL: Then what are we doing here, I ask myself.

ROS: You might well ask.

GUIL: We better get on.

ROS: You might well think.

GUIL: We better get on.

ROS *(actively):* Right! *(Pause.)* On where?

GUIL: Forward.

ROS *(forward to footlights):* Ah. *(Hesitates.)* Which way do we— *(He turns round.)* Which way did we—?

GUIL: Practically starting from scratch. . . . An awakening, a man standing on his saddle to bang on the shutters, our names shouted in a certain dawn, a message, a summons . . . A new record for heads and tails. We have not been . . . picked out . . . simply to be abandoned . . . set loose to find our own way. . . . We are entitled to some direction. . . . I would have thought.

ROS *(alert, listening):* I say—! I say—

GUIL: Yes?

ROS: I can hear—I thought I heard—music.

GUIL raises himself.

GUIL: Yes?

ROS: Like a band. *(He looks around, laughs embarrassedly, expiating himself.)* It sounded like—a band. Drums.

GUIL: Yes.

ROS *(relaxes):* It couldn't have been real.

GUIL: "The colours red, blue and green are real. The colour yellow is a mystical experience shared by everybody"—demolish.

ROS *(at edge of stage):* It must have been thunder. Like drums . . .

By the end of the next speech, the band is faintly audible.

GUIL: A man breaking his journey between one place and another at a third place of no name, character, population or significance, sees a unicorn cross his path and disappear. That in itself is startling, but there are precedents for mystical encounters of various kinds, or to be less extreme, a choice of persuasions to put it down to fancy; until— "My God," says a second man, "I must be dreaming, I thought I saw a unicorn." At

which point, a dimension is added that makes the experience as alarming as it will ever be. A third witness, you understand, adds no further dimension but only spreads it thinner, and a fourth thinner still, and the more witnesses there are the thinner it gets and the more reasonable it becomes until it is as thin as reality, the name we give to the common experience. . . . "Look, look!" recites the crowd. "A horse with an arrow in its forehead! It must have been mistaken for a deer."

ROS *(eagerly):* I knew all along it was a band.

GUIL *(tiredly):* He knew all along it was a band.

ROS: Here they come!

GUIL *(at the last moment before they enter—wistfully):* I'm sorry it wasn't a unicorn. It would have been nice to have unicorns.

The TRAGEDIANS *are six in number, including a small* BOY (ALFRED). *Two pull and push a cart piled with props and belongings. There is also a* DRUMMER, *a* HORN-PLAYER *and a* FLAUTIST. *The* SPOKESMAN *("the* PLAYER*") has no instrument. He brings up the rear and is the first to notice them.*

PLAYER: Halt!

The group turns and halts.

(Joyously.) An audience!

ROS *and* GUIL *half rise.*

Don't move!

They sink back. He regards them fondly.

Perfect! A lucky thing we came along.

ROS: For us?

PLAYER: Let us hope so. But to meet two gentlemen on the road—we would not hope to meet them off it.

ROS: No?

PLAYER: Well met, in fact, and just in time.

ROS: Why's that?

PLAYER: Why, we grow rusty and you catch us at the very point of decadence—by this time tomorrow we might have forgotten everything we ever knew. That's a thought, isn't it? *(He laughs generously.)* We'd be back where we started—*improvising.*

ROS: Tumblers, are you?

PLAYER: We can give you a tumble if that's your taste, and times being what they are. . . . Otherwise, for a jingle of coin we can do you a selection of gory romances, full of fine cadence and corpses, pirated from the Italian; and it doesn't take much to make a jingle—even a single coin has music in it.

They all flourish and bow, raggedly.

Tragedians, at your command.

ROS *and* GUIL *have got to their feet.*

ROS: My name is Guildenstern, and this is Rosencrantz.

GUIL *confers briefly with him.*

(Without embarrassment.)

I'm sorry—*his* name's Guildenstern, and *I'm* Rosencrantz.

PLAYER: A pleasure. We've played to bigger, of course, but quality counts for something. I recognized you at once—

ROS: And who are we?

PLAYER: —as fellow artists.

ROS: I thought we were gentlemen.

PLAYER: For some of us it is performance, for others, patronage. They are two sides of the same coin, or, let us say, being as there are so many of us, the same side of two coins. *(Bows again.)* Don't clap too loudly—it's a very old world.

ROS: What is your line?

PLAYER: Tragedy, sir. Deaths and disclosures, universal and particular, denouements both unexpected and inexorable, transvestite melodrama on all levels including the suggestive. We transport you into a world of intrigue and illusion . . . clowns, if you like, murderers—we can do you ghosts and battles, on the skirmish level, heroes, villains, tormented lovers—set pieces in the poetic vein; we can do you rapiers or rape or both, by all means, faithless wives and ravished virgins—*flagrante delicto* at a price, but that comes under realism for which there are special terms. Getting warm, am I?

ROS *(doubtfully):* Well, I don't know. . . .

PLAYER: It costs little to watch, and little more if you happen to get caught up in the action, if that's your taste and times being what they are.

ROS: What are they?

PLAYER: Indifferent.

ROS: Bad?

PLAYER: Wicked. Now what precisely is your pleasure? *(He turns to the* TRAGEDIANS.*)* Gentlemen, disport yourselves.

The TRAGEDIANS *shuffle into some kind of line.*

There! See anything you like?

ROS *(doubtful, innocent):* What do they do?

PLAYER: Let your imagination run riot. They are beyond surprise.

ROS: And how much?

PLAYER: To take part?

ROS: To watch.

PLAYER: Watch what?

ROS: A private performance.

PLAYER: How private?

ROS: Well, there are only two of us. Is that enough?

PLAYER: For an audience, disappointing. For voyeurs, about average.

ROS: What's the difference?

PLAYER: Ten guilders.

ROS *(horrified):* Ten *guilders!*

PLAYER: I mean eight.

ROS: Together?

PLAYER: Each. I don't think you understand—

ROS: What are you *saying?*

PLAYER: What am I saying—seven.

ROS: Where have you *been?*

PLAYER: Roundabout. A nest of children carries the custom of the town. Juvenile companies, they are the fashion. But they cannot match our repertoire . . . we'll stoop to anything if that's your bent. . . .

He regards ROS *meaningfully but* ROS *returns the stare blankly.*

ROS: They'll grow up.

PLAYER *(giving up):* There's one born every minute. *(To* TRAGEDIANS:*)* On-ward!

The TRAGEDIANS *start to resume their burdens and their journey.* GUIL *stirs himself at last.*

GUIL: Where are you going?

PLAYER: Ha-alt!

They halt and turn.

Home, sir.

GUIL: Where from?

PLAYER: Home. We're travelling people. We take our chances where we find them.

GUIL: It was chance, then?

PLAYER: Chance?

GUIL: You found us.

PLAYER: Oh yes.

GUIL: You were looking?

PLAYER: Oh no.

GUIL: Chance, then.

PLAYER: Or fate.

GUIL: Yours or ours?

PLAYER: It could hardly be one without the other.

GUIL: Fate, then.

PLAYER: Oh yes. We have no control. Tonight we play to the court. Or the night after. Or to the tavern. Or not.

GUIL: Perhaps I can use my influence.

PLAYER: At the tavern?

GUIL: At the court. I would say I have some influence.

PLAYER: Would you say so?

GUIL: I have influence yet.

PLAYER: Yet what?

GUIL *seizes the* PLAYER *violently.*

GUIL: I have influence!

The PLAYER *does not resist.* GUIL *loosens his hold.*

(More calmly.)

You said something—about getting caught up in the action—

PLAYER *(gaily freeing himself):* I did!—I did!—You're quicker than your friend. . . . *(Confidingly.)* Now for a handful of guilders I happen to have a private and uncut performance of *The Rape of the Sabine Women*—or rather woman, or rather Alfred— *(Over his shoulder.)* Get your skirt on, Alfred—

The BOY *starts struggling into a female robe.*

. . . and for eight you can participate.

GUIL *backs,* PLAYER *follows.*

. . . taking either part.

GUIL *backs.*

. . . or both for ten.

GUIL *tries to turn away,* PLAYER *holds his sleeve.*

. . . with encores—

GUIL *smashes the* PLAYER *across the face. The* PLAYER *recoils.* GUIL *stands trembling.*

(Resigned and quiet).

Get your skirt off, Alfred. . . .

ALFRED *struggles out of his half-on robe.*

GUIL *(shaking with rage and fright):* It could have been—it didn't have to be *obscene*. . . . It could have been—a bird out of season, dropping bright-feathered on my shoulder. . . . It could have been a tongueless dwarf standing by the road to point the way. . . . I was *prepared*. But it's this, is it? No enigma, no dignity, nothing classical, portentous, only this—a comic pornographer and a rabble of prostitutes. . . .

PLAYER *(acknowledging the description with a sweep of his hat, bowing; sadly):* You should have caught us in better times. We were purists then. *(Straightens up.)* On-ward.

The PLAYERS *make to leave.*

ROS *(his voice has changed: he has caught on):* Excuse me!

PLAYER: Ha-alt!

They halt.

A-al-l-fred!

ALFRED *resumes the struggle. The* PLAYER *comes forward.*

ROS: You're not—ah—exclusively players, then?
PLAYER: We're inclusively players, sir.
ROS: So you give—exhibitions?
PLAYER: Performances, sir.
ROS: Yes, of course. There's more money in that, is there?
PLAYER: There's more trade, sir.
ROS: Times being what they are.
PLAYER: Yes.
ROS: Indifferent.
PLAYER: Completely.
ROS: You know I'd no idea—
PLAYER: No—
ROS: I mean, I've *heard* of—but I've never actually—
PLAYER: No.
ROS: I mean, what exactly do you *do?*
PLAYER: We keep to our usual stuff, more or less, only inside out. We do on stage the things that are supposed to happen off. Which is a kind of integrity, if you look on every exit being an entrance somewhere else.
ROS *(nervy, loud):* Well, I'm not really the type of man who—no, but don't hurry off—sit down and tell us about some of the things people ask you to do—

The PLAYER *turns away.*

PLAYER: On-ward!
ROS: Just a minute!

They turn and look at him without expression.

Well, all right—I wouldn't mind seeing—just an idea of the kind of— *(Bravely.)* What will you do for that? *(And tosses a single coin on the ground between them.)*

The PLAYER *spits at the coin, from where he stands.*

The TRAGEDIANS *demur, trying to get at the coin. He kicks and cuffs them back.*

On!

ALFRED *is still half in and out of his robe. The* PLAYER *cuffs him.*

(To ALFRED:*)*

What are you playing at?

ROS is shamed in fury.

ROS: Filth! Disgusting—I'l report you to the authorities—*perverts!* I know your game all righ, it's all filth!

The ERS are a to leave. GUIL has remained detached.

ou ke a bet?

ally): D

GU turn and look interested. The PLAYER comes forward.*

AC

hat kind of bet did you have in mind?

walks half the distance towards the PLAYER, stops with his foot over the coin.

Double or quits.

PLAYER: Well . . . heads.

GUIL raises his foot. The PLAYER bends. The TRAGEDIANS crowd round. Relief and congratulations. The PLAYER picks up the coin. GUIL throws him a second coin.

GUIL: Again?

Some of the TRAGEDIANS are for it, others against.

GUIL: Evens.

The PLAYER nods and tosses the coin.

GUIL: Heads.

It is. He picks it up.

Again.

GUIL spins coin.

PLAYER: Heads.

It is. PLAYER picks up coin. He has two coins again. He spins one.

GUIL: Heads.

It is. GUIL picks it up. Then tosses it immediately.

PLAYER *(fractional hesitation):* Tails.

But it's heads. GUIL picks it up. PLAYER tosses down his last coin by way of paying up, and turns away. GUIL doesn't pick it up; he puts his foot on it.

GUIL: Heads.
PLAYER: No!

Pause. The TRAGEDIANS *are against this.*

(Apologetically.)

They don't like the odds.
GUIL *(lifts his foot, squats; picks up the coin still squatting; looks up):* You wer… t—h… *(Spins it, slaps his hand on it, on the floor.)* Heads I win.
PLAYER: No.
GUIL *(uncovers coin):* Right again. *(Repeat.)* Heads I win.
PLAYER: No.
GUIL *(uncovers coin):* And right again. *(Repeat.)* Heads I win.
PLAYER: *No!*

He turns away, the TRAGEDIANS *with him.* GUIL *stands up, comes close.*

GUIL: Would you believe it? *(Stands back, relaxes, smiles.)* Bet me the year of my birth doubled is an odd number.
PLAYER: *Your* birth—!
GUIL: If you don't trust me don't bet with me.
PLAYER: Would you trust *me?*
GUIL: *Bet* me then.
PLAYER: My birth?
GUIL: Odd numbers you win.
PLAYER: You're on—

The TRAGEDIANS *have come forward, wide awake.*

GUIL: Good. Year of your birth. Double it. Even numbers I win, odd numbers I lose.

Silence. An awful sigh as the TRAGEDIANS *realize that any number doubled is even. Then a terrible row as they object. Then a terrible silence.*

PLAYER: We have no money.

GUIL *turns to him.*

GUIL: Ah. Then what *have* you got?

The PLAYER *silently brings* ALFRED *forward.* GUIL *regards* ALFRED *sadly.*

Was it for this?
PLAYER: It's the best we've got.
GUIL *(looking up and around):* Then the times are bad indeed.

The PLAYER *starts to speak, protestation, but* GUIL *turns on him viciously.*

The very *air* stinks.

The PLAYER *moves back.* GUIL *moves down to the footlights and turns.*

Come here, Alfred.

ALFRED *moves down and stands, frightened and small.*

(Gently.)

Do you lose often?
ALFRED: Yes, sir.
GUIL: Then what could you have left to lose?
ALFRED: Nothing, sir.

Pause. GUIL *regards him.*

GUIL: Do you like being . . . an actor?
ALFRED: No, sir.

GUIL *looks around, at the audience.*

GUIL: You and I, Alfred—we could create a dramatic precedent here.

And ALFRED, *who has been near tears, starts to sniffle.*

Come, come, Alfred, this is no way to fill the theatres of Europe.

The PLAYER *has moved down, to remonstrate with* ALFRED. GUIL *cuts him off again.*

(Viciously.)

Do you know any good plays?
PLAYER: Plays?
ROS *(coming forward, faltering shyly):* Exhibitions. . . .
GUIL: I thought you said you were actors.
PLAYER *(dawning):* Oh. Oh well, we *are.* We are. But there hasn't been much call—
GUIL: You lost. Well then—one of the Greeks, perhaps? You're familiar with the tragedies of antiquity, are you? The great homicidal classics? Matri, patri, fratri, sorrori, uxori and it goes without saying—
ROS: Saucy—
GUIL: —Suicidal—hm? Maidens aspiring to godheads—
ROS: And vice versa—
GUIL: Your kind of thing, is it?
PLAYER: Well, no, I can't say it is, really. We're more of the blood, love and rhetoric school.
GUIL: Well, I'll leave the choice to you, if there is anything to choose between them.
PLAYER: They're hardly divisible, sir—well, I can do you blood and love without the

rhetoric, and I can do you blood and rhetoric without the love, and I can do you all three concurrent or consecutive, but I can't do you love and rhetoric without the blood. Blood is compulsory—they're all blood, you see.

GUIL: Is that what people want?

PLAYER: It's what we do. *(Small pause. He turns away.)*

GUIL touches ALFRED on the shoulder.

GUIL *(wry, gentle):* Thank you; we'll let you know.

The PLAYER has moved upstage. ALFRED follows.

PLAYER *(to TRAGEDIANS):* Thirty-eight!

ROS *(moving across, fascinated and hopeful): Position?*

PLAYER: Sir?

ROS: One of your—tableaux?

PLAYER: No, sir.

ROS: Oh.

PLAYER *(to the TRAGEDIANS, now departing with their cart, already taking various props off it):* Entrances there and there *(indicating upstage).*

The PLAYER has not moved his position for his last four lines. He does not move now. GUIL waits.

GUIL: Well . . . aren't you going to change into your costume?

PLAYER: I never change out of it, sir.

GUIL: Always in character.

PLAYER: That's it.

Pause.

GUIL: Aren't you going to—come *on?*

PLAYER: I *am* on.

GUIL: But if you *are* on, you can't *come* on. *Can* you?

PLAYER: I *start* on.

GUIL: But it hasn't *started.* Go on. We'll look out for you.

PLAYER: I'll give you a wave.

He does not move. His immobility is now pointed, and getting awkward. Pause. ROS walks up to him till they are face to face.

ROS: Excuse me.

Pause. The PLAYER lifts his downstage foot. It was covering GUIL's coin. ROS puts his foot on the coin. Smiles.

Thank you.

The PLAYER turns and goes. ROS has bent for the coin.

GUIL *(moving out):* Come on.
ROS: I say—that was lucky.
GUIL *(turning):* What?
ROS: It was tails.

He tosses the coin to GUIL *who catches it. Simultaneously—a lighting change sufficient to alter the exterior mood into interior, but nothing violent.*

And OPHELIA *runs on in some alarm, holding up her skirts—followed by* HAMLET.

OPHELIA *has been sewing and she holds the garment. They are both mute.* HAMLET, *with his doublet all unbraced, no hat upon his head, his stockings fouled, ungartered and downgyved to his ankle, pale as his shirt, his knees knocking each other . . . and with a look so piteous, he takes her by the wrist and holds her hard, then he goes to the length of his arm, and with his other hand over his brow, falls to such perusal of her face as he would draw it. . . . At last, with a little shaking of his arm, and thrice his head waving up and down, he raises a sigh so piteous and profound that it does seem to shatter all his bulk and end his being. That done he lets her go, and with his head over his shoulder turned, he goes out backwards without taking his eyes off her . . . she runs off in the opposite direction.*

ROS *and* GUIL *have frozen.* GUIL *unfreezes first. He jumps at* ROS.

GUIL: Come on!

But a flourish—enter CLAUDIUS *and* GERTRUDE, *attended.*

CLAUDIUS: Welcome, dear Rosencrantz . . . *(he raises a hand at* GUIL *while* ROS *bows—*GUIL *bows late and hurriedly)* . . . and Guildenstern.

He raises a hand at ROS *while* GUIL *bows to him—*ROS *is still straightening up from his previous bow and halfway up he bows down again. With his head down, he twists to look at* GUIL, *who is on the way up.*

Moreover that we did much long to see you,
The need we have to use you did provoke
Our hasty sending.

ROS *and* GUIL *still adjusting their clothing for* CLAUDIUS*'s presence.*

Something have you heard
Of Hamlet's transformation, so call it,
Sith nor th'exterior nor the inward man
Resembles that it was. What it should be,
More than his father's death, that thus hath put him,
So much from th'understanding of himself,
I cannot dream of. I entreat you both
That, being of so young days brought up with him
And sith so neighboured to his youth and haviour

That you vouchsafe your rest here in our court
Some little time, so by your companies
To draw him on to pleasures, and to gather
So much as from occasion you may glean,
Whether aught to us unknown afflicts him thus,
That opened lies within our remedy.

GERTRUDE: Good *(fractional suspense)* gentlemen . . .

They both bow.

He hath much talked of you,
And sure I am, two men there is not living
To whom he more adheres. If it will please you
To show us so much gentry and goodwill
As to expand your time with us awhile
For the supply and profit of our hope,
Your visitation shall receive such thanks
As fits a king's remembrance.

ROS: Both your majesties
Might, by the sovereign power you have of us,
Put your dread pleasures more into command
Than to entreaty.

GUIL: But we both obey,
And here give up ourselves in the full bent
To lay our service freely at your feet,
To be commanded.

CLAUDIUS: Thanks, Rosencrantz *(turning to* ROS *who is caught unprepared, while* GUIL *bows)* and gentle Guildenstern *(turning to* GUIL *who is bent double).*

GERTRUDE *(correcting):* Thanks, Guildenstern *(turning to* ROS*, who bows as* GUIL *checks upward movement to bow too—both bent double, squinting at each other)* . . . and gentle Rosencrantz *(turning to* GUIL*, both straightening up—*GUIL *checks again and bows again).*

And I beseech you instantly to visit
My too much changed son. Go, some of you,
And bring these gentlemen where Hamlet is.

Two ATTENDANTS *exit backwards, indicating that* ROS *and* GUIL *should follow.*

GUIL: Heaven make our presence and our practices
Pleasant and helpful to him.

GERTRUDE: Ay, amen!

ROS *and* GUIL *move towards a downstage wing. Before they get there,* POLONIUS *enters. They stop and bow to him. He nods and hurries upstage to* CLAUDIUS*. They turn to look at him.*

POLONIUS: The ambassadors from Norway, my good lord, are joyfully returned.

CLAUDIUS: Thou still hast been the father of good news.

POLONIUS: Have I, my lord? Assure you, my good liege,
I hold my duty as I hold my soul,
Both to my God and to my gracious King;
And I do think, or else this brain of mine
Hunts not the trail of policy so sure
As it hath used to do, that I have found
The very cause of Hamlet's lunacy. . . .

Exeunt—leaving ROS *and* GUIL.

ROS: I want to go home.

GUIL: Don't let them confuse you.

ROS: I'm out of my step here—

GUIL: We'll soon be home and high—dry and home—I'll—

ROS: It's all over my *depth*—

GUIL: —I'll hie you home and—

ROS: —out of my head—

GUIL: —dry you high and—

ROS *(cracking, high):* —over my step over my head body!—I tell you it's all stopping to a death, it's boding to a depth, stepping to a head, it's all heading to a dead stop—

GUIL *(the nursemaid):* There! . . . and we'll soon be home and dry . . . and *high* and dry. . . . *(Rapidly.)* Has it ever happened to you that all of a sudden and for no reason at all you haven't the faintest idea how to spell the word—"wife"—or "house"—because when you write it down you just can't remember ever having seen those letters in that order before . . . ?

ROS: I remember—

GUIL: Yes?

ROS: I remember when there were no questions.

GUIL: There were always questions. To exchange one set for another is no great matter.

ROS: Answers, yes. There were answers to everything.

GUIL: You've forgotten.

ROS *(flaring):* I haven't forgotten—how I used to remember my own name—and yours, oh *yes!* There were answers everywhere you *looked.* There was no question about it—people knew who I was and if they didn't they asked and I told them.

GUIL: You did, the trouble is, each of them is . . . plausible, without being instinctive. All your life you live so close to truth, it becomes a permanent blur in the corner of your eye, and when something nudges it into outline it is like being ambushed by a grotesque. A man standing in his saddle in the half-lit half-alive dawn banged on the shutters and called two names. He was just a hat and a cloak levitating in the grey plume of his own breath, but when he called we came. That much is certain—we came.

ROS: Well I can tell you I'm sick to death of it. I don't care one way or another, so why don't you make up your mind.

GUIL: We can't afford anything quite so arbitrary. Nor did we come all this way for a christening. All *that*—preceded us. But we are comparatively fortunate; we might have been left to sift the whole field of human nomenclature, like two blind men looting a bazaar for their own portraits. . . . At least we are presented with alternatives.

ROS: Well as from now—

GUIL: But not choice.

ROS: You made me look ridiculous in there.

GUIL: I looked just as ridiculous as you did.

ROS *(an anguished cry)*: Consistency is all I ask!

GUIL *(low, wry rhetoric)*: Give us this day our daily mask.

ROS *(a dying fall)*: I want to go home. *(Moves.)* Which way did we come in? I've lost my sense of direction.

GUIL: The only beginning is birth and the only end is death—if you can't count on that, what can you count on?

They connect again.

ROS: We don't owe anything to anyone.

GUIL: We've been caught up. Your smallest action sets off another somewhere else, and is set off by it. Keep an eye open, an ear cocked. Tread warily, follow instructions. We'll be all right.

ROS: For how long?

GUIL: Till events have played themselves out. There's a logic at work—it's all done for you, don't worry. Enjoy it. Relax. To be taken in hand and led, like being a child again, even without the innocence, a child—it's like being given a prize, an extra slice of childhood when you least expect it, as a prize for being good, or compensation for never having had one. . . . Do I contradict myself?

ROS: I can't remember. . . . What have we got to go on?

GUIL: We have been briefed. Hamlet's transformation. What do you recollect?

ROS: Well, he's changed, hasn't he? The exterior and inward man fails to resemble—

GUIL: Draw him on to pleasures—glean what afflicts him.

ROS: Something more than his father's death—

GUIL: He's always talking about us—there aren't two people living whom he dotes on more than us.

ROS: We cheer him up—find out what's the matter—

GUIL: Exactly, it's a matter of asking the right questions and giving away as little as we can. It's a game.

ROS: And then we can go?

GUIL: And receive such thanks as fits a king's remembrance.

ROS: I like the sound of that. What do you think he means by remembrance?

GUIL: He doesn't forget his friends.

ROS: Would you care to estimate?

GUIL: Difficult to say, really—some kings tend to be amnesiac, others I suppose—the opposite, whatever that is. . . .

ROS: Yes—but—

GUIL: Elephantine . . . ?

ROS: Not how long—how much?

GUIL: *Retentive*—he's a very retentive king, a royal retainer. . . .

ROS: What are you playing at?

GUIL: Words, words. They're all we have to go on.

Pause.

ROS: Shouldn't we be doing something—constructive?

GUIL: What did you have in mind? . . . A short, blunt human pyramid . . . ?

ROS: We could go.

GUIL: Where?

ROS: After him.

GUIL: Why? They've got us placed now—if we start moving around, we'll all be chasing each other all night.

Hiatus.

ROS *(at footlights):* How very intriguing! *(Turns.)* I feel like a spectator—an appalling business. The only thing that makes it bearable is the irrational belief that somebody interesting will come on in a minute. . . .

GUIL: See anyone?

ROS: No. You?

GUIL: No. *(At footlights.)* What a fine persecution—to be kept intrigued without ever quite being enlightened. . . . *(Pause.)* We've had no practice.

ROS: We could play at questions.

GUIL: What good would that do?

ROS: Practice!

GUIL: Statement! One—love.

ROS: Cheating!

GUIL: How?

ROS: I hadn't started yet.

GUIL: Statement. Two—love.

ROS: Are you counting that?

GUIL: What?

ROS: Are you counting that?

GUIL: Foul! No repetitions. Three—love. First game to . . .

ROS: I'm not going to play if you're going to be like that.

GUIL: Whose serve?

ROS: Hah?

GUIL: Foul! No grunts. Love—one.

ROS: Whose go?

GUIL: Why?

ROS: Why not?

GUIL: What for?

ROS: Foul! No synonyms! One—all.

GUIL: What in God's name is going on?

ROS: Foul! No rhetoric. Two—one.

GUIL: What does it all add up to?

ROS: Can't you guess?

GUIL: Were you addressing me?

ROS: Is there anyone else?

GUIL: Who?

ROS: How would I know?

GUIL: Why do you ask?

ROS: Are you serious?
GUIL: Was that rhetoric?
ROS: No.
GUIL: Statement! Two—all. Game point.
ROS: What's the matter with you today?
GUIL: When?
ROS: What?
GUIL: Are you deaf?
ROS: Am I dead?
GUIL: Yes or no?
ROS: Is there a choice?
GUIL: Is there a God?
ROS: Foul! No *non sequiturs,* three—two, one game all.
GUIL *(seriously):* What's your name?
ROS: What's yours?
GUIL: I asked you first.
ROS: Statement. One—love.
GUIL: What's your name when you're at home?
ROS: What's yours?
GUIL: When I'm at home?
ROS: Is it different at home?
GUIL: What home?
ROS: Haven't you got one?
GUIL: Why do you ask?
ROS: What are you driving at?
GUIL *(with emphasis):* What's your name?!
ROS: Repetition. Two—love. Match point to me.
GUIL *(seizing him violently):* WHO DO YOU THINK YOU ARE?
ROS: Rhetoric! Game and match! *(Pause.)* Where's it going to end?
GUIL: That's the question.
ROS: It's *all* questions.
GUIL: Do you think it matters?
ROS: Doesn't it matter to you?
GUIL: Why should it matter?
ROS: What does it matter why?
GUIL *(teasing gently):* Doesn't it *matter* why it matters?
ROS *(rounding on him):* What's the *matter* with you?

Pause.

GUIL: It doesn't matter.
ROS *(voice in the wilderness):* . . . What's the game?
GUIL: What are the rules?

Enter HAMLET *behind, crossing the stage, reading a book—as he is about to disappear* GUIL *notices him.*

GUIL *(sharply):* Rosencrantz!
ROS *(jumps):* What!

HAMLET *goes. Triumph dawns on them, they smile.*

GUIL: There! How was that?
ROS: Clever!
GUIL: Natural?
ROS: Instinctive.
GUIL: Got it in your head?
ROS: I take my hat off to you.
GUIL: Shake hands.

They do.

ROS: Now I'll try you—Guil—!
GUIL: —Not yet—catch me unawares.
ROS: Right.

They separate. Pause. Aside to GUIL.

Ready?
GUIL *(explodes):* Don't be stupid.
ROS: Sorry.

Pause.

GUIL *(snaps):* Guildenstern!
ROS *(jumps):* What?

He is immediately crestfallen, GUIL *is disgusted.*

GUIL: Consistency is all I ask!
ROS *(quietly):* Immortality is all I seek. . . .
GUIL *(dying fall):* Give us this day our daily week. . . .

Beat.

ROS: Who was that?
GUIL: Didn't you know him?
ROS: He didn't know me.
GUIL: He didn't see you.
ROS: I didn't see him.
GUIL: We shall see. I *hardly* knew him, he's changed.
ROS: You could see that?
GUIL: Transformed.

ROS: How do you know?
GUIL: Inside and out.
ROS: I see.
GUIL: He's not himself.
ROS: He's changed.
GUIL: I could see that.

Beat.

Glean what afflicts him.
ROS: Me?
GUIL: Him.
ROS: How?
GUIL: Question and answer. Old ways are the best ways.
ROS: He's afflicted.
GUIL: You question, I'll answer.
ROS: He's not himself, you know.
GUIL: I'm him, you see.

Beat.

ROS: Who am I then?
GUIL: You're yourself.
ROS: And he's you?
GUIL: Not a bit of it.
ROS: Are you afflicted?
GUIL: That's the idea. Are you ready?
ROS: Let's go back a bit.
GUIL: I'm afflicted.
ROS: I see.
GUIL: Glean what afflicts me.
ROS: Right.
GUIL: Question and answer.
ROS: How should I begin?
GUIL: Address me.
ROS: My dear Guildenstern!
GUIL *(quietly):* You've forgotten—haven't you?
ROS: My dear Rosencrantz!
GUIL *(great control):* I don't think you quite understand. What we are attempting is a hypothesis in which *I* answer for *him,* while *you* ask me questions.
ROS: Ah! Ready?
GUIL: You know what to do?
ROS: What?
GUIL: Are you stupid?
ROS: Pardon?
GUIL: Are you deaf?
ROS: Did you speak?

GUIL *(admonishing):* Not now—

ROS: Statement.

GUIL *(shouts):* Not now! *(Pause.)* If I had any doubts, or rather hopes, they are dispelled. What could we possibly have in common except our situation? *(They separate and sit.)* Perhaps he'll come back this way.

ROS: Should we go?

GUIL: Why?

Pause.

ROS *(starts up. Snaps fingers):* Oh! You mean—you pretend to be *him,* and *I* ask you questions!

GUIL *(dry):* Very good.

ROS: You had me confused.

GUIL: I could see I had.

ROS: How should I begin?

GUIL: Address me.

They stand and face each other, posing.

ROS: My honoured Lord!

GUIL: My dear Rosencrantz!

Pause.

ROS: Am I pretending to be you, then?

GUIL: Certainly not. If you like. Shall we continue?

ROS: Question and answer.

GUIL: Right.

ROS: Right. My honoured lord!

GUIL: My dear fellow!

ROS: How are you?

GUIL: Afflicted!

ROS: Really? In what way?

GUIL: Transformed.

ROS: Inside or out?

GUIL: Both.

ROS: I see. *(Pause.)* Not much new there.

GUIL: Go into details. *Delve.* Probe the background, establish the situation.

ROS: So—so your uncle is the king of Denmark?!

GUIL: And my father before him.

ROS: His father before him?

GUIL: No, my father before him.

ROS: But surely—

GUIL: You might well ask.

ROS: Let me get it straight. Your father was king. You were his only son. Your father dies. You are of age. Your uncle becomes king.

GUIL: Yes.

ROS: Unorthodox.
GUIL: Undid me.
ROS: Undeniable. Where were you?
GUIL: In Germany.
ROS: Usurpation, then.
GUIL: He slipped in.
ROS: Which reminds me.
GUIL: Well, it would.
ROS: I don't want to be personal.
GUIL: It's common knowledge.
ROS: Your mother's marriage.
GUIL: He slipped in.

Beat.

ROS *(lugubriously)*: His body was still warm.
GUIL: So was hers.
ROS: Extraordinary.
GUIL: Indecent.
ROS: Hasty.
GUIL: Suspicious.
ROS: It makes you think.
GUIL: Don't think I haven't thought of it.
ROS: And with her husband's brother.
GUIL: They were close.
ROS: She went to him—
GUIL: —Too close—
ROS: —for comfort.
GUIL: It looks bad.
ROS: It adds up.
GUIL: Incest to adultery.
ROS: Would you go so far?
GUIL: Never.
ROS: To sum up: your father, whom you love, dies, you are his heir, you come back to find that hardly was the corpse cold before his young brother popped onto his throne and into his sheets, thereby offending both legal and natural practice. Now why exactly are you behaving in this extraordinary manner?
GUIL: I can't imagine! *(Pause.)* But all that is well known, common property. Yet he sent for us. And we did come.
ROS *(alert, ear cocked)*: I say! I heard music—
GUIL: We're here.
ROS: —Like a band—I thought I heard a band.
GUIL: Rosencrantz . . .
ROS *(absently, still listening)*: What?

Pause, short.

GUIL *(gently wry):* Guildenstern . . .
ROS *(irritated by the repetition): What?*
GUIL: Don't you discriminate at all?
ROS *(turning dumbly):* Wha'?

Pause.

GUIL: Go and see if he's there.
ROS: Who?
GUIL: There.

ROS *goes to an upstage wing, looks, returns, formally making his report.*

ROS: Yes.
GUIL: What is he doing?

ROS *repeats movement.*

ROS: Talking.
GUIL: To himself?

ROS *starts to move.* GUIL *cuts in impatiently.*

Is he alone?
ROS: No.
GUIL: Then he's not talking to himself, is he?
ROS: Not *by* himself. . . . Coming this way, I think. *(Shiftily.)* Should we go?
GUIL: Why? We're marked now.

HAMLET *enters, backwards, talking, followed by* POLONIUS, *upstage.* ROS *and* GUIL *occupy the two downstage corners looking upstage.*

HAMLET: . . . for you yourself, sir, should be as old as I am if like a crab you could go backward.
POLONIUS *(aside):* Though this be madness, yet there is method in it. Will you walk out of the air, my lord?
HAMLET: Into my grave.
POLONIUS: Indeed, that's out of the air.

HAMLET *crosses to upstage exit,* POLONIUS *asiding unintelligibly until—*

My lord, I will take my leave of you.
HAMLET: You cannot take from me anything that I will more willingly part withal—except my life, except my life, except my life. . .
POLONIUS *(crossing downstage):* Fare you well, my lord. *(To* ROS:*)* You go to seek Lord Hamlet? There he is.
ROS *(to* POLONIUS*):* God save you, sir.

POLONIUS *goes.*

GUIL *(calls upstage to* HAMLET*)*: My honoured lord!
ROS: My most dear lord!

HAMLET *centred upstage, turns to them.*

HAMLET: My excellent good friends! How dost thou Guildenstern? *(Coming downstage with an arm raised to* ROS, GUIL *meanwhile bowing to no greeting.* HAMLET *corrects himself. Still to* ROS:*)* Ah Rosencrantz!

They laugh good-naturedly at the mistake. They all meet midstage, turn upstage to walk, HAMLET *in the middle, arm over each shoulder.*

HAMLET: Good lads how do you both?

BLACKOUT.

ACT TWO

HAMLET, ROS *and* GUIL *talking, the continuation of the previous scene. Their conversation, on the move, is indecipherable at first. The first intelligible line is* HAMLET'S, *coming at the end of a short speech—see Shakespeare Act II, scene ii.*

HAMLET: S'blood, there is something in this more than natural, if philosophy could find it out.

A flourish from the TRAGEDIANS' *band.*

GUIL: There are the players.
HAMLET: Gentlemen, you are welcome to Elsinore. Your hands, come then. *(He takes their hands.)* The appurtenance of welcome is fashion and ceremony. Let me comply with you in this garb, lest my extent to the players (which I tell you must show fairly outwards) should more appear like entertainment than yours. You are welcome. *(About to leave.)* But my uncle-father and aunt-mother are deceived.
GUIL: In what, my dear lord?
HAMLET: I am but mad north north-west; when the wind is southerly I know a hawk from a handsaw.

POLONIUS *enters as* GUIL *turns away.*

POLONIUS: Well be with you, gentlemen.
HAMLET *(to* ROS*)*: Mark you, Guildenstern *(uncertainly to* GUIL*)* and you too; at each ear a hearer. That great baby you see there is not yet out of his swaddling clouts. . . . *(He takes* ROS *upstage with him, talking together.)*
POLONIUS: My Lord! I have news to tell you.
HAMLET *(releasing* ROS *and mimicking)*: My lord, I have news to tell you. . . . When Roscius was an actor in Rome . . .

ROS *comes downstage to rejoin* GUIL.

POLONIUS *(as he follows* HAMLET *out):* The actors are come hither, my lord.
HAMLET: Buzz, buzz.

Exeunt HAMLET *and* POLONIUS.

ROS *and* GUIL *ponder. Each reluctant to speak first.*

GUIL: Hm?
ROS: Yes?
GUIL: What?
ROS: I thought you . . .
GUIL: No.
ROS: Ah.

Pause.

GUIL: I think we can say we made some headway.
ROS: You think so?
GUIL: I think we can say that.
ROS: I think we can say he made us look ridiculous.
GUIL: We played it close to the chest of course.
ROS *(derisively):* "Question and answer. Old ways are the best ways"! He was scoring off us all down the line.
GUIL: He caught us on the wrong foot once or twice, perhaps, but I thought we gained some ground.
ROS *(simply):* He murdered us.
GUIL: He might have had the edge.
ROS *(roused):* Twenty-seven—three, and you think he might have had the edge?! He *murdered* us.
GUIL: What about our evasions?
ROS: Oh, our evasions were lovely. "Were you sent for?" he says. "My lord, we were sent for. . . ." I didn't know where to put myself.
GUIL: He had six rhetoricals—
ROS: It was question and answer, all right. Twenty-seven questions he got out in ten minutes, and answered three. I was waiting for you to *delve.* "When is he going to start *delving?*" I asked myself.
GUIL: —And two repetitions.
ROS: Hardly a leading question between us.
GUIL: We got his *symptoms,* didn't we?
ROS: Half of what he said meant something else, and the other half didn't mean anything at all.
GUIL: Thwarted ambition—a sense of grievance, that's my diagnosis.
ROS: Six rhetorical and two repetition, leaving nineteen, of which we answered fifteen. And what did we get in return? He's depressed! . . . Denmark's a prison and he'd rather live in a nutshell; some shadow-play about the nature of ambition, which never got down

to cases, and finally one direct question which might have led somewhere, and led in fact to his illuminating claim to tell a hawk from a handsaw.

Pause.

GUIL: When the wind is southerly.
ROS: And the weather's clear.
GUIL: And when it isn't he can't.
ROS: He's at the mercy of the elements. *(Licks his finger and holds it up—facing audience.)* Is that southerly?

They stare at audience.

GUIL: It doesn't *look* southerly. What made you think so?
ROS: I didn't *say* I think so. It could be northerly for all I know.
GUIL: I wouldn't have thought so.
ROS: Well, if you're going to be dogmatic.
GUIL: Wait a minute—we came from roughly south according to a rough map.
ROS: I see. Well, which way did we come in? *(GUIL looks round vaguely.)* Roughly.
GUIL *(clears his throat):* In the morning the sun would be easterly. I think we can assume that.
ROS: That it's morning?
GUIL: If it is, and the sun is over *there (his right as he faces the audience)* for instance, *that (front)* would be northerly. On the other hand, if it is not morning and the sun is over *there (his left)* . . . *that* . . . *(lamely)* would *still* be northerly. *(Picking up.)* To put it another way, if we came from down there *(front)* and it is morning, the sun would be up there *(his left),* and if it is actually over *there (his right)* and it's still morning, we must have come from up *there (behind him),* and if *that* is southerly *(his left)* and the sun is really over *there (front),* then it's the afternoon. However, if none of these is the case—
ROS: Why don't you go and have a look?
GUIL: Pragmatism?!—is that all you have to offer? You seem to have no conception of where we stand! You won't find the answer written down for you in the bowl of a compass—I can tell you that. *(Pause.)* Besides, you can never tell this far north—it's probably dark out there.
ROS: I merely suggest that the position of the sun, if it is out, would give you a rough idea of the time; alternatively, the clock, if it is going, would give you a rough idea of the position of the sun. I forget which you're trying to establish.
GUIL: I'm trying to establish the direction of the wind.
ROS: There isn't any wind. *Draught,* yes.
GUIL: In that case, the origin. Trace it to its source and it might give us a rough idea of the way we came in—which might give us a rough idea of south, for further reference.
ROS: It's coming up through the floor. *(He studies the floor.)* That can't be south, can it?
GUIL: That's not a direction. Lick your toe and wave it around a bit.

ROS considers the distance of his foot.

ROS: No, I think you'd have to lick it for me.

Pause.

GUIL: I'm prepared to let the whole matter drop.
ROS: Or I could lick yours, of course.
GUIL: No thank you.
ROS: I'll even wave it around for you.
GUIL *(down* ROS*'s throat):* What in God's name is the matter with you?
ROS: Just being friendly.
GUIL *(retiring):* Somebody might come in. It's what we're counting on, after all. Ultimately.

Good pause.

ROS: Perhaps they've all trampled each other to death in the rush. . . . Give them a shout. Something provocative. *Intrigue* them.
GUIL: Wheels have been set in motion, and they have their own pace, to which we are . . . condemned. Each move is dictated by the previous one—that is the meaning of order. If we start being arbitrary it'll just be a shambles: at least, let us hope so. Because if we happened, just happened to discover, or even suspect, that our spontaneity was part of their order, we'd know that we were lost. *(He sits.)* A Chinaman of the T'ang Dynasty—and, by which definition, a philosopher—dreamed he was a butterfly, and from that moment he was never quite sure that he was not a butterfly dreaming it was a Chinese philosopher. Envy him; in his two-fold security.

A good pause. ROS *leaps up and bellows at the audience.*

ROS: Fire!

GUIL *jumps up.*

GUIL: Where?
ROS: It's all right—I'm demonstrating the misuse of free speech. To prove that it exists. *(He regards the audience, that is the direction, with contempt—and other directions, then front again.)* Not a move. They should burn to death in their shoes. *(He takes out one of his coins. Spins it. Catches it. Looks at it. Replaces it.)*
GUIL: What was it?
ROS: What?
GUIL: Heads or tails?
ROS: Oh. I didn't look.
GUIL: Yes you did.
ROS: Oh, did I? *(He takes out a coin, studies it.)* Quite right—it rings a bell.
GUIL: What's the last thing you remember?
ROS: I don't wish to be reminded of it.
GUIL: We cross our bridges when we come to them and burn them behind us, with nothing to show for our progress except a memory of the smell of smoke, and a presumption that once our eyes watered.

ROS *approaches him brightly, holding a coin between finger and thumb. He covers it with his other hand, draws his fists apart and holds them for* GUIL. GUIL *considers them. Indicates the left hand,* ROS *opens it to show it empty.*

ROS: No.

Repeat process. GUIL *indicates left hand again.* ROS *shows it empty.*

Double bluff!

*Repeat process—*GUIL *taps one hand, then the other hand, quickly.* ROS *inadvertently shows that both are empty.* ROS *laughs as* GUIL *turns upstage.* ROS *stops laughing, looks around his feet, pats his clothes, puzzled.*

POLONIUS *breaks that up by entering upstage followed by the* TRAGEDIANS *and* HAMLET.

POLONIUS *(entering):* Come sirs.
HAMLET: Follow him, friends. We'll hear a play tomorrow. *(Aside to the* PLAYER, *who is the last of the* TRAGEDIANS:*)* Dost thou hear me, old friend? Can you play *The Murder of Gonzago?*
PLAYER: Ay, my lord.
HAMLET: We'll ha't tomorrow night. You could for a need study a speech of some dozen or sixteen lines which I would set down and insert in't, could you not?
PLAYER: Ay, my lord.
HAMLET: Very well. Follow that lord, and look you mock him not.

The PLAYER *crossing downstage, notes* ROS *and* GUIL. *Stops.* HAMLET *crossing downstage addresses them without pause.*

HAMLET: My good friends, I'll leave you till tonight. You are welcome to Elsinore.
ROS: Good, my lord.

HAMLET *goes.*

GUIL: So you've caught up.
PLAYER *(coldly):* Not yet, sir.
GUIL: Now mind your tongue, or we'll have it out and throw the rest of you away, like a nightingale at a Roman feast.
ROS: Took the very words out of my mouth.
GUIL: You'd be *lost* for words.
ROS: You'd be tongue-tied.
GUIL: Like a mute in a monologue.
ROS: Like a nightingale at a Roman feast.
GUIL: Your diction will go to pieces.
ROS: Your lines will be cut.
GUIL: To dumb shows.
ROS: And dramatic pauses.
GUIL: You'll never *find* your tongue.
ROS: Lick your lips.
GUIL: Taste your tears.
ROS: Your breakfast.
GUIL: You won't know the difference.

ROS: There won't be any.

GUIL: We'll take the very words out of your mouth.

ROS: So you've caught on.

GUIL: So you've caught up.

PLAYER *(tops):* Not yet! *(Bitterly.)* You left us.

GUIL: Ah! I'd forgotten—you performed a dramatic spectacle on the way. Yes, I'm sorry we had to miss it.

PLAYER *(bursts out):* We can't look each other in the face! *(Pause, more in control.)* You don't understand the humiliation of it—to be tricked out of the single assumption which makes our existence viable—that somebody is *watching.* . . . The plot was two corpses gone before we caught sight of ourselves, stripped naked in the middle of nowhere and pouring ourselves down a bottomless well.

ROS: Is *that* thirty-eight?

PLAYER *(lost):* There we were—demented children mincing about in clothes that no one ever wore, speaking as no man ever spoke, swearing love in wigs and rhymed couplets, killing each other with wooden swords, hollow protestations of faith hurled after empty promises of vengeance—and every gesture, every pose, vanishing into the thin unpopulated air. We ransomed our dignity to the clouds, and the uncomprehending birds listened. *(He rounds on them.)* Don't you see?! We're *actors*—we're the opposite of people! *(They recoil nonplussed, his voice calms.)* Think, in your head, *now,* think of the most . . . *private* . . . *secret* . . . *intimate* thing you have ever done secure in the knowledge of its privacy. . . . *(He gives them—and the audience—a good pause.* ROS *takes on a shifty look.)* Are you thinking of it? *(He strikes with his voice and his head.)* *Well, I saw you do it!*

ROS *leaps up, dissembling madly.*

ROS: You never! It's a lie! *(He catches himself with a giggle in a vacuum and sits down again.)*

PLAYER: We're actors. . . . We pledged our identities, secure in the conventions of our trade, that someone would be watching. And then, gradually, no one was. We were caught, high and dry. It was not until the murderer's long soliloquy that we were able to look around; frozen as we were in profile, our eyes searched you out, first confidently, then hesitantly, then desperately as each patch of turf, each log, every exposed corner in every direction proved uninhabited, and all the while the murderous King addressed the horizon with his dreary interminable guilt. . . . Our heads began to move, wary as lizards, the corpse of unsullied Rosalinda peeped through his fingers, and the King faltered. Even then, habit and a stubborn trust that our audience spied upon us from behind the nearest bush, forced our bodies to blunder on long after they had emptied of meaning, until like runaway carts they dragged to a halt. No one came forward. No one shouted at us. The silence was unbreakable, it imposed itself upon us; it was obscene. We took off our crowns and swords and cloth of gold and moved silent on the road to Elsinore.

Silence. Then GUIL *claps solo with slow measured irony.*

GUIL: Brilliantly re-created—if these eyes could weep! . . . Rather strong on metaphor, mind you. No criticism—only a matter of taste. And so here you are—with a vengeance.

That's a figure of speech . . . isn't it? Well let's say we've made up for it, for you may have no doubt whom to thank for your performance at the court.

ROS: We are counting on you to take him out of himself. You are the pleasures which we draw him on to— *(he escapes a fractional giggle but recovers immediately)* and by that I don't mean your usual filth; you can't treat royalty like people with normal perverted desires. They know nothing of that and you know nothing of them, to your mutual survival. So give him a good clean show suitable for all the family, or you can rest assured you'll be playing the tavern tonight.

GUIL: Or the night after.

ROS: Or not.

PLAYER: We already have an entry here. And always have had.

GUIL: You've played for him before?

PLAYER: Yes, sir.

ROS: And what's *his* bent?

PLAYER: Classical.

ROS: Saucy!

GUIL: What will you play?

PLAYER: *The Murder of Gonzago.*

GUIL: Full of fine cadence and corpses.

PLAYER: Pirated from the Italian. . . .

ROS: What is it about?

PLAYER: It's about a King and Queen. . . .

GUIL: Escapism! What else?

PLAYER: Blood—

GUIL: —Love and rhetoric.

PLAYER: Yes. *(Going.)*

GUIL: Where are you going?

PLAYER: I can come and go as I please.

GUIL: You're evidently a man who knows his way around.

PLAYER: I've been here before.

GUIL: We're still finding our feet.

PLAYER: I should concentrate on not losing your heads.

GUIL: Do you speak from knowledge?

PLAYER: Precedent.

GUIL: You've been here before.

PLAYER: And I know which way the wind is blowing.

GUIL: Operating on two levels, are we?! How clever! I expect it comes naturally to you, being in the business so to speak.

The PLAYER's grave face does not change. He makes to move off again. GUIL for the second time cuts him off.

The truth is, we value your company, for want of any other. We have been left so much to our own devices—after a while one welcomes the uncertainty of being left to other people's.

PLAYER: Uncertainty is the normal state. You're nobody special.

He makes to leave again. GUIL loses his cool.

GUIL: But for God's sake what are we supposed to *do?!*

PLAYER: Relax. Respond. That's what people do. You can't go through life questioning your situation at every turn.

GUIL: But we don't know what's going on, or what to do with ourselves. We don't know how to *act.*

PLAYER: Act natural. You know why you're here at least.

GUIL: We only know what we're told, and that's little enough. And for all we know it isn't even true.

PLAYER: For all anyone knows, nothing is. Everything has to be taken on trust; truth is only that which is taken to be true. It's the currency of living. There may be nothing behind it, but it doesn't make any difference so long as it is honoured. One acts on assumptions. What do you assume?

ROS: Hamlet is not himself, outside or in. We have to glean what afflicts him.

GUIL: He doesn't give much away.

PLAYER: Who does, nowadays?

GUIL: He's—melancholy.

PLAYER: Melancholy?

ROS: Mad.

PLAYER: How is he mad?

ROS: Ah. *(To* GUIL:*)* How is he mad?

GUIL: More morose than mad, perhaps.

PLAYER: Melancholy.

GUIL: Moody.

ROS: He has moods.

PLAYER: Of moroseness?

GUIL: Madness. And yet.

ROS: Quite.

GUIL: For instance.

ROS: He talks to himself, which might be madness.

GUIL: If he didn't talk sense, which he does.

ROS: Which suggests the opposite.

PLAYER: Of what?

Small pause.

GUIL: I think I have it. A man talking sense to himself is no madder than a man talking nonsense not to himself.

ROS: Or just as mad.

GUIL: Or just as mad.

ROS: And he does both.

GUIL: So there you are.

ROS: Stark raving sane.

Pause.

PLAYER: Why?

GUIL: Ah. *(To* ROS:*)* Why?

ROS: Exactly.

GUIL: Exactly what?
ROS: Exactly why.
GUIL: Exactly why *what?*
ROS: What?
GUIL: *Why?*
ROS: Why what, exactly?
GUIL: Why is he mad?!
ROS: *I* don't know!

Beat.

PLAYER: The old man thinks he's in love with his daughter.
ROS *(appalled):* Good God! We're out of our depth here.
PLAYER: No, no, no—*he* hasn't got a daughter—the old man thinks he's in love with *his* daughter.
ROS: The old man is?
PLAYER: Hamlet, in love with the old man's daughter, the old man thinks.
ROS: Ha! It's beginning to make sense! Unrequited passion!

The PLAYER *moves.*

GUIL *(Fascist)*: Nobody leaves this room! *(Pause, lamely.)* Without a *very* good reason.
PLAYER: Why not?
GUIL: All this strolling about is getting too arbitrary by half—I'm rapidly losing my grip. From now on reason will prevail.
PLAYER: I have lines to learn.
GUIL: Pass!

The PLAYER *passes into one of the wings.* ROS *cups his hands and shouts into the opposite one.*

ROS: Next!

But no one comes.

GUIL: What did you expect?
ROS: Something . . . someone . . . nothing.

They sit facing front.

Are you hungry?
GUIL: No, are you?
ROS *(thinks):* No. You remember that coin?
GUIL: No.
ROS: I think I lost it.
GUIL: What coin?
ROS: I don't remember exactly.

Pause.

GUIL: Oh, that coin . . . clever.

ROS: I can't remember how I did it.

GUIL: It probably comes natural to you.

ROS: Yes, I've got a show-stopper there.

GUIL: Do it again.

Slight pause.

ROS: We can't afford it.

GUIL: Yes, one must think of the future.

ROS: It's the normal thing.

GUIL: To have one. One is, after all, having it all the time . . . now . . . and now . . . and now. . . .

ROS: It could go on for ever. Well, not for *ever,* I suppose. *(Pause.)* Do you ever think of yourself as actually *dead,* lying in a box with a lid on it?

GUIL: No.

ROS: Nor do I, really. . . . It's silly to be depressed by it. I mean one thinks of it like being *alive* in a box, one keeps forgetting to take into account the fact that one is *dead* . . . which should make all the difference . . . shouldn't it? I mean, you'd never *know* you were in a box, would you? It would be just like being *asleep* in a box. Not that I'd like to sleep in a box, mind you, not without any air—you'd wake up dead, for a start, and then where would you be? Apart from inside a box. That's the bit I don't like, frankly. That's why I don't think of it. . . .

GUIL *stirs restlessly, pulling his cloak round him.*

Because you'd be helpless, wouldn't you? Stuffed in a box like that, I mean you'd be in there for ever. Even taking into account the fact that you're dead, it isn't a pleasant thought. *Especially* if you're dead, really . . . *ask* yourself, if I asked you straight off—I'm going to stuff you in this box now, would you rather be alive or dead? Naturally, you'd prefer to be alive. Life in a box is better than no life at all. I expect. You'd have a chance at least. You could lie there thinking—well, at least I'm not dead! In a minute someone's going to bang on the lid and tell me to come out. *(Banging the floor with his fists.)* "Hey you, whatsyername! Come out of there!"

GUIL *(jumps up savagely):* You don't have to flog it to death!

Pause.

ROS: I wouldn't think about it, if I were you. You'd only get depressed. *(Pause.)* Eternity is a terrible thought. I mean, where's it going to end? *(Pause, then brightly.)* Two early Christians chanced to meet in Heaven. "Saul of Tarsus yet!" cried one. "What are *you* doing here?!" . . . "Tarsus-Schmarsus," replied the other, "I'm Paul already." *(He stands up restlessly and flaps his arms.)* They don't care. We count for nothing. We could remain silent till we're green in the face, they wouldn't come.

GUIL: Blue, red.

ROS: A Christian, a Moslem and a Jew chanced to meet in a closed carriage. . . . "Silverstein!" cried the Jew. "Who's your friend?" . . . "His name's Abdullah," replied the Moslem,

"but he's no friend of mine since he became a convert." *(He leaps up again, stamps his foot and shouts into the wings.)* All right, we know you're in there! Come out talking! *(Pause.)* We have no control. None at all . . . *(He paces.)* Whatever became of the moment when one first knew about death? There must have been one, a moment, in childhood when it first occurred to you that you don't go on for ever. It must have been shattering—stamped into one's memory. And yet I can't remember it. It never occurred to me at all. What does one make of that? We must be born with an intuition of mortality. Before we know the words for it, before we know that there are words, out we come, bloodied and squalling with the knowledge that for all the compasses in the world, there's only one direction, and time is its only measure. *(He reflects, getting more desperate and rapid.)* A Hindu, a Buddhist and a lion-tamer chanced to meet, in a circus on the Indo-Chinese border. *(He breaks out.)* They're taking us for granted! Well, I won't stand for it! In future, notice will be taken. *(He wheels again to face into the wings.)* Keep out, then! I forbid anyone to enter! *(No one comes. Breathing heavily.)* That's better. . . .

Immediately, behind him a grand procession enters, principally CLAUDIUS, GERTRUDE, POLONIUS *and* OPHELIA. CLAUDIUS *takes* ROS*'s elbow as he passes and is immediately deep in conversation: the context is Shakespeare Act III, scene i.* GUIL *still faces front as* CLAUDIUS, ROS, *etc., pass upstage and turn.*

GUIL: Death followed by eternity . . . the worst of both worlds. It *is* a terrible thought.

He turns upstage in time to take over the conversation with CLAUDIUS. GERTRUDE *and* ROS *head downstage.*

GERTRUDE: Did he receive you well?
ROS: Most like a gentleman.
GUIL *(returning in time to take it up)*: But with much forcing of his disposition.
ROS *(a flat lie and he knows it and shows it, perhaps catching* GUIL*'s eye)*: Niggard of question, but of our demands most free in his reply.
GERTRUDE: Did you assay him to any pastime?
ROS: Madam, it so fell out that certain players
We o'erraught on the way: of these we told him
And there did seem in him a kind of joy
To hear of it. They are here about the court,
And, as I think, they have already order
This night to play before him.
POLONIUS: 'Tis most true
And he beseeched me to entreat your Majesties
To hear and see the matter.
CLAUDIUS: With all my heart, and it doth content me
To hear him so inclined.
Good gentlemen, give him a further edge
And drive his purpose into these delights.
ROS: We shall, my lord.
CLAUDIUS *(leading out procession)*: Sweet Gertrude, leave us, too,

For we have closely sent for Hamlet hither,
That he, as t'were by accident, may here
Affront Ophelia. . . .

Exeunt CLAUDIUS *and* GERTRUDE.

ROS *(peevish):* Never a moment's peace! In and out, on and off, they're coming at us from all sides.

GUIL: You're never satisfied.

ROS: Catching us on the trot. . . . Why can't *we* go by *them?*

GUIL: What's the difference?

ROS: I'm going.

ROS *pulls his cloak round him.* GUIL *ignores him. Without confidence* ROS *heads upstage. He looks out and comes back quickly.*

He's coming.

GUIL: What's he doing?

ROS: Nothing.

GUIL: He must be doing something.

ROS: Walking.

GUIL: On his hands?

ROS: No, on his feet.

GUIL: Stark naked?

ROS: Fully dressed.

GUIL: Selling toffee apples?

ROS: Not that I noticed.

GUIL: You could be wrong?

ROS: I don't think so.

Pause.

GUIL: I can't for the life of me see how we're going to get into conversation.

HAMLET *enters upstage, and pauses, weighing up the pros and cons of making his quietus.*

ROS *and* GUIL *watch him.*

ROS: Nevertheless, I suppose one might say that this was a chance. . . . One might well . . . accost him. . . . Yes, it definitely looks like a chance to me. . . . Something on the lines of a direct informal approach . . . man to man . . . straight from the shoulder. . . . Now look here, what's it all about . . . sort of thing. Yes. Yes, this looks like one to be grabbed with both hands, I should say . . . if I were asked. . . . No point in looking at a gift horse till you see the whites of its eyes, etcetera. *(He has moved towards* HAMLET *but his nerve fails. He returns.)* We're overawed, that's our trouble. When it comes to the point we succumb to their personality. . . .

OPHELIA *enters, with prayerbook, a religious procession of one.*

HAMLET: Nymph, in thy orisons be all my sins remembered.

At his voice she has stopped for him, he catches her up.

OPHELIA: Good my lord, how does your honour for this many a day?
HAMLET: I humbly thank you—well, well, well.

They disappear talking into the wing.

ROS: It's like living in a public park!
GUIL: Very impressive. Yes, I thought your direct informal approach was going to stop this thing dead in its tracks there. If I might make a suggestion—shut up and sit down. Stop being perverse.
ROS *(near tears):* I'm not going to stand for it!

A FEMALE FIGURE, *ostensibly the* QUEEN, *enters.* ROS *marches up behind her, puts his hands over her eyes and says with a desperate frivolity.*

ROS: Guess who?!
PLAYER *(having appeared in a downstage corner):* Alfred!

ROS *lets go, spins around. He has been holding* ALFRED, *in his robe and blond wig.* PLAYER *is in the downstage corner still.* ROS *comes down to that exit. The* PLAYER *does not budge. He and* ROS *stand toe to toe.*

ROS: Excuse me.

The PLAYER *lifts his downstage foot.* ROS *bends to put his hand on the floor. The* PLAYER *lowers his foot.* ROS *screams and leaps away.*

PLAYER *(gravely):* I beg your pardon.
GUIL *(to* ROS*):* What did he do?
PLAYER: I put my foot down.
ROS: My hand was on the floor!
GUIL: You put your hand under his foot?
ROS: I—
GUIL: What for?
ROS: I thought— *(Grabs* GUIL.*)* Don't leave me!

He makes a break for an exit. A TRAGEDIAN *dressed as a* KING *enters.* ROS *recoils, breaks for the opposite wing. Two cloaked* TRAGEDIANS *enter.* ROS *tries again but another* TRAGEDIAN *enters, and* ROS *retires to midstage. The* PLAYER *claps his hands matter-of-factly.*

PLAYER: Right! We haven't got much time.
GUIL: What are you doing?
PLAYER: Dress rehearsal. Now if you two wouldn't mind just moving back . . . there . . . good. . . . *(To* TRAGEDIANS:*)* Everyone ready? And for goodness' sake, remember what we're doing. *(To* ROS *and* GUIL.*)* We always use the same costumes more or less, and they forget

what they are supposed to be *in,* you see. . . . Stop picking your nose, Alfred. When Queens have to they do it by a cerebral process passed down in the blood. . . . Good. Silence! Off we go!

PLAYER-KING: Full thirty times hath Phoebus' cart—

PLAYER jumps up angrily.

PLAYER: No, no, no! Dumbshow first, your confounded majesty! *(To ROS and GUIL:)* They're a bit out of practice, but they always pick up wonderfully for the deaths—it brings out the poetry in them.

GUIL: How nice.

PLAYER: There's nothing more unconvincing than an unconvincing death.

GUIL: I'm sure.

PLAYER claps his hands.

PLAYER: Act One—moves now.

The mime. Soft music from a recorder. PLAYER-KING and PLAYER-QUEEN embrace. She kneels and makes a show of protestation to him. He takes her up, declining his head upon her neck. He lies down. She, seeing him asleep, leaves him.

GUIL: What is the dumbshow for?

PLAYER: Well, it's a device, really—it makes the action that follows more or less comprehensible; you understand, we are tied down to a language which makes up in obscurity what it lacks in style.

The mime (continued)—enter another. He takes off the SLEEPER's crown, kisses it. He has brought in a small bottle of liquid. He pours the poison in the SLEEPER's ear, and leaves him. The SLEEPER convulses heroically, dying.

ROS: Who was that?

PLAYER: The King's brother and uncle to the Prince.

GUIL: Not exactly fraternal.

PLAYER: Not exactly avuncular, as time goes on.

The QUEEN returns, makes passionate action, finding the KING dead. The POISONER comes in again, attended by two others (the two in cloaks). The POISONER seems to console with her. The dead body is carried away. The POISONER woos the QUEEN with gifts. She seems harsh awhile but in the end accepts his love. End of mime, at which point, the wail of a woman in torment and OPHELIA appears, wailing, closely followed by HAMLET in a hysterical state, shouting at her, circling her, both midstage.

HAMLET: Go to, I'll no more on't; it hath made me mad!

She falls on her knees weeping.

I say we will have no more marriage! *(His voice drops to include the TRAGEDIANS, who have frozen.)* Those that are married already *(he leans close to the PLAYER-QUEEN and POISONER,*

speaking with quiet edge) all but one shall live. *(He smiles briefly at them without mirth, and starts to back out, his parting shot rising again.)* The rest shall keep as they are. *(As he leaves,* OPHELIA *tottering upstage, he speaks into her ear a quick clipped sentence.)* To a nunnery, go.

He goes out. OPHELIA *falls on to her knees upstage, her sobs barely audible. A slight silence.*

PLAYER-KING: Full thirty times hath Phoebus' cart—

CLAUDIUS *enters with* POLONIUS *and goes over to* OPHELIA *and lifts her to her feet. The* TRAGEDIANS *jump back with heads inclined.*

CLAUDIUS: Love? His affections do not that way tend,
Or what he spake, though it lacked form a little,
Was not like madness. There's something
In his soul o'er which his melancholy sits on
Brood, and I do doubt the hatch and the
Disclose will be some danger; which for to
Prevent I have in quick determination thus set
It down: he shall with speed to England . . .

Which carries the three of them—CLAUDIUS, POLONIUS, OPHELIA—*out of sight. The* PLAYER *moves, clapping his hands for attention.*

PLAYER: Gentle*men! (They look at him.)* It doesn't seem to be coming. We are not getting it at all. *(To* GUIL:*)* What did you think?

GUIL: What was I supposed to think?

PLAYER: *(to* TRAGEDIANS*)*: You're not getting across!

ROS *had gone halfway up to* OPHELIA*; he returns.*

ROS: That didn't look like love to me.

GUIL: Starting from scratch again . . .

PLAYER *(to* TRAGEDIANS*)*: It was a *mess.*

ROS *(to* GUIL*)*: It's going to be chaos on the night.

GUIL: Keep back—we're spectators.

PLAYER: Act Two! Positions!

GUIL: Wasn't that the end?

PLAYER: Do you call that an ending?—with practically everyone on his feet? My goodness no—over your dead body.

GUIL: How am I supposed to take that?

PLAYER: Lying down. *(He laughs briefly and in a second has never laughed in his life.)* There's a design at work in all art—surely you know that? Events must play themselves out to aesthetic, moral and logical conclusion.

GUIL: And what's that, in this case?

PLAYER: It never varies—we aim at the point where everyone who is marked for death dies.

GUIL: Marked?

PLAYER: Between "just desserts" and "tragic irony" we are given quite a lot of scope for our particular talent. Generally speaking, things have gone about as far as they can possibly go when things have got about as bad as they reasonably get. *(He switches on a smile.)*

GUIL: Who decides?

PLAYER *(switching off his smile)*: *Decides?* It is *written.*

He turns away. GUIL *grabs him and spins him back violently.*

(Unflustered.) Now if you're going to be subtle, we'll miss each other in the dark. I'm referring to oral tradition. So to speak.

GUIL *releases him.*

We're tragedians, you see. We follow directions—there is no *choice* involved. The bad end unhappily, the good unluckily. That is what tragedy means. *(Calling.)* Positions!

The TRAGEDIANS *have taken up positions for the continuation of the mime: which in this case means a love scene, sexual and passionate, between the* QUEEN *and the* POISONER/KING.

PLAYER: Go!

The lovers begin. The PLAYER *contributes a breathless commentary for* ROS *and* GUIL.

Having murdered his brother and wooed the widow—the
poisoner mounts the throne! Here we see him and his
queen give rein to their unbridled passion! She little
knowing that the man she holds in her arms—!

ROS: Oh, I say—here—really! You can't do that!

PLAYER: Why not?

ROS: Well, really—I mean, people want to be *entertained*—they don't come expecting sordid and gratuitous filth.

PLAYER: You're wrong—they do! Murder, seduction and incest—what do you want—*jokes?*

ROS: I want a good story, with a beginning, middle and end.

PLAYER *(to* GUIL*)*: And you?

GUIL: I'd prefer art to mirror life, if it's all the same to you.

PLAYER: It's all the same to me, sir. *(To the grappling* LOVERS:*)* All right, no need to indulge yourselves. *(They get up. To* GUIL:*)* I come on in a minute. Lucianus, nephew to the king! *(Turns his attention to the* TRAGEDIANS.*)* Next!

They disport themselves to accommodate the next piece of mime, which consists of the PLAYER *himself exhibiting an excitable anguish (choreographed, stylized) leading to an impassioned scene with the* QUEEN *(cf. "The Closet Scene," Shakespeare Act III, scene iv) and a very stylized reconstruction of a* POLONIUS *figure being stabbed behind the arras (the murdered* KING *to stand in for* POLONIUS*) while the* PLAYER *himself continues his breathless commentary for the benefit of* ROS *and* GUIL.

PLAYER: Lucianus, nephew to the king . . . usurped by his uncle and shattered by his mother's incestuous marriage . . . loses his reason . . . throwing the court into turmoil and disarray

as he alternates between bitter melancholy and unrestricted lunacy . . . staggering from the suicidal *(a pose)* to the homicidal *(here he kills "POLONIUS")* . . . he at last confronts his mother and in a scene of provocative ambiguity— *(a somewhat oedipal embrace)* begs her to repent and recant— *(He springs up, still talking.)* The King— *(he pushes forward the* POISONER/KING*)* tormented by guilt—haunted by fear—decides to despatch his nephew to England—and entrusts this undertaking to two smiling accomplices—friends—courtiers—to two spies—

He has swung round to bring together the POISONER/KING *and the two cloaked* TRAGEDIANS; *the latter kneel and accept a scroll from the* KING.

—giving them a letter to present to the English court—! And so they depart—on board ship—

The two SPIES *position themselves on either side of the* PLAYER, *and the three of them sway gently in unison, the motion of a boat; and then the* PLAYER *detaches himself.*

—and they arrive—

One SPY *shades his eyes at the horizon.*

—and disembark—and present themselves before the English king—*(He wheels round.)* The English king—

An exchange of headgear creates the ENGLISH KING *from the remaining player—that is, the* PLAYER *who played the original murdered king.*

But where is the Prince? Where indeed? The plot has thickened—a twist of fate and cunning has put into their hands a letter that seals their deaths!

The two SPIES *present their letter; the* ENGLISH KING *reads it and orders their deaths. They stand up as the* PLAYER *whips off their cloaks preparatory to execution.*

Traitors hoist by their own petard?—or victims of the gods?—we shall never know!

The whole mime has been fluid and continuous but now ROS *moves forward and brings it to a pause. What brings* ROS *forward is the fact that under their cloaks the two* SPIES *are wearing coats identical to those worn by* ROS *and* GUIL, *whose coats are now covered by their cloaks.* ROS *approaches "his"* SPY *doubtfully. He does not quite understand why the coats are familiar.* ROS *stands close, touches the coat, thoughtfully. . . .*

ROS: Well, if it isn't—! No, wait a minute, don't tell me—it's a long time since—where was it? Ah, this is taking me back to—when was it? I know you, don't I? I never forget a face— *(he looks into the* SPY's *face)* . . . not that I know yours, that is. For a moment I thought—no, I don't know you, do I? Yes, I'm afraid you're quite wrong. You must have mistaken me for someone else.

GUIL *meanwhile has approached the other* SPY, *brow creased in thought.*

PLAYER *(to* GUIL*)*: Are you familiar with this play?

GUIL: No.

PLAYER: A slaughterhouse—eight corpses all told. It brings out the best in us.

GUIL *(tense, progressively rattled during the whole mime and commentary)*: You!—What do *you* know about *death?*

PLAYER: It's what the actors do best. They have to exploit whatever talent is given to them, and their talent is dying. They can die heroically, comically, ironically, slowly, suddenly, disgustingly, charmingly, or from a great height. My own talent is more general. I extract significance from melodrama, a significance which it does not in fact contain; but occasionally, from out of this matter, there escapes a thin beam of light that, seen at the right angle, can crack the shell of mortality.

ROS: Is that all they can do—die?

PLAYER: No, no—they kill beautifully. In fact some of them kill even better than they die. The rest die better than they kill. They're a team.

ROS: Which ones are which?

PLAYER: There's not much in it.

GUIL *(fear, derision)*: Actors! The mechanics of cheap melodrama! That isn't *death! (More quietly.)* You scream and choke and sink to your knees, but it doesn't bring death home to anyone—it doesn't catch them unawares and start the whisper in their skulls that says—"One day you are going to die." *(He straightens up.)* You die so many times; how can you expect them to believe in your death?

PLAYER: On the contrary, it's the only kind they do believe. They're conditioned to it. I had an actor once who was condemned to hang for stealing a sheep—or a lamb, I forget which—so I got permission to have him hanged in the middle of a play—had to change the plot a bit but I thought it would be effective, you know—and you wouldn't believe it, he just *wasn't* convincing! It was impossible to suspend one's disbelief—and what with the audience jeering and throwing peanuts, the whole thing was a *disaster!*—he did nothing but cry all the time—right out of character—just stood there and cried. . . . Never again.

In good humour he has already turned back to the mime: the two SPIES *awaiting execution at the hands of the* PLAYER, *who takes his dagger out of his belt.*

Audiences know what to expect, and that is all that they are prepared to believe in. *(To the* SPIES*:)* Show!

The SPIES *die at some length, rather well.*

The light has begun to go, and it fades as they die, and as GUIL *speaks.*

GUIL: No, no, no . . . you've got it all wrong . . . you can't act death. The *fact* of it is nothing to do with seeing it happen—it's not gasps and blood and falling about—that isn't what makes it death. It's just a man failing to reappear, that's all—now you see him, now you don't, that's the only thing that's real: here one minute and gone the next and never coming back—an exit, unobtrusive and unannounced, a disappearance gathering weight as it goes on, until, finally, it is heavy with death.

The two SPIES *lie still, barely visible. The* PLAYER *comes forward and throws the* SPIES' *cloaks over their bodies.* ROS *starts to clap, slowly.*

BLACKOUT.

A second of silence, then much noise. Shouts . . . "The King rises!" . . . "Give o'er the play!" . . . and cries for "Lights, lights, lights!"

When the light comes, after a few seconds, it comes as a sunrise.

The stage is empty save for two cloaked figures sprawled on the ground in the approximate positions last held by the dead SPIES. *As the light grows, they are seen to be* ROS *and* GUIL, *and to be resting quite comfortably.* ROS *raises himself on his elbows and shades his eyes as he stares into the auditorium. Finally:*

ROS: That must be east, then. I think we can assume that.
GUIL: I'm assuming nothing.
ROS: No, it's all right. That's the sun. East.
GUIL *(looks up):* Where?
ROS: I watched it come up.
GUIL: No . . . it was light all the time, you see, and you opened your eyes very, very slowly. If you'd been facing back there you'd be swearing *that* was east.
ROS *(standing up):* You're a mass of prejudice.
GUIL: I've been taken in before.
ROS *(looks out over the audience):* Rings a bell.
GUIL: They're waiting to see what we're going to do.
ROS: Good old east.
GUIL: As soon as we make a move they'll come pouring in from every side, shouting obscure instructions, confusing us with ridiculous remarks, messing us about from here to breakfast and getting our names wrong.

ROS *starts to protest but he has hardly opened his mouth before:*

CLAUDIUS *(off stage—with urgency):* Ho, Guildenstern!

GUIL *is still prone. Small pause.*

ROS AND GUIL: You're wanted. . . .

GUIL *furiously leaps to his feet as* CLAUDIUS *and* GERTRUDE *enter. They are in some desperation.*

CLAUDIUS: Friends both, go join you with some further aid: Hamlet in madness hath Polonius slain, and from his mother's closet hath he dragged him. Go seek him out; speak fair and bring the body into the chapel. I pray you haste in this. *(As he and* GERTRUDE *are hurrying out.)* Come, Gertrude, we'll call up our wisest friends and let them know both what we mean to do. . . .

They've gone. ROS *and* GUIL *remain quite still.*

GUIL: Well . . .
ROS: Quite . . .
GUIL: Well, well.
ROS: Quite, quite. *(Nods with spurious confidence.)* Seek him out. *(Pause.)* Etcetera.
GUIL: Quite.
ROS: Well. *(Small pause.)* Well, that's a step in the right direction.
GUIL: You didn't like him?
ROS: Who?
GUIL: Good God, I hope more tears are shed for *us!* . . .
ROS: Well, it's *progress,* isn't it? Something positive. Seek him out. *(Looks round without moving his feet.)* Where does one begin . . . ? *(Takes one step towards the wings and halts.)*
GUIL: Well, that's a step in the right direction.
ROS: You think so? He could be anywhere.
GUIL: All right—you go that way, I'll go this way.
ROS: Right.

They walk towards opposite wings. ROS *halts.*

No.

GUIL *halts.*

You go this way—I'll go that way.
GUIL: All right.

They march towards each other, cross. ROS *halts.*

ROS: Wait a minute.

GUIL *halts.*

I think we should stick together. He might be violent.
GUIL: Good point. I'll come with you.

GUIL *marches across to* ROS. *They turn to leave.* ROS *halts.*

ROS: No, I'll come with *you.*
GUIL: Right.

They turn, march across to the opposite wing. ROS *halts.* GUIL *halts.*

ROS: I'll come with *you, my* way.
GUIL: All right.

They turn again and march across. ROS *halts.* GUIL *halts.*

ROS: I've just thought. If we both go, he could come *here.* That would be stupid, wouldn't it?

GUIL: All right—I'll stay, you go.

ROS: Right.

GUIL marches to midstage.

I say.

GUIL wheels and carries on marching back towards ROS, who starts marching downstage. They cross. ROS halts.

I've just thought.

GUIL halts.

We ought to stick together; he might be violent.

GUIL: Good point.

GUIL marches down to join ROS. They stand still for a moment in their original positions.

Well, at last we're getting somewhere.

Pause.

Of course, he might not come.

ROS *(airily):* Oh, he'll come.

GUIL: We'd have some explaining to do.

ROS: He'll come. *(Airily wanders upstage.)* Don't worry—take my word for it— *(Looks out—is appalled.)* He's coming!

GUIL: What's he doing?

ROS: Walking.

GUIL: Alone?

ROS: No.

GUIL: Not walking?

ROS: No.

GUIL: Who's with him?

ROS: The old man.

GUIL: Walking?

ROS: No.

GUIL: Ah. That's an opening if ever there was one. *(And is suddenly galvanized into action.)* Let him walk into the trap!

ROS: What trap?

GUIL: You stand there! Don't let him pass!

He positions ROS with his back to one wing, facing HAMLET's entrance.

GUIL *positions himself next to* ROS, *a few feet away, so that they are covering one side of the stage, facing the opposite side.* GUIL *unfastens his belt.* ROS *does the same. They join the two belts, and hold them taut between them.* ROS*'s trousers slide slowly down.*

HAMLET *enters opposite, slowly, dragging* POLONIUS*'s body. He enters upstage, makes a small arc and leaves by the same side, a few feet downstage.*

ROS *and* GUIL, *holding the belts taut, stare at him in some bewilderment.*

HAMLET *leaves, dragging the body. They relax the strain on the belts.*

ROS: That was close.
GUIL: There's a limit to what two people can do.

They undo the belts: ROS *pulls up his trousers.*

ROS *(worriedly—he walks a few paces towards* HAMLET*'s exit):* He *was* dead.
GUIL: Of course he's dead!
ROS *(turns to* GUIL*):* Properly.
GUIL *(angrily):* Death's death, isn't it?

ROS *falls silent. Pause.*

Perhaps he'll come back this way.

ROS *starts to take off his belt.*

No, no, no!—if we can't learn by experience, what else have we got?

ROS *desists.*

Pause.

ROS: Give him a shout.
GUIL: I thought we'd been into all that.
ROS *(shouts):* Hamlet!
GUIL: Don't be absurd.
ROS *(shouts):* Lord Hamlet!

HAMLET *enters.* ROS *is a little dismayed.*

What have you done, my lord, with the dead body?
HAMLET: Compounded it with dust, whereto 'tis kin.
ROS: Tell us where 'tis, that we may take it thence and bear it to the chapel.
HAMLET: Do not believe it.
ROS: Believe what?
HAMLET: That I can keep your counsel and not mine own. Besides, to be demanded of a sponge, what replication should be made by the son of a king?

ROS: Take you me for a sponge, my lord?

HAMLET: Ay, sir, that soaks up the King's countenance, his rewards, his authorities. But such officers do the King best service in the end. He keeps them, like an ape, in the corner of his jaw, first mouthed, to be last swallowed. When he needs what you have gleaned, it is but squeezing you and, sponge, you shall be dry again.

ROS: I understand you not, my lord.

HAMLET: I am glad of it: a knavish speech sleeps in a foolish ear.

ROS: My lord, you must tell us where the body is and go with us to the King.

HAMLET: The body is with the King, but the King is not with the body. The King is a thing—

GUIL: A thing, my lord—?

HAMLET: Of nothing. Bring me to him.

HAMLET moves resolutely towards one wing. They move with him, shepherding. Just before they reach the exit, HAMLET, apparently seeing CLAUDIUS approaching from off stage, bends low in a sweeping bow. ROS and GUIL, cued by Hamlet, also bow deeply—a sweeping ceremonial bow with their cloaks swept round them. HAMLET, however, continues the movement into an about-turn and walks off in the opposite direction. ROS and GUIL, with their heads low, do not notice.

No one comes on. ROS and GUIL squint upwards and find that they are bowing to nothing.

CLAUDIUS enters behind them. At first words they leap up and do a double-take.

CLAUDIUS: How now? What hath befallen?

ROS: Where the body is bestowed, my lord, we cannot get from him.

CLAUDIUS: But where is he?

ROS *(fractional hesitation)*: Without, my lord; guarded to know your pleasure.

CLAUDIUS *(moves)*: Bring him before us.

This hits ROS between the eyes but only his eyes show it. Again his hesitation is fractional. And then with great deliberation he turns to GUIL.

ROS: Ho! Bring in the lord.

Again there is a fractional moment in which ROS is smug, GUIL is trapped and betrayed. GUIL opens his mouth and closes it.

The situation is saved: HAMLET, escorted, is marched in just as CLAUDIUS leaves. HAMLET and his ESCORT cross the stage and go out, following CLAUDIUS.

Lighting changes to Exterior.

ROS *(moves to go)*: All right, then?

GUIL *(does not move; thoughtfully)*: And yet it doesn't seem enough; to have breathed such significance. Can that be all? And why us?—anybody would have done. And we have contributed nothing.

ROS: It was a trying episode while it lasted, but they've done with us now.

GUIL: Done what?

ROS: I don't pretend to have understood. Frankly, I'm not very interested. If they won't tell

us, that's their affair. *(He wanders upstage towards the exit.)* For my part, I'm only glad that that's the last we've seen of him— *(And he glances off stage and turns front, his face betraying the fact that* HAMLET *is there.)*

GUIL: I knew it wasn't the end. . . .

ROS *(high):* What else?!

GUIL: We're taking him to England. What's he doing?

ROS *goes upstage and returns.*

ROS: Talking.

GUIL: To himself?

ROS *makes to go,* GUIL *cuts him off.*

Is he alone?

ROS: No, he's with a soldier.

GUIL: Then he's not talking to himself, is he?

ROS: Not *by* himself. . . . Should we go?

GUIL: Where?

ROS: Anywhere.

GUIL: Why?

ROS *puts up his head listening.*

ROS: There it is again. *(In anguish.)* All I ask is a change of ground!

GUIL *(coda):* Give us this day our daily round. . . .

HAMLET *enters behind them, talking with a soldier in arms.* ROS *and* GUIL *don't look round.*

ROS: They'll have us hanging about till we're dead. At least. And the weather will change. *(Looks up.)* The spring can't last for ever.

HAMLET: Good sir, whose powers are these?

SOLDIER: They are of Norway, sir.

HAMLET: How purposed, sir, I pray you?

SOLDIER: Against some part of Poland.

HAMLET: Who commands them, sir?

SOLDIER: The nephew to old Norway, Fortinbras.

ROS: We'll be cold. The summer won't last.

GUIL: It's autumnal.

ROS *(examining the ground):* No leaves.

GUIL: Autumnal—nothing to do with leaves. It is to do with a certain brownness at the edges of the day. . . . Brown is creeping up on us, take my word for it. . . . Russets and tangerine shades of old gold flushing the very outside edge of the senses . . . deep shining ochres, burnt umber and parchments of baked earth—reflecting on itself and through itself, filtering the light. At such times, perhaps, coincidentally, the leaves might fall, somewhere, by repute. Yesterday was blue, like smoke.

ROS *(head up, listening):* I got it again then.

They listen—faintest sound of TRAGEDIANS' *band.*

HAMLET: I humbly thank you, sir.
SOLDIER: God by you, sir. *(Exit.)*

ROS *gets up quickly and goes to* HAMLET.

ROS: Will it please you go, my lord?
HAMLET: I'll be with you straight. Go you a little before.

HAMLET *turns to face upstage.* ROS *returns down.* GUIL *faces front, doesn't turn.*

GUIL: Is he there?
ROS: Yes.
GUIL: What's he doing?

ROS *looks over his shoulder.*

ROS: Talking.
GUIL: To himself?
ROS: Yes.

Pause. ROS *makes to leave.*

ROS: He *said* we can go. Cross my heart.
GUIL: I like to know where I am. Even if I don't know where I am, I like to know *that.* If we go there's no knowing.
ROS: No knowing what?
GUIL: If we'll ever come back.
ROS: We don't want to come back.
GUIL: That may very well be true, but do we want to go?
ROS: We'll be free.
GUIL: I don't know. It's the same sky.
ROS: We've come this far.

He moves towards exit. GUIL *follows him.*

And besides, anything could happen yet.

They go.

BLACKOUT.

ACT THREE

Opens in pitch darkness.

Soft sea sounds.

After several seconds of nothing, a voice from the dark . . .

GUIL: Are you there?
ROS: Where?
GUIL *(bitterly):* A flying start. . . .

Pause.

ROS: Is that you?
GUIL: Yes.
ROS: How do you know?
GUIL *(explosion):* Oh-for-God's-sake!
ROS: We're not finished, then?
GUIL: Well, we're here, aren't we?
ROS: Are we? I can't see a thing.
GUIL: You can still *think*, can't you?
ROS: I think so.
GUIL: You can still *talk*.
ROS: What should I say?
GUIL: Don't bother. You can *feel*, can't you?
ROS: Ah! There's life in me yet!
GUIL: What are you feeling?
ROS: A leg. Yes, it feels like my leg.
GUIL: How does it feel?
ROS: Dead.
GUIL: Dead?
ROS *(panic):* I can't feel a thing!
GUIL: Give it a pinch! *(Immediately he yelps.)*
ROS: Sorry.
GUIL: Well, that's cleared that up.

Longer pause: the sound builds a little and identifies itself—the sea. Ship timbers, wind in the rigging, and then shouts of sailors calling obscure but inescapably nautical instructions from all directions, far and near: A short list:

Hard a larboard!
Let go the stays!
Reef down me hearties!
Is that you, cox'n?
Hel-llo! Is that you?
Hard a port!
Easy as she goes!
Keep her steady on the lee!
Haul away, lads!
(Snatches of sea shanty maybe.)
Fly the jib!
Tops'l up, me maties!

When the point has been well made and more so.

ROS: We're on a boat. *(Pause.)* Dark, isn't it?
GUIL: Not for night.
ROS: No, not for *night.*
GUIL: Dark for day.

Pause.

ROS: Oh yes, it's dark for *day.*
GUIL: We must have gone north, of course.
ROS: Off course?
GUIL: Land of the midnight sun, that is.
ROS: Of course.

Some sailor sounds.

A lantern is lit upstage—in fact by HAMLET.

The stage lightens disproportionately—

Enough to see:

ROS *and* GUIL *sitting downstage.*

Vague shapes of rigging, etc., behind.

I think it's getting light.
GUIL: Not for night.
ROS: This far north.
GUIL: Unless we're off course.
ROS *(small pause):* Of course.

A better light—Lantern? Moon? . . . Light.
Revealing, among other things, three large man-sized casks on deck, upended, with lids. Spaced but in line. Behind and above—a gaudy striped umbrella, on a pole stuck into the deck, tilted so that we do not see behind it—one of those huge six-foot-diameter jobs. Still dim upstage. ROS *and* GUIL *still facing front.*

ROS: Yes, it's lighter than it was. It'll be night soon. This far north. *(Dolefully.)* I suppose we'll have to go to sleep. *(He yawns and stretches.)*
GUIL: Tired?
ROS: No . . . I don't think I'd take to it. Sleep all night, can't see a thing all day. . . . Those eskimos must have a quiet life.
GUIL: Where?
ROS: What?
GUIL: I thought you— *(Relapses.)* I've lost all capacity for disbelief. I'm not sure that I could even rise to a little gentle scepticism.

Pause.

ROS: Well, shall we stretch our legs?
GUIL: I don't feel like stretching my legs.
ROS: I'll stretch them for you, if you like.
GUIL: No.
ROS: We could stretch each other's. That way we wouldn't have to go anywhere.
GUIL *(pause):* No, somebody might come in.
ROS: In where?
GUIL: Out here.
ROS: In out here?
GUIL: On deck.

ROS *considers the floor: slaps it.*

ROS: Nice bit of planking, that.
GUIL: Yes, I'm very fond of boats myself. I like the way they're—contained. You don't have to worry about which way to go, or whether to go at all—the question doesn't arise, because you're on a *boat,* aren't you? Boats are safe areas in the game of tag . . . the players will hold their positions until the music starts. . . . I think I'll spend most of my life on boats.
ROS: Very healthy.

ROS *inhales with expectation, exhales with boredom.* GUIL *stands up and looks over the audience.*

GUIL: One is free on a boat. For a time. Relatively.
ROS: What's it like?
GUIL: Rough.

ROS *joins him. They look out over the audience.*

ROS: I think I'm going to be sick.

GUIL *licks a finger, holds it up experimentally.*

GUIL: Other side, I think.

ROS *goes upstage: Ideally a sort of upper deck joined to the downstage lower deck by short steps. The umbrella being on the upper deck.* ROS *pauses by the umbrella and looks behind it.* GUIL *meanwhile has been resuming his own theme—looking out over the audience—*

Free to move, speak, extemporise, and yet. We have not been cut loose. Our truancy is defined by one fixed star, and our drift represents merely a slight change of angle to it: we may seize the moment, toss it around while the moments pass, a short dash here, an exploration there, but we are brought round full circle to face again the single immutable fact—that we, Rosencrantz and Guildenstern, bearing a letter from one king to another, are taking Hamlet to England.

By which time, ROS *has returned, tiptoeing with great import, teeth clenched for secrecy, gets to* GUIL, *points surreptitiously behind him—and a tight whisper:*

ROS: I say—*he's there!*
GUIL *(unsurprised):* What's he doing?
ROS: Sleeping.
GUIL: It's all right for him.
ROS: What is?
GUIL: He can sleep.
ROS: It's all right for him.
GUIL: He's got us now.
ROS: He can sleep.
GUIL: It's all done for him.
ROS: He's got us.
GUIL: And we've got nothing. *(A cry.)* All I ask is our common due!
ROS: For those in peril on the sea. . . .
GUIL: Give us this day our daily cue.

Beat, pause. Sit. Long pause.

ROS *(after shifting, looking around):* What now?
GUIL: What do you mean?
ROS: Well, nothing is happening.
GUIL: We're on a boat.
ROS: I'm aware of that.
GUIL *(angrily):* Then what do you expect? *(Unhappily.)* We act on scraps of information . . . sifting half-remembered directions that we can hardly separate from instinct.

ROS *puts a hand into his purse, then both hands behind his back, then holds his fists out.*

GUIL *taps one fist.*

ROS *opens it to show a coin.*

He gives it to GUIL.

He puts his hand back into his purse. Then both hands behind his back, then holds his fists out.

GUIL *taps one.*

ROS *opens it to show a coin. He gives it to* GUIL.

Repeat.

Repeat.

GUIL *getting tense. Desperate to lose.*

Repeat.

GUIL *taps a hand, changes his mind, taps the other, and* ROS *inadvertently reveals that he has a coin in both fists.*

GUIL: You had money in both hands.
ROS *(embarrassed):* Yes.
GUIL: Every time?
ROS: Yes.
GUIL: What's the point of that?
ROS *(pathetic):* I wanted to make you happy.

Beat.

GUIL: How much did he give you?
ROS: Who?
GUIL: The King. He gave us some money.
ROS: How much did he give you?
GUIL: I asked you first.
ROS: I got the same as you.
GUIL: He wouldn't discriminate between us.
ROS: How much did you get?
GUIL: The same.
ROS: How do you know?
GUIL: You just told me—how do *you* know?
ROS: He wouldn't discriminate between us.
GUIL: Even if he could.
ROS: Which he never could.
GUIL: He couldn't even be sure of mixing us up.
ROS: Without mixing us up.
GUIL *(turning on him furiously):* Why don't you say something original! No wonder the whole thing is so stagnant! You don't take me up on anything—you just repeat it in a different order.
ROS: I can't think of anything original. I'm only good in support.
GUIL: I'm sick of making the running.
ROS *(humbly):* It must be your dominant personality. *(Almost in tears.)* Oh, what's going to become of us!

And GUIL *comforts him, all harshness gone.*

GUIL: Don't cry . . . it's all right . . . there . . . there, I'll see we're all right.
ROS: But we've got nothing to go on, we're out on our own.
GUIL: We're on our way to England—we're taking Hamlet there.
ROS: What for?
GUIL: What for? Where have you been?
ROS: When? *(Pause.)* We won't know what to do when we get there.
GUIL: We take him to the King.
ROS: Will *he* be there?
GUIL: No—the king of England.

ROS: He's expecting us?
GUIL: No.
ROS: He won't know what we're playing at. What are we going to *say?*
GUIL: We've got a letter. You remember the letter.
ROS: Do I?
GUIL: Everything is explained in the letter. We count on that.
ROS: Is that it, then?
GUIL: What?
ROS: We take Hamlet to the English king, we hand over the letter—what then?
GUIL: There may be something in the letter to keep us going a bit.
ROS: And if not?
GUIL: Then that's it—we're finished.
ROS: At a loose end?
GUIL: Yes.

Pause.

ROS: Are there likely to be loose ends? *(Pause.)* Who is the English king?
GUIL: That depends on when we get there.
ROS: What do you think it says?
GUIL: Oh . . . greetings. Expressions of loyalty. Asking of favours, calling in of debts. Obscure promises balanced by vague threats. . . . Diplomacy. Regards to the family.
ROS: And about Hamlet?
GUIL: Oh yes.
ROS: And us—the full background?
GUIL: I should say so.

Pause.

ROS: So we've got a letter which explains everything.
GUIL: You've got it.

ROS *takes that literally. He starts to pat his pockets, etc.*

What's the matter?
ROS: The letter.
GUIL: Have you got it?
ROS *(rising fear):* Have I? *(Searches frantically.)* Where would I have put it?
GUIL: You can't have lost it.
ROS: I must have!
GUIL: That's odd—I thought he gave it to me.

ROS *looks at him hopefully.*

ROS: Perhaps he did.
GUIL: But you seemed so sure it was *you* who hadn't got it.
ROS *(high):* It *was* me who hadn't got it!

GUIL: But if he gave it to me there's no reason why you should have had it in the first place, in which case I don't see what all the fuss is about you *not* having it.

ROS *(pause):* I admit it's confusing.

GUIL: This is all getting rather undisciplined. . . . The boat, the night, the sense of isolation and uncertainty . . . all these induce a loosening of the concentration. We must not lose control. Tighten up. Now. Either you have lost the letter or you didn't have it to lose in the first place, in which case the King never gave it to you, in which case he gave it to me, in which case I would have put it into my inside top pocket, in which case *(calmly producing the letter)* . . . it will be . . . here. *(They smile at each other.)* We mustn't drop off like that again.

Pause. ROS *takes the letter gently from him.*

ROS: Now that we have found it, why were we looking for it?

GUIL *(thinks):* We thought it was lost.

ROS: Something else?

GUIL: No.

Deflation.

ROS: Now we've lost the tension.

GUIL: What tension?

ROS: What was the last thing I said before we wandered off?

GUIL: When was that?

ROS *(helplessly):* I can't remember.

GUIL *(leaping up):* What a shambles! We're just not getting anywhere.

ROS *(mournfully):* Not even England. I don't believe in it anyway.

GUIL: What?

ROS: England.

GUIL: Just a conspiracy of cartographers, you mean?

ROS: I mean I don't believe it! *(Calmer.)* I have no image. I try to picture us arriving, a little harbour perhaps . . . roads . . . inhabitants to point the way . . . horses on the road . . . riding for a day or a fortnight and then a palace and the English king. . . . That would be the logical kind of thing. . . . But my mind remains a blank. No. We're slipping off the map.

GUIL: Yes . . . yes. . . . *(Rallying.)* But you don't believe anything till it happens. And it *has* all happened. Hasn't it?

ROS: We drift down time, clutching at straws. But what good's a brick to a drowning man?

GUIL: Don't give up, we can't be long now.

ROS: We might as well be dead. Do you think death could possibly be a boat?

GUIL: No, no, no . . . Death is . . . not. Death isn't. You take my meaning. Death is the ultimate negative. Not-being. You can't not-be on a boat.

ROS: I've frequently not been on boats.

GUIL: No, no, no—what you've been is not on boats.

ROS: I wish I was dead. *(Considers the drop.)* I could jump over the side. That would put a spoke in their wheel.

GUIL: Unless they're counting on it.

ROS: I shall remain on board. That'll put a spoke in their wheel. *(The futility of it, fury.)* All right! We don't question, we don't doubt. We perform. But a line must be drawn somewhere, and I would like to put it on record that I have no confidence in England. Thank you. *(Thinks about this.)* And even if it's true, it'll just be another shambles.

GUIL: I don't see why.

ROS *(furious)*: He won't know what we're talking about.—What are we going to *say*?

GUIL: We say—Your majesty, we have arrived!

ROS *(kingly)*: And who are you?

GUIL: We are Rosencrantz and Guildenstern.

ROS *(barks)*: Never heard of you!

GUIL: Well, we're nobody special—

ROS *(regal and nasty)*: What's your game?

GUIL: We've got our instructions—

ROS: First I've heard of it—

GUIL *(angry)*: Let me finish— *(Humble.)* We've come from Denmark.

ROS: What do you want?

GUIL: Nothing—we're delivering Hamlet—

ROS: Who's he?

GUIL *(irritated)*: You've heard of *him*—

ROS: Oh, I've heard of him all right and I want nothing to do with it.

GUIL: But—

ROS: You march in here without so much as a by-your-leave and expect me to take in every lunatic you try to pass off with a lot of unsubstantiated—

GUIL: We've got a letter—

ROS snatches it and tears it open.

ROS *(efficiently)*: I see . . . I see . . . well, this seems to support your story such as it is—it is an exact command from the king of Denmark, for several different reasons, importing Denmark's health and England's too, that on the reading of this letter, without delay, I should have Hamlet's head cut off—!

GUIL snatches the letter. ROS, double-taking, snatches it back. GUIL snatches it half back. They read it together, and separate.

Pause.

They are well downstage looking front.

ROS: The sun's going down. It will be dark soon.

GUIL: Do you think so?

ROS: I was just making conversation. *(Pause.)* We're his *friends*.

GUIL: How do you know?

ROS: From our young days brought up with him.

GUIL: You've only got their word for it.

ROS: But that's what we depend on.

GUIL: Well, yes, and then again no. *(Airily.)* Let us keep things in proportion. Assume, if you like, that they're going to kill him. Well, he is a man, he is mortal, death comes to us all, etcetera, and consequently he would have died anyway, sooner or later. Or to look at it from the social point of view—he's just one man among many, the loss would be well within reason and convenience. And then again, what is so terrible about death? As Socrates so philosophically put it, since we don't know what death is, it is illogical to fear it. It might be . . . very nice. Certainly it is a release from the burden of life, and, for the godly, a haven and a reward. Or to look at it another way—we are little men, we don't know the ins and outs of the matter, there are wheels within wheels, etcetera—it would be presumptuous of us to interfere with the designs of fate or even of kings. All in all, I think we'd be well advised to leave well alone. Tie up the letter—there—neatly—like that.—They won't notice the broken seal, assuming you were in character.

ROS: But what's the point?

GUIL: Don't apply logic.

ROS: He's done nothing to us.

GUIL: Or justice.

ROS: It's awful.

GUIL: But it could have been worse. I was beginning to think it was. *(And his relief comes out in a laugh.)*

Behind them HAMLET *appears from behind the umbrella. The light has been going. Slightly.* HAMLET *is going to the lantern.*

ROS: The position as I see it, then. We, Rosencrantz and Guildenstern, from our young days brought up with him, awakened by a man standing on his saddle, are summoned, and arrive, and are instructed to glean what afflicts him and draw him on to pleasures, such as a play, which unfortunately, as it turns out, is abandoned in some confusion owing to certain nuances outside our appreciation—which, among other causes, results in, among other effects, a high, not to say, homicidal, excitement in Hamlet, whom we, in consequence, are escorting, for his own good, to England. Good. We're on top of it now.

HAMLET *blows out the lantern. The stage goes pitch black. The black resolves itself to moonlight, by which* HAMLET *approaches the sleeping* ROS *and* GUIL. *He extracts the letter and takes it behind his umbrella; the light of his lantern shines through the fabric,* HAMLET *emerges again with a letter, and replaces it, and retires, blowing out his lantern.*

Morning comes.

ROS *watches it coming—from the auditorium. Behind him is a gay sight. Beneath the re-tilted umbrella, reclining in a deck-chair, wrapped in a rug, reading a book, possibly smoking, sits* HAMLET.

ROS *watches the morning come, and brighten to high noon.*

ROS: I'm assuming nothing. *(He stands up.* GUIL *wakes.)* The position as I see it, then. That's west unless we're off course, in which case it's night; the King gave me the same as you,

the King gave you the same as me; the King never gave me the letter, the King gave you the letter, we don't know what's in the letter; we take Hamlet to the English king, it depending on when we get there who he is, and we hand over the letter, which may or may not have something in it to keep us going, and if not, we are finished and at a loose end, if they have loose ends. We could have done worse. I don't think we missed any chances. . . . Not that we're getting much help. *(He sits down again. They lie down—prone.)* If we stopped breathing we'd vanish.

The muffled sound of a recorder. They sit up with disproportionate interest.

GUIL: Here we go.
ROS: Yes, but what?

They listen to the music.

GUIL *(excitedly):* Out of the void, finally, a sound; while on a boat (admittedly) outside the action (admittedly) the perfect and absolute silence of the wet lazy slap of water against water and the rolling creak of timber—breaks; giving rise at once to the speculation or the assumption or the hope that something is about to happen; a pipe is heard. One of the sailors has pursed his lips against a woodwind, his fingers and thumb governing, shall we say, the ventages, whereupon, giving it breath, let us say, with his mouth, it, the pipe, discourses, as the saying goes, most eloquent music. A thing like that, it could change the course of events. *(Pause.)* Go and see what it is.
ROS: It's someone playing on a pipe.
GUIL: Go and find him.
ROS: And then what?
GUIL: I don't know—request a tune.
ROS: What for?
GUIL: Quick—before we lose our momentum.
ROS: Why!—something is happening. It had quite escaped my attention!

He listens: Makes a stab at an exit. Listens more carefully: Changes direction.

GUIL *takes no notice.*

ROS *wanders about trying to decide where the music comes from. Finally he tracks it down—unwillingly—to the middle barrel. There is no getting away from it. He turns to* GUIL *who takes no notice.* ROS, *during this whole business, never quite breaks into articulate speech. His face and his hands indicate his incredulity. He stands gazing at the middle barrel. The pipe plays on within. He kicks the barrel. The pipe stops. He leaps back towards* GUIL. *The pipe starts up again. He approaches the barrel cautiously. He lifts the lid. The music is louder. He slams down the lid. The music is softer. He goes back towards* GUIL. *But a drum starts, muffled. He freezes. He turns. Considers the left-hand barrel. The drumming goes on within, in time to the flute. He walks back to* GUIL. *He opens his mouth to speak. Doesn't make it. A lute is heard. He spins round at the third barrel. More instruments join in. Until it is quite inescapable that inside the three barrels, distributed, playing together a familiar tune which has been heard three times before, are the* TRAGEDIANS.

They play on.

ROS sits beside GUIL. They stare ahead.

The tune comes to an end.

Pause.

ROS: I thought I heard a band. *(In anguish.)* Plausibility is all I presume!
GUIL *(coda):* Call us this day our daily tune. . . .

The lid of the middle barrel flies open and the PLAYER's head pops out.

PLAYER: Aha! All in the same boat, then! *(He climbs out. He goes round banging on the barrels.)* Everybody out!

Impossibly, the TRAGEDIANS climb out of the barrels. With their instruments, but not their cart. A few bundles. Except ALFRED. The PLAYER is cheerful.

(To ROS:)

Where are we?
ROS: Travelling.
PLAYER: Of course, we haven't got there yet.
ROS: Are we all right for England?
PLAYER: You look all right to me. I don't think they're very particular in England. Al-l-fred!

ALFRED emerges from the PLAYER's barrel.

GUIL: What are you doing here?
PLAYER: Travelling. *(To TRAGEDIANS:)* Right—blend into the background!

The TRAGEDIANS are in costume (from the mime): A King with crown, ALFRED as Queen, Poisoner and the two cloaked figures.

They blend.

(To GUIL:) Pleased to see us? *(Pause.)* You've come out of it very well, so far.
GUIL: And you?
PLAYER: In disfavour. Our play offended the King.
GUIL: Yes.
PLAYER: Well, he's a second husband himself. Tactless, really.
ROS: It was quite a good play nevertheless.
PLAYER: We never really got going—it was getting quite interesting when they stopped it.

Looks up at HAMLET.

That's the way to travel. . . .
GUIL: What were you doing in there?
PLAYER: Hiding. *(Indicating costumes.)* We had to run for it just as we were.

ROS: Stowaways.

PLAYER: Naturally—we didn't get paid, owing to circumstances ever so slightly beyond our control, and all the money we had we lost betting on certainties. Life is a gamble, at terrible odds—if it was a bet you wouldn't take it. Did you know that any number doubled is even?

ROS: Is it?

PLAYER: We learn something every day, to our cost. But we troupers just go on and on. Do you know what happens to old actors?

ROS: What?

PLAYER: Nothing. They're still acting. Surprised, then?

GUIL: What?

PLAYER: Surprised to see us?

GUIL: I knew it wasn't the end.

PLAYER: With practically everyone on his feet. What do you make of it, so far?

GUIL: We haven't got much to go on.

PLAYER: You speak to him?

ROS: It's possible.

GUIL: But it wouldn't make any difference.

ROS: But it's possible.

GUIL: Pointless.

ROS: It's allowed.

GUIL: Allowed, yes. We are not restricted. No boundaries have been defined, no inhibitions imposed. We have, for the while, secured, or blundered into, our release, for the while. Spontaneity and whim are the order of the day. Other wheels are turning but they are not our concern. We can breathe. We can relax. We can do what we like and say what we like to whomever we like, without restriction.

ROS: Within limits, of course.

GUIL: Certainly within limits.

HAMLET *comes down to footlights and regards the audience. The others watch but don't speak.* HAMLET *clears his throat noisily and spits into the audience. A split second later he claps his hand to his eye and wipes himself. He goes back upstage.*

ROS: A compulsion towards philosophical introspection is his chief characteristic, if I may put it like that. It does not mean he is mad. It does not mean he isn't. Very often, it does not mean anything at all. Which may or may not be a kind of madness.

GUIL: It really boils down to symptoms. Pregnant replies, mystic allusions, mistaken identities, arguing his father is his mother, that sort of thing; intimations of suicide, forgoing of exercise, loss of mirth, hints of claustrophobia not to say delusions of imprisonment; invocations of camels, chameleons, capons, whales, weasels, hawks, handsaws—riddles, quibbles and evasions; amnesia, paranoia, myopia; day-dreaming, hallucinations; stabbing his elders, abusing his parents, insulting his lover, and appearing hatless in public—knock-kneed, droop-stockinged and sighing like a love-sick schoolboy, which at his age is coming on a bit strong.

ROS: And talking to himself.

GUIL: And talking to himself.

ROS *and* GUIL *move apart together.*

Well, where has that got us?
ROS: He's the Player.
GUIL: His play offended the King—
ROS: —offended the King—
GUIL: —who orders his arrest—
ROS: —orders his arrest—
GUIL: —so he escapes to England—
ROS: On the boat to which he meets—
GUIL: Guildenstern and Rosencrantz taking Hamlet—
ROS: —who also offended the King—
GUIL: —and killed Polonius—
ROS: —offended the King in a variety of ways—
GUIL: —to England. *(Pause.)* That seems to be it.

ROS *jumps up.*

ROS: Incidents! All we get is incidents! Dear God, is it too much to expect a little sustained action?!

And on the word, the PIRATES *attack. That is to say: Noise and shouts and rushing about. "Pirates."*

Everyone visible goes frantic. HAMLET *draws his sword and rushes downstage.* GUIL, ROS *and* PLAYER *draw swords and rush upstage. Collision.* HAMLET *turns back up. They turn back down. Collision. By which time there is general panic right upstage. All four charge upstage with* ROS, GUIL *and* PLAYER *shouting:*

At last!
To arms!
Pirates!
Up there!
Down there!
To my sword's length!
Action!

All four reach the top, see something they don't like, waver, run for their lives downstage:

HAMLET, *in the lead, leaps into the left barrel.* PLAYER *leaps into the right barrel.* ROS *and* GUIL *leap into the middle barrel. All closing the lids after them.*

*The lights dim to nothing while the sound of fighting continues. The sound fades to nothing. The lights come up. The middle barrel (*ROS*'s and* GUIL*'s) is missing.*

The lid of the right-hand barrel is raised cautiously, the heads of ROS *and* GUIL *appear.*

*The lid of the other barrel (*HAMLET*'s) is raised. The head of the* PLAYER *appears.*

All catch sight of each other and slam down lids.

Pause.

Lids raised cautiously.

ROS *(relief):* They've gone. *(He starts to climb out.)* That was close. I've never thought quicker.

They are all three out of barrels. GUIL *is wary and nervous.* ROS *is light-headed. The* PLAYER *is phlegmatic. They note the missing barrel.*

ROS *looks round.*

ROS: Where's—?

The PLAYER *takes off his hat in mourning.*

PLAYER: Once more, alone—on our own resources.
GUIL *(worried):* What do you mean? Where is he?
PLAYER: Gone.
GUIL: Gone where?
PLAYER: Yes, we were dead lucky there. If that's the word I'm after.
ROS *(not a pick up):* Dead?
PLAYER: Lucky.
ROS *(he means):* Is he dead?
PLAYER: Who knows?
GUIL *(rattled):* He's not coming back?
PLAYER: Hardly.
ROS: He's dead then. He's dead as far as we're concerned.
PLAYER: Or we are as far as he is. *(He goes and sits on the floor to one side.)* Not too bad, is it?
GUIL *(rattled):* But he can't—we're supposed to be—we've got a *letter*—we're going to England with a letter for the King—
PLAYER: Yes, that much seems certain. I congratulate you on the unambiguity of your situation.
GUIL: But you don't understand—it contains—we've had our instructions—the whole thing's pointless without him.
PLAYER: Pirates could happen to anyone. Just deliver the letter. They'll send ambassadors from England to explain. . . .
GUIL *(worked up):* Can't you see—the pirates left us home and high—dry and home—drome— *(Furiously.)* The pirates left us high and dry!
PLAYER *(comforting):* There . . .
GUIL *(near tears):* Nothing will be resolved without him. . . .
PLAYER: There . . . !
GUIL: We need Hamlet for our release!
PLAYER: There!
GUIL: What are we supposed to do?
PLAYER: This.

He turns away, lies down if he likes. ROS *and* GUIL *apart.*

ROS: Saved again.
GUIL: Saved for what?

ROS sighs.

ROS: The sun's going down. *(Pause.)* It'll be night soon. *(Pause.)* If that's west. *(Pause.)* Unless we've—

GUIL *(shouts):* Shut up! I'm sick of it! Do you think conversation is going to help us now?

ROS *(hurt, desperately ingratiating):* I—I bet you all the money I've got the year of my birth doubled is an odd number.

GUIL *(moan):* No-o.

ROS: *Your* birth!

GUIL smashes him down.

GUIL *(broken):* We've travelled too far, and our momentum has taken over; we move idly towards eternity, without possibility of reprieve or hope of explanation.

ROS: Be happy—if you're not even *happy* what's so good about surviving? *(He picks himself up.)* We'll be all right. I suppose we just go on.

GUIL: Go where?

ROS: To England.

GUIL: England! *That's* a dead end. I never believed in it anyway.

ROS: All we've got to do is make our report and that'll be that. Surely.

GUIL: I don't *believe* it—a shore, a harbour, say—and we get off and we stop someone and say—Where's the King?—And he says, Oh, you follow that road there and take the first left and— *(Furiously.)* I don't believe any of it!

ROS: It doesn't sound very plausible.

GUIL: And even if we came face to face, what do we say?

ROS: We say—We've arrived!

GUIL *(kingly):* And who are you?

ROS: We are Guildenstern and Rosencrantz.

GUIL: Which is which?

ROS: Well, I'm—You're—

GUIL: What's it all about?—

ROS: Well, we were bringing Hamlet—but then some pirates—

GUIL: I don't begin to understand. Who are all these people, what's it got to do with me? You turn up out of the blue with some cock and bull story—

ROS *(with letter):* We have a letter—

GUIL *(snatches it, opens it):* A letter—yes—that's true. That's something . . . a letter . . . *(Reads.)* "As England is Denmark's faithful tributary . . . as love between them like the palm might flourish, etcetera . . . that on the knowing of this contents, without delay of any kind, should those bearers, Rosencrantz and Guildenstern, put to sudden death—"

He double-takes. ROS snatches the letter. GUIL snatches it back. ROS snatches it half back. They read it again and look up.

The PLAYER *gets to his feet and walks over to his barrel and kicks it and shouts into it.*

PLAYER: They've gone! It's all over!

One by one the PLAYERS *emerge, impossibly, from the barrel, and form a casually menacing circle round* ROS *and* GUIL, *who are still appalled and mesmerised.*

GUIL *(quietly):* Where we went wrong was getting on a boat. We can move, of course, change direction, rattle about, but our movement is contained within a larger one that carries us along as inexorably as the wind and current. . . .

ROS: They had it in for us, didn't they? Right from the beginning. Who'd have thought that we were so important?

GUIL: But why? Was it all for this? Who are we that so much should converge on our little deaths? *(In anguish to the* PLAYER:*)* Who are *we?*

PLAYER: You are Rosencrantz and Guildenstern. That's enough.

GUIL: No—it is not enough. To be told so little—to such an end—and still, finally, to be denied an explanation—

PLAYER: In our experience, most things end in death.

GUIL *(fear, vengeance, scorn):* Your experience!—*Actors!*

He snatches a dagger from the PLAYER*'s belt and holds the point at the* PLAYER*'s throat: the* PLAYER *backs and* GUIL *advances, speaking more quietly.*

I'm talking about death—and you've never experienced *that.* And you cannot *act* it. You die a thousand casual deaths—with none of that intensity which squeezes out life . . . and no blood runs cold anywhere. Because even as you die you know that you will come back in a different hat. But no one gets up after *death*—there is no applause—there is only silence and some second-hand clothes, and that's—*death*—

And he pushes the blade in up to the hilt. The PLAYER *stands with huge, terrible eyes, clutches at the wound as the blade withdraws: he makes small weeping sounds and falls to his knees, and then right down.*

While he is dying, GUIL, *nervous, high, almost hysterical, wheels on the* TRAGEDIANS—

If we have a destiny, then so had he—and if this is ours, then that was his—and if there are no explanations for us, then let there be none for him—

The TRAGEDIANS *watch the* PLAYER *die: they watch with some interest. The* PLAYER *finally lies still. A short moment of silence. Then the* TRAGEDIANS *start to applaud with genuine admiration. The* PLAYER *stands up, brushing himself down.*

PLAYER *(modestly):* Oh, come, come, gentlemen—no flattery—it was merely competent—

The TRAGEDIANS *are still congratulating him. The* PLAYER *approaches* GUIL, *who stands rooted, holding the dagger.*

PLAYER: What did you think? *(Pause.)* You see, it *is* the kind they do believe in—it's what is expected.

He holds his hand out for the dagger. GUIL *slowly puts the point of the dagger on to the* PLAYER'S *hand, and pushes . . . the blade slides back into the handle. The* PLAYER *smiles, reclaims the dagger.*

For a moment you thought I'd—cheated.

ROS *relieves his own tension with loud nervy laughter.*

ROS: Oh, very good! *Very* good! Took me in completely—didn't he take you in completely— *(claps his hands).* Encore! Encore!

PLAYER *(activated, arms spread, the professional):* Deaths for all ages and occasions! Deaths by suspension, convulsion, consumption, incision, execution, asphyxiation and malnutrition—! Climactic carnage, by poison and by steel—! Double deaths by duel—! Show!—

ALFRED, *still in his Queen's costume, dies by poison: the* PLAYER, *with rapier, kills the* "KING" *and duels with a fourth* TRAGEDIAN, *inflicting and receiving a wound. The two remaining* TRAGEDIANS, *the two* "SPIES" *dressed in the same coats as* ROS *and* GUIL, *are stabbed, as before. And the light is fading over the deaths which take place right upstage.*

(Dying amid the dying—tragically; romantically.) So there's an end to that—it's commonplace: light goes with life, and in the winter of your years the dark comes early. . . .

GUIL *(tired, drained, but still an edge of impatience; over the mime):* No . . . no . . . not for *us*, not like that. Dying is not romantic, and death is not a game which will soon be over . . . Death is not anything . . . death is not . . . It's the absence of presence, nothing more . . . the endless time of never coming back . . . a gap you can't see, and when the wind blows through it, it makes no sound. . . .

The light has gone upstage. Only GUIL *and* ROS *are visible as* ROS'S *clapping falters to silence.*

Small pause.

ROS: That's it, then, is it?

No answer. He looks out front.

The sun's going down. Or the earth's coming up, as the fashionable theory has it.

Small pause.

Not that it makes any difference.

Pause.

What was it all about? When did it begin?

Pause. No answer.

Couldn't we just stay put? I mean no one is going to come on and drag us off. . . . They'll just have to wait. We're still young . . . fit . . . we've got years. . . .

Pause. No answer.

(A cry.) We've done nothing wrong! We didn't harm anyone. Did we?

GUIL: I can't remember.

ROS pulls himself together.

ROS: All right, then. I don't care. I've had enough. To tell you the truth, I'm relieved.

And he disappears from view. GUIL does not notice.

GUIL: Our names shouted in a certain dawn . . . a message . . . a summons . . . There must have been a moment, at the beginning, where we could have said—no. But somehow we missed it. *(He looks round and sees he is alone.)*

Rosen—?
Guil—?

He gathers himself.

Well, we'll know better next time. Now you see me, now you — *(and disappears).*

Immediately the whole stage is lit up, revealing, upstage, arranged in the approximate positions last held by the dead TRAGEDIANS, the tableau of court and corpses which is the last scene of Hamlet.

That is: The KING, QUEEN, LAERTES and HAMLET all dead. HORATIO holds HAMLET. FORTINBRAS is there.

So are two AMBASSADORS from England.

AMBASSADOR: The sight is dismal;
and our affairs from England come too late.
The ears are senseless that should give us hearing
to tell him his commandment is fulfilled,
that Rosencrantz and Guildenstern are dead.
Where should we have our thanks?

HORATIO: Not from his mouth,
had it the ability of life to thank you:
He never gave commandment for their death.
But since, so jump upon this bloody question,
you from the Polack wars, and you from England,
are here arrived, give order that these bodies
high on a stage be placed to the view;
and let me speak to the yet unknowing world

how these things came about: so shall you hear
of carnal, bloody and unnatural acts,
of accidental judgments, casual slaughters,
of deaths put on by cunning and forced cause,
and, in this upshot, purposes mistook
fallen on the inventors' heads: all this can I
truly deliver.

But during the above speech, the play fades out, overtaken by dark and music.

JACK RICHARDSON

(1935–)

Gallows Humor

About the Author: Jack Richardson, born in 1935 in New York City, graduated Phi Beta Kappa from Columbia University before going to the University of Munich for graduate work. His *The Prodigal* won the Vernon Rice Award and an Obie in 1960. He followed this in the next year with a second highly acclaimed play, *Gallows Humor,* but then, after three plays in a row received less notice, he stopped writing for the theater and turned critic.

About the Play: There are two parts to *Gallows Humor,* the first featuring a condemned man in his cell and the second, his executioner in his kitchen. The two situations seem opposites of each other, and both seem extreme, outside the realm of our normal experience. The conversational references, however, are very commonplace, the stuff of our normal lives. And in both parts, the same key issues seem to be discussed: essentially, the conflict between a normal human aspiration for excitement, for feeling *alive,* and a normal human desire for the comfort of routine and habit.

This play presents its major issues in a way which pares drama down to its essentials. It presents its subject with unusual simplicity and directness. The focus of these two situations is concentrated by using uncomplicated, almost symbolic sets, representing the extremes of social situations: a prison cell and a private home. In addition, in each part there are only three characters, each of whom speaks his or her mind clearly. There are no distractions. We cannot miss the absurd inappropriateness of placing these common issues in unexpected and uncommon places. The man condemned for a crime of passion is moral, peaceful, clean. He has a work ethic. He believes in law and order. He is confronted by the morality of society in the person of a prostitute. In Part Two, the executioner is a completely routinized man who wishes he weren't. This socially sanctioned killer is the most timid of men. His wife takes her stand on the side of comfort, habit, and respectability, yet dominates him. Much of the genius of the play is in these stark yet unexpcted combinations, and in the relations between the two parts.

CHARACTERS

THE WARDEN
LUCY
WALTER

PART ONE

The lights come up upon a prison cell. There is a small washbasin to the right, and, standing close against the center wall, there is a razor-thin cot. Above the monkish bed is the room's sole window, barred into sections, through which one can see that it is night outside. At the room's left is the cell door, and behind it the beginning of an outside corridor. In this passageway, looking into the cell, stand a man and woman. Next to them, on a little portable tray, is a large platter decked with silver Queen Anne cover dishes, sauceboats, etc. The man, comfortably stout, seems expansively contented with himself. He is smiling broadly. The woman, attired in a bright yellow blouse and tight black skirt, has a thin face of angle and bone which is well covered with cosmetics. Her age is indeterminate, and she is beautiful in the way a carnival mask is so.

They are looking at Walter, who is sitting on the cell's cot. He has the jacket of his prison suit in his lap and is attending to it with needle and thread. Caught in his undershirt, he seems very pale and fragile. His face is unremarkably inoffensive, and covered with the scribbling of a fifty-year-old life. As he sews, he hums to himself.

After several seconds, the man, the Warden, and the woman, Lucy, begin to speak.

WARDEN There he is, Lucy. Let's hope this one doesn't prove too difficult for you.

LUCY Now what could someone who looks like that do to be hanged?

WARDEN *(chuckling).* He beat his wife to death with a golf club—forty-one strokes from the temple to the chin.

At this point Walter's humming rises a bit in pitch and volume.

LUCY What a nice smile he has, and how thin his arms are. They're not tattooed either.

WARDEN *(smiling, but a bit impatient).* Now, Lucy, it's romantic notions like that that get you into trouble. If you start thinking of murderers as upper-middle-class types you'll be more successful at your work.

LUCY *(indignant).* I haven't done too bad up till now. There aren't many women, even in the trade, that can take a man's mind off your gallows when he's got less than two hours to go.

WARDEN *(in an apologetic tone).* Oh, you're a professional, all right; they just don't cut them like you any more. But sometimes I wonder if you weren't better suited to those naughty houses stuffed with incense, beaded curtains, and overhead mirrors. Maybe you're just not up to making love surrounded by four gray walls.

LUCY Listen, Warden, I've had my victories in here too.

WARDEN Yes, but the state's gone to a great deal of trouble bringing your ladies up here to serve as little humanizing morsels for those it's going to hang. Your whole purpose is to make these poor fellows' last hours so heady, so full of pleasure that they just float up those stairs and smile into the dull, commonplace face of our hangman. Making love to you, Lucy, is supposed to accomplish this. And yet the last two you handed over to us behaved abominably: they shuffled by those sentimental journalists looking as if they were already dead. You know what the press can do with that; and then all our good intentions are forgotten.

LUCY I couldn't get near those two. They just weren't interested.

WARDEN *(in a slightly threatening tone).* It's your job to make them interested, Lucy.

LUCY Now what could I do? One was over seventy, after all, and the other told me he hadn't made love to anything since he saw his cat's hysterectomy scars.

WARDEN You were picked for this official work because you seemed to have experience with difficult types. Remember where you were when we found you? Standing in a doorway with a scraggly piece of fur around your neck and runs in your stockings. Even in the city's poorest section you weren't turning customers away, were you? And if you had to go back to it . . .

LUCY All right, Warden, you've made your point.

WARDEN Just a little warning, Lucy. You know how I'd hate to fire you.

LUCY All right, all right. Now, is there anything I should know about our man in there?

WARDEN Oh, you should really find him easy to deal with. He's been most cooperative since being with us: never cried when appeals were turned down, never spat his food back at the guards, never used the walls for thumbnosing little phrases at the world—no, he's been a perfect sort up till now.

LUCY Good, I don't like those who have an axe to grind. They never stop talking long enough for anything to really get going between us.

WARDEN Well, Walter there's one of the better sort, all right, that's why you were assigned to him. You used to do so well with educated types. I remembered that physicist you went after a few years ago—for six months he moped about his cell, mumbling to himself. But after you were through with him he died happily explaining the theory of subatomic particles to our executioner. You'd turned a homicidal maniac back into a useful man.

LUCY I just got his mind back on fundamentals. That seems to pep his type up.

WARDEN Well, that's what I want you to do for Walter. *(Tapping one of the cover dishes.)* I had our chef up all night working on the fried chicken in here, but I hope he'll enjoy you even more. I sort of like this one and want him to have a little fling before he's hanged.

LUCY *(flatly).* Oh, you have a big heart under that forty-dollar suit, Warden.

WARDEN Why, thank you, Lucy. Sometimes I think it goes unnoticed.

LUCY Now, shall I get to work?

WARDEN All right, we might as well start the introductions. Ah, would you wheel his dinner in to him? I think the silver trays will set you off to advantage.

The Warden extracts a key, opens the cell door, and he and Lucy enter. Walter, his sewing in his hands, jumps up abruptly to meet them. He then follows Lucy with his eyes as, smiling, she wheels the tray past him into the lower left corner of the cell.

Hello, Walter, how's it going today?

WALTER *(still trying to keep an eye on Lucy who, after leaving the tray, begins walking about the cell, tapping at the walls and poking at the cot).* Warden, nice of you to come by. Is it time already?

WARDEN Heavens, no; you still have nearly two hours. Some insects, I'm told, live an entire life through in less time—birth, copulation, and death, all counted off in seconds.

WALTER *(pleasantly, but still with an eye on Lucy who is beginning to prop up the pillow on his cot).* That sounds like a very nice arrangement.

WARDEN Right! After all, who needs years but those who have to repeat themselves?

LUCY *(stepping back from the cot and examining it).* You're talking on my time, Warden.

WARDEN Quite so, Lucy, quite so. Walter, I'd like you to meet Lucy. She's going to stay here with you until the end—compliments of the state.

WALTER With me? But I don't understand.

WARDEN No effusions of gratitude, Walter. No man should eat his last meal without a little female company.

WALTER Do you mean she's to—to . . . ?

WARDEN *(nodding).* It's an innovation in our penal program. Takes some of the sting out of anticapital punishment arguments. Sending a man out to die with a Lucy still fresh in every part of him—well, nothing cold-blooded about that, is there? Everything else about the little ceremony is, I'll admit, rather cut and dried, a bit too much so, even for my taste. That's what puts people off about it. The clack of the guard's shoes in cadence over those cobblestones, the same number of steps to be climbed, the ritual last trite phrases—no, there's not much spice in it any more. But with this new little prologue we've added—well, it seems to keep the others like you, Walter, from being swallowed up in formality. There's something touchingly human about the whole affair when Lucy and her kind deliver you back to our official hands.

LUCY *(walking back to the tray of food, she opens a cover dish).* And it keeps girls like me off the street. Hmm! This will get cold if you don't start on it, Walter.

WALTER Oh, I'm not really hungry.

WARDEN But that's fried chicken in there. With a heavy crust.

WALTER I know I ordered it, but you won't mind if I just don't begin right away.

LUCY Well, you've no complaints if I have a leg then, do you? Being up this early in the morning always gives me an *(She says the word with a seductive smile at Walter.)* appetite.

WALTER No, no; go right ahead.

WARDEN *(watching Lucy as she takes a large bite).* Look at her go after that chicken, Walter. How many men would love to be in that piece of meat's place. And you're going to get the chance.

WALTER Well, that's very nice, and I'm grateful to both of you; but I really don't . . .

WARDEN Come now, Walter, no protests. Lucy there brings a little unpremeditated dash into the dull cubes and well-scrubbed-down corridors of our prison. You've been here so long I'll bet you've forgotten what a woman like Lucy, wrapped snugly in a yellow blouse and black skirt, can mean.

WALTER *(backing away and waving his hand in protest).* Oh, no, I haven't.

LUCY *(taking a few tentative dance steps).* Do you know, it's a pity you can't have music piped in here. It would be nice to dance a bit before settling down to work, wouldn't it, Walter?

WALTER I can't dance, really.

WARDEN Well, then, she could teach you. After all, there's always time to learn something new. But now, now that a festive note's been struck in the cell, I guess I'm what they call *de trop.* Well, now, enjoy each other. *(Pointing a preceptorial finger at Walter.)* I want to see a contented face, Walter, when I return.

WALTER Doesn't it seem contented now?

WARDEN *(studying Walter's face).* It seems a little pinched and furrowed to me. Not the way one looks when Lucy's through with him.

WALTER I can smile a bit if you want.

WARDEN Save all that for the lady there. *(Stepping back and looking at the two of them.)* Ah,

actually you make a fine-looking couple together. You know, it's moments like this that make a welfare state seem worth while after all.

The Warden leaves.

LUCY *(throwing the chicken bone over her shoulder onto the floor).* God! I'd starve if he had to pimp for me.

WALTER *(quickly going over and retrieving the bone and putting it back on the tray).* Please, I'm trying to leave a tidy cell behind me.

LUCY Well, sorry!

WALTER I don't mean to be rude, but you'd be surprised how hard it is keeping a little place like this in order.

LUCY *(a little confused).* You give it a scrubbing once a day?

WALTER Yes, but that won't do it. Every time a guard comes in here, some of the lint from his uniform stays behind. *(Tracing the descent of an imaginary piece of lint with his finger.)* You can see it floating down from a sleeve or a lapel, but once it hits the gray floor it's the devil to find.

LUCY *(looking down at where Walter's finger last traced the lint).* I can see it could be a problem.

WALTER But please don't let me stop you from finishing the chicken if you want to. Just be careful the crust doesn't splatter.

LUCY But that's *your* last meal, after all, Walter.

WALTER Oh, I'm afraid I ordered that in a fit of absence of mind. Fried foods raise the deuce with my stomach.

LUCY Begins to ache?

WALTER No, just snarl. It lasts for days, and, in company, believe me, it can be very embarrassing.

LUCY *(after a pause in which she watches Walter continue his sewing).* Well, then, if no food, how about a cigarette before we begin?

WALTER No, thank you. And if you're going to, be careful of the ashes. There's a little can underneath the sink you can use.

LUCY *(returning the cigarettes to her dress pocket, she turns away from Walter).* Jesus! *(Hunching her shoulders, she shivers and takes a few halting dance steps.)* You've got to keep moving to stay warm in here.

WALTER That blouse you're wearing must be very thin.

LUCY *(brightening).* Well, finally noticing that there's a woman in here with you?

WALTER *(dropping his eyes back to the sewing).* Tell me, do you really do this sort of work often for the prison?

LUCY I've signed a five-year contract. And, as I'm not getting any younger, it's turned out to be a pretty good arrangement. In the last year, though, I've been kept a little too busy. It must have been the moon phases or something, but it seems as if everybody was cementing mothers up in the basement, shooting politicians, or setting fire to their friends. I hope things begin to calm down a bit now.

WALTER But isn't it dangerous to come into a confined place with men who are going to be hanged in a matter of hours?

LUCY *(as she sits next to Walter on the cot).* No more dangerous than the streets in the summer season. I'll take a cell with a man in it who's butchered an even dozen five-year-olds to a boulevard stuffed with tourists waving credit cards in one hand and pinching with

the other. No, by the time a man reaches this cell, Walter, the violence he had in him has wasted away. It's been used up on his victim, the judge, his childhood, his shoes, and God knows what else. There's nothing but the lamb left when I arrive.

WALTER The lamb?

LUCY I don't mean that in a bad sense now. It's just that, for a woman who doesn't like to be treated roughly, I find men who use this cell have very gentle hands.

WALTER *(looking at his hands).* Mine are a bit rough from all the floor scrubbing I've done. Prison soap isn't the best.

LUCY *(taking his hands).* They look as soft as cats' paws to me.

WALTER *(pulling his hands away, he inches back from Lucy and takes a big stitch in his sewing).* You must excuse me, but I have to finish this little job of mending.

LUCY I never thought I'd have to compete with a needle and thread, Walter.

WALTER My number-patch was loose. I was afraid it might fall off during the—well, ceremonies.

LUCY Your number-patch?

WALTER *(defensively).* It's very important that this number stays on me. This is how I'm identified in I don't know how many files and on dozens of official cards. 43556 is the key to my ending life on the proper line in the ledger, and I've grown quite fond of it.

LUCY *(humoring Walter).* 43556—it has a nice ring to it. Better than a number packed with a lot of zeros.

WALTER Well, actually, I would have preferred one with all even numbers, but it would have seemed fussy, I suppose, to insist on it.

LUCY *(moving closer to Walter and beginning to stroke his neck).* Well, now, why don't you put your sewing away and let me show you why the prison officials chose me out of over a thousand applicants for my job.

WALTER *(jumping up from the cot).* Oh, no, Lucy, that's quite out of the question.

LUCY *(just a slight touch of impatience showing).* Now listen, Walter . . .

WALTER Oh, it's certainly nothing personal. *(Staring firmly at Lucy.)* You do make that blouse and skirt seem wrapped around perfect treasures, and your skin is beautifully pale and, I'm sure, exciting to stroke for hours, even with my rather insensitive hands. *(Pulling himself together.)* But, no, I just don't wish to.

LUCY *(smoothing out her blouse).* Well, from the description, there isn't any doubt that you at least like women.

WALTER Oh I do; or, rather, I did. But that's all over now.

LUCY *(getting up and moving toward Walter).* But it doesn't have to be over. There's still a little time left. You probably have a miniature gallows dancing in front of your eyes, and you think it's numbed those important little nerves for good. But, believe me, Lucy can start them twitching again. I've done it for dozens of others far more upset about dying than you seem to be.

WALTER *(backing away from her).* But I don't want them to start twitching now.

LUCY After they begin, then you'll want, Walter.

WALTER No, no; I just want to remain peaceful.

LUCY Peaceful? How can you use that word, when, in not too much more than an hour, you'll drag yourself up those thirteen steps?

WALTER *(backed against the cell's left wall, he clutches his jacket, thread and needle in front of him).* You couldn't understand, Lucy. Being peaceful would just bore you.

LUCY Nothing bores me, Walter. That's why I'm a success in my business.

WALTER Please! Stay back a bit. I can hear you breathing.

LUCY It's a nice sound, isn't it? My lungs, in fact all the machinery inside me, Walter, work perfectly.

WALTER I'm sure; but I don't want to listen to their sounds. One of the advantages of a cell is its quiet. I've grown used to silence.

LUCY *(rubbing his arm and speaking in a coaxing voice).* But my reputation's at stake, Walter. One failure leaves a permanent mark on one in my profession. I'd have to take to deeper layers of rouge, longer eyelashes, and darker stockings. My fur coat would need more padding at the shoulders and the heels on my shoes would be raised an inch at the very least. You wouldn't want to cause that, would you, Walter? You wouldn't want to start Lucy off looking for wigs and stronger perfumes?

WALTER *(pleading).* The scent you're wearing is making me dizzy enough as it is.

LUCY There, you see, those nerves aren't dead. They're coming back to us after all.

WALTER *(trying, but not succeeding, to remove her hand).* Please, I'm just 43556; you can't expect a number to make love.

LUCY *(tripping her finger across his chest).* I'm not touching a number now, am I? No, this is the body of a man. A little out of condition, maybe, from being closed up in a cell for months, but it still reacts to my fingers, doesn't it?

WALTER *(as though suffering, he looks down at Lucy's bosom).* Oh, I've always been partial to women of your build, with your hair; and underneath that powder, I can see freckles. For me, freckles were always an irresistible aphrodisiac.

LUCY Well, those freckles, my fingers, everything's yours, Walter. Just forget where you are, and think of trombones, bourbon bottles, and streetcars crowded with wet people starting off on a Saturday night.

WALTER *(rigid, with his eyes closed).* People forgetting who, what, or where they've been. All getting into new skins, expressions, and troubles. But wanting to laugh through it all.

LUCY That's it, Walter. Laughing when you slip on the dance floor, find your socks don't match or that you can't make love more than twice a night.

WALTER *(now happily, but painfully, reminiscing).* And the Chinese restaurants you mistake for your house and the hands, often with gloves on them, you grab hold of.

LUCY *(whispering in Walter's ear).* And now stop talking, Walter, and let's . . .

WALTER *(sticking her in the back with his needle).* No! Get away from me. *(He breaks loose and moves to the center of the cell.)*

LUCY *(with a loud yell).* Why, you crazy—That was a sharp needle you stuck in me!

WALTER *(keeping the needle poised for attack).* And I'll do it again if you come after me. This is my cell—ten paces wide, twenty long. Nothing, absolutely nothing unexpected happens here.

LUCY *(feeling the wounded spot on her back).* God, I think I'm bleeding.

WALTER Oh, no; no blood, please. I've seen all the blood I ever want to see.

LUCY Then you shouldn't go about sticking people with needles or hitting them with golf clubs.

WALTER You know about that?

LUCY *(somewhat abstracted as she rubs her wound and examines her hand).* It's written right across your forehead. *(Examining and rubbing her fingers together.)* Well, I'm not bleeding after all.

WALTER I'm grateful for that at least. I'm afraid I just lost my head for a moment. I felt myself

slipping back into everything this cell protects me from, and I . . . Are you angry with me, Lucy?

LUCY *(dismissing the incident).* Oh, I've had worse done to me by clients with sort of Victorian tastes in love. But you *have* disappointed me, Walter. I thought we'd strike it off right away.

WALTER Oh, you wouldn't have found me much good anyway. My wife used to make me take pills . . .

LUCY For God's sake, no talk about the wife, especially one whose skull you split open. It's professionally insulting after being stuck with your needle.

WALTER Well, I just thought to pass the time . . .

LUCY Clients talk about their wives *after* making love. *(As if pondering a new discovery.)* Wives and postcoital depression seem to go together. *(Now back to lecturing Walter on his brothel manners.)* But before, it's themselves they take apart and it's our job to put them back together again.

WALTER Well, all my pieces are in their proper place and I don't want them disarranged.

LUCY *(sweetly).* No one wants to do that, Walter. Perhaps I did rush you a little bit; but, after all, you're the one counting the minutes and I thought you'd want them stuffed with all the things your clean little cell's been lacking.

WALTER I'd already planned how to use every second of them before you arrived: there was the number-patch to be sewn on, shoes to be polished, a final stroll four times around the cell, and then I was going to wash, which, because of the soap's poor quality, would most likely have taken me up to the time the warden and his guards came for me.

LUCY Well, it *is* asking a lot wanting you to give up all those wild plans for me.

WALTER *(nodding in agreement).* I'll already have to pass up the shoes.

LUCY Well, give up two of your laps around the room and talk a little about yourself. At least let me show you how well I've been trained as a sympathetic listener.

WALTER Why, there's nothing much to say about me.

LUCY *(coaxingly).* Oh, come on; start off with the kind of job you used to have.

WALTER Well, I was a moderately successful lawyer.

LUCY *(laughing).* A lawyer?

WALTER *(a little anxiously).* Why are you laughing?

LUCY Well, being here—that doesn't say much for your ability to sway juries, does it?

WALTER *(testily).* I didn't defend myself; and, besides, I was irrefutably guilty.

LUCY I thought it was always easier to win defending a guilty man than an innocent one.

WALTER *(slightly outraged at this).* Now, you see, it's just that sort of over-the-shoulder attitude that's turned our laws into a fool's game today.

LUCY You mean like the city ordinance against soliciting on the streets? I've always thought that one was woolly-headed.

WALTER *(wagging his head impatiently).* I'm not talking about your particular likes and dislikes, Lucy. It's the nature of the law that's been abused.

LUCY The jails seem full enough to me.

WALTER *(growing a little more excited).* No, no; laws are supposed to be as solid and immovable as these walls. At least that's what I thought when I began studying them. They weren't supposed to depend upon the judge's sinus condition, a lady juror's two Caesareans, or poor air conditioning in the courtroom. They were to be hermetically sealed—untouched by human hands.

LUCY Calm down a bit, Walter.

WALTER *(now waving his arms)*. But don't you see they weren't? They were worthless little hide-and-seek rules made up to give the neighborhood's poor children something to do in the evenings. No god had bellowed them out or burned them into a mountain.

LUCY Be careful you don't stick yourself with the needle.

WALTER *(now quite intense)*. Oh, listen to me, Lucy. Can you understand what it meant to a man devoted to the law to find out it was all one big caprice? It was as if you looked up suddenly at a night sky and saw every planet and star dancing drunkenly about.

LUCY *(smiling invitingly)*. That might be exciting, Walter. And sometimes, making love out of doors, when the weather permitted, I think I did see the stars wiggle a bit.

WALTER *(angry at Lucy's* non sequitur*)*. Wiggle, do they? Well, that's not going to happen here! Not in this cell. *(He jumps up on the cot and points to the barred window.)* Look through this window, Lucy. See how the sky's sectioned into nine perfect squares? On a clear night each square contains exactly five stars and the center one has a planet all to itself.

LUCY A planet? Which one?

WALTER A sexless one; far from the sun, always cold, but giving off a dull, dependable light. *(Patting the bars.)* No, these little bars are particular about what they let into their boundaries.

LUCY *(temporarily defeated)*. All right, let's skip love for a while.

WALTER *(somewhat calmer, he comes down from the cot)*. The law had most of my love. I believed all one had to do was match little scraps of fact against those fine, heavily punctuated sentences in the books and, like a candy machine, the right answer would come out neatly wrapped. Oh, you don't know how snugly I fitted into everything then. With those laws standing firm, all their lesser relatives, from chemistry formulas to table manners, seemed impregnable. In those days I knew exactly what to pray for, how often a month I should have sex (four times, only with my wife), and how stern I should be when my children spilled their soup. I knew who was the villain and who the virgin on the stage; I knew my laundry would come back on time without a piece missing; and I knew that every mirror would reflect at me a recognizable, satisfied face that had aged just the right amount since last being seen. Oh, Lucy, everything from constellation to subways seemed to be moving at my rhythm. And then . . . then . . .

LUCY And then?

WALTER *(bitterly)*. And then came the Gogarty trial.

LUCY A trial for murder?

WALTER *(beginning wistfully, then gradually growing more involved)*. No, a suit for damages. Mrs. Ellen Gogarty versus The Municipal Bus Company—that was its official title. The woman's son, age thirty-five, had been run over and completely mashed by one of their vehicles. The light had been with him, and the bus driver, by eyewitness account, had been drunk and singing "Little Alice Bottom" when the accident took place. I was whistling the same tune when, these bits of evidence snapped inside my brief case, I arrived at the courthouse on a morning that seemed no different from a thousand others. I even remember exchanging a joke with one of the guards and making a date with the opposing attorney, who was putting up only a token defense, for dinner that evening. Then the trial began: the judge smiled at me, the jury nodded in solemn agreement as I turned phrases and probed witnesses. With every second our case was strengthened, and, throughout the examinations, Mrs. Gogarty, wearing a new but inexpensive summer hat and asking only to be recompensed for the loss of her only son, sat soaking up sympathetic stares from everyone in the court. The case, as they say, was open and shut. Open and shut.

LUCY *(who has been sitting on the cot, listening intently).* And what happened?

WALTER *(now incensed over the memory).* Hiccups! Hiccups! Just before the jury was about to file out, Mrs. Gogarty began to hiccup. Oh, at first, it was hardly noticeable; but then they became louder and more frequent. I waved a warning finger at her to be silent, but she blinked back that she couldn't help herself; and while the jury stood stunned in their places, the gulping sounds went on jerking her frail little body this way and that. Finally, they actually came to be syncopated—two short, one long; one long, three short; two long. *(He puts his hands to his ears.)* And with the occasional change in pitch there was almost a little tune coming out of her. Sometimes I can still hear it, sounding like a street calliope; and then comes the laughter: first from the spectators in the court, then from the members of the jury, and, finally, from the judge himself. I try to speak, to read a few apposite remarks on courtroom behavior from the law book on my desk, but I'm literally drowned out with laughter. And through it all, like some devilish timpani in an orchestra, Mrs. Gogarty's hiccups, keeping up their erratic beat and brutal melody— *(He raises and drops his voice so the outline of a tune can be heard.)* One long, one short; two long, one short . . . *(Here he pauses and collects himself.)* Snorting, slapping each other's backs and nudging one another's ribs, the jury files out of the room. The wait is a very short one, and from behind the jury-chamber door come the sounds of still more snickers with an occasional imitation of my client's disorder. Finally, as if they'd been off on a party—collars open, ties askew, hair undone—the men and women who are to decide our case return and, while Mrs. Gogarty goes on with those loud little spasms, they announce a verdict against her. I can't believe it and, throwing protocol to the winds, ask why. "How can she be suffering grief worth any compensation at all when she hiccups?" so says the jury foreman. "Madness," I answer and turn to the judge. "My good sir," he says, chuckling like an idiot, "she really did hiccup out a little tune." "The law!" I cry. "Hiccups!" he answers, and the laughter starts all around again. *(Slowly now, as if looking in the narration of simple fact for a solution.)* I went to the governor himself, Lucy. I showed him there was nothing in the pertinent judicial paragraphs about this involuntary closure of the glottis and the noise produced therefrom, and *he* answered that those paragraphs were to be amended to include the peculiar Gogarty phenomenon. I knew then that it was all over, and that a sneeze, hiccup, or crooked nose could twist those impressive sentences into gibberish.

There is silence for a moment, and then Lucy rises from the cot and makes an attempt at consolation.

LUCY Maybe it's better that way. After all, that's what makes a day interesting. It's the little unexpected matters of taste, like a man going wild over a mole on your chin, that keeps the beauty contest also-rans like me in business.

WALTER *(sadly).* I knew you'd think that, Lucy; but, for me, Mrs. Gogarty's hiccups were the end of everything. I no longer knew what clubs to join, what tie to choose, what toothpaste to use, what church to go to. At home, where I always thought things went smoothly and orderly, I suddenly found my children snipping off our dog's tail an inch a day with a pair of scissors, writing obscene couplets on my shirt collars, biting my leg whenever I passed by, and singing marching songs from the War of 1812. And my wife's birthmark, a little red triangle that had always been tucked inconspicuously behind her left ear, began turning up in the center of her forehead, in the middle of her stomach, and on the soles of her feet . . .

LUCY *(now a little impatient with him).* Are we going back to the wife again?

WALTER *(growing excited again).* My life was formless, a tiny piece of chaos. What was left to me that couldn't be hiccuped out of existence? Right and left, buy and sell, love and hate—these now meant nothing to me. I found myself on the wrong trains, in the wrong beds, with the wrong people. And my neighborhood, my neighborhood that I had helped zone to perfection, became a carnival of the lowest sort, and my neighbors, whom I knew inside and out, danced about beneath layer on layer of holiday masks until I couldn't tell one from the other. And then, God knows when or where it happened, I found a mirror sending back at me a face that I had never seen before—a face with wild eyes, bristling hair, and a heavy growth of stubble—a face I would have crossed the street to avoid had I seen it coming at me in happier times. Oh, I'd been cheated, Lucy, and gradually I began to grow angry—mad, in fact—until one morning, with everything spinning about me in complete disorder, I struck back. My poor wife happened to be closest at hand, and for all I know I might have thought I was on the golf course until I felt the club make contact with her skull. I remember it sounding as if it were a good shot, and then I looked up to follow the ball's flight and found . . .

LUCY That's enough, Walter! I'm beginning to shiver.

WALTER *(recalled from his memories).* But now comes the pleasant part.

LUCY *(shaking her head as if to clear it).* No, for me, the goodies in your story are over.

WALTER No, no; don't you see? The law came back to me. Everything began falling in line again. I have my number, a room that never changes, meals that arrive punctually to the moment, and guards whose manners are perfectly predictable. *(With weak joy.)* The world has boundaries again and I know my place in it.

LUCY *(almost threateningly).* In one hour your place will be at the end of a rope.

WALTER *(with military stiffness).* But my death will take place according to a rigid schedule and then be *officially* recorded. What more could I want?

LUCY *(with desperate hope).* A little sex?

WALTER *(vexed at this).* Good God! have you understood nothing? That belongs to the dizziness on the other side of those walls. Here, in my prison, the laws hold, and I won't have them disturbed by perfume and overpowdered flesh.

LUCY *(now angry).* Oh, won't you? Do you know, if they came in this minute with a rope ready, it'd be my overpowdered flesh they'd hang? Yes, they'd be looking for something live to string up, Walter, and you certainly don't pass the test.

WALTER I know what being alive means to you.

LUCY *(beginning to unwrap the belt from around her waist).* Oh, between Mrs. Gogarty's lost case and your wife's murder you had a taste of it, all right; but it frightened you right into this cell.

WALTER *(showing apprehension).* What on earth are you doing? You're not going to undress? I promise you it won't do any good.

LUCY I'm not understanding you, Walter. And, as a client, you have a right to that from me. I'm going to try to shorten the distance between us. *(She steps upon the cot, loops one end of the belt, and fastens the other to one of the bars across the window.)*

WALTER You'll leave footprints on the pillow!

LUCY You won't be using it again, Walter. I just want to see how it'd feel with a noose around my neck. Who knows? Maybe you're right; maybe the only thing I'd worry about is that they got my name and number right on the morgue card. *(She slips the belt over her head.)* There, it's in place; the hangman's taken his hands from my shoulders, the sack's dropped over my eyes; my shoes, just polished, are shining in the morning light . . .

WALTER Stop it! Stop it! You're just pretending anyway.

LUCY *(in the tones of a spoiled little girl).* I'm in a cell with a murderer. How do I know you won't push the cot out from under me?

WALTER I might do just that.

LUCY *(with her eyes shut and her head tilted back).* I will drop down, happy that the sky I leave behind has nice equal sections, each with so many numbers of stars. I'll be content that my dying has an alphabetical standing, that my last meal came to me on time, that my cell is immaculate, that the prison day which I'll never see will be like all the others I've lived through, and that I didn't sweat, sing, throw up, or make love to a woman. So then, let the trap doors fly open underneath me. With no regrets about this life, I'll die happily. *(Pause.)* The hell I will!

WALTER *(walking up to cot and threatening to kick one of its legs).* If you don't come down, I swear I'll kick the cot out from under you, Lucy.

LUCY *(removing the belt from around her neck).* You bet I'll come down. Dying with your point of view really makes me sick to my stomach. *(She steps down and walks as far away from Walter as the confines of the cell permit.)*

WALTER *(somewhat meek and apologetic).* I'm not trying to convert you to anything, after all.

LUCY No, you're not. You're too happy curled up in your little womb to want company.

WALTER Please, no coarse talk, Lucy.

LUCY Oh, of course not. You'd like to have a conversation in algebra equations, I'll bet. Well, I'm not going to let you get away with it.

WALTER *(puzzled and on the defensive).* Why are you attacking me?

LUCY Because you remind me of a *happy* "still-life" whore, Walter. Do you know what that is? It's the last step for all of us in this business. When even the streets won't have you and you've lost your nerve for the river, then it's a twenty-four-hour-in-bed house for you. You don't own anything to wear except a grease-stained kimono the madam gives you; there's no make-up on the little table next to you, no mirror, the room's always dark, and the only sounds are the footsteps in the corridor that shuffle, with sometimes just a little hesitation, past your door that's been locked from the outside. You just lie there, Walter, waiting for the lock to click open, letting another client in at you. Oh, and there's no worry about these men like there is when you're on your own. You don't fret over whether or not he's a handsome one or if he can pay up or not. You don't have to worry about his whims or his cracking you on the jaw or his inflamed genital tract. Nothing that happens will ever move you from the room, the bed, the darkness, and the sound of footsteps. The customers will keep coming and you'll keep being fed no matter what your hair looks like or what lies you think up to tell those wheezing over you, those without faces you can ever really see. It's peaceful, all right, in a "still-life" house; and sometimes I wake up laughing at night thinking about it.

WALTER I'll bet there were times, on a December night, when business was slow on your corner, you felt such a place wouldn't be too bad.

LUCY No. I liked the cold nights. Only the really interesting ones were out when the weather was mean. The ones who must have been like you were after your Gogarty trial.

WALTER Can't you leave me out of it?

LUCY *(menacingly).* Oh, you'd like to be left out of everything, wouldn't you? Everything but the Warden's filing cabinet.

WALTER If you keep on this way, I'm going to have to ask you to leave.

LUCY *(moving toward him again).* No chance of that, Walter. Too much depends on this for me. It's your world against mine. There'll be no "still-life" house for Lucy because of you!

WALTER Must we go through this again? I was through with everything you represent when the police took the blood-stained seven-iron out of my hand.

LUCY *(speaking evenly, with a smile, and still advancing).* I don't believe you, Walter. All the talk about your little battle to keep the laws from crumbling after the Gogarty trial, I don't believe a word of it.

WALTER Well, that's really beside the point.

LUCY *(reaching into her pocket, she brings out the packet of cigarettes and extracts several).* Do you know what I believe, Walter? *(As she speaks, she begins throwing the cigarettes about the cell.)*

WALTER Here, what are you doing?

LUCY *(flipping several over her shoulder).* I'm setting up the atmosphere you really like.

WALTER *(dropping to his hands and knees to gather up the debris).* Stop it! Stop it! I may not be able to find them all before they come for me.

LUCY *(walking now to the tray of food).* Leave them, Walter. You don't mind a messy cell any more than you did finding yourself on the wrong trains. *(She opens the dish and extracts the chicken leg she'd already bitten into.)*

WALTER What are you saying? It made me sick. It made me kill my wife. And put down that chicken bone!

LUCY I think it would go well in the center of the floor. A little savage bone in the center of the cell. *(She throws the bone in the air and it lands with a clatter in the cell's center.)* And maybe a wing in the corner. *(The piece of chicken bounces off the wall and drops in the cell's corner by the washbasin.)*

WALTER I'm going to be hanged in an hour. How can you treat me this way?

LUCY Yes, Walter, you were frightened of what those hiccups touched off, all right, but it was because you were starting to enjoy that dizzy world outside. That's why your wife had her head mashed, wasn't it? You just wanted to remove yourself from temptation.

WALTER *(no longer crawling about, but still on his hands and knees).* That's not true! That's not true!

LUCY Oh, come on, Walter. Weren't you beginning to look forward to those strange beds you turned up in?

WALTER *(protesting too much).* No, they terrified me. I swear it!

LUCY *(seeing she has made a breach, she pushes on, speeding up her accusations).* And your wife's birthmark—how many times did you bet with yourself where it would pop up next?

WALTER *(now breaking a bit).* Once or twice only. But that doesn't mean . . .

LUCY And how many snips at the dog's tail did you take?

WALTER It was cruel, I know. But nothing seemed to matter in those days . . .

LUCY And you enjoyed its howls.

WALTER All my life I had an urge to torture a dog or cat. And it was just one snip. Just one!

LUCY And when you went out at night, not knowing what tie you were wearing, what streets you were walking, what name you were using, admit you were twitching with excitement.

WALTER *(feebly).* I won't; I wasn't.

LUCY *(going to the cot and picking up Walter's shirt).* Admit it, or the number goes.

WALTER I didn't, I swear I didn't.

Lucy rips the number-patch off in one short movement and Walter cries as if he's been wounded. Then she holds the piece of cloth obtrusively in front of her and lets it drop slowly to the floor. Now totally defeated, Walter watches it descend.

LUCY Now the laws are falling apart again, Walter. You're just a numberless name about to be hanged. There's a not-so-bad-looking woman in your cell. What's there to lose? Do you remember having thoughts like these?

WALTER Yes, yes, I had them. I thought for a time that all the springs, levers, and wheels of the world had broken down and I was free!

LUCY *(softening now).* And so you were, Walter.

WALTER No, there was too great a price. There were always those gray mornings when the mind took over, when you saw your crumpled clothes and cigarette pack from the night before, when your head pounded and you nibbled your lip in fear. Then you panicked for a world that made sense.

LUCY No matter how much fun you got from the world that didn't?

WALTER Oh, leave me alone.

LUCY *(helping Walter to his feet).* I'm going to bring that world back to you. After all, it's the only one there is.

WALTER *(weakly).* There's my cell.

LUCY *(drawing him toward the cot).* With the cigarettes on the floor? With the number torn from your shirt? With my perfume settling over you?

WALTER Please, don't make me start again. What I found on those mornings was death; and it's only minutes away.

LUCY Make love to me, Walter, and you won't mind the hangover of the gallows. You'll be living again when you strangle.

WALTER That's no consolation! Oh, everything was so perfect here before you came. I was just like one of the Warden's insects, living out my days unconsciously, letting the fixed rhythms of the prison carry me along.

LUCY It's too late to go back now. Look at the sky. How many stars are in your sections now?

WALTER Why, they're all bunched in two or three of them, and the planet's gone entirely.

LUCY And the cell, isn't it beginning to push in upon you?

WALTER I loved it for so long.

LUCY It's not big enough to hold a live man, Walter.

WALTER Oh, why wasn't there a glass of water next to Mrs. Gogarty in the courtroom? You would never have gotten to me then. I would have died somewhere in bed of a bad heart, thinking that a special chair had been set aside for me at an eternal dinner party where everything was properly served.

LUCY No one's lucky enough to fool himself that way forever.

WALTER But how can there ever be a contented expression on my face now when they come for me?

LUCY *(pulling him down onto the cot).* Trust Lucy for that, Walter. All those nights, beds, marching songs, toothpaste containers, and howling dogs packed into thirty minutes.

WALTER I hope so. Otherwise I think I'll break down and cry when I start up those steps.

LUCY Shall we begin, Walter?

WALTER All right, I've paid the price now. There'd better be twenty years of living in your mouth, fingertips, and breasts.

LUCY I'll lead you, Walter. You just follow.

WALTER *(bending over her).* And who knows? Maybe the rope will break? Or the hangman come down with a bad cold?

LUCY That's the way to reason, Walter. On this cot, with Lucy on it, anything and everything's now possible. *(She draws Walter to her and the cell's single light is extinguished.)*

Curtain

CHARACTERS

THE WARDEN
PHILLIP
MARTHA

PART TWO

The curtain rises on the early-morning confusion of a suburban kitchen-dining room. Phillip, the prison's executioner, and Martha, his wife, are standing at the kitchen table. Phillip is a small, erect man. He is dressed in the trousers, shirt, and tie of his official uniform. The hat and coat are placed on one of the kitchen chairs. His wife, her hair in curlers and dowdily attractive in a morning housecoat, begins busying herself at the stove. A large red pepper mill is the only conspicuous object on the table.

As the lights come up fully, the Warden is seen pacing back and forth across the table from Phillip.

WARDEN *(with rhetorical self-pity).* When I think how I stayed up nights as a boy learning the penal code by heart so someday I would be a prison warden!

PHILLIP What I asked for isn't going to prove you wasted your youth. It seems quite reasonable to me.

WARDEN Reasonable? How can you, the last and most important link in society's chain of punishment, how can you think it reasonable to want to dress up like a headsman from the Middle Ages?

PHILLIP I just want to wear a black hood over my head. I think it would lend me a little more—well, personality out there.

MARTHA *(setting a pot of coffee on the kitchen table).* Well, if you ask me, the idea of a hood, especially a black one, strikes me as a little morbid.

WARDEN There you are; from your own wife. Can you imagine what others will have to say about it? Why, it smacks of thumbscrews, iron maidens, and unsanitary dungeons.

MARTHA *(to Phillip).* I wish you'd come sit down and finish your oatmeal. *(Looking into one of the bowls set on the table.)* It's getting crusty and beginning to stick to the edges of the bowl.

PHILLIP *(a look of exasperation at Martha).* I don't want any oatmeal now. I simply want, as an employee with some twenty years' service behind him, to have a request granted. *(With a little petulance.)* I want to wear a black hood at today's execution!

WARDEN But think of what it will do to your reputation! Instead of being a finely edged instrument in a clinical, detached operation, you become a villain—a strangler—a black knight.

MARTHA *(vigorously buttering a piece of toast).* I can just imagine the treatment I'd get then from the girls in my bridge club.

PHILLIP Let them jeer and hiss at me; it's better than not being noticed or thought of at all.

WARDEN But behind a hood your face won't even be seen.

PHILLIP *(slightly angry).* My face? Don't you think I know what this collection of scribbles, bumps, and creases looks like? Any real expression I call on it to take looks ridiculous on me. But with this hood, this mask, it comes alive. My eyes, outlined by slanting black slits, crackle with perception; my mouth grows full and moist; and my chin, as if obeying a command from these other features, squares itself and, just a little arrogantly, juts forward.

MARTHA *(now beginning to pour out three cups of coffee).* It sounds as if you'd look like you were in a bad accident, Phillip.

WARDEN I think you'd frighten the men to death before you had a chance to hang them.

PHILLIP Then I would at least have some contact. *(A sigh.)* Oh, I didn't mind being your instrument when those condemned arrived like patients drowned in ether. But things have changed now. You yourself know that they come up those steps trembling, warm, talkative—exuding a scent so full of living that *my* head sometimes starts spinning because of it.

WARDEN There are rules and regulations governing these things. An executioner's uniform can be blue, black, or gray; the buttons can be bone or brass; and the cap is optional. But by no stretch of interpretation is there any mention of a black hood.

PHILLIP Hang the regulations! I'm trying to get a little color into things. *(Pleading.)* Don't you understand? I need a change.

WARDEN You have your vacation coming up in a few months. Get in some fishing, and you'll feel better. I've always found that just dangling your line in a mountain stream relaxes the muscles, improves the digestion . . .

PHILLIP I don't want to fish, Warden. For twenty years I've gone to little mountain streams on my vacation and caught nothing more interesting than a trout with one eye last summer.

WARDEN A one-eyed trout? What kind of bait were you using?

PHILLIP Don't change the subject. Now, do I or do I not wear my hood today?

WARDEN I've already given you an answer on that.

PHILLIP Just look at me in it, that's all. Just one glance.

WARDEN I couldn't be less interested.

PHILLIP All you have to say is yes or no. Just yes or no.

WARDEN *(giving in with a long sigh).* It's a waste of time; but, if you want to, go ahead.

PHILLIP Fine; it's just upstairs. *(Starting to leave.)* Oh, I may be a little time adjusting it, though. It has to sit just right, otherwise it droops a bit and I find it difficult to breathe.

MARTHA If you're just going to leave the oatmeal, should I have some scrambled eggs ready for you when you come down?

PHILLIP Forget about breakfast, Martha. *(To the Warden.)* I hope, once I'm in my hood, that I won't have to take it off until the ceremony's over with. I wouldn't want any food stains to get on it.

Phillip exits.

MARTHA He used to eat such a big breakfast on special days like this. Why, I can remember when six eggs and a quarter-pound of ham were just enough for him.

WARDEN Well, I must say I find his behavior this morning a little peculiar. The whole thing just isn't like Phillip. He's always been someone you could count on, someone who knew the importance of a good shine on his buttons and a sharp crease in his trousers.

MARTHA *(sitting down dejectedly and absently stirring her coffee).* Well, something's definitely been happening to him in the last months. If you'd been living with him every day, this business with the hood wouldn't surprise you in the least.

WARDEN I haven't noticed anything until now.

MARTHA Oh, he's kept these changes fairly well hidden, even from me. But you can't eat, sleep, and take out a joint bank account with a man without noticing the slightest change in him.

WARDEN Now that you mention it, he hasn't come to any club meetings in the last months and his weekly reports have been dotted with erasure smudges—very unlike him.

MARTHA *(putting the coffee down and nervously smoothing her hair).* It's beginning to show on the outside too? Oh, I'd hoped to keep it confined to the rooms in this house.

WARDEN *(reaching down and taking Martha's hand).* Is it something you can tell me, a very old friend? Is there another woman involved in all this?

MARTHA *(hitting the kitchen table with her free hand so that the Warden turns the other loose).* Oh, how I wish there was! How I'd love to be able to sink my nails into the flesh-and-blood reason for the way things are beginning to wobble on their legs around here! Just to see a larger bosom or a firmer behind leading Phillip down a street would let me spit at him with a clear conscience. If I just knew where the weakness was, I could make life miserable for him and then forget it!

WARDEN But you don't?

MARTHA *(rising from the kitchen table like a prosecutor at a trial).* About four months ago, after Phillip had left for work, I got up from bed and, like I do every morning the first thing, reached down for his slippers to take them to the closet. For twenty years he's always left them on his side of the bed, neatly placed next to one another, toes pointed to the wall.

WARDEN And that morning?

MARTHA One was underneath the bed and the other, after being used for an ash tray, was tucked beneath his pillow.

WARDEN *(shaking his head).* A bad sign!

MARTHA Only the first, though. In the next weeks I began making all sorts of discoveries: in his bureau drawer, tucked among his underwear, I found a book of Swedish lessons; in the hall closet, squeezed behind the Christmas decorations, I uncovered a banjo with

two of its strings missing; and under one of the sofa cushions, I turned up a pair of red socks with "World's Fair—1939" stitched down their sides. Red socks! I can't decide what to do with them, and just knowing they're sitting in the house drives me half out of my mind.

WARDEN *(approaching Martha, he puts his hands on her shoulders and speaks as the comforting male).* Go on, Martha. My home's not a happy one, either.

MARTHA Well, after that, Phillip himself began upsetting things. Since we were married, he's always slept on his stomach, one hand folded beneath his chin; but a month ago I woke up to find him snoring on his back. Then his favorite chair, that he always settled in after dinner, began being neglected; and, the dishes done, I'd come in and find him pouting in a corner or sitting cross-legged like an Arab on the floor.

WARDEN *(oozing sympathy).* And you've been suffering through all this, Martha, without a word to anyone?

MARTHA I kept hoping it would all pass over; but I see now it won't. Last night, behind a stack of bathroom towels, I discovered a box of very expensive cigars with an unpronounceable name—and then this morning the hood. *(She utters a long sigh and turns to put her head on the Warden's chest.)* Oh, Warden!

WARDEN *(a smile hinting now a little more than sympathy).* There, there. Please call me Harry.

MARTHA *(a brief smile as she pronounces the name).* Harry! *(Now the defenseless little girl.)* Oh, I just don't know what to do any longer.

WARDEN I really can't stand thinking of you being unhappy.

MARTHA Just last week Phillip refused to renew our country club membership or donate to the Red Cross.

WARDEN You need help, Martha. Can Harry, an old, old, *old* friend do anything for you?

MARTHA Don't let him wear that hood today. No matter how he coaxes, put your foot down.

WARDEN *(a vigorous nod).* You can depend on it. I'll simply tell him his pension won't be raised if he does.

MARTHA Oh, Harry, you've always been so kind. Just having you here this morning makes everything seem much easier.

WARDEN *(lifting up her chin).* We're cut from the same timber, Martha. Perhaps we can help each other. *(He starts to kiss her.)*

MARTHA *(pulling away).* No, Harry! Even if Phillip has taken to collecting red socks and turning nasty remarks about my friends, I couldn't deceive him. It would be playing his game.

WARDEN He does nothing but hurt you, Martha; and I've loved you ever since the day you came to my office to try to get a raise in salary out of me for Phillip.

MARTHA *(now enjoying being pursued).* Really? I remember coming out feeling you hadn't noticed me at all. And Phillip didn't get the raise.

WARDEN You were wearing an orange-and-blue print dress, white gloves and, as it was right after lunch, there was a little drop of mayonnaise on the left side of your chin.

MARTHA Harry! And you didn't tell me.

WARDEN *(walking up to her and speaking in a hoarse voice).* I found it terribly exciting. All the time you were going on about those extra five dollars a month, I was trying to imagine just what you could have eaten to put that tiny white mark there.

MARTHA *(pretending embarrassment).* You shouldn't talk that way. What a woman eats for lunch is an intimate matter.

WARDEN And you? Did you notice me at all?

MARTHA I'd only been married six months at the time. I wasn't noticing anyone but Phillip, such that he was.

WARDEN *(somewhat hurt).* You mean I made no impression at all?

MARTHA Well, I do recall you had on a tie with a palm tree painted on it.

WARDEN *(nostalgically).* In the dark it lit up and formed a pair of woman's legs.

MARTHA *(almost warmly).* And I noticed how bloodshot your eyes were, and I thought how hard you must work to have popped so many of those little vessels.

WARDEN Twenty years ago! Twenty years ago! If we could only have spoken frankly to each other then.

MARTHA And why didn't you?

WARDEN I thought of doing so, Martha. That very night I paced about in the dark of our five-room house, trying to decide just how bold I should be.

MARTHA And then you saw your wife asleep, her head placed at just the right angle on the pillow, and you were ashamed of your thoughts. A good wife holds on even when she's unconscious.

WARDEN Heavens no! It wasn't my wife. She'd already begun sampling the line of manual laborers that began with a teen-age elevator operator and just last week was kept going with a streetcar motorman. No, Martha, it was the twins, aged one, I think, at the time, who kept me from sending you a warm note about the stain on your chin. I wandered into their room, heard them breathing, in unison, and something made me switch on the light. I saw them: their eyes opened simultaneously, blinked once in disbelief at the questions written across my face, and gave me such a stare of clear-sighted respectability that I backed, shamefaced, from the crib. Oh, if you could have seen those accusing blue pupils daring me to jeopardize their owners' position. Martha, their plump faces were as solid as the walls of my prison, and they left me no choice but to forget your lunches and start saving for their college education.

MARTHA *(with a sigh of genuine understanding).* Well, I don't blame you for that.

WARDEN Oh, it was the right thing then when I thought you were happy with our hangman. But now . . .

MARTHA Now, now it's too late. I can't put mayonnaise on my sandwiches any longer and fit into last year's dress.

WARDEN And I wouldn't dare wear a tie with a palm tree painted on it. *(Suddenly throwing off the gloom that has settled over him and tumbling out his words.)* But my sons are almost chemical engineers and my wife never stops riding streetcars and my house is empty and no matter what size dress you wear, I love you!

He kisses Martha enthusiastically, and, for a moment, she returns in kind. Then, however, she pushes him away.

MARTHA Oh, no, Harry. No, no, no. *(She walks back to the kitchen table and steadies herself with it.)* Let me reheat your coffee or make you some toast.

WARDEN *(again advancing).* Please, don't drop back behind breakfast. We're both beyond that now.

MARTHA *(again escaping).* No, not here. Phillip may come down any minute.

WARDEN Then we must have a meeting, a rendezvous as soon as possible. Twenty years, Martha. Twenty years!

MARTHA *(after a brief pause).* All right: tomorrow, three o'clock, in front of the supermarket steps.

WARDEN Tomorrow? *(A pause and a frown, as he consults a small black engagement book.)* No, I'm afraid tomorrow's out for me. A government inspection team is coming down for the day. *(Brightening.)* But Saturday, in the afternoon, I know a little bar . . .

MARTHA But I've promised myself as a fourth in three card games that afternoon.

WARDEN Cards, Martha?

MARTHA *(with just a little less enthusiasm).* We could try Monday morning. No one suspects you of anything on a Monday.

WARDEN *(a little impatient).* That's because everyone's too busy to get into mischief. If I went away from my desk for five minutes after a weekend, it'd take me a month to catch up.

MARTHA Well, I could slip away Tuesday night and say I'm seeing a movie.

WARDEN *(dejectedly).* That's the night the twins call from school to ask for money. *(With now but faint hope.)* But Wednesday?

MARTHA *(flatly, as she checks a calendar on the kitchen wall).* Cancer Fund meeting. Thursday?

WARDEN *(in equally funereal tones).* Parole Board all day, and I visit my mother at night.

Martha turns and goes to the kitchen table where she pours a fresh cup of coffee. The Warden continues as though trying to explain something to himself rather than to her.

I've visited Mother every Thursday night since leaving her to get married. Every Thursday night, and I don't think she really enjoys seeing me at all.

MARTHA *(after a pause).* Would you like cream in your coffee, Harry?

WARDEN Black; make it as black as you can.

MARTHA *(making conversation).* Do you suppose it will rain? I always think hangings should take place in bad weather, even if it does make Phillip's back stiffen up a bit.

WARDEN *(taking up the coffee cup and staring moodily into it).* Are we back to hangings, your husband, and another official day?

MARTHA Your twins' eyes are still following us.

WARDEN *(putting down the cup).* Ah, but for a moment, for a moment . . .

MARTHA *(sharply).* We were being fools. Now drink your coffee.

WARDEN *(slinking around the table to her).* At least one more kiss, Martha. The second and last one in twenty years.

MARTHA *(dryly).* It would just be a wet sound to me now, Harry.

WARDEN But not to me.

MARTHA Your kiss would mean nothing but that I had to breathe through my nose for its duration.

WARDEN And if I don't, I'll never breathe properly again. I feel as if I'm being sealed away forever in a very small hall closet.

MARTHA And no matter what you do, I'll always be on the other side of the door. You won't even be near me, Harry.

WARDEN *(like a painful prayer).* Oh, just this once let those damned chemical engineers look the other way!

He begins kissing Martha's neck passionately while she remains immobile. After a second, Phillip, his black hood over his head, enters. His voice, because of the mask, is somewhat muffled.

PHILLIP And just what is this going on?

Martha utters a cry and jumps back from the Warden. He turns around and is equally upset by what he sees.

WARDEN Good God!

PHILLIP *(moving toward them).* I'll ask again: what were you two doing?

WARDEN *(catching his breath and paying no attention to the question).* Do you know how ridiculously ferocious you look? Your creeping in like that's sent a chill through me all the way down to my feet.

PHILLIP Your feet? What do I care about your feet? You were kissing my wife.

WARDEN What? That thing's covering your mouth and making it very hard to follow what you're excited about.

PHILLIP *(taking off the hood).* I *say* you were kissing my wife!

WARDEN It's not very well-mannered to come right out and say it that way, but I suppose I was.

PHILLIP While I was upstairs, trying to adjust this hood so you'd see it to its best advantage, you were making love to my wife. You, the Warden of the prison, who, in less than half an hour will be raising a solemn forefinger and signaling me to hang a man—you were making love to my wife in my own kitchen.

WARDEN *(really confused by all the fuss).* Man to man, Phillip, I apologize. These things happen all the time—a little slip that sets one in the bushes alongside somebody you've no business being in the bushes with. Yes, it's an unfortunate, uh, occurrence, and, as I said, I *do* apologize for it.

PHILLIP *(somewhat stunned).* Apologize? Oh, no, please don't do that. I—I couldn't accept. I don't *want* to accept.

WARDEN Now, Phillip, I understand how you feel. I've found my wife in much more than an embrace with a plumber. He was covered with grease, too, and had . . .

PHILLIP Oh, no, it's not that at all. I was a little shocked just now and perhaps I did sound like a predictable husband. It just seemed that, under the circumstances, bellowing was expected of me.

WARDEN I'm not following.

PHILLIP It's simply that, while I was in my room, I was thinking what a failure I'd be in the hood. I was thinking, Harry, that the only thing that would save me would be to turn tail on this house, this uniform, this prison—everything that keeps me jogging along in step with the rest of you. So, Harry, friend and lover of my wife, I almost opened the window, slithered down the drainpipe and slipped out of your sight forever. I was going to run away—are you listening too, Martha?—run away and find out just where those men I've been dropping through gallows' doors come from.

WARDEN Phillip, call me names, knock me down if you want to, but don't psychoanalyze yourself in public this way. At least not while you're in uniform.

PHILLIP Let me just say that it was my old, well-trained conscience that kept me off the drainpipe. I thought of you two, standing firm on this dreary morning, washing your misery down with coffee, keeping to the rules of the game, and I bowed my head, covered it with the hood, and came downstairs ready to go on as Phillip, the old executioner. But now, now that you two have kicked up your heels a little bit, I see no reason why I shouldn't follow suit. You don't know how long I've waited to find

a crack in the wall that being Martha's husband has built around me. But now that I see it's there, I'm going through it and down the drainpipe without a regret.

WARDEN Phillip, this is all impossible, you know that, don't you?

PHILLIP No more so than my finding you wrapped around my wife is impossible. If you two, at breakfast time, can stomach each other to the point of embracing, then I don't see how the line of impossibility can be drawn anywhere.

WARDEN And just who, in all honesty, is responsible for this embrace?

PHILLIP *(looking at Martha, who, during the foregoing, has folded her arms and kept her back to both of her champions).* Who, indeed?

WARDEN You, yourself. You with your black hood, your Swedish lessons, your scattered slippers, and your brooding in the corner. You sent her into my arms, Phillip.

PHILLIP *(smiling at Martha who doesn't respond).* So you did notice these things.

WARDEN Of course she has; and that's why what happened happened. It explains . . .

PHILLIP At five-thirty in the morning it doesn't explain . . .

WARDEN *(raising his arm for silence).* No! No! I am now speaking in my official capacity and I don't want to be interrupted by subordinates. *(The Warden takes the deep breath of one preparing for platitudes.)* Life, Phillip, is like a long sea voyage—the comparison's an old but apt one. We begin by deciding whether we favor temperate, tropic, or arctic waters. We decide what ports to put into with proper ceremony and what savage islands to sell trinkets and contract diseases on. We select the style of ship and the type of crew that suits us; and if one turns out to have a few leaks hidden in its bottom and the other to be bad-breathed and mutinous, we don't let that force us to drift off course. For, Phillip, staying within the latitudes and longitudes we've marked out for ourselves is all that matters. There can be no floating about to take closer looks at a curvaceous coast line or a sensual horizon. There can be no seeking out restful doldrums when your nerves get a bit frayed or poking about for a good typhoon when calm seas prove somewhat tedious. No, we keep to the prescribed path, and when other ships plow past us, flaunting well-laundered sails—well, we scrub ours up too, send every one with scurvy out of sight, keep a good mile of sea water between us and our short-lived neighbors, and leave them with the impression of nothing but that we're occupying the exact bit of ocean marked out for us. But you, Phillip, you just weren't sticking to the chart. You were sailing into harbors that weren't even marked on the maps of your second-in-command; you were tossing sensible and costly cargo overboard to make room for unmarketable baubles; you were tilting the compass to suit yourself. Now, is there any wonder, as you were approaching the dangerous waters of middle age, that Martha should lower a dinghy over the side and paddle her way to a vessel that looked, at least from a distance, to be completely shipshape? And, of course, having a good set of sea manners and seeing your wife bobbing next to me, I took her aboard, gave her, so to speak, a change of dry clothes and am now ready to return her to your schooner which, I'm sure, will be polished up and made ready for inspection. And if you don't want her to think she has to abandon ship again, tighten the hatches, throw out your World's Fair socks; secure the rigging, don't use slippers for ash trays; scrub the decks, go to club dances; check your compass hourly, burn that revolting black hood; and, finally, appear at today's execution as if you knew what your coordinates as the state's official hangman were. For remember, Phillip, no matter how attractive you find the mermaids or the rocks they wrap their appealing green tails around, the important thing is to keep sailing on course. Take that as an old captain's advice—just keep sailing on course.

The Warden, who during the speech has edged his way to the door, exits through it.

PHILLIP *(running to the door after him).* That's the same speech you gave at the club's Christmas dinner last year and the summer picnic the year before! Well, you old pirate, you'd better get your ship's lifeboats ready because there isn't going to be a hanging today. Do you hear? The person you thought you temporarily rescued is now your permanent passenger. I resign! From everything! I resign! *(Phillip pauses for a moment, comes back into the center of the kitchen, looks at his hood, then at Martha, and laughs softly.)* I'll have to admit you surprised me, Martha. It was pleasant, but a surprise nevertheless. *(Silence.)* Well, don't you have anything to say? After all, I just said I was leaving you.

MARTHA *(disinterested).* If you're not going to touch breakfast, I'll put the dishes away.

PHILLIP *(relieved).* Oh, I thought after twenty years of marriage that a little piece of flesh had begun to sprout, connecting us together like Siamese twins. You don't know how upset I was by the idea. And now, Martha, you've shown me that it's nothing but a flimsy band-aid—nothing more.

MARTHA *(beginning to remove the dishes and wash them).* A band-aid?

PHILLIP *(with real admiration in his eyes).* One that you had the courage to tear off. Oh, if I'd only known how simple it would be. There I was, trying to sneak into a black hood and leave little hints about the house.

MARTHA Hints at what?

PHILLIP Hints that I was unhappy; that I thought I'd become little more than the brass and flannel of my uniform; that I wanted to run away from everything that I was and had been. It never occurred to me that you might feel the same way. But then, seeing you pressed up against the Warden—well, Martha, I confess I underestimated you.

MARTHA And are you planning now to go out and make love to the Warden's wife?

PHILLIP Oh, no. I'm going to leave you and this little piece of the world forever. I'm going to become—to become . . .

MARTHA *(sharply).* What?

PHILLIP *(a visionary smile).* To become—to become something like those fellows I've been hanging in the last few months. Do you know, Martha, there's a light in their eyes, a pulse behind their ear that beats faster than mine, and an interest in the weather that makes me envy them. Oh, they're frightened all right, but it's a healthy fear—something I don't think I would ever have had.

MARTHA As the Warden said, they've just left those official ladies. Maybe if you didn't read all night in bed we could . . .

PHILLIP Oh, no, Martha. I need a complete and total break.

MARTHA And when do you plan to start breaking?

PHILLIP In the past a step like this would have meant travel folders, reservations, exact calculations down to the dollar. But now, Martha, I'm not even going to bother to pack. I'm walking straight out the door without a glance over my shoulder.

MARTHA *(holding out a plate to him).* Will you help dry first?

PHILLIP *(abstracted but pleasant).* What? Oh, certainly. *(Towel and plate in hand, he goes back to his vision.)* First, I'm going to a tailor. I'm going to have him make me something for every mood I'm going to try—silk vests, lace collars, green tweeds for reflective moments . . .

MARTHA *(handing him another dish).* Tweeds always make you break out in a rash.

PHILLIP *(thinking for a moment, he takes the new plate and stacks the old one).* That's true. Well, perhaps, I'll give up reflection—there won't be much time for it, I hope, anyway.

MARTHA And after the tailor, then what?

PHILLIP Ah, I want to go where the climate's very hot; where it steams, as a matter of fact; where oversized plants seem to couple with one another before your eyes and produce offspring so colorful that they look indecent.

MARTHA *(now a cup in her hand).* You never liked me to wear loud clothes: always gray, black, and brown.

PHILLIP *(taking the cup).* No offense, but you're just not a tropical plant, Martha.

MARTHA It wasn't me who had to have an air-conditioner last summer. Put the cup face down, Phillip.

PHILLIP *(he does so and receives a bowl in its place).* Now I want the heat to prevent anything from taking on too solid and sensible a shape. I want everything about me to shimmer, sway, and change in a second's time as if it were all one big sleight-of-hand trick. People, too, should melt and harden in front of you. *(He starts to put the bowl away.)*

MARTHA That still looks wet to me.

PHILLIP *(retrieving the bowl).* And, Martha, there might be mirages. Can you imagine, scenes floating about purely for your own amusement. Do you know, I think I've wanted to see a mirage for the last ten years.

MARTHA You're getting water on your trousers, Phillip. *(She opens a cupboard and takes out an apron.)* Here, put this on.

PHILLIP *(getting into the apron).* I used to try to force a mirage on myself. On days like today, when I'd see the man I was to hang being escorted toward me, I used to widen my eyes, clench my fists, and try to make my brain turn the entire scene into something else. It never worked, though: my eyes would begin to water and soon I was receiving reprimands from my superiors for what they took to be my emotional attitude while on duty.

MARTHA *(handing Phillip the last dish).* All you want, then, is to see mirages?

PHILLIP I want my pores to open and let out of me all the bubbling perspiration that's been stopped up by the civil service code. Think of it, Martha! Me, in the middle of a jungle, where everything's raw and fresh, where only the hungry and alive do the executing, where . . .

MARTHA I think some grounds are still in the coffee pot.

PHILLIP *(giving the pot another rinse).* And then, Martha, once I've filled my lungs with that wild air—well, then I'll be ready to—to . . .

MARTHA To what, Phillip?

PHILLIP *(modestly, with some embarrassment).* Oh, grow a beard perhaps.

MARTHA All this trouble just to avoid shaving?

PHILLIP No, what I mean is, once I've finally shed this old skin, I'll be ready to—to take up my old profession again with a fresh hand.

MARTHA You mean after all that sweating in the tropics you'd still want to be an executioner?

PHILLIP *(soberly).* That is my profession, my trade, the only thing I can do passably well. *(Brightening.)* But, Martha, I won't be an official piece of cloth and brass, tying the knot around living necks because someone, somewhere, has underlined their names in red ink.

MARTHA *(as if humoring someone not too sound of mind).* You're going to do free-lance work?

PHILLIP *(slowly winding the dishtowel into a strangling cord).* I'm going to have an eye peeled for all the dead branches that need pruning—for all those who want to measure away the few wild patches of weeds left to us and turn the ground, teeming with savage centipedes, into a middle-income housing development.

MARTHA *(still indulging him).* And just how do you go about determining when a branch is dead?

PHILLIP *(moving about the kitchen table, towel in hand and eyes agleam).* Oh, that won't be hard, Martha. *(He begins circling the table, his eyes on the pepper mill as if stalking it.)* Just suppose I'm standing on a busy corner at lunchtime. Oh, there'll be a lot of dead wood about, but I'll find the one beyond the help of insecticides. I'll know him: perhaps I'll notice that his tie, socks, and handkerchief match; or perhaps I'll see he doesn't cross the street until the exact moment the light blinks in his favor. Oh, I'll know him as one of those who'll spend what energy he has trying to make tomorrow a line-for-line copy of yesterday; one of those who has a favorite chair, who sees no difference but age between the woman he married and the woman he keeps. *(Phillip pauses, narrows his eyes, and moves in on the pepper mill.)* He won't notice me, but I'll be behind him all the time. I'll watch him stuff himself with just the right calorie count; I'll smile as he leaves the proper tip and takes the long way back to his office to get in a little exercise; I'll peek around a corner as he tells an off-color joke to his secretary and pats her knee. And then, when he's alone in his office, about to balance another day's equation, I'll just tiptoe up behind him, hold the loop for a moment over his head, and then—snap! *(He catches the pepper mill in the towel's knot and lifts it up level with his eyes.)* There won't be any struggle or sound. He might have just enough curiosity to turn and see just who's doing him in, but the only thing I'd find in his eyes would be the gleam of one whose funeral arrangements were planned down to the last flower, tear, and comma in his epitaph. Already dead, Martha, he'd be only too happy to lie down. *(Phillip lets the pepper mill drop to the floor.)*

MARTHA *(getting down to retrieve it).* That pepper mill was your birthday gift from my mother!

PHILLIP *(as if suddenly startled awake).* What?

MARTHA *(putting the object back on the kitchen table).* It must have cost twenty-five dollars. *(Sharply.)* Find something less expensive to play games with, Phillip.

PHILLIP *(hurt).* Games? Martha, I was trying to share a secret with you. For the first time in our marriage, I was telling you something I really felt.

MARTHA Don't be open-hearted and frank with me, Phillip.

PHILLIP But aren't you at least interested in what I'm really like?

MARTHA If I was interested in what you were really like, I don't think I'd have stayed married to you for twenty years.

PHILLIP But you might find me—well, exciting.

MARTHA *(coldly).* I've grown used to the lies, Phillip. They make up the comfortable husband I know.

PHILLIP *(realizing he's made a mistake in confiding in her).* Oh, I see. All right, then, you keep the comfortable husband! The new one, Martha, won't bother you any longer. No, he's simply going to close his eyes, turn around, and head straight through the door.

As he speaks, Phillip performs the above gestures. As he is halfway to the door, however, Martha speaks up.

MARTHA You'd better take off my apron first.

PHILLIP *(angry with himself for not having noticed it).* Oh, yes. How did I get into it in the first place?

MARTHA *(as if she were discussing a shopping list).* And another thing: I don't see how you can pick up and leave today, Phillip.

PHILLIP *(repeating the above gestures).* And why not, Martha? Why shouldn't I just close my eyes, turn around, and . . .

MARTHA Because you have a dentist appointment first thing tomorrow morning.

PHILLIP *(turning about in confusion).* Dentist? Dentist?

MARTHA *(innocently).* You remember. The molar in the back has to come out? It's infecting the gum? Because of it you can't eat sweets?

PHILLIP I don't want to eat sweets. I just . . .

MARTHA We've been invited to my sister's for dinner Friday, and you know how partial you are to her chocolate mousse.

PHILLIP *(at last rather angry).* Damn the chocolate mousse! I'm not going to your sister's for dinner anyway.

MARTHA I've already accepted. And with the weekend whirl coming up, I don't see how you can plan to leave before next Wednesday.

PHILLIP Plan? Something like this can't be planned and put on schedule. I'm giving up knowing where and what I'll be a week, a day, or even an hour ahead. I'm going to be . . .

MARTHA *(again sharp and bitter).* A man-eating, jungle plant—I know. Well, you'll have to wait until *after* my sister's dinner to start blooming. And by that time, there'll be other things popping up to detain you.

PHILLIP *(a little unnerved).* Martha, maybe you didn't understand or listen to what I was saying. I'm sweeping all the old laws, manners, and invitations under the rug. There's nothing here that can hold me now.

MARTHA Oh, yes, there is—me.

PHILLIP You? Martha, I don't want to be brutal, but if nothing else were pushing me through that door, you, in your breakfast face, would be all the reason I'd need.

MARTHA *(now in full attack).* Maybe my face won't charm you into bed, but you're going to look at it, speak to it, and—yes, even kiss it in a businesslike way every day of your life. Because, Phillip, covered with cold-cream or skin oil, it's the face of your wife. And "wife," Phillip, means a thousand obstacles for you to get over before you're free to start chopping down dead branches.

PHILLIP *(in the tones of family argument).* Wife? Hah! And were you my wife with the Warden pawing over you?

MARTHA More than ever, Phillip. That little moment with him only reminded me how snug I was with you—even with your red socks under the sofa seat. My life depends on all the little functions you perform. You're like the telephone, electricity, or underground plumbing. My life takes you for granted, but would be lost without you. Maybe we're not held together by a little piece of flesh, but there is something there even harder to snip apart. It's the word "and" in "man *and* wife." It's official and keeps us together through mistresses, dreams, bills, and burned toast. "Man *and* wife"—that's our world, Phillip; and everything in it has long ago been discovered, named, and placed in its proper corner.

PHILLIP No three-letter word's going to drag me after it. Not when I finally have the chance . . .

MARTHA You *had* the chance, Phillip. For the briefest second, when you caught the Warden and me, you had the chance. But no; you stayed and helped me with the dishes.

PHILLIP That was just habit.

MARTHA No, dear, that was the law of gravity yanking you right back to earth.

PHILLIP Well, I'm breaking the law of gravity, Martha. From now on you'll have to find someone else to eat off and dry your dishes. The first day of creation is waiting for me on the other side of the kitchen door, and all the rules of marriage or physics aren't going to keep me from it. *(He starts for the door.)*

MARTHA Touch that door and you'll find out how unpleasant the truth about yourself can be.

PHILLIP I have all the truth I need, Martha. Goodby. And if we ever meet again be careful I don't mistake you for a dead branch. *(Phillip makes to open the door, but finds it refuses to budge. He begins tugging at the knob.)* It must be the dampness has made the wood swell.

MARTHA *(taunting).* You'll never get it open, Phillip. You know too well what's on the other side.

PHILLIP *(increasing his efforts).* It's not locked. There's no reason for it to be this stubborn.

MARTHA You don't want to strain yourself, Phillip. Remember that awful rubber girdle you had to wear after cleaning out the attic last year.

PHILLIP *(more and more effort).* Shut up, Martha!

MARTHA Ha! Don't yell at *me!* You, I, and the door know on which side of it you belong.

PHILLIP *(losing all control).* I'll tear the damned thing off its hinges.

MARTHA That door's the speed of light—a permanent boundary fence. It can't be broken.

PHILLIP *(now pounding on the door).* Open, damn you! Open!

MARTHA It won't because you don't want it to. You know that all your jungle will give you is athlete's foot, diarrhea, and swollen joints.

PHILLIP *(turning from the door to Martha, he pleads with desperation in his voice).* I'm going to tear down every kitchen door in the world. I'm going to strangle, murder . . .

MARTHA You, murder? Hah! Come on, Phillip, the game's over. You're an official executioner, a little paunchy through the middle, with thinning hair and an obedient attitude. That's as close as you'll ever be to a murderer.

PHILLIP *(menacingly).* If that door doesn't open you'll be the first to know how wrong you are.

MARTHA *(with an incredulous smile).* Are you threatening me?

PHILLIP If you're keeping me in this kitchen—yes!

MARTHA Oh, poor, poor Phillip. Look at you; out of breath already and not even one step away from the house yet.

PHILLIP I won't stand you laughing at me!

MARTHA Then don't make jokes about doing me in. You're not on your gallows now; no twenty-five forms have been filled out in triplicate authorizing you to snap my neck. *(Shouting.)* You're my husband! And that makes you the most harmless person in the world as far as *I'm* concerned!

PHILLIP *(picking up the black hood from the kitchen table and beginning to knot it ominously).* For the last time: make the door open!

MARTHA How can I, Phillip? You're the one who's keeping it shut. If you really wanted to leave, it would spring open like a hungry mouth.

PHILLIP *(stepping toward her).* Then I'll have to prove I'm in earnest, Martha.

MARTHA Don't be an ass. One of the things that will make the rest of our life together

tolerable is that you can keep your mind buzzing with plans to murder me. Don't try it now and find out you can't. It'll make you sour, bitter, and even more difficult to get new hats and dresses out of than you are now.

Phillip begins testing the hood's strength and continues his advance.

MARTHA *(quite earnestly).* I'm warning you. With as much love as I can squeeze out of me after twenty years, I'm warning you not to do this to yourself.

PHILLIP As the books say: There's no good reasoning with a murderer.

MARTHA *(throwing back the challenge).* All right, murderer, if you won't listen— *(She picks up one of the kitchen table chairs, places it downstage, facing the audience, and sits in it with her neck thrust out as if for a sacrifice.)* All right then, go ahead. Try and squeeze the air out of my windpipe. Just try it! Well, what are you waiting for, Bluebeard? Come on, let me feel some of your jungle sweat dripping down the back of my neck.

PHILLIP *(a little startled by Martha's action.)* Are you just going to sit there as if you were having your hair done?

MARTHA You'll have to supply the noise and screams, Phillip. I'm just going to sit here and talk.

PHILLIP Talk? Then that's just the last bit of incentive I need. *(He knots the hood around Martha's neck and begins tightening.)*

MARTHA *(not affected at all by Phillip's attack).* Oh, you'll have to pull harder than that. I'm still getting in more than enough air to tell you that the ivy plants over our bed are all the jungle you'll ever know.

Phillip gives an extra hard tug, and Martha starts, as if tickled.

And it's your turn to water them next week. You'll take care of them every other week for as long as you're on this planet.

PHILLIP *(hopefully).* Is the blood beginning to pound in your head? Do you find it difficult to focus your eyes?

MARTHA Hah! I've never felt better. This is the closest we've come to sex in years.

PHILLIP *(increasing his efforts).* And now, Martha, is your past popping up in front of you?

MARTHA Only my future. And you, Phillip, growing stooped, absent-minded, and a little sloppy at the table, are in every minute of it.

PHILLIP *(becoming frustrated).* You should at least be gagging now, damn it!

MARTHA *(sweetly).* I don't know how to gag. But I could cough a little if it would make things easier for you.

PHILLIP *(pleading).* Please stop breathing, Martha. Please, my arms are getting tired—please stop breathing.

MARTHA At this rate, you'll stop before I will. Oh, what a story this will make at cards Saturday!

PHILLIP *(makes one last supreme effort, and then, with a groan, drops his hands).* I just can't do it. My wrists and fingers just aren't strong enough. *(He sits in one of the kitchen chairs.)* I can't even get out of the kitchen.

MARTHA *(rubbing her neck and rising from the chair).* I told you, Phillip, but you wouldn't listen, would you? Now look at you—panting and overheated. *(She takes the hood and begins mopping his brow.)* And you have to go out right away. I'm sure this will mean a cold by tomorrow.

PHILLIP *(docilely).* Go out?

MARTHA There's not fifteen minutes till the execution begins. There now, that's the best I can do. *(She takes Phillip's coat and holds it out for him.)* All right, come on, get into this. If you keep all the buttons closed there's still a chance I won't have to spend a fortune on nose drops and cough syrup.

PHILLIP So the execution's going to take place after all?

MARTHA *(buttoning up the coat).* Of course it is; and you're going to be on those gallows, stiff and tall, the way I, the Warden, and the man you're going to hang expect you to be. The whole thing will go very smoothly now, won't it?

PHILLIP I suppose it will.

MARTHA *(finishing the buttoning, Martha steps back to admire her work).* There! Now you look like my husband and the state's official executioner. You can tell at a glance that you're a fish in the right waters now.

PHILLIP I guess you can.

MARTHA *(picking up Phillip's cap).* Now, don't be so gloomy. Look on the bright side of everything to come. Think of the certificate of merit and pension bonus you'll receive when you successfully hang your thousandth man. Think of the speeches you'll be asked to give to college students on the fine prose in the penal code. Think of the jokes you'll tell at your retirement dinner and the little cottage our insurance policy's going to give us. Think how peaceful things will be when you're certain that there's only one world and one way to live in it.

PHILLIP Will that come with the retirement policy too?

MARTHA *(putting the cap on his head).* It just might, Phillip. It just might. And now, you're complete; not a wrinkle in you. *(She takes his arm and starts to lead him toward the door.)*

PHILLIP My hood? Can I at least have that?

MARTHA I'll put it under the sofa with your socks. And, on holidays, you can take them, your banjo, and the other things out to look at for a while. And on New Year's Eve, you can even sit on the floor and flip ashes into your slippers if you want to.

PHILLIP I think I'll go back to my chair. The floor's very hard.

MARTHA That *is* more sensible, I suppose.

They reach the door.

Well, come on now. Out you go.

PHILLIP But it won't open.

MARTHA *(she touches the door knob ever so lightly with the tips of her fingers and it springs open).* There's nothing holding it shut now.

PHILLIP *(taking a step toward the opening).* It is very cold this morning.

MARTHA Do you have a handkerchief with you?

PHILLIP *(feeling his pocket).* Yes.

MARTHA Well, then, you'd better be off.

PHILLIP *(turning toward Martha).* Martha, I just wanted to be . . .

MARTHA But you couldn't, Phillip. Some things just can't be broken. So you'd better just try to keep warm out there and forget all about it. Now, kiss me goodby.

PHILLIP But isn't there any chance for me at all?

MARTHA *(in a command voice and pointing to her cheek).* Kiss!

Phillip does so, and then slowly turns and leaves. Martha waits for a moment and then calls out to him.

Keep bundled up, dear. Don't work too hard. And tonight—tonight we'll have something very special for dinner. Something you really like, dear, something you really, really like.

Curtain

MARSHA NORMAN

(1947–)

Third and Oak

About the Author: A native of Louisville, **Marsha Norman** was born in 1947, went to Agnes Scott College, and earned a master's degree from the University of Louisville before teaching, working with disturbed children, and serving as book editor and reviewer for the *Louisville Times.* Her first play, *Getting Out,* won the New Playwrights Medallion and the Outer Critics Circle Award for 1977. *Third and Oak* followed in the next year. *'Night, Mother,* Norman's fifth play, received the Susan Smith Blackburn Prize in 1982 and the Pulitzer Prize for Drama in 1983 and has been made into a film. Norman continues to write plays and in 1987 published her first novel, *The Fortune Teller.*

About the Play: The play *Third and Oak* may be seen as an exercise in balancing opposites. It consists of two acts of almost exactly the same length, the first act set in a laundromat, the second in a pool hall, both presumably located at the corner of Third and Oak. There are only four characters in the entire play, but the four exemplify several possibilities for social opposition: black and white, male and female, young and old, educated and not, relatively rich and relatively poor, longtime friends and casual acquaintances. In two brief and gently comic "slices of life," Norman is able to touch a remarkably broad spectrum of human experiences.

CHARACTERS

ALBERTA, a reserved woman in her late fifties.
DEEDEE, a restless twenty-year-old.
SHOOTER, a black disc jockey in his late twenties.
WILLIE, a black man in his late fifties.

TIME AND PLACE: *The two acts of this play take place in a laundromat and the pool hall next door, at the corner of Third and Oak, in the middle of the night. The time is the late seventies.*

ACT ONE: THE LAUNDROMAT

Lights come up on a standard, dreary laundromat. There are tile floors, washers, dryers, laundry baskets on wheels, and coin-op vending machines for soaps, soft drinks and candy bars. There is a bulletin board on which various notices are posted. There is a table for folding clothes, a low table covered with dirty ashtrays and some ugly chairs littered with magazines. A clock on the wall reads three o'clock and should continue to run throughout the show. One side of the laundromat will be used as a window looking out onto the street. The song "Stand By Your Man" is playing over the radio. The door to the attendant's room is slightly ajar.

SHOOTER'S VOICE *(On the radio, over the final chords of the song):* And that's all for tonight, night owls. This is your Number One Night Owl saying it's three o'clock, all right, and time to rock your daddy to dreams of de-light. And mama, I'm comin' home. And the rest of you night owls gonna have to make it through the rest of this night by *yourself,* or with the help of *your* friends, if you know what I mean. And you know what I mean.

The radio station goes dead, music replaced by an irritating static. Alberta opens the door tentatively, looks around and walks in. She has dressed carefully and her laundry basket exhibits the same care. She checks the top of a washer for dust or water before putting her purse and basket down. She takes off her coat and hat. She walks back to the door marked Attendant, and is startled briefly when she looks in.

ALBERTA: Hello? *(Steps back, seeing that the attendant is asleep)* Sleep? Is that how you do your job? Sleep? What they pay you to do, sleep? Listen, it's fine with me. Better, in fact. I'm glad, actually. *(She leans in and turns off the radio. She walks back toward the basket, talking to herself)* Do you want him out here talking to you? *(Procrastinating)* You came to do your wash so do your wash. No, first . . . *(She takes an index card out of her purse. She tacks it up on the bulletin board. We must see that it is very important to her)* There. Good. *(She opens a washer lid and runs her fingers around the soap tray, taking out lint and depositing it in one of the coffee cans. As she does this, she accidently knocks over her purse)* It's okay. Nothing breakable. Clean it up, that's all. You've been up this late before. Nothing the matter with you, just nerves . . . and gravity.

Alberta bends down and begins to put the things back in her purse. She cannot see as Deedee backs in the door of the laundromat. Deedee is a wreck. She carries her clothes tied up in a man's shirt. She trips over a wastebasket and falls on her laundry as it spills out of the shirt.

DEEDEE: Well, poo-rats!

Alberta stands up, startled, hesitates, then walks over to where Deedee is still sprawled on the floor.

ALBERTA: Are you all right? *(She is angry that Deedee is there at all, but polite nevertheless)*

DEEDEE *(Grudgingly):* Cute, huh?

ALBERTA *(Moving the wastebasket out of the way):* Probably a wet spot on the floor. *(Goes back to her wash)*

DEEDEE: I already picked these clothes off the floor once tonight. *(No response from Al-*

berta) We been in our apartment two years and Joe still ain't found the closets. He thinks hangers are for when you lock your keys in your car. *(Still no response, though she is expecting one)* I mean, he's got this coat made of sheep's fur or somethin' and my mom came over one day and asked where did we get that fuzzy little rug. *(She is increasingly nervous)* Joe works at the Ford plant. I asked him why they call it that. I said, "How often do you have to water a Ford plant?" It was just a little joke, but he didn't think it was very funny.

ALBERTA *(Her good manners requiring her to say something)*: They probably do have a sprinkler system.

DEEDEE: Shoulda saved my breath and just tripped over the coffee table. He'd laughed at that. *(No response)* Well, *(Brightly)* I guess it's just you and me.

ALBERTA: Yes. *(Makes a move to get back to her wash)*

DEEDEE: Guess not too many people suds their duds in the middle of the night.

ALBERTA: Suds their duds?

DEEDEE: I do mine at Mom's. *(She begins to put her clothes in two washers, imitating Alberta)* I mean, I take our stuff over to Mom's. She got matching Maytags. She buys giant-size Cheer and we sit around and watch the soaps till the clothes come out. Suds the duds, that's what she says. Well, more than that. She wrote it on a little card and sent it in to Cheer so they could use it on their TV ads.

ALBERTA *(Pleasantly)*: Gives you a chance to talk, I guess. Visit.

DEEDEE: She says, "Just leave 'em, I'll do 'em," but that wouldn't be right, so I stay. Course she don't ever say how she likes seeing me, but she holds back, you know. I mean, there's stuff you don't have to say when it's family.

ALBERTA: Is she out of town tonight?

DEEDEE: No, probably just asleep. *(Alberta nods. She reads from the top of the washer)* Five cycle Turbomatic Deluxe. *(Punching buttons)* Hot wash-warm rinse, warm wash-warm rinse, warm wash-cold rinse, cold wash-cold rinse, cold wash, delicate cycle. *(Now lifts the lid of the washer)* What's this? Add laundry aids.

ALBERTA: Your mother does your laundry.

DEEDEE: You don't have a washer either, huh?

ALBERTA *(Too quickly)*: It's broken.

DEEDEE: Get your husband to fix it. *(Looking at Alberta's mound of shirts)* Got a heap of shirts, don't he?

ALBERTA: It can't be fixed.

DEEDEE: Where are *your* clothes?

ALBERTA: Mine are mostly hand wash.

DEEDEE: We just dump all our stuff in together.

ALBERTA: That's nice.

DEEDEE: Joe can fix just about anything. He's real good with his hands. *(Relaxing some now)* I've been saying that since high school. *(Laughs)* He makes trucks. God, I'd hate to see the truck I'd put together. *(Now a nervous laugh)* He had to work the double shift tonight. *(Going on quickly)* They do all kinds out there. Pickups, dump trucks . . . they got this joke, him and his buddies, about what rhymes with pickle truck, but I don't know the end of it, you know, the punch line. Goes like . . . "I'll come to get you baby in a pickle truck, I'll tell you what I'm wantin' is a— *(Stops, but continues the beat with her foot or by snapping her fingers)* See, that's the part I don't know. The end. *(Shrugs)*

ALBERTA: Overtime pays well, I imagine.

DEEDEE: It's all-the-time, here lately. He says people are buyin' more trucks 'cause farmers have to raise more cows 'cause we got a population explosion going on. Really crummy, you know? People I don't even know having babies means Joe can't come home at the right time. Don't seem fair.

ALBERTA: Or true.

DEEDEE: Huh?

ALBERTA: The population explosion is over. The birthrate is very stable now.

DEEDEE: Oh.

ALBERTA: Still, it's no fun to be in the house by yourself.

DEEDEE: See, we live right over there, on top of the Mexican restaurant. *(Going over to the window)* That window with the blue light in it, that's ours. It's a bunch of blueberries on a stalk, only it's a light. Joe gave it to me. He thinks blue is my favorite color.

ALBERTA: So the restaurant noise was bothering you.

DEEDEE: They got this bar that stays open till four. That's how Joe picked the apartment. He hates to run out for beer late. He don't mind running down. *(Broadly)* Old Mexico Taco Tavern. Except Joe says it's supposed to be Olé Mexico, like what they say in bullfights.

ALBERTA: Bullfights are disgusting.

DEEDEE: You've seen a real bullfight?

ALBERTA: We used to travel quite a bit.

DEEDEE *(Excited, curious, demanding)*: Well, tell me about it.

ALBERTA: There's not much to tell. The bull comes out and they kill it.

DEEDEE: What for? *(Putting her clothes in the washer)*

ALBERTA *(Pleased at the question)*: Fun. Doesn't that sound like *fun* to you?

DEEDEE *(Encouraged)*: Your husband works nights too?

ALBERTA: Herb is out of town. Did you mean to put that in there?

DEEDEE *(Peering into her washer)*: Huh?

ALBERTA: Your whites will come out green.

DEEDEE *(Retrieving the shirt)*: Joe wouldn't like that. No sir. Be like when Mom's washer chewed this hole in his bowling shirt. Whoo-ee! Was he hot. Kicked the chest of drawers, broke his toe. *(No response from Alberta)* And the chest of drawers too. *(No response)* Is Herb picky like that?

ALBERTA: Herb likes to look nice. *(Reaches for her soap)*

DEEDEE: Hey! You forgot one. *(Picking the remaining shirt out of Alberta's basket)* See? *(Opens it out, showing an awful stain)* Yuck! Looks like vomit.

ALBERTA: It's my cabbage soup.

DEEDEE: Well, *(Helping)* in it goes. *(Opening one of Alberta's washers)*

ALBERTA: No!

DEEDEE: The other one? *(Reaching for the other washer)*

ALBERTA *(Taking the shirt away from her)*: I don't want to . . . it's too . . . that stain will never . . . *(Enforcing a calm now)* It needs to presoak. I forgot the Woolite.

DEEDEE: Sorry.

ALBERTA: That's quite all right. *(Folding the shirt carefully, putting it back in the basket. Wants Deedee to vanish)*

DEEDEE: One of those machines give soap?

Alberta points to the correct one and Deedee walks over to it.

DEEDEE: It takes nickels. I only got quarters.

ALBERTA: The attendant will give you change. *(Pointing to the open attendant door, putting her own coins in her washers)*

DEEDEE *(Looking in the door):* He's asleep.

ALBERTA: Ah.

DEEDEE: Be terrible to wake him up just for some old nickels. Do you have any change?

ALBERTA: No.

DEEDEE: Looks like he's got a pocket full of money. Think it would wake him up if I stuck my hand in there? *(Enjoys this idea)*

ALBERTA *(Feeling bad about not helping and also not wanting the attendant awake):* Twenty years ago, maybe. *(Deedee laughs)* Here, I found some.

Deedee walks back, gives Alberta the quarters; she counts out the change.

ALBERTA: That's ten, twenty, thirty, forty, fifty.

DEEDEE *(Putting the nickels in the soap machine):* He shouldn't be sleeping like that. Somebody could come in here and rob him. You don't think he's dead or anything, do you? I mean, I probably wouldn't know it if I saw somebody dead.

ALBERTA: You'd know. *(Starts her washers)*

DEEDEE *(Pushing in the coin trays, starting her washers):* Okay. Cheer up! *(Laughs)* That's what Mom always says, "Cheer up." *(Looks at Alberta)* Hey, my name is Deedee. Deedee Johnson.

ALBERTA: Nice to meet you.

DEEDEE: What's yours?

ALBERTA: Alberta.

DEEDEE: Alberta what?

ALBERTA *(Reluctantly):* Alberta Johnson.

DEEDEE: Hey! We might be related. I mean, Herb and Joe could be cousins or something.

ALBERTA: I don't think so.

DEEDEE: Yeah. I guess there's lots of Johnsons.

ALBERTA *(Looking down at the magazine):* Yes.

DEEDEE: I'm botherin' you, aren't I? *(Alberta smiles)* I'd talk to somebody else, but there ain't nobody else. 'Cept Sleepy back there. I talk in *my* sleep sometimes, but him, he looks like he's lucky to be breathin' in his. *(Awkward)* Sleep, I mean.

ALBERTA: Would you like a magazine?

DEEDEE: No thanks. I brought a Dr. Pepper. *(Alberta is amazed)* You can have it if you want.

ALBERTA: No thank you.

DEEDEE: Sleepy was one of the seven dwarfs. I can still name them all. I couldn't tell you seven presidents of the United States, but I can say the dwarfs. *(Very proud)* Sleepy, Grumpy, Sneezy, Dopey, Doc and Bashful. *(Suddenly very low)* That's only six. Who's the other one?

ALBERTA *(Willing to help):* You could name seven presidents.

DEEDEE: Oh no.

ALBERTA: Try it.

DEEDEE: Okay. *(Takes a big breath)* There's Carter, Nixon, Kennedy, Lincoln, Ben Franklin, George Washington . . . uh . . .

ALBERTA: Eleanor Roosevelt's husband.

DEEDEE: Mr. Roosevelt.

ALBERTA: Mr. Roosevelt. That's seven. Except Benjamin Franklin was never president.

DEEDEE: You're a teacher or something, aren't you?

ALBERTA: I was. Say Mr. Roosevelt again.

DEEDEE: Mr. Roosevelt.

ALBERTA: There. Teddy makes seven.

DEEDEE: Around here? *(Alberta looks puzzled)* Or in the county schools?

ALBERTA: Ohio. Columbus.

DEEDEE: Great!

ALBERTA: Do you know Columbus?

DEEDEE: Not personally.

ALBERTA: Ah.

DEEDEE: I better be careful. No ain'ts or nuthin'.

ALBERTA: You can't say anything I haven't heard before.

DEEDEE: Want me to try?

ALBERTA: No.

DEEDEE: What does Herb do?

ALBERTA *(Too quickly)*: Is Deedee short for something? Deirdre, Deborah?

DEEDEE: No. Just Deedee. The guys in high school always kidded me about my name. *(Affecting a boy's voice)* Hey, Deedee, is Deedee your name or your bra size?

ALBERTA: That wasn't very nice of them.

DEEDEE: That ain't the worst. Wanna hear the worst? *(Alberta doesn't respond)* Ricky Baker, Icky Ricky Baker and David Duvall said this one. They'd come up to the locker bank, David's locker was right next to mine and Ricky'd say, "Hey, did you have a good time last night?" And David would say, "Yes. In Deedee." Then they'd slap each other and laugh like idiots.

ALBERTA: You could've had your locker moved.

DEEDEE: I guess, but see, the basketball players always came down that hall at the end of school. Going to practice, you know.

ALBERTA: One of the basketball players I taught . . . *(Begins to chuckle)*

DEEDEE *(Anxious to laugh with her)*: Yeah?

ALBERTA: . . . thought Herbert Hoover invented the vacuum cleaner.

Alberta waits for Deedee to laugh. When she doesn't, Alberta steps back a few steps. Deedee is embarrassed.

DEEDEE: Why did you quit . . . teaching.

ALBERTA: Age.

DEEDEE: You don't look old enough to retire.

ALBERTA: Not my age. Theirs.

DEEDEE: Mine, you mean.

ALBERTA: Actually, Mother was very sick then.

DEEDEE: Is she still alive?

ALBERTA: No.

DEEDEE: I'm sorry.

ALBERTA: It was a blessing, really. There was quite a lot of pain at the end.

DEEDEE: For her maybe, but what about you?

ALBERTA: She was the one with the pain.

DEEDEE: Sounds like she was lucky to have you there, nursing her and all.

ALBERTA: I read her *Wuthering Heights* five times that year. I kept checking different ones out of the library, you know, *Little Women, Pride and Prejudice,* but each time she'd say, "No, I think I'd like to hear *Wuthering Heights."* Just like she hadn't heard it in fifty years. But each time, I'd read the last page and look up, and she'd say the same thing.

DEEDEE: What thing?

ALBERTA: She'd say, "I still don't see it. They didn't have to have all that trouble. All they had to do was find Heathcliff someplace to go every day. The man just needed a job. *(Pause)* But maybe I missed something. Read it again."

DEEDEE: My mom thinks Joe's a bum. *(Somehow she thinks this is an appropriate response, and Alberta is jolted back to the present)* No really, she kept paying this guy that worked at Walgreen's to come over and strip our wallpaper. She said, "Deedee, he's gonna be manager of that drugstore someday." Hell, the only reason he worked there was getting a discount on his pimple cream. She thought that would get me off Joe. No way. We've been married two years last month. Mom says this is the itch year.

ALBERTA: The itch year?

DEEDEE: When guys get the itch, you know, to fool around with other women. Stayin' out late, comin' in with stories about goin' drinkin' with the boys or workin' overtime or . . . somethin'. Is that clock right?

ALBERTA: I think so.

DEEDEE: Bet Herb never did that, huh?

ALBERTA: Be unfaithful, you mean? *(Deedee nods)* No.

DEEDEE: How can you be so sure like that? You keep him in the refrigerator?

ALBERTA: Well, I suppose he could have . . . *(Doesn't believe this for a minute)*

DEEDEE: Like right now, while he's up in wherever he is. . . .

ALBERTA: Akron. *(Surprised at her need to say this)*

DEEDEE: Akron, he could be sittin' at the bar in some all-night bowling alley polishin' some big blonde's ball.

ALBERTA: No.

DEEDEE: That's real nice to trust him like that.

ALBERTA: Aren't you afraid Joe will call you on his break and be worried about where you are?

DEEDEE: You got any kids?

ALBERTA: No.

DEEDEE: Didn't you want some?

ALBERTA: Oh yes.

DEEDEE: Me too. Lots of 'em. But Joe says he's not ready. Wants to be earning lots of money before we start our family.

ALBERTA: That's why he works this double shift.

DEEDEE: Yeah. Only now he's fixin' up this '64 Chevy he bought to drag race. Then when the race money starts comin' in, we can have them kids. He's really lookin' forward to that—winnin' a big race and havin' me and the kids run out on the track and him smilin' and grabbin' up the baby and pourin' beer all over us while the crowd is yellin' and screamin' . . .

ALBERTA: So all his money goes into this car.

DEEDEE: Hey. I love it too. Sundays we go to the garage and work on it. *(Gets a picture out of her wallet)* That devil painted there on the door, that cost two hundred dollars!

ALBERTA: You help him?

DEEDEE: He says it's a real big help just havin' me there watchin'.

ALBERTA: I never understood that, men wanting you to watch them do whatever it is . . . I mean. . . . Well *(Deciding to tell this story, a surprise both to her and to us)* every year at Thanksgiving, Herb would watch over me, washing the turkey, making the stuffing, stuffing the turkey. Made me nervous.

DEEDEE: You coulda told him to get lost. *(Offers fabric softener)* Downy?

Alberta nods yes, accepting Deedee's help, but is still nervous about it.

ALBERTA: Actually, the last ten years or so, I sent him out for sage. For the dressing. He'd come in and sit down saying "Mmm boy was this ever going to be the best turkey yet" and rubbing his hands together and I'd push jars around in the cabinet and look all worried and say "Herb, I don't think I have enough sage." And he'd say, "Well, Bertie, my girl, I'll just go to the store and get some."

DEEDEE *(Jittery when someone else is talking)*: I saw white pepper at the store last week. How do they do that?

ALBERTA: I don't know.

DEEDEE: Is Dr. Pepper made out of pepper?

ALBERTA: I don't know.

DEEDEE: And what did Herb do, that you had to watch, I mean.

ALBERTA: He gardened. I didn't have to watch him plant the seeds or weed the plants or spray for pests or pick okra. But when the day came to turn over the soil, that was the day. Herb would rent a rototiller and bring out a lawn chair from the garage. He'd wipe it off and call in the kitchen window, "Alberta, it's so pleasant out here in the sunshine." And when he finished, he'd bring out this little wooden sign and drive it into the ground.

DEEDEE: What'd it say?

ALBERTA: Herb Garden. *(Pauses)* He thought that was funny.

DEEDEE: Did you laugh?

ALBERTA: Every year.

DEEDEE: He's not doing one anymore? *(Walking to the window)*

ALBERTA: No.

DEEDEE *(Looks uneasy, still staring out the window)*: Why not?

ALBERTA: What's out there?

DEEDEE: Oh nothing.

ALBERTA: You looked like—

DEEDEE: Joe should be home soon. I turned out all the lights except the blueberries so I could tell if he comes in, you know, when he turns the lights on.

ALBERTA: When is the shift over?

DEEDEE *(Enforced cheer now)*: Oh, not for a long time yet. I just thought. . . . He might get through early, he said. And we could go have a beer. Course, he might stop off and bowl a few games first.

Alberta gets up to check on her wash. Deedee walks to the bulletin board.

DEEDEE *(Reading)*: "Typing done, hourly or by the page. Cheer." What on earth?

ALBERTA: Must be cheap. *(Laughs a little)* It better be cheap.

DEEDEE *(Taking some notices down):* Most of this stuff is over already. Hey! Here's one for Herb. "Gardening tools, never used. Rake, hoe, spade and towel."

ALBERTA: Trowel.

DEEDEE *(Aggravated by the correction):* You got great eyes, Alberta. *(Continues reading)* "459-4734. A. Johnson." You think this A. Johnson is related to us? *(Laughs)* No, that's right, you said Herb wasn't doing a garden anymore. No, I got it! This A. Johnson is you. And the reason Herb ain't doin' a garden is you're selling his rakes. But this says "never used." Alberta, you shouldn't try to fool people like that. Washin' up Herb's hoe and selling it like it was new. Bad girl.

ALBERTA: Actually, that is me. I bought Herb some new tools for his birthday and then he . . . gave it up . . . gardening.

DEEDEE: Before his birthday?

ALBERTA: What?

DEEDEE: Did you have time to go buy him another present?

ALBERTA: Yes . . . well, no. I mean, he told me before his birthday, but I didn't get a chance to get him anything else.

DEEDEE: He's probably got everything anyhow.

ALBERTA: Just about.

DEEDEE: Didn't he get his feelings hurt?

ALBERTA: No.

DEEDEE: Joe never likes the stuff I give him.

ALBERTA: Oh, I'm sure he does. He just doesn't know how to tell you.

DEEDEE: No. He doesn't. For our anniversary, I planned real far ahead for this one, I'm tellin' you. I sent off my picture, not a whole body picture, just my face real close up, to this place in Massachusetts, and they painted, well I don't know if they really painted, but somehow or other they *put* my face on this doll. It was unbelievable how it really looked like me. 'Bout this tall *(Indicates about two feet)* with overalls and a checked shirt. I thought it was real cute, and I wrote this card sayin' "From one livin' doll to another. Let's keep playin' house till the day we die."

ALBERTA: And he didn't like it?

DEEDEE: He laughed so hard he fell over backward out of the chair and cracked his head open on the radiator. We had to take him to the emergency room.

ALBERTA: I'm sorry.

DEEDEE: We was sittin' there waitin' for him to get sewed up and this little kid comes in real sick and Joe he says to me, *(Getting a candy bar out of her purse and taking a big anxious bite out of it)* I brought this doll along, see, I don't know why, anyway Joe says to me . . . "Deedee, that little girl is so much sicker than me. Let's give her this doll to make her feel better." And they were takin' her right on in to the doctors 'cause she looked pretty bad, and Joe rushes up and puts this doll in her arms.

ALBERTA: They let her keep it?

DEEDEE: Her mother said, "Thanks a lot." Real sweet like they didn't have much money to buy the kid dolls or something. It made Joe feel real good.

ALBERTA: But it was your present to him. It was your face on the doll.

DEEDEE: Yeah, *(Pause)* but I figure it was his present as soon as I gave it to him, so if he wanted to give it away, that's his business. But *(Stops)* he didn't like it. I could tell. *(Walks to the window again)* They need to wash this window here.

ALBERTA: I gave Herb a fishing pole one year.

DEEDEE *(Not interested):* He fishes.

ALBERTA: No, but I thought he wanted to. He'd cut out a picture of this husky man standing in water practically up to his waist, fishing. I thought he left it out so I'd get the hint.

DEEDEE: But he didn't?

ALBERTA: Oh, it was a hint all right. He wanted the hat.

DEEDEE: Right.

ALBERTA *(Seeing that Deedee is really getting upset):* Do you like the things Joe gives you?

DEEDEE: I'd like it if he came home, that's what I'd like.

ALBERTA: He'll be back soon. You'll probably see those lights go on as soon as your clothes are dry.

DEEDEE: Sure.

ALBERTA: People just can't always be where we want them to be, when we want them to be there.

DEEDEE: Well, I don't like it.

ALBERTA: You don't have to like it. You just have to know it.

DEEDEE *(Defensive):* Wouldn't you like for Herb to be home right now?

ALBERTA: I certainly would.

DEEDEE: 'Cause if they were both home where they should be, we wouldn't have to be here in this crappy laundromat washin' fuckin' shirts in the middle of the night!

Deedee kicks a dryer. Alberta is alarmed and disturbed at the use of the word "fuckin'."

DEEDEE: I'm sorry. You probably don't use language like that, well, neither do I, very often, but I'm *(Now doing it on purpose)* pissed as hell at that sunuvabitch.

Alberta picks up a magazine, trying to withdraw completely. She is offended, but doesn't want to appear self-righteous. Now, Shooter pushes open the front door. Deedee turns sharply and sees him. She storms back and sits down beside Alberta. Both women are somewhat alarmed at a black man entering this preserve so late at night. Shooter is poised and handsome. He is dressed neatly, but casually. He is carrying an army duffel bag full of clothes, a cue case and a sack of tacos. He has a can of beer in one pocket. He moves toward a washer, sets down the duffel bag, opens the cap on the beer. He is aware that he has frightened them. This amuses him, but he understands it. Besides, he is so goddamned charming.

SHOOTER *(Holding the taco sack so they can see it):* Would either of you two ladies care to join me in a taco?

ALBERTA *(Finally):* No thank you.

SHOOTER *(As though in an ad):* Freshly chopped lettuce, firm vine-ripened New Jersey beefsteak tomatoes, a-ged, shred-ded, ched-dar cheese, sweet slivers of Bermuda onion and Ole Mexico's very own, very hot taco sauce.

DEEDEE: That's just what they say on the radio.

SHOOTER: That's because I'm the "they" who says it on the radio.

DEEDEE: You are?

SHOOTER *(Walking over):* Shooter Stevens. *(Shakes her hand)*

ALBERTA *(As he shakes her hand):* Nice to meet you.

DEEDEE: You're the Number One Night Owl?

SHOOTER *(As he said it at the beginning of the act):* . . . sayin' it's three o'clock, all right, and time to rock your daddy to dreams of de-light.

DEEDEE: You are! You really are! That's fantastic! I always listen to you!

SHOOTER *(Walking back to his laundry):* Yeah?

DEEDEE: Always. Except when . . . I mean, when I get to pick, I pick you. I mean, your station. You're on late.

SHOOTER: You got it.

DEEDEE *(To Alberta):* Terrific. *(Disgusted with herself)* I'm telling him he's on late. He knows he's on late. He's the one who's on late. Big news, huh?

SHOOTER: You a reporter?

DEEDEE *(Pleased with the question):* Oh no. *(Stands up, stretches)* Gotten so stiff sitting there. *(Walks over)* Don't you know what they put in those things?

SHOOTER: The tacos?

DEEDEE: Dog food.

SHOOTER *(Laughing):* Have to eat 'em anyway. Good business. I keep stoppin' in over there, they keep running the ad. Gonna kill me.

DEEDEE: No kidding. We take our . . . *(Quickly)* My garbage cans are right next to theirs and whatta theirs got in 'em all the time? Dog-food cans.

SHOOTER *(He smiles):* Maybe they have a dog.

ALBERTA: It could be someone else in the building.

SHOOTER: See?

DEEDEE: She didn't mean they have a dog. She meant some old person in the building's eatin' dog food. It happens. A lot around here.

SHOOTER *(To Alberta):* You her mom?

ALBERTA: No.

DEEDEE: We just met in here. She's Alberta Johnson. I'm Deedee Johnson.

ALBERTA: Shooter is an unusual name.

SHOOTER *(Nodding toward the pool hall next door):* I play some pool.

DEEDEE *(Pointing to the cue case):* What's that?

SHOOTER: My cue.

DEEDEE: You any good?

SHOOTER: At what?

DEEDEE: At pool, dummy.

SHOOTER *(Putting his clothes in the washer):* I do okay.

DEEDEE: You must do better than okay or else why would you have your own cue?

SHOOTER: Willie says, Willie's the guy who owns the place, Willie says pool cues are like women. You gotta have your own and you gotta treat her right.

DEEDEE *(Seeing a piece of clothing he's dropped in):* Did you mean to put that in there?

SHOOTER *(Pulling it back out):* This?

DEEDEE: Your whites will come out green.

SHOOTER *(Dropping it back in the washer):* Uh-uh. It's nylon.

ALBERTA: Your work sounds very interesting.

SHOOTER: Yes, it does.

DEEDEE: What's your real name?

SHOOTER: G.W.

DEEDEE: That's not a real name.

SHOOTER: I don't like my real name.

DEEDEE: Come on . . .

SHOOTER *(Disgusted):* It's Gary Wayne. Now do I look like Gary Wayne to you?

DEEDEE *(Laughs):* No.
SHOOTER: Mom's from Indiana.
ALBERTA: From Gary or Fort Wayne?
DEEDEE: Alberta used to be a teacher.
SHOOTER: It coulda been worse. She coulda named me Clarksville. *(Deedee laughs)* Hey! Now why don't the two of you come over and join us for a beer?
ALBERTA: No thank you.
SHOOTER *(Pouring in the soap):* It's just Willie and me this time of night.
ALBERTA: No.
DEEDEE *(With a knowing look at Alberta):* And watch you play pool?
SHOOTER: Actually, what we were planning to do tonight was whip us up a big devil's food cake and pour it in one of the pool tables to bake. Turn up the heat real high . . . watch it rise and then pour on the creamy fudge icing with lots of nuts.
DEEDEE: *You're* nuts.
SHOOTER: Get real sick if we have to eat it all ourselves . . .
DEEDEE: I've never seen anybody play pool.
SHOOTER: The key to pool's a . . . *(Directly seductive now)* real smooth stroke . . . the feel of that stick in your hand . . .
DEEDEE: Feels good?
SHOOTER: You come on over, I'll show you just how it's done.
DEEDEE: Pool.
SHOOTER: Sure. *(Smiles, then turns sharply and walks back to Alberta, depositing an empty soap box in the trash can)* Willie always keeps hot water. You could have a nice cup of tea.
ALBERTA *(A pointed look at Deedee):* No.
DEEDEE: Our wash is almost done. We have to—
SHOOTER: We'll be there quite a while. Gets lonesome this late, you know.
DEEDEE: We know.

And suddenly, everybody feels quite uncomfortable.

SHOOTER *(To Alberta):* It was nice meeting you. Hope I didn't interrupt your reading or anything.
DEEDEE: She used to be a teacher.
SHOOTER: That's what you said. *(Walking toward the door)* Right next door, now. Can't miss it. *(To Deedee)* Give you a piece of that fudge cake.
DEEDEE: Yeah, I'll bet you would.
SHOOTER *(Closing the door):* Big piece.

Alberta watches Deedee watch to see which direction Shooter takes.

DEEDEE *(After a moment):* I thought we'd had it there for a minute, didn't you? *(Visibly cheered)* Coulda been a murderer, or a robber or a rapist, just as easy! *(Increasingly excited)* We coulda been hostages by now!
ALBERTA: To have hostages you have to commit a hijacking. You do not hijack a laundromat.
DEEDEE: Depends how bad you need clean clothes.
ALBERTA: I didn't like the things he said to you.
DEEDEE: He was just playin'.

ALBERTA: He was not playing.

DEEDEE: Well, what does it hurt? Just words.

ALBERTA: Not those words.

DEEDEE: You don't miss a thing, do you?

ALBERTA: I'm not deaf.

DEEDEE: Just prejudiced.

ALBERTA: That's not true.

DEEDEE: If that was a white DJ comin' in here, you'd still be talkin' to him, I bet. Seein' if he knows your "old" favorites.

ALBERTA: If you don't want to know what I think, you can stop talking to me.

DEEDEE: What you think is what's wrong with the world. People don't trust each other just because they're some other color from them.

ALBERTA: And who was it who said he could be a murderer? That was you, Deedee. Would you have said that if he'd been white?

DEEDEE: It just makes you sick, doesn't it. The thought of me and Shooter over there after you go home.

ALBERTA: It's not my business.

DEEDEE: That's for sure.

Alberta goes back to reading her magazine. Deedee wanders around.

DEEDEE: You don't listen to him on the radio, but I do. And you know what he says after "rock your daddy to dreams of de-light"? He says, "And mama, I'm comin' home." Now, if he has a "mama" to go home to, what's he doing washing his own clothes? So he don't have a "mama," and that means lonely. And he's loaded, too. So if he's got a wife, she's got a washer, so don't say maybe they don't have a washer. Lonely.

ALBERTA: All right. He's a nice young man who washes his own clothes and is "friendly" without regard to race, creed or national origin.

DEEDEE: I mean, we're both in here in the middle of the night and it don't mean we're on the make, does it?

ALBERTA: It's perfectly respectable.

DEEDEE: You always do this when Herb is out of town?

ALBERTA: No.

DEEDEE: You don't even live in this neighborhood, do you?

ALBERTA: No.

DEEDEE: Know how I knew that? That garden. There ain't a garden for miles around here.

ALBERTA: You've been reading Sherlock Holmes.

DEEDEE *(Knows Alberta was insulting her)*: So why did you come over here?

ALBERTA *(Knows she made a mistake)*: I came for the same reason you did. To do my wash.

DEEDEE: In the middle of the night? Hah. It's a big mystery, isn't it? And you don't want to tell me. Is some man meetin' you here? Yeah, and you can't have your meetin' out where you live 'cause your friends might see you and give the word to old Herb when he gets back.

ALBERTA: No. *(Pauses)* I'm sorry I said what I did. Go on over to the pool hall. I'll put your clothes in the dryer.

DEEDEE *(Easily thrown off the track)*: And let him think I'm all hot for him. No sir. Besides, Joe might come home.

ALBERTA: That's right.

DEEDEE: Might just serve him right, though. Come in and see me drinkin' beer and playin' pool with Willie and Shooter. Joe hates black people. He says even when they're dancin' or playin' ball, they're thinkin' about killin'. Yeah, that would teach him to run out on me. A little dose of his own medicine. Watch him gag on it.

ALBERTA: So he *has* run out on you.

DEEDEE: He's workin' the double shift.

ALBERTA: That's what you said.

DEEDEE: And you don't believe me. You think he just didn't come home, is that it? You think I was over there waitin' and waitin' in my new nightgown and when the late show went off I turned on the radio and ate a whole pint of chocolate ice cream, and when the radio went off I couldn't stand it anymore so I grabbed up all these clothes, dirty or not, and got outta there so he wouldn't come in and find me cryin'. Well, *(Firmly)* I wasn't cryin'!

ALBERTA *(After a considerable pause)*: I haven't cried in forty years.

DEEDEE: Just happy I guess.

ALBERTA *(With a real desire to help now)*: I had an Aunt Dora, who had a rabbit, Puffer, who died. I cried then. I cried for weeks.

DEEDEE: And it wasn't even your rabbit.

ALBERTA: I loved Aunt Dora and she loved that rabbit. I'd go to visit and she'd tell me what Puffer had done that day. She claimed he told her stories, Goldilocks and the Three Hares, The Rabbit Who Ate New York. Then we'd go outside and drink lemonade while Puffer ate lettuce. She grew lettuce just for him. A whole backyard of it.

DEEDEE: Little cracked, huh?

ALBERTA: I helped her bury him. Tears were streaming down my face. "Bertie," she said, "stop crying. He didn't mean to go and leave us all alone and he'd feel bad if he knew he made us so miserable." But in the next few weeks, Aunt Dora got quieter and quieter till finally she wasn't talking at all and Mother put her in a nursing home.

DEEDEE: Where she died.

ALBERTA: Yes.

DEEDEE: Hey! Our wash is done. *(Alberta seems not to hear her)* Look, I'll do it. You go sit.

ALBERTA *(Disoriented)*: No, I . . .

DEEDEE: Let me, really. I know this part. Mom says you can't blow this part, so I do it. She still checks, though, finds some reason to go downstairs and check the heat I set. I don't mind, really. Can't be too careful.

Deedee unloads the washers and carries the clothes to the dryers. Alberta walks to the window, seeming very far away.

DEEDEE *(Setting the heat)*: Regular for you guys, warm for permos and undies. Now Herb's shirts and shorts get hot. Pants and socks get . . .

ALBERTA: Warm.

DEEDEE: What's Herb got left to wear anyhow?

ALBERTA: His gray suit.

DEEDEE *(Laughs at how positive Alberta is about this)*: What color tie?

ALBERTA: Red with a silver stripe through it.

DEEDEE *(Still merry)*: Shirt?

ALBERTA: White.

DEEDEE: Shoes?

ALBERTA *(Quiet astonishment):* I don't know.

DEEDEE: Well I'm glad. Thought you were seeing him all the way to Akron, X-ray eyes or something weird. Alberta . . .

ALBERTA: Yes? *(Worried, turning around to face her now, afraid Deedee will know her secret)*

DEEDEE: You got any dimes?

ALBERTA *(Relieved):* Sure. *(Walks to her purse)* How many do we need?

DEEDEE: Two each, I guess. Four dryers makes eight. *(As Alberta is getting them out of her wallet)* I don't know what I'd have done if you hadn't been here. I didn't think . . . before I . . .

ALBERTA: You'd have done just fine. Don't forget Sleepy back there.

DEEDEE: I wish Mom were more like you.

ALBERTA: Stuck up?

DEEDEE: Smart. Nice to talk to.

ALBERTA: Thank you, but . . .

DEEDEE: No, really. You've been to Mexico and you've got a good man.

Alberta takes off her glasses, still very upset.

DEEDEE: Mom's just got me and giant-size Cheer. And she don't say two words while I'm there. Ever. I don't blame her I guess.

ALBERTA: Well . . .

DEEDEE: Yeah.

ALBERTA *(Back in balance now):* But you're young and pretty. You have a wonderful sense of humor.

DEEDEE: Uh-huh.

ALBERTA: And you'll have those children someday.

DEEDEE: Yeah, I know. *(Gloomily)* I have my whole life in front of me.

ALBERTA: You could get a job.

DEEDEE: Oh, I got one. This company in New Jersey, they send me envelopes and letters and lists of names and I write on the names and addresses and Dear Mr. Wilson or whatever at the top of the letter. I do have nice handwriting.

ALBERTA: I'm sure.

DEEDEE: I get so bored doing it. Sometimes I want to take a fat orange crayon and scribble *(Making letters in the air)* EAT BEANS, FATSO, and then draw funny faces all over the letter.

ALBERTA: I'm sure the extra money comes in handy.

DEEDEE: Well, Joe don't know I do it. I hide all the stuff before he comes home. And I keep the money at Mom's. She borrows from it sometimes. She says that makes us even for the water for the washing machine. See, I can't spend it or Joe will know I got it.

ALBERTA: He doesn't want you to work.

DEEDEE *(Imitating Joe's voice):* I'm the head of this house.

ALBERTA: He expects you to sit around all day?

DEEDEE: I guess. *(With good-humored rage)* Oh, I can wash the floor if I want.

ALBERTA: You should tell him how you feel.

DEEDEE: He'd leave me.

ALBERTA: Maybe.

DEEDEE *(After a moment):* So what, right?

ALBERTA: I just meant, if you give him the chance to understand—

DEEDEE: But what would I say?

ALBERTA: You'd figure something out. I'm sure.

DEEDEE: I don't want to start it. I don't want to say I want a real job, 'cause then I'll say the reason I want a real job is I gotta have something to think about besides when are you coming home and how long is it gonna be before you don't come home at all. And he'll say what do you mean don't come home at all and I'll have to tell him I know what you're doing, I know you're lying to me and going out on me and he'll say what are you gonna do about it. You want a divorce? And I don't want him to say that.

ALBERTA: Now . . . you don't know—

DEEDEE *(Firmly):* I called the bowling alley and asked for him and the bartender said, "This Patsy? He's on his way, honey." I hope he falls in the sewer.

ALBERTA: Deedee!

DEEDEE: I hope he gets his shirt caught in his zipper. I hope he wore socks with holes in 'em. I hope his Right Guard gives out. I hope his baseball cap falls in the toilet. I hope she kills him. *(Pushing one of the carts, hard)*

ALBERTA: Deedee!

DEEDEE: I do. Last night, I thought I'd surprise him and maybe we'd bowl a few games? Well, I was gettin' my shoes and I saw them down at lane twelve, laughin' and all. He had one of his hands rubbing her hair and the other one rubbing his bowling ball. Boy did I get out of there quick. I've seen her there before. She teaches at the Weight Control upstairs, so she's probably not very strong but maybe she could poison him or something. She wears those pink leotards and even her hair looks thin. I hate him.

ALBERTA: I'm sure you don't really.

DEEDEE: He's mean and stupid. I thought he'd get over it, but he didn't. Mean and stupid. And I ain't all that smart, so if I know he's dumb, he must really be dumb. I used to think he just acted mean and stupid. Now, I know he really *is* . . .

ALBERTA: . . . mean and stupid.

DEEDEE: Why am I telling you this? You don't know nuthin' about bein' dumped.

ALBERTA: At least you have some money saved.

DEEDEE: For what?

ALBERTA: And your mother would let you stay with her till you got your own place.

DEEDEE: She's the *last* person I'm tellin'.

ALBERTA: I'll bet you'd like being a telephone operator.

DEEDEE: But how's he gonna eat? The only time he ever even fried an egg, he flipped it over and it landed in the sink. It was the last egg, so he grabbed it up and ate it in one bite.

ALBERTA: One bite?

DEEDEE: I like how he comes in the door. Picks me up, swings me around in the air . . .

ALBERTA *(Incredulous):* He stuffed a whole egg in his mouth?

DEEDEE: You're worse than Mom. *(Angrily)* He's gonna be a famous race car driver someday and I want to be there.

ALBERTA: To have him pour beer all over you.

DEEDEE: Yes, to have him pour beer all over me.

ALBERTA *(Checking the clothes in one of her dryers, knowing she has said too much):* He could

have come in without turning on the lights. If you want to go check, I'll watch your things here.

DEEDEE: You want to get rid of me, don't you?

ALBERTA: I do not want to get rid of you.

DEEDEE: So why don't *you* go home? Go get the Woolite for that yucky shirt you didn't wash. You not only don't want to talk to me, you didn't even want me to touch that shirt. Herb's shirt is too nice for me to even touch. Well, I may be a slob, but I'm clean.

ALBERTA: I didn't want to wash it.

DEEDEE: That ain't it at all. Herb is so wonderful. You love him so much. You wash his clothes just the right way. I could never drop his shirt in the washer the way you do it. The stain might not come out and he might say what did you do to my shirt and you might fight and that would mess up your little dream world where everything is always sweet and nobody ever gets mad and you just go around gardening and giving each other little pecky kisses all the time. Well, you're either kidding yourself or lying to me. Nobody is so wonderful that somebody else can't touch their shirt. You act like he's a saint. Like he's dead and now you worship the shirts he wore.

ALBERTA: What do I have to do to get you to leave me alone?

DEEDEE *(Feeling very bad)*: He is dead, isn't he?

ALBERTA: Yes.

DEEDEE: I'm so stupid.

ALBERTA: You . . .

DEEDEE: What? Tell me. Say something horrible.

ALBERTA *(Slowly, but not mean)*: You just don't know when to shut up.

DEEDEE: Worse than that. I don't know how. *(Hates what she has done)*

ALBERTA: But you are not dumb, child. And don't let anybody tell you you are, okay? *(Takes off her glasses and rubs her eyes)*

DEEDEE: I'm sorry, Mrs. Johnson, I really am sorry. You probably been plannin' this night for a long time. Washin' his things. And I barged in and spoiled it all.

ALBERTA: I've been avoiding it for a long time.

Deedee feels terrible, she wants to ask questions, but is trying very hard, for once, to control her mouth.

ALBERTA: Herb died last winter, the day before his birthday.

DEEDEE: When you got him the rakes.

ALBERTA: He was being nosy, like I told you before, in the kitchen. I was making his cake. So I asked him to take out the garbage. He said, "Can't we wait till it's old enough to walk?"

DEEDEE: How . . .

ALBERTA: I didn't miss him till I put the cake in the oven. Guess I thought he was checking his seedbeds in the garage. I yelled out, "Herb, do you want butter cream or chocolate?" And then I saw him. Lying in the alley, covered in my cabbage soup. It was his heart.

DEEDEE: Did you call the . . .

ALBERTA: I picked up his head in my hand and held it while I cleaned up as much of the stuff as I could. A tuna can, coffee grounds, eggshells . . .

DEEDEE *(Carefully)*: You knew he was dead, not just knocked out?

ALBERTA: He'd hit his head when he fell. He was bleeding in my hand. I knew I should get up, but the blood was still so warm.

DEEDEE: I'm so sorry.

ALBERTA: I don't want you to be alone, that's not what I meant before.

DEEDEE: Looks like I'm alone anyway.

ALBERTA: That's what I meant.

DEEDEE: Sometimes I bring in a little stand-up mirror to the coffee table while I'm watching TV. It's my face over there when I look, but it's a face just the same.

ALBERTA: Being alone isn't so awful. I mean, it's awful, but it's not that awful. There are hard things.

The dryers stop. Deedee watches Alberta take a load of clothes from the dryer, holding them up to smell them.

DEEDEE: I'd probably eat pork and beans for weeks.

ALBERTA *(Her back to Deedee)*: I found our beachball when I cleaned out the basement. I can't let the air out of it. It's *(Turning around now)* his breath in there. *(Sees Deedee is upset)* Get your clothes out. They'll wrinkle. That's amazing about the shoes.

DEEDEE: The shoes?

ALBERTA: Remember I was telling you what Herb had on? Gray suit . . .

DEEDEE: . . . white shirt, red tie with a silver stripe through it . . .

ALBERTA: I hang onto the shirt he died in, and I don't even know if he's got shoes on in his coffin.

DEEDEE: Well, if he's flyin' around heaven, he probably don't need 'em. *(Pauses)* You bought him all black socks.

ALBERTA: It was his idea. He thought they'd be easier to match if they were all the same color.

DEEDEE: Is it?

ALBERTA: No. Now I have to match by length. They may be all black, but they don't all shrink the same. I guess I don't really have to match them now, though, do I? *(Continues to match them)*

DEEDEE: I'd like to lose all Joe's white ones. *(Holding them up over the trash can, then thinking maybe it's not such a good idea)*

ALBERTA *(Going back for her last load of clothes, looking toward the window)*: Deedee . . . your lights are on. In your apartment. All the lights are on now.

DEEDEE: You sure?

ALBERTA: Come see.

Deedee walks over to the window.

DEEDEE: You're right.

ALBERTA: Yes.

DEEDEE: So what do I do now?

ALBERTA: I don't know.

DEEDEE: Should I rush right home? Ask Joe did he have a good time bowling a few games after his double shift? Listen to him brag about his score? His score he didn't make in

the games he didn't bowl after the double shift he didn't work? Well I don't feel like it. I'm going next door. Play some pool. Make him miss me.

ALBERTA: You should go home before you forget how mad you are. You don't have to put up with what he's doing. You can if you want to, if you think you can't make it without him, but you don't have to.

DEEDEE: But what should I say? Joe, if you don't stop going out on me, I'm not ever speaking to you again? That's exactly what he wants.

ALBERTA: What you say isn't that important. But there is something you have to remember while you say it.

DEEDEE: Which is?

ALBERTA: Your own face in the mirror is better company than a man who would eat a whole fried egg in one bite. *(Deedee laughs)* But it won't be easy.

DEEDEE *(Cautiously)*: Are you gonna wash that other shirt ever?

ALBERTA: The cabbage-soup shirt? No, I don't think so.

DEEDEE: Yeah.

ALBERTA *(Loading up her basket)*: Maybe, in a few months or next year sometime, I'll be able to give these away. They're nice things.

DEEDEE: People do need them. Hey! *(Leaving her laundry and going to the bulletin board)* I told you there ain't a garden for miles around here. You better hang onto these hoes. It's gettin' about time to turn over the soil, isn't it?

ALBERTA: Another two weeks or so, yes it is. Well, *(Taking the card)* that's everything. I'll just get my soap and . . .

DEEDEE *(Hesitantly)*: Mrs. Johnson?

ALBERTA: Alberta.

DEEDEE: Alberta.

ALBERTA: Yes?

DEEDEE: I'm really lonely.

ALBERTA: I know.

DEEDEE: How can you stand it?

ALBERTA: I can't. *(Pauses)* But I have to, just the same.

DEEDEE: How do I . . . how do you do that?

ALBERTA: I don't know. You call me if you think of something. *(Gives her a small kiss on the forehead)*

DEEDEE: I don't have your number.

ALBERTA *(Backing away toward the door)*: I really wanted to be alone tonight.

DEEDEE: I know.

ALBERTA: I'm glad you talked me out of it.

DEEDEE: Boy, you can count on me for that. Hey! Don't go yet. I owe you some money.

ALBERTA: No. *(Fondly)* Everybody deserves a free load now and then.

DEEDEE *(Trying to reach across the space to her)*: Thank you.

ALBERTA: Now, I suggest you go wake up Sleepy back there and see if there's something he needs to talk about.

DEEDEE: Tell you the truth, I'm ready for a little peace and quiet.

ALBERTA: Good night. *(Leaves)*

DEEDEE *(Reaching for the Dr. Pepper she put on the washer early on)*: Yeah, peace and quiet. *(Pops the top on the Dr. Pepper)* Too bad it don't come in cans.

Lights go down as she stands there looking out the window.

ACT TWO: THE POOL HALL

The pool hall is small and seedy. Plastic beer ads cover the walls. Talc is kept in empty candy-bar boxes along the window sills. There is an old bar with sacks of potato chips and other snacks. Tacky ashtrays and calendars litter the room. There is one television set and one pool table. "The Star-Spangled Banner" is playing on the television as the lights come up.

Willie is wiping off the bar. As the song ends, he turns off the TV and opens a beer. He pulls out a racing form and sits down. He looks at the clock. Shooter enters, carrying a sack of tacos, his cue case and a beer.

SHOOTER *(In greeting)*: Willie.

WILLIE *(Not looking up from the form)*: It's the man from the radio.

SHOOTER: How's it goin'?

WILLIE: Gets any busier I'll have to stand up.

SHOOTER: Or at least *look* up.

WILLIE *(Looking up now)*: Sondra just called.

SHOOTER: She knows when I get off.

WILLIE: She sure does.

SHOOTER: Where else would I be?

WILLIE: Somethin' like that.

SHOOTER: Somebody did one helluva job teaching that girl to tell the time. Tells me the time to come home, tells me the time to eat, tells me the time to go to bed.

WILLIE: Well, I told her I'd send you on soon's you finished your beer.

SHOOTER *(Indicating the racing form)*: Got any winners tomorrow?

WILLIE: Till tomorrow, they're all winners.

SHOOTER: Still betting those grays?

WILLIE: Yeah, the older I get, the more I love them gray horses.

SHOOTER: Trouble is, most of the ones you pick, gray isn't so much their color as an indication of their age.

WILLIE: Yeah, that one horse, Dusty Days, he's still runnin' from the first time I bet on him. *(Laughs)* Bout eight years now. I sit here and handicap 'em, he always comes out the winner. I can't figure it out.

SHOOTER: It's some other dude does the handicappin', Willie. Back in the stable. Finds out which ones you're layin' your money on, then ties lead weights to their legs. That's handicappin', man.

WILLIE: You're tellin' me.

SHOOTER: George go home already?

WILLIE: Sick.

SHOOTER: Bad?

WILLIE: You know any that's good? Doc says circulation.

SHOOTER: I thought I improved his circulation with that wheelchair I gave him.

WILLIE: Callin' himself the stick-shift cripple. That was nice, boy. End of the world wouldn't keep ol' George from comin' in here every night, but he sure does like havin' that motor do the work. Last six months, he gets real tired, real quick.

SHOOTER: Sondra said he wouldn't even know it was real leather, but I figured, what the hell, it's only money.

WILLIE: Oh he knew. Said, "Willie, cows got it rough, don't they? Folks lookin' at 'em seein' steak dinners and upholstery." You shoulda seen him, George doin' this dumb cow

voice, "Hey, man, you don't love me for what I am. You love me for what I'm gonna be—your suede leather shoes that walk you to get your all-beef cheeseburger which you pay for outta your genuine cowhide wallet."

SHOOTER: This dude at the surgical supply says, "Who's this for, son?" I started into this whole number like I had to explain, "Well, George, see, he's Sondra's father. Sondra, that's my wife. But George, he's also, well, my dad and George and this other man Willie, Willie he owns a pool hall, the three of them were real tight, and since Dad's gone now, one helluva pool player, my dad, anyway, George and Willie are like, well, George is family about five ways, see?" And on and on like that till finally he was givin' me this crazy look so I slapped down all those hundreds and said, "Hey, man, just give me the chair, okay?"

WILLIE: White boy in here the other night wouldn't let me lift George up to the rail to shoot. Said he had to keep one wheel on the floor.

SHOOTER: Just letting anybody in here these days.

WILLIE: Yeah. Even DJs.

SHOOTER: Little kid called me up tonight, wanted to talk to the record player. I said it don't talk, kid. He said, "No, man, you man, the record player." Over the air he said that. *(And he sets his cue case on the bar)*

WILLIE: The record player.

SHOOTER: Very funny.

WILLIE: Oh come on, boy, it don't matter what you say over the air.

SHOOTER: Thanks.

WILLIE: Folks turn on the radio to hear the music, remember?

SHOOTER *(Opening the cue case)*: I'll try to keep that in mind.

WILLIE *(Closing the cue case)*: You're hidin' out tonight, aren't you? Well, you ain't hidin' *here.*

SHOOTER *(Getting his cue out of the case)*: What you mean is you don't want nobody else hidin' in your hole. Well, the "hole" population looks pretty sparse to me.

WILLIE: Then what are you doin' here? Run outta skinny white girls?

SHOOTER: What's with you, man?

WILLIE: Go home, boy. Get outta my hall. Go home. See your wife.

SHOOTER: Ah, now we're gettin'—

WILLIE: Yeah, we're gettin'—

SHOOTER *(Looking for the felt brush)*: Nowhere, man. I've had enough of this mother-hen shit.

WILLIE: Then quit playin' rooster.

A big laugh from Shooter.

SHOOTER: Oh I'm so sorry. Did I interrupt your nap? Did I disturb your dust?

WILLIE: You're sorry all right. Did I pay for you to be born? Did I scrape up what was left of your old man when he died? Now you go home when I tell you.

SHOOTER: I'm what's left of my old man.

WILLIE: Yeah. *(Unfortunately)*

SHOOTER: And I didn't plan to be in Miami Beach when he died, it just happened. So, I'd have done it.

WILLIE: But you didn't. I identified him. I carried him to the ambulance. I bought his buryin' suit. I paid for his funeral.

SHOOTER: You got a plot out back for George when he goes? Way you tell it, those guys can't even die without you.

WILLIE: Man in here the other night said you better not die without payin' him his six thousand dollars you owe him. Said he'd come to hell to get it. Left you this note.

SHOOTER *(Crumpling up the note):* Least thanks to me, you won't have to carry George. Just dig the hole, then wheel him outta here some night, bury him wheelchair and all.

WILLIE: You can have your chair back, boy. He don't need your four-speed charity.

SHOOTER: Listen to you, giving away the cripple's chair. And charity, my man, is building a ramp *(Pointing to the door)* up to a pool hall.

WILLIE *(Pointing to the cue):* What you think you're doin' with that?

SHOOTER *(Swinging it around in a showy move):* Gonna pick my teeth.

WILLIE: Might as well, G.W., 'cause you sure as hell don't know nothin' else to do with it.

SHOOTER: Least I ain't forgot what it's for. *(And he sets the cue ball on the head spot, taps it down to the foot rail so it rolls back to hit the tip of the cue in follow-through position)*

WILLIE: And I ain't tryin' to be somethin' I ain't.

SHOOTER: I'm his kid.

WILLIE: You got his name.

SHOOTER: Yes sir. I've got the prize-winning best of the Three Blind Mice. I've got ol' Shooter's name, I've got George's only child, Sondra. And now I've got my own private pool palace.

WILLIE: Think so, huh?

SHOOTER: But not for long, right, Willie? You ain't the only nigger got spies. Man down at the station owns a part of Baskin-Robbins told me the chain needs a downtown shop and they got their eye on this place. I hear Mr. Rum Raisin makes a nice offer.

WILLIE: You heard wrong. I ain't sellin'.

SHOOTER: The hell you ain't. Come on, Willie, all the old pool players go to Asbury Park to die. Pool player's paradise. Big tournaments, best players coming through all the time. Then just eight miles up the Jersey coast you got the ponies running at Monmouth Park. And gambling in Atlantic City. Don't blame you for goin', Willie.

WILLIE: This place is a firetrap. Who'd want it?

SHOOTER: You might as well tell me, Willie, 'cause I got the picture already. Wake up about noon, spend a coupla hours with the racing form, then go for a swim, well, more like a walk in the pool. Then drive up to Monmouth, catch the daily double, collect your money and get back in time to see the hustlers do business down at Hopkins Billiards. Yes sir, racing, roulette and rack 'em up, boys, Willie's retirin' to Asbury park. I hear they even got green felt carpet in the nursing homes.

WILLIE: I'd sell this place in a minute just to keep you outta here, get you home at night.

SHOOTER: This place, got your "friend" Shooter's tracks all over the floor? This place, the only place your "friend" George got to go every night? You'd sell the only thing you got to show for your whole life just to keep me paying Sondra's cleaning lady?

WILLIE: I sure would.

SHOOTER *(As he puts the balls on the table):* Married her to please Dad and George and now I gotta keep her 'cause of you?

WILLIE: Catch right on, don't you.

SHOOTER: You're talking crazy, man.

WILLIE: You talk crazy for a living. Man gets famous talking to the air.

SHOOTER: I'm not famous.

WILLIE: But you do talk to the air.

SHOOTER: And get paid for it.

WILLIE: Well, it ain't improved your personality.

SHOOTER: When you *are* a personality, you don't have to *have* a personality.

WILLIE: Good thing.

SHOOTER: What's between Sondra and me is between Sondra and me. What do you care? She's not your baby.

WILLIE: She's George's baby and that's enough for me. And if Shooter was here—

SHOOTER: He'd be shootin' pool and that's all. 'Cause he knew—

WILLIE: 'Cause that's all he could do. Never had a job in his life. I paid for you to be born.

SHOOTER: We know.

WILLIE *(Refuses to stop)*: George paid the electric, and I paid the phone bill. George kept the grocery sendin' ham hocks, and I bought his beer.

SHOOTER: So what's that come to? I'm good for my old man's bills. *(Getting out his wallet)* You take MasterCharge?

WILLIE: It comes to more than you'll ever have.

SHOOTER: I'm rich, remember?

WILLIE: Too bad you ain't blond. I hear that's a terrific combination.

SHOOTER: Couldn't you take care of that for me, Willie? I mean, you're takin' care of George and takin' care Sondra gets her new Lincoln every year.

WILLIE: Whatever she wants. *(Then quickly)* Don't you rack those balls, boy.

SHOOTER: Uh-uh. *(Racking the balls)* What she wants, my man, is everything there is. Sable coats, suede chairs, a Cuisinart and a cook to run it, trips to wherever-it-is Hong Kong, five-hundred-dollar shoes, and fourteen-carat-gold fingernails.

WILLIE: Just things, kid. Everybody needs some things. You, you could even do with a few things.

SHOOTER: I don't need any things.

WILLIE: Your things are how you know it's your house.

SHOOTER: Then my house . . . is one of her things. I bought myself a recliner . . .

WILLIE: Yeah?

SHOOTER: She gave it away. *(Pauses)* Said it didn't go with the rest of the "things" I paid for. Marrying her was like cosigning for the national debt.

WILLIE: Marrying her was what you did.

SHOOTER: Unfortunately.

WILLIE: And you are going to stay married to her or you are going to have to answer to me.

SHOOTER: Well, the answer is no.

WILLIE: And you are going to keep her happy or you are gonna stay outta my sight. You gonna grow up if it kills you. And don't you think you can get away with one thing because I know every move you make. You screw a sheep and I'll know it.

SHOOTER: Sure you will. What else you got to do?

WILLIE: You're the one needs somethin' else to do. Somethin' else besides that gambling or dope or whatever you s'posed to owe that greasy white boy that six thousand dollars for. He shows up again, I'll kill him.

SHOOTER: It's an investment, man.

WILLIE: The hell it is.

SHOOTER: Yeah. I'm buying a mountain, a great big mountain covered in pretty red flowers. None of your business.

WILLIE: You're my business. You want somethin' I can get for you, I'll get it. Till then, I'm keepin' you from makin' the mistake of your life. You lose Sondra . . . she's a real classy lady and you like the way she looks and you know it. She reminds you where you want to get to in this world. You lose her and you're gonna lose it all. Then all you'll have left is some lousy grams of cocaine and pictures of your daddy.

SHOOTER: And won't you be happy then?

WILLIE: I will be happy—no, happy ain't got nuthin' to do with it. I will let you back in here when you stop messin' around and stay where you belong. At home. With Sondra. Your wife.

SHOOTER: Till depth do us part.

WILLIE: Now that is all I have to say to you. Get outta my hall.

SHOOTER: I don't believe you. I mean, did somebody make you Resident Caretaker and Marvelous Little Yard Man for the whole world?

WILLIE: If you don't get outta my hall—

SHOOTER: What? Huh? *(Taking his practice strokes)* What you gonna do, man? You gonna prune my hedge and trim the edges of my mile-long circular driveway? *(Now gets up quickly, poses, in an old move of his father's)* Give me a break! *(And he gets in position just as quickly and breaks the racked balls with a powerful stroke)*

WILLIE *(Has to laugh)*: Give me a break.

SHOOTER *(Pleased with his shot)*: Yeah.

WILLIE: Shooter always said that.

SHOOTER *(After a moment)*: Yeah. Give me a break.

WILLIE: Hadn't been funny for years.

SHOOTER: He's probably still sayin' it. *(And now he proceeds to run the balls in rotation)*

WILLIE *(Starting to clean up now)*: Yeah. Beer's probably hot in hell, but they got all the best pool players down there. Greenleaf, Hoppe . . . Shooter takin' 'em all on, dollar a game and the loser runs up to heaven for the cold Falls City. *(Laughs)* He was the best.

SHOOTER: Nobody even close.

WILLIE: One night he puts on this cowboy hat and glasses, wraps his left arm in a sling, rents a tux, figures to hop on down to South Side, Owensboro, pick up some fast cash. Borrows George's car, gets the word about the shortstop* there, how much money he's carrying, where he'll be standin' in the room—

SHOOTER: Who's runnin' that place now?

WILLIE: Lookin' for some one-pocket, see? So he's got on this rig. I swear he looks so strange, and walks in this joint and the bartender, swingin' a pretzel around his finger and openin' a beer, looks up, sees this bifocaled, broken-armed cowboy wearin' a tux, and says, "Hey boys, it's Shooter Stevens!" Like to died. He like to died. Got on all that crap and the first guy sees him says, "Hey boys, it's Shooter Stevens! Trip the alarm, the robber has arrived." *(Shakes his head)* Nothin', but nothin' so goddamned sad as a pool player can't get a game.

SHOOTER *(Referring to the fact that Willie won't play with him)*: Know what you mean.

WILLIE: But God, the thing he said the last night he . . . well . . .

SHOOTER: You can say it. You can say "the last night before the leap." Before the final, flyin' leap of his life.

WILLIE: Walked in. Right by a big money nine-ball goin' over there. *(Points)* Whistlin'. Not a good sign, whistlin'. Meant trouble when he was shootin', but just walkin' whistlin', I didn't worry, see?

---

*The shortstop is the best local player, the hustler's target.

SHOOTER: Wish you had, Willie.

WILLIE: Gets a Falls City and goes back to the nine-ball. Man with white shoes and his own stick, blue knitty pants says, "You in, buddy?" Man, I heard that word, "buddy," and I knew it was all over. Shooter backs up to the cues there, picks a stick not even lookin'. Mr. White Shoes says, "You don't even look?" Your ol' man gives him the ugliest scariest straight-on stare you ever seen in your life and says, "Buddy, if you can't play with any of 'em, you can't play with any of 'em." *(He laughs)* Whole place cracked up.

SHOOTER: And sure enough that night . . .

WILLIE: He couldn't play with any of 'em.

SHOOTER: Well, it had to be something else, Willie. My old man did not jump off of that bridge because of a lousy run here.

WILLIE: Sorry, boy. He did. He really did. Oh sure, maybe he knew he was losin' it, shaky stroke, no games. Hell, George was even beatin' him. So no, it wasn't this one night, but it was this goddamn game and you can bet all your fancy DJ bucks on that.

SHOOTER: All right, then, since you know so much about *my* old man, why'd he pick that side? *(He has been wanting to know the answer to this for a long time, but would prefer to have Willie think he has asked out of anger)*

WILLIE: Go for the salvage yard instead of the water?

SHOOTER: Why did he land on the '56 Chevy?

WILLIE: I got a thought about it.

SHOOTER: Well, let's hear it, Willie.

WILLIE: He was a helluva swimmer.

SHOOTER: Nice try, man.

WILLIE: I'm tellin' you, boy, your old man was so stubborn, I mean, he didn't want to give himself the slightest chance of pullin' outta that dive alive. He'd never lived it down. George'd been on him somethin' awful.

Shooter takes a shot and misses. Willie laughs.

SHOOTER: What's so funny?

WILLIE: I'm sorry. See, they called me to come get him. One of the cops knew us. Got there, nice bright mornin', spotted him soon's I got outta the car. Been layin' there all night, flat on his back, arms stretched out, legs hangin' down over the windshield. That far away, I swear to God, he looked like he was gettin' himself a suntan.

SHOOTER: Just what he always wanted.

WILLIE: Close up was different. *(Points but Shooter doesn't see him)* Needed a shorter bridge.

SHOOTER: That's enough about it, okay?

WILLIE: I'm talkin' your bridge, not his. *(Starts to walk over)* Six inches, fingers to cue tip.

SHOOTER: You start playing again, I'll start listening.

WILLIE: Shooter was the only game I had in this town. So he's gone, so why bother?

SHOOTER: It's your game, man.

WILLIE: It was his game. It killed him.

SHOOTER: You don't keep in shape, he'll be ashamed of you down at hell's pool hall. Make you watch. "But I been waitin' to play you, Shooter," you'll say, and he'll say, "Willie, I'm real glad to see you and you look real good for an old man, but this is a serious game, you know?"

WILLIE: I'll keep this place open, I'll tell you to bend from the knees and stroke from the shoulder, but unless I get some all-fired good reason, like my life depended on it, I ain't playin'.

SHOOTER: It's gonna kill you to play with me?

WILLIE: You want a beer?

SHOOTER: You just couldn't stand losin' to me.

WILLIE: What I couldn't stand, is a game that didn't mean nothin'. Don't take it personal, boy, but I went fifteen rounds with the champ, so I ain't got nothin' to prove to the challengers. Now do you want a beer or not?

SHOOTER *(Miscues):* No.

WILLIE: Boy.

SHOOTER *(Belligerent, expecting more advice):* Yeah?

WILLIE: What are you doing here?

Shooter doesn't answer. Willie turns away.

SHOOTER *(Finally):* Workin' on this bank shot.

WILLIE *(Louder):* Boy . . .

SHOOTER *(Stands up, leans on his stick):* What?

WILLIE: Look . . . *(Then deciding not to go on with this)* Don't lean on your . . . *(Tired of this too)* Oh hell. Did you ever see him shoot with an umbrella?

SHOOTER *(Going back to his game):* No.

WILLIE *(Laughs):* He lost your crib one night before he figured it out.

SHOOTER: Huh?

WILLIE: Havin' us a helluva storm, your old man comes in soaked, carryin' his umbrella, still all folded up perfect. George busts out laughin', says, "Why didn't you use that thing? Shooter you the dumbest nigger." And Shooter says, just like always, first thing popped into his head, says, " 'Cause I'm runnin' the rack with it, mother." So George says, "Let's see your green, man." Well, Shooter didn't have any, of course, so he says, "Bet the boy's bed, buddy." Now he goes real good for a while, but then he gets to the seven, and it's plumb froze to the rail. He looks it over, checks the line, sets him a sweet rail bridge, pulls back to shoot. George waits for just the right moment and says, "Do de name Ruby Begonia ring a bell?"

SHOOTER: And Dad miscued.

WILLIE: Then he hit George upside of the head.

SHOOTER: Then George went over and got my crib.

WILLIE: Bet's a bet, boy. Came draggin' it back in here, said your mama said, "George I am so tired of seein' your face carryin' out my furniture."

SHOOTER: Uh-huh.

WILLIE: So then Shooter has to learn how to shoot with that umbrella 'cause that's the only way George will give the crib back. Run the rack you get it back. Run the rack, you get it back. Wonder old George didn't die off of that bet. He could be awful mean, your daddy.

SHOOTER: The Three Blind Mice.

WILLIE: Well that's what your mama thought all right.

SHOOTER *(Singing):* They all ran after the farmer's wife.

WILLIE: You use a wafer on that tip?

SHOOTER *(Still singing):* She cut off their tails with a carving knife.

WILLIE: Need about five more pounds over your right foot.

SHOOTER *(Singing):* Did you ever see such a sight in your life as three blind mice.

WILLIE: God, your mama, that night down at the jail. *(Laughing)* God almighty.

SHOOTER: I heard that story so many times. I don't know anything like I know that story.

WILLIE: So do it.

SHOOTER *(As Mama did it, more music than narration):* See, I'm pregnant with you, boy, and paintin' on your crib one night, while your daddy and George and Willie are busy beatin' up on each other down at Willie's pool hall.

WILLIE *(Loving this):* Yeah!

SHOOTER: And I pick up the phone and, Lord have mercy, it's the police and they say they got three beat-up black men, all callin' my name. And they said would I gather up some money and come relieve them of their prisoners. And they said, it's gonna be dark when you get here, honey, 'cause the 'lectric's knocked out and the stoves ain't workin', but we fed 'em Velveeta just to hold 'em till you get here, girl.

WILLIE: She took one look at us, drunk as shit, sittin' on the floor, in the dark, eatin' cheese. She said, "I drive myself all the way down here, I give them all my money, and what do I get?"

SHOOTER AND WILLIE *(As Mama said it):* The Three Blind Mice. *(They laugh)*

WILLIE: Shooter turns on the radio on the way home and she says, "I ain't through screamin' at you yet, turn that thing off. And George, if you don't stop bleedin' on my Buick, you gonna walk!"

SHOOTER: It's a wonder she didn't drive him straight to the Red Cross, sayin', "George here's so anxious to give blood, he done started without you. Just catch a coupla pints and send him over to Willie's when he dries up."

WILLIE *(Beginning to recover from the laughing):* I'd like to see your mama again. Maybe she'll come visit. She would've walked to China for your daddy. Nearly did a coupla times. But God, did she hate George.

SHOOTER: Remember George's stick at the wedding?

WILLIE: And that big fudge cake sittin' on the table here?

SHOOTER: Mom wanted the reception at the church.

WILLIE: Sure she did.

SHOOTER: Sondra wanted it at the Palm Room.

WILLIE: Not a bad place.

SHOOTER: Her mom wanted it at the Galt House.

They both laugh.

WILLIE *(Proudly):* But we had it . . . here.

SHOOTER: Got a great picture of Dad and George holdin' their cues lookin' down real serious at this what was always their table, but what is now a high-rise fudge cake, you pourin' champagne on their heads.

WILLIE: Oh, Sondra was beautiful that day. She's the best shot ol' George ever made.

SHOOTER: She's still beautiful, man. That's not the problem.

WILLIE: She really wants a new Lincoln?

SHOOTER: Silver.

WILLIE: Used to look like the Lincoln dealership in front of this place.

SHOOTER: We can't even go to Sears driving my BMW. Gotta arrive in her Linc.

WILLIE *(Proudly):* She just looks like money.
SHOOTER: Which is why I don't have any.
WILLIE: George says they raised you to thirty grand.
SHOOTER *(Opening his sack of tacos):* Want a taco?
WILLIE: Says you can expect sixty maybe seventy in five years.
SHOOTER: And then what? You ever seen any old DJs man? You watch those records go around long enough, you start thinkin' in circles, walkin' in circles, talkin' in circles. All I learned in five years is the names of eight hundred and ninety-two singing groups and how many people don't have anybody to talk to late at night so they call up the "record player."
WILLIE: So quit.
SHOOTER: And do what?
WILLIE: You tell me.
SHOOTER: I don't know.
WILLIE: There's gotta be somethin' you like to do.
SHOOTER: I like to play pool.
WILLIE: That's not what I mean. Somethin' else.
SHOOTER: There isn't anything else.
WILLIE: Then you got a real problem, boy, 'cause pool just ain't your game.
SHOOTER: I see.
WILLIE: I mean, you do okay, but I gotta tell you—
SHOOTER *(Quietly):* No you don't.
WILLIE: Good. So tell me somethin' else you like to do.

And Willie's helpful tone only intensifies Shooter's realization.

SHOOTER *(In complete emotional panic):* There isn't anything else I like to do.

Willie backs off, stunned, but knows not to wait too long before he starts to talk again.

WILLIE: There's about a billion jobs in this world. You think there ain't one or two might make you happy?
SHOOTER *(Angry now):* How am I supposed to know what makes me happy? And what difference does it make? You don't work to be happy. You work to make money. Happy, my man . . . was one of the seven dwarfs.
WILLIE: Well, either you really do like what you do, in which case you can shut up bitchin' about it, or you hate what you do so you quit.
SHOOTER: I don't like it and I don't hate it. It pays the bills.
WILLIE: Fryin' fish would pay the bills.
SHOOTER: Not her bills.
WILLIE: I'm sick to death of you blaming her for spendin' the money you make. You quit makin' it, she'll quit spendin' it. She'd do anything for you, but you ain't told her anything except don't buy fur coats. So she's doin' what she can. Makin' you look good, and makin' your house look good. You quit work, she'll make poor look good. So you shut up about you have to work to pay her bills. Her bills are all you got to show for your work . . . *(Pauses)* best I can tell.
SHOOTER *(Stops shooting):* Well, I got something to tell you. *(Calm but firm)* And I got the

chain burns to prove it. I am a certified, wholly owned, shipped-to-the-plantation slave boy, property of . . . MasterCharge. *(And he takes a bite of his taco now)*

WILLIE: You shouldn't eat that crap.

SHOOTER: Girl next door says they're made out of dog food.

WILLIE: White girl?

SHOOTER: Come on, man, I stopped in the laundromat next door, put my clothes in the wash, and this white girl talked to me, okay?

WILLIE: Makes me sick just to look at those tacos. But George eats so many of 'em, he starts speakin' Spanish around midnight.

SHOOTER: I keep tellin' Sondra to come see him.

WILLIE: She should. He's her father. She should come in here some night and see him.

SHOOTER: I know. I told her.

WILLIE: Yeah? So tell her not to. Tell her this is the last place you want to see her sweet face. Look ugly mean. Hit the table. She'll sneak right over soon's you look the other way.

SHOOTER: Yeah. Like this other routine she's got asking should I wear the green or should I wear the red. I say green, she puts on the red. I say red—

WILLIE: On go the green.

SHOOTER: I mean, why does she bother to ask?

WILLIE: It ain't just her, boy. They all do it.

SHOOTER: Yeah, but why?

WILLIE: Well if I knew that, I'd be on Johnny Carson 'stead of runnin' this place.

SHOOTER: Yeah.

WILLIE: You get Sondra down here to see George. He needs it, but he won't ask for it, and he won't get himself over to her . . . your place, 'cause he don't feel . . . he hates that white rug.

SHOOTER: Who doesn't?

WILLIE: I know she don't feel safe comin' down, and I don't exactly blame her, it ain't safe, and she is good about callin', but you bring her down here, you hear?

SHOOTER *(Throwing away the taco sack)*: Right.

Willie watches him, perhaps begins to feel a little of Shooter's pain. Suddenly, Willie shouts.

WILLIE: Shooter! Shooter Stevens! *(And now he lines up the balls)* Wipe the sweat outta your eyes and pay attention up here, man. The boy's gonna try your favorite trick! Shooter! Hey!

Shooter doesn't understand at first, then sees that Willie is preparing one of his father's old shots.

SHOOTER: Come on . . .

WILLIE: I'll set it up for you. You can do it.

SHOOTER: This ain't my game, remember?

WILLIE *(Pointing out what should happen)*: Cue ball here, hit top center, like a clean follow. No English. Hit the one about half-ball, it goes here . . . *(Points to the middle left-hand pocket)* while the two is rotatin' its way up there. *(Points to the top right-hand pocket)* And, not to leave anybody out in the cold, the cue ball rolls across the table and drops the three in the middle. *(Middle right-hand pocket)* And, don't scratch.

SHOOTER: Of course.

WILLIE *(Reviewing):* One to here, two up there, three over there.

SHOOTER: Yeah. *(Studying the shot)* Okay. I'm ready.

WILLIE *(As Shooter is about to shoot):* Now, what about kids?

SHOOTER: Christ! You got a shopping list for my life. Milk, bread, wife, kids . . .

WILLIE: Then read me your list. What do you want?

SHOOTER: Her exact words, Willie, about kids? Her exact words, "I'm gonna blow up like a whale? Not this body, baby. Uh-uh, honey." I mean, if you could buy 'em, she'd have 'em, but she ain't buyin' havin' 'em.

WILLIE: Probably thinks she'd have to raise it by herself.

SHOOTER: If she'd have a baby, I'd stay.

WILLIE: Does she know that?

SHOOTER: But how long am I supposed to wait? If she had the boy today, I'd be forty when he's ten. He's ready to go play ball and I'm workin' up a sweat gettin' outta my chair.

WILLIE: And what you're doin' now, goin' out on her all over town, that's supposed to convince her to have your boy for you?

SHOOTER: Whoever's playing records in your head's asleep at the deck, man. Got a broken one, goin' around and around.

WILLIE: You shape up, you'll get your boy.

SHOOTER: Wanna bet?

WILLIE: Wanna try?

SHOOTER: I want to try this shot, okay?

WILLIE: Keep your stick level.

SHOOTER: All right. One for the old man. *(Shoots and misses)* Shit.

WILLIE: One to nothin', favor of the ol' man.

SHOOTER: He really could make this?

WILLIE: This shot bought you strained carrots, boy. Lotta folks thought he couldn't make this shot. Lotta folks and lotta their money said he'd miss. But he never did.

SHOOTER: Then we'll just give it another shot.

And Shooter goes around, replacing the balls. Willie adjusts them so they're in the right position.

WILLIE *(Trying another approach):* There's nothin' wrong, I mean, with you or Sondra? Doctor's got all kinds of—

SHOOTER: No.

WILLIE: There's tests.

SHOOTER: Look, Willie, she's taking the pill, using a diaphragm, I have to wear a rubber. Keeps foam just in case, I mean, this lady does not want any kids, okay?

WILLIE: Then you gotta change her mind. George needs a grandbaby.

SHOOTER: Tell that to her. Have George tell that to her.

WILLIE: Shooter needs a grandbaby.

SHOOTER: Shooter is dead. *(Now turning to face him)* Willie needs the grandbaby.

WILLIE *(As Shooter is ready to try the shot again):* You don't have any children, it's the end of the line for the Three Blind Mice.

SHOOTER: You're talking to the wrong person, Willie. I want kids. But I'll tell you something, Sondra could care less about the Three Blind Mice. Here we go. *(Shoots and misses again)*

WILLIE: That's two. Three and the ol' man crosses you off his visitin' list.
SHOOTER: Have your own kid. You got a coupla good shots left, huh?
WILLIE: I'm old, G.W.
SHOOTER: Ain't a question of old. It's a question of aim. Concentration. Bend from the hips, steady stroke, you know.
WILLIE *(Laughs)*: I know.
SHOOTER: How long's it been?
WILLIE: None of your damned business.
SHOOTER: That long, huh?

Willie gets out his keys and walks to the door.

SHOOTER: Okay. Here goes. Watch.
WILLIE: I'm watchin'.
SHOOTER *(As he misses again)*: Shit.
WILLIE: That's three.

As Willie gets to the back door, it opens, and Deedee steps in carrying a stack of folded clothes.

DEEDEE: Hello?
WILLIE: Laundry's next door, miss.
DEEDEE *(Steps in, very uncomfortable)*: Yeah, but I'm lookin' for the pool hall.
WILLIE: We're closed.
DEEDEE: Are you Willie?
WILLIE *(Grudgingly)*: Yes.
DEEDEE: See? I got Shooter Stevens' clothes. Shooter Stevens? He put 'em in over there and I figured since I didn't really have—
WILLIE: Shooter Stevens? *(Turning around to look at Shooter)* You got Shooter Stevens' clothes?
DEEDEE: It's his nickname.
WILLIE: Girl's got your old man's clothes, Gary Wayne. *(Very bitter)* Shooter Stevens' clothes.
SHOOTER *(Walking over)*: Hey, thanks.

Shooter takes the clothes from her. Deedee follows him into the room, then stops as though Willie had grabbed her.

DEEDEE: I thought they were yours, oh well, guess it don't matter now.
WILLIE: Nope. It don't matter now.
SHOOTER: You didn't have to bring me these.
DEEDEE: Your dad has nice stuff.
SHOOTER: They're mine.
DEEDEE: Can I come in?
SHOOTER: Sure. I invited you, didn't I?
DEEDEE: Don't you just love the way they smell when they come out of the dryer?
SHOOTER: You thirsty?
DEEDEE: I put in a Cling-Free. That's the smell. There any tacos left?

SHOOTER *(Walking toward the bar)*: Sorry. Chips though.
WILLIE: Dollar a bag.

Shooter stops. Willie shouldn't have said that.

DEEDEE: Mind if I look around?
WILLIE: Not much to see.
SHOOTER: Sure. I'll set up so you can see how the game goes.
DEEDEE *(To Willie)*: My name's Deedee. *(No response from Willie)* Hard to tell what year it is in here. *(Picking up an ashtray)* Hey! I been there! *(Reading from the ashtray)* See Rock City! *(Then remembering)* It wasn't much. Only thing I really wanted to see, we couldn't stop for. On the way there, kept seein' these signs . . . Giant Jungle Rat. Sure wish I coulda seen that Giant Jungle Rat.
WILLIE *(In Shooter's direction)*: Oh we got 'em come in here all the time.
SHOOTER: Really just old jungle mice.
DEEDEE: Shooter, are you hungry? There's this pancake place down on Broadway . . .
WILLIE: His name is Gary Wayne.
SHOOTER: I always wondered if that place was any good. I haven't had any pancakes since—
DEEDEE: You'd love it. They're open all night too.
WILLIE: Oh, I thought the Board of Health closed it down.
SHOOTER: Now, first you have to break. *(Gets into position, Deedee comes over to watch)* Like this.
WILLIE: Or somethin' like that. Stop by some day when we're open, you'll see what a real—

Shooter gives her the cue, and gives Willie a fierce look.

SHOOTER: This is a game of rotation. You have to hit the one ball first. Then every shot after that, you have to hit the lowest numbered ball on the table. You can sink other balls with the shot, but if you don't hit the low ball first, the other balls come out and you lose your turn. *(Now showing her how to stand)* Bend like this, let the cue just rest in your hand, somewhere around here, or so. Now . . . stand up a minute. *(Showing her a beginner's bridge)* Put your hand out on the table flat like this. Ease it up, like how an inchworm . . .
DEEDEE *(Doing it)*: That?
SHOOTER: Perfect. Now curl your index finger and slip the cue through it. *(Reaching around her to show her how it's done)* Take some practice strokes. Eye on the ball.
DEEDEE *(Straightening up suddenly)*: I got it! Your dad's name was the same as yours.
SHOOTER: Yeah.
DEEDEE: Shooter.
WILLIE: No. Stevens.
SHOOTER: And he was one helluva pool player. *(Trying to appease Willie)* Dad and Willie, here, and this other man, George—
WILLIE: The father of G.W.'s wife—
SHOOTER: Were real tight.

Deedee gets back in position and takes practice strokes.

DEEDEE: Friends.

SHOOTER: More like triplets. I ever needed anything, lunch money, rubbers, anything, didn't matter which one I asked. Seemed like it all came out of the same pocket.

WILLIE *(Not to Deedee)*: It did.

SHOOTER: Gave the same advice, wore the same clothes, drove the same cars, drank the same beer, 'bout the same age, called themselves the Three Blind Mice.

Willie does not appreciate Shooter giving away this information. That name was something they called themselves, not something they would let anybody else call them.

DEEDEE *(A little bored by this information)*: This place we did stop in, on that trip where we didn't stop in to see the Giant Jungle Rat, this place, Pete's, had this three-headed mouse in a jar. It was dead, though. A freak. *(Now concentrating on the table)* I'm ready. *(She shoots and miscues)* What happened?

SHOOTER: Aim for the middle of the ball. Loosen up your finger a little.

DEEDEE: They said it had, I mean, they, the heads . . . only had one heart. That's what killed them, it, the mouse.

SHOOTER: Yeah.

And Deedee tries to shoot on her own now, Shooter backing off a little to watch.

DEEDEE: How does this end, this rotation?

WILLIE: I could turn out the lights.

SHOOTER: First person to get sixty-one points wins the game.

DEEDEE: Could be real soon, huh?

SHOOTER: What kind of pancakes do you like?

DEEDEE: Strawberry, with whipped cream.

SHOOTER: I'll just call and have them save us some. Wouldn't want them running out before we get there.

DEEDEE *(Handing him the cue)*: Here. You get the rest of them, okay?

WILLIE: Her mother's probably worried about her, G.W.

DEEDEE: It must feel real good to like somethin' this much.

And Shooter is putting on a real show now, getting all the balls in as quickly as possible.

DEEDEE: Mom likes TV.

SHOOTER: Yeah?

DEEDEE: Joe loves his '56 Chevy.

WILLIE *(In Shooter's direction)*: Joe loves his '56 Chevy.

DEEDEE: I must love somethin'.

WILLIE: Miss . . .

SHOOTER *(Indicating, somehow, himself)*: Giant Jungle Rats?

WILLIE: Deedee . . . that's your name, Deedee?

DEEDEE: Yes.

WILLIE: Go home.

SHOOTER: Willie!

WILLIE: The pool hall is closed. And Gary Wayne has a wife to go home to, and I'm gonna see that he gets there. Now go home.

DEEDEE: No, see, we're gonna—

WILLIE: Good night.

Deedee looks at Shooter as if asking whether she should go or not. Shooter looks at Willie, then back to Deedee. This is an awkward moment, to say the least. Finally, Shooter shrugs his shoulders.

SHOOTER: It's his hall.

DEEDEE: Yeah.

SHOOTER: Need a cab?

DEEDEE *(As she walks to the door):* I just live across the street.

SHOOTER: I'll watch you out the window.

DEEDEE: That's us. *(Pointing)* See those blueberries in the window? It's a light. They're a light. I mean, I like blue, it's not my favorite color, but I like it a lot, and somebody gave it to me for, well, if the other lights were out, then you could see it real good, no, not it, them, no, it, the light better, the vines on it and everything. *(She's really chattering here)* I can't ever, well, I have to hunt all over town to find blue bulbs. I tried painting one blue, but something in the paint, I guess, made the bulb break. No, it didn't break, but it got these little holes all over the . . . *(Smacks herself to stop talking)* Don't you ever shut up, Deedee? *(Embarrassed laugh)* Mom says I could find somethin' to say to a head of cabbage.

SHOOTER: You got a cabbage at home to talk to?

DEEDEE: Yeah. I do. *(She laughs)* 'Night.

SHOOTER *(Stepping back in, door still open):* Thanks again for the laundry. Good night.

Shooter closes the door, but he is still watching her. He yells at Willie, who is returning the pool cue to its place on the wall.

SHOOTER *(Fiercely):* Just who do you think you are, man?

WILLIE: Messed up your plans, huh, boy?

SHOOTER: I can make them again, you know.

WILLIE: Not in here.

SHOOTER: It's a free country.

WILLIE: Not in here.

SHOOTER: And who knows, if she'd stayed here a little longer, you might have even picked up a cue and played with me. Anything, you'd have done just about anything to keep me from sharing a stack of strawberry pancakes with a dumb little blonde who talks to cabbages. I mean, you tell me why it is I am not allowed to talk to other people in this world without you standing there like Moses heaving your stone-tablet ten commandments down on my head. You do this to Dad? That your deal with him? I'll pay your bills, you do what I say? And when he couldn't make your trick shots anymore, he had to jump off that bridge because he never found anything else satisfying in his life 'cause you already done it all for him. Is that the real story?

WILLIE: Shooter was my friend. And I don't see that you got any friends, so you don't know nothin' about friends, so you shut up.

SHOOTER: He was my father and I'll say whatever I want. And I'll call myself Shooter if I want. And I'll dump Sondra if I want and I'll screw white women if I want.

WILLIE *(Very cold):* Go to hell.

SHOOTER: I mean, what gives you the right to run my life?

WILLIE: I'll tell you what it is, you little—

SHOOTER *(Boiling):* The Gospel According to Willie:

Thou shalt not call thyself by thy father's name because it is a holy name.

Thou shalt not try to play thy father's game because it is a holy game.

Thou shalt not give thy father-in-law George a motorized wheelchair because I, Willie, am the giver of all good things.

Thou shalt not make thy living at a radio station.

Thou shalt not refuse thy wife a new Lincoln or any other damn fool thing she wants.

Thou shalt not go home at night except that thou go straight home.

Thou shalt not talk to any other women.

Thou shalt especially not talk to white women.

WILLIE: Eight.

SHOOTER: Thou shalt not get old enough to make thy own decisions.

WILLIE *(Almost a dare):* Nine?

SHOOTER *(Particularly intense):* That's all of your gospel, Willie. The last two are mine. The last two are for you. Thou shalt not forsake, desert, skip out on, run away from, break promises to, or leave behind to die . . . thy friends.

WILLIE *(Truly confused):* What?

SHOOTER: What do you mean "What?" Thou shalt not sell this pool hall!

WILLIE: I told you—

But Shooter can't stop now. He's been wanting to deliver this lecture ever since he got here tonight. This is why he came here.

SHOOTER: Don't you know what it's going to do to George when you split for New Jersey? It's going to kill him. Where's he got to go? Nowhere. What's he got to do? Nothing. Who does he care about in the world? Nobody . . . except you. And you're selling this place, and too cheap at that, so you can go live it up at Asbury Park. *(Now as if Willie were saying it)* Well, George, old friend, I hate to leave you like this, in the wheelchair and all, but listen, you call me up sometime and we'll talk about the good old days.

WILLIE *(Calmly):* George . . .

SHOOTER: George will understand? George will not understand! Only two of the Three Blind Mice left as it is, and Willie wants to sell the hole. And you were giving me that shit about Sondra. Do your duty, keep your promises. Hang in there with those commitments, G.W., and all the time, you're deciding whether to pack your black shoes and wondering if they got Senior Citizens swimming pools.

WILLIE: Are you through?

SHOOTER: No. All my life I watched Dad and George depend on you. And maybe you got a rest coming, but you can't do it yet. If you leave now, while he's sick, then all that friends talk was just talk, and all those friends stories must be made up, and all that you-be-good-to-Sondra-because-she's-my-friend-George's-little-girl lecture is nothing but lies, because if you leave him all alone, you are not his friend and you never were.

WILLIE: My friend, George . . .

SHOOTER: Your "friend," George . . .

WILLIE: My . . . friend . . . George . . . is . . . dying.

SHOOTER: No.

WILLIE: Yes. And I am not going to Asbury Park. I am going to stay here and watch my friend George die.

SHOOTER: You said sick.

WILLIE: Yeah I said sick. Why didn't you go home when I first told you to, boy?

SHOOTER *(More gentle now)*: I didn't want to.

WILLIE *(Wearily)*: Would you go home now?

SHOOTER: No. *(Walks behind the bar)* Beer?

WILLIE: Yeah.

And Shooter opens two beers, puts one in front of Willie.

WILLIE: And a bag of chips. *(As Shooter gets one)* Uh-uh. The one at the top.

SHOOTER *(Reaching for it)*: This one?

WILLIE: Yeah. *(Taking the bag and looking at it)* We been watchin' this bag, me and George. *(Pauses)* We figure it's about a year old now.

SHOOTER: How long does he have?

WILLIE: Six months, maybe.

SHOOTER: That's not much.

WILLIE: Nope.

SHOOTER: Hospital?

WILLIE: Friday. They said he'd be more comfortable.

SHOOTER: That bad.

WILLIE: Right.

SHOOTER: And this place . . . selling this place . . . is going to pay for it.

WILLIE: Just about. *(Pause)* If he really drags his feet, it might take my car, too. *(Then standing up)* Shit, the pool hall on the mall's gettin' all the business anyway. Got pinball machines and air hockey.

SHOOTER *(With contempt)*: Pink felt tables and a ladies' john.

WILLIE *(Laughs)*: Real clean.

SHOOTER: Safe.

WILLIE: Then there's the jukebox, here. Don't exactly draw the crowd, you know.

SHOOTER: Huh?

WILLIE: Day George got his first wheelchair, hit him pretty hard, you know. I thought I told you this. *(Shooter shakes his head no)* Had me stop by Vine Records, buy all his favorites, coupla Chubby Checkers, lotta Tennessee Ernie Ford, Christ! *(Shooter laughs)* Filled up the jukebox with 'em. Left on the labels, up top here, like they were, just changed the records. Now, see, no matter what somebody picks out, they get one of George's oldies but goodies. Makes people mad. Makes me mad. Got lousy taste in music, George. Likes real crap, you know. *(Pats the machine)* Isn't all that bad, though. Funny sometimes. People punchin' up Aretha Franklin, gettin' Pat Boone.

SHOOTER: Pat Boone?

WILLIE: I told you he was sick.

SHOOTER: Know what he told me the day we got married?

WILLIE: Little fatherly advice?

SHOOTER: He said, "Boy, there's somethin' you got to know about women. *(Conspiratorial tone)* You want 'em to act nice, you want to stay outta trouble with 'em, you want 'em to love you forever?" *(Now in his own voice)* "Yeah," I'm sayin', "yeah, George, how do I do that?" And he says, "Well, when you get undressed at night . . . you got to hang up your clothes."

WILLIE: Goddamn him.

SHOOTER: Sondra must've guessed. She said George was smelling funny and that's why she wouldn't come see him.

WILLIE: She's just scared of it.

SHOOTER: Aren't you?

WILLIE: George ain't got a smell on him I ain't smelled. *(Shooter laughs)* She just don't want to know about it.

SHOOTER: Maybe.

WILLIE: She's afraid she'll be with him when it happens. He'll say somethin' smart like, "If you'll excuse me, girl, I gotta be goin'." Close his eyes and split. Go. Die.

SHOOTER: Maybe. *(Gentler about her now)* And maybe she's just a selfish, silly girl who started buying grown-up clothes but never grew into them.

WILLIE: She'll get there.

SHOOTER: I could help, with George.

WILLIE: Save it.

SHOOTER: For you?

WILLIE: I want a table, set right next to my casket, so right after "Don't he look nice," I'll hear "Little nine-ball?" I mean, if I gotta lay there dyin' for a beer, least I can have a game to watch. Boys cussin' and carryin' on, balls flyin' off the table, crushin' carnations in my wreath I'm wearin' says "Bartender."

SHOOTER: If that's the way you want it.

WILLIE: You know what I want. I want you and Sondra—

SHOOTER: Yeah, I know.

WILLIE: Right.

SHOOTER: I heard you, okay?

WILLIE: So?

SHOOTER: So what?

WILLIE: So are we gonna play or not?

Willie's offer is so unexpected, it triggers an overwhelming emotional response in both of them. They embrace, acknowledging at last their desperate need, their mutual loss, and their pure and lasting love for each other.

SHOOTER: Oh man.

WILLIE: Thought you were too old to hug me, didn't you.

SHOOTER *(Fondly)*: Just get off my neck and chalk your cue. Nine-ball. Dollar a game.

WILLIE: You're on, buddy.

Shooter gets out the balls and racks them in silence as Willie gets his cue and chalks it. Willie takes his practice, then looks up at Shooter.

WILLIE: I got to see this dollar, boy.

SHOOTER: Give me a break. *(And he slaps his dollar down on the table)*

WILLIE: What did you say? *(And he stands up, assumes old Shooter's pose)*

WILLIE AND SHOOTER *(As Shooter would have said it):* Give me a break.

And Willie breaks the balls with a powerful shot and the lights come down immediately. We hear the beginning of ad-lib exchanges as the game starts.

CHARLES FULLER

(1939–)

A Soldier's Play

About the Author: Charles Fuller is a Philadelphian. He went to Villanova University from 1956 to 1958, served in the army until 1962, then continued his education at La Salle College. His first play, *The Perfect Party,* was produced in 1968. His fifth, *A Soldier's Play,* won the Pulitzer Prize, the Drama Critics Award, the Outer Circle Critics Award, and the Theatre Club Award, all in 1982; he rewrote it for the movies, and the film *(A Soldier's Story)* was an Academy Award nominee for Best Picture of 1984.

About the Play: The play is a murder mystery. As the play begins, we see a man killed, but we are unable to identify the killers; the rest of the play involves the attempt to sift the evidence and track them down. What makes the play even more interesting than a simple "Whodunit," however, is its setting. The play takes place on an army base in the American South during World War II. The murdered man is a black sergeant in charge of a group of black recruits in the racially segregated U.S. Army. The troops, black and white, are hoping for orders to go to Europe and fight against a Nazi regime dedicated to an ideology of racial purity. The international scene provides a particularly dramatic backdrop for the conflict depicted in this play.

CHARACTERS

TECH/SERGEANT VERNON C. WATERS
CAPTAIN CHARLES TAYLOR
CORPORAL BERNARD COBB
PRIVATE FIRST CLASS MELVIN PETERSON
CORPORAL ELLIS
PRIVATE LOUIS HENSON
PRIVATE JAMES WILKIE
PRIVATE TONY SMALLS
CAPTAIN RICHARD DAVENPORT
PRIVATE C. J. MEMPHIS
LIEUTENANT BYRD
CAPTAIN WILCOX

TIME: 1944

PLACE: Fort Neal, Louisiana

SCENE: *The inner shell of the stage is black. On the stage, in a horseshoe-like half circle, are several platforms at varying levels.*

On the left side of this horseshoe is a military office arrangement with a small desk (a nameplate on the desk reads: CAPTAIN CHARLES TAYLOR*), two office-type chairs, one straight-backed, a regimental, and an American flag. A picture of F.D.R. is on the wall.*

On the right side of the horseshoe, and curved toward the rear, is a barracks arrangement, with three bunk beds and footlockers set in typical military fashion. The exit to this barracks is a freestanding doorway on the far right. (This barracks should be changeable—these bunks with little movement can look like a different place.) On the edge of this barracks is a poster, semi-blown up, of Joe Louis in an army uniform, helmet, rifle, and bayonet. It reads: PVT. JOE LOUIS SAYS, "WE'RE GOING TO DO OUR PART—AND WE'LL WIN BECAUSE WE'RE ON GOD'S SIDE."

On the rear of the horseshoe, upstage center, is a bare platform, raised several feet above everything else. It can be anything we want it to be—a limbo if you will.

The entire set should resemble a courtroom. The sets, barracks and office, will both be elevated, so that from anywhere on the horseshoe one may look down onto a space at center stage that is on the stage floor. The levels should have easy access by either stairs or ramps, and the entire set should be raked ever so slightly so that one does not perceive much difference between floor and set, and the bottom edges of the horseshoe. There must also be enough area on both sides of the horseshoe to see exits and entrances.

Lighting will play an integral part in the realization of the play. It should therefore be sharp, so that areas are clearly defined, with as little spill into other areas as possible. Lights must also be capable of suggesting mood, time, and place.

As the play opens, the stage is black. In the background, rising in volume, we hear the song "Don't Sit under the Apple Tree," sung by the Andrews Sisters. Quite suddenly, in a sharp though narrow beam of light, in limbo, TECH/SERGEANT VERNON C. WATERS, *a well-built, light-brown-skinned man in a World War II, winter army uniform, is seen down on all fours. He is stinking drunk, trying to stand and mumbling to himself.*

WATERS *(repeating):* They'll still hate you! They still hate you . . . They still hate you!

WATERS *is laughing as suddenly someone steps into the light. (We never see this person.) He is holding a .45 caliber pistol. He lifts it swiftly and ominously toward* WATERS's *head and fires.* WATERS *is knocked over backward. He is dead. The music has stopped and there is a strong silence onstage.*

VOICE: Le's go!

The man with the gun takes a step, then stops. He points the gun at WATERS *again and fires a second time. There is another silence as limbo is plunged into darkness, and the barracks is just as quickly lit.*

We are in the barracks of Company B, 221st Chemical Smoke Generating Company, at Fort Neal. Five black enlisted men stand at "parade rest" with their hands above their heads and submit to a search. They are: CORPORAL BERNARD COBB, *a man in his mid to late twenties, dressed in a T-shirt, dog tags, fatigues, and slippers.* PRIVATE JAMES WILKIE, *a man in his early forties, a career soldier, is dressed in fatigues from which the stripes have been removed, with a baseball cap on, and smoking a cigar.* PRIVATE LOUIS HENSON, *thin, in his late twenties or early thirties, is wearing a baseball T-shirt that reads "Fort Neal" on the front and "#4" on the back, with fatigues and boots on.* PFC MELVIN PETERSON, *a man in his late twenties, wearing glasses, looks angelic. His shirt is open but he does not look sloppy; of all the men, his stripe is the most visible, his boots the most highly polished.* PRIVATE TONY SMALLS, *a man in his late thirties, a career man, is as small as his name feels. All five men are being searched by* CORPORAL ELLIS, *a soldier who is simply always "spit and polish."* ELLIS *is also black, and moves from man to man, patting them down in a police-like search.* CAPTAIN CHARLES TAYLOR, *a young white man in his mid to late thirties, looks on, a bit disturbed. All the men's uniforms are from World War II.*

TAYLOR: I'm afraid this kind of thing can't be helped, men—you can put your arms down when Ellis finishes. *(Several men drop their arms.* ELLIS *is searching* PVT. HENSON*)* We don't want anyone from Fort Neal going into Tynin looking for red-necks.

COBB: May I speak, sir? *(*TAYLOR *nods)* Why do this, Captain? They got M.P.'s surrounding us, and hell, the Colonel must know nobody colored killed the man!

TAYLOR: This is a precaution, Cobb. We can't have revenge killings, so we search for weapons.

PETERSON: Where'd they find the Sarge, sir?

TAYLOR: In the woods out by the Junction—and so we don't have any rumors. Sergeant Waters was shot twice—we don't know that he was lynched! *(Pause)* Twice. Once in the chest, and a bullet in the head. *(*ELLIS *finishes with the last man)* You finished the footlockers?

ELLIS: Yes, sir! There aren't any weapons.

TAYLOR *(relaxes):* I didn't think there would be. At ease, men! *(The men relax)* Tech/Sergeant Waters, in my opinion, served the 221st and this platoon in particular with distinction, and I for one shall miss the man. *(Slight pause)* But no matter what we think of the Sergeant's death, we will not allow this incident to make us forget our responsibility to this uniform. We are soldiers, and our war is with the Nazis and Japs, not the civilians in Tynin. Any enlisted man found with unauthorized weapons will be immediately subject to summary court-martial. *(Softens)* Sergeant Waters's replacement won't be assigned for several weeks. Until that time, you will all report to Sergeant Dorsey of C Company. Corporal Cobb will be barracks N.C.O.—any question?

PETERSON: Who do they think did it, sir?

TAYLOR: At this time there are no suspects.

HENSON: You know the Klan did it, sir.

TAYLOR: Were you an eyewitness, soldier?

HENSON: Who else goes around killin' Negroes in the South?—They lynched Jefferson the week I got here, sir! And that Signal Corps guy, Daniels, two months later!

TAYLOR: Henson, unless you saw it, keep your opinions to yourself! Is that clear? *(*HENSON *nods)* And that's an order! It also applies to everybody else!

ALL *(almost simultaneously):* Yes, sir!

TAYLOR: You men who have details this afternoon, report to the orderly room for your assignments. The rest of you are assigned to the Colonel's quarters—clean-up detail. Cobb, I want to see you in my office at 1350 hours.

COBB: Yes, sir.

TAYLOR: As of 0600 hours this morning, the town of Tynin was placed off-limits to all

military personnel. *(Slight groan from the men)* The Friday night dance has also been canceled— *(All the men moan.* TAYLOR *is sympathetic)* O.K., O.K.! Some of the officers are going to the Colonel—I can't promise anything. Right now, it's canceled.

ELLIS: Tenn-hut!

The men snap to. The CAPTAIN *salutes. Only* COBB *salutes him back. The* CAPTAIN *starts out.*

TAYLOR: As you were!

The CAPTAIN *and* ELLIS *exit the barracks. The men move to their bunks or footlockers.* WILKIE *goes to the rear of the bunks and looks out.*

COBB: They still out there, Wilkie?

WILKIE: Yeah. Got the whole place surrounded.

HENSON: I don't know what the hell they thought we'd go into that town with—mops and dishrags?

WILKIE: Y'all recruits know what Colonel's clean-up detail is, don't you? Shovelin' horseshit in his stables—

COBB: Ain't no different from what we been doin'. *(He lies down and begins scratching around his groin area)*

PETERSON *(to* COBB*)*: Made you the barracks Commander-in-Chief, huh? *(*COBB *nods)* Don't git like ole Stone-ass—What are you doin'?

COBB: Scratchin'!

HENSON *(overlapping)*: Taylor knows the Klan did it—I hope y'all know that!

SMALLS *(sudden)*: Then why are the M.P.'s outside with rifles? Why hold us prisoner?

PETERSON: They scared we may kill a couple peckerwoods, Smalls. Calm down, man!

WILKIE *(quickly)*: Smalls, you wanna play some coon-can?

SMALLS *shakes his head no. He is quiet, staring.*

COBB *(examining himself)*: Peterson, you know I think Eva gave me the crabs.

HENSON: Cobb, the kinda women you find, it's a wonda your nuts ain't fell off—crabs? You probably got lice, ticks, bedbugs, fleas—tapeworms—

COBB: Shut up, Henson! Pete—I ain't foolin', man! *(He starts to open his pants)*

PETERSON: Get some powder from the PX.

WILKIE *(almost simultaneously)*: Which one of y'all feels like playin' me some cards? *(He looks at* HENSON*)*

HENSON: Me and Peterson's goin' down the mess hall—you still goin', Pete?

PETERSON *(nods)*: Wilkie? I thought all you could do was play go-fer?

HENSON *(slyly)*: Yeah, Wilkie—whose ass can you kiss, now that your number-one ass is dead?

COBB *(laughing)*: That sounds like something C.J. would sing! *(Looks at himself again)* Ain't this a bitch? *(Picks at himself)*

WILKIE *(overlapping, to* HENSON*)*: You know what you can do for me, Henson—you too, Peterson!

PETERSON: Naughty, naughty!

WILKIE *moves to his bunk, justifying.*

WILKIE: I'm the one lost three stripes—and I'm the only man in here with kids, so when the man said jump, I jumped!

HENSON *(derisively):* Don't put your wife and kids between you and Waters's ass, man!

WILKIE: I wanted my stripes back!

COBB: I'm goin' to sick call after chow.

WILKIE *(continuing):* Y'all ain't neva' had nothin', that's why you can't understand a man like me! There was a time I was a sergeant major, you know!

HENSON *waves disdainfully at him, turning his attention to* COBB.

HENSON: Ole V-girl slipped Cobb the crabs! How you gonna explain that to the girl back home, Corporal? How will that fine, big-thighed Moma feel, when the only ribbon you bring home from this war is the Purple Heart for crab bites? *(*HENSON *laughs as* SMALLS *stands suddenly)*

SMALLS: Don't any of you guys give a damn?

PETERSON: What's the matta', Smalls?

SMALLS: The man's dead! We saw him alive last night!

COBB *(quickly):* I saw him, too. At least I know he died good and drunk!

SMALLS *(loud):* What's the matter with y'all?

HENSON: The man got hisself lynched! We're in the South, and we can't do a goddamn thing about it—you heard the Captain! But don't start actin' like we guilty of somethin'. *(Softens)* I just hope we get lucky enough to get shipped outta this hellhole to the war! *(To himself)* Besides, whoever did it, didn't kill much anyway.

SMALLS: He deserved better than that!

COBB: Look, everybody feels rotten, Smalls. But it won't bring the man back, so let's forget about it!

PETERSON *moves to pat* SMALLS *on the back.*

PETERSON: Why don't you walk it off, man?

SMALLS *moves away to his bunk.* PETERSON *shrugs.*

HENSON: Yeah—or go turn on a smoke machine, let the fog make you think you in London!

SMALLS *sits down on his bunk and looks at them for a moment, then lays down, his face in the pillow.*

WILKIE *(overlapping):* Let Cobb bring his Eva over, she'll take his mind off Waters plus give him a bonus of crabs!

The men laugh, but SMALLS *doesn't move as the lights begin slowly to fade out.*

HENSON *(counting):* —an' blue-balls. Clap. Syphilis. Pimples! *(*COBB *throws a pillow at* HENSON*)* Piles! Fever blisters. Cockeyes. Cooties!

The men are laughing as the lights go out. As they do, a rather wiry black officer wearing glasses, CAPTAIN RICHARD DAVENPORT, *walks across the stage from the wings, dressed sharply in an M.P. uniform, his hat cocked to the side and strapped down, the way airmen wear theirs. He is carrying a briefcase, and we are aware of a man who is very confident and self-assured. He is smiling as he faces the audience, cleaning his glasses as he begins to speak.*

DAVENPORT: Call me Davenport—Captain, United States Army, attached to the 343rd Military Police Corps Unit, Fort Neal, Louisiana. I'm a lawyer the segregated Armed Services couldn't find a place for. My job in this war? Policing colored troops. *(Slight pause)* One morning, during mid-April 1944, a colored tech/sergeant, Vernon C. Waters, assigned to the 221st Chemical Smoke Generating Company, stationed here before transfer to Europe, was brutally shot to death in a wooded section off the New Post Road and the junction of Highway 51—just two hundred yards from the colored N.C.O. club—by a person or persons unknown. *(Pauses a little)* Naturally, the unofficial consensus was the local Ku Klux Klan, and for that reason, I was told at the time, Colonel Barton Nivens ordered the Military Police to surround the enlisted men's quarters—then instructed all his company commanders to initiate a thorough search of all personal property for unauthorized knives, guns—weapons of any kind. *(Slight pause)* You see, ninety percent of the Colonel's command—all of the enlisted men stationed here are Negroes, and the Colonel felt—and I suppose justly—that once word of the Sergeant's death spread among his troops, there might be some retaliation against the white citizens of Tynin. *(Shrugs)* What he did worked—there was no retaliation, and no racial incidents. *(Pause)* The week after the killing took place, several correspondents from the Negro press wrote lead articles about it. But the headlines faded— *(Smiles)* The NAACP got me involved in this. Rumor has it, Thurgood Marshall ordered an immediate investigation of the killing, and the army, pressured by Secretary of War Stimson, rather randomly ordered Colonel Nivens to initiate a preliminary inquiry into the Sergeant's death. Now, the Colonel didn't want to rehash the murder, but he complied with the army's order by instructing the Provost Marshal, my C.O., Major Hines, to conduct a *few* question-and-answer sessions among the men of Sergeant Waters's platoon and file a report. The matter was to be given the lowest priority. *(Pause)* The case was mine, five minutes later. It was four to five weeks after his death—the month of May. *(He pauses as the light builds in* CAPTAIN TAYLOR*'s office.* TAYLOR *is facing* DAVENPORT, *expressionless.* DAVENPORT *is a bit puzzled)* Captain?

TAYLOR *(starts back to his desk and sits on the edge of it, as* DAVENPORT *starts into the office a bit cautiously)*: We'll be getting some of you as replacements, but we don't expect them until next month. Sit down, Davenport. *(*DAVENPORT *sits)* You came out of Fort Benning in '43?

DAVENPORT: Yes.

TAYLOR: And they assigned a lawyer to the Military Police? I'm Infantry and I've been with the Engineers, Field Artillery, and Signal Corps—this is some army. Where'd you graduate law school?

DAVENPORT: Howard University.

TAYLOR: Your daddy a rich minister or something? *(*DAVENPORT *shakes his head no)* I graduated the Point— *(Pause)* We didn't have any Negroes at the Point. I never saw a Negro until I was twelve or thirteen. *(Pause)* You like the army, I suppose, huh?

DAVENPORT: Captain, did you see my orders?

TAYLOR *(bristling slightly)*: I saw them right after Colonel Nivens sent them to Major Hines. I sent my orderly to the barracks and told him to have the men waiting for you.

DAVENPORT: Thank you.

TAYLOR: I didn't know at the time that Major Hines was assigning a Negro, Davenport. *(DAVENPORT stiffens)* My preparations were made in the belief that you'd be a white man. I think it only fair to tell you that had I known what Hines intended I would have requested the immediate suspension of the investigation—May I speak freely?

DAVENPORT: You haven't stopped yet, Captain.

TAYLOR: Look—how far could you get even if you succeed? These local people aren't going to charge a white man in this parish on the strength of an investigation conducted by a Negro!—and Nivens and Hines know that! The Colonel doesn't give a damn about finding the men responsible for this thing! And they're making a fool of you—can't you see that?—and—take off those sunglasses!

DAVENPORT: I intend to carry out my orders—and I like these glasses—they're like MacArthur's.

TAYLOR: You go near that sheriff's office in Tynin in your uniform—carrying a briefcase, looking and sounding white, and charging local people—and you'll be found just as dead as Sergeant Waters! People around here don't respect the colored!

DAVENPORT: I know that.

TAYLOR *(annoyed)*: You know how many times I've asked Nivens to look into this killing? Every day, since it happened, Davenport. Major Hines didn't tell you that!

DAVENPORT: Do you suspect someone, Captain?

TAYLOR: Don't play cat-and-mouse with me, soldier!

DAVENPORT *(calmly)*: Captain, like it or not, I'm all you've got. I've been ordered to look into Sergeant Waters's death, and I intend to do exactly that.

There is a long pause.

TAYLOR: Can I tell you a little story? *(DAVENPORT nods)* Before you were assigned here? Nivens got us together after dinner one night, and all we did was discuss Negroes in the officer ranks. We all commanded Negro troops, but nobody had ever come face to face with colored officers—there were a lot of questions that night—for example, your quarters—had to be equal to ours, but we had none—no mess hall for you! *(Slight pause)* Anyway, Jed Harris was the only officer who defended it—my own feelings were mixed. The only Negroes I've ever known were subordinates—My father hired the first Negro I ever saw—man named Colfax—to help him fix the shed one summer. Nice man—worked hard—did a good job, too. *(Remembering; smiles thoughtfully)* But I never met a Negro with any education until I graduated the Point—hardly an officer of equal rank. So I frankly wasn't sure how I'd feel—until right now—and— *(Struggles)* I don't want to offend you, but I just cannot get used to it—the bars, the uniform—being in charge just doesn't look right on Negroes!

DAVENPORT *(rises)*: Captain, are you through?

TAYLOR: You could ask Hines for another assignment—this case is not for you! By the time you overcome the obstacles to your race, this case would be dead!

DAVENPORT *(sharply)*: I got it. And I *am* in charge! All your orders instruct you to do is cooperate!

There is a moment of silence.

TAYLOR: I won't be made a fool of, Davenport. *(Straightens)* Ellis! You're right, there's no need to discuss this any further.

ELLIS *appears on the edge of the office.*

ELLIS: Yes, sir!

TAYLOR: Captain Davenport will need assistance with the men—I can't prevent that, Davenport, but I intend to do all I can to have this so-called investigation stopped.

DAVENPORT: Do what you like. If there's nothing else, you'll excuse me, won't you, Captain?

TAYLOR *(sardonically):* Glad I met you, Captain.

DAVENPORT *salutes and* TAYLOR *returns salute. For an instant the two men trade cold stares, then* DAVENPORT *gestures to* ELLIS, *and the two of them start out of the office by way of the stage.* DAVENPORT *follows* ELLIS *out. Behind them,* TAYLOR *stares after them as the lights in his office fade out.* DAVENPORT *removes his glasses.*

ELLIS: We heard it was you, sir—you know how the grapevine is. Sad thing—what happened to the Sarge.

DAVENPORT: What's on the grapevine about the killing?

The two men stop as slowly, almost imperceptibly, on the right the barracks area is lit. In it, a small table and two chairs have been set up. ELLIS *shrugs.*

ELLIS: We figure the Klan. They ain't crazy about us tan yanks in this part of the country.

DAVENPORT: Is there anything on the grapevine about trouble in the town before Sergeant Waters was killed?

ELLIS: None that I know of before—after, there were rumors around the post—couple our guys from the Tank Corps wanted to drive them Shermans into Tynin—then I guess you heard that somebody said two officers did it—I figure that's why the Colonel surrounded our barracks.

DAVENPORT: Was the rumor confirmed—I didn't hear that! Did anything ever come of it?

ELLIS: Not that I know of, sir.

DAVENPORT: Thanks, Ellis—I'd better start seeing the men. *(They start into the barracks from the stage floor)* Did you set this up? *(*ELLIS *nods)* Good— *(He sets his briefcase on the table)* Are they ready?

ELLIS: The Captain instructed everybody in the Sarge's platoon to be here, sir. He told them you'd be starting this morning.

DAVENPORT *smiles.*

DAVENPORT *(to himself):* Before he found out, huh?

ELLIS *(puzzled):* Sir?

DAVENPORT: Nothing. Call the first man in, Corporal—and stay loose, I might need you.

ELLIS: Yes, sir! Sir, may I say something? *(*DAVENPORT *nods)* It sure is good to see one of us wearin' them Captain's bars, sir.

DAVENPORT: Thank you.

ELLIS *salutes, does a sharp about-face, and starts out.*

ELLIS *(loud):* Private Wilkie!

WILKIE *(offstage):* Yes, sir! *(Almost immediately,* WILKIE *appears in the doorway. He is dressed in proper uniform of fatigues, boots, and cap.)*

ELLIS: Cap'n wants to see you!

WILKIE: Yes indeedy! *(Moves quickly to the table, where he comes to attention and salutes)* Private James Wilkie reporting as ordered, sir.

DAVENPORT: At ease, Private. Have a seat. *(To* ELLIS *as* WILKIE *sits)* That will be all, Corporal.

ELLIS: Yes, sir.

ELLIS *salutes and exits.* DAVENPORT *waits until he leaves before speaking.*

DAVENPORT: Private Wilkie, I am Captain Davenport—

WILKIE *(interjecting):* Everybody knows that, sir. You all we got down here. *(Smiles broadly)* I was on that first detail got your quarters togetha', sir.

DAVENPORT *nods.*

DAVENPORT *(coldly):* I'm conducting an investigation into the events surrounding Sergeant Waters's death. Everything you say to me will go in my report, but that report is confidential.

WILKIE: I understand, sir.

DAVENPORT *removes pad and pencil from the briefcase.*

DAVENPORT: How long did you know Sergeant Waters?

WILKIE: 'Bout a year, sir. I met him last March—March 5th—I remember the date, I had been a staff sergeant exactly two years the day after he was assigned. This company was basically a baseball team then, sir. See, most of the boys had played for the Negro League, so naturally the army put us all together. *(Chuckles at the memory)* We'd be assigned to different companies—Motor Pool—Dump Truck all week long—made us do the dirty work on the post—garbage, clean-up—but on Saturdays we were whippin' the hell out of 'em on the baseball diamond! I was hittin' .352 myself! And we had a boy, C. J. Memphis? He coulda hit a ball from Fort Neal to Berlin, Germany—or Tokyo—if he was battin' right-handed. *(Pauses, catches* DAVENPORT*'s impatience)* Well, the army sent Waters to manage the team. He had been in Field Artillery—Gunnery Sergeant. Had a croix de guerre from the First War, too.

DAVENPORT: What kind of man was he?

WILKIE: All spit and polish, sir.

At that moment, in limbo, a spotlight hits SERGEANT WATERS. *He is dressed in a well-creased uniform, wearing a helmet liner and standing at parade-rest, facing the audience. The light around him, however, is strange—it is blue-gray like the past. The light around* DAVENPORT *and* WILKIE *abates somewhat. Dialogue is continuous.*

DAVENPORT: Tell me about him.

WILKIE: He took my stripes! *(Smiles)* But I was in the wrong, sir!

WATERS *stands at ease. His voice is crisp and sharp, his movements minimal. He is the typical hard-nosed N.C.O.—strict, soldierly.*

WATERS: Sergeant Wilkie! You are a noncommissioned officer in the army of a country at war—the penalty for being drunk on duty is severe in peacetime, so don't bring me no po'colored-folks-can't-do-nothin'-unless-they-drunk shit as an excuse! You are supposed to be an example to your men—so, I'm gonna send you to jail for ten days *and* take them goddamn stripes. Teach you a lesson—You in the army! *(Derisively)* Colored folks always runnin' off at the mouth 'bout what y'all gonna do if the white man gives you a chance—and you get it, and what do you do with it? You wind up drunk on guard duty—I don't blame the white man—why the hell should he put colored and white together in this war? You can't even be trusted to guard your own quarters—no wonder they treat us like dogs—Get outta' my sight, *Private!*

Light fades at once on WATERS.

DAVENPORT: What about the other men?

WILKIE: Sometimes the Southern guys caught a little hell—Sarge always said he was from up North somewhere. He was a good soldier, sir. I'm from Detroit myself—born and raised there. Joe Louis started in Detroit—did you know that, sir?

DAVENPORT: What about the Southerners?

WILKIE: Sarge wasn't exactly crazy 'bout 'em—'cept for C.J. Now C.J. was from the South, but with him Sarge was different—probably because C.J. was the best ball player we had. He could sing too! *(Slight pause)* Sarge never got too close to nobody—maybe me—but he didn' mess with C.J., you know what I mean? Not like he did with everybody else.

In limbo the spotlight illuminates C. J. MEMPHIS, *a young, handsome black man. He is in a soldier's uniform, cap on the side. He is strumming a guitar.* WATERS *is watching him, smiling. Their light is the strange light of the past.* C.J. *begins to sing, his voice deep, melodious, and bluesy.*

C.J.: It's a low / it's a low, low / lowdown dirty shame! Yeah, it's a low / it's a low, low / lowdown dirty shame!

WILKIE *(before* C.J. *finishes):* Big Mississippi boy!

WILKIE *and* C.J. *simultaneously sing.*

C.J. AND WILKIE: They say we fightin' Hitler! But they won't let us in the game!

C.J. *strums and hums as* WATERS *looks on.*

WILKIE: Worked harder and faster than everybody—wasn' a man on the team didn't like him. Sarge took to him the first time he saw him. "Wilkie," he says.

WILKIE AND WATERS *(simultaneously):* What have we got here?

WATERS: A guitar-playin' man! Boy, you eva' heard of Blind Willie Reynolds? Son House? Henry Sims?

C.J. *nods to everything.*

C.J. *nods to everything.*

C.J.: You heard them play, Sarge?

WATERS: Every one of 'em. I was stationed in Mississippi couple years ago—you from down that way, ain't you?

C.J.: Yes, sah!

WATERS: Well, they use ta play over at the Bandana Club outside Camp J. J. Reilly.

C.J.: I played there once!

WATERS *(smiles):* Ain't that somethin'? I'd go over there from time to time—people use ta come from everywhere! *(To* WILKIE*)* Place was always dark, Wilkie—smoky. Folks would be dancin'—sweatin'—guitar pickers be strummin', shoutin'—it would be wild in there sometimes. Reminded me of a place I use ta go in France durin' the First War—the women, the whiskey—place called the Café Napoleon.

C.J.: You really like the blues, huh?

WATERS: No other kind of music—where'd you learn to play so good? I came by here yesterday and heard this pickin'—one of the men tol' me it was you.

C.J.: My daddy taught me, Sarge.

WATERS: You play pretty good, boy. Wilkie, wasn' that good?

WILKIE: Yes indeed, Sarge. (to DAVENPORT) I mostly agreed with the Sarge, sir. He was a good man. Good to his men. Talked about his wife and kids all the time— *(*WATERS *starts down from the limbo area, as the lights around* C.J. *fade out.* WATERS *pulls a pipe from his pocket, lights it as he moves to the edge of the* CAPTAIN*'s office and sits on the edge of the platform supporting it. He puffs a few times.* WILKIE*'s talk is continuous)* Use ta write home every day. I don't see why nobody would want to kill the Sarge, sir.

WATERS *smiles.*

WATERS: Wilkie? *(*WILKIE *rises and walks into the blue-gray light and the scene with* WATERS. DAVENPORT *will watch)* You know what I'ma get that boy of mine for his birthday? One of them Schwinn bikes. He'll be twelve—time flies, don't it? Let me show you something?

WILKIE *(to* DAVENPORT*):* He was always pullin' out snapshots, sir.

WATERS *hands him a snapshot.*

WATERS: My wife let a neighbor take this a couple weeks ago—ain't he growin' fast?

WILKIE: He's over your wife's shoulder! *(Hands it back.* WATERS *looks at the photo)*

WATERS: I hope this kid never has to be a soldier.

WILKIE: It was good enough for you.

WATERS: I couldn't do any better—and this army was the closest I figured the white man would let me get to any kind of authority. No, the army ain't for this boy. When this war's over, things are going to change, Wilkie—and I want him to be ready for it—my daughter, too! I'm sendin' bot' of 'em to some big white college—let 'em rub elbows with the whites, learn the white man's language—how he does things. Otherwise, we'll be left behind—you can see it in the army. White man runnin' rings around us.

WILKIE: A lot of us didn't get the chance or the schoolin' the white folks got.

WATERS: That ain't no excuse, Wilkie. Most niggahs just don't care—tomorrow don't mean nothin' to 'em. My daddy shoveled coal from the back of a wagon all his life. He couldn't read or write, but he saw to it we did! Not havin' ain't no excuse for not gettin'.

WILKIE: Can't get pee from a rock, Sarge.

WATERS *rises abruptly.*

WATERS: You just like the rest of 'em, Wilkie—I thought bustin' you would teach you something—we got to challenge this man in his arena—use his weapons, don't you know that? We need lawyers, doctors—generals—senators! Stop thinkin' like a niggah!

WILKIE: All I said—

WATERS: Is the equipment ready for tomorrow's game?

WILKIE: Yeah.

WATERS: Good. You can go now, Wilkie. (WILKIE *is stunned)* That's an order!

WILKIE *turns toward* DAVENPORT. *In the background, the humming of* C.J. *rises a bit as the light around* WATERS *fades out.*

WILKIE: He could be two people sometimes, sir. Warm one minute—ice the next.

DAVENPORT: How did you feel about him?

WILKIE: Overall—I guess he was all right. You could always borrow a ten-spot off him if you needed it.

DAVENPORT: Did you see the Sergeant any time immediately preceding his death?

WILKIE: I don't know how much before it was, but a couple of us had been over the N.C.O. club that night and Sarge had been juicin' pretty heavy.

DAVENPORT: Did Waters drink a lot?

WILKIE: No more than most— *(Pause)* Could I ask you a question, sir? (DAVENPORT *nods)* Is it true, when they found Sarge all his stripes and insignia were still on his uniform?

DAVENPORT: I don't recall it being mentioned in my preliminary report. Why?

WILKIE: If that's the way they found him, something's wrong, ain't it, sir? Them Klan boys don't like to see us in these uniforms. They usually take the stripes and stuff off, before they lynch us.

DAVENPORT *is quiet, thoughtful for a moment.*

DAVENPORT: Thank you, Private—I might want to call you again, but for now you're excused.

WILKIE *rises.*

WILKIE: Yes, sir! *(Sudden mood swing, hesitant)* Sir?

DAVENPORT: Yes?

WILKIE: Can you do anything about allotment checks? My wife didn't get hers last month.

DAVENPORT: There's nothing I can do directly—did you see the finance officer? (WILKIE *nods)* Well—I'll—I'll mention it to Captain Taylor.

WILKIE: Thank you, sir. You want me to send the next man in?

DAVENPORT *nods.* WILKIE *salutes, does an about-face, and exits.* DAVENPORT *returns the salute, then leans back in his chair thoughtfully. In the background, the humming of* C.J. *rises again as the*

next man, PFC MELVIN PETERSON, *enters. Dressed in fatigues, he is the model soldier. He walks quickly to the table, stands at attention, and salutes. The humming fades out as* DAVENPORT *returns the salute.*

PETERSON: Private First Class Melvin Peterson reporting as ordered, sir!

DAVENPORT: Sit down, Private. *(*PETERSON *sits)* Do you know why I'm here?

PETERSON: Yes, sir.

DAVENPORT: Fine. Now, everything you tell me is confidential, so I want you to speak as freely as possible. *(*PETERSON *nods)* Where are you from?

PETERSON: Hollywood, California—by way of Alabama, sir. I enlisted in '42—thought we'd get a chance to fight.

DAVENPORT *(ignores the comment):* Did you know Sergeant Waters well?

PETERSON: No, sir. He was already with the company when I got assigned here. And us common G.I.'s don't mix well with N.C.O.'s.

DAVENPORT: Were you on the baseball team?

PETERSON: Yes, sir—I played shortstop.

DAVENPORT: Did you like the Sergeant?

PETERSON: No, sir.

Before DAVENPORT *can speak,* ELLIS *enters.*

ELLIS: Beg your pardon, sir. Captain Taylor would like to see you in his office at once.

DAVENPORT: Did he say why?

ELLIS: No, sir—just that you should report to him immediately.

DAVENPORT *(annoyed):* Tell the men to stick around. When I finish with the Captain, I'll be back.

ELLIS: Yes, sir!

ELLIS *exits.*

DAVENPORT *(to* PETERSON*):* Feel like walking, Private? We can continue this on the way. *(Begins to put his things in his briefcase)* Why didn't you like the Sergeant?

DAVENPORT *and* PETERSON *start out as the light begins to fade in the barracks. They go through doorway, exit, and reenter the stage in full view.*

PETERSON: It goes back to the team, sir. I got here in—baseball season had started, so it had to be June—June of last year. The team had won maybe nine—ten games in a row, there was a rumor that they would even get a chance to play the Yankees in exhibition. So when I got assigned to a team like that, sir—I mean, I felt good. Anyway, ole Stone-ass—

DAVENPORT: Stone-ass?

PETERSON: I'm the only one called him that—Sergeant Waters, sir.

As the two of them pass in front of the barracks area, the light begins to rise very slowly, but it is the blue-gray light of the past. The chairs and table are gone, and the room looks different.

DAVENPORT: Respect his rank, with me, Private.

PETERSON: I didn't mean no offense, sir. *(Slight pause)* Well, the Sergeant and that brown-nosin' Wilkie? They ran the team—and like it was a chain gang, sir. A chain gang!

The two men exit the stage. As they do, C.J. MEMPHIS, HENSON, COBB, *and* SMALLS *enter in their baseball uniforms. T-shirts with "Fort Neal" stamped on the fronts, and numbers on the back, and baseball caps. They are carrying equipment—bats, gloves.* C.J. *is carrying his guitar.* SMALLS *enters tossing a baseball into the air and catching it. They almost all enter at once, with the exuberance of young men. Their talk is locker-room loud, and filled with bursts of laughter.*

HENSON: You see the look on that umpire's face when C.J. hit that home run? I thought he was gonna die on the spot, he turned so pale!

They move to their respective bunks.

SMALLS: Serves the fat bastard right! Some of them pitches he called strikes were well ova' my head!

C.J. *strums his guitar.* COBB *begins to brush off his boots.*

COBB: C.J.? Who was that fine, river-hip thing you was talkin' to, homey?

C.J. *shrugs and smiles.*

HENSON: Speakin' of women, I got to write my Lady a letter. *(He begins to dig for his writing things)*

COBB: She looked mighty good to me, C.J.

SMALLS *(overlapping):* Y'all hear Henson? Henson, you ain't had a woman since a woman had you!

HENSON *makes an obscene gesture.*

C.J. *(overlapping* SMALLS*):* Now, all she did was ask me for my autograph.

COBB: Look like she was askin' you fo' mor'n that. *(To* SMALLS*)* You see him, Smalls? Leanin' against the fence, all in the woman's face, breathin' heavy—

HENSON: If Smalls couldn't see enough to catch a ground ball right in his glove, how the hell could he see C.J. ova' by the fence?

SMALLS: That ball got caught in the sun!

HENSON: On the ground?

COBB *(at once):* We beat 'em nine to one! Y'all be quiet, I'm askin' this man 'bout a woman he was with had tits like two helmets!

C.J.: If I had'a give that gal what she asked fo'—she'da give me somethin' I didn' want! Them V-gals git you a bad case a' clap. 'Sides, she wasn' but sixteen.

SMALLS: You shoulda introduced her to Henson—sixteen's about his speed.

HENSON *makes a farting sound in retaliation.*

C.J.: Aroun' home? There's a fella folks use ta call, Lil' Jimmy One Leg—on account of his thing was so big? Two years ago—ole young pretty thing laid clap on Jimmy so bad, he los' the one good leg he had! Now folks jes' call him Little!

Laughter.

C.J.: That young thing talkin' to me ain' look so clean.

HENSON: Dirty or clean, she had them white boys lookin'.

COBB: Eyes popin' out they sockets, wasn' they? Remind me of that pitcher las' week! The one from 35th Ordnance? The one everybody claimed was so good? Afta' twelve straight hits, he looked the same way!

PETERSON *enters, carrying two baseball bats.*

SMALLS: It might be funny ta y'all, but when me and Pete had duty in the Ordnance mess hall, that same white pitcher was the first one started the name-callin'—

HENSON: Forget them dudes in Ordnance—lissen to this! *(*HENSON *begins to read from a short letter)* "Dear, Louis"—y'all hear that? The name is Louis—

COBB: Read the damn letter!

HENSON *(makes obscene gesture):* "Dear, Louis. You and the boys keep up the good work. All of us here at home are praying for you and inspired in this great cause by you. We know the Nazis and the Japs can't be stopped unless we all work together, so tell your buddies to press forward and win this war. All our hopes for the future go with you, Louis. Love Mattie." I think I'm in love with the sepia Winston Churchill—what kinda' letter do you write a nut like this?

COBB: Send her a round of ammunition and a bayonet, *Louis!*

HENSON *waves disdainfully.*

PETERSON: Y'all oughta listen to what Smalls said. Every time we beat them at baseball, they get back at us every way they can.

COBB: It's worth it to me just to wipe those superior smiles off they faces.

PETERSON: I don't know—seems like it makes it that much harder for us.

C.J.: They tell me, coupla them big-time Negroes is on the verge a' gittin' all of us togetha'—colored and white—say they want one army.

PETERSON: Forget that, C.J.! White folks'll neva' integrate no army!

C.J. *(strums):* If they do—I'ma be ready for 'em! *(Sings)* Well, I got me a bright red zoot suit / And a pair a' patent-leatha' shoes / And my woman she sittin' waitin' / Fo' the day we hea' the news! Lawd, lawd, lawd, lawd, / Lawd, lawd, lawd, lawd!

SERGEANT WATERS, *followed by* WILKIE, *enters, immediately crossing to the center of the barracks, his strident voice abruptly cutting off* C.J.*'s singing and playing.*

WATERS: Listen up! *(To* C.J.*)* We don't need that guitar playin'-sittin'-round-the-shack music today, C.J.! *(Smiles)* I want all you men out of those baseball uniforms and into work clothes! You will all report to me at 1300 hours in front of the Officers Club. We've got a work detail. We're painting the lobby of the club.

Collective groan.

SMALLS: The officers can't paint their own club?

COBB: Hell no, Smalls! Let the great-colored-clean-up company do it! Our motto is: Anything you don't want to do, the colored troops will do for you!

HENSON *(like a cheer)*: Anything you don't want to do, the colored troops will do for you! *(He starts to lead the others)*

OTHERS: Anything you don't—

WATERS: That's enough!

The men are instantly silent.

HENSON: When do we get a rest? We just played nine innings of baseball, Sarge!

SMALLS: We can't go in the place, why the hell should we paint it?

COBB: Amen, brother!

There is a moment of quiet before WATERS *speaks.*

WATERS: Let me tell you fancy-assed ball-playin' Negroes somethin'! The *reasons* for any orders given by a superior officer is none of y'all's business! You obey them! This country is at war, and you niggahs are soldiers—nothin' else! So baseball teams—win or lose—get no special privileges! They need to work some of you niggahs till your legs fall off! *(Intense)* And something else—from now on, when I tell you to do something, I want it done—is that clear? *(The men are quiet)* Now, Wilkie's gonna' take all them funky shirts you got on over to the laundry. I could smell you suckers before I hit the field!

PETERSON: What kinda colored man are you?

WATERS: I'm a soldier, Peterson! First, last, and always! I'm the kinda colored man that don't like lazy, shiftless Negroes!

PETERSON: You ain't got to come in here and call us names!

WATERS: The Nazis call you schvatza! You gonna tell them they hurt your little feelings?

C.J.: Don't look like to me we could do too much to them Nazis wit' paint brushes, Sarge.

The men laugh. The moment is gone, and though WATERS *is angry, his tone becomes overly solicitous, smiling.*

WATERS: You tryin' to mock me, C.J.?

C.J.: No, sah, Sarge.

WATERS: Good, because whatever an ignorant, low-class geechy like you has to say isn't worth paying attention to, is it? *(Pause)* Is it?

C.J.: I reckon not, Sarge.

PETERSON: You' a creep, Waters!

WATERS: Boy, you are something—ain't been in the company a month, Wilkie, and already everybody's champion!

C.J. *(interjecting)*: Sarge was just jokin', Pete—he don't mean no harm!

PETERSON: He does! We take enough from the white boys!

WATERS: Yes, you do—and if it wasn't for you Southern niggahs, yessahin', bowin' and scrapin', scratchin' your heads, white folks wouldn't think we were all fools!

PETERSON: Where you from, England?

Men snicker.

HENSON *(at once):* Peterson!

WATERS *(immediately):* You got somethin' to say, Henson?

HENSON: Nothin', Sarge.

HENSON *shakes his head as* WATERS *turns back to* PETERSON.

WATERS: Peterson, you got a real comic streak in you. Wilkie, looks like we got us a wise-ass Alabama boy here! *(He moves toward* PETERSON*)* Yes, sir— *(He snatches* PETERSON *in the collar)* Don't get smart, niggah!

PETERSON *yanks away.*

PETERSON: Get your fuckin' hands off me!

WATERS *smiles, leans forward.*

WATERS: You wanna hit ole Sergeant Waters, boy? *(Whispers)* Come on! Please! Come on, niggah!

CAPTAIN TAYLOR *enters the barracks quite suddenly, unaware of what is going on.*

HENSON: Tenn-hut!

All the men snap to.

TAYLOR: At ease! *(He moves toward* WATERS, *feeling the tension)* What's going on here, Sergeant?

WATERS: Nothin', sir—I was going over the *Manual of Arms.* Is there something in particular you wanted, sir? Something I can do?

TAYLOR *(relaxed somewhat):* Nothing— *(To the men)* Men, I congratulate you on the game you won today. We've only got seven more to play, and if we win them, we'll be the first team in Fort Neal history to play the Yanks in exhibition. Everyone in the regiment is counting on you. In times like these, morale is important—and winning can help a lot of things. *(Pause)* Sergeant, as far as I'm concerned, they've got the rest of the day off.

The men are pleased.

WATERS: Begging your pardon, sir, but these men need all the work they can get. They don't need time off—our fellas aren't getting time off in North Africa—besides, we've got orders to report to the Officers Club for a paint detail at 1300 hours.

TAYLOR: Who issued that order?

WATERS: Major Harris, sir.

TAYLOR: I'll speak to the Major.

WATERS: Sir, I don't think it's such a good idea to get a colored N.C.O. mixed up in the middle of you officers, sir.

TAYLOR: I said, I'd speak to him, Sergeant.

WATERS: Yes, sir!

TAYLOR: I respect the men's duty to service, but they need time off.

WATERS: Yes, sir.

Pause.

TAYLOR: You men played a great game of baseball out there today—that catch you made in center field, Memphis—how the hell'd you get up so high?

C.J. *(shrugs, smiles):* They say I got "Bird" in mah blood, sir.

TAYLOR *is startled by the statement, his smile is an uncomfortable one.* WATERS *is standing on "eggs."*

TAYLOR: American eagle, I hope. *(Laughs a little)*

C.J.: No, sah, crow— *(*WATERS *starts to move, but* C.J. *stops him by continuing. Several of the men are beginning to get uncomfortable)* Man tol' my daddy the day I was born, the shadow of a crow's wings—

TAYLOR *(cutting him off):* Fine—men, I'll say it again—you played superbly. *(Turns to* WATERS*)* Sergeant. *(He starts out abruptly)*

WATERS: Tenn-hut!

WATERS *salutes as the men snap to.*

TAYLOR *(exiting):* As you were.

TAYLOR *salutes as he goes. There is an instant of quiet. The men relax a little, but their focus is* C.J.

WATERS *(laughing):* Ain't these geechies somethin'? How long a story was you gonna tell the man, C.J.? My God! *(The men join him, but as he turns toward* PETERSON, *he stiffens)* Peterson! Oh, I didn't forget you, boy. *(The room quiets)* It's time to teach you a lesson!

PETERSON: Why don't you drop dead, Sarge?

WATERS: Nooo! I'ma drop you, boy! Out behind the barracks—Wilkie, you go out and make sure it's all set up.

WILKIE: You want all the N.C.O.'s?

WATERS *nods.* WILKIE *goes out smiling.*

WATERS: I'm going outside and wait for you, geechy! And when you come out, I'm gonna whip your black Southern ass—let the whole company watch it, too! *(Points)* You need to learn respect, boy—how to talk to your betters. *(Starts toward the door)* Fight hard,

hea'? I'ma try to bust your fuckin' head open—the rest of you get those goddamn shirts off like I said!

He exits. The barracks is quiet for a moment.

COBB: You gonna fight him?
HENSON *(overlapping):* I tried to warn you!
PETERSON: You ain't do nothin'!
SMALLS: He'll fight you dirty, Pete—don't do it!

PETERSON *goes to his bunk and throws his cap off angrily.*

COBB: You don't want to do it?
PETERSON: You wanna fight in my place, Cobb? *(He sits)* Shit!

Slight pause. HENSON *pulls off his shirt.*

C.J.: I got some Farmers Dust—jes' a pinch'll make you strong as a bull—they say it comes from the city of Zar. *(Removes a pouch from his neck)* I seen a man use this stuff and pull a mule outta a sinkhole by hisself!
PETERSON: Get the hell outta here with that backwater crap—can't you speak up for yourself—let that bastard treat you like a dog!
C.J.: 'Long as his han's ain't on me—he ain't done me no harm, Pete. Callin' names ain't nothin', I know what I is. *(Softens)* Sarge ain't so bad—been good to me.
PETERSON: The man despises you!
C.J.: Sarge? You wrong, Pete—plus I feel kinda sorry for him myself. Any man ain't sure where he belongs must be in a whole lotta pain.
PETERSON: Don't y'all care?
HENSON: Don't nobody like it, Pete—but when you here a little longer—I mean, what can you do? This hea's the army and Sarge got all the stripes.

PETERSON *rises, disgusted, and starts out.* SMALLS *moves at once.*

SMALLS: Peterson, look, if you want me to, I'll get the Captain. You don't have to go out there and get your head beat in!
PETERSON: Somebody's got to fight him.

He exits. There is quiet as SMALLS *walks back to his bunk.*

C.J. *(singing):* It's a low / it's a low, low / lowdown dirty shame! It's a low / it's a low, low / lowdown dirty shame! Been playin' in this hea' army / an ain't even learned the game! Lawd, lawd, lawd, lawd—

C.J. *begins to hum as the lights slowly fade out over the barracks. As they do, the lights come up simultaneously in the* CAPTAIN*'s office. It is empty.* PETERSON *(in proper uniform) and* DAVENPORT *enter from off-stage. They stop outside the* CAPTAIN*'s office.*

PETERSON: He beat me pretty bad that day, sir. The man was crazy!
DAVENPORT: Was the incident ever reported?

PETERSON: I never reported it, sir—I know I should have, but he left me alone after that. *(Shrugs)* I just played ball.

DAVENPORT: Did you see Waters the night he died?

PETERSON: No, sir—me and Smalls had guard duty.

DAVENPORT: Thank you, Private. That'll be all for now. *(PETERSON comes to attention)* By the way, did the team ever get to play the Yankees?

PETERSON: No, sir. We lost the last game to a Sanitation Company.

He salutes. DAVENPORT returns salute. PETERSON does a crisp about-face and exits. Slowly DAVENPORT starts into the CAPTAIN's office, surprised that no one is about.

DAVENPORT: Captain? *(There is no response. For a moment or two, DAVENPORT looks around. He is somewhat annoyed)* Captain?

He starts out. TAYLOR enters. He crosses the room to his desk, where he sits.

TAYLOR: I asked you back here because I wanted you to see the request I've sent to Colonel Nivens to have your investigation terminated. *(He picks up several sheets of paper on his desk and hands them to DAVENPORT, who ignores them)*

DAVENPORT: What?

TAYLOR: I wanted you to see that my reasons have nothing to do with you personally—my request will not hurt your army record in any way! *(Pause)* There are other things to consider in this case!

DAVENPORT: Only the color of my skin, Captain.

TAYLOR *(sharply)*: I want the people responsible for killing one of my men found and jailed, Davenport!

DAVENPORT: So do I!

TAYLOR: Then give this up! *(Rises)* Whites down here won't see their duty—or justice. They'll see *you!* And once they do, the law—due process—it all goes! And what is the point of continuing an investigation that can't possibly get at the truth?

DAVENPORT: Captain, my orders are very specific, so unless you want charges brought against you for interfering in a criminal investigation, stay the hell out of my way and leave me and my investigation alone!

TAYLOR *(almost sneering)*: Don't take yourself too seriously, Davenport. You couldn't find an officer within five hundred miles who would convey charges to a court-martial board against me for something like that, and you know it!

DAVENPORT: Maybe not, but I'd—I'd see to it that your name, rank, and duty station got into the Negro press! Yeah, let a few colored newspapers call you a Negro-hater! Make you an embarrassment to the United States Army, Captain—like Major Albright at Fort Jefferson, and you'd never command troops again—or wear more than those captain's bars on that uniform, Mr. West Point!

TAYLOR: I'll never be more than a captain, Davenport, because I won't let them get away with dismissing things like Waters's death. I've been the commanding officer of three outfits! I raised hell in all of them, so threatening me won't change my request. Let the Negro press print that I don't like being made a fool of with phony investigations!

DAVENPORT *(studies TAYLOR for a moment)*: There are two white officers involved in this, Captain—aren't there?

TAYLOR: I want them in jail—out of the army! And there is no way *you* can get them charged, or court-martialed, or put away! The white officers on this post won't let you—they won't let me!

DAVENPORT: Why wasn't there any mention of them in your preliminary report? I checked my own summary on the way over here, Captain—nothing! You think I'ma let you get away with this? *(There is a long silence.* TAYLOR *walks back to his desk as* DAVENPORT *watches him.* TAYLOR *sits)* Why?

TAYLOR: I couldn't prove the men in question had anything to do with it.

DAVENPORT: Why didn't you report it?

TAYLOR: I was ordered not to. *(Pause)* Nivens and Hines. The doctors took two .45 caliber bullets out of Waters—army issue. But remember what it was like that morning? If these men had thought a white officer killed Waters, there would have been a slaughter! *(Pause)* Cobb reported the incident innocently the night before—then suddenly it was all over the Fort.

DAVENPORT: Who were they, Captain? I want their names!

TAYLOR: Byrd and Wilcox. Byrd's in Ordnance—Wilcox's with the 12th Hospital Group. I was Captain of the Guard the night Waters was killed. About 2100 hours, Cobb came into my office and told me he'd just seen Waters and two white officers fighting outside the colored N.C.O. club. I called *your* office, and when I couldn't get two M.P.'s, I started over myself to break it up. When I got there—no Waters, no officers. I checked the officers' billet and found Byrd and Wilcox in bed. Several officers verified they'd come in around 2130. I then told Cobb to go back to the barracks and forget it.

DAVENPORT: What made you do that?

TAYLOR: At the time there was no reason to believe anything was wrong! Waters wasn't found until the following morning. I told the Colonel what had happened the previous night, and about the doctor's report, and I was told, since the situation at the Fort was potentially dangerous, to keep my mouth shut until it blew over. He agreed to let me question Byrd and Wilcox, but I've asked him for a follow-up investigation every day since it happened. *(Slight pause)* When I saw you, I exploded—it was like he was laughing at me.

DAVENPORT: Then you never believed the Klan was involved?

TAYLOR: No. Now, can you see why this thing needs—someone else?

DAVENPORT: What did they tell you, Captain? Byrd and Wilcox?

TAYLOR: They're not going to let you charge those two men!

DAVENPORT *(snaps):* Tell me what they told you!

TAYLOR *is quiet for a moment. At this time, on center stage in limbo,* SERGEANT WATERS *is staggering. He is dressed as we first saw him. Behind him a blinking light reads: 221st N.C.O. Club. As he staggers toward the stairs leading to center stage, two white officers,* LIEUTENANT BYRD, *a spit-and-polish soldier in his twenties, and* CAPTAIN WILCOX, *a medical officer, walk on-stage. Both are in full combat gear—rifles, pistol belts, packs—and both are tired.* TAYLOR *looks out as if he can see them.*

TAYLOR: They were coming off bivouac.

The two men see WATERS. *In the background is the faint hum of* C.J.*'s music.*

TAYLOR: They saw him outside the club.

He rises, as WATERS *sees* BYRD *and* WILCOX, *and smiles.*

WATERS: Well, if it ain't the white boys!

WATERS *straightens and begins to march in a mock circle and then down in their direction. He is mumbling, barely audibly: "One, two, three, four! Hup, hup, three, four! Hup, hup, three, four!"* BYRD*'s speech overlaps* WATERS*'s.*

BYRD: And it wasn't like we were looking for trouble, Captain—were we, Wilcox?

WILCOX *shakes his head no, but he is astonished by* WATERS*'s behavior and stares at him, disbelieving.*

WATERS: White boys! All starched and stiff! Wanted everybody to learn all that symphony shit! That's what you were saying in France—and you know, I listened to you? Am I all right now? Am I?

BYRD: Boy, you'd better straighten up and salute when you see an officer, or you'll find yourself without those stripes! *(To* WILCOX *as* WATERS *nears them, smiling the "coon" smile and doing a juba)* Will you look at this niggah? *(Loud)* Come to attention, Sergeant! That's an order!

WATERS: No, sah! I ain't straightenin' up for y'all no more! I ain't doin' nothin' white folks say do, no more! *(Sudden change of mood, smiles, sings)* No more, no more / no more, no more, noooo! No more, no more / no more, no more, noooooo!

BYRD *faces* TAYLOR *as* WATERS *continues to sing.*

BYRD *(overlapping):* Sir, I thought the man was crazy!

TAYLOR: And what did you think, Wilcox?

BYRD *moves toward* WATERS, *and* WATERS, *still singing low, drunk and staggering, moves back and begins to circle* BYRD, *stalk him, shaking his head no as he sings.* WILCOX *watches apprehensively.*

WILCOX *(at once):* He did appear to be intoxicated, sir—out of his mind almost! *(He turns to* BYRD*)* Byrd, listen—

BYRD *ignores him.*

DAVENPORT *(suddenly):* Did they see anyone else in the area?

TAYLOR: No. *(To* BYRD*)* I asked them what they did next.

BYRD: I told that niggah to shut up!

WATERS *(sharply):* No! *(Change of mood)* Followin' behind y'all? Look what it's done to me!—I hate myself!

BYRD: Don't blame us, boy! God made you black, not me!

WATERS *(smiles):* My daddy use ta say—

WILCOX: Sergeant, get hold of yourself!

WATERS *(points):* Listen!

BYRD steps toward him and shoves him in the face.

BYRD: I gave you an order, niggah!

WILCOX grabs BYRD, and stops him from advancing, as WATERS begins to cry.

WATERS: My daddy said, "Don't talk like dis'—talk like that!" "Don't live hea'—live there!" *(To them)* I've killed for you! *(To himself; incredulous)* And nothin' changed!

BYRD pulls free of WILCOX and charges WATERS.

BYRD: He needs to be taught a lesson!

He shoves WATERS onto the ground, where he begins to beat and kick the man, until he is forcibly restrained by WILCOX. WATERS moans.

WILCOX: Let him be! You'll kill the man! He's sick—leave him alone!

BYRD pulls away; he is flush. WATERS tries to get up.

WATERS: Nothin' changed—see? And I've tried everything! Everything!

BYRD: I'm gonna bust his black ass to buck private!—I should blow his coward's head off! *(Shouts)* There are good men killing for you, niggah! Gettin' their guts all blown to hell for you!

WILCOX pulls him away. He pulls BYRD off-stage as the light around WATERS and that section of the stage begins to fade out. As it does, a trace of C.J.'s music is left on the air. WATERS is on his knees, groveling, as the lights go out around him.

DAVENPORT: Did they shove Waters again?

TAYLOR: No. But Byrd's got a history of scrapes with Negroes. They told me they left Waters at 2110—and everyone in the officers' billet verifies they were both in by 2130. And neither man left—Byrd had duty the next morning, and Wilcox was scheduled at the hospital at 0500 hours—both men reported for duty.

DAVENPORT: I don't believe it.

TAYLOR: I couldn't shake their stories—

DAVENPORT: That's nothing more than officers lying to protect two of their own and you know it! I'm going to arrest and charge both of them, Captain—and you may consider yourself confined to your quarters pending my charges against *you!*

TAYLOR: What charges?

DAVENPORT: It was *your* duty to go over Nivens's head if you had to!

TAYLOR: Will you arrest Colonel Nivens too, Davenport? Because he's part of their alibi—he was there when they came in—played poker—from 2100 to 0300 hours the following morning, the Colonel—your Major Hines, "Shack" Callahan—Major Callahan, and Jed Harris—and Jed wouldn't lie for either of them!

DAVENPORT: They're all lying!

TAYLOR: Prove it, hotshot—I told you all I know, now you go out and prove it!

DAVENPORT: I will, Captain! You can bet your sweet ass on that! I will!

DAVENPORT *starts out as the lights begin to fade, and* TAYLOR *looks after him and shakes his head. In the background, the sound of "Don't Sit under the Apple Tree" comes up again and continues to play as the lights fade to black.*

ACT TWO

SCENE: *As before.*

Light rises slowly over limbo. We hear a snippet of "Don't Sit under the Apple Tree" as DAVENPORT, *seated on the edge of a bunk, finishes dressing. He is putting on a shirt, tie, bars, etc., and addresses the audience as he does so.*

DAVENPORT: During May of '44, the Allies were making final preparations for the invasion of Europe. Invasion! Even the sound of it made Negroes think we'd be in it—be swept into Europe in the waves of men and equipment—I know I felt it. *(Thoughtfully)* We hadn't seen a lot of action except in North Africa—or Sicily. But the rumor in orderly rooms that spring was, pretty soon most of us would be in combat—somebody said Ike wanted to find out if the colored boys could fight—shiiit, we'd been fighting all along—right here, in these small Southern towns— *(Intense)* I don't have the authority to arrest a white *private* without a white officer present! *(Slight pause)* Then I get a case like this? There was no way I wouldn't see this through to its end. *(Smiles)* And after my first twenty-four hours, I wasn't doing too badly. I had two prime suspects—a motive, and opportunity! *(Pause)* I went to Colonel Nivens and convinced him that word of Byrd's and Wilcox's involvement couldn't be kept secret any longer. However, before anyone in the press could accuse him of complicity—I would silence all suspicions by pursuing the investigation openly—on his orders— *(Mimics himself)* "Yes, sir, Colonel, you can even send along a white officer—not Captain Taylor, though—I think he's a little too close to the case, sir." Colonel Nivens gave me permission to question Byrd and Wilcox, and having succeeded sooo easily, I decided to spend some time finding out more about Waters and Memphis. Somehow the real drama seemed to be there, and my curiosity wouldn't allow me to ignore it.

DAVENPORT *is dressed and ready to go as a spotlight in the barracks area opens on* PRIVATE HENSON. *He is seated on a footlocker. He rises as* DAVENPORT *descends to the stage. He will not enter the barracks, but will almost handle this like a courtroom interrogation. He returns* HENSON*'s salute.*

DAVENPORT: Sit down, Private. Your name is Louis Henson, is that right?
HENSON: Yes, sir.

HENSON *sits, as* DAVENPORT *paces.*

DAVENPORT: Tell me what you know about Sergeant Waters and C. J. Memphis. *(*HENSON *looks at him strangely)* Is there something wrong?
HENSON: No, sir—I was just surprised you knew about it.
DAVENPORT: Why?

HENSON: You're an officer.

DAVENPORT *(quickly)*: And?

HENSON *(hesitantly)*: Well—officers are up here, sir—and us enlisted men—down here. *(Slight pause)* C.J. and Waters—that was just between enlisted men, sir. But I guess ain't nothin' a secret around colored folks—not that it was a secret. *(Shrugs)* There ain't that much to tell—sir. Sarge ain't like C.J. When I got to the company in May of las' year, the first person I saw Sarge chew out was C.J.! *(He is quiet)*

DAVENPORT: Go on.

HENSON's expression is pained.

HENSON: Is that an order, sir?

DAVENPORT: Does it have to be?

HENSON: I don't like tattle-talin', sir—an' I don't mean no offense, but I ain't crazy 'bout talkin' to officers—colored or white.

DAVENPORT: It's an order, Henson!

HENSON nods.

HENSON: C.J. wasn' movin' fast enough for *him*. Said C.J. didn' have enough *fire-under-his-behind* out on the field.

DAVENPORT: You were on the team?

HENSON: Pitcher. *(Pause. DAVENPORT urges with a look)* He jus' *stayed* on C.J. all the time—every little thing, it seemed like to me—then the shootin' went down, and C.J. caught all the hell.

DAVENPORT: What shooting?

HENSON: The shootin' at Williams's Golden Palace, sir—here, las' year!—way before you got here. Toward the end of baseball season. *(DAVENPORT nods his recognition)* The night it happened, a whole lotta gunshots went off near the barracks. I had gotten drunk over at the enlisted men's club, so when I got to the barracks I just sat down in a stupor!

Suddenly shots are heard in the distance and grow ever closer as the eerie blue-gray light rises in the barracks over the sleeping figures of men in their bunks. HENSON is seated, staring at the ground. He looks up once as the gunshots go off, and as he does, someone—we cannot be sure who—sneaks into the barracks as the men begin to shift and awaken. This person puts something under C.J.'s bed and rushes out. HENSON watches—surprised at first, rising, then disbelieving. He shakes his head, then sits back down as several men wake up. DAVENPORT recedes to one side of the barracks, watching.

COBB: What the hell's goin' on? Don't they know a man needs his sleep? *(He is quickly back to sleep)*

SMALLS *(simultaneously)*: Huh? Who is it? *(Looks around, then falls back to sleep)*

DAVENPORT: Are you sure you saw someone?

HENSON: Well—I saw something, sir.

DAVENPORT: What did you do?

The shooting suddenly stops and the men settle down.

HENSON: I sat, sir—I was juiced— *(Shrugs)* The gunshots weren't any of my business—plus I wasn't sure what I had seen in the first place, then out of nowhere Sergeant Waters, he came in.

WATERS enters the barracks suddenly, followed by WILKIE. HENSON stands immediately, staggering a bit.

WATERS: All right, all right! Everybody up! Wake them, Wilkie!

WILKIE moves around the bunks, shaking the men.

WILKIE: Let's go! Up! Let's go, you guys!

COBB shoves WILKIE's hand aside angrily as the others awaken slowly.

WATERS: Un-ass them bunks! Tenn-hut! *(Most of the men snap to. SMALLS is the last one, and WATERS moves menacingly toward him)* There's been a shooting! One of ours bucked the line at Williams's pay phone and three soldiers are dead! Two colored and one white M.P. *(Pauses)* Now, the man who bucked the line, he killed the M.P., and the white boys started shootin' everybody—that's how our two got shot. And this lowdown niggah we lookin' for got chased down here—and was almost caught, 'til somebody in these barracks started shootin' at the men chasin' him. So, we got us a vicious, murderin' piece of black trash in here somewhere—and a few people who helped him. If any of you are in this, I want you to step forward. *(No one moves)* All you baseball niggahs are innocent, huh? Wilkie, make the search. *(PETERSON turns around as WILKIE begins)* Eyes front!

PETERSON: I don't want that creep in my stuff!

WATERS: You don't talk at attention!

WILKIE will search three bunks, top and bottom, along with footlockers. Under C.J.'s bed he will find what he is looking for.

WATERS: I almost hope it is some of you geechies—get rid of you Southern niggahs! *(To WILKIE)* Anything yet?

WILKIE: Nawwww!

WATERS: Memphis, are you in this?

C.J.: No, sah, Sarge.

WATERS: How many of you were out tonight?

SMALLS: I was over at Williams's around seven—got me some Lucky Strikes—I didn't try to call home, though.

COBB: I was there, this mornin'!

WATERS: Didn't I say *tonight*—uncle?

WILKIE: Got somethin'!

WILKIE is holding up a .45 caliber automatic pistol, army issue. Everyone's attention focuses on it. The men are surprised, puzzled.

WATERS: Where'd you find it?

WILKIE *points to* C.J., *who recoils at the idea.*

C.J.: Naaaawww, man!
WATERS: C.J.? This yours?
C.J.: You know it ain't mine, Sarge!
WATERS: It's still warm—how come it's under your bunk?
C.J.: Anybody coulda' put it thea', Sarge!
WATERS: Who? Or maybe this .45 crawled in through an open window—looked around the whole room—passed Cobb's bunk, and decided to snuggle up under yours? Must be voodoo, right, boy? Or some of that Farmers Dust round that neck of yours, huh?
C.J.: That pistol ain't mine!
WATERS: Liar!
C.J.: No, Sarge—I hate guns! Make me feel bad jes' to see a gun!
WATERS: You're under arrest—Wilkie, escort this man to the stockade!

PETERSON *steps forward.*

PETERSON: C.J. couldn't hurt a fly, Waters, you know that!
WATERS: I found a gun, soldier—now get out of the way!
PETERSON: Goddammit, Waters, you know it ain't him!
WATERS: How do I know?
HENSON: Right before you came in, I thought I saw somebody sneak in.
WATERS: You were drunk when you left the club—I saw you myself!
WILKIE: Besides, how you know it wasn't C.J.?
COBB: I was here all night. C.J. didn't go out.

WATERS *looks at them, intense.*

WATERS: We got the right man. *(Points at* C.J., *impassioned)* You think he's innocent, don't you? C. J. Memphis, playin' cottonpicker singin' the blues, bowin' and scrapin'—smilin' in everybody's face—this man undermined us! You and me! The description of the man who did the shooting fits C.J.! *(To* HENSON*)* You saw C.J. sneak in here! *(Points)* Don't be fooled—that yassah boss is hidin' something—niggahs ain't like that today! This is 1943—he shot that white boy!

C.J. *is stunned, then suddenly the enormity of his predicament hits him and he breaks free of* WILKIE *and hits* WATERS *in the chest. The blow knocks* WATERS *down, and* C.J. *is immediately grabbed by the other men in the barracks.* COBB *goes to* WATERS *and helps him up slowly. The blow hurt* WATERS, *but he forces a smile at* C.J., *who has suddenly gone immobile, surprised by what he has done.*

WATERS: What did you go and do now, boy? Hit a noncommissioned officer.
COBB: Sarge, he didn't mean it!
WATERS: Shut up! *(Straightens)* Take him out, Wilkie.

WILKIE grabs C.J. by the arm and leads him out. C.J. goes calmly, almost passively. WATERS looks at all the men quietly for a moment, then walks out without saying a word. There is a momentary silence in the barracks.

SMALLS: Niggah like that can't have a mother.

HENSON: I know I saw something!

PETERSON: C.J. was sleepin' when I came in! It's Waters—can't y'all see that? I've seen him before—we had 'em in Alabama! White man gives them a little ass job as a servant—close to the big house, and when the boss ain't lookin', old copycat niggahs act like they the new owner! They take to soundin' like the boss—shoutin', orderin' people aroun'—and when it comes to you and me—they sell us to continue favor. They think the high-jailers like that. Arrestin' C.J.—that'll get Waters another stripe! Next it'll be you—or you. He can't look good unless he's standin' on you! Cobb tol' him C.J. was in all evening—Waters didn't even listen! Turning somebody in *(mimics):* "Look what I done, Captain Boss!" They let him in the army 'cause they know he'll do anything they tell him to—I've seen his kind of fool before. Someone's going to kill him.

SMALLS: I heard they killed a sergeant at Fort Robinson—recruit did it—

COBB: It'll just be our luck, Sarge'll come through the whole war without a scratch.

PETERSON: Maybe—but I'm goin' over to the stockade—tell the M.P.'s what I know—C.J. was here all evening. *(He starts dressing)*

SMALLS: I'll go with you!

COBB: Me too, I guess.

They all begin to dress as the light fades slowly in the barracks area. HENSON rises and starts toward DAVENPORT. In the background, C.J.'s music comes up a bit.

DAVENPORT: Could the person you thought you saw have stayed in the barracks—did you actually see someone go out?

HENSON: Yes, sir!

DAVENPORT: Was Wilkie the only man out of his bunk that night?

HENSON: Guess so—he came in with Sarge.

DAVENPORT: And Peterson—he did most of the talking?

HENSON: As I recall. It's been a while ago—an' I was juiced!

DAVENPORT rises.

DAVENPORT: Ellis!

ELLIS appears at the door.

ELLIS: Sir!

DAVENPORT: I want Private Wilkie and Pfc Peterson to report to me at once.

ELLIS: They're probably on work detail, sir.

DAVENPORT: Find them.

ELLIS: Yes, sir!

ELLIS exits quickly and DAVENPORT lapses into a quiet thoughtfulness.

HENSON: Is there anything else?—Sir?

DAVENPORT *(vexed):* No! That'll be all—send in the next man.

HENSON *comes to attention and salutes.* DAVENPORT *returns salute as* HENSON *exits through the barracks.* C.J.*'s music plays in background. There is a silence.* DAVENPORT *rises, mumbling something to himself.* COBB *appears suddenly at the doorway. He watches* DAVENPORT *for a moment.*

COBB: Sir? *(*DAVENPORT *faces him)* Corporal Cobb reporting as ordered, sir. *(He salutes)*

DAVENPORT: Have a seat, Corporal. *(*COBB *crosses the room and sits)* And let's get something straight from the beginning—I don't care whether you like officers or not—is that clear?

COBB *looks at him strangely.*

COBB: Sir?

Pause. DAVENPORT *calms down somewhat.*

DAVENPORT: I'm sorry—Did you know Sergeant Waters well?

COBB: As well as the next man, sir—I was already with the team when he took over. Me and C.J., we made the team the same time.

DAVENPORT: Were you close to C.J.?

COBB: Me and him were "homeys," sir! Both came from Mississippi. C.J. from Carmella—me, I'm from up 'roun' Jutlerville, what they call snake county. Plus, we both played for the Negro League before the war.

DAVENPORT: How did you feel about his arrest?

COBB: Terrible—C.J. didn't kill nobody, sir.

DAVENPORT: He struck Sergeant Waters—

COBB: Waters made him, sir! He called that boy things he had never heard of before—C.J., he was so confused he didn't know what else to do— *(Pause)* An' when they put him in the stockade, he jus' seemed to go to pieces. *(Lowly in the background,* C.J.*'s music comes up)* See, we both lived on farms—and even though C.J.'s daddy played music, C.J., he liked the wide-open spaces. *(Shakes his head)* That cell? It started closin' in on him right away. *(Blue-gray light rises in limbo, where* C.J. *is sitting on the edge of a bunk. A shadow of bars cuts across the space. His guitar is on the bunk beside him)* I went to see him, the second day he was in there. He looked pale and ashy, sir—like something dead.

C.J. *faces* COBB.

C.J.: It's hard to breathe in these little spaces, Cobb—man wasn' made for this hea'—nothin' was! I don't think I'll eva' see a' animal in a cage agin' and not feel sorry for it. *(To himself)* I'd rather be on the chain gang.

COBB *looks up at him.*

COBB: Come on, homey! *(He rises, moves toward* C.J.*)*

C.J.: I don't think I'm comin' outta here, Cobb—feels like I'm goin' crazy. Can't walk in

hea'—can't see the sun! I tried singin', Cobb, but nothin' won't come out. I sure don't wanna die in this jail!

COBB *(moving closer):* Ain't nobody gonna die, C.J.!

C.J.: Yesterday I broke a guitar string—lost my Dust! I got no protection—nothin' to keep the dog from tearin' at my bones!

COBB: Stop talkin' crazy!

C.J. is quiet for a moment. He starts forward. Slowly, in center stage, WATERS *emerges. He faces the audience.*

C.J.: You know, he come up hea' las' night? Sergeant Waters?

WATERS *smiles, pulls out his pipe, lights it.*

WATERS *(calmly):* You should learn never to hit sergeants, boy—man can get in a lot of trouble doin' that kinda thing durin' wartime—they talkin' 'bout givin' you five years—they call what you did mutiny in the navy. Mutiny, boy.

C.J.: That gun ain't mine!

WATERS: Oh, we know that, C.J.! *(C.J. is surprised)* That gun belonged to the niggah did the shootin' over at Williams's place—me and Wilkie caught him hidin' in the Motor Pool, and he confessed his head off. You're in here for striking a superior officer, boy. And I got a whole barracks full of your friends to prove it! *(Smiles broadly, as C.J. shakes his head)*

DAVENPORT *(to* COBB, *at once):* Memphis wasn't charged with the shooting?

COBB: No, sir—

WATERS: Don't feel too bad, boy. It's not your fault entirely—it has to be this way. The First War, it didn't change much for us, boy—but this one—it's gonna change a lot of things. Them Nazis ain't all crazy—a whole lot of people just can't fit into where things seem to be goin'—like you, C.J. The black race can't afford you no more. There use ta be a time when we'd see somebody like you, singin', clownin'—yas—sah—bossin'—and we wouldn't do anything. *(Smiles)* Folks liked that—you were good—homey kinda' niggah—they needed somebody to mistreat—call a name, they paraded you, reminded them of the old days—corn-bread bakin', greens and ham cookin'—Daddy out pickin' cotton, Grandmammy sit on the front porch smokin' a pipe. *(Slight pause)* Not no more. The day of the geechy is gone, boy—the only thing that can move the race is power. It's all the white respects—and people like you just make us seem like fools. And we can't let nobody go on believin' we all like you! You bring us down—make people think the whole race is unfit! *(Quietly pleased)* I waited a long time for you, boy, but I gotcha! And I try to git rid of you wherever I go. I put two geechies in jail at Fort Campbell, Kentucky—three at Fort Huachuca. Now I got you—one less fool for the race to be ashamed of! *(Points)* And I'ma git that ole boy Cobb next! *(Light begins to fade around* WATERS*)*

DAVENPORT *(at once):* You?

COBB: Yes, sir. *(Slight pause)*

DAVENPORT: Go on.

C.J.: You imagin' anybody sayin' that? I know I'm not gittin' outta' hea', Cobb! *(Quiets)* You remember I tol' you 'bout a place I use ta go outside Carmella? When I was a little

ole tiny thing? Place out behind O'Connell's Farm? Place would be stinkin' of plums, Cobb. Shaded—that ripe smell be weavin' through the cotton fields and clear on in ta town on a warm day. First time I had Evelyn? I had her unda' them plum trees. I wrote song a for her— *(Talks, sings)* My ginger-colored Moma—she had thighs the size of hams! *(Chuckles)* And when you spread them, Momaaaa! / *(Talks)* You let me have my jelly roll and jam! *(Pause, mood swing)* O'Connell, he had a dog—meanes' dog I *eva'* did see! An' the only way you could enjoy them plum trees was to outsmart that dog. Waters is like that ole dog, Cobb—you gotta run circles roun' ole Windy—that was his name. They say he tore a man's arm off once, and got to likin' it. So, you had to cheat that dog outta' bitin' you every time. Every time. *(Slowly the light begins to fade around* C.J.*)*

COBB: He didn't make sense, sir. I tried talkin' about the team—the war—ain't nothin' work—seem like he jes' got worse.

DAVENPORT: What happened to him?

COBB *looks at him incredulously.*

COBB: The next day—afta' the day I saw him? C.J., he hung hisself, sir! Suicide—jes' couldn't stand it. M.P.'s found him hung from the bars.

DAVENPORT *is silent for a moment.*

DAVENPORT: What happened after that?

COBB: We lost our last game—we jes' threw it—we did it for C.J.—Captain, he was mad 'cause we ain't git ta play the Yankees. Peterson was right on that one—somebody needed to protest that man!

DAVENPORT: What did Waters do?

COBB: Well, afta' we lost, the commanding officer, he broke up the team, and we all got reassigned to this Smoke Company. Waters, he started actin' funny, sir—stayed drunk—talked to hisself all the time.

DAVENPORT: Did you think you were next?

COBB: I ain't sure I eva' believed Waters said that, sir—C.J. had to be outta' his head or he wouldna' killed hisself—Sarge, he neva' came near me afta' C.J. died.

DAVENPORT: What time did you get back the night Waters was killed?

COBB: I'd say between 2120 and 9:30.

DAVENPORT: And you didn't go out again?

COBB: No, sir—me and Henson sat and listened to the radio till Abbott and Lou Costello went off, then I played checkers with Wilkie for 'notha' hour, then everybody went to bed. What C.J. said about Waters? It ain't botha' me, sir.

DAVENPORT *is silent.*

DAVENPORT: Who were the last ones in that night?

COBB: Smalls and Peterson—they had guard duty.

TAYLOR *enters the barracks area and stops just inside the door when he sees* DAVENPORT *isn't quite finished.*

DAVENPORT: Thank you, Corporal.

COBB *rises at attention and salutes.* DAVENPORT *returns salute and* COBB *starts out. He nods to* TAYLOR, *who advances toward* DAVENPORT.

TAYLOR *(smiling):* You surprise me, Davenport—I just left Colonel Nivens. He's given you permission to question Byrd and Wilcox? *(*DAVENPORT *nods)* How'd you manage that? You threatened him with an article in the Chicago *Defender*, I suppose.

DAVENPORT: I convinced the Colonel it was in his best interests to allow it.

TAYLOR: Really? Did he tell you I would assist you?

DAVENPORT: I told him I especially didn't want you.

TAYLOR: That's precisely why he sent me—he didn't want you to think you could get your way entirely—not with him. Then neither Byrd or Wilcox would submit to it without a white officer present. That's how it is. *(There is a rather long silence)* But there's something else, Davenport. The Colonel began talking about the affidavits he and the others signed—and the discrepancies in their statements that night. *(Mimics)* He wants me with you because he doesn't want Byrd and Wilcox giving you the wrong impression—he never elaborated on what he meant by the wrong impression. I want to be there!

DAVENPORT: So you're not on *that* side anymore—you're on *my* side now, right?

TAYLOR *(bristles):* I want whoever killed my sergeant, Davenport!

DAVENPORT: Bullshit! Yesterday you were daring me to try! And today we're allies? Besides, you don't give that much of a damn about your men! I've been around you a full day and you haven't uttered a word that would tell me you had any more than a minor acquaintance with Waters! He managed your baseball team—was an N.C.O. in your company, and you haven't offered *any* opinion of the man as a soldier—sergeant—platoon leader! Who the hell was he?

TAYLOR: He was one of my men! On my roster—a man these bars make me responsible for! And no, I don't know a helluva lot about him—or a lot of their names or where they come from, but I'm still their commanding officer and in a little while I may have to trust them with my life! And I want them to know they can trust me with theirs—here and now! *(Pause)* I have Byrd and Wilcox in my office. *(*DAVENPORT *stares at him for a long moment, then rises and starts out toward center stage)* Why didn't you tell Nivens that you'd placed me under arrest?

DAVENPORT *stops.*

DAVENPORT: I didn't find it necessary.

They stare at one another. TAYLOR *is noticeably strained.*

DAVENPORT *(starts away):* What do you know about C. J. Memphis?

TAYLOR *follows.*

TAYLOR *(shrugs):* He was a big man as I recall—more a boy than a man, though. Played the guitar sometimes at the Officers Club—there was something embarrassing about him. Committed suicide in the stockade. Pretty good center fielder—

DAVENPORT *stops.*

DAVENPORT: Did you investigate his arrest—the charges against him?

TAYLOR: He was charged with assaulting a noncommissioned officer—I questioned him—he didn't say much. He admitted he struck Waters—I started questioning several of the men in the platoon and he killed himself before I could finish—open-and-shut case.

DAVENPORT: I think Waters tricked C.J. into assaulting him.

TAYLOR: Waters wasn't that kind of a man! He admitted he might have provoked the boy—he accused him of that Golden Palace shooting—

Behind them, the CAPTAIN*'s office is lit. In two chairs facing* TAYLOR*'s desk are* LIEUTENANT BYRD *and* CAPTAIN WILCOX*, both in dress uniform.*

TAYLOR: Listen, Waters didn't have a fifth-grade education—he wasn't a schemer! And colored soldiers aren't devious like that.

DAVENPORT: What do you mean we aren't devious?

TAYLOR *(sharply):* You're not as devious—! *(*DAVENPORT *stares as* TAYLOR *waves disdainfully and starts into the office)* Anyway, what has that to do with this? *(He is distracted by* BYRD *and* WILCOX *before* DAVENPORT *can answer.* TAYLOR *speaks as he moves to his desk)* This is *Captain* Davenport—you've both been briefed by Colonel Nivens to give the Captain your full cooperation.

DAVENPORT *puts on his glasses.* TAYLOR *notices and almost smiles.*

BYRD *(to* DAVENPORT*):* They tell me you a lawyer, huh?

DAVENPORT: I am not here to answer your questions, Lieutenant. And I am Captain Davenport, is that clear?

BYRD *(to* TAYLOR*):* Captain, is he crazy?

TAYLOR: You got your orders.

BYRD: Sir, I vigorously protest as an officer—

TAYLOR *(cuts him off):* You answer him the way he wants you to, Byrd, or I'll have your ass in a sling so tight you won't be able to pee, soldier!

BYRD *backs off slightly.*

DAVENPORT: When did you last see Sergeant Waters?

BYRD: The night he was killed, but I didn't kill him—I should have blown his head off, the way he spoke to me and Captain Wilcox here.

DAVENPORT: How did he speak to you, Captain?

WILCOX: Well, he was very drunk—and he said a lot of things he shouldn't have. I told the Lieutenant here not to make the situation worse and he agreed, and we left the Sergeant on his knees, wallowing in self-pity. *(Shrugs)*

DAVENPORT: What exactly did he say?

WILCOX: Some pretty stupid things about us—I mean white people, sir.

BYRD *reacts to the term "sir."*

DAVENPORT: What kind of things?

BYRD *(annoyed):* He said he wasn't going to obey no white man's orders! And that me and Wilcox here were to blame for him being black, and not able to sleep or keep his food down! And I didn't even know the man! Never even spoke to him before that night!

DAVENPORT: Anything else?

WILCOX: Well—he said he'd killed somebody.

DAVENPORT: Did he call a name—or say who?

WILCOX: Not that I recall, sir.

DAVENPORT *looks at* BYRD.

BYRD: No— *(Sudden and sharp)* Look—the goddamn Negro was disrespectful! He wouldn't salute! Wouldn't come to attention! And where I come from, colored don't talk the way he spoke to us—not to white people they don't!

DAVENPORT: Is that the reason you killed him?

BYRD: I killed nobody! I said "where I come from," didn't I? You'd be dead yourself, where I come from! But I didn't kill the—the *Negro!*

DAVENPORT: But you hit him, didn't you?

BYRD: I knocked him down!

DAVENPORT *(quickens pace):* And when you went to look at him, he was dead, wasn't he?

BYRD: He was alive when we left!

DAVENPORT: You're a liar! You beat Waters up—you went back and you shot him!

BYRD: No! *(Rises)* But you better get outta my face before I kill you!

DAVENPORT *stands firm.*

DAVENPORT: Like you killed Waters?

BYRD: No! *(He almost raises a hand to* DAVENPORT*)*

TAYLOR *(at once):* Soldier!

BYRD: He's trying to put it on me!

TAYLOR: Answer his questions, Lieutenant.

DAVENPORT: You were both coming off bivouac, right?

WILCOX: Yes.

DAVENPORT: So you both had weapons?

BYRD: So what? We didn't fire them!

DAVENPORT: Were the weapons turned in immediately?

WILCOX: Yes, sir—Colonel Nivens took our .45's to Major Hines. It was all kept quiet because the Colonel didn't want the colored boys to know that anyone white from the Fort was involved in any way—ballistics cleared them.

DAVENPORT: We can check.

BYRD: Go ahead.

TAYLOR: I don't believe it—why wasn't I told?

WILCOX: The weapons had cleared—and the Colonel felt if he involved you further, you'd take the matter to Washington and there'd be a scandal about colored and white soldiers—as it turned out, he thinks you went to Washington anyway. *(To* DAVENPORT*)* I'd like to say, Captain, that neither Lieutenant Byrd or myself had anything

whatsoever to do with Sergeant Waters's death—I swear that as an officer and a gentleman. He was on the ground when we left him, but very much alive.

TAYLOR: Consider yourselves under arrest, *gentlemen!*

BYRD: On what charge?

TAYLOR: Murder! You think I believe that crap—

DAVENPORT: Let them go, Captain.

TAYLOR: You've got motive—a witness to their being at the scene—

DAVENPORT: Let them go! This is still my investigation—you two are dismissed!

BYRD rises quickly. WILCOX follows his lead.

WILCOX: Are we being charged, sir?

DAVENPORT: Not by me.

WILCOX: Thank you.

WILCOX comes to attention, joined by a reluctant BYRD. They both salute. DAVENPORT returns salute.

BYRD: I expected more from a white man, Captain.

TAYLOR: Get out of here, before I have you cashiered out of the army, Byrd!

Both men exit quietly, and for a moment TAYLOR and DAVENPORT are quiet.

TAYLOR: What the hell is the matter with you? You could have charged both of them—Byrd for insubordination—Wilcox, tampering with evidence.

DAVENPORT: Neither charge is murder—you think Wilcox would tell a story like that if he didn't have Hines and Nivens to back it up? *(Slightly tired)* They've got a report.

TAYLOR: So what do you do now?

DAVENPORT: Finish the investigation.

TAYLOR: They're lying, dammit! So is the Colonel! You were ordered to investigate and charge the people responsible—charge them! I'll back you up!

DAVENPORT: I'm not satisfied yet, Captain.

TAYLOR: I am! Dammit!—I wish they'd sent somebody else! I do—you—you're afraid! You thought you'd accuse the Klan, didn't you?—and that would be the end of it, right? Another story of midnight riders for your Negro press! And now it's officers—white men in the army. It's too much for you—what will happen when Captain Davenport comes up for promotion to major if he accuses white officers, right?

DAVENPORT: I'm not afraid of white men, Captain.

TAYLOR: Then why the hell won't you arrest them?

DAVENPORT: Because I do what the facts tell me, Captain—not you!

TAYLOR: You don't know what a fact is, Davenport!

ELLIS enters suddenly and salutes.

ELLIS: Begging your pardon, sir.

TAYLOR: What is it, Corporal?

ELLIS: Ah—it's for Captain Davenport— *(To DAVENPORT)* We found Private Wilkie, sir. We

haven't located Pfc Peterson yet. Seems him and Private Smalls went out on detail together, and neither one of 'em showed up—but I got a few men from the company lookin' for 'em around the N.C.O. club and in the PX, sir.

DAVENPORT: Where's Wilkie?

ELLIS: He's waiting for you in the barracks, Captain.

DAVENPORT nods, and ELLIS goes out after saluting. The lights come up around WILKIE, who is seated in a chair in the barracks reading a Negro newspaper. DAVENPORT is thoughtful for a moment.

TAYLOR: Didn't you question Wilkie and Peterson yesterday? *(DAVENPORT starts out)* Davenport? *(DAVENPORT does not answer)* Don't you ignore me!

DAVENPORT: Get off my back! What I do—how I do it—who I interrogate is my business, Captain! This investigation is mine! *(Holds out the back of his hand, showing TAYLOR the color of his skin)* Mine!

TAYLOR: Don't treat me with that kind of contempt—I'm not some red-neck cracker!

DAVENPORT: And I'm not your yessirin' colored boy either!

TAYLOR: I asked you a question!

DAVENPORT: I don't have to answer it!

There is a long silence. The two men glare at one another—TAYLOR in another time, disturbed.

TAYLOR: Indeed you don't—*Captain.*

Pause.

DAVENPORT: Now, *Captain*—what if Byrd and Wilcox are telling the truth?

TAYLOR: Neither one of us believes that.

DAVENPORT: What if they are?

TAYLOR: Then who killed the goddamn man?

DAVENPORT: I don't know yet. *(Slight pause)* Is there anything else?

TAYLOR shakes his head no as DAVENPORT starts toward center stage, headed toward WILKIE.

TAYLOR: No, hotshot. Nothing.

DAVENPORT enters the barracks area. WILKIE quickly puts his paper aside and snaps to attention and salutes. DAVENPORT returns salute but remains silent, going right to the desk and removing his pad and pencil. The light around the office fades out.

DAVENPORT *(snapping at WILKIE)*: When did you lose your stripes? *(He is standing over WILKIE)*

WILKIE: Couple months before they broke up the team—right after Sergeant Waters got assigned to us, sir.

DAVENPORT: Nervous, Wilkie?

WILKIE *(smiles haltingly)*: I couldn't figure out why you called me back, sir? *(Laughs nervously)*

DAVENPORT: You lost your stripes for being drunk on duty, is that correct?

WILKIE: Yes, sir.

DAVENPORT: You said Waters busted you, didn't you?

WILKIE: He got me busted—he's the one reported me to the Captain.

DAVENPORT: How did you feel? Must have been awful— *(DAVENPORT paces)* Weren't you and the Sergeant good friends? Didn't you tell me he was all right? A nice guy?

WILKIE: Yes, sir.

DAVENPORT: Would a nice guy have gotten a friend busted?

WILKIE: No, sir.

DAVENPORT: So you lied when you said he was a nice guy, right?

WILKIE: No, sir—I mean—

DAVENPORT: Speak up! Speak up! Was the Sergeant a nice guy or not?

WILKIE: No, sir.

DAVENPORT: Why not? Answer me!

WILKIE: Well, you wouldn't turn somebody in over something like that!

DAVENPORT: Not a good friend, right?

WILKIE: Right, sir—I mean, a friend would give you extra duty—I would have—or even call you a whole buncha' names—you'd expect that, sir—but damn! Three stripes? They took ten years to get in this army, sir! Ten years! I started out with the 24th Infantry—I—

DAVENPORT: Made you mad, didn't it?

WILKIE: Yeah, it made me mad—all the things I did for him!

DAVENPORT *(quickly)*: That's right! You were his assistant, weren't you? Took care of the team— *(WILKIE nods)* Ran all his errands, looked at his family snapshots *(WILKIE nods again)*, policed his quarters, put the gun under C.J.'s bed—

WILKIE looks up suddenly.

WILKIE: No!

DAVENPORT *(quickly)*: It was you Henson saw, wasn't it, Wilkie?

WILKIE: No, sir!

DAVENPORT: Liar! You lied about Waters, and you're lying now! You were the only person out of the barracks that night, and the only one who knew the layout well enough to go straight to C.J.'s bunk! Not even Waters knew the place that well! Henson didn't see who it was, but he saw what the person did—he was positive about that—only you knew the barracks in the dark!

WILKIE *(pleadingly)*: It was the Sarge, Captain—he ordered me to do it—he said I'd get my stripes back—he wanted to scare that boy C.J.! Let him stew in jail! Then C.J. hit him—and he had the boy right where he wanted him— *(Confused)* But it backfired—C.J. killed hisself—Sarge didn't figure on that.

DAVENPORT: Why did he pick Memphis?

WILKIE: He despised him, Captain—he'd hide it, 'cause everybody in the company liked that boy so much. But underneath—it was a crazy hate, sir—he'd go cold when he talked about C.J. You could feel it.

In limbo, the blue-gray light rises on C.J. and WATERS. C.J. is humming a blues song and WATERS is standing smiling, smoking a pipe as he was in Act One. WATERS turns away from C.J. His speech takes place over C.J.'s humming.

WATERS: He's the kinda boy seems innocent, Wilkie. Got everybody around the post thinking he's a strong, black buck! Hits home runs—white boys envy his strength—his

speed, the power in his swing. Then this colored champion lets those same white boys call him Shine—or Sambo at the Officers Club. They laugh at his blues songs, and he just smiles—can't talk, barely read or write his own name—and don't care! He'll tell you they like him—or that colored folks ain't supposed to have but so much sense. *(Intense)* Do you know the damage one ignorant *Negro* can do? *(Remembering)* We were in France during the First War, Wilkie. We had won decorations, but the white boys had told all the French gals we had tails. And they found this ignorant colored soldier. Paid him to tie a tail to his ass and parade around naked making monkey sounds. *(Shakes his head)* They sat him on a big, round table in the Café Napoleon, put a reed in his hand, a crown on his head, a blanket on his shoulders, and made him eat bananas in front of them Frenchies. And ohhh, the white boys danced that night—passed out leaflets with that boy's picture on them—called him Moonshine, King of the Monkeys. And when we slit his throat, you know that fool asked us what he had done wrong? *(Pause)* My daddy told me, we got to turn our backs on his kind, Wilkie. Close our ranks to the chittlin's, the collard greens—the corn-bread style. We are men—soldiers, and I don't intend to have our race cheated out of its place of honor and respect in *this* war because of fools like C.J.! You watch everything he does—*everything!*

Light fades slowly around WATERS *and* C.J., *and as it does,* C.J. *stops humming.*

WILKIE: And I watched him, sir—but Waters—he couldn't wait! He wouldn't talk about nothin' else—it was C.J. this—C.J. all the time!

DAVENPORT *(troubled)*: Why didn't he pick Peterson—they fought—

WILKIE: They fought all the time, sir—but the Sarge, he likes Peterson. *(Nods)* Peterson fought back, and Waters admired that. He promoted Pete! Imagine that—he thought Peterson would make a fine soldier!

DAVENPORT: What was Peterson's reaction—when C.J. died?

WILKIE: Like everybody else, he was sad—he put together that protest that broke up the team, but afta' that he didn' say much. And he usually runs off at the mouth. Kept to himself—or with Smalls.

Slight pause.

DAVENPORT: The night Waters was killed, what time did you get in?

WILKIE: Around nine forty-five—couple of us came from the club and listened to the radio awhile—I played some checkers, then I went to bed. Sir? I didn't mean to do what I did—it wasn't my fault—he promised me my stripes!

Suddenly, out of nowhere, in the near distance, is the sound of gunfire, a bugle blaring, something like a cannon going off. The noise is continuous through scene. DAVENPORT *rises, startled.*

DAVENPORT: I'm placing you under arrest, Private!

ELLIS *bursts into the room.*

ELLIS: Did you hear, sir? *(DAVENPORT, surprised, shakes his head no)* Our orders! They came down from Washington, Captain! We're shippin' out! They finally gonna let us Negroes fight!

DAVENPORT is immediately elated, and almost forgets WILKIE as he shakes ELLIS's hand.

DAVENPORT: Axis ain't got a chance!
ELLIS: Surrrre—we'll win this mother in six months now! Afta' what Jesse Owens did to them people? Joe Louis?

HENSON bursts in.

HENSON: Did y'all hear it? Forty-eight-hour standby alert? We goin' into combat! *(Loud)* Look out, Hitler, the niggahs is comin' to git your ass through the fog!
ELLIS: With real rifles—it's really O.K., you know?
HENSON: They tell me them girls in England—woooow!

DAVENPORT faces WILKIE as COBB enters, yelling.

COBB: They gonna let us git in it! We may lay so much smoke the Germans may never get to see what a colored soldier looks like 'til the war's over! *(To HENSON)* I wrote my woman jes' the otha' day that we'd be goin' soon!
ELLIS: Go on!
HENSON *(overlapping)*: Man, you ain't nothin'!

DAVENPORT begins to move WILKIE toward ELLIS.

HENSON: If the army said we was all discharged, you'd claim you wrote that! *(He quiets, watching DAVENPORT)*
COBB *(quickly)*: You hea' this fool, sir?
HENSON: Shhhhh!
DAVENPORT *(To ELLIS)*: Corporal, escort Private Wilkie to the stockade.
ELLIS *(surprised)*: Yes, sir!

ELLIS starts WILKIE out, even though he is bewildered by it. They exit.

HENSON: Wilkie's under arrest, sir? *(DAVENPORT nods)* How come? I apologize, sir—I didn't mean that.
DAVENPORT: Do either of you know where Smalls and Peterson can be located?

HENSON shrugs.

COBB: Your men got Smalls in the stockade, sir!
DAVENPORT: When?
COBB: I saw two colored M.P.'s takin' him through the main gate. Jes' a while ago—I was on my way ova' hea'!

DAVENPORT goes to the desk and picks up his things and starts out.

COBB: Tenn-hut.

DAVENPORT stops and salutes.

DAVENPORT: As you were. By the way—congratulations!

DAVENPORT exits the barracks through the doorway.

HENSON: Look out, Hitler!
COBB: The niggahs is coming to get yo' ass.
HENSON AND COBB: Through the fog.

The lights in the barracks go down at once. Simultaneously, they rise in limbo, where SMALLS is pacing back and forth. He is smoking a cigarette. There is a bunk, and the shadow of a screen over his cell. In the background, the sounds of celebration continue. DAVENPORT emerges from the right, and begins to speak immediately as the noises of celebration fade.

DAVENPORT: Why'd you go AWOL, soldier?

SMALLS faces him, unable to see DAVENPORT at first. When he sees him, he snaps to attention and salutes.

SMALLS: Private Anthony Smalls, sir!
DAVENPORT: At least—answer my question!
SMALLS: I didn't go AWOL, sir—I—I got drunk in Tynin and fell asleep in the bus depot—it was the only public place I could find to sleep it off.
DAVENPORT: Where'd you get drunk? Where in Tynin?
SMALLS: Jake's—Jake's and Lilly's Golden Slipper—on Melville Street—
DAVENPORT: Weren't you and Peterson supposed to be on detail? *(SMALLS nods)* Where was Peterson? Speak up!
SMALLS: I don't know, sir!
DAVENPORT: You're lying! You just walked off your detail and Peterson did nothing?
SMALLS: No, sir—he warned me, sir—"Listen, Smalls!" he said—
DAVENPORT *(cutting him off):* You trying to make a fool of me, Smalls? Huh? *(Loud)* Are you?
SMALLS: No, sir!
DAVENPORT: The two of you went A-W-O-L together, didn't you? *(SMALLS is quiet)* Answer me!
SMALLS: Yes!
DAVENPORT: You left together because Peterson knew I would find out the two of you killed Waters, didn't you? *(SMALLS suddenly bursts into quiet tears, shaking his head)* What? I can't hear you! *(SMALLS is sobbing)* You killed Waters, didn't you? I want an answer!
SMALLS: I can't sleep—I can't sleep!
DAVENPORT: Did you kill Sergeant Waters?
SMALLS: It was Peterson, sir! *(As if he can see it)* I watched! It wasn't me!

The blue-gray light builds in center stage. As it does, SERGEANT WATERS staggers forward and falls on his knees. He can't get up, he is so drunk. He has been beaten, and looks the way we saw him in the opening of Act One.

SMALLS: We were changing the guard.

WATERS: Can't be trusted—no matter what we do, there are no guarantees—and your mind won't let you forget it. *(Shakes his head repeatedly)* No, no, no!

SMALLS *(overlapping):* On our way back to the Captain's office—and Sarge, he was on the road. We just walked into him! He was ranting, and acting crazy, sir!

PETERSON emerges from the right. He is dressed in a long coat, pistol belt and pistol, rifle, helmet, his pants bloused over his boots. He sees WATERS and smiles. WATERS continues to babble.

PETERSON: Smalls, look who's drunk on his ass, boy! *(He begins to circle WATERS)*

SMALLS *(to DAVENPORT):* I told him to forget Waters!

PETERSON: Noooo! I'm gonna' enjoy this, Smalls—big, bad Sergeant Waters down on his knees? No, sah—I'm gonna' love this! *(Leans over WATERS)* Hey, Sarge—need some help? *(WATERS looks up; almost smiles. He reaches for PETERSON, who pushes him back down)* That's the kinda help I'll give yah, boy! Let me help you again—all right? *(Kicks WATERS)* Like that, Sarge? Huh? Like that, dog?

SMALLS *(shouts):* Peterson!

PETERSON: No! *(Almost pleading)* Smalls—some people, man—If this was a German, would you kill it? If it was Hitler—or that fuckin' Tojo? Would you kill him? *(Kicks WATERS again)*

WATERS *(mumbling throughout):* There's a trick to it, Peterson—it's the only way you can win—C.J. could never make it—he was a clown! *(Grabs at PETERSON)* A clown in blackface! A niggah!

PETERSON steps out of reach. He is suddenly expressionless as he easily removes his pistol from his holster.

WATERS: You got to be like them! And I was! I was—but the rules are fixed. *(Whispers)* Shhhh! Listen. It's C.J.— *(Laughs)* I made him do it, but it doesn't make any difference! They still hate you! *(Looks at PETERSON, who has moved closer to him)* They still hate you! *(WATERS laughs)*

PETERSON *(to SMALLS):* Justice, Smalls. *(He raises the pistol)*

DAVENPORT *(suddenly, harshly):* That isn't justice!

SMALLS almost recoils.

PETERSON *(simultaneously, continuing):* For C.J.! Everybody!

PETERSON fires the gun at WATERS's chest, and the shot stops everything. The celebration noise stops. Even DAVENPORT in his way seems to hear it. PETERSON fires again. There is a moment of quiet on stage. DAVENPORT is angered and troubled.

DAVENPORT: You call that justice?

SMALLS: No, sir.

DAVENPORT *(enraged):* Then why the fuck didn't you do something?

SMALLS: I'm scared of Peterson—just scared of him!

PETERSON has been looking at WATERS's body throughout. He now begins to lift WATERS as best he can, and pull him off-stage. It is done with some difficulty.

SMALLS: I tried to get him to go, sir, but he wanted to drag the Sergeant's body back into the woods—

Light fades quickly around PETERSON, as DAVENPORT paces.

SMALLS: Said everybody would think white people did it.

DAVENPORT *(somewhat drained):* Then what happened?

SMALLS: I got sick, sir—and Peterson, when he got done, he helped me back to the barracks and told me to keep quiet. *(Slight pause)* I'm sorry, sir.

There is a long pause, during which DAVENPORT stares at SMALLS with disgust, then abruptly starts out without saluting. He almost flees. SMALLS rises quickly.

SMALLS: Sir?

DAVENPORT turns around. SMALLS comes to attention and salutes. DAVENPORT returns salute and starts out of the cell and down toward center stage. He is thoughtful as the light fades around SMALLS. DAVENPORT removes his glasses and begins to clean them as he speaks.

DAVENPORT: Peterson was apprehended a week later in Alabama. Colonel Nivens called it "just another black mess of cuttin', slashin', and shootin'!" He was delighted there were no white officers mixed up in it, and his report to Washington characterized the events surrounding Waters's murder as "the usual, common violence any commander faces in Negro Military units." It was the kind of "mess" that turns up on page 3 in the colored papers—the Cain and Abel story of the week—the headline we Negroes can't quite read in comfort. *(Shakes head and paces)* For me? Two colored soldiers are dead—two on their way to prison. Four less men to fight with—and none of their reasons—nothing anyone *said,* or *did,* would have been worth a life to men with larger hearts—men less split by the madness of race in America. *(Pause)* The case got little attention. The details were filed in my report and I was quickly and rather unceremoniously ordered back to my M.P. unit. *(Smiles)* A style of guitar pickin' and a dance called the C.J. caught on for a while in Tynin saloons during 1945. *(Slight pause)* In northern New Jersey, through a military foul-up, Sergeant Waters's family was informed that he had been killed in action. The Sergeant was, therefore, thought and unofficially rumored to have been the first colored casualty of the war from that county and under the circumstances was declared a hero. Nothing could be done officially, but his picture was hung on a Wall of Honor in the Dorie Miller VFW Post #978. *(Pause)* The men of the 221st Chemical Smoke Generating Company? The entire outfit—officers and enlisted men—was wiped out in the Ruhr Valley during a German advance. *(He turns toward TAYLOR, who enters quietly)* Captain?

TAYLOR: Davenport—I see you got your man.

DAVENPORT: I got him—what is it, Captain?

TAYLOR: Will you accept my saying, you did a splendid job?

DAVENPORT: I'll take the praise—but how did I manage it?

TAYLOR: Dammit, Davenport—I didn't come here to be made fun of— *(Slight pause)* The men—the regiment—we all ship out for Europe tomorrow, and *(hesitates)* I was wrong, Davenport—about the bars—the uniform—about Negroes being in charge. *(Slight pause)* I guess I'll *have* to get used to it.

DAVENPORT: Oh, you'll get used to it—you can bet your ass on that. Captain—you will get used to it.

Lights begin to fade slowly as the music "Don't Sit under the Apple Tree" rises in the background, and the house goes to black.

CARYL CHURCHILL

(1938–)

Vinegar Tom

About the Author: Caryl Churchill was born in London and educated in Montreal and Oxford. She has been writing plays for the past twenty years, increasingly on radical and feminist topics, and she has come to be perceived as one of England's most important and influential playwrights. *Vinegar Tom* was written in collaboration with an all-woman theater company called Monstrous Regiment (a name taken from the title of an essay warning against females by the sixteenth-century Scots churchman John Knox, *First Blast of the Trumpet against the Monstrous Regiment of Women).*

About the Play: The play is set in seventeenth-century Europe during a period of witch hunting. It is not really about witches, however, but about women: There are no witches in the play—only women accused of witchcraft. The treatment of the witches is, in a sense, an exaggerrated manifestation of what has often passed for "normal" treatment of women in western civilization. The point is underscored by the songs which are sung between several of the scenes. In the original production, all roles were played by women, and cast members who were not currently on stage would remove their costumes and sing the songs in modern dress. Like an ancient Greek Chorus, therefore, these songs comment upon or react to the action; however, the chorus here is made up not of people contemporary with the characters but with people contemporary with us in the audience, implying that the seventeenth-century actions being played out are also applicable to our own world.

Although many of the claims about the power of witches presented here will seem bizarre to modern readers, these claims are not invented but are the result of Churchill's historical research. The claims can all be found in published works well known in earlier centuries, the best known of which was the *Malleus Maleficarum,* a Latin work whose title in English would be *The Hammer of Witches.* In the play's final scene, the coauthors of the *Malleus,* two churchmen named Kramer and Sprenger, come on stage and quote passages from their work, words which provide an explanation of some aspects of the thinking that made persecution of women as witches possible.

This is in many ways a shocking play: shocking in its language, shocking in the events depicted. (Many of the most shocking examples, by the way, come directly from *The Hammer of Witches.*) The play shocks in order to get our attention (so invisible has the underlying misogyny of our culture become) and in order to dramatize a sense of outrage over this treatment of women. And yet at the center of the play is not a desire to shock but a desire to educate. In this respect and in its style, it is in the tradition of "epic theater" associated with Bertold Brecht. (See the headnote to his play, *Mother Courage and Her Children.*) What it attempts to dramatize through the treatment of a few women accused of witchcraft in one anonymous village are the root causes of misogyny, hostility to women, which Churchill implies are all too much still with us: roots which go deep into the social, economic, psychological, and religious values with which we have structured our world.

CHARACTERS

ALICE, a village girl, early 20s
SUSAN, her married friend, early 20s
JOAN, Alice's mother, a poor widow, 50
MARGERY, Joan's neighbour, a farmer's wife, 40
JACK, Margery's husband, a tenant farmer, 40
BETTY, the landowner's daughter, 16
ELLEN, a cunning woman, 35
GOODY, Packer's assistant, 45
PACKER, a witchfinder, 35
MAN, a gentleman, 30
DOCTOR, a professional, 50
BELLRINGER, a local, any age
KRAMER and SPRENGER—authors of the *Malleus Maleficarum, The Hammer of Witches,* a book highly thought of in the seventeenth century; they appear in top hat and tails as performers in a music hall.

The play takes place in and around a small village over a period of a few weeks in the seventeenth century. The songs take place in the present.

Production Note The songs, which are contemporary, should if possible be sung by actors in modern dress. They are not part of the action and not sung by the characters in the scenes before them. In the original company all the actors could sing so it was no problem for some members of the company to be out of costume at any time to be in the band. Obviously this may not always be possible. But it is essential that the actors are not in character when they sing the songs.

The first verse of "Nobody Signs" was left out in the original production because the song seemed too long. I've put it back because I like the song being about a first period as well as about getting old. It could be left out again in performance, or verse 3 or 4 could be dropped instead.

SCENE ONE: *Roadside.*

MAN: Am I the devil?
ALICE: What, sweet?
MAN: I'm the devil. Man in black, they say, they always say, a man in black met me in the night, took me into the thicket and made me commit uncleanness unspeakable.
ALICE: I've seen men in black that's no devils unless clergy and gentlemen are devils.
MAN: Have I not got great burning eyes then?
ALICE: Bright enough eyes.
MAN: Is my body not rough and hairy?
ALICE: I don't like a man too smooth.
MAN: Am I not ice cold?

ALICE: In a ditch in November.

MAN: Didn't I lie on you so heavy I took your breath? Didn't the enormous size of me terrify you?

ALICE: It seemed a fair size like other men's.

MAN: Didn't it hurt you? Are you saying I didn't hurt you?

ALICE: You don't need be the devil, I been hurt by men. Let me go now, you're hurting my shoulder.

MAN: What it is, you didn't see my feet.

ALICE: You never took off your shoes. Take off your shoes if your feet's cloven.

MAN: If you come with me and give me body and soul, you'll never want in this world.

ALICE: Are you saying that as a man?

MAN: Am I saying it as the devil?

ALICE: If you're saying it as a man I'll go with you. There's no one round here knows me going to marry me. There's no way I'll get money. I've a child, mind, I'll not leave the child.

MAN: Has it a father?

ALICE: No, never had.

MAN: So you think that was no sin we did?

ALICE: If it was I don't care.

MAN: Don't say that.

ALICE: You'd say worse living here. Any time I'm happy someone says it's a sin.

MAN: There's some in London say there's no sin. Each man has his own religion nearly, or none at all, and there's women speak out too. They smoke and curse in the tavern and they say flesh is no sin for they are God themselves and can't sin. The men and women lie together and say that's bliss and that's heaven and that's no sin. I believe it for there's such changes.

ALICE: I'd like to go to London and hear them.

MAN: But then I believe with Calvin that few are saved and I am damned utterly. Then I think if I'm damned anyway I might as well sin to make it worthwhile. But I'm afraid to die. I'm afraid of the torture after. One of my family was burnt for a Catholic and they all changed to Protestant and one burnt for that too. I wish I was a Catholic and could confess my sins and burn them away in candles. I believe it all in turn and all at once.

ALICE: Would you take me to London? I've nothing to keep me here except my mother and I'd leave her.

MAN: You don't think I'm sent you by the devil? Sometimes I think the devil has me. And then I think there is no devil. And then I think the devil would make me think there was no devil.

ALICE: I'll never get away from here if you don't take me.

MAN: Will you do everything I say, like a witch with the devil her master?

ALICE: I'll do like a wife with a husband her master and that's enough for man or devil.

MAN: Will you kiss my arse like the devil makes his witches?

ALICE: I'll do what gives us pleasure. Was I good just now?

MAN: In Scotland I saw a witch burnt.

ALICE: Did you? A real witch? Was she a real one?

MAN: She was really burnt for one.

ALICE: Did the spirits fly out of her like black bats? Did the devil make the sky go dark? I've

heard plenty of tales of witches and I've heard some called witch, there's one in the next village some say and others say not, but she's nothing to see. Did she fly at night on a stick? Did you see her flying?

MAN: I saw her burnt.

ALICE: Tell then. What did she say?

MAN: She couldn't speak, I think. They'd been questioning her. There's wrenching the head with a cord. She came to the stake in a cart and men lifted her out, and the stake held her up when she was tied. She'd been in the boots you see that break the bones.

ALICE: And wood was put round? And a fire lit just like lighting a fire? Oh, I'd have shrieked, I cry the least thing.

MAN: She did shriek.

ALICE: I long to see that. But I might hide my face. Did you hide your face?

MAN: No, I saw it.

ALICE: Did you like seeing it then?

MAN: I may have done.

ALICE: Will you take me with you, to London, to Scotland? Nothing happens here.

MAN: Take you with me?

ALICE: Please, I'd be no trouble . . .

MAN: A whore? Take a whore with me?

ALICE: I'm not that.

MAN: What are you then? What name would you put to yourself? You're not a wife or a widow. You're not a virgin. Tell me a name for what you are.

ALICE: You're not going? Stay a bit.

MAN: I've stayed too long. I'm cold. The devil's cold. Back to my warm fire, eh?

ALICE: Stay with me!

MAN: Get away, will you.

ALICE: Please.

MAN: Get away.

[*He pushes her and she falls.*]

ALICE: Go to hell then, go to the devil, you devil.

MAN: Cursing is it? I can outcurse you.

ALICE: You foul devil, you fool, bastard, damn you, you devil!

MAN: Devil take you, whore, whore, damned strumpet, succubus,* witch!

ALICE: But come back. I'll not curse you. Don't you curse. We were friends just now.

MAN: You should have behaved better.

ALICE: Will I see you again?

MAN: Unless I see you first.

ALICE: But will I see you? How can I find you?

MAN: You can call on me.

ALICE: How? Where? How shall I call on you?

MAN: You know how to curse. Just call on the devil.

ALICE: Don't tease me, you're not the devil, what's your name?

***succubus:** Female demon who has sexual relations with a man while he sleeps.

MAN: Lucifer, isn't it, and Beelzebub.
ALICE: No, what's your name?
MAN: Darling was my name, and sweeting, till you called me devil.
ALICE: I'll not call you devil, come back, what's your name?
MAN: You won't need to know it. You won't be seeing me.

SCENE TWO: *Inside* JACK *and* MARGERY'*s.*

JACK: The river meadow is the one to get.
MARGERY: I thought the long field up the hill.
JACK: No, the river meadow for the cattle.
MARGERY: But Jack, for corn. Think of the long field full of wheat.
JACK: He's had a bad crop two years. That's why he can't pay the rent.
MARGERY: No, but he's got no cattle. We'd be all right.
JACK: If we took both fields.
MARGERY: Could we? Both?
JACK: The more we have the more we can afford.
MARGERY: And we'll pray God sends us sunshine.
JACK: Who's that down by the river?
MARGERY: That Alice, is it, wandering about?
JACK: I'm surprised Mother Noakes can pay her rent.
MARGERY: Just a cottage isn't much.
JACK: I've been wondering if we'll see them turned out.
MARGERY: I don't know why she's let stay. If we all lived like her it wouldn't be the fine estate it is. And Alice . . .
JACK: You can't blame Alice.
MARGERY: You can blame her. You can't be surprised. She's just what I'd expect of a girl brought up by Joan Noakes.
JACK: If we rent both fields, we'll have to hire a man to help with the harvest.
MARGERY: Hire a man?
JACK: That's not Alice.
MARGERY: It's not Miss Betty out by herself again?
JACK: I wouldn't be her father, not even to own the land.
MARGERY: That's a fine idea, hire a man.
JACK: She's coming here.
MARGERY: What we going to do?
JACK: Be respectful.
MARGERY: No, but shall we take her home? She's not meant to. She's still shut up in her room, everyone says.
JACK: I won't be sorry to see her.
MARGERY: I love to see her. She was always so soft on your lap, not like ours all hard edges. I could sit all afternoon just to smell her hair. But she's not a child, now, you can have run in and out and touch her. She's in trouble at home and we shouldn't help her do wrong.
JACK: We can't stop her, can we, if she walks in?

[*They wait and in a moment* BETTY *does come in.*]

MARGERY: Miss Betty, how nice.
BETTY: I came to see you milking the cows.
JACK: We finished milking, miss. The cows are in.
BETTY: Is it that late?
MARGERY: You want to get home before dark.
BETTY: No, I don't. I want to be out in the dark. It's not late, it's dark in the day time. I could stay out for hours if it was summer.
JACK: If you want to come and see the farm, Miss Betty, you should ask your father to bring you one morning when he's inspecting the estate.
BETTY: I'm not let go where I like.
JACK: I've business with your father.
MARGERY: We're going to take on the river meadow for the cattle.
JACK: And the long field up the hill.
BETTY: I used to play here all day. Nothing's different. Have you still got Betty's mug?
MARGERY: That's right, she had her special mug.
BETTY: I milked the red cow right into it one day. I got milk in my eye.
JACK: She died, that red cow. But we've four new cows you've not seen.
MARGERY: Died last week. There's two or three cows died in the neighbourhood.
BETTY: I wish she hadn't.
JACK: That don't matter, losing one, we're doing well enough.
MARGERY: And you're doing well, I hear, miss.
BETTY: What?
MARGERY: I hear you're leaving us for better things.
BETTY: No.
MARGERY: I was only saying yesterday, our little Miss Betty that was and now to be a lady with her own house and . . .
BETTY: They lock me up. I said I won't marry him so they lock me up. Don't you know that?
MARGERY: I had heard something.
BETTY: I get out the window.
MARGERY: Hadn't you better have him, Betty, and be happy? Everyone hopes so. Everyone loves a wedding.
BETTY: Margery, can I stay here tonight?
MARGERY: They'd worry for you.
BETTY: Can I? Please?
JACK: There's no bed fit for you, miss.
BETTY: On my way here I climbed a tree. I could see the whole estate. I could see the other side of the river. I wanted to jump off. And fly.
MARGERY: Shall Jack walk home with you, miss, now it's getting dark?

SCENE THREE: *Inside* JOAN*'s.*

JOAN: Alice?
ALICE: No need wake up, mum.
JOAN: You'll catch cold out all night in this weather.
ALICE: Don't wake up if it's only to moan at me.
JOAN: Who were you with?

ALICE: Did he wake up?
JOAN: No, not a sound.
ALICE: He's sleeping better. Not so much bad dreams.
JOAN: Come on, child, there's some broth left.
ALICE: I couldn't eat.
JOAN: You stay out half the night, you don't even enjoy it. You stay in with the boy. You sit by the fire with no one to talk to but old Vinegar Tomcat. I'll go out.
ALICE: You go out?
JOAN: Funny, isn't it? What would I do going out?
ALICE: I'll stay in if you like.
JOAN: Where would I go? Who wants an old woman?
ALICE: You want me to stay with you more?
JOAN: An old woman wandering about in the cold.
ALICE: Do you want some broth, mum?
JOAN: Who were you with this time? Anyone I know?
ALICE: Oh mum, I'm sick of myself.
JOAN: If we'd each got a man we'd be better off.
ALICE: You weren't better off, mum. You've told me often you're glad he's dead. Think how he used to beat you.
JOAN: We'd have more to eat, that's one thing.

Nobody Sings

I woke up in the morning,
Blood was on the sheet,
I looked at all the women
When I passed them in the street.
Nobody sings about it
But it happens all the time.

I met an old old woman
Who made my blood run cold.
You don't stop wanting sex, she said,
Just because you're old.
Oh nobody sings about it,
but it happens all the time.

I could be glad of the change of life,
But it makes me feel so strange.
If your life is being wanted
Do you want your life to change?
Oh nobody sings about it,
but it happens all the time.

Do you want your skin to wrinkle
And your cunt get sore and dry?
And they say it's just your hormones
If you cry and cry and cry.

Oh nobody sings about it,
but it happens all the time.

Nobody ever saw me,
She whispered in a rage.
They were blinded by my beauty, now
They're blinded by my age.
Oh nobody sings about it,
but it happens all the time.

SCENE FOUR: JACK *and* MARGERY*'s barn.*

MARGERY *is churning.*

JACK: Hurry up with that butter, woman.
MARGERY: Butter won't come.
JACK: There's other work to do.
MARGERY: Butter won't come.
JACK: You don't churn. You sit gossiping.
MARGERY: Who would I talk to?
JACK: I heard your voice now.
MARGERY: Mother Noakes.
JACK: Always hanging about.
MARGERY: Her girl's no better.
JACK: Was her girl here? No.
MARGERY: I told her be on her way. Mother Noakes.
JACK: You tell her.
MARGERY: I told her.
JACK: Get on now with the butter and don't be always gossiping.

[JACK *goes.* MARGERY *churns and sings very quietly.*]

MARGERY: Come butter come, come butter come. Johnny's standing at the gate waiting for a butter cake. Come butter come, come butter come. Johnny's standing at the gate waiting for a butter cake. Come butter come, come butter come. Johnny's standing at the gate . . .

[*She stops as she realises* JOAN NOAKES *has come in and is standing behind her.*]

JOAN: Just passing by.
MARGERY: Again.
JOAN: I wonder could you lend me a little yeast? I've no yeast, see. I'm fresh out of yeast. I've no bread in the house and I thought, I thought . . . I'll do a little baking now and brew a little beer maybe . . . and I went to get some yeast and I've no yeast. Who'd have thought it? No yeast at all.
MARGERY: You'd be better without beer.
JOAN: I thought a little yeast as I was passing.
MARGERY: You get drunk. You should be ashamed.

JOAN: To bake a couple of little small loaves.

MARGERY: I've no yeast.

JOAN: A couple of little small loaves wouldn't take much yeast. A woman comfortable off with a fine man and a nice field and five cows and three pigs and plenty of apples that makes a good cider, bless you, Margery, many's the time . . . you'd not grudge a neighbour a little loaf? Many's the good times, eh, Margery? I've my own flour, you know, I'm not asking for flour.

MARGERY: I gave you yeast last week.

JOAN: A little small crumb of yeast and God will bless you for kindness to your poor old neighbour.

MARGERY: You're not so badly off, Joan Noakes. You're not on the parish.

JOAN: If I was I'd be fed. I should be on relief, then I'd not trouble you. There's some on relief, better off than me. I get nothing.

MARGERY: What money you get you drink.

JOAN: If you'd my troubles, Margery, you'd be glad of a drink, but as you haven't, thank God, and lend me a little yeast like a good woman.

MARGERY: I've no yeast.

JOAN: I know you, Margery.

MARGERY: What do you know?

JOAN: I know you've got yeast. My eyes are old, but I see through you. You're a cold woman and getting worse and you'll die without a friend in this parish when if you gave yeast to your good neighbours everyone would bless you . . .

MARGERY: I've no yeast.

JOAN: But you don't give and they say what a mean bitter woman and curse you.

MARGERY: There's nobody curses me. Now get out of my dairy. Dirty old woman you are, smelling of drink, come in here day after day begging, and stealing, too, I shouldn't wonder . . .

JOAN: You shouldn't say that.

MARGERY: . . . and your great ugly cat in here stealing the cream. Get out of my dairy.

JOAN: You'll be sorry you spoke to me like that. I've always been your friend, Margery, but now you'll find I'm not.

MARGERY: I've work to do. Now get out. I'm making my butter.

JOAN: Damn your butter to hell.

MARGERY: Will you get out?

JOAN: Devil take you and your man and your fields and your cows and your butter and your yeast and your beer and your bread and your cider and your cold face . . .

MARGERY: Will you go?

[JOAN *goes.* MARGERY *churns.*]

MARGERY: Come butter come, come butter come. Johnny's standing at the gate waiting for a butter cake. Come butter . . . It's not coming, this butter. I'm sick of it.

[JACK *comes.*]

JACK: What's all this? You're a lazy woman, you know that? Times are bad enough. The little black calf don't look well.

MARGERY: Butter won't come. Mother Noakes said damn the butter to hell.

JACK: Lazy slut, get on with it.

MARGERY: Come butter come. Come butter come. Come butter come. Come butter come. Come butter come. Come butter . . . Mother Noakes come begging and borrowing. She still got my big bowl I give her some eggs in that time she was poorly. She makes out I've treated her bad. I've been a good neighbour to that woman years out of mind and no return. We'll get that bowl back off her. Jack, do you hear me? Go over Mother Noakes and get my bowl. And we'll heat a horseshoe red hot and put it in the milk to make the butter come.

SCENE FIVE: *Outside* JOAN'S.

SUSAN: Don't always talk of men.

ALICE: He knew what he was doing.

SUSAN: You'll know what he was doing in a few months.

ALICE: No, it never happens. The cunning woman put a charm inside me.

SUSAN: Take more than a charm to do me good.

ALICE: Not again? Does he know?

SUSAN: He wants it. I know the night it was. He said, 'Let's hope a fine child comes of it.'

ALICE: And what did you say?

SUSAN: Devil take it.

ALICE: What he say to that?

SUSAN: He don't like me swearing.

ALICE: But the baby's not a year.

SUSAN: Two weeks late, so.

ALICE: But the baby's not weaned.

SUSAN: The boy wasn't weaned when I fell for the baby.

ALICE: You could go see the cunning woman.

SUSAN: What for?

ALICE: She's a good midwife.

SUSAN: I don't want a midwife. I got my mother, anyway. I don't want to think about it. Nearly died last time. I was two days.

ALICE: Go and see the cunning woman. Just go see.

SUSAN: What for?

ALICE: She could say for certain.

SUSAN: I'm sure for certain.

ALICE: She could give you a charm.

SUSAN: They do say the pain is what's sent to a woman for her sins. I complained last time after churching, and he said I must think on Eve who brought the sin into the world that got me pregnant. I must think on how woman tempts man, and how she pays God with her pain having the baby. So if we try to get round the pain, we're going against God.

ALICE: I hate my body.

SUSAN: You mustn't say that. God sent his son . . .

ALICE: Blood every month, and no way out of that but to be sick and swell up, and no way out of that but pain. No way out of all that till we're old and that's worse. I can't bear to see my mother if she changes her clothes. If I was a man I'd go to London and Scotland and never come back and take a girl under a bush and on my way.

SUSAN: You could go to the cunning woman.
ALICE: What for?
SUSAN: Charm.
ALICE: What for?
SUSAN: Love charm bring him back.
ALICE: I don't want him back.
SUSAN: Did he look wonderful, more than anyone here, that he's got you so low?
ALICE: It was dark, I wouldn't know him again.
SUSAN: Not so much how he looked as how he felt?
ALICE: I could do with it now, I can tell you. I could do with walking across that field again and finding him there just the same. I want a man I can have when I want, not if I'm lucky to meet some villain one night.
SUSAN: You always say you don't want to be married.
ALICE: I don't want to be married. Look at you. Who'd want to be you?
SUSAN: He doesn't beat me.
ALICE: He doesn't beat you.
SUSAN: What's wrong with me? Better than you.
ALICE: Three babies and what, two, three times miscarried and wonderful he doesn't beat you.
SUSAN: No one's going to marry you because they know you here. That's why you say you don't want to be married—because no one's going to ask you round here, because they know you.

[They move apart. JACK *has been lingering in the background a while, and now comes up to* ALICE.*]*

JACK: It's not you I've come to see.
ALICE: Never thought it was.
JACK: You should have done then.
ALICE: Why?
JACK: You know why.
ALICE: You've come to see my mum, have you?
JACK: I've business with her, yes. That's why I came.
ALICE: She's somewhere around. I'll get her.
JACK: No hurry. Wait a bit. Never seem to talk.
ALICE: Nothing to talk about.
JACK: I'm forgetting. I brought something.

[He gives her two apples.]

ALICE: Thank you. What then?
JACK: Am I not handsome enough, is that it?
ALICE: I don't want trouble.
JACK: No one's to know.
ALICE: If I say you're not handsome enough, will you go away?
JACK: Alice, you must. I have dreams.
ALICE: You've a wife.

JACK: I'm no good to my wife. I can't do it. Not these three months. It's only when I dream of you or like now talking to you . . .
ALICE: Mum. There's someone to see you.
JACK: Alice, have some pity . . .
ALICE: Do you hear me? Mum? She'll be out to see you.

[*She moves away.* JOAN *comes.*]

JOAN: What's the matter?
JACK: I've come for the bowl.
JOAN: Bowl? Bowl?
JACK: Bowl my wife gave you some eggs in, you ungrateful old hag.
JOAN: You're asking for the bowl? You think I wouldn't give you back your bowl? You think I'm stealing your bowl? When have I ever kept anything? Have your bowl. I'll get your bowl and much good may it do you.
JACK: Then get it, damn you, and quick or you'll feel my hand.

[*She goes.*]

ALICE: Why treat her like that?
JACK: Don't speak to me. Let me get the bowl and go.
ALICE: And don't come back.
JACK: Alice, I'd be good to you. I'm not a poor man. I could give you things for your boy . . .
ALICE: Go away to hell.

[JOAN *comes back.*]

JOAN: Here's your bowl, Jack, and the devil go with it. Get away home and I hope you've more trouble there than I have here.
JACK: I'll break your neck if you speak to me.
JOAN: You lift your hand to me, may it drop off.
ALICE: Go home away to hell, man.

[JACK *goes.*]

JOAN: Away to hell with him. Never liked the man. Never liked the wife.
ALICE: Don't think on them, mum. They're not worth your time. Go in by the fire, go on, go in and be warm.

[JOAN *goes.* SUSAN *approaches.*]

Nobody likes my mother. That's what it is why nobody wants me.
SUSAN: I'm sorry for what I said, Alice.
ALICE: Going to see the cunning woman then?
SUSAN: Are you going for a love charm?
ALICE: It's something to do, isn't it? Better than waiting and waiting for something to happen.

If I had a charm I could make him just appear in front of me now, I'd do anything. Will you come?

[ALICE *gives* SUSAN *an apple.*]

SUSAN: I'll keep you company then. Just tell her my trouble. There's no harm.

Oh Doctor

Oh, doctor, tell
me, make me well.
What's wrong with me
the way I am?
I know I'm sad.
I may be sick.
I may be bad.
Please cure me quick,
oh doctor.

SCENE SIX: *The landowner's house.*

BETTY *tied to a chair. The* DOCTOR *is about to bleed her arm.*

BETTY: Why am I tied? Tied to be bled. Why am I bled? Because I was screaming. Why was I screaming? Because I'm bad. Why was I bad? Because I was happy. Why was I happy? Because I ran out by myself and got away from them and—Why was I screaming? Because I'm bad. Why am I bad? Because I'm tied. Why am I tied? Because I was happy. Why was I happy? Because I was screaming.

DOCTOR: Hysteria is a woman's weakness. Hysteron, Greek, the womb. Excessive blood causes an imbalance in the humours. The noxious gases that form inwardly every month rise to the brain and cause behaviour quite contrary to the patient's real feelings. After bleeding you must be purged. Tonight you shall be blistered. You will soon be well enough to be married.

Oh Doctor

Where are you taking my skin?
Where are you putting my bones?
I shut my eyes and I opened wide,
But why is my heart on the other side?
Why are you putting my brain in my cunt?
You're putting me back all back to front.

Stop looking up me with your metal eye.
Stop cutting me apart before I die.
Stop, put me back.
Stop, put me back.
Put back my body.

Who are you giving my womb?
Who are you showing my breath?

Tell me what you whisper to nurse,
Whatever I've got, you're making it worse.
I'm wide awake, but I still can't shout.
Why can't I see what you're taking out?

Stop looking up me with your metal eye.
Stop cutting me apart before I die.
Stop, put me back.
Stop, put me back.
Put back my body.

Oh, doctor, tell
me, make me well.
What's wrong with me
the way I am?
I know I'm sad
I may be sick.
I may be bad.
Please cure me quick,
oh doctor,
What's wrong with me the way I am?
What's wrong with me?

I want to see myself.
I want to see inside myself.
Give me back my head.
I'll put my heart in straight.
Let me out of bed now.
I can't wait
To see myself.
Give me back my body.
I can see myself.
Give me back my body.
I can see myself.

SCENE SEVEN: JACK *and* MARGERY*'s barn.*

MARGERY: Jack, Jack, come quick—Jack.
JACK: What's the matter now?
MARGERY: The calves. Have you seen the calves?
JACK: What's the woman on about?
MARGERY: The calves are shaking and they've a terrible stench, so you can't go near them and their bellies are swollen up. [JACK *goes off.*] There's no good running. There's nothing you can do for them. They'll die like the red cow. You don't love me. Damn this stinking life to hell. Calves stinking and shaking there. No good you going to see, Jack. Better stand and curse. Everything dying on us. Aah. What's that? Who's there? Get out, you beast, get out. [*She throws her shoe.*] Jack, Jack.
JACK: Hold your noise.
MARGERY: That nasty old cat of Mother Noakes. I'll kill that cat if I get it, stinking up my clean dairy, stealing my cream. Where's it gone?

JACK: Let it go.
MARGERY: What you think of those calves then? Nothing to be done is there? What can we do? Nothing. Nothing to be done. Can't do nothing. Oh. Oh.
JACK: Now what is it?
MARGERY: Jack!
JACK: What is it? Don't frighten me, woman.
MARGERY: My head, oh, my stomach. Oh, Jack, I feel ill.

[*She sits on the ground.*]

JACK: Get up, woman. It's no time. There's things to do.
MARGERY: Nothing.
JACK: Lie there a bit then. You'll maybe feel better. I can hardly stir myself. What have I done to deserve it? Why me? Why my calves shaking? Why my wife falling down?
MARGERY: It's passing now.
JACK: Why me?
MARGERY: That was a terrible pain. I still feel it. I'm shaking, look.
JACK: Other people sin and aren't punished so much as we are.
MARGERY: We must pray to God.
JACK: We do pray to God, and he sends afflictions.
MARGERY: It must be we deserve it somehow, but I don't know how. I do my best. I do my best, Jack, God knows, don't I, Jack? God knows I do my best.
JACK: Don't other people sin? Is it just me?
MARGERY: You're not a bad man, Jack.
JACK: I must be the worst man.
MARGERY: No, dear.
JACK: Would God send all this to a good man? Would he? It's my sins those calves shaking and stinking and swelling up their bellies in there.
MARGERY: Don't talk so.
JACK: My sins stinking and swelling up.
MARGERY: Unless it's not God.
JACK: How can I bear it?
MARGERY: If it's not God.
JACK: What?
MARGERY: If it's not God sends the trouble.
JACK: The devil?
MARGERY: One of his servants. If we're bewitched, Jack, that explains all.
JACK: If we're bewitched . . .
MARGERY: Butter not coming. Calves swelling. Me struck in the head.
JACK: Then it's not my sins. Good folk get bewitched.
MARGERY: Good folk like us.
JACK: It can happen to anyone.
MARGERY: Rich folk can have spells against them.
JACK: It's good people the witches want to hurt.
MARGERY: The devil can't bear to see us so good.
JACK: You know who it is?
MARGERY: Who?

JACK: The witch. Who it is.

MARGERY: Who?

JACK: You know who.

MARGERY: She cursed the butter to hell.

JACK: She cursed me when I got the bowl.

MARGERY: She said I'd be sorry I'd spoken to her.

JACK: She wished me trouble at home.

MARGERY: Devil take your man and your cows, she said that, and your butter. She cursed the calves see and she's made them shake. She struck me on the head and in the stomach.

JACK: I'll break her neck.

MARGERY: Be careful now, what she might do.

JACK: I'm not afraid of an old witch.

MARGERY: You should be. She could kill you.

JACK: I'll kill her first.

MARGERY: Wait, Jack. Let's meet cunning with cunning. What we must do is get the spell off.

JACK: She's not going to take it off for asking. She might for a few hard knocks.

MARGERY: No, wait, Jack. We can take the spell off and never go near her. Serve her right.

JACK: What we do then? Burn something?

MARGERY: Burn an animal alive, don't we? Or bury it alive. That takes witchcraft off the rest.

JACK: Burn the black calf then shall we? We'll get some straw and wood and put it in the yard and the calf on top and set it on fire.

MARGERY: Will it walk?

JACK: Or I'll carry it.

MARGERY: It stinks terrible.

JACK: Stink of witchcraft it is. Burn it up.

MARGERY: We must pray to God to keep us safe from the devil. Praying's strong against witches.

JACK: We'll pray God help us and help ourselves too.

MARGERY: She'll see the fire and smell it and she'll know we're fighting her back, stinking old witch, can't hurt us.

Something to Burn

What can we do, there's nothing to do,
about sickness and hunger and dying.
What can we do, there's nothing to do,
nothing but cursing and crying.
  Find something to burn.
  Let it go up in smoke.
  Burn your troubles away.

Sometimes it's witches, or what will you choose?
Sometimes it's lunatics, shut them away.
It's blacks and it's women and often it's Jews.
We'd all be quite happy if they'd go away.
  Find something to burn.
  Let it go up in smoke.
  Burn your troubles away.

SCENE EIGHT: ELLEN*'s cottage.*

ELLEN: Take it or leave it, my dear, it's one to me. If you want to be rid of your trouble, you'll take it. But only you know what you want.

SUSAN: It's not what I came for.

ALICE: Of course it is.

SUSAN: I wanted to know for certain.

ALICE: You know for certain.

SUSAN: I want a charm against pain.

ELLEN: I'll come as your midwife if you send for me near the time and do what I can, if that's all you want.

ALICE: She wants to be rid of it. Well, do you want it?

SUSAN: I don't want it but I don't want to be rid of it. I want to be rid of it, but not do anything to be rid of it.

ELLEN: If you won't do anything to help yourself you must stay as you are.

SUSAN: I shall pray to God.

ALICE: It's no sin. You just give yourself the drink.

SUSAN: Oh, I don't know.

ELLEN: Let her go home. She can come back. You have your charm safe, Alice? I could do more if you could come at the young man and give him a potion I'd let you have.

ALICE: If I could come at him he wouldn't need potion.

ELLEN: And you're sure you've nothing of his?

ALICE: He gave me nothing.

ELLEN: A few hairs or a drop of blood makes all the difference. It's part of him and the powers can work on it to call him.

ALICE: I'll pull a few hairs out next time I've a lover. Come on, Susan.

ELLEN: For your heartache I'll give you these herbs to boil up in water and drink at night. Give you a sound sleep and think less of him.

ALICE: Don't want to think less of him.

ELLEN: You have your sleep. There'll be other men along if not that one. Clever girl like you could think of other things.

ALICE: Like what?

ELLEN: Learn a trade.

ALICE: Nothing dangerous.

ELLEN: Where's the danger in herbs?

ALICE: Not just herbs.

ELLEN: Where's the danger in healing?

ALICE: Not just healing, is it?

ELLEN: There's powers, and you use them for healing or hurt. You use them how you like. There's no hurt if you're healing so where's the danger? You could use them. Not everyone can.

ALICE: Learn the herbs?

ELLEN: There's all kinds of wisdom. Bit by bit I'd teach you.

ALICE: I'd never thought.

ELLEN: There's no hurry. I don't want you unless it's what you want. You'll be coming by to leave a little something for me in a few days, since I have to live and wouldn't charge you. You can tell me how you've got on with your young man and what you're thinking.

ALICE: Yes, I'll be coming by. Goodnight then. What are you standing there for, Susan?

SUSAN: Maybe I'll take some potion with me. And see when I get home whether I take it.

ELLEN: Don't be afraid if it makes you sick. It's to do you good.

SCENE NINE: ELLEN'*s cottage.*

BETTY: I don't know what I'm here for. I've had so much treatment already. The doctor comes every day.

ELLEN: You know what you're here for.

BETTY: The doctor says people like you don't know anything. He thinks he's cured me because I said I would get married to stop them locking me up. But I'll never do it.

ELLEN: Do you want a potion to make you love the man?

BETTY: I'd rather have one to make him hate me so he'd leave me alone. Or make him die.

ELLEN: The best I can do for you is help you sleep. I won't harm him for you, so don't ask. Get some sleep and think out what you want.

BETTY: Can I come again sometimes just to be here? I like it here.

ELLEN: Come when you like. I don't charge but you'll bring a little present.

BETTY: I'll give you anything if you can help me.

ELLEN: Come when you like.

SCENE TEN: ELLEN'S *cottage.*

ELLEN: I'm not saying I can't do anything. But if I can't, it's because you've left it too late.

JACK: Lift your hand to me, she said, may it drop off. Then next day it went stiff.

MARGERY: We want to be certain. I've talked to others and they've things against her too. She's cursed and scolded two or three, and one's lame and the other lost her hen. And while we were talking we thought of her great cat that's always in my dairy, stinking it up and stealing the cream. Ah what's that, I said crying out, didn't I, and that was the cat, and I was struck down with a blow inside my head. That's her familiar sent her by Satan.

JACK: I've seen a rat run out of her yard into ours and I went for it with a pitchfork and the spikes were turned aside and nearly went in my own foot by her foul magic. And that rat's another of her imps.

MARGERY: But you don't like to think it of your neighbour. Time was she was neighbourly enough. If you could tell us it was true, we could act against her more certain in our minds.

JACK: I shouted at her over the fence, I said I'll have you hanged you old strumpet, burnt and hanged, and she cursed me again.

MARGERY: We burnt a calf alive to save our calves but it was too late. If I knew for certain it was her I'd be easier.

ELLEN: I've a glass here, a cloudy glass. Look in the glass, so, and see if any face comes into it.

[*She gives them a mirror.*]

MARGERY: Come on, Jack, don't be afraid.

JACK: I don't like it.

MARGERY: Come on, it's good magic to find a witch.

ELLEN: Look in the glass and think on all the misfortunes you've had and see what comes.

MARGERY: Nothing yet. Do you see anything?

JACK: No.

MARGERY: Nothing still.

JACK: Don't keep talking.

MARGERY: Look.

JACK: What?

MARGERY: Did something move in the glass? My heart's beating so.

JACK: It's too dark.

MARGERY: No. Look.

JACK: I did see something.

MARGERY: It's the witch.

JACK: It's her sure enough.

MARGERY: It is, isn't it, Jack? Mother Noakes, isn't it?

JACK: It was Mother Noakes in that glass.

ELLEN: There then. You have what you came for.

MARGERY: Proves she's a witch then?

ELLEN: Not for me to say one's a witch or not a witch. I give you the glass and you see in it what you see in it.

JACK: Saw Mother Noakes.

MARGERY: Proves she's a witch.

ELLEN: Saw what you come to see. Is your mind easy?

SCENE ELEVEN: ELLEN'*s cottage.*

JACK: Want to ask you something private. It's about my . . . [*He gestures, embarrassed.*] It's gone. I can't do anything with it, haven't for some time. I accepted that. But now it's not even there, it's completely gone. There's a girl bewitched me. She's daughter of that witch. And I've heard how witches sometimes get a whole boxful and they move and stir by themselves like living creatures and the witch feeds them oats and hay. There was one witch told a man in my condition to climb a tree and he'd find a nest with several in it and take which he liked, and when he took the big one she said no, not that one, because that one belongs to the parish priest. I don't want a big one, I want my own back, and this witch has it.

ELLEN: You'd better go and ask her nicely for it.

JACK: Is that all you can say? Can't you force her to give it me?

ELLEN: It's sure to come back. You ask the girl nicely, she'll give it you back. I'll give you a little potion to take.

JACK: Kill her else.

SCENE TWELVE: *Outside* JACK *and* MARGERY'*s.*

JOAN: That's a foul stink. I don't know how you can stay there. Whatever is it?

MARGERY: Do you know why you've come?

JOAN: I was passing.

MARGERY: Why were you passing?

JOAN: Can't I pass by your door now? Time was it was always open for me.

MARGERY: And what's that?

JOAN: A foul stink. Whatever are you making? I thought I'd come and see you as I was passing. I don't want any trouble between us. I thought, come and see her, make it all right.

MARGERY: You come to see me because of that. That's my piss boiling. And two feathers of your chicken burning. It's a foul stink brings a witch. If you come when I do that, proves you've a spell on me. And now I'll get it off. You know how?

JOAN: Come and see you. Make it all right.

MARGERY: Blood you, that's how.

[MARGERY *scratches* JOAN*'s head.*]

JOAN: Damn you, get away.

MARGERY: Can't hurt me now. And if that doesn't bring the spell off I'll burn your thatch.

If Everybody Worked as Hard as Me

If everybody worked as hard as me,
if our children's shirts are white,
if their language is polite,
if nobody stays out late at night,
Oh, happy family.
Oh, the country's what it is because
the family's what it is because
the wife is what she is
to her man.
Oh I do all I can.
Yes, I do all I can.
I try to do what's right,
so I'll never be alone and afraid in the night.
And nobody comes knocking at my door in the night.
The horrors that are done will not be done to me.

Nobody loves a scold,
nobody loves a slut,
nobody loves you when you're old,
unless you're someone's gran.
Nobody loves you
unless you keep your mouth shut.
Nobody loves you
if you don't support your man.
Oh you can,
oh you can
have a happy family.

If everybody worked as hard as me,
sometimes you'll be bored,
you'll often be ignored,
but in your heart you'll know you are adored.

Oh, happy family.
Your dreams will all come true.
You'll make your country strong.
Oh the country's what it is because
the family's what it is because
the wife is what she is
to her man.
Oh please do all you can.
Yes, please do all you can
Oh, please don't do what's wrong,
so you'll never be alone and afraid in the night.
So nobody comes knocking at your door in the night.
So the horrors that are done will not be done to you.

Yes you can.
Yes you can.
Oh the country's what it is because
the family's what it is because
the wife is what she is
to her man.

SCENE THIRTEEN: *Outside* JACK *and* MARGERY*'s.*

SUSAN: You're sure it was him? You said you wouldn't know him.
ALICE: I did when I saw him.
SUSAN: Riding? Couldn't see him close.
ALICE: Close enough to be spattered with his mud. He saw me.
SUSAN: But he didn't show he knew you.
ALICE: Pretended not to.
SUSAN: It wasn't him.
ALICE: It was him.
SUSAN: And you don't know the beautiful lady?
ALICE: I'll know her again. Scratch her eyes if I come at her.
SUSAN: What was she wearing?
ALICE: What was she wearing? How should I know? A fine rich dress made her beautiful, I suppose. Are you trying to plague me?
SUSAN: Was he in black still?
ALICE: Blue velvet jacket.
SUSAN: Blue velvet.
ALICE: Yes, damn you, I said that before. Are you stupid? [*Silence.*] For God's sake, now what is it? Are you crying? Shouldn't I be crying?
SUSAN: It's not your fault, Ally. I cry all the time.
ALICE: You're still weak, that's what it is. It's the blood you lost. You should rest more.
SUSAN: I don't want him to know.
ALICE: Doesn't he know?
SUSAN: He may guess but I don't dare ask. He was out all day that day and I said I'd been ill, but not why.
ALICE: It's done anyway.

SUSAN: Can't be undone.
ALICE: You're not sorry now?
SUSAN: I don't know.
ALICE: You'd be a fool to be sorry.
SUSAN: I am sorry. I'm wicked. You're wicked.

[*She cries.*]

ALICE: Oh, Susan, you're tired out, that's all. You're not wicked. You'd have cried more to have it. All the extra work, another baby.
SUSAN: I like babies.
ALICE: You'll have plenty more, God, you'll have plenty. What's the use of crying?
SUSAN: You were crying for that lover.
ALICE: I'm not now. I'd sooner kill him. If I could get at him. If thoughts could get at him he'd feel it.
SUSAN: I'm so tired, Ally.
ALICE: Do you think it's true thoughts can reach someone?
SUSAN: What are you thinking of?
ALICE: Like if I had something of his, I could bring him. Or harm him.
SUSAN: Don't try that.
ALICE: But I've nothing of his. I'd have to make a puppet.
SUSAN: Don't talk so. Oh, don't, Alice, when I'm so tired.
ALICE: Does it have to be like? Is it like just if you say it's like?
SUSAN: Alice!
ALICE: If I get this wet mud, it's like clay. There should be at least a spider or some ashes of bones, but mud will do. Here's a man's shape, see, that's his head and that's arms and legs.
SUSAN: I'm going home. I'm too tired to move.
ALICE: You stay here and watch. This is the man. We know who though we don't know his name. Now here's a pin, let's prick him. Where shall I prick him? Between the legs first so he can't get on with his lady.
SUSAN: Alice, stop.
ALICE: Once in the head to drive him mad. Shall I give him one in the heart? Do I want him to die yet? Or just waste till I please.
SUSAN: Alice . . .

[SUSAN *tries to get the mud man, it falls on the ground and breaks.*]

ALICE: Now look. You've broken him up. You've killed him.
SUSAN: I haven't.
ALICE: All in pieces. Think of the poor man. Come apart.
SUSAN: I didn't. Alice, I didn't. It was you.
ALICE: If it was me, I don't care.
SUSAN: Alice, what have you done? Oh Alice, Alice.
ALICE: It's not true, stupid. It's not him.
SUSAN: How do you know?

ALICE: It's a bit of mud.
SUSAN: But you said.
ALICE: That's just words.
SUSAN: But . . .
ALICE: No. I did nothing. I never do anything. Might be better if I did. [*They sit in silence.*] You're crying again. Here, don't cry.

[ALICE *holds* SUSAN *while she cries.*]

SUSAN: Little clay puppet like a tiny baby not big enough to live and we crumble it away.

[JACK *comes.*]

JACK: Witch.
ALICE: Are you drunk?
JACK: Give it back.
ALICE: What?
JACK: Give it back.
ALICE: What now, Jack?
JACK: Give it me back. You know. You took it from me these three months. I've not been a man since. You bewitched me. You took it off me.
ALICE: Is he mad?
SUSAN: What is it?
ALICE: Susan's ill, will you leave us alone?
JACK: Everyone comes near you is ill. Give it back, come on, give it back.
ALICE: How can I?
JACK: She said speak nicely to you. I would, Alice, if you were good to me. I never wanted this. Please, sweet good Alice, give it back.
ALICE: What? How can I?
JACK: Give it me.

[*He grabs her round the neck.* SUSAN *screams.*]

ALICE: Damn you!
SUSAN: You'll kill her.
JACK: Give it me.
SUSAN: Let her go, she'll give it you whatever it is, you'll kill her, Jack.

[JACK *lets go.*]

JACK: Give it me then. Come on.
SUSAN: Wait, she can't move, leave her alone.
JACK: Give it me.

[ALICE *puts her hand between his thighs.*]

ALICE: There. It's back.

JACK: It is. It is back. Thank you, Alice. I wasn't sure you were a witch till then.

[JACK *goes.*]

SUSAN: What you doing, Alice? Alice? Alice?

[ALICE *turns to her.*]

ALICE: It's nothing. He's mad. Oh my neck, Susan. Oh, I'd laugh if it didn't hurt.

SUSAN: Don't touch me. I'll not be touched by a witch.

SCENE FOURTEEN: *Public square.*

BELLRINGER: Whereas if anyone has any complaint against any woman for a witch, let them go to the townhall and lay their complaint. For a man is in town that is a famous finder of witches and has had above thirty hanged in the country round and he will discover if they are or no. Whereas if anyone has any complaint against any woman for a witch, let them go . . .

MARGERY: Stopped the butter.

JACK: Killed the calves.

MARGERY: Struck me in the head.

JACK: Lamed my hand.

MARGERY: Struck me in the stomach.

JACK: Bewitched my organ.

MARGERY: When I boiled my urine she came.

JACK: Blooded her and made my hand well.

MARGERY: Burnt her thatch.

JACK: And Susan, her friend, is like possessed screaming and crying and lay two days without speaking.

MARGERY: Susan's baby turned blue and its limbs twisted and it died.

JACK: Boy threw stones and called them witch, and after he vomited pins and straw.

MARGERY: Big nasty cat she has in her bed and sends it to people's dairies.

JACK: A rat's her imp.

MARGERY: And the great storm last night brought a tree down in the lane, who made that out of a clear sky?

PACKER: I thank God that he has brought me again where I am needed. Don't be afraid any more. You have been in great danger but the devil can never overcome the faithful. For God in his mercy has called me and shown me a wonderful way of finding out witches, which is finding the place on the body of the witch made insensitive to pain by the devil. So that if you prick that place with a pin no blood comes out and the witch feels nothing at all.

[PACKER *and* GOODY *take* JOAN, *and* GOODY *holds her, while* PACKER *pulls up her skirts and pricks her legs.* JOAN *curses and screams throughout.* PACKER *and* GOODY *abuse her: a short sharp moment of great noise and confusion.*]

GOODY: Hold still you old witch. Devil not help you now, no good calling him. Strong for your age, that's the devil's strength in her, see. Hold still, you stinking old strumpet.

PACKER: Hold your noise, witch, how can we tell what we're doing? Ah, ah, there's for you devil, there's blood, and there's blood, where's your spot, we'll find you out Satan.

JOAN: Damn you to hell, oh Christ help me! Ah, ah, you're hurting, let go, damn you, oh sweet God, oh you devils, oh devil take you.

PACKER: There, there, no blood here, Goody Haskins. Here's her spot. Hardly a speck here.

GOODY: How she cries the old liar, pretending it hurts her.

PACKER: There's one for hanging, stand aside there. We've others to attend to. Next please, Goody.

[GOODY *takes* ALICE. PACKER *helps, and her skirts are thrown over her head while he pricks her. She tries not to cry out.*]

GOODY: Why so much blood?

PACKER: The devil's cunning here.

GOODY: She's not crying much, she can't feel it.

PACKER: Have I the spot though? Which is the spot? There. There. There. No, I haven't the spot. Oh, it's tiring work. Set this one aside. Maybe there's others will speak against her and let us know more clearly what she is.

[ALICE *is stood aside.*]

PACKER: If anyone here knows anything more of this woman why she might be a witch, I charge them in God's name to speak out, or the guilt of filthy witchcraft will be on you for concealing it.

SUSAN: I know something of her.

PACKER: Don't be shy then, girl, speak out.

ALICE: Susan, what you doing? Don't speak against me.

SUSAN: Don't let her at me.

ALICE: You'll have me hanged.

[SUSAN *starts to shriek hysterically.*]

GOODY: Look, she's bewitched.

MARGERY: It's Alice did it to her.

ALICE: Susan, stop.

SUSAN: Alice. Alice. Alice.

PACKER: Take the witch out and the girl may be quiet.

[GOODY *takes* ALICE *off.* SUSAN *stops.*]

MARGERY: See that.

JACK: Praise God I escaped such danger.

SUSAN: She met with the devil, she told me, like a man in black she met him in the night and did uncleanness with him, and ever after she was not herself but wanted to be with the devil again. She took me to a cunning woman and they made me take a foul potion

to destroy the baby in my womb and it was destroyed. And the cunning woman said she would teach Alice her wicked magic, and she'd have powers and not everyone could learn that, but Alice could because she's a witch, and the cunning woman gave her something to call the devil, and she tried to call him, and she made a puppet, and stuck pins in, and tried to make me believe that was the devil, but that was my baby girl, and next day she was sick and her face blue and limbs all twisted up and she died. And I don't want to see her.

PACKER: These cunning women are worst of all. Everyone hates witches who do harm but good witches they go to for help and come into the devil's power without knowing it. The infection will spread through the whole country if we don't stop it. Yes, all witches deserve death, and the good witch even more than the bad one. Oh God, do not let your kingdom be overrun by the devil. And you, girl, you went to this good witch, and you destroyed the child in your womb by witchcraft, which is a grievous offence. And you were there when this puppet was stuck with pins, and consented to the death of your own baby daughter?

SUSAN: No, I didn't. I didn't consent. I never wished her harm. Oh if I was angry sometimes or cursed her for crying, I never meant it. I'd take it back if I could have her back. I never meant to harm her.

PACKER: You can't take your curses back, you cursed her to death. That's two of your children you killed. And what other harm have you done? Don't look amazed, you'll speak soon enough. We'll prick you as you pricked your babies.

SCENE FIFTEEN: *Public square.*

GOODY *takes* SUSAN *and* PACKER *pulls up her skirt.*

GOODY: There's no man finds more witches than Henry Packer. He can tell by their look, he says, but of course he has more ways than that. He's read all the books and he's travelled. He says the reason there's so much witchcraft in England is England is too soft with its witches, for in Europe and Scotland they are hanged and burned and if they are not penitent they are burnt alive, but in England they are only hanged. And the ways of discovering witches are not so good here, for in other countries they have thumbscrews and racks and the bootikens which is said to be the worst pain in the world, for it fits tight over the legs from ankle to knee and is driven tighter and tighter till the legs are crushed as small as might be and the blood and marrow spout out and the bones crushed and the legs made unserviceable forever. And very few continue their lies and denials then. In England we haven't got such thorough ways, our ways are slower but they get the truth in the end when a fine skillful man like Henry Packer is onto them. He's well worth the twenty shillings a time, and I get the same, which is very good of him to insist on and well worth it though some folk complain and say, 'what, the price of a cow, just to have a witch hanged?' But I say to them think of the expense a witch is to you in the damage she does to property, such as a cow killed one or two pounds, a horse maybe four pounds, besides all the pigs and sheep at a few shillings a time, and chickens at sixpence all adds up. For two pounds and our expenses at the inn, you have all that saving, besides knowing you're free of the threat of sudden illness and death. Yes, it's interesting work being a searcher and nice to do good at the same time as earning a living. Better than staying home a widow. I'd end up like the old women you see, soft in the head and full of spite with their muttering and spells. I keep healthy keeping the country healthy. It's an honour to work with a great professional.

SCENE SIXTEEN: ELLEN*'s cottage.*

BETTY: I'm frightened to come any more. They'll say I'm a witch.

ELLEN: Are they saying I'm a witch?

BETTY: They say because I screamed that was the devil in me. And when I ran out of the house they say where was I going if not to meet other witches. And some know I come to see you.

ELLEN: Nobody's said it yet to my face.

BETTY: But the doctor says he'll save me. He says I'm not a witch, he says I'm ill. He says I'm his patient so I can't be a witch. He says he's making me better. I hope I can be better.

ELLEN: You get married, Betty, that's safest.

BETTY: But I want to be left alone. You know I do.

ELLEN: Left alone for what? To be like me? There's no doctor going to save me from being called a witch. Your best chance of being left alone is marry a rich man, because it's part of his honour to have a wife who does nothing. He has his big house and rose garden and trout stream, he just needs a fine lady to make it complete and you can be that. You can sing and sit on the lawn and change your dresses and order the dinner. That's the best you can do. What would you rather? Marry a poor man and work all day? Or go on as you're going, go on strange? That's not safe. Plenty of girls feel like you've been feeling, just for a bit. But you're not one to go on with it.

BETTY: If it's true there's witches, maybe I've been bewitched. If the witches are stopped, maybe I'll get well.

ELLEN: You'll get well, my dear, and you'll get married, and you'll tell your children about the witches.

BETTY: What's going to happen? Will you be all right?

ELLEN: You go home now. You don't want them finding you here.

[BETTY *goes.*]

I could ask to be swum. They think the water won't keep a witch in, for Christ's baptism sake, so if a woman floats she's a witch. And if she sinks they have to let her go. I could sink. Any fool can sink. It's how to sink without drowning. It's whether they get you out. No, why should I ask to be half drowned? I've done nothing. I'll explain to them what I do. It's healing, not harm. There's no devil in it. If I keep calm and explain it, they can't hurt me.

If You Float

If you float you're a witch.
If you scream you're a witch
If you sink, then you're dead anyway.
If you cure you're a witch
Or impure you're a witch

Whatever you do, you must pay.
Fingers are pointed, a knock at the door,
You may be a mother, a child or a whore.
If you complain you're a witch
Or you're lame you're a witch
Any marks or deviations count for more.
Got big tits you're a witch
Fall to bits you're a witch
He likes them young, concupiscent and poor.
Fingers are pointed, a knock at the door,
They're coming to get you, do you know what for?
So don't drop a stitch
My poor little bitch
If you're making a spell
Do it well
Deny it you're bad
Admit it you're mad
Say nothing at all
They'll damn you to hell.

SCENE SEVENTEEN: *A prison.*

ALICE *is tied up, sitting on the floor,* GOODY *is eating and yawning.*

GOODY: You'd better confess, my dear, for he'll have you watched night and day and there's nothing makes a body so wretched as not sleeping. I'm tired myself. It's for your own good, you know, to save you from the devil. If we let you stay as you are, you'd be damned eternally and better a little pain now than eternal . . . [*She realises* ALICE *is nodding to sleep and picks up a drum and bangs it loudly. She gives it several bangs to keep* ALICE *awake.* PACKER *comes in.*] She's an obstinate young witch, this one, on her second night. She tires a body out.

PACKER: Go and sleep, Goody, I'll watch her a while.

GOODY: You're a considerate man, Mr Packer. We earn our money.

[GOODY *goes.*]

PACKER: I'm not a hard man. I like to have my confession so I'm easy in my mind I've done right.

ALICE: Where's my boy?

PACKER: Safe with good people.

ALICE: He wants me.

PACKER: He's safe from the devil, where you'll never come.

ALICE: I want him.

PACKER: Why won't you confess and make this shorter?

ALICE: It isn't true.

PACKER: Tell me your familiars. Tell me your imps' names. I won't let them plague you for telling. God will protect you if you repent.

ALICE: I haven't any. [PACKER *drums.*] I want my boy.

PACKER: Then you should have stayed home at night with him and not gone out after the devil.

ALICE: I want him.

PACKER: How could a mother be a filthy witch and put her child in danger?

ALICE: I didn't.

PACKER: Night after night, it's well known.

ALICE: But what's going to happen to him? He's only got me.

PACKER: He should have a father. Who's his father? Speak up, who's his father?

ALICE: I don't know.

PACKER: You must speak.

ALICE: I don't know.

PACKER: You must confess.

[PACKER *drums.*]

ALICE: Oh my head. Please don't. Everything's drumming.

PACKER: I'll watch. Your imps will come to see you.

ALICE: Drumming.

[PACKER *suddenly stops.*]

PACKER: Ah. Ah. What's this? A spider. A huge black one. And it ran off when it saw a godly man. Deny if you can that spider's one of your imps.

ALICE: No.

PACKER: Then why should it come? Tell me that.

ALICE: I want my boy.

PACKER: Why? Why do you keep on about the boy? Who's his father? Is the devil his father?

ALICE: No, no, no.

PACKER: I'll have the boy to see me in the morning. If he's not the devil's child he'll speak against you. [ALICE *cries.*] I'll watch you. I've watched plenty of witches and hanged them all. I'll get that spider too if it comes back.

SCENE EIGHTEEN: *A prison.*

GOODY *is shaving* SUSAN *under the arm.*

GOODY: There, that's the second arm done, and no mark yet. Devil hides his marks all kinds of places. The more secret the better he likes it. Though I knew one witch had a great pink mark on her shoulder and neck so everyone could see. And a woman last week with a big lump in her breast like another whole teat where she sucked her imps, a little black one she had and a little white one and kept them in wool in a bottle. And when I squeezed it first white stuff came out like milk and then blood, for she fed those horrid creatures on milk and blood and they sucked her secret parts in the night too. Now let's see your secret parts and see what the devil does there.

[*She makes* SUSAN *lie down, and pulls up her skirt to shave her.* PACKER *comes in.*]

PACKER: What devil's marks?

GOODY: No need to shave the other for she has three bigs in her privates almost an inch long like great teats where the devil sucks her and a bloody place on her side where she can't deny she cut a lump off herself so I wouldn't find it.

PACKER: Such a stinking old witch I won't look myself. Is there nothing here?

GOODY: She's clean yet but we'll shave her and see what shameful thing's hidden.

PACKER: Though a mark is a sure sign of a witch's guilt having no mark is no sign of innocence for the devil can take marks off.

JOAN: And the devil take you.

PACKER: You'll be with the devil soon enough.

JOAN: And I'll be glad to see him. I been a witch these ten years. Boys was always calling after me and one day I said to a boy, 'Boy boy you call me witch but when did I make your arse to itch.' And he ran off and I met a little grey kitling and the kitling said, 'you must go with me' and I said, 'Avoid, Satan.' And he said, 'You must give me your body and soul and you'll have all happiness.' And I did. And I gave him my blood every day, and that's my old cat Vinegar Tom. And he lamed John Peter's son that's a cripple this day, that was ten years ago. And I had two more imps sent me, crept in my bed in the night, sucked my privy parts so sore they hurt me and wouldn't leave me. And I asked them to kill Mary Johnson who crossed me and she wasted after. And everyone knows Anne that had fits and would gnash her teeth and took six strong men to hold her. That was me sent those fits to her. My little imps are like moles with four feet but no tails and a black colour. And I'd send them off and they'd come back in the night and say they did what I said. Jack is lucky I didn't bewitch him to death and Margery, but she was kind to me long ago. But I killed their cows like I killed ten cows last year. And the great storm and tempest comes when I call it and strikes down trees. But now I'm in prison my power's all gone or I'd call down thunder and twist your guts.

PACKER: Is there any reason you shouldn't be hanged?

JOAN: I'm with child.

GOODY: Who'd believe that?

SCENE NINETEEN: *Public square.*

JOAN *and* ELLEN *are hanged while* MARGERY *prays.*

MARGERY: Dear God, thank you for saving us. Let us live safe now. I have scrubbed the dairy out. You have shown your power in destroying the wicked, and you show it in blessing the good. You have helped me in my struggle against the witches, help me in my daily struggle. Help me work harder and our good harvests will be to your glory. Bless Miss Betty's marriage and let her live happy. Bless Jack and keep him safe from evil and let him love me and give us the land, amen.

SCENE TWENTY: *Public square.*

JOAN *and* ELLEN *hanging.*

SUSAN: Alice, how can you look? Your poor mother. You're not even crying.

ALICE: She wasn't a witch. She wouldn't know how.

SUSAN: Alice, she was.

ALICE: The cunning woman was, I think. That's why I was frightened of her.

SUSAN: I was a witch and never knew it. I killed my babies. I never meant it. I didn't know I was so wicked. I didn't know I had that mark on me. I'm so wicked. Alice, let's pray to God we won't be damned. If we're hanged, we're saved, Alice, so we mustn't be frightened. It's done to help us. Oh God, I know now I'm loathsome and a sinner and Mr Packer has shown me how bad I am and I repent I never knew that but now I know and please forgive me and don't make me go to hell and be burnt forever—

ALICE: I'm not a witch.

SUSAN: Alice, you know you are. God, don't hear her say that.

ALICE: I'm not a witch. But I wish I was. If I could live I'd be a witch now after what they've done. I'd make wax men and melt them on a slow fire. I'd kill their animals and blast their crops and make such storms, I'd wreck their ships all over the world. I shouldn't have been frightened of Ellen, I should have learnt. Oh if I could meet with the devil now I'd give him anything if he'd give me power. There's no way for us except by the devil. If I only did have magic, I'd make them feel it.

Lament for the Witches

Where have the witches gone?
Who are the witches now?
Here we are.

All the gentle witches' spells
blast the doctors' sleeping pills.
The witches hanging in the sky
haunt the courts where lawyers lie.
Here we are.

They were gentle witches
with healing spells
They were desperate witches
with no way out but the other side of hell.

A witch's crying in the night
switches out your children's light.
All your houses safe and warm
are struck at by the witches' storm.
Here we are.
Where have the witches gone?
Who are the witches now?
Here we are.

They were gentle witches
with healing spells.
They were desperate witches
with no way out but the other side of hell.
Here we are.

Look in the mirror tonight.
Would they have hanged you then?
Ask how they're stopping you now.

Where have the witches gone?
Who are the witches now?
Ask how they're stopping you now.
Here we are.

SCENE TWENTY-ONE

SPRENGER: He's Kramer.
KRAMER: He's Sprenger.
KRAMER/SPRENGER: Professors of Theology
KRAMER: delegated by letters apostolic
SPRENGER: (here's a toast, non-alcoholic).
KRAMER: Inquisitors of heretical pravities
SPRENGER: we must fill those moral cavities
KRAMER: so we've written a book
SPRENGER: *Malleus Maleficarum*
KRAMER: *The Hammer of Witches.*
SPRENGER: It works like a charm
KRAMER: to discover witches
SPRENGER: and torture with no hitches.
KRAMER: Why is a greater number of witches found in the fragile feminine sex than in men?
SPRENGER: Why is a greater number of witches found in the fragile feminine sex than in men?
KRAMER: 'All wickedness is but little to the wickedness of a woman.' Ecclesiastes.
SPRENGER: Here are three reasons, first because
KRAMER: woman is more credulous and since the aim of the devil is to corrupt faith he attacks them. Second because
SPRENGER: women are more impressionable. Third because
KRAMER: women have slippery tongues and cannot conceal from other women what by their evil art they know.
SPRENGER: Women are feebler in both body and mind so it's not surprising.
KRAMER: In intellect they seem to be of a different nature from men—
SPRENGER: like children.
KRAMER: Yes.
SPRENGER: But the main reason is
KRAMER/SPRENGER: she is more carnal than a man
KRAMER: as may be seen from her many carnal abominations.
SPRENGER: She was formed from a bent rib
KRAMER: and so is an imperfect animal.
SPRENGER: Fe mina, female, that is fe faith minus without
KRAMER: so cannot keep faith.
SPRENGER: A defect of intelligence.
KRAMER: A defect of inordinate passions.
SPRENGER: They brood on vengeance.
KRAMER/SPRENGER: Wherefore it is no wonder they are witches.
KRAMER: Women have weak memories.
SPRENGER: Follow their own impulses.

KRAMER: Nearly all the kingdoms of the worlds have been overthrown by women.

SPRENGER: as Troy, etc.

KRAMER: She's a liar by nature

SPRENGER: vain

KRAMER: more bitter than death

SPRENGER: contaminating to touch

KRAMER: their carnal desires

SPRENGER: their insatiable malice

KRAMER: their hands are as bands for binding when they place their hands on a creature to bewitch it with the help of the devil.

SPRENGER: To conclude.

KRAMER: All witchcraft

SPRENGER: comes from carnal lust

KRAMER: which is in woman

KRAMER/SPRENGER: insatiable.

KRAMER: It is no wonder there are more women than men found infected with the heresy of witchcraft.

SPRENGER: And blessed be the Most High, which has so far preserved the male sex from so great a crime.

Evil Women

Evil women
Is that what you want?
Is that what you want to see?
On the movie screen
Of your own wet dream
Evil women.

If you like sex sinful, what you want is us.
You can be sucked off by a succubus.
We had this man, and afterwards he died.

Does she do what she's told or does she nag?
Are you cornered in the kitchen by a bitching hag?
Satan's lady, Satan's pride.
Satan's baby, Satan's bride,
A devil woman's not easily satisfied.

Do you ever get afraid
You don't do it right?
Does your lady demand it
Three times a night?
If we don't say you're big
Do you start to shrink?
We earn our own money
And buy our own drink.

Did you learn you were dirty boys, did you learn
Women were wicked to make you burn?

Satan's lady, Satan's pride,
Satan's baby, Satan's bride,
Witches were wicked and had to burn.

Evil women
Is that what you want?
Is that what you want to see?
In your movie dream
Do they scream and scream?
Evil women
Evil women
Women.

On Drama

ARISTOTLE

(384–322 B.C.)

The Poetics (Excerpts)

TRANSLATED BY S. H. BUTCHER

About the Author: Aristotle was, with Socrates and Plato, one of the three famous philosophers of ancient Greece who have, by and large, determined the direction of western philosophy. In his work, usually referred to in English by the title *Poetics,* Aristotle turned his analytical methodology on works of literature, especially on drama, and within drama, especially on tragedy. As in other fields of philosophy, the questions Aristotle raised here remain central to literary criticism and literary theory. Because of its position at the beginning of this tradition, we have excerpted a few brief passages from this text.

FROM BOOK VI

Tragedy, then, is an imitation of an action that is serious, complete, and of a certain magnitude; in language embellished with each kind of artistic ornament, the several kinds being found in separate parts of the play; in the form of action, not of narrative; through pity and fear effecting the proper purgation of these emotions. . . .

FROM BOOK VIII

Unity of plot does not, as some persons think, consist in the unity of the hero. For infinitely various are the incidents in one man's life which cannot be reduced to unity; and so, too, there are many actions of one man out of which we cannot make one action. Hence the error, as it appears, of all poets who have composed a Heracleid, a Theseid, or other poems of the kind. They imagine that as Heracles was one man, the story of Heracles must also be a unity. But Homer, as in all else he is of surpassing merit, here too—whether from art or natural genius—seems to have happily discerned the truth. In composing the Odyssey he did not include all the adventures of Odysseus—such as his wound on Parnassus, or his feigned madness at the mustering of the host—incidents between which there was no necessary or probable connexion: but he made the Odyssey, and likewise the Iliad, to centre round an action that in our sense of the word is one. As therefore, in the other imitative arts, the imitation is one when the object imitated is one, so the plot, being an imitation of an action, must imitate one action and that a whole, the structural union of the parts being such that, if any one of them is displaced or removed, the whole will be disjointed and disturbed. For a thing whose presence or absence makes no visible difference, is not an organic part of the whole.

FROM BOOK IX

It is, moreover, evident from what has been said, that it is not the function of the poet to relate what has happened, but what may happen,—what is possible according to the law of probability or necessity. The poet and the historian differ not by writing in verse or in prose. The work of Herodotus might be put into verse, and it would still be a species of history, with metre no less than without it. The true difference is that one relates what has happened, the other what may happen. Poetry, therefore, is a more philosophical and a higher thing than history: for poetry tends to express the universal, history the particular. By the universal I mean how a person of a certain type will on occasion speak or act, according to the law of probability or necessity. . . .

Of all plots and actions the epeisodic are the worst. I call a plot 'epeisodic' in which the episodes or acts succeed one another without probable or necessary sequence. Bad poets compose such pieces by their own fault, good poets, to please the players; for, as they write show pieces for competition, they stretch the plot beyond its capacity, and are often forced to break the natural continuity.

But again, Tragedy is an imitation not only of a complete action, but of events inspiring fear or pity. Such an effect is best produced when the events come on us by surprise; and the effect is heightened when, at the same time, they follow as cause and effect. The tragic wonder will then be greater than if they happened of themselves or by accident; for even coincidences are most striking when they have an air of design. We may instance the statue of Mitys at Argos, which fell upon his murderer while he was a spectator at a festival, and killed him. Such events seem not to be due to mere chance. Plots, therefore, constructed on these principles are necessarily the best.

FROM BOOK X

Plots are either Simple or Complex, for the actions in real life, of which the plots are an imitation, obviously show a similar distinction. An action which is one and continuous in the sense above defined, I call Simple, when the change of fortune takes place without Reversal of the Situation and without Recognition.

A Complex action is one in which the change is accompanied by such Reversal, or by Recognition, or by both. These last should arise from the internal structure of the plot, so that what follows should be the necessary or probable result of the preceding action. It makes all the difference whether any given event is a case of *proper hoc* or *post hoc.*

FROM BOOK XI

Reversal of the Situation is a change by which the action veers round to its opposite, subject always to our rule of probability or necessity. Thus in the Oedipus, the messenger comes to cheer Oedipus and free him from his alarms about his mother, but by revealing who he is, he produces the opposite effect. . . .

Recognition, as the name indicates, is a change from ignorance to knowledge, producing love or hate between the persons destined by the poet for good or bad fortune. The best form of recognition is coincident with a Reversal of the Situation, as in the Oedipus. There are indeed other forms. Even inanimate things of the most trivial kind may in a sense be objects of recognition. Again, we may recognise or discover whether a person has done a thing or not. But the recognition which is most intimately connected with the plot and action is, as we have said, the recognition of persons. This recognition, combined with Reversal, will produce either pity or fear; and actions producing these effects are those which, by our definition, Tragedy represents. Moreover, it is upon such situations that the issues of good or bad fortune will depend. Recognition, then, being between persons, it may happen that one person only is recognised by the other—when the latter is already known—or it may be necessary that the recognition should be on both sides. . . .

FROM BOOK XIII

As the sequel to what has already been said, we must proceed to consider what the poet should aim at, and what he should avoid, in constructing his plots; and by what means the specific effect of Tragedy will be produced.

A perfect tragedy should, as we have seen, be arranged not on the simple but on the complex plan. It should, moreover, imitate actions which excite pity and fear, this being the distinctive mark of tragic imitation. It follows plainly, in the first place, that the change of fortune presented must not be the spectacle of a virtuous man brought from prosperity to adversity: for this moves neither pity nor fear; it merely shocks us. Nor, again, that of a bad man passing from adversity to prosperity: for nothing can be more alien to the spirit of Tragedy; it possesses no single tragic quality; it neither satisfies the moral sense nor calls forth pity or fear. Nor, again, should the downfall of the utter villain be exhibited. A plot of this kind would, doubtless, satisfy the moral sense, but it would inspire neither pity nor fear; for pity is aroused by unmerited misfortune, fear by the misfortune of a man like ourselves. Such an event, therefore, will be neither pitiful nor terrible. There remains, then, the character between these two extremes,—that of a man who is not eminently good and just, yet whose misfortune is brought about not by vice or depravity, but by some error or frailty. He must be one who is highly renowned and prosperous,—a personage like Oedipus, Thyestes, or other illustrious men of such families.

A well constructed plot should, therefore, be single in its issue, rather than double as some maintain. The change of fortune should be not from bad to good, but, reversely, from good to bad. It should come about as the result not of vice, but of some great error or frailty, in a character either such as we have described, or better rather than worse. The practice of the stage bears out our view. At first the poets recounted any legend that came in their way. Now, the best tragedies are founded on the story of a few houses,—on the fortunes of Alcmaeon, Oedipus, Orestes, Meleager, Thyestes, Telephus, and those others who have done or suffered something terrible. A tragedy, then, to be perfect according to the rules of art should be of this construction. . . .

SUSANNE K. LANGER

The Comic Rhythm

Of all the arts, the most exposed to nonartistic interpretation and criticism are prose fiction and the drama. As the novel has suffered from being treated as a psychobiographical document, drama has suffered from moralism. In the theater, most people—and especially the most competent spectators—feel that the vision of destiny is the essence of the work, the thing that unfolds before their eyes. In critical retrospect they forget that this visibly growing future, this destiny to which the persons in the play are committed, is the artistic form the poet set out to make, and that the value of the play lies in this creation. As critics, they treat the form as a device for conveying a social and moral content; almost all drama analysis and comment is concerned with the moral struggle involved in the action, the justice of the outcome, the "case" of society against the tragic hero or the comic villain, and the moral significance of the various characters.

It is true that tragedy usually—perhaps even always—presents a moral struggle, and that comedy very commonly castigates foibles and vices. But neither a great moral issue, nor folly inviting embarrassment and laughter, in itself furnishes an artistic principle; neither ethics nor common sense produces any image of organic form. Drama, however, always exhibits such form; it does so by creating the semblance of a history, and composing its elements into a rhythmic single structure. The moral content is thematic material, which, like everything that enters into a work of art, has to serve to make the primary illusion and articulate the pattern of "felt life" the artist intends. . . .

It is commonly assumed that comedy and tragedy have the same fundamental form, but differ in point of view—in the attitude the poet and his interpreters take, and the spectators are invited to take, toward the action.[1] But the difference really goes deeper than surface treatment (i.e., relative levity or pathos). It is structural and radical. Drama abstracts from reality the fundamental forms of consciousness: the first reflection of natural activity in sensation, awareness, and expectation, which belongs to all higher creatures and might be called, therefore, the pure sense of life; and beyond that, the reflection of an activity which is at once more elaborate, and more integrated, having a beginning, efflorescence, and end—the personal sense of life, or self-realization. The latter probably belongs only to human beings, and to them in varying measure.

The pure sense of life is the underlying feeling of comedy, developed in countless different ways. . . . This human life-feeling is the essence of comedy. It is at once religious and ribald, knowing and defiant, social and freakishly individual. The illusion of life which the comic poet creates is the oncoming future fraught with dangers and opportunities, that is, with physical or social events occurring by chance and building up the coincidences with which individuals cope according to their lights. This ineluctable future—ineluctable because its countless factors are beyond human knowledge and control—is Fortune. Destiny in the guise of Fortune is the fabric of comedy; it is developed by comic action, which is the upset and recovery of the protagonist's equilibrium, his contest with the world and his triumph by wit, luck, personal power, or even humorous, or ironical, or philosophical acceptance of mischance. Whatever the theme—serious and lyrical as in *The Tempest,* coarse slapstick as in the *Schwänke* of Hans Sachs, or clever and polite social satire—the immediate sense of life is the underlying feeling of comedy, and dictates its rhythmically structured unity, that is to say its organic form.

---

[1]Cf., for instance, the letters of Athene Seyler and Stephen Haggard, published under the title: *The Craft of Comedy.* Miss Seyler writes: ". . . comedy is simply a point of view. It is a comment on life from outside, an observation on human nature. . . . Comedy seems to be the standing outside a character or situation and pointing out one's delight in certain aspects of it. For this reason it demands the cooperation of . . . the audience and is in essence the same as recounting a good story over the dining-table." (P. 9.)

Comedy is an art form that arises naturally wherever people are gathered to celebrate life, in spring festivals, triumphs, birthdays, weddings, or initiations. For it expresses the elementary strains and resolutions of animate nature, the animal drives that persist even in human nature, the delight man takes in his special mental gifts that make him the lord of creation; it is an image of human vitality holding its own in the world amid the surprises of unplanned coincidence. The most obvious occasions for the performance of comedies are thanks or challenges to fortune. What justifies the term "Comedy" is not that the ancient ritual procession, the Comus, honoring the god of that name, was the source of this great art form—for comedy has arisen in many parts of the world, where the Greek god with his particular worship was unknown—but that the Comus was a fertility rite, and the god it celebrated a fertility god, a symbol of perpetual rebirth, eternal life. . . .

. . . The natural vein of comedy is humorous—so much so that "comic" has become synonymous with "funny." Because the word "comic" is here used in a somewhat technical sense (contrasting "the comic rhythm" with "the tragic rhythm"), it may be well to say "comical" where the popular sense is intended. There are all degrees of humor in comedy, from the quick repartee that elicits a smile by its cleverness without being intrinsically funny at all, to the absurdity that sets young and old, simple or sophisticate, shouting with merriment. Humor has its place in all the arts, but in comic drama it has its home. Comedy may be frivolous, farcical, ribald, ludicrous to any degree, and still be true art. Laughter springs from its very structure.

There is a close relation between humor and the "sense of life," and several people have tried to analyze it in order to find the basis of that characteristically human function, laughter; the chief weakness in their attempts has been, I think, that they have all started with the question: What sort of thing makes us laugh? Certainly laughter is often evoked by ideas, cognitions, fancies; it accompanies specific emotions such as disdain, and sometimes the feeling of pleasure; but we also laugh when we are tickled (which may not be pleasurable at all), and in hysterics. Those predominantly physiological causes bear no direct relation to humor; neither, for that matter, do some kinds of pleasure. Humor is one of the causes of laughter.

Laughter, or the tendency to laugh (the reaction may stop short of the actual respiratory spasm, and affect only the facial muscles, or even meet with complete inhibition) seems to arise from a surge of vital feeling. This surge may be quite small, just so it be sudden enough to be felt distinctly; but it may also be great, and not particularly swift, and reach a marked climax, at which point we laugh or smile with joy. Laughter is not a simple overt act, as the single word suggests; it is the spectacular end of a complex process. As speech is the culmination of a mental activity, laughter is a culmination of feeling—the crest of a wave of felt vitality.

A sudden sense of superiority entails such a "lift" of vital feeling. But the "lift" may occur without self-flattery, too; we need not be making fun of anyone. A baby will laugh uproariously at a toy that is made to appear suddenly, again and again, over the edge of the crib or the back of a chair. It would take artful interpretation to demonstrate that this fulfillment of his tense expectation makes him feel superior. Superior to whom? The doll? A baby of eight or nine months is not socialized enough yet to think: "There, I knew you were coming!" and believe that the doll couldn't fool him. Such self-applause requires language, and enough experience to estimate probabilities. The baby laughs because his wish is gratified; not because he believes the doll obeyed his wishing, but simply because

the suspense is broken, and his energies are released. The sudden pleasure raises his general feeling tone, so he laughs.

In so-called "gallows humor"—the harsh laugh in distress—the "lift" of vital feeling is simply a flash of self-assertion. Something similar probably causes the mirthless laughter of hysterics: in the disorganized response of a hysterical person, the sense of vitality breaks through fear and depression spasmodically, so that it causes explosive laughter, sometimes alternating with sobs and tears.

Laughter is, indeed, a more elementary thing than humor. We often laugh without finding any person, object, or situation funny. People laugh for joy in active sport, in dancing, in greeting friends; in returning a smile, one acknowledges another person's worth instead of flaunting one's own superiority and finding him funny.

But all these causes of laughter or its reduced form, smiling, which operate directly on us, belong to actual life. In comedy the spectator's laugh has only one legitimate source: his appreciation of humor in the piece.

(Many dramatic critics today—inspired by Bergson's little book on laughter, and supported by Freud's essay on wit—hold that we laugh at the characters directly, because their folly or discomfiture makes us feel superior.)

Humor, then, would be a by-product of comedy, not a structural element in it. And if laughter were elicited thus by the way, it should not make any difference to the value of the work where it occurred; a stage accident, a bad actor who made every amateur actor in the audience feel superior, should serve as well as any clever line or funny situation in the play to amuse the audience. We do, in fact, laugh at such failures; but we do not praise the comedy for that entertainment. In a good play the "laughs" are poetic elements. Its humor as well as its pathos belongs to the virtual life, and the delight we take in it is delight in something created for our perception, not a direct stimulus to our own feelings. It is true that the comical figures are often buffoons, simpletons, clowns; but such characters are almost always sympathetic, and although they are knocked around and abused, they are indestructible, and eternally self-confident and good-humored.

. . . In comedy the stock figure of the buffoon is an obvious device for building up the comic rhythm, i.e., the image of Fortune. But in the development of the art he does not remain the central figure that he was in the folk theater; the lilt and balance of life which he introduced, once it has been grasped, is rendered in more subtle poetic inventions involving plausible characters, and an *intrigue* (as the French call it) that makes for a coherent, over-all, dramatic action. Sometimes he remains as a jester, servant, or other subsidiary character whose comments, silly or witty or shrewd, serve to point the essentially comic pattern of the action, where the verisimilitude and complexity of the stage-life threaten to obscure its basic form. Those points are normally "laughs"; and that brings us to the aesthetic problem of the joke in comedy.

Because comedy abstracts, and reincarnates for our perception, the motion and rhythm of living, it enhances our vital feeling, much as the presentation of space in painting enhances our awareness of visual space. The virtual life on the stage is not diffuse and only half felt, as actual life usually is: virtual life, always moving visibly into the future, is intensified, speeded up, exaggerated; the exhibition of vitality rises to a breaking point, to mirth and laughter. We laugh in the theater at small incidents and drolleries which would hardly rate a chuckle off-stage. It is not for such psychological reasons that we go there to be amused, nor are we bound by rules of politeness to hide our hilarity, but these trifles at which we laugh are really funnier *where they occur* than they would be elsewhere; they are employed in the play, not merely brought in casually. They occur where the tension of dialogue or other action reaches a high point. As thought breaks into speech—as the wave breaks into form—vitality breaks into humor.

Humor is the brilliance of drama, a sudden heightening of the vital rhythm. A good comedy, therefore, builds up to every laugh; a performance that has been filled up with jokes at the indiscretion of the comedian or of his writer may draw a long series of laughs, yet leave the spectator without any clear impression of a very funny play. The laughs, moreover, are likely to be of a peculiar sameness, almost perfunctory, the formal recognition of a timely "gag."

The amoral character of the comic protagonist goes through the whole range of what may be called the comedy of laughter. Even the most civilized products of this art—plays that George Meredith would honor with the name of "comedy," because they provoke "thoughtful laughter"—do not present moral distinctions and issues, but only the ways of wisdom and of folly. Aristophanes, Menander, Molière—practically the only authors this most exacting of critics admitted as truly comic poets—are not moralists, yet they do not flaunt or deprecate morality; they have, literally, "no use" for moral principles—that is, they do not use them. Meredith, like practically all his contemporaries, labored under the belief that poetry must teach society lessons, and that comedy was valuable for what it revealed concerning the social order.[2] He tried hard to hold its exposé of foibles and vindication of common sense to an ethical standard, yet in his very efforts to justify its amoral personages he only admitted their amoral nature, and their simple relish for life, as when he said: "The heroines of comedy are like women of the world, not necessarily heartless from being clear-sighted. . . . Comedy is an exhibition of their battle with men, and that of men with them. . . ."

There it is, in a nutshell: the contest of men and women—the most universal contest, humanized, in fact civilized, yet still the primitive joyful challenge, the self-preservation and self-assertion whose progress is the comic rhythm.

This rhythm is capable of the most diverse presentations. That is why the art of comedy grows, in every culture, from casual beginnings—miming, clowning, sometimes erotic dancing—to some special and distinctive dramatic art, and sometimes to many forms of it within one culture, yet never seems to repeat its works. It may produce a tradition of dignified drama, springing from solemn ritual, even funereal, its emotional movement too slow to culminate in humor at any point; then other means have to be found to lend it glamor and intensity. The purest heroic comedy is likely to have no humorous passages at all, but to employ the jester only in an ornamental way reminiscent of tragedy, and in fact to use many techniques of tragedy. It may even seem to transcend the amoral comic pattern by presenting virtuous heroes and heroines. But their virtue is a formal affair, a social asset; as Deane remarked of the French classic heroes, they do not submit to ordinary morality;

[2]His well-known little work is called *An Essay on Comedy, and the Uses of the Comic Spirit.* These uses are entirely nonartistic. Praising the virtues of "good sense" (which is whatever has survival value in the eyes of society), he says: "The French have a school of stately comedy to which they can fly for renovation whenever they have fallen away from it; and their having such a school is the main reason why, as John Stuart Mill pointed out, they know men and women more accurately than we do." (Pp. 13–14.) And a few pages later: "The *Femmes Savantes* is a capital instance of the uses of comedy in teaching the world to understand what ails it. The French had felt the burden of this new nonsense [the fad of academic learning, new after the fad of excessive nicety and precision in speech, that had marked the *Précieuses*]; but they had to see the comedy several times before they were consoled in their suffering by seeing the cause of it exposed." (Pp. 19–20.)

their morality is "heroism," which is essentially strength, will, and endurance in face of the world. Neither have the divinities of oriental drama any "ordinary morality"; they are perfect in virtue when they slay and when they spare, their goodness is glory, and their will is law. They are Superman, the Hero, and the basic pattern of their conquest over enemies whose only wickedness is resistance, is the amoral life pattern of fencing with the devil—man against death.

Humor, then, is not the essence of comedy, but only one of its most useful and natural elements. It is also its most problematic element, because it elicits from the spectators what appears to be a direct emotional response to persons on the stage, in no wise different from their response to actual people: amusement, laughter.

The phenomenon of laughter in the theater brings into sharp focus the whole question of the distinction between emotion symbolically presented, and emotion directly stimulated; it is, indeed, a *pons asinorum* of the theory that this distinction is radical, because it presents us with what is probably the most difficult example. The audience's laugh at a good play is, of course, self-expressive, and betokens a "lift" of vital feeling in each laughing person. Yet it has a different character from laughter in conversation, or in the street when the wind carries off a hat with the "hair-do" attached, or in the "laugh house" at an amusement park where the willing victims meet distorting mirrors and things that say "boo." All these laughs of daily life are direct responses to separate stimuli; they may be as sporadic as the jokes bandied in a lively company, or may be strung along purposely like the expected and yet unforeseen events in the "laugh house," yet they remain so many personal encounters that seem funny only if one is in the mood for them. Sometimes we reject witticisms and are bored with tricks and clowning.

It is different in the theater: the play possesses us and breaks our mood. It does not change it, but simply abrogates it. Even if we come in a jovial mood, this does not notably increase our appreciation of humor in the play; for the humor in a good comedy does not strike us directly. What strikes us directly is the dramatic illusion, the stage action as it evolves; and the joke, instead of being as funny as our personal response would make it, seems as funny as its occurrence in the total action makes it. A very mild joke in just the right place may score a big laugh. The action culminates in a witticism, an absurdity, a surprise; the spectators laugh. But after their outburst there is not the letdown that follows an ordinary laugh, because the play moves on without the breathing spell we usually give our own thought and feeling after a joke. The action carries over from one laugh to another, sometimes fairly far spaced; people are laughing *at the play,* not at a string of jokes.

Humor in comedy (as, indeed, in all humorous art) belongs to the work, not to our actual surroundings; and if it is borrowed from the actual world, its appearance in the work is what really makes it funny. Political or topical allusions in a play amuse us because they are *used,* not because they refer to something intrinsically very comical. This device of playing with things from actual life is so sure to bring laughs that the average comic writer and improvising comedian overdoes it to the point of artistic ruin; hence the constant flood of "shows" that have immense popularity but no dramatic core, so they do not outlive the hour of their passing allusions.

Real comedy sets up in the audience a sense of general exhilaration, because it presents the very image of "livingness" and the perception of it is exciting. Whatever the story may be, it takes the form of a temporary triumph over the surrounding world, complicated, and thus stretched out, by an involved succession of coincidences. This illusion of life, the stage-life, has a rhythm of feeling which is not transmitted to us by separate successive stimulations, but rather by our perception of its entire *Gestalt*—a whole world moving into its own future. The "livingness" of the human world is abstracted, composed, and presented to us; with it the high points of the composition that are illuminated by humor. They belong to the life we see, and our laugh belongs to the theatrical exhilaration, which is universally human and impersonal. It is not what the joke happens to mean to us that measures our laughter, but what the joke does in the play.

For this reason we tend to laugh at things in the theater that we might not find funny in actuality. The technique of comedy often has to clear the way for its humor by forestalling any backsliding into "the world of anxious interest and selfish solicitude." It does this by various devices—absurd coincidences, stereotyped expressions of feeling (like the clown's wails of dismay), a quickened pace of action, and other unrealistic effects which serve to emphasize the comic structure. As Professor Fergusson said, "when we understand a comic convention we see the play with godlike omniscience. . . . When Scaramouche gets a beating, we do not feel the blows, but the idea of a beating, at that moment, strikes us as funny. If the beating is too realistic, if it breaks the light rhythm of thought, the fun is gone, and the comedy destroyed."

That "light rhythm of thought" is the rhythm of life; and the reason it is "light" is that all creatures love life, and the symbolization of its impetus and flow makes us really aware of it. The conflict with the world whereby a living being maintains its own complex organic unity is a delightful encounter; the world is as promising and alluring as it is dangerous and opposed. The feeling of comedy is a feeling of heightened vitality, challenged wit and will, engaged in the great game with Chance. The real antagonist is the World. Since the personal antagonist in the play is really that great challenger, he is rarely a complete villain; he is interesting, entertaining, his defeat is a hilarious success but not his destruction. There is no permanent defeat and permanent human triumph except in tragedy; for nature must go on if life goes on, and the world that presents all obstacles also supplies the zest of life. In comedy, therefore, there is a general trivialization of the human battle. Its dangers are not real disasters, but embarrassment and loss of face. That is why comedy is "light" compared to tragedy, which exhibits an exactly opposite tendency to general exaggeration of issues and personalities.

The same impulse that drove people, even in prehistoric times, to enact fertility rites and celebrate all phases of their biological existence, sustains their eternal interest in comedy. It is in the nature of comedy to be erotic, risqué, and sensuous if not sensual, impious, and even wicked. This assures it a spontaneous emotional interest, yet a dangerous one: for it is easy and tempting to command an audience by direct stimulation of feeling and fantasy, not by artistic power. But where the formulation of feeling is really achieved, it probably reflects the whole development of mankind and man's world, for feeling is the intaglio image of reality. The sense of precariousness that is the typical tension of light comedy was undoubtedly developed in the eternal struggle with chance that every farmer knows only too well—with weather, blights, beasts, birds, and beetles. The embarrassments, perplexities, and mounting panic which characterize that favorite genre, comedy of manners, may still reflect the toils of ritual and taboo that complicated the caveman's existence. Even the element of aggressiveness in comic action serves to develop a fundamental trait of the comic rhythm—the deep cruelty of it, as all life feeds on life. There is no biological truth that feeling does not reflect, and that good comedy, therefore, will not be prone to reveal.

But the fact that the rhythm of comedy is the basic rhythm of life does not mean that biological existence is the "deeper meaning" of all its themes, and that to understand the play is to interpret all the characters as symbols and the story as a parable, a disguised rite of spring or fertility magic, performed four hundred and fifty times on Broadway. The stock characters are probably symbolic both in origin and in appeal. There are such independently symbolic factors, or residues of them, in all the arts,[3] but their value for art lies in the degree to which their significance can be "swallowed" by the single symbol, the art work. Not the derivation of personages and situations, but of the rhythm of "felt life" that the poet puts upon them, seems to me to be of artistic importance: the essential comic feeling, which is the sentient aspect of organic unity, growth, and self-preservation.

[3]E.g., the symbolization of the zodiac in some sacred architecture, of our bodily orientation in the picture plane, or of walking measure, a primitive measure of actual time, in music. But a study of such nonartistic symbolic functions would require a monograph.

CHAPTER

FIVE

Voices in the Essay

Mary Jane Dickerson and Richard Sweterlitsch

Introduction

Historically, the essay finds its roots in classical literature, where it developed as epistles (letters), commentaries, or, simply, histories. In later literatures, the essay appeared as treatises, tracts, discourses, and themes. It was not until the sixteenth century that the French writer Michel Montaigne proposed "essay" as a name for the form.

In following centuries, novelists and poets often wrote lengthy essays as prefaces to their published fictions and poems; political firebrands found the genre congenial to their efforts of persuading the masses to action; journalists wrote extended analyses of news events, often inserting their own experienced judgment. Today, the essay is an extremely malleable genre, yet the ancient discourses of Plato and the modern essays of Joan Didion have much in common and may be studied critically for their aesthetic qualities as well as for their rhetorical value.

The artistry in an essay may be enjoyed with the same appreciation for language, imagery, figure of speech, structure, rhythm, and sound that we learn to value in poetry, drama, and fiction. We invite you to use whatever you have learned about these genres and apply it whenever appropriate to the essay.

We suggest, in what follows, a somewhat different approach to the essay. We think it can have equal application to other literary genres as well. Our introductory essay stresses the idea of voice. This concept emphasizes the presence of the author in the essay. We chose to develop our discussion of the essay around voice because, in the process of composing, essayists ostensibly write in a voice that they create, manipulate, and sustain throughout the work. In doing so, they provide an authorial presence that we are acutely conscious of through our reading. When we read an essay, we enter into dialogue with this authorial

voice, more intensely and more directly than we often do in the fictive genres. The voice we read and hear in any essay is that of the author, created for the essay. Of course, an author's voice may vary from essay to essay and may even switch within a single essay. But voice is partly a matter of expressing convincingly ideas and attitudes to readers.

This may sound complex, but in the following pages, we hope to clarify the concept of voice in the essay and to suggest ways of becoming more sensitive to literary voice. We will discuss its role in the essay and suggest ways in which you can experiment with voice in your own writing. Throughout our discussion, we have integrated some suggestions for writing, hoping to encourage you to try developing your own sense of voice in your own writing.

WHAT IS AN ESSAY?

> They are young welterweight boxers so evenly matched they might be twins—though one has a redhead's pallor and the other is a dusky-skinned Hispanic. Circling each other in the ring, they try jabs, tentative left hooks, right crosses that dissolve in midair or turn into harmless slaps.

With these opening words to her essay "On Boxing," Joyce Carol Oates places us ringside in what she calls "the drama of life in the flesh." We are hooked, leaning toward the ring to see what happens next.

For those of us living in New England, Donald Hall is our own witness to certain seasonal truths in his essay "Winter."

> In New Hampshire we know ourselves by winter—in snow, in cold, in darkness. For some of us the first true snow begins it; for others winter begins with the first bruising assault of zero weather; there is yet another sort, light-lovers, for whom winter begins with dark's onset in mid-August.

Essays such as these tell us from their very beginning that something is about to happen. They also show us how two different voices re-create parts of their lives and worlds for our understanding and pleasure. As we read, we connect our lives to the essayists' words, images, and ideas. When we respond to them with our own words, we link ourselves with their voices. And, if we decide to write essays of our own, we can re-create place or season or occasion to extend its meaning to others who read and hear our voices.

The essay is a way of keeping in touch with others and with the boundless stretches of the human imagination as it engages the here and now. The verb "to essay"—from which the noun "essay" comes—even means to test, to explore an idea, to observe and then reflect on what you see. What's more, the essay offers us a readily available way to answer back to what's going on around us if we decide to give in to the urge to write.

It's no wonder, then, that reading and writing essays are crucial in American education because, for both students and teachers, these are ways of acquiring new visions and of adding our insights to the store of knowledge. The essay has long been a most democratic and inclusive literary form, one that has always attracted poets, dramatists, and fiction writers when they want to speak directly to us in their own voices.

CONVERSATIONS WITH THE SELF

The act of writing an essay sets conversations into motion: a more intimate conversation between writer and reader, and a larger social conversation that takes place between self and society. For example, as we read and respond to "Winter," Hall shares with us his tough but clear-eyed love and respect for New England weather; we, in turn, as readers extend this dialogue to recall how our own place and seasons have altered and shaped our ways of living. Our conversation with Hall widens to take in people from his past and present—his grandparents, his mother and her sisters as children, and a "we" that includes his wife and sometimes his children. In the course of this extended conversation, we may also evoke family and friends in remembering our own wintry seasons, past and present.

Likewise, Oates's descriptions of one fight calls up for her the scene of many others that she has watched, particularly the ones she most associates with her father's love for boxing. Our own knowledge of Americans' fascination with sports enters into her elevation of boxing into "one of those legendary magical spaces." While reading and responding to Oates as she tells us what goes on in the boxing ring, we cement our own relationships to the sports-minded culture we live in.

Whether we are the author or the reader, the essay allows us to talk with ourselves as well as to the world. Consider the personal reflection that lies at the heart of Maureen Turley's essay "Women's Studies: My Right to an Education." As a sophomore at the University of Vermont, Turley explores memories and experiences evoked by dialogues with her parents and teachers and with writers she has been studying in a literature survey course. These help her reflect on the detail and shape of her whole educational process:

> It seems my education has always been strictly divided into male and female subjects. I remember in high school telling my mother that I might be interested in being a veterinarian. She frowned at this and told me I wouldn't really like being around sick animals. . . . While my parents and teachers forgave my incompetence in mathematics, they supported and encouraged my interest in literature.

Through her dialogue with books she has read, this essayist explores how her education has shaped her self-image.

> I remember reading Whitman's *Leaves of Grass,* where the poet encouraged that the truth for all men was to see a part of himself in every profession, as male and female, black and white. It strikes me this feeling of infinitude is predominantly a male feeling, especially regarding professions. During our education, women are largely absent or viewed in traditional roles such as teachers and nurses. We grow up thinking we cannot be writers, lawyers, doctors, or politicians. Unlike Whitman, most women have a much harder time feeling multitudinous.

Essays encourage writers to make connections by responding to the words of others and by engaging in conversation with the self.

A distinctive quality of the essay is the way the voice of the essayist is quickly identified with the speaking voice. A writer of essays appears to communicate directly with readers. For example, many American readers know Donald Hall as a poet who speaks in many voices decidedly not his own. He assumes or takes on in his poetry the voice of an Arctic explorer or of an early American farmer. Yet, it's the voice of Donald Hall himself who

re-creates what it's like to go through the rigors of a New Hampshire winter or to carry on a lifelong love affair with baseball. The same is true of Joyce Carol Oates, who also writes novels and short stories. But when she's writing about boxing, she's Joyce Carol Oates, a resident of Princeton, New Jersey, not a fictive voice speaking in a novel set in the late nineteenth century in a house high above the banks of the Hudson River.

Speaking straight—sounding the way others expect us to sound—is a mark of the essay. Artists who excel in other genres, as Hall and Oates do, also enjoy essays because they are able to address us in a more straightforward manner, as themselves, as if we are equals with whom they wish to start and carry on conversations.

In contrast, poetry, drama, and fiction encourage authors to create a fictive voice that keeps plot, character, and image in the realm of the imagined even when their work is based on actual experience. The voice of the novelist or the poet is metaphorical in a way the essayist's voice never is. Dickens says this is the world *as if I were* David Copperfield; Frost says this is the world *as if I were* a swinger of birches. But Katherine Anne Porter says in her essay "St. Augustine and the Bullfight": "I intend to write something about my life, here and now, and so far as I am able without one touch of fiction, and to hope to keep it as shapeless and unforeseen as the events of life itself from day to day." In other words, she will write about this world as she has seen it and lived it.

Here again is the voice of Maureen Turley speaking to us from her experience as a contemporary college student. Hers is no imaginary voice either; since what she has to say matters deeply, she puts herself on the line.

> The problem with including women writers in undergraduate English courses is that the professor wants to communicate cultural assumptions about society and about the human condition through writers in different eras. Since women writers often depart from those assumptions to provide insights about how the other half of the human race survives, they don't portray the true emotional and intellectual climate of an age. They don't represent the recognized interpretation of an era in their works. So the educational system either distorts women so they fit the norm or omits them entirely. In anthologies, women writers exist only in the briefest of excerpts and their contributions lose value and importance. While Woolf's contributions are presented cosmetically, Dickinson is regarded as being totally cloistered from the real world.

There is concern and anger in Turley's voice, and her straightforward honesty gives power to her ideas. Her urgent voice brings her essay to life.

INFORMAL WRITING: PRIVATE WRITING

1. Begin a conversation with yourself about what you have read so far by writing at least a full page of reflections on what interests you about the essay. Write as you would speak (as nearly as you can). Then, after you've written down these observations and reflections, write a second brief observation in which you describe what your voice sounds like in that first short, informal essay. Is it straightforward and honest? Is it probing and open to new ideas? Maybe it sounds unfinished and uncertain. Does it have the ring of finality or the expectant sound of open-endedness, with more yet to come?
2. Read Hall's "Winter," Oates's "On Boxing," or Turley's "Women's Studies: My Right to an Education." Then write a character sketch of the author—everything you can find

out about the author, relying only on the voice you hear as your guide. Compare your description to a classmate's. Did different readers hear different voices?

CONVERSATIONS WITH OTHERS

We have spoken of the everpresent, straightforward voice of the author, but we recognize, too, that an essay may freely incorporate other genres and other voices within its text. In doing so, authors establish a dialogue with other essayists or sometimes with their own other voices. For example, in her essay "In Search of Our Mothers' Gardens," Alice Walker includes a poem that is a tribute to her own mother as a powerful way to end her essay about creative black women: "This poem is not enough, but it is something, for the woman who literally covered the holes in our walls with sunflowers." Here Alice Walker poet joins Alice Walker essayist.

In a more general sense, authors may write in response to newspaper articles they have read, or movies or boxing matches they have seen. They draw the voices, visions, and experiences of others into their essays, thus establishing a conversation. In this way, too, the essay becomes what we call an intertextual genre, or a kind of collaborative effort. But the collaboration does not end there. Writers write for readers. When we read an essay, we not only hear the voice of the author and overhear the ongoing dialogue the writer carries on with the self and with others past and present, but we also enter the language of the essay, adding our voices as readers thinking and maybe even writing in response. We become part of the dialogue set into motion by the essayist.

Some essayists incorporate into their work the process of dialogue with other voices, which becomes, in turn, part of the dialogue the essayist is carrying on with the reader of the moment. Such intertextual freedom and collaboration is what Ursula Le Guin describes as happening to her essay "The Fisherwoman's Daughter." In tracing its origins as a speech given several times at colleges around the country to its publication in the *New York Times Book Review,* and finally to its present form in her book *Dancing at the Edge of the World,* she notes that her essay is "a collaboration, which is what I saw myself doing as I pieced together the works and words of so many other writers—ancestors, strangers, friends."

Roger Angell shows us the origins of his essay "In the Country": "Baseball is a family for those who care about it, and members of close families like to exchange letters. Three years ago, I received a letter from a woman named Linda Kittell, who was living in Clinton, Montana." Angell includes large chunks of Linda's letter, giving the history of her love affair with baseball and with a minor league pitcher named Ron Goble. "I answered this letter, needless to say, and in time Linda wrote back." Linda's letters eventually become Angell's way of seeing what baseball is like in the hinterlands. Through a series of coincidences Ron and Linda end up near Burlington, Vermont, with Ron playing for the Burlington A's, a local semipro team. Angell visits them during the summer of 1981. It's as if the whole essay is a collaboration of three different voices, with Linda's and Ron's voices heard most distinctly, telling the story of baseball in all the remote corners of a vast country full of baseball diamonds. Angell's voice holds the essay together and provides a distance that allows us to watch and admire Linda and Ron's frankness about the sport.

If essays allow for such communities of writers, we add to this a community of readers. As we speak to you in this chapter about the essay, we address you as unnamed college students enrolled in literature courses on unfamiliar campuses. But as we speak, we also conjure up students whose names and faces we do know because we talk to them each day about the literature we are reading and writing about. Sprinkled throughout our conversation with you are the voices of many writers such as Le Guin and Angell, including essays written by our students and many other professional writers we have read through our years of teaching. Our voice is deliberately and consciously speculative as much as an actual conversation is apt to be, because we are exploring a literary genre that resists easy categorizing and defining. Instead, it's as if the essay as a genre insists on remaining in the process of becoming much like a writer who is speaking, whose voice we hear and respond to as we read and write.

Many essays in this anthology originated as lectures or speeches. This public speech connection with the essay helps to account for its relatively short prose form and its relatively plain language—a kind of literary lecture taken in at a sitting. Reading an essay is witnessing verbal performance, much as one experiences at a lecture.

In "Why I Write" Joan Didion reemphasizes the power of speech and the importance of this sound as it resonates from the printed page:

> Of course I stole the title for this talk from George Orwell. One reason I stole it was that I like the sound of the words: *Why I Write.* There you have three short unambiguous words that share a sound, and the sound they share is this:
>
> *I*
> *I*
> *I*

What alerts us to this verbal performance is Didion's very casual use of the ordinary and everyday phrase "of course." We're immediately within the range of her speaking voice, marked as well by her reference to her writing as a "talk." Notice her repetitious use of the words "sound" and "I." They affect us as readers and remind us that her essay is "I," Joan Didion, sounding herself. Later in the same essay, she writes: "In many ways writing is the act of saying *I,* of imposing oneself upon other people, of saying *listen to me, see it my way, change your mind."* Through the words she uses, by her conscious arrangement of them on the page, with her allusion to Orwell's essay, we find ourselves, as we read, in the presence of Didion's verbal performance.

With its emphases on voice and dialogue, it is not surprising that the essay is emerging as an increasingly vital form of American literature. Its history is firmly rooted in the work of such writers as Benjamin Franklin, Margaret Fuller, Ralph Waldo Emerson, Harriet Beecher Stowe, and Henry David Thoreau. The writings of the "new journalists," such as Tom Wolfe, Joan Didion, and Norman Mailer, have rekindled interest in the form for contemporary readers while broadening its meaning by blurring the line between fiction and essay, between what's imagined and what's real. The recently inaugurated yearly anthology *Best American Essays* affirms the essay's rightful place in the literary canon.

It is appropriate that all of us share in the study of the literary form that is most available for our own continued self-education—in and beyond the college and university. As Elizabeth Hardwick says in her introduction to the first volume of the *Best American Essays* series, the essay is "not a closed shop"; it's open to all of us. Series editor Robert Atwan even characterizes it as "a gutsy form." Annie Dillard draws a neat distinction when she asserts that "the essay can do everything a poem can do, and everything a short story can do—everything but fake it."

INFORMAL WRITING: STARTING DIALOGUES

1. Read Didion's essay "Why I Write" and Michelle Cliff's essay "If I Could Write This in Fire, I Would Write This in Fire." Although Didion is best known for new journalism, or the art of "personal reportage," and Cliff writes autobiographically, the essayists share a common dialogue as they explore why they write. Expand on this dialogue by writing a response exploring how writing works for you and why you write. What concerns about writing do you, Didion, and Cliff share? Where might there be some friendly disagreements? Compare your opinions and ideas about why you write with others in the class. Do they write for any of the same reasons?
2. Read any essay from the collection. Write a response based on one or more of the following questions. What does the essay make you think about, especially as it may touch your own experience? How does the writer engage you in dialogue? Does the essayist carry on a dialogue with identifiable others, such as the reader, friends, memories of past experiences, and other writers? Does convoking these other voices add to the essay? Why or why not?

VOICES THAT SHAPE THE ESSAY

Earlier we alerted you to the many voices from which a single writer may select, much as each of us may speak differently in a letter to a parent or another authority figure than we might in a letter to an intimate friend. An essayist's reputation revolves around the ability to forge a recognizable personality on paper so that we feel as if we are in that person's presence each time we read what she or he has written. At the same time, if we have read widely through that writer's essays, we begin to understand the essayist's different slants and ways of thinking over the course of time and how the writing has been affected by shifting historical, social, and personal conditions.

For example, the Alice Walker who wrote "The Civil Rights Movement: What Good Was It?" at the age of twenty-three is not the same person who wrote "Beauty: When the Other Dancer Is the Self" at age thirty-eight. In "The Civil Rights Movement: What Good Was It?," Walker is responding to those who doubt that the marches and sit-ins that characterized the sixties have made any differences in the lives of Americans. Her language is forceful and precisely chosen to mix polemical assertion with illustrative example and detail. Near the end, she writes:

> What good was the Civil Rights Movement? If it had just given this country Dr. King, a leader of conscience, for once in our lifetime, it would have been enough. If it had taken black eyes off white television stories, it would have been enough. If it had fed one starving child, it would have been enough.

While describing a precious moment when her daughter Rebecca helped her see beyond the disfiguring scar tissue on her eye, Alice Walker's language becomes personal, even full of wonder: "There *was* a world in my eye. And I saw that it was possible to love it; that, in fact, for all it had taught me of shame and anger and inner vision, I *did* love it." One voice is more tuned to the public; the other retains the essence of the private voice that we are allowed to overhear.

Essayists write to inform readers about something of significance, to argue a position, to express their own personal response, to discover what they really believe, to explain why something is as it is or how it works, why something is important enough for them and for us to spend our time discussing. Whatever circumstances give rise to an essay, whether they are personal reflections or issues of public concern, authors have certain purposes in mind as they write. Sometimes authors even alert us to their intentions through an essay's title much as Virginia Woolf does in "How Should One Read a Book?" We call these intentions the voices that shape the essay.

What follows is a brief discussion of some of the voices essayists have used. It does not exhaust all the possibilities, since the essay, as we suggest, continues to change and reshape itself to fit the everchanging interests and needs of writers.

Voices of Meditation

When Michel Montaigne wrote what has been recognized as the first essay (at least, the first one called by that name), he created a vehicle for sharing personal reflections written in an informal manner. His declared subject is himself: "Meditation is a powerful and full study for anyone who knows how to examine and exercise himself vigorously: I would rather fashion my mind than furnish it." This personal quality of the essay remains a powerful trait of the genre, although the essay today varies widely over a broad spectrum from serious formality—such as the American Declaration of Independence—to the informality found in popular journals and even daily newspapers. But Montaigne's essays exhibited an immediacy and lightness that have entertained centuries of readers even in translation.

In addition, Montaigne's essays are expressions of personal opinions and views: in "Of Smells" he writes that "the best condition they [bodies] may have is to be free of smell." Their format suggests that these essays were reflections or meditations on various subjects that struck the author as worth interest, first of all to himself, and then to his public.

Taking a lead from Montaigne, imitators retained this meditative quality of the essay. Above all, the meditative voice is a personal one. Essayists find it appropriate as they turn inward and present to the world what they find out about themselves, about their feelings, sentiments, and attitudes. The meditative essay may deal with a person's own tastes in music, sports, or fiction, or with religious beliefs, or with attitudes toward sexuality. It may focus on the author's fear of riding roller coasters or making a love commitment or on his or her anger over environmental pollution or pride in receiving a coveted award. What makes these essays interesting to readers is that their meditative quality challenges us to look at our own values and perhaps to respond positively or negatively to those of the author.

Like Montaigne's self-examination, the contemporary essayist Annie Dillard's essay "Sight into Insight" allows us to witness her meditation on the subtleties of seeing and what different angles of seeing mean for daily living: "There are lots of things to see, unwrapped gifts and free surprises. . . . What you see is what you get." She takes us along as she surveys her local landscape, meditating on what it yields to the watchful eye: "It's all a matter of keeping my eyes open. Nature is like one of those line drawings that are puzzles for children."

One of the delights in reading a meditative essay like Dillard's is the way it allows us to follow the turns of an original and penetrating mind on an almost intimate footing. This essay's exploratory nature shapes its structure so that the writer almost free-associates by lighting on first one angle of the subject, then another. For example, Dillard begins with a childhood memory of hiding pennies and providing clues for someone to see this "free gift from the universe" and then explores the implications of nature as "a now-you-see-it, now-you-don't-affair." Sometimes she sticks close to the earth's surface, examining creek water "in a white china bowl," then skyward where she "can see two million light-years to the Andromeda galaxy." She ends the essay by pondering her own search for " 'the tree with the lights in it.' " The vision came one day when she was not thinking of anything at all and saw a cedar tree "transfigured" by light—"a gift and a total surprise."

The spontaneity of Dillard's observations takes on added richness as we begin to see the carefully developed pattern of metaphors on which the essay builds itself. In her penetration into "what you see is what you get," Dillard takes us on a visual journey from "pennies cast broadside from a generous hand" and "the bright coppers at the roots of trees" to "the backyard cedar buzzing with flame."

Dillard's meditations are not developed into any arguments or recommendations for us to disagree with or to follow. Rather, it's as if we have been asked to take a series of explorations to examine what it means to see the lights illuminating the world we live in. Our landscapes are necessarily different, but we look up from her pages better equipped to use our eyes and our minds on what's out there.

INFORMAL WRITING: PRIVATE REFLECTIONS

1. Read Annie Dillard's "Sight Into Insight" and Charles Simic's "Reading Philosophy at Night." One essay offers a meditation on the nature of seeing, the other on the nature of a certain kind of reading. In a free-flowing way, write a reflection on one of your most significant activities in order to follow where it takes you toward self-examination and self-knowledge. For example, in Chapter 7, "Writing Personal Essays," a student makes a connection in his informal writing between Annie Dillard's momentary vision of "the tree with the lights in it" and the bursts of energetic highs he occasionally experiences while he is running.
2. Read over what you came up with in your reflection. Write a brief description of what you notice about your voice as you undergo such self-reflection: a note of wonder, surprise, jubilation, or wry humor. What does this reveal about yourself that you may not have been aware of?

Voices of Response

We live in a world where situational forces shape the human condition. These may be environmental or physical; social, political, historical, or economic. Sometimes the force may be simply a friend who takes issue with something we've said or an ad on TV that draws our attention for thirty seconds. Like the rest of us, essayists respond to these forces. For Virginia Woolf, "the art of writing has for backbone some fierce attachment to an idea." Occasionally essayists are affected so intensely by these cultural forces that they wish to explore their own response and to present it for readers to evaluate.

Although essayists are not necessarily trying to persuade us to agree with their reactions or to convince us they responded correctly to the situation at hand, the general intent of the responding voice reminds us that to react to what's going on around us is an

important part of day-to-day living. This kind of essay reinforces a link between human beings as sensitive and caring.

Several years ago the biographer and essayist William Manchester was invited to participate in a Flag Day ceremony at Okinawa, commemorating one of the bloodiest battles in the Pacific during World War II. Manchester fought and was wounded in that battle. He intended to go to Okinawa. "But," he writes in his essay "Okinawa: The Bloodiest Battle of All," "when I learned that Japanese were also participating, I quietly withdrew. There are too many graves between us, too much gore, too many memories of too many atrocities." His response to the invitation prompts a very personal and frank essay in which Manchester exposes an intensely deep anguish and an unforgiving rage. He writes in part:

> On Okinawa today, the ceremony will be dignified, solemn, seemly. It will also be anachronistic. If the Japanese dead of 1945 were resurrected to witness it, they would be appalled by the acceptance of defeat, the humiliation of their emperor—the very idea of burying Japanese near the barbarians from across the sea and then mourning them together. Americans, meanwhile, risen from their graves, would ponder the evolution of their own society, and might wonder, What ever happened to patriotism?

No feigned patriotic fiction sentimentalizes this essay. Manchester recalls the phony patriotism portrayed in motion pictures dealing with World War II and ponders his experience that soldiers wage what they think are decisive battles only to discover that the folks at home can't pronounce their names. He criticizes those veterans who served in the military but never saw frontline action, yet in Memorial Day parades aggrandize themselves as war heroes. Combat itself is not worthy of praise; it is instead "cruel and squalid," Manchester writes, incorporating the words of Winston Churchill in his own essay. For this essayist, the war experiences continue to fuel a "primitive rage" that lingers within him and occasionally surfaces in response to meetings or chance invitations.

> In 1978, revisiting Guadalcanal, I encountered a Japanese businessman who had volunteered to become a kamikaze pilot in 1945 and was turned down at the last minute. Mutual friends suggested that we meet. I had expected no difficulty; neither, I think, did he. But when we confronted each other, we froze.
>
> I trembled, suppressing the sudden, startling surge of primitive rage within. And I could see, from his expression, that this was difficult for him, too. Nations may make peace. It is harder for fighting men. On simultaneous impulse we both turned and walked away.

This is a responsive although bitter voice growing out of a dialogue with his memory and reflection. The essayist is not willing to accept the irony that a political peace tries to force upon former combatants. His experiences will not allow it. Neither is the voice of the essayist trying to persuade us to accept its position nor to apologize for it. The anecdotes and brief descriptions of war scattered throughout the essay serve to measure the author's anguish.

This essay shows a responding voice in which the author discovers more about himself during the process of writing, a link with the meditative voice. The invitation occasioned a response. But it also brought back memories of the war and feelings aroused by public shows of patriotism and private personal experiences, all of which Manchester must sort out in his essay and in his life. He chose not to do this in a private diary or in a conversation with a close friend. He did not choose to write his response as a short story with some invented narrative voice. Instead, he preferred to use the public forum of the essay which he published for all to read. Through the medium of the essay, we vicariously share his response, even though we may or may not agree with it.

Dr. Martin Luther King, Jr.'s "Letter from Birmingham Jail" is another responsive essay. In a footnote King explains that eight Alabama clergymen published a statement in which they criticized the timing of his activities on behalf of the civil rights movement. In the first paragraph, King speaks to the clergymen, explaining to them and to us why he wrote his essay: "But since I feel that you are men of genuine good will and that your criticisms are sincerely set forth, I want to try to answer your statement in what I hope will be patient and reasonable terms." The concerns published by the clergymen offered a challenge that needed answering, and they provided an immediate context in which King reviews his reasons for taking the civil rights movement into Birmingham.

This essay also tells us a great deal about King himself. Early on he partly defines himself by comparison to the prophets and the Apostle Paul, who often found themselves persecuted for their actions and radical beliefs. He speaks, too, as the conscience of a people at war with themselves—"We are caught in an inescapable network of mutuality, tied in a single garment of destiny. Whatever affects one directly, affects all indirectly." Trained in the traditional rhetoric of the black preacher, King's voice in the essay responds to his critics:

> Perhaps it is easy for those who have never felt the stinging darts of segregation to say, "Wait." But when you have seen vicious mobs lynch your mothers and fathers at will and drown your sisters and brothers at whim; when you have seen hate-filled policemen curse, kick and even kill your black brothers and sisters; when you see the vast majority of your twenty million Negro brothers smothering in an airtight cage of poverty in the midst of an affluent society; when you suddenly find your tongue twisted and your speech stammering as you seek to explain to your six-year-old daughter why she can't go to the public amusement park that has just been advertised on television, and see tears welling up in her eyes when she is told that Funtown is closed to colored children, and see ominous clouds of inferiority beginning to form in her little mental sky, and see her beginning to distort her personality by developing an unconscious bitterness toward white people; . . . then you will understand why we find it difficult to wait. There comes a time when the cup of endurance runs over, and men are no longer willing to be plunged into the abyss of despair. I hope, sirs, you can understand our legitimate and unavoidable impatience.

Here, the essay's voice is responding to situational forces on several levels. Essentially, King is vindicating his actions in response to a letter published by the religious leaders who accused him of acting in an an "unwise and untimely" manner. But the essay also provides King with a context in which to outline the broader social and political forces that also prompted his coming to Birmingham, including bombings, failures at negotiating a just settlement, and the denial of constitutional and what he calls "God-given rights."

It is worth noting how King uses verb tenses—moving back and forth between the present situation and injustices that took place at different moments in the past. By choosing to render time so precisely, King emphasizes that his letter addresses past events and circumstance that have forced him to respond as he does: the forces of history itself shape this essay. King makes only passing reference to his present incarceration, instead focusing on the daily lives of those who continue to live with the degradation of segregation, and makes no direct argument, only a plea in passing, for future change. His intent throughout

the essay is to justify his actions as not being unwise or untimely, but as being appropriate to the present situation and moment in history.

INFORMAL WRITING: ANSWERING IDEAS

1. This section has provided a general overview of the Manchester and King essays. Read the selections carefully and note how each author shapes his essay by maintaining a dialogue with himself, with others whom he cites (or alludes to), and with readers.
2. Both King and Manchester write out of anger, but they justify it by inferring the legitimacy of certain social and moral values. In your journal briefly describe some incident on campus that provoked you to anger. Then try in a paragraph or two to explain how the incident assaulted some value you consider important. Finally, write a longer journal entry in which you reflect on the importance of that value in your life and why your anger was appropriate. At this point, consider revising the entry into a letter to the editor of your campus newspaper.

Voices of Dissent

In the June 26, 1989, issue of the *New Yorker* an essay appeared that addressed the American response to the Chinese student protest that eventually led to a military action killing numerous demonstrators. Many Americans watched on their televisions the brutal night attack on the students in Beijing's Tiananmen Square. To many Americans, what happened in China proved again the superiority of the American political system and allowed them to gloat over China's political failings. The essay took a different stance, however, arguing that Americans should not be so self-righteous. In part its author argued:

> Our system of government and the centuries of continuity that our nation has enjoyed are powerful forces of resistance against mass political violence. But our system is something we inherited; we aren't by definition better than other people because of it. Each of us in the United States today watching the events in China has reason for sadness and reason for gratitude, but no one has reason to feel superior. It's appropriate for us to refrain from helping oppressive leaders. It's appropriate for us to express grief. But it's not our job to punish others, verbally or in any other way, and when a punitive tone creeps into our responses we no longer ring true.
>
> Our founding fathers were idealistic, yet so were the founders of Communism. Our good fortune lies in that fact that ours were less ambitious, and more realistic about the corrupting nature of power, and wiser about the limitations of government in changing the human condition. We have been lucky. It is our job to realize that, and to stay clear of the blinding light of moral superiority.

The essayist argues that Americans might better temper their reaction to the China massacre by appealing to patriotism tempered by a historical perspective. This essay's method of argumentation is typical of the hundreds of editorials which appear daily in newspapers and magazines. The most successful persuasive essays meld convincing arguments with the artistry of solid prose. The enjoyment we derive from them ranges from the simple pleasure of reading well-wrought words to the intellectual satisfaction of having the essayists actually convince us of the merits of their argument.

A classic dissenting voice is that of Jonathan Swift, best remembered for raising political satire to such a high level that we continue to read his bitterly ironic essay "A Modest Proposal." This enduring argumentative essay appalled the credulous and provoked considerable consternation throughout England and Ireland. Even today, modern readers can be deceived by the serious tone that pervades the essay. They fail to catch Swift's ironic voice that, in turn, creates his argumentative voice.

In a departure from usual essayistic practice, Swift creates a fictive "I" who seems basically decent and compassionate. This narrator recognizes that something has to be done to alleviate the horrible suffering plaguing the Irish populace, especialy the children. Wringing hands won't help, so, out of compassion, "I" responds with a plan. Seeing the huge number of starving Irish children and having been told "by a very knowing American of my acquaintance in London, that a young healthy Child, well nursed, is, at a Year old, a most delicious, nourishing and wholesome Food, whether Stewed, Roasted, Baked, or Boiled; and, I make no doubt that it will equally serve in a Fricassee, or Ragout," the speaker proposes creating an industry to raise and market children as food.

The success of this essay and its real message derive from the interplay between "I" and the second voice, that of essayist Swift. An ironic tension—saying one thing but meaning another—provides the lifeblood of this essay. The overt message of "A Modest Proposal" is outrageous and yet coolly, calmly, and logically written. While we cannot sympathize with the speaker's position, we do find ourselves siding with the bitter voice of Jonathan Swift and his covert plea for political action.

Two hundred and sixty years after Swift penned his "Modest Proposal," Chris Bouffard, a first-year student at the University of Vermont, read the essay and was drawn to it. He began a dialogue with Swift and eventually developed his own essay, which, out of indebtedness to Swift, he called "A New and Improved Modest Proposal."

Since Chris especially liked Swift's fictive "I," he adopted it to his own purposes to express his concern over problems facing contemporary society. "Upon reading 'A Modest Proposal,' " Chris writes, "it occurred to me that although Jonathan Swift's plan was appropriate for Dublin in the eighteenth century, it is much too outdated to be considered at the end of the twentieth century. This does not mean, however, that we should disregard its concepts altogether. If we can adapt parts of the proposal, society will be greatly improved." Chris suggests that criminals in prison may themselves be an excellent food source for other prisoners; ditto for folks in mental institutions and the homeless. The arguments and the voice in Bouffard's essay result from his encounter with Swift's essay and his own visions about pressing issues in American society. Neither essay proposes a workable solution, but both argue that some action must be taken.

INFORMAL WRITING: TAKING EXCEPTION

1. Read Swift's essay. Select the paragraph or passage that appeals to you most. Using a current controversy on your campus, write about it in an exact imitation of Swift's paragraph, following the sentence structure and patterns as closely as you can and speaking in the same voice that Swift uses. What have you learned about Swift's style and his tone of voice?
2. Consider revising your earlier letter to the editor by adopting an ironic voice.

Voices of Explanation

Essays frequently serve as vehicles to provide specific information and to explore ideas. Informative essays are written by people who think they have unique knowledge—perhaps they are even leading authorities in a field or they have investigated and researched a topic in depth—and take it upon themselves to inform others who happen to read their essays.

Essays written as class assignments are very often explanatory or expositional in nature. For example, as you study and master the literature in this anthology, you may be asked to compose essays in which you explain how a certain character's actions bring together the meaning in a play or why certain images control the way a poem should be read. As you write about what you read, you will be practicing literary criticism, a form of the essay in which readers—call them critics—explain their interpretations and understandings of a work.

A unique quality of this kind of essay is the authoritative voice of writers who speak because they are certain of what they write. Listen to Virginia Woolf as she asks us to consider her answers to the questions she raises in her essay "How Should One Read a Book?" She suggests to us: "Do not dictate to your author; try to become him. Be his fellow-worker and accomplice. . . . reading is a longer and more complicated process than seeing." As Woolf relies on her background as a book reviewer for newspapers and magazines, the expositional writer often draws directly upon experiences. They may come firsthand through personal observation and knowledge, through interviews of credible witnesses or other authorities, or through research and reflection on evidence. What makes the explanatory essay such a powerful literary form is the way it marries knowledge and personality.

What the explanatory voice does for readers is to bring them into ways of considering many subjects from unique perspectives. To explain things without condescension is what this voice aims for, just as Randall Jarrell does in "The Other Frost":

> Frost's seriousness and honesty; the bare sorrow with which, sometimes, things are accepted as they are, neither exaggerated nor explained away; the many, many poems in which there are real people with their real speech and real thoughts and real emotions—all this, in conjunction with so much subtlety and exactness, such classical understatement and restraint, makes the reader feel that he is not in a book but in a world, and a world that has in common with his own some of the things that are most important in both.

In his dialogue with us, Jarrell assumes we are sensitive readers well able to read Frost's poetry. He also has expressed his own opinion by explaining what he considers significant to the experience of reading Frost. In the process of writing a critical essay, he opens up something of himself, and he has drawn each of us into the critical process as well. If we are actively engaged participants in what the essayist intends, we have learned something about Robert Frost, Randall Jarrell, and ourselves.

INFORMAL WRITING: TELLING WHY

1. In your journal or reading notebook, explain very simply and directly what you consider to be most interesting or compelling about your favorite poem in Chapter 3. Try to get us to see some feature of this poem (and its poet) that might not strike us at first reading.

2. Read Woolf's essay "How Should One Read a Book?" Evaluate the effectiveness of her voice. Try rewriting the above explanation about a poem adapting Woolf's deliberately conversational tone of voice. Even try imitating her opening with "In the first place" to get into her casual voice.

Voices of Storytelling

At first it may seem to be a paradox to juxtapose "story" with "essay." Somehow, storytelling seems to be more properly a part of the world of fiction. It is important to remember, however, that not all short stories are fictions. Some essays may be shaped by a narrative voice. Traditionally, literary studies explore fictive narratives. In the fiction section of this book, you can read the life history of a short story by David Huddle. Much of what Huddle wrote was based on actual experiences, thus transforming reality into fiction. The narrative essay avoids the transformation and presents the reality as it appears to exist for the writer.

Autobiography may provide the backbone upon which an essay is constructed. James Seilsopour, born in America in 1962, spent a considerable part of his early life in Iran, living with his Iranian father. When militants seized the American embassy in Teheran in November 1979, holding the occupants hostage, Seilsopour was living in California and attending high school. In "I Forgot the Words to the National Anthem," he writes of his experiences during that time. The essay is a collage of autobiographical narratives and poignant anecdotes, and a quiet cry of anger. One incident centers on school:

> On this particular day, he [the photography teacher] decided to show a film about Iran, knowing full well that my father was Iranian and that I grew up in Iran. During the movie, this teacher encouraged students to make comments. Around the room, I could hear "Drop the bomb" and "Deport the mothers." Those words hurt. I felt dirty, guilty. However, I managed to laugh and assure the students I realized they were just joking. I went home that afternoon and cried.

This is only one of the incidents that collectively shape the essay. In it, there is comment, reflection, and opinion, but essentially Seilsopour is narrating what happened. As readers, we become witnesses to the same happenings and we begin to understand the world from the essayist's perspective. In doing so, we broaden our own experiences.

A classic narrative essay is George Orwell's "Shooting an Elephant." While the author was a local police officer in a Burmese village, an elephant went berserk, killing residents and rampaging through the bazaar. Officer Orwell is called upon to slay the beast.

> But I did not want to shoot the elephant. I watched him beating his bunch of grass against his knees with that preoccupied grandmotherly air that elephants have. It seemed to me that it would be murder to shoot him. At that age I was not squeamish about killing animals, but I had never shot an elephant and never wanted to. (Somehow it always seems worse to kill a *large* animal.)

The storyteller's voice dominates this entire essay, and indeed, part of what Orwell is doing is simply telling a good story. But the reader perceives something else. In this essay, Orwell uses the incident in which a maverick elephant is slain to explore colonialism with its inherent racism and political subjugation. We finish the narrative entertained, but we also retain a deeper understanding of the racial arrogance that is a part of colonialism. Indeed,

we come to view the shooting of the elephant as a symbolic act whose implications continue to shape world politics today.

In the passage from the Orwell essay is the parenthetic aside "Somehow it always seems worse to kill a *large* animal." David Leith, a student at our university, was struck by these words. It marked the beginning of a literary dialogue with Orwell. David thought about those words and about Orwell's feelings over shooting the elephant. He compared them with feelings he had had when he was forced to shoot a much smaller animal, and he disagreed with Orwell's aside: it is no easier to kill a small animal.

David began working on a narrative recounting a personal experience of killing a raccoon. In his early drafts, David wrote in the first person, but he eventually found that he could treat his material more effectively by casting the narrative in the third, "he" rather than "I." Nevertheless, "Where the Heart Should Be" is an autobiographical narrative essay, with David as "the boy."

One of the boy's chores is to gather eggs. One day he goes to the chicken house and notices that the hens seem somewhat unsettled and skittish. At first he pays no attention, but then

> opening the other laying box, the boy started as he saw a large raccoon eating eggs. It was a greasy mess of brown fur, its glassy eyes set into a black mask. A large raccoon about three feet long, it must have weighed over forty-five pounds. Without blinking, the raccoon, still clutching an eggshell in its front paws, looked up and hissed, snapping his jaw to reveal two rows of moist yellow teeth. The boy slammed down the laying box lid.

With a sense of certainty about what he must do, the boy goes for a gun. But as the essay unfolds, his efforts to kill the raccoon test his determination, and his initial failures test his own sense of self. Finally, he must confront his failure.

Leith's essay recounts what happened, but the telling, in its simplicity and directness, is a pleasure to read. Killing the raccoon becomes secondary to the story, which, like the Orwell piece that prompted Leith's essay, presents and develops character. We observe Orwell and the boy defining themselves by recalling in their essays their actions in demanding situations. And we respond to what they have written. Narrative provides the events and situations that essayists need in order to test and explore themselves in dialogue with the readers.

INFORMAL WRITING: NARRATING ESSAY

1. Read Seilsopour's "I Forgot the Words to the National Anthem" with an eye toward discriminating between narrative, or story, and essay. What impact would the essay have without the narratives, or with a simple summary of the narratives instead? How would you describe Seilsopour's voice when it is not narrating incidents?
2. Review the informal writing that you have done as you have been reading and thinking about essays. Have you told any stories in these informal mini-essays? If so, rewrite a piece so that you sharpen the story's effect and significance and so that you distinguish between the narrating voice and any other voice you may be using. *Or,* if you have not told any stories along the way, attempt to tell a story about something of significance that happened to you during a high school or college class.

Other Voices

By this point, you've probably figured out for yourself that the essay "takes as many shapes as weather or daylight," to borrow the writer Maureen Howard's words, and there are many more voices giving shape to those essays than those we've described in this chapter. In our discussion we have explored some of the main characteristics that help us distinguish the essay from other literary genres. But we have surely not been able to pinpoint all the essay's characteristics, just those that appear major to us. Likewise, we have examined what seem to us to be major voices that shape the essay, but, once again, our discussion has not been exhaustive. Because the essay is such a vital form of contemporary literature, it is impossible to pigeonhole its process of disclosing the riches of human curiosity and self-creation.

We believe that essays begin out of very private observations or curiosities or experiences. Essayists do not remove themselves from the reality, but instead forge an authorial identity centering on the personal "I." Beyond that, the individual writer has many options in shaping the essay. Sometimes authors speak of "trying to find the right voice" that appropriately conveys and reflects their attitude toward their subject. The "I" shapes, speaks, and reaches out to engage its readers in dialogue, but it never loses its authority by compromising the accuracy of its material.

READING ESSAYS/WRITING ABOUT ESSAYS

More and more people are getting into the act of essay writing, often beginning by keeping a journal or diary. More and more colleges are suggesting that students keep journals in which they can reflect on paper about their studies.

Consider keeping your own journal or diary in which you continue your part of the dialogue with authors you are reading. Perhaps your entries can be developed into essays to be shared with others in class. Your entries may contain the bud of an idea that eventually blossoms into an essay, given a little cultivation.

Journal entries normally do not undergo much revising because they are personal, spontaneous, and quite informal. Entries we may want to share with others we often revise, if for no other reason than we want to make them and our voice sound better.

Being a democratic and self-liberating literary form, the essay encourages its readers to participate in the craft. How one chooses to respond to an essay's challenge is purely personal. Sometimes, we write an essay responding to a particular viewpoint suggested by the way an author's voice shaped her on his commitment to an idea. Still other times, we write in direct response to the ideas offered for consideration by an essay. In all cases, however, we create voices for ourselves and through them express something of ourselves. We define our attitude toward our subject matter, and we inform our readers as to our sincerity. One of the hardest things to do when writing an essay is to be untrue to our readers and ourselves. Finding the right voice is deciding not only how we are going to present ideas, but also what those ideas are going to mean to us.

As you read the following five essays, note what interests you or what you don't understand. After you have finished, consider the suggestions in "On Becoming an Essayist" (page 1602).

E. B. WHITE

(1899–1985)

Death of a Pig

About the Author: Whether in a gently humorous or subtly simple voice, White's essays place him squarely in the tradition of Emerson and Thoreau in his search for a modern American identity. In "Death of a Pig," White blends the humorous voice with a serious purpose that brings us into the community of human and animal interrelationships.

I spent several days and nights in mid-September with an ailing pig and I feel driven to account for this stretch of time, more particularly since the pig died at last, and I lived, and things might easily have gone the other way round and none left to do the accounting. Even now, so close to the event, I cannot recall the hours sharply and am not ready to say whether death came on the third night or the fourth night. This uncertainty afflicts me with a sense of personal deterioration; if I were in decent health I would know how many nights I had sat up with a pig.

The scheme of buying a spring pig in blossomtime, feeding it through summer and fall, and butchering it when the solid cold weather arrives, is a familiar scheme to me and follows an antique pattern. It is a tragedy enacted on most farms with perfect fidelity to the original script. The murder, being premeditated, is in the first degree but is quick and skillful, and the smoked bacon and ham provide a ceremonial ending whose fitness is seldom questioned.

Once in a while something slips—one of the actors goes up in his lines and the whole performance stumbles and halts. My pig simply failed to show up for a meal. The alarm spread rapidly. The classic outline of the tragedy was lost. I found myself cast suddenly in the role of pig's friend and physician—a farcical character with an enema bag for a prop. I had a presentiment, the very first afternoon, that the play would never regain its balance and that my sympathies were now wholly with the pig. This was slapstick—the sort of dramatic treatment that instantly appealed to my old dachshund, Fred, who joined the vigil, held the bag, and, when all was over, presided at the interment. When we slid the body into the grave, we both were shaken to the core. The loss we felt was not the loss of ham but the loss of pig. He had evidently become precious to me, not that he represented a distant nourishment in a hungry time, but that he had suffered in a suffering world. But I'm running ahead of my story and shall have to go back.

My pigpen is at the bottom of an old orchard below the house. The pigs I have raised have lived in a faded building that once was an icehouse. There is a pleasant yard to move about in, shaded by an apple tree that overhangs the low rail fence. A pig couldn't ask for anything better—or none has, at any rate. The sawdust in the icehouse makes a comfortable bottom in which to root, and a warm bed. This sawdust, however, came under suspicion when the pig took sick. One of my neighbors said he thought the pig would have done better on new ground—the same principle that applies in planting potatoes. He said there might be something unhealthy about that sawdust, that he never thought well of sawdust.

It was about four o'clock in the afternoon when I first noticed that there was something wrong with the pig. He failed to appear at the trough for his supper, and when a pig (or a child) refuses supper a chill wave of fear runs through any household, or ice-household. After examining my pig, who was stretched out in the sawdust inside the building, I went to the phone and cranked it four times. Mr. Dameron answered. "What's good for a sick pig?" I asked. (There is never any identification needed on a country phone; the person on the other end knows who is talking by the sound of the voice and by the character of the question.)

"I don't know, I never had a sick pig," said Mr. Dameron, "but I can find out quick enough. You hang up and I'll call Henry."

Mr. Dameron was back on the line again in five minutes. "Henry says roll him over on his back and give him two ounces of castor oil or sweet oil, and if that doesn't do the trick give him an injection of soapy water. He says he's almost sure the pig's plugged up, and even if he's wrong, it can't do any harm."

I thanked Mr. Dameron. I didn't go right down to the pig, though. I sank into a chair and sat still for a few minutes to think about my troubles, and then I got up and went to the barn, catching up on some odds and ends that needed tending to. Unconsciously I held off, for an hour, the deed by which I would officially recognize the collapse of the performance of raising a pig; I wanted no interruption in the regularity of feeding, the steadiness of growth, the even succession of days. I wanted no interruption, wanted no oil, no deviation. I just wanted to keep on raising a pig, full meal after full meal, spring into summer into fall. I didn't even know whether there were two ounces of castor oil on the place.

Shortly after five o'clock I remembered that we had been invited out to dinner that night and realized that if I were to dose a pig there was no time to lose. The dinner date seemed a familiar conflict: I move in a desultory society and often a week or two will roll by without my going to anybody's house to dinner or anyone's coming to mine, but when an occasion does arise, and I am summoned, something usually turns up (an hour or two in advance) to make all human intercourse seem vastly inappropriate. I have come to believe that there is in hostesses a special power of divination, and that they deliberately arrange dinners to coincide with pig failure or some other sort of failure. At any rate, it was after five o'clock and I knew I could put off no longer the evil hour.

When my son and I arrived at the pigyard, armed with a small bottle of castor oil and a length of clothesline, the pig had emerged from his house and was standing in the middle of his yard, listlessly. He gave us a slim greeting. I could see that he felt uncomfortable and uncertain. I had brought the clothesline thinking I'd have to tie him (the pig weighed more than a hundred pounds) but we never used it. My son reached down, grabbed both front legs, upset him quickly, and when he opened his mouth to scream I turned the oil into his throat—a pink, corrugated area I had never seen before. I had just time to read the label while the neck of the bottle was in his mouth. It said Puretest. The screams, slightly muffled by oil, were pitched in the hysterically high range of pigsound, as though torture were being carried out, but they didn't last long: it was all over rather suddenly, and, his legs released, the pig righted himself.

In the upset position the corners of his mouth had been turned down, giving him a frowning expression. Back on his feet again, he regained the set smile that a pig wears even in sickness. He stood his ground, sucking slightly at the residue of oil; a few drops leaked out of his lips while his wicked eyes, shaded by their coy little lashes, turned on me in disgust and hatred. I scratched him gently with oily fingers and he remained quiet, as though trying to recall the satisfaction of being scratched when in health, and seeming to rehearse in his mind the indignity to which he had just been subjected. I noticed, as I stood there, four or five small dark spots on his back near the tail end, reddish brown in color, each about the size of a housefly. I could not make out what they were. They did not look troublesome but at the same time they did not look like mere surface bruises or chafe marks. Rather they

seemed blemishes of internal origin. His stiff white bristles almost completely hid them and I had to part the bristles with my fingers to get a good look.

Several hours later, a few minutes before midnight, having dined well and at someone else's expense, I returned to the pighouse with a flashlight. The patient was asleep. Kneeling, I felt his ears (as you might put your hand on the forehead of a child) and they seemed cool, and then with the light made a careful examination of the yard and the house for a sign that the oil had worked. I found none and went to bed.

We had been having an unseasonable spell of weather—hot, close days, with the fog shutting in every night, scaling for a few hours in midday, then creeping back again at dark, drifting in first over the trees on the point, then suddenly blowing across the fields, blotting out the world and taking possession of houses, men, and animals. Everyone kept hoping for a break, but the break failed to come. Next day was another hot one. I visited the pig before breakfast and tried to tempt him with a little milk in his trough. He just stared at it, while I made a sucking sound through my teeth to remind him of past pleasures of the feast. With very small, timid pigs, weanlings, this ruse is often quite successful and will encourage them to eat; but with a large, sick pig the ruse is senseless and the sound I made must have made him feel, if anything, more miserable. He not only did not crave food, he felt a positive revulsion to it. I found a place under the apple tree where he had vomited in the night.

At this point, although a depression had settled over me, I didn't suppose that I was going to lose my pig. From the lustiness of a healthy pig a man derives a feeling of personal lustiness; the stuff that goes into the trough and is received with such enthusiasm is an earnest of some later feast of his own, and when this suddenly comes to an end and the food lies stale and untouched, souring in the sun, the pig's imbalance becomes the man's vicariously, and life seems insecure, displaced, transitory.

As my own spirits declined, along with the pig's, the spirits of my vile old dachshund rose. The frequency of our trips down the footpath through the orchard to the pigyard delighted him, although he suffers greatly from arthritis, moves with difficulty, and would be bedridden if he could find anyone willing to serve him meals on a tray.

He never missed a chance to visit the pig with me, and he made many professional calls on his own. You could see him down there at all hours, his white face parting the grass along the fence as he wobbled and stumbled about, his stethoscope dangling—a happy quack, writing his villainous prescriptions and grinning his corrosive grin. When the enema bag appeared, and the bucket of warm suds, his happiness was complete, and he managed to squeeze his enormous body between the two lowest rails of the yard and then assumed full charge of the irrigation. Once, when I lowered the bag to check the flow, he reached in and hurriedly drank a few mouthfuls of the suds to test their potency. I have noticed that Fred will feverishly consume any substance that is associated with trouble—the bitter flavor is to his liking. When the bag was above reach, he concentrated on the pig and was everywhere at once, a tower of strength and inconvenience. The pig, curiously enough, stood rather quietly through this colonic carnival, and the enema, though ineffective, was not as difficult as I had anticipated.

I discovered, though, that once having given a pig an enema there is no turning back, no chance of resuming one of life's more stereotyped roles. The pig's lot and mine were inextricably bound now, as though the rubber tube were the silver cord. From then until the time of his death I held the pig steadily in the bowl of my mind; the task of trying to deliver him from his misery became a strong obsession. His suffering soon became the embodiment of all earthly wretchedness. Along toward the end of the afternoon, defeated in physicking, I phoned the veterinary twenty miles away and placed the case formally in his hands. He was full of questions, and when I casually mentioned the dark spots on the pig's back, his voice changed its tone.

"I don't want to scare you," he said, "but when there are spots, erysipelas has to be considered."

Together we considered erysipelas, with frequent interruptions from the telephone operator, who wasn't sure the connection had been established.

"If a pig has erysipelas can he give it to a person?" I asked.

"Yes, he can," replied the vet.

"Have they answered?" asked the operator.

"Yes, they have," I said. Then I addressed the vet again. "You better come over here and examine this pig right away."

"I can't come myself," said the vet, "but McFarland can come this evening if that's all right. Mac knows more about pigs than I do anyway. You needn't worry too much about the spots. To indicate erysipelas they would have to be deep hemorrhagic infarcts."

"Deep hemorrhagic what?" I asked.

"Infarcts," said the vet.

"Have they answered?" asked the operator.

"Well," I said, "I don't know what you'd call these spots, except they're about the size of a housefly. If the pig has erysipelas I guess I have it, too, by this time, because we've been very close lately."

"McFarland will be over," said the vet.

I hung up. My throat felt dry and I went to the cupboard and got a bottle of whiskey. Deep hemorrhagic infarcts—the phrase began fastening its hooks in my head. I had assumed that there could be nothing much wrong with a pig during the months it was being groomed for murder; my confidence in the essential health and endurance of pigs had been strong and deep, particularly in the health of pigs that belonged to me and that were part of my proud scheme. The awakening had been violent and I minded it all the more because I knew that what could be true of my pig could be true also of the rest of my tidy world. I tried to put this distasteful idea from me, but it kept recurring. I took a short drink of the whiskey and then, although I wanted to go down to the yard and look for fresh signs, I was scared to. I was certain I had erysipelas.

It was long after dark and the supper dishes had been put away when a car drove in and McFarland got out. He had a girl with him. I could just make her out in the darkness—she seemed young and pretty. "this is Miss Owen," he said. "We've been having a picnic supper on the shore, that's why I'm late."

McFarland stood in the driveway and stripped off his jacket, then his shirt. His stocky arms and capable hands showed up in my flashlight's gleam as I helped him find his coverall and get zipped up. The rear seat of his car contained an astonishing amount of paraphernalia, which he soon overhauled, selecting a chain, a syringe, a bottle of oil, a rubber tube, and some other things I couldn't identify. Miss Owen said she'd go along with us and see the pig. I led the way down the warm slope of the orchard, my light picking out the path for them, and we all three climbed the fence, entered the pighouse, and squatted by the pig while McFarland took a rectal reading. My flashlight picked up the glitter of an engagement ring on the girl's hand.

"No elevation," said McFarland, twisting the thermometer in the light. "You needn't

worry about erysipelas." He ran his hand slowly over the pig's stomach and at one point the pig cried out in pain.

"Poor piggledy-wiggledy!" said Miss Owen.

The treatment I had been giving the pig for two days was then repeated, somewhat more expertly, by the doctor, Miss Owen and I handing him things as he needed them—holding the chain that he had looped around the pig's upper jaw, holding the syringe, holding the bottle stopper, the end of the tube, all of us working in darkness and in comfort, working with the instinctive teamwork induced by emergency conditions, the pig unprotesting, the house shadowy, protecting, intimate. I went to bed tired but with a feeling of relief that I had turned over part of the responsibility of the case to a licensed doctor. I was beginning to think, though, that the pig was not going to live.

He died twenty-four hours later, or it might have been forty-eight—there is a blur in time here, and I may have lost or picked up a day in the telling and the pig one in the dying. At intervals during the last day I took cool fresh water down to him and at such times as he found the strength to get to his feet he would stand with head in the pail and snuffle his snout around. He drank a few sips but no more; yet it seemed to comfort him to dip his nose in water and bobble it about, sucking in and blowing out through his teeth. Much of the time, now, he lay indoors half buried in sawdust. Once, near the last, while I was attending him I saw him try to make a bed for himself but he lacked the strength, and when he set his snout into the dust he was unable to plow even the little furrow he needed to lie down in.

He came out of the house to die. When I went down, before going to bed, he lay stretched in the yard a few feet from the door. I knelt, saw that he was dead, and left him there: his face had a mild look, expressive neither of deep peace nor of deep suffering, although I think he had suffered a good deal. I went back up to the house and to bed, and cried internally—deep hemorrhagic intears. I didn't wake till nearly eight the next morning, and when I looked out the open window the grave was already being dug, down beyond the dump under a wild apple. I could hear the spade strike against the small rocks that blocked the way. Never send to know for whom the grave is dug, I said to myself, it's dug for thee. Fred, I well knew, was supervising the work of digging, so I ate breakfast slowly.

It was a Saturday morning. The thicket in which I found the gravediggers at work was dark and warm, the sky overcast. Here, among alders and young hackmatacks, at the foot of the apple tree, Lennie had dug a beautiful hole, five feet long, three feet wide, three feet deep. He was standing in it, removing the last spadefuls of earth while Fred patrolled the brink in simple but impressive circles, disturbing the loose earth of the mound so that it trickled back in. There had been no rain in weeks and the soil, even three feet down, was dry and powdery. As I stood and stared, an enormous earthworm which had been partially exposed by the spade at the bottom dug itself deeper and made a slow withdrawal, seeking even remoter moistures at even lonelier depths. And just as Lennie stepped out and rested his spade against the tree and lit a cigarette, a small green apple separated itself from a branch overhead and fell into the hole. Everything about this last scene seemed overwritten—the dismal sky, the shabby woods, the imminence of rain, the worm (legendary bedfellow of the dead), the apple (conventional garnish of a pig).

But even so, there was a directness and dispatch about animal burial, I thought, that made it a more decent affair than human burial: there was no stopover in the undertaker's foul parlor, no wreath nor spray; and when we hitched a line to the pig's hind legs and dragged him swiftly from his yard, throwing our weight into the harness and leaving a wake of crushed grass and smoothed rubble over the dump, ours was a businesslike procession, with Fred, the dishonorable pallbearer, staggering along in the rear, his perverse bereavement showing in every seam in his face; and the post mortem performed handily and swiftly right at the edge of the grave, so that the innards that had caused the pig's death preceded him into the ground and he lay at last resting squarely on the cause of his own undoing.

I threw in the first shovelful, and then we worked rapidly and without talk, until the job was complete. I picked up the rope, made it fast to Fred's collar (he is a notorious ghoul), and we all three filed back up the path to the house, Fred bringing up the rear and holding back every inch of the way, feigning unusual stiffness. I noticed that although he weighed far less than the pig, he was harder to drag, being possessed of the vital spark.

The news of the death of my pig traveled fast and far, and I received many expressions of sympathy from friends and neighbors, for no one took the event lightly and the premature expiration of a pig is, I soon discovered, a departure which the community marks solemnly on its calendar, a sorrow in which it feels fully involved. I have written this account in penitence and in grief, as a man who failed to raise his pig, and to explain my deviation from the classic course of so many raised pigs. The grave in the woods is unmarked, but Fred can direct the mourner to it unerringly and with immense good will, and I know he and I shall often revisit it, singly and together, in seasons of reflection and despair, on flagless memorial days of our own choosing.

[1948]

ALICE WALKER

(1944–)

In Search of Our Mothers' Gardens

About the Author: Walker, who won the Pulitzer Prize in 1983 for her novel *The Color Purple,* is also an accomplished poet and essayist. Her voice speaks of black pride, of individualism, and of revolution, but is always tempered by the compassion and understanding we hear in the essay "In Search of Our Mothers' Gardens."

> I described her own nature and temperament. Told how they needed a larger life for their expression. . . . I pointed out that in lieu of proper channels, her emotions had overflowed into paths that dissipated them. I talked, beautifully I thought, about an art that would be born, an art that would open the way for women the likes of her. I asked her to hope, and build up an inner life against the coming of that day. I sang, with a strange quiver in my voice, a promise song.
>
> —*Jean Toomer, "Avey,"* CANE

The poet speaking to a prostitute who falls asleep while he's talking—

When the poet Jean Toomer walked through the South in the early twenties, he discovered a curious thing: black women whose spirituality was so intense, so deep, so *unconscious,* that

they were themselves unaware of the richness they held. They stumbled blindly through their lives: creatures so abused and mutilated in body, so dimmed and confused by pain, that they considered themselves unworthy even of hope. In the selfless abstractions their bodies became to the men who used them, they became more than "sexual objects," more even than mere women: they became "Saints." Instead of being perceived as whole persons, their bodies became shrines: what was thought to be their minds became temples suitable for worship. These crazy Saints stared out at the world, wildly, like lunatics—or quietly, like suicides; and the "God" that was in their gaze was as mute as a great stone.

Who were these Saints? These crazy, loony, pitiful women?

Some of them, without a doubt, were our mothers and grandmothers.

In the still heat of the post-Reconstruction South, this is how they seemed to Jean Toomer: exquisite butterflies trapped in an evil honey, toiling away their lives in an era, a century, that did not acknowledge them, except as "the *mule* of the world." They dreamed dreams that no one knew—not even themselves, in any coherent fashion—and saw visions no one could understand. They wandered or sat about the countryside crooning lullabies to ghosts, and drawing the mother of Christ in charcoal on courthouse walls.

They forced their minds to desert their bodies and their striving spirits sought to rise, like frail whirlwinds from the hard red clay. And when those frail whirlwinds fell, in scattered particles, upon the ground, no one mourned. Instead, men lit candles to celebrate the emptiness that remained, as people do who enter a beautiful but vacant space to resurrect a God.

Our mothers and grandmothers, some of them: moving to music not yet written. And they waited.

They waited for a day when the unknown thing that was in them would be made known; but guessed, somehow in their darkness, that on the day of their revelation they would be long dead. Therefore to Toomer they walked, and even ran, in slow motion. For they were going nowhere immediate, and the future was not yet within their grasp. And men took our mothers and grandmothers, "but got no pleasure from it." So complex was their passion and their calm.

To Toomer, they lay vacant and fallow as autumn fields, with harvest time never in sight: and he saw them enter loveless marriages, without joy; and become prostitutes, without resistance; and become mothers of children, without fulfillment.

For these grandmothers and mothers of ours were not Saints, but Artists; driven to a numb and bleeding madness by the springs of creativity in them for which there was no release. They were Creators, who lived lives of spiritual waste, because they were so rich in spirituality—which is the basis of Art—that the strain of enduring their unused and unwanted talent drove them insane. Throwing away this spirituality was their pathetic attempt to lighten the soul to a weight their work-worn, sexually abused bodies could bear.

What did it mean for a black woman to be an artist in our grandmothers' time? In our great-grandmothers' day? It is a question with an answer cruel enough to stop the blood.

Did you have a genius of a great-great-grandmother who died under some ignorant and depraved white overseer's lash? Or was she required to bake biscuits for a lazy backwater tramp, when she cried out in her soul to paint watercolors of sunsets, or the rain falling on the green and peaceful pasturelands? Or was her body broken and forced to bear children (who were more often than not sold away from her)—eight, ten, fifteen, twenty children—when her one joy was the thought of modeling heroic figures of rebellion, in stone or clay?

How was the creativity of the black woman kept alive, year after year and century after century, when for most of the years black people have been in America, it was a punishable crime for a black person to read or write? And the freedom to paint, to sculpt, to expand the mind with action did not exist. Consider, if you can bear to imagine it, what might have been the result if singing, too, had been forbidden by law. Listen to the voices of Bessie Smith, Billie Holiday, Nina Simone, Roberta Flack, and Aretha Franklin, among others, and imagine those voices muzzled for life. Then you may begin to comprehend the lives of our "crazy," "Sainted" mothers and grandmothers. The agony of the lives of women who might have been Poets, Novelists, Essayists, and Short-Story Writers (over a period of centuries), who died with their real gifts stifled within them.

And, if this were the end of the story, we would have cause to cry out in my paraphrase of Okot p'Bitek's great poem:

O, my clanswomen
Let us all cry together!
Come,
Let us mourn the death of our mother,
The death of a Queen
The ash that was produced
By a great fire!
O, this homestead is utterly dead
Close the gates
With *lacari* thorns,
For our mother
The creator of the Stool is lost!
And all the young women
Have perished in the wilderness!

But this is not the end of the story, for all the young women—our mothers and grandmothers, *ourselves*—have not perished in the wilderness. And if we ask ourselves why, and search for and find the answer, we will know beyond all efforts to erase it from our minds, just exactly who, and of what, we black American women are.

One example, perhaps the most pathetic, most misunderstood one, can provide a backdrop for our mothers' work: Phillis Wheatley, a slave in the 1700s.

Virginia Woolf, in her book *A Room of One's Own,* wrote that in order for a woman to write fiction she must have two things, certainly: a room of her own (with key and lock) and enough money to support herself.

What then are we to make of Phillis Wheatley, a slave, who owned not even herself? This sickly, frail black girl who required a servant of her own at times—her health was so precarious—and who, had she been white, would have been easily considered the intellectual superior of all the women and most of the men in the society of her day.

Virginia Woolf wrote further, speaking of course not of our Phillis, that "any woman born with a great gift in the sixteenth century [insert "eighteenth century," insert "black woman," insert "born or made a slave"] would certainly have gone crazed, shot herself, or ended her days in some lonely cottage outside the village, half witch, half wizard [insert "Saint"], feared and mocked at. For it needs little skill and psychology to be sure that a highly gifted girl who had tried to use her gift for poetry would have been so thwarted and

hindered by contrary instincts [add "chains, guns, the lash, the ownership of one's body by someone else, submission to an alien religion"], that she must have lost her health and sanity to a certainty."

The key words, as they relate to Phillis, are "contrary instincts." For when we read the poetry of Phillis Wheatley—as when we read the novels of Nella Larsen or the oddly false-sounding autobiography of that freest of all black women writers, Zora Hurston—evidence of "contrary instincts" is everywhere. Her loyalties were completely divided, as was, without question, her mind.

But how could this be otherwise? Captured at seven, a slave of wealthy, doting whites who instilled in her the "savagery" of the Africa they "rescued" her from . . . one wonders if she was even able to remember her homeland as she had known it, or as it really was.

Yet, because she did try to use her gift for poetry in a world that made her a slave, she was "so thwarted and hindered by . . . contrary instincts, that she . . . lost her health. . . ." In the last years of her brief life, burdened not only with the need to express her gift but also with a penniless, friendless "freedom" and several small children for whom she was forced to do strenuous work to feed, she lost her health, certainly. Suffering from malnutrition and neglect and who knows what mental agonies, Phillis Wheatley died.

So torn by "contrary instincts" was black, kidnapped, enslaved Phillis that her description of "the Goddess"—as she poetically called the Liberty she did not have—is ironically, cruelly humorous. And, in fact, has held Phillis up to ridicule for more than a century. It is usually read prior to hanging Phillis's memory as that of a fool. She wrote:

> The Goddess comes, she moves divinely fair,
> Olive and laurel binds her *golden* hair.
> Wherever shines this native of the skies,
> Unnumber'd charms and recent graces rise. [My italics]

It is obvious that Phillis, the slave, combed the "Goddess's" hair every morning; prior, perhaps, to bringing in the milk, or fixing her mistress's lunch. She took her imagery from the one thing she saw elevated above all others.

With the benefit of hindsight we ask, "How could she?"

But at last, Phillis, we understand. No more snickering when your stiff, struggling, ambivalent lines are forced on us. We know now that you were not an idiot or a traitor; only a sickly little black girl, snatched from your home and country and made a slave; a woman who still struggled to sing the song that was your gift, although in a land of barbarians who praised you for your bewildered tongue. It is not so much what you sang, as that you kept alive, in so many of our ancestors, *the notion of song.*

Black women are called, in the folklore that so aptly identifies one's status in society, "the *mule* of the world," because we have been handed the burdens that everyone else—*everyone* else—refused to carry. We have also been called "Matriarchs," "Superwomen," and "Mean and Evil Bitches." Not to mention "Castraters" and "Sapphire's Mama." When we have pleaded for understanding, our character has been distorted; when we have asked for simple caring, we have been handed empty inspirational appellations, then stuck in the farthest corner. When we have asked for love, we have been given children. In short, even our plainer gifts, our labors of fidelity and love, have been knocked down our throats. To be an artist and a black woman, even today, lowers our status in many respects, rather than raises it: and yet, artists we will be.

Therefore we must fearlessly pull out of ourselves and look at and identify with our lives the living creativity some of our great-grandmothers were not allowed to know. I stress *some* of them because it is well known that the majority of our great-grandmothers knew, even without "knowing" it, the reality of their spirituality, even if they didn't recognize it beyond what happened in the singing at church—and they never had any intention of giving it up.

How they did it—those millions of black women who were not Phillis Wheatley, or Lucy Terry or Frances Harper or Zora Hurston or Nella Larsen or Bessie Smith; or Elizabeth Catlett, or Katherine Dunham, either—brings me to the title of this essay, "In Search of Our Mothers' Gardens," which is a personal account that is yet shared, in its theme and its meaning, by all of us. I found, while thinking about the far-reaching world of the creative black woman, that often the truest answer to a question that really matters can be found very close.

In the late 1920s my mother ran away from home to marry my father. Marriage, if not running away, was expected of seventeen-year-old girls. By the time she was twenty, she had two children and was pregnant with a third. Five children later, I was born. And this is how I came to know my mother: she seemed a large, soft, loving-eyed woman who was rarely impatient in our home. Her quick, violent temper was on view only a few times a year, when she battled with the white landlord who had the misfortune to suggest to her that her children did not need to go to school.

She made all the clothes we wore, even my brothers' overalls. She made all the towels and sheets we used. She spent the summers canning vegetables and fruits. She spent the winter evenings making quilts enough to cover all our beds.

During the "working" day, she labored beside—not behind—my father in the fields. Her day began before sunup, and did not end until late at night. There was never a moment for her to sit down, undisturbed, to unravel her own private thoughts; never a time free from interruption—by work or the noisy inquiries of her many children. And yet, it is to my mother—and all our mothers who were not famous—that I went in search of the secret of what has fed that muzzled and often mutilated, but vibrant, creative spirit that the black woman has inherited, and that pops out in wild and unlikely places to this day.

But when, you will ask, did my overworked mother have time to know or care about feeding the creative spirit?

The answer is so simple that many of us have spent years discovering it. We have constantly looked high, when we should have looked high—and low.

For example: in the Smithsonian Institution in Washington, D.C., there hangs a quilt unlike any other in the world. In fanciful, inspired, and yet simple and identifiable figures, it portrays the story of the Crucifixion. It is considered rare, beyond price. Though it follows no known pattern of quilt-making, and though it is made of bits and pieces of worthless rags, it is obviously the work of a person of powerful imagination and deep spiritual feeling. Below this quilt I saw a note that says it was made by "an anonymous Black woman in Alabama, a hundred years ago."

If we could locate this "anonymous" black woman from Alabama, she would turn out to be one of our grandmothers—an artist who left her mark in the only materials she could afford, and in the only medium her position in society allowed her to use.

As Virginia Woolf wrote further, in *A Room of One's Own:*

> Yet genius of a sort must have existed among women as it must have existed among the working class. [Change this to "slaves" and "the wives and daughters of sharecroppers."] Now and again an Emily Brontë or a Robert Burns [change this to "a Zora Hurston or a Richard Wright"] blazes out and proves its presence. But certainly it never got itself on to paper. When, however, one reads of a witch being ducked, of a woman possessed by devils [or "Sainthood"], of a wise woman selling herbs [our root workers], or even a very remarkable man who had a mother, then I think we are on the track of a lost novelist, a suppressed poet, of some mute and inglorious Jane Austen. . . . Indeed, I would venture to guess that Anon, who wrote so many poems without signing them, was often a woman. . . .

And so our mothers and grandmothers have, more often than not anonymously, handed on the creative spark, the seed of the flower they themselves never hoped to see: or like a sealed letter they could not plainly read.

And so it is, certainly, with my own mother. Unlike "Ma" Rainey's songs, which retained their creator's name even while blasting forth from Bessie Smith's mouth, no song or poem will bear my mother's name. Yet so many of the stories that I write, that we all write, are my mother's stories. Only recently did I fully realize this: that through years of listening to my mother's stories of her life, I have absorbed not only the stories themselves, but something of the manner in which she spoke, something of the urgency that involves the knowledge that her stories—like her life—must be recorded. It is probably for this reason that so much of what I have written is about characters whose counterparts in real life are so much older than I am.

But the telling of these stories, which came from my mother's lips as naturally as breathing, was not the only way my mother showed herself as an artist. For stories, too, were subject to being distracted, to dying without conclusion. Dinners must be started, and cotton must be gathered before the big rains. The artist that was and is my mother showed itself to me only after many years. This is what I finally noticed:

Like Mem, a character in *The Third Life of Grange Copeland,* my mother adorned with flowers whatever shabby house we were forced to live in. And not just your typical straggly country stand of zinnias, either. She planted ambitious gardens—and still does—with over fifty different varieties of plants that bloom profusely from early March until late November. Before she left home for the fields, she watered her flowers, chopped up the grass, and laid out new beds. When she returned from the fields she might divide clumps of bulbs, dig a cold pit, uproot and replant roses, or prune branches from her taller bushes or trees—until night came and it was too dark to see.

Whatever she planted grew as if by magic, and her fame as a grower of flowers spread over three counties. Because of her creativity with her flowers, even my memories of poverty are seen through a screen of blooms—sunflowers, petunias, roses, dahlias, forsythia, spirea, delphiniums, verbena . . . and on and on.

And I remember people coming to my mother's yard to be given cuttings from her flowers; I hear again the praise showered on her because whatever rocky soil she landed on, she turned into a garden. A garden so brilliant with colors, so original in its design, so magnificent with life and creativity, that to this day people drive by our house in Georgia—perfect strangers and imperfect strangers—and ask to stand or walk among my mother's art.

I notice that it is only when my mother is working in her flowers that she is radiant, almost to the point of being invisible—except as Creator: hand and eye. She is involved in work her soul must have. Ordering the universe in the image of her personal conception of Beauty.

Her face, as she prepares the Art that is her gift, is a legacy of respect she leaves to me, for all that illuminates and cherishes life. She has handed down respect for the possibilities—and the will to grasp them.

For her, so hindered and intruded upon in so many ways, being an artist has still been a daily part of her life. This ability to hold on, even in very simple ways, is work black women have done for a very long time.

This poem is not enough, but it is something, for the woman who literally covered the holes in our walls with sunflowers:

They were women then
My mama's generation
Husky of voice—Stout of
Step
With fists as well as
Hands
How they battered down
Doors
And ironed
Starched white
Shirts
How they led
Armies
Headragged Generals
Across mined
Fields
Booby-trapped
Kitchens
To discover books
Desks
A place for us
How they knew what we
Must know
Without knowing a page
Of it
Themselves.

Guided by my heritage of a love of beauty and a respect for strength—in search of my mother's garden, I found my own.

And perhaps in Africa over two hundred years ago, there was just such a mother; perhaps she painted vivid and daring decorations in oranges and yellows and greens on the walls of her hut; perhaps she sang—in a voice like Roberta Flack's—*sweetly* over the compounds of her village; perhaps she wove the most stunning mats or told the most ingenious stories of all the village storytellers. Perhaps she was herself a poet—though only her daughter's name is signed to the poems that we know.

Perhaps Phillis Wheatley's mother was also an artist.

Perhaps in more than Phillis Wheatley's biological life is her mother's signature made clear.

[1974]

CAROL BLY

(1930–)

Growing Up Expressive

About the Author: Bly writes fiction and poetry, as well as essays, often focusing on the plight of rural Americans. In "Growing Up Expressive," Bly's voice seeks not simply to describe what it sees as problems in American education, but to bring about change.

Love, death, the cruelty of power, and time's curve past the stars are what children want to look at. For convenience's sake, let's say these are the four most vitally touching things in life. Little children ask questions about them with relish. Children, provided they are still little enough, have no eye to doing any problem solving about love or death or injustice or the universe; they are simply interested. I've noticed that as we read aloud literature to them, about Baba Yaga, and Dr. Doolittle, and Ivan and the Firebird, and Rat and Mole, children are not only interested, they are prepared to be vitally touched by the great things of life. If you like the phrase, they are what some people call "being as a little child." Another way of looking at it is to say that in our minds we have two kinds of receptivity to life going on all the time: first, being vitally touched and enthusiastic (grateful, enraged, puzzled—but, at all events, *moved*) and, second, having a will to solve problems.

Our gritty society wants and therefore deliberately trains problem solvers, however, not mystics. We teach human beings to keep themselves conscious only of problems that *can* conceivably be solved. There must be no hopeless causes. Now this means that some subjects, of which death and sexual love come to mind straight off, should be kept at as low a level of consciousness as possible. Both resist problem solving. A single-minded problem solver focuses his consciousness, of course, on problems to be solved, but even he realizes there is a concentric, peripheral band of other material around the problems. This band appears to him as "issues." He is not interested in these issues for themselves; he sees them simply as impacting on the problems. He will allow us to talk of love, death, injustice, and eternity—he may even encourage us to do so because his group-dynamics training advises him to let us have our say, thus dissipating our willfulness—but his heart is circling, circling, looking for an opening to *wrap up* these "issues" so he can return attention to discrete, solvable problems. For example, a physician who has that mentality does not wish to be near dying patients very much. They are definitely not a solvable problem. If he is wicked, he will regard them as a present issue with impact on a future problem: then he will order experimentation done on them during their last weeks with us. It means his ethic is toward the healing process only, but not toward the dying person. His ethic is toward problem solving, not toward wonder. He will feel quite conscientious while doing the experiments on the dying patient, because he feels he is saving lives of future patients.

To return to little children for a second: they simply like to contemplate life and death. So our difficulty, in trying to educate adults so they will be balanced but enthusiastic, is to keep both streams going—the problem solving, which seems to be the mental genius of our species, and the fearless contemplation of gigantic things, the spiritual genius of our species.

The problem-solving mentality is inculcated no less in art and English classes than in mathematics and science. Its snake oil is hope of success: by setting very small topics in front of people, for which it is easy for them to see the goals, the problems, the solutions, their egos are not threatened. They feel hopeful of being effective. Therefore, to raise a generation of problem solvers, you encourage them to visit the county offices (as our sixth-grade teachers do) and you lead them to understand that this is citizenship. You carefully do not suggest that citizenship also means comparatively complex and hopeless activities like Amnesty International's pressure to get prisoners in far places released or at least no longer tortured. Small egos are threatened by huge, perhaps insoluble problems. Therefore, one feeds the small ego confidence by setting before it dozens and dozens of very simple situations. The ego is nourished by feeling it understands the relationship between the county recorder's office and the county treasurer's office; in later life, when young people find a couple of sticky places in county government, they will confidently work at smoothing them. How very different an experience such problem solving is from having put before one the spectacle of the United States' various stances and activities with respect to germ warfare. Educators regularly steer off all interest in national and international government to one side, constantly feeding our rural young people on questions to which one can hope for answers on a short timeline. We do not ask them to exercise that muscle which bears the weight of vast considerations—such as cruelty in large governments. By the time the average rural Minnesotan is eighteen, he or she expects to stay in cheerful places, devote some time to local government and civic work, and "win the little ones." Rural young people have a repertoire of pejorative language for hard causes: "opening that keg of worms," "no end to that once you get into it," "don't worry—you can't do anything about that from where you are," "we could go on about that forever!" They are right, of course: we could, and our species, at its most cultivated, does go on forever about love, death, power, time, the universe. But some of us, alas, have been conditioned by eighteen fashionably to despise those subjects because there are no immediate answers to all the questions they ask us.

The other way we negatively reinforce any philosophical bent in children is to pretend we don't see the content in their artwork. We comment only on the technique, in somewhat the same way you can scarcely get a comment on rural preachers' sermon content: the response is always, He does a good (or bad) job of speaking. "Well, but what did he say?" "Oh, he talked really well. The man can preach!"

The way to devalue the content of a child's painting is to say, "Wow, you sure can paint!" The average art teacher in Minnesota is at pains to find something to say to the third grader's painting of a space machine with complicated, presumably electronic equipment in it. Here is the drawing in words: A man is sitting at some controls. Outside his capsule, fire is flying from emission points on his ship toward another spaceship at right, hitting it. Explosions are coming out of its side and tail. What is an art teacher to do with this? Goodness knows. So he or she says, "My goodness, I can see there's a lot of action there!" It is said in a deliberately encouraging way but anyone can hear under the carefully supportive comment: "A lot of work going into nothing but more TV-inspired violence." One might as well have told the child, "Thank you for sharing."

I once attended a regional writers' group at which a young poet wrote about his feelings of being a single parent and trying to keep his sanity as he cared for his children. In his poem, he raced up the staircase, grabbed a gun, and shot the clock. When he finished reading it aloud to us, someone told him, "I certainly am glad you shared with us. I'd like to really thank you for sharing."

If we are truly serious about life we are going to have to stop thanking people for sharing. It isn't enough response to whatever has been offered. It is half ingenuous, and sometimes it is insincere, and often it is patronizing. It is the *dictum excrementi* of our decade.

I would like to keep in mind for a moment the art works described above: the child's painting of a spaceship assaulting another spaceship, and the harrowed father's racing up the staircase and shooting the clock. Here is a third. It is a twelve-year-old's theme for English class.

> They were their four days and nights before anyone found them. It was wet and cold down there. As little kids at the orphanage, they had been beaten every night until they could scarcely make it to bed. Now they were older. Duane and Ellen leaned together. "I love you forever," she told him. He asked her, "Even though my face is marked from getting scarlett fever and polio and small pox and newmonya and they wouldn't take decent care of me, not call the doctor or anything, so the marks will always be on me?" "You know I love you," Ellen told him. "You know that time they tortured me for information and I was there but I didn't talk and later I found out it was your uncle who did it. I didn't talk because I remembered the American flag." Just then they heard someone shout, "Anyone alive down there in this mess?" You see a bomb had gone off destroying a entire U.S.A. city where they lived. Duane had lived with his cruel uncle who took him out of the orphanage to get cheap labor and Ellen lived at a boardinghouse where there were rats that ate pages of her diary all the time. Now they both looked up and shouted "We're here!" A head appeared at the top of the well into which they had fallen or they would of been in 6,500 pieces like all the other men and ladies even pregnant ones and little kids in that town. Now this head called down, "Oh—a boy and a girl!" then the head explained it was going for a ladder and ropes and it ducked away and where it had been they saw the beginnings of stars for that night, the stars still milky in front of the bright blue because the sky wasn't dark enough yet to show them up good.

The English teacher will typically comment on this story by observing that the spelling is uneven, and adjectives get used as adverbs. In rural Minnesota (if not elsewhere) an English teacher can spend every class hour on adjectives used as adverbs: it is meat and potatoes to a nag. But when we discuss spelling, syntax, and adverbs, we are talking method, not content. The child notices that nothing is said of the story's *plot.* No one remarks on the *feelings* in it. Now if this happens every time a child hands in fiction or a poem, the child will realize by the time he reaches twelfth grade that meaning or feelings are not worth anything, that "mechanics" (note the term) are all that matter.

It is rare for a public school English teacher to comment on a child's content unless the material is *factual.* Minnesota teachers encourage writing booklets about the state, themes on ecology and county government, on how Dad strikes the field each autumn, on how Mom avoids open-kettle canning because the USDA advises against it. In this way, our children are conditioned to regard writing as problem solving instead of contemplation, as routine thinking instead of imaginative inquiry.

How can we manage it otherwise?

I would like to suggest some questions we can ask children about their artwork which will encourage them to grow up into lovers, lobby supporters, and Amnesty International members, instead of only township officers and annual protestors against daylight saving time. Let us gather all the elements of the three artworks presented in this Letter: the little boy's spaceship-war painting, the young divorced father's narrative poem, and the twelve-year-old girl's story of love in a well. We have a set of images before us, then:

Man directing spaceship fire
Another aircraft being obliterated

Staircase, man shooting a clock; children
Cruel orphanage
Torture
Last survivors of a decimated city

Let us, instead of lending the great sneer to these images, be respectful of them. It may help to pretend the painting is by Picasso, that Flaubert wrote the father/clock scene, and that Tolstoy wrote the well story. It helps to remember that Picasso felt the assault of historical events on us—like Guernica; Flaubert, as skillfully as Dostoyevsky and with less self-pity, was an observer of violent detail; and the Tolstoy who wrote *Resurrection* or the scene of Pierre's imprisonment in *War and Peace* would turn to the well/love story without qualm.

We know we would never say to Picasso, Flaubert, or Tolstoy, "Why don't you draw something you know about from everyday life? Why don't you write about something you know about? You say Anna was smashed beneath a train? Thank you for sharing!"

The fact is that a child's feelings about orphanages and torture and love are things that he does know about. They are psychic realities inside him, and when he draws them, he is drawing something from everyday life. Sometimes they are from his night life of dreaming, but in any event they are images of passion and he is drawing from his genuine if garbled experience. A few years ago there was a stupid movement to discourage children's reading of Grimms' fairy tales. Later, with a more sophisticated psychology, we learned that the stepmother who is hostile and overweening is a reality to all children; the cutting-off of the hero's right hand and replacing of it with a hand of silver is a reality to all children. Spaceships, witches' gingerbread houses, orphanages, being the last two people to survive on earth—all these are part of the inner landscape, something children know about. Therefore, in examining their artwork, we need better sets of questions to ask them. Young people who are not repressed are going to lay their wild stuff in front of adults (hoping for comment of some kind, praise if possible) until the sands of life are run, so we had better try to be good at responding to them. And unless we want to raise drones suitable only for conveyor-belt shifts, we had better be at least half as enthusiastic as when they tell us, Mama, I got the mowing finished.

Here are some questions to ask our young artist. How much of that electronic equipment is used for firepower and how much just to run the ship? After the other spaceship is blown up and the people in it are dead, what will this man do? Will he go home somewhere? Were the stars out that night? You said he'll go home to his parents. Did the other man have parents? How soon will that man's parents find out that his spaceship was destroyed? Could you draw in the stars? You said they were out—could you draw them into the picture some way? but don't ruin anything you've got in there now. Also, that wire you said ran to the solar plates, will you darken it so it shows better? Don't change it—just make it clearer. Yes—terrific! Can you see the planet where the other man would have returned to if he had lived till morning?

The young father's story: There is an obvious psychic complication to this story: the violence in his shooting out the clock face is gratuitous, and the plea for attention on the part of the author directed at the reader is glaring: clock faces as psychological symbols are in the public domain. Anyone who tells a friend (or a group of strangers) I am going to shoot up a clock face at 11 P.M. is asking for psychological attention. In a civil world, to ask is to receive, so if we are civilized we have to pay attention and ask the young author: Why does

the father in the story blast the clock? And, when he replies, we have to ask some more. If there was ever an instance in which it was O.K. to say, "Thanks for sharing," this is not it.

I should like to add that this will be especially difficult for rural teachers because the traditional country way to treat any kind of mental problem is to stare it down. It didn't happen. I didn't hear that insane thing you just said, and you know you don't really hate your mother. What nice parent would shoot a clock? We uniformly do what Dr. Vaillant in *Adaptations to Life* would call a denial adaptation. It takes a brave questioner when the young person brings in a crazy story.

The well/love story: Did you know there really are such orphanages? There are orphanages where the children have to get up at four-thirty to work in the dairy, and the girls work hours and hours in the kitchens, and the children's growth is stunted. Did you make the girl so brave on purpose? Were they a lucky couple or an unlucky couple, or is that the sort of a question you can't ask? You made a point of telling us they'd been through a lot of hardship. What would it have been like for them if they hadn't? Do you want to talk about what blew up the city? Did you imagine yourself in the well?

Those are not brilliant questions; they are simply respectful, because the art works described are concerned with death by violence; cruelty by institutions; treachery by relations; bravery (or cowardice—either one is important); sexual love, either despite or encouraged by dreadful circumstances.

They are some of the subjects in *War and Peace,* in Dürer's etchings, paintings, and woodcuts, and in *Madame Bovary.*

It is a moot question in my mind which of two disciplines will be the more useful in helping people stay vitally touched by the Great Things: psychology might do it—and English literature in high school might do it (instruction on the college level is generally so dutiful to methodology that it seems a lost cause to me. "How did D. H. Lawrence foreshadow this event?" and "What metaphors does Harold Rosenberg use in his discussion of Action Painting?" are the questions of technocrats, not preservers of spirit. It is as if we got home from church and the others said, "How was church?" "We had Eucharist," we tell them. "Well, how was it?" they ask. "Pretty good," we reply. "Bishop Anderson was there. He held the chalice eight inches above the rail so no one spilled, then he turned and wiped the chalice after each use so no germs were passed along. People who had already communed returned to their benches using the north aisle so there was no bottlenecking at the chancel.")

I don't think churches will be helpful in preserving the mystical outlook as long as they see life and death as a *problem*—a problem of salvation—with a solution to be worked at. Churches have an axe to grind. They might take the father running up the staircase to be an impact subject: they would wish to use their program to solve his problem. Churchmen often appear to be companionable counselors, but the appearance is largely manner and habit. Under the manner, the clergyman's mindset is nearly always to see a disturbed or grieving person's imagery as *the issues.* From there, he swings into psychological problem solving.

I would like to commend this responsibility to our English teachers: that they help our children preserve pity, happiness, and grief inside themselves. They can enhance those feelings by having young children both write and draw pictures. They can be very enthusiastic about the children's first drawings of death in the sky. Adults, particularly mature ones who have *not* got children in school at the moment, should make it clear that we expect this of English teachers and that we don't give a damn if LeRoy and Merv never in their lives get the sentence balance of past conditional and perfect subjunctive clauses right. We need to protect some of the Things Invisible inside Leroy and Merv and the rest of us.

This is my last Letter from the Country. That is why it is so shrill. Gadflies are always looking out a chance to be shrill anyway, so I jumped to this one and have shouted my favorite hope: that we can educate children not to be problem solvers but to be madly expressive all their lives.

[1979]

BARRY NEWMAN

Fisherman

About the Author: A roving foreign correspondent for the *Wall Street Journal,* Newman has also found ways to pursue his interest in what the essay yields even under journalistic constraints. Such needs may help explain his sensitivity for cultural subtleties as he gives voice to the experiences of others.

Leigh, England—Kevin Ashurst's maggot farm—a cinder block shed attached to an air scrubber—is a mile outside this old mill town, in a field of pink wildflowers.

"Looking for work?" a tatooed man calls when a visitor drives up on a hot morning. In the yard, some dead sheep nourish a new generation of bluebottle flies. Two workers, bent over the carcasses, scoop the maggots into plastic tubs. The smell is about as bad as a smell can get.

Ashurst, a meaty man of 43, wipes his hand on his dungarees to clean off the offal, and extends the same hand in greeting. Then he reaches into a tub and brings up a sample of his finest produce—moist, white and writhing.

"See, that's the size of 'em, like," he says. "Them's good maggots, quality maggots. They'll keep like this for a week in the 'fridge."

Who keeps maggots in the 'fridge? Coarse fishermen do. Kevin Ashurst sells maggots to coarse fishermen. He's a coarse fisherman himself, and a good one. Coarse fishermen bait their hooks with maggots to catch coarse fish—like barble, dace, bleak and roach. Coarse fish live in murky waters, are mostly tiny and make awful eating. Game fishermen, who catch salmon and trout, think of them as vermin. Some think the same of coarse fishermen.

Until about ten years ago, British upper-class fishermen succeeded in keeping the upper-class fish to themselves. The working class had to fish in abandoned gravel pits and industrial canals. The sport wasn't refined, but it was diverting enough, once money got involved.

Fishermen pay to line up on a bank and vie for the weightiest total catch. The winner throws back his fish and takes home the kitty. The basic strategy hasn't changed much since the first competition in 1903: Catch tiddlers. Tiddlers add up, ounce by ounce. This technique requires a hook the size of a mosquito's leg, a line as fine as a spider's web—and a rod that ought to be about thirty-six-feet long.

Coarse fishing is big in Britain, bigger than snooker. Almost four million people do it,

and many others watch. Fishing matches get on television here, though fishing doesn't come across on the screen quite as well as darts does. Coarse fishing is big on the Continent, too, and in the Eastern Bloc. The world championship is held every year. Some have pulled in crowds of twenty thousand.

Last year's event took place on the Newry Canal in Northern Ireland. The winner was Kevin Ashurst, the maggot farmer from Leigh. In five hours of intensive fishing, he caught thirteen roach and one small bream, amassing the lowest winning weight on record: one pound, ten ounces.

"It came right for me," he told the announcer on national television. "It didn't come right for the other lads."

Ashurst quits work early this day and goes off to dig for gnat larvae, a variety of bait known around here as bloodworm. There's an evening match on the Bridgewater Canal. He has to prepare. Meanwhile, his wife serves tea to a visitor in their home on one of Leigh's back lanes, and shows off her husband's trophies: shelves full of brandy snifters, loving cups and statues of fish.

"I don't know what Kevin would do if he couldn't go fishing," Shirley Ashurst says. "Not that it relaxes him. If he isn't catching, he wants to know why. He racks his brain. He comes home and relives the match all over again." She takes an inscribed hunk of crystal from a shelf and wipes off a fingerprint. "It's a beauty, that," she says.

Shirley Ashurst's father mined coal. Kevin Ashurst used to fish with him, she remembers, and that's how Kevin and Shirley met. Ashurst's father was a coal miner, too. But after a bad accident, he quit to farm maggots. Kevin runs the farm now. He and Shirley have a twenty-one-year-old son. Someday, if he wants it, the maggot farm will be his.

"Do you hear something dripping?" Shirley Ashurst says. She puts down her teacup and dashes up the stairs. "He's got bloodworm in the bathtub."

After a while, Ashurst pulls up outside in a truck from the maggot farm and sets himself to sorting his new haul of worms in the garage. "See, that's come out of the muck, like," he says, displaying a squirming red mass in a bucket.

In T-shirt and baggy pants, he is redolent of maggot. His forehead is creased, his eyes tired. He has a Lancashire accent so thick an outsider can often make out only one word, transcribed here as "flipping," as in:

"I wish fishing were as popular as flipping darts. I'd be a flipping big star. I'd be riding around in a flipping limousine."

For the time being, Ashurst settles for a couple of maggot trucks and a station wagon. At 6 P.M., he loads the wagon with his rod (in ten sections) and his tackle box, which resembles a small refrigerator. He drives to the Royal Oak, a pub in Leigh, to draw a position on the banks of the canal for the three-hour competition.

The little pub is filled with coarse fishermen when he arrives. Pint glasses and bags of maggots line the bar. Ashurst pays the entrance fee and picks a number out of a box. He gets peg fifty-four. After thirty years of fishing the Bridgewater Canal, he knows it's a spot the fish don't fancy.

"You'll win anyway, Kevin," says the match official.

The canal runs right through Leigh and on through the countryside to the Liverpool docks. Its banks are flanked by the blackened brick remains of Victorian textile mills gone broke. The water, forty feet across and four-feet deep, is sluggish and green. For a mile along the towpath, hard by the old mills, coarse fishermen bait up.

Ashurst lugs his box to a piling and sits on it. He puts on his cap and assembles his rod,

which is made of carbon fiber and costs $750. It doesn't have a reel; the line is tied to the tip. An angler has to take the whole thing apart again to bring in a fish, and he can do that often. Ashurst once caught 861 fish in five hours. They weighed a total of eighteen pounds, twelve ounces.

"Whatcha using?" shouts a man at the next peg.

"Worm," Ashurst shouts back.

For a maggot farmer, this seems extraordinary. But Kevin Ashurst senses a piscine appetite for bloodworm on the Bridgewater Canal tonight. Everyone else sticks to maggots. The next man skewers one on his hook and shoots a few more into the water with a slingshot. Ashurst rolls a wormball and lobs it into the murk.

"You have to remember where that landed," he says. "Then you lay your hook on the bottom. The fish congregate. You can overfeed them or underfeed them. Something's always wrong. There's a lot into this. Great anglers have to think."

Tenderly he threads one worm onto the hook. He swings the pole out and lowers the bait. And then he sits, concentrating on the peacock-quill float, holding the rod like a pole vaulter getting set for his next jump. "It strains the eyes," he says. "It's why I don't read much." For half an hour, as a gallery gathers behind him, Ashurst gets nary a nibble.

"Is that the lucky hat?" somebody says.

"Yeah," Ashurst mumbles. "Not much good, though."

"Should have had one by now, lad," says somebody else.

The quill twitches. Ashurst jerks the rod upward and out of the water comes a roach, battling for its life. It is two inches long and weighs about an ounce. Ashurst draws in the rod across his lap, twisting off section after section, and drops the fish into his keep net.

Now the worms are at work. Here comes another roach, and another, and a four-ounce bream. Ashurst hits stride: He can hook a fish, swing it to the bank, break down the rod, grab the fish, pluck out the hook, thread another worm, rebuild the rod, and be fishing again in twenty seconds. "If I maintain this, like, I'm gonna catch three pounds," he says.

Up and down the canal in the deepening twilight, anglers get fidgety. Nobody can match the world champion's pace. Desperate to win with one huge fish, they sling maggots with a fury. But Kevin Ashurst sticks to his worms and his strategy: Catch tiddlers. He sits on his box and stares stolidly at his quill until the official's final shout: "All out!"

"All out," Ashurst says softly to himself, and he pulls in his rod. A judge comes by to weigh the catch. Ashurst has sixteen fish. They tip the scales at three pounds, one ounce. "Well," Ashurst says, stepping briefly behind a bush, "that's flipping done with."

Back at the Royal Oak, coarse fishermen crush against the bar, ordering pints, noisily discussing the ones that got away. A thin voice rises at the far end of the bar to announce the winner. Conversation stops in a moment of shock. Somebody called I. Cunliffe caught a four-pound eel. He wins $94.95.

"It's a lie," somebody says.

"It were a good catch," says Kevin Ashurst.

But next morning at the maggot farm, Ashurst's eyes are even more tired than they were the day before.

"Couldn't sleep," he says, resting on his shovel. "Kept thinking I had a chance to win last night. Should have used a lighter float." He sprinkles some chicken heads into a box of dead fish. "Once you've had success," he says, "you can't let it stop. It isn't the money. It's prestige."

[1983]

GUILLERMO GÓMEZ-PEÑA

Documented/Undocumented

TRANSLATED BY RUBÉN MARTÍNEZ

About the Author: A visual artist, Gómez-Peña joins a growing group of American essayists who are giving voice to multicultural concerns. His essay "Documented/Undocumented" expresses the dislocations of geography and culture that Latinos in the United States face in their everyday lives.

I live smack in the fissure between two worlds, in the infected wound: half a block from the end of Western Civilization and four miles from the start of the Mexican-American border, the northernmost point of Latin America. In my fractured reality, but a reality nonetheless, there cohabit two histories, languages, cosmologies, artistic traditions, and political systems which are drastically counterposed. Many "deterritorialized" Latin American artists in Europe and the U.S. have opted for "internationalism" (a cultural identity based upon the "most advanced" of the ideas originating out of New York or Paris). I, on the other hand, opt for "borderness" and assume my role: My generation, the *chilangos* [slang term for a Mexico City native], who came to "el norte" fleeing the imminent ecological and social catastrophe of Mexico City, gradually integrated itself into otherness, in search of that other Mexico grafted onto the entrails of the et cetera . . . became Chicano-ized. We de-Mexicanized ourselves to Mexi-understand ourselves, some without wanting to, others on purpose. And one day, the border became our house, laboratory, and ministry of culture (or counterculture).

Today, eight years after my departure [from Mexico], when they ask me for my nationality or ethnic identity, I can't respond with one word, since my "identity" now possesses multiple repertories: I am Mexican but I am also Chicano and Latin American. At the border they call me *chilango* or *mexiquillo;* in Mexico City it's *pocho* or *norteño;* and in Europe it's *sudaca.* The Anglos call me "Hispanic" or "Latino," and the Germans have, on more than one occasion, confused me with Turks or Italians. I walk amid the rubble of the Tower of Babel of our American post-modernity.

The recapitulation of my personal and collective topography has become my cultural obsession since I arrived in the United States. I look for the traces of my generation, whose distance stretches not only from Mexico City to California, but also from the past to the future, from pre-Columbian America to high technology and from Spanish to English, passing through "Spanglish."

As a result of this process I have become a cultural topographer, border-crosser, and hunter of myths. And it doesn't matter where I find myself, in Califas or Mexico City, in Barcelona or West Berlin; I always have the sensation that I belong to the same species: the migrant tribe of fiery pupils.

My work, like that of many border artists, comes from two distinct traditions, and because of this has dual, or on occasion multiple, referential codes. One strain comes from Mexican popular culture, the Latin American literary "boom," and the Mexico City counterculture of the '70s . . . the other comes directly from fluxus (a late-'60s international art movement that explored alternative means of production and distribution), concrete poetry, conceptual art, and performance art. These two traditions converge in my border experience and they fuse together.

In my intellectual formation, Carlos Fuentes, Gabriel García Márquez, Oscar Chávez, Felipe Ehrenberg, José Agustín, and Enrique Cisneros were as important as Burroughs, Foucault, Fassbinder, Lacan, Vito Aconci, and Joseph Beuys.

My "artistic space" is the intersection where the new Mexican urban poetry and the colloquial Anglo poetry meet; the intermediate stage somewhere between Mexican street theater and multimedia performance; the silence that snaps in between the *corrido* and punk; the wall that divides *"neográfica"* (a 1970s Mexico City art movement involved in the production of low-budget book art and graphics) and graffiti; the highway that joins Mexico City and Los Angeles; and the mysterious thread of thought and action that puts pan-Latin Americanism in touch with the Chicano movement, and both of these in touch with other international vanguards.

I am a child of crisis and cultural syncretism, half hippie and half punk. My generation grew up watching movies about *charros* and science fiction, listening to *cumbias* and tunes from the Moody Blues, constructing altars and filming in Super-8, reading the *Corno Emplumado* and *Artforum,* traveling to Tepoztlán and San Francisco, creating and de-creating myths. We went to Cuba in search of political illumination, to Spain to visit the crazy grandmother and to the U.S. in search of the instantaneous musico-sexual Paradise. We found nothing. Our dreams wound up getting caught in the webs of the border.

Our generation belongs to the world's biggest floating population: the weary travelers, the dislocated, those of us who left because we didn't fit anymore, those of us who still haven't arrived because we don't know where to arrive at, or because we can't go back anymore.

Our deepest generational emotion is that of loss, which comes from our having left. Our loss is total and occurs at multiple levels: loss of our country (culture and national rituals) and our class (the "illustrious" middle class and upper middle). Progressive loss of language and literary culture in our native tongue (those of us who live in non-Spanish-speaking countries); loss of ideological meta-horizons (the repression against and division of the left) and of metaphysical certainty.

In exchange, what we won was a vision of a more experimental culture, that is to say, a multi-focal and tolerant one. Going beyond nationalisms, we established cultural alliances with other places, and we won a true political conscience (declassicization and consequent politicization) as well as new options in social, sexual, spiritual, and aesthetic behavior.

Our artistic product presents hybrid realities and colliding visions within coalition. We practice the epistemology of multiplicity and a border semiotics. We share certain thematic interests, like the continual clash with cultural otherness, the crisis of identity, or, better said, access to trans- or multiculturalism, and the destruction of borders therefrom; the creation of alternative cartographies, a ferocious critique of the dominant culture of both countries, and, lastly, a proposal for new creative languages.

We witness the borderization of the world, by-product of the "deterritorialization" of vast human sectors. The borders either expand or are shot full of holes. Cultures and languages mutually invade one another. The South rises and melts, while the North descends dangerously with its economic and military pincers. The East moves west and vice-versa. Europe and North America daily receive uncontainable migrations of human beings, a majority of whom are being displaced involuntarily. This phenomenon is the result of multiple factors: regional wars, unemployment, overpopulation, and especially in the enormous disparity in North/South relations.

The demographic facts are staggering: The Middle East and Black Africa are already in Europe, and Latin America's heart now beats in the U.S. New York and Paris increasingly resemble Mexico City and São Paulo. Cities like Tijuana and Los Angeles, once socio-urban aberrations, are becoming models of a new hybrid culture, full of uncertainty and vitality. And border youth—the fearsome "cholo-punks," children of the chasm that is opening between the "first" and the "third" worlds, become the indisputable heirs to a new *mestizaje* (the fusion of the Amerindian and European races).

In this context, concepts like "high culture," "ethnic purity," "cultural identity," "beauty," and "fine arts" are absurdities and anachronisms. Like it or not, we are attending the funeral of modernity and the birth of a new culture.

In 1988, the unigeneric and monocultural vision of the world is insufficient. Syncretism, interdisciplinarianism, and multi-ethnicity are sine qua nons of contemporary art. And the artist or intellectual who doesn't comprehend this will be banished and his or her work will not form part of the great cultural debates of the continent.

Art is conceptual territory where everything is possible, and by the same token there do not exist certainties nor limitations within it. In 1988, all the creative possibilities have been explored, and therefore they are all within our reach.

Thanks to the discoveries and advancements of many artists over the last fifteen years, the concept of *metier* is so wide and the parameters of art so flexible that they include practically every imaginable alternative: art as political negotiation (Felipe Ehrenberg—Mexico), as social reform (Joseph Beuys—Germany), as an instrument of multicultural organization (Judy Baca—Los Angeles), or as alternative communication (*Post Arte*—Mexico, and Kit Galloway & Sherri Rabinowitz—USA). Others conceive art as a strategy of intervention aimed at mass media, or as citizen-diplomacy, social chronicle, a popular semiotics, or personal anthropology.

In 1988, our artistic options in terms of the medium, methodology, system of communication, and channels of distribution for our ideas and images are greater and more diverse than ever. Not understanding and practicing this freedom implies operating outside of history, or, worse yet, blindly accepting the restrictions imposed by cultural bureaucracies.

Our experience as Latino border artists and intellectuals in the U.S. fluctuates between legality and illegality, between partial citizenship and full. For the Anglo community we are simply "an ethnic minority," a subculture, that is to say, some kind of pre-industrial tribe with a good consumerist appetite. For the art world, we are practitioners of distant languages that, in the best of cases, are perceived as exotic.

In general, we are perceived through the folkloric prisms of Hollywood, fad literature and publicity; or through the ideological filters of mass media. For the average Anglo, we are nothing but "images," "symbols," "metaphors." We lack ontological existence and anthropological concreteness. We are perceived indistinctly as magic creatures with shamanistic powers, happy bohemians with pretechnological sensibilities, or as romantic revolutionaries born in a Cuban poster from the '70s. All this without mentioning the more ordinary myths, which link us with drugs, supersexuality, gratuitous violence, and terrorism, myths that serve to justify racism and disguise the fear of cultural otherness.

These mechanisms of mythification generate semantic interference and obstruct true intercultural dialogue. To make border art implies to reveal and subvert said mechanisms.

The term *Hispanic,* coined by techno-marketing experts and by the designers of political campaigns, homogenizes our cultural diversity (Chicanos, Cubans, and Puerto Ricans become indistinguishable), avoids our indigenous cultural heritage and links us directly with Spain. Worse yet, it possesses connotations of upward mobility and political obedi-ance.

The terms *Third World culture, ethnic art,* and *minority art* are openly ethnocentric and necessarily imply an axiological vision of the world at the service of Anglo-European culture. Confronted with them, one can't avoid asking the following questions: Besides possessing more money and arms, is it that the "First World" is qualitatively better in any other way than our "underdeveloped" countries? That the Anglos themselves aren't also an "ethnic group," one of the most violent and antisocial tribes on this planet? That the five hundred million Latin American *mestizos* that inhabit the Americas are a "minority"?

Between Chicanos, Mexicans, and Anglos there is a heritage of relations poisoned by distrust and resentment. For this reason, my cultural work (especially in the camps of performance art and journalism) has concentrated itself upon the destruction of the myths and the stereotypes that each group has invented to rationalize the other two.

With the dismantling of this mythology, I look, if not to create an instantaneous space for intercultural communication, at least to contribute to the creation of the groundwork and theoretical principles for a future dialogue that is capable of transcending the profound historical resentments that exist between the communities on either side of the border.

Within the framework of the false amnesty of the Immigration Reform and Control Act and the growing influence of the North American ultra-right, which seeks to close (militarize) the border because of supposed motives of "national security," the collaboration among Chicano, Mexican, and Anglo artists has become indispensable.

Anglo artists can contribute their technical ability, their comprehension of the new mediums of expression and information (video and audio), and their altruist/internationalist tendencies. In turn, Latinos (whether Mexican, Chicano, Caribbean, Central or South American) can contribute the originality of their cultural models, their spiritual strength, and their political understanding of the world.

Together, we can collaborate in surprising cultural projects but without forgetting that *both should retain control of the product,* from the planning stages up through to distribution. If this doesn't occur, then intercultural collaboration isn't authentic. We shouldn't confuse true collaboration with political paternalism, cultural vampirism, voyeurism, economic opportunism, and demogogic multiculturalism.

We should clear up this matter once and for all:

We (Latinos in the United States) don't want to be a mere ingredient of the melting pot. What we want is to participate actively in a humanistic, pluralistic and politicized dialogue, continuous and not sporadic, and that this occur between equals that enjoy the same power of negotiation.

For this "intermediate space" to open, first there has to be a pact of mutual cultural understanding and acceptance, and it is precisely in this that the border artist can contribute. In this very delicate historical moment, Mexican artists and intellectuals as well as Chicanos and Anglos should try to "recontextualize" ourselves, that is to say, search for a "common cultural territory," and within it put into practice new models of communication and association.

[1988]

ON BECOMING AN ESSAYIST

Most of you are reading this material for a literature class, and you will be asked to write an essay about material relevant to the course. We would like to make a couple of suggestions that our students have found particularly helpful in writing their own papers.

We suggest that you keep a journal in which you ask yourself questions about the readings and enter into a dialogue with the voices in the essays. Over the years we have generated a series of topics students have told us were very useful beginning points that they developed first, very informally in their journals, and then a little more formally for class presentation. These journal topics are particularly designed to help you generate material that may lead you to an interesting and stimulating dialogue focus for your essay.

Some of our students did not find the journal useful, but instead wanted to follow the more traditional approach to writing, beginning with a rather free and open draft, which was refined into a final paper. Ideally, the first attempt should result in a rich discovery draft (a rough draft in which you write down everything that seems related to a particular aspect of the essay that you want to pursue without worrying about organization, sentence structure, spelling, and so on).

The following suggestions may be questions you ask yourself in the course of writing this first draft. As you make these entries, be alert to where these questions may lead you. Feel free to add questions if you see another direction to explore. If certain entries seem to overlap, move along and select only those that yield the most substantial information for your essay.

INFORMAL WRITING: RESPONDING TO READING

Entry 1: Select the essay you like best and respond to what it makes you think about, especially as it may touch on your own experience.

Entry 2: Identify what the writer seems most concerned with in the essay and tell what she or he does to make this concern known to the reader.

Entry 3: Does the essay stem from an occasion or a specific situation? How does your knowledge of this occasion or situation affect the way you respond to the essay? To its meaning?

Entry 4: Identify the way the voice of the essay works. For example, is the voice intimate, objective, humorous, playful, elegiac, or nostalgic? What seems to be the author's intention in writing the essay? For example, is the essayist conducting an argument, exploring an idea or concept, rendering an experience, or portraying a person? What alerts you to the essayist's voice? What does the essayist's voice add to the meaning of the essay?

Entry 5: Does the essayist engage you in any kind of dialogue? If so, what kind of response does the essay elicit from you? For example, does the writer assume that you share an idea, belief, or experience? How does that response affect the way you read the essay? Does the essayist also carry on a dialogue with identifiable others, such as specified readers, writers, friends, members of the writer's family? Does convoking these other voices add to the essay? Why or why not?

Entry 6: Does the essayist call on you to consider your memory or knowledge of other literary genres, other times, other cultural material? Does this add to or interfere with your reading or understanding of the essay? How?

Entry 7: Where does the essay begin and end in time? Does time matter? Why? Is there a narrative structure other than a chronology that moves the essay from the beginning to the end? For example, does the essayist disclose an attitude or a significance through an accumulation of details in figurative language (simile and metaphor)? How does this arrangement of material work to add pleasure and meaning to the essay? Does the essayist digress? If so, describe why she or he chooses to digress and how the digression affects the essay.

Entry 8: Select your favorite passage. Copy it word for word. Now write about something from your own experience, following the sentence structure and patterns in the passage as closely as you can. Briefly note what you learned about the author's handling of language by imitating his or her style.

Entry 9: Read over your earlier entries; select the one that pleases you most and that you are interested in exploring further. For this entry, write a new draft on the same topic to see what you can add to it. Compare the drafts and, making use of material in both, write another in which you try to find a focus for a formal analysis of the essay. For this draft, add appropriate quoted material from the text as evidence for each point you're making about the way the essay is written and the way you've chosen to read it.

Entry 10: Are there any pertinent passages from other essays, poems, plays, or stories that you could cite to give your essay more authority? If so, include the material in such a way that it works smoothly into your own text. Notice how many of the writers in this section embed the words and works of others in their own essays.

INFORMAL WRITING: RESPONDING TO YOUR WORLD

The following questions are designed to help you explore the connections that exist between you and the people, places, facets of culture (art, film, books, and so on), and myriad events that have shaped your life. Since this list contains only a few of the many possibilities, feel free to add your own topics and questions. The purpose of this assignment is to provide you with a body of material from which you can select to shape a finished essay of your own. Be alert to what could happen, to where these questions might lead you.

Entry 1: What are your main habits? Tastes in music/books/movies/friends? What do these activities or interests contribute to your life?

Entry 2: Describe the major landscapes (interior and exterior) of your life so far, the main place(s) you associate with your childhood, the place you live now. How do you respond to each of these? What season do you prefer, and how would you describe its effect on you? (See Donald Hall's essay "Winter" on page 1680 for an example of such a description.)

Entry 3: Describe your mother and father as concretely as possible. What particular senses and/or physical objects do you associate most strongly with each of your parents?

Entry 4: What other members of your family have had a profound influence on you? Provide visual scenes and details of each person. Who is the most important person outside your family? Again, provide details.

Entry 5: What is your earliest recollection? Other early memories? First book read to you or by you? What events were most important and vivid in passing from childhood to adulthood? Before starting school? In elementary school, high school, college? Render scenes as vividly as possible.

Entry 6: What are your major pleasures and fears, and how have they affected you? Trace these back to childhood as far as you can.

Entry 7: What are your attitudes toward money, love, sex, violence, career, sports, family life, education, work, food, animals, and so on? How do these attitudes affect your life?

Entry 8: What are the major issues in your life? What choices are open to you?

Entry 9: Read over your earlier entries; select the one that pleases you most and that you are interested in exploring further. For this entry, write a new draft on the same topic to see what you can add to it. Compare the drafts and, making use of material in both, write another in which you try to find an angle of vision to shape your material.

Entry 10: Are there any other voices you would like to include in order to create a dialogue—from letters, poems, other essays or stories, or from real or imagined conversations? Take this as the opportunity to embed these words into the flow of your essay. Be sure to identify the voices.

WORKS CITED

Angell, Roger. "In the Country." *Late Innings.* New York: Simon & Schuster, 1982.

Atwan, Robert. "Foreword." *Best American Essays 1987.* Ed. Gay Talese. New York: Ticknor & Fields, 1987.

Bouffard, Chris. "A New and Improved Modern Proposal." Unpublished. University of Vermont, Spring 1989.

Dillard, Annie. "Introduction." *Best American Essays 1988.* Ed. Annie Dillard. New York: Ticknor & Fields, 1988.

Hardwick, Elizabeth. "Introduction." *Best American Essays 1986.* Ed. Elizabeth Hardwick. New York: Ticknor & Fields, 1986.

Le Guin, Ursula. "The Fisherwoman's Daughter." *Dancing at the Edge of the World: Thoughts on Words, Women, Places.* New York: Grove Press, 1989.

Leith, David. "Where the Heart Should Be." *The Burlington Review* (1983): 5–6.

Montaigne, Michel de. *The Complete Works of Montaigne.* Trans. Donald M. Frame. Stanford, CA: Stanford University Press, 1957.

"Notes and Comment" from "The Talk of the Town." *The New Yorker* (June 26, 1989): 25–26.

Porter, Katherine Anne. "St. Augustine and the Bullfight." *The Collected Essays and Occasional Writings of Katherine Anne Porter.* New York: Delacorte Press, 1970.

Woolf, Virginia. "The Modern Essay." *The Common Reader First Series.* New York: Harcourt Brace Jovanovich, 1984.

Further Readings

FRANCIS BACON

(1561–1626)

Of Marriage and Single Life

About the Author: The voice of the philosopher-moralist dominates Bacon's writings. "Of Marriage and Single Life" is meditative in tone, but modern readers may enjoy it as an insight into early seventeenth-century morality, a sharp contrast to today's values.

He that hath wife and children hath given hostages to fortune; for they are impediments to great enterprises, either of virtue or mischief. Certainly the best works, and of greatest merit for the public, have proceeded from the unmarried or childless men, which both in affection and means have married and endowed the public. Yet it were great reason that those that have children should have greatest care of future times, unto which they know they must transmit their dearest pledges. Some there are who, though they lead a single life, yet their thoughts do end with themselves, and account future times impertinences. Nay, there are some other that account wife and children but as bills of charges. Nay more, there are some foolish rich covetous men that take a pride in having no children, because they may be thought so much the richer. For perhaps they have heard some talk, "Such an one is a great rich man," and another except to it, "Yea, but he hath a great charge of children"; as if it were an abatement to his riches. But the most ordinary cause of a single life is liberty, especially in certain self-pleasing and humorous minds, which are so sensible of every restraint, as they will go near to think their girdles and garters to be bonds and shackles. Unmarried men are best friends, best masters, best servants, but not always best subjects, for they are light to run away, and almost all fugitives are of that condition. A single life doth well with churchmen, for charity will hardly water the ground where it must first fill a pool. It is indifferent for judges and magistrates, for if they be facile and corrupt, you shall have a servant five times worse than a wife. For soldiers, I find the generals commonly in their hortatives put men in mind of their wives and children; and I think the despising of marriage amongst the Turks maketh the vulgar soldier more base. Certainly wife and children are a kind of discipline of humanity; and single men, though they be many times more charitable, because their means are less exhaust, yet, on the other side, they are more cruel and hard-hearted (good to make severe inquisitors), because their tenderness is not so oft called upon. Grave natures, led by custom, and therefore constant, are commonly loving husbands, as was said of Ulysses, *Vetulam suam prætulit immortalitati.* Chaste women are often proud and forward, as presuming upon the merit of their chastity. It is one of the best bonds, both of chastity and obedience, in the wife if she think her husband wise, which she will never do if she find him jealous. Wives are young men's mistresses, companions for middle age, and old men's nurses, so as a man may have a quarrel to marry when he will. But yet he was reputed one of the wise men that made answer to the question when a man should marry: "A young man not yet, an elder man not at all." It is often seen that bad husbands have very good wives; whether it be that it raiseth the price of their husbands'

kindness when it comes, or that the wives take a pride in their patience. But this never fails, if the bad husbands were of their own choosing, against their friends' consent; for then they will be sure to make good their own folly.

[1612]

JONATHAN SWIFT

(1667–1745)

A Modest Proposal

FOR PREVENTING THE CHILDREN OF IRELAND FROM BEING A BURDEN TO THEIR PARENTS OR COUNTRY; AND FOR MAKING THEM BENEFICIAL TO THE PUBLICK

About the Author: Although a clergyman and a poet, Swift, the author of *The Tale of a Tub, Gulliver's Travels,* and *The Battle of the Books,* is best known as a satirist. His essay "A Modest Proposal" has long been regarded the classic example of satire in English.

It is a melancholly Object to those, who walk through this great Town or travel in the Country; when they see the Streets, the Roads, and Cabbin-doors crowded with Beggars of the Female Sex, followed by three, four, or six Children, all in Rags, and importuning every Passenger for an Alms. These Mothers, instead of being able to work for their honest Livelyhood, are forced to employ all their Time in strolling to beg Sustenance for their helpless Infants; who, as they grow up, either turn Thieves for want of Work; or leave their dear Native Country, to fight for the Pretender in Spain, or sell themselves to the Barbadoes.

I think it is agreed by all Parties, that this prodigious number of Children in the Arms, or on the Backs, or at the Heels of their Mothers, and frequently of their Fathers, is in the present deplorable state of the Kingdom, a very great additional Grievance; and therefore, whoever could find out a fair, cheap, and easy Method of making these Children sound and useful Members of the Commonwealth, would deserve so well of the Publick, as to have his Statue set up for a Preserver of the Nation.

But my Intention is very far from being confined to provide only for the Children of professed Beggars: It is of a much greater Extent, and shall take in the whole Number of Infants at a certain Age, who are born of Parents in effect as little able to support them, as those who demand our Charity in the Streets.

As to my own Part, having turned my Thoughts, for many Years, upon this important Subject, and maturely weighed the several Schemes of other Projectors, I have always found them grossly mistaken in their Computation. It is true, a Child, just dropt from its Dam, may be supported by her Milk, for a Solar Year with little other Nourishment; at most not above the Value of two Shillings; which the Mother may certainly get, or the Value in Scraps, by her lawful Occupation of Begging: and it is exactly at one Year old that I propose to provide for them in such a manner, as, instead of being a Charge upon their Parents or the Parish, or wanting Food and Raiment for the rest of their Lives; they shall, on the contrary, contribute to the Feeding and partly to the Cloathing, of many Thousands.

There is likewise another great Advantage in my Scheme, that it will prevent those voluntary Abortions, and that horrid practice of Women murdering their Bastard Children, alas! too frequent among us; Sacrificing the poor innocent Babes, I doubt, more to avoid the Expence than the Shame; which would move Tears and Pity in the most Savage and inhuman breast.

The number of Souls in Ireland being usually reckoned one Million and a half; of these I calculate there may be about Two hundred Thousand Couple whose Wives are Breeders; from which number I subtract thirty Thousand Couples, who are able to maintain their own Children, although I apprehend there cannot be so many under the present Distresses of the Kingdom; but this being granted, there will remain an Hundred and Seventy Thousand Breeders. I again Subtract Fifty Thousand, for those Women who miscarry, or whose Children die by Accident, or Disease, within the Year. There only remain an Hundred and Twenty Thousand Children of poor Parents, annually born: The Question therefore is, How this Number shall be reared, and provided for? Which, as I have already said, under the present Situation of Affairs, is utterly impossible, by all the Methods hitherto proposed: for we can neither employ them in Handicraft or Agriculture; we neither build Houses, (I mean in the Country) nor cultivate Land: They can very seldom pick up a Livelyhood by Stealing until they arrive at six Years old; except where they are of towardly Parts; although, I confess, they learn the Rudiments much earlier; during which Time, they can, however be properly looked upon only as Probationers; as I have been informed by a principal Gentleman in the County of Cavan, who protested to me, that he never knew above one or two Instances under the Age of six, even in a part of the Kingdom so renowned for the quickest Proficiency in that Art.

I am assured by our Merchants, that a Boy or a Girl before twelve Years old, is no saleable Commodity; and even when they come to this Age, they will not yield above Three Pounds, or Three Pounds and half a Crown at most, on the Exchange; which cannot turn to Account either to the Parents or the Kingdom; the Charge of Nutriment and Rags, having been at least four Times that Value.

I shall now therefore humbly propose my own Thoughts; which I hope will not be liable to the least Objection.

I have been assured by a very knowing American of my Acquaintance in London, that a young healthy Child, well nursed is, at a Year old, a most delicious, nourishing and wholesome Food, whether Stewed, Roasted, Baked, or Boiled; and I make no doubt that it will equally serve in a Fricasie, or Ragoust.

I do therefore humbly offer it to publick Consideration, that of the Hundred and Twenty Thousand Children, already computed, Twenty thousand may be reserved for Breed; whereof only one Fourth Part to be Males; which is more than we allow to Sheep, black Cattle, or Swine; and my Reason is, that these Children are seldom the Fruits of Marriage, a Circumstance not much regarded by our Savages; therefore, one Male will be sufficient to serve four Females. That the remaining Hundred thousand, may, at a Year old be offered in Sale to the Persons of Quality and Fortune, through the Kingdom; always advising the Mother to let them suck plentifully in the last Month, so as to render them

plump, and fat for a good Table. A child will make two Dishes at an Entertainment for Friends; and when the Family dines alone, the fore or hind Quarter will make a reasonable Dish; and seasoned with a little Pepper or Salt, will be very good Boiled on the fourth Day, especially in Winter.

I have reckoned upon a Medium, that a Child just born will weigh Twelve Pounds; and in a Solar Year, if tolerably nursed, increaseth to 28 Pounds.

I grant this Food will be somewhat dear, and therefore very proper for Landlords; who, as they have already devoured most of the Parents, seem to have the best Title to the Children.

Infant's Flesh will be in Season throughout the Year; but more plentiful in March, and a little before and after; for we are told by a grave Author an eminent French Physician, that Fish being a prolific Dyet, there are more Children born in Roman Catholick Countries about Nine Months after Lent, than at any other Season: Therefore reckoning a Year after Lent, the Markets will be more glutted than usual; because the Number of Popish Infants, is, at least, three to one in this Kingdom; and therefore it will have one other Collateral advantage; by lessening the Number of Papists among us.

I have already computed the Charge of nursing a Beggar's Child (in which List I reckon all Cottagers, Labourers, and Four fifths of the Farmers) to be about two Shillings per Annum, Rags included; and I believe no Gentleman would repine to give Ten Shillings for the Carcase of a good fat Child; which, as I have said, will make four Dishes of excellent nutritive meat, when he hath only some particular Friend, or his own Family, to dine with him. Thus the Squire will learn to be a good Landlord, and grow popular among his Tenants; the Mother will have Eight Shillings net Profit, and be fit for Work till she produceth another Child.

Those who are more thrifty (as I must confess the Times require) may flay the Carcase; the Skin of which artificially dressed, will make admirable Gloves for Ladies, and Summer Boots for fine Gentlemen.

As to our City of Dublin; Shambles[1] may be appointed for this Purpose, in the most convenient Parts of it, and Butchers we may be assured will not be wanting; although I rather recommend buying the Children alive, and dressing them hot from the Knife, as we do roasting Pigs.

A very worthy Person, a true Lover of his Country, and whose Virtues I highly esteem, was lately pleased, in discoursing on this Matter, to offer a Refinement upon my Scheme. He said, that many Gentlemen of this Kingdom, having of late destroyed their Deer; he conceived that the Want of Venison might be well supplied by the Bodies of young Lads and Maidens, not exceeding fourteen Years of Age, nor under twelve; so great a Number of both Sexes in every County being ready to Starve, for want of Work and Service: And these to be disposed of by their Parents, if alive, or otherwise by their nearest Relations. But with due Deference to so excellent a Friend, and so deserving a Patriot, I cannot be altogether in his Sentiments. For as to the Males, my American Acquaintance assured me from frequent Experience, that their Flesh was generally tough and lean, like that of our School-boys, by continual Exercise, and their Taste disagreeable; and to fatten them would not answer the Charge. Then, as to the Females, it would, I think, with humble Submission, be a Loss to the Publick, because they soon would become Breeders themselves: And

1. Slaughterhouses.

besides it is not improbable, that some scrupulous[2] People might be apt to censure such a Practice, (although indeed very unjustly) as a little bordering upon Cruelty; which, I confess, hath always been with me the strongest Objection against any Project, how well soever intended.

But in order to justify my Friend; he confessed, that this Expedient was put into his Head by the famous Salmanaazor, a Native of the Island Formosa, who came from thence to London, above twenty Years ago, and in Conversation told my Friend, that in his Country, when any young Person happened to be put to Death, the executioner sold the Carcase to Persons of Quality, as a prime Dainty, and that, in his Time, the Body of a plump Girl of fifteen, who was crucified for an Attempt to poison the Emperor, was sold to his Imperial Majesty's prime Minister of State, and other great Mandarins of the Court, in Joints from the Gibbet, at Four hundred Crowns. Neither indeed can I deny, that if the same Use were made of several plump young girls in this Town, who, without one single Groat to their Fortunes, cannot stir Abroad without a Chair, and appear at the Play-house, and Assemblies in foreign fineries, which they never will pay for; the Kingdom would not be the worse.

Some Persons of a desponding Spirit are in great Concern about the vast Number of poor People, who are Aged, Diseased, or Maimed; and I have been desired to imploy my Thoughts what Course may be taken, to ease the Nation of so grievous an Incumbrance. But I am not in the least Pain upon that Matter; because it is very well known, that they are every Day dying, and rotting, by Cold and Famine, and Filth, and Vermin, as fast as can be reasonably expected. And as to the younger Labourers, they are now in almost as hopeful a Condition: They cannot get Work, and consequently pine away for Want of Nourishment, to a Degree, that if at any Time they are accidentally hired to common Labour, they have not Strength to perform it; and thus the Country, and themselves, are in a fair Way of being delivered from the Evils to come.

I have too long digressed; and therefore shall return to my Subject. I think the Advantages by the Proposal which I have made are obvious, and many, as well as of the highest Importance.

For First, as I have already observed, it would greatly lessen the Number of Papists, with whom we are Yearly overrun; being the principal Breeders of the Nation, as well as our most dangerous Enemies; and who stay at home on Purpose, with a Design to deliver the Kingdom to the Pretender;[3] hoping to take their Advantage by the Absence of so many good Protestants, who have chosen rather to leave their Country, than stay at home, and pay Tithes against their Conscience, to an idolatrous Episcopal Curate.[4]

Secondly, The poorer Tenants will have something valuable of their own, which, by Law, may be made liable to Distress,[5] and help to pay their Landlord's Rent; their Corn and Cattle being already seized, and Money a Thing unknown.

Thirdly, Whereas the maintenance of an Hundred Thousand Children, from two Years old, and upwards, cannot be computed at less than ten Shillings a Piece per Annum, the Nation's Stock will be thereby encreased Fifty Thousand Pounds per Annum; besides

---

2. "Over-nice or meticulous in matters of right and wrong" *(Oxford English Dictionary).*
3. James Francis Edward Stuart claimed ("pretended to") the British throne by right of succession from his father, James II. He attempted to win it by force of arms in 1715.
4. To a minister of the Church of England.
5. Impoundment for debt.

the Profit of a new Dish, introduced to the Tables of all Gentlemen of Fortune in the Kingdom, who have any Refinement in Taste; and the Money will circulate among ourselves, the Goods being entirely of our own Growth and Manufacture.

Fourthly, The constant Breeders, besides the Gain of Eight Shillings Sterling per Annum, by the Sale of their Children, will be rid of the Charge of maintaining them after the First Year.

Fifthly, This Food would likewise bring great Custom[6] to Taverns, where the Vintners will certainly be so prudent, as to procure the best Receipts[7] for dressing it to Perfection; and consequently, have their Houses frequented by all the fine Gentlemen, who justly value themselves upon their Knowledge in good Eating; and a skillful Cook, who understands how to oblige his Guests, will contrive to make it as expensive as they please.

Sixthly, This would be a great Inducement to Marriage, which all wise Nations have either encouraged by Rewards, or enforced by Laws and Penalties. It would encrease the Care and Tenderness of Mothers towards their Children, when they were sure of a Settlement for Life, to the poor Babes, provided in some Sort by the Public, to their annual Profit instead of Expence. We should soon see an honest Emulation among the married Women, which of them could bring the fattest Child to the Market. Men would become as fond of their Wives, during the Time of their Pregnancy, as they are now of their Mares in Foal, their Cows in Calf, or Sows when they are ready to farrow; nor offer to beat or kick them (as is too frequent a Practice), for fear of a Miscarriage.

Many other Advantages might be enumerated. For instance, the Addition of some Thousand Carcases in our Exportation of barrel'd Beef: The Propagation of Swine's Flesh, and Improvement in the Art of making good Bacon; so much wanted among us by the great Destruction of Pigs, too frequent at our Tables, and are no way comparable in Taste, or Magnificence, to a well-grown, fat yearling Child; which, roasted whole, will make a considerable Figure at a Lord Mayor's Feast, or any other publick Entertainment. But this, and many others, I omit; being studious of Brevity.

Supposing that one Thousand Families in this City, would be constant Customers for Infants Flesh, besides others who might have it at merry Meetings, particularly Weddings and Christenings; I compute that Dublin would take off, annually, about Twenty Thousand Carcases; and the rest of the Kingdom (where probably they will be sold somewhat cheaper) the remaining Eighty Thousand.

I can think of no one Objection, that will possibly be raised against this Proposal; unless it should be urged, that the Number of People will be thereby much lessened in the Kingdom. This I freely own; and it was indeed one principal Design in offering it to the World. I desire the Reader will observe, that I calculate my Remedy for this one individual Kingdom of Ireland, and for no other that ever was, is, or, I think, ever can be upon Earth. Therefore, let no man talk to me of other Expedients: Of taxing our Absentees[8] at five Shillings a Pound: Of using neither Cloaths, nor Household Furniture, except what is of our own Growth and Manufacture: Of utterly rejecting the Materials and Instruments that promote foreign Luxury: Of curing the Expensiveness of Pride, Vanity, Idleness, and

6. Business.
7. Recipes.
8. Absentee landlords; that is, those who owned estates in Ireland but lived in England.

Gaming in our Women: Of introducing a Vein of Parsimony, Prudence and Temperance: Of learning to love our Country, wherein we differ even from Laplanders, and the Inhabitants of Topinamboo: Of quitting our Animosities, and Factions; nor act any longer like the Jews, who were murdering one another at the very Moment their City was taken: Of being a little cautious not to sell our Country and Consciences for nothing: Of teaching Landlords to have, at least, one Degree of Mercy towards their Tenants. Lastly, of Putting a Spirit of Honesty, Industry, and Skill into our Shopkeepers; who, if a Resolution could now be taken to buy only our native Goods, would immediately unite to cheat and exact upon us in the Price, the Measure, and the Goodness; nor could ever yet be brought to make one fair Proposal of just Dealing, though often and earnestly invited to it.

Therefore I repeat, let no Man talk to me of these and the like Expedients; till he hath, at least, a Glimpse of Hope, that there will ever be some hearty and sincere Attempt to put them in Practice.

But, as to my self; having been wearied out for many Years with offering vain, idle, visionary Thoughts; and at length utterly despairing of Success, I fortunately fell upon this Proposal; which, as it is wholly new, so it hath something solid and real, of no Expence and little Trouble, full in our own Power; and whereby we can incur no Danger in disobliging England: For this Kind of Commodity will not bear Exportation; the Flesh being of too tender a Consistence, to admit a long Continuance in Salt; although, perhaps, I could name a Country, which would be glad to eat up our whole Nation without it.

After all, I am not so violently bent upon my own Opinion, as to reject any Offer, proposed by wise Men, which shall be found equally innocent, cheap, easy, and effectual. But before something of that Kind shall be advanced in Contradiction to my Scheme, and offering a better; I desire the Author, or Authors, will be pleased maturely to consider two Points. First, As Things now stand, how they will be able to find Food and Raiment, for a Hundred Thousand useless Mouths and Backs? And Secondly, There being a round Million of Creatures in human Figure, throughout this Kingdom; whose whole Subsistence, put into a common stock, would leave them in Debt two Million Pounds Sterling; adding those, who are Beggars by Profession, to the Bulk of Farmers, Cottagers and Labourers, with their Wives and Children, who are Beggars in Effect; I desire those Politicians, who dislike my Overture, and may perhaps be so bold to attempt an Answer, that they will first ask the Parents of these Mortals, Whether they would not at this Day think it a great Happiness to have been sold for Food at a Year old, in the Manner I prescribe; and thereby have avoided such a perpetual Scene of Misfortunes, as they have since gone through; by the Oppression of Landlords; the Impossibility of paying Rent, without Money or Trade; the Want of common Sustenance, with neither House nor Cloaths, to cover them from the Inclemencies of the Weather; and the most inevitable Prospect of intailing the like, or greater Miseries upon their Breed for ever.

I profess, in the Sincerity of my Heart, that I have not the least personal Interest, in endeavouring to promote this necessary Work, having no other Motive than the publick Good of my Country, by advancing our Trade, providing for Infants, relieving the Poor, and giving some Pleasure to the Rich. I have no Children, by which I can propose to get a single Penny; the youngest being nine Years Old and my Wife past Child-bearing.

[1729]

JOHN CLARE

(1793–1864)

The Natural World

About the Author: The son of a Northamptonshire, England, farmer, John Clare became famous as a peasant poet, writing descriptions of the land and animals in a voice that rings true today.

I often pulled my hat over my eyes to watch the rising of the lark, or to see the hawk hang in the summer sky and the kite take its circles round the wood. I often lingered a minute on the woodland stile to hear the woodpigeons clapping their wings among the dark oaks. I hunted curious flowers in rapture and muttered thoughts in their praise. I loved the pasture with its rushes and thistles and sheep-tracks. I adored the wild, marshy fen with its solitary heronshaw sweeping along in its melancholy sky. I wandered the heath in raptures among the rabbit burrows and golden-blossomed furze. I dropt down on a thymy molehill or mossy eminence to survey the summer landscape . . . I marked the various colours in flat, spreading fields, checkered into closes of different-tinctured grain like the colours of a map; the copper-tinted clover in blossom; the sun-tanned green of the ripening hay; the lighter hues of wheat and barley intermixed with the sunset glare of yellow charlock and the sunset imitation of the scarlet headaches; the blue corn-bottles crowding their splendid colours in large sheets over the land and troubling the cornfields with destroying beauty; the different greens of the woodland trees, the dark oak, the paler ash, the mellow lime, the white poplars peeping above the rest like leafy steeples, the grey willow shining chilly in the sun, as if the morning mist still lingered on its cool green. I loved the meadow lake with its flags and long purples crowding the water's edge. I listened with delight to hear the wind whisper among the feather-topt reeds, to see the taper bulrush nodding in gentle curves to the rippling water; and I watched with delight on haymaking evenings the setting sun drop behind the Brigs and peep again through the half-circle of the arches as if he longed to stay . . . I observed all this with the same rapture as I have done since. But I knew nothing of poetry. It was felt and not uttered.

[1820]

SAMUEL L. CLEMENS

(1835–1910)

Advice to Youth

About the Author: Clemens, better known as Mark Twain, remains one of America's premier humorists. Throughout his career, he traveled widely across the United States giving lectures in which he honed his comic voice, sounding much as it does in "Advice to Youth."

Being told I would be expected to talk here, I inquired what sort of a talk I ought to make. They said it should be something suitable to youth—something didactic, instructive, or something in the nature of good advice. Very well. I have a few things in my mind which

I have often longed to say for the instruction of the young; for it is in one's tender early years that such things will best take root and be most enduring and most valuable. First, then, I will say to you, my young friends—and I say it beseechingly, urgingly—

Always obey your parents, when they are present. This is the best policy in the long run, because if you don't they will make you. Most parents think they know better than you do, and you can generally make more by humoring that superstition than you can by acting on your own better judgment.

Be respectful to your superiors, if you have any, also to strangers, and sometimes to others. If a person offend you, and you are in doubt as to whether it was intentional or not, do not resort to extreme measures; simply watch your chance and hit him with a brick. That will be sufficient. If you shall find that he had not intended any offense, come out frankly and confess yourself in the wrong when you struck him; acknowledge it like a man and say you didn't mean to. Yes, always avoid violence; in this age of charity and kindliness, the time has gone by for such things. Leave dynamite to the low and unrefined.

Go to bed early, get up early—this is wise. Some authorities say get up with the sun; some others say get up with one thing, some with another. But a lark is really the best thing to get up with. It gives you a splendid reputation with everybody to know that you get up with the lark; and if you get the right kind of a lark, and work at him right, you can easily train him to get up at half past nine, every time—it is no trick at all.

Now as to the matter of lying. You want to be very careful about lying; otherwise you are nearly sure to get caught. Once caught, you can never again be, in the eyes of the good and the pure, what you were before. Many a young person has injured himself permanently through a single clumsy and illfinished lie, the result of carelessness born of incomplete training. Some authorities hold that the young ought not to lie at all. That, of course, is putting it rather stronger than necessary; still, while I cannot go quite so far as that, I do maintain, and I believe I am right, that the young ought to be temperate in the use of this great art until practice and experience shall give them that confidence, elegance, and precision which alone can make the accomplishment graceful and profitable. Patience, diligence, painstaking attention to detail—these are the requirements; these, in time, will make the student perfect; upon these, and upon these only, may he rely as the sure foundation for future eminence. Think what tedious years of study, thought, practice, experience, went to the equipment of that peerless old master who was able to impose upon the whole world the lofty and sounding maxim that "truth is mighty and will prevail"—the most majestic compound fracture of fact which any of woman born has yet achieved. For the history of our race, and each individual's experience, are sown thick with evidence that a truth is not hard to kill and that a lie told well is immortal. There is in Boston a monument of the man who discovered anaesthesia; many people are aware, in these latter days, that that man didn't discover it at all, but stole the discovery from another man. Is this truth mighty, and will it prevail? Ah no, my hearers, the monument is made of hardy material, but the lie it tells will outlast it a million years. An awkward, feeble, leaky lie is a thing which you ought to make it your unceasing study to avoid; such a lie as that has no more real permanence than an average truth. Why, you might as well tell the truth at once and be done with it. A feeble, stupid, preposterous lie will not live two years—except it be a slander upon somebody. It is indestructible, then, of course, but that is no merit of yours. A final word: begin your practice of this gracious and beautiful art early—begin now. If I had begun earlier, I could have learned how.

Never handle firearms carelessly. The sorrow and suffering that have been caused through the innocent but heedless handling of firearms by the young! Only four days ago, right in the next farmhouse to the one where I am spending the summer, a grandmother, old and gray and sweet, one of the loveliest spirits in the land, was sitting at her work, when her young grandson crept in and got down an old, battered, rusty gun which had not been touched for many years and was supposed not to be loaded, and pointed it at her, laughing and threatening to shoot. In her fright she ran screaming and pleading toward the door on the other side of the room; but as she passed him he placed the gun almost against her very breast and pulled the trigger! He had supposed it was not loaded. And he was right—it wasn't. So there wasn't any harm done. It is the only case of that kind I ever heard of. Therefore, just the same, don't you meddle with old unloaded firearms; they are the most deadly and unerring things that have ever been created by man. You don't have to take any pains at all with them; you don't have to have a rest, you don't have to have any sights on the gun, you don't have to take aim, even. No, you just pick out a relative and bang away, and you are sure to get him. A youth who can't hit a cathedral at thirty yards with a Gatling gun in three-quarters of an hour, can take up an old empty musket and bag his grandmother every time, at a hundred. Think what Waterloo would have been if one of the armies had been boys armed with old muskets supposed not to be loaded, and the other army had been composed of their female relations. The very thought of it makes one shudder.

There are many sorts of books; but good ones are the sort for the young to read. Remember that. They are a great, an inestimable, an unspeakable means of improvement. Therefore be careful in your selection, my young friends; be very careful; confine yourselves exclusively to Robertson's Sermons, Baxter's *Saint's Rest, The Innocents Abroad,* and works of that kind.

But I have said enough. I hope you will treasure up the instructions which I have given you, and make them a guide to your feet and a light to your understanding. Build your character thoughtfully and painstakingly upon these precepts, and by and by, when you have got it built, you will be surprised and gratified to see how nicely and sharply it resembles everybody else's.

[1882]

JOHN MUIR

(1838–1914)

A Wind-Storm in the Forests

About the Author: Born in Dunbar, Scotland, Muir was an early advocate of the significance of wilderness, particularly in his efforts to save Yosemite from destruction by commercial exploitation. "A Wind-Storm in the Forests" is one of the essays in his well-known volume *The Mountains of California* (1894).

The mountain winds, like the dew and rain, sunshine and snow, are measured and bestowed with love on the forests to develop their strength and beauty. However restricted the scope of other forest influences, that of the winds is universal. The snow bends and trims the upper forests every winter, the lightning strikes a single tree here and there, while avalanches mow down thousands at a swoop as a gardener trims out a bed of flowers. But the winds go to every tree, fingering every leaf and branch and furrowed bole; not one is forgotten; the Mountain Pine towering with outstretched arms on the rugged buttresses of the icy peaks, the lowliest and most retiring tenant of the dells; they seek and find them all, caressing them tenderly, bending them in lusty exercise, stimulating their growth, plucking off a leaf or limb as required, or removing an entire tree or grove, now whispering and cooing through the branches like a sleepy child, now roaring like the ocean; the winds blessing the forests, the forests the winds, with ineffable beauty and harmony as the sure result.

After one has seen pines six feet in diameter bending like grasses before a mountain gale, and ever and anon some giant falling with a crash that shakes the hills, it seems astonishing that any, save the lowest thickset trees, could ever have found a period sufficiently stormless to establish themselves; or, once established, that they should not, sooner or later, have been blown down. But when the storm is over, and we behold the same forests tranquil again, towering fresh and unscathed in erect majesty, and consider what centuries of storms have fallen upon them since they were first planted,—hail, to break the tender seedlings; lightning, to scorch and shatter; snow, winds, and avalanches, to crush and overwhelm,—while the manifest result of all this wild storm-culture is the glorious perfection we behold; then faith in Nature's forestry is established, and we cease to deplore the violence of her most destructive gales, or of any other storm-implement whatsoever.

There are two trees in the Sierra forests that are never blown down, so long as they continue in sound health. These are the Juniper and the Dwarf Pine of the summit peaks. Their stiff, crooked roots grip the storm-beaten ledges like eagles' claws, while their lithe, cord-like branches bend round compliantly, offering but slight holds for winds, however violent. The other alpine conifers—the Needle Pine, Mountain Pine, Two-leaved Pine, and Hemlock Spruce—are never thinned out by this agent to any destructive extent, on account of their admirable toughness and the closeness of their growth. In general the same is true of the giants of the lower zones. The kingly Sugar Pine, towering aloft to a height of more than 200 feet, offers a fine mark to storm-winds; but it is not densely foliated, and its long, horizontal arms swing round compliantly in the blast, like tresses of green, fluent algæ in a brook; while the Silver Firs in most places keep their ranks well together in united strength. The Yellow or Silver Pine is more frequently overturned than any other tree on the Sierra, because its leaves and branches form a larger mass in proportion to its height, while in many places it is planted sparsely, leaving open lanes through which storms may enter with full force. Furthermore, because it is distributed along the lower portion of the range, which was the first to be left bare on the breaking up of the ice-sheet at the close of the glacial winter, the soil it is growing upon has been longer exposed to post-glacial weathering, and consequently is in a more crumbling, decayed condition than the fresher soils farther up the range, and therefore offers a less secure anchorage for the roots.

While exploring the forest zones of Mount Shasta, I discovered the path of a hurricane strewn with thousands of pines of this species. Great and small had been uprooted or wrenched off by sheer force, making a clean gap, like that made by a snow avalanche. But hurricanes capable of doing this class of work are rare in the Sierra, and when we have explored the forests from one extremity of the range to the other, we are compelled to believe that they are the most beautiful on the face of the earth, however we may regard the agents that have made them so.

There is always something deeply exciting, not only in the sounds of winds in the woods, which exert more or less influence over every mind, but in their varied waterlike

flow as manifested by the movements of the trees, especially those of the conifers. By no other trees are they rendered so extensively and impressively visible, not even by the lordly tropic palms or tree-ferns responsive to the gentlest breeze. The waving of a forest of the giant Sequoias is indescribably impressive and sublime, but the pines seem to me the best interpreters of winds. They are mighty waving goldenrods, ever in tune, singing and writing wind-music all their long century lives. Little, however, of this noble tree-waving and tree music will you see or hear in the strictly alpine portion of the forests. The burly Juniper, whose girth sometimes more than equals its height, is about as rigid as the rocks on which it grows. The slender lash-like sprays of the Dwarf Pine stream out in wavering ripples, but the tallest and slenderest are far too unyielding to wave even in the heaviest gales. They only shake in quick, short vibrations. The Hemlock Spruce, however, and the Mountain Pine, and some of the tallest thickets of the Two-leaved species bow in storms with considerable scope and gracefulness. But it is only in the lower and middle zones that the meeting of winds and woods is to be seen in all its grandeur.

One of the most beautiful and exhilarating storms I ever enjoyed in the Sierra occurred in December, 1874, when I happened to be exploring one of the tributary valleys of the Yuba River. The sky and the ground and the trees had been thoroughly rain-washed and were dry again. The day was intensely pure, one of those incomparable bits of California winter, warm and balmy and full of white sparkling sunshine, redolent of all the purest influences of the spring, and at the same time enlivened with one of the most bracing wind-storms conceivable. Instead of camping out, as I usually do, I then chanced to be stopping at the house of a friend. But when the storm began to sound, I lost no time in pushing out into the woods to enjoy it. For on such occasions Nature has always something rare to show us, and the danger to life and limb is hardly greater than one would experience crouching deprecatingly beneath a roof.

It was still early morning when I found myself fairly adrift. Delicious sunshine came pouring over the hills, lighting the tops of the pines, and setting free a stream of summery fragrance that contrasted strangely with the wild tones of the storm. The air was mottled with pine-tassels and bright green plumes, that went flashing past in the sunlight like birds pursued. But there was not the slightest dustiness, nothing less pure than leaves, and ripe pollen, and flecks of withered bracken and moss. I heard trees falling for hours at the rate of one every two or three minutes; some uprooted, partly on account of the loose, water-soaked condition of the ground; others broken straight across, where some weakness caused by fire had determined the spot. The gestures of the various trees made a delightful study. Young Sugar Pines, light and feathery as squirrel-tails, were bowing almost to the ground; while the grand old patriarchs, whose massive boles had been tried in a hundred storms, waved solemnly above them, their long, arching branches streaming fluently on the gale, and every needle thrilling and ringing and shedding off keen lances of light like a diamond. The Douglas Spruces, with long sprays drawn out in level tresses, and needles massed in a gray, shimmering glow, presented a most striking appearance as they stood in bold relief along the hilltops. The madroños in the dells, with their red bark and large glossy leaves tilted every way, reflected the sunshine in throbbing spangles like those one so often sees on the rippled surface of a glacier lake. But the Silver Pines were now the most impressively beautiful of all. Colossal spires 200 feet in height waved like supple goldenrods chanting and bowing low as if in worship, while the whole mass of their long, tremulous foliage was kindled into one continuous blaze of white sun-fire. The force of the gale was such that the most steadfast monarch of them all rocked down to its roots with a motion plainly perceptible when one leaned against it. Nature was holding high festival, and every fiber of the most rigid giants thrilled with glad excitement.

I drifted on through the midst of this passionate music and motion, across many a glen, from ridge to ridge; often halting in the lee of a rock for shelter, or to gaze and listen. Even when the grand anthem had swelled to its highest pitch, I could distinctly hear the varying tones of individual trees,—Spruce, and Fir, and Pine, and leafless Oak,—and even the infinitely gentle rustle of the withered grasses at my feet. Each was expressing itself in its own way,—singing its own song, and making its own peculiar gestures,—manifesting a richness of variety to be found in no other forest I have yet seen. The coniferous woods of Canada, and the Carolinas, and Florida, are made up of trees that resemble one another about as nearly as blades of grass, and grow close together in much the same way. Coniferous trees, in general, seldom possess individual character, such as is manifest among Oaks and Elms. But the California forests are made up of a greater number of distinct species than any other in the world. And in them we find, not only a marked differentiation into special groups, but also a marked individuality in almost every tree, giving rise to storm effects indescribably glorious.

Toward midday, after a long, tingling scramble through copses of hazel and ceanothus, I gained the summit of the highest ridge in the neighborhood; and then it occurred to me that it would be a fine thing to climb one of the trees to obtain a wider outlook and get my ear close to the Æolian music of its topmost needles. But under the circumstances the choice of a tree was a serious matter. One whose instep was not very strong seemed in danger of being blown down, or of being struck by others in case they should fall; another was branchless to a considerable height above the ground, and at the same time too large to be grasped with arms and legs in climbing; while others were not favorably situated for clear views. After cautiously casting about, I made choice of the tallest of a group of Douglas Spruces that were growing close together like a tuft of grass, no one of which seemed likely to fall unless all the rest fell with it. Though comparatively young, they were about 100 feet high, and their lithe, brushy tops were rocking and swirling in wild ecstasy. Being accustomed to climb trees in making botanical studies, I experienced no difficulty in reaching the top of this one, and never before did I enjoy so noble an exhilaration of motion. The slender tops fairly flapped and swished in the passionate torrent, bending and swirling backward and forward, round and round, tracing indescribable combinations of vertical and horizontal curves, while I clung with muscles firm braced, like a bobolink on a reed.

In its widest sweeps my tree-top described an arc of from twenty to thirty degrees, but I felt sure of its elastic temper, having seen others of the same species still more severely tried—bent almost to the ground indeed, in heavy snows—without breaking a fiber. I was therefore safe, and free to take the wind into my pulses and enjoy the excited forest from my superb outlook. The view from here must be extremely beautiful in any weather. Now my eye roved over the piny hills and dales as over fields of waving grain, and felt the light running in ripples and broad swelling undulations across the valleys from ridge to ridge, as the shining foliage was stirred by corresponding waves of air. Oftentimes these waves of reflected light would break up suddenly into a kind of beaten foam, and again, after chasing one another in regular order, they would seem to bend forward in concentric curves, and disappear on some hillside, like sea-waves on a shelving shore. The quantity of light reflected from the bent needles was so great as to make whole groves appear as if covered with snow, while the black shadows beneath the trees greatly enhanced the effect of the silvery splendor.

Excepting only the shadows there was nothing somber in all this wild sea of pines. On the contrary, notwithstanding this was the winter season, the colors were remarkably beautiful. The shafts of the pine and libocedrus were brown and purple, and most of the foliage was well tinged with yellow; the laurel groves, with the pale undersides of their leaves turned upward, made masses of gray; and then there was many a dash of chocolate color from clumps of manzanita, and jet of vivid crimson from the bark of the madroños, while the ground on the hillsides, appearing here and there through openings between the groves, displayed masses of pale purple and brown.

The sounds of the storm corresponded gloriously with this wild exuberance of light and motion. The profound bass of the naked branches and boles booming like waterfalls; the quick, tense vibrations of the pine-needles, now rising to a shrill, whistling hiss, now falling to a silky murmur; the rustling of laurel groves in the dells, and the keen metallic click of leaf on leaf—all this was heard in easy analysis when the attention was calmly bent.

The varied gestures of the multitude were seen to fine advantage, so that one could recognize the different species at a distance of several miles by this means alone, as well as by their forms and colors, and the way they reflected the light. All seemed strong and comfortable, as if really enjoying the storm, while responding to its most enthusiastic greetings. We hear much nowadays concerning the universal struggle for existence, but no struggle in the common meaning of the word was manifest here; no recognition of danger by any tree; no depreciation; but rather an invincible gladness as remote from exultation as from fear.

I kept my lofty perch for hours, frequently closing my eyes to enjoy the music by itself, or to feast quietly on the delicious fragrance that was streaming past. The fragrance of the woods was less marked than that produced during warm rain, when so many balsamic buds and leaves are steeped like tea; but, from the chafing of resiny branches against each other, and the incessant attrition of myriads of needles, the gale was spiced to a very tonic degree. And besides the fragrance from these local sources there were traces of scents brought from afar. For this wind came first from the sea, rubbing against its fresh, briny waves, then distilled through the redwoods, threading rich ferny gulches, and spreading itself in broad undulating currents over many a flower-enameled ridge of the coast mountains, then across the golden plains, up the purple foot-hills, and into these piny woods with the varied incense gathered by the way.

Winds are advertisements of all they touch, however much or little we may be able to read them; telling their wanderings even by their scents alone. Mariners detect the flowery perfume of land-winds far at sea, and sea-winds carry the fragrance of dulse and tangle far inland, where it is quickly recognized, though mingled with the scents of a thousand land-flowers. As an illustration of this, I may tell here that I breathed sea-air on the Firth of Forth, in Scotland, while a boy; then was taken to Wisconsin, where I remained nineteen years; then, without in all this time having breathed one breath of the sea, I walked quietly, alone, from the middle of the Mississippi Valley to the Gulf of Mexico, on a botanical excursion, and while in Florida, far from the coast, my attention wholly bent on the splendid tropical vegetation about me, I suddenly recognized a sea-breeze, as it came sifting through the palmettos and blooming vine-tangles, which at once awakened and set free a thousand dormant associations, and made me a boy again in Scotland, as if all the intervening years had been annihilated.

Most people like to look at mountain rivers, and bear them in mind; but few care to look at the winds, though far more beautiful and sublime, and though they become at times about as visible as flowing water. When the north winds in winter are making upward sweeps over the curving summits of the High Sierra, the fact is sometimes published with flying snow-banners a mile long. Those portions of the winds thus embodied can scarce be wholly invisible, even to the darkest imagination. And when we look around over an agitated forest, we may see something of the wind that stirs it, by its effects upon the trees. Yonder it descends in a rush of water-like ripples, and sweeps over the bending pines from hill to hill. Nearer, we see detached plumes and leaves, now speeding by on level currents, now whirling in eddies, or, escaping over the edges of the whirls, soaring aloft on grand, upswelling domes of air, or tossing on flame-like crests. Smooth, deep currents, cascades, falls, and swirling eddies, sing around every tree and leaf, and over all the varied topography of the region with telling changes of form, like mountain rivers conforming to the features of their channels.

After tracing the Sierra streams from their fountains to the plains, marking where they bloom white in falls, slide in crystal plumes, surge gray and foam-filled in boulder-choked gorges, and slip through the woods in long, tranquil reaches—after thus learning their language and forms in detail, we may at length hear them chanting all together in one grand anthem, and comprehend them all in clear inner vision, covering the range like lace. But even this spectacle is far less sublime and not a whit more substantial than what we may behold of these storm-streams of air in the mountain woods.

We all travel the milky way together, trees and men; but it never occurred to me until this stormday, while swinging in the wind, that trees are travelers, in the ordinary sense. They make many journeys, not extensive ones, it is true; but our own little journeys, away and back again, are only little more than tree-wavings—many of them not so much.

When the storm began to abate, I dismounted and sauntered down through the calming woods. The storm-tones died away, and, turning toward the east, I beheld the countless hosts of the forests hushed and tranquil, towering above one another on the slopes of the hills like a devout audience. The setting sun filled them with amber light, and seemed to say, while they listened, "My peace I give unto you."

As I gazed on the impressive scene, all the so-called ruin of the storm was forgotten, and never before did these noble woods appear so fresh, so joyous, so immortal.

[1894]

VIRGINIA WOOLF

(1882–1941)

How Should One Read a Book?

About the Author: One of the most important stylistic innovators of fiction in the first half of the twentieth century, Woolf brought the essay to new heights in her *Common Reader* series. The essay "How Should One Read a Book?" takes us into the act of reading so that we glimpse the possibilities opening out before us as we read.

In the first place, I want to emphasise the note of interrogation at the end of my title. Even if I could answer the question for myself, the answer would apply only to me and not to you. The only advice, indeed, that one person can give another about reading is to take no

advice, to follow your own instincts, to use your own reason, to come to your own conclusions. If this is agreed between us, then I feel at liberty to put forward a few ideas and suggestions because you will not allow them to fetter that independence which is the most important quality that a reader can possess. After all, what laws can be laid down about books? The battle of Waterloo was certainly fought on a certain day; but is *Hamlet* a better play than *Lear*? Nobody can say. Each must decide that question for himself. To admit authorities, however heavily furred and gowned, into our libraries and let them tell us how to read, what to read, what value to place upon what we read, is to destroy the spirit of freedom which is the breath of those sanctuaries. Everywhere else we may be bound by laws and conventions—there we have none.

But to enjoy freedom, if the platitude is pardonable, we have of course to control ourselves. We must not squander our powers, helplessly and ignorantly, squirting half the house in order to water a single rose-bush; we must train them, exactly and powerfully, here on the very spot. This, it may be, is one of the first difficulties that faces us in a library. What is "the very spot"? There may well seem to be nothing but a conglomeration and huddle of confusion. Poems and novels, histories and memoirs, dictionaries and blue-books; books written in all languages by men and women of all tempers, races, and ages jostle each other on the shelf. And outside the donkey brays, the women gossip at the pump, the colts gallop across the fields. Where are we to begin? How are we to bring order into this multitudinous chaos and so get the deepest and widest pleasure from what we read?

It is simple enough to say that since books have classes—fiction, biography, poetry—we should separate them and take from each what it is right that each should give us. Yet few people ask from books what books can give us. Most commonly we come to books with blurred and divided minds, asking of fiction that it shall be true, of poetry that it shall be false, of biography that it shall be flattering, of history that it shall enforce our own prejudices. If we could banish all such preconceptions when we read, that would be an admirable beginning. Do not dictate to your author; try to become him. Be his fellow-worker and accomplice. If you hang back, and reserve and criticise at first, you are preventing yourself from getting the fullest possible value from what you read. But if you open your mind as widely as possible, then signs and hints of almost imperceptible fineness, from the twist and turn of the first sentences, will bring you into the presence of a human being unlike any other. Steep yourself in this, acquaint yourself with this, and soon you will find that your author is giving you, or attempting to give you, something far more definite. The thirty-two chapters of a novel—if we consider how to read a novel first—are an attempt to make something as formed and controlled as a building: but words are more impalpable than bricks; reading is a longer and more complicated process than seeing. Perhaps the quickest way to understand the elements of what a novelist is doing is not to read, but to write; to make your own experiment with the dangers and difficulties of words. Recall, then, some event that has left a distinct impression on you—how at the corner of the street, perhaps, you passed two people talking. A tree shook; an electric light danced; the tone of the talk was comic, but also tragic; a whole vision, an entire conception, seemed contained in that moment.

But when you attempt to reconstruct it in words, you will find that it breaks into a thousand conflicting impressions. Some must be subdued; others emphasised; in the process you will lose, probably, all grasp upon the emotion itself. Then turn from your blurred and littered pages to the opening pages of some great novelist—Defoe, Jane Austen, Hardy. Now you will be better able to appreciate their mastery. It is not merely that we are in the presence of a different person—Defoe, Jane Austen, or Thomas Hardy—but that we are living in a different world. Here, in *Robinson Crusoe,* we are trudging a plain high road; one thing happens after another; the fact and the order of the fact is enough. But if the open air and adventure mean everything to Defoe they mean nothing to Jane Austen. Hers is the drawing-room, and people talking, and by the many mirrors of their talk revealing their characters. And if, when we have accustomed ourselves to the drawing-room and its reflections, we turn to Hardy, we are once more spun round. The moors are round us and the stars are above our heads. The other side of the mind is now exposed—the dark side that comes uppermost in solitude, not the light side that shows in company. Our relations are not towards people, but towards Nature and destiny. Yet different as these worlds are, each is consistent with itself. The maker of each is careful to observe the laws of his own perspective, and however great a strain they may put upon us they will never confuse us, as lesser writers so frequently do, by introducing two different kinds of reality into the same book. Thus to go from one great novelist to another—from Jane Austen to Hardy, from Peacock to Trollope, from Scott to Meredith—is to be wrenched and uprooted; to be thrown this way and then that. To read a novel is a difficult and complex art. You must be capable not only of great fineness of perception, but of great boldness of imagination if you are going to make use of all that the novelist—the great artist—gives you.

But a glance at the heterogeneous company on the shelf will show you that writers are very seldom "great artists"; far more often a book makes no claim to be a work of art at all. These biographies and autobiographies, for example, lives of great men, of men long dead and forgotten, that stand cheek by jowl with the novels and poems, are we to refuse to read them because they are not "art"? Or shall we read them, but read them in a different way, with a different aim? Shall we read them in the first place to satisfy that curiosity which possesses us sometimes when in the evening we linger in front of a house where the lights are lit and the blinds not yet drawn, and each floor of the house shows us a different section of human life in being? Then we are consumed with curiosity about the lives of these people—the servants gossiping, the gentlemen dining, the girl dressing for a party, the old woman at the window with her knitting. Who are they, what are they, what are their names, their occupations, their thoughts, and adventures?

Biographies and memoirs answer such questions, light up innumerable such houses; they show us people going about their daily affairs, toiling, failing, succeeding, eating, hating, loving, until they die. And sometimes as we watch, the house fades and the iron railings vanish and we are out at sea; we are hunting, sailing, fighting; we are among savages and soldiers; we are taking part in great campaigns. Or if we like to stay here in England, in London, still the scene changes; the street narrows; the house becomes small, cramped, diamond-paned, and malodorous. We see a poet, Donne, driven from such a house because the walls were so thin that when the children cried their voices cut through them. We can follow him, through the paths that lie in the pages of books, to Twickenham; to Lady Bedford's Park, a famous meeting-ground for nobles and poets; and then turn our steps to Wilton, the great house under the downs, and hear Sidney read the *Arcadia* to his sister; and ramble among the very marshes and see the very herons that figure in that famous romance; and then again travel north with that other Lady Pembroke, Anne Clifford, to her wild moors, or plunge into the city and control our merriment at the sight of Gabriel Harvey in his black velvet suit arguing about poetry with Spenser. Nothing is more fascinating than to grope and stumble in the alternate darkness and splendour of Elizabethan London. But there is no staying there. The Temples and the Swifts, the Harleys and the St. Johns beckon

us on; hour upon hour can be spent disentangling their quarrels and deciphering their characters; and when we tire of them we can stroll on, past a lady in black wearing diamonds, to Samuel Johnson and Goldsmith and Garrick; or cross the channel, if we like, and meet Voltaire and Diderot, Madame du Deffand; and so back to England and Twickenham—how certain places repeat themselves and certain names!—where Lady Bedford had her Park once and Pope lived later, to Walpole's home at Strawberry Hill. But Walpole introduces us to such a swarm of new acquaintances, there are so many houses to visit and bells to ring that we may well hesitate for a moment, on the Miss Berrys' doorstep, for example, when behold, up comes Thackeray; he is the friend of the woman whom Walpole loved; so that merely by going from friend to friend, from garden to garden, from house to house, we have passed from one end of English literature to another and wake to find ourselves here again in the present, if we can so differentiate this moment from all that have gone before. This, then, is one of the ways in which we can read these lives and letters; we can make them light up the many windows of the past; we can watch the famous dead in their familiar habits and fancy sometimes that we are very close and can surprise their secrets, and sometimes we may pull out a play or a poem that they have written and see whether it reads differently in the presence of the author. But this again rouses other questions. How far, we must ask ourselves, is a book influenced by its writer's life—how far is it safe to let the man interpret the writer? How far shall we resist or give way to the sympathies and antipathies that the man himself rouses in us—so sensitive are words, so receptive of the character of the author? These are questions that press upon us when we read lives and letters, and we must answer them for ourselves, for nothing can be more fatal than to be guided by the preferences of others in a matter so personal.

But also we can read such books with another aim, not to throw light on literature, not to become familiar with famous people, but to refresh and exercise our own creative powers. Is there not an open window on the right hand of the bookcase? How delightful to stop reading and look out! How stimulating the scene is, in its unconsciousness, its irrelevance, its perpetual movement—the colts galloping round the field, the woman filling her pail at the well, the donkey throwing back his head and emitting his long, acrid moan. The greater part of any library is nothing but the record of such fleeting moments in the lives of men, women, and donkeys. Every literature, as it grows old, has its rubbish-heap, its record of vanished moments and forgotten lives told in faltering and feeble accents that have perished. But if you give yourself up to the delight of rubbish-reading you will be surprised, indeed you will be overcome, by the relics of human life that have been cast out to moulder. It may be one letter—but what a vision it gives! It may be a few sentences—but what vistas they suggest! Sometimes a whole story will come together with such beautiful humour and pathos and completeness that it seems as if a great novelist had been at work, yet it is only an old actor, Tate Wilkinson, remembering the strange story of Captain Jones; it is only a young subaltern serving under Arthur Wellesley and falling in love with a pretty girl at Lisbon; it is only Maria Allen letting fall her sewing in the empty drawing-room and sighing how she wishes she had taken Dr. Burney's good advice and had never eloped with her Rishy. None of this has any value; it is negligible in the extreme; yet how absorbing it is now and again to go through the rubbish-heaps and find rings and scissors and broken noses buried in the huge past and try to piece them together while the colt gallops round the field, the woman fills her pail at the well, and the donkey brays.

But we tire of rubbish-reading in the long run. We tire of searching for what is needed to complete the half-truth which is all that the Wilkinsons, the Bunburys, and the Maria

Allens are able to offer us. They had not the artist's power of mastering and eliminating; they could not tell the whole truth even about their own lives; they have disfigured the story that might have been so shapely. Facts are all that they can offer us, and facts are a very inferior form of fiction. Thus the desire grows upon us to have done with half-statements and approximations; to cease from searching out the minute shades of human character, to enjoy the greater abstractness, the purer truth of fiction. Thus we create the mood, intense and generalised, unaware of detail, but stressed by some regular, recurrent beat, whose natural expression is poetry; and that is the time to read poetry when we are almost able to write it.

Western wind, when wilt thou blow?
The small rain down can rain.
Christ, if my love were in my arms,
And I in my bed again!

The impact of poetry is so hard and direct that for the moment there is no other sensation except that of the poem itself. What profound depths we visit then—how sudden and complete is our immersion! There is nothing here to catch hold of; nothing to stay us in our flight. The illusion of fiction is gradual; its effects are prepared; but who when they read these four lines stops to ask who wrote them, or conjures up the thought of Donne's house or Sidney's secretary; or enmeshes them in the intricacy of the past and the succession of generations? The poet is always our contemporary. Our being for the moment is centred and constricted, as in any violent shock of personal emotion. Afterwards, it is true, the sensation begins to spread in wider rings through our minds; remoter senses are reached; these begin to sound and to comment and we are aware of echoes and reflections. The intensity of poetry covers an immense range of emotion. We have only to compare the force and directness of

I shall fall like a tree, and find my grave,
Only remembering that I grieve,

with the wavering modulation of

Minutes are numbered by the fall of sands,
As by an hour glass; the span of time
Doth waste us to our graves, and we look on it;
An age of pleasure, revelled out, comes home
At last, and ends in sorrow; but the life,
Weary of riot, numbers every sand,
Wailing in sighs, until the last drop down,
So to conclude calamity in rest,

or place the meditative calm of

whether we be young or old,
Our destiny, our being's heart and home,
Is with infinitude, and only there;

With hope it is, hope that can never die,
Effort, and expectation, and desire,
And something evermore about to be,

beside the complete and inexhaustible loveliness of

The moving Moon went up the sky,
And nowhere did abide:
Softly she was going up,
And a star or two beside—

or the splendid fantasy of

And the woodland haunter
Shall not cease to saunter
When, far down some glade,
Of the great world's burning,
One soft flame upturning
Seems, to his discerning,
Crocus in the shade,

to bethink us of the varied art of the poet; his power to make us at once actors and spectators; his power to run his hand into character as if it were a glove, and be Falstaff or Lear; his power to condense, to widen, to state, once and for ever.

"We have only to compare"—with those words the cat is out of the bag, and the true complexity of reading is admitted. The first process, to receive impressions with the utmost understanding, is only half the process of reading; it must be completed, if we are to get the whole pleasure from a book, by another. We must pass judgment upon these multitudinous impressions; we must make of these fleeting shapes one that is hard and lasting. But not directly. Wait for the dust of reading to settle; for the conflict and the questioning to die down; walk, talk, pull the dead petals from a rose, or fall asleep. Then suddenly without our willing it, for it is thus that Nature undertakes these transitions, the book will return, but differently. It will float to the top of the mind as a whole. And the book as a whole is different from the book received currently in separate phrases. Details now fit themselves into their places. We see the shape from start to finish; it is a barn, a pig-sty, or a cathedral. Now then we can compare book with book as we compare building with building. But this act of comparison means that our attitude has changed; we are no longer the friends of the writer, but his judges; and just as we cannot be too sympathetic as friends, so as judges we cannot be too severe. Are they not criminals, books that have wasted our time and sympathy; are they not the most insidious enemies of society, corrupters, defilers, the writers of false books, faked books, books that fill the air with decay and disease? Let us then be severe in our judgments; let us compare each book with the greatest of its kind. There they hang in the mind the shapes of the books we have read solidified by the judgments we have passed on them—*Robinson Crusoe, Emma, The Return of the Native.* Compare the novels with these—even the latest and least of novels has a right to be judged with the best. And so with poetry—when the intoxication of rhythm has died down and the splendour of words has faded, a visionary shape will return to us and this must be compared with *Lear,* with *Phèdre,* with *The Prelude;* or if not with these, with whatever is the best or seems to us to be the best in its own kind. And we may be sure that the newness of new poetry and fiction is its most superficial quality and that we have only to alter slightly, not to recast, the standards by which we have judged the old.

It would be foolish, then, to pretend that the second part of reading, to judge, to compare, is as simple as the first—to open the mind wide to the fast flocking of innumerable impressions. To continue reading without the book before you, to hold one shadow-shape against another, to have read widely enough and with enough understanding to make such comparisons alive and illuminating—that is difficult; it is still more difficult to press further and to say, "Not only is the book of this sort, but it is of this value; here it fails; here it succeeds; this is bad; that is good". To carry out this part of a reader's duty needs such imagination, insight, and learning that it is hard to conceive any one mind sufficiently endowed; impossible for the most self-confident to find more than the seeds of such powers in himself. Would it not be wiser, then, to remit this part of reading and to allow the critics, the gowned and furred authorities of the library, to decide the question of the book's absolute value for us? Yet how impossible! We may stress the value of sympathy; we may try to sink our own identity as we read. But we know that we cannot sympathise wholly or immerse ourselves wholly; there is always a demon in us who whispers, "I hate, I love", and we cannot silence him. Indeed, it is precisely because we hate and we love that our relation with the poets and novelists is so intimate that we find the presence of another person intolerable. And even if the results are abhorrent and our judgments are wrong, still our taste, the nerve of sensation that sends shocks through us, is our chief illuminant; we learn through feeling; we cannot suppress our own idiosyncrasy without impoverishing it. But as time goes on perhaps we can train our taste; perhaps we can make it submit to some control. When it has fed greedily and lavishly upon books of all sorts—poetry, fiction, history, biography—and has stopped reading and looked for long spaces upon the variety, the incongruity of the living world, we shall find that it is changing a little; it is not so greedy, it is more reflective. It will begin to bring us not merely judgments on particular books, but it will tell us that there is a quality common to certain books. Listen, it will say, what shall we call *this?* And it will read us perhaps *Lear* and then perhaps the *Agamemnon* in order to bring out that common quality. Thus, with our taste to guide us, we shall venture beyond the particular book in search of qualities that group books together; we shall give them names and thus frame a rule that brings order into our perceptions. We shall gain a further and a rarer pleasure from that discrimination. But as a rule only lives when it is perpetually broken by contact with the books themselves—nothing is easier and more stultifying than to make rules which exist out of touch with facts, in a vacuum—now at last, in order to steady ourselves in this difficult attempt, it may be well to turn to the very rare writers who are able to enlighten us upon literature as an art. Coleridge and Dryden and Johnson, in their considered criticism, the poets and novelists themselves in their unconsidered sayings, are often surprisingly relevant; they light up and solidify the vague ideas that have been tumbling in the misty depths of our minds. But they are only able to help us if we come to them laden with questions and suggestions won honestly in the course of our own reading. They can do nothing for us if we herd ourselves under their authority and lie down like sheep in the shade of a hedge. We can only understand their ruling when it comes in conflict with our own and vanquishes it.

If this is so, if to read a book as it should be read calls for the rarest qualities of imagination, insight, and judgment, you may perhaps conclude that literature is a very

complex art and that it is unlikely that we shall be able, even after a lifetime of reading, to make any valuable contribution to its criticism. We must remain readers; we shall not put on the further glory that belongs to those rare beings who are also critics. But still we have our responsibilities as readers and even our importance. The standards we raise and the judgments we pass steal into the air and become part of the atmosphere which writers breathe as they work. An influence is created which tells upon them even if it never finds its way into print. And that influence, if it were well instructed, vigorous and individual and sincere, might be of great value now when criticism is necessarily in abeyance; when books pass in review like the procession of animals in a shooting gallery, and the critic has only one second in which to load and aim and shoot and may well be pardoned if he mistakes rabbits for tigers, eagles for barndoor fowls, or misses altogether and wastes his shot upon some peaceful cow grazing in a further field. If behind the erratic gunfire of the press the author felt that there was another kind of criticism, the opinion of people reading for the love of reading, slowly and unprofessionally, and judging with great sympathy and yet with great severity, might this not improve the quality of his work? And if by our means books were to become stronger, richer, and more varied, that would be an end worth reaching.

Yet who reads to bring about an end, however desirable? Are there not some pursuits that we practise because they are good in themselves, and some pleasures that are final? And is not this among them? I have sometimes dreamt, at least, that when the Day of Judgment dawns and the great conquerors and lawyers and statesmen come to receive their rewards—their crowns, their laurels, their names carved indelibly upon imperishable marble—the Almighty will turn to Peter and will say, not without a certain envy when He sees us coming with our books under our arms, "Look, these need no reward. We have nothing to give them here. They have loved reading."

[1932]

GEORGE ORWELL

(1903–1950)

Shooting an Elephant

About the Author: Equally acclaimed as a novelist *(1984)* and essayist *(Shooting an Elephant and Other Essays),* Orwell committed himself as a writer to the causes of personal freedom and social justice. "Shooting an Elephant" keeps us aware of the heritage of racism and oppression that colonialism has left behind.

In Moulmein, in lower Burma, I was hated by large numbers of people—the only time in my life that I have been important enough for this to happen to me. I was sub-divisional police officer of the town, and in an aimless, petty kind of way anti-European feeling was very bitter. No one had the guts to raise a riot, but if a European woman went through the bazaars alone somebody would probably spit betel juice over her dress. As a police officer I was an obvious target and was baited whenever it seemed safe to do so. When a nimble Burman tripped me up on the football field and the referee (another Burman) looked the other way, the crowd yelled with hideous laughter. This happened more than once. In the end the sneering yellow faces of young men that met me everywhere, the insults hooted

after me when I was at a safe distance, got badly on my nerves. The young Buddhist priests were the worst of all. There were several thousands of them in the town and none of them seemed to have anything to do except stand on street corners and jeer at Europeans.

All this was perplexing and upsetting. For at that time I had already made up my mind that imperialism was an evil thing and the sooner I chucked up my job and got out of it the better. Theoretically—and secretly, of course—I was all for the Burmese and all against their oppressors, the British. As for the job I was doing, I hated it more bitterly than I can perhaps make clear. In a job like that you see the dirty work of Empire at close quarters. The wretched prisoners huddling in the stinking cages of the lock-ups, the grey, cowed faces of the long-term convicts, the scarred buttocks of the men who had been flogged with bamboos—all these oppressed me with an intolerable sense of guilt. But I could get nothing into perspective. I was young and ill-educated and I had had to think out my problems in the utter silence that is imposed on every Englishman in the East. I did not even know that the British Empire is dying, still less did I know that it is a great deal better than the younger empires that are going to supplant it. All I knew was that I was stuck between my hatred of the empire I served and my rage against the evil-spirited little beasts who tried to make my job impossible. With one part of my mind I thought of the British Raj as an unbreakable tyranny, as something clamped down, in *saecula saeculorum,* upon the will of prostrate peoples; with another part I thought that the greatest joy in the world would be to drive a bayonet into a Buddhist priest's guts. Feelings like these are the normal by-products of imperialism; ask any Anglo-Indian official, if you can catch him off duty.

One day something happened which in a roundabout way was enlightening. It was a tiny incident in itself, but it gave me a better glimpse than I had had before of the real nature of imperialism—the real motives for which despotic governments act. Early one morning the sub-inspector at a police station the other end of the town rang me up on the 'phone and said that an elephant was ravaging the bazaar. Would I please come and do something about it? I did not know what I could do, but I wanted to see what was happening and I got on to a pony and started out. I took my rifle, an old .44 Winchester and much too small to kill an elephant, but I thought the noise might be useful *in terrorem.* Various Burmans stopped me on the way and told me about the elephant's doings. It was not, of course, a wild elephant, but a tame one which had gone "must." It had been chained up, as tame elephants always are when their attack of "must" is due, but on the previous night it had broken its chain and escaped. Its mahout, the only person who could manage it when it was in that state, had set out in pursuit, but had taken the wrong direction and was now twelve hours' journey away, and in the morning the elephant had suddenly reappeared in the town. The Burmese population had no weapons and were quite helpless against it. It had already destroyed somebody's bamboo hut, killed a cow and raided some fruit-stalls and devoured the stock; also it had met the municipal rubbish van and, when the driver jumped out and took to his heels, had turned the van over and inflicted violences upon it.

The Burmese sub-inspector and some Indian constables were waiting for me in the quarter where the elephant had been seen. It was a very poor quarter, a labyrinth of squalid bamboo huts, thatched with palm-leaf, winding all over a steep hillside. I remember that it was a cloudy, stuffy morning at the beginning of the rains. We began questioning the people as to where the elephant had gone and, as usual, failed to get any definite information. That is invariably the case in the East; a story always sounds clear enough at a distance, but the nearer you get to the scene of events the vaguer it becomes. Some of the people said that the elephant had gone in one direction, some said that he had gone in another, some professed not even to have heard of any elephant. I had almost made up my mind that the whole story was a pack of lies, when we heard yells a little distance away. There was a loud, scandalized cry of "Go away, child! Go away this instant!" and an old woman with a switch in her hand came round the corner of a hut, violently shooing away a crowd of naked children. Some more women followed, clicking their tongues and exclaiming; evidently there was something that the children ought not to have seen. I rounded the hut and saw a man's dead body sprawling in the mud. He was an Indian, a black Dravidian coolie, almost naked, and he could not have been dead many minutes. The people said that the elephant had come suddenly upon him round the corner of the hut, caught him with its trunk, put its foot on his back and ground him into the earth. This was the rainy season and the ground was soft, and his face had scored a trench a foot deep and a couple of yards long. He was lying on his belly with arms crucified and head sharply twisted to one side. His face was coated with mud, the eyes wide open, the teeth bared and grinning with an expression of unendurable agony. (Never tell me, by the way, that the dead look peaceful. Most of the corpses I have seen looked devilish.) The friction of the great beast's foot had stripped the skin from his back as neatly as one skins a rabbit. As soon as I saw the dead man I sent an orderly to a friend's house nearby to borrow an elephant rifle. I had already sent back the pony, not wanting it to go mad with fright and throw me if it smelt the elephant.

The orderly came back in a few minutes with a rifle and five cartridges, and meanwhile some Burmans had arrived and told us that the elephant was in the paddy fields below, only a few hundred yards away. As I started forward practically the whole population of the quarter flocked out of the houses and followed me. They had seen the rifle and were all shouting excitedly that I was going to shoot the elephant. They had not shown much interest in the elephant when he was merely ravaging their homes, but it was different now that he was going to be shot. It was a bit of fun to them, as it would be to an English crowd; besides they wanted the meat. It made me vaguely uneasy. I had no intention of shooting the elephant—I had merely sent for the rifle to defend myself if necessary—and it is always unnerving to have a crowd following you. I marched down the hill, looking and feeling a fool, with the rifle over my shoulder and an ever-growing army of people jostling at my heels. At the bottom, when you got away from the huts, there was a metalled road and beyond that a miry waste of paddy fields a thousand yards across, not yet ploughed but soggy from the first rains and dotted with coarse grass. The elephant was standing eight yards from the road, his left side towards us. He took not the slightest notice of the crowd's approach. He was tearing up bunches of grass, beating them against his knees to clean them and stuffing them into his mouth.

I had halted on the road. As soon as I saw the elephant I knew with perfect certainty that I ought not to shoot him. It is a serious matter to shoot a working elephant—it is comparable to destroying a huge and costly piece of machinery—and obviously one ought not to do it if it can possibly be avoided. And at that distance, peacefully eating, the elephant looked no more dangerous than a cow. I thought then and I think now that his attack of "must" was already passing off; in which case he would merely wander harmlessly about until the mahout came back and caught him. Moreover, I did not in the least want to shoot him. I decided that I would watch him for a little while to make sure that he did not turn savage again, and then go home.

But at that moment I glanced round at the crowd that had followed me. It was an immense crowd, two thousand at the least and growing every minute. It blocked the road for a long distance on either side. I looked at the sea of yellow faces above the garish clothes—faces all happy and excited over this bit of fun, all certain that the elephant was going to be shot. They were watching me as they would watch a conjurer about to perform a trick. They did not like me, but with the magical rifle in my hands I was momentarily worth watching. And suddenly I realized that I should have to shoot the elephant after all. The people expected it of me and I had got to do it; I could feel their two thousand wills pressing me forward, irresistibly. And it was at this moment, as I stood there with the rifle in my hands, that I first grasped the hollowness, the futility of the white man's dominion in the East. Here was I, the white man with his gun, standing in front of the unarmed native crowd—seemingly the leading actor of the piece; but in reality I was only an absurd puppet pushed to and fro by the will of those yellow faces behind. I perceived in this moment that when the white man turns tyrant it is his own freedom that he destroys. He becomes a sort of hollow, posing dummy, the conventionalized figure of a sahib. For it is the condition of his rule that he shall spend his life in trying to impress the "natives," and so in every crisis he has got to do what the "natives" expect of him. He wears a mask, and his face grows to fit it. I had got to shoot the elephant. I had committed myself to doing it when I sent for the rifle. A sahib has got to act like a sahib; he has got to appear resolute, to know his own mind and do definite things. To come all that way, rifle in hand, with two thousand people marching at my heels, and then to trail feebly away, having done nothing—no, that was impossible. The crowd would laugh at me. And my whole life, every white man's life in the East, was one long struggle not to be laughed at.

But I did not want to shoot the elephant. I watched him beating his bunch of grass against his knees, with that preoccupied grandmotherly air that elephants have. It seemed to me that it would be murder to shoot him. At that age I was not squeamish about killing animals, but I had never shot an elephant and never wanted to. (Somehow it always seems worse to kill a *large* animal.) Besides, there was the beast's owner to be considered. Alive, the elephant was worth at least a hundred pounds; dead, he would only be worth the value of his tusks, five pounds, possibly. But I had got to act quickly. I turned to some experienced-looking Burmans who had been there when we arrived, and asked them how the elephant had been behaving. They all said the same thing: he took no notice of you if you left him alone, but he might charge if you went too close to him.

It was perfectly clear to me what I ought to do. I ought to walk up to within, say, twenty-five yards of the elephant and test his behavior. If he charged, I could shoot; if he took no notice of me, it would be safe to leave him until the mahout came back. But also I knew that I was going to do no such thing. I was a poor shot with a rifle and the ground was soft mud into which one would sink at every step. If the elephant charged and I missed him, I should have about as much chance as a toad under a steam-roller. But even then I was not thinking particularly of my own skin, only of the watchful yellow faces behind. For at that moment, with the crowd watching me, I was not afraid in the ordinary sense, as I would have been if I had been alone. A white man mustn't be frightened in front of "natives"; and so, in general, he isn't frightened. The sole thought in my mind was that if anything went wrong those two thousand Burmans would see me pursued, caught, trampled on and reduced to a grinning corpse like that Indian up the hill. And if that happened it was quite probable that some of them would laugh. That would never do. There was only one alternative. I shoved the cartridges into the magazine and lay down on the road to get a better aim.

The crowd grew very still, and a deep, low, happy sigh, as of people who see the theatre curtain go up at last, breathed from innumerable throats. They were going to have their bit of fun after all. The rifle was a beautiful German thing with cross-hair sights. I did not then know that in shooting an elephant one would shoot to cut an imaginary bar running

from ear-hole to ear-hole. I ought, therefore, as the elephant was sideways on, to have aimed straight at his ear-hole; actually I aimed several inches in front of this, thinking the brain would be further forward.

When I pulled the trigger I did not hear the bang or feel the kick—one never does when a shot goes home—but I heard the devilish roar of glee that went up from the crowd. In that instant, in too short a time, one would have thought, even for the bullet to get there, a mysterious, terrible change had come over the elephant. He neither stirred nor fell, but every line of his body had altered. He looked suddenly stricken, shrunken, immensely old, as though the frightful impact of the bullet had paralysed him without knocking him down. At last, after what seemed a long time—it might have been five seconds, I dare say—he sagged flabbily to his knees. His mouth slobbered. An enormous senility seemed to have settled upon him. One could have imagined him thousands of years old. I fired again into the same spot. At the second shot he did not collapse but climbed with desperate slowness to his feet and stood weakly upright, with legs sagging and head drooping. I fired a third time. That was the shot that did for him. You could see the agony of it jolt his whole body and knock the last remnant of strength from his legs. But in falling he seemed for a moment to rise, for as his hind legs collapsed beneath him he seemed to tower upward like a huge rock toppling, his trunk reaching skywards like a tree. He trumpeted, for the first and only time. And then down he came, his belly towards me, with a crash that seemed to shake the ground even where I lay.

I got up. The Burmans were already racing past me across the mud. It was obvious that the elephant would never rise again, but he was not dead. He was breathing very rhythmically with long rattling gasps, his great mound of a side painfully rising and falling. His mouth was wide open—I could see far down into caverns of pale pink throat. I waited a long time for him to die, but his breathing did not weaken. Finally I fired my two remaining shots into the spot where I thought his heart must be. The thick blood welled out of him like red velvet, but still he did not die. His body did not even jerk when the shots hit him, the tortured breathing continued without a pause. He was dying, very slowly and in great agony, but in some world remote from me where not even a bullet could damage him further. I felt that I had got to put an end to that dreadful noise. It seemed dreadful to see the great beast lying there, powerless to move and yet powerless to die, and not even to be able to finish him. I sent back for my small rifle and poured shot after shot into his heart and down his throat. They seemed to make no impression. The tortured gasps continued as steadily as the ticking of a clock.

In the end I could not stand it any longer and went away. I heard later that it took him half an hour to die. Burmans were bringing dahs and baskets even before I left, and I was told they had stripped his body almost to the bones by the afternoon.

Afterwards, of course, there were endless discussions about the shooting of the elephant. The owner was furious, but he was only an Indian and could do nothing. Besides, legally I had done the right thing, for a mad elephant has to be killed, like a mad dog, if its owner fails to control it. Among the Europeans opinion was divided. The older men said I was right, the younger men said it was a damn shame to shoot an elephant for killing a coolie, because an elephant was worth more than any damn Coringhee coolie. And afterwards I was very glad that the coolie had been killed; it put me legally in the right and it gave me a sufficient pretext for shooting the elephant. I often wondered whether any of the others grasped that I had done it solely to avoid looking a fool.

[1945]

RANDALL JARRELL

(1914–1965)

The Other Frost

About the Author: Although generally known as a poet, Jarrell has the distinction of having written extremely readable essays on his fellow poets in the collection *Poetry and the Age.* Essays such as "The Other Frost" offer valuable instruction on how to read poetry as well as understand a major American poet—the teaching voice at its best.

Besides the Frost that everybody knows there is one whom no one even talks about. Everybody knows what the regular Frost is: the one living poet who has written *good* poems that ordinary readers like without any trouble and understand without any trouble; the conservative editorialist and self-made apothegm-joiner, full of dry wisdom and free, complacent, Yankee enterprise; the Farmer-Poet—this is an imposing private rôle perfected for public use, a sort of Olympian Will Rogers out of *Tanglewood Tales;* and, last or first of all, Frost is the standing, speaking reproach to any other good modern poet: "If Frost can write poetry that's just as easy as Longfellow you can too—you do too." It is this "easy" side of Frost that is most attractive to academic readers, who are eager to canonize any modern poet who condemns in example the modern poetry which they condemn in precept; and it is this side that has helped to get him neglected or depreciated by intellectuals—the reader of Eliot or Auden usually dismisses Frost as something inconsequentially good that *he* knew all about long ago. Ordinary readers think Frost the greatest poet alive, and love some of his best poems almost as much as they love some of his worst ones. He seems to them a sensible, tender, humorous poet who knows all about trees and farms and folks in New England, and still has managed to get an individualistic, fairly optimistic, thoroughly American philosophy out of what he knows; there's something reassuring about his poetry, they feel—almost like prose. Certainly there's nothing hard or odd or gloomy about it.

These views of Frost, it seems to me, come either from not knowing his poems well enough or from knowing the wrong poems too well. Frost's best-known poems, with a few exceptions, are not his best poems at all; when you read (say) the selections in Untermeyer, you are getting a good synopsis of the ordinary idea of Frost and a bad misrepresentation of the real Frost. It would be hard to make a novel list of Eliot's best poems, but one can make a list of ten or twelve of Frost's best poems that is likely to seem to anybody too new to be true. Here it is: "The Witch of Coös," "Neither Out Far Nor In Deep," "Directive," "Design," "A Servant to Servants," "Provide Provide," "Home-Burial," "Acquainted with the Night," "The Pauper Witch of Grafton" (mainly for its ending), "An Old Man's Winter Night," "The Gift Outright," "After Apple-Picking," "Desert Places," and "The Fear."

Nothing I say about these poems can make you see what they are like, or what the Frost that matters most is like; if you read them you will see. "The Witch of Coös" is the best thing of its kind since Chaucer. "Home-Burial" and "A Servant to Servants" are two of the most moving and appalling dramatic poems ever written; and how could lyrics be more ingeniously and conclusively merciless than "Neither Out Far Nor In Deep" or "Design"? or more grotesquely and subtly and mercilessly disenchanting than the tender "An Old Man's Winter Night"? or more unsparingly truthful than "Provide Provide"? And so far from being obvious, optimistic, orthodox, many of these poems are extraordinarily

subtle and strange, poems which express an attitude that, at its most extreme, makes pessimism seem a hopeful evasion; they begin with a flat and terrible reproduction of the evil in the world and end by saying: It's so; and there's nothing you can do about it; and if there were, would *you* ever do it? The limits which existence approaches and falls back from have seldom been stated with such bare composure.

Frost's virtues are extraordinary. No other living poet has written so well about the actions of ordinary men: his wonderful dramatic monologues or dramatic scenes come out of a knowledge of people that few poets have had, and they are written in a verse that uses, sometimes with absolute mastery, the rhythms of actual speech. Particularly in his blank verse there is a movement so characteristic, so unmistakably and overwhelmingly Frost's, that one feels about it almost as Madame de Guermantes felt about those Frans Halses at Haarlem: that if you caught just a glimpse of them, going by in the street-car, you would be able to tell they were something pretty unusual. It is easy to underestimate the effect of this exact, spaced-out, prosaic rhythm, whose objects have the tremendous strength—you find it in Hardy's best poems—of things merely put down and left to speak for themselves. (Though Frost has little of Hardy's self-effacement, his matter-of-fact humility; Frost's tenderness, sadness, and humor are adulterated with vanity and a hard complacency.) Frost's seriousness and honesty; the bare sorrow with which, sometimes, things are accepted as they are, neither exaggerated nor explained away; the many, many poems in which there are real people with their real speech and real thoughts and real emotions—all this, in conjunction with so much subtlety and exactness, such classical understatement and restraint, makes the reader feel that he is not in a book but in a world, and a world that has in common with his own some of the things that are most important in both. I don't need to praise anything so justly famous as Frost's observation of and empathy with everything in Nature from a hornet to a hillside; and he has observed his own nature, one person's random or consequential chains of thoughts and feelings and perceptions, quite as well. (And this person, in the poems, is not the "alienated artist" cut off from everybody who isn't, yum-yum, another alienated artist; he is someone like normal people only more so—a normal person in the less common and more important sense of *normal.*) The least crevice of the good poems is saturated with imagination, an imagination that expresses itself in the continual wit and humor and particularity of what is said, in the hand-hewn or hand-polished texture of its saying. The responsibility and seriousness of Frost's best work—his worst work has an irresponsible conceit, an indifference to everything but himself, that appalls one—are nowhere better manifested than in the organization of these poems: an organization that, in its concern for any involution or ramification that really belongs to its subject, and in its severity toward anything else, expresses that absorption into a subject that is prior even to affection. The organization of Frost's poems is often rather simple or—as people say—"old-fashioned." But, as people ought to know, very complicated organizations are excessively rare in poetry, although in our time a very complicated disorganization has been excessively common; there is more successful organization in "Home-Burial" or "The Witch of Coös—one feels like saying, in indignant exaggeration—than in the *Cantos* and *The Bridge* put together. These titles will remind anyone of what is scarcest in Frost: rhetoric and romance, hypnotic verbal excitement, Original Hart Crane. Frost's word-magic is generally of a quiet, sober, bewitching sort, though the contrasts he gets from his greyed or unsaturated shades are often more satisfying to a thoughtful rhetorician than some dazzling arrangements of prismatic colors. Yet there are dazzling passages in Frost.

Frost has written, as everybody knows: "I never dared be radical when young/ For fear it would make me conservative when old." This is about as truthful as it is metrical: Frost *was* radical when young—he was a very odd and very radical radical, a much more interesting sort than the standard *New Republic* brand—and now that he's old he's sometimes callously and unimaginatively conservative. Take his poems about the atomic bomb in *Steeple Bush;* these amount, almost, to a very old and a very successful man saying: "I've had my life—why should you worry about yours?" The man who called himself "the author/ Of several books against the world in general"; who said that he had learned from Marlowe's Mephistopheles to say his prayers, "Why this is Hell, nor am I out of it"; who said to Henry Hudson, drowned or frozen somewhere in Hudson's Bay: "You and I and the Great Auk"; who could be annoyed at a hornet for not recognizing him as "the exception I like to think I am in everything"; who in poems like "A Servant to Servants," "Home-Burial," and "The Witch of Coös" had a final identifying knowledge of the deprived and dispossessed, the insulted and injured, that one matches in modern poetry only in Hardy—this poet is now, most of the time, an elder statesman like Baruch or Smuts, full of complacent wisdom and cast-iron whimsy. But of course there was always a good deal of this in the official rôle that Frost created for himself; one imagines Yeats saying about Frost, as Sarah Bernhardt said about Nijinsky: "I fear, I greatly fear, that I have just seen the greatest actor in the world."

Sometimes it is this public figure, this official rôle—the Only Genuine Robert Frost in Captivity—that writes the poems, and not the poet himself; and then one gets a self-made man's political editorials, full of cracker-box philosophizing, almanac joke-cracking—of a snake-oil salesman's mysticism; one gets the public figure's relishing consciousness of himself, an astonishing constriction of imagination and sympathy; one gets sentimentality and whimsicality, an arch complacency, a complacent archness; and one gets Homely Wisdom till the cows come home. Often the later Frost makes demands on himself that are minimal: he uses a little wit and a little observation and a little sentiment to stuff—not very tight—a little sonnet; and it's not bad, but not good enough to matter, either. The extremely rare, extremely wonderful dramatic and narrative element that is more important than anything else in his early poetry almost disappears from his later poetry; in his later work the best poems are usually special-case, rather than all-out, full-scale affairs. The younger Frost is surrounded by his characters, living beings he has known or created; the older Frost is alone. But it is this loneliness that is responsible for the cold finality of poems like "Neither Out Far Nor In Deep" or "Design."

Frost's latest books deserve little more than a footnote, since they have had few of his virtues, most of his vices, and all of his tricks; the heathen who would be converted to Frost by them is hard to construct. *Steeple Bush* has one wonderful poem, "Directive"; a fairly good, dazzlingly heartless one, "The Ingenuities of Debt"; and nothing else that is not done better somewhere else in Frost. Most of the poems merely remind you, by their persistence in the mannerisms of what was genius, that they are the productions of someone who once, and somewhere else, was a great poet. But one stops for a long time at "Directive."

A Masque of Mercy, though no great shakes—as you see, its style is catching—is a great improvement on the earlier *A Masque of Reason,* which is a frivolous, trivial, and bewilderingly corny affair, full of jokes inexplicable except as the contemptuous patter of an old magician certain that *he* can get away with anything in the world: *What fools these readers be!* Besides, Frost has long ago divorced reason for common sense, and is basking complacently in his bargain; consequently, when common sense has God justify His ways to Job by saying, "I was just showing off to Satan," the performance has the bleak wisdom of Calvin Coolidge telling you what life comes to at 2½%.

The plot of *A Masque of Mercy* is as simple as that of *Merope,* but it is a plot that is more likely to get Frost recognized as one more precursor of surrealism than it is to get him looked askance at as one of Arnold's Greeks. A bookstore-keeper named My Brother's Keeper has a wife named Jesse Bel; one night Jonah—who, having forgotten both his gourd and what God taught him by it, is feeling for New York City all the hatred that he used to feel for Nineveh—seeks refuge in the bookstore; after a little talk from Saint Paul (Jesse Bel's psychiatrist) and a lot of talk from Keeper (a character who develops so much that he finally develops into Robert Frost), Jonah comes to realize that "justice doesn't really matter."

Frost lavishes some care and a good deal more self-indulgence on this congenial subject. He has a thorough skepticism about that tame revenge, justice, and a cold certainty that nothing but mercy will do for *us.* What he really warms to is a rejection beyond either justice or mercy, and the most felt and moving part of his poem is the "unshaken recognition"—that is to say, the willing assertion—that

> *Our sacrifice, the best we have to offer,*
> *And not our worst nor second best, our best,*
> *Our very best, our lives laid down like Jonah's,*
> *Our lives laid down in war and peace, may not*
> *Be found acceptable in Heaven's sight.*

To feel this Fear of God and to go ahead in spite of it, Frost says, is man's principal virtue, courage. He treats Paul very sympathetically, but gives him speeches that are ineffectual echoes of what he really said; and Frost makes about him that sorry old joke which finds that he "theologized Christ out of Christianity." Paul ends in jokes like this, Columbus in chains; these are the rewards of discovery.

[1953]

MARTIN LUTHER KING, JR.

(1929–1968)

Letter from Birmingham Jail*

About the Author: As a leader in the civil rights movement, King often personally confronted segregation laws and policies in an effort to change them. On several occasions he was jailed, but even then his voice would not be stilled, as exemplified by "Letter from Birmingham Jail."

---

*Author's note: This response to a published statement by eight fellow clergymen from Alabama (Bishop C. C. J. Carpenter, Bishop Joseph A. Durick, Rabbi Hilton L. Grafman, Bishop Paul Hardin, Bishop Holan B. Harmon, the Reverend George M. Murray, the Reverend Edward V. Ramage and the Reverend Earl Stallings) was composed under somewhat constricting circumstances. Begun on the margins of the newspaper in which the statement appeared while I was in jail, the letter was continued on scraps of writing paper supplied by a friendly Negro trusty, and concluded on a pad my attorneys were eventually permitted to leave me. Although the text remains in substance unaltered, I have indulged in the author's prerogative of polishing it for publication.

April 16, 1963

My Dear Fellow Clergymen:

While confined here in the Birmingham city jail, I came across your recent statement calling my present activities "unwise and untimely." Seldom do I pause to answer criticism of my work and ideas. If I sought to answer all the criticisms that cross my desk, my secretaries would have little time for anything other than such correspondence in the course of the day, and I would have no time for constructive work. But since I feel that you are men of genuine good will and that your criticisms are sincerely set forth, I want to try to answer your statement in what I hope will be patient and reasonable terms.

I think I should indicate why I am here in Birmingham, since you have been influenced by the view which argues against "outsiders coming in." I have the honor of serving as president of the Southern Christian Leadership Conference, an organization operating in every southern state, with headquarters in Atlanta, Georgia. We have some eighty-five affiliated organizations across the South, and one of them is the Alabama Christian Movement for Human Rights. Frequently we share staff, educational and financial resources with our affiliates. Several months ago the affiliate here in Birmingham asked us to be on call to engage in a nonviolent direct-action program if such were deemed necessary. We readily consented, and when the hour came we lived up to our promise. So I, along with several members of my staff, am here because I was invited here. I am here because I have organizational ties here.

But more basically, I am in Birmingham because injustice is here. Just as the prophets of the eighth century B.C. left their villages and carried their "thus saith the Lord" far beyond the boundaries of their home towns, and just as the Apostle Paul left his village of Tarsus and carried the gospel of Jesus Christ to the far corners of the Greco-Roman world, so am I compelled to carry the gospel of freedom beyond my own home town. Like Paul, I must constantly respond to the Macedonian call for aid.

Moreover, I am cognizant of the interrelatedness of all communities and states. I cannot sit idly by in Atlanta and not be concerned about what happens in Birmingham. Injustice anywhere is a threat to justice everywhere. We are caught in an inescapable network of mutuality, tied in a single garment of destiny. Whatever affects one directly, affects all indirectly. Never again can we afford to live with the narrow, provincial "outside agitator" idea. Anyone who lives inside the United States can never be considered an outsider anywhere within its bounds.

You deplore the demonstrations taking place in Birmingham. But your statement, I am sorry to say, fails to express a similar concern for the conditions that brought about the demonstrations. I am sure that none of you would want to rest content with the superficial kind of social analysis that deals merely with effects and does not grapple with underlying causes. It is unfortunate that demonstrations are taking place in Birmingham, but it is even more unfortunate that the city's white power structure left the Negro community with no alternative.

In any nonviolent campaign there are four basic steps: collection of the facts to determine whether injustices exist; negotiation; self-purification; and direct action. We have gone through all these steps in Birmingham. There can be no gainsaying the fact that racial injustice engulfs this community. Birmingham is probably the most thoroughly segregated city in the United States. Its ugly record of brutality is widely known. Negroes have experienced grossly unjust treatment in the courts. There have been more unsolved bombings of Negro homes and churches in Birmingham than in any other city in the nation. These are the hard, brutal facts of the case. On the basis of these conditions, Negro leaders

sought to negotiate with the city fathers. But the latter consistently refused to engage in good-faith negotiation.

Then, last September, came the opportunity to talk with leaders of Birmingham's economic community. In the course of the negotiations, certain promises were made by the merchants—for example, to remove the stores' humiliating racial signs. On the basis of these promises, the Reverend Fred Shuttlesworth and the leaders of the Alabama Christian Movement for Human Rights agreed to a moratorium on all demonstrations. As the weeks and months went by, we realized that we were the victims of a broken promise. A few signs, briefly removed, returned; the others remained.

As in so many past experiences, our hopes had been blasted, and the shadow of deep disappointment settled upon us. We had no alternative except to prepare for direct action, whereby we would present our very bodies as a means of laying our case before the conscience of the local and the national community. Mindful of the difficulties involved, we decided to undertake a process of self-purification. We began a series of workshops on nonviolence, and we repeatedly asked ourselves: "Are you able to accept blows without retaliating?" "Are you able to endure the ordeal of jail?" We decided to schedule our direct-action program for the Easter season, realizing that except for Christmas, this is the main shopping period of the year. Knowing that a strong economic-withdrawal program would be the by-product of direct action, we felt that this would be the best time to bring pressure to bear on the merchants for the needed change.

Then it occurred to us that Birmingham's mayoral election was coming up in March, and we speedily decided to postpone action until after election day. When we discovered that the Commissioner of Public Safety, Eugene "Bull" Connor, had piled up enough votes to be in the run-off, we decided again to postpone action until the day after the run-off so that the demonstrations could not be used to cloud the issues. Like many others, we waited to see Mr. Connor defeated, and to this end we endured postponement after postponement. Having aided in this community need, we felt that our direct-action program could be delayed no longer.

You may well ask: "Why direct action? Why sit-ins, marches and so forth? Isn't negotiation a better path?" You are quite right in calling for negotiation. Indeed, this is the very purpose of direct action. Nonviolent direct action seeks to create such a crisis and foster such a tension that a community which has constantly refused to negotiate is forced to confront the issue. It seeks so to dramatize the issue that it can no longer be ignored. My citing the creation of tension as part of the work of the nonviolent-resister may sound rather shocking. But I must confess that I am not afraid of the word "tension." I have earnestly opposed violent tension, but there is a type of constructive, nonviolent tension which is necessary for growth. Just as Socrates felt that it was necessary to create a tension in the mind so that individuals could rise from the bondage of myths and half-truths to the unfettered realm of creative analysis and objective appraisal, so must we see the need for nonviolent gadflies to create the kind of tension in society that will help men rise from the dark depths of prejudice and racism to the majestic heights of understanding and brotherhood.

The purpose of our direct-action program is to create a situation so crisis-packed that it will inevitably open the door to negotiation. I therefore concur with you in your call for negotiation. Too long has our beloved Southland been bogged down in a tragic effort to live in monologue rather than dialogue.

One of the basic points in your statement is that the action that I and my associates have taken in Birmingham is untimely. Some have asked: "Why didn't you give the new city administration time to act?" The only answer that I can give to this query is that the new Birmingham administration must be prodded about as much as the outgoing one, before it will act. We are sadly mistaken if we feel that the election of Albert Boutwell as mayor will bring the millennium to Birmingham. While Mr. Boutwell is a much more gentle person than Mr. Connor, they are both segregationists, dedicated to maintenance of the status quo. I have hope that Mr. Boutwell will be reasonable enough to see the futility of massive resistance to desegregation. But he will not see this without pressure from devotees of civil rights. My friends, I must say to you that we have not made a single gain in civil rights without determined legal and nonviolent pressure. Lamentably, it is an historical fact that privileged groups seldom give up their privileges voluntarily. Individuals may see the moral light and voluntarily give up their unjust posture; but, as Reinhold Niebuhr has reminded us, groups tend to be more immoral than individuals.

We know through painful experience that freedom is never voluntarily given by the oppressor; it must be demanded by the oppressed. Frankly, I have yet to engage in a direct-action campaign that was "well timed" in the view of those who have not suffered unduly from the disease of segregation. For years now I have heard the word "Wait!" It rings in the ear of every Negro with piercing familiarity. This "Wait" has almost always meant "Never." We must come to see, with one of our distinguished jurists, that "justice too long delayed is justice denied."

We have waited for more than 340 years for our constitutional and God-given rights. The nations of Asia and Africa are moving with jetlike speed toward gaining political independence, but we still creep at horse-and-buggy pace toward gaining a cup of coffee at a lunch counter. Perhaps it is easy for those who have never felt the stinging darts of segregation to say, "Wait." But when you have seen vicious mobs lynch your mothers and fathers at will and drown your sisters and brothers at whim; when you have seen hate-filled policemen curse, kick and even kill your black brothers and sisters; when you see the vast majority of your twenty million Negro brothers smothering in an airtight cage of poverty in the midst of an affluent society; when you suddenly find your tongue twisted and your speech stammering as you seek to explain to your six-year-old daughter why she can't go to the public amusement park that has just been advertised on television, and see tears welling up in her eyes when she is told that Funtown is closed to colored children, and see ominous clouds of inferiority beginning to form in her little mental sky, and see her beginning to distort her personality by developing an unconscious bitterness toward white people; when you have to concoct an answer for a five-year-old son who is asking: "Daddy, why do white people treat colored people so mean?"; when you take a cross-country drive and find it necessary to sleep night after night in the uncomfortable corners of your automobile because no motel will accept you; when you are humiliated day in and day out by nagging signs reading "white" and "colored"; when your first name becomes "nigger," your middle name becomes "boy" (however old you are) and your last name becomes "John," and your wife and mother are never given the respected title "Mrs."; when you are harried by day and haunted by night by the fact that you are a Negro, living constantly at tiptoe stance, never quite knowing what to expect next, and are plagued with inner fears and outer resentments; when you are forever fighting a degenerating sense of "nobodiness"—then you will understand why we find it difficult to wait. There comes a time when the cup of endurance runs over, and men are no longer willing to be plunged into the abyss of despair. I hope, sirs, you can understand our legitimate and unavoidable impatience.

You express a great deal of anxiety over our willingness to break laws. This is certainly a legitimate concern. Since we so diligently urge people to obey the Supreme Court's decision of 1954 outlawing segregation in the public schools, at first glance it may seem rather paradoxical for us consciously to break laws. One may well ask: "How can you advocate breaking some laws and obeying others?" The answer lies in the fact that there are two types of laws: just and unjust. I would be the first to advocate obeying just laws. One has not only a legal but a moral responsibility to obey just laws. Conversely, one has a moral responsibility to disobey unjust laws. I would agree with St. Augustine that "an unjust law is no law at all."

Now, what is the difference between the two? How does one determine whether a law is just or unjust? A just law is a man-made code that squares with the moral law or the law of God. An unjust law is a code that is out of harmony with the moral law. To put it in the terms of St. Thomas Aquinas: An unjust law is a human law that is not rooted in eternal law and natural law. Any law that uplifts human personality is just. Any law that degrades human personality is unjust. All segregation statutes are unjust because segregation distorts the soul and damages the personality. It gives the segregator a false sense of superiority and the segregated a false sense of inferiority. Segregation, to use the terminology of the Jewish philosopher Martin Buber, substitutes an "I–it" relationship for an "I–thou" relationship and ends up relegating persons to the status of things. Hence segregation is not only politically, economically and sociologically unsound, it is morally wrong and sinful. Paul Tillich has said that sin is separation. Is not segregation an existential expression of man's tragic separation, his awful estrangement, his terrible sinfulness? Thus it is that I can urge men to obey the 1954 decision of the Supreme Court, for it is morally right; and I can urge them to disobey segregation ordinances, for they are morally wrong.

Let us consider a more concrete example of just and unjust laws. An unjust law is a code that a numerical or power majority group compels a minority group to obey but does not make binding on itself. This is *difference* made legal. By the same token, a just law is a code that a majority compels a minority to follow and that it is willing to follow itself. This is *sameness* made legal.

Let me give another explanation. A law is unjust if it is inflicted on a minority that, as a result of being denied the right to vote, had no part in enacting or devising the law. Who can say that the legislature of Alabama which set up that state's segregation laws was democratically elected? Throughout Alabama all sorts of devious methods are used to prevent Negroes from becoming registered voters, and there are some counties in which, even though Negroes constitute a majority of the population, not a single Negro is registered. Can any law enacted under such circumstances be considered democratically structured?

Sometimes a law is just on its face and unjust in its application. For instance, I have been arrested on a charge of parading without a permit. Now, there is nothing wrong in having an ordinance which requires a permit for a parade. But such an ordinance becomes unjust when it is used to maintain segregation and to deny citizens the First-Amendment privilege of peaceful assembly and protest.

I hope you are able to see the distinction I am trying to point out. In no sense do I advocate evading or defying the law, as would the rabid segregationist. That would lead to anarchy. One who breaks an unjust law must do so openly, lovingly, and with a willingness to accept the penalty. I submit that an individual who breaks a law that conscience tells him is unjust, and who willingly accepts the penalty of imprisonment in order to arouse the conscience of the community over its injustice, is in reality expressing the highest respect for law.

Of course, there is nothing new about this kind of civil disobedience. It was evidenced sublimely in the refusal of Shadrach, Meshach and Abednego to obey the laws of Nebuchadnezzar, on the ground that a higher moral law was at stake. It was practiced superbly by the early Christians, who were willing to face hungry lions and the excruciating pain of chopping blocks rather than submit to certain unjust laws of the Roman Empire. To a degree, academic freedom is a reality today because Socrates practiced civil disobedience. In our own nation, the Boston Tea Party represented a massive act of civil disobedience.

We should never forget that everything Adolf Hitler did in Germany was "legal" and everything the Hungarian freedom fighters did in Hungary was "illegal." It was "illegal" to aid and comfort a Jew in Hitler's Germany. Even so, I am sure that, had I lived in Germany at the time, I would have aided and comforted my Jewish brothers. If today I lived in a Communist country where certain principles dear to the Christian faith are suppressed, I would openly advocate disobeying that country's antireligious laws.

I must make two honest confessions to you, my Christian and Jewish brothers. First, I must confess that over the past few years I have been gravely disappointed with the white moderate. I have almost reached the regrettable conclusion that the Negro's great stumbling block in his stride toward freedom is not the White Citizen's Counciler or the Ku Klux Klanner, but the white moderate, who is more devoted to "order" than to justice; who prefers a negative peace which is the absence of tension to a positive peace which is the presence of justice; who constantly says: "I agree with you in the goal you seek, but I cannot agree with your methods of direct action"; who paternalistically believes he can set the timetable for another man's freedom; who lives by a mythical concept of time and who constantly advises the Negro to wait for a "more convenient season." Shallow understanding from people of good will is more frustrating than absolute misunderstanding from people of ill will. Lukewarm acceptance is much more bewildering than outright rejection.

I had hoped that the white moderate would understand that law and order exist for the purpose of establishing justice and that when they fail in this purpose they become the dangerously structured dams that block the flow of social progress. I had hoped that the white moderate would understand that the present tension in the South is a necessary phase of the transition from an obnoxious negative peace, in which the Negro passively accepted his unjust plight, to a substantive and positive peace, in which all men will respect the dignity and worth of human personality. Actually, we who engage in nonviolent direct action are not the creators of tension. We merely bring to the surface the hidden tension that is already alive. We bring it out in the open, where it can be seen and dealt with. Like a boil that can never be cured so long as it is covered up but must be opened with all its ugliness to the natural medicines of air and light, injustice must be exposed, with all the tension its exposure creates, to the light of human conscience and the air of national opinion before it can be cured.

In your statement you assert that our actions, even though peaceful, must be condemned because they precipitate violence. But is this a logical assertion? Isn't this like condemning a robbed man because his possession of money precipitated the evil act of robbery? Isn't this like condemning Socrates because his unswerving commitment to truth and his philosophical inquiries precipitated the act by the misguided populace in which they made him drink hemlock? Isn't this like condemning Jesus because his unique God-consciousness and never-ceasing devotion to God's will precipitated the evil act of cruci-

fixion? We must come to see that, as the federal courts have consistently affirmed, it is wrong to urge an individual to cease his efforts to gain his basic constitutional rights because the quest may precipitate violence. Society must protect the robbed and punish the robber.

I had also hoped that the white moderate would reject the myth concerning time in relation to the struggle for freedom. I have just received a letter from a white brother in Texas. He writes: "All Christians know that the colored people will receive equal rights eventually, but it is possible that you are in too great a religious hurry. It has taken Christianity almost two thousand years to accomplish what it has. The teachings of Christ take time to come to earth." Such an attitude stems from a tragic misconception of time, from the strangely irrational notion that there is something in the very flow of time that will inevitably cure all ills. Actually, time itself is neutral; it can be used either destructively or constructively. More and more I feel that the people of ill will have used time much more effectively than have the people of good will. We will have to repent in this generation not merely for the hateful words and actions of the bad people but for the appalling silence of the good people. Human progress never rolls in on wheels of inevitability; it comes through the tireless efforts of men willing to be co-workers with God, and without this hard work, time itself becomes an ally of the forces of social stagnation. We must use time creatively, in the knowledge that the time is always ripe to do right. Now is the time to make real the promise of democracy and transform our pending national elegy into a creative psalm of brotherhood. Now is the time to lift our national policy from the quicksand of racial injustice to the solid rock of human dignity.

You speak of our activity in Birmingham as extreme. At first I was rather disappointed that fellow clergymen would see my nonviolent efforts as those of an extremist. I began thinking about the fact that I stand in the middle of two opposing forces in the Negro community. One is a force of complacency, made up in part of Negroes who, as a result of long years of oppression, are so drained of self-respect and a sense of "somebodiness" that they have adjusted to segregation; and in part of a few middle-class Negroes who, because of a degree of academic and economic security and because in some ways they profit by segregation, have become insensitive to the problems of the masses. The other force is one of bitterness and hatred, and it comes perilously close to advocating violence. It is expressed in the various black nationalist groups that are springing up across the nation, the largest and best-known being Elijah Muhammad's Muslim movement. Nourished by the Negro's frustration over the continued existence of racial discrimination, this movement is made up of people who have lost faith in America, who have absolutely repudiated Christianity, and who have concluded that the white man is an incorrigible "devil."

I have tried to stand between these two forces, saying that we need emulate neither the "do-nothingism" of the complacent nor the hatred and despair of the black nationalist. For there is the more excellent way of love and nonviolent protest. I am grateful to God that, through the influence of the Negro church, the way of nonviolence became an integral part of our struggle.

If this philosophy had not emerged, by now many streets of the South would, I am convinced, be flowing with blood. And I am further convinced that if our white brothers dismiss as "rabble-rousers" and "outside agitators" those of us who employ nonviolent direct action, and if they refuse to support our nonviolent efforts, millions of Negroes will, out of frustration and despair, seek solace and security in black-nationalist ideologies—a development that would inevitably lead to a frightening racial nightmare.

Oppressed people cannot remain oppressed forever. The yearning for freedom eventually manifests itself, and that is what has happened to the American Negro. Something within has reminded him of his birthright of freedom, and something without has reminded him that it can be gained. Consciously or unconsciously, he has been caught up by the *Zeitgeist,* and with his black brothers of Africa and his brown and yellow brothers of Asia, South America and the Caribbean, the United States Negro is moving with a sense of great urgency toward the promised land of racial justice. If one recognizes this vital urge that has engulfed the Negro community, one should readily understand why public demonstrations are taking place. The Negro has many pent-up resentments and latent frustrations, and he must release them. So let him march; let him make prayer pilgrimages to the city hall; let him go on freedom rides—and try to understand why he must do so. If his repressed emotions are not released in nonviolent ways, they will seek expression through violence; this is not a threat but a fact of history. So I have not said to my people: "Get rid of your discontent." Rather, I have tried to say that this normal and healthy discontent can be channeled into the creative outlet of nonviolent direct action. And now this approach is being termed extremist.

But though I was initially disappointed at being categorized as an extremist, as I continued to think about the matter I gradually gained a measure of satisfaction from the label. Was not Jesus an extremist for love: "Love your enemies, bless them that curse you, do good to them that hate you, and pray for them which despitefully use you, and persecute you." Was not Amos an extremist for justice: "Let justice roll down like waters and righteousness like an ever-flowing stream." Was not Paul an extremist for the Christian gospel: "I bear in my body the marks of the Lord Jesus." Was not Martin Luther an extremist: "Here I stand; I cannot do otherwise, so help me God." And John Bunyan: "I will stay in jail to the end of my days before I make a butchery of my conscience." And Abraham Lincoln: "This nation cannot survive half slave and half free." And Thomas Jefferson: "We hold these truths to be self-evident, that all men are created equal. . . ." So the question is not whether we will be extremists, but what kind of extremists we will be. Will we be extremists for hate or for love? Will we be extremists for the preservation of injustice or for the extension of justice? In that dramatic scene on Calvary's hill three men were crucified for the same crime—the crime of extremism. Two were extremists for immorality, and thus fell below their environment. The other, Jesus Christ, was an extremist for love, truth and goodness, and thereby rose above his environment. Perhaps the South, the nation and the world are in dire need of creative extremists.

I had hoped that the white moderate would see this need. Perhaps I was too optimistic; perhaps I expected too much. I suppose I should have realized that few members of the oppressor race can understand the deep groans and passionate yearnings of the oppressed race, and still fewer have the vision to see that injustice must be rooted out by strong, persistent and determined action. I am thankful, however, that some of our white brothers in the South have grasped the meaning of this social revolution and committed themselves to it. They are still all too few in quantity, but they are big in quality. Some—such as Ralph McGill, Lillian Smith, Harry Golden, James McBride Dabbs, Ann Braden and Sarah Patton Boyle—have written about our struggle in eloquent and prophetic terms. Others have marched with us down nameless streets of the South. They have languished in filthy, roach-infested jails, suffering the abuse and brutality of policemen who view them as "dirty nigger-lovers." Unlike so many of their moderate brothers and sisters, they have recognized the urgency of the moment and sensed the need for powerful "action" antidotes to combat the disease of segregation.

Let me take note of my other major disappointment. I have been so greatly disappointed with the white church and its leadership. Of course, there are some notable exceptions. I am not unmindful of the fact that each of you has taken some significant stands on this issue. I commend you, Reverend Stallings, for your Christian stand on this past Sunday, in welcoming Negroes to your worship service on a nonsegregated basis. I commend the Catholic leaders of this state for integrating Spring Hill College several years ago.

But despite these notable exceptions, I must honestly reiterate that I have been disappointed with the church. I do not say this as one of those negative critics who can always find something wrong with the church. I say this as a minister of the gospel, who loves the church; who was nurtured in its bosom; who has been sustained by its spiritual blessings and who will remain true to it as long as the cord of life shall lengthen.

When I was suddenly catapulted into the leadership of the bus protest in Montgomery, Alabama, a few years ago, I felt we would be supported by the white church. I felt that the white ministers, priests and rabbis of the South would be among our strongest allies. Instead, some have been outright opponents, refusing to understand the freedom movement and misrepresenting its leaders; all too many others have been more cautious than courageous and have remained silent behind the anesthetizing security of stained-glass windows.

In spite of my shattered dreams, I came to Birmingham with the hope that the white religious leadership of this community would see the justice of our cause and, with deep moral concern, would serve as the channel through which our just grievances could reach the power structure. I had hoped that each of you would understand. But again I have been disappointed.

I have heard numerous southern religious leaders admonish their worshipers to comply with a desegregation decision because it is the law, but I have longed to hear white ministers declare: "Follow this decree because integration is morally right and because the Negro is your brother." In the midst of blatant injustices inflicted upon the Negro, I have watched white churchmen stand on the sideline and mouth pious irrelevancies and sanctimonious trivialities. In the midst of a mighty struggle to rid our nation of racial and economic injustice, I have heard many ministers say: "Those are social issues, with which the gospel has no real concern." And I have watched many churches commit themselves to a completely otherworldly religion which makes a strange, un-Biblical distinction between body and soul, between the sacred and the secular.

I have traveled the length and breadth of Alabama, Mississippi and all the other southern states. On sweltering summer days and crisp autumn mornings I have looked at the South's beautiful churches with their lofty spires pointing heavenward. I have beheld the impressive outlines of her massive religious-education buildings. Over and over I have found myself asking: "What kind of people worship here? Who is their God? Where were their voices when the lips of Governor Barnett dripped with words of interposition and nullification? Where were they when Governor Wallace gave a clarion call for defiance and hatred? Where were their voices of support when bruised and weary Negro men and women decided to rise from the dark dungeons of complacency to the bright hills of creative protest?"

Yes, these questions are still in my mind. In deep disappointment I have wept over the laxity of the church. But be assured that my tears have been tears of love. There can be no deep disappointment where there is not deep love. Yes, I love the church. How could I do otherwise? I am in the rather unique position of being the son, the grandson and the great-grandson of preachers. Yes, I see the church as the body of Christ. But, oh! How we have blemished and scarred that body through social neglect and through fear of being nonconformists.

There was a time when the church was very powerful—in the time when the early Christians rejoiced at being deemed worthy to suffer for what they believed. In those days the church was not merely a thermometer that recorded the ideas and principles of popular opinion; it was a thermostat that transformed the mores of society. Whenever the early Christians entered a town, the people in power became disturbed and immediately sought to convict the Christians for being "disturbers of the peace" and "outside agitators." But the Christians pressed on, in the conviction that they were "a colony of heaven," called to obey God rather than man. Small in number, they were big in commitment. They were too God-intoxicated to be "astronomically intimidated." By their effort and example they brought an end to such ancient evils as infanticide and gladiatorial contests.

Things are different now. So often the contemporary church is a weak, ineffectual voice with an uncertain sound. So often it is an archdefender of the status quo. Far from being disturbed by the presence of the church, the power structure of the average community is consoled by the church's silent—and often even vocal—sanction of things as they are.

But the judgment of God is upon the church as never before. If today's church does not recapture the sacrificial spirit of the early church, it will lose its authenticity, forfeit the loyalty of millions, and be dismissed as an irrelevant social club with no meaning for the twentieth century. Every day I meet young people whose disappointment with the church has turned into outright disgust.

Perhaps I have once again been too optimistic. Is organized religion too inextricably bound to the status quo to save our nation and the world? Perhaps I must turn my faith to the inner spiritual church, the church within the church, as the true *ekklesia* and the hope of the world. But again I am thankful to God that some noble souls from the ranks of organized religion have broken loose from the paralyzing chains of conformity and joined us as active partners in the struggle for freedom. They have left their secure congregations and walked the streets of Albany, Georgia, with us. They have gone down the highways of the South on tortuous rides for freedom. Yes, they have gone to jail with us. Some have been dismissed from their churches, have lost the support of their bishops and fellow ministers. But they have acted in the faith that right defeated is stronger than evil triumphant. Their witness has been the spiritual salt that has preserved the true meaning of the gospel in these troubled times. They have carved a tunnel of hope through the dark mountain of disappointment.

I hope the church as a whole will meet the challenge of this decisive hour. But even if the church does not come to the aid of justice, I have no despair about the future. I have no fear about the outcome of our struggle in Birmingham, even if our motives are at present misunderstood. We will reach the goal of freedom in Birmingham and all over the nation, because the goal of America is freedom. Abused and scorned though we may be, our destiny is tied up with America's destiny. Before the pilgrims landed at Plymouth, we were here. Before the pen of Jefferson etched the majestic words of the Declaration of Independence across the pages of history, we were here. For more than two centuries our forebears labored in this country without wages; they made cotton king; they built the homes of their masters while suffering gross injustice and shameful humiliation—and yet out of a bottomless vitality they continued to thrive and develop. If the inexpressible cruelties of slavery could

not stop us, the opposition we now face will surely fail. We will win our freedom because the sacred heritage of our nation and the eternal will of God are embodied in our echoing demands.

Before closing I feel impelled to mention one other point in your statement that has troubled me profoundly. You warmly commended the Birmingham police force for keeping "order" and "preventing violence." I doubt that you would have so warmly commended the police force if you had seen its dogs sinking their teeth into unarmed, nonviolent Negroes. I doubt that you would so quickly commend the policemen if you were to observe their ugly and inhumane treatment of Negroes here in the city jail; if you were to watch them push and curse old Negro women and young Negro girls; if you were to see them slap and kick old Negro men and young boys; if you were to observe them, as they did on two occasions, refuse to give us food because we wanted to sing our grace together. I cannot join you in your praise of the Birmingham police department.

It is true that the police have exercised a degree of discipline in handling the demonstrators. In this sense they have conducted themselves rather "nonviolently" in public. But for what purpose? To preserve the evil system of segregation. Over the past few years I have consistently preached that nonviolence demands that the means we use must be as pure as the ends we seek. I have tried to make clear that it is wrong to use immoral means to attain moral ends. But now I must affirm that it is just as wrong, or perhaps even more so, to use moral means to preserve immoral ends. Perhaps Mr. Connor and his policemen have been rather nonviolent in public, as was Chief Pritchett in Albany, Georgia, but they have used the moral means of nonviolence to maintain the immoral end of racial injustice. As T. S. Eliot has said: "The last temptation is the greatest treason: To do the right deed for the wrong reason."

I wish you had commended the Negro sit-inners and demonstrators of Birmingham for their sublime courage, their willingness to suffer and their amazing discipline in the midst of great provocation. One day the South will recognize its real heroes. They will be the James Merediths, with the noble sense of purpose that enables them to face jeering and hostile mobs, and with the agonizing loneliness that characterizes the life of the pioneer. They will be old, oppressed, battered Negro women, symbolized in a seventy-two-year-old woman in Montgomery, Alabama, who rose up with a sense of dignity and with her people decided not to ride segregated buses, and who responded with ungrammatical profundity to one who inquired about her weariness: "My feets is tired, but my soul is at rest." They will be the young high school and college students, the young ministers of the gospel and a host of their elders, courageously and nonviolently sitting in at lunch counters and willingly going to jail for conscience' sake. One day the South will know that when these disinherited children of God sat down at lunch counters, they were in reality standing up for what is best in the American dream and for the most sacred values in our Judaeo-Christian heritage, thereby bringing our nation back to those great wells of democracy which were dug deep by the founding fathers in their formulation of the Constitution and the Declaration of Independence.

Never before have I written so long a letter. I'm afraid it is much too long to take your precious time. I can assure you that it would have been much shorter if I had been writing from a comfortable desk, but what else can one do when he is alone in a narrow jail cell, other than write long letters, think long thoughts and pray long prayers?

If I have said anything in this letter that overstates the truth and indicates an unreasonable impatience, I beg you to forgive me. If I have said anything that understates the truth

and indicates my having a patience that allows me to settle for anything less than brotherhood, I beg God to forgive me.

I hope this letter finds you strong in the faith. I also hope that circumstances will soon make it possible for me to meet each of you, not as an integrationist or a civil-rights leader but as a fellow clergyman and a Christian brother. Let us all hope that the dark clouds of racial prejudice will soon pass away and the deep fog of misunderstanding will be lifted from our fear-drenched communities, and in some not too distant tomorrow the radiant stars of love and brotherhood will shine over our great nation with all their scintillating beauty.

Yours for the cause of Peace and Brotherhood,
MARTIN LUTHER KING, JR.
[1964]

ANNIE DILLARD

(1945–)

Sight into Insight

About the Author: In 1975 Dillard won the Pulitzer Prize for nonfiction for *Pilgrim at Tinker Creek.* Much of her work echoes the voice of someone deeply concerned with the environment and with our ability to see and perceive what's around us.

When I was six or seven years old, growing up in Pittsburgh, I used to take a penny of my own and hide it for someone else to find. It was a curious compulsion; sadly, I've never been seized by it since. For some reason I always "hid" the penny along the same stretch of sidewalk up the street. I'd cradle it at the roots of a maple, say, or in a hole left by a chipped-off piece of sidewalk. Then I'd take a piece of chalk and, starting at either end of the block, draw huge arrows leading up to the penny from both directions. After I learned to write I labeled the arrows "SURPRISE AHEAD" or "MONEY THIS WAY." I was greatly excited, during all this arrowdrawing, at the thought of the first lucky passerby who would receive in this way, regardless of merit, a free gift from the universe. But I never lurked about. I'd go straight home and not give the matter another thought, until, some months later, I would be gripped by the impulse to hide another penny.

There are lots of things to see, unwrapped gifts and free surprises. The world is fairly studded and strewn with pennies cast broadside from a generous hand. But—and this is the point—who gets excited by a mere penny? If you follow one arrow, if you crouch motionless on a bank to watch a tremulous ripple thrill on the water, and are rewarded by the sight of a muskrat kit paddling from its den, will you count that sight a chip of copper only, and go your rueful way? It is very dire poverty indeed for a man to be so malnourished and fatigued that he won't stoop to pick up a penny. But if you cultivate a healthy poverty and simplicity, so that finding a penny will make your day, then, since the world is in fact planted in pennies, you have with your poverty bought a lifetime of days. What you see is what you get.

Unfortunately, nature is very much a now-you-see-it, now-you-don't affair. A fish flashes, then dissolves in the water before my eyes like so much salt. Deer apparently ascend

bodily into heaven: the brightest oriole fades into leaves. These disappearances stun me into stillness and concentration; they say of nature that it conceals with a grand nonchalance, and they say of vision that it is a deliberate gift, the revelation of a dancer who for my eyes only flings away her seven veils.

For nature does reveal as well as conceal: non-you-don't-see-it, now-you-do. For a week this September migrating red-winged blackbirds were feeding heavily down by Tinker Creek at the back of the house. One day I went out to investigate the racket; I walked up to a tree, an Osage orange, and a hundred birds flew away. They simply materialized out of the tree. I saw a tree, then a whisk of color, then a tree again. I walked closer and another hundred blackbirds took flight. Not a branch, not a twig budged: the birds were apparently weightless as well as invisible. Or, it was as if the leaves of the Osage orange had been freed from a spell in the form of redwinged blackbirds; they flew from the tree, caught my eye in the sky, and vanished. When I looked again at the tree, the leaves had reassembled as if nothing had happened. Finally I walked directly to the trunk of the tree and a final hundred, the real diehards, appeared, spread, and vanished. How could so many hide in the tree without my seeing them? The Osage orange, unruffled, looked just as it had looked from the house, when three hundred red-winged blackbirds cried from its crown. I looked upstream where they flew, and they were gone. Searching, I couldn't spot one. I wandered upstream to force them to play their hand, but they'd crossed the creek and scattered. One show to a customer. These appearances catch at my throat; they are the free gifts, the bright coppers at the roots of trees.

It's all a matter of keeping my eyes open. Nature is like one of those line drawings that are puzzles for children: Can you find hidden in the tree a duck, a house, a boy, a bucket, a giraffe, and a boot? Specialists can find the most incredibly hidden things. A book I read when I was young recommended an easy way to find caterpillars: you simply find some fresh caterpillar droppings, look up, and there's your caterpillar. More recently an author advised me to set my mind at ease about those piles of cut stems on the ground in grassy fields. Field mice make them; they cut the grass down by degrees to reach the seeds at the head. It seems that when the grass is tightly packed, as in a field of ripe grain, the blade won't topple at a single cut through the stem; instead, the cut stem simply drops vertically, held in the crush of grain. The mouse severs the bottom again and again, the stem keeps dropping an inch at a time, and finally the head is low enough for the mouse to reach the seeds. Meanwhile the mouse is positively littering the field with its little piles of cut stems into which, presumably, the author is constantly stumbling.

If I can't see these minutiae, I still try to keep my eyes open. I'm always on the lookout for ant lion traps in sandy soil, monarch pupae near milkweed, skipper larvae in locust leaves. These things are utterly common, and I've not seen one. I bang on hollow trees near water, but so far no flying squirrels have appeared. In flat country I watch every sunset in hopes of seeing the green ray. The green ray is a seldom-seen streak of light that rises from the sun like a spurting fountain at the moment of sunset; it throbs into the sky for two seconds and disappears. One more reason to keep my eyes open. A photography professor at the University of Florida just happened to see a bird die in midflight; it jerked, died, dropped, and smashed on the ground.

I squint at the wind because I read Stewart Edward White: "I have always maintained that if you looked closely enough you could see the wind—the dim, hardly-made-out, fine débris fleeing high in the air." White was an excellent observer, and devoted an entire

chapter of *The Mountains* to the subject of seeing deer: "As soon as you can forget the naturally obvious and construct an artificial obvious, then you too will see deer."

But the artificial obvious is hard to see. My eyes account for less than 1 percent of the weight of my head; I'm bony and dense; I see what I expect. I just don't know what the lover knows; I can't see the artificial obvious that those in the know construct. The herpetologist asks the native, "Are there snakes in that ravine?" "No, sir." And the herpetologist comes home with, yessir, three bags full. Are there butterflies on that mountain? Are the bluets in bloom? Are there arrowheads here, or fossil ferns in the shale?

Peeping through my keyhole I see within the range of only about 30 percent of the light that comes from the sun; the rest is infrared and some little ultraviolet, perfectly apparent to many animals, but invisible to me. A nightmare network of ganglia, charged and firing without my knowledge, cuts and splices what I do see, editing it for my brain. Donald E. Carr points out that the sense impressions of one-celled animals are *not* edited for the brain: "This is philosophically interesting in a rather mournful way, since it means that only the simplest animals perceive the universe as it is."

A fog that won't burn away drifts and flows across my field of vision. When you see fog move against a backdrop of deep pines, you don't see the fog itself, but streaks of clearness floating across the air in dark shreds. So I see only tatters of clearness through a pervading obscurity. I can't distinguish the fog from the overcast sky; I can't be sure if the light is direct or reflected. Everywhere darkness and the presence of the unseen appalls. We estimate now that only one atom dances alone in every cubic meter of intergalactic space. I blink and squint. What planet or power yanks Halley's Comet out of orbit? We haven't seen it yet; it's a question of distance, density, and the pallor of reflected light. We rock, cradled in the swaddling band of darkness. Even the simple darkness of night whispers suggestions to the mind. This summer, in August, I stayed at the creek too late.

Where Tinker Creek flows under the sycamore log bridge to the tear-shaped island, it is slow and shallow, fringed thinly in cattail marsh. At this spot an astonishing bloom of life supports vast breeding populations of insects, fish, reptiles, birds, and mammals. On windless summer evenings I stalk along the creek bank or straddle the sycamore log in absolute stillness, watching for muskrats. The night I stayed too late I was hunched on the log staring spellbound at spreading, reflected stains of lilac on the water. A cloud in the sky suddenly lighted as if turned on by a switch; its reflection just as suddenly materialized on the water upstream, flat and floating, so that I couldn't see the creek bottom, or life in the water under the cloud. Downstream, away from the cloud on the water, water turtles smooth as beans were gliding down with the current in a series of easy, weightless push-offs, as men bound on the moon. I didn't know whether to trace the progress of one turtle I was sure of, risking sticking my face in one of the bridge's spider webs made invisible by the gathering dark, or take a chance on seeing the carp, or scan the mudbank in hope of seeing a muskrat, or follow the last of the swallows who caught at my heart and trailed it after them like streamers as they appeared from directly below, under the log, flying upstream with their tails forked, so fast.

But shadows spread and deepened and stayed. After thousands of years we're still strangers to darkness, fearful aliens in an enemy camp with our arms crossed over our chests. I stirred. A land turtle on the bank, startled, hissed the air from its lungs and withdrew to its shell. An uneasy pink here, an unfathomable blue there, gave great suggestion of lurking beings. Things were going on. I couldn't see whether that rustle I heard was

a distant rattle-snake, slit-eyed, or a nearby sparrow kicking in the dry flood debris slung at the foot of a willow. Tremendous action roiled the water everywhere I looked, big action, inexplicable. A tremor welled up beside a gaping muskrat burrow in the bank and I caught my breath, but no muskrat appeared. The ripples continued to fan upstream with a steady, powerful thrust. Night was knitting an eyeless mask over my face, and I still sat transfixed. A distant airplane, a delta wing out of nightmare, made a gliding shadow on the creek's bottom that looked like a stingray cruising upstream. At once a black fin slit the pink cloud on the water, shearing it in two. The two halves merged together and seemed to dissolve before my eyes. Darkness pooled in the cleft of the creek and rose, as water collects in a well. Untamed, dreaming lights flickered over the sky. I saw hints of hulking underwater shadows, two pale splashes out of the water, and round ripples rolling close together from a blackened center.

At last I stared upstream where only the deepest violet remained of the cloud, a cloud so high its underbelly still glowed, its feeble color reflected from a hidden sky lighted in turn by a sun halfway to China. And out of that violet, a sudden enormous black body arced over the water. Head and tail, if there was a head and tail, were both submerged in cloud. I saw only one ebony fling, a headlong dive to darkness; then the waters closed, and the lights went out.

I walked home in a shivering daze, up hill and down. Later I lay openmouthed in bed, my arms flung wide at my sides to steady the whirling darkness. At this latitude I'm spinning 836 miles an hour round the earth's axis; I feel my sweeping fall as a breakneck arc like the dive of dolphins, and the hollow rushing of wind raises the hairs on my neck and the side of my face. In orbit around the sun I'm moving 64,800 miles an hour. The solar system as a whole, like a merry-go-round unhinged, spins, bobs, and blinks at the speed of 43,200 miles an hour along a course set east of Hercules. Someone has piped, and we are dancing a tarantella until the sweat pours. I open my eyes and I see dark, muscled forms curl out of water, with flapping gills and flattened eyes. I close my eyes and I see stars, deep stars giving way to deeper stars, deeper stars bowing to deepest stars at the crown of an infinite cone.

"Still," wrote Van Gogh in a letter, "a great deal of light falls on everything." If we are blinded by darkness, we are also blinded by light. Sometimes here in Virginia at sunset low clouds on the southern or northern horizon are completely invisible in the lighted sky. I only know one is there because I can see its reflection in still water. The first time I discovered this mystery I looked from cloud to no-cloud in bewilderment, checking my bearings over and over, thinking maybe the ark of the covenant was just passing by south of Dead Man Mountain. Only much later did I learn the explanation: polarized light from the sky is very much weakened by reflection, but the light in clouds isn't polarized. So invisible clouds pass among visible clouds, till all slide over the mountains; so a greater light extinguishes a lesser as though it didn't exist.

In the great meteor shower of August, the Perseid, I wail all day for the shooting stars I miss. They're out there showering down committing hara-kiri in a flame of fatal attraction, and hissing perhaps at last into the ocean. But at dawn what looks like a blue dome clamps down over me like a lid on a pot. The stars and planets could smash and I'd never know. Only a piece of ashen moon occasionally climbs up or down the inside of the dome, and our local star without surcease explodes on our heads. We have really only that one light, one source for all power, and yet we must turn away from it by universal decree. Nobody here on the planet seems aware of this strange, powerful taboo, that we all walk about carefully averting our faces, this way and that, lest our eyes be blasted forever.

Darkness appalls and light dazzles; the scrap of visible light that doesn't hurt my eyes hurts my brain. What I see sets me swaying. Size and distance and the sudden swelling of meanings confuse me, bowl me over. I straddle the sycamore log bridge over Tinker Creek in the summer. I look at the lighted creek bottom: snail tracks tunnel the mud in quavering curves. A crayfish jerks, but by the time I absorb what has happened, he's gone in a billowing smoke screen of silt. I look at the water; minnows and shiners. If I'm thinking minnows, a carp will fill my brain till I scream. I look at the water's surface: skaters, bubbles, and leaves sliding down. Suddenly, my own face, reflected, startles me witless. Those snails have been tracking my face! Finally, with a shuddering wrench of the will, I see clouds, cirrus clouds. I'm dizzy, I fall in.

This looking business is risky. Once I stood on a humped rock on nearby Purgatory Mountain, watching through binoculars the great autumn hawk migration below, until I discovered that I was in danger of joining the hawks on a vertical migration of my own. I was used to binoculars, but not, apparently, to balancing on humped rocks while looking through them. I reeled. Everything advanced and receded by turns; the world was full of unexplained foreshortenings and depths. A distant huge object, a hawk the size of an elephant, turned out to be the browned bough of a nearby loblolly pine. I followed a sharp-shinned hawk against a featureless sky, rotating my head unawares as it flew, and when I lowered the glass a glimpse of my own looming shoulder sent me staggering. What prevents the men at Palomar[1] from falling, voiceless and blinded, from their tiny, vaulted chairs?

I reel in confusion: I don't understand what I see. With the naked eye I can see two million light-years to the Andromeda galaxy. Often I slop some creek water in a jar, and when I get home I dump it in a white china bowl. After the silt settles I return and see tracings of minute snails on the bottom, a planarian or two winding round the rim of water, roundworms shimmying, frantically, and finally, when my eyes have adjusted to these dimensions, amoebae. At first the amoebae look like *muscae volitantes,* those curled moving spots you seem to see in your eyes when you stare at a distant wall. Then I see the amoebae as drops of water congealed, bluish, translucent, like chips of sky in the bowl. At length I choose one individual and give myself over to its idea of an evening. I see it dribble a grainy foot before it on its wet, unfathomable way. Do its unedited sense impressions include the fierce focus of my eyes? Shall I take it outside and show it Andromeda, and blow its little endoplasm? I stir the water with a finger, in case it's running out of oxygen. Maybe I should get a tropical aquarium with motorized bubblers and lights, and keep this one for a pet. Yes, it would tell its fissioned descendants, the universe is two feet by five, and if you listen closely you can hear the buzzing music of the spheres.

Oh, it's mysterious, lamplit evenings here in the galaxy, one after the other. It's one of those nights when I wander from window to window, looking for a sign. But I can't see. Terror and a beauty insoluble are a riband of blue woven into the fringe of garments of things both great and small. No culture explains, no bivouac offers real haven or rest. But it could be that we are not seeing something. Galileo thought comets were an optical illusion. This is fertile ground: since we are certain that they're not, we can look at what

1. An astronomical observatory in California.

our scientists have been saying with fresh hope. What if there are *really* gleaming, castellated cities hung up-side-down over the desert sand? What limpid lakes and cool date palms have our caravans always passed untried? Until, one by one, by the blindest of leaps, we light on the road to these places, we must stumble in darkness and hunger. I turn from the window. I'm blind as a bat, sensing only from every direction the echo of my own thin cries.

I chanced on a wonderful book called *Space and Sight,* by Marius Von Senden. When Western surgeons discovered how to perform safe cataract operations, they ranged across Europe and America operating on dozens of men and women of all ages who had been blinded by cataracts since birth. Von Senden collected accounts of such cases; the histories are fascinating. Many doctors had tested their patients' sense perceptions and ideas of space both before and after the operations. The vast majority of patients, of both sexes and all ages, had, in Von Senden's opinion, no idea of space whatsoever. Form, distance, and size were so many meaningless syllables. A patient "had no idea of depth, confusing it with roundness." Before the operation a doctor would give a blind patient a cube and a sphere; the patient would tongue it or feel it with his hands, and name it correctly. After the operation the doctor would show the same objects to the patient without letting him touch them; now he had no clue whatsoever to what he was seeing. One patient called lemonade "square" because it pricked on his tongue as a square shape pricked on the touch of his hands. Of another post-operative patient the doctor writes, "I have found in her no notion of size, for example, not even within the narrow limits which she might have encompassed with the aid of touch. Thus when I asked her to show me how big her mother was, she did not stretch out her hands, but set her two index fingers a few inches apart."

For the newly sighted, vision is pure sensation unencumbered by meaning. When a newly sighted girl saw photographs and paintings, she asked, " 'Why do they put those dark marks all over them?' 'Those aren't dark marks,' her mother explained, 'those are shadows. That is one of the ways the eye knows that things have shape. If it were not for shadows, many things would look flat.' 'Well, that's how things do look,' Joan answered. 'Everything looks flat with dark patches.' "

In general the newly sighted see the world as a dazzle of "colorpatches." They are pleased by the sensation of color, and learn quickly to name the colors, but the rest of seeing is tormentingly difficult. Soon after his operation a patient "generally bumps into one of these colour-patches and observes them to be substantial, since they resist him as tactual objects do. In walking about it also strikes him—or can if he pays attention—that he is continually passing in between the colours he sees, that he can go past a visual object, that a part of it then steadily disappears from view; and that in spite of this, however he twists and turns—whether entering the room from the door, for example, or returning back to it—he always has a visual space in front of him. Thus he gradually comes to realize that there is also a space behind him, which he does not see."

The mental effort involved in these reasonings proves overwhelming for many patients. It oppresses them to realize that they have been visible to people all along, perhaps unattractively so, without their knowledge or consent. A disheartening number of them refuse to use their new vision, continuing to go over objects with their tongues, and lapsing into apathy and despair.

On the other hand, many newly sighted people speak well of the world, and teach us how dull our own vision is. To one patient, a human hand, unrecognized, is "something bright and then holes." Shown a bunch of grapes, a boy calls out, "It is dark, blue and shiny.

. . . It isn't smooth, it has bumps and hollows." A little girl visits a garden. "She is greatly astonished, and can scarcely be persuaded to answer, stands speechless in front of the tree, which she only names on taking hold of it, and then as 'the tree with the lights in it.' " Another patient, a twenty-two-year-old girl, was dazzled by the world's brightness and kept her eyes shut for two weeks. When at the end of that time she opened her eyes again, she did not recognize any objects, but "the more she now directed her gaze upon everything about her, the more it could be seen how an expression of gratification and astonishment overspread her features; she repeatedly exclaimed: 'Oh God! How beautiful!' "

I saw color-patches for weeks after I read this wonderful book. It was summer; the peaches were ripe in the valley orchards. When I woke in the morning, color-patches wrapped round my eyes, intricately, leaving not one unfilled spot. All day long I walked among shifting color-patches that parted before me like the Red Sea and closed again in silence, transfigured, wherever I looked back. Some patches swelled and loomed, while others vanished utterly, and dark marks flitted at random over the whole dazzling sweep. But I couldn't sustain the illusion of flatness. I've been around for too long. Form is condemned to an eternal danse macabre with meaning: I couldn't unpeach the peaches. Nor can I remember ever having seen without understanding; the color-patches of infancy are lost. My brain then must have been smooth as any balloon. I'm told I reached for the moon; many babies do. But the color-patches of infancy swelled as meaning filled them; they arrayed themselves in solemn ranks down distance which unrolled and stretched before me like a plain. The moon rocketed away. I live now in a world of shadows that shape and distance color, a world where space makes a kind of terrible sense. What Gnosticism[2] is this, and what physics? The fluttering patch I saw in my nursery window—silver and green and shape-shifting blue—is gone; a row of Lombardy poplars takes its place, mute, across the distant lawn. That humming oblong creature pale as light that stole along the walls of my room at night, stretching exhilaratingly around the corners, is gone, too, gone the night I ate of the bittersweet fruit, put two and two together and puckered forever my brain. Martin Buber tells this tale: "Rabbi Mendel once boasted to his teacher Rabbi Elimelekh that evenings he saw the angel who rolls away the light before the darkness, and mornings the angel who rolls away the darkness before the light. 'Yes,' said Rabbi Elimelekh, 'in my youth I saw that too. Later on you don't see these things anymore.' "

Why didn't someone hand those newly sighted people paints and brushes from the start, when they still didn't know what anything was? Then maybe we all could see color-patches too, the world unraveled from reason, Eden before Adam gave names. The scales would drop from my eyes; I'd see trees like men walking; I'd run down the road against all orders, hallooing and leaping.

Seeing is of course very much a matter of verbalization. Unless I call my attention to what passes before my eyes, I simply won't see it. If Tinker Mountain erupted, I'd be likely to notice. But if I want to notice the lesser cataclysms of valley life, I have to maintain in my head a running description of the present. It's not that I'm observant; it's just that I talk too much. Otherwise, especially in a strange place, I'll never know what's happening. Like a blind man at the ball game, I need a radio.

When I see this way I analyze and pry. I hurl over logs and roll away stones; I study

2. Pretension to esoteric spiritual knowledge.

the bank a square foot at a time, probing and tilting my head. Some days when a mist covers the mountains, when the muskrats won't show and the microscope's mirror shatters, I want to climb up the blank blue dome as a man would storm the inside of a circus tent, wildly, dangling, and with a steel knife claw a rent in the top, peep, and, if I must, fall.

But there is another kind of seeing that involves a letting go. When I see this way I sway transfixed and emptied. The difference between the two ways of seeing is the difference between walking with and without a camera. When I walk with a camera I walk from shot to shot, reading the light on a calibrated meter. When I walk without a camera, my own shutter opens, and the moment's light prints on my own silver gut. When I see this second way I am above all an unscrupulous observer.

It was sunny one evening last summer at Tinker Creek; the sun was low in the sky, upstream. I was sitting on the sycamore log bridge with the sunset at my back, watching the shiners the size of minnows who were feeding over the muddy sand in skittery schools. Again and again, one fish, then another, turned for a split second across the current and flash! the sun shot out from its silver side. I couldn't watch for it. It was always just happening somewhere else, and it drew my vision just as it disappeared: flash! like a sudden dazzle of the thinnest blade, a sparking over a dun and olive ground at chance intervals from every direction. Then I noticed white specks, some sort of pale petals, small, floating from under my feet on the creek's surface, very slow and steady. So I blurred my eyes and gazed toward the brim of my hat and saw a new world. I saw the pale white circles roll up, roll up, like the world's turning, mute and perfect, and I saw the linear flashes, gleaming silver, like stars being born at random down a rolling scroll of time. Something broke and something opened. I filled up like a new wineskin. I breathed an air like light; I saw a light like water. I was the lip of a fountain the creek filled forever; I was ether, the leaf in the zephyr; I was flesh-flake, feather, bone.

When I see this way I see truly. As Thoreau says, I return to my senses. I am the man who watches the baseball game in silence in an empty stadium. I see the game purely; I'm abstracted and dazed. When it's all over and the white-suited players lope off the green field to their shadowed dugouts, I leap to my feet, I cheer and cheer.

But I can't go out and try to see this way. I'll fail, I'll go mad. All I can do is try to gag the commentator, to hush the noise of useless interior babble that keeps me from seeing just as surely as a newspaper dangled before my eyes. The effort is really a discipline requiring a lifetime of dedicated struggle; it marks the literature of saints and monks of every order east and west, under every rule and no rule, discalced and shod. The world's spiritual geniuses seem to discover universally that the mind's muddy river, this ceaseless flow of trivia and trash, cannot be dammed, and that trying to dam it is a waste of effort that might lead to madness. Instead you must allow the muddy river to flow unheeded in the dim channels of consciousness; you raise your sights; you look along it, mildly, acknowledging its presence without interest and gazing beyond it into the realm of the real where subjects and objects act and rest purely, without utterance. "Launch into the deep," says Jacques Ellul, "and you shall see."

The secret of seeing, then, is the pearl of great price. If I thought he could teach me to find it and keep it forever I would stagger barefoot across a hundred deserts after any lunatic at all. But although the pearl may be found, it may not be sought. The literature of illumination reveals this above all: although it comes to those who wait for it, it is always, even to the most practiced and adept, a gift and a total surprise. I return from one walk knowing where the killdeer nests in the field by the creek and the hour the laurel blooms. I return from the same walk a day later scarcely knowing my own name. Litanies hum in my ears; my tongue flaps in my mouth, *Alim non,* alleluia! I cannot cause light; the most I can do is try to put myself in the path of its beam. It is possible, in deep space, to sail on solar wind. Light, be it particle or wave, has force: you rig a giant sail and go. The secret of seeing is to sail on solar wind. Hone and spread your spirit till you yourself are a sail, whetted, translucent, broadiside to the merest puff.

When her doctor took her bandages off and led her into the garden, the girl who was no longer blind saw "the tree with the lights in it." It was for this tree I searched through the peach orchards of summer, in the forests of fall and down winter and spring for years. Then one day I was walking along Tinker Creek thinking of nothing at all and I saw the tree with the lights in it. I saw the backyard cedar where the mourning doves roost charged and transfigured, each cell buzzing with flame. I stood on the grass with the lights in it, grass that was wholly fire, utterly focused and utterly dreamed. It was less like seeing than like being for the first time seen, knocked breathless by a powerful glance. The flood of fire abated, but I'm still spending the power. Gradually the lights went out in the cedar, the colors died, the cells unflamed and disappeared. I was still ringing. I had been my whole life a bell, and never knew it until at that moment I was lifted and struck. I have since only very rarely seen the tree with the lights in it. The vision comes and goes, mostly goes, but I live for it, for the moment when the mountains open and a new light roars in spate through the crack, and the mountains slam.

[1974]

JOAN DIDION

(1934–)

Why I Write

About the Author: In many of her essays, Didion voices fear over the fragmentation of American social morals and her concern for the resultant cultural chaos. In "Why I Write," she explains the role that writing plays in her life.

Of course I stole the title for this talk from George Orwell. One reason I stole it was that I like the sound of the words: *Why I Write.* There you have three short unambiguous words that share a sound, and the sound they share is this:

I
I
I

In many ways writing is the act of saying *I,* of imposing oneself upon other people, of saying *listen to me, see it my way, change your mind.* It's an aggressive, even a hostile act. You can disguise its aggressiveness all you want with veils of subordinate clauses and qualifiers and tentative subjunctives, with ellipses and evasions—with the whole manner of intimating rather than claiming, of alluding rather than stating—but there's no getting around the fact

that setting words on paper is the tactic of a secret bully, an invasion, an imposition of the writer's sensibility on the reader's most private space.

I stole the title not only because the words sounded right but because they seemed to sum up, in a no-nonsense way, all I have to tell you. Like many writers I have only this one "subject," this one "area": the act of writing. I can bring you no reports from any other front. I may have other interests: I am "interested," for example, in marine biology, but I don't flatter myself that you would come out to hear me talk about it. I am not a scholar. I am not in the least an intellectual, which is not to say that when I hear the word "intellectual" I reach for my gun, but only to say that I do not think in abstracts. During the years when I was an undergraduate at Berkeley I tried, with a kind of hopeless late-adolescent energy, to buy some temporary visa into the world of ideas, to forge for myself a mind that could deal with the abstract.

In short I tried to think. I failed. My attention veered inexorably back to the specific, to the tangible, to what was generally considered, by everyone I knew then and for that matter have known since, the peripheral. I would try to contemplate the Hegelian dialectic and would find myself concentrating instead on a flowering pear tree outside my window and the particular way the petals fell on my floor. I would try to read linguistic theory and would find myself wondering instead if the lights were on in the bevatron up the hill. When I say that I was wondering if the lights were on in the bevatron you might immediately suspect, if you deal in ideas at all, that I was registering the bevatron as a political symbol, thinking in shorthand about the military-industrial complex and its role in the university community, but you would be wrong. I was only wondering if the lights were on in the bevatron, and how they looked. A physical fact.

I had trouble graduating from Berkeley, not because of this inability to deal with ideas—I was majoring in English, and I could locate the house-and-garden imagery in *The Portrait of a Lady* as well as the next person, "imagery" being by definition the kind of specific that got my attention—but simply because I had neglected to take a course in Milton. For reasons which now sound baroque I needed a degree by the end of that summer, and the English department finally agreed, if I would come down from Sacramento every Friday and talk about the cosmology of *Paradise Lost,* to certify me proficient in Milton. I did this. Some Fridays I took the Greyhound bus, other Fridays I caught the Southern Pacific's City of San Françisco on the last leg of its transcontinental trip. I can no longer tell you whether Milton put the sun or the earth at the center of his universe in *Paradise Lost,* the central question of at least one century and a topic about which I wrote 10,000 words that summer, but I can still recall the exact rancidity of the butter in the City of San Francisco's dining car, and the way the tinted windows on the Greyhound bus cast the oil refineries around Carquinez Straits into a grayed and obscurely sinister light. In short my attention was always on the periphery, on what I would see and taste and touch, on the butter, and the Greyhound bus. During those years I was traveling on what I knew to be a very shaky passport, forged papers: I knew that I was no legitimate resident in any world of ideas. I knew I couldn't think. All I knew then was what I couldn't do. All I knew then was what I wasn't, and it took me some years to discover what I was.

Which was a writer.

By which I mean not a "good" writer or a "bad" writer but simply a writer, a person whose most absorbed and passionate hours are spent arranging words on pieces of paper. Had my credentials been in order I would never have become a writer. Had I been blessed with even limited access to my own mind there would have been no reason to write. I write

entirely to find out what I'm thinking, what I'm looking at, what I see and what it means. What I want and what I fear. Why did the oil refineries around Carquinez Straits seem sinister to me in the summer of 1956? Why have the night lights in the bevatron burned in my mind for twenty years? *What is going on in these pictures in my mind?*

When I talk about pictures in my mind I am talking, quite specifically, about images that shimmer around the edges. There used to be an illustration in every elementary psychology book showing a cat drawn by a patient in varying stages of schizophrenia. This cat had a shimmer around it. You could see the molecular structure breaking down at the very edges of the cat: the cat became the background and the background the cat, everything interacting, exchanging ions. People on hallucinogens describe the same perception of objects. I'm not a schizophrenic, nor do I take hallucinogens, but certain images do shimmer for me. Look hard enough, and you can't miss the shimmer. It's there. You can't think too much about these pictures that shimmer. You just lie low and let them develop. You stay quiet. You don't talk to many people and you keep your nervous system from shorting out and you try to locate the cat in the shimmer, the grammar in the picture.

Just as I meant "shimmer" literally I mean "grammar" literally. Grammar is a piano I play by ear, since I seem to have been out of school the year the rules were mentioned. All I know about grammar is its infinite power. To shift the structure of a sentence alters the meaning of that sentence, as definitely and inflexibly as the position of a camera alters the meaning of the object photographed. Many people know about camera angles now, but not so many know about sentences. The arrangement of the words matters, and the arrangement you want can be found in the picture in your mind. The picture dictates the arrangement. The picture dictates whether this will be a sentence with or without clauses, a sentence that ends hard or a dying-fall sentence, long or short, active or passive. The picture tells you how to arrange the words and the arrangement of the words tells you, or tells me, what's going on in the picture. *Nota bene:*

It tells you.

You don't tell it.

Let me show you what I mean by pictures in the mind. I began *Play It as It Lays* just as I have begun each of my novels, with no notion of "character" or "plot" or even "incident." I had only two pictures in my mind, more about which later, and a technical intention, which was to write a novel so elliptical and fast that it would be over before you noticed it, a novel so fast that it would scarcely exist on the page at all. About the pictures: the first was of white space. Empty space. This was clearly the picture that dictated the narrative intention of the book—a book in which anything that happened would happen off the page, a "white" book to which the reader would have to bring his or her own bad dreams—and yet this picture told me no "story," suggested no situation. The second picture did. This second picture was of something actually witnessed. A young woman with long hair and a short white halter dress walks through the casino at the Riviera in Las Vegas at one in the morning. She crosses the casino alone and picks up a house telephone. I watch her because I have heard her paged, and recognize her name: she is a minor actress I see around Los Angeles from time to time, in places like Jax and once in a gynecologist's office in the Beverly Hills Clinic, but have never met. I know nothing about her. Who is paging her? Why is she here to be paged? How exactly did she come to this? It was precisely this moment in Las Vegas that made *Play It as It Lays* begin to tell itself to me, but the moment appears in the novel only obliquely, in a chapter which begins:

> Maria made a list of things she would never do. She would never: walk through the Sands or Caesar's alone after midnight. She would never: ball at a party, do S-M unless she wanted to, borrow furs from Abe Lipsey, deal. She would never: carry a Yorkshire in Beverly Hills.

That is the beginning of the chapter and that is also the end of the chapter, which may suggest what I meant by "white space."

I recall having a number of pictures in my mind when I began the novel I just finished, *A Book of Common Prayer.* As a matter of fact one of these pictures was of that bevatron I mentioned, although I would be hard put to tell you a story in which nuclear energy figured. Another was a newspaper photograph of a hijacked 707 burning on the desert in the Middle East. Another was the night view from a room in which I once spent a week with paratyphoid, a hotel room on the Colombian coast. My husband and I seemed to be on the Colombian coast representing the United States of America at a film festival (I recall invoking the name "Jack Valenti" a lot, as if its reiteration could make me well), and it was a bad place to have fever, not only because my indisposition offended our hosts but because every night in this hotel the generator failed. The lights went out. The elevator stopped. My husband would go to the event of the evening and make excuses for me and I would stay alone in this hotel room, in the dark. I remember standing at the window trying to call Bogotá (the telephone seemed to work on the same principle as the generator) and watching the night wind come up and wondering what I was doing eleven degrees off the equator with a fever of 103. The view from that window definitely figures in *A Book of Common Prayer,* as does the burning 707, and yet none of these pictures told me the story I needed.

The picture that did, the picture that shimmered and made these other images coalesce, was the Panama airport at 6 A.M. I was in this airport only once, on a plane to Bogotá that stopped for an hour to refuel, but the way it looked that morning remained superimposed on everything I saw until the day I finished *A Book of Common Prayer.* I lived in that airport for several years. I can still feel the hot air when I step off the plane, can see the heat already rising off the tarmac at 6 A.M. I can feel my skirt damp and wrinkled on my legs. I can feel the asphalt stick to my sandals. I remember the big tail of a Pan American plane floating motionless down at the end of the tarmac. I remember the sound of a slot machine in the waiting room. I could tell you that I remember a particular woman in the airport, an American woman, a *norteamericana,* a thin *norteamericana* about 40 who wore a big square emerald in lieu of a wedding ring, but there was no such woman there.

I put this woman in the airport later. I made this woman up, just as I later made up a country to put the airport in, and a family to run the country. This woman in the airport is neither catching a plane nor meeting one. She is ordering tea in the airport coffee shop. In fact she is not simply "ordering" tea but insisting that the water be boiled, in front of her, for twenty minutes. Why is this woman in this airport? Why is she going nowhere, where has she been? Where did she get that big emerald? What derangement, or disassociation, makes her believe that her will to see the water boiled can possibly prevail?

> She had been going to one airport or another for four months, one could see it, looking at the visas on her passport. All those airports where Charlotte Douglas's passport had been stamped would have looked alike. Sometimes the sign on the tower would say "Bienvenidos" and sometimes the sign on the tower would say "Bienvenue," some places were wet and hot and others dry and hot, but at each of these airports the pastel concrete walls would rust and stain and the swamp off the runway would be littered with the fuselages of cannibalized Fairchild F-227's and the water would need boiling.

"I knew why Charlotte went to the airport even if Victor did not."
"I knew about airports."

These lines appear about halfway through *A Book of Common Prayer,* but I wrote them during the second week I worked on the book, long before I had any idea where Charlotte Douglas had been or why she went to airports. Until I wrote these lines I had no character called "Victor" in mind: the necessity for mentioning a name, and the name "Victor," occurred to me as I wrote the sentence. *I knew why Charlotte went to the airport* sounded incomplete. *I knew why Charlotte went to the airport even if Victor did not* carried a little more narrative drive. Most important of all, until I wrote these lines I did not know who "I" was, who was telling the story. I had intended until that moment that the "I" be no more than the voice of the author, a 19th-century omniscient narrator. But there it was:

"I knew why Charlotte went to the airport even if Victor did not."
"I knew about airports."

This "I" was the voice of no author in my house. This "I" was someone who not only knew why Charlotte went to the airport but also knew someone called "Victor." Who was Victor? Who was this narrator? Why was this narrator telling me this story? Let me tell you one thing about why writers write: had I known the answer to any of these questions I would never have needed to write a novel.

[1976]

MAUREEN TURLEY

Women's Studies: My Right to an Education

About the Author: A native of New Jersey, Maureen Turley graduated from the University of Vermont in 1983. She wrote "Women's Studies: My Right to an Education" as an exploration of the process of higher education.

It seems my education has always been strictly divided into male and female subjects. I remember in high school telling my mother that I might be interested in being a veterinarian. She frowned at this and told me I wouldn't really like being around sick animals. I began to wonder if my fondness for biology was abnormal because even though dissecting a crayfish was not a milestone in my life, my parents trivialized my enthusiasm about it in comparison to the praise they lavished on my maudlin poetry and oil paintings. While my parents and teachers forgave my incompetence in mathematics, they supported and encouraged my interest in literature.

I even ended up majoring in English in college, but although I was comfortable as an English major, I wondered how practical this field was for me. How many women writers were there, anyway? I could count the women writers I had been exposed to: Jane Austen; Charlotte and Emily Brontë, whose major women characters either died or got married at the ends of their novels; Elizabeth Barrett Browning, an invalid who wrote about love; Emily Dickinson, a reclusive spinster; and Sylvia Plath, who wrote about women's lack of

identity. With only this handful of female models to learn from, it is not surprising that I felt a lack of connection with what I was studying. Although my classes were full of women, in some ways English seemed no more feminized than any other field of study.

My college introductory course in British and American literature contained a token selection of poems and essays by women. While we spent four classes on Wordsworth's *Prelude,* we spent only one class on Virginia Woolf. While we read Hemingway's *The Sun Also Rises,* we ignored *Jacob's Room, Mrs. Dalloway, The Waves,* and *To the Lighthouse.* Instead we read Woolf's essays, "A Room of One's Own" and "Professions of Women." In doing so, we acknowledged Woolf as a woman who wrote and not as the innovative writer of fiction that she is. Ironically, even though Woolf has a small chapter in the *Norton Anthology of English Literature,* she can be, like Shakespeare's sister, a "lost novelist" because of the perfunctory treatment she receives in the classroom.

Such marginal treatment of women writers angered me, but to trivialize and distort women writers was even worse. Once, after a lecture on Emily Dickinson, I heard a classmate comment that Dickinson was a "manic depressive." I took offense, not because Emily Dickinson may have been neurotic and I didn't want her to be, but because no one had ever blasphemed Thoreau or Whitman in such a way, even though both of these writers had unusual backgrounds. No one bothered to dredge up rumors of Whitman's homosexuality or Thoreau's attachment to his mother, but our professor emphasized Dickinson's bizarre, autobiographical material.

In fact, his lecture echoed Emily Dickinson's introduction in the *Norton Anthology:* "She dressed all in white"; "She never left her yard"; "She avoided strangers," and communicated even with good friends "through cryptic notes and fragments of poems"; she would only let a doctor examine her through "a partially opened door." By using this type of information in the first paragraph of their introduction, the editors single Dickinson out as an anomaly in the world of literature. In effect they are saying, "Look, here's a woman writer, but she was very strange." They ignored examination of the restrictions women lived under during the 1800s and the fact that Dickinson had an education that separated her from most women in the mid-nineteenth century. Both would have helped to interpret Dickinson's unusual life, but the *Anthology* merely cautions us that "to think of Emily Dickinson as *only* an eccentric recluse is a serious mistake" (emphasis mine).

In contrast, the *Anthology*'s editors describe Thoreau as an "eccentric social experimenter," a hero, who hid himself away in a cabin by Walden Pond for two years. But unlike Emily Dickinson, Thoreau's purpose was to show disdain for society's materialistic values. Even though both Dickinson and Thoreau may have been seeking to avoid the desperation of modern life, Thoreau's behavior represents a noble "rebellion" while Dickinson's is a frail "retreat."

The problem with including women authors in undergraduate English courses is that the professor wants to communicate cultural assumptions about society and about the human condition through writers in different eras. Since women writers often depart from those assumptions to provide insights about how the other half of the human race survives, they don't portray the true emotional and intellectual climate of an age. They don't represent the recognized interpretation of an era in their works. So the educational system either distorts women so they fit the norm or omits them entirely. In anthologies, women writers exist only in the briefest of excerpts, and their contributions lose value and importance. While Woolf's contributions are presented cosmetically, Dickinson is regarded as being totally cloistered from the real world.

However unintentional neglecting women in literature and other humanities may be, it limits awareness and aborts potential. Women remain on the outside, discouraged and insecure about their pursuits in a world dominated by men. I remember reading Whitman's *Leaves of Grass,* where the poet encouraged that the truth for all men was to see a part of himself in every profession, as male and female, black and white. It strikes me this feeling of infinitude is predominantly a male feeling, especially regarding professions. During our education, women are largely absent or viewed in traditional roles such as teachers or nurses. We grow up thinking we cannot be writers, lawyers, doctors, or politicians. Unlike Whitman, most women have a much harder time feeling multitudinous. We know women are gradually working their way into untraditional fields, but to pursue such a field one needs psychological freedom. Virginia Woolf said the obstacles against women "are still immensely powerful—and yet they are very difficult to define. . . . Outwardly, what obstacles are there for a woman rather than for a man? Inwardly, I think, the case is very different; she has still many ghosts to fight, many prejudices to overcome."

To overcome these ghosts, these prejudices, women must examine the way their assumptions developed. Ideally, treatment of women's roles in history and society should be integrated into all courses in the humanities, but this involves a reexamination of history, literature, religion, and art. According to the 1981 College Blue Book, only 25 out of over 3000 two- and four-year colleges and universities offer bachelor's degrees for Women's Studies. Six offer associate degrees, five have master's programs, and one has a doctorate program. As people recognize these statistics, publicly accepted neglect of Women's Studies becomes increasingly intolerable, for to critique culture within the humanities and exclude women results in a half-truth. It is like reading all of Norman Mailer's *An American Dream* and one page out of Marilyn French's *The Women's Room.* We should at least read an entire chapter, if not the whole book.

During the past two decades women have held regional conferences to spread educational ideas. For people interested in teaching Women's Studies, syllabi collections are available. Perhaps it is a good thing that teaching remains a major occupation for women, because we are beginning to explore and integrate feminist scholarship into the educational system. But this integration involves more than just a reeducation of the existing faculty. In a discussion with a feminist scholar in the English department of my university, the subject of reeducation surfaced: "People make remarks," she said, "like Women's Studies is not a real discipline or Women's Studies isn't rigorous enough." She says this results from people not wanting to consider the insights feminist scholarship addresses, or just plain resistance to a new way of approaching various disciplines. "Some of my colleagues say they don't *do* women. They don't *do* women," she mimics incredulously.

The question of rigor has emerged in several of my Women's Studies courses. Before an exam in my Women's History course, the professor warned us that her grading on exams was harsh and that enthusiasm for the subject and a good grade don't always correspond. She said that because she taught a Women's Studies course composed of mostly women, many assumed there was some kind of "shared bond of sympathy" within the class which manifested in good grades. We laughed. How absurd—this was a class like any other, not a cult.

In addition, feminist scholars have been criticized for lacking a universal theory that ties Women's Studies together as a discipline. As in the Women's Movement, disparity exists between theories about how to approach Women's Studies programs. Some feel that Women's Studies should exist independently as a major field of study, that women's studies

should separate or "come into its own" as biology once did. Others feel it should be an interdisciplinary field because of its scope. The lack of unity behind women's issues including theories about Women's Studies can be linked to their novelty. This is a formative period of women's politics, and women's alignment with different strategies is in a continual state of flux. Consequently, women seem more divided, more pluralistic, but also more willing to admit there may be more than one truth, more than one theory about how to attain their goals. They can build bridges between groups because they know regardless of how it is attained, we have a lot of catching up to do if we are ever to fill in the other half of human knowledge and achievement.

Intellectual integration from grammar school through college is most important. It took until 1948 for women to gain the legal right to learn as stated in the United Nations Declaration of Human Rights. Not only should everyone have the right to education, but "education shall be directed to the full development of the human personality and the strengthening of respect for human rights and fundamental freedoms." I wonder how long it will take until the world decides that Women's Studies, as a discipline, should be instrumental in the development of these rights and freedoms.

[1983]

JAMES SEILSOPOUR

(1962–)

I Forgot the Words to the National Anthem

About the Author: Born in California to an American mother and an Iranian father, Seilsopour spent many of his early years in Iran. He wrote "I Forgot the Words to the National Anthem" while attending Riverside City College.

The bumper sticker read, "Piss on Iran."

To me, a fourteen-year-old living in Teheran, the Iranian revolution was nothing more than an inconvenience. Although the riots were just around the corner, although the tanks lined the streets, although a stray bullet went through my sister's bedroom window, I was upset because I could not ride at the Royal Stable as often as I used to. In the summer of 1979 my family—father, mother, brothers, sister, aunt, and two cousins—were forced into exile. We came to Norco, California.

In Iran, I was an American citizen and considered myself an American, even though my father was Iranian. I loved baseball and apple pie and knew the words to the "Star-Spangled Banner." That summer before high school, I was like any other kid my age; I listened to rock'n'roll, liked fast cars, and thought Farrah Fawcett was a fox. Excited about going to high school, I was looking forward to football games and school dances. But I learned that it was not meant to be. I was not like other kids, and it was a long, painful road I traveled as I found this out.

The American embassy in Iran was seized the fall I started high school. I did not realize my life would be affected until I read that bumper sticker in the high school parking lot which read, "Piss on Iran." At that moment I knew there would be no football games or school dances. For me, Norco High consisted of the goat ropers, the dopers, the jocks, the brains, and one quiet Iranian.

I was sitting in my photography class after the hostages were taken. The photography teacher was fond of showing travel films. On this particular day, he decided to show a film about Iran, knowing full well that my father was Iranian and that I grew up in Iran. During the movie, this teacher encouraged the students to make comments. Around the room, I could hear "Drop the bomb" and "Deport the mothers." Those words hurt. I felt dirty, guilty. However, I managed to laugh and assure the students I realized they were just joking. I went home that afternoon and cried. I have long since forgiven those students, but I have not and can never forgive that teacher. Paranoia set in. From then on, every whisper was about me: "You see that lousy son of a bitch? He's Iranian." When I was not looking, I could feel their pointing fingers in my back like arrows. Because I was absent one day, the next day I brought a note to the attendance office. The secretary read the note, then looked at me. "So you're Jim Seilsopour?" I couldn't answer. As I walked away, I thought I heard her whisper to her co-worker, "You see that lousy son of a bitch? He's Iranian." I missed thirty-five days of school that year.

My problems were small compared to those of my parents. In Teheran, my mother had been a lady of society. We had a palatial house and a maid. Belonging to the women's club, she collected clothes for the poor and arranged Christmas parties for the young American kids. She and my father dined with high government officials. But back in the States, when my father could not find a job, she had to work at a fast-food restaurant. She was the proverbial pillar of strength. My mother worked seventy hours a week for two years. I never heard her complain. I could see the toll the entire situation was taking on her. One day my mother and I went grocery shopping at Stater Brothers Market. After an hour of carefully picking our food, we proceeded to the cashier. The cashier was friendly and began a conversation with my mother. They spoke briefly of the weather as my mother wrote the check. The cashier looked at the check and casually asked, "What kind of name is that?" My mother said, "Italian." We exchanged glances for just a second. I could see the pain in her eyes. She offered no excuses; I asked for none.

Because of my father's birthplace, he was unable to obtain a job. A naturalized American citizen with a master's degree in aircraft maintenance engineering from the Northrop Institute of Technology, he had never been out of work in his life. My father had worked for Bell Helicopter International, Flying Tigers, and McDonnell Douglas. Suddenly, a man who literally was at the top of his field was unemployable. There is one incident that haunts me even today. My mother had gone to work, and all the kids had gone to school except me. I was in the bathroom washing my face. The door was open, and I could see my father's reflection in the mirror. For no particular reason I watched him. He was glancing at a newspaper. He carefully folded the paper and set it aside. For several long moments he stared blankly into space. With a resigned sigh, he got up, went into the kitchen, and began doing the dishes. On that day, I know I watched a part of my father die.

My father did get a job. However, he was forced to leave the country. He is a quality control inspector for Saudi Arabian Airlines in Jeddah, Saudi Arabia. My mother works only forty hours a week now. My family has survived, financially and emotionally. I am not bitter, but the memories are. I have not recovered totally; I can never do that.

And no, I have never been to a high school football game or dance. The strike really

turned me off to baseball. I have been on a diet for the last year, so I don't eat apple pie much anymore. And I have forgotten the words to the national anthem.

[**1984**]

MICHELLE CLIFF

(1946–)

If I Could Write This in Fire, I Would Write This in Fire

About the Author: In the tradition of many essayists, Cliff's published work ranges from poetry to autobiography, with her best-known piece a collection of prose and poetry, *The Land of Look Behind.* "If I Could Write This in Fire, I Would Write This in Fire" hints at the direct voice that expands the boundaries of the conventional contemporary essay.

I

We were standing under the waterfall at the top of Orange River. Our chests were just beginning to mound—slight hills on either side. In the center of each were our nipples, which were losing their sideways look and rounding into perceptible buttons of dark flesh. Too fast it seemed. We touched each other, then, quickly and almost simultaneously, raised our arms to examine the hairs growing underneath. Another sign. Mine was wispy and light-brown. My friend Zoe had dark hair curled up tight. In each little patch the riverwater caught the sun so we glistened.

The waterfall had come about when my uncles dammed up the river to bring power to the sugar mill. Usually, when I say "sugar mill" to anyone not familiar with the Jamaican countryside or for that matter my family, I can tell their minds cast an image of tall smokestacks, enormous copper cauldrons, a man in a broad-brimmed hat with a whip, and several dozens of slaves—that is, if they have any idea of how large sugar mills once operated. It's a grandiose expression—like plantation, verandah, out-building. (Try substituting farm, porch, outside toilet.) To some people it even sounds romantic.

Our sugar mill was little more than a round-roofed shed, which contained a wheel and woodfire. We paid an old man to run it, tend the fire, and then either bartered or gave the sugar away, after my grandmother had taken what she needed. Our canefield was about two acres of flat land next to the river. My grandmother had six acres in all—one donkey, a mule, two cows, some chickens, a few pigs, and stray dogs and cats who had taken up residence in the yard.

Her house had four rooms, no electricity, no running water. The kitchen was a shed in the back with a small pot-bellied stove. Across from the stove was a mahogany counter, which had a white enamel basin set into it. The only light source was a window, a small space covered partly by a wooden shutter. We washed our faces and hands in enamel bowls with cold water carried in kerosene tins from the river and poured from enamel pitchers. Our chamber pots were enamel also, and in the morning we carefully placed them on the steps at the side of the house where my grandmother collected them and disposed of their contents. The outhouse was about thirty yards from the back door—a "closet" as we called it—infested with lizards capable of changing color. When the door was shut it was totally dark, and the lizards made their presence known by the noise of their scurrying through the torn newspaper, or the soft shudder when they dropped from the walls. I remember most clearly the stench of the toilet, which seemed to hang in the air in that climate.

But because every little piece of reality exists in relation to another little piece, our situation was not that simple. It was to our yard that people came with news first. It was in my grandmother's parlor that the Disciples of Christ held their meetings. Zoe lived with her mother and sister on borrowed ground in a place called Breezy Hill. She and I saw each other almost every day on our school vacations over a period of three years. Each morning early—as I sat on the cement porch with my coffee cut with condensed milk—she appeared: in her straw hat, school tunic faded from blue to gray, white blouse, sneakers hanging around her neck. We had coffee together, and a piece of hard-dough bread with butter and cheese, waited a bit and headed for the river. At first we were shy with each other. We did not start from the same place.

There was land. My grandparents' farm. And there was color.

(My family was called *red.* A term which signified a degree of whiteness. "We's just a flock of red people," a cousin of mine said once.) In the hierarchy of shades I was considered among the lightest. The countrywoman who visited my grandmother commented on my "tall" hair—meaning long. Wavy, not curly.

I had spent the years from three to ten in New York and spoke—at first—like an American. I wore American clothes: shorts, slacks, bathing suit. Because of my American past I was looked upon as the creator of games. Cowboys and Indians. Cops and Robbers. Peter Pan.

(While the primary colonial identification for Jamaicans was English, American colonialism was a strong force in my childhood—and of course continues today. We were sent American movies and American music. American aluminum companies had already discovered bauxite on the island and were shipping the ore to their mainland. United Fruit bought our bananas. White Americans came to Montego Bay, Ocho Rios, and Kingston for their vacations and their cruise ships docked in Port Antonio and other places. In some ways America was seen as a better place than England by many Jamaicans. The farm laborers sent to work in American agribusiness came home with dollars and gifts and new clothes; there were few who mentioned American racism. Many of the middle class who emigrated to Brooklyn or Staten Island or Manhattan were able to pass into the white American world—saving their blackness for other Jamaicans or for trips home; in some cases, forgetting it altogether. Those middle-class Jamaicans who could not pass for white managed differently—not unlike the Bajans in Paule Marshall's *Brown Girl, Brownstones*—saving, working, investing, buying property. Completely separate in most cases from Black Americans.)

I was someone who had experience with the place that sent us triple features of B-grade westerns and gangster movies. And I had tall hair and light skin. And I was the granddaughter of my grandmother. So I had power. I was the cowboy, Zoe was my sidekick, the boys we knew were Indians. I was the detective, Zoe was my "girl," the boys were the robbers. I was Peter Pan, Zoe was Wendy Darling, the boys were the lost boys. And the terrain around the river—jungled and dark green—was Tombstone, or Chicago, or Never-Never Land.

This place and my friendship with Zoe never touched my life in Kingston. We did not correspond with each other when I left my grandmother's home.

I never visited Zoe's home the entire time I knew her. It was a given: never suggested, never raised.

Zoe went to a state school held in a country church in Red Hills. It had been my mother's school. I went to a private all-girls school where I was taught by white Englishwomen and pale Jamaicans. In her school the students were caned as punishment. In mine the harshest punishment I remember was being sent to sit under the *lignum vitae* to "commune with nature." Some of the girls were out-and-out white (English and American), the rest of us were colored—only a few were dark. Our uniforms were blood-red gabardine, heavy and hot. Classes were held in buildings meant to recreate England: damp with stone floors, facing onto a cloister, or quad as they called it. We began each day with the headmistress leading us in English hymns. The entire school stood for an hour in the zinc-roofed gymnasium.

Occasionally a girl fainted, or threw up. Once, a girl had a grand mal seizure. To any such disturbance the response was always "keep singing." While she flailed on the stone floor, I wondered what the mistresses would do. We sang "Faith of Our Fathers," and watched our classmate as her eyes rolled back in her head. I thought of people swallowing their tongues. This student was dark—here on scholarship—and the only woman who came forward to help her was the gamesmistress, the only dark teacher. She kneeled beside the girl and slid the white web belt from her tennis short, clamping it between the girl's teeth. When the seizure was over, she carried the girl to a tumbling mat in a corner of the gym and covered her so she wouldn't get chilled.

Were the other women unable to touch this girl because of her darkness? I think that now. Her darkness and her scholarship. She lived on Windward Road with her grandmother; her mother was a maid. But darkness is usually enough for women like those to hold back. Then, we usually excused that kind of behavior by saying they were "ladies." (We were constantly being told we should be ladies also. One teacher went so far as to tell us many people thought Jamaicans lived in trees and we had to show these people they were mistaken.) In short, we felt insufficient to judge the behavior of these women. The English ones (who had the corner on power in the school) had come all this way to teach us. Shouldn't we treat them as the missionaries they were certain they were? The creole Jamaicans had a different role: they were passing on to those of us who were light-skinned the creole heritage of collaboration, assimilation, loyalty to our betters. We were expected to be willing subjects in this outpost of civilization.

The girl left school that day and never returned. After prayers we filed into our classrooms. After classes we had games: tennis, field hockey, rounders (what the English call baseball), netball (what the English call basketball). For games we were divided into "houses"—groups named for Joan of Arc, Edith Cavell, Florence Nightingale, Jane Austen. Four white heroines. Two martyrs. One saint. Two nurses. (None of us knew then that there were Black women with Nightingale at Scutari.) One novelist. Three involved in white men's wars. Two dead in white men's wars. *Pride and Prejudice.*

Those of us in Cavell wore red badges and recited her last words before a firing squad in W. W. I: "Patriotism is not enough. I must have no hatred or bitterness toward anyone."

Sorry to say I grew up to have exactly that.

Looking back: To try and see when the background changed places with the foreground. To try and locate the vanishing point: where the lines of perspective converge and disappear. Lines of color and class. Lines of history and social context. Lines of denial and rejection. When did *we* (the light-skinned middle-class Jamaicans) take over for *them* as oppressors? I need to see when and how this happened. When what should have been reality was overtaken by what was surely unreality. When the house nigger became master.

"What's the matter with you? You think you're white or something?"

"Child, what you want to know 'bout Garvey for? The man was nothing but a damn fool."

"They not our kind of people."

Why did we wear wide-brimmed hats and try to get into Oxford? Why did we not return?

Great Expectations: a novel about origins and denial. about the futility and tragedy of that denial. about attempting assimilation. We learned this novel from a light-skinned Jamaican woman—she concentrated on what she called the "love affair" between Pip and Estella.

Looking back: Through the last page of *Sula.* "And the loss pressed down on her chest and came up into her throat. 'We was girls together,' she said as though explaining something." It was Zoe, and Zoe alone, I thought of. She snapped into my mind and I remembered no one else. Through the greens and blues of the riverbank. The flame of red hibiscus in front of my grandmother's house. The cracked grave of a former landowner. The fruit of the ackee which poisons those who don't know how to prepare it.

"What is to become of us?"

We borrowed a baby from a woman and used her as our dolly. Dressed and undressed her. Dipped her in the riverwater. Fed her with the milk her mother had left with us: and giggled because we knew where the milk had come from.

A letter: "I am desperate. I need to get away. I beg you one fifty-dollar."

I send the money because this is what she asks for. I visit her on a trip back home. Her front teeth are gone. Her husband beats her and she suffers blackouts. I sit on her chair. She is given birth control pills which aggravate her "condition." We boil up sorrel and ginger. She is being taught by Peace Corps volunteers to embroider linen mats with little lambs on them and gives me one as a keepsake. We cool off the sorrel with a block of ice brought from the shop nearby. The shopkeeper immediately recognizes me as my grandmother's granddaughter and refuses to sell me cigarettes. (I am twenty-seven.) We sit in the doorway of her house, pushing back the colored plastic strands which form a curtain, and talk about Babylon and Dred. About Manley and what he's doing for Jamaica. About how hard it is. We walk along the railway tracks—no longer used—to Crooked River and the post office. Her little daughter walks beside us and we recite a poem for her: "Mornin' buddy/Me no buddy fe wunna/Who den, den I saw?" and on and on.

I can come and go. And I leave. To complete my education in London.

II

Their goddam kings and their goddam queens. Grandmotherly Victoria spreading herself thin across the globe. Elizabeth II on our TV screens. We stop what we are doing. We quiet down. We pay our respects.

1981: In Massachusetts I get up at 5 A.M. to watch the royal wedding. I tell myself maybe the IRA will intervene. It's got to be better than starving themselves to death. Better to be a kamikaze in St. Paul's Cathedral than a hostage in Ulster. And last week Black and white people smashed storefronts all over the United Kingdom. But I really don't believe

we'll see royal blood on TV. I watch because they once ruled us. In the back of the cathedral a Maori woman sings an aria from Handel, and I notice that she is surrounded by the colored subjects.

To those of us in the commonwealth the royal family was the perfect symbol of hegemony. To those of us who were dark in the dark nations, the prime minister, the parliament barely existed. We believed in royalty—we were convinced in this belief. Maybe it played on some ancestral memories of West Africa—where other kings and queens had been. Altars and castles and magic.

The faces of our new rulers were everywhere in my childhood. Calendars, newsreels, magazines. Their presences were often among us. Attending test matches between the West Indians and South Africans. They were our landlords. Not always absentee. And no matter what Black leader we might elect—were we to choose independence—we would be losing something almost holy in our impudence.

WE ARE HERE BECAUSE YOU WERE THERE
BLACK PEOPLE AGAINST STATE BRUTALITY
BLACK WOMEN WILL NOT BE INTIMIDATED
WELCOME TO BRITAIN . . . WELCOME TO SECOND-CLASS CITIZENSHIP
(slogans of the Black movement in Britain)

Indian women cleaning the toilets in Heathrow airport. This is the first thing I notice. Dark women in saris trudging buckets back and forth as other dark women in saris—some covered by loosefitting winter coats—form a line to have their passports stamped.

The triangle trade: molasses/rum/slaves. Robinson Crusoe was on a slave-trading journey. Robert Browning was a mulatto. Holding pens. Jamaica was a seasoning station. Split tongues. Sliced ears. Whipped bodies. The constant pretense of civility against rape. Still. Iron collars. Tinplate masks. The latter a precaution: to stop the slaves from eating the sugar cane.

A pregnant woman is to be whipped—they dig a hole to accommodate her belly and place her face down on the ground. Many of us became light-skinned very fast. Traced ourselves through bastard lines to reach the duke of Devonshire. The earl of Cornwall. The lord of this and the lord of that. Our mothers' rapes were the things unspoken.

You say: But Britain freed her slaves in 1833. Yes.

Tea plantations in India and Ceylon. Mines in Africa. The Cape-to-Cairo Railroad. Rhodes scholars. Suez Crisis. The white man's bloody burden. Boer War. Bantustans. Sitting in a theatre in London in the seventies. A play called *West of Suez.* A lousy play about British colonials. The finale comes when several well-known white actors are machine-gunned by several lesser-known Black actors. (As Nine Simone says: "This is a show tune but the show hasn't been written for it yet.")

The red empire of geography classes. "The sun never sets on the British empire and you can't trust it in the dark." Or with the dark peoples. "Because of the Industrial Revolution European countries went in search of markets and raw materials." Another geography (or was it a history) lesson.

Their bloody kings and their bloody queens. Their bloody peers. Their bloody generals. Admirals. Explorers. Livingstone. Hillary. Kitchener. All the bwanas. And all their beaters, porters, sherpas. Who found the source of the Nile. Victoria Falls. The tops of

mountains. Their so-called discoveries reek of untruth. How many dark people died so they could misname the physical features in their blasted gazetteer. A statistic we shall never know. Dr. Livingstone, I presume you are here to rape our land and enslave our people.

There are statues of these dead white men all over London.

An interesting fact: The swear word "bloody" is a contraction of "by my lady"—a reference to the Virgin Mary. They do tend to use their ladies. Name ages for them. Places for them. Use them as screens, inspirations, symbols. And many of the ladies comply. While the national martyr Edith Cavell was being executed by the Germans in 1915 in Belgium (called "poor little Belgium" by the allies in the war), the Belgians were engaged in the exploitation of the land and peoples of the Congo.

And will we ever know how many dark peoples were "imported" to fight in white men's wars. Probably not. Just as we will never know how many hearts were cut from African people so that the Christian doctor might be a success—i.e., extend a white man's life. Our Sister Killjoy observes this from her black-eyed squint.

Dr. Schweitzer—humanitarian, authority on Bach, winner of the Nobel Peace Prize—on the people of Africa: "The Negro is a child, and with children nothing can be done without the use of authority. We must, therefore, so arrange the circumstances of our daily life that my authority can find expression. With regard to Negroes, then, I have coined the formula: 'I am your brother, it is true, but your elder brother.' " (*On the Edge of the Primeval Forest,* 1961).

They like to pretend we didn't fight back. We did: with obeah, poison, revolution. It simply was not enough.

"Colonies . . . these places where 'niggers' are cheap and the earth is rich." (W. E. B. DuBois, "The Souls of White Folk")

A cousin is visiting me from Cal Tech where he is getting a degree in engineering. I am learning about the Italian Renaissance. My cousin is recognizably Black and speaks with an accent. I am not and do not—unless I am back home, where the "twang" comes upon me. We sit for some time in a bar in his hotel and are not served. A light-skinned Jamaican comes over to our table. He is an older man—a professor at the University of London. "Don't bother with it, you hear. They don't serve us in this bar." A run-of-the-mill incident for all recognizably Black people in this city. But for me it is not.

Henry's eyes fill up, but he refuses to believe our informant. "No, man, the girl is just busy." (The girl is a fifty-year-old white woman, who may just be following orders. But I do not mention this. I have chosen sides.) All I can manage to say is, "Jesus Christ, I hate the fucking English." Henry looks at me. (In the family I am known as the "lady cousin." It has to do with how I look. And the fact that I am twenty-seven and unmarried—and for all they know, unattached. They do not know that I am really the lesbian cousin.) Our informant says—gently, but with a distinct tone of disappointment—"My dear, is that what you're studying at the university?"

You see—the whole business is very complicated.

Henry and I leave without drinks and go to meet some of his white colleagues at a restaurant I know near Covent Garden Opera House. The restaurant caters to theatre types and so I hope there won't be a repeat of the bar scene—at least they know how to pretend. Besides, I tell myself, the owners are Italian *and* gay; they *must* be halfway decent. Henry and his colleagues work for an American company which is paying their way through Cal Tech. They mine bauxite from the hills in the middle of the island and send it to the United States. A turnaround occurs at dinner: Henry joins the white men in a sustained mockery

of the waiters: their accents and the way they walk. He whispers to me: "Why you want to bring us to a battyman's den, lady?" (*Battyman* = *faggot* in Jamaican.) I keep quiet.

We put the white men in a taxi and Henry walks me to the underground station. He asks me to sleep with him. (It wouldn't be incest. His mother was a maid in the house of an uncle and Henry has not seen her since his birth. He was taken into the family. She was let go.) I say that I can't. I plead exams. I can't say that I don't want to. Because I remember what happened in the bar. But I can't say that I'm a lesbian either—even though I want to believe his alliance with the white men at dinner was forced: not really him. He doesn't buy my excuse. "Come on, lady, let's do it. What's the matter, you 'fraid?" I pretend I am back home and start patois to show him somehow I am not afraid, not English, not white. I tell him he's a married man and he tells me he's a ram goat. I take the train to where I am staying and try to forget the whole thing. But I don't. I remember our different skins and our different experiences within them. And I have a hard time realizing that I am angry with Henry. That to him—no use in pretending—a queer is a queer.

1981: I hear on the radio that Bob Marley is dead and I drive over the Mohawk Trail listening to a program of his music and I cry and cry and cry. Someone says: "It wasn't the ganja that killed him, it was poverty and working in a steel foundry when he was young."

I flash back to my childhood and a young man who worked for an aunt I lived with once. He taught me to smoke ganja behind the house. And to peel an orange with the tip of a machete without cutting through the skin—"Love" it was called: a necklace of orange rind the result. I think about him because I heard he had become a Rastaman. And then I think about Rastas.

We are sitting on the porch of an uncle's house in Kingston—the family and I—and a Rastaman comes to the gate. We have guns but they are locked behind a false closet. We have dogs but they are tied up. We are Jamaicans and know that Rastas mean no harm. We let him in and he sits on the side of the porch and shows us his brooms and brushes. We buy some to take back to New York. "Peace, missis."

There were many Rastas in my childhood. Walking the roadside with their goods. Sitting outside their shacks in the mountains. The outsides painted bright—sometimes with words. Gathering at Palisadoes Airport to greet the Conquering Lion of Judah. They were considered figures of fun by most middle-class Jamaicans. Harmless—like Marcus Garvey.

Later: white American hippies trying to create the effect of dred in their straight white hair. The ganja joint held between their straight white teeth. "Man, the grass is good." Hanging out by the Sheraton pool. Light-skinned Jamaicans also dredlocked, also assuming the ganja. Both groups moving to the music but not the words. Harmless. "Peace, brother."

III

My grandmother: "Let us thank God for a fruitful place."

My grandfather: "Let us rescue the perishing world."

This evening on the road in western Massachusetts there are pockets of fog. Then clear spaces. Across from a pond a dog staggers in front of my headlights. I look closer and see that his mouth is foaming. He stumbles to the side of the road—I go to call the police.

I drive back to the house, radio playing "difficult" piano pieces. And I think about how I need to say all this. This is who I am. I am not what you allow me to be. Whatever you decide me to be. In a bookstore in London I show the woman at the counter my book and she stares at me for a minute, then says: "You're a Jamaican." "Yes." "You're not at all like our Jamaicans."

Encountering the void is nothing more nor less than understanding invisibility. Of being fogbound.

Then: It was never a question of passing. It was a question of hiding. Behind Black and white perceptions of who we were—who they thought we were. Tropics. Plantations. Calypso. Cricket. We were the people with the musical voices and the coronation mugs on our parlor tables. I would be whatever figure these foreign imaginations cared for me to be. It would be so simple to let others fill in for me. So easy to startle them with a flash of anger when their visions got out of hand—but never to sustain the anger for myself. It could become a life lived within myself. A life cut off. I know who I am but you will never know who I am. I may in fact lose touch with who I am.

I hid from my real sources. But my real sources were also hidden from me.

Now: It is not a question of relinquishing privilege. It is a question of grasping more of myself. I have found that in the real sources are concealed my survival. My speech. My voice. To be colonized is to be rendered insensitive. To have those parts necessary to sustain life numbed. And this is in some cases—in my case—perceived as privilege. The test of a colonized person is to walk through a shantytown in Kingston and not bat an eye. This I cannot do. Because part of me lives there—and as I grasp more of this part I realize what needs to be done with the rest of my life.

Sometimes I used to think we were like the Marranos—the Sephardic Jews forced to pretend they were Christians. The name was given to them by the Christians, and meant "pigs." But once out of Spain and Portugal, they became Jews openly again. Some settled in Jamaica. They knew who the enemy was and acted for their own survival. But they remained Jews always.

We also knew who the enemy was—I remember jokes about the English. Saying they stank. saying they were stingy. that they drank too much and couldn't hold their liquor. that they had bad teeth. were dirty and dishonest. were limey bastards. and horse-faced bitches. We said the men only wanted to sleep with Jamaican women. And that the women made pigs of themselves with Jamaican men.

But of course this was seen by us—the light-skinned middle class—with a double vision. We learned to cherish that part of us that was them—and to deny the part that was not. Believing in some cases that the latter part had ceased to exist.

None of this is as simple as it may sound. We were colorists and we aspired to oppressor status. (Of course, almost any aspiration instilled by Western civilization is to oppressor status: success, for example.) Color was the symbol of our potential: color taking in hair "quality," skin tone, freckles, nose-width, eyes. We did not see that color symbolism was a method of keeping us apart: in the society, in the family, between friends. Those of us who were light-skinned, straight-haired, etc., were given to believe that we could actually attain whiteness—or at least those qualities of the colonizer which made him superior. We were convinced of white supremacy. If we failed, we were not really responsible for our failures: we had all the advantages—but it was that one persistent drop of blood, that single rogue gene that made us unable to conceptualize abstract ideas, made us love darkness rather than despise it, which was to be blamed for our failure. Our dark part had taken over: an inherited imbalance in which the doom of the creole was sealed.

I am trying to write this as clearly as possible, but as I write I realize that what I say may sound fabulous, or even mythic. It is. It is insane.

Under this system of colorism—the system which prevailed in my childhood in Jamaica, and which has carried over to the present—rarely will dark and light people co-mingle. Rarely will they achieve between themselves an intimacy informed with identity. (I should say here that I am using the categories light and dark both literally and symbolically. There are dark Jamaicans who have achieved lightness and the "advantages" which go with it by their successful pursuit of oppressor status.)

Under this system light and dark people will meet in those ways in which the light-skinned person imitates the oppressor. But imitation goes only so far: the light-skinned person becomes an oppressor in fact. He/she will have a dark chauffeur, a dark nanny, a dark maid, and a dark gardener. These employees will be paid badly. Because of the slave past, because of their dark skin, the servants of the middle class have been used according to the traditions of the slavocracy. They are not seen as workers for their own sake, but for the sake of the family who has employed them. It was not until Michael Manley became prime minister that a minimum wage for houseworkers was enacted—and the indignation of the middle class was profound.

During Manley's leadership the middle class began to abandon the island in droves. Toronto. Miami. New York. Leaving their houses and businesses behind and sewing cash into the tops of suitcases. Today—with a new regime—they are returning: "Come back to the way things used to be" the tourist advertisement on American TV says. "Make it Jamaica again. Make it your own."

But let me return to the situation of houseservants as I remember it: They will be paid badly, but they will be "given" room and board. However, the key to the larder will be kept by the mistress in her dresser drawer. They will spend Christmas with the family of their employers and be given a length of English wool for trousers or a few yards of cotton for dresses. They will see their children on their days off: their extended family will care for the children the rest of the time. When the employers visit their relations in the country, the servants may be asked along—oftentimes the servants of the middle class come from the same part of the countryside their employers have come from. But they will be expected to work while they are there. Back in town, there are parts of the house they are allowed to move freely around; other parts they are not allowed to enter. When the family watches the TV the servant is allowed to watch also, but only while standing in a doorway. The servant may have a radio in his/her room, also a dresser and a cot. Perhaps a mirror. There will usually be one ceiling light. And one small square louvered window.

A true story: One middle-class Jamaican woman ordered a Persian rug from Harrod's in London. The day it arrived so did her new maid. She was going downtown to have her hair touched up, and told the maid to vacuum the rug. She told the maid she would find the vacuum cleaner in the same shed as the power mower. And when she returned she found that the fine nap of her new rug had been removed.

The reaction of the mistress was to tell her friends that the "girl" was backward. She did not fire her until she found that the maid had scrubbed the teflon from her new set of pots, saying she thought they were coated with "nastiness."

The houseworker/mistress relationship in which one Black woman is the oppressor of another Black woman is a cornerstone of the experience of many Jamaican women.

I remember another true story: In a middle-class family's home one Christmas, a relation was visiting from New York. This woman had brought gifts for everybody, including the housemaid. The maid had been released from a mental institution recently, where they had "treated" her for depression. This visiting light-skinned woman had brought the dark woman a bright red rayon blouse and presented it to her in the garden one afternoon, while the family was having tea. The maid thanked her softly, and the other woman moved toward her as if to embrace her. Then she stopped, her face suddenly covered with tears, and ran into the house, saying, "My God, I can't, I can't."

We are women who come from a place almost incredible in its beauty. It is a beauty which can mask a great deal and which has been used in that way. But that the beauty is there is a fact. I remember what I thought the freedom of my childhood, in which the fruitful place was something I took for granted. Just as I took for granted Zoe's appearance every morning on my school vacations—in the sense that I knew she would be there. That she would always be the one to visit me. The perishing world of my grandfather's graces at the table, if I ever seriously thought about it, was somewhere else.

Our souls were affected by the beauty of Jamaica, as much as they were affected by our fears of darkness.

There is no ending to this piece of writing. There is no way to end it. As I read back over it, I see that we/they/I may become confused in the mind of the reader: but these pronouns have always co-existed in my mind. The Rastas talk of the "I and I"—a pronoun in which they combine themselves with Jah. Jah is a contraction of Jahweh and Jehova, but to me always sounds like the beginning of Jamaica. I and Jamaica is who I am. No matter how far I travel—how deep the ambivalence I feel about ever returning. And Jamaica is a place in which we/they/I connect and disconnect—change place.

[1985]

JOYCE CAROL OATES

(1938–)

On Boxing

About the Author: Although she is best known as a poet and fiction writer, Joyce Carol Oates is developing a reputation as one of the most careful chroniclers of modern American culture. "On Boxing" continues a particular American tradition of giving voice to the ways sport enters our lives.

They are young welterweight boxers so evenly matched they might be twins—though one has a redhead's pallor and the other is a dusky-skinned Hispanic. Circling each other in the ring, they try jabs, tentative left hooks, right crosses that dissolve in midair or turn into harmless slaps. The Madison Square Garden crowd is derisive, impatient. "Those two! What'd they do, wake up this morning and decide they were boxers?" a man behind me says contemptuously. (He's dark, nattily dressed, with a neatly trimmed mustache and tinted glasses. A sophisticated fight fan. Two hours later he will be crying, "Tommy! Tommy! Tommy!" over and over in a paroxysm of grief as, on the giant closed-circuit television screen, middleweight champion Marvelous Marvin Hagler batters his challenger, Thomas Hearns, into insensibility.)

The young boxers must be conscious of the jeers and boos in this great cavernous space reaching up into the $20 seats in the balconies amid the constant milling of people in the aisles, the smells of hotdogs, beer, cigarette and cigar smoke, hair oil. But they are locked desperately together, circling, jabbing, slapping, clinching, now a flurry of light blows, clumsy footwork, another sweaty stumbling despairing clinch into the ropes that provokes a fresh wave of derision. Why are they here in the Garden of all places, each fighting what looks like his first professional fight? What are they doing? Neither is angry at the other. When the bell sounds at the end of the sixth and final round, the crowd boos a little louder. The Hispanic boy, silky yellow shorts, damp, frizzy, floating hair, strides about his corner of the ring with his gloved hand aloft—not in defiance of the boos, which increase in response to his gesture, or even in acknowledgment of them. It's just something he has seen older boxers do. He seems to be saying "I'm here, I made it, I did it." When the decision is announced as a draw, the crowd's derision increases in volume. "Get out of the ring!" "Go home!" Contemptuous male laughter follows the boys in their robes, towels about their heads, sweating, breathless. Why had they thought they were boxers?

How can you enjoy so brutal a sport, people ask. Or don't ask.

And it's too complicated to answer. In any case, I don't "enjoy" boxing, and never have; it isn't invariably "brutal"; I don't think of it as a sport.

Nor do I think of it in writerly terms as a metaphor for something else. (For *what* else?) No one whose interest in boxing began in childhood—as mine did as an offshoot of my father's interest—is likely to suppose it is a symbol of something beyond itself, though I can entertain the proposition that life is a metaphor for boxing—for one of those bouts that go on and on, round following round, small victories, small defeats, nothing determined, again the bell and again the bell and you and your opponent so evenly matched it's clear your opponent *is* you and why are the two of you jabbing and punching at each other on an elevated platform enclosed by ropes as in a pen beneath hot crude all-exposing lights in the presence of an indifferent crowd: that sort of writerly metaphor. But if you have seen five hundred boxing matches, you have seen five hundred boxing matches, and their common denominator, which surely exists, is not of primary interest to you. "If the Host is only a symbol," the Catholic writer Flannery O'Connor said, "I'd say the hell with it."

Each boxing match is a story, a highly condensed, highly dramatic story—even when nothing much happens: then failure is the story. There are two principal characters in the story, overseen by a shadowy third. When the bell rings no one knows what will happen. Much is speculated, nothing known. The boxers bring to the fight everything that is themselves, and everything will be exposed: including secrets about themselves they never knew. There are boxers possessed of such remarkable intuition, such prescience, one would think they had fought this particular fight before. There are boxers who perform brilliantly, but mechanically, who cannot improvise in midfight; there are boxers performing at the height of their skill who cannot quite comprehend that it won't be enough; to my knowledge there was only one boxer who possessed an extraordinary and disquieting awareness, not only of his opponent's every move or anticipated move, but of the audience's keenest shifts in mood as well—Muhammad Ali, of course.

In the ring, death is always a possibility, which is why I prefer to see films or tapes of fights already past—already crystallized into art. In fact, death is a statistically rare possibility of which no one likes to think—like your possible death tomorrow morning in an automobile crash, or in next month's airplane crash, or in a freak accident involving a fall on the stairs—a skull fracture, subarachnoid hemorrhage.

A boxing match is a play without words, which doesn't mean that it has no text or no language, only that the text is improvised in action, the language a dialogue between the boxers in a joint response to the mysterious will of the crowd, which is always that the fight be a worthy one so that the crude paraphernalia of the setting—the ring, the lights, the onlookers themselves—be obliterated. To go from an ordinary preliminary match to a "Fight of the Century"—like those between Joe Louis and Billy Conn, Muhammad Ali and Joe Frazier, most recently Marvin Hagler and Thomas Hearns—is to go from listening or half-listening to a guitar being idly plucked to hearing Bach's "Well-Tempered Clavier" being perfectly played, and that too is part of the story. So much is happening so swiftly and so subtly you cannot absorb it except to know that something memorable is happening and it is happening in a place beyond words.

The fighters in the ring are time-bound—is anything so excruciatingly long as a fiercely contested three-minute round?—but the fight itself is timeless. By way of films and tapes, it has become history, art. If boxing is a sport, it is the most tragic of all sports because, more than any human activity, it consumes the very excellence it displays: Its very drama is this consumption. To expend oneself in fighting the greatest fight of one's life is to begin immediately the downward turn that next time may be a plunge, a sudden incomprehensible fall. *I am the greatest,* Muhammad Ai says. *I am the greatest,* Marvin Hagler says. You always think you're going to win, Jack Dempsey wryly observed in his old age, otherwise you can't fight at all. The punishment—to the body, the brain, the spirit—a man must endure to become a great boxer is inconceivable to most of us whose idea of personal risk is largely ego related or emotional. But the punishment, as it begins to show in even a young and vigorous boxer, is closely assessed by his rivals. After junior-welterweight champion Aaron Pryor won a lackluster fight on points a few months ago, a younger boxer in his weight division, interviewed at ringside, said: "My mouth is watering."

So the experience of seeing great fighters of the past—and great sporting events are always *past*—is radically different from having seen them when they were reigning champions. Jack Johnson, Jack Dempsey, Joe Louis, Sugar Ray Robinson, Willie Pep, Rocky Marciano, Muhammad Ali—as spectators we know not only how a fight ends but how a career ends. Boxing is always particulars, second by incalculable second, but in the abstract it suggests these haunting lines by Yeats:

Everything that man esteems
Endures a moment or a day.
Love's pleasure drives his love away,
The painter's brush consumes his dreams;
The herald's cry, the soldier's tread
Exhaust his glory and his might:
Whatever flames upon the night
Man's own resinous heart has fed.
—from "The Resurrection"

The referee, the third character in the story, usually appears to be a mere observer, even an intruder, a near-ghostly presence as fluid in motion and quick-footed as the boxers themselves (he is frequently a former boxer). But so central to the drama of boxing is the referee that the spectacle of two men fighting each other unsupervised in an elevated ring would appear hellish, obscene—life rather than art. The referee is our intermediary in the fight. He is our moral conscience, extracted from us as spectators so that, for the duration

of the fight, "conscience" is not a factor in our experience; nor is it a factor in the boxers' behavior.

Though the referee's role is a highly demanding one, and it has been estimated that there are perhaps no more than a dozen really skilled referees in the world, it seems to be necessary in the intense dramatic action of the fight that the referee have no dramatic identity. Referees' names are quickly forgotten, even as they are announced over the microphone preceding a fight. Yet, paradoxically, the referee's position is one of crucial significance. The referee cannot control what happens in the ring, but he can frequently control, to a degree, *that* it happens: he is responsible for the fight, if not for the individual fighter's performance. It is the referee solely who holds the power of life and death at certain times; whose decision to terminate a fight, or to allow it to continue, determines a man's fate. (One should recall that a well-aimed punch with a boxer's full weight behind it can have an astonishing impact—a blow that must be absorbed by the brain in its jelly sac.)

In a recent heavyweight fight in Buffalo, 220-pound Tim Witherspoon repeatedly struck his 260-pound opponent, James Broad, caught in the ropes, while the referee looked on without acting—though a number of spectators called for the fight to be stopped. In the infamous Benny Paret–Emile Griffith fight of March 24, 1962, the referee Ruby Goldstein was said to have stood paralyzed as Paret, trapped in the ropes, suffered as many as 18 powerful blows to the head before he fell. (He died ten days later.) Boxers are trained not to quit; if they are knocked down they will try to get up to continue the fight, even if they can hardly defend themselves. The primary rule of the ring—to defend oneself at all times—is both a parody and a distillation of life.

Boxing is a purely masculine world. (Though there are female boxers—the most famous is the black champion Lady Tyger Trimiar with her shaved head and tiger-striped attire—women's role in the sport is extremely marginal.) The vocabulary of boxing is attuned to a quintessentially masculine sensibility in which the role of patriarch/protector can only be assured if there is physical strength underlying it. First comes this strength—"primitive," perhaps; then comes civilization. It should be kept in mind that "boxing" and "fighting," though always combined in the greatest of boxers, can be entirely different and even unrelated activities. If boxing can be, in the lighter weights especially, a highly complex and refined skill belonging solely to civilization, fighting seems to belong to something predating civilization, the instinct not merely to defend oneself—for when has the masculine ego ever been assuaged by so minimal a gesture?—but to attack another and to force him into absolute submission. Hence the electrifying effect upon a typical fight crowd when fighting emerges suddenly out of boxing—the excitement when a boxer's face begins to bleed. The flash of red is the visible sign of the fight's authenticity in the eyes of many spectators, and boxers are right to be proud—if they are—of their facial scars.

To the untrained eye, boxers in the ring usually appear to be angry. But, of course, this is "work" to them; emotion has no part in it, or should not. Yet in an important sense—in a symbolic sense—the boxers *are* angry, and boxing is fundamentally about anger. It is the only sport in which anger is accommodated, ennobled. Why are boxers angry? Because, for the most part, they belong to the disenfranchised of our society, to impoverished ghetto neighborhoods in which anger is an appropriate response. ("It's hard being black. You ever been black? I was black once—when I was poor," Larry Holmes has said.) Today, when most boxers—most good boxers—are black or Hispanic, white men begin to look anemic in the ring. Yet after decades of remarkable black boxers—from Jack Johnson to Joe Louis to Muhammad Ali—heavyweight champion Larry Holmes was the object of racist slurs and insults when he defended his title against the over-promoted white challenger Gerry Cooney a few years ago.

Liberals who have no personal or class reason to feel anger tend to disparage, if not condemn, such anger in others. Liberalism is also unfairly harsh in its criticism of all that predates civilization—or "liberalism" itself—without comprehending that civilization is a concept, an idea, perhaps at times hardly more than a fiction, attendant upon, and always subordinate to, physical strength: missiles, nuclear warheads. The terrible and tragic silence dramatized in the boxing ring is the silence of nature before language, when the physical *was* language, a means of communication swift and unmistakable.

The phrase "killer instinct" is said to have been coined in reference to Jack Dempsey in his famous early fights against Jess Willard, Georges Carpentier, Luis Firpo ("The Wild Bull of the Pampas"), and any number of other boxers, less renowned, whom he savagely beat. The ninth of eleven children born to an impoverished Mormon sharecropper and itinerant railroad worker, Dempsey seems to have been, as a young boxer in his prime, the very embodiment of angry hunger; and if he remains the most spectacular heavyweight champion in history, it is partly because he fought when rules governing boxing were somewhat casual by present-day standards. Where aggression must be learned, even cultivated, in some champion boxers (Tunney, Louis, Marciano, Patterson, for example), Dempsey's aggression was direct and natural: Once in the ring he seems to have wanted to kill his opponent.

Dempsey's first title fight in 1919, against the aging champion Jess Willard, was called "pugilistic murder" by some sportswriters and is said to have been one of boxing's all-time blood baths. Today, this famous fight—which brought the nearly unknown twenty-four-year-old Dempsey to national prominence—would certainly have been stopped in the first minute of the first round. Badly out of condition, heavier than Dempsey by almost sixty pounds, the thirty-seven-year-old Willard had virtually no defense against the challenger. By the end of the fight, Willard's jaw was broken, his cheekbone split, nose smashed, six teeth broken off at the gum, an eye was battered shut, much further damage was done to his body. Both boxers were covered in Willard's blood. Years later Dempsey's estranged manager Kearns confessed—perhaps falsely—that he had "loaded" Dempsey's gloves—treated his hand tape with a talcum substance that turned concrete-hard when wet.

For the most part, boxing matches today are scrupulously monitored by referees and ring physicians. The devastating knockout blow is frequently the one never thrown. In a recent televised junior-middleweight bout between Don Curry and James Green, the referee stopped the fight because Green seemed momentarily disabled: His logic was that Green had dropped his gloves and was therefore in a position to be hurt. (Green and his furious trainer protested the decision but the referee's word is final: No fight, stopped, can be resumed.) The drama of the ring begins to shift subtly as more and more frequently one sees a referee intervene to embrace a weakened or defenseless man in a gesture of paternal solicitude that in itself carries much theatrical power—a gesture not so dramatic as the killing blow but one that suggests that the ethics of the ring are moving toward those that prevail beyond it. As if fighter-brothers whose mysterious animosity has somehow brought them to battle are saved by their father. . . .

In the final moment of the Hagler-Hearns fight, the dazed Hearns—on his feet but clearly not fully conscious, gamely prepared to take Hagler's next assault—was saved by the referee from what might well have been serious injury, if not death, considering the

ferocity of Hagler's fighting and the personal anger he seems to have brought to it that night. This eight-minute fight, generally believed to be one of the great fights in boxing history, ends with Hearns in the referee's protective embrace—an image that is haunting, in itself profoundly mysterious, as if an indefinable human drama had been spontaneously created for us, brilliantly improvised, performed one time and one time only, yet permanently ingrained upon our consciousness.

Years ago in the early 1950s, when my father first took me to a Golden Gloves boxing tournament in Buffalo, I asked him why the boys wanted to fight one another, why they were willing to get hurt. My father said, "Boxers don't feel pain quite the way we do."

Gene Tunney's single defeat in an eleven-year career was to a flamboyant and dangerous fighter named Harry Greb ("The Human Windmill"), who seems to have been, judging from boxing literature, the dirtiest fighter in history. Low blows, butting, fouls, holding and hitting, using his laces on an opponent's eyes—Greb was famous for his lack of interest in the rules. He was world middleweight champion for three years but a presence in the boxing world for a long time. After the first of his several fights with Greb, the twenty-four-year-old Tunney had to spend a week in bed, he was so badly hurt; he'd lost two quarts of blood during the fifteen-round fight. But as Tunney said years afterward: "Greb gave me a terrible whipping. He broke my nose, maybe with a butt. He cut my eyes and ears, perhaps with his laces. . . . My jaw was swollen from the right temple down the cheek, along under the chin and part way up the other side. The referee, the ring itself, was full of blood. . . . But it was in that first fight, in which I lost my American light-heavyweight title, that I knew I had found a way to beat Harry eventually. I was fortunate, really. If boxing in those days had been afflicted with the commission doctors we have today—who are always poking their noses into the ring and examining superficial wounds—the first fight with Greb would have been stopped before I learned how to beat him. It's possible, even probable, that if this had happened I would never have been heard of again."

Tommy Loughran, the light-heavyweight champion from 1927 to 1929, was a master boxer greatly admired by other boxers. He approached boxing literally as a science—as Tunney did—studying his opponents' styles and mapping out ring strategy for each fight. He rigged up mirrors in his basement so that he could see himself as he worked out—for, as Loughran realized, no boxer ever sees himself quite as he appears to his opponent. But the secret of Loughran's career was that he had a right hand that broke so easily he could use it only once in each fight: It had to be the knockout punch or nothing. "I'd get one shot, then the agony of the thing would hurt me if the guy got up. Anybody I ever hit with a left hook, I knocked flat on his face, but I would never take a chance for fear if my left hand goes, I'm done for."

Both Tunney and Loughran, it is instructive to note, retired from boxing before they were forced to retire. Tunney was a highly successful businessman and Loughran a successful sugar broker on the Wall Street commodities market—just to suggest that boxers are not invariably illiterate, stupid, or punch-drunk.

One of the perhaps not entirely acknowledged reasons for the attraction of serious writers to boxing (from Swift, Pope, Johnson to Hazlitt, Lord Byron, Hemingway, and our own Norman Mailer, George Plimpton, Wilfrid Sheed, Daniel Halpern et al.) is the sport's systematic cultivation of pain in the interests of a project, a life-goal: the willed transposing of the sensation called "pain" (whether physical or psychological) into its opposite. If this is masochism—and I doubt that it is, or that it is simply—it is also intelligence, cunning, strategy. It is the active welcoming of that which most living beings try to avoid and to flee. It is the active subsuming of the present moment in terms of the future. Pain now but control (and therefore pleasure) later.

Still, it is the rigorous training period leading up to the public appearance that demands the most discipline. In this, too, the writer senses some kinship, however oblique and one-sided, with the professional boxer. The brief public spectacle of the boxing match (which could last as little as sixty seconds), like the publication of the writer's book, is but the final, visible stage in a long, arduous, fanatic, and sometimes quixotic, subordination of the self. It was Rocky Marciano who seems to have trained with the most monastic devotion, secluding himself from his wife and family for as long as three months before a fight. Quite apart from the grueling physical training of this period and the constant preoccupation with diet and weight, Marciano concentrated on only the upcoming fight, the opening bell, his opponent. Every minute of the boxer's life was planned for one purpose. In the training camp the name of the opponent was never mentioned and Marciano's associates were careful about conversation in his presence: They talked very little about boxing.

In the final month, Marciano would not write a letter. The last ten days before a fight he saw no mail, took no telephone calls, met no new acquaintances. The week before the fight he would not shake hands with anyone. Or go for a ride in a car. No new foods! No envisioning the morning after the fight! All that was not *the fight* was taboo: when Marciano worked out punching the bag he saw his opponent before him, when he jogged early in the morning he saw his opponent close beside him. What could be a more powerful image of discipline—madness?—than this absolute subordination of the self, this celibacy of the fighter-in-training? Instead of focusing his energies and fantasies upon Woman, the boxer focuses them upon the Opponent.

No sport is more physical, more direct, than boxing. No sport appears more powerfully homoerotic: the confrontation in the ring—the disrobing—the sweaty, heated combat that is part dance, courtship, coupling—the frequent urgent pursuit by one boxer of the other in the fight's natural and violent movement toward the "knockout." Surely boxing derives much of its appeal from this mimicry of a species of erotic love in which one man overcomes the other in an exhibition of superior strength.

Most fights, however fought, lead to an embrace between the boxers after the final bell—a gesture of mutual respect and apparent affection that appears to the onlooker to be more than perfunctory. Rocky Graziano, often derided for being a slugger rather than a "classic" boxer, sometimes kissed his opponents out of gratitude for the fight. Does the boxing match, one almost wonders, lead irresistibly to this moment: the public embrace of two men who otherwise, in public or in private, could not approach each other with such passion. Are men privileged to embrace with love only after having fought? A woman is struck by the tenderness men will express for boxers who have been hurt, even if it is only by way of commentary on photographs: the startling picture of Ray (Boom Boom) Mancini after his second losing fight with Livingstone Bramble, for instance, when Mancini's face was hideously battered (photographs in *Sports Illustrated* and elsewhere were gory, near-pornographic); the much-reprinted photograph of the defeated Thomas Hearns being carried to his corner in the arms of an enormous black man in formal attire—the "Hit Man" from Detroit now helpless, only semiconscious, looking precisely like a black Christ taken from the cross. These are powerful, haunting, unsettling images, cruelly beautiful, very much bound up with the primitive appeal of the sport.

Yet to suggest that men might love one another directly without the violent ritual of

combat is to misread man's greatest passion—for war, not peace. Love, if there is to be love, comes second.

Boxing is, after all, about lying. It is about cultivating a double personality. As José Torres, the ex-light-heavyweight champion who is now the New York State Boxing Commissioner, says: "We fighters understand lies. What's a feint? What's a left hook off the jab? What's an opening? What's thinking one thing and doing another . . . ?"

There is nothing fundamentally playful about boxing, nothing that seems to belong to daylight, to pleasure. At its moments of greatest intensity it seems to contain so complete and so powerful an image of life—life's beauty, vulnerability, despair, incalculable and often reckless courage—that boxing *is* life, and hardly a mere game. During a superior boxing match we are deeply moved by the body's communion with itself by way of another's flesh. The body's dialogue with its shadow-self—or Death. Baseball, football, basketball—these quintessentially American pastimes are recognizably sports because they involve play: They are games. One *plays* football; one doesn't *play* boxing.

Observing team sports, teams of adult men, one sees how men are children in the most felicitous sense of the word. But boxing in its elemental ferocity cannot be assimilated into childhood—though very young men box, even professionally, and numerous world champions began boxing when they were hardly more than children. Spectators at public games derive much of their pleasure from reliving the communal emotions of childhood, but spectators at boxing matches relive the murderous infancy of the race. Hence the notorious cruelty of boxing crowds and the excitement when a man begins to bleed. ("When I see blood," says Marvin Hagler, "I become a bull." He means his own.)

The boxing ring comes to seem an altar of sorts, one of those legendary magical spaces where the laws of a nation are suspended: Inside the ropes, during an officially regulated three-minute round, a man may be killed at his opponent's hands but he cannot be legally murdered. Boxing inhabits a sacred space predating civilization; or, to use D. H. Lawrence's phrase, before God was love. If it suggests a savage ceremony or a rite of atonement, it also suggests the futility of such rites. For what atonement is the fight waged, if it must shortly be waged again . . . ?

All this is to speak of the paradox of boxing—its obsessive appeal for many who find in it not only a spectacle involving sensational feats of physical skill but an emotional experience impossible to convey in words; an art form, as I have suggested, with no natural analogue in the arts. And of course this accounts, too, for the extreme revulsion it arouses in many people. ("Brutal," "disgusting," "barbaric," "inhuman," "a terrible, terrible sport"—typical comments on the subject.)

In December 1984, the American Medical Association passed a resolution calling for the abolition of boxing on the principle that it is the only sport in which the *objective* is to cause injury. This is not surprising. Humanitarians have always wanted to reform boxing—or abolish it altogether. The 1896 heavyweight title match between Ruby Robert Fitzsimmons and Peter Maher was outlawed in many parts of the United States, so canny promoters staged it across the Mexican border four hundred miles from El Paso. (Some three hundred people made the arduous journey to see what must have been one of the most disappointing bouts in boxing history—Fitzsimmons knocked out his opponent in a mere ninety-five seconds.)

During the prime of Jack Dempsey's career in the 1920s, boxing was illegal in many states, like alcohol, and like alcohol, seems to have aroused a hysterical public enthusiasm.

Photographs of jammed outdoor arenas taken in the 1920s with boxing rings like postage-sized altars at their centers, the boxers themselves scarcely visible, testify to the extraordinary emotional appeal boxing had at that time, even as reform movements were lobbying against it. When Jack Johnson won the heavyweight title in 1908 (he had to pursue the white champion Tommy Burns all the way to Australia to confront him), the special "danger" of boxing was also that it might expose and humiliate white men in the ring. After Johnson's victory over the "White Hope" contender Jim Jeffries, there were race riots and lynchings throughout the United States; even films of some of Johnson's fights were outlawed in many states. And because boxing has become a sport in which black and Hispanic men have lately excelled, it is particularly vulnerable to attack by white middle-class reformers, who seem uninterested in lobbying against equally dangerous but "establishment" sports like football, auto racing, and thoroughbred horse racing.

There is something peculiarly American in the fact that, while boxing is our most controversial sport, it is also the sport that pays its top athletes the most money. In spite of the controversy, boxing has never been healthier financially. The three highest paid athletes in the world in both 1983 and 1984 were boxers; a boxer with a long career like heavyweight champion Larry Holmes—forty-eight fights in thirteen years as a professional—can expect to earn somewhere beyond $50 million. (Holmes said that after retirement what he would miss most about boxing is his million-dollar checks.) Dempsey, who said that a man fights for one thing only—money—made somewhere beyond $3,500,000 in the ring in his long and varied career. Now $1.5 million is a fairly common figure for a single fight. Thomas Hearns made at least $7 million in his fight with Hagler while Hagler made at least $7.5 million. For the first of his highly publicized matches with Roberto Duran in 1980—which he lost on a decision—the popular black welterweight champion Sugar Ray Leonard received a staggering $10 million to Duran's $1.3 million. And none of these figures takes into account various subsidiary earnings (from television commercials, for instance) which in Leonard's case are probably as high as his income was from boxing.

Money has drawn any number of retired boxers back into the ring, very often with tragic results. The most notorious example is perhaps Joe Louis, who, owing huge sums in back taxes, continued boxing well beyond the point at which he could perform capably. After a career of seventeen years he was stopped by Rocky Marciano—who was said to have felt as upset by his victory as Louis by the defeat. (Louis then went on to a degrading second career as a professional wrestler. This, too, ended abruptly when 300-pound Rocky Lee stepped on the forty-two-year-old Louis's chest and damaged his heart.) Ezzard Charles, Jersey Joe Walcott, Joe Frazier, Muhammad Ali—each continued fighting when he was no longer in condition to defend himself against young heavyweight boxers on the way up. Of all heavyweight champions, only Rocky Marciano, to whom fame and money were not of paramount significance, was prudent enough to retire before he was defeated. In any case, the prodigious sums of money a few boxers earn do not account for the sums the public is willing to pay them.

Though boxing has long been popular in many countries and under many forms of government, its popularity in the United States since the days of John L. Sullivan has a good deal to do with what is felt as the spirit of the individual—his "physical" spirit—in conflict with the constrictions of the state. The rise of boxing in the 1920s in particular might well be seen as a consequence of the diminution of the individual vis-à-vis society; the gradual attrition of personal freedom, will, and strength—whether "masculine" or otherwise. In the

Eastern bloc of nations, totalitarianism is a function of the state; in the Western bloc it has come to seem a function of technology, or history—"fate." The individual exists in his physical supremacy, but does the individual matter?

In the magical space of the boxing ring so disquieting a question has no claim. There, as in no other public arena, the individual as a unique physical being asserts himself; there, for a dramatic if fleeting period of time, the great world with its moral and political complexities, its terrifying impersonality, simply ceases to exist. Men fighting one another with only their fists and their cunning are all contemporaries, all brothers, belonging to no historical time. "He can run, but he can't hide"—so said Joe Louis before his famous fight with young Billy Conn in 1941. In the brightly lighted ring, man is *in extremis,* performing an atavistic rite or agon for the mysterious solace of those who can participate only vicariously in such drama: the drama of life in the flesh. Boxing has become America's tragic theater.

[1985]

DONALD HALL

(1928–)

Winter*

About the Author: The poet Donald Hall has increasingly turned his talents to the possibilities of the essay. Along with baseball, the subtleties of seasonal changes in New Hampshire engage Hall's reflective voice; in "Winter" we see and hear that season in new ways.

In New Hampshire we know ourselves by winter—in snow, in cold, in darkness. For some of us the first true snow begins it; for others winter begins with the first bruising assault of zero weather; there is yet another sort, light-lovers, for whom winter begins with dark's onset in mid-August. If we wake as we ought to at 5:30, we begin waking in darkness; and dawn turns throaty with the ululations of photophiliacs, noctophobics, some of whom are fanatical enough to begin lamentation late in the month of June—when dawn arrives at 4:32 A.M. and yesterday it arrived at 4:31:30. On June 22 my wife exchanges postcards of commiseration with a fellow in Michigan who is another amorist of light. Fortunately this mountain has an upside as well as a downside. When in January daylight lasts half a minute longer every day, Jane's faint green leaves take on color, she leans south toward Kearsarge and the low, brief but lengthening pale winter sun; an observer can spy the faint buds that will burst into snowdrops in April, daffodils in April, tulips in May . . .

Some of us, on the other hand, are darkness-lovers. We do not *dislike* the early and late daylight of June, whippoorwill's graytime, but we cherish the gradually increasing dark of November, which we wrap around ourselves in the prosperous warmth of woodstove, oil, electric blanket, storm window, and insulation. We are partly tuber, partly bear. Inside our warmth we fold ourselves in the dark and the cold—around us, outside us, safely away from us; we tuck ourselves up in the long sleep and comfort of cold's opposite, warming ourselves by thought of the cold, lighting ourselves by darkness's idea. Or we are Persephone gone

*A version of this essay also appeared in *Harper's Magazine.*

underground again, cozy in the amenities of Hell. Sheltered between stove and electric light, we hollow islands of safety within the cold and dark. As light grows less each day, our fur grows thicker. By December 22 we are cozy as a cat hunkered under a Glenwood.

Often October has shown one snow flurry, sometimes even September. For that matter, it once snowed in New Hampshire every month of the year. In 1816, it snowed and froze in June, in July, in August—the Poverty Year, season of continuous winter when farmers planted over and over again, over and over again ripped out frozen shoots of corn and pumpkin. A volcanic eruption in the South Seas two years earlier did it, though at the time our preachers thought the source more local and divine wrath explicit.

Winter starts in November, whatever the calendar says, with gray of granite, with russet and brown of used leaves. In November stillness our stonewalls wait, attentive, and gaunt revenant trunks of maple and oak settle down for winter's stasis, which annually mimics and presages death for each of us and for the planet. November's palette, Braque's analytic cubism, static and squared with fieldstones, interrupts itself briefly with the bright-flapped caps of deer hunters and their orange jackets. Always it is modified by the black-green fir, enduring, hinting at permanence. Serious snow begins one November afternoon. Gradually Mount Kearsarge, south of us, disappears into white gauzy cloud, vanishing mountain, weather-sign for all of us to its north. For one hundred and eighty years the people of this house have looked south at dawn's light and again at sunset to tell the coming weather, reliable in 1802 when the first builder put in the south windows, reliable still. When Kearsarge disappears, the storm comes closer. Birds gather at the feeder, squabbling, gobbling their weight. When they are full they look for shelter, and we do the same, or at least we bring wood from the shed to stack beside the old Glenwoods and the new Jøtul.

Every year the first snow sets us dreaming. By March it will only bring the grumps, but November snow is revenance, a dreamy restitution of childhood or even infancy. Tighten the door and settle a cloth snake against the breeze from the door's bottom; make sure the storms are firmly shut; add logs to the stove and widen the draft. Sit in a chair looking south into blue twilight that arrives earlier every day—as the sky flakes and densens, as the first clear flakes float past the porch's wood to light on dirt of the driveway and on brown frozen grass or dry stalks of the flower border. They seem tentative and awkward at first, then in a hastening host a whole brief army falls, white militia paratrooping out of the close sky over various textures making them one. Snow is white and gray, part and whole, infinitely various yet infinitely repetitious, soft and hard, frozen and melting, a creaking underfoot and a soundlessness . . . But first of all it is the reversion of many into one. It is substance, almost the idea of substance, that turns grass, driveway, hayfield, old garden, log pile, Saab, watering trough, collapsed barn, and stonewall *into the one white.*

We finish early in November the task of preparing the house for snow—tacking poly over the low clapboards, raking leaves against the foundations as high as we can rake them. When the first real snow arrives, no dusting half inch but a solid foot, we complete the insulation, for it is snow that keeps us warm. After a neighbor's four-wheel-drive pickup, plow bolted in front, swoops clean our U-shaped driveway, and after we dig out the mailbox for Bert's rural delivery, it is time to heap the snow over leaves and against poly, around the house, on all sides of the house, against the granite foundation stones. Arctic winds halt before this white guard. When bright noon melts inches of snow away from the house, reflecting heat from the snowy clapboard, it leaves cracks of cold air for us to fill when new snow falls all winter long.

But November, although it begins winter, is only winter's approach, with little snow and with cold that announces itself only to increase. The calendar's winter begins at the

solstice, Advent's event: the child's birth who rises from winter to die and rise again in spring. November is autumn's burial and the smoke of victims sacrificed is thanks for harvest and magic as we go into ourselves like maples for winter's bear-sleep. We make transition by way of feast and anticipatory snow, toward the long, white, hard hundred days of the true winter of our annual death. We wait for December to feel the *cold,* I mean COLD, like thirty-five degrees below zero Fahrenheit. Seldom does it stay *cold,* or COLD, for longer than a week, but we are ready now for snow.

The first *big* snow accumulates one night. Kearsarge may disappear at noon, and darkness start early. In teatime twilight, big flakes slowly, as if hesitant, reel past the empty trees like small white leaves, star-shaped and infrequent. By bedtime, driveway and lawn turn shaggy with the first cover. It is good to go to bed early in winter, and tonight as we sleep our dreams take punctuation from the thudding of snowplows as they roll and bluster all night up and down Route 4, shaking the house yet comforting our sleep: Someone takes care, the solitary captains in their great snowships breasting through vast whiteness, fountaining it sideways into gutter drifts. If we stir as they thump past, we watch revolving yellow lights flash through our windows and reflect on the ceiling. We roll over and fall back into protected sleep. In a house full of cats we sleep not alone, for the snowplows that reassure us frighten our animals like thunder or riflefire; they crawl between our warm bodies under warmer electric blankets.

When we become aware, by the plows' repeated patrols, that the first deep snow accumulates; when the first intense and almost unbreakable sleep finishes and we enter the frangible second half of the night's house, I pull myself out of bed at two or three in the morning to inspect the true oncoming of winter's work. I walk through the dark house from one vantage to another—parlor window that looks west toward pond, kitchen from which I look toward Kearsarge, dining room that gives on the north, and if I twist, back to the slope of Ragged Mountain rising east above us. The night's flaking air breaks black sky into white flecks, silent and pervasive, shuttering the day's vista. This snow fills the air and the eyes, the way on spring nights peepers fill the ears. Everywhere I look, limited by snow-limits, cold dewy whiteness takes everything into itself. Beside the covered woodshed, side by side, I see the shapes of two small cars rounded and smooth like enormous loaves of dead-white bread. Where the woodpile waits for final stacking in the shed, a round mound rises with irregular sticks jagging out of it. Up on the hill the great cowbarn labors under a two-foot layer of snow, its unpainted vertical boards a dark upright shadow in all the whiteness, like the hemlocks above it on Ragged's hill. Although snowplows keep Route 4 passable, they do not yet scrape to the macadam: In the darkness the highway is as white as the hayfields on either side. Down the road white cottage disappears against white field, green shutters a patch of vacancy in the whiteness. In the stillness of two A.M., in a silent unlit moment with no plows thudding, I regard a landscape reverted to other years by the same snow—and I might be my great-grandfather gazing from the same windows in 1885. Or it might be his mother's eyes I gaze from, born on a Wilmot hill in 1789. Or maybe I look, centuries earlier, from the eyes of a Penacook wintering over the pond. If I squint a little I cannot see that this depression is a road.

But now the snowplow's thunder signals itself, and I watch the revolving yellow light reflect upward into white prodigious air, and hear the great bruising barge roar and rumble past the house, 1985 and grateful, as a steel prow swooshes high waves of whiteness up and over the gutter almost to the front of the house, and buries the mailbox.

One year the first great snow came Christmas Eve after the family had struggled to bed. When we lit the tree in the morning, the day was thick and dark past the windows, and as

we opened our presents the snow deepened in yard and hayfield outside, and on Christmas Day, all day, the great plows of state and town kept Route 4 clear. Snow stopped at three in the afternoon, and when Forrest rolled in to plow the driveway in the early blue twilight, Jane heaped slices of turkey between homemade bread to comfort him in his cab as he drove over the countryside digging people out.

The next morning was cold, thirty below, cold enough to notice. January is the coldest month, in fact, although many would argue for February. Usually our cold is dry, and it does not penetrate so much as damp cold. December of 1975, our first full winter here, I tried starting the Plymouth one morning with normal confidence in the old six and without cold-weather precautions; I flooded it. When I looked at the thermometer I was astonished to find it minus seventeen degrees, for my face and forehead had not warned me that it was *cold.* I had lived in Michigan where the winters were damp, and Ann Arbor's occasional zero felt harsher than New Hampshire's common twenty below. Later that winter we did not complain of the mildness. In January of 1976, morning after morning was thirty below; one morning on the porch the thermometer read thirty-eight degrees under—a temperature we did not equal again until 1984. My grandmother had just died at ninety-seven, and she had spent most of her late winters going south to Connecticut. The house had grown unaccustomed to winter, the old heavy wooden storm windows broken, no central heat, and no insulation. Jane and I had never lived without central heat. Now we had a parlor Glenwood stove for heating, two kerosene burners in the kitchen, and on occasion an electric oven with the door left open. This twelve-room house, in January of 1976, dwindled to a one-room house, with a kitchen sometimes habitable. Working at the dining room table, twenty feet from the living room's Glenwood, I felt chilly. At the time, we were too excited or triumphant to complain. We were camping out; we were earning our stripes. The next summer we added aluminum combination storms and screens together with some insulation; we added two more small woodstoves, one for each study so that we could each work despite the winter. My grandparents survived with only two woodstoves because they bustled around all day; in our work we sat on our duffs and required extra stoves. When February came we learned we had passed our initiation, for it had been the coldest January since New Hampshire started keeping records more than a hundred years earlier. In all my grandmother's ninety-seven Januarys she had not known so cold a month.

My grandfather worked all day without any heat except for the bodies of his cows. When he sat at morning and evening between two great steaming black-and-white Holstein hulks, pulling the pale thin tonnage of blue milk from their cud-chewing bodies, he was warm. I can remember him, on my winter visits to the farm as a boy, scurrying into the house for a warm-up between his other daily chores, rubbing his hands together, opening the drafts of one of the woodstoves and looming over it for a moment. Early and late, he moved among cold sheds and unheated barns. In the cowbarn, he fed the cattle hay, grain, and ensilage, and provided his horse Riley with oats and hay and water. He let the Holsteins loose to wander stiff-legged to the old cement watering trough next to the milk room, from which he first removed a layer of ice. Their pink muzzles dipped one by one into the near-freezing water. And he fed the sheep in sheepbarn and sheepyard. From the sheep's trough he dipped out water for the hens, who lived next door to the sheep, and carried feed for his hens from the grainshed beside the cowbarn.

He would start these chores early, most days of deep winter, rising at four-thirty, perhaps three hours before the sun, to do half the daily chores of feeding and watering, of milking and readying milk for the trucker, because the special daily chores of winter were the year's hardest. The pains of minus twenty were exacerbated by pains of hard labor. To

chop wood for next year's stove the farmer stalked with his ax into his woodlot after chores and breakfast, and often marched far enough so that he carried with him his bread and butter, meat and pie, and thermos of coffee for dinner. Setting out with a great ax, usually working alone, the farmer chopped the tree down, trimmed branches, cut the trunk into four-foot sections, and stacked it. Later he would hitch oxen to the sledge and fetch the cordwood downhill for cutting in the barnyard to stove-length pieces, and for splitting. Maybe ten cord of a winter for the house—more for the sugaring in March.

In January he harvested another winter crop—the crop that people forget when they think of the needs of an old farm—which was the harvest of ice, cut in great oblongs two or three feet thick from Eagle Pond, ox-sledded up to the icehouse in back of the cowbarn's watering trough, packed against warm weather six months hence. Each winter the farmer waited for a cold stretch, augering through the pond ice to check its thickness. Then he cut checkerboard squares with his ice saws. He kept himself heavily mittened not only against cold and wind rattling over the open desert lake, but also against the inevitable clasp of near-frozen water. A crew of them—neighbors cooperated to fetch ice—sawed and grappled, lifted and hauled, hard work and cold work. In the icehouse they stacked layers of ice, thickly insulated with sawdust, to last from the earliest warmth of April through hot spells of June and the long summer hay days of July and August through autumn with its Indian summer until the ice froze again. In the hot months my grandfather brought one chunk a day downhill from the icehouse, great square balanced with ice-tongs on his shoulder, to the toolshed behind the kitchen where my grandmother kept her icebox, drip drip. Most ice went to cool the milk, hot from the udders of Holsteins, so that it would not spoil overnight in the hot summer. July and August, I was amazed every time we dug down through the wet sawdust in the cool shade of the icehouse to find cold winter again—packed silvery slab of Eagle Pond preserved against summer, just as we hayed to preserve for the winter-cattle summer's hay. On the hottest days when we returned sweaty from haying, my grandfather cracked off a little triangle of ice for me to suck on. Every January when he dug down in the icehouse to bury his crop of new ice, he found old ice underneath it. After all, you never wanted to find yourself all out; some years, there might be hot days even in November when you would require a touch of ice. One long hot autumn, he found at the bottom of the ice shed, further than he ever remembered digging, a small coffin-shaped remnant from times past, ice that might have been five years old, he told me; maybe older . . .

And my grandfather told me how, in the state of Maine especially, in the old days, clipper ships loaded up ice and sawdust, at the end of winter, and sailed this cargo—transient mineral, annual and reproducible reverse-coal tonnage—down the East Coast to unload its cool for the South that never otherwise saw a piece of ice: ice by the ton for coastal cities like Charleston, South Carolina. Sometimes they sailed all the way to the West Indies with their perishable silvery cargo: Maine ice for the juleps of Charleston, northern January cooling Jamaica's rum.

By tradition the hard snow and heavy cold of January take a vacation for the eldritch out-of-time phenomenon of January thaw. Sometimes the January thaw comes in February, sometimes it never arrives at all, and on the rarest occasions it starts early and lasts all winter . . . Mostly the January thaw lives up to its name. Some strange day, after a week when we dress in the black of twenty below, we notice that we do not back up to the fire as we change our clothing. Extraordinary. Or at midday we pick up the mail in our shirtsleeves, balmy at forty-two degrees. (It is commonplace to observe that a temperature which felt Arctic late in August feels tropical in mid-January.) Icicles drip, snow slides off the south roof in

midday sun, and mud season takes over the driveway. Snow melts deeply away from clapboard and poly. Or the January thaw comes with warm rain. ("If this was snow we'd have twelve feet . . .") And if warm rain pours for three January days, as I have known it to do, Ragged's melt floods our driveway, snow vanishes from all hayfields, and water drowns the black ice of Eagle Pond. Our small universe confuses itself with false spring. Bears wake perplexed and wander looking for deer-corpses or compost heaps, thinking that it's time to get on with it. I remember fetching the newspaper one morning at six o'clock (I pick up the *Globe* outside a store nearby that does not open for customers, slugabeds, until eight o'clock) on the third day of a warm rain. Chugging through deep mud in my outboard Nissan, I pulled up at the wet porch to see a huge white cat rooting about in perennials beside the walk, a white pussycat with black spots . . . Oh, no . . . Therefore I remained in the front seat, quietly reading the paper, careful not to make a startling sound or otherwise appear rude—until the skunk wandered away.

Until we replaced rotten sills three years ago, a family of skunks lived in our rootcellar every winter. We never *saw* them, but we found their scat; we found the holes by which they entered and exited; we confirmed their presence by another sense. In the spring they sometimes quarreled, possibly over the correct time and place for love, and we could hear them snapping at each other, and, alas, we discovered that skunks used on each other their special skunk-equipment: Once a year in February or March we threw our windows wide open. On one occasion, Ann Arbor friends visited in March, dear friends notable for the immaculateness of their house in a culture of unspotted houses. When we brought them home with their skis from the airport, and opened the door, we discovered that our rootcellar family had suffered a domestic disagreement; therefore we opened all downstairs windows, although it was of course fifteen below. As we prepared to take our friends upstairs to their bedroom, where the air would be purer, we opened the doorway upstairs to discover a dead rat on the carpet, courtesy of a guardian cat. Welcome to the country.

January thaw is dazzling, but it is a moment's respite. If this were January in England we would soon expect snowdrops; here we know enough to expect replacement battalions of snow's troopers following on coldness that freezes the melt, covering it with foot upon foot of furry whiteness and moon-coldness. We return to the satisfactions of winter, maybe even to the deliverance and delirium of a full moon.

In New Hampshire the full moon is remarkable all year long, because we suffer relatively little from garbage-air and even less from background light. The great cloudless night of the full moon is werewolf time, glory of silver-pale hauntedness whenever it happens—but in winter it is most beautiful. I set the internal alarm, maybe three or four nights in a row, and wander, self-made ghost, through pale rooms in the pewter light while the moon magnifies itself in bright hayfields and reflects upward, a sun from middle earth, onto shadowy low ceilings. High sailing above, higher than it has a right to, bigger, the February full moon, huge disc of cold, rides and slides among tatters of cloud. My breathing speeds, my pulse quickens; for half an hour I wander, pulled like a tide through the still house in the salty half-light, more asleep than awake, asleep not in house or nightshirt in 1985 but in moon, moon, moon . . . What old animal awakens and stretches inside the marrow of the bones? What howls? What circles, sniffing for prey?

It's no winter without an ice storm. When Robert Frost gazed at bent-over birch trees and tried to think that boys had bent them playing, he knew better: "Ice storms do that." They do that, and a lot more, trimming disease and weakness out of the tree—the old tree's friend, as pneumonia used to be the old man's. Some of us provide life-support systems for our precious shrubs, boarding them over against the ice; for the ice storm takes the young

or unlucky branch or birch as well as the rotten or feeble. One February morning we look out our windows over yards and fields littered with kindling, small twigs and great branches. We look out at a world turned into one diamond, ten thousand karats in the line of sight, twice as many facets. What a dazzle of spinning refracted light, spider webs of cold brilliance attacking our eyeballs! All winter we wear sunglasses to drive, more than we do in summer, and never so much as after an ice storm with its painful glaze reflecting from maple and birch, granite boulder and stonewall, turning electric wires into bright silver filaments. The snow itself takes on a crust of ice, like the finish of a clay pot, that carries our weight and sends us swooping and sliding. It is worth your life to go for the mail. Until sand and salt redeem the highway, Route 4 is quiet; we cancel the appointment with the dentist, stay home, and marvel at the altered universe, knowing that midday sun will strip ice from tree and roof and restore our ordinary white winter world.

Another inescapable attribute of winter, increasing in the years of postwar affluence, is the ski people, cold counterpart of the summer folks who have filled New Hampshire's Julys and Augusts ever since the railroad came in the 1840s. Now the roads north from Boston are as dense on a February Friday as they are on a July; and late Sunday afternoon Interstate 93 backs up from the tollbooth. On twenty thousand Toyotas pairs of skis ride north and south every weekend. At Christmas vacation and school holidays every hotel room fills all week with families of flatlanders. They wait in line at the tows, resplendent in the costumes of money, booted and coifed in bright petrochemical armor. They ride, they swoop, they fall, they drink whiskey . . . and the bonesetter takes no holiday on a New Hampshire February weekend, and the renter of crutches earns time and a half. Now that cross-country rivals downhill, the ski people grow older and more various; tourism, which rivals the yard sale as major north country industry, brings Massachusetts and New York money for the thin purses of the cold land. And by the fashionable areas—much of Vermont, and the Waterville Valley in New Hampshire's White Mountains—restaurants and boutiques, cute-shops and quiche-cafés buzz like winter's blackflies.

The snowmachine breaks trails for cross-country, and it is also the countryman's ski outfit. Few natives ski, though some have always done, and in our attic there are wide heavy wooden skis from the time of the Great War on which my mother and her sisters traipsed all winter, largely doing cross-country but perfectly willing to slide down a hill. Old-timers remember the horse as ski-tow, pulling adventurers uphill.

The motorcycle roar of snowmachines, from a distance indistinguishable from chainsaws, interrupts the down-quiet of midweek evenings, as kids roar along disused railroad tracks and over the surface of frozen lakes. Mostly kids. The older folks, men mostly, park their bobhouses on thick ice of winter lakes, saw holes in the ice, light a fire, warm themselves with a pint of whiskey, and fish for the wormless perch of winter. Like deer-hunting in November, of course, this fishing is not mere sport; it fills the freezers of ten thousand shacks, trailers, and extended farmhouses. On Eagle Pond just west of us we count six or a dozen bobhouses each winter, laboriously translated by pickup and pushed or slipped across the ice to a lucky spot. Most springs it seems one fisherman waits too late. How many little houses, some with tin stoves flaking away, raise a freshwater Davy Jones's condominium on the bottom of Eagle Pond?

After the labor of cordwood and ice in the old days, in March, as the winter ended, followed the great chore of maple sugaring. It still arrives, though without so much labor. Usually it comes in March, one stretch, but on occasion the conditions for sap turn right for two weeks in February, go wrong for twenty days, then right again—a split season of

sugaring. Right conditions are warm days when the snow melts followed by cold nights when it freezes. Nowadays people suction sap from the sugarbush with miles of plastic tubing. In the old time, you pounded the spigot into the tree—several of them in a good-sized three-hundred-year-old maple—and hung a bucket from each for the sap to drip into. My grandfather trudged from tree to tree every day, wearing a wooden yoke across his shoulders; long pails hung from the ends of it, narrow on top and wide on bottom, for collecting sap from each bucket. He emptied these yoke-pails into a great receptacle sledged by an ox—oxen were especially useful in the winter, slow but unbothered by snow—and when he filled this great sledge-kettle, his ox pulled it to a funnel and pipe whence the sap flowed downhill to a storage tank behind the saphouse.

Gathering sap was a third of the work, or maybe a quarter. There was cordwood to cut and burn under the trays boiling the sap down. Someone had to tend the fire day and night, and to watch and test the sap on its delicate journey to syrup. In 1913 my grandfather corked five hundred gallons at a dollar a gallon, big money in 1913, with the help of his father-in-law Ben Keneston, cousin Freeman, and Ansel the hired man. When we remember that it takes about forty gallons of sap, boiled down, to make one gallon of syrup, we begin to assess the labor required.

But the sweetness of the task was not only the cash crop. With honey from the beehive next to the barn and the hollyhocks, my grandfather and grandmother grew and produced their own sweetening. With the cash from the syrup—sometimes from wool and baby lambs—they bought land and paid taxes. Often their tax was little or nothing, for in the old days many farmers paid their taxes by doing road work—scraping and rolling the dirt roads, filling in with hardpan, and in winter rolling down the snow on the road to make it fit for the runners of sleighs, taking on a mile of Wilmot's Grafton Turnpike.

March was always the month for blizzards. Still is. It is the time when we all tell ourselves: *We've had enough of winter.* Old folks come back from Florida and Hilton Head; younger ones, fed up, head off for a week where the weather performs like May or June in New Hampshire. Every morning the *Globe* measures a word from Florida: *baseball* . . . In New Hampshire, tantalizing melt is overwhelmed with four feet of snow, drifts to twelve feet . . . We comfort each other, when we use the form of complaint for our boasting, that even if we lost the old outhouse yesterday, or the '53 Buick that the chickens use for summer roosting, what comes quick in March goes quick in March, and three or four days from now it'll melt to reveal the lost Atlantis of the family barnyard. Of course three or four days later, we find another four feet.

Blizzards happen in March, like the great one of '88, which the old people still bragged about in the 1940s. My Connecticut grandfather and my New Hampshire one, who shared little, shared the blizzard of '88: a great watershed for bragging, or for telling lies about. And in the 1980s I still ask old people what they remember that *their* old people told them about '88, much as the '88ers themselves asked their old-timers about the Poverty Year of 1816. Great weather makes great stories. Paul Fenton told me a story he heard as a boy, not about '88 but just about "the big snows we used to have, back in the old days." It seems that a bunch went out after a heavy snow, dragging the roads with the help of oxen so that people could use their sleighs and sledges, when one of the oxen slipped and got stuck, couldn't move at all; got a hoof caught in something . . . Well, they dug down, dug around, trying to free the ox's hoof, and what do you know . . . That ox had stuck its foot into a chimney!

Now, the blue snow of 1933 is *not* a lie. I am sure of it, because of the way Ansel Powers tells me about it, because his wife Edna confirms it, because Les Ford from Potter Place, who has never been known to collaborate on a story, remembers it just as well and tells the same stories. It may be hard to believe: *but it was blue.* You stuck a shovel in it, and it was *blue,* blue as that sky, blue as a bachelor's button. It fell in April, a late snow, and it fell fast. Les remembers that he'd been to a dance at Danbury, and when he went to bed at midnight the sky was clear and full of stars; when he woke up in the morning, there was three feet of blue snow. The snowplows were disassembled for summer; the road agent had to start up the old dozer and go up and down the road with it, to clear a way for the Model T's—and a few shiny Model A's. Nobody *saw* it snow except Sam Duby, the same blacksmith who made the first snowplows in Andover. He woke up at two or three in the morning and had to do something, you know; well, the outhouse was across the road in the barn, and he came out on the porch and it was snowing to beat the band and he just dropped a load right there . . . He's the only one who saw it snow; the rest of us went to bed under stars, woke up to the sun shining in three feet of *blue snow.*

In *The Voyage of the Beagle* Charles Darwin wrote about finding red snow, *Protococcus nivalis,* on the Peuquenes Ridge in Chile in 1835. "A little rubbed on paper gives it a faint rose tinge mingled with a little brick-red." When he examined it later, Darwin found "microscopical plants." As far as I know, no one took our blue snow into a laboratory.

Of course it snows in April, every year, most often white, but you cannot call it winter anymore. Snow sticks around, in the north shade, most years until early in May, but it is ragged and dirty stuff, and we overlook it as we gaze in hopeful amazement at this year's crop of daffodils. Every year the earlier daffodils fill with snow, bright yellow spilling out white crystals, outraged optimism overcome by fact. And the worst storm I have driven through, after ten New Hampshire winters, occurred a few years back on the ninth day of May.

But annual aberration aside, March is the end of winter, and the transition to spring is April's melt. One year not long ago we had an open winter, with very little snow, *no* snow we all said; we exaggerated a little for we had an inch here and an inch there. The winter was not only dry but mild, which was a good thing, for an open winter with cold weather destroys flowers and bushes and even trees, since snow is our great insulator. As it was, in our open winter we suffered one cold patch—twenty below for a week—and in the spring that followed, and in the summer, we discovered winterkill: A few rose bushes and old lilacs, plants and bulbs that had survived for decades, didn't make it that year. When spring came without a melt, when mild days softened with buttery air and the protected daffodils rose blowing yellow trumpets, we felt uneasy; all of us knew: Lacking the pains of winter, we did not deserve the rapture and the respite of spring.

Our annual melt is the wild, messy, glorious loosening of everything tight. It is gravity's ecstasy as water seeks its own level on every level, and the noise of water running fills day and night. Down Ragged Mountain the streams rush, cutting through ice and snow, peeling away winter's cold layers. Rush, trickle, rush. Busy water moves all day and all night, never tired, cutting away the corrupt detritus of winter. Fingers of bare earth extend down hillsides. South sides of trees extend bare patches farther every day. Root-patterned rivulets melting gather downhill to form brief streams. Dirt roads slog, driveways turn swamps, cars smithereen transmissions. Rural delivery, which survives ten thousand blizzards, sticks in the mud of April.

Then it dries. Last snow melts. Trees bud green. Soft air turns. Who can believe in winter now?

All of us. We know that winter has only retreated, waiting. When the bear comes out of its winter sleep, winter itself goes into hibernation, sleeping off the balmy months of peeper-sing until the red leaf wakes it again and the white season returns with the New Hampshire by which we know ourselves.

[1986]

WILLIAM MANCHESTER

(1922–)

Okinawa: The Bloodiest Battle of All

About the Author: A reporter and foreign correspondent, Manchester has been an eyewitness to the events shaping our world. In "Okinawa: The Bloodiest Battle of All," Manchester speaks from his experience in the Marine Corps.

On Okinawa today, Flag Day will be observed with an extraordinary ceremony: two groups of elderly men, one Japanese, the other American, will gather for a solemn rite.

They could scarcely have less in common. Their motives are mirror images; each group honors the memory of men who tried to slay the men honored by those opposite them. But theirs is a common grief. After forty-two years the ache is still there. They are really united by death, the one great victor in modern war.

They have come to Okinawa to dedicate a lovely monument in remembrance of the Americans, Japanese and Okinawans killed there in the last and bloodiest battle of the Pacific war. More than 200,000 perished in the 82-day struggle—twice the number of Japanese lost at Hiroshima and more American blood than had been shed at Gettysburg. My own regiment—I was a sergeant in the 29th Marines—lost more than 80 percent of the men who had landed on April 1, 1945. Before the battle was over, both the Japanese and American commanding generals lay in shallow graves.

Okinawa lies 330 miles southwest of the southernmost Japanese island of Kyushu; before the war, it was Japanese soil. Had there been no atom bombs—and at that time the most powerful Americans, in Washington and at the Pentagon, doubted that the device would work—the invasion of the Nipponese homeland would have been staged from Okinawa, beginning with a landing on Kyushu to take place November 1. The six Marine divisions, storming ashore abreast, would lead the way. President Truman asked General Douglas MacArthur, whose estimates of casualties on the eve of battles had proved uncannily accurate, about Kyushu. The general predicted a million Americans would die in that first phase.

Given the assumption that nuclear weapons would contribute nothing to victory, the battle of Okinawa had to be fought. No one doubted the need to bring Japan to its knees. But some Americans came to hate the things we had to do, even when convinced that doing them was absolutely necessary; they had never understood the bestial, monstrous and vile means required to reach the objective—an unconditional Japanese surrender. As for me, I could not reconcile the romanticized view of war that runs like a red streak through our literature—and the glowing aura of selfless patriotism that had led us to put our lives at forfeit—with the wet, green hell from which I had barely escaped. Today, I understand. I was there, and was twice wounded. This is the story of what I knew and when I knew it.

To our astonishment, the Marine landing on April 1 was uncontested. The enemy had set a trap. Japanese strategy called first for kamikazes to destroy our fleet, cutting us off from supply ships; then Japanese troops would methodically annihilate the men stranded ashore using the trench-warfare tactics of World War I—cutting the Americans down as they charged heavily fortified positions. One hundred and ten thousand Japanese troops were waiting on the southern tip of the island. Intricate entrenchments, connected by tunnels, formed the enemy's defense line, which ran across the waist of Okinawa from the Pacific Ocean to the East China Sea.

By May 8, after more than five weeks of fighting, it became clear that the anchor of this line was a knoll of coral and volcanic ash, which the Marines christened Sugar Loaf Hill. My role in mastering it—the crest changed hands more than eleven times—was the central experience of my youth, and of all the military bric-a-brac that I put away after the war, I cherish most the Commendation from General Lemuel C. Shepherd, Jr., U.S.M.C., our splendid division commander, citing me for "gallantry in action and extraordinary achievement," adding, "Your courage was a constant source of inspiration . . . and your conduct throughout was in keeping with the highest tradition of the United States Naval Service."

The struggle for Sugar Loaf lasted ten days; we fought under the worst possible conditions—a driving rain that never seemed to slacken, day or night. (I remember wondering, in an idiotic moment—no man in combat is really sane—whether the battle could be called off, or at least postponed, because of bad weather.)

Newsweek called Sugar Loaf "the most critical local battle of the war." *Time* described a company of Marines—270 men—assaulting the hill. They failed; fewer than 30 returned. Fletcher Pratt, the military historian, wrote that the battle was unmatched in the Pacific war for "closeness and desperation." Casualties were almost unbelievable. In the 22d and 29th marine regiments, two out of every three men fell. The struggle for the dominance of Sugar Loaf was probably the costliest engagement in the history of the Marine Corps. But by early evening on May 18, as night thickened over the embattled armies, the 29th Marines had taken Sugar Loaf, this time for keeps.

On Okinawa today, the ceremony will be dignified, solemn, seemly. It will also be anachronistic. If the Japanese dead of 1945 were resurrected to witness it, they would be appalled by the acceptance of defeat, the humiliation of their emperor—the very idea of burying Japanese near the barbarians from across the sea and then mourning them together. Americans, meanwhile, risen from their graves, would ponder the evolution of their own society, and might wonder, What ever happened to patriotism?

When I was a child, a bracket was screwed to the sill of a front attic window; its sole purpose was to hold the family flag. At first light, on all legal holidays—including Election Day, July 4, Memorial Day and, of course, Flag Day—I would scamper up to show it. The holidays remain, but mostly they mean long weekends.

In the late 1920s, during my childhood, the whole town of Attleboro, Massachusetts, would turn out to cheer the procession on Memorial Day. The policemen always came first, wearing their number-one uniforms and keeping perfect step. Behind them was a two-man vanguard—the mayor and, at his side, my father, hero of the 5th Marines and Belleau Wood, wearing his immaculate dress blues and looking like a poster of a Marine, with one magnificent flaw: the right sleeve of his uniform was empty. He had lost the arm in the Argonne. I now think that, as I watched him pass by, my own military future was already determined.

The main body of the parade was led by five or six survivors of the Civil War, too old to march but sitting upright in open Pierce-Arrows and Packards, wearing their blue uniforms and broad-brimmed hats. Then, in perfect step, came a contingent of men in their fifties, with their blanket rolls sloping diagonally from shoulder to hip—the Spanish-American War veterans. After these—and anticipated by a great roar from the crowd—came the doughboys of World War I, some still in their late twenties. They were acclaimed in part because theirs had been the most recent conflict, but also because they had fought in the war that—we then thought—had ended all wars.

Americans still march in Memorial Day parades, but attendance is light. One war has led to another and another and yet another, and the cruel fact is that few men, however they die, are remembered beyond the lifetimes of their closest relatives and friends. In the early 1940s, one of the forces that kept us on the line, under heavy enemy fire, was the conviction that this battle was of immense historical import, and that those of us who survived it would be forever cherished in the hearts of Americans. It was rather diminishing to return in 1945 and discover that your own parents couldn't even pronounce the names of the islands you had conquered.

But what of those who *do* remain faithful to patriotic holidays? What are they commemorating? Very rarely are they honoring what actually happened, because only a handful know, and it's not their favorite topic of conversation. In World War II, 16 million Americans entered the armed forces. Of these, fewer than a million saw action. Logistically, it took nineteen men to back up one man in combat. All who wore uniforms are called veterans, but more than 90 percent of them are as uninformed about the killing zones as those on the home front.

If all Americans understood the nature of battle, they might be vulnerable to truth. But the myths of warfare are embedded deep in our ancestral memories. By the time children have reached the age of awareness, they regard uniforms, decorations and Sousa marches as exalted, and those who argue otherwise are regarded as unpatriotic.

General MacArthur, quoting Plato, said: "Only the dead have seen the end of war." One hopes he was wrong, for war, as it had existed for over four thousand years, is now obsolete. As late as the spring of 1945, it was possible for one man, with a rifle, to make a difference, however infinitesimal, in the struggle to defeat an enemy who had attacked us and threatened our West Coast. The bomb dropped on Hiroshima made the man ludicrous, even pitiful. Soldiering has been relegated to Sartre's theater of the absurd. The image of the man as protector and defender of the home has been destroyed (and I suggest that that seed of thought eventually led women to re-examine their own role in society).

Until nuclear weapons arrived, the glorifying of militarism was the nation's hidden asset. Without it, we would almost certainly have been defeated by the Japanese, probably by 1943. In 1941 American youth was isolationist and pacifist. Then war planes from Imperial Japan destroyed our fleet at Pearl Harbor on December 7, and on December 8 recruiting stations were packed. Some of us later found fighting rather different from what had been advertised. Yet in combat these men risked their lives—and often lost them—in hope of winning medals. There is an old soldier's saying: "A man won't sell you his life, but he'll give it to you for a piece of colored ribbon."

Most of the men who hit the beaches came to scorn eloquence. They preferred the 130-year-old "Word of Cambronne." As dusk darkened the Waterloo battlefield, with the French in full retreat, the British sent word to General Pierre Cambronne, commander of

the Old Guard. His position, they pointed out, was hopeless, and they suggested he capitulate. Every French textbook reports his reply as "The Old Guard dies but never surrenders." What he actually said was *"merde."*

If you mention this incident to members of the U.S. 101st Airborne Division, they will immediately understand. "Nuts" was not Brigadier General Anthony C. McAuliffe's answer to the Nazi demand that he hoist a white flag over Bastogne. Instead, he quoted Cambronne.

The character of combat has always been determined by the weapons available to men when their battles were fought. In the beginning they were limited to hand weapons—clubs, rocks, swords, lances. At the Battle of Camlann in 539, England's Arthur—a great warrior, not a king—led a charge that slew 930 Saxons, including their leader.

It is important to grasp the fact that those 930 men were not killed by snipers, grenades or shells. The dead were bludgeoned or stabbed to death, and we have a pretty good idea how this was done. One of the facts withheld from civilians during World War II was that Kabar fighting knives, with seven-inch blades honed to such precision that you could shave with them, were issued to Marines and that we were taught to use them. You never cut downward. You drove the point of your blade into a man's lower belly and ripped upward. In the process, you yourself became soaked in the other man's gore. After that charge at Camlann, Arthur must have been half drowned in blood.

The Battle of Agincourt, fought nearly one thousand years later, represented a slight technical advance: crossbows and long bows had appeared. All the same, Arthur would have recognized the battle. Like all engagements of the time, this one was short. Killing by hand is hard work, and hot work. It is so exhausting that even men in peak condition collapse once the issue of triumph or defeat is settled. And Henry V's spear carriers and archers were drawn from social classes that had been undernourished for as long as anyone could remember. The duration of medieval battles could have been measured in hours, even minutes.

The Battle of Waterloo, fought exactly four hundred years later, is another matter. By 1815, the Industrial Revolution had begun cranking out appliances of death, primitive by today's standards, but revolutionary for infantrymen of that time. And Napoleon had formed mass armies, pressing every available man into service. It was a long step toward total war, and its impact was immense. Infantrymen on both sides fought with single-missile weapons—muskets or rifles—and were supported by (and were the target of) artillery firing cannonballs.

The fighting at Waterloo continued for three days; for a given regiment, however, it usually lasted one full day, much longer than medieval warfare. A half century later, Gettysburg lasted three days and cost 43,497 men. Then came the marathon slaughters of 1914–1918, lasting as long as ten months (Verdun) and producing hundreds of thousands of corpses lying, as F. Scott Fitzgerald wrote afterward, "like a million bloody rugs." Winston Churchill, who had been a dashing young cavalry officer when Victoria was queen, said of the new combat: "War, which was cruel and magnificent, has become cruel and squalid."

It may be said that the history of war is one of men packed together, getting closer and closer to the ground and then deeper and deeper into it. In the densest combat of World War I, battalion frontage—the length of the line into which the 1,000-odd men were squeezed—had been 800 yards. On Okinawa, on the Japanese fortified line, it was less than 600 yards—about 18 inches per man. We were there and deadlocked for more than a week in the relentless rain. During those weeks we lost nearly 4,000 men.

And now it is time to set down what this modern battlefield was like.

All greenery had vanished; as far as one could see, heavy shellfire had denuded the scene of shrubbery. What was left resembled a cratered moonscape. But the craters were vanishing, because the rain had transformed the earth into a thin porridge—too thin even to dig foxholes. At night you lay on a poncho as a precaution against drowning during the barrages. All night, every night, shells erupted close enough to shake the mud beneath you at the rate of five or six a minute. You could hear the cries of the dying but could do nothing. Japanese infiltration was always imminent, so the order was to stay put. Any man who stood up was cut in half by machine guns manned by fellow Marines.

By day, the mud was hip deep; no vehicles could reach us. As you moved up the slope of the hill, artillery and mortar shells were bursting all around you, and, if you were fortunate enough to reach the top, you encountered the Japanese defenders, almost face to face, a few feet away. To me, they looked like badly wrapped brown paper parcels someone had soaked in a tub. Their eyes seemed glazed. So, I suppose, did ours.

Japanese bayonets were fixed; ours weren't. We used the knives, or, in my case, a .45 revolver and M1 carbine. The mud beneath our feet was deeply veined with blood. It was slippery. Blood is very slippery. So you skidded around, in deep shock, fighting as best you could until one side outnumbered the other. The outnumbered side would withdraw for reinforcements and then counterattack.

During those ten days I ate half a candy bar. I couldn't keep anything down. Everyone had dysentery, and this brings up an aspect of war even Robert Graves, Siegfried Sassoon, Edmund Blunden and Ernest Hemingway avoided. If you put more than a quarter million men in line for three weeks, with no facilities for the disposal of human waste, you are going to confront a disgusting problem. We were fighting and sleeping in one vast cesspool. Mingled with that stench was another—the corrupt and corrupting odor of rotting human flesh.

My luck ran out on June 5, more than two weeks after we had taken Sugar Loaf Hill and killed the seven thousand Japanese soldiers defending it. I had suffered a slight gunshot wound above the right knee on June 2, and had rejoined my regiment to make an amphibious landing on Oroku Peninsula behind enemy lines. The next morning several of us were standing in a stone enclosure outside some Okinawan tombs when a six-inch rocket mortar shell landed among us.

The best man in my section was blown to pieces, and the slime of his viscera enveloped me. His body had cushioned the blow, saving my life; I still carry a piece of his shinbone in my chest. But I collapsed, and was left for dead. Hours later corpsmen found me still breathing, though blind and deaf, with my back and chest a junkyard of iron fragments—including, besides the piece of shinbone, four pieces of shrapnel too close to the heart to be removed. (They were not dangerous, a Navy surgeon assured me, but they still set off the metal detector at the Buffalo airport.)

Between June and November I underwent four major operations and was discharged as 100 percent disabled. But the young have strong recuperative powers. The blindness was caused by shock, and my vision returned. I grew new eardrums. In three years I was physically fit. The invisible wounds remain.

Most of those who were closest to me in the early 1940s had left New England campuses to join the Marines, knowing it was the most dangerous branch of the service. I remember them as bright, physically strong and inspired by an idealism and love of country they would have been too embarrassed to acknowledge. All of us despised the pompousness and pretentiousness of senior officers. It helped that, almost without exception, we admired and respected our commander in chief. But despite our enormous pride in being Marines, we saw through the scam that had lured so many of us to recruiting stations.

Once we polled a rifle company, asking each man why he had joined the Marines. A majority cited *To the Shores of Tripoli,* a marshmallow of a movie starring John Wayne, Randolph Scott and Maureen O'Hara. Throughout the film the uniform of the day was dress blues; requests for liberty were always granted. The implication was that combat would be a lark, and when you returned, spangled with decorations, a Navy nurse like Maureen O'Hara would be waiting in your sack. It was peacetime again when John Wayne appeared on the silver screen as Sergeant Stryker in *Sands of Iwo Jima,* but that film underscores the point; I went to see it with another ex-Marine, and we were asked to leave the theater because we couldn't stop laughing.

After my evacuation from Okinawa, I had the enormous pleasure of seeing Wayne humiliated in person at Aiea Heights Naval Hospital in Hawaii. Only the most gravely wounded, the litter cases, were sent there. The hospital was packed, the halls lined with beds. Between Iwo Jima and Okinawa, the Marine Corps was being bled white.

Each evening, Navy corpsmen would carry litters down to the hospital theater so the men could watch a movie. One night they had a surprise for us. Before the film the curtains parted and out stepped John Wayne, wearing a cowboy outfit—ten-gallon hat, bandanna, checkered shirt, two pistols, chaps, boots and spurs. He grinned his aw-shucks grin, passed a hand over his face and said, "Hi ya, guys!" He was greeted by a stony silence. Then somebody booed. Suddenly everyone was booing.

This man was a symbol of the fake machismo we had come to hate, and we weren't going to listen to him. He tried and tried to make himself heard, but we drowned him out, and eventually he quit and left. If you liked *Sands of Iwo Jima,* I suggest you be careful. Don't tell it to the Marines.

And so we weren't macho. Yet we never doubted the justice of our cause. If we had failed—if we had lost Guadalcanal, and the Navy's pilots had lost the Battle of Midway—the Japanese would have invaded Australia and Hawaii, and California would have been in grave danger. In 1942 the possibility of an Axis victory was very real. It is possible for me to loathe war—and with reason—yet still honor the brave men, many of them boys, really, who fought with me and died beside me. I have been haunted by their loss these forty-two years, and I shall mourn them until my own death releases me. It does not seem to much to ask that they be remembered on one day each year. After all, they sacrificed their futures that you might have yours.

Yet I will not be on Okinawa for the dedication today. I would enjoy being with Marines; the ceremony will be moving, and we would be solemn, remembering our youth and the beloved friends who died there.

Few, if any, of the Japanese survivors agreed to attend the ceremony. However, Edward L. Fox, chairman of the Okinawa Memorial Shrine Committee, capped almost six years' campaigning for a monument when he heard about a former Japanese naval officer,

Yoshio Yazaki—a meteorologist who had belonged to a four-thousand-man force led by Rear Admiral Minoru Ota—and persuaded him to attend.

On March 31, 1945, Yazaki-san had been recalled to Tokyo, and thus missed the battle of Okinawa. Ten weeks later—exactly forty-two years ago today—Admiral Ota and his men committed seppuku, killing themselves rather than face surrender. Ever since then Yazaki has been tormented by the thought that his comrades have joined their ancestors and he is here, not there.

Finding Yazaki was a great stroke of luck for Fox, for whom an Okinawa memorial had become an obsession. His own division commander tried to discourage him. The Japanese could hardly be expected to back a memorial on the site of their last great military defeat. But Yazaki made a solution possible.

If Yazaki can attend, why can't I? I played a role in the early stages of Buzz Fox's campaign and helped write the tribute to the Marines that is engraved on the monument. But when I learned that Japanese were also participating, I quietly withdrew. There are too many graves between us, too much gore, too many memories of too many atrocities.

In 1978, revisiting Guadalcanal, I encountered a Japanese businessman who had volunteered to become a kamikaze pilot in 1945 and was turned down at the last minute. Mutual friends suggested that we meet. I had expected no difficulty; neither, I think, did he. But when we confronted each other, we froze.

I trembled, suppressing the sudden, startling surge of primitive rage within. And I could see, from his expression, that this was difficult for him, too. Nations may make peace. It is harder for fighting men. On simultaneous impulse we both turned and walked away.

I set this down in neither pride nor shame. The fact is that some wounds never heal. Yazaki, unlike Fox, is dreading the ceremony. He does not expect to be shriven of his guilt. He knows he must be there but can't say why. Men are irrational, he explains, and adds that he feels very sad.

So do I, Yazaki-san, so do I.

[1987]

CHARLES SIMIC

(1938–)

Reading Philosophy at Night

About the Author: Simic has won fame for his highly inventive poetry and essays. Images of the everyday world that fathom existential themes often direct his voice. In "Reading Philosophy at Night" he plays with the act of meditating while in solitude.

It is night again around me; I feel as though there had been lightning—for a brief span of time I was entirely in my element and in my light.

—Nietzsche

The mind loves the unknown. It loves images whose meaning is unknown, since the meaning of the mind itself is unknown.

—Magritte

I wore Buster keaton's expression of exaggerated calm. I could have been sitting on the edge of a cliff with my back to the abyss trying to look normal.

Now I read philosophy in the morning. When I was younger and lived in the city it was always at night. "That's how you ruined your eyes," my mother keeps saying. I sat and read late into the night. The quieter it got, the more clearheaded I became—or so it seemed to me. In the sparsely furnished room above the Italian grocery, I would be struggling with some intricate epistemological argument which promised a magnificent insight at its conclusion. I could smell it, so to speak. I couldn't put the book away, and it was getting very late. I had to be at work in the morning. Even had I tried to sleep my head would have been full of Immanuel Kant. So, I wouldn't sleep. I remember well such moments of decision: The great city that had suddenly turned quiet, the open book, and my face reflected dimly in the darkened windowpane.

At such hours I thought I understood everything. The first time it happened I was twenty. It was six o'clock in the morning. It was winter. It was dark and very cold. I was in Chicago riding the El to work seated between two heavily bundled-up old women. The train was overheated, but each time the door opened at one of the elevated platforms, a blast of cold air would send shivers through us. The lights, too, kept flickering. As the train changed tracks, the lights would go out and I would stop reading the history of philosophy I had borrowed the previous day from the library. "Why is there something rather than nothing?" the book asked, quoting Parmenides. It was as if my eyes were opened. I could not stop looking at my fellow passengers. How incredible, I thought, being here, existing.

I have a recurring dream about the street where I was born. It is always night. I'm walking past vaguely familiar buildings trying to find our house, but somehow it is not there. I retrace my steps on that short block of only a few buildings, all of which are there except the one I want. The effort leaves me exhausted and saddened.

In another version of this same dream, I catch a glimpse of our house. There it is, at last, but for some reason I'm unable to get any closer to it. No lights are on. I look for our window, but it is even darker there on the third floor. The whole building seems abandoned. "It's not possible," I tell myself.

Once in one of these dreams, many years ago, I saw someone at my window, hunched over, watching the street intently. That's how my grandmother would wait late into the night for us to come home, except this was a stranger. Even without being able to make out his face, I was sure of that.

Most of the time, however, there's no one in sight during the dream. The facades of buildings still retain the pockmarks and other signs of the war. The streetlights are out and there's no moon in the sky so it's not clear to me how I am able to see all that in complete darkness.

Whoever reads philosophy reads himself as much as he reads the philosopher. I am in a dialogue with certain decisive events in my life as much as I am with the ideas on the page. Meaning is the matter of my existence. My effort to understand is a perpetual circling around a few obsessive images.

Like everyone else, I have my hunches. All my experiences make a kind of untaught ontology which precedes all my readings. What I am trying to conceptualize with the help of the philosopher is that which I have already intuited.

That's one way of looking at it.

> The Meditation of yesterday filled my mind with so many doubts that it is no longer in my power to forget them. And yet, I do not see in what manner I can resolve them; and, just as if I had all of a sudden fallen into very deep water, I am so disconcerted that I can neither make certain of setting my feet on the bottom, nor can I swim and so support myself on the surface. I shall nevertheless make an effort and follow anew the same path as that on which I yesterday entered, i.e. I shall proceed by setting aside all that in which the least doubt could be supposed to exist, just as if I had discovered that it was absolutely false; and I shall ever follow in this road until I have met with something which is certain, or at least, if I can do nothing else, until I have learned for certain that there's nothing in the world that is certain. Archimedes, in order that he might draw the terrestrial globe out of its place, and transport it elsewhere, demanded only that one point should be fixed and immovable: in the same way I shall have the right to conceive high hopes if I am happy enough to discover one thing only which is certain and indubitable.

I love this passage of Descartes; his beginning again, his not wanting to be fooled. It describes the ambition of philosophy in all its nobility and desperation. I prefer this doubting Descartes to his famous later conclusions. Here everything is still unsettled. The poetry of the moment still casts its spell. Of course, he's greedy for the absolute, but so is his reader.

There's an Eastern European folk song which tells of a girl who tossed an apple higher and higher in the air until she tossed it as high as the clouds. To her surprise the apple didn't come down. The cloud got it. She waited with arms outstretched, but the apple stayed up there. All she could do is plead with the cloud to return her apple, but that's another story. I like the first part when the impossible happens.

I remember lying in a ditch and looking at some pebbles while German bombers were flying over our heads. That was long ago. I don't remember the face of my mother nor the faces of the people who were there with us, but I still see those perfectly ordinary pebbles.

"It is not *how* things are in the world that is mystical, but that it exists," says Wittgenstein. I had a feeling of great clarity. Time had stopped. I was watching myself watching the pebbles and trembling with fear. Then time moved on.

The pebbles stayed in their otherness, staved forever as far as I am concerned. I'm talking about the experience of heightened consciousness. Can language do it justice? Speech is always less. When it comes to consciousness, one approximates, one speaks poorly. Competing phenomenologies are impoverishments, splendid poverties.

Wittgenstein puts it this way: "What finds its reflection in language, language cannot represent. What expresses *itself* in language, we cannot express by means of language." We are not, most certainly, thinking about the same thing, nor were he and his followers subsequently very happy with this early statement of his, but this has been my experience on a number of occasions.

I knew someone who once tried to persuade me otherwise. He considered himself a logical positivist. There are people who tell you, for example, that you can speak of a pencil's dimension, location, appearance, state of motion or rest but not of its intelligence and love of music. The moment I hear that the poet in me rebels and I want to write a poem about an intelligent pencil in love with music. In other words, what they regard as nonsense, I suspect to be full of unknown imaginative possibilities.

There's a wonderful story told about Wittgenstein and his Cambridge colleague, the Italian economist Piero Sraffa. Apparently they often discussed philosophy. "One day," as Justus Hartnack has it, "when Wittgenstein was defending his view that a proposition has the same logical form as the fact it depicts, Sraffa made a gesture used by Neapolitans to express contempt and asked Wittgenstein what the logical form of that was. According to Wittgenstein's own recollection, it was this question which made him realize that his belief that a fact could have a logical form was untenable."

As for my logical friend, we argued all night. "What cannot be said, cannot be thought." And then again, after I blurted out something about silence being the language of consciousness, "you're silent because you have nothing to say." It got to the point where we were calling each other "you dumb shit." We were drinking large quantities of red wine, misunderstanding each other liberally, and only stopped bickering when his disheveled wife came to the bedroom door and told us to shut up.

Then I told him a story.

One day in Yugoslavia, just after the war, we made a class trip to the town War Museum. At the entrance we found a battered German tank which delighted us. Inside the museum one could look at a few rifles, hand grenades and uniforms, but not much else. Most of the space was taken up by photographs. These we were urged to examine. One saw people hanged and people about to be hanged; people on tips of their toes. The executioners stood around smoking. There were piles of corpses everywhere. Some were naked. Men and women with their genitals showing. That made some kid laugh.

Then we saw a man having his throat cut. The killer sat on the man's chest with a knife in his hand. He seemed pleased to be photographed. The victim's eyes I don't remember. A few men stood around gawking. There were clouds in the sky.

There were always clouds, as well as blades of grass, tree stumps, bushes and rocks no one was paying any attention to. At times the earth was covered with snow. A miserable, teeth-chattering January morning and someone making someone's life even more miserable. Or the rain would be falling. A small hard rain that would wash the blood off the hands immediately, that would make one of the killers catch a bad cold. I imagined him sitting that same night with his feet in a bucket of hot water and sipping tea.

That occurred to me much later. Now that we had seen all there was to see, we were made to sit on the lawn outside the museum and eat our lunch. It was poor fare. Most of us had plum jam spread on slices of bread. A few had lard sprinkled with paprika. One kid had nothing but bread and scallions. Everybody thought that was funny. Someone threw his thick slice of black bread in the air and got it caught in a tree. The poor fellow tried to get it down by throwing pebbles at it. He kept missing. Then, he wanted to climb the tree. He kept sliding back. Even our teacher who came over to take a look thought it was hilarious.

As for the grass, there was plenty of it, each blade distinct and carefully sharpened, as it were. There were also clouds in the sky and many large flies of the kind one encounters at slaughterhouses that kept interrupting our thoughts and our laughter.

And here's what went through my head just the other night as I lay awake in the dark:

The story had nothing to do with what you were talking about.

The story had everything to do with what we were talking about.

I can think of a hundred objections.

Only idiots want something neat, something categorical . . . and I never talk unless I know!

Aha! You're mixing poetry and philosophy. Bertrand Russell wouldn't give you the time of day. . . .

"Everything looks very busy to me," says Jasper Johns, and that's the problem. I remember a strange cat, exceedingly emaciated, that scratched on my door the day I was scratching my head over Hegel's phenomenology.

Who said, "Whatever can be thought must be fictitious"?

You got me there! Error is my first love. I'm shouting her name from the rooftops.

Still and all! And nevertheless! And above all! Let's not forget "above all."

"The Only Humane Way to Catch a Metaphysical Mouse" is the name of the book I work on between three and four in the morning.

Here's what Nietzsche said to the ceiling: "The rank of the philosopher is determined by the rank of his laughter." But he couldn't really laugh. No matter how hard he tried he couldn't laugh.

I know because I'm a connoisseur of chaos. All the good looking oxymorons come to visit me in my bed. . . .

Wallace Stevens has several beautiful poems about solitary readers. "The House Was Quiet and the World Was Calm" is one. It speaks of a "truth in a calm world." It happens! The world and the mind being so calm that truth becomes visible.

It must be late night—"where shines the light that lets be the things that are"—which might be a good description of insomnia. The solitude of the reader and the solitude of the philosopher drawing together. The impression that one is on the verge of anticipating another man's next turn of thought. My own solitude doubled, tripled, as if I were the only one awake on the earth.

Understanding depends upon the relation of what I am to what I have been. The being of the moment, in other words. Consciousness waking up conscience—waking up history. Consciousness as clarity and history as the dark night of the soul.

The pleasures of philosophy are the pleasures of reduction—the epiphanies of saying in a few words what seems to be the gist of the matter. It pleases me, for instance, to think of both philosophy and poetry as concerned with Being. What is a lyric poem, one might say, but an acknowledgment of the Being of beings. The philosopher thinks Being; the poet in the lyric poem re-creates the experience of Being.

History, on the other hand, is antireductive. Nothing tidy about it. Chaos! Bedlam! Hopeless tangle! My history and the History of this century like a child and his blind mother on the street—and the blind mother leading the way! You'd think the sole purpose of history is to stand truth happily upon its head.

Poor poetry! For some reason I can't get Buster Keaton out of my mind. Poetry as imperturbable Keaton alone with the woman he loves on an ocean liner set adrift on the stormy sea. Or, poetry as that kid throwing stones at a tree to bring down his lunch. Wise enough to play the fool, perhaps?

And always the dialectic: I have Don Quixote and his windmills in my head and Sancho Panza and his mule in my heart.

That's a figure of speech—one figure among many other figures of speech. Who could live without them? Do they tell the truth? Do they conceal it? I don't know. That's why I keep going back to philosophy.

It is morning. It is night. The book is open. The text is difficult, the text is momentarily opaque. My mind is wandering. My mind is struggling to grasp the always elusive . . . the always hinting . . . What do you call it?

It, it, I keep calling it. An infinity of *it* without a single antecedent—like a hum in my ear.

Just then, about to give up, I find the following on a page of Heidegger:

> No thinker has ever entered into another thinker's solitude. Yet it is only from its solitude that all thinking, in a hidden mode, speaks to the thinking that comes after or that went before.

And it all comes together: poetry, philosophy, history. I see—in the sense of being able to picture and feel the human weight of another's solitude. So many of them. Seated with a book. Day breaking. Thought becoming image. Image becoming thought.

[1987]

On the Essay

VIRGINIA WOOLF

(1882–1941)

The Modern Essay*

As Mr Rhys truly says, it is unnecessary to go profoundly into the history and origin of the essay—whether it derives from Socrates or Siranney the Persian—since, like all living things, its present is more important than its past. Moreover, the family is widely spread; and while some of its representatives have risen in the world and wear their coronets with the best, others pick up a precarious living in the gutter near Fleet Street.† The form, too, admits variety. The essay can be short or long, serious or trifling, about God and Spinoza, or about turtles and Cheapside. But as we turn over the pages of these five little volumes, containing essays written between 1870 and 1920, certain principles appear to control the chaos, and we detect in the short period under review something like the progress of history.

Of all forms of literature, however, the essay is the one which least calls for the use of long words. The principle which controls it is simply that it should give pleasure; the desire which impels us when we take it from the shelf is simply to receive pleasure. Everything in an essay must be subdued to that end. It should lay us under a spell with its first word, and we should only wake, refreshed, with its last. In the interval we may pass through the most various experiences of amusement, surprise, interest, indignation; we may soar to the heights of fantasy with Lamb or plunge to the depths of wisdom with Bacon, but we must never be roused. The essay must lap us about and draw its curtain across the world.

So great a feat is seldom accomplished, though the fault may well be as much on the reader's side as on the writer's. Habit and lethargy have dulled his palate. A novel has a story, a poem rhyme; but what art can the essayist use in these short lengths of prose to sting us wide awake and fix us in a trance which is not sleep but rather an intensification of life—a basking, with every faculty alert, in the sun of pleasure? He must know—that is the first essential—how to write. His learning may be as profound as Mark Pattison's, but in an essay it must be so fused by the magic of writing that not a fact juts out, not a dogma tears the surface of the texture. Macaulay in one way, Froude in another, did this superbly over and over again. They have blown more knowledge into us in the course of one essay than the innumerable chapters of a hundred text-books. But when Mark Pattison has to tell us, in the space of thirty-five little pages, about Montaigne, we feel that he had not previously assimilated M. Grün. M. Grün was a gentleman who once wrote a bad book. M. Grün and his book should have been embalmed for our perpetual delight in amber. But the process

---

*Originally published in a slightly different form in 1922, this essay draw upon the publication of Ernest Rhys's *Modern English Essays, 1870–1920* [5 vols., London, 1922]. Virtually every proper name in this essay refers to an essayist included in Rhys's anthology.

†London's newspaper publishing district.

is fatiguing; it requires more time and perhaps more temper than Pattison had at his command. He served M. Grün up raw, and he remains a crude berry among the cooked meats, upon which our teeth must grate for ever. Something of the sort applies to Matthew Arnold and a certain translator of Spinoza. Literal truth-telling and finding fault with a culprit for his good are out of place in an essay, where everything should be for our good and rather for eternity than for the March number of the *Fortnightly Review.* But if the voice of the scold should never be heard in this narrow plot, there is another voice which is as a plague of locusts—the voice of a man stumbling drowsily among loose words, clutching aimlessly at vague ideas, the voice, for example, of Mr Hutton in the following passage:

> Add to this that his married life was brief, only seven years and a half, being unexpectedly cut short, and that his passionate reverence for his wife's memory and genius—in his own words, 'a religion'—was one which, as he must have been perfectly sensible, he could not make to appear otherwise than extravagant, not to say an hallucination, in the eyes of the rest of mankind, and yet that he was possessed by an irresistible yearning to attempt to embody it in all the tender and enthusiastic hyperbole of which it is so pathetic to find a man who gained his fame by his 'dry-light' a master, and it is impossible not to feel that the human incidents in Mr Mill's career are very sad.

A book could take that blow, but it sinks an essay. A biography in two volumes is indeed the proper depository; for there, where the licence is so much wider, and hints and glimpses of outside things make part of the feast (we refer to the old type of Victorian volume), these yawns and stretches hardly matter, and have indeed some positive value of their own. But that value, which is contributed by the reader, perhaps illicitly, in his desire to get as much into the book from all possible sources as he can, must be ruled out here.

There is no room for the impurities of literature in an essay. Somehow or other, by dint of labour or bounty of nature, or both combined, the essay must be pure—pure like water or pure like wine, but pure from dullness, deadness, and deposits of extraneous matter. Of all writers in the first volume, Walter Pater best achieves this arduous task, because before setting out to write his essay ('Notes on Leonardo da Vinci') he has somehow contrived to get his material fused. He is a learned man, but it is not knowledge of Leonardo that remains with us, but a vision, such as we get in a good novel where everything contributes to bring the writer's conception as a whole before us. Only here, in the essay, where the bounds are so strict and facts have to be used in their nakedness, the true writer like Walter Pater makes these limitations yield their own quality. Truth will give it authority; from its narrow limits he will get shape and intensity; and then there is no more fitting place for some of those ornaments which the old writers loved and we, by calling them ornaments, presumably despise. Nowadays nobody would have the courage to embark on the once famous description of Leonardo's lady who has

> learned the secrets of the grave; and has been a diver in deep seas and keeps their fallen day about her; and trafficked for strange webs with Eastern merchants; and, as Leda, was the mother of Helen of Troy, and, as Saint Anne, the mother of Mary . . .

The passage is too thumb-marked to slip naturally into the context. But when we come unexpectedly upon 'the smiling of women and the motion of great waters', or upon 'full of the refinement of the dead, in sad, earth-coloured raiment, set with pale stones', we suddenly remember that we have ears and we have eyes, and that the English language fills a long array of stout volumes with innumerable words, many of which are of more than one syllable. The only living Englishman who ever looks into these volumes is, of course, a gentleman of Polish extraction. But doubtless our abstention saves as much gush, much rhetoric, much high-stepping and cloud-prancing, and for the sake of the prevailing sobriety and hard-headedness we should be willing to barter the splendour of Sir Thomas Browne and the vigour of Swift.

Yet, if the essay admits more properly than biography or fiction of sudden boldness and metaphor, and can be polished till every atom of its surface shines, there are dangers in that too. We are soon in sight of ornament. Soon the current, which is the life-blood of literature, runs slow; and instead of sparkling and flashing or moving with a quieter impulse which has a deeper excitement, words coagulate together in frozen sprays which, like the grapes on a Christmas-tree, glitter for a single night, but are dusty and garish the day after. The temptation to decorate is great where the theme may be of the slightest. What is there to interest another in the fact that one has enjoyed a walking tour, or has amused oneself by rambling down Cheapside and looking at the turtles in Mr Sweeting's shop window? Stevenson and Samuel Butler chose very different methods of exciting our interest in these domestic themes. Stevenson, of course, trimmed and polished and set out his matter in the traditional eighteenth-century form. It is admirably done, but we cannot help feeling anxious, as the essay proceeds, lest the material may give out under the craftsman's fingers. The ingot is so small, the manipulation so incessant. And perhaps that is why the peroration—

> to sit still and contemplate—to remember the faces of women without desire, to be pleased by the great deeds of men without envy, to be everything and everywhere in sympathy and yet content to remain where and what you are—

has the sort of insubstantiality which suggests that by the time he got to the end he had left himself nothing solid to work with. Butler adopted the very opposite method. Think your own thoughts, he seems to say, and speak them as plainly as you can. These turtles in the shop window which appear to leak out of their shells through heads and feet suggest a fatal faithfulness to a fixed idea. And so, striding unconcernedly from one idea to the next, we traverse a large stretch of ground; observe that a wound in the solicitor is a very serious thing; that Mary Queen of Scots wears surgical boots and is subject to fits near the Horse Shoe in Tottenham Court Road; take it for granted that no one really cares about Æschylus; and so, with many amusing anecdotes and some profound reflections, reach the peroration, which is that, as he had been told not to see more in Cheapside than he could get into twelve pages of the *Universal Review,* he had better stop. And yet obviously Butler is at least as careful of our pleasure as Stevenson; and to write like oneself and call it not writing is a much harder exercise in style than to write like Addison and call it writing well.

But, however much they differ individually, the Victorian essayists yet had something in common. They wrote at greater length than is now usual, and they wrote for a public which had not only time to sit down to its magazine seriously, but a high, if peculiarly Victorian, standard of culture by which to judge it. It was worth while to speak out upon serious matters in an essay; and there was nothing absurd in writing as well as one possibly could when, in a month or two, the same public which had welcomed the essay in a magazine would carefully read it once more in a book. But a change came from a small

audience of cultivated people to a larger audience of people who were not quite so cultivated. The change was not altogether for the worse. In volume iii, we find Mr Birrell and Mr Beerbohm. It might even be said that there was a reversion to the classic type, and that the essay by losing its size and something of its sonority was approaching more nearly the essay of Addison and Lamb. At any rate, there is a great gulf between Mr Birrell on Carlyle and the essay which one may suppose that Carlyle would have written upon Mr Birrell. There is little similarity between *A Cloud of Pinafores,* by Max Beerbohm, and *A Cynic's Apology,* by Leslie Stephen. But the essay is alive; there is no reason to despair. As the conditions change so the essayist, most sensitive of all plants to public opinion, adapts himself, and if he is good makes the best of the change, and if he is bad the worst. Mr Birrell is certainly good; and so we find that, though he has dropped a considerable amount of weight, his attack is much more direct and his movement more supple. But what did Mr Beerbohm give to the essay and what did he take from it? That is a much more complicated question, for here we have an essayist who has concentrated on the work and is without doubt the prince of his profession.

What Mr Beerbohm gave was, of course, himself. This presence, which has haunted the essay fitfully from the time of Montaigne, had been in exile since the death of Charles Lamb. Matthew Arnold was never to his readers Matt, nor Walter Pater affectionately abbreviated in a thousand homes to Wat. They gave us much, but that they did not give. Thus, some time in the nineties, it must have surprised readers accustomed to exhortation, information, and denunciation to find themselves familiarly addressed by a voice which seemed to belong to a man no larger than themselves. He was affected by private joys and sorrows, and had no gospel to preach and no learning to impart. He was himself, simply and directly, and himself he has remained. Once again we have an essayist capable of using the essayist's most proper but most dangerous and delicate tool. He has brought personality into literature, not unconsciously and impurely, but so consciously and purely that we do not know whether there is any relation between Max the essayist and Mr Beerbohm the man. We only know that the spirit of personality permeates every word that he writes. The triumph is the triumph of style. For it is only by knowing how to write that you can make use in literature of your self; that self which, while it is essential to literature, is also its most dangerous antagonist. Never to be yourself and yet always—that is the problem. Some of the essayists in Mr Rhys' collection, to be frank, have not altogether succeeded in solving it. We are nauseated by the sight of trivial personalities decomposing in the eternity of print. As talk, no doubt, it was charming, and certainly the writer is a good fellow to meet over a bottle of beer. But literature is stern; it is no use being charming, virtuous, or even learned and brilliant into the bargain, unless, she seems to reiterate, you fulfil her first condition—to know how to write.

This art is possessed to perfection by Mr Beerbohm. But he has not searched the dictionary for polysyllables. He has not moulded firm periods or seduced our ears with intricate cadences and strange melodies. Some of his companions—Henley and Stevenson, for example—are momentarily more impressive. But *A Cloud of Pinafores* has in it that indescribable inequality, stir, and final expressiveness which belong to life and to life alone. You have not finished with it because you have read it, any more than friendship is ended because it is time to part. Life wells up and alters and adds. Even things in a book-case change if they are alive; we find ourselves wanting to meet them again; we find them altered. So we look back upon essay after essay by Mr Beerbohm, knowing that, come September or May, we shall sit down with them and talk. Yet it is true that the essayist is the most

sensitive of all writers to public opinion. The drawing-room is the place where a great deal of reading is done nowadays, and the essays of Mr Beerbohm lie, with an exquisite appreciation of all that the position exacts, upon the drawing-room table. There is no gin about; no strong tobacco, no puns, drunkenness, or insanity. Ladies and gentlemen talk together, and some things, of course, are not said.

But if it would be foolish to attempt to confine Mr Beerbohm to one room, it would be still more foolish, unhappily, to make him, the artist, the man who gives us only his best, the representative of our age. There are no essays by Mr Beerbohm in the fourth or fifth volumes of the present collection. His age seems already a little distant, and the drawing-room table, as it recedes, begins to look rather like an altar where, once upon a time, people deposited offerings—fruit from their own orchards, gifts carved with their own hands. Now once more the conditions have changed. The public needs essays as much as ever, and perhaps even more. The demand for the light middle not exceeding fifteen hundred words, or in special cases seventeen hundred and fifty, much exceeds the supply. Where Lamb wrote one essay and Max perhaps writes two, Mr Belloc at a rough computation produces three hundred and sixty-five. They are very short, it is true. Yet with what dexterity the practised essayist will utilise his space—beginning as close to the top of the sheet as possible, judging precisely how far to go, when to turn, and how, without sacrificing a hair's-breadth of paper, to wheel about and alight accurately upon the last word his editor allows! As a feat of skill it is well worth watching. But the personality upon which Mr Belloc, like Mr Beerbohm, depends suffers in the process. It comes to us not with the natural richness of the speaking voice, but strained and thin and full of mannerisms and affectations, like the voice of a man shouting through a megaphone to a crowd on a windy day. 'Little friends, my readers', he says in the essay called 'An Unknown Country', and he goes on to tell us how—

> There was a shepherd the other day at Findon Fair who had come from the east by Lewes with sheep, and who had in his eyes that reminiscence of horizons which makes the eyes of shepherds and of mountaineers different from the eyes of other men. . . . I went with him to hear what he had to say, for shepherds talk quite differently from other men.

Happily this shepherd had little to say, even under the stimulus of the inevitable mug of beer, about the Unknown Country, for the only remark that he did make proves him either a minor poet, unfit for the care of sheep, or Mr Belloc himself masquerading with a fountain pen. That is the penalty which the habitual essayist must now be prepared to face. He must masquerade. He cannot afford the time either to be himself or to be other people. He must skim the surface of thought and dilute the strength of personality. He must give us a worn weekly halfpenny instead of a solid sovereign once a year.

But it is not Mr Belloc only who has suffered from the prevailing conditions. The essays which bring the collection to the year 1920 may not be the best of their authors' work, but, if we except writers like Mr Conrad and Mr Hudson, who have strayed into essay writing accidentally, and concentrate upon those who write essays habitually, we shall find them a good deal affected by the change in their circumstances. To write weekly, to write daily, to write shortly, to write for busy people catching trains in the morning or for tired people coming home in the evening, is a heart-breaking task for men who know good writing from bad. They do it, but instinctively draw out of harm's way anything precious that might be damaged by contact with the public, or anything sharp that might irritate its

skin. And so, if one reads Mr Lucas, Mr Lynd, or Mr Squire in the bulk, one feels that a common grayness silvers everything. They are as far removed from the extravagant beauty of Walter Pater as they are from the intemperate candour of Leslie Stephen. Beauty and courage are dangerous spirits to bottle in a column and a half; and thought, like a brown paper parcel in a waistcoat pocket, has a way of spoiling the symmetry of an article. It is a kind, tired, apathetic world for which they write, and the marvel is that they never cease to attempt, at least, to write well.

But there is no need to pity Mr Clutton Brock for this change in the essayist's conditions. He has clearly made the best of his circumstances and not the worst. One hesitates even to say that he has had to make any conscious effort in the matter, so naturally has he effected the transition from the private essayist to the public, from the drawing-room to the Albert Hall. Paradoxically enough, the shrinkage in size has brought about a corresponding expansion of individuality. We have no longer the 'I' of Max and of Lamb, but the 'we' of public bodies and other sublime personages. It is 'we' who go to hear the *Magic Flute*; 'we' who ought to profit by it; 'we', in some mysterious way, who, in our corporate capacity, once upon a time actually wrote it. For music and literature and art must submit to the same generalisation or they will not carry to the farthest recesses of the Albert Hall. That the voice of Mr Clutton Brock, so sincere and so disinterested, carries such a distance and reaches so many without pandering to the weakness of the mass or its passions must be a matter of legitimate satisfaction to us all. But while 'we' are gratified, 'I', that unruly partner in the human fellowship, is reduced to despair. 'I' must always think things for himself, and feel things for himself. To share them in a diluted form with the majority of well-educated and well-intentioned men and women is for him sheer agony; and while the rest of us listen intently and profit profoundly, 'I' slips off to the woods and the fields and rejoices in a single blade of grass or a solitary potato.

In the fifth volume of modern essays, it seems, we have got some way from pleasure and the art of writing. But in justice to the essayists of 1920 we must be sure that we are not praising the famous because they have been praised already and the dead because we shall never meet them wearing spats in Piccadilly. We must know what we mean when we say that they can write and give us pleasure. We must compare them; we must bring out the quality. We must point to this and say it is good because it is exact, truthful, and imaginative:

> Nay, retire men cannot when they would; neither will they, when it were Reason; but are impatient of Privateness, even in age and sickness, which require the shadow: like old Townsmen: that will still be sitting at their street door, though thereby they offer Age to Scorn . . .

and to this, and say it is bad because it is loose, plausible, and commonplace:

> With courteous and precise cynicism on his lips, he thought of quiet virginal chambers, of waters singing under the moon, of terraces where taintless music sobbed into the open night, of pure maternal mistresses with protecting arms and vigilant eyes, of fields slumbering in the sunlight, of leagues of ocean heaving under warm tremulous heavens, of hot ports, gorgeous and perfumed . . .

It goes on, but already we are bemused with sound and neither feel nor hear. The comparison makes us suspect that the art of writing has for backbone some fierce attachment to an idea. It is on the back of an idea, something believed in with conviction or seen with precision and thus compelling words to its shape, that the diverse company which includes Lamb and Bacon, and Mr Beerbohm and Hudson, and Vernon Lee and Mr Conrad, and Leslie Stephen and Butler and Walter Pater reaches the farther shore. Very various talents have helped or hindered the passage of the idea into words. Some scrape through painfully; others fly with every wind favouring. But Mr Belloc and Mr Lucas and Mr Squire are not fiercely attached to anything in itself. They share the contemporary dilemma—that lack of an obstinate conviction which lifts ephemeral sounds through the misty sphere of anybody's language to the land where there is a perpetual marriage, a perpetual union. Vague as all definitions are, a good essay must have this permanent quality about it; it must draw its curtain round us, but it must be a curtain that shuts us in, not out.

[1925]

ELIZABETH HARDWICK

(1916–)

Its Only Defense: Intelligence and Sparkle

About the Author: One of North America's major essayists, Elizabeth Hardwick edited the inaugural volume of the *Best American Essays* series. Hers has been an innovative voice helping to forecast the directions of the contemporary essay through attention to craft and through critical reflection.

The essay? Thousands of pages of prose are published each month and not many of them are given to fiction. Perhaps most of the pages are information about the events of the day or the week and are not to be thought of as essays. What is this thunder and hail of newsprint felling the forests of the world? Journalism? Not quite, not nowadays. The knowing would not restrict the word "journalism" to mere information, if information can be thought of as *mere.* Nowadays journalism is a restless and predatory engagement, having established its imperial mandate under the phrase "new journalism," established its claim with such occupying force that the phrase itself is no longer needed, no longer defining.

If we cannot be sure we are reading journalism according to the rules of the professional schools, we are even less certain that we are reading the elevated essay. Still, there is something called the essay, and volumes by individual writers are published under the title. Even then the term does not provide a serenity of precision, it is not altogether genuine in its shape, like fiction or poetry. It does not even have the advantage of pointing to scale, since some essays are short and many are long and most incline to a condition of unexpressed hyphenation: the critical essay, the autobiographical essay, the travel essay, the political—and so on and so on.

There is a self-congratulatory sense in the essay. It wants to signify that what has been offered is not a lesser offering, not just a review, a sketch, a "piece"—odd, useful word—summoned to feed the hungry space of periodicals. Sometimes the vagrant coinage "essayistic" appears in the press, and this is bad news for the language, since it indicates an extension of murky similarity to what is itself more than a little cloudy. Of course, we always know what a barbarism is trying to say, its nature is to indicate the struggle for definition.

To be like an essay, if not quite the real thing, means that, in a practical bit of prose, attention has been paid to expressiveness and that to gain expressiveness certain freedoms have been exercised, freedoms illicit in the minds of some readers, freedoms not so much exercised as seized over the border. Essays are aggressive even if the mind from which they come is fair, humane and, when it is to the point, disinterested. Hazlitt, in an essay on the poets living in his own time, writes: "Mrs. Hannah More is another celebrated modern poetess, and I believe still living. She has written a great deal which I have never read." It might take Mrs. More, if indeed she lived still, some time to figure out just what was being said.

The aggressiveness of the essay is the assumption of the authority to speak in one's own voice, and usually the authority is earned by previous performance. We see a name on the cover or inside the pages and we submit to the reading with some eagerness, which may be friendly eagerness or not. One of the assumptions of the essayist is the right to make his own mistakes, since he speaks only for himself, allowing for the philosopher's cunning observation that "in my opinion" actually asserts "all reasonable men will agree." This claim is sometimes disputed by an elected authority, the editor, who may think too many villages have been overrun by the marauder. Since the freedom of the open spaces is the condition of the essay, too much correction and surgical intervention turns the composition into something else, perhaps an article, that fertile source of profit and sometimes pleasure in the cultural landscape.

William Gass, in what must be called an essay, a brilliant one, about Emerson, an essayist destined from the cradle, makes a distinction between the article and the essay. Having been employed by the university and having heard so many of his colleagues "doing an article on," Mr. Gass has come to think of the article as "that awful object" because it is under the command of defensiveness in footnote, reference, coverage, and would also pretend that all must be useful and certain, even if it is "very likely a veritable Michelin of misdirection." If the article has a certain sheen and professional polish, it is the polish of "the scrubbed step"—practical economy and neatness. The essay, in Mr. Gass's view, is a great meadow of style and personal manner, freed from the need for defense except that provided by an individual intelligence and sparkle. We consent to watch a mind at work, without agreement often, but only for pleasure. Knowledge hereby attained, great indeed, is again wanted for the pleasure of itself.

We would not want to think of the essay as the country of old men, but it is doubtful that the slithery form, wearisomely vague and as chancy as trying to catch a fish in the open hand, can be taught. Already existing knowledge is so often required. Having had mothers and fathers and the usual miserable battering of the sense of self by life may arouse the emotional pulsations of a story or a poem; but feeling is not sufficient for the essay. Comparisons roam about it, familiarity with those who have plowed the field before, shrewdness concerning the little corner or big corner that may remain for the intrusion of one's own thoughts. Tact and appropriateness play a part. How often we read a beginner's review that compares a thin thing to a fat one. "John Smith, like Tolstoy, is very interested in the way men interact under the conditions of battle." Well, no.

Fortunately, the essay is not a closed shop, and the pages do vibrate again and again with the appearance of a new name with no credentials admired or despised. An unknown practitioner of the peculiar animation of the prose of an essay takes up the cause. It is an occasion for happiness, since it is always astonishing that anyone will write an essay. Some write them not once but more or less regularly. To wake up in the morning under a command to animate the stones of an idea, the clods of research, the uncertainty of memory, is the punishment of the vocation. And all to be done without the aid of end rhyme and off rhyme and buried assonance, without an imagined character putting on a hat and going into the street.

Those with the least gift are the most anxious to receive a commission. It seems to them that there lies waiting a topic, a new book, a performance, and that this is known as material. The true prose writer knows there is nothing given, no idea, no text or play seen last evening, until an assault has taken place, the forced domination that we call "putting it in your own words." Talking about, thinking about a project bears little relation to the composition; enthusiasm boils down with distressing speed to a paragraph, often one of mischievous banality. To proceed from musing to writing is to feel a robbery has taken place. And certainly there has been a loss; the loss of the smiles and ramblings and discussions so much friendlier to ambition than the cold hardship of writing.

Essays are addressed to a public in which some degree of equity exists between the writer and the reader. Shared knowledge is a necessity, although the information need not be concrete. Perhaps it is more to be thought of as a sharing of the experience of reading certain kinds of texts, texts with omissions and elisions, leaps. The essayist does not stop to identify the common ground; he will not write, "Picasso, the great Spanish painter who lived long in France." On the other hand, essays are about something, something we may not have had reason to study and master, often matters about which we are quite ignorant. Elegance of presentation, reflection made interesting and significant, easily lead us to engage our reading minds with Zulus, herbaceous borders in the English garden, marriage records in 18th-century France, Japanese scrolls.

In the contemporary essay, as in contemporary fiction, the use of the first-person narrator or expositor has become so widespread it must be seen as a convenience. This is a puzzle having to do, perhaps, not with self-assertion to fill every available silence, but with modesty, a fear of presumption. In fiction a loss of movement is accepted by the choice of "I" in order to gain relief from knowing and imagining without the possibility of being there to know. That at least may be one of the esthetic considerations. Also, the dominance of the first-person narrator in current fiction seems to reflect uncertainty about the classical conception of character; often the contemporary psyche is not seen as a lump of traits so much as a mist of inconsistencies, flights, constant improvisations. It is more agreeable to this sense of things to write "It seemed to me" rather than "It was."

In the essay we find the intrusion of the "I" even where little is autobiographical. In my mind I imagine a quite obscure reflection beginning, "I pulled into the filling station with my wife in the front seat and the kids restless and hungry in the back, and there I saw an interesting commercial logo, a sort of unicorn-horse that recalled to me certain medieval illuminated texts." What will follow is as it is, learned, perhaps difficult. How to account for the filling station, except as a fear of presumption about the subject, a search for immediacy, a loosening of the boundaries of prose? Of course it doesn't always work. There are many things worth knowing that cannot be made familiar.

De Quincey in his memoir about the Lake Poets tells of a Mr. Wedgwood, a gifted, loved, quite rich young man, patron of Samuel Coleridge, the tormented genius who very much needed a patron. Mr. Wedgwood sought to distract himself from feelings of depression and lassitude by buying a butcher shop, where the wrangling abuse would force him to a high level of response. The experiment was not happy. There is a certain kind of

polemical essay around that is a butcher shop of raw, hacked opinion which arouses a sure relief from torpor by encouraging dissent and violent rebuttal.

Intemperance in political writing has its hacks and its celebrated practitioners. As Hugh Trevor Roper writes in his introduction to a volume of essays by the great Macaulay, "Macaulay could be very unjust to persons. He could also be vindictive. His essay on Boswell's 'Life of Johnson' is both. He is unjust to Johnson, unjust to Boswell, and positively vindictive to the editor, Croker, who was not only a Tory but a member of parliament who enraged Macaulay by opposing him in the debates on parliamentary reform." Macaulay was a Whig. It is nearly always useful to be aware of the mindset of essayists because a determined coloration of belief may spread itself far and wide and land not only on the political field but on the head of the novelist, the film maker, the historian. So it has been; so it is yet. The mastery of expository prose, the rhythm of sentences, the pacing, the sudden flash of unexpected vocabulary, redeem polemic, and, in any case, no one is obliged to agree. But ill-written, pompously self-righteous, lamely jocular forays offend because an air of immature certainty surrounds them. Too great a degree of exhortation and corrective insistence makes us wish for the tone of the earlier English "familiar essay," with its calm love of nature and tolerance of human frailty.

The essay form exists in so many shapes and sizes and is directed to every point of the compass. It is nothing less than the reflection of all there is: art, personal experience, places, literature, portraiture, politics, science, music, education—and just thought itself in orbit. Roland Barthes has written an essay on wrestling, the spectacle of it; Hazlitt composed "The Fight": "Reader, have you ever seen a fight? If not you have pleasure to come, at least if it is a fight between the Gas-man and Bill Neate." Proust wrote an essay "On Reading"; Sartre has written two essays on Faulkner, and thousands have been written on Proust and Sartre and again on Faulkner.

There is nearly always a time when the novelist and poet will stand aside to create something other. This will be an imaginative essay, and often among the most beautiful and arresting we know. Such essays tend to be offhand and intuitive, flashing and yet exacting—D. H. Lawrence's, for example. Knowing how to write—there is no substitute for that. The writer may be said to precede the material, and that is why academic writing, where the material is the fundamental capital, is so often like hoeing a hard field in winter. However, being a professor and knowing a great deal about some things does not make one an academic writer. Only the withholding gods can accomplish that.

So there is no end to the essay, and no beginning. Walter Benjamin makes a visit to Moscow: "Each thought, each day, each life lies here as on a laboratory table." The poet Jules Laforgue goes to Berlin to be in the service of the Empress: "She has been bored, she is still bored, and she still dreams." Joan Didion has been to Alcatraz in California: "Alcatraz Island is covered with flowers now: orange and yellow nasturtiums, geraniums, sweet grass, blue iris, black-eyed Susans. Candytuft springs up through the cracked concrete in the exercise yard."

The essay, at least in reduction, is to be thought of as popular. Think of the number published. In the lightest examples—short sentences, short altogether, with photographs surrounding the shortness—it appears that words here and there about celebrities are gratifying in the gross. This cannot be the search for information, since there is little information in them. Libel is the handmaiden of information about the living. The appeal of celebrity journalism seems to rest upon a promise and the acceptance of the fact that the promise will again and again be unfilled. To know the sanitized items, in almost infinite repetition, about the famous indicates an overwhelming appetite. Born somewhere, lives somewhere, may have a "wonderful" child, possibly a mate to whom, for the time being, everything is owed. Parents somewhere and, nearer, the career itself. "I want to improve my acting." All of this is prose of some kind, a commission arranged and concluded.

The true essay, making as it does a contribution to the cultural life, is not so simple. Its celebrities are likely to be long-dead painters, writers and thinkers; living ones not memorable in photographs, and not in a synopsis. Insofar as essays give information, and of course they do in their way, a peculiar condition of reciprocity, reader participation, prevails. Wit, the abrupt reversal, needs to strike a receptive ear or eye or else the surprise is erased, struck down. Expressiveness is an addition to statement, and hidden in its clauses is an intelligence uncomfortable with dogmatism, wanting to make allowances for the otherwise case, the emendation.

A well-filled mind itself makes the composition of essays more thorny rather than more smooth, with everything readily available. There is seldom absolute true assertion unless one is unaware. Words and phrases, ideas and opinions, invading the vast area of even the narrowest topic must fall back on a fluency of reference, reference sometimes merely hinted, if the convincing is to be achieved. Conviction itself is partial and the case is never decided. The essay is not the ground of verdicts. It rests on singularity rather than consensus.

Montaigne: can there be a reflection upon the essay without the dropping of this sacred name? Emerson finds Montaigne a "representative man" under the description, the skeptic, as Shakespeare is the poet. A close reading of the essay will show that Emerson writes around Montaigne rather than about him. However much he may admire the French master's candor and "uncanonical levity," the men are not attuned, differences in temperament being too great. Mr. Gass, in his essay on Emerson, slides into a diversion on Montaigne and notes, "Have we digressed, however? I hope so." Hannah Arendt in her writing on the great modern essayist, Walter Benjamin, remarks upon the difference in the social station of the modern essayist when compared with the world of the classical European man of letters.

The world of the American essay is a democratic one, a meritocracy. And much more so now than in the time of Emerson, a man from the old Harvard, well educated in a nation commonly much less so. The tones of "Self-Reliance" and even of "Compensation" would not appear to be suitable orchestration today. Confidence it has, if very different from the given, worldly self-confidence of Montaigne. Emerson's confidence, his attraction to enlightened sermonizing, is addressed to an audience still small enough for instruction. "The man must be so much, that he must make all circumstances indifferent."

Modes of conduct—except for that of foreign policy, which is impersonal in spite of pleas to view it as a burning pan on the stove in the kitchen of every citizen—commend themselves as a subject mostly to cranks and uplifters and health fiends. If we would in the manner of Lord Chesterfield tell a young gentleman how to behave, the pages might take the form of case histories of drug addicts, dropouts, and statistics on earning power. The American essay, the contemporary one, is personal in its manners, as a display, and also as a wrestling with means, how to shape the exposition. Little is proposed as a model. The personality of the literary critic is sharp and—with the most gifted—eccentric, but it wishes to reveal a difference in itself, not to promote imitation in manner, but only imitation in opinion, since every opinion loves a follower.

A collection of essays is a collection of variations. The theme or the plot is not an

imaginary construction, as in the novel, but arises from some factuality of history, culture, politics, personal experience, and above all from general ideas. Yet the most interesting essays will have the self-propelled interior life of imaginative literature, and this is true even when they are responses to an occasion. Expertise, an acquisition promoted by usefulness, is less cogent to the essay than passion, less to the point than is the soloist's personal signature flowing through the text. Such is the art of the essay.

[1986]

PHILLIP LOPATE

(1943–)

The Essay Lives—in Disguise

About the Author: A novelist and poet, Phillip Lopate is probably best known for his astute commentary on contemporary American middle-class life. His essays, as well as his examinations of the essay as a literary form, put us back in touch with much of the world around us.

The informal or familiar essay is a wonderfully tolerant form, able to accommodate rumination, memoir, anecdote, diatribe, scholarship, fantasy and moral philosophy. It might have an elegant form or an amoebic shapelessness, held together by little more than the author's voice. Working in it liberates you from the structure of the "well-made" short story and allows you to ramble in a way that reflects the mind at work. You have an added freedom at this historical moment, because no one is looking over your shoulder. Nobody much cares. Commercially, essay volumes rank even lower than poetry.

I know, because my last book, a personal essay collection called "Bachelorhood," received lovely critical notices but was less welcomed by booksellers, who had trouble figuring what niche or category to put it in. Autobiography? Short fiction? Self-help? I felt like telling them, "Hey, this category has been around for a long time—Montaigne, Addison and Steele, Hazlitt, remember? I didn't invent it." Yet, realistically, they were right: what had once been a thriving popular tradition had ceased being so. Readers who enjoyed the book often told me so with some surprise, because they didn't think they would like "essays." For them, the word conjured up those dread weekly compositions they were forced to write on the gasoline tax or the draft.

Essays are usually taught all wrong: instead of being celebrated for their delights as literature, they are harnessed to rhetoric and composition, in a two-birds-with-one-stone approach designed to sharpen the students' skills at argumentative persuasion. Equally questionable is the anthology approach, which assigns an essay apiece by a dozen writers along our latest notion of a representative spectrum. It would be much better to read six apiece by two writers, since the essay (particularly the familiar essay) is so rich a vehicle for displaying personality in all its willfully changing facets.

Essays go back at least to classical Greece and Rome, but it was Michel de Montaigne, generally considered the "father of the essay," who first matched the word to the form around 1580. Reading this contemporary of Shakespeare (whom the Bard himself is rumored to have read), we are reminded of the original, pristine meaning and intention of the word, from the French verb *essayer:* to attempt, to try, to make an experimental leap into the unknown. Montaigne understood that, in an essay, the track of a person's thoughts struggling to achieve some understanding of a problem *is* the plot, is the adventure. The essayist must be willing to contradict himself (for which reason an essay is not a legal brief), to digress, and even to end up in an opposite place from where he started. Particularly in Montaigne's magnificent late essays, freefalls that go on for a hundred pages or more, it is possible for the reader to lose all contact with the shore, ostensible subject, top, bottom, until there is nothing to do but follow the companionable voice of Montaigne, thinking alone in the dark. Eventually, one begins to share his confidence that "all subjects are linked with one another," which makes "any topic equally fertile."

It was Montaigne's peculiar project, which he claimed rightly or wrongly was original, to write about the one subject he knew best: himself. As with all succeeding literary self-portraits—or stream-of-consciousness, for that matter—success depended on having an interesting consciousness, and Montaigne was blessed with an undulatingly supple, learned, skeptical, sane and self-attentive one. In point of fact, he frequently strayed onto other subjects, giving his opinion on everything from cannibals to coaches, but we do learn a lot of odd things about the man, down to his bowels and kidney stones. "Sometimes there comes to me a feeling that I should not betray the story of my life," he writes. On the other hand: "No pleasure has any meaning for me without communication."

A modern reader may come away thinking that the old fox still kept a good deal of himself to himself. This is partly because we have upped the ante on autobiographical revelation, but also partly because Montaigne was writing essays, not confessional memoirs; and in an essay it is as permissible, as candid, to chase down a reflection to its source as to confess some past misdeed. In any case, having decided that "the most barbarous of our maladies is to despise our being," he did succeed via the "Essays" in learning to accept himself, by making friends with his mind.

Montaigne's generous development of the essay form, taking it to its outer limits right away, was also daunting. Afterward came an inevitable specialization, which included the very un-Montaigne split between formal and informal essays. It is difficult even now to draw a firm distinction between the two, because elements of one often turn up in the other, and because most of the great essayists were adept at both modes. However, the official version states that the formal essay derived from Francis Bacon and is (to quote the New Columbia Encyclopedia) "dogmatic, impersonal, systematic and expository" and written in a "stately" language, while the informal essay is "personal, intimate, relaxed, conversational, and frequently humorous."

Informal, familiar essays tended to seize on the parade of everyday life: odd characters, small public rituals, vanities, fashions, love and disappointment, the pleasures of solitude, reading, going to plays, walking the streets. It is a very urban form, and it enjoyed a terrific vogue in the coffeehouse London society of the 18th and early 19th centuries, when it enlisted the talents of such stylists as Jonathan Swift, Dr. Johnson (in his "Rambler" series), Addison and Steele, Charles Lamb, William Hazlitt, and the visiting American, Washington Irving. This golden age of the familiar essay was given a boost by the phenomenal growth of newspapers and magazines, all of which needed "smart" copy (of the kind inaugurated by the Spectator papers) that functioned as instructions on manners for their largely middle-class readership.

Much of the casual, *feuilleton* journalism of this period was not as memorable as Addison and Steele—it was, in fact, cynical hackwork. However, the journalistic situation was still fluid enough to afford original thinkers a platform within the public press. The British tolerance for eccentricity seemed especially to encourage their commentators to develop idiosyncratic, independent voices. No one was as cantankerously marginal, in his way, or as willing to write against the grain, as Hazlitt. His energetic prose registered a temperament that passionately, moodily swung between sympathy and scorn. Anyone capable of writing such a bracingly candid essay on "The Pleasures of Hating" could not—as W. C. Fields would say—be all bad. At the same time, Hazlitt's enthusiasms could transform the humblest topic, such as going on a country walk or seeing a prizefight, into descriptions of visionary wholeness.

What many of the best essayists have had—what Hazlitt had in abundance—was quick access to their own blood reactions, so that the merest flash of a prejudice or taste-discrimination might be dragged into the open and defended. Hazlitt's readiness to pass judgment, combined with his receptivity to new impressions, made him a fine critic of painting and the theater; but he ended by antagonizing all of his friends, even the benign, forgiving Charles Lamb. Not that Lamb did not have his contrary side. He too was singled out for "his perverse habit of contradiction," which helped give his prose its peculiar bite. Lamb's "Elia" essays are among the most pungent and funny in the English language.

How I envy readers of the London Magazine, who could pick up a copy in 1820 and encounter a new essay by Hazlitt, Lamb, or both. After their deaths, the familiar essay continued to attract gifted practitioners, like Robert Louis Stevenson, Thomas DeQuincey and Mark Twain, but somehow a little of the vitality seeped out of it, and by the turn of the century it seemed rather toothless and played out. As Stevenson confessed, "Though we are mighty fine fellows nowadays, we cannot write like Hazlitt," Perhaps the very triumph of the early essayists in exploiting the familiar essay form so variously contributed to its temporary decline.

The modernist esthetic was also not particularly kind to this sort of writing, relegating it to some genteel, antiquated nook, "belles lettres"—a phrase increasingly spoken with a sneer, as though implying a sauce without the meat. If "meat" is taken to mean the atrocities of life, it is true that the familiar essay has something obstinately nonapocalyptic about it; the very act of composing such an essay seems to implicate the writer in rationalist-humanist assumptions, which have come to appear suspect under the modernist critique.

Still, it would be unfair to pin the rap on modernism, which Lord knows gets blamed for everything else. One might as well "blame" the decline on what happened to the conversational style of writing. Familiar essays were fundamentally, even self-consciously, conversational: it is no surprise that Swift wrote one of his best short pieces on "Hints Toward an Essay on Conversation"; that Addison and Steele were always analyzing true and false wit; that Hazlitt titled his books "Table Talk," "The Plain Speaker" and "The Round Table"; that Montaigne wrote his own "Of the Art of Discussion" or that Oliver Wendell Holmes actually cast his familiar essays in the form of breakfast table dialogues. Why would a book like Holmes's "The Autocrat of the Breakfast Table," a celebration of good talk that was so popular in its time, be so unlikely today?

I cannot go along with those who say, "The art of conversation has died," because I have no idea what such a statement means. If it did pass on, it happened long before I came on the scene; and I hope I may be forgiven by those with longer memories for not knowing the difference between the real article and those pleasurable verbal exchanges in my life. No, conversation grows and changes as does language; it does not "die." What has departed is conversationally-flavored writing, which implies a speaking relationship between writer and reader. How many readers today would sit still for a direct address by the author? To be called "Gentle Reader" or *"Hypocrite lecteur,"* to have one's arm pinched while dozing off, to be called to attention, flattered, kidded like a real person instead of a privileged fly on the wall—wouldn't most current readers find such devices archaic, intrusive, even impudent? Oh, you wouldn't? Good, we can go back to the old style, which I much prefer.

Maybe what has collapsed is the very fiction of "the educated reader," whom the old essayists seemed to be addressing in their conversational remarks. From Montaigne onward, essayists until this century have invoked a shared literary culture: the Greek and Latin authors and the best of their national poetry. The whole modern essay tradition sprang from quotation. Montaigne's "Essays" and Robert Burton's "The Anatomy Of Melancholy" were essentially outgrowths of the "commonplace book," a personal journal in which quotable passages, literary excerpts and comments were written. Though the early essayists' habit of quotation may seem excessive to a modern taste, it was this display of learning that linked them to their educated reading public and ultimately gave them the authority to speak so personally about themselves.

Such a universal literary culture no longer exists; we have only popular culture to fall back on. While it is true that the old high culture was never really "universal," excluding as it did a great deal of humanity, it is also true that, without it, personal discourse has become more barren. Not only is popular culture not strong enough to cleanse the air of narcissism, but the writer's invocation of its latest bandwagon successes, be it "Indiana Jones" or cabbage patch dolls, comes off as a pandering to the audience.

The average reader of periodicals becomes conditioned to digest pure information, up-to-date, with maybe a smattering of viewpoint disguised as objectivity, and is ill equipped to follow the rambling, cat-and-mouse game of contrariety played by the great essayists of the past. Very few American periodicals today (shall we say none?) support house-essayists to the tune of letting them write regularly and at comfortable length on whatever topics they may choose, however, non-topical. The nearest thing we have to that are columnists. The best of these, like Russell Baker, Ellen Goodman and Leon Hale, are in a sense carrying on the Addison and Steele tradition; they are so good at their professional task of hit-and-run wisdom that I only wish they had the space sometimes to try their essayistic wings for real. The problem with the column format is that it becomes too tight and pat: One idea per piece.

Fran Lebowitz, for instance, is a very clever writer and one not afraid of presenting a cranky persona; but her one-liners have a cumulative sameness of effect that inhibits a true essayistic movement. In the future, I hope, her structures may become more receptive to self-surprise, so that she might say, with Lamb, "I do not know how, upon a subject which I began treating half seriously, I should have fallen upon a recital so eminently painful."

From time to time, I see hopeful panel discussions offered on "The Resurgence of the Essay." Yes, it would be very nice, and it may come about yet. The fact is, however, that very few American writers today are essayists primarily. A good number of the essay books issued each year are essentially random collections of book reviews, speeches, articles and prefaces by authors who have made a name for themselves in other genres. The existence of these collections owes more to the celebrated authors' desire to see all their words between hard covers than it does to any real devotion to the essay form. A tired air of grudgingly graceful civic duty hovers over many of these performances. Still, there are exceptions, like Cynthia Ozick, who seems to have brought her freshest energies to the essays in "Art and Ardor."

I do not want to overstate the case for decline. While any boom in the essay will be

held back by its commercial sluggishness, at the same time the form seems to have powerful attractions, esthetically at least, for many good writers working today. The essay offers the chance to wrestle with one's own intellectual confusion and to set down one's ideas in a manner both more straightforward and more exposed than in fiction (where it is always possible to attribute opinions to the characters or narrator instead of the author).

As for the familiar essay, it is very much alive today, if you choose to track it down under its various disguises. Shards of the form, more or less complete, appear in the work of newspaper columnists, as mentioned; under the protective umbrella of New Journalism (Joan Didion being the most substantial personal essayist to emerge from that training ground); in autobiographical-political meditations (Richard Rodriguez, Adrienne Rich, Ntozake Shange, Norman Mailer); naturalistic and regional essay-writing (John Graves, Wendell Berry, Lewis Thomas, Edward Abbey, Annie Dillard); humorous pieces (Max Apple, Roy Blount Jr., Calvin Trillin); literary criticism (Susan Sontag, Cynthia Ozick, Vivian Gornick, Seymour Krim); and travel writing (Mary McCarthy, Eleanor Clark and Paul Theroux). E. B. White is in a class of his own, as was the late William Saroyan. I am sure I have left out some other first-rate essayists and regret not having the space here to analyze the individual contributions of those listed; the point is, however, to indicate the range of activity and continuing viability of the form, especially when linked to a compelling subject that makes the reader temporarily overlook his or her hostility to essays.

In Europe, the essay stayed alive by taking a turn toward the speculative or philosophical, as seen in writers like Walter Benjamin, Theodor Adorno, Simone Weil, E. M. Cioran, Albert Camus, Roland Barthes, Czeslaw Milosz and Nicola Chiaramonte. All are offspring of the epigrammatic, belletristic side of Nietzsche, in a sense. This fragmented, aphoristic, critical tradition of essay writing is only now beginning to have an influence on American writing. One sees it, curiously, in much of the experimental new fiction—in Renata Adler, William Gass, Donald Barthelme, Elizabeth Hardwick, John Barth. Their novelistic discourse often reads like a broken essay, personal and philosophical, intermixed with narrative elements. The tendency of many post-modernist storytellers to parody the pedantry of the essay voice speaks both to their intellectual reliance on that tradition and their unsureness about adapting the patriarchal stance of the Knower. This is why the essay must remain "broken" for the time being.

In one of the most penetrating discussions of the essay form, Georg Lukacs put it this way: "The essay is a judgment, but the essential, the value-determining thing about it is not the verdict (as is the case with the system) but the process of judging." Uncomfortable words for a non-judgmental age. The familiar essayists of the past may have been non-specialists—indeed, it was part of their attraction—but they knew how to speak with a generalist's easy authority.

That is precisely what we contemporary essayists have a hard time doing; we are too well aware of the superiority experts have over us in technical information. The last generalist-essayist who seemed able to write comfortably, knowledgeably, opinionatedly on everything under the sun was Paul Goodman; we may not see his like again soon.

Still, the willingness of contemporary writers to try the form, if not necessarily commit themselves to it, speaks well of its chances for survival. If we do offend, we can always fall back on Papa Montaigne's "Que scay-je?": What do I know?

[1984]

CHAPTER

SIX

Writing Critical Essays

Robyn Warhol

When literature professors assign you to "write a paper," what exactly do they want you to do? Some instructors are precise about assignments: they may specify a topic or even a thesis; they may supply the evidence on which you are to comment. Often, though—especially in more advanced English courses—the assignment is "open." What, then, is your professor looking for?

Probably he or she expects you to write a "critical essay," a relatively brief paper in which you will apply your ingenuity, creativity, and analytical skills to confronting and explaining a literary text. A paper qualifies as a critical essay when it makes an original observation about a work of literature while answering the question, "Well, so what?"

You may find yourself a bit overcome at the prospect of coming up with something original to say about a work by William Shakespeare, or Emily Dickinson: haven't professional scholars been writing everything that could possibly be said, for decades if not for centuries? Intimidated by this assumption, many students go to the library and look up what "the critics" have said before trying to work on criticism of their own. I don't think that's a good way to go about it. Even if you are assigned to write a research paper (which differs from a critical essay in that it requires you to consult and cite other scholars' work), you will find the writing less difficult if you work out your own critical position on a text before consulting other sources. You can always revise your ideas and your essay as your understanding of the text increases. For this, after all, is the purpose of writing critical essays: to come to a more complete understanding of a given work of literature and to communicate that understanding to another reader.

WHAT CRITICAL ESSAYS DO

"Critical," in literary matters, does not carry the negative connotations of "finding fault" that the word has in common usage. Most critical essays either imply or express a great deal of enthusiasm for the works they discuss. The reason is simple: it's much more productive to spend time thinking and writing about a poem, play, story, or novel you enjoyed reading than to dwell on one you didn't like in the first place. Devoting the necessary hours to tearing apart a work you found boring or offensive or amateurish can be depressing.

In literary study, critical essays usually have one of three main goals. They can aim primarily to *describe, evaluate,* or *interpret* a text. All essays will combine some elements of each activity. For instance, "evaluation" is implicit in every critical essay. Even if you don't set out to prove how good a particular text is, you imply that it has value when you choose it as the subject for critical study. Still, every essay's main point, or *thesis,* should focus on one of these three main questions: How does this text work? Is this text any good? What does this text mean?

The Descriptive Critical Essay

When you write a descriptive critical essay, the main question you are trying to answer is: How does this literary text work? How does it get its meaning across? The broad term for this kind of study is "poetics" or—as Jonathan Culler has defined it—the study of the codes and conventions, the recurring patterns and familiar structures, that make it possible for literary texts to have "meaning" (37). In student writing, the descriptive critical essay usually focuses on specific features of one text, and sometimes compares a given text to a model of the genre, or type of literature, it belongs to.

For example, if you are writing about a Shakespearean sonnet, you may want to describe the ways it conforms to and deviates from the Elizabethan sonnet form. Does it have the proper number of lines, arranged in a typical sonnet rhyme scheme? Does its meter conform strictly to iambic pentameter? Is its imagery limited to typical sonnet conventions? Does it follow a line of argument common to sonnets? Sometimes the answer will be no. It's in the nature of texts to deviate somewhat from their generic models: often, in understanding a poem's uniqueness, we can understand the poem itself more clearly. If an author is writing within a certain genre and chooses to violate some of the "rules" of that genre, you can infer some significance from that choice.

Depending on how long the essay is to be, you may have to select a particular feature of the text to describe. Say you are writing about the formal features of *Huckleberry Finn.* You might want to describe the way Mark Twain uses dialect to characterize the people in the novel. Or you might be interested in describing the effect that Huck's narration has on the perspective of the story. Or you might look at the placement of the chapter breaks and their impact on the novel's pace. Or you might want to examine the effect of Twain's juxtaposing scenes of humor with scenes of pathos. These are only a few of the possible topics you might develop for a descriptive critical essay on this novel—pursuing any one of them will bring you closer to an understanding of how *Huckleberry Finn* works and, by extension, how novels work in general. Sometimes you can gain added insight by combining two descriptive approaches to one text: for instance, you could consider the role dialect plays in humorous scenes.

The advantage of the descriptive essay is that it gives you an entry into the workings of the text you are studying. The conventions and anticonventions you describe are not difficult to uncover and are relatively easy to defend or "prove"—there they are, in black and white, between the covers of the book. As you understand their workings in one text, you come to understand the genre more clearly. The disadvantage of writing a descriptive essay is that it can be tricky to develop your topic into an argument or thesis, an answer

to the question, "So what?" When you are accounting for the obvious, as many critics so fruitfully do, some creative thinking is necessary for placing your observations in an interesting, provocative context.

The Evaluative Critical Essay

This kind of essay asks about a literary text, "Is it any good?" It's a question that has no trouble addressing the "So what?" of criticism—if the poem, play or novel is "good," it's worth reading; if it's "bad," it's a waste of time, right? What keeps evaluative criticism alive, of course, is that no two readers' standards are ever exactly the same.

The most common form of evaluative essay is the book review, of the kind professional critics write to help prospective readers decide whether to buy a book now, wait until it's out in paperback, look for it in a casual way at the library, or forget about it altogether. Teachers seldom expect students to write evaluative criticism of this kind: if a book is listed on a syllabus, the instructor undoubtedly feels it's worth reading. Sometimes, though, you may be writing to disagree with an instructor's choice; or you may want to propose a defense for a text that is not on the list. Sometimes too, instructors ask you to explain in an essay why you like or dislike a particular work they have assigned.

The number-one requirement for evaluative criticism is that you must make your standards of judgment explicit. Maybe you have a gut reaction to a particular book: reading *The Yellow Wallpaper* might make you feel elated or irritated, excited or bored. To explain why you "love" it or "hate" it, however, you need to explore the textual reasons for your response: you need to identify the formal features of texts that you do like, and compare the work in question to your model of "good literature." Simply to say that you like certain features of the text is not to make an argument, however; you need to demonstrate how the text achieves the effects you admire.

Therefore, spell out your standards. If you object to the form of an e. e. cummings poem, what is the model of good poetry you contrast with it? For example: Does good poetry need rhyme and meter? Why? If you admire the complexity of the narrative structure in an experimental story, what kind of story do you think it improves upon? For example: Are there advantages to scrambling chronology, quoting dialogue without clearly attributing it to characters, and otherwise departing from the conventions of more traditional short stories? Why? If you think Fitzgerald's use of symbolism in *The Great Gatsby* is effective, what ideals of symbolism are you assuming? For example: Should symbolism be clear and repetitive, or subtle? Should symbolic images carry easily recognizable, "universal" significances, or should they be idiosyncratic and obscure? Why?

Many reviewers leave their esthetic standards implicit, operating on the assumption that all educated readers can agree upon some unspoken, universal standard of literary quality. Literary criticism, though, has become more self-conscious, recognizing that all critics' judgments are colored by their subjectivity and by the position from which they are speaking: the esthetic standards of a Chicana poet are likely to differ from those of an Oxford don, but they are no less valid. If you want to judge the artistic value of a text, then, you must be clear about your own position.

Of course, your evaluation of a literary work might depend on extraliterary elements, such as political or religious attitudes. If D.H. Lawrence's "The Horse Dealer's Daughter" takes a stance on women's roles that offends you, you need to explain your own position before you can evaluate Lawrence's; the same is true if you approve of the attitudes you

think Lawrence's story endorses. Before you can argue that a text is good or bad, you must establish the values you are following. Readers who don't share your values will be inclined to disagree with your point. The challenge of evaluative criticism is to write it persuasively, alluding to the possibilities for opposition to your argument, and answering potential objections with specific commentary on passages from the text.

The Interpretive Critical Essay

In this, the most common kind of student essay, the main question you are asking is, "What does this text mean?" As my illustrations of descriptive and evaluative arguments show, a critical essay always raises questions about meaning. To write a descriptive essay is to address the question: *How* does this work transmit meaning? To write an evaluative essay is to ask: *Why* is it worthwhile to think about this text's meaning? And to write an interpretive essay is directly to ask: *What* does this work mean? Whether the work you are interpreting is on the scale of a haiku verse or *Moby Dick,* the question is never a simple one. How you find and present a meaning will depend on the strategy of interpretation you choose to apply.

The literary-academic world is made up of what Stanley Fish has called "interpretive communities" (11). These are unofficial groups of readers who agree on the best way or ways to get at the meaning of texts. Your instructor—whether or not he or she advertises or even realizes it—belongs to one or more of these communities; so do you. The study of literature is partly the process of discovering which of the communities you want to embrace.

The best interpretive essays do three things: (1) They establish the strategy by which you, the essayist, choose to find meaning. They might do this explicitly, by saying something like "I propose to do a Marxist reading of *Hamlet* in order to examine the assumptions about class relations exhibited in the text," or they may be more subtle, announcing the strategy through certain key words. If, for example, an essay's thesis paragraph refers to "desire," "the mirror stage," and "libidinal impulses," it is almost certainly drawing on psychoanalytic modes of interpretation. (2) They "read," or interpret, the work in question according to that strategy, giving lots of specific examples from the text. And (3) They make a point or an argument. Simply paraphrasing the work in your own words is not the same as interpreting it, because a paraphrase will not answer the question, "So what?" You need to place the work's ideas in some context, in order to write persuasively about it. Being self-consciously explicit about your interpretive strategy can help you develop a thesis.

GETTING STARTED

Doubtless you will begin working on a critical essay unofficially for some time before you actually write anything. Some people do their best thinking in the shower, or on the jogging trail, or in conversation with friends. Working out a thesis in circumstances like these is not procrastination, but rather an important stage in the process of getting ready to write. To ensure that an argument will come to you early enough to be useful, however, you should pace yourself by going through certain steps on your way toward writing the paper. These steps may intersect and may be repeated at different stages of the process, but I have listed

Some Modern Interpretive Strategies

Historicist criticism finds meaning by looking at a text within the framework of the prevailing ideas, assumptions, and discourse of its historical era, or by considering its contents within the context of "what really happened" during the period that produced the text.

Literary-historical criticism finds significance in the ways a particular work resembles or differs from other works of its period and/or genre. (This interpretive strategy relies heavily on the techniques of descriptive poetics, differing from poetics in its main goal: to determine what a text means, rather than "how it means.")

Biographical criticism looks for a text's significance in terms of its author, either by comparing events and attitudes in the text with those in the author's life, or by comparing textual features with the author's other works.

Political criticism looks at the ideas in a text through an explicit overlay of political ideology (for example, Marxism or feminism) to find meaning.

Psychoanalytic criticism adopts the systems of explanation suggested by Freud (or later theorists who have built upon Freud's work, such as Lacan or the feminist psychoanalysts) to interpret what a text signifies.

Formalism finds meaning in the direct relation between a text's ideas and its form, the connection between *what* a text says and the *way* it's said. Formalists may find tension, irony, or paradox in this relation, but they usually resolve it into unity and coherence of meaning.

Deconstruction, too, looks at the relation of a text's ideas to the way the ideas are expressed. Unlike formalists, though, deconstructionists find meaning in the ways the text breaks down: for instance, in the ways the rhetoric contradicts the ostensible message.

them here in the order in which I try to go through them myself, when writing literary criticism.

Take Notes. As you read and reread the text, you should underline, highlight, star, or otherwise mark all the passages that interest you. When I am working on a long text, I keep track of the interesting passages by making notes to record page numbers for examples of themes or techniques that appeal to me. I like to make these notes on the blank pages and inside covers of my paperback edition of the text. This way I don't lose them, and I'm always glad to recover my previous work when I return to the same text for another project.

Use Your Journal. If you are keeping a reading journal, either by choice or assignment, it will be an ideal source of inspiration (see Chapter 1).

Ask Questions. As you read, consult your own intellectual and emotional response to the text. Watch yourself reading, and mark any parts of the text that you found especially moving, persuasive, confusing, or difficult. Write out your questions as they occur to you;

for instance, "Why does this passage make me cry?" or "Why is this description so difficult to visualize?" or "What is this novel's position on racism?" or "Why is this dialogue so hilarious?" Such questions can lead you to a thesis for any of the three modes of critical essays I have described.

Look at the Text's Form. Try to analyze the structure of the text. If it is a poem, consider its rhyme scheme, meter, verse form, and arrangement of ideas; if it is a novel, describe for yourself its point of view, sequence of events, chapter divisions, and narrative voice. Ask yourself: To what subgenre does the structure conform? (A text that fits the genre novel, for instance, might be a Gothic romance, a "social problem novel," a *roman à clef,* a work of fantasy or science fiction, an epistolary novel, an "experimental novel," a work of psychological realism, a historical novel, a "novel of sentiment," a mystery novel—or, most likely, a unique combination of some features of several subgenres.) In what ways does it diverge from the expected model? (Texts always do.) What is the significance of the author's having chosen this particular structure to convey the ideas in this work? For some guidance on appropriate questions to ask about particular kinds of texts, see the chapters in this book on drama, poetry, and fiction.

Look for Familiar Moves. Identify the literary conventions in the text. Does the sonnet's persona claim that the poem will make his beloved immortal? Does the novel's narrator say the heroine is too beautiful to describe? Does the hero of the play sometimes address himself to the audience, in asides? If so, the writers are following conventions of the genres in which they are writing. The more literature you have read, the more readily you will recognize the habits that typify the period and genre you are studying. Ask yourself (and your instructor) where you have seen certain patterns of conventions before. If the work you are studying is either remarkably conventional or noticeably unconventional in any respect, this might lead you to a thesis.

Interpret Figures of Speech. Think about any imagery or figurative language you have noticed in the text. What symbolic patterns emerge? What are the vehicle and tenor of any metaphors you find? (If you are unfamiliar with the intricacies of figurative language, consult a literary handbook or your instructor.) Is there any way to read the text as an allegory for ideas that it doesn't mention directly? Make notes of your answers: abstract ideas like these can be easy to lose track of or forget.

Look Up Unfamiliar Words. Especially if you are working on a poem, and especially if it was written before the twentieth century, you should make sure that you understand the sense in which each word is being used. Words that appear in seventeenth-century poetry, for instance, may look like modern words, but may have carried meanings or connotations that have become obsolete. For example, when John Donne mentions "trepidation of the spheres," he does not mean that the planets are alarmed or frightened; for Donne, "trepidation" also referred to a Ptolemaic explanation for planetary movements. The modern denotation might also be there, and might be relevant to your interpretation, but it's important not to overlook the original meaning.

The *Oxford English Dictionary,* available in every library, is the best source for the history of individual words in the language. It arranges definitions chronologically and provides many examples from literary and common language, so you can use it to determine exactly what meanings the word had during the era in which your author was writing.

MAKE CONNECTIONS

As you take notes and look over the passages that you have marked, try to establish any meaningful patterns among the material you have collected. How you determine the significance of these patterns (or the point that you want to make about them) will depend, of course, on the interpretive strategy or critical stance you adopt. Not coincidentally, your strategy will have shaped your selection of examples as well, so the move between the "collecting" and "connecting" steps will not be as tricky as you might think.

At the connecting stage, a good idea is to play a little game of "Jeopardy" with yourself: look at the data you've collected from the text and figure out what questions they might be the answers to. This is also the stage at which you will begin eliminating some of the data as less relevant to the questions you find yourself raising. Put those data aside, and think about them again when you must write a research paper or essay exam for this course. Concentrate for now on the patterns that emerge as you begin to think about your data in terms of your general questions.

What do I mean by looking for "patterns"? I mean that you should look at the examples you have collected and try to see what they might have in common with one another: the parallels among them will be your key to a thesis. A pattern might look perfectly consistent, or it might have irregularities. In either case, it can direct you to an argument. At this point you should try to decide whether you are most inclined to describe, evaluate, or interpret the work in your essay.

Your decision will depend on the patterns you have noticed and on your own critical inclinations. Say, for example, you are studying a sonnet and you have noticed that the meter in some lines varies drastically from iambic pentameter. If you want to interpret the sonnet and you are inclined to do a formalist reading, you can ask yourself, "Why is the metric variation appropriate to the ideas expressed in these lines? Why might the poet have wanted to draw special attention to these particular moments in the poem? How does that attention color the poem's meaning?"

"So What?": Create a Thesis

Once you have begun collecting some of your examples under the banner of one main question, you should begin to see the general answer that will account for the examples you want to use. This answer will become your thesis: the statement about the text that you will support with examples throughout your essay. The thesis statement you develop at this stage will probably not be identical to the one that controls the final draft of your paper. It will evolve as you think in more detail about your data and your question; you will be continually reconceiving and rephrasing your thesis as you draft your essay, and you will probably have to rewrite the thesis statement several times toward the end of the writing process, to make sure it reflects the argument you are making in your essay's final draft. Nevertheless, it's important to formulate your main argument now, as a tentative guide to writing your essay.

Generate Some Ideas. This is the point where techniques of brainstorming can be very helpful, especially the approach that composition theorists have called "focused free writing." In spite of its liberated-sounding name, free writing is a strictly rule-governed exercise that can help you work through frustrating blocks which may be delaying your arrival at a thesis.

Here's the technique: write one of the questions you asked during the "collect" stage at the top of a clean piece of paper. Set a timer or alarm clock to ring in five or ten minutes. Once the time period has begun, set your pen or pencil to the page and explore possible answers to that question. Write rapidly, without stopping or even slowing down, until all the time has elapsed. *Do not pause* to make corrections, cross out words, reread what you've written, or collect your thoughts. Just keep writing, and try to make as accurate a record as possible of what passes through your mind. If you can't think of anything to say, write "I can't think of anything to say," over and over, until you think of something. (This quickly becomes very boring and motivates you efficiently to *think* of something to say.)

Free writing in many ways resembles the techniques Toby Fulwiler describes in this book's chapter on journal writing, and it carries many of the same benefits. If you repeat the exercise several times, preferably over a period of a few days, you will amost certainly come up with original and arguable answers to your questions, one of which can become your thesis. The technique is tiring and leads to temporary bouts with writers' cramp. But, like aerobic exercise, it can produce benefits (such as self-discipline and a way to conquer writer's block) that are probably worth the discomfort.

Formulate the Thesis. Perhaps the best way to go about developing your thesis at this point is to talk it over with others. By all means, take advantage of any in-class workshops or discussions your instructor may have planned for this purpose, but if you can, you should find as many opportunities as possible to explore your ideas for the paper in conversations. Visit your professor during office hours, make appointments with any teaching assistants or writing tutors available to you, or discuss your ideas with friends and classmates. Read your free writings to any willing listener, and talk over the possibilities for basing an argument on them.

At this juncture, one of the most useful questions you can ask of others is: What are some plausible arguments *against* the point I am trying to make? If there are no such arguments, then your point is probably too obvious and will make a weak thesis. If plausible arguments do exist, be glad. Your thesis is controversial enough to be interesting and you will want to refute or concede those arguments in the course of writing an essay that is persuasive, as all good essays should be.

Finding a thesis that is controversial will help you develop an answer to the big "So what." For instance, this statement would not make an arguable thesis: "In *The Great Gatsby,* Fitzgerald explores and examines the American Dream through the perspective of his narrator, Nick Carraway and the experience of his hero, Jay Gatsby." Anyone who has read the novel would probably agree that this statement is true—the novel does other things, too, but among the things it does are "exploring and examining the American Dream." To answer "So what?" an argumentative thesis must go into the *how* or *why,* must make a point.

Possible arguments for descriptive essays on this topic might be: "Through the use of narrative flashbacks, Fitzgerald reveals Nick's and Jay's parallel disillusionment with the American Dream," or "The symbolic images Fitzgerald associates with the American

Dream combine with the movement of the plot to reveal ambivalence about the attractiveness of the Dream." Possibilities for an evaluative essay might include: "The narrator's eye for descriptive detail and ear for believable conversation make *Gatsby* an enjoyable spoof of the humorous side of the American Dream," or "Fitzgerald's tendency to slip into caricature—in the names, personalities, and appearances of his characters—prevents an otherwise realistic novel from being a serious critique of the American Dream." The possibilities for interpretive theses are endless: whatever strategy you choose, you will find yourself accounting for *how* or *why* Fitzgerald does what he does with the American Dream in this novel. For instance, a biographical critic might argue, "Jay Gatsby's pursuit of the American Dream parallels Fitzgerald's own experience and predicts his personal fate"; a historical critic might say, "The treatment of the American Dream in *Gatsby* simultaneously exemplifies and exposes prevailing attitudes in the 1920s toward the equation of prosperity with happiness." A feminist critic given to archetypal criticism might argue that "The portrayals of Daisy Fay and Jordan Baker as bitch-goddesses points to the misogyny at the heart of Fitzgerald's American Dream." For each of these theses there are potential counterarguments. None of them is safely "right" or strictly "wrong"—their strength will depend on the quality of evidence you bring to bear in proving them.

When you think you know what you want to argue, write the thesis out in as coherent a form as possible. You may not want to state it so directly in your essay, but you should have a firm idea of it in your own mind and in your notes. This is as true for someone writing a scholarly book as for someone writing a critical essay: you need a clear, interesting answer to the question "What's it about and why does it matter?"

When you eventually do develop the thesis into an introduction for your essay, remember to phrase it in an arguable form. If you shrink from beginning an essay with a statement such as "In this essay I will argue that Fitzgerald uses the color green in *The Great Gatsby* to symbolize hope, envy, and the future," your instincts are good. Such a sentence is not a thesis: it is an announcement of the paper's topic. Instead, try to make a direct statement about how or why Fitzgerald uses the symbol, along the lines of the examples I proposed above. This would be a debatable statement, and therefore a thesis or an argument. But it doesn't need a label like, "My thesis is x" or "In this essay I will argue y." In a short critical paper, self-reference isn't necessary and can sometimes be too obvious.

This is not to say, however, that you shouldn't use the word "I." Not every professor would agree with me, but I think you should use it. Why pretend to be objective? Since your argument depends in every way on your selections—of a topic, of examples, of interpretive strategies—it has to reflect you, and it should be written in a voice that is recognizably yours. If you are making a statement that refers to your own experience, your own feeling, your own judgment, it only makes sense to attribute it to yourself. Remember, however, that (unless you are writing a particularly subjective kind of reader-response criticism) *you* are not the topic of the paper, even if you are its "subject"; the poem, play, story, or novel is the object you have in view, and your essay should focus attention on the text, rather than on itself. And even if you can't be objective as you write about a text, you can and should be logical. Try, therefore, not to fall back on using "I" as an excuse for faulty reasoning: rather than using disclaimers such as "I'm not really sure, but I get the feeling that Fitzgerald is trying to say something about the American Dream . . .," work on figuring out what you do think about the topic and presenting appropriate evidence to support your idea.

Organize the Essay

Unless you've had so much experience writing from formal outlines that you are addicted to using them, don't make yourself do it. Instead, arrange your ideas informally, in a list or even a chart or map, to sketch out the order in which you want to bring them up. This will allow you the flexibility to develop new connections and slants on your examples as you write.

Shape your Argument. Decide now what rhetorical strategy you will use in the arrangement of your essay. Will it be deductive—that is, begin with a general statement of your point, then proceed to illustrate it with specific examples arranged around subpoints? Or will it be inductive, arguing through specific examples that "build" to a concluding statement?

Some student writers prefer the inductive form for the element of suspense it injects into essays, but I suspect that few teachers appreciate the approach. If you arrange your argument deductively, you make it much easier for your reader to determine how well you are making your point. You also give the impression that you know what you are talking about from the start.

For the strongest rhetorical effect in a deductive essay, you can follow certain conventions for arranging your evidence. Put the most convincing points in the most memorable positions: the beginning and the end of the argument. Less persuasive evidence can be "buried" in the middle. You have to consult your own conscience as to whether each piece of evidence is strong enough to be used at all.

Build in Transitions. In determining the order of your arguments, you should also think about the transitions you can make among individual points. Sometimes the same example will illustrate two points; if so, it would be a good "pivot" between them. Sometimes one of your points will qualify, alter, or even contradict another. Take these relations among your ideas into account as you work out the initial organization.

Don't Suppress Conflict. If you find that your argument doesn't "work" perfectly, that certain aspects of the text cannot be reconciled with it or that in some ways it is self-contradictory, do your best not to ignore or bury the problem. Confront it, think about it, write about it—you may even decide to incorporate it into the final draft. I believe that a paper which recognizes, acknowledges, and attempts to deal with its difficulties is much more interesting and valuable for the writer and the reader than a paper which oversimplifies issues in order to gloss over problems. Writing literary criticism is never easy. It's perfectly all right for an essay to reflect this fact of academic life, as long as it does so intelligently and self-consciously.

CONVENTIONS OF WRITING ON LITERARY TOPICS

Of course, once you have settled on an argument and a basic organization for your paper, you will write the critical essay as you would any formal written assignment: everything you know about composing, revising, and editing holds true for writing about literature. There are only a few respects in which the actual writing of literary criticism may diverge from your writing in other fields.

Verb Tense

When writing about actions that occur in a literary work, use the present tense ("Hamlet cannot decide whether to take action," not "Hamlet could not decide . . ."). When writing about events that occurred in history, use the past tense ("Shakespeare composed his plays for a dramatic company in which he sometimes acted."). When attributing ideas to an author through what he or she says in a literary work, use the present tense ("Shakespeare writes that 'all the world's a stage'.").

Quotations

Be sure that quotations are perfectly accurate: check them against the text. If a quotation is four or more lines long, indent each line ten spaces from the left margin in order to set the passage off from your own prose. When you indent a quotation, omit the quotation marks. If it is shorter than four lines, enclose it in quotation marks and treat it typographically as part of your own sentence. If you quote fewer than four consecutive lines from a poem, indicate the line breaks with a slash (/).

In writing about literature, as in all kinds of writing, you should be very careful, when you use quotations, to integrate them into your argument. Introduce every quotation from a primary source with at least one sentence or phrase that establishes its connection to what you have said in the paragraph so far (use phrases such as "in a typical example," or "in one exceptional case," or "for instance"). Then, after reproducing the quotation, be sure to comment on it specifically, pointing out the details that support your argument (this might mean paraphrasing the quotation in your own words to relate it to your argument, or it might mean drawing your reader's attention to the text's use of certain vocabulary, images, rhetorical moves, metric variations, or whatever you mean to highlight by using the quotation).

Documentation and Use of Sources

Consult the new *MLA Handbook for Writers of Research Papers* (third edition) for the simplest, most streamlined rules of documentation in literary essays. Generally speaking, a critical essay should have few or no footnotes. List the editions you are using under "Works Cited" at the end of the paper. Directly after each quotation you use as evidence, give the page number (for fiction), line number (for poetry), or act, scene and line number (for drama) in parentheses. Punctuate your sentences containing quotations like this:

> Ernest Hemingway provides readers with most of the background information they need to understand the central character in ''Soldier's Home'' in the story's opening line: ''Krebs went to the war from a Methodist college in Kansas'' (145).

Remember to comment on the quotation after citing it; be sure to specify your reasons for claiming the quotation makes the point you claim it makes.

If you paraphrase ideas you found in other critics' work without quoting them directly, be careful to avoid charges of plagiarism by attributing the ideas to their source within your essay. You can use a formula like: "As Mary Poovey has pointed out, early nineteenth-century women's novels tend simultaneously to reinforce and to subvert the image of the

'Proper Lady.' " (You should attribute ideas and phrases to critics who have published work on them, even if the idea occurred to you before reading the criticism.) If you are paraphrasing a general idea from someone else's work, you will list the secondary source under "works cited" at the end of your essay. If you are borrowing a phrase or idea that occurs on a particular page, you will give that page number in parentheses in your text—"(Poovey 38)." If your context makes it clear which writer's work you are referring to, you can eliminate the author's name and give just the page number: "(38)."

Following the new MLA format, you use superscript footnotes or endnotes *only* for "content notes" that explain, qualify, or elaborate upon points in your essay that you do not want to develop within the body of the paper. Remember, the traditional footnote form that relied on *ibid.* and *op cit.,* so difficult to compose and so tiresome to follow, is obsolete in literary studies. Learn to operate within the new system. Once you've mastered it, documentation becomes much easier for both the writer and the reader to use (see Chapter 10, Writing Research, for more information on documentation).

WHY ARE YOU WRITING A CRITICAL ESSAY?

Admittedly, the process I am describing requires an enormous amount of time, energy, and concentration. Perhaps you doubt that all these steps are really what instructors expect from you when they tell you to "write a paper." I am willing to concede that we don't always *expect* to find evidence of all this work when we sit down to grade a paper, but I think most of us do *hope* to find it. From our point of view it's the process of writing a paper that will contribute to your education, more than the product that comes out of that process. A polished student essay is valuable primarily as a sign of the work and thought that went into it.

Why, after all, do you write critical essays? The superficial answer is "to fill a requirement; to earn a grade." But why do we grade you on this particular assignment? Why are critical essays such an important part of the English curriculum, taking priority in most courses over quizzes and exams? A high grade on an examination signifies mastery of the material of a course, but a high grade on an essay shows that you have mastered the modes of thought that operate in literary studies as a discipline. Your knowledge of narrative forms and poetic devices, of authors' lives and literary periods, will probably have no direct relevance to what you do in later life, unless you teach English (as only a small minority of students of literature decide to do). But your mastery of literary thinking, of the ways that critics approach and decipher texts, is an important indicator of the flexibility of your mind. And writing critical essays is the best way—in some courses, the only way—both to develop and express that mastery.

WORKS CITED

Culler, Jonathan. *The Pursuit of Signs: Semiotics, Literature, Deconstruction.* Ithaca: Cornell UP, 1981.

Fish, Stanley. *Is There a Text in This Class?* Cambridge: Harvard UP, 1980.

Gibaldi, Joseph, and Walter S. Achtert. *MLA Handbook for Writers of Research Papers,* 3rd ed. New York: The Modern Language Association, 1988.

CHAPTER

SEVEN

Writing Personal Essays

Mary Jane Dickerson

As a college freshman in 1955, when I was assigned to read Faulkner's story "A Rose for Emily," I immediately recognized that not only was I reading about a character in a small town in rural Mississippi but I was also reading about a woman who lived as close as two houses down the road in my own rural North Carolina. What I was in the act of reading merged with details of my own existence. It was as if from that moment on, writing about a work of literature was no longer an abstract exercise, but held possibilities of knowing unlike any other I had ever encountered. Since I first glimpsed these connections through reading, I have also written about those characters who peopled my childhood by filling the spaces of my poems with them. Writing and living have continued to overlap through both reading and writing.

All serious readers undergo such shocks of recognition and find themselves forever altered by what they read. No matter whether we are writing about a fictional life, an actual life, or indeed our own lives, we undergo a process of change as we write. We make connections with the voices in fiction, in autobiography, in poetry, in our own various texts, and of those people surrounding us as part of our everyday lives. We keep reading, we keep listening, and we keep writing.

William Faulkner's representations and visions of reality have offered me ways to make sense of my own "postage stamp of the universe." Perhaps you can name the writer who has done the same for you. Although I have never recovered from that powerful initiation, the "I" who writes occasionally about Faulkner and other American authors has undergone transformations and has learned to listen to the many potential and possible voices that enable writing literary criticism as well as poems, essays, letters, and journals as the need and desire arise.

PERSONAL ESSAYS

Let's pause for a moment to list some things to keep in mind when writing personal responses to literature:

- Autobiographical: Use "I" frequently even when autobiography is not central.
- Conversational: Create a friendly sense of equality between yourself and your reader (or audience).
- Exploratory: Be reflective, even imaginative, rather than explanatory or analytical (or persuasive).
- Creative: Whenever appropriate, consider how reflecting on the act of writing might allow you to participate in the creative process of the literary work—in the production of meaning itself.
- Open: Rather than coming to a conventional kind of conclusion that ties things together, try, instead, to follow where the central idea might lead you toward other possibilities, thereby encouraging the play of ideas that resists the finality of usual conclusion or closure.

AUTOBIOGRAPHY

To stimulate a rich identification between students and their literary subjects, I often distribute an autobiographical questionnaire to help students generate their responses during the entire semester as part of their course journal. For my literature courses, autobiography encourages students to connect the narratives they see within their own lives to the narratives that they are reading in various literary genres. Responding to these questions can stimulate richly conceived essays in which you actively integrate your experience into your interpretation of others' texts. Questions about the self can arm you with a powerful invention tool to create textual forms that may more uniquely represent your writerly identity. At least, posing such questions is worth a try. Here is a list of questions that you can use as a guideline and add to as you read.

AUTOBIOGRAPHICAL QUESTIONNAIRE

1. Is there any dominant physical trait, gesture, or feature in a character that gives you special insight into yourself? Of others close to you? How does this recognition affect your response to the character? The work?
2. Is there a character who comes close to being like you in important ways? Describe the similarities.
3. What physical objects in your reading do you associate with yourself, your parents, or other family members? What does their appearance make you think about?
4. What things that you are most passionate about appear in your reading? How does this recognition affect your response?
5. What of your major fears do you also find in literary characters? What inhibitions or desires?
6. What patterns or events in your own life are reflected in the literature you are reading? What similarities and/or differences are there in the events selected?
7. What are the motivating forces of your own life that set up particular responses to the literary work?
8. Which place or setting (interior, landscape, street, building) in your reading do you identify with most and why?

9. What have you found most disturbing or disquieting (or pleasurable and satisfying?) about what you are reading? Why?
10. What connections do you see between some aspect of political or social life in the present and political and social life in an earlier work?
11. How do you see the past affecting the present in your own life? In the lives of characters you are reading about?
12. What is your earliest memory of reading or being read to? Do you remember the book's title? What are your favorite books and the ones that remain most vividly a part of you? How might these earlier reading experiences have affected your responses to literature in the present?

What follows are some journal explorations students have made in response to the autobiographical questionnaire; in each case, the writer found possibilities for the personal essay. One student describes his obsession with running in answer to the question about being altered in some way by what he is reading, in this case Annie Dillard's *A Pilgrim at Tinker Creek:*

> The syllable ME was not the center of my thoughts this fine October afternoon. Orange, red, and brown captured my imagination. I stared at the sun through the trees. Looking up at the sun, patches of color registered in my head. I felt daring enough to close my eyes for an instant; imprinted on my eyelids were kaleidoscopic images of the leaves. The death grey bark of the white birch, which is my favorite tree, reminded me of winter. I had found my own ''tree with the lights in it.'' It had come in the form of loosely connected observances and recollections. My ''tree'' was not as profound or cohesive as Dillard's, but that did not matter. It was my own.
>
> Adrian

This material from his own daily experience finally turned into an exploratory essay titled "Running After Dillard," in which Dillard's book altered Adrian's running attitudes and habits.

In another journal entry, a student describes the experience of hearing Hayden Carruth read his own poetry:

> I had never gone to hear a poet speak or read his poetry before in person. But I got what I expected. I expected to feel special because I was in the same room as an excellent poet. I expected to hear other works not in the book we read and to get more meaning from poems I had already read because he would be speaking the voice that originally spoke them before they were written down on paper.
>
> You know, after reading the above paragraph I wonder about myself. My ability to communicate is almost nonexistent in that paragraph.
>
> Brian

Most of us would probably disagree with Brian and regard his intense experience of seeing, hearing, and remembering coupled with the writing and reading in his journal as a revelation of what it means to experience a poetry reading. Using oneself as a vehicle to explore the meanings of literary texts makes reading a co-creative act: acts of reading *and* writing the self. Brian later wrote an essay in which he used his own knowledge and performance of jazz to explore its influence on the composition of many of Carruth's poems in *Brothers, I Loved You All.*

CONVERSATION

Since writing about literature is like engaging in a personal dialogue with writers and their texts, this sense of conversation, with its strong use of "I," creates a friendly relationship between writer and audience. One of the most powerful places for such dialogues to occur is in the journals described in Chapter 1. The many and varied conditions of journal writing provide an even larger framework that encourages free-ranging writing activities that involve the self. It's as if the autobiographical journals create ideal conditions for conversations to take place between you and what you're reading—between who you are and what you think. These conversations, in turn, help bridge the gap between reading and writing that all of us experience to some degree whenever we are faced with a writing assignment.

When we write as frequently as we read, we enlarge our potential to make connections with facets of our own lives. Many writers acknowledge the pleasure they get when readers communicate just how much their works have affected their lives. Surely Alice Walker would appreciate what this reader expresses in a journal entry about how sharing *The Color Purple* with her mother enriched that reading experience for her:

> I haven't had much in common with my mother for a while, and that seemed to crumble away this weekend. She has read The Color Purple and we spent the whole day talking about women, her relationship with my father, her job, her education and all that she feels about such things. For the first time in a while I found myself caring about her thoughts and listening to what she said. She talked about the book and how she would like to borrow mine to read more by Alice Walker. I told her that I would send her some of her own which I promptly did when I got back to Burlington. I sent her Once and inscribed it with one of A. W.'s musings from ''Mississippi Winter II'':
>
> When you remember me, my child,
> be sure to recall that Mama was
> . . . . .
> not happy
> with fences.
>
> I think I started to really love my mother again this weekend.
>
> Patti

For Patti, discussing her reading of Alice Walker encourages her to engage in conversation with communities of voices outside those she hears in the novel: she creates an informing context to enrich her own reading experience. Through reflection on the novel in her journal, she gets in touch with her own mother's life and reestablishes a vital connection.

Alice Walker's voice sets into play the voices of a mother and daughter that found an outlet through a journal entry. But what's even more significant here is that the student's major piece of writing for the semester turned into an examination of the nurturing and inspiring influence that earlier writer Zora Neale Hurston has had on the contemporary writer Alice Walker—another variation of mother-daughter relationships. For Patti, reflecting on the role of family as she reads Walker, whose fiction and poetry speak to all women as they explore their bonds with both their real and their adopted mothers, provides her with a perspective for writing an essay about Hurston's influence on Walker. Patti's conversation with her mother gave her an idea for an essay in which she explores the way Zora Neale Hurston and Alice Walker use story-telling traditions from African-American culture. Through using your journal as the site for personal explorations about the literature you read, you practice the kinds of conversations that enable you to speak about yourself in the act of reading in equally powerful ways.

EXPLORATION

Since you may not be trying to prove a point about a literary work, the form of the personal essay may take on a different shape than the exposition you are more accustomed to in which you develop a thesis and marshal support toward a persuasive and reasoned conclusion. Consider the following scenario. Your teacher might make an assignment similar to one given recently asking students to write a personal response to their reading of a Wordsworth poem. This assignment demanded a careful reading of the poem, but the interpretation must also be informed by the student's own life.

In response to Wordsworth's urging that we can learn much of value from nature in "I Wandered Lonely as a Cloud," you might open your essay with a description of a memorable instance of productive inner reflection or daydreaming. From this personal anecdote, you might compare the progress of Wordsworth's own process of learning from nature in a state of daydreaming as he narrates it in his poem. You might interweave other scenes from your own childhood and schooling that show how children learn from their environments as well as from formal education. In the ending of your essay, you might speculate on what we might learn from Wordsworth's poem as contemporary educators consider lengthening the school day and going to a year-round schedule.

For a similar kind of assignment, another student recognizes in Maxine Hong Kingston's *Woman Warrior: Memoir of a Chinese Childhood Among Ghosts* implications for his own cultural identity:

> Since I am a third generation Chinese-American, I am further removed than Kingston from a Chinese past. Both of my parents speak Chinese, but I lost my ability to speak Chinese as I grew up . . . and now I am unable to have any lengthy conversation with my grandmother. She does not speak English and I do not speak Chinese. We

> communicate through limited vocabulary and creative sign language. . . . I really feel a tremendous loss. Now I am learning the Chinese language and searching for my roots. For the first time in my life I am considering myself Chinese.
>
> Jason

As Jason considered his reading of his own life alongside reading Kingston's memoir, his choice of representing himself as author through the writerly "I" became a natural, even an inevitable act as he faced the dimension of loss in his own life. He could not write an authentic critical essay about the nature of Maxine Hong Kingston's search for gender, familial, and cultural identity without exploring and acknowledging his own Chinese-American history. It's as if these autobiographical connections create the conditions for conversations to take place between writers and readers so that readers also become writers of their own stories in the flexible form of the personal essay.

Whenever we write, we are engaged in making meanings, but these meanings are never fixed or static on the page (or on the screen or the world, for that matter); they become texts constantly undergoing construction as readers read and remake them through the lenses of their own realities. Writing through such awareness of what happens is akin to what Joan Didion describes in the opening lines of her essay, "Why I Write":

> Of course I stole the title for this talk from George Orwell. One reason I stole it was that I like the sound of the words: *Why I Write.* There you have three short unambiguous words that share a sound, and the sound they share is this:
>
> I
I
I (257)

Didion continues the exploration of her preoccupation with the sound of her own voice and its significance for her identity as a writer. By acknowledging her debt to Orwell's essay, she places herself in the company of those who see writing as a process of creating the "I."

ENGAGING THE CREATIVE PROCESS

Student Charles Baraw took full advantage of the creative process to shape an essay he called "Purgatory," in which he writes his own autobiography against reading Virginia Woolf's *A Room of One's Own* and Dante's *Divine Comedy.* Here is how he opens the piece: "Virginia Woolf—that was the name embossed on the tattered binder of the slim black book. It was strange the significance the name and the book had taken in my life."

Baraw traces his memory of hearing about this book from earlier high school years when "I was excited to add her to my growing list of 'must reads.' She joined Milton, Melville, and Hemingway." In college, Hemingway remained prominent while Woolf remained unread, but Baraw's involvement with women friends whose growing interests in feminist ideas and issues began to affect him as well—often in spite of himself: "A few months later Deidre took *A Room of One's Own* out [of the library] in my name, read it, and left it on my desk. I asked her about it. I wanted her to sum up the answers it contained and hand them to me ready for consumption."

After a period of time had passed with the loss of Deidre as lover and friend, Virginia

Woolf's book remained as yet unread until "I started to read" these words: " 'But, you may say, we asked you to speak about women and fiction—what has that got to do with a room of one's own?' I nearly slammed the book shut in my shock. What was this woman doing—talking directly to me? I hadn't asked anything. Shouldn't she just leave me alone and let me read her story and take it as I wish? Something was obviously wrong here."

He examines his own relationships with and attitudes toward women through his responses to the constant sound of Virginia Woolf's voice. The autobiographical essay takes on the shape of a dialogue between aspiring male writer and authoritative female writer.

> Virginia Woolf, with her casual yet firm voice, seemed to be offering her hand to anyone who was willing to undertake the journey. Convinced I would not reach the end without her as my guide, I took hold of her hand. Mine was sweaty.
>
> No sooner had we begun than Virginia asserted, ''Fiction here is likely to contain more truth than fact. . . . I need not say what I am about to describe has no existence.''
>
> I squeezed her hand tighter—no existence—for she deemed the earth below my feet to be imaginary, and it sank away. Before my vertigo subsided, I found we were walking along the venerable turf of Oxford University, surrounded by its ancient buildings, sacred churches, and revered libraries—this was something of a comfort.

In this excerpt we can see how Charles Baraw makes use of the imagined experience to mingle with details of his reality and the language of Woolf's text to organize meaning into a text of his own.

Several features distinguish the form of "Purgatory" in addition to its references to other works. First, the author keeps the piece firmly grounded in place. He describes his scene of reading as follows and keeps referring to that place until the end of reading *A Room of One's Own:*

> I picked it up one day, and lay beneath a tall, strong maple tree which was caressed by an unusually brilliant sun. Its leaves were just beginning to ignite; some on top were unusually bright red, and the rest were in various stages of combustion—orange, yellow, and green. I was as happy as I could hope, under the circumstances, under the tree on the thick grass on a fine September day.
>
> I started to read.

The second most important feature of Charles's essay is the way he relies on dialogue to advance the narrative and its revelatory power. The central dialogue is the one he carries on with Virginia Woolf as his mentor, using her actual language in combination with his imagined (yet real!) language:

> All through lunch Virginia's insistent question, ''why, why are men so angry?'' rang in my head. It was driving me crazy. Meanwhile Virginia read the newspaper. Suddenly she announced, ''The most transient visitor to

> this planet must see that England is under the rule of a patriarchy.'' I perked up. The ringing question stopped. This was common ground. I agreed enthusiastically, remembering my paper on Milton, ''Paradise Lost: A Poetical Rationalization of Patriarchy.'' Yes, the domination of women is a key to upholding social hierarchies, the state, and . . .

The dialogue with Virginia Woolf and the memories of and references to other writers are constantly punctuated by Charles's dialogues with his sister and with Deidre and other women in his life. In these remembered conversations, Baraw realizes the many connections between Woolf's words and his own relationships with women and his attitudes about male and female in art and as artists.

> Virginia returned to the question. Why are men angry? Her calm voice shattered my careful logical constructions. ''Life for both sexes . . . is arduous, difficult, a perpetual struggle . . . it calls for confidence in oneself. And how can we generate this imponderable quality most quickly? By thinking that people are inferior to oneself?'' I nearly choked. . . . ''Women have served all these centuries as looking-glasses possessing the magic and delicious power of reflecting the figure of man at twice the natural size.''
>
> Sheri, my little sister, not yet five, sat across from me on the floor. She looked in a toy mirror and pretended to apply makeup. I sauntered over and knocked it out of her hands.

True to memory and true to the way memory operates in time, the third feature Baraw's writing displays so vividly is that, although a narrative, his autobiography moves around in time so that the contemporary consciousness becomes intrinsic to the development of the self. He writes:

> Virginia kept pushing further and further, memory after memory crowded my mind.
>
> ''The looking-glass vision is of supreme importance because it changes the vitality; it stimulates the nervous system. Take it away and a man may die like a drug fiend deprived of his cocaine.''
>
> COCAINE! cooo-caine. . . . Karla, my high school girlfriend . . . sat on my bed. . . .
>
> ''Yeh, Karla, let's do another line—I still have to write that paper.''
>
> ''But I have to drive home, and the roads are terrible.''

This scene also continues as Baraw recognizes yet another painful instance of his exploitation of women, especially with regard to writing—a recurring theme in this self-examination.

Moving around in time and evoking many voices in literature and in his own life in fully developed scenes and settings enable Baraw to create a textual form that, although clearly linked to what writers in the past from Dante to Woolf have done with the actual circumstances of their own lives, expresses what he sees himself as being at this time in his education. It's a marvelous blend of reader response literary criticism and of autobiography that calls the self into being while making a text. Through writing "Purgatory," with its intertextual resonances with Dante and with Woolf, Baraw expands his knowledge of autobiography as literature, the lives of women and men as writers, and the emerging contours of his own capacity for creating voices through which to give voice to his world.

OPEN-ENDED

While it may not be appropriate on all writing occasions to use "I" as personally as I have shown it being used in this chapter, knowing more ways to incorporate your own life experience into the life of what you read whenever you write about literature gives you more choices about which voice to select for expressing yourself. Much of what I've suggested is close to William Stephany's advice in his chapter, "Imaginative Writing and Risk Taking." Much of what I've suggested also has links to Toby Fulwiler's "Journal Writing" and Robyn Warhol's "Writing Critical Essays." It's as if the personal response to literature falls somewhere between the informality of journal writing and the more formal structures of the critical essay.

Perhaps I've altered the way you will regard yourself as a writer about literature while you are reading literature. You are, after all, an author whenever you write, and just *who* you are signifies a great deal for your ongoing process of self-creation. The autobiographical element in all texts is what makes each of us anxious when we show what we have written to another reader, no matter how sympathetic that reader might be: it is always as if we are being judged along with our words—our words *are* us in an important way as we seek to join a community of readers and writers through literary study. Writing autobiographically is exploratory and, for that reason, risky. You may often ask, as Charles Baraw does at the end of his essay, "But how, how, I wondered, would I squeeze this onto paper? Virginia Woolf had one more answer. 'So long as you write what you wish to write, that's all that matters, and whether it matters for ages or hours, nobody can say.' I walked on."

WORKS CITED

Didion, Joan. "Why I Write." *Eight Modern Essayists.* Ed. William Smart. 4th ed. New York: St. Martin's 1985.

Woolf, Virginia. "A Sketch of the Past." *Eight Modern Essayists.* Ed. William Smart. 4th ed. New York: St. Martin's 1985.

CHAPTER

EIGHT

Imaginative Writing and Risk Taking

William A. Stephany

In most cases, writing an analytical or interpretive paper will be the way you can best demonstrate the quality of your reading and thinking about a work of literature. However, if that is by far the most common and usually the most appropriate form for your writing, it is by no means the only one. There may be times when the best way for you to respond to a work might be to write a parody or an imitation of it or to write some other form of imaginative or playful paper. Recently, when I assigned a paper in a survey of British literature, in addition to four traditional topics for analytical essays, I offered students the following option:

> Congratulations! You have just been awarded a one-month trial membership in the Scriblerus Club. Now that you have read some of the works of your fellow club members Jonathan Swift and Alexander Pope, perhaps you would like to try your hand at a similar act of creation. Perhaps you would like to bring Lemuel Gulliver out of retirement and compose a portion of his fifth voyage, one which would reveal something about our world. Or perhaps you have found some of the lost couplets of Alexander Pope, originally intended for inclusion in any of his poems assigned for class.
>
> Or perhaps you'd like to try your hand at a parody of the conventions, style, or concerns of any writer or work covered this semester. Try your hand at a metaphysical conceit or Miltonic blank verse or heroic couplets. Remember that parodists often strive for a disparity between content and parodied form: part of the fun of the Dunciad and "Rape of the Lock" lies in the heroic treatment of inherently non-heroic subjects.

In response to this assignment, several students wrote chapters from an imagined fifth Book of *Gulliver's Travels,* and most of them did an excellent job of maintaining a tone akin to Swift's. One, for example, caught the spirit of Swift's use of gratuitous detail to imply, tongue-in-cheek, that these clearly fantastic voyages actually happened:

> . . . I left with a crew of sixty-five aboard the <u>Devonshire</u> well equipped for most difficulties I would encounter. It had been four years since my last voyage. . . . First mate Lou Noonford spotted land at 3:15 on the twenty-second day, so we sailed south until we reached the rocky shore where we were met by what appeared to be a friendly fisherman.
>
> Andy

Only someone who had entered into the pleasure of reading *Gulliver's Travels* could emulate the style in this way. Because of the way it brings one element of the work to the foreground, Andy's imitation may itself be considered a form of interpretation.

An imaginative paper can also demonstrate an understanding of a work's thematic concerns. In his version of a fifth book, another student, Jim, extended one of the patterns through which Swift presents Gulliver's increasing misanthropy. In Book I, Gulliver is shipwrecked; in Book II, he is abandoned; in Book III, he is set adrift by pirates; in Book IV, he is the victim of mutiny. The motivation for his "journeys" gets worse and worse. In Jim's paper, Gulliver, whom we had left hating humans and loving horses at the end of Book IV, murders a man who is whipping a horse, and so begins his final adventure by fleeing in an open boat from a lynch mob.

A creative response to an assigned reading can also use the form of the original to comment on some aspect of our contemporary world. A third student wrote about Gulliver's journey to a fictional "land of excessive knowledge," where he encounters a native named Dalloway:

> The inhabitants are much like humans, but supposedly better because of their capacity to take in verbal and written knowledge. . . . Lessons are taught by educators who speak at sixty words per ciab. A ciab is almost equal to ten seconds. These people have existed for nearly two trillion years, so in each education period almost two thousand years are covered. . . . [Knowledge] is served to them at such a quick pace that they neither can retain nor recall much of it. Dalloway also conveyed to me that the thirst for knowledge is so great that most pupils interpret it in the wrong way.
>
> Phil

Phil is here recalling Swift's own thematic concerns, especially in Book III, in which he satirizes inappropriate approaches to knowledge. His imagined world allows him to make his point about the frustrations of taking a lecture-format survey, one covering British literature from the seventh through the eighteenth centuries in one semester. Since his parody is true to the spirit and form of Swift's work (and includes quotations from and mock scholarly annotations on Shakespeare), he also demonstrates how much he has learned from his reading, a technique that inherently confers credibility to his implied critique of the course format.

"RULES" FOR RISK TAKING

However attractive an option of this sort might seem, let us acknowledge from the outset that novelty of approach is no guarantee that a paper will be written well, and if you've never tried this kind of writing before, you will probably welcome some guidelines before beginning. You will realize, I assume, that none of the suggestions I'm about to make should be regarded as hard-and-fast rules for writing this kind of paper. It would be ironic for me to propose in one paragraph that you expand the possibilities for writing about literature, only to begin limiting those possibilities in the next one. I would like to describe what some of my students have done, in order to suggest the wide range of what is possible and also to generalize about why certain kinds of writing have worked.

There are, however, three principles which are so universally applicable that I'd suggest you *should* consider them to be absolute.

Careful Reading

Rule number one is important for any kind of writing about literature: *Know your subject matter.* In order to do a good job writing the kind of paper I am proposing, you need to have read the text closely, to have thought about it deeply, to have internalized for yourself its form, its themes, its structure, its rhythms, both verbal and conceptual, its relationship to the other readings in the course. If your paper is to be effective, it must be more than just a clever reaction to the text; it must be an interpretation of it. Whether your purpose is to mimic a writer's stylistic quirks (as Andy does in his parody of *Gulliver*), or to cast light on his or her subject matter (as Jim does), or to illuminate our own world as mediated through the assigned text (as Phil does), you need a clear sense of your purpose as a writer and a solid understanding of the original text in order to write an effective paper.

Voice

Rule number two is more specifically appropriate for an imaginative paper: *Maintain a consistent voice.* If your paper requires you to adopt a voice or a point of view, don't shift ground in the middle to explain what you're doing; allow the voice to develop. Swift himself provides an excellent model for this principle in his famous essay "A Modest Proposal." As an Irish patriot, he had already written a wide range of pamphlets protesting the economic abuses England had been inflicting on Ireland in the early eighteenth century. The suggestions he made in these "analytical essays" were all ignored, so he finally circulated anonymously a pamphlet written in the style of a "Projector," the term used in his day to describe people who proposed projects for implementation of economic or social policy. In this case, the project being advanced is one which would allegedly cure the country of its crippling poverty. Only after we've read several pages of cool, deadpan calculation about the scope of the problem does the full horror of the project become clear—that the infants of the poor be fattened for the first year of their lives and then slaughtered, their meat offered for sale to the wealthy. A bit later still, the pamphlet's underlying figure of speech becomes clear:

since the landlord class has been metaphorically consuming the parents, they may as well literally consume the children. The chilling effect of the whole piece depends on Swift's relentless consistency in maintaining the speaker's matter-of-fact voice. With his concentration on mathematical finesse and blind logic, the speaker implicitly condemns those like himself who would treat a human crisis as if it were an intellectual problem.

Revision

Rule number three actually applies to any kind of writing, not just to writing about literature: *Revise.* Your paper will assume its final polish and its final point only as a result of several revisions. The point seems obvious but needs to be made, since a creative paper might often begin life as a journal entry or free writing. While this might be a thoroughly appropriate and normal way for the idea, or even for an entire draft, to be generated, such a draft, if left unrevised, will almost surely be inadequate as a final paper. Be prepared for the possibility that you may be too close to your original draft immediately after completing it to assume editorial objectivity toward it: it's difficult—indeed, for most of us, it's impossible—to be creative and critical at the same time. Let at least a day pass after you've written your draft before you return to it to revise it, and then try to read it objectively, as someone else will read it. Better still, find someone else to whom you can read your work, ideally a friend who is also in the course for which you're preparing the paper. Such a person has read the text you're writing about and shares with you a familiarity with the dynamics of the class and the concepts that have been considered. As you read your paper aloud to such an audience, you will hear the parts of the paper that work well or poorly; your friend will hear more.

CREATIVE CHOICES

There are several ways in which you might write creatively about a work of literature. Here are a few:

Imitation of Form

Parody is the term used for writing that imitates the style of another, usually famous, piece of work, and sometimes this imitation of form can be extremely close, maintaining the exact rhyme scheme of a poem, for example, or the syntax of the original's sentences.

The sixteenth-century writer Christopher Marlowe's poem, "The Passionate Shepherd to his Love," inspired two well-known parodies of this sort. Marlowe begins his poem:

> Come live with me and be my love,
> And we will all the pleasures prove
> That valleys, groves, hills, and fields,
> Woods, or steepy mountain yields. (813)

In this famous pastoral poem, Marlowe's shepherd invites his beloved nymph to live with him a simple life of uncomplicated pleasure. Several of his contemporaries wrote poems in response to Marlowe's, two of which are themselves quite famous. Walter Raleigh's

"Nymph's Reply to the Shepherd" repeats many of the same words and deals with many of the same concepts, but in order to make the opposite point. For Raleigh's nymph, time and deception make it impossible to accept the offer of a world without responsibilities. He begins:

> If all the world and love were young,
> And truth in every shepherd's tongue,
> These pretty pleasures might me move
> To live with thee and be thy love. (782)

If Raleigh's response is serious, John Donne's is comic. He begins his poem, "The Bait," by inviting his love to live with him so they can go fishing together:

> Come live with me and be my love,
> And we will some new pleasures prove,
> Of golden sands and crystal brooks,
> With silken lines and silver hooks. (1074)

In response to the assignment reproduced earlier in this chapter, three students wrote close parodies of poems studied during the semester. Like Raleigh's, the first matches the serious tone of the original; like Donne's, the other two are lighter in tone, though also serious. Shakespeare's Sonnet 73 appears on the next page with Melissa's parody below it.

The rhyme schemes of the two poems are the same (though the logical structure of Shakespeare's first twelve lines consist of three groups of four lines, and Melissa's consists of four groups of three). As in Shakespeare's poem, Melissa's speaker is conscious of aging and speaks of what one can see in her, but in contrast to the relatively tranquil resolution in Shakespeare's poem, where advancing age increases the intensity of love, Melissa's sonnet presents a terrifying view of aging. "In me thou seest what soon shall be thy fate," says her speaker, and the result is a rejection which isolates the elderly from loved ones.

Another student, Peter, achieves a delightfully comic effect by dealing with a relatively trivial topic in the style of a poem dealing with a serious one. John Donne's poem "The Good Morrow" celebrates the wonders of "awakening" to true sexual intimacy; Peter calls his parody, celebrating a love affair with a lawn mower, "The Good Toro." See page 1745 for the first stanzas of the two poems.

A third student, Cullen, also writes a comic parody, but one with some bite to it. She recasts Marvell's "To His Coy Mistress" in a hip contemporary slang in a way that may imply a criticism of the male speaker's arrogance in both poems. See page 1746 for the first verse paragraphs of the two poems.

Parodies

Parodies of specific works need not follow the form of the originals as closely as these examples do. Students of mine have written a wide range of imitations which have in various ways illuminated either the original text, our modern world, or both. They have written modern versions of Old English riddles, dramatic monologues imagined to have been spoken by Beowulf, and a "boasting speech" by Mohammed Ali in the style of an Anglo-Saxon hero, all following the conventions of Old English poetry. Several students in my Chaucer courses have written imitations of "The General Prologue" to *The Canterbury Tales,* usually in iambic pentameter couplets, sometimes even attempting to use Chaucer's Middle English.

If you do attempt a parody of this sort, try to be as faithful as you can to the style of the original. Show your reader how thoroughly you have interiorized its poetic conventions and "intellectual tics." At its best, writing of this sort is not only elegant and fun, but incisive literary criticism: you teach your reader to see the work, at least the parts you parody, as you do. Mohammed Ali's boast, for example, even while it showed a familiarity with the forms and conventions of Old English poetry, suggested something about the survival in an

Original

That time of year thou mayst in me behold
When yellow leaves, or none, or few, do hang
Upon those boughs which shake against the cold,
Bare ruined choirs, where late the sweet birds sang.
In me thou seest the twilight of such day
As after sunset fadeth in the west;
Which by and by black night doth take away,
Death's second self that seals up all in rest.
In me thou seest the glowing of such fire,
That on the ashes of his youth doth lie,
As the deathbed whereon it must expire,
Consumed with that which it was nourished by.
This thou perceiv'st, which makes thy love more strong,
To love that well, which thou must leave ere long.

William Shakespeare

Parody

That time of year thou mayst in me behold
When yellow teeth, or none, or few do stay
In softened gums which chatter 'gainst the cold.
A halo of hair, yet sparse and bristly grey
In me thou seest, and yet thou failst to see
My heart, that hasn't changed inside.
Inside I'm more than how I look to thee.
My body's weak, but my soul shall never die.
In me thou seest what soon shall be thy fate.
My mind a mix of thoughts half done,
Cherished loves shriveled to bitter hate,
Awaiting friends who oft forget to come.
This thou perceiv'st, which keeps thee from my side,
And chokes thy love until the day I've died.

Melissa

Original: The Good Morrow

I wonder, by my troth, what thou and I
Did, till we loved? Were we not weaned till then,
But sucked on country pleasures, childishly?
Or snorted we in the seven sleepers' den?
'Twas so; but this, all pleasures fancies be.
If ever any beauty I did see,
Which I desired, and got, 'twas but a dream of thee.
John Donne

Parody: The Good Toro

I wonder, by my blade, what thou and I
Did, till we cut? Had I no machine till then,
But cut country lawns, so primitively?
Or pushed and snipped I for neighborhood Men?
'Twas so; but then, Sears' catalog was sent me.
If ever any mower I did see,
Which I desired, and got, 'twas but a dream of thee.
Peter

analogous modern context of the Anglo-Saxon warrior's spirit of assertiveness on the brink of battle. Parodies, by the way, are very often acts of love; people rarely devote this much time and effort to a work that is not worth it.

Imitation of Modern Literary or Cultural Forms

I have also had students devise modern alternates to Chaucer's "General Prologue" as a means for presenting characters in a quasi-encyclopedic format. One wrote about arriving in Canterbury with Chaucer's group of Pilgrims in the style of an article for *The New York Times* travel section. Another wrote a mock yearbook with invented biographies, student activities, and quotations, imagining for each pilgrim the high school characteristics that would develop into the characters as we have them. In both cases, the fun and value came from the writer's ability to invent specific details which recalled and reacted to details from Chaucer's text. The intent was not to escape from, but rather to illuminate, the literary work dealt with. One student imagined the sexually aggressive Wife of Bath on a television talk show; another, in a *Playboy* interview. Another dealt with "The Clerk's Tale," in which the improbably patient Griselda endures one affront after another from her increasingly obsessive husband, as an episode in the soap opera "Patience Place."

Finally, several students have written modern variants of Chaucer's *Troilus and Criseyde,* a romance about two young lovers in the doomed city of ancient Troy. Jennifer rewrote the story as a modern "romance" of the type you'd find on the shelves near the supermarket checkout, beginning her version as follows:

To His Coy Mistress

Had we but world enough, and time,
This coyness, lady, were no crime.
We would sit down, and think which way
To walk, and pass our long love's day.
Thou by the Indian Ganges' side
Shouldst rubies find; I by the tide
Of Humber would complain. I would
Love you ten years before the Flood,
And you should, if you please, refuse
Till the conversion of the Jews.
My vegetable love should grow
Vaster than empires, and more slow;
An hundred years should go to praise
Thine eyes, and on thy forehead gaze;
Two hundred to adore each breast,
But thirty thousand to the rest;
An age at least to every part,
And the last age should show your heart.
For, lady, you deserve this state,
Nor would I love at lower rate.

Andrew Marvell

To His Prude Babe

If we had more time after school,
Your Prudeness, Chick, would be real cool.
We could cruise and rap about stuff
Like cars—we'd never get enough.
You'd strut the Charles the whole night through
And count the street lamps. I'd follow you
On Storrow Drive real bummed. I'd leer
A long time before Senior year.
You could slam lockers in my face
Till insects are the human race.
My bulging feelings get real big,
More rockin' than our band's last gig.
Skip nights with the dudes to applaud
Your swinging hips, your gorgeous bod.
Sit home—picture your chest
For weeks—knowing you're the best.
A month or more for your behind.
The last month—here's to your mind.
'Cause smart Chicks should be treated fine;
My love, a slow buzz like good wine.

Cullen

> The tall and glamorous Criseyde glided into the fashionable hall, located in the exciting Greenwich Village section of New York City. Her flowing black gown enhanced the shimmering clear blue of her electric eyes. She slid into an elegant mahogany chair, the color of which contrasted darkly with her golden tresses. Crossing her shapely legs, she glanced across the <u>Palladium,</u> the most popular club in the Big Apple. Criseyde, the young and beautiful widow, glistened like a brilliant diamond among rough stones. . . .

In Chaucer's romance, the Palladion is the name of the annual celebration of Pallas Athena, goddess of Wisdom, at which Troilus first sees Criseyde and falls in love with her. In reconceiving the encounter as taking place in a singles bar, and the form as the modern "romance" of soft-core sexploitation, Jennifer is able to suggest something about the diminution of the term "romance" in our own culture, while simultaneously suggesting a sinister dimension to what is going on in Chaucer's poem as well.

Greg's response to the *Troilus* was a made-for-television movie called "Trevor and Chrissie" as seen through the eager eyes of Randall, Jr., an eleven-year-old who "has seen previews for it throughout the week and also read the *TV Guide* review that called it 'a hot and steamy romance.' " What Greg presents is an indirect commentary on Chaucer's use of an intrusive narrator who interrupts his story, particularly at moments of sexual interest, in a way that breaks the emotional spell he is creating. In the following passage, Greg is approaching his conclusion:

> Chrissie rolls her black silk stocking off of her well-formed calves. Trevor kisses her neck. ''I'm crazy about you!'' he says. He kisses her shoulder and reaches for the tassled silk strap that holds on her nightgown. He begins to pull it below her shoulder. Randall, Jr., has stopped breathing. He sits trembling, his eyes focused on the screen. Trevor pulls the strap even lower and starts on the other. Chrissie arches her back and licks her lips.
>
> The screen goes blank for a half second.
>
> ''NEW CHEESE WIZ, NOW IN MICROWAVABLE CONTAINER!''

The intrusion of the commercial and the eleven-year-old's voyeurism both create effects very much analogous to those of the *Troilus*'s narrator. As such, the parody is itself an act of interpretive analysis.

Rewriting the Text

You might rewrite a passage from a piece of fiction from an alternative point of view. If it is written in the third person, for example, rewrite it as if it were narrated by one of the characters. This would require you to be confident about the limits of the character's knowledge and about the peculiar qualities that would affect how this character would serve as a filter or center of consciousness through which the story could be told. You might also rewrite a work in a different genre: if it's a narrative, rewrite it as dialogue; if it's a play, retell it through a narrator. With any of these topics, what you would probably discover and should be sure to demonstrate is the way in which fundamental artistic choices limit subsequent decisions and predetermine the range of esthetic effects.

Rewriting the Ending

Sometimes students have told me that they really don't like the way a play or short story ends. Usually I've let remarks of this sort pass, but in doing so, I now realize, I've missed an opportunity. What I should say is, "If you don't like the ending, rewrite it." If someone asked you to do this, you would need to think about the work's structure, its themes, its effect. In order to figure out why you don't like the ending, you'd first have to figure out very carefully just why the work *does* end as it does and how that ending affects you.

Creating Dialogues

One way to demonstrate your mastery of the subject matter in a course is to create imagined discussions. For example, imagine an encounter between two or more of the writers whose works you're reading in a course. Or between two or more characters, perhaps from different works. Or between a writer and one or more of his or her characters.

Some Final Examples

For her paper on *Troilus and Criseyde,* Lisa wrote an imagined letter from Criseyde to Helen of Troy, composed after the fall of the city when she and Helen are both safely back in Greece, in which she presents her side of the story which Chaucer tells. Since Helen puts in a cameo appearance in Chaucer's romance, Lisa's premise is not really far-fetched, especially since Troilus and Criseyde exchange letters both before they become lovers and after they are separated, and these letters become one of the ways in which Chaucer himself presents their characters. Lisa's letter, in fact, filled with specific references to episodes in Chaucer's romance all as perceived by Criseyde, is really a creative variant of the traditional paper analyzing a character.

I'll end with two more examples from the survey course. One student transformed the quarreling of Adam and Eve, a moment of epic grandeur in Book IX of *Paradise Lost,* into a dispute among the actors on the set of the fictional soap opera, "Paradise Tossed." In this imagined dialogue, the actress, Eve, was protesting the role which the creator (presumably God) and the writer of the series (Milton) had conspired for her to play. Another student wrote a poem in blank verse, imitating Milton's form, with the capitalized first words of each line forming an acrostic, spelling out vertically down the left margin the words "OF PARADISE LOST AND REGAINED." (We had seen Milton use this technique on one occasion in his poem.) The subject matter of the student's poem, however, was not adapted from Milton, but from Chaucer: it imagined the emotional reaction of the maiden who is raped in the initial episode of "The Wife of Bath's Tale." Either of these students might have written about the cultural basis of gender roles or about the cultural distortion inherent in the canon of exclusively male-authored texts enshrined in the traditional *Beowulf* to 1800 survey course. In a way, both did.

THE EXPERIMENTAL TRADITION

If some of the student papers I've been discussing in this chapter seem too experimental to you, I would suggest that they are in many ways similar to works we normally think of as "great" literature. When works become accepted as influential or significant within our cultural tradition, it is easy for us to forget that often they were originally daring. Perhaps you have recognized this playful quality in some of the works I've mentioned already in this chapter: Swift's "Modest Proposal" and *Gulliver's Travels* and Donne's "The Bait" come readily to mind. But did you think of how outrageous Dante was in the *Comedy* in claiming that he's telling us about a journey he took through hell, purgatory, and heaven, conducted at first by the ancient Roman poet Virgil, then by a woman he had once loved, and finally by St. Bernard? Does Chaucer's conceptual daring occur to you when he insists that he was only a reporter traveling on the pilgrimage to Canterbury Cathedral, thereby denying authorial responsibility for the tales he narrates? His lesser known *Troilus and Criseyde* is equally daring in its insistence that the narrator is a pedantic scholar, innocent of sexual intimacy, who is translating from Latin into English a lost history of the Trojan War at the center of which is a story of passionate love. When the story he is translating turns erotic, he becomes alternately flustered and voyeuristic; when it turns tragic, he feels dread at his obligation to be true to a "history" he can't alter.

What all these texts share is their fundamental "bookishness." They are incorporating, reacting against, even rewriting earlier works from the culture in which they share, and in so doing they are contributing to a tradition which goes back to antiquity. Mark Twain, for example, is so much of an American institution as a humorist that we might overlook his brilliance in putting his Connecticut Yankee into King Arthur's court, thereby intersecting the worlds of modern scientific skepticism and medieval magic, the traditional concepts of military courtesy and chivalry found in Arthurian romance and the technological horrors of American Civil War weapons. In our own time, John Gardner's novel *Grendel* presents a book-long stream-of-consciousness monologue of the thoughts of the monster from *Beowulf.* Grendel's mind is filled with specific echoes from the Anglo-Saxon epic as re-imagined from his point of view, but the book's real focus seems to be to provide a commentary on certain twentieth-century philosophical and political ideologies to which the monster's ideas bear a disquieting similarity.

The central premise of Tom Stoppard's play *Rosencrantz and Guildenstern Are Dead* is that its audience is already familiar with Shakespeare's play *Hamlet.* The two plays deal with exactly the same characters, and the events of both are going on simultaneously, so that what happens onstage of one play is off-stage of the other. When characters exit from one play, they enter the other. By keeping the focus on minor characters, on powerless functionaries with no clear sense of separate identity, rather than on the royal family and the highly individualistic Hamlet, Stoppard indirectly comments on the lack of potential for heroic—or even significant—action in the contemporary world. Perhaps he suggests something about the nature of the power relations that lie just under the surface of Shakespeare's play, as well.

What all of these writers are doing is playing with and interpreting the inherited literary tradition, while finding ways to let it speak to their own worlds. There are times when you might choose to do the same. In fairness to you and your teachers, however, I have to conclude by reminding you that the kind of paper I've been talking about is not always appropriate. It's important for you to ascertain whether such an approach would be acceptable before submitting such a paper. Nevertheless, if you're keeping a course-related journal, either as a requirement or on your own, it would be perfectly natural for you to explore this kind of writing there. Moreover, remember that writing about literature need not always be a command performance and that your teacher need not be your only audience. Why not write something like this to show to your friends? And if the paper works, consider showing it to your teacher even if it doesn't count as part of a grade. Writing for an audience rather than for a grade might be an important step in your development as a writer.

As a teacher, when I approach a stack of student papers, I want to be taught. As a result of your paper, I want to read the work you're writing about in a new way. The kind of paper I've been discussing in this chapter can have the effect of "de-familiarizing" a work of literature. Works that were startling when they were originally written—and startling for me when I originally read them—can come to seem normal, tame, familiar, after they've been processed through the forms and formulas of academia year after year. Your paper can help make the work's original lightning visible, both for you and for me. Finally, it can help you incorporate those works into your own consciousness—of yourself, your literary tradition, and your world—in a playful way, and for those of us who love literature, our tradition can appropriately be considered our playground.

CHAPTER

NINE

Examining the Essay Examination

Tony Magistrale

Please write on two of the following topics. You will have 50 minutes to complete this examination. Write only in the examination book provided.

1. In "Out of the Cradle Endlessly Rocking" the discovery of worldly pain and death forms a connection to the self-discovery of a poet. Is this relationship between the awareness of death and the birth of a poetic spirit a convincing assertion? (20 minutes)
2. Discuss the importance of the father's character in Hemingway's short story "Soldier's Home." (20 minutes)
3. Compare Emily Dickinson's view on immortality in the poem "I've known a Heaven, like a Tent" to her perspective on this subject in any of her other poems studied this semester. (25 minutes)

When I showed these exam topics to several of the authors of the other chapters in this book, each one gave me a similar response: relief at not having to answer any of the questions. If English professors are glad to be free of such an ordeal, why do they put their students through it? Is the essay examination an educational rite of passage? A testing routine teachers are reluctant to give up? A fundamental illustration of the profession's tendency toward sadistic behavior? Maybe a little of each. But it is also something more.

Sid Poger, co-author of the poetry chapter, told me that he assigns essay examinations out of a desire to "help the student discover for him- or herself the major theme of the course throughout the term. That idea is what the essay will address, and I hope the student who has been in class, in mind as well as body, will come to recognize what's been going on." Another colleague, Tom Simone, feels that an essay exam is "the place for a student to shine. If he or she has been paying attention and has been thinking about the class material, my essays are always open-ended enough to allow him or her to show off." Bill Stephany, our medievalist, reminded me that he looks for "connections that surprise the teacher . . . giving information on topics I want to know more about." Editor Toby Fulwiler often sees essay exams as "more like 'free writes' than methodically structured prose."

If you look carefully at the reasons each of these professors gives for assigning essay questions, it is clear that exams are always more than a means for establishing a grade. Each of these teachers seeks to test your ability to interpret aspects of specific literary works or to synthesize disparate material covered in class into a more comprehensive whole. Sometimes, as in the Dickinson question above, a writing task may also ask you to recognize similarities and differences between two or more characters, themes, symbols, or individual texts. In any event, your instructor is interested not only in how much you know about a particular subject, but also about the course as a whole.

In a very real way, you begin to prepare for an exam on the first day of class, as you notice your professor's assignments, biases, and perspectives. Since essays are usually written for an audience of one—your teacher—what you say on an exam might be viewed as an intellectual dialogue with a person you know quite well. This doesn't mean that your writing should get chummy or informal, but it does suggest that you pay attention to your professor's beliefs. If you intend to present an opinion or perspective that will run contrary to your teacher's, be prepared to back it up especially well. In other words, be aware of your instructor's position and clearly acknowledge this awareness somewhere in the essay. Then go ahead and strike out on your own. Remember Professor Stephany's request for "surprises." You won't surprise any professor by writing safe answers, by simply reiterating interpretations from a lecture. On any given essay examination, I expect at least half the answers to do this, and quite frankly, after reading thirty attempts to reconstruct my lectures, it is always refreshing to discover someone saying something unique—especially if it is an articulate and supported reassessment of my interpretation.

But be careful here. Exam surprises can be both good and bad. The kind of surprise Bill Stephany encourages gets a teacher excited about what you have to say; it demonstrates not only a solid understanding of a poem or a novel, but also shows that you have spent some time considering its larger connections to the course and to your own life. In contrast, a student who disagrees with me without much thought and merely for the sake of saying something different or who goes off into a new interpretation without adequate support for the position is surely going to give me a surprise, but it will be one I probably will not enjoy.

WRITING UNDER PRESSURE

Composing answers to an essay examination may appear difficult enough when you are given several days to construct responses. The assignment becomes all the more challenging, however, when you must write in a short, predetermined period of time, usually surrounded by other students who seem to possess magical pens that seldom rise from the exam book's page. Writing under a time restraint demands even more concision and discipline than ordinarily employed in producing a research paper or a critical essay over an extended period of days or weeks. Time restraints preclude the luxury of multiple drafts or the leisure of returning to the work after an elapsed length of time. Perhaps this is one reason why so many teachers continue to assign in-class essay exams and believe they are important; as is often the case in contexts outside the classroom, we do not always have the opportunity to polish language until it says exactly what we want it to. We are often required to think quickly, to use words spontaneously yet accurately. And although this is a difficult activity, there are a few tricks you might learn.

One of the most common (and natural) reactions to an hour essay exam is panic. My own students reminded me of the anxiety and tension associated with this type of writing when I asked them to list their own attitudes toward the experience: "sweating palms, faint nausea," "a mixture of excitement and apprehension," "a pressing urge to go to the bathroom," and "a desire to hurry up and start the exam in order to get it over with."

On the typical examination, you have about twenty or thirty minutes per essay, so there is little room for mistakes. Your answers must get to the point immediately and concisely. You can't easily cross out or start over. Therefore, you must compose essays which are clearly written and, most important, carefully organized to answer the question being asked. But before considering a general procedure for structuring answers to essay questions, let's consider a few fundamental points to keep in mind prior to the actual writing.

Preliminary Steps and Some Practical Advice

An essay exam is first and foremost an essay. As such, it is important to decide what to include, what to exclude, how to arrange, and what to emphasize.

1. Before beginning any writing, you should read the entire test. What choices, if any, does the exam allow? What specific kinds of information does each essay require?
2. Which of the questions do you feel most comfortable answering? (It might help to start with the easiest and work your way to the most difficult.)
3. Allot yourself a certain period of time per answer and hold yourself to it. Instructors seldom sympathize with an indication you have run out of time.
4. Plan on building in enough time to read the exam over before handing it in. Simple qualifications to central arguments as well as mistakes in diction are hard to recognize in a first draft, but may be captured in revision.
5. Finally, when you feel ready to begin the actual writing, keep the following points in mind to help in organizing and presenting the essay: (a) circle core issues, concepts, and requests in the exam question itself; (b) use frequent paragraph breaks (each new paragraph is the place to make new arguments to recapture a tired professor's attention); (c) leave space on the left side of your paper or exam book for second thoughts and revisions; (d) write on every other line, as this will make it easier for your professor to read and for you to make changes directly into the text of your answer.

Types of Information Requests

The key to performing well on an essay examination is to understand completely what the questions are asking. The language of a given assignment will often contain hidden clues which reveal directions toward composing a potential answer. Consider, for example, this examination question from a recent literature midterm:

> Like many fiction writers, Ann Beattie acknowledges the influence of Ernest Hemingway on her writing. ''I sound like someone talking in The Sun Also Rises,'' says a character in ''The Lawn Party.'' Compare Beattie's narrative style to that of Hemingway.

First, notice how much information is already supplied in the question itself: an argument that suggests a firm connection between Beattie and Hemingway. The exam question identifies the connection through the quotation from "The Lawn Party," and then goes on to ask the student to elaborate upon an *already stated* position. Often if you read an examination question carefully, it is possible to sense at least an initial direction for writing. In this case, the teacher is interested in having the student pursue further the comparison between Beattie and Hemingway. But notice that this comparison is stated in specific terms: it asks for a discussion of *style*—that is, sentence structure, language exchanges between characters, word choice. It would not do, then, to approach the question by arguing that Beattie and Hemingway had common thematic concerns—similar perspectives about war, or the relationship between the sexes, or alcoholic consumption—unless these issues were directly connected to how Hemingway and Beattie actually tell their stories. An enterprising student may want to talk about these thematic issues—indeed, they are present in both authors—but would need to do so within the context of perhaps what is left unsaid in their spare, often dull sentences and platitudinous conversations. Hemingway and Beattie manage in their best stories to make us feel that there is something interesting beyond the simple declaratives that their characters utter. The writer of this exam question would want to discuss why the language is interesting and give examples of where it occurs.

On the other hand, suppose the student wished to disagree with the connection between Beattie and Hemingway. Is there room in the exam question for a writer to head in this direction? Yes. The word "compare" in the question allows flexibility. The term "comparison" usually calls for a larger, more inclusive approach to the topic that may include both similarities and differences. Only if you were asked to "contrast" Beattie with Hemingway, would you need to emphasize the differences. Therefore, any question that asks you to compare or contrast may be requesting (1) the differences between two or more things, (2) the similarities between generally dissimilar things, (3) an explanation of one thing in relation to something else, (4) a basis for evaluation and/or argument. All these comparisons and contrasts require you to go beyond individual positions, theses, or texts—to think about the *interrelationships* between characteristics of two or more concepts.

If an essay examination does not request some type of a comparison or contrast between individual works or concepts, it will generally ask you to *analyze* a single literary text or some aspect of it.

```
Discuss the symbolic functions of the plaster statue in
Flannery O'Connor's short story ''The Artificial
Nigger.''
```

This question asks you to explain the relationship between parts and a larger whole. By first identifying and then explaining the significance of a literary text's components—considering what, where, why, and how they operate—we gain a fuller appreciation of how individual elements work together to produce structural unity. To understand the role of O'Connor's statue in this story, the writer must establish the specific connection between the Artificial Nigger and the events which have occurred to the protagonists in the course of the story. It is important to highlight the statue in light of this context, so that it rightfully occupies center stage in your analysis. The answer you eventually write should focus on this end—everything you say about this story should in some way relate back to the statue. Otherwise, you may distract your reader from the real purpose of the writing and thus weaken your analysis.

Planning

Once you understand the type of information the exam question requests, you should plan a response to it. First, make a simple list of main ideas. This will generate new concepts at the same time as it will help in formulating the language you will need to construct a coherent argument. Second, use a written plan to keep your writing focused on the subject. After you have composed such a plan, check it against the examination request. Are the topics you intend to discuss in your answer relevant to what is being asked? Below is an outline Nancy used to help her address the midterm examination question raised at the beginning of this chapter, "Compare Emily Dickinson's view on immortality in the poem 'I've known a Heaven, like a Tent' to her perspective on this subject in any one of her other poems studied this semester." Nancy's literature class had not studied this poem prior to the exam, so it was reproduced under the topic assignment.

NANCY'S PLAN
INTERPRET POEM: —"heaven" as circus tent
—circus tent as symbol of afterlife
COMPARE TO: "I heard a Fly buzz—when I died"
—human isolation
—lost vision, taken away
—same conclusion: no hope/light

Looking at Nancy's plan, it becomes clear that she has constructed an excellent framework for composing an essay answer. She chooses first to analyze the poem cited in the exam, "I've known a Heaven, like a Tent," emphasizing the use of a departed circus as a metaphor for describing the loss of heaven. (Pay particular attention to the manner in which she will blend her reading of the poem with specific excerpts from the poem itself, thereby making her interpretation all the more persuasive.) From there, she then seeks to complete the assignment by comparing it to another Dickinson poem, "I heard a Fly buzz." Because the exam asked for a comparison, Nancy elected to work with a poem that has a perspective similar to "I've known a Heaven, like a Tent." She could just as well have gone

I've Known a Heaven, Like a Tent

I've known a Heaven, like a Tent—
To wrap its shining Yards—
Pluck up its stakes, and disappear—
Without the sound of Boards
Or Rip of Nail—Or Carpenter—
But just the miles of Stare—
That signalize a Show's Retreat—
In North America—

No Trace—no Figment of the Thing
That dazzled, Yesterday,
No Ring—no Marvel—
Men, and Feats—
Dissolved as utterly—
As Bird's far Navigation
Discloses just a Hue—
A plash of Oars, a Gaiety—
Then swallowed up, of View.

in the opposite direction, choosing a poem to contrast with the exam selection. Finally, notice that in both the plan and the essay that emerge, Nancy maintains her critical attention on the unifying thesis of the issue at hand: how each of these poems reflects a comparable attitude toward the theme of immortality.

> In the poem ''I've known a Heaven, like a Tent,'' Emily Dickinson in her own way is describing her idea of heaven. It seems as though she breaks a childhood myth with this poem. The myth being that heaven is a visible place that awaits us with its great pearly gates and its angels waiting to take you in and check your name off this great ledger that some old white-haired man is seated in front of. This ''Heaven'' she has ''known,'' may refer to a glimpse of God's happy place, or perhaps she is recalling a special ''heavenly'' moment or event that profoundly touched her life. In either event, myth or reality, this recollected image of heaven is now gone, and it is significant that she ties its departure to a circus show ''That dazzled, Yesterday.'' The carnival is a visual image from childhood (perhaps invoking the poet's earlier, innocent perception of heaven?) that promises fun and excitement, but in this poem those promises are unfulfilled, as the tent ''wrap[s] its shining Yards—/Pluck[s] up its stakes, and disappear[s]—.'' What was here yesterday, her heaven or hope of attaining this place, has gone without a figment or trace—utterly dissolved and ''Then swallowed up, of View.''

I Heard a Fly Buzz

I heard a Fly buzz—when I died—
The Stillness in the Room
Was like the Stillness in the Air—
Between the Heaves of Storm—

The Eyes around—had wrung them dry—
And Breaths were gathering firm
For that last Onset—when the King
Be witnessed—in the Room—

I willed my Keepsakes—Signed away
What portion of me be
Assignable—and then it was
There interposed a Fly—

With Blue—uncertain stumbling Buzz—
Between the light—and me—
And then the Windows failed—and then
I could not see to see—

> Dickinson now interprets heaven as a vast emptiness, just a ''View.'' She discovers that heaven cannot be traced with empirical evidence, that it is just an eternity: ''No Trace—no Figment of the Thing,'' leaving only ''just the miles of Stare.'' This theme of disillusionment with heaven, of eternal loneliness and emptiness, can be traced throughout her poetry.
>
> In ''I heard a Fly buzz—when I died,'' when the speaker began the poem in the process of dying, she rose above herself and was aware of <u>everything</u> going on around her: the ''Breaths gathering firm,'' the ''Eyes wrung dry,'' and the ''Keepsakes—Signed away.'' But when she finally dies—at the moment of death—''the windows failed—and then/ I could not see to see,'' meaning that she could no longer see anything ahead of her. Just as in the exam poem, the afterlife portrayed in ''I heard a Fly buzz'' is unattainable, the ''Heaven'' remains unseen, a mere suffocating darkness. As her ''Heaven'' in the circus poem just dissolves, in ''I heard a Fly buzz'' there is no hope for a beautiful or fulfilling afterlife. Her view in both these poems is filled with the dark despair of a Melville or a Hawthorne, rather than the unqualified faith in the future of a transcendentalist.

Nancy's analysis is a good illustration of how the act of writing helps the mind not only to clarify concepts, but also to develop new insights and parallels. Her answer is a study in the art of discovery. It starts by working through the complex details of a poem she has never seen before and concludes by reconnecting to information in "I heard a Fly buzz," which is a work she knows quite well. Notice that in writing about both of these poems Nancy not only discovers some similarities they share, but also goes on to enlarge her understanding of Dickinson as a nineteenth-century American poet.

The concluding sentence of her essay is different—in diction and scope—from the rest of her response. Here is evidence of the "surprise" Stephany mentioned earlier when explaining his reason for assigning essay topics. Nancy's final sentence jumps at the reader because it extends her analysis of these two Dickinson poems to include an important assertion about the poet's relationship to her literary contemporaries. If Nancy were able to revise this essay, or if it were a take-home examination, this final sentence might well become her first sentence, as it is a large thesis statement that is supported in the act of interpreting the two poems. In any event, as this concluding sentence represents the culmination of Nancy's effort to understand the poetry of Emily Dickinson, she might highlight it in a new paragraph or by somehow distinguishing it from the rest of the essay.

STRUCTURING ESSAY ANSWERS

Under the tense and circumscribed conditions of a timed examination, most students tend to write too much: by saying as much as they can about a particular text or a writer, they trust that the torrent of information will sufficiently impress the teacher or somehow manage to strike upon a response relevant to the question. Consider, for example, Ken's response to a midterm examination question asking him to discuss the significance of Madeline Usher's role in Poe's tale "The Fall of the House of Usher":

> Poe's tales have no apparent logic to them. He was a writer from the period of dark romanticism and his stories often show a person's inability to control experiences that exist psychologically and from his personal negative motivations. Poe hated women, or at least he didn't trust them very far, so all his male characters rebel against them. Poe's own relationship to women was influenced by his mother's rejection of him at an early age and he spent the rest of his life trying to find someone to take her place. The male characters in his stories take drugs and use exotic settings to forget tragic love affairs that are similar to the ones Poe himself experienced with women in his own life. For them, time is always an enemy—it is there as a reminder of frustration and ultimate death. Madeline Usher is a symbol of Poe's women. She is all the things her brother hates, all the things out of his control. She suffers from the same kind of illness that is killing Usher.

What can we say is strong in this essay? Ken demonstrates a wide-ranging understanding of Poe. Many of the points he makes in this essay are valid. He knows, for instance, that Poe was a dark romantic, that the writer's feelings toward women were ambivalent, that his male protagonists are deeply troubled individuals subject to compulsive and aberrant behavior, that time is a symbol of human destruction throughout Poe's stories, and finally, that Madeline is a constant source of irritation for her brother. What are the problems with this essay? A central one is within its organization or structure; Ken wanders around the subjects of Poe's fiction in a manner painfully reminiscent of Roderick himself wandering the corridors of the Usher mansion. His writing has neither direction nor thesis; he never really comes to terms with Madeline's role in the story, and thus produces more of a collection of assertions rather than a cohesive essay. Instead of pursuing only material relevant to answering the exam question, Ken tries to impart everything he knows about Poe's fiction. He doesn't really begin to answer the question until line 14 of a 17-line response.

There are several places in this answer where the writer might have "turned the corner" to commence a more focused analysis of "The Fall of the House of Usher," and Madeline's character specifically. What, for instance, are "all the things her brother hates, all the things out of his control"? If Madeline is symbolic of these restrictive elements, a more detailed explanation of (1) exactly what these elements are and (2) how they are embodied in Madeline would help the reader to see the connection between her character and the rest of the story. Once Madeline's relationship to Roderick is ascertained and clarified, then a discussion of the larger issue of Poe's general attitude toward women—either in other stories or as biographical criticism—makes more sense. But unless these issues are tied directly to the discussion of Madeline's relationship with her brother, the examination question remains essentially unanswered. Rather than simply "leaping into" an essay answer on an exam, and thereby encouraging your thoughts to wander in a number of directions, as in Ken's example above, it is better to keep your writing focused. Here's where some sort of writing plan can prove particularly useful, since long, meandering responses suggest imprecise, fuzzy thinking, even if relevant information is embedded somewhere in your response.

Once you have decided exactly what the exam question requires and the plan is

completed, you are ready to begin writing. But how? Your written plan contains pertinent information for developing an essay, but in what order should these points be presented? What form should the answer take? What should come first?

In the comparison-contrast example Nancy supplied earlier, the writer saved the actual comparison until the end, after she had focused individual attention on each of the Dickinson poems. On the one hand, I think her essay is organized in such a way that the material is presented clearly and concisely (and organization is one of the most difficult accomplishments in writing an essay exam, since good insights may occur late in the writing). On the other hand, Nancy could have structured things differently and still achieved similar results. Employing the same ideas listed under her plan, the major points of the essay could easily be reorganized to introduce the comparison between the two poems at the beginning, rather than at the end.

In discussing strategies for structuring essay exams, several of my English department colleagues suggested that the strongest part of any essay should be its beginning. Since professors read hundreds of essays in a rush, students should give them what they want up front, and certainly within the first paragraph. Consequently, Nancy might have inverted the form of her essay—starting with a few sentences to introduce the most important points of comparison between the two poems, then a paragraph or two describing how each poem connects to the theme of immortality, and concluding with a summary that brings the two poems together again.

Nancy's writing illustrates that the form an essay takes is often less important than the information it provides and the degree to which that information responds accurately to what the examination question asks. Other instructors may feel differently. It would be well within the province of a teacher to argue that Nancy's answer does not confront the issue of an actual comparison between two of Dickinson's poems until the final paragraph, and as a consequence her response is not so complete as it should be. Some instructors might feel that since the request for a comparison is at the heart of the examination question, language directly addressing this issue should appear within the essay's opening paragraph.

Thus, the standard advice in structuring essays is to create some version of a "funnel"

A Noiseless Patient Spider

A noiseless patient spider,
I mark'd where on a little promontory it stood isolated,
Mark'd how to explore the vacant vast surrounding,
It launch'd forth filament, filament, filament, out of itself,
Ever unreeling them, ever tirelessly speeding them.

And you O my soul where you stand,
Surrounded, detached, in measureless oceans of space,
Ceaselessly musing, venturing, throwing, seeking the spheres to
connect them,
Till the bridge you will need be form'd, till the ductile anchor hold,
Till the gossamer thread you fling catch somewhere, O my soul.

shape: start broadly by stating and defining the most important elements, or thesis, of your argument. Then, gradually narrow or specify your main argument through examples and illustrations of the points raised initially in the broad thesis statement. In this way, your examples and analyses will refer to concepts you have established, and your supporting evidence can be tailored to fit the major points which began the essay. This principle can be illustrated in the paragraphs that follow, taken from a midterm examination in which Susan was asked to relate the theme of Walt Whitman's short poem "A noiseless patient spider" to his larger poetic vision:

> Walt Whitman was a poet who wrote about the unity of all things. He took Emerson's doctrines to their furthest extremes, believing that not only were the diverse and individual elements of the universe related to one another but, in fact, that they were reflective of the same identical thing.
>
> Whitman's themes were about everything—a blade of grass, a prostitute, a dying man alone on a battlefield—and he believed sincerely that no one thing was better, or worse, than another. A spider (which before this class I would probably squash) is only a small part of the ''whole,'' yet is still connected to the ''whole,'' just as one human being is representative of a larger humanity.
>
> The spider is isolated, as are those individual men and women who fail to explore and learn from their surroundings and others, but the difference is that the spider creates a web which ''connects'' things together. Whitman's verse accomplishes the same sort of connecting. He unifies everything and everybody in poetic song. In the first half of ''Song of Myself'' the poet takes all of life's experiences and makes them his own—he observes and studies them—and then seeks to understand how they are connected to one another.
>
> In ''A noiseless patient spider'' he asks his soul the same question: ''Where do I stand?/ Surrounded, detached, seeking spheres to connect them.'' Only by ''connecting'' himself to everything and everyone he observes can the poet, like the spider's web, ''form a bridge'' that will link him to the rest of the world.

In the opening paragraph, Susan begins her analysis with a broad assessment of Whitman's poetry; she even includes a mention of Emerson's influence on his work. After establishing the unity theme in Whitman's poetry, she ends her first paragraph by tying this concept to "A noiseless patient spider": "A spider (which before this class I would probably squash) is only a small part of the 'whole,' just as one human being is representative of a larger humanity."

In the second paragraph, Susan's analysis becomes more specific, centering on the relationship between the metaphor of the spider's web and Whitman's broader poetic principles: ". . . the spider creates a web which 'connects' things together. Whitman's verse accomplishes the same sort of connecting. He unifies everything and everybody in poetic song." The connection between "A noiseless patient spider" and Whitman's canon is made explicit in her reference to "Song of Myself," and here she is careful to stress common themes found in both poems. The use of the "funnel" structure as an organizing metaphor in this essay aids Susan in developing her argument in a systematic and coherent manner. As the answer unfolds, she gradually narrows her analysis from the general to the specific, so that by the conclusion Whitman's poetic vision and the symbolic spider web become synonymous in purpose: "Only by 'connecting' himself to everything and everyone he observes can the poet, like the spider's web, 'form the bridge' that will link him to the rest of the world."

PREPARATION FOR A TIMED ESSAY EXAMINATION

Here's some good advice if you can follow it: A week or two before an examination, get together with several of your classmates and write three or four potential essay questions based upon lecture notes and textbook information. Compose answers to one or two of the questions posed by your classmates under exam conditions; allot the same amount of time your professor intends to allow. Once you have completed the essays, share your writing with the group, and suggest improvements for one another. This activity will help acquaint you with the process of having your work evaluated, at the same time as it will broaden your knowledge of the material in the course. You may even find yourself practicing an answer that will be similar (or, great joy, identical) to the very exam topic your professor poses.

THE TAKE-HOME EXAMINATION

A well-written essay—whether composed during a timed in-class examination or in response to a take-home assignment—reflects the strengths described in this chapter: it is organized and focused; it demonstrates the ability to analyze and/or engage comparative thought; it shows the capacity to assemble and assess information; and it indicates an understanding of course material and the capability to shape this understanding into writing appropriate to the exam topic. The take-home essay is closely related to its in-class brethren in form, content, and purpose. However, since they are each composed under different circumstances, there are some slight variations in their manner of production. Primarily, a take-home examination affords the chance to edit, to revise, and to rethink what you have composed. Furthermore, the take-home exam provides the opportunity to incorporate research—class notes, quotes, journals, and sometimes published scholarship—directly into the composition. It is, of course, a fatal mistake not to acknowledge citations used in a take-home exam. Richard Sweterlitsch and Robyn Warhol provide assistance in their chapters for avoiding plagarism, and their advice should be applied to take-home exams as well as to the composition of more formal research projects.

Using Class Notes and Journals

As Toby Fulwiler suggests in his chapter, journals are an excellent source for helping you to study for examinations, to assemble information for conducting research, and as a place to generate ideas through informal prose. Before writing a given essay assignment, read through your journal entries and class notes on areas germane to the topic. Sometimes you may discover whole sections or passages that require only slight modification for inclusion into the essay. Often a sentence or two, even the seed of an idea currently in undeveloped form, can point you in the direction for further writing.

Aside from generating ideas to use in composing a response, the journal is also the

place to begin the actual writing of the essay itself. Since a take-home exam affords you a certain amount of flexible time, use the journal to freewrite about your subject. The journal will not only help to start the flow of writing itself, but a couple of good entries may become the basis for your essay.

Revising and Editing

Since the take-home examination typically allows you several days to produce an essay, the sooner you get started writing, the more chance you will have to polish and improve its contents. Once a first draft of the essay is complete, reread it from start to finish, paying particular attention to logic and overall organization. Is your thesis clear, and is it developed throughout the length of the essay? Does it answer the question? Do individual paragraphs fit together, or would the thesis be more coherent if the order of presentation were rearranged?

When the revisions are completed, read the work aloud to a friend before typing it. The very act of reading an essay aloud can often reveal places where language might be improved, or where the logic of the argument needs to be strengthened. I often dictate my own prose into a tape recorder; the act of hearing my thoughts forces me to concentrate on how the writing sounds—from the overall development of a thesis to the way in which individual words work (or do not work) harmoniously with one another.

Preparation for a Take-Home Essay Examination

A few days before the exam is distributed, spend a couple of hours marking passages in texts and journals that you consider significant. This activity will accomplish two things. First, it will refresh your memory by helping you to refocus material studied weeks ago. Second, like the outline plan described earlier in this chapter, these recollections will get you thinking about the most important aspects of a writer's canon. Instead of beginning the exam on the day you receive it, your preparation will place relevant information at your fingertips, giving you an obvious head start on assembling evidence. (This process is especially valuable prior to in-class open-book examinations. Premarked notations and quotes will save you precious minutes during the exam itself.)

BEGINNING AT THE END: IN MEMORY OF BELLS

Last year I returned to my undergraduate alma mater, Allegheny College, for the first time since graduation a decade earlier. I arrived on campus on a day late in May—one of those glorious spring afternoons filled with promise when even the earth of the western Pennsylvania snowbelt is refreshed in light. It was warm and final examinations were in session, so all the windows of Arter Hall, home of the English Department, were open to the afternoon. As I strolled alongside the building, bemused by the torrent of recollections each step seemed to summon, a series of bells sounded from inside indicating the start of a final exam. All the old feelings returned—the nervous fingers, the twitch somewhere near the base of my stomach. The exam bell removed the brightness of that May afternoon. I was back in the dim grey air of Arter Hall, blue book open on the desk in front of me, three exam topics measuring the distance between my pen and summer vacation. I may well have decided at that very moment to write the chapter you have just finished reading.

CHAPTER

TEN

Writing Research

Richard Sweterlitsch

Last spring in my American Literature course, I assigned a paper that was to draw upon research. To most of the students, this meant "research paper," and off they went to the library to look through the card catalogue. One student, Marsha, remembered that her high school teacher talked about how much Fitzgerald's relationship with Zelda affected *The Great Gatsby.* So she checked out Arthur Mizener's *The Far Side of Paradise,* Sara Mayfield's *Exiles from Paradise: Zelda and F. Scott Fitzgerald,* and *Zelda: A Biography* by Nancy Milford. She skimmed the first chapters of each book and found enough material about the stormy relationship to fill a dozen or so index cards. She returned to her room and spent an afternoon arranging her notes; these she connected into a flowing essay, linked by her own transitions. The next day she added her endnotes and a bibliography, making sure that all the correct forms were followed. Her work was simple, to the point, and a waste of time.

Writing a paper based on research is nothing new for most students. Somewhere in high school or college, everyone has written a research paper, and many do what Marsha did. They scour the library card catalogue, find a couple of books and magazine articles related to their topic, and skim through them, taking down some notes. Writing the paper means piecing together quotes from various sources, writing footnotes and bibliography correctly, and turning in the paper for a grade. This is not research writing. Marsha's paper had nothing to offer other than a demonstration of her ability to stitch together a patchwork from diverse sources. While she took a stab at researching a particular topic, she went no further than reproducing ideas from other scholars. Her voice was not heard; there was no sense of personal excitement over researching some curiosity she had about the novel. The paper offered no new insights and had no fresh purpose. Her research, sketchy as it was, reinforced something she already knew, but she had nothing new to share with me or anyone else in the class. It was all so very little.

Writing up one's research is not a mindless task of regurgitating critics' opinions. It is personal writing. The voice of the writer—the "I"—should come through loudly and clearly. The "I think" and "I believe" have a place in the research paper. Too often, research writing degenerates into an impersonal treatise with no sense of the personal curiosity that prompted the search in the first place or the personal excitement the writers felt when they resolved their questions. The very personal critical writings that characterize much of the

literary criticism and research writings in the late nineteenth and early twentieth centuries have been replaced by the disinterested and sterile—and too often boring—voice of the clinician, as literary scholars try to sound like something they are not—scientists.

After all, literary research is a type of humanistic inquiry. It is not meant to be an alienating experience. Researchers become thinkers by synthesizing their findings with their own ideas in order to produce new knowledge. They become writers when they present that knowledge in essays to the scholarly community. So, research reinforces the relationship between acquiring information and sharing new insights.

Research is a handmaid to a variety of approaches to studying literature. A critical essay may draw upon the insights other critics present in published essays. But we should not think that the only reason for undertaking research is to write a critical, analytic paper. Novelists, poets, and playwrights often do research to provide themselves with ideas and details they want to use in their work. For instance, playwright Tom Stoppard turned to Shakespeare's *Hamlet* for situations, characters, and themes when he was writing his own *Rosencrantz and Guildenstern Are Dead.* Another example: several years ago, a colleague writing a novel asked me—a folklorist by training—for some information about an Irish custom related to horses. I gave him a copy of *Irish Folk Ways* by E. Estyn Evans. My colleague wanted to be sure he had presented a particular tradition in his novel accurately. All conscientious writers want to know that their allusions are accurate, and so they research them carefully before finally integrating them into their writing.

Whether one is writing an analytical paper, a play, a poem, short story, novel, or book review, knowing how to do effective research is an important skill. It is fitting that research and writing based on research be an integral part of every class. In this chapter, I emphasize the kind of research one undertakes in order to write critical and analytic papers, the kinds generally discussed in this book.

GETTING STARTED

Writing a paper based primarily on research is different from other types of literary writing, but it does share some of the concerns of critical writing. In her chapter, Robyn Warhol points to the three main goals of critical writing: to describe, to evaluate, and to interpret a text. The only difference is that research writing includes reaching out to the findings of other scholars.

The primary task with literary research is finding a subject to write about and then narrowing it down to a topic and then a thesis. As students of literature, we have one advantage: we usually have a specific text to deal with. Obviously knowing the text well is a good place to start, asking questions of and about the text sets up a dialogue, as it were, between yourself and the text. Read the text looking for something that strikes you. Jot down questions and notes to yourself as you read, either in a journal, or as I usually do, right on the text itself. Give your ideas free rein; let them float around in your head for a while. Do some free writing.

The questions you may ask are as endless as there are ways of answering them. For example, literary scholarship has gathered about itself a number of modes of inquiry. Historical questions can be asked about a text:

- When was it written?
- Under what circumstances was it written?

- What impact did it have on literature when it first appeared? On later writers?
- Are there different versions of a text and what significance do the variations have on the reading of a text?

For example, Martin Luther King's essay "Letter from Birmingham Jail" was written in response to an appeal by several prominent Birmingham, Alabama, clergymen, who hoped that Dr. King would not lead a civil rights march in their city. King did come and was arrested during the march. He claims to have begun writing his response to their appeal while in jail. He had a copy of the clergymen's appeal and wrote his initial response on its margins. After he was released from jail, he finished the essay and polished it for publication. This essay takes on a unique meaning when it is read knowing something about the civil rights movement in the early 1960s. Equally interesting would be the opportunity to read earlier drafts of the essay in order to watch King develop his argument.

Students of literature are also concerned with sources and analogues that influence writers and their works:

- What sources influenced a work or an author?
- How did the source influence the author?
- Why is one work in a particular period similar to or different from others in the same genre?
- Was an author familiar with a particular piece of literature?

The way King wrote his essay suggests the way Henry David Thoreau penned his famous essay "Civil Disobedience" in 1848. A close reading of Thoreau's essay points to its influence on King's own logic in his essay. Both essayists argue that by breaking the law they were responding to moral law which both saw as a law higher than political law. That moral law may take precedence over a political law lies at the heart of arguments expressed in many documents, including the Declaration of Independence and the writings of American patriots such as Samuel Adams and Thomas Jefferson, and the essays of Gandhi and Ralph Waldo Emerson.

Researchers very often go beyond a work and look for psychological, historical, cultural, and environmental factors that affected authors and their works, at the time they were first published and afterward.

- Are there autobiographical motifs in a work?
- Is the text based on historical fact?
- What ethnic and social concerns does the work raise?

Again, King's essay "Letter From Birmingham Jail" may serve as an example. King himself experienced racial prejudice in his youth, but it intensified as he became a more prominent actor in the civil rights movement. Yet his essay addresses not only the issue of rights for African-Americans but also of the fundamental rights of all persons protected by the Constitution and moral law. In reading his essay, moreover, we can deduce much about King and his personality. He compares himself in this essay to the epistolist Paul, who wrote a number of letters to small Christian communities during the first century A.D. In fact, much of the rhetorical structure of King's letter parallels the letters that Paul wrote. What

does this comparison say about King's sense of his mission as leader of the Southern Christian Leadership Conference? Later in his essay, he compares his and other civil rights leaders' extremism to the extremism of Jesus, of the prophet Amos, of Martin Luther, and of Abraham Lincoln. These are very consciously made comparisons, and they suggest much about Dr. King's vision of himself and his role in the civil rights movement.

Asking questions of a text, as we have just done, raises curiosity, and being curious is the very state to be in when beginning to undertake research. Don't do what Marsha did when she wrote about Fitzgerald and Zelda. She knew what she was going to say before she started her research. You may not know in the beginning where your curiosity will take you, and that lack of the known is one of the most exciting things about research.

Finding an Overview

When first approaching a potential topic, many researchers often turn to an encyclopedia or similar broad study. These resources lack the detail the serious researcher needs, but they are useful places to begin researching a problem. Among the more helpful are Margaret Drabble's *The Oxford Companion to English Literature* (5th ed., New York: Oxford UP, 1985) and James D. Hart's *The Oxford Companion to American Literature* (5th ed., New York: Oxford UP, 1983). Two older general studies which weaned a number of scholars are Albert Baugh's *A Literary History of England* (2nd ed., Englewood Cliffs, NJ: Prentice-Hall, 1967) and Robert Spiller's *Literary History of the United States* (4th ed., New York: Macmillan, 1974). The *Oxford History of English Literature* series, begun in 1945, is very helpful because each volume is written by a specialist and each provides an excellent overview of literary periods and their major authors. Each book also has an important bibliography, albeit somewhat dated.

The purpose of your research at this stage is essentially exploratory: What have others to say about the topic I'm interested in pursuing? Perhaps you will discover that one of these studies will satisfy your curiosity and you won't want to pursue it any further. In any case, if these sources have something to say which you think is worth saving, make a note of the information and be sure to indicate to yourself exactly where you found it. You may want to return to it later.

At this stage too, don't forget your teacher and classmates. Research on a government project might need to be kept secret, but in literary circles, secrecy is often the bane of successful research. Your teacher might have some information to share with you or maybe some advice about where you can turn for information. Classmates are often thinking along the same lines. In their research they might come up with a lead worth your investigating.

Following Leads

A couple of years ago, I assigned a research paper on any work by Faulkner. Tom, a sophmore majoring in economics, liked *As I Lay Dying.* In particular, he was curious about the bizarre behavior of Darl, the novel's major character. Tom had taken Psychology 1, and he remembered that schizophrenia was discussed in the course. From what Tom could recall, Darl seemed to exhibit some of the symptoms. First Tom put up a trial balloon: in class, he asked me what I thought. Frankly, I liked the idea, but I couldn't offer much help other than suggesting he look in one of the Faulkner bibliographies to see what has been written about Darl. Some of the others in class agreed with Tom's ideas about Darl; others didn't, saying that Darl was probably the most sane of the whole Bundren clan. So Tom began some formal research.

He went first to his former psychology professor, who suggested an essay for Tom to read. That article whetted his curiosity even further. He was sure he was on to something, but he knew he needed to undertake some additional research. He looked through a Faulkner bibliography, which turned up a couple of useful articles, and he interviewed a social worker at a local mental health center. Armed with a much better understanding of what the mental illness was and what its outward signs were, Tom was prepared to analyze Darl and write the paper. The central thesis of the paper was Tom's—Darl was a schizophrenic—and his argument was his own, but now it was supported with information he gathered during his research.

Three summers ago, when I was teaching a course on Vermont literature, Donna, a sophomore, decided to research the background of "Marjorie Grey," a poem by a nineteenth-century Vermont local-color writer, Julia Dorr. The poem, set in the early 1800s, depicts the hardships suffered by a Rockingham, Vermont, woman who lost her way and wandered for several months in the forests before she stumbled upon a settlement. Dorr claimed her poem was not based on fact. But when Donna drove to Rockingham, she found a descendant of Marjorie Grey who said the poem was an accurate depiction of what had happened. Why would Dorr say she invented the plot? Donna discovered too that the story of Marjorie Grey had been set to music sometime in the nineteenth century by an unknown balladeer and is found in oral circulation in Vermont. Had Dorr really written the poem, or had she based it on a ballad already in existence? Perhaps the descendant of Grey told Donna a bit of family lore that was shaped more by the poem and the ballad than by history. Donna's initial field research raised some important questions about Dorr's sources and about analogues to the poem and about the influence of art on family history. She eventually wrote a textual comparison between the "folk" texts and Dorr's poem, and she outlined the historical and literary contexts of both. A little curiosity, an afternoon trip to Rockingham, and a chance meeting marked the beginning of some original research.

Starting research may or may not derive from a request or an assignment, but it does come from an honest admission—"I don't know, but I would like to know." Admitting ignorance isn't a problem. Someone once told me that it's impossible to know everything, but everyone ought to know how to find out everything. Remember the student who wanted to write about Fitzgerald and Zelda? The problem was that she already knew what she would write. As a result, her paper suffered from a lack of excitement. In literary scholarship, we probably begin with a curiosity about an author, the text, and/or the reading of a text by an audience. Broad beginnings, admittedly, but a start just the same. Tom wanted to know if Darl was a schizophrenic—a question of how he read the text. Donna began with a historical interest in a poem, but her fieldwork opened up whole new issues worth pursuing. They both reached out for help and in return were able to give something back to the community of scholars in the form of their essays.

The types of research we undertake are limited by our imagination and the amount of time we have to work on a project. Tom and Donna each spent about about two weeks researching; Marsha spent a couple of hours. They all used the library. Marsha learned nothing new and contributed nothing new to the scholarly community. Tom and Donna finished their projects a little wiser about their subjects and could take pride in making a scholarly contribution.

FIELD RESEARCH AND INTERVIEWING

The library, as I mentioned, is probably the resource literary researchers use most often, but it is not necessarily the only or best source of information. Innovative researchers discover their own best resource, and sometimes even generate their body of data. Linda was in an English course that touched on the idea of the affective nature of literature, how texts affect readers. She found herself crying over parts of *Uncle Tom's Cabin,* but wanted to know why she was so moved and whether she was alone in her reaction. She made up a questionnaire and took it along with a particularly emotionally moving passage from the novel to a group of freshmen. They read the passage and then filled out the questionnaire, which asked about how they were affected by the passage. Linda was generating her own data. Based on it, she wrote a very intriguing paper about readers' identification with characters and how this identification affects their sentiments as they read the passage.

Ken Macrorie writes: "The worse place you can begin your search is at the card catalogue in the library. Go to people. They're alive this year, up to date—and the books listed in the file cards aren't" (89). He is speaking about what he calls the "I-search" paper, but with only slight reservation, what he asserts is good advice for the literary research writer.

Unlike library research, the interview gives the researcher the opportunity to question writers and critics about their works, their studies, and their lives. Undergraduates should not ignore the possibility of interviewing local writers, and scholars, and guest visitors to the campus. College campuses have faculty who are experts in various fields. Tom's interviews with a professor and a social worker provided him with ideas that helped shape his thinking and his writing. Within every English Department there are specialists who are generally more than willing to be interviewed.

Some simple advice expedites a successful interview:

1. Contact interviewees several days in advance. A phone call is all it usually takes. Explain what you are doing and why you wish to interview them. Be specific. Tell them what topic you are researching. If you plan on tape-recording the interview, ask for approval ahead of time.

2. Prepare yourself for the interview. Do a little research and create an extended list of questions. If you plan on interviewing professionals on campus, ask the department secretary for the interviewees' professional vitae and read over the relevant material they published. As a folklorist, I am often interviewed by freshmen for their writing courses. Both of us find the interview frustrating and less than productive if the interviewer is not prepared with a substantial list of well-conceived questions. Two or three questions is nowhere near enough. Remember that an interview is not a conversation, an informal bull session, or a fishing expedition. Don't expect your experts to lead the interview. You want particular information. Go prepared to conduct the interview confidently. A good list of specific questions can help provide that confidence.

3. If your interviewees are agreeable and you plan to tape the interview, know your equipment—especially the quirks of microphones—beforehand. Without getting into technical difficulties, I should mention that different mikes function best in special settings. Spend some time learning how well the microphone you will use picks up voices at various distances and with different background noises. Avoid using batteries. They seemed to be programed to fail when needed.

4. Be on time for the interview, and don't forget paper and a pencil. If the recording

equipment becomes a distraction or is not functioning properly, put it aside at once and be thankful you brought paper and pencil. In addition, it's always wise to take notes during the interview. You will want to write down unusual terms and the spelling of names and places. At the very beginning, jot down the time, date, and place where the interviewed is conducted, and the names of those present. Then begin asking questions and listening carefully to the answers. Don't interrupt your interviewees, even if they aren't answering your question. Wait until they are done, and rephrase the question. If you talk over their voice the tape will become gibberish; the machine cannot distinguish between voices as well as the human ear. Ask the questions you have prepared, but always be ready to follow another line of questioning if something worth pursuing comes up. Then return to the next question on your list. But remember, no matter how famous or intimidating your interviewees are, you are in charge of the interview. Ask questions forthrightly. Don't hesitate to ask how to spell unusual terms and proper names. If your interviewees start using "they" or "it," make it clear to whom or what "they" or "it" refers. And before you leave, get your interviewees' permission to quote them. Get it in writing, or at least on the tape.

5. Immediately after the interview, sit down with your notes and tape, if you have one, and review the interview. Does what you heard an hour ago still make sense? Do you have the correct spelling of proper names and unusual terms? Once again, check to make sure that the "they's" and "she's" and "there's" and "then's" are clear. If you are missing vital information, call your interviewees and get the information straight. Maybe you might even want to make a follow-up visit just to clarify obscure points.

Attending public readings and lectures is another method of research. Poets sometimes take questions during or after their presentation. Guest scholars present public lectures on campus. Even class lectures are contexts for doing research. Go, listen, and take notes. Ask questions directly related to the topic and get your professor's perspective. If you want to tape a lecture or poetry reading, or any public presentation, always get permission from the speaker and the sponsoring organization beforehand. And always note the date and place of the interview or lecture. This is information you will need when you document your research in your paper.

USING THE LIBRARY

The library is fundamentally a research facility at the service of a college's students and faculty. The basic tools for research include the card catalogue, which may be available on index cards, on CD disks, or on-line as part of a computer network, and various indices, as well as specialized checklists and bibliographies. The last is particularily useful to the researcher. A bibliography is a list of works related to a particular subject (such as modern fiction or Renaissance drama), or author (like Twain or Poe), or sometimes a particular genre within a period of literature (such as medieval English sermons or modern Irish fiction). There are hundreds of bibliographies and even bibliographies of bibliographies. Each, however, is there to serve the interests of researchers who want to save a lot of time and energy in trying to locate particular articles or books. Approaching these sources may at first seem intimidating, but learning to use these resources early in your research work will lessen both anxiety and footwork.

A couple of very general research tools can point toward specific sources for literary research. For example, if you want to know where to turn to get some information about

sources for studies on Walt Whitman or Sylvia Plath, a number of guides can help. One is Richard Altick and Andrew Wright's *Selective Bibliography for the Study of English and American Literature* (6th ed., New York: Macmillan, 1979). Although dated, this book lists all journals, reference guides, and bibliographies that you would probably need for your research. Knowing the period or author you wish to work with, you simply consult the *Selective Bibliography* for the names of particular journals and books that deal with the period or author. Another more recent resource is Robert H. Miller's *Handbook of Literary Research* (Metuchen, NJ: Scarecrow Press, 1987). It is a practical guide to the major English and American literature bibliographies.

The *Cambridge Bibliography of English Literature,* edited by F. W. Bateson (5 vols., Cambridge: Cambridge UP, 1940–57) and its successor *The New Cambridge Bibliography of English Literature,* edited by George Watson and Ian Willison (5 vols., Cambridge: Cambridge UP, 1969–77) are important catalogues arranged according to literary periods and genres within those periods. For American authors, consult Jacob Blanck's *Bibliography of American Literature* (New Haven: Yale UP, 1955–) and *American Literary Scholarship: An Annual* (Durham: Duke UP, 1963–).

The most formidable bibliography, simply because of its size and thoroughness, is *The MLA International Bibliography of Books and Articles on the Modern Languages and Literature,* published annually since 1963 by the Modern Language Association. It's the successor to the association's *Annual Bibliography* (1956–62), which was preceded by *American Bibliography* (1921–53). The *International* is an extremely comprehensive bibliography arranged according to national literatures and subdivided into literary periods. You could, for example, look up American literature, subsection nineteenth century, subsection Henry David Thoreau, and find a list of the many articles published that year regarding Thoreau.

I haven't mentioned much about the card catalogue because it is such an obvious source and one you probably already know about. Many libraries have put their card catalogues on computer and allow for rapid research of titles and authors and subject. I recommend that you play around with computer searches so that you can learn the strengths and limitations of the system. Remember, too, that the card catalogue is useful for books and manuscripts, but less helpful for journals and periodicals. Articles and essays in journals are not normally listed in card catalogues, but they are included in bibliographies, many of which have been put on CD systems.

What about note taking? I'm not going to stress the subject because you have heard about it since grade school. Moreover, every college writing handbook has a section devoted to note taking, explaining how to write down the title, author, publisher, place and date of publication, and page numbers. Similar advice is given for journals and periodicals. It's obvious that if you're planning to cite a source, you need all the publication information in order to make a thorough and accurate statement about exactly where the idea or quote came from. Some people write down such material on index cards; those who use the photocopier write the source information on the back of the copies. If you are using an archive with its own catalogue system, note how one could find the artifact or manuscript you have viewed. The secret is to get all the information down before you begin reading the text, so that if you do use ideas or words from it, you will have all the information at your fingertips.

Failure to offer readers complete and accurate information about sources undermines your own paper and measurably weakens its power to inform or argue. Everything about research writing—your ideas and the ideas from your sources—should be able to withstand serious scrutiny. Research-based papers with weak or inadequate documentation fail to live

up to the expectations of a critical audience. Even if you don't use a source directly, you might still want to list it as a work you know about and consulted. Inadequate note taking becomes particularly frustrating when, after you have written the body of the paper and are about to write in the citations or create the list of works consulted, your notes are incomplete. What should be a very simple task if adequate notes were taken in the beginning turns into a mad scramble back in the library.

DOCUMENTATION

With your research finished, you are ready to begin writing the paper. I'm not going to review the writing and revising of a paper, but I want to comment on documenting sources. There are two basic questions: What should be documented in a paper? How can quotes be incorporated into a text?

In regard to the first question, Walter S. Achtert and Joseph Gibaldi, authors of *The MLA Style Manual,* write:

> In scholarly writing, everything derived from an outside source requires documentation—not only direct quotations and paraphrases but also information and ideas. Of course, good judgment as well as ethics should guide you in interpreting this rule. Although you rarely need, for example, to give sources for familiar proverbs . . . , well known quotations . . . , or common knowledge . . . , you must indicate the origin of any appropriated material that readers might otherwise mistake for your own. (163)

"Good judgment," "ethics," and "appropriated material" are key phrases. Tom appropriated into his paper ideas from his interviews with the social worker and his psychology professor. He gave them credit in his paper for two reasons: what he quoted were their ideas, and he didn't want to take responsibility for the ideas if they were wrong. There is no justification for authors/researchers/scholars to misrepresent the source of an idea that is not their own; it is simply a matter of professional ethics.

This spring Mark, a junior majoring in religion, wrote a brief paper on "The Hippopotamus" by T. S. Eliot. It's a short poem, nine quatrains long. There is, of course, a Latin quotation from St. Ignatius's letter to the Traillians, but the rest is Eliot's poem. As Mark read it, he realized that Eliot compares the "True Church" to the lazy, gluttonous hippo. Mark found the sarcasm particularly interesting, but he was aware that Eliot was not the first to attack abuses within the Catholic Church. The lines "While the True Church can never fail / For it is based upon the rock," Mark felt, particularly emphasize the Church's smugness, and he writes:

> Eliot writes these lines with absolute sarcasm to emphasize the whole theme of the poem—that the Church has indeed failed and is lacking in some of the basic ideals of Christianity as Christ taught it. This challenge to the Church is not new to Eliot, however, as we have seen other writings such as Goliardic literature of the Middle Ages which were songs and poems in praise of love and wine. These were written in direct rebellion against the Church because the writers felt that the Church had become too wealthy and pompous (Jesus was never rich or pompous). When papal power had reached a peak under Innocent III in the late 12th

> century, new movements of criticism were aimed at the Church by such groups as the Waldensians and Albigensians. They made many of the same claims against the Church as Eliot did in ''The Hippopotamus.'' What makes ''The Hippopotamus'' a great poem is not that it presents a new theme, but that it presents an old theme in a new way. (3)

Mark presented information he had learned in a medieval history course, and he didn't need to cite a source for it because the material was truly part of his own knowledge and expressed in his own words. For someone who gathered this information about the medieval Church, a source would have to be cited.

Citations

Before providing some examples of ways of incorporating source material into an essay, I want to present some of the rationale behind documentation procedures. A quotation is the reproduction of the words of another voice in your paper. It may come from an interview or from print. It might be the words of a TV advertisement or a recorded song. In any case, they are not your words and should not be presented as such in your paper.

It is stylistically preferable to cite the author's name and source right in the text. The former may be repeated throughout the text whenever necessary, but there is no need to give the title every time you quote the source, if by omitting it there is no confusion. Following each quotation, put a page reference. That is what the "(3)" at the end of my quotation from Mark's paper is. If you are using more than one source by the same author, include in the parentheses shortened titles along with the page number(s).

For the sake of demonstration, I am using a passage from the introduction to the book *This Song Remembers: Self-Portraits of Native Americans in the Arts.* The introduction was written by Jane B. Katz, who also edited the book.

The first example indicates that I have taken Katz's idea and put it into my own words, a kind of paraphrase:

> Jane Katz in her Introduction to <u>This Song Remembers</u> stresses the variety of art forms which children in American Indian and Eskimo cultures learn at home (1).

The advantage of the paraphrase is that I can condense my source's ideas and use only the essential parts of them. After all, the purpose of having sources in the first place is for the ideas they express and not necessarily the actual words, unless, of course, the words are particularly significant.

Sometimes, however, I may want to use the words of the source. I can incorporate them into my own sentences:

> In her Introduction to <u>This Song Remembers</u>, Jane Katz states that unlike Western society, Native American societies ''foster the child's innate creativity'' (1). Families and communities with their heritage help their ''young people learn a wide variety of art forms at home.''

Note that I provided only one citation for two quotes. In doing so, I am saying that the second came from the same source as the first. If the quotation is less than four typed lines (about thirty-five to forty words), incorporate it directly into your own text as I have done above. If the quotation is longer, indent it about ten spaces from the left margin:

> Jane B. Katz in her Introduction to <u>This Song Remembers</u> points to the important early experience Native American children have with their heritage:
>
> > American Indian and Eskimo cultures, as distinct from Western society, foster the child's innate creativity. In communities and in families that have preserved their tribal heritage, young people learn a wide variety of art forms at home. The Pueblo child makes pots and jewelry; the Navajo learns weaving, basketry, and silversmithing; woodcarving is the hallmark of the Northwest tribes; Eskimos carve in ivory, bone, and stone; beadwork, drawing, and painting are almost universal. (1)

When quoting a statement of another person, quote only what is specifically relevant. Quote directly only when the words are strikingly important, if you are unable to present the idea in any better way. Otherwise, paraphrase the idea in your own words, but be sure to give credit for the idea to its source.

Had I not cited Katz's name, I would include it in the parentheses, preceding the page number and not separated from it by any punctuation: (Katz 1). If I happen to have other works by Katz cited elsewhere in my text, I make clear in my text or in my citation the source I am citing. This is usually done with a shortened title of the book or article: (Katz, *This Song* 1).

Poetry is quoted differently because of its form. Like a prose quote, try to weave the author and title into your text, at least the first time you quote from a particular poem. One line of poetry is simply written in quotation marks without any indentation:

> Shelley begins his elegiac poem ''Adonais'' with a force unmatched in literature: ''I weep for Adonais--he is dead!'' (line 1).

Two or three lines are written into your text with a "space-slash-space" separating the verses:

> Shelley' elegiac poem ''Adonais'' begins with the poet expressing his intense grief for the fallen god: ''I weep for Adonais--he is dead! / Oh, weep for Adonais! though our tear / Thaw not the frost which binds so dear a head!'' (lines 1-3)

For more than three lines, indent ten spaces from the left and begin each verse on a new line:

> In ''Adonais,'' Shelley expressed his grief for the fallen god and invites all to weep for him:

```
I weep for Adonais--he is dead!
Oh, weep for Adonais! though our tears
Thaw not the frost which binds so dear a head!
And thou, sad Hour, selected from all years
To mourn our loss, rouse thy obscure compeers,
And teach them thine own sorrow! (lines 1-6)
```

What about interviews? material from phonograph records? photographs? survey results? Weave into your text pertinent source material as much as possible:

```
When I interviewed Professor O'Bryan he stated: ''Shelley
began ''Adonais'' following the elegiac formula
established in classical literary tradition.''
```

Remember, the purpose of the citations in the text is to make a quick source identification, but the reader may refer to the list of sources cited at the end of the paper for more complete reference information. Fuzzy citations weaken the plausibility of a research paper, and suggest that the authors do not have control over their research or their information.

Is there a limit to the number of quotations a research paper should have? The answer is no, but common sense and stylistic concerns should be taken into account. A page of typed text that has ten citations looks rather silly, unless there is a particular point in terms of the sources themselves which the writer of the paper is trying to make. But there is no hard and fast rule: Just don't detract from your paper by making it look silly with too many references crowded together.

Footnotes

Footnotes have not vanished from scholarly writing, although writers tend to replace them with endnotes, not to be confused with lists of works cited or consulted. For years, all citations were put in footnotes at the bottom of a page or in endnotes placed after the text but before the bibliography. With the shortened internal forms I have described becoming more widely used, notes are limited more often to what is called informational or content notes. If you need to explain something about your text—perhaps you used an unusual research method that needs some explaining or you want readers to be aware of a particular idea or problem—but don't feel that the information properly belongs in the text itself, use a content note. Place a superscript number in the text where you think the reader needs to have the explanation and put that information at the bottom of the page or at the end of the text, identifying it with the same superscript number. Perhaps you wish to describe some field research procedures you used in your paper. Your text reads:

```
Besides exploring my own responses to Uncle Tom's Cabin,
I sought information about how others respond.[1]
```

Your footnote or endnote reads:

```
[1]On April 30, 1987, I distributed 75 questionnaires to
students enrolled in English 3, sections 3, 7, and 12. A
copy of the questionnaire is in Appendix One. Appendix
Two details all of the responses to the questionnaire. I
```

```
also gave each student a copy of ''The Slave Warehouse''
chapter of Uncle Tom's Cabin, and their responses to the
questionnaire dealt with their reading of that chapter.
```

Most writers avoid using these notes at all, reasoning that if the information is important enough, they will work it into the text.

Works Cited

Once the main part of the paper is written, you need to create a list showing where your sources may be found. You have given an author, title, and page number, but that isn't enough information. Your reader may want to know dates, editions, volume numbers, and so forth.

The term "Bibliography" is no longer used in research circles; it has been replaced by "Works Cited" and "Works Consulted." The difference between the latter two is simple: the former lists only the sources you actually paraphrased, quoted from, or took ideas from; "Works Consulted" lists sources that may have influenced your thinking, but in a less specific way. You found these helpful, and although you did not particularly rely upon them, you want readers to know you consulted them. Most of my students are content with only a list of works cited, but most critical readers, including teachers, want to see how thorough the research was and like to see "Works Consulted."

Here are examples of various types of citations. I have not tried to be exhaustive, but to present those my students most commonly need to follow. For a more complete set of examples, English students should refer to *The MLA Style Manual* or to the forms prescribed by the class instructor.

Nonwritten Sources

Interview

Feldman, Henry. Personal interview. 29 June 1988.

Phonograph Recording

MacArthur, Margaret. "When the Wind's in the West." *An Almanac of New England Farm Songs.* Green Linnet, SIF 1039, 1982.

Art Works (if you are using the original, otherwise treat reproduction in book like an essay from a collection)

Lachaise, Gaston. "The Mountain." Metropolitan Museum of Art, Alfred Stieglitz Collection.

Written Sources

Books

Basic format

Katz, Jane (ed.). *This Song Remembers: Self-Portraits of Native Americans in the Arts.* Boston: Houghton Mifflin Co., 1980.

Two or three authors

Barzum, Jacques, and Henry F. Graff. *The Modern Researcher.* Rev. ed. New York: Harcourt, Brace & World, 1970.

Republished texts

Twain, Mark. *Adventures of Huckleberry Finn.* 1885. Berkeley: University of California Press, 1985.

Essay reprinted in a collection

Lewis, C. S. "What Chaucer Really Did to *Il Filostrato.*" *Essays and Studies by Members of the English Association* 17 (1932): 56–75. Rpt. in *Troilus and Criseyde & The Minor Poems.* Vol. 2 of *Chaucer Criticism.* Eds. Richard J. Schoech and Jerome Taylor. South Bend: University of Notre Dame Press, 1961. 16–33.

JOURNALS AND PERIODICALS

BASIC FORM FOR SCHOLARLY JOURNAL

Clements, William M. "The Ethnic Joke as a Mirror of Culture." *New York Folklore Quarterly* 12.3–4 (1986): 87–97.

NEWSPAPER

Shaw, Kent. " 'Amazing' Daisy Turner Nearly 104." *Burlington Free Press* 3 June 1987, 1A+.

POPULAR JOURNAL

Robison, Mary. "Seizing Control." *The New Yorker* 25 May 1987: 35–36.

All this concern over correct citations and lists of works consulted is not particularly formidable. With practice, most of it becomes automatic. But researchers usually keep *The MLA Style Manual* handy, and every college library has at least one copy. Research projects ought not to become bogged down in prescriptions; they are simply means by which a student of literature can pursue scholarly interests. Learning how to undertake and to use research in one's writing and for intellectual growth is part of becoming a professional in the field.

WORKS CITED

Achtert, Walter S., and Joseph Gibaldi. *The MLA Style Manual.* New York: Modern Language Association, 1985.

Katz, Jane (ed.). *This Song Remembers: Self-Portraits of Native Americans in the Arts.* Boston: Houghton Mifflin, 1980.

Macrorie, Ken. *Searching Writing.* Upper Montclair, NJ: Boynton/Cook, 1984.

McNiff, Mark. Manuscript of "Eliot and the Church." Department of English, University of Vermont [Spring 1987].

Shelley, Percy Bysshe. "Adonais." Rpt. in *How Does a Poem Mean?* Eds. John Ciardi and Miller Williams. 2nd ed. Boston: Houghton Mifflin, 1975. 176–87.

Glossary

Act A major division of a drama, like an inning in a baseball game or a period in a football or basketball game.

Alliteration The repetition of initial consonant sounds, as "On the bald street breaks the blank day." **Consonance** refers to the repetition of consonant sounds from any position in the word.

Allusion A reference to a person, place, or event outside a work of literature. It is a kind of shorthand whereby the recalling of something outside the work supplies an emotional or intellectual context, such as a reference in a poem about current political conditions which calls up the memory of George Washington.

Antagonist A character or force which opposes the main character, or **protagonist**, in a plot. In *Lysistrata,* the antagonist is first the men of Greece, later the sexual desires of the women themselves.

Aside In drama, a remark spoken directly to the audience which supposedly is not audible to the other characters on stage, as when Iago explains to the audience what his motives are in taking Roderigo in while Roderigo himself is on the stage.

Atmosphere The mood or emotional aura of a story or drama. It is the air, the impression, given off by the work, established in part by the setting or landscape. The atmosphere in Venice is different from that of Cypress in *Othello.*

Audience Those to whom writing is directed. In drama, it is those observers present in the theater who view the play. The audience is an important consideration in any piece of writing.

Autobiography The story of all or part of someone's life as written by that person. Various autobiographical forms are journals, memoirs, diaries, letters, and the narrative essay.

Character The people in fictional or dramatic narratives, as Othello, Eveline, and the Duke in "My Last Duchess." They are revealed or developed through **speech, diction, physical description, actions,** etc. Some characters **develop** or are **dynamic:** they change under the pressure of events; others are **revealed:** they do not change, but

growing knowledge of them changes our perception of them; a third group is **static:** they do not change nor does our knowledge of them grow. A **universal character** is understandable and appealing to readers of all times and places.

Chorus In Greek drama, a group of actors which moves and speaks in unison and which represents some group of people affected by the play's actions, as the Chorus of Old Women in *Lysistrata.*

Climax (a) A moment of emotional or intellectual intensity, as when Katarin in *Mother Courage* warns the city of its destruction; (b) a turning point in the plot at which one opposing force gains control over another and the conflict is headed toward its resolution, as when Mother Courage decides not to go with the Cook but remains with Katarin.

Comedy A form of drama which aims primarily to amuse and which ends happily, as *Lysistrata.*

Conflict A struggle between opposing forces or characters, as between Othello and Iago. On one side is the principal character or **protagonist**; on the other side, the **antagonist**, taking the form of another character, nature, society, or an aspect of the protagonist's character.

Connotation What a word suggests beyond its dictionary meaning. Although two words may seem to mean the same thing, they may be very different, as the difference between "naked" and "nude," or the difference between "young" and "immature."

Conventions The structures through which literary texts create meaning, as the dramatic aside or the Shakespearean soliloquy.

Critical essay A relatively brief paper whose aim is to describe, evaluate, or interpret a text.

Denotation The dictionary definition of what a word means: its primary meaning.

Dialogue Conversation between two or more people. Dialogue is one of the main devices of drama, in which characters speak to each other. Another kind of dialogue, in which the author speaks to the reader, is used in the essay.

Diction The choice of particular words whose educational, social, and situational levels help create meaning. The diction of Emily Dickinson creates a different set of meanings than that of Wanda Coleman.

Discovery or recognition When a character in drama learns the significance of a person or thing previously unknown or inadequately understood, as when Oedipus discovers that he is the son as well as the murderer of King Laius.

Discovery draft A rough draft, usually of an essay, in which one writes out everything that comes to mind without worrying about organization, sentence structure, spelling, etc. Also called **focused free writing**.

Dramatic compression A device which creates the feeling that a great deal of exposition and action has been packed into a few minutes.

Dramatic irony The knowledge possessed by members of the audience but not by the characters in a drama, as when Oedipus is ignorant of his parentage in *Oedipus Rex.*

Documentation The form by which one gives credit for materials taken from other sources, as footnotes or citations in the text.

Exposition Language which explains the nature of an object, an idea, or a theme. In fiction, it explains what has gone before, the relation between characters, the setting forth of a theme, etc. In drama, a passage which provides background information about the play's plot and characters.

Farce A form of comedy exciting laughter through exaggerated or improbable situations.

Figurative language Language which deviates from the literal in order to suggest additional meanings or effects. Metaphors and similes are examples of figurative language.

Flashback A device in drama, fiction, or film which presents a scene that occurred prior to the opening scene of the work. It is a way of presenting exposition dramatically.

Foil character Any character who, through strong contrast, underscores the distinctive characteristics of another, as Cassio is set off by the evil Iago.

Imagery Language which appeals directly to one of the five senses, as the sensuous language in the poems of Keats.

In medias res Literally, "in the midst of things." This term refers to when a piece of fiction, a drama, or a poem begins in the middle of an action, then uses other devices such as the **flashback** for exposition. *Othello* begins in this way.

Intertextuality This term goes beyond **allusion** to suggest the dialogue between two separate texts. An allusion refers to something as a kind of shorthand; intertextuality encompasses a broader context in which two texts establish a larger dialogue. For example, the title of Archibald MacLeish's poem, "You, Andrew Marvell," alludes to Marvell's poem "To His Coy Mistress"; the rest of MacLeish's poem sets up a dialogue between Marvell's attempt to grasp pleasures as actively as possible and MacLeish's more passive lying on the shores of Lake Michigan waiting for the coming on of night.

Irony The discrepancy between reality and the masking appearance. Often, this term is defined as saying one thing and meaning another, as when the narrator of "A Modest Proposal" does not really mean that people should eat the children of Ireland.

Journals Notebooks kept by writers for themselves as a means of methodically locating, collecting, and making sense of their thoughts. Diaries are a private form of journals; class notebooks an objective and public record. You might lend your class notebooks to someone who missed a class; you would rarely lend your diaries to another.

Juxtaposed scenes Two scenes in drama placed beside each other which gain additional meaning from their placement.

Katharsis In drama, a purgation through pity and terror. Our feelings at the end of *Othello* are drained through the experience of the play.

Lyric A fairly short, concentrated, and song-like poem (originally sung to a lyre). E. A. Robinson's "Richard Cory" has been set to music by Simon and Garfunkle; Coleridge's "Kubla Khan" is a lyric whose appeal lies in its musical qualities.

Metaphor An implied comparison in which the figurative word is substituted for the literal term, as opposed to the explicit comparison of the **simile**. "He is a lion in the field" is a metaphor.

Meter The recurrence of rhythmic beats, of a regular pattern, in a poem, as in Frost's "Stopping by Woods."

Monologue Speech by one person alone on stage in which the person reveals or discovers things either to him- or herself or to the audience. A character may also reveal motivation, or lack thereof, as Iago does when he discusses his motives for hating Othello. In drama, often called a **soliloquy**.

Narrator The teller of a story, as the voice of the younger brother in Huddle's "The Summer of the Magic Show."

Omniscient narrator A narrator who is capable of seeing, knowing, and telling whatever he or she wishes and exercises this freedom at will. In **total omniscience**, the story is told as if seen through the eyes of God; most stories are told through **limited omniscience** in which the narrator is consciously limited to a knowledge of only certain places or times, or the minds of certain characters.

Parody Writing which imitates the style, form, or theme of another, usually serious, work in order to ridicule in nonsensical fashion or criticize by brilliant treatment. Nash's "Mighty Like a Whale" parodies Byron's "The Destruction of Sennacharib."

Past tense narrative A method of narration which tells the story as if it had happened in the past, as Huddle's "The Summer of the Magic Show."

Personification Giving human attributes to an animal, inanimate object, or abstract concept. This allows the writer to give the world life and motion, which creates a more understandable context for emotions or actions, as when Keats refers to the season of Autumn as if it were a farm worker.

Plot The significant order of events in a narrative or drama, often comprising one important action: what happens to the narrator of "Summer of the Magic Show." A **subplot** is a subordinate or complicating action which helps set off, reinforce, or contrast with the main action: what happens to the older brother in that story.

Point of view A term used in fiction to describe the way in which the narrator perceives and presents the materials of the story. **First person point of view**, or **character-narration**, features an "I" who tells the story. Such a narrator cannot know the thoughts of other people or can only speculate on them. A **retrospective narrator** tells a story which occurred some time before.

Present tense narrative A method of narration which pretends that the story is happening at the present time.

Protagonist The main character of a plot, as the narrator in "The Yellow Wallpaper."

Reversal When the fortunes of a character take a sharp turn, the tragic character suddenly losing his good fortune, as when Peyton Farquhar thinks he escapes from his captors in "An Occurrence at Owl Creek Bridge"; the comic, suddenly gaining hers back, as when Lysistrata triumphs at the end of her play.

Rhyme The close similarity or identity of sounds between accented syllables. A regular rhyme consists of the repetition of the last stressed vowel and all following consonants, as "soon," "June," "honeymoon." Regularly recurring combination of **alliteration** and **consonance**.

Rhythm The passage of equivalent time intervals between definite events in a story or drama or the recurrence of specific sounds or the recurrence of stressed and unstressed syllables in poetry. In poetry it is distinguished from **meter**, which is a more limited rigid way of measuring rhythm.

Satire A form of comedy in which a character or society is held up to some standard of behavior and is found wanting, as the picture of Athenian society in *Lysistrata.*

Scansion The way of determining **meter** by analyzing the number and kinds of metrical feet in a line of poetry.

Scene The basic unit of drama, it consists of an action staged as if in a single physical space and during an unbroken period of time. A scene takes place before the governing body of Venice at which Brabantio accuses Othello of betrayal and Othello is appointed head of the armies of defense.

Setting Where a story or drama takes place.

Simile An explicit comparison which uses the words "like," "as," "than," "similar to," "resembles," or "sees"; distinguished from **metaphor**. "He is like a lion in the field" is a simile.

Soliloquy A form of the **monologue** which appears in drama. A character, alone on the stage, speaks aloud about his or her inmost thoughts for the audience to hear, as when Hamlet ponders over the possibility of suicide in "To be or not to be."

Sonnet A fourteen-line iambic pentameter poem which follows, or refers to, specific rules of rhyming and thought. The two main types are the Shakespearean, or English, sonnet and the Petrarchan, or Italian, sonnet. See the poems of Shakespeare or Claude McKay in the anthology.

Story All that happens during a fictional narrative. It is developed through **plot, character, setting**, etc.

Structure The general plan or form of a piece of literature. The structure of a sonnet is discussed in the "so what?" section of the chapter on poetry.

Style The particular way in which a writer uses words, including diction, abstract and concrete language, imagery, syntax, and tone. The style of Hawthorne creates a different world than that of Huddle.

Symbol A figure of speech which combines a literal, concrete existence with a suggestive, abstract dimension. It gains its value because of the way it is used or talked about. A symbol can be anything which refers to something else, as Desdemona's handkerchief becomes a symbol of her chastity and faithfulness to Othello.

Theme What a work of literature means or is about, its central idea, is its **thematic concern**. In fiction and drama, these concerns are expressed through character, action, and image. In poems, they are also expressed through language, both literal and figurative. The thematic concern seeks to communicate something, to express some intellectual or emotional attitudes of the author.

Thesis An attitude or position on a problem taken by a writer with the purpose of proving or supporting it.

Time In fiction, the organization of **plot** which determines in what order the reader learns of the events. Many stories are organized in a simple, linear fashion. Other methods include the **flashback** and **in medias res**.

Tone An author's attitude toward the subject and audience. Tone is often revealed through

diction, point of view, narrative distance from the action, etc. The tone of Whitman's "To a Locomotive in Winter" is much more heroic than that of Dickinson's "I Like to See It Lap the Miles."

Tragedy A form of drama which shows a unified and significant action which is treated with great dignity and seriousness. A tragedy involves the fall of a great or representative person such as Othello or Willie Loman.

Voice The way in which an author communicates with a reader. A **fictive** or **pretend voice** narrates fictive works; the essay strives for an authentic-sounding voice, concentrating on what the reader hears. The essay often uses a **meditative voice** which encourages the reader to examine values as the author of the essay examines his or her own. The **responding voice** shows the reaction of the essayist to what goes on in day-to-day living.

ACKNOWLEDGMENTS

The following works are protected by the copyright laws of the United States and international copyright laws. Permission was kindly granted to McGraw-Hill, Inc., for reprinting in this publication.

Prelude: Reading and Writing in College

Biddle, Arthur, and Toby Fulwiler. Chapter is adapted from "Prelude," pp. 1–11, in Arthur Biddle and Toby Fulwiler, eds., *Reading, Writing, and the Study of Literature.* Copyright © 1989 by Random House, Inc. All rights reserved. Reprinted by permission of McGraw-Hill, Inc.

Chapter 1: Journal Writing

Fulwiler, Toby. Chapter is adapted from Chapter 1, "Journal Writing," pp. 15–26, in Arthur Biddle and Toby Fulwiler, eds., *Reading Writing, and the Study of Literature.* Copyright © 1989 by Random House, Inc. All rights reserved. Reprinted by permission of McGraw-Hill, Inc.

Chapter 2: The Story of a Story

Adams, Alice. "Tide Pools" from *After You're Gone.* Copyright © 1989 by Alice Adams. Reprinted by permission of Alfred A. Knopf, Inc.

Anderson, Sherwood. "Death in the Woods." Copyright 1926 by The American Mercury, Inc., renewed 1953 by Eleanor Copenhauer Anderson. Reprinted by permission of Harold Ober Associates, Inc.

Baldwin, James. "Sonny's Blues," from *Going to Meet the Man.* Copyright 1965 by The Dial Press. Reprinted by permission of The Dial Press, a division of Bantam Doubleday Dell Publishing Group, Inc.

Bambara, Toni Cade. "Gorilla, My Love" from *Gorilla, My Love.* Copyright © 1960, 1963, 1964, 1965, 1968, 1970, 1971, 1972 by Toni Cade Bambara. Reprinted by permission of Random House, Inc.

Beattie, Ann. "The Burning House" from *The Burning House.* Copyright © 1979, 1980, 1981, 1982 by Irony and Pity, Inc. Reprinted by permission of Random House, Inc.

Broughton, T. Alan. "Duck Season" from *The Jesse Tree.* Copyright © 1988 by T. Alan Broughton.

Carver, Raymond. "Cathedral" from *Cathedral.* Copyright © 1981, 1982, 1983 by Raymond Carver. Reprinted by permission of Alfred A. Knopf, Inc.

Chekhov, Anton. "A Dead Body" from *The Image of Chekhov.* Translated by Robert Payne. Copyright © 1963 by Alfred A. Knopf, Inc. Reprinted by permission of Alfred A. Knopf, Inc.

Diaz, Rony. "Death in a Sawmill" from *Modern Philippine Short Stories.* By permission of David McKay Publishers.

Erdrich, Louise. "Fleur" from *Esquire,* August 1986. Copyright © 1986 by Louise Erdrich. Published by arrangement with the author.

Faulkner, William. "Barn Burning" from *The Collected Short Stories of William Faulkner.* Copyright 1950 by William Faulkner. Copyright renewed 1977 by Jill Faulkner Summers. Reprinted by permission of Random House, Inc.

García Márquez, Gabriel. "Balthazar's Marvelous Afternoon" from *No One Writes to the Colonel and Other Stories.* English translation copyright © 1968 by Harper and Row, Publishers, Inc. Reprinted by permission of HarperCollins Publishers.

Hannah, Barry. "Testimony of Pilot" from *Airships.* Originally published in *Esquire.* Copyright © 1978 by Barry Hannah. Reprinted by permission of Alfred A. Knopf, Inc.

Hemingway, Ernest. "Soldier's Home" from *In Our Time.* Copyright 1925 by Charles Scribner's Sons, renewed 1953 by Ernest Hemingway. Reprinted with permission of Charles Scribner's Sons, an imprint of Macmillan Publishing Company.

Hilberg, David. "Mask." Copyright © 1989 by David Hilberg.

Hinojosa-Smith, Rolando. "Sometimes It Just Happens That Way, That's All." Reprinted by permission of Rolando Hinojosa-Smith.

Huddle, David. "The Summer of the Magic Show" from *Only the Little Bone.* Copyright © 1986 by David Huddle. Reprinted by permission of David R. Godine, Publisher, and by permission of Grand Street Publications.

Hughes, Langston. "One Friday Morning" from *The Crisis.* Also in *American Negro Short Stories* (Hill and Wang). Reprinted by permission of Harold Ober Associates Inc. Copyright 1959 by Langston Hughes. Copyright renewed 1980 by George Houston Bass.

Joyce, James. "Eveline" from *Dubliners.* Copyright 1916 by B. W. Huebsch, Inc. Definitive text copyright © 1967 by The Estate of James Joyce. Reprinted by permission of Viking Penguin, a division of Penguin Books USA, Inc.

Lavin, Mary. "Frail Vessel" from *The Stories of Mary Lavin.* Copyright © 1964 by Mary Lavin. Reprinted by permission of Mary Lavin and Constable Publishers.

Lawrence, D. H. "The Horse Dealer's Daughter" from *The Complete Short Stories of D. H. Lawrence.* Copyright 1922 by Thomas Seltzer, Inc., 1950 by Frieda Lawrence. Reprinted by permission of Viking Penguin, a division of Penguin Books USA, Inc.

Mansfield, Katherine. "The Garden Party" from *The Short Stories of Katherine Mansfield.* Copyright 1922 by Alfred A. Knopf, Inc., renewed 1950 by John Middleton Murry. Reprinted by permission of publisher.

Mishima, Yukio. "Swaddling Clothes," translated by Ivan Morris, from *Death in Midsummer, and Other Stories.* Copyright © 1966 by New Directions Publishing Corporation. Reprinted by permission of New Directions Publishing Corporation.

Moravia, Alberto. "The Secret" from *The Atlantic Monthly,* CCII (December 1958), 126–128. Translation by Helene Cantarella. Reprinted by permission of the author, Casa Editrice Valentino Bompiani Co., and their agent, James Brown Associates, Inc., and Intercultural Publications Inc. and *The Atlantic Monthly.* Copyright © 1958 by Alberto Moravia.

Naylor, Gloria. "Etta Mae Johnson" from *The Women of Brewster Place.* Copyright © 1980, 1982 by Gloria Naylor. Reprinted by permission of Viking Penguin, a division of Penguin Books USA, Inc.

Nicol, Abioseh. "As the Night the Day" from *Modern African Prose.* Copyright © 1964 by Abioseh Nicol. Reprinted by permission of Abioseh Nicol.

Oates, Joyce Carol. "Where Are You Going, Where Have You Been?" from *The Wheel of Love.* Copyright © 1965, 1966, 1967, 1968, 1969, 1970 by Joyce Carol Oates. Reprinted by permission of John Hawkins and Associates, Inc.

O'Connor, Flannery. "Good Country People" from *A Good Man Is Hard to Find.* Copyright © 1955 by Flannery O'Connor, renewed © 1983 by Regina O'Connor. Reprinted by permission of Harcourt Brace Jovanovich, Inc.

O'Connor, Frank. "First Confession" from *Collected Stories.* Copyright © 1951 by Frank O'Connor. Reprinted by permission of Joan Daves and Alfred A. Knopf, Inc.

Quammen, David. "Walking Out" from *Triquarterly,* Spring 1980. Copyright © 1980 by David Quammen.

Robison, Mary. "I Get By" from *Believe Them.* Copyright © 1988 by Mary Robison. Reprinted by permission of Alfred A. Knopf, Inc. Excerpted from *The New Yorker,* July 21, 1986.

Rosa, João Guimãraes. "The Third Bank of the River," translated by William Grossman, from *Modern Brazilian Short Stories.* Copyright © 1967 by The Regents of The University of California.

Updike, John. "A Sense of Shelter" from *Pigeon Feathers and Other Stories.* Copyright © 1962 by John Updike. Reprinted by permission of Alfred A. Knopf, Inc.

Welty, Eudora. "Powerhouse" from *A Curtain of Green and Other Stories.* Copyright © 1941, renewed © 1969 by Eudora Welty, reprinted by permission of Harcourt Brace Jovanovich, Inc. "A Place in Fiction" from *The Eye of the Story: Selected Essays and Reviews,* by Eudora Welty. Copyright © 1978 by Eudora Welty. Reprinted by permission of Random House, Inc.

Chapter 3: Why Poetry Matters: Singing a New Song, Dancing an Old Dance

Ai. "Why Can't I Leave You?" from *Cruelty.* Copyright © 1970, 1973 by Ai. Reprinted by permission of Houghton Mifflin Company.

Alta. "I Don't Have No Bunny Tail On My Behind" from *Poems and Prose by Alta,* "The Art of Enforced Deprivation" from *I Am Not a Practicing Angel,* "I Never Saw a Man in a Negligee" from *No Visible Means of Support.* Copyright 1971, 1991 by Alta Gerrey. Reprinted by permission of Alta.

Alvarez, Julia. "Homecoming" and "Dusting" from *Homecoming: Poems by Julia Alvarez.* Copyright © 1984 by Julia Alvarez. Reprinted by permission of Grove Press, Inc.

Ammons, A. R. "Corsons Inlet" from *Collected Poems, 1951–1971.* Copyright © 1972 by A. R. Ammons. Reprinted by permission of W. W. Norton and Company, Inc.

Ampah, Hadiza Lantana. "When the Clouds Gather" from *Dandali* vol. 1 (1986). By permission of Forum for the Creative Arts, Zaria, Nigeria.

Angelou, Maya. "Phenomenal Woman" from *And I Still Rise.* Copyright © 1978 by Maya Angelou. Reprinted by permission of Random House, Inc.

Auden, W. H. "As I Walked Out One Evening," "Musée des Beaux Arts" from *Collected Shorter Poems 1927–1957.* Copyright © 1976 by Edward Mendelson, William Meredith, and Monroe K. Spears, executors of the estate of W. H. Auden. Reprinted by permission of Faber and Faber, Ltd., from *W. H. Auden: Collected Poems,* edited by Edward Mendelson by permission of Random House, Inc. "The Shield of Achilles," reprinted from *W. H. Auden: Collected Poems,* edited by Edward Mendelson, by permission of Random House, Inc., and from *The Shield of Achilles,* by W. H. Auden, by permission of Faber & Faber, Ltd. "O What Is the Sound," reprinted from *Collected Poems,* by W. H. Auden, by permission of Faber & Faber, Ltd., and from *W. H. Auden: Collected Poems,* by permission of Random House, Inc. Copyright © 1976 by Edward Mendelson, William Meredith, and Monroe K. Spears, executors of the estate of W. H. Auden.

Awonoor, Kofi. "Song of War," "The Weaver Bird," "The First Circle." Copyright © 1991 by Kofi Awonoor. Reprinted by permission of Kofi Awonoor.

Baraka, Imamu Amiri. "Poem for Half White College Students" from *The Black Poets.* Copyright © 1969 by Imamu Amiri Baraka. Reprinted by permission of Sterling Lord Literistic, Inc.

Biddle, Arthur W. "Grandfather." Copyright by Arthur Biddle. Reprinted by permission of the author.

Bishop, Elizabeth. "The Fish" from *The Complete Poems 1927–1979.* Copyright © 1940 by Elizabeth Bishop. Copyright © 1979, 1983 by Alice Helen Methfessel. Reprinted by permission of Farrar, Straus & Giroux, Inc.

Bly, Robert. *The Teeth Mother Naked at Last,* excerpt from Part II. Copyright Robert Bly. Reprinted by permission of Robert Bly.

Brooks, Gwendolyn. "The Blackstone Rangers," "Kitchenette Building," "The Lovers of the Poor," "the mother," "We Real Cool" from *Blacks.* Copyright © 1987 by Gwendolyn Brooks Blakely. Published by The David Company, Chicago. Reprinted by permission of Gwendolyn Brooks.

Coleman, Wanda. "Women of My Color," "Sweet Mama Wanda Tells Fortunes for a Price," "Drone," "Doing Battle with the Wolf" from *African Sleeping Sickness.* Copyright © 1979 by Wanda Coleman. Reprinted by permission of Black Sparrow Press. "Rape" from *Imagoes.* Copyright © 1983 by Wanda Coleman. Reprinted by permission of Black Sparrow Press.

Crane, Hart. "Voyages II" from *The Complete Poems and Selected Letters and Prose of Hart Crane,* edited by Brom Weber. Copyright 1933, © 1958, 1966 by Liveright Publishing Corporation. Reprinted by permission of Liveright Publishing Corporation.

cummings, e. e. "the Cambridge ladies who live in furnished souls" from *Tulips and Chimneys,* edited by George James Firmage. Copyright 1923, 1925 and renewed 1951, 1953 by e. e. cummings. Copyright © 1973, 1976 by the Trustees for E. E. Cummings Trust. Copyright © 1973, 1976 by George Firmage. Reprinted by permission of Liveright Publishing Corporation. "Raise the shade will youse dearie?" from *Tulips and Chimneys,* edited by George James Firmage. Copyright 1923, 1925 and renewed 1951, 1953 by e. e. cummings. Copyright © 1973, 1976 by the Trustees for the E. E. Cummings Trust. Copyright © 1973, 1976 by George James Firmage. Reprinted by permission of Liveright Publishing Corporation. "if everything happens that can't be done" from *Complete Poems 1913–1962.* Copyright © 1923, 1925, 1931, 1035, 1938, 1939, 1940, 1944, 1945, 1946, 1947, 1948, 1949, 1950, 1951, 1952, 1953, 1954, 1955, 1956, 1957, 1958, 1959, 1960, 1961, 1962 by the Trustees for the E. E. Cummings Trust. Copyright © 1961, 1963, 1968 by Marion Morehouse Cummings. Reprinted by permission of Liveright Publishing Corporation. "in Just—" from *Tulips and Chimneys,* edited by George James Firmage. Copyright 1923, 1925 and renewed 1951, 1953 by e. e. cummings. Copyright © 1973, 1976 by the Trustees for the E. E. Cummings Trust. Copyright © 1973, 1976 by George James Firmage. Reprinted by permission of Liveright Publishing Corporation. "next to of course god america i," "she being brand" from *Is 5,* edited by George James Firmage. Copyright © 1985 by E. E. Cummings Trust. Copyright 1926 by Horace Liveright. Copyright © 1954 by e. e. cummings. Copyright © 1985 by George James Firmage. Reprinted by permission of Liveright Publishing Corporation. "l(a" from *Complete Poems of E. E. Cummings, 1913–1962,* Vol. 2 (1936–1962). Copyright renewed. Reprinted by permission of Liveright Publishing Corporation.

de la Mare, Walter. "The Listeners" from *The Norton Anthology of Poetry,* 3d ed., edited by Alexander W. Allison et al., 1983. Copyright The Literary Trustees of Walter de la Mare and The Society of Authors. Reprinted by permission of The Literary Trustees of Walter de la Mare and The Society of Authors as their representative. "Silver" from *The Random House Book of Poetry for Children,* Jack Prelutsky ed., 1983. Copyright The Literary Trustees of Walter de la Mare and The Society of Authors.

Delanty, Greg. "Out of the Ordinary." Copyright Greg Delanty. Reprinted by permission of Greg Delanty.

Dickinson, Emily. "Because I could not stop for Death," "I heard a Fly buzz—when I died," "I Like to See It Lap the Miles," "A narrow Fellow in the Grass," "Tell all the Truth, but tell it slant," "There's a certain Slant of light," "A Bird came down the Walk" from *The Poems of Emily Dickinson,* edited by Thomas H. Johnson. Copyright 1951, © 1955, 1979, 1983 by the President and Fellows of Harvard College. Reprinted by permission of The Belknap Press of Harvard University Press and the Trustees of Amherst College.

Diop, David Mandessi. "The Vultures" from *Coups de Pilou.* Presence Africaine 1973. Reprinted by permission of Presence Africaine, Paris.

Djoubali, Leila. "For My Torturer, Lieutenant D—" from *Voices from Twentieth-Century Africa: Griots and Towncriers.* Reprinted by permission of Faber & Faber, Ltd.

The Doors. "L.A. Woman" by Jim Morrison, Ray Manzarek, John Densmore, and Robby Krieger. Copyright © 1971 by Doors Music Company. All rights reserved. Reprinted by permission.

Eberhart, Richard. "Long Term Suffering" and "Reading Room, the New York Public Library" from *Collected Poems 1930–1986.* Copyright © 1960, 1976, 1988 by Richard Eberhart. Reprinted by permission of Oxford University Press, Inc.

Eliot, T. S. "The Hippopotamus," "Preludes," excerpt of "The Waste Land" from *Collected Poems 1909–1962.* Copyright 1936 by Harcourt Brace Jovanovich, Inc., copyright © 1963, 1964 by T. S. Eliot. Reprinted by permission of Harcourt Brace Jovanovich, Inc. "The Love Song of J. Alfred Prufrock" from *Collected Poems 1909–1962.* Copyright 1936 by Harcourt Brace Jovanovich, Inc., © 1964, 1963 by T. S. Eliot. Reprinted by permission of Harcourt Brace Jovanovich, Inc., and Faber & Faber, Ltd.

Engels, John. "Vivaldi in Early Fall" from *Vivaldi in Early Fall.* Copyright © 1981 by John Engels. Reprinted by permission of John Engels.

Ferlinghetti, Lawrence. "Constantly Risking Absurdity" from *A Coney Island of the Mind.* Copyright © 1958 by Lawrence Ferlinghetti. Reprinted by permission of New Directions Publishing Corporation. "Lost Parents" from *Who Are We Now?* Copyright © 1976 by Lawrence Ferlinghetti. Reprinted by permission of New Directions Publishing Corporation.

Finkel, Donald. "They" from *A Mote in Heaven's Eye.* Copyright © 1975 by Donald Finkel. Reprinted by permission of Donald Finkel.

Frost, Robert. "The Death of a Hired Man" excerpt, "Design," "Mending Wall," "The Silken Tent," "Stopping by Woods on a Snowy Evening" from *The Poetry of Robert Frost,* edited by Edward Connery Lathem. Copyright 1923, 1930, 1939, © 1969 by Holt, Rinehart and Winston. Copyright 1936, 1942, 1951, © 1958 by Robert Frost. Copyright © 1964, 1967, 1970 by Lesley Frost Ballantine. Reprinted by permission of Henry Holt & Company. "The Figure a Poem Makes," from *Selected Poems of Robert Frost.* Copyright © 1963 by Holt, Rinehart & Winston. Reprinted by permission of Henry Holt & Company.

Giovanni, Nikki. "My Poem" from *Black Feeling, Black Talk, Black Judgement.* Copyright © 1968, 1979 by Nikki Giovanni. Reprinted by permission of William Morrow and Company, Inc. "The True Import of Present Dialogue: Black vs. Negro" from *The Black Poets.* Reprinted by permission of William Morrow and Company, Inc.

Ginsberg, Allen. "To Aunt Rose" from *Collected Poems 1947–1980.* Copyright © 1958 by Allen Ginsberg. Reprinted by permission of HarperCollins Publishers. "A Supermarket in California" from *Collected Poems 1947–1980.* Copyright © 1955 by Allen Ginsberg. Reprinted by permission of HarperCollins Publishers.

Hall, Donald. "Kicking the Leaves," "Names of Horses" from *Kicking the Leaves.* Copyright © 1978 by Donald Hall. Reprinted by permission of HarperCollins Publishers.

Hayden, Robert. "Frederick Douglass," "Those Winter Sundays" from *Angel of Ascent, New and Selected Poems.* Copyright © 1975, 1972, 1970, 1966 by Robert Hayden. Reprinted by permission of Liveright Publishing Corporation.

Healy, Eloise Klein. "Los Angeles." Copyright Eloise Klein Healy. Reprinted by permission of Eloise Klein Healy.

Heaney, Seamus. "Death of a Naturalist," "Digging" from *Death of a Naturalist.* Reprinted by permission of Faber & Faber, Ltd. "Digging," "Mid-Term Break" from *Poems 1965–1975.* Copyright © 1966, 1969, 1972, 1980 by Seamus Heaney. Reprinted by permission of Farrar, Straus and Giroux, Inc. "Requiem for the Croppies" from *Door into the Dark.* Reprinted by permission of Faber & Faber, Ltd.

Housman, A. E. "Epilogue," "Loveliest of Trees," "With Rue My Heart Is Laden," "Terence, This Is Stupid Stuff," "When I Was One-and-Twenty" from "A Shropshire Lad," Authorised Edition, *The Collected Poems of A. E. Housman.* Copyright 1939, 1940, © 1965 by Holt, Rinehart and Winston. Copyright © 1967 by Robert E. Symons. Reprinted by permission of Henry Holt & Company.

Huddle, David. "Going, 1960–1970" from *Paper Boy.* Copyright © 1979 by David Huddle. Re-

printed by permission of University of Pittsburgh Press. "Stopping by Home" reprinted by permission of David Huddle.

Hughes, Langston. "I, Too" from *Selected Poems of Langston Hughes* by Langston Hughes. Copyright 1926 by Alfred A. Knopf, Inc., and renewed 1954 by Langston Hughes. Reprinted by permission of Alfred A. Knopf, Inc. "Freedom's Plow." Copyright 1942 by Langston Hughes. Reprinted by permission of Alfred A. Knopf, Inc. Copyright Langston Hughes. "Dream Deferred" ("Harlem") excerpt from *The Panther and the Lash.* Copyright 1951 by Langston Hughes. Reprinted by permission of Alfred A. Knopf, Inc.

Hugo, Richard. "Landscapes" from *What Thou Lovest Well Remains American.* Copyright © 1975 by W. W. Norton and Company Inc. Reprinted by permission of W. W. Norton and Company Inc.

Jacinto, Antonio. "Poem of Alienation," "Monangamba" from *When Bullets Begin to Flower.* Reprinted by permission of East African Publishing House, Nairobi, Kenya.

Jeffers, Robinson. "Hurt Hawks" from *Selected Poetry of Robinson Jeffers.* Copyright 1938 and renewed 1966 by Donnan Jeffers and Garth Jeffers. Reprinted by permission of Random House, Inc. "To the Stone-Cutters" from *Selected Poetry of Robinson Jeffers.* Copyright 1938 and renewed 1966 by Donnan Jeffers and Garth Jeffers. Reprinted by permission of Random House, Inc.

Justice, Donald. "Men at Forty" from *Night Light.* Copyright © 1966 by Donald Justice. Reprinted by permission of Wesleyan University Press.

Kennelly, Brendan. "The Silent Pits" from *Cromwell.* Blood Axe Books, 1987. Reprinted by permission of Blood Axe Books, Ltd.

Kinnell, Galway. Excerpt from "The Dead Shall Be Raised Incorruptible" from *Mortal Acts, Mortal Words.* Copyright © 1980 by Galway Kinnell. Reprinted by permission of Houghton Mifflin Company.

Knight, Etheridge. "The Idea of Ancestry" from *Belly Song and Other Poems.* Copyright © 1973 by Etheridge Knight. Reprinted by permission of Broadside Press.

Koch, Kenneth. "Variations on a Theme by William Carlos Williams" from *Thank You and Other Poems.* Copyright © 1962, 1985 by Kenneth Koch. Reprinted by permission of Kenneth Koch.

Koertge, Ronald. "For My Daughter," "Two Men," "Orientation Week," "Panty Hose" from *Life on the Edge of the Continent.* Copyright 1982 by Ronald Koertge. Reprinted by permission of University of Arkansas Press.

Kumin, Maxine. "After Love" from *Our Ground Time Here Will Be Brief.* Copyright © 1969, 1970 by Maxine Kumin. Reprinted by permission of Viking Penguin, a division of Penguin Books USA, Inc.

Larkin, Philip. "Church Going" from *The North Ship.* Copyright Philip Larkin. Reprinted by permission of Marvell Press, Ltd. "A Study of Reading Habits," "This be the Verse" from *The Whitsun Weddings.* Reprinted by permission of Faber & Faber, Ltd.

Lawrence, D. H. "Piano" from *The Complete Poems of D. H. Lawrence.* Copyright © 1964, 1971 by Angelo Ravagli and C. M. Weekley, executors of the estate of Frieda Lawrence Ravagli. Reprinted by permission of Viking Penguin, a division of Penguin Books USA, Inc. "Snake" from *The Complete Poems of D. H. Lawrence.* (Viking Penguin). Copyright © 1964, 1971 by Angelo Ravagli and C. M. Weekley, executors of the estate of Frieda Lawrence Ravagli. Used by permission of the publisher Viking Penguin, a division of Penguin Books USA, Inc.

Lee, Don L. (Haki R. Madhubuti). "A Poem to Complement Other Poems" from *Don't Cry, Scream.* Third World Press. Copyright © Haki R. Madhubuti. Reprinted by permission of Broadside Press.

Lehrer, Tom. "When You Are Old and Gray" from *Too Many Songs by Tom Lehrer with Not Enough Drawings by Ronald Searle.* Copyright © 1953 by Tom Lehrer. Copyright renewed. Reprinted by permission of Tom Lehrer.

LeSueuer, Meridel. "The Village" from *A Geography of Poets: An Anthology of the New Poetry,* ed. Edward Field (Bantam Books, 1979). Reprinted by permission.

Levertov, Denise. "Libation" from *The Freeing of the Dust.* Copyright © 1975 by Denise Levertov. Reprinted by permission of New Directions Publishing Corporation.

Levine, Philip. "My Son and I" from *The Names of the Lost.* Copyright © 1976 by Philip Levine. Reprinted by permission of Philip Levine.

Lowell, Robert. "Jonathan Edwards in Western Massachusetts" and "For the Union Dead" from *For the Union Dead* by Robert Lowell. Copyright © 1960, 1962, 1964 by Robert Lowell. Reprinted by permission of Farrar, Straus and Giroux, Inc.

MacLeish, Archibald. "Ars Poetica," "The End of the World," "Memorial Rain," "You, Andrew Marvell" from *New and Collected Poems 1917–1982* by Archibald MacLeish. Copyright © 1985 by the estate of Archibald MacLeish. Reprinted by permission of Houghton Mifflin Company.

McKay, Claude. "America," "Baptism," "The Harlem Dancer," "If We Must Die," "The White House," from *Selected Poems of Claude McKay.* Copyright 1953 and reprinted by permission of Twayne Publishers, a division of G. K. Hall and Company, Boston.

Magistrale, Tony. "Vanishing Point." Copyright by Tony Magistrale. Reprinted by permission of the author.

Mapanje, Jack. "On Being Asked to Write a Poem for 1979" from *Of Chameleons and Gods.* Reprinted by permission of Heinemann Educational Books, Ltd.

Mnthali, Felix. "The Stranglehold of English Lit." from *Echoes From Ibadan* (privately printed, 1961). Copyright by Felix Mnthali. Reprinted by permission of Felix Mnthali.

Montague, John. "The Cage" from *A Chosen Light.* Copyright John Montague.

Moore, Marianne. "The Steeple-Jack" from *Collected Poems.* Copyright 1951 by Marianne Moore, renewed 1979 by Lawrence E. Brinn and Louise Crane. Reprinted by permission of Macmillan Publishing Company. "Poetry" from *Collected Poems.* Copyright 1935 by Marianne Moore, renewed 1963 by Marianne Moore and T. S. Eliot. Reprinted by permission of Macmillan Publishing Company.

Moss, Howard. "The Refrigerator" from *A Swim Off the Rocks.* Copyright by Howard Moss. Reprinted by permission of the estate of Howard Moss.

Mueller, Lisel. "A Voice From Out of the Night" from *The Need to Hold Still.* Copyright © 1980 by Lisel Mueller. Reprinted by permission of Louisiana State University Press.

Nash, Ogden. "Very Much Like A Whale" from *Verses from 1929 On.* Reprinted by permission of Little, Brown & Co. (Inc.)

Neto, Augustnho. "The Grieved Lands," "African Poem." Copyright by the author.

Ochester, Ed. "The Gift" from *Dancing on the Edges of Knives.* Copyright © 1973 by the curators of the author. Reprinted by permission of University of Missouri Press.

Okara, Gabriel. "Once Upon a Time" from *Black Orpheus.* "Piano and Drums" from *Black Orpheus,* reprinted in Gerald Moore and Ulli Beier, eds., *Modern Poetry from Africa,* published by the Penguin Group, London. Both reprinted by permission of African Universities Press, Lagos.

Olds, Sharon. "Sex Without Love" from *The Dead and the Living.* Copyright © 1983 by Sharon Olds. Reprinted by permission of Alfred A. Knopf, Inc.

Orth, Ghita. "Secrets of the Rain Forest" and "What Didn't Happen in Arizona." Copyright by Ghita Orth. Reprinted by permission of Ghita Orth.

Owen, Wilfred. "Dulce et Decorum Est," "Anthem for Doomed Youth," "Strange Meeting" from *The Collected Poems of Wilfred Owen.* Copyright © 1963 by Chatto & Windus, Ltd. Reprinted by permission of New Directions Publishing Corporation and by permission of Chatto & Windus, Ltd.

p' Bitek, Okot. "The Graceful Giraffe Cannot Become A Monkey" from *Song of Lawine/Song of Ocol.* Reprinted by permission of Hayanga and Company, Nairobi, Kenya.

Piercy, Margaret. "To the Pay Toilet" from *Circles on the Water.* Reprinted by permission of Alfred A. Knopf, Inc.

Plath, Sylvia. "Daddy," "Death and Co." from *The Collected Poems of Sylvia Plath,* edited by Ted Hughes. Copyright © 1963, 1965, 1981 by Ted Hughes. Reprinted by permission of HarperCollins Publishers and by permission of Olwyn Hughes.

Pomeroy, Ralph. "Looking at the Empire State Building" from *The Geography of Poets,* published by

New Directions Publishing Corporation. Copyright by Ralph Pomeroy. Reprinted by permission of Ralph Pomeroy.

Pound, Ezra. "In a Station of the Metro" from *Personae.* Copyright 1926 by Ezra Pound. Reprinted by permission of New Directions Publishing Corporation.

Ransom, John Crowe. "Bells for John Whiteside's Daughter" from *Selected Poems,* 3d ed., Revised and enlarged. Copyright 1924 by Alfred A. Knopf, Inc., renewed 1952 by John Crowe Ransom. Reprinted by permission of Alfred A. Knopf, Inc. "Piazza Piece" from *Selected Poems,* 3d ed., Revised and enlarged by John Crowe Ransom. Copyright 1927 by Alfred A. Knopf, Inc., and renewed 1955 by John Crowe Ransom. Reprinted by permission of Alfred A. Knopf, Inc.

Reed, Henry. "Judging Distances," "Naming of Parts," excerpts from "Lessons of the War" from *A Map of Verona.* Reprinted by permission of the Peters Fraser and Dunlop Group, Ltd.

Reed, Ishmael. "badman of the guest professor" from *New and Collected Poems.* Copyright © 1972, 1988 by Ishmael Reed. Reprinted by permission of Atheneum Publishers, an imprint of Macmillan Publishing Company.

Replansky, Naomi. "The Mistress Addresses the Wife" first appeared in *Poetry,* February 1954. Copyright 1954 by The Modern Poetry Association. Reprinted by permission of the *Poetry* and Naomi Replansky.

Rich, Adrienne. "Aunt Jennifer's Tigers" from *The Fact of a Doorframe: Poems Selected and New, 1950–1984.* Copyright © 1984 by Adrienne Rich. Copyright © 1975, 1978 by W. W. Norton and Company, Inc. Copyright © 1981 by Adrienne Rich. Reprinted by permission of W. W. Norton & Company.

Robinson, Edwin Arlington. "Mr. Flood's Party" from *Collected Poems.* Copyright 1921 by Edwin Arlington Robinson, renewed 1949 by Ruth Nivison. Reprinted by permission of Macmillan Publishing Company.

Roethke, Theodore. "Frau Bauman, Frau Schmidt, and Frau Schwartze" from *The Collected Poems of Theodore Roethke.* Copyright 1952 by Theodore Roethke. Reprinted by permission of Doubleday, a division of Bantam Doubleday Dell Publishing Group, Inc. "The Waking" from *The Collected Poems of Theodore Roethke.* Copyright 1948 by Theodore Roethke. Reprinted by permission of Doubleday, a division of Bantam Doubleday Dell Publishing Group, Inc. "My Papa's Waltz," from *The Collected Poems of Theodore Roethke.* Copyright 1942 by Hearst Magazines, Inc. Reprinted by permission of Doubleday, a division of Bantam Doubleday Dell Publishing Group, Inc.

Rubadiri, David. "An African Thunderstorm" from *Penguin Book of Modern African Poetry.* Copyright by David Rubadiri. Reprinted by permission of David Rubadiri.

Sédar-Senghor, Léopold. "Visit," "New York," reprinted in *The Penguin Book of Modern African Poetry.* By permission of Editions du Seuil.

Sexton, Anne. "Woman with Girdle," "All My Pretty Ones" from *All My Pretty Ones* by Anne Sexton. Copyright © 1962 by Anne Sexton. Reprinted by permission of Houghton Mifflin Co.

Shapiro, Harvey. "Riding Westward" from *National Cold Storage Company: New and Selected Poems.* Copyright by Harvey Shapiro. Reprinted by permission of Wesleyan University Press.

Smith, Stevie. "Not Waving But Drowning," "Our Bog Is Dood" from *Collected Poems of Stevie Smith.* Copyright © 1972 by Stevie Smith. Reprinted by permission of New Directions Publishing Corporation.

Snodgrass, W. D. "A Flat One" from *After Experience.* Copyright W. D. Snodgrass. Reprinted by permission of W. D. Snodgrass.

Snyder, Gary. "The Bath" from *Turtle Island.* Copyright © 1972 by Gary Snyder. Reprinted by permission of New Directions Publishing Corporation.

Soyinka, Wole. "Telephone Conversation" and "Massacre, October '66" from *The Penguin Book of Modern African Poetry.* By permission of the author.

Spender, Stephen. "My parents kept me from" (also called "Rough") from *Collected Poems: 1928–*

1953. Copyright 1934 by The Modern Library, Inc. Copyright 1930, 1942, 1947, 1949, 1952, 1955 by Stephen Spender. Reprinted by permission of Random House, Inc.

Stevens, Wallace. "The Motive for Metaphor," "So-And-So Reclining on Her Couch" from *The Collected Poems of Wallace Stevens.* Copyright 1947 by Wallace Stevens. Reprinted by permission of Alfred A. Knopf, Inc. "The Snow Man," "The Emperor of Ice-Cream," "Anecdote of the Jar" from *The Collected Poems of Wallace Stevens.* Copyright 1923 and renewed 1951 by Wallace Stevens. Reprinted by permission of Alfred A. Knopf, Inc.

Tate, Allen. "Ode to the Confederate Dead" from *Collected Poems 1919–1976.* Copyright © 1977 by Allen Tate. Reprinted by permission of Farrar, Straus & Giroux, Inc.

Thomas, Dylan. "Fern Hill," "Do Not Go Gentle into That Good Night" from *Poems of Dylan Thomas.* Copyright 1945 by the Trustees for Copyrights of Dylan Thomas, 1952 by Dylan Thomas. Reprinted by permission of New Directions Publishing Corporation and by permission of David Higham Associates, Ltd.

Urdang, Constance. "Safe Places" from *The Lone Woman and Others.* Copyright © 1980 by Constance Urdang. Reprinted by permission of University of Pittsburgh Press.

Voigt, Ellen Bryant. "The Lotus Flowers" from *The Lotus Flowers, Poems by Ellen Bryant Voigt.* Copyright © 1987 by Ellen Bryant Voigt. Reprinted by permission of W. W. Norton & Company.

Walker, Alice. "Women" from *Revolutionary Petunias and Other Poems.* Copyright © 1970 by Alice Walker. Reprinted by permission of Harcourt Brace Jovanovich, Inc.

Williams, William Carlos. "At the Ball Game," "The Dance," "This Is Just to Say," "Tract," "Danse Russe" from *The Collected Poems of William Carlos Williams, 1909–1939,* vol. 1. Copyright 1938 by New Directions Publishing Corporation. Reprinted by permission of New Directions Publishing Corporation. *Paterson* (excerpt). New Directions Publishing Corporation 1963.

Wilson, Keith. "The Arrival of My Mother" from *White Dancing Feet Shatter the Earth.* Copyright © 1978 Keith Wilson.

Winner, Robert. "Miss Alderman." Copyright © 1977 by NEW LETTERS. Reprinted by permission of Sylvia Winner.

Wright, James. "Lying in a Hammock at William Duffy's Farm in Pine Island, Minnesota" from *Collected Poems.* Copyright © 1971 by James Wright. Reprinted by permission of Wesleyan University Press and University Press of New England.

Yeats, W. B. "Lapis Lazuli," "The Circus Animals' Desertion" from *The Poems of W. B. Yeats: A New Edition,* edited by Richard J. Finnerman. Copyright 1940 by George Yeats, renewed 1968 by Bertha Georgie Yeats, Michael Butler Yeats, and Anne Yeats. Reprinted by permission of Macmillan Publishing Company. "A Prayer for My Daughter" from *The Poems of W. B. Yeats: A New Edition,* edited by Richard J. Finneran. Copyright 1924 by Macmillan Publishing Company, renewed 1952 by Bertha Georgie Yeats. Reprinted by permission of Macmillan Publishing Company. "The Wild Swans at Coole," "The Lake of Innisfree" from *The Poems of W. B. Yeats: A New Edition,* edited by Richard J. Finneran. Copyright 1919 by Macmillan Publishing Co. Renewed 1947 by Bertha Georgie Yeats. Reprinted by permission of Macmillan Publishing Company.

Zimmer, Paul. "The Day Zimmer Lost Religion," "What Zimmer Would Be," "Zimmer Envying Elephants," "Zimmer in Grade School" from *The Zimmer Poems.* © 1976 by Paul Zimmer. Published by Dryad Press, Washington, D.C. Reprinted by permission of Paul Zimmer.

Chapter 4: Reading Script into Play

Aristophanes. *The Lysistrata of Aristophanes: An English Version* by Dudley Fitts. Copyright 1954 by Harcourt Brace Jovanovich, Inc., and renewed 1982 by Cornelia Fitts, Daniel H. Fitts, and Deborah W. Fitts. Reprinted by permission of Harcourt Brace Jovanovich. *Caution:* All rights,

including professional, amateur, motion picture, recitation, lecturing, public reading, radio broadcasting and television are strictly reserved. Inquiries on all rights should be addressed to Harcourt Brace Jovanovich, Inc., Permissions Department, Orlando, Florida 32887.

Brecht, Bertold. *Mother Courage and Her Children.* Translated by Eric Bentley. From *Seven Plays by Bertold Brecht,* Grove Press. Copyright © 1955, 1959, 1961 by Eric Bentley.

Churchill, Caryl. *Vinegar Tom.* Reprinted by permission of Methuen & Company, Ltd., London. International copyright secured. All rights reserved, including the right of public performance.

Friel, Brian. *Philadelphia, Here I Come!* from: *Philadelphia, Here I Come!* Copyright © 1965 by Brian Friel. Reprinted by permission of Faber & Faber, Ltd.

Fuller, Charles. *A Soldier's Play.* Copyright © 1981 by Charles Fuller. Reprinted by permission of Hill and Wang, a division of Farrar, Straus and Giroux, Inc. *Caution:* Professionals and amateurs are hereby warned that *A Soldier's Play* is subject to a royalty. It is fully protected under the copyright laws of the United States of America, and of all countries covered by the International Copyright Union (including the Domain of Canada and the rest of the British Commonwealth), and of all countries covered by the Pan-American Copyright Convention and the Universal Copyright Convention, and of all countries with which the United States has reciprocal copyright relations. All rights, including professional, amateur, motion picture, recitation, lecturing, public reading, radio broadcasting, television, and the rights of translation into foreign languages, are strictly reserved. Particular emphasis is laid upon the question of readings, permission for which must be secured from the author's agent in writing. All inquiries concerning rights (other than stock and amateur rights) should be addressed to William Morris Agency, 1350 Avenue of the Americas, New York, NY, 10019. The stock and amateur production rights for *A Soldier's Play* are controlled exclusively by Samuel French. No stock or amateur performance of the play may be given without obtaining in advance the written permission of Samuel French, Inc., and paying the requisite fee.

Hansberry, Lorraine. *A Raisin in the Sun.* Copyright © 1958 by Robert Nemiroff, as an unpublished work. Copyright © 1959, 1966, 1984 by Robert Nemiroff. Reprinted by permission of Random House, Inc.

Ibsen, Henrik. "The Wild Duck" from *Modern Drama.* Translated by Otto Reinhart. Copyright © 1966 by Little Brown & Co., Inc. Copyright 1961, 1962, 1963 by Little Brown & Company, Inc. Reprinted by permission of Otto Reinhart.

Norman, Marsha. *Third and Oak* from *Four Plays* by Marsha Norman. *Third and Oak* copyright © 1978 by Marsha Norman. Reprinted by permission of Theatre Communications Group, New York.

Richardson, Jack. *Gallows Humor,* E. P. Dutton. Copyright © 1961 Jack C. Richardson. Reprinted by permission of Jack Richardson.

Shakespeare, William. *Hamlet, Othello* from *Shakespeare: Major Plays and the Sonnets,* edited by G. B. Harrison, copyright 1948 by Harcourt Brace Jovanovich, Inc., and renewed 1976 by G. B. Harrison. Reprinted by permission of Harcourt Brace Jovanovich, Inc.

Sophocles. *The Oedipus Rex of Sophocles: An English Version* by Dudley Fitts and Robert Fitzgerald, copyright 1949 by Harcourt Brace Jovanovich, Inc., and renewed 1977 by Cornelia Fitts and Robert Fitzgerald, reprinted by permission of the publisher. *Caution:* All rights, including professional, amatuer, motion picture, recitation, lecturing, public reading, radio broadcasting, and television are strictly reserved. Inquiries on all rights should be addressed to Harcourt Brace Jovanovich, Inc., Permissions Department, Orlando, Florida 32887.

Stoppard, Tom. *Rosencrantz and Guildenstern Are Dead.* Copyright © 1967 by Tom Stoppard. Reprinted by permission of Grove Press, Inc., and by permission of Faber & Faber, Ltd.

Williams, Tennessee. *The Glass Menagerie.* Copyright 1945 by Tennessee Williams and Edwina D. Williams and renewed 1973 by Tennessee Williams. Reprinted by permission of Random House, Inc.

Chapter 5: Voices in the Essay

Bly, Carol. "Growing Up Expressive" from *Letters from the Country.* Copyright © 1979 by Carol Bly. Reprinted by permission of HarperCollins Publishers.

Cliff, Michelle. "If I Could Write This in Fire, I Would Write This in Fire" from *The Land of Look Behind.* Copyright Michelle Cliff. Reprinted by permission of Firebrand Books, Ithaca, New York.

Didion, Joan. "Why I Write" from *The New York Times Book Review* (subsequently published in *Eight Modern Essayists,* 4th ed., Harper and Row). Copyright © 1976 by Joan Didion. Reprinted by permission of The Wallace Literary Agency, Inc.

Dillard, Annie. "Sight into Insight." First published in *Harper's Magazine,* February, 1974. Copyright © 1974 by Annie Dillard. Reprinted by permission of the author and her agent, Blanche C. Gregory, Inc.

Gómez-Peña, Guillermo. "Documented/Undocumented," copyright © 1988 by Guillermo Gómez-Peña. Reprinted by permission of Guillermo Gómez-Peña.

Hall, Donald. "Winter" originally appeared in the exhibition catalogue *Winter,* published by the Hood Museum of Art, Dartmouth College, in the Winter of 1986, available through the University Press of New England, Hanover, New Hampshire. Subsequently published in *The Best American Essays 1987.* Reprinted by permission of Hood Museum of Art.

Hardwick, Elizabeth. "Its Only Defense: Intelligence and Sparkle." Copyright Elizabeth Hardwick. Reprinted by permission of Elizabeth Hardwick.

Jarrell, Randall. "The Other Frost" from *Poetry and the Age.* Copyright Mary Jarrell. Reprinted by permission of Mary Jarrell.

King, Martin Luther, Jr. "Letter from Birmingham Jail" from *Why We Can't Wait.* Copyright © 1963, 1964, by Martin Luther King, Jr. Reprinted by permission of HarperCollins Publishers.

Lopate, Phillip. "The Essay Lives—In Disguise" from *The New York Times Book Review,* November 18, 1984. Reprinted by permission of the Julian Bach Literary Agency.

Manchester, William. "Okinawa: The Bloodiest Battle of All," *New York Times Magazine,* June 14, 1987. Copyright © 1987 William Manchester. Reprinted by permission of Don Congdon Associates, Inc.

Newman, Barry. "Maggots in Icebox, Bloodworm in Tub, Roach on the Hook," *The Wall Street Journal,* September 13, 1983. Reprinted by permission.

Oates, Joyce Carol. "On Boxing" from *New York Times Magazine.* Subsequently published in *The Best American Essays 1986.* Copyright © 1985 by The Ontario Review, Inc.

Orwell, George. "Shooting an Elephant" from *Shooting an Elephant and Other Essays.* Copyright 1945, 1946, 1949, 1950 by Sonia Brownell Orwell, renewed 1978 by Sonia Pitt-Rivers. Reprinted by permission of Harcourt Brace Jovanovich, Inc.

Seilsopour, James. "I Forgot the Words to the National Anthem" from *Student Writers at Work: The Bedford Prizes,* edited by Nancy Sommers and Donald McQuade. Copyright © 1984. Reprinted with permission of St. Martin's Press, Inc.

Simic, Charles. "Reading Philosophy at Night" from *Wonderful Worlds, Silent Truth,* University of Michigan Press, 1990. First appeared in *Antaeus,* No. 59, 1987. Reprinted by permission of Charles Simic.

Turley, Maureen. "Women's Studies: My Right to an Education." Copyright Maureen Turley Sara.

Walker, Alice. "In Search of Our Mothers' Gardens" from *In Search of Our Mothers' Gardens.* Copyright © 1974 by Alice Walker. Reprinted by permission of Harcourt Brace Jovanovich, Inc.

White, E. B. "Death of a Pig" from *Essays of E. B. White.* Copyright 1947 by E. B. White. Reprinted by permission of HarperCollins Publishers.

Woolf, Virginia. "How Should One Read a Book?" from *The Common Reader: Second Series.* Copyright 1932 by Harcourt Brace Jovanovich, Inc., and renewed 1960 by Leonard Woolf. Reprinted

by permission of Harcourt Brace Jovanovich, Inc., The Estate of Virginia Woolf, and Hogarth Press. "The Modern Essay" from *The Common Reader: Second Series.* Copyright 1925 by Harcourt Brace Jovanovich, Inc., and renewed 1953 by Leonard Woolf. Reprinted by permission of Harcourt Brace Jovanovich, Inc., and by permission of Random Century Group, Ltd.

Chapter 6: Writing Critical Essays

Warhol, Robyn. Chapter is adapted from Chapter 6, "Writing Critical Essays," pp. 95–11, in Arthur Biddle and Toby Fulwiler, eds., *Reading, Writing, and the Study of Literature.* Copyright © 1989 by Random House, Inc. All rights reserved. Reprinted by permission of McGraw-Hill, Inc.

Chapter 7: Writing Personal Essays

Dickerson, Mary Jane. Chapter is adapted from Chapter 7, "Writing Personal Essays," pp. 112–116, in Arthur Biddle and Toby Fulwiler, eds., *Reading, Writing, and the Study of Literature.* Copyright © 1989 by Random House, Inc. All rights reserved. Reprinted by permission of McGraw-Hill, Inc.

Chapter 8: Imaginative Writing and Risk Taking

Stephany, William A. Chapter is adapted from Chapter 8, "Imaginative Writing and Risk Taking," pp. 127–210, in Arthur Biddle and Toby Fulwiler, eds., *Reading, Writing, and the Study of Literature.* Copyright © 1989 by Random House, Inc. All rights reserved. Reprinted by permission of McGraw-Hill, Inc.

Chapter 9: Examining the Essay Examination

Magistrale, Tony. Chapter is adapted from Chapter 9, "Examining the Essay Examination," pp. 141–164, in Arthur Biddle and Toby Fulwiler, eds., *Reading, Writing, and the Study of Literature.* Copyright © 1989 by Random House, Inc. All rights reserved. Reprinted by permission of McGraw-Hill, Inc.

Chapter 10: Writing Research

Achtert, Walter S., and Joseph Cibaldi. "Documentation," from *The MLA Style Manual,* p. 163. Reprinted by permission of the Modern Language Association.

Sweterlitsch, Richard. Chapter is adapted from Chapter 10, "Writing Research," pp. 155–174, in Arthur Biddle and Toby Fulwiler, eds., *Reading, Writing, and the Study of Literature.* Copyright © 1989 by Random House, Inc. All rights reserved. Reprinted by permission of McGraw-Hill, Inc.

INDEX

of Authors, Titles, and First Lines

Selection titles appear in italics, and first lines of poems appear in roman type. Numbers in roman indicate the opening page of a selection; italic numbers indicate discussion of a selection.